13 45

W9-BCL-760

MEMORIAL LIBRARY
LUTHERAN THEOLOGICAL
SOUTHERN SEMINARY
COLUMBIA, S. C.

a dictionary of COMPARATIVE RELIGION

a dictionary of COMPARATIVE RELIGION

General Editor
S.G.F.BRANDON MA DD
Professor of Comparative Religion
in the University of Manchester

WEIDENFELD & NICOLSON
5 Winsley Street London W1

© 1970 by S. G. F. Brandon

All rights reserved. No part of this publication may be reproduced, stored in a retrieval system, or transmitted, in any form or by any means, electronic, mechanical, photocopying, recording or otherwise, without the prior permission of the Copyright owner.

SBN 297 00044 6

Printed in Great Britain by C. Tinling and Company Limited, London and Prescot

General Editor

and Editor of
PREHISTORIC, ANCIENT NEAR EASTERN, GREEK and ROMAN RELIGIONS AND CHRISTIANITY

S. G. F. Brandon

Sectional Editors

BUDDHISM

T. O. Ling, MA, PhD
Senior Lecturer in Comparative Religion
University of Leeds

HINDUISM

N. Smart, MA, BPhil
Professor of Religious Studies
University of Lancaster

ISLAM

J. Robson, MA, DLitt, DD
Professor Emeritus and formerly Professor of Arabic
University of Manchester

CHINA AND THE FAR EAST

D. Howard Smith, BA, BD
Formerly Lecturer in Comparative Religion (Chinese Cults and Philosophies)
University of Manchester

CONTENTS

* A list of those religions which are described in single comprehensive articles in the Dictionary can be found on the following page.

PREFACE

The comparative study of religion has now become an established subject in the Humanities' curriculum of university education. 'Comparative Religion', as it is more popularly and conveniently named, has been a recognised field of study for more than a century; but it has been slow in acquiring independent status. For too long it was regarded as a handmaid to Theology, concerned primarily with the task of showing how other religions were destined to find their completion in Christianity. This theological involvement inevitably resulted in the evaluation of Comparative Religion as a discipline based on theological presuppositions and with confessionist interests. But now, due to a variety of causes, the claim of Comparative Religion to be considered as an academic discipline in its own right, concerned with the scientific investigation and assessment of the relevant data, is generally acknowledged. And with this acknowledgement has come an increasing appreciation of its importance in a liberal education. It is realised that to have an intelligent understanding of our common humanity and its problems today, it is necessary to know something of its religions as well as its political and economic affairs, its scientific and cultural achievements. For, whatever may be one's evaluation of the metaphysical aspects of religion, the significance of religion as a social phenomenon is fundamental. The ways in which other peoples today and in the past have sought to solve the problem of human nature and destiny have a deep and abiding interest, even when they may amaze or shock by their superstition, intolerance or cruelty. Moreover, the problem, which others have thus tried to solve, is a continuing one and it confronts each of us, whatever our age or the society in which we live.

It is to meet the increasing demand for information, reliable and current, about the religious beliefs and practices of mankind that this *Dictionary* has been prepared. It is planned to provide this service in five ways: (1) The alphabetic arrangement of subjects affords both easy reference and reveals the fascinating variety and complexity of the subject-matter of Comparative Religion. (2) The bibliographies attached to each entry will help the reader to pursue subjects that are, necessarily, treated briefly here. (3) The cross-referencing (→) is designed to show the interrelationship of topics or themes and to facilitate comparative study. (4) The General Index lists names and subjects not allotted an individual entry, and indicates under what head-word reference to them occurs. (5) The Synoptic Index lists all entries relating to the specified major religions, thus enabling the reader to obtain both a detailed and comprehensive account of any particular religion with which he may be specially interested. The lesser religions are treated in single comprehensive articles.

The compilation of this one-volume dictionary has made the editor very appreciative of the immense achievement of the *Encyclopaedia of Religion and Ethics*, edited by J. Hastings; but it has also made him sadly aware how much this great work needs revision in the light of subsequent research and new orientations of outlook. Its first volume appeared in 1908 and its final (twelfth) volume of text in 1921; consequently, although it remains a treasure-house of strange and fascinating material, it can be safely used only with informed circumspection. The *E.R.E.* abides as a superb memorial to a past generation of scholars, and a challenge to their successors today. The challenge has been partially met by the third edition (1957–62) of the great German encyclopaedia, *Die Religion in Geschichte und Gegenwart* (6 vols., and Index vol.). However, although it is indeed comprehensive in scope, this great corpus gives the impression of being more concerned with Christianity than with the other religions, either when considered individually or as whole. The aim of the present *Dictionary*, though so much smaller in size, is to treat the various religions proportionately to their significance in the history of human culture.

In order to include the maximum amount of material in one manageable volume, of easily legible type, abbreviation of various kinds has been used here; but care has been taken to keep the text clear and readable. (In the entries concerning Islamic matters dates are shown according to both the Muslim and Christian eras. Thus 1/622 denotes the first year from the → Hijra, and the year 622 of the Christian era.)

The editor is indebted to the sectional editors for their ready co-operation in the planning of the work as a whole, and he is grateful also to those other scholars who have helped to give the *Dictionary* its comprehensive scope by contributing articles on subjects in which they specialise. It has been his policy to leave the sectional editors, and the other contributors, to select or emphasise those aspects of their subjects which they considered to be most important or relevant to the comparative study of religion. As general editor, he has endeavoured to interrelate their work by cross-referencing. The author of each entry can be identified by the appended initials.

The editor welcomes this opportunity of expressing his gratitude to Mrs Elizabeth Farrow for her efficient typing of the major part of the work, and for her great assistance in compiling the indexes; he is also indebted to Miss Gillian Shepherd for her valuable clerical help in the earlier stages of the project. To his wife he owes the transcribing and indexing of the initial lists of suggested subjects for the contributors, a tedious but necessary task which she cheerfully undertook.

The University of Manchester S. G. F. Brandon
6 January 1970

LIST OF CONTRIBUTORS

(*key to initials*)

S.G.F.B.	S. G. F. Brandon, M.A., D.D. Professor of Comparative Religion, Manchester University
F.F.B.	F. F. Bruce, M.A., D.D. Rylands Professor of Biblical Criticism and Exegesis, Manchester University
C.A.B.	C. A. Burland Fellow of the Royal Anthropological Institute; Membre de la Sociétè des Américanistes de Paris; formerly on staff of British Museum
G.H.S.B.	G. H. S. Bushnell, M.A., Ph.D. Reader in New World Archaeology and Curator of the University Museum of Archaeology and Ethnology, Cambridge
H.C.-J.	The Rev. H. Cunliffe-Jones, B.A., B.Litt., D.D. Professor of Theology, Manchester University
B.D.	The Rev. B. Drewery, B.A., M.A. Bishop Fraser Lecturer in Ecclesiastical History, Manchester University
K.C.D.	The Rev. K. C. Dykes, M.A., B.D. Formerly Principal of the Northern Baptist College, Manchester
J.M.F.	The Rev. J. M. Fennelly, B.Sc., B.D., Ph.D. Assistant Professor, Beirut College for Women, Lebanon
A.H.F.	The Rev. Rabbi A. H. Friedlander, Ph.D. Wembley and District Liberal Synagogue
J.H.-T.	The Rev. J. Heywood-Thomas, D.D. Reader in Divinity, Durham University
F.K.	The Rev. F. Kenworthy, M.A., B.D. Principal of the Unitarian College, Manchester
T.O.L.	Trevor O. Ling, M.A., Ph.D. Senior Lecturer in Comparative Religion, Leeds University
D.H.J.M.	D. H. J. Morgan, B.Sc., M.A. Lecturer in Sociology, Manchester University

D.A.P.	The Rev. D. A. Pailin, M.A., Ph.D. Lecturer in the Philosophy of Religion, Manchester University
E.G.P.	E. G. Parrinder, M.A., D.D. Reader in Comparative Religion, London University
R.H.P.	The Rev. Canon R. H. Preston, B.Sc., M.A. Special Lecturer in Christian Ethics, Manchester University
W.G.R.	The Rev. W. Gordon Robinson, B.A., M.A., B.D., Ph.D. Formerly Principal of the Northern Congregational College, Manchester
J.R.	James Robson, M.A., D.Litt., D.D. Professor Emeritus, formerly Professor of Arabic, Manchester University
A.R.	Anne Ross, M.A., Ph.D. (Celtic Studies and Archaeology)
E.G.R.	The Rev. E. Gordon Rupp, M.A., D.D. Professor of Ecclesiastical History, University of Cambridge
B.L.S.	B. L. Sansom, B.A. Lecturer in Social Anthropology, Manchester University
E.J.S.	Eric J. Sharpe, M.A., Th.D. Lecturer in Comparative Religion, Manchester University
N.S.	Ninian Smart, M.A., B.Phil. Professor of Religious Studies, University of Lancaster
D.H.S.	D. Howard Smith, B.A., B.D. Formerly Lecturer in Comparative Religion (Chinese Cults and Philosophies), Manchester University
D.L.S.	D. L. Snellgrove, M.A., Ph.D. Reader in Tibetan, School of Oriental and African Languages, University of London
F.B.W.	The Rev. F. B. Welbourn, M.A. Lecturer in the Study of Religion, University of Bristol; formerly Senior Lecturer in Religious Studies, Makerere University College, Uganda
D.W.	Douglas Woodruff, C.B.E., M.A. Formerly Editor of *The Tablet*
D.N. de L.Y.	The Rev. D. N. de L. Young, M.A. Lecturer in Comparative Religion (Buddhist Studies), Manchester University

PRONUNCIATION OF WORDS IN NON-EUROPEAN LANGUAGES

Comparative Religion involves the use of names and terms in many unfamiliar languages, which are often written in a non-Roman script. These words are transliterated into English with the use of diacritical marks and symbols to indicate their approximate pronunciation in English. Often the sounds concerned can be indicated only by a very elaborate phonetic apparatus. In view of the complexity of the matter, brief general guidance only can be given here.

In the *Dictionary* Pali and Sanskrit words are shown with diacritical marks when they appear as head-words to entries; thereafter they are often printed in a more popular form: e.g. the Hindu god Śiva is written as Shiva. The vowels in these two languages are as in German or Italian, except that the short *a* has the sound of *u* as in *but.* The consonants are generally pronounced as in English, with *g* always hard (as in *garden*), and *c* as the *ch* in *church*: *t* and *d* etc. are true dentals and should be pronounced with tongue against teeth; *ṭ* and *ḍ* etc. are pronounced with tongue against the hard palate. The aspirated letters, *th, ph,* etc., represent two distinct sounds as, e.g., the *th* and *ph* in *pothole* and *shepherd. Ṛ* is a short vowel, being pronounced as *ri* as in *rich. Ś* and *ṣ* are generally pronounced as *sh* in *ship.*

The pronunciation of Arabic is equally complicated, with many national variations from its classical form. The following points may be briefly noted. Consonants: *ḍ* is an emphatic *d*; *dh* as *th* in English *the*; *gh* is a strongly guttural *g; ḥ* is an emphatic smooth guttural *h*; *j* as in *John*; *kh* as *ch* in Scottish *loch*; *q* is guttural *k*; *sh* as in *ship*; *ṭ* is an emphatic *t*; *th* as *th* in *through*; *w* as in English. A glottal stop is indicated by '; a guttural sound with no English equivalent is shown as '. The long vowel *ā* is variously pronounced: e.g. as in *sand, dart* and *hall*; *ī*, as in *ee* in *meet*; *ū* as *oo* in *boot.* The diphthongs *ay*, as *i* in *tide*; *aw* as *ow* in *town.* It is to be noted that Arabic names, such as al-Ghazālī, are listed under appropriate initial letter. Thus al-Ghazālī appears under 'G' as -Ghazālī. As with Pali and Sanskrit words, the diacritical marks of Arabic words are shown in the head-words; in the articles they sometimes appear without this apparatus.

The Romanisation of Chinese and Japanese words is so complicated, and various systems have been used, that reference should be made to the sections on China and Japan in the *Handbook of Oriental History*, ed. C. H. Philips (Royal Historical Society, London, 1951), to which reference may be usefully made on the other eastern languages.

For Aztec names the following points may be noted. The *Tl* is similar to the Welsh *Ll* as in *Llangollen*; the *X* is a guttural like the Scottish *ch* in *loch*; but is usually softened to *sh. H* is not usually sounded; it serves to divide syllables. *J* is pronounced as *h*. The dipthongs *oa* and *ua* are like *wāh*; *uei* as *way*; *huit* sounds like *wit*; *ou* as the *o* in *Pole*. The accent falls on the penultimate syllable.

Ancient Egyptian and Sumerian words have been printed according to the generally accepted conventional forms, as has also been done with ancient Greek, Persian, Hittite and Etruscan words. In the article on Scandinavian religion the Old Norse þ has the value of *th* unvoiced; ð represents the *th* voiced. For a concise account of the difficulties attending the rendering of Tibetan scripts see D. Diringer, *The Alphabet* (1948) pp. 352ff.

ABBREVIATIONS

I GENERAL

Abp.	Archbishop
acc. to	according to
add.	addition
adj.	adjective
attr.	attribute(d)
anc.	ancient
Ar.	Arabic
b.	born
B.C.	Before Christian Era
Bhm.	Buddhism
Bp.	bishop
Buddh.	Buddhist(s)
C.	Central
c.	*circa*, about
C.E.	Christian Era
C. of E.	Church of England
cent.	century
Ch.	Church
ch.	chapter(s)
Chi.	Chinese
Chr.	Christian
cmp.	compare
comy.	commentary
d.	died
doc.	doctrine, doctrinal
E.	East, Eastern
eccles.	ecclesiastical
ed.	edited, editor
Eg.	Egyptian
Eng.	English
esp.	especially
estab.	establish(ed)
E.T.	English translation
ex	from, derived from
excl.	exclude(d), excluding
fig.	figure
gen.	general(ly)
gov.	government
grad.	gradual(ly)
Grk.	Greek
Heb.	Hebrew
hist.	history, historical
import.	important, importance
imposs.	impossible
incl.	include(d), including
indic.	indicate(s), indicating
intro.	introduce(d), introduction
J	Yahwist
Jap.	Japan, Japanese
Lat.	Latin
lit.	literally, literature
m.	million
Md.	Muḥammad
Mhy.	Mahāyāna
mil.	millennium
mod.	modern
N.	North, Northern
n.d.	no date
orig.	origin(s), originally
partic.	particular(ly)
passim	continually dealt with
phil.	philosophy, philosophical
pl.	plural
p.m.	*post-mortem*
prob.	probable, probably
poss.	possible (possibly)
publ.	published
Paleo.	Paleolithic
R.C.	Roman Catholic
ref.	refers, reference
rel.	related, relative
relig.	religion, religious

repr.	represent(ed) or reprint, acc. to context
S.	South, Southern
sing.	singular
Skt.	Sanskrit
s.v.	*sub voce*, under word (subject)
syn.	synonym(ous)
Thv.	Theravādin(s)
trad.	tradition(ally)
trans.	translation
univ.	universal(ly)
v. vv.	verse(s)
W.	West, Western
Zor.	Zoroaster, Zoroastrianism
→	cross reference
→→	cross reference to subjects named
‖	parallels

II BIBLIOGRAPHICAL

A.	*Al-Andalus*
Abbott, *Papyri*	N. Abbott, *Studies in Arabic Literary Papyri*, II, *Qur'anic Commentary and Tradition*, Chicago, 1967
Acts	*Acts of the Apostles*
A.E.C.W.	*Atlas of the Early Christian World*, by F. van der Meer and C. Mohrmann, E. T. London, 1958
Ae.R.T.B.	*Die ägyptische Religion in Texten und Bildern*, by G. Roeder, 4 Bände, Zürich/Stuttgart, 1959–61
A.J.S.L.	*American Journal of Semitic Languages*
Albright, *Y.G.C.*	Albright, W. F. *Yahweh and the Gods of Canaan*, London, 1968
Ali, *Qur'ān*	Maulana Muhammad Ali, *The Holy Qur'ān* (Arabic text, E.T., and comm.), 5th edn., Lahore, 1963
A.L.U.O.S.	*Annual of Leeds University Oriental Society*
A.N.	*Aguttara-Nikaya*
A.N.C.L.	*Ante-Nicene Christian Library*
A.N.E.T.	*Ancient Near Eastern Texts relating to the Old Testament*, ed. J. B. Pritchard, Princeton University Press, 2nd edn., 1955
A.O.T.S.	*Archaeology and Old Testament Study*, ed. D. Winton Thomas (1967)
Arberry,	
Doctrine	A. J. Arberry, *The Doctrine of the Sufis* (1935)
Koran	*The Koran interpreted*, 2 vols. (1955)
Revelation	*Revelation and Reason in Islam* (1957)
A.S.E.	*Annales du Service de l'Égypte*, Le Caire
A.V.	Authorised Version of Bible
B.A.	*The Biblical Archaeologist*, Cambridge, Mass.
B.A.S.O.R.	*Bulletin of the American Schools of Oriental Research*
B.C.	*The Beginnings of Christianity*, ed. F. J. Foakes Jackson and Kirsopp Lake, 5 vols., London, 1920–33
Bell,	
Introduction	R. Bell, *Introduction to the Qur'ān* (1953)
Qur'an	*The Qur'ān, trans. with critical rearrangement of the surahs*, 2 vols., 1937–9
Bilderatlas	*Bilderatlas zur Religionsgeschichte*, hrg. H. Haas, Leipzig/Erlangen, 1924–30
B.J.R.L.	*Bulletin of the John Rylands Library*, Manchester
Blachère, *Coran*	R. Blackère, *Le Coran*, 2 vols., French trans. chronologically arranged, with notes (1949–50)
	Le Coran (1957)—normal order of Suras, shorter notes
B.M.F.E.A.	*Bulletin of Museum of Far Eastern Antiquities*, Stockholm

Brandon, *C.L.*	Brandon, S. G. F. *Creation Legends of the Ancient Near East*, London, 1963
Brandon, *M.D.*	Brandon, S. G. F. *Man and his Destiny in the Great Religions*, Manchester University Press, 1962
R.A.H.	*Religion in Ancient History*, New York 1969
Brenk, *W-G*	Brenk, Beat *Tradition u. Neuerung in der christlichen Kunst des ersten Jahrtausends: Studien 3. Geschichte des Weltgerichtsbildes*, (Wiener Byzantische studien, Band III), Wien, 1966.
Broadhurst, *Ibn Jubayr*	R. J. C. Broadhurst, *The Travels of Ibn Jubayr*, E. T. (1952)
Bruce, *N.T.H.*	Bruce, F. F. *New Testament History* (1969)
B.S.O.A.S.	*Bulletin of the School of Oriental and African Studies*, London
Burton, *Pilgrimage*	Sir Richard F. Burton, *Personal Narrative of a Pilgrimage*, 2 vols. (1913)
C.A.H.	*Cambridge Ancient History*
C.H.B.	*The Cambridge History of the Bible* (from 1963)
Canaan, *Aberglaube*	T. Canaan, *Aberglaube u. Volksmedizin im Lande der Bibel* (Hamburg, 1914)
C.C.	*The Crucible of Christianity*, ed. A. Toynbee (1969)
C.E.	*The Catholic Encyclopedia* (1907–22)
I, II *Chron.*	1st and 2nd *Books of Chronicles*
C.H.	*Corpus Hermeticum*
C.H.I.	*Cambridge History of Iran*
Charles, *A.P.*	*The Apocrypha and Pseudepigrapha of the Old Testament*, ed. R. H. Charles, 2 vols., 1913
Charnay, *Normes*	J.-P. Charnay (ed.) *Normes et valeurs dans l'Islam contemporain* (1966)
Clemen, *P.R.*	Clemen, C. *Die phönikische Religion nach Philo von Byblos* (Leipzig, 1939)
C.M.H.	*Cambridge Mediaeval History*
Cor. I, II	*St. Paul's Epistle to the Corinthians*, Books I or II
Coulson, *Law*	N. J. Coulson, *A Hist. of Islamic Law* (Edinburgh, 1964)
Cragg, *Counsels*	K. Cragg, *Counsels in Contemporary Islam* (1965)
Dome	*The Dome and the Rock* (1964)
Minaret	*The Call of the Minaret* (1956)
C.R.	*Classical Review*
C.T.	*The Egyptian Coffin Texts*, ed. A. de Buck, vols. I-VII, Chicago University Press, 1935–61
Cumont, *R.O.*[4]	Cumont, Fr. *Les religions orientales de la paganisme romain*, 4th edn., Paris, 1929
Dan.	*Daniel*
D.C.C.	*The Oxford Dictionary of the Christian Church* ed. F. L. Cross, London, 1958
De Boer, *Philosophy*	T. de Boer, *The Hist. of Philosophy in Islam* (1903)
Deut.	*Deuteronomy*
Dhorme, *R.B.A.*	Dhorme, E. *Les religions de Babylonie et d'Assyrie*, Paris, 1945
D.I.	*Der Islam*
Dickson, *Arab of Desert*	H. R. P. Dickson, *The Arab of the Desert* (1949)
D.H.I.	*Dictionary of the History of Ideas*, ed. P. P. Wiener, New York
D.N.	*Digha-Nikaya*
Donaldson,	
Ethics	D. M. Donaldson, *Studies in Muslim Ethics* (1953)
Shi'ite	*The Shi'ite Religion* (1933)
Doutté, *Magie*	E. G. Doutté, *Magie et religion dans l'Afrique du nord* (Algiers, 1909)

D.P.P.N.	*Dictionary of Pali Proper Names*
D.T.C.	*Dictionnaire de Théologie Catholique*, ed. A. Vacant *et alii*, 15 vols. 1903–50
D.T.Z.	*The Dawn and Twilight of Zoroastrianism*, by R. C. Zaehner, London, 1961
Dupont-Sommer, *E.E.*	Dupont-Sommer, A. *Les écrits esséniens découverts près de la Mer Morte*, Paris, 1959
Dussaud, *Les religions*	R. Dussaud, *Les religions des Hittites et des Hourrites, des Phéniciens et des Syriens* (coll: Mana), Paris, 1945
E.	Elohist (writer)
Ebeling, *T.L.*	Ebeling, E., *Tod und Leben nach den Vorstellungen der Babylonier*, Band I, Berlin/Leipzig, 1931
E.B.	*Encyclopaedia Britannica*
E.I.	*Encyclopaedia of Islam*, 4 vols., and Supplement, Leiden/London, 1913–38
E.I.^{2}	*Encyclopaedia of Islam*, new edn. in progress Leiden/London, from 1954
E.J.R.	*Encyclopedia of the Jewish Religion*, ed. R. J. Zwi Werblowsky and D. Wigoder, London, 1965.
Eliade, *F-S.*	*Myths and Symbols: Studies in Honor of M. Eliade*, ed. J. M. Kitagawa and C. H. Long (Chicago Univ. Press, 1969)
Ep. Heb.	*Epistle to the Hebrews*
E.R.E.	*Encyclopaedia of Religion and Ethics*, ed. J. Hastings, 12 vols. and Index vol., Edinburgh, 1908–26
Ex.	*Exodus*
Fyzee, *Creed*	A. A. A. Fyzee, *A Shi'ite Creed* (1942)
G.A.L.	C. Brockelmann, *Geschichte der arabischen Literatur*, 2 vols., new edn., Leiden, 1943–9. Supplement 3 vols. (1937–42), abbrev. S = Supplement
Gaudefroy-Demombynes,	
Institutions	M. Gaudefroy-Demombynes, *Muslim Institutions*, E.T. (1950)
Mahomet	*Mahomet* (Paris, 1957)
G.B.	*The Golden Bough*, by J. G. Frazer, 12 vols., London
G.C.S.	*Die griechischen christlichen Schriftsteller der ersten drei Jahrhunderte*
G.D.E.T.^{2}	H. Stephan/M. Schmidt, *Geschichte d. deutschen evangelischen Theologie*, 2. Aufl., Berlin, 1965
Gen.	*Genesis*
Goldziher, *M.S.*	I. Goldziher, *Muhammedanische Studien*, 2 vols. (Halle 1888–90). An E.T. is in process of publication by C. R. Barber and S. M. Stern
Grabar, *B.C.A.*	Grabar, A. *The Beginnings of Christian Art*, E.T. (1967)
Gressmann, *O.R.*	Gressmann, H. *Die orientalischen Religionen im hellenistisch-römischen Zeitalter*, Berlin/Leipzig, 1930
Guillaume, *Life*	A. Guillaume, *The Life of Muhammad*, trans. of Ibn Isḥāq's *Sīrat Rasūl Allāh* (Oxford, 1955)
Traditions	*The Traditions of Islam* (1924)
Hamīdullah, M. *Prophète*	*Le Prophète de l'Islam*, 2 vols., Paris, 1959
Harnack, *H.D.*	Harnack, A., *History of Dogma*, 7 vols., E.T., repr. of 3rd edn., New York, 1961
Harrison, *Prolegomena*	J. Harrison, *Prolegomena to the Study of Greek Religions*, 3rd edn., New York, 1955
H.B.	*Hinduism and Buddhism*, 3 vols., by Sir C. Eliot (1921, repr. 1954)
H.D.B.^{2}	*Dictionary of the Bible*, ed. J. Hastings, 2nd edn., 1963
H.G.R.	*Histoire générale des religions*, ed. M. Gorce et R. Mortier, 5 tomes, Paris, 1947–52
Hitti, *History*	P. K. Hitti, *Hist. of the Arabs* (4th rev. edn., 1949)
Hourani, *Averroes*	G. F. Hourani, *Averroes on the Harmony of Religion and Philosophy*, E.T. (1961)

Hourani, *Thought*	A. Hourani, *Arabic Thought in the Liberal Age*, 1798–1939 (1962)
H.R.	*History of Religions*, Chicago University Press
H.Th.R.	*Harvard Theological Review*
Hughes	T. P. Hughes, *A Dictionary of Islam* (1885, frequent repr. to 1964)
I.A.A.M.	*The Intellectual Adventure of Ancient Man*, by H. and H. A. Frankfort, J. A. Wilson, T. Jacobson and W. A. Irwin, Chicago University Press, 1946
Ibn Khallikan	*Ibn Khallikan's Biographical Dictionary*, E.T. Baron MacGuckin de Slane, 4 vols., Paris (1843–71)
I.C.	*Islamic Culture*, Hyderabad
I.E.J.	*Israel Exploration Journal* (Jerusalem)
I.I.	*Index Islamicus 1906–55*, by J. D. Pearson (1958), *Supplement*, *1956–60* (1962); *Second Supplement*, *1961–65* (1968)
I.L.	*Islamic Literature*, Lahore
I.L.N.	*Illustrated London News*
I.Q.	*The Islamic Quarterly*, London
I.R.	*The Islamic Review*, Woking
Is.	*Isaiah*
I.S.	*Islamic Studies*, Karachi
Ivanow, *Creed*	W. Ivanow, *A Creed of the Fatimids* (Bombay, 1936)
Guide	*A Guide to Ismā'īlī Literature* (London, 1933)
J.A.	*Journal Asiatique*
J.A.O.S.	*Journal of American Oriental Society*
Jastrow, *Aspects*	M. Jastrow, *Some Aspects of Religious Belief and Practice in Babylonia and Assyria*, New York, 1911
J.B.L.	*Journal of Biblical Literature*, Philadelphia (Penn.)
J.B.R.A.S.	*Journal of the Bombay Branch of the Royal Asiatic Society*
J.E.	*Jewish Encyclopedia* (1901–06)
J.E.A.	*Journal of Egyptian Archaeology*, London
J.E.H.	*Journal of Ecclesiastical History*
Jeffery, *Materials*	A. Jeffery, *Materials for the Hist. of the Text of the Qur'ān* (Leiden, 1937)
Vocabulary	*The Foreign Vocabulary of the Qur'ān* (Baroda, 1938)
J.f.A.C.	*Jahrbuch für Antike und Christentum*, Münster
Jn.	*Gospel acc. to St. John*
J.N.E.S.	*Journal of Near Eastern Studies*, University of Chicago Press
Jones, *Mosque*	Jones, Bevan, L. *The People of the Mosque* (London, 1932)
J.R.A.S.	*Journal of the Royal Asiatic Society of Great Britain*
J.S.S.	*Journal of Semitic Studies*, Manchester University Press
J.T.S.	*Journal of Theological Studies*
Kamal, *Sacred Journey*	Ahmed Kamal, *The Sacred Journey* (1964)
Kautzsch, *A.P.*	*Die Apokryphen und Pseudepigraphen des Alten Testaments*, hrg. E. Kautzsch, 2 vols., Tübingen, 1900
Kees, *T.*[2]	*Totenglauben und Jenseitsvorstellungen der alten Aegypter*, 2. Aufl., Berlin, 1956
Kgs. I, II	*Kings*, Book I, or II
Kidd, *Docs.*	Kidd, E. J., *Documents Illustrative of the Hist. of the Church*, 2 vols., London, 1932–3
K.N.	*Khuddaka-Nikaya*
Kleine Pauly	*Der Kleine Pauly Lexikon der Antike*, Stuttgart (from 1962)
Lammens, *L'Islam*	H. Lammens, *L'Islam* (Beyrouth, 1926)

Lane, *Egyptians*	E. W. Lane, *The Manners and Customs of the Modern Egyptians* (Everyman Library edn.)
Lexicon	*An Arabic-English Lexicon,* 8 vols., last ed. S. Lane-Poole, London, 1863–93
Lane-Poole, *Dynasties*	S. Lane-Poole, *Muhammadan Dynasties* (Westminster, 1894)
Lev.	*Leviticus*
Levy, *Social Structure*	R. Levy, *The Social Structure of Islam* (1957)
Lk.	*Gospel acc. to St. Luke*
L.R-G	*Lehrbuch der Religionsgeschichte* (Chantepie de la Saussaye, hrg. A. Bertholet u. Edv. Lehmann), 4 Aufl., 2 Bände, Tübingen, 1925
LXX	Septuagint
Macdonald,	
Aspects	D. B. Macdonald, *Aspects of Islam* (New York, 1911)
Attitude	*The Religious Attitude and Life in Islam* (Chicago, 1909)
Theology	*Development of Muslim Theology* (New York, 1926)
Macdonald, *Eschatology*	J. Macdonald, Trans. of a collection of traditions on eschatology, in *I.S.*, III–V, 6 parts (1964–66)
Massignon, *Hallaj*	L. Massignon, *La passion . . . d'al-Hallaj,* 2 vols. (Paris, 1922)
Masson, *Coran*	D. Masson, *Le Coran* (French trans. and notes), Paris, 1967
M.A.W.	*Mythologies of the Ancient World,* ed. S. N. Kramer, New York, 1961
Mez, *Renaissance*	A. Mez, *The Renaissance of Islam,* E.T. (1937)
Miller, *Bāb*	W. McE. Miller, *al-Bâbu 'l-Ḥâdî 'Ashar* (E.T. of treatise on principles of Shi'ite theology by al-Hillī), London, 1928, repr. 1958
Mishkāt	Baghawī, *Mishkāt al-maṣābīḥ* (a collection of Muslim traditions), E.T., with explanatory notes by J. Robson, 4 vols., Lahore, 1963–5 (revision by al-Tibrīzī)
Mk.	*Gospel acc. to St. Mark*
M.N.	*Majjhima-Nikaya*
Mt.	*Gospel acc. to St. Matthew*
Muir, *Caliphate*	Sir Wm. Muir, *The Caliphate: rise, decline and fall,* ed. T. H. Weir (1915)
Life	*The Life of Mohammad,* ed. T. H. Weir (1912)
M.W.	*The Muslim World,* Hartford, Conn.
N.C.M.H.	*New Cambridge Modern History*
Nicholson,	
L.H.A.	R. A. Nicholson, *Literary Hist. of the Arabs,* 2nd edn. (1930)
Mystics	R. A. Nicholson, *The Mystics of Islam* (repr. 1963)
Studies	*Studies in Islamic Mysticism* (1921)
Nöldeke, *Geschichte*[2]	Th. Nöldeke, *Geschichte des Korans,* 2nd edn. Schwally *et alii,* 3 vols. (Leipzig, 1909–38)
N.T.	New Testament
N.T.S.	*New Testament Studies,* Cambridge University Press
Nu.	*Numbers*
Numen	*Numen* (International Review of the History of Religions), Leiden, from 1954
O.C.D.	*The Oxford Classical Dictionary,* Oxford, 1949
Oesterley-Box, *L.R.M.J.*	Oesterley, W. O. E. and Box, C. H., *A Short Survey of the Literature of Rabbinical and Mediaeval Judaism,* London, 1920
O'Leary, *Arabia*	De Lacy O'Leary, *Arabia before Muhammad* (1927)
O.T.	Old Testament
P	Priestley (writer)
Pareja	F. M. Pareja *et alii, Islamologie* (Beyrouth, 1957–63)

Paret, *Koran*	R. Paret, *Der Koran*, German trans. (Stuttgart, 1963–6)
Parrinder, *Jesus*	G. Parrinder, *Jesus in the Qur'ān* (1965)
P.C.^{2}	*Peake's Commentary on the Bible*, 2nd edn., 1962
P.G.	*Patrologia Graeca*, ed. J. Migne
P.L.	*Patrologia Latina*, ed. J. Migne
P.M.H.R.	*Problèmes et méthodes d'histoire des religions. Mélanges*, publ. par la Section des Sciences religieuses à l'occasion du centaire de l'École pratique des Hautes Études (Paris, 1968).
P.R.E.^{3}	*Realencyklopädie für protestantische Theologie u. Kirche*, bgt. J. J. Herzog; 3rd edn. A. Hauck, 24 vols. 1898–1913
Ps	*Psalms*
P.T.	*Pyramid Texts*
P.T.S.	*Pali Text Society*
P.W.	Pauly, A., Wissowa, G., Kroll, W. *Real-Encyclopädie d. klassischen Altertumswissenschaft*
Querry	A. Querry, *Droit musulmane*, 2 vols., Paris, 1871–2
Qur	*Qur'ān*
R.A.C.	*Reallexikon für Antike und Christentum*, hrg. T. Klauser, Stuttgart (from 1950)
R.Ae.R-G	*Reallexikon der ägyptischen Religionsgeschichte*, by H. Bonnet, Berlin, 1952
Rahman, *Islam*	Fazlur Rahman, *Islam* (1966)
R.A.P.H.	*Recherches d'archéologie, de philologie et d'histoire*, Le Caire
Rev.	*Revelation of St. John*
R.G.G.^{3}	*Die Religion in Geschichte und Gegenwart*, 3. Aufl., hrg. K. Galling, Bände I–VI, 1957–62, Tübingen
R.-G.L.	*Religionsgeschichtliches Lesebuch*, hrg. A. Bertholet, 1908, 2. Aufl., 1926–9
R.H.P.R.	*Revue d'histoire et de philosophie religieuse*, Strasbourg
R.H.R.	*Revue de l'histoire des religions*, Paris
R.M.E.	*Religion in the Middle East*, ed. A. J. Arberry, 2 vols., Cambridge, 1969
Robson, *Introduction*	J. Robson (ed.), *An Introduction to the Science of Tradition*, E.T., with notes, of Ḥākims *Madkhal* (London, 1953)
Rom.	*St. Paul's Epistle to the Romans*
Rosenthal, *Ibn Khaldun*	*Ibn Khaldun, The Muqaddimah* (*an Intro. to History*), E.T. by F. Rosenthal, 3 vols. (1958)
Rosenthal, *Political Thought*	E. I. J. Rosenthal, *Political Thought in Medieval Islam* (1958)
R.Q.	*Revue de Qumran*, Paris
R.S.V.	American Revised Standard Version of the Bible
Rutter, *Holy Cities*	E. Rutter, *The Holy Cities of Arabia*, 2 vols. (1928)
R.V.	Revised Version of the Bible
Sale, *Qurán*	E. M. Wherry, *A Comprehensive Commentary on the Qurán; comprising Sale's trans. and preliminary discourse*, 4 vols., London, 1896
I, II Sam	*Samuel*, Books I or II
S.B.E.	*Sacred Books of the East*
Schacht, *Jurisprudence*	J. Schacht. *The Origins of Muhammadan Jurisprudence* (1950)
Schürer, *G.J.V.*	*Geschichte des jüdischen Volkes im Zeitalter Jesu Christi*, by E. Schürer, 3 Bände, Leipzig, 1898–1901
Seale, *Theology*	M. S. Seale, *Muslim Theology* (1964)
S.I.	*Studia Islamica*
Siddiqi, *Hadith*	M. A. Siddiqi, *Hadith Literature* (Calcutta, 1961)
S.L.S.	*Studies in the Lankavatara Sutra*, by D. T. Suzuki

Smith, *Early Mysticism*	Margaret Smith, *Studies in Early Mysticism in the Near and Middle East* (1931)
Ghazali	*Al-Ghazālī, the Mystic* (1944)
Smith, *Modern History*	W. C. Smith, *Islam in Modern History* (Princeton, 1957)
S.N.	*Saṁyutta-Nikaya*
S.O.	*Sources orientales.* A series comprising volumes, variously entitled and by various contributors from 1959, Paris
Stanton, *Teaching*	Stanton, H.U., Weitbrecht, *The Teaching of the Qur'ān*, London/New York, 1919
Sweetman, *I.C.T.*	J. W. Sweetman, *Islam and Christian Theology*, 2 parts, 2 vols. each; numbered here as vols. I to IV (1945–67)
Syn.	Synoptic Gospels
T.G.U.O.S.	*Transactions of Glasgow University Oriental Society*
Th. Wb.	*Theologische Wörterbuch zum Neuen Testament*, begr. V. G. Kittel, hg. V.G. Friedrich, from 1933
Trimingham,	
Ethiopa	J. S. Trimingham, *Islam in Ethiopia* (1952, repr. 1965)
History	*Hist. of Islam in W. Africa* (1962)
Sudan	*Islam in the Sudan* (1949, 1965)
West Africa	*Islam in West Africa* (1959)
Tritton, *Non-Muslims*	A. S. Tritton, *The Caliphs and their Non-Muslim Subjects* (1930)
Turchi, *Fontes*	Turchi, N. *Fontes Historiae Mysteriorum Aevi Hellenistici*, Roma, 1923
Van den Bergh, *Tahāfut*	S. Van den Bergh, *Averroes*, '*Tahāfut al-tahafut*', E.T., 2 vols. (1954)
Watt,	
Acquisition	W. M. Watt, 'The Origin of the Islamic Doctrine of Acquisition', in *J.R.A.S.* (1943), pp. 234ff.
Free Will	*Free Will and Predestination in Early Islam* (1948)
Ghazali	*Faith and Practice of al-Ghazālī* (1953)
Mecca	*Muhammad at Mecca* (1953)
Medina	*Muhammad at Medina* (1956)
Philosophy	*Islamic Philosophy and Theology* (1962)
Wellhausen, *Reste*	J. Wellhausen, *Reste arabischen Heidentums*, 2nd edn. (Berlin/Leipzig, 1927)
Wensinck,	
Creed	J. Wensinck, *The Muslim Creed* (1932)
Handbook	*A Handbook of Early Muhammadan Tradition* (1927)
W.I.	*Die Welt des Islams*
Widengren, *R-P.*	Geo Widengren, *Religionsphänomenologie*, German trans. (1969) of *Religionens värld*
Z.A.	*Zeitschrift für Assyriologie u. verwandte Gebiete*
Z.A.W.	*Zeitschrift für die alttestamentliche Wissenschaft*
Z.Ae.S.A.	*Zeitschrift für ägyptische Sprache und Altertumskunde*
Z.D.M.G.	*Zeitschrift der deutschen morgenländischen Gessellschaft*
Zimmer, *M.S.*	Zimmer, H. *Myths, and Symbols in Indian Art and Civilization*, New York (ed. 1962)
Z.N.T.W.	*Zeitschrift für die neutestamentliche Wissenschaft u. die Kunde der älteren Kirche*

A

A and Ω (alpha and omega) First and last letters of Grk. alphabet, used in Rev. 1:8, 21:6, 22:13 to denote completeness and eternity of God, manifest in → Jesus Christ. Symbol was much used later in Chr. art and inscriptions. Similar ideas of deity as comprehending whole Time-process occur in anc. Egypt., Grk., and Indian relig. S.G.F.B.

E.R.E., I, *s.v.; R.A.C.*, I, *s.v.;* S. G. F. Brandon, *History, Time and Deity* (1965), pp. 1ff., 31ff.

Aaron Brother of → Moses and a → Levite acc. to Heb. trad. (Ex. 4:14); name poss. of Egypt. orig. as was Moses. A. is a problematic figure in Heb. trad.: he and his descendants are appointed priests by → Yahweh (Ex. 28 and 29; Num. 8 and 18), he performs miracles (Ex. 7:9ff.), but leads worship of golden calf (Ex. 32:1–6), and opposes Moses (Num. 12); his exclusive priesthood is challenged (Num. 16). Scholars see in this conflict of trad. evidence of opposition to exclusive claims of an Aaronic dynasty to highpriesthood, perhaps at expense of the kingship repr. by Moses. → Qumran lit. ref. to two Messiahs, of 'Aaron' and 'Israel' respectively: the former was to be the eschatological anointed highpriest. As mediator between God and man acc. to → Torah, A. was seen as prototype of Christ in Ep. Heb. S.G.F.B.

F. S. North, 'A's Rise in Prestige' (*Z.A.W.* 66, 1954); *R.G.G.*[3], I, *s.v.*; K. G. Kuhn, *Scrolls and N.T.*, ed. K. Stendahl (1958), pp. 54–64.

Aaronic blessing Threefold, rhythmically constructed blessing, used in Jew. and Chr. worship, *ex.* Num. 6:24–6. Rarely used in Middle Ages, it was generally adopted by Prot. Reformers. S.G.F.B.

Abaddon Lit. 'destruction'. Used in Job 26:6; Prov. 15:11 as equivalent of → Sheol. In Rev. 9:11 it is name of angel of → Abyss, whose Grk. name was → Apollyon ('Destroyer'). S.G.F.B.

Ab, 9th day of Jew. fast day commemorating two destructions of Jerusalem → Temple, in 586–7 BC and CE 70. Occurs about beginning of August. S.G.F.B.

Abba → Aramaic for 'father'; acc. to Mk. 14:36, Rom. 8:15, used as current expression for God. S.G.F.B.

'Abbās Son of → 'Abd al-Muṭṭalib, and uncle of → Muḥammad, was a late convert to Islam, taking Md.'s side during march to Mecca in 8/630. He had fought against him at → Badr. The 'Abbasid dynasty traced its descent to him, so he is spoken of highly by 'Abbasid historians. He had been a wealthy merchant in Mecca; later he settled in Medina, but held no administrative post. d. 30/653. J.R.

E.I.[2], I, pp. 8f; Watt, *Mecca*, index; Watt, *Medina*, index.

'Abbāsids (132/750—656/1258), the caliphate with longest nominal rule. The family were descended from → al-'Abbās, uncle of → Muḥammad, and claimed inherent right to office. The 'Alids made similar claim, as → 'Alī was Md.'s cousin. The 'A. propaganda was conducted in name of Md.'s family, which made the 'Alids think they were being supported. The 'A. thus used their help; but when the → Umayyads were defeated, Abu 'l-'Abbās was appointed Caliph with title al-Saffāḥ. In 136/754 he was succeeded by al-Manṣūr, founder of Baghdad, which became centre of a highly developed culture. Scholars here and elsewhere trans. many Greek books into Arabic, a work which had already begun in Umayyad times. These trans. had great influence on Muslim theology and philosophy, in addition to making contributions to medicine and the sciences. The greatest cultural develop. took place in time of Caliphs Hārūn al-Rashīd (170/786—193/809) and al-Ma'mūn (198/813—218/833). After al-Mutawakkil (232/847—247/861), the Caliphate came more and more under power of Turkish and Buwayhid rulers, so that its rule was a mere shadow. The 'A. realm never had extended so widely as the Umayyad. Various rulers in the W set up independent states, and the same applied in the E. The only difference was that the East. rulers liked to receive formal authorisation from Caliph. He thus became a mere figurehead, the real rule being divided among different kingdoms. Hūlāgū finally brought this Caliphate to an end. J.R.

E.I.[2], I, pp. 15–23; Muir, *Caliphate*, index; Hitti, *History*, index; Levy, *Social Structure*, index.

Abbess Female head of community of nuns, corresponds to → Abbott. Title (Lat. *abbatissa*) current from 514. Acc. to Council of → Trent, a nun must be at least 40 yrs. old and 8 yrs. professed to qualify for election. Office held for life, except in → Franciscan order. A. is entitled to ring, staff and abbatial cross. Some medieval A.s had great powers: e.g. hearing confessions, attending eccles. councils, presiding over communities of monks (gen. in double monasteries in Saxon England). Such extraordinary powers were ended by Council of Trent. Buddhist nuns have never enjoyed similar eminence (→ Monasticism, Buddhist). S.G.F.B.

R.A.C., I (1950), 126–8 ('Aebtissin'); *D.C.C.*, *s.v.*: J. Godfrey, *Church in Anglo-Saxon England* (1962), pp. 157–61 (*E.R.E.*, VIII, p. 779a).

Abbot Title *ex.* Grk. *abbas* = Syriac *Abba*, meaning 'father', given to older, more experienced Chr. ascetic (from 4th cent.), who guided others seeking to live ascetical life (→ Asceticism) in Egypt. desert. A.s became important figures in → monasticism and eccl. government in Middle Ages. Acc. to Rule of → St. Benedict, A. was father and head of his monastery, with wide powers over monks. Method of appointment of A.s varied: some were elected by monks concerned, more often by high eccl. or secular authorities. The filling of a vacant abbacy was frequent occasion of bitter conflict between various rival authorites. A.'s insignia of office are same as → bishop's: mitre, crozier, ring, pectoral cross. Powers of A.s outside their monasteries varied greatly in Middle Ages, and was often disputed by bishops and civil authorities; some A.s sat in Eng. Parliament. A.s were originally laymen, but later were gen. in priests' orders: *abbates nullius* (*sc.* dioecesis) had certain episcopal powers, e.g. to confirm and ordain to minor orders → Hierarchy (Christian). It is difficult to compare Chr. A. with heads of Buddhist monasteries, owing to the essentially hierarchical structure of Chr. → Church. The Bud. A. naturally has some disciplinary powers, but gen. the → Sangha is a democratic community, not a monarchically ruled organisation as is Chr. monastery (→ Monasticism (Buddhist)). S.G.F.B.

R.A.C., I, 52–5; *E.R.E.*, I, *s.v.*; *D.C.C.*, *s.v.*; D. Knowles, *The Monastic Order in England* (1950), pp. 395–410.

Abbot of Unreason Scottish title for burlesque figure known elsewhere as Lord of Misrule. Many medieval examples are known of such mimic dignitaries, having mimic trappings and court of an → abbot. A. of U. was monastic counterpart of Boy Bishop. These figures were connected with Feast of Fools, celebrated during → Christmas season. This licensed burlesquing of high eccl. offices prob. derived from Roman → *Saturnalia*, and may reflect policy of early Church to 'Christianise' pagan customs. S.G.F.B.

E.R.E., I, *s.v.;* G. G. Coulton, *Medieval Panorama* (1938), pp. 606–7.

'Abd al-Jabbār on Christianity considerable interest was caused in 1966 by the publication by S. Pines of an art. entitled 'The Jewish Christians of the Early Centuries of Christianity acc. to a New Source' (*Israel Academy of Sciences and Humanities Proceedings*, II). Pines argued that an Arabic work '*The Establishment of Proofs for the Prophethood of Our Master Mohammed*', by 10th cent. C/E → Mu'tazilite theologian 'Abd al-Jabbār, incorporated a trans. of a Jew. Christian treatise of the 5th-6th cent. CE. Acc. to Pines, this work affords valuable evidence of → Jew. Christian teaching about Jesus and Paul. This interpretation has been opposed by S. M. Stern (*J.T.S.*, XVIII (1967), XIX (1968)), who maintains that the document on which 'Abd al-Jabbār drew was in fact a refutation of Christianity by the 9th cent. 'Alī b. Rabban al-Ṭabarī, a → Nestorian Christian converted to Islam. This specialist debate will doubtless continue; it is significant, however, that, whatever the origin of the source concerned, it emphasises the essential Jewishness of Jesus and the first Christians and Paul's part in transforming the movement into a Gentile (Roman) relig. (→ Christians (*Naṣārā*)). S.G.F.B.

'Abdallāh b. al-'Abbās Born 3 years before the → Hijra and died *c.* 68/687–8. Took part in some military expeditions and for a time was → 'Ali's governor of Basra. He later changed his allegiance to Mu'āwiya (→ Umayyads) and settled down to scholarly pursuits in the Ḥijāz. He is credited with being one of earliest authorities on Qur. interpretation, → Ḥadīth, canon law, pre-Islamic hist. and poetry. Because of his learning, he is called *Ḥibr al-umma* (doctor of the community). J.R.

*E.I.*², I, pp. 40f; *G.A.L.*, I, p. 203; S.I., p. 331; Guillaume, *Life*, index. Schacht, *Jurisprudence*, pp. 249ff; Abbot (N.), *Papyri*, index; Robson, *Introduction*, index.

'Abdallāh b. 'Umar b. al-Khaṭṭāb (d. 73/693) is said to have been prevented by → Muḥammad from taking part in battle of → Uḥud, because he was only fourteen, but to have been allowed to fight the following year at battle of the Trench. Though he took part in a number of battles, he held aloof from the civil strife which arose, and refused to accept any public office. He is quoted as authority for many traditions, his client Nāfi' being a transmitter of his trads. to → Mālik b. Anas. J.R.

Guillaume, *Life*, index; *E.I.*², I, pp. 53f; Ibn Khallikān, I, pp. 567f; III, p. 521; Mas'ūdī, *Murūj* (text and French trans., Paris, 1851–77); Robson, 'Non-resistance,' *T.G.U.O.S.* ix (1941), pp. 5–7; N. Abbott, *Papyri*, index.

'Abd al-Muṭṭalib b. Hāshim Paternal grandfather of → Muḥammad. Hāshim had married Salmā bint 'Amr of the Banī al-Najjār, rel. to Khazraj in Yathrib (Medina), and she and her son and daugher stayed there. After Hāshim died, his brother al-Muṭṭalib brought his nephew 'A. al-M. to Mecca. Muslim writers say he got this name because he was mistaken for a slave (*'abd*) of al-Muṭṭalib. Is said to have become leading man in Mecca and to have been such when → Abraha made his ill-fated expedition from Ṣan'ā' to destroy the → ka'ba. He is also said to have cleared the well → Zamzam. When Md.'s mother died he took Md., then six years old, under his care. Two years later he died. J.R.

*E.I.*², I, p. 80; Watt, *Mecca*, index; Guillaume, *Life*, pp. 45, 62–4.

'Abd al-Qādir al-Jīlānī (Jīlī) (470/1077—561/1166), a Ḥanbalite theologian who adopted → Sufism, and a noted preacher. To him is traced the widely-spread Qādiriyya order (→ Sufi Orders). His tomb at Baghdad is visited by many seeking blessing of his mediation. J.R.

*E.I.*², I, pp. 69f.; *G.A.L.*, I, pp. 560; *S.I.*, pp. 777f.; Pareja, pp. 774, 780, 804, 810. *E.R.E.*, I, pp. 10–2.

Abel Acc. to Gen. 4:2, son of Adam and Eve, A. was a pastoralist, his brother Cain an agriculturalist. The account of killing of A. by Cain prob. combines two aetiological (→ Aetiology) motives: to explain first murder; to show pastoral life is preferred by → Yahweh. S.G.F.B.

S. G. F. Brandon, *C.L.*, p. 141.

Abelard, Peter (1079–1142) More accurate form of name is Abailard. Theologian and philosopher, whose tragic romance with Heloïse has given him greater human appeal than that of other medieval Schoolmen (→ Scholasticism). His contribution to medieval theological thought is notable for its fresh vigour and independence. His *Sic et Non* was collection of apparently contradictory statements from Scripture and Fathers. His philosophy, opposed to both Realism and Nominalism, was known as Conceptualism, and maintained that universals acquired reality only by being predicated of things. His intellectual boldness aroused opposition of → St. Bernard, and many of his views were condemned as unorthodox. A. exercised great influence in Paris; Arnold of Brescia and John of Salisbury were among his pupils. S.G.F.B.

J. G. Sikes, *Peter Abélard* (1932); E. Gilson, *Hèloïse et Abélard* (1938); G. Leff, *Medieval Thought* (1958).

Abercius, Inscription of Grk. epitaph apparently placed over his future tomb by Abercius Marcellus, Bp. of Hieropolis, in Phrygia Salutaris (d. *c.* 200), now in Lateran Museum. Text records visits to Rome and Nisibis, and refers, in symbols of fish, wine and bread, to widespread celebration of → Eucharist. Earlier attempts to interpret Inscr. as referring to pagan → mystery relig. now abandoned. S.G.F.B.

J. B. Lightfoot, *The Apostolic Fathers* (1889), II, i. pp. 492–501; J. Quasten, *Monumenta Eucharistica et Liturgica Vetustissima* (1935), I, pp. 21–4; *R.A.C.*, I (1950), 12–7; B. J. Kidd, *Documents*, I, 64.

Abgar, Legend of Acc. to 3rd cent. legend, → Jesus wrote to Abgar V, king of Edessa (4 BC–CE 50), in reply to A.'s request for healing. → Eusebius gives letter in *Eccl. Hist.* I. xiii. A later version of legend tells that Jesus also sent his portrait, miraculously imprinted on canvas. Legend was prob. inspired by conversion of Abgar IX (179–214). S.G.F.B.

D.C.C., *s.v.;* M. R. James, *Apocryphal New Test.* (1926), pp. 476–7.

Abhidhamma (Pali); (Skt.) **Abhidharma** Thematic arrangement and logical development of Buddha's teaching. Whereas the doc. of Buddha contained in → *Sutta-Pitaka* is discursive (in form of parables, anecdotes, metaphors, etc.), and refers to persons and places, the A. is entirely abstract, precise and impersonal. The beginning of schematization of ideas is found in → *Anguttara-Nikaya*, part of *Sutta-Pitaka*, and prob. repr. an early form of A. Such lists of topics for mnemonic or catechetical purposes known as *mātikā* were used by monks in earliest period; from these developed the A. The A. is concerned mainly with analysis of psychical or mental phenomena and their inter-relationships. The many poss. different states of consciousness are described and their mental and moral constituent elements enumerated, being classified acc. to their capacity to produce wholesome or unwholesome → *karma.* These elements or *dhammas* are regarded as always being in state of interdependence with other *dhammas* within vast relational net. The study of A. requires considerable application, powers of memory, and perseverence, and is trad. the occupation of monks. It is intensively studied at certain monasteries. A. is spec. assoc. with the → Theravada. Burma has long reputation for A. studies. Strong interest in A. has developed in Ceylon also in mod. times, partly stimulated by European converts. (→ *Abhidhamma-Piṭaka*). T.O.L.

Nyanaponika, *Abhidhamma Studies* (1949); H. V. Guenther, *Philosophy and Psychology in the Abhidharma* (1957); Lama Anagarika Govinda, *The Psychological Attitude of Early Buddhist Philosophy* (1961); W. F. Jayasuriya, *The Psychology and Philosophy of Buddhism* (1963).

Abhidharma-Kośa An import. Buddh. treatise of → *Sarvāstivādin* sch.; attr. to → Vasubandhu. A.K.

consists of two parts: *A.K.-Kārikā*, a collection of 600 verses, and *A.K.-Bhāsya*, a prose commentary on these verses. The whole forms a compendium of the → *Abhidharma* of the Sarvāstivāda, and is arranged under nine heads: elements (*dhātu*); faculties (*indriya*); world (*loka*, i.e., forms of existence and varieties of living beings); action (*karma*); proclivities or inclinations (*anusaya*); stages in removal of defilement (*pudgala-marga*); types of knowledge (*jñāna*); types of meditation (*samādhi*); lastly, an exam. of theories of the 'person' (*pudgala-viniścaya*). This last section is an independent treatise intended to refute in partic. idea of individual → *ātman*, advocated by → Brahman philosophers and by the Buddh. Vatsiputrīyas, a sect who affirmed reality of individual *pudgala*, or person (Pudgala-vādins). In monasteries in India, in time of → I-Tsing, the A.K. was used as intro. to study of Buddh. thought. While it is a compendium of Sarvastivādin Abh. doc. (as the → Abhidhammatha-sangaha is of → Theravādin), A.K. offers also an interpretation recognised as moving in direction of the → Sautrantikas, and thus towards → Mahāyāna Buddhism. It was an import. instrument of propagation of Buddhism in China, and produced much commentarial literature. The text of A.K. is in Skt., the original of which was lost in India; it has been preserved in Chinese and Tibetan trans. From Chinese versions a French trans. was made by L. de la Vallée Poussin (6 vols., Paris, 1923–31). In 1934 and 1936 a Skt. version was discovered in Tibetan monasteries by Indian scholar Rahula Sanskrityayana. Text of *Karika* portion was pub. by V. V. Gokhale (*The Text of the Abhidharmakośakārikā of Vasubandhu*, *JBRAS*, vol. 22). T.O.L.

Abhidharma-Piṭaka (Sarvāstivādin) A-P. of the → Sarvastivadin school differs completely from → *Abhidhamma Piṭaka* of Thv. in names of books it contains, although some of subject-matter coincides. The seven books of this school's A-P. are: (1) *Sangiti-pariyaya-pada;* (2) *Dharma-skandha;* (3) *Dhatukaya-pada;* (4) *Prajnapti-pada;* (5) *Vijnana-pada;* (6) *Prakarana-pada;* (7) *Jnana-prasthana.* Of these the closest in content to a Thv. Abh. text is (2), which has chapters coinciding with 14 of the 18 chapters of the Thv. *Vibanga.* Whereas language of Thv. A-P. is Pali, that of the Sarvastivadins was Skt; but now is preserved in Chinese and Tibetan trans. only. T.O.L.

Abhidharma-Piṭaka (Theravādin) Third section of Buddh. Pali canonical scriptures, or → *Ti-piṭaka.* Preserved by Thvs. of S. E. Asia, this is one of two extant collections of Abh. texts. The other is that of the → Sarvastivadins. Thv. A-P. consists of seven books: (1) *Dhammasangani* (enumeration of *dhammas,* or entities); (2) *Vibhanga* (the treatises); (3) *Dhātu-kathā* (discussion about *dhatus,* or elements); (4) *Puggala-paññatti* (categories of individuals); (5) *Kathā-Vatthu* (areas of dispute, or points of controversy): (6) *Yamaka* (the pairs); and (7) *Patthāna* (causality). Of these (1) and (7) are together said to present quintessence of Abh. (1) follows the analytical method of reducing all phenomena to ultimate constituent entities or *dhamas*; while (7) is concerned with synthesis, or causal relationships which exist between *dhammas* in actual human existence, which are not necessarily the same as 'common-sense' relationships which appear on surface of life. (2) is a collection of 18 treatises, each of which deals with some fundamental category of B. analysis: the 5 → Khandhas, the 12 → *ayatanas,* the 18 → *dhatus,* the → 4 noble truths, etc. (3) comprises hundreds of questions and answers rel. to the *khandhas, ayatanas* and *dhatus.* (4) is smallest of books of A-P. and differs from other works in dealing with a popular or 'common-sense' concept, that of the 'individual', a concept not regarded as valid or even helpful in B. thought gen. (→ Anatta); the main body of work consists of enumeration and brief definition of over 300 different human types. (5) deals with controversies which had arisen among Buddhists by about mid. of 3rd cent. BC, e.g., whether in any absolute sense a human individual (*puggala*) could be said to exist, each question being followed by the unorthodox answer and its refutation; the book is trad. attr. to Thera Moggalipputta-Tissa, who is said to have recited it at 3rd Buddh. Council held at → Pataliputra in time of → Ashoka. (6) is a work on logic, in so far as it consists of Abh. propositions, each of which is examined in its reverse form. Since Thv. and Sarvastivadin A-Ps. differ in list of books which each contains, the compiling of the A-P. was, in each case, prob. carried out after separation of these 2 schools, *c.* 300 BC, since the Vinaya and Sutta Ps. of the 2 schools are the same. → *Abhidharma-Pitaka* (Sarvāstivādin). T.O.L.

Nyanatiloka Mahathera, *Guide through the Abhidhamma-Piṭaka* (1957).

Abhidhammika (Buddh.) Buddh. monk who is specialist in study of → *Abhidhamma.* This does not mean that he is unacquainted or unconcerned with the other two → Pitakas of Buddh. canon, but that he has specially mastered the *Abh.* The Buddha is described in → *Atthasalini* as first A.; this is an anachronism since development of → *Abh. Pitaka* took place some time after Buddha's decease. In anc. Buddhism, A.s were among → Theravadins held in higher esteem than other monks. The Chinese Buddh. pilgrim → Fa-hsien mentions a → stupa built in honour of the *Abh.* at which A.s performed devotions on Buddh. holy days. T.O.L.

Abhidhammattha-Saṅgaha (Buddh.) Compendium (*saṅgaha*) of meaning (*attha*) of → *Abhidhamma*. → Theravada B. work of 12th cent. by → Anuruddha. Has been and still is most widely used primer and handbook for Abh. study in Thv. countries. Since material is presented in extremely condensed form, it has produced crop of commentaries espec. in Burma and Ceylon. Was trans. into English by S. Z. Aung of Burma and ed. by Mrs. Rhys Davids as *Compendium of Philosophy* (1910, 1956). T.O.L.

Abhiññā Supernatural knowledge or insight, accord. to Buddh. thought, possessed by Buddha and by those who have reached advanced stage of spiritual development. It is super-natural in so far as not characteristic of generality of men, but only of those who have transcended certain ordinary human limitations. Is mentioned in Buddh. scriptures as seventh in series of nine results of apprehension of → 4 holy truths; its position in series indic. its importance, the eighth and ninth being enlightenment and *nibbana* (D.III.XXIX). Is frequently attr. to Buddha in Pali scriptures; by his A. or insight, Buddha has knowledge of realities not immediately apparent to ordinary men. He 'knows the universe, with its devas, with → Mara, with → Brahma, the whole creation, with recluse and → brahman, the world of men and devas, by his own *abhinna* he knows'. (D.I.87 etc.) T.O.L.

T. O. Ling, *Buddhism and the Mythology of Evil* (1962), pp. 68, 96, etc.

Ablution (*wuḍū'*) A necessary preliminary to prayer. Qur. v, 8f. says, 'O you who have believed, when you stand up for prayer wash your faces and your hands up to the elbows, and wipe your heads and your feet up to the ankles, and if you are polluted purify yourselves. If you are sick or on a journey, or if one of you comes from the privy, or if you have touched women and do not find water, sand yourselves (*tayammamū*) with dry, good [sand] and rub your faces and your hands with it.' Mosques provide facilities for A. Trad. says that when a believer washes his face, hands and feet, every sin connected with these parts of body will come out as result of A. Another tells that → 'Uthmān performed A., pouring water over his hands 3 times, rinsing his mouth and snuffing up water, washing the right arm 3 times up to the elbow, then the left, then wiping the head, then washing the right and the left foot 3 times; after which he said he had seen → Muḥammad doing it thus. Many keep strictly to details in the Qur. passage quoted above. If one is unaware of any minor pollution since previous prayer, A. may be omitted. There is dispute about wiping over shoes (or, leather socks). Orthodox schools allow it 3 times a day for travellers and once for others. → Khārijites and → Shi'ites do not allow it. The intention (*niyya*) must be expressed before A. to make it valid. This A. suffices for minor defilements; but various forms of sexual pollution require bathing (*ghusl*) of whole body. J.R.

E.I., IV, p. 1140; Hughes, pp. 3f. (ablution); p. 693 (*wuẓū'*); Gaudefroy-Demombynes, *Institutions*, pp. 71f.; *Mishkāt*, Book III; Querry, I, pp. 1ff.

Ablutions (Christ. and General) (i) Term used to describe various ritual washings of sacred vessels and hands of celebrant during →→ Mass or Eucharist. Custom can be traced back to 10th or 11th cent., and prob. orig. from increasing concern for sanctity of Eucharistic elements. Ritual rinsings of the mouth both before and after reception of Eucharistic sacrament have been practised by priests and laymen in various parts of the Catholic Church. *C.E.*, *D.C.C.*, *s.v.* (ii) Washing has been practised in many primitive religions as ritual cleansing from contagion of death or other forms of ritual impurity, e.g. sexual intercourse, childbirth, menstruation, or before offering sacrifice. Water is usual means of such A.s, but use of sand and blood is known. → Purification (Islam). S.G.F.B.

E.R.E., X, pp. 463b–6a.

Abode (Buddh.) → Vihāra (*Pali*) T.O.L.

Abomination of Desolation In Mk. 13:14; Mt. 24:15, presence of a sacrilegious object in Jerusalem → Temple that would herald → Parousia of Christ. Idea came from violation of Temple in 168 BC by Antiochus Epiphanes' erection of altar to → Zeus (Dan. 11:31). A. of D. was poss. seen in Caligula's attempt to put statue of Zeus in Temple (CE 39–40). Mk. 13:14 prob. refers to violation of Temple in CE 70 by Roman troops' sacrificing to their standards there. S.G.F.B.

V. Taylor, *The Gospel acc. to St. Mark* (1952), pp. 511ff.; S. G. F. Brandon, *Jesus and the Zealots* (1967), pp. 88–9, 230–3.

Abortion Destruction of human embryo has been variously evaluated by different peoples and at different times. In Assyria it was severely punished by law. Its condemnation in →→ Hinduism, Zoroastrianism, and Islam is gen. a vague prohibition, without adducing specific reasons. Buddhist condemnation stems from opposition to destroying any form of life. A. was prob. condemned in → Orphism, but for what reason is unknown: poss. it was thought to interfere with → metempsychosis. Its condemnation in Christianity resulted from Chr. doc. of → Man. Acc. to 2nd cent. *Apoc. of* → *Peter*, women guilty of A. were specially punished in Hell. Tertullian held that A. was murder, since embryo is a potential man (*Apol.* 9). Problem for later theologians was to determine when → soul entered foetus. Roman jurists held it was 40th day after conception. Hence → Augustine ruled killing of animated foetus was murder. During Middle Ages women guilty of A. were condemned on capital charge. Later Papal Bulls punished A. with → excommunication. In recent times civil law, which had gen. reflected eccl. view in modified form, has taken more tolerant attitude to therapeutic A. Catholic theologians hold therapeutic A. to be unlawful, but the issue is still much debated, esp. in view of recent civil legislation to authorise it. S.G.F.B.

E.R.E., VI (1913), *sub* 'Foeticide'; L. Delaporte, *La Mésopotamie* (1923), p. 316; *D.C.C., s.v.; R.A.C.*, I (1950), 55–60 ('Abtreibung'); *R.G.G.*[3], V, 1588–9 ('Schwangerschaftsunterbrechung').

(Buddh. view) Act of A., i.e. terminating life of a foetus, is explicitly mentioned in Buddh. canonical scriptures, in the → *Vinaya Pitaka*, as a grave offence. If A. is brought about by Buddh. monk, or if he is in any way a party to the procuring of an A., by offering advice as to the method, or supplying abortive medicine, penalty is expulsion from monkhood. This is in accord. with Buddh. view that destruction of life is a moral transgression. T.O.L.

Aboth de Rabbi Nathan Exposition of →→ Mishnah treatise, *Pirke* Ābōth. One of two recensions is usually appended to the Babylonian → Talmud. (→ Judaism). S.G.F.B.

W. O. E. Oesterley and G. H. Box, *Short Survey of Lit. of Rabbinical and Mediaeval Judaism* (1920), p. 97; *E.J.R.*, p. 51.

Abracadabra Magical formula, its letters being arranged in form of triangle, enabling them to be read in many different ways. Paper, inscribed with A., was folded in form of cross and used as prophylactic → amulet against evil spirits, and to cure fevers and other maladies. First recorded mention by Serenus Sammonicus, 2nd cent CE. S.G.F.B.

Abraha Abyssinian leader, who invaded Arabia, and was signally defeated in CE 570 in attack on → Mecca, the year of → Muhammad's birth. A. was a Christian, and built cathedral at Ṣan'ā', called al-Qulays (= Grk. *ekklesia*) in pre-Islamic Arabia. S.G.F.B.

E. Ullendorff, *The Ethiopians* (1960), p. 56.

Abraham Heb. patriarch, whose career is recorded in Gen. 11:10–25:10. Narrative comprises various traditions which → Yahwist writer skilfully combined to present A. as progenitor of Israelite people, to whom → Yahweh promised land of Canaan (Gen. 12:1–3). By repr. A. as father of → Isaac, and grandfather of → Jacob, whose 12 sons become eponymous ancestors of 12 tribes of → Israel, the Yahwist gave the various Semite tribes, which formed confederation for conquest of Canaan, a history attesting their common ancestry. A's name, explained in Gen. 17:5 as meaning 'Father of a multitude of nations', is a personal theophoric name of N. Semitic origin, poss. meaning 'the Father (God) is exalted'. It has been suggested that A. was orig. a deity. This seems unlikely; but he was certainly a figure of folk-legend, connected with many sanctuaries in Canaan, whom the Yahwist could well present as common ancestor to various Semite tribes that had relations with north Syria, Mesopotamia, and Canaan. In later Jew. thought A. repr. ideal of faithful obedience to God, his willingness to sacrifice Isaac (Gen. 22) being the signal example of his trust. Name of A. also occurs in magical formulae and in → astrology in Graeco-Roman paganism. A. has been important in Chr. thought. His example was invoked by → Paul in his doc. of justification by faith (Rom. 4:1ff.) A.'s sacrifice of Isaac provided Patristic writers with a typology of Christ's sacrifice. In → Islam A. has played important role, esp. as 'the → *Hanīf*'. (→ Judaism). S.G.F.B.

G. von Rad, *Genesis* (E.T. 1961); K. Galling, *Die Erwählungstraditionen Israels* (1928); *R.G.G.*[3], I (1957), 68–71; *R.A.C.*, I (1950), 18–27; *H.D.B.*[2], *s.v.*

(in Islam) (Ar. Ibrāhīm). Qur. vi, 74 calls his father Āzar (?from name of his servant Eleazar). → Muḥammad, like → Paul, recognised A. as the father of the faithful. Qur. iii, 60 says, 'A. was neither a Jew nor a Christian, but was a → *ḥanīf*, a Muslim.' (cf. ii, 134). Claiming A. as a *ḥanif*, Md. was able to look on him as founder of Arab religion. In vi, 74ff. A. renounces idols, finds worship of star, moon and sun unsatisfactory, so turns to worship their Creator. A longer story is followed by prayer for a son, telling of his purpose to sacrifice him some years later (xxxvii, 81ff.). Son is unnamed, but Muslims hold A. proposed to sacrifice → Ishmael. A. and Ishmael together take part in rebuilding the → ka'ba; A. is credited with founding Meccan cult (ii, 118ff., cf. xiv, 38ff.). The Qur. knows of angels visiting A. on their way to Sodom and their announcing birth of son to Sarah (xi, 72ff.; cf. xv, 51ff.; xxix, 30; li, 24ff.). Ref. is made to scriptures called 'sheets' given to A. (liii, 37f.; lxxxvii, 19). A's relig. is to be followed (xvi, 124; cf. iv, 124). Those most closely attached to A. are Md. and the believers (iii, 61). God took A. as a friend (*khalīl*—iv, 124). Hebron, where A's tomb is reputed to be, gets name al-Khalil after him. Many details are added by Tha'labī and Kisā'ī in their books, both called *Qiṣaṣ al-anbiyā'* (Stories of the prophets); no trans. J.R.

E.I., II, pp. 431f.; Bell, *Introduction*, index; Stanton, *The Teaching of the Qur'ān* (1919), index.

Abraham, Apocalypse of Early 2nd cent. CE writing,

orig. in Heb. or Aramaic, surviving only in Slavonic trans. A Jew. composition, later ed. for Chr. use. Chapters 1–8 describe A's conversion from idolatry. Main section deals with A's journey through 7 heavens, where past and future are revealed to him, esp. → Fall and its ultimate result in destr. of → Temple (CE 70). A.A. is important for angelology of →→ Qumran and Gnosis. S.G.F.B.

E. Schürer, *G.J.V.*, III, pp. 336ff.; G. H. Box, *The Apoc. of Abr.* (1919); G. Quispel in *The Jung Codex*, ed. F. L. Cross (1955), pp. 71ff.

Abraham's Bosom Expression occurs in Parable of Dives and Lazarus (Lk. 16:22), and was evidently a current Jew. image of blissful afterlife. Idea is not found in early Rabbinic lit; in early Chr. lit. it had two meanings: (i) place of rest (not Heaven) for Abraham and other righteous persons who died before coming of Christ (ii) place of eternal bliss = Heaven. In medieval → Dooms A.B. repr. → Heaven, being depicted realistically as seated figure of A. holding souls in bosom. S.G.F.B.

R.A.C., I (1950), 27–8; *H.D.B.*², *s.v.;* S. G. F. Brandon, *The Judgment of the Dead* (1967), pp. 111, 119, 127.

Abraham, Testament of Orig. Jew. writing of 2nd cent. CE, worked over by Chr. scribe; it exists in two Grk. versions, and Coptic, Arab., Ethiop., Rumanian trans. Acc. to A.T., Abraham, being afraid to die, is conducted through next world by Archangel → Michael. A.T., which was prob. written in Egypt, reflects anc. Egypt. ideas in two-way route to underworld, and weighing of souls. Ref is also made to legend of d. of → Moses. The Copt., Arab., and Ethiop. versions are supplemented by *Test. of Isaac* and *Test. of Jacob.* (→→ Eschatology, Egypt.; Psychostasia). S.G.F.B.

M. R. James, 'The Test. of Abr.', in *Cambridge Texts and Studies,* ii, no. 2 (1892); Schürer, *G.J.V.*, III, pp. 338f.; G. H. Box, *The Test. of Abr.* (1927); S. G. F. Brandon, *The Judgment of the Dead* (1967), pp. 122ff.

Abrahamites (i) 9th cent. sect of Syrian heretics, stemming from or reviving teaching of Paulianists. A. denied divinity of Christ; they were named after founder, Ibrahim or Abraham of Antioch. (ii) Bohemian sect of → Deists, who claimed to follow religion of Abraham before his circumcision. They repudiated → Trinity and → Bible, except → Ten Commandments and Lord's Prayer. Appearing in 1782, they claimed to be followers of John Huss (→ Reformation). They were forcibly suppressed. S.G.F.B.

*R.G.G.*³, I, 71–2.

Abraxas, or Abrasax Secret divine name, frequently found in magical papyri and on gems, prob. invented by the Gnostic → Basilides. Its efficacy lay partly in fact of its containing 7 letters, of which the numerical value = 365, the number of spiritual powers ruling cosmos acc. to system of Basilides. S.G.F.B.

Kleine Pauly, I (1964), 17–8; E. A. W. Budge, *The Mummy* (1925), plate XXIV, pp. 331–2.

Abrogation (Islam) (Ar. *nāsikh wa-mansūkh* = abrogating and abrogated). Qur. ii, 100: 'For whatever verse we abrogate or cause to be forgotten we bring a better, or its like.' Commentators have gen. agreed that certain Qur. verses were abrogated by others revealed later; but, although verses are mentioned, no one would dare to delete them. Suyūṭī gives a list of 20 verses with those which abrogate them (cf. Hughes, 520). Muhammad 'Alī ('Alī: *Qur'ān*, n. 152), expressing an → Aḥmadiyya view, while admitting existence of abrogated verses is gen. accepted, says Qur. ii, 100 is misunderstood. He says those who believe in A. do not agree about number of the verses. He holds that the Qur. verse refers to the Jewish law being abrogated by Qur., which gives something of similar type, but better. A. may apply also to trads. Sometimes, when two trads. seem contrary, it may be known that one was later than other, so it obviously was meant to abrogate earlier one. Only a trad. can abrogate a trad. J.R.

E.I., II, p. 1065; Bell, *Introduction*, pp. 98f.; Goldziher, *M.S.*, II, p. 148; Nöldeke, *Geschichte,*² index (*al-mansūḫ, mansūḫāt*).

Absolute, The (Buddh.) In Pali Buddh., nearest approach to West. philosophical notion of the A. is that which is ref. to in canon as the unconditioned (*asankhata*). Certain other negative adjectives also are used in this connection: not-born (*ajātam*), not-become (*abhūtam*), and not-made (*akatam*). Thus the Buddha is repr. as saying, 'Monks there is that which is not-born, not-become, not-made and unconditioned. If this not-born, not-become, not-made and unconditioned were not, then there would be apparent no release from that which is born, become, made and conditioned.' (*Udāna*, VIII: 3) Since it is to → *nibbāna* that adj. 'unconditioned' is applied elsewhere (AN I:152; SN IV:359 etc.), it may be assumed that it is *nibbāna* which is to be understood as the A. in Pali Buddh.

In Mhy. Buddh. it is the universal 'void' or → *śūñyatā*, which becomes the A, espec. as repr. in → Nagarjuna's doc. In the further development, or poss. synthesis, repr. by Asanga's → Yogācāra system of thought, it was the → *ālayavijñāna*, the abode of consciousness, which repr. the A. In all these cases, the A., however represented, was identified with goal of Buddh. relig. life. T.O.L.

Absolution Acc. to Cath. doctrine, Church possesses authority to pronounce A. of sins, through Christ to repentant sinners. This authority is committed to bishops and priests, empowering them to pronounce A. at appointed places in divine service or privately to individuals in sacrament of → Penance. Two forms of A. are used: (i) the *indicative* as in formula 'I absolve thee from thy sins' (ii) the *precatory*, where priest prays formally that God will absolve an individual or congregation. The sacerdotal power to give A. derives from doc. of → Apostolic Succession, and is current in those Churches claiming such Succession. It is repudiated by Prot. Churches, together with doc. of Apos. Succession. The term A. is used in → Presbyterian Church of Scotland to denote declaration of Kirk session releasing a person from eccles. interdict placed upon him for notorious delinquency. S.G.F.B.

E.R.E., I (1908), *s.v.; D.C.C.*, *s.v.;* K. E. Kirk, *The Vision of God* (1950), pp. 288–92, 534–40.

Absolutions of the Dead Service, of medieval origin, in R.C. Church, following Requiem → Mass, in which corpse is censed and asperged with holy water, and prayers said for departed soul. S.G.F.B.

Abstinence Cath. trad. term signifying A. from certain specified foods at certain seasons or in preparation for certain relig. rites. In R.C. Church 'days of abstinence' are distinguished from 'days of fasting': the former being occasions for A. from meat; the latter involving both A. from meat and reduction of, or total abstention from, other food. Such forms of self-denial may be part of disciplinary practice of Church, being prescribed in → Calendar, or voluntary acts of asceticism. (→→ Asceticism; Fasting). In some religions it means abstaining from sexual intercourse on certain religious occasions. S.G.F.B.

W. K. L. Clarke (ed.), *Liturgy and Worship* (1932), pp. 245–6; *D.C.C.*, *s.v.*

Abū Bakr First → Caliph, staunch friend and supporter of → Muḥammad. A merchant in Mecca, slightly younger than Md., who suffered considerable decrease in his means because of faithfulness to him. He was Md.'s only companion at the → hijra. Md. strengthened bonds of friendship by marrying A.B.'s daughter → 'Ā'isha. A.B. was a valued counsellor. He was appointed to lead Pilgrimage in 9/637, and lead prayers in the Medina mosque during Md.'s last illness. After Md.'s death, there was short period of uncertainty, but the people were persuaded to appoint A.B. Caliph. Arab tribes throughout Arabia refused to pay taxes to Medina or to obey its officials. This movement has been called the → apostasy, but the term (*ridda*) is too strong. Many honestly believed they had sworn allegiance to Md. and not to his successors; but A.B. insisted that Md. had initiated a new relig. on which system of government was based, so his death made no change. He, therefore, engaged in warfare to bring the tribes back to obedience, with notable success. During his brief period of rule Muslim forces began to spread into Iraq and Syria. A.B. d. 13/634 and was buried beside Md. A man of wise counsel, resolute purpose and unselfish service, he was an excellent choice to succeed Md. J.R.

*E.I.*², I, pp. 109–11; Guillaume, *Life*, index (Bakr, abu); Watt, *Mecca*, index, and *Medina*, index; Hitti, *History*, pp. 140–5 and index, Muir, *Life*, index, and *Caliphate*, index.

Abū Dāwūd al-Sijistānī (202/817—275/889), a traditionist who came from Sijistān and settled in Basra. His great distinction is his *Kitāb al-sunan*, a collection of Muslim trads. which came to be recognised by → Sunnīs as one of the six canonical works. He was first to add notes at end of a number of trads., showing his opinion of their value. J.R.

*E.I.*², I, p. 114; *G.A.L.*, I, pp. 168f.; *S.I.*, pp. 266f.; Goldziher, *M.S.*, II, pp. 250f., 255f.; *J.A.*, 1900, pp. 330, 902f.; *B.S.O.A.S.*, 1952, pp. 579ff.

Abū Ḥanīfa (*c.* 80/699—150/767), theologian and relig. lawyer of recognised authority who lived in Kufa. One of the four Sunnī legal schools, the Hanafī (→ Muslim Law) is traced to him. He wrote no law books, but his doc. was discussed by him with pupils and is to be found in works by Abū Yūsuf and Shaibānī, commonly ref. to as the two doctors. A. is typified by his reasoning. Personal judgment (*ra'y*) and analogy (*qiyās*) were used by him, but to no exceptional degree; yet later generations have accused him of depending too much on own opinion and neglecting trad. In this they have been unfair. The Ḥanafī school has prevailed in C. Asia, India, Turkey, Lower Egypt; but in mod. times modifications are being made in most countries. A.Ḥ. was an influential theologian with → Murji'ite tendencies. It is notable that while his *Fiqh Akbar* I (see Wensinck, *Creed*, 102ff.) contains articles against some parties, there is nothing against Murji'ites. A.Ḥ. was imprisoned in Baghdad by Caliph Manṣūr; the reason for this is not clear. J.R.

*E.I.*², I, pp. 123f.; Ibn Khallikān, III, pp. 555ff.; I, Goldziher, *Die Zāhiriten* (1884), 2, pp. 12ff.; Wensinck, *Creed*, index; Schacht, *Jurisprudence*, index.

Abū Hurayra (d. *c.* 58/678) became a Muslim less than 4 years before → Muhammad's death, yet more trads. are recorded through him than through any other. This does not mean that he was responsible for all, but simply that his name was attached to give authority. There are even trads. explaining why he transmitted more trads. than others. J.R.

*E.I.*², I, p. 129; Goldziher, *M.S.*, II, index; N. Abbott, *Papyri*, index; Ṣiddīqī, *Ḥadīth*, index.

Abū Lahab Son of → 'Abd al-Muṭṭalib, uncle of →

Muḥammad. A.L. rejected Md.'s message and was hostile to him. Qur. cxi is directed against A., declaring that he and his wife are doomed to hell. He died not long after battle of → Badr, in which he did not take part. Two of his sons became Muslims in year of Conquest of Mecca. J.R.

*E.I.*², I, pp. 136f.; Hughes, p. 8; Watt, *Mecca*, index.

Abuna (*Abun*, if not followed by the name). Title of Patriarch of → Ethiopic Church, meaning 'our father' in Eth. and Arabic. Sometimes used as courtesy prefix for the most senior clerics of Eth. Church. S.G.F.B.

Abū Ṭālib Son of → 'Abd al-Muṭṭalib, uncle of → Muḥammad. Seems to have been head of clan of Hāshim. On his father's death, he undertook the care of Md. Although A.T. did not accept Md.'s message when he claimed to be a prophet, he continued to give him protection, even when his clan was boycotted by the Quraysh clans. He d. *c.* CE 619. His sons 'Alī and Ja'far accepted Md.'s teaching, and → 'Alī became fourth Caliph. J.R.

*E.I.*², I, pp. 152f.; Goldziher, *M.S.*, II, p. 107; Watt, *Mecca*, index; Hitti, *History*, index.

Abydos Town in Upper Egypt of great antiquity, being burial place of early kings (*c.* 3200–2780 BC). Its religious importance derives from cult of → Osiris, located there. Acc. to legend, head of Osiris was buried at A., thus making it place of → pilgrimage. Ritual plays were periodically celebrated, commemorating death and resurrection of Osiris. Royal munificence built and endowed sanctuary, and a representative of king supervised the 'mysteries' of Osiris. Because of its sanctity, multitudes sought to be buried at A. or have a cenotaph erected there. S.G.F.B.

H. Bonnet, *Reallexikon*, *s.v.; Ae.R.T.B.*, I, pp. 232ff.

Abyss *Ex.* Grk. word *abyssos* signifying a bottomless or boundless deep. In LXX version of Gen. 1:2 *abyssos* = Heb. *tĕhōm*, which prob. = Bab. → Ti'āmat, personification of the primordial deep of waters, existent before creation of world. Egypt. → cosmogony had similar concept in Nun. From being primordial deep or chaos, A. became identified with → Sheol and Tartarus (LXX Job 41:24), which latter was, in Grk. mythology, the murky prison of notorious opponents of → Zeus. The Book of → Enoch makes A. place of punishment for fallen → angels. In the N.T., the A. is abode of demons (Lk. 8:31) and → Hades (Rom. 10:7), where the → Devil is imprisoned (Rev. 20:2). The → Gnostics made A., under name of Bythus, into divine first principle, source of all existence, thus repr. a return to original concept. S.G.F.B.

E.R.E., I, *s.v.; R.A.C.*, I, *s.v.;* S. G. F. Brandon, *C.L.*, pp. 16–7, 46–7, 99–101, 147ff., 169ff.

Abyssinian Church → Ethiopic Church. S.G.F.B.

Acacian Schism During controversy over → Monophysitism, schism occurred between Rome and the East. It arose in 482, following promulgation by Emp. Zeno of *Henoticon* of → Acacius, Patr. of Constantinople, in which concessions were made to Monophysitism, and lasted to 519. S.G.F.B.

Acacius (1) of Caesarea: exponent of → Arianism, who became bp. of Caesarea in Palestine in 340. Deposed by Council of Sardica (343), A. was a leading repres. of the → Homaeans, proposing a Homaean Creed at Council of Seleucia (359). He signed Creed of → Nicaea at Antioch in 363, but returned to Arianism. He was deposed by Synod of Lampsacus in 365 and d. 366. Little of his voluminous works survived; his followers ('Acacians') formed a theological party (357–61).

(2) Of Constantinople, Patriarch (471). At first anti-Chalcedon (→ Chalcedon, Council of), he advised Emp. Zeno (474–91), in his attempt to unite Eastern Church, by a Chalcedonian formula (*Henoticon*), which was rejected by Rome and caused → Acacian Schism. S.G.F.B.

*R.G.G.*³, I, 1957, 82–3; *D.C.C.*, *s.v.*

Academy Park and gymnasium near Dipylon Gate of Athens, where → Plato established school *c.* 385 BC. Organised as corporate body orig. to train men for service of State, it continued as centre of philosophical study until dissolution by Justinian in CE 529. In 3rd cent. BC, under Arcesilaus and Carneades, A. became chief school of → Scepticism. After period of obscurity, A. emerged in 5th cent. CE as centre of → Neoplatonism, under leadership of Proclus. A. was also concerned with commentaries on Plato and → Aristotle. S.G.F.B.

O.C.D., *s.v.; R.A.C.*, I, 204–11.

Ācārya (Hindu) Sometimes transliterated *āchārya*, term means 'teacher', and is used as honorific suffix to names of some prominent Hindu theologians, such as →→ Sankara (Sankaracarya); Yamuna (Yamunacarya); Ramanuja (Ramanujacarya). In partic. the term became assoc. with institution of headship of a sect or centre of relig. life, e.g. at Srirangam in S. India, the centre of Vaisnavite → Visistadvaita, where Ramanuja was recognized as *acarya.* The succession of *acaryas* in Sri Vaisnavism after Ramanuja became divided as between the → Vadagalai and the Tengalai sub-sects. There is also a succession of *acaryas* among the → *Smartas* (followers of Sankara). N.S.

R. G. Bhandarkar *Vaishnavism, Shaivism and Minor Religious Systems* (1928).

Ācārya (Skt); Acariya (Pali) in Buddhism. In Buddhism the teacher or instructor (*ācārya*) plays an indispensable role. As it has existed historically, Buddhism has always involved social relationship, even when this is at minimum level of teacher and pupil: the 'solo' Buddh. is a rare exception. *Ācārya* is one of 2 main types of teacher; other is *upadhyaya* (Skt), or *upajjhāya* (Pali.) Orig. A. was teacher of → *dhamma* or doctrine, while *upajjhāya* was moral preceptor, whose function it was to encourage and correct learner-monk. A. was thus custodian of Buddh. viewpoint or trad. doc., and it was his responsibility to ensure its preservation and accurate transmission. In early period, the role of *upajjhāya* was regarded as more import.; this reflected primary importance within the Buddh. community of moral discipline. When transmission of essential Buddh. teaching became more difficult by reason of unsettled conditions of times, role of A. was regarded as having an importance equal to that of *upajjhāya*. When → Buddhaghosa's *Visuddhimagga* was composed, role of A. had become even more import. than that of *upajjhāya* (*Vis.* 81, etc.).

Relationship between A. as teacher and junior monk as pupil, or *antevāsika*, was similar to that expected between father and son, i.e., one of reciprocal confidence and respect. T.O.L.

Acca Larentia Roman goddess of obscure orig. and nature. Her name suggests she may have been *Mater Larum*, 'Mother of the → Lares'; but her festival, the Larentalia, on 23 December, was more than a festival of dead. Roman legend makes A.L. mother of → Arval Brothers and adopted-mother of Romulus, legendary founder of Rome; it also connected her with → Hercules, and, by repr. her as a prostitute (*lupa* = she-wolf), provides euhemerist explanation (→ Euhermerus) of legend of suckling of Romulus and Remus by the Roman she-wolf. S.G.F.B.

Kleine Pauly, I (1964), *s.v.;* E. Pais, *Anc. Legends of Roman History* (E.T. 1906), pp. 60ff.

Accaophori Christ. sect that used water instead of wine in → Eucharist: also called Hydroparastatae. S.G.F.B.

Acceptilation Term *ex* Roman Law, used to describe → soteriology of Duns Scotus (*c.* 1264–1308), who taught sacrifice of Christ was graciously accepted by God as sufficient satisfaction for sins of mankind, though it was not a full equivalent. S.G.F.B.

Access-Concentration (*Upacāra Samādhi*) Term used in Buddhism for a stage of meditation in which concentration on a moral object has reached the degree that precedes entrance into state of absorption, or → *jhāna* (→ Samadhi) T.O.L.

Accident *Ex* Lat. *accidentia*, term used in medieval philosophy, which, following → Aristotle, conceived of any entity as consisting of a *substantia* or essence, and a varying group of attributes: e.g. size, shape, colour. The distinction between → *substantia* and A. was utilised in doc. of → Transubstantiation. Acc. to → Aquinas, after action of consecration in → Mass, the *substantiae* of the bread and wine changed into Body and Blood of Christ, but A.s continued to exist and be perceptible by the senses. This interpretation was rejected by Reformers. Council of → Trent maintained doc. of Transubstantiation without ref. to A.s. S.G.F.B.

A. Harnack, *H.D.*, VI, pp. 235ff.; *D.C.C.*, *s.v.; E.R.E.*, I (1908), *s.v.*

Accidie *Ex* Grk. *akēdeia* = 'negligence', 'indifference'. Term used in Chr. moral theology to denote spiritual torpor, sloth, listlessness and melancholy, which frequently afflict monks and nuns and others concentrating on spiritual devotion. It is dealt with by many theologians and spiritual writers, incl. → Cassian and → Aquinas. S.G.F.B.

E.R.E., I (1908), *s.v.; R.A.C.*, I, 62–3 ('Acedia').

Acephalos, Acephali Headless being or beings. Depiction of A. occurs in Palaeolithic art (→ Palaeolithic relig.), evidently having some magic. or relig. meaning. A. attacked by great black birds are depicted in sanctuary at → Çatel Hüyük. In Egypt. mythology → Osiris was beheaded by → Set, and head buried at → Abydos A. are shown in Egypt. depictions of *p.m.* punishment. Grk. magic. papyri ref. to 'strong Headless One', who is supreme Creator God. Osiris is connected with this conception. Grk. demonology knew headless demon Phonos = Death. A. figure in relig. and folklore of European peoples; medieval Chr. art shows many headless saints, often holding their heads. Idea of A. prob. stems from primitive fear of decapitated dead. (→ Celtic Relig.). S.G.F.B.

R.A.C., I (1950), 211–5; S. G. F. Brandon, *The Judgment of the Dead* (1967), pp. 2–5.

Acheron River of Thesprotia in S. Epirus, which ran through gloomy gorges and disappeared underground in places: consequently thought to lead to → Hades. Acc. to Virgil (*Aen.* VI), souls of dead gathered on its banks. → Dante and Virgil cross A. in *Inferno* of Dante. The idea of an infernal river passed into later Jew. apocalyptic lit. (→ Apocalyptic); in Chr. lit. as the Acherusian lake, it assumed a propitious aspect and repr. → Elysium (cf. Apoc. of Peter, cf. M. R. James, *Apocryphal New Test.* (1925), p. 518). (→ Styx, The). S.G.F.B.

Kleine Pauly, I, 45–6; *R.A.C.*, I, 71–2.

Acolyte Highest of the four Minor Orders of Latin Church, first mentioned in Rome in 251. Duties of A.s are to assist at → Mass, esp. by lighting altar candles, carrying candles in procession, and preparing the wine and water needed for the celebration. (→ Hierarchy, Chr.). S.G.F.B.

Acquisition (Islam) (*Kasb*), doc. developed by Muslim theologians to attempt reconciliation between idea of man's responsibility for actions and doc.

that God is prime Agent. (→ Free-will and predestination). J.R.

Watt, *Acquisition*; Wensinck, *Creed*, index (*kasb*); Sweetman, *I.C.T.*, II, IV, index (*kasb*); Pareja, index (*kasb*, *iktisāb*).

Actaeon In Grk. mythology, hunter who surprised → Artemis when bathing; he was transformed by angry goddess into a stag and killed by own hounds (Ovid, *Met.* 3, ll. 138ff.). There are other variant versions of his offence. The story may originate from → tabus surrounding a virgin goddess: she (or her image) must not be seen (naked?) by a man. A similar fate befell → Teiresias. However, this story dates from Hellenistic period and is prob. later than other less picturesque versions. There is much conflicting evidence concerning orig. of A., suggesting that he was a 'faded god'. S.G.F.B.

H. J. Rose, *A Handbook of Greek Mythology* (1928), pp. 185, 195; *Der Kleine Pauly*, I (1964), 223–4 ('Aktaion').

Acts of the Apostles Purports to be narrative account, in Grk., of development of → Church from foundation (2:1ff.) to arrival of Apostle → Paul in Rome (*c.* CE 62). Acc. to preface (1:1–2), it repr. sequel to an earlier work, i.e. Gospel of → Luke. The A.-A. contains no explicit statement about its author; early trad. (Irenaeus) assigns it to Luke, a companion of Paul. The book is clearly a literary composition, based on various sources: e.g. some passages, known as 'We-sections' (16:10–7; 20:5–15; 21:1–17; 27:1–28.16) appear to be diary-extracts of a travel-companion of Paul. The extant Grk. text exists in two recensions: a shorter text given by most great Uncial MSS., e.g. Codices →→ Sinaiticus, Vaticanus and Alexandrinus; a longer text, known as the 'Western text', in → Codex Bezae. The latter is gen. regarded as expanded version, made in 2nd cent. of orig. text. The date of A.-A. is problematical: no ref. is made to d. of Paul (*c.* CE 65), nor to Epistles of Paul; a chronological error in 5.36–7 could indicate dependence on *Jew. Ant.* of → Josephus, and imply a *post*-CE 93 date; critical opinion gen. favours *c.* CE 80–90. A.-A. has certain distinctive themes, and does not give balanced comprehensive account of Chr. Origins. It presents Christianity as divinely-guided movement from beginnings in Jerusalem to establishment at Rome, capital of anc. world: it is an idealised picture, glossing over serious controversies among Chr. leaders. Paul is repr. as the Apostle *par excellence*, and progress of Christianity coincides with his journeys, i.e. north-westwards from Judaea. A.-A. ignores orig. of Christianity in Egypt, and shows hostility to Ch. of → Alexandria. Its strange silence about antecedents of → James, the Lord's brother, who became head of Ch. of → Jerusalem, and reticence about relations between James and Paul, suggest there were aspects of Chr. Origins which A.-A. preferred not to disclose. Since A.-A. is the only extant account of Chr. Origins, its influence has been immense; its character and motives must be critically evaluated for more balanced estimate. S.G.F.B.

F. J. Foakes Jackson and K. Lake (eds.), *The Beginnings of Christianity*, 5 vols. (1920–33); *R.G.G.*³, I, 501–8; F. F. Bruce, *The Acts of the Apostles* (1951); S. G. F. Brandon, *The Fall of Jerusalem and the Christian Church*,² (1957); *H.D.B.*², pp. 596ff.; H. Conzelmann, *Die Apostelgeschichte* (1963).

Act of Supremacy Passed in Nov. 1534 confirming to Henry VIII and his successors title of 'the only supreme head in earth of the Church of England, called *Anglicana Ecclesia*'. Title amended under Elizabeth I (1559) to: 'the only supreme governor of this realm . . . as well as in all spiritual or ecclesiastical things or causes as temporal'. → Church of England. S.G.F.B.

D.C.C., p. 1306.

Acts of the Martyrs The sufferings of Chr. martyrs (→ Martyr) naturally commanded admiration and reverence of their brethren, and written records of them were highly prized. The earliest A.-M. are gen. brief and factual: e.g. the *Acta Proconsularia* of St. → Cyprian. Early accounts written by Christians known as *Passiones* (e.g. *P. of St. Perpetua and St. Felicitas*), were based on eye-witness reports and the miraculous element is restrained. → Eusebius of Caesarea prob. made first collection of A.-M., of which only a fragment survives. Later A.-M. are characterised by their legendary nature and love of miracle (e.g. A. of St. Catherine of Alexandria or St. Thecla). The Bollandists published most comprehensive collection of A.-M. under title *Acta Sanctorum.* Pagans also produced A.-M. (→ Persecution Relig.). S.G.F.B.

*R.G.G.*³, IV (1960), 592–3 ('Märtyrerakten'); *D.C.C.*, *s.v.;* H. Musurillo, *The Acts of the Pagan Martyrs* (1954).

Actual Sin In Chr. theology, a sinful act, whether of commission or omission, that results from free personal choice of individual concerned. It is contrasted with → Original Sin. S.G.F.B.

'Ād A prosperous anc. S. Arabian people mentioned several times in Qur. They rejected prophet → Hūd and were destroyed by a violent wind (cf. Qur. vii, 63ff.; xxvi, 123ff.; xlvi, 20ff.; li, 41f.) Some scholars have doubted their existence. Wellhausen mentioned phrases 'from the time of 'Ād', and 'from al-'Ād', suggesting that 'Ād was word meaning 'ancient time' which was misinterpreted. Stories about 'Ad's prosperity, which later developed, are presumably legends amplifying Qur. references. J.R.

*E.I.*², I, p. 169; J. Horovitz, *Koranische Untersuchungen* (1926), 125f.

Adad Storm god of Akkad and Assyria. The Sumerians had similar deity named Ishkur. Thunder was voice of A. and lightning his weapon. Although feared for his destructive powers, A. had benevolent aspect as provider of rain for good harvests. In Epic of → Gilgamesh, A. directs → Flood, ordered by → Enlil. (→→→ Assyrian; Babylon; Mesapot. Religs.). S.G.F.B.
E. Dhorme; *R.B.A.*, pp. 96–102, 126–8.

Adalbert of Bremen *c.* 1000–72, Archbp. of Bremen-Hamburg, who promoted missionary work in Scandinavia, Iceland, Greenland and the Orkneys. App. by Pope Leo IX in 1053 as Papal Vicar and Legate of the Nordic nations. S.G.F.B.

Adam Name used by → Yahwist writer for first man in creation legend in Gen. 2:4ff. Since Adam (*'ādhām*) is formed by → Yahweh out of clay (*'ădhāmāh*), an essential relationship may be suggested acc. to Yahwist doc. of Man, which precluded belief in *post-mortem* survival. In subsequent account of Temptation and Fall of Adam, orig. of death and mortal nature of Man are explained (3:19). Subsidiary aetiological motifs are also embodied in story: orig. of Woman and her subjection to Man (2:18–24; 3:16), (→ Eve); of clothes (3:20); childbirth (3:16); → agriculture and its toil (3:17–9). No significant ref. is made to A. elsewhere in O.T. In the → Apocrypha idea that mankind shared in A.'s sin through seminal identity with him is adumbrated in 2 Esdras 3:21, 7:46–56. Interest in A. increases in later Jew. → Pseudepigrapha (e.g. Enoch 30:8ff.); there once existed a *Book of Adam.* Rabbinic lit. taught that A.'s sin brought penalty of death on his descendants (*Sabbath*, fol. 55a–55b). In N.T. → Paul draws parallel and contrast between A. and Christ (Rom. 5:12–21; I Cor. 15:20–2, 45:9), as First Man, who brings death and Second Man who brings resurrection from death. In Chr. theology A.'s → Fall became basis of doc. of → Original Sin. There was much speculation about A.'s fate: it was believed that, in his → Descent into Hades, Christ rescued A. first. Acc. to legend, Christ's cross was raised over A.'s grave, so that Redeemer's blood first touched first sinner and progenitor of mankind. A. and Eve appear in Chr. art from time of → Catacombs. A. figures much in → Islam, and was connected with the → Ka'ba at Mecca. As the → 'Urmensch', A. has parallels in other religs.: e.g. →→ Adapa; Enkidu; Deucalion; Yama; Yima. S.G.F.B.
E.R.E., I (1908), *s.v.;* N. P. Williams, *The Ideas of the Fall and of Original Sin* (1927), *passim;* E. A. W. Budge, *The Book of the Cave of Treasures* (1927); Brandon, *C.L.*, pp. 122ff.; *H.D.B.*², p. 9.
(In Islam) Qur. speaks of A. as a vicegerent, whom God tells angels he is going to place in earth (ii, 28). In xv, 28 God speaks of A. as human being made of clay, of mud fashioned into shape, and tells angels to do obeisance to him. All agree except Iblīs (→ Spirits and demons), who is cast out of Garden and cursed (cf. xxxviii, 71). → Jesus is in same position as A., being created of dust (iii, 52). A. and his spouse are called parents of all mankind (cf. vii, 189f.). They are to inhabit the Garden, but to avoid a certain tree. Iblīs tempts them, they eat of it, and God expels them and sends them down to earth (vii, 18ff.; cf. ii, 33ff.; xx, 115ff.). A. asks forgiveness and God shows compassion, promising peace of mind if he follows guidance (ii, 35f.; xx, 120ff.). Muslim trad., influenced by Jew. and Christ. sources, considers A. a prophet. The → Ismā'īlīs have held him to be first of seven, others being Noah, Abraham, Moses, Jesus, Muhammad, and Ismā'īl's son Muḥammad. Each had a helper (*waṣy*), Adam's being Seth. Trad. says that when first parents were expelled from Garden, A. landed in Ceylon and Eve at Jidda. They met at 'Arafāt (→ 'Arafa or 'Arafāt); after → Black Stone was sent down, A. built → ka'ba at Mecca. J.R.
Massignon, *Hallaj*, index; Nicholson, *Studies*, index; L. Ginzberg, *The legends of the Jews* (1909), I, pp. 47ff.; H. Speyer, *Die biblischen Erzählungen im Qoran* (Gräfenhainichen, 1931), pp. 41ff.; D. B. Macdonald, *Theology*, index; Sweetman, *I.C.T.*, I, II, IV, index; *E.I.*², I, pp. 176–8.
Book of → Adam. S.G.F.B.

Adamites Gnostic sect mentioned by → Epiphanius, whose members tried to live as Adam before the Fall. They renounced marriage, and worshipped in complete nudity. Name was later given to Waldenses, Dutch → Anabaptists, and others who have professed similar principles. (→ Nudity, Ritual). S.G.F.B.
R.G.G., I (1957), 91–2 ('Adamiten'); A. G. Dickens, *Reformation and Society in Sixteenth Century Europe* (1966), ill. 98.

Adamnan, St. (*c.* 624–704, Abbot of Iona), and one of its greatest scholars. At the Synod of Tara (697), he secured adoption of a law, the 'Canon of A.', forbidding women and children to be made prisoners of war. A. wrote an account of a pilgrim's visit to Palestine, entitled *De Locis Sanctis.* A. is venerated in Ireland as St. Eunan. S.G.F.B.
Bede, *Eccl. Hist.* V. 15f.; *D.C.C.*, *s.v.*

Adapa Anc. Mesopot. hero of city of Eridu. Acc. to myth, existent in fragmentary form, A. broke wings of South Wind and was summoned by → Anu, god of heaven, to answer for offence. A.'s patron god → Ea advised him to refuse any food or drink offered to him when he appeared before Anu, since they would prove fatal. Anu forgave

A., and offered him 'the food of life' and 'the water of life', which A. refused, thus, unwittingly depriving himself of immortality. The myth has caused much speculation, since ref. is made therein to the 'ill that A. has brought upon men'. Some scholars have seen A. myth as Mesopot. prototype of Heb. myth of Adam's → Fall. This view is difficult to sustain: it is not certain that A. was regarded as progenitor of mankind; moreover, A.'s loss of immortality resulted from his deception by Ea, and not from his own fault. The myth in its extant form was used in a healing ritual. S.G.F.B.

A. Heidel, *The Epic of Gilgamesh and Old Test. Parallels*[2] (1949), pp. 122–6; Brandon, *M.D.*, pp. 87–9.

Adeste Fideles Famous Christmas hymn, of anonymous authorship, dating prob. from 17th or 18th cent., and orig. in either France or Germany. John Reading, organist of Winchester Cathedral, in 17th cent., may have written its most popular tune. S.G.F.B.

Adhān (Announcement), technical term for call to prayer made by *mu'adhdhin* (muezzin) before five daily times of Muslim worship. Not long after → *hijra*, Muḥammad is said to have decided on this method on hearing of dream of 'Abdallah b. Zayd, wherein he saw someone calling Muslims to prayer from mosque roof. It is prob. that by time the A. was instituted, Md. felt it necessary to have different method from Jews and Christians of summoning people to worship. The words of the A. are: 'God is most great (4 times); I testify that there is no deity but God (twice); I testify that Md. is God's messenger (twice); come to prayer (twice); come to salvation (twice); God is most great (twice); there is no deity but God.' In the morning 'Prayer is better than sleep' (twice) is added after 'Come to salvation'. Shī'īs add 'Come to the best work' after 'Come to salvation'. Those who hear call should listen reverently and repeat words. At worship in a mosque words are repeated when people have lined up, and end with words 'the worship is now ready'. This is the *iqāma*. J.R.

E.I.[2], I, pp. 187f.; Wensinck, *Handbook*, s.v. *adhān*; *Mishkāt*, pp. 130ff.; Hughes, pp. 28f.; Querry, I, pp. 68ff.; Cragg, *Minaret*, Part II.

Adi-Buddha Term used in → Mhy. Buddhism, espec. in Nepal and Tibet, for the 'primordial Buddha', the Buddha without beginning. Necessity for such concept arises within context of developments in Mhy. Buddhism, where, as Snellgrove comments, the term A.-B. 'serves to distinguish the basic idea of buddha-hood from secondary buddha-forms'. Since term is found in Java as well as Nepal and Tibet, it is considered that it may have originated in the Mhy. of Bengal and thence have spread to both these regions. It was in connection with esoteric, → Tantric Buddhism, that concept was first developed; although embryo of concept can be found in earlier Buddh. thought. When notion of a plurality of Buddhas had developed in Tantric Buddhism, where there is belief in 5 Buddhas, thought of as different co-existent forms of one principle rather than (as in earlier Buddh. thought) forming an hist. succession, this led in turn to re-emphasis on one original Buddha who is central principle of Buddha-hood. It is this conception which receives name A.-B. The term *Svayambhu* (self-existent) is used synonym for A.-B. It has been suggested that this constitutes an approach to concept of a creator god, in that the A.-B. alone is held to be self-existent. Creative activity is not, however, a characteristic of A.-B.; he is not thought of as creating the five Buddhas, but as constituting their central principle. Other names by which A.-B. is known in Nepal support this view of the matter: *Adinatha*, or 'first protector' and *Svayambhulokanatha*, or 'self-existent protector of the world'; i.e., A.-B. is most characteristically *natha*, 'protector' rather than primeval creator-god. Linking of A.-B. and *Adinatha* may mean that for lay people A.-B. is assimilated to Hindu → Shiva (since *Adinatha* is title of Shiva); but this still does not imply that A.-B. is thought of as a creator. T.O.L.

Earliest evidence of concept of A.-B. is found in the *Namasangiti*, a book dating poss. to 7th cent. CE, in which bodhisattva → *Manjusri* is ref. to as A.-B.

Eliot, (*Hinduism and Buddhism*, III, 387) suggests that A.-B. concept developed as Buddh. Asia's attempt to come to terms with Islamic monotheism, and to show that monotheism was already contained in Buddh. thought. T.O.L.

D. Snellgrove, *Buddhist Himalaya* (1957); C. Eliot, *Hinduism and Buddhism* (1921, repr. 1957).

Adonai Heb. word *ex.* *'ādhōn* = 'Lord', used for Divine name in O.T. Jews read it as substitute for unutterable name of → Yahweh, which in Heb. text was usually pointed with vowels of A. Name of a Gnostic → aeon. (→ Kyrios). S.G.F.B.

R.G.G.[3], I, 97 ('Adonaj'); J. Doresse, *The Secret Books of the Egyptian Gnostics*, E.T. (1960), pp. 38, 56, 202.

Adonis Orig. Syrian or Phoenician vegetation-fertility god, whose Grk. name prob. derived from Semitic title 'Adon' ('Lord'), or 'Adoni' ('my Lord'). A. was assoc. as son or lover with fertility-goddess → Astarte, his chief cult-centre being Byblus; the annual staining of nearby river Adonis was regarded as commemorative of his death. Texts found at → Ugarit indicate currency of myth there (*c.* 1500 BC) concerning death of → Baal and lamentation of goddess → Anat, which was prob. prototype of A. myth, and Canaanite (→ Canaanite religion) version of the vegetation-fertility myth-and-ritual pattern (→ Myth and Ritual) widespread in anc. Near East. Cult of A. entered Graeco-Roman world, prob. via Cyprus, and myth became poetically elaborated. A. was repr. as beautiful youth, beloved of → Aphrodite, who was killed by boar, or as infant, entrusted by Aphrodite to → Persephone, who was permitted by → Zeus to spend part of each year alternatively above ground with Aphrodite and in underworld with Persephone. Alternating death and resurrection of A., doubtless derive from his orig. nature of vegetation deity (→→ Agriculture, Dying-Rising Gods). Annual rites of A. were similar to those of → Tammuz, and consisted of ritual lamentation, gen. by women, over effigy of dead god, and subsequent rejoicing at his resurrection. Acc. to Theocritus (*Idylls*, 15), at → Alexandria marriage of A. and Aphrodite was ritually enacted, followed next day by carrying of A.'s image to seashore amid lamentation. 'Gardens of A.', consisting of forced growth of seedlings, symbolising resurrection of A., were known both in → Athens and → Israel (Is. 17:10–1). A. became target of early Chr. polemic against paganism. A.'s relations with Aphrodite were espec. attacked; it was also argued that his death by a wild boar proved he was not divine. A.'s chief temple at Aphaka was destroyed by → Constantine, and a church was later erected on its site (→ Attis). S.G.F.B.

W. W. Baudissin, *Adonis und Esmun* (1911); J. G. Frazer, *Adonis, Attis, Osiris* (*G.B.*), I (1936³); *R.A.C.*, I (1950), *s.v.;* G. Contenau, *La civilisation phénicienne* (1948), pp. 94–5; J. Leipoldt (ed.), Bilderatlas, 9–11 (1925), pp. XII–XV, Abb. 94–108; *Kleine Pauly*, I (1964), *s.v.; R.G.G.*³, I (1957), *s.v.;* J. Gray, *The Canaanites* (1964), pp. 122–4, 133–4.

Adoptianism Spanish heresy of 8th cent., acc. to which Christ, in his humanity, was not true, but adoptive, Son of God. Elipandus, Abp. of Toledo, one of its chief exponents, taught that the → Logos, the true eternal Son of God, had adopted humanity in the nature, and not person of Christ. This doctrine was poss. intended to be acceptable to Moors of Toledo. Elipandus was supported by Felix, Bp. of Urgel (d. 818), against whom Alcuin wrote his *Contra Felicem*. A. provoked much opposition and Papal condemnation; it disappeared after d. of Elipandus. A modified form of A. was revived in 12th cent. by → Abelard and others; it was reflected later in attempts of Duns Scotus, Suarez, and others to provide an orthodox interpretation of Jesus as the adopted Son of God. S.G.F.B.

E.R.E., I (1908), pp. 104a–5b; *D.C.C.*, *s.v.*

Adoptionism This term should be used to distinguish a primitive form of → Christology from → Adoptianism. As Acts 2:36 shows, the orig. → Jew. Christians regarded Jesus as a man whom God made 'both Lord and Christ'. → Paul introduced an alternative explanation in I Cor. 2:6ff., acc. to which, a pre-existent divine being was incarnated in the person of Jesus. The former explanation was consistent with current Jew. belief, and it survived among the → Ebionites. A. Harnack, in his *Hist. of Dogma*, used A. to describe similar, but more sophisticated, interpretation found in → Hermas, Paul of Samosata, Theodore of Mopsuestia, → Nestorius, and the → Antiochene School. S.G.F.B.

Harnack, *H.D.*, I, p. 191, n. 3, and *passim* in other vols.; *E.R.E.*, I (1908), pp. 103a–4a; *R.G.G.*³, I (1957), 98–100; S. G. F. Brandon, *History, Time and Deity* (1965), pp. 164ff.

Adoration *Ex.* Lat. *adoratio*, which derived from *ad oro* = 'I pray to', and was equivalent of Grk. *latreia*, denoting act of worship to God alone. It was used more loosely (e.g. in Roman imperial court etiquette), in sense of Grk. *proskunēsis*, for acts of veneration addressed to persons or sacred objects. *Proskunēsis* could be used also for worship of God, as e.g. in Mt. 4:10. By 5th cent. Christians felt need of defining more exactly what was meant by A., prob. as result of Iconoclastic Controversy. The 2nd Council of → Nicaea (787) reserved *latreia* for worship of God alone, leaving *proskunēsis* to describe veneration of creatures. In Western Church *latria* was accepted for adoration of God, and *dulia* (*ex.* Grk. *douleia*) for veneration of creatures, incl. → Virgin Mary. A. has become current term in R.C. Church, and sometimes in → C. of E., for a service in which Eucharistic elements are adored, acc. to doc. of Real Presence of Christ in these elements. S.G.F.B.

Kleine Pauly, I (1964), 72–3 ('Adoratio'); *D.C.C.*, *s.v.; C.E.*, I, *s.v.*

(of Cross) The tendency appeared early among Christians to worship the → Cross of Christ. The *latreia* of C. was forbidden by 2nd Council of → Nicaea (787); but Thomas → Aquinas taught that *latria* (→ Adoration) could be paid to Cross. A ceremony of the A.-C. is observed in R.C. Church on → Good Fridays. The worshippers kiss a crucifix and adore it on their knees. S.G.F.B.

E.R.E., I (1908), p. 120a; *R.G.G.*³, IV (1960), 52 ('Kreuzfest').

Adultery (Babylon) Code of Hammurabi (*c.* 1728 BC) legislates carefully about marriage and A. Penalties for A. are severe: the offended husband could punish wife and paramour himself or bring them before a court; he could require their deaths, or mutilation or free them. A Bab. proverb equated the sexual organs of the adulterer and

adulteress, and disease could result from A., at the hand of the god Urash. S.G.F.B.
H. W. F. Saggs, *The Greatness that was Babylon* (1962), pp. 213, 431, 464; L. Delaporte, *La Mésopotamie* (1923), pp. 84, 314–6.
(Buddhism) Adultery is mentioned in Buddh. texts as one of number of forms of similar sexual misconduct. Thus, a monk who is guilty of A. is to be excommunicated from Order; but this is so in any case of sexual intercourse in which a monk is wilfully involved, irrespective of whether woman is married or not. For laymen sexual intercourse is forbidden with any woman who is under any form of protection—whether that of parents, or guardians, or husband. However, in one of oldest texts, the *Sutta* → *Nipata*, sexual intercourse with other men's wives is repr. as the most grave in series of examples of misconduct (*Sn.* 106–8). It is also regarded as serious cause of evil → *karma*, the effects of which would persist beyond present life and bring serious retribution (S. II:259). T.O.L.
(China and Far East) Acc. to Confucian ethic, which had predominant influence in China and throughout Far East, and which devised most stringent rules to govern relationships between the sexes, A. was one of seven causes for divorce, the first being failure of wife to produce a male heir. Chastity was made obligatory only on the female. Strictly speaking a man had only one legal wife, but society tolerated extra-marital sexual indulgence on part of male, and polygamy and concubinage were tolerated. Marriage being contract between families, and filial piety taking precedence over the mutual relations of husband and wife, adultery was fairly common. To avoid public scandal and expense of litigation, condign punishment for A. was often meted out by family concerned, guilty parties being beaten, maimed or disfigured. A wife found guilty of A., having been divorced and abandoned by her husband's family, had resource to suicide, servitude or the brothel. In modern times the legal status of women in Far Eastern countries has been immeasurably improved. A. by male or female often results in divorce granted by courts of law. D.H.S.
J. D. Ball, *Things Chinese* (5th ed. 1925), p. 185.
(Christian) In the Sermon on the Mount → Jesus is repr. as (i) going behind prohibition of A. in 7th Commandment to condemn an adulterous disposition of mind; (ii) as allowing divorce of a wife only on grounds of her unchastity (*porneia*, which must = *moicheia*, 'adultery' here); (iii) as equating marriage with a divorced woman with A. (Mt. 5:27, 31–2). Although parallel passages in Mk. 10:2–12 and Lk. 16:18 omit the exceptive clause in Mt. 5:32, Church has decreed A. as constituting cause for divorce. Severe penance was imposed for A. by Council of Elvira (305). Christian emperors Constantine and Constans revived earlier capital penalty for A. Death penalty for man was confirmed by Justinian (d. 565), and life imprisonment in nunnery was decreed for an adulteress, whose husband did not receive her back within two years. (→ Adultery, Roman). S.G.F.B.
E.R.E., I, pp. 131b–3b; *C.M.H.*, II, p. 106.
(Egypt) Anc. Egyptians from *c.* 1500 BC, regarded A. as sin: chap. 125 of → *Book of the Dead* incl. A. among offences punishable in *post-mortem* judgment (→ Judgment of Dead). Egypt. wisdom literature contains warnings against A. Women gen. enjoyed equal status with men; but extant evidence suggests that women could be punished severely for A., incl. burning: nothing is said of penalty incurred by men. S.G.F.B.
E.R.E., I, pp. 126b–7a; A. Erman u. H. Ranke, *Aegypten* (1923), pp. 176ff.; W. M. F. Petrie, *Social Life in Anc. Egypt* (1923), pp. 112ff.
(Greek) Extant evidence is mostly from Athenian sources, but it prob. indicates attitude towards A. elsewhere in Greece. This attitude resulted from importance of family in social structure. Since a wife's A. might introduce alien blood into family, her conduct was treated with great severity. If her A. was proved, her husband was obliged to repudiate her. She was excluded from temples: if she attempted to enter, she could be assaulted by any citizen and stripped of her clothing and ornaments, but not maimed or killed. The husband could kill her paramour, if caught in act, or choose some lesser punishment, incl. money compensation. A. of husband was condoned by law, unless it infringed rights of another family. S.G.F.B.
E.R.E., I, pp. 127a–b; H. Licht, *Sexual Life in Anc. Greece* (E.T. 1949), pp. 59ff.
(Hebrew) Heb. legislation contains both categorical and detailed probitions of A. (e.g. Ex. 20:14; Lev. 18:20; Deut. 22:22–9). The penalty for both parties (with some variations) is death by stoning. This legislation is cited as having divine authority: in Deut. 22:22 the reason for death penalty is explained—'so you shall purge the evil from Israel'. In Heb. lit. A. is used as metaphor for Israel's unfaithfulness to → Yahweh. In Num. 5:11–31 prescription is made for ordeal of the 'water of bitterness', to which a wife might be subjected by her jealous husband. In Rabbinic law punishment for A. was modified into the divorce of wife, who lost all her dowry rights: the offending man was scourged. The ordeal of the 'water of bitterness' was also abolished. A. was regarded as irrevocably meriting Gehenna (*Sota*, 4b). S.G.F.B.
E.R.E., I, pp. 130a–1a, 135a–7a; J. Pedersen, *Israel* (1926), I–II, p. 415, 427, 547–52.

(Islam) (*Adultery and Fornication*). Arabic uses *zinā'* for both forms of illegal sexual intercourse, but punishment differs. The Qur. denounces fornication (cf. xvii, 34; xxv, 68), and lays down certain rules about punishments—not so clear as one might desire. iv, 19 says that women who, on evidence of four witnesses, have committed *fāḥisha* are to be confined to their houses for remainder of their lives, or till God appoints a way for them. It is argued that *fāḥisha* here means some form of indecency short of sexual intercourse; but that is not clear because word is used in verse 30 obviously meaning adultery. That verse ref. to slavewomen whose punishment is to be half that of free women. xxiv, 2 prescribes 100 stripes for both parties guilty of fornication. A trad. says → 'Umar declared the Qur. contained a verse regarding stoning of married men and women convicted of adultery; there is no evidence of its existence. Trad. has much to say about punishment of adulterers and fornicators. One, given by → Muslim, says unmarried people shall receive 100 lashes and be banished for a year, but married people will receive 100 lashes and be stoned to death. To prove A. or fornication, four competent witnesses who have seen act being committed are necessary; if their evidence is unsatisfactory, they are liable to receive 80 lashes. Confession by a guilty party is accepted as full evidence, some holding it must be uttered on four separate occasions; but if the confession is withdrawn punishment may not be inflicted. J.R.

E.I., II, p. 606 (*ḳadhf*); IV, pp. 1227f. (*zinā'*); Hughes, pp. 11, 130f., 479 (*qazf*); Nöldeke, *Geschichte*[2], I, pp. 248ff.; *Mishkāt*, pp. 757ff.; Lane, *Egyptians*, chs. vii and xiii.

(Primitive Peoples) In primitive societies, since woman is gen. regarded as property of her husband, A. is essentially an infringement of his property rights, and offending wife and her paramour are punished accordingly. Punishments are various, incl. death and mutilation. Rarely has wife redress against her husband's A. In so far as A. has a relig. or magic. significance, it is in terms of pollution it causes. Among the Nuer of southern Sudan, rituals are performed on behalf of husband to prevent sickness resulting from wife's A. (E. E. Evans-Pritchard, *Nuer Religion*, 1956, pp. 185–7). S.G.F.B.

E.R.E., I, pp. 122–6b.

(Roman) The Romans distinguished between *adulterium* (sexual intercourse of wife with any man other than husband, or of husband with married woman) and *struprum* (husband's misconduct with other than married women). During Republic, husband could kill wife for A. A. in the Empire was dealt with under the *Lex Julia*, sponsored by Augustus. Roman law then first recognised A. as civil offence, and allowed others than father or husband concerned to prosecute. Adulteress lost one half of dowry and one third of property; an adulterer forfeited half of property. Death penalty was excluded from orig. form of *Lex Julia*. Adulteress could not remarry. A father could still kill daughter and paramour, if caught in act; but right was withdrawn from husband of thus killing wife. The *Lex Julia* continued until amended by Constantine, under Christian influence, when death penalty was intro. for adulterer. This was confirmed by Justinian, who added lifelong imprisonment in a nunnery for adulteress, unless reclaimed by husband. (→ Adultery, Christ.). S.G.F.B.

E.R.E., I, pp. 134b–5a; O. Kiefer, *Sexual Life in Anc. Rome* (E.T. 1934), pp. 31ff.

Advaita Vedānta 'Non-Dualistic Vedanta' is most influential of schools of → Vedanta, in the Hindu trad. It was given its main shape by → Sankara (CE ? 788–820), though he was influenced by → Gaudapada. Accord. to Advaita, there is a strict identity between ultimate reality (*Brahman*) and the → Atman or self, i.e. the eternal element within man (and other living beings). Thus the Upanisadic formula → *tat tvam asi* ('That art thou') is to be interpreted strictly. It follows that if the Self and *Brahman* are identical, there is but one Self. Liberation occurs through realisation that one's Self is identical with *Brahman*: this realisation does not bring about the identity, which was always there, but it releases the person from implication in the illusory world and from the round of → rebirth. Until this happens, individuals conceive themselves as separate entities and more widely conceive the world itself as distinct from ultimate reality. Thus they are victims of ignorance (→ *avidya*) and illusion (→ *maya*). But from standpoint of higher truth, revealed in experience of realisation and pointed to by such scriptural statements as *tat tvam asi*, both individuality and notion of a real world independent of *Brahman* must be transcended. The idea that there is a 'higher truth' distinct from 'common-sense or ordinary truth' Sankara owed in part to → Madhyamika Buddhism; the distinction enabled him to work out a systematic exegesis of Vedic scriptures and the *Brahmasutra*, normative for exponents of Vedanta. The higher level of truth is complemented by a lower level in which ordinary judgments implying reality of world, etc., have provisional validity. At a third and even lower level there are ordinary illusions, like mistaking a coiled rope for a snake; the relationship between the first and second level is like that between the second and third—so that with experience of identity with *Brahman* one perceives the illusory and mistaken nature of ordinary, empirical knowledge. At the empirical level, however, *Brahman* can be conceived as personal Creator of world and as object of worship: at this level it appears as the → *Isvara*. But from higher standpoint he is seen as implicated in the illusoriness of the world which he creates. Hence one transcends the idea of a personal object of devotion when one attains the higher identity-experience. This application of two levels of truth to relig. life forms basis of Sankara's system of exegesis. For those texts which point to the identity are treated as belonging to the higher level: those which talk of sacrificial duties and the fabric of ritual and devotional religion belong to lower level. In this way, the tensions existing in the → Upanisads and other texts are resolved. However, the system of exegesis implied that Brahmanical relig. itself belongs to the empirical, illusory level and so needs to be transcended—an implication which made Sankara seem revolutionary to his Brahmin contemporaries and caused him to be accused of being a 'crypto-Buddhist' by some of the orthodox. Sankara's theology made sense of the trad. distinction between *saguṇam* and *nirguṇam Brahman—Brahman* with and without qualities (attributes). *Brahman* with qualities is the *Isvara; Brahman* without qualities is the indefinable ultimate reality, the nature of which, however, is summed up as consisting of *saccidānanda*—being, consciousness and bliss (being, because it is of the nature of undifferentiated reality; consciousness, because it is undifferentiated consciousness, the *Atman*; bliss, because it is of the nature of liberation, etc.). Sankara elaborated this system as a method of exegesis, but backed it also by philosophical arguments. His work was carried on by a number of import. writers, notably Maṇḍana Miśra, Śureśvara, and Vācaspati Miśra (of the 9th cent. CE); *Śrīharṣa* (12th cent.); and Madhusūdana and Appaya Dikṣita (16th cent.). Sriharsa and others evolved a dialectical method of presenting Advaita, through the attempt to expose contradictions in opposing positions, and indeed in all positions attempting to describe the nature of *nirgunam Brahman* (this was analogous to the dialectical method implicit in Madhyamika). Although Sankara was not properly speaking a subjective idealist, since within the realm of empirical truth the world has objective reality, there were tendencies to interpret Advaita in a subjective idealist sense, by the 'subjective-creationist school' (the *dṛṣṭisṛṣṭivāda*), which held that the 'world' is the product of subjective perceptions. In mod. times there has been a considerable revival of Advaita, partly because of apparent congruence between Advaitin absolutism and → Hegelian idealism; partly because theory of levels of truth could be extended in interests of a synthesis between levels and forms of religion—it being felt that the special genius of Hinduism lay in its ability to produce unity out of plurality (in contradistinction to Christianity, which appeared to create relig. disunity, by criticising and seeking to supplant other faiths). To a substantial extent, Advaita has provided basis of mod. Hindu ideology; among notable exponents of the new Vedanta have been →→ Vivekananda and Radhakrishnan. N.S.

S. N. Dasgupta, *A History of Indian Philosophy*, vols. 1 and 2 (1922, 1932); S. K. Murthy, *Revelation and Reason in Advaita Vedanta* (1959); S. Radhakrishnan, *Indian Philosophy*, 2 vols. (1958); W. S. Urquhart, *The Vedanta and Modern Thought* (1928); S. M. Srinivasa Chari, *Advaita and Visistadvaita* (1961); S. Radhakrishnan *The Brahma Sutra* (1960).

Advent *Ex.* Lat. '*adventus*' = '*coming*'. In anc. Grk. relig. it was believed that deities periodically visited various sanctuaries dedicated to them. Their advent or *epidēmia* was celebrated as festival. In Christianity, A. is an annual period of preparation for → Christmas, during which theme is Christ's Second Coming in judgment. Observance of A. in W. Church dates from 6th cent., and period includes the 4 Sundays before Christmas. In → E. Church A. lasts 40 days. A. is a penitential season, when purple is the liturgical colour, but is kept with less strictness than Lent. A. Sunday marks beginning of eccl. year. (→ Parousia). S.G.F.B.

R.A.C., I (1950), *s.v.; R.G.G.*³, I (1957), *s.v.; D.C.C.*, *s.v.*

Adventists, Second Sect founded by William Miller (1781–1849) in U.S.A., in expectation of Second Coming of Christ, which was fixed for 1843–4. Date was changed many times subsequently. The orig. 'Evangelical Adventists' died out: the movement is now repr. by 'Second Advent Christians', and 'Seventh Day Adventists'. (→ Parousia). S.G.F.B.

*R.G.G.*³, I, 101–3.

Advocatus Diaboli The 'Devil's Advocate' is appointed to put objections, if any, to → canonisation of a person of saintly reputation in R.C. Church. He opposes the Advocatus Dei who proposes canonisation. S.G.F.B.

Adyton Grk. word for most sacred part of temple, accessible only to priests. It was closely assoc. with *abaton*, Grk. term denoting place made → holy by presence of a numinous being (→ Numen), and, therefore, treated as → tabu. S.G.F.B.

Kleine Pauly, I, 5 ('Abaton').

Aegean Religion Expression used to describe relig. in an homogeneous cultural area, comprising Crete, Cyprus, Cyclades, Grk. mainland, and, sometimes, adjoining coastal area of Asia Minor and Syria, in pre-Hellenic period (before 1200 BC). Since subject is better dealt with under → Cretan-Mycenaean Relig., gen. character of primitive form of A.-R. only will be noted here. From Neolithic period and early Bronze Age many figurines of nude women have been found, mostly in tombs throughout area. This fact, together with prominence of a goddess in later Cretan religion suggest that A.-R. was characterised by cult of a goddess connected with fertility and death (→ Great Goddess). The presence of such a cult on Asiatic mainland, with which Aegean area had close contacts, offers further confirmation (→ Cybele). There is some Cypriot evidence also of a ritual involving a goddess, a god or priest, female dancers, and serpents. Cretan religion is doubtless to be seen, in its later stages, as an elaboration of a relig. trad. common to Aegean area. (→→ Eleusinian Mysteries; Greek Relig.). S.G.F.B.

G. Glotz, *La civilisation égéenne* (1937), p. 263; C. Picard, *Les religions préhelléniques* (1948), pp. 46ff.; *Bilderatlas*, 7 (G. Karo), 1925; J. Charbonneaux in *H.G.R.*, II, pp. 3–6; S. Casson, *Ancient Cyprus* (1937), pp. 19ff.; S. Hood, *The Home of the Heroes* (1967), pp. 17ff. S.G.F.B.

Aegis Attribute of →→ Zeus and Athene, repr. as goatskin, but prob. orig. conceived as storm-cloud, due to similarity of *aix* ('goat') and *kataigis* ('hurricane'). A. was regarded as invincible protection, capable also of inspiring terror. Athene is depicted with A. form mid 6th cent. BC; it has form of short cloak, edged with snakes and → Gorgon's head in centre. S.G.F.B.

O.C.D., *s.v.; Kleine Pauly*, I, 164–5 ('Aigis').

Aelia Capitolina New city built by Emperor Hadrian (*c.* CE 130) on site of → Jerusalem, after its destruction in CE 70. A.C. was named after Emperor (P. Aelius Hadrianus) and → Jupiter Capitolinus. Statues of Hadrian and Jupiter were erected → Temple area. The topography of A.C., still not exactly known, is important for determining Chr. holy sites, esp. Calvary and the Holy Sepulchre. S.G.F.B.

H. Vincent and F. M. Abel, *Jérusalem Nouvelle*, 4 vols. (1914–26); M. Join-Lambert, *Jerusalem* (E.T. 1966[2]), pp. 102ff.; K. M. Kenyon, *Jerusalem* (1967).

Aeneas Trojan hero, son of Anchises and goddess → Aphrodite. In Homer's *Iliad* (→ Homer), → Poseidon prophesies A. and his descendants would rule over Trojans (20.307). A. escapes from destruction of Troy, with his father, Ascanius, his son, and ancestral gods (→ Penates). Later Grk. writers repr. A. as visiting or founding many places in Greece, as well as Delos and Crete. Hellanicus (b. 500 BC) brings him to Latium. Early Latin writers, seeking a founder of Roman state, make him founder of Lavinium, head of the Latin League, and connect him also with Dido, queen of Carthage (→ Carthaginian Religion). Virgil fashioned these legends into epic of the *Aeneid*, presenting A. as divinely appointed founder of Rome's *imperium*. In *Aeneid*, Virgil develops Homer's emphasis on A.'s piety into Roman ideal of *pietas*, i.e. devotion to parents, gods, and destiny of Rome. Virgil thus assisted Augustus' policy of strengthening trad. Roman virtues and relig. S.G.F.B.

O.C.D., *s.v.; Kleine Pauly*, I, 173–5 ('Aineias'); F. Altheim, *Hist. of Roman Religion* (E.T., 1938), pp. 35, 39, 153, 206.

Aeon(s): Grk. *Aiōn* Concept of great importance in relig. and philosophical speculation of Graeco-Roman world, but of considerable complexity and variety of use. Its primary meaning, 'life', 'lifetime' (Homer, *Il.* 16:453), was extended to mean long periods of time, i.e. ages. It could also denote eternity. A. was used by Presocratic philosophers for space-time (e.g. Anaximander, frg. 10). In → Orphism, A. was personified as son of → Chronos. Grk. conception of A. was prob. influenced by Iranian idea of → Zurvan, in its two forms of *Zurvan akarana* ('infinite Time') and *Zurvan dareghō-chvadāta* ('Time of the Long Dominion'). → Mithraism furthered these conceptions: images of a lion-headed monster in the *mithraea* prob. repr. *Zurvan dareghō-chvadāta*, and were identified with A. *Zurvan akarana* influenced conception of A. as supreme deity, and led to its adoption as tutelary deity of → Alexandria. Further transformation of concept occurred in Alex., prob. owing to native Egypt. ideas of Time and assoc. of A. with → Sarapis and → Agathos-Daimon. Birth of A. was celebrated annually on night of 5–6 January at Alex., which gave rise to esoteric idea of A. as Eternity perpetually extended in a series of *aiōnes*. From Alex. in 1st cent. BC, A. came to Rome, where it was assimilated with → Janus, and inspired conception of → Aeternitas. In Gnostic speculation (→ Gnosticism), A. underwent strange metamorphosis. In → Hermetic lit., A. as the *deuteros theos* ('second god'), creates the World (*kosmos*) and Time ('*chronos*'). From idea of a transcendental deity, who was 'king of the A.s' (*basileus tōn aiōnōn:* I Tim. 1:17), poss. in terms of A. at Alex., arose conception of A.s as entities mediating between supreme deity and material world. Hierarchies of such A.s constituted the → Pleroma of certain Gnostic systems. Time-aspect of A. finds expression in esoteric form in the N.T.: Paul conceives both of a series of A.s and a present A. (I Cor. 2:6–8); Mt. 12:32 envisages 'this (present) A' and 'the A. to come'. (→ Time). S.G.F.B.

R.A.C., I (1950), pp. 193–204 ('Aion'); *Kleine Pauly*, I, pp. 185–8 ('Aion'); S. G. F. Brandon, *History*, *Time and Deity* (1965), ch. 3.

Aeschylus Grk. dramatist (525–456 BC), often called 'Father of Tragedy', is notable for moral tension manifest in his plays between trad. Grk. concept of the gods and his own sense of tragedy of human life. In early plays → Zeus is gen. presented as omnipotent and inscrutable, but just. There is some suggestion also of an impersonal universal order, to which Zeus is subordinate and of which he is the personal embodiment. The *Oresteia* treat double problem of hereditary criminality and blood-guiltiness. The inevitable penalty of blood has to be paid, despite innocent suffering involved: 'while Zeus abides on his throne . . . the doer must suffer; this is the eternal law' (*Ag.* 1563–4). The theological situation in his *Prometheus* is strikingly different. Here Zeus is shown as an arbitrary tyrant, torturing the benefactor of mankind. A.'s originality lay in attempt to moralise trad. beliefs; but he was unable to break free from their intellectual constriction; → *hubris* remains for him the unforgivable sin. (→ Prometheus). S.G.F.B.

E.R.E., I, *s.v.; Kleine Pauly*, I, pp. 192–8 ('Aischylos'); *O.C.D.*, *s.v.;* G. Nebel, *Weltangst und Götterzorn* (1951), pp. 51ff.

Aesculapius Lat. form of Grk. Asklepios. In Grk. mythology the 'blameless physician', son of → Apollo and Coronis. A. was taught the healing art by Chiron, and killed by → Zeus for restoring Hippolytus to life. His daughter Hygieia was personification of Health. A. was orig. either a → chthonian deity or deified hero: his snake-'familiar' indic. some chthonian orig. Cult of A. orig. in Thessaly, but achieved its fame elsewhere, espec. at Epidauros: other notable centres were at Pergamon, Cos, and Rome (on the Insula Tiberina). In Egypt., A. was identified with → Imhotep. The cult of A. was very popular. Exvotos attest numbers of those who sought cures in his temples: the method used was → incubation, supported by various therapeutic means, incl. dietetic regimens, baths and exercise. In a paean to A. at Epidauros was a thrice repeated invocation: 'Hail, Lord, Great Saviour, Saviour of the world'. In art, A. was depicted as a mature bearded man, similar to Zeus, but of more benign expression: his attributes are the staff and snake; the latter often coiled about the staff. (→ Healing Gods). S.G.F.B.

Kleine Pauly, I, pp. 644–8 ('Asklepios'); *R.A.C.*, I, 795–9 ('Asklepios'); *O.C.D.*, 16b; 106b; 106b–7.

Aeternitas Lat. personification of eternity. Repr. on Roman coins from reign of Vespasian (CE 69–79), its most notable image is on column of Antonius Pius (CE 86–161), depicting → apotheosis of emperor: A. is shown as heroic male fig., with eagle's wings, holding a serpent-encircled globe. A. was closely associated with *mystik* of Rome's imperial destiny in twofold sense of *aeternitas populi Romani* and *aeternitas imperii* → Aion). S.G.F.B.

R.A.C., I, 197–200; *Kleine Pauly*, I, 103–4.

Aetiology Explanation given in terms of causes. Many myths are aetiological, in that they explain origin or cause of things: e.g. wearing of clothes in Gen. 3:21; temple of Marduk at Babylon (→ Enuma elish). A. has been an important topic in metaphysics since early Grk. philosophers sought cause for existence of universe. (→ Myth and Ritual). S.G.F.B.

E.R.E., I, *s.v.*

Afghāni → Jamāl al-Dīn al-Afghānī. J.R.

Afghanistan (Buddhism) Area known today as Afghanistan was formerly known by such names as Gandhāra, Kandahar, and Balkh. By beginning of Christ. era this was strongly Buddh. area: Archaeological research in 20th cent. has demonstrated existence of a flourishing Buddh. culture which began to decline in 7th cent. CE; it had virtually ended by beginning of 10th cent., when Islam finally displaced it. (→ Gandhāra). T.O.L.

Africa, East: Ritual Cults and Beliefs The indigenous people of Kenya, Uganda and Tanzania fall into six main groups (Goldthorpe and Wilson, 1960)—orig. inhabitants (e.g. Dorobo) still found in small pockets: Nilotes (e.g. Acholi, Luo); Hamites (e.g. Somali, Galla); Nilo-Hamites (e.g. Maasai, Markweta); Sudanic (e.g. Madi, Lugbara); and Bantu (e.g. Ganda, Nkore). They are subdivided into about 150 tribes, each having distinctive features. About many of them reliable information is not available. This article attempts to describe only four, sufficiently contrasting, groups in detail. Much research remains to be done; none of the accounts must be regarded as complete. Many cults and beliefs have been modified by impact of West. But few are wholly extinct; and present tense is used throughout.

(1) Maasai are nomadic pastoralists, organised primarily into age-grades. Boys, through → circumcision, become *moran*—the fighting force. *Moran*, through further ritual, become elders, entitled to marry; there are two further grades of elders, entered through rituals which confer right to administer, respectively, domestic and tribal rituals. Girls become adult through clitoridectomy. God is Enk Ai. (In other contexts *enk ai* means 'rain'. But here, as elsewhere, there is no confusion between God and material phenomenon which gives him a name). In the beginning Enk Ai set Maasinda on earth (though there is no myth of creation of natural order). His four sons became founding fathers of Maasai (owners of all cattle), forest hunters, agriculturalists and smiths. In course of long migration, the Maasai came to the precipitous escarpment of Kerio river. Only the strongest reached the top; and Enk Ai is addressed, 'O thou who broughtest us up from

Kerio'. After first two groups to be initiated as *moran* when ascent was done, he is named 'Enk Ai of Ilkitilik and Ilkuarri'. He is dynamically involved at every point of life, preserving order and punishing injustice and ensuring effectiveness of deserved blessings and just curses. Daily prayer by individuals, as well as corporate prayer on special occasions, is spontaneous feature of Maasai life. His chief intermediaries are *iloibonok* (sing., *oloiboni—aibon*, 'to make medicine'), who come from particular clan and whose hereditary powers are traced back for ten generations to first who fell, full-grown, from sky, married Maasai woman and sent his sons to practise among other tribes. While all Maasai may address Enk Ai direct in prayer, *iloibonok* are in direct communication with him through dreams, trances or pebbles poured from horn. His sanction, through them, must be obtained before any import. social event. But all executive power rests with elders. *Iloibonok* are credited with remarkable powers of foresight. They can make and unmake rain. They prescribe ritual measures to be taken against social and individual troubles. They act against sorcerers, treat disease and prob. have genuine surgical skill. They may practise sorcery against rival or to pursue a grudge. But such anti-social activity gives bad repute and is rare. Other members of same sub-clan can stop rain and are skilled sorcerers. There are no demi-gods or nature spirits. The dead are normally left in the bush to be eaten by hyenas; there is no belief in personal survival after death. Very old and rich men, or women who have borne many children, may be buried under heap of stones. The eldest son tries to live near; and the 'life' of such a man may return to commingle with his cattle and cause their increase. With marginal exception of trances of *iloibonok*, behaviour is not interpreted in terms of spirit-possession. Hysterical and cataleptic symptoms, experienced by women during tribal fertility rite, would certainly be regarded in many African societies as spirit-possession: but not by the Maasai. Sorcery is widely used to ensure safe return from journey, guard homes, protect and increase cattle. It is also widely suspect as cause of ill-luck and sickness and can be countered only through consultation with *oloiboni*. A curse may be used (a) against unknown miscreant, e.g. thief or murderer; the consequences for him are so severe that he will ultimately confess in order to receive just punishment and restoration to tribe (b) by seniors against juniors who misbehave (c) by whole society against member who has become public danger. A just curse is sustained by Enk Ai and is always effective. It can be removed only through reconciliation, followed by blessing of cursed by curser. Curse of man, not withdrawn before his death, has no remission. Unjust curse has no effect. The → evil eye, on the other hand, is entirely arbitrary in its effects. It is hereditary; one clan is partic. notorious. Although its possessor may use his power with deliberate evil intent, its effect is normally involuntary. Simply to look at another may cause him to faint or, in extreme case, die. Only cure is for 'owner' of eye to spit on victim; a stranger, entering house where there are children, spits on them as prophylactic measure. Exceptional beauty, courage or wealth are potentially dangerous to their possessors. Simply to be admired and talked about may itself bring disaster.

(2) The Markweta, one of Kalenjin group of tribes, are settled agriculturalists. Totemic clans are more import. than among Maasai. But age-grades are fundamental part of social organisation; → initiation of both young men and girls is necessary prelude to adulthood. Without it, Markweta is still a 'boy' and unable, at death, to enter society of ancestors. Although surgical operation of circumcision is focal to male rite, complete rite occupies six months and is introduction, through provocation to shame and fear, considerable hardship and bullying, to essential tribal *mores*. God is Asis ('sun'), 'daughter of the day', 'one who shines', 'man of the sky', 'one who crosses sky'. He is omnipotent, omniscient arbiter of all things and guarantor of right. He is directly addressed only in major crises and has no immediate effect on day-to-day activities. But his presence is deeply felt. The common cosmology is that things have always been as they are. But one story tells how, in the beginning, Asis and the Moon lived on earth with Man and the animals. The first two became suspicious of Man and escaped to sky. Too late animals found that Man was killer and fled to forest. Asis has active agent, Ilat, spirit of thunder, lightning and waters. He may strike house or stock, or drown children or stock. But, though he cannot restore dead, he may be influenced by prayer to return what he has taken (e.g. people or cattle, swept away by floods, may be found alive). If he strikes piece of ground, burning grass, he is offered beer. Undetected criminal may be cursed, and Ilat will reveal him by striking his house or stock. During drought, sacrifices are offered to Ilat, asking him to send rain. If the living are not to be troubled by ghost of dead person, corpse must be buried acc. to trad. rites. As it is carried to grave, a man follows behind, throwing stones to drive away ghosts, which are said to be coming to call living to join dead. All involved in burial must, before again putting on their clothes, wash away 'ghost' from their bodies; deceased's ornaments are ritually washed with beer, while ghosts are

driven away with cry, 'Go away. This man has been made sweet'. Markweta are nevertheless on intimate terms with ghosts of their relatives, who visit them in dreams to give advice or simply chat. Each child is named after ghost who, in ritual held at end of mother's confinement, 'agrees' to its name being used. Ghostly advice must be followed, or failure of crops may ensue. There are large number of rites, both domestic and public, related to individual development and crises, and to welfare of society, of crops and stock. For most part they are administered by experienced elder. In some, Asis is addressed directly; in all his presence is intensely felt. But, even when sheep is killed, rites often seem to be automatic in their action rather than sacrifices to personal god. In case of unresolved dispute (e.g. legal prosecution in which there are no impartial witnesses, theft, when there are many potential suspects) all parties take oath which surrenders judgment to Asis. The consequences to guilty are expected to be extremely severe; recourse to this oath is discouraged unless no other solution is apparent. There are at least four types of ritual specialist: (a) *Reed-blowers,* whose skill is passed from father to eldest son among allied Endo people and who travel widely, seeking custom. They divine and curse humans, animals and thieves, and drive away owls of ill-omen from homesteads (b) *Herbalists,* most of whom are women. They use knowledge acquired through experience and passed on by older practitioners. They are guided by their toes in finding herbs they seek. Skill of each is usually limited to curing symptoms of partic. types (c) *Diviners,* who use variety of material means to divine cause of troubles which have not yielded to empirical treatment (d) *Orgoy,* who may be consulted about prospects of war or weather but are regarded as very jealous, so that great care is taken not to offend them. Although they do not advertise their services, they are supposed to acquire great wealth. Sorcery is widely feared as source of misfortune and protective charms are carried. Convicted sorcerer is killed. Evil eye takes much same form as among Maasai.

(3) Nkore are mixture of settled agriculturalists and invading nomadic pastoralists, from whom come ruling family. There is little intermarriage. But the two groups live in peaceful symbiosis, speak same language, share same totemic, patrilineal clans and have fundamentally same relig. beliefs. Ruhanga, the Creator, made all things and is known as 'Creator', 'Giver', 'Lord of Sun'. His presence can be felt in thunder and lightning. His glory is shown in rainstorms and black clouds. His is above all things, omnipresent, moving like sun across whole earth. He sustains both the natural and social order. But, though it is customary to draw his attention to import. ritual acts, and prayer may be said to him by individuals, he is not expected to intervene in human affairs. The order which he made may may be disrupted. But consequences are automatic, impersonal. It is not poss. to speak of offending him, or to feel guilty towards him. Probably most import. cult is that of Cwezi *emandwa,* ghosts of legendary dynasty of kings. Six are named; and each family has three as guardian spirits, derived from lineages of husband, wife and husband's mother. Each has shrine at which regular offerings are made by member of family (of any age and either sex), 'chosen' by *emandwa* and initiated in a three-day rite of great brutality. Their function is to preserve well-being of family and its property. But, as often as not, they are neglected until crisis occurs, when diviner is consulted to find cause and advise appropriate ritual action. Other *emandwa* are responsible, e.g., for epidemics of smallpox or look after interests of specialist groups such as hunters or diviners. After burial, eldest son is responsible for making regular offerings to father's ghost. Special sheep or goat is dedicated to him and must be replaced if it dies. Small shrine is built, in which are placed spear, beer pot and food basket. Every evening food is taken to shrine with the prayer, 'Care for me. Care for my children. Care for my home.' Or ghost's help may be asked against junior kin who lack respect for their elders. If the food is eaten by animals, it is sign that ghost (or, in other cases, *emandwa*) has accepted offering and shared it with others. Each new moon a cow or goat is killed at shrine with same prayer. But, in practice, ghosts are experienced as wholly malevolent. They may continue active for up to three generations. Ghost of any member of household (incl. children and non-kin) may interfere in wholly arbitrary manner with survivors or their stock. The head of household then makes offering, prescribed by diviner, at shrine. Both → witchcraft and sorcery are widely suspect as causes of misfortune. The curse is used primarily as means of enforcing kinship obligations. Evil eye is hereditary, esp. in one clan. Diviners are consulted to discover non-empirical agent of misfortunes and use grasshoppers, seeds of plants or guts of chicken: or become possessed by *emandwa.* In certain cases of illness, in add. to prescribing ritual action, they refer patient to herbalist. The king is centre of tribal unity. His name is not spoken during his reign nor after his death; he is known by such titles as 'he who bestrides the earth'. He has supreme power over his people. His spit is major blessing. He must not be hurt, nor be seen to be old. If he feels his powers failing, he must commit suicide by special

royal poison. At his death there is total cessation of work throughout kingdom. His corpse is left to rot in forest. He is reborn as maggot from corpse; this turns into a lion cub. Only then can his successor sit on throne and rival claimants offer battle. The continuing symbol of kingship—poss. superior to individual kings—is royal drums (the only drums in kingdom), to which daily offerings of milk are made from sacred herd of cattle. King himself is subject to *emandwa* and ghosts and needs-diviners and sorcers to help him in business of life.

(4) The Ganda are organised in segmental, patrilineal, totemic clans, membership of which provides very deep sense of identity. The head of each segment is personification of all his predecessors and can, at same time, address them in prayer—often through means of deceased's lower jawbone, preserved in special shrine. At death, each ghost visits Walumbe, spirit of death, and then returns to clan burial ground, where his corpse must be buried. An heir (even for children) must be proclaimed or ghost is angry. For ghosts of men shrines are built and supplied regularly with beer and warmth; in general, ghosts are active in promoting welfare of their kin or, if neglected, in causing sickness. Great care is taken to ensure that ghosts of evil sorcerers, suicides and abnormal births cannot return to trouble the living. Ghosts of outstanding men may become incarnate in animal and act as guardians of a clan-segment or a locality; there is widespread cult of spirits of natural objects. There is also large selection of *balubaale*—hero- and nature-spirits—available in principle to every member of tribe. They are responsible, between them, for almost every eventuality and have temples served by priests, mediums and many attendants. Three of them may orig. have been → 'high gods'. But, by middle of 19th cent., they had been absorbed into the gen. cult. So far as poss., all *balubaale* are fitted into human genealogies; it is said that they are ghosts of exceptional men—princes, soldiers, sorcerers—who continued to practise their powers after death. This makes them, mythologically, inferior to king. Ganda stories of origin begin with coming of first king. All Ganda—even if their clans were in country when he arrived—are his 'grandchildren'. Each king, who (like a clan head) is personification of all his predecessors, is not only 'head of all men' but 'head of all clan heads'. He is holder of supreme power and source of all authority and values. At his death, his jawbone is separated and kept in special shrine, along with his umbilical cord, where his ghost can regularly be consulted by successors. The rest of corpse is buried elsewhere, along with some of his widows and import. members of his private household; tomb is kept in repair and tended *in perpetuo* by kin of orig. guardians. There is no suggestion that king is 'divine' (*vide* Irstam, 1944). But he is certainly 'sacred'—the greatest of all men and therefore, probably, greatest of all beings. Priests of *balubaale* are appointed, and their temples built, only with his permission; in past he killed their servants, and destroyed their property, if they offended him. At same time, he has to keep on good terms with them, may be harmed by sorcerers and employs sorcerers to achieve his ends. Sorcery (attr. to anger or jealousy) is widely suspect of causing misfortune. Every death, whatever the natural cause recognised, is attr. *also* to sorcery. Convicted evil sorcerer is burnt alive outside village. 'Night-prowlers' go about naked, muttering hoarsely, eating human flesh and doing much wholly arbitrary mischief. The curse—esp. of father or paternal aunt—is effective way of enforcing kinship obligations. Diviners are widely consulted and some of them become very rich. They are possessed by one of the *balubaale*, who speak through them; they also use material means of divination recommended by *balubaale*. They often prescribe both ritual and empirical curse for sickness, and may, on either count, refer patient to specialist. F.B.W.

C. Cagnolo, *The Akikuyu: Their Customs, Traditions and Folklore* (1933); J. E. Goldthorpe—F. B. Wilson, *Tribal Maps of East Africa* (*East African Studies*, No. 18, 1960); T. Irstam, *King of the Ganda* (Ethnographical Museum of Sweden, 1944); J. Kenyatta, *Facing Mount Kenya* (1938, 1960); L. P. Mair *An African People in the Twentieth Century* (1965); J. Middleton, *Lugbara Religion* (1960); J. Middleton—E. G. Winter, *Witchcraft and Sorcery in East Africa* (1963); J. Roscoe, *The Baganda* (1965); J. K. Russell, *Men without God?* (1967); F. B. Welbourn, 'Some aspects of kiganda religion', *Uganda Journal*, 26.2, pp. 171–82 (1962), 'Emandwa Initiation in Ankole', *Uganda Journal*, 29.1, pp. 13–25 (1965), *Religion and Politics in Uganda*, E. African Publ. House (1965); M. Wilson, *Rituals of Kinship among the Myakyusa* (1957), *Communal Rituals of the Myakyusa* (1959), *Divine Kings and the Breath of Men* (1959).

Africa, South: Religious Cults This article concerns the trad. relig. system of the Bantu-speaking peoples who inhabit Africa S. of 10° latitude. This line is an approx. boundary that separates cultures of Congo and E. Africa from Bantu culture of South. For relig. of S. African Bushmen → Bushman Relig.

The Bantu of the South are divided into tribes and congeries of tribes distinguished by differences in language, culture and social organization. Each division has its partic. system of belief and ritual practice. Yet, just as S. Bantu languages are members of one family, the separate tribal religs. all bear family resemblance. Bantu belief systems are compounded of similar elements. Relig. practices vary as they are articulated in social structure of different tribes. The common elements of S. Bantu belief can be abstracted and types of social structure classified in order to build up systematic overview of relig. in S. Bantu region.

Belief: Summarily described, S. Bantu relig. is one of → ancestor worship modified by presence of other mystical agencies. Chief among these are witches and sorcerers (→ Witchcraft). The cult of tendance on ancestors is universal among S. Bantu.

A creator god is gen. recognised but (with notable exception of Rhodesian Shona) is neither worshipped nor credited with any aptitude for regular intervention in affairs of men. The existence of a creator god explains orig. of things, and he is occasionally invoked to account for events whose causes are not attr. to other agencies. The Zulu Tikdoshe, a malevolent dwarf with one leg and single buttock, repr. a devil or incarnation of evil that has counterparts in most tribes. Such beings can become witches' familiars.

The personified beings of S. Bantu belief exist in universe governed by two related principles. One is the gen. notion of mystical causation; the other is belief in mystical power or force which is imminent in beings and things. In his *Bantu Philosophy*, Tempels argues that idea of a power or 'vital force' that pervades all things is fundamental to Bantu ideas of reality. Super-added to observable attributes, everything contains power or force that acts on a mystical plane. Men, animals and spirits can be ranked in terms of quota of force imminent in them. Among men, those in authority have greater charges of vital force than their subordinates. Further, the strength of certain things or beings is specific, and their use is prescribed for partic. purposes. These two gen. principles underwrite specific beliefs and have consequences for social action.

For Bantu, there are two avenues of recourse to mystical plane of causation. On one hand, spirits —esp. ancestors—can be approached and asked to look after supplicant's interests. On the other, powerful substances with inherent mystical force can be used to effect desired ends. In many rituals these means are used conjointly. Thus, in annual *incwala* rite of the Swazi, the King 'strengthens' his person and hence the nation with magical substances and later participates in sacrifice to spirits of past kings. Both acts are prescribed, and both are essential to secure future of kingship and nation. Because → magic and spirits are mutually involved in safeguarding personal and group destiny, magical practice complements tendance of ancestors. Belief in magic and belief in ancestors are inseparably woven into single cosmology.

Ancestors and their living descendants are linked in relationship of mutual dependence. Men succour forebears with sacrifice and libation: the stature of an ancestral ghost among ghosts is determined by attention it receives from its cult—a congregation of the living. Unremembered ghosts become impotent, oblivious and irrelevant. To ensure remembrance, ancestral spirits can punish living for neglect. Ancestors can become indifferent and withdraw their protective influence. Or they may send misfortune or illness. The ancestors are also concerned with morality and proper management of descent groups of which they are founders. Thus dissension or moral lapses among descendants can provoke ancestral wrath. In add., most S. Bantu recognize that ancestors may use powers capriciously, provoking living into soothing testy spirit with supernumary sacrifice. The gen. attitude towards ancestors is thus not one of unmitigated respect and reverence. Ancestors are like elderly monied uncles who make demands on unwilling nephews who must obey, or take consequences.

Ancestral protection assists men in their efforts to counteract malevolence of sorcerers and witches. These are persons who seek to bring misfortune to others by using magic or familiars. The S. Bantu conception of a witch is not that of person imbued with 'the inherent power of evil'. Bantu witches know good from evil and are conscious of their moral position. They may be likened to perverts, and are often described as having been recruited to witchcraft by seduction. The mythology of witchcraft varies greatly from tribe to tribe, but cannibalism and sexual perversion are recurrently attr. to witches. Witches may also be credited with ability to use souls of sleeping men to do their bidding. However, the significant gen. feature is that anyone can learn black magic and become a witch/sorcerer.

S. Bantu gen. distinguish between 'white' and 'black' magic, though they do not phrase distinction in this way. White magic involves use of substances whose effects are protective and preventative: hence it is legitimate and socially approved. In contrast, black magic brings harm to others. Harm may be intention of sorcerer's act: accident, death or disease may be the aim. But substances to ensure success are also suspect. Success is often won at expense of another's failure. Thus self-seeking sorcerer can bring misfortune to others by supercharging own powers with 'success medicines'. In both black and white magic there is emphasis on substances or 'medicines'. Spells play little part. Black magic potions often incorporate 'body filth' of victims (sweat, excrement, nail parings, hair) to make their potential for harm specific. The efficacy of white protective medicines similarly derives from power inherent in their constituent substances.

Ancestor spirits and witches have been identified as two types of agent capable of bringing misfortune to men. The symptoms of witchcraft-attack and of visitation of ancestral wrath are the same. Either may bring illness, accident or misfortune, though ancestors do not normally kill outright as witches may do. It is also poss. that some misfortune is result of combined assault by witch and ancestor spirit. In any case, witches who strike home have somehow by-passed vigilance of ancestor spirits: ancestors repay attention with attention.

Given a plurality of poss. causes of misfortune, a decision on operative cause in each case of accident must be made. Only then can remedy be found. → Divination supplies the answers. Methods vary through S. Africa from throwing bones and interpreting meaning of each cast, to consulting oracles of many types. Spectacularly the Cewa used a poison oracle which, allegedly, would kill witches and be vomited up by innocent. Whatever the method, the intention in divination is to reduce or eliminate ambiguity. Witch or ancestor spirit? is a frequent initial question. If this is answered, further questioning may at best reveal precise cause of trouble. Alternatively, a short list of likely causes of misfortune may be produced.

Divination is prelude to remedial action and is one way in which relig. and magical belief is integrated into the moral order. Seances of divination are often scenes of confession and allocation of moral responsibility. An angry ancestor is identified. What could have provoked his displeasure? In face of question, a member of cult that tends the ghost may admit to a moral lapse. Any wrong may then be righted and sin purged in sacrifice. Alternatively parties may agree to differ and redefine their relations accordingly. Schism of a group, dissolving of partnerships, recognition of new statutes, are often remedial acts when relationships concerned breed unmanageable animosities. Suppressed animosities among kin are made evident and breaches in relations sealed in common worship.

Similarly, witchcraft beliefs are tied to morality. Persons accused of witchcraft are not rarities. Those who have shown open hatred or resentment towards others who later become victims of misfortune are likely to be formally accused of witchcraft. In most tribes, only the persistent witch is drastically punished. Again, witchcraft-accusation can lead to reassessment of social relations which have become strained and difficult. Witchcraft, too, can be purged and thus in some instances, those defined as witches are like confessed sinners.

Divination, so far considered as diagnosis after misfortune, can be used in another way. A man can consult diviner before embarking on import. project to see whether conditions are propitious. In this, emphasis is not on prophesy of coming events: it is a testing of contemporary mystical climate. Estranged ancestors or persons contemplating witchcraft are identified. Ancestors can be placated and magical or secular means used to daunt potential witch. Divining, even when future is at stake, is diagnostic. A diviner's prognostication, like that of Western medical practitioner, is conditional. Before project is completed, mystical climate may change; failure to predict misfortune does not lead to questioning of diviner's competence.

Divining is one of the few specialist occupations in S. Bantu communities. Often diviner is a 'doctor' as well, offering remedies for both sickness and misfortune. His *materia medica* incl. herbs which, when administered, have palpable results, acting e.g. as emetics and purges. However, distinction between 'magic' and 'medicine' is foreign to the culture, for all substances derive their potency from mystical power latent within them. The diviner is a ritual and magical practitioner. In his role, the worlds of spirits and magic are again brought together. Diviners are consultants with special knowledge and skills. They are not priests; for S. Bantu, priesthood is an aspect of kinship and political relations.

In describing Bantu diviners and divination, European observers have consistently resorted to language of Western medical practice. The 'witch-doctor' diagnoses and 'treats' patient who consults him. Similarly the diviner 'doctors' fields, house sites and animals with protective medicine. This analogue can be further extended because S. Bantu relig. thought, while not scientific, propounds notions about causes and limitations of intervention that have counterpart in modern medical practice. But these ideas are not limited to consideration of health and illness, they are generalized over whole field of practical living.

In mod. medicine a state of health is posited to describe 'normal' human condition. Disease or injury intervene to disturb normal and healthy state. Similarly, for S. Bantu, there is a gen. idea of normal expectation. Farmers should be moderately successful with crops and herds. Husbands should have reasonable relations with wives and so on. When things go awry, the resultant crisis is akin to illness: a state of social morbidity or crisis is recognized.

Pursuing this metaphor, much of Bantu religs. and magical practice is brought into perspective.

The Western medical man is called in at times of crisis to diagnose a condition, and treat patient. But medicine also seeks to prevent crises from arising. Prophylaxis anticipates crisis; every hygenic practice may be seen as catering specific or gen. threats. S. Bantu rituals share these characteristics.

Crisis and the occasion of ritual: Ritual among S. Bantu is performed at time of present or impending crisis. Crises are turning points, fraught with danger and demanding of decision. The causes and types of crisis are manifold. There are periodic ritual performances that correspond to regular crises in human activity. The seasonal crises among S. Bantu, who are subsistence farmers combining farming with cattle-herding where they can, produce rites attendant on harvesting, tilling and sowing. Signal points in the individual life cycle (e.g. birth, → initiation into adulthood, marriage, death) evoke life crises rituals. These are typically in form of rites of passage that mark changes from one social status to another. Then there are other tribe-wide crises of crop failure, famine, war, or epidemic that evoke collective response. Finally, contingent crises that beset individuals and bring them to cult groups or diviner, are of limited relevance in the community and are ritualized by small groups.

In Christ. rites, crises are expressed against background of regular weekly worship. There are special occasions, high days, holidays, and services of special intention. In this sense, S. Bantu rituals are always 'special'. Because rituals are rituals of crisis, they reflect ebb and flow of human activity with precision. There is no church, if the 'church' is considered as an independent institution with own specialist officers and calendrical observance. Instead, there are congregations who gather for specific purposes. These congregations, in size, composition, and in the chosen venue for their meetings, reflect nature of events toward which their ritual activities are directed. Worship in church has a certain inertia of its own, while, in contrast, Bantu congregations are produced by social events and processes. Thus there is always an immediate sense of relevance and purpose to ritual gatherings that relates primarily to the business of men and only secondarily to the supernatural. The crises inherent in living precipitate men into ritual performance; relig. teaching does not impose a total pattern of observance.

Symbols and meaning: S. Bantu relig. is expressed in action rather than dogma. The intricacy of ritual, involving manipulation of sacred objects, contrasts with paucity of myth and other verbal expression. Part of explanation is that Bantu culture is non-literate. But Bantu oral expression is limited compared with that of other non-literate peoples. The emphasis on notion of power inherent in objects, which is a peculiar part of S. Bantu belief, accounts for lack of development of verbal ritual. Knowledge of specific powers is given through ritual participation more than by verbal instruction. Thus, in a Pedi initiation ceremony, initiates are scalded by steam that is piped onto them from boiling pot. In background, men chant phrase that denotes woman's sexual parts: this signifies dangers inherent in sexual relations. Initiation admits boys into manhood, and proper sexual conduct is a theme in these rites. But the facts of life are symbolically expressed in many 'mysteries' involving the elements of fire and water. In a final mystery, the 'eyes of the initiate are opened' by sight of a fire burning on a raft that floats in a pool. The initiate is gruffly told that he can now 'found a house'. Having comprehended mystical union of maleness and femaleness symbolically expressed by fire floating on water, the initiate gains right to set up house over which he will preside as master and, eventually, as ancestral ghost.

Little overt interpretation of symbols is made during rituals, for the ritual actions form a language on their own. Older men can explain more esoteric features, but powers of explanation vary with individual interest and articulateness. Exegesis of S. Bantu ritual symbolism requires an almost native knowledge of wealth of meanings assoc. with actions and objects in various contexts, both secular and sacred. V. Turner's *Forest of Symbols*, which deals with the Ndembu of Zambia, is one of few works in which the richness of symbolic meaning and significance in S. Bantu ritual has been explored.

Relig. and Social Structure: Consideration of authority and descent illustrates interpenetration of S. Bantu relig. and social structure. Descent provides import. principle for continuity in Bantu society. Heirs inherit estates and right to administer them. They may also succeed to political office. The major lines of descent for secular purposes correspond with those recognized when defining relig. obligations to kin and ancestors. People who share rights and obligations in family estates tend to be drawn into membership of a single cult. Matriliny, patriliny or other principles of descent emphasized in partic. tribes, recruit people to membership of groups in which relig., economic and political ties reinforce one another.

Temporal power is backed by relig. authority. In families, fathers are family priests; village headmen are custodians of material and spiritual welfare of their people. Chiefs are high priests of their tribes. An import. distinction can be made between ancestors of chiefs and those of commoners. Chiefly ancestors are concerned with fate of entire chiefdoms and can only be approached by members of chiefly houses. Chiefship, in its priestly aspect, is essential for mystical welfare of tribe. Chiefs have ritual prerogatives in their rights to *sacra* that symbolize authority and mark them off from ordinary men. Some chiefs, through access to spirits and/or medicine, are rainmakers; fertility is ultimately dependent on an office that combines political and ritual authority.

The volumes of the Ethnographic Survey published by the International African Institute (ed. D. Forde) provide excellent accounts of religs. of S. Bantu tribes outside Republic of S. Africa. *The Bantu-Speaking Tribes of South Africa* ed. by I. Schapera (1956), is the standard work on tribes of Republic of S. Africa. B.L.S.

Africa, West: Ritual Cults and Beliefs Among W. African peoples, from Senegal to the Congo, over 2000 languages and dialects have been recorded. Past tribal distinctions were accentuated by isolation or warfare, and remain important. Yet there are similarities of relig. belief and mythology, and there have been contacts through migrations. There are differences in belief and cultus between W. and E. or S. Africa. Unfortunately there are no scriptures of these religions, since writing was unknown in the tropical and southern regions till mod. times. The general model of a pyramid for African religion places a Supreme Being at apex, cults of gods and ancestors on the two sides, and magico-relig. practices at base. But cults of nature and personal gods are more highly developed in W. Africa than elsewhere in continent. They have been compared with the pantheon of → Egypt; but there is no clear evidence of connection, and they fit into a gen. polytheistic pattern. The African relig. attitude is life-affirming, with reincarnation, where it is held, welcomed as a return to this warm world, to strengthen the family and perpetuate its names.

Belief in a creating → High God is found in nearly all W. Africa. Not all the peoples of this vast region have been studied; but investigations have underlined this belief, though there are variations in cultus. The names for God overlap mod. political frontiers which are an inheritance from imperialism; thus God is called Olorun by the Yoruba of Nigeria and Dahomey, Mawu by the Ewe of Dahomey and Togo, Nyame in Ghana and the Ivory Coast, Amma by the Dogon of Upper Volta, Yataa by the Kono and Ngewo by the Mende of Sierra Leone, Soko by the Nupe and Chukwu by the Ibo of Nigeria.

Mythologies show basic resemblances but regional differences. In Dogon myth, Amma made sun and moon like pots surrounded by rings of red and white copper respectively; the stars were pellets of clay flung into space; the earth a further lump which spread out flat, and other spirits and mankind came from union of Amma with the earth. In Yoruba myth, Olorun lived in sky with other divinities, the earth below was a marsh and Olorun sent a divine agent with a snail shell in which was earth, which he poured out and had it scattered by a pigeon and a hen till solid ground was formed. Mawu for the Fon of Dahomey sometimes alone and supreme, and sometimes as female with a male consort, Lisa. These divine twins created other gods in seven pairs, but Mawu also travelled about on a great snake, making the earth and mountains and tracing out rivers. The snake still supports the earth on thousands of coils. A snake swallowing its tail is a common motif in art, and symbolizes eternity and vitality.

God is creator and sustainer of universe and judge of men at death. Myths may speak of his wife and family, yet he is never represented in art. More remarkably, he has few temples and little cultus, and among many peoples none at all. The Dogon have shrines for Amma, and the Ashanti have a few mud temples with priests, and a number of forked sticks which hold bowls with gifts for Nyame. But Olorun, Chukwu, Soko and the rest have no temples or formal worship. God is transcendent and this is expressed in many myths, found all over Africa, which speak of his retirement from earth. Often a woman is blamed for withdrawal of the sky, which here is virtually identified with God. Yet despite his present distance, and absence of cultus, God is invoked in prayers which laymen utter without intermediary. Salutations at different times of day use the divine name, ordinary speech has many phrases in which he is mentioned, and oaths are sworn by him.

God fulfils other functions in mythology. Death is thought to be unnatural and its coming due to fault of messengers from God, dog or chameleon, which delayed bringing a divine promise of immortality. In some stories this was stolen by the snake, which sheds its skin but goes on living. There is little eschatology, in sense of an end of world; but God closes the lives of men and judges them, and is the ultimate sanction for morality. Further, in offerings made to other gods the name of the Supreme Being is often first invoked; some priests say that the essence of all sacrifices goes to him through his intermediaries. God is not so remote as may appear, and he is more than an occasional or henotheistic deity.

Next to the Supreme Being are countless gods who are spirits of nature, or deified human beings or both. Their cults are declining in many places; but in southern Dahomey they are still particularly well organized and little affected by Islam or Christianity. Innumerable small shrines receive offerings for them; many priests are dedicated to their service and trained by months or years of instruction.

The spirits are sometimes distinguished acc. to regions: sky, earth, water, forest. Of → sky gods Shango of the Yoruba is particularly interesting. He was fourth king of the old town of Oyo, but because of cruelty was banished by his subjects. He retired to forest and brought down lightning on his enemies. Then he either hanged himself or ascended to heaven by a chain, and henceforth was identified with the storm. Shango has many temples today, with altars enclosing thunderstones, primitive celts. He is served by priests who impersonate him in festivals, and claim to be able to invoke or avert lightning and thunderbolts.

Spirits of the earth are assoc. with soil and crops, hills and rocks, and sometimes with diseases such as smallpox. Asase Yaa of the Shanti receives libations when ground is hoed or a grave dug, and work on land is forbidden on her sacred day of Thursday; but she has no temples or regular cultus. But Ala of the Ibo is the greatest force in tribal life, repr. in many temples by a human figure with a child in her arms, and receiving sacrifices regularly, especially at planting, first fruits and harvest. Ala is also mother of dead, who are buried in her womb, and is custodian of morality.

Water spirits are assoc. with lakes, rivers, wells and the sea. Tano is a river of central Ghana, but its cultus is also found far from that locality due to popularity of the god. Brass pans are placed on wooden stands for his altars, and white-robed priests serve him in more elaborate temples. In anc. kingdom of Benin the god of the sea, Olokun, is believed to live in an underwater palace with human and fishlike attendants; there are stories of his attempts to win the earth by flood. The Songhay of the upper Niger have many myths of water spirits, called Zin, perhaps the → jinns of Islam; despite more than 500 years of Muslim relig. in the area, every week dances are held in which water spirits are believed to possess their devotees.

The forest spirits are less clearly identified and have irregular cults. The forest is held to be abode of dangerous and uncanny spirits, from ghosts of those who have died without burial to spirits of twins. Hunters are assiduous in propitiation of the dryads, and place offerings beside stones or streams in forest connected with them. They claim to receive medicinal and magical powers from them, as well as knowledge of nature and ability to cause or prevent rain.

Other gods are connected with oracles and magic. There are many systems of → divination in popular usage, some of which may be derived from Islamic or even older sources, and others are local inventions. One of the most popular is the cult of Ifa, centred in S.W. Nigeria but spread from Ghana to Cameroun. It is said that Ifa was a wise man who brought knowledge of divination to the town of Ifé and founded line of priest-diviners who passed on their supernatural knowledge to others. Ifa is now name for the oracle god, also know as Orunmila, 'heaven knows salvation', who is still one of most popular deities. The oracle is consulted in infancy and adolescence, to provide horoscope for a child, before marriage and family events, at appointment of chiefs, and at times of special private or public need. Often assoc. with oracular deities are other intermediaries, messengers to the gods, guardians of houses and villages, and tricksters who are dangerous but can be propitiated. At lower levels are many other spirits, which express the Vital Force or Dynamism that underlies many African relig. ideas. This animism may be expressed personally, in gods that have names and local shrines, or impersonally in the manipulations of magic. But the term → Animism is not adequate to incl., in W. Africa, the whole range of relig. belief and practice, for the Supreme Being and the ancestors can hardly be included under this title.

In E. and S. Africa → ancestor-cults occupy most of relig. field; but in W. Africa the cults of gods and greater prominence of the Supreme Being provide a wider range of relig. devotion. Yet ancestors are of great importance here, and survival of death is universally believed. Great attention is given to funerals; there is a first burial a day or two after death, necessitated by hot damp climate, and a second funeral some weeks later when all the relatives have assembled. The dead person is addressed by name, his belongings are buried with him, and food or drink are placed at his grave at regular intervals. In family-ceremonies the senior or oldest member officiates; not usually a priest. The recent dead, and other outstanding past members of the family, are recalled by name but grad. memory fades. The dead provide a cloud of witnesses which warn or help their descendants. Their will is believed to be made known through dreams or misfortunes. In disease or accident the diviner is asked which ancestor is bringing trouble, and offerings are made to him accordingly. As senior members of family, the dead are consulted on questions of property, often by casting nuts on ground and judging reply from way they fall. The dead are asked to bless crops; with the earth-gods, they receive a portion of first-fruits. Their help may also be sought to influence weather, in storm, flood or drought. Their particular concern is the family, birth of children and health of everyone; they oppose → witchcraft, which may prevent childbirth and reincarnation and so destroy the family line.

Ancestral cults are specially prominent in the many masquerades and 'secret societies' connected with both dead and living. The most numerous and popular products of African art are the wooden masks which represent ancestors, animals and other powers. These are sometimes naturalistic, sometimes highly stylized, to indicate power and awe of supernatural beings. In many places there are regular and annual ceremonies when masqueraders appear to represent the dead, visit their relatives, and give messages from other world. 'Secret societies' may be small groups, but more gen. they incl. whole adult male population; there are also women's societies. The purpose of the society is to intro. youths into social responsibility, usually by isolating them for long period and imposing endurance tests upon them. They may be → circumcised at this time, though some tribes do not know this practice. Youths are instructed in sexual and social matters, and finally initiated by older members in masks and robes. The Poro of Sierra Leone and Guinea for boys, and Sande for girls, are two of the best known of such societies. Myths are told of origin of Poro, but the purpose is perpetuation of ancestral customs and initiation of youths. → Initiation into manhood, as in many other African societies, is a symbolical rebirth in which young people are said to be swallowed by the Poro spirit when leaving their parents, and returned to them later as adults.

There are no great stone temples in W. Africa, for there is little soft stone for building, and in past no explosives for harder rock. Temples are made of clay, though this is often decorated with geometrical patterns when soft, or coloured plates are set in it, or pictures of human and animal figures may be painted on walls in primary colours. The temples are small, sometimes tiny, and normally only priests enter them to place offerings on low earthen altars. Lay attendants stand outside and prayers are made for them, or by them, invoking spirits in general and particular deity of temple, for blessings on nation, chief, family and children. The use of images varies considerably. African carvings have become famous and are made above all in wood, though many bronze, ivory and stone carvings are known; the use of stone being chiefly in Sierra Leone, Nigeria and the Congo. The Ibo of eastern Nigeria have countless clay images of Ala and her child, and on occasion they build special houses for many images of all kinds of beings, under presidency of Ala; these are made by concerted effort but then are allowed to fall into ruin. Their neighbours, the Yoruba of W. Nigeria have produced more wooden and bronze sculptures than any other African people; but while many of these are relig., in sense that they are attendants on the gods, there are few representations of the gods themselves. Some of the commonest are simply images of twins (*ibeji*). The Dogon and Bambara of W. Sudan, and many other Africans, make representations of snakes and abstract figures in their shrines, and few anthropomorphic figures, though of course this does not apply to the innumerable masks of ancestors.

In temples and ancestral shrines stools are often used, notably in Ghana. The Ibo make clay images of dead, and in Benin carved poles stand at grave, and wooden or bronze heads represent departed. The stools are carved in many patterns which always have a meaning. On the stools stand brass pans or clay pots for offerings; when animal sacrifices are made, portions are placed in the pots and rubbed on the stools. There are annual festivals in which the stools are taken to rivers for 'soul-washing' cleansing. Human sacrifices, which used to be notorious in old kingdoms of Kumasi, Abomey and Benin, were not relig. sacrifices; the killing of wives and retainers of dead chiefs, was practised both at funerals and at annual and special occasions when they were remembered. These have long since ceased; but nails and hair of these people may be buried along with their master. A few other human sacrifices used to be made at foundation of a gate or town, and in times of national danger. (→ Foundation Sacrifice).

Offerings made to ancestors and gods differ little, and prayers made to them are similar, so that, although some people maintain that ancestral cults are not truly relig., yet their function resembles that of gods. The commonest offerings are libations of water or alcohol, and the gift of a little maize, beans or oil. Animal sacrifice is common, though some gods are said to have a taboo, a thing 'hateful' to them, of blood and they prefer snails or vegetables. On great occasions a sheep or even a bull may be sacrificed; the blood and entrails are offered, and the remainder cooked and eaten by assistants. Simple prayers are made daily, at dawn and dusk. Many gods have special day of week for their worship; there are annual festivals. There is no obligation for layman to attend a temple, though he may do so in time of special need. Most homes have small shrines, cared for by elder members. Worship is both private and public. Events in agricultural year, and in customs of ancestors and village affairs, call for public celebration. In families there are the 'rites of passage', when individuals pass through the crises of conception, birth, naming, adolescence, marriage and death. In all of these ancestors are interested, tutelary gods are invoked, and oracles consulted.

In modern times great changes have come from imperialism, political independence, new communications, great cities, money economy, education and missionary religions. Many old temples have disappeared, but ancestral customs continue. Most significant are the independent African churches, split off from the missions, but reflecting health as well as spiritual well-being. The idea of the Supreme Being has been enlarged in both Islam and Christianity, and belief in life after death given fuller detail; but these religions need still more adaptation to African beliefs and needs. The old religion is declining, though its practice is still widespread and its influence upon ideas will last for centuries. Christianity and Islam have the greater appeal of history, sacred books and universal membership; but they are still foreign religions to many people in W. Africa. E.G.P.

G. Dieterlen, *Les Âmes des Dogons* (1941), *Essai sur la Religion Bambara* (1951); M. J. Field, *Religion and Medicine of the Gâ People* (1937); D. Forde, ed., *African Worlds* (1954); M. Griaule, *Conversations with Ogotemmêli* (1965); M. J. Herskovits, *Dahomey* (1938); E. B. Idowu, *Olódùmarè, God in Yoruba Belief* (1962); K. L. Little, *The Mende of Sierra Leone* (1951); S. F. Nadel, *Nupe Religion* (1954); E. G. Parrinder, *West African Religion* (1961); R. T. Parsons, *Religion in an African Society* (1964); R. S. Rattray, *Ashanti* (1923); J. Rouch, *La Religion et la Magie Songhay* (1960); E. W. Smith and E. G. Parrinder, eds., *African Ideas of God* (1950–1966); J. S. Trimingham, *Islam in West Africa* (1959); S. G. Williamson, *Akan Religion and Christian Faith* (1965).

Afterlife → Eschatology. S.G.F.B.

Āgama A title used in Mahāyāna Buddhism for collection of scripture, roughly equivalent to term → *Nikaya* in Pali. There are 4 *Āgamas* in the Skt. canon, as there are 4 *Nikāyas* in → Pali canon. The names of 4 Skt. A.s are: *Dirghāgama, Madhyamāgama, Samyuktāgama, Ekottarikāgama.* As in Pali canon, these together constitute one of the three divisions of the → *Tri-pitaka*, namely, the *Sutra-pitaka.* Different schools had their own A.s, and in 7th cent. CE there existed seven different collections. There is, now, no complete orig. Skt. *Ā.* text extant; they exist, however, in Chinese trans. T.O.L.

Agapē Grk. 'love'. Term used for a common religious meal ('love-feast') in Early Church. It was orig. closely assoc. with the → Eucharist, and could lead to abuses (I Cor. 11:17–34). In 2nd cent., A. was held in evening, the Eucharist in morning. A. gradually became a kind of charity-supper for poor, and eventually fell into disuse. The word also describes funeral or commemorative feats held at tombs of martyrs, and poss. repr. Chr. version of pagan *parentalia* or festival in honour of dead relatives. Eccl. authorities were often concerned with abuses that occurred during their celebration. (→ Charity). S.G.F.B.

E.R.E., I, *s.v.; R.G.G.*[3], I, pp. 169–70 ('Agapen'); *D.C.C., s.v.; Th. Wb.*, I, pp. 20ff.; C. Spicq, *Agapē dans le Nouveau Test.*, 3 vols. (1955–9).

Agapetai and Agapetoi Grk. meaning 'beloved women' and 'beloved men'. The custom of men and women living together in a 'spiritual marriage' is praised in the *Shepherd of Hermas* (→ Hermas) in 2nd cent. Its existence is attested at Antioch and Constantinople. The women were also known as *suneisaktoi* (Grk.) or *subintroductae* (Lat.). The practice had obvious dangers and was forbidden officially, e.g. at Council of → Nicaea (325). A similar practice existed later in Irish mixed monasteries of monks and nuns. → Philo ascribes such a custom to the → Therapeutae. S.G.F.B.

E.R.E., I, pp. 177b–80a; *D.C.C.*, p. 1300 ('Subintroductae').

Agatha, St. Chr. virgin martyred at Catania in Sicily (251 ?), whose cult already reached Rome by *c.* 470, and became popular elsewhere, poss. because of dramatic nature of her legend. Her cult contains many elements that suggest incorporation of pagan traditions, and is connected with eruptions of Mt. Etna. Because of amputation of her breasts during martyrdom, she is invoked by sufferers of diseases of breast, and severed breasts are her attributes in relig. art. She is patroness of virgins, shepherdesses, and bell-founders. (→ Breast). S.G.F.B.

R.A.C., I, 179–84; G. Ferguson, *Signs and Symbols in Christian Art* (1961), pp. 46, 102.

Agathos Daimon Grk. = 'Good Daimon' (→ Demons, Greek). Gen. designation of a nameless *numen* (→ Numen), regarded as friendly and helpful. A libation of wine was often made to A.-D. after meals. A.-D. was also designated protecting spirit of house, conceived as serpent. In Hellenist. Egypt a cult of A.-D. developed as the 'good serpent', and was connected with that of *Agathē Tychē* ('Good Fortune') → Tychē. S.G.F.B.

Kleine Pauly, I, *s.v.;* E. A. W. Budge, *The Mummy* (1925), p. 332; J. Doresse, *Secret Books of the Egypt. Gnostics* (E.T. 1960), pp. 315ff.

Ages of the World (General) Most religions incl. a specific view about past, present and future, in terms of divine purpose. This present world-order is gen. thought to have had a beginning and will have an end. Other world-orders or ages may have existed before this one, and others will replace it. Often the past is believed to have been a Golden Age, and hope is expressed for return to it; sometimes the Golden Age is in the future (→→ Apocalyptic; Messianism). Where the time-process is conceived as cyclic, the world-order is conceived as perpetually repeating itself (→ Aeon). A linear view of time-process usually implies that present world-order is unique, and that time started with it and will cease at its ending (→→ Eschatology; Time). S.G.F.B.

M. Eliade, *Traité d'histoire des religions* (1949); E.T., *Patterns of Comparative Religion* (1958), ch. XI, *Le mythe de l'éternel retour* (1949); G. Van der Leeuw, *Le religion* (1948), pp. 375ff.; S. G. F. Brandon, *History, Time and Deity* (1965).

(China-Japan) At least from time of Tsou Yen (*c.* 305–240 BC) the Chinese held a cyclical theory of history, commencing with separation of Heaven and Earth, and governed by evolutions of → Yin-Yang, and rise and fall of influence of the Five Powers or Movers (→ Wu Hsing) which controlled all universal events and historical processes in rotation. → Buddhism, with its theory that world is ever passing through recurring sequence of four kalpas or world-periods, had a considerable influence on neo-Confucian theories of cosmic evolution, conspicuously developed by Shao Yung (CE 1011–77). In his *Huang-chi Ching-shih* or *Cosmological Chronology*, periods of time are expressed in terms of cycles, epochs, revolutions and generations. 1 cycle = 12 epochs = 360 revolutions = 4320 generations = 129,600 years (a generation being reckoned as 30 years). Equating Shao's theory with Western chronology, present world cycle began in 67,017 BC and will end in CE 62,583, when new and identical cycle will begin, to be followed by others. However, the idea that world will be sometime destroyed and replaced by new world is alien to trad. C. thought, with its strong emphasis on recorded history and aversion to mythological speculation. D.H.S.

Fung Yu-Lan, *Hist. of Chinese Philosophy* (1953), vol. 2 (espec. ch. 11).

(Japan) The early Shinto chronicles record seven generations of gods, ending with → Izanagi and Izanami, who produce the present world, gods who correspond to manifestations of nature, Isles of Japan and Japanese people. There is no concept of Ages of the World, except as introduced by Buddhism. (→ Chronology). D.H.S.

(Christ.) Christianity inherited Heb. → *Heilsgeschichte* in taking over O.T. as its sacred scriptures. The way was paved by → Paul, who saw Church as the true Israel. Delay of the → Parousia caused Christians to contemplate possibility that Church had an extended mission in this world. Since pagan society valued antiquity, Chr. scholars, sensitive about newness of their faith, developed Paul's view of Church as true Israel by designating Heb. scriptures as record of God's Old Covenant or Testament, which was replaced by New Testament made by Christ. The canon of Chr. writings was eventually called → New Testament. Hence Christians began to view time-process as having two parts or ages, divided by → Incarnation of Jesus Christ. In 525 custom began of designating period after Incarnation as *anni Domini* ('years of the Lord'). The reckoning of past backwards from Incarnation as era BC did not become general until 18th cent. As first age had begun with Creation and ended with Incarnation, so it was believed that second age, starting with First Coming of Christ would end with his Second Coming (→ Advent), which would also terminate present world-order. S.G.F.B.

R.A.C., III (1957), pp. 58–9 ('Chronologie'); S. G. F. Brandon, *History, Time and Deity* (1965), ch. 6.

(Egyptian) Egyptian cosmogonies (→ Cosmogony, Egyptian) envisaged a motionless watery chaos (*Nun*) before creation of world. Time began with emergence of first land and creator god from Nun. This was 'first time' (*sp tpy*), and was a kind of Golden Age. A passage from → *Book of the Dead* expresses belief that ultimately primordial state of Nun would return. Manetho (*c.* 280 BC) in his hist. of Egypt placed an age of the gods and an age of demi-gods before pharaonic times. In → Hermetic lit., end of Egypt. civilisation is contemplated (*Lat. Asclepius*, III, p. 25). S.G.F.B.

Brandon, *C.L.*, ch. 2 (with bibliography).

(Greek and Roman) In 8th cent. BC → Hesiod presented the past as succession of five generations or ages. They began with golden generation (*genos*) or age, followed by silver, bronze, generation of heroes, and iron age. These ages or generations repr. declension from happy state of mortal life to grim age in which Hesiod was living. Although → Zeus or other gods are responsible for creation of these five generations, no reason is given for fact that each is made inferior to its predecessor. Hesiod's Five Ages was modified in 3rd cent. BC by Aratus. He envisaged a Golden Age of simplicity and peace, when Justice (*Dikē*) lived on earth; a Silver Age, more sophisticated, with Justice in retirement; a Brazen Age, when swords are first made and Justice leaves earth. Another division of ages prob. preserved some memory of Minoan civilisation: an age of → Kronos was followed by age of Zeus and → Olympian gods. Virgil made age of Saturn = Kronos into Golden Age, and age of Zeus = Jupiter he identified with the present, the difficulties of which → Jupiter had planned as necessary for growth of man's character and abilities. Ovid, in his *Metam.* 89–162, presented scheme of four past Ages (Gold, Silver, Bronze, and Iron), the last being destroyed by a Flood, and replaced by present age.

These series of Ages presuppose a linear view of time. A cyclic view was also current, finding expression in →→ Pythagoreanism and Orphism, and in philosophies of →→ Plato, Aristotle and the → Stoics. The Stoic 'great year' was an immense period of time, at end of which the present world-order would be destroyed by fire, and replaced by another, reproducing its pattern for a similar period. Virgil's *4th Eclogue* was based on a like idea of a *saeculum*, the ending of which would bring the Golden Age. (→ Time). S.G.F.B.

E.R.E., I, pp. 192a–200b; M. Eliade, *Le mythe de l'éternel retour* (1949), pp. 183ff.; S. G. F. Brandon, *C.L.*, ch. V; *History, Time and Deity* (1965), pp. 84–96.

(Hebrew) The O.T. incorporates an → *Heilsgeschichte*, based on a linear view of time. Beginning with Creation, it describes a Golden Age before disobedience of → Adam and → Eve brought death and evil into world. The settlement of Israel in Canaan fulfilled first stage of → Yahweh's promise to → Abraham; subsequent misfortune caused prophets to proclaim that Yahweh would restore his people. This restoration was presented as a supernatural event (→ Apocalyptic), heralding a new Messianic Age (→ Messiah). Although the imagery used is confused, this new Age seems to imply destruction of existing world-order and creation of a new one. The new Age would last for ever; but in some versions it would be preceded by a millennial rule of Messiah (→ Chiliasm). Rabbinic lit. contains much speculation about Messianic Age. (→ Ante-diluvian). S.G.F.B.

E.R.E., p. 203a–5a; S. G. F. Brandon, *History, Time and Deity* (1965), ch. 5.

(Iranian) → Zoroastrianism, in its later forms, incorpor. an → *Heilsgeschichte*, which comprised four ages or periods of trimillennia, through which the divine purpose was grad. achieved. Acc. to the → *Bundahishn*, 'Time was *for* twelve thousand years'. During first 3,000 years, the creative and destructive principles of cosmos, personified as → Ohrmazd and → Ahriman prepare for their coming struggle. The succeeding three trimillennia mark, severally, different stages in the cosmic struggle between Ohrmazd and Ahriman. The final overthrow of Ahriman, the Resurrection, Judgment, and Final Rehabilitation occur in 12th millennium, after which 'Time of the Long Dominion' (→ Zurvan) ends. From standpoint of the faithful these final events still lay in future. The events that occur during the four trimillennia are mythological in character, and, with exception of birth of → Zoroaster, none are related to history. The origin of this time-scheme is unknown. It is preserved in late documents but ref. to the trimillennia-pattern is made by Theopompos (*c.* 378 BC). (→ Eschatology, Iran). S.G.F.B.

R. C. Zaehner, *D.T.Z.*, pp. 248ff.); *E.R.E.*, I, pp. 205a–10a; S. G. F. Brandon, *History, Time and Deity* (1965), pp. 140–6.

(Mesopotamian) Sumerians thought of a kind of Golden Age, after creation of world, when the gods →→ Enki and Enlil invented basic elements of civilisation, incl. mankind. Babylonian belief, set forth in the → *Enuma elish*, conceived of a primordial age of two stages: (i) birth of the gods from primordial chaos of the sweet and salt waters (ii) defeat of primaeval chaos and fashioning of world from its carcass by → Marduk, followed by creation of mankind. The New Year Festival at Babylon (→ Akitu) ritually commemorated or represented these events. The Sumerian King List, divided past into two ages, divided by → Flood, after which 'kingship was lowered (again) from heaven'. Acc. to → Berossos, present world would be destroyed by fire. (→→ Antediluvian; Mesopot. Relig.). S.G.F.B.

S. G. F. Brandon, *C.L.*, ch. 3 (with bibliography).

Agha Khan Title of the *imāms* of Nizārīs (→ Assassins). It was given to Ḥasan 'Alī Shāh in 1250/1834 by Shah of Persia. After trouble in Kirman, he had to fly to Sind in 1256/1840. Later he settled in Bombay, which became headquarters of movement. He died in 1299/1881 and was succeeded by son, who was succeeded on death in 1303/1885 by his son, Sulṭān Muḥammad (1294–1377/1877–1957). He took active part in politics and social reform, exerting influence outside his community as well as within. He was succeeded by his grandson Karīm, the present A.Kh. The leader has great influ. over followers, mostly Nizārīs, incl. a class of Indians, mainly business men, called → Khojas, in Syria, Persia, India and E. Africa. They make him huge contributions, enabling him to carry on charitable and cultural activities. The A.K. is a supreme head, descended from → Muḥammad, and considered to some extent to be the abode of divinity. Among followers, some criticisms have been uttered in recent times of large contributions which are made to A.K. J.R.

*E.I.*², I, p. 246; Pareja, pp. 842f. and index; E. Bevan Jones, *The People of the Mosque* (1932), p. 135.

Agnes, St. A Roman martyr, whose cult dates from 4th cent. Her name derives from Grk. *Hagnē*, i.e. 'the chaste', and, in absence of well attested account of her martyrdom, it has been suggested that A. was orig. personification of the ideal of virginal chastity. In one version of her death, A.'s modesty parallels that of pagan virgin Polyxena. The lamb is her emblem in art ('Agnes' sugg. Lat. *agnus*), and from wool of two lambs dedicated annually in her basilica at Rome, on her feast-day (21st Jan.), the archiepiscopal pallium is made. S.G.F.B.

R.A.C., I, 184–6; *D.C.C.*, *s.v.*

Agni Hindu god of fire; of central import. in → Vedic relig., partly because of crucial role of fire in sacrificial ritual. Thereby he is mediator between men and gods; and he is the all-pervading power in universe. A. is sometimes identified with → Indra and Surya the sun god, since the thunderbolt (Indra's weapon) and the sun are forms of atmospheric and celestial fire respectively. However, A. is essentially a god of the terrestrial region (→ gods, Hindu), and is perpetually born in the making of sacrificial fire. Trad., ritual fire had five forms: first, the holy fire which arises during sacrifice itself; second, the fire handed over to the student (→ *brahmacarin*) when he is initiated and invested with the sacred thread, and with this he performs the *agnihotra* offering; third, the householder's fire, installed after marriage and the focus of domestic rituals (→ *gṛhastha*); fourth, the 'southern fire', placed at southern entrance to sacrificial hall to honour ancestors, exorcize evil spirits, etc.; fifth, the funeral fire. Thus in numerous ways A. is assoc. with and implicit in the divine rites. N.S.

A. Danielou *Hindu Polytheism* (1964); A. Hillebrandt *Vedische Mythologie* (1927–9).

Agnosticism Name given for opinion that a Divine Being, a supernatural world, and human immortality, are subjects that cannot be proved acc. to accepted means of rational demonstration. T. H. Huxley is said to have invented word in 1869. A. is often used in wider sense to denote scepticism; but true A. should mean profession of ignorance about reality of what cannot be apprehended by the human senses. (→→ Agnosticism, Buddhist; Sceptics). S.G.F.B.

E.R.E., I, *s.v.;* A. W. Brown, *The Metaphysical Society* (1947), p. 223.

Agnostos Theos Grk. = 'unknown god': altar inscriptions have only plural form. Dedication of Grk. altars 'to the unknown gods' was prob. due to fear, resulting from increasing → syncretism, that some deities might be neglected. The inscr. to the A.-T. in Acts 17:23 is unusual, and, in view of its monotheistic implication, its authenticity has been much debated. An anonymous 'Great God' was known in → Egypt. religion, and Egypt. god → Amun, was called the 'hidden god'. (→ Deus absconditus). S.G.F.B.

Kleine Pauly, I, *s.v.*

Agnus Dei Lat. 'Lamb of God'. In Chr. imagery → Christ, as Divine Victim of human sin, has been equated with the Pascal Lamb (→ Passover): I Cor. 5:7, Rev. 5:6. A.-D. also denotes threefold invocation, beginning 'O Lamb of God', recited by celebrant in the Latin → Mass, shortly before the Communion. A wax medallion, bearing fig. of lamb, blessed by Pope in 1st yr. of his pontificate and every 7th yr. after, is known also as an A.-D., and is an object of devotion. The image of the A.-D. is sometimes stamped on the large → Host, used by celebrant at Mass. S.G.F.B.

D.C.C., *s.v.; C.E.*, I, *s.v.*

Agrapha Sayings of Jesus unrecorded in four canonical Gospels. The N.T. has two (I Thess. 4:15f.; Acts 20:35); others are found in various early Chr. writings: to determine their authenticity presents many complicated problems. S.G.F.B.

E. Klostermann: *Apocrypha II. Gospels* (1904); M. R. James, *The Apocryphal New Test.* (1926); R. Dunkerley, *Beyond the Gospels* (1957); *R.G.G.*[3], I, *s.v.;* J. B. Bauer, in *Evangelien aus dem Nilsand* (ed. W. C. Van Unnik, 1959), pp. 180ff.

Agriculture The earliest forms of human culture (*c.* 30,000–10,000 BC), were based on a food-gathering economy, chiefly hunting (→ Palaeolithic Religion). During Neolithic period (from *c.* 7,000–5,000 BC) a change was grad. effected to a food-producing economy by invention of agriculture. The process has aptly been called the 'Neolithic Revolution', because it revolutionised human culture, incl. relig. Man now became profoundly concerned with fertility of earth and life-cycle of vegetation. J. G. → Frazer in *The Golden Bough* showed how greatly some fundamental ideas and practices of relig. reflect this concern. The earth was conceived as a goddess needing to be fertilised, to produce vegetation (→ Earth Mother). Vegetation, espec. in terms of corn, was personified as off-spring of earth, being born each year at spring, cut down at harvest, reborn and resurrected in next spring. Hence evolved such deities as →→ (?)Osiris, Attis, Adonis, and also a myth-and-ritual pattern found in many religs. (→ Myth and Ritual). In → Yahwist trad., A. was seen as punishment for → Fall of Adam (Gen. 3:17–19; cf. 4:2ff.); (→ Abel). S.G.F.B.

J. G. Frazer, *The Dying God* (1911[3]), *Adonis, Attis, Osiris*, 2 vols. (1914[3]), *Spirits of the Corn of the Wild*, 2 vols. (1912[3]); V. G. Childe, *Man Makes Himself* (1941); G. Clark, *World Prehistory* (1961); J. Mellaart, *Earliest Civilizations of the Near East* (1965).

Ahiṁsā 'Non-injury' or 'non-violence', a concept central to ethics of → Jainism, prominent in → Buddhism and import. in Hinduism. Prob. the earliest form of prohibition against taking life was the Jain, and here it is applied with characteristic thoroughness. The monk, for instance, strains drinking water so as not to destroy the animalcules in it, sweeps ground softly to prevent death of insects, treads softly so as not to crush minute forms of life in soil, etc. Laymen are forbidden to enter occupations necessarily involving taking of life. Non-injury was given prominence in the edicts of → Asoka, who favoured Buddhists and other mendicant sects; and it figures not only in the five precepts of Buddhism, but also in analogous five in classical → Yoga. It was import. also in → Bhagavata Vaisnavism. In recent times it was given new applications by → Gandhi, as method of peaceful struggle against colonial domination, castism, etc., and as a positive interior virtue, involving desire for welfare of and aversion from injury of other living beings. Emphasis upon non-injury in relation to animals has conduced to spread of vegetarianism in India, esp. among Brahmins, though early Vedic writings depict meat-eating, animal sacrifice, etc. A. was a main motive for condemnation of sacrificial ritual by Jains, Buddhists and others; one cause of virtual disappearance of animal sacrifice within Hinduism (→ sacrifice, Hindu). N.S.

Chakravart Nayanar, *The Religion of Ahimsa* (1953); I. C. Sharma, *Ethical Philosophies of India* (1965); M. K. Gandhi *Hindu Dharma* (1950), *Non-Violence in Peace and War* (1948).

Ahl al-suffa, or, aṣḥāb al-ṣuffa (people of the portico). A name trad. explained as being given to certain poor and pious people in Medina in Muḥammad's time, who lived in portico of the mosque and engaged in study and worship. That they voluntarily adopted an ascetic life is now questioned, it being more prob. that they had no patron to provide them with accommodation, and so lived at mosque. → Abū Hurayra, whose authority is quoted most frequently for trads., is mentioned among the A. The name → Ṣūfī was sometimes said to be derived from *ṣuffa*, an imposs. derivation; it really comes from *ṣūf* (wool) with ref. to the woollen cloak the Ṣūfīs. wore. J.R.

*E.I.*², I, pp. 266f.; Hughes, p. 24; Hujwīrī, *Kashf*, p. 81; Arberry, *Doctrine*, pp. 2, 5, 9.

Ahl-i Ḥaqq (The people of God), a secret sect chiefly in W. Persia. They are often incl. among the → 'Alī Ilāhīs; but this appears to be an error, for 'Alī is not the chief object of worship. They speak of the twelve → *imāms*; but they are distinct from the Twelvers (→ *imām*). They believe that God has manifested himself seven times, the fourth of the theophanies being as Sulṭān Ṣohāk (9th/15th cent.). While they give 'Alī some worship, their devotion is mainly directed to Sulṭān Ṣohāk. They believe in → reincarnation and a final → judgment, when the good will be admitted to paradise and evil annihilated. To be a full member, the head of each initiate must be ceremonially commended to a → *pīr*. They hold assemblies at which offerings of food and animals are made. A three days' fast is observed every winter. The background of their beliefs seems to owe something to → Manichaeanism; and some people have suggested Christ. influences also. The movement is largely popular, the members being nomads, villagers and poorer class townspeople. J.R.

*E.I.*², I, pp. 260–3; Pareja, pp. 845f.; C. R. Pittman, *The final word of the Ahl-i-Haqq*, in *MW* xxvii (1937), pp. 147–63.

Aḥmad b. Ḥanbal (164–241/780–855) Famous theologian and traditionist of Baghdad; a man of strongly held convictions on account of which he suffered persecution when the Caliph Ma'mūn tried to enforce the → Mu'tazilite doc. A. refused to accept the doc. that the Qur. is created. Under Caliph Mu'taṣim he suffered beating and imprisonment, and though later released, he did not resume teaching till Mu'tazilite doc. was renounced by Mutawakkil. A.'s collection of trads. (*Musnad*) was arranged and published by his son 'Abdallah. It is a work of several volumes containing trads. arranged under name of the orig. authority for their transmission. A.'s theological doc. was strict. He did not write much, but his followers have elaborated on his doc. and produced a system based fundamentally on the Qur. and the Tradition (→ *Ḥadīth*). The Ḥanbalī school of canon law is followed by the → Wahhābīs of Arabia, and has had some influence in mod. times on the → Salafiyya in Egypt. J.R.

*E.I.*², I, pp. 272–7; *G.A.L.*, I, p. 93; *S.I.*, pp. 309f.; Pareja, p. 635 and index (Ibn Ḥanbal); D. B. Macdonald, *Theology*, index; Wensinck, *Creed*, index.

Aḥmad al-Badawī (b. *c.* 596/1199–1200) Most popular Muslim saint in Egypt. He traced ancestry to → 'Alī b. Abū Ṭālib. At an early age he went from Fez, with family, on pilgrimage to Mecca. His father died there, and A. remained, enjoying himself for a number of years; but about 627/1230 he had a change of heart and devoted himself to relig. studies and asceticism. After visit to Iraq, he went in 634/1236–7 to Tanta in Egypt, obeying an order received in a vision. He spent long periods standing on a roof-top and observed long silence, alternated with periods of screaming. He superseded the other saints in Egypt. He wrote prayers and some gen. admonitions, but was not of high intellectual calibre. He d. in 675/1276; his successor 'Abd al-'Āl built a mosque over his tomb. → Pilgrimages were made there; although efforts were made to stop them, they continued. The Ṣūfī order called the Aḥmadiyya after A. has many branches in Egypt. Like other saints, A. has miracles attr. to him, performed both in his lifetime and after death at his tomb. Some people *en route* for Mecca first visit his tomb. J.R.

*E.I.*², I, pp. 280f.; Pareja, pp. 774, 780; Lane, *Egyptians*, pp. 77, 246f., 249.

Aḥmadiyya Movement Estab. by Mīrzā Ghulām Aḥmad (*c.* 1251–1326/1835–1908) of Qadian in

Panjab. He longed for regeneration of Islam and spent years studying his own and other religions. In 1307/1889 he claimed to have received revelation giving him right to receive homage; during subsequent years, he claimed to be the → Messiah, the → Mahdī, the world teacher expected by Zoroastrians, Hindus and Buddhists, an avatar of → Krishna, and to have come in spirit of → Muḥammad. He held that Qur. lxi, 6 speaks of him when it says Jesus foretold coming of a messenger called Aḥmad. He taught that Jesus was crucified, but was taken from Cross alive and resuscitated, then went to Kashmir to preach and d. there aged 120, his tomb being there with the name Yūs Āsaf. Ghulām A.'s claims led to his being called an infidel. Among these was claim to be a prophet, which contradicted the normal Muslim doc. that Muḥammad was the final prophet. He claimed his personality had been merged with that of Muḥammad, so to call himself a prophet did not contradict Muslim belief. He claimed to perform signs and miracles. In gen. his teaching was orthodox; but his insistence that revelation did not cease with Muḥammad failed to find favour, although he said such revelation was not on level with the Qur. He taught that mere formal observance of relig. rites was valueless. He upheld polygamy and the pardah system, but rejected doc. of warlike → *jihād*. He banned tobacco. Some of his teaching seems to echo parts of St. John's Gospel. He admitted new members personally, but instituted *Ṣadr Anjumān-i Aḥmadiyya* (Chief A. society) to administer movement's affairs. On his death, Maulvi Nūr al-Dīn was appointed *khalīfa* (successor); when he d. in 1332/1914, Ghulām Aḥmad's son Bashīr al-Dīn Maḥmūd Aḥmad was appointed *khalīfa* in Qadian, after which a split took place. A party set up a separate branch with Lahore as centre. The Qadian party has always held that founder was a prophet: the Lahore party insist he made no such claim, but was a *mujaddid* (reformer). The Qadian party removed to Rabwah in Pakistan in 1367/1947, as Qadian was on Indian side of new border. It has always been a close-knit society with a strong missionary incentive. Its missions have spread to many parts of world; its literature is widespread. While there has been some success, Muslims gen. consider it heretical; some of its missionaries have suffered death. Its aggressive propaganda has often caused trouble, e.g. see the Munir Report on the Lahore disturbances in 1373/1953. Bashīr al-Dīn d. in 1385/1965 and was succeeded by son Hafiz Mirza Nasir Ahmad. During 1967 the new *khalīfa* paid a visit to Europe, visiting the Hague, Copenhagen (where he inaugurated first mosque in Scandinavia), London, Oxford (where he had studied at Baliol), and Glasgow. The Lahore party is more moderate in doc. and method. It too produces much lit. and carries on missionary work; but it does not keep itself separate from the gen. community of Islam as the Rabwah party does. It is difficult to estimate number of followers of movement. There are no accurate census reports, and claims of numbers in different countries are gen. questioned. But there is no question of devotion of both sections of movement, and their assurance that Islam as they interpret it is the only rational religion. J.R.

Ghulam Ahmad, *The Teachings of Islam* (Muhammad 'Ali's trans.), 5th edn. (Lahore), 1963. The above with appendix, Rabwah, 1959 (called *Philosophy of Islam*); Bashīr al-Dīn, *Intro. to study of Holy Quran*, 1949, *Ahmadiyyat or the true Islam*, 5th edn. (Rabwah), 1959; *E.I.*[2], I, pp. 301–3; H. J. Fisher, *Aḥmadiyyah*, (1963), Phoenix, *His Holiness* (criticism by a Muslim), repr. Lahore (1958); H. Walter, *The Aḥ. Movt.* (1918); J. S. Trimingham, *Islam in West Africa* (1959), esp. App. IV; *Report of court of enquiry . . . into the Punjab disturbances of* 1953 (Munir report), (1954); Zafrulla Khan, *Islam, its meaning for modern man* (1962); Pareja, pp. 850–3; *M.W.*, indexes I-XXV and XXVI-L, thereafter quarterly indexes.

Aḥmad Khān *Sir Sayyid* (1232–1316/1817–98), descended from import. Delhi family, took service with E. Indian Company after father's death. Following the Mutiny, he wished his community acquitted of charge of being chief culprit, and that it should find its salvation in new learning. A visit to Europe in 1286/1869 impressed him with West. progress. In 1295/1878 he founded the Muhammadan Anglo-Oriental College at Aligarh. In 1339/1920 it became the Muslim University of Aligarh. His purpose was to train men who would preach gospel of free enquiry, of large-hearted tolerance and pure morality. He sought to bring Islam into line with mod. West. learning, ethics and economics. He held Islam was not unprogressive. In 1304/1886 he founded the All-India Muhammadan Educational Conference to promote learning among Muslims. He held the individual had right to private judgment regarding Islamic revelation, and upheld reason against authority. He pled for more sympathy between Muslims and Christians. He worked for social reforms and challenged purdah system. His efforts had a degree of success, but were opposed by reaction in favour of older type of Muslim thought and life. Followers of his have taught that present-day Islam is not true Islam, and have been anxious to sweep away trad. and legal ordinances standing in way of progress. Such men have strongly opposed polygamy. Khuda Bakhsh (d. 1350/1931) has called it destructive alike of domestic peace and social purity.

As a result of A.Kh's work, improvements were made and desire for education spread. The most notable instance was founding of the Osmaniya University in Hyderabad (1336/1917). A develop. not so much in accord. with his ideas was the founding of the All-India Muslim League in 1324/1906, to uphold Muslim political interests. J.R.

*E.I.*², I, pp. 287f.; p. 403 (Aligarh); Pareja, pp. 504ff.; J. M. S. Baljon, *Reforms and religious ideas of Sir Sayyid A. Kh.*, Leiden, 1949 (with full bibliog.); A. Hourani, *Thought*, pp. 124f.; W. C. Smith, *Modern history*, index; Hafeez Malik, 'The relig. liberalism of Sir Sayyid A. Kh., *M.W.*, LIV (1964), pp. 160ff.

Ahriman In later → Avesta name for principle of Evil, *ex.* → Angra Mainyu, used by → Zoroaster in → Gāthās for same concept (→ Dualism, Iranian). Owing to later identification of → Ohrmazd with the Spenta Mainyu ('Holy Spirit'), A. became opponent of Ohrmazd. (→ Zurvan). S.G.F.B.

J. Duchesne-Guillemin, *Ormazd et Ahriman* (1953), pp. 26ff.; R. C. Zaehner, *D.T.Z.*, *passim.*

Ahura Mazdah Title meaning the 'Wise Lord', used by → Zoroaster for supreme creator deity. Behind A.-M. prob. lies anc. Indo-Iranian sky-god (named → Varuna in → Rig-Veda), combining attributes of life and death, light and darkness. Zoroaster made this ambivalent deity into a beneficent creator, and personified the two aspects of its nature as the Spenta Mainyu ('Holy Spirit') and the → Angra Mainyu ('Destructive Spirit'). S.G.F.B.

R. C. Zaehner, *D.T.Z.*, pp. 66ff.; J. Duchesne-Guillemin, *Zoroastre* (1948), pp. 87ff.; G. Widengren, *Hochgottglauben in alten Iran* (1938), p. 252, in *Numen*, I (1954), pp. 21ff.; G. Dumézil, *Les dieux des Indo-Européens* (1952), pp. 15ff.

Ainus A primitive, small-statured people, living in Hokkaido and parts of Saghalien in N. Japan, numbering about 16,000. Remnants of a pre-historic, probably proto-nordic race which was widely spread over N. Asia, occupied in hunting and fishing. Their animistic religion is without known historical beginnings. They believe in supreme High-God who dwells in the highest Heaven, and in multitude of inferior deities: sun, moon, fire, rain, processes of vegetation etc. Also in hostile deities who created disease and death and every kind of evil. Hence a dualism pervades their religious thinking. The use of fetishes, divination, exorcism and magic is integral part of their religion, together with ancestor-worship, prayers to dead and propitiation of demons. Communion with their deities is sought, espec. in the important bear-festival, when bear, kept previously in a cage for about three years, is killed and eaten. They believe in a future life, and in a judgement before the supreme God, at which chief witness is the fire-goddess. D.H.S.

J. Batchelor in *E.R.E.*, I, pp. 239–52; *The Ainu and their folklore* (1901); J. M. Kitagawa, 'Ainu Bear Festival (Iyonmante)', in *H.R.*, I (1961).

'Ā'isha Daughter of → Abū Bakr (q.v.), was born in Mecca *c.* 614 CE. Betrothed to → Muḥammad when about 6 years old, she went to live with him in Medina some 4 years later. She was very beautiful and was Muḥammad's favourite wife. On an expedition in 5/627, in which she had accompanied Muḥammad, she was inadvertently left behind when the caravan, on last stage to Medina, moved ahead, and was found by a young man who brought her to Medina. This caused great scandal, but was eventually settled by a Qur. revelation (xxiv, 11ff.). In his final illness Muḥammad asked his wives to be allowed to remain in 'Ā.'s apartment and this was granted. He d. there and was buried under the floor. 'Ā. was left a childless widow at age of 18, and could not remarry, this being forbidden to Muḥammad's wives. She lived in Medina till assassination of → 'Uthmān in 35/656, when she went to Mecca. Along with Ṭalḥa and al-Zubayr and an army of about 1,000 she went to Basra a few months later. → 'Alī, who had removed from Medina to Kufa, came out and won victory at the Battle of the Camel, in which Ṭalḥa and al-Zubayr were killed and 'Ā. was captured and treated with respect. She returned to live in Mecca, where she is reputed to have transmitted trads. of Muḥammad. She had also reputation for knowledge of poetry, Arab history, etc. She died in 58/678. J.R.

*E.I.*², I, pp. 307f.; Pareja, index; N. Abbott, *Aishah the beloved of Mohammed* (1942); *Papyri*, index.

Ajantā An anc. Buddh. monastic site in Aurangabad dist. Bombay state, India. Neglected and forgotten for more than a thousand years, it was rediscovered in 1819. The monastic dwelling halls (→ *vihāra*) and shrine rooms (*chaitya*) are in form of caves, hewn from rock of valley-side to similate wooden buildings of early Buddh. period; there are 30 altogether. The shrine rooms contain, as central feature, a sacred relic-mound or → *stupa.* Many of caves are decorated with paintings on walls, pillars and ceilings. In some there are also inscriptions in early Brāhmi script of 2nd cent. BC. Other of the paintings and inscriptions are of 5th-6th cents. CE. The scenes depicted illustrate stories of former lives of the Buddha, i.e. the → *Jātakas.* They thus deal with palace and court life, kings, queens and princesses; rural scenes which incl. wide range of animal and bird life—buffaloes bulls, horses, elephants, lions, swans, geese, etc.; processions, dances, musicians, lovers—in fact an acutely observed panorama of Indian life in pre- and early Christ. era. There is also considerable sculptural work, a feature of which is the intense portrayal of human emotions. Besides illustrating the *Jātakas*, many of the most magnificent paintings and sculptures deal with life of historical Buddha. as it is known from the *suttas*: the prince Siddhartha confronted by the three signs of old age, disease and death; the temptation by → *Māra*; and various other incidents of his life, together with final scene, the → *parinirvāṇa*. The murals of A. are of importance to art historian, since development of styles over period of 1,000 years can be traced here. T.O.L.

Benjamin Rowland, *The Art and Architecture of India* (1959); Sukumar Dutt, *Buddhist Monks and Monasteries of India* (1962).

Ajātasattu King mentioned in Pali Buddh. scriptures, who reigned over the kingdom of → Magadha during last 8 years of the Buddha's life, and for 24 years after that. His name means 'enemy (*sattu*) while still unborn (*ajata*)'. This is said to ref. to ante-natal desire of his mother to drink blood from her husband's knee, interpreted by astrologers to mean that the child she was bearing would kill his father → Bimbisara, and seize the kingdom. An alternative explanation of name is 'he against who there has arisen no foe'. A. is repr. as having been ambitious prince who could not wait for his father's death to inherit the kingdom, plotted to murder him. In this he had co-operation of → Devadatta, the Buddha's cousin, who through vain self conceit wished to oust Buddha and become leader of the Sangha. Bimbisara was a supporter of Buddha., hence a double plot was formed: Devadutta was to murder Buddha, while A. murdered his father King Bimbisara. The plot was discovered; Bimbisara pardoned his son and abdicated in his favour. However, A., unsafe while his father was still alive, imprisoned him and starved him to death. One visit of A. to Buddha is recorded: the king recounts that he has visited six other ascetics and outlines their various doctrines; he then asks Buddha. concerning his doc. and its advantages, Buddha expounds to him advantages of the ascetic life. (→ *Samannaphala Sutta*). One further connection between A. and Buddha. is of importance. His ambition as ruler led him to plan attack on the territory of the Vajjian confederacy of tribes; in connection with this he sent Vassakara, his brahman chief minister, to obtain Buddha's views on his chances of success. His reply concerning security of the → *Vajjis* is occasion for an import. piece of Buddh. teaching on virtues of democratic confederacy in general, and the Sangha's role as preserver of this form of organisation, which at that time was fast disappearing before advancing autocratic monarchy, such as that of A. (*Mahāparinibbāna Su.*). While there is no further evidence of any continued interest on the part of A. in teaching of Buddha, the trad. records that after Buddha's death, A. obtained share of his ashes and erected a *stupa* over them in Rajagaha. (*Mahāparinibbāna Su*, pp. 164–6). Acc. to the → *Mahāvastu*, A. was then approached by members of the Sangha, who were planning a gen. council for reciting of entire teaching of Buddha, for the king's assistance. This was readily given, acc. to this Skt. source: the king ordered an enormous hall to be built, 'like the assembly-hall of the gods', imposingly furnished with lofty seats for president and reciting monk. Acc. to trad., the Council of Rajagaha was then held, under patronage of king, and lasted seven months. (→ Councils). Nevertheless, acc. to a Thv. recorded by → Buddhaghosa, A.'s evil deeds caused him to be reborn in hell, where he was to suffer torment for 60,000 years before rebirth as a → *pacceka-buddha*. T.O.L.

Malalasekera, DPPN, '*Ajatasattu*'; *Sacred Books of the Buddhists*, vol. II (1899), pp. 56ff.; *S.B.E.*, vol. II, pp. 131–4; vol. 19, p. 248; vol. 20, pp. 233–8, 241–3, 377; vol. 21, p. 6; vol. 22, pp. XIVff.; vol. 49 (II), pp. 161–4.

Ājīvikas Relig. movement headed by Makkhali Gosala, a contemporary of → Mahavira. Early Buddhism took the A. very seriously as a rival teaching, but very little of the writings of latter has survived. There is some doubt as to meaning of name; it prob. derives from *ājīva*, 'mode of life', 'profession'. The chief doc. of Gosala was determinism. Virtue and vice are not due to human effort, and living beings are fated to undergo an immense series of → rebirths before they attain liberation. One's destiny is controlled by fate, *niyati*. This karmic predestinationism, however, did not result in antinomianism, and the A. mendicants preached great austerity (such austerity being symptom rather than cause of one's fitness for liberation), though their rivals accused them of laxity. Some of their practices were similar to those in → Jainism: e.g. at initiation into the A. order the novice has his hairs plucked out one by one; the medicants went round naked (→ Nudity, ritual); some of their saints ended their lives by self-starvation. The movement lasted until medieval period, when it became absorbed within the Pancaratra sect of Hinduism. This was facilitated by developments within S. Indian Ajivikism (it survived longest in the S.) of views analogous to those of → Mahayana Buddhism → Gosala being elevated to quasi-divine status, and the world being considered illusory. N.S.

A. L. Basham *Hist. and Doctrines of the Ajivikas: a vanished Indian Religion* (1951).

Akephaloi → Acephalos, Acephali. S.G.F.B.

Akh Anc. Egypt. designation for 'glorified dead', i.e. those on whose behalf the necessary funerary ritual had been performed (→ Funerary Rites, Egypt.). The Egyptians distinguished the *akhu* (pl.) from the (ordinary) dead. S.G.F.B.

H. Kees, *T.*, pp. 37–8; *R.Ae.R.-G.*, p. 4 ('ach'); S. G. F. Brandon, *M.D.*, pp. 44–5.

Akhenaten (Amenhotep IV) Egypt. king (1372–1354 BC), son of Amenhotep III and husband of the famous Nefertiti, who attempted to reform Egypt. relig. A. sponsored already existing movement, prob. stemming from → Heliopolis, to break power of priesthood of → Amun by replacing Amun as chief state-deity by the → Aten. A. proceeded in stages with his reform, these being marked by change of his orig. name Amenhotep = 'Amun is satisfied' to Akhenaten = 'It is pleasing to the Aten', and by building a new capital called Akhetaten = 'The Horizon of Aten'. He aimed at complete extirpation of cult of Amun, even removing deity's name from monuments. A. prob. intended to establ. the Aten as sole god of Egypt: on the monotheistic character of his movement → Aten. A. appears to have been a man of strange genius. At Akhetaten (modern Tell el-Amarna) he inspired new form of art, and he seems personally to have composed the *Hymn to the Aten*, which has survived. His movement failed: the powerful priesthood of Amun hated him, and his neglect of Egypt's empire antagonised the army. After his death, his successor Tut-Ankh-Amen made his peace with Amun and returned the capital to Thebes. A.'s memory was execrated; the destruction of his monuments has seriously reduced available evidence of the first-known relig. reformer. S.G.F.B.

R.Ae.R.-G., pp. 59–71 ('Aten'); S. G. F. Brandon, *Religion in Ancient History* (1969), chap. 9; A. Gardiner, *Egypt of the Pharaohs* (1961), pp. 212ff.; C. Aldred, *Akhenaten* (1968).

Akiba ben Joseph Celebrated rabbi (CE 50–135) who played important part in Jew. life after the destr. of Jerusalem, CE 70. A. is regarded as the true Father of → Talmud, because it was his exposition of Scripture as basis for → Halakhah, that laid foundation for this later rabbinic achievement. A. actively supported the revolt of → Bar Cochba, and, after its suppression was executed by the Romans. (→ Judaism). S.G.F.B.

E.R.E., I, *s.v.; R.G.G.*³, I, *s.v.*

Akitu New Year festival held at Babylon. It lasted 11 days, during which the → *Enuma elish* was twice recited liturgically, thus connecting the New Year with creation of world. The theme of *Enuma elish* was → Marduk's acquisition of authority to decide destinies; at the A. it was believed that Marduk cast the destiny of Babylon for coming year. The A. consisted of many ceremonies, one of which was the ritual humiliation of king. Some enigmatic evidence has been interpreted as indicating that the A. incl. a ritual presentation of death and resurrection of Marduk; but this interpretation, favoured by the → Myth and Ritual school, remains doubtful. A. festivals were celebrated elsewhere in Mesopotamia. A. was also a designation for a pavilion used during New Year festival at Babylon. S.G.F.B.

S. A. Pallis, *The Babylonian Akîtu Festival* (1926); S. H. Hooke, *Myth, Ritual and Kingship* (1958), pp. 1–11; Brandon, *C.L.*, pp. 91ff.

Akkad (Accad), Akkadian (Accadian) Before the rise of → Babylon, southern Mesopotamia was divided into two provinces: Sumer (south); Akkad (north). The latter took its name from the city of Agade. Akkadian was the Semitic language of people of A., and is now generally applied to the languages of Babylon and → Assyria. S.G.F.B.

G. R. Driver, *Semitic Writing* (1948), pp. 2ff.

Ālaya-Vijñāna Term used by Buddh. school of → Yogācāra, usually trans. into Eng. as 'store-consciousness', the basic consciousness or persisting element which is subject of successive births and deaths. This doc. was developed by → Asanga, the 4th cent. CE authority and exponent of the Yogacara school. T.O.L.

Alb Long white linen garment, secured at waist by girdle, worn by ministers at Mass. It derived from under-tunic worn in Graeco-Roman world, and was used in Chr. worship from early date. S.G.F.B.

Albertus Magnus Albert the Great, medieval theologian (*c.* 1200–1280), who entered → Dominican order and taught at many centres of learning, incl. Cologne, when Thomas → Aquinas was his pupil. A man of vast learning, influenced by Jew. and Arab. writers as well as by → Aristotle, he pointed the way to the great synthesis of philosophy and theology achieved by Aquinas. A.M. was canonised (→ Canonisation) and proclaimed a *doctor ecclesiae* in 1931. S.G.F.B.

D.C.C., s.v.; E. Bréhier, *La philosophie du Moyen Age* (1949) pp. 296ff.; G. Leff, *Medieval Thought.* (1958), 206ff.

Albigenses Heretical sect, named after city of Albi, in Languedoc, S. France, which was centre of movement; Toulouse and Carcassonne were also important strongholds. Sect first appeared in 11th cent., and prob. stemmed from → Cathari, estab. in Bulgaria. The A. professed a form of → Manichaean dualism, acc. to which spirits were created by an eternal good principle and matter by an eternal evil principle. Spirits which fell from orig. goodness became imprisoned in material bodies, passing through succession of incarnations (→ Metempsychosis) until they purged their evil and merited heaven (→ Gnosticism). A. regarded Christ as angel with a phantom body (→ Docetism), and held that Catholic Church had erred and become corrupt by taking N.T. allegories literally. Rejecting orthodox → soteriology, A. sought salvation through esoteric knowledge and → asceticism, even incl. suicide by starvation in certain circumstances. The moral standard of their lives gen. compared favourably with that of Cath. clergy. Regarded as both spiritually and socially dangerous, the A. were condemned by various eccl. Councils (e.g. 4th Lateran C., 1215). After unsuccessful attempts to convert them by → Cistercians and St. → Dominic, → Innocent III launched → Crusade against them, led by Simon de Montfort. A. were subdued with great cruelty; the war later assumed a political aspect for incorp. of Languedoc into France. In 1233 Dominican → Inquisition was charged to extirpate remnants of heresy, which vanished by end of 14th cent. S.G.F.B.

E.R.E., I, *s.v.; D.C.C., s.v.; R.G.G.*[3], I, 217; S. Runciman, *The Medieval Manichee* (1955), pp. 109, n.1, 116ff.

Alchemy Word derives *via* Arabic from Grk. *chēmeia*, which might in turn come from anc. Egypt. *kēme* = black (Egypt was called *kēmet* = the 'black land'). This latter derivation is disputed; but Egypt was certainly assoc. with beginnings of A. Early knowledge of chemistry in Egypt, Mesopot. and Greece led to speculations about essential nature of things and ways of transmuting them. Practical interest found expression in attempts to change base metals into gold. The association of the 4 Elements (fire, earth, water, air) with the planets Mercury, Saturn, Jupiter, Mars, connected A. with →→ astrology and astralism. Belief in a *materia prima*, from which everything was formed, also assisted A. The oldest documents of A. are two Grk. papyri, found near Thebes in Egypt, and deal with transmuting of metals, purple-dyeing, alloying, colouring metals, glass and precious stones. It was in Egypt during Graeco-Roman era, that A. developed its mystical side, and was assoc. with → Hermes Trismegestos. A. provided useful material for → Gnostic speculations, esp. on constitution of the Primal Man. This trad. of A. was taken over by Islamic scholars; Spain became an important centre of its study, whence it passed to Chr. Europe. Many medieval ecclesiastics and scholars were interested with various aspects of A., among them Pope Sylvester II (999–1003), →→ Albertus Magnus, Aquinas, Roger Bacon. Medieval A. was much concerned with finding an 'elixir' that would prolong life and the 'Philosopher's stone', which would transform baser metals into gold. A. survived into 17th cent., when it was gradually replaced by exact sciences of chemistry and biochemistry. Although it produced much superstition and esoteric speculation, A. repr. a necessary stage *en route* to more exact knowledge about constitution of matter. (→ Taoism). S.G.F.B.

E.R.E., I, *s.v.* (pp. 287b–98a); *R.G.G.*[3], I, 219–23; *Kleine Pauly*, I, 237–9; J. Doresse, *The Secret Books of the Egyptian Gnostics* (1960), pp. 99ff.; H. Butterfield, *The Origins of Modern Science* (1949); E. J. Holmyard, *Alchemy* (1957); *R.A.C.*, I, 239–60; G. E. Monod-Herzen, *L'alchimie méditerranéenne* (1963).

Alcheringa Name given by the Arunta, Kaitish, and Unmatjera tribes in Central Australia to a mythical past when their ancestors were created and their ritual customs instituted. At this time, or prior to it, a Supreme Being, an → All Father is believed to have lived on earth (→ Austral. Aborig. Relig.). S.G.F.B.

Alcohol (Buddhist attitude) One of the 5 moral rules (→ Morality, Buddh.) binding upon all Buddhists, monks and lay people, is the requirement to abstain from all intoxicating liquor; this incl. intoxicants and drugs of all kinds, whether made from grain, fruit, sugar, yeast or in any other way. The precept here, as in other four cases, takes form of voluntary vow of abstinence: 'I take upon me the vow to abstain from taking intoxicants and drugs such as wine, liquor, etc. since they lead to moral carelessness'. T.O.L.

(Hindu attitudes to) Over a very long period Brahmins have been required by relig. law not to consume alcohol, though the intoxicating beverage → Soma figured prominently in anc. Vedic rites. In mod. times there has been a wider attempt to impose abstention from alcohol, culminating in prohibition in Ahmedabad pre-war (then under a Congress gov. and place of Gandhi's ashram), and in a number of states in India since independence in 1947. However, it has been trad. for many non-Brahmins to drink alcohol; even when Indian society was under considerable Buddh. influence, the fifth precept of Buddhism, prohibiting use of intoxicants, was not taken very seriously. Moreover, the festival of *dīvalī* saw a lifting of taxation on alcohol and restrictions on private brewing, etc. Tendencies towards 'temperance' in the last few cents. have been reinforced by presence of a substantial Muslim population in the sub-continent and in this cent. by attitude of Gandhi. (→→ Sikhism, Tantrism). N.S.

J. Auboyer *Daily Life in Ancient India* (1961).

Alcuin English scholar (*c.* 735–804), who inspired revival of learning in Europe during reign of Charlemagne. A native of York, A. became master of its cathedral school, before becoming Abbot of Tours in 781, where he established important school and library. Using dialogue form, A. based his instruction on works of →→ Boethius, Augustine and the grammarians. Among his famous pupils was Rabanus Maurus. A. wrote educat. manuals, poetry, and on theological (→ Adoptianism) and liturgical subjects. S.G.F.B.

R. L. Poole, *Medieval Thought and Learning* (1932), pp. 18ff.; *D.C.C., s.v.; R.G.G.*[3], I, 237; G. Elland, *Master Alcuin* (1956).

Aleut Religion Few traces of indigenous relig. of people of the Aleutian Islands (S.W. of Alaska) now remain. Settled by Russians in 18th cent. and transferred to U.S. in 1867, the Al. Is. have long been field of Chr. missionary work, first by Russian Orthodox and more recently by Protestants. The Al. themselves declined sharply in numbers during this period. They are branch of → Eskimo family, but have distinctive language and social structure, their original economy being based entirely on the sea. Much of Al. relig. is now obscure, but Jochelson reports belief in a → High God, Aleuxta-Agudax^{c} (*agudax^{c}* = doer). Among Al. origin legends was one of a dog-mother, Mahakh, and another of two half-human, half-fox creatures, the male being called Acagnikakh—these inviting comparison with Eskimo legends. Al. relig. practice may be classified as form of → shamanism. There were no temples, but numbers of cult sites, at which ceremonies were carried out to propitiate and control the spirits (*kugan*); at these centres human images were sometimes set up. Among common cult-objects were the drum (an integral part of shamanism) and what Jochelson calls the *calumet*, a pair of wooden or reed staffs from 1½ to 4 ft. long, painted and decorated with symbolic objects; amulets were also widely used, and a fluid prepared from tissues of a dead body was a powerful unguent. Ceremonies connected with puberty (esp. of girls) are still occasionally carried out: the girl is isolated, and kept from entering church; she is placed under care of old women, and certain foods are forbidden. The whole process lasts for 50 days, during which time the girl is thought to have healing powers (→ tabu). Al. mortuary practices seem orig. to have comprised exposure, followed by preservation of remains in rock-shelters; beliefs concerning human destiny resembled those of Eskimos. E.J.S.

E.R.E., I, pp. 303a–5b; W. Jochelson, *History, Ethnology and Anthropology of the Aleut* (1933); C. I. Shade, in *Amer. Anthrop.* (1951), pp. 145ff.; G. H. Marsh, *A Comparative Survey of Eskimo-Aleut Religion* (Anthropol. Papers of Univ. of Alaska III, 1954).

Alexander VI (Pope) Rodrigo Borgia (1431–1503), who became Pope in 1492, is the most notorious holder of the → Papacy. He was mostly concerned with politics and the advancement of his family, espec. his son Caesare, and was unscrupulous in his methods. He succeeded in destroying → Savonarola. A. is also notable for dividing the New World between Spain and Portugal (1493–4). He was a generous patron of the arts. S.G.F.B.

D.C.C., s.v.; N.C.M.H., I (1957), pp. 77ff.

(of Abonutichos) Relig. charlatan of 2nd cent. CE, who took his name from small city in Paphlogonia. Information about A. comes almost exclus. from Lucian, famous for his cynicism about popular relig. Acc. to Lucian, A. succeeded in imposing himself as semi-divine prophet of → Aesculapius on people of Abonutichos. There he manipulated an → oracle in form of large snake with human head, supposedly a manifestation of Aesculapius. A cult was instituted of the deity under name of Glycon. Its fame became widespread and survived A.'s death. A. also estab. mysteries (→ Mystery religions), lasting 3 days, connected with Aescul.-Glycon. A. was hostile to Christians and → Epicureans, and at beginning of mysteries warning was given: 'If there be any atheist or Christian or Epicurean here spying upon our rites, let him depart in haste; and let all such as have faith in the god be initiated and all blessing attend them.' The career and achievement of A. are significant for understanding popular relig. in Graeco-Roman world. S.G.F.B.

H. W. and F. G. Fowler (eds.), *The Works of Lucian of Samosata* (1905), II, pp. 212ff.; A. D. Nock, *Conversion* (1933), pp. 93ff.; *R.A.C.*, I, 260–1.

(the Great) Third Macedonian king of this name, A. (356–323 BC) merited title 'great' by military genius, organising ability and dynamic personality, which made him ruler of anc. world by time of early death at 32. In a series of victories, he destroyed Persian Empire, and led army triumphantly into N.W. India. His career changed political situation in Near East for nearly 3 cents.: his generals divided empire after his d.; Seleucus founding a dynasty ruling over Mesopot. and Syria; Ptolemy a line of rulers in Egypt until 30 BC. A.'s activities, espec. his founding of cities throughout his empire, greatly assisted Hellenisation of Near East. The spread of Grk. language and culture in turn fostered relig. → syncretism, and paved way for universalist cults such as → Christianity and → Mithraism. A.'s relig. beliefs and policy are important. While in Egypt, he made difficult journey to oracle of Ammon (→ Amun) in oasis of Siwah, where he was recognised as son of Ammon (Zeus). In 324 A. officially requested Grk. cities to treat him as a god, and he was much concerned to emulate →→ Heracles and Dionysus. He seems also to have conceived of a cosmopolitan empire, based on fundamental unity of mankind. A.'s amazing career produced a rich abundance of legend in India, Persia, Arabia, Israel and elsewhere. The A. romance has eighty versions, in twenty-four languages, and can be traced even in China and Malaya. In → Ethiopian Christianity A. became a saint; in Jew. legend he is the 'Two-horned', the precursor of the → Messiah, and, as Dhulcarnein (the 'Two-horned'), he is one of the heroes of Islam. S.G.F.B.

W. W. Tarn, *Alexander the Great*, 2 vols. (1948), and chs. 12 and 13 in *C.A.H.*, VI (1927); *O.C.D.*, *s.v.;* P. Jouguet, *L'impérialisme macédonien et l'hellénisation de l'orient* (1926); F. Schachermeyr, *Alexander der Grosse* (1949), pp. 204ff., 467ff.; *R.A.C.*, I, 261–70; *Kleine Pauly*, I, 247–9.

Alexandria (in Egypt) Founded by → Alexander the Great in 332–331 BC, who was also buried there, A. became 2nd greatest city of Mediterranean world in anc. times. It was essentially a Grk. city, and in Hellenistic age supplanted → Athens as centre of Grk. culture, possessing a Museum and a library of 900,000 vols. It was distinguished for its science and lit., and magnificence of its buildings. A great manufacturing and commercial city, through which flowed much of trade with India and the East, A. inevitably became centre of relig. → syncretism. Many Grk. and Egypt. gods were worshipped there, and the cult of → Sarapis epitomised this syncretism. A large Jew. population made A. the leading centre of Hellenistic Judaism, and many relig. documents, incl. LXX (→ Septuagint) were written there; → Philo endeavoured to synthesis Heb. relig. and Grk. philosophy. A. became important Chr. centre (→ Alexandria, Church of), and also of Chr. → Gnosticism (→→ Clement of Alex.; Origen). A. passed into world of → Islam with Arab conquest of Egypt in 642. (→ Coptic Church). S.G.F.B.

R.A.C., I, 271–83; H. I. Bell, *Cults and Creeds in Graeco-Roman Egypt* (1953); P. D. Scott-Moncrieff, *Paganism and Christianity in Egypt* (1913).

(Church of) A curious silence invests the origins of Christianity in → Alex. A late legend (→ Eusebius, *eccl. hist.* II. xxiv) makes St. Mark first bishop of Alex. The earliest ref. to Christianity there occurs in mention of → Apollos in Acts 18:24ff., which seems to denigrate Alex. → Christology as defective acc. to → Paul's teaching. A letter sent by Emp. Claudius to Alexandrians (CE 41) may indic. that Christianity had already reached there. There is some evidence for thinking that Ch. of A. was orig. Jew. Chr. (→ Jewish Christianity), and so was opposed to Paul's doctrine. It is poss. that Gospel of → Matthew, Ep. to → Hebrews, Ep.s of →→→ James, Barnabas, and II Clement were products of Ch. of A., reflecting grad. transition from orig. Jew. Christianity to early Alex. Gnostics (→→ Cerinthus, Basilides) and → Clement. The works of → Philo were prob. preserved by Ch. of A. From time of Clement (*c.* 150–*c.* 215), Alex. grad. became one of chief centres of Christianity, distinguished alike for its theology (→ Alexandrian Theology), and great personalities (→→ Origen, Athanasius, Cyril). S.G.F.B.

R.A.C., I, 281–2; H. I. Bell, *Cults and Creeds in Graeco-Roman Egypt* (1953), pp. 78ff.; *R.G.G.*[3], I, 121–3, 476 ('Apollos'); S. G. F. Brandon, *The Fall of Jerusalem and the Christian Church* (1957[2]), pp. 24ff., 224ff.; *Jesus and the Zealots* (1967), pp. 196ff., 291ff.

Alexandrian Theology The distinctive thought of Chr. theologians at → Alexandria from late 2nd to 5th cent. Alexandria's trad. of learning embraced Hellenic schools of relig. philosophy, Hellenistic → Judaism, the orientalised Hellenism of Chr. → Gnostics, and Hellenistic Christianity itself, thus providing a complex of presuppositions: abstract transcendentalism and absolute monism in idea of God; mediating powers, spirits, or → aeons to bridge gap between heaven and earth; a depreciation of matter as inherently evil; → asceticism as pathway to knowledge of God and immortality. Such a *Weltanschauung* resulted from synthesis of East and West at Alexandria; it is already perceptible in the → LXX (*c.* 130 BC), the *Wisdom of Solomon* (prob. 1st cent. BC), and preeminently in → Philo. The influence of Philo on → Clement and → Origen has hardly even yet been given its due. The researches of Koetschau, Stählin *et alii* in their critical editions of the Chr. Alexandrians (in *G.C.S.*) lay bare their vast indebtedness, both in idea and expression, to Philo's scholarship and relig. philosophy. Of espec. importance were his docts. of God's utter transcendence—even above being, virtue and knowledge—aligned with his providence (as Father) over all his creation, the link being the → Logos, who combines the quasi-hypostatised Word-Wisdom of Jew. trad. with the immanent universal Reason of → Stoic pantheism. The Logos is the principle of differentiation in universe and of individuality in man, the archetype, i.e., of human reason; but it hardly achieves individuality. Philo's transcendentalism implies a kind of *via negativa*, which leads to God through progressively stripping from our idea of him all that marks our finite human existence; the highest grade of relig. life is spiritual → ecstasy, and the supreme blessedness is 'to stand steadfastly in God alone'. Philo's mysticism leaves no place for resurrection of the flesh. Philo was primarily a Biblical exegete, and his docts. (*prima facie* so alien to O.T.) were derived from it by → allegory. The origins of allegory are currently much debated. (cf. Hanson,

R. P. C., *Allegory and Event*, pp. 11ff.). It is, however, clear that, whatever ascription of priorities we prefer, allegory follows naturally from the kind of *Weltanschauung* dominant in Alex. The depreciation of matter led to depreciation of literal meaning of the sacred text; it inspired an exaggerated 'sacramentalism' of exegesis, which at its best afforded genuine insight into spiritual truth, and at its worst a refuge for educated men who were attached to an 'established' religion but wished to evade absurdities and immoralities in its sacred documents. The early hist. of Christianity in Alex. is shrouded in mystery (→ Alexandria, Church of). It has been conjectured that Matthew's Gospel may have had an Alex. orig.; more certain is the Alex. orig. of the so-called Epistle of Barnabas (*c.* 70–100), which turns the weapons of Philonic allegory into an all-out attack on Judaism itself. The early succession lists of Church incl. no Alex. bishops—prob. because earliest prominent Alexandrians were Gnostics (so Turner, H. E. W., *Pattern of Christian Truth*, p. 57). The greatest schools of Gnosticism (→ Valentinus, → Basilides) were Alexandrian, and reached their culmination in 2nd cent. CE. Our previous fragmentary knowledge of Gnostics (derived mainly from their orthodox adversaries) is being vastly extended by gradual publication of the → Nag Hammadi discoveries. Here we can only note that their immense variety stems from common grounding in the Alex. *Weltanschauung*, and their enormous and fantastic super-structures of speculation often disguise their essential concurrence with thought of their Chr. successors, espec. Clement and Origen. In their efforts to destroy Gnosticism, the latter incurred the charge of Gnosticism themselves. From the later 2nd cent. there existed at Alex. something new in the Chr. world, i.e., the Catechetical School, designed not only to train Chr. catechumens but propagate Gospel by intellectual debate with cultured Jews and pagans. Of its first Principal, Pantaenus (d. *c.* 200) we know little; the second was Clement (*c.* 150–*c.* 215). Cultured and able, Clement lacked the power to systematise: his significance for development of Alex. theology lies in (a) his vindication of philosophy as a *praeparatio evangelii* for the Greeks (like the Law for Jews), at a time when reaction against Gnosticism had brought philosophy as such into disfavour with Christians (cf. Tertullian's *haereses a philosophia subornantur*, *Praescr.* 7); (b) his personalising of the → Logos, in which he moves from Philonic relig. metaphysics to a decisively Chr. presentation of Logos, supremely incarnate in Christ, while yet agent of creation and 'world-soul' of the Stoics; (c) his → Christology as incarnational rather than soteriological: Christ the Logos is supremely the Educator: baptism is the 'washing of illumination', which initiates into the true mysteries: salvation is not so much redemption by Cross as attainment of immortality; (d) his ideal of the perfect Christian as the true 'gnostic', the principle of whose life is knowledge or illumination, based upon but higher than faith, which is a *prolepsis* ('anticipation') of things unseen. As a philosopher, Clement gives the marks of the true Gnostic as *apatheia* and deiformity or even deification; as a Christian he adds → *agape*, and sets the whole in framework of revelation and faith—the faith of the Church, with its Apostolic trad., open and secret, the latter being prob. the allegoric exegesis of the Bible, through which the esoteric philosophy of the true Gnostic is imparted. Clement's work culminates in his successor Origen (*c.* 186–*c.* 255), who curiously never mentions him. Here the orig. Alex. *Weltanschauung* is expanded to limit by a scholar and thinker of professional genius, one of the half-dozen greatest the Church has produced. As a Biblical exegete, he is the supreme allegorist, and much of his work constitutes a *reductio ad absurdum* of this highly questionable and subjective procedure. But his chief significance for our purpose lies elsewhere. With a far wider range of philosophic learning than Clement, and a mastery of Bible as a whole and in detail unequalled until → Luther, he turns his untiring mind to task of constructing a systematic Chr. philosophy, which will outclass the Greeks at their own game, and at same time be strictly faithful to totality of the Apostolic trad. Enigmas such as the doc. of the Person of Christ and work of Spirit, at which Clement merely glances, are squarely faced. That Origen's solutions were often found later to be unacceptable is partly the penalty of the pioneer, partly the limitations imposed by the Alex. *Weltanschauung*, which made assimilation of the Gospel with his eclectic stoicised-Platonism a task beyond even his powers. He was often content to lay side by side insights, derived from his philosophy, with those of a thinking and praying churchman; hence in a later generation, when dogma had become more defined, he could be accused of fathering quite inconsistent heresies. His insistence on unity and transcendence of God led to charge of subordinationism; yet his doc. of the eternal generation of the Son far removed him from anything like the vulgar → Arianism of the 4th cent. As a philosopher, he insisted that prayer may only be offered to the supreme God; as a Chr. worshipper, he prayed to Jesus Christ. Indeed, his pursuit of the full Biblical truth about all three Persons of → Trinity foreshadowed the later Alex. trend towards tritheism. Creation to him, as a philosopher, was the automatic issue of evil in the spirit-world; as a churchman, he rejoices in creation as the spontaneous self-giving of God. The Stoic *apatheia* is an axiom, and O.T. refs. to God's wrath and 'repentance' are all allegorised away; yet the Biblicist can write movingly of God's love and mercy. Origen developed an impressive doc. of providence, approx. to the heights of Biblical theology yet sufficiently grounded in current philosophical polemic to repel attacks of men like Celsus with ease. He presented Christ the Logos under different *epinoiai* ('attributes'), varying with the grade of spiritual attainment of believer, and developed the 'double standard', foreshadowed by Clement, into a non-Biblical separation of the sanctified, for whom Cross is no longer necessary and Christ can serve as Word and Wisdom—who also alone qualify for work of Holy Spirit. Yet Origen expounded the → Atonement, as expiatory sacrifice of Christ, the High-priest, and revelation of God's eternal redemption for all mankind, in a way that might well have precluded the crude 'substitutionary transactionism' of later theology, had he not spoilt it by (for once) an over-literal theorising on the N.T. 'ransom' motif: the Cross being the 'fish-hook' to catch the devil. His ideas of the soul's preexistence and of resurrection are again a blending of philosophy and theology; his → eschatology, based in part on his conviction that all punishment is disciplinary, not retributive, leads him to → *apocatastasis* and universal salvation—not, however, as a dogma, but as a hope. His → mysticism, leading to ideal of deification as goal of the purified and enlightened soul, is as much Platonic as Biblical. The later theology of Alex. was dominated by Origen, but developed in specific rivalry to the school of Antioch. The latter, comprising Paul of Samosata, Lucian, Marcellus, → Chrysostom, Theodore, → Nestorius, Theodoret, emphasised the historical against the allegorical interpret. of Scripture, and tended to an 'economic' doctrine of the → Trinity (*oikonomia* = 'plan of salvation', i.e. the Persons are distinguished merely as 'modes of operation' of the one God, which are necessary for men's salvation). Further, Christ had two natures, linked not by *henōsis* (union) but *synapheia* (conjunction), not *kath' hypostasin* (hypostatically) but *kat' eudokian* (by union of the will). Alex. theology, under men like → Athanasius, → Apollinarius and → Cyril, continued the Origenistic trad. of allegory and a Trinitarianism that tended to become tritheistic in the insistence on essential god-head of all three Persons; its Christology leaned heavily on Divine nature of Christ, whereas Antioch emphasised his humanity. Both these schools of theology ran to seed in heresies that the Councils of Ephesus and → Chalcedon condemned: it is clear, however, that the predominant voice throughout was that of Alexandria, and many have seen even in the Chalcedon decisions the unhealthy prevalence of Alex. limitations and presuppositions, which really go back to the *Weltanschauung* with which we began. (→ Antiochene Theology). B.D.

A. Adam, *Lehrbuch der Dogmengeschichte*, I (1965), pp. 212ff.; C. Bigg, *Christian Platonists of Alexandria* (ed. Brightman 1913); E. Molland, *Conception of the Gospel in the Alexandrian Theology* (1938); R. V. Sellers, *Two Ancient Christologies* (1940); *Council of Chalcedon* (1953). See also bibliogs. for Philo, Clement, Origen.

'Alī 'Abd al-Rāziq (b. 1307/1888) An Egyptian who published in 1344/1925 *Islām wa-uṣūl al-ḥukm* (Islam and the principles of government), in which he argued that Islam did not require a → Caliph, that → Muḥammad's mission was purely relig., and that therefore Islam should separate religion from politics. He held that Caliphate was contrary to true Islam. Admitting that Muḥammad had engaged in → *jihād* to further his relig. mission, 'Ā. explained this on ground that evil is sometimes necessary to produce good. His book was condemned and he was expelled from teaching at al-Azhar (→ Education), and from office of judge in → *sharī'a* courts. J.R.

G.A.L., S III, pp. 329f.; Adams, *Modernism*, pp. 251–3, 259–68; Lammens, *l'Islam*, pp. 121f.; Grunebaum, *Essays*, pp. 198ff.; E. I. J. Rosenthal, *Islam*, pp. 85ff.; Cragg, *Counsels*, pp. 69–72.

'Alī b. Abū Ṭālib Cousin of → Muḥammad and 4th Caliph. One of earliest believers in Muḥammad. He married Muḥammad's daughter, → Fāṭima, who bore al-Ḥasan and al-Ḥusayn. 'A. took part in many warlike expeditions, and also served Muḥammad on disciplinary and diplomatic missions. He showed some disagreement with his three predecessors in the Caliphate; but it is not clear that he claimed right to follow Muḥammad as first → Caliph. His behaviour during the rising against → 'Uthmān suggests he was prepared to become Caliph, though unwilling to support the insurgents openly. On becoming Caliph after 'Uthmān's murder, he weakened his position by failing to punish the rebels, and so gave reason to Mu'āwiya (→ Umayyads) to rise against him. 'A. is reputed to have been an intrepid warrior, but an unwise ruler. He was grad. superseded by Mu'āwiya. In 40/661 he was assassinated by a → Khārijite. The → Shī'a hold he should have been first Caliph, and different degrees of dignity have been accorded him. He was intensely relig. even inclined to extreme strictness; but he would never have admitted the extravagant docs. of divinity, or of possessing a divine light which his followers have applied to him. The Imāmīs

(→ Shī'a) do not admit of such extreme views, but 'Alī has a high position as an → *imām*. J.R.

*E.I.*², I, pp. 381–6; Pareja, index; Watt, *Mecca*, index; *Medina*, index; E. L. Petersen, *'Alī and Mu'āwiya in early Arabic tradition* (1964); Donaldson, *Shi'ite*, index.

'Alī Ilāhīs (Deifiers of → 'Alī), name applied to a number of extreme → Shī'a sects in Asia Minor, Persia, Turkestan, Afghanistan, India. Some have incl. the → Ahl-i Ḥaqq among them, but this is questionable. The → Nuṣayrīs, however, do seem to qualify for the title. The chief characteristic is the divine honours paid to 'Alī. J.R.

*E.I.*², I, p. 392; Pareja, p. 846; Mirza Karam, 'The sect of the Ali Ilahis or the Ahl-i Haqq', in *M.W.*, xxix (1939), pp. 73–8.

Allah → God (Islam). J.R.

Allatum Akkadian name of goddess of Mesopot. underworld. A. = *Ir-kal-la*, i.e. personification of underworld. Another title was Eresh-ki-gal = 'Lady of the kigallu', i.e. the 'great land'. S.G.F.B.

E. Dhorme, *R.B.A.*, pp. 39, 52.

Allegory, Allegorical Interpretation To regard any specific text as containing an A. presupposes that the text concerned contains another meaning, usually a more significant one, than the literal meaning. It is often asserted that A.I. started when pious Greeks, shocked by attacks on the gods of → Homer and → Hesiod made by certain philosophers, sought a new meaning behind their texts. But A.I. was used by anc. Egyptians at least from mid. 2nd mill. BC, as chap. 17 of → *Book of the Dead* clearly shows. However, from *c.* 5th cent. BC, Grk. A.I. of Homeric writings estab. an approved trad., to which Jew. and Chr. scholars gladly resorted later in interpretation of sacred texts, espec. of difficult passages such as that of serpent tempting Eve or → Tower of Babel. → Philo is a notable Jew. exponent of A.I. → Paul set the example for Chr. use of A.I., which was much practised, espec. by Alexandrian scholars (→→ Clement, Origen). Its use continued throughout Middle Ages: St. Bernard's interpretation of Song of Solomon is a classical example. A.I. was rejected by Prot. Reformers. S.G.F.B.

E.R.E., *s.v.; R.A.C.*, I, 283–93; *R.G.G.*³, I, 238–40; J. Pepin, *Les deux approches du Christianisme* (1961).

Alleluia (Hallelujah) Heb. expression = 'Praise ye Yah' (→ Yahweh), occurring in many → Psalms (e.g. Pss. 111–17) where its liturgical use is indicated. It was adopted into Chr. worship at an early date, being used both in liturgical offices and in hymns. S.G.F.B.

L. Duchesne, *Christian Worship* (E.T. 1927), pp. 114, 167ff.; *R.G.G.*³, III, 38–9; *R.A.C.*, I, 293–9.

All Fools' Day Name for First of April, which was commemorated by fooling of various kinds from 16th cent. Once a firmly estab. folk-custom, the origin of A.F.D. is obscure. Various explanations have been offered, e.g. that it derives from Roman *Cerealia*, kept at begin. of April, or from anc. Celtic Spring Festival. Similar fooling marks the First of April at the Holī Festival in India. S.G.F.B.

E.R.E., I, *s.v.*

All Saints' Day Festival commemorating all saints, known or unknown, kept in West. Church on 1 Nov., and on first Sunday after → Pentecost in East. Church. First mention of such a feast is made by Ephrem Syrus (d. 373). Its observance of 1 Nov. dates from time of Pope Gregory III (d. 741); before then it was kept on 13 May. S.G.F.B.

D.C.C., *s.v.; R.G.G.*³, I ('Allerheiligenfest'); *R.A.C.*, I, p. 299.

All Souls' Day Commemoration on 2 Nov. of souls of departed Christians. Odilo of → Cluny promoted its observance by ordering, in 998, all Benedictine monasteries under his jurisdiction to keep it annually. The commemoration has a penitential aspect, black being the liturgical colour and the → Dies Irae being recited at Mass. (→→ Eschatology, Christ.; Soul). S.G.F.B.

D.C.C., *s.v.; R.A.C.*, I, 300.

Almighty Omnipotence or possession of all power has been ascribed to many deities: e.g. →→ Amun-Re; Marduk; Yahweh; Zeus; Allah; Vishnu; Chr. God the Father. Such ascription results from belief that supreme Deity must mean supreme power over everything. The logical implications raise many theological difficulties: if God is A. and also good, how is → Evil to be explained? can human freewill be real, if God is A.? (→ Predestination). There are also metaphysical ques.: does omnipotence mean that God can act contrary to his nature? Such problems do not arise where Supreme Deity was regarded as both Creator and Destroyer (→ Dualism); but such ambivalence involves other metaphysical and theological problems. S.G.F.B.

E. O. James, *The Concept of Deity* (1950); *R.G.G.*³, IV, 564–9 ('Macht'); Brandon, *M.D.*, *passim*, in *D.H.I.*, *s.v.*, 'God'.

Almohads (*Al-Muwaḥḥidūn*—the Unitarians), movement initiated by → Ibn Tūmart, which developed into a brief Caliphate. His pupil 'Abd al-Mu'min, who conquered N. Africa up to borders of Egypt but d. (559/1163) before effecting conquest of Spain, assumed title of → Caliph. The → Almoravids were overthrown by the A., but the two successors of 'Abd al-Mu'min, Abū Ya'qūb Yūsuf and Abū Yūsuf Ya'qūb (558–580/1163–84 and 580–95/1184–99 respectively) were the only other Caliphs of note. The most interesting feature of their reigns was their attitude to philosophy. The A. relig. doc. was strict and did not allow of private judgment; but these rulers allowed scholars to hold whatever views they pleased, so long as they did not make them public and undermine faith of the common people, who must follow the letter of the Qur. and the A. interpret. of it, observe Islamic rites faithfully, take part in war against Christians in Spain, but not think for themselves. Notable scholars in this period were → Ibn Ṭufayl and → Averroes. A fine example of architecture of period is the Giralda tower, which was built as minaret of the mosque in Seville, to which the A.s transferred their capital. The dynasty finally came to end in Spain in 667/1269; the last vestiges of A. power had disappeared in the Maghrib by 674/1275. J.R.

E.I., I, pp. 314–8; Pareja, pp. 162–4 and index; Hitti, *History*, pp. 546–9 and index; D. B. Macdonal, *Theology*, pp. 246–57, 261–5 and index; F. Rosenthal, *Ibn Khaldun*, index.

Almoravids (*Al-Murābiṭūn*—defending warriors), relig. brotherhood, mainly of tribe Lamtūna, set up by 'Abdallāh b. Yāsīn in 5th/11th cent. in fortified monastery (*ribāṭ*) on island in the Senegal river. When their numbers grew, they came out to fight to propagate Islam. Their conquests spread through NW Africa and eventually to Spain. In 454/1062 Yūsuf b. Tāshfīn founded Marrakesh. His later conquests incl. Fez and Algiers. The help of the A. was asked against the Christians in Spain by local Muslim dynasties. They responded; then made it clear they meant to stay. Fighting broke out with local dynasties and by 493/1099–1100, the A. had control of almost all Muslim Spain. In cultured Spain the arrival of the A. was like a relapse into barbarism. In relig. they were strictly orthodox, acknowledging only the Mālikī school (→ Muslim Law). They abolished all taxes not sanctioned by the Qur.; the common people were glad to accept both their orthodoxy and fiscal policy. Jews and Christians suffered hardship under their strict rule. Although philosophy was disapproved, → Avempace lived during their period. He was b. in Zaragoza, was for a time *wazīr* to governor of Granada, but was put to death in Fez in 533/1138 on a charge of atheism. The A. rule was short. By 541/1147 the → Almohads had conquered their African possessions; all that was left being a feeble hold on parts of Spain which the Almohads eventually took from them. The story of the A. illustrates common Islamic characteristic of combination of relig. and rule. A relig. movement almost inevitably becomes political one as well. J.R.

E.I., I, pp. 318ff.; Pareja, pp. 160f. and index; Hitti, *History*, pp. 537, 540ff.; F. Rosenthal, *Ibn Khaldun*, index.

Almsgiving (Buddhist) → Dāna. T.O.L.

(China–Japan) Though benevolence heads list of Confucian virtues, almsgiving in early China was to great extent obviated by the strong bonds of clan and family and the five social relationships. The duty of a family was to care for all its members; the duty of emperor and magistrate to see that all were adequately fed. To give to others without adequate return was contrary to propriety (→ *li*). → Mo-tzŭ, with his doctrine of universal love, was condemned by orthodox Confucians. Throughout Chinese history frequent famines, floods and wars brought beggary and destitution. At such times public relief was organized by magistrates, who called upon the charity and good-will of the wealthy. → Buddhism in China led to almost universal belief that great merit accrued to oneself and descendants by giving alms to the needy. This doctrine led to great increase in almsgiving, not only by Buddhists but by Confucians and Taoists. Giving alms to poor and needy, doing acts of public benefit, helping people in times of special need or trouble, all helped in producing honour in this world and merit for afterlife. It also resulted in making beggary an organized profession, at times so troublesome to the charitable that those desirous of distributing alms often arranged with a shop or temple to distribute relief tickets to the genuine poor. Since the Communist revolution in China organized beggary has been practically stamped out.

Buddhist influence in Japan resulted in charity being considered one of the three divine virtues; the bead for charity is one of the three insignia of the throne. Buddhism, with its teaching of charity and compassion to all living creatures, did much to foster almsgiving, and Buddhist monks were often active in organization of relief to the needy and destitute. D.H.S.

(Christ.) Although Jesus condemned ostentatious A. (Matt. 6:1–4), he is repr. as being at one with rabbis in commending A. Acc. to Acts 4:34ff., primitive Chr. community at Jerusalem lived on a communistic economy, sharing possessions. A. figures much in Paul's letters, and a weekly collection was ordered (I Cor. 16:2). Acc. to Ep. of James 1:27: 'Pure religion and undefiled before our God and Father is this, to visit the fatherless and widows in their affliction, and to keep oneself unspotted from the world'. The Ep. to the Hebrews (13:16), describes A. as a sacrifice pleasing to God. This stress on A. continues in Early Church, the collection of alms and distribution of relief being entrusted to deacons. Collections made at → Eucharist were called oblations: given in form of bread and wine for the celebration, what was superfluous was given to poor. When Christianity became official relig.

of Roman Empire, charity began to be organised on vast scale. Hospitals and orphanages were established; endowments were made, so that a person's charity could continue to benefit the deserving after his death. Monasteries (→ Monasticism) became recognised centres of poor relief in Middle Ages; their suppression in countries converted to Protestantism had grave consequences for poor. The succour of poor and needy has continued to characterise Christianity, and in modern times has led to organisation of charitable action on a world-wide scale, using modern methods of advertisement for attraction of funds. S.G.F.B.

E.R.E., III, pp. 381a–b, 382b–6b; *R.A.C.*, I, 302–7.

(Egyptian) In tomb inscriptions, dating *c.* 2400 BC, charitable deeds are listed as commending the deceased to the 'Great God'. The formula: 'I gave bread to the hungry, clothing to the naked, I ferried him who had no boat', becomes traditional, and is found in the → *Book of the Dead*. From *c.* 2000 BC the belief is also expressed that in *post-mortem* judgment a man's good and bad deeds will be assessed. (→ Judgment of the Dead, Egypt). S.G.F.B.

S. G. F. Brandon, *The Judgment of the Dead* (1967), ch. 2.

(Greece and Rome) Grk. relig. and philosophy provided no strong impetus to charitable action. Strangers, incl. beggars, were under protection of → Zeus Xenios, and the account of Odysseus' reception, when disguised as a beggar, is significant (*Odyssey*, 17.227ff.). Athens had a state system for relief of infirm paupers, who doubtless had to be citizens. → Stoicism encouraged sense of responsibility towards others which finds expression later in dictum of the Stoic Emperor of Rome: 'Revere the gods, save mankind' (Marcus Aurelius, vi. 30), (→ Marcus Aurelius). Roman magnates were much concerned with public charities, but gen. the motive was political ambition. The institution known as *alimenta* was much encouraged in Empire period. These foundations were to provide for poor children; but here also political motive operated, in that concern was felt about declining population. Burial clubs existed for mutual aid of members. S.G.F.B.

E.R.E., III, pp. 386b–7b, 391a–2b; IV, pp. 485ff.; *O.C.D.*, *s.v.* 'Alimenta'; *R.A.C.*, I, 301–2.

(Islam) → Hospitality and Almsgiving. J.R.

(Israel) Helping the poor and unfortunate is clearly presented as a fundamental relig. duty thoughout the O.T. Acc. to Ex. 23:11, produce of fallow land during Sabbatical year was to be reserved, 'that the poor of thy people may eat'. Corners of fields were not to be reaped, but left for poor to glean. Job claims God's mercy because of his charitable deeds—helping the poor, widows and orphans (31:16ff.). It is significant that → LXX uses word *eleēmosyn* for succouring the poor: therefrom our word 'alms' derives, denoting pitifulness and kindly feeling as motives. Later → Judaism continued this trad., with perhaps even greater emphasis. Acc. to *Midrash Tehellim* to Ps. 118–19, at → Last Judgment the soul will be asked about its deeds of charity. Poor-relief was well organised in Talmudic period, and it has continued a feature of Jew. society ever since. S.G.F.B.

E.R.E., III, pp. 380a–1a, 389–91a; I. Epstein, *Judaism* (1959), pp. 150ff.

(Mesopot.) There is an absence of emphasis on charitable action in Mesopot. texts. Rules of personal conduct are of negative character, though condemnation for omitting to release prisoners indicates a more positive attitude (M. Jastrow, *Religious Belief in Babylonia and Assyria* (1911), p. 308). The pessimistic nature of Mesopot. → eschatology caused cynicism about doing good: 'Behold the skulls of the latter and the former ones—which is now an evil doer, which now a benefactor?' (*A.N.E.T.*, pp. 437f.). S.G.F.B.

S. G. F. Brandon, *The Judgment of the Dead* (1967), ch. 3.

Alobha (Pali) 'Greedlessness': in Buddhism one of the three wholesome roots, or morally conditioning factors (→ *mūla*), which produce good → *karma*. T.O.L.

Altaic Religion The Altaic peoples comprise a group, poss. linguistically related, which incl. Turks, Mongols and those speaking Tungus-Manchu languages. Various nomadic peoples from C. Asia were known to Anc. World as Scythians, Sarmatians, and Huns. The characteristic native form of A.-R. is → Shamanism. Behind this cultus was a → cosmogony which conceived of heaven as a tent supported by poles or pillars. A sky-god, variously named, was recognised; also an → earth-goddess: the sun was 'Mother Sun', the moon 'Father Moon'; thunder was regarded as an evil spirit in dragon-form. The soul was believed to be independent of body, which it leaves on certain occasions. The dead were variously disposed of: buried, burnt, exposed to animals. Mortuary equipment was customary; the next world was envisaged as a mirrored reflection of this, thus having a reversed order. The A. peoples were variously influenced by Iranian relig., Christianity (→ Nestorian), Manichaeism, Islam, Buddhism. S.G.F.B.

R.G.G.[3], I, 248–51; J. Auboyer, *H.G.R.*, I, pp. 477–83; P. Masson-Oursel, *H.G.R.*, IV, pp. 441–7; A. Pallisen, 'Die alte Relig. der Mongolen und der Kultus Tschingis-Chans', *Numen*, III (1956); J.-P. Roux, 'Tängri. Essai sur le Ciel-Dieu des peuples altaïques', *R.H.R.*, 149–50 (1956), 'La religion des Turcs de l'Orkhon', *R.H.R.*, 161 (1962); *La mort chez les peuples altaïques anciens et médiévaux* (1963), in *S.O.* 7 (1966), pp. 207ff.; E. Lot-Falck, 'A propos d'Autügän: déesse mongole de la terre', *R.H.R.*, 149 (1956); T. Talbot Rice, *Anc. Arts of Central Asia* (1965); K. Czeglédy, 'Das sakrale Königtum bei den Steppenvölkern', *Numen*, XIII (1966).

Altar (General) In offering → sacrifice, common practice has been (except in Africa and S. America) to use an elevated surface, formed of a rock or artificially constructed: the analogy of a table is prob. not accidental, since appropriate level facilitates manipulation and in some instances suggests a table of the gods. Analysis of words used for A. in Semitic languages indic. place where victim was slaughtered; in Indo-Germanic languages place where sacrifice was burned. There has also been a widespread custom of hanging offerings to gods on sacred trees. A.'s may gen. be said to be orientated sky-wards; but, when concerned with cults of → chthonian deities or the dead, A.'s had holes and conduits to take blood into ground. In these cults the A. is in effect a door to tomb or → underworld: in anc. Crete A.'s were sometimes placed in tombs. When located in temples, A. could constitute sacred hearth (→ Altar, Greek and Roman); in anc. German relig. it was regarded as throne of deity. The A., because of its assoc. with deity was → holy and was usually protected by → tabus; its construction was often carefully prescribed (e.g. in Jew. relig. Ex. 20:24ff.). (→ American Religious, anc.). S.G.F.B.

E.R.E., I, pp. 333a–5a; *R.G.G.*³, I, 251–3.

(China) From earliest hist. times A.'s for worship of Heaven and Earth and gods of land and grain (*shê-chi-t'an*) formed one of the twin foci of Chinese relig., the other being the ancestral temples on whose A.'s sacrifices were made to ancestral spirits. Chinese emperors worshipped the Supreme God (Shang Ti) on mountain-tops, or on circular A.'s, of which the A. of Heaven in Peking is most famous example. This impressive structure of white marble is situated in a beautiful park in the s. suburb. It rises under the open sky to a height of 27 ft., and comprises 3 circular terraces, 210 ft., 150 ft. and 90 ft. in diameter respectively. It is approached by 4 flights of steps, corresponding to 4 points of compass. Nearby are the Temple of the Prosperous Year, the Hall of Abstinence and other buildings deemed necessary for the cult. Until end of Empire, the most awe-inspiring and magnificent ceremony of Chinese relig. was conducted here at the winter solstice by the emperor (Son of Heaven), surrounded by his princes and ministers.

The worship of Earth was conducted on a square mound in the n. suburb, with 2 marble terraces of 100 ft. and 60 ft. diameter respectively. Other important A.'s were those of Agriculture and the Shê-chi-t'an associated with the T'ai Miao, in which dynastic ancestors were worshipped.

Local A.'s, on which sacrifices to the spirits of the land and grain were periodically offered, consisted of low mounds about 5 ft. square.

In temples, whether Confucianist, Buddhist or Taoist, the A. was a central feature, consisting of stone, rectangular table on which were placed censers, candlesticks and vases of bronze, porcelain or stone.

Permanent A.'s were often erected in front of tombs for sacrifices to spirits of dead. Private houses contained small A.'s, where incense was burned and food presented to spirits of deceased or to popular Buddhist or Taoist divinities. D.H.S.

(Christ.) Earliest A.'s were tables in private houses, and so were of wood: wooden altars were still in use in 4th and 5th cents. Early custom of celebrating → Eucharist on tombs of → martyrs led to stone being regarded as proper material for A.'s; this view was prob. supported by accounts of stone-A.'s in Heb. sacred law (→ Altar, Israel). In early cents. churches had each only one A.; but medieval custom of private → Masses caused intro. of additional A.'s, and led to main A. being designated High A. Absence of private Masses in E. Church has meant that each church has only one A., although some have a 'fasting A.' In → Reformation-countries stone-A.'s were gen. destroyed, and name often denounced, owing to its assoc. with doc. of Sacrifice of the Mass (→ Eucharist). Before 10th cent. candles and cross were not placed on A. Acc. to modern R.C. requirements, an A. must contain a *mensa* ('table'), which is unbroken piece of stone. Portable altars are used in R.C. church. S.G.F.B.

R.A.C., I, 336–54; *D.C.C.*, *s.v.; E.R.E.*, I, pp. 338a–42a; *R.G.G.*³, I, 255–66.

(Egypt.) In Egypt. temples few A.'s have survived; but it seems that great state-gods (→ Re, → Aton, → Amun) had large stone altars—that at Deir el-Bahari measures 16 by 13 ft. Such an A. was called a *ḫꜣwt*; the hieroglyph repr. a bivalve shell, poss. used for offerings. The gen. sign for 'table of offerings' (*hotep*) shows a loaf on board or mat. Many other types of A., in form of tables for offerings, sometimes holding jars, are shown in sculptures and paintings. A tall stand with flaming vessel, sometimes depicted, poss. repr. A. for burnt offerings. In Amarna there existed small house-altars, similar to great-stepped altar in temple of → Aton. S.G.F.B.

E.R.E., I, pp. 342–3; *R.Ae.R.-G.*, pp. 14a–7a, 123–5.

(Greek, Roman) A.'s were used in both family and public worship. A distinction drawn between an A. called a *bōmos*, used for → Olympian gods and another called *eschara* for heroes or chthonic beings, was often disregarded in Grk. lit. A sacred place in Greece usually comprised a temple, an A., and a precinct; although focus of attention in temple was statue of the deity, the ritual focus was the A. A.'s varied greatly in size and form, from the immense sculptured A. of → Zeus at Pergamon to the A. of → Apollo at Delos, said to be made of horns of sacrificed victims, or to the great A. of → Athene on the Acropolis, Athens, which was a mass of natural rock. A.'s were also set up in homes (→→ Lares, Penates), market-places, graves, caves or besides sacred springs. Various offerings were made upon them, acc. to deity worshipped: sometimes fruit, flowers, and libations of wine; sometimes portions of slaughtered victim, which would be burnt. Some A.'s were erected as memorials of notable events, this being partic. so in Rome. Small portable A.'s, cylindrical or rectangular were also used. The hearth was regarded as an A.: on the sacred hearth at Athens sacrifice was regularly offered as on altar of Hestia (→ Fire-cult). In Rome, → Vestal Virgins tended the perpetual fire in temple of Vesta as being the hearth of city. Acc. to Roman custom, tombs frequently had form of altars, and were assoc. with offerings to dead. S.G.F.B.

E.R.E., I, pp. 342b–5a, 349a–50a; *R.A.C.*, I, 310–29.

(Hindu) Because of frequency of sacrifice, A.'s are import. in Hinduism. In → Vedic times the A. was orig. a trench of varying shape, dug in earth, to hold sacrificial fire. It was called *Vedi* (Skt. for A.). The shape was very import.; special Skt. manuals (*śulbasutrās*) prescribed shape and construction. Some A.'s had form of falcon, two triangles, etc. These were built up of earth. In mod. India A.'s, made of earth and clay, are designed to hold sacred fire into which clarified butter and parched grain are thrown. They are used for most ritual occasions incl. marriage. S.G.F.B.

E.R.E., I, pp. 295–6.

(Iran) Herodotus (I. 131ff.) and Strabo (XV, iii, 13) assert that early Persians had no A.'s or temples. It is prob. that these writers had large Grk. A.'s in mind: however, sacrifices were offered, trenches being dug over which victim was slaughtered. Acc. to Herodotus, the Persians worshipped on mountain tops; it is poss. that these repr. their A.'s. Better documented are their fire-A.'s; early examples consisted of massive plinth or pedestal, bearing a stone slab *Adōsht* on which stood the *Ātash-dān*, the 'fire-container'. Portable fire-A.'s were also known. Fire-A.'s, used by → Parsis, preserve the two features of earlier examples, namely, the *Adōsht* and *Ātash-dān* (→ Fire-worship). S.G.F.B.

E.R.E., I, pp. 346a–8b; Zaehner, *D.T.Z.*, plates 9, 15, 16–17, 36, 42; B. Goldman, 'Persian Fire Temples or Tombs', *J.N.E.S.*, 24 (1965); D. Stronach, 'The Kūh-i-Shahrak Fire Altar', *J.N.E.S.*, 25 (1966).

(Israel) Archaeological research in Palestine and adjacent cultural areas have revealed variety of A.'s, with which early Israelites were doubtless familiar and used. Rough cairns of unhewn stones on hill tops, with surrounding trenches, repr. primitive A.'s. At Gezer an A. of earth was found, beneath which were human skulls: Ex. 20:24–6 mentions an earth A. Another notable type of A. was the *maṣṣebāh*, a stone phallus-shaped column, on which fat and oil were rubbed. As a *bethel* (Gen. 28:17ff.), it was also dwelling-place of a god: an interesting instance of cultic use of *maṣṣebāh* occurs in II Sam. 18:18. Rock-cut A.'s at ritual high-places appear to be development of primitive cairn A.'s. A notable example was found at Petra, where the rock-cut A. was part of a ritual complex for sacrifice. The top of this A. had depressions for fire-pans; an adjoining platform, prob. used for preparation of sacrifices, was equipped with basins for blood and conduit to carry it away. Many portable A.'s of incense have been found in different places. Heb. lit. contains much about A.'s; some of it relating to Tabernacle (Ex. 27) prob. repr. later speculation of priestly writers. A detailed acc. is given of a great bronze A. and other sacrificial equipment ordered by Solomon in his temple (II Chron. 4:1ff.); the dimensions are prob. exaggerated. II Kgs. 16:10ff. describes stone-A. made by King Ahaz for → Temple; it was copied from one seen in Damascus. Ref. is made in Heb. lit. to 'horns of the A'. These were projections at corners, and appear on an A. found at Megeddo: various theories account for their origin, which is still uncertain. (→ Stones, Sacred). S.G.F.B.

E.R.E., I, pp. 350–2b, 353b–4a; *R.A.C.*, I, 330–4; *H.D.B.*², *s.v.;* A. Lods, *Israel* (1949), *passim*, pl., I-III, IV, VI, XI.

(Japan) In → Shinto the A. possessed no special sanctity. In the greater shrines offerings were placed on tables of unpainted wood, whilst in smaller shrines they were placed on mats on the ground. In homes, domestic A.'s, known as *kamidana*, were the repository of Shinto pictures, tokens or other objects of devotion. In Buddhist temples, stands known as *kōdan* or *kodzukuya* (incense tables) were provided for burning of incense, whilst the domestic A.'s were in nature of shrines for image of Buddha. A doctrine of the Shinto sect, Tenri-kyō, is that of the unfinished A. A certain spot in Tamba-Ichi called *jiba* (lit.

ground-place) was revealed to founder of sect as the centre of world and place where God consummated his creation. Central to an area of some 20 acres, in which the sect has its headquarters, lies a sacred spot, open to the sky, where an A. is slowly being built through the years, and cannot be completed till the teaching has been proclaimed throughout world and all men made brethren in the service of God and one another. D.H.S.

E.R.E., I, pp. 337–8, 346; D. C. Holtom, *The National Faith of Japan* (1938), p. 282.

(Mesopot.) Acc. to Herodotus (I. 183), there were two kinds of A. in temple of → Marduk at Babylon: a small one of gold and a large of unspecified material. These doubtless repr. A.'s of incense and A.'s of burnt-offering respectively. A large A. of sun-dried brick, measuring 13 ft. by 8 ft., was found at Nippur. Small incense-A.'s were of various shapes. Bronze A.'s are also known, having form of table: acc. to reliefs on bronze gates of Balawat, such an altar was used by army for burnt sacrifices when campaigning. Another A. of completely different type is that surmounted by two eyes in the Brak Eye Temple, *c.* 3000 BC (M. E. L. Mallowan, *Early Mesopot. and Iran*, 1965, ill. 38). (→ Eye-Goddess). S.G.F.B.

E.R.E., I, pp. 352b–3a; *R.A.C.*, I, 329–30; B. Meissner, *Babylonien u. Assyrien*, II (1925), pp. 73ff., 88ff.

Ālvārs Sometimes transliterated Āṟvārs: the twelve great poet saints of Tamil Vaisnavism. They lived between 7th and 10th cents. CE, or a little earlier. In the 10th cent. their poems were collected into a scripture, the *Prabandham* or *Nālāyiram* ('Four Thousand') by Nāthamuni, the first → *acarya* of S. Vaisnavas. Nathamuni caused the verses to be used in temple worship at Srirangam and elsewhere; images of the A. were also incorporated into the cultus. Thus the *Prabandham* acquired similar status to → Veda. The poetry of the collection expresses a very strong and emotional → *bhakti* directed towards → Krishna; its composition ran parallel to develop. of → Saivite *bhakti* poetry among the Nāyaṉārs or 'Teachers'. Among the A. were numbered people of different classes, incl. outcastes and a woman. The most import. part of *Prabandham* is constituted by four poems of Nammālvār, most famous of the poet-saints. They are sometimes ref. to by Sri Vaisnavas as the 'four Vedas in Tamil dress'. The theology expressed in the *Prabandham* is highly personalistic. God is infinite (and even described as creator of → Brahma and → Rudra-Siva—the poems are definitely sectarian, for this doc. implies superiority of → Vaisnavism over → Saivism). But though infinite, God is willing to limit himself by manifesting himself through *avataras*, and even through dwelling secondarily in images; he does this out of love for men and desire to give them access to salvation through his grace. The response of the devotee is self-surrender (*prapatti*). Such a response is open to all people, however humble; it is not restricted by considerations of relig. orthodoxy, purity, etc. Thus the A. succeeded in creating an indigenous and relig. egalitarian cult to set side by side with upper class orthodoxy, and of equal validity. A synthesis between this fervent Tamil *bhakti* and Vedantin orthodoxy, and between the forms of worship, was effected through the Sri Vaisnava movement, notably by first of the → *acaryas*, Nathamuni; but culminating in the theology of → Ramanuja. However, Ramanuja's successors divided along linguistic and cultural lines, and over interpretation of doc. of grace, into the → Vadagalai and → Tengalai schools. N.S.

J. S. M. Hooper (tr.), *Hymns of the Alvars* (1929); H. Bhattacharyya, *The Cultural Heritage of India*, vol. 4 (1956); T. A. Gopinath Rao, *Hist. of Sri Vaisnavas* (1923); J. E. Carpenter, *Theism in Medieval India* (1921); M. S. Purnalingam Pillai, *Tamil Literature* (1929).

Amana Society Chr. sect, sometimes called Community of True Inspiration, founded in Germany in 1714, and repr. → Pietist views and belief in present-day inspiration. Many members settled at Amana, Iowa, U.S.A., in 1842, where they survive as small communistic society. S.G.F.B.

E.R.E., I, pp. 358a–69a; *R.G.G.*³, I, 303; J. Montgomery, *Abodes of Love* (1962), pp. 48ff.

Amarapura The Amarapura is one of the three major communities (*nikāya*) of Buddh. monkhood in → Ceylon. It takes its name from city of Amarapura, in Burma. In late 18th cent. it became difficult for Sinhalese who were not of the *goigama* caste (→ Caste, Buddh. Attitude) to obtain higher ordination (*upasampadā*) (→ Ordination, Buddh.), owing to restrictive decree made by the king of Kandy, Kīrti Shrī Rājasiṃha. In 1799, Naṇavimalatissa, a monk of the *salāgama* caste, together with five novices left Ceylon and in 1802 reached Amarupura, the Burmese capital, where they were received by Buddhist king, Bodawpaya, and given higher ordination by a Burmese *mahāthera*. Together with some Burmese monks, they returned to Ceylon and were able to give higher ordination to Sinhalese novices not of the *goigama* caste. From this beginning has grown present A. community of monkhood, divided into 18 sub-communities, numbering in 1959 more than 3,000 monks (Buddha Sāsana Commission Report, Government of Ceylon, 1959). T.O.L.

Amarna Tablets Cuneiform tablets found at Tell el-Amarna, site of capital of → Akhenaten. A.T. were archives of Eg. Foreign Office, and provide invaluable information of contemporary situation in Palestine and Syria. S.G.F.B.

A.N.E.T., pp. 453ff.; A. Gardiner, *Egypt of the Pharaohs* (1961), pp. 207ff.; *A.O.T.S.*, pp. 3ff.

Amarāvatī Anc. city of S. India, once a great centre of Buddh. culture, now small village on S. bank of R. Krishna (Kistna), about 80 miles from coast. The city was the east. capital of the Sātavāhana rulers and was known as Dhānya-kataka; the name A., 'habitation of the immortals', seems to have been acquired in Buddh. times; its importance for Buddhists was on account of the Mahā Chaitya, the great shrine or → *stupa*, about ½ mile to E. of city, which, acc. to some Buddh. trad. contained relics of Buddha himself. The discovery of an Ashokan pillar-edict at A. has strengthened belief that the *stupa* was built by emperor → Ashoka (third cent. BC). It was main object of veneration of the Mahāsanghika school, known as the Chaityakas; pilgrims are said to have come to it from as far as Pātaliputra (Patna). The Chinese pilgrim → Hsuan-tsang, in 7th cent. CE, recorded that there were about 20 flourishing Buddh. monasteries there, though there were others which had been deserted. The site was rediscovered at end of 18th cent.; the numerous sculptures which have survived provide valuable evidence of develop. of Buddh. art. The style is said to be partly derived from that of Mathurā and Sānchī, but with distinctively orig. features of S. Indian kind. It is a style which has evidently had a widespread influence, partic. the type of Buddha figure, evidence of which is found in Ceylon, Thailand and Indonesia. T.O.L.

D. E. Barrett, *Sculptures from Amaravati in the British Museum* (1954); Philippe Stern and Mireille Beniste, *Evolution du Style Indien d'Amaravati* (1961); D. Seckel, *The Art of Buddhism* (1964).

Amaterasu-Omikami 'The Heaven-shining-great-deity'. Old Yamato sun-goddess, in modern Japan called Tenshō-daijin, and conceived of as a general Providence who watches over human affairs, and espec. over welfare of the Mikado and his government. She is the divine-ancestress, the progenitress of the Japanese imperial family. Traditionally, the first emperor, Jimmu-Tennō, is deemed to be her direct descendant. She is the central figure of Shinto worship, the symbol of the state, the mighty ruler of the spirit-world, the guardian of the Japanese nation. Acc. to Jap. mythology, she was born of the sky-father, → Izanagi-no-mikoto, and his wife, the earth-mother, Izanami-no-mikoto. Her chief shrine is at Ise, where, as in other Shinto shrines, her representation → (shintai) or dwelling-place is a mirror, i.e. a sun symbol. (→ Shinto). D.H.S.

D. C. Holtom, *The National Faith of Japan* (1938), pp. 123–51.

Amazons In Grk. mythology a warrior race of women: refs. always locate them as dwelling beyond frontiers of Greece, usually in N. and W. Asia Minor. Peculiar customs were ascribed to them, e.g. mating with men of neighbouring tribe for a season; killing male offspring and training female for war. The etymological explan. of name: *a-mazos* = 'without breast', and attr. of custom of amputating right breast to facilitate handling of bow, is gen. now abandoned. A.'s were always shown in art with two breasts. A.'s were closely assoc. with Thracian god → Ares and goddess → Artemis. Many Grk. heroes were connected with them: e.g. Achilles, → Herakles, Theseus. The many graves of A.'s in Greece, e.g. at Athens, where there was also an Amazoneion, suggest some anc. chthonian cult. Many attempts have been made to explain origin of A. myth: acc. to a recent theory, the myth preserves memory of anc. conflict with Asiatic matriarchal tribes. S.G.F.B.

O.C.D., *s.v.*, *E.R.E.*, I, *s.v.; Kleine Pauly*, I, 291–3; C. Picard, *Les religions préhelléniques* (1948), pp. 75 n. 6, 206.

Ambo A raised platform used in early Chr. → basilicas for reading of Scriptures and other liturgical lections. Orig. one only was used, but later a second was intro., so the Epistle and Gospel at → Eucharist could be read respectively from south and north sides. A. gen. replaced by pulpit from 14th cent. S.G.F.B.

R.A.C., I, 363–5 ('Ambon').

Ambrose, St. (*c.* 339–97) Famous Bishop of Milan; he was elected to the see by popular acclaim while still unbaptised. Distinguished already as a magistrate, his statesmanlike qualities enabled him to champion the Church successfully against the civil power, paganism and → Arianism. His moral sense, however, caused him to protest against execution of → Priscillianist heretics, and to excommunicate Emp. Theodosius for a massacre. A. had an important part in conversion of → Augustine of Hippo. Among his many theological works was the *De Officiis Ministrorum*, an important treatise on ethics. A. also composed some well known Latin hymns. He is one of the four traditional Doctors of Latin Church. S.G.F.B.

D.C.C., *s.v.;* 365–73.

Ambrosia In Grk. mythology A., with Nectar, were respectively the food and drink of the gods. They had the virtue of conferring immortality, and even of preserving a corpse from decay (*Iliad*, 19.38–9). A. was very fragrant and sweet. On similar 'food of the gods' →→ Adapa; Haoma; Soma. S.G.F.B.

O.C.D., *s.v.; Kleine Pauly*, I, 295–6.

Ambrosian Rite Anc. rite, used in archiepiscopal prov. of Milan, which has survived against powerful Roman rite. Name ex → Ambrose, though prob. having no orig. connection with him. A.R. differs much from Roman rite, though using Roman Canon of → Mass. Its origins have been much discussed. S.G.F.B.
D.C.C., s.v.

Ambrosiaster Name given by Erasmus to unknown author of Lat. commentaries of 13 Ep. of Paul; ascribed in Middle Ages to → Ambrose. A. is important witness to pre-Vulgate (→ Vulgate) text. S.G.F.B.
D.C.C., s.v.; R.G.G.[3], I, 307.

Amen Heb. word, *via* Grk., meaning 'verily'. Used O.T. and N.T. to express assent (e.g. Deut. 27:15ff.; I Cor. 14:16), and adopted into Christianity as trad. formula at end of prayers, hymns, and creeds. S.G.F.B.
R.A.C., I, 378–80; *D.C.C., s.v.; Jahrbuch* für *Antike u. Christentum*, I (1958), pp. 152ff.
(Egypt. god) → Amun. S.G.F.B.

Amenhotep (or Amenophis) Egyptian who acquired great honour and reputation as 'Overseer of buildings of the King' to Amenhotep III (1408–1372 BC). In some obscure way, poss. through statues dedicated to him or erection of his mortuary temple by King, A. became deified at Thebes, poss. to offset deification of Memphite → Imhotep. His cult developed during Graeco-Roman period; at Der el Bahri he shared shrine with Imhotep as gods of healing. A. was famous also for his wisdom. S.G.F.B.
R.Ae.R.-G., pp. 21a–2b.

Amentet (Amenti) Egypt. goddess of the West. Since dead were gen. buried in desert on western side of Nile, A. became both goddess and personification of → underworld. (→ Allatum). S.G.F.B.
R.Ae.R.-G., pp. 22–3.

American Religions (ancient) The religs. of the native peoples of Mexico, Guatemala, British Honduras, and San Salvador were closely related, and appear to have had a common origin, as yet unidentified. The most import. information was collected from the Aztecs, ruling nation of Mexico at time of Spanish Conquest of 1518 to 1521. A distinct variation of same relig. occurred among the Maya (*q.v.*) from whom information was collected in mid 16th cent. (→ Inca Relig.).

Much of mythology and ritual of region shows influences stemming from N. American cultures and is prob. very anc. in origin. The Aztecs intro. some modifications, incl. elaborations of warrior cults which reinforced this north. trad. Of pre-Aztec belief we have very few trads., but sculptured and painted monuments and some of the painted religious books (*codices*, painted on prepared skin in leporello format) give evidence of unity of basic belief through time and across tribal and linguistic barriers.

The basic cosmic image of this relig. was of a flat expanse of earth overshadowed by several layers of heavens (13 in one account and 9 in another), and resting above similar series of underworlds. The whole was conceived of as *Anahuac* (between the waters), and was believed to be sustained in hand of a supreme being known to Aztecs as Ometecuhtli (Two-Lord). This deity was at once male and female, repr. in himself the two aspects of all living and fruitful nature. He was a high philosophical concept, and can so far be traced only by his image in relig. books which do not go back far before Conquest, but probably have Toltec (750–1000 AD) origins. Ometecuhtli had no temples on earth: it was presumed that he had no need of them because he was in all living things. His partic. manifestation on earth was in moment of conception of new life. In the codices his image is often accompanied by representation of a couple in coitus. (→ Fertility Cults) He was closely assoc. with the Fire God; the hearth in every home was in some way regarded as a linkage with him (→ Fire Gods). Some accounts of fate of the soul suggest that, after long period in Land of the Dead, the soul might reach the Central Fire and ascend once again to the Lord of Life.

The gods of the material universe were not at all of same philosophic grandeur. They had different aspects as powers of nature, as constellations or planets, and as repr. aspects of human behaviour when they possessed individuals and influenced their actions. These deities were not eternal. There had been three previous creations, each of which built up a race of beings who displeased the gods, but of whom two individuals survived from each destruction to become parents of the newly designed race. The previous creations each had an individual sun, which was destroyed at the appointed time. The present sun was regarded as the Olin-Tonatiuh, Earthquake-sun, which would eventually be destroyed by a terrible earthquake. Nobody knew if a fifth sun would be created. There is some confusion in legends, but the gen. view was that each sun lasted about 6,000 years. The present sun had been created at Teotihuacan, which would mean that at time of fall of Mexico it was a little under 2,000 years old. At this event the gods were believed to have come to earth as individuals travelling from afar. They sat in council to determine who was to be the new sun. On the fourth day Nanautzin, a poor and ailing god, arrived. On hearing of need for a new sun to illuminate the new creation he willingly threw himself into the fire, whence his heart ascended as Tonatiuh, the Sun. Later on another god who was envious jumped into the sinking fire, but he only partially burnt up and his bones circle the earth as the white moon.

This legend is a contradiction of another series of legends more characteristic of Aztec belief, in which the hero is the → demiurge Tezcatlipoca (Smoking mirror). In this version, the 400 (many) star gods, hearing their Great Mother was pregnant, were jealous and plotted to destroy the new child. In a dark cave they were kept at bay until the birth. Then Tezcatlipoca leapt forward as a fully-armed warrior and destroyed his enemies, incl. his only helper, his sister Golden Bells (Coyolxauhqui). Unable to save her, he cut off her head and threw it into the sky where it lives as the moon. In this Tezcatlipoca-cycle, the god is the sun, seen in four forms as yellow (East) blue (South) Red (West) and Black (North). It is a cosmological myth which explains existence of moon even in daylight, and disappearance of stars at dawn. The sun-aspects repr. the colours of sky when sun is in each of the four quarters of heavens. It had ritual expression in the sacrifice of a cock quail (a bird with black feathers speckled white) at every sunrise to symbolise the 'killing' of the stars each morning.

The Tezcatlipoca-cycle was very import. to Aztecs, since the Blue Tezcatlipoca, the High-flying sun in south. sky was named Huitzilpochtli (Blue humming-bird on left foot). This deity was patron god of Aztec nation. He came from their temple in Aztlan, their anc. home, to lead them on migration at the end of which he promised them a great empire. To confirm promise, he would appear at the chosen seat of power as an eagle holding a serpent in his talons while perched on a cactus growing on a rocky islet. This was to be the Aztec capital city, Cactus Rock (Tenochtitlan, now called Mexico City, after Aztec proper tribal name Méxica).

Tezcatlipoca was gen. regarded as patron god of young warriors, as a great magician capable of terrifying cruelties, and as demiurge who drew Earth goddess from the waters of creation. In his struggle with the earth-mother in her form as a gigantic alligator (Cipactli), he lost left foot but succeeded in tearing off her lower jaw so that she could not sink back into primaeval ocean. Then she became the earth, of which the mountains are ridges of her scaly reptilian coat. The Kundalini-like earth also appears as goddess in human form in the codices, and was regarded with great affection as mother of mankind and of all food. She was too holy for any individual to claim any part of her as personal property, but might be farmed on a temporary basis for benefit of community.

In gen. the goddesses in Anc. Mexico were earth- or moon spirits. The → Earth Mother was progenitrix of vegetation spirits. Others were personifications of plants incl. the seed-maize and young corn (although the maize itself, as a whole, was regarded as male spirit Cinteotl). The flowering and fruitful surface of earth was realm of the Lady Precious Jewel (Chalchihuitlicue), who was also goddess of young women, of whirlpools and unpredictable happenings. There was a fertility goddess Xochiquetzal, the first mother of twins. She was much loved by Aztec women, and her little pottery images wearing two plumes of Quetzal feathers in hair are commonly found in excavations in all parts of country. On marriage Aztec women plaited their hair and coiled it round their heads with two little 'tails' standing over their temples as symbols of their hope for children from the goddess. Other goddesses were the Salt goddess; the lady Tozi (Grandmother) patroness of healing, espec. of the sweat-baths which were dedicated to her: others repr. healing herbs, and also there was the Lady Chantico who seems to have been a fire-goddess, and earthly counterpart of feminine half of Supreme Deity. A very special goddess was the fourfold-goddess Tlazolteotl (Lady of Filth) who was counterpart of the four phases of moon. She was patroness of sexual temptation, of gambling, of witchcraft in its dangerously black aspects, and yet of cleansing and forgiveness of past evil doing. Confession of sins was made to her priests and forgiveness was obtained. However, this cleansing ritual could not be repeated; it was delayed till late in life when easier to preserve ritual cleanliness.

The Aztec attitude to sex was that of a simple warrior tribe and terribly puritanical. It was evil for a warrior to be seen to have any sex-life, since it weakened the Aztec reputation. Adultery was social crime punishable by death. Nakedness was deeply shocking, and, though tolerated in visitors from tropical lands, was not permitted to Aztecs. In penitential rituals the ears and tongue were pierced for offering blood, and also the prepuce of penis was pierced and torn, especially by priests. It was an aspect of a specifically Aztec and poss. Toltec attitude to life in a warrior society, which does not seem to have been shared by their neighbours.

The gods were not so generalised as goddesses, and they were not so limited to the earth and moon. The Aztecs had tendency to organise their deities with ref. to the four directions of universe, as do many of N. American Indian peoples. The cardinal point was the Sunrise. This is natural cardinal point in all simple societies who have no means of determining North with any exactitude, and indeed have no reason for doing so. In Codex Fejervary Mayer (Liverpool City Museums), there is a diagram showing deities of the four quarters of world. In centre is fire-god Xiuhtecuhtli as surrogate of the Supreme Duality. To him flows the constant stream of blood offered from the quarters of universe, which are marked by the portions of dismembered body of the god Tezcatlipoca. The directions each enshrine a pair of gods who were thought of as standing on edge of earth.

East is place of the sun: its gods are the yellow-haired Piltzintecuhtli (?Mercury), and Itztli, who is the stone knife of sacrifice. This refers to the little planet as herald of sun, and the stone knife by which continual blood offerings made in order to quench terrible thirst of sun, who was continually burning for sake of humanity. West is marked by the fire-bowl on the earth, into which sun sank at night. Its patrons are two goddesses. In some way they repr. the powers of women as receivers of the male and as comforters. There is also a somewhat Freudian linkage with the sunset and place of the Dead. The goddesses are opposed in character, one being the beautiful lady of green vegetation, the other the Lady of Witchcraft and darkness. The southern edge of earth is place of the height of sun and hence of symbols of richness. Its gods are Tlaloc, Lord of the fruitful rains, and Tepeyollotl who guards the riches under the earth. North really relates to land of the Dead, it was called Mictlampa, and the patron gods were naturally the God of the Dead, Mictlantecuhtli, and the maize god Cinteotl. This was quite natural, since the seed of maize has to die and be buried until it bursts out of its skin to resurrection in Spring.

From this arrangement we see that major gods of the Mexican pantheon were linked with concepts of the directions of earth's surface. They were also linked with passage of → time. The same diagram in Codex Laud is surrounded by four groups of 5 days, thus dividing the 20 named days of Mexican system with the four directions; the diagram is framed in a rayed cross which is marked with same day-names arranged as twenty groups of 13 days, thus making up the 260-day period known as the Tonalpouhalli. This figure is a mathematical concept arrived at through system used in naming days. Each of the 20 named days was accompanied by a numeral, and the two series of 20 names and the numerals limited from 1 to 13, completed their poss. permutations in 260 days. Since each day was linked with a patron god, and each numeral also had its patron, there was wide range of influences from which one could judge the fortune assoc. with a day. The quality of a day was determined by its patron gods, one of whom influenced the total fortune of day, beginning from sunset; the other modified the quality of period from sunrise to end of day. The gods who were involved in this time-machine were known as the 13 gods of day and the 9 Lords of night. They kept their sequence unendingly in the ritual *tonalpouhalli,* which repeated continuously through time. Every human being was thought to be conditioned by the gods of his birthday; although rituals might mitigate extremities of fortune, the basic decree of fate was really immutable.

The *tonalpouhalli* ran its continuous course in parallel with another time system, in which all the day-names were similar but the basic divisions were recurring series of 20 days (with their numeral coefficients). Each period of 20 days was under influence of a pair of deities who usually repr. a contrast of personalities. It is normal to find that of each pair one was dominant. There were eighteen of these 20-day periods, each of them commencing with a great relig. festival. At completion of the eighteen groups of days, a further group of 5 days was added to complete series of 365 days needed for agricultural calendar. These 5 days were the *nemontemi,* or nothing-days, on which one performed as few actions as poss. This agricultural year began with Spring (though it appears that some tribal groups may have chosen different days to coincide with festival of some favourite tribal god). Naturally the sequence of 20-day festivals reflected passage of agricultural year, partic. through worship of the deities of different aspects of developing maize plant. But interwoven with them was a complex pattern, which brought in groups of festivals for the weather gods and warrior gods, partic. Tezcatlipoca.

Since every year began with a day named in the Tonalpouhalli system, which did not exactly fit the Solar year at any point, it was poss. to name years after their initial day. There were only four possible day-names for year-beginning days, these were *Acatl* (Reed), *Tecpatl* (Stoneknife), *Calli* (House), *Tochtli* (Rabbit). With them the thirteen numbers could fully combine. In Aztec times the Calendrical cycle began with a year 2 Acatl, and it was complete when the combination of day and number once again came to 2 Acatl. This happened every 52 years, and was an occasion of great rejoicing. An intercalary fast was held at this point in time to bring civil calendar into true line with solar time. After fast of 13 days, in which all household utensils and clothing were destroyed, the priests set out to a sacred hill near Mexico to watch procession of the stars. The chosen moment was when Alcyone of the Pleiades crossed Meridian at midnight. First, the triangle of stars in Taurus, with the fiery star Aldebaran, passed. The priests sacrificed a human victim, and laid firesticks across cavity whence they had cut his heart. Then they made new fire with the sticks. As the new fire burst forth the 'Market Place of the Stars' passed the zenith, and the new fire was given to runners who carried blazing torches to all local temples. Thence in turn new fire was carried to homes of the fasting people. There was great rejoicing. New clothing was woven, new household goods were made and world resumed its course. Each such festival was period of anxiety, since at one of them the stars would halt and present world face its doom in the great earthquake.

The complexities of calendar made it imperative that among priests there should be a class of trained astronomical observers. The last Aztec Emperor, Moctecuzoma, was one of them. By watching constellations and noting movements of planets and of shooting stars, they were in touch with rhythms of Universe and estimated fate of each day as it approached. This was all conditioned by belief that the major gods all had houses in the heavens, which were marked by constellations. Of course, the most import. ones marked the four quarters of heavens. These were not the same as those of earth, since it was seen that they revolved through the sky. The East. house of the sky was Leo, of which the crook was the staff of Quetzalcoatl, who as Morning star was worshipped as a protective power. When his stars crossed zenith at midnight in February, it was said that he was come to bring winds to sweep land clear for the rain gods to come in, to prepare land for Spring. The Scorpion, known by same name in Mexico, marked the May-midnight. Pegasus and Aquarius combined to make a starry image of Rain God, Tlaloc, and marked the August quarter of sky. Finally, fiery Aldebaran marked the November midnight of the year-changing. It will be noticed, in the context of primitive astronomy, that the stars which crossed zenith at midnight were those which rose on the east. horizon at sunset. They repr. constellations opposite to those in which sun was placed in daytime.

The planets repr. gods; and it was no contradiction that the same gods repr. days in calendar, had special temples on earth and also homes among constellations of the zodiac. Mercury seems to have been Piltzintecuhtli, the Young Prince, always close to sun. Venus was known as a whole as Tlauizcalpantecuhtli, Lord of the Palace of Dawn, a demonic being; as evening star Venus repr. the distorted and evil creature Xolotl, who thrust sun down into darkness; but as Morning Star the planet was Quetzalcoatl, god of breath of life, the wind, and once also an earthly king. Mars, Jupiter and Saturn were observed, but it is not quite certain which gods were represented. Astronomy was well developed, and it has recently been shown that the famous Calendar Stone in Mexico City can be used for predicting solar eclipses forward and backward in time. There are a few monuments which record observations of transits of Venus from periods earlier than observation of this event in Europe. The obsession with magical aspects of Venus has resulted in inscriptions of immense importance in establishing import. events in historical time. In Codex Vindobonensis a record of a solar eclipse near mid-day, with Venus in ascendant, has dated whole section on Toltec history in that document.

The expression of the complex relig. with its nature deities, often raw and direct expressions of universal archetypes in human personality, and its interest in the rhythms of time took form in dramatic ritual performances. These were accomplished in courtyards and on long stairways ascending the great stepped pyramids, which supported the sacrificial stone in front of a god-house on summit. The priests were celibate, and trained under conditions of extreme asceticism. They were usually painted black and dressed in white gowns, except when ceremonies demanded that they should impersonate gods in glorious raiment of coloured capes and headdresses of tropical plumage and gold.

At most festivals there were ceremonial dances and a ritual in which hymns were sung; long chants described stories of the gods whose festival was being celebrated. → Incense was used, and much music, espec. rhythmic music on wooden drums and pottery flutes, which set mood of occasion. There was not a universal need for human sacrifice, since at some festivals fruits and flowers were the acceptable offerings, espec. those for the god Quetzalcoatl and the fertility spirits. But on most of the festival commencements of 20-day periods humans were sacrificed. Women were sometimes decapitated, or roasted and skinned. Men were stretched over a stone rather like a low round topped cone, and their hearts cut out quickly and neatly by a single stroke of a stone knife. For the victims, this was a sure path to heaven of the gods, to whom they were sacrificed. To the priests, it was a gift of life to the gods from whom all life was given sustenance. For the congregation, it was a chance of absorbing some of power of the god through eating a tiny portion of body which had been blessed by presence of the god within the sacrifice.

The saddest of sacrifices was in early Spring when a few small children were drowned to bring the rains. It was necessary to call the gods, but everybody wept. The most glorious was the midsummer festival of warrior nobles when the war-god Huitzilopochtli came in his temples and magically showed his footprint in an untouched bowl of maize flour. Then warriors were sacrificed; but for all it was a happy and glorious occasion of national pride. On all these great occasions there were public holidays and everyone participated in one way or another in the processions and dances, though only qualified people were allowed to take part in the ritual; very few indeed ever entered the temple buildings. Participation at all social levels was necessary, for then the gods had support of whole population who were all equally their protégès.

Priests were drawn from whole population. Suitable boys were sent for training in the *calmecac*, the house of learning. There they learned the ritual of abstinence and fasting, rising grad. towards high rank of Sacrificing Priest. At top of priestly pyramid was the Tlaloc Tlamacazqui, the High Priest. He was a member of supreme Council of Four who ruled nation; his duties were regulation of all relig. ceremonies and keeping of nation on path of blessing from the gods. Questions of social rank at birth were not considered in his selection. The High Priest was chosen for his holiness of life and powers of communicating with mind of the gods. There were also a great range of relig. specialists, women who cared for the temple buildings and prepared food for priests and made ceremonial garments; women who specialised in medicine and midwifery; men who were technicians of the gods, carvers of images and painters of sacred books; and prophets, who were individuals who suffered visions and were sometimes possessed by gods so that they prophesied.

The sacrificial rituals were not so excessive as is often thought. A town could keep in a state of holiness by offering about forty human lives a year. It must be remembered that all Aztecs and their kindred peoples believed that all life was a sacrifice, and that the pains and sorrows of everyday were given by the gods as a means of suffering in return for blessings of life. The ghastly atrocity by which the Aztec war-leader Ahuitzotl sacrificed entire manpower of a group of Mixtec tribes at dedication of the great temple in Mexico city was not characteristic of relig. as a whole. It is well authenticated that several days were taken up in slaying 20,000 victims. It is also clear that many great men in Mexico disapproved, and that name of Ahuitzotl, a prince famed for his love of flowers and all beauty, afterwards became a synonym for hideous cruelty.

There is reason to think that relig. of Mexico was always concerned to some extent with heart-sacrifice; but it was intensified at some period of Toltec regime when trad. says that the fertility-god and earthly king, Quetzalcoatl, was driven out by the terrible shadow, the Prince of this world Tezcatlipoca. It is equally clear that the peculiar Aztec temperament, with its passion for beauty and poetry contrasting with its grim asceticism, must lead to increases of spectacular cruelty. We may say that development of the rituals was towards increasing ferocity.

Historically there is some possibility of tracing a sequence of development of this relig. system through archeological time. The comparisons to be made between Aztec and Toltec art are not always in favour of the much revered Toltecs. However, it is quite clear that the trad. representations of the gods derive directly from Toltec originals, and that the structure of temples and palaces also belonged to Toltec trad. This artistic continuity links with recognisable calendrical symbols, showing direct continuity from Toltec to Aztec calendars. An earlier form of same system of reckoning dates comes from last temple at Xochicalco, where not only dates but some artistic symbols, in partic. the great feathered serpents which are assoc. with Quetzalcoatl, can be linked from this monument of 6th cent. CE with later Mexican Art of early 16th cent. The calendrical continuity can be traced further back, but not in cen. Mexico; it stems from inscriptions around Sta. Cotzumahualpa, Guatemala, which, incl. a record of a transit of Venus in late 5th cent. CE, are linked with gods of earth and sky showing symbols which identify them and link them directly with Toltec and Aztec relig. system.

There is considerable disparity between the Toltec-Aztec relig. system and that of the S.W. Mexican peoples, the Zapotecs and Mixtecs, though the Mixtec painted books often show deities which can be equated with Mexican system. Also they use same calendrical system, which in some cases, but not all, can be shown to run exactly parallel with Aztec calendar. The Zapotecs used a calendrical system of which the glyphs are only newly deciphered. They show that there was close similarity to Toltec system. However, Zapotec art, basically independent and with a slightly differing pantheon, had close contact at one period (3rd to 4th cent. CE) with the great cen. Mexican culture of Teotihuacan (2nd cent. BC to 7th cent. CE). Teotihuacano art is radically different in style, and often in technique from that of later periods in cen. Mexico. However, careful analysis of images of gods, partic. in wall paintings, shows that difference is only in style, and that symbols decorating the figures have the same balance and meanings as in later times. It is poss. to identify the majority of gods of Aztec pantheon in the art of Teotihuacan. However, the few pictures of ritual show emphasis on agricultural gods, and in partic. it is quite clear that most import. deity of the Teotihuacanos was rain god Tlaloc. Trad. states that the enormous earthern pyramid at Teotihuacan was dedicated to Sun and a smaller one to Moon. A courtyard is decorated with masks of feathered earth-wind serpent and of rain god, thus showing linkage of Quetzalcoatl with coming of rains mentioned in later legend.

Earlier than the Teotihuacanos were a people of south. coast of Mexican Gulf who are designated Olmec, on ground that the later people living there were named Olmecs (People of the Rubber-growing country). They date from 9th to 4th cent. BC, have a unique, nearly realist art style which spread widely in Mexico, and left behind a good deal of fine sculpture. This contains images which may be rather vaguely related to later gods, but identifications are never quite certain as yet. They used carefully oriented temple mounds, and erected stone stelae with elaborate pictorial compositions. There are also huge stone heads apparently repr. deities, perhaps stellar beings. But since we cannot read the few syllabic symbols they employ and the iconography is very different from that of later cultures, we cannot make any definite statements about nature of relig. among these mysterious Olmec peoples.

The Maya repr. a highly specialised variant of C. American culture. Not only did they form a closely knit physical and linguistic group, but were unique in possessing a phonetic syllabary for writing. Their attitude towards the powers of nature was rather more free than that of peoples of Mexican highlands, and was prob. conditioned by their habitat, the tropical forests of E. Guatemala and S. Mexico, together with dry limestone peninsula of Yucatan. The great period of the Maya reaches from 2nd cent. CE to early 10th cent. They had rapidly advanced from a village-dwelling group of tribes to a people having a loose unity between their fine city-states, which not only displayed magnificent relig. buildings but were decorated with sculpture and painting which gives many clues to nature of their religion. Basically they were interested in judicial → astrology to an almost unprecedented degree. They counted in periods of 20 days (the day-names being very similar in meaning to Mexican ones). The next time unit was the Tun (or stone) of 360 days. This was lengthened by multiples of twenty. This kind of calculation was a mathematician's delight. The astrologers could deal with calculations in days which amounted to millions of years. As with Mexicans, each day and each period (incl. a *tzolkin* which was exactly parallel to the Mexican *tonalpouhalli*) was under divine protection. Hence Maya astrological predictions could be carried to great detail, bringing in data from vast periods of time which were necessary to pursue planetary data to some regular rhythmic conclusion. There was a continual adjustment of dates in Maya inscriptions, since the *tun* of 360 days had to be adjusted to suit solar year of 365¼ days. Hence every lengthy Maya inscription has special 'distance numbers', which bring the precise date of monument into relationship with solar year. The stone faced-pyramids, and great courtyards of Maya ceremonial centres are often sprinkled with large stone stelae or else images of the Earth-toad, which are really time-markers, recording astrological calculations in periods of time—usually Katuns of 360 by 20 days.

Many of these monuments incl. figures of deities; the gigantic, monstrous, frog-like Earth-Mother, and such recognisable beings as the maize god (equated with the Mexican Xipe by some of his symbols), the Goddess of the South, wearing her skirt of jade beads, the death god of the North, and a god of the East who is Kukulkan (equiv. to Quetzalcoatl).

The remaining few painted books (Codices) incl. pictures which show an abundance of deities, having special functions with regard to arts and crafts as well as agriculture. There appears to have been something like a cult of → Saktism, since in the Dresden Codex a series of pictures shows godesses *in coitu* with sky-god Itzamna. In Codex Troano-Cortesianus there are pictures of day to day activities connected with the gods, and a table which shows divisions of the *tzolkin* (260 day period), divided acc. to the four directions of earth. Codex Peresianus gives us some astrological information, and shows that the sky-band was divided into 13 constellations, presumably the regions traversed by moon in journey through the year. This sky-band is often shown on sculptured stelae as being held across their chests by the Bacabs, gods who guard the four directions of universe. These gods are obviously regarded as gigantic beings towering from earth to sky and then beyond, in a way not made clear in any Mexican painting. Also from the ruined Maya city of Tikal there is a carved wooden lintel (now in Basel, Switzerland), in which the god Kukulkan (= Quetzalcoatl) is shown as god, as the planet Venus, and as the mysterious Moan bird, which is the flying planet in sky. The triple symbolism of this carving shows a rich theology which is much more advanced intellectually than anything shown in Aztec or Toltec art in Cen. Mexico, though it coincides in some ways with poems said to have been made by Mexican King of Tezcuco, the wise Nezahualcoyotl.

Thus we see that although Maya relig. was a branch of the common relig. and calendrical system of Middle America, it had special features which make it worthy of special study. More information will be undoubtedly forthcoming in near future as decipherment of Maya hieroglyphic writing becomes more precise: C.A.B.

(The various works and editions listed here all

contain full bibliographies) (1) Orig. accounts of 16th century missionaries: Landa, Bishop Diego de, *Relacion de las Cosas de Yucatan.*, ed. and trans. by A. M. Tozzer, (Peabody Museum Papers, XVIII, 1941); Motolinia, Fray Toribio de Venavente, *Hist. of the Indians of New Spain*, trans. E. A. Foster, (Cortes Society, 1950); Sahagún, Fray Bernardino de, *General Hist. of the Things of New Spain*, Nahuatl text trans. by A. J. O. Anderson and C. Dibble, 12 vols. (School of American Research Santa Fe, and Univ. of Utah, Salt Lake City in progress 1961). (2) Modern Works: Anders, F. *Das Pantheon der Maya* (1963); Burland, C. A., *The Gods of Mexico* (1966); Caso, A., *The Aztecs, People of the Sun* (1958); Cooper-Clark, J., *Codex Mendoza*, 3 vols. (1940); Morley, S. G., *The Ancient Maya*, 3rd ed. rev. by G. W. Brainerd (1956); Paddock, J. (ed.), *Ancient Oaxaca* (1966); Sejourne, L., *Burning Water* (1957); Seler, E., *Gesammelte Abhandlungen zur amerikanischen Sprach- und Altertunskunde*, 5 vols. Reprint (1960–1); Vaillant, G. C., *The Aztecs of Mexico*, rev. ed. by S. B. Vaillant (1962). →→ N. Amer. Relig.; Inca Relig.

Amesha Spentas In → Zoroastrianism, designation meaning 'Immortal Bounteous Ones', given to six spiritual entities: Good Mind (*Vohu Manah*), Good Order (*Arta*), Dominion (*Xshathra*), Devotion (*Ārmaiti*), Welfare (*Haurvatāt*), Immortality (*Ameretāt*). Zoroaster assigned A.S. as companions or attributes to → Ahura Mazdah. They were prob. orig. Indo-Iranian functional deities, and Zoroaster thus transformed them in interests of his monotheistic concept. of deity. S.G.F.B.

G. Widengren, in *Numen*, I (1954), p. 23; J. Duchesne-Guillemin, *Zoroastre* (1948), pp. 57–80, 146–7; G. Dumézil, *Naissance d'Archanges* (1945), pp. 57–98; Zaehner, *D.T.Z.*, pp. 45ff., 63ff., 257ff.

'Am Ha-Ares Rabbinic Heb. designation meaning 'people of the land', given to those ignorant of → Torah or careless about its observance. S.G.F.B.

E.R.E., I, p. 385b–6b; *H.D.B.*², p. 749.

Amice (ex Lat. *amictus*). Linen cloth, gen. square, with strings, worn as part of Eucharist → vestments in Western Church. Origin obscure. S.G.F.B.

D.C.C., *s.v.*

Amida Name used in Japan. Buddhism for Amita, a transcendental Buddha. In the → Mahāyāna of India, this transcendental Buddha. was known both as *Amitayus* (external Life) and *Amitābha* (eternal Light). Main Mhy texts which ref. to Amita, are greater and smaller *Sukhāvatīvyūha Sūtras* and *Amitāyur-dhyāna Sutra* (see *S.B.E.*, vol. 49). *Sukhāvatī* is 'the happy land' or paradise, to which Amita was believed to be able to bring his devotees. The worship of A. in Mahāyāna appears to be traceable back to just before time of → Nāgārjuna i.e. to about begin. of 2nd cent. CE, since Nāgārjuna is said to have derived his knowledge of cult of A. from his teacher Saraha. The Greater *Sukhāvatīvyūha Sūtra*, which was trans. into Chinese about begin. of second half of 2nd cent. CE, relates story of Dharmākara, who is repres. as having lived many aeons ago, and who, although he could have entered into Buddahood, chose not to do so, but made vow that he would wait until he could achieve such Buddhahood as would make him lord of a paradise (*sukhāvatī*), to which all who meditated upon this paradise ten times should be admitted. This he achieved as the Buddha. Amitābha. The *Amitāyur-dhyāna Sūtra* describes series of sixteen meditations (*dhyāna*) upon *Amitāyus* which are said to lead to admission to his paradise. In Indian Mahāyāna, the cult of A. appears to have been of relatively minor importance, even though so eminent a figure as Nāgārjuna was among his devotees. In → Tibet and Nepal, A. is one among many Buddhas worshipped. By time of development of idea of the → *Adi-Buddha*, Amita had come to be regarded as one of the five principle Buddhas or Jinas, who are emanations of the Adi-Buddha. → Vasubandhu also composed a 'Discourse on Paradise' based on *Sukhāvatīvyūha Sūtra*; his discourse begins 'I take refuge single heartedly in Amita and pray to be reborn in his Paradise'. It was in China and Japan, however, that the cult of Amita had its greatest success and became one of predominant forms of Buddhism in those countries. (→ Amida, Jap.). T.O.L.

(Jap.): **Amitabha** (Skt.); **A-mi-t'o fo** (China). The → Buddha. of infinite (*amita*) light (*ābhā*). Also known as Amitayus, i.e. of infinite (*amita*) life-span (*āyuh*). Personification or mode of manifestation of the primordial, self-existent Buddha., (→ Adi-Buddha.), whose creative activity is symbolised under seven Dhyāna-Buddhas., of which A. is fourth. The cult of A. shows strong Iranian influence, and is only prominent in northern (Mahāyāña) Buddhism, being practically unknown in Siam (Thailand), Burma and Ceylon. It was introduced into China by Chih Ch'ien, of Indo-Scythian origin, by the trans. of the *A-mi-t'o ching* (*Sukhāvatīvyūha sūtra*) in the period CE 220–52. By end of 4th cent., the cult was well established under the influence of → Hui Yüan.

As personification of infinite mercy, compassion, wisdom and love, figure of A. became the supreme object of devotion and faith in the → Pure Land sects which developed in China and Japan, i.e. → Jodo and → Shin. About middle of 7th cent. in China, A. superseded Shakyamuni and Maitreya as the supreme object of popular devotion. He was regarded as intermediary between Supreme Reality and mankind. Faith in him ensured rebirth in his Western Paradise (Sukhāvati). Associated with A. were the two great → bodhisattvas, → Mahāsthāmaprāpta and → Avalokitesvara (Kuan Yin). (→ Amida (1)). D.H.S.

E. Conze, *Buddhism* (1951); E. Zurcher, *The Buddhist Conquest of China* (1959); K. L. Reichelt, *Truth and Tradition in Chinese Buddhism* (1927); E. T. C. Werner, *Dictionary of Chinese Mythology* (1932).

Amish Chr. sect of → Anabaptist type, orig. in late 17th cent. The A. are named after Jacob Amman, a Swiss → Mennonite Bishop, who insisted on stricter *Meidung* (separation) from wordly influences than did other Mennonites. Emigration of A. to America took place throughout 18th cent., esp. to Lancaster County, Pennsylvania, which is still main centre of A. influence. The 'Old Order' A. are an extremely conservative, rural people, wearing beards and 18th cent. costume, refusing to use motor cars or electricity, or to permit marriage with non-A. They have no church buildings, worship taking place in houses; celebrate the → Holy Communion twice yearly, with foot washing; and have threefold ministry of Bishop (*Volle Diener*), Preacher (*Diener zum Buch*) and Deacon (*Armen Diener*), all chosen by lot. There are less conservative A. groups which have broken away from the 'Old Order' parent body. E.J.S.

C. G. Bachman, *The Old Order Amtsh of Lancaster County* (Pennsylvania German Society, vol. 60, 1961).

Ammonius Saccas Christian of 3rd cent. → Alexandria, who returned to paganism, and taught a mystical kind of philosophy. Among his pupils were → Origen and Plotinus; because of his influence on latter he ranks as a founder of → Neoplatonism. S.G.F.B.

O.C.D., *s.v.*

Amorites Name frequently used in O.T. as designation both for pre-Israelite inhabitants of Palestine, and for anc. inhabitants of west and east Jordan cultural areas. A. is never used to describe a precise people or dwellers in a precise place. The name is related to → Akkadian 'Amurru' = 'western': 'Amurru-land'—Syria-Palestine. S.G.F.B.

*R.G.G.*³, I, 327–8; K. M. Kenyon, *Amorites and Canaanites* (1966).

Amos, Book of Earliest of canonical prophets of O.T., *c.* 760–750 BC. A.'s message is notable for assoc. → Yahweh with concern for social justice, and proclaiming 'Day of Yahweh' as coming judgment on Israel as on other nations. Although not explicitly monotheistic, A. presents Yahweh as Lord of nature and of nations, and so points way to teaching of → Deutero-Isaiah. S.G.F.B.

R. H. Pfeiffer, *Intro. to Old Test.* (1948), pp. 577ff., 869–70; W. O. E. Oesterley-T. H. Robinson, *Hebrew Religion* (1930), pp. 204ff.; *R.G.G.*³, I, 328–31.

Amphiaraos Local Boeotian god, whose → chthonic cult derives from Aegean past (→ Aegean Religion). Name has been found on Mycenaean tablets. A. figures as celebrated hero and seer in Grk. mythology, espec. in connection with legend of the Seven against Thebes. His chthonian nature is reflected in story of his death: Zeus opens earth with lightning flash and A., in his chariot, descends. His cult was also connected with dream interpretation and healing. S.G.F.B.

M. P. Nilsson, *The Mycenaean Origin of Greek Mythology* (1932), pp. 115ff.; *Kleine Pauly*, I, 308–10.

Amphictionies *Ex.* Grk. word meaning 'dwellers around', used to designate leagues of tribes or cities connected with temples and maintenance of their cults. Most celebrated was the Amphictionic League, comprising 12 tribes, associated with temple of → Apollo at → Delphi. A. League had political significance: it could proclaim a sacred war. The idea of A. has been used (notably by M. Noth, *A Hist. of Israel*, E.T., 1960), to account for organisation of 12 Tribes of Israel (→ Israel). S.G.F.B.

O.C.D., *s.v.; Kleine Pauly*, I, 311–3; *E.R.E.*, I, 394a–9a.

Amulets Objects, believed to possess magical virtue, have been used, from remote antiquity and in all parts of world, to give protection or power to owner. Usually amulets are small and can be worn: but larger examples are known, e.g. wolf's snout affixed to door (Pliny, *Hist. nat.* 28.157). They can be of all kinds of material or colour, though often their efficacy might reside in their substance (e.g. → jade, to prolong life). A.'s might give protection from all forms of peril, natural and supernatural: e.g. the → evil-eye, or they could give good fortune (e.g. lucky charms). Often they were given significant shapes (e.g. → ankh, hand, cross, phallus, vulva); sometimes they were inscribed with relig. or magical formula (→→ Abracadabra; phylacteries). They could derive their value from origin (e.g. bones of saints, → Relics). Use of A.'s may go back to Palaeolithic era: e.g. pieces of mammoth bone found in some graves perhaps gave protection to dead. A.'s were extensively used in anc. Egypt, espec. in → funerary ritual. A.'s have been officially recognised in some religions (e.g. by blessing in R.C. Church); otherwise they are repr. of folk-belief. (→→ Cicada, Charms). S.G.F.B.

E.R.E., III, pp. 392–472; *R.G.G.*, I, 345–7; *R.Ae.R.-G.*, pp. 26–31; B. Meissner, *Babylonien u. Assyrien*, II (1925), pp. 205ff.; *R.A.C.*, I, 397–411; E. A. W. Budge, *The Mummy* (1925), pp. 276ff., *Amulets and Talismen* (1930).

Amun, (Amen, Amon) Egypt. deity who became chief state-god during New Kingdom (1580–1100 BC). A. first appears in neighbourhood of → Thebes at begin. of Middle Kingdom (*c.* 2130 BC). His origins are obscure; he was poss. one of 8 creator deities of Hermopolis (→ Cosmogony (Egypt)). He seems to have been assoc. with air or wind; he was also known as 'the hidden one'. The rise of princes of Thebes to royal power at begin. of New Kingdom led to exaltation of A., who was identified with anc. sun-god → Re as Amun-Re. Many New King. pharaohs ascribed their foreign victories to A., and built and endowed the vast temples that still survive at Karnak and Luxor (site of anc. Thebes). The power and prestige of A., and his priesthood, provoked unsuccessful reformation of → Akhenaten. Eventually High Priests of A. took over royal power. Cult of A. spread to Libyan oasis (→ Alexander visited A.'s oracle at Siwa), and Ethiopian kings adopted A. as state-god. The destruction of Thebes by Assyrians in 664 BC ended supremacy of A. In art A. was depicted in human form, sometimes with ram's head. Mut, local Theban goddess, and moon-god Khons, were assoc. with A. as wife and son respectively. S.G.F.B.

R.Ae.R.-G., pp. 31–7; S. A. B. Mercer, *Religion of Anc. Egypt* (1949), pp. 157ff.; S. G. F. Brandon, *C.L.*, pp. 46ff.

Amyraldists Followers of Moses Amyrant, French Protestant divine and Professor at Saumur (1633–64). Although a Calvinist (→ Calvin), and interested in docs. of Predestination and Grace, A. held that salvation, which depended essentially on faith in Christ, is possible for all men through grace of God. A.'s teaching led to formation, among French and Swiss Protestants, of a sect of so-called 'Hypothetical Universalists'. S.G.F.B.

*R.G.G.*³, I, 347–8.

Anabaptists Name, derived from Grk. word meaning 'to baptise again', given to Prot. sect that emerged in 16th cent. They disapproved of infant baptism, and required adults so baptised to be rebaptised. Movement was also characterised by radical social views, tending to egalitarianism and community of goods. A.'s owed their origin largely to Thomas Müntzer (1485–1525), a Lutheran preacher of Zwickau, in Saxony. Müntzer became leader of a peasants' revolt and was executed at Mühlhausen, 1525. In 1534 A.'s set up a 'Kingdom of Saints' at Münster, having gained possession of city. During ensuing siege, fanatical excesses, incl. a form of polygamy, brought A.'s into ill repute, and hardened attitude of authorities to A.'s elsewhere. A.'s were condemned by →→ Luther, Calvin, and Zwingli. Menno Simons (1496–1561) reorganised A.'s, after Münster episode, in Holland, where sect prospered in 17th and 18th cents., being named Mennonites. To their belief about believers' baptism, they added rejection of participation in civil magistracy and non-resistance. Mennonites were in close contact with English A.'s. A.'s exist today also in various parts of Europe, incl. Russia, and in America. (→→ Amish, Baptists). S.G.F.B.

E.R.E., I, pp. 406–12; *D.C.C.*, *s.v.* and 'Mennonites'; *N.M.C.H.*, II, pp. 119ff.; E. Troeltsch, *Social Teaching of the Christ. Churches* (E.T. 1931), II, pp. 694ff.

Anāgāmin Term used in Buddhism for the 'non-returner', i.e. one who has reached third stage of spiritual development: next stage before becoming an → *arahant*. The two previous stages of spiritual progress recognised in → Theravada are: the 'stream-enterer' (→ *Sotāpanna*), and the 'once-returner' (→ Sakadāgāmin). The non-returner is one who has gone beyond the spiritual attainments of the two earlier stages, having overcome the five 'fetters' which bind humans to sphere of senses, viz: (1) belief in an enduring entity (2) doubt (3) belief in value of rules and rituals (4) sensuous desire (5) ill-will. He is thus free from the 'bond of craving' (*Kāma-yoga*), but has yet to become free of the 'bond of existence' (*bhava-yoga*). Existence for him will continue, but in a heavenly or super-sensual sphere; it is to sphere of sensual existence that he is a non-returner. In the heavenly sphere (*deva-loka*), or, acc. to → Buddhaghosa (*Visuddhimagga*), in the 'Pure Abodes', he will attain → Nibbāna. Attainment of the non-returner stage is often ref. to in the Pali canon, in words attr. to the Buddha. (*Itivuttaka* 39; 40; *AN.* V. 108; *SN.* V. 177, 178). In the *Mahāparinibbāna Su.* Buddha ref. to some Buddh. monks already deceased, who 'have all attained the state of non-returner and will attain *parinibbāna* without returning to this world again'. (*DN.* II, 92). The A. concept is found also among the → Sarvāstivādins; it is ref. to in the → *Abhidharmakosa-sāstra* as third of four stages on the spiritual path, from which there is no return to sphere of sensuality. The concept thus passed into → Mahāyāna; but by Mahāyānists it is held that, if an A. wishes to return to help another being who is still in sphere of sensuality to attain Enlightenment he may do so by returning to sphere of sensuality in a 'spiritual' or 'blissful' body (→ *Sambhoga-Kāya*). T.O.L.

Anagārika Term used in anc. India for one who was not (*an*) a householder (*agārika*), i.e., one who had gone forth from home to homelessness, renouncing comforts of life to become a holy man, pursuing the holy life (*brahmacariya*). There were numerous groups or schools of such A.'s in anc. India, each having its own form of teaching or discipline. One of these was the Buddha. → Sangha. Such groups of A.'s depended on householders or laymen for supply of food, and were thus sometimes in competition with one another; the Buddh. scriptures contain accounts of plots hatched against the Sangha by non-Buddh. groups, jealous of popularity enjoyed by the former. (→ *Saṃyutta Nikaya*, I, p. 122). T.O.L.

Anagarika Dharmapala → Maha-Bodhi Society. T.O.L.

Anahita (Grk. Anaitis) Iranian fertility goddess, who 'purifies the seed of males and the womb and the milk of females' (*Vidēvdāt*, vii, 16; *Yast* v, 5). A. is prob. to be identified with Canaanite goddess → Anat and Mesopot. goddess → Ishtar. It is significant that → Zoroaster ignores her, as he does → Mithra, with whom she was associated. The cult of A. was diffused throughout Persian Empire: in her sanctuary at Erēz in Akilisene sacred → prostitution was practised. The Greeks identified A. with both →→ Athene and Aphrodite, thereby recognising her warlike and fertility character respectively. At Tauropolis, A. was prob. associated with the → taurobolium. S.G.F.B.

E.R.E., I, pp. 414b–5b; L.-I. Ringbom, *Zur Ikonographie der Götten Ardvi Sura Anahita* (1957); Zaehner, *D.T.Z.*, pp. 145ff.; M. Chaumont, *R.H.R.*, 153 (1958), pp. 154ff.

Analects of Confucius → Lun Yü. D.H.S.

Analogy Method employed in Chr. theology whereby concepts, derived from normal human experience, are taken as guides to understanding those aspects of the divine nature in which some similarity is discerned: e.g. from the idea of human justice something significant may be inferred as to the 'justice' of God. By a disciplined use of analogy, it is believed that danger of anthropomorphising God may be avoided. 'Analogues' assume that two specific objects are basically dissimilar, while having some similarity. The method of A. is to be contrasted with that of symbolism, which presupposes total dissimilarity. (→ Philosophy of Relig.). S.G.F.B.

E.R.E., I, pp. 415b–9b; D. Cupitt, 'The Doctrine of Analogy in the Age of Locke', in *J.T.S.*, XIX (1968).

Analogy of Religion, The Title of famous work by J. Butler, Bishop of Durham, pub. in 1736, in which analogical method is used in a closely knit argument. It proved a powerful weapon against contemporary → Deism, although intention is not formally admitted. In ch. 6 Butler enunciated the celebrated proposition: probability is the guide of life. S.G.F.B.

D.C.C., *s.v.*

Anamnesis Grk. word meaning 'memorial', used to designate commemoration of Passion of Christ in the Words of Institution, in Canon of the → Eucharist (*v.* I Cor. 11:24f.). S.G.F.B.

Liturgy and Worship (1932), pp. 118, 123, 346–9; *D.C.C.*, *s.v.*

Ānanda One of foremost disciples of the Buddha. His name means 'joy', and he was so called acc. to commentary on the Theragāthā, because he brought joy to his kinsmen. A member of the Sākya clan and first cousin of Buddha., A. entered the Buddh. Order in second year after the Buddha had begun to preach his doc. From begin., A. was closely assoc. with Buddha; for the last 25 yrs. of his life was his personal attendant. This function A. agreed to perform on condition that he was to derive no personal benefits or comforts from his special position, so that none should say it was for these things that he ministered to the Buddha; his service was to be expression of personal devotion only. The great care with which he ministered, sparing no effort, and devoting himself tirelessly to Buddha's comfort and protection is emphasised in Pali canonical and commentarial lit. It was A. who foiled → Devadatta's plot to murder Buddha (→ Ajātasattu). A. was entrusted also by the Buddha with task of teaching the doc. Having given a short outline discourse, he would leave it to A. to provide for hearers of full exposition of what had been said. When the report of A.'s preaching reached Buddha, he praised A.'s perceptiveness and understanding. A. was a partic. close friend of Sariputta, Buddha's chief disciple. He was also champion of the women's cause. Buddha's step-mother, Pajāpati Gotamī, made request to him that women should be admitted to an Order. The Buddha at first firmly refused. A., finding the women weeping over the reply, then asked Buddha on their behalf that they should be admitted. When he maintained his refusal, A. asked him if women were capable of attaining the relig. goal of the Buddh. way. Buddha replied that they were; A. then repeated his plea that they be allowed to enter the Order, subject to special conditions. Buddha then agreed, although not without prediction that with admission of women the Buddh. Order would now last only half the time it would have lasted otherwise. A. is regarded in Buddh. trad. as having remained a *sekha*, that is not having achieved goal of → arantship, until after Buddha's death, when by a great spiritual effort he at last attained that state. It was by A. that the words of the Buddha's discourses are said to have been preserved with faultless accuracy. In first four → *Nikayas* of Pali canon, the phrase 'Thus have I heard' frequently occurs as an intro. to some words of Buddha. In this phrase, the 'I' is understood as being spoken by A.

After Buddha's death, A.'s last years were

spent in teaching, preaching, encouraging and guiding younger monks. He was, however, at the Council of monks, held immediately after Buddha's death charged, with certain previous faults, namely, that he had failed to ascertain from Buddha which were minor precepts only, which the monks could revoke if necessary (D. II, 154); that he had failed to request Buddha to live on for a further → *kalpa* (D. II, 115); that he had unneccessarily prevailed on Buddha to allow women to be admitted (Vin. II, 253). His reply was that he regarded these acts not as a fault, but would confess them as such out of respect for his fellow-monks. The Suttas of Pali canon which mention A., and together testify to his eminence, are listed by → Buddhaghosa as follows: the *Sekha, Bāhitiya, Āmanjasappāya, Gopaka-Moggallāna, Budhudatāka, Cūlasunnata, Mahāsunnata, Acchariyabbhuta, Bhaddekaratta, Mahānidāna, Mahāparinibbāna, Subha, Cūlaniyalokdhātu Suttas*. His death is not mentioned in Pali canon, but the Chinese pilgrim, → Fa Hsien, records anc. trad. that A.'s death took place in mid-river between domains of → Ajāta-Sattu, King of Magadha, and the chiefs of Vesāli, and that both parties took a share of his ashes and built *cetiyas* for their enshrinement.
T.O.L.

Anaphora Grk. word, meaning 'offering', used to designate central prayer of Eucharist Liturgy, embracing the Consecration, → Anamnesis, and → Communion. It begins with the Sursum Corda. The A. dates back to Apostolic Tradition of Hippolytus (3rd cent.). S.G.F.B.

R.A.C., I, 422–7.

Anat Canaanite fertility goddess: she is named on a stele from Bethshan, in Egypt. hieroglyphs 'Anit Queen of Heaven and Mistress of all the gods'. A. is gen. depicted nude, with sexual attributes emphasised. She figures prominently in mythological texts of → Ugarit as sister and lover of → Baal, whose death she mourns and avenges (→ Adonis). S.G.F.B.

T. Gray, *The Canaanites* (1964), pp. 123ff., 133ff.

Anāthapindika Wealthy man of the Buddha's time who is remembered in Buddh. trad. for his great generosity. At great expense he purchased the Jetavana grove near Sāvatthi, and built there a monastery for the use of Buddha and his monks. For this, and other acts of generosity, he was remembered as the chief of alms-donors (A.I. 25). His name was Sudatta, but he was referred to as Anāthapindika (feeder of the poor) in recognition of his generosity. A number of suttas found in the *Anguttara Nikaya* are addressed to A. One of these, the *Velāma Sutta*, consists of Buddha's words of encouragement to A., when as result of loss of his wealth, he was no longer able to provide food for the monks (A. IV, 392ff.). T.O.L.

Malalasekere, *DPPN*, vol. I, pp. 67–72.

Anathema Grk. word, meaning 'suspended', which = Heb. word *chāram*, meaning 'to cut off', 'curse', 'destroy'. In O.T. it was used of things devoted to → Yahweh, and, therefore, not for common use: Joshua 6:17ff. affords graphic example of custom and its consequences. Later practice involved exclusion from community and loss of goods of person incurring penalty. In N.T., Paul uses A. to denote separation from Chr. community (Gal. 1:8). Earliest eccles. use of A. against offenders is at Council of Elvira (*c.* 306). It subsequently became regular procedure against heretics; but was frequently used by one ecclesiastic against another. It was regarded from 6th cent. as a more serious penalty than excommunication; but the distinction was grad. lost.
S.G.F.B.

J. Pedersen, *Israel* (1940), III, pp. 29ff.; *D.C.C., s.v.; R.A.C.*, I, 427–30.

Anatta (Pali) **Anātma** (Skt) Buddh. doctrine that there is not (*an*) a permanent self (*atta*) within each individual being. This is third of the '3 characteristic marks of existence' (→ *ti-lakkhaṇa*), and is a doc. entirely peculiar to Buddhism, distinguishing it from all other relig. and philosoph. schools of anc. India. Without proper appreciation of meaning of *anatta*, it is imposs. to understand Buddh. thought. The Buddha's teaching on this point was a denial of reality of a self or soul inhabiting the individual, a perdurable entity which is the agent of the individual's actions. Instead, the individual is seen as a temporary collocation of five → *Khandhas*, or groups of constituent factors. The *Khandhas* themselves are not enduring, but are series of momentary events; each such event standing in a casual relationship to next. While there is thus a flux of constantly changing factors in any given empirical 'individual', there is also a certain continuity in the process—sufficient to give the appearance, both at physical and psychological levels, of individuality. The recognition of such continuity, and use of everyday terms and proper names to denote particular individuals, is allowed as concession and aid to economy of language. 'These are wordly usages, wordly language, wordly terms of communication, wordly descriptions by which a Tathāgata communicates without misapprehending them.' (D.I. 195f.). The doc. of A. is regarded in Buddh. trad. as the most difficult truth of all to apprehend, since the notion of a permanent 'self' is deeply rooted in everyday habits of thought. The idea of an individual self was re-introduced and affirmed by the → *pudgala-vādins*, whose views were not accepted as true by other Buddh. schools. T.O.L.

E. Conze, *Buddhist Thought in India* (1962).

Anaxagoras Grk. philosopher, born *c.* 500 BC, at

Clazomenae, in Ionia. A. is notable for using concept of Mind (*nous*) as principle that produced the cosmos out of primordial chaos. He also had distinction of being charged at Athens with impiety, in that he denied divinity of sun and moon, by asserting that the one was a burning stone and the other earth. He was exiled to Lampsacus, where he died *c.* 430 BC. A memorial was erected to him, having on one side the word *Nous* and on the other *Alētheia* ('Truth').
S.G.F.B.

G. S. Kirk and J. E. Raven, *The Presocratic Philosophers* (1960), pp. 362ff.; W. Jaeger, *The Theology of the Early Greek Philosophers* (1947), pp. 155ff.; A. B. Drachmann, *Atheism in Pagan Antiquity* (1922), pp. 25ff.

Ancestor Cults (Introductory) This term covers two forms of belief and practice often confused. Where dead are regarded as divine, their cult becomes worship and can be designated ancestor-worship. However, there are many instances in which dead, though not divinised, are thought to be potent beings whose needs must be served. Either form of A.C. presupposes that dead survive death in some effective sense. They are gen. regarded as living in their graves or below ground, and as retaining many physical needs of this life, e.g. need of food and drink. Palaeolithic burials (→ Palaeolithic Religion) indic. such tendance of dead. The burial of some bodies beneath domestic hearth in caves may attest an A.C.; but extant evidence does not permit assumption that a definite A.C. was gen. practised by Palaeolithic peoples. Portrait skulls found beneath floors in → Jericho, dating from *c.* 7000 BC, may witness to A.C., as may skulls found at → Çatal Hüyük. A.C. can be inspired by both trust and fear of dead: located below ground, ancestors have often been assoc. with fertility; they could also be considered malevolent, causing disease, if not carefully served. An attempt was made by → Euhemerus to find origin of relig. in ancestor-worship; he was followed by H. Spencer (1820–1903). Some deities have indeed so originated (→ Amenophis, → Imhotep); but the theory is inadequate as total explanation of origin of relig. (→ Religion, Origin). S.G.F.B.

E.R.E., I, pp. 425–32; J. G. Frazer, *The Belief in Immortality and the Worship of the Dead*, 3 vols. (1913–22); E. Bendann, *Death Customs* (1930), pp. 264ff.; S. G. F. Brandon, *M.D.*, pp. 8ff., 50, 275ff., 309ff., 354ff. → Africa (East, South, West).

(China–Japan) Cult of ancestors is most ancient and persistent element in Chinese relig. There is lack of evidence as to whether common people in anc. China sacrificed to ancestor spirits, but hereditary aristocracy believed that spirits of their ancestors supervised human destinies, rewarded and punished, and demanded the service and obedience of their descendants. They were consulted on all important occasions, their wishes made known through divination, and elaborate sacrifices were made to them in ancestral temples. Confucianism, with its doctrine of filial piety which in some schools became summit of all virtues, promoted A.-C. and elaborated rituals of burial, mourning and sacrifice to ancestors. 'While they are alive, serve them (parents) according to the ritual; when they die, bury them acc. to the ritual; and sacrifice to them acc. to ritual' (Ana. 2:5).

In anc. times, representatives of the dead, chosen from grandsons, took seats of honour at clan feasts, and received on behalf of the spirits, who were believed to indwell them, prayers and sacrifices. During Chou Dynasty, prob. *c.* BC 350, the custom began of erecting tablets to dead. These ancestral tablets, oblong pieces of hard wood about 12 in. by 3 in. bearing name and date of birth of deceased, were set up in ancestral temples. In case of a sovereign, these were 7 in number with the tablet of founder of dynasty occupying central position. The other six were the immediate ancestors of sovereign, and all other tablets were relegated to a store. At prescribed times, elaborate ceremonies were performed and sacrifices made before the tablets. Much of domestic worship of the people centred in clan temples to ancestors, and a careful register was kept of all members of clan. In ordinary families, the tablets of the 3 preceding generations were kept in house of senior member. (→ Confucius).

Buddhism in China promoted A.-C. by practice of chanting masses for dead and in popular festival of Departed Spirits (Yü Lan P'ên Hui) held on the 15th of the 7th moon. Popular throughout China was the spring festival at the tombs, → Ch'ing Ming at the end of the 2nd moon when the departed spirits were worshipped at the tombs.

The cult of ancestors was so important to the Chinese that when deprived of a male heir, adoption was resorted to in order to ensure the continuance of the family sacrifices. D.H.S.

D. H. Smith, *Chinese Religions* (1968), *passim.*

Primitive → Shinto, acc. to earliest evidence available (→ Kojiki, → Nihongi and early → Noritos) did not possess a developed cult of ancestors. There was a vague belief in continuance after death, and of the need to supply the departed with sustenance. Confucianism, introduced from China in 5th cent. CE, strengthened, if it did not create, early Japanese A.-C., and promoted a strong family sentiment. This resulted in national worship of the imperial ancestors, together with worship of clan and family ancestors, so that A.-C. became and remained an integral and fundamental aspect of Shinto religion. The great goddess → Amaterasu was worshipped as the divine progenitrix, and practically all the great ancient → kami were recognised by Shintoists as the racial heads of recognised clans and families, and as such received worship. Buddhism in Japan taught that spiritual communion embraced the souls of dead, and promoted the practice of setting up memorial stones and tablets on which were recorded prayers for sake of dead. Though in theory the sentiment of filial piety inculcated by Buddhism in Japan was but an exercise in religious piety, in practice it corresponded to A.-C. D.H.S.

(Egypt) There is no evidence of A.-C. as such in Egypt., although tendance of dead was essentially a family responsibility. The son of deceased was primarily charged with funerary service of father, the divine example being → Horus who had accomplished all necessary for resurrection and *post-mortem* welfare of his father → Osiris. Since dead were believed to live in their tombs, it was necessary that family should arrange for regular supply of mortuary offerings. The dead were ritually identified with Osiris; but they were not consequently worshipped as divine (→ Funerary Rites, Egypt). Seti I is repr. at Abydos as offering incense to long rows of cartouches of past pharaohs; but this scarcely implies worship since all Egypt. kings, incl. Seti, were regarded as divine. S.G.F.B.

R.Ae.R.-G., pp. 9b–11a; Kees, *T., passim;* E. A. W. Budge, *The Mummy* (1926), pp. 432ff.; E. A. E. Reymond, 'Worship of the Ancestor Gods at Edfu'. in *Chronique d'Egypte*, 38 (1963); S. G. F. Brandon, *History, Time and Deity* (1965), plate X.

(Greece) The family's responsibility for performing proper funerary rites for deceased member was accepted, as in other cultures, as basic and essential duty. Evidence of a distinctive A.-C., however, is problematic. The strongly established → hero-cult prob. stemmed from a primitive A.-C. The hero, although gen. a chthonic daemon (→ Demons (Greek)) was regarded as orig. human; he dwelt in tomb and possessed power for good or ill, and was, accordingly, worshipped (→ Altars, Greek and Roman). The *genos* (clan or family) in Grk. society often had an eponymous ancestor of hero-status. The hero-cult was prob. pre-Hellenic Cretan. The famous painted sarcophagus of Hagia Triada may depict a Minoan A.-C., and richly equipped burials at Mycenae suggest currency of an A.-C. there (→→ Aegean, Cretan, Mycenean Religs.; Anthesteria; Funerary Rites, Greek). S.G.F.B.

S. Marinátos, *Crete and Mycenae* (E.T. 1960), plates XXVII–XXX, pp. 151–2 (Haghia Triada), pp. 90ff.; E. Rohde, *Psyche* (1898), I, pp. 157ff., 167ff.

(Iranian) The → Fravashi, described in Yasna 13 as the Holy Fravashi 'who are under the earth since the time of their decease', were venerated as potent beings able to confer fertility on man and beast, but who needed tendance of the living. In later → Zoroastrianism the last five days of the period Hamaspathmaēdaya (March 10–20) were consecrated to their service; they were also commemorated on 19th of each month. S.G.F.B.

E.R.E., I, pp. 454b–5b; Brandon, *M.D.*, pp. 274–5, 283; Zaehner, *D.T.Z.*, pp. 146–7, 269ff.

(Israel) The extant evidence, esp. for earlier period, is difficult to interpret, owing to policy of → Yahwism. Acc. to Yahwist doc. of Man in Gen. 2:19, death was complete dissolution, though the → Sheol-eschatology taught a form of *post-mortem* existence. However, many words and custom attest to an A.-C. The dead, or certain of them, were called → *elohim*, implying some kind of divinity (Is. 8:19b), or *rephaim*, an obscure term meaning a kind of daemonic being. The sepulchres of certain notable persons were clearly sanctuaries: e.g. those of Sarah (Gen. 13:18), Deborah (Gen. 35:8). The mysterious → *terāphim*, were prob. household gods linked with head of family (Gen. 31:19). The much-used expression of 'sleeping with his fathers' (e.g. I Kgs. 1:21) suggests that at burial a man joins his ancestors in the tomb. The statement in Mt. 27:52 that, at death of Jesus, 'many bodies of the saints who had fallen asleep' emerged from their tombs, doubtless witnesses to current belief that dead were still alive in some form in tomb. The custom of → Levirate marriage also suggests an A.-C. (→ Eschatology, Israel). S.G.F.B.

E.R.E., I, pp. 444b–50a, 457b–61a; W. O. E. Oesterley, *Immortality and the Unseen World* (1921), pp. 95ff.; J. Jeremias, *Heiligengräber in Jesu Umwelt* (1958); S. G. F. Brandon, *M.D.*, pp. 110ff.

(Mesopot.) There was no A.-C. among the Mesopot. peoples; but their eschatology required careful tendance of dead, which naturally devolved upon family concerned. As Tablet 12 of the Epic of → Gilgamesh shows, the wretched condition of dead could be somewhat alleviated by a regular supply of mortuary offerings. If offerings were not made, dead were reduced to living on filth, and so became vengeful and punished their neglectful relatives. (→ Eschatology, Mesopot.). S.G.F.B.

Brandon, *M.D.*, pp. 72ff. (bibliog.).

(Roman) The Romans called dead the *Di Manes*, 'good gods', but their divinity was of a nominal kind. At death a shadowy entity left the body, and, at burial, descended below ground and joined indistinct mass of dead. Its shade acquired individuality only on ritual occasions of revisiting its family. The dead had to be properly buried:

it was naturally family's duty to arrange the elaborate funerary rites, which incl. a sacrifice to Tellus (the 'earth'), and funeral banquet for the dead. Lack of proper burial meant ghost had no proper place in underworld, and would be vengeful towards living. In Rome the *mundus*, i.e. opening to underworld, was uncovered twice yearly for dead to return to earth. The *Lemuria* (Feb. 13–21), which ended with ritual expulsion of ghosts, was a primitive apotropaic rite, and may be cmp. with Grk. → Anthesteria, and Chr. → All souls Day. The *Parentalia* (May 9–13) was a festival of *parentes*, when families decorated graves of ancestors and made offerings. Roman mortuary customs were essentially connected with family. The concept of the → *genius* was epitomised in the *genius* of the *paterfamilias*, and families preserved masks of ancestors. It should also be noted that the *genius* of the Emperor, worshipped during life, was elevated to company of state-gods after death (→ Apotheosis) and assigned a cult and priesthood (→ Ruler Worship). Sepulchral monuments were, significantly, dedicated: *Dis Manibus Sacrum.* (→ Funerary Rites, Roman). S.G.F.B.

E.R.E., I, pp. 461–6; A. Grenier, *Les religions étrusque et romaine* (1948), pp. 117ff. 132; *The Roman Spirit* (E.T. 1926), pp. 37, 94ff.; *O.C.D.*, *s.v.* 'Genius', 'Manes'.

Anchorite; Anchoress Name derived from Grk. word 'to withdraw', and used to describe persons, male or female, who withdrew from society to devote themselves to solitary ascetic life of prayer. Although orig. covering both → coenobites and → hermits, A. came to mean one confined strictly to cell. In Middle Ages A.'s cell was sometimes attached to parish church, and A. was officially enclosed by bishop. S.G.F.B.

R. M. Clay, *Hermits and Anchorites of England* (1914); *D.C.C.*, *s.v.*

Andjty (or Anezti) Very ancient patron-deity of 9th nome of Lower Egypt (later Busiris), who became incorporated into → Osiris. A. is repr. on nome-standard as a schematic human fig., with attributes of royalty: these were adopted into iconography of Osiris. S.G.F.B.

A. Moret, *Le Nil et la civilisation égyptienne* (1926), pp. 91ff.; S. A. B. Mercer, *Religion of Anc. Egypt* (1949), pp. 109ff.; *R.Ae.R.-G.*, p. 38.

Andrewes, Lancelot (1555–1626) Bishop of Winchester, who played important part in English eccles. life and theological controversy during reigns of Elizabeth I and James I. A. was one of the translators of the Authorized Version of Bible, and was largely responsible for formation of distinctive Anglican theology (→ Church of England). His *Preces Privatae*, a collection of private devotions, have been much valued and used. S.G.F.B.

D.C.C., *s.v.; R.G.G.*³, I, 369.

Andrew, St. An → apostle of Jesus who, though not of 'the inner three', figures in several incidents (Jn. 1:35–42; Mt. 4:18–20; Mk. 13:3ff.). A late and unreliable trad. places his martyrdom at Patras, in Achaia, in 60. Trad. that he was crucified on a diagonal cross (X) appears only in 14th cent. Patron saint of Scotland since *c.* 750. S.G.F.B.

D.C.C., *s.v.*

(Acts of) Apocryphal work, dating prob. from 3rd cent., describing missionary journeys, miracles and martyrdom of St. A. Prob. of → Gnostic origin. Survives only in fragmentary form. S.G.F.B.

M. R. James, *The Apocryphal New Test.* (1924), pp. 337ff.; *D.C.C.*, *s.v.; R.G.G.*³, I, 368 ('Andreasakten').

Angel(s) *Ex.* Grk. word *angelos*, which in → LXX trans. Heb. *mal'akh*, meaning 'messenger'. Term denotes characteristic function of A.'s in Heb. and Ch. thought. But idea of supernatural messengers or servants of the gods or God occur in many religs.: e.g. anc. Mesopotamians conceived of giant winged genii as divine ministrants; the → Amesha Spentas of → Zoroastrianism were ministers of → Ahura Mazdah; → Zeus sends 'wind-footed, swift Iris' as messenger to men, and → Hermes acted as divine herald in Grk. mythology. In Heb. lit. a primitive concept. of A.'s finds expression in Gen. 6:1ff. as 'sons of God' (*beni ha-Elohim*). In → Job 1:6ff., the *beni ha-Elohim* appear as members of court of → Yahweh. In early Heb. trad. the 'Angel (*mal'akh*) of Yahweh' seems at first only an aspect of Yahweh (Ex. 3:2–4). Acc. to Is. 6:1ff. → Seraphim serve as A.'s. The → Cherubim were another type of A.; images of them adorned → Ark of Yahweh (Ex. 25:18ff.). After → Exile, Jew. angelology was greatly elaborated, prob. due both to foreign influence and increasing emphasis on transcendence of Yahweh: such mediators were necessary for his dealings with men. A.'s now acquire names, e.g. Gabriel, → Michael. A.'s were identified by → Philo with Grk. → daemons. There was much speculation about the angelic nature: acc. to Mk. 12:18ff., A.'s were regarded as sexless. A.'s were estimated to number 7 divisions, each under an archangel and comprising 496,000. Belief in A.'s finds abundant expression in N.T., and passed into Christianity. The idea of a revolt of A.'s occurs in Book of → Enoch, and in → Rev. (12:7–9), where rebel A.'s, under → Satan, are cast out of heaven. Chr. theologians speculated much about A.'s, drawing up elaborate hierarchy of angelic orders. The idea of personal guardian-A.'s appears in 2nd cent. CE; Pope Paul V (d. 1621) decreed a festival of Guardian A.'s, on Oct. 2nd. Chr. repr. of A.'s as winged human-forms derive from Roman art: cf. winged figures (Etruscan) in tomb of Volumni, Perugia, or the winged 'Victories'. (→→ Angels, Islam; Gabriel, Islam). S.G.F.B.

R.A.C., V, *s.v.* 'Engel' (53–322); *E.R.E.*, IV, pp. 578a, 584, 594a–601; *R.G.G.*[3], II, 465–9; S. G. F. Brandon, *Religion in Ancient History* (1969), chap. 24; C. D. C. Müller, *Die Engellehre der Koptischen Kirche* (1959).

(China-Japan) If by A. is meant a ministering spirit, a divine messenger, a spiritual being attendant upon a supreme deity, and ever-ready to do his bidding, A.'s are a constant theme in Chi. and Jap. mythology, folk-lore and Buddhist and Taoist religs. In the prevailing polytheism of the East they are classified as 'gods' (Chi. '*shên*'), who occupy subordinate and inferior positions in a spiritual hierarchy. They are in close and constant relationship with human world. The → bodhisattvas of Buddhism, the 'immortals' of Taoism, the glorified saints and heroes of pop. relig. are conceived of, not only as enjoying felicity in spiritual world, but as agents of a supreme Being (Buddha or Yü Huang) in bringing healing, succour, guidance, and meting out rewards and punishments to men, or guiding souls of men to their appropr. destiny and judgement in underworld.

The doc. of A.'s in →→ Zoroastrianism, Islam, Christianity and Manichaeism seems to have had considerable influence on Chi. relig. thought. Tombstones of the Yüan Dynasty (of → Nestorian, R.C., and poss. Manichaean provenance) have been discovered at Ch'üan-chou and other centres, depicting winged A.'s, bearded and dressed in Mongol style, flying to present gifts to the Cross. (See Wu Wên-liang, *Ch'üan-chou tsung-chiao shih-k'o*, Peking, 1957). D.H.S.

K. L. Reichelt, *Truth and Tradition in Chinese Buddhism* (1927); H. Maspero, 'The Mythology of modern China' and S. Eliseev, 'The Mythology of Japan' in J. Hackin (ed.), *Asiatic Mythology* (1932).

(Islam) (*Malā'ika*). The Qur. frequently mentions A. They have 2, 3 or 4 pairs of wings (xxxv: 1). They worship God (xvi: 51; xxxix: 75; xl: 7, etc.). Some record men's deeds (vi: 61; xliii: 80; lxxxii: 10); 1, 16 speaks of two, one on each side. In later writing the one on right records good deeds; the one on left evil. But since this verse follows a ref. to God's being nearer than the jugular vein, the commentator Baiḍāwī says God knows matters which may escape recording angels. A. pray God to pardon believers (xl: 7), or mankind (xlii: 3). They take the soul at death (vi: 93; viii: 52; xvi 30; xlvii: 29). These verses, against unbelievers, speak also of punishment by A. The A. will gather the righteous on Day of → Judgment with words of comfort (xxi: 103; cf. xiii: 24; xxxiii: 43). Some carry God's Throne (xl: 7). On Day of Judgment, 8 will carry it (lxix: 17). At last judgment, they will stand in rows with the *Rūḥ* (spirit) (lxxviii: 38; cf. lxxxix: 23). The Qur. mentions by name two archangels: Gabriel (ii: 91; lxvi: 4) and Michael (ii: 92). It mentions, without name, the angel of death (xxxii: 11), who in later lit. is called Izrā'īl. The last trump is to be blown by Isrāfīl (not mentioned in Qur.). The Qur. mentions Hārūt and Mārūt, said to have come to Babylon, who first warned people they were trying to mislead them, and taught demons to cause mischief (ii: 96). Mālik is the angel in charge of hell (xliii: 77). There are also said to be 19 A. in charge (lxxiv: 30f.), elsewhere (lxvi: 6) an unspecified number of huge and powerful A. Trad. says A. are made of light. Theologians have discussed relative rank of men and A. A. are considered superior to mankind in gen. but inferior to prophets. In exorcism A. with strange names are invoked. (→→ Adam; Examination in the tomb). J.R.

E.I., III, pp. 189–92; Wensinck, *Theology*, index; Sweetman, *I.C.T.*, I, II, IV, index; J. Macdonald, *Eschatology*, passim; Canaan, *Aberglaube*, pp. 6f., 11f.

Anger (Buddh.) In B. thought one of the three main morally unwholesome states, based on the mistaken notion of a 'self' within the individual. → *Dosa*. T.O.L.

Angkor → Cambodia, Hinduism in. T.O.L.

Anglican Communion The term has come into gen. use to designate a number of churches, professing principles of → Anglicanism, in communion with the primal see of Canterbury of → Ch. of England. The churches concerned are: Ch.s of Ireland and Wales, Episc. Ch. of Scotland, Prot. Episc. Ch. in U.S.A., Ch.s of Pakistan, India, Burma, Ceylon, Canada, W. Indies, Australia, New Zealand, S. Africa, W. Africa, the Nippon Sei Ko Kwai (Japan), and various missionary bishoprics. Although existence of many of these churches reflect past pattern of British Empire, the Ch. of England only has an official connection with Crown and Constitution of Great Britain. The A.-C. is in communion with various parts of → Eastern Orthodox Church. S.G.F.B.

D.C.C., s.v.; R.G.G.[3], I, 380–4.

Anglicanism The system of doctrine and practice professed by Churches of → Anglican Communion. A., which is a product of relig. hist. of England, repr. the *via media* between → R.C. Catholicism and Calvinist Protestantism (→→ Calvin; Reformation). It is claimed that doctrine and liturgical practice of A. are based jointly on testimony of Scripture and teaching of Church during first four centuries. A. lays essential emphasis on its claim to preserve → Apostolic

Succession, and hence on validity of its Orders of Bishop, Priest, and Deacon (→ Hierarchy, Christ.). S.G.F.B.

D.C.C., *s.v.* ('Anglican Ordinations', 'Anglicanism'); *R.G.G.*[3], I, 376–80; J. W. C. Wand, *Anglicanism in Hist. and Today* (1961).

Anglo-Catholicism Name given to movement in → Ch. of England which emphasises Catholic tradition of that Ch. in faith and practice. It stemmed from 19th cent. Oxford Movement for Church reform. S.G.F.B.

D.C.C., *s.v.; R.G.G.*[3], I, 384–5.

Angra Mainyu In Gâthic Avestan (→ Avesta) = 'Enemy Spirit'. In → *Gâthâs*, Zoroaster contrasts A.-M. with → Spenta Mainyu ('Holy Spirit'), the two repr. the two opposing principles of Good and Evil that ceaselessly struggle for mastery in universe. A.-M. seems to be equated with the Drūj, i.e. the 'Lie', in *Gâthâs* (→→ Ahriman; Dualism (Iranian); Zoroaster). S.G.F.B.

E.R.E., I, pp. 237–8 ('Ahriman'); J. H. Moulton, *Early Zoroastrianism* (1913), pp. 135ff.; Zaehner, *D.T.Z.*, *passim.*

Anguttara-Nikāya (Buddh.) One of the five nikayas or collections of *suttas*, or discourses which together make up the Buddh. Pali → *Sutta-Pitaka.* The *A.-N.* is so arranged that first section deals with topics which occur in 'ones'; the next section of topics which occur in pairs; the next, topics in trios; the next, in fours; and so on up to topics which form groups of eleven, there being eleven sections in all to the *A.-N.* These eleven sections comprise some 2,308 suttas, or separate discourses, or by another reckoning 2,344; by yet another, that of the book itself, it contains 9,557 suttas. There is a good deal of overlap with other sections of the Pali canon; for instance, the description of 8 kinds of assembly is found here in the 'eights' section; it occurs also in the *Mahāparinibbāna Sutta* of the → *Dīgha-Nikaya.* The scheme used in the *A.-N.*, of progressive numerical classification is one which in a later and more developed form is basis of the → Abhidhamma lit. T.O.L.

W. Geiger, *Pali literature and language* (1956); B. C. Law, *A History of Pali literature* (1933); F. L. Woodward and E. M. Hare (trs.), *The Book of the Gradual Sayings*, 5 vols. (1932–6, repr. 1953–65).

Anicca Buddh. doc. of the impermanence of all things; the first of the '3 characteristic marks of existence' (→ *ti-lakkhaṇa*). It is a feature of all mundane existence; it is empirically observable at the physical levels in human body, whose constituent elements are in constant flux, quite apart from the more obvious bodily impermanence observable in difference between infancy, childhood, youth, maturity and old age. Even more impermanent, however, in the Buddh. view, is cognisance, mind, or consciousness, which arises and ceases from moment to moment. (S. II:94–5). Whereas impermanence of physical things is readily observable empirically, impermanence of consciousness is not so readily discerned, until it is pointed out (i.e., in the course of Buddh. teaching). 'The characteristic of impermanence does not become apparent because, when rise and fall are not given attention, it is concealed by continuity. . . . However, when continuity is disrupted by discerning rise and fall, the characteristic of impermanence becomes apparent in its true nature.' (*Vism.* XXI:3). It is the notion of 'rise and fall', or coming into being followed by dissolution, which is at root of notion of impermanence. Body and mind are alike regarded as scenes of events, bodily or mental. Each moment of consciousness is regarded as being formed from cause and condition and as being unstable, and therefore immediately dissolving. The analogy of the sound of a lute is used: this does not come from any 'store' of sounds, nor does it go anywhere when it has ceased; rather, from not having been, it is brought into existence by the lute and the player's effort, and then, having been, it vanishes (S. IV:197). So with all material and mental events: they come to be, and having been, vanish.

This inevitable dissolution of whatever is brought into being, or *anicca*, provides subject matter for contemplation for Buddhists: *aniccānupassanā* or 'contemplation of impermanency' is one of three major ways in Buddh. meditation to achieve insight (→ *vipassanā*). The others are contemplation of → *dukkha*, and contemplation of → *anatta.* T.O.L.

Animals, Worship of Animals have naturally concerned men from earliest times. This concern has had many motives: fear, admiration, dependence on them for food. Palaeolithic cave-art indicates cults connected with A.'s; the picture of so-called Dancing Sorcerer (of the Trois Frères cave) may attest worship of a 'Lord of the Beasts', repr. as hybrid form of man and beast (→ Palaeolithic Religion). A bull-cult is attested at → Çatel Hüyük *c.* 7000 BC. In religs. of Anc. World, esp. → Egypt. Relig., there was much A.-W. It has found expression elsewhere, partic. in cults of primitive peoples (→ Totemism); it still has an important role in → Hinduism today. S.G.F.B.

E.R.E., I, pp. 483–535; *R.Ae.R.-G.*, pp. 812–24 ('Tiercult').

Animatism Theory advanced as modification of → animism, acc. to which primitive man must have conceived of a single animating force, diffused throughout universe, before he personified it in separate entities. Such a concept. seemed to be attested by idea of → mana. R. R. Marett used term 'supernaturalism' for this earlier conception.

It is not possible to establish either a pre-animistic or an animistic stage in hist. of religions. S.G.F.B.

R. R. Marett, *The Threshold of Religion* (1914); E. O. James, *Comparative Religion* (1938), pp. 27ff.; G. Vander Leeuw, *La religion* (1948), pp. 13ff.

Animism Theory about origin of relig. advanced by Sir E. B. Tylor. Acc. to Tylor's 'minimum definition', relig. is 'belief in Spiritual Beings'. He held that, from experience of sleep, dreams, ghosts and phenomenon of breathing, primitive man conceived of an *anima,* i.e. an immaterial animating principle that indwelt the body and left it at death. Such an *anima* was attributed to all entities that moved and appeared to live: hence rivers, trees, sun, moon, etc. were thought to possess *animae.* Since many such entities were immensely powerful and impressive, man began to worship them, the degree of his veneration corresponding to the measure of his fear, respect, or need of them. A. became a popular designation for so-called 'primitive religion'. S.G.F.B.

E. B. Tylor, *Primitive Culture,* 2 vols. (1871); *E.R.E., s.v.* ('Animism'); L. H. Jordan, *Comparative Religion* (1905), pp. 259ff.; *R.G.G.*³, I, 389–91; G. Van der Leeuw, *La religion* (1948), pp. 75ff.

Ankh (Also called the *crux ansata*). Anc. Egypt. symbol of life; having form of cross, with a loop-shaped top, origin of the A. is unknown. Deities are repr. holding A. or holding it to mouth and nostrils of devotees, thus imparting life. The rays of the → Aten end in hands holding A., and the resurrected deceased in → *Book of the Dead* holds A. in each hand. The A. appears in Chr. Coptic art (→ Coptic Church). S.G.F.B.

R.Ae.R.-G., pp. 418–20 ('Lebensschleife'); M. Cramer, *Das altägyptische Lebenszeichen* (1955).

Annam → Vietnam. D.H.S.

Anna Perenna Roman goddess of obscure origin. Her festival on 15 March was occasion of merry-making. She has been explained as a year-goddess or an Etruscan form of → Ceres. A.P. had no mythology. S.G.F.B.

O.C.D., s.v.; Kleine Pauly, I, 357–8.

Anne, St. Mother of → Virgin Mary. No mention is made of her in Bible; her legend is given in 2nd cent. *Protoevangelium of James.* A church was dedicated to her in Constantinople by Emp. Justinian I (d. 566). The cult of A. became very popular in Middle Ages, and she is frequently repr. in art; but was condemned by the Reformers. Her feast day is kept in both R.C. and Eastern Churches. S.G.F.B.

D.C.C., s.v.

Annihilation (Buddh.) Term sometimes mistakenly used in West in connection with the Buddh. *Nirvāṇa.* The Buddha expressly rejected notion of 'annihilationism' (*uccheda-ditthi*) as a false or misleading idea, since its use presupposes existence of an individual entity which can be annihilated; a supposition which is contrary to the basic. Buddh. tenet of → *anatta.* (→→ Nibbāna; Uccheda-Vāda). T.O.L.

Anno Domini Lat. = 'in the year of the Lord'. A system of dating devised by Dionysius Exiguus (d. 550), based upon a reckoning of year of Christ's birth that is now known to be at least 4 years too late. The system, although orig. having definite Chr. theological significance, has now been gen. adopted throughout world (→ Chronology). S.G.F.B.

D.C.C., s.v.; R.A.C., III, 58–9; S. G. F. Brandon, *History, Time and Deity* (1965), pp. 149ff.

Anointing Relig. use of oils and unguents has been widespread throughout mankind. Many substances have been used, incl. blood and saliva; the A. material was often perfumed. The motives behind practice are complex: a division can be drawn between cosmetic and sacral use of A. It would seem that A. of statues of gods in anc. Egypt was part of a courtly ritual, and thus primarily cosmetic. The sacral use is very diverse; but essential purpose seems to be that imparting, by A., some supernatural or spiritual virtue. A. is used at great crises of life: e.g. birth, initiation (incl. Chr. → baptism), consecration to special office (priests, kings), death (Cath. rite of Extreme → Unction). The act of A. is often accompanied by recitation of some formula, indic. its purpose. The classic instance of A. conferring a charismatic character is Heb. idea of the → Messiah (Christos) = 'Anointed' One. S.G.F.B.

E.R.E., I, pp. 549–57; *D.C.C., s.v.; R.G.G.*³, V, 1330–4 ('Salbung'); E. Kutsch, *Salbungals Rechtsakt im alten Israel u. im alten Orient* (1963).

Anquetil de Perron, Abraham Hyacinth (1731–1805) French philologist who brought first mss. of the → Avesta to Europe, and translated them. In 1801 he produced a Latin trans. of some → Upanishads, the reading of which greatly impressed → Schopenhauer. S.G.F.B.

J. Duchesne-Guillemin, *The Western Response to Zoroaster* (1958), pp. 14ff.

Anselm, St. (*c.* 1033–1109) Native of Aosta, Italy, A. became Archbp. of Canterbury, and played an important part in controversy between Church and State. His chief fame lies in his work as theologian and philosopher in the Platonic trad. A. propounded the Ontological Argument for existence of God. His *Cur Deus Homo?* repr. a landmark in theology of → Atonement. A. interpreted the Atonement in terms of satisfaction due to outraged majesty of God by human sin, and repudiated trad. interpretation of Devil's rights over fallen man. S.G.F.B.

E.R.E., I, *s.v.; D.C.C.*, *s.v.; R.G.G.*³, I, 397–9; G. Leff, *Medieval Thought* (1958), pp. 98ff.; M. J. Charlesworth, *St. Anselm's Proslogion* (1965); J. McIntyre, *St. Anselm and his Critics* (1954).

Ante-diluvian 'Before the Flood'. The Sumerian King-List. is divided by → Flood into two parts: a primaeval age of 241,000 years that ran from 'when kingship was lowered from heaven' to the Flood; a post-diluvian age, commencing 'After the Flood had swept over (the earth), . . . when kingship was lowered (again) from heaven . . .'. Heb. tradition knew a similar A. and post-diluvian chronology (Gen. 6:11ff.). S.G.F.B.

A.N.E.T., p. 265; R. C. Dentan (ed.), *The Idea of History in Anc. Near East* (1955), pp. 50ff.; Brandon, *C.L.*, pp. 142ff.

Anthesteria Spring festival of flowers held at Athens on 12th Anthesterion. It had two parts: 1st day devoted to → Dionysos, who was thanked for new wine; 2nd day pots of food were put out for dead → (*kēres*), who were solemnly dismissed at end (→ Ancestor Cults, Greek). S.G.F.B.

E. Rohde, *Psyche*, I (1898), pp. 236–9; Harrison, *Prolegomena*, pp. 32–55; *Kleine Pauly*, I, 372–4.

Anthropology Although Anthropology has had a relatively short history as an academic discipline, its roots may be traced back to the Enlightenment and beyond. A., as now understood is, however, a development of the late 19th and early 20th cents., during which period it has passed through a series of well-defined phases. Its methodology and, to some extent, terminology have also varied from country to country, making a broad general account difficult. Thus what is known in the English-speaking world as 'physical A.' is often ref. to on Continent as A. pure and simple; the British term 'social A.' is known in America as 'cultural A.'; terms such as ethnology and sociology are frequently taken to ref. to substantially same area of study as A.

Orig., A. denoted simply and lit. 'the science of man'; its first flowering at end of last cent. reflected this universal perspective. Subsequent refinement of methodology, and the increasing volume of material requiring treatment, led to division of field into e.g. physical A., cultural/social A., economic A., etc. Here, following British terminological usage, we shall confine our account to the development of *social A.* as it bears upon the study of → Comp. Relig. Social A. has been defined by Evans-Pritchard as 'a branch of sociological studies, that branch which devotes itself to primitive societies'. Hence in its relig. application it has to do primarily (but not exclusively) with the religs. of pre-literate peoples, i.e. with those rites, beliefs, actions, behaviour patterns which, in so-called primitive societies, have to do with what is regarded as being the sacred and the supernatural.

We may also note, by way of preliminary observation, that the term A. is occasionally used by students of Comp. Relig. and others to denote the comparative or phenomenological study of beliefs and practices rel. to nature and destiny of man (See e.g. C. F. Bleeker (ed.), *Anthropologie religieuse* (1955)). While it may be allowed that study of this type may well touch upon field of A. proper, it is not normally regarded by anthropologists as being a legitimate branch of their own discipline, being concerned largely with the conceptual analysis of bodies of trad. relig. material. The use of term A. in this connection reflects, however, something of the uncertainty as to frames of ref. which has always attended A.

In its first phase, A. was thought of in the West as being 'the science of man *in evolution*', and therefore as a hist. discipline. The chapter-headings in an early text-book of A. (Marett, 1911) were: Antiquity of Man, Race, Environment, Language, Social Organization, Law, Religion, Morality and Man the Individual. Of course, studies of man, his physical characteristics, social organization, religion, etc., had been carried on for generations. But all were more or less haphazard for want of a suitable principle of classification. In the task of assembling material, the Germans were far ahead of other scholars: the work of C. Meiners, G. Clemm (*Allgemeine Cultur-Geschichte*, 1843) and T. Waitz (*Anthropologie der Naturvölker*, 1858–1871) should be mentioned. But two theories in partic. helped to place anthropological studies gen. on a new, systematic footing. The first of these was the 'three-age' system for classifying prehistory, introd. by the Danes Thomsen and Worsaae. The second was the Darwinian theory of evolution, not least as popularized by Spencer and Huxley, which brought whole of human experience within scope of a single law: 'From the standpoint of evolution, the entire organic world, not excluding man, reveals a unity, a harmony, and a grandeur never before disclosed under any system of speculative philosophy (*E.R.E.*, I, p. 572b). R. R. Marett was thus able to write in 1911 that 'A. is the whole history of man as fired and pervaded by the idea of evolution . . . A. is the child of Darwin. Darwinism makes it possible. Reject the Darwinian point of view, and you must reject A. also'. (*Anthropology*, p. 8).

If evolutionism provided first theoretical framework of A., its material came on one hand from prehistoric archaeology, and on other from the growing body of facts and opinions collected among the 'primitive' races of mankind. The study of prehistory, although fascinating in itself, left large gaps in anthropologist's knowledge of early technology; on subject of early supernaturalism and relig. it could say very little. The problem was solved by theory of 'survivals'—by making an equation between the primeval savage and modern 'primitive' peoples, and by using information derived from latter to illustrate life and beliefs of former. It became (and has to a great extent remained) axiomatic that e.g. → Australian Aborigines provide a living example of Stone Age culture.

For more than a generation, the anthropological problem *par excellence* was problem of origins—the → origins of relig. not excepted. This crystallised into a double concern. First, an interest in physical origins of *homo sapiens*, and his evolution from ape-like 'ancestors'. And, secondly, concern for details of primitive culture, within which relig. was at once seen to play a vital role.

At time of emergence of A. as an academic discipline in Europe, the most widely-held theory of origins of relig. was that of the philological school of Max Müller—that relig. had orig. in a primeval *sensus numinis*, and mythology in a 'disease of language'. Against this theory, a group of British anthropologists (soon becoming known as the 'Anthropological School') advanced evidence to show that this could not poss. be the case, not least since Müller's work had been done entirely on basis of Indo-European languages. E. B. Tylor (1832–1917), father of British A., first put forward his theory of → animism in 1866, though its best-known statement is to be found in his book *Primitive Culture* (1871); he became Reader in Anthropology at Oxford in 1884. His successor at Oxford, R. R. Marett (1866–1943), went a step further with his theory of → animatism or pre-animism (*The Threshold of Religion*, 1909) (→ Mana). At Cambridge, J. G. → Frazer (1854–1941), in successive volumes and editions of his monumental work *The Golden Bough*, brought forward an overwhelming mass of evidence in support of thesis that an age of magic had preceded an age of relig., and that latter had developed out of former. The 'amateur' of the company, the ubiquitous Scotsman Andrew Lang (1844–1912), having been largely responsible for discrediting the philological speculations of Max Müller (see his art. 'Mythology', in *E.B.*, 9th ed., 1884), later subjected Tylor's animistic theories to critical scrutiny in his book *The Making of Religion* (1898). His counter-theory of primeval → high gods, though virtually ignored during own lifetime, was eventually to prove of more than lasting significance once it had been taken up by the Austrian Wilhelm Schmidt (1877–1934). Lang was also deeply interested in subject of → folklore, which he defined as 'the study of survivals'. In this area he was able transmit to English-speaking world many of the concerns of the German pioneers, the brothers Grimm, Mannhardt and others. Among other British anthropologists of period, who were interested in problems of relig., may be mentioned W. Robertson Smith, Sidney Hartland and J. F. McLennan.

The British 'Anthropological School' suffered, however, from a number of unavoidable deficiences. Although their intellectual honesty would not be called in question, in spirit of late 19th cent. they treated relig. solely from the individual point of view. Primitive man, partic. in his relig. life, they regarded as a rudimentary rationalist. Hence they were unable to take adequate account of either the collective or the irrational in experience of primitive man. More seriously, they were forced for most part to make use of second-hand material, none having had any extended experience of field-work.

The first two decades of 20th cent. saw breakdown of A. as orig. conceived into the component parts already mentioned. The study of prehistoric man became a discipline in itself, a department of archaeology. Other areas of study, first regarded as merely contributing to overall hist. of evolution of man, had perforce to secede and subdivide—a process which has gone on unchecked down to present day. At same time, a revolution in thought was also taking place, as the optimistic generalizations of evolutionists were replaced by more narrowly defined and detailed descriptive accounts. For sake of completeness we must here mention the 'Diffusionist School', anti-evolutionists who regarded similarities in relig. as having been produced either by migration or diffusion from centres of culture. The *Kulturkreislehre* of Austrians Gräbner and Fr. Schmidt, and the 'Pan-Egyptian' theories of Englishmen Elliott Smith and Perry, are no longer taken seriously. In case of Fr. Schmidt we must, however, draw distinction between his work on subject of primeval high gods (which is still worthy of study) and his theory of 'culture-circles' (which is not). Broadly speaking, though, the trend of period immediately following World War I was in direction of the inductive, as opposed to deductive method, and a turning away from pure theorizing (whether about relig. origins or anything else) to a pure and dispassionate analysis of functions, incl. relig. functions in primitive society.

Some formative influences in this reorientation may be mentioned briefly. First, on theoretical level, the work of the French school of sociologists, Durkheim, Hubert, Mauss and others, provided necessary counterbalance to individualism of British anthropologists. Drawing on

Australian Aborigines for material, Durkheim stressed role of social unit as formative element in relig. (→ totemism); relig. he regarded as virtually an apotheosis of society. Few anthropologists since his time have been able entirely to ignore this perspective. Secondly must be mentioned the work of psychologist Sigmund → Freud. Concerned in his own way with origins of relig., Freud impelled a whole generation of anthropologists to seek elsewhere than in customary places for their material. Malinowski in partic. (see below) owed much to Freud's theories.

But the most import. new departure was recognition that the day of the semi-amateur, dilettante, armchair anthropologist was over. In recent years it has been fashionable to decry work of such men as Tylor and Frazer on ground that they had no first-hand experience of the primitives they were describing in such detail. This is hardly fair. Frazer in partic. went to great lengths to gather material from reputable and accurate sources. But a new generation arose, in which three concerns were stressed: (1) it was necessary to break decisively with work of Victorian intellectuals (2) it was necessary to gain first-hand experience of primitives at all costs (3) it was necessary to abandon customary concentration on beliefs, and turn instead to what could be observed and recorded, to rites and rituals. It might be argued that none of these was really a new concern: all may be observed, however embryonically, in work of earlier anthropologists. But together they constituted a revolution in A.

In America, the Indian tribes, though fast diminishing, provided anthropologists with a convenient object of study and field-work. Pioneers in Indian studies, from mid-19th cent. on, incl. such men as H. R. Schoolcraft and J. W. Powell, while the Smithsonian Museum in Washington D.C. became responsible for publication of much material. Among fathers of Amer. A. two names in partic. are deserving of mention. Lewis H. Morgan (1818–1881) worked among the Iroquois, and not unnaturally concentrated on such problems as → totemism and kinship; his book *Ancient Society* (1877) gained unexpected fame as one of sources of economic theories of → Marx and Engels. Of incomparably greater importance was work of Franz Boas (1858–1942). Boas was trained in Germany, being one of first anthropologists of any nation to combine thorough scientific training and complete familiarity with all theoretical aspects of discipline with capacity for painstaking field-work—in this case largely among Indian tribes of North-West. He was also responsible for training virtually a whole generation of anthropologists: a list of Boas' pupils would incl. practically all best-known names of older generation of Amer. anthropologists, incl. Spier, Lowie, Goldenweiser and Radin, Ruth Benedict and Margaret Mead. Boas recognised that apparent lack of rationality in primitive cultures was less a defect than a fundamentally different way of making associations and explaining concepts. On relations between → myth and ritual, he held that ritual is the primary factor: myth serves merely to sanction performance of ritual. On subject of totemism, while recognizing its importance, he refused to generalise unduly, regarding the phenomenon as neither so simple nor so unified as many before him had supposed. This was characteristic of all Boas' work. He was not a theorist. To him, the empirical approach was all-important; the actual nature of material must not be allowed to be distorted or forced to fit *a priori* theory. He did not found a school of A. in strict sense, but few Amer. anthrs. would fail to acknowledge their debt to him partic. in area of method.

Following Boas, the subject of totemism continued to exercise minds of Amer. scholars, import. studies being publ. by Goldenweiser and Lowie. Lowie and Radin also publ. comprehensive works on primitive relig. But tendency was in direction of more specialized monographs dealing with specific areas of primitive culture, partic. of N. Amer. Indians. Characteristic of Amer. approach has remained an openness to significance of history—a feature which became less marked in Europe after World War I.

In U.K., the development of A. in 20th cent. is bound up above all with names of A. R. Radcliffe-Brown (1881–1945) and Bronislaw Malinowski (1884–1942).

Radcliffe-Brown was disciple of Durkheim. He had done field-work in the Andaman Is., Australia and S. Africa. His theories are characterized as 'structural functionalism', and based on analysis of the three terms 'structure', 'process' and 'function' in primitive society. Every feature of social life, incl. relig., has a function in society; the task of A. is to discover interrelations of separate functions within overall structure of society. Relig., he claimed, serves to bind society together by stressing non-rational cohesive elements, and by perpetuating those elements by way of trad. While Radcliffe-Brown was thus concerned with the function of, e.g., a certain custom within social structure and needs of society, Malinowski was more interested in function of that same custom in respect of culture—'a specifically human form of biological adjustment'—and human needs. He and Radcliffe-Brown together are thus regarded as founders in Britain of 'functionalist school' of A. Malinowski's method has been described as 'total immersion', in this case the fullest poss. identification with members of the Melanesian society within which he worked (although it seems from posthumously publ. papers that he had little fellow-feeling with the Melanesians). No feature of their daily life was too trivial to record. Although not concerned with relig. in any exclusive sense, he drew working distinction between relig. and → magic: magic being a technique intended as complement to practical knowledge and compensation for practical inadequacy; relig. being an end in itself, expressed in rituals carried out in times of emotional stress. It is in this area that influence of Freud is to be seen, though this element should not be overemphasized.

Neither Radcliffe-Brown nor Malinowski was concerned with history. To them, as to majority of social anthrs. since, the empirical method is only satisfactory approach. A. is a process of measurement, observation and recording; the anthr. must collect all that can be collected having any bearing on activities and institutions of a given people at a given time. He must then describe what has been collected, leaving all speculation aside. The positive gains of this approach have been enormous. What has been called the 'Malinowskian cult of field-work' has provided scholars with a vast assembly of monographs and articles describing individual societies, compiled with care and accuracy. On negative side, it has been objected that general and comparative studies have tended to be neglected as result—although there are certain prominent exceptions, e.g. work of Lévi-Strauss on interpretation of myths (a subject we cannot go into here).

It is not easy to summarize present state of A. studies and methods in their bearing on Comp. Relig. While it is clear, on one hand, that we have more material at our disposal than ever before, it is equally clear, on the other, that very few anthrs. are prepared to do more than describe a narrow segment of their chosen field. There is no longer any synoptic vision such as was once provided by the evolutionary comparative method. A leading British anthr., E. E. Evans-Pritchard, sums up situation in these words: 'Instead of attempting to paint on a grand scale the development of the notion of responsibility, or the development of the state, in the whole human race, the anthropologist of today concentrates on such small problems as can be investigated by direct inquiry and observation, such as the function of the feud, or the position of chieftainship of a certain kind, in societies where social activities centred around these institutions can be seen and studied. . . . The view-point in social anthropology today may be summed up by saying that we now think we can learn more about the nature of human society by really intensive and observational studies, conducted in a series of a few selected societies with the aim of solving limited problems, than be attempting generalizations on a wider scale from literature.' (*Social Anthropology*, 1951, pp. 91f.). The relevance of this summary statement for the study of relig., partic. in pre-literate societies, will be evident. Indeed, many of the underlying methodological assumptions of this statement are already widely accepted by students of relig. phenomena, though most would wish to accord history greater significance than is here implied.

Finally a recent survey of trends in A. of period 1930–60 indic. the following present-day lines of inquiry: (1) interest in societies undergoing rapid change. (2) application of anthr. methods to study of relig. in complex and literate societies. (3) analysis of symbolism in relig. and myth. (4) Attempts to develop new and more precise methods for study of relig. and myth. (5) application of new fields in A. to study of relig. phenomena: ethnomedicine and ethnolinguistics are mentioned; ethnomusicology might be added. None of these diverse aims can fail to be of significance for the student of relig. E.J.S.

The literature is vast, and growing. Most early gen. works now have little more than hist. interest; see e.g. *E.R.E.*, I, pp. 561a–73a; E. B. Tylor, *Anthropology* (1881); R. R. Marett, *Anthropology* (1911). A useful compendium of extracts is W. A. Lessa and E. Z. Vogt (eds.), *Reader in Comparative Religion: An Anthropological Approach*² (1965). Other gen. works incl. (alphabetical order): F. Boas, *Primitive Art* (1927), *Race, Language and Culture* (1940); R. Benedict, *Patterns of Culture* (1934); E. E. Evans-Pritchard, *Social Anthropology* (1951), *Theories of Primitive Religion* (1965); R. Firth (ed.), *Man and Culture* (1957) (an appraisal of work of Malinowski); A. Goldenweiser, *Anthropology* (1942); I. C. Jarvie, *The Revolution in Anthropology* (1964); R. H. Lowie, *An Intro. to Cultural Anthropology* (1934), *The History of Ethnological Theory* (1937); B. Malinowski, *Magic, Science and Religion* (1925); D. F. Pocock, *Social Anthropology* (1961); A. R. Radcliff-Brown, *Structure and Function in Primitive Society* (1952); S. Tax and others (eds.), *An Appraisal of Anthropology Today* (1953); A. de Waal Malefijt, *Religion and Culture* (1968).

Anthropomorphism Grk. philosopher Xenophanes (*c.* 545 BC) perceived fallacy of making God in man's image. He observed that if animals could draw or carve, they would repr. gods after their own form. A. in relig. inevitably follows from fact that man can conceive of deity only in terms of his own mental categories. A. is more obvious in some relig. than others (e.g. Grk. and Roman relig.). It finds frequent expression in the higher religs. (e.g. Hebr. relig., Christianity, Islam); but theologians have been aware of fact and guarded against its grosser forms. A. has been definitely encouraged in some religs.: Grk. art sought to express divinity in perfect human form, and the doc. of Christ's → Incarnation meant presentation of deity in human form: (→ Ikon). Hindu art, while anthropomorphic, has sought to portray divine attributes by adding extra arms. S.G.F.B.

E.R.E., I, *s.v.; R.A.C.*, I, 446–50; G. Van der Leeuw, *La Religion* (1948), pp. 171ff., 441ff.; H. Zimmer, *Myths and Symbols in Indian Art and Civilization* (1946), *passim.*

Anthroposophy Religio-philosophical system, composed by R. Steiner (1861–1925), from many elements, incl. neo-Indian theosophy, →→ reincarnation, occultism (symbolism of colours), astralism. As name indicates, attention is centred on man, not God. A. has adherents in Germany, America and Britain, and sponsors of a specific form of education. S.G.F.B.

*R.G.G.*³, I, 425–31; *D.C.C.*, *s.v.* and p. 1289 (Steiner, R.).

Antichrist From 2nd cent. BC belief appears in Jew. lit. that a powerful being would oppose God in the last days (Dan. 7:8ff., 11:40). The belief doubtless reflects dualistic tendency current in Judaism at this time (→ Dualism). There were many variations of belief. This enemy might be → Satan or → Belial (*Ass. Moses* 10:1; *Test. Levi* 18:12). The Qumran sectaries (→ Qumran) believed that Belial would lead the Sons of Darkness against Sons of Light (Y. Yadin, *The Scroll of the War of the Sons of Light against the Sons of Darkness* (1962), pp. 232ff.). The enemy might be human: poss. Caligula, who threatened to desecrate the → Temple in 39–40 CE or a Hero *redivivus*, were cast for role. Since Jews looked forward to coming of the → Messiah ('Christ'), this opponent, whether human or daemonic, became an Antichrist. The belief in A. finds expression in the N.T. (e.g. Mk. 13:14; II Thess. 2:3ff.; I Jn. 2:18ff.; Rev. 17:8), where the A. seems to be either Caligula, Titus, or Nero. Belief in A. became established in Christianity, flourishing esp. in times of trouble, when various enemies were identified as A. (e.g. Arius (→ Arianism), → Muhammad, Emp. Frederich II, the → Papacy). (→ Chilarism). S.G.F.B.

E.R.E., I, *s.v.*, *R.G.G.*³, I, 431–6; *R.A.C.*, I, 450–7.

Antinomianism Term of abuse, deriving from charge made by → Paul's opponents that his emphasis upon grace as opposed to the Mosaic Law led to licentiousness. It was subsequently used to describe teaching of many → Gnostic sects, and, later that of the → Anabaptists. S.G.F.B.

E.R.E., I, *s.v.*

Antioch Capital of Syria, founded in 300 BC by Seleucus I. It became the third city of the Roman Empire, and an important centre of Hellenistic culture: the temple of → Apollo in nearby Daphne was world-famous. A. had large Jew. pop., and for this reason perhaps attracted early Chr. missionaries. The name of 'Christian' was first used in A. (Acts 11:26). The Antiochene Church was one of the most important centres of theological thought during early period (→→ Antiochene Theology; Ignatius; Nestorius). S.G.F.B.

O.C.D., *s.v.*, *R.A.C.*, I, 461–9; *D.C.C.*, *s.v.; R.G.G.*³, I, 452–4; G. Downey, *Hist. of Antioch in Syria from Seleucus to Arab Conquest* (1961); A.-J. Festugière, *Antioch païenne et chrétrenne* (1959).

Antiochene Theology The theology of Church of Antioch in Patristic period was sometimes complementary and sometimes opposed to that of Church of Alexandria (→ Alexandrian Theology). It embodied a Syrian-Hebraic trad. of study, and theological reflection with emphasis on the historical and on process of revelation. The Alex. Church had a metaphysical approach, derived from Grk. sources, and stressed upshot of revelation in theological conviction. The trad. of A.-thinking is to be found in both heretics and orthodox alike—in Paul of Samosata and Marcellus of Ancyra as well as Theodore of Mopsuestia and John → Chrysostom. In interpret. of Bible they followed an exegetical-critical line as opposed to allegorical-mystical one. The allegorical interpet. was, they believed, illegitimate. Where the spiritual message was not clear, the key was through insight (*theoria*). For this the literal sense must be kept; there must be real correspondence between spiritual truths seen, and historical fact, and the two must be grasped as unity. The chief names here are Diodore of Tarsus (*c.* 330–*c.* 390), Theodore of Mopsuestia (*c.* 350–*c.* 428), and Theodoret (*c.* 393–*c.* 460), though the A.-method in its practical working is clearly seen in sermons of St. John Chrysostom (347–407). Chrysostom is remarkable for seeing the spiritual meaning of an author, and his ability to find immediate practical application of what he has seen. This is the more striking because he turns away from allegorical to liberal exegesis, to find the spiritual meaning. The A.-approach affected whole attitude to theology; but it is in → Christology that the A.-theologians specially made their mark. Here essentially they stood for a Word-Man Christology, in which the Word (→ Logos) was united with a whole human nature as against a Word-

Flesh Christology, in which the term 'flesh' was either undefined, or indic. a truncated humanity. The tendency of the A.- school was to incline towards belief in a loose union of the divine and human natures in Christ; and this looseness appeared to their opponents to be even greater than it actually was because of certain technical ambiguities.

Paul of Samosata (bp. of Antioch *c.* 260–*c.* 270) undoubtedly belonged to A.-school. It is unfortunate that we have none of his own works by which to judge his standpoint; we know him only by the comments of his opponents. His chief interest was in Christology; in this apparently he taught that Christ differed only in degree from the prophets. Marcellus of Ancrya (d. *c.* 274) was early linked with Paul of S.; but his main interest was in the → Trinity. He denied that the Logos was generated by God. Before all ages the Logos was in God as his immanent reason identical with him. The kingdom of Christ would come to an end—this was repudiated at the Council of Constantinople (381)—but the Logos was eternal. Diodore of Tarsus (d. *c.* 390) was the pioneer of developed A.-Christology. He was named in 381 by Theodosius I as one of the bishops, with whom communion was a test of orthodoxy. His teaching shows a process of transition. He started from and remained influenced by Word-Flesh presuppositions; but he attacked the Monophysite tendency of → Apollinarianism, and so was led to distinguish the Son of God and son of David. In contrast with the prophets, the son of David was completely filled with glory and wisdom of God. Theodore of Mopsuestia (*c.* 350–*c.* 428), the great teacher of A.-theology, was a notable Biblical scholar. He made his opposition to the Apollinarian mutilation of Christ's humanity his starting point. He insisted that the Word took not only a body, but a complete man composed of a body and an immortal soul. The Lord's created soul was the principle of life and activity in him, and so of the bringing about of man's Redemption. His solution of problem of nature of union of the Word and humanity was that it was a permanent union *kat'eudokian*, i.e. by favour or grace. (The Alex. alternative was *kat'ousian:* the one does full justice to the humanity, but finds it difficult to do justice to the godhead; the other does full justice to the godhead, but finds it difficult to do full justice to the humanity). The upshot of his teaching is that the perfect conjunction of two natures have brought about one *prosōpon*, a single person; but he has clearly not thought through the nature of the conjunction nor the implications of their being one *prosōpon*. The *enfant terrible* of A.-theology was → Nestorius, bp. of Constantinople (428–49). He was a careful scholar but a tactless and politically naive patriarch. He alienated popular sympathy by condemning out of hand the expression *theotokos*, 'Mother of God'. He also alienated the unscrupulous, but politically skilled, → Cyril, patriarch of Alexandria (412–44). The two men misunderstood one another. Cyril thought that Nestorius held that there were two persons artificially linked together; whereas Nestorius thought that Cyril mixed up the two natures together. Nestorius himself insisted that the two natures in the Incarnate Christ remained unaltered and distinct in the union. The way in which they were one in the Person of Christ—and he firmly held that they were one—was a question on which he had not thought through to a clear position. But it is clear now that he did not himself hold the heresy of Nestorianism that there were two separate Persons in the Incarnate Christ—the one, Divine, and the other, human. In the upshot Nestorius was condemned; and the moderate Antiochenes, led by Theodoret (*c.* 393–*c.* 458), and Cyril of Alex. came to a crucial agreement known as the *Symbol of Union*, 432: 'We confess, therefore, our Lord Jesus Christ, the only begotten Son of God, perfect God and perfect man composed of a rational soul and a body, begotten before the ages from his Father in respect of his divinity, but likewise in these last days for us and our salvation from the Virgin Mary in respect of his manhood, consubstantial with the Father in respect of his divinity and at the same time consubstantial with us in respect of his manhood, for a union of two natures has been accomplished. Hence we confess one Christ, one Son, one Lord.' This was the basis for the Chalcedonian Statement of Faith (451), which was the high water mark of influence of A.-theology in the General Councils of Church. Here, though the Alex. position was victorious, it was victorious only after taking into itself and being modified by the fundamental truths contained in the A.-position. Thereafter, though in the East the → Monophysite position was officially condemned, it was widely influential; while in West, the full implications of Chalcedon were not realised, and a more Alex. interpretation, minimising the human nature of Christ, became widely prevalent. On the other side, the Nestorian churches have survived in Iran to perpetuate the condemned extreme development of the A.-thinking. Later developments in history of Chr. theology have an analogy to the A.-trad. One of these is to be found in → Reformation theology. The Reformers turned away from the multiple senses of Scripture to concentrate on its literal hist. meaning. → Calvin, in partic., is noted for the careful accuracy of hist. perception. Another analogy is to be found in development in 19th cent. of historical-critical Biblical study with all the resources of scientific scholarship. One aspect of this is the understanding of Scriptures against their Semitic background. Both developments are links with the Antiochenes. In fact, analogies to both A. and Alex. approaches can be discerned in contemporary discussion of Biblical interpretation and theological construction. H.C.J.

J. N. B. Kelly, *Early Christian Doctrines* (1958); R. V. Sellars, *Two Ancient Christologies* (1940); A. R. Vine, *The Nestorian Churches* (1937); Alfred Adam, *Lehrbuch der Dogmengeschichte*, I, (1965).

Antipas Herod Herod Antipas (→ Herodian Dynasty). S.G.F.B.

Antisemitism An attitude of hostility towards Jews can be traced back as far as 3rd cent. BC, in the writings of Manetho, an Egypt. priest. Apion, an Alexandrian grammarian (1st cent. CE) wrote against the Jews, and was answered by → Josephus in his *Contra Apionem.* Lat. writers (Tacitus, Horace, Juvenal and Martial) show A. Main grounds of complaint at this period were hatred of mankind (because of Jew. social exclusiveness), and → atheism (Jew. refusal to worship pagan gods). The fanaticism of the → Zealots during Jew. War against Rome (CE 66–73), and the later revolt under → Bar Cochba caused further A. A. took on a new character with rise of Christianity. Some N.T. writings (e.g. →→ Mk.; Jn.; Acts) are strongly antisemitic. But cause of this A. is Jew. rejection of → Jesus as → Messiah. The Gos. of → Mt. inadvertently provided apparent justification for future Chr. A. by making Jews accept responsibility for death of Christ (Mt. 27:24ff.). Regarded as murderers of Christ, in medieval Christendom Jews were a depressed class and ever subject to persecution. Their exclusion from the professions drove them into trade and commerce, in which they gen. prospered, thus providing further cause for hatred. Massacres of Jews occurred in many European lands, esp. during time of → Crusades; they were often victims of the → Inquisition. Scandalous tales were told of their impious practices, incl. ritual murder of Chr. children. The growth of relig. toleration and secularism helped the Jews. The French Revolution first gave them equal rights in France; their civil disabilities were grad. withdrawn in other countries. Modern A., which began to emerge in Germany towards end of 19th century, was inspired by racial and economic motives; it reached its most terrible form during the Nazi régime, which was pledged to extermination of the Jews. Chr. reaction against A. found significant expression in decree of → Vatican Council (1965–6), formally exonerating Jews from guilt of crucifying Christ. A. still finds expression in Europe and elsewhere. Arab hostility of Jews cannot rightly be designated A.; it stems from estab. of State of Israel in Palestine in 1948. The continuing currency of the so-called 'Protocols of the Elders of Zion' is significant in this connection. S.G.F.B.

E.R.E., I, *s.v.; R.A.C.*, I, 469–76; *R.G.G.*[3], I, 456–9; M. Simon, *Verus Israel* (1948), pp. 239ff., 273ff.; B. Blumenkranz, *Les auteurs chrétiens du Moyen Age sur les Juifs et la Judaïsm* (1963), *Le Juif médiéval au miroir de l'art chrétien* (1966); J. Trachtenberg, *The Devil and the Jews* (1943); C. Sykes, 'The Protocols of the Elders of Zion', *History Today*, XVII (1967); D. D. Runes, *The War against the Jew* (1968); S. G. F. Brandon, *The Trial of Jesus of Nazareth* (1968).

Antony, St. (251?–356) Egypt. hermit, whose reputation for holiness and austerities attracted others to join him. This community of hermits was organised under a rule, thus anticipating later → monasticism, although very different from that later institution in life and purpose. A. used his influence to support Nicene party against → Arianism, and was closely assoc. with → Athanasius, who was reputed to have written the *Vita Antonii.* S.G.F.B.

W. H. Mackean, *Christian Monasticism in Egypt* (1920), pp. 69ff.; R. Draguet, *Les Pères du désert* (1949), pp. 1ff.; *D.C.C., s.v.; R.G.G.*[3], I, 461.

Anu Sumerian sky-god (in Akkadian: Anum), head of Mesopot. pantheon. Although a rather shadowy figure, A.'s primacy was always acknowledged (e.g. on Code of Hammurabi). His consort was the goddess Antum. (→ Sumerian Relig.). S.G.F.B.

C.-F. Jean, *La religion sumérienne* (1931), pp. 30ff.; E. Dhorme, *Les religions de Babylonie et d'Assyrie* (1945), pp. 12ff., 22ff.

Anubis Anc. Egypt. mortuary god, gen. repr. with jackal's head and human body. A. was prob. a deification of wild dogs or jackals living in desert where dead were buried: hence assoc. with dead, espec. as guide to underworld. A. was early incorpor. into mortuary cult of → Osiris as chief embalmer of corpse; he also attended the scales in weighing of the heart (→ Judgment of the Dead, Egyp.). In funerary ritual A. was repr. by priest wearing mask of jackal. The cult of A. continued into Graeco-Roman period; A. was identified with → Hermes Psychopompos. S.G.F.B.

R.Ae.R.-G., pp. 40–5; S. A. B. Mercer, *Religion of Anc. Egypt* (1949), pp. 146ff.

Anuruddha (1) A prominent monk of the Buddh. → Sangha in time of Buddha, mentioned many times in the Pali canon and in the → *Mahāvastu.* A. appears as close and loyal comrade of Buddha. He was present at his death, and was active in strengthening and exhorting the other monks. To him is attr. the reciting and preserving of the → *Aṅguttara Nikaya.* T.O.L.

Malalasekere, *D.P.P.N.*, vol. I, pp. 85–90; *Vinaya Pitaka*, II, pp. 180–3, *Mahāvastu*, iii, 177f.; *D.N.*, II, pp. 156–7; Thag. 908.

(2) Author of the Pali work, → *Abhidhammattha-sangaha,* who is believed to have been incumbent of the Sinhalese *Mūlasoma-vihāra* (monastery). Little else is known of him. His name appears in list of saintly men of S. India; and he is believed to have composed at Kāñcipura (Conjevaram) another learned Buddh. work, the *Paramattha-vinicchaya.* His dates are not known with certainty: prob. after 8th and before 12th cent. CE. T.O.L.

Anurādhapura Anc. capital of Ceylon until 10th cent. CE, where was situated the Great Monastery (*Mahāvihāra*) which had been stronghold of → Theravada Buddhism in Ceylon, since its intro. in 3rd cent. BC. Also in A. was the rival Abhayaggiri Vihāra, a centre of liberal Buddhism of the Mahāyāna type. When capital was moved to Polonnaruwa, A. was abandoned and its many temples, monasteries and pagodas fell into ruins. Rediscovered in 19th cent., it is now recognised as valuable repository of early Sinhalese Buddh. art and architecture. (→ Ceylon). T.O.L.

Anussati Pali Buddh. term for 'recollection'. The conventional list of six objects of recollection, each recommended as a form of meditational exercise, consists of: recollection of the Buddha (*buddhānussati*); of his doctrine (*dhammānussati*); his community (*sanghānussati*); morality (*silānussati*); detachment (*cāgānussati*); the heavenly sphere (*devānussati*). Any of these types of recollection is regarded as effective in bringing the meditator to → Access-Concentration (*upacāra-samādhi*). T.O.L.

Aphrodite Grk. goddess of sexual love and fertility. Origin of name uncertain; recent opinion is inclined to assoc. it with → Astarte, name of Semitic goddess whose cult was estab. in Cyprus, trad. home of A. In Cyprus A. was assoc. with → Adonis. The Hellenisation of A. was already well developed by time of → Homer, who makes her daughter of → Zeus and Dione. In Greece the public cult of A. was decorous; but she was served by sacred → prostitutes at Corinth. The dove and myrtle were sacred to A. Grk. art of 5th cent. BC portrayed A. as a grave and majestic type of female beauty. In 4th cent. BC. Praxiteles produced the A. of Cindos, the supreme example of female nude in Anc. World (→ Venus).
S.G.F.B.

O.C.D., s.v.; Kleine Pauly, I, 425–31; O. E. James, *The Cult of the Mother Goddess* (1959), pp. 147ff.; H. J. Rose, *Handbook of Greek Mythology* (1928), pp. 122ff.; H. Licht, *Sexual Life in Anc. Greece* (E.T. 1949), *passim*; J. Harrison, *Prolegomena*, pp. 307ff.

Apocalyptic Literature Grk. word *apokalypsis*, meaning 'revelation' has been applied to a class of Jew. and Chr. lit. purporting to reveal, in terms of God's purpose, what is to happen in future. Such revelation was orig. connected with Israel's salvation from heathen oppression. Acc. to the Heb. → *Hellsgeschichte*, → Yahweh fulfilled his promise to → Abraham by settling Israel in Canaan. Later disasters (e.g. Babylonian Exile) seemed to contradict Yahweh's purpose. To justify Yahweh, the later → prophets explained Israel's sufferings as punishment for sin and promised future restoration. The Book of → Daniel is earliest example of A.-L., and was prob. written to comfort Jews suffering under Antiochus Epiphanes (175–163 BC). From that time A. writing increases. A. books are pseudonymous, being attrib. to great heroes of past. Among most important are Book of → Enoch, Apocalypse of → Baruch, 4th Book of → Ezra, Assumption of → Moses, Book of Jubilees, and Testament of the Twelve Patriarchs. The most important Chr. A. writings are Rev. and Apocalypse of → Peter. A. passages also occur in Mt. 24–5, Mk. 13, Lk. 21:5f. S.G.F.B.

R. H. Charles, *A.P.*, 2 vols.; R. H. Pfeiffer, *Hist. of New Test. Times* (1949), pp. 74ff.; E. Schürer, *G.J.V.*, III, pp. 181ff.; H. H. Rowley in *Peake's Commentary*[2] (1962), pp. 484ff.; *R.A.C.*, I, 504–10; D. S. Russell, *The Method and Message of Jewish Apocolyptic* (1964).

Apocatastasis Grk. word used for doc. that all creatures, i.e. men, angels and devils, will ultimately be saved. Doc. is found in →→ Origen, Clement of Alexandria, and Gregory of Nyssa, and was opposed by → Augustine of Hippo and formally condemned by Council of Constantinople in 543. In its modern form, A. is known as Universalism. S.G.F.B.

D.C.C., s.v.; R.A.C., I, 510–6.

Apocrypha Grk. word, meaning 'the hidden (things)', used as trad. designation for certain writings received by Church as part of Grk. version of O.T. (→ LXX), but excluded from Heb. Bible (→ Canon). These writings, some of which are Grk. trans. of Heb. originals, date from *c.* 300 BC–CE 100. They are of fundamental importance for study of Jew. life and thought during this period, and also for Christ. Origins. The Jews distinguished between canonical books and those 'to be hidden from all except the wise' (2 Esd. 14:44–7), and such books were excl. when canon was finally fixed at Synod of Jamnia *c.* 100 CE. Although there was some diversity of opinion in Early Church about which books of A. were to be accepted, the following became canonical and formed part of → Vulgate, and the A.V. and

R.V.: I Esdras, Tobit, Judith, the Rest of Esther, Wisdom of Solomon, Ecclesiasticus, Baruch with Epis. of Jeremy, Song of the Three Children, Hist. of Susanna, Bel and the Dragon, Prayer of Manasses, I and II Maccabees. At → Reformation the Prot. leaders refused status of inspired Scripture to A., though gen. agreeing that 'the Church doth read (them) for example of life and instruction of manners; but yet it doth not apply them to establish any doctrine' (Art. 6 of Ch. of England's 39 Articles). The Council of → Trent (1548) confirmed canonicity of A. for R.C.s. The A. is also of great importance for understanding Chr. thought and art during Early Church period and Middle Ages. S.G.F.B.

R. H. Charles, *A.P.*, I (1913), *Religious Development between Old and New Testaments* (1914); *New Commentary on Holy Scripture*, ed. C. Gore, H. L. Goudge, A. Guillaume (1929), part II; E. Schürer, *G.J.V.*, III, pp. 135ff.; R. H. Pfeiffer, *Hist. of New Test. Times* (1949), pp. 233ff.; *D.C.C.*, *s.v.; R.A.C.*, I, 516–20 (on idea of *apocryphos*); *H.D.B.*², *s.v.;* L. H. Brockington, *A Critical Intro. to the Apocrypha* (1961).

Apocryphal New Testament This expression has become a gen. designation for certain early Chr. writings, some dating from 2nd cent., concerning Jesus and other N.T. figures, which were never incl. in → canon of N.T. Despite lack of canonicity, they have great value for understanding early Chr. life and thought, espec. at popular level. These writings form four groups: (i) so-called Gospels. Some of these, such as that *acc. to the Hebrews* and *Gospel of → Thomas* may contain early oral trad. Others were produced in response to popular desire to know more about childhood of Jesus, and other events of his life (e.g. *Childhood Gospel of Thomas, Gospel of Nicodemus, the Protoevangelium, Hist. of → Joseph the Carpenter*) (ii) so-called *Acts*, e.g. of Peter, Paul, John, etc. (iii) so-called *Epistles* (e.g. correspondence of Christ and → Abgar; Paul's lost Ep. to the Laodiceans; Letter of → Lentulus). (iv) *Apocalypses*, e.g. of → Peter. The A.-N.-T. is also important for study of Chr. → art. The documents discovered at → Nag Hammadi reveal popularity of such writings. S.G.F.B.

M. R. James, *The Apocryphal New Test.* (1926): gives trans. of all relevant writings; E. Hennecke, *Neutestamentliche Apokryphen*³, 2 vols. (1959, 1964), E.T. *New Test. Apocrypha*, 2 vols.; *R.G.G.*³, I, 473–4; P. Carrington, *The Early Christian Church* (1957), II, pp. 351ff.; W. Van Unnik, *Evangelien aus dem Nilsand* (1960).

Apollinarianism Name given to teaching of Apollinarius (*c.* 310–90), Bishop of Laodicea. A. was first great Christological heresy (→ Christology). A. asserted that Christ had a human body and soul, but that the → Logos replaced the human mind. Hence Christ possessed perfect godhead, but lacked complete manhood. A. was condemned at Council of Constantinople in 381. It was objected, *inter alia*, that what Christ did not have (i.e. human mind), he could not redeem. S.G.F.B.

E.R.E., I, *s.v.; D.C.C.*, *s.v.;* A. Harnack, *Hist. of Dogma*³ (E.T. 1961), IV, pp. 149ff.

Apollo Grk. god, depicted in art as ideal type of young hero. A. was assoc. with music, archery, prophecy, medicine and care of cattle; he was also regarded as patron of Hellenic culture. Through his chief shrine at → Delphi and its oracle, A. became essentially a panhellenic deity. The origin of his name and cult is uncertain: he had an anc. connection with N. Greece; the theory that he was orig. a sun-deity is not now gen. held. A. had a complex mythology: he acquired his sanctuary at Delphi by killing Pytho, the dragon that guarded it. He and his sister → Artemis were born at Delos, their mother being Leto, a Titaness. He had many liaisons with human women (e.g. Daphne, the → Sibyl of Cumae). There was a grim side to A.; he could both cause and stop plague. A. was worshipped by the → Etruscans (a famous statue at Veii survives). At Rome he was a god of healing; Augustus raised a splendid temple to him on the Palatine in thanksgiving for his victory at Actium, where A. had a temple. S.G.F.B.

H. J. Rose, *Handbook of Greek Mythology* (1928), pp. 114ff., 134ff.; W. K. C. Guthrie, *The Greeks and their Gods* (1950), pp. 73ff.; 183ff.; *Kleine Pauly*, I, 441–8.

Apollonius of Tyana Neophythagorean philosopher of 1st cent. CE, whose ascetic wandering life and miraculous power won for him a great reputation: his career was recorded by Philostratus. A. was cited as a parallel to Christ by anti-Christian writers. S.G.F.B.

Philostratus' *Vita Apolloni* is published in Loeb Classical Library, 2 vols. *Kleine Pauly*, I, 451–2; *R.A.C.*, I, 529–33.

Apollos A 'learned' Jew of Alexandria, who, though a Christian, knew only the 'baptism of John' and needed instruction from Paul's friends (Acts 18:24ff.). This acc. of A.'s defective Christianity provides a significant clue to the Pauline view of Alexandrian Christianity (→ Alexandria, Church of). The attribution of the Wisdom of Solomon and Ep. to the → Hebrews has not been estab. S.G.F.B.

S. G. F. Brandon, *The Fall of Jerusalem and the Christian Church* (1957²), pp. 17ff., 139ff.; *Jesus and the Zealots* (1967), pp. 192ff.; *H.D.B.*², *s.v.*

Apologetics From Grk. word *apologetikos*, meaning 'defence'. Before its victory over paganism in 4th cent., reasoned defences of Christianity against various charges were composed (→ Apologists).

During period of Christianity's cultural and political predominance in Europe such defences were not needed; a change set in from 18th cent. The rise of modern science and the secularisation of society began to stir Chr. scholars to produce reasoned defences of relig. interpretation of reality and to defend the supernatural character of Christianity. A. will sometimes take form of stripping Christianity of what is regarded as outmoded ideas and forms of expression (→ Demythologising). (→ Christian Ethics). S.G.F.B.

E.R.E., I, *s.v.;* L. E. Elliott-Binns, *English Thought*, 1860–1900, *the Theological Aspect* (1956), pp. 32ff.; *R.G.G.*³, I, 485–95.

Apologists Name given to early Chr. writers who sought to defend Christianity from pagan calumnies and win toleration of civil authorities. The → Acts of the Apostles is really the first *apologia* for Christianity; but the A.'s are usually reckoned to start in 2nd cent. with Aristides, Quadratus, → Justin Martyr. Later A.'s incl. Tatian, Athenagoras, Tertullian, and → Origen. Some A.'s addressed their works to reigning Emperor; but it is doubtful whether he ever saw them. The A.'s are gen. concerned to show Christianity to be morally and culturally superior to paganism and politically harmless. Sometimes they made extravagant claims: e.g. Tertullian claimed that Roman archives proved that Emp. Tiberius was convinced of Christ's divinity (*Apol.* V. 3). A.'s writings are invaluable for revealing how early Christians evaluated their faith *vis-à-vis* paganism; what they say of pagan faith and practice has, however, to be carefully evaluated. S.G.F.B.

D.C.C., *s.v.; R.A.C.*, I, 533–43 ('Apologetik'); *R.G.G.*³, I, 477–85; H. M. Gwatkin, *Early Church Hist.* (1912), I, ch. XI; A. A. T. Ehrhardt, *Politische Metaphysik von Solon bis Augustin* (1959), II, pp. 71ff.

Apophis In Egypt. relig., the serpent-monster of darkness that daily threatened → Rē, the sun-god, as he sought to arise from underworld to illuminate world above. In Egypt. thought each dawn was achieved only after sun's victory over darkness. A. was prob. also the personification of primeval chaos which ever threatened the ordered universe. (→ Light and Darkness). S.G.F.B.

R.Ae.R.-G., *s.v.;* R. T. Rundle Clark, *Myth and Symbol in Anc. Egypt* (1959), pp. 208ff.

Apostasy (Christ) The abandonment of Christianity, either voluntarily or under compulsion, was regarded as most heinous. In Early Church it was first deemed unforgivable; but large-scale A. under stress of persecution caused less rigorist policy, although leniency was strongly opposed and led to schism (→ Donatism). In Middle Ages A. was punished by death. In modern R.C. Church A. is used in three senses: A. from faith; from Holy Orders by a cleric; from their vows by monk or nun. S.G.F.B.

E.R.E., I, pp. 623–5; *D.C.C.*, *s.v.; R.A.C.*, I, 550–1; W. H. C. Frend, *Martyrdom and Persecution in the Early Church* (1965), pp. 415ff.

(Islam) It has always been held that those who have been brought up Muslims, and those who have accepted Islam later in life, are committed to it; therefore A. cannot be recognised. The legal schools agree that punishment, at least so far as male adults are concerned, is death; but sentence should not be carried out till condemned has rejected opportunities of returning to Islam. It has been customary to confine women apostates till they recanted or died. Minors are kept under surveillance till they become adult, when they are dealt with. But those who have apostatised under duress are not to be punished (cf. Qur., xvi: 108). A. automatically leads to dissolution of marriage, though theoretically if a woman apostatised to → Judaism or → Christianity, her marriage would be capable of being continued, for Muslim men can marry women who are people of the Book; but Muslim women can marry only Muslims. In more mod. times European influ. has led to mitigation of law; but it has been said that, in spite of this, some apostates have mysteriously disappeared, and must have been subject to persecution. In 1903 and 1924 some → Ahmadiyya members were stoned to death in Afghanistan, on ground of being apostates. But in gen., while law still remains, it is not normally put into effect. It is, however, very difficult for a Muslim to change his relig. An example of this is the law in Malaya, a Muslim country, that while liberty of relig. is given to all, no attempt to convert Muslims to another relig. is permissible. The rising which took place in Arabia after → Muhammad's death is commonly called the A. (*ridda*), but this is not really accurate (→ Abū Bakr). J.R.

Pareja, pp. 669f. and index; S. M. Zwemer, *The law of apostasy in Islam* (1924); Querry, II, pp. 528–33; Lane, *Egyptians*, pp. 111f.

Apostle *Ex.* Grk. word *apostellein* = 'to send'. Title used for the Twelve Disciples selected and commissioned by Jesus (Mt. 10:1ff.). The title seems soon to have acquired authoritative significance: Paul's claim to be an A. was challenged (II. Cor. 12:11–2). Acc. to Cath. belief, Christ conferred special grace and authority upon the A.'s, which they handed on to successors (→ Apostolic Succession). S.G.F.B.

R.A.C., I, 553–5; *D.C.C.*, *s.v.; R.G.G.*³, I, 497–9.

Apostles' Creed → Creeds.

Apostolic Age Modern designation for period to *c.* CE 100, this being the presumed life-time of the

Apostles of Christ. Sometimes a sub or post A.A. is distinguished, running into 2nd cent., corresponding to lifetime of those who personally knew the Apostles. S.G.F.B.

(Fathers) Title used from later 17th cent. for certain Chr. writers of period subsequent to Apostolic Age, whose works were regarded as repr. of orthodox belief. They are →→ Clement of Rome, Ignatius, and Hermas, Polycarp, Papias, and authors of → Ep. of Barnabas and '2 Clement', and → Didache. S.G.F.B.

J. B. Lightfoot, *The Apostolic Fathers* (1891); K. Lake, *The Apostolic Fathers*, 2 vols. (1917–9); *D.C.C.*, *s.v.;* L. W. Barnard, *Studies in the Apost. Fathers and their Background* (1966).

(Succession) Doctrine that the authority and sacramental grace which Christ conferred on his → Apostles were passed by them to successors, who were believed to be first or second bishops of churches estab. during Apostolic Age. These in turn transmitted this authority and grace to their successors, or to bishops they consecrated to newly estab. churches. Thus each see could claim a succession of apostolic grace and authority reaching back to Apostles: the classic example is the see of Rome which has preserved a trad. list of bishops back to St. → Peter. This A.-S., in turn, is held to guarantee a valid sacerdotal ministry, with authority and grace to administer the → sacraments. A.-S. is regarded as essential to Catholicity. Prot. churches, except → Ch. of England, repudiated the doc. A.-S. has now become an issue of basic importance for the → ecumenical movement. A.-S. repr. theological theory rather than historical fact. The origins of the Chr. → hierarchy is a subject of much complexity, on which there is diversity of expert opinion. S.G.F.B.

E.R.E., I, *s.v.; D.C.C.*, *s.v.; R.G.G.*³, VI, 521; A. A. T. Ehrhardt, *The Apostolic Succession* (1953).

Apotheosis Grk. word meaning deification of a human being, usually after death. Oldest form occurs in Egypt. mortuary cult (from *c.* 2500 BC), where deceased was assimilated with → Osiris. In *Story of Sinhue* (*c.* 1900) the dead pharaoh is united with sun-god. Grk. mythology has many examples (→ Heracles), and so has Grk. history (→ Alexander the Great). A. was decreed by Roman Senate to deceased emperors. The A. of Emp. Antoninus and his wife Faustina is graphically repr. on sculptured panel at base of his column in Rome. It has been suggested that Chr. practice of → canonisation is form of A.; the medieval use of Lat. *divus* for saint has been cited in support. However, where A. has been used in Chr. lit., it means union with God, not deification. (→ Ancestor Cult, Roman). S.G.F.B.

R.Ae.R.-G., pp. 856–60 ('Vergöttlichung'); *Kleine Pauly*, I, 458–60; *D.C.C.*, *s.v.; R.A.C.*, III, 284–94 ('Consecratio II'); L. Curtius and A. Nawrath, *Das Antike Rom* (1944), Abb. 144.

Apotropaic Term (*ex.* Grk. adjective meaning 'averted') used to describe magical rites or articles (→ Amulets) designed to avert evil of various kinds. One of → Apollo's titles was *Apotropaios.* S.G.F.B.

A. Bertholet, *Wör‚erbuch der Religionen* (1952), pp. 35–6.

Apsu In anc. Mesopot. mythology, the primaeval deep of sweet waters. Through union of A. with → Ti'āmat (the sea), the gods of Mesopot. pantheon were born (→ Cosmogony, Mesopot.). The god → Ea killed A., and his temple at Eridu was supposed to be built upon the A. S.G.F.B.

C.-F. Jean, *La religion sumérienne* (1931), p. 46; Brandon, *C.L.*, pp. 71ff.

Apuleius Born *c.* CE 123 at Madauros, N. Africa, of local renown as philosopher, poet, and rhetorician. A.'s importance for hist. of relig. lies in his authorship of the *Metamorphoses* or *The Golden Ass.* Written in Lat., this work describes, vividly and imaginatively, the adventures of one Lucius, who dabbles in black magic. Having been changed into an ass, Lucius is restored to human form by goddess → Isis. The latter part of book describes Lucius' initiations into mysteries of Isis and → Osiris (→ Mystery Religions). A. prob. writes of his own experiences and beliefs here: what he says reveals how profoundly an initiate into these mysteries could be moved, and how real Isis could be to a devotee. The *Metamorphoses* also contains beautiful myth of Cupid and → Psyche. S.G.F.B.

Apuleius: *The Golden Ass* (Loeb Classical Library, 1935); A. D. Nock, *Conversion* (1933), ch. IX; *O.C.D.*, *s.v.; Kleine Pauly*, I, 471–3.

Aquinas, St. Thomas The great systematist of W. medieval Scholasticism. A. was born *c.* 1225 at Roccasecca, youngest son of Count Landulf of Aquino. At age of five he was sent to neighbouring Benedictine school of Montecassino, where he was destined by his parents for the Abbacy. In 1240 he proceeded to Naples to finish his Arts course. Here he was attracted to ideal of an intellectual apostolate and resolved to seek admission to recently founded → Dominican Order. This was against opposition of family; but in April he joined the order. A. came to Paris where he came under the influence of → Albertus Magnus, who had intro. him to → Aristotle and with whom he went to Cologne. 1252–9 he was in Paris; 1259–69 in Italy; 1269–72, he was recalled to work in Paris again. He died on 7th March 1274 at the Cistercian Monastery of Fossanuova, on his way to the Council of Lyons. A.'s writings incl. many philosophical works: his two most import. writings were the *Summa*

Contra Gentiles, which was a text-book for missionaries, and the *Summa Theologica*, his greatest theological work. He made a discriminating synthesis of the whole of trad. up to that time and incl. the newly discovered corpus of Aristotle's writings. The whole Scriptural-Platonic-Augustinian-Pseudo-Dionysian trad. he welded together with use of method and teaching of Aristotle, whom he thought was the type of the natural philosopher. The method of the *Summa Theologica* is the answering of separate questions, with separate subordinate articles or questions under them. The result is that it consists of thousands of minute points, with no overall discussion of theme to bring them into focus, though the pattern is ordered in the author's mind. The result of this method is that he is enabled to make very sharp distinctions; but these must not be emphasized too much, because in process of argument he is able very nearly to approximate his antitheses together.

Fundamental to A.'s teaching is his sharp distinction between reason and faith—i.e., between reason and acceptance of authority of revelation on authority of God himself. Over a large area, natural reason is able to probe questions that the theologian needs to answer. Such truths as existence of God, his eternity and simplicity, his creative power and providence can be discovered by natural reason altogether apart from revelation. The ordinary person needs revelation here, because these truths can only be discovered after much difficulty and with many errors. But the work of the natural philosopher is quite competent in this sphere. Chr. verities, truths such as the → Trinity and Incarnation, Creation of World in → Time, → Original Sin, → Purgatory, → Resurrection of Body, etc., lie wholely beyond capacity of natural reason. This sharp distinction between natural reason and true revelation led, in time, to possibility, realised in 18th cent., of accepting natural reason alone as capable of giving all truth that human mind wanted relating to God, thereby neglecting truths of revelation (so much more import. to A., and which dominated and crowned his teaching on natural reason).

For A., knowledge of God necessarily set out from sense-perception, not from abstract thinking, since man is a corporeal as well as an intellectual being; from the contingent facts of empirical world he finds five ways of knowing that there is a necessary being which is God. In beings other than God there are various degrees of potency and act. God, however, who is source of all being, is complete realised perfection (*purus actus*). This perfection is beyond distinction between essence and existence; we know it by analogy. Matter is the principle of individuation in the universe. In knowledge the mind strips off what is individual and grasps the essence or nature, which is real in its own right. As matter is entirely lacking in the → angels, each angel is necessarily a complete species in himself. Reason and order throughout universe reflect the unchanging mind and law of God.

In theology A. stressed the Vision of God, → Incarnation, → Atonement and the → Sacraments. The Vision of God (seeing of God in his Essence) is that which human nature requires for its satisfaction but cannot of itself supply. Only through revelation can we think of any attaining to it in this life. He maintained, against the → Franciscans, that the Incarnation would not have taken place apart from → Fall, and that the Virgin → Mary was not immaculately conceived.

In rel. to the Atonement he brought out clearly that, while man's salvation is solely due to grace of Christ, God's grace in Christ is so generous that he transforms man by his grace so that he is able to live a good life and by grace of Christ merit his own salvation. He held that all seven Sacraments were instituted by Christ, and that these culminated in the → Eucharist. To elucidate the doc. of → trans-substantiation, which had been formally defined at fourth Lateran Council of 1215 shortly before his time, A. made use of Aristotelian philosophy of substance and accident. The presence of both body and blood of Christ together in each Eucharistic species gave him a theological justification for practice of giving communion in one kind only.

As a patient and discriminating analysis of existing trad., and a weaving of it into one whole, A.'s work is of a masterly type and remains a great teaching instrument. He used Aristotle very considerably, but was not afraid to modify his teaching where it seemed to conflict with Chr. assumptions. What he did not answer was the critical problems of that same trad. that were to follow later. The R.C. Church has accepted the substance of A.'s teaching as official doctrine. Leo XIII in his encyclical *Aeterni Patris* (1879) enjoined study of A. on all theological students; Pius XI in 1923 reaffirmed his authority. H.C.J.

Text: The Leonine Edition (Rome, 1882ff.). A good working text and trans. of *Summa Theologica* is given in new Dominican translation (1963–); valuable are those by E. Gilson, 5th ed. Paris, 1944; M. C. D'Arcy, S. J., 1930. Cf. *St. Thomas Aquinas* (papers read at celebration of Sixth Centenary of Canonization of St. Thomas Aquinas, held in Manchester in 1924), 1925; C. C. J. Webb, *Studies in the History of Natural Theology* (1915), pp. 33–91; David Knowles, *The Evolution of Medieval Thought* (1962), pp. 255–68.

'Arafa (or *Arafāt*), site of chief ceremony of annual → Pilgrimage, is about 13 miles E. of Mecca.

The ceremony takes place round a granite hill about 200 ft. high, called Jabal al-Raḥma (the mount of mercy). A minaret stands at top. From a platform near top the sermon is preached on 9th Dhul Ḥijja. The arid plain surrounding hill becomes an enormous camp site. The ceremony of the *wuqūf* (standing) lasts from time of midday sermon till after sunset, when pilgrims hasten to Muzdalifa. It is said that the greatest sinner is one who stands at 'Arafāt and thinks his sins are not forgiven. J.R.

*E.I.*², I, p. 604; Burton, *Pilgrimage*, ch. xxix; Broadhurst, *Ibn Jubayr*, pp. 176–83 and index; Rutter, *Holy Cities*, I, ch. xii.

Arahant Term used in Pali Buddhism for one who reached final stage of spiritual progress; lit. 'the worthy'. The word A. was used gen. in anc. India to indic. respect, not unlike the Eng. usage 'his worship'. In the → *Ṛg-veda* the term is used of the god → Agni (II, 3.3). It was also used as an epithet of → Mahāvira, the founder of the Jain community. It was applied to the Buddha also by his contemporaries. Later it came to have a specialised meaning in Buddh. usage. Four stages of spiritual attainment were distinguished: first that of the → *sotāpanna*, or 'stream-enterer'; the → *sakadāgāmi*, or 'once-returner'; the → *anāgāmī* or 'non-returner'; and, finally, the *arahant*. The A. was regarded as one in whom all the → *āsavas*, or 'influxes', which produced further → *karma* and thus continuance of existence in the sensuous sphere, had been extinguished. While attainment of first 3 stages was poss. for lay people, attainment of 4th by a layman was regarded as very unusual and extremely difficult. This view is expressed, e.g. in the → *Milindapañha* (*SBE*.36, p. 56). Among Ceylon Buddhists it is held that a layman who attains arahantship should immediately enter the monastic Order (*sangha*). Acc. to the Buddha, women were equally capable with men of becoming A.'s Many examples of nuns (*therīs*) who attained A.ship are given in the → Therīgāthā. In time of Buddha and immediately after, A.'s were neither expected nor encouraged to withdraw from human society, as is clear from Buddha's own example. The trad. of Indian asceticism was, however, strongly in favour of withdrawal, and early Buddhism provides examples of the solitary A. Normally, the A. continued to live disinterestedly within human society. Among → Theravadins the A. tended to be regarded with great reverence; the → Mahāsanghika school, however, criticised this exaltation of the A., and maintained that some who were held to be A.'s in fact exhibited various imperfections. This criticism was voiced by → Mahādeva. Criticism of A. ideal was continued by the Mahāyāna schools, on ground that the *nirvāṇa* which the A.'s reached was merely cessation of the *āsavas* and not full enlightenment (*sambodhi*). Superior to the A. ideal was, according to Mahāyāna Buddhists, the → *bodhisattva* ideal. The Mahāyāna work *Saddharma-pundarīka*, e.g., maintains that A.'s, having extinguished the *āsavas*, must go on to seek supreme enlightenment, i.e. become a Buddha. T.O.L.

Kindred Sayings (PTS) III, 68ff.; V. 170; 181ff.; E. Lamotte, *Histoire du Bouddhisme Indien*, pp. 300ff.; E. Conze, *Buddhist Thought in India* (1962), pp. 166–9; 234–6.

Ārāma Term used in anc. India for a park or grove, and partic. for such places when set aside for use of Buddh. monks as places of quiet retreat, and, eventually of residence. T.O.L.

(→ Monasteries, Buddh.).

Aramaeans A Semitic people first heard of in Euphrates area *c.* 2000 BC. They occupied territory stretching from Harran into the Hauran and Syria (A.'s are often called 'Syrians' in A.V. and R.V.). Their language was → Aramaic. The relig. of A.'s was a complex of many other religs. (incl. →→ Mesopot., Canaanite, Hittite, Hurrite religs.). It was polytheistic: →→ Atargatis and Hadad being prominent deities. S.G.F.B.

A. Dupont-Sommer, *Les Araméens* (1949); *H.D.B.*², s.v.; *R.G.G.*³, I, 531–2.

Aramaic A (Semitic) language of the → Aramaeans. It became widely diffused in Near East, incl. Palestine, through commercial and diplomatic use. In later O.T. period it so largely superseded Heb. in Palestine that Aramaic paraphrases in the Heb. Scriptures were needed by Jew. people (→ Targums). A. was prob. used gen. by → Jesus, and A. modes of thought, forms of expression, and words can be discerned in Grk. N.T. There is also a large Christ. lit. in the A. dialect called Syriac. S.G.F.B.

H. H. Rowley, *The Aramaic of the Old Test.* (1929); G. Dalman, *Jesus-Jeshua* (E.T. 1929); M. Black, *An Aramaic Approach to the Gospels and Acts* (1946); A. Dupont-Sommer, *Les Araméens* (1949); G. R. Driver, *Semitic Writing* (1948); *R.G.G.*³, I, 532–4; W. B. Stevenson, *Grammar of Palestinian Jewish Aramaic* (1962²).

Arcana Discipline (*arcani disciplina*) (Lat. *arcana* = secret). Term invented in 17th cent. to describe custom of Church in 4th and 5th cents. of forbidding presence of uninitiated, i.e. unbaptised at → Baptism and → Eucharist. The custom was prob. taken over from the → Mystery Religions, which had carefully defined stages of initiation before full membership. S.G.F.B.

*R.G.G.*³, I, 606–8 ('Arkandisziplin'); *R.A.C.*, I, 667–76; *E.R.E.*, I, *s.v.* 'Arcani Disciplina'.

Architecture (Religious) There is much reason for saying that relig. created A. In the great cultures of antiquity, earliest examples of A. are temples and tombs. Stone-built sanctuaries at → Jericho and → Çatal Hüyük date from 7th mil. BC. The Step Pyramid of Zoser and its mortuary temple, erected *c.* 2700 BC, were products of an already long trad. of Egypt. tomb and temple building. In Mesopotamia relig. structures date back into 5th mil. In early Near East. civilisations temples were largest and most durable edifices built. Not only did their construction demand both high technical ability and outlay of considerable economic resources, their adornment also required skills of sculptors, painters, wood and metal workers. In later civilisations, e.g. in Graeco-Roman world, India, China, Japan, pre-Columban America, temples and sometimes tombs were the most notable achievements of A. Even among less developed peoples, e.g. in Prehistoric Britain and → Malta, relig. needs produced notable monuments (e.g. Stonehenge and stone temples in Malta). In medieval Christendom cathedral and church constituted the most impressive structures of countryside, as did also mosques of → Islamic lands. Relig. A. has been basically functional. The lay-out of a sanctuary, whether temple or church, was dictated by ritual needs; this was true of tombs in many religs. The Gothic cathedral was a veritable epitome in stone of Chr. faith and practice. Relig. A. also produced its own partic. styles, often quite distinct from contemporary domestic and military A. A. has gen. reflected the peculiar ethos of relig. concerned (cmp., e.g. Hindu temple with Islamic mosque). The apparent failure to produce a satisfactory modern relig. A. in Europe and America has been interpreted as due to lack of vital creative relig. spirit in contemporary society. (→→ Pyramids; Temple; Basilica; Cathedrals; Mosques; Pagoda; Americ. Relig. anc.). S.G.F.B.

E.R.E., I, pp. 677–774; *R.A.C.*, I, 1225–59 ('Basilika'); H. Frankfort, *The Art and Architecture of Anc. Orient* (1954); B. Rowland, *The Art and Architecture of India* (1953); O. von Simson, *The Gothic Cathedral* (1956); J. Harvey, *The Gothic World*, 1100–1600 (1950); E. Panofsky, *Gothic Architecture and Scholasticism* (1957); D. T. Rice, *Islamic Art* (1965); G. H. S. Bushnell, *Ancient Art of the Americas* (1965); J. Finegan, *Archeology of World Religions* (1952); A. Malraux, *The Metamorphosis of the Gods* (E.T. 1960).

(China–Japan) The construction and form of Chi. buildings has varied little through history. Trad. patterns were followed with exceptional scrupulousness. Both site and construction were governed by → Fêng Shui. The chief material being wood, few A. remains from anc. China have been preserved. A small stone chapel at Hsiao-t'ang-shan (Shantung) may be dated from 1st cent. CE. 3 or 4 masonry pagodas remain from 6th cent. CE, and the 1st authentic wooden building dates from 9th cent. CE. Refs. in literature, and clay and pottery funerary models and bas-reliefs from Han Dynasty onwards, supply what knowledge we possess of ancient Chinese A. The rituals of anc. China centred in the Ming T'ang (Hall of brightness) of the ruler, the T'ai Miao or Great Ancestral Temples of the nobility, and the simple Earth → Altars. Evidence respecting their construction is conflicting and unreliable.

The construction of temples, whether Confucian, Buddhist or Taoist, was similar in design through the ages, and matched the formality of the imperial palaces. The group design was based on spacious courtyard, entered through formal gateway and dominated by main hall. The main structures, two or three in number of simple rectilinear construction, were solidly framed buildings standing on masonry terraces, and were crowned by tiled roofs. They faced S. on a rigidly symmetrical plan. Dwellings for monks and other subsidiary buildings were built at sides or behind and connected by numerous ornamented corridors.

The roofs of temples, palaces and halls are the chief feature, beautifully tiled and with graceful curves and skyward-pointing eaves. The beams and the complicated bracketing of roof structure rest on massive wooden pillars. Ceilings, beams and pillars are superbly decorated by skilful use of design in paint, lacquer and gilt. The spaces between external pillars are usually filled with brick, plastered mud and decorative lattice-work.

Pagodas, numerous throughout China, are among most graceful specimens of Chi. A. These tower-like structures, rising 7, 9, 11 or even 13 stories in form of a polygonal obelisk, and often assoc. with temples and monasteries, preserved relics of Buddhas or saints, and were believed to exert a propitious influence on the neighbourhood. Commemorative triple arches, erected to memory of famous scholars, saints, heroes or virtuous women, called '*p'ai lo*', are found all over China. They consist of lofty columns supporting a more or less elaborate rooflet, and are made of wood, brick or stone. The mosques of Islam in China are similar in style to temples, but are distinguished by plan and interior arrangement. The → Minbar is placed at right-hand corner of rear hall. There is neither dome nor minaret.

Chinese tombs are simply low, artificial mounds; but tombs of wealthy have monumental stones, often accompanied by stone figures of men and animals. Chinese domestic architecture possesses a drabness and uniformity of style, particularly in the N., where cities and dwellings

are surrounded by high walls. Within the walls is the same formal arrangement of courtyards and buildings, the main buildings made of brick and tiled and facing S. D.H.S.
L. Sickman and A. Soper. *The Art and Architecture of China* (1956); *E.R.E.*, I, pp. 693ff.; J. Dyer Ball, *Things Chinese*, 5th ed. (1925), pp. 33ff.; 440ff.

Shinto. The most archaic type of shrine was simply primitive hut made of wood and thatched with reeds or straw, in a definite enclosure of land surrounded by a sacred fence. It was intended as house for a god. Though Buddhist influence led to some elaboration, Shinto shrines are usually characterised by great simplicity. They are not meant for communal or congregational worship. A characteristic feature is the *torii*, or ceremonial gateways, which adorn approaches to shrines. These usually consist of two upright pillars of wood, tied by cross-beam with another beam resting on top and projecting beyond the pillars. The building itself consists of a worship-sanctuary (*haiden*), and the chief sanctuary (*honden*), in which is housed the → shintai of the god. (→ Shinto).

Buddhism. Jap. secular architecture and the great Buddhist temples and monasteries were, in the first place, almost wholly dependent on Chinese influence and inspiration. In Nara period (CE 710–782) Chi. T'ang Dynasty A. was meticulously copied as to design and construction. (*Vide* the Hōryūji temple at Nara). It was only during the Heian Period (CE 782–1068) that there occurred in A. a resurgence of Jap. national taste. In the great mountain monasteries of → Tendai and → Shingon the formal Chinese layout was impossible, whilst the needs of large lay congregations and tantric rituals led to development of great individual halls of worship. These demanded experiments in new forms of A., and the development in Japan of temple constructions less dependent on traditional Chinese patterns. Nevertheless, throughout Jap. hist. the influence of China on A. has been immense. → Art, Sacred (Buddh.), D.H.S.
E.R.E., I, p. 773; R. T. Paine and A. Soper, *The Art and Architecture of Japan* (1955); Jean Herbert, *Shinto* (1967), pp. 92ff.

Archōn (pl. **Archontes**) Grk. word, orig. meaning political magnates (*Kleine Pauly*, I, 517–20), which acquired in Jew.-Hellenist. relig. thought a twofold meaning: (i) supernatural powers (e.g. → angels) serving God, esp. as mediators between God and mankind (ii) daemonic hostile powers, often identified with planets, who controlled destinies of men (→ Astrology). A.'s had important role in → Gnosticism, and in Paul's theology (e.g. I Cor. 2:6ff.). S.G.F.B.
R.A.C., I, 631–3; A.-J. Festugière, *La révélation d'Hermès Trismégiste*, I (1950), pp. 89–96; R. Bultmann, *Urchristentum in Rahmen der antiken Religionen* (1949), pp. 211ff.

Ares Grk. war-god, perhaps of Thracian orig. Since there was no distinctive cult of A., except poss. at Thebes, it has been thought A. was essentially a deification of murderous warfare. He was an unpopular god in → Homer. In mythology A. is assoc. with violence in both war and love; he is the paramour of → Aphrodite, who had a warlike side to her nature as did other of great goddesses (→→ Astarte; Ishtar). A. was identified with the Roman → Mars. S.G.F.B.
O.C.D., *s.v.; Kleine Pauly*, I, 526–9.

Aretalogies *Ex.* Grk. *aretai* = 'virtues', usually of miraculous kind, *logoi* = 'accounts'. Compilations of virtues and miracles of particular deities, made by their devotees for propagation of cult, during Hellenistic Age. The A. of → Isis are esp. notable. The term was often used pejoratively. S.G.F.B.
M. P. Nilsson, *Geschichte der griechischen Religion*, II[2] (1961), pp. 228, 535: F. C. Grant, *Hellenistic Religions* (1953), pp. 131ff.; *P.W.*, II(i), pp. 670–2.

Ariadne Orig. a Minoan vegetation-goddess (→ Cretan relig.), prob. to be identified with the *labyrinthoio potnia* in Linear B. texts. In Grk. mythology she is connected with Theseus and → Dionysos. The many complicated legends concerning A. may result from supersession of cult of an anc. Aegean deity by Grk. cults (→ Aegean relig.). One curious custom of cult of A. may be noted. At Amathus (Cyprus) the pregnancy of A. was annually commemor. by a young man imitating woman in childbed. S.G.F.B.
Kleine Pauly, I, 543–5; M. P. Nilsson, *The Mycenaean Origin of Greek. Mythology* (1932).

Arianism Chr. heresy taking name from Arius (*c.* 250–*c.* 336), an Alexandrian priest who was its chief exponent. A. resulted from problem caused by deification of Jesus Christ relative to monotheistic trad., which Church inherited from → Judaism (→ Monotheism). Acc. to A., Christ as Son of God was not eternal but created by God the Father (→ Trinity), his deity being bestowed by the Father. This made Christ an inferior deity. A. was condemned as heretical, → Athanasius being the chief exponent of orthodoxy. In ensuing controversy, political factors as well as theological operated. The Emp. Constantine and his successors sought to impose peace on disputants in interest of consolidating Empire. At Council of → Nicaea, 325, orthodox position was defined by use of Grk. term *homoousios*, meaning that Christ as Son was coeternal and coequal with the Father, because he was of same substance or essence (Grk. *ousia*). The supporters

of A. were banished. The controversy, however, dragged on with varying fortunes for opposing sides until final victory of orthodoxy at Council of Constantinople in 381. A. survived for another cent. among Teutonic tribes who were first converted to that form of Christianity. S.G.F.B.
The subject is dealt with at length in all the larger histories of Chr. doctrine and of Church during period: e.g. A. Harnack, *Hist. of Dogma*; H. Lietzmann, *Gesch. der Alten Kirche*, III, IV; *The Church in the Christian Roman Empire* by J. R. Palanque *et alii* (E.T. 1949), I. Cf. *D.C.C.*, *s.v.; E.R.E.*, I, *s.v.; R.G.G.*^{3}, I, 593–5; *R.A.C.*, I, 647–52; A. A. T. Ehrhardt, *Politische Metaphysik von Solon bis Augustin*, II (1959), ch. 7; T. E. Pollard, 'The Origins of Arianism', *J.T.S.*, IX (1958).

Aristeas of Prokonnesos A reputed wonder-worker of *c.* 7th cent. BC, who was supposed to have possessed gift of constant ecstasy and → bilocation. S.G.F.B.
Kleine Pauly, I, 555.

Aristeas, Letter of An account, in Grk., of the miraculous trans. of Heb. Scriptures into Grk., known as the → Septuagint. The L.-A. is supposed to have been written by an official at court of Ptolemy Philadephus (285–247 BC); it is dated between 200 BC–CE 33. S.G.F.B.
Kleine Pauly, I, 555–6; *R.G.G.*^{3}, I, 596; *D.C.C.*, *s.v.*

Aristobulus of Paneas (3rd–2nd cent. BC) Jew. philosopher of → Alexandria, who sought to reconcile Jew. relig. and Grk. philosophy by allegorical interpretation (→ Allegory), based on thesis that O.T. was source of much Grk. philosophy. A. wrote a commentary on → Pentateuch, known only by quots. of Early Chr. Fathers. (→ Philo). S.G.F.B.
E. Schürer, *G.J.V.*, III, pp. 512–22; *Kleine Pauly*, I, 563–4; *O.C.D.*, *s.v.;* P. Dalbert, *Die Theologie der hellen.-jüd. Missions-Literatur unter Ausschluss von Philo u. Josephus* (1954), pp. 102ff.

Aristotle, Aristotelianism Grk. philosopher (384–22 BC), whose influence on subsequent West. thought has been profound and continuous. In 367 A. was a disciple of → Plato at Athens; later, joining Macedonian court, he became tutor to future → Alexander the Great. Returning to Athens, he opened at the Lyceum a rival school to Plato's Academy, the headship of which he had failed to obtain on Plato's death. For next 12 yrs. he taught at Lyceum. A. was more attracted to biology than mathematics, on which stress was laid in the Academy. For hist. of relig., the *Nicomachean Ethics*, *Eudemian Ethics*, and *Metaphysics* are the most important of A.'s many works. A. differed from Plato in his interpretation of reality. Instead of Plato's hierarchy of ideas, presided over by 'Idea of the Good', these ideas imparting reality to each instance of their accidental manifestation, A. maintained that each entity, being a union of 'form' and 'matter', had its own individual reality. This thesis involved a theory of causation to account for union of form and matter in its multitudinous variety of occurrence in universe. A., accordingly, posited a 'First Cause', which is the Unmoved Mover, i.e. God. He distinguished four kinds of cause: 'formal', 'material', 'final', 'efficient', which are the essential constituents of an event. In his *Ethics*, A. conceived of the good life as one of moderation between two opposing extremes of action.

Early Chr. thinkers preferred Plato's philosophy to A.'s, believing latter to be materialistic. Knowledge of A. only became available to medieval scholars, through Arabic trans. in 12th cent.; it became very influential, because →→ Albertus Magnus and Thomas Aquinas built their systems on an Aristotelian basis. S.G.F.B.
Editions and trans. of Aristotle are manifold. The Loeb Classical Library provides convenient eds. of text and trans. to many works. Cf. *E.R.E.*, I, pp. 786–91; *O.C.D.*, *s.v.;* L. Robin, *La pensée grecque* (1928), pp. 288ff.; *C.A.H.*, VI, ch. XI; B. Russell, *A Hist. of Western Philosophy* (1946), pp. 182ff., 474ff.; *R.A.C.*, I, 657–67; *D.C.C.*, *s.v.; Kleine Pauly*, I, 582–91; *R.G.G.*^{3}, I, 597–606; G. Leff, *Medieval Thought* (1958), pp. 171ff.

Arius → Arianism. S.G.F.B.

Ariya-Sacca (Pali); **Arya-Satya** (Skt.) → Truths, Four Holy. T.O.L.

Arjun The fifth → Sikh → Guru, who led the community from 1581 to 1606. Apart from building the Harimandir (Golden Temple) at Amritsar (later to be rebuilt in present form by Ranjit Singh → Sikhism) and helping to consolidate community, he compiled first authoritative version of the scriptures (→ *Granth, Adi*). This was later completed and finalized by → Gobind Singh, who included, among other extra material, hymns written by A. The new prosperity of the community under A. marked a consciousness of identity of the Sikhs as a separate group in the Panjab, but it attracted unfavourable attention from Akbar's successor, Jehangir, who suspected A. of favouring his son Khusrao, who had raised a rebellion against him. From this time onward there was considerable hostility on the part of the Mughals to the Sikhs, driving the latter under Gobind to organize themselves as a military community. A. himself was arrested and imprisoned in Lahore, where he was severely tortured. Ultimately, having been given permission to wash in the river Ravi, beside the prison, he was overcome by shock and carried away by the waters. N.S.

Ark (of Noah) The large vessel built by Noah (Gen.

6:14ff.), to save himself, family, selection of animals from the → Flood, had its prototype in ship that served same purpose in Mesopot. Flood legend. The A. was subject of allegorical speculation in Judaism and Christianity. Because of its saving function, it was seen as a symbol of Church: if often appears in early Chr. art. S.G.F.B.

A. Heidel, *The Gilgamesh Epic and Old Test. Parallels* (1949), pp. 232ff.; *R.A.C.*, I, 597–602; *D.C.C., s.v.*

(of Yahweh) Also called 'Ark of God' and 'Ark of the → Covenant'. Acc. to Dt. 10:1ff., a chest of acacia wood, containing stone tablets of Covenant. A. localised presence of Yahweh; it was focus of ritual, and was carried into battle. Solomon put A. in the → Temple; its ultimate fate is unknown. The orig. nature and significance of the A. are obscure: one hypothesis is that it was throne-seat of Yahweh during nomadic period of Israel's hist. The 'Ark of the Covenant' was interpreted by Chr. Fathers as symbol of Christ. S.G.F.B.

H.D.B.[2], p. 53; *E.R.E.*, I, *s.v.; D.C.C., s.v.;* J. Leven, *The Hebrew Bible in Art* (1944), pp. 63ff.; H. H. Rowley, *Worship in Anc. Israel* (1967), pp. 53ff.

Armageddon (R.V. gives Har-Magedon) Name given in Rev. 16:16 for place where the forces of evil will fight battle against God. A. is gen. identified with Megiddo in Palestine, which had been site of many great battles. S.G.F.B.

H.D.B.[2], *s.v.*

Armenia, Armenians The name Armenia is first met in cuneiform inscript. of the Achaemenian period (*c* 6th–5th cent. BC); it formed part of anc. state of Urartu, of which the capital was Tuspas, the modern Van. Acc. to Vannic inscriptions (840–640 BC), the chief god was Khaldis, with whom local deities were identified. Gods of sun and air were assoc. with Khaldis, thus forming a divine triad. The vine seems to have been esp. venerated; inscripts. give long lists of animals sacrificed to Khaldis. These Vannic peoples were not → Aryan, but Aryans gained control of A. highlands by end of 7th cent. BC. These Aryan invaders became the A.'s of history. They orig. called themselves *Hayy*: they prob. came from E. Anatolia. A. became subject to Iranian influence, and a form of → Zoroastrianism was estab., the goddess Anahit (→ Anahita) being very prominent. This Zoroastrianism lacked many characteristic features, in partic. there was no developed → dualism; it was in fact a polytheism. The A.'s were the first nation to accept Christianity, being converted by Gregory the Illuminator in 3rd cent. The dogmas of A. Church are similar to those of Orthodox Church, although A. Church is reputed to be → Monophysite. Some A.'s are in communion with R.C. Church. The A.'s have often been terribly persecuted, partic. by Turks and Soviets. There are A. communities in England and America. The A. version of N.T. was trans. in 3rd–4th cents., prob. from Old Syriac version: it was later corrected to standard Grk. version. S.G.F.B.

E.R.E., I, pp. 793–807; B. B. Piotrovskh, *The Kingdom of Van and its Art* (E.T. 1967); R. N. Frye, *The Heritage of Persia* (1962), pp. 65ff.; *D.C.C., s.v.; R.A.C.*, I, 678–89; *R.G.G.*[3], I, 610–6; S. Runciman, *The Medieval Manichee* (1955), pp. 26ff.; N. Zernov, *Eastern Christendom* (1961), pp. 72ff., 168ff.; S. D. Nersessian, in *The Dark Ages*, ed. D. T. Rice (1965), ch. 4; K. Sarkessian, *The Council of Chalcedon and the Armenian Church* (1965); *R.M.E.*, I, ch. 9.

Arminianism A theological reaction, named after its initiator Jacobus Arminius (1560–1609), against strict determinism of Calvinism (→ Calvin). A. upheld belief that sovereignty of God was compatible with human free-will, and that Christ died for all men and not only for the elect. Since A. was Dutch in origin, it became involved in contemporary Dutch politics and was persecuted, until a more tolerant attitude prevailed in 1630. A. doctrine was formally set forth in the Remonstrance of 1610. A. had considerable influence of formation of modern Prot. theology. In 17th cent. England anti-Calvinism was termed A., though its connection with orig. Dutch movement is unclear. John → Wesley held A. outlook. S.G.F.B.

E.R.E., I, *s.v.; D.C.C., s.v.; R.G.G.*[3], I, 620–2.

Art, Sacred (General) Relig. or magical needs prob. provided the orig. impetus to A. in both its plastic and linear forms. In earliest human culture, *c.* 30,000 BC, painting and sculpture were used in hunting and fertility magic (→ Cave Painting) and attempts were prob. made to repr. deities (→ Palaeolithic Religion). In Neolithic culture relig. used art forms (e.g. portrait-skulls at → Jericho; murals in sanctuary at → Çatal Hüyük). This earliest relig. A. was functional, not decorative. The linear or plastic depiction of an object was intended to utilise its potency either by making it perpetually present (→ Ritual Perpetuation of Past) or to effect what it represented: e.g. image of 'Venus' of Laussel (→ Palaeolithic Relig.), with emphasised breasts and womb, or that of the pregnant goddess with emphasised naval at → Çatal Hüyük, were prob. intended to promote fertility; or Palaeolithic pictures of animals pierced with darts to promote a successful hunt.

If A. was created to serve religio-magical needs, it also reacted upon relig. Once the image of a specific deity was created, that image profoundly influenced subsequent popular ideas of the deity concerned. In most religs. an iconographic trad. became estab., it being often regarded as sacrosanct (e.g. in →→ Egypt. Relig.; → Hinduism, → Buddhism; of Chr. → Ikon). Veneration of divine images does not depend usually on their artistic worth. Other factors can operate: their antiquity, supposed divine origin or miraculous power. But high quality can count: e.g. statue of → Zeus by Pheidias at Olympia was found inspiring. Another import. aspect of relig. art was repr. of ritual acts on walls of temples or tombs (esp. in Egypt). The motive was prob. magical: the person so depicted is ever before the gods in adoration and prayer. Mortuary art has also had great significance. In Egypt it was vital to future life of deceased (→ Funerary Ritual, Egypt); elsewhere it has been commemorative (e.g. Grk.-Roman, Etruscan, Christian mortuary A.). Sometimes relig. art has been protective (e.g. winged monsters guarding Assyrian temples; the Chinese → *t'ao-t'ieh*). Relig. art has often been didactic, imparting instruction by depicting sacred truths, e.g. the vignettes of Egypt. → Book of the Dead; medieval Christ. art (→ Dooms, medieval). A. has also served in the honouring of deity. Temples, cathedrals and churches, mosques and pagodas have been lavishly constructed and adorned, acc. to resources of contemporary A., as offerings to, and sometimes as abodes of, the divinities concerned (→ Architecture).

The needs of relig. have also encouraged the minor arts of metal-working, jewellery, textiles (→→ Vestments, Opus anglicanum), stained glass, calligraphy (esp. in Islam). (→→ Drama, Relig.; Music). S.G.F.B.

E.R.E., I, pp. 817–88; S. Giedon, *The Eternal Present* (1962); T. G. E. Powell, *Prehistoric Art* (1966); S. G. F. Brandon, *History, Time and Deity* (1965); R. Hamann, *Aegyptische Kunst* (1944); H. Frankfort, *The Art and Architecture of the Ancient Orient* (1954); K. Woermann, *Geschichte der Kunst*, I (1915); *R.G.G.*[3], IV, 126–81; *Bilderatlas zur Religionsgeschichte* (1924); Lübke-Pernice, *Die Kunst der Griechen* (1948); A. de Ridder and W. Deonna, *L'art en Grèce* (1924); *O.C.D.*, p. 102; D. Talbot Rice, *The Beginnings of Christian Art* (1957); F. van der Meer and C. Mohrmann, *Atlas of the Early Christian World* (1958); A. Grabar, *Beginnings of Christian Art* (E.T. 1967), *Byzantium* (E.T. 1966); E. I. Watkin, *Catholic Art and Culture* (1947); E. Mâle, *L'art religieux du XIIe. siècle en France* (1953), *L'art religieux du XIIIe. siècle en France* (1947), *Religious Art: from 12th to 18th cent.* (1949); A. Katzenellenbogen, *The Sculptural Programs of Chartres Cathedral* (1959); H. Focillon *The Art of the West in the Middle Ages*, 2 vols. (1963); D. T. Rice, *Art of the Byzantine Era* (1963); G. H. S. Bushnell, *Ancient Arts of the Americas* (1965); B. Rowland, *The Art and Architecture of India* (1953); D. Talbot Rice, *Islamic Art* (1965); F. Sierksma, *The Gods as We Shape Them* (1960); E. Panofsky, *Tomb Sculpture* (1964); A. Hauser, *The Social History of Art*, I (1951); G. Van der Leeuw, *Sacred and Profane Beauty* (E.T. 1963); E. Bevan, *Holy Images* (1940); H. Zimmer, *Myths and Symbols in Indian Art and Civilization* (1946); W. Willets, *Chinese Art*, 2 vols. (1958); A. Malraux, *The Metamorphosis of the Gods* (E.T. 1960).

(Buddhist) Much of the art of Buddh. countries has been directly inspired by Buddh. ideas and practices, although very little (unless lit. is incl.) has been work of Buddh. monks: the production of works of art has been primarily done by Buddh. laymen. Sculpture, painting and architecture are the major fields; music is not encouraged in Buddh. devotional contexts and is not used by monks, whose corporate chanting of suttas in devotional services bears some slight similarity to European plain-chant but is basically a reciting aloud. In field of sculpture, however, Buddhism has a rich record, partic. in develop. of the → *rupa*, or Buddha-statue, from early beginnings in N.W. India to its mod. forms in S.E. Asian countries, notably in Thailand. The painting of murals on walls of monasteries and temples has also had a long develop. and has produced many different styles; the principal subjects have been, and still are, scenes from life of Buddha, and from → Jātaka stories. In field of architecture the → *stupa* has provided ample scope for rich develop., culminating in such structures as the pagodas of S.E. Asia, notably the Shway Dagon, in Rangoon; monasteries and temples have also provided outlet for rich creative skills, the results of which are to be seen throughout Buddh. Asia from Ceylon to Japan. The subject is a vast one; the reader must be ref. to specialist works on subject, a few of which are mentioned below →→ Ajanta: Gandhara). T.O.L.

B. Rowland, *The Art and Architecture of India* (1959); A. K. Coomeraswamy, *Elements of Buddhist Iconography* (1935); S. Kramrisch, *The Art of India* (1954); H. Zimmer, *The Art of Indian Asia*, 2 vols. (1955); R. Le May, *Buddhist Art in Siam* (1967); R. T. Paine and A. Soper, *The Art and Architecture of Japan* (1955); D. Seckel, *The Art of Buddhism* (1964).

(Islam) The → '*ulamā*' have gen. expressed disapproval of art which represented living creatures, both in painting and statuary. Qur. v, 92, which incl. *al-anṣāb* (→ idolatry) among forbidden practices, has been adduced as argument against representations; but the argument is questionable, for *al-anṣāb* are part of heathen worship whereas works of art need not become idols. The Qur. condemns idols (e.g. xxvi: 70ff.; xxi: 52ff., etc.), but this does not necessarily incl. works of art. Trad. is more precise. It speaks of → angels refusing to enter house where there are representations (*Mishkāt*, p. 940); of God on Day of Resurrection rebuking those who have made representations and telling them to give life to their creation (*Mishkāt*, pp. 940f.). But a trad. which says that those who make representations will receive the severest punishment from God (*Mishkāt*, p. 941) is interpreted by some as meaning those who make them to be worshipped. The '*ulamā*' have allowed representations of trees and inanimate objects, but not of human beings and animals. Yet while they have condemned art widely, apart from calligraphy and formal designs, it has always flourished in some regions, notably Persia, India and Turkey. Even in early period in Syria under the → Umayyads, and Baghdad under the → 'Abbasids, art was valued. In Spain, and Egypt under the → Fāṭimids, art was highly cultivated. In relig. circles it appears that real objection to art was connected with fear of idolatry, and of presuming to copy God in his creative work. But while conservative leaders may still use old arguments expressing their disapproval of artistic representations of living creatures, one need only look at the stamps of modern Muslim states to see how fear of representing human beings has gone. Yet, while Islamic art of great beauty has been produced in many regions, there has always been tendency among many sincere people to consider it with suspicion. J.R.

E.I., IV, pp. 561ff. (*ṣūra*), pp. 682f. (*taṣwīr*); *M.W.*, XLV (1955), pp. 250ff. ('Muslims and Taṣwīr'), trans. of article from the journal of al-Azhar; J. Berque, 'L'art musulman', in Charnay, *Normes*, pp. 101ff.; Pareja, pp. 660f.

Arta (Asha) 'Righteous Order' acc. to → Zoroaster. A. was Iranian counterpart of Vedic → Rta, being the principle of cosmic order. The concept had moral implications: it could connote truth and righteousness (→ Maat). S.G.F.B.

J. Duchesne-Guillemin, *Zoroastre* (1948), pp. 59–62; L. von Schroeder, *Arische Religion*, I (1914), pp. 346–52; Zaehner, *D.T.Z.*, pp. 285ff.

Artapanos 2nd cent. BC Jew. writer who sought to show that famous Jews, such as → Abraham, Joseph and → Moses, were the tutors of the Gentiles in astronomy, agriculture, technology, philosophy and worship of God. Frags. of his *Peri Ioudaiōn* are preserved by → Eusebius, *Praep. ev.* 9, 8.23, 27. S.G.F.B.

P. Dalbert, *Die Theologie der hellenistisch-jüdischen Missions-Literatur unter Ausschluss von Philo u. Josephus* (1954), pp. 42ff.; *Kleine Pauly*, I, 614–5.

Artemis Grk. goddess, but prob. pre-Hellenic: her name appears on Pylos tablets. A. seems orig. to have been connected with the earth, and wild places and animals, being a 'lady of wild things' (*potnia thērōn*). She was a fertility goddess, assoc. with child-birth, and was prob. a mother-goddess before Grks. venerated her as a virgin goddess. Her mythology is meagre, and, despite later legend, she prob. had no orig. connection with → Apollo. She was worshipped with strange rites in many places. A. was identified with several foreign goddesses, incl. great goddess of → Ephesus. In Rome she was identified with → Diana. (→ Ariadne). S.G.F.B.

O.C.D., s.v.; Kleine Pauly, I, 618–25; W. K. C. Guthrie, *The Greeks and their Gods* (1950), p. 99.

Arthur, Arthurian Legend The cycle of legend concerning A. is not only intrinsically interesting and important: it affords instructive example of how legend can grow about a folk-hero. The A.-L. provides a medieval parallel to Sumerian legend-cycle of → Gilgamesh. The oldest mention of A. is by Nennius (9th cent. CE), who calls him *Dux bellorum*, in British resistance against invading Saxons. Many scholars have thought that A. was, therefore, a historical person who played heroic role during obscure period of post-Roman Britain. However, in Welsh lit., esp. the *Mabinogion*, which preserves much anc. Celtic folklore, A. appears as a beneficent giant, battling with witches and monsters, and journeying into Underworld. The connection between this mythical folk-hero, an historical 6th cent. British leader, and the courtly King Arthur of English, French, and German romance, with all the trappings of medieval chivalry, is a subject of continuing archaeological and literary research. S.G.F.B.

G. and T. Jones (trs.), *The Mabinogion* (1949); E. K. Chambers, *Arthur of Britain* (1927); *E.R.E.*, II, *s.v.;* N. K. Chadwick, *Celtic Britain* (1963), pp. 45ff.

Arūpa-Loka (or Dhātu, or -Bhava) → Cosmology, Buddhist. T.O.L.

Aruru Babylonian goddess, who assisted → Marduk in creation of mankind (→ Cosmogony, Mesopot.). S.G.F.B.

Arval Brothers Anc. Roman fraternity concerned with a primitive agricultural ritual: their most import. ceremony was held in May in honour of goddess Dea Dia. The Emp. → Augustus restored fraternity *ante* 21 BC, which caused A.-B. to become concerned for welfare of imperial house. A hymn of the A.-B., the *Carmen Arvale*, has been preserved. (→ Acca Larentia) S.G.F.B.

W. Warde Fowler, *The Religious Experience of the Roman People* (1911); *O.C.D.*, *s.v.* ('Fratres Arvales'); *Kleine Pauly*, I, 629–31.

Arya Samāj (Noble/Aryan Society') a mod.

reforming group within Hinduism founded by → Dayananda Sarasvati. The Society was founded in 1875 in Bombay, but in fact had its greatest influence in Lahore and the → Panjab generally, where conversions were made from → Sikhism, as well as among Hindus. The teachings of the A. S. were unitarian, egalitarian and somewhat nationalistic, repr. in part a reaction to the forces of Christ. mission and mod. science intro. into India under the Eng. Raj. It was also strongly scripturally oriented: the truth was to be seen in the Veda. However, Dayananda Sarasvati interpreted Vedic hymns in a strictly monotheistic sense, and was opposed to idolatry and cult of gods—Vedic relig. had not made use of temple-worship or of images. But some strain was required to interpret the hymns monotheistically, and the A. S. was also keen to see the germs of mod. science, etc., contained already in the Veda. The movement was strongly proselytizing, though it was involved in schism after founder's death, in 1883. However, it continued fairly vigorously and promoted educational institutions, charities, etc. Its present headquarters are in Delhi. N.S.

Dayananda Sarasvati, *Light of Truth* (1932); G. P. Upadhyaya, *The Origin, Scope and Mission of the Arya Samaj* (1940); P. D. Padale, *The Endowed Arya Samaj in Hinditown* (1953); J. N. Farquhar, *Modern Religious Movements in India* (1919); H. Bhattacharyya, ed., *The Cultural Heritage of India*, vol. 4 (1956).

Āryadeva Younger contemporary and pupil of → Nāgārjuna, who was founder of the Mādhyamika Buddh. → Mādhyamika system. A. is sometimes ref. to simply as Deva; sometimes as Bodhisattva Deva. His activity as an exponent of Mādhyamika should prob. be dated during 1st half of 3rd cent. CE. The sources of information for his life are: the biography trans. into Chinese by → Kumārajīva (4th–5th cent. CE); the Chinese pilgrim → Hsüan-tsang's travel diary, and two Tibetan histories, those of → Bu-ston and Taranatha. A great deal of the material in these sources is, however, legendary. Acc. to Hsüan-tsang, A. was one of the 'four suns' who illumined the world, the other 3 being → Asvaghosa, Nāgārjuna, and → Kumāralabhda. Hsüan-tsang records also that he was a native of Ceylon. This is confirmed by 6th cent. CE writer Candrakīrti, in his commentary on A.'s. *Catuḥśataka*. A. left Ceylon for S. India, poss. because the Mahāyānist trend of thought, to which he was attracted, had more congenial environment in S. India than in predominantly → Theravādin Ceylon. There were close contacts at that time between these 2 areas, espec. between Ceylon and Nāgārjunikonda, the centre of Nāgārjuna's teaching activity. Nāgārjuna and A. are trad. connected also with → Nālanda, the great monastic centre of learning in N.E. India.

A.'s principal written work is the *Catuḥśataka*, the '400' treatise (i.e. the treatise of 400 verses), the complete text of which is preserved in Tibetan trans. the Skt. orig. surviving only in fragments. The Skt. text has been reconstructed from the Tibetan by V. S. Bhattacharya (Vishva Bharati Series, 1931). The 1st half of work deals with the Madhyamika system of thought and its discipline; the 2nd half is devoted to refutation of the → Abhidharma, and of 2 of the six Indian (non-Buddhist) philosophical systems, the → Saṃkhya and → Vaiseśika. Other works attr. to A. are: the *Akṣara Śatakam*, a treatise expounding some 20 propositions of Mādhyamika philosophy; and the *Hasta-vāla-prakaraṇa* (the Hand Treatise), a summary of Mādhyamika doc. A restored Skt. text of this was pub. by F. W. Thomas in *J.R.A.S.*, 1918, (pp. 267–310).

A. was not only an import. literary exponent of the Mādhyamika school; he was also a powerful debater. Adherents of other contemporary schools of thought are said to have been frequently defeated in public debate with him. Acc. to Chinese sources this brought about his death: he was murdered by a disciple of a non-Buddh. teacher who had been worsted in debate. T.O.L.

T. R. V. Murti, *The Central Philosophy of Buddhism* (1955), pp. 92–5; H. Winternitz, *Hist. of Indian Literature*, vol. 2; E. Obermiller (tr.) *Bu-Ston's History of Buddhism in India and Tibet*; V. S. Bhattacharya, *The Catuḥśataka of Aryadeva* (1931).

Aryans (Aryan Religion) The development of comparative philology in 19th cent. led to idea of an orig. racial group whose language was source of a number of related languages (Sanskrit, Old (Avestan) Persian, Greek, etc.). This racial group was called Aryan (*ex.* Sanskrit = noble') or Indo-European. Situated orig. in the Pontic and Caucasian Steppes, the group broke up during 2nd mil. BC, its migrating members settling eventually in Anatolia, Iran, N.W. India, Greece, Italy, and W. Europe. From comparative study, initiated esp. by Max Müller, of mythology of → *Rig-Veda*, → *Avesta*, and Grk. lit., attempts were made to reconstruct an orig. A.-R. It was held to have centred round a sky-god, perhaps called *deiwos*, whose memory was preserved in Sanskrit *dyáus pitā*, Grk. → Zeus, Lat. → Jupiter, and Teutonic Tiu. The origin of the A. is still much discussed, with new archaeological data coming to light. The problem of A.-R. entered a new stage with the studies of G. → Dumézil, who has sought, *inter alia*, to show by comparative philology, that A. society was tripartite, comprising priests, warriors, and agriculturists. He has also laid stress on duality of deity in the pair → Varuna-Mitra. (→ Mithras). Some scholars have welcomed Dumézil's theories, but others remain unconvinced. (→ Scandinavian Relig.). S.G.F.B.

V. G. Childe, *The Aryans* (1926); *E.R.E.*, II, pp. 11–57; G. Dumézil, *Les dieux des Indo-Européens* (1952); *Mitra-Varuna* (1948); *R.H.R.*, 152 (1957), pp. 8ff.; J. Duchesne-Guillemin, *The Western Response to Zoroaster* (1958), pp. 33ff.; E. O. James, *The Worship of the Sky-God* (1963), pp. 67ff.; R. N. Frye, *The Heritage of Persia* (1962), pp. 19ff.; E. D. Philips, *The Royal Hordes* (1965), pp. 39ff.

(in Hinduism) Term derives from the Sanskrit *ārya*, lit. 'noble', which was used in the Vedic corpus to ref. to the people among whom Vedic culture had arisen. They conceived themselves as 'noble' in relation to the inhabitants of N. India whom they conquered. Thus 'Aryans' is typically used to ref. to the Indo-European-language-speaking groups who entered India from the northwest during early and middle part of 2nd mill. BC. The A. traversed Iran before entering India, and there are similarities between early Iranian relig. and that of the Vedic hymns. There are also broad similarities to other branches of Indo-European speakers, such as the Romans, Greeks and Celts, e.g. a similar division of society into three classes, extended to four and then in effect five (→ *varnas*) among the A. in India, due to the domination of successive elements in the indigenous population. The A. were lighter skinned than the latter; distinction between the upper classes, esp. the Brahmins, and, e.g., the Dravidian-speaking population of S. India, still is in part maintained. *Arya* was also used as an honorific term in early Buddhism, e.g. to ref. to the noble eightfold path. N.S.

V. Gordon Childe *The Aryans* (1926); P. L. Bhargava *India in the Vedic Age* (1956); A. L. Basham *The Wonder that was India* (1954).

Āsana Yogic posture or mode of sitting. The practice of cultivating certain bodily postures is the third member of eightfold technique of Hindu → Yoga, and it is closely coupled with → breathing control (*pranayama*). Both are central to that aspect of Yoga (Hatha Yoga) which deals with physiological processes, and are a preliminary to mental control culminating in → *samadhi*. Different treatises describe differing numbers of *asanas* (one, e.g., describes as many as thirty-two). The most common posture is the *padmāsana* or 'lotus-posture', in which left foot is placed on right thigh and right foot on left thigh. Such postures are not only used in the Yoga school of Hinduism, but also in other relig. movements (e.g. Buddhism); they also play an import. part in Indian iconography. N.S.

Asaṇga Indian Buddh. philosopher of 4th cent. CE, founder of the → Yogācāra or Vijñāna-vāda school. His most import. work was the *Yogācārabbhūmi-Śāstra*. It is held that A. had no human teacher (hence his name: A-sanga, 'unattached'), but had received his doc., that of Yogācāra, direct from the heavenly Buddha → Maitreya. This 'supernatural' teacher has, however, been identified by some mod. scholars with a human preceptor, an hist. personage named Maitreya-natha, regarded as orig. author of the *Yogācārabhūmi-Śāstra*. Others, notably Demiéville, have rejected this identification, on grounds that attempt to find in Maitreya a human teacher is due to a 'manie historiciste introduite de l'Occident', and a basic misunderstanding of relig. psychology, espec. that of → Mahāyāna Buddhism, where it is customary to attr. doctrines to supernatural inspiration, often that of Maitreya. Not all mod. scholars are convinced by Demiéville's objections: T. R. V. Murti maintains that Maitreya-natha's historicity is now firmly estab. S. Dutt takes a similar view. A. is gen. held to have been eldest of three brothers, born in Purusapura (mod. Peshawar, in W. Pakistan). The second brother was → Vasubandhu; the third was Viriñcivatsa, of whom little is known, except that he became an → arahant. Acc. to Paramartha's *Life of Vasubandhu*, main source of information about A., Vasubandhu's criticism of Mahāyāna doctrines grieved A.; but when these were properly expounded to Vasubandhu by his brother, he was converted from the → Sarvāstivāda school, and became a Mahāyānist. In order to compensate for his earlier criticisms, he then began, at instigation of A, to devote himself to an acute and skilful exposition of the Yogācāra doctrines.

A.'s own works expounding Yogācāra are, principally, the *Mahāyāna-saṇgraha*, the *Yogācārabhūmi-Śāstra* (unless this is attr. to an hist. Maitreya-natha), and the *Mahāyānasūtrālankāra*. The second of these sets out the 17 stages, or → bhumi, by which the → Bodhisattva achieves Buddahood. These, acc. to A., consist of intellectual and spiritual attainments; these 17 *bhūmis* taken together are called *Yogācārabhūmi*.' The first part of text has been ed. by V. S. Sastri (*The Yogācāra-Bhūmi of Acarya Asanga*, Calcutta University 1957). The *Mahāyānasūtrālankāra* has been ed. by Sylvain Levi, and trans. into French. Levi notes that there is in this work an element of → Manichean and → neo-Platonic thought. The area in which A. lived, namely → Gandhāra, had been one of strong Graeco-Roman influence since time of Alexander the Great. Another work, which has been connected with A.'s name, is the Tantric Buddh. work, *Guhya Samāja Tantra*. If the connection is accepted, A. is seen as an important leader of the Tantra, or → *Vajrayāna*. T.O.L.

G. Tucci, *On some Aspects of the Doctrines of*

Maitreya (*nātha*) *and Asanga* (1930); E. Frauwallner, *On the date of the Buddhist Master of the Law Vasubandhu* (Serie Orientale Roma III) (1951); P. Demiéville, La Yogācārabhūmi de Sangharaksa', in *Bulletin de l'Ecole Francaise d'Extreme Orient, XLIV*, fasc. 2 (1954).

Āsava (Pali); **Āsrava** (Skt.) The 'influxes' or 'taints', 4 in number, which in Buddh. thought are regarded as intoxicating the human mind and preventing spiritual progress. The 4 influxes are *kāmāsava*, sensuality; *bhav-ā.*, lust for life (rebirth); *ditth-ā.*, false view or speculation; *avijj-ā.*, ignorance. The 4 together are frequently mentioned in the *Sutta* → *Pitaka.* In some cases 3 only are mentioned; *ditth-ā.* being omitted. This may represent earlier usage; *ditth-ā.* having been added later. The extinction of the A.'s was held to constitute arahantship, hence a syn. for the → arahant is *anāsava*, i.e. one in whom there is no (*an-*) *asāva.* Another such syn. is *khīnāsava*, i.e. one whose A.'s are destroyed (*khīna*). The A.'s are ref. to also as 'floods' (*ogha*) and as 'yokes' (*yoga*). T.O.L.

Ascension of Christ Recorded in Lk. 24:51; Acts i:9: trad. located on Mt. of Olives. The A.-C. constitutes the definitive end of incarnational life of Christ. His A. into the sky implies belief in a celestial Heaven, whence he had descended to earth. In terms of Comparative Relig., A.-C. is a form of → Apotheosis, and it parallels withdrawal of → Osiris from world after his resurrection and justification. Although raised from death, neither Osiris nor Christ resume their *antemortem* life. Heb. trad. records other ascensions: e.g. of Enoch, Elijah. The feast of A.-C. has been kept from later part of 4th cent.; a → basilica was built on trad. site in 325. S.G.F.B.

*H.D.B.*², *s.v.; D.C.C., s.v.; R.G.G.*³, III, 333–6; C. Kopp, *The Holy Places of the Gospels* (E.T. 1963), pp. 405ff.

Ascetical Theology Theological discipline concerned with advancing the spiritual life by estab. modes. A.S. is distinguished from Moral Theology and Mystical Theology. The *Spiritual Exercises* of Ignatius → Loyola is a notable and much used treatise on A.T. (→ Theology). S.G.F.B.

F. P. Harton, *The Elements of the Spiritual Life* (1932); *D.C.C., s.v.*

Asceticism (General) Grk. word *askēsis*, from which A. derives, means 'exercise', 'training'; but it denotes one aspect only of customs, practices, and ideas to which A. is gen. applied. To acquire self-control by discipline of body and mind is an obvious notion, widely adopted for both relig. and secular ends: e.g. in war and sport. Such discipline can be positive or negative; hard physical tests or mental concentration; abstention from food, sleep, sexual intercourse. Relig. A. has also been motivated by a low estimate of body, often regarding it as contaminating prison of soul (→ Dualism II). On this view, A. is designed to subjugate body to soul, and often takes form of punishing body e.g. by flagellation (→ Flagellants). A. of this kind can be pathological in character. Such A. has sometimes been thought to confer supernatural power (e.g. Hindu → *tapas*), or win merit (e.g. Jew. fasting, cf. Lk. 18:12), make atonement (e.g. Flagellants), propitiate deity (e.g. scourging of boys at altar of Artemis Orthia). The practice of A. has been both individual and communal. A good example of linking of two occurs in legend of → Buddha; seeking enlightenment by his own ascetical life, his reputation quickly led six other ascetics to join him (→ Antony, St.). Communally organised A. produced → monasticism. The Buddhist → Sangha, and poss. → Pythagorean communities are oldest forms of organised A. The → Therapeutae and → Essenes (→ Qumran) were Jew. communities of ascetics. A. in → Stoicism was essentially discipline of self-control, designed to make mind impervious to irrational promptings of emotions.

Where A. connotes contempt of body, a this-world-denying attitude is gen. assoc.: this has been notably so in →→ Buddhism; Christianity; Gnosticism; Manichaeism. Sometimes contempt of body has produced an inverted A., i.e. insulting body by subjecting it to abominable uses, usually of sexual kind. A. has been absent from those religs. having a this-world-affirming outlook or a *carpe-diem* attitude (e.g. Egypt., Mesopot., Israelite, Greek (Classical), Zoroastrianism). S.G.F.B.

E.R.E., II, pp. 63–111; *R.G.G.*³, I, 639–42; *R.A.C.*, I, 749–58.

(Buddhist) The practice of physical austerities was a familiar feature of India in the Buddha's time. Contemporary ascetics are ref. to in the Pali canon by various names. In the *Mahāsihanāda Sutta* (MN. I.77ff.), Buddha tells Sariputta of his own experience as an ascetic during period before his enlightenment. He had engaged in bodily self-mortification as means to spiritual attainment; but gaining no spiritual benefit he abandoned these practices. (→→ Buddha, Gotama). In gen., therefore, the Buddh. attitude towards A. is to avoid this extreme, and, avoiding also opposite extreme of hedonism, to follow the Middle Way between the two. The life of the Buddh. monk, as prescribed in the → *Vinaya*, is one of self discipline; extreme asceticism is forbidden. A list of some 13 practices of self-humbling kind, mentioned separately at various places in Pali canon, is given in the → *Visuddhimagga* II; these are recommended as helping to promote right attitudes of mind. They are as follows: (1) wearing patched up robes; (2) wearing no more than minimum of 3 robes; (3) going for alms-food; (4) not discriminating between houses on alms-food round; (5) eating one meal only each day; (6) eating from alms bowl only; (7) declining further offers of food; (8) living in the forest; (9) living at the foot of tree; (10) living under open sky; (11) living in a graveyard; (12) being satisfied with one's dwelling; (13) sleeping in sitting position rather than lying down. Even in following such practices, however, it is emphasised that monk must do so for sake of frugality, contentedness, purity etc., rather than for praise; otherwise they will be of no value: mere external performance is not real self-discipline. (*Puggala-paññatti*, P.T.S. 1883, 275–84). T.O.L.

(China–Japan) A. finds practically no place in the native religs. of China and Japan. → Confucianism, with its pronounced humanism, frowned upon all forms of self-mortification and abstinence, except that officiants at sacrifices were expected to prepare themselves by a period of purification and fasting. Certain schools of → Taoism, in their search for the prolongation of life, taught the need for strict physiological disciplines and abstinence from certain foods. Taoist recluses and adepts seem at times to have practised extreme forms of A. Some Taoist lay societies imposed on their members strict abstinence from meat, wine etc.

Refs. to early → Shinto in Japan speak of men called 'abstainers', who were not allowed to comb hair, wash, eat flesh or approach women. The hereditary priestly corporation of 'Imbe' (root—*imi*, to abstain), whose function was to prepare offerings to the gods, had to abstain from all defilement or impurity. Abstinence was a common form of preparation for relig. festivals. → Buddhism, imported into China and Japan, taught a strict discipline of body and mind, and certain sects not only forbade eating of meat but all forms of self indulgence. Many monks in Buddhist monasteries practised A. along with intense meditation.

The life-affirming attitude of China and Japan was, on the whole, not conducive to A. D.H.S.

E.R.E., II, pp. 96–7.

(Christ.) The ascetical ideal is firmly estab. in the N.T. Acc. to Mk. 8:34, Jesus called men to self-denial, and Paul compared Chr. life to games in which 'every man that striveth . . . is temperate in all things' (I Cor. 9:25). With such exhortations went a low evaluation of body and an exaltation of virginity. A., in form of abstinence, fasts, vigils, characterised life of early Christians, and was closely linked with expectation of → martyrdom. After estab. of Christianity as official relig. of Roman Empire and cessation of → persecution, A. found expression increasingly in → monasticism. The monastic threefold vow of poverty, chastity and obedience constituted a permanent form of A., which was supplemented by organised ascetic. practices of abstinence, fasting, vigils, manual labour and austere conditions of living. The Renaissance and → Reformation resulted in widespread rejection of A. Monasticism, and its ideals, ended in Prot. lands, and humanist values, stemming from revival of pagan antiquity, produced unsympathetic ethos in many Cath. countries. However, ascetical ideal was upheld by Council of Trent (1545–63), and new relig. orders were formed. Puritanism repr. a kind of A., and ascetical practices were promoted by early → Methodism and the Oxford Movement. Within Christianity extravagant forms of A. were professed by certain sects, e.g. Montanists, →→ Gnostics; Manichaeans; Albigenses; Cathari; Waldenses. S.G.F.B.

E.R.E., II, pp. 73–80; *D.C.C.*, *s.v.; R.A.C.*, I, 758–95; *R.G.G.*[3], I, 642–8.

(Hindu, Jain, etc.) The relig. of the Vedic hymns was not notably ascetic, but there is mention of groups of ascetics—the *muṇis* or 'silent ones' and the *vrātyas*, who also practised a fertility cult (→ *Atharvaveda*). In late Vedic period the power of A. (→ *tapas*, lit. 'heat', is a key term for ascetic practices) is recognized; for austerities give a person magical powers surpassing even those of the gods. Assoc. with *tapas* was practice of meditation and → yoga. These forces were assimilated into Brahmanical relig. in the → Upanishads; the eremitical ideal was enshrined in the 'stages of life' or four → *asramas* by period of classical Hinduism. Whether ascetic practices can be traced back to → Indus Valley Civilization is not altogether clear; but since there are evidences of → yoga there, it is probable. At time of the Buddha, there was a wide class of *parivrājakas* or wandering teachers of various persuasions; and six → *sramaṇas* heading sects are mentioned. Among the import. ascetic movements were → Jainism and the → Ajivikas. Even some → Carvaka materialists practised A., despite their disbelief in rebirth, etc. Later texts describe large number of types of ascetic. Some were married, while others were celibate—though sometimes assoc. with A. were orgiastic practises of a sexual kind, often orig. in fertility rites. Thus the Kapalikas, predecessors of the more recent Aghoris, practised orgiastic copulation in graveyards, etc., and lived in part off human flesh. A common garb of the ascetic was the ochre or red coloured ragged robe, adopted in Buddhism, but there was also a large class of naked ascetics, incl. the Ajivikas and the → *Digambara* Jains. Others clad themselves in bark. Variety of beliefs existed among them in classical period; inscriptions ref. to *Bhagavatas* (→ *Bhakti*) who worship

Kesava, others who follow → *sruti*, as well as to groups already mentioned. Saivite ascetics gen. wore matted hair, like Shiva himself; while removal of hair from body was practised by Ajivikas and Jains (and moderately by Buddhists). The Ajivika initiation in this respect was peculiarly severe, as the initiate was buried up to neck and the hairs pulled out. Though much A. was geared to interior exercises (→ Mysticism, Hindu), there is evidence from early times of more exhibitionist kinds of self-mortification, incl. holding one's arms above head till they withered, staring at sun till one went blind; while the five-fire *tapas* was quite common, Ascetics gen. controlled their diet in various ways: some regulating eating by phases of moon, others by eating only berries, etc., available in forest, others eating cow dung; and most getting food by begging. The respect in which they were mostly held derived partly from recognition of their supernormal and magic powers, incl. power to burn up enemies, to fly through air, remember past lives, know mental states of other people, and render oneself invisible. (Such *siddhis* also played part in Buddhism; the notion of *Siddhas* or perfected ones remains an import. feature of N. Indian folklore). In medieval Hinduism, the development of → monasticism encouraged a moderate A. comparable to that of Buddhism, but it never dominated the complex of ascetic orders, etc.; and India has remained a country of wandering *sādhus*. In late medieval times there emerged some orders of fighting ascetics, degenerating ultimately into gangs, and these were suppressed under British rule. The major festival for → *sannyasins* is the Kumbha Mela at Prayag (Allahabad: → Festivals, Hindu). As a sign of the ascetic's not belonging to → Aryan society, for he has transcended it, it is typical for him to be buried rather than cremated. N.S.

J. W. Hauer, *Der Vratya* (1927); J. C. Oman, *The Mystics, Ascetics and Saints of India* (1903); J. N. Farquhar, 'Organization of the Sannyasis of the Vedanta', *J.R.A.S.* (1928), p. 15ff., and 'The Fighting Ascetics of India', *B.J.R.L.*, vol. ix (1925), p. 431ff.; A. L. Basham, *History and Doctrines of the Ajivikas: A Vanished Indian Religion* (1951); M. Eliade, *Yoga: Immortality and Freedom* (1958).

(Islam) *Zuhd* (self-denial) developed from idea of abstinence from sin to complete A., which was practised by some in early cents. of Islam, the ascetics being forerunners of the → Ṣūfīs. A famous ascetic of Khurāsān was Ibrāhīm b. Adham (d. 160/777) who renounced his wealth to become a wandering ascetic, and taught abstention from all worldly possessions beyond barest necessities, and complete trust in God. → Rābi'a of Basra (d. 185/801) was so wrapped up in her love of God that she abjured all human pleasures. She refused offers of marriage because she belonged to God. Ghazālī, in *al-maqṣad al-asnā*, Cairo, n.d., 33, says true abstinence makes one think this world and the next of no importance and concentrate on God alone. To practise A. in this world merely to gain reward in next is declared by him to be on level of a commercial transaction. Ascetics considered struggle against human passions the greater → *jihād*, as resisting desires is more import. than fighting infidels. While *zuhd* has remained a principle among Ṣūfīs, it has not always been interpreted so stringently, but is treated as a stage on the Ṣūfī path. J.R.

E.I., IV, p. 1239; Pareja, pp. 744ff.; Nicholson, *Mystics*, index; Arberry, *Sufism*, ch. 4; J. M. Abun-Nasr, *The Tijaniyya* (1965), pp. 46ff.; M. Smith, *Rābi'a the Mystic* (1928), *passim.*

-Ash'arī 'Alī b. Ismā'īl (260–324/873–935), pupil of al-Jubbā'ī, leading → Mu'tazilite in Basra, left party *c.* 300/912 and moved to Baghdad *c.* 323/935. He adopted the docs. of → Aḥmad b. Ḥanbal, who held closely to trad., but applied rational arguments. He countered Mu'tazilite doc., holding that God possesses eternal attributes, that the Qur. is God's speech, therefore uncreated, that good and evil are created by God who is omnipotent, that a Muslim guilty of serious sin is still a believer, but will be punished in hell for a time. He held that, while Qur. references to God's hand, face, his sitting on Throne, and the beatific vision in paradise were not to be understood as attrib. corporeality to God, they were to be accepted as read though we do not understand them. He gathered disciples, with result that a school was developed. It had its vicissitudes, but came grad. to be recognised as almost the orthodox doc. in Sunnī Islam; yet it had its opponents who disapproved of philosophical arguments. J.R.

*E.I.*², I, pp. 694f.; Pareja, index (al-Aš'arī); D. B. Macdonald, *Theology*, index; Wensinck, *Creed*, index; Watt, *Philosophy*, index, and bibliography, pp. 90, 113; Sweetman, *I.C.T.*, II (index of authors), IV (index of proper names); *G.A.L.*, I, pp. 207f., *S.I.*, pp. 345f.

Ash'arites → Ash'arī had attracted followers who developed his doc. and became a definite school. They had their difficulties for a time, as they were not looked on with approval; but later, under the Saljūqs, they came into favour. The famous wazīr Niẓām al-Mulk (410–485/1019–20–1092) gave them every encouragement, and their learned men taught in the colleges he founded. The earliest member of school, some of whose works are available, is al- → Bāqillānī. Some members came to differ from Ash'arī by treating anthropomorphic terms in Qur. metaphorically.

Among distinguished members of school were → Juwaynī and → Ghazālī. Qushayrī (376–465/986–1072), another famous A., is noted as writer on → Sufism, his *Risāla* being a standard work. Within Sunnī Islam, the A. came to be recognised practically as representatives of orthodoxy; but in mod. times there are tendencies to move away from some of the strict docs. J.R.

*E.I.*², I, p. 696; Gardet and Anawati, *Introduction à la théologie musulmane* (1948); Watt, *Philosophy*, index; Sweetman, *I.C.T.*, II, IV, index; Pareja, index (aš'arites).

Ashes Used ritually in many religs. either as a purificatory substance, of apotropaic kind, or as sign of mourning and humiliation. (→ Ash Wednesday). S.G.F.B.

E.R.E., II, *s.v.; H.D.B.*², *s.v.*

Asherah O.T. designation for Canaanite goddess Athirat, a creatrix and consort of → El, who appears in → Ugaritic texts as mother of the gods. Her cult, of a fertility kind, was condemned by Heb. prophets. A. could also mean sacred trees or poles, used ritually as symbols of goddess. (→ Ashtart). S.G.F.B.

T. Gray, *The Canaanites* (1964), pp. 15ff.; R. Dussaud, *Les religions des Hittites et des Hourrites, des Phéniciens et des Syriens* (1945), pp. 362ff.; *H.D.B.*², *s.v.;* R. Patai, 'The Goddess Asherah', in *J.N.E.S.*, 24 (1965).

Ashkenazim Jew. designation, of medieval origin, (*ex.* Gen. 10:3; I Chr. 1:6), for Jews of German- and Slavonic-speaking lands, distinguishing them from the Sephardim, i.e. Spanish and Portuguese Jews. Yiddish was spoken by the A. Medieval Jews mistakenly took 'Ashkenaz' to mean Germany. S.G.F.B.

*H.D.B.*², *s.v.;* H. J. Zimmels, *Ashkenazim and Sephardim* (1958).

Ashrams, Hindu The ashram (term also used for a 'stage of life', → *asramas*) as a centre of relig. teaching and spiritual living has been more characteristic of trad. Hinduism than regular → monasticism. The anc. practice of forest-dwelling (→ *vanaprastha*), as a means of withdrawal from world, and the common ideal of living as a holy recluse, lie behind institution of the A. Students (→ *brahmacarin*) would come for instruction in Vedic lore to Brahmanical forest-dwellers, while more gen. the recluse (→ *sramana*) would tend to attract disciples. Import. A. tend to attract pilgrims, and conversely places of pilgrimage acquire A., as in the Himalayan centres of Rishikesh and Hardwar. Among famous mod.A. is that of Gandhi at Sevagram; the largest and most highly organised is the → Sri Aurobindo A. at Pondicherry. A number of Christian A. have been started, to indigenize Christianity (→ Christianity in India). N.S.

Ashtart (Astarte) Canaanite fertility goddess, whom Hebrews called Ashtoreth, vocalising name with vowels of *bōsheth* ('shame'). In O.T., A. is confused with → Asherah; but → Ugaritic texts distinguish between latter and A., who is consort of → Baal. The cult of A. was condemned by Heb. prophets both because it challenged supremacy of → Yahweh, and for licentious character of its rites: A. was served by sacred → prostitutes. A., and prob. Asherah are Canaanite forms of great Mesopot. goddess → Ishtar (→ Anat). A. was later identified with → Aphrodite and → Isis. S.G.F.B.

*H.D.B.*² ('Ashtoreth'); *E.R.E.*, II, pp. 115–8; J. Gray, *The Canaanites* (1964), pp. 121ff.; D. Harden, *The Phoenicians* (1962), pp. 87ff.; *R.A.C.*, I, 806–10.

Ashtoreth → Ashtart. S.G.F.B.

Ashur (Assur) Name of both state god and anc. capital of Assyria, and of Assyria itself. (→ Assyrian relig.). S.G.F.B.

'Āshūrā' The 10th day of Muḥarram, first month of lunar year, was adopted from Jews by → Muḥammad as a fast day when he went to Medina. Later Ramaḍān (→ fasting) replaced it both in length of fast and manner of its observance. The 'A. is still held as a fast by many orthodox Muslims. In N. Africa it seems to have adopted old agrarian rites which are observed. Amongst the → Shī'a, the 10th of Muḥarram is celebrated by passion plays representing the death of → al-Ḥusayn at Karbalā in 61/680. This concludes period of ten days' mourning. *Ta'ziyas*, representations of his tomb, are carried in procession. A horse with coverlets spattered with red and arrows fixed in its harness is led to indicate Ḥusayn's horse. The *ta'ziyas* are commonly broken up after the procession. 40 days later another period is observed, when the horse is decked up and story of Ḥusayn is repeated, with outbursts of weeping by the hearers. J.R.

*E.I.*², I, p. 705; Pareja, pp. 647, 649, 654; Hughes, p. 25; Watt, *Medina*, pp. 199, 203, 307; *Mishkāt*, pp. 409, 433f., 437f.; Wensinck, *Handbook*, p. 26.

Ash Wednesday In Christ. calendar, first day of → Lent. Name derives from anc. ceremony of putting ashes on foreheads of faithful as sign of penitence. S.G.F.B.

D.C.C., *s.v.*

Asmodaeus Evil demon in Jew. *Book of Tobit* (3:17), who prob. derives from Iranian demon of wrath, *Aēshmā daēva*. S.G.F.B.

*H.D.B.*², *s.v.; R.G.G.*³, I, 649 ('Asmodi').

Aśoka (Ashoka) Ruler of Mauryan empire of N. India in 3rd cent. BC who, after conquest of Kalinga, became a Buddhist. The founder of the Maurya dynasty, Chandragupta, in wake of Alexander the Great's invasion of N.W. India, had extended the Magadhan kingdom into W. half of N. India. His son, Bindusāra extended it yet further; Ashoka, by his conquest of Kalinga gave it a S.E. seaboard, so that it extended across India from sea to sea. This last campaign, with its terrible bloodshed, produced in Ashoka a psychological crisis. He embraced the faith which had made its appearance in Magadha 2 centuries earlier, that of the Buddha; in his own words, there was heard thenceforth in his domains no longer the sound of the drum, but the sound of the *Dhamma* (*Dhammaghosa*). The main sources of information about A. are 2-fold: (1) Pali chronicles produced by Buddh. monks, which portray him as a Buddh. emperor; (2) archaeological evidence in form of rock and pillar-edicts and epigraphs, for which A. himself was responsible. Whereas the Pali chronicles repr. A.'s empire as Buddh., and A. himself as a missionary enthusiast seeking to propagate the Buddh. faith outside his realm, the edicts reveal a monarch who, while he himself a Buddhist, with personal contacts with the → Sangha, nevertheless encouraged and patronised various relig. communities as natural part of his duty as an Indian ruler. The edicts frequently mention the → *Dhamma,* which A. wished his subjects to follow and to practise. But it is not certain that this word, of widespread use in anc. India before it was given a special meaning by Buddhists, here denotes the Buddha-Dhamma. T.O.L.

G. P. Malalasekere, *D.P.P.N.*, vol. I, pp. 216–9; V. Smith, *Asoka* (3rd edn. 1920); S. Dutt, *Buddhist Monks and Monasteries of India* (1962), pp. 107–14; E. Lamotte, *Histoire du Bouddhisme Indien* (1958); A. Sen, *Asoka's Edicts* (1956).

Asperges Ritual sprinkling of altar and congregation with → Holy Water at principal Mass on Sundays in R.C. Church. Ceremony dates from 9th cent.; its orig. purpose was prob. to → exorcise demons. (→ Absolutions of Dead). S.G.F.B.

D.C.C., s.v.

Āśramas, Four Four stages of life in trad. Hinduism, which provided a scheme of living permitting ascetic withdrawal from world without implying monasticism as practised in Buddhism, Jainism, etc. The theory of the A. was indeed a defence against the Buddhist challenge to Brahmanical religion, seeing that many younger men and women were attracted by monastic existence. The first stage of life, from → initiation until marriage was that of the celibate student (*brahmacārin*). Next there was the period as → *grhastha* or householder. At an age when household responsibilities could devolve on the next generation, the householder becomes hermit (*vānaprastha*), practising → asceticism and acting as preceptor of young. Finally the person becomes a wandering recluse (→ *sannyasin*), sustaining his frugal existence by begging, and hoping to gain final liberation. This ideal pattern applied primarily to → Brahmins. The scheme was meant to ensure orderly completion of a man's family, relig. and social duties before moving on to deep spiritual exploration, and contrasts with pattern evident in lives of the Buddha, Mahavira and others. However, Hinduism did make provision for → monasticism; it is clear that for most of Indian history the four stages were gone through only by a minority. N.S.

Assassins Branch of → Ismā'īlī section of the → Shī'a, which had period of strength in Persia and parts of Iraq and Syria till their independent rule was brought to end by Hūlāgū, under whom the grand-master of Alamūt was put to death in 654/1256, and by Baybars, the Mamlūk sultan of Egypt, who finally captured their fortresses by 671/1273. The founder was al-Ḥasan b. al-Ṣabbāḥ, who went from Persia to Egypt in 471/1078. He supported Nizār, eldest son of al-Mustanṣir, for succession to the → Fāṭimid Caliphate; but it went to a younger son. Though movement is called Nizārī, al-Ḥasan was real head. He occupied fortress of Alamūt, N.W. of Qazwīn, by 483/1090, and it remained chief centre till 654/1256. 'Assassins' is derived from *hashshāshiyyūn* (Indian hemp smokers). The purpose of practice was to produce ecstasy and make devotees ready for any act of disobedience to governors. Assassination was a common weapon, not confined to this party. The docs. of sect are really unknown. They prob. followed in gen. Ismā'īlī teaching. There were various degrees, the grand-master, the initiates, headmen of districts, propaganda agents, and fanatics called *fidā'is* (suicide squad), ready to risk lives by assassinating those marked down for that end. There are still remnants of the Nizaris in India, Persia, C. Asia, Syria and E. Africa, whose head is the → Agha Khān. He is treated with extreme deference. J.R.

E.I., I, pp. 491f. (Assassins); *E.I.*², I, pp. 352–4 (Alamūt); Pareja, index (Alamūt, assassins, Nizāriyya); Hitti, *History*, index; B. Lewis, *The Assassins* (1967); Juvayni, *Tarīkh-i-Jahān-Gushā*, trans. J. A. Boyle, 2 vols (1958), index.

Assumption of Virgin Mary Belief that the → Virgin Mary at death, or three days after, was taken up, both body and soul, into heaven, first appears in N.T. apocrypha at end of 4th cent. The doc. was first formulated in W. Church by Gregory of Tours (d. 594), and was gen. accepted in E. Church by 7th cent. It was defended by → Albertus Magnus and Thomas → Aquinas. In 1950 Pope Pius XII officially defined doc. and provided new Mass for Feast. The N.T. contains no evidence of belief; it repr. a natural development of cult of Virgin Mary, following precedent of → Ascension of Christ and of Enoch and Elijah. S.G.F.B.

D.C.C., s.v.; R.G.G.[3], IV, 789 (d).

Assyrian Religion Assyria, which dominated Fertile Crescent during 12th–7th cent. BC, was a Semite state partaking of gen. culture of Mesopotamia. Its relig. embodied beliefs and practices that stemmed from → Sumerian relig. The chief A. god was Ashur, whose name designated both the land and its capital city. During their hegemony, Assyrians replaced → Marduk, supreme god of Babylon, by their god Ashur, thus making him creator of universe and mankind. Ashur was depicted as a warrior god. After Ashur, → Ishtar was next import. deity, her military aspect predominating. Other leading Mesopot. gods took their place in A. pantheon (→→ Sin; Shamash; Adad; Bel-Marduk; Nabu; Nergal). A. temples followed Sumerian-Akkadian pattern; priesthood had same ritual duties, incl. study of → omens. The cult incl. same practices: prayers, offerings and sacrifices. Magic played an import. role, partic. in private life. Fear of gods was basis of A.-R., as of Babylon. relig. The A. doc. of man was similar: gods would reward piety with prosperity and long life; the eschatology was of same pessimistic kind as Babyl. and Sumerian. (→→ Eschatology, Mesopot.; Mesopot. Relig.). S.G.F.B.

L. Delaporte, *Le Mésopotamie* (1923), pp. 345ff.; B. Meissner, *Babylonien u. Assyrien*, II (1925); M. Jastrow, *Aspects*, pp. 41ff.; E. Dhorme, *R.B.A.*, pp. 156ff. For Assyrian texts see *A.N.E.T.*

Astral Religion Modern designation for a complex of faith and practice, current in Graeco-Roman society, connected with the stars. There was no A.-R. organised as such, with priesthood, creeds and sacred lit.; but there was a discernible pattern of belief that was widely diffused and influential. Relig. significance of astral phenomena is very anc. In the → Pyramid Texts immortality was achieved by joining the circumpolar stars. Union at death with sun-god → Re was also a long estab. Egypt. belief. Worship of heavenly bodies long existed in Mesopot., which was also home of → astrology. The importance of Mesopot. in this connection led earlier scholars of so-called Pan-Babylonianism to locate origin of all A.-R. there. Present opinion finds origins rather in Ptolemaic Egypt, prob. under stimulus of Iranian-Mesopot. cultural influences. Mystic writings, prob. composed in → Alexandria *c.* 150 BC, and ascribed to fictitious king Nechepso and priest Petosiris, became profoundly influential in promoting A.-R. in Graeco-Roman world. These apocryphal writings were powerfully reinforced by → Hermetic lit. Elaborate chronological systems relating astral phenomena, divisions of time, and human destinies, were worked out. The stars were divinised, sometimes being identified with trad. deities, and even the hours had their own gods. A hierarchy related to zodiac, incl. 10 Decans, and 360 *Monomoiriai* was constructed. Astrology was utilised, and → horoscopes were of primary importance. Star-gods were thought to inhabit their stars. The planets in partic. were regarded as ruling world and deciding fates of men (→ Archōn(tes)). A.-R. became closely assoc. with → mystery religions, and also with Jew. angelology (→ Angels). The N.T. reflects contemporary A.-R. Paul ascribes crucifixion of Christ to the *archontes* (I Cor. 1:6ff.), and repr. → salvation as deliverance from astral forces (e.g. Gal. 4:3); astralism is prominent in *Rev. of John*. Traces of A.-R. can be found in early and medieval Christ. thought, owing to influence of astrology. A.-R. had an important place in → Gnosticism. S.G.F.B.

F. Cumont, *Astrology and Religion among Greeks and Romans* (E.T. 1912); *Les religions*, ch. VII; *R.Ae.R.-G.*, pp. 749–51; A.-J. Festugière, *La révélation d'Hermès Trismègiste*, I (1950); *R.A.C.*, I, 810–7; *R.G.G.*[3], I, 662–4; J. Seznec, *La survivance des dieux antiques* (1940); J. Doresse, *The Secret Books of the Egyptian Gnostics* (E.T., 1960); J. Bidez and F. Cumont, *Les Mages hellénisés* (1938), I, pp. 133ff., II, pp. 274, n. 10, 283; M. P. Nilsson, *Numen*, I (1954), pp. 106ff.

Astrology To anc. Mesopotamians stars were the 'writing of Heaven', and they believed that destinies of nations and men were written there. Consequently a science of interpreting astral phenomena was evolved. Careful record was kept of position of various heavenly bodies coincident with notable events, in expectation that with similar astral conjunctions similar events would again occur. Ref. to the zodiac, of basic importance for A., dates from 700 BC. It was also believed that individual destinies could be forecast by studying position of stars at time of birth: a cuneiform text exists giving horoscope of a child born on 29 April 410 BC. This 'Chaldaean' science spread far afield. It became popular in Graeco-Roman world, and was closely related to → Astral Religion. It naturally tended to produce a sense of fatalism. A. also became connected with → Alchemy through identification of planets with specific metals. The foretelling of Christ's birth by a star (Mt. 2:2) helped to commend A. to Christians, though many warnings against it were given by various Fathers. It continued into Middle Ages, being used even by Popes, and it survived the Reformation. Belief in A. grad. declined as astronomy became more scientifically based; but it still continues as a form of folk-belief in W. Society. A. became firmly estab. in Islam, India, and China: it would seem likely that Mesopot. A. reached both India and China, although later developments in both lands were indigenous. (→ Americ. Relig. anc.). S.G.F.B.

E.R.E., XI, *s.v.* ('Sun, Moon and Stars'); B. Meissner, *Babylonien und Assyrien*, II (1925), pp. 247ff., 400ff.; H. W. F. Saggs, *The Greatness that was Babylon* (1962), pp. 489ff.; O. Neugebauer, *The Exact Sciences in Antiquity* (1957); *R.A.C.*, I, 817–31; *Kleine Pauly*, I, 660–4; *R.G.G.*[3], I, 664–6; J. Needham, *Science and Civilisation in China*, II (1956), 351ff.; R. Eisler, *The Royal Art of Astrology* (1964); J. W. Montgomery, 'L'astrologie et l'alchemie luthériennes à l'époque de la Réforme', in *R.H.P.R.*, 46 (1966). See Bibliography to Astral Religion.

Astronomy/Astrology, Hindu Study of *jyotiṣa*, combining both what would be counted as astronomy and astrology in the West, was early recognized as important in Hindu tradition; it was one of the six *Vedangas* (→ *Veda*) or sciences subsidiary to the study of scripture required of the Vedic student. *Jyotisa* was necessary for calendrical purposes, in connection with the timing and execution of complicated rituals. The calendar was worked out on a lunar basis, though a solar calendar was known from time of the Maurya dynasty. In classical and medieval Hinduism, *jyotisa* became increasingly import. for fixing of rites such as marriage, and for prediction of successes and disasters, horoscopes, etc., and remains a pervasive feature of mod. Indian life. Sometimes planets were considered to influence fruits of → *karma*, a theory synthesizing astrology and *karma*-doctrine, and were identified, e.g., with different *avataras* of → Visnu. Most of the trad. held a geocentric view of the solar system (→ cosmology, Hindu). N.S.

Details of how to compute the highly complex Hindu calendar and eras are given in A. L. Basham, *The Wonder that was India* (1954); *Aryabhatiya, an Ancient Indian Work on Mathematics and Astronomy* (1930).

Asuras The 'antigods' of Vedic and post-Vedic Hinduism. *Asura* is equivalent to the Iranian *ahura* (→ Ahura Mazda) and was orig. honorific term applied to deities such as →→ Indra and Varuna. It came, however, to be used of evil gods at war with the → Aryans and threatening human life, such as Vṛtra, who witholds the rain. Sometimes, in the Vedas, the *Mahabharata* and elsewhere it is hard to distinguish between the A. as antigods and the A. as worshippers of the antigods. Thus some categories of A. such as *piśācas* (raw flesh eaters) and *dasyus* (barbarians), undoubtedly are groups against whom the Aryans fought in their gradual conquest of N. India. There are also accounts of intermarriage between Aryans and A. The opposite of A. is the *devas*, favourable gods. N.S.

A. Danielou, *Hindu Polytheism* (1964); J. Dowson, *A Classical Dictionary of Hindu Mythology* (1891).

(Buddh.) Common term for demons in anc. India, *asuras* are mentioned almost always collectively in Pali canon as a spirit-host, hostile to all forces of goodness. The word A. is cognate with *ahura* in Iranian, where, however, it denotes a good spirit. In Pali canon A.'s are usually mentioned in assoc. with their counterparts, the → *devas*, or heavenly beings, with whom they wage continual war. A.'s are incl. within whole range of living being subject to renewed existence; but are regarded as very low in the scale, being one of the four forms of evil rebirth poss. to human beings. The lord of the A.'s (*asurinda*) is Rāhu (AN. II, 17). Another name for this 'lord' is Vepacitti (SN, IV, 202). T.O.L.

Aśvaghosha Name of a Buddh. writer, or writers. To an A. of 1st/2nd cent. CE is attributed authorship of → *Buddha Carita*, *Saundarānanda*, and *Śariputra-Prakarana*. The Mhy. work, '*The Awakening of Faith*' (*Śraddhotpāda Śāstra*), preserved in Chinese, has also been attr. to this A.; but Murti considers that ideas elaborated in this work are post-Nāgārjuna (4th cent. CE), and therefore work of another A., of 5th cent. CE. S. Dutt has suggested that on grounds of style, manner, and contents the works commonly attr. to A. may be ascribed to 3 diff. authors. '*The Awakening of Faith*' is title of a trans. by D. T. Suzuki and T. Richard of the *Śraddhotpāda*; in this summary of Chinese and Tibetan, legends concerning A. are given, one of which speaks of no less than 6 A.'s who flourished at various times. A. thus seems likely to have been a name assumed by, or applied to, a number of different authors of various periods. Acc. to Tibetan trad., a man of this name was a leading figure at first Mhy. Council, convened by emperor → Kaniska, and was called upon to give precise formulation of doctrines agreed by the Council. T.O.L.

Aśvamedha The horse sacrifice, a Vedic and Hindu rite, which was the solemn culmination of consecration of king. The aim was to bring prosperity to him and to the people. A specially selected horse was released to wander for a year, accompanied by a group of → *ksatriyas*. The territory it traversed was deemed to belong to the kingdom (a theory which sometimes proved the occasion for clashes between neighbouring principalities). Under the protection of the *ksatriyas*, the horse returned to the orig. place of release at end of year. The horse itself was, among often a large number of animal and other offerings to → Agni, sacrificed. As part of the fertility ritual implicit in festival, the queen lay beside the dead horse. In post-Vedic times the sacrifice was performed by, among others, the Gupta emperors, and is last recorded in 9th cent. CE. N.S.

Jeannine Auboyer, *Daily Life in Ancient India* (1961); P. E. Dumont *L'Asvamedha* (1927).

-Aswad Born *Ka'b al-'Ansī*, called Dhul khimār (the veiled one), rose against Muḥammad in the Yemen. In 10/632 he led tribesmen and drove two of Muḥammad's agents from Najrān, then occupied Ṣan'ā'. -A. is said to have been a false prophet, prob. rather a soothsayer (*kāhin*) and magician; but his rising seems to have been more political than relig. Dissension broke out soon after; he was killed in 11/632 before Muḥammad's death. His movement was called the first apostasy (*ridda*) (→ apostasy) in the Yemen. Soon after the more famous *ridda* took place and was soon crushed by → Abū Bakr's forces. J.R.

*E.I.*², I, p. 728; Muir, *Life*, pp. 478f.; Watt, *Medina*, pp. 128–30 and index; Guillaume, *Life*, p. 648; *Mishkāt*, p. 964.

Asylum *Ex.* Grk. and Lat. words meaning 'refuge', 'sanctuary'. The custom has been widespread among mankind of allowing refugees (usually criminals), and sometimes animals, to remain unmolested in certain specific places, usually of a sacred nature, e.g. temple, sacred grove, or tomb. The right of A. existed among many primitive peoples of modern world (e.g. in C. Australia, Hawaii, N. America, India, Africa, Morocco). In anc. Israel altars (Ex. 21:13ff.) and later six cities (Dt. 4:41ff.) were A.'s. Certain Phoenician, Syrian, Grk. and Roman temples gave A., and it existed among pagan Slavs and Teutons. The custom was accepted by Christianity, and many churches had right of sanctuary, though it was increasingly restricted. Various reasons have been suggested for institution. Since it was invariably connected with sanctuaries, it would seem to be relig. in origin. Poss. it stemmed from idea that a refugee becomes guest of deity in whose sanctuary he seeks A., and thus can claim guest-rights, usually held to be sacred. S.G.F.B.

E.R.E., II, *s.v.; R.A.C.*, I, 836–44; *R.G.G.*³, I, 666–8; *D.C.C.*, *s.v.; Kleine Pauly*, I, 670–1.

Atargatis The 'Syrian Goddess', whose name compounds 'Atar = Ashtart and 'Ate' (?). A fertility goddess, A.'s chief temple was at Hieropolis-Bambyce, in Syria. Her consort was → Hadad; at Ascalon she was repr. as half-woman, half-fish. Her cult spread in 3rd cent. BC to Egypt and Macedon, and later to many other areas, incl. Britain. Grks. recognised A. as form of → Aphrodite. A. was identified with constellation Virgo, and thus was assoc. with → astrology. Like the Canaanite → Astarte, A. was doubtless a local Syrian form of → Ishtar. S.G.F.B.

E.R.E., II, *s.v.; O.C.D.*, *s.v.; R.A.C.*, I, 854–60; *Kleine Pauly*, I, 1400–3 ('Dea Syria').

Ate Grk. personification of divine temptation or infatuation that caused a person to pursue conduct that must inevitably prove fatal. Homer (*Il.* 19:90ff.) uses concept, personifying it as daughter of → Zeus, in dealing with problem of divine moral responsibility. S.G.F.B.

E. R. Dodds, *The Greeks and the Irrational* (1951), pp. 2–8, 37–41; *Kleine Pauly*, I, 673–4.

Aten (Aton) Egypt. word for sun's disc. In reign of Amenhotep III (d. *c.* 1367 BC), the sun's disc, hitherto symbol of → Rē, the sun-god, became personalised. The change was poss. due to reaction of priests of → Heliopolis, anc. sanctuary of Rē, against exaltation of → Amun, god of Thebes. To be free of anthropomorphic associations, they presented A. alone as image of sun-god. The next king → Akhenaten attempted to make the A. supreme god of Egypt, thus supplanting Amun. In art, the A. is shown as disc, subtending rays, which end as hands caressing king and his family, or touching them with → ankh. Akhenaten composed hymns to the A., and built a great temple to it in his new capital at Tell el-Amarna. His conception of the A. was a noble one, and was monotheistic in character. The cult of the A. ceased after d. of Akhenaten. S.G.F.B.

R.Ae.R.-G., pp. 59–71; S. G. F. Brandon, *R.A.H.*, ch. 9; C. Aldred, *Akhenaten* (1968).

Athanasian Creed Formal statement of Chr. belief about the →→ Trinity and Christology. Its attribution to → Athanasius is not now gen. accepted. It was orig. written in Latin, and prob. dates between 381–428. It has been widely used in W. Christendom, but more rarely in E. Its → anathemas have been found distasteful by many modern Christians. The A.-C. is used in R.C. and Anglican Churches on certain prescribed occasions. It is also known as the *Quicumque vult* from its opening words in Latin. S.G.F.B.

D.C.C., *s.v.;* W. K. Clarke (ed.), *Liturgy and Worship* (1932), pp. 280ff.; J. N. D. Kelly, *The Athanasian Creed* (1960).

Athanasius (*c.* 296–373) The great champion of what became Cath. orthodoxy in controversies concerning divinity of Christ. A. became bishop of → Alexandria in 328, from when until his death he suffered many vicissitudes of fortune in opposing → Arianism. He laid foundations for ultimate triumph of orthodoxy at Council of Constantinople in 381. Besides maintaining essential deity of Christ, A. also upheld deity of the → Holy Spirit. A. had close relations with St. → Antony. S.G.F.B.

D.C.C., *s.v.; E.R.E.*, II, *s.v.; R.A.C.*, I, 860–6.

Atharvaveda Last of the four collections of → Vedic hymns, the A. comprises the magic lore of the 'Atharvans', a class of priestly magician. It contains large number of spells, together with stanzas and hymns appearing in the → *Rgveda*, and with prose sections in style of → *Brahmanas*, one of which is devoted to topic of the mysterious *vratyas*, a class of early ascetics, prob. of non-

Aryan provenance. Indeed much of the material in the A. arises out of magical and medicinal practices seemingly prevalent in the indigenous culture in process of being Aryanized. At same time, there are many incantations and formulae for use in domestic rituals, reflecting customs of lower-class → Aryans, etc. Spells used in connection with use of herbs for curing variety of diseases provide knowledge of early stage of Indian medicine (*ayurveda*), later fully developed classically by Caraka (1st cent. CE). There are also spells for the warding off of evil spirits, long life, protection of crops and cattle, victory for king in battle, success in gambling, compelling love, happy marriage, the destruction of rivals, expiation of moral and ritual transgressions, the procreation of children, prosperity, etc. A group of hymns are of greater philosophical and theological interest, in which various forces (Desire, *Kāma*; Time, *Kāla*; Breath, *Prāṇa*, etc.) are hypostatized. The attempt to identify various entities with ultimate reality (*Brahman*) in these hymns is analogous to speculations of the → *Upanisads*. Orig. the Veda was known as threefold, comprising the other three collections (just as Aryan society itself was composed of three classes, to which an assimilated fourth and lowest class was added); assimilation and expansion account for inclusion of fourth Veda. The inclusion of hymns from the *Rgveda* in it, together with *Brahmana*-like material and speculative Upanishad-like hymns just mentioned helped its elevation to equality of status with the other collections. N.S.

W. D. Whitney and C. R. Lanman (trs.), *Atharva Veda Samhita*, 2 vols. (1906); M. Bloomfield, *Hymns of the Atharva Veda* in M. Müller (ed.), *S.B.E.*, vol. 42 (1897); and *The Atharvaveda* (1899); N. J. Shende, *Religion and Philosophy of Atharvaveda* (1952); L. Renou *Religions of Ancient India* (1953).

Atheism (China–Japan) Since the rise of neo-Confucianism (→ Chu Hsi) in 10th cent. CE educated Confucians have been, in the main, atheistic, believing only in a supreme and universal Moral Law. Hence the materialistic and atheistic philosophy of Marxist Communism found ready acceptance in China. Popular religion, on the other hand, whether Taoist or Buddhist inspired, is incurably polytheistic, yet invariably accepting the reality of a Supreme Being over a hierarchy of gods and spirits. Islam and Christianity, with their belief in God, have exerted a considerable influence.

The Chinese from earliest times appear to have been almost incapable of thinking of spirit as existing apart from matter. Confucianism, though grounded in the theism of the early Chou Dynasty, became in main an ethical system to which were attached the worship of Heaven by the ruler, and the ancestral rites practised by most families. About the time of → Confucius (6th cent. BC) agnosticism rather than A. rose to challenge the earlier theism, though → Hsün-tzu, who exerted great influence, had no place in his system for a personal God. The Tao of → Taoism, a supreme, eternal, unknowable cosmic principle, became the generally accepted belief.

The populace of China as a whole cannot be termed A. → Buddhism and relig. Taoism developed a strong belief in a spiritual world and in life after death. D.H.S.

G. Wint (ed.), *Asia* (1965), pp. 308ff.

Though → Buddhism, as a philosophical system is averse to idea of a Supreme God, the great Amidist Jodo and Shin sects undoubtedly worship Amida Buddha in that capacity. → Zen Buddhism is non-theistic. The → Shinto sects which since the war have replaced National Shinto are almost all theistic. Among the educated, except for militant Marxists, agnosticism rather than A. seems to be the approved order. D.H.S.

(Indian) Some trad. Indian relig. and philosophical systems exclude belief in a Creator or in a supreme personal Object of worship, without however denying existence of gods and spirits as supernatural inhabitants of the cosmos. Thus the →→ Samkhya and Mimamsa schools of Hinduism, together with anti-Brahmanical movements such as →→ Jainism, the Ajuvikas and Theravada Buddhism have been averse to doc. of Creation and relatively indifferent to worship and sacrificial rituals directed towards God, *Brahman*, etc. Nevertheless, these schools and movements were deeply concerned about salvation, etc., and were not therefore atheistic in an anti-relig sense. They are thus to be distinguished from the → Carvaka (anc. Indian materialism), which explicitly denied concepts such as eternity of soul, efficacy of sacrifice, existence of God, possibility of salvation, etc. For the relig. atheistic system, the Indologist H. Zimmer coined the term 'transtheism', to indic. that they transcend belief in the gods, since liberated souls and great teachers are superior to the gods. Sometimes the term *nāstika*, used to ref. to unorthodox schools in Indian trad., i.e. those not accepting validity of Vedic revelation (→ revelation, Hindu), has been translated 'atheistic'; but this is inaccurate, since some orthodox schools are atheistic. N.S.

H. Zimmer, *Philosophies of India* (1956); but see N. Smart, *Doctrine and Argument in Indian Philosophy* (1964); D. Riepe, *The Naturalistic Tradition in Indian Thought* (1960); D. Chattopadhyaya, *Lokayata, Ancient Indian Materialism* (1959).

(Westernş ancient and modern) Word derives from Grk. *atheos*, 'without God', for it is in

Greece that W. trad. of A. begins. → Xenophanes held that men had created gods in their own image. → Anaxagoras was charged with A. for denying divinity of sun and moon. Teaching of various other Grk. philosophers tended to A., either by criticising myths of gods or presenting intellectual concepts of deity, as did → Aristotle, which negated idea of personal gods. A. was also used as term of abuse for Jews (→ Antisemitism) and early Christians, because of their non-acceptance of Roman state gods. Until invention of term → agnosticism in 19th cent., A. was used for all kinds of doubt about trad. theism. Modern A. can cover three different attitudes: philosophical agnosticism, which maintains that evidence is not sufficient for asserting or denying existence of God; pantheism which merges deity with universe; materialism which identifies material phenomena with reality. These three attitudes are lit. atheistic only when a definite denial of existence of God is made. Such denial is gen. made by materialists, esp. by supporters of Dialectical Materialism of Communism (→ Marx, K.). S.G.F.B.

E.R.E., II, pp. 173–83, 184–5a, 187–8; A. B. Drachmann, *Atheism in Pagan Antiquity* (1922); *O.C.D.*, *s.v.*, *D.C.C.*, *s.v.; R.G.G.*³, I, 670–7; G. van der Leeuw, *La religion* (1948), pp. 172ff., 582ff.; E. Frank, *Philosophical Understanding and Religious Truth* (1945), *passim.*

Athena (Name often prefixed by 'Pallas'). Patron goddess of Athens, who was also worshipped in other parts of Greece. A. was prob. a pre-Hellenic deity (→ Aegean Religion), being assoc. with a Mycenaean palace ('house of Erechtheus') on the Acropolis. A virgin goddess, she was closely connected with war, like many other goddesses of the Levant (→ Aphrodite, Astarte, Ishtar). A. was regarded as patroness of arts and crafts, and personified wisdom. Acc. to myth, her birth took form of her leaping fully armed from head of → Zeus when split by an axe. Her chief epithet *glaukōpis* ('owl-faced') has led to unconfirmed theory that she orig. from a → totem animal: the owl was indeed assoc. with her. A.'s most famous shrine was the Parthenon on Acropolis of Athens. The origin of her title 'Pallas' is obscure; many interpretations are current. It could well mean a *Virago*. Linear B texts give A.'s name with title *Atana potinija*. S.G.F.B.

C. Picard, *Les religions prehélléniques* (1948); W. K. C. Guthrie, *The Greeks and their Gods* (1950), pp. 106ff.; *O.C.D.*, *s.v.; Kleine Pauly*, I, 681–6; *R.A.C.*, I, pp. 870–81; L. A. Stella, 'La religione greca nei testi micenei', in *Numen*, V (1958), pp. 31ff.

Ātman (Hinduism) 'Self'—a key concept in Hinduism. The word prob. derives from the root *an* 'to breathe'. The term means 'self' in the ordinary sense, but in relig. and philosophical works it typically ref. to the eternal self or soul underlying physical and psychological processes. Most schools of Hindu philosophy and theology believe in a plurality of eternal selves, but in → Advaita Vedanta, there is only one Self, which is identical with → *Brahman* or ultimate reality. Thus, on this view, all living beings share (so to say) the one Self. The basis of the Advaitin view is the Upanishadic teaching that in some sense *Atman* is *Brahman* (→ *tat tvam asi*). In denying existence of many individual eternal selves, Advaita had an analogy to Buddhism, but the latter's *anātmavāda* or non-self doc. also excluded a single Absolute Self. Differing conceptions of selves or souls were held in various schools; indeed alternative terms to *ātman* were used by → Samkhya-Yoga (→ *purusa*) and → Jainism (*jiva*). However, it is characteristic of Indian trad. to treat the eternal self as different from the mind or discursive consciousness; the mental side of the individual is regarded as a subtle form of matter. This subtle matter is illuminated by the self, which is of the nature of pure consciousness. It thus lies 'behind' the normal psychological states that constitute the inner aspect of the individual's life. Typically, it is considered that the way to discover or have an existential realisation of the *atman* is by contemplative techniques, when consciousness is emptied of discursive thoughts, perceptions, etc. The *Brahman-atman* identification in the → Upanishads can be seen, therefore, as a synthesis between a relig. search based on sacrificial religion, which sees *Brahman* as the holy power pervading and sustaining the outer world, and the religion of → yoga and inner meditation, which seeks ultimate reality within. Though a rigorous application of the identification, as propounded in Advaita, was influential, there was also the intermediate interpretation of Visistadvaita, namely the view that souls are offshoots of the divine Being, partaking in large measure of latter's nature. The doc. of an eternal self was sometimes used to explain the continued identity of individual from one life to another, in the process of → reincarnation. The term *Atman* is also used in Upanishads and elsewhere for the Self animating universe, and the term *paramātman* ('supreme Self') is frequently a synonym for God (→ *Isvara*). → Anatta. N.S.

S. N. Dasgupta, *A History of Indian Philosophy*, vol. 1 (1922); Sarasvati Chennakesavan, *The Concept of Mind in Indian Philosophy* (1960); G. Tucci, *Storia della filosofia indiana* (1957).

Atomic Theory Orig. a theory advanced by Grk. philosophers Leucippus and Democritus (5th cent BC) to explain orig. and nature of universe. Acc. to A.-T., atoms of various kinds and size, falling through an infinite void, by mutual contacts and relations form the world. The → soul is composed of smooth round atoms, like fire, which penetrate body and vitalise it. The A.-T. was accepted by → Epicurus as providing explanation of universe without interference of gods. Forms of A.-T. were current in Indian thought, Islam, and medieval European thought. (→ Vaiśeṣika). S.G.F.B.

E.R.E., II, *s.v.;* G. S. Kirk and J. E. Raven, *The Presocratic Philosophers* (1960) pp. 400ff.; W. Jaeger, *Theology of Early Greek Philosophers* (1948), pp. 180ff.

Atonement 'At-one-ment'. The etymology of this English word well denotes its appropriateness in Chr. theology: i.e. the putting of man 'at one' with God through sacrificial death of Christ. The doc. of A. constitutes essence of Christianity; but it has never been officially defined, and various interpretations have been advanced concerning nature and mode of the A. achieved by Christ. The idea of A. is deeply rooted in O.T. (→ Atonement, Day of). It was integrated with sacrificial ritual: the offering of life of victim, symbolised by its outpoured blood, both propitiated → Yahweh and cleansed sinners, thus effecting reconciliation. The blood of → martyrs for Israel could be thought of in this way. The orig. → Jew. Christians prob. regarded death of Jesus thus. But → Paul saw death of Jesus as effecting → salvation of all mankind. In his Epistles, Paul suggests two main ways in which Christ's death saved men. One is indicated in I Cor. 2:6ff., whereby men are rescued from daemonic slavery (→→ Archon(tes); Soteriology), nothing being said of A. with God. The other invokes Jew. sacrificial ritual. Christ is equated with Paschal Lamb (I Cor. 5:7), expiation is made by his blood (Rom. 3:25), and by offering of his life men are reconciled to God (Rom. 5:10). Paul never formulated these suggestions into a doc. of A.; but they formed basis of subsequent interpretations. Some Fathers saw Christ's death as ransom paid to → Devil for man. → Anselm interpreted death of Christ as being the only adequate satisfaction for sin against God, on principle that sin is an infinite offence and requires an infinite satisfaction; only thus could A. be achieved, Christ taking place of man in the transaction. A new line was developed by → Abelard, whereby exemplary effect of Christ's death moves sinner to contrition and so makes A. → Luther taught that Christ was vicarious victim for man, and → Calvin developed an even stronger version of this 'penal theory' of A. Mod. interpretations gen. tend to be exemplarist, with notable except. of → Barth's. (→ sacrifice). S.G.F.B.

E.R.E., V, pp. 641b–50b, 653b–9a; A. Harnack, *H.D.*, 7 vols., *passim*; J. F. Bethune-Baker, *Intro. to Early Hist. of Christ. Doctrine* (1903), pp. 327ff.; L. W. Grensted, *A Short Hist. of Doctrine of Atonement* (1920); G. Aulén, *Christus Victor* (E.T. 1931); *D.C.C.*, *s.v.; R.G.G.*³, II, 586–99 ('Erlösung'); Brandon, *M.D.*, pp. 201ff.; *R.A.C.*, VI, *s.v.* ('Erlösung').

(China–Japan) In the sense in which the term is used in Christ. theologies, A. is practically non-existent in Chi. and Jap. religs. D.H.S.

(Day of) Known as *Yomā*, 'the Day', the impressive ritual transactions of D.-A. repr. culmination of sacrificial system of Jew. relig. The ritual of D.-A. is described in Lev. 16 (cf. 23:26–32, Nu. 29:7–11, Ex. 30:10). All three refs. are post-Exilic; but the rites were certainly practised long before this time, though poss. not integrated into the impressive ceremonies of Lev. 16. The D.-A., observed by strict fast and cessation from work, took place on 10th day of 7th month (Tishri). Its essential purpose was solemn purification of high priest, sanctuary, and people from contagion of sin, thus restoring rightful relations of Israel with → Yahweh, its god. The ritual, performed by high-priest, was complex and had two distinctive parts. The first consisted of sacrifice of a bullock and goats, and purification of → Ark, within Holy of Holies, by sprinkling victim's blood and burning of incense. The second part took form of high priest's making solemn confession of nation's sins over another goat, allotted to → Azazel. After this ritual transference of guilt, the → scape-goat was led out into desert: in N.T. times it was pushed to its death over a cliff 12 miles E. of Jerusalem. The high priest, and all who had touched the sacrosanct animals, had subsequently to bathe and wash their clothes. With necessary adaptations, the D.-A. remains most solemn and widely observed of all festivals of Jew. year. The D.-A. has been connected with ritual of Babylonian New Year Festival (S. H. Hooke, *The Origins of Early Semitic Ritual* (1938), pp. 52ff.; → Akitu). S.G.F.B.

*H.D.B.*², *s.v.;* J. Pedersen, *Israel*, III–IV (1940), pp. 359ff., 453ff.; R. H. Pfeiffer, *Intro. to Old Test.* (1948), pp. 266ff.; A. Lods, *Les prophètes d'Israël* (1935), pp. 332ff.; H. H. Rowley, *Worship in Anc. Israel* (1967), pp. 92ff., 133ff.; *E.J.R.*, *s.v.*

Atra-hasis Name of hero of the recently reconstructed Babylonian account of the → Flood. S.G.F.B.

Atthakathā (Buddh.) Pali term meaning 'a commentary' on Buddhist canonical scriptures. Acc. to → Buddhaghosa, there was in existence in → Ceylon in his day an anc. A. which, acc. to trad., had been brought from India by → Mahinda when Buddhism was intro. into island, and which he used as basis of his own work. He mentions that the version he received was in

Sinhalese, and that he trans. it into Pali. Nothing is known to have been directly preserved of this ancient, A., which may have existed in several sections, since Buddhaghosa refers to the 'composers' of the A. (*Atthakathācariyā*). The hist. portions of the A. provided the basic source for the later compilation known as the → Dipavamsa ('The Island Chronicle'), or hist. of Ceylon. There is evidence that the old A. was in existence in Ceylon as late as 12th cent. CE. T.O.L.

W. Geiger, *Pali Literature and Language*, 2nd edn. (1956), pp. 25f.

Atthasālini Name of commentary in Pali by → Buddhaghosa on the → Dhammasangani, first book of the → Abhidhamma Pitaka, of Buddh. Pali Canon. It is gen. held to have been composed in Ceylon, and may have been based on an earlier commentary by same writer and bearing same title, written while he was in India. The A. has itself been subject of further commentaries (*Tikā*) by Ceylonese and Burmese Buddh. writers from 12th cent. CE onwards. T.O.L.

Attis Youthful lover of → Cybele, the Great Mother, in anc. Phrygian relig. The cult of Cybele and A. spread through Asia Minor to Greece and Rome. There are variant versions of myth of A. explaining his self-castration and death, thus making him prototype of the eunuchs ('galli') who served Cybele (→ Castration). A. was orig. a vegetation god (→→ Adonis; Tammuz), whose death and resurrect. were ritually commemorated at equinoctial spring festival, with which → taurobolium was assoc. In art, A. appears as effeminate youth, with Phrygian cap and trousers, often with genitals exposed. The → *criobolium*, i.e. sacrifice of ram to A., poss. involving blood-baptism, with consequent purification and regeneration of initiate, paralleled taurobolium. The pine was sacred to A., thus suggesting orig. as tree-spirit. The 3rd day of festival of A. (March 24) was 'Day of Blood', when Archigallus presented own blood as offering. S.G.F.B.

J. G. Frazer, *Adonis, Attis, Osiris* (G.B.), I (1936), pp. 261ff.; Gressmann, *O.R.*, pp. 91ff.; *O.C.D.*, *s.v.; Bilderatlas* 9–11, Lief., Abb. 134–59; *R.A.C.*, I, 889–99; Ch. Picard, 'Sur quelques documents nouveaux concernant les cultes de Cybele et d'Attis', *Numen*, IV (1957); M. J. Vermaseren, *The Legend of Attis in Greek and Roman Art* (1966).

Attitude to other religions (China–Japan) In general the Chinese are tolerant of other religs. They are regarded as different ways to sagehood, and no way is absolute. Though the state sought to exercise tight control, and forbade relig. expression believed to be inimical to Confucian morality and good order, there have been no relig. wars and few relig. persecutions. At times (notably in CE 845), fierce persecution of → Buddhism and other foreign religs. was engineered by Confucian and Taoist scholars. Anti-Muslim and anti-Christian movements had political rather than religious motivation. From 10th cent. CE onwards, eclectic and syncretistic tendencies prevailed. Institutionalized relig. was comparatively weak. Indifference to relig. characterised the scholar-class, whilst popular relig. became an amalgam of beliefs and practices drawn from Confucianism, Buddhism and Taoism, and latterly from Islam and Christianity. D.H.S.

Chun I T'ang, 'Confucian and Chinese Religs.' in *Relations among Religs. Today*, ed. M. Jung et al. (1963).

Throughout Jap. hist. there are only exceptional instances of persecution and relig. wars. → Shinto and → Buddhism learned mutual tolerance, and syncretistic Ryobu Shinto developed. The most cruel and violent persecution of Christianity in early CE 17th cent. was politically motivated. The chauvinistic revival of national Shinto in 18th and early 19th cents. led to persecution of Buddhism towards the end of Tokugawa era and the Meiji restoration (1868). Freedom of relig. belief is accepted today, and the numerous sects of Shinto and Buddhism show remarkable mutual tolerance. (→ Mission). D.H.S.

M. Anesaki. *Hist. of Japanese Relig.* (1930); D. C. Holtom. *The National Faith of Japan* (1938).

Atum Local god of anc. Egypt. city of *Iunu* (O.T. Ōn; Grk. Heliopolis). Meaning of name A. uncertain, but connected with 'completion': in → Coffin Texts (141e) A. is described as 'the not-yet-Completed One, who will attain completion'. A. was identified with → Rē, the sun-god, and in → Pyramid Texts is presented as self-existent-Creator who emerged out of primordial waters of Nun, at Heliopolis, and created deities who personified main parts of universe (→ Cosmogony, Egypt.). Atum-Re was later eclipsed by Theban god → Amun-Re, and priests of Heliopolis prob. initiated worship of → Aten as counter-measure (→ Akhenaten). A. was usually repr. in human form. S.G.F.B.

R.Ae.R.-G., pp. 71–7; S. A. B. Mercer, *The Religion of Anc. Egypt* (1949), pp. 262ff.; Brandon, *C.L.*, pp.16ff.

Augurs, Augury Ex. Lat. *augures* = official Roman diviners, who formed official *collegium*. Etymology of term uncertain. It was duty of A. to observe and interpret signs (*auguria*) indicat. of divine will about some proposed undertaking. The action of chickens or wild birds were gen. so watched. Observations preceded import. public or private actions; but augural advice could be rejected (→ Divination). S.G.F.B.

O.C.D., *Kleine Pauly*, I, 734–6.

Augustine, St. Aurelius Augustinus (354–430),

bishop of Hippo Regius 396–430, was prob. greatest of Fathers of West. Church. Born in Tagaste in N. Africa of pagan father and Chr. mother, he was trained in rhetoric. He was → Manichaean for nine years from age of 19 to 28; he then found → Neoplatonism the gateway to Christianity. He was baptised at Easter 387. The primary importance of A., and secret of his dominance in W. Christendom until 17th cent., is that he was the Father of Western piety. He was not only a great theologian but a great expositor. In his exposition he is steeped in a highly articulate emotional response to God. His piety draws on combination of profound knowledge of Bible with a doc. of God which is joint product of Chr. and Neoplatonic materials. His *Confessions* is his most widely celebrated work; but his expositions, notably of Psalms, have been extremely influential. During his episcopate, A. had to deal with three heresies. One was → Manichaeanism (belief that the created world was evil and product of an evil agency opposed to a good God). A. insisted that the good God was creator of all things and sustained them in being, which was essentially good—evil being privation of the goodness of being. His decisive formal repudiation of Manichaeism is clear; but some scholars see in some of his docs. traces of the Manichaeism of his formative years. The second heresy was → Donatism, concerning the holiness and unity of Church: is Church holy, if it contains unholy members?; is it a mixed community of holy and unholy? A. held that Church is one through mutual love of its members; and is holy, not because its members are holy, but because its purposes are holy. In wrestling with nature of Church, A. repudiated → Cyprian's conception of invalidity of → sacraments outside the Church; he held that they were valid but not efficacious. His thinking here has influenced all subsequent discussion. Under pressure of controversy, A. was led to accept need for compulsion against heretics, with use of power of state to support authority of Church. This view had widespread influence in later cents., endorsing persecution by Church and state of heretics (→ Heresy).

One of A.'s most famous works was the *De Civitate Dei* (*City of God*) in 22 books, written over many years (413–26), to counteract consternation caused by Fall of Rome in 410. The first 10 books contain his victorious attack on the uncertainties, contradictions, absurdities, and immoralities of paganism. Thereafter he depicts two cities—the city of Earth and the city of God—in which the rival systems of paganism and Christianity are incorporated. They persist in interaction and rivalry with one another. God's judgment is operative in history, but is not finally vindicated until the → last judgment. The idea of the city of God for A. is a concept much wider than that of the Church—though there are passages in the *City of God* where he identifies the two.

A.'s teaching on the Church has been influential, partly because he did not iron out its incompatibilities. On one hand, the authority of the visible historic Church constrained him. On the other, he drew a distinction between the visible and invisible Church, which alone had true authority. Here, too, there is an unresolved distinction between the invisible Church, as composed of those devoted to Christ and manifesting his spirit; and the invisible Church as comprising the fixed number of the elect known to God alone. Both Catholics and Protestants have found in A.'s preaching the source of their opposing doctrines.

The third main controversy was against → Pelagianism. Pelagius was primarily a moralist. A.'s prayer, 'give what thou commandest and command what thou wilt' suggested to him that men were puppets wholly determined by divine grace. Against this, Pelagius insisted on man's capacity to choose freely either good or evil, the grace of God instructing his mind what he ought to choose. Against this, A. stressed man's co-responsibility for Adam's sin, and his consequent loss of liberty to avoid sin and do good. Before man can even hope for what is good, God's → grace must be in his heart. This is prevenient grace; there is also co-operating grace, by which God assists our active will; there is sufficient grace, which should have sufficed for Adam—but is no longer sufficient for fallen humanity; and efficient grace which alone will save, but which is given only to the predestined. Apart from question of pre-destination, A. has done a great service to Chr. theology in stressing the initiative of God's grace, and intimacy of God's action in stirring, helping and cooperating with man to respond to him. Yet in his exaggerated picture of the helplessness of man in sin, he does not leave sufficient room for freedom and responsibility of man for which Pelagius so rightly contended.

It is often said that A.'s 15 books *On the Trinity* constituted his finest theological achievement—but this is unlikely. Here his thinking derives from initial premise of the unity and simplicity of God, and is a philosophical attempt to find permanent distinctions—subsisting relations—within that unity. Some at least will think that the approach of the Cappadocian Fathers from the persons to the unity, is nearer to experience and biblical reality, and so nearer to that relig. response to God, which was A.'s own primary concern.

H.C-J.

E.T. of works by P. Schaff in the *Nicene and*

Post-Nicene Fathers, 8 vols. (1887–92); A. Harnack, *Outlines of the History of Dogma* (E.T. 1893), Book II, ch. 4; G. Bonner, *St. Augustine of Hippo* (1963); J. Burnaby, *Amor Dei: A study of the religion of St. Augustine* (1938); P. Brown, *Augustine of Hippos* (1967).

Augustus Title bestowed by Senate of Rome on Octavian in 27 BC, which had relig. connotation, and contrasted with *humanus*. A. became title of Roman Emperors (exc. Vitellius). The wife of Emperor had title of Augusta. S.G.F.B.

O.C.D., p. 124a; *R.A.C.*, I, 994–5.

Aurelius → Marcus Aurelius Antoninus. S.G.F.B.

Aurobindo, Sri Aurobindo Ghose (1872–1950), commonly styled Sri Aurobindo, was founder of a vigorous mod. Hindu movement with headquarters in Pondicherry, formerly French India. He was educated almost entirely in England, his father being a strong anglophile, and read classics at Cambridge. On return to India, he was for a time in the educational service of Baroda; then in Bengal. Arrested for alleged implication with militant Bengali nationalists, he underwent a mystical experience in gaol; and, after his release, withdrew to Pondicherry, to pursue search for spiritual truth. His modest → ashram eventually grew to substantial proportions, and A. acquired a wide following. His major writing is *The Life Divine*, which seeks to integrate trad. Hindu thought with mod. evolutionary ideas. The shape of his system bears some resemblance to that of → Teilhard de Chardin; both composed their major works about same time, during and after the First World War, but, of course, independently. Accord. to A., there is a progressive evolution of the divine Being through matter to higher spiritual forms, and the Aurobindo movement is held to represent vanguard of this evolutionary process in our own times. A. practised and taught an 'integral yoga', in which meditative and spiritual exercises are integrated with physical, cultural and intellectual pursuits. Though its main inspiration can be said to be Hindu, the movement is cosmopolitan, missionary and inter-religious, and a number of Westerners belong. The Ashram in Pondicherry has little resemblance to trad. Indian ashrams: it is a large community of people, many married, with its own printing-works, stadium, university, dairy, garages, etc. After A.'s death, the Ashram has continued under aegis of the Mother, a Frenchwoman of vigour and ability who joined him in the 1920's and was largely responsible for expansion of Ashram and diffusion of knowledge of A.'s teachings. A. wrote poetical and other works, as well as relig. and metaphysical works. N.S.

Sri Aurobindo, *The Life Divine* (1960); *Essays on the Gita* (1950); *Synthesis of Yoga* (1953); *The Mother* (1928); *On the Veda* (1956); H. Chaudhuri and F. Spiegelberg, eds., *The Integral Philosophy of Sri Aurobindo* (1960); Morwenna Donnelly, *Founding the Life Divine* (1956).

Auspices *Ex.* Lat. *auspicia*, term used for signs given by birds believed to indicate pleasure or displeasure of gods on an undertaking: closely assoc. with *auguria* (→ Augurs). A. were taken on public and private occasions, but later became reduced to weddings. S.G.F.B.

O.C.D., s.v.; Kleine Pauly, I, 734–6 ('Augures').

Australian Aborigine Religion Australian Aborigines first became object of serious scientific study in last quarter of 19th cent. Since then, while our understanding of their relig. has been greatly increased, the relig. data themselves have all too often been used to reflect presuppositions and support theories—more so than in almost any other field of relig. study. Early observers were often convinced that the A.'s had no relig. at all. Evolutionists, believing A. race to be 'a survival into modern times of a protoid form of humanity incapable of civilization' (Stanner), were unwilling to credit them with any but the most rudimentary forms of relig. sensibility. Andrew Lang's book *The Making of Religion* (1898), with its claim that even seemingly 'savage' races (among them the A.) knew of high moral deities, aroused immediate and bitter controversy—though he was later to find a powerful, if extreme, champion in Wilhelm Schmidt. The researches of → Frazer into → magic, and Durkheim into → totemism, were also responsible for clouding the basic issue of real nature of indigenous Aust. relig. in interests of *a priori* theories. Only with the researches of anthropologists A. P. Elkin, R. M. and C. H. Berndt, E. A. Worms, T. G. H. Strehlow, W. E. H. Stanner and others since the 1920's has the subject been placed on firm footing. In the meantime, however, the A.'s themselves have suffered greatly from the depredations of 'civilisation', making new observation and verification of earlier, unsystematically gathered material virtually imposs. in many areas.

E. A. Worms has said that 'The Aboriginal relig. represents in its essentials an organic whole, consisting of the same fundamental concepts of faith . . . throughout the whole of Australia'. Allowing for local variations, this involves (i) belief in a → sky-god, and in auxiliary spirit-beings, often functioning as → Culture Heroes (ii) belief in 'sacramental' nature of visible universe, as repr. and containing power of the sacred (iii) belief in efficacy of rites and rituals to re-present and renew creative work of spirits *in illo tempore* (iv) initiation practices (v) institution of a form of → shamanism and (vi) 'totemism'. It must not be supposed, however, that these are in any way mutually exclusive categories; they rather repr.

various facets of a basic and all-inclusive *Weltanschauung* motivated by conviction of the wholeness and design of life, the design having been estab. once and for all in past by supernatural forces.

Controversy over existence or otherwise of belief in a Supreme Being among the A.'s having now largely subsided, it can be seen that most Aust. tribes knew of a sky-being, Supreme Being, or → High God, though he was often respected rather than worshipped. He appears under a wide variety of names, among them Nurrundere, Nurelli, Bunjil, Baiame, Daramulun, Mungan-ngaua, Djamar, Nogämain and Wallanganda (names often connoting fatherhood). In Aranda-speaking areas of Cen. Aust. it was trad. believed that earth and sky had always existed. In the sky lived an emu-footed, eternally young Great Father (Knaritja), with many wives, sons and daughters; they dwelt amid flowers and fruits, immortal and unconcerned about what was happening on earth. Communications between heaven and earth once existed, but are now irreparably broken. Long ago there was neither life nor death on earth; but below earth's surface there slept a mass of supernatural beings, among them sun, moon and stars. In time these emerged, taking various forms, some human, some animal (but with interchangeable functions). These were 'totemic ancestors', and they wandered about, shaping the earth, making man and teaching him the arts of survival. Their work done, they subsided once more into sleep. The period of their wanderings the Aranda call the Dream Time, or Dreaming (*alcheringa*)—a concept paralleled in other tribes. Thus, while the Great Father himself is inaccessible and unconcerned (*a → deus otiosus*), the Dream Time, the primordial paradise in which totem ancestors walked the earth, is a subject of intense nostalgia. That was the period of beginnings, in which the Abor. world was shaped and estab.; and throughout the continent, relig. while comparatively unconcerned with Supreme Being as such, has as its objective the temporary reactualisation of events of the Dream Time. 'The "primordiality" of the Great Father was not of immediate relevance to the Aranda's existence; once communication with heaven had been interrupted and death come into world, it was not very helpful to know about immortality of Altjira's family or of those who had ascended to heaven. The only "immortality" accessible to the Aranda and to other Australian tribes was the reincarnation, the perennial return to life of the primordial ancestors . . .' (Eliade).

Since, during period of their wanderings on earth, the totemic ancestors had given form to pre-existent matter, the world in which the A.'s lived was seen as reflecting supernatural activity. There was a multiplicity of sacred rites. Chthonian supernatural beings were assoc. with definite sacred centres, as were all ceremonies, sacred songs and magical practices: 'Each centre had its own separate cycle of ceremonies which in the old days could be performed nowhere else—on pain of death—but at that particular site' (Strehlow). Again, ceremonies were designed to recall orig. events which had taken place at a partic. site, and thus to maintain link with seminal past. The efficacy of such rituals was held to depend on all actions being performed in exact pattern instituted by the supernaturals themselves. The Aranda myth of Numbakulla and the sacred pole (*kauwa-auwa*), on which it was recorded, *inter alia*, that the ancestors set up *kauwa-auwa* when entering new territory, is thought by Eliade to repr. the sanctification of space and its 'organisation' around a centre, joining earth to heaven. At all events the A.'s, once initiated, knew earth as former site of activities of the supernaturals: 'The whole countryside is his living, age-old family tree' (Strehlow).

The theme of → fertility is of great importance in Aust. relig. The myth-cycle of Djangawwul tells how, in the Dream Time, two men and two women landed on coast of Arnhem Land, in N. Australia—Djangawwul, his two sisters, and a second man, Bralbral (who is not significant). Djangawwul maintained his sisters in state of perpetual pregnancy, and from them were born ancestors of A.'s. These supernaturals were also believed to be responsible for institution of fertility rituals, in which women still play an import. role. Among cult objects used in these rituals is the *rangga*, symbolizing the phallus. Orig. brought by the Djangawwul sisters, the *rangga* were stolen by men to enable them to carry out sacred dances on their own; some present-day *rangga* are believed to be copies of these originals, while others may represent totemic objects and species, human organs and ancestral people. 'They are often stylized, made from various hard woods, cane or paperbark, bound with jungle-fibre twine, painted with clan totemic designs, and ornamented with colourful feathered strings' (Berndt). The Kunapipi (Mother) Cult of Arnhem Land is a similar expression of same concern for cycle of fertility. Kunapipi herself is a perpetually pregnant woman, from whose womb all men were born in the Dream Time, and who is responsible for continual renewal of natural species. Her 'consort' is the Rainbow Snake—another symbol. Her cult makes use of → bullroarer (a pierced wooden object swung on string to produce deep and penetrating sound); belief that the dancing-ground is uterus of Mother; the setting up of symbolic repres. of male and female organs;

and exchange of wives and gifts, with ceremonial intercourse. In this way is maintained the rhythm of human procreation, and of seasons. (→ Phallic Cults).

Aust. → initiation rites are excl. concern of males. Women and children are excl. from all contact with sacred actions and objects, on pain of death; they must even stay out of earshot of men's singing. The ceremonies themselves involve such features as painting, dancing, → circumcision, the knocking out of teeth and abstention from certain foods. Most import. is, however, the imparting to neophyte of sacred trads. of tribe, incl. myths of the Dream Time, the significance of sacred rites and functions of cult-objects (esp. bullroarer). This makes youth into full and active participant in life of his people. 'In learning what took place in the Dream Time, the initiate also learns what must be done in order to maintain the living and productive world ... The world in which the initiate henceforth moves is a meaningful and "sacred" world, because Supernatural Beings have inhabited and transformed it' (Eliade). But to the uninitiated, 'sacred' objects and narratives are invested with strict → tabus, and may not even be approached. The women have their own secret ceremonies, songs and rites; the main concern of these is with 'love magic', though other aims incl. healing sick and repairing quarrels. From these rites adult men and (usually) children are excl., since they would impair efficacy of rite. Other female ceremonies, to which tabus are attached, have to do with e.g. sub-incision and menstruation. A further curious feature is that some male ceremonies are widely believed to have been property of women: 'We women had everything first, all the *mareiin* (= sacred, cf. → *mana*); it was ours. Men had no *mareiin* at all ... men got it by stealing ...' (Elcho Is. Abor. woman 1961, rep. by C. H. Berndt).

The sphere of the sacred is gen. the concern of the 'medicine man' or shaman, who mediates between people and supernatural world (→ Shamanism). Little is known of his training, though the individual often believes his powers to depend upon stones (usually quartz) secreted in his body by the spirits, following a 'death' and rebirth; he may have been taken by spirits on a dream-journey into sky. His functions are threefold: (i) He diagnoses and cures illnesses, which are almost always believed to be result of sorcery or other malignancy, and involve the loss of the free-soul. His methods involve simple remedies, suggestion, and 'soul-retrieval'. (ii) he maintains contact with spirit-world, with spirits of departed. (iii) he carries out 'inquests' to determine cause of an individual's death, i.e. origin of the fatal sorcery. He may dream of the 'murderer', or he may interpret signs on or near grave or place of death. When revenge is called for, he will carry out rites to ensure success. The customary distinction between black and white → magic may be observed in these activities, the medicine man being employed to undo work of sorcerer and institute new positive action. (→ Witchcraft). The complex of ideas surrounding death and the dead are of partic. significance. Although A. views on nature and destiny of man are not consistent, death itself is always regarded as having magical cause. After extravagant demonstrations by next of kin, the medicine man is called in to fix cause of the evil. Mortuary practices are determined by forms of social organisation, and vary greatly. They may be confined to simple burial; or may involve prior exposure of body in tree and subsequent disposal of bones; or interment, followed by disinterment and final disposal. (A form of mummification is occas. practised). In former case, it is believed that soul lives on in grave, and grave-gods are provided; in latter case, that soul remains in grave until final disposal of bones (or until cause of death has been determined), after which soul may proceed to its own place in sky, beyond sea or on an island. In some cases man is believed to have two souls—a pre-existent 'eternal dream-time soul' (Elkin) which may be reincarnated, and a free-soul which may become a malevolent ghost, and against which protective measures must be taken.

→ Frazer once described Aust. as 'the great mother-land of totemism'—an expression to which Stanner in partic. has taken exception, pointing out that Aust. 'is just a continent with a lot of totems'. Frazer's error—and the error of other scholars—was that of too strict systematization. The term '→ totemism' is perhaps unavoidable (though the commonest Aust. word is *kobong*), but the phenomenon is very complex. It involves idea, expressed in symbolic form and maintained by strict rules, of a close connection between individuals and groups and other existents ('totems'). For the A., the maintenance of life itself is dependent on these relationships being kept in good repair, since they were estab. in the Dream Time by the supernaturals, and thus belong in total context of A. relig. understanding. Totems may be individual, social or cultic. Practically any natural phenomenon, object, plant or animal may serve as totem, and they may reveal themselves to individuals or groups in a number of ways, among them inheritance, dream and augury (→ North American Indian Religion). Totems as a rule belong to separate geographical sites and regions, though some have wider application; some are universal. They are more cosmological than cosmogonical: 'they have less to do with the setting up of the world than with the instituting of relevances within it' (Stanner)—and thus again refer back to events of the Dream Time. The rites in which they are celebrated are strictly localised, and in many cases strictly personal or tribal. Dancers imitate totem animal or object (in Kunapipi fertility ritual the yam, opossum, wild honey, rat, wallaby, iguana, native companion and kangaroo), with ultimate purpose of securing continuation of species. At these 'increase ceremonies' the *kobong* is ritually eaten. As Elkin has said, totemism (and this judgment could well be applied to Aust. relig. as a whole) 'is a view of nature and life, on the universe and man, which colours and influences the Aborigines' social groupings and mythologies, inspires their rituals and links them to the past'. E.J.S.

J. Greenway, *Bibliography of the Australian Aborigines* (1963); A. P. Elkin, *The Australian Aborigines* (1948); R. M. Berndt, *Kunapipi* (1951); E. A. Worms, 'Religion', in H. Sheils (ed.), *Australian Aboriginal Studies* (1963), pp. 231ff.; W. E. H. Stanner, 'Religion, Totemism and Symbolism', in R. M. and C. H. Berndt (ed.), *Aboriginal Man in Australia* (1965), pp. 207ff.; M. Eliade, 'Australian Religions', in *H.R.*, vol. 6 (1966), vol. 7 (1967–8).

Avadāna Type of Buddh. literature which repr. transitional stage between lit. of → Hinayāna schools and that of the → Mahāyāna. A notable feature is its tendency to glorification of the → Bodhisattva ideal. The word A. means 'a note-worthy deed', gen. in a good sense (though occasionally the reverse also), to indic. a relig. meritorious feat, such as sacrifice of one's life for others, or giving of something very precious for erection of a Buddh. sanctuary. The general theme of the A. lit. is to show that 'black deeds bear black fruits, while white deeds bear white fruits', and is thus homiletic in intention. The stories, which bear such morals, are usually intro. as though told by the Buddha (in stylised manner like that used in the → *Jātakas*). Stories of this type occur throughout the canonical scriptures; but they are also collected together into anthologies in the A. lit. Among such anthologies are, e.g., the *Avadana-Sataka*, 'the 100 A.'s' which was trans. into Chinese in 1st half of 3rd cent. CE. (→ Divyāvadāna). T.O.L.

M. Winternitz, *Hist. of Indian Literature* (1933), vol. 2, pp. 284ff.

Avalokiteśvara One of most prominent → Bodhisattvas in Mhy. Buddhism. The name may be regarded as being formed from two Skt. words: *Avalokita*, he who looks down upon human world, i.e. with compassion, and *Isvara*, the Lord (a common word for God in Indian relig.). This 'looking down' in compassion is from the Tusita heaven where A. is regarded as dwelling. It is equally poss. however that *avalokita* means 'he who is looked to' (for help). A. thus repres. one of two major aspects of the Buddha-nature, viz compassion (→ *karunā*), the other being → wisdom (*prajñā*); the latter is repres. in Mhy. mythology by the Bodhisattva → Mañjuśrī. One of A.'s epithets is *Mahākarunā*—the great Compassion. With A.'s compassion is linked, in Mhy. thought, his miraculous power to help human beings, when they call upon him in times of difficulty or distress. In his cosmic aspect A. is sovereign lord of universe; hence he possesses absolute power to protect men from natural disasters such as storms; on the other hand, to grant fertility to childless women. This cult of A. has been described as 'the Buddhism of Faith', in contrast to earlier doc. of human self-reliance and disavowal of heavenly aid. In his final development, in → Vajrayāna Buddhism, A. becomes magician, who works by means of *mantras* or spells. In accordance with notion that the great Buddh. ruler is an incarnation of a Bodhisattva, it is held that ruler of → Tibet, the Dalai Lama, is an incarnation of A. The various transformations of which A. is capable, in order to guide and help men, are described in the Mhy. Skt. treatise, the → *Saddharmapundarīka Sūtra* (Eng. trsl. by H. Kern, *S.B.E.*, vol. 21). T.O.L.

C. Eliot, *Japanese Buddhism* (1935), pp. 117–24; *Hinduism and Buddhism*, vol. 2 (1921), pp. 13–9.

Āvāsa Name used in anc. India for Buddh. monks' dwelling place during rainy season. (→ Monasteries, Buddh.). T.O.L.

Avatāra (Sometimes rendered 'avatar' in English). A 'descent' or incarnation of God, as understood primarily in the Vaisnavite trad. within Hinduism. There are analogies to doc. outside → Vaisnavism, in that the distinction between divine and human is somewhat fluid. The orig. notion was that God manifested himself from time to time, typically with the intent of restoring virtue and true religion; such manifestations of → Viṣṇu came to be considered as descents of the God, so that he is really present in such incarnations. In the later elaborated theory there were not merely full descents, but partial (and partial partial) *avatāras* (e.g. Kapila, the legendary founder of → Samkhya). The ten avatars of Vishnu are: the Fish (Matsya), who saved → Manu from a universal flood; the Tortoise (Kūrma), who served as a support for Vishnu's churning-rod; the Boar (Varāha), who raised the earth from the oceans; the Man-Lion (Nṛsiṁha), who slew the evil king Hiraṇyakaśipu; the Dwarf (Vāmana), who gained dominion of world for Vishnu from the king Bali; Rama-with-the-Axe (Paraśu-Rāma), who restored society after the → *ksatriya* class had tried to gain control from the Brahmins; → Rama, the hero of the → *Ramayana*; → Krishna (Kṛṣṇa), celebrated in the *Harivaṁśa* and the → *Mahabharata*; the Buddha, who oddly comes into the sequence, supposedly to mislead men of low birth and to hasten decline of religion in present age, the → *kaliyuga*, and so to hasten the restoration; and Kalki, at end of age, who will come in glory to estab. a golden age, judge men, destroy world and recreate a new mankind. Overwhelmingly, the two most import. avatars are Rama and Krishna, the latter in partic. being the focus of fervent → bhakti. The accounts of the various *avataras* are portrayed in → *Puranas* and the epics, a class of literature widely available, through recitation, dramatic performance, etc., to the masses. The theory of periodic restorations of → *dharma* is parallel to → Jain and Buddhist trads. of the sequence of → Tirthamkaras and Buddhas, and it is prob. that the doc. of avatars derived in part from them. N.S.

J. Estlin Carpenter, *Theism in Medieval India* (1921); R. G. Bhandarkar, *Vaisnavism, Saivism and Minor Religious Systems* (1913); J. Gonda, *Aspects of Early Visnuism* (1954); A. Danielou, *Hindu Polytheism* (1964); M. N. Dutt, *A Prose Translation of Harivamsha* (1897).

Avempace (Ibn Bājja), of Zaragoza, d. 533/1138 in Fez, where he is said to have been poisoned on ground of being an atheist. A noted philosopher, he was versed in natural philosophy, astronomy, mathematics, medicine. He argued that isolation and self-knowledge will lead philosopher to knowledge of God. This is developed in his work *Tadbīr al-mutawaḥḥid* (The [self-] direction of the solitary). He recognised two ways by which the human intellect can come into contact with the Active Intellect: (1) study and philosophy (2) messengers and prophets. But God has given man reason and intends him to use it as means of drawing near to himself. The approach to union with God is different from that of the → Ṣūfīs, for it is a purely rational method. A. does not deny revelation, but holds that the philosopher can reach knowledge of God independent of it. (→ Almoravids). J.R.

G.A.L., I, p. 601; *S.I.*, p. 830; *E.I.*, II, p. 366; Pareja, p. 998; De Boer, pp. 175ff.; Watt, *Philosophy*, pp. 137f., 144; E. I. J. Rosenthal, *Political thought*, pp. 158ff. and index. Trans. of *Tadbīr*: Spanish by Asin, *El régimen del solitario* (1946); Eng. by D. M. Dunlop, in *J.R.A.S.* (1945), pp. 61ff.

Averroes (Abul Walīd b. Rushd; 520–595/1126–1198), with same name as his distinguished grandfather (d. 520/1126), was a member of influential family in Cordova. He had a wide education, being equipped in law, medicine and philosophy. He served as → *qāḍī* in both Seville and Cordova. → Ibn Ṭufayl intro. him to Caliph Abū Ya'qūb Yūsuf (→ Almohads), who encouraged him in his philosophical work. A. was noted as commentator of works by → Aristotle, his commentaries being so greatly valued that they were trans. into Hebrew and Latin. In these his aim was to expound Aristotle's meaning, not to express his own docs., which could be found in other works of his. One of his famous works is *Tahāfut al-tahāfut*, a reply to Ghazālī's *Tahāfut al-falāsifa* ('the incoherence of the philosophers'). → Ghazālī, to whom no one had previously ventured to reply was dead before A. was born. A. defends reason as a source of knowledge and strongly denounces Gh.'s arguments. Another work of importance is his *Faṣl al-maqāl* ('the decisive treatise'), dealing with connection between relig. and philosophy. A. not only had legal training, he had also written legal text books; he uses his familiarity with law to support his thesis, boldly entitling first chapter, 'The law makes philosophical studies obligatory'. He holds that there is nothing in philosophy opposed to Islam; but he realises danger of teaching philosophical interpretations of scripture to the common people. He declares that the Qur. itself shows how people should be taught and should understand it, and insists on danger of allegorical interpretations. He was an acute thinker, but while his influ. was great in medieval Europe, it was very slight among his co-religionists. He was a convinced Muslim; but for a time Caliph Abū Yūsuf Ya'qūb had to send him into semi-exile in the Maghrib in deference to the → *fuqahā'*, who accused A. of atheism; but later he took him back to favour. J.R.

E.I., II, pp. 410–3; *E.R.E.*, II, pp. 262–6; *G.A.L.*, I, pp. 604–6; *S.I.*, pp. 833–6; Pareja, pp. 990f. and index; Van den Bergh, *Tahafut*; G. Hourani, *Averroes*; De Boer, *Philosophy*, pp. 187ff.; Watt, *Philosophy*, pp. 139ff.; E. I. J. Rosenthal, *Political thought*, pp. 175ff. and index; Sweetman, *I.C.T.*, IV, pp. 73–210.

Avesta Word of uncertain origin, perhaps meaning 'wisdom' or 'knowledge' used to designate sacred scriptures of → Zoroastrianism. The A. is only a small remnant of anc. Iranian sacred lit.; in present form, it repr. recension made in reign of Shāhpūhr II (CE 309–80) from earlier material. The A. comprises three principal divisions (1) *Yasna*, liturgical hymns, incl. → *Gāthās*, gen. considered the work of Zoroaster. The *Gāthās* form oldest A.-material, and are written in an archaic form of language (2) *Yashts*, i.e. hymns addressed to various deities (3) *Vidēvdāt* or 'Law against the Demons'. S.G.F.B.

The standard ed. is that of K. F. Geldner, 3 vols. (1895); E.T. by J. Darmesteter and L. H. Mills in *S.B.E.* IV, XXIII, XXXI, *E.R.E.*, II, *s.v.; R.G.G.*[3], I, *s.v.;* Zaehner, *D.T.Z.*, pp. 25ff., 339ff.

Avicenna (Ibn Sīnā; 370–429/980–1037) belonged to neighbourhood of Bukhārā. In youth he was an assiduous student, going through normal course of Qur. and assoc. studies (→ Education), to which he added medicine, science and philosophy. Aristotle's *Metaphysics* gave him great trouble. After reading it 40 times without understanding it, his difficulties were eventually removed by a commentary written by → Fārābī. A. lived in an unsettled period and had to make many moves; but while he had to undertake official government work to earn living, this did not hinder him from his studies and writing. He was an outstanding scholar in different fields. His *Qānūn*, a medical encyclopaedia, was a standard work for cents., and his writings in science, philosophy and relig. had influ. among European scholars. His outlook was in main → Aristotelian, but influenced by → Neoplatonism. While he emphasised use of reason, he was essentially a faithful Muslim, and accordingly gave prophecy an import. place. He held that, as the prophet is under divine guidance, he is superior to philosopher whose knowledge is attained by reasoning. The prophet also brings the → *sharī'a*, which guides mankind for their good both in this world and the next. In addition to upholding Muslim doc., A. gave import. place to → mysticism, doubtless influenced by Neoplatonism, holding that contemplation of God's essence is goal set before mankind, and its realisation is man's greatest reward. J.R.

E.I., II, pp. 419ff.; *G.A.L.*, I, pp. 589–99; *S.I.*, pp. 812–28; *E.R.E.*, II, pp. 272ff.; Pareja, pp. 986f. and index; De Boer, index; A. J. Arberry, *Avicenna on theology* (1951); L. Gardet, *La pensée religieuse d'Avicenne* (1951); Watt, *Philosophy*, index; Sweetman, *I.C.T.*, I–IV, index; E. I. J. Rosenthal, *Political thought*, pp. 143ff. and index; G. Hourani, 'Ibn Sina, Secret of destiny', in *M.W.*, LIII (1963), pp. 138–40.

Avidyā (Hindu) 'Ignorance', the explanation, in → Advaita Vedanta, of the condition of individuals involved in round of → rebirth: another term also used is *ajñāna* 'nescience'. The state of living beings is due to a kind of primordial ignorance, the lack of spiritual perception which gives a true grasp of nature of reality. This perception is to be found in the existential realisation of the Self's identity with → *Brahman*, and this brings about liberation and release from grip of illusory world. For → Sankara, A. has no causal explanation, because it is beginningless, and because causal explanations themselves lie within realm of empirical world and therefore within realm of → *maya* or illusion, which is, so to say, the 'objective' counterpart of the ignorance clouding the Self. In a rather different context, Buddhism also traces back suffering to ignorance, since craving (*taṇhā*), which binds living beings to round of rebirth, has its ultimate origin in ignorance. The emphasis in Advaita and elsewhere on ignorance is the counterpart of the high valuation of a mystical, or contemplative knowledge or gnosis, in gaining insight into ultimate reality and so liberation. N.S.

(Buddhist) (Skt.); **Avijjā** (Pali), Ignorance, in the Buddh. view, is failure to see true nature of things, and is a primary root of ordinary man's unsatisfactory condition. It is one of the → *āsavas*, and in the cycle of renewed mundane existence is one of critical 'links' where whole process may poss. be interrupted, by following of the Buddh. way. Ignorance is also called *moha*, delusion, one of basic 3 roots of evil, the other two being *lobha* (greed) and *dosa* (hate). T.O.L.

Avis Locutius Lat. = the 'sayer' or 'speaker', an otherwise nameless → *numen*, whose voice gave warning of invasion of the Gauls in 390 BC. A *sacellum* (shrine) and *templum* (precinct) was later dedicated on the Nova Via, Rome, to A.-L. S.G.F.B.

Kleine Pauly, I, 210–1.

Āyatana Term used in Buddhism for basis of a sensation, these bases being arranged in 6 pairs: eye and visible object; ear and sound; nose and odour; tongue and tastable object; body and tactile object; mind and mental object. The *āyatanas* together thus constitute a preliminary classification of factors involved in sensual existence, as basis for further analysis. For a discussion of the 12 A.'s, see *Vsm. XV*. T.O.L.

Axe, Double Axe, with two flanges, appears as estab. relig. emblem or symbol in anc. → Cretan relig. It seems, acc. to scenes on painted sarcophagus of Hagia Triads, to have been import. constituent of a sanctuary: it is depicted standing upright, and of a size that precludes its practical use; birds perch upon it. D.-A. appears between horns of bulls on vases and gems, and multitudes of miniature bronze models have been found suggesting votive use. Origin and meaning of D.-A. has been much discussed. Since Lydian word for D.-A. was *labrys*, the D.-A. has been connected with trad. weapon of → Zeus of Labraunda and the Labyrinth of Knossos. Zeus of Labraunda was Hellenised form of Hittite weather god Teshub, whose D.-A. has been seen as symbol of Thunder God (e.g. Thor). However, in Crete D.-A. is symbol of the household goddess. The D.-A. was prob. weapon used for slaughtering sacrificial bulls; but D.-A.'s seem also to have been tools of woodmen and carpenters. There is some Mycenaean evidence of a male deity's connection with the D.-A. (→→ Hittite Relig.; Scandinavian Relig.). S.G.F.B.

E.R.E., II, *s.v.;* C. Picard, *Les religions préhelléniques* (1948), pp. 199–201; R. W. Hutchinson,

Prehistoric Crete (1962), pp. 224–5; S. Marinatos, *Crete and Mycenae* (1960): numerous illus.; *Kleine Pauly*, III, 431–2.

Azazel Heb. name of desert demon to whom was consigned the goat, on which Israel's sins on → Day of Atonement were ritually placed and led into desert (Lev. 16:8–10). The meaning of A. is uncertain: the demon was prob. a desert satyr. Why the 'scape-goat' should be sent to A. is not clear; for it meant that the priestly legislators of Lev. 16 thereby assigned import. status to a demon. The idea of ritual transmission of pollution or bad luck occurs in many religs. (→ Scapegoat); but not its consignment to a specific demon. A. appears in *Book of* → *Enoch* (6.7, 10.4f.) as prince of fallen angels. S.G.F.B.

*H.D.B.*², *s.v.; R.G.G.*³, V, *s.v.* ('Sündenboch'); *E.R.E.*, II, *s.v.;* J. G. Frazer, *The Scapegoat* (*G.B.*, 1933), pp. 31ff.; W. O. E. Oesterley, *Immortality and the Unseen World* (1930), pp. 38–9.

-Azhar → Education. J.R.

Aztecs → American Relig. (ancient)

Azymites Grk. designation for Western Christians used contemptuously by the Easterns at time of 1054 schism: it referred to their use of unleavened bread (*azuma*) in → Eucharist, which E. rejected. S.G.F.B.

B

Ba Anc. Egypt. word for an essential element in human nature that is often misleadingly trans. 'soul'; but Egyptians did not distinguish an ethereal entity as the essential self, distinct from body. In art, the B. is repr. as a human-headed bird; it is often shown perched on tomb or flying down tomb-shaft to visit embalmed body. In → Pyramid Texts deceased king met his B. in heaven; but → Coffin Texts suggest that B. issued forth from body at death, conserving individual's essential powers. The bird-like form prob. indic. that Egyptians believed B. was a free-moving entity after death, independent of body but sentimentally attached to it. A Middle Kingdom document repr. a man conversing with his B. during life. The B. seems orig. to have connoted supernatural power: → Rē had 7 B.s (→ Ka). S.G.F.B.

R.Ae.R-G., pp. 74–7; Kees, *T.;* pp. 39–45; Sainte Fare Garnot, in *Anthropologie religieuse* (ed. C. J. Bleeker, 1955), pp. 22–3; Brandon, *M.D.*, pp. 42ff.

Baal (pl. *Baalim*) Heb., meaning 'possessor' or 'lord', applied to local Canaanite gods as manifestations of Baal, fertility-god of Canaan (→ Canaanite Religion). This Baal was really the → Amorite god of winter rain and storm, known as → Adad or → Hadad ('the thunderer'). In texts of → Ugarit, B. figures as dying-rising god of myths about annual conflict between vegetation and drought. In art, B. is repr. as a warrior-god. As fertility-god, B. was worshipped with licentious rites, which Heb. prophets denounced. Israelites tended either to serve Canaanite baals or identify → Yahweh with B. (→ Baalzebub). S.G.F.B.

E.R.E., II, *s.v.; H.D.B.*², *s.v.*, G. R. Driver, *Canaanite Myths and Legends* (1956), pp. 10ff.; J. Gray, *The Canaanites* (1964), pp. 121ff.; A. S. Kapelrud, *Baal in the Ras Shamra Texts* (1952).

Baalzebub, Beelzebul Acc. to 2 Kings 1:2ff., a Philistine god at Ekron was named Baalzebub, meaning 'lord of flies'. In N.T. (e.g. Mt. 10:25) Beelzebul was prince of demons. An explanation of much discussed problem of relations of these two names has been found in Ugaritic tablets (→ Ugarit). The title 'Baalzebul' occurs, meaning 'lord of the mansion', as epithet for great Syrian (Canaanite) god → Baal. Beelzebub was prob. derisive Jew. distortion of Baalzebul. S.G.F.B.

*H.D.B.*², *s.v.;* T. Gray, *The Canaanites* (1964), p. 122: cf. *E.R.E.*, II, *s.v.*

Babel, Tower of In Gen. 11:1–9, the T-B. legend is used by → Yahwist writer to account for break-up of orig. unity of human race and its dispersal into different nations, speaking different tongues. The legend effects transition from universalist theme of Primaeval History (Gen. 1–10:32) to nationalist theme of Patriarchal History (Gen. 11:26–50:26). Evidence of a Sumerian legend attr. end of Golden Age to → Ea's diversification of language has recently been found. 'Babel', name of Babylon (→ Babylon. Relig.) suggested Heb. *balal*, 'to confuse'. S.G.F.B.

A. von Rad, *Genesis* (E.T. 1961), pp. 143ff.; *H.D.B.*², pp. 1007–8; S. G. F. Brandon, *History, Time and Deity* (1965), pp. 108, 129; S. N. Kramer, *From the Tablets of Sumer* (1956), p. 260; *The Times*, 25 March 1967, p. 3 ('New light shed on the Tower of Babel').

Bābīs A Sect founded by 'Alī Muḥammad of Shiraz (1235–66/1819–50), who proclaimed himself *Bāb* (gate) in 1260/1844, the millenary by the Muslim calendar of disappearance of the twelfth → *imām* in 260 A.H. Versions in Arabic and Persian of the Bāb's book *al-Bayān* are the sacred books of the new revelation. Some laws of the → *sharī'a* are abrogated, eschatological terms in the Qur. are spiritualised, the Bāb's abode is made the → *qibla*, and promise is made of a prophet who is to come. The number 19 has great significance. A calendar of 19 months, each with 19 days was estab., the last month being the fast. The sexes were declared equal; while divorce was allowed, it was looked on with disapproval. Alcoholic drinks, begging and giving private charity are forbidden. Two years before the Bāb was shot at Tabriz the B.s publicly declared their secession from Islam and the *sharī'a*. The hist. of movement has largely been record of persecution. The Bāb's body was cast away unceremoniously, but eventually disinterred, and, after some years, placed in mausoleum on Mount Carmel. Yaḥyā Nūrī, entitled Ṣubḥ-i Azal (dawn of eternity), and his older half-brother Ḥusayn 'Alī Nurī, entitled Bahā' Allāh (splendour of God) were leaders. The former claimed the Bāb had appointed him as successor, but in 1279/1863 the latter said he was the prophet whom the Bāb foretold. So a split arose. The Azalīs remained the minority; the followers of Bahā' Allāh became a new movement → (Bahā'īs). J.R.

*E.I.*², I, pp. 833ff., 846f.; Pareja, pp. 846–9; A. L. M. Nicolas, *Le béyan arabe, le livre sacré du Babysme* (Trans. of work by the Bāb) (1905); *Le Béyan persan* (Persian trans. of same), 4 vols. (1911–14); Shoghi Effendi, *The Dawn Breakers* (trans. of work giving early narrative of movement) (1932); *God passes by* (1950); E. G. Browne, *Materials for the study of the Babi religion* (1918).

Babylonian Religion The city of Babylon became capital of anc. provinces of Sumer and Akkad under its king Hammurabi (*c.* 1728 B.C.). It inherited both culture and relig. of Sumer (→ Sumerian Religion); but priests of Babylon were concerned to exalt their own local god → Marduk as head of trad. pantheon. The way they achieved this finds significant expression in the → *Enuma elish*, the Creation Epic which was ritually recited at New Year Festival (→ Akitu). Although chronological priority of Sumerian gods was accepted, which made Marduk the son of → Ea, the *Enuma elish* tells how Marduk acquired supremacy by defending the older gods against the primaeval monster → T'iâmat. The Epic also repr. Marduk as creating universe and mankind; the other gods build. his great temple (Esagila) at Babylon as token of their gratitude, having recognised his plenary authority. The Babylonians took over Sumerian doctrine of man, with its pessimistic eschatology (→ Eschatology, Mesopot.). It was prob. in Babylon that the Epic of → Gilgamesh was composed, which presents a pessimistic philosophy of life. The gods, esp. Marduk, were served for reward of long life and prosperity, and protection from demons. → Magic, → divination, → astrology had important roles in B-R., and influenced other religions. The Persian conquest of Babylon in 539 B.C., and subsequent political misfortune resulted in gradual decay of Babylonian culture and relig. S.G.F.B.

B. Meissner, *Babylonien u. Assyrien*, II (1925); E. Dhorme, *R.B.A.;* J. Bottéro, *La religion babylonienne* (1952); M. Jastrow, *Some Aspects of Religious Belief and Practice in Babylonia and Assyria* (1911); Brandon, *M.D.*, ch. III, *C.L.*, chap. III; H. W. F. Saggs, *The Greatness that was Babylon* (1962), ch. 10. For trans. of Babylonian relig. texts see *A.N.E.T.*

Bacchae → Maenads. S.G.F.B.

Bacchanalia Lat. name of orgiastic rites of → Dionysus; they are esp. notable for severe measures taken by Roman Senate in 186 B.C. to suppress them. The B. came to Rome from S. Italy: orig. a cult for women, men were later initiated. B. were held at night; they produced undesirable forms of → ecstasy and moral disorder. The Senate decree forbade participation in B. on pain of death: acc. to Livy, 7,000 suffered this penalty. The official cult of Dionysus was not suppressed; it became very influential in Italy. The phallic element in B. prob. resulted from identification of Lat. fertility god Libera with Bacchus-Dionysus. S.G.F.B.

O.C.D., s.v.; Kleine Pauly, I, 799; *R.A.C.*, I, 1149 (II); Cumont, *R.O.*, pp. 196ff.

Bacchus Lydian name of → Dionysus. S.G.F.B.

Badr 20 miles SW of Medina, where first battle between → Muhammad and the Meccans took place (2/624); the Muslims with over 300 defeated about 1,000 Meccans. Md. declared that angels had fought on the Muslim side. The victory was of great significance, helping Md. towards estab. his position. The names of those present are recorded, and are held in greatest honour. J.R.

*E.I.*², I, pp. 867f.; Guillaume, *Life*, pp. 289–360; Watt, *Medina*, pp. 10–21 and index.

Bahā'īs Bahā' Allāh (1233–1309/1817–92) founded a new relig., developed out of that of the Bāb → Bābīs), known as Bahaism. He suffered imprisonment and exile, during which his assurance was strengthened that he was the prophet the Bāb had foretold. In later years of his life, he lived at Bahji near Acre, where he wrote *Kitāb-i Aqdas* ('the most holy book'), the basic work of his relig. After his death, his son 'Abbās Effendi, known as 'Abd al-Bahā', was recognised as interpreter of his writings, and undertook missionary work in Europe and America. The movement has spread widely in Europe, America, Africa and in eastern countries. The administrative centre is at Haifa, though largest group is still found in Persia, in spite of fact that they are not officially recognised and are subject to periodic persecution. God is held to be transcendant and unknowable; but makes himself manifest by his creation and espec. by prophets who are a mirror in which God is reflected. Earlier prophets are recognised, but in Bahā' Allah a new era, to last five millennia, has begun. Paradise and hell are symbols: paradise, of the journey to God; hell, of that to annihilation. Prayer for dead is recommended. The movement seeks universal peace, holding to unity of human race, advocating removal of prejudice, and teaching that all religs. have an essential unity. The desire for peace leads B. to reject military service, at least in countries where conscientious objection is respected. While there are no stated services of worship, B. should meet on first day of each of the 19 day months (→ Bābīs), when prayers and reading of scriptures are observed. Scriptures of other religs. may be used. Weekly meetings are held in towns in the West. Building temples, open for prayer to people of other religs. is recommended. There are various local assemblies and national assemblies elected from them. The aim is to have eventually a world assembly. All matters affecting members, no matter how private, should be dealt with by local assembly. A system of instruction is an import. part of movement's work. Alcohol is prohibited, but not tobacco, although non-smoking is preferred. The sexes being equal, monogamy is rule; although divorce is allowed, it is disapproved. → Bābīs. J.R.

*E.I.*², I, pp. 911, 915–8; Pareja, pp. 849f.; S. G. Wilson, *Bahaism and its claims* (1915); Aqa 'Abdu 'l-Ahad-i Zanjani, *New materials for history of Bahaism* (1916); J. E. Esslemont, *Baha'ullah and the new era* (1923); G. Rosenkranz, *Die Baha'i* (1949); Baha' Allah, *al-kitab al-aqdas*, trans. and ed. by E. E. Elder and W. McE. Miller (1961); → bibliography in Bābīs; *J.R.A.S.* (1921), pp. 443–70.

Baḥīra Monk said to have had cell near Buṣrā in Syria. Though reputed normally to have paid no attention to passing caravans, when Muḥammad as a boy came with his uncle → Abū Ṭālib, he noticed that a cloud was shadowing Md. and that when he stopped under a tree the branches came round to shade him. He invited the company to a meal; when Md. was eventually brought, he questioned him and received answers in keeping with the description of him in a book he had inherited. He also saw the → seal of prophecy, where the book said it would be. He advised Abū Ṭālib to guard his nephew, for if the Jews knew what he knew they would try to harm him. J.R.

*E.I.*², I, pp. 922f.; Guillaume, *Life*, pp. 79–81; Watt, *Mecca*, pp. 36–8.

Bala Buddh. term meaning 'power' (Skt. plur. *balāni*). In → Pali canon a frequent group of 5 moral powers are: faith (*saddhā*), energy (*viriya*), mindfulness (*sati*), concentration (*samādhi*) and wisdom (*paññā*). Other 'powers', e.g. moral shame, and moral dread, etc. are mentioned in Pali texts, singly or in groups. In Mhy. Buddhism there is a conventional list of ten 'powers' with which a → Bodhisattva is said to be endowed. They are: *āsayabala*, having mind strongly turned away from worldliness; *adhyāsaya°*, having faith growing ever stronger; *prayoga°*, power of disciplining oneself in exercises of Bodhisattvahood; *prajnā°*, intuitive power of understanding minds of all beings; *pranidhāna°*, power of having every prayer fulfilled; *carya°*, power of working until end of time; *yāna°*, power of creating varieties of vehicles (*yana*) of salvation, while remaining true to Mhy.; *vikurvana°*, power to make a pure world in every pore of skin; *bodi°*, power of awakening every being to enlightenment; *dharmacakrapravartana°*, power of uttering one phrase of universal appeal. T.O.L.

Balances (Islam) (*Mawāzīn*, pl. of *mīzān*, or *mawzūn*). Qur. xxi:48 says, 'We shall set up just balances on the day of resurrection, and no one will suffer any wrong; if it be but the weight of a grain of mustard-seed we shall produce it. We are sufficient as reckoners.' Here *mawāzīn* is clearly 'balances'. In vii:7; xxiii:104f.; ci, 5f., where the ref. is to the *mawāzīn* being light or heavy, some (e.g. Blachère, Masson, Muhammad 'Ali) treat it as pl. of *mawzūn* (lit. what is weighed), and understand it to ref. to good deeds of person being judged. The common view has been that actual scales will be set up to weigh good and evil deeds. A trad. tells of God's giving a man a paper on which was written, 'There is no deity but God; Muḥammad is God's messenger', with the assurance that it would outweigh all his evil deeds. Deeds are all recorded, and it is sometimes said that each man's books are weighed to see whether the good or evil deeds are heavier. Many Muslims, however, have understood the B. as figurative. See Masson, *Coran*, n. on vii:8, ref. to anc. Egyptian belief that deceased's heart is weighed, and Zoroastrian belief that his actions are weighed; Brandon, *The Judgment of the Dead* (1967), index (→ Psychostasia). J.R.

Hughes, pp. 353f.; Wensinck, *Creed*, index (Balance); D. B. Macdonald, *Theology*, pp. 296, 306, 311; Sweetman, *I.C.T.*, II, p. 148; IV, pp. 25, 49f.; *Mishkāt*, pp. 1176f.

Balts, Religion of the The word Balts denotes people orig. speaking 'Baltic' languages—Old Prussian, Lithuanian, Lettish, Curonian, Semigallian and Selian, of which only Lith. and Lettish still survive as living tongues. This linguistic group belonged to Indo-European family, and their relig. appears to have reproduced gen. pattern of → Aryan relig. It is known today chiefly through accounts of medieval Chr. writers, folklore and archeological data. The chief deity was Dievas (Lith.), 'god of the shining sky', to be equated with → Dyaus, Zeus, Jupiter. Perkūnas (Lith.) was thunder-god; Saule, sun-goddess; Mėnuo, moon-god; Kalvaitas, the divine smith (→ Hephaetus). Except Dievas and Perkūnas, other deities were little anthropomorphised. Laima was goddess of fate. The Earth Goddess, of whom men were born, was *Zemes māte* ('mother earth') in Lettish; Žemyna (Lith.). The dead were preserved for period before cremation; funerary ritual was elaborate, with rich mortuary equipment and funerary games. The dead were often accompanied by victims who were close relatives and their horses. At death two entities survived: the *vėlė* sought the land of the dead, imagined as high sandy hill, steep-sided, on which Dievas dwelt. The *Siela* (vital principle) remained on earth, being re-incarnated in trees, animals, etc. A cosmic tree was imagined, roofed and topped with symbols of sun, moon and stars, with its base guarded by stallions and snakes (cf. Yggdrasil → Scandinavian Relig.). Remains of temples (e.g. at Tuskemlja and Gorodok, near Smolensk) indic. use of ritual post, prob. surmounted by skull of horse or bull. A green snake, Žaltys (Lith.) was connected with fertility; there is evidence of a fire-cult (→ Agni; Fire gods). S.G.F.B.

M. Gimbutas, *The Balts* (1963); *R.G.G.*[3] I, 856–9.

Ban → Anathema. S.G.F.B.

Banāras (Benares) The most holy city in India (→ sacred cities, Hindu), and also import. in Buddhism (Buddha having preached first sermon in Sarnath, on outskirts); sometimes spelt *Benares*, it is also known by names Vārānasī and Kāśī. It has immemorially been centre of pilgrimage, and has been long import. for Sanskrit learning. It owes its preeminence partly from situation on the → Ganges (it is held to lie at intersection of the heavenly Ganges, i.e. the milky way, the earthly Ganges, and the invisible underground Ganges). It contains large numbers of temples, but few are old, because of repressive policy of Aurangzeb, who built a large mosque now dominating sky line, beside the stump of a pillar erected by → Asoka. The river front is lined with bathing steps or *ghats*, among which are numbered the *Dasasvamedha Ghat* (where anciently a ten-horse-sacrifice was performed, → *asvamedha*) and the Tulsi Das Ghat, named after poet who rendered the → Ramayana into Hindi. Among import. relig. teachers orig. in B. was → Kabir. The river itself is focus of import. pilgrimages, as well as daily ablutions; the ghats are occupied by relig. teachers and the pious, incl. many widows. The area round B. is also sacred; the circuit of fifty miles along the *panchkosi* road, starting and ending in B. itself, is an esp. meritorious pilgrimage. Also in B. is the B. Hindu University, whose foundation owed something to Annie Besant the → Theosophist, and expresses Hindu trad. in a mod. manner. N.S.

Baptism *ex.* Grk. *baptizein* = 'to dip', i.e. in water. Word in N.T. denotes a rite of immersing in water. Ceremonial washing was an already estab. Jew. custom in 1st. cent. CE. It was used as an initiatory ritual for → proselytes, in a purificatory sense, and as a purificatory ritual at → Qumran; → John the Baptist used it sacramentally as token of repentance, in preparation for kingdom of God. In Rom. 6:3ff. → Paul set forth another, and more significant, interpretation of B. By descent into water the neophyte was ritually assimilated to Christ in his death, thus to be reborn to a new spiritual life in the Resurrected Christ. Hence B. became the initiatory ritual of Christianity which mystically regenerated the neophyte. This meaning of B. was dramatically repr. in early ritual of B. The neophytes were baptised naked, thereby symbolising their dying to their former selves. They often received a new name, were reclothed in white robes, and given mystic food of milk and honey, thus symbolising their rebirth to new life in Christ. This regenerating aspect of Chr. B. had its phenomenological prototype in anc. Egypt. mortuary ritual (→ Funerary Rites, Egypt). The corpse was lustrated both as act of purification and of revivification. In funerary papyri the deceased is depicted under two streams of water which are sometimes repr. as chains of life-giving → ankhs. The idea of regeneration was prob. present also in the → Taurobolium of cult of → Cybele. B., as an initiatory rite, was practised in many → Mystery Religions, e.g. → Eleusinian, and of → Isis: but purpose was purificatory. B. as ritual purification occurs in birth and initiatory rites in many other anc. religs. and those of primitive peoples of modern world. (→→ Initiation; Nudity, ritual; Bathing, ritual).

(2) Chr. baptismal practice, based on Mt. 28:19, made B. in name of → Trinity the essential formula of valid B. Whether infant B. was practised in Apostolic Age is uncertain: it is poss. implied by Mt. 19:14, Acts. 16:33, I Tim. 2:4. Adult B. was normal in early cents., being conferred by → bishop only at Easter and Pentecost. B. was followed by → Confirmation and → Eucharist. During first 4 cents., B. was often delayed till death, for fear of responsibilities incurred: the custom gradually ceased as infant baptism increased: Chr. parents naturally wanted their children baptised, thus to be saved. A theology of B. was developed, being closely connected with doc. of → Original Sin, the logic of which condemned unbaptised infants to Hell. The grace of B. was regarded as produced → *ex opere operato*, which led to essential emphasis being placed upon use of correct 'form' and 'matter'; since B. was the essential initiatory → sacrament, proper reception of other sacraments depended upon its acceptance. Some Fathers accepted 'baptism of blood' of unbaptised martyrs for Chr. faith as constituting valid B. B. was gen. continued, with various doctrinal qualifications, by Prot. Reformers; but → Anabaptists and → Baptists became distinguished by rejection of infant B. and insistence

on adult believers' B. by immersion. Modern theology tends to present B. more as signifying incorporation into Church then effecting regeneration. S.G.F.B.

E.R.E., II, *s.v.*, pp. 367–412; *D.C.C.*, *s.v.; R.G.G.*³, VI, 626–60 ('Taufe'); *H.D.B.*), *s.v.;* G. Wagner, *Das religionsgeschichtliche Problem von Römer* 6.1–11 (1962); S. G. F. Brandon, *The Saviour God* (1963), pp. 22ff.; *Bilderatlas*, 9–11 Lief., 1926 (J. Leipoldt) Abb. 2; L. Duchesne, *Christian Worship* (E.T. 1927), ch. IX; J. Jeremias, *Die Kindertaufe in den Ersten Vier Jahrhunderten* (1958); *R.A.C.*, I *s.v.* 'Baptisterium (1158–67), 'Baptistes' (1167–76); F. van der Meer and C. Mohrmann, *Atlas of the Early Christian Church* (E.T. 1958), pp. 125ff.; N. Zernov, *Eastern Christendom* (1961), pp. 249ff.; J. Z. Smith, 'The Garments of Shame', *H.R.*, V (1965); M. Eliade, *Images and Symbols* (E.T. 1952), pp. 151ff.; J. D. C. Fisher, *Christian Initiation: Baptism in the Medieval West* (1965).

(by Blood) → Baptism (2); → Taurobolium. S.G.F.B.

(Infant) → Baptism (2). S.G.F.B.

Baptists As their name suggests, the characteristics distinguishing B. from other Christians centre on the rite of initiation. They contend that → baptism should be administered only to those who confess faith in Christ for themselves. Whereas in most Chr. Churches the subjects of baptism are normally infants, in Baptist churches they are always believers. The mode of baptism is usually immersion; but how one is baptised is secondary to who is baptised. The sacramental nature of rite is expounded chiefly from point of view of a means whereby one who has already laid hold of the Grace of God by repentance and faith is able, through obedience, to enter more fully into the gracious action of God for man's → salvation. The burial and rising dramatised in immersion are seen as identification of believer with Christ, in accord. with → Paul's teaching in Romans 6. That in final resort faith is deemed more vital than baptism may be inferred from fact that it is poss. to join some B. churches simply on confession of faith. Implicit in Believers' Baptism is doc. of Church as fellowship of believers. Concern about Church and Society being co-terminous, and many citizens being but nominal church members, orig. led to revaluation of Church and the gateway into it.

The relation of children of believing parents to Church has never been stated very clearly by Baptists. Much has been said somewhat polemically about infants' not needing baptism to wash away → original sin and save them from damnation. Positively, the service B. hold for blessing of infants and dedication of parents indicates that children of believing parents are regarded as a kind of → catechumenate.

Implicit in Believers' Baptism is an intensely personal conception of what it means to be a Christian. One must decide for oneself. There is no escaping a solitary encounter with Christ. Bound up with this emphasis on responsibility of individual is a witness to freedom of conscience and a plea for relig. toleration, which have meant much in struggle for human rights. It was a Baptist, Thomas Helwys, who in 1612 wrote the first plea for full relig. liberty to be published in England. In '*A short Declaration of the Mistery of Iniquity*' he declared, 'Men's religion to God is betwixt God and themselves; the king shall not answer for it, neither may the king be judge between God and man. Let them be heretics, Turks, Jews or whatsoever, it appertains not to the earthly power to punish them in the least measure.'

If the secular power may not coerce in relig., the only eccles. authority which can be acknowledged is one to which free consent is given. → Creeds are not commonly used in B. worship, though they are quoted in some of the historic Confessions of Faith. The reason appears to be that believing in Christ transcends believing this or that doc. about Christ. Conscience must not be coerced with respect to docs. Nevertheless B. have frequently been in bondage to the letter of Bible and often appear very conservative theologically, due no doubt to their reliance on the N.T. as sole authority for their position. The love of freedom is reflected in the ordering of the Church. The government is congregational. Believers assembled in Church Meeting claim Christ's presence and authority to order their worship and witness. Presiding over church is a minister who is assisted by lay deacons; both minister and deacons being elected by the members. The provision of an adequate ministry led B. early in their hist. to form county associations of local churches and then national unions. Today the policy may best be described as one of inter-dependency, where local self-governing churches advise one another and help each other financially, certain ministers being available to guide the churches of an area. Ministers, occasionally women, are those who are deemed to have gift for preaching, pastoral work and leadership of churches. Trained academically and vocationally, they are ordained in name of Christ and his Church by representatives of the churches of an area. The whole Church is a ministering community in which certain functions are normally, but not always, undertaken by ordained men.

The above sketch indic. that, in classification of Chr. Churches, B. must be put under heading of Protestant and the sub-division 'Free'. Within a decade of commencement of → Reformation, Grebel and Manz were involved in controversy with → Zwingli in Zürich and took momentous step of 'baptising again'. The name → Anabaptist was given in scorn to a medley of left-wing reformers, not all of whom were concerned with Chr. initiation and its implications for structure of Church. The movement grew rapidly, but was decimated by ruthless persecution. Notable survivors were those of a quietist outlook, the Mennonites, who sought refuge in Holland. It was in Amsterdam that the English Separatist, John Smyth, and members of his congregation in exile, founded in 1609 what is regarded as the first Baptist church. In 1612 Helwys, who had been with Smyth, formed a B. church in London. Smyth and Helwys revealed that their ancestry was on left wing of Reformation by departing from the Augustinian teaching on man and sin. The → Arminian strain is apparent in their contention that Christ died not for a particular number but had effected a general redemption. These 'General Baptists' were followed in the 1630's by emergence of 'Particular Baptists' from an Independent Church. The study of scripture convinced a number of members that, with → Calvinistic theology and congregational church government, they must combine believers' baptism. These Particular B. were destined to become by far the larger body, though today the issue of limited or universal atonement is not a live one. Landmarks in spread of the B. into all five continents were: a settlement in Rhode Island in 1639; the formation of missionary societies which in 1793 took Carey from England to India and twenty years later Judson from America to Burma; and the estab. of a German B. Church at Hamburg in 1834, with its outreach to N. Europe and Russia. Today B. have a world membership of over 20 millions, half of them being in the south. states of U.S.A. The national unions maintain contact with one another through the Baptist World Alliance formed in 1905. K.C.D.

G. R. Beasley-Murray, *Baptism in the New Testament* (1962); A. Gilmore (ed.) *Christian Baptism* (1959); W. L. Lumpkin, *Baptist Confessions of Faith* (1959); E. A. Payne, *The Fellowship of Believers* (1944); R. G. Torbet, *A History of the Baptists* (1950).

-Bāqillāni Muḥammad b. al-Ṭayyib (d. 403/1013), of Basra, an → Ash'arī theologian, belonging to the Mālikī school (→ Muslim law), settled in Baghdad. He was a → *qāḍī* and a skilful debater. Ibn Farḥūn (d. 799/1397) says he was dubbed 'the *shaikh* of the → *sunna* and the tongue of the community' (*umma*). He has commonly received high praise for his propagation of Ash'arite dogma, but most of the works with which he is credited are no longer available, which makes accurate estimate of his importance difficult. He is notable for his argument regarding miracles, holding that God alone can perform miracles which may be used to support a prophet's claims. The supreme miracle is the Qur. (→ *i'jāz*). J.R.

*E.I.*², I, pp. 958f.; *G.A.L.*, I, p. 211; *S.I.*, p. 349; A. S. Tritton, *Muslim theology* (1948); Gardet et Anawati, *Introd. à la théologie musulmane* (1948); R. J. McCarthy, *Theology of Ash'ari* (1953), *passim;* Watt, *Philosophy*, pp. 107–9; Sweetman, *I.C.T.*, IV, index of authors; Ibn Khallikān, II, pp. 671f.

Barabbas 'Son of Abbas'. Jew. revolutionary, prob. a → Zealot, who, acc. to Mk. 15:6ff. and Syn. parallels, was chosen by Jews for release at Passover instead of Jesus. The episode involves fundamental problems about circumstances of Crucifixion. Acc. to a variant reading for Mt. 27:16, B. may also have been called 'Jesus'. S.G.F.B.

P. Winter, *On the Trial of Jesus* (1961), pp. 91ff.; S. G. F. Brandon, *Jesus and the Zealots* (1967), pp. 258–64; *The Trial of Jesus of Nazareth* (1968); J. Blinzer, *Der Prozess Jesu* (1969), pp. 301ff.

Baraitha Designation for additions to → Mishnah, meaning lit. 'external', i.e. outside canon. The B.s are Tannaite traditions (→→ Tannaism; Judaism). S.G.F.B.

W. O. E. Oesterley–G. H. Box, *Short Survey of Literature of Rabbinical and Mediaeval Judaism* (1920), pp. 111ff.; *E.J.R.*, p. 57.

Barbelo-Gnostics Form of → Gnosticism so designated by Irenaeus (*c.* 130–200), although it seems to have differed little from other Gnostic systems. Acc. to Irenaeus, Barbelo was a primordial Virginal Spirit or → Aeon, to whom the 'unnameable Father' revealed himself. B. was first of a series of aeons, and produced Light, which the Father anointed as Christ. The orig. of B. is unknown, but concept could stem from Alexandrian identification of → Isis with Sophia (Wisdom). In the B.-G. → pleroma, B. is distinguished from Sophia; however, behind these ideas of a primordial female principle doubtless lies concept of → Great Mother goddess, exemplified in →→ Isis; Ishtar; Atargatis; Cybele; Anahita; Astarte. Irenaeus derived his account from Grk. text of '*Secret Book of John*'; B. appears in → Nag Hammadi *Apocryphon of John* equated with primaeval Thought (*Ennoia*). S.G.F.B.

R.A.C., I, 1176–80; *R.G.G.*³, I, 869–70; R. M. Grant, *Gnosticism* (1961), pp. 49ff.; J. Doresse, *The Secret Books of the Egypt. Gnostics* (E.T. 1960), *passim;* W. C. van Unnik, *Evangelien aus dem Nilsand* (1959), pp. 85, 190ff.

Bardesanes (154-222) Syrian theologian with → Gnostic tendencies (Syr. name, Bardaisan), who lived at court of Abgar IX of Edessa, where Syrian, Iranian and Hellenistic influences intermixed. B., who wrote in Syriac, was interested in other nations and wrote the *Book of the Laws of the Lands*. He opposed dualism of → Marcion and denial of freewill in → astrology, but he was influenced by latter and its concept of Destiny (*heimarmenē*). His cosmology was regarded as Gnostic, and his → Christology as → Docetist. His son, Harmonius, deepened Gnostic elements in teaching of B., which was also propagated by his hymns. S.G.F.B.

D.C.C., s.v.; R.G.G.[3], I, 870–1; *R.A.C.*, I, 1180–6.

Bar Hebraeus (1226–86) Syrian bishop and philosopher of Jew. descent, whose real name was Abû-l-Farag. He was last of great Syrian encyclopaedists, and his voluminous works, mostly in Syriac, contain a vast erudition culled from writings of predecessors. Among his writings was hist. of world from creation. S.G.F.B.

D.C.C., s.v.; R.G.G.[3], I, *s.v.*

Bar-Kochba Jew. leader in revolt against Rome, CE 132–5. His Aramaic name meant 'son of a star': cf. Num. 24:17. He was recognised as → Messiah by celebrated rabbi Akiba. The revolt was prob. occasioned by building of Roman city of → Aelia Capitolina on site of ruined Jerusalem. B.-K. perished after a fierce guerrilla war. Recent excavation has revealed many relics of B.-K. and his companions: an operation order was found signed 'Shimon Bar Kochba, Prince over Israel'. In Rabbinic sources B.-K. is called Simon. S.G.F.B.

E. Schürer, *G.V.J.*, I, pp. 682ff.; M. Noth, *The Hist. of Israel* (E.T. 1960), pp. 449ff.; *I.L.N.*, 4, 11 Nov., 2 Dec. 1961.

Barlaam and Joasaph A Chr. romance drawn indirectly from legend of → Buddha. J. is a prince, whom his father seeks to shield from knowledge of suffering. He is won to the ascetic life by a Chr. hermit B., and performs many miracles. J. is a corruption of → Bodhisattva. The story prob. was transmitted to Byzantine world through → Manichaean sources, either in Syriac or Pahlavi, undergoing much transformation *en route*. The present Grk. version is designed both as Chr. apologetic and to edify: its orig. trans. was prob. made by John Damascene. Its popularity resulted in → canonisation of B. and J. in both E. and W. Churches. S.G.F.B.

St. John Damascene, *Barlaam and Joasaph*, Loeb Class. Lib. (1953); *D.C.C., s.v.; R.G.G.*[3], I, *s.v.;* T. W. Rhys Davids, *Buddhist Birth Stories*[2], pp. xxxiiiff.; E. J. Thomas, *The Life of Buddha as Legend and Hist.* (1952), pp. 287–8; H. Peri, *Der Religionsdisput der Barlaam-Legend* (1959); *R.A.C.*, I, 1193–200; P. M. Lang, *The Balavarian*, E.T. of Old Georgian version (1966).

Barnabas, Epistle of Chr. writing, in Grk., ascribed by → Clement of Alexandria, doubtless wrongly, to Apostle Barnabas. It was prob. written in Alexandria between CE 70–100 against Jews or Jew. Christians. Jew. institutions such as Temple and sacrificial system are condemned as due to Jew. blindness, and O.T. is interpreted as confirming Christianity. S.G.F.B.

Text and trans. in J. B. Lightfoot, *The Apostolic Fathers* (1891); *D.C.C., s.v.; R.G.G.*[3], I, 880–1; *R.A.C.*, I, 1212–7.

Barsom Collection of small metal-wire rods, bound by girdle, used in → Parsee ritual, being frequently sprinkled with holy water or milk. The B. derives from bundle of sacred twigs, comprising 3 to 33, used in anc. Iranian ritual on variety of occasions. It has been suggested that B. symbolises straw cushion on which Vedic gods were supposed to sit. Ezekiel (8:16–7) refers, in condemnation, to practice of holding twigs to face when worshipping sun, but the connection was prob. with cult of Mesopot. sun-god → Shamash. S.G.F.B.

E.R.E., II, *s.v.;* H. W. F. Saggs, 'The Branch to the Nose', *J.T.S.*, XI (1960).

Bath, Karl (1886–1968) Swiss Prot. theologian. B. was for 12 years a minister in pastoral charge; for 10 years (1911–21) at Safenwil on border of Switzerland where he could hear guns of opposing armies in First World War. B. became a theological professor at Göttingen, Münster, and Bonn, where he was deprived in 1935 of his chair because he refused to take an oath of unconditional allegiance to Hitler. He returned to Switzerland and held the professorship of Theology at Basel until he retired. B. has two major achievements to his credit: (i) he decisively changed the emphasis in theological reflection and discussion from an anthropocentric to a theocentric one (ii) he has elaborated a vast, flexible and unfinished *Church Dogmatics*, centred in → Christology, with many orig. features, in which is a running discussion with the past hist. of theology and contemporary discourse.

The First World War was a profound shock to the young Barth. He was horrified the find his German liberal Prot. teachers endorsing standpoint of German Emperor; this led him to question their whole theology, and to find in it no authentic word of God as he sought to preach to his Swiss congregation under the shadow of war. He read → Kierkegaard, who led him to the Bible and → Luther and → Calvin and Dostoievsky. He discovered that you do not speak of God by speaking of man in a loud voice. He discovered what he called 'the strange new world of the Bible'. He came to believe that there was no road from man to God, and that even man's relig. left man self-enclosed. But into man's world, God spoke and came, coming not horizontally but vertically, striking paradoxically and shatteringly into the world of man's pride and presumption. The outcome of this period was B.'s *Commentary on the Epistle to the Romans* (1918, E.T. 1926[2]), in which the paradoxical character of his new awareness of God (in which 'redemption is invisible, inaccessible, impossible for it meets us only in hope'), found passionate and striking expression. The impact of this book—whether it horrified, or found welcome, or seemed a one-sided version of an emphasis that needed to be recovered—changed the Prot. theological atmosphere. The extreme eschatological position of B. lasted only till about 1925; then his thinking and achievement changed to the construction of a Church-based Christ-centred Dogmatic, in which the links between God and man, though estab. from God's side, are real. The starting-point for B.'s *Church Dogmatics* is to be found most simply in the 1st article of the *Theological Declaration* of the Synod of Barmen of May 31st, 1934. This reads: 'Jesus Christ, as He is attested to us in Holy Scripture, is the one Word of God, which we have to hear and which we have to trust and obey in life and death'. The points at which other Chr. theologians might dissent from B. are whether the one Word is an inclusive or an exclusive one, and what is meant by 'attested to us in Holy Scripture'. B. believes that he has found a method by which the Word of God can be heard undistorted by human weakness. 'At each point', he says, 'I listen as unreservedly as possible to the witness of Scripture and as impartially as possible to that of the Church, and then consider and formulate whatever may be the result'. This he calls 'theological exegesis'. This is absolute truth —though his own theological opinions are as fallible as those of other theologians. The satisfactoriness of this starting-point is disputed not least by his contemporary German-speaking Prot. theologians—notably P. → Tillich (1884–1966) and R. → Bultmann (1884–): the one disputing in partic. B.'s attitude to philosophy; the other partic. his attitude to Bible. But the theological construction which B. built on this basis is an enduring stimulus, full of orig. suggestions and profound clarification. B. is at once deeply steeped in theological trad. and not afraid to dissent from it radically—as in his rewriting of → Calvin's doc. of double → predestination, insisting that Jesus Christ is both the elected and the reprobated one. His starting-point for all theological reconstruction is the concrete fact of the Incarnate Christ; and he works out, as never before, what it means to have a theology in which everything is derived from the grace of Christ. The structure of his theology is essentially simple—the Word of God, God, God the Creator, God the Reconciler, God the Redeemer. He insists that we must not isolate any moment in the action of God—even the → Atonement—as having a reality apart from God Himself. 'Who and what God is, His freedom, His sovereignty and His glory cannot be merely the premise or conclusion to the doctrine of the atonement, nor can it be merely provisionally, incidentally or consequentially included in the framework of an exposition of what takes place between the gracious God and sinful man'. In his doc. of God, his Christological centrality, his affirmative attitude to the created world, his orig. doc. of calling of Church as the provisional representation of whole of humanity, and his insistence that the command of God and obedience of man to it in practical life is an essential part of Christian dogmatics, B. has much to say to any constructive theology. Criticism will persist on his denial of natural theology, his attitude to Scripture, to human freedom, the doc. of Atonement, and the theological achievement of last three cents. But both in his prophetic and in his dogmatic significance, B. occupies an import. place in 20th cent. Chr. theology. H.C-J.

Epistles to the Romans (E.T. 1932), *Church Dogmatics* (E.T. 1936–); *Karl Barth's Church Dogmatics*, Selections by H. Gollwitzer (E.T. 1961); *The Humanity of God* (E.T. 1961); T. F. Torrance, *Karl Barth: An Intro. to his early theology* 1910–1931 (1962); H. Hartwell, *The Theology of Karl Barth: An Intro.* (1964); H. A. Meynell, *Grace versus Nature* (1965).

Bartholomew, Massacre of St On St Bartholomew's Day, 24 Aug. 1572, Catherine de Medici, regent of France, organised massacre of Huguenots in Paris. More than 4,000 perished; further slaughter occurred in provinces. The Pope commemorated event with special medal. S.G.F.B.

D.C.C., s.v.; J. N. Neale, *The Age of Catherine de Medici* (1963), pp. 51ff.

Baruch, Book of A book of the → Apocrypha, to which is attached the Epistle of Jeremy. It is gen. regarded as being written or adapted for liturgical use in cycle of Sabbaths commemorating national disasters, a custom which began after fall of Jerusalem in CE 70. S.G.F.B.

R.G.G.[3], I, 900–1 (gen. on Baruch lit.); R. H. Pfeiffer, *Hist. of New Test. Times*, pp. 409ff.

(Greek Apocalypse) A Jew. apocryphal work, prob. dating from 2nd cent. CE, edited for Christ. use. The extant MS describes the vision made allegedly to B. of five of the seven heavens of Jew. cosmology. A Slavonic version also exists. S.G.F.B.

E. Schürer, *G.J.V.*, III, pp. 223–7; Charles, *A.P.*, II, pp. 527–41; Kautzsch, *A.P.*, II, pp. 402–4, 446–57.

(Syriac Apocalypse of) Jew. apocryphal writing attributed to Baruch, the disciple of Jeremiah. It is a Pharisaic work, compiled shortly after CE 70 to encourage Jews dejected by fall of Jerusalem; it deals with earlier capture of Jerus. in 586 BC. Close parallels exist with IV Ezra (II → Esdras); it is an important document for study of Jew. → eschatology. Among other apocryphal works attr. to Baruch is: *The Rest of the Words of B.*, a Jew. work of 2nd cent. CE, with Chr. adds. S.G.F.B.

Charles, *A.P.*, II, pp. 470–526; Kautzsch, *A.P.*, II, pp. 402–46; E. Schürer, *G.J.V.*, III, pp. 223–7; *H.D.B.*², p. 823a; *R.G.G.*³, I, 901–2.

Barzakh (Barrier). Qur. xxiii:102 speaks of the unrighteous asking after death to be sent back to earth to perform some good. This is imposs. because of the B. behind them, till the day they are raised up. It is explained either as period between death and resurrection, or place (some say the grave) where man stays between death and judgment. It is to be noted, however, that Qur., ii: 149 and iii: 163–5 say those killed in → *jihād* are alive. J.R.

*E.I.*², I, pp. 1071f.; Hughes, pp. 38f.; Wensinck, *Creed*, p. 119; Jeffery, *Vocabulary*, p. 77; Cragg, *Dome*, pp. 206f.

Basil, St. (*c.* 330–79) Called 'the Great', B. played a leading role in Church during latter period of Arian controversy (→ Arianism). After living as hermit, he became bp. of Caesarea in 370. Of great learning and personal holiness, B. was also a vigorous controversialist and good organiser. He clashed both with Eunomius, leader of Arian extremists, with the Pneumatomachi (who denied divinity of → Holy Spirit), and with Bps. of Rome and Alexandria because of his support of Meletius, whose orthodoxy these questioned. B. wrote many important theological works, incl. three against Eunomius, and the *Philocalia* (excerpts from → Origen) with Gregory of Nazianzus. He endeavoured to reconcile semi-Arans by showing that their key-word *homoiousios* ('like substance to the Father') implied same as orthodox *homoousios* ('of one substance'). To ending of Arian controversy at Council of Constantinople in 381/2 he contributed greatly. B. was later suspected of → Apollinarianism, due to his stress on unity of Person of Christ (→ Christology). B. is one of the three so-called Cappadocian Fathers, the others being his brother Gregory of Nyssa and Gregory of Nazianzus. The feast-day of B. is 14 June. S.G.F.B.

L. Hodgson, *Essays on the Trinity and Incarnation* (ed. A. E. J. Rawlinson, 1933), pp. 280ff.; J. F. Bethune-Baker, *Intro. to Early Hist. of Christ. Doctrine* (1903), pp. 217ff.; A. Grillmeier, *Christ in Christ. Tradition* (E.T. 1965), pp. 278ff.; W. Bright, *The Age of the Fathers*, I (1903), ch. xix; *D.C.C.*, *s.v.; R.A.C.*, I, 1261–5.

(Liturgy of) → Liturgy. S.G.F.B.

(Rule of) Monastic rule of life, forming basis of that still current in E. Church, which → St. Basil set forth in 358–64. It also required poverty and chastity as in W. monasticism, and was gen. strict, while avoiding stimulating extreme austerities. Hours of liturgical prayer, and manual and other forms of work were carefully prescribed. Arrangements were made for training children for monastic life, and care of the poor was enjoined. S.G.F.B.

E. F. Morison, *St. Basil and his Rule: a study in Early Monasticism* (1912); P. de Labriolle, in *The Church in the Christian Roman Empire*, II (E.T. 1952), pp. 475ff.; *D.C.C.*, *s.v.*

Basilica A Roman form of building, used for law-court and commercial exchange, adopted by early Christians for communal worship. The Chr. B. usually had three distinct parts. An outer courtyard ('atrium'), with colonaded cloister; a 'narthex', or narrow porch, leading by three or more doorways into main structure, i.e. the church proper, which was divided by two lines of arcading into central nave and two aisles (sometimes four). Above arcading was the clerestory pierced by windows. The B. was usually orientated, with east end forming semi-circular apse. The → altar stood on chord of apse, surmounted by canopy. Beneath altar was '*confessio*', or chapel, often containing body of saint. The bishop sat on throne behind altar, and celebrated → Eucharist facing west. The title 'basilica' is given by Pope to certain privileged churches. S.G.F.B.

D.C.C., *s.v.;* F. van der Meer and C. Mohrmann, *Atlas of Early Christian World* (1958), pp. 135ff.; *R.A.C.*, I, 1225–59; Grabar, *B.C.A.*, pp. 169ff.

Basilides An Alexandrian → Gnostic *c.* CE 130/140. Acc. to Irenaeus, B. sought to account for world and man's situation therein by regarding the God of the Jews as chief of lowest order of hierarchy of → angels or emanations who created this lower world. When God of Jews sought to subjugate other nations to Jews, the higher entities opposed him. These had at their head an unbegotten Father, from whom was born Nous ('Mind'), who in turn produced → Logos; from Logos came Phronesis ('Understanding'), who generated Dynamis ('Power') and Sophia ('Wisdom'); these produced a descending order of virtues, powers and angels, grouped severally in 365 heavens. To frustrate design of God of

Jews, the Father sent his first-born Nous = Christ to free those faithful to him. Nous (Christ) was incarnated as Jesus, and worked many miracles. Acc. to B., at Crucifixion Jesus assumed form of Simon of Cyrene (cf. Mk. 15:21–4), who suffered instead of him (→ Docetism). Knowledge (*gnōsis*) of this and of names of angels wins salvation, which is for the → soul alone. The 365 heavens had astrological (→ Astrology) significance, and → Abraxas was incorporated into system. An even more esoteric, but prob. less accurate, version of B.'s teaching is given by Hippolytus. S.G.F.B.

R. M. Grant, *Gnosticism* (1961), pp. 33–5; R. McL. Wilson, *The Gnostic Problem* (1958), pp. 123ff.; *D.C.C.*, *s.v.; E.R.E.*, I, *s.v.; R.G.G.*³, I, 909–10; *R.A.C.*, I, 1217–25; W. Foerster, 'Das System des Basilides', *N.T.S.*, 9 (1963).

Basmala Abbrev. for the Arabic phrase *bismi 'llāhi 'l-raḥmāni 'l-raḥīm*, usually trans. 'In the name of God, the Merciful, the Compassionate'; but perhaps more correctly, '[I begin] with the name of God. . . .' Each *sūra* of the Qur., except 9th, begins with this phrase. Some treat it as separate v., but normally, with exception of *sūra* i, this is not so. These words are written at begin. of books and spoken before food, or when begin. any undertaking. But when an animal is being slaughtered, one says, in place of 'the Merciful, the Compassionate', 'God is most great'. The phrase is credited with magical powers and so is often found in → charms. The contraction B. is also used by Christians, but it is among them short for 'In the name of the Father and of the Son and of the Holy Ghost'. J.R.

Hughes, p. 43; Lane, *Lexicon*, *s.v. bi*, Book I, Part I, p. 141.

Bastet Local goddess of Bubastis in Lower Egypt. Depicted as a cat, B. was assoc. or identified with many deities, e.g. Tefnut, the lion-goddess Sekmet, → Hathor, and later with the → Isis cult. Cats were popular in anc. Egypt. S.G.F.B.

R.Ae.R-G., pp. 80–2; G. Posener, *Dictionary of Egypt. Civilization* (E.T. 1962), *s.v.* ('Cat'); S. A. B. Mercer, *The Religion of Anc. Egypt* (1949), p. 210.

Bathing, Ritual (China-Japan) There is little evidence that B.R. formed a distinctive part of purification rituals of Confucians. → Mencius indicates (iv. b. 25) that those who sacrificed to God on High prepared themselves by ritual bathing.

The most important of → Shinto observances was that of purity, and ablution in ceremonies as well as in daily life. The earliest known purification process was by ablution of naked body of defiled person in waters of sea or of rivers. Thus, the male deity, → Isanagi, washes himself in the sea as first act on escaping from land of Yomi. At Shinto shrines rinsing of hands and mouth is symbolic of the earlier complete ablution of body. Ceremonial purity colours rituals and doctrines of all modern Shinto sects, espec. Shinshu Kyō, and rests on fear of pollution.

There is no evidence of ritual bathing being practised by Buddhists in China or Japan. (→ Baptism). D.H.S.

Bāṭinites → Ismā'īlīs. J.R.

Baubo Name of woman of Eleusis, who, acc. to → Clement of Alexandria (*Protp.* ii), caused the mourning → Demeter to smile by exposing her private parts. Clement cites unknown poem of → Orpheus: the incident appears differently in *Homeric Hymn to Demeter*. This exposure of female *pudenda* has produced much discussion, since Clement relates it to → Eleusinian mysteries, thereby suggesting that it repr. a feature of the rites. The name B. has been explained as meaning female *pudenda*; also that B. is a personification of the vulva. (→ Nudity, Ritual). B. has been identified as female daemon, assoc. with → Hekate. S.G.F.B.

Kleine Pauly, I, 843–5; W. K. C. Guthrie, *Orpheus and Greek Religion* (1952), pp. 135ff.; H. Licht, *Sexual Life in Anc. Greece* (E.T. 1949), p. 501; G. E. Mylonas, *Eleusis and the Eleusinian Mysteries* (1961), pp. 291ff.

Baur, Ferdinand Christian (1792–1860) German Prot. theologian, founder of so-called Tübingen School. A disciple of → Schleiermacher, B. became Professor of Theology at Tübingen in 1826. He was much influenced by → Hegel's theory of history, seeing Primitive Christianity as evolving through conflict of opposing views. He helped to lay foundations of modern hist. of dogma by treating subject historically instead of systematically acc. to estab. custom. His book *Paulus, der Apostel Jesu Christi* (1845; E.T. 1873–5), caused great controversy because it presented Paul in violent opposition to older disciples. After a period of eclipse, B.'s work is now being increasingly appreciated. S.G.F.B.

D.C.C., *s.v.;* H. Stephan, *Geschichte der deutschen evangelischen Theologie* (1960), pp. 147ff.; *R.G.G.*³, I, 935–8; P. C. Hodgson, *The Formation of Historical Theology* (1966).

Bear Cult Skeletal remains of cave-bears, dating from Early Palaeolithic era (*c.* 100,000 BC), found at various sites in Alpine area have been interpreted as indic. existence of a B-C., incl. propitiatory sacrifice to a hypothetical 'Lord of the beasts', to ensure future successful hunts. This interpretation has been influenced by B-C.'s existing in modern world among circumpolar peoples in Europe, Asia and N. America, and the → Ainus of Japan. These modern B-C.'s involve elaborate mimetic ritual, incl. dancer wearing head and skin of dead bear, which is exhorted not to be sad or angry. Skin and head are set in place of honour, presiding over feast on victim's flesh. The bones and other remains are ceremonially buried, perhaps to ensure its resurrection as new bear. S.G.F.B.

J. Maringer, *The Gods of Prehistoric Man* (E.T. 1960), pp. 26ff.; *R.G.G.*[3], I, 841–2 ('Bärenfest'); J. M. Kitagawa, 'Ainu Bear Festival', in *H.R.*, I (1961), pp. 95ff.

Beatification Process of conferring title of 'Blessed' on a person of saintly reputation after death, ordered by Pope. It permits public veneration in specific church or area; sometimes permission is made universal. Before 12th century, local bishops were accustomed to beatify persons in their own dioceses. A similar process exists in Russian Church (→ Canonisation). S.G.F.B.

D.C.C., s.v.; E.R.E., II, *s.v.; C.E.*, II, *s.v.*

Beatific Vision, The Acc. to Chr. theology, the consummation of destiny of redeemed mankind is to see God. The nature and conditions of the B-V. became subject of much intricate dispute in later Middle Ages. It has been believed that certain persons have enjoyed the B-V. during lifetime: e.g. → Moses (Ex. 34:28–35), St. → Paul (II Cor. 12:2–4), and Thomas → Aquinas. See → Dante's vision of the Rose of God (*Paradiso*, xxxi:1–30). S.G.F.B.

D.C.C., s.v.; K. E. Kirk, *The Vision of God* (1950), pp. 1ff.

Bede, the Venerable (*c.* 673–735) Monk and scholar of Anglo-Saxon Church, often called 'Father of English History'. B. spent his life from age of 7 in monasteries of Wearmouth and Jarrow, where he devoted himself to study, teaching and writing. Among his many works (all in Lat.), is the *De Temporum Ratione*, which promoted custom of dating events from Incarnation (→ Chronology), and the *Historia Ecclesiastica Gentis Anglorum*, which is chief source of early English history. The title 'Venerable' was conferred within a cent. of his death; his bones are buried in Durham Cathedral. B.'s life and works attest to vigour and high quality of contemporary monastic life. S.G.F.B.

For convenient ed. of text and trans. of historical works see Baedae, *Opera Historica*, 2 vols. (Loeb Classical Library). *D.C.C., s.v.;* J. Godfrey, *The Church in Anglo-Saxon England* (1962), pp. 207ff.

Beelzebub → Baalzebul. S.G.F.B.

Bekṭāshīs → Ṣūfī Orders. J.R.

Bel Akkadian word meaning 'lord of . . .'; orig. an epithet of → Enlil, the title was later acquired by → Marduk, and Ashur (→ Assyrian Relig.). Enlil was differentiated as the 'old Lord'. Bel was also name of chief god of Palmyra whom some scholars identify with Marduk, others with → Baal or → Hadad. The temple of B. at Palmyra is remarkable for its relig. sculptures. S.G.F.B.

Dhorme, *R.B.A.*, pp. 26–7, 146–7; R. Dussaud, *Les religions des Hittites, et des Hourrites, des Phéniciens et des Syriens* (1945), pp. 404–13; *R.A.C.*, II, 1084 (49); → Parthian Relig.

Bel and the Dragon Book of the → Apocrypha, containing two legendary exploits of → Daniel, in which he exposes deceit of priests of → Bel (Marduk) and kills a dragon worshipped by Babylonians. Of unknown authorship and date (prob. 2nd cent. BC). S.G.F.B.

R. H. Charles, *A.P.*, I, pp. 652–4; *D.C.C., s.v.;* Schürer, *G.V.J.*, II, pp. 452ff.; *R.G.G.*[3], I, 1017.

Belial (Beliar) Heb. word of uncertain etymology. It prob. means 'land without return', like → Sheol, and → *kur-nu-gi-a.* In O.T. it is usually employed adjectivally for 'base', 'wicked'. In inter-Testamental lit. and N.T. (2 Cor. 6:15) it is used as proper noun. S.G.F.B.

H.D.B.[2], *s.v.*

Bellona Roman war-goddess, assoc. with → Mars. B. had no *flamen* or festival; her temple was in the Campus Martius, near altar of Mars. In Imperial times B. was identified with → Mâ. S.G.F.B.

O.C.D., s.v.; Kleine Pauly, I, 858–9; *R.A.C.*, II, 126–9.

Bells Widely used in various religs. They prob. orig. in China *c.* 1,000 BC, and spread westward. Their relig. use has been various: → apotropaic-exorcist, devotional, invitatory, significatory. The Chr. use of bells in Middle Ages, to note hours of prayer, and the 'passing-bell' denoting death, reflected Chr. preoccupation with significance of → Time. The Chr. use of B. dates from about 5th–6th cent. From 8th cent. B. were blessed by bishop with holy water and chrism ('baptism of bells'). (→ Music, China–Japan). S.G.F.B.

R.G.G.[3], II, 1621–6; *D.C.C., s.v.;* O. Spengler, *The Decline of the West* (E.T. 1945), I, pp. 14ff.; L. Mumford, *Technics and Civilization* (1934), pp. 12ff.

Beltane Fires Lit in honour of Celtic sun-god Bâl on May-day Eve, Midsummer Eve, and All Hallow-e'en. The custom was widespread in Celtic lands, and continued as a folk custom into recent times (→ Celtic Relig.). S.G.F.B.

J. Vendryes, *La religion des Celtes* (1948), pp. 273–4, 312–3; J. G. Frazer, *Balder the Beautiful* (*G.B.*), I (1936), pp. 146ff.

Beltis Goddess of Palmyra, assoc. with → Bel. S.G.F.B.

Benedict, St.; Benedictine Order Little is known of life of B. (*c.* 480–*c.* 550), who was born at Nursia, and educated at Rome. After living as hermit at Subiaco, and founding 12 monasteries, he moved to Monte Cassino (*c.* 525), where he stayed until his death. Here he planned reform of → monasticism and composed his Rule, to regulate life of his monks. Drawing on Rules of John → Cassian and → Basil, B.'s Rule aimed at life of balanced austerity centred on performance of Divine Office (the *opus Dei*), with work, study and private devotion completing daily activity. The abbot has full authority, and monk must reside in one place. The B-O. grad. expanded in Europe, being intro. into England (597) by Augustine of Canterbury, and into Germany by → Boniface. In 817 Benedict of Aniane, by his *Capitulare Monasticum* tried to weld B-O. into closer corporate union. Successive attempts at centralisation and greater austerity gave rise to other orders: → Cluny, Carthusian, → Cistercian. B-O. suffered much from → Reformation and French Revolution; but present cent. has seen revival in Europe and America; there is also a B-O. in Anglican Church. Benedictine nuns, estab. by B. and his sister St. Scholastica, live acc. to Rule. The habit of both B. monks and nuns is black. S.G.F.B.

D.C.C., pp. 152, 155; G. G. Coulton, *Five Centuries of Religion*, I (1923), pp. 198ff.; D. Knowles, *The Monastic Order in England* (1950), pp. 3ff.; *R.A.C.*, II, 130–6; *R.G.G.*³, I, 1033–5.

Beni Israel Lit. 'sons of Israel'. Designation of community of Jew. descent settled in Bombay and other places in W. India. B.I. keep → Sabbath strictly, practise → circumcision, observe great Jew. festivals, and abstain from fish. S.G.F.B.

E.R.E., II, *s.v.; R.M.E.*, I, pp. 193ff.

Ben Sira 'The son of Sira'. Name often used for Jesus ben Sira, the author of → Ecclesiasticus. S.G.F.B.

Berakah Heb. = 'blessing'. Jew. prayer, taking form of blessing or thanksgiving to God. It has been suggested that Grk. word → Eucharist derives from Chr. adaptation of Jew. B. recited over cup of wine. S.G.F.B.

W. O. E. Oesterley-G. H. Box, *Short Survey of Literature of Rabbinical and Mediaeval Judaism* (1920), pp. 146–7; *D.C.C.*, *s.v.; E.J.R.*, pp. 61ff.

Berkeley, George (1685–1753) Philosopher and bishop of Cloyne (1734–52), B. is chiefly famous for his metaphysical doctrine, known as Subjective Idealism, acc. to which he held that reality of material world depends upon our perception of it (*esse est percipi*). When not observed by men, material world continues to exist because it is conceived in mind of God. S.G.F.B.

E.R.E., II, *s.v.;* B. Russell, *Hist. of Western Philosophy* (1946), ch. XVI.

Bernadette, St. (1844–79) Peasant girl of → Lourdes, who in 1858 received the first of eighteen visions of Virgin Mary, manifesting herself as the → 'Immaculate Conception'. B. joined the Sisters of Notre-Dame at Nevers, where she lived to her death. She was canonised in 1933, 18 Feb. being her feast-day in France. S.G.F.B.

D.C.C., *s.v.*

Bernard, St. (1090–1153): as abbot of Clairvaux, which he made a chief centre of → Cistercian Order, B. became one of the most influential Churchmen of his day. He prob. drew up Rule of the Knights → Templar, and he preached the Second → Crusade. A champion of orthodoxy, he condemned, among others, → Abelard (1140). His works on → mysticism are more significant than those on theology: his *De Diligendo Deo* is a most important work of medieval mysticism. S.G.F.B.

E.R.E., II, *s.v.; D.C.C.*, *s.v.; R.G.G.*³, I, 1067; G. G. Coulton, *Five Centuries of Religion*, I (1923), chs. 18–9.

Berosus or Berossus Priest of → Bel (Marduk), in 2nd cent. BC, who wrote history of Babylon in Greek. His work gives version of Babyl. creation myth and Flood as current at this late period (→ Cosmogony, Mesopot.). S.G.F.B.

P. Schnabel, *Berossos u. die babylonisch-hellenist. Literatur* (1923); *E.R.E.*, II, *s.v.;* Brandon, *C.L.*, pp. 107, 111ff.

Bes Egypt. god, repr. as grotesque, dwarf-like figure. Preeminently a god of the people, B. protected men against various evils, e.g. reptiles and demons, and helped women in childbirth. He was depicted on stelae, vases, and amulets: often he is ithyphallic (→ Ithyphallic gods). He was also assoc. with music and dancing. B. sometimes appeared in pantheistic form. A female form of B., called Beset, is known. B. seems to have individualised a group of good genii of popular belief. No particular sanctuary of B. is known. S.G.F.B.

R.Ae.R-G., pp. 101–9, 116–8; *Bilderatlas*, 2.–4. Lief., Abb. 42, 43; S. A. B. Mercer, *The Religion of Anc. Egypt* (1949), p. 189.

Bestiality Anc. Semitic myth seems to envisage a primordial state, perhaps before creation of woman, when man lived with animals, having sexual relations with them. Thus the wild man Enkidu in → Epic of Gilgamesh consorts with beasts until he is civilised by sacred courtesan; acc. to Gen. 2:18–24, God created Eve for → Adam because animals were not sufficient 'helpers' for him. In Heb. lit. (Lev. 20:15–6), → Yahweh prohibits B. → Baal had intercourse with cow and fathered a bull-calf (*A.N.E.T.*, p. 139a). Grk. myth provides many instances of divine amours which take form of B. (e.g. Europa and the Bull; Leda and the Swan—the act was realistically portrayed in art). B. occurred in Hindu ritual with *membrum virile* of sacrificed sacred horse. In primitive societies there was prob. no conscious distinction between man and beast: the Palaeolithic picture of Dancing Sorcerer (→ Palaeolithic Religion) indicates close kinship, and drawings from the Trois Frères Cave (Ariège) may depict ritual intercourse between masked dancer and cow. S.G.F.B.

E.R.E., II, *s.v.;* H. Breuil, *Four Hundred Centuries of Cave Art* (1952), pp. 163–5, 173; *A.N.E.T.*, pp. 74ff.; H. Licht, *Sexual Life in Anc. Greece* (E.T. 1949), pp. 157ff., 504. (→ Celtic Relig.)

Bethel Heb. 'house of God'. Orig. Luz, about 12 miles north of Jerusalem, excavations have shown occupation of site of B. from *c.* 2,000 BC. The → Ark was placed there before → Temple was built at Jerusalem. After division of kingdom, Jeroboam I made B. rival shrine to Jerus. Temple (I Kgs. 12, 28ff.). The 'golden calves' of Jeroboam prob. formed pedestal for presence of → Yahweh, who was thus identified with Canaanite → Baal. S.G.F.B.

*H.D.B.*², *s.v.; R.G.G.*³, I, 1095–6.

Bethlehem Native city of King David and birthplace of Christ (Mt. 2:1; Lk. 2:4). The church, covering traditional cave of Nativity, is one of the oldest in Christendom, having been founded by Constantine I in 330, and restored by Justinian in 6th cent. S.G.F.B.

R. W. Hamilton, *The Church of the Nativity, Bethlehem* (1947); *R.G.G.*³, I, 1097–8; *H.D.B.*), *s.v.; R.A.C.*, II, 224–8; C. Kopp, *Holy Places of Gospels* (E.T. 1963).

Bhagavadgītā The 'Song of the Lord' is the most famous and popular of Hindu relig. writings, though it does not belong to the Vedic canon (→ revelation, Hindu), but rather to auxiliary writings known as *smṛti.* It has this status because of its forming part of the epic → Mahabharata, in which it is an interpolation, and the epics were treated as *smṛti.* It was prob. composed shortly before the Christ. era (though there have been wildly differing estimates of its date: some, having detected N.T. influence on it, without good reason, have assigned it to the 2nd cent. CE or later; some, incl. → S. N. Dasgupta, have considered it pre-Buddhistic, on grounds of lack of ref. in it to anything Buddhistic). Its incorporation in the *Mahabharata* has helped its popularity, since the epics were a medium of both entertainment and relig. instruction, and were available to lower classes, unlike the Veda. The work has attracted a large number of commentaries, the most import. being those of → Sankara, Yamuna, teacher of → Ramanuja, Ramanuja and → Madhva. It had a strong influence on → Gandhi, whose disciple and successor Vinoba Bhave has also written a commentary on it. The teachings of the *Gita* are not totally unified, since it draws on differing strands of thought and relig. sentiment; and it has been poss. to interpret it from a variety of points of view (thus Sankara could make it → Advaitin, while Ramanuja and Madhva emphasised its theism). However, the main trend of the *Gita*'s teachings is fairly clear. First, it places a personal God at centre of picture, and though it makes use of the concept of → *Brahman*, this idea is essentially subordinate to that of the → *Isvara*, personal Lord. God is also ref. to as the *Paramātman* or Supreme Soul; but is distinguished from imperishable element, the → *atman* or *purusa*, residing in individual. The distinction is sometimes obscured by the strongly immanentist account of God ('I am intelligence of the intelligent, majesty of the majestic', etc.—vii:10). God, being creator of all things and working within them, is source of both good and evil; but there is no systematic attempt in *Gita* to deal with problem of evil. God's personal nature and majesty is brought out vividly in the shattering theophany vouchsafed to the hero Arjuna in ch. xi, perhaps the most intense expression of the numinous in relig. literature. The relation of the Lord to men's salvation has to be understood in context of problem posed to Arjuna at start of book: he is about to take part in a great battle, and will be killing his relatives—yet will not the performance of his duties bind him to the painful round of → rebirth? The latter doc. is much more strongly emphasised in *Gita* than in → Upaniṣads; and the poem evidently is strongly influenced by ideas drawn from → Samkhya, though it uses these in a special way. The initial resolution of Arjuna's dilemma is to reject view that only way to escape rebirth and attain higher liberation is by inaction—the austerity and quietism practised by the yogin. The performance of action without regard for its fruits is itself a mode of detachment. Thus a distinction is drawn between the *karmayoga* and the *jnanayoga*—the method or discipline of action (i.e. in the world) and the method of knowledge (i.e. liberating knowledge gained by philosophical contemplative, e.g. the follower of → Samkhya-Yoga). Thus a justification is provided for Arjuna's continuance with his social duties as a *ksatriya* (and in any event, the eternal soul cannot be killed by a sword). The detachment poss. in *karmayoga* is given, however, a deeper interpretation and related to person of God. Beyond *karmayoga* there is the method or discipline of *bhakti* (*bhaktiyoga*), whereby renunciation of fruits of action is given a positive significance, for the agent does what he does for sake of God and in devotion to him. The devotee is promised salvation by the Lord. The way of *bhakti* is easier and more embracing than the way of *jnana*. The latter's validity is not denied, though there are hints that the bliss of the *bhakta* is superior to liberation achieved by austerity and inner contemplation. The practice of orthodox Vedic ritual is viewed tolerantly; but *Gita* declares that salvation is open to all classes. The cosmology is influenced by Samkhya; though *Gita*'s understanding of Samkhya is somewhat different from that of classical Samkhya school (as also with its use of *yoga*). The ethics of poem emphasise control of senses, of a moderate kind, as distinguished from severe austerity (→ *tapas*), and are in many respects analogous to those of Buddhism. However, though → *ahimsa* is mentioned, it is not given much prominence; Arjuna is encouraged to fight. The prehistory of the ideas in *Gita* is not altogether clear; but elements are drawn from the Upanishads (e.g. part of its eschatology and the concept of *Brahman*), from early Samkhya and above all from the Bhagavata movement. Already in the *Gita* some main features of later → Vaisnavism are present: the theory of → *avataras*, cult of → Krishna, importance of *bhakti*, openness of God's saving work to all classes of men, and use of Samkhya categories to delineate God's creative activity. Although use of Upanishadic ideas and conceptions such as → *maya* (used, however, infrequently) made Sankara's Advaitin interpretation feasible, there is not much doubt that the theistic exegesis of Ramanuja and others is nearer essential spirit of *Gita*. The emphasis on God's grace, etc., accounts for earlier and mistaken Western theories that poem owed something to Christ. influence. N.S.

F. Edgerton, *The Bhagavad Gita*, 2 vols. (1944) (includes Sir Edwin Arnold's famous translation of the *Gita*); S. Radhakrishnan, *The Bhagavad Gita* (1948); Swami Nikhilananda, *The Bhagavad Gita* (1944); R. C. Zaehner, *The Bhagavad Gita* (1969); N. Macnicol, *Hindu Scriptures* (1938); F. Edgerton, *The Beginnings of Indian Philosophy* (1965); S. N. Dasgupta, *A History of Indian Philosophy*, vol. 2 (1932).

Bhakti Attitude of loving adoration towards God in Hinduism (one can also speak of B. in some phases of Indian Buddhism). The *bhaktimārga* or 'way of devotion' has been one of most import. features of Hinduism since classical times, and finds its first main expression in the → *Bhagavadgītā*. B. contrasts with the sacrificial ritualism characterising much of Vedic relig. and later Brahmanical relig.; with the somewhat analogous sacramentalism of → Tantrism; and with the pursuit of *jnana* or gnosis through yogic techniques, etc.—though it could combine with these other forms of relig. The rise of B. devotionalism dates from last cents. before Christian era, with appearance of the *Bhāgavatas*, i.e. those devoted to the *Bhagavat* or 'Lord' (the word is related to *bhakti*, so that the Lord is the adorable one). An import. cult was that of the god Vasudeva in W. India, who came to be identified with →→ Vishnu and Krishna. Thus the *Bhāgavatas* represent beginning of → Vaisnavism, which throughout its later hist. remained strongly devotional in flavour. Another school which ultimately evolved an extensive literature, and which may have orig. in Kashmir, was the *Pāñcarātra;* it claimed Vedic roots, though it was strongly opposed by Brahmanical orthodoxy, and regarded world as due to a series of emanations out of the godhead, Vishnu. Evident in the *Pāñcarātra* teachings was the cult of gods, such as Aniruddha, conceived as lower manifestations of Vishnu. It was to be characteristic both of Vaisnavism and → Saivism to assimilate a variety of cults under aegis of the master-faith. An instance of this was the elaboration of theory of incarnations, → *avataras*, in Vaisnavism. Also vital in rise of devotionalism was cult of Krishna, which may have owed something to Dravidian influence. By time of *Bhagavadgītā* devotion to Krishna, Vasudeva and Vishnu had been synthesised. Further, the idea of B. was complemented by that of → grace of God in bringing salvation. However, the devotionalism of the *Gita* was less tender than that which was later to develop, esp. in south. The Krishna of the *Gita* is terrifying, powerful, imperious, though merciful. But there were other elements in Krishna legend—his playful sport with the cowgirls, etc.—which were to lend themselves to allegorical account of mutual love been God and souls. Meanwhile, devotionalism oriented towards → Śiva was expressed by movement known as the *Pāśupatis*, named after Pāśupati ('Lord of beasts'), an epithet of Shiva. In Tamil Saivism the term *pasu* was used to symbolise the soul: the Lord of animals is the Lord of souls (→ *Saiva Siddhanta*). The greatest growth of B. was in early medieval period, through vernacular hymns of Tamil and other poets (notably the → Alvars). This fervent and loving devotionalism emphasised humility and love of one's fellows; and like most other B. movements had egalitarian tendencies. This was partly because devotionalism was expressed in hymns and writings lying outside orthodox canon, and repr. in part reaction against formalism of Brahmins. Nevertheless, Brahmanical sacramentalism and B. were repeatedly in differing ways synthesised. Thus → Ramanuja, drawing on piety of southern Vaisnavism, presented an interpretation of Vedanta in conformity with the docs. of a personal God and salvation by grace, while earlier → Sankara had at least conceded place for pietism at the 'lower' level of truth (devotional hymns are ascribed to him). Also, B. could provide framework for inner contemplation, where aim is communion with divine, rather than attainment of Self or of isolated liberation, as in → Yoga; this was a feature of the relig. taught by → Madhva, among Vaisnavites, and of the Saiva Siddhanta. In early 16th cent., → Caitanya was the preacher of devotionalism in Bengal, where it became popular and widespread. The coming of Islam into India also had its effects, in its strong monotheism and repudiation of castism. The interplay between it and Hinduism provided impulse for shaping of an inter-religious B. developed by →→ Kabir, Nanak and others. One can thus say that → Sikhism repr. an essentially devotional relig. with roots in Hindu B. Though the major foci of B. have been deities represented as male, there has also been a not unimportant type of worship, → Saktism, oriented to goddesses, e.g. Kali, esp. in Bengal (it formed essential ingredient in faith of → Ramakrishna, for instance). But prob. the classical form of B. is summed up in Ramanuja's Vaisnavism, with its stress on God's grace and on self-surrender (*prapatti*) to God. The resemblances between spirit of this faith and that of Christianity, esp. Protestantism, have made it natural for Hindus to classify Christianity as type of *bhaktimarga*. Devotionalism has not been as evident in mod. Hindu reforming movements as might have been anticipated, though it was prominent in the lives of both → Ramakrishna and Gandhi. This was partly because of strongly rationalistic element in nineteenth cent. movements (→→ Brahmo Samaj; Arya Samaj); and partly because of increasing influence of neo-Advaita as a unifying ideology. B. is here seen as a means towards end of self-realisation, and thus essentially a lower level of spirituality. N.S.

W. G. Archer, *The Loves of Krishna* (1957); J. E. Carpenter, *Theism in Medieval India* (1921); Sir George Grierson, '*Bhaktimarga*', in *E.R.E.*, II; N. Smart, *The Yogi and the Devotee* (1968).

Bhaktiyoga The way or discipline of *bhakti* as described in the → *Bhagavadgita*, and as contrasted with the *karmayoga* or way of action (through fulfilment of one's ethical and relig. duties in the world) and to the *jnanayoga* or way of knowledge (→ *jnanamārga*), attained through gnosis consequent upon the practice of → yoga, etc. Action in the world can lead to salvation, if it is done in spirit of self-renunciation; but best if it is combined with *bhaktiyoga*, i.e. devotion to the Lord. Thus the one who reveres God is described as the 'most perfectly disciplined' man. N.S.

F. Edgerton, *The Bhagavad Gita*, 2 vols. (1944).

Bhūmi (Skt.) Lit. 'earth': term occurs in cpd. form *bhūmisparshamudrā*—the earth-touching gesture of certain → *Buddha-rūpas*. Used also in specialised sense in Mhy Buddhism as 'stage', in upward spiritual progress of a → Bodhisattva; there are conventionally 10 such 'stages'. T.O.L.

Bible *Ex.* Grk. word *biblia*, 'books'. Used orig. to designate 'Holy Scriptures', the Lat. word *Biblia* came to be used as a sing. and thus passed into modern language in sense of the 'Book'. In Chr. usage the B. denotes two distinctive collections of writings (i) Jew. sacred scriptures, distinguished theologically as the Old Testament, (ii) Christian sacred writings similarly distinguished as the New Testament. The Heb. books comprising the O.T. received canonical status for Jews prob. at Council of Jamnia (*c.* CE 100). This Jew. canon excl. many writings, contained in Greek O.T. (→ LXX), which form the → Apocrypha in Chr. B. Until the N.T. was formed, the Greek O.T. constituted the sacred scriptures of Church. The → canon of N.T. was formally fixed in W. Church together with Chr. O.T. canon (based on LXX), by publication of a Lat. version of B., known as → Vulgate, *c.* 404, which was trans. by → Jerome. Other anc. versions of B. exist in Syriac, Coptic, Ethiopic and Armenian.

The oldest Heb. MS of O.T. is that of Isaiah, dating from 2nd cent. BC, found at → Qumran: it confirmed accuracy of trad. → Massoretic text. The oldest MS of N.T. is a fragment of St. John's Gospel, now in John Rylands Library, Manchester, dating from 2nd cent. The oldest MSS of Greek B. are the →→ Codex Sinaiticus and Codex Vaticanus, dating from 4th cent. CE. The oldest MS of Samaritan → Pentateuch (→ Samaritans) dates from 10th cent. CE, but it preserves a text, independent of Massoretic trad., dating from 4th cent. BC.

The B. has been trans., as a whole or in part, into almost every existing language. Among most notable English versions is the Authorised Version (A.V.), commissioned by King James I, dated 1611; Rheims-Douai version (R.C.) of 1609; Revised Version (R.V.), 1881–5; American Standard Version (1901); Revised Standard Version (R.S.V.), 1946–52; New English Bible (N.T. only, 1961). The importance of B. for Judaism and Christianity is fundamental. The Jew. study and interpretation of Heb. B. produced an immense literature, of which the → Mishnah and Talmud are the most notable memorials (→ Judaism). In Christianity the B. has been regarded as embodying divine revelation concerning the faith; its study and exegesis has ever been a major preoccupation of Christians. It has also been source of much controversy.

All the Prot. Reformers appealed to B. as authority and confirmation for their own particular views. Private interpretation of B. has been productive of multitudinous and often strange versions of Christianity. (→ Biblical Research). S.G.F.B.

*H.D.B.*², arts. entitled Bible, Canon of N.T., Canon of O.T., English Versions, Greek Versions of O.T., Papyri and Ostraca, Text of O.T., Text of N.T.; *E.R.E.*, II, *s.v.; R.G.G.*³, I, 1118–56, 1166–74; F. Gladstone Bratton, *Hist. of the Bible* (1961); *R.A.C.*, I, 354–63; *P.C.*), pp. 24ff., 73–91, 671–82; *Kleine Pauly*, I, 883–91; J. W. C. Weiser, *Intro. to O.T.* (E.T. 1961); R. H. Pfeiffer, *Intro. to O.T.* (1948); *Hist. of N.T. Times* (1949); O. Eissfeldt, *The O.T.* (E.T. 1965); *E.J.R.*, pp. 65–71.

(in Islam) The Qur. shows no knowledge of B. as such, but refers to the →→ Tawrāt, Zabūr, and → Injīl. The trads. contain many phrases obviously of biblical origin, and not only from Pentateuch, Psalms, or Gospels. They may have come through Jew. and Christ. converts to Islam. Trans. of B. were fairly early made into Arabic. Later writers were able to quote the B. and point out inconsistencies, a notable example was → Ibn Ḥazm. For trans. cf. Sweetman, *I.C.T.*, iii:179. J.R.

Hughes, pp. 440ff.; F. Rosenthal, *Ibn Khaldūn*, index; Sweetman, *I.C.T.*, II, p. 131; III and IV, index, *The Bible in Islam* (1953); Syed Ahmad Khan, *The Mohammedan commentary on the Holy Bible* (1862).

Biblical Research Study of the Bible in earlier centuries was inspired by theological and devotional motives, and it so continues among both Jews (with Heb. Bible) and Christians of all denominations. This kind of study was sometimes pursued with a measure of critical awareness (e.g. the formation of both a Jew. and Chr. → canon of Scripture involved some critical assessment of many anc. writings and rejection of certain of them). However, critical investigation of Bible as historical documents and not sacred scripture began only in 17th cent. with R. Simon's *Histoire critique du Vieux Testament* (1678). From that time research has progressed, using every available means (e.g. philology, archaeology, anthropology, comparative religion). Attention has been concentrated upon various topics: e.g. textual research (called 'Lower Criticism') which aims at finding orig. form of text behind existing MS trad.; the investigation of sources underlying orig. text (called 'Higher Criticism'); an extension of this activity, known as → *Formgeschichte*, which is concerned with problem of formation of oral trad., preceding earliest written forms. From study and debate of many generations of scholars certain gen. accepted conclusions are now regarded as reasonably estab.: most notably that the → Pentateuch combines four distinctive trads. (→→ Yahwist; Elohist; Priestly Source; Deuteronomist); that Gospels of Mt. and Lk. incorporate material from Mk. and → Q (→ Synoptic Problem). For hist. of religions B.-R. has been of profound importance. It has promoted study of Heb. relig. with ref. to other religs. of anc. Near East, revealing features common and distinctive. It has also developed techniques of research in comparative philology, archaeology and comparative myth-and-ritual that have charted lines of research in other cultures. There is, indeed, no corpus of sacred lit. that has been so intensively studied. The repercussions of B.-R. for orthodox Judaism and Christianity have been profound, and parties and movements within each faith reflect variety of reaction. B.-R. is largely the work of Chr. scholars of various denominations, and has often been inspired by conflicting motives of apologetic and desire to understand origins of faith: hence tension is often manifest in writings of many scholars between the findings of their research and the relation of them to their personal faith. S.G.F.B.

E.R.E., II, pp. 592b–601; *H.D.B.*², *s.v.* ('Criticism, Biblical'); *R.G.G.*³, I, 1184–92; R. H. Pfeiffer, *Intro. to Old Test.*, 1948, pp. 11ff.; H. H. Rowley (ed.), *The Old Test. and Modern Study* (1952); J. Bright in *The Bible and the Anc. Near East* (1961); A. Schweitzer, *The Quest of the Historical Jesus* (E.T. 1910); J. Moffatt, *An Intro. to Literature of New Test.* (1933); S. Neill, *The Interpretation of the New Test., 1861–1961* (1964); H. Stephan, *Gesch. d. deutschen evangel. Theologie*² (1960), pp. 341ff.; H. M. Orlinsky-R. M. Grant in *Religion*, ed. P. Ramsey (Humanistic Scholarship in America: Princeton Studies, 1965); J. P. Hyatt (ed.), *The Bible in Modern Scholarship* (1966); M. Metzger, *Annotated Bibliog of Textual Criticism of N.T.* (1955). See also B. Smalley, *Study of Bible in Middle Ages* (1952²); *A.O.T.S.*, *C.H.B.*

Bibliolatry The word can be used in several senses: (1) worship or excessive veneration of a sacred book. It is doubtful whether in any relig. a sacred book has actually been worshipped. However, in the ceremonial reading of sacred books, the copy used is often treated with great veneration, being carried in procession, censed, kissed, bowed or genuflected to (varieties of such reverence occur in Judaism, Parseeism, Christianity, Islam, Sikhism). (2) the giving of plenary authority to a sacred book as the Word of God (e.g. → Torah in Judaism, Bible with some Christians, the → *Qur'ān, Science and Health* with → Christian Scientists). (3) as

referring excl. to Bible as evaluated by certain Prot. Christians, e.g. in statement of W. Chillingworth (1602–44): 'The Bible, and the Bible only, is the religion of Protestants'. (→→ Granth, The; Mormons). S.G.F.B.
E.R.E., II, *s.v.*

Bigotry (China-Japan) The Chinese, obsessed by superiority of their civilisation and culture, and of Confucianism as a system, often manifested blind and unreasoning B., an attitude which has been carried into Chinese Communism. The Japanese, on the other hand, with their early indebtedness to Confucianism and Buddhism, and more latterly open to European and American influence, have shown little B. D.H.S.

Bilocation Alleged simultaneous presence of a person in two widely separated places. Such miraculous manifestation was ascribed in anc. world to → Pythagoras, Aristeas, → Apollonius of Tyana, and in Chr. Church to St. Antony of Padua, Francis Xavier, Alphonsus Liguori. B. seems to be attrib. to Risen Christ (Lk. 24:33–5). The power of B. is also claimed by → shamans. S.G.F.B.
E. R. Dodds, *The Greeks and the Irrational* (1963), pp. 140ff.; J. A. MacCulloch, *Medieval Faith and Fable* (1932), p. 174.

Bimbisāra A king of → Magadha at time of the Buddha, and 5 yrs his junior. At age of 30, B. is said to have heard Buddha preach and have become a Buddh. lay adherent and supporter. For remaining years of life he piously observed duties of a layman and used his power in support of Buddha and his community. His death was brought about by his son → Ajātasattu., in whose favour B. had already abdicated, and at instigation of Devadatta, the notorious enemy of Buddha. T.O.L.
Malalalasekere, *D.P.P.N.*, vol. II, pp. 285–9.

Binding and Loosing In Mt. 16:19, 18:18, Christ gives, severally, to Peter and to all the Apostles power of B.-L. In its orig. context this power prob. = that of → rabbis in insisting on or dispensing from obligation of certain ritual requirements. Chr. trad. soon connected B.-L. with apostolic power to forgive or withhold forgiveness of sins (Jn. 20:23). Mt. 16:19 became basis of Papal claim to B.-L. (→ Papacy). S.G.F.B.
E.R.E., II, *s.v.; R.A.C.*, II, 374–80.

Birth The earliest human culture (Upper Paleolithic, *c.* 30,000 BC) evidences man's preoccupation with mystery of B.: e.g. by female figurines with emphasised maternal features and depictions of pregnant animals (→→ Cave Art; Paleolithic Religion). Biological ignorance made B. a mystery of basic significance: it repr. new life or renewal of life, offsetting negation of life in death and replacing the dead. The earliest literate societies show that B. was treated as a crisis necessitating careful ritual action. A sculptured repr. of divine B. of King Amenhotep III (1405–1370 BC) at Luxor records Egypt. ideas of B. Coincident with act of coition, the god → Khnum makes infant and his → ka on potter's wheel, and goddess → Hathor animates them. The actual B. is shown with mother on birth-stool, assisted by women and deities. Later, the infant is presented to his (divine) father, while attendant-goddess determines his destiny. In many religs. B. is surrounded by → tabus designed to protect new-born and mother, and to ensure future well-being. The awe stirred by blood, esp. in menstruation, attaches to B., thereby demanding ritual control and subsequent purification. A notable custom among certain primitive peoples is the *couvade*, or 'man—childbed', whereby father imitates weakness of pregnancy. The custom has been variously interpreted: it might estab. kinship between father and new-born child. The actual moment of B. was deemed critical for future destiny: omens were observed, and horoscopes compiled (→ Astrology). Sometimes new-born child was ritually laid on the earth (e.g. in China). The afterbirth had to be protected, lest it should be used magically against child. After B., various rites are necessary to purify child and mother and incorporate them into community after their critical experience. S.G.F.B.
E.R.E., II, pp. 635–66; *R.G.G.*³, II, 1239–40; Brandon, *M.D.*, pp. 14ff.; *R.Ae.R-G.*, pp. 208ff.; A. M. Blackman, *Luxor and its Temples* (1923), pp. 162ff. (b. of Queen Hatshepsut).

Birth Control (Sterilisation; Contraception) There are three forms of birth control: in descending order of gravity they are → abortion, sterilisation and contraception.

Sterilisation: this may be defined as deprivation of capacity for reproduction. It used to be considered almost entirely in terms of → castration, or removal of sexual organs, but today this would only occur when organs are diseased, and no great ethical problem is involved. Now male sterilisation is by a simple operation, vasectomy, which prevents the passage of spermatozoa into the seminal fluid; female sterilisation in its simplest form is the tying or cauterisation of the Fallopian tubes, best done within a day or two of childbirth. Experiments are being made with non-surgical means of sterilisation such as irradiation or use of chemicals (e.g. the contraceptive pill). As distinct from castration, these mod. forms of sterilisation do not interfere with sexual desire or activity, or with secondary sexual characteristics.

The ethical problem consists in relating gen. ethical considerations (usually derived from a basic relig. or philosophical world-view) to the partic. facts of sterilisation. Sometimes theologians have been tempted to reason solely in terms of abstract considerations; Christ. moral teaching sometimes gives this impression. Its gen. assumptions are: (1) man is crown of God's creation and intended to exercise responsible freedom in it (2) the creation, incl. the body is basically good (3) because of (2), man should not mutilate his own body or that of another except in grave necessity. The problem arises in deciding what is grave necessity, and how far changing empirical factors modify what is thought to be covered by the phrase.

Traditionally sterilisation has been considered under three heads: (1) *Therapeutic:* e.g. case of the diseased organ; case where there is threat to life or health of mother through child-bearing (and where contraception is not thought reliable enough); case of simple desire of a married couple to have no more children. Moral theologians have tended to be against allowing any but first case; opinion is becoming less rigorist. Moral theologians are much less prone to advocate abstinence from coitus in second and third cases, because they are more aware of its impracticability in many social and domestic circumstances, and because they are more aware of the relational importance of coitus in married life. (2) *Eugenic:* there has been concern about the breeding of physically and mentally subnormal children by those who are themselves sub-normal and liable to transmit a serious defect; but greater knowledge of biology of inheritance has shown that sterilisation is largely an inappropriate remedy, and in partic. that the feeble-minded are less, not more, fertile than the 'normal'. (3) *Punitive*, (a) *retributive:* there seems no case for this in a society which has got beyond the 'eye for an eye and tooth for a tooth' view of punishment (b) *protective:* on the whole this is not an effective way of protecting society against the 'sex maniac', whose desires are not diminished by it.

The moral problem involved is complicated by two new factors: (1) the operation in males is in most cases reversible, and so no longer has the decisiveness it once had (2) the 'population-explosion' produced by success of mod. medicine in lands without economic resources to carry burden. The Indian Government has, since 1955, been promoting campaigns for voluntary sterilisation, esp. since the physical and cultural level of so many Indians makes use of contraceptives unlikely. Moral theologians begin to feel the logic of such a case.

Should sterilisation ever be compulsory? St. Thomas → Aquinas held that it could be on ground that State was entitled to remove genital organs of a diseased citizen as the body could legitimately be deprived of a diseased member. Moralists have been unwilling to follow him, and, with 20th cent. totalitarian States in mind, have been loathe to allow this power to State. But it is now seen that necessity must incl. social as well as personal factors; of these the State is partial guardian, so that it is difficult to rule out its action in principle, though it is likely to be inexpedient.

Contraception: this is prevention of conception as result of coitus by (1) a device worn by man or woman which stops the male sperm fertilising female ovum (2) a pill which halts process of ovulation or stops growth of fertilised ovum (3) the practice of '*coitus interruptus*', or withdrawal before orgasm (this last is widely condemned as leading to unsatisfactory sexual relationship in marriage).

For most of history the struggle has been to maintain population in face of hazards of life. Even a cent. ago in Britain it was necessary to have five children to ensure that two would survive to 21. Now, rise in standards of living in industrial countries has led to smaller families (though not too small as was feared), through use of contraception. In other lands mod. medicine has produced the population-explosion, and here contraception is often advocated. Is it legitimate? A number of relig. trads. are hostile to it. In Christianity much of the discussion has taken place in terms of theory of Natural (Moral) law, which is held to indic. that the practice is 'unnatural'. Against this it is pointed out (1) that nature does not restrict coitus to occasions when conception is poss. (2) that man is not subject to nature in ways that animals are with their mating seasons (3) that coitus has a relational as much as a procreative role in human marriage. The first reasoned change in Christ. thought came with the Lambeth Conference of Bishops of Anglican Communion in 1958; in 1959 a consultation of the World Council of Churches came to a similar view (the East. Orthodox dissenting). Since then there has been an acute debate in the R.C. Church, which is still not resolved. That Church allows coitus to be separated from conception in intention by use of the 'safe period' (i.e. avoiding the middle 14 days of menstrual cycle), but holds that 'artificial' means of doing so are 'unnatural'. This means that it should be evidently so to men in general; since it is not so evident, the R.C. Church has to invoke her own authority in declaring something unnatural which is not gen. seen to be so. This is perhaps why much evidence suggests that many R.C.'s do not follow teaching of their Church at this point. In 1968 the Pope issued an Encyclical *Humanae Vitae* which reiterated trad. teaching and rejected the majority report of a Commission on subject which he had appointed and which had advocated a modification of it; the publication of the Encyclical provoked widespread controversy in the R.C. Church.

Contraception as a means of family planning can be seen as an aid to responsible decisions in marriage. It leaves mutual courtesy and restraint as still required. Since it greatly reduces unwanted pregnancies, it means that relig. standards of sexual behaviour must be positively promoted and not by fear. R.H.P.

Birth-Rites (China) Customs vary widely throughout China. Elaborate preparations are made previous to birth, charms are worn by mother, and worship made before household gods and ancestral tablets, not only to ensure safety of mother and child, but to prevent death before delivery, which would involve the mother in endless torment in the 'Lake of Blood', a department of the Underworld. On birth of child, a charm procured from a temple is fastened round child's neck, and a piece of raw ginger hung up at street door to keep away evil spirits and strangers. On 3rd day the child is usually ceremonially bathed; when the baby is clothed an open lock is passed over its body from head to foot, and when it reaches the ground it is locked, thus binding the child to this world. White paper money is burned, and offerings of cakes etc. made to deities who preside over the bed. Very early in life a diviner is called to cast a horoscope (→ Astrology). On 29th or 30th day, the ancestors are worshipped by the mother-in-law, carrying the child, and offerings and thanksgivings made in the ancestral hall. Eggs, dyed red, and presents are sent by relatives and friends, who are invited to a feast. D.H.S.

E.R.E., II, pp. 645–6; J. Dyer Ball, *Things Chinese*, 5th ed. (1925); J. Cormack, *Chinese Birthday*, *Wedding*, *Funeral and other Customs* (1923).

(Japan) Four months before the expected birth, at time when the soul is believed to enter the foetus, the ceremony of *Iwata-obi* takes place, when a piece of unbleached silk is wound round body of expectant mother. In former times four ceremonies followed birth, on the evening of the birth and on 3rd, 5th, and 7th days. On 7th day, in absence of mother, the baby is introduced to relatives and friends and receives its name, usually chosen by a 'god-parent'. A feast is prepared consisting of rice cooked with red beans, seabream and sake. D.H.S.

J. Herbert, *Shinto* (1967), pp. 161, 165.

Bishop *Ex.* Grk. *episcopos*, 'overseer'. Origins obscure in N.T.: *episcopos* and *presbyter* ('elder') seem interchangeable (e.g. Acts 20:17; 20:28). By early 2nd cent. → Ignatius knows hierarchy of B.'s, Presbyters, and → Deacons. By mid. 2nd cent. all main churches had B.'s. → Apostolic Succession is invested in B.'s, who have power to ordain → priests and other orders. B.'s receive consecration at hands of a metropolitan (i.e. archbishop or primate) and 2 other B.'s. Mode of election and appointment varies in different Churches: in R.C. Church it is normally by Pope. The chief duties of B. are administration of → sacraments of → Confirmation and Ordination, and, unless he is a suffragan or assistant B., oversight of diocese. In Middle Ages B.'s often held civil office; in England a number of B.'s have seats in House of Lords. The B.'s see or throne (*cathedra*) is in his → cathedral. The chief insignia of a B. are mitre, pastoral staff, pectoral cross and ring. At → Reformation, of Prot. Churches the Ch. of England alone retained trad. order of B.'s; certain other Prot. Churches kept title, without claiming Apostolic Succession. (→ Hierarchy, Christ.) S.G.F.B.

D.C.C., *s.v.; R.G.G.*[3], I, 1300–11; *R.A.C.*, II, 394–407; A. A. T. Ehrhardt, *The Apostolic Succession* (1953); T. Klauser, *Der Ursprung der bischöflichen Insignien u. Ehrenrechte* (1950).

Black Mass A Satanic parody of the → Mass, gen. connected with → Witchcraft. All symbolism and ritual are inverted, and the Sacrifice of the Mass is offered to the → Devil instead of God. Information about the B.-M. is usually obscure and often suspect, as it is concerning all forms of → Satanism and witchcraft. The term B.-M. is also a popular expression for Requiem Mass for the dead, at which the → vestments are black. S.G.F.B.

M. Summers, *Witchcraft and Black Magic* (1945), pp. 208ff.; H. E. Wedeck, *A Treasury of Witchcraft* (1961), ch. V.

Black Muslims Sect in U.S.A., which teaches overthrow of white race by year 2,000, when the Nation of Islam, i.e. the Black Nation, will bring in a new civilisation. W. D. Fard is said to have come to U.S.A. from Arabia about 1930 as a travelling salesman. He concentrated on negroes of Detroit, speaking of the 'lost found' nation of Islam; by 1934, when he disappeared, an effective organisation had been estab. Elijah Muhammad (b. 1897) was Fard's closest assistant and successor. He teaches that Allah has come to U.S.A. in person of Fard, called the great Mahdi, and appointed him as prophet. He says his office is mentioned in Bible and Qur. (Malachi, iv, 5f.; Qur. lxii, 2). The racial element with its mythology is strong. The black race was the original, but a genius called Yakub created people of different shades, and eventually produced a white man. The white races are inherently wicked, so the black will overthrow them. White people are excl. from B.M. temples, but no violence is used. A para-military body called Fruit of Islam has so far acted peacefully. Members wear in their lapels buttons with star and crescent. Excellent work is done in reclaiming criminals and drink and drug addicts. Rules of conduct are strict: no alcohol, tobacco, drugs, cosmetics, gambling, dancing, sport, sexual immorality, idleness, or long holidays. Cleanliness, thrift, respect for women, and sense of personal dignity are emphasised. There are also dietary laws. Attendance twice weekly at temple meetings is compulsory, unless permission for absence is given beforehand. Members are supposed to observe the five Muslim times of prayer daily; but evidently normal Muslim prayer-ritual is not strictly followed. When Malcolm X., Elijah Muhammad's second in command, visited Mecca, he was embarrassed to find that he, a leader in the Nation of Islam, did not know the prayer-ritual. In temples prayer is in Eng., but occasionally in Arabic, and is said silently after the minister. But it incl. prayer for 'blessing on Muhammad here in the wilderness of N. America', which can be interpreted only as ref. to Elijah Muhammad. Both Bible and Qur. are used in temples, but Elijah Muhammad's interpretation is all-import. He teaches that God is the only eternal being, so man has no immortality. Heaven and hell are 'two conditions on earth which reflect one's state of mind, his moral condition and actions'. The movement has helped lower class members of the Black Nation, giving them sense of purpose, and by education and business projects giving them new hope. But can it properly be called Muslim when it teaches that Allah has appeared in human form, that there is no life for man after death, and upholds racialism which Islam repudiates? Malcolm X. left movement to found one of his own, after doubting Elijah Muhammad's teaching about Yacub, and experiencing real → Islam in Muslim lands. He was assassinated in 1965. J.R.

S. Eric Lincoln, *The Black Muslims in America*, 6th print. (1964); E. U. Essien-Udom, *Black Nationalism*, 2nd imp. (1963); *M.W.*, LV (1965), pp. 344f.; Malcolm X., *Autobiography* (with A. Harley) (1966).

Black Stone (*Al-ḥajar al-aswad*), prob. an aerolite, set in E. corner of the → Ka'ba. Legend says Gabriel gave it to → Ishmael; but it is also said to have been sent down in → Adam's time. It has had chequered career. It was damaged in time of Ibn al-Zubayr (1st/7th cent.); in 4th/10th cent. the → Qarmaṭians took it to al-Aḥsā' in E. Arabia, where it remained for 21 years. Al-Ḥākim, → Fāṭimid Caliph in Egypt (5th/11th cent.) sent a man to destroy it, but he was quickly stopped after splintering it slightly. It shows signs of repair, though worn smooth by pilgrims who have kissed it for cents. It is in a silver casing, showing diameter of about 10″. The practice of kissing it was retained from pagan times; but one must not consider that Muslims treat it as an object of worship. J.R.

E.I., II, p. 585; Hughes, pp. 154f.; Burton, *Pilgrimage*, index; Rutter, *Holy Cities*, I, pp. 220–2.

Blasphemy *Ex.* 2 Grk. words: *blaptein*, 'to damage', and *phēmē*, 'reputation'. Speech or action derogatory to God. In O.T. (Lev. 24:16), B. was punished by stoning. In Christianity, B. was regarded as → mortal sin, and canon and civil law prescribed severe penalties. From the Enlightenment attitude to B. became grad. less severe, and legislation was correspondingly adjusted and administered. In England and America tendency is to treat B. less as sin against God than as conduct liable to cause offence against peace and good order of society. S.G.F.B.

E.R.E., II, pp. 669–72; *D.C.C.*, *s.v.; H.D.B.*², *s.v.; R.G.G.*³, II, 1804–5 ('Gotteslästerung').

Blessing In primitive thought verbal pronouncements can have magical efficacy. Anc. gods such as → Ptah, → Ea, → Yahweh created by power of their *fiat*. Similarly, it was believed that a deity's pronouncement of well-being or reverse (→ Cursing) on any person or thing would be effective, unless countered by a stronger power. Such efficacy, with suitable modification, could attach to words of men of great sanctity or spiritual authority. The O.T. and N.T. abound with examples of B. The Church incorporates formulae of B. in its liturgy: pronouncement of B. is usually accompanied by ritual action, namely, raising of right hand and making sign of cross. Sometimes B. is mediated by laying hands on head of recipient. S.G.F.B.

E.R.E., IV ('Cursing and Blessing'); *D.C.C.*, *s.v.; H.D.B.*², pp. 109–10.

Blest, Abode of the (China-Japan) → Confucianism had little concern with the after-life. Early literature speaks of souls of deified rulers being associated with → T'ien on high, and dwelling in region of the Pole Star. → Taoism conceived of 36 heavenly grottoes and 72 Happy Lands, the most famous being K'un Lun Shan in extreme W., and P'êng Lai Shan (or Isles of the Blest) situated E., off coast of Shantung. The W. paradise of K'un Lun was presided over by Hsi Wang-Mu (the W. Royal Mother), and was peopled by immortals, who with perfected bodies continually live a life of ease and pleasure. P'êng Lai, situated in the E. sea, is the home of the → Eight Immortals and of a great host who have attained immortality.

Buddhism in China first accepted belief in the Tushitā paradise of the future Buddha, → Maitreya; but under influence of the *Lotus Sūtra* and the → Pure Land Sect, belief in Hsi T'ien or the W. Paradise of → Amitābha became almost universal. This blissful land, in which sorrow, grief and pain are for ever banished, is described in extravagant language, and for the masses at least supplanted → Nirvāna as final goal. Souls who attain the W. Paradise are released from subsequent birth. These Abodes of the Blest are contrasted with the Buddhist and Taoist hells, where souls of sinful work out in torment their evil → *karma*. D.H.S.

C. H. Plopper, *Chinese Relig. seen through the Proverb* (1926); E. T. C. Werner, *A Dictionary of Chinese Mythology* (1932).

→ Shinto, except as influenced by Buddhism, has little to say regarding a future state. Acc. to early records, → Izanagi, when he died, went to a blessed island, or, acc. or another account, to → Heaven where he dwelt in palace of the sun. '*Ame*' or Heaven, where the gods dwell, is place to which deified men (Mikados, heroes, the wise and virtuous) go at death. 'Toko-yo no kuni' (the Eternal Land) is described as an island paradise, a land of immortality, often sought but rarely found by mortals.

Among the Abodes of Bliss of Japanese Buddhism are the Paradise of Vulture Peak, the Tushitā Paradise of the future Buddha, Maitreya, and the W. Paradise of the Pure Land Sects, ruled over by → Amida. D.H.S.

W. G. Aston, *Shinto* (1905); M. Anesaki, *Hist. of Japanese Buddhism* (1930); *E.R.E.*, II, pp. 700–2.

Blood To the primitive mind B. was the 'soul-substance'. The idea is succinctly expressed in the Heb. phrase: 'the blood is the life' (Dt. 12:23: 'life' here = 'soul'). The ritual significance of B. finds prob. expression in Paleolithic custom of using red pigment in burials: red being colour of B., the corpse might be revitalised by application of red pigment. Acc. to Homer, the shades of dead gained momentary vitality by partaking of blood (*Od.* XI:152–3). The offering of victim's blood was an important part of ritual of sacrifice: the idea finds expression in Chr. soteriology in the blood of Christ (→ Atonement). The drinking of sacramental blood of Christ effects communion between devotee and Saviour God in the → Eucharist. S.G.F.B.

E.R.E., II, *s.v.; R.G.G.*³, I, 1327–32; *R.A.C.*, II, 459–73; E. O. James, *The Origins of Sacrifice* (1933), pp. 21ff.; L. Dwer, 'The Biblical Use of term "Blood" ', *J.T.S.*, IV (1953).

Bodhi Indian term used espec. in Buddhism, meaning 'enlightenment' or 'awakening', from *budh:* to awake, become conscious. B. is held to be of 3 kinds, that of the disciple, or hearer of the Buddha, that of an isolated enlightened one, or → *pacceka-Buddha*, which is independently gained; and that of the universal Buddha, the *samma-sambuddha*, which is independently gained, but also proclaimed to others. → Buddha (as a generic title). T.O.L.

Bodhidharma (*c.* CE 470–543). In Chinese = Ta Mo. An Indian Buddhist monk, who went to China and is credited with the estab. of → Ch'an or the Meditation Sch. of Buddhism. The date of his arrival in China is generally given as CE 520, and he soon acquired an outstanding influence. The accounts of his life are largely legendary. He based his teachings on the *Lankāvatāra Sūtra* (E.T. by D. T. Suzuki, London, 1932), and his message was summarised in the famous stanzas:

A special transmission outside the Scriptures,
No dependence upon words or letters,
Direct pointing at the soul of man,
Seeing into one's own nature and attainment of Buddhahood. D.H.S.

E. Wood, *Zen Dictionary* (1962).

Bodhisatta (Pali); **Bodhisattva** (Skt.) Term used in Buddhism for one who aspires to → *Bodhi* (enlightenment), i.e. one who is a Buddha-to-be. Orig. term appears to have been used to denote → Gotama the Buddha's state prior to becoming a Buddha: cf. phrase found in Pali texts such as *Mahāpadāna Sutta* (DN. ii, 13), 'in the days before my Enlightenment when I was as yet only a Bodhisatta . . .' Interest in 'previous lives' of Buddha thus developed, and stories concerning the B. Gotama were brought together in the → *Jātakas*. Speculation concerning state of life of a B. is also discernable in → Pali canon; acc. to the *AN.* (iv, 127; viii, 70), the B., before being born on earth in his last existence, i.e. as a Buddha, dwells in place of bliss, the *Tusita*-heaven, where he may live as long as 6 million years. As speculation developed further, so concept of the B. became further conventionalised: his career as a B. was held to begin with his making a formal resolution to become a Buddha, for welfare of all beings. This was the B.'s *abhinīhāra*, and its ultimate realisation depended on fulfilling of 8 conditions, viz. that the aspirant (1) was a human (2) male (3) able to become an → *arahant* during existence in which resolution was made (4) a recluse, (5) declared his resolution to a Buddha (6) was able to attain state of → *jhāna* (7) was prepared for absolute self-sacrifice (8) was unswerving in his resolve (*Buddhavamsa* ii, 59).

The concept of B. received a greatly increased importance in Mhy., where it replaced *arahant* ideal as goal of Buddh. life. In Har Dayal's classic work, *The Bodhisattva Doctrine*, it is argued that the B. ideal was revival of the orig. genius of Buddhism, which had become obscured by too self-centred attitude of monks who were seeking lesser goal of arahantship. The distinction made by Mahāyānists is that the B. aims at enlightenment of all beings without distinction of 'self' and 'not-self'; whereas the *arahant* aimed only at self-enlightenment. The quality of compassion is emphasised equally with wisdom in the Mhy., whereas the → Hīnayāna had emphasised wisdom more than compassion. The B. ideal was thus of a universalist character. The question when one can justifiably be called a B. was answered by → Nāgārjuna (1st cent. CE) as follows: 'This change from an ordinary being to a Bodhisattva takes place when his mind has reached the stage when it can no longer turn back on enlightenment. Also, he has by then gained five advantages: he is no more reborn in the States of woe, but always among gods and men; he is never again born in poor or low-class families; he is always a male and never a woman; he is always well-built, and free from physical defects; he can remember his past lives, and no more forgets them again.' (*Mahāprajñā-paramitā-sāstra* 86.C–89.C; Conze's trans., *Buddhist Scriptures*, pp. 30f.). Acc. to the *Lankāvatāra Su*, an important work of → Yogācāra school, the B. is characterised by 9 endeavors: (1) to rid himself of all perverted views of existence; (2) thereby to liberate himself from fetters of conventional concepts; (3) to penetrate unreality of a so-called external world of particulars; (4) to attain position where → *samsāra* and → *nirvāna* are understood as 2 aspects of one and the same reality; (5) to cultivate a compassionate heart and skilful means; (6) to perform effortless deeds; (7) to cultivate contemplation (*samādhi*) which sees beyond all forms; (8) to have perfect wisdom (*prajñā*); (9) finally, to manifest the Buddha-body. When these all have been achieved, the B. will have come to Buddhahood.

Since this is a path open to all, acc. to Mhy., the concept of B. implies poss. of existence within world of many B.'s. Those who were regarded as having reached penultimate stage of existence in the *Tusita* heaven, were thought of as heavenly beings, upon whom ordinary mortals could call for help, confident that the compassionate B. would not fail them. In such terms were regarded the major B.'s, such as →→ Avalokitesvara, Manjusri, Maitreya, Samantabhadra and Kshitigarbha. In this way the Mhy. philosophy was able to provide what in Mhy. Buddh. view was a respectable rationale for a popular cult.

The term B. was not, however, confined to 'celestial' beings. Great teachers, e.g. →→ Nagarjuna and Asanga, were referred to as B.'s. It was also a convention of Buddhists in S. E. Asia to regard their kings as B.'s, since they were beings whose great efforts were directed towards securing welfare of the many. → Kings (Buddhist). T.O.L.

Malalasekere, *D.P.P.N.*, vol. II, pp. 322–9; Conze, *B. Thought in India* (1962), pp. 234ff.; Eliot, *H.B.*, II, ch. XXVII; H. Sarkisyanz, *The Buddhist Backgrounds of the Burmese Revolution* (1965); Pe Maung Tin, *B. Devotion and Meditation* (1964), pp. 56–8.

Bodhi-Tree (Bodhirukkha) The *aśvattha* (*ficus religiosus*) tree under which, acc. to Buddh. trad., the Buddha attained enlightenment, at Uruvelā, on bank of the Neranjara river, near modern Gāya. The Pali texts recount propagation of other *bodhi* trees from this parent one. The people of → Sāvatthī are said to have asked Buddha's disciple Ānanda, for provision of a shrine where they might make their offerings of flowers and incense in honour of Buddha at times when he was absent from the place. After consulting him, Ānanda is said to have obtained a seed of the *Bodhi*-tree of Uruvelā, and to have planted it in front of the Jetavana monastery which Anāthapindika had built at Sāvatthi for Buddha and his disciples. The tree, which sprang from the seed, was hallowed by Buddha's spending a night beneath it in meditation. From its planting by Ānanda, this second b. tree became known as the *Ānanda bodhi.* Another descendant of the Uruvelā B.-T. is said to be that at Anurādhapura in → Ceylon. Acc. to Pali chronicle (*Mahāvaṃsa* XVII, pp. 46f.), a cutting was taken to Ceylon in reign of → Devanampiya Tissa and planted there with royal ceremony. From the seed saplings are said to have been raised at various other places in Ceylon.

It has been suggested that the connection of the *aśvattha* tree with Buddha's enlightenment has no hist. foundation, since the most continuous and detailed account of events surrounding the enlightenment, viz., the *Mahāsaccaka Sutta* (*MN.* 36), does not mention the matter of the tree. (S. Dutt, *Buddha and 5 After Centuries*, pp. 40ff.). The veneration of sacred → trees was a common feature of anc. Indian life, long before time of Buddha; this primitive tree-cult may have made its way into Buddh. trad. The veneration of *aśvattha* tree was perhaps provided by Buddh. piety with a legendary connection with Buddha enlightenment; an actual *aśvattha* tree at Uruvela was then identified with tree of legend. T.O.L.

Malalasekere, *D.P.P.N.*, vol. I, p. 275; vol. II, pp. 319–22; S. Dutt, *Buddha and 5 After Centuries* (1957).

Bodies of the Buddha → Buddha-Kāya. T.O.L.

Body and Soul It is unknown when idea first emerged that man was compounded of B. and S. Acc. to theory of → Animism, the idea appeared very early in evolution of culture. Archaeological evidence for idea in Paleolithic era is uncertain. In earliest Egypt. records (→ Pyramid Texts), man was already regarded as a psycho-physical organism of many constituents (→→ Akh; Ba; Ka; Heart). But the body was deemed essential for proper personal life; hence attempts to preserve corpse (→ Mummification). The term → 'soul' can be misleading, unless carefully defined in relation to specific religs., because it connotes great variety of concept. In many religs. (e.g. Mesopot., anc. Heb., Greek, Chinese), the soul was closely connected with animating breath, which became, after death, shadowy replica of living person. On such a view, proper personal life required both B. and S. as an integrated whole; consequently, life after death necessitated → Resurrection of physical body. Where soul was conceived as a preexistent spiritual entity, constituting inner essential self (e.g. in →→ Hinduism; Pythagoreanism; Orphism), body was regarded as temporary, and often contaminating, dwelling-place of soul, from which latter was freed at death: sometimes the body was regarded as intrinsically evil (→ Manichaeism). Christianity sought to combine Heb. and Orphic docs. of man, incl. corporeal resurrection. → Islam and → Zoroastrianism teach resurrection of body, but conception of soul is not well defined. → Buddhism regards B. and S. as temporary combination of certain physical and psychical entities. (→→ Dualism; Man, Doc. of). S.G.F.B.

E.R.E., II, pp. 755–74; C. J. Bleeker (ed.), *Anthropologie religieuse* (1955); Brandon, *M.D.*, *passim.*

Body of Christ → Corpus Christi. S.G.F.B.

Boehme, Jakob (1575–1624) German mystic (→ Mysticism), whose relig. background was → Lutheranism. His many theosophical (→ Theosophy) writings use Chr. terminology, but his thought seems basically to have been either pantheistic (→ Pantheism) or dualist (→ Dualism): his meaning is gen. difficult to comprehend, because of esoteric imagery and vocabulary. His influence was far reaching, affecting such as → Hegel, W. Law and Isaac Newton. S.G.F.B.

E.R.E., I, *s.v.; D.C.C.*, *s.v.; R.G.G.*[3], I, 1340–2.

Boethius, Anicius Manilius Severinus (*c.* 480–524) Philosopher and statesman, chiefly famous for his *De Consolatione Philosophiae*, written in prison while awaiting execution, which shows how the soul can attain the vision of God through philosophy. The work was very popular: King Alfred trans. it into Anglo-Saxon. The attrib. to B. of a work on the → Trinity (*De sancta trinitate*) and another on → Christology seems now to have settled question whether B. was a Christian. His execution by Arian emperor Theodoric led to B.'s canonisation as St. Severinus. S.G.F.B.

Boethius' chief works are ed. and trans. in Loeb Classical Library, by H. F. Stewart and E. K. Rand. *C.M.H.*, II, pp. 448ff.; *O.C.D.*, pp. 139–40; *R.G.G.*[3], I, 1344–5; *Kleine Pauly*, I, 915–6; *R.A.C.*, II, 482–8.

Bogomiles Dualistic sect in Balkans and Asia Minor in early Middle Ages. Name prob. derives from founder Bogomile, who was burnt in 1118 on order of Emp. Alexis Comnenus. Sect has → Gnostic affinities, and was related to Paulicians, Euchites, and → Catharists. Their → dualism took form of ascribing creation of world and Adam to Satanael, the rebel son of God, who gave to Adam his soul. To save mankind from bondage to Satan(ael), God sent his second son, Jesus, into world in human form. Jesus returned to heaven, after victory over Satan, leaving → Holy Spirit to assist B., the only true Christians, who were transformed into ethereal bodies at death. B. accepted N.T., but rejected parts of O.T. as work of Satan, infant baptism, marriage, all prayers except the 'Our Father', and other orthodox beliefs and customs. Sect disappeared in late 14th cent. S.G.F.B.

D. Obolensky, *The Bogomiles* (1948); *E.R.E.*, II, *s.v.; D.C.C.*, *s.v.;* S. Runciman, *The Medieval Manichee* (1955), ch. IV.

Bohorās Muslim community mainly in W. India, with section in the Yemen. The Indian B. are descendants of Hindu converts to → Ismā'īlī Islam, with a mixture of Yemeni blood. The sect is connected with those who upheld claims of Musta'lī (487–95/1094–1101) as successor of Fāṭimid Caliph Mustanṣir (→ Assassins). B. is not a sect name, for some Hindus and Jains are registered as B. Neither are all Muslim B. Ismā'īlīs, for some are → Sunnīs, the former mainly merchants, the latter peasants. The *dā'ī* (head) was in Yemen up to 946/1539, when he migrated to India. A schism took place in 996/1588, forming Dā'ūdīs and Sulaymānīs, after names of their leaders; the former with their head in Bombay, the latter with theirs in Yemen and his representative in Baroda. The relig. beliefs are kept secret; they keep themselves separate from other Muslims. J.R.

E.I.[2], I, p. 1265; Pareja, p. 841; Jones, *Mosque*, p. 134, S. T. Lokhandwalla, 'The Bohras: A Muslim community of Gujarat', *S.I.* (1955), pp. 117–35.

Bon and Tibetan Pre-Buddh. Relig. Pre-Buddh.

relig. in Tibet is ref. to in earliest texts simply as the 'sacred conventions' (*lha-chos*) or the 'pattern of heaven and earth' (*gnam sa'i lugs*). Relig. officiants were known as *Bon* ('invokers') and as *gShen* ('sacrificers'). It was only later on, when early indigenous relig. began to be permeated with Buddhism, that the relig. itself came to be known as Bon, and the practisers of this new composite relig. known as *Bonpo*. Retrospectively all pre-Buddh. beliefs and rites were called Bon; this causes some confusion.

A special feature of the early relig. was cult of the royal dead, who were entombed under mounds together with certain possessions and even accompanied by close companions, who were seemingly bound under oath to die with king. By 7th cent. this practice was sufficiently humanised to permit officials concerned to live at the tomb but keeping out of contact with other living men and women. Acc. to often recited myths, king was conceived of as divine being descended from celestial spheres. Orig. kings were supposed to have returned to zenith by means of celestial cord, thus not leaving bodies behind on earth. It is told in legend how cord came to be cut, and from then on kings had tombs on earth. In Yarlung Valley, east of Lhasa, there is group of ten royal tombs dating from 7th and 8th cents. CE. Until Buddhism taught otherwise, there is no suggestion of another life in heavens or hells. Deceased belonged to realm of dead, prob. rather like a kind of Hades. In gen. pre-Buddh. relig. in Tibet, like so much of the relig. of simple people throughout whole Buddh. period, was primarily concerned with affairs of this life. Its purpose was to discover by means of sortilege or astrological calculation, causes of human misfortunes, and then prescribe suitable cures. Main causes of misfortune were local gods, demons and sprites of various kinds; usual ways of counteracting their attacks were by ransom offerings. Such practices were soon taken over by Bhuddh. in Tibet in order to win lay support from already entrenched indigenous priests. There was an import. cult of powerful local gods, often conceived of as mighty warriors with host of fighting attendants. Some were explicitly connected with certain mountains; one may note that first king of Tibet was thought of as having descended from heavens onto mountain know as Yar-lha-sham-po. Ransom offerings took the form in early period of sacrificial victims, and acc. to Chinese reports, even human beings were once sacrificed. But from the hist. period (7th cent. CE onwards) there is no proof of this. Like early kinds of sortilege and rites, many local divinities were accepted by Buddh. clergy as protecting divinities who had sworn to defend the new Buddh. relig. This whole class of local 'converted' gods were known as *dam-can*, the 'oath-bound'; from now on they began to receive their offerings as part of elaborate Buddh. rituals. Special sacrificial cakes made of barley-flour, but shaped and coloured to look like flesh-offerings, were offered to them; this continues right up to 20th cent.

While Buddh.s were adopting non-Buddh. practices, priests of old relig. grad. organised themselves into a new relig. order, incorporating all they could of Buddh. docs. and practices. They began to build temples and later monasteries on Buddh. pattern. Writing was intro. into Tibet from 7th cent. as part of limited court interest in Buddhism; hence nearly all lit. intro. and trans. was Buddh. in inspiration. No other philosophy was known in Tibet; the Bonpos, as they were now called, developed their own sets of philosophical works, which they took over from Buddh. with occasional changes of terminology. They developed their own sets of → tantras, interesting since they centre on Bon divinities; but in content and intention they correspond with Buddh. tantras. They developed systems of → yoga and meditation, and produced their own treatises and manuals. Thus by 14th cent. they were fully organised as special kind of Buddhism, unorthodox in that they persisted in claiming that their teachings had not come orig. from India, but from W. Tibet (known by old name of Shang-shung), and orig. from even further west, from land of *sTag-gzigs* (? modern Tadzhig) identified vaguely with pre-Muslim Persia. The founder of their relig., Mi-bo gShen-rab, was supposed to have come from there; an elaborate biography was grad. put together from early mythological materials, but shaped on model of the historical or quasi-historical biography of → Shākyamuni. In their conventional set of 'Nine Ways of Bon' they grouped their early teachings on prognostics, ransom-offerings, placating gods and demons together with tantric rituals, → stūpa-worship, practice of the ten (Buddh.) virtues, relig. asceticism, higher tantric practice of using mystic circles as means towards spiritual integration, and finally highest reaches of yoga, where all theories and methods are transcended. Later they copied the dGe-lugs-pas in a new insistence on strictness of monastic life, in the study of philosophy and logic, and even in awarding the degree of *dGe-bshes* (a kind of doctorate) for skill in logical and philosophical debate. In this they even went beyond the older orders of → Tibetan Buddhism, who do not seem to have followed dGe-lugs-pas in this. Some writers have referred to Bon as → 'shamanism'; but, although pre-Buddh. relig. in Tibet may have had certain features vaguely classifiable under such heading, it comprised very much else besides; in its subsequent develop., it loses any shamanistic affiliations it might once have had, becoming merely a special kind of Tibetan Buddhism. D.L.S.

Helmut Hoffmann, *The Religions of Tibet* (E.T. 1961); D. L. Snellgrove, *Nine Ways of Bon* (1967).

Bona Dea 'The Good Goddess', Roman deity, whose proper name was prob. Fauna. The B.-D. was worshipped excl. by women, her official rites being celebrated at night in house of chief magistrate, whose wife presided, assisted by → Vestal Virgins. There was a temple of B.-D. on the Aventine, and a sow was customarily sacrificed to her. The myrtle was tabu in her worship, the reason being variously explained in legend. S.G.F.B.

O.C.D., s.v.; Kleine Pauly, I, 925–6.

Bonhoeffer, Dietrich (1906–45) Studied at Berlin under such liberal theologians as Harnack, Lietzmann and Seeberg. His two theses, however, reveal influence of → Barth's dialectical theology: in *Communio Sanctorum* (1927) he attempted to understand nature of Church as a living community through insights given by sociology; in *Act and Being* (1930) he sought to define epistemology of Chr. faith by relating it to contrasting epistemologies of act (as in → Kant) and of being (as in Heidegger). In 1930 B. was appointed to teach theology in Berlin. From 1931 he engaged in ecumenical activity; he also became a leading representative of those Christians in Germany who refused to compromise with Nazi authorities, and formed the Confessing Church. From 1933 he served as pastor to two German congregations in London, but returned to Germany in 1935 to take charge of an 'illegal' seminary of the Confessing Church. He continued to lecture in Berlin until banned by the authorities in 1936. In 1937 he published *The Cost of Discipleship*, a study of the Chr. life based on Sermon on the Mount. He attacked 'cheap grace'—the undemanding view of Chr. life which sees it in terms of man-made dogmas, rites and institutions. He argued that authentic discipleship involves total commitment to Christ to point of suffering and death. In *Life Together* (1939) B. used his experiences of close community life in seminary at Finkenwalde to offer practical guidance to others who wanted to take seriously the Chr. life as part of a fellowship. In 1939 he made a short visit to U.S.A., but was unwilling to take opportunity thus created for him to escape the fate of Germany. He returned to Germany shortly before war broke out. Although banned from teaching, public speaking and publishing, he helped to sustain the Confessing Church. He gave up his pacificism as an illegitimate escape, and became involved in German Resistance movement against Hitler. Through influential friends, he was able to travel and visited Sweden, to contact Bishop of Chichester on behalf of German Resistance. In April 1943 he was arrested, and on 9th April 1945 was executed. Before his arrest he had been working on a book on *Ethics*. Some fragments survived the war and have been published. They develop B.'s earlier thought and deal with total demand of Christ as Lord over every part of world's life. B.'s greatest influence, however, has been through publication of his *Letters and Papers from Prison*. In some of these letters he criticises theologians of post-liberal movement, and seeks a new way forward which recognises thorough secularity of mod. world. The develop. of certain ideas, only hinted at in earlier writings, suggests that in prison B.'s thought was radically changing. He holds that 'religion', described as a metaphysical, individualistic and subjective matter, is not significant for contemporary man who finds no need of a 'God of the gaps', either in thought or practice. This situation of the 'maturity' of man is acc. to will of God. What is now needed is a 'religionless Christianity'. B. offers certain enigmatic suggestions about poss. nature of such a Chr. faith. Since these letters were published in 1951, they have exercised powerful influence upon radical Prot. theology. D.A.P.

J. D. Godsey, *The Theology of Dietrich Bonhoeffer* (1960); M. E. Marty, *The Place of Bonhoeffer* (1963); J. A. Phillips, *The Form of Christ in the World* (1967); R. G. Smith (ed.), *World Come of Age: A Symposium on Dietrich Bonhoeffer* (1967).

Boniface, St. (680–754) Often called the 'Apostle of Germany', and orig. named Wynfrith, B. was born at Crediton, England, and made first missionary journey to Frisia in 716. Increasing success won B. full Papal support, which he repaid by spreading Papal influence. A notable event of his missionary career was felling of Oak of Thor at Geismar. B. founded famous abbey of Fulda (*c.* 743), and became Archbishop of Mainz, *c.* 747. He was martyred in Frisia. Feast day, 5 June. S.G.F.B.

D.C.C., s.v.; R.G.G.[3], I, 1355–6; J. Godfrey, *The Church in Anglo-Saxon England* (1962), pp. 230ff.

Bonzes Japanese *Bonzō*, or *Bonzi;* Chinese *fan-sêng* (a 'religious'). A term applied by Europeans to Buddh. monks and priests of Japan and other Far Eastern countries. D.H.S.

Book of Common Prayer Official service book of → Church of England, designed for use of clergy and laity. It contains forms of services for

administration of chief → Sacraments, for daily Morning and Evening Prayer, and for chief occasions of Christ. life, e.g. Marriage, Burial of Dead; it also incl. various official regulations concerning belief (→ Thirty-Nine Articles), and the 'Ornaments of the Church and the ministers'. The B.C.P. is a memorial of the English Reformation, and it characterises the ethos of → Anglicanism. Its first version appeared in 1548 as 'First Prayer Book of Edward VI'; thereafter it underwent a number of revisions due to contemporary political and relig. changes. The final form was achieved in 1662. Attempts made to revise B.C.P. in 1927 and 1928 caused much controversy, chiefly on ground that a more Catholic form of belief and practice was intended, and failed to obtain Parliamentary sanction.
S.G.F.B.

D.C.C., pp. 317–8; *E.R.E.*, X, pp. 205–9; W. K. Lowther Clarke and C. Harris (ed.), *Liturgy and Worship* (1932), *passim.*

Book of the Dead From 18th Dynasty (*c.* 1580 BC) down to Roman era, it was customary to put in Egypt. tombs papyrus scrolls containing magical texts designed to secure for dead a blessed after-life. These texts comprise a great variety of trad. material: libretto of mortuary rituals, hymns, prayers, incantations, spells, myths. Some of it can be traced back through → Coffin Texts to → Pyramid Texts. The number of texts incl. varies in the versions; certain texts or chapters were regarded as essential and were always incl. The more sumptuous versions of B.-D. were illustrated by vignettes depicting funerary scenes or *post-mortem* experience of deceased: most notable among these scenes is the weighing of the heart (→ Judgment of Dead, Egypt). The finest illustrated example of B.-D. is the *Papyrus of Ani* in British Museum. The B.-D. is an invaluable source-book for Egypt. relig. The title B.-D. is modern; the anc. title was *Chapters of Coming Forth by Day*, being thus expressive of Egypt. mortuary faith. (→ Eschatology, Egypt.). S.G.F.B.

E. Naville (ed.), *Das aegyptische Totenbuch*, 2 vols. (1886); E. A. W. Budge, *The Book of the Dead*, text, 3 vols. (1898), trans. 2nd ed. (1953); *The Book of the Dead: Facsimile of the Papyrus of Ani* (Brit. Mus.², 1894); T. G. Allen, *The Egyptian Book of the Dead* (1960); *R.Ae.R-G.*, pp. 824–8 ('Totenbuch').

Book of Life The idea of a written record concerning a person's *post-mortem* destiny occurs in anc. Egypt in the Osirian Judgment: the verdict of weighing the heart was recorded by the god Thoth (→ Judgment of Dead, Anc. Near East). In O.T. there are many refs. to a divine record of citizens of (future) theocratic community (e.g. Ex. 32:32ff.; Is. 4:3); in N.T., ref. is made to 'names written in heaven' (Heb. 12:23), and to the Lamb's 'book of life' (Rev. 13:8). Ref. is also made to books containing records on which dead will be judged (Rev. 20:12). A book of fate recording the individual's life is mentioned in the → Qur'ān, 17:14ff. S.G.F.B.

R.A.C., II, 725–30; *H.D.B.*), p. 111; S. G. F. Brandon, *The Judgment of the Dead* (1967), *passim.*

Book, Heavenly In German a specialist expression for books of supernatural character: they comprise three kinds (1) Books of Fate (2) Books of Deeds or records of personal conduct (3) Books of Life. Earliest example of (1) occurs in Mesopot. mythology where 'Tablets of Destiny', possessed by → Marduk, signified authority to order future events. The Sibylline *libri fatales* is a notable Roman example of this type of H.-B. (→ Sibylline Oracles). The idea of a divine record of human deeds had important place in anc. Egypt. belief in → judgment of dead. The verdict of weighing the heart was recorded in writing by scribe-god → Thoth. A supernatural account of human deeds figures in Christianity (Rev. 20:12), in Islam, and Hinduism. The idea appears to derive from commercial accountancy. The 'Book of Life' occurs in Jew. thought and takes form of nominal roll of Elect (Ex. 32:32); in N.T. (Rev. 20:12) a 'Book of Life' is produced at Last Judgment. A similar idea found expression in early custom of remembering names of faithful at → Eucharist on the so-called diptych.
S.G.F.B.

L. Koep, *Das himml. Buch in Antike u. Christentum* (1952); *R.A.C.*, II, 725–31; S. G. F. Brandon, *The Judgment of the Dead* (1967)—'records of dead'; F. F. Bruce (ed.), *Holy Book and Holy Tradition* (1968).

Books, Sacred The art of writing was closely linked with relig. from its beginnings. The earliest forms of writing served relig. needs (e.g. → Pyramid Texts (Egypt.), earliest texts of Sumerians, Chinese → Oracle Bones), and scribes were usually priests or assoc. with temples. Writing had thus a sacred character; even when it was used first for economic purposes, it was often to record temple property. The earliest texts, the Pyramid Texts, were wholly concerned with mortuary needs of pharaohs; they gen. have form of divine pronouncements or dialogues between deities. The Pyramid Texts constituted a sacred trad. which produced later forms of S.-B.: →→ Coffin Texts, Book of the Dead. Although divine orig. is gen. assumed, the claim is explicitly made that Chap. 30 of Book of Dead was found under statue of → Thoth, the scribe-god. Tacit assumption of sacred origin or authority seems similarly to have been made in other religs. about certain texts (e.g. the Babylonian → Enuma elish; Hindu → Rig-Veda; → Hermetic lit.; the → Gāthās; the Book of the → Law (II Kgs. 22:8ff.); the → Sibylline Oracles). Apart from sacred writings of this kind, there exist S.-B. that are consciously regarded as specific revelations of divine will. These claims are sometimes explicitly made in the books concerned, but gen. the claim is integrated into the theology of the related religion, and forms a basic datum of its *raison d'être*. The most notable examples are: →→ Bible; Qūr'an; Book of Granth; Book of Mormon (→ Mormons). S.G.F.B.

E.R.E., VIII, pp. 81–113 ('Literature'); *A.N.E.T.*, *passim;* S. N. Kramer, *From the Tablets of Sumer* (1956); S. Morenz, *Aegyptische Religion* (1960), ch. X; W. J. Leipoldt-S. Morenz, *Heilige Schriften* (1953); A. A. Macdonell, *Hist. of Sanskrit Literature* (1928); D. Diringer, *The Alphabet* (1947); *R.G.G.*³, V, 1537–8; *R.A.C.*, II, 688–717; G. Lanczkowski, *Heilige Schriften* (1956).

Bosch, Hieronymus (*c.* 1450–1516) Netherland painter whose work is a remarkable amalgam of medieval Christianity, esoteric and often pathological imagery. B. seems to have been a reforming but orthodox Catholic. His paintings were collected by kings and nobles, and much copied. Interest in his work has greatly increased in recent times: it commands the attention of historians of art, of medieval relig., and psychologists. S.G.F.B.

J. Combe, *Jerome Bosch* (1946); C. de Tolnay, *Hieronymous Bosch* (1966).

Bouphonia Athenian sacrifice of ox to → Zeus Polieus, performed acc. to a peculiar ritual. Ox had to approach altar 'of its own accord' and eat corn upon it. The priest who killed ox, fled into voluntary exile, and the axe used was adjudged guilty and thrown into sea. After eating flesh of ox, its hide was stuffed and yoked to plough. The ritual was prob. apotropaic, the sacrifice being regarded as murder of the ox. S.G.F.B.

O.C.D., p. 788 (V); Harrison, *Prolegomena*, pp. 111ff.

Boy Bishop Medieval custom, esp. popular in England, of electing on St. Nicholas Day (Dec. 6) a boy who would perform in church various episcopal functions until Holy Innocents' Day (Dec. 28). Custom was gen. abolished at Reformation (→ Abbot of Unreason). S.G.F.B.

D.C.C., *s.v.*

Brahmā Creator God in Hinduism (→ creation, Hindu), commonly assoc. with → Viṣṇu and → Śiva as one of the three primary forms of the divine being (→ *trimurti*). B. is first mentioned in the → *Brahmanas*. In the Vedic hymns the Creator is known as Prajapati or as Hiranyagarbha. The word 'Brahmā' is the masculine form of the neuter → *Brahman* (sacred power, ultimate reality). Though in principle he is equal to Vishnu and Shiva, he is not the object of a special cult, and so does not attract the → *bhakti* focussed on the other two. He thus has some of the properties of the → 'high god' of other cultures. In later Hinduism, creation tended more and more to be associated, not with B. but with the female principle, → *sakti*. N.S.

Brahmācārin First of the trad. four → *asramas* in trad. Hinduism: the stage of life in which the young → Aryan is a student, learning Vedic lore under teacher, typically a *vanaprastha*. This period ideally lasts twelve years, between initiation or *upanayana* and the assumption of household responsibilities through marriage (→ *grhastha*). The student is required to remain celibate: hence the noun *brahmacārya* was also used more gen. for the virtue of maintaining correct sexual relations, in partic. celibacy. Though the student had to obey and serve his teacher or → *guru*, he was also free to change teachers. The custom has largely lapsed in mod. times, and was primarily observed since classical Hinduism by the members of the → Brahmin class. N.S.

Brahma-Cariya In Buddh. usage this term denotes 'holy living', i.e. life of the monk, with enlightenment as ultimate goal. It can be applied also to relig. life of the lay Buddh., who undertakes to observe not the 5 moral precepts (→ *pañca-sila*) only, but the additional three, and undertakes to refrain from sexual misconduct in lieu of vow of complete chastity. T.O.L.

Brahma-Vihāra (Buddh.) 'The Spiritual Abodes', or 'Heavenly Abodes', are, in B. thought, the four universal virtues: loving kindness (*metta*); compassion (*karunā*); sympathetic or altruistic joy (*muditā*); equanimity (*upekkha*). They are fully expounded by → Buddhaghosa in his *Visuddhimagga*, ch. IX. The Buddh. is exhorted frequently, in the Suttas, to cultivate these virtues in such a way as to embrace all beings in every direction throughout world. For this reason, these 4 virtues are known also as 'Illimitables'. T.O.L.

S.B.E., vol. XI, pp. 201ff., 272ff.

Brahman A neuter term (the masculine form is → Brahmā), sometimes transliterated into English as *Brahma. Brahman* orig. ref. to the sacred or magical power implicit in and created through the sacrificial ritual in Vedic relig. The word is derived from a root meaning 'to grow'; and in turn is at basis of word *Brāhmaṇa* (→ Brahmin), for it was the priestly class which administered, controlled and released the sacred power. By a development of thought in period leading up to principal → Upaniṣads, during which speculative identifications of this power with a variety of phenomena (the sun, food, etc.) were made, B. came to mean the holy power implicit in the whole universe, the processes of which were sometimes treated as a grand cosmic sacrifice. Thus eventually the term came to ref. to ultimate reality or the 'holy power' underlying the visible world, and thus became standard expression for the Absolute or God in the Hindu trad. In some Upanishads, B. is identified with the → *Atman* or eternal Self lying within man, and also thought of as pervading world (→ *tat tvam asi*). However, B. was also treated in some Upanishads as a personal God or → Isvara. This personalistic theme was taken up in medieval Hinduism by theistic theologians such as → Ramanuja, Madhva and others, since it was congruent with the by then highly developed → *bhakti* forms of Hindu piety. For → Sankara, on the other hand, the supreme B. is not the personal Lord, but is 'without attributes' (*nirguṇam*). Although in the Upanishads and elsewhere B. is sometimes (apparently) identified with universe (*sarvam idam*), it is misleading to treat this as implying pantheism: rather, the formed world was seen as being an expression or part of the holy power. Since B. was described so differently by various interpreters in the later Vedantin trad., it in effect bifurcates into a number of different concepts, defined by varying theologies and metaphysics. N.S.

J. Charpentier, *Brahman: eine sprachwissenschaftlich-exegetisch-religionsgeschichtliche Untersuchung* (1932); J. Gonda, *Notes on Brahman* (1950); L. Renou, *Religions of Ancient India* (1953).

Brāhmaṇas Prose works appended to collections of Vedic hymns, and devoted to instructions and exegesis about sacrificial ritual. They have, as appendices, the *Āraṇyakas* or 'forest treatises', which themselves merge into the → *Upaniṣads*. (Indeed the *Brhadaranyaka Upanisad* is essentially part of the *Śatapathabrāhmana*, the *Brahmana* of a 'hundred discourses'.) The *Brahmanas* were composed after the *Rgveda*, and prob. date from about 1000 BC and onwards. N.S.

A. B. Keith (tr.), *Rigveda Brahmanas, the Aitareya and Kausitaki Brahmanas* (1920); J. Eggeling (tr.), *The Satapatha-Brahmana*, 5 vols., in Max Müller, *S.B.E.*, vols. 12, 26, 51, 53, 54 (1882–1900); W. Caland, *Pancavimsa-brahmana* (1931); A. B. Keith, *The Religion and Philosophy of the Veda and Upanishads*, 2 vols. (1925).

Brahmanism This term has been used in a variety of ways: to ref. to form of relig. found in later Vedic writings (*Brahmanas, Upanisads*), by contrast with earlier 'Vedism'; to ref. to relig. carried on from that time and administered by → Brahmin priesthood, by contrast with 'popular Hinduism'; and even as a synonym of Hinduism. Although it is true that distinction can be made between the Hindu trad. as interpreted by Brahmanical trad. and the wider synthesis and interplay of cults emerging after the Upanishadic period, i.e. in classical Hinduism, there are objections to the contrast between B. and popular Hinduism; first, because in fact the Brahmins have played an import. part in temple-worship, village relig., etc.; second, because Brahmanical theology has been considerably moulded by non-Vedic forms of worship and belief, e.g. through recognition of the → *Puranas* as → *smrti*, the incorporation of → *bhakti* sentiments into theology, etc.; third, because, however dominant in it, the Brahmins are essentially part of the total caste fabric constituting Hindu society. The term, then, is not an altogether useful one, and where one wishes to ref. to specifically Brahmanical practices and ideas, it is best simply to speak of 'Brahmanical religion' (as one might also speak of 'Vaisnavite religion', etc.). N.S.

Brahmasūtra The B. ('Aphorisms about *Brahman*'), sometimes called the *Brahma Sutras* or *Vedanta Sutras* (or *Vedantasutra*, etc.) and ascribed to Bādarāyaṇa, is the root text of the → Vedanta school of Hindu → philosophy and exegesis. It has, therefore, attracted extensive commentary by leading exponents of Vedanta, notably →→ Sankara, Ramanuja and Madhva; and a typical form of presenting Vedantin docs. has been through such a commentary. The aphoristic nature of exegesis of Upanishadic teaching in the → *sutra* has enabled different sub-schools within Vedanta to assign highly diverse meanings to the text. It is uncertain when the B. was composed, but since it has refs. to other schools, etc., it is prob. after turn of the millennium, and prob. 2nd or 3rd cent. CE. The commentarial literature upon it preceded Sankara, though earlier commentaries are no longer available; but it was during medieval period, from Sankara onwards, that most flourishing activity of exegesis dates. One or two commentaries from 17th and 18th cents. are also of some importance. In view of variety of interpretations, of which Sankara's proved most influential, and of the rather cryptic nature of the aphorisms in the B., it is not altogether certain how the position of Badarayana should be characterised; but most prob. it was a form of *bhedābheda* or the doc. of 'identity in difference', i.e. the identity and yet difference between → *Brahman*, the world and souls (selves), which might be described as a less personalistic precursor of theology of → Visistadvaita (Qualified Non-Dualism). The work is divided into four sections. The first deals with interpretation of the Upanishads. The second relates this interpretation to conclusions of other schools. Thus there are refutations of → Samkhya, → Yoga, certain Buddh. schools (the → *Sarvastivada*) and the Bhagavatas. The third section concerns the practice of realising *Brahman*, the practice of meditation, the condition of the → *sannyasin*, etc. The final section deals chiefly with forms of liberation, in which the soul attains non-separation with *Brahman*. The commentaries on the B. tend to follow a stylised form, owing something to procedures of disputation in classical and medieval India. The topic is stated; then objections to view to be presented are stated; and then the counter arguments to the objections. There follows a coherent account of thesis thus established. N.S.

G. Thibaut (tr.), *The Vedanta-Sutras*, in Max Müller, ed., *S.B.E.*, vols. 34, 38, 48 (1890–1904), incl. the commentaries of Sankara and Ramanuja; S. N. Dasgupta, *A History of Indian Philosophy*, vol. 2 (1932); S. Radhakrishnan, *The Brahma Sutra* (1960).

Brahmins 'Brahmin' is an anglicised version of Sanskrit *Brāhmaṇa*, lit. 'one endowed with → *Brahman*', i.e. with the sacred power implicit in sacrificial ritual administered by Brahmins. They were the highest of the four classes or → *varnas* in Vedic society and have retained dominant social position within the → caste structure of Hinduism. The B. is *par excellence* the custodian of sacred knowledge (→ *Veda*) and has hereditary right to perform orthodox rituals. B. are also employed in some cases for ceremonies performed on behalf of unorthodox relig. groups (e.g. → the Jains). In Upanishadic period B. were coupled with, and to some extent contrasted with → *sramanas*, wandering teachers and ascetics (e.g. the → Buddha and his followers), with whom they shared prestige and whose → asceticism needed to be matched by them. At same time, there were indications of attempt to erode Brahmanical authority, some teachers cited in the Upanishads, e.g. being → *ksatriyas*. The main criticisms of the B., however, came from unorthodox schools; with evolution of classical Hinduism characteristically different from Buddhism, Jainism, etc., the B. maintained their function as mediators of Vedic truth and ritual. For their partic. priestly functions → priests, Hindu. Though in principle the priestly class, B. came to pursue variety of occupations, from civil servants to cooks. As most literate group, they were a chief instrument in gradual sanskritisation of Indian peninsula, incl. the Dravidian-speaking south, which was long outside ambit of Indo-Aryan culture. The intro. of English as medium of learned communication and resurgence of vernacular languages have somewhat eroded their classical status. The B. class is trad. supposed to maintain stricter attitude to food, drink, etc., than other classes, e.g. to maintain vegetarianism (though there are fish-eating B. in Bengal, etc.) and to abstain from alcohol. N.S.

Jeannine Auboyer, *Daily Life in Ancient India* (1961); L. Dumont, *Homo Hierarchicus* (1966); J. H. Hutton, *Caste in India* (1961); G. M. Carstairs, *The Twice-Born* (1958).

Brāhmo Samaj The Brahmo or Brāhma Samāj is a reforming movement within mod. Hinduism, founded by → Ram Mohan Ray in 1828. Its principles were unitarian, and it was opposed to temple-cults, etc., of Hinduism. Roy himself was a strong campaigner against suttee (→ *sati*) and for intro. of Western education, etc., into India. Both he and his followers regarded present state of Hinduism as representing a degeneration from earlier monotheism. A few years after Roy's death, the leader of movement became Debendranath Tagore (d. 1905); but a more dynamic organiser, Keshab Chandra Sen (1838–84), came to dominate it; his followers formed the Sadharan Brahmo Samaj or 'General' Brahmo Samaj, Debendranath's followers being left with the rump, the Adi or 'Original' Brahmo Samaj. The tendency of the new leadership was to assimilate movement more to Christ. → Unitarianism; while Debendranath saw the society more as means of purifying Hinduism and propagating monotheism. However, Keshab intro. further elements into his creed towards end of life, and this issued in a third split after his death. It was the General Brahmo Samaj that continued most vigorously thereafter. The movement, though small in number, has proved relatively influential, since it has recruited largely from the intelligentsia and has promoted social works. Its basic rationalism never gave it wide appeal. N.S.

P. K. Sen, *Biography of a New Faith* (1950); S. Sastri, *History of the Brahmo Samaj*, 2 vols. (1911–2); J. N. Farquhar, *Modern Religious Movements in India* (1919).

Breast The human female B. has been a symbol of relig. significance from the Paleolithic era: B.'s were carefully depicted on Paleolithic female figurines (→ Paleolithic Religion), and were sometimes repr. independently. The Neolithic sanctuary at → Çatal Hüyük was adorned with frieze of B.'s moulded of plaster, within which were placed skulls of vultures, foxes, and lower jaw-bones of wild boars, thus seemingly combining symbols of fertility and death. Egypt. kings were repr. as being suckled by goddesses. Figurines of Mesopot., Canaanite, Hittite and Aegean goddesses show them offering their B.'s, and the B. was a symbol of → Isis. A statue of → Astarte, found in Spain, had the nipples of B.'s replaced by holes through which liquid might flow into bowl held by the goddess. The Great Goddess of → Ephesus, identified with → Artemis, was repr. in art as multi-breasted woman. The Dionysiac murals in Villa of the Mysteries, Pompeii, show a young girl suckling a kid (→ Dionysus). B.'s are sculptured on the Iron Age Tressé *allée couverte*. The ambivalent nature of Hindu goddess → Kali, personifying fertility and death, is repr. by her full B.'s. The blessing invoked on B.'s of the → Virgin Mary (Lk. 11:27f.) marks beginning of *motif* of considerable importance in cult of Mary, which finds expression in → *Deisis* of the medieval → Doom. (→ Agatha, St.). S.G.F.B.

S. Giedon, *The Eternal Present* (1962), pp. 211ff.; *R.A.C.*, II, 657–64; *Bilderatlas*, Lief. 7, Abb. 1–16, Lief. 9–11, Abb. 50, 55, 130, 131; D. Harden, *The Phoenicians* (1962), p. 104, pl. 72; V. C. C. Collum, *The Tressé Iron-Age Megalithic Monument* (1935); H. Zimmer, *Myths and Symbols in Indian Art and Civilization* (1962), pp. 211ff.; C. Picard, *Les religions préhelléniques* (1948), p. 75, n. 6; F. Sierksma, *The Gods as We Shape Them* (1960), ill. pp. 59, 81–2.

Breastplate of St. Patrick Anc. Irish hymn, current before 9th cent., and attr. to St. Patrick. It invokes aid of Trinity, Angels, Prophets, the powers of heaven and earth, and, finally, Christ, against the power of evil. S.G.F.B.

D.C.C., *s.v.*

Breathing Control Breathing control or *prāṇāyāma* constitutes part of the techniques of the → Yoga school: similar techniques are also used outside Hindu trad., in → Buddhism and → Taoism. *Pranayama* is the fourth of eight elements or stages of Yoga, and involves rhythmic breathing, designed to bring about very low rates of respiration, so low as to make poss. in some cases such wonder-working tricks as being buried alive for a short period. One effect is attainment of cataleptic trance. The technique in principle subserves spiritual aim of total physiological and psychical control leading up to *samadhi*, the final state of Yogic meditation, issuing in liberation. The slowing down of usual breathing processes is supposed to induce diminution in sleep, excretions and other bodily functions and to increase perspiration—one reason for assoc. austerity or *tapas* with heat—and levitation. The system of *pranayama* is assoc. with mythic concept of *prāṇa*, breath, which figures prominently in Upanishadic speculation as being central to living and conscious processes. Consequently the term *pranayama* is sometimes used, e.g. in the *Mahabharata* to ref. not just to breathing control but more widely to gen. withdrawal of senses which is central to practice of yogic contemplation. N.S.

M. Eliade, *Yoga: Immortality and Freedom* (1958); Arthur H. Ewing, 'The Hindu Conceptions of the Functions of Breath', *J.A.O.S.*, vol. xxii, 1901, pp. 249ff.; A. Koestler, *The Lotus and the Robot* (1959); F. Edgerton, *Beginnings of Indian Philosophy* (1965).

Breviary Collection of Psalms, hymns, lessons, etc. arranged for daily recitation through Chr. year. Modern B.'s are usually in four volumes, acc. to seasons. It is duty of all R.C. priests and members of most relig. orders to recite appropriate parts of B. daily. S.G.F.B.

D.C.C., *s.v.; R.G.G.*[3], VI, 432–5; *C.E.*, II, *s.v.*

Bridges At the Pons Sublicus, Rome's oldest bridge, an annual ceremony was performed, in which human effigies (*Argei*) were thrown into river. The exact orig. of rite has been much discussed; but it seems most prob. that it repr. some anc. propitiatory rite to river-god, affronted by building of bridge. Customs and legends connected with B. elsewhere suggest widespread anc. belief of similar kind, involving orig. human sacrifice. B. also feature in the → eschatology of many religs. The passage of them usually constitutes test of ritual or moral fitness of dead for *post-mortem* blessedness. Notable examples are → Chinvat Bridge in → Zoroastrianism, and that of → Ṣirāṭ in → Islam, the Gjallar Bridge in → Scandinavian Religion. An interesting Chr. version of belief is the medieval N. English idea of the 'Brig o' Dread' or 'Brig o' Death'. Some memory of primitive attitude to B. is preserved in Lat. word *pontifex*, meaning one skilled in magic of bridge-making. (→ Styx). S.G.F.B.

E.R.E., II, *s.v.;* W. Warde Fowler, *Roman Festivals* (1899), pp. 111ff.; A. Grenier, *Les religions étrusque et romaine* (1948), pp. 118ff.; *Kleine Pauly*, I, 532–3; *O.C.D.*, *s.v.* ('Argei', 'Pontifex, Pontifices').

Brimo, Brimos Name or title, perhaps meaning 'strong', variously assigned to Grk. goddesses Rhea, → Demeter, → Persephone, → Hekate. Acc. to Hippolytus (*Haer.* 5.8.40), during celebration of → Eleusinian mysteries announcement was made: 'Holy Brimo has borne a sacred child Brimos'. The identity of both B. and Brimos has been much discussed. It seems likely that Hippolytus wrongly attrib. to Eleusis an episode of rites of Rhea-Cybele, and Brimos should be identified with → Attis. (→ Cybele). S.G.F.B.

G. E. Mylonas, *Eleusis and the Eleusinian Mysteries* (1962), pp. 305ff.; *Der Kleine Pauly*, I, 1463.

British Israel Theory Theory invented to provide divine sanction for imperialist destiny of British people. It was based on assumption that British were descended from the ten tribes of Israel that disappeared after taken into captivity by Assyria in 721 BC. The theory has no basis in historical, archaeological or ethnological fact, and was held by a small, though enthusiastic, minority chiefly between the two World Wars. It became involved with esoteric speculation about the Great Pyramid. S.G.F.B.

H. L. Goudge, *The British Israel Theory* (1922).

Britomartis 'Sweet virgin', *ex.* Cretan *britu* = 'sweet'. B. was prob. huntress-deity figured on certain Minoan seal-stones. She was identified with → Artemis, and, acc. to legend, to escape attentions of Minos, she leaped off cliff into the sea, but was saved by fishermen's nets; hence her title Diktynna (*diktys* = net). (→ Cretan Relig.). S.G.F.B.

H. J. R. Rose, *Handbook of Greek Mythology* (1928), pp. 117ff.; W. K. C. Guthrie, *The Greeks and their Gods* (1950), pp. 105–6; R. W. Hutchinson, *Prehistoric Crete* (1962), pp. 207–8.

Buber, Martin (1878–1965) Jew. relig. thinker, born in Vienna, actively concerned with Zionism, who taught at universities of Frankfurt and Jerusalem. Of his many writings a small treatise entitled *Ich und Du* (1923), E.T. *I and Thou* (1937), has profoundly influenced Prot. theologians. It is a study of relationship between man and things ('I-It') and man and God ('I-Thou'). (→ Judaism). S.G.F.B.

M. Buber, *Schriften z. Bibel* (1964); *Schriften z. Chassidismus* (1963); *R.G.G.*[3], I, 1452–3.

Bucranion Grk. = 'ox-skull'. Anc. temples and altars were often decorated with skulls of sacrificed victims (later repr. in sculpture), prob. as memorial of sacrifices made to deity and because they were regarded as being efficacious against evil. (→ Altar, Greek). S.G.F.B.

E.R.E., II, pp. 888b–9a.

Buddha (as generic title) In Buddh. thought, 'an enlightened one' or 'awakened one', and thus a man distinguished from all others by his knowledge of the Truth (*Dhamma*). As P.T.S. Dictionary points out, Buddha is an appellative, not a proper name. In Buddh. theory, the perfect knowledge, made known by a Buddha, eventually becomes lost to world, and has then to await emergence of a new Buddha, in order to be known and proclaimed again. Such a being is ref. to more precisely as *Sammā-sambuddha*, a universal, perfectly enlightened being. It is the same doc. which is proclaimed by all these successive Buddhas, namely, the 4 holy truths proclaimed and expounded by → Gotama the *Buddha*. A being who is enlightened and discovers the truth, and is thus *buddha*, but who does not proclaim it, is termed an isolated or 'private' Buddha (→ *Pacceka-buddha;* Skt. *pratyeka-*). Related to concept of a Buddha is that of the → *Bodhisattva*, a state of being which precedes final state of Buddhahood. Once this final state has been reached, the Buddha endures as such only as long as his physical life lasts; after that he has no further relations with world of space and time, acc. to → Theravādin thought. But in the → Mhy., Buddhas are held to be transcendental beings to whom appeal for help can be made by mortal men. T.O.L.

(Gotama) (Gautama-Skt.) Concerning dates and life-story of Gotama, the Buddha, there is no hist. certainty. Not until → Asvaghosa, in 1st/2nd cent. CE, composed his → *Buddha-carita* (*Acts of the Buddha*) was a comprehensive account of his life produced. Evidence of earlier kind is found in many biographical references to Buddha in the Pali canon of scripture, both the → *Vinaya-pitaka*, and in various scattered details in the 5 *Nikayas* of the *Sutta* → *Pitaka.* Acc. to the → Theravāda school of Burma and Ceylon, the dates of Buddha's life are 623–543 BC; in Cambodia, Laos and Thailand, 624–544. The → Mhy. and most mod. scholars prefer the dates *ca.* 566–486, or 563–483. It will be seen that all these give a life-span of 80 years. From biographical details provided by Pali literature, an outline of Buddha's life emerges as follows. A member of the Sakya tribe, who inhabited the Himalayan foothills and were subjects of the Kosalan king, G. was the son of Suddhodana, ruler of → *Kapilavatthu,* and his chief consort Mahā Māya. He was of the Gotama-clan, and his personal name was Siddhattha (same as that of 16th of the 24 preceding Buddhas → Buddhas (other than Gotama). Thus he was known, by personal and clan name together, as Siddhattha Gotama. (Skt. Siddhattha Gautama). He was known also as the 'sage' (*muni*) of the *Sakya* tribe, i.e. *Sakyamuni.* His birth is regarded in the trad. as having been surrounded by miraculous features. Without at the time having marital relations with her husband, Mahā Māya had a dream of the → Bodhisatta (Buddha-to-be), as a white elephant, entering her womb; she then ceased to have any desire for sexual pleasure. The birth, which took place in consequence, is thus properly described as parthogenetic (but not necessarily a virgin birth). The birth occurred in the → *Lumbinī* grove, while Mahā Māya was journeying between Kapilavatthu and her parents' home. The courtiers attending her, escorted mother and child back to Kapilavatthu; Mahā Māya died seven days later. Acc. to trad., Gotama lived an easy and protected life in childhood and youth, married and had a son; then, at the age of 29, he renounced home and comforts and adopted the ascetic life. Certain incidents had provoked dissatisfaction with his old life of ease: the sight of a man suffering from extreme old age; a sick man; a corpse being carried out to burning ghat. On the full-moon day he saw also a holy man, and became convinced of virtues of ascetic life. He himself, after the Renunciation or going forth (*pabbajjā*), i.e. from home, spent six years engaging in the most austere of ascetic practices and was brought to point of death, without deriving spiritual benefit. He then decided to abandon extreme asceticism, and, on the full moon day of *Vesākha* (May), he sat down in meditation at foot of the → Bodhi tree, at Uruvelā, beside river Neranjarā (tributary of the Ganges), near modern Gaya; he determined to remain there until he had attained Enlightenment. The trads. tell of efforts made by → *Māra*, the Evil One, to deflect him from his purpose, but to no avail. The night was spent in deep meditation; at dawn his Enlightenment came. The truth, which he had supernaturally perceived, he then sought to teach to others. His first discourse was addressed to certain ascetics who had formerly been his companions; it is known as the 'Discourse of the Setting in Motion of the Wheel of *Dhamma*' (→ *Dhamma-cakkappavattana Sutta*) (*SN*. V. 420). This sermon certainly contains some of fundamental principles of early Buddh. thought and practice; in its present form, it is a product of later times. Acc. to trad., it was delivered in the Deer Park of Benares. Grad. the Buddha, as he now was, began to gain disciples and the → *Sangha* or assembly (i.e. of monks) was formed. For next 20 yrs. some kind of chronology can be worked out on basis of the Pali texts; it has been done, e.g. by G. P. Malalasekere in his *D.P.P.N.* (Gotama). These years were spent by Buddha and his monks in various places of middle Ganges basin of N.E. India: → Benares, Uruvelā, → Rājagaha, → Vesālī, → Sāvatthi, Kosambī, and → Kapilavatthu. The 3 months of rainy season each year were spent in a rains-retreat, often a monastic shelter provided by wealthy supporters; the remainder of year was devoted to travelling from village to village, staying a little while in each, and preaching to all and sundry and engaging in discussion with → Brahmins and with other relig. communities. For last 25 years of the Buddha's life no consecutive chronology can be constructed. Devadatta's plot to kill him appears to belong to 8th year before his decease (→→ Ajatasuttu; Devadatta). A fairly full account of last year of Buddha's life is given in the → *Mahāparinibbāna Sutta*, which describes the events leading up to his decease at Kusinārā and his entry into *parinibbāna* at the age of 80. Acc. to trad., Buddha's last words to disciples were: 'Decay is inherent in all compounded things; work out your salvation with diligence.' The cremation was carried out seven days after the decease, and was accompanied by highly honorific ceremonies. After the cremation, the relics of Buddha were divided among eight claimant parties; these were then carried off and → *stupas* were built over them in various places, (→ Dead, The, Disposal of). T.O.L.

Malalasekere, *D.P.P.N.* ('Gotama'); Sukumar Dutt, *The Buddha and Five After-Centuries* (1957), pp. 1–56; Ashvaghosha, *Buddhacarita*, trans., *S.B.E.*, vol. 49, and by E. H. Johnston, *Acta Orientalia* (1937); E. J. Thomas, *The Life of Buddha as Legend and History*, 3rd edn. (1949); H. Oldenberg, *Buddha, sein Leben, Seine Lehre, seine Gemeinde*, 9th edn. (1921, E.T. 1882); E. Lamotte, *Histoire du Bouddhisme Indien* (1958).

(Gotama) (Historicity) Since mid. of 19th cent. orientalists have assessed in varying ways the evidence for the historicity of Gotama, the → Buddha. Some have considered the data provided by Buddh. trad., both Pali and Skt., to be largely legendary. H. H. Wilson, in 1856, suggested that the life of the B. in the trad. accounts was an allegory of Indian philosophical school of → *Sāmkhya*, of which Buddhism was seen by him as a variant derivative form. E. Senart of Paris and H. Kern of Leyden regarded the trad. life as a solar myth, seeing in the 'turning of the wheel of the Law' (*Dhamma-cakkappavattana Sutta*) (*DN*. V. 420), a solar symbol of the universal monarch. Senart's theory, propounded in 1875, was challenged by H. Oldenberg in 1882, in his '*Life of the Buddha*,' based on Pali sources, from which he maintained that it was poss. to reconstruct an authentic hist. account. While Kern did not deny that some such hist. personage as Gotama may have existed, he argued that all trad. stories about him are mythological descriptions belonging to a corpus of solar myths. A mythological interpretation has recently been re-argued by Paul Levy. Edward Conze, a European Buddhist, has affirmed that the hist. existence of Gotama as an individual is a matter of no importance, although he does not deny his hist. existence. The B., he says, is 'a kind of archetype which manifests itself in the world at different periods, in different personalities, whose individual particularities are of no account whatsoever' (*Buddhism*, pp. 34f.). Similarly, Murti: 'though Gotama is a hist. person he is not the only B. . . . The Mahayana religion escapes the predicament of having to depend on any particular hist. person as the founder. . .'

The gen. opinion nowadays is, as A. Bareau points out, that there really existed a man to whom may be att. the founding of Buddhism, an hist. personage, the principal features of whose life and personality can be retraced, thanks to mod. critical appreciation of the data. T.O.L.

H. H. Wilson, *Buddha and Buddhism, J.R.A.S.*, t. XVI (1856), pp. 248ff.; E. Senart, *Essai sur la legende du Buddha* (1875); H. Oldenberg, *Buddha, sein Leben, sein Lehre, sein Gemeinde* (1881); E. Conze, *Buddhism*, 3rd edn. (1957), pp. 34ff.; P. Levy, *Buddhism, A Mystery Religion?* (1957); A Bareau, *Les Religions de L'Inde* (1966).

Buddhacarita A Mhy. Buddh. work in Skt. by 1st/2nd cent. CE poet → Aśvaghosha. The title may be trans. 'Acts of the Buddha'. Earliest known consecutive life-story of the → Buddha Gotama. Of the orig. 28 cantos only 17 are preserved in Skt.; poss. only 13 of these authentic. Exists in Tibetan trans. in 28 cantos. The Chinese Buddh. pilgrims to India of 7th cent. CE recorded that it was then widely read or sung throughout India. Acc. to Murti, it reflects a trend in 1st cent. India towards 'Buddha-bhakti', or the glorification of Buddha as a cult figure, and thus towards greater popularisation of Buddhism. (*Central Philosophy of Buddhism*, pp. 79f.). T.O.L.

Buddhadatta Thv. Buddh. monk-scholar, native of Uragapura in S. India, contemporary with → Buddhaghosa; like latter an important commentarial writer. Acc. to Pali trad., he met Buddhaghosa, and like him lived and studied in Great Monastery (Mahāvihāra) at Anurādhapura in Ceylon. His two principal works are the *Vinaya-Vinicchaya* and the *Abhidhammāvatāra*, being commentaries on the → *Vin.* and → *Abh. Pitakas* respectively. T.O.L.

Buddha-Gaya A location in N.E. India, Sacred to Buddh. → Gaya. T.O.L.

Buddhaghosa → Theravāda Buddh. monk-scholar of Ceylon of 4th/5th cents. CE, famous for commentaries on Pali canon of scripture, espec. his great compendium of Buddh. thought and practice, the → *Visuddhimagga* (The Path of Purification). In Thv. countries B. is regarded as greatest exponent and interpreter of canonical scriptures; emphasis is laid on fact that his name means 'the voice of the Buddha'. Nothing is known with certainty of date or place of his birth. The Sinhalese trad., contained in 2 Pali works, the → *Culavamsa* and the *Buddhaghosuppatti* (a collection of legends about the great man), is that he was a native of → *Magadha* in N. India, a → brahman by birth who was early attracted to Buddhism by contact with a learned Buddh. monk named Revata; he was ordained into the → Sangha, and travelled to Ceylon, settling in Great Monastery (*Mahāvihāra*) or Anurādhapura, where he spent most of life in study of scriptures and writing; he returned at end of life to his native Magadha and died at Gaya. Burmese trad. claims him as a native of Burma, who, having studied in Ceylon and there composed his great work, the *Visuddhimagga*, intro. this and complete Pali canon of scripture into Burma, thus inaugurating what Burmese regard as a new era in Buddhism of their country. Mod. research, using internal evidence of his works and archaeological evidence, suggests Andhra, in S. India, as his place of birth. B.'s writings reveal close familiarity with the Andhra of that time, whereas his refs. to N. India contain inaccuracies difficult to reconcile with theory of his Magadhan origin (e.g. his ref. to Patna (Pātaliputta) as sea-port). Beside the *Visuddhimagga*, B. wrote commentaries on (1) the → *Vinaya-Pitaka*, (2) → *Sutta-Pitaka*, and (3) → *Abhidhamma-Pitaka*. These are as follows: (1) on the *Vinaya: Samantapāsādikā* and *Kankhāvitarani;* (2) on *Sutta-Pitaka; Sumangalavilāsini* (on the *DN*), *Papañcasūdanī* (on the *MN*), *Sāratthapakāsinī* (on the *SN*), *Manorathapurāni* (on the *AN*), *Paramatthajotika* (on the *KN*); (3) on → *Abh. Pitaka; Atthasālinī*, *Sammohavinodani*, and *Pancappakaranaṭṭha-katha.* His great achievements were: the new status he gave Pali scholarship at time when Skt. in India had become the prestige language among Buddh., as well as among brahmans; the develop. of a coherent and systematic Theravāda school of philosophy. T.O.L.

The *Culavamsa*, E.T., C. Mabel Rickmers, 2 vols. (1953); B. C. Law, *The Life and Work of Buddhaghosa* (1923) (new edn. 1946); Nyanoponika, *The Path of Purification* (1964); S. Dutt, *Buddhist Monks and Monasteries of India* (1962), pp. 249–60.

Buddha-Kāya In Buddh. thought, since the Buddha is equated with the → Absolute, as well as being one who is concerned with welfare of world, the conception of the three *Buddha-kāya*, or Buddha-bodies, has been developed to express relationship of one aspect of the Buddha-nature to the other. The 'three-bodies' doc. (*Tri-kāya*) affirms that Buddha exists as (1) *Dharma-kāya;* (2) *Sambhoga-kāya;* (3) *Nirmāna-kāya.* The *Dharma-kāya*, Dharma-body, or Truth-body, is also known as *sva-bhāva-kāya*, or 'self-being-body', because it is self-existent; it is the Dharma, or reality, remaining within its own nature. It is in this sense, says Suzuki, 'the absolute aspect' of the Buddha-nature (*op. cit.*, 308). (2) The *Sambhoga-kāya*, or 'Bliss-body', is the celestial manifestation of the Buddha-nature, i.e. as it is perceived by celestial, or non-mortal beings. There is also in this term the sense of 'Enjoyment-body', i.e. that which is 'enjoyed' by the Awakened One (Buddha); a well-deserved 'enjoyment' of fruit of spiritual discipline. These two notions converge in another poss. trans. of *sambhoga-kāya*—viz, 'Glorious-body' or 'body of glory'.

It is says, Murti, 'the concrete manifestation to himself and to the elect (of) the power and splendour' of the Buddha-nature. (3) the *Nirmāna-kāya* is the 'Assumed-body'. This body is necessitated, says Suzuki, because 'the Dharmakāya is too exalted a body for ordinary mortals to come into any conscious contact with. As it transcends all forms of limitations, it cannot become an object of sense or intellect. . . . The essence of Buddhahood is the Dharmakāya, but as long as the Buddha remains such, there is no hope for the salvation of a world of particulars. The Buddha has to abandon his original abode, and must take upon himself such forms as are conceivable and acceptable to the inhabitants of this earth.' (*Op. cit.*, 310). The *nirmāna-kāya* is thus the hist. manifestation of the Buddha-nature as a man, e.g. as → Gotama. This doc. of the Triple-Body of Buddha is a late development in → Mhy. Buddhism, although the germs of doc. were present long before it was thus given systematic form. The formal affirmation of the doc. is assoc. with the crystallising of the → *Yogācara* philosophy into a system by → Asanga and his disciples in the 4th cent. CE. T.O.L.

D. T. Suzuki, *Studies in the Lankāvatāra Sutra* (1930), pp. 308–38; T. R. V. Murti, *The Central Philosophy of Buddhism* (1955), pp. 284–7.

Buddhas (other than Gotama) The Buddh. idea that, when truth (*dhamma*) is lost to men, it needs to be re-proclaimed by a new Buddha, is reflected in belief that there had been earlier Buddhas in the world before appearance of Gotama the Buddha. The Pali canon, in its → *Khuddaka-Nikaya*, incl. a book entitled *Buddha-vaṃsa*, or the Buddha-lineage. This gives accounts of lives of 24 Buddhas prior to Gotama, and incl. him as the 25th. Of these 24, the last seven are mentioned in earlier works found in Pali canon, *viz.* in the *Dīgha-Nikaya* (II, pp. 5ff.), the *Samyutta-Nikaya* (II, pp. 5f.), and *Vinaya-pitaka* (II, p. 110). These seven are Vipassi, Sikhi, Vessabhu, Kakusandha, Konagamana, Kassapa and Gotama. (On these, see further, *Mahāpadāna Sutta*.) These 7 are incl. in the *Buddha-vaṃsa*, together with the preceding 18 (Dipankara, Kondanna, Mangala, Sumana, Revata, Sobhita, Anomadassi, Paduma, Narada, Padumuttara, Sumedha, Sujata, Piyadassi, Atthadassi, Dhammadassi, Siddhattha, Tissa and Phussa). The 27th ch. of this book mentions a further 3, who preceded Dipankara, *viz.* Tanhankara, Medhankara and Saranankara. In the Skt. literature of the Mhy., the number is further increased: the → *Lalitavistara* has a list of 54, and the *Mahāvastu* of over a hundred. It should be noted, to avoid confusion, that the names given above are not exclusively those of previous Buddhas, but are frequently used by other individuals, and are, e.g. often taken as the 'religious' names assumed by Buddh. monks, in a fashion similar to that by which Catholic children are given names of saints.

In addition to Gotama, and Buddhas who preceded him, the *DN* of the Pali canon mentions also those Buddhas who will follow him, i.e. those who are yet to come, after the present Buddha-era. 10 of these are named in the *Cakkavatti-Sihanāda Sutta* (*DN*, III, pp. 75ff.): Metteya, Uttama, Rama, Pasenadi, Kosala, Abhibhu, Dighasoni, Sankacca, Subbha, Todeyya, and Nalagiripalaleyya. Of these the most important in Buddh. thought is the next successor to Gotama, the coming Buddha, → Metteya. Acc. to Pali trad. the Buddha is born only in Jambudīpa (India), one of the 4 great continents in Indian cosmology (see → Cosmology), and only in the *Majjhima-desa* region of that land, i.e. the 'middle-country', approx. the region, where Buddhism orig. and developed historically. Not only does every Buddha preach the truth (*dhamma*) which has been lost by men; he also founds an Order (→ *Sangha*) and does not pass into → *nibbāna* until the relig. (*sāsana*) is well-estab. (*DN*, III, p. 122). T.O.L.

Buddha-Sāsana Term commonly used in Asian countries for the 'religion' of the Buddha (lit. 'the Buddha-discipline'). The term implies whole scheme of moral precepts, devotional practices, meditation, and social relationships which is regarded as owing its origin to Buddha. A more specialised meaning is that of the ninefold Buddha-S. (*navanga Buddha-sāsana*) in → Thv. Buddhism, by which is meant nine forms in which teaching of Buddha is found, viz: discourse (*sutta*); mixed prose (*geyya*); exegesis (*veyyākarana*); verse (*gātha*); solemn utterance (*udāna*); sayings (*itivuttaka*); previous-birth-stories (*jātaka*); marvels (*abhuta-dhamma*); analysis (*vedalla*). T.O.L.

Buddha-Vaṃsa 'The Buddha-lineage', a Buddh. canonical text of the Pali canon. (→ Buddhas (other than Gotama).) T.O.L.

Buddhism, General Survey Buddhism is the West. name for what in Asia is gen. known as the *Buddha-Sāsana*, i.e. the relig., or, lit., 'discipleship' of the Buddha, or Awakened One. (→ Buddha, as generic title.) The relig. thus named orig. in N.E. India, in region now known as Bihar, in 6th cent. BC, as result of experience of Gotama (or Gautama) (→ Buddha, Gotama), a young 'prince', or more exactly, son of a ruler of the → Sakya tribe. His home was in → Kapilavatthu, in the foothills of the Himālayas; but his 'awakening' or 'enlightenment' occurred at a place now known as Budh-Gaya, on banks of one of the south. tributaries of the Ganges

(→ Buddha-Gaya.) The doc. which he then began to preach is known as the → Dhamma (or Dharma); it consists of an analysis of the human situation, of nature of human existence, and structure of human personality, and a setting forth of means whereby the suffering and mortality, which is common lot of mankind, may be transcended and a new state of being achieved (→→ Dukkha; Anicca; Anatta; Holy Truths; Nibbana). Acc. to Buddh. trad., the first proclamation of this doc. was at Sarnath; the discourse has come to be known as the → Dhamma Cakkappavattana Sutta. The Buddha's personality and preaching attracted disciples, who were subsequently organised into community of those who followed the way of Buddha, and known collectively as the → Sangha. The doc. was independent of any belief in a supreme creator god (→ Creator, Doctrine of), and of priestly rites or functions. It was regarded by contemporary → brahman priests as heretical; in many discourses (→ Sutta) the Buddha is repr. as engaging in controversy with brahmans. The new community of the Sangha was an egalitarian society in which caste differences were entirely disregarded. (→ Caste, Buddh. Attitude). The doc. gained for Buddha and his community the sympathy and support of the king of → Magadha, viz., → Bimbisara. By time of Buddha's death at age of 80 (→ Kushinagara), the Buddh.s, i.e. both members of Sangha, and lay-followers, had become a large and growing body, drawn mainly from land owning, merchant, and labouring classes; a few brahmans had also become Buddh. Among principal disciples of Buddha was → Ananda, who is credited with having had responsibility of preserving the orig. form of a number of most import. discourses of Buddha, which now form the → Digha Nikaya, one of main sections of the → Pali canon of scripture (→ Tipitaka). The suttas, together with rules for monastic order, (i.e. the Sangha), later codified in the → Vinaya Pitaka, were rehearsed and their correctness endorsed at council held immediately after Buddha's death, at → Rajagaha (→ Councils, Buddh.). Differences of opinion among monks concerning keeping of these rules developed about a cent. after Buddha's death and were reason for convening of second council, at → Vesali. A further difference of opinion, this time on matters of doc., developed in 3rd cent. BC, during reign of emperor → Asoka, who had by this time become a Buddh. (in revulsion against violent campaigns he had waged earlier). A third council was held to deal with these doc. differences, at imperial capital of → Pataliputta (Patna). As result of this, a section of monks who held the → Sarvāstivāda view, as against trad. view of the elders or Sthaviras (→ Schools of Thought, Buddh.) moved away from lower Ganges plain N.W.-wards towards → Madhura, which became their stronghold. Out of these differences, and criticisms of lowered spiritual standards of traditionalists, a new movement within Buddhism eventually emerged, which called itself the 'Great Means' to salvation (→ Mahāyāna); by this was meant the wider scope of their concern for salvation of men, as this was understood by Buddh.s. They gave older school the name → Hīnayāna, or 'Lesser Means' to salvation (→ Yāna). The strength of new Mhy. school was in N.W. of India, in area that was influenced by Graeco-Roman culture, through Greek Bactrian Kingdom on N.W. borders of India (→ Gandhāra). The new school's much greater emphasis on virtue of compassion, as well as on wisdom, (which had been principally emphasised by Hīnayāna School) has led to suggestion that Christian influences may have had some part in development of the Mhy., since at that time trade between India and Roman world was also a vehicle for traffic of ideas, eastwards and westwards. Another feature of the Mhy. school was their new emphasis on the → Bodhisattva (or Buddha-to-be) as one whose function towards men in gen. was virtually that of a saviour. It was this form of Buddhism which spread northwards into C. Asia in 1st cent. CE, and in 2nd cent. from there onwards into China, where also it began, from end of 2nd cent. CE to meet with increasing acceptance. A feature of the Mhy. was use of → Sanskrit, language of the brahman Hindu priests; in this prestige-language many new writings of the Mhy. Buddhism were composed. In India the 2nd cent. CE saw development of further stage in unfolding of the analytical principles of Buddh. thought, viz. the emergence of the → Madhyamika school, with its doc. of *śūñyā*, in which Buddh. logical analysis reached its ultimate and most highly sophisticated form. The founders of this school, which is regarded by some as climax of develop. of Mahāyāna, were → Arya Deva and → Nagarjuna. Its over-sophistication brought about a certain reaction, or turning away from the extreme intellectualism and logical analysis which characterised Madhyamika, towards greater emphasis on direct apprehension of spiritual truth through cleansing and clarifying of consciousness; this new develop., led by → Asanga and his brother → Vasubandhu in 4th cent. CE was known as → Yogacara, so far as its practical emphasis on methods of meditation (*yoga*) were concerned, or as Vijnāna-Vāda, so far as its doc. of the permanent and supreme reality of consciousness (*vijñāna*) was concerned. The final stage of develop. in Mhy.

was that of the absorbing of much non-Buddh. material in the way of *mantras*, symbols, and cultic practices of various kinds in a process which in gen. was characterised by aim of spiritual enlightenment through use of these various devices and practices, and was known, first as → Mantrayana and later as → Vajrayana, or Tantra. It made its way to China as the Chenyen, and to Japan as → Shingon, and in 9th and 11th cents. CE to Tibet, where it persisted as dominant form of Buddhism. Meanwhile Buddhism had spread, by agency of missionary monks, over much of rest of India, first the Deccan and west. side of sub-continent, then the S.; in time of Asoka, in Hīnayāna form it had travelled to → Ceylon. Its spread eastwards across Bay of Bengal to → Burma and what is now → Thailand also took place during early cents. of CE; at first in the Mhy. form; later this was displaced by Pali or → Theravada form from Ceylon. The Theravāda was one of 18 schools into which the Hīnayāna had developed; it is only school which has persisted to mod. times. From Ceylon, and Thailand, Theravāda Buddhism spread to Cambodia and Laos, in 13th and 14th cents. CE, while from China the Mhy. form travelled into Vietnam. (→ South East Asia, Buddhism in). In India the Tantric or Vajrayāna form of Buddhism (*vide supra*) was followed by gradual decline in strength of the Buddh. community, and eventually it was displaced at popular level by various Hindu → bhakti and → Tantric cults. The → Monasteries declined, and finally, by 13th cent., Buddhism had virtually disappeared from India, except for a few pockets of survival on N.E. frontiers, notably in the Chittagong area of E. Bengal. In Ceylon, however, about 60% of population still adhere to Buddhism; in Burma, Thailand, Laos and Cambodia about 90%. From Ceylon knowledge of Buddhism, in its Pali form, came to Europe and America in 19th cent. Since then interest in the docs. and way of life of the Buddha has increased grad. and steadily in West. countries, notably England, Germany and U.S.A.; Buddh. monks from Ceylon, Thailand, Burma and Tibet are now found living in these countries; Buddh. societies of West. lay people are also increasing in number from year to year; some West. nationals have also taken → ordination in Sangha. Another feature of mod. hist. of Buddhism has been its revival in India, land of its origin; this has taken 2 forms: (1) increased interest on part of Indian intellectuals in this feature of their own heritage, esp. among those dissatisfied with Hindu relig.; (2) a mass movement to Buddhism among the Scheduled Classes (the former 'untouchables') led by conversion to Buddhism of their leader, Dr. B. R. Ambedkar, Minister of Law in Govt. of India, in 1956. (→ Cambodia–Laos.) T.O.L.

(in China) Chinese B. is usually classified as belonging to the Northern or → Mahāyāna form of B.; but from its inception Hīnayānist texts, trans. from Sanskrit exerted considerable influence, espec. on monastic discipline through the Vinaya, and in the Dhyāna or meditation schools. B. infiltrated along the central Asian silk roads about beginning of CE, and till close of Han Dynasty (*c.* CE 220) was largely confined to scattered groups of foreigners. Influence on court circles about middle of 2nd cent. CE is recorded. At first Taoist scholars assisted as translators, Taoist terms were used to trans. B. ideas, and similarities between the two religs. were emphasised. Early Chinese B. was an urban phenomenon, and till end of 3rd cent. CE the hist. of Chinese B. is largely that of translators whose work gave the literati access to speculative ideas of Mahāyāna. Weakness and disunity consequent on downfall of Han Dynasty led to invasion of N. China by non-Chinese peoples, who controlled vast areas during ensuing 300 years. The ruling princes of the N. looked favourably on B. relig. and B. monks became diplomatic, military and political advisers. They also gained great reputation among populace for thaumaturgical and magical practices. Fo T'u-têng (d. 349) and other indefatigable B. preachers converted nearly whole of N. China to B., whilst a famous school of translators under → Kumarajiva (CE 344–413) worked at the capital, Ch'ang-an. The minds of Chinese scholars were thus opened to great ideas of the Indian masters of Mahāyāna.

In CE 399, Fa Hsien left Ch'ang-an on his famous pilgrimage to India, inaugurating a pilgrim movement to centres of Indian B., which proved a source of perennial inspiration. In S. China, the 4th cent. witnessed penetration of B. into 'gentry' circles. Educated and wealthy lay patrons assisted the → Sangha, helped to pay for trans. work, founded monasteries and temples, and accepted the five rules of B. morality. Two trends developed in S. China; the dhyāna school of meditation, control of the mind and suppression of passions, Hīnayānist in inspiration; the prajñā school, interested in questions of ultimate reality, in trans. of the great Mahāyāna sūtras, and in fostering close connection between the sangha and the literati.

In this period of B. development in China, the central figures were → Tao An (312–85), → Hui Yüan (344–416) and Tao Shêng (360–434). Under their influence, great monastic foundations were estab., the Vinaya rules translated, and the speculative ideas of Mahāyāna widely disseminated. In works of these great Chinese B.

masters we see germ of ideas which developed into the distinctive Mahāyānist schools of the Sui and T'ang dynasties. The teachings of Confucian and Taoist classics were wedded to the Mahāyāna B. of Ashvaghosha, Nagarjuna, Vasubandhu and Asanga, and thus led to a distinctive Chinese B. trad. This flowered espec. in the T'ien T'ai, Pure Land, Hua Yen and Ch'an schools, which reached their maturity in the T'ang Dynasty. It is estimated that by *c.* CE 420 there were 1,786 temples and some 24,000 B. monks and nuns in China. The growing wealth and court influence of the B. clergy, together with doctrines which seemed to undermine stability of family and Confucian morality, gave rise to acute criticism, and outbreaks of persecution.

In the T'ang Dynasty (CE 618–907), B. in China reached its maturity. The dynasty was on the whole favourable to B. Contacts opened up with central Asia and India brought many foreigners into China. When → Hsüan-tsang (*c.* 596–664), the famous B. scholar and pilgrim, returned to China from 13 years spent in India, he received a hero's welcome. He exerted immense influence, and left behind a prodigious work of trans. By middle of 9th cent. Chinese B. had reached peak of its influence. The power, wealth, influence and splendour of its monastic establishments, inevitably leading to corruption, finally provoked great persecution of B. under emperor Wu-tsung (CE 845), a persecution from which Chinese B. never recovered. It is estimated that some 4,000 temples were sequestered or destroyed, and some 250,000 monks and nuns forced back into secular life. Priceless B. treasures of art, and extensive libraries perished in the flames of destruction. During the T'ang Dynasty some eight or ten major schools of B. flourished in China; but gradually a process of syncretism obliterated salient features of doctrine and practice, so that by the Sung Dynasty only the Pure Land and Ch'an schools remained active.

With estab. of Mongol (Yüan) Dynasty, Tibetan or Lama Buddhism (→ Lamaism) became prominent in China; but for past 700 years, apart from monks confined to ascetic life in monasteries, B. became largely absorbed in a popular relig., in which Buddh. and Taoist elements combined. This popular relig. of the masses was tolerated by the literati, but despised as a mass of crude superstitions.

The late 19th cent. and early 20th cent. brought an intellectual awakening and moral reform to Chinese B., notably under T'ai Hsü (1890–1947). But with rise of militant Communism, B. is once more under a cloud. → also Fa Hsien; Hsüan Tsang; Hua Yen School; Hui Yüan; I Tsing; Tien T'ai School; Ch'an; Hui Nêng; Tun Huang; Amida; Bodhidharma. For the Chinese Buddhist Canon → Tripitaka—Chinese. D.H.S.

D. H. Smith, *Chinese Religions* (1968), ch. 10; E. Zurcher, *The Buddhist Conquest of China* (1959); A. F. Wright, *Buddhism in Chinese History* (1959); K. L. Reichelt, *Truth and Tradition in Chinese Buddhism* (1927); K. K. Ch'en, *Buddhism in China* (1964).

(in South-East Asia) While the Buddhism of Burma, Thailand, Cambodia and Laos has, in each case, been shaped to some extent by hist. of country concerned, certain features of the relig. are common to these Buddh. countries of continental S.E. Asia. In each case the early form appears to have been much more strongly of the → Mahāyāna trad. than is case now; often there were considerable → Tantric elements. The influence of the Sinhalese form of Theravāda Buddhism has, however, become so strong that it is this form which provides → ecumenical framework of Buddhism in S.E. Asia: all four countries use same → Pali canon of scriptures, their monks are of Theravāda order, adhering closely to rules of the → Vinaya; they can pass from monasteries of one country to those of another with greatest ease (except where political conditions at present provide barrier), and Pali is their common language. Each country has in course of its hist. been a monarchy, whose ruler was trad. a Theravādin Buddh., and in each case there developed the office of chief monk, or supervisor of whole monastic order throughout country (*Sangharāja*, in Burma *Thathanabaing*). Moreover, in each country there has been accommodation to local indigenous forms of relig., notably belief in → spirits who must be placated, and in → astrology and numerology. These local beliefs have, in each case, been fused with Buddhism at popular level to produce distinctive national amalgams which should properly be described as Burmese Buddhism; Thai Buddhism, etc. (→→ Burma; Cambodia; Festivals; Holy Days, Buddhist; Laos; Thailand). T.O.L.

(Political Power) In hist. of Buddhism four patterns of relationship with State can be distinguished: (i) easy co-existence between Buddhism and the State; (ii) State patronage of Buddhism; (iii) identity of Buddh. → Sangha with State; (iv) persecution of Buddhism by State. Examples of (i) occurred during lifetime of Buddha and reign of → Bimbisara, king of Magadha, in certain periods in hist. of Chinese and Japanese Buddhism, and present situation in → Ceylon. Examples of (ii) are → Asoka in anc. India; Medieval Ceylon, Burma, Thailand and Cambodia, under such kings as Parakamma Bahu, and Anawratha; mod. → Thailand and

Cambodia. Tibet until time of Chinese invasion in 1950 provides almost only example of (iii); from 1950 the same country provides a clear example of (iv); Chinese Buddhism also provides examples of State persecution, notably that which occurred in early part of 7th cent. CE under first emperor of T'ang dynasty, Kao Tsu, and the more severe persecution of CE 845, ordered by emperor Wu-Tsung, who commanded that some 45,000 temples and small shrines should be destroyed and a quarter of million monks and nuns ejected from monastic life. (→ Buddhism in China). The experience of Buddh. Sangha in those Asian countries which fell under European imperial domination from 16th cent. onwards was in some cases that of direct persecution, as in Ceylon under Portuguese in 16th cent., and in other cases disablement, due to indirect attack or to social, economic or legal discrimination, as in cases of Ceylon and Burma. It was largely because of such disablement that Buddh. monks in Burma and Ceylon under British rule became allies of those of their compatriots who were agitating for freedom from foreign rule. Even in medieval Burma, however, under conditions of State patronage of Buddhism, Burmese monks did not hesitate to reject or oppose decisions or actions of king if they considered these to be contrary to spirit of the Buddha-Dhamma. An attitude of protest against a secular government hostile to Buddhism is seen in the → self-immolation of monks and nuns in Vietnam in recent times. T.O.L.

Buddhist (Pali) Literature Buddh. Pali lit. falls into 2 categories: (a) canonical, (b) non-canonical. (a) *Canonical lit.:* this consists of the Ti-pitaka, or '3-baskets', viz. Vinaya-pitaka, Sutta-pitaka and Abhidhamma-pitaka. (→ Tipitaka). To these is added, in Ceylon, as part of canon, a supplement known as the *Paritta* (Sinhalese *pirit*), a collection of canonical chants use in certain popular rituals, such as building of new house, at funerals, in times of sickness, etc. These are used in Burma also in ceremonies and rituals for lay-people.

(b) *Non-canonical lit.:* this consists of (1) chronicles, (2) commentaries on canonical texts, (3) compositions based on canonical texts and presented as compendiums or manuals of Buddh. life or philosophy. The chronicles are → *Dipavamsa*, i.e. 'the Island Chronicle' (the island being Ceylon); this is oldest of the chronicles; → *Mahāvamsa*, 'the Great Chronicle'; → *Culavamsa*, 'the Little Chronicle'; → *Mahābodhivamsa*, 'the Chronicle of the Bodhi-tree'; → *Thupavamsa*, 'the Chronicle of the Stupa'; → *Dathavamsa*, 'the Chronicle of the Sacred Relic' (i.e. the Buddha's Tooth); → *Sāsanavamsa*, 'The Chronicle of the Religion', a work composed in 19th cent. in Burma. The commentaries are far too numerous to list, these being not only commentaries upon various books of Tipitaka, but also commentaries and sub-commentaries upon the commentaries. Some of the more import. of these may be noted, viz. those composed by → Buddhaghosa: on the Vinaya-pitaka, *Samantapāsādikā;* on the Digha-Nikaya, *Sumangala-vilāsini;* on the *Dhammasangani* (1st book of the Abh.-pitaka, *Atthasālinī.* The third type of non-canonical lit., the compendiums or manuals, incl. import. works such as Buddhaghosa's → *Visuddhimagga;* the → *Malindapanha;* the → *Abhidhammatthasangaha.* T.O.L.

Trans. into Eng. of many of these non-canonical texts may be noted: *The Great Chronicle of Ceylon* (Mahavamsa) (1912, repr. 1964); *Minor Chronicles of Ceylon* (Culavamsa), 2 vols. (1929–30); *The Sāsanavamsa* (1952); *The Expositor* (Buddhaghosa's Atthasālinī), 2 vols. (1920–1, repr. 1958); *The Path of Purification* (Visuddhimagga) (1964); *Compendium of Philosophy* (Abhidhammattha-sangaha) (1910, repr. 1963); *Inception of Discipline* (intro. to Samantapāsādikā) (1962); *Milinda's Questions* (Malindapanha), 2 vols. (1963–4).

Buddhist Schools of Thought The first major division in the Buddh. → Sangha is trad. connected with the Council of Vesali (→ Councils, Buddh.), approx. 100 years after decease of the Buddha (*c.* 383 BC). Disagreement arose concerning degree of strictness with which monastic discipline (→ Vinaya Pitaka) was to be observed. The dissentient body, who disagreed with the stricter, more conservative *Sthaviras* or Elders, henceforth became known as the → *Mahāsanghikas*, i.e. the Great Sangha Party, since they claimed a greater following for their more liberal interpretation of the rules. The *Sthaviras* subsequently divided into 18 schools, among the more important of which were the → Puggalavādins, Vibhajyavādins, → Sarvāstivādins, and Theravādins (→ Theravāda). The *Mahāsanghikas* also divided into number of separate schools, among whom the more import. were the Lokottaravādins (→ Mahāvastu), Prajñaptivādins and the Caitiyas. Relationships between these other schools are shown on p. 168. The develop. of the → Mahāyāna from within the Mahāsanghika trad. is, as Conze says, 'wrapped in obscurity' (*Buddhist Thought in India*, 1962, pp. 198f.). The 2 principal Mahāyāna schools in India were the → Mādhyamikas and the → *Yogācaras.* In China and Japan, Mahāyāna developed into a number of schools peculiar to those countries, notably the T'ien-t'ai or →→ Tendai, Ch'an or Zen, Chen-yen or Shingon, the Pure Land, and the Nichiren. (→ Buddhism in China). T.O.L.

Buddhist Scriptures → *Tipitaka*. T.O.L.

-Bukhārī Muḥammad b. Ismā'īl (194–256/810–870), a famous Muslim traditionist from Bukhārā, whose collection of traditions, *al-Ṣaḥīḥ* (the sound), is considered by most → Sunnīs to be book next in importance to the Qur. B. travelled widely in search of trads. and claimed to have heard from 1,000 authorities. He took 16 years to compile his *Ṣaḥīḥ*, showing care with which he made his selection. Many commentaries have been written on it. Though recognised gen. as outstanding traditionist, praised for his detailed knowledge and perspicacity in detecting faults, B. fell into disgrace with the authorities towards end of life. He was expelled from Naysābūr on ground of heterodoxy and went to Bukhārā. There he got into trouble with governor because he refused to bring his books to his house, or give private instruction to his children; he had to leave Bukhara, and ended his days among relatives in village of Khartank near Samarqand. J.R.

*E.I.*², I, pp. 1296f.; *G.A.L.*, I, pp. 163–6; *S.I.*, pp. 260–5; Goldziher, *M.S.*, II, pp. 234–45; J. Fück, 'Beiträge zur Überlieferungsgeschichte von Buḫārī's Traditionssammlung', *Z.D.M.G.*, 92 (1938), pp. 60–87.

Bull, Apis As an incarnation of divine procreativity, the A.-B. was worshipped at Memphis (Egypt) from early times, being identified with → Ptah, god of Memphis. In art the A.-B. carries the sun's disk between its horns, thus assoc. it with sun-god → Re. Later it was identified with → Osiris, and so acquired mortuary significance. When the A.-B. died, it was solemnly buried in catacombs of the Serapaeum at Sakkara; but it was also believed that the A.-B. was immediately reborn, and priests searched for a bull calf, showing special marks. The Mnevis Bull of → Heliopolis was assoc. with → Atum-Re. (→ Sarapis). S.G.F.B.

R.Ae.R-G., pp. 46–51; S. A. B. Mercer, *The Religion of Anc. Egypt* (1949), pp. 233–4.

Bull-cult From Paleolithic era the bull has been admired and reverenced for its strength, ferocity and virility. A B.-C. was practised at → Çatal Hüyük, closely assoc. with Mother Goddess in 7th mil. BC. It was a well developed institution in Egypt (→ Apis Bull, Mnevis Bull); also in Crete with the → Minotaur (→ Cretan Relig.). Acc. to Ex. 32; I Kgs. 12:28ff., → Yahweh was prob. worshipped under image of bull, as was also → Baal. The → Taurobolium in cult of → Cybele was a regenerating baptism in blood of sacrificed bull. The sacrifice of the cosmic Bull was supreme cultic act of → Mithra. → Zoroaster condemned → Yima for slaying Primordial Bull. S.G.F.B.

E.R.E., II, pp. 887–9; *R.G.G.*³, VI, 372–3 ('Stierdienst'); *H.D.B.*², p. 119 ('Calf, Golden'); M. Eliade, *Traité d'histoire des religions* (1949), pp. 84ff., *Patterns in Comparative Religion* (E.T. 1958), pp. 86ff.

Bull-roarer Designation for instrument that emits roaring sound when whirled through air. Objects of this kind have been widely used (New Mexico, Australia, Africa) in primitive rituals of various kinds. The anc. Greek *kōnos* was prob. of a similar character; there is some evidence of use of B. in Paleolithic times. S.G.F.B.

E.R.E., II, *s.v.;* J. Maringer, *The Gods of Prehistoric Man* (E.T. 1960), pp. 60ff.; E. O. James, *Comparative Religion* (1938), pp. 57ff.

Bultmann, Rudolf Karl (1884–) Import. in mod. Christ. thought, because, on basis of immense learning and ability, he combines roles of N.T. scholar and apologist in close interrelation. B. studied at Marburg, where he was specially influenced by Jühlicher, Weiss, and Hermann; at Tübingen where he responded to Müller; and at Berlin where his mentors were Gunkel and Harnack. He linked himself with → Barth in revolt against liberal theology of Harnack and the 'Jesus of History' school. In N.T. study he developed the *form-critical* method, started by Johannes Weiss. Using 20th cent. standards of hist. evidence, he came to very sceptical conclusions about element of hist. fact in the N.T. Acc. to → Form Criticism, the Gospels primarily give us a glimpse into the period after Jesus' death, when the primitive Church was clarifying content of its own preaching, and coming to terms with its environment. This refers only to isolated anecdotes and sayings; the linkages and situations of the Gospel stories are all conventional afterthoughts. Christianity today agrees with Christianity then in relying on the → *Kerygma* to be found in Rom. 1:3–4, 6:3–4, 10, 9; I Cor. 11:23–6, 15:3–7; Phil. 2:6–11; Acts 2:21–4, 3:13–5, 10:37–42, 13:26–31. To B. almost nothing can today be certainly known about life and personality of Jesus, since the Chr. sources did not show any interest in these things, and further are very fragmentary and over-grown with legend. The pronouncements which the N.T. make about Jesus are not about his *nature*, but about his significance, i.e. about what God says to man through him (The trad. discussion of his nature involves use of categories applicable to inanimate objects to describe the living). Within the N.T. itself, knowledge of nature of Christ unaccompanied by knowledge of oneself is that possessed by the evil spirits in the Markan Gospel or by the demons in the Epistle of James. The centre of the Chr. story lies in death and resurrection of Jesus Christ. B. says of the Crucifixion that it is not the saving-event because it is the Cross of Christ; rather, is it the Cross of Christ because it is the saving-event. The Resurrection is not an objective event which is an hist. happening. But it is a living experience here and now. This means entering into a new dimension of existence, the being-set-free from guilt, care and the past, and made open to one's fellow men in love. B. believes that the hist. facts have been irreparably changed into a story of a pre-existent divine being who became incarnate and atoned by his blood for the sins of men, rose from the dead, ascended into heaven, and would shortly return on the clouds to judge world and inaugurate the new age. These ideas belong to 'myth'. B. gives two definitions of myth: (1) myth is a mode of thought, in which what belongs to the other world is pictured as belonging to this world—and the transcendent as immanent. Thus, e.g., God's transcendence is conceived of as one of spacial remoteness; (2) mythical thinking regards world and world-events as 'open'—i.e., open for intrusion of transcendent powers, and so not water-tight from point of view of scientific thought. This type of thinking has become utterly imposs. for scientifically-influenced 20th cent. man. And we cannot, acc. to B., pick and choose from the mythical picture—the mythical view of world must be accepted or rejected in its entirety.

But B. believes that hidden in the myth is a *Kerygma*, a divine word addressed to men. This can be heard and obeyed, only if it is set free from its mythical framework. The process of doing this he calls *demythologizing*. This is not a repudiation of the myth, but the translation of its content into a possibility of human existence, for which we are summoned to decide. This is most clearly to be seen in the Pauline picture of contrast between the sinner unable to fulfil law of God, and the redeemed man in Christ. Essentially the N.T. confronts us with a choice between authentic and unauthentic existence. That this choice is available to men is due to the decisive eschatological act of God in Christ. B. insists that to speak in this way is not mythological thinking but analogical thinking, resting on an actual hist. event. To find God's action in nature is incompatible with the uniformity of natural science, and the impulse to find it there is sinful. But, in the hist. fact of the Cross, God's grace becomes manifest. We know this because God meets us in our own concrete existence through grace. So we speak of God's action as a fact we know in our human existence.

To provide the framework of the concepts that we need to expound this new human possibility, B. turns to the philosopher Martin Heidegger's Analysis of Existence. Every individual stands before his imminent end—his own death. In his everyday decisions, he works out a judgment on his own life, as he lays hold of or turns away from his authentic being. So applied to individual life, the ideas of the myth are alive and urgent as we make unrepeatable decisions in fact of the end which is coming. The Chr. *Kerygma* summons men to decisions of faith, by which they die to world in order to live by the unseen reality of God. B.'s interpret. of the N.T. and his apologetic theology are both subjects of active controversy. The chief points in dispute are: (1) is B.'s judgment on the hist. element in Gospels realistic or unnecessarily sceptical? (2) is it a fault or a necessary element in sound thinking to apply to living things some categories which also apply to inanimate things? (3) is B. right in thinking that myth must be accepted or rejected as a whole, and in finding no direct truth in it? (4) is B. right in exempting any conception of God at all from mythological thinking, and is he right on his own assumptions in speaking of the action of God? (5) (of least importance) is B. right in making use of philosophy to expound the Gospel in its contemporary meaning? If so, is Heidegger's the right philosophy to use? H.C-J.

For Bultmann's writings and the controversy they have aroused see his *Theology of the New Testament*, E.T., 2 vols. (1952, 1955), *Kerygma and Myth* (1953, 1962); C. W. Kegley (ed.), *The Theology of Rudolf Bultmann* (1966), with full bibliography; J. McQuarrie, *The Scope of Demythologizing* (1960); I. Henderson, *Myth in the New Testament* (1952), *Rudolf Bultmann* (1965); D. Cairnes, *A Gospel without Myth?* (1960).

Bundahishn 'Original creation', a Pahlavi Book, dating from 9th or 10th cent. CE, dealing with Zoroastrian cosmogony, cosmology and eschatology. It exists in two recensions. (→ Zoroastrianism). S.G.F.B.

Trans. E. West, *S.B.E.*, V (1880); R. C. Zaehner, *Zurvan* (1955), pp. 81ff.

Bunyan, John (1628–88) Born at Elstow, Bedfordshire, of poor parents, his mastery of English language came from reading Bible. He joined the Parliamentary side in the Civil War (1644–6), and became an → Independent at Bedford in 1653, acquiring reputation as preacher. While in prison (1660–72), as result of Royalist repressive measures after Restoration, B. wrote autobiography *Grace Abounding to the Chief of Sinners* (1666), the *Pilgrim's Progress* (1678), and the *Holy War* (1682). His last (posthumous) work was anti-R.C. treatise *Antichrist and her Ruin*. B.'s writings, esp. the *Pilgrim's Progress*, reveal a deep evangelical piety which saw life in this world as exclusively a spiritual warfare or pilgrimage, of which the sole concern should be salvation of the soul. B.'s attitude was similar to the this world-denying of early anchorites and monks. S.G.F.B.

E.R.E., II, *s.v.; D.C.C.*, *s.v.; R.G.G.*³, I, 1526.

-Burāq Name of winged animal on which Muḥammad is said to have ascended to heaven on night of the → *Mi'rāj.* A trad. in Muslim's collection says it was white and long, larger than a donkey but smaller than mule. The distance of its footsteps was equal to range of its vision. J.R.

*E.I.*², I, pp. 1310f.; Hughes, p. 44; Guillaume, *Life*, p. 182; *Mishkāt*, pp. 1264, 1267, 1290.

Burial (General) The burial of his dead is a practice that differentiates man from other species: it was practised by *homo sapiens*' precursor, the so-called Neanderthal or Mousterian Man. From that time the custom has been universal, except where it has been replaced by cremation or exposure to birds of prey (→ Funerary Rites, Zoroastrian). Paleolithic B.'s indicate that purpose was not utilitarian, but ritual. Depositing of food, implements and ornaments in grave suggests belief that dead had need of such. Fear of dead may also have operated: many bodies were tightly bound before B. (→ Paleolithic Religion). In early ages, and in primitive communities, B. has gen. had two interrelated motives: (1) it put the dead *en route* for land of dead, to which they now belonged; (2) not to be buried left them between worlds of living and dead, which predicament made them malevolent towards the living; thus fear of dead further prompted proper funerary care. Anc. Mesopot. divinationary texts show how real this fear could be. B.-customs have varied much: sometimes important persons were buried with servants, thus sacrificed to minister to their master in next world (e.g. at Ur of Chaldees and Anyang, China). The Egypt. belief that deceased lived in tomb led to → mummification of body (→ Funerary Rites, Egypt.). Change from B. to cremation does not necessarily repr. change of belief about condition of dead, e.g. ascent of soul to sky instead of residence in underworld. Ashes of dead were frequently buried. A subterranean land of dead could be assoc. with cremation (e.g. Greek → Hades), and B. with celestial afterlife (e.g. Egypt). Orientation of body in grave could be significant (e.g. Chr. custom of facing east to meet Christ at Last Day. The crouched posture of many Paleolithic B.'s has been interpreted as implying rebirth (→ Paleolithic Relig.). In medieval Christendom the custom of burying heart, and sometimes other parts of body, of important people, in different places, existed. Chr. B.-practice has theological justification (Gen. 3:19, I Cor. 15-35ff.). (→ Funerary Rites, various). S.G.F.B.

E.R.E., IV, pp. 411–511; E. Bendann, *Death Customs* (1930); E. O. James, *Prehistoric Religion* (1957), pp. 17ff.; E. A. W. Budge, *The Mummy* (1925), pp. 396ff; *R.Ae.R-G.*, pp. 257–60 ('Grab'); W. Watson, *China, before the Han Dynasty* (1961), pp. 69ff.; *Kleine Pauly*, I, 873–6; *R.G.G.*³, I, 959–67; *R.A.C.*, II, 194–219; F. Cumont, *After Life in Roman Paganism* (1922), pp. 66ff.; Brandon, *M.D.*, *passim;* E. Panofsky, *Tomb Sculpture* (1964); P. Lacroix, *Military and Religious Life in Middle Ages*, ed. (1964), pp. 447ff.

(Chinese) (→ Funerary Ritual, → Mortuary Cult, → Mourning Customs.) The Chinese have always buried their dead (except for cremation of Buddhist monks and nuns), and, apart from children and unmarried persons, the requirements of → filial piety and → the ancestor cult demanded scrupulous observance of elaborate rites as regards the preparation of corpse, the actual burial, mourning and post-mortem care of the dead.

From earliest hist. times (Shang Dynasty *c.* 1766–1154 BC), princes and nobles were buried in elaborate pits of tamped earth; with the coffin were placed food, weapons, ornaments, utensils, etc., together with immolated servants, retainers and relatives. The custom of burying servants and attendants alive seems to have almost died out by time of → Confucius, and straw and paper effigies were substituted. The ancient B. customs, as recorded in the *Li Chi* (vide *S.B.E.* vols. 27–8), modified by local usage and practice and by Buddhist influence, have continued to modern times. The corpse, washed and dressed, was placed in heavy wooden coffin, and remained in the home for several days, burial often taking place on 49th day, whilst elaborate mourning ceremonies were conducted by Taoist and Buddhist priests, and the chief mourners. The elaborateness of funeral depended on age and rank of deceased and social standing of family.

The dead are usually buried in ancestral graveyards or some carefully chosen spot on the family lands, in shallow pits over which mounds of earth are erected, which are renovated each year at spring festival of → Ch'ing Ming. The ceremonies attached to B. in China are primarily designed to emphasise the honour, prestige and social standing of deceased and his family, and to provide for his comfort and safety in the afterlife. After burial, periodical ceremonies, with offerings of drink and food, are performed at grave, whilst the spirit-tablet of the deceased in the ancestral shrine keeps alive his memory. D.H.S.

E.R.E., IV, pp. 450ff.; J. J. M. de Groot, *The Religious System of China*, vol. 2 (1892); *S.B.E.*, vols. 27–8 (1888, 1899).

(Islam) After a death, the women wail loudly for a period with most disconcerting sounds. The corpse is washed, clothed in its shroud and turned facing Mecca. Some vv. of the Qur. may be recited then. In some places the corpse is carried on a bier to the mosque, in others direct to cemetery. This is done at a quick pace to chanting of 'There is no deity but God; Muḥammad is God's messenger,' men taking turns at carrying. To accompany a cortege is a meritorious deed. The imām leads mourners in prayers, praising God, praying for blessing on Muḥammad, praying that the living may be kept alive in Islam and that those God causes to die may die in Islam. The people spend some time seated in silent prayer for the dead, and then the corpse is buried. The grave is so made that the corpse can be laid facing Mecca; when it is properly placed, the grave is filled in. The people recite the → *Fātiḥa* on behalf of dead; after they have gone a short distance, they recite it again, then present food to poor people. For some nights following, recitation of the Qur. takes place at home of bereaved on behalf of deceased. (→ Mourning for dead). J.R.

Hughes, pp. 44–7; Pareja, p. 659; *Mishkāt*, pp. 337–59; Levy, *Social Structure*, pp. 187f.; Lane, *Egyptians*, ch. xxviii; Gaudefroy-Demombynes, *Institutions*, pp. 171ff.; Dickson, *Arab of desert*, ch. xiv; H. Granquist, *Muslim death and burial* (1965); A. S. Tritton, 'Muslim funeral customs', *B.S.O.A.S.* (1938), pp. 653–61; cf. *M.W.*, vii, p. 205; xxxi, p. 418.

(Japanese) (→ Funerary Ritual, → Mortuary Cults, → Mourning Customs). In ancient times the corpses of princes and nobles, enclosed in stone, wooden or earthenware coffins, were first placed temporarily in a building called a *moya* (mourning house), whilst a megalithic vault was prepared, over which was placed a huge mound of earth. The corpses were buried with food, weapons, ornaments, pottery, etc., as in China, and eulogies were pronounced over them and music performed. Human → sacrifices were often made at the tombs of Mikados and princes. With the common people, B. was called *no-okuri* (sending to a moor or waste place), and was a simple interment or perhaps exposure at a distance from habitable dwellings. Offerings consisted of rice and water.

Cremation was introduced by → Buddhism in CE 703, and became a common practice among Buddhists. In → Shinto, the coffin is buried in the grave with few or no ceremonies. Death is regarded as source of pollution, and after a burial both the house of deceased and the mourners are submitted to purification rites. D.H.S.

W. G. Aston, *Shinto* (1905); *E.R.E.*, IV, pp. 485ff.

Burma, Buddhism in as elsewhere in S.E. Asia, has two aspects: monastic and lay; these two aspects are organically connected, and neither could exist apart from other. The Buddhism of the monasteries is predominately of kind which looks to Pali canonical and commentarial lit. (→ Literature, Buddhist, Pali) for its norms and standards, and is known as → Theravāda. There are, however, a few very small, isolated monasteries adhering to the → Mahāyāna; these are supported by, and minister to, local Gurkha and Chinese communities; the former in some hill areas of north, and the Shan States of E. Burma; the latter in Rangoon.

Historically the Mahāyāna has lost ground in Burma. Archaeological evidence indic. that in earlier period Skt. Buddhism, both Mahāyāna and → Sarvāstivādin, had considerable influence. B. of some kind may have existed in Burma as early as 3rd cent. CE, if evidence of an early Chinese source can be accepted. Certainly from 5th cent. CE there is epigraphical and other archaeological evidence of a fairly flourishing Buddh. life, which appears to have been closely connected with N.E. India, and poss. also with Andhra, on east coast of S. India. Fragments of the Buddh. Pali canon have been discovered at Prome, dating poss. from as early as 5th cent. CE. By 7th cent., for which evidence is available in accounts given by Chinese pilgrims, both the Theravāda and Sarvāstivāda forms existed. From 8th and 9th cents. CE the Mahāyāna form appears to have existed in lower Burma, notably at Prome, where it was intro. from N.E. India (Bengal). Before long this had followed the Indian course of develop., and became markedly Tantric (→ Vajrayāna). A new era for Burmese B. began in 11th cent. CE with coming of a ruler of Pagan named An-aw-ra-hta (the Burmese form of *Aniruddha*), who became king of upper Burma in 1044. Converted to Theravāda B. by a monk, he set out to reform the relig. from extreme form of → Tantrism into which it had developed under control of the *Aris* (or Aryas), a corrupt Tantric priesthood which dominated upper Burma. Having extended domain eastwards to Thaton, he opened up Burmese Kingdom to strong Theravāda influence emanating from the Mons who at that time inhabited S.E. Burma. It is from this time that Theravāda became dominant form of B. practised by Burmese of the central river valley regions; from this, says Coedès, sprang the civilisation, lit. and art of the Burmese, which have persisted to mod. times. The Aris, however, were not completely suppressed; they managed to maintain their corrupt form of B. (incl. the eating of meat, drinking of spirits, use of spells, and sexual licence) until as late as 18th cent. Nor did

Theravāda B., though it had royal patronage, succeed at once in transforming the earlier indigenous worship of spirits, or Nats; it grad. made its way, transforming local beliefs and practices and producing through the cents. the amalgam of Theravāda B. and local trad. which is peculiar to Burma, and to which the name Burmese B. must be given. When this was first discovered by Europeans, it was declared to be a thin veneer of Buddhism covering the 'real' religion of Burma, viz. Nat-worship. More recently, however, it has been argued (by E. M. Mendelson and others) that Burmese B. is properly understood as a spectrum, at one end of which are the indigenous cults and beliefs, at the other the authentic Theravāda B. of the Pali Canonical scriptures practised in the monasteries; between these two extremes is a continuum in which the transition from one to the other is made, with a steady growth of the authentic Theravāda element. At this level there has been communication with other Theravāda countries, notably → Ceylon, from time to time. Burma has become noted for its → Abhidhamma studies, and in recent centuries has attracted monks from Ceylon to the monasteries where this is specially studied. The British conquest of Burma in 19th cent. and imposition of Brit. imperial rule seriously damaged trad. structure of → Sangha organisation; when Burma achieved independence in 1947, the task of recovering a great deal of lost ground confronted the Sangha. U Nu, prime minister of independent Burma until 1962 attempted to fill the role of the Buddh. kings of pre-colonial days in acting as protector of B. In 1956, the 2500th anniversary (acc. to Theravāda chronology) of the Buddha's entry into *nibbāna* was celebrated by holding of a great 'Buddh. Council', with reciting and revision by monks of entire text of the → Tipitaka, in a vast cave-auditorium outside Rangoon specially constructed for purpose from public funds. In 1961 a measure was passed in the Rangoon Parliament making B. the official relig., but without discrimination against other religs., which together account for the approx. 20% non-Buddh. portion of pop. of Burma. This was subsequently rescinded by military government under Gen. Ne Win, who took over control of Burma in March 1962.

Burma has many monasteries. Through the heartland of Burmese civilisation (the river valleys) they are to be found in almost all small towns and villages, where they provide centres of influence, moral and educational, for the local people. Burma, like other Theravāda countries of Asia, has a high rate of literacy. The → pagodas, built and furnished by Kings and lay people are found attached to monasteries in most towns; some of the more magnificent of these, such as the pagodas of Mandalay and the *Shwe Dagon Pagoda* at Rangoon, covered with gold leaf donated by Buddh.-laypeople, are famous as centres of pilgrimage, and provide places of assembly for vast crowds on festival days. T.O.L.

G. Coedès, *Les Peuples de la Peninsule Indochinoise* (1962); *Les États Hindouisés d'Indochine et d'Indonésie* (new ed., 1964); N. R. Ray, *Sanskrit Buddhism in Burma* (1936); E. Sarkisyanz, *The Buddhist Backgrounds of the Burmese Revolution* (1965); E. M. Mendelson, 'Religion and Authority in Modern Burma', in *The World Today* (March, 1960), 'Buddhism and the Buddhist Establishment', in *Archives de Sociologie des Religions*, 1964, No. 17.

Bushidō The Way of the Samurai. A moral discipline, controlling the life and death of ruling class of Japan. It required propriety of behaviour acc. to prescribed standards, inculcating dignity, valour, honour, obedience and reverence. Though not a religion itself, it possessed its cult of family worship and the strict observance of → Shinto festivals. D.H.S.

M. Anesaki, *Hist. of Japanese Relig.* (1930), pp. 262ff.

Bushman Religion (note: Bushman languages are 'click' languages. The five clicks are indicated by signs; two such are used here: // and !).

There are considerable variations in belief and relig. practice between Bushmen tribes, a declining race of S. African hunters and food-gatherers; but the following common features may be noted. All B. believe in a supreme creator spirit, in lesser spiritual beings and in spirits of the dead. These spirits can intervene in human affairs; some have power to modify weather and movements of animals. The spirits of the dead usually act punitively, attacking those guilty of breaches of the moral order. B. thus fear their dead and avoid graves where ghosts may linger. All groups recognise that some of their number have special powers that can be used to counter attacks from the spirit world. Most B. are reported to address personifications of Sun, Moon and Rain in attempts to mitigate harsh weather conditions or bring good fortune. This, a casual practice in most groups, was elaborated into sidereal worship in the now extinct B. culture of the Cape Province. B. oral folklore is extensive; it provides myths of origin and creation; tales that detail the actions and attributes of spirits and many examples of beast-fable mythology.

Once the sole inhabitants of the area south of the Zambesi river, the Bushmen were later decimated, first by incoming Bantu tribesmen and later by white settlers who regarded B. as vermin. Many B. became servants of Bantu or white masters and lost, or modified their relig. and culture. Surviving groups, whose culture remains intact, are found in the less coveted regions of S. Africa, notably in arid zones of S.W. Africa, in the Kalahari Desert and S. Angola.

Traditionally, the B. are divided into a large number of named tribes, each distinguished by its distinctive language or dialect. Tribes, in turn are divided into small independent bands necessarily limited in size by paucity of resources provided by a harsh environment. The band is the largest political unit, for there is no form of central or tribal government. The band is also the largest congregation that gathers for relig. purposes.

Accounts of relig. in the various tribes are fragmentary and incomplete, and systematic inter-tribal comparison is imposs. However, Silberbauer has recently provided first authoritative study of the relig. of a single B. tribe, the G/wi of the C. Kalahari. Here G/wi religion is described to exemplify B. belief and practice.

G/wi believe in two opposed spiritual beings; N!odima, the creator of the world, and G//awama who seeks to disrupt N!odima's creation and to wreak evil. N!odima now lives 'in a state of semi-retirement'; he continues work of creation by quickening the foetus in women in fifth month of pregnancy. He sometimes favours men by appearing as advisor in dreams. N!odima may sometimes take back a life, if a man shows himself unworthy by persistent wrongdoing. All living creatures belong to N!odima; therefore it is wrong to harm them. Wild animals may be killed for meat or in self-defence, but any form of wilful killing is wrong. G/wi express respect and reverence for N!odima by respecting and reverencing his creations.

G//awama is a semi-anthropomorphic figure, weaker than N!odima and subject to many of same limitations as man. Men can temporarily thwart G//awama's attempts to harm them, but he cannot be permanently defeated. He is resisted with the means N!odima provides. These are charms made up on principles of analogous magic, and, more importantly, a dance of exorcism. G//awama may be cursed; G/wi delight in tales that tell of his discomfiture—a python once bit G//awama, who suffered thirst, pain and sickness as he limped through the desert in search of water.

The ghosts of the dead are, for G/wi, a third spiritual force. While there is no doctrine of reward and punishment in the after-life, ghosts would rather be alive as men. The ghost pines for company of his family and band, though, with passage of time it becomes resigned to its new state and joins the other ghosts. After a burial, the grave is marked with the deceased's possessions, camp is broken, and the grave abandoned. Graves are places of danger, for ghosts are malicious and resentful beings who will try to capture family or band-members to join them in death. Younger people, less resigned to death, make more dangerous ghosts than the elderly, who are better able to accept loneliness of the grave.

Ghosts are dangerous in another way. The dead can be unleashed from their home below ground, if taboos are broken. The breaking of taboos opens way for ghosts to emerge with their anger and resentment re-awakened. Angry ghosts can destroy the people and property of a band in whose territory the taboo has been broken. Belief in these ghostly activities acts as a general sanction that reinforces the observance of custom. The → taboos involved concern relations of men and women and proper arrangement of sexual and procreative activity.

By refraining from wrong action, the wrath of ghosts or of N!odima may be avoided. G//awama, on the other hand, is gratuitously vindictive and some defence against his action is necessary. The central communal rite of the G/wi band is a dance of exorcism designed to drive out G//awama's evil. G//awama sits in the sky and shoots down invisible arrows of evil which may strike and enter into women. Women, in turn, may contaminate men with this injected evil, which can affect both the physical and moral wellbeing of the band. In the course of the Iron or Gemsbok dance, men take the evil out of women by laying on of hands. Male dancers then rid themselves of the evil, which is felt as a chest pain, by entering a state of trance. The trance, in some, is cataleptic; the entranced dancer is brought back to a normal state by friends who massage his body and manipulate his limbs. Silberbauer writes that a night of dancing purges band-members of tension and repressed emotions. The sense of achievement, which follows the dance, has a significant unifying effect on the band.

A second important ritual among the G/wi is the girl's puberty ritual, with which the public announcement of a girl's wedded state is combined; G/wi betrothals precede puberty. This ritual follows classic pattern of a rite of passage (→ Initiation). During ritual, the girl's husband participates and unity of the couple is expressed.

G/wi are typical of Bushmen in that their beliefs picture a world that is inherently good, and would continue to be so save for intervention of a senseless and indiscriminate force of evil. Though misfortune can come because the ghosts or N!odima are angered, evil is more likely to be the working of G//awama. The band does not unite to worship or placate spiritual beings. Nor are individuals singled out as sinners and held responsible for bringing evil to the band. Instead there is a merging of the individual with his fellows in the collective fight against G//awama, the common foe. B.S.

The standard work on Bushman ethnography is I. Schapera, *The Khoisan Peoples* (1930); G/wi religion is described by G. Silberbauer in *The Bushman Report* (Bechuanaland Govt., Gaborone`, 1965).

Bu-Ston Tibetan Buddh. Scholar and historian: b. CE 1290; d. CE 1322, who is credited with collection and arrangement of Buddh. Tibetan canon; author of commentaries on import. Buddh. treatises. Best known for *History of Buddhism*, in two parts, trans. by E. Obermiller (Heidelberg, 1931–2). T.O.L.

Butterfly Because of its transformation from apparent death in its chrysalis stage, the B. became a symbol of → soul and its rebirth. It appears frequently in Minoan and Mycenaean art. The soul (→ Psychē) was repr. as a B. in Grk. art from late 5th cent. BC. A 3rd cent. CE sarcophagus, now in the Museo Capitolino, Rome, shows → Prometheus fashioning men and → Minerva inserting soul in form of B. Grk. word *psychē* could also mean B. or moth. S.G.F.B.

L.R-G., I, p. 113; C. Picard, *Les religions pré-helléniques* (1948), *passim;* Brandon, *C.L.*, pl. X.

Byzantium Grk. city founded in 667 BC at entrance of Bosphorus. Because of strategic position, Emp. Constantine founded a New Rome there in CE 330 which was called after its founder 'Constantinople'. The fall of Western Roman Empire, centred on old Rome, to northern barbarians, left B. unchallenged centre of Graeco-Roman civilisation, as well as capital of Eastern Roman or Byzantine Empire. In 451 the bishopric of B.-Constantinople was raised to status of patriarchate, and because of power and prestige of city, its holders became rivals of Pope. Owing to presence of Emperor, Patriarchs of B.-Const. never acquired power and independence enjoyed by Popes. After years of conflict, a breach finally came in 1054 between W. Church, under Pope, and E. Church, led by Patriarch, who was recognised as Oecumenical Patriarch of the E. from 6th cent. Despite many vicissitudes of fortune, incl. capture and sacking by 4th → Crusade, B. remained centre of a sophisticated Grk. Chr. civilisation, preserving continuity with anc. Graeco-Roman culture in language and literature. It finally fell to Turkish attack in 1453, when most of its anc. churches, incl. the famous Hagia Sophia, were turned into mosques. The Patriarchs continued to reside in city, and were recognised by Turkish government as head of Grk Chr. community. B. developed a distinctive art and architecture which influenced both Christian West and Islam. S.G.F.B.

N. H. Baynes-H. St. L. B. Moss, *Byzantium* (1948); L. Bréhier, *Vie et Mort de Byzance* (1947), *Les Institutions de l'Empire byzantin* (1949), *La Civilisation byzantine* (1950); D. T. Rice, *Art of the Byzantine Era* (1963); *Kleine Pauly*, I, 979–82; D. T. Rice (ed.), *The Dark Ages* (1965), chs. V, VI; N. Zernov, *Eastern Christendom* (1961), pp. 39ff.; S. Runciman, *The Fall of Constantinople, 1453* (1965).

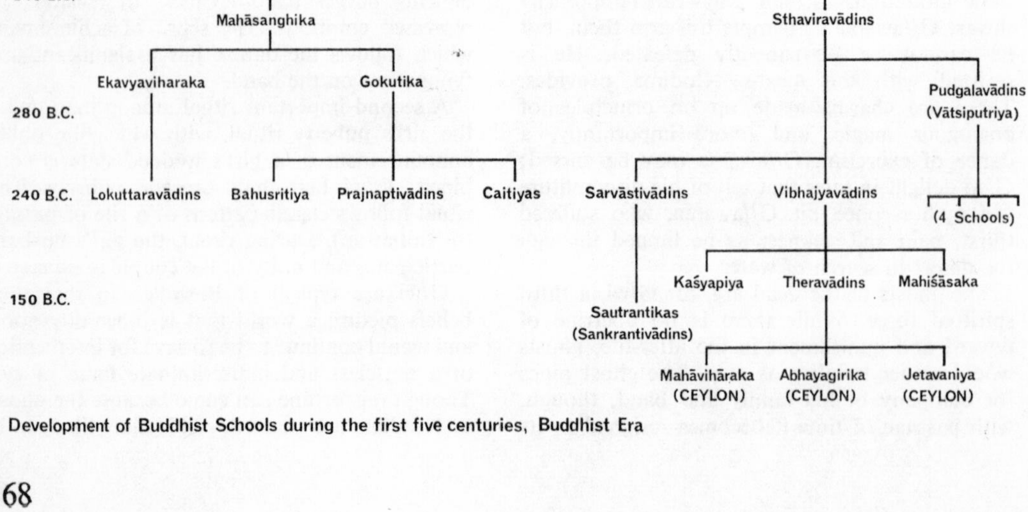

Development of Buddhist Schools during the first five centuries, Buddhist Era

C

Cabbala (Kabbala) Heb. = 'tradition'. A Jew. system of esoteric mystical thought, orig. in the Middle Ages, based on Heb. Bible, but incorp. diverse traditions drawn from →→ Philo, Gnosticism, Pythagoreanism, and Neoplatonism. The text of Heb. Bible was regarded as a complex code concealing profound secrets about God and the world: the interpretation of this code depended upon understanding the significance of the arrangement of letters of text and their numerical value. The chief work of the C. is the *Zohar*. A Chr. form of the C. was developed in 15th-16th cents., partic. by J. Reuchlin and Paracelsus. (→ Judaism). S.G.F.B.
E.R.E., VII, pp. 622–8 ('Kabbala'); Oesterley-Box, *L.R.M.J.*, pp. 235ff.; G. G. Scholem, *Major Trends in Jew. Mysticism* (1946) *Zur Kabbala und ihrer Symbolik* (1960); J. L. Blau, *The Christ. Interpretation of the Cabbala in the Renaissance* (1944); *R.G.G.*[3], III, 1078–9; A. Safran, *La Cabale* (1960).

Cabiri → Chthonian deities, prob. of Phrygian or Phoenician origin, concerned with fertility and protection of sailors. Their cult-centre was Samothrace, where mysteries were celebrated (→ Mystery Religions). The number of the C. varied; where they were thought of as two, they tended to be identified with → Dioscuri. S.G.F.B.
O.C.D., *s.v.*, W. K. C. Guthrie, *Orpheus and Greek Religion* (1952[2]), pp. 123ff.; L. Gernet-A. Boulanger, *Le génie grec dans la religion* (1932), pp. 325, 469; N. Turchi, *Fontes*, pp. 103–15.

Caesaropapism Form of government where an absolute monarch claims and exercises supreme control over Church in matters of faith and practice. C. characterised the Byzantine emperors (→ Byzantium); in W. Christendom Charlemagne and Maximilian I acted thus, and so did Henry VIII in England. S.G.F.B.
L. Bréhier, *Les Institutions de l'Empire byzantin* (1949), chs. I, II; *R.G.G.*, I, 1582, III, pp. 1093–9; N. H. Baynes-H. St.L. B. Moss, *Byzantium* (1948), *passim.*

Caitanya (Sometimes transliterated 'Chaitanya'): a Hindu relig. teacher of 16th cent. (b. 1485 in Bengal). He organised a movement of intense Vaisnavite → *bhakti*, on basis of cult of → Krishna. At age of 24 he became a *samnyasin* and went to Puri in Orissa, and thereafter toured India preaching. He identified himself with Rādhā, the beloved of Krishna—a symbol of the love of man for God and conversely. → Brahman, acc. to C.'s theology, is a personal being who becomes manifest to men in perfect form of the *avatara* Krishna: the theology otherwise is a version of Dvaita (→ Dualism). Salvation follows from true love of Krishna, which is expressed in worshipping and praising God and in humility and forebearingness towards others. C. was concerned to promote a form of fervid congregational worship (*sankīrtana*); out of this arose a whole new genre of vernacular relig. literature. An aspect of the Caitanya school's thought which, though perhaps not orig., is the emphasis on eagerness of God to save men. There was also strong opposition to concept of *sāyujya* or merging of saved soul in → *nirgunam* Brahman, on ground that it obliterated individuality of worshipper and thus made nonsense of eagerness of God to save him. The focussing of faith on Krishna made C. Vaisnavism place special emphasis on concept of → *avatara* and on idea of God's play (*līlā*), the sport symbolized in the Krishna legend, where the cow-maidens represent souls in love with God. The → Tagore family, among other mod. Bengali intellectuals, were influenced by the C. movement's literature and spirit. N.S.
M. T. Kennedy *The Chaitanya Movement* (1925); S. K. De *Early History of the Vaishnava Faith and Movement in Bengal*, 2nd edn. (1961); H. Bhattacharyya *The Cultural Heritage of India*, vol. 4 (rev. edn., 1956).

Cakkappavattana → Dhamma-Cakkappavattana Sutta. T.O.L.

Calendar, Religious Origins The cyclic character of the time-process and its relation to cosmic phenomena must soon have been appreciated by man and utilised in planning his affairs. Agriculture demands calculation of right times for its operations. The moon's phases prob. provided earliest form of time-reckoning, and, since the moon was deified, chronology was thus linked with relig. The Sumerian moon-God → Sin was known as 'lord of the month' (→ Sumerian Religion). Because agriculture in Egypt depended on annual inundation of the Nile, this event had to be calculated in advance. A solar calendar was invented at least as early as 2776 BC, based on coincidence of beginning of inundation with the heliacal rising of Sothis, the Dog-star. This C. was closely related to relig. festivals, some assoc. with legend of → Osiris, whose death and resurrection symbolized life-cycle of vegetation (→ Agriculture). The start of the New Year was regarded as critical occasion, and in many religs. special rituals dealt with it (e.g. the Mesopot. → Akitu). It might be said gen. that needs of agriculture, causing invocation of divine aid, inevitably linked C. with relig. in terms of periodic festivals of supplication or thanksgiving. This pattern became diversified in many religs. in various ways: e.g. by commemoration of notable events such as the Exodus with → Passover in Jew. C., b. and d. of Jesus in Chr. C., and b. and d. of Muhâmmad in Islamic C. (→→ Chronology; Festivals; Americ. Rel. anc.). S.G.F.B.

V. G. Childe, *Man Makes Himself* (1941), pp. 103, 135ff.; O. Neugebauer, *The Exact Sciences in Antiquity* (1957), pp. 81ff.; J. W. S. Sewell in *The Legacy of Egypt*, ed. S. R. K. Glanville (1942), pp. 1ff.; A. L. Basham, *The Wonder that was India* (1954), pp. 492ff.; J. Needham, *Science and Civilisation in China*, II (1956), pp. 269ff.; J. T. Frazer (ed.), *The Voices of Time* (1966), pp. 100ff., 402ff.; G. Van der Leeuw, *La Religion* (1948), 7,6; 55,2; S. G. F. Brandon, *History, Time and Deity* (1965), *passim*. Detailed accounts of calendars and festivals in various religs. are given in *E.R.E.*, II, pp. 61–140, V, pp. 835–94; E. O. James, *Seasonal Feasts and Festivals* (1961).

Caliph (Caliphate) When Muḥammad died, → Abū Bakr was appointed head of community by popular vote in Medina and was called *khalīfa rasūl Allah* (successor of God's messenger). This title ref. to his authority in government, with no suggestion of divine inspiration such as was possessed by Md. → 'Umar, who succeeded him, adopted title *Amir al-mu'minin* (commander of the faithful), which remained ever after as distinctive title of C. The centre was first in Medina. 'Alī, fourth C., moved to Kufa in Iraq; Mu'āwiya, the first → Umayyad C., made Damascus his capital. The → 'Abbasids founded Baghdad, which became capital during most of their period, till Hulagu sacked city in 656/1258; a member of the 'Abbasid family was set up as C. in Egypt. Later, the Turks claimed that the rights had been transferred to them, and the C. remained in their hands till 3rd March 1924, when the Turkish National Assembly abolished it. Ḥusayn, king of the Hijaz, then claimed the C., but in same year Ibn Saud expelled him from his kingdom, since when no serious claim to title has been made, and the office has passed away. The → Zaydī imams, who ruled in the Yemen till recent times, used title *Amīr al-mu'minīn*, but such a local claim had no influ. in the Muslim world at large. In earlier times there was an Umayyad C. in Spain alongside the 'Abbasid; for a time there was a third in Egypt, the → Fatimid, a → Shi'a one brought to end by Saladin. The C. should not be compared with the → Pope. He was head of community in all its affairs; but had no power to decide matters of faith, being only its defender. During long period the C. had no real power when C.s were controlled by other rulers; but there was a certain mystical aura about office, which made rulers value recognition of their position by C.s. (→ 'Alī 'Abd al-Rāziq). J.R.

E.I., II, pp. 881–5, T. W. Arnold, *The Caliphate* (1924); Gaudefroy-Demombynes, *Institutions*, ch. VII; Levy, *Social Structure*, ch. VII.

Calvary A.V.'s rendering of → Vulgate's *locus calvariae*, 'place of the skull' (Lk. 23:33) as designation of site of Christ's crucifixion. The other Gospels use the Aramaic *Gulgultā* ('Golgotha'), having same meaning. The trad. site in Church of Holy Sepulchre dates from 4th cent. (→ Jerusalem). S.G.F.B.

*H.D.B.*², p. 339; A. Parrot, *Golgotha and the Church of the Holy Sepulchre* (E.T. 1957); C. Kopp, *The Holy Places of the Gospels* (E.T. 1963), pp. 374ff.

Calvin, John (1509–63) In the person of C. and city of Geneva, the emerging Reformed trad. of the cities of Switzerland and Rhineland became articulate and consolidated. Geneva at time was in process of freeing itself from feudal overlords, and was entangled with and overshadowed by Bern. The → Reformation was intro. there by William Farel (1489–1565), Antoine Froment and Peter Viret. The years 1532–6 witnessed struggle there with Catholic forces which led to premature victory of Reformers, who, on May 21 1536, met with Council in the Cathedral and swore to live by the Word of God.

C. was born in Noyon, in Picardy. He attended Univ. of Paris, studying under Mathurin Cordier and John Major, and acquiring fluent sensitive style in Latin and French. He took degree in Law at Orleans and returned to humanistic studies, laying foundation of his immense learning in Bible and the Fathers. In the uproar surrounding the Rectorial address of Nicholas Cop in Univ. of Paris (1st. Nov. 1533), C. had to go into hiding, where he wrote his first theological tract the *Psychopannychia*, attacking the → Anabaptist doctrine of the sleep of souls after death. In 1534 he went to Basle, where, at house of Thomas Platter, he printed first small ed. of his *Christianae*

Religionis Institutio. C. went on to Geneva, intending to study scholarly pursuits, but was conjured into assisting reformation by pious imprecations of Farel. The attempt to carry through thoroughgoing reformation in Geneva being held up by interference of Bern and claims of city council, in 1538 C. and Farel left the city. C. then spent three fruitful years in Strasbourg as pastor of French congregation, where he learned much from what he saw and from thought of Martin Bucer about Church, ministry and liturgy. In 1541 he produced a marvellously lucid French ed. of his now enlarged and ever enlarging *Institutes* and a tract on the Lord's Supper (1540), which was something between the Lutheran and Zwinglian positions. At request of the Genevan magistrates, he returned in 1541, and they accepted his blue print for reformation, the *Ordonnances Ecclésiastiques*. C. found in Scripture a four-fold ministry of pastors, teachers, elders and deacons, and, though he had to fight hard and long for it, he insisted on leaving discipline in hands of Church. He now published his simplified liturgy and a catechism, and in the next years came to dominate spiritual and moral life of city, though content to be simply a member of the 'company of pastors' who gathered round him. He cared greatly for education, and brought the best teachers he could find to Geneva; in this work, as in much else, he found an able colleague and successor in Théodore Béza.

Such a man and such a career must inevitably create opposition and enemies, and there was always a party opposed to C. in Geneva. In addition, there were theological conflicts with Caroli and Castellio. Most tragic of these conflicts was with the anti-Trinitarian Spanish scholar Servetus, who was captured in Geneva, and executed, after a long theological inquisition from C. and the pastors, and with approval of most of Prot. and Cath. world. Under C., Geneva itself became a training ground for exiles from France, Scotland and England; in the 1560's both C. and Béza kept in constant touch with happenings in France. In 1559 the *Institutes* was given its final massive shape of 84 chapters, constituting an immensely learned Prot. *summa*, embodying Scripture, the Fathers, → Luther and Calvin's own theology. This, together with C.'s more dynamic conception of Chr. obedience and more democratic Church polity, created a new form of Protestantism capable of extension and development in other lands in succeeding centuries. E.G.R.

T. H. L. Parker, *A Portrait of Calvin* (1954); J. T. McNeill, *History and Character of Calvinism* (1954); W. Niesel, *Calvin's Theology* (1956).

Cambodia and Laos (Buddhism in) Like other countries of S.E. Asia, Cambodian relig. was, in earlier period of medieval history a mixture of → Brahmanism and Mhy. Buddhism. The Khmer kingdom, of which mod. Cambodia is survival, with its centre at Angkor, was in former times of great influence and importance in the Indo-Chinese peninsula and was strongly Hindu in culture. The description of Cambodian affairs in years 1296–7 given by a Chinese envoy, Chao Ta-Kuan (French trans. by P. Pelliot, *Bulletin de l'École française d'Extrême-Orient*, II, 123), shows at end of 13th cent. Theravāda Buddh. monks were one of 3 principal relig. groups in country (the others being Hindu → brahmans and → Saivites). In 14th cent., as result of growing influence of the Thais, who had now estab. Ayudhaya (see Thailand, Buddhism in) as capital, and accepted the Sinhalese, → Theravāda form of Bhm., Cambodia became more predominantly Theravādin and has continued so until present. From Cambodia, Ther. Bhm. was intro. into newly founded state of Laos in 14th cent. A Thai prince, brought up by a Buddh. monk in old Cambodian capital at Angkor, and himself son-in-law of king of Cambodia proclaimed himself king at Lan Ch'ang (modern Luang Prabang) in 1353; he founded the state of Laos, which also, since 14th cent., been a predominantly Ther. Buddh. country, having strong links with the Buddh. Order in neighbouring Thailand (the Lao people themselves being of same ethnic group as Thais). T.O.L.

G. Coedès, *Les États hindouisés D'Indochine et d'Indonésie* (1964); *The Making of South-East Asia* (1966); D. Deydier, *Introduction à la connaissance du Laos* (1952); M. L. Manich, *History of Laos* (1967).

(Hinduism in) The area covered by mod. state of Cam. was one of earliest in S.E. Asia to become Hinduised → (*Hinduism: Intro. into S.E. Asia*). Chinese dynastic chronicles of 2nd cent. CE ref. to a kingdom of Fu-nan situated in area of Mekong delta. The name Fu-nan is Chinese form of word *bnam*, or *phnom*, frequently found in this part of Indochina, meaning 'mountain'. The full title of ruler of state was *kurung-bnam*, 'the king of the mountain'; a title commonly assumed also by Hindu kings in India, e.g. Pallava kings of S. India, and appears to have been a ref. to cult adopted by king, the cult of a mountain deity who was pre-eminent above other local deities. In its Skt. form, Shailendra or Shailaraja, the title occurs later in connection with other S.E. Asian dynasties. From what is said in Chinese chronicles it appears that state of Fu-nan was organised largely along Indian lines. Evidence of practice of Hindu cults in Fu-nan has been found in Sanskrit inscriptions which ref. to worship of 'the god Maheshvara (i.e. the great god, or → Shiva)' and to cult of → Vishnu. (G. Coedès, 'Deux inscriptions sanskrites du Fou-nan', *Bulletin de l'École française d'Extrême-Orient*, XXXI, 1.) Statues of Vishnu-Krishna belonging to period of Fu-nan kingdom have been found at Angkor Borei, the kingdom's last capital (R. Le May, *The Culture of S.E. Asia*, p. 113). At end of 5th cent. CE a Buddhist monk from Fu-nan, on visit to emperor of China, reported to him that both Buddhist and Brahman forms of relig. were practised in Fu-nan.

By beginning of 9th cent. CE Fu-nan's control of territory was challenged by the Khmers, a people living in upper Mekong valley in what had until then been the tributary kingdom of Chan-la. Its kings also bore Sanskritic names, from at least time of 6th cent. Khmer King Bhavavarman, who was a prince of Fu-nan kingdom. By 9th cent. the Khmer King Jayavarman II controlled whole area now known as Cambodia, and moved its capital to N. of great lake Tonle Sap. He estab. a Khmer dynasty which was to rule Kambuja for next six cents. The Khmers inherited Indianised royal culture of Fu-nan kings, and of their neighbours, the Chams whose kingdom extended over E. coastal area of what is now Vietnam. This entailed principally worship of Shiva and recognition of king as human representative of god, a role which king entered upon by means of ceremony carried out by Brahman priests at summit of a temple-mountain or pyramid, in which the → *linga*, or stone phallic symbol of god Shiva, became also symbol of king's divinity. The royal Shaivite cult of Khmer kingdom centred upon rituals connected with linga-sanctuary at summit of temple. Excavations have revealed a number of such temples used by Khmer kings before building of those at Angkor, in 12th cent. CE. Like Angkor temples, these earlier Khmer sacred 'mountains' appear to have been surmounted by a monolith, testifying to continuity of cult of *linga* from earlier period, when, as we noted, ruler's title was 'king of the sacred mountain'. The pattern of Khmer kingship seems to have combined Indian features with indigeneous features, incl. ancestor worship. The temple-mountain was replica of Mount Meru, which in Indian mythology was centre of cosmos, and from which → Indra or Shiva reigned as supreme god. But Khmer sanctuaries were also mausoleums, which would become abode of king when he died; the worship which centred upon it would combine personal name of king with the supreme deity, Indra, Shiva or Vishnu, or even a → *bodhisattva* of Mahāyāna Buddhism. After death of king, it would thus become, for his successors, a centre of ancestor worship. Such a cult was elaborate and expensive, and would have made great demands on resources of kingdom; it indic. a centralised authoritarian power which could command these resources from the people. In return the king was their protector, the guarantor of property and welfare. The economic basis of Hinduised Khmer has been investigated by B. Ph. Groslier (*Angkor et le Cambodge au XVIe siècle d'apres les sources portugaises et espagnoles*, Paris, 1958), who finds that it was of a kind known elsewhere as 'hydraulic civilisations' (see Karl A. Wittfogel, *Oriental Despotisms*, 1957), i.e., it was based on centralised and rationalised use of all available water-supplies, administered centrally by authoritarian ruler. 'La religion fondamentale de la société Khmère, sous son brillant manteau indien, fut le culte des eaux et du sol.' (Groslier *op. cit.*, 116). The acceptance by Khmers of Hindu cults of Shiva and Vishnu, and even of Mahayana *bodhisattvas*, prestigious as these were in S. Asian world, may thus be seen as having also been facilitated by fact that they could so readily be harmonised with indigenous relig. economic factors, and which, as D. G. E. Hall says, 'hark back to a condition of society anterior to any impact of Indian influence' (*A History of S.E. Asia*, 125). So far as the people were concerned, it is prob. that their relig. beliefs and practices continued largely undisturbed in the spirit- and ancestor-worshipping trad. common to much of S.E. and E. Asia, apart from such demands as would have been made upon them by this aristocratic cult of the divine king. The results of this situation were seen in end of Khmer kingdom, in 15th cent. CE, when it was overthrown by the Thais, who had been moving into the Menam valley during previous cents. For, combined with expansion of Thai political power, another process had been going on at a more popular level: → Theravada Buddhism, which had for cents. been practised by the Mon peoples in the west of S.E. Asian mainland, was penetrating eastwards among people of Menam valley, and had now reached the Khmer people. 'This religion was economical, its ministers were pledged to poverty, contenting themselves with a straw roof and a handful of rice, a moral religion whose principles assured peace of soul and social tranquility.' (Louis Finot, qu. by G. Coedès, *Angkor: An Introduction*, 1963, p. 107). As D. G. E. Hall points out the monks of Theravāda Buddhism 'were in direct contact with the people, and they undermined completely the old state religion and all that went with it.' (*op. cit.*, p. 119).

The Khmer relig. pattern of the god-king, the *Deva-rāja*, which in outward forms had been so strongly influenced by Hinduism, and whose administrants had been Brahman priests, was thus superseded by Theravāda Buddhism, which has remained principal relig. trad. of C., though not without the continuance to present day of much of Hindu mythology and cosmology which had become part of Cambodian culture during Khmer period, esp. those features which are harmonious with Theravāda Buddhism. (→→ *Hinduism: Introduction into S.E. Asia*). T.O.L.

G. Coedès, *Pour Mieux Comprendre Angkor* (1943, 2nd edn., 1947), tr. (condensed) by E. F. Gardiner, *Angkor: An Introduction* (1963); *Les États Hindouisés d'Indochine et d'Indonésie*, 3rd edn. (1964); *The Making of S.E. Asia* (1966); B. Ph. Groslier, *Indochina: Art in the Melting Pot of Races* (1962); D. G. E. Hall, *A History of South-East Asia* (1964).

Canaanite Religion The Canaanites occupied territory later known as Palestine and Syria from *c.* 3,000 BC. They were Semites, and closely akin to Hebrews, who were profoundly influenced by them in both relig. and culture, as the O.T. indicates and archaeology attests. C-R. was little known until discovery of Execration Texts at Luxor and Sakkara and ritual and mythological texts at → Ugarit. C-R. was polytheistic, and chiefly of a fertility kind. The senior god was El (= 'god'), who was described as 'the Father of Men': in art he is shown as seated, wearing bull's horns, signifying strength. El is a passive figure comp. with → Baal, who personified divine power in conflict with forces of chaos and disorder, being young and vigorous. 'Baal' was actually the title of Hadad, god of the fertilising autumn rains. Baal was son of → Dagon, a corn deity. Fertility goddesses were → Anat, → Ashera, and → Astarte. They were usually repr. nude, with emphasised sexual features, and were served by sacred → prostitues. Less prominent deities were Reshef, Horon, Athtar, and those of sun and moon. Worship centred around sacrifice of animals (sheep and cattle), incl. act of communion by ritual eating of part of victim by devotees. The Ugarit texts record myths concerning Baal's contest with power of chaotic water, prob. related to New Year festival (autumn), and with Mot, who personified drought and sterility. The latter myth tells of Baal's death and resurrection, and of concern of Anat, who slays Mot, treating him as grain. The legends of Krt and Aqht, found at Ugarit, record fortunes of heroes and providence of deities for them. At a New Year festival the king prob. underwent ritual humiliation as in Babylonian → Akitu. (→→ Ugarit; Phoenician Relig.). S.G.F.B.

C. F. A. Schaeffer, *The Cuneiform Texts of Ras Shamra-Ugarit* (1939); G. R. Driver, *Canaanite Myths and Legends* (1956); R. Dussaud, *Les religions des Hittites et des Hourrites, des Phéniciens et des Syriens* (1945), pp. 355ff.; J. Gray, *The Canaanites* (1964), ch. V; *Legacy of Canaan* (1965), *R.G.G.*³, I, 1109–13; *A.N.E.T.*, pp. 128–55; R. De Langhe, in *Myth, Ritual and Kingship*, ed. S. H. Hooke (1958), ch. V; C. H. Gordon, *M.A.W.*, pp. 181ff.; K. M. Kenyon, *Amorites and Canaanites* (1966); Albright, *Y.G.C.*

Cannibalism The relig. significance of C. finds its earliest literary expression in the → Pyramid Texts. The dead pharaoh is acclaimed as one who devours gods: 'He it is that eateth their magic and swalloweth their lordliness' (A. Erman, *Literature of Anc. Egyptians*, E. T., 1927, pp. 6ff.). Among primitive peoples, from Paleolithic era, there is evidence of ritual C., obviously inspired by idea that by eating one's enemy, or a powerful person, his strength and abilities could be absorbed. Skulls were similarly used as drinking vessels. C. has often been connected with human sacrifice (e.g. with Maoris and anc. Mexicans), the motive then perhaps being that of achieving communion with victim sacrificed to the deity. (→ American Relig. anc.). S.G.F.B.

E.R.E., II, *s.v.*; E. O. James, *Origins of Sacrifice* (1937), chs. 3 and 4.

Canon Law Chr. eccles. rules or laws, concerning matters of faith, morals, and discipline, issued by various Councils and authorities of high repute. In 12th cent. a collection was made by Gratian, a monk of Bologna, to which were added Decretals of Pope Gregory IX, to form the *Corpus Iuris Canonici*, which remained chief corpus of C-L. in R.C. Church until 1917, when it was superseded by the *Codex Iuris Canonici*. Canons were issued in Ch. of → England in 1603–4; a reviewed set is still under consideration. The relation between C-L., or Church law, and civil law varies from country to country, and is usually very involved. S.G.F.B.

D.C.C., pp. 228, 230, 307, 346; *R.G.G.*³, III, 1501–10; IX, pp. 56ff.; H. Hess, *The Canons of Council of Sardica, AD 343* (1958); R. C. Mortimer, *Western Canon Law* (1953).

Canon of New Testament The Grk. word 'canon', meaning 'rod for measuring', is first used of books of N.T. by Amphilochius, bishop of Iconium (end of 4th cent.). Thus used, it meant list of books officially recognised as suitable for reading at public worship. Implicit in this recognition was evaluation of such books as authoritative for Chr. faith and practice. The formation of the C. was a gradual process. The heretic → Marcion (*c.* 140) had a C. comprising Gospel of Luke and 10 Epistles of Paul. Such a collection suggests that an orthodox C. of some kind already existed. The liturgical use of Gospels, which implied selection, is attested by → Justin Martyr (*c.* 150). The oldest extant list of

N.T. books is the 'Muratorian Fragment', prob. dating from end of 2nd cent., recording C. at Rome. It appears to know the 4 Gospels, Acts, and 13 Epistles of Paul, and includes Jude, 2 Epistles of John and Revelation. It also contains Book of → Wisdom and → Apocalypse of → Peter, and commends → Hermas for private reading. In writings of subsequent Fathers a list of accepted books approx. to those of N.T. grad. emerges. The process of definition was finally completed in 5th cent. due to recognition of present C. by → Augustine of Hippo, whose personal influence was immense, and → Jerome, whose → Vulgate was accepted as standard version of Bible by W. Church. No General Council, however, pronounced on C.; the Council of → Trent did so in 16th cent. The inclusion of some books in C., e.g. Ep. to Hebrews and Revelation, was for long doubtful. The C. rests mainly on trad. and usage. S.G.F.B.

B. F. Westcott, *A General Survey of Hist. of Canon of New Test* (1870); *P.C.*², pp. 679ff.; *H.D.B.*), pp. 123–7; *R.G.G.*³, III, 1119–22; *D.C.C.*, pp. 229–30; A. A. T. Ehrhardt, *The Framework of the New Test. Stories* (1964), pp. 11–36.

(of Old Testament) → Bible. S.G.F.B.

(of Scripture, Buddhist) → Tipitaka. T.O.L.

Canonisation In early Church veneration of martyrs was a natural reaction, which grad. developed to include other saintly persons. Local bishops controlled cults in their own areas, though often fame of saint spread elsewhere. The first attested case of Papal C. was that of Ulrich of Augsburg in 993. From 12th cent. Popes claimed sole right to canonise, and provision was accordingly made in → Canon Law. C. is distinguished from → Beatification, in that Pope formally declares that a person, formerly beatified, has already entered eternal glory, and ordains a public cult throughout R.C. Church. C. authorises dedication of churches in saint's memory, festivals and masses in his or her honour, invocation in public prayers, pictorial representation adorned with halo, veneration of relics. In → E. Church C. is authorised in an autocephalous church, and other autocephalous churches are informed. S.G.F.B.

E.R.E., II, *s.v.; D.C.C.*, *s.v.; R.G.G.*³, III, 171–5, 175–6 ('Heiligsprechnung'); N. Zernov, *Eastern Christendom* (1961), pp. 233ff.; *C.E.*, II, *s.v.* ('Beatification and C').

Canterbury Owing to fact that C. was capital of King Ethelbert of Kent, who received evangelising mission from Rome, headed by Augustine in 597, it became the primatial see of Church of England instead of London, with Augustine as its first Archbishop. The see of C. has continued to hold this primacy ever since: the Archbp. of C. has unique position in English Church and State, being chief ministrant at coronation of monarch. C. Cathedral was famous in Middle Ages for shrine of St. Thomas Becket. The principal residence of Archbp. of C. is at Lambeth Palace, London. S.G.F.B.

*D.C.C., s.v.; R.G.G.*³, I, 1610; J. Godfrey, *The Church in Anglo-Saxon England* (1962), pp. 71ff.; H. Batsford-C. Fry, *The Cathedrals of England*⁶ (1944), pp. 14ff.

Canopic Jars Trad. name given to four jars in which principal organs of a deceased person were placed, acc. to anc. Egypt. mortuary practice. The C-J. were deposited in tomb, usually in a special chest. Each jar had a lid repr. one of the sons of → Horus, who protected contents. (→ Funerary Rites, Egypt.) S.G.F.B.

E. A. W. Budge, *The Mummy* (1925), pp. 240–6⁶ *R.Ae.R-G.*, pp. 365–8.

Cargo Cults Cults of Messianic (→ Messianism) and nationalist character which arose among many peoples of Melanesia. (→ Melanesian Relig.) after Second World War. The spectacle of Japanese and American forces arriving on their shores in vessels packed with equipment and food inspired idea that ancestors of tribes would so come, bringing vast cargoes of goods to estab. an age of plenty and well-being. S.G.F.B.

M. Mead, *New Lives for Old* (1956); P. Worsley, *The Trumpet Shall Sound: a study of Cargo Cults in Melanesia* (1957).

Carnival Period of festivity in R.C. countries of 3 days preceding Ash Wednesday. Name is often explained as derived from *carne vale*, i.e. 'flesh, farewell', thus relating it to Lenten fast, which started on Ash Wednesday. In Germanic countries C. is called *Fastnacht*, a term having similar meaning. There is also reason for thinking that C. may derive from Roman words *car navale*, commemorating ship-cart used in procession connected with cults of → Isis and → Dionysus. A pre-Christian origin of the C. is prob.; but many pagan trads. have contributed to it. incl. a spring festival concerned with cult of dead, current in Greece and Rome and among anc. Celts and Germans. S.G.F.B.

E.R.E., II, *s.v.; R.G.G.*³, II, 887 ('Fastnacht').

Carpe diem Lat. expression 'seize the day', used to describe attitude to life, based on disbelief in immortality, which counsels the exploiting of joys of this life to fullest. C.D. finds earliest lit. expression in Egypt and Mesopot: cf. Egypt. 'Song of the Harper' (*c.* 2000 BC) and Epic of → Gilgamesh. It occurs in many other cultures: e.g. Heb. Wisdom lit.; Grk. lit. and philosophy (→ Epicurus); Rome; India; China. C.D. repr. an inevitable deduction about human life, when uninspired by a powerful eschatology that convinces men of a significant *post-mortem* existence. S.G.F.B.

Brandon, *M.-D.*, *passim* (with bibliog.).

Carpocrates Reputed founder of Gnostic sect of Carpocratians: (his existence has been doubted by some scholars). C.'s son, Epiphanes, who died aged 17, was apparently worshipped as a deity at Cephalonia: there is poss. some connection here with Egypt. cult of Harpocrates (→ Horus). Acc. to Chr. writers, C. taught that world was created by → Archon(tes), to whom souls of men were enslaved. The soul of Jesus had been able to crush passions that subject men to the Archons. The enlightened (i.e. Carpocratians) could have same or even greater power. The C. believed in → reincarnation, and were alleged to have sought every kind of experience, incl. sexual promiscuity, on principle that reincarnation ceases only when total experience is achieved. Acc. to → Irenaeus, the doc. of C. was propagated with much success in Rome by Marcellina, when Anicetus was Pope (*c.* 155). Irenaeus also records that Carpocratians venerated images of →→ Christ, Pythagoras, Plato and → Aristotle. The obviously tendentious accounts of Chr. writers indic. eclectic form of → Gnosticism, with a Chr. veneer. S.G.F.B.

Irenaeus, *adv. haer.*, I, 25; Clement of Alex. *Strom.*, III, 5, 2ff.; R. M. Grant, *Gnosticism* (1961), pp. 36–40; *R.G.G.*³, III, 1159.

Carthaginian Religion Carthage founded by Phoenicians in 814 BC, flourished greatly, challenging Rome for empire in Mediterranean world in 3rd and 2nd cents. BC. After its fall in 146 BC, Carthaginian influence remained strong in N. Africa and C. language (Punic) survived for many cents. The Phoenic. colonists took their relig. to N. Africa, and a relig. link between C. and Phoenicia was long preserved (→ Phoenician Religion). The chief gods of C. were Baal Hammon (who may repr. an assimilation of a Phoenic. → Baal and Egypt. Ammon of Siwa oasis (→ Amun)); Tanit, who was prob. → Astarte; Melqart, the god of Tyre, whom Greeks identified with → Heracles; → Eshmun (→ Adonis); Reshuf, Phoenic. storm god. These deities, exc. Reshuf, were later given Roman names, respectively as → Saturn, Caelestis, → Aesculapius and Hercules. Tanit is usually called in inscriptions 'Tanit Pene Baal' (lit. 'Tanit Face of Baal'): the title is explained as either 'reflection of Baal' or as local name. Baal Hammon and Tanit are often linked as pair. Tanit was distinguished by enigmatic symbol of triangle, surmounted by disc, with a cross-arm dividing the two figures: it is somewhat reminiscent of Egypt. → *ankh*. Egypt. deities were known, → Bes being esp. popular. There was also a cult of → Demeter/Kore. The precinct of Tanit at C. has provided abundant evidence, extending over long period, of infant sacrifice by fire. The calcined bones were placed in urns and marked by stone stelae; the inscriptions are *ex-voto* to Tanit Pene Baal and Baal Hammon (→ Moloch). Sanctuaries were served by priests and priestesses, from aristocratic families. The dead were carefully buried in elaborately excavated tombs, and equipped with grave goods. An Hellenisation of C-R. can be traced from mid. 5th cent. BC. S.G.F.B.

S. Gsell, *Histoire ancienne de l'Afrique du Nord*, IV (1929); G.-G. Lapeyre-A. Pellegrin, *Carthage punique* (1942), pp. 125ff.; G. C. Picard, *Les religions de l'Afrique antique* (1954), pp. 26ff.; D. Harden, *The Phoenicians* (1962), ch. VII.

Cārvāka Principal name given to philosophical materialism in the Indian trad.: the name derives from that of the legendary founder of school. The doc. was also called *lokāyata*, i.e. the view that there is no world beyond the *loka*, the empirical cosmos, and *svabhāvavāda* or naturalism (lit. 'the doc. that things come to be on their own'). Materialists tended to criticise relig. beliefs and institutions vigorously, and were active from at least the 6th cent. BC. The school remained import. until medieval period, when it virtually disappeared. In early period, since non-Brahmanical movements (such as → Jainism) explained change in the world by recourse to principle of *karma*, rather than creation by God, the materialists produced arguments against belief in the soul and in rebirth: thus consciousness was explained as an emergent property arising out of a particular type of blend of material elements (just as alcoholic potency arises as a new property when certain materials are blended). Materialists were also esp. critical of ritual and privileged position of → Brahmins. The classical materialist texts have largely disappeared, but there survives the 7th cent. CE *Tattvapaplasimha* ('Lion assaulting all philosophical principles'). N.S.

Dale Riepe *The Naturalistic Tradition in Indian Thought* (1960); D. Chattopadhyaya *Lokayata: Ancient Indian Materialism* (1959).

Cassian, John (*c.* 360–435) Monk of Levantine orig., who settled at Marseilles, where he founded two monasteries. C.'s *Institutes* deals with ordering and problems of monastic life, and was largely influential in W. monasticism: St. → Benedict used it. C. was prob. founder of semipelagianism (→ Pelagius). He is regarded as saint in E. Church, but was never officially canonised in W. S.G.F.B.

*D.C.C., s.v.; R.G.G.*³, I, 1626.

Caste (Buddhist attitude) Caste, of Indian type, has strictly no place in Buddh. social structure. In rejecting role of → brahmans as guardians and transmitters of sacrificial system, the Buddha implicitly rejected their claim to pre-eminent social status, and ritual hierarchical structure of Indian society of which brahman supremacy was key-stone. Early disciples of Buddha were from various social strata: a few brahmans, some → kshatriyas ('landed gentry'), a large number from vaishya (merchant) class, and some from shudra or labourer class. In becoming a disciple of Buddha, one shed former hereditary lineage (*gotra*) and became member of (spiritual) lineage of Buddha. (*Vis. IV:* 74). Within the early → *Sangha* there were no distinctions on grounds of former caste membership; honour was accorded to those who were spiritually advanced, or who were seniors, or 'elders' → *Thera,* in terms of years of membership of Sangha. This attitude to caste distinctions continued to characterise Sangha throughout most of its hist.; in Ceylon, however, a caste-system exists among Buddhists, both of cen. Kandyan highlands, and of lowlands. The highest and most numerous caste is the Goigama; the caste incl. not only Buddhist laymen, but also monks whose family are of this caste. The tendency of Goigama to separate themselves from others even in matters of Buddh. devotion at local temple is, however, even by them occasionally seen to be basically inconsistent with Buddh. principles (Cf. Ryan, *op. cit.*, pp. 121ff.). T.O.L.

D. D. Kosambi, *The Culture and Civilization of Ancient India* (1965), ch. 5; Nyanamoli, *The Path of Purification* (1964), pp. 142ff.; R. Pieris, *Sinhalese Social Organisation* (1956); Ryan, B., *Caste in Modern Ceylon* (1953), *Sinhalese Village* (1958); Nur Halman, 'The Flexibility of Caste Principles in a Kandyan Community', in E. R. Leach (ed.), *Aspects of Caste in S. India, Ceylon, and N.W. Pakistan* (1960).

Caste system (Hindu) The caste-system of trad. Hinduism has various roots. First, in Vedic times there was a division of people into four classes or → varnas (lit. 'colours'). The upper three, →→ Brahmins, Ksatriyas and Vaisyas were 'twice-born', and so fully initiated into the → Aryan community. The fourth class, the Sudras, was drawn from the subjugated population. In theory the classes were tied to social function and were, within certain limits, endogamous—hypergamy (a woman marrying a man of higher class), however, being permitted. Second, there was the development of endogamy and commensality, relatively late in evolution of classical Hinduism, among craft and professional groups within the four varnas. Third, there was the gradual assimilation of tribal and other groups (such as adherents of unorthodox relig. movements, such as → Jainism) into the gen. social structure. The formation of a pan-Indian structure was facilitated by spread of Sanskrit as the literary and administrative medium of the upper classes and the consequent reinforcement of the position of Brahmins, as mediators of Sanskrit. The first and third of the above factors were prob. the most important, since notions of ritual purity were increasingly influential with spread of Brahmanical ritual, which itself depended on division between Brahmins and others; while clan groups of tribal origin were maintained in village society, and were naturally tied, with the differentiation of economic roles, to craft and manual occupations. Perhaps the Portuguese term *casta,* which is at basis of the English 'caste', was not an altogether mistaken one to use, for the Portuguese, on coming to India, saw Indian society as a system of exclusive clan and family groups. While the ancient Sanskrit law-books (→ Law of Manu) were primarily concerned with varna, the later writings concentrated more on caste proper. A caste is a wider group than the family, is normally tied to craft or occupation and typically involves endogamy and commensality. The caste groups are more immediately import. than the varnas, and are controlled in a guild-like way, having power to expel members, with dire social effects. With spread of Sanskrit culture and dominance of the four earlier classes, a fifth class came into existence, the 'untouchables'—later to be dubbed Harijans by Gandhi. Among these the best known group is that of the Caṇḍālas, who had the most impure occupations. In theory also the foreigner or *mleccha* was also untouchable; but such outsiders were often assimilated to the appropriate varna (e.g. Greek rulers having the status of ksatriyas). The castes themselves tended to change relative status up and down. Within groups theoretically outside the caste-system, caste phenomena (naturally modified considerably) tended to develop, e.g. among Muslim and Christ. converts. Some of the caste rules, e.g. regarding commensality, proved hard to follow in the mod. era, with railways, industrialisation, urbanisation, etc.; and a further impetus to change was given by Gandhi's campaign on behalf of the untouchables. However, caste groups can acquire new functions in an urban environment, where a wider-than-family organisation is a form of insurance against poverty and a means of promoting education, etc., for members of group. The survival of such an elaborate system is partly due to way in which it provided a framework for the living together of very diverse social and religious groups. This is reflected in manner in which religious duties, etc., depend much on caste allegiance—one reason for the continuance of the great diversity of beliefs and practices within Hinduism. N.S.

J. H. Hutton *Caste in India* (1961); J. Jolly *Hindu Law and Custom* (1928); L. Dumont *Homo*

Hierarchicus (1966); G. S. Ghurye *Caste, Class and Occupation* (1962); J. M. Mahar *India: A Critical Bibliography* (1964).

Castration The most notable instance of C. in connection with relig. is in cult of → Cybele. A twofold problem is involved here: acc. to legend of → Attis, the youthful lover of Cybele castrated himself; the priests of Cybele (*galli*) *actually* castrated themselves in honour of goddess. It is possible that self-C. of Attis is aetiological, to explain self-emasculation of priests of Cybele. The orig. purpose of such ritual C. has been much debated. C. G. Jung even suggested that it resulted from guilt or fear of incest. The action seems prob. connected with fact that the *galli* wore female attire, which may indicate that male devotees of Great Mother sought by C. and attire to assimilate themselves to her. The alleged custom of burying the severed parts in earth also suggests some fertility motif, since Cybele was goddess of fertility. C. of youths has occurred among some primitive peoples of modern world, poss. in connection with phallic worship. The C. of deities in cosmogonic myths (→ Cosmogony) occurs in Hittite and Greek mythology (e.g. Kumarbi gives birth to Hittite gods through swallowing genitals of Anu; Cronos castrates → Uranos, and is in turn castrated by → Zeus). C. could also have another significance: it excluded from 'assembly of Yahweh' (Deut. 23:1.), and it disqualifies from Catholic priesthood. Self-C. has been known in Christianity, the most celebrated case being of → Origen, who took Mt. 19:12 literally. C. was practised by Russian heretical sect of Skoptzy, who also mutilated female genitals and breasts. The C. of boys, to preserve their voices for Papal choir, was finally condemned by Pope Benedict XIV. The making of eunuchs for social purposes has occurred among many peoples; it has also been decreed as penalty for rape and adultery in many legal codes. S.G.F.B.

E.R.E., V, pp. 579–85 ('Eunuch'); C. G. Jung, *Symbols of Transformation* (E.T. 1952), pp. 204, 426ff.; H. G. Güterbock in *M.A.W.*, pp. 156ff.; Brandon, *C.L.*, pp. 171ff.; H. Licht, *Sexual Life in Anc. Greece* (E.T. 1949), pp. 507ff.; *R.A.C.*, V, p. 357–8.

Casuistry Term used in R.C. moral theology for application of gen. moral principles to particular cases. The development of private → Confession made the art or science of C. necessary for giving guidance and assessing penance. The subject has also been dealt with by some Anglican divines, notably Bp. J. Taylor and Bp. K. E. Kirk. (→ Christ. Ethics) C. was used by Jew. rabbis in determining application of → Torah. S.G.F.B.

E.R.E., III, *s.v.; D.C.C.*, pp. 244, 770; *R.G.G.*³, III, 1166–71.

Catacombs The Chr. C.s at Rome are most notable for their part in Early Chr. life, and for evidence they provide of that life. Because Roman law protected burial-places, Christians used C. both for burial of their dead and worship during → persecutions. The C. are situated outside city, and consist of labyrinths of galleries excavated from soft rock. Niches (*loculi*) were made in walls for bodies, and were then sealed with stone slab, inscribed with name of deceased, some relig. formula and symbols. Many martyrs were buried in C., and → Eucharist was celebrated there on their anniversaries. Use of C. declined in 5th cent., and relics of martyrs were transferred to churches. The C. were rediscovered in 16th cent., and their subsequent exploration has provided many paintings, inscriptions, and sarcophagi. Jew. C. at Rome have provided much archeological evidence. S.G.F.B.

L. Hertling–E. Kirschbaum, *The Roman Catacombs and their Martyrs* (E.T. 1960); *D.C.C.*, *s.v.;* F. Grossi Grande, *I Monumenti cristiani* (1923), pp. 274ff.; *R.G.G.*³, III, 1171–4.

Çatal Hüyük Recent excavations of this Anatolian site have revealed the largest Neolithic settlement in Near East, dating from 7th mil. BC. It is esp. notable for forty shrines distributed over nine building levels, thus indicating long continuity of cult. The chief deity was a goddess, manifested as a young woman, mother in childbirth, and old woman. A male deity appears as youth, son or lover of goddess, and as bearded figure assoc. with bull. Decoration of shrines also suggests bull-cult, and concern with death: murals show large black vultures menacing headless bodies, and models of female breasts contain symbols of death (→ Breast); skulls were also found. Ç-H. suggests beginnings of cult of Mother Goddess that later became widespread in Asia Minor and Aegean area (→ Great Goddess). S.G.F.B.

J. Mellaart, *Earliest Civilizations of the Near East* (1965), pp. 77ff.; *Çatal Hüyük* (1967).

Catechism *Ex.* Grk. *katēkein*, 'to make to hear', i.e. 'to instruct'. C. orig. meant oral instruction in Chr. faith given to candidates for → Baptism. Later term was used for book of elementary instruction in faith. There have been many such. Medieval C.s incl. explanations of Lords' Prayer and → Creed, and lists of mortal sins etc. → Reformation saw great proliferation of C.s, e.g. → Luther's *Kleiner Katechismus* (1529); Calvinist *Heidelberger Katechismus* (1563); C. in → Book of Common Prayer as preparation for → Confirmation (1549, 1604); R.C. C.s of St. Peter Canisius, *Summa Doctrinae Christianae* (1554), and *A Catechism of Christian Doctrine*, known as the 'Penny Catechism' (1898). S.G.F.B.

E.R.E., III, *s.v.; D.C.C.*, *s.v.;* W. K. L. Clarke,

Liturgy and Worship (1932), pp. 429ff.; *R.G.G.*³, III, 1175–88; *C.E.*, V, pp. 85ff.

Catechumens *Ex.* Grk. *katēchoumenoi*, designation of those undergoing instruction for → Baptism in Early Church. They formed a distinct group, owing to long preparation for Baptism, administered usually only at Easter. The C. were permitted to attend first part (i.e. to the → Anaphora) of → Eucharist or Mass, which was known as *Missa Catechumenorum* in contrast to the whole *Missa Fidelium*, which the baptised attended. S.G.F.B.

D.C.C., *s.v.; R.G.G.*³, III, 1189–90.

Cathari Grk. *katharoi* = 'pure'. The term was applied by → Augustine of Hippo to a Manichaean group (→ Manichees). It is best known as a designation for medieval heretical sect in Germany in 12th cent., called in S. France → Albigenses. The C. prob. orig. from the → Bogomils. Movement first known in France in 11th cent. Pope Innocent III sought to suppress it; it finally disappeared from Italy at end of 14th cent., after much persecution. S.G.F.B.

J. A. MacCulloch, *Medieval Fact and Fable* (1932), pp. 211ff.; *D.C.C.*, *s.v.; E.R.E.*, I, *s.v.* ('Albigenses'); *R.G.G.*³, III, pp. 1192–3; S. Runciman, *The Medieval Manichee* (1955), pp. 116ff.; C. Thouzellier, *Catharisme et Valdéisme en Languedoc* (1966).

Cathedral A church containing the *cathedra* or throne of → bishop of diocese. From alternative Lat. word *sedes*, 'seat', the Eng. word 'see' derives. The bishop's *cathedra* orig. stood behind the high altar, facing W.; it is now gen. located on N. side of sanctuary. C.s were gen. the largest and most splendid church in diocese. The medieval Gothic cathedral was designed to symbolise in structure and ornament the complex structure of the Chr. faith. S.G.F.B.

D.C.C., *s.v.;* O. von Simson, *The Gothic Cathedral* (1956); E. Mâle, *The Gothic Image* (1961), pp. 27ff.; A. Katzenellenbogen, *The Sculptural Programs of Chartres Cathedral* (1959).

Catholic, Catholicism, Catholicity These words, deriving from Grk. *kath' holou*, 'on the whole', 'in general', have a distinctive eccl. connotation which is very ancient. 'Catholic' was orig. used of universal Church, esp. to indicate belief or practice accepted 'everywhere, always, and by all' (acc. to Vincent of Lérins, *ante* 450). Hence it acquired meaning of 'orthodox' as opposed to 'heretical' or 'schismatical'. After the schism of 1054, the W. Church called itself 'Catholic', and the → E. Church 'Orthodox'. Since → Reformation, the R.C. Church has regarded itself as exclusively Catholic; but Anglicans (→ Anglicanism) and → Old Catholics have also claimed title on ground that they possess → Apostolic Success. and continuity of Catholic faith and practice: in this sense, 'Catholic' contrasts with 'Protestant'. (→→ Ecumenical Movement; Vatican Council II). S.G.F.B.

E.R.E., III, *s.v.; D.C.C.*, *s.v.; R.G.G.*³, III, 1206–27; N. Zernov, *Eastern Christendom* (1961), pp. 227ff.; *C.E.*, III, *s.v.;* W. van Loewenich, *Modern Catholicism* (ET 1959).

Catholic Apostolic Church Sometimes called the 'Irvingites', as being disciples of E. Irving (1792–1834). The movement, orig. of revivalist nature, and largely initiated by H. Drummond (1786–1860), aimed at preparing for Second Coming of Christ by reviving primitive offices of Church. The ornaments, vestments and ritual of R.C., Greek, and Anglican Churches were adopted by C-A-C. It had considerable success during 19th cent. in Britain, Holland, Germany and U.S.A. It has since declined, and only small groups survive. S.G.F.B.

E.R.E., VII, pp. 422–8; *D.C.C.*, pp. 251, 423, 702; *R.G.G.*³, III, pp. 1196–7.

Catholic Epistles First mentioned by → Eusebius (*c.* 310) in a way that suggests a collection of N.T. writings so designated already existed. Eusebius includes under title the seven epistles now known as C-E.: Epistles of → James, I and II → Peter, I, II and III → John, and → Jude. In what sense these epistles were 'Catholic' has been disputed: it could mean that they were considered as addressed to Christians in general, in contrast to Paul's Epistles which were addressed to specific Churches or individuals, or that they were 'Catholic' in that they were accepted by Cath. Church as → 'authoritative'. The cath. character of the various Epistles was only gradually recognised prior to Eusebius' attestation. S.G.F.B.

*P.C.*², pp. 1020–1; *R.G.G.*³, III, 1198–9.

Causation, Chain of, in Buddhist thought → *Paticca-Samuppada.*

Cave Art In cave-systems in S.W. France, the Pyrenees, N.W. Spain, and (to a minor degree) in Sicily and S. Urals, paintings and engravings dating from the Upper Paleolithic era (*c.* 15,000 BC) have been found. The subjects of this art are invariably animals: e.g. bison, horses, rhinoceros, deer, mammoths. These depictions, since they are situated in places of difficult access, far from natural light, were obviously not intended for display. The fact that many animals are shown as pierced by darts or pregnant suggests that this cave-art was magical: to achieve success in hunting or ensure birth of animals (→ Magic). The sexual significance of C.-A. has been recently emphasised by two French prehistorians, who also claim to discern complex mythic patterns. Humans are rarely depicted, and then only in schematic form and with animal features. The so-called 'Dancing Sorcerer' in the Trois Frères Cave (Ariège) may represent either a masked dancer or 'embryonic' deity. A bird-headed man, slain by a wounded bison, depicted at Lascaux, may be earliest known instance of 'black magic'. This C.–A. is of primary importance for study of → Paleolithic Religion. S.G.F.B.

H. Breuil, *Four Hundred Centuries of Cave Art* (E.T. 1952); P. Wernert, 'La signification des cavernes d'art paléolithique', in *H.G.R.*, I; H. Kuhn, *Die Felsbilder Europas* (1952); A. Laming, *Lascaux* (E.T. 1959); Brandon, *M.D.*, pp. 16ff.; S. Giedon, *The Eternal Present* (1962), pp. 275ff.; T. G. E. Powell, *Prehistoric Art* (1966), ch. I; G. Clark, *The Stone Age Hunters* (1967); P. J. Ucko–A. Rosenfeld, *Palaeolithic Cave Art* (1967); A. Laming-Emperaire, *La signification de l'art rupestre paléolethique* (1962); A. Leroi-Gourham, *Art et religion au Paléolithique Supérieur* (1963).

Caves From the dawn of human culture C. have been used as dwellings, sanctuaries and tombs. The Paleolithic peoples so used them (→→ Cave Art; Paleolithic Religion). The practical usefulness of C. for shelter is obvious: their ritual use was prob. due to their mysterious character, suggestive of entrance to → underworld. The following examples may be cited of C. as sanctuaries: temple at Abu Simbel dedicated by Rameses II to → Rē and → Amun; Idaean Cave, Crete, assoc. with b. of → Zeus; C. of the Lupercal, Rome; the Kārlī, Ajanta, and Ellorā cave-temples in India; C. of the Thousand Buddhas at Tun-Huang, China; the rock-temples of Petra; cave-sanctuaries of → Mithra; the cave birth-place of Christ at Bethlehem. The purchase of C. of Machpelah by → Abraham for burial (Gen. 23:8ff.) is a notable example of mortuary use of C. The famous pharaonic tombs in Valleys of Tombs of Kings and Queens near Thebes were not caves, but specially excavated, and were prob. thus located for security. The Church of the Holy Sepulchre, Jerusalem, is the supreme monument of veneration of sacred cave-tomb. S.G.F.B.

E.R.E., III, *s.v.;* R. W. Hutchinson, *Prehistoric Crete* (1962), pp. 203, 336ff.; *O.C.D.*, p. 177; *H.D.B.*², p. 129; A. L. Basham, *The Wonder that was India* (1954), pp. 352ff.; J. Finegan, *Archeology of World Religions* (1952), pp. 308ff.; F. Cumont, *The Mysteries of Mithra* (E.T.² 1956), p. 30; H. T. F. Duckworth, *The Church of the Holy Sepulchre* (1922), pp. 33ff.; R. W. Hamilton, *The Church of the Nativity, Bethlehem* (1947), pp. 9ff., 84ff.; C. Kopp, *The Holy Places of the Gospels*, E.T. (1963), *s.v.* ('Grottos').

Cecrops Either a → chthonian deity or eponymous hero of extinct tribe once inhabiting Athens, C. was assoc. with oldest sanctuary on Acropolis, situated beneath the Erectheum, and with cult of → Zeus (Hypatos). S.G.F.B.

E.R.E., III, *s.v.;* M. P. Nilsson, *The Mycenean Origin of Greek Mythology* (1963), p. 163; C. Picard, *Les religions préhelléniques* (1948), pp. 115, 120, 239.

Celibacy *Ex.* Lat. *caelebs*, 'unmarried', 'single'. Abstension from sexual relations either for prescribed period or permanently has occurred in many religs. (→ Asceticism). The reasons have been various: to maintain ritual purity, consecration to divine service, to remove distractions from pursuit of salvation. The following examples show variety of expression: the priests of Cybele castrated themselves (→ Castration); breach of C. meant expulsion of Buddhist monk from the → Sangha; the → Vestal Virgins were entombed alive, if they lost their virginity. The growth of anthropological → dualism in Graeco-Roman world exalted virgin state, by regarding body as contaminating prison of soul. This dualism finds expression in earliest Chr. writings: e.g. → Paul exalts virginity (I Cor. 7:8ff.), Mt. 19:4ff.12ff. commends those who are eunuchs for 'the kingdom of heaven's sake'. In Early Church this tendency grew stronger, esp. as → monasticism increased its appeal. After various limited injunctions about C. of clergy, Pope Siricius prescribed absolute C. for higher clergy (385). This and subsequent decrees were resisted by many clergy. The Grk. Church finally decided that bishops must accept C., but parochial clergy may marry before ordination, though not after. C. continued to be imposed on all clergy in W. Church throughout Middle Ages; but it was never willingly accepted by all. The Reformation saw strong reaction against C.: e.g. → Luther, a former monk, married a nun. In R.C. Church the Council of Trent (→ Counter-Reformation) made C. of clergy a dogma; so it has continued to present day, when its universal compulsory character for all clergy is now being questioned in some circles. C. for women ideally repr. consecration of their virginity to Christ: some nuns receive ring as token of their solemn profession. S.G.F.B.

E.R.E., III, pp. 271–7, 817–9 ('Concubinage, Christian'); *D.C.C.*, pp. 255–6; *R.C.G.*³, VI, 1923–7; K. E. Kirk, *The Vision of God* (1932), pp. 184ff.; *C.E.*, III, *s.v.*

Celtic Christianity During Roman occupation of Britain, Christianity was introduced, perhaps in 2nd or 3rd cent., prob. from Gaul. It was sufficiently estab. to send delegates to Synod of Arles in 314; it produced a martyr in St. Alban, prob. in Diocletian persecution, *c.* 305, and a heretic in → Pelagius. The ending of Roman rule and the Saxon invasions of 5th cent. led to elimination of Christianity in eastern parts of country, and to its survival among the (Celtic) Britons in Cornwall, Wales, and Strathclyde. This C.-C., cut off from Roman Church, turned its missionary endeavour to other Celtic lands, i.e. Ireland, Scotland and Brittany, where it founded flourishing churches. C.-C. was loosely organised, being centred largely upon monasteries, of which that at Bangor Iscoed once had 2,000 monks. The Celtic Christians made no attempt to convert Saxons, and they became hostile to Roman Christianity, when brought into England by mission of Augustine in 597. C.-C. was distinguished from Roman Christianity by its attachment to earlier customs that had become superseded in W. Church, e.g. date of Easter and form of tonsure. C.-C. played import. part later in conversion of Saxons of Northumbria. In 664 at Synod of Whitby, the Celtic Church submitted to Roman Christianity, as organised from Canterbury, partly through political pressure. An independent C.-C. lingered on in Wales, Scotland and Ireland for several centuries. C.-C. was distinguished for the learning and artistic skill of its monks, and their missionary zeal. The artistic tradition of C.-C. affected Saxon eccl. art, and produced such masterpieces as the *Lindisfarne Gospels*. S.G.F.B.

N. K. Chadwick, *Studies in the Early British Church* (1958), *Celtic Britain* (1963); M. and L. de Paor, *Early Christian Ireland* (1958); J. Godfrey, *The Church in Anglo-Saxon England* (1962); F. M. McNeill, *Iona* (1949³); J. H. Cockburn, *The Celtic Church of Dunblane* (1954); W. Delius, *Gesch der irischen Kirche von ihren Anfänge bis zum 12 Jahrhundert* (1954).

Celtic (Pagan) Religion *Sources of Evidence*: Celtic society was tribal and aristocratic. The priests (Druids) and knights were import. element, common people of little interest, according to Caesar. The C. priests did not commit their sacred lore to writing. This was deliberate policy on their part, and Caesar remarks that Druids 'were unwilling, first, that their system of training should be bruited abroad among the common people and second, that the student should rely on the written word and neglect the exercise of his memory.' As result of this attitude to writing, there are no direct sources of evidence for pagan C.-R. Much of our knowledge is therefore inevitably inferential, and with many gaps. Even so, such evidence as exists demonstrates unequivocally that the Celts were deeply conscious of relig.; also that, in spite of great geographical and temporal differences in the C. world and its duration, there is fundamental similarity of relig. cults which makes it possible to speak of C. relig. as something individual, distinctive and remarkably persistent. The sources of evidence that can be employed are three-fold. When used with caution and collated with each other, they can be seen to be of considerable value and validity. The evidence of archaeology is most reliable, but is limited to bare fact and can provide little in way of detail. The comments of Greek and Roman ethnographers are often enlightening. The vernacular lit.s of the British Isles contain mythological legends and poems, but committed to writing under aegis of Chr. Church, their relig. content is not always obvious, and the material requires careful and critical analysis.

Temples, Sanctuaries and Cult Sites: there is little evidence for temples of classical kind in early C. world. Recent excavations do, however, suggest, that built structures of some kind may have been more common than has previously been supposed. It is clear from these that sanctuaries of an artificial and fairly substantial nature did exist in C. countries. These consisted of earthen banks and ditches, enclosing in some cases sacrificial platforms paved with stone and ritual pits filled with offerings of bones, pottery and other objects. One example of such a site is at Libenice, near Kolin, in Czechoslovakia. Other shrine-like structures, consisting of shafts or pits, sometimes reaching a great depth, and filled with bones and cult-offerings of many kinds, turn up widely in the C. world. In some instances there are traces of buildings that enclosed them; in others they are found inside rectilinear earthwork enclosures, known as *viereckshanzen*. These may be fore-runners of later double square Romano-Celtic temples. In S. France alone there are remains of stone temples of Mediterranean type, and these are essentially alien to the Celts. They occur, e.g. at Roquepertuse and Entremont. In gen., shrines and sanctuaries of the Celts seem to have consisted of simple earthworks, deep shafts round which ritual must have been carried out, and natural sites made holy by long use. Later, under influence of Rome, double square, circular or multangular stone temples were constructed, in which both C. and Roman gods were worshipped, and images and dedications set up in classical fashion.

The Celts believed certain natural features to be in some way connected with their deities; their focus for ritual was often a hill or a well, the source of a river, a grove of trees, a burial mound or a standing stone. There is some evidence for use of simple wickerwork structures, in which cult-objects were presumably housed, and shown to people by priests at correct ritual time. The actual rites, in which the people, participated, must have been performed in the open, in proximity to some feature made sacred by cult-legend. The Celts believed that entrance to otherworld lay in a variety of places: inside a burial mound or hill; at the bottom of a well or the sea; on an island across the ocean (→ Styx); in a cave, like the sinister Cave of Cruachan, Ireland. Mortals could gain access to otherworld in a number of ways. They could make love to an immortal being, and so earn right to enter lover's territory; they could assist some deity in fighting a battle, for the gods sometimes called upon heroes for aid against their divine foes; or they could enter by trickery, for the Celts believed that their gods were capable of treachery, and this must be matched by equal cunning. On *Samuin*, the night preceding 1 November, perhaps most potent relig. festival of the C. year, otherworld was thought to become visible to mortals who could enter it at will. Several Irish tales are concerned with adventures of people in otherworld, and tricks played on them there by the gods. One way in which otherworld was never attained was as reward for good behaviour. Ethics did not enter into C.-R.; the clever, not the good, were suitably rewarded. It is, then, at such places, where mankind was supposedly best able to communicate with divine powers, that we must envisage cult sites of the early C. peoples.

The Priests: the priests, known as Druids, have acquired a popular status—due to the writings of early antiquarians—which is not substantiated by evidence. Actual information about this relig. order is slight; it is derived primarily from remarks of classical writers—in which context political prejudice is apparent—at a time when the C. priests had lost real power they undoubtedly once held. Caesar provides most detailed account of Druidic order. He notes that they were concerned with worship of the gods, with sacrifice, and with passing on learning to young; that they could ban people from attending sacrifices—a dreaded punishment, for it placed wrongdoer outside tribal sanctions and protection. Certain aspects of the law were also apparently the concern of this order. The Druids met annually at site believed to be centre of Gaul; and Caesar also mentions existence of a chief Druid. The order was believed to have orig. in British Isles, and there is growing archaeological support for such supposition. The Druids took no part in war; nor did they pay taxes. There is no evidence to support widely-held belief that Druidic doc. contained subtle and sophisticated philosophy. There is nothing in what we can now learn of it to differentiate it from the teaching of any barbarian priesthood. There is only one written reference to Druids in Britain, and this is in description by Tacitus of attack by Paulinus on Druidic stronghold in the Island of Anglesey in CE 62. The account of the fearful appearance of screaming, black-clad women, the awful imprecations of the Druids, and the ghastly groves bloody with sacrifice makes dramatic reading. Paulinus wiped out the stronghold, destroyed the sacred woods; and we hear no more of Druids in Britain.

Apart from Druids, there were apparently other priests, but it is not easy to determine whether these had an existence prior to Roman conquest of C. lands, or had come into being as direct result of it. Priests called *gutuatri* and *antistes* are mentioned, and Lucan refers to a *sacerdos* who officiated in the sacred grove near Marseilles.

Celtic Ritual: foremost in C.-R. was the import. ritual of sacrifice, human as well as animal. The Druids presided over sacrifices, and, since human sacrifice had long ceased in classical world, this practice was used as pretext by the Romans for destroying the politically dangerous power of the Druids. The sacrificial victims were usually criminals; but in times of tribal or national distress innocent persons were also offered up to the gods. Caesar mentions great figures of interwoven branches made by some tribes, in which men and beasts alike were enclosed and offered to the gods for burning. Although there are no actual accounts of human sacrifice in Ireland, the Chr. Church being anxious to suppress any reference to pagan practice of this kind, there are plenty of instances which indicate that there, as elsewhere in C. world, it was customary. The ritual would no doubt be performed at some sacred site where idols, like the crude wooden figure from Ralaghan, Co. Cavan, or some stone head or figure, would be set up; the sacrificial offering and rites would no doubt be followed by festivity and games of all kinds, music-making and horse-racing, drinking and commercial exchanges, all under aegis of the deity of place or tribe. Offerings in form of agrarian produce would be made, as well as living victims; the priests would preside over all, ranking with kings in social status.

An extraordinary example of late survival of ritual practice in Ulster occurs in a 12th-cent. source. The enthronement of a new king was accompanied by his ritual mating with a white mare, symbolic of the earth-fertility goddess. The beast was then killed and cooked, and new king had to bathe in the broth, lap some up like an animal, and eat some flesh. Parts of horses, espec. skulls, found in British graves, may echo this ritual, the horse being a sacrificial animal in C., as in Teutonic cults.

The Calendar Festivals: the Celts divided their year into four main parts, each demarcated by ritual. They reckoned time in terms of lunar months, and in nights, not days. The most import. of these feasts was *Beltain*, 1st May, when beasts were ritually purified by fire by priests. Beltain marked beginning of pastoral year, when animals were taken up to summer grazings. It is prob. to be connected with ancient C. god Belenos, a god of healing and thermal waters. *Samuin*, the night before Nov. 1st, was night when supernatural forces were very active and hostile to man. The beasts had been brought down from summer pastures; those that could not be wintered would be slaughtered, perhaps in honour of presiding god; after the sacrifices, festivity would ensue. But festivity tempered by fear, for the gods do not seem to have looked kindly on mankind at this season, and required propitiation. The two other major feasts of C. year were *Imbolc* (1st Feb.) and *Lughnasa* (1st Aug.). In Roman Gaul, the festival of Emperor Augustus replaced ancient feast held (acc. to Irish trad.) by the god Lugh in honour of the goddess Tailtiu. This festival is one which has survived widely, in vestigial form, throughout C. countries. C. tales contain many refs. to rules laid down for celebration of these tribal festivals, which lasted several days; punishment for disturbing the peace was instant death. Ritual objects such as sacred weapons and tools, crowns and sceptres would be displayed, and ritual postures, some of which are described in the lit., adopted.

The Gods: as the Celts were a tribal society, ancestors were important. They traced their ultimate ancestry to an eponymous deity, father of tribe, leader in war, giver of peace, fertility, and all good things. So each tribe must have its own father-god, and the multiplicity of dedicatory names demonstrates just how local these deities were—local in name, that is, but universal in function and import. There are well over 300 different god-names in C. epigraphy; of these some 260 occur once only. But, although these gods held basically similar positions in tribal society, certain patterns or cults are discernible; traces of these are to be found in various legends as well as in iconography. Because of lack of written C. relig. documents, it is not easy to determine how much of an official state relig. there was in C. countries. There is, however, a certain amount of evidence to suggest that there were gods whose influence was national rather than simply tribal. Some of these gods have a wider distribution than others; their names, or names closely similar, also occur in the literatures. This may, of course, simply indic. tribal movement, but it is perhaps more explicable in terms of powerful gods patronised by the Druids themselves; there is some evidence of hierarchy of deities in Irish tales which may support this hypothesis. A god such as *Belenos*, with some two score dedications, mentioned by classics and apparently appearing in insular trad., is suggestive of ancient C. pastoral deity. Another god, whose name appears only once, but whose iconographic appearances are numerous, is [*C*] *ernunnos*, 'The Horned One', the squatting, antler-bearing god, with ram-headed serpent attribute. His main spheres of influence seem to have been those of fertility and prosperity of all kinds; under Roman influence he was likened to → Mercury, god of commerce and leader of souls of dead to underworld. He can be detected in the insular legends; he survived as a symbol of anti-Christ into medieval contexts.

A triad of deities occurs in Gaul whose names, acc. to the scholiasts on Lucan, were *Esus*, 'Lord, Master'; *Taranis*, 'Thunderer'; and *Teutates*, 'God of the Tribe'. Whether these were really three powerful universal C. gods or not, it is difficult to say; but their epigraphic distribution is limited, and it may be more realistic to see in them local manifestations of the basic C. concept of the tribal god in triple form, well-attested in Irish sources. *Lugus*, the Irish *Lugh* and Welsh *Lleu*, again seems to have had an import. beyond that of a partic. tribe or geographical locality. It appears from Irish sources that he was a late-comer to pantheon there, an innovator, subtle, intellectual, using his wits rather than his brute force to achieve success in combat. He is recommended in the name *Lugudunum*, 'Fort of Lugus' (Lyons), and at Carlisle, *Luguvalium*, 'Strong in the God Lugus'. His name occurs widely in place-names. He is invoked in plural form in Switzerland and Spain, while in an Irish trad. he is regarded as having been born at one birth with two brothers of same name. Another god, whose distribution seems to have been more than purely local—national rather than tribal, is *Sucellos*, 'Good Striker', with his mallet or hammer and dish or barrel attributes. He is often accompanied by a dog. He has been equated by some with venerable Irish father-god, the *Dagda*, 'Good God'; he seems to have been ancestor-deity of the *Dis Pater* type. There are about 100 monuments portraying *Sucellos*, and about 6 inscriptions bearing his name; he appears as elderly, benign and portly man. There are about a score of dedications to the god *Grannos*, whose name may indicate some solar assoc. and a connection with thermal waters. Some gods are local only to N. Britain, where they are widely invoked—*Belatucadros*, *Cocidius* and *Vitiris*, for example.

The Goddesses: the lit. evidence for the C. goddesses is more helpful and detailed than that of iconography, where female deities are often portrayed in form of threefold mother-goddesses or as consort of some god, with attributes which make little contribution to our knowledge of their real, individual spheres and functions. The evidence suggests that whereas goddesses were as plentiful and as loyal as gods, they were more static. The gods seem to have moved with the tribes, destroying or mating with the goddesses of new regions; whereas tribal goddesses seem to have remained, more concerned with the land than with the tribe itself, meting out fertility and well-being from their own special localities. The local goddess is commemorated in the *Dindshenchas*, the place-name legends of Ireland, which do much to testify to her espec. connection with the soil and with a limited but powerful territory. The mother-goddesses, usually three in number, figure in iconography; these we may take to have been concerned with the women of the tribe, their fertility and their success in child-birth, as well as with comforting sick warriors on their military exploits, and seeing to fertility of soil. The king-elect mated with local or tribal earth-mother, and so attempted to secure well-being of tribe by her favour. The goddesses are repr. as being sensual, and in some cases their sexual appetite is almost insatiable. Over and above these universal divine mothers there is some evidence for a C. *Magna Mater*, Mother of the gods themselves. This again brings in the question of a C. hierarchy of deities. Women held high status in C. society; that the chief of all the gods should be the Mother, the female, is in keeping with their social attitudes. The gods of the Irish are known as *Tuatha De Danann*, 'People of the Goddess Danu'; her equivalent in Welsh trad. is Don. Certain goddesses, like the Irish *Medb*, 'Intoxication', actually took part in battle, fighting with weapons. Others, like the triple raven goddesses influenced outcome of war by magic and treachery; they were sinister prognosticators, powerful enemies, rewarding allies to mankind. Some C. goddesses were partic. connected with pursuits such as hunting, and protection of wild things. In Ireland *Flidais*, woodland goddess, filled this role, and there is ample evidence for similar female deities from the Continent. Other goddesses are repr. as being in charge of pleasures and delights of happy otherworld, owning magical singing-birds which healed all pain and conferred every joy to mankind.

The goddess frequently mated with a mortal, luring him to her domain by means of a magical branch, and keeping him there indefinitely. She could take on bird form, or appear as beautiful fawn, in order to win love or mate with king-elect, and so bless him. Nymph goddesses abound, either extremely local or of wider import. like *Coventina* of N. Britain, also known from Europe. Most of goddesses have some connection with water, and this coheres well with the great reverence Celts everywhere had for springs and pools. Several of Irish calendar festivals were held in honour of a goddess; many of the female deities, who are commemorated in some tale or place-name legend, have survived in mod. folk trad. both in British Isles and on Continent. Some goddesses, like *Epona*, the horse goddess, achieved wide popularity with Romans and natives alike; others, like *Damona*, goddess of cattle, and *Rosemerta*, appear several times in epigraphy. The C. tribal goddess, then, was divine epitome of all that ideal womankind stands for—sexuality, maternity, the conveyor of delight, the healer of all sorrow.

Cult of the Head: the entire deity was frequently portrayed cryptographically as a head, sometimes having features linking it to some specific cult or sphere. The severed head stood for many things in C.-R. It was held to be seat of the soul; it was believed capable of everything the Celts desired—prophetic wisdom, divine knowledge, sweet music, perfect hospitality. It could allegedly move and speak and sing in its independent state. It could promote fertility, most import. in a pastoral society. It was indeed the symbol of divinity, the god-head. It is perhaps the best attested cult or symbol for whole of C.-R. It impressed classical writers so that they commented upon it; archaeology amply testifies to it; the vernacular lit. add striking detail to what other sources suggest. It is a motif taken over by hagiography and popular trad., and one which persists to a striking degree in folk tale and popular belief down to present day. All cults of individual deities are portrayed in symbolism of human head. Their attributes speak for themselves; where they are lacking, the enigmatic, mask-like features seem to stand as a symbol of the *concept* of divinity, nameless and remote, a symbol, not a portrait.

Animals and Birds: animals and birds play an import. part in C. mythology. The relationship between the divine being and the beast seems to have been fundamental; what iconography suggests in this respect is well borne out by written evidence. Gods, as well as Druids, were believed to have powers of shape-shifting, to take on animal form for some purpose of their own; and to have their partic. cult-animal, by which they were accompanied and served. Gods, having animal parts, occur in iconography of C. world; Irish tales are full of refs. to characters who either stem from animal ancestors or belong to a tribe of bird-warriors, or have horns or other animal characteristics. *Cernunnos*, the antler-bearing stag-god, is best example of this. The most sacred animal among the Celts was the boar. There is much evidence for hunting of supernatural boar, sometimes having human origins; but there are few traces of a divine bull-hunt. The pig was most prized of all meat animals, and the theme of magic pigs, sometimes malevolent or beneficial to mankind, occurs in all the early lits. There are traces of a divine bull-legend in great Irish epic tale, the *Cattle Raid of Cualgne*. In iconography, the sacred bull sometimes has three horns, sometimes knobbed horns; it seems to have been espec. assoc. with venerated waters. Dogs, the ram—espec. in form of ram-headed serpent—and the horse, play import. parts in pagan C.-R.; the sacred animal was also the sacrificial animal, as in other relig.s. Birds abound in every aspect of C. trad. They were regarded as servants and companions of the gods, as their messengers, and form for metamorphosis. The sanctity accorded to birds, espec. water birds, can be seen in proto-C. contexts as early as late Bronze Age in Europe, and it persists into mod. folklore and belief. Omens were drawn from bird behaviour by Druids; certain birds were believed to be lucky or friendly to mankind, others to be sinister and hostile. Gods, embarking on amorous exploits, sometimes took on goose or swan form. The crane was assoc. with women of evil character, and with defeat in battle. Gods in bird shape led mortals into their territory. Birds indic. to men intentions of their divine masters. Birds and animals, then, played a major role in pagan C.-R., and constitute a distinctive and typically C. feature of the entire mythology. A.R.

A full bibliography of main works on Celtic religion is contained in Anne Ross, *Pagan Celtic Britain* (1967). [See also *L.R.-G.*, II, pp. 601–35; *R.-G.L.*, 13 (W. Krause); *E.R.E.*, III, pp. 277–304; J. Vendryes, *La religion des Celtes* (Coll: Mana, Paris 1948); T. G. F. Powell, *The Celts* (1959); S. Piggott, *The Druids* (1968). Ed.]

Cerdo Syrian → Gnostic, in Rome *c*. 140. Acc. to →→ Irenaeus and Hippolytus, C. was teacher of Marcion, and contrasted the 'just' god of the O.T. with the 'good' Father of Jesus Christ. S.G.F.B.

R. M. Grant, *Gnosticism: an Anthology* (1961), p. 9; E. E. Blackman, *Marcion and his Influence* (1948), pp. 68ff.; *R.G.G.*[3], I, 1632.

Cereberus In Grk. mythology a monstrous three-headed dog guarding entrance to → Hades; orig. of name is obscure. In anc. thought, the dog had a twofold eschatological role. (1) As Grk. underworld monster threatening dead, who had to offer him honey-cakes to pass. Poss. this aspect stems from idea of dog or jackal eating corpses. The feat of → Heracles in dragging C. to upperworld was prob. intended to show that the Saviour-hero's power extended to realm of dead. (2) The dog or jackal as → psychopompos is most notably repr. in → Anubis. The beneficient character of Anubis in anc. Egypt. mortuary cultus seems to have changed in Graeco-Roman period to a more sinister role. Acc. to Macrobius, an image of → Sarapis in Alexandria was accompanied by image of three-headed monster, the heads being severally those of lion, wolf and dog and repr. three aspects of → Time. C. appears in Chr. eschatological imagery. S.G.F.B.

R.A.C., II, 973–90; S. G. F. Brandon, *History, Time and Deity* (1965), pp. 58ff.

Ceres *Ex*. Lat. *creare*, *crescere*, ('to increase'), anc. Italian corn-goddess, identified with Grk. → Demeter; she was also assoc. with anc. Roman earth goddess Tellus Mater, and had other underworld connections. In Rome, there was a temple of C. on the Aventine, where she was worshipped with Liber and Libera, thus constituting a triad prob. after Eleusinian pattern of Demeter, → Kore, and Iacchus (→ Eleusinian Mysteries). S.G.F.B.

F. Altheim, *Hist. of Roman Religion* (E.T. 1938), pp. 98ff.; *O.C.D., s.v.; Kleine Pauly*, I, 1113–5; H. Le Bonniec, *Le culte de Cérès à Rome* (1958).

Cerinthus (*fl. c.* 100) → Gnostic heretic from Asia Minor who taught that world was not created by supreme God, but by a → Demiurge, ignorant of supreme God; that Jesus was ordinary man upon whom Christ descended at baptism: at Crucifixion only Jesus suffered, since Christ was impassible (→ Impassibility). S.G.F.B.

E.R.E., III, *s.v.;* R. M. Grant, *Gnosticism: an Anthology* (1961), p. 41; *R.G.G.*[3], I, 1632.

Cetiya Earthen mound or tumulus, reverenced as cult-object in pre-Buddh. India. → Stupa. The name survives in Siamese name for a Buddh. pagoda, viz.; '*chedi*', or more properly '*Phra Chedi*', (*Phra* being a term of respect) → *Pagoda*, Buddh.) T.O.L.

Ceylon, Buddhism in Acc. to the *Mahāvamsa*, 5th cent. CE Pāli chronicle, the → Buddha made three visits to island of Ceylon. Once he went to the top of Sumanakata (now known as Adam's Peak), and there left his footprint. The story has no historical basis; but the footprint remains one of the great centres of pilgrimage in C., and is a potent symbol of popular belief that C. is the *dhammadipa*, the island which is the guardian of Buddha's teaching.

The hist. advent of Buddhism in Ceylon was result of embassy sent by Tissa, king of C., to Indian emperor → Ashoka. In his reply, Ashoka commended the Buddh. relig. and arranged for his son, the *bhikkhu* (→ Ord. Bhd.) Mahinda, to visit C. and instruct Tissa. This is the *Mahāvamsa's* account, which is confirmed in part by Ashokan inscriptions. In these Ashoka claims to be supreme over many countries, incl. Tambapanni (Ceylon), and to have sent embassies to estab. Buddhism in all his dominions. The *Mahāvamsa* account surrounds embassy of Mahinda with various legendary elements, but behind them a kernel of hist. truth may be discerned. Tissa accepted the new relig.; with Mahinda, he arranged for a *vihāra* to be built in the capital city, Anurādhapura. Here were accommodated members of the → sangha who had arrived in C. with Mahinda. This community of *bhikkhus* was forerunner of the Mahāvihāra which for many cents. was leading sect in C. The ruins of Anurādhapura have recently been uncovered, incl. one of most striking moments of the Mahāvihāra, the Ruwanvali *dāgaba*, built prob. by king Dutthagāmani in 1st cent. BC. The fame of the Mahāvihāra is confirmed by → Buddhaghosa, who came to C. in 5th cent. CE and lived as member of Mahāvihāra community. He rewrote in Pāli the Sinhalese commentaries on the → Tripitaka; and these works, together with his comprehensive summary of Buddh. teaching and practice, the *Visuddhimagga*, have been of great import. in shaping the → Theravāda trad. found in C.

The close connection between rulers of C. and the sangha goes back to time of Mahinda and Tissa. From advent of Buddhism to occupation of Kandy by British in 1815, it was required that ruler of country should be Buddhist. It may have been the close relationship between court and sangha, and custom of court gifts to sangha, which was responsible for growth of different sects. A king of 1st cent. BC arranged for a gift to be made, not to the Mahāvihāra, but to an individual *bhikkhu*, and from this beginning sprang the Abhayagiri sect. Although there was at first no difference in teaching or discipline, the new *vihāra* became centre of foreign influence. The Mahāvihāra *bhikkhus* were conservative guardians of Theravādin orthodoxy; the Theravāda Tripitaka had been committed to writing in 1st cent. BC before rise of the Abhayagiri. The new sect welcomed ideas from abroad, and studied both Theravāda and → Mahāyāna teaching. The link between Abhayagiri and Buddhism in India is confirmed by fact that when the Tooth relic was brought from Kalinga to C. in 3rd cent. CE it was given into custody of Abhayagiri *bhikkhus*. From this time dates the cultus of the Tooth (claimed to be a left eye-tooth of Buddha). The Chinese pilgrim → Fa-Hsien, who visited C. at beginning of 5th cent. CE described in detail the Anurādhapura of this period, giving a picture in which the Abhayagiri and cultus of Tooth relic overshadow the Mahāvihāra.

A third sect, the Jetavana, was formed in much the same way as the Abhayagiri, and finally seceded from them in 3rd cent. CE. These three sects remained foundation of sangha during succeeding cents. in which period there was a great deal of S. Indian and Hindu influence. An 8th cent. CE king is said to have repaired many old *devālayas* (temples of Hindu gods); temples to → Visnu and → Siva have been found at Polonnaruwa, dating from 11th or 12th cent CE. A great revival of national independence and Buddhism was begun by 11th cent. CE king Vijaya, and carried to completion in next cent. by Parākrama Bāhu. Under Vijaya the various sects of sangha were united into one group, accepting orthodox Theravādin teaching. Parākrama Bāhu stressed importance of Tooth relic for well-being of C., together with another relic, the alms-bowl of Buddha which has now been lost. During succeeding cents. the Tooth relic moved with capital and court. The Portuguese claimed to have captured and destroyed it in 16th cent. CE; but Sinhalese maintain that this was a replica, and that original was eventually taken to Kandy, where it is still housed today.

Popular Buddhism in C. is centred on the *vihāras* which are both dwelling places for *bhikkhus* and shrines for Buddh. devotees. The first *vihāras* on C. consisted of *bhikkhus*' living quarters, together with *dāgaba* in which a relic was buried. Usually a bo-tree was grown also. The bo-tree, which still stands in Anuradhapura, is said to have been grown from cutting of tree at → Bodh Gayā under which Buddha attained enlightment, and brought to C. by sister of Mahinda. From 4th cent. CE onwards, image-houses became regular feature; together with the *dāgaba* and bo-tree, it forms part of most *vihāras* in C. today. One further development in the *vihāra* took place from 12th cent. CE onwards, when the *devālayas* came to be more closely assoc. with the *vihāras*. By the 15th cent. CE *devālayas* were being constructed in same building as the image-house. The gods who are besought in the *devālayas* incl. pre-Buddh. deities such as Sumana, guardian of Adam's Peak, and Hindu deities such as Bishnu. In popular imagination, propitiation of such deities is often of greater importance than reverence payed to Buddha.

The popular relig. of Ceylonese people incl. pre-Buddh. practices such as use of devil-dancers to cure sick and of *kattādiyas* or exorcisers to cast off spells. Much use is also made of astrologers, another pre-Buddh. practice. Some of Buddh. customs betray pre-Buddh. background, such as *pirit*, the chanting of suttas from Tripitaka to ward off evil spirits. More firmly Buddh. is customs of *dāna*, the giving of food to *bhikkhus*, by which means much merit accrues to donor.

Buddh. festivals enjoy great popular support, esp. festival of Wesak, which commemorates three great events in life of Buddha—the renunciation, enlightenment, and entry into *parinib-*

bāna. Even more powerful in popular imagination is annual *perahara* held in Kandy, during which Tooth relic is carried in procession. This procession also incl. the representatives of four of the popular deities worshipped in the *devālayas*. Once in 10 yrs. the relic itself, normally carried in casket, is exposed; multitudes of pilgrims pass through the *Māligāva* where relic is housed.

The sangha today is divided into three major communities or *nikāyas*, in add. to which there are some smaller communities. The leading community, the Siam Nikāya (so-called because it received its authority from Siam in 18th cent. CE) is distinguished chiefly by caste, only members of highest Ceylonese caste being admitted. The Amarapura Nikāya incl. members of other castes, while the Rāmanya Nikāya is distinguished by slightly stricter discipline. There is no difference in teaching between the *nikāyas*.

Although sangha maintained its numbers during occupation of C. by Portuguese, Dutch and British, during this period Buddhism fell to low ebb. It was revived only towards end of 19th cent. Since visit to C. of theosophist Col. Olcott, there has been steady increase in Buddh. study and learning. The two Buddh. universities of Vidyalankāra and Vidyodaya were founded to stimulate Buddh. education. Since independence of country in 1947, there has been growing sense of cultural and national identity linked with revival of Buddhism. The Buddh. missions estab. by C. in Europe and America bear witness to C.'s self-conscious role as the *dhammadipa*, the country which is bearer of Buddha's message to mod. world. D.N. DE L.Y.

W. Geiger (tr.), *The Mahavamsa* (1912); R. S. Copleston, *Buddhism Primitive and Present in Magadha and Ceylon* (1892); E. W. Adikaram, *Early Hist. of Buddhism in Ceylon* (1946); W. Rahula, *Hist. of Buddhism in Ceylon* (1956); E. F. C. Ludowyck, *The Footprint of the Buddha* (1958).

Chalcedon, Council (CE 451) Reckoned as 4th Oecumenical Council, the C.-C. is notable for its presentation of orthodox → Christology. It condemned teaching of Eutyches and → Nestorius, and endorsed ascription of title *Theotokos* ('God-bearer') to Virgin Mary, as attesting both Divinity and Humanity of Christ. In effect, the C.-C. met dilemma that logically stemmed from concept of God incarnated as man, by asserting that in Christ one person existed in two natures (divine and human), which in their union remained unconfused and unchanged, while the person was essentially one and undivided. The concepts and terminology derived from Grk. metaphysical thought, and the problem was basically one of trying to reconcile Chr. belief in deity of the incarnated Christ with logical implications of Grk. psychology. The 'Definition of Chalcedon' did not end → Monophysitism or → Monothelitism; but it was gen. received as orthodoxy in both E. and W. Church. The so-called Tome of Pope Leo I (d. 461) was accepted by C.-C. as an authoritative statement of Catholic doc. of Incarnation. S.G.F.B.

D.C.C., s.v.; pp. 259; 1346; A. Grillmeier-H. Bacht, *Das Konzil von Chalcedon*, 3 vols. (1951–4); R. Sellera, *The Council of Chalcedon* (1953); A. Grillmeier, *Christ in Christian Tradition* (E.T. 1965), pp. 480ff.; K. Sarkessian, *The Council of Chalcedon and the Armenian Church* (1965).

Chaldaens Orig. inhabitants of land of Kaldu, a part of S.E. Babylonia. Because of anc. assoc. of Babylon with → astrology and astronomy, the word C. became a designation in one word for oriental astrologers, magicians, and practitioners of occult arts. This use of C. is found in *Dan.* 1:4. Owing to their assoc. with astrology, esp. horoscopes, the C. were also called *mathematici*. S.G.F.B.

J. Bidez-Fr. Cumont, *Les Mages hellénisés*, 2 vols. (1958); *R.A.C.*, II, 1006–21; F. Cumont, *Astrology and Religion among the Greeks and Romans* (1912, 1960), Lect. I, *Kleine Pauly*, I, 1123–4.

Ch'an (→ Zen). A school of Chinese Buddhism and undoubtedly one of most distinctive and original products of the Chinese mind. The character '*ch'an*' is derived from the Sanskrit *dhyāna*, and hence the school was designated the Meditation School. It aims at an immediate awareness of Reality in which subjective and objective are transcended; a state of being in which there is no duality. This goal is referred to as *prajnā*, *nirvāna*, *bodhi* etc. Ch'an taught that the only reality is the Buddha-mind, which cannot be apprehended by philos. or relig. thought, meditation or practice of ritual or magic. It cannot be taught, or transmitted by books or teachers. Ch'an stressed 'realisation' by a kind of spiritual illumination which comes when thought and sense-perception have ceased. Everything being a manifestation of the Buddha-mind; → *samsāra is* → *nirvāna*, my mind *is* the Buddha-mind, pure consciousness *is* wisdom.

Ch'an has affinities with Tibetan Mahāmudra. → Tao-an and → Hui-yüan had early emphasised the importance of dhyāna exercises; but the beginnings of Ch'an are attributed to → Bodhidharma (*c.* CE 520), whose teaching is summed up in the lines:

A special transmission outside the scripture.
No dependence upon words or letter.
Direct pointing to the soul of man.
Seeing into nature and attainment of Buddhahood.

Bodhidharma emphasised the teachings of the → *Lankāvatāra Sūtra.*

With Hung-jên (CE 601–74), the 5th patriarch, and his two outstanding disciples, Shên-hsiu (605–706) and Hui-nêng (638–713), Ch'an began to develop divergent tendencies concerned with interpretation and method. Whereas Shên-hsiu and the N. school distinguished between pure and false mind, and taught the need to eliminate all false thinking and gradually reach the point of absolute quietude, Hui-nêng and the S. school refused to make this distinction and sought realisation in sudden awareness of Absolute Truth.

Hui-nêng is credited with authorship of the only Chinese Buddhist writing to be honoured with the rank of *sūtra* (*ching*), the famous *Platform Sūtra* of Hui-nêng, which became a basic text of Ch'an. Soon after Hui-nêng's death (CE 713), the meditation hall came into use in Ch'an monasteries. At the same time Buddhist laymen and lay women were encouraged to practise Ch'an meditation in their homes. By 10th cent. CE the Kung-an (→ Koan) came to be recognised and used extensively as a device for attainment of enlightenment.

Ch'an did not object to conceptual knowledge as such, but to the clinging to intellectualization. Nor did Ch'an meditation preclude vigorous and creative physical activity. The search for direct communication with the inner nature of things and the vision of a world beyond all opposites led to a great outpouring of creative art in China and Japan. Ch'an also had a profound influence on the neo-Confucian movement of the Sung Dynasty, and as → Zen in Japan it exerted untold influence on Japanese civilisation. D.H.S.

W. T. Chan, *Source Book in Chinese Philosophy* (1963), ch. 26; Fung Yu-lan, *Hist. of Chinese Philosophy*, vol. 2 (1953), pp. 386ff.

Chance The unforeseen factor in life was deified by Grks. as Tychē (= Lat. Fortuna). Tychē was primarily venerated as 'good fortune', and in Graeco-Roman times was patroness of various cities. Many writers conceived of Tychē only as the incalculable factor in life (e.g. Thucydides, Plato, Aristotle, Polybius). Fortuna was prob. orig. a goddess of fertility. S.G.F.B.

O.C.C., pp. 368, 929–30; S. G. F. Brandon, *M.D.*, pp. 173–5.

Chang (Tao) Ling d. CE 157–178. Is regarded by Taoists as the founder and spiritual head of an important Taoist sect, the Sect of Right Unity. Little is known of C. historically, but he is the subject of numerous Taoist legends. He is believed to have studied → alchemy and produced the pill of immortality, to have received a mysterious book containing recipes for spiritualisation which he handed on, together with various talismans, a seal and a magic sword. He possessed remarkable gifts of healing, and started a healing cult which rapidly developed into a politico-relig. movement towards the middle of 2nd cent. CE in Szêchuan (W. China). Thousands of peasants joined his movement, which became hierarchical in structure with an hereditary head. Each family paid cult-dues annually of five pecks of rice. Hence his enemies called him the 'rice thief', and the movement was known as 'The Way of the Five Pecks of Rice' (*Wu-tou-mi-tao*). His son, Chang Hêng, and grandson, Chang Lu, carried on the movement. The origins of his title, Celestial Master (T'ien Shih) is variously ascribed to the 5th and 8th cents. A claim by Chang Chêng-sui to be his direct descendant was recognised in 1016 by the emperor Chên Tsung, when a vast hereditary establishment was provided near the Dragon and Tiger mountain in Kiangsi. This remained an important Taoist centre till 1927, when the reputed 63rd descendant of Chang Ling was evicted by communists and his lands given to peasants. The present Celestial Master lives in Taiwan, where Taoism flourishes. The priests of this sect marry, do not confine themselves to monasteries, nor restrict themselves to vegetable diet. They move among the masses, selling charms, telling fortunes, performing relig. ceremonies, and dealing in → astrology, → divination and the like. The Celestial Master is regarded as a great sorcerer, and Chang Ling himself as an immortal. D.H.S.

E. T. C. Werner, *Dictionary of Chinese Mythology* (1932); H. Maspero (*Le Taoisme* (1950); H. Welch, *The Parting of the Way* (1957).

Changes, Book of → I Ching. D.H.S.

Chanukkah Jew. Dedication Festival, lasting 8 days from 25th of month. Kislev, commemorating rededication of Temple after desecration by Antiochus Epiphanes in 165 BC. It is called festival of lights by → Josephus (Ant. XII: 323), prob. because ceremonial lighting of candles recalled relighting of sacred lamp in Temple. (→ Judaism). S.G.F.B.

E.R.E., V, pp. 865–6; *E.J.R.*, p. 172.

Chaos Grk. word meaning 'gape, gap, yawn'. Acc. to → Hesiod, 'at first Chaos came to be'. His use of idea as primordial state is puzzling since it implies some pre-existent substance that 'split' or 'gaped'. Hesiod prob. derived his concept from Hittite cosmogony. Most anc. cosmogonies (e.g. Egypt., Mesopot., Heb., Grk.) imagined a primordial situation that was featureless and without order, and that divine Creation intro. order, turning 'chaos' into 'cosmos' (→ Cosmogony). S.G.F.B.

E.R.E., III, *s.v.; R.A.C.*, II, 1031–40; S. G. F. Brandon, *C.L.*, *passim.*

Charites In Grk. mythology, three goddesses,

daughters of → Zeus, personifying charm, grace, beauty. From Lat. trans. of C. by *Gratiae* comes Eng. 'Graces'. As repr. of beauty and grace, the C. were naturally assoc. with → Aphrodite. They always appear in art as a triad; in Graeco-Roman period they were depicted nude. S.G.F.B.
O.C.D., s.v.; E.R.E., III, *s.v.; Kleine Pauly*, I, 1135–7; J. Seznec, *La survivance des dieux antiques* (1940), *passim.*

Charity *Ex.* Lat. *caritas*, the → Vulgate trans. of orig. Grk. *agapē*, 'love'. *Agapē* is exalted by → Paul (I Cor. 13) as supreme Chr. virtue. *Agapē* contrasted with *eros* = sexual love, and it has been cmp. with Hindu → *bhakti*. In Chr. theology it is evaluated as greatest of the 'theological virtues', i.e. those that form basis of Chr. life in contradistinction to 'cardinal' or natural virtues. (→ Agapē). S.G.F.B.
Th. Wb., I, 34ff.; *R.G.G.*[3], IV, 364–7; A. Nygren, *Agape and Eros* (E.T. 1936); *H.D.B.*[2], p. 131; *P.C.*[2], p. 962; *E.R.E.*, III, *s.v.*

Charms A charm (*ex.* Lat. *carmen*, 'song') is a magical formula sung or recited to achieve some beneficial end: it may also be inscribed on some portable object or enclosed therein (→ Amulets). S.G.F.B.
(Islamic) (*ḥirz, ḥamāla*, pl. *ḥurūz, ḥamā'il*). These are of different kinds. Qur. vv. are used in popular Islam for various purposes. Many have disapproved of this, but Tradition tells of Muḥammad's approval of using C., or spells, for healing and deliverance from evil powers. The last two suras of Qur. are obviously meant to be used this way. A number of Qur. vv. called *āyāt al-ḥifẓ* (vv. of guarding) may be used in times of danger. The *āyāt al-shifā'* (vv. of healing) are used as cures, the words being written out, then obliterated in liquid, rose-water being a favourite, and drunk. A group known as the *futūḥ al-Qur'ān* (Qur. vv. with the root *fatḥ* = opening, bestowing, or victory), when written and carried as C. guarantees adequate provision. Other vv. may be used for various purposes, such as to overcome an enemy, keep women chaste, protect travellers, make land fertile, give business success, get husband for an unmarried daughter, get information about what people are doing, find hidden treasure. Sometimes elaborate performances are necessary to make the vv. exert desired effect. Two vv. (iii, 148; xlviii, 29) containing every letter of alphabet are very effective for any disease, internal or external, used as an ointment, drink, a C. to be worn, or when recited. C., with names of God and with letters which appear at beginning of 29 suras, are popular. Magic squares are common: some of them being perfect numerical squares in which total is same whether one adds vertically, horizontally, or diagonally; some squares of at least 16 numbers, where every contiguous group reaches same total. Others are made up from names of God, or their numerical value, or from Qur. vv. Some are combined with names of angels, or certain magic symbols called the seven seals. → 'Alī's sword is another symbol which may appear on charms with words: 'There is no hero but 'Alī; there is no sword but Dhul Fiqār.' C. should properly be written by one reputed to have sufficient expertise, but many printed C. are produced. C. are usually sewn into leather case and worn like a locket, or tied to a limb. Children and animals are supplied with C. to avert the → evil eye. The subject is not considered a branch of → magic, which is condemned in orthodox circles; but many rites which are observed cannot easily be dissoc. from magic. (→ Amulets). J.R.
E.I., IV, pp. 409–17 (*siḥr*), p. 767 (*tilsam*); Hughes, pp. 14f., 72–8, 303–5; Pareja, pp. 785–7; Canaan, *Aberglaube, passim.;* Doutté, *Magie, passim.;* Trimingham, *West Africa*, pp. 111ff.; W. B. Stevenson, 'Some specimens of Moslem charms', in *Studia Semitica et Orientalia* (1920); J. Robson, 'The magical use of the Koran,' *T.G.U.O.S.*, VI (1934), pp. 51ff.; *Mishkāt*, pp. 945ff.

Charon In Grk. mythology, the aged boatman who ferried souls of dead across infernal river (→ Acheron or → Styx) to Hades. He was paid by a coin placed in mouth of corpse. The Etruscans had a death-god called Charun (→ Etruscan Religion). Sanctuaries of C. existed in places exuding mephitic vapours. Anc. Egypt. eschatology also knew a ferryman who performed a similar service, but, like C., was irascible or churlish. In the Epic of → Gilgamesh, the hero is ferried over the 'water of death', by 'Urshanabi, the boatman', who has a curiously ambivalent role. Michelangelo repr. C. in his Sistine 'Last Judgment'. S.G.F.B.
O.C.D., s.v.; R.A.C., II, 1040–61; *R.Ae.R-G.*, pp. 333–4 ('Jenseitsfährmann'); J. G. Frazer, *Adonis Attis, Osiris*, I (1936), pp. 204ff.

Chassidism (Hasidim) *Ex.* Heb. = 'pious', name of Jew. sect founded in first half of 18th cent. by Rabbi Israel ben Elieser (1698–1759), which spread in Hungary, Rumania, and Russia. It repr. reaction against aridity of → Talmud and rooted itself in the → Cabbala. The C. sought union with God through ecstatic prayer, and tended in pantheism. It was popular among the poor. (→ → Hasidaeans; Judaism). S.G.F.B.
R.G.G.[3], I, 1644–6; I. Epstein, *Judaism* (1959), pp. 270ff.; *E.J.R.*, pp. 174–6.

Chastity Abstention, either temporary or permanent, from sexual intercourse for relig. or magical motives has been practised by various peoples throughout the ages. Sexual potency has been regarded with relig. awe, and its use in primitive societies has often been carefully controlled by → tabus. A dual attitude to sex has gen. found expression: (1) as a sacred potency or strength that the individual must expend with discretion; (2) as a cause of pollution. Accordingly, on certain critical occasions in primitive society, e.g. hunting and war, C. is obligatory. C. has often been regarded as conferring spiritual or magical strength, e.g. with Hindu, Buddh. and Chr. ascetics. Abstension from sexual intercourse with certain social groups or on certain occasions has sometimes been demanded, e.g. in caste systems; during menstruation and pregnancy. Certain persons having special relig. status or duties had to observe C., e.g. priests while occupied in sacred ministry, → Vestal Virgins. The low evaluation of body which characterised early Christianity led to exaltation of C. as superior spiritual state comp. with that of marriage. (→ Celibacy). S.G.F.B.

E.R.E., III, pp. 474–503; *R.G.G.*³, III, 1257–61; K. E. Kirk, *The Vision of God* (1932), pp. 184; G. Van der Leeuw, *La Religion* (1948), pp. 224ff.

Cherubim Acc. to O.T., winged beings who acted as guardians of → Yahweh or bearers of his throne. They had several faces; acc. to Ezk. 10:14, of a cherub, man, lion and eagle. Images of two C. protected → Ark (Ex. 25:10ff.), and two colossal images of C. stood in Solomon's Temple (I Kgs. 6:23). The C. were prob. Assyrian in origin, akin to the *lamassu* or *šedu*, repr. as winged bulls or lions with human faces, that guarded entrances to temples and palaces. In later Jew. angelology, C. ranked among higher orders of angels. The conception passed into Christianity, and high status was accorded to C. in the Heavenly Host (→ Angels). S.G.F.B.

R.A.C., I, 62–3, 78–9, 92(c), 172ff.; *H.D.B.*), p. 133.

Chiliasm *Ex.* Grk. *chilia* = 1,000. Chronological speculation based on millennia occurs in → Zoroastrianism, and certain Grk. and Roman writers, e.g. →→ Plato, Virgil. C. gen. relates to Jew. and Chr. eschatological belief. Some rabbis taught that the → Messiah would reign on earth 1,000 years. In Christianity, C. took form of belief that earthly reign of Christ (a kind of Golden Age) would last 1,000 years from → resurrection of righteous to resur. of wicked, and would be followed by general judgment. C. disappeared by 5th cent., but was revived at Reformation by various Prot. sects, and has appeared sporadically since then in various places (→ Christadelphians). Another name for C. is Millenarianism, ex. Lat. *mille* = 1,000 (→ Chronology). S.G.F.B.

R.A.C., I, 1073–8; *H.D.B.*², *s.v.; R.G.G.*³, I, 1651–3; J. A. MacCulloch, *Medieval Faith and Fable* (1932), pp. 287ff.; N. Cohn, *Pursuit of the Millennium* (1957).

Chinese Religions It has been customary to speak of the Three Relig.s of China as → Confucianism, → Taoism and → Buddhism. Though in the past these three great systems of belief, ritual practices and organisational relationships designed to deal with ultimate matters of human life have exercised a profound influence, as definite relig. systems they have, for several centuries, had only a historical interest.

In anc. China relig. was a political function conducted by officially appointed shaman-diviners, and contained four leading elements: the cult of ancestors; the worship of Heaven and its subordinate nature-deities; → divination; and → sacrifice. With the estab. of empire, an ethico-political Confucian orthodoxy was linked to the anc. cult, and Confucian scholars, versed in tradition, ritual and customary law, became under the emperor the 'priests' of the cult. This 'official' relig. continued throughout history till the fall of the Chinese monarchy.

It was only with the rise of relig. Taoism (2nd cent. CE) and the intro. of Buddhism into China (from 1st cent. CE) that for the first time (except perhaps for → Mohism) membership in a consciously organised relig. was based on conversion and the voluntary choice of the individual believer. Through several centuries Taoism and Buddhism developed as distinct religs., with trained priests, vast monastic foundations, numerous temples and millions of adherents. They lacked, however, centralised authority and cohesive national organisation. Syncretistic and eclectic tendencies, and mutual borrowings characterised Chi. religs. From the Sung Dynasty (CE 980–1279) onwards the three religs., Confucianism, Taoism and Buddhism, were in large measure merged into a Popular Relig., permeating almost every aspect of Chi. life, which for the past 700 years has been the relig. of the majority of the Chi. people.

Though there are millions of Chi. who might be correctly labelled Confucian, Buddhist or Taoist (together with some 15 million Muslims and 3 million Christians), for the vast majority of Chi. a Popular Relig. suffices, grounded in an anc. nature-worship linked to a cult of → ancestors, and borrowing various features from all three religs., such as Confucian ethics, the Buddhist belief in transmigration and concern for the after-life, the Taoist pantheon with its supreme deity and a host of deified saints and heroes, its belief in divination, magic and sorcery, and faith-healing. The popular relig., weak in formal organisation, is catered for by a host of Buddhist monks and Taoist priests and sorcerers, and exercises a diffused and pervasive influence in every major aspect of Chi. social life.

The permeation of Chi. society by the popular relig. is everywhere evidenced: by the number and variety of temples and wide range of functions which they serve; by festivals, → pilgrimages, ceremonies etc. of a relig. character; by the spirit-tablets, images and pictures of deities to be found in every traditional Chi. home; and by the rituals of relig. brought to bear on every major event of social or family life. Belief in the supernatural is an outstanding mark of Chi. popular relig., but its main concern is to seek the help of these supernatural agencies, whether they be gods, Buddhas, immortals or mere tutelary and nature spirits, to avoid or overcome the ills of life, and guarantee a happier existence in the future. Yet, through a combination of Confucian ethics, Taoist mysticism, Buddhist discipline and techniques of meditation, relig. has proved to be a most potent factor in the development of Chi. civilisation. D.H.S.

W. E. Soothill, *The Three Religions of China* (1923); E. R.-K. Hughes, *Religion in China* (1950); K. L. Reichelt, *Religion in Chinese Garment* (1951); C. K. Yang, *Religion in Chinese Society* (1961); D. H. Smith, *Chinese Religions* (1968).

Ching Chinese character used for classic books; e.g. *Wu Ching*—the five books which make up the Confucian Canon; *Hsin Ching*—the *Heart Sūtra* (Buddhist); *Shêng Ching*—the Holy Bible (Chr.). D.H.S.

Ch'ing Ming Chinese spring festival (lit.—'Pure and Bright') falls usually in 3rd month of lunar year. Now an → All Souls' Festival, when the ancestral graves are visited, repaired and decorated, and offerings of food etc. are made to spirits of dead. Its origins go back to an orgiastic life-renewing and spring-mating festival. It is preceded by eating of cold food (*han shih*), when no fires are lighted for twenty-four hours. As late as T'ang dynasty, new fire was produced by rubbing two willow sticks together. An alternative name, Chih-shu-chieh (Tree-planting festival), also indicates its primitive origin. D.H.S.

Ching T'u → Pure Land School (Buddhist). D.H.S.

Chinvat Bridge → Bridges. S.G.F.B.

Chou I → I Ching. D.H.S.

Christ *Ex.* Grk. *Christos*, 'anointed', which trans. Heb. *māshîah*, i.e. → Messiah, the divinely appointed deliverer of Israel, acc. to Jew. apocalyptic hope. As Mk. 8:27ff. shows, the disciples of → Jesus of Nazareth recognised him as the C., and there can be little doubt that he was popularly so regarded, and that he was executed as a Messianic pretender, as were many others, by the Romans. The Gospels give no certain evidence that Jesus claimed himself to be C., though many of his actions (e.g. Triumphal Entry into Jerusalem) imply such a claim. In Apostolic Age, the title C. quickly became so closely assoc. with Jesus as to be used as personal designation, without article, i.e. 'Jesus Christ' or 'Christ Jesus'. Paul's use of both together in letters to Gentiles reveals basic premise of his theology that the → Old Testament or Covenant with Israel was completed in incarnation of C. in person of Jesus. This view led to re-interpretation of orig. Jewish idea of Messiah (→→ Christianity; Christology, Jesus Christ). S.G.F.B.

*H.D.B.*², pp. 646, 653ff.; *P.C.*², pp. 739ff.; *R.A.C.*, I, 1250–62; *R.G.G.*³, I, 1745–62; *B.C.*, I, pp. 345ff.; J. Klausner, *Jesus of Nazareth* (E.T. 1929), pp. 293; S. G. F. Brandon, *Jesus and the Zealots* (1967), pp. 175–82.

Christadelphians Chr. sect founded in America in 1848 by John Thomas. C. accept Bible as infallible revelation, reject doc. of → Trinity, and expect return of Christ to estab. → theocracy for 1,000 yrs. They teach → baptism by immersion only, annihiliation of wicked, exclusion of those ignorant of Divine Will from → resurrection. They have no ministers. (→ Chiliasm). S.G.F.B.

E.R.E., III, *s.v.; D.C.C.*, *s.v.*

Christian Ethics *Basis*: Chr. Ethics derives from belief that God has revealed his nature and purpose for men in → Jesus Christ; it is the way of life appropriate to that disclosure. The → Bible is regarded as the authoritative witness to that disclosure: the O.T. by way of preparation, the N.T. to Jesus himself and early years of community which resulted from his mission and message. Jesus Christ is thus the key to the Scriptures: he fulfils and in part negates O.T.; the N.T. derives from him. The Gospels are, therefore, of key importance for faith and ethics. The whole weight of Scripture is profoundly ethical, growing out of deepening ethical understanding of God in O.T., and involving a moral renewal of those who follow Christ. This renewal is at once personal and corporate: the Christian is a member of a new community in Christ, i.e. the Church, intended to be moral leaven in the world. Christians were orig. known as followers of a 'Way (of life)'.

Characteristics: the word most used to summarise C.-E. is *love*. This one word in Eng. has to cover wide range of meanings (1) *Libido* or fundamental instinctive drives (2) *philia* or brotherly affection (3) *eros* or yearning for satisfaction, from the coarse level (which adjective 'erotic' now suggests) to desire for beauty, truth and goodness; (4) *agape*, the distinctively Chr. word (though C.-E. allows for other three). → *Agape* is a noun coined from a rather colourless Grk. verb to describe new quality of life brought into world by Jesus. St. → Paul describes it in *I Cor.* 13; it is taught in 'farewell discourses' of

John's Gospel (14–7), and 1st Epistle of John; in → Synoptic Gospels, Jesus says that love to God and neighbour constitute epitome of → Torah, his parables and actions being designed to disclose radical goodness of the God who is to be loved. This is done largely in terms of Kingdom or Rule of God which Jesus sees as drawing near in his ministry, as an earnest of God's final purpose for world. God's power and rule are seen to be highly paradoxical from normal way of thinking: Jesus seeks out the lost; deals with wrongdoers, not by punishment but by forgiveness and bearing consequences of the wrongdoing; he calls into question the goodness of 'good' people and finds the bad not nearly as bad as the 'good' think them; he will not admit restrictions on the neighbour who is to be loved. (Lk. 10:29ff). In Matthew's Gospel a long section of Jesus' ethical teaching has been put together in chs. 5–7, forming 'Sermon on the Mount'. It begins with the Beatitudes, which strike a radical note comp. with Jew. ethics; it goes on to demand absolute trust, obedience and sincerity as the ethic of Kingdom of God, and on ground of what God is like and how he treats us. A moral goodness is disclosed, and demanded by Jesus, which is inexhaustible—the more we know of it, the more we find there is to know. It should be noted that ethical criticisms are sometimes made of certain words and actions of Jesus (usually on ground that they fall short of his own best). There can be no final answer to those who do not find Jesus morally good; but most criticisms arise from misunderstanding the background of Gospels, which the study of any modern commentary would resolve.

Motive: the key motive in C.-E. is a joyful response to love of God revealed in Jesus Christ; it involves any outgoing love to others, which is, in fact, the way by which the self finds its true fulfilment. But negation of self is not part of C.-E.: rather, 'Freely ye have received, freely give', or 'Love as I have loved you'. There is another motive in the Gospels: the hope of rewards (in heaven) or fear of loss (in hell). This motive is frequently said by those who dislike it to be mainspring of C.-E.; but it is not so. It is, however, a secondary motive. Even so, it is much misunderstood by those who think men should do what is right without thought of reward. Rewards in the Chr. life are a by-product for those who live by the first motive, and not its direct object. If God is as Jesus believed, then the pure in heart must in the end 'see' him; i.e. Christ-like conduct must bring men to God. But the reward is no reward to those who are not pure in heart, nor could they receive it: it can only come to those who follow Christ for love's sake, not the reward's sake.

Relation to other ethical systems: (1) *Everyday ethics*: the contrast here is striking, for this is broadly on a basic of reciprocity, 'do good to those who do good to you'. Jesus' ethic is non-reciprocal, e.g. Peter is told to forgive not 7 times but 70 × 7, i.e. to an unlimited extent (Mt. 18:22). Jesus explicitly contrasts his ethic with that of everyday ethics and adds the challenge: 'What do you more than others?' (Mt. 5:47). This is a further instance of the radical goodness revealed by him; it is so far-reaching that it has been called 'an impossible possibility', i.e. no limits can be set to possibilities of its realisation, for it will always transcend and challenge any empirical achievement. Some have criticised it on grounds that a more practicable teaching, e.g. that of → Islam, is more useful. (2) *Moral Philosophy*: C.-E. pre-supposes in some sense freedom of will, a complex issue much discussed in theology and philosophy (e.g. controversy between St. → Augustine and → Pelagius). Beyond this, moral philosophy has tended to fall into two types: the deontological, which stresses duty without regard to consequences of actions; the teleological, which stresses estimated consequences (evaluated by criterion which itself has to be vindicated) as basis of moral choice. Advocates of each of these have never convinced those of other. C.-E. has a deontological side, with its stress on a life of loving obedience to God, and a teleological side when it comes to deciding precisely what to do. Here estimated consequences are judged in light of Chr. criteria, derived from Chr. understanding of nature and destiny of man. In so far as Moral Philosophy eschews either of these types and confines itself to analysis of the logical structure of ethical discourse, C.-E. must submit to this in its own search for clarity of articulation. In so far as Moral Philosophy insists on a logical break between what *is* the case and what *ought* to be, C.-E. agrees that moral judgment cannot be reduced to factual ones, but queries the contention that facts have no bearing on them. There are signs that the 'naturalistic fallacy', which has been widely accepted in recent Anglo-Saxon moral philosophy, is being challenged; but for moment, if the Chr. moralist is required to make this sharp logical distinction, he will say that he makes two assumptions: (a) that God is at least as Jesus believed him to be (b) that it is right to do what accords with the nature of such a God. (3) *Other religions and ethical systems*: these include the → Stoic and → Epicurean systems of antiquity, ethics of the ethnic faiths, and ethics of the two great comprehensive views of life in the mod. world, Marxism and various kinds of humanism. There are similarities at certain levels with the ethics of the ethnic faiths, though none quite arrive at *agape* as Christians understand it. Similarly, resemblances between Stoic and Chr. Ethnic were noted in early cent. of Church, though again *agape* is distinctive. Often different metaphysical background gives different flavour to what verbally seems very similar: e.g. Buddhist compassion and *agape*. Mod. humanism shares many ethical insights with Christianity, which is not surprising as it has grown out of it, usually accepting the ethic but repudiating the doctrine behind it. (Some humanists reject the ethic too, e.g. Nietzsche.) Marxism is interesting, because, theoretically, it is 'scientific socialism' and a repudiation of all religions. In fact, a full critique of Marxism would show that it is much more a series of Biblical concepts clothed in a scientific dress, so that there are many ethnical attitudes in Marxist ethics which are close to Chr. ones, partic. the prophetic protests in O.T. against social corruption, which are taken over in N.T. The resemblances between so many ethical traditions are usually accounted for in Chr. theology by the concept of *Natural Law*. This notion, which is confusing in its name and history, needs careful delimitation, for it cannot be dispensed with altogether. It stands for a capacity in man as man to recognise basic moral distinctions, and to know that he ought to follow what he judges to be right, even if it is against his immediate interests. He works it out in partic. instances by his conscience (another fundamental term in C.-E); This concept was taken over from Stoicism, and given a wider meaning by Paul and other N.T. writers to cover man's reason in its apprehension of matters of right and wrong, in order to make moral choices, and pass judgment on them after they have been acted on. The education of conscience is a vital matter in Chr. life, since a man should obey his conscience (such as it is), but should also set out to grow in maturity and sensitivity of judgment. Christians do not believe in infallibility of conscience, for they so often fail both in insight and action that the phenomenon of the 'bad' conscience is very familiar—indeed so familiar that some theologians have mistakenly restricted the meaning of the term to it.

History: in the N.T. we see a new community of a strikingly creative nature, endeavouring to rule its life by the radical ethic of Jesus. At first it expected the end of time (→ *parousia*) very soon. It had no power or position in the State. Its horizons were therefore restricted and foreshortened. In the N.T. there are many partic. ethical judgments given at this time by Paul which must be read in their context; *1 Corinthians* is esp. illuminating for this. Later, when the *parousia* did not happen, gen. advice was given on standard domestic relationships (the only gen. ethical problems Christians had to deal with). The State was obeyed, unless it required what Christians regarded as idolatrous worship. There was not, and could not be, any worked-out theory of civil society and public responsibility. A drastic change came after conversion of the Emperor Constantine in CE 313, when Christians found themselves in control of the huge and rickety Roman state. From that time until recently, Christianity has been built into European civilisation and its offshoots in other parts of world.

Since the Chr. ethic in the Gospels is worked out in personal and not collective terms, acute problems have been raised as to how it should be related to structure of life, e.g. marriage and the family, daily work in the economic order, political life and citizenship in a locality and in the State; beyond that, in problems of international order. These orders, structures, institutions, mandates (to use the various terms given to them) have come to be seen as areas of obedience given by God for good of mankind. They must be influenced to run in a humane and just way, because they provide framework which moulds men and within which they have to act. All this has caused much reflection on relation of justice to *agape*, and it can roughly be said that it is the expression of *agape* in collective relationships.

In the course of nearly 2,000 years there have been several characteristic Chr. theologies of life, all stemming from same Biblical basis. There has been a 'pietist' turning away from world, sometimes in a pessimistic spirit, sometimes in form of optimistic colonies of 'pure' Christians; there has been the great medieval synthesis with Chr. theology controlling whole of life in an ordered hierarchy; there has been a sharp separation made between world of the Church and that of public life, both being affirmed; and there has been a dynamic understanding of need for Christianity to be an agent of creative change. Only this last insight is adequate for the world of continuous and rapid social change of today; it is this which is characteristic of all Churches, influenced by movement towards unity, known as the → Ecumenical Movement.

Method: since aim of C.-E. is to act from right motive and to find right action in each case, empirical information is vital. But, because of inevitable uncertainties over facts and estimated consequences of actions, there is room for much legitimate differences of opinion among Christians on partic. issues. The study of bearing of a gen. position on a partic. situation is called → *casuistry;* it is often thought to be the special province of *Moral Theology* (as distinct from C.-E. as a more gen. study), though there is no agreed terminology. Casuistry has a bad name because it was used in the → Counter-Reformation to find the least that had to be done without committing grave sin, instead of what was the best thing to do in each circumstance; it has also been too *a priori* in method. But casuistry cannot be avoided, so it is important to estab. it on a right basis which requires attention to the empirical data. R.H.P.

There are no single volumes covering whole range of subject; there are an immense number covering aspects of it. The following deal with most aspects and offer significantly different approaches: R. Schnackenburg, *The Moral Teaching of the New Testament* (E.T. 1965); E. Brunner, *The Divine Imperative* (E.T. 1937); K. E. Kirk, *The Vision of God* (1931); B. Häring, *The Law of Christ*, 3 vols. (E.T. 1961–); Richard Niebuhr, *Christ and Culture* (1951); Reinhold Niebuhr, *An Interpretation of Christian Ethics* (1935); G. F. Thomas, *Christian Ethics and Moral Philosophy* (1955).

Christianity Seen in context of hist. of religions, C. is a saviour-god relig., incorporating trads. of faith and practice current in → Judaism and cults of Graeco-Roman world. It orig. as a Jew. Messianic movement, inspired by and centred on → Jesus of Nazareth. So far as evidence goes, Jesus was concerned only with preparing Israel for coming of Kingdom of God. His crucifixion by the Romans for sedition would prob. have ended movement, as the deaths of the claimants ended other Messianic movements between CE 6 and 66; that it did not was due to conviction of certain disciples that Jesus had risen from death. Inspired by this conviction, the movement revived in new form: the Risen Jesus would return again with supernatural power to complete his Messianic vocation to 'restore the kingdom to Israel' (Acts 1:6). The conversion of → Paul led to transformation of this orig. Jew. Christ. gospel (→ Jewish Christians). Paul explained Crucifixion not as martyrdom for Israel, but as God-planned event to save mankind from enslavement to daemonic forces, which ruled world (→ Archōn), by a pre-existent divine being incarnated in person of Jesus (I Cor. 2:6). Paul, accordingly, presented Christ as divine Saviour of mankind rather than as → Messiah of Israel. The obliteration of Jew. Christ. community of Jerusalem in 70 ensured that Paul's gospel should form basis of Cath. Christianity. It also meant that C. would develop in Graeco-Roman society, and that doctrines of C. would be thought out in terms of Grk. metaphysical thought. This process resulted in doctrine of → Trinity, whereby essential divinity of Jesus was formulated, and his nature as God incarnate was defined (→→ Councils of Nicaea and Chalcedon, → Christology). The doc. of → Atonement, though never officially defined, presented d. of Jesus as only covenanted means of → salvation; the doc. of → Original Sin meant all men needed such salvation. The establishment of C. as official relig. of Roman Empire, and subsequent success of Church in converting barbarian peoples of Europe, produced the rich culture of medieval Christendom, with C. permeating every aspect of life in Europe. The Renaissance and → Reformation shattered supremacy of medieval Church and initiated a gradual process of decline of C. that has continued to present day. Maritime exploration from 15th cent., and consequent spread of European political influence and commercial enterprise, enabled C. to be established in new lands (America, Australia, New Zealand) and in Asia and Africa. Since Reformation, Chr. sects have proliferated, and many, and often strange, varieties of C. now exist throughout world. From 19th cent., Prot. C. produced a trad. of liberal scholarship that has endeavoured to relate Chr. faith and practice to modern knowledge and outlook. The 20th cent. has witnessed a large-scale movement for reunion of Christendom (→ Ecumenical Movement). On so vast and important a subject the following works indicate the complexity of the data and variety of interpretation. S.G.F.B.

E.R.E., I, pp. 579–600; *R.G.G.*, I, 1685–1729; A. Harnack, *History of Dogma*, 7 vols. (E.T. 1900, 1961); Ed. Meyer, *Ursprung und Anfänge des Christentums*, 3 vols. (1921–2); *B.C.*, 5 vols.; *R.A.C.*, II, 1138–59; M. Goguel, *The Life of Jesus* (E.T. 1933), *The Birth of Christianity* (E.T. 1953), *The Primitive Church* (E.T. 1964); M. Werner, *Die Entstehung des christlichen Dogmas* (1941), *The Formation of Christian Dogma* (E.T. 1958); P. Martinetti, *Jésus Christ et le Christianisme* (1942); R. Bultmann, *Primitive Christianity in its contemporary setting* (E.T. 1956); *H.G.R.*, vols. III, IV; F. van der Meer–C. Mohrmann, *Atlas of the Early Christian World* (E.T. 1958); S. G. F. Brandon, *The Fall of Jerusalem and the Christian Church*[2] (1957); *M.D.*, ch. VI; *Jesus and the Zealots* (1967); *Trial of Jesus of Nazareth* (1968); G. G. Coulton, *Five Centuries of Religion*, 4 vols. (1923–50); N. Zernov, *Eastern Christendom* (1961); *N.C.M.H.*, II (1958); B. J. Kidd, *The Counter Reformation* (1933); K. S. Latourette, *Hist. of Expansion of Christianity*, 7 vols. (1937–45); H. Stephan–M. Schmidt, *Gesch. d. deutschen evangelischen Theologie*[2] (1960); L. E. Elliott-Binns, *English Thought* (1860–1900), *The Theological Aspect* (1956); P. Ramsey (ed.), *Religion* (1965); K. Adam, *Catholicism* (E.T. 1929); T. Corbishley, *Roman Catholicism* (1950); *The Crucible of Christianity*, ed. A. Toynbee (1969).

Christians Acc. to Acts 11:26, name was first used

at Antioch by outsiders for followers of Christ, *c.* 40–4. Tacitus (*Annals*, XV:44) indicates that name was already current in Rome at time of Neronian persecution, CE 64. The coining of name, implying leadership of Christ, suggests that C. were perhaps orig. regarded as members of a quasi-political movement. S.G.F.B.

B.C., V, pp. 383ff.; *R.A.C.*, II, 1131–5; *D.C.C.*, *s.v.; H.D.B.*[2], pp. 137–9; H. B. Mattingly, 'The Origin of the Name *Christiani*', *J.T.S.*, IX (1958).

(Nasārā) The Qur. refers both favourably and unfavourably to C.: v, 85 says, 'You will certainly find those nearest in affection to them (i.e. Muslims) the ones who say: We are C.'; iv: 156 condemns C. for saying Jesus was slain, for he was not crucified. They are also blamed for belief in → Trinity (v: 77). Jesus is said to have declared, when questioned by God, that he had not told people to take him and his mother as gods apart from God (v: 116). Within the Muslim state, C. were allowed to practise their relig., and, at least at first, although they were allowed to repair old churches, they were not allowed to build new ones. This did not remain a hard and fast rule. C. were subject to the Muslim state, and had to pay → *jizya* (→ Protected peoples). Many C. rose to positions of influence, notably under the → 'Abbasids. In early days of → Caliphate, when conquests were being made, the local officials were still retained; it was some time before Arabic took place of languages of the conquered countries. (→ 'Abd al-Jabbār on Christianity). J.R.

E.I., III, pp. 848–54; Hughes, pp. 53–6; Wellhausen, *Reste*, pp. 230–4; Tritton, *Non-Muslims*, *passim*; Levy, *Social Structure*, index; F. Rosenthal, *Ibn Khaldun*, index, Parrinder, *Jesus*, index.

Christian Movements in India Christianity was trad. founded in India by the disciple Thomas himself, who is supposed to have preached in various parts of India and been martyred, his tomb being in Mylapore, a suburb of Madras. Though the trad. is doubtful, it cannot be wholly discounted, and the Mar Thoma Church is certainly very ancient. For a long time its bishops were consecrated through Persia; but formal allegiance was transferred to the Jacobite Patriarch of Antioch in mid-17th cent. This resulted from crises arising out of relations with Rome, after coming of Cath. missionaries in 16th and 17th cent. The Syrian Christians of Mar Thoma Church had been induced to recognise papal authority, but in 1633 a substantial body revolted and reasserted independence, in affiliation with Antioch. The coming of Prot. missions in 19th cent. helped to reinvigorate Syrian Church, but also brought about further fragmentation. Some organised themselves as the totally independent Mar Thoma Syrian Church; others ultimately merged with the united Church of South India. But though contact with the West had these effects, it also prevented Syrian Christians from becoming a quasi-caste within the Hindu social fabric—in effect, their position in 15th cent. The use of Syriac in the liturgy, the thoroughly indigenous nature of Church and its antiquity give it a special place in Indian Christianity. Its chief strength is in Kerala and W. Mysore (where it may have had some influence on → Madhva). The first Cath. missionary to India was St. Francis Xavier (1577–1656). Jesuit and other orders were very active during period of Portugese ascendancy, operating chiefly out of Goa. By consequence, the main centres of Cath. strength are in S. and W. India. The methods of Roberto di Nobili (1577–1656), however, who adopted the style of a → *sannyasin* and expounded Christianity in trad. Indian terms, did not attract papal approval, and an import. experiment in indigenisation was not pursued. Prot. missions, apart from those estab. in Danish enclaves, Tranquebar in south and Serampore in Bengal, were excl. by British East India Company, fearing disturbances that might ensue on missionary activity, until early 19th cent. Thereafter there was considerable activity, its impact somewhat weakened by denominational divisions. A substantial part of Western-style education came through mission foundations; and this was to develop an interplay between Christianity and Hinduism among intelligentsia. Many mod. movements of Hinduism (such as the →→ Brahmo Samaj, the Arya Samaj, etc.) were stimulated in this way. The first major success in removal of denominational barriers came with formation of Church of S. India, embracing most Prot. denominations, in 1947. Hindu influences on Christianity can be seen in founding of Christ. → *ashrams* (the first at Tirupattur in S. India in 1921); while → Gandhi both influenced and was influenced by a member of prominent Christians (C. F. Andrews, Foss Westcott, *et al.*) in 1920's and 1930's N.S.

A. E. Medlycott, *India and the Apostle Thomas* (1905); P. Thomas, *Christians and Christianity in India and Pakistan* (1954); L. W. Brown, *The Indian Christians of St Thomas* (1954); J. W. Pickett, *Christian Mass Movement in India* (1933); F. A. Plattner, *Christian India* (1957); S. F. Bayne (ed.), *Ceylon, North India, Pakistan: A Study in Ecumenical Decision* (1960).

Christian Science A faith-healing movement founded in America by Mrs. Mary Baker Eddy (1821–1910). Healed from chronic ill health by a mesmerist, P. P. Quimby, Mrs. Eddy became convinced that illness results from false thinking, esp. in taking matter for reality. She believed that Christ had healed by spiritual influence, and she claimed that she had learnt the secret of this influence. Her ideas and healing methods were set forth in her book *Science and Health* (1875), which enjoyed immense success and is regarded as sacred literature by adherents of C.-S. Her third marriage, in 1877, to Mr. Eddy put his business experience at the service of the movement, which from then began to flourish. In 1879 the 'First Church of Christ Scientist' was opened in Boston, Mass. C.-S. has became estab. in many countries. Its *Christian Science Monitor* is a well-informed newspaper. The tenets of C.-S. are gen. rejected by other Chr. denominations. S.G.F.B.

E.R.E., III, *s.v.;* H. A. L. Fisher, *Our New Religion* (1933); *R.G.G.*³, I, 1732–6; *D.C.C.*, *s.v.*

Christmas The exact time of year of Jesus' birth is not indicated in Gospels. Earliest mention of its commemoration on 25 Dec. is in Philocalian Calendar, showing Roman custom in 336. The date was prob. chosen to offset pagan festival, held at that time, of *Natalis Solis Invicti* ('Birthday of the Unconquered Sun'). In E. Church, C. on 25 Dec. superseded → Epiphany (6 Jan.) by mid. 5th cent. The merrymaking connected with mid-winter festival in many lands, incl. Roman → *Saturnalia*, was naturally transferred to C. S.G.F.B.

E.R.E., III, pp. 601–10; *D.C.C.*, *s.v.; R.G.G.*³, VI, 1564–71 ('Weihnachten'; 'Weihnachtsspiele').

Christology Study of nature of Jesus Christ as God incarnated in person of historical Jesus. Paul's teaching that Christ was divine inevitably raised problem of reconciling this belief with fundamental doc. of → monotheism. Since there could not be two deities, the divinity of Christ had to be related in some way to the unique divinity of God the Father. The problem led to Arian controversy (→ Arianism). The orthodox position was defined at Council of → Nicaea (325) by using metaphysical concept of *homoousios*, 'being of one substance'. Christ was declared to be '*homoousios* to the Father', thus asserting his essential divinity without his being a kind of 'second God'. But the apparent solution of Christ's relation to God the Father raised another question: if he were truly God, how could he also be truly Man, i.e. have a real human nature? Further controversy followed as various interpretations were advanced (→→ Apollinarianism; Monophysitism; Monothelitism; Nestorianism). The basic dilemma, acc. to current Grk. anthropology, was to decide whether Christ had two natures (divine and human), or, two spirits, or two wills. The orthodox view was formulated at Council of → Chalcedon (451) as holding 'one . . . Christ . . . in two natures, without confusion, without change, without division, without separation'. This formula, although it safeguarded the Chr. conviction that Christ was both God and Man, did not explain how a human being could also be God. Among modern attempts at explanation of this problem, the Kenotic theory may be mentioned. 'Kenotic' derives from Grk. word meaning 'to empty'; the theory elaborates the suggestion in Phil. 2:7, that Christ 'emptied himself' of his divine attributes on being born in the likeness of man.' S.G.F.B.

A. Harnack, *H.D.*, 7 vols. (E.T. 1900), *passim;* O. Cullmann, *Die Christologie des Neuen Test.* (1957); R. P. Casey, 'The Earliest Christologies', *J.T.S.*, IX (1958); A. Grillmeier, *Christ in Christian Tradition* (E.T. 1965); *R.G.G.*³, I, 1745–89.

Chronology In many cultures the time-process has been divided into eras related to relig. events. The Sumerian King List had two eras divided by the → Flood, 'when kingship was (again) lowered from heaven' (*A.N.E.T.*, pp. 265–6). Egypt. C., acc. to Manetho, had eras of gods, demi-gods and spirits of dead, before dynastic era. Heb. C. had ante- and post-diluvian periods, closely related to divine providence; in Judaism, time has been reckoned from Creation. In Chr. C. the era → AD was intro. in 5th cent. and that of BC begame gen. in 18th cent. The Muslim era begins with the → Hirja, i.e. Muhammad's flight from Mecca, CE 622. The Five Ages of → Hesiod did not become estab. as a Grk. chronological scheme. The → Stoics, conceiving of time as cyclic, imagined a Great Year which ended with universal conflagration followed by rebirth of new cosmic order. Hindu and Buddhist C., are based on cyclic view of time: 1,000 *mahayugas*, each containing 12,000 'years of the gods', make one *kalpa*, which equals one day of → Brahma. Zoroastrian C. comprised a consequential series of four trimillennia, during which struggle between Good and Evil takes place. The Aztecs used a 52 year period, which was related to a cyclic pattern of fate (→ Americ. Relig. anc.). (→→ Calendar; Time). S.G.F.B.

E.R.E., I, pp. 183–210; *R.A.C.*, III, 30–60; S. G. F. Brandon, *History, Time and Deity* (1965).

Chronos Grk. word for 'time'. Personified by Pindar (*Ol.* 2:19) as 'the father of all', and conceived as one of three primordial agents in cosmic creation by Pherecydes (*c.* 550 BC). Similarity of C. → Kronos led to identification, also with → Aion (Aeon) (→ Time). S.G.F.B.

S. G. F. Brandon, *History, Time and Deity* (1965), pp. 47, 59; *Kleine Pauly*, I, 1166.

Chthonian Deities *Ex.* Grk. *chthōn* = earth. C.-D were Grk. gods or demi-gods who dwelt in the *chthōn*, being connected with both fertility and the dead. They prob. derive from → Aegean Relig., and contrast with Olympic Gods (→ Greek Relig.). There was a Zeus Chthonios, prob. repr. a Hellenising of an Aegean C.-D. Amphiaros and Trophonios were typical C.-D. The → hero-cult was closely assoc. with C.-D. S.G.F.B.

W. K. C. Guthrie, *The Greeks and their Gods* (1950), ch. IX; *E.R.E.*, V. pp. 129–31.

Chuang-tzŭ (Chuang Chou) *c.* 369–286 BC. Taoist philosopher and Chinese mystic, an outstanding interpreter of Taoist thought. A native of Meng in the state of Sung, he held a small governmental post at Ch'i Yüan. A contemporary of → Mencius, though neither mentions the other. His teachings are found in a book of 33 chapters which bears his name and imprint of his mind. Most scholars accept first seven chapters as C.'s own work. C.'s concepts of Tao and Tê are practically the same as those of the → *Tao Tê Ching*. He taught that Tao is an all-embracing first principle. By its spontaneous action everything in nature is produced, and is in constant flux and transformation. The individual should seek tranquility along with spontaneous and natural activity, sageliness within and kingliness without, thus achieving a perfectly balanced life. Happiness lies in knowing one's own nature, in nourishing it and conforming it to the universal and spontaneous process. This can only be done in freedom, hence the recognition of the liberty and equality of all things. Good and evil are relative to one's standard. Life and death are all part of a universal process of endless transformation. When the individual becomes perfectly one with the universal Tao, he reaches a state of pure experience and absolute freedom. In general Confucianists have been critical of C., but he has had great influence on → Buddhism in China, espec. → Ch'an, and was an inspiration to Chi. naturalism, in poetry, painting etc. D.H.S.

Y. L. Fung, *Hist. of Chinese Philosophy* (1937), vol. I, ch. X; W. T. Chan, *Source Book in Chinese Philosophy* (1963), ch. 8; H. A. Giles, *Chuang-tzŭ* (rev. ed. 1961).

Chu Hsi (Also known as Chu Tzŭ, Chu Yüan Hui, Shushi (Japan)): CE 1130–1200. Most celebrated Chi. scholar of Sung dynasty, who through his prolific writings and commentaries on Confucian classics systematised and synthesised the works of earlier neo-Confucians (Chou Tun-i, Shao Yung, Chang Tsai and the Ch'êng brothers), into one all-embracing rationalistic Confucian philosophy which was to remain orthodox till 20th cent. In early life C. studied → Buddhism and → Taoism, but renounced them in favour of → Confucianism. At 19 he passed the governmental exam., and thereafter occupied a succession of official posts; his official life was intermittent and turbulent, as he strongly criticised officials and policies and opposed making peace with the invading enemy. Towards end of life he suffered disgrace, and his teachings were for a short time prohibited. Posthumously he was ennobled as a duke, and in 1241 had his tablet placed in the Confucian temple. His brilliant interpretation and commentaries on the → Four Books (Analects, Mencius, Great Learning and Doctrine of the Mean), which he grouped together, became the basis of a social and ethical philosophy which from 1313–1905 was fundamental in education. D.H.S.

J. P. Bruce, *Chu Hsi and his masters* (1923); Y. L. Fung, *Hist. of Chinese Philosophy* (1953), vol. 2, ch. 13; W. T. Chan, *Source Book of Chinese Philosophy* (1963), ch. 34.

Ch'un Ch'iu (*Spring and Autumn Annals*). One of the 5 Confucian Classics, and attributed to → Confucius himself. It is a brief year by year chronicle of the State of Lu from 722–481 BC. The text is extremely concise and at times obscure, and its value as a hist. record of the times has been greatly enhanced by the commentary known as the *Tso Chuan*. Later, two other valuable commentaries were made; the *Ku-liang Chuan* and the *Kung-yang Chuan*. From early times the C.–C. has been a subject for Confucian instruction, to 'encourage goodness and censure evil'. D.H.S.

J. Legge (tr.), *The Chinese Classics*, vol. 5 (1895); Fung Yu-Lan, *Hist. of Chinese Philosophy* (1937), vol. 1.

Church Eng. word derives ultimately from Grk. *kyriakon*, '(something) belonging to the Lord'. The Lat. *ecclesia* (hence Eng. adj. 'ecclesiastical'. comes from Grk, *ekklésia*, meaning 'assembly') In → LXX, *ekklésia* trans. Heb. *qāhāl*, used for 'assembly' or 'congregation' of Israelites. *Ekklésia* appears in Paul's Epistles, in sing. or plur., for whole Church or local churches respectively. In N.T., C. is already conceived under various mystical concepts: e.g. as Christ's Body (Col. 1:24), Bride (Eph. 5:25ff.), Temple (I Cor. 3:16). Increasing stress was laid on divine constitution and vocation of C. Its four trad. 'notes' were defined as unity, holiness, catholicity, apostolicity (→→ Apostolic Succession; Catholic). The Prot. Reformers sought to re-define nature of C., laying stress on its assoc. with Word of God, not on its sacramental aspect and function. The claim is made by almost every Chr. sect to be, or to belong to, the true C. Acc. to Paul, the C. was the New Israel (Rom. 9:6ff.); hence O.T. was taken over and interpreted as sacred lit. of C. S.G.F.B.

D.C.C., *s.v.; H.D.B.*², pp. 160–2; *E.R.E.*, III, *s.v.; R.G.G.*³, III, 1296–1323; M. Goguel, *L'Église primitive* (1947, E.T. 1964).

Church of England When Christianity was first intro. into Britain is unknown: a Church was estab. before 314, when British bishops attended Council of Arles. The pagan Anglo-Saxons, from 5th cent., obliterated Christianity in parts they conquered; but it survived and flourished in western areas (→ Celtic Christianity). The conversion of Anglo-Saxon England started with mission sent by Pope Gregory, under leadership of Augustine, in 597, and was completed in north by Celtic missionaries from Scotland. The Anglo-Saxon Church was vigorous: it produced a distinctive art and poetry, scholars such as → Bede, and missionaries such as → Boniface. The Norman conquest brought English Church more closely into Continental Church life. The change was marked by building of great cathedrals, the stronger organisation of dioceses and parishes, and intro. of French monasticism (→ Cistercian Order). During Middle Ages there were frequent conflicts between interests of Church and State, the most notable instance leading to martyrdom of Thomas Becket, Archbp. of Canterbury (1170). English kings gen. resisted Papal jurisdiction in England, esp. in matters of finance and eccl. appointments: often this resistance was connected with international politics, particularly the age-long struggle with France. There was much popular criticism of eccl. wealth and corruption, and Papal exactions: the monastic orders also frequently aroused resentment. Desire for reform found effective expression in teaching of Wycliffe and → Lollards. The English Reformation was immediately occasioned by Henry VIII's divorce of Queen Catherine; but its ready acceptance by the people proved that it was welcome, and they resisted attempt of Mary I to undo it. The vicissitudes of the Reformation settlement were closely related to the Tudor dynastic succession. Pressure was strong to bring the C. of E. into line with Continental Protestantism, esp. by abolishing episcopacy. Elizabeth I resisted, and, chiefly through teaching Bp. Jewel and R. Hooker, idea of C. of E. as the 'Via Media' between Rome and Geneva emerged. During the Commonwealth a Puritan victory seemed prob., but restoration of Charles II (1660) finally ensured that C. of E. would be legally estab. form of Christianity in England. The quiescence of C. of E. during 18th cent. led to → Methodist secession, also to an Anglican Evangelical revival. The 19th cent. saw a renewed emphasis on Cath. character of C. of E. in the Oxford Movement, the effects of which have been widespread and continuous. The same period also witnessed great controversy resulting from new scientific theories (e.g. Evolution of Species) and Biblical criticism, and the emergence of a liberalising theology. Rejection by Parliament of C. of E.'s proposed revisions of → Book of Common Prayer in 1927 and 1928 caused much questioning of relations of Church and State, but without change resulting. British imperial expansion during 18th and 19th cents. led to estab. of autonomous churches of C. of E. trad. in many parts of world (→ Anglicanism).

The Elizabethan ideal of the Via Media still characterises C. of E., enabling it to play a special role in modern → ecumenical movement. Its innate comprehensiveness permits it to incl. members whose theological views and practice may be emphatically Catholic, Evangelical or Modernist. It still preserves its trad. connection with the monarchy, which finds dramatic expression in the Coronation ceremony. S.G.F.B.

E.R.E., III, *s.v.; D.C.C.*, *s.v.; R.G.G.*[3], I, 376–85; J. Wand, *Anglicanism in History and Today* (1961); J. R. H. Moorman, *Hist. of the Church in England* (repr. 1958); P. E. More–F. L. Cross, *Anglicanism* (repr. 1957); *Doctrine in the Church of England* (1938); *Official Year Book of the Church of England* (current ed.).

Churinga Ritual instruments used by Central Australian tribes. They were pieces of wood or polished stone, gen. oval or oblong. They could be used as → bull-roarers. They were totemic objects, and were tabu to women and boys. They were housed in a sacred place, and were believed to have magical power. C. were closely assoc. with ancestors, either as residence of soul or image of body. (→ Australian Aborigine Relig.). S.G.F.B.

E.R.E., IV, pp. 365a–6; E. O. James, *Comparative Religion* (1938), pp. 57ff.; M. Eliade in *H.R.*, 6 (1966), pp. 130ff.

Cicada Regarded in China from anc. times as symbol of → resurrection and → immortality. The insect, most frequently *Cicada Atrata* of the order Hemiptera, is very common in China. The young larva passes four years underground, after which it emerges as a mobile pupa which turns into the perfect insect. This rising, as it were, from the grave was noticed in ancient times, when pieces of jade, carved in shape of cicada, were placed in mouths of corpses before burial. The C. is also in China a symbol of happiness and eternal youth. D.H.S.

C. A. S. Williams, *Outlines of Chinese Symbolism* (1931).

Circumcision The cutting off of foreskin or prepuce of male genital organ is undertaken in modern surgical practice for hygienic reasons. Hygiene, however, was not orig. purpose of this anc. practice. The earliest evidence of C. comes from Egypt. It was practised by many Semite peoples (not Babylonians or Assyrians), by some African and Polynesian peoples, by the Aztecs, Maya and Peruvians and some American Indians. The origin of so widespread a custom has been much discussed and various theories offered. Gen. it would seem that C. has been an initiatory rite (age varies from shortly after birth to puberty). An element of sacrifice was prob. involved: offering of part of genital organ to a deity. Peoples practising C. usually despised those who did not: anc. Egyptians amputated genitals of uncircumcised Libyans, but did not thus violate circumcised corpses. With the Hebrews, C. became essential rite of Covenant-relationship with → Yahweh (Gen. 17:10ff.), and has so continued. It is obligatory in Islam. The necessity of C. for Gentile converts to Christianity was an important issue in Primitive Church: Paul's championship of Gentile freedom from C. was successful. Female C., as an initiatory rite, has been practised by some peoples. The Chr. Calendar commemorates C. of Christ on 1 Jan. Roman law forbad C. of non-Jews. (→ Africa, E: Ritual Cults). S.G.F.B.

E.R.E., III, pp. 659–80; *R.G.G.*^{3}, I, 1090–1; *R.A.C.*, II, 159–69; G. Posener (ed.), *Dictionary of Egyptian Civilization* (1962), *s.v.; H.D.B.*^{2}, *s.v.*

(Islam) It seems to have been custom in pre-Islamic Arabia to circumcise both males and females. The Qur. does not refer to C., but practice is mentioned in the traditions. There is even a trad. that Muḥammad was born circumcised. The legal books do not devote much space to C.; but practice is gen. among Muslims, the time varying from age of 7 to 13 in case of boys. Most commonly it is not performed earlier than 7. It has been customary to hold processions preceding C., with the boy to be circumcised partly veiled. The Shāfi'ī school (→ Muslim Law, schools of) consider C. obligatory; but the Mālikī and others treat it as → *sunna*. Whether treated as obligatory or customary, it is universally practised; but not in case of girls. When they are circumcised, it is usually at an earlier age than boys, and no ceremonies are observed. Male converts to Islam who are uncircumcised are expected to undergo rite; but this is not always made obligatory. J.R.

E.I., II, pp. 957–60; Pareja, pp. 657f.; Lane, *Egyptians*, pp. 511ff.; Dickson, *Arab of desert*, pp. 175–8, 507, 518; Wensinck, *Handbook*, p. 44.

Cistercian Order In 1098 Robert of Molesme founded the C.-O., or White Monks, at Cîteaux in Burgundy. Their rule was a very strict form of the → Benedictine Rule, incl. austere diet, silence, and manual labour. Their churches were plain, and ornaments and vestments simple. C. abbeys were usually founded in remote places, and played important part in development of agriculture, and in England of sheep farming. St. → Bernard of Clairvaux was a distinguished C. monk. Each house regulated its life in acc. with ordinances of annual General Chapters at Cîteaux. After 13th cent. influence of C.-O. declined. The 17th cent. saw reform movements the most notable being that of La Trappe, hence the 'Trappists' or Reformed Cistercians of the Strict Observance. (→ Cluny, Order of). S.G.F.B.

D.C.C., pp. 292, 1372; G. G. Coulton, *Five Centuries of Religion*, I (1923), chs. 20–2, 26, 29; D. Knowles, *The Monastic Order of England* (1949), chs. 12–4.

Cit Sometimes transliterated *chit:* consciousness, or the essential property of the eternal self (→ *atman*) in Hindu thought. It is also one of the three crucial attributes of → *Brahman*, together with being and bliss. Typically *cit* is distinguished from transient psychological states, etc.; i.e. the mind as functioning in body belongs to material world, though it is illuminated by *cit*. N.S.

Citta An import. term in the Buddh. analysis of human existence; sometimes trans. as 'consciousness', sometimes as 'mind'. It is regarded as a characteristic of all beings above level of plant life. C. is used as collective term for whole stream or series of momentary mental states (somewhat after manner of the individual 'frames' in a film, which, when shown quickly and successively, give impression of continuous action). The systematic analysis of the → *Abhidhamma* distinguishes in all phenomena three elements: *citta:* the quality of the citta, or that which 'accompanies' it (*cetisakā*); the material shape or corporeality (*rūpa*).

Every C., or individual momentary state of consciousness, is characterised by pain, pleasure or indifference; sensation of sight, hearing, taste, etc.; whether morally wholesome or unwholesome etc. C.s. are distinguished also acc. to whether they are 'states of consciousness' in the material-sensory world (*kāma-loka*), the world of pure form (*rūpa-loka*), world of formlessness (*arūpa-loka*), or transcendental world. Acc. to the → Thv. *Abhidhamma* there are altogether 121 different types of C.s. Each of these is capable of occurring in combination with any of 52 mental properties or concomitants (*cetasikā*), thus making poss. a great variety of poss. mental events.

In → Mahāyāna Buddhism, C. is identified by the → Yogācārins with the 'store-consciousness' or → *ālaya-vijñāna*. It is thus, acc. to the → *Lankāvatāra Sutra*, that which 'gathers up *karma*'; '*karma* is gathered up by *citta*'. In gen., in Buddh. usage, C. is virtually a synonym of → *Vijñāna*, also trans. 'consciousness'. T.O.L.

S. Z. Aung, *Compendium of Philosophy*, PTS. 1910 (repr. 1956); D. T. Suzuki, *Studies in the Lankāvatāra Sutra* (1930), pp. 176, 180ff., 398–402.

Clean and Unclean Among primitive peoples distinction has been made between objects and events that confer ritual impurity and those that do not. This distinction is not based upon sanitary considerations, but stems from religio-magical evaluation. An object or event imagined to have some supernatural or numinous quality must be guarded by → tabus, and is often regarded as → holy. Contact with such can be dangerous both to the person concerned, and, through his contamination, affect others. Sometimes only certain persons, such as priests or → shamans, can safely have commerce with such things: for others contact is fatal, as, e.g. Uzzah who touched the → Ark (II Sam. 6:6ff.). Heb. relig. law set out careful regulations about what was ritually unclean or made unclean, and the means of ritual purification. The items concerned fall into five groups: sexual activity of various kinds; blood, esp. menstrual blood (Lev. 15:19ff.); certain food; death; leprosy. The idea finds significant expression also in Jew. definition of a sacred book as one that 'defiles the hands', i.e. hands had to be ceremonially washed after touching it. The distinction between C. and U., and rules for purification became excessively elaborated among Jews (Mk. 7:1–5), and was condemned by Jesus (Mt. 15:1ff.). S.G.F.B.

*H.D.B.*², pp. 165–7; *R.G.G.*³, V, 940–4; *E.R.E.*, X ('Purification'); E. R. Dodds, *The Greeks and the Irrational* (1951), pp. 35ff.

Cleanthes (331–232 BC) Celebrated Stoic teacher, whose → Stoicism was permeated with a religious fervour that finds noble expression in his *Hymn to Zeus*. S.G.F.B.

E. Bevan, *Later Greek Religion* (1927), pp. 9–15; *E.R.E.*, III, *s.v.;* A.-J. Festugière, *La révélation d'Hermès Trismégeste*, II (1949), pp. 310ff.

Clement of Alexandria (*c.* 150–*c.* 215 AD) Chr. theologian; b. prob. at Athens, of pagan parents. After conversion (details unknown), C. spent several years studying Christianity and philosophy in Italy, Syria, Palestine. He finally became pupil and successor of Pantaenus, first head of Catechetical School of Alexandria, of whom he writes (*Strom.* I:1): 'When I came upon the last teacher (in ability, the first), having tracked him down in Egypt, I found rest. He, the true Sicilian bee, gathering the spoil of the flowers of the prophetic and apostolic meadow, engendered in his hearers a deathless element of knowledge'—the description might well apply to C.'s own subsequent achievement. The persecution of Septimius Severus (202/3) forced C. to leave Egypt for Cappadocia; he never returned, and was succeeded as head of School by → Origen. C.'s many writings illustrate development of Early Chr. thought in rel. to its cultural environment. His *Exhortation to the Greeks* (*Protrepticus*) is an attack on pagan beliefs and relig. practices; it presents the → Logos of the world as incarnate in Christ, who brings redemption and immortality. Christianity is, thus, the only true *philosophy;* for the Logos had through world-history educated mankind and now in Christ offered knowledge that saves. '*The Tutor*' (*Paidagōgos*) assumes that the *Exhortation* has done its work and offers instruction to the converted. There should have been a third treatise, forming a trilogy, presumably entitled '*The Teacher*' (*Didaskalos*), i.e. systematic doc. and ethics (cf. Origen's later *De Principiis*); but C. had not the gifts for this, and instead produced his '*Stromateis*', i.e. 'carpet-bags', a contemporary genre of philosophers and litterateurs, sometimes called 'tapestries', 'meadows', 'banquets', being unsystematic discussions of all sorts of themes. Its main concern is relation of Chr. → Gnosis to Grk. philosophy. C. continues 2nd cent. Apologetic trad. (in contrast to → Tertullian) of evaluating Grk. philosophy positively as providential *praeparatio evangelii* for Greeks, as was the Law for Jews: he ranked the Law as logically and temporarily prior. C. (with little acknowledgement) was heavily dependent on → Philo. *Quis Dives Salvetur?* is a short homily on Mk. 10:17ff. *Excerpta ex Theodoto, Eclogae Propheticae* contain C.'s extracts for his own studies from Gnostics, from whom he seeks (not always successfully) to dissociate his own 'Christian Gnosticism'. Fragments only survive of his *Hypotyposeis* ('sketches'), i.e. allegorical interpretations of passages of Scripture and some disputed writings (e.g. *Ep. of → Barnabas*). C., who sat loose to ecclesiastical ties, was the father of Chr. humanism, cultured, unsystematic, hospitable to the truth wherever he found it. He valued the faith and sacraments of Church as supreme instruments of the Logos, who, nevertheless, was source of all human reason and of the partial insights of paganism and heresy. B.D.

Text: Migne, *P.G.*, vols. 8, 9; Stählin, *G.C.S.*, 4 vols., new edn. by Früchtel (crit. ed. with useful notes and refs.). C. Bigg, *Christian Platonists of Alexandria*, ed. F. E. Brightman (1913); E. Molland, *Conception of the Gospel in Alexandrian Theology* (1938). Full bibliog. of immense mod. work on C., esp. Continental and journals, in J. Questen, *Patrology*, vol. II (1953), pp. 5ff. *Trans.:* W. Wilson, *A.N.L.* (1867–72); A. E. de Genoude, *Les Pères de l'Église*, vols. 4, 5 (1839); Stählin, *Bibliothek der Kirchenväter* (1934 *et seq.*).

Clement, Epistles of First Ep. of C. was written by C., Bishop of Rome, *c.* 96. It was addressed, in name of Roman Church, to Christians of Corinth, to deal with fierce dissensions there. It affords valuable evidence of Chr. life and institutions at both Rome and Corinth at this early period. The so-called Second Ep. of C. is really a homily, by another (unknown) author, prob. of Corinth. S.G.F.B.

J. B. Lightfoot, *The Apostolic Fathers* (1891), pp. 1–94; J. Weiss, *Earliest Christianity* (E.T. 1959), II, pp. 849ff.; *R.A.C.*, III, 188–206.

Clementine Literature Several writings were current in Early Church ascribed to Clement of Rome, of which only the First Epistle of → C. is genuine. Under title of C.-L. the two most notable documents are the *Clementine Homilies* and *Recognitions:* they are often called the '*Pseudo-Clementines*'. The former is a kind of relig. romance, arranged in 20 discourses, purporting to have been sent by C. to → James, the Lord's brother, at Jerusalem. They are chiefly concerned with St. → Peter's conflict with → Simon Magus. The discourses are prefaced by two letters from Peter and C. to James. The *Recognitions* largely covers same ground as *Homilies*, with addition of account of final reunion, subsequent on their 'recognition', of separated member of C.'s family. The orig. of C.-L. has been much discussed: in their present form (*Recognitions* exists only in Lat. trans. of orig. Grk.) they prob. date from 4th cent., but derive from early 3rd cent. source. The C.-L., or its source, incorporates much earlier material, poss. the *Kerygma Petrou*, which may derive from → Ebionite tradition. S.G.F.B.

Text in *G.C.S.*, 42 (1953), 51 (1965), ed. B. Rehm; E.T., in *A-N.L.*, III, XVII; O. Cullmann, *Problème littéraire et historique du roman pseudo-clementin* (1930); *R.A.C.*, III, 197–206; *R.G.G.*[3], V, 693–4; H. J. Schoeps, *Theologie u. Gesch. d. Judenchristentums* (1949); G. Strecker, *Das Judenchristentum in den Pseudo-Clementinen.*

Clergy (Islam) There are no clergy in Islam, unless we can say there is such in the → Ṣūfī orders. The imam, who leads worship in a mosque, has no priestly function, but is merely the one who leads the congregation. Any Muslim of full age, sound mind, and good character is eligible to lead others in worship. It is convenient to have a regular imam in mosque. But while the imam of a large mosque is looked on with respect, his office is not a priestly one. (→ Hierarchy). J.R.

M.W., LI (1961), pp. 197ff. (A. W. Sadler, 'Islam: the parish situation'); Cragg, *Minaret*, p. 125.

Cluny, Order of The monastery of Cluny, Burgundy, founded in 910, became source of monastic reform which profoundly affected W. Church from 10th to 12th cent. Its second Abbot, Odo (927–42) laid foundations of its influence, which stemmed from strict observance of → Benedictine Rule, personal holiness, and emphasis on choir office. The Cluniac Order was highly centralised: heads of subject houses were priors, not abbots. It attracted many members of noble families, and was greatly respected by kings and popes. When consecrated in 1131–2, the mother Church of Cluny was largest in Europe; the C.-O. patronised development of art and architecture. Its influence greatly declined in later Middle Ages. (→ Cistercian Order). S.G.F.B.

D.C.C., s.v.; G. Zarnecki in *The Flowering of the Middle Ages*, ed. J. Evans (1966), pp. 63ff.; G. G. Coulton, *Five Centuries of Religion*, I (1923), ch. XXI; D. Knowles, *The Monastic Order in England* (1950), ch. XVI.

Codex Alexandrinus An early 5th cent. MS. of Grk. Bible, presented by Patriarch of Constantinople to James I (1603–25); now in British Museum. C.-A. includes the two. Ep. of → Clement. It was prob. written in Egypt; in critical apparatus it is designated 'A'. S.G.F.B.

F. G. Kenyon, *Our Bible and the Ancient Manuscripts*[3], pp. 128–32; *D.C.C., s.v.;* T. S. Skeat, 'The Provenance of Codex Alex.', *J.T.S.*, VI (1955).

Bezae A Grk.-Lat. MS. of Gospels, Acts and part of III John, dating prob. from 5th cent., given to Univ. of Cambridge in 1581 by T. Beza. It is principal representative of Western text (→ Text of N.T.). In critical apparatus it is designated 'D'. S.G.F.B.

D.C.C., s.v.; F. G. Kenyon, *Our Bible and the Ancient Manuscripts*[3], pp. 139–44; *B.C.*, III, pp. lviff.

Sinaiticus Famous MS. of Grk. Bible discovered by C. Tischendorf in monastery of St. Catherine on Mt. Sinai in 1844; it was purchased from Soviet Government in 1933 and is now in British Museum. Besides O.T. and N.T., C.–S. contains Ep. of → Barnabas and part of the Shepherd of → Hermas'. It was prob. written in Egypt in latter 4th cent. C.S. decisively affected text followed in R.V. of N.T. in 1881. In critical apparatus it is designated 'א'. S.G.F.B.

F. G. Kenyon, *Our Bible and the Ancient Manuscripts*[3], pp. 121–8; *D.C.C., s.v.*

Vaticanus A 4th cent. MS. of Grk. Bible that has been in Vatican Library since at least 1481. The N.T. text is missing after Heb. 9:14. It was prob. written in → Alexandria; with Codex Sinaiticus, it constitutes what is known as the Neutral Text of N.T., i.e. a text supposedly the less corrupted by editorial revision. In critical apparatus it is designated 'B'. (→ Text of N.T.). S.G.F.B.

F. G. Kenyon, *Our Bible and the Ancient Manuscripts*[3], pp. 132–7; *D.C.C., s.v.*

Coffin Texts, The During the Middle Kingdom (2160–1580 BC) it was customary in Egypt to paint mortuary texts on sides of large wooden coffins for use of deceased. Many C.-T. derive from → Pyramid Texts; together with other material, they document the development of mortuary cult and other aspects of Egypt. relig. In partic. they witness to a democratisation of the royal mortuary ritual, the increasing import. of → Osiris, and develop. of idea of judgment of dead. Certain coffins from El-Bersheh give a variant form of C.-T., known as the *Book of the Two Ways*, constituting a veritable guide-book to next world. S.G.F.B.

A. De Buck, *The Egyptian Coffin Texts*, 7 vols. (1935–61); *R.Ae.R-G.*, *s.v.* ('Sargtexte'); J. Vandier, *La religion égyptienne* (1949[2]), pp. 86ff.; L. Speleers, *Textes des cercueils du Moyen Empire égyptienne* (1947).

Colossians, Epistle A letter supposedly written from Rome by → Paul to Christians at Colossae, a city in Phrygia. It is chiefly notable for its evidence concerning a form of astral → Gnosticism current at Colossae, which had seriously affected Christians there. Pauline authorship of writing has been questioned: critical opinion seems gen. prepared to accept it as substantially of Paul's authorship. (→ Astralism). S.G.F.B.

P.C.[2], pp. 990ff.; *H.D.B.*[2], pp. 169–70; *R.G.G.*[3], III, 1727–8; F. F. Bruce, 'The Epistle to the Colossians', *B.J.R.L.*, 48 (1966).

Colours—Religious Meaning (China-Japan) The 5 primary colours, acc. to Chinese gradation are red, yellow, azure, white and black, and are emblematic of rank, authority, virtue and vice, joys and sorrows. Azure was assoc. with worship of Heaven; yellow, of Earth, red, of the Sun; white, of the Moon. Red is symbolic of happiness and virtue; black, of guilt and vice. Red is used at weddings and festivals; white clothing a symbol of mourning. White also indicates purity. Charms against evil spirits are written on yellow paper.

In Japan, red and white are considered to be auspicious colours, red being espec. obnoxious to devils. Among gifts offered to gods at → Shinto shrines are *mochi* cakes, placed in sets of two, one white and one red. Black, being colour of rain-clouds, offerings of black animals are made when praying for rain. D.H.S.

C. A. S. Williams, *Outlines of Chinese Symbolism* (1931); W. G. Aston, *Shinto* (1905).

Companions of Prophet (*Ṣaḥāba*, or *aṣḥāb*, sing. *ṣaḥābī*). Muslims hold Muḥammad's companions in high esteem. Those who deserve this title are people who accepted Islam in Muḥammad's lifetime and accompanied him, however short the period may have been; but some hold that a period of a year is required to qualify. Some of those who are reckoned C. were still in childhood when Muhammad died. C. are gen. considered to be above criticism; when one mentions one of them it is usual to say, 'God be pleased with him.' The Traditions are presented as transmitted through C., but through a comparatively small number of total. The number of C. may have reached 100,000. While → Sunnīs respect the C. → Shī'īs are inclined to criticise them, sometimes even violently, because they accepted first three caliphs, so defrauding → 'Alī, as they feel, of his right. There are a number of biographical dictionaries of the C., but none are trans. from the Arabic. J.R.

E.I., I, pp. 447f. (Aṣḥāb); Goldziher, *M.S.*, II, pp. 240f.; D. B. Macdonald, *Theology*, index; Wensinck, *Creed*, index; Siddiqi, *Hadith*, pp. 21ff.; *Mishkāt*, pp. 1317ff. and index (miscellaneous items).

Communion, Holy In most forms of sacrifice involving offering of victim's life, part of the body was burnt on altar, to convey it to deity concerned; the rest was eaten by those offering the sacrifice. This ritual-eating constituted an act of communion between deity and devotees. Such an interpretation of the ritual commemoration of the Last Supper seems to be made by → Paul in I Cor. 10:16–21: *koinōnia* ('participation', 'communion') is effected by consuming 'the blood' and 'the body of Christ'. The sacrificial aspect of the → Eucharist is thus primitive, and reception of the sacramental Body and Blood of Christ by officiant and people after act of consecration constitutes H.-C., in terms of the trad. sacrificial pattern. Prot. churches, which rejected doc. of Eucharistic Sacrifice, retained act of H.-C., though assigning to it various meanings. (→→ Mystery Religions, Omphagia). S.G.F.B.

H. Lietzmann, *An Die Korinther*, I, II (1923), pp. 48–51; J. F. Bethune-Baker, *Intro. to Early Hist. of Christian Doctrine*, pp. 393ff.; M. Goguel, *L'Église primitive* (1947), pp. 350ff.; *The Primitive Church* (1964), E.T., 325ff.; J. Jeremias, *The Eucharistic Words of Jesus* (E.T. 1955), pp. 153ff.; *R.G.G.*[3], I, 11–4, 19–21; C. Clemen, *Religionsgeschichtliche Erklärung des N.T.* (1924), pp. 174ff.; A. Loisy, *Les mystères païens et le mystère chrétien* (1914), pp. 286ff.; *Th. Wb.*, III, pp. 730ff.

Communism The absence of private property and community of goods have often been regarded as an idyllic state of society in a mythical Golden Age. Such idealised C. has characterised many relig. movements. The Buddhist → Sangha was communist, and C. has been an essential characteristic of Jew. and Chr. → monasticism (→→ Essenes; Qumran). It has also been practised in the Hindu *Ashram*, i.e. small community of disciples gathered around their *guru* ('teacher').

The original Chr. community at Jerusalem practised C., and Acts 2:42ff.; 4:32ff., 5:1ff. give a graphic account of its nature and consequences. Certain Chr. sects, e.g. →→ Albigenses, Cathari, Levellers were C. In Persia a Zoroastrian C. appeared under Mazdah: it was suppressed in 528 (→ Mazdahism). (→ Marx, K.) S.G.F.B.

*R.G.G.*³, III, 1733–7; E. Troeltsch, *The Social Teaching of the Christian Churches* (E.T. 1931), I, pp. 115ff.; *E.R.E.*, III, *s.v.;* D. M. Mackinnon (ed.), *Christian Faith and Communist Faith* (1953).

Comparative Religion Designation that has become trad. for the comparative study of religion. C.-R. can be traced back to → Xenophanes (6th cent. BC), who noted that Thracians and Ethiopians each depicted gods after their own facial characteristics. Awareness of significance of similarity in religs. is shown by several Grk. and Lat. writers; but scientific interest dates from 18th cent., J. Lafitau being a notable pioneer by comparing relig. customs of N. American Indians, Graeco-Roman paganism and Christianity. Interest in C.-R. greatly increased in 19th cent., being stimulated by study of oriental languages, decipherment of anc. Egypt. and Mesopot. tongues, and ethnology, and deeply influenced by the evolutionary concept. Among chief exponents then were F. Max Müller (1823–1900), who initiated the *S.B.E.* series, Sir E. B. Tylor (1832–1917), who advanced theory of → animism, and Sir J. G. → Frazer. The subject gained academic recognition, chairs were instituted at various universities, and journals started, one of the most notable being the *Revue de l'histoire des religions* (1880). In Germany the subject took form more of hist. of religs. → (*Religionsgeschichte*). There was a tendency to regard C.-R. as an adjunct to Chr. theology: today the subject is regarded increasingly as a discipline in its own right, and one that has an essential place in the corpus of the humanities. The 'International Association for the Hist. of Religions' (founded 1900) holds an internat. Congress at five-yearly intervals, and sponsors the journal *Numen* (from 1954) and other publications. (→ Phenomenology of Religion). S.G.F.B.

L. H. Jordan, *Comparative Religion: its genesis and growth* (1905), *Comparative Religion: its adjuncts and allies* (1915); *Chantepie de la Saussaye, Lehrbuch der Religionsgeschichte*, hrg. A. Bertholet u. E. Lehmann, 2 vols. (1925); E. O. James, *Comparative Religion* (1938); H. Pinard de la Boullaye, *L'Étude comparée des religions*, 2 vols. (1925); G. Mensching, *Vergleichende Religionswissenschaft* (1949); G. Van der Leeuw, *La Religion* (1948); M. Eliade, *Traité d'histoire des religions* (1949), E.T., *Patterns in Comparative Religion* (1958), *From Primitives to Zen* (1967); J. Wach, *The Comparative Study of Religions* (1958); S. G. F. Brandon, *Man and his Destiny in the Great Religions* (1962); *Religion in Geschichte und Gegenwart*³, 6 vols. and index vol. (1957–65); J. G. Frazer, *The Golden Bough*³, 13 vols. (1936); J. Hastings, *Encyclopaedia of Religion and Ethics*, 13 vols. (1908–26); P. H. Ashby, The History of Religions', in *Religion* (The Princeton Studies. ed. P. Ramsey (1965); H. Ringren–A. V. Ström, *Religions of Mankind* (E.T. 1967); Widengren, *R-P.* (1969). Journals: *Revue de l'histoire des religions; Journal of Religion; Zeitschrift für Religions—und Geistesgeschichte; Numen; Review of Religion; History of Religion; Religious Studies*. Bibliography: Bibliographie générale', by H. Ch. Puech in *Mana*, I (1949), together with J. Vandier, *La religion égyptienne; International Bibliography of the History of Religions* (from 1952, pub. by The International Association for the History of Religions).

Compassion (Buddh.) One of the 4 'illimitable' or universal virtues in Buddh. thought, described also by Conze as the social emotions' (*Buddh. Thought in India*, 1962, ch. 6). C. (*karunā*) follows loving kindness, i.e. it is a resultant of cultivation of attitude of loving kindness; and in the Buddh. order it precedes 'sympathetic joy'. In → Mhy. Buddhism, compassion is elevated to place of importance equal to that of wisdom (*prajñā*); in → Hīnayāna Buddhism, compassion was subordinate to wisdom. In the Mhy. the term *karunā* denotes partic. the 'infinite grace of the Buddhas and Bodhisattras for beings' (Murti, *Central Philosophy of Buddhism*, 1955). (→ Brahma-Vihara). T.O.L.

Compitalia Popular Roman festival, in honour of the *lares compitales* (→ Lares). Of rural orig., celebrated at end-Dec.-begin.-Jan., it became urbanised; its celebration was located at meeting-points of *insulae* (blocks of houses), orig. at cross-roads. A notable custom of C. was hanging up puppets and bells repr. freeman and slaves respectively of households concerned: purpose was prob. not substitute for human sacrifice, but part of a purificatory ritual. S.G.F.B.

Kleine Pauly, I, 1265–6; *O.C.D.*, *s.v.* ('Lares').

Conceit (Buddh.) In Buddh. thought, 3 types of conceit (*māna*) are distinguished: 'superiority-conceit'; 'equality-conceit'; 'inferiority-conceit'. In Buddh. view, it is characteristic of those who believe in a permanent, enduring → ego to entertain such conceits. All those who rely on idea of a permanent individual self imagine, 'Better am I', or 'Equal am I', or 'Worse am I'; all these imagine thus through not understanding reality (SN.XII:49). C. is thus a 'fetter', which is broken only at attainment of → Arahantship. T.O.L.

Conception, in Buddh. thought (1) The conception

by mind of an object, in Buddh. thought, is result of operation of 3 distinguishable mental properties, or → *cetasika*: *vitakka* (directing of attention to object); *vicāra* (sustaining of attention upon object); *adhimokkha* (decision to go on attending to that one object out of many presented to the consciousness). (2) Physical conception in womb of mother, acc. to B. thought, takes place when three conditions are fulfilled: (a) when intercourse has taken place (b) when time is auspicious for mother (c) when some → *karma*-energy (i.e. from some previous existence) is ready to enter upon a new life. When these 3 conditions are fulfilled an embryo is produced; this is known as *okkanti* (lit. 'descent'). In B. countries, it is usual to reckon age of child from time of conception, which is regarded as re-beginning of life-process (*jāti*), rather than from time of birth. In some S.E. Asian B. countries, e.g. Thailand, concep. is gen. welcomed, since it is regarded as a blessing from the Buddha. T.O.L.

Conditional Immortality Belief that the → soul is not intrinsically immortal, but must prove itself worthy thereof; otherwise it is annihilated. C.-I. was held by 4th cent. N. African Chr. Arnobius; it was condemned by 5th Lateran Council in 1513. It has found favour among certain Chr. writers in 19th and 20th cent., but is still officially rejected. S.G.F.B.

E.R.E., III, *s.v.; D.C.C., s.v.*

Confession Acknowledgement of faults, either moral or ritual, to a deity, as a necessary expression of penitence finds early expression in relig. In → Mesopot. relig. C. was frequent, gen. concerning ritual offences, to avert divine wrath, and was accompanied by ritual acts, mostly of propitiatory nature. Some formularies of C. refer to unknown offences, since consequences of such could also be dire. The Egypt. → Book of the Dead contains what are often called 'Negative Confessions'. addressed by deceased respect. to → Osiris and 42 other gods. The descript., which is modern, is misleading, since the formularies are really detailed declarations of innocence. C.'s of sins, addressed to various gods, are found in Egypt. texts. C. was a regular feature of Heb. relig.: the Psalms provide numerous expressions of individual C. made directly to God; corporate C. was prescribed most notably in ritual of Day of → Atonement. In Christianity, C. was a natural consequence of power of forgiving sins given to apostles acc. to Jn. 20:22ff.; practice of C. is inculcated in James 5:16 and I Jn. 1:9. The practice of public C. was regular in Early Church, and was part of system of → Penance. In W. Church, public C. was suppressed by Pope Leo I (d. 461), and custom of private C. became normal. This change was marked by appearance in E. and W. Church, mostly from 7th cent., of *Penitentials*, prescribing for administration of penance. In R.C. Church, C. is necessary before receiving Holy Communion, and it must be made at least once a year. The hearing of C.'s is carefully prescribed, and special confessional places are erected in churches. C.'s can only be heard by bishop or priest, and absolution given. The inviolable secrecy of C. is enjoined on confessor, and severest penalties are prescribed for breaking 'seal of C.'. In → Anglican Church, C. is recommended but not commanded. Private C. to priest is regularly prescribed in E. Church; it is rejected by Prot. Churches, though Salvation Army and some sects have forms of public C. (→ Inca Relig.). S.G.F.B.

E. Dhorme, *R.B.A.*, p. 239; Ch. Maystre, 'Les déclarations d'innocence', *R.A.P.H.*, 8 (1937); S. G. F. Brandon, *The Judgment of the Dead* (1967), ch. 2; *E.R.E.*, III, pp. 825–31; IX, pp. 711–20; *R.G.G.*[3], VI, 505–6; K. E. Kirk, *The Vision of God* (1950), pp. 279ff.; N. Zernov, *Eastern Christendom* (1961), pp. 251ff.

Confirmation Chr. rite, given sacramental status (→ Sacrament), whereby grace of → Holy Spirit is conferred in some new or fuller way than in → Baptism. The orig. of C. is obscure, and there is considerable diversity of theological opinion about its nature and purpose. By 4th cent. it seems that anointing with oil, formerly part of baptismal ritual, became separate rite. Baptism was henceforth usually administered by priest, and anointing became separate rite performed by bishop or priest using oil consecrated by bishop. It has become custom in E. Church for priest to anoint infant immediately after baptism, thus retaining orig. close connection of C. with baptism. In W. Church, anointing or C. was deferred until candidate could be presented to bishop. The custom now in R.C. Church is to confer C. after 7th birthday, by anointing. In C. of E., it is necessary to give adolescents special course of instruction in faith preparatory to C., which is administered by laying on of bishop's hands, without anointing. (→ Unction). S.G.F.B.

D.C.C., s.v.; N. Zernov, *Eastern Christendom* (1961), pp. 250–1; *E.R.E.*, IV, *s.v.; C.E.*, IV, *s.v.;* L. Vischer, *La confirmation au cours des siècles* (1959).

Confucianism Called in Chinese *Ju Chiao* ('The Teaching of the Scholars') and *K'ung Chiao* ('The Teaching of Confucius'). → Confucius. The roots of C. are earlier than Confucius and lie in teachings of a scholar class, known as *Ju* who, in anc. China, were experts in rituals and ceremonials of an official cult in which sacrifices were made and prayers offered to Heaven and Earth, a host of nature deities and the *manes* of the ancestors (→ Ancestor worship).

After the death of Confucius (479 BC), his ethico-political teachings became increasingly influential, and by Han Dynasty (206 BC–CE 225) these teachings, linked to the imperial ceremonies, the worship of Heaven by emperor, and the ancestral rites practised by most families, became official cult of scholar-class and remained so until fall of Chinese monarchy in CE 1912. There were, however, long periods when imperial favour bestowed on → Taoism and → Buddhism resulted in neglect of Confucian cult.

The official relig. imposed the public worship of Confucius on all officials in administrative districts throughout China, and a Confucian temple (*Kung Miao* or *Wen Miao*) was maintained in all cities. Though from CE 1382 onwards, statues or images of Confucius have been forbidden in temples, their place was taken by his spirit-tablet, which occupies a place of honour behind the central altar, facing S. His tablet is accompanied by those of his four principal disciples, whilst place is found in the temples for tablets of all the greatest Confucian scholars. Twice a year, in mid-spring and mid-autumn great feasts in honour of Confucius were held, attended by civil and military officials of each district, together with scholars and students. Offerings and prayers were presented to Confucius to accompaniment of solemn music and dancing. Offerings were also presented twice a month at full moon and new moon.

With estab. of the Republic, and until Communists gained control, although the great rituals for the worship of Heaven fell into abeyance, the honours paid to Confucius continued, and an abortive attempt was made to make C. into a state relig.

The questions as to whether C. may be regarded as a relig. has been hotly debated. Certainly there is no church organisation, no specialised priesthood, no obligatory creeds or dogmas. For past 700 years, since → Chu Hsi and → neo-Confucian revival, most Confucian scholars have been agnostic as regards belief in God and an after-life. C. has always considered perfection of social and individual life in this world as of paramount importance, and its emphasis has been on ethics, education and political and social stability. Yet Confucius has undoubtedly been worshipped and honoured for over 2000 years of Chi. hist. as a superior being, as the Holy and Wise Sage co-equal with Heaven and Earth, and prayers and sacrifices have been regularly made to him. In C. a cosmic ruling power and transcendent spiritual values have been generally recognised, so that, if relig. is broadly defined, C. may be classified as one of the important and most influential of religs. of mankind. D.H.S.

D. H. Smith, *Chinese Religions* (1968), chs. 3, 8 and 11.

Confucius: *c.* 551–479 BC. Lat. form of K'ung Fu Tzŭ (The Master or Philosopher K'ung). Chi. name is K'ung Ch'iu, styled Chung Ni. Born at Tsou in the state of Lu (part of modern Shantung), all trads. concerning his ancestry and parentage are late and unreliable. Orphaned at an early age, he grew up in poverty. He acquired a good education, and from age of 15 devoted himself to study. Married at 19, we know nothing of his wife. He had an elder brother, a son who pre-deceased him, and a daughter. He occupied minor posts in Lu as keeper of stores and then as superintendent of pastures. Ambitious for political success, C. believed that he had mission to bring about peace and good government by reaffirming the virtues of anc. sages. His ideals of government, based on deep concern for wellbeing of all men, confidence in inherent goodness of human nature and belief in power of example, had little appeal to the reigning princes. Having no talent for political intrigue, and temperamentally unfitted for a successful political career, he devoted his energies to study and teaching. As an educator he was highly successful. training young men for political office. His students became his disciples, bound to him by affection, loyalty and devotion. He kindled in them an enthusiasm for literature, history, philosophy and moral training. About the age of 50, C. was given office in the state council, but trad. that he became chief justice and prime minister of Lu is unreliable. Craving for recognition and for a position in which he could give practical effect to his ideas, led C. to embark on 13 years of exile, wandering from court to court through the states of Wei, Ch'ên and Sung, where he encountered much hardship. Finally in 483 BC, he returned to Lu where discouraged by his seeming failure and distressed by death of his favourite disciple, he gave himself up to study and teaching. He died in comparative obscurity in 479 BC.

C. is distinguished as an ethical rather than a relig. teacher. In main, he accepted and approved the trad. relig. of his time, placing great emphasis on relig. rituals and holding firm belief in an over-ruling Providence, T'ien. T'ien was an overruling cosmic power which appointed to men and all things their destinies. His central concept was that of the Way (*Tao*) of Heaven, a Way in which all men should strive to walk. Hence his ethical emphasis. He ascribed great importance to sincerity, loyalty to principles, the cultivation of human-heartedness (*jên*) and good character, and taught that inward goodness finds full expression in all human relationships through cultivation of propriety, decorum and observance of rites (*li*). True nobility was not inherited, but all men could become noble (*chün tzŭ*). The marks of true nobility are human-heartedness, filial piety, loyalty, reciprocity, propriety and a harmonious balance between extremes. Though never claiming to be an innovator, but simply a follower and interpreter of the anc. sages (*shêng jên*), C. was mainly responsible for firmly estab. the ethical principles which undergird family, social and political life in China.

C., except perhaps for bare text of the *Spring and Autumn Classic* (→ *Ch'un Ch'iu*), left behind no writings. Very little in the five Confucian Classics can be attributed to him. His teachings are enshrined in the *Analects of Confucius*, and in scattered sayings found elsewhere. Soon after his death his influence began to grow, notably through the teachings of his disciple, → Tsêng Tzŭ, his grandson → Tzŭ Ssŭ, and his greatest followers, → Mencius and → Hsün-Tsŭ. Temporarily eclipsed during short-lived Ch'in dynasty, C. came to his own in Han dynasty, when attempts were even made to deify him. From that time onwards he has been generally recognised as China's greatest sage, and has had a paramount influence on Chi. life and thought. D.H.S.

H. G. Creel, *Confucius, the Man and the Myth* (1951); Shigeki Kaizuka, *Confucius*, E.T., G. Bownas (1956); A. Waley, *The Analects of Confucius* (1938); J. Legge, *The Life and Teaching of Confucius* (1875).

Congregational Church C. Churches, alternatively called Independent even after word Congregational came into use about 1640, arose out of movements of → Reformation in England in mid. 16th cent., when companies of men and women separated themselves from national Church, chose their own ministers, elders and deacons (after pattern of → Calvinism), administered the Dominical → sacraments, and bound themselves together by covenants undertaken by committed Christians. They claimed autonomy for each local company, and that the Church was truly to be found in the 'gathered church' of the local congregation. Contrary to a gen. accepted view, they did not claim that each 'particular' church was completely independent of every other such church, but (as is seen in first statement of faith, the Savoy Declaration of 1658, and in other writings) that churches must help and advise each other without imposing authority from outside.

Churches were formed in Norwich (by Robert Browne and Robert Harrison), in London (e.g. under Richard Fitz and Francis Johnson), in Scrooby and Gainsborough, and elsewhere; but persecution following upon the Acts of 1593 brought about execution of such leaders as Henry Barrow, John Greenwood, and John Penry. The movement was driven underground or abroad, where it was estab. in Holland. From Leyden, in 1620, the Pilgrim Fathers sailed via Plymouth to America, and there the Congregational Way began to exercise considerable influence in New England. The days of the first two Stuart kings were extremely difficult, but during and after Civil War the Independents were the backbone of Cromwell's army and asserted their beliefs and polity, though unsuccessfully, against → Presbyterians in the *Apologetical Narration* to the Westminster Assembly in 1643. With the restoration of monarchy in 1660 and Act of Uniformity of 1662, C.'s, as other Nonconformists or Dissenters, were objects of discriminatory laws; they persisted under persecution until the so-called Act of Toleration of 1689 lifted some penalties against dissent and gave some limited privileges. The 18th cent., which produced hymn-writers Isaac Watts and Philip Doddridge, saw C. beginning to flourish, taking a lead in education in Dissenting Academies (when University education was not available to Dissenters), combating the threat of → Socinianism in mid-century, at first being resistant to the Evangelical Revival and then advancing in influence and taking full part in mod. Prot. missionary movement overseas and at home. The former is seen notably in leading part played by C.'s in formation of London Missionary Society in 1793; the latter in the founding of County Unions, each with a concern for evangelising town and rural areas, and in co-operation with evangelical Anglicans in societies such as the Religious Tract Society, and, in 1804, the British and Foreign Bible Society. Desire for fellowship and mutual assistance between C. churches was implicit from beginning, as is seen in writings of Robert Brown and John Robinson, in the *Apologetical Narration*, the Savoy Declaration, and works of John Owen. The organisation of associations of churches was proposed in 18th cent. (e.g. by Doddridge), and developed by end of cent. in the County Unions. Out of these latter the Congregational Union of England and Wales was formed in 1832, with no legislative authority but with aim of channelling the efforts of churches to help each other and to evangelise. It produced a Declaration of Faith and Order designed 'not to be an imposition upon any', but serving to set out accepted views of doc. and church government. This was superseded by a new Statement of Faith, re-written in mod. terms, in the 1960's, by which time (1966) the C. *Union* of England and Wales had become the C. *Church* in England and Wales, with a new and more firmly knit organisation based upon a covenant relationship between individual churches and new stress on importance of groups of churches and their common kind.

In C., the ministry is non-episcopal, ordination being almost eithout exception into a local church with consent and approval of the national Church and of local churches. Its doct. is not marked by insistence upon acceptance of creeds and formulations of faith; these are regarded as useful affirmations but not to be used as tests. Its confessions of faith and order have moved from moderate Calvinism into mod. re-statements, whilst claiming to be within mainstream of Chr. orthodox belief. In polity it still insists on the 'particularity' of the visible Church, seen in the local gathered-churches, espec. when manifested in intimate relationships with other local churches. Its worship is in the Reformed trad. of Geneva and → Calvinism.

The International C. Council was formed in 1881; it has since then brought together into a voluntary fellowship unions of C. churches in England and Wales, Scotland, Ireland, the Brit. Commonwealth (where churches had been estab. by emigration or by missionary activity), in the U.S.A. (where C.'s, espec. in New England, U.S.A. have a long history), in Continental churches where there is a C. ethos in Sweden, Finland, the Netherlands, Czechoslovakia, and in some parts of S. America. C.'s have united this cent. to form part of United Churches in China, Japan, S. India, in the U.S.A. and Canada. In England and Scotland there is a strong movement towards union with Presbyterians. W.G.R.

Williston Walker, *Creeds and Platforms of Congregationalism* (1893 and 1960); R. W. Dale (ed. A. W. W. Dale), *Hist. of English Congregationalism* (1907); G. G. Atkins–F. L. Fagley, *Hist. of American Congregationalism* (1942); A. Peel, *The Congregational Two Hundred*, 1530–1948 (1948); H. Escott, *Hist. of Scottish Congregationalism* (1960); R. Tudor Jones, *Congregationalism in England*, 1662–1962 (1962); Glynmor John, *Congregationalism in an Ecumenical Era* (1967).

Consciousness (Buddhist) → Citta. T.O.L.

Constantine the Great (274 or 288–337) The Roman emperor who first (313) accorded Christianity legal recognition and encouraged its estab. as relig. of Roman Empire. At battle of Milvian Bridge (312), where he defeated Emp. Maxentius who persecuted Christians, C. adopted the → Labarum standard. Looking to Christianity as an integrating force within Empire, C. both patronised the Church and intervened in its affairs. He summoned Council of Nicea in 325 (→ Arianism). His transference of centre of Roman government from Rome to → Byzantium (Constantinople) had effect of promoting influence of → Papacy in West, a process which was assisted by so-called → Donation of Constantine. C. deferred → baptism until just before death. In E. Church, C. is canonised, as is also his mother Helena, celebrated for her discovery of → Cross at Jerusalem. S.G.F.B.

Eusebius, *Vita Constantini;* J. Burckhardt, *Die Zeit Konstantins des Grossen* (1853; cf. Phaidon illus. ed.); A. Alfölde, *The Conversion of Constantine and Pagan Rome* (E.T. 1948); A. H. M. Jones, *Constantine and the Conversion of Europe* (1948); H. Kraft, *Kaisar Konstantins religöse Entwicklung* (1955); A. A. T. Ehrhardt, *Politische Metaphysik von Solon bis Augustin* (1959), II, pp. 259ff.

Coptic Church The native church of Egypt: the name 'Copt' derives from Grk. word *Aigyptioi* = 'Egyptians'. Its members spoke Coptic, which descends from anc. Egypt. language, being written in Grk. with seven additional signs. The Church of → Alexandria was Grk. in speech and culture, but Christianity in Egypt proper was Coptic. A considerable Chr. lit. exists in Coptic, which has been notably increased by finds at → Nag Hammadi. → Monasticism flourished greatly in C.-C. From 5th cent. C.-C. became → Monophysite, and thus was increasingly isolated from rest of Christendom. With Arab conquest of Egypt in 642, C.-C. gradually became minority faith among Muslim population. Arabic was gen. adopted, Coptic becoming the liturgical language: service books have Arabic trans. The C.-C. has had long connection with → Ethiopic Church. S.G.F.B.

E.R.E., IV, *s.v.;* D. Lacy O'Leary in *The Legacy of Egypt*, ed. S. R. K. Glanville (1942), pp. 317ff.; *R.G.G.*[3], IV, 6–13; *D.C.C., s.v.;* W. H. Mackean, *Christian Monasticism in Egypt* (1920); W. C. Till, *Koptische Grammatik* (1955); J. Beckwith, *Coptic Sculpture* (1963); E. R. Hardy, *Christian Egypt* (1952); M. Cramer, *Das christliche koptische Aegypten* (1959); A. Badawy, *Les premières églises d'Égypte* (1947); C. D. C. Müller, *Die Engellehre der koptischen Kirche* (1959); A. S. Atiya et alii, *Hist. of Patriarchs of Egypt. Church*, 3 parts (1943–59); K. Wessel, *Coptic Art* (E.T. 1965); *R.M.E.*, I, ch. 8.

Corban Heb. word used in Ezk. 20:28 and → Priestly Code for 'offering', oblation', in sense of something devoted to altar, and thus to God. Acc. to Mk. 7:11, in time of Jesus C. was used as excuse to evade duty to parents and was condemned by him. Pontius Pilate violated Temple Treasury known as '*Korbōnas*', acc. to Josephus, *War* ii: 175. S.G.F.B.

H.D.B.[2], *s.v.;* V. Taylor, *Gospel acc. to St. Mark* (1952), pp. 341ff.

Corinthians, Epistles to Two such Epistles are ascribed to Paul in N.T. The integrity of these Epistles has been much discussed. The gen. consensus of critical opinion seems to regard I Cor.

as substantially one letter written by Paul; but II Cor. is held to comprise at least four fragments of different letters of Paul. These documents are of primary importance for study of Chr. origins. They provide evidence about Paul himself, his teaching and life and problems of a primitive Chr. community set in a Grk. city; they also reveal difficulties of adjusting Jew. theological concepts to those of Grk. trad. S.G.F.B.

H.D.B.[2], pp. 177–82; *P.C.*[2], pp. 954–72; *R.G.G.*[3], IV, 17–24; W. L. Knox, *St. Paul and the Church of the Gentiles* (1939), pp. 111ff.; H. Leitzmann, *An die Korinther*, I, II[2] (1923); Ed. Meyer, *Ursprung u. Anfänge des Christentums* (1923), pp. 438ff.

Corn Spirits J. G. → Frazer entitled two volumes of *The Golden Bough* (1933[3]), *Spirits of the Corn and of the Wild.* In them he describes how the corn has been both personified and deified under various images in the religs. of many peoples. There have been Corn-mothers (e.g. → Demeter) and Corn-maidens (→ Persephone). Many of the so-called → 'dying-rising gods' have been personifications of corn or vegetation (e.g. →→ Adonis; Attis; Osiris). In harvest rituals the last-sheaf has often been regarded as embodying the C.-S., and has been known as the 'Old Woman' or 'Old Man'. The ritual slaying of the C.-S. has been enacted in many agric. rites, and human sacrifice has sometimes accompanied it. In some rituals the new corn was eaten sacramentally as the body of C.-S. Such ideas and customs testify to the profound influence → agriculture has had on relig. faith and practice throughout the world. S.G.F.B.

Corpus Christi Lat. = 'Body of Christ'. Feast of C.-C., on first Thurs. after Trinity Sunday, was decreed by Papal bull in 1264. It commemorates institution of → Eucharist. The services for C.-C. were drawn up by Thomas → Aquinas. The feast is closely assoc. with doc. of → Transubstantiation, and the → Host is adored when carried in procession on that day. In the N.T. the Body of Christ' is also a mystical image for → Church (Eph. 5:23). S.G.F.B.

D.C.C., *s.v.; R.A.C.*, III, pp. 437–53.

Cosmogony (China) Early Chi. philosophical interest was centred on human affairs; it was not till beginning of Han Dynasty (2nd cent. BC) that Chi. C. theories, as found in the *I Ching* and *Huai-nan-tzŭ* were fully developed. These works borrowed ideas from → Lao-tzŭ, → Chuang-tzŭ, and the → Yin-yang and → Five Elements (*Wu Hsing*) schools. Their C's. were purely naturalistic. The *I Ching* taught that origin of all things lay in the Great Ultimate (*T'ai Chi*), which produced two forces (Yin and Yang). These combined to form four emblems (*hsiang*), which in turn produced the Eight Trigrams (*Pa Kua*) from which all phenomena resulted. Acc. to the *Huai-Nan-tzŭ*, before Heaven and Earth took shape there was only undifferentiated and formless vacuity out of which arose a universe of space and time, which in turn produced a primal vapour (*yüan ch'i*) in constant flux. The more clear and light particles drifted upwards to form Heaven. The heavy and turgid particles, taking longer to congeal, formed Earth. From the essence of Heaven and Earth, the Yin and the Yang were produced and from their constant interaction, transformation and change all things came into existence. These C. ideas were the basis of orthodox → Confucian doctrine throughout Chi. hist.

The Sung Dynasty → Neo-Confucian philosophers sought to elucidate origin of universe. Chou Tun-I (CE 1017–73) composed his *Diagram of the Supreme Ultimate*, with explanations in which he propounded the theory that all things are produced from the interaction of movement and quiescence in the Supreme Ultimate. The two ethers, Yin and Yang, by their interaction produce phenomena, which in their turn produce and reproduce in a process of transformation and change which continues without end. The Neo-Confucian C. reached its most developed form with → Chu Hsi, who maintained that the Supreme Ultimate consists of 'Principle' (*li*) and 'Ether' (*ch'i*), and that creation is the result of union of Principle, which gives all things their nature, and Ether, which gives all things their form. Principle lacks volition and plan and has no creative power. Ether creates the world of shapes and forms, using the individualising principles which are contained in Principle. The creation of man depends simply on the union of Principle with Ether. Men are endowed with the Principle of the universe to give them their form. Chu Hsi envisages a time before the Supreme Ultimate when an earlier world existed, a cycle of creation and destruction which continues eternally.

The creation myth of P'an Ku, who chiselled the universe out of chaos, and whose bones were changed to rocks; his flesh to earth; his marrow, teeth and nails to metals; his breath to wind; his veins to rivers; his hair to trees and herbs; and his four limbs to the pillars which marked the boundaries of the universe, is of comparatively late origin, certainly not earlier than 4th cent. CE, and probably introduced from Siam. (→ Creation, China-Jap.). D.H.S.

Fung Yu-lan, *Hist. of Chinese Philos.* (1953), vol. 2, pp. 19ff.; 99ff.; 139ff.; 426ff.; 546ff.; W. T. Chan, *Source Book in Chinese Philos.* (1963), pp. 305ff.; 462.; 484; 496; 593; C. B. Day, *The Philos. of China* (1962), pp. 200–2; E. T. C. Werner, *Dictionary of Chinese Mythology* (1932), p. 355; M. Kaltenmark, 'La naissance du monde en Chine', *S.O.*, I (1959); D. Bodde in *M.A.W.*, pp. 382ff.

(Egypt) C. in Egypt was motivated by desire of various priesthoods to show that their own particular god was the Creator of other gods, and that their temple stood on site of orig. scene of creation. The earliest C., in → Pyramid Texts, presented → Atum as creator and → Heliopolis as the place. Similar claims were made for → Ptah of Memphis, → Hermopolis, → Amun of → Thebes, Neith at Esna. The first event in time was imagined as emergence of a hill out of the primaeval watery chaos of Nun, on which creator-deity stood to begin his work. Since Egypt. C.'s were concerned to relate gods in order of precedence, little attention was paid to creation of mankind. Men were usually imagined as being created out of clay on a potter's wheel by → Khnum. Cosmic creation is conceived either in terms of biological acts (e.g. copulation, masturbation) or by divine *fiat* (→ Memphite Theology). S.G.F.B.

S. G. F. Brandon, *Creation Legends of Ancient Near East* (1963), ch. 2 (with biblio.).

(Greek) There is no clearly defined C. in → Grk. relig.; but Grk. philosophy from beginning was much concerned with accounting for origin and constitution of universe. In → Homer brief ref. is made to Oceanus, the primordial water, as 'the begetter of all'. The chief of the Olympic gods, → Zeus, is never presented as Creator, thus reflecting consciousness of an earlier order of things (→ Aegean Relig.). In his *Theogony*, → Hesiod presents a C., in terms of relations of personified cosmic phenomena and virtues. It prob. repr. rationalisation of an alien C., poss. Hittite (→ Hittite Religion). Hesiod also explains evolution of mankind as series of Five Ages (→ Ages of World, Grk.). The → Orphics had a C. which prob. derived from Egypt. and Iranian sources. A late trad. attributes creation of man to → Prometheus. S.G.F.B.

E.R.E., IV, pp. 145–51; Brandon, *C.L.*, ch. 5 (with biblio.).

(Hebrew) The first two chaps. of *Genesis* contain two C.'s: that in 1:1–2:4a comes from the later P or Priestly trad. (→ Pentateuch); the earlier J or → Yahwist, starting at 2:4b, deals with creation and fall of → Adam (→ Hebrew Relig.), and omits cosmic creation. It is poss. that J's acc. of creation of world was removed by editor who fused P and J into continuous narrative of divine creation. P's cosmogony, which shows traces of Mesopot. and poss. Egypt. cosmological ideas, repr. creation of universe by divine fiat—'God said, "Let there be light"; and there was light'. J. repr. → Yahweh making man of clay, as → Khnum does in Egypt. C. and Mami in Mesopot. C. J's C. is aetiological, explaining orig. of animals, woman, clothes, death, agriculture, etc. In other parts of O.T. there are signs of a primitive C., involving Yahweh's conquest of primaeval dragon, as in → Enuma elish. S.G.F.B.

E.R.E., IV, pp. 151–5; Brandon, *C.L.*, ch. 4 (with biblio.).

(Hindu) The trad. Hindu term for creation (by God) is *sṛṣṭi*, from the root *sṛj*, to 'let down'. Various myths of creation are to be found in the *Ṛgveda* and the *Upaniṣads*, while more philosophical accounts are given by the trad. schools. The earlier stories of creation do not envisage the cyclical alternation between periods of cosmic quiescence (*pralaya*) and creation, a cosmological framework which came to dominate the Indian imagination and prob. derived from non-Brahmanical sources. The incorporation of the cyclical idea into Hindu cosmology meant that the older Vedic myths of creation were fitted into it. One of most import. of latter is contained in the 'Hymn of Primeval Man', the *Puruṣasūkta* (→→ *purusa*), where Prajāpati (Lord of Beings), also later termed → *Brahmā*, is identified with a cosmic man whose divine body is sacrificed; it is out of this rite that there emerges the manifold variety of the formed world. This motif is carried on in the Vedic notion that the cosmos is a kind of sacrificial process, controlled by the sacred ritual power of → Brahman. In other hymns Prajapati impregnates the primeval waters and becomes manifest in them as a golden embryo (*Hiraṇyagarbha*), out of which the cosmos develops. It is later called the Brahmāṇḍa or Brahmā egg. Creative power is also ascribed to the austerity (*tapas*) of Prajapati, since practice of austerity was widely believed to give the ascetic great power. The most striking Vedic account, however, is the 'Hymn of Creation' (*Ṛgveda* x. 9), which graphically depicts an orig. nothingness in which One breathed, born of the power of heat; through desire, the forces of cosmic formation are released. Even the gods do not know secret of how creation began, since they postdate it. The hymn ends on a sceptical note: even he who is supposed to be Creator may not know how it occurred. Among Upanisadic accounts of creation (which tend to speak of universe as somehow evolving out of the One Being→ Brahman or the cosmic → Atman), that in *Bṛhadāraṇyaka Upaniṣad*, 1.4.1ff. starts with the Self who sees around him only himself and declares 'I am' (*aham asmi*), this being the origin of self-consciousness. He is afraid, being alone; and creates out of his own substance a female counterpart. From embraces between the two, living beings are born. Because the Self has produced the cosmos, he is this cosmos; thus is expressed a panentheistic world-picture. With the emergence of the cyclical view of cosmic creation, these myths were used to explain the periodic re-formation of universe out of chaos. In later Vaisnavite and Saivite schools, the creative power of God is often identified with his female consort or → *sakti.* At the theological and philosophical level, the evolutionary account of formation of cosmos found in → Samkhya (itself, however, atheistic) was incorporated into theistic, and esp. Vaisnavite, descriptions of the creative process. The cyclical view, however, raised problems as to why creation should be renewed. Why should the divine Being, having reabsorbed the universe into his inner substance, bring it forth again? One main answer is that the kinetic forces which determine the future existences of living beings are latent in period of cosmic quiescence, and reactivate the divine Being, much as a resolve to wake up at such and such a time will bring about one's waking up. The relapse into quiescence at end of a period is sometimes explained conversely as allowing living beings a time of rest from the cycle of → *samsara.* Another motif in the variety of creation myths is the picture of Śiva as *nāṭarāja* or 'king of the dance', who dances out the universe, out of sheer exuberance. There is less emphasis in Hindu trad. than in the Judeo-Christian on the ulterior purposiveness of creation: it is more a matter of God's self-expression. Also, the successive acts of divine creation presuppose that world has no beginning, but has always existed, either in manifest form or, in periods of quiescence, latently. Moreover, because of the cyclical view, God is conceived as destroyer as well as creator. N.S.

S. Radhakrishnan *The Principal Upaniṣads* (1953); A. Danielou, *Hindu Polytheism* (1964); N. Smart, *Doctrine and Argument in Indian Philosophy* (1964). (→ Creation, Buddh. view).

(Iranian) The fundamental dualism of Iranian relig. thought appears in the → *Gāthās*, the oldest Iranian writing concerned with C. From the beginning 'two primal Spirits', repr. Life and Not-life, Good and Evil, are in opposition: the relation of these rivals to a greater deity, Zoroaster's → Ahura Mazdah, is obscure. Acc. to Eudemos of Rhodes (4th cent. BC), Iranians conceived of a primordial Space-Time, from which a good and an evil deity derived. The *Bundahishn* (7th cent. CE), contains the most complete statement of Zoroastrian C. At start of first of four trimillennia, which constitute the whole time-process, → Ohrmazd, who is identified with Time (→ Zurvan), is supreme. The opposing principle, → Ahriman, is inactive and in primordial darkness. The world, with its mixture of good and ill, results from creative activities of Ohrmazd and Ahriman as they struggle for supremacy. Iranian lit. also reveals existence of myths about fortunes of a primordial man, → Yima, or a primordial pair, Mâshya and Mâshyôî. (→ → Zoroastrianism; Urmensch). S.G.F.B.

Brandon, *C.L.*, ch. 6 (with biblio.); *E.R.E.*, IV, pp. 161–2; *M.A.W.*, pp. 337ff.

(Islam) The Qur. frequently states that when God wishes to bring anything into existence he says 'Be', and it thereupon exists (ii:111; xvi:42; xl:70, etc.). He created the heavens and earth in six days (vii: 52; cf. xli:8–11). There are 7 heavens and 7 earths (lxv:12). Creation is one of God's signs (xlii:28). His control of his creation is continuous. In his hands are life and death (xv:16–25; lxxxi:12–19). Though the Qur. says C. took 6 days, a trad. in Muslim's *Ṣaḥiḥ* says God created the earth on Saturday, mountains on Sunday, trees on Monday, objectionable things on Tuesday, light on Wednesday, animals on Thursday, and Adam late on Friday (*Mishkāt*, p. 1227f.). The Qur doc. seems clearly to teach *creatio ex nihilo*, but xli, 10 seems to suggest that heaven was created from smoke. The scholastic theologians (→ *mutakallimūn*) taught *creatio ex nihilo;* they also held an atomistic theory, for, unlike the → Mu'tazilites, they could not admit of man being the creator of anything. God is the only creator. So they did not believe in cause and effect; e.g. burning does not take place because of fire, for God created fire and he created burning with no necessary connection between the two; so it is God and not fire which produces burning. This means that God's creative activity is continuous, for all action, whether it seems to be produced by man or otherwise, is really God's (→ Acquisition). Some Mu'tazilites explained C. in terms of God's foreknowledge, his thought causing the reality of things without a specific act of C. It is gen. agreed that God is dissimilar to his C. Even a → Sufi like Kalābādhi can hold that God has eternal names and attributes, 'without resembling creation in any respect' → Ghazālī can say categorically, 'Nothing is like him and he is not like anything else'. J.R.

E.I., II, pp. 891–3; D. B. Macdonald, *Theology*, index; Wensinck, *Creed*, index; Arberry, *Doctrine*, pp. 14ff.; Sweetman, *I.C.T.*, I–IV, index.

(Jain) As → Jainism is → atheistic, there is no doc. of creation by God. The cosmos is considered to be everlasting and indestructible, and composed of living and material substances, in constant change. The immediate environment of men undergoes periodic progress and decline, a cyclical movement analogous to the periods of cosmic formation and destruction in other Indian systems. The Jains hold that there is no need to postulate a Creator, since change, etc., can be accounted for by the principle of → karma. Jainism does not, also, emphasise cults of worship and sacrifice, and hence, religiously, there is no need for a supreme personal Being on whom world is dependent. N.S.

G. Della Casa, *Il Giainismo* (1962); J. Jaini, *Outlines of Jainism* (1941).

(Japan) Jap. cosmogonic mythology has its beginnings in myth of → Izanagi and Izanami, recorded in the → *Kojiki* and the → *Nihongi.* The opening of the *Nihongi*, however, borrows from the Chi. the concept of → Yin and Yang, which by their interaction form Heaven and Earth. → Shinto C, presents a tripartite division of universe: the upper world of gods and everlasting bliss; the middle world of men on surface of earth; and the lower world of darkness (Yomi), where evil spirits live under rule of the earth-mother. From 6th cent. CE → Buddhism influenced Jap. C. ideas. In particular, the world of forms was believed to be constituted from emanations proceeding from the Dhyani-Buddha, → Vairochana, with whom, in → Ryobu-Shinto, the sun-goddess, → Amaterasu, was identified as a temporal manifestation. (→ Creation, China-Jap.). D.H.S.

D. C. Holtom, *The National Faith of Japan* (1938), pp. 21, 101ff.; J. Hackin (ed.), *The Mythology of Modern Japan* (1932, 1963), p. 415; E. Dale Saunders in *M.A.W.*, pp. 411ff.

(Mesopot). Sumerian C. (→ Sumerian Religion) was more concerned to explain orig. of mankind and fundamental needs of civilisation than creation of world. Legends tell how gods → Enlil and → Enki were responsible for inventing basic implements such as the brick-mould and pick-axe, and determining use of plants for food. Mankind was created out of clay, to serve gods by building temples and offering sacrifices. The great Babylonian creation legend (→ Enuma elish) was designed to exalt Babylon's own god → Marduk as creator of world and lord of destiny. Marduk is represented as slaying Ti'âmat, personification of the sea, and fashioning world out of its carcass. In the *Enuma elish* men are out of blood of Kingu, a rebel god. S.G.F.B.

Brandon, *C.L.*, ch. 3 (with biblio.).

Cosmology (Buddh.) Not all schools of Buddhism have concern with cosmology: the → *Mādhyamika*, e.g., with its view of unreality of external world and exclusive concern with questions of ontology, had relatively little interest in cosmological schemes. Among 3 schools, where there was interest in phenomenology, a broadly similar C. was (and is) affirmed. These 3 are (1) the → Theravādin (2) the → Sarvāstivādin (3) the → Yogācāra. In many respects this C. was that of → brahmans of anc. India, in which an infinite number of worlds was affirmed, the cosmography of each being basically similar to that of this world, which had as central point a huge mountain, Mt. Meru, on 4 sides of which were 4 territories, each ruled over by a Great King, or guardian. The southern territory or continent was called Jambūdvipa; it was this which the anc. Indians believed they inhabited (→ Cosmology, Hindu). Since there were unlimited numbers of similarity structured worlds, a scheme of classification of these worlds was developed. In B. cosmology, the entire universe is divided into 3 spheres, or *dhātus: kāma-dhātu* ('sensual' sphere); *rūpa-dhātu* ('sphere of form' only); *arūpa-dhātu* (sphere of 'formlessness'). The word *loka* (world) may occur in these 3 compounds instead of *dhātu*. Another syn. for *dhātu* is *bhava* (existence); this term occurs most frequently in the *Suttas* of Pali canon, where considerable ref. is made to this 3-fold cosmology. The lowest of the 3 spheres is the *Kāma-dhātu* (or *K-loka*, or *K-bhava*), the sensual world. This ranges from, at very lowest, a vast number of hells, upwards through the realms of ghosts (*pretas*), of animals, and of men, to realm of the inferior 'deities', the → *asuras*, on to the heavens of superior 'deities', the *devas*, at highest point of sensual-world. The whole of this world is inhabited by beings with six senses—sight, hearing, taste, smell, touch, and mental impression (the last name is regularly regarded in B. thought as one of 6 senses). In the various hells are beings who are suffering in various degrees of previous wickedness. Some hells are dark, some cold, some hot; each type has eight grades in rank-order from bad to worst (in the hottest hell, e.g. there is no intermission of pain whatsoever). The surface of earth is realm of animals and mankind. The *asuras* belong partly to surface of earth, partly to upper regions. The *devas* inhabit highest plane of sensual-world, viz., the heavens above summit of Mt. Meru. Here is the Heaven of the Thirty Three Gods (*Trayastrimsa*); the Heaven of → Yāma, where it is never night; the Tusita Heaven, where resides → Metteya, the Buddha-to-be; and the two highest heavens where even a wish or a thought (without action) can generate new → *karma;* the highest heaven is the abode of → Māra, the Evil One, who is thus supreme over whole sensual-world. A notable feature of the *deva*-heavens is that no women are there; rebirth there is always as male. The second world, the *Rūpa dhātu* (or *R-loka*, or *R-bhava*) (sometimes trans. 'Fine-material world') is characterised by absence of 3 senses of taste, smell and touch; here there is only sight, hearing and mental impression. The inhabitants of this world still have shape, or form (*rūpa*), which at this level is still indispensable to their existence. The *Rūpa*-world is divided into a number of heavens: 17 acc. to the → *Abh. Kosa* of Vasubandhu; 16 acc. to the Thv. and 18 acc. to the Yogācāra. Connected with these heavens, are various stages of Jhāna → (Dhyāna), or contemplation: the practice of the 1st Jhāna gives access to the 1st 3 *Rūpa*-heavens (sometimes called *Brahma-loka* or Brahma-world); the practice of 2nd Jhāna, the next 3; the 3rd Jhāna to next 3; the final Jhāna to last 8. Above the *Rūpa*-world is the third major division of the cosmos, the *Arūpa-dhātu* (*°loka*, or *°bhava*). In this 'formless' or 'immaterial' world, sight and sound are absent; there is only mental impression, or, in Yogācāra terms, consciousness-only. All schools agree in a list of 4 heavens in the Formless World: the heavens of boundless space; of infinite consciousness; of nothingness or non-existence; of neither consciousness nor unconsciousness. To these heavens come beings, whose rebirth follows meditation on one of the 4 illimitables or → Brahma-vihāra. These two upper worlds (the Fine material (*Rūpa-dhātu*), and the Immaterial (*Arūpa-dh.*)) are sometimes ref. to collectively as the *Brahma-loka*, or spiritual world, although, as already mentioned, this term is sometimes used in a more partic. sense of the 3 heavens of the *Rūpa-dh.*

The → Hinayāna and → Mhy. cosmology is approx. the same up to this point. But beyond the 3 worlds *Kāma*, *Rūpa*, and *Arūpa*, the Mhy. points existence of yet another realm, the *Buddha-Ksetras* (lit. the 'Buddha-fields'). Each is field of influence of a supremely Enlightened One (or Buddha), (→ *Buddhas other than Gotama*); each Buddha is regarded by Mahayanists as able to secure rebirth in his own heaven of all men who call on his name in perfect faith. Women also may be reborn there, but it will be as men; just as only male beings inhabit the *deva* heavens of *Kāma-dhātu* (see above). In Mhy. Buddhism, espec. in China and Japan, rebirth in the Buddha-land becomes for lay people the real relig. goal, displacing → *nirvāna* as the ultimate hope. (→ Creation, Buddh.).

The lit. sources in which the C., outlined above, is most prominent are: (1) for Theravadin school, certain Abh.-works, notably the *Vibhanga* (last chapter) and *Dhamma Sangani;* there are cosmological refs. in the *Kathā-vathu;* beyond the canonical lit., Buddhaghosa's *Visuddhimagga* is on this, as on other import. B. topics, the standard authy. (2) the Sarvāstivādin views are repr. in the *Abh.-Kosa* of Vasubandhu (3) the Yogācārin system is repr. in the *Vidyāmātra Siddhi* of → Dharmapala. T.O.L.

R. Spence Hardy, *Manual of Buddhism* (1853; 1st Indian edn. 1967); Nyanamoli, *The Path of Purification* (1964); W. M. McGovern, *A Manual of Buddhist Philosophy*, vol. I, *Cosmology* (1923).

(Hindu) There is some difference between the cosmology of the Vedic hymns and that of classical Hinduism, which took over the cyclical view of cosmos found in non-Brahmanical systems (such as → Buddhism). In the Vedas there is a three-decker universe. Above, there is heaven, where the heavenly gods move and live; below this there is the atmospheric region, which is realm of the weather gods, etc. (e.g. → Indra and Vayu); then there is the earth, conceived as flat and circular, which is home not merely of gods, spirits, etc., but also of such import. gods as → Agni. At this stage of thinking, the cosmos was thought of as a relatively small affair; but in classical Hinduism a more elaborate picture is found. Not only is cosmos everlasting, though subject to periodic destruction and recreation; but it is immense in extent. Our world-system is only one among a vast number, distributed at great distances through the cosmos. Each world-system has an egg-like shape, being composed of the *Brahmanda* or 'Brahma-egg' (→ creation, Hindu concept of); and is split into 21 regions. Above the earth are six heavens, the most beatific being at top; below the earth are seven regions of *Pātāla*, the sphere of various kinds of spirits; below these again are the seven regions of *Naraka*—these are purgatories, the ghastliest being the lowest. Living beings circulate, by action of → karma, throughout the zones, rising and falling in the cosmic hierarchy in acc. with their deeds. The gods dwell in the heavens, chiefly; but have their signs and representatives on earth (e.g. the *lingam*, images, incarnations). The centre of our world system is Mount Meru, vaguely in the Himalayas, which is 168,000 *yojanas* high (roughly, 700,000 miles) and deep. This is the axis on which world spins, and its upper reaches are the playground of the gods. To south of Mount Meru is the continent of Jambudvipa; and that part of it which is south of the Himalayas is the *Bhāratavarṣa*, the 'region of the sons of Bharata', i.e. India. There are variations on this scheme in the → *Puranas.* Also, the → Mimamsa school denied the periodic destruction and re-creation of cosmos, in order to preserve the eternity and thus authority of the Vedas. Trad. Indian astronomy was sometimes in conflict with the trad. mythic cosmology, and various attempts to reconcile the systems were made. The main function, however, of the cosmology was to provide a picture of man's involvement in the immensities of the living hierarchy, perpetually being reborn. N.S.

A. L. Basham, *The Wonder that was India* (1954); A. Danielou, *Hindu Polytheism* (1964); W. E. Clark (tr.), *Aryabhatita*, *an ancient Indian*

Workon Mathematics and Astronomy (1930).

Councils (Buddh.) Acc. to Buddh. trad., there have been, in the course of Buddh. hist., a number of councils: the number accepted as authentic varies from country to country. Ceylon and Burma, e.g. acknowledge 6; the 6th having been held in Rangoon in CE 1956. Thailand acknowledges 10, the Rangoon C. in this case being reckoned as 10th. All, however, are agreed on first 3. These are (1) at Rajagṛha (Rājagaha), in monsoon season following Buddha's decease, *c.* 483 BC (2) at Vesāli, about a cent. later (3) at Pātaliputra (Patna) during reign of emperor → Ashoka, poss. *c.* 250 BC. These are all locations within India, in the lower Ganges valley. A 4th C. was held in N.W. India, under auspices of the Kushan emperor → Kanishka. The date of this C. is uncertain, as K's own dates are matter of controversy. The Pali chronicles of the Thv. school do not take this 4th C. into account; although it is not certain that Thv. monks did not take part. It was held, acc. to some authorities, at Jālandhar; acc. to others, in Kashmir. The Thai Buddh. trad. reckons the 4th C. to have been one held at → Anuradhapura in Ceylon, convened by King of Ceylon, Devanam Piya Tissa *c.* 220 BC. Burmese and Sinhalese trads., however, reckon as the 4th the C. held at the Aloka Vihara in Ceylon, convened by King Vatthagāmini *c.* CE 90. Acc. to Thai trad., the 6th and 7th C.'s were also held in Ceylon, in 27 BC and CE 1044 respectively; the latter being convened by the great king Parakrama, at Pulatthi-nagara. Thai trad. claims that 8th and 9th were held in Thailand, in CE 1477 at Chiengmai (N. Thailand) and CE 1788 at Bangkok, respectively; the latter being convened by Rāma I, King of Thailand. Acc. to Sinhalese trad. the 5th C. was held in CE 1865 at Ratnapura in Ceylon, the royal patron being Basnayaka Nilama. Acc. to Burmese trad. (which at this point only differs from the Sinhalese), the 5th was the C. held at Mandalay in CE 1871, convened by Min-don-min, King of Upper Burma.

The occasion for assembling of these C.'s was gen. a need to agree upon text of the Buddh. scriptures, or commentaries thereon. Thus the 1st C., acc. to unanimous trad. of all Buddh. schools, met to estab. text of the → *Vinaya Pitaka* and → *Sutta Pitaka*. Mahākassapa is held to have presided, and a monk named Upali to have supplied the definitive version of the *Vinaya*, and → Ananda that of the *Sutta Pitaka*. The text thus agreed was recited in chorus; hence the Pali name for the assembly, '*saṇgīti*', a 'singing-together'; this word is repr. in Eng. as 'council'. The historicity of this 1st C. has been challenged by mod. scholars, notably by Oldenberg, and is still held by some to be purely legendary; however, a considerable body of scholarly opinion, in both East and West, supports the view that such an assembly did take place shortly after the Buddha's decease. Acc. to Buddh. trads., the 1st C. was held in a large cavern in a hillside, near Rajgṛha (the mod. Rajgir), though the site has not been identified. The trads. agree that 500 monks took part. The basic account of 1st C. is found in the → *Cullavagga*, which is followed in the Pali extra-canonical lit. of the → *Dipavaṃsa* and *Mahāvaṃsa*. Other accounts are those of the → *Mahāvastu* (the *Vinaya* of the Lokuttara-vadins) of → Ashvaghosha, and the Tibetan *Dulva*. Other accounts such as → Buddhaghosa's *Samantapāsādikā* and that of Chinese pilgrim → Hsüan-Tsang, though much later compositions, may embody anc. trads.

The 2nd C., held at Vesali, was occasioned by growth of irregular practices among certain monks in that area. A highly venerable monk named Yasa, disciple of Ananda, reproached them with ten breaches of Buddh. monastic discipline. They replied with counter-accusations against Yasa. Another highly respected and venerable monk, Revata, of great repute for learning and piety, was appealed to by all concerned. He gave his verdict in support of Yasa, and at his suggestion a C. of 700 monks was convened at Vesali to settle the dispute. This C. appointed a committee of 8 monks, 4 from the 'western territory' and 4 from the 'eastern territory'. The committee reported unanimously in condemnation of practices of monks of Vesali. Acc. to Pali trad. of Buddhaghosa, this was followed by recital by all the monks of a new arrangement of the *Vinaya* and *Suttas*. The royal patron of this 2nd C. is held to have been Kālāṣoka, a descendent of King Ajātasattu. This C. is last event in hist. of Buddhism which is commonly recorded in all the various versions of the *Vinaya-pitaka*, i.e. both Pali and Skt. The accounts of 2nd C., like 1st, were regarded by Oldenberg as unhistorical; but majority of mod. scholars accept historicity of 2nd C. more readily than that of 1st.

The 3rd C. is assoc. with name of the great Mauryan emperor, Ashoka. The emperor himself had become a Buddh. in revulsion against carnage involved in his early conquests; as ruler, his primary concern was not partisan, but rather maintenance of harmony among his subjects and discouragement of sectarian quarrels. The → Theravādin trad., which repr. him as actively promoting harmony by agreeing to convening of a C. to deal with a variant form of Buddh. teaching, whose exponents were called → Sarvāstivādins, has therefore a large element of hist. authenticity. The Sarvāstivādin doc., that not only present states of mind (→ *citta*) are real but also past and future states, was repudiated by the orthodox, who called themselves *Vibhajya-vādins*, 'those who make distinctions' (? between present, and past/future states). The growth of the Sārvāstivādin view was apparently causing dissension in the → Sangha, and at instigation of the venerable Mogalliputta → Tissa, a defender of orthodoxy of those who adhered to teaching of the Elders (the *Sthaviras*, as the orthodox were also known), Ashoka agreed to convene a C. of a thousand monks at Patna, capital city of the Mauryan empire. At this 3rd C., Tissa is said to have recited the → *Kathāvatthu*, a work composed by him in refutation of various heresies; it subsequently became part of Theravādin → *Abh. Pitaka.* Ashoka is reputed to have favoured Tissa and the Vibhajya-vādins; in consequence the Sarvāstivādin groups withdrew from region of Patna northwestwards, and made first Mathura and then Kashmir their strongholds. Acc. to Thv. chroni. 80,000 heretical monks were expelled from the Patna region after the Ashokan C., because of their refusal to subscribe to Vibhajya-vādin doc. Certain rock edicts of Ashoka, condemning monks who were guilty of causing dissensions and therefore expelled, are held to provide epigraphical evidence in support of the Thv. trad. (J. Bloch, *Les Inscriptions D'Asoka*, Paris 1950, pp. 152f.).

Of the 4 C.'s held in Ceylon and reckoned by Thai Buddhists as the 4th, 5th, 6th and 7th C.'s, only that of 90 BC at Aloka-Vihara is reckoned by Ceylon Buddhists. The 5th by Thai reckoning, it is known in Ceylon as 4th C. (that of Kanishka in N.W. India being disregarded by the Thv.). This 4th C. was for purpose of revising commentaries on the → *Tipitaka.* At end of C., the entire *Tipitaka*, with its commentaries, are said to have been committed to writing: they were inscribed on palm-leaves and submitted to extensive checking and counter-checking. The other 3 Ceylon C.'s (by Thai reckoning) were not C.'s in the true sense, but concerned only with revision of commentaries.

5 C.'s belong to the period of mod. history: that of 1477 at Chiengmai, N. Thailand (then the Thai capital), lasted for a year; it was convened by Thai King to estab. Buddhism more firmly in that country; that of 1788 also in Thailand, at newly estab. capital of Bangkok under King Rāma I, was prelude to a purification of the Sangha and a revival of Buddhism in Thailand; the Ceylon C. of 1865 at Ratnapura, which lasted for 5 months, is reckoned by Sinhalese as 5th C., whereas that of 1868–71 at Mandalay, when the entire *Tipitaka* was recited and subsequently inscribed on 729 marble tablets, is reckoned by Burmese as the 5th. The occasion for the so-called '6th' C. in 1956 in Rangoon was celebration of 2500th anniversary (acc. to Thv. chronology) of the Buddha's entry into *pari-nibbāna* in 543 BC. It was held under patronage of the Buddh. prime minister of Burma, U Nu. 500 Burmese monks, with collaboration of learned monks from India, Ceylon, Nepal, Cambodia, Thailand, Laos and Pakistan, were charged with task of revising text of the *Tipitaka.* Greetings to the C. in warmest terms were received from the President of India, and from the prime minister of India, Jawaharlal Nehru. At end of C., the entire text of the Pali *Tipitaka*, and its commentarial literature, was recited by assembled monks in the vast auditorium built to similate the cave-assembly of anc. India: The revised edition of text was subsequently published (in Burmese characters) by the Burmese authorities. T.O.L.

E. Lamotte, *Histoire du Bouddhisme Indien* (1958); M. Hofinger, *Étude sur le concile de Vaisāli* (1946); A. Bareau, *Les premiers counciles bouddhiques* (1955); N. R. Ray, *Theravāda Buddhism in Burma* (1946), pp. 245–9; P. V. Bapat (ed.), 2500 *years of Buddhism* (1956), ch. IV.

Councils, Christian →→ Chalcedon; Counter-Reformation; Creed (Christian); Vatican II.

Counter-Reformation, The Name for 16th-17th cent. revival of R.C. Church through internal reformation and aggressive evangelism, motivated by reaction to Prot. → Reformation; but orig. in Cath. discontent with administrative and ethical abuses from late Med. and Renaissance periods. The first overt sign of C.-R. was the foundation of new relig. orders: Theatines (1524), Capuchins (1529), Barnabites (1530), and, above all, the → Jesuits (1536) under S. Ignatius Loyola, who became spear-head of attack on Protestantism in Europe and paganism abroad. The situation, however, called clearly for a Universal Council; but this demand was repeatedly frustrated by dissensions between Pope, Emperor and the French. Eventually the XIXth Ecumenical Council met at Trent in 1545. Its 25 sessions were extended over three periods: (1545–7, 1551–2, 1562–3), and five papacies. It was interrupted by political tensions and by revolts within Holy Roman Empire; its progress was marked by grad. triumph of → Papacy over those who sought reconciliation with Protestantism, and those (esp. from France and Spain) who sought moderation of Papal power. The influence of Prot. Reformation was shown in choice of subjects dealt with (e.g. Decrees on → Original Sin, Justification, the seven → Sacraments, → Penance, → Indulgences). The substance of the decrees betrayed at time little concession to → Luther and → Calvin; but recent R.C. scholarship (e.g. Hans Kung) has seen in them underlying trends which became visible in First → Vatican Council (1869–70), and, espec. in Second (1962 *et. seq.*), thus showing that insights of the Prot. Reformers had their effect. Of greater immediate importance were the practical regulations on appointment of bishops, on synods, preaching, the training of priesthood, etc. The work of Council was later completed by such measures as issue of → Catechism (1566) and revision of → Breviary (1568); by founding of Congregation of the → Index (Liborum Prohibitorum), responsible for additions and revisions to Index (first issued 1557); by revision of → Vulgate (concluded 1592). The all-important renewal of discipline throughout Church and efficiency in Papal Curia, were completed by later 16th cent. Popes, reinforced by growing power of Spain under Philip II, who became the Cath. secular champion; the Italian → Inquisition (1542) increasingly mirrored the Spanish model. Thus disciplined, the reformed R.C. Church won back Poland and S. Germany from Prots. consolidated its strength everywhere, and advanced (esp. through Jesuits) to a new era of evangelistic conquest. Perhaps, however, the abiding significance of the C.-R. lies rather in the renewal of apostolic devotion in men like S. Francis de Sales and the Spanish Mystics, in the birth and growth of relig. orders, and in the firm doctrinal platform estab. for the faithful everywhere by Council of Trent. B.D.

L. von Ranke, *Hist. of the Popes* (1834ff.); A. W. Ward, *The Counterreformation* (1889); B. J. Kidd, *The Counter-Reformation* (1933); L. Christiani, *L'Église à l'époque du concile de Trente* (1948); vol. 17 of Fliche and Martin's *Church History*. On Council of Trent see the Decrees in Danzinger, *Enchiridion Symbolorum* (edn. 1952), nos. 782ff.; for modern bibliog., G. Schreiber (ed.), *Das Weltkonzil von Trient* (1951), with discussions and bibliogs. in H. Kung, *Justification* (E.T. 1959). Cf. W. M. Abbott (ed.), *Documents of Vatican II*.

Couvade → Birth. S.G.F.B.

Covenant Idea of C. between → Yahweh and Israel is basic to Heb. → *Heilsgeschichte*. The Heb. word *b^erîth* ('covenant') meant agreement between two parties, pledging them to mutual loyalty. Acc. to Heb. belief, Yahweh made a C. with → Abraham, progenitor of Israel: it was confirmed by sacrifice (Gen. 15:7ff.). This C. foreshadowed that made at Sinai, where whole nation of Israel entered into a C. relationship with Yahweh (Ex. 19:5ff.), who promised to estab. Israel to Canaan: the C. was confirmed by sacrifice (Ex. 24:3ff.). This idea of a C.-relationship characterises Heb. relig., and was constantly invoked by the prophets. The idea passed over into Christianity, where it was effectively utilised in Chr. apologetic *vis-à-vis* Judaism. Paul refers to → Church as the 'new covenant', using Grk. *diathēkē*, which trans. Heb. *b^erîth* in → LXX. Hence emerged idea of God's providence finding successive expression in an Old C. or Testament and a New C. or Testament. The wine at the Last Supper reinforced idea of a new C., confirmed by sacrifice, being described in Christ's words as 'the new covenant in my blood' (I Cor. 11:25; cf. Mk. 14:24). The C. idea had an important role in theology of → Qumran. S.G.F.B.

H.D.B., pp. 183–5; *R.G.G.*³, I, 1512–8; W. Beyerlin, *Herkunft und Geschichte der ältesten Sinaitraditionen* (1961); S. G. F. Brandon, *History, Time and Deity* (1965), pp. 130, 176–7, 190ff.; *R.A.C.*, III, 982–90 ('Diatheke').

Cow, Sanctity of in Hinduism A large variety of animals are revered in Hinduism, but cow has come to hold very special position. In → Vedic and later times there is evidence of cow-sacrifice, and even → Asoka did not forbid killing of cows. By about beginning of Christ. era a ban on cow slaughter had become widespread. The penalties for killing cow were severe, and equivalent to those incurred for killing high-class person. Expiations incl. such requirements as that killer had to live with herd of cows, clad in skin of dead animal, for long period, during which he subsisted on a kind of barley-gruel. The sanctity of cow has had its effect on intensifying some caste distinctions, since those who act as tanners, eat beef, etc., are regarded as esp. unclean by upper castes. The five hundred products of the cow (the *pañcagavya*) are by contrast regarded as having purifying properties: these are milk, curd, butter, urine and dung. With gradual decimation of India's forests, the last has come to be used widely as fuel. Respect for cows is incorporated in guiding principles of constitution of Republic of India; the Government has encouraged methods of improving stock, since cow-sanctity has resulted in very heavy, but relatively unproductive, cow population in subcontinent. The bull, in shape of Nandi, is the mount of → Śiva, a cult which may go back as far as → Indus Valley Civilisation. N.S.

Craving (*Tanhā*, Pali; *Tṛṣṇā*, Skt.) Acc. to the 2nd of the Buddh. → Holy Truths, craving is the root of all suffering entailed in mortal existence. C. (or lit. 'thirst') is closely linked, in Buddh. analysis, with → Ignorance (*avijjā*), and → Karma, as forces which perpetuate sorrowful existence, i.e. continue the cycle of re-birth. In the Buddha's first sermon (*SN*, V, pp. 420ff.; *Vin*, 1:10), it is proclaimed that C. must be got rid of, if → *nibbāna* is to be attained. 3 kinds of C. are distinguished: (1) for sensuous pleasure (2) for rebirth (3) for no further rebirth. Thus, even so long as *nibbāna* is the object of C., it cannot be attained; all C. of any kind whatsoever is regarded as a sign of imperfection. In some passages in Buddh. scripture, C. is spoken of as having another 3 aims: C. for sensual existence (*kāma*); for fine-material existence (*rūpa*); for non-material existence (*a-rūpa*). In Buddh. mythology C. is the 4th member of → Māra, the Evil One's army. C. has a 6-fold source: it arises in connection with visible objects, sounds, odours, tastes, bodily contacts and mental impressions. The term is used more extensively in passages where language is popular, picturesque or poetic; is less often used in passages of philosophical analysis, although C. is mentioned in famous formula of Chain of Causation (→ *Paticca-Samuppāda*). The most common syn. for C. in the Buddh. *Suttas* is greed (*rāga* or *lobha*). T.O.L.

Piyadassi Thera, *The Buddha's Ancient Path* (1964), ch. 4.

Creation (Buddh. view) The doc. of a personal God who created the universe *ex nihilo* is not found in Buddhism. Such a being is neither explicitly affirmed nor denied. In so far as Brahmanic theology asserted a doc. of creation by → Brahma, and that Brahma was proud of his achievement, this was met by the Buddh. counter-assertion that such a being, victim of self-conceit, must be morally inferior to the Buddha. But on larger question of how universe originated the Buddh. attitude is one of agnosticism. The Buddhist views the attempt to answer question as futile, and having no relig. importance in comparison with prior task confronting men, i.e. of spiritual progress and elimination of moral evil, acc. to way opened up by the Buddha. Buddhist thought is positive in emphasising that world has existed for such an incredibly long duration as to make it tantamount to being datum from which human knowledge starts; consequently the question: 'How did the universe begin?' is virtually ruled out as beyond scope of proper human concern. Buddh. thought conceives of world-history in terms of *kalpas* (Skt) or *kappas* (Pali), each of which is, to all intents and purposes, an eternity; of such world-periods there have already been many hundred thousands. 'Inconceivable, O Monks', said Buddha, 'is this → *Samsāra;* not to be discovered is any first beginning of beings.' (*SN*. XV. pp.5). (→ Cosmogony; Cosmology, Buddh.). T.O.L.

Creation (Chinese and Japanese) The Chinese have no distinctive doc. of creation, but only a concept of cosmic evolution out of a primaeval unity. The creation myth of P'an Ku (→ Cosmogony, Chinese) is of comparatively late origin and prob. dates from 4th cent. CE. Acc. to Chi. author Jên Fang, the myth was brought to China from Siam in 6th cent. CE. P'an Ku was regarded as offspring of → Yin and Yang. He is pictured as dwarf, clothed in bearskin or merely in leaves, holding in hands a hammer and chisel. He is attended by four supernatural creatures—the unicorn, phoenix, tortoise and dragon. Sometimes he is depicted with sun and moon in his hands, the first fruits of his labours. His task occupied 18,000 yrs., after which he dissolved into the various components of universe. (→ Cosmogony, various entries).

For Japanese creation myths → Izanagi–Izanami. D.H.S.

E. T. C. Werner, *Dict. of Chinese Mythology* (1932) p. 355; W. G. Ashton, *Shinto* (1905), ch. 6; J. Herbert, *Shinto* (1967), *passim*.

Creed (Buddh.) The nearest Buddh. approach to a formal creed in Christ. sense is the 3-fold affirmation, 'I go to the Buddha for refuge; I go to the Dhamma (Doctrine) for refuge; I go to the Sangha (Order of monks) for refuge.' This is the most widely used devotional formula among Buddh.s, and forms preliminary invocation to daily recital of the *Pansil*, or affirmation of five basic moral precepts by laymen and monks alike. Apart from this, no formal statement of faith is binding upon Buddh. In → Theravādin countries of S.E. Asia, there is tacit acceptance of the Doctrine (→ *Dhamma*) of the Buddha, as this is contained in the Pali canon; but even this is to be accepted on authority only tentatively as first step towards experimental verification of its truth. Without intention of practical verification, intellectual acceptance of doc. is not regarded as in itself of any ultimate value. The *Kālāma Sutta* teaches that there should be no acceptance of propositions on authoritative grounds alone. (→ Faith, Buddh.). T.O.L.

K. N. Jayatilleke, *Early Buddhist Theory of Knowledge* (1963), ch. VIII.

(China and Japan) The indigenous religs. of China and Japan never attempted to formulate or define a body of doctrine. Buddh., both in China and Japan, in general with Buddh. everywhere, accepted the Four Noble Truths, the Three Refuges, and the Eightfold Path as being the foundation of the Buddha's teaching (→ Buddhism). D.H.S.

(Chirst.) Christianity is distinguished among the great religs. by its use in instruction and worship of precisely formulated statements of belief. → Judaism provides nearest parallel in the *Thirteen Principles of the Faith*, orig. formulated in 12th cent. by Maimonides and incl. in authorised prayer books. The Muslim *kalima* is an authoritative affirmation of belief in uniqueness of Allah and status of Muhammad; but it defines nothing more of Islamic doctrine. The Chr. creeds reflect speculation and controversies that attended the grad. develop. of doctrine in terms of current Grk. metaphysic. C. began as short formulas of belief for → baptism candidates. By 4th cent. the so-called Apostles Creed had emerged, and by early Middle Ages was in gen. use in W. at baptism and daily services. This C., which was attr. to 12 Apostles, affirms main doctrines, but without theological definition. The so-called Nicene Creed is not that drawn up by Council of Nicaea in 325: its orig. is obscure; it prob. derives from Baptismal Creed of Jerusalem (early 4th cent.). Its use in → Eucharist began at Antioch towards end of 5th cent., and grad. spread in both E. and W. Church. The carefully defined clauses on divinity of Christ reflect → Arian controversy and connect it with Council of Nicaea. The → Filioque clause was added in early Middle Ages in W. only. The longer → Athanasian C. reflects later Christological controversy. (→ Creed). S.G.F.B.

E.R.E., IV, pp. 231–48; G. Van der Leeuw, *La religion* (1948), pp. 433ff.; *D.C.C.*, pp. 72, 354, 952; J. N. D. Kelly, *Early Christian Creeds* (1950); *R.G.G.*[3], I, 988–94; J. Wach, *The Comparative Study of Religions* (1958), pp. 73ff.; A. J. Wensinck, *The Muslim Creed* (1932.)

(Islam) There is no universally acceptable C. in Islam, unless one applies term to the profession of → faith in the one God and → Muḥammad as his messenger. This expresses the essence of Islam; but while Muslims accept and continually repeat this brief statement of belief, other more formal statements have been drawn up with much greater detail. Macdonald, *Theology*, pp. 293ff. gives a trans. of four C.'s. Among the articles in → Ash'arī's are rejection of allegorical interpret. of the → Qur., belief that Qur. is uncreated, that everything good and bad happens in accord. with God's will, that God is the only creator, so man's deeds are created and predestined by God, that believers will experience the beatific vision on day of resurrection, that God will not leave in hell any who have believed in his unity, that the teaching of the Traditions is reliable and that first four Caliphs are to be accepted. → Ghazālī's C. is more theological in statements regarding God. It mentions his attributes and supreme control, then speaks of Muḥammad and his statements about what happens after death. The high rank of first four Caliphs and excellence of the Prophet's → Companions are asserted. A C. by Nasafī contains all the elements mentioned with some change of emphasis in places. A more mod. C. by Fuḍalī gives 50 articles incumbent on all Muslims, 41 relating to God and 9 to his messengers. Wensinck, *Creed* is a very import. work, discussing basic beliefs and practice of Islam and develop. of theology, also views of different parties. A full trans. with comm. is given of three creeds, and summaries of later ones are given. The above refers to → Sunnī doc. For other sects →→ Mu'tazilites, Isma'īlīs, Khārijites, Shī'a. J.R.

E.I.[2], I, pp. 332ff.; Watt, *Free-will;* Sweetman, *I.C.T.;* Fyzee, *Creed;* Miller, *Bāb.*

Cremation (Buddh.) → Dead, The: Disposal of (Buddh.). T.O.L.

(China and Japan). The Chinese in gen. buried their dead and were averse to cremation, believing that filial piety demanded that body should return to ancestors in its wholeness. Buddh. monks and nuns in China practised cremation, and through the influence of → Buddhism in Japan, C. gradually became fairly general from the 8th cent. onwards. (→ Burial: Chinese; Japan). D.H.S.

Crescent (Islam) The crescent, orig. assoc. with moon-worship, was a symbol used in Byzantium and said to have been taken over by Turks after conquest of city in 857/1453. Though formerly a Greek, Roman, and later a Christ. symbol, it has come to be accepted as a Muslim one. It appears on flags of some modern Muslim states as well as on the Turkish flag, always accompanied by a star; it sometimes appears on stamps. In Muslim lands, the body parallel to the Red Cross is the Red Crescent. (→ Moon). J.R.

E.I.[2], III, pp. 379–85 (*hilāl*)*;* Hughes, p. 63; *E.R.E.*, pp. 12, 145.

Cretan-Mycenaean Religion It is customary to treat these religs. together in view of extant evidence, although they were faiths of two distinct peoples, of different racial origs. Cretan or Minoan culture dates back to *c.* 3,000 BC; it is known only by archeological data, since the 'Linear A' tablets are not yet deciphered. Mycen. culture is documented both by archeology and 'Linear B' tablets, now deciphered. Earliest Cretan shrines were in caves or mountain tops, and such sites continued to be used. No large temple has been found. Worship of settled communities took place in open air shrines, signified by double axes (→ Axe, Double), as depicted on Hagia Triada sarcophagus, or in domestic chapels. Sacrifices of animals were offered, and libations made. The chief deity was a vegetation goddess, assoc. with a tree-cult. She, or her priestesses, are depicted in contemporary Cretan female attire, with bare breasts, and holding snakes. The goddess is often attended by young male deity, and lions. A bull-cult is evidenced by many repres. of bulls, symbolic use of bull's horns, and prob. by ritual contest with bulls performed by young men and women:

some memory thereof seems to be preserved in legend of → Minotaur. The dead were buried with symbolic grave equipment, and were prob. thought to be in care of goddess, who also had chthonian attributes. The Hagia Triada sarcophagus may indic. belief also in a transmarine realm of dead. The Mycenaean period (*c.* 1,600–1,100 BC) reveals intermixture of Cretan relig. with that of Indo-European invaders. Cultic scenes on Mycen. objects reproduce those of Crete, but Linear B tablets show that names of some Olympian deities were current. Mycen. burials differ from Cretan in having real, not symbolic, equipment (→ Funerary Rites, Crete-Mycen.). It is prob. that the → Eleusinian Mysteries derived from a pre-Hellenic cult of goddess(es) connected with corn, earth, and the dead. (→ Aegean Relig.). S.G.F.B.

M. P. Nilsson, *The Minoan-Mycenaean Religion and its Survival in Greek Religion*² (1950); C. Picard, *Les religions préhelléniques* (1948); R. W. Hutchinson, *Prehistoric Crete* (1962); Lord William Taylour, *The Mycenaeans* (1964); S. Marinatos, *Crete and Mycenae* (1960); L. A. Stella, 'La religione greca nei testi micenei', in *Numen*, V (1958); S. Hood, *The Home of the Heroes* (1967); *Antiquity*, XLIII (1969).

Criobolium Sacrifice of ram in rites of → Cybele. The word *bolos* prob. derived from lasso used in capturing victim for sacrifice. S.G.F.B.

Cumont, *R.O.*, pp. 63ff., 229; R. Duthoy, *The Taurobolium* (Leiden 1969).

Cross In varying forms, the C. is an anc. and widespread relig. symbol. occurring in both the Old and New Worlds. Apart from its Chr. significance, two forms of C. may be specially noticed: the Egypt. sign of life, the *crux ansata* or → *ankh;* the gammate cross or *swastika* which had wide currency both as solar symbol and sign of life or blessing. In Christianity, the C. became the symbol *par excellence* of sacrificial d. of Christ. It prob. had already acquired significance as symbol of martyr's death among → Zealots: hence saying of Jesus about C.-bearing, Mk. 8:34 (S. G. F. Brandon, *Jesus and the Zealots* (1967), pp. 57, pp. 103ff.). → Paul was first to lay primary emphasis on C. of Christ as soteriological symbol (e.g. I Cor. 1:17 ff.; Gal. 6:14). In Chr. art, hymns and devotional lit., the C. has always figured prominently, and there are legends about the tree from which C. was made. The C. was alleged to have been found by St. Helena, mother of Emp. Constantine (d. 337) close to trad. site of Golgotha. The Chr. Calendar commemorates this event and recovery of C. from Persians in 629, by two feasts, the 'Invention' and the 'Exhaltation of the Cross'. In R.C. Church, the C. is venerated at a special ceremony on → Good Friday, known as 'Creeping to the C.'. (→ Crucifixion). S.G.F.B.

E.R.E., IV, *s.v.; D.C.C.*, pp. 480, 698, 1411; *R.G.G.*³, IV, 45–7, 52; M. Cramer, *Das ältagyptischen Lebenszeichen im christlichen (koptischen) Aegypten* (1955); *A.E.C.C.*, pp. 411–5; E. A. W. Budge (tr.), *The Book of the Cave of Treasures* (1927), pp. 224ff.; C. Kapp, *The Holy Places of the Gospels* (E.T. 1963), pp. 382ff.

Crucifixion This mode of death prob. orig. in Phoenicia; it was adopted by Romans as punishment of slaves, foreigners and criminals of lowest class—Tacitus refers to C. as 'supplicium servile' (*Hist.*, ii, 72). During 1st cent. CE, the Romans crucified Jew. rebels: Josephus records numerous cases. Jesus was crucified for sedition against Roman gov. in Judea (Mk. 15:15ff.). Representations of C. of Jesus first appear in Chr. art in 5th cent. S.G.F.B.

*H.D.B.*², *s.v.;* P. Winter, *On the Trial of Jesus* (1961), p. 107; S. G. F. Brandon, *Jesus and the Zealots* (1967), *Trial of Jesus of Nazareth* (1968); *R.G.G.*³, IV, 47–9; *A.E.C.W.*, p. 145.

Crusades When Jerusalem was captured by Seljuk Turks in 1071, Chr. pilgrimage to the holy places, which had continued after their possession by Islam in 637, became impossible. In 1095 Pope Urban II summoned Chr. forces to recover the Holy Land. Those who 'took the cross', symbolised by a cross on their clothing, were called Crusaders, and various spiritual benefits were promised to them. The First C. was surprisingly successful, and Jerusalem was captured in July, 1099: the victory was marred by massacre of Muslim and Jew. inhabitants. A Latin kingdom of Jerusalem was estab. until city was recaptured by Muslims under Saladin in 1187. There were eight C., the last being in 1270. The last six were all unsuccessful; the 4th C. was deflected to Constantinople, capital of E. Christendom, which was stormed and a Latin Emperor set up and E. Church forcibly reunited with Rome. The success and failure of the C. demonstrated both strength and limitations of medieval Papacy. The C. also greatly affected chivalry of Europe, esp. of France, whose nobility played a leading role; they deepened hostility felt by E. Church towards Papacy, and increased hatred between Christianity and Islam. The C. produced the military monastic orders of the Knights → Hospitaller and → Templar. S.G.F.B.

S. Runciman, *A. Hist. of the Crusades*, 3 vols. (1951–4); P. Alphandèry, *La Chrétienté et l'idée de Croisade* (1954); L. E. Browne, *The Eclipse of Christianity in Asia* (1933); E. Barker in *The Legacy of Islam*, ed. T. Arnold–A. Guillaume (1931), pp. 40ff.; *E.R.E.*, IV, *s.v.; R.G.G.*³, IV, 54–9; M. Join-Lambert, *Jerusalem*

(E.T. 1958), pp. 144ff.; J. J. Saunders, *Aspects of the Crusades* (1962).

Culavaṃsa 'The Short Chronicle', a continuation of 'Great Chronicle' (→ *Mahāvaṃsa*), or Buddh. history of Ceylon. The titles 'Mahāvamsa' and 'C.' are not found in work itself: they were intro. by W. Geiger, who edited Pali text of whole chronicle; his terminology has been adopted by other western writers. The Sinhalese use only the title *Mahāvaṃsa* for whole history, from intro. of Buddhism to Ceylon in 3rd cent. BC to arrival of authorship at ch. 37.51 (point at which the '*Culavaṃsa*', acc. to Geiger, begins). The earlier chapters of *Mahāvaṃsa* (1–37.50) are attr. to a monk called Mahānāma, who lived at Anurādhapura *c.* 5th cent. CE. The section beginning at ch. 37.51 is attr. to a monk of 13th cent. CE, named Dhammakitta, who prob. lived at Polonnaruwa. The chs. dealing with period after 13th to 18th cents. (90–100) are gen. held to have been added in latter part of 18th cent.; ch. 101, dealing with arrival of British, is a yet later addition. (→ Ceylon). T.O.L.

Culavaṃsa (Pali text, 2 vols., ed. by W. Geiger, with German trans. 1935; E.T. by Mrs. C. Mabel Rickmers, 1953); W. Geiger, *Pali Literature and Language* (2nd edn. 1956); Walpola Rahula, *History of Buddhism in Ceylon: the Anurādha period* (1956).

Cullavagga → *Vinaya Pitaka*. T.O.L.

Culdees Name given to certain Irish and Scottish monks in 8th cent. and onwards, deriving prob. from old Irish *céle dé*, 'companion'. The C. seem orig. to have been groups of anchorites, comprising each thirteen members on analogy of Christ and his Apostles. Except at Armagh, by 11th cent. C. were superseded by secular canons. In settled eccl. establishments C. took part in choral side of worship, and were assoc. with care of sick and poor and distribution of alms. S.G.F.B.

E.R.E., IV, *s.v.;* K. Hughes in *The Early British Church*, ed. N. K. Chadwick (1958), p. 264; J. H. Cockburn, *The Celtic Church in Dunblane* (1954), ch. XII.

Culture Hero(es) Term used for legendary figures regarded in folklore as the inventors or initiators of various objects or institutions essential to civilisation: e.g. agriculture, the vine, olive, implements (brick-mould, pick-axe), sacrifice, divination. The following appear as C.H.: →→ Osiris, Adam, Cain and Abel, Tubal-Cain, Noah, Ea, Prometheus. C.H. may be deities or divinised → heroes. The German term 'Kulturbringer' is more descriptive. S.G.F.B.

Cursing The idea that by pronouncing words expressive of harm, directed against some person or thing, or of good as in → blessing, what is intended will come to pass, doubtless stems from primitive belief in magical efficacy of words. The custom is universal. The Shabaka Stone (→ Memphite Theology), shows that already in 3rd mil. BC, Egyptians conceived of creation by divine *fiat*. The efficacy of C., as of blessing, depended on power or authority of person pronouncing it: hence both C. and blessing take form of invocation of divine or demonic powers to effect what is thus desired. Often C. is accompanied by ritual action deemed appropriate to occasion or intent: e.g. in Chr. use of → anathema, after bishop pronounced sentence, lighted candles were thrown to ground. S.G.F.B.

E.R.E., IV, pp. 367–74; *R.G.G.*³, V, 1648–52; G. Van der Leeuw, *La Religion* (1948), pp. 394 ff.

Cybele The great mother-goddess of Anatolia. Pessinus, in Phrygia, was her chief sanctuary, where her symbol or image, in form of small meteoric stone, was venerated. C. was a fertility-goddess, assoc. with a young lover → Attis, and thus akin to similar goddesses in anc. Near East (→→ Astarte; Aphrodite; Ishtar; → Cretan-Mycen. Religion). She was connected with mountains and animals. In art she appears enthroned and draped, wearing a mural crown, and flanked by attendant lions. She prob. had chthonian attributes and was assoc. with care of dead. In Greece, C. was early assoc. with → Demeter. Her cult came to Rome in 205–4 BC. Her spring festival was mainly a ritual commemoration of death and resurrection of Attis. She was served by priests (*galli*) who castrated themselves for her service (→ Castration). The *taurobolium* (→ crioboloium) was connected with cult of C., and orig. in Asia Minor. It was an initiation rite, prob. with regenerating virtue; it took form of bathing recipient in blood of sacrificed bull. The cult of C. spread throughout Roman Empire, being esp. popular in Gaul and Africa. There was a later tendency to identify C. and Attis with celestial powers. S.G.F.B.

O.C.D., *s.v.;* F. Cumont, *Les religions*, ch. III; Gressmann, *O.R.*, pp. 56ff.; N. Turchi, *Fontes*, pp. 215ff.; J. Carcopino, *Aspects mystiques de la Rome païenne* (1943), pp. 49ff.; Ch. Picard, *Numen*, IV (1957), pp. 1ff.; M. J. Vermaseren, *The Legend of Attis in Greek and Roman Art* (1966); R. Duthoy, *The Taurobolium* (Leiden 1969).

Cynics Derisory name given to followers of Diogenes of Sinope (*c.* 400–325 BC), because he recommended their rejection of all conventions, thus to live like dogs (*kynes*). The C. were never organised as a school, professing a distinctive doctrine. The C. way of life was to reduce possessions to bare necessities, to avoid all social entanglements, so as to gain personal independence and serenity. The movement, having gradually declined, took on new vigour in 1st cent CE. Some C. beggar-philosophers brought movement into disrepute, but there were many educated men who lived sincerely acc. to C. principles. S.G.F.B.

D. R. Dudley, *A History of Cynicism* (1938); L. Robin, *La pensée grecque* (1928), pp. 199ff.; *E.R.E.*, IV, *s.v.; O.C.D.*, *s.v.*

Cyprian, St. (d. 258) A pagan rhetorician who, two years after conversion, was elected bishop of Carthage. C. became involved in question whether, or on what terms, those who lapsed during → persecution could be restored to membership of Church. C. decided that *lapsi* could be restored after suitable penance. He was also involved in controversy with Stephen, Bp. of Rome, by his demanding rebaptism of schismatics. C. died a martyr's death *c.* 258. His numerous writings are important as evidence of Chr. faith and practice: they have also been much used in later controversy about Papal claims. S.G.F.B.

R.A.C., III, 463–6; *D.C.C.*, *s.v.*, P. de Labriolle, *Hist. and Literature of Latin Christianity* (E.T. 1884), pp. 131ff.

Cyril of Alexandria (d. 444) Becoming Patriarch of Alex. in 412, C. played a leading part in theological controversies until his d., and his influence was effective for some time after, e.g. at Council of → Chalcedon (451). C. was protagonist of Alex. theology against that of Antioch, the condemnation of whose Patriarch, → Nestorius, he secured at Council of Ephesus (431), and posthumously at Chalcedon (451). C. was indirectly responsible for murder of celebrated pagan philosopher Hypatia, and his conduct at Council of Ephesus was not irreproachable. A vigorous controversalist, his writings are important theological documents. Certain aspects of his terminology caused him later to be cited by exponents of → Monophysitism. (→ Alex., → Antioch. Theology).

R.A.C., III, 499–515; *D.C.C.*, *s.v.;* W. Bright, *The Age of the Fathers* (1903), vol. II.

D

Dābbat al-arḍ (The beast of the earth). One of signs of the resurrection (→ Hour). Qur., xxvii: 84 says it will appear and declare that mankind has no belief in God's signs. Trad. elaborates on this, the only Qur. ref., saying the beast has body composed of parts of different animals. It will mark believers and unbelievers to distinguish them. Masson in his n. on the v. (82 in his numbering) refers to Revelation xi:7; xiii:11; xix:19f.; but if there is a connection, it must be due to imperfect knowledge of passages. *E.I.*² mentions only xiii, 11 and throws doubt on assimilation. 'Alī, *Qur'ān*, n. 1863, makes the curious statement that the beast repr. 'the materialistic nations of the West who have lost all sense of the higher values of life'. J.R.

*E.I.*², II, p. 71; Hughes, pp. 64, 539; *Mishkāt*, p. 1143; Sale, *Qur'ān*, I, pp. 131f.; Wensinck, *Handbook*, p. 100.

Dādūpanthīs Hindu reforming sect founded by Dādū (CE 1544–1603), who was influenced by → Kabir. His main sphere of preaching was south of Delhi and in Jaipur state. His docts. were a radical application of reforming inter-relig. ideals expressed also by Kabir, → Nanak and others. He rejected both authority of Veda and of → *Qur'ān*, criticised ritualism, cult of images, caste distinctions, pilgrimages and other divisive and external marks of piety, and gave a euhemeristic explanation of gods →→ Brahma, Viṣṇu and Śiva. There is one God who is supreme Teacher and Creator. Dadu considerably watered down doc. of → rebirth, considering that rebirth as an animal, etc., was symbolic representation of kind of mood or disposition of individual. A strong exponent of → *bhakti*, he emphasised need to cling to God in love and hope. His writings were collected in scriptures known as the *Bānī*, which antedated the *Adi* → *Granth* and thus is earliest of 'modern' scriptures of India. Though Dadu lived life of a householder and did not consider life in world as evil (but rather worldliness), a substantial number of Dadupanthis were celibate monks and mendicants, incl. a group of fighting ascetics in Jaipur state (→ Asceticism, Hindu). The later cult had many of characteristics of → Sikhism, incl. reverence to the *Bani*. N.S.

J. C. Oman, *Mystics, Ascetics and Saints of India* (1903); William G. Orr, *A Sixteenth-Century Indian Mystic* (1947).

Dagan (Dagon) Anc. Semitic deity, whose cult dates from before 2400 BC in Mesopotamia. D. was worshipped at many places in Syria and Palestine: he had a temple at → Ugarit, where he was named father of → Baal. D. was an agricultural deity: the rare Heb. word *dāghān* meant 'corn'. His cult was adopted by the Philistines. S.G.F.B.

E.R.E., IV, *s.v.;* E. Dhorme, *R.B.A.*, pp. 165ff.; *H.D.B.*², *s.v.*

Dāgaba (Buddh.) Name used, espec. in Ceylon, for a Buddh. reliquary mound. The word is a compound of → *dhātu* (element, essence, and hence 'a sacred relic') and *garbha* (a chamber, or cavern); thus a chamber for a sacred relic. The D. usually has the architectural form of → *Stupa* or memorial-mound, though the two words are not, as sometimes assumed, completely interchangeable. Not all *stupas* are D.'s, i.e. they do not all contain a relic chamber. A secondary meaning which has been seen in word D. is derived from usage of *dhātu*, to mean element in the sense of 'seed', and *gharbha* in sense of 'womb': a D. is thus a place of sacred potential, the seed in the womb. The word 'pagoda' may possibly be a Europeanisation (Portugese and Eng.) of *dāgaba*, though this is uncertain. (→ Pagoda). T.O.L.

Daibutsu (Great Buddha): Name given to several large images of → Buddhas and → bodhisattvas in Japan, usually made of bronze, in a sitting or standing posture. The three most important D. are at Nara, Kyoto and Kamakura. The colossal D. at Nara was erected under patronage of zealous Buddh. emperor, Shōmu Tennō (CE 724–48) to be perpetual memorial of successful attempt to plant Buddhism in Japan and to ally it with the native → Shinto. It was completed in CE 754. The image, in a sitting posture 53 ft high, stands in the Todaiji temple at Nara. The Kyoto D., a sitting figure of Lochana-Buddha 58½ ft in height, was begun for self-glorification by Hideyoshi and completed early in 17th cent. by his son Hideyori. It was destroyed by earthquake in 1662; the copper used for coinage. The present Kyoto D. dates from 1801. The D. at Kamakura, though smaller than that at Nara, is better known. It is an image of → Amida Buddha 49 ft 7 in. in height. Erected in 1252, it marks the success of the great Amidist (Pure Land) sects. Originally it was housed in a temple, twice destroyed in 1369 and 1494 and since then never rebuilt. D.H.S.

D. Lloyd in *E.R.E.*, IV, pp. 389–90.

Dainichi Japanese name for Mahā-Vairochana Buddha, the Great Illuminator whose body was deemed to comprise the whole cosmos, and whose body, speech and thought make up the life of the universe. Acc. to → Shingon, all deities and demons of Buddhist pantheon are but manifestations of D. D.H.S.

M. Anesaki, *Hist. of Japanese Buddhism* (1930), pp. 125ff.

-Dajjāl One-eyed monster who will appear as one of the signs before the last → Hour. It is sometimes said that he will have the letters K F R = *kāfir* (infidel) on forehead. Some trads. say a contemporary of → Muḥammad, Ibn Ṣayyād, was the D. Sometimes D. is called *al-masīḥ al-dajjāl* (the *antichrist*). It is commonly said he will appear from the East; some stories locate him in Indonesia. He is to rule for 40 days before end of world, one like a year, one like a month, one like a week, and the rest like ordinary days. → Jesus will then descend 'at the white minaret in the E. of Damascus'. He will pursue the D. to gate of Ludd and kill him there. This happens before the inroads of → Gog and Magog. A trad. given by Bukhārī and Muslim says about 30 lying D.'s will be sent forth before last Hour. (→ Antichrist). J.R.

*E.I.*², II, pp. 76f.; Hughes, p. 64; *Mishkāt*, pp. 1129–33, 1143–58 and index (miscellaneous items); Wensinck, *Creed*, index (Anti-Christ).

Dakhmas 'Towers of silence': Specially constructed towers on which naked corpses are laid to be devoured by birds of prey, acc. to → Zoroastrian and Parsi funerary custom. D. are regarded as awful and impure places, and have special attendants. S.G.F.B.

E.R.E., IV, pp. 503–4; *Numen*, I (1954), pp. 56–7.

Dalai Lama → Tibet, religion of. T.O.L.

Damascus Fragments, The Two fragments of Heb. MS. found by S. Schechter in the Cairo Genizah in 1910. The discovery of fragments of same work at → Qumrân has helped to elucidate problem which the D.-F. formerly constituted. The work tells of a Jew. sect of 'Sons of Zadok' (hence sometimes called the 'Zadokite Work'), or of the 'New Covenant', which had settled in Damascus and was distinguished by certain customs and beliefs (e.g. in a 'Teacher of Righteousness', and the 'Messiah of Aaron and Israel'). It is gen. agreed that sect was identical, or closely related, to the Qumrân Covenanters: some scholars would interpret 'Damascus' as 'Qumrân' (→ Qumrân). S.G.F.B.

H. H. Rowley, *The Zadokite Documents and the Dead Sea Scrolls* (1952); A. Dupont-Sommer, *Les écrits esséniens découvertes près de la Mer Morte* (1959), ch. V; C. Rabin, *The Zadokite Documents* (1958²).

Dāna (Buddh.) The Pali word D. means lit. 'giving'; this is one of the major B. virtues. Generosity is encouraged as an essential B. attitude, and as best way of offsetting human tendency to individualistic self-centredness. It is also regarded as a form of renunciation, open to all, laymen as well as monks, and hence is first of three major ways of making merit (*puñña*); the other two, in ascending order of value, being observance of moral precepts (*sila*) and meditation (*bhāvanā*) (DN.33; Itivuttaka 60). For the monk, if he is a hermit-ascetic, such as are found in some places in Ceylon, he has no possessions whatever to give; if he is a village-monk, however, as are vast majority in Ceylon and S.E. Asia, 'giving' for him means giving of time and service to village community in form of teaching, counselling etc. For the layman practice of generosity has been cast in certain routine forms since earliest days of Buddhism, and consists largely in economic reciprocation of monks' services to villagers. Thus, merit is gained by the layman in giving food to monks, either daily when the monks make their almsround, or on special occasion when monks are invited to ceremonial meal; it is gained also in giving of robes, money (often to head of monastery, for the community's needs), and sometimes land, or materials, or labour, for building of new monastery or pagoda. In some B. countries (e.g. Burma) there is a recognised hierarchy of merit-making by D., as follows (in descending order of value): (1) to build a new pagoda (2) act as sponsor for a novice-monk (3) build and donate a monastery; (4) donate a well to a monastery (5) feed a group of monks on a special occasion (6) feed monks in normal way (7) give hospitality to laymen. T.O.L.

M. M. Ames, 'Magical Animism and Buddhism: a Structural Analysis of the Sinhalese Religious System', in *J.A.S.* (1964); Manning Nash, *The Golden Road to Modernity* (1965), ch. 4.

Dance of Death, The The later Middle Ages were characterised by preoccupation with death, which found expression in both lit. and art. The D.-D. depicted Death as a skeleton dragging away living persons repr. of various occupations or stations in life. It emphasised ubiquity of Death

and its unexpected approach; it is poss. that the Black Death stimulated this morbidity. Many orig. depictions of the D.-D. exist in various places in Europe; it is also well known through woodcuts of Hans Holbein (1538). S.G.F.B.
T. Tindall Wildridge, *The Dance of Death* (1887); *D.C.C.*, *s.v.; R.G.G.*³, VI, 957–8; J. Huizanga, *The Waning of the Middle Ages* (E.T. 1924), ch. XI; J. Nohl, *The Black Death* (1961 edn.), pp. 89ff.

Dance, Sacred Paleolithic → cave art poss. provides evidence in such a figure as the 'Dancing Sorcerer' of the Trois Frères Cave (Ariège) of magical dances performed by men in animal disguise: such dances were prob. mimetic and designed to promote a successful hunt or propitiate slain animal. Similar rites were performed by the → Ainus. Ritual dances are well attested in anc. Egypt: they were performed on many occasions both in divine worship and mortuary rites. Heb. lit. provides abundant evidence of S.-D. (e.g. II Sam. 6, vv. 14ff.; Ex. 15:20–1ff.); so also does Grk. lit. (e.g. acc. to Aristotle, Grk. tragedy and comedy derived from the Dithyramb, a leaping, inspired dance performed in Spring festival connected with → Dionysos; the ecstatic dance of the → Maenads was notorious). The S.-D. has been an estab. form of Chr. worship in some Churches (e.g. of → Ethiopia); but in W. Church it was gen. regarded as devilish, and many medieval legends tell of fate of dancers; the Chr. Middle Ages also witnessed epidemics of dancing-mania (St. John's Dance at Aix; St. Vitus' Dance). Dancing has been a universal phenomenon; in its anc. and primitive forms it invariably had a relig. or magical character. Many types of S.-D. can be distinguished: e.g. magical, ecstatic, liturgical, pantomimic. Acc. to C. Sachs, 'The dance can be sacrifice, prayer, magic act. It invokes or combats the forces of nature, heals sickness, establishes contact between dead and living; assures the harvest, successful hunt and victory; it creates, maintains, orders and protects.' He defines the essence of the dance as 'life at a degree of high intensity.' (→→ Dance of Death; Drama; Sacred, Labyrinth). S.G.F.B.
C. Sachs, *Histoire de la Danse* (1938); J. G. Frazer, *The Magic Art* (*G.B.*), I, pp. 137ff.; J. E. Harrison, *Ancient Art and Ritual* (1935); *E.R.E.*, X, pp. 358ff.; J. A. MacCulloch, *Medieval Faith and Fable* (1932), pp. 24ff., 256ff.; M. A. Johnstone, *The Dance in Etruria* (1956); *R.G.G.*, VI, 612–6; G. Van der Leeuw, *Sacred and Profane Beauty* (E.T. 1963), pp. 9ff.; W. O. E. Oesterley, *The Sacred Dance* (1923); *Les danses sacrées* (*S.O.*, VI, 1963).

Daniel, Book of Written partly in Heb. and Aramaic, expert opinion gen. regards B.-D. as a work, dating *c.* 164 BC, designed to encourage Jews to remain faithful to their relig. during oppression of Antiochus Epiphanes. It was prob. ascribed to Daniel, a renowned hero of Jew. folklore, to win attention; earlier material was used in its composition, and unity of extant work has been questioned. For hist. of relig., the B.-D. is notable for being earliest example of fully developed *Apocalypse*, and for providing earliest evidence of belief in a post-mortem → judgment, subsequent on resurrection of dead (only of martyrs and apostates). It also witnesses to incorporation of angelology in Jew. relig. (→ Apocalyptic Lit.). S.G.F.B.
J. A. Montgomery, *Critical Commentary on Book of Daniel* (1927); *P.C.*², p. 603; *H.D.B.*², *s.v.; R.A.C.*, III, 575–85; H. H. Rowley, *Darius the Mede and the Four World Empires in Book of Daniel* (1959).

Dante (1265–1321) Italian poet, whose chief work, the *Divina Commedia*, is a noble and significant presentation of faith of medieval Christendom, set forth in poetic form. Dante's life was unhappy: having identified himself ardently with anti-Papal faction in his native Florence, he was exiled on its defeat and never returned home. D. was much concerned with struggle between → Papacy and Holy Roman Empire, and in his *De Monarchia* (*c.* 1313) he presented his ideal of a universal temporal monarchy, with Pope as supreme spiritual authority. The *Divina Commedia*, written towards end of life, describes Dante's visionary pilgrimage through → Hell and → Purgatory until he is granted a glimpse of → Beatific Vision in Paradise. Dante's consciousness of classical past is symbolized in → Virgil who guides him through Hell and Purgatory. The descriptions of Hell and Purgatory are vivid and realistic; Paradise is etherealized, and, therefore, not so graphically presented. The whole poem is replete with refs. and allusions indic. of contemporary medieval culture, partic. of scholastic theology. It has been highly valued from time of its publication. S.G.F.B.
The classical E.T. is by H. F. Cary (3 vols., 1814); more recent is that of Dorothy L. Sayers in Penguin Book series (1943 on). *E.R.E.*, V, pp. 394–8; *R.G.G.*³, II, 32–8; G. G. Coulton, *Medieval Panorama* (1938), pp. 207ff.; R. L. John, *Dante* (1946).

Dār al-Ḥarb; Dār al-islām → Jihād. J.R.

Darśana The trad. Indian term for a philosophical system. From the root *dṛś* ('to see') the term is best trans. 'viewpoint'. In Hinduism, the schools have usually been classified into six: the *saḍdarśana* or 'six viewpoints', viz. →→ Samkhya, Yoga, Nyaya, Vaisesika (Purva) Mimamsa and Vedanta. In fact, there are as import. differences within Vedanta as between it and other schools, and there are philosophical systems such as

Saiva Siddhanta, lying outside the trad. six, so that the scheme is somewhat artificial (→ Hindu philosophy). N.S.

Dasgupta, S.N. Surendra Nath Dasgupta (1885–1952) is greatest of historians of Indian philosophy, and, though doing little directly to promote the mod. Hindu renaissance, nevertheless did much to stimulate consciousness of philosophical and theological achievements of past. In addition to monumental *A History of Indian Philosophy*, 5 vols. (1922–62) (the last volume being edited by widow and publ. posthumously), he wrote extensively on mysticism, etc., e.g. in his *Hindu Mysticism* (1929) and *Yoga Philosophy in Relation to other Systems of Indian Thought* (1930). N.S.

David 2nd king of Israel, whose achievements made him ideal king in Jew. trad. Although his career is vividly recorded in I Sam. 16:3–I Kgs. 2:11, I Chron. 11:1–29.30, it is evident that various conflicting trads. existed concerning D. There are three different accounts of his entry into public life (I Sam. 16:1–13; I Sam. 16:14–23; I Sam. 17); even his famous killing of Goliath is attributed to Elhanan (II Sam. 21:19). D. was a fervent devotee of → Yahweh, who designated him Saul's successor, and his reign achieved Israel's frontiers acc. to Yahweh's promise (Gen. 15:18–21; II Sam. 24:5–7; cf. von Rad, *Das Formgesch. Problem des Hexateuchs* (1939), pp. 67–8). D.'s character is repr. as brave and generous, but capable of such crimes as murder of Uriah (II Sam. 11:2f.). D.'s capture of Jebusite city of → Jerusalem, which he made his capital, bringing the → Ark there, and his plan to build → Temple of Yahweh there, were of profound consequence for Jew. relig. (II Sam. 6:12ff.). The attr. of the → Psalms to David is trad., but it prob. reflects memory of an assoc. with psalmody. Since D.'s reign repr. zenith of Israelite political power, restoration of such hegemony inspired later → Messianism; the → Messiah would be the 'Son of David' (thus Davidic descent of → Jesus is stressed in Mt. 1:1ff., 21.9; Rom. 1:3; Rev. 5:5). David figures prominently in Christ. art as royal musician and as ancestor of Christ. in so-called Jesse Windows. S.G.F.B.

*H.D.B.*², *s.v.; R.A.C.*, III, 594–603; *D.C.C.*, pp. 374–5, 722; M. Noth, *Hist. of Israel* (E.T. 1960), pp. 179ff.; S. Mowinckel, *He That Cometh* (E.T. 1956), pp. 155ff.

Dayanand Sarasvati Founder of → Arya Samaj, a reforming movement within Hinduism in 19th cent. Born in 1824 in Kathiawar, he was son of a → Brahmin and received strict orthodox upbringing. Dissatisfied with forms of temple worship, etc., which he experienced, he left home at 21 to become wandering ascetic (→ *sannyasin*), and eventually took relig. name of Dayanand Sarasvati. In 1866, he started preaching against idolatry, and eleven years later launched the Arya Samaj, which soon attracted much interest. He taught that there is one God only; that image worship is wrong; that the Vedic scriptures are revelation of God. In effect, he was preaching a Hindu unitarianism. His method of interpreting the → Veda, in support of his conviction that they taught monotheism, was to treat apparent refs. to partic. gods, such as → Agni, etc., in symbolic sense. His main writings were a Hindi work on religion, education, etc.; a commentary on Veda—the *Vedabhaṣya*, and a further commentary on the → *Rgveda*. He attacked caste practices, institutions such as child-marriage and welcomed Western science and engineering. In this, and to some extent in his relig. teachings, he repr. a syncretism between Western and Christ. ideas and those of his Hindu heritage. He considered that defects of Hinduism arose from falling away from orig. pure teaching as found in Vedic revelation. He died in 1883. N.S.

J. N. Farquhar, *Modern Religious Movements in India* (1919); L. Lajpat Rai, *The Arya Samaj* (1915); Har Bilas Sarda, *Life of Dayanand Sarasvati* (1940).

Deacon, Deaconess Office in Chr. ministry next below that of priest. Name comes from Grk. *diakonein* ('to serve'), and institution of diaconate is recorded in Acts 6:1–6, to relieve apostles from service of poor, in order to concentrate on spiritual work. In Early Church, D.'s collected and distributed alms and assisted bishop and priests at → Eucharist, reading the Epistle and Gospel and helping in distribution of Holy Communion. Their concern with economic resources of Church produced office of archdeacon as bishop's chief administrative officer. In Rome seven Cardinal D.'s are closely assoc. with Pope. The office of D. diminished in importance in Middle Ages, becoming merely a stage in preparation for priesthood. In Cath. churches a D. cannot celebrate Eucharist, pronounce Blessing, give absolution in private or public → Confession, and can preach and baptise only by special permission. The vestments of D. are dalmatic and stole, worn over left shoulder; ordination to office is performed by bishops. The office of D. exists, in varying forms, in certain Prot. churches. The office of Deaconess is ancient, and was orig. concerned with ministering to female sick and poor, and esp. assisting at → Baptism of women, which involved disrobing. With decline of adult baptism, need of deaconesses diminished. The office was eventually abolished; it was revived, in modified form, in C. of E. and certain Prot. churches in the 19th cent. S.G.F.B.

D.C.C., pp. 376–8; *R.A.C.*, III, pp. 888–928.

Dead, Disposal of → Funerary Rites. S.G.F.B.

(Offerings to) → Funerary Rites.

(Prayers for the) (China–Japan) In the ancestral cult, prayers were made *to* rather than *for* the dead, yet concept of family solidarity, comprising both dead and living, included care of and concern for the ancestor spirits. In Japan → Shinto gods are invariably prayed to for material blessings. It was through Buddh. influence, both in China and Japan, that P.-D. became common practice. → Mahāyāna Buddhism, with its belief in → *karma* and rebirth, its numerous heavens and hells, and its compassionate Buddhas and → bodhisattvas, gave great impetus to belief in efficacy of **P.-D.** The → Nestorian Christians, entering China in 7th cent. held regular solemn masses for living and dead. With Amogha Vajra (Chinese—Pu K'ung Chink'ang. d. CE 772) there was a rapid development in Chinese Buddhism of masses for the dead and the institution on the 15th of 7th month of Feast of Wandering Souls, the main object being to conduct souls as rapidly and safely as possible over the sea of sorrow into which they had been plunged by their sins. In the popular relig., Buddh. or Taoist, priests are engaged to recite P.-D., particularly during 49 day period immediately following death. (→ Ancestor Worship). See also Indulgences; Mass. D.H.S.

K. L. Reichelt, *Truth and Tradition in Chinese Buddhism* (1927), espec. ch. 4.

(Prayers for) (Christ.) → Indulgences; Mass; Purgatory.

(Prayers for) (Islam) It is customary for Muslims to hold funeral service at which prayers are offered for deceased. Although Islam teaches that death ends every chance of repentance, and the → examination in grave indic. that one's destination in next world is already fixed, Muslims still continue practice of praying for dead in hope that this will bring them blessedness. A trad. tells of Muḥammad praying at a funeral and incl. among petitions for deceased, 'O God, forgive him, show him mercy, grant him security, pardon him, grant him a noble provision and a spacious lodging, wash him with water, snow and ice, purify him from sins . . . cause him to enter paradise and preserve him from the trial in the grave and the punishment in hell.' But the Qur. teaches that each one is responsible for his own actions, which suggests that P.-D. should be ineffective. There is, on other hand, a strong belief in → intercession of Muḥammad for his people on day of judgment. (→ Burial of the dead; Mourning; Rosary). J.R.

Mishkāt, pp. 348ff.; Pareja, p. 659; Hughes, pp. 471f.; see also Indulgences; Mass.

Dead Sea Scrolls → Qumrân. F.F.B.

Dead, State of (Buddh.) In Buddh. lit. unhappy spirits of departed, who are unable to find rebirth in embodied form, are ref. to by anc. Indian term *preta* (Pali, *peta*). Their wretched existence is regarded as enduring until their evil → *karma* is exhausted, when they will achieve further, poss. more happy, rebirth. They are held to inhabit region immediately below surface of earth; sometimes they are found on surface; but certainly in a situation somewhat superior to that of inhabitants of the various hells, in bowels of the earth. (→→ Cosmology (Budd.), Petavatthu). T.O.L.

(China–Japan) Both → Confucianism and → Shinto are without an → eschatology, and have only vague and contradictory ideas regarding the S.-D. Earliest ideas conceived of soul descending into the earth. In China, the → Yin-Yang dualism led to development of belief in two soul elements (→ *hun* and → *p'o*) and early records speak of kings and princes ascending on high to become → *shên*, assoc. with → T'ien. Confucianism, as it developed, was gen. agnostic in regard to life after death. → Chuang-tzŭ and other early Taoist writers speak of a transformation at death, in which the elements which compose personality undergo change into some other form of existence. Relig. Taoism taught that certain adepts were transformed into → *hsien* (immortals), and accepted Buddh. teaching re heavens and hells. Under Buddh. influence, in China and Japan, belief in a soul, subject to → *karma* and rebirth, became general. Retribution in various hells, and reward in various heavens were meted out in strict accordance with evil and good done in this life. The aim of popular relig. was to assure release from the karmic process which involved all sentient beings, and final entrance upon an endless life of bliss. (→ Eschatology). D.H.S.

(Christ.) →→ Eschatology; Indulgences; Judgment of Dead; Mass; Purgatory.

(Islam) → Death (Islam). J.R.

Deae Matres Divinities worshipped in Roman provinces of Gaul, Britain, Germany, and, rarely, in Spain and Rome. Monuments relating to them date from 1st cent. CE. D.-M. are repr. in triads of draped female figures, seated under canopy, often holding baskets of fruit. Their exact significance is unknown; they were doubtless connected with fertility and plentitude; whether they were Celtic or Germanic in origin, or commonly derived from Indo-European past, continues to be debated. (→ Celtic (Pagan) Relig.). S.G.F.B.

O.C.D., *s.v.; E.R.E.*, IV, *s.v.;* J. Vendryès, *La religion des Celtes* (Coll: Mana, 2, 1948), pp. 249ff.; 275ff.; T. G. E. Powell, *The Celts* (1959), pp. 124ff.; A. Ross, *Pagan Celtic Britain* (1967), pp. 204ff.

Dea Syria → Atargatis. S.G.F.B.

Death In primitive thought D. is not gen. regarded as a natural event, but due to mischance or attack of some malevolent being. Sometimes it has been explained, in terms of 'myth of the overcrowded earth', as necessitated by growth of population: the way to land of dead had to be found for the aged. In many religs., D. has been personified as a death-god (e.g. Uggae in → Mesopot. relig.; Yama in → Hinduism); a demon (e.g. Charun in → Etruscan relig.); an angel (Sammael in Jew. relig.). In Egypt. relig. → Set, murderer of → Osiris, became god of evil, if not actually death-god. Grk. art depicts D. as winged youth with sword (Thanatos), and as a → *kēr*. D. is personified by → Paul (I Cor. 15:26), and in Rev. 6:8; in myth of Christ's → Descent into Hades, D. becomes identified with → Devil. In Chr. medieval art, D. was repr. as skeleton, with dart, and is gradually assoc. with → Time (→ Zurvan). (→ Eschatology). S.G.F.B.

S. G. F. Brandon, 'The Personification of Death in Some Anc. Religions', in *B.J.R.L.*, 43 (1961); *History, Time and Deity*, ch. 3; J. Zandee, *Death as an Enemy acc. to Anc. Egyptian Conceptions* (E.T. 1960); H. Schwarzbaum, 'The Overcrowded Earth', in *Numen*, IV (1957); G. E. Lessing, 'Wie die Alten den Tod gebildet' (*Samtliche Schriften*, 1895, XI); E. Bendann, *Death Customs* (1930).

(Buddh. recollection of) In Buddhism one of the four Recollections (→ Anussati), which are sometimes added in B. lists to the 6 basic R.'s described in the *Suttas* (the other 3 are the → Body, → Breathing, → Peace). The recollection of D. consists in monk's frequent calling to mind, every evening and every dawn, the many risks which surround human life, and thus how easily D. may come upon him. He must then consider unsubdued evil states within him, which could lead to prolonged future suffering should he die thus. 'If he understands that this is the case, he should use his utmost resolution, energy, effort, endeavour, steadfastness, attentiveness and clear-mindedness in order to overcome these evil unwholesome things'. T.O.L.

(*A.N.*, VIII, p. 78).

(Buddh. view of) Acc. to Buddhism, the death of any living being is inherent in its nature as a compounded entity: it is the dissociation of the constituent elements of a being. 'For the born there is no such thing as not dying' (*S.N.*, II). D. is thus a natural function of the ongoing process of life. For just as a birth leads inevitably to a death, so a death leads inevitably to a birth. Of the five → *khandhas*, the most import. is consciousness. At death of an individual these five khandhas contract, so to speak, to a zero-point; the momentum of life itself, however, carries the constituent elements on beyond this zero-point, to open out into new life; thus consciousness becomes assoc. yet again with another *rupa*, or form, another series of feelings, perceptions, etc. For this reason, the last state of consciousness of one 'life' is held to be of great import. for first state of consciousness of the ensuing one; if it was wholesome (*kusala*), this will produce a 'wholesome' inauguration of new life. Similarly, if it was *akusala*, unwholesome, the ensuing new life will be unwholesomely inaugurated. It is not this last state only which determines the character of the new life; the whole previous life has produced a momentum of a wholesome or unwholesome kind, in varying degrees, which will inevitably have effects upon the ongoing course of life. T.O.L.

(Interpretation) (China) Chi. philosophers, Confucian and Taoist, have in general conceived of D. as the disassociation of those vital elements (→ yin and yang; → *shên* and *kuei;* → *hun* and *p'o*) which, coming together at birth, constitute a living human being. As birth is a beginning, so death is an end. Those elements which, in association, make up a human personality, though in themselves indestructible, evolve into new forms of relationship. The personality as such no longer exists. Though agnostic as regards life after death, existence of a post-mortem spirit is generally assumed, but it is difficult to determine if such existence is necessarily or in all cases immortal. The elaborate ceremonies connected with death and burial have, as their underlying motive, reverence for ancestors. The Chinese have always regarded it as a duty of the living to show affection, respect and gratitude for the departed, and have worshipped the departed, and sacrificed to them 'as if' they were sentient beings. The practice of 'calling back the soul', mentioned in the → *Li Chi*, reveals that from very early times the Chinese believed that at death an invisible spirit left the body, and early Chi. texts speak of deceased kings as being associated with a supreme God on high, and able to counsel and guide, punish and reward their descendants. The Chi. people, in general, regarded D. as entrance upon a state of being not very dissimilar from that which existed on earth. In a spiritual hierarchy, presided over by a supreme deity, the spirits of dead were awarded rank and status in acc. with their merit. Heroes and worthies were deified, and all the spirits of dead continued to interest themselves in affairs of living.

The intro. of → Buddhism into China with its doctrines of → *karma* and rebirth, both modified native belief and reinforced it, so that popular relig. in China accepted notion that all spirits at death went for → judgement before a divine tribunal, and from thence to their appointed destiny. But their state, whether in heaven or hell was never considered to be irrevocable. Powerful deities could be induced to intercede on their behalf. Hence need for services of Buddhist and Taoist priests, to give them a safe and comfortable passage to other world, to provide masses for their souls suffering in hades, and to intercede for divine help and protection. Hence also the frequent offerings made at tombs or before the spirit-tablets.

The elaborate preparations for burial and the whole mortuary cult were motivated by fear and love. There was fear that any neglect might incur displeasure of the dead, also that the uninhabited corpse might be seized upon by some disembodied demon. Love expressed itself in a willingness to do everything possible to assist spirit of dead to make a favourable impression before the judge of hades. The dead must be dressed in their best robes, their rank clearly recorded, and they must be provided with everything necessary to maintain their dignity and status in the next world. Not only were food and drink provided for their sustenance, but paper and straw effigies of all articles of necessity and luxury, which they had found useful in this life, were burned to provide for their wants in the after-life. (→ Ancestor Worship). D.H.S.

D. H. Smith, 'Chinese Concepts of the Soul', in *Numen*, V (1958); N. Vandier-Nicolas, 'Le jugement des morts en Chine', in *S.O.*, IV (1961); S. G. F. Brandon, *The Judgment of the Dead*, ch. IX (1967).

(Interpretation) (Japan) Anc. Japanese records say little of condition of the dead. The doc. of the immortality of soul is nowhere taught explicitly. There are no prayers for the dead or for happiness in a future life. The great megalithic vaults of anc. Japan in which princes and nobles were buried, together with food, weapons, ornaments and other valuables (→ Burial—Japanese) indicate some vague belief in a post-mortem existence. Older → Shinto regarded death as corruption and a source of pollution, and avoided everything connected with it. Yomi (darkness), which corresponds to Hades, was a metaphor for state of the dead, and in modern times was identified with Jigoku, the Buddh. place of torture for wicked. The interpretation of death was influenced by Confucian → Ancestor-worship, and particularly by intro. of → Buddhism into Japan. The doctrines of karmic retribution and rebirth were popularly accepted, along with the Mahāyāna teachings concerning the 'self' as being indestructible and the only reality. Death was but a transformation into a different state of being; for heroes and worthies—deification, for the Buddh. faithful—translation into paradise of → Amida Buddha, and for the erring and sinful, removal to a place of purgation leading to rebirth. The ultimate goal of all sentient beings, through a cycle of births and deaths, was → Nirvana. D.H.S.

W. G. Aston, *Shinto* (1905), pp. 53ff.; *E.R.E.*, IV, pp. 485ff.; R. Sieffiert, 'De quelques répresentations du jugement des morts chez les Japonais', in *S.O.*, IV (1961); S. G. F. Brandon, *The Judgment of the Dead* (1967), ch. X.

(Islam) The Qur. teaches that all must die (iii:182); but that God gives a respite and does not punish immediately for sin, as he has appointed when everyone will die (xvi:63). Trad. makes it clear that one should not wish for D.; but it commends those who court death in → *jihād*. (→→ Barzakh; Burial of dead; Examination in grave; Mourning for dead; Tombs). J.R.

'Death of God' Phrase taken from Nietzsche's story of the madman in *The Gay Science* and used by various theologians to label set of radical positions which aroused considerable popular interest, esp. in United States, in the 1960's. The main positions so labelled are: (1) that language about God is dead (e.g. in Paul van Buren, *The Secular Meaning of the Gospel*, 1963). It is claimed that the word 'God' has no significance today, both because it is internally incoherent and because it implies unacceptable metaphysical and supernatural connotations. God-talk is translated into talk about perspective from which an individual values and understands his world. This position properly belongs to attempts to understand relig. language from standpoint of linguistic analytical philosophy. (2) that God is not experienced by man today (e.g. M. Buber, *Eclipse of God*, 1953; W. Hamilton, *The New Essence of Christianity*, 1961). Here it is asserted that God is not at present experienced by man either as personal presence or as supernatural agent influencing natural events. Opinions vary about whether this is a temporary or more permanent state and, if former, about reasons for it. (3) that God is not a cultural idol (e.g. G. Vahanian, *The Death of God, The Culture of our Post-Christian Era*, 1961, and *Wait Without Idols*, 1964). Vahanian interprets godlessness of contemporary culture from a Barthian (→ Barth, K.) standpoint as making poss. in future true recognition of transcendent, non-objective nature of God in place of false, man-constructed idol which has dominated previous Western culture and relig. (4) that God has withdrawn so that man can be free and responsible (e.g. W. Hamilton, *op. cit.*, H. Cox, *The Secular City*, 1965). This theological affirmation of power and maturity of modern man is esp. influenced by some thoughts in → Bonhoeffer's *Letters and Papers from Prison*. The crucifixion of

→ Jesus Christ is regarded as revelation both of God's refusal to coerce man and intervene in human affairs, and of his will that man should find fulfilment in controlling world in accord. with his love. (5) that God is immanently involved in contemporary reality (e.g. T. J. J. Altizer, *The Gospel of Christian Atheism*, 1966). Altizer is partic. influenced by work of Mircea Eliade and own study of Eastern religs., esp. atheistic forms of → Buddhism, and by his understanding of dialectial process described in Hegelian philosophy (→ Hegel.). The life and death of Jesus Christ are here viewed as self-negation of transcendent God, who is believed to stand over against man as a life-denying threat (and is identified by William Blake as Satan), and proclamation of reality of God as a dynamic, incarnate spirit which is creatively active within processes of reality. God, therefore, is to be located in whatever forces are now leading towards life-enhancement, wherever such are to be found within worlds of man and nature. Underlying the various and sometimes conflicting 'death of God' positions is concern to understand Christ. theism in a way that is clearly relevant to, and coherent with, the self-understanding and experience of contemporary, scientifically-orientated, self-consciously autonomous, Western man. Although slogan of 'the death of God' had largely been dropped by late 1960's, this concern continues to be basis of radical theological work. D.A.P.

To books mentioned in article, the following may be added: T. J. J. Altizer and W. Hamilton, *Radical Theology and the Death of God*, 1966 (contains very full bibliography of relevant lit.); T. J. J. Altizer (ed.), *Towards a New Christianity* (1967); J. C. Cooper, *The Roots of the Radical Theology* (1967), B. Murchland (ed.), *The Meaning of the Death of God* (1967).

Death, Personification of

(Personification) → Death. S.G.F.B.

(Personification) (Buddh.) → Māra, the evil one. T.O.L.

(China) in China Yama was taken over from Hindu mythology to become → Yen-lo Wang, who presided over realm of dead, and was later demoted to become king of the fifth hell. When a person's destined span of life is accomplished, Yen-lo Wang sends his messenger, Wu Ch'ang, to summon him to the underworld. Wu Ch'ang, as the Chinese characters imply, is really the personification of the Buddh. doc. of impermanence, as there is growth and decay, life and death in all creatures. Wu Ch'ang is represented in two forms: Yang Wu Ch'ang which is male, and Yin Wu Ch'ang which is female; their images stand on right and left of Yen-lo Wang in temple of the city's guardian god (Ch'eng Wang Miao). Accompanied by two demons. 'Horse-face' (*Ma Mien* and 'Ox head' (*Niu T'ou*), Wu Ch'ang is guided to home of dying by local earth-spirit (T'u Ti). The spirit of the dead man is seized, bound and conveyed to the city-god and thence to court of the god of the Eastern Peak, where his good and evil deeds are assessed before he is carried off into Hades. D.H.S.

E. T. C. Werner, *Dictionary of Chinese Mythology* (1932), p. 568.

Decalogue, The Known also as the Ten Commandments. Acc. to Ex. 20, the D. was proclaimed verbally by → Yahweh on Mt. Sinai, apparently to all Israel (Ex. 19:25, 20:18). Ex. 32:15ff. implies that D. was written on two tables of stone in the 'writing of God', and delivered to → Moses, who broke them in anger at Israel's idolatry. They were re-written, and subsequently put in → Ark (Deut. 10:1–5). The text of D. is given, in closely similar versions, in Ex. 20:1–17 and Deut. 5:6–21. The D. concerns both moral and relig. duties; the reason given for sabbath observance (Ex. 20:11) suggests relation with post-Exilic P source (→ Pentateuch). An older code of laws, prob. of → J origin, is given in Ex. 34:14–29, and is also recorded as being delivered to Moses on Mt. Sinai and written on two stone tables. The origin of D. and its relation to Moses is uncertain. The D. may be usefully comp. with 'Declarations of Innocence' in Egypt. → Book of Dead. The D. was incl. in instruction to → catechumens by time of → Augustine of Hippo, and was much used in popular systems of instruction by the Reformers. In C. of E. the D. replaced → Kyrie Eleison in Holy Communion service. S.G.F.B.

*H.D.B.*², *s.v.; D.C.C.*, p. 316; *E.R.E.*, IV, *s.v.;* H. H. Rowley, 'Moses and the Decalogue', in *Men of God* (1963); *R.G.G.*³, IV, 69–72; W. Beyerlin, *Herkunft u. Geschichte der ältesten Sinaitraditionen* (1961), pp. 59ff.

Ded-column A symbolic object closely assoc. with → Osiris. Its orig. nature and significance are unknown: it has been identified as either a human back-bone or tree, with branches removed. A large D.-C. was ritually raised to upright position annually in ceremony commemorating resurrection of Osiris. Amulets of the D.-C. were widely used, partic. in funerary ritual: it repr. stability or duration. S.G.F.B.

R.Ae.R-G., pp. 149–53; A. M. Blackman in *Myth and Ritual*, ed. S. H. Hooke (1933), pp. 21ff.; S. A. B. Mercer, *The Religion of Anc. Egypt* (1949), pp. 107ff.

De-eschatologisation Trans. of German *Enteschatologisierung*, term used by M. Werner for process necessitated by non-fulfilment of → Parousia-hope, which profoundly affected evolution of Christ. doctrine. S.G.F.B.

M. Werner, *Die Entstehung des christlichen Dogmas*[2] (1953); E.T., *The Formation of Christian Dogma* (1957).

Defilement, in Buddh. thought There is in the Buddh. system no conception of *ritual* defilement which needs ritual cleansing, as there is in some relig. systems. The practice of the Buddh. way of life is, however, described as purification (*visuddhi*); this implies a condition from which men need to be purified. In Buddh. thought this is a condition of mind; the natural man is at mercy of influxes (→ *Asava*) which have to be overcome by insight, sense-control, avoidance of occasion of their arising, right use of food, sleep etc. More commonly the → *Kilesas* are trans. by Eng. word 'defilements'. These are the morally defiling passions, the extinction of which constitutes → *Arahantship* or the attainment of holiness. The extinction of these defilements is first aspect of → *nibbāna*, and is sometimes ref. to as *Kilesa-nibbana*. T.O.L.

Deification The making of a person, animal or thing into a deity is an ancient and widespread practice. The implied transformation is conditioned by concept of deity involved. The process is easier and less notable in a polytheistic (→ Polytheism) than a monotheistic (→ Monotheism) culture. In primitive systems of thought, attributes of deity are vague (e.g. in → Totemism, or Lat. → numen). That men could be deified was perceived by → Euhemerus in 3rd cent. BC. Many examples thereof can be cited: → Imhotep in Egypt, → Alexander the Great, Roman Emperors (→ Apotheosis). The → Buddha has been deified, despite orig. atheistic character of his doctrine. The most notable instance of D. is that of the historical → Jesus of Nazareth as incarnation of Second Person of → Trinity. (→ Ruler Worship). D in →→ Gnosticism, Mystery Religs., and sometimes in Early Chr. writers is really assimilation or communion with Deity. S.G.F.B.

E.R.E., IV, *s.v.;* G. van der Leeuw, *La Religion* (1948), pp. 170ff.; *R.Ae.R-G.*, pp. 856–60 'Vergöttlichung'); K. E. Kirk, *The Vision of God* (1932[2]), *passim.;* A.-J. Festugière, *La révélation d'Hermès Trismégiste*, III (1953), *passim.*

Dēisis Grk. meaning 'intercession'. Term used to describe scene in medieval → Doom, of Virgin Mary and St. John interceding with Christ at Last → Judgment. S.G.F.B.

J. Fournée, *Le jugement dernier* (1964), ch. X; S. G. F. Brandon, *The Judgment of the Dead* (1967), ch. 6.

Deism A term, derived from Lat. *Deus*, 'God', used to designate movement that rejected revealed relig., for 'natural religion', i.e. one based on man's intuitions about, and inferences from, the world of experience. D. orig. in England in late 17th cent., and spread to Continent; it was essentially a reaction against Christianity's claims that its doctrines were divinely revealed. J. Locke, though rejecting title 'Deist', profoundly influenced movement by his *Reasonableness of Christianity* (1695). Two other influential works were J. Toland's *Christianity not Mysterious* (1696) and M. Tindal's *Christianity as Old as Creation* (1730). Despite variations, D. was characterised by belief in a Divine Creator, who did not intervene in world he had created, and scepticism about *post-mortem* rewards and punishment. Bishop J. Butler's *Analogy of Religion* (1736) was directed against D. In France, Voltaire, Rousseau and the Encyclopaedists were exponents of D., which also became influential in Germany. D. is reflected in views of Reimarus and → Kant. S.G.F.B.

E.R.E., IV, *s.v.; D.C.C.*, *s.v.; R.G.G.*[3], II, 57–68; E. O. James, *The Concept of Deity* (1950), pp. 133ff.

Delphi, Delphi Oracle Most famous sanctuary in Greece, impressively situated on slopes of Mt. Parnassus. Pre-Hellenic sanctuary of a → chthonian deity, called Python, D. became cult-centre of → Apollo, whose temple dominated complex of sacred buildings there. D. also contained the *omphalos*, or 'navel' of the earth, which was marked by carved circular stone. D.'s chief claim to fame was its Oracle, which attracted both individuals and cities, seeking advice about future. The Oracle took form of responses of priestess, the 'Pythia', while in state of frenzy, to questions mediated by a prophet, who interpreted them to the enquirer. The Pythia's ecstasy was supposedly induced by Apollo: it was prob. assisted by use of drugs. The D. Oracle played import. part in directing Grk. colonisation, and priesthood controlling it acquired considerable political influence. On private matters the Oracle promoted high standard of ethical behaviour. D. also furthered cult of → Dionysus, and was recognised centre for *katharsis*, i.e. ritual purification. Among a people noted for their disunity, D. exercised unifying influence not only through its Oracle and cult of Apollo, but also by its Pythian Games and as centre of powerful → amphictyony. The cult was finally suppressed in 390 by edict of Theodosius, in favour of Christianity. S.G.F.B.

H. W. Parke, *A Hist. of the Delphic Oracle* (1939); *O.C.D.*, pp. 261–2, 624; *Kleine Pauly*, I, 1450–5; W. K. C. Guthrie, *The Greeks and their Gods* (1950), pp. 183ff.; G. Tarsouli, *Delphi* (Athens, n.d.); *E.R.E.*, IX, p. 432 ('Omphalos'); J. Defradas, *Les thèmes de la propagande delphique* (1954).

Deluge → Flood Legends. S.G.F.B

Demeter Grk. corn-goddess. Last two syllables of name make Grk. word for 'mother'; but first syllable has never been satisfactorily explained. D. was concerned with fruits of earth, but esp. with bread-corn. She was usually assoc. with a maiden goddess (→ Korē, or → Persephone), who personifies the corn. In anc. *Homeric Hymn to Demeter*, D. is mother of Korē, who is carried off by → Hades to his subterranean realm. D. seeks for Korē, neglecting her function as corn-goddess, until → Zeus arranges that Korē spends part of year with D. and part with Hades. This myth was prob. based on phases in life of seed-corn, i.e. seed-time, harvest, and storage in underground silos. The *Homeric Hymn to Demeter* connects her with institution of → Eleusinian Mysteries. The cult of D. prob. came from Thessaly and Thrace. D. had chthonian associations; the dead were referred to as 'Demeter's people'. S.G.F.B.

O.C.D., s.v.; H. J. Rose, *Handbook of Greek Mythology* (1928), pp. 91ff.; *Kleine Pauly*, I, 1459–64; *R.A.C.*, III, 682–94; G. E. Mylonas, *Eleusis and the Eleusinian Mysteries* (1961), pp. 14ff. G. Méautis, *Les dieux de la Grèce* (1959).

Demiurge *Ex.* Grk. *demiurgos* orig. meaning, in pl., 'public workers', e.g. metal-workers, potters, masons. Plato used word for Creator of world, and its currency in this sense was thus estab. Although → LXX gen. uses *ktistēs* for God as Creator, D. was employed by Hellenised Jews, partic. → Philo. The term passed into Christianity, being used in Heb. 11:10 and by many Grk. Fathers. D. denoted an important concept in → Gnosticism; for owing to its basic → dualism, creation of material world had to be attr. to a being lower than God. S.G.F.B.

R.A.C., III, 694–711; A.-J. Festugière, *La révélation d'Hermès Trismégiste*, IV (1954), pp. 275ff.; R. M. Grant, *Gnosticism* (1961), pp. 170ff.; R. McL. Wilson, *The Gnostic Problem* (1958), pp. 130ff.; Brandon, *C.L., passim.*

Demons (General) The earliest literate cultures (Egypt and Mesopot.) reveal belief in supernatural beings, feared as horrific and hostile. Such belief prob. goes back to Palaeolithic era, for some figures in Capsian art look demonic. The conception of such beings doubtless stems from man's instinctive fear of the unknown, the strange and horrific. It is significant that belief in evil spirits or D. can exist without idea of the → Devil, i.e. the personification of principle of evil in a single being (e.g. in → Mesopot. Relig.; Taoism). In →→ Judasim, Christianity, Islam, Zoroastrianism, Manichaeism, D. have been regarded as minions of Devil or Spirit of Evil, who leads them in unceasing struggle against God and his servants (→ Dualism). In pre-scientific cultures disease, both mental and physical, and misfortune are gen. attr. to demonic agency. (→ African Relig.s). S.G.F.B.

E.R.E., IV, pp. 565–8; *R.G.G.*[3], II, 1298–1301; A̱d. E. Jensen, *Mythos u. Kult bei Naturvölhern* (1951), pp. 368ff.; G. Van der Leeuw, *La Religion* (1948), pp. 129ff., 236–7.

(Buddh.) Belief in demons does not constitute a primary or essential feature of Buddh. thought. Such beliefs were, however, common in anc. India at time of the rise of Buddhism and was accepted by early Buddh. as part of cosmic 'scenery'; refs. to demons of various kinds are not uncommon in B. sacred texts, where they have approx. same doctrinal status (or lack of it) as refs. to demons in early Christ. texts. One of more prominent roles of the demons, such as → *yakkhas*, → *pisacas*, etc., was their supposed activity of causing distraction to B. monks (and nuns) in their meditation, by causing loud or frightening noises, often by assuming guise of some wild bird or beast. Demons are thought of in early Buddhism as beings whose doleful and malevolent condition is due to bad → *karma* of some previous existence. Wherever Buddhism has spread, it has accommod. itself to indigenous popular demonology in a gen. tolerant spirit, not openly denying existence or function of demons, but by its own characteristic docs. directing focus of attention away from such conceptions to moral and psychological roots of human evils; B. thought is not tied to such demonology; and can easily disperse with it. (→→ Mara, the evil one; Asuras). T.O.L.

J. Masson, *La Religion Populaire dans le Canon Bouddhique Pali* (1942); T. O. Ling, *Buddhism and the Mythology of Evil* (1962).

(and Demonology) (Chinese) In Chinese popular relig. four orders of beings are considered superior to men: → *shên* (gods), → *kuei* (demons), → *hsien* (genii) and → *Fo* (Buddhas). Under the term *kuei-shên* (variously trans. as 'demons and spirits' or 'demons and gods') are included all inhabitants of spiritual world of the Chinese, the various objects of relig. worship and superstitious fear. Strictly speaking, the *kuei* are the departed spirits of humans and animals who have returned from the visible to the invisible world; they are considered capable at times of assuming animal or human form to beguile, mislead or wreak vengeance on the living. But since, from earliest times, the Chinese have believed in supernatural beings dwelling in or assoc. with natural objects, such as rivers, mountains, rocks, trees, animals, etc., as well as various kinds of fairies, elves, goblins and sprites, these are all included under the general title of *kuei.* Chi. folklore and popular literature is full of stories of activities of these 'demons', witnessing to an almost universal belief. The multiplication of deities and a pervasive dread of demons are mainly connected with → Taoism; but → Buddhism has also been influential in peopling spirit world with a host of beneficient and malevolent beings. Demons in China are considered to be ubiquitous, capable of animating dead bodies, haunting cemeteries, cross roads and the homes of relatives. Some live in Hades in the service of → Yen-lo Wang; others inhabit the air, and some, visible only at night, dwell among men. Many are hungry ghosts, the spirits of those who have had no proper burial or who have no descendants to feed them by sacrifices. The Hindu ceremony of feeding hungry ghosts was brought to China by Amogha (*c.* CE 733) and, engrafted upon the native ancestral worship, obtained immense popularity.

The extraordinary precautions to ward off maleficient influences of demons has resulted in development of a pseudo-science, of which Taoist priests in particular are recognised as expert practitioners. By spells and incantations, prescriptions, charms and amulets, they are able to control the activities of demons and give protection to the individual and his home. Many forms of mental and physical illness are attr. to demon-possession. Hence the need for exorcism, and immense popularity of → Fêng-shui necromancy, and spiritism. The basis of Chi. demonology lies in belief in close relation existing between the human, the natural and supernatural worlds, and that everything, including man, is spirit-fraught. D.H.S.

E.R.E., IV, pp. 576–8; J. J. M. de Groot, *The Religious System of China*, 6 vols. (new ed. 1964); H. A. Giles, *Strange Stories from a Chinese Studio* (3rd edn. 1916); C. H. Plopper, *Chinese Religion seen through the Proverb* (1926), pp. 82ff.

(Christ.) Christianity inherited O.T. demonology, to which was added belief that pagan gods were D. (e.g. I Cor. 10:20ff.) (→ Demons, Greek). Converts to Christianity naturally continued to believe in D. of their pagan past. → Coptic Christianity provides many examples. → Hermas taught that every person had two guardian → angels, severally inspiring good and evil. Theological interest in D. was understandably subordinate to that in → Devil, who had a fundamental role in Chr. → soteriology. Peter Lombard (d, 1164) devoted ten sections of his *Sententiae* to good and evil spirits, and Thomas → Aquinas endorsed trad. view that D. were angels, fallen from orig. state through pride and envy: they abode both in → Hell, where they tormented damned, and in air where they troubled men. Apocryphal lit. such as *Apocalypses of* → *Peter* and of *Paul* and Coptic *Hist. of Joseph the Carpenter* describe D. and their activities. Medieval lit. reveals widespread folk-belief in D., which was also connected with → witchcraft. Medieval art provides abundant evidence of current ideas of D., esp. in → Dooms. How horrific conception of D. could be is graphically shown in paintings of H. → Bosch. Belief in D. was accepted by Reformers. J. Milton's *Paradise Lost* is eloquent proof of Puritan view. The development of more scientific outlook has diminished belief in D., partic. in Prot. countries. The office of exorcist still exists in R.C. Church, and exorcizing of evil spirits is provided for in both R.C. and E. Churches. S.G.F.B.

E.R.E., IV, pp. 578–83; *R.G.G.*[3], II, 1303; J. A. MacCulloch, *Medieval Faith and Fable* (1932), ch. IV; G. G. Coulton, *Five Centuries of Religion*, I (1923), pp. 29ff.; S. G. F. Brandon, *The Judgment of the Dead* (1967), ch. 6.

(Egypt) The Egyptians, although filling underworld with D., had no special name for them and gen. denoted them in writing by determinative sign for deity. Where particular designations are given, they often describe functions, e.g. 'Breaker of bones', Am-mut, 'Eater of dead' (hybrid monster that attended → Judgment of the Dead). D. were depicted in either animal or human form, or mixture of both, and given fearsome attributes, e.g. knife or fire-spitting. In underworld they supervise punishment of sinners. The more notable of demonic beings were Apophis, giant serpent that daily threatened the sun-god → Re; Bebon or Babi, D. of darkness; Nebed, D. of darkness assoc. with → Set. Less information exists on D. in this world; but many rituals and customs were inspired by fear of D. which brought disease and other ills (→ Bes). S.G.F.B.

R.Ae.R-G., pp. 146–8; S. A. B. Mercer, *The Religion of Anc. Egypt* (1949), pp. 191–3; *E.R.E.*, IV, pp. 584–90.

(Greek) The Eng. word 'demon' derives from Grk. *daimōn*, pl. *daimōnes*. The opprobrious sense which 'D'. has for us is due to its early Chr. use for pagan gods. In Grk. thought, D. had ambivalent connotation. → Hesiod, in his acc. of the Four Ages, explains that, after death, those of the Golden Age became *daimōnes* (*Works and Days*, 109ff.). The term was used of spirits of dead, partic. of ancestors, and often with favourable ref. as 'good D.'. The idea of a 'good D.', as a guardian-spirit to each person, was widely held: Socrates' refs. to his D. are notable (Plato, *Apol.* 31D, 40A). The notion naturally led to belief in both good and bad D. There was much speculation about relation of D. to gods (*theoi*); some thinkers regarded former as a kind of demi-gods (cf. Plutarch, *De Is. et Os.*, pp. 361ff.). Plutarch explains that →→ Isis and Osiris, →→ Heracles and Dionysus, were translated, because of their virtues, from good D. into gods. The Apostle → Paul significantly refers to pagans' offering of sacrifice to D., meaning thereby to pagan gods (I Cor. 10:20). Grk. relig. also knew of horrific beings: e.g. Alastor (an avenging D.), Eurynomous (corpse-eating D.), the → Sphinx, Harpies (death-angels), → Erinyes (avenging spirits), the Sirens. *Kēres*, ghosts of the dead, were also dreaded as sources of evil. S.G.F.B.

E.R.E., IV, pp. 590–4; J. Harrison, *Proleg.*, pp. 4–7, 165ff.; *Kleine Pauly*, I, 1361–2; E. R. Dodds, *The Greeks and the Irrational* (1963), pp. 39ff.

(Hebrew) Although pre-Exilic lit. gives no clear indic. of a demonology, the Hebrews prob. conceived of D. haunting desert (→ Azazel and Lilith were doubtless conceptions from pre-Exilic period). In Is. 34:14 ref. is made to *se'irim*, i.e. 'hairy ones', trans. R.V. and R.S.V. as 'satyrs', which were demonic beings inhabiting ruins (comp. Arab. *jinn*), and to Lilith, the 'night-hag', prob. identifiable with Mesopot. Lilitu. There are refs. also to Rahab and Leviathan, demoniac monsters deriving from some primeval dragon of Chaos like the Bab. → T'iâmat or Egypt. Apophis. Before belief in → Devil or → Satan, evil was attributed to → Yahweh as well as good (Is. 45:7). After Exile, prob. due to influence of Persian → dualism, idea of a spirit of Evil, served by demonic minions, became estab. Demonology develops more elaborate forms in → Apocalyptic lit. In → Enoch, *Parables* (37–71), origin of D. is found in myth preserved in Gen. 6:2–4, thus repr. them as fallen angels. Satan, demoted from court of Heaven (Job 1:2), becomes leader of D., and is defeated by → Michael and the heavenly host (Rev. 12:7ff.). Asmodaeus (Persian, *Aēšma*), → Beliar, and → Beelzebub, are notable in later demonology. The Gospels witness to contemporary Jew. belief both in Devil and D., the latter being regarded esp. as able to possess human beings (e.g. Mk. 5:2ff.). D. figure prominently in → Qumran texts. The word *shēdîm*, used in Deut. 32:17 for Canaanite deities, is widely used for D. in Rabbinic lit., which attests to continuity of belief in D. (→ Demons, Mesopot.). S.G.F.B.

E.R.E., IV, pp. 594–601, 612–3; *H.D.B.*², *s.v.;* W. O. E. Oesterley, *Immortality and the Unseen World* (1930), pp. 24ff.; Ad. Lods, *Israël* (1949), pp. 274ff.; H. W. Huppenbauer, *Der Mensch zwischen zwei Welten* (1959); *J.E.*, IV, *s.v.*

(Iranian) In pre-Zoroastrian Iran there were prob. two types of deity, akin to → Rig-Vedic *asuras* and *devas*. The Iranian form of latter, i.e. *daēvas*, were regarded as D. by → Zoroaster. Zoroastrian → dualiasm found expression in an elaborate demonology. The principle of Evil, called the *Drūj* ('Lie') in the → *Gāthās*, engages in unceasing conflict with the Good, and D. spring from evil thought, deceit and pride (*Yasna* 32:3). Acc. to the → *Bundahishn* (i:10, xxviii:1–46), → Ahriman (i.e. Evil) created D. and noxious beasts as allies in struggle against → Ohrmazd (i.e. Good). In later → Zoroastrianism, a hierarchy of D. was constructed: most notable is the arch-D. Aēšma, demon of fury, rapine and lust, who figures in Heb. Book of Tobit as Asmodoeus. Iranian D. were male; but there were female D. (*drujes*), derived from the *Drūj*, which was a fem. abstract noun. D. were thought of as spirits, gen. haunting dark and foul places, esp. → dakhmas. There were demonic monsters such as Azhi Dahāka, from whose shoulders two snakes emerge. Acc. to Zoroastrian → eschatology, D. would finally be involved in defeat of Ahriman by Ohrmazd. In → Zurvanism, concupiscence was personified as Āz, a female D. and plays an important role. Āz passed into → Manichaeism. (→ Vidēvdat). S.G.F.B.

E.R.E., IV, pp. 619–20; J. Duchesne-Guillemin, *Ormazd et Ahriman* (1953), pp. 26ff.; R. C. Zaehner, *D.T.Z.*, pp. 37ff., 101ff., 223ff., 257ff.; G. Widengren, *Mani and Manichaeism* (E.T. 1963), pp. 59ff.

(Islam) →→ Jinn; Spirits and Demons (Islam).

(Japan) Jap. beliefs concerning demons can usually be traced to Chinese and Buddh. sources. Like the Chinese, the Japanese believe that the spiritual world, peopled by innumerable supernatural beings, lies close to the material world, and that men, plants, animals, mountains and other inanimate objects have their spiritual counterparts. The spirits of foxes and other animals have power to assume phantom bodies or to intrude into the bodies of humans. In → Shinto, the Oni or demons are associated with disease, calamity and misfortune. They have no individual names. They often assume human form with addition of bull's horns and a tiger's skin thrown round the loins. The ceremony of Tsuina or Oni-yarahi (demon-expelling) is a sort of drama, performed on last day of year, in which personified diseases, ill-luck and calamities are driven off with threats and a show of violence. The mysterious beings known as Tengu (heavenly dog), depicted in form of birds with beaks, wings and talons, are considered to be subject to sacerdotal powers of the Buddh. priesthood. Tengu-possession, however, is not accompanied by the mischief and devilry assoc. with the Oni. Many forms of exorcism are in vogue, and the → Nichiren sect holds periodical retreats for driving out of evil spirits of all kinds. D.H.S.

E.R.E., IV, pp. 608ff.; W. G. Aston, *Shinto*

(1905), p. 308; Jean Herbert, *Shinto* (1967), pp. 188ff.

(Mesopotamia) Belief in D. was a potent factor in → Mesopot. relig. D. were of two kinds: non-human beings and vengeful dead. The first comprised many types: monsters that lurked in dangerous places, e.g., deserts and graveyards—the *labartu*, a female D. of mountains or marshlands attacked children in particular. The *šêdu* and *lamassu* were ambivalent, being both evil and guardian-spirits. Namtaru was the plague D.; Pazuzu a wind-demon; Lilitu a succubus who visited men at night, from which unions *alû* and *gallû*, faceless monsters, were born. The ghosts (*etimmu*) of those who had died by mischance were greatly feared, and many texts are concerned with exorcizing them. The following extract is typical: 'a ghost hath appeared and devoured me! From my body may he be released! I will bring to him an offering for the dead: water of the mortuary offering will I give him to drink.' Sickness and misfortune were attr. to demonic attack, espec. of *etimmu*. The gods protected their devotees from such attack, but withdrew their protection from those remiss in their service. Texts concerned with exorcism form a large part of cuneiform tablets found on Mesopot. sites; protective amulets are numerous. Depictions of D. gen. show horrific beings, some semi-human, some animal: Lilitu, however, was repr. as beautiful nude female, winged, but with talons for feet (H. Frankfort, *The Art and Architecture of the Anc. Orient* (1954), Pl. 56). Acc. to → Enuma elish, Ti'âmat created demonic monsters to help her against the gods. S.G.F.B.

R. C. Thompson, *Devils and Evil Spirits of Babylonia*, 2 vols. (1903–5); *E.R.E.*, IV, pp. 568–71; C.-F., Jean, *La religion sumérienne* (1931), pp. 123ff.; E. Dhorme, *R.B.A.*, pp. 264ff.; E. Ebeling, *Tod und Leben nach den Vorstellungen der Babylonier* (1931), pp. 122ff.; H. W. F. Saggs, *The Greatness that was Babylon* (1962), pp. 302ff.

Demythologisation Trans. of German *Entmythologisierung*, term used by R. → Bultmann for process of ridding N.T. of 1st cent. mythical concepts in order to get at essential message of Christianity. See Bibliography to art. on Bultmann. S.G.F.B.

Dengyō Daishi (CE 767–822). Posthumous name of great and learned Buddh. priest Saichō, who, having studied in China the idealistic teachings of T'ien T'ai, formulated by Chih-i (536–97), intro. them into Japan as → Tendai. Tendai became a unifying force in Japanese → Buddhism, teaching that supreme object of all mysteries, virtues and wisdom is to realise Buddhahood in one's own consciousness. Though not distinguished as an original thinker, D. D. expounded the *Lotus sūtra* (*Saddharma-pundarika*), and made its idealistic teachings the basis of a practical relig. system, influential for centuries. D. D. had great influence at court, and built a monastery on Mt. Hiei near Nara, a centre of Buddh. learning and ecclesiastical power. He and Kōbō Daishi were the two most influential Buddh. of the Heian period. D.H.S.

Dēnkart 'Acts of Religion', a Pahlavi work of encyclopedic character concerning Persian relig. beliefs and traditions. It constitutes chief source of information about relig. in the Sassanian period (CE 226–651). S.G.F.B.

R. C. Zaehner, *Zurvan: a Zoroastrian Dilemma* (1955), *passim;* acc. to Zaehner (*D.T.Z.*, p. 341), the trans. of the D. by E. W. West in *S.B.E.* is now out of date; Edv. Lehmann in *L.R-G.*, II, p. 210.

Descent into Hades The idea of a deity or man visiting underworld occurs in many religs. In Mesopot. mythology → Ishtar descended into underworld for an undefined reason and had to be rescued therefrom. Tablet XII of Epic of → Gilgamesh tells of Enkidu's fatal descent, and an Assyrian text records visit of Kummaya and his dreadful experience. The legend of Satmi and Senosiris graphically describes anc. Egypt. underworld. Grk. lit. provides examples of Odysseus' descent, and those of Heracles (to rescue Alcestis), and → Orpheus (to bring back Eurydice). → Virgil tells of Aeneas' descent. Buddh. lit. provides examples (the *Yü li ch'ao chuan*), also Japan. lit. (the *Kojiki*). The most notable example of *motif* is Christ's descent. The purpose of legend was theological, not to describe underworld as in most other instances. Acc. to I Peter 3:19ff., Christ, having died, 'went and preached to the spirits in prison'. The exact meaning of passage has been much debated; it was certainly interpreted to mean that Christ descended into Hades to save O.T. saints who lived before his incarnation, and to cast → Satan into Tartarus. The transaction is graphically described in 4th cent. *Gospel of Nicodemus* (cf. M. R. James, *The Apocryphal New Test.* (1926), pp. 117ff.), and was frequently depicted in art. It has been suggested that theme was elaborated to offset pagan legend of → Heracles as saviour from death. Chr. lit. contains many accounts of visits to Hades or Hell, most notably the *Apocalypse of* → *Peter* and → Dante's *Inferno*. S.G.F.B.

A.N.E.T., pp. 97–9, 106–10; F. L. Griffith, *Stories of the High Priests of Memphis* (1900), pp. 44–50; *E.R.E.*, IV, pp. 648–63; *R.G.G.*[3], IV, 408–11; C. Clemen, *Religionsgesch. Erklärung des Neuen Test.* (1924), pp. 91ff.; J. Kroll, *Gott und Hölle* (1932); M. Simon, *Hercule et le Christianisme* (1955), pp. 112ff.

Desire (Tanhā/Trsnā), in Buddh. thought → Craving (Buddh.). T.O.L.

Destiny →→ Fate; Man, Doctrine of.

Determinism (Buddh. rejection) The B. view that human existence is a continuous psycho-physical stream, in which birth of any one so-called 'individual' is conditioned by previous human actions and attitudes might be thought to imply a closed determinism with regard to human conduct. In fact, this is not so. The deterministic view was known in early Buddhism as *Niyati-vāda*; it is explicitly rejected by Buddha at several places in the canonical scriptures. Thus, in the *A.N.* ('Book of the Threes,' §61) Buddha examines view, held and taught by some recluses and → brahmans, who say that 'whatever weal or woe or neutral feeling is experienced, all that is due to some previous action. His reply to them is that for those who hold such a view there is no motive for desiring or striving to do any action or for abstaining from that action, and that they have in fact no logical reason at all for the pursuit of life of a recluse: 'they live in a state of bewilderment' (*A.N.*, III:173). The view, that all that happens to a man is 'due to what was previously done', is examined in the *Devadaha Sutta* also (*M.N.*, II:214–28), where again it is rejected by Buddha on ground that such a view of the human situation leaves out of account the real effect of present 'effort and striving'. In the → *Jataka*, the view of the Non-Causationists is rejected: if human action has no element of free-choice, then there is also no human responsibility for evils suffered. It is rejected on ground that it is untrue to say that human action has in it no element of moral choice (*Jat.*, V:237). It is because the B. analysis begins from premise, that conscious beings have freedom of moral choice, that deterministic views are rejected. Starting from same premise, Buddhists reject also any doc. of divine predestination of life of man. (→ *Predestination, Divine: Buddh. attitude*). The Buddha rejected both the view called Determinism—that the course of human events is unalterably fixed and determined by antecedent factors, and that of complete Indeterminism—that all which man suffers occurs as matter of chance without causal connection with antecedent moral choices. T.O.L.

K. N. Jayatilleke, *Early Buddhist Theory of Knowledge* (1963), pp. 410–1, 444–6, 469; Piyadassi Thera, *The Buddha's Ancient Path* (1964), pp. 62–4; I. B. Horner, *The Middle length Sayings* (1959), vol. 3, pp. 3–14; E. M. Hare, *The Book of the Gradual Sayings* (repr. 1953), vol. 3, pt. III, ch. VII, 'The Great Chapter'.

Deucalion In Grk. legend the son of → Prometheus, who warned him of intention of → Zeus to destroy mankind by a → flood. Advised by his father, D. and his wife Pyrrha escaped by building an ark (*larnax*). When the waters subsided, they repopulated earth by casting stones ('bones' of their Mother Earth) over their shoulders. S.G.F.B.

H. J. Rose, *Handbook of Grk. Mythology*, pp. 56, 257; *Kleine Pauly*, I, 1498–1500.

Deus absconditus Lat. = the 'hidden god'. A concept occurring in → mysticism. The Egypt. god → Amun was known as 'the hidden one'. S.G.F.B.

Deus otiosus Lat. = 'unoccupied, quiet, or retired god'. Expression used to denote type of deity, gen. a → High or Creator God, who is regarded as having grown old and withdrawn from world, but still omnipotent. An Egypt. myth pictures → Re as becoming senile. →→ Dyaus-pitri, An(u), and the Australian 'high-god' (→ Austral. Aborig. Relig.) are other examples. S.G.F.B.

Deutero-Isaiah Designation given to chapters 40–55 of Book of Isaiah, regarded by O.T. scholars as constituting a distinct work from Isaiah 1–39, and the so-called Trito-Isaiah, chaps. 56–66. D.-I. is dated for later years of Exile (549–538 BC). S.G.F.B.

*H.D.B.*³, p. 427; *P.C.*², pp. 516ff.; R. H. Pfeiffer, *Intro. to the Old Test.* (1948), pp. 449ff.

Deuteronomy, Book of Fifth and last book of → Pentateuch, attr. to → Moses. Title derives from Grk. *Deuteronomion*, 'repetition of the Law'. D. dates prob. from early 7th cent. BC; it reflects influence of 8th cent. prophets, and was doubtless connected with Josiah's reform (621 BC). It teaches unique sovereignty of → Yahweh, holiness of Israel, one sanctuary (i.e. Jerusalem → Temple) and one priesthood. D. epitomised belief and purpose of → Yahwism, and exercised profound influence upon subsequent Jew. relig. (→ Judaism). S.G.F.B.

*H.D.B.*², *s.v.; P.D.*², pp. 269ff.; R. H. Pfeiffer, *Intro. to the Old Test.* (1948), pp. 178ff.; C. R. North in *The Old Test. and Modern Study*, ed. H. H. Rowley (1951), pp. 48ff.; G. Von Rad, *Deuteronomy* (E.T. 1966).

Deva (Buddh.) Pali and Skt. term meaning 'a heavenly being' or lit. 'a shining one' (rel. to Lat. *deus*). Used in B. cosmology for beings who inhabit the heavenly sphere, invisible to mortals. D.'s are not strictly 'gods' in any absolute sense, since they are not 'eternal', but are subject, together with all other sentient beings, to law of rebirth. Acc. to B. → Cosmology, D.'s are found in all three realms into which universe is divided: *Kāma-dhātu; Rūpa-dh.* and *Arūpa-dh.*; although they are most usually thought of as inhabiting highest level of first of these, i.e. the sensual world, or *kāma-dhātu*. They are opposed by the → *Asuras*, disembodied spirits gen. of an evil or hostile disposition. Acc. to the B. *Suttas*, when the hosts of D.'s increase and the hosts of Asuras decrease, this is a happy situation for mortal men, just as it is inauspicious when reverse occurs. (→ Demons (Iran)). T.O.L.

J. Masson, *La Religion Populaire dans la Canon Bouddhique Pali* (1942); T. O. Ling, *Buddhism and the Mythology of Evil* (1962).

Devadatta A cousin of the → Buddha who, hearing him discourse on his return to Kapilavatthu after his Enlightenment, was converted and joined the → Sangha. He became a highly honoured member of Sangha, but about 8 years before Buddha's death he grew jealous of him, and won over the King of Magadha, → Ajatasattu as his ally in conspiring to bring about his death: three attempts were made, once with a gang of assassins, who were overcome by Buddha's presence and converted; once by D.'s hurling a stone at him of which only a splinter struck his foot; once by letting loose a wild elephant, which was calmed and subdued by the Buddha. D. then set about causing dissension in the Sangha; he advocated a more strict ascetisism than Buddha favoured, who replied that those who wished might follow such rules but he would not make them binding upon all monks. D. then began to proclaim that Buddha was not a true ascetic, and was given to luxurious living; he thus succeeded in drawing away 500 newly ordained Vajjian monks from Vesālī. D. died of an internal injury which caused blood to come from his mouth; acc. to the commentaries, in his last moment he declared that his only refuge was the Buddha. Acc. to trad., he was destined to suffer a long period in hell before being reborn. His story is told in the *Cullavagga* of the → *Vinaya-Pitaka;* he is mentioned also in the → *Saddharma-Pundarika*, and in the commentary on the → *Dhammapada*. T.O.L.

Malalasekere, *D.P.P.N.*, vol. I, pp. 1106ff.

Deva-Dūta (Buddh.) In B. thought, the 3 *devadūtas* or messengers to man from the heavenly beings (→ Deva) are age, disease and death. These remind man of his mortal condition, and serve to encourage him to seek more earnestly the holy life. Acc. to trad. account of life of the Buddha, it was when, as a young man, he saw, on the same day, a very old man, a sick man and a corpse being carried out to the burning ghat, that he was stirred to consider the meaning of human striving. (→ Buddha, The, Gotama). T.O.L.

Devānam-Piyatissa (Buddh.) (Lit. 'Tissa, beloved of the gods'). The honorific title of the King of Ceylon (247–207 BC), under whose patronage Buddhism was introduced into → Ceylon. The connotation of title would be, perhaps, 'His sacred majesty, Tissa'. He is credited with having had various important B. buildings erected, notably the 'Great Monastery' (Mahā Vihāra) at → Anuradhāpura, which was for cents. the home of the orthodox → Theravādins. The events of the D.'s reign, which marked beginning of B. hist. of Ceylon, are described in the Pali → *Mahāvamsa*. T.O.L.

Devil, The Explanation of world in terms of divine creation and providence raises problem of source of → evil. The hist. of relig. records two different solutions: (1) that supreme deity is of ambivalent nature, being both creator and destroyer: →→ Shiva, Vishnu, Zurvan are examples. (2) that universe is creation of opposing forces of Good and Evil, ever contending for mastery: → Zoroastrianism provides classic example of such → dualism, the evil principle, → Ahriman, is in effect a D. In Egypt. relig. → Set acquired such a role, as did → Māra in Buddhism. The word D. derives from Grk. *diabolos* = 'slanderer', and denotes personification of evil in → Judaism and → Christianity. The Jew. conception of D. is post-Exilic and was prob. influenced by Iranian dualism. In pre-Exilic period, → Yahweh was source of good and evil (e.g. Is. 45:7). After 538 BC, → Satan appears as 'the Adversary' (Zech. 3:1–2), and in Job. 1:6ff. he slanders and torments Job. In 1st cent. BC, the D. is identified with serpent of Temptation story (Gen. 3:1ff.), and blamed for bringing death into world. The N.T. and → Qumran scrolls reveal dualistic outlook, with D. under various names, leading forces of evil against God. In Temptation of Christ, D. is repr. as ruler of world (Lk. 4:5–6). Early Chr. → soteriology interpreted death of Christ as divinely-planned means to save mankind from D., or as ransom paid to D. to redeem mankind (→ Atonement). Christ's → Descent into Hades was explained as conquest of D. in his own house (Mt. 12:29). During Middle Ages, the D. was closely assoc. with → witchcraft, being worshipped by witches; he was naturally the focus of → Satanism and the → Black Mass. The iconography of D. has been various. He was gen. conceived anthropomorphically, and black in colour. Acc. to Dante, he had three heads. The familiar horned figure, with tail and cloven hooves, prob. derived from → Pan and satyrs, with poss. some memory of Celtic horned-god Cerunnos (→ Celtic (Pagan) Relig.). Belief in D. has gen. been abandoned or reinterpreted by modern Christians. S.G.F.B.

D.C.C., *s.v.; H.D.B.*[2], pp. 888–9 ('Satan'); *R.G.G.*[3], VI, *s.v.* ('Teufel'); Rene Bruno de Jesus-Marie (ed.), *Satan* (1951); T. Ling, *Buddhism and the Mythology of Evil* (1962); R. C. Zaehner, *Zurvan: a Zoroastrian Dilemma* (1955); M. Summers, *Witchcraft and the Black Art* (1932); J. A. MacCulloch, *Medieval Faith and Fable* (1932); S. G. F. Brandon, *History, Time and Deity* (1965), 'The Devil in Faith and History', in *R.A.H.* (1969), ch. 23.

(Buddh.) → Māra, the evil one. T.O.L.

Devotions (Buddh.) Acts of devotion constitute import. part of the Buddh. relig. life, both for monks and laymen, as the many popular manuals and books of worship pub. in Asian countries such as Ceylon and Burma testify. Such a manual has recently been published in Eng. for Western Buddhists. B. devotion consists primarily of recollection of greatness and honour of Buddha, his Doctrine (→ Dhamma), and his Order (→ Sangha), i.e. the 'three jewels' (*tiratna*), the praising of them, and commitment of oneself to them. Such an act of devotion, together with affirming of the 5 moral precepts, is the common daily practice of both monks or laymen. This may be performed, in case of laymen, at a small shrine in house or in a public place such as pagoda or temple. Often, and espec. at the pagoda, to such devotions will be added the offering of flowers, lights and incense, together with reciting of verse which connects what is offered with some specific B. intention: thus 'I offer this good light in memory of the Enlightened One; by meritorious action I would dispel the darkness'. The posture for devotion is usually kneeling, with hands placed in front of face, palms together, and at certain points in the devotions there will be complete prostration, with forehead touching ground. Corporate devotions, with chanting of verses, often from scripture or from devotional writings, take place in the monastic assembly hall; in these the monks take part daily, in morning and evening; on B. holy days (full moon and new moon) lay people may join in the special devotions of day. There is no set form for these; the length and order of devotions may be left to senior monk who conducts them. On holy days there will also frequently be a sermon, in which a senior monk explains some aspect of B. teaching or reminds his hearers of moral disciplines of the B. life. T.O.L.

K. Wells, *Thai Buddhism* (1960); Pe Maung Tin, *Buddhist Devotion and Meditation* (1964); Saddhatissa Mahathera, *Handbook of Buddhists* (1956); T.O. Ling, *Buddha, Marx and God* (1966), ch. 6.

Devotee, Lay (Buddh.) → Upāsaka. T.O.L.

Dhamma (Pali); **Dharma** (Skt.)—**Buddh.** Word occurring frequently and in many connections in Buddhism; it has no one gen. applicable meaning. D. is trans. into Eng. variously as religion, truth, doctrine, righteousness, virtue, essence, elemental ultimate constituent or 'atom', phenomena, nature, law, norm, property, and entity. Some meanings are common usage in Indian relig. gen.; others are peculiar to Buddhism (e.g. 'ultimate constituent'). The Skt. root *dhṛ*, from which it is derived, has sense of 'bearing', 'upholding', 'supporting', 'that which forms a foundation'. → Buddhaghosa, in his commentary on the *D.N.*, distinguishes 4 meanings of D.: (1) having ref. to good conduct (2) moral instruction (3) doc. of Buddha as contained in the scriptures (4) cosmic law, (*D.A.*, I, 99). In his comy. on the → *Dhamma-Sanganī*, he gives another list of four meanings: (1) doctrine (2) condition, or causal antecedent (3) moral quality (4) what is 'phenomenal', as opp. to what is 'noumenal' or 'substantial'. The primary meanings in B. usage are, therefore, doctrine, righteousness, condition and phenomenon. Of these, most prominent is the first; by this is understood the Dhamma (Dharma) of the Buddha, one of the *three jewels* (Tri-ratna) of the B. system: the Buddha, the Dhamma, the → Sangha. In this usage, D. means the universal truth proclaimed by Buddha. The D. is itself ontologically anterior even to the Buddha, who is also the expression or historical manifestation of the D. (→ Trikāya Doctrine). Buddhas appear, at intervals, in course of time; they come and go, but the D., as it were, goes on for ever. In this usage, D. corresponds in some sense to Gk. concept of the *Logos*. It is in the D., in this sense, that the Buddh. 'takes refuge' (→ *Tri-Ratna*). The discourses of Buddha, since they set forth this ultimate reality, or truth, of the D., are referred to collectively as the D.; the meaning here being that of 'doctrine' or 'teaching'. A life lived consonantly with the truth, set forth by Buddha, is a life characterised by D. or, in this case, 'righteousness'.

The sense of 'that which is ultimate' underlies also the special usage of *dhamma* (usually repr. by a small initial letter) by the Theravādin school, who signify by this 'an ultimate constituent', i.e. of human existence. The → Theravādins hold that there is a certain fixed and limited number of such 'atoms' of existence (some being material, but the majority psychological); it is this view-point which is repr. in their → Abhidhamma lit., a view for which they were criticised by the Mahāyāna schools (see → Mādhyamika). T.O.L.

The Pali Text Society's Pali-English Dictionary (1921), p. 171; W. Geiger, *Pali Dhamma* (1920) (for philology); E. Conze, *Buddhist Thought in India* (1962), pt. I, sect. 7; D. T. Suzuki, *Studies in the Lankavatara Sutra* (1930), pp. 154–6.

Dhammapada An import. and widely known book of the Thv. Buddh. Pali canon; it is incl. in the 5th (*Khuddaka*) *Nikaya* of the *Sutta Pitaka*. It consists of 423 verses, each verse consisting of a proverb or pithy saying concerning the Buddh. life. The verses are arranged in 26 chapters, acc. to types of verses, or subject: e.g. ch. 1, 'The Twin-Verses', where verses are paired, dealing with opposite aspects of a single statement; 2nd ch. deals with 'Vigilance'; 3rd with 'Thought', and so on. The whole book is an anthology of sayings; it is the work of a fairly early editor; many verses occur in other canonical texts. The word *dhammapada* means lit. 'a line of the → *Dhamma*' (i.e. the Doctrine), or a portion thereof. The sayings or proverbs, of which book consists, are well known in Buddh. countries, espec. those of → Thv. school of S.E. Asia, being memorised by monks; often by lay people also, who may possess copies of book. Thv. Buddhists regard the D. as brief summary of essent. teaching of Buddha. The Pali text was ed. by Suriyogoda Sumangala, and pub. in Roman script by the PTS in 1914. E.T.'s have been made by Max Müller (*S.B.E.*, vol. X, 1898), by S. Radhakrishnan, 1950 (repr. 1958) and various others.

The D. is also title of a similar collection of Buddh. proverbs in Gandhārī Prakrit, partly recovered in mod. times and ed. by J. Brough; about $\frac{3}{8}$ of orig. text is still missing. Brough has estimated that the Pali and Prakrit versions had a common nucleus of about 330 verses, and considers that both collections had an earlier, common source, which different schools have used, each having 'to a greater or less degree modified, re-arranged or expounded a common fund of inherited materials'. T.O.L.

W. Geiger, *Pali Literature and Language* (1956); P. V. Bapat (ed.), 2500 *Years of Buddhism* (1959), pp. 156–8; S. Radhakrishnan, *The Dhammapada:* Pali Text (E.T. and Notes) (1950, repr. 1958); John Brough, *The Gandhārī Dharmapada* (1962).

Dhamma Cakkappavattana Sutta Name of Buddh. Sutta which is trad. regarded as the Buddha's first sermon, viz. 'The setting in motion (*pavattana*) of the wheel (*cakka*) of the Dhamma.' This is said to have been preached in the Deer Park at Isipatana, near Benares, on full moon day of the month of Āsālha. The discourse contains the fundamental teaching of the Buddha, viz., (1) the necessity for avoidance of the two extremes of sensual indulgence and fanatical ascetism (both of these were features of the anc. Indian scene) (2) the → Four Holy Truths and → Eightfold Path; although latter is regarded by some scholars as a formulation of Buddh. scheme of life, developed somewhat later as an elaboration of the earlier three-fold way. The *Sutta* occurs in the Pali canon in the *Samyutta-Nikaya* (V:420) and in the *Vinaya* (I:10f.); the name, *Dhammacakkappavattana*, however, is applied to it as a title only in refs. to it in later Pali literature, e.g. in *Jāt.* I:82; in commentary on the *Dīgha Nikaya* I:2, etc. Skt. versions of it are found in the → *Lalitavistara*, and in the → *Mahāvastu*. The 'setting in motion' or 'Turning' of the 'wheel of Dhamma' is regarded as one of the 4 great events of Buddha's life, the other 3 being the birth, enlightenment, and passing into *parinibbāna*. (→ Wheel (*Cakka*)). T.O.L.

Dhamma-Sanganī (Buddh.) Pali B. work of the Theravādin school. It forms part of third section of the canonical writings, viz. the → *Abhidhamma Pitaka*, of which it is the 1st of 7 books. The title means, lit. a 'recital of *dhammas*'. It consists of an enumeration of various poss. psychic elements, or → *dhammas*, and brings together into systematic arrangement terms which occur throughout earlier books of the → *Sutta Pitaka*. The terms are arranged in numerical groups, in twos, threes, and fours; the primary concern is with the ethical significance of these terms. It is said to have been trans. into Sinhalese by King Vijayabahu of Ceylon, but this trans. is now lost. It was trans. by Mrs. Caroline Rhys-Davids into Eng. as 'A Buddhist Manual of Psychological Ethics'. A commentary on the D.-S. was composed by the great Theravādin writer → Buddhaghosa, entitled *Atthasālinī*. T.O.L.

Nyanatiloka, *Guide through the Abhidhamma-Pitaka* (1957), pp. 12–23.

Dharma, Hindu *Dharma* means 'law' or 'sacred law' in Hindu trad., and can be used for 'religion': Hindu relig. is the *sanatana dharma* or 'everlasting law'. In → Vaisnavism, the *avataras* of Vishnu come to restore D. after period of decadence, etc. The word is used with rather different emphasis in → Buddhism (also the plural is used in Buddhism to mean 'events'; while, as a technical term in → Jainism, it means 'motion'). The idea of D. as sacred law has some analogy to earlier → *rta* in Vedic hymns, → Varuna. The formulation of code of sacred law occurred through composition of the *Kalpasutras*, which are collections of three → *sutras*, each work dealing respectively with sacrificial ritual, domestic ritual (*Grhyasutras*) and conduct (*Dharmasutras*). The last date from *c.* 5th to 2nd cent. BC. Later were composed more extensive expositions of law, the *Dharmasāstras*, most import. of which is Law Book of → Manu, the *Mānavadharmaśāstra*, also known as the *Manusmrti* (→ *smrti*). These works on D. were held to belong to auxiliary canon, together with epics and → *Puranas*. They lay down in considerable detail duties of men in society, with some mention of gen. obligations applicable to all men, but with much greater emphasis on the *varnasramadharma* (→ *varna*, → *asrama*), i.e. codes applicable to different classes or castes and at different stages of life. The following of D. is what constitutes virtue, and is thus one of four ends of life in Hinduism (→ Ethics, Hindu). It was trad. considered to be duty of king to uphold law, and he had at his disposal forces of punishment (*daṇḍa*) (→ Dhamma). N.S.

P. V. Kane, *Hist. of Dharmasastra*, 5 vols. (1930–62); G. Buhler (tr.), *The Sacred Laws of the Aryas*, 2 vols., in Max Müller (ed.), *S.B.E.*, vols. 2 and 14 (1879–82); and *The Laws of Manu*, *S.B.E.*, vol. 25 (1886); N. C. Sen Gupta, *Evolution of Ancient Indian Law* (1953).

Dharma-kāya In Buddh. thought, one of the 3 aspects of the Buddha-nature; (→ Buddha-Kāya). T.O.L.

Dharmapada → Dhammapada. T.O.L.

Dhātu (Buddh.) Term widely used in Buddhism, meaning gen. 'an element', being etymologically closely rel. to → *dhamma*. It is used in various different senses, of which principal ones are: (A) the physical 'elements', which in pop. B. thought were earth, water, fire and wind, were regarded as primary forms of matter (B) the 18 D.'s or psycho-physical elements of consciousness, viz: (1) eye (2) ear (3) nose (4) tongue (5) body (6) visible object (7) audible object (8) odorous object (9) gustative object (10) tactile object (11) visual consciousness (12) aural consciousness (13) olfactory consciousness (14) gustatory consciousness (15) touch-consciousness (16) the mind (17) mental object (18) mental consciousness. (C) the 3 'elements' or spheres into which cosmos is divided in B. thought, viz: (1) *Kāma-dhātu*, the sensual sphere (2) *Rūpa-d.*, the fine-material sphere (3) *Arūpa-d*, the immaterial sphere (→ Cosmology, Buddh.). The word is used also of group of 6 'elements', viz: solid, liquid, heat, motion, space and consciousness; also of remains of mortal body after cremation. In this latter sense of 'relic', the word is a component of *dhātu-garbha* i.e. 'relic-chamber', which in its shortened form is known as → *dagoba*. T.O.L.

Dhātu-Kathā Name of a book of the Pali canonical scriptures of the Theravāda Buddh. It is one of the 7 books of third section of canon, i.e. of the → *Abhidhamma Piṭaka*, and is usually listed as 5th. The title means 'Discussion of the → *Dhātus* or 'elements', which in this case means largely the psychological elements occurring in the more spiritually advanced. The book serves as a supplement to the → *Dhammasanganī;* it may have been designed as such. A commentary on the *D.-K.* was composed by → Buddhaghosa. T.O.L.

Dhātuvaṃsa Pali Buddh. work, attr. to writer named Dhamma-kitti. The work, which is in form of poem, tells story of sacred tooth-relic of the Buddha, said to have been taken to Ceylon from India at begin. of 4th cent. In addition to narrative-material derived from the → *Mahāvaṃsa*, the poem makes use of other local trads. of Ceylon, and was prob. composed in early part of 13th cent. CE. The text was published in Roman script by Rhys-Davids in 1884 in *Journal of the Pali Text Society*. T.O.L.

Dhikr (Remembering). A practice carried out in → Sūfī fraternities, consisting of repetition of certain phrases such as 'There is no deity but God', 'Praise be to God', 'Glory be to God', 'God is most great', or simply 'Allāh'. This may be a monotonous chanting, often accompanied by musical instruments and rhythmic movements to induce → ecstasy. (Cf. Lane, *Egyptians*, for descriptions). Among Sūfīs the novice is taught by his *shaykh* how to perform the *dhikr*, and must follow him carefully, saying the words mentally while the *shaykh* repeats them aloud. Besides the corporate D. there is the individual, when a devout person may practise the remembrance of God by repeating, either aloud or mentally, the usual phrases, commonly using a → rosary as help to observing conventional number of times phrases should be repeated. The rosary is commonly used for repetition of the 99 attributes, or 'beautiful names' of God (→ God, 99 names of). When one has recited the normal number of repetitions of phrases, it is usual to spend some time quietly meditating on some Qur. vv. J.R.

*E.I.*², II, pp. 223–7; Lane, *Egyptians*, index (Zikrs); D. B. Macdonald, *Aspects*, index, *Attitude*, index; Arberry, *Sufism*, index; Rice, *Persian Sufis*, pp. 88–97.

Dhimmī → Protected peoples. J.R.

Dhul Ḥijja 12th month of Muslim lunar year, on certain days of which the annual pilgrimage to Mecca and certain places in neighbourhood is observed (→ Pilgrimage). J.R.

Dhul Nūn (d. 246/861). Of Egypt, an import. ascetic and → Sūfī. He has been credited with intro. the doc. of → gnosis (*ma'rifa*); but it has been pointed out that this was known earlier. He has been considered a *quṭb* (→ Saints). He travelled widely, coming in touch with other Sufis and teaching his ascetic and mystical doctrines. J.R.

*E.I.*², II, p. 242; Hujwīrī, *Kashf*, pp. 100ff.; Arberry, *Doctrine*, index; M. Smith, *Early mysticism*, pp. 191ff., 230ff., etc.

Dhyāna (Buddh.) → *Jhāna*. T.O.L.

(Hindu) The practice of meditation, prescribed as seventh element in path to liberation of → Yoga school of Hinduism; but more widely used as interpreted in Hindu trad. (as well as in →→ Buddhism and Jainism, etc.) to cover attempt to fix mind on ultimate reality, etc. It is sometimes equated with *upāsanā*, kind of meditative worship described in the → *Upaniṣads* and later trad. In Yoga it stands between *dhāraṇā* and → *samadhi*, and involves stage of expertise where adept can fix his attention at will upon some object, such as → Viṣṇu, and penetrate to its inner essence, thus appropriating it to himself. Eventually aim is to transcend use of an object, and to attain non-dual state of consciousness in higher *samadhi*. The notion that in D. one attains a kind of identity with object gave D. a role in worship as understood in → Tantrism, as a counterpart to external purification and sacramental use of formulae transforming worshipper into a divinised counterpart of object of his worship. In general, the nature of meditation in Hinduism was understood against background of diverse theologies—e.g. in → Madhva's *Dvaita dhyana* is seen as concentration of mind on qualities of God. D. is most gen. term for practice of meditation; and thus is integral part of yoga, and can be roughly contrasted with the attitude of → *bhakti* and practice of works (*karmamārga*). (→ Mysticism, Hindu.) D. is typically a means to → *jnana*. N.S.

M. Eliade, *Yoga: Immortality and Freedom* (1958); S. N. Dasgupta, *Hindu Mysticism* (1959); and *Yoga as Philosophy and Religion* (1924); N. Smart *The Yogi and the Devotee* (1968).

Diamond Sūtra Name of a Mahāyāna Buddh. treatise, belonging to type of lit. known as → *Prajnā-Pāramitā Sūtras*. T.O.L.

Diana Italian goddess. The root DI in name may signify 'bright one'. D. was a fertility goddess, partic. honoured by women. She was connected with woods, and her most famous temple near Aricia, on shore of Lake Nemi, stood in a grove; another important shrine was on Mt. Tifata, the name meaning 'holm-oak-grove'. Attached to her shrine at Aricia was the *Rex Nemorensis*, 'king of the grove'. The holder of this priestly office obtained it by killing his predecessor, after challenge of plucking a branch, thus violating sanctity of grove. These priest-kings were gen. escaped slaves. J.B. → Frazer in his *G.B.*, I, attempted to explain significance of institution. D. was identified with → Artemis; whether she was a moon-goddess is debated. S.G.F.B.

W. Warde Fowler, *The Religious Experience of the Roman People* (1911), pp. 234ff.; F. Altheim, *A Hist. of Roman Religion* (E.T. 1938), pp. 166, 178ff., 250ff.; *O.C.D.*, pp. 274, 765; *Kleine Pauly*, I, 1510–2; *R.A.C.*, III, 963–72.

'Diana of the Ephesians' Title well-known in Eng. owing to A.V. and R.V. trans. of orig. Grk. 'Artemis' by 'Diana' in Acts 19:24ff. However, the name → Artemis was an ancient misnomer, for the Ephesian goddess had little in common with classical Grk. Artemis. The origin of the goddess is obscure. She was prob. a form of great Asiatic mother-goddess (→ Great Goddess), whose cult was adopted by Ionian Grks., who identified her with Artemis: 'Ephesia' was her local name. Her great temple, begun in 6th cent. BC, was one of wonders of anc. world. The episode recorded in Acts 19:24ff. attests popularity of cult. In art the goddess was repr. in stiff upright posture, the top part of body being covered with breasts (→ Breast). Her chief priest was a eunuch, and bore Persian title of Megabyzos. Plutarch compared her maiden priestesses with the Roman → Vestals. S.G.F.B.

L. R. Taylor, 'Artemis of Ephesus', in *B.C.*, V, pp. 251ff.; H. Gressmann, *O.R.*, pp. 78ff.

Diaspora, The Grk. word for 'dispersion', used partic. for dispersion of Jews, which started with Assyrian and Babylonian deportations (722 and 597 BC). The process continued voluntarily, so that by 1st cent. CE there were Jew. communities in most parts of Roman Empire eastward from Italy. There were about one million Jews in Egypt. The D.-Jews were mainly Grk.-speaking and influenced by Grk. culture; but they remained faithful to their faith, visited Jerusalem for festivals and sent offerings. As Acts. and Epistles of Paul show, the D. was an import. factor in early propagation of Christianity. The D.-Jews were not gen. popular with their Gentile neighbours, and were often persecuted (→ Philo; → Septuagint). S.G.F.B.

E. Schürer, *G.J.V.*, III (1909), pp. 1–188; R. H. Pfeiffer, *Hist. of New Test. Times* (1954), pp. 166ff.; J. Juster, *Les Juifs dans l'Empire romain* (1914); *R.A.C.*, III, 972–82.

Diatessaron, The An edition of four Gospels in a continuous narrative, made by Tatian, *c.* 150. It circulated among Syriac-speaking churches, and may have been written in Syriac, Grk. or Lat. It is significant, *inter alia*, for showing desire to harmonise the four Gospels: that it did not establish a widespread custom attests reputation early acquired by four canonical Gospels. S.G.F.B.

B. F. Westcott, *General Survey of Hist. of Canon of New Test.* (1870), pp. 288ff.; *D.C.C.*, *s.v.;* R. M. Grant, *The Earliest Lives of Jesus* (1961), pp. 22ff.

Didachē, The Grk. word meaning 'Teaching', used as abbrev. for early Chr. tractate entitled 'Teaching of the Lord through the Twelve Apostles'. The only known MS. of D. was discovered in 1875; there is a partial Lat. trans. Having previously been dated for 90–150, more recent opinion places its composition later, even in 3rd cent. It is gen. regarded as emanating from Palestine or Syria. Chs. 1–6 describe the 'Way of Life' and the 'Way of Death'. The remaining 10 chs. deal with matters of faith and practice incl. →→ baptism (by immersion), Eucharist, prophets, bishops, and deacons, fasting. The D. is of great import. as evidence of early Chr. life; the fact that fragments exist in Coptic, Syriac, Arab., and Georgian, and that it was used in → Didascalia attests its influence. S.G.F.B.

Convenient editions of text and trans. are J. B.

Lightfoot-J. R. Harmer, *The Apostolic Fathers* (1891); K. Lake, *The Apostolic Fathers* (Loeb Classical Library, 1912–3), F. E. Vokes, *The Riddle of the Didache* (1938); *D.C.C., s.v.; R.A.C.*, III, 1009–13; *R.G.G.*[3], I, p. 508 ('Apostellehre'); *Kleine Pauly*, II, 3–4; P. Nautin, *R.H.R.*, 155 (1959), pp. 191ff.

Didascalia Apostolorum Chr. writing, composed by Jew. convert, in N. Syria in first half of 3rd cent. It deals with variety of topics concerning Chr. faith and practice. Written orig. in Grk., it survives in a Syriac version and frags. of Lat. version. S.G.F.B.

D.C.C., s.v.; Kleine Pauly, II, 5–6; *R.G.G.*[3], p. 189. L. Duchesne, *Christian Worship* (E.T., 1927), pp. 56–7.

Dies Irae Lat. 'Day of Wrath'. Opening words of hymn concerning → Last Judgment, used in → Mass for the Dead. It was prob. written by a 13th cent. Franciscan friar. There are several Eng. trans. e.g. in *The English Hymnal*. The D.-I. is a significant expression of medieval → eschatology. S.G.F.B.

D.C.C., s.v.; J. Evans (ed.), *The Flowering of the Middle Ages* (1966), p. 226.

Digambaras The 'Sky-clad', a main sect of → Jainism, together with the → *Svetambaras*, or 'White-clad'. The chief difference from *Svetambaras* is that they in principle practice → nudity, among monks, as a sign of total renunciation of worldly goods and values. Although there is little in way of doctrinal divergence between the sects, the D. are rather more conservative and do not recognise written canon, on ground of its being hopelessly corrupt in transmission (a view in line with Jain belief in progressive decline of relig. until end of the present world-cycle). D. temple worship is also more conservative, and is not, as often in the other sect, administered by non-Jains. N.S.

Dīghanikaya (Pali), **Dirghāgama** (Skt.) 1st of the 5 major divisions (→ *Nikayas*) of the Buddh. *Sutta Pitaka*, or Discourse-Collection, which in turn is second of 3 main divisions of canonical scriptures of Thv. (Pali) Buddhism. The *D.N.* consists of 34 basic lit. units known as *suttas*, or 'connected discourses', i.e. usually of Buddha. The Mhy. collection, the *Dirghagama*, which exists in a Chinese version, consists of 30 sutras; 27 of these are common to both collections. The title *Digha/Dirgha*, meaning 'long', refs. to fact that the DN/DA contain some of the longest *suttas*, although not all are long compared with *suttas* contained in other *Nikayas;* about 16 of the *suttas* of the DN are 'long'. The 34 *Suttas* of DN. are arranged in 3 sections, or *vaggas*. The first *vagga* contains 13 *suttas;* whose titles are as follows: (1) Brahmajāla (2) Samannaphala (3) Ambattha (4) Sonadanda (5) Kutadanta (6) Mahali (7) Jaliya (8) Kassapasihanāda (9) Potthapāda (10) Subha (11) Kevaddha (12) Lohicca (13) Tevijja. The second *vagga* contains 10 *Suttas:* (14) Mahāpadāna (15) Mahānidāna (16) Mahāparinibbāna (17) Mahāsudassana (18) Janavasabha (19) Mahā-Govinda (20) Mahā-samaya (21) Sakkapanha (22) Mahā-Satipaṭṭhāna (23) Pāyāsi. The third *vagga* contains 11 *Suttas:* (24) Pātika (25) Udambarika-sīhanāda (26) Cakkavatti-sīhanāda (27) Agganna (28) Sampasadaniya (29) Pāsādika (30) Lakkhaṇa (31) Singālovāda (32) Ātānātiya (33) Sangīti (34) Dasuttara. The better known and more import. of these are (1) the Brahmajala, which enumerates both popular superstitions and pastimes of anc. India in early Buddh. period; also 62 different philosophical theories of same period; (2) the Samanna-phala, which sets out doctrines of six other non-Buddh. teachers of the time, and the great benefits or fruits (*phala*) of life of the Samanna, or Buddh. monk; (3) (4) and (5) are all concerned with refuting claims of the → brahmans of anc. India to be a social and relig. elite; (14), which sets forth legends of the six Buddhas reputed to have preceded Gotama the Buddha; (15), which provides exposition of Law of Dependent Origination (→ Paticca-Samuppada); and poss. most import. of all (16), which describes in detail events of last few weeks of Buddha's life, his entry into 'final' → *nibbāna*, or *pari-nibbāna*, the ceremonial cremation of his body and distribution of remains and building of → Stupas over them. (31) is import., espec. for Buddh. lay people, since it contains what are set out as proper duties to be observed by them in their various roles as parents, children, masters, servants, teachers, pupils, etc. (→→ Mahāparinibbāna Sutta; Mahāpadāna Sutta). T.O.L.

Dialogues of the Buddha, 3 vols., trans. and ed. by T. W. and C. A. F. Rhys-Davids (1899–1921, repr. 1956–66); A. A. G. Bennett, *Long Discourses of the Buddha*, I–XVI, n.d.

Dikē Grk. word for justice. Personified, D. reports wrong-doings of men to → Zeus and punishes injustice. Alternatively, D. was identified with constellation of Virgo (hence the scales), having left earth at commencement of Bronze Age. Refs. to D. in Grk. lit. show great variety of concept, owing to her essentially abstract character. S.G.F.B.

O.C.D., s.v.; Kleine Pauly, II, 24–6.

Dionysius, the Pseudo-Areopagite So-called because a corpus of mystical theology, written by unknown author *c.* 300, was attr. to Dionysius the Areopagite converted by Paul acc. to Acts 17:34. The writings concerned repr. an attempt to synthesize Chr. dogma and → Neo-Platonism. Their aim is to achieve union of soul with God and progressive → deification (*theiōsis*) of man. They exercised a profound influence on medieval theology in both W. and E. Churches: their high reputation declined in 16th cent. S.G.F.B.

D.C.C., pp. 402–3; *R.A.C.*, III, 1075–1121; R. Roques, *L'Universe dionysien. Structure hierarchique du monde selon le Pseudo-Denys* (1954); J.-M. Hornus, 'Les recherches dionysiennes de 1955 à 1960'; *R.H.P.R.*, 41 (61).

Dionysos Origin and nature of this god constitutes a great problem in study of Grk. relig. D. was widely influential over a long period; but he was not one of the → Olympian gods, and differed greatly from them in being object of a very emotional relig. He was god of wine; his influence, however, did not stem from this role. The name D. has been explained as *Dios vusos* = 'Son of Zeus'. In mythology, D. was offspring of → Zeus and Semele. The name D. has been identified on a Mycenaean (Pylos) tablet; also that of → Zagreus, another name of D., and a tablet from Knossos gives alternative name for Semele. This evidence has been interpr. as attesting Aegean origin of D. (→ Aegean Relig.). One trad. brings D. from Asia Minor, and repr. him as god of vegetation, partic. of fruit and vines. His name of Bacchus was Lydian. Another trad. locates orig. of D. in Thrace, and repr. cult as ecstatic in character and feminine in appeal. Myths tell of frenzied devotees (→ 'maenads'), whirling in dance, rending and devouring living animals and children during their *orgia*. This → omophagy was a sacramental meal by which devotees made communion with D. The cult of D., incl. *orgia*, was estab. at → Delphi, but in milder form. D. became closely assoc. with → Orphism, partic. through myth of Zagreus, and thus with immortality and rebirth, as murals of the Villa of the Mysteries, Pompeii, and many sculptured sarcophagi show. In art until 5th cent. D. was repr. as mature, bearded man, later as effeminate youth, usually nude. The → phallus was frequent object in his cult, but D. is never portrayed ithyphallic as are his attendant Sileni and Satyrs. D. was also closely connected with the → Anthesteria and orig. of → drama. S.G.F.B.

O.C.D., *s.v.;* W. K. C. Guthrie, *The Greeks and their Gods* (1950), pp. 145ff.; N. Turchi, *Fontes*, pp. 1–39; Cumont, *R.O.*, pp, 195ff.; V. Macchioro, *Zagreus* (1930), *passim;* M. P. Nilsson, *Gesch. d. griech Relig.*, I (1955²), pp. 564ff.; L. A. Stella, 'La religione greca nei testi micenei', in *Numen*, V (1958), p. 34; *Kleine Pauly*, II, 77–85; I. A. Richmond, *Archeology, and the After-Life in Pagan and Christian Imagery* (1950), pp. 29ff.; G. Zuntz, 'On the Dionysiac Fresco in the Villa dei Misteri at Pompeii', *Proc. Brit. Acad.*, 49; *Bilderatlas*, 13/14 Lief., Ab. 15–17, 63–5.

Dioscuri 'The Sons of Zeus', named Castor and Polydeuces (Lat. Pollux): twin brothers of Helen. Their nature and origin are obscure. Evidence can be cited for regarding them as either → chthonic beings or celestial (astral) deities. *Od.* XI, pp. 300ff. states that 'the corn-bearing earth holds them', yet they were identified with constellation of Gemini. They have a rich mythology, which assoc. them, *inter alia*, with war and horses (cf. the Vedic Asvins). They are often confused with the → Cabiri. S.G.F.B.

O.C.D., *s.v.; R.A.C.*, III, 1122–38; *Kleine Pauly*, II, 92–4.

Dipankara (Buddh.) Name of a legendary Buddha, reputed to have lived long ages ago; the first of 24 Buddhas who are held to have preceded Gotama the Buddha (→ Buddhas (other than Gotama)). The details concerning him are all of gigantic kind: he was 80 cubits tall, always attended by 84,000 saints (*arahants*), he lived for 100,000 years; the *stupa* in which his remains were enshrined was 36 yoganas high. He is remembered espec. for fact that, acc. to legend, it was while D. was Buddha that Gotama, who became the Buddha in 6th cent. BC, and was then an ascetic named Sumedha, made his vow to become a Buddha. T.O.L.

Buddhavamsa, II, pp. 207f.; Malalasekere, *D.P.P.N.*, vol. I, p. 1087; *Mahāvastu*, I, pp. 231–9; E. Conze, *Buddhist Scriptures* (1959), pp. 20–4.

Dīpavamsa (Buddh.) The oldest of B. Pali hist. chronicles. The title means 'The Island Lineage (or Chronicle)', and indic. contents of work, viz. the hist. of island of → Ceylon; the work tells of intro. of Buddhism to island and continues story up to end of reign of Mahāsena (CE 325–52). It is thought to have been compiled some time after 352 and before *c.* 450. The compiler appears to have used an older work, the → *Atthakathā*, as main source. The hist. reliability of the D. has been questioned in mod. times (e.g. by R. O. Franke); but Geiger held that its frequent agreements with contemporary trads. of India was sufficient guarantee that it was 'the vehicle of an old hist. tradition'. It is recorded that a 5th cent. King of Ceylon, Dhatusena (460–78), provided endowment for regular recitals of the D. T.O.L.

W. Geiger, *Pali Literature and Language* (2nd edn. 1956), pp. 27f.; G. R. Malalasekere, *D.P.P.N.*, vol. I, p. 1088.

Discipline (Buddh. Monastic) The disciplinary code which governs life of the Buddh. monastic community, or → Sangha, is contained in the *Pātimokkha*, (lit. 'that which is binding'), an anc. text which forms part of the B. → *Vinaya-Pitaka*. The *P.-Sutta* is gen. held to be nucleus and oldest part of the Pali *Vinaya-Pitaka*. It is extant also in Skt. versions (*Prātimokṣa-Sūtra*), which have been discovered in mod. times. It has 2 parts: one set of rules for monks, the *Bhikkhu-patimokkha;* and another for nuns, the *Bhikkhuni-p*. The scheme followed is an enumeration of offences in descending order of seriousness: first, those for which penalty is expulsion from community viz: sexual misconduct, theft, murder, boasting of power to perform miracles; second, those which merit temporary suspension (with poss. of re-admission, if offender was subsequently found worthy), and which incl. offences concerned with improper relations between men and women, independent setting-up of a hermitage, making of false accusations, causing dissension and so on. The 3rd section (2 kinds of offences), the 4th (26 offences), the 5th (92 offences), the 6th (4 offences) all require restitution (where applicable and formal confession of guilt before community as proper method of dealing with offences concerned. The 7th section consists virtually of advice on matters of etiquette—how to eat inoffensively, enter a sick-room etc. The 8th section sets out seven ways for settling disputes within community. The complete set of these rules is to be recited by monks in full assembly on full-moon and new-moon days every month. (→ Monasticism). T.O.L.

S.B.E., vol. XIII, pp. 1–69; P. V. Bapat (ed.), 2500 *Years of Buddhism* (1959), pp. 163–5; S. Dutt, *Buddhist Monks and Monasteries of India* (1962).

(China–Japan) Confucian: → Confucianism, possessing no church-organisation with distinctive priesthood and rules for membership, has nothing analogous to D. in the Chr. Church. Yet such were the effects of Confucian ethics, with priority given to filial piety, reverence and respect for authority, and the patriarchal organisation of Chinese society, that the life of a Confucian scholar was regulated from early childhood by a strict code of D. All human relationships, and indeed relations with the spiritual world, were ruled by → Li (propriety, rites, good manners etc.). Confucian D. was not only imposed by the social *mores*, but by a state whose supreme head was regarded as Son of Heaven, Vice-regent of Heaven on earth, and parent of all the people. The Board of Rites (*Li Pu*) had power, under the emperor, to D. and punish any Confucian official for failure to exercise his relig. duties. Within the Confucian family, D. was inculcated, not so much by relig. sanctions as by reverence for ancestors and duty and obedience to parents and elders.

Taoist: → Taoism has always been so loosely organised that each monastery or relig. society was left to impose its own measures to secure purity and spiritual well-being of its members. During 2nd and 3rd cents. CE, the semi-relig. and semi-political organisations imposed a fairly strict D. on priests and adherents alike. This involved payment of cult dues; imposition of prohibitions against lying, stealing and debauchery; rules of abstinence, and vows of obedience to Taoist rules. Similar D.'s have been characteristic of Taoist secret societies and Taoist lay movements ever since. In 6th cent. CE celibacy was estab. in Taoist monasteries, and standards of moral and spiritual proficiency were attested by issue of certificates. But corruption and abuse nullified in large measure all attempts at organised D. Taoism always taught the need for self-D. on part of the adept who sought perfection in → Tao, or strove to attain immortality.

Chinese and Japanese Buddhism: Except for its ethical codes and its teaching concerning need for self-D., → Buddhism imposed no formal D. on the laity. Within the Buddh. order, each monastery took over training and D. of its novices and monks. The large corpus of Vinaya rules was studied, and generally observed, incl. the 250 prohibitions of the Pratimoksa and the 58 prohibitions of the *Sūtra of Brahma's Net.* But many of the D.-rules devised for Indian Buddhism were found impracticable in China and Japan and were tacitly ignored, e.g. rules concerning money, the holding of personal property, the duty of begging etc. The *Pure Rules of Pai Chang* (*Pai Chang Ch'ing Kuei*) composed by a Ch'an monk of 9th cent. CE (d. 814), revised and re-edited frequently during subsequent cents., exerted great authority in Buddh. monasteries down to present day. In addition, each monastery drew up its own code of rules (*kuei yüeh*). In gen., the D. of → Ch'an (Zen) monasteries was harsher and more exacting than that of → Pure Land monasteries. Certain monasteries became famous for strictness of their D., e.g. Chin Shan and Kao-min-Ssu in China. Punishment for offences took various forms and varied from monastery to monastery. In some, corporal punishment was common. The heaviest penalty was expulsion from the monastery, normally the prerogative of the abbot. H. Welch, *The Practice of Buddhism in China*, 1900–1950 (1967), pp. 105ff.

Shinto: The object of spiritual D. is generally described as 'pacifying the soul' (*mitama-shizuma*). Exercises, aimed at transformation of inner-self, are preceded by others of a more material and mechanical nature, which aim at purification (*misorgiharai*). The rules of D. vary with the sects and schools, but generally include a vegetable diet, abstinence from alcohol, tea and coffee, and ritual bathing. (→ Confession). D.H.S.

J. Herbert, *Shinto* (1967), pp. 79ff.

(Christ.) →→ Abstinence; Fasting; Penance.

(Islam) In earlier times the → *muḥtasib* dealt

with offences of various kinds. Nowadays there is greater laxity; but in some countries, such as Saudi Arabia, Malaya, Morocco, account is taken of neglect of relig. duties, such as attending at the → Friday noon prayer, and observing fast of Ramaḍān (→ Fasting). Muslims in Malaya can be fined up to 80 dollars for failure to attend Friday noon prayer. Note is taken of people absent on three consecutive Fridays (*M.W.*, LVII:159). In most Muslim countries nowadays public opinion counts for more than any D. Where people are slack in observance no stigma seems to be attached to non-observance of duties; but elsewhere, though no official punishment may be meted out to offenders, people observe duties because it is respectable thing to do. When the writer lived at Sheikh Othman, near Aden, it was common to see people eating in public in Ramaḍān as month progressed, though this was not seen at begin. or end of the month. In Lahej, not far away, people were imprisoned when found breaking the fast. (→ Confession). (→→ *Ḥadd; 'Ulamā'; Muḥtasib*). J.R.

Disease (Buddh. thought) Acc. to popular B. trad., disease is one of the 'messengers' (*dūta*) from the heavenly beings (*devas*), reminding man of his mortal condition. (→ Deva-Dūta; → Medicine, in). Buddhism. T.O.L.

Disease and Medicine (China–Japan) In the popular religs. of E. Asia, whether originating in → Taoism, → Buddhism or → Shinto, nervous disorders and diseases are usually attr. to supernatural agencies. Consequently, in their cure, though medicines are extensively used, they are supplemented by such practices as faith-healing, exorcism, spiritism and provision by priests of charms, amulets, magical potions and the like.

The art of healing in China is said to have originated with the legendary emperor Shênnung (*c.* 2838 BC), who discovered the principles governing nature and the virtues of herbs and other medicinal remedies. The prime duty of a physician was to keep in harmony the five elements (→ Wu Hsing), of which a man's body is composed and to restore their equilibrium when upset. The chief Chinese medical work, the *Pên Ts'ao* or Herbal shows that drugs were mainly selected for their symbolical or emblematical significance: e.g. various parts of the peach, symbol of immortality and springtime and emblem of marriage, were believed to be efficacious for a variety of diseases; the wood of the peach tree was made into seals by Taoist priests for their talismen and amulets, and its branches used to strike fever patients to expel the spirit of fever. The fruit is a chief ingredient in the *elixir vitae* of the Taoists. Peach stones, carved in the shape of locks, are used as amulets, to secure children from disease and death. Other 'medicines', used for their symbolical significance, are the *ling-chih* or plant of immortality, ginseng, cinnabar, tiger's bones, bear's gall, hedgehog skins, turtle shells, and many dried insects. Taoism had its celestial ministry of medicine, presided over by Yao Wang, the king of medicine, who was assisted by numerous specialists and celebrities, the deified physicians of Chi. hist. Pien Ch'iao, reputed to have lived in 6th cent. BC, is worshipped by apothecaries and doctors, who offer incense to him as god of medicine. Yao Shih Fo, or the Buddha Physician (*Baishajyaguru*) is worshipped by Buddh. in China, Japan, Tibet and Manchuria. Having received healing powers from → Gautama, he dispenses spiritual medicine to those who worship him.

The arts of medicine were introduced into Korea and Japan by Buddh. monks, who took over Chi. medical practice. Until intro. of Western medicine, Chi. theories concerning disease and its cure were gen. accepted throughout Far East. Even today much of influence of modern Buddh. and Shinto sects in Japan is attributable to reputation of their practitioners for success in faith-healing, exorcism and the like. D.H.S.

S. W. Williams, *The Middle Kingdom*, 2 vols. (1883 and 1965), vol. 2, pp. 119–21; S. Couling, 'Pharmacopaeia', in *Encycl. Sinica* (1917 and 1965); E. T. C. Werner, *Dictionary of Chinese Mythology* (1932), 'Yao Wang' *et al.;* C. A. S. Williams, *Outlines of Chinese Symbolism* (1931), 'Medicine'. (→ Healing Divine).

Ditthi (Pali); **Dṛsti** (Skt.) Lit. 'a view', word used in Buddhism for a speculative opinion; it normally refers to one that is discountenanced, on ground that it is based not on reason, but on desire. Most prominent example is belief in the permanent, individual ego, or *atta*, ref. to as *atta-ditthi*, against which B. teaching was partic. directed. This (wrong or perverted) view takes 2 forms, acc. to B. teaching: either, the 'eternity-belief' (*sassata-ditthi*), i.e. that there is an eternal individual ego which is independent of physical and mental processes and persists eternally; or the 'annihilation-belief' (*uccheda-ditthi*), i.e. that human existence is nothing other than physical and mental processes, and will, at death of individual, be annihilated. The 1st *Sutta* in the → *Dīgha-Nikaya* of the Pali *Sutta Pitaka*, entitled *Brahma-jāla Sutta*, sets out 62 different false speculative 'views' or theories concerning nature of human existence, based on the initial false premise of existence of a permanent self or ego. T.O.L.

Nyanatiloka, *Buddhist Dictionary* (1956), pp. 47–8; T. W. Rhys Davids, *Dialogues of the Buddha*, *S.B.B.*, vol. II (1899), pp. 1–55.

Divination Man's time-consciousness, from dawn of culture, has caused preoccupation with the future. Man plans for foreseen contingencies, but is aware that much of future is menacingly unknown. He has naturally sought to penetrate this unknown by various means. As Eng. word, *ex.* Lat. *divinare*, indicates, these means have been of a supernatural kind. D. has been a widespread practice, and is traceable from first literate cultures. The means used divide into two main types (1) automatic (2) interrogation of divine intent. Under (1) may be grouped → astrology, → augury, → auspices. The principle involved is that pattern of future events is adumbrated in various ways, e.g. in celestial phenomena, the entrails of sacrificial victim, flight of birds, or forms taken by oil when dropped in water (Mesopot. practice). The omens given by such required expert interpretation. In Mesopot., where D. was ancient and elaborate, records of omens were kept and interpreted by professional diviners. The variety of such forms of D. are immense. Some approx. to (2), as, e.g. the *sortes sanctorum*, where Bible is opened at random to indicate divine will (thus St. → Francis of Assisi found his *Rule*), others depend on chance as in tossing a coin. D. under (2) presupposes that future is determined by god(s). A classic example is → Marduk's acquisition of Tablets of Destiny, implying Babylonian belief that deity had authority over future of world. It was assumed that deity might be willing to indicate or advise on future. Among such forms of D. are: oracles (→ Delphi); → dreams, often received while sleeping in temple (→ Aesculapius, Samuel's dream, I Sam. 3:1ff.); by drawing lots after prayer, as in Acts 1:23ff.; by some mechanical means, e.g. → Ephod, → Urim and Thummin. Another form of D. related to (2) was → necromancy, as in Odysseus' consulting of the dead Teiresuas (*Od.*, X, pp. 494–5) or Saul's learning future from the dead Samuel (I *Sam.*, 28:2ff.). (→→ Incubation; Africa, E. and W. Ritual Cults). S.G.F.B.

E.R.E., IV, pp. 775–830 (detailed survey of D. in various religs.); C. Conteneau, *La divination chez les Assyriens et les Babyloniens* (1940); *O.C.D.*, *s.v.; R.Ae.R-G.*, pp. 560–4 ('Orakel'), pp. 835–8 ('Traum'); *R.G.G.*^{3}, IV, 727–9 ('Mantik'); A. Guillaume, *Prophecy and Divination* (1938); G. Van der Leeuw, *La religion* (1948), pp. 219ff., 371ff.; M. Granet, *La pensée chinoise* (1950), pp. 173ff.; C. S. Burne, *Handbook of Folklore* (1914), pp. 124ff.; *S.O.*, II (1959), *Les songes et leur interpretation; S.O.*, VII (1966), *Le monde du sorcier, passim.; La divination en Mésopot.*, anc. etc. (XIVe Recontre assgr. internat., Strasbourg, 1965), Paris 1966.

Divorce (China–Japan) Until modern times, in China and Japan marriage was considered to be a contract between two families, and could be terminated without recourse to legal proceedings by the joint request and consent of the contracting parties. A woman could not divorce her husband, but might obtain redress for gross cruelty or neglect either through public opinion or recourse to law. The divorce of a woman by her husband was governed by Confucian teaching, enshrined in an ancient text known as the *Chia Yü* or *Sayings of Confucius.* Seven reasons were given for divorce—barrenness, adultery, jealousy, talkativeness, thieving, disobedience to husband's parents and leprosy. Divorce was not permitted, if (1) the woman had no parental home to return to, (2) if she had mourned the customary three years for her husband's parents, (3) if the husband, once poor, had become rich. In China, secondary wives and concubines had no such protection. In Japan divorce was common, especially among the lower classes. No reliable statistics are available concerning China, but under Communism, with female emancipation, and sexual equality, legal divorce proceedings could be instituted by both men and women, and this has led to an extra-ordinary increase in the divorce rate. D.H.S.

Guy Wint (ed.), *Asia* (1965), pp. 585–6; B. H. Chamberlain, *Things Japanese* (5th edn. 1905), pp. 503, 309–10; J. D. Ball, *Things Chinese* (5th edn. 1925), pp. 184–6. (→ Adultery).

(Islam) (*Talāq*). The Qur. mitigated pre-Islamic custom which allowed husband to cast off wife at any time, by instituting waiting period (*'idda*) of three menstrual courses; or, if at time of divorce wife was pregnant, until child was born. During this period the husband had to maintain her. There was also time for poss. reconciliation. If the divorce is final, the husband cannot remarry his divorced wife before she has been married to another and been divorced by him (Qur., II, 230). In → Sunnī law a man can repudiate his wife orally or in writing, and this is binding. The approved repudiation (*ṭalāq al-sunna*) may be by one utterance of repudiation which is revocable till end of *'idda* period, followed by two in subsequent months after first. The third makes the D. irrevocable. The disapproved variety (*ṭalāq al-bid'a*, i.e. of innovation) may be by uttering the repudiation three times one after the other, or declaring a single repudiation to be final. Though disapproved, this is legally binding. The → *sharī'a* normally gives right of divorce to husband; but wife may obtain divorce in certain circumstances. This is known as *khul'* (release in return for a payment made by wife). The husband must be agreeable to accept it, for wife cannot claim right to her freedom.

Some countries have made modifications in mod. times. By principle of *takhayyur* (selection), practices in different schools have been considered and adopted when thought suitable. The right of wives to D. has been instituted acc. to certain circumstances, such as husband's impotence, his suffering from a disease liable to harm wife, failure to maintain her, desertion, cruelty. In 1953 Syria enacted law that wives repudiated without just cause could be granted maintenance from husband up to a year. Tunisia in 1957 made D. by husband outside a court of law invalid, though court had to grant D. if he insisted. But wives were put on equality in this respect, so their claim for D. must be granted. A wife could, in addition, receive compensation for damage sustained through being divorced.

The → Shī'a Twelvers insist that repudiation must be expressed orally in presence of two witnesses, using *ṭalāq*, or another part of root. They have form of marriage (*mut'a*) not allowed by Sunnis or Shi'a Seveners. Instead of dower (*mahr*) paid to woman in a regular marriage, remuneration (*ujra*) is given, and period during which marriage is to last is specified. At end of period the marriage automatically ends, but either party may end it earlier. If it is husband who wants to end it, he can make no claim on any part of the *ujra* he paid; if it is woman, she must pay a proportionate amount of *ujra* to husband for period not fulfilled. J.R.

E.I., IV, pp. 636–40; Pareja, pp. 675f.; Coulson, *Law*, index; Gaudefroy-Demombynes, *Institutions*, ch. viii; Dickson, *Arab of Desert*, ch. viii, Querry, I, pp. 708ff.; II, pp. 1ff.; J. N. D. Anderson, 'The dissolution of marriage', *M.W.*, XLI (1951), pp. 271ff. (→ Adultery).

Divyāvadāna Buddh. anthol. of stories of the → *Avadāna* type; title means 'the heavenly Avadānas'. The collection incls. very old material derived from → Hīnayāna schools. The D., as it stands, is confused and disorderly, being work of a compiler who borrowed *verbatim* from number of earlier sources. One of more import. of these appears to have been entitled 'The Book of King Asoka', which is thought to have orig. in → Mathurā approx. 150–50 BC, and is known only in Chinese trans. Other materials are taken from lit. of various periods, the work of compilation having been carried out at some time during 4th cent. CE. One of best known and most import. stories is the strange tale of how → Māra, the Evil One, was 'converted' by a Buddh. monk named Upagupta; this is thought to have been based on a popular 'morality play' or Buddh. drama, well known in the early cents. T.O.L.

M. Winternitz, *Hist. of Indian Literature* (1933), vol. II, pp. 284–90.

Docetism Designation, from Grk. *dokein*, 'to seem', for tendency in Early Church to believe that Christ did not actually, but only seemed to, suffer and die on cross. The tendency, general among → Gnostics, stemmed from idea that Christ was wholly spirit and that his incarnate form was not real. D. was rejected as heretical. → Muhammad held a 'Docetic' view of crucifixion of Jesus (*Qur'ān*, IV, 156–7). (→ Jesus in Islam). S.G.F.B.

E.R.E., IV, *s.v.;* Kidd, *Docs.*, I, pp. 120–1; S. G. F. Brandon, *History, Time and Deity* (1965), pp. 189ff.

Doctrine, Buddh. → Dhamma. T.O.L.

Dōgen (CE 1200–53). Founder of the Sōtō division of the → Zen sect of Japanese Buddhism centred in the Eiheiji temple in the province of Echizen. The greatest figure in Jap. Zen, and venerated by all Japanese Buddh.s as a → bodhisattva. A man of incorruptible integrity, genuine humanity, creative thought and relig. intuition. Of noble parentage, he was orphaned when 7 years of age. Was ordained in CE 1213, and journeyed to China in 1223, where after much searching he achieved enlightenment under the famous → Ch'an master, Ju-ching (1163–1268). Returned to Japan in 1227; under his leadership the first fully independent Zen monastery, the Kōshōhōringji, was built in 1236. Here D. attracted many gifted disciples, including numerous lay people, both men and women. Teaching that the essence of man and all things is the Buddha-nature, which is realised by purification of the ego, the elimination of all selfish desires and complete surrender of self, D. gave precedence above all else to relig. practice. He cultivated the practice of Zazen, or sitting upright with legs crossed in meditation. He saw in Zazen the realisation and fulfilment of the whole law of Buddhism, since the unity of practice and enlightenment is rooted in the one Buddha-nature. Philosophically, his monistic pantheism equated the phenomenal world with the Absolute, leaving no room for transcendence; but, as a great religious leader, he stressed the importance of faith and relig. devotion to the Buddha. D. eliminated the endless stages on the way to salvation by finding in Zen a way of perfect unity. Unlike many Zen masters, D. advocated the diligent reading of the sūtras, the respectful veneration of sacred Buddh. objects, and considered the → kōan as of secondary importance. He condemned the sectarianism of Buddhism, and refused to recognise existence of the Sōtō sect as such. His outstanding literary work is the *Shōbōgenzō*, of which a modern edition was published in Tokyo in 1939–43. D.H.S.

H. Dumoulin, *A Hist. of Zen Buddhism* (1963).

Dogma *Ex.* Grk. *dogma*, 'opinion', from *dokein*, 'to

seem'. Orig. meaning was 'that which seems good'. In Chr. theology it came to mean relig. truth, estab. by divine revelation, and recognised and defined as such by Church. S.G.F.B.
R.A.C., III, 1257–60.

Dolichenus Orig. Hittite-Hurrite storm-god Teshub who survived into Roman times as → Jupiter Dolichenus; he is repr. as bearded man, flourishing a double-axe, mounted on bull. Related to Syrian god → Hadad. Cult of D. in Roman Empire was spread by slaves, merchants, and army. S.G.F.B.
R. Dussaud, *Les religions*, pp. 342, 392–3; *Kleine Pauly*, II, 115–6; F. Cumont, *R.O.*, pp. 104ff.

Dominic, St.; Dominican Order Dominic (1170–1221), a Spaniard, estab. special order of preachers for conversion of → Albigenses. A man of heroic, though austere, sanctity, D. was canonised (→ Canonisation) in 1234. His order (Ordo Praedicatorum, abbrev. O.P.), is known as Dominicans or Black → Friars, from black cloak worn over white habit. They are specially devoted to preaching and study. They staffed the → Inquisition, and their zeal against heretics earned title of *Domini canes*, 'dogs of the Lord'. The D. have been distinguished for their learning (→→ Albertus Magnus and Thomas Aquinas were D.'s), and the distinguished École Biblique, Jerusalem, is a D. institution. S.G.F.B.
D.C.C., pp. 413–4; G. G. Coulton, *Five Centuries of Religion*, II (1927), pp. 137ff.; D. Knowles, *The Religious Orders of England*, I (1950), pp. 146ff.; H. C. Lea, *The Inquisition of the Middle Ages* (1963 edn.), pp. 77ff.

Donation of Constantine During 8th–9th cent. a document was fabricated, showing that Constantine, regarded as first Chr. emperor, had conferred on Pope Sylvester I (314–35) primacy over all other patriarchs and bishops, dominion over Italy and Western regions, and had appointed him judge of all clergy. This so-called D. of C. was accepted as authentic and greatly strengthened papal claims to supremacy. Its falsity was first demonstrated in 15th cent. (→ Papacy). S.G.F.B.
D.C.C., pp. 414–5; *R.A.C.*, III, 376–8; *C.M.H.*, II, pp. 585ff.; D. Maffei, *La Donazione di Constantino nei Giuristi Medievali* (1964).

Donatism Schismatic movement formed in N. African Church in 4th cent.; it derived name from chief leader, Donatus. D. was theologically rigorist, holding that validity of → sacraments to be impaired by unworthiness of minister; it orig. in refusal to accept ministry of *traditores* (i.e. those who had surrendered Scriptures during Diocletian → Persecution). D. was also a political separatist movement of Africans from Roman rule. The movement engendered violent fanaticism, and though attacked by state and condemned by orthodox theologians such as → Augustine, it survived until Arab conquest of N. Africa in 7th–8th cent. S.G.F.B.
W. H. C. Frend, *The Donatist Church* (1952); *R.A.C.*, IV, 128–47.

Dooms Name given to medieval depictions of → Last Judgment. They were either sculptured on tympana of cathedrals and churches, or painted on interior walls, or in glass of windows. They followed a gen. pattern of presentation, gen. comprising three tiers of scenes: Advent of Christ; separation of the saved and damned; resurrection of dead. S.G.F.B.
J. Fournée, *Le Jugement Dernier* (1964); S. G. F. Brandon, *The Judgement of the Dead* (1967), ch. 5.

Dōshō (CE 629–700). The most prominent Buddh. leader in Japan in 7th cent., who went to China and studied → Yogacara teachings under the famous → Hsüan-tsang, and introduced the relig. philosophy of → Hossō to Japan. Though he left no writings, D. was a pioneer in Japan of Buddh. philosophy, practised mystical meditation, and spent the last years of his life in actively promoting the building of Buddh. monasteries, almshouses etc. He was a pioneer in the practice of → cremation in Japan. D.H.S.
M. Anesaki, *Hist. of Japanese Relig.* (1930).

Doukhobors Name of Russian sect founded towards end of 18th cent.: name means 'spirit-wrestlers'. S. Kapoustin, an early leader, claimed to be incarnation of Christ. Their beliefs are difficult to define; they are not orthodox and seem to incl. → metempsychosis: they are characterised by rejection of all civil authority and a tendency to communism. Persecuted, funds were found by philanthropists, incl. L. Tolstoi, to enable D. to leave Russia and settle in Canada, 1898. Their leader, Peter Verigin, changed their name to 'Christian Community of Universal Brotherhood'. Internal disputes caused splits: an extremist group calls itself 'Sons of Freedom'. Though hard-working and puritanical, their anarchism has caused Canadian authorities much trouble. The D. have gained notoriety by resorting to arson and nudism in protesting against authority. S.G.F.B.
E.R.E., IV, *s.v.;* J. Montgomery, *Abodes of Love* (1962), pp. 134ff.; S. Holt, *Terror in the Name of God* (1964); G. Woodcock and I. Abakumović, *The Doukhobors* (1969).

Dragon (China–Japan) Unlike the ferocious and evil creature of European mediaeval mythology, the D. in China and Japan is gen. a beneficient deity and held in high regard. He is the controller of the productive forces of moisture, the emblem of royalty and the symbol of greatness. D.'s are tutelary deities ruling over all rivers, marshes, lakes and seas, and exercising dominion over all fishes and reptiles. Their palaces are at bottom of ocean, N. of Mt. Meru. They have infinite powers of transformation, and of rendering themselves visible or invisible. As water-gods, they soar into the clouds and release the blessings of rain on the parched earth. They live in the heavens in the spring, returning to the deeps in autumn. From earliest times in China, the D. featured in relig. mythology and folk-lore of the people as most famous of symbolic animals, and chief of the 4 spiritual animals—the D., Phoenix, Unicorn and Tortoise. The character for D. (*lung*) is frequently found on the → Oracle Bones of the 2nd mil. BC.

There are many kinds of D.'s, which serve in many capacities. The great host of D.-kings were assimilated by the Chinese Buddhs. and Lamas with the mythical serpents (*naga*) of Hindu myths. In Buddh. and other writings there are long lists of D-kings: Celestial D.'s, who protect and support the palaces of the gods; Spiritual D.'s, who produce the wind and rain; D.'s, which guard Buddh. temples and care for Buddha's worship; D.'s, which dwell in the 5 regions of universe and in the 4 seas; D.'s, which guard the hidden wealth concealed from human eyes.

The D. is depicted with animal head, body and tail of a snake, 4 legs with bird-like claws, and wings. The fiery ball which he chases is variously described as the sun, moon, symbol of rolling thunder, emblem of → Yin and Yang, pearl of productivity. Since the Han Dynasty, the 5-clawed D. has been recognised as symbol of imperial majesty and power: the emperor's throne was called the D.-throne, and his robes and household articles were designed with the D.-motif. Temples erected in honour of the D.-king (*lung-wang miao*) were common throughout N. China. The D.-boat festival, on 5th of the 5th moon, popularly believed to have been instituted in memory of the poet-statesman, Ch'ü Yüan (*c.* 295 BC), probably owes origin to far more anc. ceremonies for propitiation of the D.-king in the hope that he would send the fructifying rains.

Japanese beliefs concerning the D. are derived from Chinese sources. D.H.S.

C. H. Plopper, *Chinese Relig. seen through the Proverb* (1926), pp. 44ff.; J. J. M. de Groot, *The Relig. System of China*, vol. 3, pp. 1194ff.; E. T. C. Werner, *Dictionary of Chinese Mythology* (1932), pp. 285ff.; C. A. S. Williams, *Outlines of Chinese Symbolism* (1931), pp. 109ff.

Drama, Relig. D. orig. from mimetic ritual; its earliest forms are repr. in Palaeolithic depictions of masked dancers prob. miming movements of animals (→ Cave Art). Anc. Egypt provides abundant evidence of ritual D. The mortuary ritual represented the sacred hist. of → Osiris (→ Abydos; → Ritual Perpetuation of Past), incl. poss. → judgment of dead. The → Shabaka Stone contains libretto of sacred D. performed at Memphis. The principle involved was that of sympathetic or imitative → magic, that 'like will produce like'. From such imitative action, designed to induce sense of communion with → Dionysos, Grk. D. prob. arose. The principle can be traced in sacred D. of many other peoples. The elaboration of primitive ritual D. into sophisticated forms such as Athenian D. and the Japanese 'No' repr. combining of relig. and entertainment motives. The comedy element, often very salacious, gen. derived from primitive fertility rituals with joy at rebirth of Nature. In its degenerate form in Roman Empire, D. still kept something of its relig. orig., thus meriting condemnation of Tertullian in his *De spectaculis* (*c.* 200). Chr. medieval D., in form of Mystery or Miracle Plays, combined instruction and entertainment. Their plots were taken from Bible, and often comprised series repr. hist. of man's salvation: the York, Chester and Wakefield cycles are most notable Eng. examples. Moral plays were also presented, dramatising moral conflict and man's destiny: *Everyman* is most famous example, and is related to the Flemish *Elckerlyc*. S.G.F.B.

E.R.E., IV, pp. 889–907; *R.G.G.*[3], II, 262–4; J. Harrison, *Ancient Art and Ritual* (1935); S. G. F. Brandon, 'Ritual Technique of Salvation in Anc. Near East', in *The Saviour God* (1963); Th. Gaster, *Thespis: Ritual, Myth and Drama in Anc. Near East* (1950); *O.C.D.*, pp. 216ff., 299ff., 915ff.; K. Young, *The Drama of the Medieval Church*, 2 vols. (1933); A. C. C. Cawley, *Everyman and Medieval Miracle Plays* (1956); M. D. Anderson, *Drama and Imagery in English Medieval Churches* (1963); *D.C.C.*, *s.v.;* E. O. James, *Christian Myth and Ritual* (1933); R. Merkelbach, *H.R.*, 3 (1964), pp. 175ff.

(China) The origin of relig. D. in China is found by some writers in the songs, dances and miming which accompanied relig. and court ceremonies in pre-Confucian days. Great festivals were accompanied by performances in which joys of harvest, triumphs of war, pleasures of peace, etc. were represented. In 8th cent. CE the T'ang emperor Ming Huang founded a college known as the Pear Garden for training of singers and dancers of both sexes. Whether these court entertainers were actors is uncertain; but 'youths of the pear garden' became term to designate the dramatic fraternity in China. It was during the T'ang dynasty that Buddh. monks propagated and popularised the faith by enacted scenes from Buddh. history and legend (similar to Christ. miracle plays), in towns and villages throughout the land.

But D., as repres. in mod. Chinese stage-play was not indigenous to China; it was intro. prob. from Tartar sources, during the Yüan (Mongol) Dynasty (1280–1368) CE. The greatest plays date from this period. They were mythological, hist. relig. and domestic in character. They inculcate justice and morality, and in their written form seldom, if ever, stray beyond bounds of decency. It was customary, in towns and cities, for wealthy patrons to engage troupes of actors to entertain the guests; but in villages dramatic performances are usually arranged by public subscription and assoc. with the village temples, the plays being performed in honour of the god's birthday.

From the days of the emperor Ch'ien Lung (CE 1736–96) until 20th cent., women were debarred from stage, and actors regarded as socially inferior. In mod. times these disabilities have ceased, and under Communism plays enacted by male and female cadres are devised to promote Communist ideology, patriotism and communal solidarity, and to pour scorn on what are deemed to be the superstitions of religion. The heroes are communist liberators, peasant patriots, ill-used women etc., whilst the villains are oppressive landlords, capitalists, immoral aggressors or idle and unproductive Buddh. and Taoist priests. D.H.S.

E.R.E., IV, pp. 878–9; H. A. Giles, *Hist. of Chinese Literature* (1927), pp. 256ff.; J. D. Ball, *Things Chinese* (5th edn. 1925), pp. 656ff.

(Japan) Drama in Japan was in its beginning closely associated with relig. It grew out of the pantomimic dance, known as *Kagura*, performed from antiquity at → Shinto festivals to sound of music. When dance and music were supplemented by spoken dialogue, the result was *Nō* drama, which, dating from about the 14th cent. CE, drew its inspiration from the Buddhism of the Nara period, and from Chinese and Indian influences. At first the Nō plays were purely relig. performances acted at temples and shrines and intended to propitiate Shinto and Buddh. divinities. Later Nō theatres came under the patronage of the shoguns. The librettos of most plays were the work of Buddh. monks or persons impregnated with the spirit of Buddhism. Embracing within their scope legendary lore, relig. sentiment and classical poetry, their object was to promote piety. The *kyōgen* or satirical farce, though acted on the same stage as the Nō, was different in character and had different actors. Whilst the Nō are permeated with relig. idealism, the *kyōgen* reflect a more secular realism.

It was late in the 16th cent. that the popular *Kabuki* theatres arose; through the great historical plays and dramas of life and manners produced by Chikamatsu (1653–1724) and others, the Jap. stage was influential in forming popular ideas of morality and relig. and inculcating the principles underlying → Bushidō, forming the ideal of the hero,—brave, loyal, patient under trial, quick to defend his honour. Yet, under the Shogunate, the Kabuki actors were despised and theatres considered too vile for gentlemen to enter. It was not till 1868 that Kabuki actors ceased to be ostracised. Since that time the theatre has won for itself a recognised and influential place in the Jap. world. D.H.S.

E.R.E., IV, pp. 888ff.; W. G. Aston, *Hist. of Japanese Literature* (1898), pp. 197ff.; B. H. Chamberlain, *Things Japanese* (5th edn. 1905), pp. 462ff.

Dravidians The Dravidian-speaking peoples of S. India have contributed importantly to develop. of Hinduism, esp. in relation to the → *bhakti* movement. The principal D. languages are Tamil, spoken in Madras state (Tamilnad) and N. → Ceylon; Canarese (or Kannaḍa) in Mysore State; Telugu in Andhra Pradesh; and Malayalam in Kerala. The existence of a pocket of Dravidian-speakers, the Brahuis, in Baluchistan in N.W. India, has suggested that → Indus Valley Civilisation was Dravidian; there are difficulties in the hypothesis, and presence of Muṇḍa-speaking peoples in N. India before the → Aryans complicates issue. There is doubt as to whether the D. languages are related to any other; but there is some ground for relating them distantly to the Finno-Ugrian group. The gradual Aryanisation of S. India superimposed a Sanskrit literary culture on the vernaculars, but at same time the D. may have contributed to N. Indian cults—e.g. worship of → Krishna may be, at least in part, of D. origin. The hymns of the → Alvars and others contrib. to a fervent pietism which was synthesized with Vedanta in medieval period by →→ Ramanuja, Madhva, Nimbarka and other import. relig. teachers of sourthern origin. The egalitarian → Lingayat sect expressed reaction against → Brahmin dominance; in recent times there has emerged a southern (esp. Tamil) nationalism which is to some extent anti-Brahmin (since Brahmins claim to be *par excellence* of Aryan descent). The D. style of → temple architecture differs somewhat from that of north. N.S.

Dreams The mysterious nature of the dream has naturally led to its being regarded as supernatural or numinous experience. It prompted belief that man could leave his body and have experiences apart from it. The fantastic, yet vivid nature of dream-imagery inevitably impresses the unsophisticated mind with conviction of having made contact with another order of existence. Anc. Egypt. lit. provides much evidence of such reaction: a notable instance is Thothmes IV's dream, under shadow of the Sphinx, of appearance of the sun-god who requested him to free his image (the Sphinx) for encroaching sand. Keys for interpretation of D. as foretelling future were produced in Egypt. Similarly Mesopot. lit. attests relig. importance of D. The Sumerian word Ma-Mu meant 'creation of the night', and was closely rel. to sleep and death. In Epic of → Gilgamesh, Enkidu dreams of his coming death. Gudea of Lagash practised → incubation to learn will of god Ningirsu concerning building of a temple. Elaborate keys to dream-interpretation were also compiled. Belief in D. as warnings of future abound in Bible (e.g. Joseph's dream and his ability as dream-interpreter (Gen. 40:5ff.); Paul's dreams (Acts 23:11; 27:23)). Grk. lit. provides abundant testimony to belief that D. had divine origin and were prophetic: the custom of → incubation was well estab. Dreams figure much in medieval Chr. lit., and could have either divine or demonic orig.; dreams of sexual nature were attrib. to latter source. S.G.F.B.

E.R.E., V, pp. 28ff.; *Les songes et leur interprétation* (*S.O.*, III, 1959); *R.G.G.*, VI, 1001–4; J. A. MacCulloch, *Medieval Faith and Fable* (1932), pp. 55, 183ff.; *E.J.R.*, p. 120; *H.D.B.*², *s.v.:* J. A. Hadfield, *Dreams and Nightmares* (1961).

(China) From anc. times popular relig. in China has emphasised importance of dreams for → divination, and as a channel of communication of warnings and messages from the spiritual world. The shaman-diviners of anc. China and their successors, the Taoist magicians, had a reputation for interpretation of dreams. A poem of the → *Shih Ching* (2:4:5) says:

'Divine for me my dreams. What dreams are lucky?
I dreamt of bears and snakes. The chief diviner divines thereon. The bears are omens of male children.
The snakes are omens of female children.'

Two theories lie at basis of Chi. belief in significance of D. The first is that human personality is constituted of same principles and forces which comprise the universe (→→ Yin-Yang; Wu Hsing). A sympathy and harmony exist between the human microcosm and the cosmic macrocosm. Celestial and terrestrial phenomena, the external visible signs of cosmic change, are reflected in the individual and during the quiescence of sleep produce D.'s. Therefore, the correct interpretation of dreams was of such importance as to warrant the appointment of special officials to enquire into dreams of emperors and officials. The second theory is that man possesses two souls, the → Hun and the → P'o, and during dreams the superior soul (*Hun*) leaves the body, and things dreamed are true objective realities which the soul encounters during its wanderings. The cosmic rhythms of Yin and Yang apply to the human personality, to the activities of day and waking and the quiescence of night and sleep. → Mencius (6a: 8, 2) speaks of the restorative powers of sleep upon the mind, so that, in the morning period between night and day, the mind feels most strongly those desires and aversions which are proper to humanity. D.H.S.

L. Wieger, *Hist. of Relig. Beliefs and Philos. Opinions in China*, (E.T. 1927), pp. 89–90; M. Soymié, 'Les songes et leur interprétation en Chine', *S.O.*, II (1959).

(Islam) Arabic uses *ru'ya* for 'vision', *ru'ya ṣāliḥa* for 'a good vision', *manām* gen. for a good dream and *ḥulm* for bad one. *Ru'ya* is used in Qur. xii:4, 101 of Joseph's dream; in xxxvii:105 of Abraham's vision; in xvii:62 of → Muḥammad's vision (? the → *Isrā'*); in xlviii:27 of Muhammad's vision of conquest of Mecca. Trad. reports Muhammad as saying, 'A good vision is a forty-sixth part of prophecy'; 'He who has seen me in a dream (*manām*) has seen me, for the devil does not appear in my form'; 'A good vision comes from God and a dream (*ḥulm*) from the devil'. Bad dreams should not be told; good dreams should be told only to a friend. J.R.

Mishkāt, pp. 962–8; Dickson, *Arab of Desert*, ch. xxiv; Canaan, *Aberglaube*, pp. 43f.; Wensinck, *Handbook*, pp. 61f.; T. Fahd, *S.O.*, II (1959).

(Japan) The → *Kojiki* and the → *Nihongi* have many instances of gods appearing to men in dreams and giving them instructions. There is a common belief that through the interpretation of D.'s it is possible to predict the future. D.H.S.

W. G. Aston, *Shinto* (1905), pp. 345–6; R. Sieffert, 'Les songes et leur interprétation au Japon', *S.O.*, II (1959).

Dress (Relig.) → Vestments. S.G.F.B.

Dress, Relig. (Buddh.) The primary feature of Buddh. relig. dress is its simplicity. The only distinctive dress used is that of the *bhikkhu* or monk, which in India and Ceylon and S.E. Asia is a saffron coloured cotton robe. This is usually presented to him by relatives or friends at his → Ordination, and renewed by laymen at annual ceremony when robes are presented to the → Sangha: the materials for these robes are usually spun and woven in course of one night by lay women of local village or township; the ceremony is a great social occasion. The robes consist of (1) the *antaravāsaka*, or sarong, which covers lower half of body from the waist (2) the *uttarasanga*, or upper garment, which in Thailand, is called also the *cīvara* (elsewhere gen. term for monks' clothing) (3) the *sanghāti*, a long piece of cloth about 8 ft. by 10 ft., folded into 12 folds, somewhat in shape of a stole, and worn over left shoulder, above the *uttarāsanga;* this is worn at relig. ceremonies, and only by fully ordained monks, not by novices. T.O.L.

(China) Much attention was given to the ceremonial robes in which the emperor, accompanied by high dignitaries and Confucian officials, performed the imperial sacrifices. The head-dress, the designs on the robes and the ornaments were all highly symbolical. Official costumes were coloured red, yellow, purple, blue or black, acc. to rank. A dragon design, on an embroidered plaque over the chest and also incorporated into the head-dress, was a symbol of kingly authority and power and reserved for imperial families. The phoenix design, symbol of peace and prosperity, was reserved for the empress. Each rank had its own distinctive design.

White is the colour of mourning, and during mourning ceremonies white or unbleached calico is worn, the head-dress being built up of folded strips of white linen.

Buddh. monks are distinguished by long flowing robes of yellow or sulphur green or black, with enormous sleeves and black collar. The head is shaven. The ceremonial robes of Lama priests have an outer garment of yellow cotton, collar and sleeves edged with blue. The under garment is red or purple. The robes of Taoist priests are usually blue, but other colours are allowed. Collar and sleeves are edged with black with small squares. The hair is gathered into a knob held together by a simple pin. D.H.S.

C. A. S. Williams, *Outlines of Chinese Symbolism* (1931), pp. 79–82; Anon., *Chinese Costumes* (1932).

(Japan) *Shinto.* Outside → Shinto temples the priestly robes are only worn for performance of sacred rites and ceremonies. Otherwise, in ordinary life, priests and laymen are indistinguishable. The priestly costume dates from the Heian period. A wide-split skirt (*hakama*), of which the colour may vary,—white, light-blue, and, for high dignitaries, purple silk—falls down to ankles. The upper part of the dress is a kimono with wide and long sleeves, over which other garments, similar in shape, may be worn. An informal outer robe of white silk or cotton (*jō-e*) may be worn by laymen on pilgrimage and on various other occasions. There is considerable diversity of headgear, the simplest type being the black *eboshi*. Black lacquer clogs are worn by priests, made from pawlonia wood, and worn when proceeding to ceremonies. For treading on very sacred ground both priests and laymen wear a special type of sandal (*waragi*), with a grass sole. The Shinto priests carry a flat wooden sceptre called *shaku*, and the way this is held and handled when officiating is minutely regulated by a strict ritual.

J. Herbert, *Shinto* (1967), pp. 143ff.

Buddhist. In anc. times silk and brocade were forbidden for priests because of interdiction against unnecessary taking of life; but in modern times ceremonial robes of Buddh. clergy are rich and ornate. In certain sects scarves are worn, into which are sewn sacred words deemed to possess magic power to ward off evil spirits. Certain of the more beautiful robes, worn by distinguished Buddh. officials, were determined by imperial decree. Purple is freely used for the outer garments of the superior clergy. Priests always carry a → rosary. D.H.S.

R. C. Armstrong, *Buddhism and Buddhists in Japan* (1927), pp. 24ff.

Drinks (Sacred) →→ Ambrosia, Haoma; Soma; Eleusimian Mysteries (*kykeon*).

(Sacred) (China–Japan) There is nothing analogous to the Aryan deification of → Soma in India and → Haoma in Persia. Wine and fermented liquors were considered to be gifts of the gods or deified ancestors to men; at the sacrificial feasts to gods and ancestors they were used as libations. In both China and Japan weddings were solemnised by the drinking of wine by bride and bridegroom from the nuptial cups. D.H.S.

Druj, The 'The Lie', → Zoroaster, Zoroastrianism. S.G.F.B.

Druids → Celtic (Pagan) Religion. S.G.F.B.

Druzes Movement connected with the → Fāṭimid Caliph al-Ḥākim (386–411/966–1021), who claimed to be a divine incarnation and who is believed to be in occlusion with promise of a return. The name Druze is connected with a Persian follower, al-Darazī, but another Persian follower, Ḥamza b. 'Alī, had a greater influ. on doc. The D. call themselves *Muwaḥḥidūn* (Unitarians). Ḥamza developed organisation of different classes of propagandists to whom ordinary believers were subordinate. Egypt proving an infertile soil for movement, it transferred to Syria where it provided background for peasant revolts. The chief D. districts are now in mountains of Lebanon and anti-Lebanon and in Ḥawrān; present-day numbers being estimated at about 200,000. Owing to being a close-knit community which allowed no intermarriage with outsiders, the D. have developed a distinct racial type. For cents. they have engaged in no proselytising. There are two main classes, the *'uqqāl* (sages) and *juhhāl* (ignorant). To belong to former involves daily relig. exercises, abstention from use of stimulants, and high moral character. This class wears distinctive dress with white turban. The most pious and learned are *shaykhs*, from whom each district has its chief (*ra'īs*) appointed. Weekly services are held on Thursday evenings. Their scriptures consist of number of letters from Ḥamza and others—*Rasā'il al-ḥikma* (letters of wisdom)—which were formed into a canon. Though secret, copies have been acquired and are in some libraries, but they are said to vary considerably. The rules applicable to gen. membership demand speaking truth to one another, mutual defence, renunciation of former religions, separation from unbelievers, recognition of unity of al-Ḥākim (called *mawlānā*—our lord), and submission to his orders. The most peculiar item in their faith is the → reincarnation of souls. D. do not take part in Islamic rites such as the → Pilgrimage or observance of fast of Ramaḍān; but they hold to → Shi'a practice of *taqiyya* (caution, dissimulation), whereby they may pretend to be Muslims when there is danger of persecution. They practise monogamy; divorce is not looked on with favour. J.R.

*E.I.*², II, pp. 631ff.; Pareja, p. 840; *A.J.S.L.*, LVI (1939), pp. 388ff.; LVII (1940), pp. 75ff.; S. de Sacy, *Exposé de la religion des Druzes*, 2nd edn. (1838); P. K. Hitti, *Origins of the Druze people and religion* (1928); N. Bouron, *Les Druzes, histoire du Liban et de la montagne haournaise* (1930); J. N. D. Anderson, 'Personal law of Druze community', *W.I.*, N.S. 1 (1952), pp. 1ff., 83ff.; M. G. S. Hodgson, 'al-Darazi and Hamza in origin of Druze religion'; *J.A.O.S.*, LXXXII (1962), pp. 5–20; J. R. Buchanan, 'The Druzes: their origins and development'; *T.G.U.O.S.*, XIX (1963), pp. 41ff.

Dualism The term can be used in two senses: (1) for interpretation of universe as battleground of principles of Good and Evil (2) for strict division of human nature into Spirit and Matter. The classic example of (1) is → Zoroastrianism. But Zoroaster separated into two contending principles an anc. Indo-Iran. conception of deity as ambivalent: e.g. →→ Varuna-Mitra; Zurvan; Vayu. In Hinduism → Shiva and → Vishnu are ambivalent, in that they are, each, creator and destroyer. → Yahweh orig. had an ambivalent aspect (e.g. Is. 45:7). After Exile, prob. due to Persian influence, → Judaism became dualistic owing to idea of the → Devil. This D., like the Zoroastrian, was not a logically consistent D., since it was believed that eventually Good or God would overcome Evil or Devil. Christianity inherited this modified Jew. D., regarding Devil as active until → Advent of Christ. An incipient D. found expression in Egypt in → Set, murderer of → Osiris, and in Apophis, dragon that nightly threatened sun-god. Phenomenologically, D. repr. man's reaction to ambivalent experience of world: modified D., such as Zoroast., and Jew.-Christ., reflect hope that Good will ultimately triumph. D. of (2) type first emerges in India in → Upanishads, in idea of → samsara. In the West, it first appears in 6th cent. in → Pythagoreanism and → Orphism, and was elaborated by → Plato. This D. was succinctly stated in Orphic saying: *sōma, sēma*, 'the body, a tomb'. The idea affected → Diaspora Jews (e.g. → Philo), and is reflected in teaching of → Paul, and → Gnosticism. The Chr. doc. of → Man repr. compromise between Jew. trad. of man as a psycho-physical organism and Orpheo-Platonic view. The most extreme form of (2) is found in → Manichaeism (→→ Albigenses; Catharists). This form of D. invariably regarded body as evil or contaminating to soul. The idea gen. underlies → metempsychosis. S.G.F.B.

E.R.E., V, pp. 100–14; *R.G.G.*³, 272–6; *R.A.C.*, IV, 334–50; G. Van der Leeuw, *La religion* (1948), pp. 302ff., 583ff.; Brandon, *M.D.*, *passim*, *History, Time and Deity* (1965), pp. 38–9, 63ff.; Zaehner, *D.T.Z.*, *passim;* J. Duchesne-Guillemin, *Ormazd et Ahriman: l'aventure dualiste dans l'antiquité* (1953); H.-C. Puech, *Le Manichéisme* (1949); H. W. Huppenbauer, *Der Mensch zwischen zwei Welten* (1959); U. Bianchi, *Il dualismo religioso* (1958), 'Le dualisme en histoire des religions', *R.H.R.*, 159 (1961); S. Aalen; *Die Begriffe 'Licht' und 'Finisternis' im Alten Test., im Spätjudentum und im Rabbinismus* (1951).

Dukkha (Pali); **Duhkha** (Skt.) Term used in Buddh. trad. for one of the 3 characteristic marks of existence or → Ti-Lakhana. Variously trans. into Eng. as 'suffering', 'ill', 'evil', 'unsatisfactoriness', the term covers all these meanings. The affirmation that all human existence is characterised by D. is the first of the Buddh. → Four Holy Truths. T.O.L.

Dumézil, G. Professor of Indo-European civilisation at the Collège de France, Paris, since 1949, is distinguished for the interpretation of → Indo-European society and relig. which he has propounded in many books. His method is that of comparative linguistics, by which he claims to discern two basic aspects of Indo-European ideology: (1) a tripartite organisation of society into sacerdotal and warrior castes and common people (2) a duality of nature and function in deity between light and darkness, order and violence, benevolence and malevolence, the priestly and the martial. D. has applied his thesis to →→ Iranian, Hindu, Greek, Roman, Celtic religs.; his chief books are mentioned in the relevant bibliogs. and under 'Aryans'. D.'s views have won the enthusiastic support of some scholars and the vigorous opposition of others. S.G.F.B.

J. Duchesne-Guillemin, *Western Response to Zoroaster* (1958), pp. 33ff.; R. N. Frye, 'Georges Dumézil and the Trans. of the Avesta', *Numen* (1960); F. B. J. Kuiper, 'Some Observations on Dumézil's Theory', *Numen* 8 (1961); C. S. Littleton, *The New Comparative Mythology, An*

Anthropological Assessment of Theories of G. Dumézil (1966).

Dumuzi → Tammuz. S.G.F.B.

Duty, Religious and Moral (China–Japan) Individual and social life, both in China and Japan, has been governed by → Confucian teaching of moral obligation, duty imposed by moral ordering of universe, by reverence for ancestors, and by the individual's position and status within various social groupings. Man's true wisdom and happiness are only to be found in a life of virtue, in which humanity, sincerity, loyalty, courage and temperance are stressed. Every human being is bound in a nexus of 5 social relationships, each with its appropriate duties: those of ruler and subject, father and son, elder and younger, husband and wife, friend and friend. In China the concept of → Li (Propriety etc.), and in Japan → Bushidō, inculcated a strong sense of moral duty among the ruling classes. → Buddhism in China and Japan taught that, though there was an unfailing law of retribution, whether in fate of individual or fortunes of family, it was the duty of each individual by strenuous effort to endeavour to overcome the fetters of → Karma by forsaking forgetfulness and delusion, and by renouncing 'self' for a universal self-hood. Linked to Confucian duty of obedience, the self-renunciation taught by Buddhism led to practice of virtues of tolerance and forbearance, and not infrequently to a passive resignation to circumstances. D.H.S.

Dvaita The dualist school of → Vedanta, whose chief exponent was → Madhva (13th cent. CE). As name implies, D. broke with any appearance of monism or non-dualism, and is thus strongly contrasted with doc. of → Sankara. The reason for this dualistic theology was in part desire to preserve Vaisnavite → *bhakti* religion, since notion of non-dualism, i.e. non-difference between the self and → *Brahman* or the divine reality made practice of worship ultimately meaningless. Acc. to D., God, selves and material objects are essentially distinct from one another. In regard to its cosmology and account of a plurality of heavens and hells, D. may have owed something to → Jainism, which had been strong in region of W. India from which Madhva came. The chief difference between God, on the one hand, and the world and eternal selves, on the other, is that God is self-dependent, while the others are 'other-dependent'. That is, they are subject to change and control by God, who brings about periodic re-creation of world, etc. (→ cosmology, Hindu). It is God who controls destinies of eternal selves, arranging for their various states of liberation or damnation. Since individuals have different characteristics, their careers are determined in different ways by → *karma;* but latter is an expression of God's predestinating activity. Some souls end up in varying grades of communion with → Viṣṇu; others undergo various forms of purgatory; others again are destined to everlasting damnation. This last idea is unique to D. among Hindu schools, which elsewhere treat → hells, however horrifying, as purgatorial in nature (where people work out effects of previous → *karma*). This is one among a number of features of D. belief which have suggested Christ. influence upon Madhva (St. → Thomas Christians were to be found along the West coast of India); an import. role is assigned to → Vayu ('Wind', 'Spirit') as intermediary between man and God, and some miracles ascribed to Madhva are reminiscent of those in N.T. But it is more prob. that such features can be explained otherwise. Thus idea of everlasting damnation is consequence of thesis that different souls ought to have different ultimate destinies, in accord. with their characteristics, while Vayu is of Vedic provenance. Like → Visistadvaita, D. is realist and combats illusionism of classical Advaita (→ *maya*): for if world is illusory, distinction between it and God collapses—it needs independent existence for God to stand in contrast to it. As well as encouraging devotionalism, D. emphasises importance of meditation directed towards communion with God. Among Dualist philosophers and theologians after Madhva, the most import. was the logician Jayatīrtha (13th cent. CE). As a relig. movement, D. gained great popularity in Kanara-speaking country, partly through its saints and hymnwriters known as *Dāsas*, lit. 'slaves', sc. of God, who preached loving dependence on Lord and a relig. egalitarianism breaking down caste distinctions. N.S.

J. Estlin Carpenter, *Theism in Medieval India* (1921); B. N. K. Sharma, *A History of Dvaita School of Vedanta*, 2 vols. (1960–2); H. von Glasenapp, *Madhwas Philosophie des Vishnu Glaubens* (1923).

Dvi-yāna → Yāna. T.O.L.

Dying-Rising Gods Descriptive title for deities, invariably male, whose *mythoi* tell of their deaths (accidental) and subsequent resurrections. Most D-R.G. are personifications of annual cycle of vegetation (→ Agriculture). They were usually assoc. with a Mother-Virgin goddess (→ Great Goddess), and their death and res. were ritually commemorated annually, together with sacred → marriage. Notable examples of D-R.G. are →→ Adonis; Attis; Osiris; Tammuz. (→ Myth and Ritual). S.G.F.B.

J. G. Frazer, *The Dying God* (1936), *Adonis, Attis, Osiris*, 2 vols. (1936), in *G.B.;* S. H. Hooke (ed.), *Myth and Ritual* (1932), *Myth, Ritual and Kingship* (1958).

E

Ea, Enki Mesopot. god of the waters, Enki being his more primitive name. E. ranked third in Mesopot. pantheon, and was in orig. a Sumerian god (→ Mesopot. Religion). He was a popular deity, and figured prominently in Sumerian creation myths, but rather as creator of mankind and inventor of civilisation than as cosmic creator. He was also god of wisdom and magic. His chief cult-centre was Eridu. He was father of → Marduk, and appears prominently in the → Enuma elish. He warned Uta-Napishtim of the → Flood. (→→ Adapa; Sumerian Relig.). S.G.F.B.

C.-F. Jean, *La religion sumérienne* (1931), pp. 45ff.; S. N. Kramer, *Sumerian Mythology* (1944), *passim;* E. Dhorme, *R.B.A.*, pp. 31ff.; Brandon, *C.L.*, ch. 3.

Earth-Mother It was natural that the earth should be imagined as feminine and be deified. It has been suggested that Paleolithic custom of crouched burials symbolised laying of dead in womb of E.-M. for rebirth. Most great goddesses have been assoc. with earth and its fecundity: e.g. the Grk. Gaia or Gē, →→ Demeter; Persephone; Ashtart; Atargatis; Cybele; Ishtar; Bona Dea; Ceres; Terra Mater; the Vedic Prthivi; the Aztec Coatlicue; the Teutonic Nerthus. The E.-M., besides being source of vegetation, was mistress of dead who rested within her (→→ Eleusinian Mysteries; → Metempsychosis). In many religs., a → Sky-Father impregnates, as rain, the E.-M. to produce crops, and ploughing and sowing were conceived as sex acts. → Egypt. relig. provides a curious exception to usual pattern: earth was a god, → Geb, and sky a goddess, → Nut. (→ Marriage, Sacred). (→ Great Goddess, The). S.G.F.B.

E.R.E., IV, pp. 129–31; *R.G.G.*[3], II, 548–9; A. Dieterich, *Mutter Erde* (1925[3]); E. O. James, *The Cult of the Mother Goddess* (1959); J. Przyluski, *La Grande Déese* (1950); M. Eliade, *Traité d'histoire des religions* (1949), pp. 211ff., E.T., *Patterns of Comparative Religion* (1958), pp. 239ff.; *R.Ae.R.-G.*, pp. 167, 201ff., 536ff.; *R.A.C.*, V, 1119–33.

Easter Acc. to → Bede, name derives from Anglo-Saxon spring goddess Eostre. E. was also widely known as Pasch, Lat. *Pascha*, from → Aramaic *Pasḥa* → 'Passover'. E. commemorating → Resurrection of Christ is oldest and greatest Chr. feast. It has a long liturgical preparation in Lent and Passion-tide. In R.C. and E. Churches, E. is preceded by vigil on Holy Saturday. In Early Church → catechumens were baptised early on E. day. The date of E. is determined by Paschal Full Moon; since it can vary from 21 Mar. to 25 Apr., there are current plans to fix it by law. E. customs are many and various, incl. exchanging of → eggs; the liturgical colour of E. is white. S.G.F.B.

D.C.C., s.v.; R.G.G.[3], IV, 1735–9; L. Duchesne, *Christian Worship* (E.T. 1927[5]), pp. 235ff.

Easter Island This mid-Pacific island is famous for its giant stone figures, the orig. of which has caused much discussion and speculation. Acc. to recent research of Thor Heyderdahl, the hist. of human settlement dates from *c.* CE 300, and was made by a non-Polynesian people. They worshipped a sun-deity, and erected stone images of medium size. Various aspects of their culture, incl. masonry, suggests a pre-Inca Peruvian origin. About 1100 this culture was suddenly replaced by another characterised by erection of giant stone images and cult of a bird-man. Earlier statues were overthrown and sometimes incised with image of bird-man. The statues, prob. of deified ancestors were erected on a *ahu* or burial platform, and had cylindrical crowns of red volcanic scoria. This so-called Middle Period ended *c.* 1680; its culture, despite break with that of Early Period, shows basic kinship therewith. Polynesians arrived *c.* 1500, and finally dominated island. The Late Period, *c.* 1680–1864, is marked by overthrowing of statues and decadence. Custom began of storing property in family caves, protected by guardian ancestral spirits called *aku-aku*. Despite intro. of Christianity, cult of the *aku-aku* continues. (→ Inca Religion). S.G.F.B.

T. Heyerdahl, 'Navel of the World', in E. Bacon (ed.), *Vanished Civilizations* (1963), *Aku-Aku* (E.T. 1958); *E.R.E.*, IV, *s.v.; Reports of Norwegian Archaeol. Exped. to Easter Island and East Pacific*, T. Heyerdahl *et al.*, 2 vols. (1961, 1965).

Eastern Church, The The designation has both a geogr. and hist. connotation. Geogr. it means that organised form of Christianity current in E. part of Roman Empire as divided by Emp. Constantine. It incl. the anc. patriarchates of Antioch, Alexandria, Jerusalem, and Constantinople, the last having been metropolis of the E. Empire (→ Byzantium), together with many national churches that resulted from political changes, and the Church of Russia, which was never part of the E. Roman Empire. Historically, the E.-C. means that part of Church which rejected pretensions of Papacy, causing schism between E. and W. Churches from 1054. The E.-C. is organised as a number of autocephelous Churches, sharing same faith and liturgical practice, although using various languages. It has carefully preserved → Apostolic Succession, which guarantees validity of → Sacraments. Owing to fact that E. Roman Empire was largely conquered by → Islam, the E.-C. suffered grave losses and in many lands its members lived as oppressed minority under Muslim rule. Consequently, theology of E.-C. was largely cut-off until modern times from challenge of modern scientific thought which has so profoundly affected W. theology. Closer relations have been fostered with non-R.C. Churches of W., esp. with → Anglican Church. The E.-C. also calls itself the Orthodox Church (→ Orthodoxy), thereby stressing its claim to preserve continuity of faith and practice with Early Church. Restoration of unity has recently been initiated by Pope Paul and the Patriarch of Constantinople. S.G.F.B.

E.R.E., IV, *s.v.; R.G.G.*[3], IV, 1705–19; L. E. Browne, *The Eclipse of Christianity in Asia* (1933); N. H. Baynes and H. St. L. B. Moss (ed.), *Byzantium* (1948); N. Zernov, *Eastern Christendom* (1961); Metropolit Seraphim, *Die Ostkirche* (1952); P. S. Sherrard, *The Greek East and the Latin West* (1959); E. Hammerschmidt *et al.*, *Symbolik des orthodoxen u. oriental, Christentums* (1962), *Symbolik des oriental Christentums*, Tafelband (1966); J. Danzas, *H.G.R.*, III, pp. 309ff.; *R.M.E.*, I, ch. 6.

Ebionites Name used first by → Irenaeus (*adv. haer.* I. 26:2) for Jew. Chr. heretics living in E. Jordan. The name prob. derives from Heb. *ebyōn*, 'poor', and may indic. some orig. connection with pre-70 Chr. community of Jerusalem (→ Jerusalem, Church of), whom Paul refers to as 'poor' (Rom. 15:26): such a designation was assumed in some Jew. pietistic sects. Although Jerus. Church perished in destruction of city in year 70, there were other Jew. Chr. communities in Palestine from which E. prob. descended. Since surviving evidence of E. comes from garbled and prejudiced accounts of later orthodox Chr. writers, or is inferred from → Clementine lit., the hist. and beliefs of E. are obscure but it is known that their → Christology was of → Adoptionist type and regarded as unorthodox. They were also hostile to Paul, and reported to use only Gosp. of Mt. The evidence is gen. consistent with what is known of orig. Jew. Christianity, which rejected Paul's Christology. Isolated from Cath. Christianity, the E. gradually disappeared. It is possible that → Muhammad acquired his knowledge of Christianity from E. (→→ Jew. Christianity; Nazaraeans). S.G.F.B.

E.R.E., V, pp. 139ff.; H. J. Schoeps, *Theologie u. Gesch. des Judenchristentum* (1949); *R.G.G.*, 297–8; G. Strecker, *Das Judenchristentum in den Pseudoklementinen* (1958); *R.A.C.*, IV, 487–500; S. G. F. Brandon, *The Fall of Jerusalem and the Christian Church* (1957[2]), *Jesus and the Zealots* (1967); L. E. Keck, 'The Poor among the Saints in Jew. Christianity and Qumran', in *Z.N.T.W.*, 57 (1966).

Ecclesiasticus Written orig. in Heb., prob. in Palestine, *c.* 180 BC, and trans. into Grk. Its author was Jesus, son of Sirach; hence work is also known as 'Ben Sira' or 'Sirach'. E. is incl. in → Apocrypha. An example of Jew. → Wisdom lit., E. is esp. significant as evidence of trad. → Yahwist outlook in 2nd cent. BC. S.G.F.B.

R. H. Pfeiffer, *Hist. of New Test. Times* (1954), pp. 352ff.; *D.C.C.*, *s.v.;* Schürer, *G.J.V.*, III, pp. 157ff.; S. G. F. Brandon, *M.D.*, pp. 145ff.

Ecclesiastes, Book of Title repr. Grk. and Lat. attempts to render Heb. title 'Qoheleth', meaning 'speaker in an assembly'. E. is trad. ascribed to Solomon. Dating from begin. of 2nd cent. BC, E. repr. the pessimistic estimate of life to which logic of → Yahwist doc. of Man led. The text was later emended to lighten this pessimism. S.G.F.B.

R. H. Pfeiffer, *Intro. to Old Test.* (1948), pp. 724ff.; *H.D.B.*[2], *s.v.; P.C.*[2], pp. 458ff.; Brandon, *M.D.*, pp. 144ff.; C. C. Forman, 'The Pessimism of Ecclesiastes', *J.S.S.*, 3 (1958).

Ecstasy Grk. word signifying state of being outside of body, a psychic condition known in cult of → Dionysos. Such abnormal states of consciousness, in which mind becomes both unaware of external stimuli and subject to extraordinary experiences, occur in many religs. The state can be induced by various means: e.g. drugs (→ Peyot Religion), orgiastic dancing (→ Dionysos), → flagellation, self-hypnotisation, rhythmic breathing (→ Yoga), gazing at bright light. In Cath. mystical theology it is recognised as a proper stage in mystic life, and many saints are recorded to have experienced it (→ Neoplatonism; Shamanism). S.G.F.B.

E.R,E., IV, *s.v.; D.C.C.*, *s.v.; R.A.C.*, IV, 944–87; M. Eliade, *Images and Symbols* (E.T. 1961), pp, 85ff,

Ecumenical Movement (Grk. *hē oikomenē*, 'the inhabited world'). Name for 20th cent. attempt to achieve Christ. unity on world-wide scale. The conscience of Church was never easy in face of disruption and secession. Attempts to heal breaches might be listed from early times to 2nd → Vatican Council (1962–66): e.g. the mediating theologians in → Arian controversy; the *Henoticon* of → Acacius of Constantinople (482) which vainly sought to reunite → Monophysites with Chalcedonian orthodoxy; Council of Florence, designed to reunite E. and W. (1438–45) when Turks were nearing → Constantinople; in → Reformation times, the work of Erasmus on the Roman and Melanchthon on the Lutheran side; within the new Prot. bodies, the Colloquuy of Marburg (1529), which tried unsuccessfully to heal sacramental rift between → Luther and → Zwingli, and Formula of Concord (1577), which, in spite of title, really sealed division of Lutheran and Calvinist. In Britain, abortive Savoy Conference of 1661 (Anglican-Presbyterian); the schools of thought within → Anglicanism, during last three cents., which have looked for reunion with Rome on one side and Nonconformist bodies on the other; the Lambeth Quadrilateral (1888), which gave four minimum essentials (in Anglican eyes) for reunion (Scripture, the Apostles' and Nicene → Creeds, the two Dominical → Sacraments, the Historic Episcopate); Anglican links with → Eastern Church (e.g. Anglican and Eastern Orthodox Churches Union, founded 1906), which led to recognition by E. Church of Anglican orders as being 'as valid as those of Rome'; the ill-fated Malines Conversations (Anglican-R.C.) 1921–5; the estab. of full communion between C. of E. and → Old Catholics (1932). The E.M. proper dates from the Edinburgh World Missionary Conference (1910), repr. almost all Prot. denominations, and setting itself the ideal of world-evangelism. Here were first heard famous names like J. H. Oldham (General Secretary), John R. Mott. The Conference created the Edinburgh Continuation Committee, which changed its name in 1921 to the International Missionary Council; this was finally merged with World Council of Churches (abbr. W.C.C.) at New Delhi in 1961.

Edinburgh initiated reversal of 1900 years of Chr. divisions. The impetus it unleashed was channeled into two main streams, 'Faith and Order' and 'Life and Work', world-conferences of former being held at Lausanne (1927), Edinburgh (1937), Lund (1952), Montreal (1963), and of latter in 1925 (Stockholm, where Archbp. Söderblom persuaded Ecumenical Patriarch of Constantinople to be joint President), and Oxford (1937)—this last, under challenge of Nazism, devoting itself to 'Church, Community and State', and marking final commitment of Anglicanism to the E.M. Archbp. Lang celebrated at corporate Communion for all delegates, proclaiming subsequently in St. Paul's Cathedral, London, the new conception of Church as 'one body in ideal if not yet in actual fact, with one life, one faith, one mission to the world'. In 1938 the W.C.C. was born, when at Utrecht a provisional constitution was adopted, with a Committee of which William Temple, master-mind of the E.C., was chairman. Into the W.C.C. were merged Faith and Order and Life and Work movements. Its first assembly was delayed by 2nd World War, through which however it was active; its delegates met Council of Evangelical Church in Germany at Stuttgart in Sep. 1945, where that Church made its famous declaration of war guilt. At Amsterdam (1948), the first assembly of W.C.C., with its Gen. Secretary, Visser t'Hooft, adopted as basis, 'a fellowship of Churches which accept our Lord Jesus Christ as God and Saviour', which was expanded at New Delhi (1961) into more comprehensive formula: 'a fellowship of Churches which confess the Lord Jesus Christ as God and Saviour acc. to the Scriptures and therefore seek to fulfil together their common calling to the glory of the one God, Father, Son and Holy Spirit' (N.B. the explicit refs. to Bible and → Trinity). Here certain Pentecostal Churches (largely American) were incl.

Actual church reunions achieved during this period incl. the United Church of Canada (1925—Presbyt., Methodist, Congreg.); reunion of various → Presbyterian bodies with C. of Scotland (1929); → Methodist Union in Gt. Britain (1932); estab. of C. of S. India (1947—Anglican, Presb., Meth., Cong.). Negotiations are in progress between → Congregational and Presbyt. (England) churches, the C. of E. and C. of Scotland, the C. of E. and Meth. Church (Gt. Britain), N. India and Ceylon, various African provinces. Other landmarks incl. the 1920 Lambeth Conference (Anglican) 'Appeal to all Christian People'; the 1946 Cambridge Sermon of Archbp. Fisher, suggesting that non-episcopal Churches might 'take episcopacy into their system' to prepare way for intercommunion; the 1964 Nottingham Youth Conference of British Counc. of Churches, demanding all-round reunion by 1970. However, rejection of scheme to implement reunion between C. of E. and Meth. Church by Convocation of Canterbury and York in July 1969, revealed continuing strength of causes of separation.

The causes of E.M. are many and various. The orig. impetus at Edinburgh, 1910, was missionary and evangelical: it was later intensified by the two world wars, attesting need of reconciliation as heart of Chr. faith; by rise of aggressive evangelism among other potential world-religions in 20th cent.; by birth of new national Chr. churches (e.g. S. India), where hist. propulsions to disunity in West. world are gen. irrelevant; by threat to relig. belief in gen. of mankind's 'coming of age' (→ Bonhoeffer), i.e. of 20th cent. mastery of material resources, facilitated by revolution in world-communications, and leading to agnostic humanism, in face of which a divided Christendom feels itself increasingly impotent.

The R.C. Church held aloof from E.M., at most keeping itself privately informed of proceedings from Edinburgh Confer. to that at New Delhi. A new era, seems to have been opened by short papacy of John XXIII and 2nd Vatican Council. Pope John asked for observers from Prot. and Orthodox Churches, and estab. a 'Secretariat for Promoting Christian Unity' under Cardinal Bea, which drew up 'Concilian Decree on Ecumenism' (*Unitatis Redintegratio*), seen by Pope John in draft before his death, and promulgated by successor Paul VI. The chapter-headings are: Catholic Principles on Ecumenism; the Practice of Ecumenism; Churches and Ecclesiastical Communities separated from Roman Apostolic See (East. and West.). It is wholly premature to assess full significance of this Decree, or to forecast its ultimate effects. It should be contrasted, e.g., with the Encyclical *Mortalium Animos* (1928) and the *Monitum* (1948) of the → Holy Office, which it supersedes. The following points are clear: (1) whole atmosphere has changed from isolated aloofness to brotherly and evangelical concern (2) emphasis is no longer on return to Rome as only poss. movement toward unity, but on common 'pilgrim' movement towards Christ (3) acceptance of non-Romans as 'communities' rather than mere individuals, and of work of → Holy Spirit within such communities (4) explicit recognition that for great hist. divisions 'men of both sides were to blame' (5) strong emphasis on centrality of Scripture in trad., and concern for biblical studies unfettered by dogmatic prescriptions. Conversely there is (perhaps inconsistently) no relaxation of claim that 'it is through Christ's Catholic Church alone . . . that the fulness of the means of salvation can be obtained', or of primacy of successors of St. Peter in jurisdiction over whole Church.

The abiding significance of E.M. may be thus summarised: (1) whole atmosphere, and, to some extent, visible pattern, of the Chr. Churches in their relations to one another has been decisively changed. This is most evident in united Chr. prayer (cf. the R.C. *Octave for Christian Unity* (18 Jan. *et seq*), now shared by almost all Christians) and work, espec. for social welfare and above all on Mission Field (2) the problems confronting E.M. lie in fields of *faith, church order*, and certain '*non-theological factors*', the whole lying within larger context of a hist. process which has tended of itself to harden and exacerbate Chr. divisions. Question of *faith* have always been recognised as fundamental (cf. Faith and Order, 1937: 'none is to be asked to . . . compromise its convictions . . . Irreconcilable differences are to be recorded as honestly as agreements', and the Vatican Decree's warning against a 'false conciliatory approach which harms the purity of Catholic doctrine'). But ecumenism, by forcing Churches to clarify their beliefs, has indirectly caused a resurgence of 'Confessionalism' on world-scale, and problem of relating this to quest for unity is unsolved. Questions of *order* (→ episcopacy, → Sacraments, authority of Bible and Tradition etc.) remain formidable divisive factors, esp. for those churches which link them closely with the faith itself. The fundamental barrier of episcopal/non-episcopal has been surmounted in S. India. The question of Papal supremacy remains for future. *Non-theolog. factors* (social and economic divisions, inherited habits and conventions of worship etc.) are more potent in historic Churches of West than elsewhere, and are losing their importance as secular context changes. The ultimate goal of E.M. remains undefined: either, one organic universal Church, or a small number of international Confessions in full communion and working in harmony. Uniformity (in expressions of faith, in Church order, ethics etc.) is everywhere disclaimed, and *variety in unity* is made target of ecum. endeavour. This, along with universal call for reunion through internal renewal, marks present stage and achievement of E.M. B.D.

G. K. A. Bell (ed.), *Documents on Christian Unity* (1st, 2nd, 3rd series), (1924–48); *Christian Unity: the Anglican Position* (1948); A. C. Headlam, *The Doctrine of the Church and Christian Reunion* (1920); R. Rouse and S. C. Neill (eds.), *A History of the Ecum. Movt., 1517–1948* (1954); K. D. MacKenzie (ed.), *Union of Christendom*, 2 vols. (1938); W. M. Abbott, S. J. (ed.), *The Documents of Vatican II* (1966); H. R. T. Brandreth, *Unity and Reunion. A Bibliography* (2nd edn., 1948); Journals, esp. *Irénikon, Oecumenica, The Ecum. Review; International Review of Missions.*

Education, Buddh. → Monasteries, Buddh. T.O.L.

(Islam) Islam has always emphasised importance of E.; but it has never been universal, and there has always been tendency to disapprove of educating girls in conventional school subjects, although there are records of erudite women from early times. Nowadays E. of girls is more general, even up to University standard. On other hand, as recently as Sept., 1964, the first girls' school in hist. of the Yemen was opened (*MW*, 1965, p. 174). The elementary school (*kuttāb*) was primarily for teaching pupils the Qur. by heart. Other subjects were reading, writing and elementary arithmetic. No attempt was made to explain meaning of Qur., the whole purpose being to learn parts, or whole, by heart. Such schools remain to present day; but west. methods of E. are mainly followed in most Muslim countries. Perhaps because of unintelligent nature of trad. elementary E., teachers in such schools were a despised class. More advanced E. incl. grammar, Qur. exegesis, Tradition, legal studies, in preparation for official career, or relig. leadership. In early times students frequently travelled to study under distinguished scholars. Interest in Greek philosophy, medicine and science developed in early Islam, and there was great activity in trans. works into Arabic. Institutions were later estab. in different countries. Niẓām al-Mulk founded the Nizamiyya College in Baghdad in 459/1067. He also founded colleges in Naysabur and other towns. The Mustanṣiriyya (631/1234) founded in Baghdad was also famous. Colleges were founded throughout Muslim world. Earlier institutions were connected with mosques. The Azhar mosque in Cairo, founded by Fāṭimid Caliph al-'Azīz (d. 386/996), was completed in 361/972; the educat. institution there has been famous down to mod. times. Students come from all parts of the Muslim world. Allowance has been made for teaching of the docs. of the four → Sunni legal schools; while for long it was a centre of conventional Islamic studies, in recent times scientific studies have been intro. Its head, al-Marāghī (d. 1365/1945) held that, while there was no desire to train scientists and physicians, it was useful to study mod. science and learn how it may be used in defence of faith. French and Eng. as well as Arabic are used for instruction. Women students have been accepted. J.R.

E.I., III, pp. 350–68; *E.R.E.*, V, pp. 198–207; Bayard Dodge, *al-Azhar, a millennium of Muslim learning* (1961), *Muslim education in medieval times* (1963); E. H. Douglas, 'The Muslim college of Malaya', *M.W.* (1967); pp. 57f.; H. J. Fisher, 'Early Muslim-Western education in West Africa', *M.W.* (1961), pp. 288ff.; A. M. M. Mackeen, 'Islamic studies: a university discipline', *M.W.* (1965), pp. 246ff., 297ff.; Y. B. Mathur, 'Muslim education in India (1765–1928)', *I.C.* (1967), pp. 173–83 (well documented); A. S. Tritton, *Muslim education in the Middle Ages* (1957).

Edwards, Jonathan (1703–58) Probably greatest and most influential thinker in early American Christianity, E. was also a devoted pastor, dedicated to → Calvinist trad. At an early age, he showed remarkable philosophical ability, apparently working out a complete system of Idealism before reading → Berkeley. Ordained to → Congregational church at Northampton, Massachusetts, in 1727, E. exercised powerful ministry, which was marked by a 'Great Awakening' of religious life in 1735, thus anticipating the 'Great Awakening' occasioned by visit of George Whitefield. During his 23 years ministry at Northampton there were many 'revivals', which E. carefully studied in his *Treatise concerning Religious Affections* (1746), which has been described as a masterpiece of 'spiritual diagnostics'. A strict Calvinist, E. became increasingly disturbed about genuiness of the 'conversion' of certain members of his church, and finally forbad their attendance at → Holy Communion. The decision led to dismissal in 1749; he settled at Stockbridge to work as missionary to Housatonic Indians and serve as pastor to small white community. There he wrote his most import. theological works: *Inquiry into the Modern Prevailing Notions respecting that Freedom of the Will which is supposed to be essential to Moral Agency;* on *Original Sin; Dissertation concerning the Nature of True Virtue; History of Redemption* (unfinished). In 1757 E. became President of the College of New Jersey, Princeton, but died following year. E. worked hard to stem the contemporary drift towards → Arminianism; after his death a 'New England Party' of philosophical Calvinists carried on his teaching. S.G.F.B.

E.R.E., V, pp. 221–7; *R.G.G.*³, II, 309–10; H. Shelton Smith, R. T. Handy, Lefferts A. Loetscher, *American Christianity*, I (1960), pp. 310ff.; W. S. Hudson, *Religion in America* (1965), pp. 64ff.

Egg The E. has been used in many religs. as (1) cosmogonic symbol (2) as symbol of rebirth or resurrection. Examples of (1) occur in Egypt. creation legend at → Hermopolis where sun-god emerged from E. provided by eight primordial beings, and in Orphic cosmogony (→ Orphism). Under (2) may be cited Etruscan tomb-paintings showing deceased holding E., and Chr. custom of giving Easter-E.s Connected with (2) is widespread folk-custom of giving E.s at spring festival, a fertility motif being involved. E.s also had purificatory value. S.G.F.B.

*R.G.G.*³, II, 342–3; M. Eliade, *Traité d'histoire des religions* (1949), pp. 353, E.T., *Patterns of Comparative Religion* (1958), pp. 413ff.; Brandon, *C.L.*, pp. 44ff., 184ff.; *R.A.C.*, IV, 731–45; *R.Ae.R.-G.*, pp. 162–4; E. Bacon (ed.), *Vanished Civilizations* (1963), ill. 19, 27; J. G. Frazer, *The Magic Art* (*G.B.*), II (1936), pp. 65, 78, 81ff.; *O.C.D.*, *s.v.;* Zimmer, *M.S.*, pp. 37, 104, 116.

Ego (in Buddhist Thought) → Anatta. T.O.L.

Egyptian Religion Egypt shares with Mesopot. the

distinction of providing the earliest written evidence of relig. The → Pyramid Texts and Shabaka Stone (→ Memphite Theology), dating *c.* 2400 BC, not only reveal current faith and practice, but preserve earlier trad. These texts are supplemented by much archeological data from temples and tombs: evidence for later periods is gen. varied and abundant. A brief outline of main features of E.-R. only is given here. E.-R. was polytheistic, but with tendency to → henotheism. Most deities were of local orig. and often had animal or → fetish forms. But cosmic deities (e.g. →→ Rē, sun-god; Nut, sky-goddess) appear in earliest records, together with abstract deities such as →→ Atum, Tefnet, 'moisture'. Of anc. but unknown orig. was → Osiris, → dying-rising god of the dead, who was always repr. as embalmed human figure. Often ref. is made, without specification, to the 'Great God', who was prob. Rē or Osiris. The priests of great sanctuaries composed cosmogonies designed to show precedence of their own god over others (→ Cosmogony, Egypt.). The state-god *par excellence* was Rē, but he was assoc. with gods of cities that attained political hegemony; e.g. Atum-Rē of Heliopolis; → Amun-Rē of Thebes. The priests of → Ptah of Memphis claimed that their god was actually Egypt itself. Rē had various forms, the most import. being that of → Horus, repr. as hawk or hawk-head man; (→ Scarab). The state-relig. was closely assoc. with kingship. The king was regarded as incarnation of son of Rē, being his vicegerent and chief minister. He was identified also with solar-Horus and Horus, son of Osiris. The exaltation of Amun in New Kingdom (1580–1098 BC) caused unsuccessful attempt of → Akhenaten to replace him by the → Aten. The ending of last native dynasty in 391 BC did not end state relig. The Ptolemies (330–30 BC) assumed relig. functions of pharaohs: the intro. of → Sarapis was intended to provide a deity uniting Egyptians and Greek settlers. Although state cult was assiduously served, the spiritual needs of Egyptians became centred on Osiris. By ritual identification with Osiris in the mortuary ritual, it was believed that resurrection from death could be achieved (→ Funerary rites, Egypt.). Osiris was also judge of dead (→ Judgment of Dead, Near East). There were many goddesses; most notable were → Isis and → Hathor.

E.-R. was highly organised, with professional priesthood and numerous temples, some of immense size. It was also many-sided. Magic flourished, while a → Wisdom lit. presented realistic view of life; there was also a trad. of → scepticism. The prospect of *post-mortem* judgment made for moral consciousness.

In Graeco-Roman times cult of Isis and Osiris spread to many other lands, assuming form of a → mystery-religion. E.-R. was finally suppressed in favour of Christianity by edict of Emp. Theodosius in CE 384; its influence on Christianity was considerable. (See Synoptic Index under 'Egypt'). S.G.F.B.

R.Ae.R.-G.; A. Erman, *Die Religion der Aegypter* (1934); *Bilderatlas*, 2–4 Lief. (1924); E. A. W. Budge, *The Mummy* (1925); J. H. Breasted, *The Development of Religion and Thought in Ancient Egypt* (1912); J. Černý, *Anc. Egypt. Religion* (1952); J. Vandier, *La religion égyptienne* (1949); H. Kees, *Totenglauben u. Jenseitsvorstellungen der alten Aegypter* (1956^2), *Der Götterglaube im alten Aegypter* (1941), 'Aegypten' in *R.-G.L.*, 10 (1928); S. Morenz, *Aegyptische Religion* (1960); S. A. B. Mercer, *The Religion of Anc. Egypt* (1949); H. Idris Bell, *Cults and Creeds in Graeco-Roman Egypt* (1953); Brandon, *M.D.*, ch. 2 (with biblio.); *C.L.*, ch. 2 (with biblio.); R. Anthes, 'Egypt. Theology in Third Mil. B.C.', *J.N.E.S.*, 18 (1959); W. B. Emery, *Archaic Egypt* (1961).

Eightfold Path (Buddh.) The holy, or noble, (*arya*) Eightfold Path (*atthangika-magga*) is a schematic description of the Buddh. life. It has been noted that this 8-fold exposition of the Buddh. way is not found in some of earliest Buddh. sacred texts, e.g. the → Sutta-Nipāta, and that it may therefore, be a later expansion of what in earlier texts is the *three*fold scheme of Buddh. life, viz: (1) initial faith, (*saddha*) which ultimately becomes wisdom (*pannā*); (2) morality (*sīla*); (3) concentration, or meditation (*samādhi*). Each of these aspects is subdivided: faith, into right understanding and right thought; morality, into right speech, right bodily action, and right livelihood; meditation, into right (spiritual) effort, right mindfulness and right concentration. At a more advanced stage of Buddh. practice, what was initially an attitude of faith, namely the way of understanding and thinking, accepted on trust from the Buddha, becomes, because of experiential verification, direct perception of what was initially accepted in faith, i.e. wisdom. The diversification of the orig. threefold scheme may be set out as follows:

8-*fold path*

(i) *faith*
- 1. right understanding
- 2. right thought

} = (iv) *wisdom*

(ii) *morality*
- 1. right speech
- 2. right bodily action
- 3. right livelihood

(iii) *meditation*
- 1. right effort
- 2. right mindfulness
- 3. right concentration

The items of the 8-fold path are not to be understood as steps or stages, each of which must be mastered before one can progress to next. The progression, if there is any, is from the initial, preliminary attitude of faith to moral living as a whole; thence (without passing beyond, or abandoning, moral living) to meditation, which is possible on basis of precedent faith and moral living. Within the groups of items, e.g. *morality*, the separately listed items are to be practised concurrently; thus also with items under *meditation*. The 3-fold structure of the Buddh. way is ref. to in the → *Mahā Parinibbāna Sutta* (I.12), where the Buddha, during last days, is repr. as discoursing to the monks 'on the nature of *sīla* (morality), *samādhi* (meditation), and *paññā* (wisdom)'—'great is the fruit, great the advantage of *meditation*, when surrounded by *morality*; great the advantage, great the fruit of *wisdom*, when surrounded by *meditation*.' This formula occurs in the *M.P.Sutta*, as Rhys-Davids comments, 'as if it were a well-known summary' and is constantly repeated in the *Sutta*.

The amplification of these 3 items into the 8-fold scheme may be seen as a natural process of expansion and exposition, for benefit of Buddh. disciples. By *faith* is meant (1) acceptance of the kind of *understanding*, derived from Buddha, viz. understanding the world and human existence in terms of the → 4 Holy Truths, and (2) right mental attitudes, viz, a turning away from attitudes based on sensuous desire, malice, and cruelty. By *morality* is meant (3) right speech, viz., saying nothing that is untrue; (4) right bodily action, viz., abstaining from taking life, from stealing, from unlawful sexual pleasure; (5) right livelihood, viz. avoidance of such occupations as that of butcher, trader in arms, or in intoxicants, or drugs, or any other occupation out of keeping with Buddh. principles. By *meditation* is thus meant: (6) right effort, viz, the effort to avoid evil and unwholesome states of mind, and to develop and maintain wholesome states; (7) right mindfulness, viz, a true awareness of physical body and of feelings (agreeable, disagreeable, or neutral) and of mental impressions; (8) right concentration, viz, the practice of 'one-pointedness' of mind (→ Samādhi). The outcome of practice of this 8-fold way is held to be the attainment of state of *wisdom*, that is state when right understanding and right mental attitudes become direct and immediate, where formerly they were based on *faith*. The 8-fold path is thus a systematic setting out of way that the tiniest germ of right understanding, beginning as an attitude of faith in the Buddha's knowledge, can grow eventually to highest state of enlightenment. T.O.L.

Eisai (Zenchō Kokushi, CE 1141–1215). The founder of Japanese → Zen Buddhism, who became a monk when still a boy, and was trained at the Tendai monastery on Mt. Hiei. Twice visited China (1168 and 1187), where, deeply impressed by the spirit of Ch'an, he became convinced that it could contribute towards a Buddhist awakening in Japan. E. received enlightenment in the Lin-chi sect, which he transplanted to Japan as Rinzai, building the first Rinzai temple, Shōfukuji, at Hakata in S. island of Kyushu in 1191. Opposed by Tendai monks on Mt. Hiei, he received protection and help from Shogun Minamoto Yoriie, who appointed him head of the Kenninji temple in Kyoto, built in 1202, which harboured Tendai and Shingon as well as Zen. E. intro. the Zen trad. to Kamakura, and became abbot of 3rd Rinzai temple, Jūfukuji. There he combined relig. fervour with national aspiration, expounded Zen meditation, and strove for recognition of Zen as an independent school. He composed a treatise on 'The Spread of Zen for the protection of the country'. Though not the first to introduce tea into Japan, he is regarded as the father of Jap. tea culture. D.H.S.

E. Takeda, 'Eisai', in *Gendai Zen-Kōza* (2nd edn. 1956), pp. 198–205; H. Dumoulin, *Hist. of Zen Buddhism* (1963).

Eka-Yāna → Yāna. T.O.L.

El Heb. word for God, meaning 'power'. In O.T., it is used in compounds such as El Shaddai (Gen. 17:1) = 'God Almighty'. El was also name of an import. Canaanite deity and appears often in → Ugarit texts, where he is creator and head of pantheon (→ Canaanite Religion). S.G.F.B.

*H.D.B.*², p. 334; R. Dussaud, *Les religions*, pp. 358ff.; J. Gray, *The Canaanites* (1964), pp. 70ff.; R. de Langhe, in S. H. Hooke (ed.), *Myth, Ritual and Kingship* (1958), pp. 135ff.; C. H. Gordon, in *M.A.W.*, pp. 185ff.

Elders (Buddhist) → Thera. T.O.L.

Election (Divine) Theological term for process whereby, it is believed, God has elected or selected certain people for → salvation or some glorious destiny. The most notable belief in E. occurs in O.T., acc. to which → Yahweh elected → Israel as his Chosen People. The call of → Abraham and the Sinai → Covenant form the basic episodes of the → Heilsgeschichte, in which the belief is embodied. A variation of idea is that of the Godly Remnant (e.g. I Kings 19:18), acc. to which, not the whole nation but only a faithful minority were elect. Christianity took over idea, esp. through → Paul, who identified Christians as the New Israel which inherited the E. of the Old Israel. The number of the elect was thought to be small (Mt. 22:14). In Chr. theology the doc. of E. has been closely related to that of → Predestination: the problem of those obdurate to the Gospel was solved on supposition that some were chosen by God for salvation and some not. The doc. of E. was basic to teaching of → Calvin, and characterised → Puritans. The idea also occurs in Islam, → Free-will (Islam). S.G.F.B.

H. H. Rowley, *The Biblical Doc. of Election* (1950); *H.D.B.*², pp. 238ff.; 841; K. Galling, *Die Erwählungstraditionen Israels* (1928); H. Wildberger, *Jahwes Eigentumsvolk* (1960); *R.G.G.*³, II, 610–21; W. Helfgott, *The Doc. of Election in Tannaitic Lit.* (1954).

Eleusinian Mysteries Celebrated at Eleusis, near Athens, from remote antiquity; prob. surviving from → Aegean relig. Acc. to *Homeric Hymn to Demeter* (7th cent BC), → Demeter instituted the E.-M. to commemorate her visit to Eleusis in quest of → Persephone. The rites, held annually, were elaborate and impressed initiates with sense of participating in divine mysteries concerning the gods, life and death. They were given assurance of a blessed afterlife, prob. in subterranean paradise since Demeter and Persephone were → chthonian deities. Information about the rites and their meaning in relevant texts is meagre and unreliable (much is Chr. polemic); excavation of site has added little. It is known, however, that initiation had three stages and lasted two years. The final stage (*epopteia*) incl. a culminating revelation. The E.-M. doubtless served spiritual needs not met by → Olympian gods: they survived until forcible suppression of paganism in 4th cent. in favour of Christianity (→ Mystery Religions). Our lack of information is prob. due to initiates keeping vow of secrecy. S.G.F.B.

N. Turchi, *Fontes*, pp. 41ff.; G. E. Mylonas, *Eleusis and the Eleusinian Mysteries* (1961); *R.A.C.*, IV, 1100–05; *Kleine Pauly*, II, 243–5; C. Picard, *Les religions préhelléniques* (1948).

Elkesaites Jew. Chr. → Gnostic sect, orig. in E. Jordan *c.* 100. They claimed special revelation given by a human or supernatural being called Elkesai, prob. meaning 'hidden power', which was embodied in *Book of Elkesai*. The E. held Docetic view of Christ (→ Docetism), carefully kept Mosaic Law, rejected Paul's Epistles, and emphasised redeeming efficacy of → baptism. Knowledge of them comes chiefly from Chr. sources, mostly from →→ Hippolytus and Epiphanes, and is prob. distorted. Relation of E. to → Ebionites is obscure. They may poss. be related to Sabeans mentioned in the → Qur'ān. S.G.F.B.

E.R.E., IV, *s.v.; R.A.C.*, IV, 1171–86; H. J. Schoeps, *Theologie u. Gesch. des Judenchristentums* (1949), pp. 325ff.; *R.G.G.*³, II, 435.

Elohim Heb. word meaning 'gods', but used in O.T. for 'God', and syntactically treated as sing. The pl. form thus used prob. developed from regarding one god as repr. all gods, as in use of Akkadian pl. *ilâni* 'gods' in → Amarna tablets. E. was also used for superhuman beings or powerful dead as in case of Samuel (I Sam. 28:13). S.G.F.B.

W. O. E. Oesterley and T. H. Robinson, *Hebrew Religion* (1930), pp. 117, 132–3; J. Pedersen, *Israel*, IV (1940), pp. 499ff.; *H.D.B.*², p. 334.

Elohist, or E Term used in O.T. research for a literary trad. characterised by use of → Elohim for → Yahweh. E. is regarded as work of member of N. Kingdom of Israel, dating from *c.* 8th cent. BC. This E. hypothesis, which is gen. accepted as explaining one of the sources of → Pentateuch, is rejected by → Scandinavian School. (→ Yahwist). S.G.F.B.

R. H. Pfeiffer, *Intro. to Old Test.* (1948), ch. 4; W. Rudolph, *Der 'Elohist' vom Exodus bis Joshua* (1938); *H.D.B.*², pp. 745ff.; *P.C.*², 136f., 139b.

Elyon Heb. word meaning 'most high'. It is used in Gen. 14:18ff. with → El as 'God Most High', and was prob. name of Jebusite god of → Jerusalem. In Deut. 32:8 a significant distinction is made between E. and 'sons of El' (*P.C.*², 243c). E., named 'Elioun', is given Grk. title of *Hypsistos*, 'Highest' by Philon of Byblos, and repr. as patron-god of Byblos. E. was assimilated with → Yahweh in development of Heb. relig. S.G.F.B.

Dussaud, *Les religions*, pp. 358ff.; *P.C.*², 157d; *Kleine Pauly*, II, 226–8; Clemen, *P.R.*, pp. 24, 60f.

Emigrants (*Muhājirūn*). Term used of those who left Mecca for Medina because of their faithfulness to → Muḥammad's teaching. There was an earlier emigration to Abyssinia, said to be due to persecution. Some returned to Mecca after a time; others remained, and later many came to Medina. The emigration to Medina was the import. one, the → *Hijra*, from which the Muslim calendar is reckoned. The Qur. speaks in commendation of the E. e.g. ii:215 says, 'Those who have believed and those who have emigrated and striven in God's way have hope of God's mercy'; ix:20, a later passage, speaks more strongly: 'Those who have believed and emigrated and striven with goods and person in God's cause are of higher rank in God's estimation. They are the blessed'; viii:76 indicates that term E. applies not only to those who emigrated at time of *Hijra*, but incl. people who accepted Islam later and emigrated. Acc. to many trads., no one could claim title after conquest of Mecca, if he had not possessed it before. It is said that at first a system of brotherhood was instituted in Medina by which → Helpers made brothers of poor E. as means of providing support for them; but some at least of the E. preferred to be independent. When Muhammad died, the two sections had retained their individuality, as the suggestion was made that each party should appoint its own leader, a disastrous suggestion which was soon rejected, followed by appointment of → Abū Bakr as Caliph. J.R.

E.I., III, p. 640; Guillaume, *Life*, pp. 221ff.,

234f. and *passim*; Watt, *Mecca*, index, *Medina*, index; Wensinck, *Handbook*, pp. 98, 156f.

Empedocles (*c.* 493–433 BC) A native of Acragas, Sicily, E. combined many roles: philosopher, scientist, statesman, and mystagogue, claiming divine powers and honours; it is evident that he soon became a legendary figure. For hist. of relig., E. is import. for assoc. with → Orphism and belief in → metempsychosis. The latter belief, expressed in his *Purifications*, conflicts with explanation of universe, in *On Nature*, which negates idea of immortal soul. Various theories have been given for this contradiction. E.'s theology is really a deification of universal principles discerned in cosmic phenomena, together with belief that human nature incorporates something divine. S.G.F.B.

G. S. Kirk and J. E. Raven, *The Presocratic Philosophers* (1960), pp. 320ff.; W. Jaeger, *The Theology of the Early Greek Philosophers* (1947), pp. 128ff.; *Kleine Pauly*, II, 258–60.

Emperor Worship → Ruler Worship. S.G.F.B.

'Emptiness' (Buddh. doc.) → Śūñya. T.O.L.

Encratites Grk. designation given to Chr. sects, mostly heretical, professing extreme forms of → asceticism, incl. abstention from flesh-meat and wine, and sometimes from marriage. Many →→ Gnostic, Ebionite, and → Docetic sects were so described. S.G.F.B.

E.R.E., IV, *s.v.; R.G.G.*³, II, 494; *R.A.C.*, V, 343–65.

Engishiki Or 'Ceremonies of Engi'. Jap. collection of 50 books originating in the Engi era (CE 901–22), and first published in 927. It is a principal source of information for ceremonies of → Shinto, giving minute descriptions of Shinto rituals. It incl. 27 ancient *norito* or ritualistic prayers, read by officiating priests in services before the deities of Shinto shrines. D.H.S.

W. G. Aston, *Shinto, the Way of the Gods* (1905); D. C. Holtom, *The National Faith of Japan* (1938); Jean Herbert, *Shinto* (1967), pp. 38ff.

Enlightenment (Buddhist) → Bodhi. T.O.L.

Enlil The second god of Sumerian pantheon. Of unknown orig. (En-lil means 'lord of breath, or spirit'), E. was regarded as divine ruler of world. His cult-centre was Nippur. E. is gen. presented as a fierce deity in texts, and was responsible for the → Flood: he does appear in more benevolent guise in certain Sumerian culture myths. His consort was Nin-lil ('Lady of heaven and earth'). E. seems to be displaced by → Marduk in the → Enuma elish. (→ Sumerian Relig.). S.G.F.B.

S. N. Kramer, *Sumerian Mythology*, *passim;* C.-F. Jean, *La religion sumérienne* (1931), pp. 36ff.; Jastrow, *Aspects*, *passim;* B. Meissner, *Babylonien u. Assyrien*, II (1925), *s.v.* ('Ellil'); E. Dhorme, *R.B.A.*, pp. 18ff.

Ennin (CE 794–864). Third patriarch of great Buddhist monastery on Mt. Hiei in Japan, he emphasised the occult mysticism of → Shingon. His diaries, containing account of his travels in T'ang Dynasty China, provide an important source for study of Chinese → Buddhism at period of its great expansion in that country. D.H.S.

E. O. Reischauer, *Ennin's Travels in T'ang China* (1955).

Enoch, Books of Pseudepigraphic writings, attr. to O.T. patriarch Enoch (Gen. 5:24), who prob. derived from Mesopot. trad., were composed in 1–2 cents. BC (→ Pseudepigrapha). Three collections of these survive: (1) 'Ethiopic Book of Enoch', so-called from Eth. trans. of Heb. or Aramaic orig., in which it is alone wholly preserved. It purports to record revelations given to E. about orig. of → evil, → angels, nature of → Gehenna and Paradise. The work is composite. The section called 'Parables' or 'Similitudes' (chs. 37–71) is important for N.T. study because of refs. to → 'Son of Man'. (2) 'Slavonic E.', also called 'The Book of the Secrets of E.'. The orig. Grk. survives only in Slav. trans. It describes E.'s ascent to heaven and visions there. (3) so-called 'Third E.', in Heb., deals, *inter alia*, with angels and → Sheol. It shows signs of → Gnosticism and anti-Chr. polemic. S.G.F.B.

Charles, *A.P.*, II (1913); *The Book of Enoch* (1921); R. H. Pfeiffer, *Hist. of New Test. Times* (1949), pp. 75ff.; E. Schürer, *G.J.V.*, III, pp. 190ff.; *D.C.C.*, *s.v.; R.G.G.*³, III, 222–5; M. Black, 'Eschatology of the Similitudes of Enoch', *J.T.S.*, III (1952).

Enthusiasm *Ex.* Grk. word *enthousiasmos*, meaning state of being possessed or inspired by God, and akin to *entheos* and *enthous*, 'having God in oneself'. The idea prob. orig. from cult of → Dionysos; later in → mystery-religions and mystical philosophy, *enthousiasmos* became a theological conception. In 17th cent. CE word was used in connection with sects claiming divine inspiration, and, owing to much undesirable phenomena, it acquired an opprobrious meaning. S.G.F.B.

E.R.E., IV, pp. 316–21; R. A. Knox, *Enthusiasm; A Chapter in the Hist. of Religion* (1950); *R.A.C.*, IV, 955 (g)ff.

Enûma Elish Opening words, meaning 'When on high', of Babylonian Creation Epic, by which it was known. The Epic was composed at Babylon in honour of → Marduk, and was recited ritually twice during the → *akitu* or New Year Festival. An Assyrian version substitutes → Ashur for Marduk. Date of composition is unknown: recent opinion puts it in Kassite period (*c.* 1750–1171 BC) rather than 1st Babyl. dynasty (1894–1712). The E.-E. envisages primordial situation as a watery chaos called Ti'âmat (sea) and Apsû (sweet-water). These entities are personified, and from their union the gods are born. Consequent on killing of Apsû by → Ea, Ti'âmat prepares to destroy the gods. They are saved by Marduk, who kills Ti'âmat, and makes world from her body. The creation of man is described, and the building of Marduk's great temple at Babylon. The E.-E. is, in effect, an *apologia* for precedence of Marduk over older gods, and reflects Babylon's hegemony in Mesopot. S.G.F.B.

A.N.E.T., pp. 60ff.; A. Heidel, *The Babylonian Genesis* (1951²); H. W. F. Saggs, *The Greatness that was Babylon* (1962), pp. 409ff.; Brandon, *C.L.*, pp. 91ff.; B. Landsberg and J. V. Kinnier Wilson, *J.N.E.S.*, XX (1961), pp. 154ff.; W. G. Lambert and S. B. Parker, *Enuma Eliš, the Bab. Epic of Creation: the Cuneiform Text* (1966).

Envy (Buddh. view) Envy (Pali, *issā*) is regarded in Buddh. trad. as a mental factor (*cetasika*), producing unwholesome → Karma. It comes 9th in a list of 14 unwholesome mental factors given in the → *Abhidhammattha-Sangaha*, (Pt. II, §2, III). T.O.L.

Ephesians, Epistle to Trad. attr. to → Paul during his captivity in Rome, the authenticity of this Epistle is much questioned by modern scholars, chiefly because of its differences in style and teaching from Paul's other Epistles: there is also doubt whether it was orig. addressed to Ephesus. It has been suggested that it was composed by editor of Paul's writings as a preface to the collection at end of 1st cent. S.G.F.B.

*H.D.B.*², *s.v.; P.C.*², pp. 980ff.; *R.G.G.*, II, 517–20.

Ephod In later Priestly lit. (→ Pentateuch), the E. was part of high priest's ornaments (e.g., Ex. 28:6ff.), but in older sources it seems to be an object or garment connected with → Divination (Heb.). At → Ugarit an *'pd* was the garment of a deity. It is poss. that after condemnation of images in Israel, the E. served as surrogate for image of → Yahweh, in divination. (→ Urim and Thummin). S.G.F.B.

R.G.G., II, 521–2; M. Burrows, *What Mean These Stones?* (1957), p. 216.

Epictetus (*c.* CE 55–135) Stoic philosopher, once a slave. He taught in Rome, until 89, when Emp. Domitian banished philosophers; he continued teaching in Nicopolis (Epirus) until his death. E. was more interested in → Stoicism as philosophy of life than as metaphysics. He addressed himself to all men, seeking to make them self-reliant and immune to vicissitudes of fortune. He saw Divine Providence in unity and order of nature: hence, man must accept pain and death as part of pattern of universe. E.'s teaching was preserved in his *Manual* (*Encheiridion*), which greatly influenced → Marcus Aurelius; it is also important for study of begin. of Christianity. S.G.F.B.

The Discourses of Epictetus, trans. and ed. W. A. Oldfather (Loeb Class. Library, 1926, 2 vols.); *O.C.D.*, p. 324; *E.R.E.*, V, *s.v.; R.A.C.*, V 599–681.

Epicureans, Epicurus, (342–271 BC) Grk. philosopher, who settled in his native Athens in 306 and opened school of philosophy. He lived quiet retired life with pupils, who venerated him. A small part only of his voluminous works have survived. Adapting atomic theory of Democritus, E. analysed universe into atoms and the void. Everything, incl. gods and men, consists of atoms moving in various patterns in void. Death is dispersal of atoms constituting a person: hence it involves personal extinction. The gods, made of finest atoms, live in blessed serenity outside world and untroubled by it. E. aimed at freeing men from fear of death and the gods. He advised a quietism, avoiding causes of fear and trouble: imperturbability (*ataraxia*) was the desired state. E.'s greatest disciple was Lat. poet → Lucretius (*c.* 94–55 BC), who expounded E.'s philosophy in his didactic poem *De Rerum Natura.* Lucretius regarded E. as the saviour of men for freeing them from relig. (e.g. *op. cit.*, I:62ff.); he (L.) uses 28 arguments against immortality of soul. The Apostle → Paul encountered E.'s at Athens (Acts 17:18). S.G.F.B.

E.R.E., V, *s.v.;* VIII ('Lucretius'); *O.C.D.*, *s.v.; Kleine Pauly*, I, 314–8; *R.A.C.*, V, 681–819; A.-J. Festugière, *Epicurus et ses dieux* (1946).

Epiphanius (*c.* 315–403) Bp. of Salamis, whose writings, despite their gen. unreliable nature, contain much valuable historical material. Most notable are: the *Panarion* or 'Refutation of all the Heresies', and the *De Mensuris et Ponderibus.* S.G.F.B.

Grk. text in Migne, *P.G.*, xli–xliii; K. Holl, Epiphanius-Ausg. (*Ancoratus* and *Panarion*, *G.C.S.*, pp. 25, 31, 37 (1915–33); J. E. Dean, *Epiphanius' Treatise on Weights and Measures* (1935); *R.A.C.*, V, pp. 909–27.

Epiphany *Ex.* Grk. word *epiphaneia*, meaning 'manifestation'. Chr. feast held on 6 Jan., which orig. in E. in 3rd cent. to commemorate baptism of Christ. From 4th cent. E. ranked with → Easter and → Pentecost as chief Christ. festivals. In W. Church, E. was assoc. with manifestation of Christ to Gentiles, repr. by the → Magi. The idea of *epiphaneia* had a long hist. and found expression in many forms in the religs. of the anc. Near East. S.G.F.B.

D.C.C., *s.v.; R.A.C.*, V, 832–909.

Erinyes Avenging spirits in Grk. mythology. Their origin is obscure: assoc. with blood-guilt suggests they were ghosts of the slain; or they may have orig. as personifications of → curses which were regarded as having baleful potency. S.G.F.B.

O.C.D., *s.v.;* E. Rohde, *Psyche*, I (1898), pp. 268ff.; E. R. Dodds, *The Greeks and the Irrational*

(1963), pp. 6–8, 21 (37), 38ff.; *Kleine Pauly*, II, 358–9.

Erōs Grk. god of sexual love, both between sexes and homosexual. In → Homer, E. is violent physical desire that 'looses the limbs and damages the mind'. → Hesiod makes E. one of oldest and most powerful of gods, and Parmenides conceives him as a cosmic principle. The concept of E. is import. in thought of → Plato. Hellenistic poets depicted E. in a lighter, and often frivolous, manner. His bow and arrows are first mentioned by → Euripides. E. appears in idyllic form in beautiful myth of → Psyche given by → Apuleius (*Met.* 4.28). E.'s assoc. with → Aphrodite is as old as Hesiod: at Athens they had a joint sanctuary, in which → phallic symbols have been found. In art, E. seems to grow younger: starting as youth, he is depicted as playful putto in Hellenistic times. S.G.F.B.

O.C.D., *s.v.; Kleine Pauly*, II, 361–3; *R.A.C.*, VI, 306–42; Brandon, *C.L.*, pp. 167ff.; E. Panofsky, *Studies in Iconology* (1962), pp. 95ff.

Eschatology Term, *ex.* Grk. *eschata*, 'last things', used to denote beliefs concerning death, judgment, purgatory, heaven and hell. With variations, this eschatological pattern occurs in all religs. and is essential part of doctrine of → Man. S.G.F.B.

E.R.E., V, *s.v.; R.G.G.*³, II, 650–5.

(Buddh.) Buddhism has no E. in the strict sense of term, as this is understood in Christianity, since there are no ultimately 'last things' so far as cosmos as whole is concerned (→ Eternity, Buddh.). So far as individual human existence is concerned, acc. to Buddh. thought, the consummation of this is in the 'deathless' state of → Nibbāna. Buddh. → cosmology has its heavens and hells, but no one is condemned to eternal existence in these; eventually the inhabitants of both the Buddh. heavens and hells will return to other levels of existence; in this respect the Buddh. hell is more akin to Christ. → Purgatory. Only human beings can achieve *nibbāna*, hence the only strictly 'eschatological' moment for the Buddhist is moment when a man achieves awakening or enlightenment. (→ Bodhi). T.O.L.

(China–Japan) (→ Ages of the World; → Blest, the abode of; → Death, Interpretation of). Confucianism is without an eschatology. There is no teaching concerning a Day of → Judgement, or of a catastrophic end to world and its renewal, and no millennial ideas (→ Chiliasm). Such E. ideas as the Chinese possess were intro. into China by → Buddhism, and largely taken over and adapted by Taoists. Buddhism, with its concept of rebirth, and cyclical view of → Time, envisaged great cosmic cycles (*kalpas*) through which the soul proceeds in countless rebirths until its final absorption in → Nirvana. Both Buddhism and → Taoism teach that the soul, immediately after death, is led before tribunal of ten judges of the dead, who decide its fate with strict impartiality, after which it is taken to live for a period in one of the heavens or hells of Buddhist or Taoist mythology. Millennialist theories, connected with Chinese Buddhism, grew up with cult of → Maitreya (Mi Lo Fo), intro. into China in 4th cent. CE. Acc. to these theories, 3,000 years after the Buddha, Buddhism will have reached such a state of decline that Maitreya will appear and establish his millennial kingdom, and a new cycle of life with hope of redemption for all living creatures. It is thus that Chi. Buddhism inculcates hope that, at the last hour of a final dispensation (*mo-fa*), a great saviour and renewer will descend from the → Tushita heaven to establish on earth a new era, leading to universal salvation. D.H.S.

K. L. Reichelt, *Truth and Tradition in Chinese Buddhism* (1927), pp. 87; 186ff.

→ Shinto is without an eschatology, having but vague ideas concerning the state of the dead. Buddhist E. ideas were similar to those of Chinese Buddhism. (→ Death, Interpretation of (Japan)). D.H.S.

(Christ.) The first Christians believed that the → Parousia was imminent, at which world would end, the dead be raised, and judgment follow, with its consequences of Heaven or Hell. Nonfulfilment of Parousia led to idea of Immediate Judgment for each person after death, expiation in → Purgatory, until Second → Advent of Christ (→ De-eschatologisation). Then the dead would be resurrected for the → Last Judgment, at which the eternal fate of all, in Heaven or Hell, would be decided. (→ Judgment of Dead, Christian). S.G.F.B.

R. H. Charles, *Eschatology* (1913²); J. A. Fischer, *Studien z. Todesgedanken in der alten Kirche*, I (1954); A. Stuiber, *Refrigerium Interim: die Vorstellungen vom Zwischenzustand u. die früh christliche Grabeskunst* (1957); *R.G.G.*³, II, 665–80; S. G. F. Brandon, *M.D.*, ch. 6; *The Judgment of the Dead* (1967), ch. 6; P. Hoffmann, *Die Toten in Christus* (1966).

(Egypt) E. constituted a major concern of → Egypt. Relig. Egyptians believed that resurrection from death could be achieved (→ Funerary rites, Egypt), that there was a judgment of the dead, followed, if condemned, either by a second death or eternal punishment, or, if justified, by eternal beatitude in company of either → Rē or → Osiris. (→ Judgment of Dead, Near East). S.G.F.B.

Kees, *T.*; S. Morenz, *Aegyptische Religion* (1960), pp. 192ff.; E. A. W. Budge, *The Mummy* (1925); S. A. B. Mercer, *The Religion of Anc. Egypt* (1949), ch. 19; Brandon, *M.D.*, ch. 2; *The Judgment of the Dead* (1967), ch. 2.

(Greek) The trad. view of human destiny, deriving from → Homer, was that the personality disintegrated at death, and only the shade (*eidōlon*) descended to a miserable consciousless existence in → Hades. The → Eleusinian Mysteries, however, promised a happy afterlife, while → Orphism and → Plato taught that → metempsychosis was the common lot, from which the initiated or philosopher won deliverance. Belief in *post-mortem* judgment was vague and diverse in imagery and purpose. (→ Judgment of Dead, Greek; →→ Epicurus; Stoicism). S.G.F.B.

E. Rohde, *Psyche*, 2 vols. (1898); G. Pfannmüller, *Tod, Jenseits u. Unsterblichkeit in der Religion, Literatur u. Philosophie der Griechen u. Römer* (1953); F. Cumont, *After Life in Roman Paganism* (1959 edn.); Brandon, *M.D.*, ch. 5; *The Judgment of the Dead* (1967), ch. 5.

(Hebrew) → Yahwism orig. taught that death irreparably ended life in any significant sense, and that what survived went to a joyless existence in → Sheol. Since this was the common lot, there was no *post-mortem* judgment. Towards end of 2nd cent. BC, belief in a resurrection and judgment of dead was estab. in certain circles, and after 70 CE became orthodoxy. This E. was bound up with → Apocalyptic, with emphasis more on Israel's redemption and punishment of Gentiles than on individual destiny. Resurrection was physical, acc. to Heb. doctrine of → Man. E. also involved idea of → Messiah, whose advent would end existing world-order. Sheol was grad. transformed into place of punishment. (→ Judgment of Dead, Jew.). S.G.F.B.

R. H. Charles, *Eschatology* (1913²); E. Schürer, *G.J.V.*, II, pp. 496ff.; Ch. Guignebert, *Le monde juif vers le temps de Jésus* (1935), pp. 162ff.; *R.G.G.*³, II, 655–65; Brandon, *M.D.*, ch. 4; *The Judgment of the Dead* (1967), ch. 4.

(Hindu Ideas) Vedic ideas of the afterlife were transformed by Upanisadic and later Hindu adoption of doc. of → rebirth. In the → Vedic hymns a distinction is drawn between those who go to heavenly world of the fathers, transported by purifying power of → Agni, the fire-god active in cremation of dead (→ Funeral Customs, Hindu), and those who go below to darkness of the house of clay. The ideal of heaven (*svarga*), as the goal, persisted in the → *Mimamsa* school, though it tended to be replaced more gen. by ideal of → *moksa* as belief in rebirth spread. The possibility of re-death is canvassed in the *Bṛhadāraṅyaka* → *Upaniṣad*, where for first time the new E. came explicitly into the Brahmanical trad. Henceforth, the afterlife is conceived within framework of operation of → *karma*, and souls are destined for rebirth on mundane plane or in some heaven or hell (purgatory). Nearly all these states are impermanent, however long the soul may suffer torment in one of the *narakas* (→ hells, Hindu) or enjoy bliss in the lower heavens. The growth, however, of → *bhakti* religion elevated idea of heaven as abode of God and locus of liberation to a prime position. However, upper-class Hindu (→ twice-born) funeral customs implied earlier Vedic picture of the afterlife, since offerings made to dead and ancestors were regarded as a mode of sustaining them on their upward journey and preventing their unlucky and inauspicious lapse into status of ghosts (*preta*). N.S.

(Iran) → Zoroaster spoke of 'Chinvat Bridge' (→ Bridges) as the awful ordeal facing dead, and of a *post-mortem* retribution of molten metal. In later → Zoroastrianism, this E. was greatly elaborated: after crossing Chinvat Bridge, the soul met its conscience, beautiful or hideous acc. to its conduct. The cosmic struggle between → Ohrmazd and → Ahriman would end with resurrection of dead, judgment, and punishment of wicked, after which all would undergo an ordeal of molten metal, though the just would not suffer. Finally Evil would be destroyed and all, incl. purified sinners, be renewed for eternity. (→→ Ages of World, Iran; Judgment of Dead, Iran). S.G.F.B.

R. C. Zaehner, *D.T.Z.*, chs. 1, 15; J. D. C. Pavry, *The Zoroastrian Doctrine of a Future Life* (1929); Brandon, *M.D.*, ch. 8; *The Judgment of the Dead* (1967), ch. 7; M. Molé, 'Ritual et eschatologie dans le mazdéisme', *Numen*, VII (1960).

(Islam) →→ Balances; Barzakh; Dābbat a'-arḍ; Dajjāl; Hell; Hour (Last); Jesus Christ; Judgment of dead; Intercession; Paradise; Resurrection; -Ṣirāṭ. J.R.

(Mesopot.) The Mesopotamians, although they thought the gods had withheld immortality from men, believed that the dead, horribly transformed, went to *kur-nu-gi-a*, 'Land of No-return', where they lived joylessly in dust and darkness. This was the common lot: hence there was no *post-mortem* judgment or hope of heaven. (→→ Mesopot. Relig.; Gilgamesh, Epic; → Judgment of Dead, Mesopot.). S.G.F.B.

A. Heidel, *The Gilgamesh Epic and Old Test. Parallels* (1949²); Ebeling, *T.L.*, I, *passim*; M. Jastrow, *Aspects*, pp. 351ff.; B. Meissner, *Babylonien und Assyrien*, II (1925), pp. 142ff.; Brandon, *M.D.*, ch. 3; *Judgment of the Dead* (1967), ch. 3.

Esdras, Books of Considerable confusion exists in enumeration of books attr. to E., owing to different ordering in → LXX, → Vulg. and Eng. trans. (Esdras is Grk. for → Ezra). The → Apocrypha, A.V., R.V., R.S.V. entitle them as I and II E. (1) I E. = I Esdras in LXX = III Esdras in Vulg. This is a composite Grk. work taken from Heb. Bible, and an unknown source, dating *c.* 200–50 BC (2) II E. = III Esdras in LXX = IV Esdras in

Vulg. A composite work, its most notable part lies in chs. 3–14, known as the 'Ezra' or 'Salathiel Apocalypse': it is post-CE 70 and reflects Jew. reaction to destr. of → Jerusalem (70); section 7.30–98 is important for Jew. Chr. → Eschatology. The LXX II Esdras = Heb. books of Ezra-Nehemiah. S.G.F.B.

D.C.C., *s.v.; H.D.B.*², pp. 40, 882–3; R. H. Pfeiffer, *Hist. of New Test. Times* (1949), pp. 81ff., 233ff.; *R.A.C.*, VI, 595–611; *R.G.G.*³, II, 694–700; Schürer, *G.J.V.*, III, pp. 232ff., 326ff.

Eshmun God of Sidon (Phoenicia), assimilated by Greeks with Asklepios (→ Aesculapius). E. was → chthonic fertility god, assoc. with → Astarte. He became an important god at Carthage (→ Carthaginian Relig.). (→ Adonis). S.G.F.B.

D. Harden, *The Phoenicians* (1962), p. 86; W. W. Baudissin, *Adonis and Esmun* (1911); G. Contenau, *La civilisation phénicienne* (1949), pp. 92ff.; G.-G. Lapeyre and A. Pellegrin, *Carthage punique* (1942), pp. 137, 140; G. Charles-Picard, *Les religions de l'Afrique antique* (1954), pp. 125ff.

Eskimo Religion The Eskimo, or *Innuit* ('people', 'men') form a distinctive race of N. American aborigines. Their origin has been sought in Asia, and there are small groups in E. Siberia; otherwise they occupy an area extending from Alaska to E. Greenland, Labrador and Newfoundland. They are closely related to the Aleuts (→ Aleut Religion). Their culture and relig. were until recently determined by their Arctic and sub-Arctic environment, being based on hunting and fishing. E. relig. is centred on fundamental concept that every object is endowed with a spirit, or *inua* (lit. 'his man': 3rd pers. poss. of *inuk*, 'man'). There were various classes of *inua*, the most powerful being Sila (*silap inua*, 'The inua of the air'), who possessed many characteristics of a → High God; independent spirits were called *tornat*. These did not, however, receive worship. The two most import. deities, around which the cult was centred, were concerned with land and sea-creatures respectively. Aningákh was a moon-god, lord of land-animals and patron of hunting; Sedna, the most clearly defined of E. deities, was mistress of the seas. The myth of Sedna tells how she lived with her father, rejecting all suitors. Finally she married a man-animal, first in form of a dog and then in form of a petrel. Her father rescued her from the petrel, and took her away in his kayak, but the petrel caused a great storm to spring up; in fear her father threw her overboard and as she clung to the gunwale, he cut off her fingers, one by one. These became the sea creatures—seals, walruses and whales. Sedna herself sank into the sea, becoming the guardian of the creatures. For purposes of cult, she has to be propitiated in order to release the hunters' prey. She is easily annoyed, partic. by breaches of → taboo (partic. the many taboos involving women) and must then be placated by a shaman. The cult was almost entirely in the hands of professional shamans, or *angakkut* (sing. *angakok*). The E. shamans were believed to have guardian spirits at their command, and be able to project themselves in spirit to regions of the living and dead (incl. the depths of sea). They had no special costume, but did have their own language, a mixture of archaic Eskimo and gibberish; their main item of equipment was the drum, through which contact was made with spirit-world (→ Shamanism). Every part of human body was believed to be endowed with soul-force, sickness being a sign of loss of soul; the lost soul might then be sought, and the sickness cured, by the shaman. Otherwise the E. seem to have believed in the dual soul (→ North American Indian Religion), one soul passing on death to land of the dead, while the other might be reincarnated; there was little consistency on these points. The Alaskan E. believed that the fortunate dead had their home in the Aurora Borealis, and held periodical 'Inviting-in Feasts', to which the souls of dead were called. E.J.S.

G. H. Marsh, *A Comparative Survey of Eskimo-Aleut Religion* (Anthropol. *Papers of the Univ. of Alaska* III, 1954); *E.R.E.*, V, pp. 391–5; *R.G.G.*³, II, 690f.

Essenes Jew. ascetic sect dwelling in W. area of Dead Sea, recorded by →→ Philo, Josephus, and Pliny. Organised on monastic lines, the E. prob. orig. in 2nd cent BC and were exterminated during Jew. War of CE 66–70. They zealously observed ritual laws of → Torah, observed strict discipline of life, incl. three years' novitiate, and had goods in common. Though orthodox Jews, they are alleged to have reverenced sun and believed in → metempsychosis. The E. have been identified by many scholars with the Qumran Covenanters (→ Qumran). S.G.F.B.

E.R.E., V, *s.v.;* Schürer, *G.J.V.*, II, pp. 556ff.; *Kleine Pauly*, II, 375–8; *H.D.B.*², *s.v.;* A. Dupont-Sommer, *Les écrits ésséniens découvertes près de la Mer Morte* (1959), pp. 31ff.; J. Klausner, *Jesus of Nazareth* (E.T. 1929), pp. 207ff.; *R.G.G.*³, II, 701–3; S. Wagner, *Die Essener in der wissenschaftlichen Diskussion vom Ausgang des* 18 *bis zum Beginn. des* 20 *Jahrhunderts* (1960).

Etana Acc. to Sumerian King List, E. was king of Kish, 'who ascended to heaven'. The legend of his ascent on an eagle is preserved in Akkadian and Assyr. texts. Its motif may be aetiological: E. sought the 'plant of birth', to found a dynasty. S.G.F.B.

A.N.E.T., pp. 114ff., 265; B. Meissner, *Babylonien u. Assyrien*, II (1925), pp. 189ff.; Dhorme, *R.B.A.*, pp. 312ff.

Eternity (Buddh.) The nearest approach to conception of eternity in Buddh. thought is the *kappa* (Pali) *kalpa* (Skt.), which is an inconceivably long period of time. The k. is divided into 4: period of world-dissolution; period of chaos; period of world-formation; period of world-continuation (*AN.IV.*156). A simile, used in a discourse of Buddha. (*SN.*XV.5) is as foll: 'Suppose, O monks, there was a huge rock of one solid mass, one mile long, one mile wide, one mile high, without split or flaw. And at the end of every 100 years a man should come and rub against it with a silken cloth. Then that huge rock would wear off and disappear quicker than a *Kappa.*' Of such world-periods (*kappas*), acc. to Buddha there have been many hundred thousands. In the Buddh. view of things there is no termination to process of world-dissolution, chaos, world-formation, continuation, nor to the number of Buddhas who will appear in course of this process. (→→ Buddhas (other than Gotama), Creator (Buddh.)). (→ Ages of the World). T.O.L.

W. M. McGovern, *Manual of Buddhist Philosophy*, vol. 1, *Cosmology* (1923).

Ethics (Buddh.) In Buddh. trad. the principles governing human conduct relate the characteristic *condition* of humanity (suffering, unease, ill (→ Dukkha), caused by the basic evil of → Desire) to the recognised *goal* of Buddh. endeavour, viz. complete enlightenment and → nirvana. Buddh. ethics thus favours those attitudes and kinds of behaviour which help humanity towards ultimate goal of transcendental enlightenment; as an intermediate criterion, the goal of auspicious and wholesome rebirth is import.: whatever is conducive to this end is to be encouraged; whatever detracts is to be discouraged or renounced. The outworking of the Buddh. ethic is seen at the most elementary level in the 5 basic moral precepts, binding upon all Buddhists, monastic and lay; to these may be added, by lay people, a further 3, and by monks a further 5 (→ Morality). It is explicated more fully in the formula called the → Eightfold path, for both monks and laymen: for the monk it is set out in detail in the monastic rule of life called the *Patimokka* (Pali)/*Pratimoksha* (Skt.). (→ Discipline, Buddh. Monastic). For laypeople the outworking of the ethical principles governing their domestic and social inter-relationships is set forth in the well-known → *Sigālovāda Sutta.* T.O.L.

(Chinese) The ideals for human character and conduct and the system of morality which, throughout Chinese history and until China became Communist, have governed all social relationships and national legislation and administration, were fundamentally Confucian. Taoists and Buddhists, though undoubtedly influenced by → Buddhist ethics, have gen. accepted the Confucian ethic as normative for life. → Confucius himself was pre-eminently a teacher of practical morality, but he never gave a systematic interpretation of his ethical theories. For him the ideal of virtue was the Perfect Sage (*Shêng Jên*), exemplified in the sage-kings of anc. times, and the Princely Man (*Chün-tzŭ*), whose inner virtues of benevolence (*jên*) and righteousness (*i*) found expression in propriety (*li*), sincerity (*ch'êng*), loyalty (*chung*), reciprocity (*shu*), wisdom (*chih*) and filial piety (*hsiao*). His ethical teachings, set forth by disciples in the → *Analects*, were developed by later Confucians in such works as the *Doctrine of the Mean* (*Chung Yung*), the *Great Learning* (*Ta Tsüeh*), → Mencius and → Hsün-tzŭ.

Confucianists hold that there are five virtues: *jên* (human-heartedness, love, benevolence, goodness); *i* (righteousness, justice); *li* (propriety); *chih* (wisdom); and *hsin* (faithfulness). In his teaching concerning '*jên*', Confucius sometimes spoke of it as greatest of all virtues, sometimes as the sum of all virtues. He enunciated the → Golden Rule in the form 'do not do to others what you would not wish done to yourself'; but he suggested that injury should be requited by justice, kindness by kindness. In the teaching of Mencius the ideal of righteousness or justice assumed unprecedented importance, whereas Hsün-tzŭ, with his doctrine that man's original nature is evil, laid great stress on need to control human nature by means of laws and rules of propriety (*li*). Confucianists taught that it is through wisdom (*chih*) that men learn distinction between right and wrong, learn to know men, and come to knowledge of truth. Faithfulness (*hsin*) is the basis of all human intercourse. Mencius, recognised as greatest of Confucius' followers, taught that man's orig. nature is fundamentally good (a doctrine challenged by Hsün-tzŭ), and given him by Heaven. If men follow their natural feelings of pity, shame, reverence, and of approval and disapproval they will develop the fundamental virtues of human-heartedness, righteousness, propriety and wisdom. Every man, by the constitution of his nature is capable of goodness and of becoming a Sage. Failure to do so is due to man's refusal to follow that in his nature which distinguishes him as a human being. Morality, therefore, has no supernatural sanction, and virtue constitutes its own reward. The Confucians have argued the superiority of their own ethical system over those based on relig. sanctions, on one's duty to God and the inevitability of rewards and punishments in an after-life.

As the family lies at basis of Chi. social structure, the virtues of filial piety (*hsiao*) and brotherly affection (*t'i*) came to occupy a dominant place in Confucian ethics. A paramount duty, acc. to Confucius, is to serve and obey one's parents acc. to propriety when they are alive, and to bury them, mourn for them and sacrifice to them acc. to propriety when they are dead. Hence importance of → Ancestor cult. Confucian E., based on patriarchal organisation of society, was not concerned with social equality. Each had his or her own position, status and grade within family and society. Morality consisted in acting in a manner appropriate to one's status. It was incumbent on rulers and elders to display kindness and justice; on subjects, women and younger people to be dutiful, loyal and obedient. All should be governed by strict rules of propriety.

Confucian morality taught that sphere of women should be confined to the home. The position of a wife was one of dependence, owing a first duty to her husband's parents. A virtuous woman served them and her husband uncomplainingly, gave them male descendants to continue the ancestral sacrifices, was frugal, modest, chaste and decorous in all her conduct, and refused to marry again on death of her husband.

Though the Confucian ethics moulded and shaped Chi. civilisation, the ethical teachings of Confucius have been severely criticised by the Communists as feudal, patriarchal and unjust to underprivileged, and therefore inimical to a democratic and egalitarian society. D.H.S.

E.R.E., V, pp. 466ff.; W. E. Soothill, *Three Religs. of China* (1923), pp. 33–5; 186ff.; D. H. Smith, *Chinese Religs.* (1967), pp, 43ff., 65, 69, 325.

(Christ.) → Christian Ethics. R.H.P.

(Hindu) Hindu ethics have been worked out against a theory of ends or aims of life and system of law determining duties of different groups acc. to their caste or class status (→ *dharma*, → *varṇas*). This has been supplemented for upper class Hindus by theory of four stages of life (→ *asramas*), in which one's obligations differ in accord. with stage of life one has reached. The four ends of life are *kama*, pleasure; *artha*, economic gain; *dharma*, duty or virtue; and → *mokṣa*, liberation. For the householder (*gṛhastha*), living in world, the first three ends are predominant, and are in ascending order of importance. It is assumed that both pursuit of pleasure and economic gain occur within framework of moral obligation. The details of latter are closely interwoven with relig. rites laid upon men; there is in this sense no distinction between relig. and moral law. However, the →→ *Upaniṣads*, *Bhagavadgītā*, law books, the epics, etc., have quite a lot to say about gen. principles and spirit of right behaviour. Thus the *Muṇḍaka Upaniṣad* ref. to five virtues of austerity (→ *tapas*), giving, right conduct, non-injury (→ *ahiṁsā*) and truthfulness; while the *Bṛhadāraṇyaka Upaniṣad* sums up morals as the three *das* (the opening syllable of the three words employed) of self-control, giving and mercy. Virtue is related to highest relig. aim in same Upaniṣad, where Yājñavalkya teaches that all values and loves (for husband, wife, possessions, etc.) are subsumed under love of supreme Self. The growth of → *bhakti* relig. tended to relate goodness of God to kind of conduct expected of men, though this tendency is not yet strong in the *Bhagavadgita*. There the major emphasis is upon self-control and unselfishness, for it is through renouncing fruits of action that liberation is gained: one's actions are performed for sake of God. A contrast is drawn between the good and the demoniac: the latter are characterised by arrogance, self-confidence, lust, anger, etc., and are condemned to → rebirth, while former practice self-control, generosity, non-injury, etc. Though *ahimsa* is ref. to in *Gita*, it is not given much prominence, esp. because solution of Arjuna's dilemma is to go on with battle in spirit of indifference and loyalty to the Lord. The → *Mahābhārata* inculcates ethical attitudes partly through characters of its heroes—Arjuna is, e.g., an ideal *kṣatriya*, brave and generous; Yudiṣṭhira, righteous and good; and so on. Among other things, the epic teaches the → Golden Rule. The figure of → Rama in the *Ramayana* is attractive, though his suspicions of Sita's faithfulness are perhaps overplayed. The later *bhakti* movement, esp. in → Dravidian south and, under such figures as → Kabir and Nanak, in late medieval times in N. India, made a solid connection between God's love and compassion for men and the duty of latter to show love and compassion to one another. This trend was assisted by egalitarian tendencies in *bhakti*, stemming from fact that it gained its greatest strength outside Hindu upper classes. Esp. in the north, *bhakti* relig. was anti-ascetic; though codes of Hindu practice were in mod. times to diffuse more widely some puritanical elements of trad. Brahmanical relig.—e.g. the ban of → alcohol, vegetarianism and (partly through Muslim influence, *via* the practice of purdah) the strict regulation of sexual expression. The ferment created by imposition of British rule and influx of missionaries and Western-style values and education encouraged rationalistic reforming movements (→→ Ram Mohan Roy, Arya Samaj), and reappraisal of customs such as → *sati* (suttee), child marriage and untouchability. The last was most effectively tackled by → Gandhi, who drew both on the egalitarianism implicit in *bhakti* religion and trad. of *ahimsa* in his concern to eliminate foreign oppression and internal injustice. A marked feature of mod. Hindu attitudes has been stress on virtue of tolerance (in part a reaction against divisiveness of relig. evangelism and attitudes of European superiority). This virtue flowed from mod. conception of Hinduism as the synthetic, all-embracing faith, expressing its own version of ultimate unity of all religions—a conception at basis of Indian idea of the secular State. N.S.

E. W. Hopkins, *Ethics of India* (1924); Dhairyabala P. Vora, *Evolution of Morals in the Epics* (1959); R. W. Scott, *Social Ethics in Modern Hinduism* (1953); I. C. Sharma, *Ethical Philosophies of India* (1965); S. Radhakrishnan, *The Hindu View of Life* (1927); K. M. Panikkar, *Caste and Democracy* (1933); M. K. Gandhi (M. H. Desai (tr.), *The Gita according to Gandhi* (1951).

(Jain) Since → Jainism aims at release through austerity and contemplation, which are centrally pursued through monastic life, it makes distinction between rules applicable to monks and those required of laity. For ascetics, there are five precepts: non-injury (→ *ahiṃsā*), i.e. not taking any form of life; truthfulness; non-stealing; sexual continence; and non-possession. These are supplemented by sub-rules: (1) caution in walking to prevent injury to living beings that might be crushed underfoot; (2) control over speech, so as not to cause verbal injury to others; (3) checking food to make sure that it has not been specially prepared by donor; (4) using certain articles (e.g. a gauze veil over the mouth) to avoid injury to living beings; (5) throwing away unnecessary articles with caution, for same reason. The monk is hereby encouraged to be strongly preoccupied with duty of *ahimsa* in its most detailed applications, since injury to life has specially bad effects on karmic condition of individual. Householders are not so rigorously controlled, but they are encouraged to take vows against killing, suicide, abortion, violence, cruelty and practice of untouchability (Jainism not recognising caste system). The vow against suicide is not in contradiction with heroic ideal of death by self-starvation, practised by → Mahavira and others; since this is only permitted to those who have attained the equanimity, etc., necessary, and other forms of suicide are selfish. Laymen have duty to support monks by gifts of food, etc. They are also encouraged to prepare themselves for ascetic life, e.g. by abstaining from sexual intercourse for 20 days a month. The rules governing layman's life determine occupations properly open to Jains, since, e.g., agriculture necessarily involves taking of life. In general, laymen attempt to follow five precepts laid down for the monks, within conditions imposed by mode of life. N.S.

I. C. Sharma, *Ethical Philosophies of India* (1965); J. Jaini, *Outlines of Jainism* (1940); Chakravarti Nayanar, *The Religion of Ahimsa* (1957).

(Japanese) → Shinto has no recognised ethical code. The supreme virtue is to follow the Way of the → Kami (*kannagara-no-michi*), to conform one's life to will of the Heavenly Kami and to emulate lives of those men who have themselves become great kami. Morality has been dominated by anc. Shinto mythology, which represents Japan and its people as the creation of the gods, and the emperor and people as the living descendants of the gods. If men follow the pattern bequeated by their divine ancestors, they need no codified rules of conduct. Virtue is love of Japan, expressed in implicit loyalty, obedience to emperor, dutifulness to parents and superiors, gratitude, and submission which results in action and valour. As regards individual virtues, basic to all is sincerity (*makoto*), which is regarded as the source of beauty, truth and goodness, and stems from awareness of the divine. It includes righteousness (*seigi* or *nahoki-koto*), honesty (*shojiki*), purity and cheerfulness of heart (*seimei*), and thankfulness to the kami, the nation, society and family (*kansha*). Great stress is laid on industriousness (*tsui-shin*). Such virtues are deemed to belong to the true nature of man. There is little concern in Shinto for the problems of sex and drink.

For the past 17 centuries E. in Japan have been greatly influenced by Confucian E. teaching (→ E., Chinese), and by → Buddhism. Buddhism, with its doctrine of → Karma and rebirth, of impermanence and of the fundamental unity and inter-connection of all things, gave effect to its teaching in a practical morality which included the 5 precepts (to abstain from murder, theft, fornication, lying and use of intoxicants) and the 6 *paramitas* (charity, morality, patience, fortitude, meditation and knowledge). When → Bushido developed in 12th and subsequent cents. as a moral system for the military class, inculcating virtues of loyalty, filial piety, benevolence, courage and magnanimity, it was reinforced by Buddhist teachings concerning unselfishness and freedom from desire. → Zen Buddhism regarded morality as a test of spiritual achievement and the natural expression of a noble loftiness of mind. D.H.S.

E.R.E., V, pp. 498ff.; J. Herbert, *Shinto* (1967), pp. 68ff.; D. C. Holtom, *The National Faith of Japan* (1938), pp. 125ff.

(Muslim) The best qualities of pre-Islamic ethics and morality were absorbed by Islam. While reinforcing such pre-Islamic virtues as courage, loyalty, hospitality, self-control, the Qur. emphasised man's obedience to God's will rather than tribe's. The final → judgment which all will experience is an overpowering element in the doc.; so man must both fear and obey God. Faithfulness to trusts is linked with faithfulness to God and his messenger (viii:27). Believers must settle their differences justly; if one party acts oppressively towards another, the oppressors should be fought 'till they return to God's affair' (xlix:9), oppression of a believer being ranked as departure from God's law. Believers are brethren, so piety towards God is shown by settling differences between them (xlix:10). The passage xlix, 6–13, which emphasises right behaviour towards fellow-Muslims, is summed up in 'the most noble among you in God's eyes is the most pious.' Forgiveness when angry is commended (xlii:35). While an evil deed deserves similar recompense, forgiveness results in reward from God (xlii: 38f.). The Qur. further inculcates such virtues as returning evil with good (xli:34), modesty (xlii:35); xxxiii:35 lists number of classes of men and women who will receive forgiveness and reward from God. The Trad. develops in detail the ethical characteristics demanded of a Muslim. These cover every sphere of life, and present a body of instruction which has been influential. Cf. *Mishkāt*, Book XXIV and *passim*, →→ Adultery; Discipline; Divorce; Food; Hospitality; Almsgiving; Muḥtasib.

In mod. apologetic writing emphasis is laid on → Muḥammad as a model: e.g. Kamal al-Din, in *The Ideal Prophet* (Woking, 1925), calls him 'The man who brought to perfect perfection the best of that of which human nature is capable.' Muhammad is considered superior to → Jesus because of comprehensiveness of his qualities. He has kindly qualities as well as qualities of resolution; he has been married, showing what is normal life for man; he has engaged in warfare, proving himself to be a good soldier. He has been a ruler of men, showing diplomatic qualities. He discouraged both asceticism and luxury, emphasising moderation in possessions. Connected with ethics is subject of *adab* (good manners), on which many books have been written. All the *muṣannaf* (→ Ḥadīth) collections of Trad. have section on this subject; many books have been written giving suitable advice. J.R.

*E.I.*², I, pp. 325–8; Hughes, pp. 10 (Adab), 12 (Akhlāq); R. Levy, *A mirror for Princes* (1951), *Social Structure*, ch. V; Donaldson, *Ethics*; Khan, *Islam*, ch. VI; Lane, *Egyptians*, ch. xiii (*passim*).

(Pre-Islamic) The inhabitants of Arabia were predominantly nomadic; their morals were influenced by their surroundings. Society was tribal and the tribe's interests were paramount. The chief must be obeyed in time of war, but otherwise he was little more than *primus inter pares*. Qualities which comprised virtue (*muruwwa*) incl. courage, loyalty, hospitality, endurance. Courage was shown in defence of tribe, and in raiding which was like a national sport; but this was not unmixed with discretion. In raids it was foolish to hold out against superior strength, for someone might be killed, and that demanded a life in return. The blood-revenge (*tha'r*) was a duty, for it was commonly felt to be disgraceful to accept payment in compensation for a death. Many a son recognised that he must avenge his father's death, and he sought out and killed a member of the killer's tribe, not necessarily the killer himself. Loyalty to tribe was essential, for it provided protection, so one was dependent on its goodwill. To be cast out of tribe was depth of disgrace, in addition to being deprived of the one means of security. Loyalty had an individual side also, exemplified notably in story of Samau'al b. 'Adī who, when threatened with death of his son if he did not hand over to an assailant weapons which had been entrusted to his care, refused to betray his trust even to save his son's life. Endurance (*ṣabr*) was a quality naturally developed by hard life of people amid rigours of desert, and may well have been looked on less as a virtue than a necessity. An import. quality was self-control (*ḥilm*), shown by lofty characters, in contrast with roughness (*jahl*) shown by many. Generosity was characteristic, sometimes going to what one feels a ridiculous extent. The chief must be noted for hospitality, a virtue practised by many members of the tribe. Strangers could count on hospitality up to three nights. Feasts were provided on special occasions, and poor benefited. These were often assoc. with the gambling game of *al-maisir*, when lots were cast by means of arrows for shares in a camel to be slaughtered for feast. Wine-drinking was evidently common. The Qur. speaks against *al-maisir* and wine (ii:216; v:92f.), the former passage admitting they have advantages, the latter prohibiting them outright. The pre-Islamic Arabs are criticised for killing female infants. Qur. lxxxi:8 speaks of girl buried alive, (but see Blachère, *Coran*, in note ref. to a v.1); xvii:33 prohibits killing children (*awlād*) for fear of want; this cannot mean merely females. xvi:61 speaks of disappointment felt when a female is born, and of hesitation whether to keep child or hide it in the dust. This suggests female infanticide. vi:138 refers more gen. to human sacrifice. The pre-Islamic good qualities are still shown in the nomadic communities, being absorbed among gen. Muslim virtues. J.R.

(→→ Jāhiliyya; Months sacred in pre-Islamic times). Lyall, *Poetry*, pp. xxiff.; Nicholson, *L.H.A.*, pp. 82ff.; Lammens, *l'Islam*, pp. 12ff.; Goldziher, *M.S.*, I, pp. 1ff., 219ff.; I. Lichtenstädter, *Women in the Aiyam al-'Arab* (1935); Dickson, *Arab of Desert*, *passim*; Watt, *Mecca*, pp. 20ff.

Ethiopic Church Christianity was brought into Ethiopia in 4th cent. by St. Frumentius and Edesius of Tyre. Its orig. assoc. with Egypt caused E.-C. to become → Monophysite. During Middle Ages, E.-C. suffered many vicissitudes of fortune, owing to dynastic struggles and pressure of → Islam. Attempts were made, without lasting success, by → Papacy to win E.-C. to R. Catholicism. In 1948 agreement was reached with → Coptic Church that henceforth → Abuna would be an Ethiopian, not an Egypt. Copt. The canon of Scriptures of E.-C. contain some apocryphal works, e.g. → Enoch, Shepherd of → Hermas. Many Jew. customs are kept, incl. → circumcision. In recent times there have been serious → Christological controversies. S.G.F.B.

E.R.E., I, pp. 57–9; *Jahrbuch f. Antike u. Christentum*, I (1958), pp. 143–50; *D.C.C., s.v.;* E. Ullendorff, *The Ethiopians* (1960), pp. 97ff.; E. Tisserant, *H.G.R.*, III, pp. 305ff.; *R.M.E.*, I, ch. 9.

Etruscan Religion E.-R. shares obscurity that invests the origins and culture of the Etruscans. This is due mainly to our ignorance of E. language: information has to be gleaned from archeological data and refs. of Grk. and Lat. authors. Roman writers mention many E. relig. books: they seem to have dealt chiefly with → divination. Etruscans were expert in divining from liver of sacrificial victims and fall of thunderbolts. Their chief god was Tinia, prob. a storm-god. Many E. gods were equated with Grk. gods, e.g. Tinia = Zeus; Fufluns = Dionysos; Turan = Aphrodite. Etruscans buried dead in house-like tombs, decorated with paintings. This mortuary art shows increasing morbidity: the dead are menaced by awful demons such as Charun (→ Charon) and Tuchulcha. Roman gladiatoral games prob. orig. from E. funerary games, and also use of funerary masks. S.G.F.B.

M. Pallottino, *The Etruscans* (1955), p. 154; F. Altheim, *Hist. of Roman Religion* (E.T. 1938), pp. 46ff.; *E.R.E.*, V, *s.v.;* A. Grenier, *Les religions étrusque et romaine* (1948); *O.C.D.*, pp. 759–61; *Kleine Pauly*, II, 383–91; J. Heurgon, *Daily Life of the Etruscans* (E.T. 1964); G. Bendinelli, *Compendio di storia dell'arte etrusca e romana* (1931); A. Stenico, *Roman and Etruscan Art* (E.T. 1963); E. Hrkal, *Der detruskische Gottesdienst* (1947); D. Strong, 'The Etruscan Problem', in E. Bacon (ed.), *Vanished Civilizations* (1963).

Eucharist The Grk. word *eucharistia* 'thanksgiving' was used from early 2nd cent. for chief act of Chr. worship. The rite orig. from Jesus' action at Last Supper. Paul's statement in I Cor 11:20ff. is earliest evidence of its ritual commemoration: the problem of relating this statement to orig. intention of Jesus has been much discussed, but, owing to nature of evidence, can never be solved. The E., from earliest period, was regarded as divinely instituted means of communion with Christ and as a → sacrifice. How the bread and wine became Body and Blood of Christ began to be debated in early Middle Ages, and led to doctrine of → Transubstantiation. The sacrificial aspect of E. came to be regarded as propitiatory, and led to its being offered for specific purposes in → Masses for Dead. The E. became subject of great controversy at Reformation, because of medieval abuses. In varying modified forms, the E. has been retained by most Prot. Churches, and it continues the chief act of worship in →→ R.C., Eastern and Anglican Churches (→→ Communion (Holy), Mass). S.G.F.B.

D.C.C., s.v.; E.R.E., V, pp. 540–70; J. F. Bethune-Baker, *Intro. to Early Hist. of Christian Doctrine* (1903), ch. 21; M. Goguel, *L'Église primitive* (1947), pp. 343ff.; A. Harnack, *H.D.*, 7 vols., *passim; R.G.G.*[3], I, 'Abendmahl', 10–51; J. Jeremias, *The Eucharistic Words of Jesus* (E.T. 1955); M. de la Taille, *Mysterium Fidei* (1921); N. Zernov, *Eastern Christendom* (1961), pp. 238ff.; E. O. James, *Christian Myth and Ritual* (1933), ch. V; J. Betz, *Die Eucharist in der Zeit der griechischen Väter* (1955).

Euhemerus of Messine (*fl.* 311–298 BC) Notable for theory of orig. of gods, expounded in form of a travel-romance. E. related how he had seen an inscription, on an island in Indian Ocean, which told how → Zeus and other gods were orig. great kings and conquerors whom men, out of gratitude, had deified. Chr. writers cited. E. in attacks on paganism. 'Euhemerism' has become term for explanations of orig. of relig. along similar lines (→→ Ancestor Cults; Imhotep). S.G.F.B.

O.C.D., s.v.; Kleine Pauly, II, 414–5; G. Van der Leeuw, *La religion* (1948), pp. 100, 170ff., 441ff.; H. Pinard de la Boullaye, *L'étude comparée des religions*, I (1925), pp. 33ff.

Eusebius of Caesarea (*c.* 260–340) E. has distinction of being first to write a consequential record of past with progress of Christianity as its theme. His *Ecclesiastical History*, though not critical in its use of sources, is of primary importance for early hist. of Church. Written when the Emp. Constantine's patronage gave Church peace and victory, E. records its previous hard struggle to survive → persecution of pagan state. E. was much involved in → Arian controversy, and, though orthodox, did not fully support → Athanasius. E. wrote many other works, incl. a *Life of Constantine*. S.G.F.B.

Convenient ed. and trans. of *The Eccl. Hist.* by K. Lake in Loeb Class. Library, 2 vols. *D.C.C., s.v.;* R. L. P. Milburn, *Early Christian Interpretations of History* (1954), pp. 54ff.; A. Momigliano, *The Conflict between Paganism and Christianity in the Fourth Century* (1963), pp. 79ff.; *R.A.C.*, VI, 1052–88; K. Mras (ed.), *Eusebius: Praeparatio Evangelica* (1954).

Eve In Heb. *Ḥawwāh*, prob. denoting 'life' or 'life-giving'. It is poss. that behind figure of E. in *Gen.* 2:21ff. there may be anc. myth of the 'Great Mother' of all living. E.'s part in → Adam's downfall recalls idea of the *femme fatale* portrayed in courtesan of → Ishtar who indirectly causes death of Enkidu in Epic of → Gilgamesh, and → Pandora. (→ Mary, Cult). S.G.F.B.

E.R.E., V, *s.v.;* K. Buddhe, *Die biblische Paradiesesgeschichte* (1932), p. 75; Brandon, *C.L.*, pp. 131ff.

Evil, in Buddh. Thought There is no term in Buddh. usage which exactly corresponds to the term 'evil' in West. relig. usage; the nearest is → *dukkha* variously trans. 'ill' 'suffering' 'unsatisfactoriness' 'evil'. Buddh. thought on subject of E. does not concern itself with origins; the fact of E. inclinations and attitudes is recognised, the reality of E. is affirmed, and way to overcoming and negating of such E. is proclaimed. In Buddh. thought, E. is most characteristically seen in its three basic roots: *lobha*, *dosa*, *moha* (greed, hatred, illusion). The degree to which these factors are present in the human mind, in varying degrees and combinations, determines from moment to moment the 'given' situation in which a human individual acts. The presence of the evil factors, at any given moment, is regarded as result of previous actions and attitudes (just as is also the presence of the opposite, good factors, in varying degrees). The situation is not envisaged, however, as one of mechanistic determinism. At each moment, confronted by a given combination of such factors produced by previous events, or finding himself in a certain given moral state, each individual is free to act; his action may perpetuate the moral state he is in, or change it, for better or worse, so that the immediately succeeding moment, the result of the preceding one, may be characterised by an intensification of the evil condition, or its alleviation. (→ Māra, The Evil One). T.O.L.

Evil Eye Belief that harm could be wrought by the eye is anc. and widespread. An Egypt. myth tells how the eye of Rē, the sun-god, slaughtered mankind; the eye of the → Gorgon could petrify. The Egypt. Udzat-eye symbol was put on coffins to ward off evil. Folk belief that certain persons had an E.-E. is universal, and antidotes, esp. in form of → amulets, are found among many peoples. The belief doubtless stems from psychological significance of the eye. (→ E. African Ritual Cults). S.G.F.B.

E.R.E., V, *s.v.; R.Ae.R.-G.*, *s.v.* ('Sonnenauge', 'Uzatauge'); E. A. W. Budge, *The Mummy* (1925), pp. 316ff.

(Islam) Belief in the E.-E. is widespread among the common people in Muslim lands, but is not confined to them alone. The → Qur. refers to belief: 'Those who disbelieve almost cause you to slip by their looks' (lxviii:51); ciii:5 mentions among evils from which deliverance is sought, 'the evil of an envier when he envies'. The E.-E. is connected with envy. One should never praise a child, an animal, or anything belonging to another, unless qualified by a phrase like *mā shā'llāh* (as God wills). People have often been surprised to receive a valuable gift, not realising they have given the article unqualified praise, so the owner is glad to get rid of it, as it has been smitten with the E.-E. A trad. given by → Muslim tells that → Gabriel applied a charm to → Muḥammad 'from the evil of every evil eye, or eye of an envious one'. → Bukhārī tells that Muhammad used God's words in commending al-Ḥasan and al-Ḥusayn to God's protection 'from every devil and poisonous creature and from every E.-E.' (*Mishkāt*, p. 322). An evil influ. may proceed from the eye without anything being said, but matters are worse when look and words are combined. Blue eyes are commonly considered harmful (perhaps due to memories of Crusaders), so blue pearls are often used as → charm. Other protections are artificial eyes, bright gems, glass and metal, alum and 'the hand of Fāṭima'. Boats often have an eye painted on them to ward off harm. The hand, related to Venus in anc. times and to Mary among superstitious Christians, is by Muslims connected with Muhammad's daughter. Hands, or simply five lines, may be used as charms to be worn, or may be drawn on houses for protection. J.R.

Canaan, *Aberglaube*, pp. 28–32; Doutté, *Magie*, pp. 317ff. and *passim*; *E.I.*², I, p. 786 (Ayn).

Evil, Origin The comparative study of relig. shows that mankind is basically agreed on what constitutes evil: namely, pain and death. Pain is experienced in an infinite variety of ways: disease, hunger, injury, old age, fear, being the chief forms. Such experiences have rarely been accepted as part of the natural pattern of existence (→ Stoicism), and supernatural causes have been found for both pain and death. These causes may be grouped under three headings: (1) divine action (2) cosmic → dualism (3) human sin or ignorance. Mesopot. mythology supplies examples of: (1) the gods purposely withheld immortality from mankind, and in their sport made prototypes of the aged and diseased. (→ Mesopot. Relig.). Under (2) → Zoroastrianism provides classic examples of personified Evil creating all that afflicts man. As examples of (3) the Heb. myth of → Fall of Adam accounts for death and hard toil of agriculture as due to sin; the doctrines of → metempsychosis in Hinduism, Buddhism, and Orpheo-Platonism attr. cause of evil entailed to human ignorance of true nature of soul or self. Ambivalent concepts of deity (e.g. →→ Śiva, Vishnu, Zurvan) may be noted as coming under (1), for they attr. Evil to a divine source, even though it is also the source of Good. (→→ Death; Original Sin; Sin). S.G.F.B.

C. J. Bleeker (ed.), *Anthropologie religieuse* (1955); Brandon, *M.D., passim; C.L., passim; History, Time and Deity*, chs. 1–3.

(China–Japan) Chinese philos. found no positive source of E. in universe. → Confucianism sought origin and nature of E. in negative deflection from the → Mean. The principles of man's nature react to external phenomena in such a way that they no longer accord with the Mean; the result is moral E. In same way the interactions of natural phenomena in universe produce aberrations from the Mean which produce physical evils. To Taoist thinkers (i.e. → Lao-tzŭ and → Chuang-tzŭ) good and evil are purely relative. What is good in one condition is evil in another. Both Chi. → Buddhism and → Taoism regarded good and evil as due to response of the mind to external stimuli. The → Neo-Confucians made a distinction between orig. nature, which is good, and physical nature due to interaction of material forces in which good and evil are always at work.

→ Shinto mythology sees good and evil at work in activities of the deities who created universe. The Storm-god is often identified with the mighty evil spirit ruling the invisible world; one of his sons, Oh-Magatsumi, is the great Evil-doer, the source of all evils. But the souls of deities and human beings are considered to be composed of two parts: *nigi-mitama* which is mild, refined and good; and *ara-mitama*, which is rough, brutal and evil. This dualism pervades the universe.

Though in Buddhism there is no satisfactory explanation of origin of evil, the view that E. is the entail of → *karma* and must persist through rebirths, till one finds release from the karmic process and rises above good and evil, has had great influence in China and Japan. It not only explains human tendencies to moral corruption, but also the E. suffered through no seeming fault of one's own. D.H.S.

Fung Yu-lan, *Hist. of Chinese Philos* (1953), vol. 2, pp. 378–82; 446–7; 515–9; 552–6. M. Anesaki, *Hist. of Japanese Relig.* (1930), pp. 27–30; W. G. Aston, *Shinto* (1905), pp. 6, 9, 139, 314.

(Islam) The → Qur. is not clear about origin of E., or whether E. has an entity; it is more interested in evil deeds which deserve punishment, or may be pardoned. It speaks of the soul which incites to E. (xii:53), seemingly laying responsibility for evil on man. On other hand, it can speak of God guiding some and leading others astray (cf. vii:154, xvi:95); xvii:17 says that when God intends to destroy a town he gives the rich command and they act viciously, producing a just sentence followed by the city's destruction; yet other vv. merely say that God does not guide evildoers (cf. ix:81, 110; lxii:5), with the suggestion that the E. they have produced makes them forfeit God's guidance. The problem is whether God, who is creator of all things, is creator of E. The → Mu'tazilites denied this, holding that God must do what is best for his creatures, and that he has commanded them to call people to what is reputable and forbid what is disreputable (cf. Qur. iii:100; ix:72; xxxi:16, etc.). Those who were later recognised as orthodox theologians taught that while obligatory and supererogatory acts resulted from God's will, decision, decree, creation, etc., the obligatory also being commanded, evil acts were only by God's will, decision, decree, creation, knowledge, abandoning and recording. This may seem to make distinction between his relation to good and to E., but it still acknowledges that he creates E. E.g., in spite of a modifying doc. like *kasb* (→→ Acquisition; Freewill and Predestination), a theologian like → Ash 'arī still held that what God wills comes to pass and what he does not will does not. In spite of attempts to lay responsibility on man, it is difficult to see how this can logically be done while holding that God creates man's evil acts, however much he may disapprove of them. One reason why theologians have emphasised God's activity is because they cannot admit of an absolute good or E., as this detracts from God's supreme position. What is good or E. is so because God says it is. In mod. times the common people are still greatly influenced by a kind of fatalism which attributes all good and evil to God; but the educated classes show growing tendency to emphasise human responsibility and treat man as author of his E. They can find grounds for this in the Qur., if not always in the docs. of theologians. J.R.

Wensinck, *Creed*, index; Watt, *Free will*, ch. II; Sweetman, *I.C.T.*, II and IV, index; Levy, *Social structure*, pp. 205ff.; Pareja, ch. 13, *passim*.

Examination in the grave Muslim trad. attr. to → Muḥammad details of what happens to the dead when the funeral party retires. Qur. authority is claimed, e.g. xlvii:29 ('How then when the angels take them away, beating them before and behind?'); vi:93 ('the angels are . . . saying; . . . Today you shall receive the punishment of humiliation'). Two angels, Munkar and Nakīr, then come to question the deceased on his religion. The believer gives satisfactory answers, the grave is expanded and he is surrounded by light, or, alternatively, shown the place he is to occupy in paradise after the resurrection, then told to sleep till then. The unbeliever gives unsatisfactory answers and receives a severe beating, feels the grave pressing in on him and, in one version, is shown the place he is to be debarred from in paradise and place in hell where he is to be punished. J.R.

E.I., III, pp. 724f. (Munkar wa-Nakīr); Pareja, p. 659; Hughes, pp. 27f.; *Mishkāt*, pp. 35f.; Wensinck, *Creed*, index (Punishment); J. Macdonald, *Eschatology* (1965), pp. 74f.

Excommunication (Buddh.) The only kind of excommunication practised by Buddhists is that which is applied in case of fully ordained monk who is found guilty of one of the offences mentioned in the *Patimokkha* (→ Discipline, Buddh. Monastic), for which prescribed penalty is permanent expulsion from the Order (→ Sangha); sexual misconduct, theft, murder, boasting of supernatural powers. For offences of serious nature, other than these, the offender may be temporarily suspended, with prospect of readmission later, if found worthy. It will be noted that there is no E. on grounds of heretical beliefs; the unity of the Order is regarded as consisting primarily in a common discipline of life and standard of morality, rather than in a confession of belief. The four offences, for which the penalty is expulsion, are known as *pārājikā*, i.e., 'involving defeat': this may mean moral defeat suffered by individual concerned; it may refer also to defeat which has to this extent been suffered by Order as a whole, and threat to its proper nature which has been sustained. T.O.L.

S.B.E., vol. XIII, pp. 1ff.; S. Dutt, *Buddhist Monks and Monasteries of India* (1962), pp. 68f.

Exercises, Spiritual (Buddh.) →→ Devotions (Buddh.); Meditation (Buddh.). T.O.L.

Existentialism It has been said that E. is a style of philosophy as old as St. → Augustine, if not as old as Greek Sophists. Another common opinion is that E. has its beginning in thought of → Kierkegaard. These views repr. not so much difference of opinion about phenomenon of E. as difference in emphasis on certain aspects of this philosophical movement. Those who wish to emphasise way in which E. is philosophy born of introspection call attention to similarity between this kind of thinking and that of Augustine. But by their desire to estab. longevity of this kind of philosophy, these writers often reveal weakness of their case, when, e.g., they argue that such philosophy is found in Bible. This is a *reductio ad absurdum*; and throughout argument a confusion is manifest in way philosophy is understood. However, those who view existentialist philosophy as philosophy of existence call attention to fact that it was Kierkegaard who first formulated a technical use of term 'existence'. The impact of his personality and outlook has been greatest single cultural influence operating on later developments. Thus Kierkegaard has gained title of father of E.

Two things must be said before talking of Kierkegaard as initiator of E. The first is that Kierkegaard's philosophy, though it was a highly orig. production, did not arise in a vacuum. It can only be understood in context of anti-Hegelian movement in German philosophy in second half of 19th cent. Thus → Tillich points out that hist. of E. goes back to 1840–50, 'when its main contentions were formulated by thinkers like Schelling, Kierkegaard and Marx in sharp criticism of the reigning rationalism or panlogism of the Hegelians'. (*Theology of Culture*, p. 76). Tillich was fond of saying that Schelling was real source of modern E.; careful examination of his influence on Kierkegaard leads one to doubt whether this is so. Schelling was an important, but not the most important, influence on Kierkegaard; there is too little of the characteristic existentialist twist in Schelling to justify regarding him as initiator of E. But Kierkegaard had evidently gone to Berlin in 1841 in expectation that Schelling would teach him something like this. So, though we cannot say that it began with him, the question of the relation of Schelling to E. remains open. It has been suggested that Kierkegaard found inspiration in the work of strange German philosopher, J. G. Hamann; and it is certainly true that in Hamann's chaotic writings he would find a passionate rejection of rationalism and seeds of full-blooded philosophy. We see, then, that, though it is true to say that Kierkegaard is father of E., he too had a pedigree in the form of his debt to the anti-Hegelian philosophy that flourished in Germany from 1830 onwards. The second point is more briefly made. This is that Kierkegaard made very sparing use of terms 'existence' and 'existential' in his own writings, and never once talked of E. He did not use the term 'existential' until 1845, in conclusion to *Stages on Life's Way*. He had no intention of founding school of philosophy, nor did he regard himself as belonging to philosophical party. To regard E. as such is contrary to orig. inspiration in Kierkegaard.

Kierkegaard's conception of philosophy as existential was born of his impatience with pretentiousness of philosophy as understood by → Hegel. Hegel's intention was to construct a scheme of thought in which the System would be indistinguishable from reality itself: reality was essentially rational. His ideal was to incl. everything within scope of his philosophy. Everything, therefore had meaning for Hegel only as moments within evolution of universal Idea. As against this emphasis on speculation and objectivity, Kierkegaard advanced thesis that truth is subjectivity. Kierkegaard brought the person into philosophy and changed the emphasis from objective world of ideas to person who has those ideas. Philosophy, he contended, had been too much concerned with knowledge and too little concerned with existence: the one thing that Hegel had not learned was what it meant to exist. Speculative philosophy for Kierkegaard is incomplete philosophy, because it does not do justice to individual. The Hegelian attempt to philosophise on basis of purely undetermined notion of being is nothing more than a trick. There is no presuppositionless philosophy. We must remember creaturely conditions of knowledge, and our starting point must be man in his concrete existence. This does not mean that for Kierkegaard philosophy develops into autobiography; for there is in his work an abundance of theoretical discussion of the modes of being and nature of knowledge and of matters such as aesthetics, ethics and religion.

After this striking emergence of Existentialist philosophy, impulse of movement subsided; it was replaced by Neo-Kantian idealism or naturalistic empiricism. Feuerbach and Marx were interpreted as dogmatic materialists, Kierkegaard remained completely unknown, and Schelling and other critics of Hegel were contemptuously referred to in a few sentences in the Histories of Philosophy. But a new impulse to existential philosophy came from the *Lebensphilosophie* of the 1880s, the philosophy assoc. with names of Nietzsche, Dilthey and Bergson. The 'Philosophy of Life' is not identical with E., but it does incl. some of its distinctive emphases. More import. in the develop. of E. is the next step in its history, the rise of the Phenomenological Movement introduced by Husserl. Neither the German nor French Existentialists can be understood without reference to Husserl. Heidegger was Husserl's pupil, and Jaspers accepted the phenomenological method for his psychology, while in France Sartre and Merleau-Ponty were both profoundly influenced by Husserl. Husserl used the term 'phenomenology' to mean an analysis of certain basic types of human consciousness. These he held to be correlated with objective contents, the essences or 'structures' of which may be revealed to disinterested reflection. One of Husserl's guiding principles was that 'consciousness is always consciousness of something'. The phenomenological answer to problem of how consciousness comes to know a world outside consciousness is the link between Kierkegaard and Heidegger; for Heidegger not only used Kierkegaard, but he also set out to criticise Husserl.

So we come to the contemporary Existentialists, in whom the motives of the Kierkegaardian thought return: but they return depersonalised and emptied of their relig. content. Heidegger takes Kierkegaard's use of term 'existence' as denoting something essentially personal, and he follows very closely Kierkegaard's analysis of dread in his analysis of human existence (*Dasein*); but he is an ontologist of existence. For Heidegger human existence is concern. It is open toward future, and, as I confront possibility, I am filled with *angst*. Unlike Kierkegaard, Heidegger does not refer to God. He does not deny that God exists: God is just absent from Heidegger's world. Man is thrown into being, and the authentic existence of man is his existing for death. The other great figure—and indeed in opinion of some authors, the originator—of the German school of E. is Karl Jaspers. Jaspers argues that, since Kierkegaard, it has become imposs. to imagine that one can comprehend Truth, the whole scheme of things, in a System. So Jaspers rejects both metaphysics and science as complete world-views. Jaspers' attitude to both science and rationalism is really quite different from that of Kierkegaard. Kierkegaard's genuine mistrust of system led him to regard all thought as necessary fragmentary and incomplete. Jaspers believes that philosophy can be an attempt to grasp being as such. Jaspers makes great use of concept of the transcendent, and by this he seems to mean God. Man is aware of transcendent in those crucial experiences which he calls 'limit-situations'. His final assessment of life is no more optimistic than Heidegger's. We must accept shipwreck. Sartre is a much more import. philosopher than either Heidegger or Jaspers; in a way the work of Germans derives importance from fact that it coloured Sartre's essentially French philosophy. His work could be said to start with the Cartesian emphasis on the 'I think', and to incorporate German phenomenology and Heidegger's doc. of the Nothing. He takes his basic ontology from Heidegger. The world is divided into two kinds of being—*être-en-soi* (being-in-itself), and *être-pour-soi* (being-for-itself). The former is the being of things; latter the being of persons. Things simply are, and, therefore, and complete in themselves; whereas persons are incomplete because they are open toward the future, the future that is unmade. Confronted with this, man feels anxiety and nausea. Man is a project. Life is absurd, and death is just another absurdity thrown in for good measure. Sartre is quite explicitly atheistic. The idea of God is self-contradictory, since it is the idea of a being who is both a being-for-itself and a being-in-itself. There is no God, and man seeks to be God. Marcel, on the other hand, is a theistic philosopher. Orig. a disciple of Royce's personal idealism, Marcel can be called an existentialist because of his preoccupation with a philosophy of existence. His method is very near the empirical trad., but his philosophy is shot through with realisation of the essential mystery of life. One of his most import. contributions has been distinction between problems and mysteries. Problems are those puzzles to which we can offer a solution; but mysteries are those problems of which we ourselves are part and are not capable of solution.

In conclusion, we can mention four characteristics of E. First, it is protest against rationalism in any form, because rationalist claims that reality can be grasped primarily or exclusively by means of intellect alone. Thus thesis of Kierkegaard is repeated that, though a logical system is poss. an existential system is imposs. Secondly, E. is a protest against all views of man which reduce him to status of a thing, an assortment of functions and reactions. So it is equally opposed to mechanism and naturalism, and those political philosophies which elevate the state above the individual and make latter a mere function of the state. Thirdly, E. makes sharp distinction between subjective and objective truth and gives priority to former. It is import. to realise that use of the word 'subjective' here derives from special meaning that Kierkegaard gave it and does not mean something purely psychological. It has to do rather with contrast between those activities, where information-gathering and problem-solving are relevant, and those where such procedures are irrelevant. Finally, E. is always characterised by its stress on the ambiguities of life which arise from man's freedom. The human situation is for the Existentialist full of contradictions and tensions which cannot be resolved by thought. Many questions, which have been the trad. problems of philosophy, have been discussed only by Existentialist philosophers in the 20th cent. J.H-T.

M. Heidegger, *Being and Time* (E.T. 1962); K. Jaspers, *Perennial Scope of Philosophy* (E.T. 1950); Jaspers, *Way to Wisdom* (E.T. 1951); J.-P. Sartre, *Being and Nothingness* (E.T. 1957); *Existentialism and Humanism* (E.T. 1948); G. Marcel, *The Mystery of Being*, 2 vols. (E.T. 1950–1); Marcel, *Homo Viator* (E.T. 1951). Cf. W. Barrett, *Irrational Man, A Study in Existential Philosophy* (1960); H. J. Blackham, *Six Existentialist Thinkers* (1952); F. H. Heinemann, *Existentialism and the Modern Predicament* (1953); I. Murdoch, *Sartre, Romantic Rationalist* (1953); P. A. Schilpp (ed.), *The Philosophy of Karl Jaspers* (1958).

Exodus The 'coming out' of Israel from bondage in Egypt, facilitated by miraculous events, is described in Book of Exodus. The narrative combines two literary trads. (→ Pentateuch); no mention is made of E. in extant Egypt. texts. The E. is gen. accepted as historical, though greatly transformed in later Heb. imagination: it is dated somewhere between 1580 and 1215 BC. The E. has ever been the supreme event of Jew. → Heilsgeschichte, and is commemorated annually in → Passover; it has also greatly influenced Chr. thought and imagination. S.G.F.B.

H. H. Rowley, *From Joseph to Joshua* (1950); *R.G.G.*[3], II, 831–2; *H.D.B.*[2], *s.v.;* M. Noth, *Hist. of Israel* (E.T. 1960), pp. 110ff.; S. G. F. Brandon, *History, Time and Deity* (1965), pp. 109ff.; G. Fohrer, *Überlieferung u. Gesch. des Exodus* (1964); *E.J.R.*, p. 139.

Ex Opere Operato Lat. term used by Cath. theologians since 13th cent. in connection with → sacraments. In order to ensure validity of sacramental grace from dependence on worthiness of officiating minister, it is maintained that the grace stems from the proper enactment of rite concerned, acc. to God's will. The term may also be used to explain operation of all ritual and magical action, i.e., the appropriate potency is generated by the actual doing of a rite and not through the faith of officiant or some other agency (divine or demonic). S.G.F.B.

Exorcism → Demons and Demonology; → Hierarchy, Christ.

Expiation The notion stems from fear of divine anger, incurred by ritual or moral trespass, and instinct to placate the angered deity by some action such as →→ sacrifice, fasting, penance. E. is found in various forms in all religs. It is related to → Atonement; but latter repr. higher form of relig. reaction, since it aims at being 'at-one' again with offended deity. E. stops at placation. Both ideas occur in Jew. sacrificial cultus, and are not always distinguished; the same obtains in Chr. doc. of Atonement (→ Purgatory). S.G.F.B.

E.R.E., V, pp. 635–71; *H.D.B.*, *s.v.; R.G.G.*[3], VI, 474–6.

Extinction (Buddh.) Where term 'extinction' occurs in Buddh. trad. it refers to E. of feeling and perception in the special state of meditation achieved only by one who attained mastery of the 8 → Jhānas, and is an → Anāgami or an → Arahant. It is incorrectly used in connection with state of *nirvāṇa*, if it is applied to the one who has achieved *n.* The state thus achieved is not one of 'extinction' or 'annihilation' of all existence; what has suffered total extinction, acc. to the Buddh. view, are the passions, greed, hatred, and illusion, which are the roots of all evil and suffering. (→ *nibbāna*, i.e. *nirvāṇa*). T.O.L.

Eye-God (Goddess) At Brak, N. Mesopot., evidence has been found, dating *c.* 2500 BC, of cult of a deity (*c.* 2500) symbolised by a stylised pair of eyes. Multitudes of 'eye-idols' were unearthed in the temple; similar objects have been found at Ur, Mari and Lagash. One idol is engraved with a stag, symbol of Sumerian goddess of childbirth, Nin-hur-sag, which may indicate that the deity was female. Stylised symbols of eyes appear on objects elsewhere, e.g. an Early Bronze Age drum-shaped idol found at Folkton, Yorks. The attr. of many eyes to deities is widely attested as symbol of omniscience. S.G.F.B.

M. E. L. Mallowan, *Early Mesopotamia and Iran* (1965), pp. 46ff.; R. Pettazoni, *The All-Knowing God* (E.T. 1956), pp. 16ff., 82ff.; O. G. S. Crawford, *The Eye Goddess* (1956).

Ezekiel, Book of Although many aspects of its composition and its relation to prophet E. are problematic, it provides invaluable evidence of Jew. relig. in early years of Babylon. Exile. The fall of → Jerusalem in 586 BC seems to divide situation in chs. 1–24 from that in chs. 25–48. E., a prophet-priest, sought to re-adapt trad. → Yahwism to needs of downcast Israel. In promising that → Yahweh would restore broken nation, he uses imagery of → resurrection in ch. 37 which is important for develop. of Jew. → eschatology. E. stresses individual responsibility, and envisages restored Israel as a → theocracy. The theophany in ch. 1 is important for comparative iconography; 8:14 attests cult of → Tammuz at Jerusalem. S.G.F.B.

G. A. Cooke, *Ezekiel* (I.C.C., 1936); *H.D.B.*², *s.v.; P.C.*², *s.v.;* H. H. Rowley, 'The Book of Ezekiel in Modern Study', in *Men of God* (1963).

Ezra Jew. priest and scribe, whose reform of → Judaism towards end of 5th cent. BC, made it essentially an exclusive national faith. Pursuing ideals of → Ezekiel, E. invested → Torah with a new sanctity and influence, and his prohibition of foreign marriages ensured that Jews would retain racial identity as holy people of their national god → Yahweh. The career of E. is recorded in Books of E. and Nehemiah, these being later compositions that embody earlier sources. S.G.F.B.

*H.D.B.*², pp. 285ff.; *P.C.*², pp. 370ff.; H. H. Rowley, *Men of God* (1963), pp. 211ff.

F

Fa Hsien Famous Chinese Buddhist monk and pilgrim. Surname—Shih. Born in Shansi, he was trained at Buddhist centre in Ch'ang-an, the W. capital of China. He left Ch'ang-an in CE 399 with several companions, to visit India and Buddhist countries of W., in search of a complete canon of Buddhist scriptures. After 6 years of adventurous travel through C. Asia, he finally arrived in India with one disciple, Tao Chêng. There he spent another 6 years in travel and sojourn, and collected and copied sacred texts of various schools. He returned by sea from Ceylon, visiting Sumatra, arriving home in CE 414. He inaugurated a period of intensive trans. work on Buddhist scriptures. He wrote famous account of his travels, known as the *Fa Hsien Chuan* ('The narrative of Fa Hsien'), and later as the *Fo Kuo Chi* ('Record of the Buddhist Countries'), trans. into Eng. by S. Beal (1869, and 1884), by J. Legge (1886), by H. A. Giles (1923). D.H.S.

H. A. Giles, *The Travels of Fa Hsien* (1923, 3rd impr. 1959); *E.R.E.*, XII, pp. 841, 843.

Faith (Buddh.) Faith (*saddhā*, Pali/*sraddhā*, Skt.) has an import. place in the Buddh. scheme, both at the entry upon the Buddh. way, and in perseverance in the way. F. is said to be a factor assoc. with any karmically wholesome state of consciousness whatsoever, at any stage of the relig. life. In a more formal analysis, F. is said to be one of the 5 *balas*, or powers assoc. with the Buddh. life (→ Powers), the other 4 being energy, mindfulness, concentration and wisdom. The initial adoption of the 2 preliminary Buddh. attitudes, described in the → Eightfold Path as right understanding and right thought, is that stage of relig. life only poss. in faith; later, what is accepted in faith is apprehended directly, and experientially confirmed. Primarily F. has the → Buddha, the → Dhamma, and → Sangha as its objects; but always with the eventual confirming of faith by direct apprehension in view. F. never depends on authority alone; experiential verification as the vindicating of F. is always held to be part of the intention of F. Jayatilleke describes this as 'provisional acceptance . . . for the purposes of verification.' The same writer has analysed F., in the Buddh. context, as of 3 kinds: affective, conative, and cognitive. Affective F. is very close to → *bhakti* or devotion, and produces serene pleasure (*pīti*); conative faith produces spiritual energy (*viriya*); cognitive faith, or 'belief', is the antidote to doubt (*vicikiccha*) and delusion (*moha*), since it is a rational faith. T.O.L.

K. N. Jayatilleke, *Early Buddhist Theory of Knowledge* (1963), pp. 383–401.

(China–Japan) The Chinese character *hsin*, depicting a man standing by his word, is used both as substantive—truth, sincerity, confidence—and as a verb—to believe in, to trust. F., as the duty of fulfilling one's trust, is recognised as one of the 5 principal virtues. Relig. F. is manifest in two ways: trust in the trad. teachings enshrined in sacred writings, and dependence on, trust in and worship of Higher Power or Powers.

The → Mahayana Buddhism of China and Japan, and in particular the → Amida sects, developed a doctrine of salvation by F. A distinction is made between the Buddha's grace and our F., both being recognised as essential. As in Christianity, the question was even raised as to whether F. is not itself the free gift of grace. The centrality of Saving F. is notably developed in the treatise, *Ch'i Hsin Lun* (*Awakening of Faith in the Mahayana*, E.T. D. T. Suzuki, 1900, Y. S. Hakeda, 1967) which has had an immense influence in Chi. and Jap. Buddhism. There it is argued that 'fundamental' F. is joyous recollection of 'Suchness' (*chen ju*). Such 'fundamental F.' is finally attained by (1) F. in the illimitable merits of Buddha, resulting in worshipping and reverencing him, (2) F. in the benefits of → Dharma, leading to practice of charity, morality, patience, energy and tranquillity with insight, and (3) F. in the → Sangha in which one's identity with all the Buddhas and → bodhisattvas is realised. D.H.S.

(Christian) Term has two distinctive uses: (1) as body of beliefs and practices, gen. set forth in → Creeds, that constitute orthodox Christianity (2) as first, but not greatest, of three 'Theological Virtues' defined by → Paul in I Cor. 13:13. Paul, prob. owing to his reaction to → Judaism, contrasted F. with 'Works', by making F. essential for → salvation. Later theology presented F. as gift of God (→ Grace), in sense of wholehearted trust in and commitment to Christ's Gospel, not intellectual acceptance of it. At Reformation, F. was re-emphasised, esp. by → Luther, in a reaction to medieval sacerdotalism similar to that of Paul's against → Torah-observance in Judaism. S.G.F.B.

E.R.E., V, pp. 689ff.; *D.C.C.*, *s.v.; H.D.B.*², *s.v.; R.G.G.*³, II, 1586–1611; Harnack, *H.D.*, *passim.*

(Islam) F. = *Imān.* Qur. xlix:14 criticises the Bedouin who say, 'We have believed' (*āmannā*), telling them to say rather, 'We have submitted' (*aslamnā*), for *al-imān* has not yet entered their hearts. The following verse describes believers (*mu'minūn*) as those who believe in God and his messenger, then do not doubt, and who strive with their property and persons in God's way. F. is obviously more than mere acceptance of beliefs; it involves appropriate action. In accord. with this the Qur. makes it clear that waiting till one's deathbed to declare one's faith is of no avail (cf. vi:159). At same time it says no one can believe except by God's permission (cf. x:100). The → Kharijites held that a sinner did not have faith; but the → Murji'ites held that sin did not annul faith. The first article of the *Fiqh Akbar* I (cf. Wensinck, *Creed*, 103) says, 'We do not consider anyone to be an infidel on account of sin; nor do we deny his faith'. This prob. goes back to some of → Abū Ḥanīfa's answers to questions. A Trad. tells of → Gabriel's asking → Muḥammad what faith is and approving his reply: 'It means that you should believe in God, his angels, his books, his messengers, and the last day, and that you should believe in the decreeing of both good and evil.' Another says, 'F. has over 70 branches, the most excellent of which is the declaration that there is no deity but God, and the humblest of which is the removal from the road of what is injurious. And modesty is a branch of F.' But another attributes to Md. the saying, 'None of you believe till I am dearer to him than his father, his child, and all mankind.' In another, Md. tells a deputation that F. in God alone incl. the testimony that there is no deity but God and that Md. is God's messenger, the observance of → prayer, the payment of *zakāt* (→ Legal alms), the → fast of Ramaḍān, and giving a fifth of the booty. This clearly indic. that F. involves action as well as belief. J.R.

E.I., II, pp. 474f.; Hughes, pp. 204f.; D. B. Macdonald, *Theology*, index (Iman); Wensinck, *Creed*, pp. 125, 131ff. and index (Faith, Iman); W. M. Watt, 'The conception of īmān in Islamic theology', *D.I.*, Band 43 (1967), pp. 1–10; M. A. Rauf, 'Islam and Iman', *M.W.*, LVII (1967), pp. 94ff.; *Mishkāt*, pp. 5ff.

Faith-healing (China–Japan) The healing of sickness and disease by relig. attitudes and ceremonies has usually been accompanied by magical prescriptions, exorcism, and the like. Sickness and disease are commonly attr. to demons or other maleficent influences, and can be cured by invoking assistance of powerful and merciful divinities. An import. feature assoc. with the rise of relig. → Taoism 2nd cent. CE) was prominence given to F.-h. Sickness and disease were attr. to sin, and at great public ceremonies, by means of music, holy water, incense, fasting, prayers, chanting etc. such fervour was generated that believers were led to ecstatic repentance resulting in the expiation of sin and curing of disease.

F.-h. is a dominant interest in several → Shinto sects of Japan, notably →→ Kurozumi-kyō, Konkō-kyō, and Tenri-kyō: e.g. in Tenri-kyō physical and mental sickness are attr. to uncleanness which may be swept away by exercise of a sincere faith in God. D.H.S.

H. Maspero, *Le Taoïsme* (1950), pp. 150ff.; D. C. Holtom, *The National Faith of Japan* (1938), pp. 245, 278ff. (→→ Christ. Science; Healing Divine).

Fall of Man, The story of → Adam's disobedience to his Creator in Gen. 3:1ff., is used by → Yahwist to account for orig. of death and toil of agriculture. → Paul's use of myth (Rom. v:12ff.) provided basis for Chr. doc. of → Original Sin, by arguing that sinning, initiated by Adam, put mankind in state of perdition. The attempt to find a Mesopot. prototype of F.-M. in myth of → Adapa is mistaken since motifs involved are different. The idea of a lost Golden Age figures in many religs.; but only in Heb. and Chr. religs. has it acquired theological significance. Idea of → metempsychosis in →→ Hinduism, Buddhism, Orphism implies a primaeval error. (→ Gnosticism). S.G.F.B.

N. P. Williams, *Ideas of the Fall and of Original Sin* (1927); Brandon, *C.L.*, pp. 122ff.; *M.D.*, pp. 87ff., 123ff., 211ff.; *R.G.G.*³, VI, 489–93, 1208–11.

Family (Chinese) Throughout history and until modern times Chinese society has been predominantly patriarchal, and the F. the norm of social organisation. The F. was more than the social unit on which the structure of Chi. civilisation rested; it was a living organism linking generations of ancestors with generations as yet unborn. It can only be understood in relation to the → Ancestor Cult. Though in actual practice the average Chi. F. unit differs little in size from the average F. in Europe or America, the ideal Chi. F. consists of 3 or 4 generations, with wives, children and dependents, often scores of individuals, all living in one homestead under authoritarian control of eldest male acc. to primogeniture. The ideal F. was governed acc. to the principles of strict Confucian morality. Benevolence, justice and strict impartiality were expected of the head; duty, obedience and respect (i.e. → Filial Piety) from all subordinates. So long as F. remained united, property was held and used in common, and each individual contributed his or her earnings to the common purse. When an inheritance came to be divided, each received a share, but eldest son was given a larger portion. Each member of F. had his or her appropriate duties and status. In general women were considered as of inferior status, kept to their own quarters (wives were called *nei jên*, i.e. the persons within), and partook of meals apart from and after the men. Legally the head of F. had considerable disciplinary powers, and it was considered a disgrace for F.-affairs to come into the law courts. Marriages were considered as contracts, arranged often without consent of individuals concerned through go-betweens. The function of a wife was to bear children and to render service and obedience to husband and his parents. A husband was considered to owe a greater loyalty to his parents than to his wife, and, as most women were limited in education, they were often unfitted to be companions to their husbands. Little children were treated with affection and indulgence, and boys remained, largely undisciplined, in care of the women until formal education began. When children were lacking, it was common practice to provide for the succession by adoption. An extension of F. was the kinship group, consisting of all those who recognised a common ancestor, usually all with same surname, the bond of union being a common ancestral temple and burial ground.

Much of Chi. relig. expression was centred in the F., primarily in cult of Ancestors but also in worship of household gods and tutelary deities assoc. with the land. In modern times many forces have combined to undermine the paramount importance of F. in Chi. civilisation. These include process of urbanisation and industrialisation, rapid growth of nationalism, communism with its experiments in communalisation, and priority given to state-controlled education.

→→ Adultery, Ancestor Worship, Divorce, Filial Piety. D.H.S.

E.R.E., V, pp. 730ff.; A. H. Smith, *Village Life in China* (1900), pp. 237ff.

(Japanese) In anc. Japan the *uji* or household was the unit of society, an organisation not only of blood relationships but bound by social, economic and political interests as well. As families increased, they became sub-divided, but all were under the authority of the central *uji*. Economically the *uji* were important, as professions, occupations and trades were usually hereditary. As political groups, they constituted the material and machinery of government. Theoretically all *uji* were but branches of the central *uji*, of which the emperor was head. In those early days women held a place of greater importance than at later times. With the general acceptance of Chinese cultural and social patterns, the Confucian ideal of F. (→ F., Chinese) came to predominate, with its patriarchal system, the dominance of ancestor worship, the acceptance of filial piety as the chief obligation, and the inferior position given to women. From the dawn of the Meiji era (1868), espec. among the educated and in urban areas, the penetration of Western ideas led to more individualistic type of family, composed of husband, wife and children, in which women and children have far greater freedom of individual choice and decision. D.H.S.

E.R.E., V, pp. 740ff.

Family and Social Duties (Buddh.) For the Buddh. monk the relig. life means renunciation of home and family life, and membership instead in the 'clan' of the Buddha. For the Buddh. layman, however, the relationships of family life are subject of specific guidance from Buddha. For Buddhists of S. Asia this is set forth in its best-known form in the *Sigālovāda Sutta* (part of → *Digha Nikaya*). This consists of advice reputedly given by Buddha to the 'young householder' on his duty in various social roles: duty to parents, to teachers, to wife and children, to friends and companions, to servants and to relig. perceptors. In each case, 5 responsibilities are mentioned: (1) towards parents, to support them, perform duties for them, keep trad. of the family, maintain family lineage, and make oneself worthy of them (2) towards children; in showing love for them, he must restrain them from vice, exhort them to virtue, train them for a profession, contract suitable marriages for them and in due time hand over to them their inheritance (3) towards teachers, in order to honour them, he must rise in salutation, attend upon them, show eagerness to learn, offer personal service and pay attention when being taught; (4) concerning pupils, he should pass on to them the learning or training which he has himself received, ensure that they retain what they are taught, make them thoroughly conversant with every art, speak well of them among friends and companions, and provide for their safety. Husbands and wives have reciprocal responsibilities; the husband is to respect his wife, be courteous to her, be faithful, hand over authority to her, and provide her with adornment; the wife is to see that her duties are well performed, offer hospitality to both his and her kin, be faithful, watch over her husband's goods and show skill and industry in business. Similarly, reciprocal responsibilities are laid upon masters and servants: masters are to assign their servants work acc. to their strength, to supply them with food and wages, to care for them in sickness, share any unusual delicacies with them, and grant them leave of absence from time to time; servants, in return, are to rise before their master in the morning, go to rest after he does at night, to be content with what they receive, do their work well, and maintain their master's good reputation. Similar reciprocity of generosity, courtesy, benevolence, fairness and keeping of promises is enjoined upon friends and companions. Finally, the reciprocal roles of relig. preceptors and householders are described: the householder is to show affection to his preceptors in act and word and thought, offer them hospitality, and supply their temporal needs; the relig. preceptor is to restrain householder from evil, exhort him to good, be kindly disposed towards him, teach him what he does not know, correct him when he makes mistakes and reveal to him the way to heaven.

The responsibilities of a young wife to her husband are described at length in the *Uggaka Sutta*, found in the → *Anguttara Nikaya*. A gen. dissertation on social duties is found in the *Mahāmangala Sutta* of the → Sutta–Nipāta. In Mhy. Buddhism the ideal householder is described in the *Vimala-kirti-nirdesa Sūtra;* this ideal has strongly influenced social life of Buddh. China and Japan. T.O.L.

R. Gard, *Buddhism* (1961), ch. VI; T. W. Rhys-Davids, *Dialogues of the Buddha*, vol. III, pp. 180–3; E. M. Hare, *Gradual Sayings*, vol. III (1934, repr. 1952), pp. 29–30; E. M. Hare *Woven Cadences* (2nd edn. 1948), pp. 40–2; Tsunoda R., de Bary and Keene, *Sources of the Japanese Tradition* (1958), pp. 101–6.

Fanaticism (China–Japan) Religs. in China, being organisationally weak and laying little emphasis on distinctive creeds and dogmas, have been remarkably free from F., which has in main been politically inspired. The populace, however, has on several occasions been roused to relig. F., e.g. in 2nd cent. CE with the rise of relig. → Taoism; in 9th cent. CE at suppression of → Buddhism and other 'foreign' faiths; in the cruel suppression of Muslims in 19th cent.; in the T'ai p'ing rebellion; and in the fanatical communist-inspired 'Red Guards' of modern times.

F. has seldom been manifest in either → Shinto or Buddhism, the two religs. of Japan. For over 1000 years they have lived side by side in mutual tolerance and with mutual borrowings as in → Ryobu Shinto. → Nichiren and his followers displayed fanatical opposition to other Buddhist sects; but F. in general has been inspired and motivated by the government. In 16th and 17th cents. CE, fanatical opposition to Christianity resulted in its total suppression. Later, state Shinto inculcated a fanatical loyalty to the emperor, and a fanatical belief in Japan's mission and destiny, resulting in the debacle of Second World War. D.H.S.

Fang Shih Chinese name given to → Taoist practitioners, versed in arts of healing and preparation of prescriptions (*fang-tzŭ*). They were concerned with alchemy, and espec. the production of the elixir or pill of immortality. Considered to be magicians, possessed of divine powers, they gained great influence, not only among populace, but at courts of several Taoist-inclined emperors. One of earliest and most famous was Li Shao-chün who persuaded the Han emperor, Wu Ti (140–87 BC), to seek immortality by transmuting cinnabar into gold. D.H.S.

Homes Welch, *The Parting of the Way* (1957), pp. 99ff.

Faqīr (Poor). Used in a material and in a spiritual sense. It is an ordinary word for a poor man. → Sūfīs and → ascetics give it a spiritual sense, expressing one's need of God. *Faqr* (poverty) is one of the Sufi stations. Asceticism is involved; but the true F. thinks most of his need of God, and belongs to an order (→ Sūfī Orders). F. is also used in expressing merely a relig. mendicant. J.R.

E.I., II, p. 46 (*fakīr*); IV, p. 1239 (*zuhd*); Hughes, pp. 115ff.; Arberry, *Doctrine*, ch. xxxviii; Smith, *Early mysticism*, p. 172; Lane, *Egyptians*, pp. 251–3. (→ Ebionites).

-Fārābī, Abū Naṣr Muḥammad b. Muḥammad (d. 339/950, aged *c.* 80), a famous Muslim philosopher of Turkish origin. He studied first in Khurasan, then in Baghdad, where he settled. In 330/942 he received patronage of Sayf al-Dawla of Aleppo, which became his main home till death. Because of his commentaries on → Aristotle he was called 'the second teacher'. In his philosophy he was Aristotelian, but with admixture of → Neoplatonism. In political theory, he was influenced by → Plato's *Republic* and *Laws*. He held that reason was superior to relig. faith; but while he held that prophecy was auxiliary to rational faculty, he insisted that prophets had an import. function to fulfil. He wrote many books, classified in *G.A.L.*, *S.I.* under headings of logic, ethics and politics, mathematics, astrology, alchemy, music, miscellanea, writings on Aristotle. J.R.

*E.I.*², II, pp. 778–81; *G.A.L.*, I, pp. 232ff.; *S.I.*, pp. 375ff., 957f.; D. M. Dunlop (trans. and ed.), *Al-Fārābī: Fuṣūl al-madanī* (Aphorisms of the statesman) (1961); H. G. Farmer, *The sources of Arabian music*, index, 2nd edn. (1965); I. Madkour, *La place d'Al-Fārābī dans l'école philosophique* (1934); Pareja, index; N. Rescher, *Al-Fārābī: An annotated bibliography* (1962); E. Rosenthal, *Political thought*², pp. 122ff. and index; Watt, *Philosophy*, index.

Fasting, Fasts Voluntary abstention from food, for relig. or magical reasons, prob. stems from fact that F. is naturally assoc. with times of stress and grief, while feasting is a natural expression of joy. Three forms of F. may be distinguished: (1) preparatory to initiation (e.g. of adolescents in primitive societies, in → Mystery Religions, for → baptism, knighthood, admission to → hierarchy); also in prep. for communion with deity (e.g. Ex. 34:28, Lk. 4:1–2, and before → Holy Communion). The reason (unconscious) has prob. been to avoid pollution through eating. (2) F. as act of mourning for dead: motives seem to be various, e.g. sorrow, propitiatory to deceased, to avoid contagion of death. (3) F. as act of penitence: the belief that voluntary affliction by abstaining from food will placate offended deity is natural and has been universally practised. In many religs., periods of F. are officially prescribed (e.g. Jew. Day of → Atonement; Chr. Lent; Muslim → Ramaḍān). (→→ Abstinence; Asceticism). S.G.F.B.

E.R.E., V, *s.v.; R.G.G.*[3], II, 881–5; *R.Ae.R.-G.*, pp. 744ff. ('Speiseverbote'); *H.D.B.*[2], *s.v.; O.C.D.*, *s.v.; D.C.C.*, p. 495; G. Widengren, *Mani and Manichaeism* (E.T. 1965), p. 98; M. Jastrow, *Aspects*, pp. 320ff.

(Buddh.) Fasting, in a Buddh. context, normally refers to practice, enjoined by monastic regulations, of taking no food between mid-day and following morning. This is the regular daily custom of Buddh. monks; the drinking of water during time of fasting is, however, allowed. This practice is followed also by some lay people as a specially meritorious discipline; is usually undertaken on the Buddh. holy day (at new moon or full moon). One of the ten points of indiscipline of which the Vajjian monks were accused at the 2nd Council at Vesali (→ Councils, Buddh.) was that of taking food when sun was past zenith. In gen. the Buddh. attitude is one which favours restraint in taking of food rather than long periods of complete fasting. Among the 13 practices which are regarded as aids to the holy life, or 'means of purification' (*dhutanga*), and which are to be observed for short or long periods, 3 concern food, viz., eating one meal a day, eating only from alms-bowl, declining 'second-helpings'. The import. of an accompanying good moral intention is emphasised in connection with such habits of restraint; mere external performance is in itself of no value (*Puggala-paññatti* 275–84); they are useful only 'if they are taken up for sake of frugality, contentedness, purity, etc.' T.O.L.

(China–Japan) → Asceticism. D.H.S.

(Islam) (*ṣawm*, or *ṣiyām*). At first the Muslims observed the → *'Ashūrā'* as a fast, following the Jew. *yōm kippūr*. In Medina the fast of Ramaḍān, 9th month of lunar year, was substituted. Qur. ii:181 says, 'God wishes to make it easy for you', which suggests that the month's 29 days were considered easier than the 40 days of Chr. Lent. But the fast, which is incumbent on all who have reached puberty, are sane, in good health, and not travelling, must be observed rigorously from dawn till after sunset. Food, drink and all bodily enjoyments are to be avoided during hours of fasting. When it ends a snack is taken, then after the night prayer a full meal. Another full meal should be taken as near dawn as poss. Illness and travel give respite, but the number of days should be made up when obstacle is removed. The supererogatory *tarāwīḥ* prayers of 20 → *rak'as* are commonly observed during the night, the *imām* in the mosque also reciting Qur. passages. Ramaḍān is the obligatory fast. To atone for some offences, F. is prescribed. Otherwise voluntary fasts may be observed, but none should last more than three consecutive days. F. is held in esteem as means of obeying God's commands and of gaining control over bodily cravings. Nowadays in most places the begin. and end of Ramaḍān are decided by calendar. Previously, and still in some parts, it has been custom to look for new moon, and when the *qāḍī* was satisfied that it had been seen by reliable witnesses, the month began. The same process was observed at end of month. When next new moon had been seen by reliable witnesses, the month ended and was followed by the lesser festival (→ *Īd al-fiṭr*) In many countries it has been customary to punish people caught breaking the fast, but this is not common nowadays (→ Discipline). In Tunisia the Ramaḍān fast is no longer officially compulsory; but this does not prevent many from observing it. J.R.

E.I., IV, pp. 192–9; Hughes, pp. 124f. (Fasting), 533–5 (Ramazan); Pareja, pp. 647–9; *Mishkāt*, pp. 417ff.; Wensinck, *Creed*, index (*Tarāwīḥ*); Gaudefroy-Demombynes, *Institutions*, pp. 102ff.; Levy, *Social Structure*, index.

Fatalism (Buddh. Rejection) → Determinism (Buddh.). T.O.L.

(China) → Fate (*Ming*). D.H.S.

Fate, or Destiny From Man's time-consciousness stems a sense of fundamental insecurity: the future is known to hold change, old-age and death. Man tries by various means to avoid or delay these dreaded experiences. The notion of F. witnesses to a gen. recognition that, whatever plans may be made, inscrutable powers ultimately decide nature and length of a person's life. The conception of these powers varies acc. to form of relig. professed. Monotheistic faiths logically require that length of life is determined by God, and its nature, good or bad, reflects what the individual morally deserves. Experience, however, does not confirm this view of life: the case of → Job, in Heb. relig., is a notable example of clash between idea of divine omnipotence and justice and undeserved suffering. Similar problems exist in polytheistic faiths, though not so acutely: → Homer repr. → Zeus in several contradictory ways relat. to men's fate (e.g. *Iliad*, 24:527ff., 16:431ff.). Misfortune and death in many religs. are attr. to → demons; such a view gen. implies a cosmic → dualism. Sometimes F. is imagined as an impersonal force greater than the gods (e.g. in Grk. idea of → *Moira*, and Stoic concept of *Anankē* ('Necessity'), or in the fatalistic Islamic → *ḥadīth*: 'what reaches you could not possibly have missed you, and what misses you could not possibly have reached you'). → Astrology implied similar impersonal determinism. The Mesopot. concept of destiny reveals a significant difference of evaluation: destiny was essentially *raison d'être*, each man having a destiny so long as the gods had purpose for him; when they ceased to have it, he died. In Christianity, the issue became one of Free Will and → Predestination: it repr. logical dilemma of believing in both God's omniscience and man's moral responsibility. → Metempsychosis (Hindu, Buddh. and Orphic) implies each person's F. is determined by past action, but it is capable of future change. If F. is thought of in terms of Lat. *fatum*, 'that which has been spoken', it differs from Destiny, which means rather achievement of purpose for which man is created. (→ Evil, Origin). S.G.F.B.

E.R.E., V, pp. 771–96; *O.C.D.*, *s.v.;* M. David, *Les dieux et le destin en Babylonie* (1949); *R.Ae.R.-G.*, pp. 680–1; *R.G.G.*^{3}, V, 1404–10; R. B. Onians, *The Origins of European Thought* (1951), pp. 303ff.; C. J. Bleeker in *Numen*, 2 (1955), pp. 28ff.; S. G. F. Brandon, *M.D.*, *passim; History, Time and Deity*, *passim;* W. M. Watt, *Free Will and Predestination in Early Islam* (1948); *Fatalistic Beliefs in Religion, Folklore, and Literature*, ed. H. Ringren (Stockholm, 1967).

(Chinese) *Ming* = Destiny, appointment, degree or will of Heaven. The Chinese character *Ming* seems to be derived from pictogram of a vassal kneeling in his lord's ancestral hall to receive title to his fief; hence = that which Heaven confers. The early Chou kings (*c.* 900 BC) proclaimed doctrine that they ruled by Mandate or Decree of Heaven, and this had a profound influence on subsequent Chi. thought. In general the Chinese accepted Confucian attitude to F. or destiny, advocated by → Confucius and → Mencius, that it is incumbent on every man to develop his moral nature, but that there is much that is beyond his control and determined by F., i.e. 'that which happens without man's causing it to happen' (Mencius 5A:6). One must do good with singlemindedness and cultivate one's personal life, and wait for F. to take its course, realising that success or failure, longevity or brevity of life are matters of F. A fatalistic view, however, developed, which taught that man's destiny is fixed and unchangeable; it was opposed by → Mo-tzŭ (*fl.* 473–38 BC) on grounds of its disastrous moral effect. Others taught a moral determinism, that Heaven always encourages virtue and punishes vice. → Hsün-tzŭ (*c.* 298–38 BC) completely ruled out influence of supernatural forces, and advocated view that F. is result of purely natural causes working automatically.

The modern Chi. attitude to F. was influenced by Buddh. doctrine of → karma, summed up in Chi. proverb, 'One's destiny is decided at birth'. Birth, marriage, death, prosperity or misfortune are all decreed. Man can only try to cooperate with F., whose decrees can be known through astrologers, fortune-tellers and the like. In general, the belief is held that one's F. cannot be altered but can be mitigated by one's understanding of it and attitude towards it. D.H.S.

E.R.E., V, pp. 783–5; C. H. Plopper, *Chinese Relig. seen through the Proverb* (1926), ch. 11; W. T. Chan, *Source Bk. in Chinese Phil* (1963), p. 78.

(Japan) Buddhism brought to Japan the concept of great cosmic cycles, predetermined and independent of human volition and moral effort. The ultimate destiny of each individual, however, is determined by his own will and moral purpose, his fate being the result of his own deeds whether good or evil. Through a series of rebirths, his destiny is being shaped by his deeds until he learns to perform action without desire or 'clinging'. Then the entail of → *karma* is broken and he attains → Nirvāna. In Jap. Buddhism the attainment of this final destiny can be powerfully assisted by the example, encouragement and aid of a whole hierarchy of supernatural beings.

From the 17th cent. onwards a form of → Messianism was associated with National → Shinto. The destiny of the individual was bound up with that of the Jap. race, descended from the gods and destined to relig., moral, intellectual and political superiority over all other races. A peculiar doctrine of Fate, called the 'Truth of Causality', is assoc. with modern Shinto sect, → Tenri-kyō. All things are predetermined for man by two kinds of fate, one evil or black, the other good or white. Evil fate is the accumulated evil of all human history and previous incarnations. Good fate is all the achieved virtue of the race, individual and social, reaching back to creation itself. Tenri-kyō is a way of turning black fate into white fate, by establishing open channels of communication between the spirit of God and man, when the natural, divinely ordered conditions of health are re-established, and evil fate is miraculously transformed into good fate. D.H.S.

D. C. Holtom, *The National Faith of Japan* (1938), pp. 280ff.

Fātiḥa (the opening [*sūra*]), the first *sūra* of the → Qur., called also *fātiḥat al-kitāb* (the opening [*sūra*] of the Book), which is held in special reverence. It is in form of a prayer. In ritual worship every → *rak'a* contains it near the beginning (→ Prayer). The number of vv. is said to be seven; but this means incl. the → Basmala as a v. xv:87 is commonly treated as ref. to the F. in the phrase 'seven of the *mathānī*', using an Arabic word never satisfactorily explained (cf. Bell, *Introduction*, 120). The F. is used also in various circumstances, e.g. when visiting a shrine, praying for dead, even in connection with commercial dealings. As a → charm it is common. When written and carried, or when the writing is obliterated with water which is then drunk, or when used in squares called *jadwal*, its effect is potent for cure and for warding off harm. J.R.

E.I.[2], II, p. 841; Hughes, p. 125; Nöldeke, *Geschichte*[2], I, pp. 110ff.; Pareja, index.

Fāṭima Daughter of → Muḥammad, married → 'Alī b. Abū Ṭālib. The → Shi'a imams are direct descendants of Md. through this marriage. Their sons al-Ḥasan and al-Ḥusayn succeeded 'Ali, and the remaining imams were descendants of al-Ḥusayn. F. did not long survive her father. When he d., she made a claim to some property at Khaybar, but → Abū Bakr rejected claim, holding that property belonged not to Md. but to the community. She was therefore ill-disposed to A.-B., and it is said that 'Ali did not recognise him as → Caliph till after F.'s death. F., her father and the twelve → imams form in Shi'a belief the pleroma of the 14 most pure ones. A Shi'a trad. says God created F. from the light of his greatness. When the angels were dazzled, God told them this light he had created would be brought forth from the loins of the prophet he favoured most, and that from this light imams would be brought forth to guide mankind. (al-Ḥurr, *Jawāhir*, 240). In certain Shi'a circles F. has become an object of devotion, similar to the Virgin → Mary in the R.C. Church. Prayers are offered to her and feasts are held in her honour. She will be first to enter paradise after resurrection of dead. The amulet in form of five fingers, called by Christians in the Levant the hand of Mary, is called by Muslims the hand of F. (→ Evil eye). J.R.

E.I.[2], II, pp. 841–50; Hughes, p. 125; Pareja, index; Charnay, *Normes*, p. 42; Canaan, *Aberglaube*, pp. 64f.; *Mishkāt*, index of proper names.

Fāṭimids A F. → Caliphate was founded in Tunisia by 'Ubaydallah, who claimed to be descendant of → Muhammad's daughter → Fāṭima, and to be the → *mahdī*. It was a → Shī'a movement of the → Ismā'īlī branch, which later spread eastward to Egypt and Syria. The dynasty lasted from its beginnings in Tunisia in 297/910 to its overthrow in Egypt by Saladin in 567/1171. It left its mark chiefly on Egypt which, during a considerable period, was centre of high culture. Fine works of art and magnificent buildings still witness to this. The Azhar mosque was built in 361/972; a few years later the Caliph al-'Azīz (365–86/975–96) estab. it as an academy (→ Education). J.R.

E.I.[2], pp. 850–62; Pareja, index; Hughes, pp. 125–7; F. Rosenthal, *Ibn Khaldūn*, index; Hitti, *History*, index.

Fatwā → Muftī. J.R.

Feeling (Buddh. analysis) Feeling (*vedanā*) is one of the 5 primary groups of aggregates, or → *khandhas*/*skandhas*, into which human 'personality' is divided. It is, in Buddh. literature, formally divided into 5 kinds: (1) physically agreeable (2) physically disagreeable (3) mentally agreeable (4) mentally disagreeable (5) neutral or indifferent. There is also a 6-fold classification of feeling in terms of the senses, viz: sight, hearing, smelling, tasting, touch, and mental impression. T.O.L.

Fêng Shui (Lit. wind and water). The Chinese term used to define a geomantic system, elevated into a pseudo-science about 12th cent. CE, by which orientation of sites of houses, temples, graves etc., and their form, are determined to ensure prosperity and good fortune of their inhabitants. It is based on beliefs of an anc. Chinese nature cult in a universally active cosmic breath or life force (*ch'i*), the interaction of → *yin* and *yang*, and of five primary elements: wood, fire, earth, metal and water, which resulted therefrom. The activities of these forces are modified within a locality by topographical features, natural or artificial. The forms of hills and direction of water-courses, being outcome of moulding influences of wind (*fêng*) and water (*shui*) within a district, may prove to be lucky or unlucky for its inhabitants; any artificial alteration to natural forms will bring prosperity or calamity, acc. to the new form produced. It is of special interest to the living to secure and preserve an auspicious environment for ancestral graves and temples, since the dead are affected by cosmic currents and can use them for benefit of the living. As *fêng-shui* can make or mar the happiness and well-being of an individual, a family or a locality, Chi. thought tried to create a system to control it. Hence need for the geomancer or *fêng-shui* expert.

The *fêng-shui* practitioner is expert in interpretation of the → Pa Kua (or eight trigrams), which reveal workings of cosmic forces. He uses a mirror in which to see the emanations or influences, an astrological compass and a dowsing-rod. He suggests modifications in shaping the ground, in siting a grave or in planning and erecting a building, by which the forces of *fêng-shui* may be regulated for benefit of men. The repair or building of a pagoda is often suggested to ward off evil and life-destroying forces.

The first historic mention of *fêng-shui* is in the *Lun Hêng* (see chs. 23 and 25) by Wang Ch'ung, a first century CE sceptic philosopher, who characterised it as 'a superstitious belief in aerial currents and subterranean water-courses which bring good or bad fortune'. *Fêng-shui* is said to have been first applied to graves by Kuo P'o (d. CE 324), and to house building by Wang Ch'i (11th cent.); but → divination to determine auspicious sites goes back at least to the beginning of Chou dynasty (*c.* 1000 BC). From the Sung dynasty onwards *Fêng-shui* was an import. element in the popular syncretistic relig. of the Chinese. D.H.S.

J. J. M. de Groot, *The Relig. System of China*, 6 vols. (new ed. 1964), *passim*; H. Doré, *Recherches sur les Superstitions en Chine*, 15 vols. (1914–29), *passim*; C. H. Plopper, *Chinese Relig. seen through the Proverb* (1926), pp. 118ff.; C. A. S. Williams, *Outlines of Chinese Symbolism* (1932), p. 144; J. D. Ball, *Things Chinese*, 5th edn. (1925), pp. 269ff.

Fertility F. in man, animals and (later) fields, has been a basic human concern from dawn of culture. This concern has found relig. expression in a rich variety of idea and practice. Paleolithic images of women, with maternal features emphasised, adumbrate concept of → Great Goddess. Repr. of pregnant animals in → Cave Art prob. attest F.-magic. The development of agriculture had profound effect on relig., producing F.-rituals, based on idea of a Sacred → Marriage between → Earth Goddess and → Sky-god or → Corn Spirit. This sacred marriage was often ritually enacted by king and queen or priest and priestess (→ Myth and Ritual). The temples of some goddesses (e.g. → Ishtar) had sacred courtesans, who assisted F. of their divine mistress by prostituting themselves (→ Prostitution, sacred). Sexual symbols are found in many religs., partic. Egypt., Grk., Hinduism (→ phallic cults, → lingam, → ithyphallic gods, → breast, → yoni). F., because of its assoc. with life, has gen. been regarded as sacred and subject to → tabu; however, it has obviously been impossible to divorce it from eroticism. F.-cults and customs are still a feature of folk relig. among many Chr. peoples, esp. R.C. and E. Christians. (→ Festivals). S.G.F.B.

G. Van der Leeuw, *La religion* (1948), pp. 82ff.; M. Eliade, *Traité d'histoire des religions* (1949), chs. 7–9, E.T., *Patterns of Comp. Religion* (1958), chs. 7–9; E. Lehmann in *L.R.–G.*, I, pp. 25ff.; *R.G.G.*[3], II, pp. 1166–8; E. O. James, *Comparative Religion* (1938), pp. 33ff., 86ff.; J. Maringer, *The Gods of Prehistoric Man* (E.T. 1960), pp. 97ff.; *M.A.W.*, pp. 184ff., 253ff.; J. Mellart, *Earliest Civilizations of the Near East* (1965), pp. 92ff.; W. K. C. Guthrie, *The Greeks and their Gods* (1950), pp. 30ff.; J. B. Frazer, *G.B.*, *passim*; P. J. Ucko and A. Rosenfeld, *Palaeolithic Cave Art* (1967), *passim*; G. R. Levy, *The Gate of Horn* (1948), *passim*; J. Gonda, *Die Religionen Indiens*, I (1960), *s.v.* ('Fruchtbarkeit').

Festival(s): anc. World; Christian The term has a wide connotation. F. derives from 'feast', and is used both in apposition to, and as substitute for, it. Strictly, F. means a relig. anniversary of joyous kind, as opp. to → Fasts; but it is often employed for non-joyous occasions. F. are gen. annual and related to → Calendar; but some occur at longer intervals (e.g. Grk. Olympic Games every 4 yrs., Heb. Jubilee (50 yrs.), R.C. Holy Year (25 yrs.)). Calendar F. are gen. connected with the seasons; many prob. orig. from seasonal crises affecting pastoral or agric. life. F. commemorating events of a sacred history, such as →→ Easter; Passover, often have seasonal aspect. The following are notable F. of religs. of anc. Near East and Europe:

Egypt: New Year F., connected orig. with coincidence of rising of Sothis (Dog-star) and inundation of Nile: Sothis was identified with → Isis. F. of Opet, in honour of → Amun, held during inundation; it had a fertility aspect. F. of Min, fertility-god of Koptos (→ ithyphallic gods) was harvest-F. In winter-month of Khoiak, F. of death and resurrection of → Osiris were kept: these F. were connected with ploughing and sowing of fields. The Sed-F. was a royal F., celebrated periodically as a ritual renewal of kingship.

Mesopot.: (1) New Year or → Akitu F. (2) F. of Dumuzi or → Tammuz, commemorating death and resurrection of god of vegetation. (3) There were also monthly F. connected with phases of moon (→ Sin).

Hebrew: (1) → Passover and → Mazzoth were Spring F. (2) Feast of Weeks or Pentecost was agricult. F. at start of wheat harvest. (3) *Sukkoth* (Tabernacles) or Feast of Ingathering, an autumn vintage F., which assumed character of New Year F. at Jerusalem: it became connected with *Rosh hash Shanah*, 'Feast of Trumpets', on 1st day of 7th month, Tishri (Oct.), prob. marking begin. of New Year. (4) F. of Purim, commemorating a notable occasion of Israel's deliverance during Persian period. (5) F. of Dedication (→ *Chanukkah*), in memory of purification of Temple after desecration by Antiochus Epiphanes (168 BC). (6) F. of Wood Offering (15 April), recalling offerings of wood for Temple (Neh. 10:34, 13:31). (8) *Yōm Kippūr* (Day of → Atonement). (→ Judaism).

Greek: (1) Thesmorphia: performed by women

in honour of → Demeter at time of autumn sowing. (2) Skirophoria: fertility ritual performed by maidens at time of threshing, and assoc. with → Aphrodite and → Athena. (3) Thalysia: harvest-F. assoc. with Demeter. (4) Thargelia: orig. expiation rite, designed to expel past evil and sin of killing corn-spirit preparatory to harvest. Rite consisted of expelling the → *pharmakos*, and presenting to → Apollo the *thargelia*, first-fruits of harvest. (5) → Anthesteria. (6) Lenaia: phallic procession, connected with → Dionysos, held at Athens in Jan. to promote fertility of fields. (7) the Greater Dionysia: Athenian F. in honour of Dionysos, held in March. Orig. a spring dithyrambic ritual, it provided occasion for production of tragedies and comedies of the great Athenian dramatists. (8) F. (public) connected with → Eleusinian Mysteries, having agrarian significance and concerned with fertility. (9) Panathenaia, held in summer, honouring birthday of → Athena. Homer's epics were then recited publicly. The procession is repr. on frieze of Parthenon. (10) Hyakinthia: held in May at Amyklai, in Lakonia, in honour of Apollo and Hyakinthos. Latter was prob. a pre-Hellenic vegetation deity of Adonis-Attis type, since F. commemorated his death and resurrection. (11) The Olympic Games, held in honour of Olympian Zeus, and Pythian Games at Delphi, held every 8th yr., and connected with cult of Apollo. (→ Greek Relig.).

Rome: the following were anc. native agric. F.: (1) processions of the Salii, armed dancers, held in March, in honour of → Mars, an agric. and war god. (2) at the *Fordicidia*, 15 April, a cow in calf (*forda*) was sacrificed to → Earth Mother (Tellus Mater). (3) *Parilia*, lustral rite, held on 21 April, to purify cattle and herdsmen. It also marked trad. birthday of Rome. (4) *Robigalia*, procession and apotropaic sacrifice on 25 April to Robigus, god of wheat-mildew. (5) *Floralia* (28 April–3 May) in honour of Flora, goddess of flowering plants. Its licentious character prob. derived from orig. concern with fertility. (6) *Vestalia* (9 June) in honour of → Vesta. (7) F. of → Bona Dea (1 May). (8) *Lemuria* (9, 11, 13 May) in honour of the *lemures*, ghosts of dead, regarded as dangerous owing to lack of funerary rites. (9) *Parentalia* (13–22 Feb.), private commemoration of ancestral dead. (10) *Saturnalia*, at winter solstice. Saturnus was prob. anc. god of sowing and seed-corn, identified with Grk. → Kronos. F. began with sacrifice of pig in temple of Saturn. It was a time of merry-making, with reversal of roles (masters serving slaves), and election of mock-king (→ Abbot of Misrule). (11) *Lupercalia:* anc. F., combining motifs of fertility and expiation. held on 15 Feb. by priests called Luperci: orig. name of deity concerned was forgotten. A notable feature of F. was the striking of women, to make them fertile, by near-naked youths with whips made from hide of sacrificed victim. (12) *Terminalia* (23 Feb.): sacrifices made at boundary stones to Terminus, god of boundaries. In Rome annual F. of imported cults were celebrated: → Bacchanalia, and F. of →→ Cybele; Isis; Mithras. (→ Roman Relig.).

Hittite: eighteen F. are mentioned on a ritual tablet, some named after seasons. One major F. called *purulliyas* was a spring-F., at which myth concerning slaying of the Dragon Illuyankas was liturgically recited, in honour of weather-gods of Hatti and Zippalanda and a chthonic goddess Lilwani (→ Enuma elish). (Hittite Relig.).

Iran: the two great F. of → Zoroastrianism are Naurūz (New Year) and Mihrajān (F. of → Mithra); the latter also appears to have been orig. a New Year F. There is evidence of four seasonal F.: Mihrajān or Magophonia (autumn equinox); Xurram (winter solstice); Naurūz (vernal equinox); Tīragān (summer solstice).

Christian: the two major F. which commemorate events in life of Christ are also related to seasons: (1) → Easter occurs in spring; (2) → Christmas is close to winter solstice. Pentecost, commemorating descent of → Holy Spirit, derives from Heb. → Feast of Weeks. Other F. relate to career of Christ: →→ Advent, Circumcision, Ephiphany, Lent, Holy Week, Ascension; or life of → Virgin Mary and saints. There are theological F., e.g. →→ Corpus Christi, Trinity Sunday. S.G.F.B.

E.R.E., V, pp. 835–94; E. O. James, *Seasonal Feasts and Festivals* (1961); *R.G.G.*, II, 906–23; *H.D.B.*², pp. 294ff.; I. Epstein, *Judaism* (1959), pp. 170ff.; *O.C.D.*, p. 360; *R.Ae.R.-G.*, pp. 185ff.; Dhorme, *R.B.A.*, pp. 234ff.; O. R. Gurney, *The Hittites* (1952), pp. 151ff.; T. H. Gaster, *Thespis* (1961), pp. 95ff.; G. Van der Leeuw, *La religion* (1948), pp. 380ff., 546ff.; M. Eliade, *Traité d'Histoire de religion* (1949), ch. 11; E.T., *Patterns in Comparative Religion* (1958), ch. 11; Brandon, *History, Time and Deity* (1965), pp. 65ff.; E. Uphill, 'The Egyptian Sed-Festival Rites', *J.N.E.S.*, 24 (1965); H. H. Rowley, *Worship in Anc. Israel* (1967); *E.J.R.*, pp. 144ff.

(Buddh.) Public celebration of relig. occasions is a prominent feature of Buddh. countries. The major occasions are (1) regular annual → Holy Days in Buddh. calendar, together with (2) such others as occur intermittently in course of life of monastery and its neighbourhood, such as ordinations to monkhood, special days of merit-making, the giving of new robes to monks, and other similar occasions. The most universally celebrated is *Vesākha*, which belongs to first category; it is a celebration of birth, enlightenment, and passing into final *nibbāna* of Buddha.

This is a monastery-centred festival, of great importance for monks, but an occasion in which entire neighbourhood also participates.

In rural areas of continental S.E. Asia this festival spreads over three days, from 14th to 16th day of sixth month (by Buddh. calendar). The festival is marked by public reading of lessons concerning life of Buddha, hearing of sermons preached by monks, expounding significance of the day, and by public processions in open air, with circumambulation of local Buddh. shrine. In urban areas the festival is limited to one day. In Bangkok a royal procession circumambulates the Royal Chapel, or *Bōd*, of the Emerald Buddha; the king and queen of Thailand take part in this, leading royal family and officials; the procession takes place in evening of full moon; the people carry lighted tapers, and the *Bōd* is decorated with candles and lights and flowers. Similar ceremonies are held in villages, where abbot of monastery leads other monks and lay-people 3 times round the *Bōd*. As they go, they chant stanzas of praise to Buddha. When the 3 circumambulations are completed, monks and people usually enter the sanctuary for further devotions and readings, which may go on until late hour of night. Similar ceremonies may be held on *Māgha Pūja*, 3 months earlier, which commemorates Buddha's promulgation of monastic code of discipline, the → Vinaya. An import. festival which comes at end of Buddh. 'Lent' or *Vassa* is that connected with presentation by lay-people of new robes to monks. This is called *Kathina* (i.e., 'cloth') ceremony. The gift of robes may be sponsored by a number of villagers, or by one wealthy person, or a local business firm. Since occasion marks end of Lenten period, it is noisiest and gayest of popular festivals. In add. to robes, it is usual for other gifts to be presented to monks (candles, soap, tea, note books etc.). Various kinds of entertainment for lay people are also provided, and stalls are set up to provide food. (See H. K. Kaufman, *Bankhuad* (1960), pp. 185–9; Manning Nash, *The Golden Road to Modernity* (1965), pp. 132–7.) A further occasion for public festivity is → ordination of a local inhabitant into Buddh. Sangha. This will be preceded by procession, sometimes led by local band of musicians, and followed by outdoor entertainment and feasting. The considerable expense of such festivities is often shared by the guests, who make contributions. In rural areas, therefore, ordinations are often, though not always, held after rice-harvest, when funds are more plentiful. Fund-raising efforts on behalf of local temple are also occasions for celebrations and parades; the relig. significance of event is 'merit-making', which it entails for all donors (in Thailand, '*tham-bun*'; in Ceylon, a '*pin-kama*').

Various other festivals are observed in Buddh. countries of S. Asia, which vary from country to country, such as New Year's Day, Rice-Pagoda Ritual, First-Fruits Ritual, the celebration connected with → *paritta*, or ceremonial changing of protective formulae on some special occasion: these enjoy varying prominence and importance, and some are only marginally Buddh. (→ Holy Days, Buddh.). T.O.L.

J. G. Scott, *The Burman: His Life and Notions* (1903, repr. 1963); W. A. Graham, *Siam*, 2 vols. (1924); B. Ryan, *Sinhalese Village* (1958); (for Burma) Manning Nash, *The Golden Road to Modernity* (1965); (for Thailand) H. K. Kaufman, *Bangkhuad: A Community Study in Thailand* (1960); Phra Anuman Rajadhon, *Life and Ritual in Old Siam* (1961); K. E. Wells, *Thai Buddhism* (1959); (general) Manning Nash et alii, *Anthropological Studies in Theravāda Buddhism* (1966).

(Chinese) Apart from modern festivals of political significance, such as May Day and the 10th of the 10th month to mark the founding of the Republic, there are numerous relig. or semi-relig. festivals throughout the year to mark birthdays of Buddhist and Taoist deities, and deified heroes and scholars. Each temple has its own festival in honour of its principal deity, often assoc. with annual fair and theatrical performances, and commenced by appropriate relig. ceremonies. Six great F.'s are universally observed throughout China in course of agricultural or Moon year. Three are F.'s of the living (*Jên Chieh*, from *jên*—man), and three are F.'s of the dead (*Kuei Chieh*, from *kuei*—spirit). These six annual festivals are of great antiquity, and all have profound relig. significance. The greatest of all F. is New Year, celebrated over fifteen days and preceded by great preparations. Ancestors and household gods are honoured and worshipped, families united, friends visited, debts paid, homes garnished; a time of general festivity and feasting. The Dragon-boat festival on 5th of 5th moon (→ Dragon), and the great autumn or harvest F. on 15th of 8th moon have now lost most of their relig. significance. The F. of the dead are → Ch'ing Ming, celebrated early in the 3rd moon, when graves are visited and repaired and sacrifices made at the graves; the F. of Hungry Ghosts or All Souls' Day on 15th of 7th moon, a F. which goes back to a primitive spirit-worship but which from 8th cent. onwards became identified with popular Buddh. F. called *Yü-lan-p'ên* (Ullambana) and characterised by masses for souls of dead; and finally a F. on 1st of 10th moon when graves are visited and bundles of clothing burned to provide warm clothing for the spirits. Apart from giving relief in relaxation and gaiety from burden of endless toil and drudgery, the main function of F. in China was to emphasise family and social (and now, national) solidarity, embracing both living and dead. D.H.S.

Bredon and Mitrophanow, *The Moon Year* (1927); D. Bodde (tr.), *Annual Customs and Festivals in Peking* (1965); K. L. Reichelt, *Relig. in Chinese Garment* (1951), pp. 68ff., 149ff.; M. Granet, *Festivals and Songs of Ancient China* (1932), pp. 147ff.

(Hindu) The Hindu scheme of festivals has a double complexity: first, there is a large number of sacred days, fixed by ref. (chiefly) to the lunar calendar; second, there are different practices in different regions. The most import. period for festivities are spring and autumn. The best known festival of spring is the Holī, orig. connected with the god of love, Kāma, and in which caste and other tabus are broken down. It sometimes merges with the *dolā* or swing festival, e.g. at Puri in Orissa, during which images of the god are swung. One of the chief autumn celebrations is the Diwali or Dīpāvali, festival of lights in October-November, in which there is worship of Kali and (more widely) Laksmi. The winter solstice is period for bathing at Prayaga (Allahabad), which every twelve years has the Kumbha Mela, in which vast congregations of holy men gather to bathe at confluence of the Jumna and Ganges (→ Sacred rivers, Hindu). There are similar bathing festivals at Hardwar, Ujjain, Nasik, etc. The gathering of harvest in late autumn is occasion for a first-fruits festival, at which rice is boiled and cattle are garlanded, and is preceded by autumn celebrations known in Bengal as the *Durga puja* (worship of Durga), the tenth night of which (Dusserah) is occasion of chief festivities, incl. enactments of story of the → Ramayana, known as the Rāmalīlā (Rama play). Another import. day is that of Sarasvati, goddess of learning, celebrated in January-February. As well as these fairly widespread feasts, there are regional and local occasions, often of great splendour and excitement, such as the drawing of local deity in procession on a carriage (*rathayātrā*). The most famous of these is festival of Jaggannath at Puri and Orissa, but those at Kanci, Rameswaram and Madurai (where it is Śiva's local spouse Mīnakṣī, who has most famous S. Indian temple devoted to her, who is honoured) are also splendid. The celebration of such festivals in different parts of India stimulates → pilgrimages. In add. to gods, famous spiritual teachers are commemorated ritually, such as birthdays of → Sankara, Ramanuja, Ramananda, etc.; different sects and castes have their special holy days. N.S.

Muriel M. Underhill, *The Hindu Religious Year* (1921); P. V. Jagadis Ayyar, *South-Indian Festivities* (1921); D. K. Roy *Kumbha; India's Ageless Festival* (1955); A. C. Mukerji, *Ancient Indian Fasts and Feasts* (1932).

(Islam) → *'Īd al-aḍḥā; 'Īd al-fiṭr.* J.R.

(Japanese) The main F.'s of Japan are intimately connected with → Shinto. The times of their celebration were originally based, as in China, on a lunar calendar and assoc. of each F. with a particular season has in large measure been destroyed by intro. of European calendar in 1873, as New Year is now five or six weeks earlier than formerly. The F.'s legally recognised as national holidays are 12 in number, and divided into two classes: Fete-days and Grand Relig. F.'s. They are designed to emphasise national solidarity, honour and prestige of imperial family and divine emperor, and gratitude to gods and ancestors for benefits bestowed on nation and people. In relig. ceremonies and worship conducted at the imperial shrines on F. days the emperor himself was chief officiant, whilst similar ceremonies were conducted on his behalf at principal shrines throughout nation. The chief relig. F.'s are those of New Year, the vernal and autumnal equinoxes, anniversary of death of the first emperor, Jimmu Tennō Sai, and F.'s of first-fruits and harvest thanksgiving, when worship is offered to gods who have given the harvest. Besides these national F.'s there are numerous popular F.'s, celebrated throughout year in honour of various Shinto deities, and the famous Buddh. festivals of Buddha's birthday on 8 April, and *Bon* or All Souls' Day in middle of July. Numerous local F.'s of great importance are held in special localities. In all, underlying dominant theme of joy and gratitude, is sense of need to keep on good terms with the invisible spiritual powers. D.H.S.

B. H. Chamberlain, *Things Japanese*, 5th edn., pp. 159ff.; D. C. Holtom, *The National Faith of Japan* (1938); *E.R.E.*, III, pp. 116–7; J. Herbert, *Shinto* (1967), pp. 168ff.

Fetish, Fetishism F. is derived from Portuguese *feitico*, *ex.* Lat. *factitius*, meaning 'skilfully made'. Term was orig. used by Portug. sailors for objects venerated by W. Africans. C. de Brosses added term to vocab. of Compar. Relig. through his book *Du culte des dieux fétiches* (1760). He used it for cult of various objects, natural or artificial, endowed with supernatural virtue, current among primitive peoples. Later scholars extended its use so widely that it has rather lost its value as a definition. Examples of F. incl. →→ Churingas; Ark of Yahweh; icons. S.G.F.B.

E.R.E., V, pp. 894–906; G. Van der Leeuw, *La religion* (1948), pp. 23ff., 441ff.; M. David, *R.H.R.*, 171 (1967), pp. 207ff.

Filial Piety (China and Japan) Though recognised as important virtue in pre-Confucian China, it was only after time of → Confucius that Filial Piety came to be accepted as the supreme virtue. The *Hsaio Ching* or *Classic of Filial Piety* (trans.

by J. Legge: *S.B.E.*, vol. 3, 1899), erroneously attr. to Tsêng-tzŭ, a disciple of Confucius, was probably composed early in Han dynasty, and has exerted immense influence ever since. F.-P. required that a man should serve his parents while they are alive, mourn for them for 3 years when they die and continue thereafter to worship them and sacrifice to them accord. to prescribed ritual. Confucius made it clear that F.-P. does not consist merely in adequate support of parents, but includes obedience and dutiful compliance with their wishes, and care to cause them no anxiety. F.-P. also demanded provision of a male heir to continue the → ancestor-cult. (→ Ethics). D.H.S.

A. H. Smith, *Chinese Characteristics*, 2nd edn. (1895), pp. 171ff.; J. D. Ball, *Things Chinese*, 5th edn. (1925), pp. 238f.

Confucian morality has exercised great influence in Japan over past thirteen centuries, and loyalty and F.-P. came to be recognised as root of all virtues. D.H.S.

B. H. Chamberlain, *Things Japanese*, 5th edn. (1905), pp. 165–6.

'Filioque' Clause Lat. doctrinal formula meaning 'and the Son', added by W. Church to Nicene-Constantinopolitan Creed immediately after words 'the Holy Ghost Who proceedeth from the Father'. It affirmed belief in 'Double Procession of the Holy Ghost'. The formula was never accepted by → E. Church, and became a chief issue between E. and W. Church. The → C. of E. has followed W. trad. (→ Creeds). S.G.F.B.

D.C.C., *s.v.;* N. Zernov, *Eastern Christendom* (1961), pp. 89ff.

Finno-Ugric Religion Under heading of F.-U. R. are incl. the relig. beliefs and practices of many E. European and N. Asiatic peoples: the Baltic Finns, Lapps, Esthonians and Hungarians (Magyars) in Europe; the Mordvins, Cheremiss, Votiaks, Ostiaks, Voguls, Samoyeds and others in Asiatic Russia. Subject to Christ. influence from an early date, few traces now remain of the orig. relig. of the Finns, Lapps and Magyars; more has survived among the Asiatic peoples.

The deities of the F.-U. peoples comprised a hierarchy, supreme among them being a → High God (sky-god) known in Finland as Jumala. In hist. times he appears to have been a → *deus otiosus*, to whom no sacrifices were offered, though he might be anthropomorphised, e.g. by the Cheremiss, in folk poetry. A god of atmospheric phenomena was the Finnish Ilmarinen (cf. Votiak In(m) and Ostiak Ilem or Item). In the → *Kalevala* (which in present form dates from 19th cent.) Ilmarinen is a blacksmith, perhaps indic. an orig. connection with lightning. Most import. among the great gods was, however, the god of thunder (cf. Thor in → Scandinavian Religion); called Ukko ('old man', 'grandfather') by the Finns, his cult remained important in Finland well into Middle Ages. Other heavenly deities incl. personifications of sun and moon, wind, frost and clouds. Among lesser deities, gods (or spirits) of forest were partic. import.; these were many and various, some being assoc. with animals, such as the bear and wolf: the bear was esp. venerated. → Sacrifice was made to forest spirit(s) for wellbeing of cattle and for success in hunting. The rituals were carried out in sacred groves, or before sacred trees, and were entrusted to priests or shamans. Sacrifice was also made by the Lapps to stones or wooden objects, called *seitar*; these were often placed on hills, and may have had some orig. connection with cult of dead.

F.-U. beliefs concerning nature and destiny of man show broad similarity with those of other pre-literate peoples. It seems that man was thought to possess two 'souls', a free-soul (Cheremiss *ört*, Votiak *urt*), which might leave body in dream or trance; and a life-soul (Ostiak *lil*, Vogul *lili*, Esthonian *leil*), which left body only on death. The free-soul might assume, either before or after death, other forms, e.g. those of a butterfly or bird; or it might reveal itself as a *Doppelgänger* (Finnish *haltija*): 'the dead themselves do not walk, it is their *haltijas* which appear as ghosts'. All natural objects were believed to possess a *haltija*: thus the Finnish forest spirit was called *Metsänhaltija* ('Forest ruler', cf. Swedish *skogsrå*), and might be thought of either as an old man with a coat of lichen, or as a woman. Mortuary customs had dual purpose of speeding dead on way into the beyond, and of preventing their return. There was no clear conception of future state of dead, though the *Kalevala* speaks of kingdom of Tuoni (Tuonela), to which the dead hero Lemminkäinen is carried along the dark river, in terms reminiscent of the tale of Balder in → Scandinavian Religion. The customary grave-goods were provided, and periodical offerings made to ensure continued help of departed. Among the Lapps, and to a lesser extent among other F.-U. peoples, the shaman (Lapp. *nåjd*) acted as mediator between spirit-world and world of men (→ Shamanism). E.J.S.

U. Holmberg, *The Mythology of All Races IV: Finno-Ugric, Siberian* (1928); I. Paulson, *et al.*, *Die religionen Nord-eurasiens und amerikanische Arktis* (1962); I. Paulson, 'Seelenvorstellungen u. Totenglaube der permischen und wolga-finnischen Völker', *Numen*, XI (1964).

Fiqh (Orig. knowledge, understanding). Came to be applied partic. to jurisprudence. It was felt that F. must regulate matters of worship, belief, family law, social behaviour, political affairs, indeed all aspects of human life. One might say of it *nihil humanum a me alienum puto*. The theory was that all matters must be controlled by the relig. law

(→ sharī'a); but as time went on it became more and more of a theory, for many aspects of subject were little more than matters of scholarly debate. J.R.

*E.I.*², II, pp. 886–91; Levy, *Social Structure*, index; Coulson, *Law*, pp. 75, 83; Gaudefroy-Demombynes, *Institutions*, pp. 68f.; Pareja, index; F. Rosenthal, *Ibn Khaldun* index (Jurisprudence); Rahman, *Islam*. pp. 101–3.

Fire-cult The ability to kindle and use fire is a unique characteristic of *homo-sapiens*. To anc. Egyptians F. had ambivalent significance: it was element of purification and *post-mortem* punishment. In Grk. mythology F. was withheld from men by → Zeus, but → Prometheus stole it and gave it to them. In the → Gāthās, F. is symbol of Truth, and → Zoroaster confirmed its cult; he also depicts F. as an eschatological ordeal. The hearth-fire was deemed sacred, being personified and worshipped by Greeks as Hestia, by Romans as → Vesta. Although fire-gods existed in many religs. (e.g. the Mesopot. Nusku; Grk. → Hepaestus; Rom. Vulcan), with exception of the Vedic → Agni, none achieved major status. Fire has been a means of eternal punishment in many eschatologies (e.g. Jew., Chr. Islamic); in Chr. belief the fires of → Purgatory were purgatorial. F. was also means of → apotheosis (e.g. of Heracles). The myth of the phoenix, rejuvenating itself by fire, is prob. a Grk. transformation of Egypt. Benu-bird, the → ba of → Rē. (→ Altar, Iran). S.G.F.B.

E.R.E., VI, pp. 26ff.; *R.Ae.R.-G.*, pp. 189ff.; Dhorme, *R.B.A.*, pp. 59, 111ff.; Zaehner, *D.T.Z.*, *passim*; L. Séchan, *Le mythe de Prométhée* (1951). J. G. Frazer, *Adonis, Attis, Osiris*, (*G.B.*), I, pp. 110ff.

Firstborn The Heb. custom of dedicating F. of man and beast to God (Ex. 13:11ff.) prob. orig. as prophylactic act on behalf of later offspring at nomadic stage of culture. The ritual 'redeeming' of F. poss. repr. later substitution for orig. sacrifice (cf. II Kg. 3:27; Mic. 6:7; → Carthaginian Relig.). The acc. of → Abraham's sacrifice of Isaac (Gen. 22) may reflect memory of sacrifice of F. S.G.F.B.

*H.D.B.*², *s.v.; P.C.*², pp. 159c; *E.R.E.*, VI, pp. 31–6.

First Sermon, of Buddha → Dhamma-Cakkappavattana Sutta. T.O.L.

Fish, Symbol of From 2nd cent. the F. was used in Chr. art and lit. as symbol of Christ, and sometimes of the newly baptised. The orig. and meaning of symbol are obscure. The Grk. word for F., *Ichthus*, forms acrostic = *Iesous Christos, Theou Usios Sōtēr* ('Jesus Christ, Son of God, Saviour'); but it is not certain whether symbol derived from acrostic or *vice versa*. The F. had long pre-Chr. trad. as a relig. symbol (e.g. assoc. with → Osiris). In 4th cent. the F. also became emblem of the → Eucharist. (→ Atargatis). S.G.F.B.

F. J. Dolger, *ΙΧΘΥC*, Bd. 1–5 (1910–43); *D.C.C., s.v.;* F. Grossi Gondi, *I monumenti cristiani* (1923), pp. 51ff.; R. Eisler, *Orpheus, the Fisher* (1921); *R.G.G.*³, II, 968; *R.Ae.R.-G.*, pp. 191–4; E. R. Goodenough, *Jewish Symbols in Greco-Roman Period*, V–VI (1958).

Five Elements (Chinese) The F.E. theory was prob. the earliest Chi. attempts to account for structure of physical universe. The theory first appears in the Hung Fan or Great Plan, attrib. to 12th cent. BC and incorpor. into the → Shu Ching. The F.E. were considered to be fundamental forms of matter: wood, fire, earth, metal and water. In post-Confucian times, partic. with Tsou Yen (*c*. 350–270 BC), the theory came to be assoc. with that of → Yin and Yang, and became theoretical basis for a whole science of → divination: belief in intimate relation between laws of nature and human affairs, and a cyclical interpret. of nature and history. The F.E. were interpreted in terms of 'powers, agents or forces', which in turn came to dominate the processes of natural evolution and influenced course of history and government. From Han Dyn. onwards the Yin-Yang and F.E. theories, systematized and amplified, formed basis of Chi. → cosmogony. The theory was developed further by the neo-Confucians of Sung Dyn., who expounded a scheme of cosmogenic genealogy as follows: the Supreme Ultimate (T'ai Chi) gave rise to Yin and Yang from which arose the F.E., which in turn produced the Manifold of Nature. Acc. to → Chu Hsi, the F.E. are not identical with wood, fire, earth, metal and water; but are subtle essences, whose nature is best exemplified by these objects. (→ Wu Hsing). D.H.S.

S. Couling, *Encycl. Sinica* (new edn. 1964), pp. 183f.; C. B. Day, *The Philosophers of China* (1962) *passim*; Fung Yu-lan, *Hist. of Chinese Philosophy*, 2 vols. (1927 and 1953), *passim*.

Flagellants Self-scourging as act of penance had long been practised by Chr. ascetics. In 1259, suddenly but doubtless in reaction to gen. psychological tension, in Perugia a mass-feeling of penitence found expression in public flagellation. It had an epidemic effect, and spread rapidly outside Italy. Again in 1349, prob. under threat of Black Death, mass flagellation broke out in Germany. Penitents formed themselves into a Brotherhood of the F. They believed that 33½ days of flagellation would cleanse soul from all sin. The Church soon realised danger of such fanaticism, esp. since it implied claim of individual to free himself of sin without eccles. mediation. The F. were condemned by Church and civil authority, and the movement grad. disappeared. S.G.F.B.

E.R.E., VI, *s.v.;* J. A. MacCulloch, *Medieval Faith and Fable* (1932), pp. 251ff.; *R.G.G.*[3], II, 971–2; J. Nohl, *The Black Death* (E.T. 1961), ch. 10.

Flood, The Legends of a catastrophic F. exist among many peoples, incl. anc. Grks., American Indians, Chinese, Polynesians, and in India and Iran; the most notable examples are the Mesopot. and Heb. Various theories have been advanced in explanation: the legends seem gen. to have a local orig., though most assign cause of F. to divine anger or an evil being. The Mesopot.-F. legend is Sumerian in orig., and prob. arose from experience of floods in delta of Tigris and Euphrates: there is archeological evidence of severe flooding in the area. A frag. text tells how Ziusudra, learning of divine plan to drown mankind, escaped by building a great boat. After F., Ziusudra offered sacrifice, and → Anu and → Enlil conferred immortality on him. In Sumerian King List the F. is used for chronological demarcation. The Akkadian F.-legend is preserved on Tab. XI of Epic of → Gilgamesh. It is cleverly inserted there to show Gilgamesh that his quest for immortality was hopeless. Utanapishtim, whom he had consulted, explains his own immortality as due to his survival of Flood. Acc. to his account, Enlil ordered F. to punish mankind. U., warned by → Ea, escaped, with 'the seed of all living things', in a great ship. The F., which lasts six days and nights, is vividly described. After ship grounds on Mt. Nisir, U. sends out, in turn, a dove, swallow and raven, before emerging. He offers sacrifice, and Enlil rewards him and wife with immortality. The Heb. F.-legend (Gen. 6:11ff.) which evidently derives from Mesopot. sources, is inserted by → J. into his Primaeval History at cost of obscuring role of Noah as foretold in Gen. 5:28–9. The F. is explained as divine punishment (Gen. 6:11–13). In Chr. imagery, deliverance from F. signified → Baptism, and Noah's → Ark repr. Church. (→ Ante-diluvian). S.G.F.B.

A.N.E.T., pp. 42ff., 72ff., 265; *E.R.E.*, IV, *s.v.* ('Deluge'); S. N. Kramer, *Sumerian Mythology* (1961), pp. 97ff.; A. Heidel, *The Gilgamesh Epic and Old Test. Parallels* (1949[2]); *M.A.W.*, pp. 118ff., 398ff.; Brandon, *C.L.*, pp. 87ff., 142ff.; A. Parrot, *Déluge et Arche de Noé* (1953); *H.G.R.*, V (1952), pp. 59ff.; W. G. Lambert and A. R. Millard, *Atra-hasis: the Babylonian Story of the Flood* (1969); M. Civil, *Sumerian Flood Story* (1969).

Fo Chinese term for → Buddha, but it is a mistake always to equate Fo with the historical Buddha, who is known in China as *Shih-chia-mou-ni Fo* (Sakyamuni). The Chi. equivalent of → Tathāgata is *Ju-lai Fo* (Thus-come Buddha), who is regarded as all-powerful and omniscient; he is usually repres. as gilded image, seated cross-legged upon a lotus blossom, his eyes half-closed in contemplation. The most universally worshipped Fo is → Amitabha (*O-mi-t'o Fo*), whilst → Maitreya (*Mi-lo-Fo*) is regarded as the Buddha who is to come and his image, repres. in nearly all temples, is easily recognised by his laughing and hope-inspiring face. In Chi. → Mahāyāna Buddhism, every intelligent person who has broken through bondage of sense, perception and self, knows unreality of all phenomena and is ready to enter into → Nirvana, is reckoned as a Fo. The term is often used as a honorific for some person who is noted for saintliness or kingly virtue. D.H.S.

E. T. C. Werner, *Dictionary of Chinese Mythology* (1932), pp. 130ff.

Folklore The term was coined in 1846 by W. J. Thomas to replace earlier expression 'popular antiquities'. It is now gen. used to denote 'traditional Beliefs, Customs, Stories, Songs, and Sayings current among backward peoples, or retained by the uncultured classes of more advanced peoples'. There are Folklore societies in many countries, with journals (Brit.: *Folk-Lore;* U.S.A.: *Journ. of Amer. Folklore*). S.G.F.B.

C. S. Burne, *The Handbook of Folklore* (new edn. 1957); L. H. Jordan, *Comparative Religion: its Genesis and Growth* (1905), pp. 308ff.; *R.G.G.*[3], VI, pp. 1462–9; E. O. James, 'The Influence of Folklore on Hist. of Relig.', *Numen*, IX (1962); *H.G.R.*, V (1952), pp. 9ff.; R. M. Dorson, *Amer. Folklore* (1959).

Food, Rules (Buddh.) The most import. single rule with regard to food, in Buddh. trad., is, espec. for the monk, that of restraint in eating, which covers also obligation not to eat after 12 noon. (→ Fasting, Buddh.). Apart from this, alcohol of any kind is forbidden 'as tending to cloud the mind'. (→ Morality). The vow, incumbent on all Buddhists, monastic and lay, not to take life, causes them to be vegetarian in their food habits, though with varying degrees of strictness. Among Buddhists, emphasis is laid on wrongfulness of killing an animal (since it is a sentient being), rather than on eating its flesh when dead. The onus of bad → *karma* comes upon the slayer rather than the eater—a somewhat different attitude from that found among Hindus, who regard eating of meat as equally fraught with bad karmic consequences. T.O.L.

(China–Japan) → Confucianism is remarkably free from food restrictions. All food is acceptable and may be offered to gods and ancestor-spirits in sacrifice. In → Taoism, certain schools of hygiene taught that the adept must eliminate from diet grains, wine and meat, which were offensive to the interior gods who ruled within the personality. Most Buddhist monks in China and Japan are strictly vegetarian. → Buddhism seems to have been more successful in

Japan than in China in imposing restrictions on laity against eating meat, though even there eating of fish is tolerated. In both China and Japan lay devotees often take vows to eat no meat or join vegetarian societies; pilgrims, while on pilgrimage to shrines, will take only a vegetarian diet. Behind the prohibition of meat lies the Buddh. rule against taking of life. Muslims in China are distinctive because of their strict prohibition against eating pork. D.H.S.

(Islam) Islam has regulations about forbidden food and drink. Qur. ii, 167f., after telling to eat of the good things God has provided and give thanks, mentions that carrion, blood, swine flesh, and anything over which the name of another god has been invoked are forbidden; but it adds that, if anyone eats such under constraint, he is not guilty of sin. In add. to this Qur. prohibition, it is considered that carnivorous animals, and birds which seize their prey with talons are prohibited. While the flesh of the domestic ass is prohibited, the ban is not so clear on horse flesh. The ban is extended to any animal not killed properly by cutting the windpipe, carotid arteries and gullet with knife, while saying *Bismi 'llāhi. Allāh akbar* (I begin with God's name. God is most great → Basmala). These words should also be used when shooting birds or animals to make it lawful to eat them. In Qur. v, 92 wine is associated with gambling, idols and divination as an abomination and part of Satan's work. Wine (*khamr*) is mentioned; but ban is applied to all alcoholic drinks, the standard being that if a large amount causes intoxication, the smallest amount is forbidden. The ban is extended to drugs, and by some to tobacco. In the past people have been put to death for drinking coffee; now it is practically a national drink. Instructions about eating speak of using fingers of right hand, the left hand being unclean; but now in many places eating is conducted in W. style, using cutlery. Grace before and after meat is regarded as necessary. Before and after eating hands should be washed. When washed before meat, one should say, 'I begin with God's name'; after eating one should say, 'Praise be to God. (→ Judaism). J.R.

Wensinck, *Handbook*, pp. 80ff. (food), 251ff. (wine); Pareja, pp. 659f.; Querry, II, pp. 228ff.; *Mishkāt*, pp. 877–83, 886–911; Levy, *Social structure*, index (drugs, foods, wine-drinking).

Formgeschichte German term, trans. 'Form Criticism'. F. is a method of research most notably applied to → Gospels. It seeks to distinguish behind the written sources earlier oral trad. This oral trad. has recognisable forms such as 'Pronouncement Sayings', 'Controversial Speeches', etc. F. orig. in Germany shortly after World War I, → Bultmann being one of its most notable exponents. The method is now also gen used in N.T. research elsewhere. F. has been applied to O.T. (e.g. G. Von Rad, *Das formgeschichtliche Problem des Hexateuchs*, 1930). S.G.F.B.

*P.C.*², p. 683; V. Taylor, *The Formation of the Gospel Tradition* (1945); S. Neill, *The Interpretation of the New Test.* (1964), ch. 7; R. Bultmann, *Die Geschichte der synoptischen Traditionen* (1957³), Ergänzsheft (1958); K. Koch, *Was ist Formgeschichte?* (1964).

Formosa → Taiwan. D.H.S.

Foundation Rites The erection of a building, esp. a temple or bridge, has been regarded by many peoples as a critical occasion, demanding performance of rites, mostly of propitiatory character. Selection of site is often a matter for → divination (→ Feng-Shui). F. sacrifices have been widespread, sometimes of humans (Josh. 6:26 refers to F. sacrifices of infants). Portrait-skulls found under floors at Jericho may repr. F. sacrifices. The purpose of F.-sacrifices was prob. to propitiate → chthonic deities, whose domain was thus infringed. Human images found under buildings (e.g. in Mesopot.) may substitute human victims. The custom of F.-deposits, still existent, can be traced back to Egypt and Mesopot. S.G.F.B.

E.R.E., VI, pp. 109–15; Dhorme, *R.B.A.*, pp. 182ff.; *R.Ae.R.-G.*, pp. 264ff.; E. B. Tylor, *Primitive Culture* (1913⁵), pp. 104ff.; J. Pedersen, *Israel*, III–IV (1940), p. 348; K. M. Kenyon, in *Antiquity*, 30 (1956), pp. 186ff.

Four Holy Truths (Buddh.) the Eng. trans. of the Buddh. *cattarī-ariya-saccāni* (Pali)/*catvari-ārya-satyāni* (Skt) as 'four holy truths' is somewhat inadequate. These are, in fact, 4 principles concerning human existence, which, when apprehended in *experience*, are said to be recognized by Buddh.s as together constituting ultimate truth or reality. Through realisation of this 4-fold set of principles Buddha gained enlightenment, so it is claimed. It is for this reason that they are called *ariya*, i.e. 'holy' (sometimes trans., inadequately, 'noble'). In form in which they are found in Pali Buddh. scriptures (in the → *Mahāparinibbāna Sutta* of the → Dīgha Nikāya), they are as follows: 'The holy truth concerning ill; the holy truth concerning the cause of ill; the holy truth concerning the cessation of ill; the holy truth concerning the path which leads to that cessation. When these holy truths are apprehended and known, the craving for further rebirth is rooted out, that which leads to renewed becoming is destroyed, and there is no more rebirth.' (DN.II.90). The 1st. *H.T.* sets forth nature of human existence—that it is characterised by → *dukkha*. This incl. suffering, i.e. physical pain or mental distress, and also the gen. unsatisfactory quality of existence where all joy is fleeting and life is repeated process of descent into death. This principle (that all existence is *dukkha*) may not be immediately apparent to the 'worldling' (*putthujana*); it is proclaimed as part of truth revealed by Buddha. The 2nd *H.T.* offers explanation of how *dukkha* comes to be conditioning factor of all life. Human existence is seen as a continuous causal process (described in terms of 12 related phases in the formula known as → *paticca-samuppāda*. The process repeats continually, and thus forms a cycle; but the phase in cycle which is of partic. importance, since it provides as it were the motive power to keep process going, is *tanhā* (Pali) or *tṛṣṇā* (Skt.), i.e. thirst, → craving, or desire. It is this which initiates new → *karma*, and continues process, producing resultant states of being which are conditioned by antecedent *tanhā*. Since they are *tanhā*-conditioned, they have no absolute nature, they are impermanent, and the process of decay and re-death is repeated. The 3rd *H.T.* affirms that this *dukkha*-characterised life can be brought to an end; that there is a way out of the apparently endlessly repeated cycle, and that another kind of life is poss., viz., that of → *nibbāna/nirvāna*. The 4th *H.T.* points to means by which this freedom, this new life, can be achieved, viz., the 'way' of the Buddha, the holy → eightfold path. The following of this way incl. in itself full realisation of 1st *H.T.*, understanding of 2nd *H.T.*, and the actualising of what is promised in 3rd *H.T.* T.O.L.

Walpola Rahula, *What the Buddha Taught* (1962); Piyadassi Thera, *The Buddha's Ancient Path* (1964); Th. Stcherbatsky, *The Conception of Buddhist Nirvāna* (1927).

Francis of Assisi, St.; Franciscan Order Francis (1181/2–1226), prob. best-known and attractive of medieval saints, profoundly affected life of W. Church. His simple but passionate devotion to God, his love of both men and natural world are vividly portrayed in early writings such as the *Little Flowers*. His *Regula Primitiva*, approved by Pope Innocent III in 1209/10, provided foundation of his 'friars minor' (*fratres minores*). The Order quickly grew, and its evangelical zeal revived faith of many. The ideals of F. moved St. Clare, a lady of Assisi, to found a similar, though enclosed, order for women. In 1221, F. founded an order of Tertiaries, for those desirous of practising his ideals while living normal life. F.'s intense mysticism produced the 'Stigmata', i.e. the reprod. in his body of marks of Christ's crucifixion. After his death, F.'s ideal of complete poverty caused long-standing dissension in Order; there was also rivalry with → Dominicans. The F.-O., one of most notable in R.C. Church, has always cultivated popular preaching and foreign missions. There is a small F.-O. in the → Ch. of Eng. F. was buried in native town of Assisi, which has many memorials of him. S.G.F.B.

D.C.C., pp. 520–1, 523, 1292, 1333; *R.G.G.*³, II, 1057–8, 1061–4; D. Knowles, *The Religious Orders in England*, I (1950), pp. 114ff.; G. G. Coulton, *Five Centuries of Religion*, II (1927), chs. 8, 10–13; J. Moorman, *Hist. of Franciscan Order* (1968).

Fravashi Ancestral spirits in Iranian relig. The term is not used by → Zoroaster, but it clearly repr. an anc. concept akin to → Rig-Vedic *pitṛs*, being also connected with fertility. Acc. to Zaehner, the F. were pre-existent, and constituted man's 'external soul'. S.G.F.B.

E.R.E., VI, *s.v.;* G. Widengren, *Numen*, I (1954), p. 33; J. Duchesne- Guillemin, *Zoroaster*, pp. 39ff.; Zaehner, *D.T.Z.*, pp. 146ff.; *R.G.G.*³, II, 1089.

Frazer, Sir James G. (1854–1941) Trained as classical scholar, F. became one of the greatest exponents of → anthropological approach to study of relig. He was concerned to illustrate → Hegel's theory that an 'Age of Magic' preceded the 'Age of Religion', and that agriculture had profoundly conditioned relig. concept and practice. His *magnum opus* was *The Golden Bough*, 12 vols., Suppl. *Aftermath* (1936). Other important works were *Totemism and Exogamy*, 4 vols.; *Belief in Immortality and the Worship of the Dead*, 3 vols.; *Folk-Lore in the O.T.; Creation and Evolution in Primitive Cosmogonies*. His works remain treasures of data for Comp. Relig. S.G.F.B.

Th. Besterman, *A Bibliog. of Sir J. G. Frazer* (1934); R. A. Dounie, *J.G.F., the Portrait of a Scholar* (1940); J. G. Frazer, *Man, God and Immortality* (1927); L. H. Jordan, *Comparative Religion* (1905), pp. 268ff.; *The New Golden Bough*, ed. T. H. Gaster (1959).

Free Will → Predestination (general). S.G.F.B.

(Buddh.) →→ Determinism (Buddh. Rejection), Predestination (Buddh.) A. T.O.L.

(China) → Fate. D.H.S.

(Islam) In 1st cent. of Islam some Muslims called Qadarites, owing to their insistence on God's justice, held belief in free-will. Others, called Jabrites (*jabr* = compulsion) held a strict doc. of predestination. Both parties could quote the Qur. in their favour; for while it clearly speaks of man's responsibility for actions, it also at other times seems to teach that God is the only agent. These people were not to be considered sects. Theologians developed a doc. of → acquisition, which speaks of man acquiring his actions, though God is prime agent. God's almighty power is upheld; but theology in gen. did not uphold a doc. approaching fatalism, although many common people have been practical fatalists. *Min Allah* (from God) has been common explanation of calamities, both natural and moral, with suggestion that man is helpless. The doc. of acquisition (*kasb*) may seem largely a matter of words, but it did uphold some degree of human responsibility while asserting God's power. It also assured men of God's justice. On other hand, even such a scholar as → Ghazali could argue that injustice can be predicated only of one who deals wrongly with things he does not own. This cannot be said of God; for he owns everything and so can do as he wishes with his possessions. Another point of view is indic. in a trad. recorded by Muslim which tells of Adam and Moses disputing in God's presence. Moses told Adam he had been shown great honour, but because of his sin mankind were sent down to earth. Adam asked how long before his (Adam's) birth this was written in the → Torah; Moses replied it was forty years. So Adam asked, 'Do you then blame me for doing a deed which God had decreed for me forty years before he had created me?' J.R.

Watt, *Free Will*, 'Acquisition', *J.R.A.S.* (1943), pp. 234ff., 'Philosophy', pp. 86f.; D. B. Macdonald, *Theology*, index; Wensinck, *Creed*, index; *Mishkāt*, pp. 23ff.

Friday (Islam) The day of assembly (*yaum al-jum'a*), is not to be compared with the Jew. → Sabbath; but in mod. times some Muslim countries observe day as a weekly holiday so far as offices and educational establishments are concerned. Qur. lxii, 9f. gives authority for special observance on F. People are to come to mosque when call to prayer (→ *adhān*) is made; afterwards they may resume their business. This is interpreted as ref. to the noon prayer. Then a sermon is preached in two parts, between which the preacher descends from pulpit and he and congregation offer silent prayers. The sermon should contain exhortation and prayers for → Muḥammad, his → Companions and ruler of the time. After sermon, the preacher descends and the people engage in a two *rak'a* prayer. If the preacher is → imam, he leads the worship. A sign of rebellion was the omission of ruler's name from sermon, with prob. the name of someone else in his place. (→ Discipline, Islam). J.R.

E.I.[2], II, pp. 592–4; *Mishkāt*, pp. 284–7; Wensinck, *Handbook*, pp. 83f.; Hughes, pp. 274–7 (khuṭbah).

Friends, Society of Founded by G. Fox in 1668; also called Quakers. Their relig. beliefs were set forth in classic work of R. Barclay, *Theologiae Verae Christianae Apologia* (1676). The central doctrine is the 'Inner Light', coming directly from God into the soul, and being thus superior to Scriptures and Church. Its reality should be manifest in simplicity, purity and truthfulness of personal life. With such guidance, there is no need for → sacraments, a ministry or set forms of worship. Meetings of F. are characterised by periods of silence. Until growth of toleration, the F. suffered much persecution; their refusal of military service has caused conflict with civil authorities. However, their high standards of personal life, and world-wide social and educational work have earned them great respect. Elizabeth Fry (1780–1845), a pioneer for prison-reform, was a F. The name 'Quakers' seems to have a two-fold explanation: it was given to Fox for demanding that Justice trembled before Word of God; it denoted spiritual trembling manifested at relig. meetings by eary 'Quakers'. S.G.F.B.

E.R.E., VI, *s.v.; D.C.C.*, *s.v.*

Fujiyama Mt. Fuji—venerated as most sacred mountain of Japan, and an important deity in → Shinto pantheon. The earliest known organiser of worship of F. was Takematsu Hasegawa, gen. known as Kakugyo (b. CE 1541), from whose teachings developed the Shinto sects of Jikkō-kyō and Fusō-kyō. He taught that Japan was chief of all nations and centre of world, and that F. was earthly dwelling-place of supreme God. Through his influence a large number of organisations of F. pilgrims arose during Tokugawa period, each with its leader and guides. The sacred spirit-mountain was regarded as guardian of nation, only to be ascended after purification of body and mind, accompanied by penance and relig. austerities. It is estimated that over 100,000 pilgrims make the journey to top of F. each year in July and August. D.H.S.

D. C. Holtom, *The National Faith of Japan* (1938), pp. 215ff.; J. Herbert, *Shinto* (1967), pp. 473ff.

Fundamentalism The term F. is used widely, if vaguely, today to denote type of conservative Prot. Christ. orthodoxy resting on belief in literal infallibility of Bible, Virgin Birth of Christ, his Substitutionary Atonement, Resurrection and Second Coming. However, few of those who accept these docs. would accept term F., preferring instead to call themselves 'Evangelicals' or 'Conservative Evangelicals'.

Although impact of Biblical criticism and theory of evolution was felt throughout Protestantism in last quarter of 19th cent., opposition was more vehement in America than elsewhere. One effect of Civil War (1861–5) had been to postpone conflict; when it came, it came with extraordinary violence. The debate was well under way when there appeared, just before First World War, a series of twelve pamphlets entitled *The Fundamentals: A Testimony to the Truth*, written by leading conservative churchmen on both sides of Atlantic. Their subject-matter was by no means limited to question of Biblical infallibility, though this was basic presupposition of all writers; all united in condemning →

'Modernism' or 'liberalism', by which they meant application of evolutionary theory and higher criticism to study of Bible. Rome, → Mormonism and → Christ. Science were also criticised. It seemed to the writers that to disturb any one stone in Biblical edifice would be to destroy the whole: 'Let us then, by repudiating this modern criticism, show our condemnation of it. What does it offer us? Nothing. What does it take away? Everything. Do we have any use for it? No!' (IV, pp. 89f.). Evolutionism, by casting doubts on the historicity of Genesis, was condemned equally, as '... the law of human progress apart from God, and under the leadership of the prince of this world system who originated it' (VIII, p. 32).

It was theory of evolution which finally brought controversy between Fundamentalists and Modernists to a head in America. In 1925, J. T. Scopes, a school teacher of Dayton, Tennessee, was prosecuted for teaching evolutionism (at that time banned by State law). The Fundament. leader William Jennings Bryan attended the trial, and, although he won 'his' case, suffered greatly in prestige as result of cross-examination by the 'atheist' Clarence Darrow, appearing for defence. This notorious 'monkey trial' had effect of bringing the controversy before public eye on a unparalleled scale; the issues it raised had to be faced in all Prot. Churches of America. That the passions aroused at that time have not completely subsided, though their focus has shifted somewhat, and tone of debate has moderated, is attested by activities of many right-wing Prot. Churches and sects in America today. Evolutionism is still occasionally attacked, along with Biblical criticism; but Communism and World Council of Churches have joined these trad. issues as matters subversive of true faith. Similar phenomena and similar attitudes, though on much smaller scale, may be observed in Europe, Asia, Africa and Latin America, often in connection with Pentecostal and similar movements. E.J.S.

The Fundamentals: A Testimony to the Truth I–XII (1911ff.); N. F. Furniss, *The Fundamentalist Controversy*, 1918–31 (1954); H. Shelton Smith R. T. Handy and Lefferts A. Loetscher, *American Christianity* (1963), II, pp. 294ff.; W. S. Hudson, *Religion in America* (1965), pp. 363ff.

Funerary Rites (General) Burial of the dead is a distinctive human practice: no other animals so care for their dead. The practice is very anc. (→ F.-R., Paleolithic); it was evidently not due orig. to sanitary motives, for most burials are ritual, i.e. rites were performed and food and other equipment placed in grave. F.-R. gen. attest belief in some kind of afterlife; but their practice may continue after orig. purpose has been forgotten, e.g. Chr. custom of burying dead facing east preparatory to Second → Advent of Christ. Cremation does not necessarily imply belief that dead ascend into sky, nor does burial imply subterranean afterlife. Funerary customs naturally express sorrow; but many are also → apotropaic, being designed to avert contagion of death, to propitiate dead (often regarded as jealous of the living), or despatch dead to realm of dead. (→ Styx). S.G.F.B.

E.R.E., IV, pp. 411–44; E. Bendann, *Death Customs* (1930); J. G. Frazer, *The Belief in Immortality and the Worship of the Dead*, 3 vols. (1913–22); Brandon, *M.D.;* E. Panofsky, *Tomb Sculpture* (1964).

(Buddh.) The methods of disposing of dead practised by Buddhists are those inherited from Indian culture. The Buddha was cremated with honours customarily given to a great king, acc. to the → *Mahāparinibbāna* Sutta. The cremation was carried out by the Malla tribes-people of Kusinagara, where he died, after they had enquired of → Ananda his personal attendant and disciple, how the remains of a → Tathāgata or Buddha should be dealt with. (*S.B.E.*, 11, pp. 125ff.). After 7 days of ceremonial homage, the body was wrapped in 500 layers of new cloth, placed in an iron sarcophagus, filled with oil, and placed on funeral pyre, made of many kinds of fragrant wood. They were unable to ignite the pyre, however, until 500 Buddh. monks led by Mahā Kassapa had arrived and reverenced the Buddha's body. After that, the pyre is said to have burst into flames spontaneously. When the fire had died down, only the bones were left: 'the body of the Blessed One burned itself away... neither soot nor ash was seen'. For 7 days the closely guarded bones were honoured 'with dance and song and music, and with garlands and perfumes'. King → Ajātasuttu, hearing of Buddha's death and cremation, proposed to build a → *stupa* over the remains. The Licchavis, the Sakiyas, the Bulis, the Koliyas, and the Mallas and a brahman of Vethadipa also claimed a right to build the *stupa*. The remains were, therefore, divided into 8 parts, and 8 *stupas* were built, by the various claimants in their respective territories. This building of 8 *stupas* is considered by mod. scholars a later embroidery of the narrative, in the interests of providing a justification for the *stupa*-cult, as it had developed by time of → *Ashoka* (→ Stupa).

That the Buddha was cremated indicates not that this is universal practice among Buddhists, but rather his status as a great man. At that time in India, as now, not all dead bodies are cremated; those of children, and of holy men, and of very poor are notable exceptions: these are buried, or even left in a charnel field to be devoured by beasts and birds of prey. Bodies thus disposed of, and in various stages of decomposition are mentioned in Buddh. scriptures as subjects for meditation by monks, espec. those who by their nature are tempted to sensuality. Practice among Buddhists varies nowadays in disposal of dead. In Ceylon, e.g. espec. in villages, burial is more usual: Ryan estimates only 1 case in 25 is dealt with by cremation; this where family is sufficiently wealthy. In S.E. Asia, both burial and cremation are used, but cremation is more usual. This will take place from 3 to 7 days after death, and is occasion more than any other in the human life-cycle when Buddhist monks have an import. relig. role. Various ceremonies take place throughout the 7 days after death, in which groups of monks take part; these ceremonies are partly expressive of non-Buddh. ideas, such as aiding transition of dead man's spirit, and partly occasions for monks to offer solace and comfort to bereaved, and to remind them of Buddh. doctrines. Where, as in Burma and Thailand, the population is predominantly Buddh., the funerary rites provide occasion for communal participation, both financial and devotional, for the villagers; in doing so they are considered to gain merit. Cremation, the more usual method in S.E. Asia, is carried out on unused open ground outside village; in more urban areas, within compound of Buddh. temple. T.O.L.

S.B.E., vol. XI, pp. 122–36; S. Dutt, *Buddha and 5 After Centuries* (1957), pp. 168–71; B. Ryan, *Sinhalese Village* (1958), pp. 103–4; J. E. de Young, *Village Life in Modern Thailand* (1955), pp. 68–74; Manning Nash, *The Golden Road to Modernity: Village Life in Contemporary Burma* (1965), pp. 151–6.

(China) → Burial (China). D.H.S.

(Christian) The Early Chr. attitude to death was one of joy; for a martyr, of victory. In the words of → Origen (*Comm. on Job.*): 'We celebrate the day of death because those who seem to die do not really die'. Christians wore white at funerals, not black, and had no fear of contact with corpse (→ Relics), as in many other religs.; → Jerome observes that Christians do not then lament but sing psalms. They called burial places *coemeteria*, 'sleeping-places'. The funeral procession, acc. to Chrysostom, was a *propompē*, 'triumphal procescesion', with waving palm-branches and cries of 'Alleluia'; the → Eucharist was also celebrated. The names of dead were recorded on diptychs and read out at celebrations of Eucharist; their anniversaries were kept at their graves by holding an → agape. About CE 1000, for various reasons, a change of attitude occurred; the note of glad confidence changed to one of fear, with increasing emphasis upon God's → judgment. F.-R. became sombre and penitential. The dying were exhorted to confess and repent in preparation for judgment; they were anointed when *in extremis* (→ unction). At funeral, priests' vestments and mourners' clothing were black; penitential psalms were chanted. Special Requiem → Mass was celebrated, at which the → *Dies Irae* was recited, followed by Absolutions of the Dead, the body being censed and asperged. The actual internment was a sombre ceremony, accompanied by solemn tolling of church bell. Arrangements were made, acc. to resources, for Masses to be said for repose of dead on specified occasions. The *Officium pro defunctis* incl., as part of preparation for actual obsequies, Vespers of the Dead. F.-R. in Reformed Churches omitted most of medieval ritual, incl. Requiem Mass; but the simplified services, consisting of psalms and lections of Scriptures, retained sombre character of medieval rites. Christians, from earliest period, have gen. buried their dead. Tombs of martyrs and saints became cult-centres, and often attracted masses of pilgrims (→ Pilgrimage). S.G.F.B.

A. S. Duncan-Jones in *Liturgy and Worship*, ed. W. K. L. Clarke (1932), pp. 616ff.; *E.R.E.*, III, *s.v.;* ('Commemoration of the Dead'), V, pp. 456–8; *D.C.C.*, *s.v.* ('Absolutions of the Dead', 'Requiem', 'Unction', 'Viaticum'); P. Lacroix, *Military and Religious Life in the Middle Ages* (1874, 1964), pp. 447ff.; I. A. Richmond, *Archaeology and the After-Life in Pagan and Christian Imagery* (1950); E. Panofsky, *Tomb Sculpture* (1964); B. Kötting, *Der frühchristliche Reliquienkult und die Bestattung im Kirchengebaude* (1965); *R.A.C.*, II, 208–11.

(Crete and Mycenae) Evidence from Cretan tombs indicates belief that dead lived underground, prob. in realm of → Great Mother Goddess: arrangements were made for offerings and libations (directed into tomb by conduit); funerary equipment was gen. of symbolic character. Tholoi-ossuaries were used for many generations. The painted sarcophagus of Hagia Triada depicts elaborate F.-R., but also suggests, in showing the offering of a boat, that dead made transmarine journey to next world. Mycenaean burials, with rich equipment, indicate belief that dead lived in tomb, and prob. originated later Grk. → hero-cult. Evidence of fire in graves has been explained as attempt to dry corpse, to free *psychē*. (→ Cretan Religion). S.G.F.B.

C. Picard, *Les religions préhelléniques* (1948), pp. 162ff.; M. P. Nilsson, *Minoan-Mycenaean Religion and its Survival in Greek Religion* (1950²), pp. 427ff.; *Gesch. d. griech. Religion*, I (1955²), pp. 325ff.; R. B. Onians, *The Origins of European Thought* (1951), pp. 258ff.; Brandon, *M.D.*, pp. 155ff.; R. W. Hutchinson, *Prehistoric Crete* (1962), pp. 141ff.; S. Marinatos and M. Hirmer, *Crete and Mycenae* (1960), pp. 48ff., 81ff.

(Egypt) Provision for death and afterlife was a main preoccupation of the anc. Egyptians. Believing that immortality could be achieved by ritual assimilation to → Osiris, F.-R. were basically a re-enacting on behalf of deceased of actions believed to have effected resurrection of Osiris. Since body was regarded as essential for afterlife, it was ritually embalmed, as body of Osiris had been, and its faculties magically restored (→ Mummification). After burial, the dead lived on in tomb, and needed, besides funerary equipment, regular mortuary offerings, for which provision was made acc. to individual resources: pharaohs had mortuary temples erected, provided with priesthoods to perform this mortuary service. (→→ Book of Dead; Coffin Texts; Egypt. Relig.; Judgment of Dead, Egypt.). S.G.F.B.

Kees, *T.*, *passim*; E. A. W. Budge, *The Mummy* (1925); *E.R.E.*, IV, pp. 458–64; J. Spiegel, 'Das Auferstehungsritual der Unaspyramide', *A.S.E.*, 53 (1956); G. Thausing, *Der Auferstehungsgedanke in ägyptischen religiosen Texten* (1943); J. Sainte Fare Garnot, 'Les formules funéraires des stèles egyptiennes', *H.G.R.*, I; *R.Ae.R.-G.*, pp. 90–100, 257–64, 341–55, 482–90, 550–9; Brandon, *M.D.*, pp. 33ff., 'The Ritual Technique Salvation in anc. Near East', in *The Saviour God*, ed. S. G. F. Brandon (1963); G. Roeder, *Ae.R.T.B.*, V (1961); H. Kees, *R.-G.L.*, 10 (1928), pp. 47ff.

(Greek) In → Homer, cremation is estab. custom. The funeral of Patroklos is described in detail in *Iliad*, 23:175ff.: its F.-R. incl. human and animal sacrifice, libations, funerary meal and games. After cremation, bones were placed in urn and buried in mound, which was marked by a pillar. Such elaborate F.-R. were doubtless for import. persons. In classic period, deceased was carried for burial with face exposed: excessive weeping and lamentation were prohibited by law. Funerary equipment of food and articles of personal use was placed in tomb: at late period it was customary to put money in mouth of dead to pay → Charon, and honey-cakes for → Cerberus. A funeral meal followed burial, and sacrifices made on 3rd and 9th day. Mourning could last 30 days, and was denoted by black garments and cutting of hair. Funerary epitaphs are characterised by their brevity and restraint. (→ Greek Relig.). S.G.F.B.

E.R.E., IV, pp. 472–5; *O.C.D.*, pp. 255ff.; E. Rohde, *Psyche* (1898²), I, pp. 22ff., 215ff., II, 336ff.; H. L. Lorimer, *Homer and the Monuments* (1950), pp. 103ff.; R. B. Onians, *The Origins of European Thought* (1951), pp. 234ff.; *Kleine Pauly*, I, 837–46; *R.A.C.*, II, 200–7.

(Hindu) Cremation has become the dominant method of disposing of the dead in Hinduism. The rites practised today are essentially similar to those of → Vedic religion, though ref. is made in the → *Rgveda* to alternatives to cremation. The → Indus Valley Civilisation practised burial, while it has been common for children and ascetics to be buried rather than cremated, being technically outside the → Aryan community. The burial of ascetics in yogic position, and covered by a mound or → *lingam*, later liable to become site of a temple, played part in evolution of Indian temple architecture. Among other groups not practising cremation are the → Lingayats (who may have been influenced by Islam in this) and some southern Indian castes. Death by exposure to wild animals, etc., was anciently quite common, and descriptions of charnel grounds in Buddh. and other texts indic. that burning was not always thorough. The main change in orthodox rites since classical times has been tendency to consign final remains after cremation to waters of a river, etc.; whereas previously it was usual to bury them in a funerary pot in cemetery. Further, cow and other animal sacrifices at the funeral no long occur, though once common. In principle the ceremonial period lasts for ten days, during which relatives are barred from normal contacts and activities, being impure. The cremation itself is performed by officiating priest and by the → *gṛhastha*, head of family, e.g. eldest son. Trad., the pyre is hedged in by three fires, one to northwest, another to southwest, the third to southeast. Depending on which fire's flames reach the pyre first, prognostications are made about destined → rebirth of deceased. After corpse is consumed, the mourners leave; theoretically it is only three days later that the bones are gathered up and consigned to river (but often the sequence is telescoped). For the ten days after cremation offerings of rice balls are made to dead, and thereafter there are periodic offerings made. However, at end of ten days, the worst threats both to dead and to survivors are over. If offerings are not made, the deceased may remain a homeless *preta*, miserable himself and causing misery to his relatives. Because of pollution conveyed by death, the *caṇḍālas* who looked after cremation ground, acted as undertakers, etc., were regarded as peculiarly unclean. On the other hand, ascetics were wont to frequent cremation grounds, to meditate on death, etc. (even to eat flesh of exposed corpses) (→ asceticism, Hindu). The practice of → *sati* (suttee) at one time was not uncommon, and allowance was made at funeral ceremonial for occasion on which the widow could or could not signify her willingness to join her deceased husband. N.S.

A. Hillebrandt, 'Death and Disposal of the Dead, Hindu', in *E.R.E.;* J. C. Oman, *The Mystics, Ascetics and Saints of India* (1903); J. Auboyer,

Daily Life in Ancient India (1961); R. B. Pandey, *Hindu Samskaras, A Socio-Religious Study of the Hindu Sacraments* (1959).

(Jewish) The archeology of Palestine attests continuity of burial practice indicat. of belief that dead dwelt in tomb and needed offerings of food and drink. Incidental refs. in O.T. reveal F.-R. of propitiatory kind (e.g. Jer. 16:6); the custom of → Levirate marriage also suggests that dead survived and needed tendance of living. This evidence shows that → Yahwist denial of survival in Gen. 3:19 did not repr. popular faith. Burial was regarded as essential: acc. to Deut. 21:22ff., even corpses of criminals were to be buried. Both corpse and tomb were regarded as ritually unclean (Nu. 5:2, Lev. 21:11), prob. due to idea of contagion of death. Mourning consisted of lamentation, rending of garments, wearing sackcloth and → fasting. Burial was often in caves or tombs excavated from rock. In N.T. period dead were wrapped in linen bandages (Jn. 11:44, 20:6–7). Rabbinical trad. enjoins seven days of strict mourning; the Jew. Prayer Book provides for repetition by sons of the *Ḳaddish* for eleven months after death of parent. (→→ Israelite Relig.; Judaism). S.G.F.B.

E.R.E., IV, pp. 497–500; R. A. S. Macalister, *A Century of Excavation in Palestine* (1925), pp. 258ff.; S. A. Cook, *The Religion of Anc. Palestine in the Light of Archaeology* (1930), pp. 35ff.; A. G. Barrois, *Manuel d'archéologie biblique*, II (1953), pp. 280ff.; W. F. Albright, *The Archaeology of Palestine* (1949), *passim*; J. Jeremias, *Heiligengräber in Jesu Umwelt* (1958); A. Lods, *Isräel* (1932), pp. 256ff.; J. Pedersen, *Israel*, IV (1940), pp. 481ff.; Brandon, *M.D.*, pp. 110ff.; *H.D.B.*[2], *s.v.* ('Mourning Customs', 'Tomb'); I. Epstein, *Judaism* (1959), p. 178.

(Islam) → Burial (Islam). J.R.

(Japan) → Burial (Jap.). D.H.S.

(Mesopot.) Mesopot. burials from earliest period show that dead were equipped with food, tools, utensils and weapons, thus implying an afterlife having such needs. The 'royal tombs', excavated by Sir L. Woolley at Ur suggest that royal persons were buried with their possessions and retinue, so to form a court in next world. This evidence of funerary practice seems to contradict view of afterlife expressed in texts, which visages the dead as all doomed to a wretched existence in 'Land of No-return' (→→ Death; Eschatology, Mesopot.). However, as 12th Tablet of Epic of → Gilgamesh shows, the lot of the dead was somewhat alleviated by regular mortuary offerings made by their survivors. Proper burial was also essential, so that ghost (*etimmu*) could depart to land of dead. The 'royal' burials of Ur have not been satisfactorily explained in relation to gen. eschat. trad. in Mesopot. Cremation was also practised in anc. Sumer and Akkad. S.G.F.B.

A. Parrot, *Archéologie mésopotamienne*, I (1946), pp. 276ff.; A. Heidel, *The Gilgamesh Epic and Old Test. Parallels* (1949[2]), pp. 137ff.; *E.R.E.*, IV, pp. 444–6; L. Woolley, *Ur Excavations, II, The Royal Cemetery* (1934), *Ur: the First Phases* (1946), pp. 22ff.; Jastrow, *Aspects*, pp. 360ff.; *R.A.C.*, II, 196–8; Brandon, *M.D.*, pp. 72ff.; M. E. L. Mallowan, *Early Mesopot. and Iran* (1965), pp. 89ff.; Ebeling, *T.L.*, I, *passim*.

(Palaeolithic) The so-called Neanderthal Man, precursor of *homo sapiens*, i.e. present human species, buried his dead ritually. Paleolithic burials (*c.* 30,000–12,000 BC) reveal elaborate funerary equipment (tools, food, ornaments), and some variety of F.-R.: (1) bodies were gen. buried in crouched posture, interpreted by some scholars as evidence of belief in rebirth (2) many burials show use of red pigment, perhaps indict. attempt at magic revivification (3) instances of preservation of skulls only may indicate cult of skulls (→ Paleolithic Relig.). S.G.F.B.

H. Breuil and R. Lantier, *Les hommes de la Pierre Ancienne* (1951); P. Wernert, 'Le culte des crânes à l'époque paleolithique', 'Les hommes de l'Age de la Pierre représentaient-ils les esprits des défunts et des ancetres?', both in *H.G.R.*, I; J. Maringer, *The Gods of Prehistoric Man* (E.T. 1960); Brandon, *M.D.*, ch. 1 (ii); G. Clark, *The Stone Age Hunters* (1967).

(Roman) Information is more ample for F.-R. of wealthy in 1st cent. CE: they were very elaborate and costly; other classes, as is usual in most societies, tried to imitate them acc. to their means. Death was marked by the *conclamatio*, perhaps orig. an attempt to call back the spirit. During preparatory rites, the body was dressed in full insignia, and a wax mask taken of face to join those of ancestors. A branch of cypress or pine at entrance to house denoted death. The funeral procession (3–7 days after death) incl. family, special officers, professional musicians and dancers; the death-masks of ancestors were also carried. After the *laudatio* in Forum, body was cremated at an appointed place. After cremation, the *os resectum* (prob. severed finger-joint) was buried, an act symbolic of anc. inhumation, and a funeral meal was held. The ashes were placed in tomb after 9 days of mourning. The custom of putting coin in mouth to pay passage over → Styx was gen, observed (→ Charon). Memorial festivals were held on various appropriate occasions: they consisted of visiting tomb, lighting lamps, funeral banquets and offerings to gods and *manes* (spirits of dead). Freedman and artisans formed *collegia funeraticia* to ensure proper funeral and rites. Cremation and inhumation were alternative means of disposal at all times. S.G.F.B.

E.R.E., IV, pp. 505–7; *R.A.C.*, II, 200–7; F. Cumont, *After Life in Roman Paganism* (1959 edn.); W. Warde Fowler, *The Religious Experience of the Roman People* (1911), pp. 385ff.; A. Grenier, *The Roman Spirit in Religion, Thought, and Art* (E.T. 1926), pp. 14ff., 94ff.; *Les religions étrusque et romaine* (1948), pp. 75ff.; V. E. Paoli, *Vita romana* (1942[3]), ch. 13; I. A. Richmond, *Archaeology and the After-Life in Pagan and Christian Imagery* (1950).

(Zoroastrian) Acc. to → Zoroastrianism, the death of a believer is a victory to Evil in its continuous conflict with Good (→ Dualism). F.-R. are motivated by fear of contagion of death and belief that neither fire nor earth must be polluted by corpse. F.-R. are elaborate. After death, the body, washed and clothed in white and girded with sacred cord is set in a special place in house, prescribed prayers being said. The corpse, being now in danger of attack by corpse-demon, the Druj Nasu, may only be touched by special officials. A curious feature of F.-R. is the *sag-dīd*, which is repeated at intervals. It takes form of bringing a dog near corpse in belief that its look will frighten the Druj Nasu. The body is next carried by special officials, accomp. by priests and relatives, to the → dakhma, where it is exposed to birds of prey. The relatives, on their return home, have to bathe, and place where corpse lay is → tabu for a period, a lamp being lighted there. The family abstains from meat for three days from the death. S.G.F.B.

E.R.E., IV, pp. 502–5; J. D. C. Pavry, *The Zoroastrian Doctrine of a Future Life* (1929); J. J. Modi, *The Religious Ceremonies and Customs of the Parsees* (1937[2]).

G

Gabriel (Islam) Held to be medium through whom the → Qur. was revealed to → Muhammad. The Qur. mentions him twice by name (ii:91; lxvi:4). The phrases 'the spirit of holiness' (→ Holy Spirit) (ii:81, 254; v:109; xvi:104), 'the faithful spirit' (xxvi:193), and 'one terrible in power' (liii:5) are taken as ref. to him. In xix:17, concerning annunciation to → Mary, the Qur. says, 'We sent to her our spirit', but does not indic. whether G. is intended. In ii:81, 254; v:109 the spirit of holiness is said to have supported → Jesus and other messengers, and in xvi:104 to have conveyed the Qur. revelations. In xxvi:193 the faithful spirit is medium of Qur. revelation. liii:5, which speaks of a vision Muhammad had of one terrible in power, is normally interpreted as ref. to G., but Bell suggests that God himself is intended. Trad. has no doubt about G.'s being medium of revelation. It has much to say about him also as appearing and speaking to Muhammad apart from transmission of revelation. J.R.

*E.I.*², II, pp. 362–4; Hughes, p. 133; Pareja, index; *Mishkāt*, index of miscellaneous items; Jeffery, *Vocabulary*, pp. 100f.; Bell, *Introduction*, index; Sweetman, *I.C.T.*, I, II, IV, index; Doutté, *Magie*, pp. 159ff.

Galatians, Epistle to Addressed by → Paul to his converts in either Galatia in interior of Asia Minor, or Roman province of Galatia: it dates about 50 or 57–8—it may be the earliest extant Ep. of Paul. the Ep., though raising many problems, is of great importance for the light it throws on Paul and his difficult relations with Church of → Jerusalem. S.G.F.B.

*H.D.B.*², *s.v.; P.C.*², pp. 973ff.; *R.G.G.*³, II, pp. 1187–9; H. Schlier, *Der Brief an die Galater* (1962).

Gandhabbas (Pali); **Gandharvas** (Skt) A class of celestial beings in anc. Indian cosmology, whose existence is taken for granted in early Buddh. world-view reflected in canonical scriptures. They are regarded as lowest class of → *Devas*, and are mentioned in conjunction with → *Asuras*. Rebirth as a G. is regarded as result of observance of the minimum moral precepts only. G. are credited with being musicians of the heavenly realm; they also serve as attendants upon the higher Devas. The *Ātānātiya Sutta* of the → Dīgha Nikāya mentions that they are a source of disturbance to monks and nuns engaged in meditation. It is sometimes asserted that they are effective agents in human conception; but this is a misunderstanding of statements on subject in Pali Buddh. scriptures, where it is said that one factor in conception is presence of a karma-complex or 'being', ready to enter into a new embodiment (e.g. *M.N.*, I, pp. 157; 265f.). It is explained in Pali commentaries that what is meant here by G. is a being who is ready to enter a human womb to be born. (→ *Conception in Buddh. thought* (2)). T.O.L.

T. W. and C. A. F. Rhys-Davids *Dialogues of the Buddha*, vol. II (1910, repr. 1966), pp. 288, 308; vol. III (1921, repr. 1965), pp. 142f., 188f.

Gandhāra (Kandahar) Region to extreme N.W. of India (now southern Afghanistan), notable in connection with develop. of the Buddh. → Mahāyāna and Buddh. art. The region came under Indian control, when the Hellenistic Syrian ruler Seleucid ceded it by treaty to the Mauryan emperor Chandragupta in 4th cent. BC. G. was open to Buddh. influence at least from time of emperor → Ashoka, since Ashokan edicts have been discovered there, the latest (in Greek Aramaic) in 1958; the region is mentioned in other Ashokan records as a frontier-region to which Buddh. missions were sent during his reign. G. had also been, and continued to be, subject to Graeco-Roman cultural influence. It was here (and at Mathurā, on the Jumna, S. of Delhi) that use of a statue, image, or ikon to repr. the Buddha developed. It is gen. recognised that the G. type of image, the portrayal of an idealised human form, was to large extent a reflection of kind of anthropomorphic representations of the divine, characteristic of east. part of Roman empire, but with a distinctive Indian contribution (→ Rūpa). Under the Kusāna kings (→ Kanishka), i.e. during approx. the first 3 cents. CE, this area was one of flourishing and vigorous Buddh. culture, with many monastic centres of learning; the most import. was Taksasilā (Taxila). Many of these centres have been uncovered by archaeological research in mod. times. The large number of monasteries indicates substantial lay Buddh. pop. at the time, since monasteries were (and are) built with funds or labour provided by lay supporters; many donors in G. were prob. wealthy merchants, since it was a transit-centre of international trade. During 2nd cent. CE and after, G. was an area which nourished Buddh. missionary expansion N.-wards and then E.-wards into China. The multi-storied pagoda, which emperor Kanishka built at Peshawar, was regarded as one of the wonders of world at that time; it prob. had import. influence on evolution of the Chinese type of pagoda. Among the more famous of learned Buddh.-monks of region were the two Mahāyāna writers and teachers, the brothers → Asanga and → Vasubandhu, whose home was at Purusapura (Peshāwar). Many monasteries of G. were devastated in 5th cent. CE during the Hūna invasions. By 7th cent., when the Chinese pilgrim → Hsuan-tsang visited India, the prosperity and splendour of this Buddh. region was of the distant past: Buddhism was in decline there; most monasteries were 'deserted and in ruins . . . filled with wild shrubs, and solitary to the last degree. . . .' T.O.L.

S. Dutt, *Buddhist Monks and Monasteries of India* (1962); Dietrick Seckel, *The Art of Buddhism* (1964), pp. 30–7.

Gandhi, M. K. Mohandas Karamchand Gandhi (1869–1948), known as Mahatma (title meaning 'great-souled') was, with Nehru, chief architect of Indian independence, and gave the Indian Congress Party its policy of non-violent resistance. G. was influenced by writings of Tolstoy and by Sermon on the Mount, and drew upon, and reinterpreted, the anc. Indian concept of → *ahimsa*, giving it a political and social dimension as part of struggle to reform Indian society and remove foreign domination. He first experimented with non-violent tactics in S. Africa, in leading campaign for better treatment for Indians there. His combination of political acumen, → asceticism and simplicity won a large following among the masses, a factor which the Congress was able to maintain in the independence struggle. His major effort at reform of Hinduism was his campaigning for the untouchables, whom he christened 'Harijans' (sons of God —Hari being a title of → Viṣṇu). G. was not primarily a relig. teacher, and did not have a systematic theology, but he was strongly influenced by → *bhakti*. He also considered that truth was to be found in all religs., and preferred to speak of God as Truth—a concept connected with his use of key term *satyagraha*, or 'holding to truth', to describe the spirit and method of non-violent reform. Strongly opposed to inter-relig. hostility, he struggled hard against waves of communal violence before and after the partition of India in 1947: the partition he disapproved of, as it was the death of his ideal of a harmonious India in which both Muslim and Hindu could share. This brotherly regard for Muslims was a factor in his death at hands of a militant right-wing Hindu assassin. Apart from his stress on non-violence, G.'s ethical teachings were puritanical and encouraged a return to values of village life (his economics, scarcely implemented by Republic of India, involved a kind of village autarchism). Largely under G.'s influence, prohibition was tried out in Gujarat (alcoholism being a problem among millworkers of Ahmedabad, where G. had his ashram), and was later more widely implemented by Indian government. The wearing of homespun white cloth, as symbol of simple self-sufficient life, became a badge of Congress. His work has been carried on by Vinoba Bhave, who has promoted *bhūdān* (bhoodan), the giving of land to help the landless. G. has also been influential among Christians and others in struggles for civil rights in America, S. Africa, etc. N.S.

M. K. Gandhi, *An Autobiography; or the Story of my Experiments with Truth* (1959); *Hindu Dharma* (1950); *My Religion* (1955); *Satyagraha* (1951); also, *Collected Works*, 6 vols. continuing (1958–); P. K. Prabhu (ed.), *What Jesus Means to Me* (1959); D. M. Datta, *The Philosophy of Mahatma Gandhi* (1953); L. Fischer, *The Life of Mahatma Gandhi* (1950); P. G. Deshpande, *Gandhiana: A Bibliography of Gandhian Literature* (1948).

Ganeṣa (or Ganesh). Popular Hindu god, son of → Śiva and Pārvatī (→ Kālī), and also called Ganapati or Lord of Ganas (a species of attendant on Śiva). He is repr. as elephant-headed, and may be a survival of some early theriomorphic cult, though a comparative latecomer to prominence in Hindu pantheon. He is now highly popular, and reckoned to be the shifter of obstacles (*Vighneśvara*); hence he is prayed to before undertaking of all sorts of enterprises (and so is well-regarded among businessmen). Though tracing his descent from Śiva, G. is widely worshipped by → Vaisnavites, and is regarded as symbolizing unity of opposites—being part human, part elephant, he symbolizes identity between man and God as expressed in formula → *tat tvam asi*. A late → Upaniṣad is devoted to him, as well as a → *Purana*, also late. N.S.

A. Danielou, *Hindu Polytheism* (1964); Alice Getty, *Ganesa* (1936).

Ganges The *Gaṅgā* or Ganges is the most sacred of rivers of India, partly because it is main river running through anc. heartland of Hinduism. Mythologically, the G. is supposed to have orig. from foot of → Viṣṇu, whence it flows across the heavens as the Milky Way: it descends to earth from locks of → Śiva, and so emerges through

Himālaya range, itself the abode of the gods, into the plain. Hardwar, on its upper reaches, and → Banaras are specially sacred places of pilgrimage, as well as Prayāga or Allahabad, which is at confluence of G., the Humna and mythic underground river, the Sarasvati. It is the scene of some notable → festivals; it is esp. efficacious and sacred to have one's ashes scattered on its waters. Bathing in the G. is the prototype of bathing rituals widespread in temple-worship in Hinduism—for such purposes any body of water can be deemed to be the G. The pre-eminence of Banaras is sometimes explained mythically because of its being at point of intersection of the three Ganges —the Milky Way, the earthly Ganges, and an underground Ganges flowing south. Other import. sacred rivers are the Godavari, Narmada, Kistna and Kaveri. Despite its grandeur, the Brahmaputra has not attracted the same reverence, partly because of its distance from the heartland. Gaṅgā is also personified as a deity, the cause and symbol of purity. N.S.

Gāthās, The Oldest writings of → Avesta, the G. are 17 'hymns' or 'songs', forming part of liturgy called the *Yasna*. They are gen. accepted as being compositions of → Zoroaster, and, are, therefore, of primary importance as evidence of his teaching. The G. are written in archaic form of the Avestan language, so that their interpretation is difficult and uncertain. Many trans. have been made in various European languages. S.G.F.B.

J. Duchesne-Guillemin, *The Hymns of Zoroaster* (1952), being trans. of orig. French version in *Zoroastre* (1948); J. H. Moulton, *Early Zoroastrianism* (1913), pp. 343ff.; C. Bartholomae, *Die Gathas des Awesta* (1905); Zaehner, *D.T.Z.*, pp. 25ff., 339ff.

Gāya A town in Bihar, N. India, near to the → bodhi-tree which was the scene of the → Buddha's enlightenment. The Chinese pilgrim → Fa-Hsien recorded (in 5th cent. CE) that the bodhi-tree was 3½ miles from the town. The place is mentioned as having been visited again on several occasions by Buddha. in the course of his ministry. Buddhagaya, the scene of the enlightenment, is one of the 4 places of Buddh. pilgrimage (→ Holy Places, Buddh.). An import. monastery, 'The Great Enlightenment Monastery' (*Mahābodhi Sanghārāma*), was built at Buddhagaya by a King of Ceylon; monks from Ceylon used to stay there. Inscriptions made by Burmese and Chinese pilgrims have also been found, recording repairs and offerings made at the *Mahā bodhi* temple on various occasions. Acc. to the Sinhalese chronicles, the great teacher → Buddhaghosa left Ceylon at end of life to go to Gaya, where he died. T.O.L.

P. V. Bapat (ed.), *2500 Years of Buddhism* (1956, repr. 1959), pp. 308–11.

Gāyatrī The most sacred verse of the → *Rgveda*, which is mandatorily the central utterance in many Hindu prayers and rites. It is addressed to the sun-god, Savitṛ. and is used in ceremonies of initiation, marriage, etc., as well as in daily worship of upper-class (i.e. the → twice-born Hindu). The verse means: 'Let us dwell on the beautiful glory of the god Savitṛ, that he may inspire our minds'. Only the twice-born may rightly utter verse, and should do so three times a day. There is, however, a 'lower-class' version of the *G.*, the *Brahmagayatri* which can be used universally. N.S.

Gayōmart In Iranian mythology, the Primal Man (→ Urmensch), who, together with the Primal Bull, was slain by → Ahriman. From seed of dying G., the first human pair, Mashyē and Mashyanē, were born. The myth of G. is very complex, and it has been variously interpreted by scholars (→ Yima). S.G.F.B.

S. S. Hartmann, *Gayōmart: étude sur le syncretisme dans l'ancien Iran* (1953); H. Güntert, *Der arische Weltkönig und Heiland* (1923), pp. 346f.; Zaehner, *D.T.Z.*, pp. 72, 131, 262ff.

Geb Egypt. earth-god. In Egypt. → cosmogony, G. orig. lay in close embrace with → Nut, the sky-goddess: their separation by Shu, the air-god, formed the universe. The idea of a recumbent earth-god impregnating sky-goddess may have orig. from customary posture in sexual intercourse. G. was symbolized by a goose in hieroglyphic. S.G.F.B.

R.Ae.R.-G., pp. 201ff.; S. A. B. Mercer, *The Relig. of Anc. Egypt* (1949), pp. 264ff.; Brandon, *C.L.*, pp. 23ff.

Gehenna *Ex.* Grk. transcription of Heb. *Gê-Hinnōm*, name of valley s. of → Jerusalem, where refuse was burnt and Ahaz had sacrificed his children to → Moloch (II Chron. 28:3). Its sinister past and constant fires led to adoption of its name for place of eternal punishment of wicked in Jew. lit. and N.T. S.G.F.B.

H.D.B.², *s.v.;* R. H. Charles, *Eschatology* (1913), pp. 161ff., 474ff.

Gemara Name (= 'what has been learned') used for 2nd part of → Talmud, being a commentary on 1st part, which comprises the → Mishnah. The G. of Babylonian Talmud is in E. Aramaic, that of Palestinian Talmud in W. Aramaic. (→ Judaism). S.G.F.B.

Oesterley and Box, *L.R.M.J.*, pp. 85ff.

Genesis, Book of This title of first book of O.T., derives from → LXX; the Heb. title is *Bereshith*, 'in the beginning', which is the opening word. In its present form, G. is post-Exilic (→ Pentateuch), comprising three main literary sources: → P, and the pre-Exilic → J and → E (→ Scandinavian School). J provides orig. framework, presenting his philosophy of → history in two parts (a) Primaeval History, 2:4–11:9 (b) Patriarchal History, 12:1 to end. Thus, starting with creation of Man, J traces → Yahweh's providential action down to settlement of Israel's eponymous ancestors in Egypt. G. provided Chr. theology with Biblical basis for docs. of Creation, → Fall of Man, and → Original Sin. S.G.F.B.

R. H. Pfeiffer, *Intro. to Old Test.* (1948), pp. 130ff., 142ff.; *H.D.B.*², *s.v.; P.C.*², pp. 175ff.; G. von Rad, *Genesis* (E.T. 1961); *R.G.G.*³, II, 1377–9; S. G. F. Brandon, *History, Time and Deity* (1965), pp. 106ff.

Genku → Honen. D.H.S.

Genshin (CE 942–1017). Better known in Japan as Eshin-Sōzu, G. was a great exponent of cult of → Amida Buddha. He emphasised idealistic tenets of → Tendai philosophy, and sought to purify Buddhism from abuses of mystic ritualism. His writings and paintings, combining vivid imagination with mystic vision, depicted various resorts of transmigration, states of perdition or spiritual beatitude, and glories of Amida's paradise, and proved to be a great inspiration to Buddhist faith in Japan throughout succeeding cents. D.H.S.

M. Anesaki, *Hist. of Japanese Buddhism* (1930), pp. 151ff.

Geomancy (China) → Fêng Shui. D.H.S.

Germanic Relig. → Scandinavian Relig.

-Ghazālī Abū Ḥāmid (450–505/1058–1111), famous Muslim scholar and mystic, b. at Ṭūs in N.E. Persia. He had conventional Muslim → education. In 470/1077 he went to Nizamiyya College at Naysabur to study under al-Juwayni, and remained there till → Juwayni's death in 478/1085, as student, and latterly as teacher. In 484/1091 he was appointed professor at Nizamiyya College, Baghdad; in 488/1096 he resigned this office to adopt life of a → Sūfī. He wrote a record of his spiritual pilgrimage, *al-munqidh min al-ḍalāl* ('the deliverer from error'). See trans. in Watt, *Ghazali*. With his wide learning, G. was able to discuss various approaches to knowledge, all of which he declares to contain weakness except that of Sufis who have true knowledge. After eleven years of solitude, G. was persuaded to resume teaching at Naysabur. Later he went to Ṭūs, where he d. He was a voluminous writer. His *magnum opus* was *Iḥyā' 'ulūm al-dīn* ('the revivifying of the religious sciences'), various parts of which have been trans. into Eng. He has been called the greatest Muslim after → Muḥammad, but has not always received as much honour from Muslims as from W. scholars. J.R.

G.A.L., 535–46, I; *S.I.*, pp. 744–56; *E.I.*², II; 1038–41, Pareja, index (Gazzālī); M. Smith, *Ghazali*; D. B. Macdonald, *Theology*, index; Van den Bergh, *Tahafut*; Watt, *Ghazali Muslim Intellectual* (1962); Sweetman, *I.C.T.*, indexes, esp. IV; S. A. Kamali, *Tahafut* (E.T. 1958).

Gilgamesh Hero of anc. Mesopot. legend and folklore. He appears on early → Sumerian seal-stones engaged in heroic labours; he is mentioned in Sumerian King List as reigning 126 yrs. at Kullab (a district of Erech), and he figures in certain Sumerian epic tales. He is best known as hero of the Epic of → Gilgamesh. He was reputed to be partly human and partly divine, but was mortal by nature. S.G.F.B.

A.N.E.T., pp. 44ff., 266; S. N. Kramer, *From the Tablets of Sumer* (1956), pp. 209ff.; L. Delaporte, *La Mésopotamie* (1923), *passim.*

(Epic of) The text in its completest form exists on 12 clay tablets, in Assyrian and was found at Nineveh: it dates from 7th cent. BC. Fragments of older versions exist in Sumerian and Akkadian: Assyrian version may derive from a Babylonian orig. of *c.* 2000 BC. The Epic has been described as 'a meditation on death, in the form of a tragedy' (A. Heidel). The author has used the adventures of G. as means of presenting a philosophy of life acc. to the Mesopot. view of → Man. G. and his friend Enkidu perform heroic deeds until they offend the goddess → Ishtar. The gods decide that Enkidu's life must be forfeited. His death has a devastating effect on G., who sees in it a presage of his own demise. He determines to learn secret of immortality from the only man who had achieved it, Utanapishtim, hero of the → Flood. The Flood legend is used in Epic to show G. the hopelessness of his quest. However, Uta. tells G. where to get a plant giving eternal youth. He obtains it, only to lose it to a serpent. Disconsolately, G. returns to Erech, where he settles down to fulfil his proper destiny as ruler. The moral of Epic is that men must accept their lot and not seek the impossible; for the gods had made men mortal, being immortal themselves. The Epic is used to comment on other matters; partic. state of man before civilisation as exemplified in Enkidu. The 12th Tablet contains an unrelated episode (→ Funerary Rites, Mesopot.). S.G.F.B.

A.N.E.T., pp. 72–99; A. Heidel, *The Gilgamesh Epic and Old Testament Parallels* (1949²); W. G. Lambert, *Babylonian Wisdom Literature* (1960); H. W. F. Saggs, *The Greatness that was Babylon* (1962), pp. 390ff.; Brandon, *M.D.*, pp. 89ff.; 'The Epic of Gilgamesh: a Mesopot. Philosophy of Life', in *R.A.H.*, ch. 10; G. Furlani, *Miti babilonesi e assiri* (1957); P. Garelli, *Gilgames et sa legende* (1960).

Glossolalia *Ex.* Grk. *glōssa*, 'tongue', and *lalia*, 'talking'. Term used to denote 'talking with tongues', a psychical phenomenon current among primitive Christians (Acts 2:4ff., I Cor. 12:10ff.). It was a form of ecstatic utterance, needing interpretation. Similar phenomena occur frequently in relig. revivalist movements. In Acts 2:4ff., the G. is taken to be speaking in foreign languages, perhaps with some idea of reversal of confusion of tongues at Tower of → Babel. S.G.F.B.

*H.D.B.*², *s.v.* ('Tongues, Gift of'); H. Lietzmann, *An die Korinther I, II* (1923²), pp. 69ff.

Gnosticism, Gnostics A religio-philosophical movement current in Graeco-Roman world. G. comprised many sects in various places, under various leaders. Despite many differences of presentation and imagery, these G. sects merited their designation by each claiming a secret *gnosis* ('knowledge') about constitution of universe, human nature and destiny. Basically they repr. a widespread desire to account for human nature as being compounded of an immortal ethereal → soul and a mortal material body. This situation was gen. emphasised in terms of a cosmogony, acc. to which the world was made by a → Demiurge, who was an inferior being to the Supreme Being, who was often equated with Mind ('*Nous*'), Life (*Zōe*), and Light (*Phōs*). Between Supreme Being and world were a series of entities (→ *aeons*), among which were the → *archontes*, daemonic powers, inhabiting the planets, and being immediate rulers of world. Mankind stemmed from union with Nature (*Phusis*) and an archetypal Man (*Anthropos*), who had descended from the Supreme Being. Hence mankind had a dual nature: the spiritual element came from the divine Man and the material from Nature. In this world, men were subject to the planets, i.e. the *archontes*. They could be saved from their wretched state by acquiring true knowledge (*gnosis*) of their real nature, and by following a prescribed discipline, which would free their souls to return to communion with Supreme Being. Belief in → metempsychosis was usually a basic tenet. The origins of G. are obscure. It was prob. closely allied to, if it did not actually derive from, → Orphism; it incorporated many other esoteric trads., incl. Bab. → astralism, Persian → dualism, Jew. angelology (→ angels), and was closely akin to → Hermeticism. It formed an effective factor in cultural environment of Early Christianity. → Paul instinctively thought in G.-terms as I Cor. 2:6ff. shows. The incarnation of Christ could be readily explained in G.-imagery as descent of a divine aeon from Supreme Being to mediate to men a saving *gnosis*. In Early Church there were many Chr. Gnostics: →→ Basilides; Cerinthus; Clement of Alexandria; Valentinus; Marcion. G. was opposed most notably by →→ Irenaeus; Tertullian; Hippolytus, who emphasised reality of Christ's sufferings (→ Docetism), and rejected G. identification of → Demiurge with God of O.T. Until discovery of the → Nag Hammadi documents, most of our knowledge of G. came from works of its Chr. opponents. Full publication and extended study of these documents will doubtless greatly increase our knowledge of G. → Manichaeism may also be regarded as G., and so may beliefs of the → Albigenses and → Cathari. S.G.F.B.

E.R.E., VI, *s.v.; R.G.G.*², II, 1648–61; R. M. Grant, *Gnosticism and Early Christianity* (1959), *Gnosticism: an Anthology* (1961); R. McL. Wilson, *The Gnostic Problem* (1958); C. Quispel, *Gnosis als Weltreligion* (1951); 'Der gnostische Anthropos und die jüdische Tradition', in *Eranos-Jahrbuch*, 22 (1955); F. L. Cross (ed.), *The Jung Codex* (1955); W. C. van Unnik, *Evangelien aus dem Nilsand* (1960); J. Doresse, *The Secret Books of the Egyptian Gnostics* (E.T. 1960); C. H. Dodd, *The Bible and the Greeks* (1935), pp. 99ff.; H. Schlier, 'Der Mensch im Gnostizismus', in C. J. Bleeker (ed.), *Anthropologie religieuse* (1955); A.-J. Festugière, *La révélation d'Hermès Trismégiste*, III (1953), pp. 33ff., IV (1954), *passim*; 'Hermétisme et Gnose païenne', in *H.G.R.*, III; H. J. Schoeps, *Urgemeinde, Judenchristentum, Gnosis* (1956); Brandon, *M.D.*, pp. 190ff., 213ff.; R. Bultmann, *Das Christentum im Rahmen der antiken Religionen* (1949), pp. 181ff.; E.T., *Primitive Christianity* (1960), pp. 193ff.; *Gnosis* (E.T. 1952); J. Zandee, 'Gnostic Ideas on the Fall and Salvation', *Numen*, XI (1964); H. Jonas, *Gnosis u. spätantiker Geist* (1964³); *Kleine Pauly*, II, 830–9; U. Bianchi (ed.), *Le Origini delle Gnosticismo* (1967).

Gobind Singh Tenth of the → Sikh → Gurus, who gave the community (*Khalsa*) its present shape and finalized the scriptures (→ *Granth*). Son of Tegh Bahadur, the ninth Guru, whom he succeeded in 1675, at the age of nine, Gobind received an extensive education and was a noted writer of hymns and other genres, the collection known as the *Dasan Granth* being ascribed to him (his writings are not however incl. in the *Adi Granth*). To avenge father's death at hands of Mughals and to give Sikhs power to resist persecution, he organised an army, and in 1699 instituted the new community, baptising five disciples to form nucleus of the 'pure' (*Khalsa*). The sacrament of initiation involved drinking from same bowl (to break caste tabus) and renunciation of previous relig. loyalties. His followers were given name of 'Singh', to symbolize both that this was a new family cutting across social divisions and that it was a martial group. He also ordained taking of five emblems, known as the five 'k's (→ Sikhism), as outer signs of allegiance. Gobind reemphasised creed of → Nanak, and repudiated → asceticism. Mass initiations followed founding of new order, and Gobind swiftly created a strong and distinctive community

in the Panjab. It was not, however, until early 19th cent. that the Sikhs came to dominate region militarily. Gobind was assassinated, for reasons unknown, in 1708. Before death he asked followers to accept the *Granth* as their Guru, and thus he himself was last of the human Gurus. N.S.
Khushwant Singh, *A History of the Sikhs*, vol. 1 (1963).

God, Concept of See also entries under specific religions and deities. S.G.F.B.

(Buddh.) → Deva. T.O.L.

(China–Japan) Fundamental to Chinese and Japanese religs., whether Confucian, Buddh., Taoist or Shinto, is belief that at basis of all created and manifested existence is an underlying unitary, spiritual Reality, the absolute spiritual source of all things. For this Reality it is doubtless incorrect to use the term 'God', with its Chr., Jewish and Islamic connotations. Philosophically this supreme being is conceived of in impersonal or rather supra-personal terms: in → Confucianism as cosmic counterpart of moral principle in man; in → Taoism as unnameable and unknowable → Tao, the source and sustainer of all that is; in → Mahāyāna Buddhism of China and Japan as the → Adi-Buddha or the → Dharmakāya (Body of righteousness). The Supreme Reality, however conceived, is considered to be beyond reach of finite intelligence, and Far East. philosophies are pervaded by spirit of agnosticism. Yet recognition that the life-principle, permeating whole of nature, is fundamentally one with the Supreme Reality, leads to belief that man, by penetrating to depths of his own nature, may arrive at an intuitive recognition of Supreme Reality. In Confucianism this is achieved through full development of one's own moral nature; in Taoism, by a return to Tao; in Buddhism, by a realisation of one's Buddha-nature.

In practical relig. expression a theistic tendency is observable in all Far East. religs. Popular relig. is incurably polytheistic, and worship is given to a whole hierarchy of spiritual beings,—gods, Buddhas and deified men and animals; but at head of this hierarchy is a Supreme Being, worshipped and honoured under different names; the → Shang Ti or → T'ien of Confucianism; the Yü Huang of relig. Taoism; the → Amitabha Buddha of Buddhism; and → Amaterasu in Shintō.

Shang Ti or T'ien in Confucianism was considered to be such an august being that only the emperor, as Son of Heaven, was worthy to render adequate worship and homage to him in an elaborate State Cult. All others offered worship to various deities who, in a spiritual hierarchy, were agents of his supreme will and intermediaries between God and man. Though no worship was offered to him in temples of popular relig., almost every Chi. peasant recognised his supremacy under name Lao T'ien Yeh.

Though it is true to say that Buddhism, including the Mahāyāna of China and Japan, philosophically speaking denies existence of a Creator God who controls destinies of mankind, in practical relig. expression the Dharmakāya of the Adi-Buddha, manifest supremely in → Amitabha (Amida), is regarded as supreme Deity, endowed with personality, will, intelligence and love. By millions of Buddhists in China and Japan, Amitabha is regarded as supreme God with attributes of grace, mercy, omniscience and omnipotence. In all the → Pure Land sects he is regarded as supreme object of homage and worship. In relig. Taoism and in Shinto the same theistic tendencies are apparent. (→ Yü Huang; → Konkyo-kyō; → Kurozumi-kyō.) D.H.S.

E.R.E., VI, pp. 269ff.; 294–5; D. H. Smith, *Chinese Religion* (1968), pp. 33ff.; 50ff.; 138ff.; 263ff.; D. C. Holtom, *National Faith of Japan* (1938), pp. 123ff.; 171ff.; 292–3; W. G. Aston, *Shinto* (1905) pp. 69ff.; 121ff.; M. Anesaki, *Hist. of Japanese Buddhism* (1930), pp. 170ff.

(Christian) Christianity inherited Heb. conception of God as unique creator and ruler of universe. It also took over Heb. → Heilsgeschichte, which was adapted to belief that Jesus was incarnated Son of God and his death planned for man's salvation (→ Soteriology). The adjusting of orig. Heb. monotheistic conception to accommodate belief in Christ's divinity led to Christological controversies of first 4 cents. and resulted in doc. of → Trinity. In this process Greek metaphysics were influential, incl. idea of divine → impassibility and immutability (→ Christology). The influence of → Plato is apparent in teaching of → Augustine of Hippo, and that of → Aristotle in the work of Thomas → Aquinas. The Reformers, although reacting strongly against medieval scholasticism, continued in the estab. philosophical presentation of God, despite their constant use of Scriptural imagery. Since Reformation, the Chr. concept of God has been continuously affected by current philosophical thinking (→→ Kant; Hegel), although → Schleiermacher's repudiation of metaphysics in favour of intuition initiated movement that is still strongly repr. though variously presented, by modern theologians. The moral character of God, antithetically presented as his 'love' and 'justice', has been variously emphasised in → soteriology, with gen. tendency to emphasise justice of God and love of Christ. Presentation of God as exclus. beneficient Creator raises problem of origin of → evil as a fundamental issue, esp. relat. to scientific view of universe. (→ Philosophy of Relig.). S.G.F.B.

The lit. is immense: Harnack, *H.D.*, *E.R.E.*, VI,

pp. 252–69, XII, *s.v.* ('Theism'); *D.C.C.*, pp. 566ff.; *R.G.G.*[3], II, 1715–45; J. K. Mozley, *The Impassibility of God* (1926); F. R. Tennant, *Philosophical Theology*, II (1930), chs. 6–9; K. E. Kirk, *The Vision of God* (1932); Barth, K., *The Doctrine of God*, (*Church Dogmatics, II*), 2 vols. (E.T. 1967); E. L. Mascall, *He Who Is* (1962).

(Hebrew) During nomadic stage of Heb. culture, power, in various forms of manifestation, was essence of deity. → Yahweh was assoc. with storm, fire and war: the imagery was always anthropomorphic and continued so. After settlement in Canaan, the concept of Yahweh became fused with those of Canaanite → El and → Baal, thus acquiring concern with fertility of fields. The → Yahwist policy to make Yahweh the only god of Israel resulted in a monotheistic conception, implying universal onmipotence: he was also portrayed as sole creator of universe. The concomitant emphasis on Yahweh's moral character led to problem of innocent suffering epitomized in → Job. In later period, increasing stress was laid on Yahweh's holiness. The ethnic factor has always remained basic: Yahweh is essentially the god of Israel, with whom he has unique → covenant relation. (→→ Israel; Apocalyptic; Eschatology, Heb.; Judaism). S.G.F.B.

H.D.B.[2], *s.v.* ('God'); *E.R.E.*, VI, pp. 253–6, 295–9; *R.G.G.*[3], II, 1705–15; J. Pedersen, *Israel*, III–IV (1940), pp. 524ff.; H. H. Rowley, *The Faith of Israel*, ch. 2; A. Lods, *Israël* (1949), *Les prophètes d'Israël* (1935), *passim*; G. von Rad, *Old Testament Theology*, 2 vols. (E.T. 1962–5); W. Eichrodt, *Theology of the Old Test.*, 2 vols. (E.T. 1961–7); C. J. Labuschagne, *The Incomparability of Yahweh in the O.T.* (1966).

(Hindu Conceptions) Divine beings and spirits, together with humans and animals given divine status, form wide spectrum in Hinduism. The many gods (→ Gods, Hindu, *asuras*), incarnations (→ *avataras*) and other beings regarded as worthy of worship are, however, usually seen, from classical → Hinduism onwards, and already in the → Upaniṣads, as connected in one way or another with a supreme Being, interpreted either as personal (→ *Iśvara*) or as semi-personal. Much of classical and medieval Hindu theology turns on right estimate of nature of the holy power or ultimate reality designated as → *Brahman*. Polytheistic elements in Hindu culture are thus subsumed under theism or absolutism. The idea of a supreme God appears in three main theological forms, and is mythologically worked out in two main trads. (→→ Vaisnative and Saivite). First, God is treated as a 'lower' manifestation of *Brahman*, as in → Advaita Vedanta. Acc. to this conception, the personal Creator and focus of worship belongs to lower level of reality than the Absolute, the *nirgunam Brahman* or 'ultimate reality without attributes', identified with the → *Atman*. Mod. variations of this picture assign series of levels of reality to various conceptions of God—thus God as incarnated belongs to lower level than that of Creator, etc. This theory is basis of attempt at a unified ideology of religions. Second, God is conceived both as Creator and object of worship, as in →→ Visistadvaita, Dvaita, etc., and in gen. in → *bhakti* cults. Third, God is treated as Lord, but not as Creator, as in → Yoga school. Mythologically, the two import. streams of worship focus on →→ Viṣṇu and Śiva respectively, and it is gen. assumed that these figures are alternative symbols of the one underlying reality (they are also assoc. with → Brahmā in a → 'trinity' (→ *trimurti*). The chief difference between two is that Vaisnavism has well-developed cult of *avataras*, the most import. being →→ Rama and Krishna. Since gods in Hinduism tend to have consorts, the great Gods do also: → Laksmi in case of Viṣṇu, → Kālī (Durga, etc.) in case of Siva. These are usually taken to repr. creative power or *śakti* of God. It is commonly agreed among Vedantin schools that God's nature can be summed up in formula *saccidananda*, viz. *sat*, 'being'; *cit*, 'consciousness' and *ānanda*, 'bliss'. The chief theologies setting forth nature of God/*Brahman* are Advaita (→ Śankara), → Visistadvaita and → Dvaita, expressing non-dualistic (monistic), qualified non-dualistic and dualistic views of relation between ultimate reality and the self (soul) respectively. Also import. is the → Śaiva Siddhanta, setting forth a Saivite theism, independently of Saivite-influenced forms of Vedanta (notably Śankara's). There is in much of Hindu thought a strong tendency to treat world as kind of emanation of God, or to think of divine Being as lying 'within' what surrounds us. This immanentist approach to description of relation between world and God has sometimes been treated as → pantheism: but it is doubtful whether this judgment is correct—it is rather that Hindu images of way in which God transcends world have differed from those more typical in West. The *bhakti* schools have been strongly theistic, though the theism has different style from that discoverable in the Semitic religions, since it has coexisted with the cults of many 'lower' gods: it thus is a kind of theism transcending → polytheism, or 'transpolytheistic theism', as distinguished from a → monotheism which plainly rejects polytheistic elements. With regard to semi-personal view of ultimate reality, as in Advaita, comparisons have been made with the *deitas* of Eckhart (by Rudolf Otto) and with conception of God in → pseudo-Dionysius. In add. to theistic and absolutistic schools within orthodox Hinduism, there are others (e.g. →

Samkhya) which are atheistic, denying a personal Lord; and for long → Carvaka materialism, which was both anti-relig. and atheistic, was moderately influential in Indian trad. The → Nyaya-Vaisesika school of Hindu philosophy was main proponent of → classical arguments for God's existence, somewhat in style of Christ. natural theology (but → Ramanuja was a critic of arguments, though a powerful exponent of devotional theism). N.S.

J. E. Carpenter, *Theism in Medieval India* (1921); Bharatan Kumarappa, *The Hindu Conception of the Deity* (1934); A. Danielou, *Hindu Polytheism* (1962); N. Smart, *Doctrine and Argument in Indian Philosophy* (1964); R. Otto, *Mysticism East and West* (1957).

(Indian arguments about existence of) Parallel to discussions in Christ. trad. about whether God's existence can be proved, there has been an import. series of arguments in Hindu, and more widely, Indian philosophy. The classical collection of proofs of God's existence is to be found in the *Kusumāñjali* ('Handful of Flowers') of Udayana (10th cent. CE), who belonged to the → Nyaya-Vaisesika school. Counter-arguments were used by → atheistic groups, →→ Jains, Buddhists and → Carvaka Materialists; also in very full and penetrating fashion by the theist → Ramanuja, who considered that knowledge of God does not derive from human reason. These counter-arguments he set out in commentary on the → *Brahmasutra*. The most import. 'proof' of God's existence was version of the Teleological Argument (→ Philosophy of Religion): the universe is made up of parts, and thus has analogy to artifacts; artifacts arise from intelligent agency; therefore universe arises from intelligent agency. Against this Ramanuja and others argued as follows. First, though experience shows that pots, etc., are produced by intelligent agents, we are ignorant of material causes of mountains, etc., and have no right to infer intelligent agents to account for them. Second, the argument does not show that there is a single Artificer, and there may be many, esp. as we have no right to assume that universe was created all at one time. Third, if analogy is drawn between universe and organic bodies, there is difficulty that there are as many points of dissimilarity as of similarity between them (e.g. mountains do not breathe). Fourth, intelligent agents use their bodies; if God is Creator he needs a body; but then *that* has to be accounted for, and so on *ad infinitum*. Fifth, the stronger any proof drawing upon analogies between human artificers and God, the greater the similarity between them is, and so God is turned into a finite being. Various other subsidiary counter-arguments were also employed. The Nyaya-Vaisesika also attempted to prove God's existence by appealing to need for an intelligent being to combine atoms at beginning of a period of world-Creation (→ cosmology, Hindu). A very gen. counter-argument to any attempt to prove a Creator was used by Jains and Buddhists. If the universe is considered to be an effect, God needs to be considered as such too; for if he creates universe, this repr. a change in him; this change itself needs explanation, i.e. it is of the nature of an effect; and so on. There is an argument in the *Yogabhāṣya* (commentary on the *Yogasutra*) which has been compared to the Ontological Argument of → Anselm, though strictly it is an argument to show that the most perfect being is God and is unique (it was criticised by the → Mimamsa and others, partly because the → Yoga 'proof' made use of notion of perfect knowledge or omniscience; but if such knowledge were poss. without bodily organs, what is function of latter?). The need to explain operation of → *karma* was made basis of argument for an intelligent Controller of *karma*, in the → *Saiva Siddhanta* and elsewhere; but conception of self-operative *karma* was so strongly entrenched in Indian trad. that such a 'proof' did not seem as persuasive as perhaps it ought to have seemed. Finally, it is worth mentioning the appeal to relig. experience (yogic insight, etc.) to estab. existence of a transcendent Being or state. Apart from the appeal to revelation in orthodox Hinduism; this was prob. the most widely held ground for belief in the transcendent. Problems, however, of relation between experience and interpretation did not escape attention. Thus Jains raised question of whether belief in God was not cause of an intuition of him, rather than conversely. One interesting feature of pattern of discussion in India on these matters was its degree of overlap with independently generated discussions in West. E.g., many of Hume's celebrated arguments against the Teleological Argument were closely anticipated by Ramanuja. (→ Philosophy of Relig.). N.S.

N. Smart, *Doctrine and Argument in Indian Philosophy* (1964); G. Thibaut (tr.), *The Vedanta-Sutras with the Commentary of Ramanuja* in Max Müller (ed.), *S.B.E.*, vol. 48 (1904); S. Radhakrishnan and C. A. Moore (eds.), *A Source Book in Indian Philosophy* (1957).

(Islam) (Arabic: Allah, presumably derived from *al-ilāh*—the god) was known as supreme in pre-Islamic Arabia, though for practical purposes local gods meant more to people (cf. Qur. xiii:17; xxix:61, 63, etc.). The Qur. teaches that God is Creator, by whose word 'Be' all things have come into existence (cf. ii:111; vi:72; xvi:42, etc. and → Cosmogony). He is the sole divinity, and is one in his nature. xcii is most striking assertion of God's unity and uniqueness ('He has not begotten and he has not been begotten, and no one is equal to him'). The assertion of God's unity (*tawḥīd*) is so fundamental, that to disbelieve it came to be reckoned the unforgiveable sin. The Qur. stresses God's omnipotence, such titles being used as the Overpowering (*al-jabbār*—lix:23), the Dominant (*al-qahhār*, xiii:17), the Strong (*al-qawī*, xi:69). Other names speak of his kindliness, such as the Compassionate, the Merciful (*al-raḥmān al-raḥīm*, at the begin. of every sura except ix), the Provider (*al-razzāq*, li:58), the Loving (*al-wadūd*, lxxxv:14), the Forgiving (*al-ghafūr*, xxxv:27): → God, Ninety-nine Names. God has provided 'signs' (*āyāt*) to show his power and beneficence, which call men to show thankfulness (xxx:45) and to worship him. They serve as proofs, incl. as they do his good providence in changes of seasons and day and night, and his provision for mankind (xvii:13; xli:37; xxx:19ff.; vi:95fn.). Elsewhere God speaks of his creative work and power to raise the dead (xxii:5ff.). He summons people to use their minds in contemplating his signs; but some neglect them (cf. x:16; xix:74; xlv:24; lxxxiii:13). God is sometimes repr. as calling men to believe and do what is right (ciii:2f.; iii:127ff.; xvi:34; xxxiii:35); at other times as saying he determines all men's actions (vi:107; x:100; xvi:39, 95; xxxv:9; lxxiv:34). He rewards the believers and punishes the unbelievers (ii:75f.; iv:17f.; vii:34, 40; x:27f.): → Creed; → Free-will and Predestination.

Theologians later developed a doc. of God's attributes. The seven commonly mentioned are Life, Knowledge, Power, Will, Hearing, Sight, Speech, sometimes with variation in order. These are said to belong to God's essence. In add. there are attributes belonging to his action, such as creating, sustaining, producing, renewing, making, etc. (cf. Wensinck, *Creed*, 188). Emphasis is laid on their being different from those of his creatures. The effect of this doc. is to set God apart. Worship, therefore, cannot be communion with God; for there can be no communion between beings altogether different from one another. Worship is merely a service God has commanded, but it makes no difference to him whether men worship him or not. While this is logical outcome of theology, it is not satisfying to human heart, so → mysticism continued to thrive within Islam. Though mysticism had its martyrs, → Ghazali gained for it a place within Islam. The orthodox theologians, like the Qur., emphasise God's unity and power; they try to reconcile human responsibility with God's decrees on basis of man's acquiring (*kasb*, *iktisāb*) the deeds God created within him (→ Acquisition). Islamic discussions incl. the docs. of the → Mu'tazilites, who felt that to speak of attributes being in God's essence implied a kind of multiplicity, and of those who were influenced by Greek philosophy which was mixed with → Neoplatonism. This affected Shi'a doc. to some extent, espec. that of → Isma'ilis. J.R.

*E.I.*², I, pp. 332ff. (*'aḳīda*), 406ff. (Allāh); D. B. Macdonald, *Theology*, Appendix I and index (Allah); Wensinck, *Creed*, index; Watt, *Free Will*; Gardet and Anawati, *Introduction*; Sweetman, *I.C.T.*, indexes; Stanton, *Teaching*, pp. 31ff.; Jeffery, *Vocabulary*, pp. 66f.; F. Rosenthal, *Ibn Khaldun*, index.

(Islam) Ninety-Nine Names of

1.	al-Raḥmān	The Compassionate
2.	al-Raḥīm	The Merciful
3.	al-Malik	The King
4.	al-Quddūs	The Holy
5.	al-Salām	The Source of Peace
6.	al-Mu'min	The Preserver of Security
7.	al-Muhaymin	The Protector
8.	al-'Azīz	The Mighty
9.	al-Jabbār	The Overpowering
10.	al-Mutakabbir	The Great in Majesty
11.	al-Khāliq	The Creator
12.	al-Bāri'	The Maker
13.	al-Muṣawwir	The Fashioner
14.	al-Ghaffār	The Forgiver
15.	al-Qahhār	The Dominant
16.	al-Wahhāb	The Bestower
17.	al-Razzāq	The Provider
18.	al-Fattāḥ	The Decider
19.	al-'Alīm	The Knower
20.	al-Qābiḍ	The Withholder
21.	al-Bāsiṭ	The Plentiful Giver
22.	al-Khāfiḍ	The Abaser
23.	al-Rāfi'	The Exalter
24.	al-Mu'izz	The Honourer
25.	al-Mudhill	The Humiliator
26.	al-Samī'	The Hearer
27.	al-Baṣīr	The Seer
28.	al-Ḥakam	The Judge
29.	al-'Adl	The Just
30.	al-Laṭīf	The Gracious
31.	al-Khabīr	The Informed
32.	al-Ḥalīm	The Clement
33.	al-'Aẓīm	The Incomparably Great
34.	al-Ghafūr	The Forgiving
35.	al-Shakūr	The Rewarder
36.	al-'Alī	The Most High
37.	al-Kabīr	The Most Great
38.	al-Ḥafīẓ	The Preserver
39.	al-Muqīt	The Sustainer
40.	al-Ḥasīb	The Reckoner
41.	al-Jalīl	The Majestic
42.	al-Karīm	The Generous
43.	al-Raqīb	The Watcher
44.	al-Mujīb	The Answerer
45.	al-Wāsi'	The Liberal

46. al-Ḥakīm	The Wise
47. al-Wadūd	The Loving
48. al-Majīd	The Glorious
49. al-Bā'ith	The Raiser
50. al-Shahīd	The Witness
51. al-Ḥaqq	The Real
52. al-Wakīl	The Trustee
53. al-Qawī	The Strong
54. al-Matīn	The Firm
55. al-Walī	The Patron
56. al-Ḥamīd	The Praiseworthy
57. al-Muḥṣī	The All-Knowing
58. al-Mubdi'	The Originator
59. al-Mu'īd	The Restorer to life
60. al-Muḥyī	The Giver of life
61. al-Mumīt	The Giver of death
62. al-Ḥayy	The Living
63. al-Qayyūm	The Eternal
64. al-Wājid	The Self-sufficient
65. al-Mājid	The Grand
66. al-Wāḥid	The One
67. al-Aḥad	The Single
68. al-Ṣamad	He to whom men repair
69. al-Qādir	The Powerful
70. al-Muqtadir	The Prevailing
71. al-Muqaddim	The Advancer
72. al-Mu'akhkhir	The Delayer
73. al-Awwal	The First
74. al-Ākhir	The Last
75. al-Ẓāhir	The Outward
76. al-Bāṭin	The Inward
77. al-Wālī	The Governor
78. al-Muta'ālī	The Sublime
79. al-Barr	The Amply Beneficent
80. al-Tawwāb	The Accepter of repentance
81. al-Muntaqim	The Avenger
82. al-'Afūw	The Pardoner
83. al-Ra'ūf	The Kindly
84. Mālik al-Mulk	The Ruler of the Kingdom
85. Dhul Jalāl wal Ikrām	The Lord of Majesty and Splendour
86. al-Muqsiṭ	The Equitable
87. al-Jāmi'	The Gatherer
88. al-Ghanī	The Independent
89. al-Mughnī	The Enricher
90. al-Māni'	The Depriver
91. al-Ḍārr	The Harmer
92. al-Nāfi'	The Benefiter
93. al-Nūr	The Light
94. al-Hādī	The Guide
95. al-Badī'	The First Cause (or, The Incomparable)
96. al-Bāqī	The Enduring
97. al-Wārith	The Inheritor
98. al-Rashīd	The Director
99. al-Ṣabūr	The Patient

The above list is in a trad. traced to → Abū Hurayra, given by → Tirmidhī. Slight differences are to be found in lists, but the above is gen. recognised. When making supplication, it is customary to invoke God, using a name appropriate to content of one's petition. Some lists omit No. 67 (al-Aḥad). When that is done, Allāh may be counted first of the names; but one may find al-Mu'ṭī (the Giver) following No. 89 (al-Mughnī), when al-Aḥad is omitted. J.R.

E.I.[2], I, pp. 714ff. (al-asmā' al-ḥusnā); Hughes, pp. 141f.; *Mishkāt*, pp. 483f.; Sweetman, *I.C.T.*, I, pp. 215f.

(Origin of Concept of) The subject has long been discussed and many various theories advanced. Most of the work has been of the nature of philosophical, psychological, or theological speculation, e.g. (1) E. B. Tylor's → animism (2) R. Otto's idea of the 'Numinous' (→ Holy, The); (3) W. Schmidt's theory of primeval → monotheism. The relevant evidence gen. shows that concept of deity orig. in many ways and found expression in various, and often very diverse, forms. The idea of supernatural power certainly lies behind many conceptions; but there can be striking exceptions, e.g. → dying-rising gods. Paleolithic archeology provides earliest evidence of one concept of deity, possibly of two. The sculptured figure of the so-called 'Venus of Laussel' prob. repr. deification of woman as source of life, a prototype of the → Great Goddess. The picture of the so-called 'Dancing Sorcerer' in the Trois Frères cave (Ariège) has been interpreted as repr. a divine 'Lord of the beasts' (→ Cave Art). It is significant that Paleolithic art provides no evidence of deification of sun, moon, or stars. Excavations at → Çatel Hüyük reveal cult of goddess, connected with → fertility and → death, dating from 7th mil. BC. The earliest literate cultures (in Egypt, Mesopot., India, China and Americas) attest existence already of complex concepts of deity. (→→ Euhemerus; Religion, Origin; Time). S.G.F.B.

E.R.E., V, pp. 243–7; E. O. James, *The Concept of Deity* (1950), *The Worship of the Sky-God* (1963); G. Van der Leeuw, *La religion* (1948), pp. 9ff.; L. R. Farnell, *The Attributes of God* (1925); C. H. Ratschow, *Magie und Religion* (1955), pp. 68ff.; M. Eliade, *Traité d'histoire des religions* (1949); pp. 47ff. (E.T.), *Patterns in Comparative Religion* (1958), pp. 38ff.; R. Pettazzoni, *The All-Knowing God* (E.T. 1956); H. Breuil and R. Lantier, *Les hommes de la Pierre Ancienne* (1951), pp. 312, 325ff.; J. Maringer, *The Gods of Prehistoric Man* (1956), pp. 108ff.; G. Clarke, *The Stone Age Hunters* (1967), pp. 80ff.; G. R. Levy, *The Gate of Horn* (1948), pp. 27ff.; *R.G.G.*[3], II, pp. 1701–5; Brandon, *M.D.*, pp. 14ff.; 'The Origin of Religion: in Theory and Archaeology', *R.A.H.*, ch. 1, in D.H.I., *s.v.;* P. J. Ucko and A. Rosenfeld, *Palaeolithic Cave Art* (1967), pp. 123ff.

(Sikh Conception of) A major feature of → Nanak's teaching was that the forms by which men describe God, whether as →→ Allah, Rama, Viṣṇu or etc., tend to mislead and divide them. Thus he described God as *niraṅkār* or 'formless'. On other hand, he used trad. names of God, both Muslim and Hindu; but within the context of strict → monotheism, and commonly used the designations *Sat Kartār* ('True Creator') and *Sat Nām* ('True Name'). God is the all-powerful creator of world, existing from before time, and pervading whole universe. It is inappropriate, in view of his formlessness, to represent him by images. God is also merciful, and will save those who have faith in him. However, such salvation does not occur through intermediaries, import. as guidance of Guru(s) may be. Sikhism has been opposed to the whole doc. of → *avataras* or incarnations of God, and Gurus discouraged tendencies to see them in this light. So far, the doc. of God has strong affinities with that in Islam; but some elements of trad. Hindu theism were present too in teachings of Nanak and his successors. Thus there is strong emphasis on all-pervading presence of God (as in → Vaisnavism) and on nature of world as → *maya*, a kind of illusion or beguilement. However, Sikhism did not treat this in idealistic way of → Advaita. Rather the *maya* was the outpouring of God's creative power, in which souls could easily lose themselves in forgetting their likeness to the Creator. Thus the trouble with men, and cause of their sufferings, is egoism. Once one could overcome selfishness, the other virtues would appear. This egoism is in part consequence of ignorance, in which men are unaware of divine goodness residing in them and waiting to be cultivated. Sikhism also makes use, but not in any highly formalised way, of distinction between God as *nirgunam* and as *sagunam* (without and with attributes). Prior to creation God is purely formless—a notion preserving transcendence of divine reality, complementing the strong sense of God's immanence in created world and in man. The Sikh gurus also taught doc. of → reincarnation. The overcoming of egoism and knowledge of divine radiance would free man from this, and his spirit would join God's in eternal bliss. (→→ Guru; Sikhism). N.S.

M. A. Macauliffe *et al.*, *Sikh Religion; a Symposium* (1958); Khushwant Singh, *A History of the Sikhs*. 2 vols. (1963–6).

Gods, Hindu The Hindu pantheon is immense and variegated; but the gods are typically subordinated to or seen as manifestations of a single ultimate reality (→ Brahman, → God, Hindu conceptions of). Already this trend is seen in → *Rgveda;* but it found classical form in subsumption of gods under →→ Visnu, Siva and Brahma. → Vedic relig. subscribed to theory that the gods (*devas*) numbered thirty-three; in later Hinduism number was raised to thirty-three crores (330,000,000)—a formal estimate to cover large variety of cults, village deities, etc., which had been woven into overall fabric of its socially complex piety. Since classical Hinduism emerged out of synthesis between → Aryan and non-Aryan cults, the major Vedic gods tended to lose predominance—e.g. →→ Agni, Indra, Varuna; while relatively minor Vedic deities, Viṣṇu and Śiva became central, partly through absorption of a variety of cults under their aegis, e.g. →→ Krishna, Vasudeva, Narayana. As tribal groups, too, were fitted into → caste system, and a theoretically Aryan culture spread into S. India, the gods of groups and regions were identified with major deities. Mother goddesses, such as → Kali, Uma, Parvati, were 'wedded' to male consorts. The process of unifying pantheon was assisted by regarding gods as offspring of such pairs. Thus the elephant-headed → Ganeṣa (Ganesh), now very widely revered by Hindus as 'remover of obstacles', is son of Śiva and Parvati, as is also the war-god Skanda or Subrahmanya—another orig. non-Aryan deity, identified with major god of anc. Tamils. Other deities which have become highly popular are Laksmi (→ Śrī), the consort of Viṣṇu, → Sarasvati, the consort of Brahma, Hanumant, the monkey friend of → Rama (also import. in late medieval piety, esp. in north). In add. to such gods of pan-Indian significance, there is a host of local gods and goddesses, e.g. the *grāmadevatā* or village deities, such as Mariyammai, goddess of smallpox, whose cult is widespread in south. Since all living beings exist in constantly shifting continuum in Hindu imagination, the concept of gods is fluid, and there are many spirits, demons, etc., as well as above categories of gods. Import. among these are serpent-deities (*nāgas*), tree-spirits (the *aśvattha* or pipal being esp. revered), genii (*yakṣas* and *yakṣīs*, the latter female, frequently portrayed in sculpture as delightfully sensuous), *gandharvas* and *apsarases*, male and female heavenly musicians and servants of gods, and → *asuras*, antigods. It was comparatively frequent for humans to be elevated to divine status, e.g. through theory of *avataras*; the anc. → *rishis* are looked on as divine; while cult of → *gurus* encourages ascription of god-like properties to the teacher, acting as mediator of God. Below human status are ghosts, evil spirits, etc. (*pretas*, *bhūtas*, *piśācās*, etc.), many of whom orig. as outlying or hostile tribal groups, etc., regarded as demonic. Geographical features such as rivers and mountains are often personified and divinised, such as the → Ganges, as goddess Ganga. Except in so far as they are manifestations of ultimate reality, deities are regarded as impermanent (though living longer, more splendidly and powerfully than men (or than most men: often the → yogi, e.g., is regarded as acquiring greater power than the gods, through his austerities, etc.). Thus it is common to treat a god as being successively manifested in different periods of world-creation: hence there are many Brahmas, Indras, etc. The wealth and variety of pantheon encourages some freedom in symbolism which the worshipper or devotee may adopt, though this may be determined for him by relig. and caste group to which he belongs. The chosen deity, through which a person or group approaches ultimate reality, is known as the *iṣṭadevatā*. This practice has analogies to the kathenotheism of Vedic period (→ God, Hindu conceptions). N.S.

J. Dowson, *A Classical Dictionary of Hindu Mythology* (1961); A. Danielou, *Hindu Polytheism* (1962); W. Crooke, *Religion and Folklore in Northern India*, 2 vols. (1926); H. Whitehead, *The Village Gods of South India* (1921); J. N. Banerjea, *The Development of Hindu Iconography* (1956); Alice Getty, *Ganesa* (1926); H. Zimmer, *Myths and Symbols in Indian Art and Civilization* (1962).

Godiva, Lady The legend of her famous ride, naked, through the streets of Coventry, at challenge of her husband Count Leofric, to gain remission of taxes for the citizens, has caused much speculation as to its origin. The story is first recorded at end of 12th cent. by Roger of Wendover, who doubtless drew on earlier trad. The first recorded Godiva Procession at the Corpus Christi fair took place in 1678. The earliest ref. to Peeping Tom, who was struck blind for looking at G. occurs in 1634. G. and her husband are well authenticated persons, connected with Coventry in the early 11th cent. Attempts have been made to explain the Ride, which seems unlikely to have been historical, as pagan fertility ritual (→ Nudity, Ritual), as folk-memory of some Germanic goddess (Nerthus, Holda, Perchta/Berchta), or of Eve in the Coventry miracle-plays. Similarly, Peeping Tom has been equated with → Actaeon, who saw → Artemis bathing. None of these theories is convincing, owing to lack of evidence. The legend provides significant example of how a historical person can become assoc. in folk trad. with ideas of apparent pagan origin. S.G.F.B.

K. Häfele, *Die Godivasage und ihre Behandlung in der Literatur* (1929); F. Bliss Burbidge, *Old Coventry and Lady Godiva* (1952); J. C. Lancaster (with H. R. Ellis Davidson), *Godiva of Coventry* (1967); V. Newall, 'Peeping Tom', *Folklore*, 80 (1969).

Gog and Magog (Yājūj wa-Mājūj). Fierce peoples of C. Asia, mentioned twice in the → Qur. xviii:93–7 tells of Alexander the Great (Dhul Qarnayn) blocking a valley with iron to stop their depredations; xxi:96 speaks of their bursting forth before end of world. Trad. mentions this coming of G. and M. as one of signs of the last hour. A lengthy trad. (*Mishkāt*, 1146) says → Jesus and his companions will beseech God, who will send insects to put G. and M. to death. When the earth is purged from their putrefaction by birds which will remove their bodies (cf. Ezekiel, xxxix:4), it will become fertile. The spirit of every believer will then be taken up, and the wicked will be left to be disorderly in the earth. Then the last hour will come. J.R.

E.I., IV, p. 1142; Wensinck, *Handbook*, p. 263; *Mishkāt*, p. 1142; Hughes, pp. 148f.; Masson, *Coran*, n. on xviii, p. 94; Sale, *Qurán*, I, p. 133; III, pp. 96f.

Gohei The word G. is of Chinese origin, the Japanese term being *mitegura*. The G. is both a symbolic offering and an indication that the → kami is present in a shrine. It is an upright wand, from which strips of paper, elaborately folded in a zigzag fashion, hang down on either side. The colour of the paper may vary, and sometimes thin sheets of metal are used instead. The G. stand on altars and elsewhere in → Shinto temples. Originally the G. represented clothing offered and dedicated to the deity. Today Shinto worshippers, for an offering of money, receive pieces of the G. from the temple to place them on the 'god-shelf' in their homes, in belief that they will ensure the god's protection and good fortune. They are not infrequently objects of popular worship. A means of purification is to shake the G. over person or object to be purified. D.H.S.

W. G. Aston, *Shinto* (1905), p. 216; G. F. Moore, *Hist. of Religs.*, vol. 1 (1914), pp. 101–3; J. Herbert, *Shinto* (1967), pp. 116–7.

Golden Rule, The Modern name given to pronouncement attr. to Jesus, recorded in Mt. 7:12; Lk. 6:31 (shorter version runs: 'As ye would that men should do unto you, do ye also to them likewise'). Similar statements, but in negative form, are found in Rabbinic sources (e.g. R. Hillel summarised → Torah as: 'What is hateful to yourself, do to no other', (*Sabb.* 31a)). Parallels occur in Grk. lit., and → Confucius ruled: 'What you do not like if done to yourself, do not do to others', a negative form that would have its positive side acc. to his principle of 'reciprocity'. S.G.F.B.

E.R.E., VI, *s.v.; R.G.G.*[3], II, 1688–9; C. G. Montefiore, *Rabbinic Literature and Gospel Teachings* (1930), pp. 150ff.; A. Dihle, *Die Goldene Regel* (1962).

Golden Legend (Legenda Aurea) A collection of lives of saints, composed by Jacob of Voragine, *c.* 1255–66. Its attractive anecdotes made it exceedingly popular; it was trans. into French in 14th cent., and was one of first books to be printed, being issued in several languages. It was a source of inspiration to medieval artists. S.G.F.B.

E.T. by F. S. Ellis in *The Temple Classics*, 7 vols. (1900); *D.C.C., s.v.;* E. Mâle, *The Gothic Image* (E.T. 1961 edn.), pp. 272ff.

Gongs and Bells (China–Japan) → Music, Ritual and Sacred. D.H.S.

Good Friday Friday before → Easter, observed as anniversary of Crucifixion of Jesus. Acc. to the *Peregrinatio Etheriae*, already in 4th cent. at Jerusalem, Christians solemnly venerated the Cross on that day. The custom was estab. in Rome in 7th–8th cent., together with 'Mass of the Presanctified (i.e. sacred elements consecrated on previous day). G.-F. is a fast-day, and in R.C. Church one of two days, Holy Saturday being other, when Mass is not celebrated. Many other special services are customary on G.-F., incl. the Three Hours Devotion from noon to 3 p.m. orig. introduced by → the Jesuits. (→ Cross). S.G.F.B.

L. Duchesne, *Christian Worship* (E.T. 1927), pp. 248ff., 510; *D.C.C., s.v.*

Good Life, Ideal (Buddh.) → Nibbuta. T.O.L. (China–Japan) → Ethics. D.H.S.

Good Shepherd, The Christ's statement: 'I am the good shepherd' (Jn. 10:14) naturally suggested an attractive image for early Chr. artists, and representations of G.-S. are found from 4th cent. in → catacombs and on sarcophagi. The image, however, already had a long pagan trad. It can be traced back to 3rd mil. BC in Mesopot. art, where it repr. man carrying a sacrificial animal (goat). It appears on pagan Roman sarcophagi contemporary with Chr. depictions. S.G.F.B.

A.E.C.W., p. 155; *Jahrbuch f. Antike u. Christentum*, I (1958), pp. 23ff., 819 (1965–6), pp. 126ff.

Good Works (China) → Merit. D.H.S.

Gorgo(n) or Medusa In Grk. mythology a terrible monster, whose hair was serpents and whose gaze turned beholder to stone. She had two sisters, Sthenno ('the Strong') and Euryale ('the Wide Leaping'), and lived in far West. The hero Perseus was sent by → Athena to kill G., which he did, decapitating her (the slaying is also attr. to Athena). In her death-pangs, G. gave birth to Pegasus and Chrysaor. The head of G. adorned → aegis of both → Zeus and Athena. It has been suggested that G. was an Aegean chthonian goddess whom Athena displaced, taking over her horrific aspect in form of head on her aegis. In Hellenistic art, G. was repr. as a beautiful dying maiden. Her head was widely used by Grks. and Etruscans as an apotropaic symbol. S.G.F.B.

H. J. Rose, *Handbook of Greek Mythology* (1928), pp. 29ff.; *O.C.D., s.v.; Kleine Pauly*, II, pp. 852–3.

Gospels The Old Eng. *godspel*, 'good news', trans. Grk. word *euangelion*, having same meaning. It was orig. used (e.g. Mk. 1:1) to describe accounts of career of → Jesus, written in Grk. and trad. ascribed to Matthew, Mark, Luke and John. Jesus is described as 'preaching the *euangelion* of the kingdom of God' in Mk. 1:14. *Euangelion* is used by → Paul for own interpretation of nature and work of Christ as distinct from the *euangelion* of Jerusalem Christians (Gal. 1:6ff., 2:7); but he also talks of the '*euangelion* of Christ'. The orig. sources and authenticity of the G. have been critically studied by Western scholars for more than a century, and a vast lit. has accumulated (→ Formgeschichte; →→ John; Luke; →→ Mark; Matthew, Gospels of, → Synoptic Problem). There are many so-called Apocryphal Gospels which never won canonical status (→ Canon, N.T.), a few may preserve 1st cent. trad. not incl. in canonical G. (→ Apocryphal New Test.; → Logia; → Thomas, Gospel of). (→→ Biblical Research; Kerygma). S.G.F.B.

B. H. Streeter, *The Four Gospels* (1924); J. Moffatt, *An Intro. to the Literature of the New Test.* (1933³); F. C. Grant, *The Gospels: their Origin and Growth* (1957); *R.G.G.*³, II, 749–70; *P.C.*², pp. 676ff.; *H.D.B.*², *s.v.; Th.Wb.*, II, *s.v. euangelion.*

Gotama (Pali); **Gautama** (Skt.) → Buddha, Gotama. T.O.L.

Grace, Doctrine of In N.T., *charis*, 'grace', denotes God's goodwill and help, enabling men to be well-pleasing to him: it finds expression in various ways. From N.T. refs., Chr. theologians gradually composed a very intricate doc. of G., the contrib. of → Augustine of Hippo being most important. It stemmed from doc. of → Fall and → Original Sin: if human nature was so depraved as doc. of Original Sin taught, how could man of his own accord ever turn to God and be saved? A solution was found in idea of 'prevenient grace', i.e. God freely gives prior prompting to individuals towards conversion. The notion raised other problems, much debated, of → predestination and free-will. A problem also arose in interpreting G. relative to → Sacraments. Controversy concerning G. continued through Middle Ages into Reformation period. In theology, three forms of G. are distinguished: (1) habitual or sanctifying G.: it is normally conveyed in the Sacraments (2) actual G., which is divine prompting to some good act; it may be received by unbaptised (3) prevenient G. S.G.F.B.

*H.D.B.*², *s.v.; D.C.C., s.v.; E.R.E.*, VI, 364–72; *R.G.G.*³, II, 1632–47; Harnack, *H.D.*, vols. 2–7, *passim*; N. P. Williams, *The Ideas of the Fall and of Original Sin* (1927); S. Cave, *The Christian Estimate of Man* (1944); K. E. Kirk, *The Vision of God* (1932²); R. Niebuhr, *The Nature and Destiny of Man*, II (1943).

Grace, Hindu Concept of The → *bhakti* movement

in Hinduism, with emphasis on loving reliance upon God, had profound effect on attitudes to operation of → *karma*. An early sign of this is found in the docs. of the → *Bhagavadgita*, where God in effect short-circuits effect of *karma*, since those who rely upon the Lord are assured of liberation, despite cumulative effects of previous actions. This notion was intensified in later *bhakti* cults. Salvation or → liberation occurs through grace (*prasāda*) of God. This was consequent upon the *prapatti* or self-surrender of individual to God. The doc. of grace was reconciled to that of *karma* in that latter was seen as action of God in controlling destinies of souls. Thus operation of grace could take form of kind of predestinationism, as in → Madhva's theology, where intrinsic character of an individual is worked out, through *karma*, by God towards salvation, damnation or continual → rebirth. The emphasis in Madhva's *Dvaita* on intrinsic justice of God's action had its opposite in docs. such as those of → Vallabha, who stressed inscrutability of salvation. The fact that God saves by his grace and gives bliss in this life to some rather than others is not to be explained by moral virtue, etc. Gen. speaking, *bhakti* theologians were divided between two theories, variously called: one doc. was that liberation is entirely work of the Lord; the other that moral (and also in some cases ritual) effort is necessary to qualify for grace (this division was an independent parallel of similar disputes in West, esp. during → Reformation). The school of → Ramanuja was divided on this issue, splitting into the → Tengalai and → Vadagalai. The latter party have qualified doc. of necessity of works or effort as preliminary to reception of grace. Since they follow Sanskrit rather than vernacular texts, this involves some concession to trad. requirement of ritual and ethical works as necessary to salvation. Likewise in N. Indian *bhakti* schools, such as those of → Nimbarka and → Vallabha, there was distinction between absolute and qualified grace. Except for some followers of Vallabha, there was relatively little antinomianism as consequence of extreme doc. of grace. Belief in grace tended to contrast with ideas of self-sufficient conquest of liberation, such as taught in → Samkhya-Yoga and → Advaita, and ritual and sacramental prescriptions for salvation, as in → Mimamsa, and up to a point in → Tantrism. A form of predestinationism, but divorced from concept of grace (there being no God) was found in teachings of the → Ajivikas. The → Mahāyāna Buddh. conception of transfer of merit, to account for salvation of folk prematurely (that is, in regard to their *karma*, which would imply many further lives) was not prominent in Hindu thinking, though present in a limited way in → Vaisnavism. Classically, self-surrender to God which is complemented by God's grace (though devotee does not ask for it or for salvation) is defined as state of deep prayerfulness towards Lord, conviction that he alone is Saviour and universal love and charity towards all men. In *bhakti* schools stress on inscrutable love of God tends to carry with it corollary that, since works do not save, ritual practices and distinctions are relatively or absolutely unimportant; from this it follows that salvation is open to classes other than those trad. able to benefit from sacred Vedic lore. This was an import. aspect of trend towards egalitarianism in medieval *bhakti* schools—though often equality was for relig. purposes only. The ultimate use of doc. of grace in relation to social equality was found in N. India, with preaching of →→ Kabir, Nanak and others (the egalitarianism of → Lingayats had other relig. and social roots). The dominance in mod. Indian thought of neo-Advaitin teachings has tended to obscure degree to which ideas of grace have informed most late medieval Indian relig. movements. N.S.

J. E. Carpenter, *Theism in Medieval India* (1921); B. Kumarappa, *The Hindu Conception of Deity as culminating in Ramanuja* (1934).

Grail, The Holy Object of many medieval romances, where it gen. figures as a mysterious vessel having virtue of imparting exalted spiritual experience to a person beholding it. The earliest evidence of legend is *Le Conte del Graal* of Chrétien de Troyes (1180–90). It was incorporated into → Arthurian legend by at least 1200. The orig. of concept has been widely discussed, but remains uncertain. It was identified with Cup used at → Last Supper, but this seems to be a Christianised form of a more anc. notion. The source of the legend has been traced to Celtic mythology, Coptic Egypt, and → Mystery Religs. There can be no doubt that, whatever its orig., the idea of the G. incorporated many different motifs during its wanderings; one common element, however, is that G. radiated supernatural light. S.G.F.B.

E.R.E., VI, *s.v.;* E. K. Chambers, *Arthur of Britain* (1927), *passim;* M. Williams, 'Some Aspects of the Grail Problem', *Folk-Lore*, 71 (1960), pp. 85–103.

Granth, Ādi The scriptures of → Sikhism, known also as the *Guru Granth*, since the line of → Gurus came to end with → Gobind Singh, who told his followers to accept the *Granth* henceforth as their Guru. The scriptures were first compiled in autoritative edition by fifth Guru, → Arjun, who had been installed in the Harimandir (Golden Temple) at Amritsar. However, the collection was expanded and finalized by Gobind, who incl. hymns by Arjun and Gobind's father Tegh Bahadur, the ninth Guru. A compilation of relig., philosophical and other writings attributed to Gobind is known as the *Dasam Granth*, but does not have same sacred status as the *Adi G.* though verses from it are used in Sikh worship, etc. The *Adi G.* contains about 6,000 hymns, the majority composed by first five and ninth Guru. Over 2,000 were composed by Arjun. In earlier edition the largest contributor had been → Nanak, who wrote the famous *Japji* or morning prayer, central to Sikh daily devotions. Apart from poems attr. to Gurus, there is substantial number of hymns drawn from Hindu and Muslim sources, notably from *bhaktas* and → Sufis. Among the authors are Farid (?13th cent. CE), Nam Dev (1270–1350), and → Kabir. Compositions of court bards and others have also been woven into collection. The hymns are arranged into 31 sections, corresponding to modes in which they should be sung, and so from beginning were assigned a firmly liturgical purpose. Though by now somewhat archaic, the language remains intelligible in context of mod. Panjabi. N.S.

T. Singh *et al.*, *Selections from the Sacred Writings of the Sikhs* (1960); G. S. Dardi, *Translation of the Adi Granth*, 4 vols. (1960); Jogendra Singh, *Sikh Ceremonies* (1941).

Grasping (Buddh.) Grasping (*upādāna*) or, as sometimes trans., 'clinging' is, acc. to Buddh. thought, an intensified form of *taṇhā* (→ Craving). It is of 4 kinds: (1) sensuous-clinging, i.e. clinging to sensuous desires and pleasures (2) clinging to views (i.e. false or mistaken views) (3) clinging to rules and rituals, with the idea that one may through them gain salvation (4) clinging to notion of individual personality. The → Anāgami is regarded as entirely free from all these manifestations of grasping or clinging. T.O.L.

Great Goddess, The Customary term for deification of female principle as source of life and fertility. The G.-G. gen. appears as → Earth Goddess, and is ambivalently regarded as Mother and Virgin: she is often closely assoc. with the dead. (→→ Anat; Anahita; Aphrodite; Astarte; Çatal Hüyük; Cybele; Demeter; Diana of Ephesians; Fertility; Isis; Kore; Ma; Magna Mater; Mary, Cult; Paleolithic Relig.; Venus). S.G.F.B.

I. Przyluski, *La Grande Déesse* (1950); E. O. James, *The Cult of the Mother Goddess* (1959).

Greed (Buddh. view) In Buddh. trad., G. (*lobha*) is one of the 3 morally unwholesome 'roots' of thought and action (the other 2 being hatred and illusion). It is often used as synonym of *taṇhā* (→ desire or thirst). T.O.L.

Greek Religion The earliest written evidence of G.-R. is provided by → Homeric poems, the *Iliad* and *Odyssey*, dating from 8th cent. BC, but incorporating both earlier and later material. A polytheistic relig. is depicted, evidently repr. the faith of the Indo-European peoples (→ Aryans) whose invasion of Aegean area some five cents. before had destroyed earlier culture centred on Crete (→ Aegean Relig.; → Cretan and Mycenaen Relig.). The chief deity, → Zeus, was a sky-god, who ruled world of gods and men; he was not regarded as creator-god, but was essentially upholder of cosmic order. He presided over company of deities assoc. with various parts of universe (e.g. → Poseidon, the sea) or functions (e.g. → Ares, war; → Aphrodite, sexual love). The abode of the gods was Mt. Olympus, highest mt. in Greece. In Homer the gods are depicted as super-human beings, immortal, very powerful but not omnipotent; they have human passions and often behave in immoral and undignified ways. Behind this Homeric presentation, however, signs can be discerned of more primitive and non-human conceptions. The responsibility of Zeus for human destiny is variously conceived (→ Moira). Man's lot is regarded pessimistically: a dismal existence in Hades followed death (→ Eschatology, Greek; → Hades). Homeric relig. reveals gen. structure of an Indo-Europ. sky-relig., with certain Aegean elements incorporated: e.g. such goddesses as Aphrodite, →→ Athena, Artemis, Hera, are pre-Hellenic. The *Theogony* of → Hesiod preserves memory of an earlier divine order, the Aegean. The Olympian relig., as evidenced in Homer, formed state-relig. of classical Greece. Temples to various Olympian gods existed in cities and other places (e.g. → Delphi), sacrifices being chief cultic act. The state-cults did not meet individual spiritual needs; these were catered for by → mystery religions (→→ Eleusinian Mysteries; Orphism), and philosophy (→→ Aristotle; Epicurus; Neo-Platonism; Plato; Pythagoreanism; Stoicism). The Eleus. Mysteries prob. stemmed from Aegean relig. The grad. Hellenisation of Mediterranean world, consequent on victories of → Alexander the Great, was a two-way process. The diffusion of Grk. culture also meant its fusion with Oriental cultures, esp. in relig., and spread of Oriental and Egypt. cults in Graeco-Roman society. It was in this syncretistic ethos that → Christianity emerged and its theology developed (→ Gnosticism). G.-R. was finally suppressed in favour of Christianity in 390 by Emp. Theodosius. See Synoptic Index under 'Greece'. S.G.F.B.

M. P. Nilsson, *Geschichte der griechischen Religion*, I (1955[2]), II (1950), *The Minoan-Mycenean Relig. and its Survival in Grk. Relig.* (1950[2]); *R.-G.L.*, 4 (1927[2]); W. K. C. Guthrie, *The Greeks and their Gods* (1950), *Orpheus and Grk. Relig.* (1935); Harrison, *Proleg.;* E. Rohde *Psyche: Seelencult u. Unsterblichkeitsglaube der Griechen*, 2 vols. (1898); *E.R.E.*, VI, pp. 392–425;

H. J. Rose, *Ancient Greek Religion* (1948); E. R. Dodd, *The Greeks and the Irrational* (1951); L. Gernet and A. Boulanger, *La génie grec dans la religion* (1932); Brandon, *M.D.*, ch. 5; *Bilderatlas*, 7, 9–11, 13/14 Lief.; Turchi, *Fontes;* Fr. Cumont, *R.O.;* R. Reitzenstein, *Die hellenistischen Mysterienreligionen* (1927[3]); J. Geffcken, *Der Ausgang des griechisch-römischen Heidentums* (1929); A.-J. Festugière, *Personal Religion among the Greeks* (1960).

Gṛhastha The householder, who is key figure in trad. Hindu family. The *gṛhastha* stage of life is one of the four → *asramas*, which in theory controls pattern of existence for upper-class Hindus. The householder, as head of family, leads a wider group than term 'family' implies in mod. Western countries—it incl. the wife and offspring, paternal relatives (e.g. the *G.*'s aunts and uncles), servants, etc. His role can be passed on to eldest son, and some of his ritual functions can be undertaken by wife. In early India, polygamy added to family, and the senior wife (either the first-wedded or one of highest class) assisted the *G.* ritually. The daily rites performed by him involved complex of ceremonials—offerings to domestic fire, centre of family life, being prominent; it was one of the five → sacrifices he was obligated to carry out. In theory, the householder in middle age, his son now being old enough to take over, withdraws to forest, to become a *vanaprastha*. N.S.

H. Oldenberg (tr.), *The Grihya-sutras* in Max Müller (ed.), *S.B.E.*, vols. 29, 30 (1886, 1892); J. E. Padfield, *The Hindu at Home* (1908).

Guardianship (Islam) (*Wilāya*, or *walāya*). The father is rightful guardian, and must provide for his children till boys reach puberty and girls are married. The mother is not required to contribute, even if she is rich. On father's death, G. passes to grandfather or male relative on father's side. If none, the mother may be made guardian; but if she remarries, she must give up office, though she may resume it if new husband dies or divorces her. When necessary, the *qāḍī* appoints a guardian. The Qur. has much to say about care of orphans and honest administration of their property. iv:2ff. (Medinan) deals at length with subject. See also, e.g., xvii:36 (Meccan), ii:172, 211 (Medinan). For traditions cf. Wensinck, *Handbook* (Orphans, Marriage, Walī). In → *fiqh* strict regulations are laid down regarding administration of wards' property. The guardian (*walī*) must conserve it, but may apply some of it to business projects which have prospect of profit, but not in his own business. He arranges marriages of wards. When they reach years of discretion, he must give account of his management. G. is considered a relig. duty. The question of custody (*ḥiḍāna*) of children is connected. A mother, even when divorced, has right of custody of young children; but boys at age of 7 and girls at puberty must be returned to father, failing whom, or any male of his family, the *qāḍī* may put a girl in charge of female trustee, or allow her to live alone if satisfied she is sufficiently mature. J.R.

E.I., IV, p. 1138 (Wilāya, II); Hughes, pp. 151f.; Pareja, p. 674; Coulson, *Law*, index (*ḥaḍāna*); *Mishkāt*, pp. 719f.

Gûji Jap. name for a high-priest in charge of a Shinto temple. Normally every temple (→ *jinja*) has a G. Until the Meiji era many G., in add. to spiritual function, were administrators and statesmen, wielding secular authority over vast districts. Traditionally the office was hereditary, and still remains so in many temples, in spite of efforts to abolish hereditary transmission and have G. selected by secular authority. Many G. claim direct descent from the → Kami, being regarded with awe and great veneration by populace. In most small temples served by a G. the temple income fails to maintain him and his family. Hence he engages in secular work or in service of another temple, involving long absences. In such cases the services of temple are maintained by his wife or some other member of his family. (→ Shinto). D.H.S.

J. Herbert, *Shinto* (1967), pp. 132ff.

Guṇa The *guṇas* are the three attributes, qualities or stands (trans. of term varies) postulated by → Samkhya school of Hinduism and later by → Vaisnavite theology, in so far as it made use of Samkhya categories in expounding its view of creation—to explain evolution of material world or nature (*prakṛti*). The Samkhya explanation of periodic reformation of universe, after period of chaos or dissolution (*pralaya*), is that there are three attributes or forces within nature which begin to interact once they are in state of disequilibrium. These are *sattva* (brightness, the most subtle force of three), *rajas* (force, the next most volatile) and *tamas* (darkness or mass). These are correlated to physical and psychological phenomena, since psychophysical organism has gen. been conceived as being material (i.e. even what Westerners conceive as mental functions are material in nature). With slight predominance of *sattva* in an early stage of cosmic evolution, the other *guṇas* become increasingly differentiated, and out of interplay between the three there emerge intelligences, mental faculties, organic bodies, material objects, etc. The → *Bhagavagita* and later → Vaisnavite theology made use of this scheme to exhibit processes whereby God recreates world at end of each period of dissolution (→ Creation, Hindu conceptions of), even though Samkhya school was atheistic and considered that theory of *gunas* and disequilibrium were sufficient to account for periodic recreation of cosmos. The term *guṇa* is also used more gen. to mean 'attribute' or 'quality' as applied to God or ultimate reality: thus *nirgunam Brahman* means 'Brahman without attributes' (e.g. the 'higher' *Brahman* as expounded by → Advaita Vedanta), while *sagunam Brahman* means 'Brahman with attributes', i.e. the → Iśvara or Lord, Creator of the world. N.S.

A. D. Keith, *The Samkhya System* (1949); N. Smart, *Doctrine and Argument in Indian Philosophy* (1964).

Gurdwara A → Sikh temple, which houses principally the *Adi* → *Granth*, or sacred scriptures. The latter form focus of rites in the G., taking place of image of the god in a Hindu temple. During 19th cent. hinduising influences had penetrated Sikh temples of Panjab, incl. the famous Golden Temple at Amritsar, involving use of images. Reforms, from 1890's onwards, partly stimulated as reaction to proselytizing activities of → Arya Samaj and Christianity, improved administration of the G. and brought about removal of images, etc. Orig. simple places of worship looked after by scripture-readers (*granthis*), the G. became in add. community centres, and during Mughal persecution of Sikhs, were controlled by *udāsis*, holy men belonging to a partially Sikh order, since latter were clean-shaven, etc., and not as readily identifiable as Sikhs. For this and other reasons connected with property-laws in British India, the G. were not effectively controlled by Sikhs until reform movements brought matters to a head, sometimes using militant tactics and achieving passing of Sikh Gurdwaras Act in 1925. N.S.

Khushwant Singh, *A History of the Sikhs*, vol. 2 (1966).

Guru The G. or teacher, in partic. as spiritual teacher, has played an import. role in transmission and development of Hindu and other Indian religs. In anc. India, passing on of Vedic knowledge was in hands of *guru*, gen. occupying a hermitage as a → *vanaprastha*; the student, → *brahmacarin* lived with him, learnt from him and served him. Great reverence was paid to G., though student was free to leave. In add. to passing on Veda, the G. gave instruction in subsidiary sciences known as *Vedangas*. This classical form of education shared features with wider phenomenon of eremitical and wandering relig. teachers common throughout Indian history. The importance of the G. as mediator of divine truth was marked in → Saivism (incl. → Lingayats) and in → Tantrism. The title was also given to founders and later leaders of → Sikh religion (and ultimately to Sikh scriptures as replacing human *gurus*). In the → *Saiva Siddhanta*, there is an explicit doc. of necessity for saving truth to come from one who is both God and man: so that the G. is a manifestation of Śiva; it has not been uncommon to treat relig. teachers as incarnations. In a number of Hindu sects, the G. is also responsible for initiation of adept. N.S.

Gypsies The name is a corruption of 'Egyptian'; it is found in varying form in many European languages, and reflects medieval belief that G. came from Egypt or a land called 'Little Egypt'. Refs. to G. first appear in European records in first decades of 15th cent.; but it is certain that they had lived in Balkans for many cents. before. Since their language, Romani, shows affinity to some Indian languages, it has been thought that G. orig. in N.W. India. Despite much persecution, G. have succeeded in maintaining their racial distinction and way of life in the many countries in which they have settled: their social organisation is matriarchal. Their true or orig. relig. is obscure. They have gen. accepted Christianity, and often have their children baptised; but there is some evidence of attachment to more primitive cults, incl. that of trees. The dead are not named, and their spirits are feared. Magical customs, incl. use of amulets, are prevalent. S.G.F.B.

E.R.E., VI, *s.v.;* C. J. Popp Serboianu, *Les Tsiganes: histoire, ethnographie, linguistique, grammaire, dictionnaire* (1930); B. Vesey-Fitzgerald, *Gypsies of Britain* (1953); *The Journal of the Gypsy Lore Society* (from 1888); M. Block, *Die Zegeuner, ihr Leben u. ihre Seele* (1936); *R.G.G.*[3], VI, 1908–10.

H

Habakkuk, Book of The eighth of the 'Minor Prophets', it has been dated variously between 643 and 330 BC. It appears to be work of a Judean prophet who predicts invasion of Judah by the Chaldeans in 600 BC. It has acquired greater ʇsǝɹǝʇuı since finding of Dead Sea Scrolls (→ Qumran); for one of these is a commentary on H., interpreting it in terms of more recent events in which the Qumran Covenanters were profoundly concerned. S.G.F.B.

H.D.B.[2], *s.v.; P.C.*[2], pp. 637ff.; M. Burrows, *The Dead Sea Scrolls* (1956), pp. 365ff.; Dupont-Sommer, *E.E.*, pp. 269ff.

Habiru Akkadian name for a heterogeneous people, of no fixed abode, who figure much in official records of Near East. powers from about 2000 BC as lawless bands, ready for mercenary service. Some scholars have sought to identify Hebrews as H., but identification has not been estab. (→ Judaism). S.G.F.B.

H.D.B.[2], *s.v.;* H. H. Rowley, *From Joseph to Joshua* (1951), *passim;* M. Greenburg, *The Hab/pirū* (1955).

Hachiman → Shinto war-god, but also worshipped as powerful protector of human life, as god of agriculture, and as guardian deity who gives peace and happiness to Japan. In many temples H. is worshipped as god of shipping and seafarers. Out of approx. 90,000 temples officially registered, about half are devoted to H. His first shrine was built at Usa in W. Japan. The origin of his worship is unknown, and he is not mentioned in the → *Kojiki* or → *Nihongi*. His worship came into prominence *c.* CE 720, promoted by great Minamoto clan who erected to him a temple near Kyoto *c.* CE 859–80. He was identified with the emperor Ogin-tennō (b. CE 200), whose reign was remarkable for what he did to raise cultural and living standards of the people. In CE 1039, H. was given high place in the state of relig. His cult was influenced by → Buddhism; he is first recorded instance of a Shinto god being styled *bosatsu* (→ boddhisattva) in CE 783. Both before and after Meiji reform, H. played a peculiar role as protector of Buddhism, and it was even said that H., the God of Eight Banners, symbolized the Eightfold Path of Buddh. morality. D.H.S.

W. G. Aston, *Shinto* (1905), pp. 178–9; D. C. Holtom, *The National Faith of Japan* (1938), pp. 173ff.; J. Herbert, *Shinto* (1967), pp. 426ff.

Hadad Aramean name of the Mesopot. weather (thunder) god → Adad, and the → Baal of → Canaanite Relig. S.G.F.B.

Ḥadd (Pl. *ḥudūd*, limit). Used in → Qur. and Tradition (→ Hadīth) for punishments expressly laid down by God, incl. such matters as adultery (stoning), fornication (100 stripes), false allegation of adultery (80 stripes), apostasy (death), theft above certain minimum value (cutting off hand), wine-drinking (80 stripes), highway robbery (loss of hands and feet), robbery with murder (death). These punishments are rarely enforced in mod. times. In metaphysics and in logic *Ḥadd* = definition. J.R.

E.I.[2], III, pp. 20–2; Hughes, pp. 153 (ḥadd), 476f. (punishment); Coulson, *Law*, index; Querry, II, pp. 482ff.

Hades Lord of Grk. underworld, to which all dead descended. The name means 'the Unseen'. In classical Grk., H. is never identified with underworld, which is the 'House of Hades'. His only appearance in mythology is with → Persephone. Although regarded as grim and unpitying, H. was not a devil or god of evil in Grk. classical lit. He had several titles, the best known being Pluton, the 'Rich One'. H. is used in → LXX for Heb. → Sheol. In Rev. 6:8 and → Apocryphal N.T., H. is personification of underworld and regarded as an evil demonic being, assoc. with Death: in Rev. 20:13 both are cast into 'the lake of fire'. S.G.F.B.

O.C.D., s.v.; Kleine Pauly, II, 903–5; M. R. James, *The Apocryphal New Test.* (1926), pp. 125ff.; S. Morenz, *Die Geschichte von Joseph dem Zimmermann* (1951), p. 63.

-Ḥadīth ('Talk', 'Story', then 'Tradition'). Presents material on all kinds of subject traced back to → Muḥammad. From an early period there must have been considerable interest in learning what Muhammad said and did and how he reacted to circumstances. At first this would be a matter of individual interest, but as time passed enthusiasm developed to learn more about Muhammad, and, as the Islamic realm expanded, people began to make long journeys to hear traditions. There was no corpus of Trad., for the Qur. was still sole guide, apart from local custom; but with extension of Islam circumstances were encountered for which Qur. gave no sufficient guidance. In certain circles conviction grew that a knowledge of Muhammad's practice and teaching would give the guidance required. As Islam demands a total obedience, this meant that the material of Ḥ. covered every conceivable subject. In different centres groups of traditionists arose and study of Ḥ. developed greatly, espec. in 2nd/8th and 3rd/9th cents. The Qur. speaks of Muhammad being given the Book and the Wisdom, interpreted later as meaning the Qur. and the Ḥ. Though not verbally inspired like the → Qur., the words in Ḥ. spoken by Muhammad are held to be spoken under divine guidance.

The manner in which Ḥ. came to be presented was through a chain of authorities (*isnād*), prefaced to the text (*matn*) of each trad. The *isnād* was traced back to a → Companion of Muhammad, who related some incident, or some words attributed to Muhammad. The *isnād* was an essential part. Sometimes more than one *isnād* is given with same *matn*, but each *isnād* with that *matn* is treated as a separate trad. → Bukhārī is said to have examined 600,000 trads., from which he selected about 4,000. This means he examined 600,000 *isnād* + *matn*, which would be much less than the number of separate *matns*. With growth of interest, spurious trads. arose to meet demand. Some who were troubled by laxity of the times invented trads. condemning evils, a practice so rife that it was said none were so much given to lying as the pious. Heretics tried to pass off some views in form of trads., and parties tried to uphold their opinions by same method. So criticism of trads. arose. To great extent it involved exam. of reputation of the men who appeared in *isnāds*, but criticism was not confined to the *isnād* as is often said; the *matn* was also examined. The reliability of the men in *isnāds* was an import. study, as a result of which Arabic is rich in biographical works. The views of different authorities are quoted regarding subjects of biographical notices; unfortunately they do not always agree. Dates of birth and death were import., as they showed whether the men could reasonably have met those they quoted, or have been met by those who quoted them. A perfect *isnād* must be an unbroken chain of reliable authorities. A science of Ḥ. arose, discussing types of trads. and respective reliability. There are three main groups: *ṣaḥīḥ* (sound), *ḥasan* (good) and *ḍa'īf* (weak), with subdivisions. The methods of transmission were discussed at length, incl. words used to indic. how the transmission was made, and appropriate ages at which one might begin and stop transmitting. Ḥ. came to be authority next to Qur.; therefore it was necessary to be sure of what was reliable.

The orthodox Sunnī doc. holds that there are two Ḥ. works, compiled by Bukhārī (d. 256/870) and Muslim (d. 264/875) respectively, which are completely reliable, and are called the two *Ṣaḥīḥs*. Four other books are taken along with them, though not so completely reliable, those of Abū Dāwūd (d. 275/889), Tirmidhī (d. 279/892), Nasā'ī (d. 303/915) and Ibn Māja (d. 275/889), the last being the least reliable. The authors add frequent notes about reliability of individual trads., Tirmidhī's being most import. in this respect. One may call these works canonical. There are also others which are as readily quoted. These works all arrange material acc. to subject matter, and are called *muṣannaf* (classified). Some other works, mostly earlier, arrange material acc. to the Companion to which it is attributed, and so are called *musnad*. As Companions transmitted material on variety of subjects, it is not always easy to find what one wants on a given subject. A very large work of this nature is traced to → Aḥmad b. Ḥanbal (d. 241/855), edited by his son.

Shī'ī Muslims have their own collections of Ḥ.: *al-Kāfī fī 'ilm al-Dīn* ('The Sufficient concerning knowledge of the religion') by Kulīnī (or, Kulaynī) (d. 328/939); *Kitāb man lā yaḥḍuruhu 'l-faqīh* ('The Book of him who has no legist available') by Qummī (d. 381/991); *Tahdhīb al-aḥkām* ('The Beautifying of the laws') by Ṭūsī (d. *c.* 459/1067), and a shorter version made of the same work with the title *al-Istibṣār fīmā 'khtulifa fīhi min al-akhbār* ('The Investigation into disputed traditions'). These Shi'i trads. are compiled in *muṣannaf* works, traced through → 'Ali's family.

Although serious criticism was applied and a theory of what was reliable was reached, some W. scholars have radically criticised whole subject. Goldziher pointed out many anomalies (see his MS, II), and discussed with great learning the transmission and reliability of trads. Most thoroughgoing in his criticism in recent times is Schacht (see his *Jurisprudence*, *passim*). More recently arguments have been adduced by N. Abbott (see her *Papyri*, Part I and *passim*) in favour of genuineness of many lines of transmission. Within Islam, while some are prepared to express doubts about much of the material, others hesitate to express criticism. Many, however, still uphold conventional view of reliability of transmission through the cents. from the Companions who transmitted genuine

information about Muhammad. J.R.
E.I.[2], II, p. 462 (*djarḥ*), III, pp. 23–8 (*Ḥadīth*); Hughes, pp. 639–46; Pareja, pp. 622ff.; J. Horovitz, 'Alter und Ursprung der Isnād', *D.I.*, VIII (1918), pp. 39ff.; J. Fück, 'Die Rolle des Traditionalismus im Islam', *Z.D.M.G.*, XCIII (1939), pp. 1ff.; J. Robson, 'Ibn Isḥāq's use of the isnād', *B.J.R.L.*, 38 (1956), pp. 449ff., and *Introduction;* Siddiqi, *Hadith; Mishkāt;* A. Houdas-W. Marcais, *El-Bokhari*, *Les traditions islamiques*, 4 vols. (1903–14) (trans. of Bukhari's *Ṣaḥīḥ*); F. Rahman, *Islam* (1967), ch. 3; F. Rosenthal, *Ibn Khaldun*, index.

(Qudsi) (Sacred, or divine trad.). A branch of → Ḥadīth which gives words attr. to God. They are not considered to be of same level of authority as the → Qur., held to be the unalterable, uncreated word of God. They are not necessarily revealed through → Gabriel, and they may give meaning rather than actual words of God. They may not be used in ritual prayer, and it is not necessary to wash before touching a book containing them. In quoting the Qur. one says, 'God said . . .'; in quoting Ḥ.Q. one says that this is what God said as reported by Muhammad, or that God said it as reported by Muhammad. The collections of Trad. do not arrange these trads. as separate group, but collections have been made from the six books and others. There is also a collection of them from Shi'a sources by al-Ḥurr al'Āmilī (d. 1104/1692–3), publ. in Baghdad, 1964. In a number of *isnāds* (→ -Ḥadīth) names of archangels appear. Many of these trads. suggest a Biblical source, though the words may not always be a strict trans. of O.T., or N.T. passages. J.R.
E.I.[2], III, pp. 28f.; S. M. Zwemer, 'The So-called hadith qudsi', *M.W.*, XII (1922), pp. 263ff.; repr. in his *Across the world of Islam* (1929), pp. 75ff., and trans. (*Das sogenannte Ḥadith qudsi*), in *D.I.*, XIII (1923), pp. 53ff.; J. Robson, *M.W.*, XLI (1951), pp. 261ff.

Hagar → Ishmael's mother, is not mentioned by name in the → Qur. She is mentioned in the → Ḥadīth as running about between the hills al-Ṣafā and al-Marwa at Mecca looking for water, which was revealed to her by an angel. This was the well → Zemzem, from which pilgrims drink to present day. The running between these two hills at the → Pilgrimage is interp. as repr. H.'s running when seeking water. J.R.
Hughes, p. 154; Guillaume, *Life*, p. 45; *Mishkāt*, pp. 1220f., 1289.

Haggadah Heb. term meaning 'narrative', used in Rabbinic study for exposition or interpretation of Scripture of a freer edifying kind, in contrast to Halakhah ('that by which one walks'), i.e. trad. rules of practice having binding or legal character. (→ Judaism). S.G.F.B.
Oesterley-Box, *L.R.M.J.*, pp. 60ff.; *R.G.G.*[3], III, 23, 32; *E.J.R.*, pp. 166ff.

Haggai, Book of The tenth of the 'Minor Prophets', it is concerned with situation in Judaea at time of rebuilding of → Temple (520–519 BC). Consoling his fellow-Jews on the inevitable inferiority of the restored Temple, H. prophesies that all nations will come to → Jerusalem and its Temple in the future glorious Messianic Age. S.G.F.B.
P.C.[2], pp. 643ff.; *R.G.G.*[3], III, 24–6; M. Noth, *The History of Israel* (E.T. 1960[2]), pp. 311ff.; W. O. E. Oesterley, *Hist. of Israel*, II (1939), pp. 82ff.

Haiden Hall of worship in → Shinto temple before which devotees stand for their worship and prayers, and within which rituals are performed on stated occasions by Shinto priests. In front of the H. stands a large wooden alms chest, above which is a bell to be rung by worshippers to attract attention of the → kami. D.H.S.
D. C. Holtom, *The National Faith of Japan* (1938), pp. 9, 11, 154; J. Herbert, *Shinto* (1967), p. 107.

Hakuin (CE 1685–1768). Next to → Dogen, the greatest of Japanese → Zen masters, who by his efforts towards renewal of → Rinsai laid foundations of modern Zen. Though he left home at the age of 15 to become a Buddh. monk, it was not until his 24th year that H. had his first experience of enlightenment, to be followed by a vigorous and painful training under the aged hermit and Zen master, Etan. In CE 1716, H. settled permanently at the Shōinji temple near his birthplace, which under his guidance became strongest Buddh. centre of Tokugawa period. In H. Zen enlightenment and intense ecstatic and mystical experiences were combined with genuine artistic ability. His rich humanity, deep piety, tireless zeal in study, and great gifts as preacher, writer, poet and artist drew to him a multitude of disciples. 'Through his undemanding goodness, his candour and religious enthusiasm H. won the hearts of the common people; he belongs among the greatest relig. reformers of Japanese hist.' (cf. Dumoulin, p. 247). He deprecated the 'easy way' of the → Amida Sects, and emphasised the incomparable power of Zen meditation and the → koan exercises. The core of his doc. of enlightenment, which rested in his own experience, may be summed up in a trio of mystical states: the Great Doubt, the Great Enlightenment and the Great Joy. D.H.S.
H. Dumoulin, *Hist. of Zen Buddhism* (1963), pp. 242–68.

Halakhah → Haggadah. S.G.F.B.

-Ḥallāj Al-Ḥusayn b. Manṣūr b. Maḥamma al-Bayḍāwī (b. *c.* 244/857–8; d. 309/922), an ascetic and → Ṣūfī; b. in Ṭūr and brought up in Wāsiṭ, studied *taṣawwuf* at school of Sahl al-Tusturī. When 20, he went to Basra and received the Sufi habit. He visited → Junayd in Baghdad, then travelled widely, incl. three pilgrimages to Mecca. Among countries he visited were Khurasan and India. Because of these travels he was accused of being a → Qarmaṭian propagandist. He abandoned Sufi habit and began to preach in public, to which Sufis objected, as he spoke of his secret experiences. Emphasis was laid by him on love of God, and he taught people to find God in the heart. Accusations of heterodoxy and blasphemy were made against him; for he laid stress on inner significance of ritual acts, so seeming to make the acts themselves unnecessary. In ecstatic utterance he used the phrase *ana 'l-ḥaqq* (I am the Real), suggesting that he claimed substantial union with God (→ God, 99 names, no. 51). As result of hostility he was executed. J.R.

*E.I.*², III, pp. 99–104; *G.A.L.*, I, pp. 215f.; *S.I.*, p. 355; Massignon, *Hallaj;* Arberry, *Sufism*, pp. 59f., also *Revelation*, index; Ibn Khallikān, I, pp. 423–6.

Ḥamdala Abbrev. of *al-ḥamdu lillāh* (Praise be to God!), phrase which occurs at begin. of first sura of the → Qur. It is very commonly used in everyday speech; it is natural to find that the phrase is not confined to Muslims. When one is asked about one's health, the reply should always be 'Praise be to God!' Then one is free to tell all about one's troubles. Unlike the → *Basmala*, it does not seem to be used in charms. J.R.

*E.I.*², III, pp. 122f.

Ḥanīf Occurs 12 times in the → Qur., two occasions using the plural (*ḥunafā'*). Most refs. call → Abraham a Ḥ. He is considered to have followed the orig. religion, having renounced idols and worship of sun, moon and stars, but being neither a Jew nor Christian (iii:60). There were people in → Muḥammad's time who were influenced by monotheistic beliefs without becoming Jews or Christians, to whom name Ḥ. has been applied; but the Qur. uses word mainly of Abraham and summons people to become Ḥs. xcviii:4 seems to treat word as equivalent to a follower of → Islām, doubtless on ground that Islam is held to be the true monotheistic relig. followed by Abraham. But this seems to be a peculiarly Qur'anic meaning, accepted gen. in Islam. Earlier usage suggests word meant 'heathen'. J.R.

*E.I.*², III, pp. 165f.; Hughes, pp. 161f.; Bell, *Introduction*, p. 12; also 'Who were the Ḥanīfs?', *M.W.*, XX (1930), pp. 120–4; Jeffery, *Vocabulary*, pp. 112–5.

Haoma Sacred beverage used in anc. → Iranian relig. and → Zoroastrianism, prepared from medicinal plant so-called. Many virtues were attr. to it, incl. immortality; both its preparation and drinking constituted a solemn ritual act. H. was akin to Vedic → Soma, and was deified. Zaehner interprets Zoroaster's apparent condemnation of H.-rite as due to its misuse in bull-sacrifice. In mod. → Parsee H. ritual, H. juice is consumed by priests only at first pressing. S.G.F.B.

E.R.E., VI, *s.v.;* Zaehner, *D.T.Z.*, pp. 84ff.; J. Duchesne-Guillemin, *Symbolik des Parsismus* (1961), pp. 59ff., 69ff.

Happiness, Buddh. Concept of The word *sukha* used in Buddh. lit. has the general sense of 'agreeable', 'happy', 'joyful', and is the opp. to → *dukkha*, an import. term which in Buddh. usage refers to chief characteristic of mortal existence, viz., its unsatisfactoriness, painfulness, and basic unease. *Sukha*, however, is not given such a fundamental sense; it denotes agreeable bodily or mental feeling. It is import., in Buddh. view, chiefly because it makes successful concentration, or meditation, poss. This is ref. to in a number of passages in the Suttas: 'It is a natural law that the mind of the happy one becomes concentrated'. (*A.N.*, X, 2). Apart from this, there is no Buddh. term that approx. to West. abstract notion of 'happiness'. T.O.L.

(China) The Chinese character for H. (*Fu*), meaning also 'good fortune, prosperity, blessedness', is explained as manifestation of fullness, completeness, perfection. Acc. to Confucian doctrine, neither pleasures nor honours nor wealth are the *summum bonum* which produces true H., but virtue alone. The Taoists taught that ideal happiness results from attainment of pristine perfection of the → Tao, in which all is harmonious and spontaneous. → Chuang-tzŭ, in his famous chapter (ch. 18) on 'Perfect Happiness' asks if perfect H. is found on earth, and doubts if what people call H. is true H. H., he believes, consists of 'inaction'. The Chinese Buddh. accepted doc. that true H. cannot be found within the karmic process. They looked forward to attaining H. in the paradise of → Amitabha. In gen., the Chinese believe that H. is not attained merely by human effort, but is, in a measure, designed by → Fate (*Ming*). The five constituents of H. are longevity, wealth, health, virtue, and to finish one's allotted span. The god of happiness (Fu Shên) is almost universally worshipped, and the bat (also pronounced *fu*) is everywhere used as the emblem for H. D.H.S.

W. E. Soothill, *Three Religions of China* (1923); H. A. Giles (tr.), *Chuang-tzŭ* (1889 and 1916), ch. 18; R. H. Mathews, *Chinese–Eng. Dictionary* (rev. edn. 1952).

-Haqīqat al-Muḥammadiyya, phrase ref. to first individuation from the divine essence, which is the orig. essence of → Muhammad, who is the first of God's creation. The light of Muhammad is another way of expressing the idea. This light has descended to the → imams. The doc. is a → Shi'i conception, giving Muhammad a position never claimed for him in the → Qur. J.R.

E.I., II, p. 223; *E.I.*², III, p. 75; Hughes, p. 72; Sweetman, *I.C.T.*, II, p. 112; Arberry, *Sufism*, p. 93.

Ḥaqq (What is fixed). Word used of reality (→ God's 99 names, no. 51). The opposite is *bāṭil* (vain, unreal). Among → Sūfīs, the Ḥ. of God means his essence. Ḥ. comes to mean 'truth' and 'duty', also 'a right'. These are secondary meanings deriving from idea of what is established. J.R.

E.I., II, pp. 225f.; *E.I.*², III, pp. 82f.; E. E. Calverley, 'Ḥaqq (*Truth*)', *M.W.*, LIV (1964), pp. 56ff., 122ff.; D. Rahbar, *God of Justice* (1960).

Harakiri (Japanese lit. 'belly-cutting') common name for *seppuku*. In Japan, as in China, from very anc. times voluntary sacrifice in order to follow a master or husband into other world was practised. Also, except in case of treason, royal and noble offenders were allowed self-execution to escape disgrace of public execution. H. was not mere suicide; until Criminal Code of 1873, it was a legal and ceremonial institution, invented in 12th cent. CE, by which nobles and warriors could expiate crime, apologise for errors, escape disgrace, exonerate family and relations from sharing in guilt, protest against a superior's wrongful conduct, or prove one's loyalty and sincerity. It was an honourable form of self-execution, carried out with great ceremony, usually in presence of witnesses and with a kinsman or special friend in attendance. After the ceremonial 'belly-cut' had been made, the sufferer was usually dispatched, either by cutting the throat or by beheading. H. is still practised by those seeking to avoid humiliation and disgrace, and numerous instances were recorded in World War II. D.H.S.

E.R.E., IV, p. 286; XII, pp. 351ff.

Ḥarām (Prohibited). Used in Muslim law of acts which are forbidden, and so punishable. There are four other grades of actions: obligatory, recommended, disapproved, legally indifferent (→ Sharī'a). J.R.

E.I., IV, pp. 322f.; Hughes, p. 163; Coulson, *Law*, p. 84.

Ḥaram (Sacred). Used of areas round sanctuaries in pre-Islamic times. Within such areas security was guaranteed. In Islam the chief Ḥ. areas are those round →→ Mecca and Medina; that near the Qubbat al-ṣakhra (Dome of the Rock) in → Jerusalem is another. In the Mecca area no arms may be carried and no fighting is allowed; game may not be killed, grass may not be cut, thorns may not be broken. The rules are not so strict in Medina. No non-Muslim may enter the Ḥ. of Mecca or Medina. They are called the two Ḥs. (→ Juwaynī). J.R.

*E.I.*², III, pp. 173–5 (only on Jerusalem); Hughes, p. 163; Watt, *Mecca*, index, *Medina*, index; Hitti, *History*, pp. 99f., 118, 192, 221.

Ḥarīm From root meaning 'sacred'. Ref. to parts of house forbidden to strangers, and so used both for women's quarters and for women in gen. The common Eng. spelling is 'harem'. It was customary for women of upper and middle classes to be secluded in apartments of their own, meeting no men, but husbands and male relatives, within the prohibited degrees. Nowadays this is not common in many Muslim countries. (→ Women, status of). J.R.

*E.I.*², III, p. 209; Hughes, pp. 163–7; Lane, *Egyptians*, chs. vi, vii; Dickson, *Arab of Desert*, p. 123.

Harranian Religion The city of Harran in N.W. Mesopotamia was a cult-centre of Mesopot. moon-god → Sin from at least 19th cent. BC. It remained a pagan centre in 6th cent. CE, after paganism had disappeared from rest of Roman Empire. H.R. seems to have derived from anc. → Mesopot. Relig., and was chiefly concerned with worship of planets. Three gods are mentioned in inscriptions: Sin, Marilaha, Be'el Shamin, but little is known of their conception at this period. The Arab writer → 'Abd al-Jabbār mentions that Harrians would not eat beans because they are elliptical, whereas celestial sphere is globular. Muslims called the people → Ṣābians. The Ṣābians have been identified with the → Mandaeans, but the issue is obscure. S.G.F.B.

D. Chwolson, *Die Ssabier u. der Ssabismus*, 2 vols. (1856); J. B. Segal, 'The Sabian Mysteries: the planet cult of ancient Harran', in E. Bacon (ed.), *Vanished Civilizations* (1963); S. M. Stern, *J.T.S.*, XIX (1968), pp. 159ff.

Harvest, Rites →→ Agriculture; Festivals.

-Ḥasan *-Hasan b. 'Ali*, grandson of → Muḥammad and 3rd → imam of the Shi'a. He succeeded to → Caliphate after father's assassination, but soon abdicated in favour of Mu'āwiya (→ Umayyads), who gave him ample source of income. Retiring to Medina, he lived life of ease. He is said to have been married 100 times and to have earned title *miṭlāq* (great divorcer). There is little indication of his having shown any degree of high character or of sanctity, but among the → Shi'a he is credited with having performed miracles, and in the → Muḥarram celebrations his name is chanted along with that of his brother, → al-Ḥusayn. He was poisoned about 49/669; though this is most likely to have been act of a wife, blame has been thrown on Mu'āwiya, who can hardly have felt that al-Ḥ. presented any danger to him. J.R.

*E.I.*², III, pp. 240–3; Hughes, p. 168; Pareja, pp. 84, 829, 836; Donaldson, *Shi'ite*, ch. VI and index; F. Rosenthal, *Ibn Khaldun*, index.

-Ḥasan al-Baṣrī (d. 110/728). Influential in scholarly and relig. circles in Basra. He was an ascetic who, in add. to his relig. exercises and wise moral and relig. exhortations, was skilled in jurisprudence and honoured for his wide learning. His name is assoc. with various movements of his time, which makes one suspect that people of later generations obviously felt his influence was so extensive that his name could not be left out anywhere. E.g., he has been assoc. with Qadarite (→ Free-will) doc., and his name has been connected with the circumstances which gave rise to the → Mu'tazilite beliefs; but his chief interest was in calling men to repentance. J.R.

*E.I.*², III, pp. 247f.; D. B. Macdonald, *Theology*, index; Watt, *Freewill*, index, *Philosophy*, pp. 32, 35; M. Smith, *Early mysticism*, pp. 174ff.; Seale, *Theology*, index; Pareja, pp. 696, 746f.

Hasidaeans (in A.V., Assideans) Designation, *ex.* Heb. *chasidim*, 'the pious', for devout Jews who suffered persecution in early 2nd cent. BC in opposing Hellenising policy of Antiochus IV. They supported → Maccabees; but, having no political interests, withdrew after recovery and cleansing of → Temple. The H. prob. incl. orthodox scribes; they may have been precursors of → Pharisees, → Essenes (→ Qumran). An 18th cent. E. European sect of Jew. mystics called Hasidim had no connection with H. (→→ Chassidism; Judaism). S.G.F.B.

E.R.E., VI, *s.v.;* W. O. E. Oesterley-T. H. Robinson, *Hist. of Israel*, II (1932), pp. 262ff.; M. Noth, *Hist. of Israel* (E.T. 1960²), pp. 382ff.; *E.J.R.*, pp. 173–4.

Hasmonaeans Dynastic name of → Maccabees, who founded dynasty of Jew. sacerdotal rulers, some claiming royal title (160–37 BC). S.G.F.B.

W. O. E. Oesterley-T. H. Robinson, *Hist. of Israel*, II (1932), pp. 262ff.; M. Noth, *Hist. of Israel* (E.T. 1960²), pp. 382ff.

Hathor Egypt. sky-goddess. Her name meant 'House of Horus', and she was regarded as daughter of the sun-god Rē, and mother of the solar → Horus. She figures curiously in myth as the 'eye of Rē', sent to destroy mankind. She was often repr. as a cow, sometimes suckling the pharaoh. She was gen. considered a benign deity, assoc. with love and joy; but her roles were many and often logically contradictory. (→ Nut). S.G.F.B.

R.Ae.R-G., *s.v.;* S. A. B. Mercer, *The Relig. of Anc. Egypt* (1949), pp. 203ff.

Hatred, (Dosa) in Buddh. Thought In Buddh. analysis H. is one of the 3 morally unwholesome roots, the other two being → Greed (*lobha*), and → Illusion (*moha*). The presence of these morally unwholesome qualities, or 'roots', conditions the mental attitude and volitional state; in other words, produces morally unwholesome → *karma*. H. is said to be present as result of aversion, or unwise contemplation of a repulsive object (*A.N.*, III, 68). Its range covers all degrees of hostile feeling, from annoyance to most violent extreme of wrath. In Buddh. analysis, repres. in → Abhid. lit., it is held that the 3 unwholesome roots are eradicated by deliberate encouragement of their opposites. In case of H. (*dosa*), the opp. is *adosa* or non-hatred, and means attitude of love to all sentient beings. This is held to be achieved by one who cultivates type of meditation which focuses on Universal Love (*mettā bhāvanā*). (→→ Meditation; Mūla). T.O.L.

Hawaiian Religion The Hawaiian Islands (now a state of U.S.A.) form extreme n-w. limit of Polynesia (→ Polynesian Religion), and have much in common, incl. language, with rest of area. Before the Christianization of H., gods worshipped incl. Algaloa, a → sky-god, Ukupanipo, a shark-god, and Pélé, goddess of the H. volcanoes, together with lesser deities and the potentially malignant spirits of the departed. Worship was centred on temples (*Heiau*), and was carried out through mediation of a sorcerer (*Kahuna*), who was often an exponent of black → magic, as well as a healer and interpreter of → omens. Mortuary practices were elaborate, strict measures being taken to prevent remains of dead (esp. chieftains) from falling into wrong hands; common people were interred in caves. It was believed that souls of the dead descended to kingdom of Milu, beneath the floor of the ocean, but might return to torment the living. H. has been formally Christ. since mid-19th cent., and most indigenous relig. practices have died out, some even being forbidden by law (e.g. practice of sorcery); an indeterminate amount survives in popular folk-lore. E.J.S.

E.R.E., VI, pp. 529a–32a; E. S. C. Handy, *Polynesian Religion* (1927); E. Beaglehole, *Some Modern Hawaiians* (Univ. of Hawaii, Research Pubs. 19, 1939), pp. 71ff.

Healing, Divine The natural tendency in pre-scientific cultures has been to attrib. disease to supernatural agency; healing, in turn, has been sought from gods or through magic. In some religs. disease, esp. plague, has been deified (e.g. Mesopot., India) or regarded as divine punishment. An early record of D.-H. is inscribed on an Egypt. stele (*c.* 1250 BC) by a father thanking the god → Amun for healing his son. Mesopot. texts describe healing rituals assoc.

with → Ishtar and → Tammuz. In many religs. certain gods, divine heroes or saints acquired special renown for healing (e.g. →→ Imhotep (Egypt), Aesculapius (Greece–Rome), the angel at Bethzatha (Jn. 5:22ff.), → Kuan-yin (China), various Chr. saints: Peter (Acts 5:15), → Agatha). The healing miracles of Jesus are presented in the N.T. as 'signs' of his Messiahship. Often certain places have become famous for healings: e.g. temple of Aesculapius at Epidauros; shrine of Virgin → Mary at Lourdes. The widespread custom of → pilgrimage has often been motivated by hope of healing. S.G.F.B.
E.R.E., VI, pp. 540–56; *R.G.G.*³, III, 194–8; A. Erman, *Literature of the Anc. Egyptians* (E.T. 1927), pp. 310ff.; B. Meissner, *Babylonien u. Assyrien*, II (1925), *passim;* L. S. S. O'Malley, *Popular Hinduism* (1935), pp. 151, 184; J. Leipoldt, *Vom Epidauros bis Lourdes* (1957); *S.O.*, III, *Les pèlerinages* (1960), *passim;* G. G. Dawson, *Healing, Pagan and Christian* (1935).

Health: Gods of Healing (China–Japan) → Disease and Medicine. D.H.S.

Heart In pre-scientific cultures, the H. has been regarded as centre of sentient and emotional life. It has unique status in → Egypt. relig.: it was called 'the god who is in man', being conceived as separate entity within individual that could witness against him at *post-mortem* judgment; in → Book of the Dead it is repr. as being weighed against → Maat on this fateful occasion (→ Judgment of Dead, Anc. Near East). The R.C. cult of Sacred Heart of Jesus orig. in Middle Ages and attained great popularity: although the devotion is necessarily mystical, its object is the physical heart of Jesus, and is so depicted in art. There is a feast of the S.-H., with special → Mass and Office. S.G.F.B.
A. Pianhoff, *Le 'coeur' dans le textes égyptiennes* (1930); *R.Ae.R-G.*, pp. 227ff., 296–8; Brandon, *M.D.*, pp. 45, 55, *The Judgment of the Dead*, ch. 2; *D.C.C.*, *s.v.* ('Sacred Heart').

(Sacred) → Heart. S.G.F.B.

(Sutra) The *Hrdaya Sūtra*, name of a → Mahāyāna Buddh. treatise, belonging to type of literature known as → Prajñā Pāramitā Sūtras. T.O.L.

Heaven In many primitive → cosmogonies, separation of H. (sky) and earth is an initial act of creation. H. was often regarded as solid arch-like canopy on which sun, moon and stars move; sometimes it is the 'firmament' holding back water, which seeps through as rain (Gen. 1:6–8, 7:11). The deification of sun etc. naturally led to H. being conceived as abode of the gods. In some religs. beatified dead are located in H. (e.g. in Egypt, dead might join → Re, the sun-god, or become stars). → Sky-gods, usually regarded as oldest and highest of gods, are found in many religs. (e.g. of Mesopot., India, Greece–Rome, China, Israel, Teutons, Islam). In Chr. thought, God and abode of blessed have been located in sky: the → Ascension of Christ (Acts 1:9ff.) is depicted as vertical ascent from earth. (→→ Anu; Nut; Jupiter; Shang-ti; T'ien; Varuna; Zeus). S.G.F.B.
*R.G.G.*³, III, 328–35; Brandon, *C.L.;* E. O. James, *The Worship of the Sky-God* (1963); M. Eliade, *Traité d'histoire des religions* (1949), ch. 2 E.T., *Patterns of Comparative Religion* (1958); U. Simon, *Heaven in Christian Tradition* (1958), *R.Ae.R.-G.*, pp. 302–05.

(Buddh.) → Cosmology, Buddh. T.O.L.

(Hindu conceptions of) From the three-decker universe of Vedic hymns (earth, atmosphere, heavens) there was a considerable transition to complex → cosmology of classical Hinduism, incorpor. scheme of levels of universe similar to that of Buddhism and Jainism. There was also shift of interest away from promise of *svarga* or heaven, as attainable through Vedic ritual, to ideas of → liberation from → rebirth and dissociation of soul from natural universe, incl. its heavenly aspects. However, → *bhakti* relig. implied goal of dwelling with God, beyond the lesser heavens inhabited by the gods; thus in → Vaisnavism, there is an imperishable region inhabited by Vishnu, the highest heaven called Vaikuṇṭha (place of no hindrance). Metaphysically it was argued that strictly this level of reality is non-spatial and non-temporal, though distinction could still be made there between liberated souls and God. The lower levels, including the *svarga* of → *Mimamsa* are treated as impermanent. N.S.

Hebrews, Epistle to Written in Grk., of unknown authorship and destination (none of various suggestions for both has won gen. acceptance). Its date is also unknown: some maturity of Christological development is indicated (e.g. 6:1ff., 8:1ff.); it is quoted by → Clement of Rome, *c.* 90. The familiarity implied with sacrificial ritual of Jerusalem → Temple suggests that it is addressed to a → Jew. Chr. community, whose members would understand the often obscure refs. to Jew. cults. H. provides valuable evidence for early evolution of Chr. theology, esp. of → Atonement. S.G.F.B.
*P.C.*², pp. 1008ff.; *H.D.B.*², *s.v.; R.G.G.*³, III, 106–9; T. W. Manson, *Studies in the Gospels and Epistles* (1962), pp. 242ff.

(Gospel acc. to) Apocryphal Gospel, written in Heb. or Aramaic, of which only brief quots. survive in Grk. It was prob. Gospel of a Jew. Chr. sect known as → Nazareans (hence also called 'Gospel of the N.'). → Jerome (*De vir. illus* 2) claims that he trans. it into Grk. and Latin: he quotes a passage concerning an appearance of the Risen Jesus to his brother James, to which → Paul refs. in I Cor. 15:7, but which is not recorded in canonical Gospels. The G.-H. seems to have preserved other trads. unrecorded in N.T. S.G.F.B.

M. R. James, *The Apocryphal New Test.* (1924), pp. 1ff.; *D.C.C., s.v.; R.G.G.*[3], III, 109; *Neute-Stamentliche Apokryphen*, hrg. E. Hennecke, I (1959), pp. 104ff.

Hecate Chthonian goddess, poss. pre-Hellenic, depicted with three faces. H. was gen. assoc. with the uncanny and ghosts, and was worshipped at cross-roads, trad. haunted by dead. 'Hecate suppers' (*Hekatēs deipna*) were monthly offerings made to her at cross-roads: they gen. incl. dog-flesh. H. was assoc. with the black art, and her cult survived into Middle Ages, being connected with → witchcraft. (→ Chthonian Deities). S.G.F.B.

O.C.D., s.v.; E.R.E., VI, *s.v.* ('Hecate's Suppers'); *Kleine Pauly*, II, pp. 982–3; J. Seznec, *La survivance des dieux antiques* (1940), pp. 217, 280; G. Parrinder, *Witchcraft* (1963), pp. 19, 74, 107.

Hegel, Georg Wilhelm Friedrich (1770–1831) Studied philosophy and theology at Tübingen, 1788–93; after various teaching posts, he became Professor of Philosophy at Heidelberg in 1816 and Berlin in 1818. H.'s philosophy attempted to produce synthesis of all thought and reality, potential and actual. It is culmination of classical idealist response to → Kant, found earlier in Fichte and Schelling. Opinions about its success vary from complete approval to utter condemnation. Since system is incomplete and its ideas are themselves subject to change, it is not surprising that there are considerable differences among H.'s interpreters. The basic concept is that of *Geist*, which should be trans. as 'spirit' rather than as 'mind'; for it expresses a unity of mind and power. The processes of life are relative and finite manifestations of infinite and absolute Spirit. By speaking of Spirit as 'absolute', H. is not implying that it is static; for he sees it as unsurpassably creative and dynamic. It is not separate from concrete, historical reality; but is the immanent ground and dynamic essence of these partial actualisations of itself. History is the process in which absolute Spirit comes to fulfilment, in partic. through increasing self-consciousness in man. The process follows the develop. defined in Hegelian logic, where contradictories are not regarded as mutually incompatible, but as imperfect expressions of truth which react with each other to produce a more perfect expression. Since H. holds that ultimately, in spite of appearances to contrary, what is real is rational and what is rational is real, he considers that this dialectical logic of thesis, antithesis and synthesis, applies to historical reality as much as to processes of thought. Everything, therefore, is subject to the dialectics of change—except, perhaps, H.'s philosophical system. H. considered that his system was consistent with real truth of relig. The 'God' of relig. is 'absolute Spirit' of his philosophy. The different historical religions are regarded as different ways in which man has sought to grasp his relationship to absolute Spirit. Christianity is highest form of religion, since in → Jesus Christ absolute Spirit has come to fullest self-consciousness. Theological statements express, in form of images or pictures, truths which are expressed directly in philosophy. Although pure concepts of philosophy have developed out of the stories of relig., philosophical forms are normative. Strauss and others used this view of relig. language as basis of their mythological treatment of Bible. H.'s view of history as the actualisation of divine potentiality offers a theodicy which sees the purpose of life not in terms of individuals, but in terms of working-out of an immanent, cosmic process. Immortality does not belong to individuals, but to the process. H.'s view of dialectical develop. of history was used by → Marx to interpret social history, and by certain Church historians to explain the development of Christianity. → Kierkegaard, the most radical critic of the Hegelian system, was greatly influenced by it. The existentialist concepts of alienation and estrangement come from H. Kierkegaard held that H.'s fundamental error was to consider that an existing person could ever be in a position to grasp the absolute essence of reality. There was a revival of interest in Hegel's thought at end of 19th cent. (cf. Bradley, Bosanquet and McTaggart); his influence is also to be found in the various philosophies and theologies of 'process' which have appeared in 20th cent. (→ Existentialism). D.A.P.

G. W. F. Hegel, *Phenomenology of Mind, Logic, Philosophy of History, Philosophy of Religion, On Christianity: Early Theological Writings;* J. N. Findlay, *Hegel, A Reinterpretation* (1958); W. Kaufmann, *Hegel* (1966); W. T. Stace, *The Philosophy of Hegel* (1924).

Hegesippus 2nd cent. Palestinian Chr. writer and opponent of → Gnosticism, fragments of whose writings on Primitive Church are preserved by → Eusebius. His acc. of martyrdom of → James, the Lord's brother, differs curiously from that of → Josephus, and is obviously a very garbled version of earlier trad. A list of early Roman bishops, given by Epiphanius, may come from H. S.G.F.B.

F. J. Hort, *Judaistic Christianity* (1894), pp. 164ff.; W. Telfer, 'Was Hegesippus a Jew?', *H.Th.R.*, 53 (1960); Brandon, *Jesus and the Zealots* (1967), pp. 119ff.

Heilsgeschichte German word, meaning 'Salvation-History', which has become accepted term in O.T. and N.T. scholarship. In O.T. it means presentation of past in terms of God's purpose to save Israel. This O.T. theme was re-adapted by Chr. thinkers to accommodate belief that Jesus was → Messiah, whose death and resurrection closed first part of H., and opened up second of mankind's salvation, or the 'Age of the Church'. (→ Ages of World, Chr.; → History, Philosophy of). S.G.F.B.

P.C.[2], 141a–g; O. Cullmann, *Christus u. die Zeit* (1946); Brandon, *History, Time and Deity* (1965), chs. 5, 6.

Heliopolis Grk. name, meaning 'Sun-City', for anc. Egypt. city of *Iunu*, Bibl. Ōn. H. was cult-centre of → Atum, whose priests claimed that Atum's temple stood on primaeval hill where work of creation began (→ Cosmogony, Egypt.). As the most venerable of sanctuaries, H. priesthood resented rise of Thebes, and its god → Amun, to preeminence in the New Empire (→ Akhenaten). (→ Pyramid Texts). S.G.F.B.

R.Ae.R-G., *s.v.* ('On'); Brandon, *C.L.*, pp. 15 ff. A. Gardiner, *Egypt of the Pharaohs* (1961), pp. 421ff.; G. Roeder, *Ae.R.T.B.*, I, pp. 135ff.

Helios Grk. sun-god. Except in Rhodes, H. was the object of no important cult, and plays a meagre role in Grk. mythology. In later times, prob. owing to oriental influence, he acquired greater theological significance. An early mosaic repr. Christ as H. (→ Apollo). S.G.F.B.

O.C.D., *s.v.; Kleine Pauly*, II, 999–1001; Cumont, *R.O.*, app. 106ff.; Grabar, *B.C.A.*, p. 80.

Hell Name derives through Old Eng. from Old Teut. word meaning 'the coverer-up or hider'. H. is used in Eng. trans. of Bible for →→ Sheol, Gehenna, Hades. On strength of such passages as Mt. 25:41, it denotes place of eternal punishment for those damned at → Last Judgment. Medieval art and lit. (e.g. Dante's *Inferno*) attest realistic manner in which H. was conceived. Similar conceptions of place of punishment for wicked occur in many religs. (e.g. → Eschatology: Buddh.; China–Japan; Egypt). In modern theology attempts are made to spiritualise the trad. ideas of H. S.G.F.B.

D.C.C., *s.v.; R.G.G.*[3], III, pp. 402–7; G. G. Coulton, *Five Centuries of Religion*, I (1923), pp. 67ff., 441ff.; J. A. MacCulloch, *Medieval Faith and Fable* (1932), ch. 12; A. M. Cognac, *Le jugement dernier dans l'art* (1955); S. G. F. Brandon, *The Judgment of the Dead* (1967).

(Buddh.) → Cosmology, Buddh. T.O.L.

(Islam) The Qur. has several words for place of torment in next world. The Fire (*al-nār*) occurs 66 times with ref. to H.; *Jahannam* (from Heb. Ge Hinnom, → Gehenna) 77 times; *Laẓā* (a blazing fire) once—though commonly taken as a name of H., its use in lxx:15 seems merely descriptive. *al-Ḥuṭama* (the crusher) occurs twice (civ:4f.), explained there as God's fire, whose flames overwhelm the damned. *Sa'īr* (a blaze) occurs 8 times with the definite article and 8 times without it. It seems rather a descriptive than a name. In iv:58 it is clearly descriptive of *Jahannam*. *Saqar* (from a root = to scorch) is a name occurring 4 times. *Jaḥīm* (fierce fire) occurs 23 times with the definite article and 3 times without. lxxiv:30 says it has 19 guardians. *Hāwiya* (abyss) occurs only in ci:6, where it is said to be a burning fire. The article is not used. In Qur. commentaries attempts are made to distinguish the various titles. Hughes, 171 mentions *Jahannam* as the purgatorial hell for Muslims; *Laẓā* for Christians; *al-Ḥuṭama* for Jews; *Sa'īr* for → Ṣabians; *Saqar* for the → Magi; *al-Jaḥim* for idolaters; and *Hāwiya* for hypocrites. The Qur. gives no justification for such explanations.

Orthodox Muslim doc. is that H. is eternal for those who have believed in more gods than one; those who have believed in the one God may have to go to H. to be punished for serious sins, but will eventually be taken to paradise. Note, however, should be taken of Qur. xxxii:13: 'If we willed we should cause its guidance to come to every soul; but the saying of mine is true, "Assuredly I shall fill Jahannam with jinn and men together" '; and of vii:178: 'We have created for Jahannam many from among jinn and mankind'. The description of punishment in H. is alarming. The inhabitants are chained (lxxiii:12). They are given hot water and pus to drink (xxxviii:57). They are given garments of fire, and hot water is poured over their heads (xxii:20). When their skins are properly burned, God will give them new skins so that they may feel the punishment (iv:59). While the idea of actual fire and of such tortures has commonly been believed, there have always been those who have treated the descriptions allegorically. That is done by the Ahmadis (→ Ahmadiyya Movement) at present time. They hold also that H. is not eternal for anyone, but that all will eventually be taken from it. J.R.

E.I.[2], II, pp. 381f. (Djahannam); Hughes, pp. 170–3; Wensinck, *Creed*, index; Sweetman, *I.C.T.*, I, II, IV, indexes; Jeffery, *Vocabulary*, pp. 105f. (Jahannam); J. Robson, 'Is the Mu. hell eternal?', *M.W.*, XXVIII (1938), pp. 386–93; *Mishkāt*, pp. 1210ff.

Hells (Hindu) Strictly the hells described in Hindu myth are purgatories, since, with exception of the → Madhva school, the belief is that souls do not reside there eternally; rather the *narakas* are places of great pain and suffering where some of worst effects of → *karma* can be worked off. Thereafter individual begins to take an upward course, and may ultimately attain salvation. Classical Hinduism took over general pattern of a non-Aryan cosmology, found also in Jainism and Buddhism, in which universe is conceived as hierarchy of levels. Below the earth are seven regions known as *Pātālas*, abode of lesser beings such as → *Nagas*, and below these again are the hells, typically computed as seven (but sometimes as twenty-one, etc.). The most hideous hell is the *Avīci*. N.S.

Helpers (*Anṣār*). The people of Medina who supported → Muḥammad after he left Mecca at the → *hijra*. The main Arab tribal groups were the Aws and the Khazraj. Their rivalries did not completely cease all at once; but Muhammad did succeed eventually in producing a community based on → Islām instead of tribal allegiance. The Medina Arabs, who accepted Muhammad, were proud of title *Anṣār*. A member of group was called *Anṣārī*. The other main section was formed by the → Emigrants, many of whom received help from the *Anṣār* when they came to Medina without means of subsistence. J.R.

E.I.[2], I, pp. 514f.; Watt, *Medina*, index (Anṣār); Guillaume, *Life*, pp. 234f.

Henotheism *Ex.* Grk. words '*henos*' ('one'), and '*theos*' ('god'), coined by F. Max Müller for form of relig. which, while accepting many gods (→ Polytheism), concentrates attention on a single god, often regarding this god as repr. the others. This attitude occurs, e.g., in → Egypt. relig. and early stage of → Heb. relig. H. differs from → monotheism, which is belief in one sole god. Müller also used, as alternative, 'Kathenotheism'. S.G.F.B.

Max Müller, *Chips from a German Workshop*, I (1867), pp. 27ff., 354ff.; H. Pinard de la Boullaye, *L'étude comparée des religions*, I (1925), p. 349.

Hephaistos Grk. god of fire and artificer-god. Orig. H. was prob. an Asiatic deity connected with volcanoes. → Homer repr. H. as lame and despised by other gods (his lameness recalls Nordic divine smith Völund-Wieland (→ Scandinavian Relig.)). H.'s attributes of fire, volcanoes, magical artistry or technique, and metal-working reflect a complex of religio-cultural interests naturally existent at a primitive stage of culture. H. was identified with Egypt. → Ptah (→ Vulcan). S.G.F.B.

O.C.D., *s.v.; Kleine Pauly*, II, 1024–8.

Hera Pre-Hellenic goddess, assoc. with marriage and sexual life of women. In mythology, H. is wife of → Zeus: this union may indicate compromise between strong entrenched cult of an Aegean goddess and that of sky-god of invading Indo-Europeans. Argos was H.'s most anc. cult-centre. (→ Greek Relig.). S.G.F.B.

C. Picard, *Les religions préhelléniques* (1948), *passim; O.C.D., s.v.; Kleine Pauly*, II, 1028–32; W. K. C. Guthrie, *Greeks and their Gods* (1956), pp. 66ff.

Heracles Most popular and widely worshipped of Grk. heroes (→ Hero-cult). Although sometimes regarded as a deity, the name 'Heracles' = 'Hera's glory', attests human prototype behind legend, perhaps hero of a people worshipping → Hera. Of his celebrated 12 labours, 3 significantly concern conquest of death, thus giving to H. character of a saviour (→ Soteriology): it is possible that in this role he affected development of Christology. H. was identified with several foreign deities, incl. Phoenician → Melqart. The cult of H. was first foreign cult received at Rome, where he was called Hercules. S.G.F.B.

O.C.D., pp. 413–4, 416; *Kleine Pauly*, II, 1049–52, 1054–7; U. von Wilamowitz-Moellendorf, *Der Glaube der Hellenen*, II (1931), pp. 23ff.; L. R. Farnell, *Greek Hero-Cults and Ideas of Immortality* (1921), pp. 174ff.; M. Simon, *Hercules et le Christianisme* (1955).

Hereafter (Islam) The Qur. frequently uses phrase *al-dār al-ākhira* (lit. 'the last abode') with ref. to the life after death. While it sometimes ref. to the life of the blessed, it is really a more gen. term. *al-Ākhira* by itself develops into a word for the life after death. It is opposed in the Qur. to *al-ḥayāt al-dunyā* (lit. 'the nearest life'), meaning this world. *al-Dunyā* by itself came to be used for the world. J.R.

Heresy *Ex.* Grk. *hairesis* = 'choice'. The term was applied orig. to tenets of philosophical schools; → Josephus called Jew. sects of →→ Pharisees, Sadducees, Essenes, Zealots, 'heresies' in this sense. In Christianity, the disposition to formulate orthodoxy led to condemnation of contrary opinion as H., in sense of being aberration from divine truth. Persistence in H. incurred excommunication, and, in Middle Ages, civil punishment, incl. burning to death. The R.C. Church distinguishes between 'formal' and 'material' H. The former, meaning wilful persistence in doctrinal error, is a grave sin, and merits excommunication; the latter means holding erroneous beliefs without conscious choice, and is not reckoned sinful. (→ Inquisition). S.G.F.B.

E.R.E., VI, pp. 614–24; *D.C.C., s.v.; R.G.G.*[3], III, pp. 13–21; G. Leff, *Heresy in the Later Middle Ages*, 2 vols. (1967); W. Bauer, *Rechtgläubigkeit u. Ketzerei im ältesten Christentum* (1964[2]).

(Buddh. attitude) H. is primarily a West. relig. concept; there is no exact Buddh. equivalent. The nearest approximation is → *ditthi* (Pali) *drsti* (Skt.), literally a view, usually a 'wrong' view, that is due not to reason but to

→ craving or → desire (*tanhā*). The most serious form of *ditthi*, acc. to Buddh. trad. is to assert the reality and permanence of the individual human ego, i.e. the assertion of *atta* or *ātman*. Since the West. concept of H. implies an orthodoxy capable of denouncing H. and willing to do so, the approx. of Buddh. *ditthi* to West. H. here comes to an end, since Buddhism has no authoritative hierarchy, and no sacramental sanctions. Even the most serious form of *ditthi*, assertion of reality of a permanent individual human 'self', was maintained by certain Buddh. known as → Pudgala-Vādins. They were regarded by all other Buddh. schools of thought as weaker brethren, and in error; but they maintained their existence and monastic institutions; as late as 7th cent. CE, Pudgala-vādin monks amounted to about quarter of total number of Buddh. monks in India. On the whole, the attitude of other schools seems to have been that more prolonged meditation would eventually cause them to see error involved in their view, and its abandonment. T.O.L.

E. Conze, *Buddhist Thought in India* (1962), pp. 122–31.

(China and Japan) The Chinese term for H. (*hsieh*) connotes not only that which is heterodox but what is depraved, vicious, evil. → Confucians considered as H. all doctrines opposed to trad. teachings; but, in gen., considerable licence in interpretation was permitted, and → Buddhism, → Taoism and other faiths were tolerated. Frequently, in Chinese hist., the state censors banned as H. doctrines which they considered inimical to best interests and safety of state, or which offended against public morality, and this led to vigorous persecution, and the destruction of H. books. D.H.S.

C. Goodrich, *The Literary Inquisition of Ch'ien Lung* (1935).

The rise of sectarianism in Japanese → Buddhism inevitably led to charges and counter-charges of H. This is partic. evident in → Nichiren (CE 1222–82) and his followers, whose aggressive and repressive propaganda was directed against the Amita-sects whom they considered heretical. The 15th and 16th cents. were marked by intense relig. strife, in partic. between followers of → Shinran, as represented by Ikkō (One-direction or Whole-hearted), and followers of Nichiren. Accusations of H. led to violent persecution. The degeneracy and disintegration of great Buddh. centres led to rise of schismatics and heretics, who organised themselves within churches and formed secret societies. With the 17th cent. Buddh. doctrines were systematized and respective Buddh. sects formulated their orthodox dogmas. Ecclesiastical authorities attempted to enforce orthodox teachings of Buddh. Church, and this was accompanied by a vigorous fight against H. With 18th cent. revival of → Shinto, diversion from nationalist ideas of State Shinto were considered heretical and political measures were taken to suppress all who refused to conform with the orthodox state doctrine. D.H.S.

M. Anesaki, *Hist. of Japanese Buddhism* (1930), pp. 191ff., 229ff., 305.

Hermae Orig. stone or bronze pillars (from 5th cent. BC), surmounted by bust of → Hermes, with carved erect phallus; at later period other deities were sometimes repr. H. were sacred objects, and their defacement was sacrilegious (Alcibiades was exiled from Athens 415 BC for defacing H.). H. were used as sign-posts on roads, boundary marks, and on graves. They prob. had good luck and apotropaic significance (→ Phallic Cult). S.G.F.B.

O.C.D., s.v.; Bilderatlas, 13/14 Lief. (1928), Abb. 29–30, 32; *Kleine Pauly*, II, 1065–6.

Hermaphroditos Bisexual Grk. divinity, repr. in art as either beautiful youth with female breasts or an Aphrodite with male genitals. The hybrid form has been variously explained: e.g. as derived from primitive ambivalent concept of deity (there are Hindu examples), or exchange of garments in marriage rites, or some primitive androgynous view of life. S.G.F.B.

O.C.D., s.v.; H. Licht, *Sexual Life in Anc. Greece* (E.T. 1949), pp. 124ff.; *Kleine Pauly*, II, 1066–7; H. Zimmer, *Myths and Symbols in Indian Art and Civilization* (1962), p. 216, fig. 70; M. Delacourt, *Hermaphrodote: mythes et rites de la bisexualité dans l'Antique classique* (1958).

Hermas Author of 2nd cent. Chr. writing known as the *Shepherd*. The book purports to record visions, grouped in three divisions: 5 'Visions', in which Church is personified as matron; 12 'Mandates'; 10 'Similitudes'. The work, which derives its name from the 'Angel of Penance' who appears as a shepherd, was highly esteemed in Early Church. H. affords valuable evidence of Chr. thought *c.* 150, partic. on Christology and penance. S.G.F.B.

J. B. Lightfoot-J. R. Harmer, *The Apostolic Fathers* (1891), pp. 291ff.; *D.C.C., s.v.;* P. Carrington, *The Early Christian Church*, I (1957), pp. 391ff.; *R.G.G.*[3], 242; R. Joly (ed.), *Hermas le Pasteur* (1958); M. Whittaker, *Die Apostolischen Väter I: Der Hirt der Hermas* (1956).

Hermes Grk. god of obscure origin. His assoc. with the → Hermae may indic. that orig. he was a → daimon haunting heap of stones or a stone at roadside. The phallus, characteristic emblem of H., suggests orig. connection with fertility (→Phallic Cult). In mythology, H. had role of messenger of greater gods; he is also repr. as thief and → trickster. In art he appears either as herald of gods, with winged-sandals and herald's staff, or as nude young man (e.g. Praxitele's statue). H. was also the → *Psychopompus*, as well as patron of travellers and merchants. The Romans knew him as Mercurius (→ Hermes Trismegistos). S.G.F.B.

O.C.C., pp. 417ff., 559; W. K. C. Guthrie, *The Greeks and their Gods* (1950), pp. 87ff.; *Kleine Pauly*, II, 1669–75; J. Boardman, *Greek Art* (1964), pp. 14, 148.

Hermes Trismegistos, Hermetic Literature 'Trismegistos' = 'thrice great', was Grk. rendering of Egypt. title of → Thoth, who was, quite wrongly, identified with H. Thoth was reputed author of series of revelations of a religio-philosophical kind, written in Grk. (a part exists in Lat. trans. only). These writings, known as Hermetica or Hermetic Lit., orig. in Egypt; it was formerly the gen. opinion of scholars that they contained little Egypt. material, but this view is now changing. The H. is so extensive and contains such variety of concept and aspiration that its contents defy brief definition. It may be said that, gen. in spirit and doctrine, the H. is akin to lit. of → Gnosticism, and it repr. a kind of → theosophy that synthesizes many relig. trads. of anc. Near East. The fact that a number of H. tractates were among collection of Coptic Chr. writings discovered at → Nag Hammadi attests their appreciation by Chr. Gnostics. The H. prob. dates from 2nd cent. CE, but incorp. earlier trad. S.G.F.B.

Corpus Hermeticum, ed. and trans., A. D. Nock-A.-J. Festugière, 4 vols. (1945–54); A.-J. Festugière, *L'révélation d'Hermès Trismégiste*, 4 vols. (1950–4), 'Hermétisme et Gnose païenne', *H.G.R.*, III; *E.R.E.*, VI, pp. 626–9; S. Angus, *Religious Quests of the Graeco-Roman World* (1929), ch. 19; C. H. Dodd, *The Bible and the Greeks* (1954), part II; G. van Moorsel, *The Mysteries of Hermes Trismegistus* (1955); J. Doresse, *The Secret Books of the Egyptian Gnostics* (E.T. 1960), pp. 241ff.; W. C. Van Unnik, *Evangelien aus dem Nilsand* (1960), pp. 47, 49; Ph. Derchain, 'L'authenticité de l'inspiration égyptienne dans le "Corpus Hermeticum" ', *R.H.R.*, 161 (1962).

Hermopolis Anc. city in Upper Egypt. Its Egypt. name Chmunu, 'Eight', ref. to eight primordial beings believed to have deposited → egg there, from which sun-god emerged and commenced work of creation. H. became cult-centre of → Thoth. Acc. to tomb inscription of Petosiris, a priest of H. (*c.* 300 BC), pilgrims to H. were shown relics of this cosmic egg. (→ → Cosmogony, Egypt; Relics). S.G.F.B.

G. Roeder, *Hermopolis*, 1929–1939 (1959); Brandon, *C.L.*, pp. 43ff.

Hero Cult In → Grk. relig., worship of certain real or imaginary persons of the past at their tombs. These beings were regarded as dwelling below ground, and offerings made to them were like those to → chthonian deities (→ Altar, Greek). The H.-C. prob. stemmed from → Aegean Relig., and its logic contradicted Homeric eschatology which located all the dead to a consciousless existence in → Hades. (→ Eschatology, Grk.). S.G.F.B.

L. R. Farnell, *Greek Hero-Cults and Ideas of Immortality* (1921); *E.R.E.*, VI, pp. 652–6; E. Rhode, *Psyche* (1898), I, pp. 146ff.; *O.C.D.*, *s.v.; Kleine Pauly*, II, 1103–15; A. Brelich, *Gli eroi greci, un problema storico-religioso* (1958); M. P. Nilsson, *Greek Folk Religion* (1961), pp. 18ff.

Hero Gods (China–Japan) Both in China and Japan, relig., based on primitive animism, recognised superior powers, whether in men, nature or gods, as only a matter of degree. Though, acc. to the strict principles of → ancestor-worship, each family worshipped only spirits of its own ancestors, innumerable national heroes and worthies were given place and function within a divine hierarchy. These included mythical and legendary kings and heroes of pre-hist., ancestors who had wrought mighty deeds, great scholars, inventors, benefactors, civilizers of country and military heroes. Many heroes attained merely a local fame and became minor gods, worshipped in localised temples built to their honour.

In China, noted heroes and worthies of national importance were given divine rank by imperial decree, the emperor himself petitioning the Supreme God to elevate a posthumous hero to a special place and function within spiritual hierarchy. The most famous of hero-gods of China is → Kuan Ti (also known as Kuan Yü, Wu Ti, Kuan Kung), god of war and also of literature. His temples are found in every major city. In Japan the cult of hero-gods tended to diminish as divine status of emperor was emphasised. Nevertheless, in popular cults of Japan numerous hero-gods are worshipped, a typical example being Yamato-dake, believed to have lived about CE 100, the third son of emperor Keikō. In both China and Japan the deification of heroes continued throughout the whole course of hist., and many personages were objects of a well-defined worship. D.H.S.

E.R.E., VI, pp. 646–7, 662–4; E. T. C. Werner, *Dictionary of Chinese Mythology* (1932); D. C. Holtom, *The National Faith of Japan* (1938), pp. 176–9; H. Dore, *Recherches sur les Superstitions en Chine*, vol. 4, p. 487; A. Couling, *Encyclopaedia Sinica* (1917), p. 230.

Herodian Dynasty For hist. of relig. the following members of Jew. H.-D. are notable: (1) Herod the Great (*c.* 73–4 BC), who was greatly hated by Jews for his foreign extraction, pagan tastes and cruelty; he built the most splendid of the → Temple(s); acc. to Mt. 2:1ff., he was reigning when Jesus was born. (2) Archelaus, son of H. the Great, ethnarch of Judaea from 4 BC to CE 6, he is mentioned in Mt. 2:22. When he was deposed in CE 6, Judaea was placed under direct Roman rule until 41. (3) Herod Antipas, son of H. the Great, tetrarch of Galilee from 4 BC to CE 39. He executed → John the Baptist and was involved with Jesus. (4) Herod Agrippa I, appointed king of Judaea by Emp. Claudius, CE 41. His action against Apostles James and Peter and his death (44) are recorded in Acts 12:1ff. (5) Agrippa II, son of Agrippa I (CE 17 to 100), ruler of Galilee and Peraea, before whom → Paul was tried (Acts 25:13ff.). S.G.F.B.

Schürer, *G.J.V.*, I, pp. 360ff.; A. H. M. Jones, *The Herods of Judaea* (1938); S. Perowne, *The Life and Times of Herod the Great* (1956), *The Later Herods* (1958); *Kleine Pauly*, II, 1090–4; F. F. Bruce, 'Herod Antipas', *A.L.U.O.S.*, V (1966); A. Schalit, *König Herodes* (1969).

Hesiod (*c.* 700 BC) Boeotian poet, whose works provide valuable evidence of → Grk. relig. to balance and supplement that of → Homer, who prob. lived a generation earlier. In his *Works and Days*, H. ascribes wretchedness of human life to enmity of → Zeus. This view is presented in terms of myth of → Prometheus and → Pandora; in same writing he sets forth a pessimistic interpretation of history in his 'Five Ages', again holding Zeus responsible for deterioration of his own times. The *Theogony* is earliest Grk. → cosmogony: it recognises that the Olympian gods were late-comers. S.G.F.B.

A convenient ed. and trans. of Hesiod by H. C. Evelyn White is publ. in Loeb Classical Library; *E.R.E.*, VI, *s.v.;* F. Schwenn, *Die Theogonie des Hesiodos* (1934); U. von Wilamowitz-Moellendorf, *Hesiod's Erga* (1928); N. O. Brown, *Hesiod's Theogony* (1953); *O.C.D.*, *s.v.;* Brandon, *C.L.*, pp. 166ff.; *Kleine Pauly*, II, 1113–7.

Hetu Buddh. term for a 'root-condition', viz. a morally wholesome or unwholesome primary mental state which conditions thought and action. Thus H. is not the *cause* of thought or action but the *conditioner* of the thought or action when it arises, given a cause. The 6 kinds of H. distinguished in Buddh. psychology are: (morally unwholesome), greed (*lobha*), hatred (*dosa*), and illusion (*moha*); (morally wholesome), generosity (*alobha*), non-hatred (*adosa*), and absence of illusion (*amoha*). T.O.L.

S. Z. Aung (tr.), *Compendium of Philosophy* (*Abhidhammattha-Sangaha*) (1910, repr. 1956), pp. 279–81.

Hexateuch *Ex.* Grk. *hex*, 'six', and *teuchos*, 'book'. Name given by great Biblical scholar J. Wellhausen (1876) for first six books of Bible, believing that they comprised same pattern of literary sources as → Pentateuch. The term is frequently used by some O.T. scholars, though rejected by others. S.G.F.B.

*P.C.*², 138c, 249a.

Hierarchy (General) Organised body of priests or clergy. Any relig., in so far as it has a trad. organised faith and practice, needs ministers competent to teach its doctrines and perform its rituals. Paleolithic culture reveals that already there were specialists in → cave art and hunting magic. How such functionaries acquired their knowledge and authority is unknown: → shamanism offers some instructive suggestions. H.'s may be wholly professional, partly so, or be constituted of those acquiring relig. office with civil appointments as with Grk. and Rom. magistrates. Special initiation or ordination is often required preparatory to holding office, certain disciplines (e.g. → celibacy) of tabu kind, may be imposed, and sometimes special dress worn during performance of office or permanently. H.'s may be highly organised bodies, with their own internal discipline and process of promotion (e.g. R.C. hierarchy), or may comprise one member only following a trad. regime (e.g. priest king of → Diana at Nemi). Membership may be hereditary, by election, or even purchase. (→ Priest, China, Japan). S.G.F.B.

E. O. James, *The Nature and Function of Priesthood* (1955); G. Van der Leeuw, *La religion* (1948), pp. 210ff.; *R.G.G.*, V, 569–74.

(Christ.) The Chr. H. orig. from Christ's appointment of the Twelve Apostles (e.g. Mt. 10:1ff., Jn. 20:21ff.), who had paramount status in Primitive Church, though → James, the Lord's brother, became head of orig. Jerusalem Church. → Paul lists a variety of specialised officers: apostles, prophets, teachers, miracle-workers, healers, helpers, administrators, speakers in various tongues (→ glossolalia: I Cor. 12:28). The appointment of → deacons by laying on of hands, is recorded in Acts 6:1ff.; *episkopoi*, 'overseers or bishops' are mentioned in Acts 20:28, and 'presbyters' (e.g. Acts 11:30). Out of this variety of offices there gradually evolved a recognised H. At Rome *c.* 250 there was a → bishop, presbyters, deacons, sub-deacons, acolytes, exorcists, readers and door-keepers. The presbyters have become priests, with power to celebrate → Eucharist; bishops, in addition to this power, have power of ordaining priests, and, with other bishops, of consecrating a bishop. In W. Church distinction was made between Major Orders (from bishop to sub-deacon) and Minor Orders (remaining orders of those specified above). The head of H. of R.C. Church is the → Pope, claiming divine authority for this status. The patriarchs of → E. Church, as the archbishops of R.C. and → Anglican Church, have higher jurisdictional, not spiritual, status than bishops. Candidates are initiated into their particular orders by special rituals, held to convey specific spiritual power and authority. The gift of Holy Orders is regarded as a → Sacrament. S.G.F.B.

D.C.C., pp. 987ff.; *E.R.E.*, VIII, pp. 659–74; A. Ehrhardt, *The Apostolic Succession* (1953); Harnack, *H.D., passim;* W. K. Firminger in W. K. L. Clarke (ed.), *Liturgy and Worship* (1932), pp. 626ff.; L. Duchesne, *Christian Worship* (E.T. 1927), pp. 342ff.; *R.G.G.*³, V, 578–82, I, 335–42, III, 313–4; N. Zernov, *Eastern Christendom* (1961), p. 254.

(Egypt.) Since a god was believed to indwell his cult-statue within temple, it was considered that he had to be served each day in matters of food and toilet as a king. Eg. priests, who performed this service, were known as 'servants of the god'. Theoretically they were deputies in each temple concerned for the pharaoh, who alone had authority to minister to the god on behalf of Egypt. The office was hereditary or conferred by king; the priests were supported by offerings and other revenues of temple. There were four grades of priests, of descending importance: the first, or high-priest, of a great state-god such as → Amun had great political power. There were also mortuary priests who performed funerary rites and service of the dead. Priests had to observe strict rules of physical purity, and were → circumcised. There was also a H. of priestesses, who served in various capacities, incl. singers and dancers. S.G.F.B.

E.R.E., X, pp. 293–302; S. Sauneron, *Les prêtres de l'ancienne Égypte* (1957); *R.Ae.R-G.*, pp. 596–608; W. Otto, *Priester u. Tempel im hellenist. Aegypten*, 2 vols. (1905–8).

(Greek) There was no priestly caste in Greece. Relig being essentially a civic affair, priests were in effect civil servants appointed to manage some specific state temple. Their duties were to perform the prescribed ritual, incl. sacrifice, and administer business of the temple. Even management of the → Eleusinian Mysteries, but not the secret ritual, was the concern of Athenian government. Some priesthoods (e.g. → Delphi) doubtless formed a closely organised body. S.G.F.B.

E.R.E., X, pp. 302–7; *R.G.G.*, V, 574–8; *O.C.D.*, pp. 729ff.

(Hebrew) Acc. to post-Exilic trad., → Yahweh ordered → Moses to consecrate → Aaron and his sons 'to minister in the priest's office' (Ex. 28:1). Thus divine and Mosaic authority were claimed for H. as re-constituted after Exile. There were earlier and different trads., most notably that concerning Zadok, who may have been priest of anc. Jebusite sanctuary of → Jerusalem when captured by → David. The Levites seem also to have been priests before Exile (Ex. 32:29); but, after, they became Temple ministers distinct from Aaronic priesthood, which was supposed to be hereditary. The → Priestly Code contains precise directions about sacerdotal office: its functions, discipline, privileges, → vestments. The offering of sacrifice was its *raison d'être*. The directions are given in terms of the high priest, the uniqueness of whose status is seen in Day of → Atonement ritual. With cessation of the monarchy, the high priest became both relig. and civil head of Israel, espec. with the → Hasmonaeans and under Roman gov. until CE 70. (→→ Sadducees; Sacrifice; Divination; Theocracy; Synagogue; Judaism). S.G.F.B.

*H.D.B.*², pp. 793–8; *E.R.E.*, X, pp. 307–11, 322–5; E. O. James, *The Nature and Office of Priesthood* (1955), pp. 68ff.; J. Pedersen, *Israel*, III–IV (1940), pp. 150ff.; H. H. Rowley, *Worship in Anc. Israel* (1967), *passim; E.J.R.*, pp. 184 309; J. R. Bartlett, 'Zadok and his successors at Jerusalem', *J.T.S.*, XIX (1968).

(Hindu) The major class of priests in Hinduism is drawn from the → Brahmin class. Not only have they had hereditary rights to perform sacrificial and domestic rituals, and to expound → *Veda*, together with subsidiary learned disciplines and philosophy, etc.; but they have also acquired dominant position in many popular institutions of worship, etc. Thus growth of temple-cults in classical Hinduism, though it had origin outside trad. Vedic conception of worship, gave a new dimension to activities of priesthood. Though such worship is not exclusively conducted by Brahmins, it is largely dominated by them. Similarly at village-level, Brahmins came to act not only for performance of domestic and social rites, but also as astrologers, medicine-men, etc. Already in the → *Atharvaveda* the process of syncretism between → Aryan and non-Aryan magic is apparent, and doubtless the Brahmin class itself was penetrated by non-Aryan practitioners of various kinds of ritual skills. For Vedic sacrificial rites, the complex liturgy typically demanded participation of variety of specialist priests, such as the *hotṛ*, who chanted invocations, the *udgitṛ*, who sang litany, the *adhvaryu*, who performed manual operations necessary in sacrifice, the *potṛ*, cleanser, etc. The priest who administered domestic rites was the *purohita*, who in classical times, with growth of monarchies, acquired considerable prestige, as domestic chaplain and adviser of king. Moreover, as being the trad. transmitters of sacred and secular lore and wisdom, the priesthood were much in demand as civil servants, tutors, etc. The dispersion, however, of Brahmins into variety of occupations and sub-castes, due to regional and other differences, led to dilution of respect for class, and the law books give contradictory views on whether a secularized Brahmin deserves trad. sacred respect. Gen. speaking Brahmin officiants at temple-cult (the administrators of *puja*, or *pujaris* (→ Worship, Hindu)) were less highly regarded than those who performed Vedic rituals and were learned in philosophy and other sacred sciences. Moreover, complexity of classical and medieval Hindu culture meant that many sacred functions were performed among groups and sects by people other than, or not necessarily, Brahmins. For instance, the → Lingayats had a non-Brahmin ministry, the *jangamas;* while Tantric rituals of initiation were undertaken by → *gurus,* conveying esoteric knowledge on par with that available through Vedas; while tribal groups assimilated into Hindu society maintained non-Brahmanical sacraments, etc. As relig. teachers also, the Brahmins were never capable of a monopoly, save among those who rigorously accepted obligations of 'twice-born' status, since wandering ascetics were drawn from all classes (despite attempts to restrict status of → *sannyasin* to upper classes), and were a main source of new teachings; while general trend of medieval *bhakti* cults was towards at least relig. egalitarianism, so that some of influential popular preachers were not Brahmins. The coming of Western-style higher education to India has also involved diffusion of trad. philosophical and other knowledge orig. mainly under Brahmanical control. Nevertheless, the priestly offices of the Brahmin, above all in rituals of → initiation, marriage, death, etc., remain important, esp. among upper classes (→ *varnas*). Rites are also performed by Brahmins for those who are not Hindus—notably for Jains (temple cult of the → *Svetambaras* often being performed by Brahmins). N.S.

M. Stevenson, *Rites of the Twice-Born* (1920); J. F. Staal, *Nambudiri Veda Recitation* (1961); K. Rangachari, *The Sri Vaishnava Brahmans* (1931); C. G. Diehl, *Instrument and Purpose* (1956); J. H. Hutton, *Caste in India* (1961).

(Iran) Considerable obscurity invests orig. and early development of the H. that characterised later → Zoroastrianism. The → Avestan word *āthravan* = 'priest', is derived from *ātar*, 'fire', thus indic. that priestly office was orig. connected with cult of fire. The antiquity of cult of → Haoma also suggests another pre-Zoroaster function of H. Zoroaster calls himself a *zaotar* (anc. Aryan term for 'priest'), and confirmed cult of sacred fire: but he was also in conflict with another priestly order. In post-Zoroaster era the → Magi, a priestly-caste of W. Iran, adopted Zoroastr. and formed its H. The H. reached fullest development in Sassanian period (CE 226–637); it comprised eight classes with special functions, among which fire and haoma rituals were prominent. Priesthood was hereditary; its holder was denoted by various symbols. Among → Parsees, hereditary candidates are initiated into various grades of sacerdotal office. (→ Fire-worship). S.G.F.B.

E.R.E., X, pp. 319–22; Zaehner, *D.T.Z.*, pp. 161ff.; G. Widengren, 'Stand u. Aufgaben der iranischen Religionsgeschichte'. *Numen*, 2 (1955), pp. 53ff.

(Mesopot.) The rulers of Sumer, Babylon and Assyria were theoretically chief ministers of the god(s) of their partic. state; but divine service was actually performed by a professional H., the head of which was the *urigallu*, i.e. 'grand guardian' of temple concerned. Beneath him were many other orders, incl. exorcists, diviners (→ divination). → Eunuchs served the rites of → Ishtar, as did sacred → prostitutes. There were several orders of priestesses, some high ranking and drawing their members from royal house. (→→ Nudity, ritual; Mesopot. Relig.). S.G.F.B.

M. Jastrow, *Aspects*, pp. 273ff.; B. Meissner, *Babylonien u. Assyrien* (1925), II, pp. 52ff.; Dussaud, *R.B.A.*, ch. 8; H. W. F. Saggs. *The Greatness that was Babylon* (1962), pp. 345ff.

(Roman) The various priestly colleges were regarded as an integral part of state, to serve its well-being in relig. matters. Their members performed routine duties, and, when called upon by Senate, advised on specific questions acc. to relig. trad. (e.g. consideration of prodigies by the *pontifices* and *augures*, or consultation of → Sibylline Books). The various priesthoods (*flamines*) were provided with money and personnel by State for maintenance of their cults. The → Vestal virgins were charged with maintaining sacred hearth-fire of city. Appointment was co-optation or election, and was for life, except for Vestals and Salii. In Imperial times office of *pontifex maximus* was held by the emperor. S.G.F.B.

E.R.E., X, pp. 325–35; *O.C.D.*, pp. 364, 716; W. Warde Fowler, *The Relig. Experience of the Roman People* (1911), *passim;* G. Dumézil, *Jupiter, Mars, Quirinus* (1941[2]), pp. 69ff., 100ff.

High Church Designation used from 17th cent. for group in → C. of E. that stressed its historical continuity with Catholic Christianity. H.-C. principles received fresh impetus from the Oxford Movement in 19th cent. S.G.F.B.

G. W. O. Addleshaw, *The High Church Tradition* (1941).

High God(s) Term, with its alternatives (see later),

much used by those scholars (preeminently W. Schmidt) who have sought to prove there was a universal primitive → monotheism centred on a Supreme Being, usually a → sky-god, who was also regarded as the All-Father. The religs. of many peoples, in both anc. and mod. world, provide examples of such deities. Sometimes they are so high and remote that they have no cult; others, like → Yahweh, are very potent beings, constantly intervening in affairs of this world. (→ Deus otiosus). S.G.F.B.

A. Lang, *The Making of Religion* (1898); W. Schmidt, *Der Ursprung der Gottesidee*, 12 vols. (1912–51); M. Eliade, *Traité d'histoire des religions* (1949), pp. 47ff.; E.T., *Patterns in Comp. Relig.* (1958), pp. 38ff.; R. Pettazzoni, *The All-Knowing God* (E.T. 1956), pp. 23ff.; E. O. James, *The Worship of the Sky-God* (1963), pp. 2ff.

(China) → T'ien; Shang Ti. D.H.S.

-Hijra (The Emigration). Used for → Muḥammad's emigration from Mecca to Medina (Yathrib) in 1/622. In Mecca conditions had become difficult, so when Muhammad made contact with some people from Yathrib (later called *Madīnat al-nabī* = the city of the Prophet, which afterwards was shortened to *al-Madīna* = the city) at two successive pilgrimages, he arranged for his followers to go to Medina, and he went last with → Abū Bakr. Marvellous tales are told of his escapes from pursuit by divine help. This was a turning point in Muhammad's career. Later → 'Umar b. al-Khaṭṭāb, during his Caliphate (13–23/634–44), fixed year of the H. as the first in the Muslim calendar. The year began on 16 July; the actual H. was later, as Muhammad arrived in Medina in September. But the first year of the H. counts from 16 July. J.R.

E.I.[2], III, pp. 366f.; Guillaume, *Life*, pp. 219ff.; Watt, *Mecca*, pp. 149–51, *Medina*, index.

Hillel Jewish rabbi of 1st cent. CE, who, with his disciples, taught a more liberal and less austere interpretation of → Torah in opposition to R. Schammai and his followers. R. Gamaliel, mentioned in Acts 5:34, 22:3, was a grandson of H. (→ Judaism). S.G.F.B.

E.R.E., VI, *s.v.;* Oesterley-Robinson, *L.R.M.J.*, pp. 93ff.; Schürer, *G.J.V.*, II, pp. 359ff.; G. F. Moore, *Judaism*, I (1927), pp. 72ff.; *R.G.G.*[3], III, 326–7; *E.J.R.*, p. 65.

Hīnayāna Buddh. term, used in anc. India, for one among several 'means' or methods of attaining enlightenment. H. was method of limited appeal, compared with the → Mahāyāna, held to be of universal appeal. *Yāna* = means, method. T.O.L.

→→ Yana; Theravāda.

Hinduism The relig. which has come to be called H. by Westerners is a complex product of amalgamation of various cults and beliefs within a common social framework (→ caste system). It acquired its characteristic form in period after the → Upaniṣads, with increasing importance of popular gods as objects of devotion (Vasudeva, →→ Viṣṇu, Śiva). This repr. an amalgamation of →→ Vedic and Brahmanical relig., mediated primarily by priestly class, the → Brahmins, with forms of relig. welling up from popular practice, some of which prob. had roots in → Indus Valley civilisation. One can roughly distinguish the following periods: first, the → Vedic, during which Vedic hymns were composed and collected, and lasting from latter part of 2nd mil. BC to about 800 BC; second, the → Upaniṣadic period, in which Vedic relig. evolved in monistic and monotheistic direction, and at same time acquired beliefs such as that of →→ karma and rebirth—lasting to about 400 BC; third, the classical period, i.e. that during which Hinduism acquired its classical or typical form, and lasting to about CE 500; fourth, the medieval period, import. for further evolution of → bhakti cults, esp. in Dravidian south and for elaboration of major theological and philosophical positions within orthodox trad. (→ Vedanta); finally, there is mod. period, during which H. has come to terms with impact of Western colonialism, etc. Though H. is not typically a missionary relig., for it is essentially the complex of cults, etc., characterising Indian society, it has in this last period, through such organisations as the → Ramakrishna movement, increasingly made universal claims. H. has displayed great capacities for absorption, not merely taking up into its social framework a series of populations lying outside → Aryan society, which orig. gave birth to its sacred scriptures and provided dominant priestly class, but also grad. swallowing up unorthodox movements such as → Buddhism (in India itself) and → Ajivikas. Technically, orthodoxy consists in recognition of the → Veda as authoritative → revelation: theologies and philosophies, however diverse, recognising this authority are reckoned as *astika*, and those, like Buddhism and → Jainism which do not do so are reckoned as *nastika*. But this definition of Hindu orthodoxy has its limitations, since Vedic revelation was not in fact accessible to classes lying below top three (→ twice-born). For *sudras* and untouchables, etc., the import. scriptures are epics (→→ Mahabharata, Ramayana) and the → *Puranas*. The fact that Vedic relig. was essentially restricted has led some writers in past to distinguish between popular H., on one hand, and → Brahmanism on other, using latter term to ref. to relig. administered and conveyed by Brahmins ('Brahmanism' is also used for Upanishadic relig., to distinguish it from preceding Vedism and later H.). The distinction is not very satisfactory, since one aspect of Brahmanically administered relig. is the whole system of law (→ *dharma*), which defines structure of society at large. From point of view of orthodoxy, the name of H. itself is *sanātana dharma*, the 'everlasting law'; over a long period it is misleading to think of H. as conceiving of itself as separate religion: rather, it was a pattern of living controlled by what was taken to be correct interpretation of anc. trad. In so far as there is justification for the Brahmanism—popular H. contrast, it arises from increasing split between theory of Brahmanical religion and actual shape of Hindu practices. For instance, Vedism did not involve temple cults; but by the latter part of the classical period these were widespread, and came to be of far greater significance than the anc. ritual which Brahmins in theory continued as part of ancient heritage. Again, the rise of → *bhakti* cults meant that a very different kind of relig. became dominant in many parts of India from that represented in the Upanishads. Thus medieval theology in part saw its task as providing a synthesis between Upanishadic and non-Upanishadic elements in the trad. This was notable in works of → Ramanuja and Madhva: the former, for instance, drew heavily upon Tamil pietism, but wedded it to orthodox → Vedanta. Earlier, → Sankara, though less influenced by *bhakti*, provided brilliant method of exegesis which likewise made sense of different levels of relig. present in medieval Hinduism. These were some of the ways in which orthodoxy maintained a fairly unified → Sanskrit culture overlaying, but not unaffected by, the variety of vernacular cultures in sub-continent. At same time, certain lesser relig. groups, technically outside Hindu orthodoxy, such as → Jains, in effect became parts of gen. social structure, and operated to some degree like Hindu castes. In latter part of medieval period, the Muslim invasions, followed by fairly extensive conversions to Islam, brought new problems. The new forces were too strong even for Hindu organism to digest, but had effects at its periphery. Thus a synthesis between Hindu and Muslim values was preached by → Kabir and → Nanak; this give rise to popular monotheistic sects, the most notable being the → Sikhs, who, however, came to constitute effectively a separate relig. community outside H. Less effective was attempt at synthesis by the emperor → Akbar. In British period, there were rather similar reactions at periphery—e.g. the reforming → Brahmo Samaj and the → Arya Samaj, groups tending towards a Hindu unitarianism. However, for most Hindus the cult of gods and images has remained central, and there is no strong feeling (as there has been among Muslims and Christians) about dangers, etc., of idolatry. Characteristically, the many gods are seen as manifestations of one divine reality: this interpretation tends to be accompanied by theory of levels of relig., such that villager reverencing tree-spirits or snakes, etc., has a fragmentary perception of what those at a higher level of insight perceive as one God or as → *Brahman*. Another aspect of Hindu synthesis is coexistence of alternative cults of →→ Viṣṇu and Śiva, two forms of supreme God. A similar complexity characterises → ethics and law, since the particular obligations of individuals are heavily determined by their position in caste structure, and by stage of life (→ *asramas*) they may have reached. Thus, as an extra dimension of Hindu society, there are those who have gone beyond trad. law, by taking up role of → *sannyasin*. Such ascetics have played import. role in evolution and transmission of relig., and coexist side by side with more prominent 'this-worldly' aspects of Hindu life. They are one reason for continued importance of → yoga, existing in dialectical contrast with → *bhakti*, since classical times. Apart from variety implicit in the Hindu social structure, the lack of a unified ecclesiastical organisation has encouraged diversity: saintly teachers and → gurus can start new movements, as e.g. in mod. period that of → Aurobindo. The spread of their ideas has been facilitated by the long-standing trad. of → pilgrimages. Despite complexities, one can pick out some aspects of Hindu belief as virtually universal and others as characteristic. Among former are belief in rebirth or → reincarnation and in → karma and the recognition of Veda as authoritative; among latter, Hindu theology has been predominantly either non-dualistic (→ Advaita) or theistic. N.S.

R. C. Zaehner, *Hinduism* (1962); K. Morgan (ed.), *The Religion of the Hindus* (1953); A. L. Basham, *The Wonder that was India* (1954); L. Renou, *Religions of Ancient India* (1953); Sir Charles Eliot, *Hinduism and Buddhism*, 3 vols. (1922); S. N. Dasgupta, *History of Indian Philosophy*, 5 vols. (1922–62); H. Bhattacharyya (ed.), *The Cultural Heritage of India*, vol. 4 (1956); J. M. Mahar, *India: A Critical Bibliography* (1964). (→ Philosophy, Hindu).

(Intro. into S.E. Asia) Although continental S.E. Asia (Burma, Thailand, Cambodia, Laos and Vietnam) is now largely Buddh., and Indonesian archipelago is largely Muslim, there is ample evidence of the H. which until 13th cent. CE was an import. living element in culture of this region. The process of 'Indianization' of

S.E. Asia appears to have begun in approx. the 1st cent. of Christ. era; it consisted largely of intro. of Brāhman relig. rites and worship of Hindu gods →→ Vishnu and Shiva; adoption of Hindu → cosmological ideas, esp. in connection with role and function of king; and spread of Hindu literature, art-forms and styles of architecture. Evidence of this is to be found in massive monumental remains of Hindu architecture of Angkor in Cambodia, and at Prambanan in Java; in the still widespread occurrence of Sanskritic terms and names; in extent to which Hindu cosmology and mythology, partic. that of → Rāmāyana epic, still form import. element of popular culture in Thailand and Cambodia.

When this process of Hinduisation began cannot be stated with certainty, nor is there full agreement as to exactly how it took place, although it is gen. agreed that Indian Brāhman priests were principal agents in transmission to S.E. Asia of Hindu relig. and culture. Various hypotheses have been put forward to account for this eastward expansion of Hinduism. Some mod. Indian scholars have repr. process as having been one of deliberately planned colonisation carried out by Indian political rulers, a theory which arises more from desire to estab. India as a one-time imperial power than from careful assessment of available evidence. Others have suggested that it was due to emigration from E. India of peoples who were being subjected to pressure by eastward advance of the Mauryan conqueror → Asoka into Kalinga (coastal area of India between deltas of Godavari and Mahanadi rivers). But this Mauryan conquest occurred in 3rd cent. BC, and there is no evidence of Indian cultural influence in S.E. Asia until 1st cent. CE at earliest. A similar theory is that such emigration eastwards from India occurred at time of Kushan advance into N.W. India, in 1st cent. CE. But there is no evidence from India of any such migration having been caused by Kushan conquests. Another hypothesis links beginning of Indian influence in S.E. Asia with rise of → Buddhism as popular movement in E. India. Since Buddhism disregarded Indian caste restrictions and taboos, it is argued, the rise of this movement to popularity made poss. a new freedom and mobility, and allowed Indians to travel overseas. However, this argument overlooks probability that caste rules which inhibited Hindus of later period from engaging in sea voyages had not reached so rigid a stage of develop. during early Buddh. period; the argument from alleged 'liberating' effect of Buddhism therefore loses most of its force. Moreover, it was Hindu beliefs and practices which were transmitted; the agents must clearly have been Hindus. Further, the beginnings of Indian influence in S.E. Asia appear to belong to period somewhat later than this theory would require. G. Coedès suggested that impetus to H.'s overseas expansion into S.E. Asia came from necessity to develop Indian trade with this region, to gain new source of gold and precious metals at time when other sources in W. and N.W. of India had been cut off; trading centres were estab. in S.E. Asia which eventually drew Brāhman priests, craftsmen, and other specialists from India; their presence, and inter-marriage with local women, led to dissemination of Hindu culture in regions surrounding trading centres. J. C. van Leur rejected this theory on grounds that form which Hinduisation took was, at very early stage, the Hinduising of the courts of indigenous S.E. Asian Kings. This, he argues, could not have been result of presence of Indian traders, who belonged to lower social classes. He allows that some cultural influence may have been transmitted by traders, 'But as regards the specifically Indian cultural forms—in which, as even the oldest extant unanimously bear witness, what was involved was the ritualistic, magical legitimation of the ruler, the offerings, the consecration formulae, the classical, mythological genealogy of the ruling house—it must be considered completely out of the question that traders, even if they had been rich merchant gentlemen, should have participated in such things repeatedly and in a way defined in so much detail. It can only have been the work of Brahmans' (J. C. van Leur, *Indonesian Trade and Society*, p. 99).

The impetus which set the process in motion, acc. to van Leur, came from indigenous S.E. Asian rulers who, wishing to acquire for their dynasties a prestige equal to that of great *rājas* of India, summoned Brahman priests to their courts. 'The Indian priesthood was called eastwards—certainly because of its wide renown—for the magical, sacral legitimation of dynastic interests and the domestication of subjects, and probably for the organisation of the ruler's territory into a state. Alongside the priesthood, Indian artifice came to the royal courts, and the architectural activities of the rulers and the official religious activities of those overseas states alike show the unmistakable imprint of Indian civilisation on Ceylon, Indonesia, Farther India and southern Indo-China' (*op. cit.*, p. 104).

Coedès has also moved towards this view, and somewhat modified his earlier hypothesis. He agrees with van Leur and L. de la Vallée Poussin in seeing Hinduisation as primarily a process of Brahmanisation, i.e. a process in which the Brahman's role was that of providing sacralisation for ruler (whether Indian or S.E. Asian) and assimilating local relig. cults into Sanskritic cults, first of Shiva and then of Vishnu. In this respect Hinduisation in S.E. Asia was in principle the same as process which was going on concurrently in India; it was, says de la Vallée Poussin, 'the extension overseas of the process of Brahmanisation which started long before the time of the Buddha, and which, from its area of origin in North West India, has spread and still continues to spread in Bengal and the South' (G. Coedès, *The Making of South-East Asia*, p. 55).

In first cents. of Christ. era this process was in its early stages in S. India and Bengal; it is likely that it was from these two areas principally that it was transmitted to S.E. Asia, since these were the parts of India from which communication with S.E. Asia could be most easily estab.

In course of the early cents. a number of Hinduised states came into being in S.E. Asia. The earliest known to us were kingdoms of Fu-nan and Lin-yi. These are Chinese forms of their names, since earliest evidence of them occurs in Chinese dynastic chronicles of 2nd cent. CE. Fu-nan extended over lower Mekong valley and delta; with add. of further territory, this later became kingdom of Kambuja (Cambodia). Lin-yi consisted of E. coastal strip of what is now Vietnam, and was later known by Sanskritic name Champa. In S. part of the Chao Phya (Menam) valley (in what is now Thailand) there was an Indianized kingdom known as Dvaravati, and in lower Irrawaddy valley the kingdom of Shrikshetra. In Sumatra by early 7th cent. CE there had appeared the Indianized state of Shrivijaya, whose dominance of surrounding region, incl. Malay peninsula, the Javan state of Shailendra took over in middle of 9th cent. CE.

For Fu-nan and Kambuja → *Cambodia, Hinduism in;* for Dvaravati and Shrikshetra →→ *Thailand, Burma;* for Shrivijaya and Shailendra →→ *Sumatra, Java.* T.O.L.

G. Coedès, *Les Peuples de la Péninsule Indochinoise*, 1962 (E.T. by H. M. Wright, *The Making of South East Asia*, 1966); *Les États hindouises d'Indochine et de l'Indonésie*[3] (1964); B. Ph. Groslier, *Indochina: Art in the Melting Pot of Races* (1962); D. G. E. Hall, *A History of South-East Asia*[2] (1964); R. Le May, *The Culture of South-East Asia* (1964); J. C. van Leur, *Indonesian Trade and Society* (1955).

Hippolytus (*c.* 170–236) Theologian of Roman Church, whose views and actions brought him into conflict with successive Popes but whose reputation was ultimately rehabilitated, so that he was → canonised. The most import. of his many writings is the *Refutation of all Heresies*, of which 4 books survive. H. was exponent of a doctrine of the → Logos which had ditheistic implications. The *Apostolic Tradition*, a treatise on rites current at Rome at this time, is gen. attr. to H. S.G.F.B.

D.C.C., s.v.; P. Carrington, *The Early Christian Church* (1957), II, *passim; R.G.G.*[3], III, 362. E.T. of many of Hippolytus' works are given in *A.N.C.L.*, vols. 6 and 9; J. M. Hanssens, *La liturgie d'Hippolyte* (1959); B. Botte, *La tradition apostolique de saint Hippolyte* (1963).

Hirā' A hill near Mecca where → Muḥammad used to retire for meditation and devotions in a cave. During one period there, he was first conscious of call to the prophetic office. To-day it is called *Jabal al-nūr* (Mountain of light), doubtless because it was scene of first revelation. J.R.

E.I.[2], III, p. 462; Guillaume, *Life*, pp. 104ff.; Watt, *Mecca*, pp. 40, 44.

History, Philosophy of Appreciation of significance of H. as evidence of mankind's destiny has been meagre in most religs. apart from Jew. relig. and Christianity: although → Zoroastrianism evaluated Time teleologically (→ Zurvan), little interest was shown in relating hist. events to this teleology. A notable and unique Islamic P.-H. was produced by Ibn Khaldun (1332–1406). Jew. and Chr. P.-H. are essentially → Heilsgeschichte. The → Yahwist initiated a trad. of appealing to past as evidence of → Yahweh's providence for Israel. This O.T. trad. was re-adapted by Chr. thinkers to belief that → Jesus was both → Messiah of Israel and saviour of mankind. The hist. of Israel was regarded as *Praeparatio Evangelica* for 'Age of Church'. Chr. writers began to write P.-H. (e.g. Julius Africanus, → Eusebius). The most notable composition was → Augustine's *De Civitate Dei*, written to answer pagan charges about fall of Rome to Goths in 410. The Chr. P.-H. profoundly affected W. culture; but increased knowledge of mankind's past since Renaissance has led to its obsolesence and attempts to interpret hist. along secular lines. The most notable of these has been the Marxist materialistic interpretation of hist., O. Spengler's *Der Untergang des Abendlandes* (E.T. *The Decline of the West*, 2 vols., 1926–8), A. J. Toynbee's, *The Study of History*, 10 vols. (1934–54). Together with these attempts to evaluate the hist. of mankind, there has been much study of nature of hist. S.G.F.B.

R. G. Collingwood, *The Idea of History* (1946); S. J. Case, *The Christian Philosophy of History* (1943); R. C. Denton (ed.), *The Idea of Hist. in the Anc. Near East* (1955); C. Issawi, *An Arab Philosophy of History* (1950); R. H. Walsh, *An Intro. to Philosophy of History* (1951); R. Aron, *Intro. à la philosophie de l'histoire* (1948);

K. Löwith, *Meaning in History* (1950); *R.G.G.*³, III, 369–71 ('Historismus'); A. J. Toynbee, *An Historian's Approach to History* (1956); H. S. Hughes, *Oswald Spengler: a Critical Estimate* (1952); E. H. Carr, *What is History?* (1964); C. A. Patrides, *The Phoenix and the Ladder: the rise and decline of the Christian view of History* (1964); S. G. F. Brandon, *History, Time and Deity* (1965); B. Mazlish, *The Riddle of History* (1966).

Hittite Religion The sculptured procession of deities on walls of rock-sanctuary of Yazilikaya, near H. capital Hattusas, repr. the official pantheon, *c.* 1400 BC. The two chief deities are the sun-goddess of Arinna, whose Hattian name was Wurusemu and Hurrian name Hebat, and a weather-god, whose Hurrian name was Teshub. Politically, Teshub was god who repr. Hittite state in foreign treaties. He is gen. depicted as bearded man, holding club or axe, and standing on bull (→ Adad, → Dolichemus). Behind sun-goddess, her divine son Sharma is portrayed. Among other gods in the procession, Telipinu can be discerned: he was a vegetation deity of → dying-god type. Other import. deities were the Hurrian Shaushka, identified with → Ishtar; Tarhund, a weather god, whom some scholars would identify with Etruscan Tarchon (→ Etruscan Relig.); Kubaba, who seems to have been a prototype of Phrygian → Cybele. Worship was performed in temples and open-air rock-sanctuaries. In temples, the cult-statue was accessible to few worshippers only; it was object of daily toilet-ritual and food-offering. Priests and other ministrants observed strict discipline of ritual purity, and slept in temple. Animal sacrifice was gen.; human sacrifice was occasionally made. The H. deity was essentially a deification of some aspect of natural phenomena, being always conceived of anthropomorphically. Misfortune, either personal or communal, could result from divine displeasure due to sin or to divine negligence. → Divination was widely practised, as was also practice of → magic. The dead were either cremated or buried: there is some evidence of food offerings, but H. → eschatology is unknown. Mythological texts concern death of Telipinu, the slaying of dragon Illuyanka, and theogony. (→ Festivals, Hittite). S.G.F.B.

O. G. Gurney, *The Hittites* (1952), pp. 132ff.; Dussaud, *Religions*, pp. 333ff.; *R.G.G.*³, III, 299–305; H. G. Güterbock in *M.A.W.*, pp. 139ff.; *A.N.E.T.*, pp. 120ff.; E. Cavaignac, *Les Hittites* (1950); L. Delaporte in *H.G.R.*, I; A. S. Kapelrud, *Numen*, VI (1959), pp. 32ff.; S. Lloyd, *Early Highland Peoples of Anatolia* (1967), pp. 52ff.; E. Neufeld, *The Hittite Laws* (1951).

Holy, The Holiness, in origin and essence, is the quality or character imparted to things, men, animals, places, events and actions, by contact with a mysterious, supernatural power. This power has been aptly designated the 'numinous' (R. Otto)—a term derived from anc. Roman concept of impersonal power manifesting itself in some specific way or place: the Melanesian word → mana has also been used to describe it. Holiness renders an object ritually unclean, i.e. dangerous to profane touch, and requires that it be surrounded by → tabu (→ Clean and Unclean). R. Otto (1869–1937), in his influential study, *Das Heilige* (1917), E.T. *The Idea of the Holy* (1923), described the 'Numinous' as the 'Wholly Other', that evokes the sense of awe, of the uncanny, and the eerie: he also called it the *Mysterium Tremendum.* Holiness orig. had nothing to do with moral goodness: a 'holy person' was one apart from his fellows because of his tabu-character (e.g. the → shaman). Distinction between the sacred or holy and the profane is widespread, occurring in both primitive and sophisticated cultures. (→ Numen). S.G.F.B.

E.R.E., VI, pp. 731–59; M. Eliade, *Traité d'histoire des religions* (1949), pp. 16ff.; E.T. *Patterns of Comp. Relig.* (1958), pp. 1ff.; G. Van der Leeuw, *La religion* (1948), pp. 30ff.

(Concept of) (Buddh.) It has been observed by West. scholars that while Buddhism has no place for an omnipotent personal deity of kind affirmed in theistic religions, it has a concept of the → holy, and this constitutes focal point of its relig. ideas and teachings. (Cf., e.g. E. Durkheim, *Les formes elementaires de la vie religieuse*, 1912). This concept of the holy manifests itself at one level in the → Four Holy Truths, and the → 'Holy Eightfold Path'; at another level, in popular devotional Buddh. practices, espec. veneration of the → *stupa* or → pagoda, as symbolising Buddha, and in notion of the → 'holy places', to which it is desirable that → pilgrimage should be made. T.O.L.

Holy Days, Buddh. These are of 2 kinds: those occurring monthly, and those annually. Of former, the more import. are the day of full moon, and day of new moon. On these the ceremony of reciting the → *Patimokkha*, or disciplinary code, is carried out by → Sangha in each local monastery. These two, together with the two intervening days of first quarter and last quarter of moon, together make up the four Uposattha days in every month. These days are trad. times for special relig. observances by Buddh. lay people; in theory these are days for attending the monastery and taking part in devotions led by monks (in forenoon), or hearing sermon (dhammadesina) by a monk (usually in evening). In mod. S. Asia such attendance is frequently left to women, the elderly and very young. In Ceylon these days are known as 'poya' days, and are observed as public holidays, corresponding to the Christ. Sunday; but since their incidence is determined by phases of moon they do not always fall on same day of week. In Burma and Thailand they are not public holidays; the international Sunday being observed instead. In Thailand there is trend towards using Sunday, as day free from work, for devotional services at the monastery attended by lay people or for preaching of sermons, giving of public lectures on Buddh. doc., and holding of Sunday-schools for children; lunar holy days, however, are also observed, and are still ref. to by their trad. name in Thai: 'Wan Phra' (lit. 'holy day'). The Uposattha days are trad. also the occasion for more devout lay people to take the eight moral precepts (three extra to universal five) ref. to as *attha-silā* (→ morality); in add. to fasting, they spend day at monastery in meditation; in all Buddh. countries of S. Asia, however, only a small minority of people, usually the elderly, actually do this. The eve of the Uposattha day is occasion for monks to reshave the hair of head. Nowadays Uposattha days are occasion for special radio broadcasts on relig. subjects; these have large audiences, even though only a minority attends the monastery. In rural areas, however, esp. in Thailand, a higher proportion of lay people attend Uposattha services in monastery than is case in urban areas. Of annual holy days the most import. is Vesak, or *Vesākha-pūjā* (Pali)/ *Vaiśākha-pūjā* (Skt.), which falls on full-moon day of May. On this day are commemorated jointly the Buddha's birth, his attaining enlightenment, and passing into → parinibbāna. This also is observed as public holiday in Buddh. countries of S.E. Asia; it is marked by publication of special collections of articles dealing with various aspects of Buddh. relig., as well as by special ceremonies, and popular festival activities. Three months before this, on full-moon day of February occurs Māgha Pūjā, on which promulgation by Buddha of the monastic disciplinary code, or → Vinaya, is commemorated. Another period of special relig. significance in Buddh. year is that of Vassa, sometimes referred to as the Buddh. Lent. This is season of monsoon rains in India and S.E. Asia, and is observed by Sangha as period of retreat, when monks may not travel about country as at other times of year, but must remain in own monastery. For Buddhs. it begins on first day of waning moon in eighth month (by the Roman calendar this is usually in July), it lasts until full moon of eleventh month (in Roman calendar, October). It is time specially devoted to relig. study by monks, and instruction of lay people. More people than usual are likely to attend monasteries to hear sermons. There is a considerable increase in number of monks in Sangha during Vassa, as it is customary for some to take ordination for this period even although they may return to laymen's life when Vassa is ended. A monk's seniority is measured by number of Vassas he has spent in Sangha, rather than by complete calendar years. It used to be trad. for theatrical and performances and public amusements to be suspended during Vassa period; but this is no longer strictly observed, at least in the urban areas. (→ Festivals, Buddh.). T.O.L.

Holy Places (Buddh.) Every → *stupa* or → pagoda is regarded as a place to be venerated, symbolising as it does the Buddha and his → Dhamma; but the holy places *par excellence* are the 4 sites in N.E. India connected with events of the life of the Buddha. These are (1) → Lumbini, his birth-place; (2) → Buddh-Gaya, scene of his Enlightenment; (3) → Sārnāth, where his First Sermon was preached, and thus place of 'setting in motion' of the 'wheel of Dhamma'; (4) → Kushinagara, or (by its anc. name) Kusināra, the place of his entry into *parinibbāna*. Without being identified by name, these 4 places are mentioned in the → *Māha-parinibbāna Sutta* of the Pali canon: (1) 'The place at which the believing man can say "Here the → Tathāgata was born!"; (2) the place at which (he) can say, "Here the T. attained to the supreme and perfect enlightenment!"; (3) the place at which (he) can say "Here was the wheel of the Dhamma set in motion by the T.!"; (4) the place at which (he) can say, "Here the T. passed finally away in that utter passing away which leaves nothing whatever to remain behind!" '. Each of these four places, it is said, the believer 'should visit with feelings of reverence'. (*D.N.*, II, pp. 140–1). T.O.L.

T. W. and C. A. F. Rhys Davids, *The Dialogues of the Buddha* (part II), (*Sacred Books of the Buddhists*, vol. II), 1910 (repr. 1966), pp. 153f.

Holy Spirit The Heb. word *ruach*, used in O.T. for Spirit of God, essentially denotes 'an initial awareness of air in motion, partic. "wind"' (A. R. Johnson). H.-S. is often depicted as though it were an attribute or agent of God capable of operating separately, but harmoniously, with God (e.g. Gen. 1:2ff.). The concept prob. stemmed from Heb. anthropology; as a human attribute, it described outstanding mental and physical energy, in contrast to → *nephesh*. In O.T., the H.-S. appears as a divine force inspiring men with courage, wisdom, artistic genius, and prophecy. In *Wisdom of Solomon*, H.-S. is equated with Wisdom, and almost hypostatised, its feminine gender being suggestive here: however, the monotheistic character of → Yahwism prevented its development into separate deity. In N.T., the H.-S. figures very prominently (e.g. it descends like dove as Jesus is baptised and drives him into wilderness; blasphemy against H.-S. is the ultimate sin, Mk. 3:29; it descends upon Apostles at Pentecost; for → Paul the manifestation of H.-S. is a basic factor of Chr. life). This Scriptural witness inevitably meant that status of H.-S., rel. to God the Father and Christ, became problem for Chr. theology. After much controversy, at Council of → Chalcedon, 381, the doc. of H.-S. as Third Person of → Trinity was defined as orthodoxy. S.G.F.B.

A. R. Johnson, *The Vitality of the Individual in the Thought of Anc. Israel* (1949), pp. 26ff.; *H.D.B.*³, *s.v.; D.C.C., s.v.; R.G.G.*³, II, 1270–86; *E.R.E.*, XI, pp. 784–803; Harnack, *H.D.*, *passim; E.J.R.*, p. 190; Th. Rüsch, *Die Entstehung der Lehre vom Heiligen Geist* (1952).

(Islam) In the Qur. *rūh al-qudus*, often trans. 'Holy Spirit' occurs. It would be more correct to trans. 'the spirit of holiness'. Muslims usually interpret the phrase as meaning → Gabriel. Islam has no equivalent for the Holy Spirit, third Person of Christian Trinity; so 'H.-S.' is a misleading trans. Jesus is said to have been strengthened by *rūḥ al-qudus* (ii:81, 254; v:109). Elsewhere one reads of the spirit descending on the night of power (xcvii:4). In xvii:87 the non-committal remark is made that the spirit comes at command of the Lord. God sends the spirit on whom he wills (xvi:2; xl:15). The revelation is said to come from God to → Muḥammad's heart by the faithful spirit (*al-rūḥ al-amīn*). These, and the refs. to God breathing into Mary of his spirit (xxi:91; lxvi:12) are normally interpreted by Muslims as ref. to Gabriel. J.R.

E.I., III, p. 827; Hughes, p. 177; Sweetman, *I.C.T.*, I, p. 23, II, pp. 75f.

Holy Truths (Buddh.) → Four Holy Truths, Buddh. T.O.L.

Homer The identity, birth-place, and date of H. still remain unsolved problems, as do questions concerning the sources, integrity, and authorship of the *Iliad* and *Odyssey*, ascribed to him. However, for hist of Grk. relig. these poems are of primary importance: they are the earliest extant sources (8th cent. BC), and their influence on subsequent Grk. culture was profound. They provide evidence of early Grk. concept of deity, ritual practices, the nature and destiny of man, and → eschatology. (→ Greek Relig.). S.G.F.B.

A convenient ed. of text and trans. of *Iliad* and *Odyssey*, by A. T. Murray, is publ. in Loeb Classical Library, 4 vols. Cf. *O.C.D., s.v.; E.R.E.*, VI, *s.v.; Kleine Pauly*, II, 1201–8; W. F. Otto, *The Homeric Gods* (E.T. 1954); M. P. Nilsson, *Gesch. d. griech. Relig.*, I² (1955); E. Rhode, *Psyche*, I (1898), ch. 1; H. L. Lorimer, *Homer and the Monuments* (1950), pp. 103ff., 433ff.; D. Page, *History and the Homeric Iliad* (1963); W. R. Holliday in *C.A.H.*, II, pp. 624ff.; E. R. Dodds, *The Greeks and the Irrational* (1963), pp. 2ff.; Brandon, *M.D.*, pp. 160ff.

Honden The most important building in → Shinto temple, being the sanctuary in which the → *mitama* of the → kami resides. The doors are normally kept closed. Laymen are not allowed to enter; only the high priest or his substitute. D.H.S.

D. C. Holtom, *The National Faith of Japan* (1938), pp. 9, 11; J. Herbert, *Shinto* (1967), pp. 117ff.

Honen (Also called Genku: CE 1133–1212). Founder of → Jodo sect of Jap. Buddhism in 1175. As a boy he entered the Tendai monastery on Mt. Hiei, but later withdrew to give himself up to seclusion and study. His fundamental tenet was belief in power and grace of the saviour → Amida, lord of Sukhāvati (the Western paradise). He advocated repeated invocation of Amida's name, by which anyone, ignorant or wise, high or low, could be saved. His teaching was based on that of → Hui-Yüan (Jap. -Zendō), the Chi. founder of the → Pure Land sect. His greatest disciple was → Shinran, who developed Pure Land doctrines further and founded Jodo Shin-shu or True Pure Land. Saintly, pious and of sincere conviction, H. exerted great influence, until the jealousy of his Tendai rivals led to his exile. D.H.S.

H. H. Coates and R. Ishizuka (trs.), *Hōnen, the Buddhist Saint* (Kyoto, 1925); M. Anesaki, *Hist. of Japanese Religion* (1930), pp. 170ff.

'Honest to God' Debate Heralded by an article in the *Observer*, London, 17 March 1963, which argued that 'the image of God must go', *Honest to God*, written by Dr. J. A. T. Robinson, Bishop of Woolwich, was from first a best-seller. Substantially, argument was nothing more than repetition of thought of three well-known theologians, → Tillich, → Bultmann, and → Bonhoeffer: in a sense only thing new was unexpected combination of these three theologies. However, unsatisfactory though book was thought to be by most professional theologians, it was welcomed warmly by many laymen both inside and outside Church.

Robinson set out to replace outmoded ways of talking of God by language of depth which Tillich uses. Like Bultmann, he wants to disentangle Chr. faith from its primitive world view, holding that trad. doc. of God's transcendence is nothing more than a mythological cosmology. Arguing that picture of God as 'up there' has given way to picture of Him as 'out there', he uses Bonhoeffer's 'non-religious understanding of God' to destroy idea that God is 'there'. For him, God is, instead, depth of common, non-religious experience. With regard to Jesus Christ, Robinson holds that trad. theology is thoroughly supranaturalistic. Thus problem of → Christology is put as the problem of how → Jesus can be fully God and fully man, and yet genuinely one person. This trad. supranaturalistic way of describing → Incarnation R. parodies as God's taking part for a limited time in a charade. So Christology becomes an impossible *tour de force*. Christ is, accordingly, nothing more than divine visitant from 'out there'; the entire scheme is mythical. The mythical element of the N.T. story has legitimate function—that of indicating divine depth of history—but it does not repr. a supranaturalistic interpretation of the natural. Reinterpretation of Christology must begin with claim which Jesus makes for what God is doing uniquely through him. Following Tillich, R. says that Jesus reveals God by being nothing in himself: hence, following Christ is, as Bonhoeffer put it, to participate in powerlessness of God. On subject of Chr. life R.'s position is summed up in the phrases 'worldly holiness' and 'nothing prescribed—except love'. Generally, attitude of *Honest to God* was that secular situation of world is one not far from Kingdom of God.

The book's publication was followed by vigorous and vociferous discussion, to which various mass-communications media all contributed. The → Ch. of England in partic. was disturbed; the Abp. of Canterbury, Dr. Michael Ramsey criticised R. on television and in his presidential address to the convocation of clergy. However, the Archbishop's pamphlet's *Image Old and New* was quite sympathetic and aroused considerable support for R. from several of his fellow-Churchmen. In the discussion the two most significant charges made are: first, that R.'s position is atheistic; philosophical critics pointed out the atheism in the retention of the word God, when the content itself has been translated into secular language. Secondly, R. was said to be advocating an antinomianism in flagrant contradiction to the Chr. ethic. Whilst critics were prepared to admit that the Chr. ethic is a positive ethic of life, it was emphasised that the mode proposed of Chr. behaviour and the ethic of life need not be a purely situational ethic. J.H.-T.

J. A. T. Robinson, *Honest to God* (1963), *New Morality* (1964), *Reformation Old and New* (1965), *Exploration into God* (1967). Cf. D. L. Edwards and J. A. T. Robinson, *The Honest to God Debate* (1963); O. Fielding Clarke, *For Christ's Sake* (1963); E. L. Mascall, *The Secularization of Christianity* (1965); J. I. Packer, *Keep Yourselves from Idols* (1963); A. Richardson (ed.), *Four Anchors from the Stern* (1963).

Horus Anc. Egypt. god of double nature and role. The early kings, who united Upper and Lower Egypt, worshipped a sky-god, in falcon-form, named H. This H. was identified with sun-god → Rē, and thus became royal god *par excellence*. Each king had a 'Horus-name'. The other aspect of H. orig. from the → Osiris legend, in which H. was repr. as pious son of the dead Osiris, who performed his funerary rites and punished his murderer → Set. In this context, the king was identified as the 'living H.', and his dead predecessor as Osiris. The 'Eye of Horus', which he lost in avenging Osiris, became symbol of filial duty and sacrifice. H. is often depicted as an infant nursed by his mother → Isis. In this guise he was known by Grk. name of Harpocrates = Egypt. 'H. the Child'. In iconography H. appears as falcon with sun-disc on head, or as falcon-headed man, with royal crown. S.G.F.B.

S. A. B. Mercer, *The Relig. of Anc. Egypt* (1949), ch. 4; *R.Ae.R-G.*, pp. 273ff., 307ff.; J. Gwy Griffiths, *The Conflict of Horus and Seth* (1960); B. H. Stricker, *De geboorte van Horus* (1963 continuing).

Hosea, Book of Purports to record prophecies of H., a younger contemporary of → Amos, delivered some time before fall of Samaria in 721 BC. These prophecies are notable for H.'s use of his own unhappy experiences with his wife Gomer, poss. a former sacred → prostitute, as a parable of the relations of → Yahweh and Israel. The book attests syncretistic factors operative in early Heb. relig. (e.g. 2:16–17, 3:1ff.). S.G.F.B.

*H.D.B.*², pp. 397–9; *P.C.*², pp. 603ff.

Hospitality (Islam) Islam advocates pre-Islamic virtue of H. Special ref. is made in the Qur to kindness to travellers, e.g. ii:172, 211; iv:40 xxx:37. Incl. are one's parents and kindred, orphans, people under one's protection. Trad. has much on subject: e.g. 'He who believes in God and the last day should honour his guest. Provisions for the road are what will serve for a day and a night; hospitality extends for three days; what goes beyond that is *ṣadaqa;* and it is not allowable that a guest should stay till he makes himself an encumbrance.' Here a distinction is made between H. and voluntary almsgiving (→ Legal Alms). Tirmidhī told of man consulting → Muḥammad about one who had given him no H., and asking if he should treat him in same way if he paid him a visit. Muhammad replied, 'No, give him entertainment.' Regarding almsgiving apart from legal alms, trad. emphasises necessity of attending to needs of others. First in order come one's parents and kinsfolk; but goodwill extends to whole body of Muslims, who are said in a trad. to be one body. 'When one member has a complaint, the rest of the body is united with it in wakefulness and fever' (cf. 1 Cor. xii:26). J.R.

Hughes, p. 177; Wensinck, *Handbook*, pp. 19–21; *Mishkāt*, pp. 898ff., 1024ff.; Dickson, *Arab of Desert*, index (Hospitality), Lane, *Egyptians*, pp. 296f.

Hospitallers, or Knights Hospitaller Relig. order founded in 11th cent. to care for sick pilgrims and → Crusaders in Palestine: they also constituted an armed guard for pilgrims. The H. lived under three-fold monastic vow. At end of Crusader kingdom (1291), they migrated to Cyprus and Rhodes. In 1530 they settled in Malta, which they defended against Turkish attack. The order, having later lost its military role, became a charitable relig. institution, with its H.Q. estab. at Rome in 1878. (→ Knights Templar). S.G.F.B.

F. J. King, *Knights Hospitallers in the Holy Land* (1931); *D.C.C.*, *s.v.;* S. Runciman, *Hist. of the Crusades*, II, III, (1954), *passim;* P. Lacroix, *Military and Relig. Life in the Middle Ages* (republ. 1964), pp. 172ff.

Hossō (Skt.: *dharma-lakshana*, the 'criteria of Laws and Truths') A school of Jap. Buddhism, introduced from China by → Dōshō (CE 629–700), who studied → Yogacara doctrines under the famous → Hsüan-tsang. H. philos. was highly analytical, and a peculiar combination of Idealism and Realism. It taught that ultimate reality is to be found in the mind, in the *Ālayā* or 'store-consciousness' of each individual. The store-consciousness has within it an inexhaustible store of 'seeds' (*bīja*), which manifest themselves in innumerable varieties of existences. Phenomena (*dharmas*) exist by virtue of these 'seeds', and whole cosmos is made up of various combinations of their qualities. Thus, the infinite varieties of existence all participate in the prime nature of *Ālayā* (cf. the 'unconscious' in modern psych.), and are pervaded by universal foundation (*dharmatā*) of existence. The school elaborated ten stages in mystical contemplation, which finally led to immediate realisation of innermost nature of all being. Thus the aim of an elaborate Buddh. training and discipline was to discover the ultimate entity of cosmic existence in contemplation, through investigation into the specific characteristics of all existence and realisation of fundamental nature of soul in mystic illumination, attained only by a select few. D.H.S.

E.R.E., IX, p. 870b; M. Anesaki, *Hist. of Japanese Religion* (1930), pp. 94–6.

Host Ex. Lat. *hostia* = sacrificial victim. Word used in W. Church for consecrated bread of → Eucharist (or → Mass), in accordance with doc. of Eucharistic Sacrifice. The H. became the object of much medieval superstition. S.G.F.B.

J. A. MacCulloch, *Medieval Faith and Fable* (1932), ch. 10.

Hōtoku A society which was originated in Japan by → Ninomiya Sontoki (CE 1787–1856), known as the peasant-sage of Japan. He proclaimed doc. of 'indebtedness' (*Toku*—virtue, order, benefit; *Hōtoku*—indebtedness identified with virtue and benefit). H. is not a relig., but combines elements drawn from → Confucianism, → Buddhism and → Shinto. It emphasises the indebtedness man owes to the gods, to nature, the ancestors and the emperor. This can be repaid only by conformity to cosmic order, moral sincerity and economic frugality. H. taught that self-sacrifice is a fundamental virtue, condemned the spirit of revenge, and promoted prosperity among peasants by emphasis on moral reform, mutual helpfulness, and energy and diligence in work to ensure a surplus of wealth. H. encouraged new industries, relieved distress and rewarded good deeds. Though favouring no one relig. sect, and opposed to priests as wealth-consuming, the movement was deeply relig. in character. D.H.S.

Tadasu Yoshimoto, *A Peasant Sage of Japan:* tr. from Hotoku-ki (1912); M. Anesaki, *Hist. of Japanese Relig.* (1930), pp. 302–4; *E.R.E.*, IX, pp. 274–5.

Hour, Last The end of world is commonly called The Hour in the → Qur. (e.g. vi:31; vii:186; xxii:1), and Tradition (→ Hādith). Muslim has a trad. that → Muḥammad mentioned signs which will precede it: smoke (cf. Qur. xliv:9), the → dajjāl, the beast (→ *dābbat al-arḍ*, cf. Qur. xxvii:84), the rising of sun in its place of setting, the descent of Jesus son of Mary (→ Jesus Christ in Islam), → Gog and Magog, three subsidences, one in E., one in W. and one in Arabia, after which a fire, issuing from the Yemen, will drive mankind to the place of assembly (i.e. for the Judgment). J.R.

E.I., II, pp. 1048–51; Hughes, pp. 177, 539f.; *Mishkāt*, pp. 1137ff., 1161ff.; Wensinck, *Creed*, pp. 23ff., 197, 243.

Hsien Chinese term for Taoist immortals, supposed to have partaken of elixir of immortality by which they retain all properties of living beings, and possess power to roam at will through universe. In → Taoism there are three categories of deified humans; the *shêng jên* or saints, who live in highest heaven; the *chên jên*, or perfected men, who live in second heaven; and the *hsien*, who live in mountains (as the Chi. character implies) or in perpetual happiness in Isles of the

Blest. Thousands of mortals are believed to have become H., and to have received various dignities in the celestial hierarchy. In partic., the Pa Hsien or Eight Immortals are favourite subject of repres. and romance in China. They are embodiment of ideal happiness, and repres. all sections of Chi. society, old and young, male and female, civil and military, rich and poor. Their cult is probably to be assigned to the Yüan Dynasty (CE 1280–1368), whose emperors had a preference for Taoism. D.H.S.

H. Maspero, *Le Taoisme* (1950); E. T. C. Werner, *Dict. of Chinese Mythology* (1932), arts. Chên Jên; Shêng Jên; Hsien; Pa Hsien; H. Maspero in J. Hackin (ed.), *Asiatic Mythology* (1932), pp. 348–9.

Hsüan-hsüeh Profound or mysterious learning. The name given to a highly metaphysical neo-Taoist movement which arose in China in period CE 220–420. Its chief exponents were Wang Pi (CE 226–49), Ho Yen (d. 249) and Kuo Hsiang (d. 312), who, whilst emphasising → Taoist doctrines, honoured → Confucius as the greatest sage. Their study of → Lao-tzŭ and → Chuang-tzŭ led them to assert that ultimate reality, underlying all phenomena and beyond space and time, is original 'non-being' (*pên wu*), which transcends all distinctions and descriptions. This is the unity underlying and unifying all phenomena, which exist and evolve acc. to principle of their being. The perfect sage (e.g. Confucius) acts always with natural spontaneity. The school had considerable influence on development of Confucian and Buddh. thought in China. D.H.S.

Fung Yu-lan, *Hist. of Chinese Philos.*, vol. 2 (1953), chs. 5–6; W. T. Chan, *Source Book in Chinese Philos.* (1962), ch. 19.

Hsüan Chuang → Hsüan Tsang. D.H.S.

(Tsang) (Hsüan Chuang) CE 596–664. Jap.—Genjo. The greatest Chinese pilgrim to India, and one of most import. figures in Chi. → Buddhism. Ordained at age of 13, he left for India in 629 by the C. Asian route, and arrived in 633, to spend ten years there in travel and study. He arrived back in China in 645, with 657 Buddh. texts, and was received at capital, Ch'ang-an, in triumph. The rest of his life was spent in trans. work under imperial patronage, and he completed some 75 trans., mostly → Yogācāra works. He introduced into China the teachings of → Vasubandhu (*c.* CE 420–500) and → Dharmapāla (439–507). His most famous philos. work is the *Ch'êng Wei-shih lun* ('On the establishment of the doctrine of Consciousness-only'). The *Hsi Yu Chi* (an account of the journey to the W.) is based on diaries of his travels. It is one of greatest Chi. literary treasures, and indispensable for study of Indian Buddhism. It was trans. into Eng. by S. Beal in 1884 under the title *Si-yu-ki, Buddhist Records of the W, World trans. from the Chinese of Hsien-tsiang.* 2 vols., London. D.H.S.

W. T. Chan, *Source Book in Chinese Philos.* (1963), ch. 23; Fung Yu-lan, *Hist. of Chinese Philos.*, vol. 2 (1953), pp. 299ff.

Hua Yen Import. school of Chi. → Buddhism, of which the highly metaphysical doctrines repres. highest development of Chi. Buddh. thought. The school based its principal teachings on the *Hua-yen Ching* or the *Mahāvaipulya Sūtra* (The expanded Sūtra of the adornments of the Buddha). This was accepted as first discourse of Buddha on his enlightenment, preached to → bodhisattvas, and beyond comprehension of mortals, to whom he proceeded to preach a simpler doctrine. Tu-shun (CE 557–640) is reputed to be its first Chi. master, followed by Chih-yen (601–68) and → Fa-tsang (643–712). Fa-tsang, who had been disciple of → Hsüan-tsang, was greatest exponent of Hua Yen philosophy. Whilst other Buddh. schools (e.g. → Ch'an) taught that Being and Non-Being are alike illusion and negated in the Void, Hua Yen taught a permanently immutable 'mind', which is universal in scope and basis of all phenomenal manifestations. It was thus more adaptable to indigenous Chi. thought. D.H.S.

Fung Yu-lan, *Hist. of Chinese Philos.*, vol. 2 (1953), pp. 339ff.; W. T. Chan, *A Source Book in Chinese Philos.* (1963, pp. 406–8; C. B. Day, *The Philosophers of China* (1962), pp. 172–5.

Huai Nan-tzŭ An important Taoist work, attr. to Liu-an, prince of Huai-nan and grandson of first Han Dynasty emperor, *c.* 130 BC. Though a miscellaneous compilation, it contains clearest statement of anc. Chinese cosmological ideas. D.H.S.

Fung Yu-lan, *Hist. of Chinese Philosophy*, vol. 1 (1937), pp. 395ff.

Huang-Lao Chün An important deity in Chinese Taoist pantheon. From *c.* 200 BC, in vocabulary of early philos. → Taoism, H.-L. refers to mythical emperor Huang Ti (one of early Taoist books, now lost, bore his name), and to → Lao-tzŭ, reputed author of the → *Tao Tê Ching*. By middle of 2nd cent. CE, H.-L. was reduced to a single individual, and became principal god of sect of the Yellow Turbans, conceived of as supreme divine instructor, guide to those who studied → Tao and sought immortality. He was head of triad of Taoist divinities, dwelling in Heaven and presiding over world. By 4th cent. CE, H.-L. had declined in importance, his place being taken by → Yüan Shih T'ien Tsun, a supreme deity conceived of as Principle of all beings. D.H.S.

H. Maspero, *Le Taoïsme* (1950); H. Welch, *The Parting of the Way* (1957).

Hubal Chief deity of the → Ka'ba in pre-Islamic times, was repr. by an idol, or a picture, showing a human form. It is said there were 360 idols within the Ka'ba, and that H. was tutelary deity of → Mecca: perhaps it may be more correct to say of the Ka'ba. Wellhausen notes that the tribe → Quraysh swore by → al-Lāt and → al-'Uzzā, not by H. When → Muḥammad occupied Mecca in 8/630, he destroyed all idols saying, 'Truth has come and falsehood has vanished; falsehood is apt to vanish' (Qur. xvii:83). J.R.

E.I., II, p. 327; Hughes, p. 181; Wellhausen, *Reste*, pp. 75, 221; Muir, *Life*, index.

Hubris In Grk. thought, 'the capital sin of self-assertion'. The Greeks regarded a sense of satisfaction at personal well-being as fatal, for it would provoke divine jealousy and result in catastrophic reversal of fortune. S.G.F.B.

E. R. Dodds, *The Greeks and the Irrational* (1951), *passim*.

Hūd Mentioned several times in the → Qur. as a prophet sent to people of → 'Ād. Owing to their rejection of him, they were destroyed (cf. Qur., vii:63ff.; xi:52ff.; xxvi:123ff.). The reputed tomb of H. at far end of Wādī Ḥaḍramawt is most import. place of pilgrimage in the region. J.R.

E.I., II, pp. 327f.; Hughes, pp. 181f.; Watt, *Mecca*, p. 28; Bell, *Introduction*, p. 121; D. van der Meulen, *Aden to the Hadhramaut* (1947), index.

Hui Nêng (CE 628–713). Known in S. China as Wei Lang and in Japan as Eno, he was sixth and last patriarch of → Ch'an Buddhism in China (the first being → Bodhidharma, or in Chinese—Ta Mo). As leader of S. branch of Ch'an school, he taught doc. of Spontaneous Realisation or Sudden Enlightenment, through meditation in which thought, objectivity and all attachment are eliminated. He wrote the only sacred Chi. Buddh. writing which has been honoured with the title → Ching or Sūtra, the famous *Platform Sūtra of Hui Nêng*. D.H.S.

C. B. Day, *The Philosophers of China* (1962), pp. 139ff.; E. Wood, *Zen Dict.* (1962).

Hui Yüan (CE 334–417). Surname Chia. A native of Lou-fan, in Yen-mên, Shansi, his early years were spent in study of → Confucianism and → Taoism. In his 21st year, was converted to → Buddhism and became most brilliant disciple of → Tao-an (312–85). His fame as a Buddh. master and expositor of Buddh. teachings spread far and wide. He founded the Tung-lin monastery on Lu Shan in C. China, to which he retired, and this became most famous centre of Buddhism in S. China. He drew his inspiration largely from the Greater and Lesser *Sukhāvatī-Vyūha Sūtras*, with their vivid descriptions of the → 'Pure Land' and infinite compassion of → Amitābha Buddha. In CE 402 he founded the White Lotus Society (*Pai Lien Chiao*), when he assembled monks and laymen of his community before an image of Amitābha, stressing importance of worship, the use of icons in meditation and devotion to Amitābha. In later times, this event was taken to mark beginning of Pure Land Sect, of which H.Y. is reckoned first patriarch. He carried on extensive correspondence with great Buddh. translator → Kumārajīva. These letters give insight into nature and scope of his doc. He combined Buddh. devotion and secular scholarship. D.H.S.

E. Zürcher, *Buddhist Conquest of China* (1959), pp. 204–59.

Human Sacrifice The practice, which has been widespread throughout mankind, was prompted by a variety of motives, the following being the more notable: (1) in funerary rituals, to provide the dead with companions or servants: e.g. in royal burials at Ur in Sumer (*c.* 2500 BC), and those of Shang Dynasty rulers at Anyang, China (*c.* 1200 BC), scores of retainers were buried with their deceased masters. The Hindu custom of → *suti* may also be cited. (2) as propitiatory sacrifice to gods: e.g. child-s. at Carthage (→ Carthaginian Relig.); s. of Iphigenia to → Artemis in Grk. mythology; the burying alive of four people in the Forum Boarium, Rome, during crisis in Carthaginian War; → Abraham's s. of Isaac. (3) to feed gods or promote their vitality or fertility: e.g. s. among the Aztecs (→ Americ. Relig. anc.); s. to Freyr and Nerthus in anc. → Scandinavian relig. (4) s. of war-captives 'devoted' to a god (e.g. s. of Agag to → Yahweh, I Sam. 15). (5) s. of ageing king to preserve virility and fertility of land and people (e.g. by the Shilluk of Upper Nile). (6) vicarious s., usually of → scape-goat-type (e.g. the *pharmakos* at Grk. → festival of Thargelia; as repr. by Aztec god Xipe Totec). The sacrificial death of Christ (→→ Atonement; Salvation) combines aspects of (2) and (6). Cannibalism was often part of ritual of H.-S., the participants identifying themselves with victim by eating of the body. (→→ Eucharist; Foundation Rites; Sacrifice). S.G.F.B.

E.R.E., VI, pp. 840–67; E. O. James, *The Origins of Sacrifice* (1937); J. G. Frazer, *The Scapegoat* (G.B. 1933); C. A. Burland, *The Gods of Mexico* (1967), *passim;* E. O. G. Turville-Petre, *Myth and Relig. of the North* (1964), ch. 13; W. Watson, *China before the Han Dynasty* (1961), pp. 69ff.; L. Woolley, *Excavations at Ur* (1955), ch. 3; *R.G.G.*³, IV, col. 867–8.

Humility (China) In → Confucianism, H. is a social virtue, necessary in conduct of an inferior towards his superior. In all human relations a retiring, modest, respectful, unassuming and self-deprecatory attitude is considered mark of the truly virtuous. This self-depreciation, carried to excess, has tended to produce insincerity, hypocrisy and many absurdities in language of social relationships. On principle that the weak overcomes the strong, that non-resistance is better than resistance and that the wise man puts himself in background, Taoists taught that practice of H. was a most effective technique for getting people to do what we want. D.H.S.

Hun and P'o Acc. to Chinese theory, the nature of man is essentially dualistic. He possesses two soul elements, one partaking of nature of *Yang* and the other of *Yin* (→ Yin-Yang). These two soul-elements went by different names, the most common being *hun* and *p'o*. The *hun* is *yang*, pure and intelligent; the *p'o* is *yin*, turbid and earthy. At birth they combine; at death they separate. Acc. to some late Taoist accounts, there were 3 *hun* and 7 *p'o*.

The *p'o* is the animal spirit which appertains to form, gives perception to the senses, and is ruling element in man's emotive nature. Wieger is probably right in connecting it with the sperm, so that it becomes a constituent of human nature at conception. At death it still clings to the corpse, becomes a ghost (→ *kuei*), and returns with corpse to earth, gradually to dissipate its vital force.

The *hun* enters the child with first breath at birth, and is the first to depart at death, ascending like vapour to become a spirit (→ *shên*). To die is therefore 'to sever or cut off the *hun*'. To lose one's wits is to 'lose the *hun*'. To call back the soul, and thus to be resuscitated, is to 'call back the *hun*'.

The developed doc. is set forth in the *Shu Chu Tzŭ*, a Taoist work of 13th cent. CE. There it states that 'the human personality is said to have two souls, the *hun* and the *p'o*. The *hun* is *yang*, pure and intelligent; the *p'o* is *yin*, turbid and dark. The true man nourishes the *hun*, whilst the majority of mankind nourish the *p'o*. . . . At birth the *p'o* is first produced and then the *hun*. At death the *hun* first departs, and afterwards the *p'o* is dissipated. . . . In a living man the *hun* and *p'o* live together in a harmonious relationship like husband and wife. At death they separate, the *hun* to rise, the *p'o* to descend, and they no longer have any regard for each other. . . . If a former *hun* can receive a new *p'o* it can return to life. The *p'o* of a dead man, if it can receive the vital force, can also return to life. When the bones decay, the *p'o* is also destroyed. There are cases in which a *p'o* has not been dissipated for a hundred years. No *hun* can exist for more than five generations.' (→ Kuei). D.H.S.

L. Wieger, *Hist. of Relig. Beliefs and Philos. Opinions in China* (1927), pp. 120, 680ff.; L. Wieger, *Textes Philosophiques* (1930), pp. 346ff.; D. H. Smith, 'Chinese Concepts of the Soul', Numen, vol. 2 (1958).

Hung Hsiu³ch'üan (CE 1812–64). Became leader of the T'ai P'ing rebellion. Influenced in his early days by Christ. doctrines, he became a fortune-teller and joined a society known as the Society of God. In 1836, he announced himself to be the younger brother of Jesus Christ, and formed a pseudo-Chr. sect. He began his rebellion in 1850 and styled himself Heavenly Prince (T'ien Wang), and for a while set up a theocratic form of government under the title *T'ai P'ing T'ien Kuo* ('The Great Peaceful Heavenly Kingdom'). He denounced → Buddhism and → Taoism as idolatries, and destroyed their temples. He substituted the Chr. Gospels for the Confucian Classics. He inaugurated remarkable social reforms, forbidding foot-binding and the use of opium. He sought the friendship of foreigners, regarding them as co-religionists. By his followers he was regarded as a prophet and inspired leader, raised up by God for purpose of estab. peace and virtue in the land. His movement was finally overthrown, after appalling loss of life, not by the corrupt, degenerate and reactionary Manchus who ruled over China, but through the assistance of foreign powers. D.H.S.

C. P. Fitzgerald, *China* (1935), pp. 566ff.; S. Couling, *Encycl. Sinica* (1917), p. 245.

-Ḥusayn b. 'Alī (4–61/626–80). Grandson of → Muḥammad and third → imam of the Shi'a. He lived in Medina during Mu'āwiya's Caliphate (→ Umayyads), but retired to Mecca and avoided swearing allegiance to Mu'awiya's son Yazīd. Persuaded to go to Kufa in 61/680 by promise of support from its people, Ḥ. and his small company of about 200 were surrounded at → Karbalā, about 25 miles N.W. of Kufa; when he refused to surrender, they were eliminated. Ḥ.'s head was cut off and sent to Yazīd at Damascus. The massacre took place on 10th Muḥarram, 61/10th Oct., 680, and the → Shi'a have observed this period ever since as time of mourning. Ḥ.'s death is considered as a martyrdom which has sacrificial value (→ 'Āshūrā, Karbalā). J.R.

E.I., II, p. 339; Hughes, pp. 185–7; Pareja, index; Donaldson, *Shi'ite*, ch. vii and index (Hasan and Husain); Hitti, *History*, index; F. Rosenthal, *Ibn Khaldun*, index.

Hypocrites (*Munāfiqūn*). Name frequently given in → Qur. to a party in → Medina. → Muḥammad's supporters were the → Emigrants from Mecca and the → Helpers in Medina. The H. were Medina folk who hesitated to help Muhammad, perhaps because they wished to see first how matters would turn out. In the Qur. they are rebuked for cowardice (cf. iii:150; lix:12ff.), plotting against Muhammad (cf. ii:8; xxxiii:60; ix:48, 61, 127), blindness and indifference to Muhammad's preaching (cf. ii:8; iv:141; lxiii:5f.; ix:65, 125, 128), their equivocal attitude (cf. ii:7, 13; viii:51; lxiii:1, 4; v.:45, 57). The Qur. offers pardon, if they repent (cf. iv:145; ix:75), but also threatens them with going to hell (cf. ii:9; iv:137, 139; lix:15; ix:49, 55, 67, 69, 78, 96). Clearly, while they hesitated to follow Muhammad, some opposed him. Watt suggests the H. were a party of Muslims who disagreed with Muhammad's projects; so he calls them the Muslim Opposition. That is poss., but the Qur. seems normally to suggest that they had not allied themselves with Muhammad, and so could hardly be called → Muslims. The word *munāfiqūn* comes from verb used of mouse retreating into its hole. So perhaps the H. were merely quite a typical group who hesitated to commit themselves before it was obvious which side would win. J.R.

E.I., III, pp. 722f.; Pareja, p. 69; Guillaume, *Life*, pp. 247ff.; Watt, *Medina*, index; Blachère, *Coran* and Stanton, *Teaching* give details in their indexes.

I

Iamblichos (*c.* CE 250–325) → Neoplatonist philosopher and author of philos. and mathemat. works. His *de mysteriis Aegyptiorum*, a defence of ritual magic, is significant for occult beliefs and practices of period, as is also his *peri psychēs* ('About the Soul'). S.G.F.B.

O.C.D., *s.v.; Kleine Pauly*, II, col. 1305–6; *R.G.G.*³, III, col. 528–9; F. C. Grant, *Hellenistic Religions* (1953), pp. 173ff.; A.-J. Festugière, *La révélation d'Hermès Trismégiste*, III (1953), pp. 10ff., 177–264; Jamblique, *Les mystères d'Égypte*, text and trans., Éd. des Places (1966).

Ibn al-'Arabī Muḥyī 'l-Dīn (560–638/1165–1240), a famous mystic, b. in Murcia. He spent 30 years in Seville. His studies in → *fiqh* and → *ḥadīth* were carried on there and elsewhere in Spain and N. Africa. In 598/1201–2 he went to E., where he remained. He visited a number of towns in Asia during period of years, twice making the Pilgrimage to Mecca, and finally settled in Damascus. In the E. he was called Ibn 'Arabī. He belonged to the Ẓāhirite school (→→ Muslim Law; and Ibn Ḥazm); but while he could follow its literalist doc. in matters legal and ritual, his beliefs seemed far removed from strict Muslim doc. He conformed outwardly, but held that he had special guidance and experienced revelation. He wrote on theology and mysticism in manner which suggests → pantheism. Two of his many works are espec. famous: *al-Futūḥāt al-Makkiyya* (The Meccan revelations), and *Fuṣūṣ al-ḥikam* (Philosophical gems). Besides this he wrote poetry, but his *Tarjumān al-ashwāq* (ed. R. A. Nicholson, with E.T., 1911) was so criticised for its eroticism that he had to supply commentary explaining mystical meaning of his language. In his doc. he allows only one Reality (→ *al-Ḥaqq*), namely God; but this incl. whole creation whose essence is one. Such a doc. should make it difficult to discuss satisfactorily good and evil, or freewill and predestination, but I.-'A. attempts to do this. Everything, he holds, is good; what appears to be evil is absence of a positive quality. Though everything is determined, man does not necessarily recognise this, so he must act as if he were a free agent. As God is the self of all things, he is to be worshipped as transcendant and as externalised in nature. It also follows that all religions are relatively true, although → Islām is superior to others. An eternal heaven and hell did not agree with his monism, but this did not hinder him from teaching some idea of a temporary hell. But if God alone is al-Ḥaqq, what place can there be for individual immortality, and if evil has no reality in itself, what need is there for a hell? J.R.

E.I., II, pp. 361f.; Pareja, p. 763 and index (Ibn 'Arabī); *E.R.E.*, pp. 8, 907ff.; *G.A.L.*, I, pp. 571–82; *S.I.*, pp. 790–802; D. B. Macdonald, *Theology*, pp. 261ff. and index; Asin y Palacios, *Islam and the Divine Comedy* (1926), *passim;* A. E. Affifi, *The mystical philosophy of Muhyid Din-Ibnul 'Arabi* (1939); Rom Landau, 'The Philosophy of Ibn 'Arabi,' *M.W.*, XLVII (1957), pp. 46–61, 140–60.

Ibn Bājja → Avempace. J.R.

Ibn Ḥazm (383–456/993–1064). A noted supporter of the Ẓāhirite school of → Muslim Law, came of an influential Cordovan family which had accepted Islam after the Muslim conquest of Spain. He had experience of administrative work in different centres, and had also been taken prisoner in war. Later he devoted himself to scholarship. His writings consist of belles lettres, → *fiqh*, theology, philosophy, ethics → Qur. and → Ḥadīth. He was brought up in Mālikī school of Muslim law; dissatisfied he changed to the → Shāfi'ī, and by 418/1027 to the Zahirite, of which he became an uncompromising supporter. *Ẓāhir* = outward, or literal, is used because, the school insisted on literal understanding of the words of Qur. and Ḥadīth I.Ḥ.'s theology led him into controversy. In his *Kitāb al-fiṣal fī 'l-milal wa'l-ahwā' wa'l-niḥal* ('Book of the distinctions in the religions, fanciful notions, and sects'), where he deals with varieties of views within → Islām and elsewhere, he is very strong in his condemnation of those which depart from his literal interpret. of wording of Qur. and Trad. He was bitterly opposed esp. to → Ash'arites and → Shi'ites. He castigated leaders long held in honour in the schools and accordingly made enemies. But he came up against a difficulty, when he had to reconcile his literal doc. with his objection to anthropomorphic ideas. The Qur. contains such terms, so he searched for various meanings of the words till he discovered such as enabled him to make the desired reconciliation between seemingly opposed beliefs. He is violent in his criticism of the Jew. and Christ. scriptures, of which he shows considerable knowledge. J.R.

E.I., II, pp. 384–6; *G.A.L.*, 1, pp. 505f.; *S.I.*, pp. 692–7; Pareja, pp. 707f. and index; Watt, *Philosophy*, pp. 134–6; Sweetman, *I.C.T.*, II–IV, index of authors, esp. III, pp. 178–262.

Ibn Isḥāq (85–151/704–768). Biographer of → Muḥammad, b. in Medina, assoc. with traditionists of second generation, and became recognised authority on the events of Md.'s life. As a result of jealousy on part of → Mālik b. Anas, to whom he felt superior, I.I. went to Iraq and eventually farther east. Some books on Md.'s campaigns (*maghāzī*) had been compiled, but I.I. was first to compile a complete biography (*sīra*) of Md. This work has been edited and enlarged by Ibn Hishām (d. 218/834), and is commonly called his *Sīra*; but he has carefully indicated I.I.'s material, and where he has made additions to it, so that one can see the orig. work. Guillaume has translated this along with other material by I.I. found elsewhere. J.R.

Guillaume, *Life;* Muir, *Life*, pp. lxvii–lxxix*; E.I.*, II, pp. 389f., IV, p. 442; Watt, *Mecca*, p. xii and index; J. Robson, 'Ibn Isḥāq's use of the isnād', *B.J.R.L.*, 38 (1956), pp. 449ff.

Ibn Māja Muḥammad b. Yazīd al-Qazwīnī (209–273/824–886). Was compiler of a collection of Trads., which, after some cents. came to be recognised gen. among → Sunnīs as sixth of the canonical collections. Different views have been expressed regarding its contents. Some have praised it; others have expressed dissatisfaction because some men quoted as authorities for Trads. were unreliable. (→ Ḥadīth). J.R.

E.I., II, p. 400; *G.A.L.*, I, p. 171; *S.I.*,, p. 270; Goldziher, *M.S.*, II, pp. 262ff.; Ibn Khallikān, II, p. 680; J. Robson, 'The Transmission of Ibn Majah's "Sunan",' *J.S.S.*, III (1958), pp. 129ff.; Siddiqi, *Hadith*, index.

Ibn Mas'ūd 'Abdallāh (d. 32/652–3), one of earliest Muslim converts, became noted as traditionist and Qur. authority. He went to Kufa, where he settled. He had a version of the Qur. which was superseded by the 'Uthmanic recension → (Qur'ān). It did not contain the last two suras, and some think the first was also missing; but it seems otherwise to have followed arrangement of what became official version, though there were variant readings, as indic. by refs. in a number of works. That the version was not destroyed immediately after the completion of the 'Uthmanic recension, as the conventional story suggests, is indic. by Ibn al-Nadīm (d. 385/995), compiler of the *Fihrist*, a large and famous catalogue of Arabic books, who says he had seen a 200 year old copy of I.M.'s Qur. If his information is correct, it means that it must have been transcribed in 2nd cent. of the → Hijra, very much later than time of intro. of the 'Uthmanic recension' J.R.

E.I., II, pp. 403f.; Hughes, p. 189; Pareja, pp. 605f.; Bell, *Introduction*, pp. 40f.; Nöldeke, *Geschichte*², II, pp. 39ff., III, pp. 60ff.; Jeffery, *Materials*, pp. 20ff.

Ibn Rushd. → Averroes. J.R.

Ibn Sīnā → Avicenna. J.R.

Ibn Taymiyya (661–728/1263–1328). A Ḥanbalite of great intellectual ability and force of character. He held positions of importance in Damascus, and also lectured in Cairo, but his strict views roused opposition and he suffered periods of imprisonment in Damascus and Cairo. He vigorously upheld → Hanbali doc. both in theology and law. He attacked belief in → astrology and methods of philosophical argument used by → Ash'arite theologians. He opposed the docs. of the → Ṣūfīs and their desire for union with God who, he insisted, was completely different from his creatures. He called saint-worship and honouring of saints' tombs idolatry. His teaching exerted considerable influence, and his docs., remembered by men of succeeding generations, were to bear fruit in the → Wahhabi movement. J.R.

E.I., II, pp. 421–3; *G.A.L.*, II, pp. 125–7; *S*, II, pp. 119ff.; Pareja, pp. 713ff. and index; D. B. Macdonald, *Theology*, pp. 273ff., 283ff.; Watt, *Philosophy*, index; Wensinck, *Creed*, pp. 254, 264; H. Laoust, *Essai sur les doctrines de.... Ibn Taymīya* (1939).

Ibn Ṭufayl (d. 581/1185). Became court physician of the Almohad Caliph Abū Ya'qūb Yūsuf to whom he introduced → Averroes. His fame rests mainly on his philosophical romance Ḥayy b. Yaqẓān (Alive son of Awake), which deals with an infant mothered by a gazelle on an island with no human inhabitants. The child's development is described, his confusion of mind when the gazelle dies, his acquiring a rudimentary belief in the existence of a soul, his perception of cause and effect leading to belief in God which is developed when he considers the heavenly bodies, and results in his becoming absorbed in asceticism and contemplation. Asāl, an orthodox Muslim, arrived from a neighbouring island, taught Hayy language and discovered that Hayy's philosophy was fundamentally the same as revealed relig. They went to Asal's island to teach the people their docs., but having no success they returned to Hayy's island to engage in contemplation, leaving the common people to conventional rituals. I.Ṭ. held that purpose of philosophy was to attain such union with God that truth should be attained by intuition. J.S.

E.I., II, pp. 424f.; *G.A.L.*, I, pp. 602f.; *S*, I, pp. 831f.; Pareja, p. 989 and index; De Boer, *Philosophy*, pp. 181ff.; E. Calverley, 'A brief bibliography of Arabic philosophy', *M.W.*, xxxii (1942), pp. 60–8; D. B. Macdonald, *Theology*, pp. 252–6, 261; Ibn Tufayl: *Hayy b. Yaqzan*, E.T., *The Improvement of Human Reason*, by S. Ockley (1708), revised by A. S. Fulton (1929).

Ibn Tūmart Muḥammad (d. *c.* 524/1130) set himself up as → Mahdī in the Maghrib. He had studied in the E. for a time, and returned to the Maghrib to institute a reformation. He attacked laxity of the → Almoravids. His doc. was largely → Ash'arite, but combined with suggestions of → Shi'ism. He opposed the literal interpr. of the → Qur. and all anthropomorphic doc. He trans. the Qur. into the Berber tongue and had the → *adhān* and the Prayer recited in that tongue also. From reform by teaching he moved to fighting, feeling he must lead a → *jihād* not only against infidels, but also against the Almoravids, for to him infidels were not confined to non-Muslims; they incl. → Muslims whose docs. differed from his. Eventually, in company with 'Abd al-Mu'min, he was victorious, and the dynasty of the → Almohads was founded. It held power in the Maghṛib and Spain for over a cent. J.R.

E.I., II, pp. 425–7; *G.A.L.*, I, pp. 506f.; *S.*, I, p. 697; Pareja, pp. 712f.; D. B. Macdonald, *Theology*, pp. 245ff.

I Ching (*The Book of Changes*). Also known as the *Chou I.* One of the five Confucian Classics. Modern research attr. orig. stratum of text to early days of Chou Dynasty (*c.* 1000 BC). The orig. corpus of *I.C.* was made up of famous → Pa Kua (Eight Trigrams), each composed of three whole or divided lines, and symbolising, acc. to anc. Chinese cosmology, the eight basic constituents of universe. So far as we know, the *I.C.* was first used as a book of divination. The supplementary commentaries and appendices (known as the Ten Wings) were probably written by Confucians towards close of Chou dynasty, and form basis of → Confucian philosophy and cosmology. In the *I.C.* are 64 hexagrams, made by combining the 8 trigrams, and 384 *hsiao* (the single lines which compose the hexagram). Each hexagram and each line symbolically repr. a certain object or idea, and to each a judgement is attached. These symbols were deemed to repr. in their totality, all principles of life and action in the universe, principles which when applied to human society lead to prosperity, peace and happiness. The philosophy of the *I.C.* is based on the assumption that whole universe is in a perpetual state of flux and on the mutual interaction of its parts. The process is cyclical in nature. All that happens, natural or human, is a continuous whole, a chain of natural sequences. These, it was believed, could be understood by study and interpretation of the simple symbolical representations in the hexagrams. The book has, philosophically, exercised more influence than any other Confucian Classic. A bibliography of works on the Chinese Classics, published in 1962, contains approx. 2000 titles on the *I.C.* D.H.S.

I Ching., trans. by J. Legge, ed. by Ch'u Chai–Winberg Chai (1964); *The I Ching or Book of Changes*, trans. by R. Wilhelm and rendered into Eng. by C. F. Baynes, 2 vols. (1951); Fung Yu-lan, *Hist. of Chinese Philos.*, E.T. 1937, vol. 1, ch. 15; H. Wilhelm, *Eight Lectures on the I Ching* (1960).

Icon(s) Grk. *eikōn* = image. I. are pictures of Christ, Virgin Mary, or a saint, painted gen. on a flat board, in stiff → Byzantine style. They are venerated in Grk. and Russian Church by kissing, genuflexions, and offering of incense. Many I. are alleged to work miracles. From *c.* 725–842, Grk. Church was greatly disturbed by Iconoclastic Controversy caused by those, gen. regarded as heretics, who violently opposed veneration of I. The final victory of orthodoxy greatly stimulated cult of I. The iconostasis in Grk. churches is a screen, covered with I., separating sanctuary from nave. (→ Images). S.G.F.B.

D.C.C., pp. 674–6; E. J. Martin, *Hist. of Iconoclastic Controversy* (1930); *R.G.G.*[3], III, col. 670–4; D. T. Rice, *Art of the Byzantine Era* (1963), *passim;* N. Zernov, *Eastern Christendom* (1961), ch. 11, A. Grabar, *L'iconoclasme byzantin. Dossier archéologique* (1957); *Byzantium* (E.T. 1966), pp. 185ff.; G. E. von Grunebaum, 'Byzantine Iconoclasm and the Influence of the Islamic Environment', *H.R.*, 2 (1962).

'Īd al-Aḍḥā Commonly called *al-'īd al-kabīr* (the great festival), is the festival of sacrifice celebrated on 10th Dhul Ḥijja. This essential part of the Pilgrimage rites is not confined to pilgrims but is observed everywhere. There is a period of rejoicing and holiday throughout the Muslim world, extending in some places to four days. People try to appear in new clothes, at least with some new article. This is only occasion when → Islām observes sacrifice. The occasion is traditionally connected with → Abraham's readiness to obey God's command to sacrifice his son, held by Muslims to have been → Ishmael. The site where Abraham went to sacrifice him is said to have been Mānā (→ Pilgrimage). → Gabriel substituted a broadtailed sheep for Ishmael. When a family observes the sacrifice, the animal is divided into three portions, one for relatives, one for the poor, and one for the family. J.R.

E.I., II, pp. 444f.; Hughes, pp. 192–4; Lane, *Egyptians*, p. 493; Rutter, *Holy Cities*, I, pp. 171ff., II, 272ff.; Kamal, *Sacred journey*, pp. 86–8.

'Īd al-Fiṭr Commonly called *al-'īd al-ṣaghīr* (the lesser festival), is festival of the breaking of fast observed on 1st Shawwāl when → Ramaḍān has ended. The giving of alms is prominent, and in addition people take gifts of food to friends. Large congregations gather to observe worship, and there is an air of gen. rejoicing with mutual congratulations on completion of fast. Although this is the lesser festival, the holiday may extend to four days as with → *'Īd al-aḍḥā*, and, as then, people like to have new clothes to wear. In Indonesia (→ Islam in Indonesia) young people ask parents and grandparents to forgive their offences, often kneeling down before them and asking a blessing for coming year. J.R.

E.I., II, p. 445; Hughes, pp. 194–6; Lane, *Egyptians*, pp. 484–6; Gaudefroy-Demombynes, *Institutions*, p. 104; *I.R.* (April 1966), pp. 23f., 40.

Iddhi Buddh. term for 'psychic power', said to be one of the 'higher powers' which result from → *abhiññā*, and were held to incl. power to assume many outward forms of various kinds, to make oneself impervious to bodily harm, walk on water, etc. These powers are described in → *Visuddhimagga*, XII. The power of mind to remain imperturbable amid distractions is described as *ariyā-* (or holy) *iddhi* in the *Sampasādaniya Sutta* (*D.N.*, iii, 112f.), where it is said that the monk, by means of this power, can 'remain unconscious of disgust amid what is disgusting; or conscious of disgust amid what is not disgusting; or unconscious of disgust amid what is both d. and not-d; or remain indifferent to them both as such, mindful and understanding' (*Dialogue of the Buddha*, pt. III, 1921, (trans. T. W. Rhys-Davies), p. 107). The display, before lay people, of any supernatural power which is the monk's as result of his special insight, is strictly forbidden by the Buddha (*Vinaya* II, 112). In the *Kevaddha Sutta*, Buddha is repr. as saying, 'It is because I perceive danger in the practice of mystic wonders [i.e. 'psychic powers'] that I loathe, and abhor, and am ashamed thereof' (D.N., i, 213). (See *Dialogues of the Buddha*, pt. I, pp. 276ff.). T.O.L.

Idealist School of Neo-Confucianism Known in China as Hsin Hsüeh ('the study of mind'), or school of Liu-Wang, after its chief exponents. Founded by Liu Hsiang-shan (personal name Chiu-yüan) CE 1139–93, Liu taught that purpose of study is to rid mind of all those things by which it is blinded, thus enabling it to return to its orig. pure condition; to develop inborn capacity for reflective knowledge. He equated mind with 'universal principle' (*Tao*, *Li*). The mind is fundamentally one with universe. 'The universe is in my mind and my mind in the universe.' Liu criticised → Buddhism for its escapism and refusal to be involved in the world. He taught that → Confucius estab. the Way of Man, not by withdrawing from world, but by dealing with world through following what is natural to the mind. The greatest exponent of school was → Wang Yang-ming (personal name Shou-jên) CE 1472–1529, whose teachings dominated Chi. thought during his lifetime and for 150 years thereafter. Wang's basic ideas were (1) the unity of mind and universal principle (*li*). 'Heaven and earth and all things are actually present within the mind.' (2) The development of intuitive knowledge without cognition and apart from outside corrupting influences. (3) The unity of knowledge and action, knowledge being the beginning of action and action the completion of knowledge. Although his writings reveal Buddh. influence, Wang rejected the other-worldliness of Buddhism and the contemplation of → Nirvāna. He laid stress on Confucian teachings concerning the Heaven-bestowed principles of *jên* (human-heartedness) and '*i*' (righteousness) as inherent in nature of man. The influence of school extended to Japan, where it was known as Yōmei-gaku from the 17th–19th cents. and provided strong leadership for the Meiji restoration in 1868. In early 20th cent. in China a revival of school took place under T'an Ssŭ-t'ung and Hsiung Shih-li. D.H.S.

Fung Yu-lan, *Hist. of Chinese Philosophy*, vol. 2, ch. 14 (1953), W. T. Chan, *Source Book of Chinese Philosophy*, ch. 35 (1963); C. B. Day, *The Philosophers of China*, ch. 11 (1962).

Idolatry (Chinese) Idolatry does not seem to have existed in pre-Confucian China. The extensive use of images in worship was intro. by → Buddhism, the earliest iconography showing marked Indian influence. After the intro. of Buddhism, the Chinese developed art of manufacturing idols to an extraordinary degree. When the idols are fashioned, they are consecrated by a ceremony in which the pupils of the eyes are opened (*k'ai kuang*), homage rendered to the god, after which he is deemed to have taken up his abode in the idol. Sometimes living insects or reptiles are introduced into the idol through a hole in the back, or the breasts are smeared with the blood of a cock. Though by the enlightened the images are regarded as merely visible symbols of invisible spiritual power, in popular relig. the idol itself is deemed to possess that power.

At first images were confined to repres. the great Buddhas; gradually almost every god in extensive pantheons of → Taoism and Buddhism came to be repres. by idols. Even → Confucianism for a time tolerated images in temples. The temples were full of idols, usually made of heavily-gilded clay. Idols, of metal, wood, clay and paper were kept and used in the homes. Images of Confucius came into vogue during T'ang Dynasty, and were often supplicated for the granting of posterity. Confucianism, however, never allowed images to be made of → Shang Ti, and in CE 1530 all images were ordered to be removed from Confucian temples. Ancestral temples were largely free from idols, though pictures of founders of clan were hung up on sacrificial occasions, or painted in a niche behind the Ancestral Tablets (→ Ancestor Worship). In Chi. popular relig., the majority believe that the image is continually inhabited by the god. Others believe that the god, normally engaged elsewhere, comes at time of worship to 'inform' the image, being summoned by ringing of bells or by other ritual music. A few recognise in the image nothing more than a visible, material symbol of spiritual power.

I. in its crudest form is exemplified in times of disaster (epidemic, flood, drought etc.), when the idol is taken in procession from temple to scene of disaster, there to be noisily supplicated, and at times even beaten, to induce it to give immediate relief. D.H.S.

E.R.E., VII, pp. 130–1; C. H. Plopper, *Chinese Relig. seen through the Proverb* (1926), pp. 164ff.; K. L. Reichelt, *Truth and Tradition in Chinese Buddhism* (1927), pp. 171ff.

Idolatry (Japanese) In → Shinto, except as it has been influenced by → Buddhism, there are no images to represent gods. The visible, concrete token of presence of the god, known as → Shintai, has usually no resemblance to supposed form of god whom it represents. The making of images dates from intro. of Buddhism into Japan. As in China, the Buddhas and → bodhisattvas came to be repres. by images in temples and in houses of devout Buddh.s. Among most famous images are the → Daibutsu in Nara, Kamakura and Kyoto. The image of → Kwannon, goddess of mercy, is one of most popular objects of worship. (→ Idolatry, Chinese). D.H.S.

E.R.E., VII, pp. 146ff.

Idolatry (pre-Islamic) The pre-Islamic objects of worship mentioned in the Qur., apart from →→ al-Lāt, al-'Uzzā and Manāt, are Wadd, Suwā', Yaghūth, Ya'ūq and Nasr. They served different areas. Among other objects of worship were → Hubal, Dhul Sharā, Dhul Khalaṣa, al-Fals, al-Jalsad, Sa'd. Wellhausen, *Reste*, mentions others and gives details, being dependent on Ibn al-Kalbī's *Kitāb al-aṣnām* ('Book of idols'). At al-Marwa and al-Ṣafā (→ Pilgrimage) were two idols, Iṣāf and Nā'ila. These were removed, but the → Black Stone, still an object of respect, is the one relic of idolatry left, but is no longer object of worship. The word *ṣanam* is used of a sculptured object of worship and *wathan* of something in nature of picture. Stones (*anṣāb*) were a common feature of pre-Islamic relig. Sanctuaries of objects of worship were within a sacred area (*ḥimā*) and had attendants (*sādin*, pl. *sadana*), usually hereditary. Worship consisted of circumambulation naked (→ Nudity, ritual), and sacrifice of animals whose blood was smeared on the stones. Sanctuaries had their special seasons for visiting. The Qur. says that idols can neither harm nor help (e.g. xxv, 3f.). The word al-Tāghūt occurs in xvi:38; xxxix:19, seemingly as gen. term for idols, or meaning idolatry. J.R.

E.I., III, p. 967 (nuṣb), IV, p. 147 (ṣanam); Hughes, pp. 190–2; Wellhausen, *Reste*, pp. 14ff.; Guillaume, *Life*, pp. 35ff. and index (idols); O'Leary, *Arabia*, pp. 193ff.

Ignatius, St. (*c.* 35–107) Bp. of Antioch: little is known of his life beyond martyrdom in Rome. *En route* for Rome, I. wrote letters, which have survived, to Churches of Ephesus, Magnesia, Tralles, Rome, Philadelphia, and Smyrna, and to Polycarp, Bp. of Smyrna. Besides their personal interest, these letters provide valuable information about contemporary Chr. faith and practice, and its reaction to → Docetism. S.G.F.B.

J. B. Lightfoot–J. R. Harmer, *The Apostolic Fathers* (1891), pp. 165ff. (text and trans.); B. H. Streeter, *The Primitive Church* (1929), pp. 163ff.; *R.G.G.*[3], III, col. 665–7; P. Carrington, *The Early Christian Church* (1957), I, ch. 24; H. Lietzmann, *Geschichte der Alten Kirche*, I (1937), ch. 13.

Ignorance (in Buddh. thought) → *Avidya*. T.O.L.

Iḥrām The pilgrim's dress and his state while wearing it. It consists of two seamless cloths, one (*izār*) wrapped round waist and reaching below knees, the other (*ridā'*) over left shoulder and tied at right side. Women wear long robes down to feet; while it is not necessary to veil face, some covering is commonly used. At certain places round Mecca pilgrims put on the I. They bathe, pray two → *rak'as*, declare their intention, then don the I. Sandals may be worn. The head is uncovered, but an umbrella may be used. The I. is worn high for both '*umra* and *ḥajj* (→ Pilgrimage). One may express intention of assuming the I. for the '*umra*, or for the '*umra* to be followed at proper date by the *ḥajj*, or for the '*umra* and *ḥajj*.If last form is used, the I. may not be taken off till Pilgrimage is completed. In other two instances, it may be taken off and assumed at proper time at one of the stations for purpose. While wearing the I., a pilgrim may not oil his head, use perfume, shave any part of body, or cut nails, have sexual intercourse with or kiss wife, pluck grass or cut a green tree. But he may kill a noxious animal such as a rat, snake, scorpion, or biting dog. J.R.

E.I., II, pp. 455–7; Pareja, pp. 649–51; *Mishkāt*, pp. 541–3; Burton, *Pilgrimage*, II, pp. 138ff.; Rutter, *Holy Cities*, I, pp. 96ff.; Kamal, *Sacred Journey*, pp. 14ff.

I'jāz A verbal noun from same root as *mu'jiza* (→ miracles), used of the miraculous nature of → Qur., which makes it inimitable. The Qur. makes such a claim for itself: lii:34 challenges unbelievers to produce a discourse like it; xi:16 challenges them to produce ten suras like it; x:38f. say it could not have been devised by anyone but God, and challenge those who say it has been invented by → Muḥammad to produce a sura like it (cf. ii:21); and xvii:90 makes a very strong claim: 'If mankind and jinn united to bring the like of this Qur., they could not bring the like though they should back each other up.' With such Qur. authority, it is not surprising that Muslim theologians should have strongly held the doctrine of I. The word means bafflement, indic. the Qur's uniqueness. It is the supreme miracle. J.R.

Pareja, pp. 615f.; D. B. Macdonald, *Theology*, p. 151; Watt, *Philosophy*, p. 107.

I King → I Ching. D.H.S.

Ikhwān al-Ṣafā' (The Pure—or Sincere—Brethren). An association with → Ismā'īlī views in 4th/10th cent., with its centre in Basra. It has left a compilation of 51 letters in encyclopaedic form, covering matters scientific, philosophical, theological and estoric, addressed to a popular community rather than to the learned. A large portion of their work deals with natural sciences. The letters begin with mathematics and logic, then, in addition to natural sciences, deal with metaphysics, mysticism, astrology and magic. They were readily recognised as heretical, seeming to undermine the → *sharī'a*. They raised difficulties regarding theology without attempting to resolve them, their purpose being the Isma'ili one of raising doubts regarding Islamic doc. and practice. → Ghazali accuses them of misleading the simple by incl. teaching from prophets and mystics along with their own false teaching. The uninitiated approve the truth they recognise, and are led thereby to believe the falsehood also. It is recognised that they were not so scholarly as some West. scholars imagined them to be. They were connected with a movement of underprivileged classes, whom they sought to stir up against the → 'Abbasid Caliphate; they did this by insinuating heretical teaching under guise of philosophy and learning. J.R.

E.I., II, pp. 459f.; *G.A.L.*, I, pp. 236–8; *S.*, I, pp. 379ff.; Levy, *Social Structure*, pp. 471–96; Watt, *Philosophy*, p. 102, *Ghazali* pp. 41f., 53; D. B. Macdonald, *Theology*, index; Pareja, index (Iḫwān); I. R. al-Faruqi, 'On the ethics of the Brethren of Purity', *M.W.*, L (1960), pp. 109ff., 192ff. 252ff.; LI (1961), pp. 18ff.

Image(s) As the 'Venus of Laussel' shows, man has made images of deities from the dawn of culture (→ Cave Art, → Paleolithic Relig.). I. in either plastic or linear form, occur in almost all religs.; even in the two religs. professedly aniconic, → Judaism and → Islam, depictions of sacred events are known, although the deity is not repr. I. of gods served various purposes. The actual cult-image, which was often small and portable (e.g. in Egypt), was regarded as indwelt by deity and was object of daily toilet and feeding rituals; it was carried in procession to visit temples of other deities. I. also serve as objects of pious veneration and to focus and inspire devotion of faithful (e.g. in anc. Greece and Rome, Cath. Christianity, Hinduism, Buddhism). In some religs., I. of saints and supernatural beings other than deities are also venerated (e.g. of Virgin →→ Mary; saints, and angels in Cath. Christianity; → bodhisattvas in Buddhism; → Taoist genii in China). Another type of I. existed in anc. Egypt, where → funerary rites required I. of deceased for his → *ka* to inhabit in the tomb. I. have often been regarded as endowed with miraculous powers (e.g. and I. of Egypt. god → Khons was sent to heal a princess of Baktun). I. were sometimes manipulated by priests to seem miraculous (e.g. the 'Rood of Boxley', exposed in London during Reformation). The Reformers gen. abolished I., although the crucifix continued to be used in Lutheran churches. (→→ Art; Icon). S.G.F.B.

E.R.E., VII, pp. 110–60; *H.D.B.*², pp. 412–3; G. Van der Leeuw, *La religion* (1948), pp. 441ff.; E. Mâle, *Religious Art* (1949); A. de Ridder-W. Deonna, *L'art en Grèce* (1924), pp. 60ff.; *Bilderatlas, passim; R.G.G.*³, I, col. 1268–76; *R.A.C.*, II, col. 287–41; *R.Ae.R-G.*, pp. 118–20; J. Leveen, *The Hebrew Bible in Art* (1944); *D.C.C.*, *s.v.;* F. Sierksma, *The Gods as We Shape Them* (E.T. 1960); A. Malraux, *The Metamorphosis of the Gods* (E.T. 1960); J. Gairdner, *The English Church in 16th Cent.* (1902), pp. 199, 253; E. Bevan, *Holy Images* (1940); H. Zimmer, *Myths and Symbols in Indian Art and Civilisation* (1962); A. Grabar, *Beginnings of Christ. Art* (E.T. 1967); *Christ. Iconography* (1968).

(Buddh.) → *Buddha-Rūpa.* T.O.L.

(China–Japan) → Idolatry. D.H.S.

(Hindu) Early Vedic relig. did not use temples or sculptured representations of the gods, although the → Indus Valley civilisation has left seals and statuettes of relig. significance. In Hinduism, images and buildings to house them belong to the classical, post-Upanisadic period, though no actual temple remains antedate the Gupta dynasty (4th cent. CE onwards). An image, acc. to the trad. account is an *arcā* or icon of the God. Once it is consecrated acc. to prescribed ritual, the god takes up his abode in it: i.e. he is 'specially present' in it (though he may be present elsewhere and indeed may be omnipresent). The elaborateness of many sculptures is due to the complex iconography of gestures (→ *mudras*), which comprise a visual language for the worshipper. It is common to treat images in a very human way; the god is aroused in the morning, washed, dressed, fed, etc. Though the most import. images reside in the inner sancta of temples, for some festival processions, etc., elaborate clay images are made, later to be broken up and thrown away. Some relig. teachers, notably → Kabīr, have attacked use of images from within the Hindu trad.; but the main response to Muslim, Christ. and other imputations of idolatry is that images are iconic representations of God and spiritual forces, so that it is not the images themselves which are worshipped. N.S.

S. Kramrisch, *The Art of India through the Ages* (1954); H. Zimmer, *Myths and Symbols in Indian Art and Civilization* (1946); J. N. Banerjea, *The Development of Hindu Iconography* (1956).

Imām (Leader). Used of person who leads others in worship, whether in mosque or elsewhere. This is not a priestly office, for anyone who is adult, of sound mind and good character may lead. When a number of people pray together, one of them should act as I. In mosques it is convenient to have a spec. appointed I., but this gives him no spiritual authority.

The → Shi'a party call their head I. They hold there must be an I, who is a descendant of Muhammad through his daughter → Fāṭima. This I. is held to be faultless. The Shi'a divided into two main groups, the Twelvers and the Seveners, acc. to number of I.'s they recognised, → 'Alī b. Abū Ṭālib being the first. There were other subsidiary groups. The main body is the Twelvers (→ Shi'a), much more numerous than the Seveners (→ Ismā'īlīs). The imams are:

1. 'Alī, d. 40/661

2. -Ḥasan, d. 49/669

3. -Husayn, d. 61/680.
4. 'Alī Zayn al-'Ābidīn, d. 93/712.
5. Muḥammad al-Bāqir, d. 113/731.
6. Ja'far al-Ṣādiq, d. 148/765.

7. Ismā'īl d. not long before 148/765
   Muḥammad

7. Mūsā al-Kāẓim, d. 183/799
8. 'Alī al-Riḍā, d. 203/818
9. Muḥammad al-Jawād, d. 220/835
10. 'Alī al-Hādī, d. 254/868
11. -Ḥasan al-'Askarī, d. 260/874
12. Muḥammad al-Muntaẓar, disappeared *c.* 264/878

The Seveners held that Isma'il, oldest son of Ja'far al-Sadiq, was 7th I., having been appointed by his father, who deposed him because of drunkenness. This deposition is unlawful in the eyes of Seveners, for a second son, as Mūsā was, cannot take place of older brother. They also reject statement that Isma'il died before his father, and so was unable to carry on succession. But whether or not he did die before his father, his son Muḥammad is given rank of a prophet. But Isma'il is held to be the 7th imam, and last of series. He is still guiding his followers. The Twelvers, commonly called Imāmīs, hold that the 12th I., called al-Muntaẓar (the expected one) is still alive and guiding affairs. In due time he will return. In mod. times the Parliament in Iran was stated to have been estab. under auspices of the hidden I.

I. is also applied, esp. in Pakistan and India, to great scholars, e.g. Imām Mālik, Imām al-Shāfi'ī, etc. J.R.

E.I., II, pp. 473f.; Hughes, pp. 203f.; Pareja, pp. 832ff.; D. B. Macdonald, *Theology*, index; Miller, *Bāb*, Section VI.

Imbe A hereditary corporation of Jap. → Shinto priests. Their chief business was to prepare sacrificial offerings, and, as their name implies (*imi*—avoidance, abstinence), they had to avoid all sources of impurity in doing so. They also prepared the foundations and wood for Shinto shrines. Though neither celibate nor vegetarian, they gave scrupulous attention to ritual purity. D.H.S.

W. G. Aston, *Shinto* (1905), p. 202.

Imhotep Vizier of king Zoser (*c.* 2800 BC) and prob. architect of Step Pyramid (→ Pyramids). In later ages, I. was deified as a healing-god. His cult became very popular; he was called Imuthes by the Greeks, who identified him with Asklepios (→ Aesculapius). Statues of I. show him seated, with open scroll. S.G.F.B.

R.Ae.R-G., pp. 322–4; J. B. Hurry, *Imhotep* (1926); R. C. Grant, *Hellenistic Religions* (1953), pp. 124ff.

Immaculate Conception of Virgin Mary The belief that the V.-M. had, by divine grace, been kept free from → sin from moment of her conception developed inevitably from her status as *Theotokos*

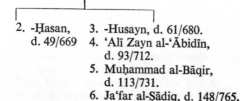

('God-bearer') and from doc. of → Original Sin. The latter made doc. of I.-C. inevitable, because, even if she had committed no actual sin, Mary would have inherited Orig. Sin at her conception —a situation deemed incompatible with her bearing the Son of God. The belief, for many cents. unofficial, was finally made a dogma by Papal decree in 1854. The Feast of the I.-C. is on 8 Dec. S.G.F.B.

D.C.C., *s.v.; E.R.E.*, VI, *s.v.;* E. D. O'Connor (ed.), *The Dogma of the Immaculate Conception* (1958).

Immolation (Buddh.) → Self-immolation, Buddh. T.O.L.

Immortality The term, without qualification, is imprecise. Deathlessness, or immunity to dying, may apply to the whole person, body and soul, or to some part only, e.g. the soul, however that entity may be defined. Belief in some form of survival of physical death is prob. instinctive in man: → funerary-rites attest it from dawn of culture. But the nature of *post-mortem* existence depends on view of human nature held: if body is regarded as essential to full life, as in many docs. of → Man, such *p.m.* existence is not I., but a kind of miserable half-life, unless amended by ultimate → resurrection of body (as →→ in Judaism, Christianity, and Islam). The anc. Egyptians believed that the whole psycho-physical organism could be magically resuscitated and made immortal. Where the → soul is evaluated as the inner essential self, independent of body, I. means immunity of soul from death. Such a conception of soul has gen. found expression in belief in → metempsychosis, as, e.g., in → Hinduism and → Orphism. Belief in I. is then based on intrinsic nature of soul. (→ Plato). S.G.F.B.

C. J. Bleeker (ed.), *Anthropologie religieuse* (1955); J. G. Frazer, *The Belief in Immortality and the Worship of the Dead* (1913); Brandon, *M.D.;* G. Van der Leeuw, *La Religion* (1949), pp. 302ff.; M. Guilmont, *R.H.R.*, 165 (1964), pp. 145ff.; 166 (1964), pp. 1ff.

(Buddh.) In Buddh. though I. or the death-less state is nirvāṇa (→ Nibbāna). One of the adjectives applied to nirvāna from earliest days is *amata*, i.e. deathless, (e.g. *Sutta Nipāta* 960). The deathless realm is considered to be gained not at end of one human individual's span of existence, but as result of spiritual refinement which may be continued throughout many generations; it is held to be outcome of process of moral and spiritual refinement initiated and pursued by free choice of the human will, when once possibility of such a goal has been heard of, through the Buddha-Dhamma.

A modification of this view occurs in the → Pure Land Buddhism of China and Japan, where an intermediate goal is introduced, attainable without long preparation through many existences necessary for nirvāna. This short-term relig. goal is rebirth in heaven of the → Bodhisattva, known as the Pure Land or Paradise. Such rebirth is made poss. by compassion, grace and spiritual power of the Bodhisattva and faith of believer. Strictly, however, this is not I., in that even such blissful rebirth must be followed by further rebirth, as human, before the ultimate goal, i.e., the absolute deathlessness of nirvāna, is reached. T.O.L.

(Chinese) In pre-Confucian China, belief in personal survival after death, at least in the case of kings and nobles, is well attested by anc. literary records (→ *Shu Ching* and *Shih Ching*), in which there are constant ref. to power and influence of deceased ancestors, who dwell on high with *Shang Ti*, and come down to receive sacrifices and oblations, having power to bless their descendants. The oldest and most persistent element in Chi. relig. is that of → Ancestor-worship, which, at least for majority of Chinese, implies belief that ancestor-spirits live on as intelligent and rational beings.

Belief in I. was greatly reinforced by intro. of → Buddhism into China, and popular Chi. interpretation of Buddh. theory of rebirth. The Chi. Buddh. belief in a soul, which does not perish at death, is actually a distortion of true Buddh. view, which denies existence of an enduring entity or soul. The vast mythological structures of Buddhism and relig. → Taoism, as they developed in China with their numerous heavens and hells, are based firmly on belief in personal survival and immortality of soul.

In gen., Chin. philosophers, both Confucian and Taoist, have been agnostic as regards an after-life. Man was thought of as a coalescence of vital forces, and his life ended with their dispersal at death, when his personality ceased to exist. What comes after death is unknown and unknowable. This life, and this life only, is what matters. From time of → Hsün-tzŭ onwards many Chi. thinkers completely rejected concept of I. of soul after death. The only I. they recognised was perpetuation of personality in and through one's descendants, and the enduring fame of those whose virtue, great deeds and teachings were kept alive in remembrance of countless generations. D.H.S.

Fung Yu-lan, *Hist. of Chinese Philos.*, vol. 1 (1937), pp. 344ff.; vol. 2 (1953), pp. 284ff.

(Japanese) → Dead, State of (Japanese). D.H.S.

Immortals, Taoist → *Hsien*. D.H.S.

Impassibility of God Grk. metaphysics required that the divine nature, being eternal and perfect, could not suffer in any form, since suffering logically implied change and imperfection. Early

Chr. theologians, educated in Grk. metaphysics, accepted the principle of God's I., which resulted in a continuing tension in Chr. theology between the Heb. and Grk. trads. of God, the former being anthropomorphic. The relat. of the suffering Christ to God the Father was also a problem. S.G.F.B.

J. K. Mozley, *The Impassibility of God* (1928); *D.C.C., s.v.*

Inari → Shinto god of rice, also called Uga-no-mitama, ('the god of food and fertility'). One of most universally popular of Jap. gods, whose shrines are found in every village and in many private houses. Gen. recognised as identical with goddess Uke-mochi (the food possessor). Though primarily worshipped as giver of agricultural prosperity, I. is conceived of as a general providence, appealed to to restore stolen property, avoid pestilence, give wealth and prosperity, unite friends. In one place he is patron of swordsmiths. The fox is his servant and messenger. His → shintai is usually a round stone. The year CE 711 seems to have been main starting-point of I. cult. Four main peculiarities distinguish I. temples: (1) they are painted bright red, whereas most Shinto temples are unpainted; (2) they are accompanied by long rows of → torii, also painted red with top beam and base of pillars black; (3) numerous small and large statues of foxes are in evidence; (3) a special pear-shaped emblem known as *hoju-no-tama* is a feature of them. D.H.S.

J. Herbert, *Shinto* (1967), pp. 504ff.

Inca Religion The word Inca in this article refers to the Inca people. The head of the state is called ruler or Emperor. The Incas came at end of a long series of prehistoric Peruvian cultures; in relig., as in much else, they doubtless owed a good deal to their predecessors. In absence of any aboriginal system of writing, it is not poss. to go very far in distinguishing between strictly I. relig. elements and those which they absorbed from others; but it is known that they removed the most import. idols of conquered peoples to Cuzco, together with priests to tend them and though the intention was primarily political, it must have affected relig. The renowned sanctuary of Pachacámac, on the coast near Lima, was an exception because the I. left it in place; but they set up a Sun temple on a hill alongside it, which dominated it and so brought it into their system. The relig. discussed here is that of the Imperial Inca Period, starting when the I. conquests began *c.* CE 1440. Much of what is known of I. relig. comes from Spanish sources of 16th and even 17th cent. An excellent summary based on these and on archaeological indications is given by J. H. Rowe in his account of I. culture in the *Handbook of South American Indians*. Many features of I. relig. showed an extraordinary capacity for survival in the face of efforts to stamp out idolatry; the Spaniards consequently studied them extensively. Rowe concludes from a study of these sources that relig. was more concerned with ritual and organisation than with mysticism and spirituality, and that its chief interests were the food supply and curing. This impression may have been accentuated by the probability that such aspects were the most likely to survive and to be detected by the Spaniards; but it is doubtless essentially true.

Supernatural Beings: at time of Spanish conquest the I. worshipped a → high god, creator of all other gods and living things, who had no name but was known by a series of titles, of which that gen. used was WIRAQOCA (gen. Hispanicised into Viracocha). Though repr. by a golden idol in human form, he was somewhat withdrawn and was thought to have delegated his authority very largely to his many deputies. Some authorities believe that his cult was on the increase in Imperial I. times, and that Pachacuti, who reigned from 1438 to 1471, had a special devotion to him; but his worship was confined to the topmost ranks of society and the idea was too subtle for the mass of the people. Since he was the source of all power, it was not thought necessary to assign lands or special temples to him. Nevertheless prayers to a lesser deity or a *huaca* were generally prefaced by one to Viracocha. After Viracocha came the heavenly bodies, the Sun, Thunder, Moon, Stars, then Mother Earth and Mother Sea. Besides his importance as the ripener and protector of the crops, the Sun was the ancestor and personal god of the ruling I. family. His idol was a golden disc with rays surrounding a face. He shared his temple in Cuzco and probably elsewhere with the male Thunder- or Weather-god, the Moon-goddess by whom the ceremonial calendar was regulated, and the Stars, some of whom watched over partic. human activities and also the flocks and certain wild animals. Mother Sea was worshipped by coastal fishermen, but had little importance to highland Indians. In addition there were multitudes of *huacas*, things and places regarded as holy in varying degrees, many of which were of merely local importance. Mountains, rocks, mummies of the dead (espec. dead rulers), tombs, springs, stones and bridges are examples. Particular places were regarded as dwellings of natural powers, e.g. a palace doorway in Cuzco was worshipped as home of the wind. Cuzco itself was holy, and there were shrines at places where it first came in sight along the roads. A very important *huaca* was a natural spindle-shaped stone, thought to be Ayar Oco, one of the brothers of Manco, legendary founder of

Cuzco. He turned himself to stone on the sacred hill of Huanacauri, where import. ceremonies took place each year. The arrangement of terraces faced with fine masonry and stone channels carrying water along them at Tampu Macchai, not far from Cuzco, was doubtless a *huaca* where water was worshipped. Men still put stones, coca-quids and other small offerings on piles of stones, a special form of *huaca* called *apacita,* which mark the summits of passes and other import. places on roads—a remarkable survival of anc. usage. Some *huacas* were small and portable. There were stone figures of men and animals, some of which were natural objects slightly 'improved', corn bobs and other vegetables, stones of unusual appearance and bezoar stones. Small, beautifully carved stone alpacas with a cylindrical hole in back are frequently found buried in fields near Cuzco. Mod. pottery versions, used in ceremonies to promote fertility of Alpacas, can still be brought in Cuzco market; the old examples doubtless had the same use. Gods and *huacas,* of whatever degree, were worshipped for benefits which might be gained from them. Neglect of obligations of worship or positive sin might lead to loss of their protection, or to bad luck. There were evil spirits also, but little is known about them; they were feared but not gen. worshipped, because they were thought to be incapable of doing any good.

Temples and shrines: ceremonies were gen. held in open air, and temples were meant chiefly for storage of images and ceremonial paraphernalia and as quarters for priests and the Chosen Women. The best example is the Temple of the Sun, the Corcancha or Golden Enclosure, at Cuzco, which also served various celestial bodies. It consisted of a series of rooms enclosing a court, some of which survive in the Dominican convent. The largest room, which occupied one side, was the hall of the Sun; after Span. Conquest, this apparently served at first as the Dominican church, but it disappeared when present church was built. Some surviving rooms have been tentatively identified as halls of the Thunder, the Stars and the Rainbow, but that of the Moon has gone. All were built of finest I. masonry, and the walls were adorned with plates of gold; they were roofed after the I. manner with thatch worked into elaborate patterns. The whole followed an ordinary domestic plan; it has been justly described as a dwelling of the gods patterned after the dwellings of men. When ceremonies were held in the great square of the city, or one of the smaller squares near temple, the cult objects and mummies of deceased rulers were brought out, to take part or at least to be present. Most *huacas* were in the open, and ceremonies of varying degrees of elaboration were carried out near them. A good example, not far from Cuzco, is a large pointed natural limestone rock called Kenco, which rises from a rectangular stone-faced terrace built round its base; this is the focus of an impressive amphitheatre enclosed by a low crenellated wall of I. masonry. It would make a magnificent setting for ceremonies before the rock, which must have been one of the more import. *huacas.*

Priests and attendants were of many types and grades. At their head was a high priest, the Wilya-Oma, gen. a close relation of ruler and a most import. official. Below him was a graded hierarchy corresponding roughly to that of the gov. officials, which cared for the official 'Sun Temples'. These were maintained from the produce of lands assigned to 'the Sun' or official relig. (lands were, in theory at least, divided into three parts, one for the Inca or government, one for relig., and one for the people; but the three were not necessarily equal). Such shrines were also served by a number of Mama-kona, selected from among the Chosen Women. The latter were picked for their beauty and freedom from blemish from various communities when young girls; some were later taken as concubines by Emperor or given as wives to nobles or successful warriors, and some, the Mama-kona, set aside in perpetual chastity for service of temples, where they wove fine textiles for priests and images and brewed chicha for ceremonies. Some were designated for sacrifice in serious emergencies such as illness or death of Emperor; it is prob. that a number of richly-dressed women found in a cemetery at Pachacámac, killed by strangulation, belonged to this class. The Mama-kona were under rule of a high priestess of noble birth who was regarded as wife of the Sun. Priests not only tended the shrines, but made sacrifices, divined in various ways, heard confessions, were curers and practised magic. It seems that some were specialists in one or other of these functions, but to what extent this was so is not clear. Those of the lower orders only spent part of their time at the shrines; when not on duty, they lived in their own villages and were not supported from lands dedicated to relig. Local shrines, which were not part of official cult, were served by at least one priest, an old man past working in the fields, and were supported by local families.

Worship: there was a regular round of public ceremonies linked with the 12 lunar months of agricultural year; but it is not known how this was brought into accord with solar year, which is about 11 days longer. There were four stone towers built in a row on the horizon both east and west of Cuzco, which marked rising and setting of sun at the times when sowing or various crops should begin; it is poss. that a similar tower marked sunrise at beginning of year, in which case it could have served as means of correcting the lunar year. The towers were observed from a platform in centre of great square at Cuzco. The four world directions, so familiar in Middle → American relig., had no place here; the only ceremonial directions were east and west because of rising and setting of sun. As well as ceremonies connected with the months, there were others daily and special for particular needs and emergencies, such as droughts, earthquakes, and illness, death or succession of Emperors. All these include sacrifice, dancing, recitation and drinking of much *chicha*, a maize beer.

Sacrifice: sacrifices were offered both by official priesthood and individuals. The things most frequently sacrificed were llamas and guinea pigs; llamas of a given colour were gen. offered to particular gods, thus brown ones were sacrificed to Viracocha and white on many occasions to the Sun. They were led round image of the god, and their throats cut after saying of a set form of words. Human victims, gen. children of Chosen Women, were reserved for times of serious crisis; they were led round image, and killed by strangling, cutting their throats or removing their hearts. The idol, or mummy-bundle of a dead ruler, was then anointed with victim's blood by drawing a line across face or by rubbing it all over. Some victims, esp. older children, were made drunk before being sacrificed. Fine textiles were offered by being burnt, as was food such as maize flour, llama fat, or the narcotic coca leaf. Chicha was poured on ground. Sea shells, whole, cut into pieces or powdered, were offered to springs. A good example is given by the daily morning sacrifice at Cuzco, which consisted of lighting at sunrise a fire of specially prepared wood, into which food was thrown with prayer to the Sun, followed by sacrifice of a llama and some coca. The priests ate the surplus food, which was also the gen. practice when individuals offered sacrifice to a *huaca*. Official sacrifices to Viracocha were not made directly by Emperor; but were offered through various *huacas* from their own resources, assigned to them from the 'church' lands and llama flocks.

Prayer: the normal position denoting reverence for god, *huaca* or Emperor, was to stand bowed from hips with arms extended forwards and hands open and slightly above level of head. After making a clicking sound with lips, the devotee kissed his finger tips. When worshipping the high gods, Viracocha, the Sun or the Thunder, he also held a switch. Prayers could be silent or aloud, and private ones were gen. extempore, but there were set forms for public ceremonies. The following is an example of a prayer said to have been addressed to Viracocha by an Emperor; it was recorded by Molina and was prob. set enough in its form to be regarded as one of the latter type.

> O conquering Viracocha!
> Ever-present Viracocha!
> Thou who art without equal upon the earth!
> Thou who art from the beginnings of the world until its end!
> Thou gavest life and valour to men, saying,
> 'Let this be a man'
> And to the woman saying
> 'Let this be a woman'.
> Thou madest them and gavest them being.
> Watch over them, that they may live in health and in peace.
> Thou who art in the high heaven,
> and among the clouds of the tempest,
> grant them long life,
> and accept this our sacrifice
> O Creator.

A common brief prayer to the Sun was:

> May you never grow old; may you ever remain young;
> may you rise every day illuminating the earth!

Sin and Confession: what was regarded as sin varied acc. to social degree of sinner; what was sin to a commoner might be permitted to a noble. To take an exteme case, murder and stealing, grave sins for the commoner, were as nothing for the Emperor, who was above the law. Purification was necessary before taking part in relig. ceremonies; this was achieved by confession and penance. Sin was also dangerous, since displeasure of the gods brought misfortune in this life and danger of banishment to inside of earth, where the sinner suffered cold and hunger after death. The righteous, and the nobility whatever their character, went to live with the Sun in the Upper World, where they had abundant food and drink and like pleasure of this life. Members of royal family confessed secretly to the Sun and subsequently bathed in a river, which was asked to carry their sins away. Others confessed to priests who were also diviners; they were bound to confess all their sins of deed or word, but some sources say that thoughts were not sinful. It is said that confessors were bound to secrecy, but it may be permitted to speculate whether this was not a reflexion of Catholic practice. The confessors employed divination to determine whether all had been confessed; if he believed that it had not, he hit the sinner on back with a stone and made him repeat the confession. Penance might take form of fasting, or prayer at the *huaca* which the confessor served, and was completed by washing in running water. It was apparently liable to be more severe for a poor man who could not pay the confessor. (→ Confession). Fasting was of varying degrees of severity, a light form being abstinence from salt and chile pepper; more severe forms including denial of meat, chicha or sexual intercourse (→ Abstinence).

Divination was used for a wide variety of purposes, from consulting the gods before taking import. decisions to diagnosing a disease or finding lost property. It took many forms. *Huacas* were consulted through their priests like oracles: the diviner, removing lungs of a sacrificed llama, blew into a vein and interpreted resulting marks on lung; on less import. occasions the same was done with a guinea pig; piles of beans, pebbles, maize kernels, etc., were also counted, the answer depending on whether number was odd or even. → Dreams, rainbows, appearance of a fire, and many other things gave good or bad auguries. A very import. method, sometimes done in presence of Emperor himself, with fasting and sacrifices, was to make a fire in two contiguous braziers, blow it up with a metal tube, invoke the spirits and listen for voices coming from the fires, prob. by ventriloquism on part of operator (→ Divination).

Injury, Disease and Curing: injuries and diseases were attr. to supernatural causes, and cured by relig. and magical means. To take but one example: injuries such as broken bones arose from anger of spirit of place where they happened, to which the curer made a series of sacrifices as part of cure. The curers, who were generally diviners also, derived their power from a vision or by having made an abnormally quick recovery from serious illness. Many plants, used in curing, were used for magical rather than physiological reasons; other substances such as maize flour and guinea pig fat were utilised. Their use still survives. When summoned to cure a sick person, the curer offered sacrifice to his vision, and divined the cause of illness. If this was, e.g., the anger of his ancestors, the sick man was ordered to put food on their tombs and offer some chicha. There were many varieties of this sort of cure; but all finished with washing, either in house, or, if the man was well enough, at junction of two rivers. If the curer thought that the sickness was caused by a foreign object in body, the essence of the cure was to suck part affected and then to produce some object such as a stone, worms, a toad, or bits of straw, blaming them for the pain.

Public Ceremonies: only a few features of ceremonies assoc. with the months can be mentioned. The months were matched very approx. with solar ones by Span. writers; the correlation will serve to show the time of year at which events took place. Names of months will be given in the usual hispanicised form. The year began with Capac Raymi, (December). There were coming-of-age ceremonies for boys of royal lineages who received their breech clouts and ear-ornaments, besides ceremonies showing interest of the Sun and other gods in I. state. During this time (about 3 weeks), all provincials had to leave the ceremonial centre of Cuzco. In Camay, (January), the same boys had a ceremonial battle in great square at Cuzco on day of new moon. Llamas, for sacrifice in next year's coming-of-age ceremonies, were consecrated. Dances were held at full moon, incl. one in which dancers carried a thick woollen rope of four colours. The ground-up bones of previous year's sacrifices were mixed with coca, flowers, various condiments and chicha, and thrown into river to be carried to Viracocha. In Ayrihua (April), in a ceremony in honour of the royal insignia, a perfect white llama, symbol of royal authority, was brought out into the plaza dressed in a red garment with golden ear-ornaments. It had been taught to eat coca and drink chicha; llamas were sacrificed in its name, and it sacrificed chicha daily by kicking over jars of it. It took part in many ceremonies, was kept until it died naturally, and was then replaced. A cast-silver llama, about 9½ inches high, with inlaid patch of red resin like a saddle cloth (restored), in the American Museum of Natural History, prob. represents this animal. The maize harvest was celebrated in Aymoray (May), when many llamas were sacrificed. Boys, who had come of age in Dec., harvested the maize crop from a sacred field, and nobles dug it over ceremonially with *tacllas* or foot ploughs. In Chahuahuarquis (July), sacrifices were offered to the *huaca* which governed the irrigation system of Cuzco valley; in Yapaquis (August), the sacred field was planted afresh with maize, and a thousand guinea pigs, sent from provinces, were sacrificed to Frost, Air, Water and Sun. In Situa (September), there was a festival against sickness, liable to arise from change of weather accompanying the first light rains. Persons with physical defects and dogs were sent out of city, and the people watched for new moon from near Temple of the Sun. When they saw it they shouted an injunction to sickness, misfortune and disaster to get out of the land, after which they shook their clothes from the doors of their houses to remove any evil. Four groups of runners, dressed as warriors, ran out along four main roads, passing the cry to others, who finally bathed themselves and their weapons in rivers, which carried the evil away. After further ceremonies, the *huacas* of conquered tribes, in Cuzco, were carried into great square to do homage to Emperor. In Cantarayquis (October), there were ceremonies to bring rain for crops, which had mostly been sown in last two months. G.H.S.B.

Betanzos, Juan de, *Suma y narración de los Incas*, ed. Marcos Jiménez de la Espada, Biblioteca Hispano-Ultramarina, vol. 5 (1880); Cieza de León, Pedro de, *Segunda parte de la crónica del Perú, que trata del senorío de los Incas Yupanquis y de sus grandes hechos y gobernación*, Book 2, chs. 27–30, ed. Marcos Jiménez de Espada, Biblioteca Hispano-Ultramarina, vol. 5 (1880); Cobo, Bernabé, *Historia del Nuevo Mundo*, Book 13; ed. Marcos Jiménez de Espada, Sociedad de bibliófilos andaluces, 4 vols. (1890–5); Means, P. A., *Ancient Civilizations of the Andes* (1931); Molina (of Cuzco), Cristobal de, *Relación de las fábulas y ritos de los Incas*, ed. T. Thayer Ojeda, *Revista Chilena de Historia y Geografía*, vol. 5, pp. 117–90 (1913); (also a translation by C. R. Markham in *Rites and Laws of the Incas*, pp. 1–64, Hakluyt Society, London, 1873); Polo de Ondegardo, Juan, *Los errores y supersticiones de los indios, sacadas de tratado y averiguación que hizo el Licenciado Polo*, ed. H. H. Urteagada–C. A. Romero. Coleccion de Libros y Documentos referentes á la historia del Peru, 1st series, vol. 3, pp. 1–43 (1916); Rowe J. H., *Inca Culture at the time of the Spanish Conquest. Religion. Handbook of South American Indians*, vol. 2, pp. 293–314, ed. J. H. Steward. Smithsonian Institution (1946).

Incarnation *Ex.* Lat. *in carne*, 'in flesh'. In relig. phenomenology, I. is of two kinds: the assuming of a physical body by (1) a deity; (2) a → soul. There are many instances of (1): in anc. Egypt it was thought that → Amun incarnated himself in the pharaoh for coition with queen, to produce heir to throne; Grk. and Hindu mythology tells of I. of gods in human or animal forms for specific purposes (e.g. → Zeus as swan to seduce Leda; → Vishnu as a charioteer in → *Bhagavad Gita*); the I. of Second Person of → Trinity as → Jesus of Nazareth for man's salvation is basic tenet of Christianity. (2) → metempsychosis involves I. of pre-existent and immortal souls in successive bodies, human and animal, and even in inanimate substances. The I. of Christ has distinction of being permanent; for acc. to doc. of → Ascension, Christ returned to heaven in incarnated form. (→ Avatāra). S.G.F.B.

E.R.E., VII, pp. 183–201; A. M. Blackman, *Luxor and its Temples* (1923), pp. 68, 163ff.; *D.C.C.*, *s.v.*, *R.G.G.*[3], III, col. 753–5; Harnack, *H.D.*, *passim; H.D.B.*[2], *s.v.*

(China–Japan) In Chi. and Jap. religs. it is impossible to draw a hard and fast line between divine and human spheres. Humans are sometimes regarded as gods and worshipped with divine honours (e.g. the Mikado). Many humans are elevated to become minor deities. On other hand, gods are deemed to take up temporary possession of certain human beings. Such 'god-possessed' ones were the founders of Shinto sects of →→ Kurozumi-kyō and Tenri-kyō. In Mahāyāna → Buddhism of China and Japan, Buddhas and → bodhisattvas often appeared and lived in human form, and were deemed capable of assuming human form at will. There are numerous stories of supernatural conceptions and births. But I., as it is understood in Chr. theology, is unknown in Chi. and Jap. relig. thought, and when Chr. missionaries intro. idea of Supreme God becoming incarnate in Jesus Christ, the idea appeared to literate Chinese as an incredible superstition. D.H.S.

Incense The burning of aromatic substances in worship is a widespread custom of great antiquity. It seems to have two motives: that pleasant odours were naturally pleasing to gods, and that rising smoke naturally suggested ascent to heaven. That the gods also appreciated the 'sweet savour' of sacrifice is mentioned in both Mesopot. and Heb. lit. Methods of using I. have been various: e.g. in curious arm-shaped censers of anc. Egypt; by casting on altars acc. to Grk. and Rom. custom; in swinging thuribles in Christ. worship. Christians who apostatised during Rom. → persecutions were called *thurificati*, for casting I. on a pagan altar as a ritual act. The use of I. in mortuary rituals (e.g. in Egypt and Christianity) is prob. purificatory. (→ Absolutions of Dead). S.G.F.B.

E.R.E., VII, *s.v.; R.Ae.R-G.*, pp. 624–6; *H.D.B.*[2], *s.v.; D.C.C., s.v.;* L. Duchesne, *Christian Worship*[1], (E.T. 1927), *passim.*

(China) I. is extensively used in both public and private cults. It is burned before the ancestral tablets and the household gods, in the daily worship offered in temples, in almost all festivals and processions. In Buddh. monasteries periods of meditation are marked by burning down of incense sticks. I. plays import. part in ceremonies connected with birth and death. D.H.S.

E.R.E., VII, pp. 204–5; K. L. Reichelt, *Truth and Tradition . . .* (1927), pp. 279ff., 294–5.

(Japan) There is no evidence in early → Shinto records of use of I., but after intro. of → Buddhism, I. came to be commonly used at Buddh. and Shinto ceremonies. The elaborate ceremony known as 'incense-sniffing' was from about CE 1500 enthusiastically taken up by the aristocracy, but seems to have had only aesthetic and not relig. significance. D.H.S.

B. H. Chamberlain. *Things Japanese*, 5th edn. (1905), p. 245.

Incubation Term used for practice current among several anc. peoples, but preeminently among the Greeks, of passing night in temple in order to receive a divine revelation or healing (→ Aesculapius). S.G.F.B.

E.R.E., VII, *s.v.; R.Ae.R-G.*, pp. 837–8; *R.G.G.*³, III, col. 755–6; *O.C.D.*, *s.v.; S.O.*, II (1959): *Les songes et leur interpretatien, passim.*

Index Librorum Prohibitorum (Lat. 'List of prohibited books'): In 1557 the Congregation of the → Inquisition first issued an Index of books which → R.C.'s must not read or possess as being contrary to faith or morals. The issue of such lists continued: an 'Index Expurgatorius' is also publ. of books expurgated of undesirable passages. Considerable modification of such censorship has resulted from → Vatican Council II. S.G.F.B.

D.C.C., *s.v.; E.R.E.*, VII, pp. 207–9; *R.G.G.*³, III, 699.

India, Buddhism in → Buddhism: general survey. T.O.L.

(Christianity in) → Christ. Movements in India. N.S.

Indian Religions Extant religions orig. in Indian sub-continent (and excl. tribal cults) are: →→ Hinduism, Buddhism, Jainism and Sikhism. Hinduism is name given complex relig. emerging in post-Upanisadic times, but regarding Vedic scriptures as authoritative, and thus is sometimes contrasted with earlier → Vedic religion (or Vedism); distinction is sometimes made between 'popular' Hinduism and → Brahmanism, the type of cult and belief mediated and continued by → Brahmin class. Buddhism has largely disappeared in Indian sub-continent, save the Himalayas and to some extent in Maharashtra. An early relig. movement, the → Ajivikas, was once influential, but no longer is extant, having disappeared during medieval period. From 11th cent. → Islam penetrated India, and it was interplay between it and Hinduism that gave rise to → Sikkhism. A number of → Zoroastrians settled in W. India after Persia was overrun by Muslims in 8th cent. CE, and formed beginning of the → Parsi community. Since 3rd century CE or perhaps earlier, Christianity has been present in India, among the St. Thomas Christians (→ Christ. Movements in India), but bulk of Indian Christianity dates from Portuguese, British and other European incursions into India (15th cent. onwards). A Jewish community in Malabar is anc. In add. to these faiths, there is a variety of tribal religs. extant in sub-continent. Religs. which have orig. in India have spread beyond it either by export of Indians and Indian culture (e.g. the Hindu kingdoms of South-East Asia: cf. pp. 331ff.) or more directly by missionary endeavours, as with Buddhism. N.S.

A. L. Basham, *The Wonder that was India* (1954); H. Bhattacharyya (ed.), *The Cultural Heritage of India*, vol. 4 (1956); J. M. Mahar, *India: A Critical Bibliography* (1956); C. J. Adams (ed.), *A Reader's Guide to the Great Religions* (1965).

Indo-China (Buddh.) Continental S.E. Asia, the peninsula formerly known as Indo-China, has a predominantly Buddh. culture, and majority of population of countries of region are Buddh. There were two underlying foreign cultural influences (prior to that of West) viz. of India, in west. part of peninsular; of China in east. part. The area of Indian cultural influence is repr. by the mod. states of →→ Burma, Thailand, Cambodia and Laos. The area of Chinese cultural influence is thus considerably smaller, and is confined to → Vietnam. With these two cultural sub-divisions goes differentiation in the types of Buddhism; in W. part the predom. trad. is that of → Theravāda, while in Vietnam it is that of → Mahāyāna, which came into country from China. The Mhy. form existed formerly in other areas of Indo-China, having been intro. there prob. from E. India; from about begin. of 11th cent. CE has been replaced by the Theravāda form. T.O.L.

Indo-Europeans → Aryans. S.G.F.B.

Indonesia (Buddh.) Bhm. had been intro. into Java some time in 1st half of 5th cent. CE. Acc. to Chinese pilgrim → Fa Hsien, who visited island in 418, at that time 'it hardly deserves mentioning'; but, later in same century, it had made much progress as result of work of Buddh. monk from India. In island of Sumatra, Bhm. became import. from latter half of 7th cent., when kings of Srivijaya became its patrons, and Srivijaya became an import. centre of learning in S. Asia, a fact which is testified by Chinese traveller → I-tsing, who visited Sumatra about 671 CE. The form of Bhm. which flourished there appears, from archaeological evidence, to have been → Mahāyana, although Ī-tsing mentions the → Hīnayāna form; this latter could have been of the → Sarvāstivāda school, a form of Hīnayāna not too dissimilar from Mhy. By end of 8th cent. the → Tantric form of Bhm. had spread to these islands from E. India. From the archipelago Mhy. Bhm. spread to Malay peninsula. It enjoyed period of great prosperity from late 8th cent. onwards under the Sailendra dynasty, rulers of a kingdom which incl. the Malay peninsular as well as much of archipelago. There were strong connections between the Sailendra kings and those of E. India; Indian Buddh. scholars appear to have moved back and forth between great centres of learning such as → Nalanda and Vikramasila in India and those of 'Suvarnadvipa', as part of Indonesia was then called. The great symbolic stone structure known as Borobudur in Java is evidence of the importance of Bhm. in island at that period. Gradually, however, the Tantric form of Bhm. was merged in

Brahmanic and Saivite relig., and with coming of Islam, finally disappeared, from Sumatra by end of 14th cent., and from Java early in 15th. T.O.L.

D. G. E. Hall, *A History of South-East Asia* (1955); G. Coedès, *Les États Hindouisés d'Indochine et d'Indonésie*, 3rd edn. (1964); Sir Charles Eliot, *Hinduism and Buddhism* (1921, repr. 1957), vol. III, ch. XL.

→ Islam in Indonesia.

Indra Indra is most import. of Vedic gods: over 250 of hymns of → *Rgveda* are addressed to him. Despite preeminence, the god underwent severe decline in classical Hinduism, though he played import. part in Buddh. mythology (as Śakra/Sakka). Evidence of his displacement by more potent deities is found in the → *Puranas*, where he is rival of → Krishna, by whom he is defeated. I.'s primary sphere of operations was the atmosphere, from whence he sends down rain and wields his thunderbolts. It is he who defeats the dragon Vṛtra and overcomes drought. He is also *par excellence* war-god of the → Aryans; his warfare against the antigods (→ *asuras*) is as effective as his assistance in destruction of the *dasyus*, the dark barbarians conquered by Aryans. Golden in colour, bearded, riding a chariot, boastful, drinker, I. is divine counterpart of Aryan warrior. He is assisted by the stormy → Maruts in chariots. He is also repr. as king of the gods, and theoretically retained this status after being overshadowed by →→ Brahma, Viṣṇu and Siva. His spouse, of no great importance, is Indrāṇī. If → Agni was chief deity for priesthood, I. was chief deity of → *ksatriyas*. N.S.

A. Danielou, *Hindu Polytheism* (1962); A. A. Macdonell, *Vedic Mythology* (1897).

Indriya Term of considerable importance in Buddh. psychology and ethics. Derived from → 'Indra', name of anc. Indian god who was the 'mighty one', 'the ruler', the term denotes 'controlling principle', 'directive force' or 'dominant'. There are many such I.'s, and various classifications and groupings are given, the most usually accepted being that found in the → Abhidhamma book, the *Vibhanga*, which gives a list of 22. First there are the sense-perception 'dominants', eye, ear, nose, tongue, and body; then the mind; femininity and masculinity; vitality; the feelings, bodily pleasure, bodily pain, gladness, sadness, and indifference; after these come the five 'spiritual' dominants, faith, energy, mindfulness, concentration and wisdom (these 5 are also called → *bala*); finally come the 3 'supermundane dominants', viz., (20) the assurance: 'I shall know what I do not know', which comes to the → *sotapana* or one newly entered on Buddh. path; (21) the dominant called 'higher knowledge', which belongs to one who has passed through Sotapana stage; finally (22), the dominant which characterises one who has attained → Arahantship. T.O.L.

Indulgences System operative in → R.C. Church by which temporal punishment in → Purgatory may be remitted by performance of specified meritorious acts and drawing upon 'treasury of merits' of Christ, the Virgin Mary, and the saints. The → Pope normally grants I., which may be 'plenary' or partial. The abuse of selling I. was an immediate cause of Reformation (→ Luther). Comparative ref. might be made to system of →→ Bodhisattvas; Prayers for Dead. S.G.F.B.

E.R.E., VII, *s.v.; D.C.C., s.v.; R.G.G.*³, III, col. 64–7.

Indus Valley Civilisation This urban-centred culture was discovered by archaeologists in 1920's and proved to be revolutionary in regard to understanding of origins of → Hinduism. Spreading along Indus Valley in N.W. India, it reached into N.E. Panjab and Kathiawar. Rather similar in style to anc. Mesopotamian culture, it dates from early part of 3rd mil. BC. A high degree of organisation is implied by finds, and a standard of material culture well in advance of existing societies in sub-continent. Moreover, it is clear that in technical advance I.V.C. was superior to culture of → Aryan invaders who came into N.W. India about 1500 BC, and whose relig. ideas are known to us through the → Vedic hymns. Before discovery of I.V.C. (also called the 'Harappā' culture, after one of earliest sites excavated—Mohenjo-Daro being another import. one), it was assumed by scholars that main features of Hinduism could be traced in one way or another to Aryan relig. This was in accord with theory of revelation implicit in → Brahmanical Hinduism. However, there are features of I.V.C., discoverable from carved seals primarily, which indic. presence of factors later import. in classical Hinduism. The seals show parallels to → Śiva, the practice of → yoga, sacredness of pipal tree, cult of → *lingam*, etc. Some identifications may be mistaken, but the pre-existence of non-Aryan factors and their re-emergence in classical Hinduism remains a plausible account of changes coming over relig. in the subcontinent during and after Upanishadic period. N.S.

S. Piggott, *Prehistoric India* (1950); E. Mackay, *Early Indus Civilizations* (1968); R. E. Mortimer Wheeler, *The Indus Civilization* (1958); *Civilizations of Indus Valley and Beyond* (1966).

Infallibility, Papal At the Vatican Council, 1870, it was officially declared that definitions of the Pope, made *ex cathedra*, in matters of faith and morals are infallible, and not dependent on consent of the Church. There is, however, uncertainty about which Papal definitions are infallible, i.e. are made *ex cathedra* ('from the throne'), and changes are made in Papal policy, despite its previous solemn promulgation. S.G.F.B.

D.C.C., p. 689; *E.R.E.*³, VII, pp. 269–78; *R.G.G.*³, III, col. 748–9; G. G. Coulton, *Papal Infallibility* (1932).

Influxes (Buddh.) → *Asava*. T.O.L.

Ingen CE 1592–1673. Jap. name for the Chi. → Zen master, Yin Yüan, who founded the → Obaku sect in Japan. When over 60 years of age, in response to repeated invitations, I. left China for Japan with 20 disciples. He stayed first in the Kōfukuji temple at Nagasaki but moved in following year to Kyoto, where he established chief temple of Obaku sect. D.H.S.

H. Domoulin, *Hist. of Zen Buddhism* (1963), p. 229.

Inheritance and Wills (Islam) The Qur. speaks of bequests and also of the portions of an estate certain heirs are to receive. ii:176–8 refer to making will on behalf of parents and near relatives. ii, 241 deals with bequest in favour of widow guaranteeing her maintenance for a year, unless she leaves house before year is up. iv:8–17 is a more precise passage, stating that male members of family get twice as much as female from parent's estate, giving details regarding number of heirs, also mentioning what a man may get from wife's estate, or a wife from husband's acc. to whether or not there are children, and what brothers and sisters may receive in event of there being no direct heir. v:105–7 deal with witnesses to a will. The rules of I. indic. that immediate family has taken place of tribe of pre-Islamic times. Opinions differ about interpret. of refs. to bequests, some holding that the precise regulations abrogate them, others holding they are allowable within limits. Trad. specifies that one may not bequeath more than a third of estate, and that a bequest may not be made to an heir, as regulations stipulate how much each heir may receive. But the Twelver section of the → Shi'a allow bequests to heirs. Trad. suggests that while → Muḥammad allowed a third to be bequeathed outside family, he considered it a lot. The legal schools differed in some degree in interpret. basic Qur. laws, some being more literal in their interpret. than others. Shi'a law differs from → Sunni by giving no distinctive place to male agnate relatives, and by laying greater emphasis on rights of immediate family. In recent times mod. states have intro. some modifications. J.R.

E.I., III, pp. 508–14 (Mīrāth); IV, pp. 1132f. (Waṣīya); *Mishkāt*, pp. 650–7; Pareja, pp. 677–9, 689; Querry, I, pp. 610ff.; Schacht, *Jurisprudence*, index, p. 342; Coulson, *Law*, index (Bequests).

Initiation Initiatory rituals occur in all cultures, and gen. involve preparatory discipline and rites designed to transform the initiate into either a new social or relig. status and character. Among many primitive peoples adolescents, at puberty, have to undergo what is aptly called a *rite de passage* to enter adult membership of their community. I. into a relig. community gen. involves, besides instruction and declaration of personal commitment, rites that confer a new spiritual character, often regarded as rebirth (→ baptism, → circumcision, → Eleusinian Mysteries, → Mystery Religions). S.G.F.B.

A. von Gennep, *Les rites de passage* (1909); *E.R.E.*, VII, pp. 314–29; *R.G.G.*³, III, col. 751–3; E. O. James, *Comparative Religion* (1938), ch. 3; (ed.) C. J. Bleeker, *Initiation* (1965).

(Buddh.) → *Ordination* (Buddh.) T.O.L.

(Chinese) 1. The anc. 'capping ceremony', recorded in the → *Li Chi* (Book 40), was import. Confucian rite by which a youth was elevated to full adult status within community. The day of ceremony was decided by divination. It was conducted at top of eastern steps of ancestral temple, before family and guests. Three caps were used, each successive one more honourable. When the capping was over, the young man received his adult name, and was then presented to his mother, brethren and cousins, after which, with appropriate gifts and courtesies, he appeared before his rulers and elders.

2. The numerous secret societies and brotherhoods in China had both relig. and political significance. Initiation was often a long and complicated process. After careful examination and a period of instruction, the ceremony of I. took place in some pre-determined and secret place. Death to the old life and rebirth to a new estate was usually symbolised by such means as shaving head, lustrations, discarding of old garments and putting on of new ones. The laws and statutes of the society having been solemnly read; gods, spirits and ancestors invoked; the candidate ratified his oaths of obedience and secrecy by drinking a mixture of blood and wine, and by various ceremonies by which his status as 'blood-brother' within the society was recognised.

3. Initiation into the Buddh. Order in China follows usual Buddh. practice. After a long novitiate under guidance of a 'master', the candidate usually presents himself for ordination to priesthood at one of the great monasteries, where elaborate ordination ceremonies are conducted. Formerly novices had to be 20 years old before they could be ordained, and a considerable time had to elapse between the three stages of ordination; for practical reasons these rules are no longer adhered to, and boys of 15, 16 or 17 are frequently ordained. For a good account

of I. ceremonies into Buddh. order see K. L. Reichelt, *op. cit.*. Rites of I. into Taoist priesthood were in large measure copied from Buddh. D.H.S.

J. Legge (tr.) *Li Chi, S.B.E.*, vol. 28 (1885, repr. 1966), ch. 40; K. L. Reichelt, *Truth and Tradition in Chinese Buddhism* (1927), ch. 8; J. D. Ball, *Things Chinese*, 5th edn. (1925), pp. 605ff.; B. Favre, *Les Sociétés Secretes en Chine* (1933), *passim.*

(Hindu) For the upper class Hindu, the most import. of the *samskaras* (→ sacraments, Hindu) has been the *upanayana* or new birth, in which a boy is admitted as full member of the → Aryan community and so become a *dvija* or 'twice-born'. The ceremony involves his being invested with the sacred thread, worn from left shoulder and passing under right arm. Theoretically age of initiation for the → Brahman is eight, for → *ksatriya* eleven and for → *vaisya* twelve; but there is some variation, and the ceremony is not universal among lower two of the three classes. In Vedic times, girls were sometimes initiated, but practice no longer exists; marriage forms kind of initiation for girls, for it is then that they acquire full status in husband's community. In theory I. is the transition to status of student or *brahmacarin*, when boy is intro. to his teacher who will then instruct him, over period of up to twelve years, in Vedic lore; nowadays instruction is largely confined to ceremonial itself, which in some cases still conforms closely to anc. rites. I. into Vedic lore is symbolised by being instructed in the → *Gayatri*, either by → *guru* or father. This may be varied to incl. name of *istadevata* or chosen deity of caste group. For many castes the essential I. into group occurs through the food-giving ceremony in first year, which estab. the commensality of infant with group (a somewhat similar ceremony accompanies upper-class *upanayana*). As well as these I.'s of essentially social character, I.'s are central feature of → Tantrism and → Saivism: the disciple is initiated by his *guru*, and is thereby reborn and intro. to secret knowledge which will carry him on path to salvation. The term used, *dikṣā*, goes back to elaborate I. necessary, acc. to the *Aitareya Brāhmaṇa*, before performance of the → *soma* sacrifice, in which officiant and wife had to fast, practise → *tapas* in seclusion; and where resultant state is explicitly compared to that of baby, after their having regressed into womb. N.S.

R. B. Pandey, *Hindu Samskaras, A Socio-Religious Study of the Hindu Sacraments* (1949); M. S. Stevenson, *The Rites of the Twice-Born* (1920).

(Japanese) In → Shinto, the first ceremony of I. takes place on 32nd or 33rd day after birth, when the child is taken to temple of the tutelary deity by a chosen relative, and there receives recognition as one of the parishioners. When the child is 120 days old, a ceremony takes place in which it is given first solid food. The next I. ceremony is the *shichi-go-san*, when boys of 3 and 5 and girls of 3 and 7 years visit the tutelary temple to pray for protection and social approval. On 9th anniversary of birth, the child is submitted to ceremony of cutting hair like that of an adult. On 13 April of the solar calendar, the yearly *jusan-mairi* takes place for boys and girls who have attained the age of 13. At that age the young → samurai was for first time allowed to buckle on two swords, indicating his arrival at manhood. D.H.S.

J. Herbert, *Shinto* (1967), p. 165.

Injīl From Grk. *euangelion* (evangel). Occurs 12 times in the → Qur. for revelation given by God to Jesus, evidently conceived of as a book. Qur. iii:43 says the angels told Mary, when announcing to her the birth of Jesus, that God would teach him the Book, the Wisdom, the → Tawrāt, the Injīl. In earlier times, largely perhaps because → Muslims were ignorant of Christ. scriptures, the I. was spoken of as book of God's revelation to Jesus, but in more mod. times it has become customary to treat the I. as the N.T. Christians, and also Jews, are accused of tampering with their scriptures. While Muslims have been told to reverence the Tawrat, Zabūr (→ Psalms) and I., this is practically a dead letter; for they hold that the books in possession of Jews and Christians are not the orig. revelations. Therefore, while the Qur. verifies and acknowledges the earlier scriptures, what we have is of no further value; so the Qur. is sufficient, as it gives God's final revelation. But controversialists, while rejecting scriptures of O.T. and N.T. now extant, quote them freely. Perhaps one could suggest that the four Gospels may seem to Muslims to take place of the → Tradition rather than that of a revelation comparable in style to the Qur. (→ Jesus Christ in Islam). J.R.

E.I., II, pp. 501–4; Hughes, pp. 211–3, 433; Jeffery, *Vocabulary*, pp. 71f.; Sweetman, *I.C.T.*, III, pp. 178ff. and index (Bible); Parrinder, *Jesus*, ch. 15 and index (Gospel).

Inquisition, The In 13th cent. a Papal organisation was estab. to search out and extirpate heresy. The inquisitors were chiefly → Dominicans and → Francisans. In 1252 Pope Innocent IV allowed use of torture in trials. On conviction, in grave cases, the heretic was handed over to secular arm for execution by fire. The Spanish I., estab. end of 15th cent., was directed orig. against apostate Jew. and Moorish converts. The I. was later directed against Protestantism. → Heresy was deemed pernicious to the good ordering of both Church and State. S.G.F.B.

H. C. Lea, *Hist. of the Inquisition in the Middle Ages*, 3 vols. (1888); A. S. Turberville, *Medieval Heresy and the Inquisition* (1920); *E.R.E.*, VII, *s.v.; R.G.G.*[3], III, col. 769–72.

In Shā'a 'llāh Commonly pronounced *Inshallah* ('If God will'), is a phrase commonly used by Muslims with ref. to the future. It has basis in Qur. xviii:23, 'Do not say about anything, "I am going to do that to-morrow", but only, "If God will".' Cf. James, iv:15. J.R.

Insight (Buddh.) →→ *Abhinna; Vipassanā.* T.O.L.

Inspiration → Prophecy. S.G.F.B.

(China–Japan) In China and Japan there survives, from animistic stage of culture, the common belief that a god or spirit is able to take possession of a person either for good or evil, and that one under such influence becomes inspired to communicate a divine message or commission. Though such divine-possession may happen to anyone, men, women and even children, those adepts (e.g. as in → Taoism) who, by means of austerities or shamanistic techniques were able to enter a state of ecstasy or hypnotic trance, were peculiarly liable to become inspired intermediaries of divine revelations. The Jap. word *kangakari* implies idea of god-possession, the literal meaning being 'god-attachment', indicating passive attitude under supernatural influence. Literature in both countries abounds in cases of god-possession, and also possession by spirits of ancestors or by spirits of animals such as foxes; in most cases the god or spirit indicates its will in some particular commission, e.g. building or restoration of a temple.

Many of the faith-healing sects of modern Japan are based upon what are believed to be divinely inspired teachings of their founders. Thus Munetada, the founder of the → Kurozumi-kyō, on 22 Dec. 1814, had ecstatic experience, in which his mind was flooded with new insight and he received the direct command of Heaven. The farmer-saint who founded → Konko-kyō declared that his teachings were given him by revelation from the divine source of truth. Miki, the woman founder of → Tenri-kyō, on 9 Dec. 1838 attained conviction that God had taken possession of her, to reveal himself through her and save the world. (→ Prophecy, Prophets; → Revelation). D.H.S.

E.R.E., X, pp. 131ff.; W. G. Aston, *Shinto* (1905), pp. 348ff.; D. G. Holtom, *The National Faith of Japan* (1938), pp. 249, 257, 269.

(Islam) Islam recognises different kinds of I. That in the → Qur. is *waḥy*, which was dictated to → Muḥammad by → Gabriel, and is the highest form. A trad. says, 'It comes to me at times like the clanging of a bell, the type which is most severe to me; it then leaves me, I having retained of it what the angel said. At times the angel appears to me in human form and speaks to me, and I retain what he says.' → 'A'isha said she had seen I. coming to Muhammad on a cold day, and when it left him his forehead was pouring with sweat. This type of I. is open to prophets. Other people may have a secondary type (*ilhām*), which may be something impressed on mind without seeing any angel, but distinguished from process of meditation or reasoning. Saints can receive *ilhām*. Muhammad is believed to have received both types, the higher in the Qur. revelation, and the lower in contents of → Tradition. Muhammad is held to have been under divine guidance in all he said in matters of religion; but in other matters he was as liable to make mistakes as anyone else, though all are not prepared to concede this. *Ilhām* is also used for natural endowments which cannot be said to result from knowledge. (→ Prophecy, Prophets; → Revelation). J.R.

E.I., II, pp. 467f. (*ilhām*), IV, pp. 1091–3 (*waḥy*); Hughes, pp. 213f.; Stanton, *Teaching*, pp. 38ff.; Bell, *Introduction*, pp. 31–6; *E.R.E.*, VII, pp. 354–7.

Intercession (*Shafā'a*). It is gen. held that on Day of Judgment → Muḥammad will be only intercessor appointed by God; but a trad. admits intercession of angels, messengers, prophets, martyrs and saints. The Qur. is less definite. Qur. xx:108 says, 'No I. shall avail on that day, except his whom the Merciful shall allow, and whose words he shall approve.' The view is that Muhammad will be able to intercede for believers in the one God who are guilty of grave sins; and, as result of his I., will be allowed to take many of his followers from → hell to heaven. It is vain to intercede for people who believed in more gods than one, for that is the unforgivable sin. The → Mu'tazilites did not accept the doc. of Muhammad's I., holding it was inconsistent with justice and retribution. They based their doc. on Qur., ii:45, 'Fear a day on which a soul shall not avail for a soul at all, nor shall any I. be accepted from them, nor shall any ransom be taken, nor shall they be helped.' Wensinck remarks that the orthodox community may have adopted the doc. of I. owing to need to counterbalance predestination (*Creed*, 180). J.R.

E.I., IV, pp. 250f.; Hughes, pp. 214f.; Pareja, 807f.; *Mishkāt* 1179ff.; D. B. Macdonald, *Theology*, index (Shafā'a); Wensinck, *Creed*, index; Miller, *Bāb*, pp. 87f.

Ippen (CE 1239–89). Known in Japan as the itinerant sage, because of his method of propagating Buddhism. An outstanding preacher and missionary of the faith in → Amita-Buddha, his missionary journeys covered nearly the whole of Japan. I. combined relief work with his preaching; he propagated practice of repeating the Buddha name, with which he linked idea that the believer is thus prepared for death at any moment. His followers formed a separate sect, called Jishū (Time doctrine), which inculcated pious thoughts at every moment, and a relig. service six times a day. D.H.S.

M. Anesaki, *Hist. of Japanese Relig.* (1930), pp. 186–7.

Iranian Religion The relig. of the Iranians before → Zoroaster is a matter of inference from writings affected by Zoroaster's reform and from → Vedic. relig., which reflects a common Indo-Iranian trad. (→ Aryans). This I.-R. was → polytheistic, its deities being personifications of cosmic phenomena. There was a chief- → sky-god, prob. of ambivalent nature = the Vedic pair Varuna-Mitra (→→ Varuna; Mithra). This god combined roles of creator and destroyer, repr. both life and death, light and darkness. Such ambivalence doubtless reflected Iran. view that world was battle-ground of opposing forces (→ Dualism). This deity has been variously identified as Vayu (wind-god), → Zurvan, and → Ahura Mazah. Fire and → haoma were objects of ritual cults. The dead (→ Fravashi) were prob. worshipped as fertility spirits (like Vedic → *pitrs*). Ritual sacrifices of bulls were performed, poss. to win → immortality. Some kind of *post-mortem* ordeal was envisaged as Zoroaster's ref. to → Chinvat Bridge shows. Other import. deities were → Mithra, and → Anahita. Much of this earlier I.-R. re-emerged in later → Zoroastrianism. (→ Amesha Spentas). (See Synoptic Index under 'Iran'). S.G.F.B.

G. Widengren, *Hochgottglauben in alten Iran* (1938), 'Stand und Aufgaben der iranischen Religionsgeschichte', in *Numen*, I (1954), II (1955), *Die Religionen Irans* (1965); H. S. Nyberg, *Die Religionen des alten Irans* (1938); J. Duchesne-Guillemin, *Zoroastre* (1948), *La religion de l'Iran ancien* (1962); G. Dumézil, *Mitra-Varuna* (1948), *Les dieux des Indo-Européens* (1952); R. C. Zaehner, *Zurvan* (1955), *D.T.Z.* (1961); M. Molé, *Culte, mythe et cosmologie dans l'Iran ancien* (1963); R. N. Frye, 'Georges Dumézil and the Translators of the Avesta', *Numen*, VIII (1961).

Irenaeus (*c.* 130–200), **Bp. of Lyons** I.'s writings are of primary import. for evolution of Cath. Christianity in opposition to → Gnosticism. Instead of producing a Chr. Gnosticism as did → Clement of Alexandria, I. emphasised trad. elements, esp, episcopacy and canon of Scripture, like → Ignatius before, I. insists on reality and fulness of → Incarnation of Christ. He taught doc. of 'recapitulation' (i.e. the culmination of human evolution in Incarnate Christ). I.'s chief work is the *Adversus omnes Haereses.* S.G.F.B.

There is an E.T. of *Adv. Haer.* in *A.N.C.L.*, 2 vols. (1868–9), *D.C.C., s.v.;* P. Carrington, *The Early Christian Church*, II (1957), pp. 307ff.; *R.G.G.*[3], III, col. 891–2; A. Benoit, *S. Irénée. Intro. à l'étude de sa théologie* (1960); J. Lawson, *The Biblical Theology of St. Irenaeus* (1948); A. Houssiau, *Le christologie de S. Irénée* (1955).

Isaiah, Book of It is gen. agreed that B.-I. in its form is composite: (1) chs. 1–35 contain prophecies of Isaiah (*c.* 700 BC), asserting supremacy of → Yahweh and promising inviolability of → Jerusalem, menaced by Assyrians. (2) chs. 36–9, mainly taken from 2 Kgs. 18:13–20:19. (3) chs. 40–5 called 'Deutero Isaiah', comprising prophecies designed to inspire Jew. exiles in Babylonia just prior to Cyrus' sanction for their return in 537 BC. This section contains → Servant Songs. (4) chs. 56–66, called 'Trito-Isaiah', deals with situations presupposing restoration of Temple (*c.* 520 BC). B.-I. has greatly affected Chr. thought, partic. by Immanual prophecy (7:14) and Servant Songs. A MS. of B.-I., dating *c.* 2nd cent. BC, was found at → Qumran. S.G.F.B.

H.D.B.[2], pp. 423–7; *P.C.*[2], pp. 489ff.; R. H. Pfeiffer, *Intro. to Old Test.* (1948), pp. 415ff.

Ishmael (*Ismā'īl*). Son of → Abraham and → Hagar, is considered to have been progenitor of N. Arabs. The Qur. calls him a prophet (xix:55, 'He was a messenger, a prophet'). He is mentioned along with Abraham, Isaac, Jacob and the patriachs (ii:134; iii:78—Moses, Jesus and God's prophets added in the latter—cf. vi:86; xxi:85; xxxviii:48). In iv:161 I. is mentioned among a number inspired by God. He helped Abraham to rebuild the → ka'ba (ii:119ff.). He, not Isaac, is gen. held to have been the son Abraham was told to sacrifice; but a trad., taken from one of the less authoritative collections, tells of advice given to man who had vowed to sacrifice himself if he were rescued from his enemy. He was told to buy a ram and sacrifice it for the poor, 'for Isaac was better than you and he was ransomed with a ram' (*Mishkāt*, 733). In Qur. xxxvii:100ff. Abraham is told in a dream to sacrifice his son, but the son is not named. Muḥammad 'Alī ingeniously argues from verse 112 which says, 'and we gave him the good news of Isaac', that this shows Isaac was not yet born at time when Abraham was told to sacrifice his son. J.R.

E.I., II, pp. 543f.; Hughes, pp. 216–20; Pareja, index (Ismā'īl); 'Alī, *Qur'ān*, note 2116.

Ishtar Known as Innina by Sumerians, I. was the great goddess of Mesopot., and was identified with → Astarte, → Ashtoreth, → Cybele, and other goddesses of Near East. She was assoc. with planet Venus, and regarded as daughter of → Sin and sister of → Shamash. I. had a dual nature: as goddess of war and goddess of love and fertility. Mythologically I. was assoc. with → Tammuz, her lover, whose death she lamented. The myth of her descent into underworld is significant for Mesopot. → eschatology. I.'s chief cult-centre was Erech (Uruk), where she was served by sacred → prostitutes. I. was also assoc. with healing rituals, in which sick were identified with Tammuz, whom I. was invoked to save. S.G.F.B.

Dhorme, *R.B.A.*, pp. 67ff.; S. N. Kramer, *Sumerian Mythology* (1961), *passim;* Jastrow, *Aspects*, pp. 127ff.; B. Meissner, *Babylonien u. Assyrian*, II (1925), pp. 26ff.; *A.N.E.T.*, pp. 52ff., 106ff.

Isipatana Name of open space near Benares, where the Buddha is reputed to have preached the famous 'First Sermon', later described as the 'Setting in motion of the Wheel of the Dhamma', (→ Dhamma Cakkappavattana Sutta). The open space known as I., trad. location of this sermon, was also noted for its deer-park, or *Migadāya*, where deer were allowed to roam in safety. The Buddha is also said to have spent the first rainy season, after enlightenment, at I. It is a place of Buddh. pilgrimage; one of the 4 → Holy Places. The location is now known as Sārnāth, 6 miles from Benares. A rock-pillar, erected by → Ashoka, stands on site, on which is inscribed the emperor's '*Sanghabhedaka*' edict, i.e. 'concerning dissension in the → *Sangha*. The remains of monasteries cover a considerable area, some of which are of great antiquity. At time of Chinese Buddh. pilgrim → Hsuang-tsang's visit in 637 CE there was a flourishing monastic community at Sarnath. There are known to have been two → *stupas* of unknown age, one of which was destroyed in 1794 by an Indian prospecting for building materials. A *vihāra* has been built at S. in mod. times by the → Maha-bodhi-society. T.O.L.

S. Dutt, *Buddhist Monks and Monasteries of India* (1962), pp. 215–7; P. V. Bapat (ed,), *2500 Years of Buddhism* (1956), pp. 311–3; Malalasekere, *D.P.P.N.*, vol. 1, pp. 323–6.

Isis Egypt. goddess, wife of → Osiris, mother of → Horus. Her symbol, hieroglyph for 'throne', has never been satisfactorily explained. I. was most beloved of Egypt. goddesses: she was ideal of wifely affection, restoring mutilated body of her husband and revivifying it, bearing his posthumous son, menaced by his murderer → Set. Her popular image was the Divine Mother suckling her Divine child, a prototype of → Virgin Mary and infant Christ. I. played an important role in Egypt. → funerary ritual. Her cult was popular in Graeco-Roman world, taking form of a → mystery religion. She was regarded as the supreme goddess, other goddesses of the anc. world being considered as localised forms of her: the devotion she could evoke is movingly recorded by → Apuleius (*Metam.* XI), and in → Aretologies. S.G.F.B.

R.Ae.R-G., pp. 326–33, 376ff.; S. A. B. Mercer, *The Relig. of Anc. Egypt* (1949), pp. 199ff.; *O.C.D.*, *s.v.;* C. J. Bleeker, 'Isis as Saviour Goddess', in S. G. F. Brandon (ed.), *The Saviour God* (1963); F. C. Grant, *Hellenistic Religions* (1953), pp. 128ff.; *Bilderatlas*, 8/11. Lief. (1926), Abb. 23–39.

-Islām Came to be used as name of relig. estab. by → Muḥammad. The root from which it comes means to surrender; fundamentally it means submitting oneself to God, which naturally incl. idea of renouncing any other object of worship. The idea of peace is assoc. with the root (cf. *salām*), so it is often said that I. means peace; but this is difficult to justify linguistically, however much one may experience peace through submission to God. *Muslim* (active participle) indic. one who submits himself to God, however defective his faith may be (cf. Qur. xlix:14). The Qur. does not confine the title to Muhammad's followers. It is applied to → Abraham (iii:60), Lot's family (li:36), the Queen of Sheba's folk (xxvii: 38, 42), the disciples of Jesus (iii:45; v:lll), the People of the Book (xxviii:53); and Moses exhorts his people to trust in God and be Muslims (x:84). (→ Muslim). J.R.

E.I., II, p. 539 (Islam), III, pp. 755f. (Muslim); Hughes, p. 220; *E.R.E.*, VII, pp. 437f.; 'Alī, *Qur'ān*, notes 156, 400; Khan, *Islam*, p. 164; Cragg, *Minaret*, pp. 29, 46, 190; J. Robson, 'Islam as a term', *M.W.*, XLIV (1954), pp. 101–9; M. A. Rauf, 'Islām and Īmān', *M.W.*, LVII (1967), pp. 94–102.

(in Indonesia) There were Muslims in Java in 6th/12th cent., the relig. being intro. by merchants from India; but the conventional view locally is that Islam was intro. by nine *awliyā'* (→ Saints), or hermits, semi-legendary missionaries in 9th/15th cent. There are two main groups of Muslims in I. called *santri*, who observe Islamic tenets strictly, and *abangan*, who combine Islamic doctrines and practices with indigenous beliefs and rituals, a blend of animism, pantheism, Hinduism and Islam. The chief Islamic influences have come from India, Hadramawt and Egypt, but these have not been able to root out many non-Islamic practices. As long as people acknowledge one God and Muhammad as his prophet, they are recognised as Muslims, which means they are free to maintain anc. customs. The *slametan*, an anc. ritual meal, is observed at import. times, such as births, marriages, deaths, agricultural celebrations, or any special occasion public or private; but a mosque official is usually invited. These occasions are enlivened by the *gamelan* (orchestra) and the *wayang* (theatrical representations containing Indo-Javanese mythology). Certain heathen practices, such as mutilating teeth and visiting idol shrines and temples are common. *Santris* are faithful in observing the prayers. Their most orthodox party is the *Dār al-Islām* (House of Islam) movement, uncompromising in its orthodoxy and treating all who differ as infidels. It advocates a theocracy, with the → Shafi'i legal school in full control. In various districts it has found support, esp. N. Sumatra and wherever anti-communist groups are found. Other sections are hostile to both nationalism and communism, arguing that Islam gives a relig. basis which delivers from secularism, and provides → *zakāt* (*pitrah* in Indonesia) which makes communism unnecessary. The *Sarekat Islam* (Islamic Union) was founded in 1328/1910 to care for economic and intellectual needs. It engaged in disturbances with Chinese at Surabaya and Surekarta in 1331/1921 and had a period of suspension. A split took place when main body denounced communism and the *Sarekat Merah* (Red Union), later called *Sarekat Rayah* (People's Union) was formed. As result of strikes and agitation, the *Sarekat* was declared illegal in Java and Sumatra in 1325/1926. The *Muhammadiyya*, founded in 1331/1912 followed the doctrines of → Muhammad 'Abduh, engaging in education and social work, their interests being relig. rather than political. The Friday sermon in the vernacular is recommended. Women's groups, called *'A'ishiyya*, wear a headdress to distinguish them from other women. They have built mosques reserved for women. The *Masjumi* (Muslim Federation), which was banned, was violently anti-communist, and at the same time seemed to support the aims of *Dar al-Islam*. Many better educated Indonesians, as well as others, are being attracted by the → Ahmadiyya propaganda. This movement claims about 10,000 members in various islands. Women have considerable freedom. Marriages are nearly all monogamous, but divorce is frequent. Many Muslims are careless about relig. duties such as prayer and → pilgrimage. Although the fast is not observed to any great extent, some being satisfied with fasting first and last days of month, → *'Īd al-fiṭr* is observed widely, except in Hindu Bali and some Christ. and pagan areas, as a holiday. Law never has followed the → *sharī'a* to any great extent, for *adat* (custom) has been main authority in matters of private law. Indonesia has over 85 million people, 90% of whom are reckoned as Muslim. J.R.

E.I., IV, pp. 551f.; Pareja, pp. 273–91, 536–8, 593f., 738f.; Clifford Geertz, *The Religion of Java* (1960); Justus M. van der Kroef, 'Recent trends in Indonesian Islam', *M.W.*, LII (1962), pp. 48–58; *I.R.* (April 1966), 'Id al-Fitr in Indonesia', pp. 23f., 40.

(in Philippines) Islam was first spread there by traders and adventurers in 8th/14th cent., but its spread was checked when Spaniards arrived in 923/1565. The Muslims put up violent resistance when they found their relig. attacked, and came to be considered savages. But after 300 years Americans adopted a more peaceful attitude, and better relations between Muslims and Christians arose, since Muslims had no longer to fight to preserve identity. As is common, Islam had adapted itself to practice of the people; so, although the → Shafi'i school of law was acknowledged, much local practice persisted and many non-Islamic customs were followed. Things are changing. Muslim missionaries have come from different countries and have found much to criticise. They have been welcomed, and as result there is a quickening within the local Islam. Many mosques and relig. schools have recently been built, Muslim societies have been founded, students go abroad to Muslim universities; the numbers who perform → Pilgrimage are growing. It is estimated that there are over 1½ million Muslims in the Philippines, with numbers presumably growing. J.R.

Pareja, index; Peter G. Gowing, 'Muslim Filipinos Today', *M.W.*, LIV (1964), pp. 39–48, 112–21 (with excellent selected billiography).

(spread of) In Muhammad's lifetime his followers were confined to Arabia, although he is reputed to have addressed letters to certain foreign rulers; after → Abū Bakr had suppressed the 'apostasy' (*ridda*) after Md.'s death, he employed tribesmen in campaigns outside Arabia. Syria was soon conquered, Damascus being taken in 14/635 and → Jerusalem in 15/636. Madā'in, the Persian capital, was taken in 16/637, and the Muslims spread E. and N. Within about a cent. after Md.'s death they had reached the borders of China. Westwards they spread through Egypt and along N. Africa. In 92/711 Spain was invaded, leading to a rapid conquest. France was entered, but the Muslims were defeated between Poitiers and Tours in 114/732 and retired southwards. They later got control in Malta, Sicily, Sardinia, and the Balearic Isles; but their conquests there and in Spain were taken from them. In 898/1492 Granada, their last capital in Spain, fell. But in 857/1453 the Turks took → Constantinople and made further conquests in E. Europe. Now little remains except E. Thrace; but Muslim communities survive, notably in Albania and Bulgaria. Muslims entered Sind in 92/711, but conquests were not estab. till time of Maḥmūd of Ghazna (360–423/969–1030). Muslim influence was permanently estab. in the Panjab and there were Muslim kingdoms in Sind. Later Muslim influence spread S. and communities were established throughout India. It should not, however, be assumed that Islam spread only by conquests, for much missionary work was also done by traders who travelled far afield. In Ceylon Islam spread slowly, but the Muslim community has been strengthened mainly by Madrasis. From India Islam spread to Malaya and from there to Sumatra, where there were Muslim communities at least in 8th/14th cent. Early in 9th/15th cent. traders from Hadramawt came to Java, where there were already Muslims, and as usual engaged in missionary work. Islam reached the → Philippines in 8th/14th cent. through Muslim traders from Malaya. It penetrated China, partly through Turkish influence, partly through traders who visited coastal regions. Till recent times there were many Muslims at least in W. China, and smaller communities in outer Mongolia, but it is imposs. to say what the position is at time of writing. In Africa the Islamisation of the Sudan in the E. was slow. In → Ethiopia there have been Muslims from early days, but official religion is Christian. In E. Africa Muslim states were estab., and they spread Islam in C. Africa. Farther W. Islam has grad. spread S. In W. Africa many converts have been made; while appreciation of Islamic doc. may be faulty in some quarters, efforts are being made to teach the people who are inclined to hold on to pagan customs. Since 9th/15th cent. N. Nigeria has been Muslim. In rivalry between Christianity and Islam in Africa much is being made in some quarters of argument that Islam is the black man's relig. In N. and S. America there are many Muslim communities, mostly emigrants from Lebanon and Syria; throughout Europe there are communities, mostly of Asiatic and African origin, but also containing a number of European converts. J.R.

E.I., II, pp. 539–41; Pareja, pp. 29ff.; T. W. Arnold, *The Preaching of Islam* (1913); Levy, *Social Structure*, pp. 1–52; Trimingham, *Sudan, Ethiopia, West Africa, History;* I. M. Lewis (ed.), *Islam in Tropical Africa* (1966); *R.M.E.*, ch. 1–12.

Israel, Israelite Religion It is customary to divide the relig. development of I. at the Exile (586–38 BC), by designating its later form → 'Judaism'. The earlier period saw evolution of I. to status of a nation, with a distinctive relig., focussed on → Temple at → Jerusalem, as its unique cult-centre. I. appears to have developed from an → amphictyony of Semite tribes, whose war-god was → Yahweh. Estab. in Canaan, these tribes grad. acquired a sense of national unity due to efforts of → Yahwist prophets and writers to provide them with a common → Heilsgeschichte. The earlier books of the O.T. record long struggle to estab. Yahweh as the only god of a settled agrarian people as Israel eventually became. The Yahwist prophets had to eliminate belief both in ancestral tribal gods and those of → Canaan. relig. This policy led to adoption of a pessimistic → eschatology, in opposing pagan cults. I.-R. was essentially an ethnic relig., centred on relat. of I., as a people, to its god Yahweh. It was, thus, inadequate as a personal faith, which fact created the tensions reflected in Book of → Job. Experience of Exile led to adjustments to meet this need (→ Ezekiel, → Jeremiah). During latter part of period, the monarchy had a certain cultic significance (→ King, Divine). I.-R. has been described as orig. → henotheism; it emerged from the Exile monotheistic. Prophetic emphasis on moral character of Yahweh caused problems for doc. of → Man, which were only solved after Exile by belief in *post-mortem* resurrection and → judgment (→ Eschatology, Jew.). (→→ Moses; Covenant, Judaism). See Synoptic Index under 'Jews'. S.G.F.B.

W. O. E. Oesterley–T. H. Robinson, *Hebrew Religion* (1930); J. Pedersen, *Israel: its Life and Culture*, I–IV (1926, 1940); H. H. Rowley, *The Faith of Israel* (1956); M. Noth, *Hist. of Israel* (E.T. 1966); J. Bright, *Hist. of Israel* (1959); A. Lods, *Israël* (1949), *Les prophètes d'Israël et les débuts du Judaïsme* (1935); G. W. Anderson, in H. H. Rowley (ed.), *The Old Test. and Modern Study* (1951); Brandon, *M.D.*, ch. 4; H. Ringgren, *Israelite Relig.* (E.T. 1967).

Ismā'īlīs This party of the → Shi'a have been called *ghulāt* (fanatics) by their opponents; also Bāṭiniyya from *bāṭin* (esoteric) because they taught the Qur. has an internal as well as external (*ẓāhir*) meaning; also Ta'līmiyya from *ta'līm* (teaching) because they claimed to derive their teachings from a hidden source which must receive absolute obedience. There were various grades of members and associates who received teaching only acc. to their capacity, the lowest grades receiving external instruction in keeping with normal Islamic practice, other grades developing to more esoteric teaching. Knowledge of the → *imām* is necessary. Though invested with an eternal light, he is still mortal; but he is so exalted that he requires an intermediary between him and humanity. This is the *ḥujja* (proof) who knows all the mysteries. The doc. worked on a series of sevens, seven prophets ending with Muhammad b. Isma'il, between each pair of which were seven *imāms*. So they are spoken of as the Seveners. Muhammad b. Isma'il is the last and greatest prophet. Their enemies accused them of denying all relig. and morality as they reached higher grades, but one cannot confidently accept such an accusation. They estab. a dynasty in Tunisia which developed into a Caliphate in Egypt (→ Fāṭimids). (→→ Agha Khān; Assassins, Bohorās; Ikhwān al-Ṣafā'; Imām; Khojas; Qarmaṭians). J.R.

E.I., Supplement, pp. 98ff.; Pareja, pp. 836ff. and index; Ivanow, *Creed, Guide;* D. B. Macdonald, *Theology*, index; B. Lewis, *The origins of Isma'il-ism* (1940); Watt, *Ghazali*, index (Bāṭinīyah, Ta'līmīyah), *Philosophy*, pp. 100ff. and index; W. Madelung, 'Das Imamat in der früher ismailitischen Lehre', *D.I.*, XXXVII (1961), 43ff.

Isrā' Qur. xvii:1 speaks of a night journey of → Muḥammad from the sacred mosque to the farthest mosque (*al-masjid al-aqṣā*), the former gen. being treated as the → ka'ba, and the latter → Jerusalem; but an older trad. connects it with heaven. See Guillaume, 'Where was al-masĵid al-aqṣā? in *A*, XVIII (1953), 323ff., indic. the poss. of its being not far from Mecca. While Md. was asleep in Mecca → Gabriel wakened him and led him to → Burāq. Some trads. say his spirit travelled, but his body remained in Mecca. He was accosted by siren voices on way to Jerusalem, but ignored them. At Jerusalem they met Abraham, Moses and Jesus, and Md. led them in prayer. Then followed the ascent (→ Mi'rāj). J.R.

E.I., II, pp. 553f.; Hughes, pp. 351f.; Pareja, pp. 793f., 803f.; Guillaume, *Life*, pp. 181ff.

Īśvara Sanskrit word for 'Lord', and term commonly used to ref. to God as supreme personal being. The short form *īsa* gives title to *Īśa Upaniṣad.* Though the Lord is usually conceived to be creator (and destroyer) of world, he need not be. Thus in → Yoga school, there is belief in an *Isvara,* but he does not create. *Isvara* is used in → *Advaita Vedanta* to signify 'lower' personal aspect of ultimate reality, who creates world of illusion and is implicated in it himself. Most commonly the Lord is identified with →→ Viṣṇu, Śiva or Brahmā, or all three as different manifestations of one ultimate reality. N.S.

Ithyphallic Deities The relig. significance of virility finds expression in the iconography of many gods who are repr. with erect phalli: e.g. (Egypt.) → Amon, Min, recumbent → Osiris, → Bes; (Grk.) →→ Herme, Pan, Priapus; (Nordic) → Thor. (→ Phallic Cults). S.G.F.B.

Bilderatlas, I Lief. p. 2, Abb. 10, 18, 26; Lief. 2/4, Abb. 93, 150; Lief. 13/14, Abb. 29, 30, 32; *R.Ae.R-G.*, pp. 32, 107, 462ff.; H. Licht, *Sexual Life in Anc. Greece* (E.T. 1949), pp. 120, 222ff.

I Tsing (I Ch'ing), 634–713 CE. A famous Chinese Buddh. pilgrim to India, Sumatra and Java, who spent 25 years abroad, collecting and copying Skt. Buddh. texts. He was partic. concerned to observe and record in minute detail the → Vinaya rules and practices of Indian monks, espec. of the → Sarvāstivāda school. He spent 10 years studying at celebrated Buddh. centre at → Nalanda. Whilst sojourning at Palembang, Sumatra, he sent home to China *A Record of the Buddhist. Relig. in India and the Malay Archipelago*, published in Chinese in 690 and trans. into Eng. by J. Takakusu in 1896. A further record, giving biographical notices of 56 Chinese monks who journeyed to India, and describing his own experiences, was trans. into French by E. Chavannes in 1894. On his return to China in CE 695, I.T. engaged in an influential trans. work under imperial patronage until his death. D.H.S.

J. Takakusu, *Record* (as above) (1896); E. Chavannes (tr.), *Voyage des pélerins bouddhistes, mémoire composé à l'époque de la grande dynastie T'ang sur les religieux éminents . . . dans les pays d'occident*, par I Tsing (1894); *E.R.E.*, XII, pp. 842f.

Izanagi-Izanami (Male-who-invites and Female-who-invites). Jap. cosmogonic mythology (→ Kojiki and → Nihongi) has its beginnings in I. and I., who at bidding of the celestial gods descend from the High Plain of Heaven, and by their union create the islands of Japan. They are universal parents, producing the land and all forms of vegetation, and are the ancestors of gods and men. It has been cogently argued that Izanagi is primarily a Sky-Father and Izanami an Earth-Mother (Cf. D. C. Holtom, below). The myth has several variants; but acc. to gen. accepted version, Izanami, at conception of Fire-god, Kagu-tsuchi, died and went down to the land of Yomi or darkness to become the personification of death. Izanagi, having sought and found her, against her wishes gazed on her corruption and was chased back to land of the living. His first act on his return was to purify himself, and from washings of his eyes and nose were born the three great deities, → Amaterasu the sun goddess, Tsuki-yomi the moon god, and → Susa-no-wo the boisterous storm god. The realm of light, incl. heaven and earth, was assigned to Amaterasu; the realm of night to the moon-god; the ocean and the realm of hidden things to Susa-no-wo. Thereupon Izanagi returned to his abode in High Heaven, or, acc. to one version, to island of Ahaji where he dwells in silence and concealment. D.H.S.

D. C. Holtom, *The National Faith of Japan* (1938), pp. 89–121; W. G. Aston (tr.), *Nihongi* (1896, 1956); M. Anesaki, *Hist. of Japanese Relig.* (1930), pp. 25–7; J. Herbert, *Shinto* (1967), *passim.*

J

Jabrites → Free-will and predestination. J.R.

Jacob In Jew. trad., son of Isaac and Rebekah, and father of 12 sons who formed eponymous ancestors of 12 Tribes of → Israel: his life is recounted in Gen. 25:21–50:13, where he appears as a distinctive personality. Whether J. was a historical person or an eponymous tribal ancestor or deity is problematic: 'Jacob-el' appears as a Palestinian place-name in a 15th cent. BC Egypt. inscription. (→ Judaism). S.G.F.B.

*H.D.B.*², *s.v.; R.G.G.*³, III, col. 517–20; *A.N.E.T.*, p. 242; *E.J.R.*, p. 208.

Jade Supposed by Chinese to have property of preserving flesh from corruption. In Chou and Han dynasties, J. amulets were buried with dead. In form of → cicada, emblem of resurrection, J. was placed on the tongue, and other apertures of body were closed with J. Sacrificial vases, incense burners, statuettes of various deities, and eight Buddh. emblems for altars were made of J. The chief Taoist deity, → Yü Huang, is called the Jade Emperor. D.H.S.

Laufer, *Jade* (new ed. 1946); S. Couling, *Encycl. Sinica* (1917, 1965), p. 254.

-Jāhiliyya Applied to the pre-Islamic period in Arabia. It is commonly trans. 'the times of ignorance', but Goldziher has argued that 'the times of barbarism' is more correct. The root *jhl* contains an element of both ideas, so one may find it convenient to trans. freely 'the Pre-Islamic period'. In central Arabia the tribal system led to feuds, and the difficulties of desert life determined what were considered good qualities. *Muruwwa* (virtue, manliness) involved bravery and generosity among other characteristics, notable among which was endurance. Vengeance for murder or any wrong was natural and right. The severe desert conditions developed a degree of hedonism, so pleasures of food and drink were indulged in when opportunity arose. Gambling was prevalent, but the game *al-maisir* proscribed in the → Qur. had an element of generosity, as it provided supply of camel meat for poor. → Muḥammad condemned evils of the J., but retained good qualities. He tried to supersede tribal system by a new people based on → Islām. He denounced polytheism. He abolished heathen sanctuaries, but retained one at Mecca which he purified, the → Ka'ba. Poetry was greatly appreciated in the J. Muhammad is often said to have condemned it, but this is a misunderstanding. His insistence that he was not a poet was not because he condemned poetry as such, but because it was believed that poets were inspired by a familiar spirit, whereas he insisted that his inspiration came from God. The fact that he employed poets shows that he had no objection to them. (→→ Ethics and morality (pre-Islamic), Months sacred in pre-Islamic times). J.R.

*E.I.*², II, pp. 383f.; Goldziher, *M.S.*, I, pp. 1ff., 219ff.; Lammens, *l'Islam*, pp. 9ff.; Watt, *Mecca*, pp. 24f. and index.

Jahmites A party which gets its name from Jahm b. Ṣafwān (executed 128/746), its alleged founder. They appear about beginning of third Muslim cent. when their docs. were spread by Bishr b. Ghiyāth al-Mārisī (d. 218/833) and others. We are largely dependent on books by opponents for knowledge of their docs. For example, Dārimī (200–280/815–893) denounced doc. of God's omnipresence by quoting chapter and verse to show God is above his creation and distinct from it. He condemns their doc. which denies distinction between God's attributes, so reducing him to a bare unity, and their teaching that God can know something only after he has created it. The J. had much in common with the → Mu'tazilites, e.g. their doc. about God's attributes, their belief that the Qur. is not eternal, their rational dealing with anthropomorphic terms; but they disagreed by denying doc. of free will. So, although they agreed with much of the Mu'tazilite doc., they were not accepted by that party. J.R.

*E.I.*², II, p. 388; Pareja, pp. 699, 720; Wensinck, *Creed*, index (Djahm); Watt, *Free Will*, pp. 96ff. and index; Gösta Vitestam, *Kitāb ar-radd 'alā l-ğahmīya des Abū Sa'īd 'Uthmān b. Sa'īd ad-Dārimī* (1960) (Arabic text with excellent intro. in German).

Jainism J., though numerically not powerful (*c.* 2 million adherents), has played import. role in hist. of Indian religs. It is of great antiquity, going back at least to → Parsva, 8th cent. BC. → Mahavira, 6th cent. BC, at one time regarded by Western scholars as founder of faith, was rather restorer and reformer of an existing anc. trad. J. was vigorous rival of early → Buddhism. At first its centre of influence remained the Ganges region, but a migration to Deccan in early 3rd cent. BC, part result of a famine, estab. the relig. in south and west of India. The migration was a factor in bringing about schism between → *Svetamabaras* and → *Digambaras*, divided primarily over question of whether monks should practise nudity. Division was finalized by end of 1st cent. CE; but in points of doc. there is little divergence, and most monks of 'Sky-clad' Digambara sect in fact wear robes in public. The concentration of Svetambaras in N. India shifted gradually; their main influence in medieval period was in Kathiawar, Rajasthan and Gujarat, while Digambara influence was strongest in Mysore. The political and cultural importance of J. was affected by resurgence of →→ Saivite and Vaisnavite relig. in late medieval period; but Jains have retained degree of influence out of proportion to numbers, since strict observance of → *ahimsa* tended to exclude them from agricultural occupations and channel them into business activities, etc. The teachings of J. have been maintained with great conservatism over immense period, even though there is disagreement about validity of canon (→ revelation, Jain). Chief change in relig. practice has been adoption of temple-worship, rather on pattern of → Hinduism, where, however, offerings of flowers, incense, etc., are made to the → Tirthamkaras. Family rites, such as marriage, are not distinctive, and use is made of services of → Brahmins. There was at one time cult of → stupas, as in Buddhism. Most notable J. monuments, apart from complex of temples at Mount Abu, are the enormous free-standing sculptures at Sravana Belgola and elsewhere, depicting *jinas* standing naked, sublimely indifferent to values and concerns of world. J. has always stressed → asceticism strongly, and struggle for liberation is accompanied by heroic self-mortification culminating, as in case of Mahavira and other great figures, in death by self-starvation. The necessity for such austerity arises from picture of → karma offered in J. The accumulation of karma, weighing the life-monad down and binding it to round of → rebirth, is to be combatted by annihilating it through external and internal asceticism, the latter culminating in practice of contemplation. But even so, there is continued danger for ascetic of acquiring injurious karma, since even unintentional taking of animal and insect life, etc., is deleterious. Since such high degree of asceticism and non-injury is only practicable for monks, the laity's chief concerns are to maintain latter and practise an approximation to ascetic ideal, which will carry them upward in long path to liberation in future lives. No help here is to be gained by appeal to God, since J. is → atheistic, though recognising a hierarchy of gods as denizens of cosmos. The universe is conceived as immense and everlasting, and as incl. various heavens and hells (→ cosmology, Jain). The heavens are regions which the gods inhabit; but latter are essentially inferior to the Tirthamkaras, who, with other liberated life-monads, occupy topmost part of cosmos. The middle level of universe, the region inhabited by men, animals and other living beings, is like flat disc, dividing heavens from millions of hells below. Living beings are categorised acc. to number of senses they possess: men have the five senses, plus a mind-organ (a 'sixth' sense involved in co-ordinating impressions derived from others); the higher animals five senses only; and so on. The atomic constituents of fire, water, etc., are thought to have one sense, that of touch. Even lower than these are infinite number of animalcules, which do not individually possess organs, but cluster together to share in processes of respiration and nutrition. The law of *karma* and circulation of life-monads through successive bodies, through process of → rebirth, are features of existence of living beings above level of animalcules. Infrequently, life-monads achieve liberation and are taken out of circulation; but from time to time some animalcules 'rise' and enter karmic circulation. This, then, is the backcloth, teeming with life, against which quest for liberation is undertaken. Despite tenacity with which J. has maintained its teachings from anc. times, it believes in progressive decline of the relig. in present age of world, and will die out (to be renewed, however, when next cycle of history commences). The world-picture of J. is supplemented with various philosophical docs. (→ philosophy, Jain). Unlike Buddhism, J. has not been strongly missionary relig., though it has certainly made converts; it has not migrated beyond India except among Indians abroad who happen to be Jains. N.S.

C. Della Casa, *Il Giainismo* (1962); J. Jaini, *Outlines of Jainism* (1940); H. von Glasenapp, *Der Jainismus* (1925); S. T. Stevenson, *The Heart of Jainism* (1915); Charavarti Nayanar, *The Religion of Ahimsa* (1957).

Jalāl al-Dīn Rūmī (604–72/1207–73). Born in Balkh. In childhood the family had to leave because of court intrigue, and, after years of wandering, settled at Qōnya (Iconium). The name Rūmī comes from settling in Asia Minor

(Rūm). Rumi studied in Damascus and Aleppo; when he returned to Qōnya he was made professor. The dervish Shams al-Dīn Tibrīzī came there and exerted considerable influence over Rumi who lodged him in his house, and spent much time learning from him, much to annoyance of his *murīds* (disciples) who resented his neglect of them. The Mawlawī (Mevlevi) order goes back, it is said, to Rumi's respect for Tibrīzī in whose memory he founded it. The name comes from *Mawlānā* (our master), a title given to Rumi. The first branches of order were formed by Rumi's son Sulṭān Walad with music and dancing as central parts of their worship. They have been known as the whirling dervishes. The order continued in Turkey till suppression of orders in 1344/1925. Rumi's most famous work is the *Mathnawī* which contains about 27,000 vv. It consists of stories interspersed with theosophical digressions, the whole being an import. mystical work. For Rumi, God is the Absolute Value, he alone really existing. The world was created for man, the microcosm which reflects God's attributes. God has given man the power of choice between good and evil, making him responsible for his actions. The rites of the relig. ritual are binding on everyone. At the same time, Rumi recognises a real unity underlying varieties of religion. Man's aim, he holds, through love of God should be to pass from individuality and be absorbed in God. Underlying his thought there is a distinct element of → pantheism. J.R.

*E.I.*², II, pp. 393–7; *E.R.E.*, 7, pp. 474f.; *G.A.L.*, *S.*, I, pp. 806f.; Hughes, pp. 118, 121; Pareja, pp. 774, 908f., 929f.; *Mathnawi*, ed. and trans. by R. A. Nicholson, 8 vols. (1925–40) (vols. 1, 3, 5 text; 2, 4, 6 trans.; 7, 8 commentary). R. A. Nicholson, *Rumi: poet and mystic*, ed. A. J. Arberry (1950).

Jamā'at-i-Islāmī Movement which was begun in India in 1360/1941 by Mawlānā Abul A'lā al-Mawdūdī, compares with the → Muslim Brethren. Mawdūdī, a journalist, came from Hyderabad, Deccan to Pathankot in 1337/1938 and removed to Lahore in 1366/1947. His movement is conservative, holding that the → *Sharī'a* cannot be superseded, but granting that law may be instituted on matters it does not cover. The movement has lent itself to violence, but that is not a main purpose of its activity. After the Panjab riots in 1372/1953 involving attacks on the → Ahmadiyya Movement, Mawdūdī spent two years in prison. The movement firmly holds to the trad. docs. of Islam and teaches that Pakistan should be governed by the *sharī'a.* In numbers it is small; but its members ardently believe in what they hold to be the pure Islamic doc., and are prepared to suffer for their faith. Mawdūdī has written many books and pamphlets in Urdu, some trans. into Eng., since 1351/1932 he has published his monthly Urdu magazine, *Tarjumān al-Qur'ān.* J.R.

Munir Report, pp. 243ff. (cf. bibliog to 'Ahmadiyya Movement'); M. J. Faruqi, *Jama'at-i-Islami* (1957); F. K. Abbott, 'Maulana Maududi on Quranic Interpretation', *M.W.*, XLVIII (1958), pp. 6ff.; Cragg, *Counsels*, index (Jama'at, Mawdūdī); W. C. Smith, *Modern History*, pp. 233ff. and index.

Jamāl al-Dīn al-Afghāni (1255–1314/1839–97). Expelled from various countries because of his relig. docs. and political activity, or had to fly for life. He was a man who seemed able to attract followers, esp. among young men. They listened eagerly to his lectures and welcomed his docs. The → '*ulamā*', however, considered him heretical. One of his docs. was need to free the E. from European influence. In relig. he argued in favour of a liberal theology. Though he was more political agent than relig. teacher, the two aspects of his propaganda cannot be altogether separated. He worked in Paris with disciple → Muhammad 'Abduh, but the journal they produced was short-lived. (→ Pan-Islam). He upheld cause of → Mahdi in the Sudan, holding view that the Mahdi would supersede → Caliph. His docs. were such as pleased neither Turks nor British. J.R.

*E.I.*², II, pp. 416–9; Pareja, index (Ğamāl-al-Dīn); W. C. Smith, *Modern History*, index; A. Hourani, *Thought*, index; Elie Kedourie, *Afghani and 'Abduh* (1966); S. A. Hanna, 'Al-Afghani: A pioneer of Islamic Socialism', *M.W.*, LVII (1967), pp. 24ff.; Cragg, *Counsels*, index.

James, brother of Jesus J. played a major role in Primitive Christianity, but a curious silence surrounds his antecedents. Acc. to → Paul, who calls him 'the Lord's brother', J. was first of three leaders of → Jerusalem Church (Gal. 1:19, 2:9, 12); in Acts 21:18, J. is obviously head of Jerus. Church, and Paul reports to him (Acts is silent about J.'s relat. to Jesus). This preeminence of J. is surprising since he was not one of Jesus' orig. → Apostles; it was prob. due to his blood-relationship to Jesus. J. was a zealous Jew, and clearly envisaged future of Chr. movement in terms of → Judaism. He was executed by Ananus (high priest), in 62, in curious circumstances. The Epistle ascribed to him in N.T. is unlikely to be his; but it is of Jew. orig. and seems to reflect his spirit. S.G.F.B.

*H.D.B.*², pp. 457ff.; *R.G.G.*³, III, col. 525–8; K. L. Carroll, 'The Place of James in the Early Church', *B.J.R.L.*, 44 (1961); S. G. F. Brandon, *Jesus and the Zealots* (1967), pp. 159ff.; 'The Death of James the Just: a new interpretation', in *Studies in Mysticism and Religion*, ed. R. J. Z. Werblowsky (1967–8).

Janus Orig. Roman *numen* of *ianua*, entrance-gate, J. became god of beginnings, and headed list of gods; the 1st month of reformed calendar was Januarius, in which his festival occurred. The closing of the monumental *Ianus geminus* in Forum signified peace. J. was repr. with two faces, each looking in opp. direction from other. S.G.F.B.

O.C.D., *s.v.; Kleine Pauly*, II, col. 1311–4; F. Gnecchi, *Monete romane* (1935), figs. 18, 30, 31.

Japan (Cultural traditions) J. consists of four major and some 3,000 small islands situated in W. Pacific, and separated from Korea and U.S.S.R. by Sea of J., with an area of some 143,000 square miles and a pop. of about 95 M. The land is mostly mountainous and largely volcanic, only one-tenth of total surface being agricultural land. 63% of pop. is urban; it is the most industrialized and highly developed country in Asia.

Though reliable hist. records do not exist before *c.* 4th cent. CE, it is almost certain that earliest inhabitants of J., → Ainus (of whom a few descendants survive in N.), were supplanted by immigrants from China, Manchuria, Korea and S.E. Asia. Their main settlements developed on two great plains, the Kanto area in E., which today possesses in Tokyo the most populous capital city of world, and the Kansai region in W., at the head of Inland Sea, with its great cities of Kyoto, Osaka and Kobe. This latter area was the heartland of the J. empire from CE 794 when Heian-kyo (now Kyoto) was estab. as capital, and remained so till 1868 CE. From earliest hist. times J. was profoundly influenced by Chinese culture, and received from China its ideographic script, Confucian ethico-political ideals, and → Buddh. relig. This latter, adapted and remoulded along distinctively J. lines, exerted profound influence over all aspects of J. culture. The indigenous faith → Shinto, with its myths of creation of J. and estab. of the imperial dynasty, continued to exist alongside Buddhism as a major relig., social and political influence.

Throughout J. hist., the emperor, by virtue of divine descent, received a unique dignity and status, but seldom exercised real powers of government. In feudalistic society of mediaeval J., government from 8th–12th cents. was in hands of a gifted family of courtiers known as the Fujiwara, and from 12th cent. until the middle of 18th cent. was exercised by a succession of military rulers known as shoguns. It was during the Kamakara period (CE 1185–1338) that Buddhism assumed a J. complexion, and the great → Jodo, → Shin and → Nichiren sects had their birth. → Zen also came to flower, to provide a perennial inspiration to J. art and culture.

From 17th cent. until the Meiji Restoration in CE 1868, the Tokugawa shogunate attempted policy of strict national seclusion, limiting foreign trade to port of Nagasaki and forbidding J. to travel abroad. Christianity, intro. into J. by Portuguese missionaries in 16th cent., after considerable initial success, was violently suppressed. A strong revival of nationalist Shinto took place. With the Meiji Restoration, the emperor became sovereign ruler, and the capital was moved to Tokyo. The policy of seclusion was abandoned, and J. became rapidly modernised along W. lines. After defeat of China (1894–5) and of Russia (1904–5), J. embarked on a policy of imperial expansion which was brought to a dramatic end by World War II. Since then, though the emperor remains as symbol of national unity, J. has become a democracy, governed by a parliament of two houses, the Lower House, elected by universal suffrage, having most power.

In the post-war years, economic growth, industrialization and technological advance have been phenomenal. There is a high degree of literacy, and the standard of living for most J. has been raised. The granting of complete relig. freedom, the removal of restrictive legislation and greater individual liberty have led to remarkable upsurge of what are known as Shinko-shukyo, the New Religions. These, mainly based in sectarian Shinto, claim the adherence of tens of millions. D.H.S.

Guy Wint (ed.), *Asia* (1965); G. B. Samson, *Japan*, rev. edn. (1946); J. E. Kidder, *Japan before Buddhism* (1959).

Japanese Religion Japan is the meeting place of four religs.: →→ Shinto, Buddhism, Confucianism and Christianity. Of these Shinto alone is native to Japan. About middle of 6th cent. CE, Buddh., Taoist and Confucian influences came into Japan from China along with Chi. culture, literature and art. The Japanese accepted the Confucian morality with its emphasis on filial piety; but it was Buddh. monks who made the greatest impact, and for 1,000 years Shinto was in large measure absorbed into the Buddh. system. Christianity came to Japan about middle of 16th cent.; after initial success it was practically obliterated until Chr. missions began again in middle of 19th cent.

→ Shinto, the indigenous relig. of Japan, has always been connected with national traditions and social institutions. Possessing a body of myths concerned with creation of Japan and estab. of the imperial dynasty, Shinto has hardly any system of doc., is poorly organised and incurably polytheistic. Yet its influence has persisted through the cents.: as National Shinto through its cult of emperor-worship, inseparable from worship of divine ancestress → Amaterasu, the sun-goddess, its divinisation of national heroes, and its influence for national unity and social solidarity; as sectarian Shinto, rooted in family and communal life, calling for faithful observance of age-old traditions, teaching reverence for nature in all its manifestations, and inculcating virtues of gratitude, loyalty, courage, justice, politeness, reserve and honour.

→ Confucianism influenced political, social, legal and educational institutions of Japan, and provided systematic teaching of morality, whilst the cosmological and metaphysical systems developed by neo-Confucians (→ Chu Hsi and → Wang Yang-ming) exerted profound influence over Jap. scholars.

But it was → Buddhism, intro. in 6th cent. CE from China, which became main relig. force in life of Jap. people. It provided a satisfying cosmology and eschatology, elaborate systems of spiritual disciplines and training, and well-organised eccles. organisations. It stimulated creative philosophical speculation, and production of magnificent works of art and literature. It provided great seats of learning, and brought to flower the relig. and aesthetic sentiments of the people. As a popular relig. of the masses, Buddhism provided, on one hand, a satisfying ritual for repose of dead; on the other hand, magical and supernatural assistance for production of mundane benefits. The great → Jodo and → Shin sects taught absolute faith and trust in → Amida Buddha. → Zen Buddhism offered discipline and guidance for those who sought enlightenment through self-reliance.

In the hist. of relig. in Japan the relation between Buddhism and Shinto has undergone great changes. In gen. it has been marked by mutual tolerance and mutual borrowings (→ Ryobu Shinto); but from 17th cent. onwards chauvinism and xenophobia exalted Shinto as a national faith, which led to severe persecution of Buddhism and burdensome restrictions upon Buddh. clergy.

When Christianity entered Japan in 16th cent., it had great initial success under the protection of powerful feudatory lords; partic. under Shogun Nobunaga (*c.* CE 1568) who hated Buddh. But, under Shogun Ieyasu (d. CE 1616) and his son Hidetada, it was completely suppressed in persecution of intense ferocity. Not until opening of Japan to W. influence in middle of 19th cent., did Chr. missionary activity again begin. Though Christianity has made a considerable impact, espec. in urban areas, and through its social, educat. and medical work, the Chr. community repr. less than 1% of population.

In modern times, all religs. in Japan have been faced with growing secularism and non-relig. attitude of the intelligentsia, and inroads made by Communist ideology. At close of World War II, National or State Shinto disappeared; since that date there has been a phenomenal proliferation of Shinto sects, usually founded by some charismatic figure, promulgating apocalyptic and eschatological teachings, practising faith-healing, spiritism, divination and the like, and inculcating virtue and mutual helpfulness. These sects are usually syncretistical, drawing their inspiration and ideas from Buddhism, Christianity, and pseudo-scientific societies. Buddhism, with its numerous sects and entrenched in traditionalism, is still a living relig. in Japan, but has lost much of its early vigour. D.H.S.

M. Anesaki, *Hist. of Japanese Religion* (1930); W. K. Bunce, *Religs. in Japan* (1955); J. M. Kitagawa, *Relig. in Japanese Hist.* (1966); J. Herbert, *Shinto* (1967); J. Boxer, *The Christian Century in Japan*, 1549–1650 (1968).

-Jassāsa Name of fabulous animal, so hairy that one could not tell its front from back, mentioned in trad. in which → Muḥammad is repr. as quoting Tamīm al-Dārī, a Christ. convert to Islam. He told of reaching an island where this animal lived after his boat had been storm-tossed for a month. Its duty was to find out information for the → dajjāl, who was chained on the island. The story is strange, for the dajjāl told the sailors he would soon be set free to roam earth. The J. has been assimilated to → *dābbat al-arḍ*, but its function seems quite different. Its name means female spy, which indic. its purpose. J.R.

*E.I.*², II, p. 486; *Mishkāt*, pp. 1149–51.

Jātaka Type of Buddh. lit., viz. a 'birth-story'. By this is meant a story of the Buddha, or of some prominent character among early Buddh., in some previous existence, or 'birth'. The principal character may appear as a man, a *deva*, a demon, or more usually, an animal. The present characteristics or situation of person concerned are supposed to be at least partly explainable in terms of his conduct in previous existence of which the J. tells. The → Pāli canon contains collection of 547 such stories, which forms part of the → *Khuddaka Nikaya*. Many stories are anc. folk tales of Indian pre-Buddh. origin, which have been taken over and adapted for Buddh. use by add. of an explanatory prologue giving the *mis-en-scéne*, often in connection with travels and preaching of → Gotama the Buddha, and with epilogue added, in which the characters in the anc. story are identified with prominent persons of time of Buddha. The most import. element in these J.'s are the verses, which sometimes express the moral of story, sometimes form part of narrative and dialogue. Strictly it is the verses alone which are regarded as canonical; the narrator was allowed certain liberty of expression in prose passages. Besides the Pali canonical collection of 547, there are several Chinese collections, based on Skt. or Prakrit originals; variant collections are known to exist in Buddh. countries of S.E. Asia, some of which have recently become known to West. scholars. From early times Buddh., e.g. → *Ajantā* have delighted in providing pictorial or *bas-relief* versions of J.'s for embellishment of pagodas and monasteries and for edification of the Buddh. populace, who thus from an early age have become familiar with the virtues regarded as admirable in Buddh. trad. Beside their familiarity with these pictorial versions of the J.'s the Buddh. lay people of S.E. Asia are usually familiar also with at least the major J.'s in their lit. or recited forms. T.O.L.

Jātaka Stories, trans. by various hands under editorship of E. B. Cowell, repr. in 3 vols (1956); T. W. Rhys-Davids, *Buddhist India*, 8th edn. (1959), ch. XI.

Java (Buddhism) → *Indonesia* (Buddhism). T.O.L.

Jehovah → Yahweh. S.G.F.B.

Jehovah's Witnesses Chr. Adventist sect, founded and developed during last two decades of 19th cent. in U.S.A. by C. T. Russell and 'Judge' I. F. Rutherford. Interpreting Bible literally, they believe that Jehovah will defeat → Satan, and the faithful, i.e. J.-W., either then alive or resurrected, will live in divine kingdom on earth. The sect has spread to Britain, Africa and elsewhere. Their principles cause them to refuse military service and blood transfusion. (→ Chiliasm). S.G.F.B.

R. Pike, *Jehovah's Witnesses* (1954); M. Cole, *Jehovah's Witnesses* (1956).

Jeremiah, Book of There are many problems concerning the composition of this book; but it is gen. accepted that it contains prophecies of J. before and after the destr. of → Jerusalem in 586 BC. Its significance for hist. of Jew. relig. lies in its evidence of how a → Yahwist prophet dealt with break-down of old sense of communal solidarity and new demand for individual significance resulting from Israel's misfortunes at this time. J. preaches individual responsibility; he extends scope of → Heilsgeschichte, and proclaims the → Messianic hope. The book reveals J.'s personality and spiritual anguish. (→ Judaism). S.G.F.B.

H.D.B.[2], pp. 465–70; *P.C.*[2], pp. 537ff.; *R.G.G.*[3], III, col. 581–90; A. Lods, *Les prophètes d'Israël* (1935), pp. 50ff.; H. H. Rowley, *Men of God* (1963), pp. 133ff.

Jericho This anc. city, which figures so dramatically in Jew. hist. (*Joshua* 2:1ff.), has acquired further distinction through recent excavations. Human settlement can be traced back there to *c.* 7800 BC. Of unique interest has been the discovery of 'portrait-skulls' (*c.* 6500 BC), prob. repr. → ancestor-cult. The cult of the Mother Goddess is also attested for this remote period. S.G.F.B.

K. M. Kenyon, 'Neolithic Portrait Skulls from Jericho', *Antiquity*, 27 (1953), *Excavations at Jericho*, I (The Tombs) (1960), *Amorites and Canaanites* (1966); J. Mellaart, *Earliest Civilizations of the Near East* (1965), pp. 22ff.; *H.D.B.*[2], *s.v.*

Jerome, St. (*c.* 342–420) Born at Strido, nr. Aquileia, J. was not only an eminent Chr. scholar, but had the distinction of knowing Hebrew. His knowledge of Heb. and Grk. enabled him to produce the Lat. trans. of Bible known as the → Vulgate, which became official version of W. Church. J. wrote other works on Biblical and eccl. subjects, and participated vigorously in current theological controversy. He was a fervent advocate of → asceticism and finally settled at Bethlehem, where he ruled a monastery. S.G.F.B.

E.R.E., VI, *s.v.; D.C.C.*, *s.v.; R.G.G.*[3], III, col. 315–6; P. de Labriolle, *Hist. and Lit. of Latin Christianity* (E.T. 1924), pp. 333ff.

Jerusalem This city, sacred to Judaism, Christianity and Islam, was orig. a Jebusite settlement; it is first mentioned in Egypt. records *c.* 1330 BC. Its Jew. hist. begins with → David's capture of it (*c.* 1000 BC). The first → Temple was built by Solomon (*c.* 970–31). Destroyed by Nebuchadnezzar, 586 BC, J. was resettled by Jews and Temple rebuilt in 516 BC. After many vicissitudes of fortune, J. and its Temple were destroyed by Romans under Titus in CE 70. Hadrian built a Roman city, → Aelia Capitolina, on site in 135. Chr. interest in J. started with estab. of Church there (→ Jerus. Church); it found concrete expression in early 4th cent., when Constantine caused Church of Holy Sepulchre to be built over alleged tomb of Christ and → Calvary. In 637, J. fell to Muslims, for whom its O.T. assocs. and connection with → Muhammad made it holy. They built the Dome of the Rock, a mosque, on site of Temple. J. was captured by → Crusaders in 1099, and remained in Chr. possession until its Muslim recapture in 1187. It was captured from Turks by British in 1917, who ruled it until end of Mandate in 1948, it was then divided between new state of Israel and Kingdom of Jordan until its capture by Israel (1967). Possession of Chr. holy-places is shared between Lat., Grk., Armenian, Coptic and Ethiopic Churches. S.G.F.B.

G. A. Smith, *Jerusalem*, 2 vols. (1907); L. H. Vincent, *Jérusalem antique* (1912); L.-H. Vincent-F. M. Abel, *Jérusalem nouvelle*, 4 vols. (1914–26); L.-H. Vincent-A. M. Steve, *Jérusalem de l'Ancien Testament*, 2 vols. (1954–6); M. Join-Lambert, *Jerusalem* (1966); *H.D.B.*[3], *s.v.;* K. Kenyon, *Jerusalem* (1967); J. Jeremias, *Jerusalem zur Zeit Jesu* (1958[2]).

(Church of) Acc. to → Paul and → Acts, the orig. community of Jesus' disciples at Jerus. formed the fount of Chr. movement and its centre of authority and trad. This evidence is suppl. by → Hegesippus and → Clementine Lit. The members of J.-C. continued to live as orthodox Jews, worshipping in → Temple; they incl. → Pharisees and priests. The head of J.-C. was → James, the Lord's brother; he was succeeded by Symeon, another relative, thus indic. dynastic leadership. The J.-C. opposed Paul's interpret. of Christianity, and prob. would have kept movement within → Judaism, if it had not been obliterated in destruc. of Jerus. in 70. It is likely that members of J.-C. had made common cause with compatriots against Rome. A later legend about their flight to Pella prob. repr. claim of Church of → Aelia Capitolina to descend from orig. C.-J., and is unhistorical. S.G.F.B.

H. J. Schoeps, *Theologie u. Gesch. des Judenchristentums* (1949), *Urgemeinde, Judenchristentum, Gnosis* (1956); G. Strecker, *Das Judenchristentum in den Pseudoklementinen* (1958); S. G. F. Brandon, *The Fall of Jerusalem and the Christian Church* (1957[2]), *Jesus and the Zealots* (1957); J. Daniélou, in *Crucible of Christianity* (1969), pp. 275ff.

Jesuits The Society of Jesus (S.J.), founded by Ignatius Loyola, former Spanish soldier, received Papal approval in 1540. It was designed to support → Papacy against heresy and convert the heathen. It was organised on military lines (its head is called General), and to usual threefold monastic vows a 4th was added: to go instantly wherever the Pope ordered. The J. soon became both an effective force in → Counter Reformation and in missions in Africa, India, China, Japan and America, where many suffered martyrdom. Enmity in Cath. countries caused suppression of Society by Pope in 1773. It was restored by Papal decree in 1814. J. work today in most countries, esp. in education missions. Their influence in R.C. Church has been very considerable. S.G.F.B.

D.C.C., *s.v.; E.R.E.*, VI, *s.v.; R.G.G.*[3], III, col. 612–8; *N.C.M.H.*, II, pp. 291ff.; L. Polgar, *Bibliography of Hist. of Society of Jesus* (1967).

Jesus of Nazareth This article deals with the historical person; for theological evaluation → Christ; → Christianity; → Christology; → Incarnation; → Soteriology. The extant evidence is almost wholly of Chr. origin, being provided by the four → Gospels: very brief refs. are made by Roman writers Tacitus and Suetonius; an account of J. by → Josephus raises many critical problems. J. was born at Bethlehem sometime before d. of Herod the Great in 4 BC (Mt. 2:1ff.). Until his 30th yr., his life was lived at Nazareth and is unrecorded, except for one incident (Lk. 2:41ff.). Acc. to early trad., his mother Mary conceived him without intercourse with her husband Joseph (→ Virgin Birth). The chronology of public career of J., as recorded in → Gospels, is obscure: it could have lasted either one or three yrs. After baptism by → John the Baptist, J. began an independent mission in Galilee. His message is summarized in Mk. 1:15: 'The time is fulfilled, and the kingdom of God is at hand: repent'. Seen in context of contemporary Jew. → apocalyptic lit., this message suggests that J.'s aim was to prepare Israel for the imminent replacement of existing social and political order by a → theocracy. His message and miracles won much popular response; but he encountered opposition of Jew. relig. authorities. J. was evidently recognised as → Messiah by many, and his action during last visit to Jerusalem suggests he so regarded himself: he appears to have arranged a Messianic entry into city (Mk. 11:1ff.). The exact significance of the events of J.'s last days in Jerus. is obscure, owing to apologetic intent of Mark's Gospel, whose record is followed by other Gospels. Thus the purpose of his 'Cleansing of the Temple' (Mk. 11:15ff.) is puzzling: it was in effect an attack on authority of the priestly aristocracy, who dealt with domestic affairs under the Romans. J.'s attack on Temple may have coincided with a revolt in which → Zealots were involved (Mk. 15:17). It seems that Jew. authorities were not strong enough to arrest J. openly, but were able to seize him at night, owing to defection of → Judas Iscariot. The disciples of J. were armed and armed resistance was offered in Gethsemane to his arrest, but unsuccessfully (Lk. 22:35ff.). J.'s trial before the → Sanhedrin is obscure, due to Mark's apologetic concern: its purpose seems to have been to get evidence of sedition preparatory to handing J. over to Pilate, who ordered his crucifixion as rebel against Roman government (yr. 30 or 33). J.'s body was buried in a rock-hewn tomb, which, acc. to Chr. trad., was found empty three days later. The disciples became convinced that they saw him alive and touched him after his death and burial. These experiences are recorded to have lasted 40 days (Acts 1:3), after which J. visibly ascended into heaven and was seen no more in this manner

(→ Ascension of J.C.). What J., as a historical person actually did and taught, is obscured in Gospels by theological and apologetical interests of their authors and those for whom they wrote. The account of J.'s death is esp. involved in this way. Mark's Gospel reveals embarrassment about J.'s relations with the Zealots, and seeks to shift responsibility for Crucifixion from Roman gov. to Jew. leaders. Recent study of Zealots is likely to cause some adjustment of trad. interpretation of J. as a hist. person. (→ Mark, Gospel). S.G.F.B.

The lit. is vast and reflects theological preconceptions. The following list is designed to give a representative estimate: A. Schweitzer, *The Quest for the Historical Jesus* (E.T. 1910); J. Klausner, *Jesus of Nazareth* (E.T. 1929); C. J. Cadoux, *The Historic Mission of Jesus* (1941); B. S. Easton, *Christ and the Gospels* (1930); F. C. Burkitt, *Christian Beginnings* (1924); A. J. Olmstead, *Jesus: in the Light of History* (1942); T. W. Manson, *The Teaching of Jesus* (1935); E. Stauffer, *Jesus and his Story* (E.T. 1960); O. Cullmann, *The State in the New Test.* (E.T. 1957); F. W. Beare, *The Earliest Records of Jesus* (1962); *R.G.G.*[3], III, col. 619–53; H. P. Kossen, *Op Zoek naar de Historische Jezus* (1960); M. Goguel, *The Life of Jesus* (E.T. 1933); Ch. Guignebert, *Jesus* (E.T. 1935); P. Winter, *On the Trial of Jesus* (1961); J. Blinzer, *The Trial of Jesus* (E.T. 1959); *H.D.B.*[2], *s.v.; P.C.*[2], p. 733; *Kleine Pauly*, II, col. 1134–54; J. M. Robinson, *A New Quest of the Historical Jesus* (1959); H. Zahrnt, *The Historical Jesus* (E.T. 1963); O. Betz, *What do we know about Jesus?* (E.T. 1968); S. G. F. Brandon, *Jesus and the Zealots* (1967), *The Trial of Jesus of Nazareth* (1968); J. Blinzler, *Der Progress Jesu* (1969[4]).

Jesus Christ (in Islam) Mentioned 25 times in the → Qur. with name 'Isā. He is also called → Messiah (*al-Masīḥ*) and son of Mary. The Qur. contains stories of Annunciation (iii:37ff.; xix:16ff.) and → Virgin Birth (xix:22ff.), of miracles such as making clay birds fly, healing dumb and leper and raising dead (iii:43; v:109f.). J. was strengthened by spirit of holiness (ii:81, 254). He came to verify → Tawrāt and give good news of coming of Aḥmad (lxi:6). People who say God is Messiah, son of Mary, have disbelieved (v:76). When questioned by God, J. denied telling men to take him and his mother as gods beside God (v:116f.). J. speaks in a Meccan sura of 'the day I was born, the day I die and the day I am raised up alive' (xix:34). In a Medina sura God says to J. 'I shall cause you to die and raise you to myself' (iii:48). The most striking passage is in a Medina sura (iv:156f.), where God speaks in condemnation of those who say they have killed the Messiah. They neither killed him nor crucified him; a substitute was put in his place and God raised J. to himself. The Qur. calls J. servant, prophet, messenger, word, spirit, and describes him as a sign, example, witness, mercy, eminent, one brought near, one of the upright and blessed. But it insists that he is no more than a prophet, though he is given titles ascribed to no other.

Trad. speaks of his second coming as just judge. He will break crosses, kill swine, and abolish the → *jizya.* His descent will be at the white minaret in the E. of Damascus. Every infidel who feels the odour of his breath will die. He will catch up with the → dajjāl at the gate of Ludd, and kill him. Another trad. says he will marry, have children, and die after a stay of 45 yrs. He will be buried in → Muḥammad's grave, and Muhammad and he will rise between → Abū Bakr and → 'Umar at the Resurrection.

Later Muslim lit. has numerous refs. to J., laying emphasis on his being an ascetic, his miracles and moral teaching. Later Islam characteristically considers him as one who abhorred world and lived as extreme ascetic. E.g., one story says J. took only a comb and jug with him; but one day he saw a man combing his beard with his fingers, so he threw away the comb. Afterwards he saw another drinking from a river with the palms of his hands, so he threw away the jug. A saying frequently quoted which is attr. to J. is, 'The world is a bridge, so pass over it and do not inhabit it.' J.R.

E.I., II, pp. 524–6; Hughes, pp. 229–35; S. M. Zwemer, *The Moslem Christ* (1912); J. Robson, *Christ in Islam* (1929); Parrinder, *Jesus;* F. Rosenthal, *Ibn Khaldun*, index; *Mishkāt*, pp. 1143, 1146f., 1159f. and index; Asin y Palacios, 'Logia et Agrapha Domini Jesu apud Moslemicos Scriptores, asceticos praesertim, usitata', in *Patrologia Orientalis*, xiii and xix.

Jewish Christianity Christianity began in Galilee as a Jew. messianic movement centred on → Jesus of Nazareth. After his crucifixion, Jerusalem became the headquarters of movement (→ Jerusalem, Church), which remained essentially Jew. and looked for triumphant return of Jesus as → Messiah to 'restore the kingdom of Israel'. Chiefly due to → Paul, a new form of the faith was propagated, outside Palestine among Gentiles, in which Jesus was presented as universal saviour-god rather than Jew. Messiah. After destruction of → Jerusalem, CE 70, in which Jerus. Church perished, remnants of J.-C. continued in various parts of Palestine and Syria. Their → Christology, being of primitive character (→ Adoptionism), and their other Jew. beliefs caused them to be regarded as heretics by Gentile Christians. They grad. died out. Some fragments of their literature survives:

→→ Clementine Lit., Hebrews, Gosp. of (→ Nazarene). S.G.F.B.

H. J. Schoeps, *Theologie u. Gesch. des Judenchristentums* (1949); J. Daniélou, *Théologie du Judéo-Christianisme* (1958); G. Strecker, *Das Judenchristentum in den Pseudoklementinen* (1958); J. Munck, 'Jew. Christianity in post-Apostolic Times', *N.T.S.*, 6 (1960); S. G. F. Brandon, *Jesus and the Zealots* (1967).

Jews (in Islām) The Qur. uses *Yahūd* (Jews) only 8 times, and only in Medina suras, the adjective *yahūdī* once. Banū Isrā'īl (Children of Israel) occurs 40 times, in Mecca and Medina suras. This shows → Muḥammad had Jew. contacts before going to Medina, from which source he gained some elementary knowledge of prophets and Israelite hist. In Medina where lived the Jew. tribes of Qurayẓa, al-Naḍīr and Qaynuqā', with prob. some minor clans, he had closer experience, and soon felt disappointment because the J. did not accept him as prophet. His emphasis on → Abraham as father of the faithful made little impression, and he grad. showed his displeasure. In 2/623 he changed the direction in which prayer was conducted (→ Qibla) from Jerusalem to Mecca; shortly after battle of → Badr, he began to deal with the Jew. tribes, first Qaynuqā', then at later dates al-Naḍīr and Qurayẓa, all the men of latter being executed. He had profited from Jew. divisions by being able to deal with tribes separately. The Jews of Khaybar, about 100 miles N. of Medina, had been plotting, so Muhammad attacked and took their settlement, leaving them to work land on condition of paying over half produce (yr. 7/628). Other Jew. settlements made treaties with Muhammad and danger of Jew. attacks was removed. Muhammad had always shown himself willing to come to terms with the J., but their hostility had led to stern measures. He could now accept them as a → protected people. During → 'Umar's Caliphate, the Jews were expelled from Arabia on ground that there must be only one relig. in the land. Elsewhere, throughout Muslim world, J. were always treated as a protected people, even being able later to return to Arabia and estab. communities in the Yemen. J. often rose to high position in state, and their contributions to learning, notably in Spain, were distinguished. They had gen. to be content with position of second class citizens; but they had freedom to observe their relig. and administer their laws within their community, subject to payment of → *jizya*. J.R.

E.I., IV, pp. 1146–8; Hughes, pp. 235–43; Pareja, index; Tritton, *Non-Muslims*, *passim;* Guillaume, *Life*, pp. 239ff., 363f., 437ff., 461ff., 510ff.; Watt, *Medina*, ch. VI and index; F. Rosenthal, *Ibn Khaldun*, index; H. G. Reissner, 'The Ummi Prophet and the Banu Israil of the Qur'an', in *M.W.*, XXXIX (1949), pp. 276ff.

Jhāna (Pali); **Dhyāna** (Skt.) Buddh. technical term for progression through certain mental states, the climax of which is a special experience of enhanced psychic vitality. The use of term may have been pre-Buddh. Usually 4 stages are distinguished: concentration of mind on single subject; mental and physical joy and ease; then a sense of ease only; finally, sense of perfect clarity and equanimity. In the → Abhidhamma lit. 5 stages are distinguished, the 1st of the 4 subdivided into two; these divisions are arbitrary and schematic only; the order of progression could be divided up into yet other stages. The 4 Jh.'s are described in a number of passages in the Pali canon, e.g. in the *Samañña-phala Sutta* (*D.N.*, i, 73ff.), (*Dialogues of the Buddha*, Pt. I, pp. 84–6). The experience thus achieved is regarded as means to further spiritual progress and not as an end in itself; from a relig. or spiritual point of view the Jh.'s as such are of neutral value. The view that achievement of the Jh.'s was equivalent to attaining spiritual state of → nirvāna is repudiated in the *Brahma-Jala Sutta* of the → Digha Nikaya (*D.N.*, i, 37ff.) (*Dialogues of the Buddha*, pt. I, pp. 50–2).

The hist. of word *jhāna/dhyāna* is noteworthy. In its Skt. form, the term passed into Chinese Buddh. usage as → Ch'an, and hence into Japanese as → Zen. A somewhat different arrangement of *dhyāna* under 4 heads is characteristic of → Mahayana, and espec. of the → Yogācāras; it is dealt with by D. T. Suzuki in his *Essays in Zen Buddhism*, Series I, pp. 81f., and *Studies in the Lankavatara Sutra* (1930). The Yogācāras laid special emphasis on experience of withdrawal from world by means of *dhyāna*. T.O.L.

Jihād (Striving). May refer to fighting with infidels, or to striving by persuasion and example to make converts. The fact that it was customary to divide world into two sections, *dār al-Islām* (the abode of Islam) and *dār al-ḥarb* (the abode of war) shows that the feeling was predominant that war must continue till Islam is the universal religion. The → Qur. clearly envisages fighting against polytheists (cf. viii:39f., which allows for forgiveness if the Meccans repent, but if not, they are to be fought till the relig. is entirely God's; ix:124, which orders harsh fighting with neighbouring unbelievers). Fighting is also ordered against Jews and Christians till they pay the → *jizya* (ix:29). → 'Umar I clearly understood that no place could be given to unbelievers when he decreed that there could be only one relig. in Arabia (→ Jews). The common phrase in Qur. is to strive in God's path (*fī sabīl Allāh*), a phrase which does not always necessarily involve fighting. Fighting was pre-eminently against polytheists; for them the choice was between Islam or the sword. In case of such people as Jews, Christians, Magians surrender and payment of *jizya* was demanded, otherwise there was no compulsion to accept Islam; they could practice their relig., but not propagate it. In course of time, with spread of Islam, Muslims learned to live alongside other peoples not orig. among those called 'People of the Book' (Scriptuaries). Regarding fighting in J., the theory is that J. is a duty, but not applicable to everyone; for the duty is fulfilled when a sufficient number who are able to fight take part in J. But it is to be noted that J. was not always conducted irrespective of conditions; favourable circumstances for it were sought. In the past → Ṣūfīs have held that the greater J. is conquest of oneself; the lesser is fighting with infidels. In more mod. times arguments have been put forward to show that fighting was conducted only in self-defence, and Qur. authority can be quoted to support this, e.g. ii:186 which exhorts the believers to fight in God's way those who fight them. But those who use this argument select their quotations. J. was fundamentally the relig. war. The → Zaydīs and the more recently instituted → Ahmadiyya reject the warlike J. J.R.

*E.I.*², II, pp. 538–40; Hughes, pp. 243–8; Pareja, index (*ǧihād*); Cheragh 'Ali, *A critical exposition of the popular 'Jihad', showing that all wars of Mohammad were defensive* (1885); Levy, *Social Structure*, index; T. W. Arnold, *Preaching of Islam* (1913); R. Amaldez, 'La guerre sainte selon Ibn Ḥazm de Cordoue', *Études d'orientalisme dédiées à la mémoire de Levi-Provençal*, II, pp. 445 ff. (1962).

Jimmu Tennō Deified in → Shinto as 1st emperor of Japan, the direct descendant of → Amaterasu and progenitor of Japanese imperial family. Acc. to Jap. hist. traditions, J.T. embarked from Kyushu on conquest of central province of Yamato; setting up his capital there, he ascended the throne in 660 BC. He reigned till 585 BC, when he died at age of 127. With him Jap. hist. is supposed to begin; but the annals of Japan for this period and for nearly 1000 years subsequently are mainly legend. A great national yearly festival on 29th day of 1st month commemorates the accession. D.H.S.

W. G. Aston, *The Way of the Gods* (1905), pp. 116ff.; *E.R.E.*, XI, pp. 466–7.

Jingū The designation 'Jingu' (*jin*—deity; *gū*—dwelling-place) is applied to Shinto shrines in Japan of special importance. It is applied to the two Ise temples, to some special temples where ancestors of emperors are enshrined, and also to a few other temples of distinguished background. (→ Jinja). D.H.S.

J. Herbert, *Shinto* (1967), p. 128.

Jinja Name officially applied to trad. shrines of state Shinto in Japan, in which the Shinto deities were supposed to live or to take up residence when summoned by appropriate ceremonies. (*Jin*—deity: *ja*—dwelling-place). The use of name was not permitted to Buddh. temples (*tera*), or shrines of Shinto sects (*kyōkai*). D.H.S.

D. C. Holtom, *The National Faith of Japan* (1938), p. 7.

Jinjō (d. 742 CE). Korean monk who introduced the → Kegon school of Buddhism into Japan. D.H.S.

Jinn (Sing. *jinnī*, anglicé, genie). Beings created of fire mentioned frequently in the Qur. (cf. xv:27, lv:14). They are mortal (xli:24; xlvi:17). Though God has created men and J. to adore him (li:56), some are unbelievers(vi:130) and will go to hell (vi:110; xi:120; xxxii:13). Some tried to suggest false ideas to → Muḥammad (vi:112). Some heard the Qur. and repented of their infidelity (lxxii:1ff.; slvi:28ff.). Solomon commanded troops of J. (xxvii:17, 29; xxxiv:11). J., as distinct from → angels, are said to have been objects of worship (xxxiv:40). Some prophets were accused by their people of being possessed by J. (xxiii:25, 72; xxxiv:8). This is an accusation of receiving their inspiration from such a source and not from God. Muhammad indignantly denied that he was a poet, because it was believed that poets were J.-possessed, this being source of their inspiration. That J. can exert harmful influence is indic. by a prayer for preservation from their evil (cxiv:6).

Acc. to popular belief, J. exist mainly in communal groups, marrying and living life comparable to that of humanity; but individuals may inhabit trees, waste places, ruined, or even inhabited houses. They are normally invisible, but can appear in human or other forms. The common people usually think of them as workers of mischief. Stories about their doings usually come at second or third hand. The present writer was told by an Arab that he had heard wedding celebrations of the J. in his neighbourhood in the Yemen, and he knew a family near Aden which had a succession of troubles attri. by neighbours to presence of a jinnī in their house. Some mod. Muslims have explained the J. in Qur. as refs. to natural forces, or causes of disease. Muhammad 'Alī, in his commentary on the Qur. usually explains them as hostile people. In lxxii:8 he considers them to be diviners and astrologers. The word *majnūn* (jinn-possessed) is used meaning insane. J.R.

*E.I.*², pp. 346ff.; Hughes, pp. 133–8; Pareja, index (*ǧinn*); *E.R.E.*, I, pp. 669f.; Wellhausen, *Reste*, pp. 148ff.; D. B. Macdonald, *Attitude*,

Lecture V; A. S. Tritton, 'Spirits and demons in Arabia', *J.R.A.S.* (1934), pp. 714ff.

Jīva One of terms used in Indian trad. for soul or life-monad, and also for empirical self. Thus in → Jainism there is a fundamental distinction between the life-monads (*jīvas*) and non-living, material world (*ajīva*)—the latter incl. human and other organic bodies. The J. undergoes successive rebirths until it attains liberation (*kevala*), when it remains motionless at summit of universe. In → Advaita Vedanta, the J. is empirical self, which is ultimately unreal. It continues to be implicated in rebirth until one gains existential realization of identity of the Self and → *Brahman*. N.S.

Jizya (Tax). Came to be used of poll-tax levied on non-Muslim protected people. If they had come to an agreement with their conquerors, they could retain their land; but if they were conquered by force, their land belonged to the Muslim community and the orig. owners were employed on it. The J. was levied acc. to financial position of those liable to pay. In the doc. of the Ḥanafī school women and children were exempt, but other schools held they should pay J. Monks and hermits, paupers and slaves were exempt. If a member of the protected people became a → Muslim he was freed from paying J., but had to pay *zakāt* (→ Legal Alms), and was liable to be put to death if he apostatised (→ Apostasy). In return for paying J., protection was guaranteed; non-Muslim subjects were not liable for military service, but they could volunteer. (→ Protected Peoples). J.R.

*E.I.*², II, pp. 559–67; Hughes, p. 248; Pareja, index (*ğizya*); Jeffery, *Vocabulary*, pp. 101f.; Levy, *Social Structure*, index.

Jñānamārga The way of *jñāna*—'knowledge', 'gnosis'. In trad. → Hinduism contrast is drawn between path of works (*karmamārga*), incl. ritual works, as means of salvation, etc.; the way of → *bhakti* (the *bhaktimārga*) and way of knowledge. The last incl. philosophy, but in principle Hindu philosophical systems are geared to attainment of → *moksa*, so that in theory the knowledge they bring is existential. Most characteristically *jnana* accrues upon meditative and yogic practices. Its opposite is *ajnana* or → *avidya*, often regarded as root cause of one's implication in suffering and round of → rebirth, since ignorance or lack of spiritual perception veils the eternal from men, and leads them to grasp for perishable goods. N.S.

A. Wayman, 'Notes on the Sanskrit Term *Jñāna*', *J.A.O.S.*, vol. 75 (1955), pp. 253ff.; F. Edgerton, 'The Upanisads: What do they seek, and why?', *ibid.*, vol. 49 (1929), pp. 97ff.

Joachim of Fiore (*c.* 1132–1202) Christ. mystic, who founded a monastery at Fiore in Calabria and whose writings were widely influential, though some of his views were officially condemned. He expounded a philosophy of → history, divided into three phases. The first two coincided with orthodox view of significance of O.T. and N.T. (→ Covenant). The third phase would start in 1260, and would see rise of new relig. orders to convert world and bring in the *Ecclesia Spiritualis*. His followers were called Joachimites. S.G.F.B.

E.R.E., VI, pp. 566–7; *D.C.C.*, *s.v.;* J. A. MacCulloch, *Medieval Faith and Fable* (1932), pp. 291ff.; G. G. Coulton, *Five Centuries of Religion*, II (1927), pp. 114ff.

Job, Book of Of unknown authorship and dated by scholars between 5th and 2nd cents. BC, the B.-J. is one of most significant books of O.T. The main part (chs. 3–46:6) is in poetical form, to which a prose Prologue (1–2) and Epilogue (46:7–17) have been added. The theme is the problem of innocent suffering. In Prologue, Job is presented as a pious and good man, whose faith God allows → Satan to test by misfortune and suffering. In poetical part, Job's plight is debated between him and his friends. No adequate answer is found in terms of trad. view that suffering is punishment for sin. Job's questioning of his lot is finally silenced by a display of divine omnipotence. The Epilogue gives a happy-ever-after ending, which is in bathetic contrast to nobility of theme. Job's agony of faith is accentuated by orthodox → Yahwist view that there is no significant after-life (→ Eschatology, Heb.). S.G.F.B.

*H.D.B.*², *s.v.; P.C.*², pp. 391ff.; R. H. Pfeiffer, *Intro. to Old Test.* (1948), pp. 660ff.; Brandon, *M.D.*, pp. 131ff.; F. Horst, *Hiob* (1960); E. Dhorme, *Book of Job* (E.T. 1967).

Jodo Jap. name for Chi. → Ching T'u or Pure Land school of Buddhism. The great → Amida-school of Jap. Buddhism, which proclaimed the Buddha of Infinite Light and Great Compassion, won adherence of the masses and became most popular form of Buddhism in Japan. Founded by → Honen in CE 1175, it was developed into Jodo-Shinshu by → Shinran (CE 1173–1263). It proclaimed the doc. of *Tāriki* ('other-effort'), or salvation by faith and grace. It encouraged practice of → *nembutsu*, the constant repetition of Amida's name by which birth in the West. Paradise was effected. Devotees were taught childlike trust in compassion and infinite merit of Amida and → Kwannon. The result was a pietistic form of relig., regarded as an easy way to salvation. There are four sects of Jodo in Japan, with minor differences: Jodo proper with about 4 m. adherents; → Shinshu with about 13 m., and Yuzunembutsu and Ji, each with a much smaller following. The principal scriptures of school are the smaller and large *Sukhāvatī-*

vyūha sūtras and the *Amatāyur-dhyāna sūtra.* D.H.S.

M. Anesaki, *Hist. of Japanese Relig.* (1930), pp. 170ff.; E. Steinilber-Oberlin, *The Buddhist Sects of Japan* (1938), chs. 9, 10; *E.R.E.*, VII, pp. 483–4.

Johanan ben Zakkai After destruc. of → Jerusalem in CE 70 Rabbi J.-Z. estab. centre of Rabbinic study (*Beth ha-Midrash*) at Jabne (*Jammia*), the pronouncements of which were accepted as authoritative by Jews in Palestine and → Diaspora. (→ Judaism). S.G.F.B.

J. Neusner, *Life of Rabban Yohanan ben Zakkai* (1962); Schürer, *G.J.V.*, I, pp. 657ff., II, pp. 366ff.; *E.J.R.*, p. 213.

John, Gospel of The Fourth Gospel, differs in many ways from the → Synoptic Gospels: e.g. it implies a three-years Ministry of Jesus instead of one as do Synoptics; it places 'Cleansing of Temple' at beginning of Ministry; it repr. Jesus engaging in long monologues contrary to impression given by other Gospels; its presentation is mystical rather than historical. Although G.-J. was attr. to Apostle John from latter part of 2nd cent., this Apostolic authorship is contested by modern scholars. G.-J. is prob. best evaluated as evidence of a certain phase of Christological interpretation at begin. of 2nd cent. (e.g. its → Logos doc. in ch. 1); it repr. a trad. that either did not know or was ready to disagree with Synoptic trad., and that may contain some authentic hist. data. S.G.F.B.

W. F. Howard, *The Fourth Gospel in Recent Criticism and Interpretation* (1955[4]); C. K. Barrett, *The Gosp. acc. to St. John* (1957); R. Bultmann, *Das Evang. d. Johannes* (1964[18]); C. H. Dodd, *Interpret. of the Fourth Gosp.* (1953), *Historical Trad. in Fourth Gosp.* (1963); *H.D.B.*[2], *s.v.; R.G.G.*[3], III, col. 840–51; *P.C.*[2], p. 844.

John, Revelation of This is only N.T. book completely concerned with → apocalyptic; its attr. to Apostle John is very improbable. Its refs. to persecution and hatred of Rome suggest that it was prob. written in reign of Emp. Domitian (81–96). Its bizarre imagery, drawn from Jew. and other sources, reveals thought-world of Christianity at this period. R.-J. exercised much influence on later Chr. → eschatology and art. S.G.F.B.

R. H. Charles, *The Revelation of St. John*, 2 vols. (1920); *H.D.B.*[2], *s.v.; P.C.*[2], pp. 1043ff.; *R.G.G.*[3], III, col. 822–36; A. Feuillet, *L'Apocalypse: État de la question* (1963); E. Mâle, *The Gothic Image* (E.T. 1961), ch. VI.

John the Baptist The → Gospels agree in starting ministry of → Jesus with his baptism by J. An ambivalent attitude is shown towards J.: (a) he is presented as divinely appointed precursor of Jesus (e.g. Lk. 1:5ff.); (b) yet he is inferior to Jesus (Lk. 3:16). There was prob. some rivalry between disciples of Jesus and of J., the latter continuing as a separate sect (Acts 19:1ff.; → Mandaeans). J. operated in neighbourhood of → Qumran, and poss. had some connection with community there. His message was → apocalyptic, his baptism being a lustration symbolic of repentance before divine judgment. Acc. to evidence of Gospels and → Josephus, J. was beheaded by Herod Antipas, whose conduct he had condemned. S.G.F.B.

H.D.B.[2], *s.v.; R.G.G.*[3], III, col. 804–8; W. H. Brownlee, 'John the Baptist in the New Light of Ancient Scrolls', in K. Stendahl (ed.), *The Scrolls and the New Test.* (1958).

Jojitsu School of Jap. Buddhism intro. from Paikche (S. Korea) by Korean monks Kwanroku and Ekwan about 625 CE. Its nihilistic teachings drew their inspiration from the Hindu patriarchs Nagarjuna and Deva, and teachings of Chinese monk → Hsüan tsang. A school of analytical study devoted to cosmological and psychological problems, its teachings were freely studied during Nara period, but school soon merged with → Sanron. It taught that both the 'ego' and all *dharmas* are equally illusions; the past and future non-existent and the present vanishing as soon as born. D.H.S.

E. Steinilber-Oberlin, *The Buddhist Sects of Japan* (1938), ch. 2.

Jonah, Book of Purpose was to teach that God is concerned for welfare of Gentiles as well as Jews, and was thus prob. post-Exilic. Its teaching is given in parable form: J., a Jew, tries to avoid God's command to warn the Ninevites, lest they should repent and be spared. J.'s deliverance from the 'whale' is used as sign of Christ's → Resurrection in N.T. The incident was much used in early Chr. art as symbolising salvation. S.G.F.B.

H.D.B.[2], *s.v.; P.C.*[2], pp. 627ff.; *A.E.C.W.*, ill. pp. 90, 107–8, 167, 579–80.

Josephus, Flavius (*c.* 37–100). Jew. historian, whose writings form chief source of information about Jew. affairs in 1st cent. CE. J. was born in Palestine, of priestly descent, and a → Pharisee. He organised defence of Galilee in war of 66–70, and was captured by Romans. He became Jew. liaison officer to Romans, and witnessed siege and fall of → Jerusalem (70). Settling in Rome, under imperial patronage, he wrote the *Jewish War*, ascribing his nation's ruin to → Zealots. Later he produced the *Antiquities of the Jews*, a survey of Jew. hist. from Creation to fatal war against Rome. It was designed to give Gentiles a better opinion of Jews. His *Contra Apionem* is a defence against → anti-Semitism; his *Life* seeks to justify his conduct in Jew. War.

Regarded as renegade by his people, J. was a complex character, fundamentally loyal to Judaism but aware of hopelessness of Israel's revolt against Rome. J.'s works were closely studied by Christians, who prob. altered his orig. account of Jesus to present version in *Ant.* 18:63–4. J. also mentions → John the Baptist and → James, brother of Jesus. A medieval Slavonic version of *Jew. War* provides many strange variants which have not yet been satisfactorily explained. S.G.F.B.

Loeb Classical Library ed. of Josephus (9 vols., 1926–65, by various scholars) provides text and trans. of all works. H. St. J. Thackeray, *Josephus: the Historian and the Man* (1929); F. J. Foakes-Jackson, *Josephus and the Jews* (1930); R. Eisler, *Iesous basileus ou basileusas*, 2 vols. (1929–30), *The Messiah Jesus and John the Baptist* (1931); *E.R.E.*, VII, *s.v.;* R. J. H. Shutt, *Studies in Josephus* (1961); *La Prise de Jerusalem de Josèphe le Juif* (Slavonic version), ed. V. Istrin, A. Vaillant, P. Pascal, 2 vols. (1934, 1938); S. G. F. Brandon, 'Josephus: Renegade or Patriot?', *R.A.H.*, ch. 20, *Jesus and the Zealots* (1967).

Judaising The orig. disciples of Jesus saw the movement he had founded as essentially concerned with salvation of Israel, and they continued to live as orthodox Jews (→ Jerusalem, Church of). When confronted with conversion of Gentiles, they required that they accepted Judaism, i.e. → circumcision and observance of → Torah. → Paul, envisaging Christ as universal saviour, opposed this requirement. His letters and the Acts reveal something of the controversy. The issue was finally resolved by fall of → Jerusalem in yr. 70 and disappearance of Jerusalem Church. S.G.F.B.

A. D. Nock, *St. Paul* (1938); *E.R.E.*, VII, *s.v.;* H. J. Schoeps, *Paul* (E.T. 1961); M. Goguel, *La naissance du Christianisme* (1946); S. G. F. Brandon, *The Fall of Jerusalem and the Christian Church* (1957²), *Jesus and the Zealots* (1967).

Judaism (1) Anc. Judaism is faith and context of the Hebrew Scriptures, a Covenant faith proclaiming God of time against neighbouring gods of space. Its beginning is trad. assigned to → Abraham, first of Hebrews. Near Eastern texts, from 20th to 12th cent. BC, speak of → *Habiru* (or *Hapiru*), nomadic Semitic wanderers, craftsmen, and mercenaries. The Hebrews were prob. related to them: Habiru are found in Larsa, less than 30 miles from Ur, in 1900 BC. Hurrian trads. are found in Bible: Rachel's → teraphim (Gen. 31) were Hurrian property deeds. Other *Habiru* groups lost their designation when they settled in a land (as Moabites, Edomites, Midianites); thus the term 'Hebrews' gave way to 'Israelites' once they were settled in Canaan.

The 1st stage of Anc. J. is patriarchal. The father ruled; the right of primogeniture prevailed. Economy was pastoral; cult still incl. animism (sacred stones, etc.). Cosmology was more complex, influenced by → Enuma Elish and → Gilgamesh epic. Break with → polytheism came at patriarchal stage. A 'covenant faith' saw the tribe entering into an exclusive agreement with the 'God of Abraham', then 'Kinsman of Isaac', then 'Champion of Jacob'—each separate → numen named for first worshipper and linked to Canaanite sanctuaries. Other gods were not denied (Gen. 31:53 'God of Nahor'); but Hebrews did not worship them. They moved through → henotheism to practice of → monotheism. Their faith was covenant and its moral demands. Their spirit was free: Abraham's challenge to his God anticipates Job's.

The 2nd stage is that of *eisodus* and *exodus:* the going into Egypt at end of 17th cent. BC, and the way out of Egypt, with fashioning of a national covenant. Older and newer trad. are blended by genius of the → Yahvist, who gave the assent of his own time to Covenant of Patriarchs and → Exodus. Hist. of the Hyksos supports biblical narrative of sojourn in Egypt. → Moses, leader of Hebrew exodus from Egypt in 13th cent., has an Egyptian name. But Covenant at Sinai is built upon monotheistic Covenant of Patriarchs and not upon Egypt. monolatry (→ Aten). During wilderness-sojourn, Moses created a people and a national relig. in which old covenant became permanent foundation of Jew. existence. He estab. 'Mosaic Law' of → Pentateuch, even though scholars cannot accept trad. view that he wrote Pentateuch. In patriarchal trad., his personal encounter with the One God led to a new name for God: Yhvh. Numerous ritual and cultic innovations stem from his time: the Tabernacle: the → Ark; priesthood. Judaism is not Mosaism; but Moses is justly recognized as *the* teacher of Jew. people. (→ Yahweh).

As Hebrews enter Canaan—with long hist. telescoped and summarised in person of Joshua —they become the Israelites. Much of sophisticated → Canaanite relig. was assimilated by Israel: local shrines, fertility figurines. Period of Judges notes struggle of Covenant-faith against pagan rites and thoughts. Joined together in loose confederation, governed by primitive democracy of 'the elders', Israel begins to achieve relig. identity based upon Mosaic law. Its ritual law is apodictic: rising out of → Covenant are dogmatic imperatives. Civil law is casuistic: it rises out of contingencies of community life. In contrast to its neighbours, Israel places sacred beyond and above secular. Eventually, there was partial surrender as kingship comes into its own, moving from Saul to → David and → Solomon. A golden period of expansion and develop. gave later ages a prototype for messianic dreams; but David's impact upon J. consists of his plans for the Temple built by his son Solomon (965–925); his personality and ethical struggles which often ended in failure; and in 'his city': → Jerusalem. David set up sacred tent in Jerusalem; and its function was taken up in Solomon's Temple. Pentateuch, based upon oral transmissions, then began to take shape. → Baal-worship and its orgiastic rites enter the ritual more freely. But even the division into two kingdoms, Judah and Israel (925 BC) did not destroy Israel's self-awareness of being covenanted people.

The kingdom of Israel was more open to alien influence: sanctuaries in Dan and → Beth-el may have contained golden calves. Judah, pledged to Davidic dynasty, was more stable. In both kingdoms, assertion of spiritual authority over secular life found its spokesmen: the → prophets. Anc. Hebrew *ro-eh* (seer) blends with *navi* (prophet), God's mouth-piece. Nathan had confronted David; Elijah conquered Baal-priests of Jezebel. But full impact of that revolutionary movement, which was heart of prophetic J., did not show itself fully until advent of → Amos (760 BC). Not a professional prophet, Amos yet built on anc. insights of Covenant with God who will enforce the moral law. The 'day of the Lord' is a judgement day—not a time of national victory; social justice, not lavish sacrifices, is valid worship of God; defects in social structure, the breakdown of personal morality—these become legitimate concerns of a relig. faith breaking away from nationalism to a true universalism.

→ Hosea, younger contemporary of Amos, enlarged this teaching with insight of God's attribute of love. Covenant becomes the marriage-contract, baal-worship is adultery, and God's attribute of mercy is gateway to forgiveness. The great poet-prophet → Isaiah (*c.* 740 BC) added dimension of holiness which is yet no aloofness: the Universal God is the God of history, using Assyria as rod to punish transgressing Israel. Prophecy reached a climax in → Jeremiah (*c.* 626–586 BC), whose personal anguish and private confessions brought vision of God within matrix of individual suffering. The prophets refashioned J., but were not its totality. In Jeremiah's time (*c.* 621 BC), the Josianic Reformation brought Deuteronomic pattern to Jewish worship: the idols were swept away, all shrines except Temple were destroyed, and priesthood was purified. The reforms were not permanent: the prophets' denunciations of idolatry continued until fall of Temple (586 BC); but the moral dynamism, with its patriarchial roots, is also found in the folk relig. which accompanied Israel into Babylonian exile. The prophetic role had its priestly function, most clearly realised in prophet-priest → Ezekiel, who was pastor and comforter of Israel in exile. Its national tragedy was countered by his teaching of individual responsibility; against all reason, Ezekiel convinced Israel that the dry bones would live again. In time, → Deutero-Isaiah could hail Cyrus as the → 'messiah' who would restore Israel to its land—Israel, who was God's suffering servant. Israel did return, and Haggai and Zechariah saw a modest Temple rise upon ruins of Jerusalem. But the ruins predominated. The time of Israel's national glory had gone.

A new stage of develop. in J. took place during the later half of 5th cent., when → Ezra, with the authority of Artaxerxes, came to reorganize Jewish community. The 'second law-giver', in pattern of Moses, Ezra reinstituted the covenant of the Torah for the people. The Torah, 'Law' or 'Teaching', is the Pentateuch: →→ Genesis, Exodus, Leviticus, Numbers, and Deuteronomy. From time of Ezra to this day, it has been the foundation of Jew. law, and is read in the Synagogue, where it is enshrined in the Holy Ark, hand-written on parchment, in its anc. form of a scroll. The holy days were observed, pagan influences rooted out, and the priestly aspects of J. were re-emphasized. Together with Nehemiah, Ezra achieved a social and relig. revival and created a Jew. theocratic state. Its clear authority was the written Torah; it had permanent, well estab. institutions: the Temple, visited on → Passover, Weeks and Tabernacles; and the → Synagogue, which eventually eclipsed it. This new institution was unique. Rising out of the assemblies of Exile, it was the great democratization of worship: no altar, no priesthood, popular education, a place of meeting, study and worship. It produced the next stage of J. Instead of individual prophets, there were scribes to bring the vision of J. to all its members, 'the people of the Book'.

In Hellenistic period, the theocratic state was replaced by a commonwealth; the Torah-constitution was reinterpreted by the liberal → Pharisees in accord. with new conditions. Persian and Greek concepts had entered Jew. thought (angelology, apocalypticism in partic.); new institutions were emerging. In confronting these situations, Israel split into a variety of groupings: the (priestly) → Sadducees, and the pious Pharisees, more repr. of the laity. The Pharisees tried to make priestly law of purity operative in ordinary life—all Israel was to be holy. Functions claimed by priests for themselves were transferred to laity; and a liberal interpret. of Torah clashed with Sadducees' insistence on a rigid interpret. The Pharisees believed in → resurrection. The Sadducees did not: it was not found in the Torah. Ultimately, the Pharisees estab. the Oral Torah (the liberal rabbinic interpretation) as an equal aspect of Divine revelation alongside the Written Torah; and this became normative J. A chain of trad. was estab., which reaches from Torah through every generation of interpreters: the commentary on the Torah (the Mishna) has its own commentary (the Gemara): together, they formed the Talmud; and Talmudic commentaries stretch all the way into contemporary J. (see below).

Other parties existed alongside the Pharisees and Sadducees. Research into the Dead Sea Scrolls (→ Qumrân) indic. existence of many sects, some patterned after → Essenes, a type of organised fellowship often practising the monastic life, asceticism, rites of purification, and a way of life rising logically out of a theology which despaired of this world and centered upon messianism. There were → Zealots and pacifists, a large unorganised group which hated Roman oppression, small groups who looked for a messiah. → Christianity emerged out of this milieu. But clearest product of that time, surviving fall of Jerusalem and destruc. of Temple (70 CE), being itself a creative amalgam of Jewry dispersed in many places, was rabbinic Judaism, the child of anc. J. (→ Israel, Israelite Relig.).

W. F. Albright, *From the Stone Age to Christianity* (1940); A. Alt, *Der Gott der Vater* (1929); Leo Baeck, *Essence of Judaism* (1948); John Bright, *Hist. of Israel;* M. Noth, *Hist. of Israel* (E.T. 1960); H. Orlinsky, *Ancient Israel* (1954).

(2) Rabbinic J. was the spiritual expression of a new structural complex which had shattered anc. forms. The loss of → Jerusalem and the → Temple (the shekel—due now went to Jupiter Capitolinus) forced the scattered Jew. community to seek a new inner centre. They could not disappear among the nations; the Roman world stressed ethnic classifications, and Jew. life itself contained deep desire for identity and cultural autonomy. Roman tolerance left room in its empire for Jew. relig., congregations, and academies. And the Pharisees (Sadducees had disappeared with Temple) supplied a new central authority.

Rabban Jochanan b. Sakkai founded an academy at Jamnia (Yavneh) after CE 70. His successors (R. Gamaliel and other descendants of Davidic House of Hillel) were granted authority of the Patriarchate by Rome (from CE 85–425). The spiritual authority of these → rabbis was clear from beginning: they emended the liturgy, so that Temple-rites became part of synagogue-worship. The Pharisaic teachings of personal commitment to holiness put national catastrophe into perspective: it was Divine chastisement, but not final rejection. Personal piety was the proper response for individual; study and prayer in synagogue (almost synonymous) was to be the community response. The Pharisees built upon estab. foundations. Palestinian Jewry had already been won for rabbinism. 200 years of Pharisees' teaching had made folk heroes of great teachers → Hillel and Shammai (1st cent. BC); synagogues abounded (Herod's Temple had been forced to incl. synagogue-chambers and services!); a viable Jew. community had survived in Palestine to serve as centre for a world community of faith.

A basic uniformity of faith, trad. and practice came to link Jews of Roman world. The catastrophe of CE 70 became a re-experience of first Temple loss (586 BC), and a reaffirmation of faith in Israel's role among the nations. Rabbinic authority built upon this experience: expounding the Torah, as the true teaching, the one and only law, which alone could give meaning to Jew. suffering. It was the Book, the Revelation; and it spoke to each generation through its interpreters. The rabbis were not charismatic, prophetic figures, but teachers and lawyers who estab. norms and rules, but not dogmas. Variant interpretations were valid: 'Both views are the words of the living God', is a rabbinic saying. The Oral Torah, interpreting and amplifying the written Torah, united the → Diaspora and its varying group experiences. Alexandrian Jewry could follow → Philo into a world where the Jew. symbols became abstractions, crystallising monotheistic thought within philosophy; the God of Abraham became the far-away transcendent First Cause. But Palestinian Jewry could not rejoice in outer world; its suffering turned it inward. God was thought of in utterly human terms: he wept with his children; he suffered in exile. However, in totality of Jew. life, both aspects of relig. found their place within the shared practices and polarities of rabbinic theology: the near and the far God, the mystery which had to be the commandment.

A new interpretive literature arose, together with a complicated system of hermeneutics. Called *Midrash*, creative interpretation, it knew that everything could be found in Torah through diligent search. Two types of Midrash existed: *Halacha* and *Aggadah. Halacha* ('the way') dominated. It was the legal exegesis, giving answers to living questions of daily conduct: What does God want us to *do?* Reverence for the particular—the respect for little things—was part of this legal questing. Ethics and ritual formed a unity; for the minutiae (e.g. of Sabbath observances) were seen as 'fence around the Law', safeguarding great visions of J. All came from Torah. Even rare new *Takkanah* (legislated ordinance) had to be woven into anc. fabric and thus became sacred.

Next to Halachic legislation stood *Aggadah* ('lore'), weaving homiletic interprets. of Bible into the new existence. In its continuum, time had no meaning: rabbis knew private thoughts of snake in Eden; Moses could visit the classroom of Rabbi Akiba; Elijah was an everyday guest. *Aggadah*, the way in which rabbis reflected upon Jew. hist. became Jew. theology. *Aggadah* and *Halacha* interpenetrated one another; the earliest homiletic collections contained much *Halacha*. But authoritative texts of Jew. life were records of Halachic legislation. Rabbi Judah 'The Prince' (CE 135–220) ed. decisions of *Tannaim* (rabbis who had preceded him) into six-volume *Mishnah* ('repetition'). Rabbis who followed Rabbi Judah, → *Amoraim*, based their interprets. on *Mishnah* text. Three cent. later, their decisions were given final form in *Gemara* ('completion'). Placed together, this vast stream of rabbinic interprets. (which incl. much Aggada together with Halacha) came to be known as *Talmud*. Two versions exist, since Palestine and Babylonia had each developed their own Gemara. But Rabbinic J., in its medieval stage, was direct outgrowth of Babylon. thinking, where a great Jew. community (its exilarchs ruled Diaspora until 11th cent.) had directed Oral Law into a confrontation with conditions of Diaspora life.

Talmud evidences rabbinic concern with all of life; the 613 direct commandments adduced from it deal with all aspects of existence. Rabbinic J. could stray into formalism; but central motif was always the quest for underlying meaning, for ethical act which sanctified God in human life. The prophetic teachings were part of all social legislation; and stress upon community never lost sight of individual. No one was cut off from the Revelation: the road of study was open to all. This incl. convert; for Rabbinic J. was universalistic and reached out to non-Jew *when this was permitted by its environment*. The *Siddur* (prayerbook) expressed rabbinic theology of near and far God ('Our Father, our King'), who was characterised by *Rachamim* (loving-mercy') and *Din* ('justice'). Universe was viewed as permeated by his moral order; and righteous action mattered more than right belief. The constant Jew. experience of → martyrdom brought the biblical 'suffering servant' into rabbinic concept of the people Israel, God's chosen covenant-folk. The rabbis, burned at stake and repeating words of Torah, were viewed as representative Jews. There is a mystic aspect to rabbinic J., even if much of it was suppressed. → Essenes and other rebel groups had left their heritage within a folk eschatology of messianism and dreams of the final days. The land had its own mystique. The rabbinic concept of Torah as ultimate revelation rendered each Torah letter sacred, containing an inner meaning open to mystic speculation. The rabbis drily said: 'If you are told the messiah has come, finish your work first and then go and see.' But thoughts of the messiah filled many minds. **(3) Jewish life in the Middle** Ages still followed the Babylon. pattern. But as → Islam arose and ruled the East, that pattern changed. → Aramaic gave way to Arabic, and that language was new key to Greek philosophy. Rabbinic J. began to reflect upon itself. The Karaite schism rejected the Oral Law of the rabbis and tried to go back to Scriptures (*Mikra*), led by Anan b. David (d. *c.* CE 800). Outside, a new world of reason challenged trad., but also gave it new weapons. In the defence of the trad., Saadia Gaon (882–942) blended philosophy with theology in his *Emunot V'Deot* ('Beliefs and Opinions'), buttressing rabbinic teachings with a rational, Islamic system called → *Kalam*. Other outside influences showed their impact later, when Bachya ibn Pakuda publ. his *Chovot Ha-Levavot* ('Duties of the Heart') in Saragossa in 1040. → Neo-Platonism and ascetic → Sufi mysticism fashioned the form of this work on personal piety and ethics, though much was moderated by Jew. trad., which kept individual firmly within community and prevented full flight into mysticism.

As Babylon. Jew. life grad. began to decline, Spain moved into foreground. The problems for J. had not changed: it had to defend itself as the true faith against Islam and Christianity; secular rational philosophy remained a rival, to be overcome and put to service of faith; Israel's role in world had to be understood. In the 'Golden Age' of Spanish Jewry, poets could be philosophers and grapple with these tasks. Solomon ibn Gabirol (1021–69) viewed God as the metaphysical absolute, united with world through his divine will. Gabirol's poem *Keter Malchut* ('Royal Crown') is still chanted in the synagogue; his masterpiece of philosophy, 'Fountain of Life', came to be studied by Christ. Churchmen, who thought the *Fons Vitae* to be of Christ. origin. Moses ibn Ezra (1080–1139) was a poet of delicate sadness, overshadowed by his great contemporary Jehuda Halevi (1086–1143). Halevi's poems sing of Israel's love of Zion and of God. His philosophic dialogue *Kuzari* is brilliant relig. polemic, telling story of the → Khazars who chose J. over Islam and Christianity. Halevi challenged the opponents of J. on basis of historic revelation given to Israel. Faith, not reason is way to God; yet

Halevi did not deny role of reason. It had its place—subordinated to faith and experience of Israel, which has known God and his miracles. The emphasis on relig. experience (partially influenced by → al-Ghazali) and Jew. life stressed special nature of Jew. people gifted with prophecy. Israel is 'the heart of the nations'; its suffering is the badge of its election.

Moses Maimonides (1135–1204) was crown of medieval J. The greatest rabbinic scholar of his era—his *Mishne Torah* is a compendium of rabbinic law up to his time—he was also the greatest Jew. philosopher. He reconciled J. with → Aristotelianism, and his *More Nevukim* ('Guide for the Perplexed') showed that faith is not opposed to reason; the chief docs. of J. can be demonstrated in a rational manner. Maimonides formulated 13 Principles of Faith, in which he stressed God's existence, unit, incorporeality, and eternity. No attributes can be ascribed to God except as a denial of imperfection. One may only say 'God is not weak, not ignorant'. Biblical anthropomorphisms are thus swept away as Jew. theology enters the *via negativa*. Maimonides' world was an Aristotelian system of concentric spheres ending (the 10th sphere) with the *sekel ha-poel*, the creative intellect which imposes form on life and also gives men faculty of prophecy. But all can develop their rational faculty through the discipline of Torah. It fosters soundness of mind and body with *all* its laws, helping man achieve the greatest good: the contemplation of God, vouchsafed to all in the messianic time. Intoxicated with intellectual love of God, reason here builds its house upon the rock of faith. Halevi, by contrast, had reared his edifice of faith with tools of reason. In other ways, their thought intertwined. And medieval J. has to be understood as the relig. which could encompass both these thinkers.

The encounter between J. and philosophy had taken place in a relatively open society. But the Diaspora, at this point, has to be seen in terms of two areas. There was that in the Mediterranean world, under Islam, which came to be known as Sephardic (Spanish) Jewry. Under the Church, in Germany and Cen. Europe, Ashkenasic (German) Jewry differed greatly. Leo Baeck defined the first as 'the piety of culture'; the latter, as 'the culture of piety'. Sephardic scholars wrote in Arabic and affirmed the outer culture. Ashkenazim wrote in Hebrew and lived within culture of Torah. The Sephardim became systemizers; the Ashkenazim commentators. The commentaries of Rashi of Troyes (1040–1105) and his successors, the Tosaphists, are concerned with the *peshat*, the clear and simple meaning of the classic text, and are as essential to the dialogue between the generations and the tradition as the great system of Maimonides. The two forms were linked by Jew. daily existence with its many and divergent observances and the one faith. Much later, Joseph Caro (1488–1575) wrote his *Shulchan Aruch* ('Prepared Table'), as guide and code to all aspects of Jew. life; and Moses Isserles (1520–72) added his *Mappah* ('Tablecloth') to adjust this code to Ashkenazic Jew. life.

Caro was a mystic. This, too, matters; for the continuous strand of Jew. mysticism is part of the weave even when invisible. Ashkenazic mysticism was individualistic; its *Sefer Hasidim* (*c.* 1200) is, above all, a book of personal ethics. Sephardic mysticism developed the great systems (speculative and practical) of the *Kabbala*. Anc. Jew. foundations, going back to speculations upon Ezekiel's chariot, dominated the many outside influences noted in Sephardic thought. In contrast to the outside forms and their quest for mystical *union*, Jew. mysticism developed *communion: d'vekut*, 'cleaving unto God', which implied *no loss of identity* (cf. G. Scholem). God was the *En Sof*, infinitely distant, the → *deus absconditus*. But in the 'Talmud of mysticism', the *Zohar* ('Illumination'), which was given its final form in 13th cent., the near God is encountered. The Ashkenazic Jew invested the small actions of daily life with a mystic glow; the Sephardi scholar hurled his mind through the universe; both were joined in their efforts to redeem the world.

That world became ever harsher. Pogroms marched in the train of every → crusade. Accusations of ritual murder and host-stabbing (→ Host) filled Christ. Europe and decimated Ashkenazi Jewry. Poland became place of refuge at time of Casimir III (1333–70); the centre of Jew. life now shifted eastward. The Sephardic community also suffered and contracted. First the Church, then the → Inquisition, came to Spain; and the Jews were expelled in 1492. The Jews became scattered, with each community turning inward, seeking its own solution; some in ritual, others in mystic thoughts. And even the sober brokers of Amsterdam sold their stock when Shabbetai Zvi, the false → messiah, announced the messianic year 1666. There were other false messiahs who stirred Jewry into frenzic hope and left it in deeper despair. Out of this turbulance, which shook both institution and teachings, we see the beginnings of modern Judaism emerge.

Salo Baron, *Social and Religious Hist. of the Jews* (2nd rev. edn. 1952); Leo Baeck, *The Essence of Judaism* (1948), *The People Israel* (1965); Leon Roth, *Moses Maimonides* (1948); J. Guttmann, *Philosophies of Judaism* (1964);

K. Kobler, *Jewish Theology* (1943); G. F. Moore, *Judaism* (1947); A. Cohen (ed.), *Everyman's Talmud* (2nd edn. 1949); S. Schechter, *Some Aspects of Rabbinic Theology* (1909); Gershon Scholem, *Major Trends in Jewish Mysticism* (1954).

(4) Modern Judaism: The pattern of world around the Jews kept changing. E. Europe, the place of refuge became a death trap, with Cossacks slaughtering multitudes of Jews. Somehow, Jew. life continued, even while sinking ever deeper into abject poverty and helplessness. Rabbinic J. was a bulwark against outside world; but, as its demands became imposs. to fulfil, for the average Jew laboured all day and had no time for study, rabbinic authority crumbled. About 1740 Israel ben Eliezer, the *Baal Shem Tov* ('The good Master-of-the-Name') became spokesman of those who had no learning but a simple piety: love of nature, music, dancing, direct communion with God. His followers told each other stories: of the peasant who recited the alphabet and asked God to order it into the proper prayer; of the boy whose whistling in the synagogue was more import. than the scholar's learning. A movement arose: *Hasidism.* Its mixture of pietism, Safed mysticism, (based upon a school of thought which arose in Safed, Palestine, in 16th cent.) and anti-rabbanism swept through Polish Jewry. While it did not keep its freshness and simplicity for long (within 50 years its leaders—*Saddikim*—claimed miraculous powers of intercession for themselves, estab. dynasties, and held court), rabbis like Shneor Zalman in Lithuania and Levi Yitzchak in Poland infused E. Jewry into a new life. The *Mitnagdim* ('Opponents') of Hasidism found their leader in Elijah, The Gaon of Vilna (1720–97), whose writings constituted the best of Jewish learning, and who placed the Hasidim under ban. But the old authority was gone. The Jew. community could not split apart in an E. Europe still living in the Middle Ages in terms of its treatment of Jews. But the internal struggles within Jewry began to shape a similar type of modern Jew to the one now coming to the fore in W. Europe.

In the West. relig. authority was dying. As the Age of Reason came into its own, the commercial middle class gained power and confidence, and there was a lowering of relig. and class barriers. A sane and ethical deism, not tied to institutions, heralded the new secular world. Men like Christian Wilhelm von Dohm and Lessing tried to open this new world to Jews. And Moses Mendelssohn (1727–86) entered it as the father of mod. J. Mendelssohn (Lessing's 'Nathan the Wise') gained fame in Europe as a great German stylist and popular philosopher. He trans. the Pentateuch and Psalms into German (using Hebrew letters and thus teaching German to the new generation) and strove to reconcile J. with the Age of Reason. J., he taught, is an absolute rational faith; its tenets are in full harmony with dictates of reason. But its practices are based on revelation—the divine legislation of the Torah. Leaving the ghetto which had been both prison and shelter, the Jew could thus maintain his trad. practices and yet feel part of mod. life.

This formula worked for some; but the next generation of German Jews found the trad. practices a barrier to gen. culture. Some resolved the conflict by changing to a nominal Christianity. Others changed Jew. practices. A new movement arose, Reform Judaism, which modernized Synagogue practices (intro. organ music; use of vernacular in shortened liturgy, men and women seated together) and discarded many trad. observances incl. dietary laws. Led first by laymen like Israel Jacobson (1768–1828), then rabbis like the scholarly Abraham Geiger (1810–74), it made a sharp break with past by rejecting Oral Law. Building upon concept of continuous develop., Reform J. was an expression of its time: rational, liberal, rejecting messianism but stressing human progress. While it had assimilatory aspects, it did in fact curb assimilation by offering a viable alternative to traditions. It became linked with a generation of young Jew. scholars, eager to find place for Jew. thought (and for themselves) in gen. culture, who were then creating a 'Jüdische Wissenschaft' (Science of Judaism). L. Zunz (1794–1886) and H. Graetz (1817–91) were part of this flowering of Jew. learning, in which J. reflected upon itself and moved towards golden age of German-Jewish creativity.

Trad. J. found its spokesman in S. R. Hirsch (1808–88) of Frankfurt, who estab. a framework of vigorous neo-Orthodoxy, in which trad. filled the Jew. home which was yet part of mod. world. Led by Hirsch, and drawing upon the great trad. learning which continued to come from E. Europe, the new Orthodoxy stressed the second part of Mendelssohn's formula: obedience to ritual law. No longer in absolute control, trad. learned to live with other interpretations within *Einheitsgemeinden* (unified congregations); at times, the Orthodox or the Reform group would break away from this unified community.

Outside of Germany, various patterns of community life emerged. In France, Napoleon's attempt to create a new Sanhedrin (1806) failed; but French Jewry was incorporated into state under a consistory system which to this day remains outwardly trad. In quieter England, there were few changes. A progressive J. developed grad., with a Reform (est. 1840) and more radical Liberal wing (est. 1902). E. European Jewry continued to suffer under medieval restrictions. When revolt against estab. relig. authority did take place there, it took on a secular form. First the *Haskalah* (Enlightenment), at turn of 19th cent., and later socialism and Zionism (movement to re-settle Palestine and create Jewish state, given its mod. format by Theodor Herzl who called together first Zionist Congress in Basle in 1897) estab. themselves within community and in Yiddish literature. There was no Reform movement of consequence in E. Europe; but a large secular community challenged Tradition. Nevertheless, trad. learning flourished in the great East. *Yeshivot* (seminaries), until Hitler's Germany destroyed European Jewry by murdering six million Jews.

The greatest Jew. community today is in the United States. Estab. initially by early influx of Sephardic Jews, the community developed in a liberal direction with large-scale immigration of German Jews (after 1848 revolution had failed). The major leaders of Reform J. were German rabbis: I. M. Wise (1819–1900), the great organiser who estab. the Hebrew Union College (1875) and the congregational union; David Einhorn (1809–79), who stressed radical aspects of Reform theology; and those who issued the Pittsburgh Platform of 1885—a strongly anti-Zionist, anti-ritual, radical statement superseded 50 years later by the Columbus Platform of 1935. The congregationlist pattern and lack of estab. church in America favoured Reform J. in the U.S. during its west. expansion. But at turn of cent., when millions of Jews fled Russian pogroms and made their way to America, the new need for urban industrial workers transplanted whole communities, their synagogues, rabbis, and trads. No central rabbinic authority could develop in America, but Orthodoxy estab. itself firmly in larger cities, with major seminaries in New York and Chicago. Trad. life in America today is marked by creativity and growth. At same time, a centre movement emerged: Conservative Judaism. Its theology stems from Reform J., its practices are trad. The Jewish Theological Seminary (est. 1886) gave the scholarly Solomon Schechter (1848–1915) an instrument to create a relig. community still gaining influence. A small splinter movement, Reconstructionism, also began at the Seminary, since its founder Mordecai Kaplan (b. CE 1881) taught there. Viewing J. as a relig. civilisation (Durkheim's influence may be noted), God as a process, and the state of Israel as basic to Jew. life, it has helped shape contemporary Jew. thought in America. The American Jew. community of 5,750,000 has perhaps one million Jews officially part of the Reform movement, one million part of Conservative Judaism, and well over a million within Orthodoxy. The large number remaining gives evidence of growing secular Jew. community which identifies with charities and liberal causes, with the state of Israel—but not with the synagogue.

The State of Israel, estab. in May 1948, now holds well over 2,000,000 Jews. Its impact upon Jew. life and thought is enormous. It must be understood that it is the culmination of a secular 'religion'—Zionism. The *Siddur* (prayerbook) has always stressed a return to Zion. Yet both trad. Judaism and Reform (now strongly pro-Israel and growing in appreciation for ritual and trad.) find difficulties in placing a restored Israel into their theology. The most anguishing problems within mod. J. are the questions asked by the Nazi Holocaust and the State of Israel. The second is no answer to the first; both ask the Jew to come to terms with his existence as God's witness to world. The thirteen million Jews, scattered over world, (except for two and a half million 'Jews of silence' isolated from rest in U.S.S.R.) have drawn much closer towards one another in quest for an answer.

(5) Jew. life and thought today are determined by classic pattern of the creative tension between Israel and the → Diaspora. Much of immediate past must still be assimilated, from great Talmudists of E. Europe to philosophers of the German-Jewish 'Golden Age'. Contemporary Jew. theology still depends on that German heritage: e.g. Martin Buber (1878–1965) and the 'I-Thou' dialogue; Franz Rosenzweig (1886–1929) and the existential faith of his *Star of Redemption* (1921); Leo Baeck (1873–1956) and his classic summation of mod. J. (*Essence of Judaism*, 1905); and the great teacher upon whom they all built, the neo-Kantian Hermann Cohen (1842–1918). The personal impact of these three men is also significant. Buber served as bridge between Jew and Christian, and tried to bring Jews and Muslims closer to each other in Israel. Rosenzweig's great *Lehrhaus* (Adult Academy) in Frankfurt helped him reach out towards the community through his years of sickness and paralysis. Baeck became leader of German Jewry in the darkest hours, taught even in the concentration camp, and lived to write *This People Israel*, in which the three thousand years of Jew. peoplehood, with their constant renewals and re-births, became a way of understanding the continuous development of J. Thus, Jew. thinkers today find their way to God through peoplehood, discovering God in man. The distinction between the sacred and the secular is not part of Jew. life; in a secular age, J. finds itself less troubled than other faiths.

The Jew today—no matter where he affiliates—differs little from his fellow Jews. S. R. Hirsch once stated that 'the Jewish calendar is the Jew's catechism'. And most Jew. lives still move through the festivals: the autumnal *Rosh Hashanah* ('New Year') and *Yom Kippur* ('Day of Atonement') celebrated in the synagogue and calling for repentance; *Sukkot* as a harvest festival of thanksgiving; *Chanukah* ('Rededication of the Temple'), the Feast of Lights in midwinter which brings eight days of presents to children; *Purim* ('Feast of Lots'), in which biblical story of Haman deals with 20th century problems; *Pesach* (Passover), in which the home table becomes altar and story of Exodus reasserts the Covenant for the mod. Jew; and *Shavuot* ('Weeks', i.e. Pentecost) marking the giving of the Ten Commandments, which has led to intensification of the confirmation ritual among Reform and some Conservative communities. There are no dogmas to be affirmed and made the key to Jew. identity: participation in the covenant community is by action more than belief. J. here comes back to its origin: it is still the proclamation of ethical monotheism, the worship of the One God through ethical action to bring about brotherhood of man and thus to estab. God's kingdom on earth. A.H.F.

Howard M. Sachar, *The Course of Modern Jewish Hist.* (1958); Joseph Blau, *Modern Varieties of Judaism* (1966); Nahum Glatzer, *The Dynamics of Emancipation* (1965); Ira Eisenstein, *Varieties of Jewish Belief* (1966); Ismar Elbogen, *Ein Jahrhundert Jüdisches Lebens* (1967); Bernard Bamberger, *The Story of Judaism* (1957). (→ Synoptic Index, Jewish).

Judas Iscariot The apostle who betrayed → Jesus to → Sanhedrin (e.g. Mk. 14:10ff.). Variant versions of his suicide are given in Mt. 27:3ff.; Acts 1:16ff. Abhorred by Christians, J. is alleged to have been venerated by Gnostic sect of Cainites. J.'s motives in betraying Jesus have been much discussed. The meaning of 'Iscariot' is obscure: it could be a corruption of *sicarius*, i.e. → Zealot extremist. S.G.F.B.

G. Dalman, *Jesus-Jeshua* (E.T. 1929), pp. 28ff.; O. Cullmann, *The State in the New Test.* (E.T. 1957), pp. 15ff.; *H.D.B.*², *s.v.;* S. G. F. Brandon, *Jesus and the Zealots* (1967), p. 204, n. 1; *Trial of Jesus of Nazareth* (1967); K. Lüthi, *Judas Iskarioth in der Gesch. der Auslegung v. der Reform. bis z, Gegenwart* (1955).

Judges, Book of Purporting to be sequel to Book of Joshua, B.-J. actually provides a more accurate account of same period. It reveals that Israelite conquest of Canaan was gradual and not the swift achievement descr. in B. of Joshua. The 'Judges' were leaders who, inspired by → Yahweh, led a faithless and defeated people, after repentance, to victory. B.-J. preserves many anc. trads. from period of Israel's settlement in Canaan. S.G.F.B.

*H.D.B.*², *s.v.; P.C.*², pp. 304ff.; M. Noth, *Hist. of Israel* (E.T. 1960), pp. 101ff.

Judgment, Final → Judgment of Dead (Christ.). S.G.F.B.

(Immediate) → Judgment of Dead (Christ.). S.G.F.B.

(of the Dead) (Anc. Near East) The idea of a J.-D. first appears in → Egypt. relig., *c.* 2400 BC, in a twofold form: (1) that dead might be accused of evil; (2) that good deeds of dead would win approval of the 'Great God', prob. → Rē. In → Coffin Texts ref. is made to scales being used in J.-D. In → Book of Dead (*c.* 1400 BC) idea finds dramatic expression in scenes of weighing → heart of deceased against → Maat (truth), in presence of → Osiris. Ch. 125 also gives two 'Declarations of Innocence' for the occasion. Belief in J.-D. continued in Egypt at least into 1st cent CE. As Egypt. evidence shows, belief in possibility of happy afterlife involved fear of *post-mortem* punishment for sins done in this world. In →→ Mesopot., Israelite, Grk.-Roman religs., because such belief did not exist, there was no basis for idea of J.-D. In Israel, the idea appeared in 2nd cent. BC with belief in *post-mortem* resurrection (→ Eschatology, Heb.); it was essentially connected with Israel's destiny and punishment of Gentiles (→→ Eschatology, Heb.; Heilsgeschichte). It also became known in Greece through → Orphism, finding expression in → metempsychosis. In the → Gāthās, → Zoroaster envisages (vaguely) a J.-D., which is elaborated later, incl. some kind of → psychostasia. Among these anc. religs. the idea of the J.-D. achieved its fullest and most impressive form in Egypt. S.G.F.B.

J. Spiegel, *Die Idee vom Totengericht in der aegyptischen Religion* (1935); *R.Ae.R-G.*, *s.v.*, 'Jenseitsgericht'; A.-M. Esnoul *et al.* (eds.), *Sources orientales*, IV, *Le jugement des morts* (1961), chs. 1–4; S. G. F. Brandon, *The Judgment of the Dead* (1967), chs. 1–4, 7 (with bibliog.).

(Christian) Christianity inherited two conceptions of J.-D. One came from Jew. → eschatology, and was a Last and General Judgment at end of world, which was believed to be imminent (Mt. 25:31ff.). The other was Immediate, i.e. it follows death of each person, as is implied in Lk. 16:19ff. The non-fulfilment of → Parousia led to an eschatology that incl. both an Immediate and Last J. After death, the dead were, each, judged on their former lives and consigned to → Purgatory, unless they at once merited

Heaven or damnation. At Second → Advent of Christ, the Last or Final J. would take place. All dead would be resurrected and judged, and their eternal destiny in Heaven or Hell decreed. Logically, Immediate J. made Last J. unnecessary; but trad. N.T. eschatology was too sacrosanct to be abandoned. Great emphasis was laid on J.-D. in Middle Ages, as is seen by the → Dooms. The → psychostasia, by → Michael, orig. connected with Immediate J., became central feature of Last J. The Prot. Reformers laid equal stress on J.-D., although rejecting doc. of Purgatory. Modern Chr. opinion about J.-D. has abandoned the medieval conception, but it seems gen. hesitant to define its own view. (→ Judgment of Dead, Anc. Near East). S.G.F.B.

J. Fournée, *Le Jugement Dernier* (1964); L. Kretzenbacher, *Die Seelenwaage* (1958); A.-M. Cocagnac, *Le Jugement Dernier dans l'art* (1955); Brenk, *W.-G.;* D. Miloševicć, *The Last Judgment* (E.T. 1967); J. P. Martin, *The Last Judgment in Protestant Theology* (1963); S. G. F. Brandon, *The Judgment of the Dead*, ch. 6 (with bibliog.).

(Islam) Qur. teaches that in the final judgment, when God himself will judge (xxii:55), justice will be done (xvi:112). A witness will be summoned from each community (xvi:86, 91; xl:54). The pages will be spread open (lxxxi:10). The Book will be placed in position, and each will find his deeds recorded there (xviii:47). The righteous will be given their book in right hand; the unrighteous theirs in left (lxix:19ff.; lxxxiv: 7ff.). Nothing will be hidden (lxxxii:4f.; xcix: 6ff.). The → Balances will be set up. Their hearing, sight and skins will testify against God's enemies (xxiv:24; xli:18ff.). On that day no one can avail for another (ii:117; vi:69; xxxii:3; lxxxii:19). Refs. are made to failure of false gods to intercede for their worshippers (cf. xxx:12; xl:19). Intercession depends on God's permission (xxxix:45). Trad. speaks of mankind assembled on a wide plain, barefoot, naked and uncircumcised. → Abraham will be first to be clothed. When → 'A'isha asked → Muḥammad if men and women would be looking at one another, he replied that the situation would be too serious to think of that. After the judgment, God will give order to bring forth from hell those who had as much faith in their hearts as a grain of mustard-seed. When people have been sent to their reward, death will be summoned and slain. The announcement that there is no more death will add joy to those in paradise and grief to those in hell. (→→ Examination in the grave; Hell; Hour (Last); Intercession; -Ṣirāṭ). J.R.

E.I., II, pp. 1048–51; Hughes, pp. 541–4; *Mishkāt*, pp. 1168ff.; Wensinck, *Creed*, index (Balance, Bridge, Hell, Intercession, Paradise, Reward, Sins); Sweetman, *I.C.T.*, I, II, IV, index; D. Sourdel, 'Le jugement des morts dans l'Islam', *S.O.*, IV (1961); S. G. F. Brandon, *The Judgment of the Dead* (1967), ch. VI.

-Junayd (d. 298/910). A famous → Ṣūfī who was born and brought up in Baghdad. He had normal education, studying Qur., → *fiqh* and → Ḥadīth. Later he was attracted by Sufism, learning from such men as Sarī al-Saqaṭī (d. *c.* 253/867) and al-Ḥārith al-Muḥāsibī (d. 243/857). Among his pupils was → Hallāj, who developed an excitability not characteristic of his teacher. J. insisted that his doc. was closely in keeping with Islamic teaching, with the Qur. and the → *sunna*. He realised that if one adopted the Sufi life without firm grounding such as he had in the regular relig. education, he was liable to go astray; but J. was firmly convinced that true Sufi doc. was in keeping with Islamic principles. He adopted an ascetic form of life, and showed both his asceticism and orthodoxy by performing the → Pilgrimage on foot three times. He had a trade as silk spinner, because of which he is called al-Khazzāz. He was leader among Sufis of his time, and one of most import. in formulating Sufi thought. He taught that everything comes from God, so must return to him, and this is achieved by *fanā'* (dying to self); but in this he did not fall into → pantheism. He held that the true Sufi was one who was made pure from all except God. Dr. Abdel Kader (see below) has provided a full and authoritative account of J.'s life and doc., and published a number of his letters with E.T. J.R.

E.I.[2], II, p.600; *G.A.L.*, I, pp. 214f.; *S.*, I, pp. 354f.; Arberry, *Doctrine*, index; 'Ali Hassan Abdel-Kader, *The life, personality and writings of al-Junayd*, Gibb Mem. Ser. (1962).

Juno Anc. Italian goddess, identified with Grk. → Hera, being also closely assoc. with life, partic. sexual, of women. Her orig. is obscure; it seems prob. that she personified the → *numen* of womanhood. As Juno Regina, J. formed one of the Roman (Capitoline) triad with → Jupiter and → Minerva. S.G.F.B.

O.C.D., *s.v.; Kleine Pauly*, II, col. 1563–8; A. Grenier, *Les religions étrusque et romaine* (1948), pp. 115ff.

Jupiter Anc. Italian → sky-god, identified with Grk. → Zeus. J. was assoc. with thunder, lightning and rain; in Rome his priest was the *flamen Dialis*. → Hierarchy, Rom.). The Etruscan kings, who intro. his cult under title of *Iuppiter Optimus Maximus*, 'the best and greatest of all Jupiters', to Rome, estab. it in temple on Capitol, together with those of → Juno and → Minerva. His oldest Roman associates, however, were → Mars and → Quirinus. As Roman state-god, J.

was assoc. with war, treaties and oaths. It was to him that a victorious general sacrificed during his triumph. S.G.F.B.

O.C.D., *s.v.;* W. Warde Fowler, *Roman Ideas of Deity* (1914), pp. 29ff.; A. Grenier, *Les religions étrusque et romaine* (1948), pp. 97ff.; G. Dumézil, *Jupiter, Mars, Quirinus* (1941[2]), *Les dieux des Indo-Européens* (1952), pp. 106ff.; E. O. James, *The Worship of the Sky-God* (1963), pp. 132ff.; *Kleine Pauly*, III, col. 1–6.

Justin Martyr, St. (*c.* 100–165) Born at Nablus, Samaria, J. became a Christian (*c.* 130), after seeking truth in pagan philosophy. He was first Chr. thinker to try to reconcile faith and reason. He held that truths, adumbrated in pagan philosophy, find their complete rational expression in Christianity. J. was most able of the → Apologists, addressing two *Apologies*, still extant, to Roman authorities. His *Dialogue with Trypho* (a Jew) shows how Christians claimed that Church had superseded Israel. J. was martyred for his faith. S.G.F.B.

Justin's works are trans. in *A.N.C.L.* (1867). A. A. T. Ehrhardt, 'Justin Martyr's two Apologies', *J.E.H.*, IV (1953), *Politische Metaphysik von Solon bis Augustin*, II (1959), pp. 75ff.; *D.C.C.*, *s.v.;* P. Carrington, *The Early Christ. Church*, II (1957), ch. 7; *R.G.G.*[3], III, col. 1076.

-Juwaynī, Abul Ma'ālī 'Abd al-Malik (419–478/1028–1085). Son of a Shafi'i scholar who taught at Naysabur. On his father's death in 438/1047 he, though still young, carried on his teaching. For a period he taught → Ash'arī doc., but when Ash'aris were denounced by the Seljuq wazīr and treated as heretics along with → Shi'is, he moved to Baghdad; in 450/1058 he came to the Ḥijāz, where he spent four years and taught in both Mecca and Medina. Because of this he became known as *Imām al-ḥaramayn* ('leading scholar of the two sacred territories'). When Niẓām al-Mulk became wazir, he invited those who had fled to return. J. went back to Naysabur, and the wazir built a fine college for him, the Nizamiyya, calling it after himself, as he did with the college in Baghdad. J. taught in Naysabur for remainder of life. His main studies were → *fiqh* and → *kalām*, but Ibn Khallikān indic. that he had a busy life; in add. to his professorial duties, he was leader of the Shafi'is, administered the *waqfs* (→ Pious foundations), acted as → imam and preacher at public prayer. One of his distinctions during last years is that he had Abū Ḥāmid, the famous → Ghazali, as pupil and assistant. In his writings he was spec. interested in the basic principles (*uṣūl*). Though an Ash'arite, he showed some → Mu'tazilite influence; he departed from strict Ash'arite teaching by treating the anthropomorphic terms in the Qur. as metaphors. J.R.

E.I.[2], II, pp. 605f.; *G.A.L.*, I, pp. 486–8; *S.*, I, pp. 671–3; D. B. Macdonald, *Theology*, index; Wensinck, *Creed*, index; H. Klopfer, *Das Dogma des Imam al-Haramain* (1958); Imam el Haramein, *El-Irchad*, French trans. by J. D. Luciani (1938) (cf. *J.A.* (1938), pp. 149ff.); Watt, *Philosophy*, index; Sweetman, *I.C.T.*, IV, index of authors.

K

Ka In anc. Egypt. anthropology a kind of double possessed by each person, serving as a protecting genius. It is imposs. to define concept exactly: refs. in Egypt. lit. are not consistent. The K. was born together with individual concerned; special provision had to be made for it after death. The sun-god Rē and the king possessed either 7 or 14 K.'s. (→→ Funerary Rites, Egypt.; Man, Concept of). S.G.F.B.

L. Greven, *Der Ka in Theologie u. Königskult der Aegypter des alten Reiches* (1952); U. Schweitzer, *Das Wesen des Ka im Diess·its u. Jenseits der alten Aegypter* (1956); *R.Ae.R-G.*, pp. 357–62; Brandon, *M.D.*, pp. 40ff.

Ka'ba A building in Mecca, *c.* 40 feet long, 33 broad, 50 to top of parapet; God's House towards which all → Muslims face in prayer. Trad. says → Adam was first builder, and that → Abraham and → Ishmael rebuilt it; later it became centre of idol worship, all signs of which → Muḥammad destroyed. The only door, seldom opened, stands in N.E. wall. The floor inside is marble; the walls are lined with marble slabs. At annual → Pilgrimage the K. gets a new black covering (*kiswa*) of silk and wool with a band of Qur. texts in fine calligraphy. Pilgrims circumambulate the K. 7 times on a broad pavement (*al-Maṭāf*). The → Black Stone, prob. an aerolite, is about 5 feet up in the E. corner of the S.E. wall, and a stone of Meccan granite is about same height in S. corner. The wall between door and Black Stone, against which pilgrims press while praying, is called *al-Multazam.* On roof of N.W. wall is a gold rain-water spout (*mīzāb*) *c.* 4 feet long. A trough (*al-Mi'jan*) set in pavement to right of door, where Abraham and Ishmael reputedly mixed mortar, is a favourite place of prayer. A semi-circular wall (*al-Ḥaṭīm*), about 4½ feet high, faces N.W. wall. The space between (*al-Ḥijr*, or *Ḥijr Ismā'īl*), said to have been part of orig. K., has two slabs marking reputed tombs of Ishmael and → Hagar. J.R.

E.I., II, pp. 584–92 (and n. by Wensinck on p. 432); Hughes, pp. 256–9; Wellhausen, *Reste*, pp. 73ff.; Burton, *Pilgrimage*, Appendix II; Rutter, *Holy Cities*, I, ch. xv; Broadhurst, *Ibn Jubayr*, pp. 77ff.; Hamidullah, *Prophète*, index; Gaudefroy-Demombynes, *Mahomet*, index; N. Abbott, *Papyri*, pp. 153f.

Kabeiroi, or Cabiri Non-Hellenic deities, prob. Phrygian, whose cult was estab. at many places in Greece, most notably at Samothrace, where mysteries were celebrated (→ Mystery Religions). The K. formed a pair, and were often confused with the → Dioscuri. The K. were of → chthonian orig. and concerned with fertility. S.G.F.B.

E.R.E., VII, *s.v.; O.C.D.*, pp. 150ff.; W. K. C. Guthrie, *Orpheus and Greek Religion* (1952²), pp. 123ff.; *R.G.G.*³, III, col. 1080–1; C. Kerényi, 'The Mysteries of the Kabeiroi', in J. Campbell (ed.), *The Mysteries* (1955); *Kleine Pauly*, III, 34–8.

Kabīr Kabīr (prob. CE 1440–1518) was a weaver in → Banaras, brought up by → Muslims and became a prominent relig. teacher and forerunner of → Sikhism, attacking external differences dividing Muslim and Hindu. A disciple of → Ramananda, he opposed cult of images and → caste system, and attracted a wide following through his preaching and relig. poetry. His teachings emphasised unity and spiritual nature of the True God, whom he also called Ram (Rāma) and → Allah, to show his indifference to trad. differences. Liberation comes from calling on name of God in faith; and Kabīr's followers were urged to live a simple, productive life in the world. After his death, some followers remained Muslims; his Hindu adherents formed the sect of Kabirpanthis, which has a substantial following (*c.* 1,000,000 people) in N. and N.W. India. His disciple → Nanak was main founder of the Sikh relig., and some of Kabīr's poems are incl. in the → Adi Granth. His works were collected into a scripture known as *Bījak*. Another notable disciple was Dādū, founder of sect of Dadupanthis. N.S.

G. H. Westcott, *Kabir and the Kabir Panth*, 2nd edn. (1953); R. Tagore (tr.), *One Hundred Poems of Kabir* (1961); F. E. Keay, *Kabir and his Followers* (1931).

Kaivalya Concept of → liberation in the → Yoga school of Hinduism. It is achieved through purification of the psycho-physical processes of the individual, by means of various physical and meditative techniques, above all → *samādhi* or contemplative rapture; these lead to purification of the *buddhi* or intellect, which in this condition perfectly reflects the → *puruṣa* or soul, which lies 'behind' all mental processes and faculties. Once the *puruṣa* is thus known by reflection, the Yogin gains mastery over it, so that it is no longer in bondage to → *prakṛti* (matter/nature) and to round of → rebirth, which is intrinsically full of suffering (*duḥkha*). The Yogin is then in a state of 'living liberation' (*jivanmukti*): previous → karma is burnt up and destroyed, so that at his death there will be no more impetus to rebirth, and the soul will be forever in a state of oneness (*kaivalya*): this means perfect quiescence and absence of suffering. This 'oneness' is not conceived as union with God or with other souls: each liberated soul exists in a state of perfect isolation. N.S.

M. Eliade, *Yoga: Immortality and Freedom* (1958); S. Dasgupta, *Yoga as Philosophy and Religion* (1924); J. H. Woods (tr.), *The Yoga System of Patanjali*, 2nd edn. (1927).

Kalām (Literally speech). Used in Muslim theological circles for discussion, and eventually developed the meaning of dogmatic theology. The → *Mutakallimūn* adopted rational arguments to support their dogmas. J.R.

E.I., II, pp. 670–5; Pareja, index; D. B. Macdonald, *Theology*, index; Wensinck, *Creed*, index; Sweetman, *I.C.T.*, IV, pp. 6ff.; F. Rosenthal, *Ibn Khaldun*, index (Theology).

Kalevala Finnish national epic in 50 songs (22,795 lines), made up of disparate trad. material collected and arranged by Elias Lönnrot (1st edn. 1835; definitive edn. 1849; abridged edn. 1862). About 1,000 lines were added by the editor. Only the orig. material, now published separately, is of significance for the study of → Finno-Ugric Religion. E.J.S.

Kālī One of commonest names of consort of → Śiva (others are Durgā, Umā, Pārvatī, Caṇḍī, etc.). Various cults have syncretised into worship of Devī, the Goddess. There are refs. to K. and other spouses of Śiva in → Upaniṣads; in the *Mahābhārata*, though a fully developed, → Śaktism (worship of divine being as female) belongs to medieval period. K. is repr. as the *śakti* or creative power of God; as goddess of → Time, she brings world to destruction. She is typically depicted of dark complexion, and commonly wears garland of skulls and skirt made of severed arms. This ferocious aspect gives way to more serene one when she symbolises the eternal night of rest and peace between periods of world-creation. Further, the very ferocity of K. is interpreted to mean that she, in embodying fear, overcomes it, so that she can grant peace to her devotees. K. is also depicted as dancing on quiescent figure of her consort, symbolising dialectic between inner self-sufficiency of Śiva and creative-destructive power of *śakti*. The fertility aspects of cult of K. in part explains its persistence and appeal, and are connected with practice of → sacrifice to her, notably in Bengal. N.S.

Kaliyuga Fourth age of the present *mahāyuga* or aeon, which is, in Hindu trad. cosmology, one of the periods into which each cycle of cosmic history is divided (→ Time, Hindu concept of). It is trad. reckoned to have started at time of the Mahabharata war, ascribed to 3102 BC. It is last phase of a general decline in relig. and society, and will end in social chaos, except in so far as the → Vaisnavite trad. looks for coming of Kalki, the last avatara, to usher in new age of justice. The *kaliyuga* is usually reckoned to last 1200 'years of the gods', each equal to 360 human years; but some reckon it to be much shorter. N.S.

Kalpa (Skt.); **Kappa** (Pali) In Buddh. usage: (1) a measure, rule or practice (2) a certain period of time—in common with all Indian thought, the Buddh. K.'s are held to be of incredibly long duration: 'an age'; 'an eternity'. (→ *Creator, Doctrine Buddh.*). T.O.L.

Kāma (Buddh.) Term used in Buddhism as in Hinduism for 'pleasure', 'sense-enjoyment', 'sensuality'. K. is used to characterise existence in all but the higher or more refined planes or 'realms'; it occurs in combination with *loka* (world) or *vacara* (sphere of existence), to designate the world in which majority of inhabitants of universe are found, i.e. kāma-loka, or *kāma-vacara* (→ Cosmology, Buddh.). K. is always regarded in Buddh. thought as first and chief obstacle to spiritual progress; it is frequently assoc. with passion (*rāga*), impulse (*chanda*) and greed (*gedha*). T.O.L.

(Desire or love)—one of the four trad. ends or aims of life in Hindu thought (together with *artha*, economic gain; → *dharma*, virtue and → *moksa*, liberation). Personalised, K. is Hindu god of love, sometimes identified with Buddh. → Mara. In → *Mahābhārata* K. is sent to distract → Siva from yogic meditation, but is burnt to ashes by magical power generated by Śiva's asceticism (→ *tapas*). Conversely, however, K. is much prized by yogis, since it is through his benevolence that they can be freed from sexual desire (erotic sculptures in holy places, therefore, serve purpose in propitiating K.). At one time K. played large part in great spring festival, Holi (→ Festivals, Hindu). N.S.

Kami Jap. term, having gen. meaning of 'above', 'superior', is the most common and comprehensive word for deity in Jap. language. It refers to everything that is sacred, strange, mysterious, fearful, powerful or beyond human comprehension. The term is used in ref. to gods and supernatural powers, to spirits and deities of nature, to ancestor-spirits, and superior human beings such as the mikado and nobles, high government officials and feudal lords. In → Shinto the Kami are worshipped, and their will made known through divination. They dispense calamity and good fortune, punish crime and reward virtue. Trad. refers to 800 myriads of *kami*, and vast and indefinable host of superhuman beings, though in recognised shrines of Shinto some 200 are worshipped. A phonetic variant of Kami is Kamu (or Kabu), and resembles both in word-form and meaning the Polynesian → Tabu (Taboo). The following terms are notable: → *Kami-gi*—sacred tree often planted in front of Shinto shrines, usually evergreen *Cleyera japonica; Kami-no-michi*—the Way of the Gods; *Kami-oroshi*—formula for 'bringing down the gods to reside temporarily in the → Gohei. D.H.S.

D. C. Holtom, *The National Faith of Japan* (1938), pp. 22–5, 171–85; W. G. Aston, *Shinto, the Way of the Gods* (1905), pp. 7–10.

Kami-dana (→ *kami, dana*—shelf). Jap. term for altar, on which the favourite *kami* of family have been enshrined. It generally consists of small cupboard in shape of a Shinto temple, in front of which are daily presented offerings of rice, salt and water, and on special days, saki, fruits and other foods. In many cases a light is kept burning before the K.-D. D.H.S.

J. Herbert, *Shinto* (1967), p. 159.

Kamma (Pali); **Karma** (Skt.) In Buddh., as in Indian thought gen., K. is the universal law of act and consequence. The primary meaning is that of *action* or *deed;* from this follows the applied meaning of deed as expressive of the doer's will, and thus the causal factor in doer's subsequent state or condition. K. thus comes to be 'a law, the working of which cannot be escaped' (PTS Pali-Eng. Dict.). Every being thus 'inherits' his own K., and also continues to produce further K., the consequences of which will be felt at some later time. In the Buddh. analysis of the human situation, however, K. does not constitute a doc. of determinism, since one is free to act for better or for worse within situation which his K. has produced; his K. does not determine his *response to* situation, it only presents him with the datum of situation itself. Moreover, it is the volition, rather than the action alone, which, in the Buddh. view, is of greatest importance in producing fresh K. The consequences of K. may be experienced during life-time of the doer, or in next birth, or in some successive birth. (A.N., VI, 63). In gen. the Buddh. view is that volition characterised by greed, hatred and delusion produces unwholesome K., while volition characterised by opposite qualities produces wholesome K.

It is sometimes assumed that belief in → rebirth was accepted by Buddha without question from earlier Indian relig. This is a controversial question, discussed at length by K. N. Jayatilleke, who argues that there is no evidence that such a belief was 'universal or even widespread prior to advent of Buddhism', or for assumption that Buddh. took such a notion for granted in sense of accepting it uncritically from prevalent trad. It is poss. that early Buddh. thought may in fact have contributed towards formulation belief. Buddh. saw difficulty of reconciling belief in K. and → transmigration with doc. of → *anatta*, yet regarded belief in *K* as essential to their position, and asserted it over against contemporary materialist thinkers and others who did not hold such a belief. T.O.L.

K. N. Jayatilleke, *Early Buddhist Theory of Knowledge*, 1963, ch. VIII.

Kanishka Buddh. ruler of Kushan empire, which lay to N.W. of India. His accession is dated variously as 78, 128 and 144 CE, the 2 latter now being regarded as more probable. A Buddh. council, reckoned by Mhy. Buddh. as the 4th (→ Councils, Buddh.) was held in his reign, at Jālandhar acc. to one trad. in Kashmir acc. to another. K. is repr. in trad. as desirous of settling disputes among various schools of Buddh. thought, and has a place in estimation of Mhy. Buddh. similar to that given to → Ashoka by Theravādins. T.O.L.

H. Winternitz, *History of Indian Literature*, vol. 2, ch. 5.

Kannushi The most common word to designate priests of → Shinto temples. A contraction of *kami-nushi*, lit. deity-master. They are also called *shinshoku*, a word derived from the Chinese. Before the Meiji Reform, the term was applied exclusively to high-priest and assistant high-priest of a Shinto temple. In a relig. sense, the emperor was the Highest K., and in social status the K. ranked above the → Samurai. In later times all Shinto priests came to be called K. Their function was to worship and serve the → Kami, thus assuring material and spiritual well-being of land and people. They were responsible for Shinto ceremonial, and upkeep and preservation of their temples. The K. are not celibate. They often combine other duties with their relig. duties, only wearing their distinctive dress when officiating. In 1962 the Shinto clergy numbered approx. 21,000; there were about 480 women-K., of whom 98 were officially recognised as → *guji*. The high-priest in charge of a temple is now uniformly called → *guji*. D.H.S.

E.R.E., XI, p. 468; W. G. Aston, *Shinto* (1905), p. 204; J. Herbert, *Shinto* (1967), pp. 134f.

Kant, Immanuel (1724–1804) Lived and taught in Könisberg. While in his later years, he ignored relig. practices, he never completely lost influence of his pietist upbringing. For most of his academic life, he was an undistinguished teacher of scientific subjects and the philosophical system that Wolff had developed from ideas of Leibniz. A radical change in his thought occurred in the 1770's as a result of reading Hume's empiricist philosophy, of discovering that contradictory propositions could both be demonstrated by applying fundamental concepts to reality, and of realising that extension of the causal nexus to cover all events denied the freedom essential to morality. The first exposition of his new position was *The Critique of Pure Reason* (1781). This was followed by discussions of the metaphysical, ethical, aesthetic and relig. aspects of the 'critical philosophy'. Kant argued that our knowledge of things is determined by certain conditions which he defined as 'forms of intuition'—namely, space and time—and the 'categories of understanding'—which incl. categories such as 'cause', 'substance', 'unity', and 'necessity'. These forms and categories are prior to all experience and provide its structure. Furthermore, they only apply to our apprehension of experience. If we attempt to apply the forms and categories to what lies beyond or behind and may be said to give rise to experience, we fall into contradiction. Thus we cannot know what things are in themselves (*i.e.* as '*noumena*'); but only as we experience and understand them in terms of these prior structures (i.e. as '*phenomena*'). K. shows that the ontological, cosmological and teleological arguments fail to demonstrate existence of God,—although he does allow some significance to the teleological argument. He further rejects all claims to know what God is like on ground that they attempt to apply to realm of the infinite and noumenal what properly belongs only to the finite and phenomenal. Since his arguments apply equally to any attempt to prove that God does not exist, K. concludes that he has shown that relig. is based on faith and not on knowledge. Within limits of reason, the concept of 'God' has some significance—though as a concept and not as a name for an existing being. For pure reason the concept of 'God', or the *ens realissimum*, acts as a 'regulative principle', i.e., it provides a theoretical goal which gives direction to our thinking. For the practical (or moral) reason, the concepts of 'God', 'freedom' and 'immortality' are 'postulates' required to make sense of the unconditional demand of morality. Religion, for Kant, is the practice or morality. History is viewed as a moral struggle, where each individual is responsible for living his own life accord. to the dictates of reason and morality. Kant's philosophy has dominated philosophy and theology since his time, espec. in the Prot. world. Although his arguments can be criticised, they are widely considered to have effectively demolished the trad. proofs for existence of God and to have raised in an acute form the questions of possibility of knowing the nature of God. D.A.P.

I. Kant, *Critique of Pure Reason; Prolegomena to any future Metaphysic; Critique of Practical Reason; Critique of Judgment; Religion within the Limits of Reason Alone:* S. Körner, *Kant* (1955); N. K. Smith, *A Commentary to Kant's 'Critique of Pure Reason'* (1918); C. C. J. Webb, *Kant's Philosophy of Religion* (1926).

Kapilavatthu (Pali); **Kapilāvastu** (Skt.) Paternal home of → Gautama the Buddha; a town in Himalayan foothills in what is now Nepal, it was in Buddha's time the capital of the → Sakya tribe. The Buddha was born at → Lumbini, near K., and spent his childhood and early manhood in K. Acc. to Pali texts (*Jat.*, I, 87ff.; *Vin.*, I, 82), the Buddha visited K. again in year after his enlightenment. He preached his doc. to the people of K., and his father → Suddhodana became a → *sotdpanna.* The Buddha's son → Rāhula, who was at this time still a child, became a → *samanera*, or novice-candidate for the → Sangha. A large number of Sakyans also entered the Sangha. The Buddha visited K. on a number of other occasions; various discourses and → Jātaka stories contained in the Pali canon are said to have been preached by him at K. Towards end of Buddha's life the town was attacked and destroyed and the Sakya people massacred by Viḍūḍabha, a Kosalan prince, in revenge for insult he received there. Nevertheless, at Buddha's death, the people of K. are said to have claimed a share of his ashes after cremation, and to have erected a shrine over them in town (D.N., II, 167). At time of the Chinese pilgrim Fa-Hsien, who visited India early in 5th cent. CE, however, there were only ruins to be seen at K.; the site of town is now unidentified. T.O.L.

Malalasekere, *D.P.P.N.*, vol. I, pp. 516–20.

Karaites Jew. sect. founded in Babylon, *c.* CE 750, by Anan b. David, hence also called Ananites. Their orig. aim was to base themselves in Scripture instead of Tradition, i.e. → Talmud; but they soon developed their own traditions, which diverged from orthodox → Judaism. The K. now exist mainly in Russia, and various places in Near East. S.G.F.B.

E.R.E., VI, *s.v.; R.G.G.*^{3}, III, pp. 1144–5.

Karbalā About 60 miles S.S.W. of Baghdad, site of massacre of → al-Ḥusayn and his small band of followers on 10th Muḥarram 61/680. It is one of the → Shi'a sacred places, containing shrine of al-Ḥusayn, a place of pilgrimage visited annually by thousands. The very soil is sacred. Small clay tablets are made from what is considered place where Ḥusayn was killed, and are normally given free, for selling them would be like selling Ḥusayn's flesh. Rosaries of 34 beads are also made from this clay. The small tablets are used in prayer, the head resting on them during prostration. The shrine has suffered damage and destruction on different occasions, the most recent being by the → Wahhābīs in 1216/1801. J.R.

E.I., III, pp. 477–9; Pareja, p. 829; Donaldson, *Shi'ite*, ch. viii; Levy, *Social Structure*, index (Kerbelā).

Karma, Hindu Concept Karma, sometimes transliterated *karman*, lit. means 'deed' or 'act', but more partic. is used to ref. to law governing deeds, whereby they have more and material effects in this life and future lives. It is thus closely connected with belief in reincarnation or → rebirth, and is related to analogous conceptions in → Jainism and → Buddhism. The belief makes first unambiguous appearance within Brahmanical trad. in the → Upanisads, and displaces earlier Vedic eschatology (though trad. exegetes of Vedic hymns, etc., see docs. of K. and rebirth as already present there). Belief in K. became virtually universal in classical → Hinduism, and only school seriously to resist doc. were → Carvaka materialists. Popularly, K. provides explanation of social differences and good and bad fortune, by connecting these with good and bad acts in this or previous lives. Spiritually, K. has been import. in relation to path to liberation (→ *moksa*). One's deeds in world are determinative of one's chances of final release from round of rebirth. In principle, it is through annihilating effects of evil acts, or more gen. of acts, whether good or bad, which bind one to world, that one gains salvation. Thus typically it is held that one has power or freedom to alter one's destiny, though one or two teachers in Indian trad., notably Makkhali Gosala, of the → Ajivika sect, propounded a deterministic doc. The means of eliminating effects of K. differ acc. to various Hindu schools. Thus for → Yoga, there is scheme of moral and meditative practices bringing about purification of consciousness. In theistic Hinduism (→→ Vaisnavism, Saivism), faith in the Lord can bring release, since God is controller of K. The → *Bhagavadgita* combines this notion with beief that if one renounces fruits of one's acts one is not bound to world by them. In Hindu theism, K. came increasingly to be seen as expression of God's continuing activity of dealing justly and mercifully with men's lives. For → Advaita Vedanta, key to liberation is knowledge of one's identity with ultimate reality, → *Brahman:* conversely, the force which binds men to world ultimately is ignorance (→ *avidya*). The operation of K. was sometimes used as argument for God's existence in medieval philosophy, on ground that only an intelligent being could apportion rewards and punishments, etc.; but argument was scarcely persuasive to non-theistic schools, since belief in K. as law of universe was so deeply entrenched in trad. There was considerable discussion, however, of exact mode in which K. operates, e.g. as to how it connects with hereditary characteristics transmitted by parents, etc. In its less specific sense, K. is used to mean 'works' → *karmayoga*. N.S.

S. Radhakrishnan, *The Brahma Sutra* (1960); N. Smart, *Doctrine and Argument in Indian Philosophy* (1964); K. Morgan (ed.), *The Religion of the Hindus* (1953). → Kamma (Pali).

(Jain Concept) In gen. form, the Jain concept of K. corresponds to, though in origin it antedates, that found in classical → Hinduism (and → Buddhism). It is presented, however, more 'materialistically'; K. is seen as subtle material force obscuring → *jiva* and weighing it down. With elimination of K. the life-monad will regain its intrinsic omniscience, etc., and gravitate upwards to still summit of universe, there to exist eternally at rest. All actions produce K., some of which takes long to work out effects, some a short time. The net effect of one's K. colours life-monad, either black, blue, grey, yellow, red or white (the *leśyās* or 'complexions' of life-monad)—the first three colours belonging to bad people, the last three to good. To gain release, one must exercise *samvara* or restraint or blocking of K. from entering soul, by good action in conformity with right moral rules (→ Ethics, Jain); and by annihilating K. through practice of → *tapas* or austerity. Even unintentional taking of life, etc., will produce K., so that considerable circumspection is demanded, above all of monks, who take detailed precautions against such accidents. But elimination of K. is not just an external matter, since it requires equanimity and eradication of passions, together with practice of contemplation. (→ Jainism, Bibliography → Kamma (Pali). N.S.

Karunā In Buddh. thought *karunā*, or compassion, holds import. place as one of the 4 'spiritual abodes', i.e. → *Brahma-vihāras*. In partic., this is the unmotivated graciousness of attitude shown by → Buddhas and → Bodhisattvas towards mortal beings. The Buddh. life is understood as consisting of cultivation of both wisdom (*prajñā*) and compassion; it is held that, without former, the emotion of compassion may be erroneously directed, i.e., it may be engaged in for unwise motives. The older, → Hīnayāna, form of Buddhism tended to lay principal emphasis on need for wisdom; the → Mahāyāna emphasised both as equally important, over against earlier emphasis on wisdom predominantly, which could, acc. to the Mhy., result in an isolated intellectualism. Eventually this emphasis on K. became the more predominant, and in later forms of Mhy. developed into concept of the 'saving grace' of the Buddha → Amitābha, which he offers to those who call upon him in faith. T.O.L.

Kasb →→ Acquisition, Free-will and Predestination. J.R.

Kathā-Vathu One of 7 books of the Pali → Abhidhamma-pitaka of the Theravāda school; considered by some authorities to be historically the most import. of the seven. Acc. to the trad. (*Mahāvamsa*, V, 278; *Dipavamsa*, VII, 41:56–8), *K.-V.* is said to have been recited by the Elder named Moggaliputta Tissa at 3rd Buddh. Council (→ Councils, Buddh.), held at Patna in reign of emperor → Ashoka. The work, in 23 chapters, consists of discussion (*kathā*), and refutation of 219 different erroneous teachings then being propounded by schismatic groups of monks. Some mod. scholars are inclined to doubt that work, as it now exists, was compiled by Moggaliputta Tissa, as some heretical views confuted are those of schools which arose some cents. later than Council of Patna. T.O.L.

S. Z. Aung-C. A. F. Rhys-Davids, *Points of Controversy* (1915, repr. 1960); Nyanatiloka Mahathera, *Guide through the Abhidhamma-Pitaka* (1957), ch. 5.

-Kawthar In Qur. cviii:1, is properly 'abundance' acc. to some authoritative commentators; but others treat it as proper name of a river in paradise, basing this on some traditions. A trad. from Anas, → Muḥammad's servant, given by → Bukhari quotes Muhammad as saying, 'While I was travelling in paradise I came to a river whose banks were domes of hollowed pearls, and when I asked God what this was he replied that it was al-Kawthar which my Lord had given me. Its soil was the most excellent musk.' Another from the same source, given by → Tirmidhi, tells that Muhammad said of al-Kawthar, 'This is a river of God given me (meaning in paradise), whiter than milk and sweeter than honey, containing birds whose necks are like the necks of sacrificial animals.' 'Alī, *Qur'ān*, n. 2807, in commenting on K., does not even mention idea of its being a river in paradise. He seems to prefer meaning of 'abundance', or 'the abundance of good'. He quotes remarks about its meaning God's promises to Muhammad, such as triumph of Islam, help against enemies, intercession for his community (→ Intercession). One statement, in reply to a question about K. being a river in paradise, says, 'the river and all (good) besides it.' J.R.

E.I., II, pp. 834f.; Hughes, p. 262 (al-Kauṡar); *Mishkāt*, pp. 1179, 1201.

Kāya (Buddh.) → Buddha-Kāya. T.O.L.

Kegon School (→ Hua Yen). This school, intro. into Japan by Korean monk, → Jinjo (d. 742) played import. role in → Buddhism of Nara period. Based on the *Avatāmsaka Sūtras*, with their doc. of the Buddhahood of all sentient beings, the identity of → nirvāna and → samsara, and wisdom and compassion of the → bodhisattvas who guide errant beings to Buddhahood, the school had considerable influence on development of → Zen. Its teaching that aim of relig. is to dispel illusion of the separate ego may be described as cosmotheism. Though its philosophical appeal was considerable, it did not exert much practical influence. D.H.S.

H. Dumoulin, *Hist. of Zen Buddhism* (1963), pp. 38ff.; M. Anesaki, *Hist. of Japanese Relig.* (1930), pp. 93ff.

Kēres (sing. Kēr) Anc. Grk. word for souls of dead, having a grisly connotation. In art the K. were repr. as little black emaciated human forms, winged. There were also other K. who brought disease, old age, and death. At the → Anthesteria the K. were annually entertained and then dismissed. (→ Psyche). S.G.F.B.

Ed. Rohde, *Psyche* (1898), I, pp. 236ff.; J. Harrison, *Prolegomena*, pp. 32ff., 165ff.; *O.C.D.*, *s.v.*; R. B. Onians, *The Origins of European Thought* (1951), pp. 399ff.; *Kleine Pauly*, III, 194–5.

Kerygma Grk. → 'preaching'. Used with ref. to 'proclamation' element in Chr. Gospel in contrast to its teaching (*didachē*) aspect. K. has been used much in modern theology to denote essential message of Apostles. S.G.F.B.

C. H. Dodd, *The Apostolic Preaching and its Developments* (1944); R. Bultmann, *Theology of the New Test.*, I (E.T. 1952), pp. 3ff.; H. W. Bartsch (ed.), *Kerygma and Myth* (E.T. 1953); C. F. Evans, 'The Kerygma', *J.T.S.*, VII (1956).

Khadīja Daughter of Khuwaylid, was a Meccan widow in comfortable circumstances who employed → Muḥammad as agent to look after her business interests in a caravan to Syria. Impressed by his personality and acumen, she offered him marriage which he accepted. She is said to have been 40 then, and Muhammad 25. Her cousin Waraqa b. Nawfal was a man of relig. nature; she may have been influenced by him, for she was able to appreciate Muhammad's spiritual development, and encouraged him. Muhammad was devoted to her and lived happily with her for 25 years till her death in CE 619. It is said that he never forgot her, and that → 'Ā'isha declared she had never been so jealous of any of Muhammad's wives as of Kh., although she had never seen her. J.R.

E.I., II, pp. 860f.; Guillaume, *Life*, index; *Mishkāt*, index; Watt, *Mecca*, index.

-Khaḍir (The green one). Later more commonly al-Khiḍr, a popular figure in Muslim legend, connected by commentators with God's servant in Qur. xviii:59ff. He acts strangely, and seemingly wickedly, when accompanied by Moses, but can justify his actions. → Ṣūfīs later used story to prove that a saint can do no wrong. Kḥ. may be connected with the prophet Elijah. J.R.

E.I., II, pp. 471 (Ilyās), 861ff. (al-Khaḍir); *E.R.E.*, VII, p. 694; Hughes, pp. 272f.; Nicholson, *Mystics*, index, *Studies*, index (p. 269).

Khālid b. al-Walīd (d. 21/641–2). Famous Muslim general who was given title *Sayf Allah* (Sword of God) by Muhammad. A Meccan, he was at first opposed to → Muḥammad; by his timely attack he was responsible for defeat of the Muslims at → Uḥud. In 8/629 he accepted Islam and was responsible for import. conquests. He was among leaders at taking of Mecca. In 11/632 he defeated → Ṭulayḥa. In 12/633 he defeated → Musaylima. He was prominent in early part of attack on Persia; then was called to help in Syrian campaign, and accomplished a remarkable crossing of desert with his forces. In 14/625 Dmascus was taken. Kh. had to take second place to Abū 'Ubayda, but continued fighting successfully. He held a governorship in Syria, but was recalled by → 'Umar and deprived of most of his wealth. Preeminently a great general, accused at times of violence, Kh. is nevertheless said to have been sent by Muhammad to Najran on a peaceful mission to convert a tribe, which he successfully accomplished. J.R.

E.I., II, pp. 878f.; Muir, *Life*, index, *Caliphate*, index; Watt, *Medina*, index; Hitti, *History*, index; Levy, *Social Structure*, index.

Khandha (Pali); **Skandha** (Skt.) Buddh. term meaning 'group' or 'aggregate' of factors. What is commonly regarded as a human 'individual' may, in Buddh. terms, be analysed into 5 K.s. The 1st group of factors is *rūpa* (form) = the physical or corporeal; 2nd: *vedanā* = sensation or feeling; 3rd: *sannā* (Pali)/*samjnā* (Skt.) = perception; 4th: *sankhāra* (Pali)/*samskāra* (Skt.) = formative principle or volition; 5th: *viññāna* (Pali)/*vijñāna* (Skt.) = consciousness. Each of these is a group, aggregate or 'bundle' of elements of that type which are continually in flux; thus the physical nature of individual is at any moment a process or flux of physical elements; similarly with sensations, perceptions, volitions and consciousness. The whole process constituted by the 5 groups is the human individual at any given moment of his life-history; at different stages in that hist. he exhibits different appearances and characteristics. This process of continual change is evident, even to the eye of 'commonsense', in the difference between the individual as a baby, a youth, a mature man, and old man. Physically the process of change is continuous; similarly, it is held, at the level of sensation-volition; and of the state or condition of consciousness. The 5 K.'s are sometimes given in a 3-fold scheme: (1) physical, viz., *rūpa;* (2) sense-perception and reaction, viz., *vedanā*, *saññā*, and *sankhāra;* (3) consciousness, or *viññāna.* In this case the 3 groups are called *rūpa*, *cetasikā* (concomitants or conditioning factors of consciousness) and *citta* (state of consciousness). This is scheme used in the → Abhidhamma; e.g. in → *Dhammasanganī* of the Theravādin Abh. Pitaka. More simply the 5 K.'s may be arranged in 2 groups: (1) *rūpa* (2) *nāma* (viz. the other 4 K.'s. There is thus nothing ultimate or absolute about the 5 K.'s; they are simply abstract classifications used in Buddh. analysis of human existence, useful as analytical categories, but themselves only concepts, just as the 'individual' is only a concept, having no abiding reality. In the Theravādin view, the ultimate elements of psycho-physical existence are the → *dhammas:* these are the 'atoms' of which the K.'s are groups or aggregates. The *dhammas* are of momentary existence only; before they arise they have no reality, when they have passed they have no reality; they are thus as it were 'flashes' of reality. The → Mādhyamika school of → Mahāyāna criticised the Theravādin for not applying relentlessly analytical method by which it was perceived that K.'s are only relative categories to the *dhammas* also, but instead, arbitrarily, stopping at *dhammas* as the 'atoms'. T.O.L.

Kharāj (Tax). Came to be used partic. of the land tax. At first only the → protected people owned land, and they had to pay this tax as well as → *jizya.* Later land came into Muslim hands, and one who owned land had to pay Kh. as well as *zakāt* (→ Legal Alms). J.R.

E.I., II, pp. 902f.; Hughes, p. 269; Levy, *Social Structure*, index; Hitti, *History*, index.

Khārijites Origin of this party has commonly been explained as the defection of some of → 'Ali's followers who disapproved of agreement to stop Battle of Ṣiffīn (37/657) between 'Ali and Mu'awiya, and put question of which of them had right to → Caliphate to arbitration. Because of their objection, they are said to have set themselves up against the constituted authorities. There was not one single party going under name of K., but rather separate groups all of fanatical nature. But it has been suggested that origin of their name may be found in Qur. ix, which speaks of people who went out (*kharaja*) to fight in God's way as opposed to those who sat (*qa'ada*) at home. This origin suggests that name Kh. refers to people who went forth to spread the faith and oppose infidels. They were for long a thorn in flesh of Caliphate. They insisted that any Muslim was eligible to become Caliph, provided he was of exemplary conduct; also that a Caliph who did not live up to their standards could be deposed. They held that faith must be proved by works, that serious sin was apostasy deserving punishment. They believed they were the only true Muslims. Most of their sects died out early. Still remaining are the 'Ibādites in Algeria, Tripolitania, Oman and Zanzibar; they are moderate in their views. They do not claim to be the only Muslims, and are ready to intermarry with other Muslims. They have views like some held by → Mu'tazilites, e.g. that the Qur. is created, that the beatific vision will not be realised, that the Qur. anthropomorphisms are to be allegorised, and that believers who die unrepentant, having committed grievous sins, will go to → hell for ever; Muhammad will not intercede for such. J.R.

E.I., II, pp. 904–8; Pareja, pp. 815ff. and index; Wensinck, *Creed*, index; D. B. Macdonald, *Theology*, index; Levy, *Social Structure*, index; Watt, *Philosophy*, ch. 2 and index; Rahman, *Islam*, index.

Khazars Tribe of Turkish or Finnish origin, which estab. kingdom in Crimea during 8th–10th cent. CE. They are notable for the conversion to → Judaism of their kings and many nobles. Judaism was made the state relig., though majority of people were Muslim, Christian or pagan. The K. disappeared in Tartar invasion of 1237. There is a problematic *Correspondence khazare*, some of it allegedly dating from 10th cent. S.G.F.B.

D. M. Dunlop, *Hist. of the Jewish Khazars* (1954); S. Szyszman, 'Les Khazars: problèmes et controverses', *R.H.R.*, 152 (1957).

Khōjas Community mainly Muslim, of whom most owe allegiance to the → Agha Khan. They are chiefly found in W. coast of India, in E. Africa, in the Panjab, and in some parts of C. Asia. In origin they were converted Hindus, and elements of Hindu practices are maintained, e.g. the marriage customs of the Bombay Kh. In gen. they follow the → Isma'ili faith; but secessions have taken place, and one group claims to belong to the Imamis (→ Shi'a). The Panjab Kh. do not recognise the Agha Khan as leader, but follow guidance of certain → Ṣūfī shaykhs. There is little or any difference between the parties in relig. belief and practice. In 1346/1927 a party in Karachi called 'The Khoja Reformers' Society' addressed petition to the Agha Khan that he should repudiate the divine honours paid him and stop accepting offerings. They felt his life was luxurious in contrast with poverty of many of his followers. J.R.

E.I., II, pp. 960–2; Pareja, pp. 843f.; Jones, *Mosque*, pp. 134f.

Khons(u) Egypt. moon-god, whose name prob. derives from word meaning 'to wander' or 'traverse', and obviously refers to moon's movements. In myth, K. was presented as son of → Amun and Mut; his chief shrine was at Thebes. He was gen. repr. as young man, with moon's disc and crescent on head. S.G.F.B.

R.Ae.R-G., pp. 140ff.; S. A. B. Mercer, *The Relig. of Anc. Egypt* (1949), pp. 153ff.; P. Derchain, *S.O.*, V (1962), pp. 40ff.

Khnum Egypt. creator-god, his role being signified by name (*ẖmnw* = 'to create'). K. was repr. as a ram-headed man; he is also depicted fashioning human infants out of clay on a potter's wheel, while goddess → Hathor animates them. K. had several sanctuaries in Egypt, that at Elephantinē being chief. S.G.F.B.

A. M. Badawi, *Der Gott Chnum* (1937); *R.Ae.R-G.*, pp. 135ff.; S. A. B. Mercer, *The Relig. of Anc. Egypt* (1949), pp. 151ff.; Brandon, *C.L.*, pp. 60ff.

Khuddaka-Nikāya Collection of Buddh. canonical books, forming 5th section of the → Sutta Pitaka of Pali canon. The name *khuddaka* designates this Nikāya as one of 'short pieces'. These are 15 in number, as follows: (1) *Khuddaka-pātha*, a miscellaneous collection of lists of moral rules, catechism questions, Buddh. formulae incl., e.g. that of taking refuge in the Buddha, Dhamma, and Sangha (→ Tri-Ratna) widely used in Buddh. devotions; (2) → *Dhammapada*; (3) → *Udāna;* (4) *Itivuttaka*, collection of miscellaneous verses dealing largely with morality, and intro. in most cases by formula '*iti vuccati*'—'thus it is said'; (5) → *Sutta Nipāta;* (6) *Vimāna-vatthu*, collection of 83 stories, arranged in 7 groups, concerning lives of → devas (heavenly beings) in their celestial palaces, where they enjoy rewards for some previous good acts; this, and (7) → *Petavatthu*, describing sad fate of those who in spirit-realm are now expiating some past misdeed, are gen. held to be later in origin than other parts of canon, largely on linguistic grounds; (8) → *Thera-gāthā*, and (9) → *Therī-gāthā* are, respectively, collections of 'songs of the Theras' (elder monks) and of the Therī (elder nuns); (10) → *Jātaka* stories; (11) *Niddesa*, a commentary on part (the *Atthakavagga*) of the → Sutta Nipāta, (which testifies to early date of latter, that it should have a canonical commentary); (12) *Patisambhida-magga*, an analytical treatise in style of the → Abhidhamma works; (13) *Apadāna*, collection of stories in verse of previous existences of certain monks and nuns; (14) → *Buddhavamsa;* and (15) *Cariyāpitaka*, selection of *Jātakas* arranged specially to illustrate certain Buddh. moral virtues, regarded by Geiger, following Winternitz, as work of a monk 'who manufactured edifying stories for the elucidation of the doctrine on the basis of the existing Jātakas'. The *KN* thus incl. a variety of types of Buddh. texts, both in contents and date of composition, embracing as it does what is undoubtedly one of the earliest Buddh. documents, the *Sutta Nipāta*, as well as some of the latest of canonical lit., such as (11), (12), (13) and (15) listed above. (→→ *Tipitaka: Sutta Pitaka*). T.O.L.

Khutba (Sermon). The Kh. is preached at noon prayer on Fridays in mosques. There is also a sermon after sunrise on morning of the two great festivals (→→ *'Īd al-aḍḥā* and *'Īd al-fiṭr*). The Kh. has been formalised. On Friday, at the noon prayer, the preacher (*khaṭib*) mounts the pulpit (*minbar*). His sermon is divided into two parts. It begins with praise of God, and, after invoking blessings on → Muḥammad and his → Companions, issues exhortations. The preacher then descends and sits on ground offering silent prayer. He then mounts pulpit and delivers second part of his sermon. This also begins with praise of God. Blessing is invoked on Muhammad, his descendants, the first four → Caliphs, and other people famous in early days of Islam. After prayer for those who help → Islām, the preacher prays for ruler of the age and exhorts the people to remember God. It is import. to pray for ruler. In earlier times this prayer was for the Caliph; the substitution of some other name was an indication of rebellion. On 7th day of → Dhul Ḥijja a sermon is preached in Mecca exhorting pilgrims to go out to perform the rites which take place outside Mecca; on 9th a sermon is preached on hill at → 'Arafat at the noon prayer. J.R.

E.I., II, pp. 980–3, Hughes, pp. 274–7; Pareja, index (*ḥuṭba*); Lane, *Egyptians*, pp. 87–92, 94, 165, 513f.; Kamal, *Sacred Journey*, pp. 68ff.; Mez, *Renaissance*, pp. 317ff.

Khuzā'a Anc. S. Arabian tribe which had occupied the sacred area about the → Ka'ba, and were eventually ousted by → Quraysh under Quṣayy. They still lived in neighbourhood, and, after → Hijra, kept in touch with → Muḥammad, with whom they later made alliance. The Conquest of Mecca was consequent on breach of ten years' truce between Muhammad and Quraysh, who were attacking Kh. J.R.

E.I., II, pp. 984f.; Guillaume, *Life*, index; Watt, *Mecca*, index.

Kierkegaard Søren Aabye (1813–55) Born in Copenhagen in 1813, son of wealthy merchant, Michael Pedersen Kierkegaard, who had retired from business dramatically at early age of 40. K. was profoundly influenced by father, and much of his life-story had to be understood in terms of his changing relationship to father. After father's death in 1838, K. finished his theological course and crowned his studies with a Master's thesis on *The Concept of Irony with Particular Reference to Socrates* (1841). Already in 1837 he had met Regine Olsen, and three years later they became engaged; but finally in October 1841 he broke with Regine, because he believed that he was called to forgo security of ordinary life. He spent some time in Berlin, where he wrote first publ. work *Either/Or*. The break with Regine tapped a well of literary talent; the remaining years of life were spent in writing. Two decisive events in these years had their effect on his authorship. The first was the attack on him by the radical humorous paper *The Corsair*, an attack which he had sought and to which he replied in a series of articles. The second was the funeral address by Martensen in which he praised Bishop Mynster as a 'Witness'. This evoked Kierkegaard's attack on official relig. K. collapsed in street in October 1855, and died a month later.

K. is import. both as philosopher and relig. writer. Philosophically his importance lies mainly in his criticism of Hegelian System. There is no more trenchant and perceptive critic of → Hegel in all 19th cent. philosophy than this lonely writer with a relig. mission. The attack on Hegelianism began with *The Concept of Irony*, which is a deliverately ironical use of Hegelian idiom and philosophy to discredit the Hegelian position. It continued in *Either/Or*, a strange collection of various writings, the significance of which Kierkegaard later said was to argue that tautology is the highest principle of thought. *Repetition* and—more obviously—*Fear and Trembling* take up the detailed criticism of the System, and in *Stages on Life's Way* Kierkegaard sums up his criticism by saying that Hegel's fundamental short-coming is his suppression of passionate features of human subjectivity. When he was to say later that subjectivity is truth, he was pointing to this kind of philosophical error, and also to fallacy that philosophy is a collection of results.

As a relig. writer Kierkegaard is equally concerned with the person of the believer. One of the main dangers of Hegelian influence on Christianity for him was that it destroyed the element of choice and risk of faith. So Kierkegaard rejects the System and its proof of religion, insisting that faith is opposite of proof. Nor does he favour historical proof: the only advantage he concedes that the first generation of disciples had was that of seeing the historical figure, and this is no advantage. The object of faith is the Paradox, the God-Man. *Training in Christianity*, one of his greatest works, is a profound analysis of the revelation in Christ and implies the concepts of paradox and offence to show a correlation of revelation and faith. Though he did not develop a Christology in the strict sense, his ideas have been very influential in modern → Christology. Similarly, his discussion of sin in its relation to human anxiety in the Concept of Dread have been influential. Finally, in several of his books he discussed problems of ethics and he made import. criticisms of Kantian and Hegelian ethics as well as developing in works devoted to Chr. ethics an account of the Chr. ethic which centres on the ideas of life and imitation of Christ. (→ Existentialism). J.H.-T.

Kierkegaard's entire authorship has been published in Danish—*Samlede Vaerker* (ed. Drachman, Heiberg, and Lange); *Papirer* (ed. Heiberg, Kuhn and Torsting); *Breve og Akstykken* (ed. Thulstrup). Oxford University Press has publ. most of the works in trans. Amongst the many works on Kierkegaard are the following: James Collins, *The Mind of Kierkegaard* (1955); H. Diem, *Kierkegaard's Dialectic of Existence* (1959); J. Heywood-Thomas, *Subjectivity and Paradox* (1957); W. Lowrie, *Kierkegaard* (1938); R. Thomte, *Kierkegaard's Philosophy of Religion* (1948); Thulstrup-Johnson, *A Kierkegaard Critique* (1962).

Kilesa (Pali); **Kleśa** (Skt.) Buddh. Term used in Buddhism for 'defilements', i.e. 'morally defiling passions'. In the → Theravadin sch., these are ten in number: (1) greed (*lobha*) (2) hatred (*dosa*) (3) delusion (*moha*) (4) conceit (*māna*) (5) speculative views (*ditthi*) (6) doubt (*vicikiccha*) (7) mental sloth (*thina*) (8) restlessness (*uddhacca*) (9) shamelessness (*ahirika*) (10) moral carelessness (*anottappa*). This list of 10 occurs first in the Thv. scriptures in the → *Abh. Pitaka*, in the *Dhammasangani*; it is thus a feature of the reflective systematic stage in hist. of B. thought. The → Sarvāstivādin school affirmed first six of these as fundamental K.'s, (acc. to the → *Abh. Kosa*), and to them added list of 10 subsidiary K.'s, viz. anger, hypocrisy, selfishness, envy, gloom, shamefulness, enmity, deceit, dishonesty and arrogance. The Mhy. school of → Yogācāra also affirmed first 6 as fundamental K.'s and added list of 20 subsidiary K.'s, (acc. to the *Vidhyāmātra Siddhi* of Dharmapāla). These 20 are virtually the 10 given in the Sarvāstivādin list with add. of: shamelessness, impudence, torpor, recklessness, lack of faith, idleness, carelessness, forgetfulness, confusion and wrong judgment. Some Yogācāra lists give 24 subsidiary K.'s. In the Yogācāra view, K. is regarded as something foreign to basic consciousness or *Ālaya-vijñāna;* a kind of 'dust' or impurity, 'spoiling the immaculate Alaya' (Suzuki), or the 'guest who is uninvited'—a somewhat different doc. of man from that reflected in Thv. phenomenology. T.O.L.

Nyanamoli, *The Path of Purification* (1964); W. M. McGovern, *Manual of Buddhist Philosophy*, vol. I (1923); D. T. Suzuki, *Studies in the Lankavatara Sutra* (1930).

-Kindī, Abū Yūsuf Ya'qūb b. Isḥāq (d. *c.* 256/870) Was called the philosopher of the Arabs, being only notable one of pure Arab descent. He enjoyed favour of the Caliph al-Mu'taṣim; but when → Mu'tazilite influence ceased under al-Mutawakkil, he suffered some degree of persecution and had his library taken from him for a time. In his philosophy he was influenced by → Neoplatonism, which at that time largely coloured study of → Aristotle. A work called 'The Theology of Aristotle', really a Neoplatonic work, was popular in its Arabic trans. K.'s knowledge was encyclopaedic, as may be inferred from consulting the list of his works given in *G.A.L.*, covering theology, philosophy, psychology, natural philosophy, astronomy, astrology, music, medicine, mathematics, geography. J.R.

E.I., II, pp. 1019f.; Pareja, pp. 981f.; *G.A.L.*, S., I, pp. 372–4; Sweetman, *I.C.T.*, III, IV, index of authors; Watt, *Philosophy*, index.

King, Divine The idea of royal divinity is very anc. and widespread; it also has many aspects, and is thus difficult to define concisely. The oldest instance is also the most highly developed; the Egypt. pharaoh was regarded as an incarnate god, son of the sun-god Rē, and his representative, on earth. The pharaonic insignia, titles and court ritual, were all expressive of king's divinity. Elsewhere, kings were often recognised as being of divine descent and vicegerents of supreme deity on earth (e.g. in Mesopot., China, Japan, Peru). Sometimes royal divinity was acquired (e.g. with Hellenistic rulers and Roman emperors). Byzantine and medieval Chr. kingship was sacred, the sacral character being conferred by coronation ritual (coronation of British monarchs still has this character); it was even believed that kings had power to heal scrofula or the King's Evil. In some primitive societies ageing kings were prob. killed, lest their decline of virility should affect fertility of land. (→ Myth and Ritual). The Israelite king held office as Yahweh's Anointed (→ Messiah); but his part in the cultus is obscure. (→ Africa, E. Ritual Cults; Ruler Worship, China–Jap.). S.G.F.B.

E.R.E., VII, pp. 708–32, 736–8 ('King's Evil'); J. G. Frazer, *The Early Hist. of Kingship* (1905); H. Frankfort, *Kingship and the Gods* (1948); *R.Ae.R-G.*, pp. 380ff.; 395ff.; A. R. Johnson, *Sacral Kingship in Anc. Israel* (1956); C. J. Gadd, *Ideas of Divine Rule in the Anc. Near East* (1948); S. H. Hooke (ed.), *Myth, Ritual and Kingship* (1958); *The Sacral Kingship* (Papers at 8th Internat. Congress for Hist. of Religions, Rome, 1955), publ. 1959; F. Heer, *Aufgang Europas* (1949), pp. 107ff.; L. Brehier, *Les institutions de l'empire byzantin* (1949), pp. 5ff., 52ff.

Kings, Books of Two narrative accounts of N. and S. Kingdoms of Israel, dating *c.* 550 BC. They develop the → Yahwist philosophy of history by showing how → Yahweh guides events, partic. as exemplified in careers of kings of Israel and Judah, in his providence for Israel, his people. S.G.F.B.

J. A. Montgomery, *The Book of Kings* (I.C.C. 1951); *H.D.B., s.v.; R.G.G.*³, III, col. 1703–6; M. Noth, *Könige* (1964).

(Buddh.) → Political Power and Buddhism. T.O.L.

Kitchen God (Chinese) Tsao Chün, one of earliest known gods of relig. → Taoism, his worship goes back at least to 2nd cent. BC. Almost every Chi. home has his image near cooking stove. He apportions the span of life, bestows wealth or poverty, and reports to Heaven the good and bad deeds of family. A universal Chi. custom is to burn his picture before the New Year in order to send him up to Heaven; at the New Year another picture is placed in position. D.H.S.

H. Doré, *Recherches sur les Superstitions en Chine* (1914–29), vol. 2, p. 901; S. Couling, *Encyl. Sinica.* (1917), 1965, p. 274.

Knots Tying and untying of K., symbolizing binding and loosing, is a concept of widespread occurrence in magic and relig. The Vedic god → Varuna is repr. as divine-magician who binds men in baleful ways, gen. connected with fate. → Homer depicts Olympian gods binding their fate upon mortals. Alternatively, evil may be bound as e.g. → Satan (Mk. 3:27; Rev. 20:2). S.G.F.B.

M. Eliade, *Images and Symbols* (E.T. 1961), pp. 92ff.; R. B. Onians, *The Origins of European Thought* (1951), pp. 310ff.; *E.R.E.*, VII, *s.v.*

Kōan (Jap.) from Chinese *kung-an*—an official record, a public notice. A technical term used in → Zen Buddhism for an exercise given by a Zen master to his disciple and designed to break through intellectual limitations and lead to a flash of sudden intuition for attainment of → satori. The kōan are often couched as problems insoluble by, and nonsensical to, the intellect. In almost all of them the striking element is the illogical or absurd act or word. Collections of kōan were made in China in the Sung Dynasty, notably the *Pi-yen-lu* and the *Wu-mên-kuan*, and they provided an effective method for systematic guidance towards enlightenment in Zen monasteries both in China and Japan. Those in actual use by Zen masters are numerous and varied, some 1700 in all. Attempts have been made to classify them into five or more groups. D.H.S.

H. Dumoulin, *Hist. of Zen Buddhism* (1963), pp. 126ff.; D. T. Suzuki, *Essays in Zen Buddhism* (2), 1933, pp. 83ff. *Studies in Zen* (1955), pp. 24ff.

Kōbō Daishi (CE 774–835). Posthumous name of Kūkai, Jap. Buddh. saint and founder of → Shingon sect of Buddhism. Having studied in China, he intro. into Japan, and brought to its final systematization, the pantheistic mysticism of the Tantric (Chên Yen or True Word) sect. Acc. to K.D.'s philosophy, the universe is the exterialised form of → Maha-Vairochana Buddha. It is his real body (*dharmakāya*), divided into two complementary constituents, the mental and the material. K.D. classified various forms of the relig. life, incl. Hinduism, Confucianism, Taoism, and other Buddh. sects, into ten grades of development, culminating in the mystic pantheism of Shingon, in which full blessedness of Buddhahood is realised. He taught an all-embracing syncretism of a highly mystical nature, and thus paved the way for → Ryōbu Shinto. K.D. had a far-reaching influence both in court circles and among the common people. He built a monastery on Mt. Kōya, which became headquarters of Shingon sect. His body is believed never to have decayed, but awaits resurrection at advent of → Maitreya Buddha. (→ Dharma-Kāya). D.H.S.

Kogoshūi Import. Jap. book of mythology, and one of chief literary sources for study of old → Shinto. Compiled by Hironari (CE 807), a Shinto priest belonging to the priestly guild of the → Imbe, it adds little to information given in the → *Kojiki* and → *Nihongi.* D.H.S.

Katō-Hoshino, *The Kogoshūi or Gleanings from Ancient Stories* (E.T. 1924).

Ko Hung Chinese Taoist philosopher, *c.* 250–330. Author of monumental work known as the *Pao P'u Tzŭ*, (completed in 317), on art of becoming → Hsien, in which he popularised the alchemistic, dietetical and magical teachings of → Taoism. He taught the temporary survival after death of two souls in man, the → *hun* and the → *p'o*, which finally re-entered into the Great Unity with consequent loss of personality. For Taoist adepts, who followed teachings of the *Pao P'u Tzŭ*, a much longer personal survival was possible through becoming a *hsien* or an immortal. K.H.'s influence on popular Taoism was immense; but he reveals a curious mixture of Taoist relig. and Confucian traditionalism, and stands outside main current of Chi. medieval thought. D.H.S.

H. Welch, *The Parting of the Way* (1957), pp. 126ff.; L. Wieger, *Hist. of Relig. Beliefs and Philos. Opinions in China* (E.T. 1927), ch. 52; L. C. Wu-T. L. Davis, tr. of Ko Hung's biography in *Lieh-hsien-chuan* in *Journal of Chemical Education* (1934).

Kojiki 'Records of Ancient Events.' The oldest

extant Jap. hist. record, compiled by imperial order from mainly oral tradition, and completed in 3 vols. in CE 712. It begins with creation myths and ends with close of reign of Empress Suiko in CE 628. With the → *Nihongi*, it is our chief literary source for study of anc. → Shinto. D.H.S.

Tr. by B. H. Chamberlain, in *Transactions of the Asiatic Soc. of Japan*, vol. 10, supplement (1882) and repr. in 1906 and 1932; W. G. Aston, *Shinto* (1905), p. 2; D. C. Holtom, *The National Faith of Japan* (1938), p. 17.

Konkyo Kyō ('Gold-lustre teaching'). One of import. modern Shinto sects of Japan, K. is farthest removed from trad. myths, popular magic and official rituals of → Shinto. Many of its tenets suggest Chr. influence, which, however, has not been proved. The founder, Kawate Bunjiro (1814–83) declared that his teaching was given him from the divine source of all truth by revelation. In early years he was intensely relig., but calamity, sickness and threatened death brought despairing conviction that he was singled out for divine punishment. A succession of revelations led him to belief in the One True God, to renewed health and to repudiation of all superstition. From 1859 to his death, he lived a frugal life of fellowship with God and ministry to his fellow men. An illiterate farmer, he wrote no books, teaching by precept and example and drawing a large following. Two years after his death, K. was organised as a sect, and the main contents of founder's teaching were gathered together in 182 precepts, which came to be regarded as sacred scripture. Proclaiming a fundamental spiritual unity beneath and within all appearances and change of the world, K. teaches the importance of spontaneous and natural communion with God through prayer. Formal rituals, ascetic practices, abstinence and reliance on magic, charms and divination all become unnecessary. K. declares that all men are brethren, teaches overcoming of evil by good, and strives for peace and mutual love. The most import. thing is a clear conscience. D.H.S.

D. C. Holtom, *The National Faith of Japan* (1938), pp. 257ff.

Korah (Qārūn) → Moses. J.R.

Korē Grk. = 'Maiden'. The Grk. earth-goddess was both 'Mother' and 'Virgin'. It was customary to ref. to a local goddess as 'the K'. In → Eleusinian Mysteries, the two aspects of earth-goddess are personified as → Demeter, the 'Mother', and → Persephone, the 'Korē'. S.G.F.B.

Harris, *Prolegomena*, pp. 271ff.; E. O. James, *The Cult of the Mother Goddess* (1959), pp. 153ff.; G. R. Levy, *The Gate of Horn* (1963), pp. 221ff.; J. Boardman, *Greek Art* (1964), pp. 76ff.

Korea Now divided into Communist N. and Nationalist S. by the 38th parallel, K. comprises a large peninsula on Pacific seaboard of Asia, separated from the N.E. Provinces of China by the Yalu and Tumen rivers. Its total area is about 83,000 square miles. The K.'s are related to all other Turanian peoples of N. Asia. Their language, Korean (Hanguk script) is agglutinative, and differs greatly from Japanese and wholly from Chinese. The K. trace their origin back some 43 cents. to a legendary and semi-divine being, Tangun, who taught the people the rudiments of civilisation. At beginning of Chi. Chou Dynasty (*c.* 1000 BC), a powerful Chi. official, Kija, came, with a large following, to K. and founded kingdom of Chosun ('Morning Calm'), and estab. a dynasty which lasted for nearly 1000 years. When it was overthrown in 193 BC, K. for a while was brought under Chi. rule; it gained independence in 37 BC, when began the era of the Three Kingdoms of Silla, Koryu and Chosun which dominated the peninsula for next 1000 years. The rise of Mongol power in 13th cent. CE led to incorpor. of K. into Chi. empire of → Kublai Khan in CE 1260. As with Japan, the chief cultural influences came from China, and, during great Chi. Ming Dynasty, K. culture reached its peak early in 16th cent. CE. Destructive Jap. invasions towards close of 16th cent. CE were followed by disastrous war with the Manchus, who ruled China till 20th cent. but left Korea virtually independent, until its annexation by Japan in 1910. Jap. dominance was bitterly resented by patriotic and nationalistic groups, seeking a return to independence. With collapse of Japan after World War 2, a power-struggle between Communists and Nationalists and a bitter and disastrous war from 1950–3 led finally to partition of country into N. and S.

The religs. of K. are → Animism, → Confucianism and → Buddhism, with some 3 mil. Christians in the S. Buddhism, intro. from China from about 4th cent. CE, was a powerful influence in court circles and grad. permeated down through all strata of population, providing in its temples and monasteries great centres of culture, and stimulating works of art, literature, philosophy and relig. But by 14th cent. CE, it was largely moribund. The influence of Confucianism was not so much relig. as political, social and ethical. The most deep-rooted relig. of K. is the ancient nature-worship, with its veneration of mountains, rivers and seas, its sacrifices in connection with agriculture, and its its altars for worship of the spirits of nature. D.H.S.

E.R.E., VII, pp. 755ff.; Guy Wint (ed.), *Asia, A Handbook* (1965).

Kosa → *Abhidharma-Kosa.* T.O.L.

Koyasan A famous Jap. monastery of → Shingon sect, S.E. of Osaka, where lies tomb of → Kōbō Daishi, where he sleeps until awakened at coming of next Buddha, Miroku. The monastery is place of pilgrimage, and the cremated remains of devout Buddh. are often sent to be deposited there. D.H.S.

Krishna (Kṛṣṇa) Lit. the name means 'Black One'. K.is most important of the incarnations (→ *avatara*) of → Viṣṇu. Born a ksatriya among the Yādavas at Mathurā, S.E. of Delhi, as son of Vāsudeva and Devakī, he was saved as a child from the destruction of all children of kingdom wrought by his cousin, king Kamsa, and was brought up by a cowherd and his wife. K. spent his childhood round Vṛṇdāvana (Brindaban), and as a youth had amorous affairs with the *gopis* (cowmaidens), among whom his favourite was Rādhā. Kamsa, however, tracked him down; and Krishna was forced to fight him. He killed him and took over kingdom. Allies of Kamsa advanced on him, and he had to migrate to Dvārakā in Kathiawar, where he set up a new kingdom. He married Rukmiṇī, a princess, and acquired a large number of other wives. The story of the → *Mahābhārata* belongs to this period of his legendary life; in it he helped the Pāṇḍavas to regain Kurukṣetra. On return to Dvaraka, fighting among the Yadavas broke out and K.'s son and brother were killed. In dejection, he wandered in forest outside city, and was there struck by a hunter's arrow in his heel, his one vulnerable spot. He died, and Dvaraka was inundated by the sea. Clearly, the legend is composed of a number of elements which have been woven together. Krishna Govinda ('Lord of Herdsmen') was prob. a non-Aryan fertility deity: analogues are found in Tamil literature and elsewhere. The story of his childhood escape from a 'massacre of the innocents' may owe something to Christ. sources, and his death to legend of Achilles. His reign as an ideal monarch may derive from Aryan sources; but it may be that this K. was an actual historical figure. There is also reference to K. Devakiputra (son of Devaki) in the *Chandogya Upaniṣad*, and some would therefore trace the story of K. back to pre-Buddh. times. The relig. most significant episodes in legend are K.'s participation in the *Mahabharata* struggle and hence his spiritual guidance as expressed in the → *Bhagavadgita;* and his period as a cowherd—the dalliance between K. and the maidens is typically taken as an allegory of relation between God and souls whom he loves and who love him. Both episodes are central in the evolution of Vaisnavite → *bhakti* religion. In later Vaisnavism, → Caitanya, K. tends to be treated as an absolute incarnation and expression of God, displacing even Vishnu from central focus of faith. The popularity of the K. cult is due to several factors: the child K. is a delightful and playful figure, appealing to maternal sentiments; the pastoral K. expresses divine tenderness, with import. fertility suggestions in background; K. as king rivals Rama as an ideal ruler; the genius of the *Bhagavadgita* gives K. a central place in the relig. lit. of India; the tragedy of his end is unique in Hindu mythology. K. is also a fertile subject of Indian painting. The main → pilgrimage centres assoc. with him are Dvaraka and Brindaban. N.S.

H. Bhattacharyya, *The Cultural Heritage of India*, vol. 4 (rev. ed. 1956); A. Danielou, *Hindu Polytheism* (1964); V. R. Ramachandra Dikshitar, *The Purana Index*, 3 vols. (1951–5); W. G. Archer, *The Loves of Krishna* (1957); R. Mukerjee, *Lord of the Autumn Moons* (1957).

Kronos Grk. God, doubtless of Aegean orig., who has confused role in Grk. mythology, which prob. preserves a distorted memory of him as predecessor of → Zeus, who castrates and supplants him. In another trad., K. is repr. as king of the Golden Age. The similarity of Kronos and → Chronos ('Time') led to K.'s identification with → Time in cosmogonic speculation. Identified with → Saturn, K. eventually became Father Time. S.G.F.B.

O.C.D., s.v.; Kleine Pauly, I, col. 1166; E. Panofsky, *Studies in Iconology* (1939, 1962), ch. 3; Brandon, *C.L.*, pp. 168ff.; *History, Time and Deity* (1965), pp. 47, 55ff.

Kṣatriyas Second of four classes (→ *varnas*, → caste system) in Vedic society. Relig. and political power was divided between the → Brahmins and K., the latter supplying the warriors, nobles and rulers. Although Brahmins came to have greater prestige among orthodox Hindus, K. had powerful prerogatives; in Upanishadic period there were a number of import. relig. teachers, notably the →→ Buddha and Mahavira, drawn from the K. class. This partly reflected incomplete Aryanisation of N. Indian society at time (→ Aryans), and partly dissatisfaction with or opposition to complex ritualism administered by Brahmins. K., though they came to pursue wide variety of occupations, retained military and aristocratic style of upbringing. N.S.

Kuan Ti (Kuan Kung; Kuan Yü; Wu Ti. Various names for one of most popular deities of official Chinese relig.). Revered in modern times as god of war, a champion who was always ready to intervene against all who disturb the peace of the realm—foreign enemies, rebels, sorcerers, evil spirits and demons—he also became patron god of literature, and a god of wealth. In mod. China there were some 1600 state temples and thousands of local shrines erected in his honour.

Kuan Yü was born in (mod.) Shensi in CE 162, and became a famous general and popular hero in the Three Kingdoms Period (3rd cent. CE), being a symbol of military valour and loyalty. He was captured and executed in 220. Some years after his death he received his first title, 'Marquis of martial dignity'. By 7th cent., he was honoured in a widespread popular cult. In the Sung Dynasty further honours were conferred upon him, and a temple built to his memory. In the Ming Dynasty (1594), he received the title 'Faithful and Loyal Great Ti, God of War'; from then onwards his popularity increased, receiving special honours and worship throughout the Ch'ing Dynasty, and even in the early decades of the Republic. Buddh. gave him the title of → *bodhisattva;* in spiritist seances he is the god who most frequently manifests himself. Special sacrifices are offered to him on 15th of the 2nd moon, and 13th of the 5th moon.

The famous saga, *San Kuo chih yen i* ('Story of the Three Kingdoms'), a perennial source of inspiration to dramatist and storyteller, assisted the widespread dissemination of his cult. D.H.S.

E. T. C. Werner, *Dict. of Chinese Mythology* (1932); H. Maspero, 'The Mythology of Modern China', in J. Hackin (ed.), *Asiatic Mythology* (1932, 1963), pp. 333ff.; S. Couling, *Encycl. Sinica* (1917, 1965), p. 280.

Kuan Kung → Kuan Ti. D.H.S.

Kuan Yin (Jap. Kwan-on, Kwannon). Chinese name for famous Buddh. → bodhisattva, → Avalokitesvara, next to → Amitābha, the most popular deity of → Pure Land Sects of Mahāyāna Buddhism throughout the Far East. The Chi. name, Kuan Yin ('the One who hears the cry'), seems to have arisen through a confusion between the Skt. words *iśvara*, 'lord' and *svara*, 'sound, noise'. The cult of K.Y. was intro. into China about 5th cent. CE. The bodhisattva is repres. in early iconography in male form, sometimes with a thousand eyes and arms, sometimes with eleven heads, or with a horse's head etc. But it was as a great female divinity, the Goddess of Mercy, that K.Y. gained a supreme place in Chi. popular relig. as the protectress of women and children, the bestower of children and the all-compassionate Mother-Goddess. Numerous legends and stories have arisen in China regarding her origin, life and saving activities. Temples in her honour are to be found all over China, and it is practically impossible to distinguish her from the Taoist-inspired T'ien Hou (Empress of Heaven), T'ien Shang Shêng Mu (The Holy Mother) and the Pi-hsia- Yüan-Chün (Princess of the Variegated Clouds). D.H.S.

H. Maspero, 'Mythology of Modern China', in J. Hackin (ed.), *Asiatic Mythology* (1932, 1963), pp. 352ff.; H. Doré, *Chinese Superstitions* (E.T. 1914), vol. 6; K. L. Reichelt, *Truth and Tradition in Chinese Buddhism* (1927), pp. 179ff.; J. H. Chamberlayne, 'The Development of Kuan Yin', in *Numen*, vol. 9 (1962).

Kuan Yü → Kuan Ti. D.H.S.

Kublai Khan (CE 1206–94). The grandson of Genghis Khan, he came to throne of Mongol Empire on death of his brother, Mangu, in 1260. He founded the Yüan (Mongol) Dynasty in China, and estab. his capital in Peking. By 1279 he had conquered whole of China from the Sung Dynasty. A fine military leader and shrewd administrator, he deliberately adopted Chi. culture. During his reign, China was wide open to foreign influences, and foreigners (Muslims, Mongols, Uighurs, Christians, etc.) were given most of import. positions in the administration. A free interchange of ideas and culture grew up between China and W. Though Korea accepted his suzerainty, his attempts to conquer Japan (1274 and 1281), Java (1293) and Annam (1283, 1285, 1287) failed disastrously. Towards all religs. K.Kh. showed the greatest tolerance, except when he sided with the Buddh.s in a great public debate in 1255; thereafter he persecuted the → Taoists and had their books destroyed. As emperor, he meticulously performed the required rituals of state → Confucianism. He employed Buddhists, Taoists, Confucians, Muslims and Christians, regardless of race or creed. His own personal preference was for → Buddhism, espec. in its Tibetan form. He protected → Nestorian Christianity, and in 1275 allowed the Patriarch of Baghdad to create an archbishopric in Peking, and in 1289 instituted a special office to deal with Chr. affairs. It was during his reign that Marco Polo lived in China, and afterwards gave a glowing account of Chi. civilisation and culture; however, acc. to C. P. Fitzgerald, *op. cit.*, 'The Mongol Dynasty, founded on terror and butchery, passed away after only 89 years, leaving behind it no lasting or valuable contribution to Chinese civilisation, but having destroyed much that was irreplaceable'. D.H.S.

R. Grousset, *The Rise and Splendour of the Chinese Empire* (E.T. 1952), ch. 26; C. P. Fitzgerald, *China* (1935, rev. edn. 1950), pp. 435ff.; L. C. Goodrich, *A Short Hist. of the Chinese People*, 2nd edn. (1957), ch. 6.

Kuei (Kwei) Chinese term used for disembodied spirits, demons, spirits of the dead, ghosts or goblins. The character, being a pictogram depicting a being of fearsome aspect, is one of oldest in the language, being frequently used on the → Oracle Bones. It is a 'primitive' or 'radical', whilst other characters used to designate the soul, the spirit or the vital breath (→ *shên*, *ch'i*, → *hun*, *p'o*, *ling* etc.) are all composite in form, which suggests that they were invented later. From very early times Chi. literature refers to spiritual beings as *kuei shên*, corresponding to the *p'o* and the *hun*, the vital elements or soul constituents of a living man. The K. were thought of as living on for a while after death with the corpse in the earth, receiving sustenance from sacrifices made to ancestor spirit. Improper burial, neglect of sacrifices, or death through unpropitious circumstances might lead to K. appearing as maleficent ghosts or demons to haunt the living. These K. became the subject of innumerable tales in Chi. folklore. D.H.S.

J. J. M. de Groot, *The Religious System of China* (1875), vol. 4, pp. 5ff.; D. H. Smith, 'Chinese Concepts of the Soul', in *Numen*, vol. 5 (1958).

Kūkai → Kōbō Daishi. D.H.S.

Kumārajīva (CE 344–413). Buddh. monk and eminent translator, also import. agent in spread to China of Indian → Mādhyamika school of Buddh. philosophy. Before 20 yrs of age, K. studied → Sarvāstivādin Abhidharma literature in Kashgar; but, on meeting a Mahāyānist named Suryasama, was converted to the → Mādhyamika views. Ordained monk at age of 20 at Kuchā, he spent some years there studying Mahāyāna literature. When about 40, K. was captured by a Chinese raiding force and taken to China, where he remained for rest of life. He learnt Chinese and trans. into this language many → Mahāyāna texts, mostly of Mādhyamika school. T.O.L.

Richard H. Robinson, *Early Mādhyamika in India and China*, 1967, ch. 3. (K. in Chi. context).

(Chinese–Fa Hu) CE 344–413. One of greatest of early translators of Buddh. scriptures from Skt. into Chinese, K. headed famous school of translators in capital city, Ch'ang-an. Born in Kuchā of Brahmin father and Kuchean princess, he studied Buddhism in Kashmir, after which he returned to Kuchā to be ordained. There for 20 yrs. he studied the Mahāyāna. Taken as a prisoner to China, he arrived in Ch'ang-an in CE 401, where he was venerated by members of ruling family and drew disciples from all quarters of empire. Through his efforts the great philosophical treatises of Mahāyāna were made comprehensible to the Chinese; in partic. works of →→ Nagarguna, Aryadeva, Vasubandhu and Asanga. He engaged in extensive correspondence with → Hui Yüan. Largely through his efforts, Buddh. philosophy came to be regarded on an equal footing with indigenous thought; to his success in trans. may be attributed much of progress of Buddhism among the gentry. D.H.S.

E. Zürcher, *The Buddhist Conquest of China* (1959), *passim*; D. H. Smith, *Chinese Religions* (1968), pp. 115f. 127f.

Kuṇḍalinī The feminine serpent-power which figures in the physiology of Hindu → Yoga and also in Buddh. Tantric writings. It is coiled round the → *lingam* and obstructs movement of vital powers upwards to the head, until it is awakened by practice of the → *āsanas* and in gen. through Haṭha Yoga. This awakening arouses powerful heat (→ *tapas*)—an inner fire which corresponds to outer significance of → Agni, God of Fire (from Upaniṣadic period onwards there is tendency to correlate microcosm and macrocosm in Yogic trad.). Through the arousal of K., the yogin traverses the various *cakras* (wheels or centres of power) distributed along the spinal column, etc., from the *mūlādhāra*, at base of trunk and the primary seat of K., to the *suṣumṇā* in apex of skull. Through rousing and controlling the forces released in this way, the yogin can gain both physiological and physical purification and power, ultimately issuing in → *kaivalya* or liberation. K. is identified with the coiled serpent-energy which when aroused gives rise to universe, after period of quiescence (*pralaya*): wound round → Śiva, it symbolizes the sleep of the cosmos. The stoppage of various functions, such as breathing and emission of semen, arouses K., and this is basis of practice of → *prāṇāyāma* (breath-control) and reabsorption of semen, which figures both in classical Yoga and in → Tantrism. N.S.

M. Eliade, *Yoga: Immortality and Freedom* (1958); A. Avalon (Sir John Woodroffe), *The Serpent Power*, 3rd edn. (1931).

Kur-nu-gi-a Sumerian name for underworld, meaning 'the land of no return'; it was also called *ki-gal*, 'the great land'. In → Akkadian these epithets were respectively *erṣet lâ târi* and *kigallu*. The proper name of the underworld was Arallŭ. Erish-ki-gal was the 'Lady of the Kigallu'. S.G.F.B.

Dhorme, *R.B.A.*, pp. 38–9; B. Meissner, *Babylonien u. Assyrien.*, II (1925), pp. 143–4; A. Heidel, *The Gilgamesh Epic and Old Test. Parallels* (1949[2]), pp. 170ff.

Kurozumi-kyō An import. sect of mod. → Shinto, founded by Kurozumi Munetada (1780–1850), who is recognised as one of great saints of early 19th cent. Japan, a man of simplicity, devotion, great moral strength, strict piety and impartial goodness. Believing that divine power of → Amaterasu had taken possession of him, he regarded Amaterasu as source of all life, the creator and sustainer of universe, whose spirit fills heaven and earth. The individual may participate in vitality of the Supreme God, and thus enjoy blessings of goodness, truth, health and beauty. These blessings are given only in so far as one recognises the essential divinity of all life, and renounces self in seeking full control of divine spirit over mind and body.

Kurozumi Munetada preached a gospel of cheerfulness, health and gratitude. It was believed that he frequently performed miracles of healing. He taught that a universal divine life manifested itself in many forms, incl. the trad. gods of Shinto, the ancestral spirits and imperial rulers. His teachings spread far and wide and even affected members of court circle. 12 years after his death, a shrine was built to his spirit in the E. suburbs of Kyoto. In 1876 the K. was organised as an independent Shinto sect, whose members bind themselves under oath to follow steps of their founder. Their devotional activities incl. early-rising, sun-bathing, deep breathing and physical exercises. They teach faith-healing and surmounting of misfortune by negation of evil, and the cultivation of joy and health in oneness with the Infinite. D.H.S.

D. C. Holtom, *The National Faith of Japan* (1938), pp. 245ff.

Kusha school School of Jap. Buddhism, long extinct, was intro. into Japan from China by two Japanese monks Chitsu and Chitatsu in CE 658. Its highly metaphysical teachings are based on the Abhidharma Kosa, attr. to celebrated Indian Buddh. sage Vasubandhu (*c.* 5th cent.). D.H.S.

Kushinagara One of the 4 Buddh. → *holy places*, location of the → Buddha's decease. The events leading up to and following the decease are recounted in detail in the → *Mahā-parinabbāna Sutta* of the Digha Nikaya; here Kushinagara, with its anc. name Kusināra, is described as an insignificant 'wattle and daub' township of the Malla tribe, 'set in the midst of jungles'. After death of Buddha, his body was taken through town, from north gate to the east, and cremated outside at a shrine of the Mallas. The trad. is that, after cremation, some of the relics were deposited in a → *stupa* at K., known as the Mukutabandhana. A large monastic settlement (*vihāra*) appears to have been built there, but was already in ruins by time the Chinese pilgrim → Hsuan-tsang visited site in 7th cent. CE. Before this, it had been place of sacred pilgrimage; the reason why it fell into ruins is unknown. The remains of *stupa*, built by the Mallas over their share of the relics, is thought to be repr. by the large ruined mound called locally 'Ramabhar'. The village, which stands on the anc. site, at junction of river Rapti and the Gondak, is known as Kasia, in the east of the Gorakhpur district, in Uttar Pradesh, to the south of the Nepal border. T.O.L.

Malalasekere, *D.P.P.N.*, vol. I, pp. 653–5; S. Dutt, *Buddhist Monks and Monasteries of India* (1962), pp. 217f.; P. V. Bapat (ed.), 2500 *Years of Buddhism* (1956), p. 314.

Kwan-On (or Kwannon) (→ Kuan Yin). Jap. name for great Buddh. *bosatsu* or → bodhisattva, most revered in Japan, to whom many great temples are consecrated. The cult of K. goes back to intro. of → Buddhism into Japan; Prince Shotoku (CE 572–621) was a fervent worshipper. K., together with Daiseishi-bosatsu, was regarded as a companion (or, acc. to → Shingon sect, as a manifestation) of → Amida. He is repres. in many forms (i.e. with six arms, or eleven heads, or with a horse's head), to indicate his infinite power, compassion, and virtue, and his purpose of salvation for all sentient beings, incl. men and animals. He is the all-compassionate Lord of Mercy, represented as healer and saviour, leading souls, in whom he has awakened piety to the paradise of Amida. Sometimes, as in China, K. is represented as a female deity. D.H.S.

E.R.E., VII, pp. 763–4; Serge Eliseev, 'The Mythology of Japan', in J. Hackin (ed.), *Asiatic Mythology* (1932), pp. 438–41.

Kyrie Eleison Grk. = 'Lord, have mercy'. A brief supplicatory prayer of pre-Chr. orig., appearing in Chr. usage in 4th cent. Syria. It survives in Latin → Mass as a remnant of (earlier) Grk. liturgy (→ Eucharist) once current in Rome. S.G.F.B.

L. Duchesne, *Christian Worship* (E.T. 1927), pp. 58, 164ff.; *D.C.C., s.v.; R.G.G.*³, IV, col. 192.

Kyrios Grk. = 'Lord'. The term had wide currency in Greek world for gods and rulers. In → LXX it was used to trans. *adhonai* (pl.), which was Heb. title used as substitute for → Yahweh. K. was an early title for → Jesus, and it clearly implied attribution of divinity (e.g. Phil. 2:11). (→→ Adonai; Adonis). S.G.F.B.

W. Foerster-G. Quell, *Lord* (E.T. 1958); *Kleine Pauly*, III, col. 413–17.

L

Labarum Military standard showing Grk. letters X and P (first two of *ΧΡΙΣΤΟΣ*, i.e., 'Christ') intersecting. Trad. relates L. to vision seen by Emp. → Constantine. The L. seems to have been adapted from Roman cavalry standard by removing pagan emblems and surmounting it with the ☧. The orig. of name is uncertain. The L. first appears on coins in 326, witnessing to triumph of Christianity. S.G.F.B.

R.G.G.[3], IV, col. 1105 ('Monogram Christi'); A. Alföldi, *The Conversion of Constantine and Pagan Rome* (1948), pp. 17, 23, 39ff.; F. J. Dolger, in *Jahrbuch für Antike u. Christentum*, 8/9 (1965–6), pp. 47ff.

Labyrinth The L., or maze-like form, is anc.; it finds various modes of expression from India through Mediterranean area to N. Europe (e.g. as historical L. at Knossos, Crete; in funerary temple of Amenemhat III, in Egypt, known to classical writers as the L.; in Scandinavian stone-circles of L. pattern; in a ceremonial dance-parade of mounted youths, described by → Virgil (*Aen*, V, 545–603) and related to Troy; as pattern on floor of medieval churches, as in Chartres Cathedral). The L. has been variously explained as orig. from → initiation ritual (*rite de passage*), ritual drama of passage from death to life, ritual dances for cosmic renewal or fertility. It has also been supposed that buildings of L-form derived from suggestion of a ritual prototype. The name L., orig. given to palace-complex at Knossos, was derived from *labrys*, the sacred double → axe. (→ Cretan Relig.). S.G.F.B.

S. H. Hooke (ed.), *The Labyrinth* (1935), ch. 1 by C. N. Deedes; *R.G.G.*[3], IV, col. 194; R. W. Hutchinson, *Prehistoric Crete* (1962), p. 104; *Kleine Pauly*, III, III, col. 433–5.

Lalita-Vistara One of most import. texts of → Mahāyāna Buddhism, although it emanated from the → Sarvāstivādin school. The title implies the viewpoint: the Buddha's life and work is seen as 'play' or 'sport' (*lalita*) of a supernatural being, of which the book is a narration (*vistara*). While narrative begins in style of early Pali suttas, 'Thus have I heard', it soon becomes markedly different in tone and character in its extravagently miraculous setting. Those portions of work, which are held to be older than main narrative, viz. the *Gāthas*, or stanzas, are in fairly close agreement with early Pali accounts of events of Buddha's life, such as that of the *Mahāvagga* of the → Vināya-Pitaka. It has, therefore, been concluded that the L. is revised form of an older narrative, poss. of Sarvāstivādin school; the revision having taken form of enlarging and embellishing details in accord. with ideas and spirit of the Mahāyāna, as, e.g., in its tendency towards Buddha-bhakti, or adoration of Buddha. When it was cast in present form is unknown; it may poss. have been in period when the art-forms of → Gandhāra were developing, as there are certain agreements and similarities between conception of the Buddha in them and in L. Since, however, it evidently contains anc. material, the L. has been regarded as import. source of evidence of anc. Buddhism. T.O.L.

M. Winternitz, *Hist. of Indian Literature* (1933), vol. 2, pp. 248–56.

Lambeth Conferences Assemblies of bishops of → Anglican Church held every ten years at Lambeth Palace, London, under presidency of Archbp. of Canterbury. The first L.-C. was in 1867. The resolutions at L.-C.'s, though not officially binding, are significant of views of Anglican episcopate on current issues. S.G.F.B.

D.C.C., *s.v.*

Lankā Anc. name for → Ceylon. T.O.L.

Lankāvatāra Sūtra One of the nine principal texts of Mhy. Buddhism (→ Sanskrit Literature). Acc. to full title, '*Ārya-saddharma-lankāvatāro-nāma-mahāyāna-sutram*', it contains the 'noble orthodox teaching (i.e. of Buddhism), given (i.e. by the Buddha) (on occasion of) entering into Ceylon'. It consists of conversations Buddha had with both Ravanna, the mythical lord of → Ceylon, who is here repr. as a good Buddh. layman; and also, at more profound level with a Bodhisattva named Mahāmati (or → Mañjuśrī). The Sutra embodies critique of Hindu philosophy, and also essays explanation of resemblance between Mhy. Buddh. and Hindu philosophy which had come to be recognised by time of composition of this work. An early form of sūtra existed in CE 420, when it was trans. into Chinese. Three subsequent trsls. into Chinese were made, the last of these in CE 704; the earlier Skt. text, on which 1st trans. was based, appears to have received some elaboration by 8th cent. The sūtra is import. source so far as Chi. and Jap. Bhm. is concerned, esp. for notions of → *ālaya-vijñāna* and docs. of → Yogācara school → Ch'an (Zen) school. It has no recognisable systematic structure; it is, acc. to Suzuki, 'a collection of notes unsystematically strung together'. T.O.L.

For summary of contents cf. E. J. Thomas, *Hist. of Buddhist Thought*, 2nd edn. (1951), pp. 230–6; see also D. T. Suzuki, *Studies in the Lankāvatāra Sūtra* (1930), *Essays in Zen Buddhism* vol. I (1927).

Laos, Buddhism in → Cambodia. T.O.L.

Lao Tzŭ (Also called Lao Chün and Lao Tan). Acc. to Taoist trad., he was an older contemporary of → Confucius, being the greatest of Taoist masters and reputed author of the → *Tao Tê Ching* (called the Book of Lao-Tzŭ). He is supposed to have lived in 6th cent. BC, and to have held post of imperial archivist at the Chou Dynasty court. → Hsün-tzŭ, the *Lü-shih-Ch'un-Ch'iu*, and → Chuang-tzŭ all attr. Taoist doctrines to Lao-tzŭ, who, however, must be regarded as a semi-legendary figure, of whom nothing is known historically. Ssŭ-ma Ch'ien, the father of Chi. hist. and author of the *Shih Chi* (1st cent. BC), attempted to write a biography (*Shih Chi*, ch. 63), in which Lao Lai-tzŭ is confused with Tan, a historian of Chou Dynasty in 4th cent. BC and a Taoist recluse called Li Erh, who seems to have been a hist. figure. Numerous legends grew up concerning Lao-tzŭ, and later, in relig. → Taoism, he was worshipped as Lao Chün, and assoc. with the mythical Huang Ti or Yellow Emperor as the author of Taoism. Most Chi. scholars believe that there was a hist. figure called Lao-tzŭ, to whom they attr. at least the substance of the *Tao tê Ching*. D.H.S.

Fung Yu-lan, *Hist. of Chinese Philos.* (1937), vol. 1, pp. 170ff.; W. T. Chan, *Source Book in Chinese Philos.* (1963), pp. 136–8; A. Waley, *The Way and its Power* (1934), pp. 101ff.

Lares In Roman relig., the L. were prob. orig. deities of farm-land, who came to be regarded as guardians of any cross-way (→ Compitalia). The connection of → Hecate with cross-ways poss. suggested that L. were ghosts of dead, as some scholars have maintained (→ Acca Larentia). S.G.F.B.

O.C.D., *s.v.;* A. Grenier, *Les religions étrusque et romaine* (1948), pp. 114ff., 150ff., 196ff.; W. R. Halliday, *Hist. of Roman Relig.* (1922), pp. 27ff.

Last Supper Acc. to → Synoptic Gospels, the L.-S., which Jesus had with disciples on night before Crucifixion, was the → Passover. The Gosp. of John, however, asserts that Crucifixion took place on the 'preparation' of the Passover (19:31), thus putting L.-S. on night before Passover, so that the meal was prob. a Kiddush, i.e. a preparatory service of sanctification for Sabbath or holy day. The → Eucharist derived from L.-S. The communal meal at → Qumran and evidence of use of different calendar there have raised new problems rel. to L.-S., on which discussion continues. (→ Communion, Holy). S.G.F.B.

D.C.C., pp. 765, 787; M. Goguel, *The Life of Jesus* (E.T. 1933), pp. 443ff.; G. Dalman, *Jesus-Jeshua* (E.T. 1929), pp. 86ff.; K. G. Kuhn, *The Scrolls and the N.T.*, ed. K. Stendahl (1958), pp. 65ff.; M. Black, *The Scrolls and Christ. Origins* (1961), pp. 102ff., 199ff.; Joh. Steinbeck, 'Das Abendmahl Jesu unter Berücksichtigung moderner Forschung', *Numen*, VI (1959).

-Lāt Goddess worshipped in pre-Islamic Arabia whose chief shrine was at al-Ṭā'if. The name is poss. the feminine of Allāh (→ God). In Qur. liii:19f. al-Lāt, → al-'Uzzā and → Manāt are mentioned. The passage goes on to ask whether God will have female issue when men have male, and says these beings are nothing but names used by earlier generations. J.R.

E.I., III, pp. 18f.; Wellhausen, *Reste*, pp. 29ff.; *Mishkāt*, pp. 1163; Watt, *Mecca*, index.

Lateran Basilica Known as S. Giovanni in Laterano, the Basilica is the cathedral church of Rome, claiming to be *mater et caput omnium ecclesiarum.* The palace that orig. stood on site and given by Emp. Constantine, was official residence (*patriarchium*) of Popes from 4th cent. until departure for Avignon (1309). Most of L. was destroyed by fire in 1308. The present building was constructed in 16–17th cent. A series of Council were held in L. Palace from 7th to 18th cents. S.G.F.B.

D.C.C., *s.v.;* A. Alföldi, *The Conversion of Constantine and Pagan Rome* (E.T. 1948), pp. 51ff., 130; *C.A.H.*, XII, p. 569, vol. of plates V, 224b; Grabar, *B.C.A.*, fig. 179.

Law (Chinese) The Confucian view that a ruler should govern by virtue and example, and without need for codified laws, has exerted profound influence in making customary morality of primary import. and legal sanctions secondary. L. in China was not conceived of as result of Divine revelation or fiat. It was a man-made institution, deemed necessary for regulation of an imperfect society. Statute L. was intended to reach only where customary law, based on Confucian morality and enshrined in the *Chou Li* and → *Li Chi*, proved ineffective.

The Chinese ascribed first promulgation of their system of laws to legendary sage-kings of 3rd mil. BC; but it was collapse of feudalism and rise of the Warring States which led to drawing up of first legal codes, and grad. transition from gov. by customary morality to gov. by law. Already in 6th cent. BC the statesman Tzŭ-ch'an of the state of Ch'êng is credited with drawing up a penal code and having it inscribed on metal tripods. The advent of written laws was strongly opposed by conservative scholars, who believed that such written laws for all to read would only promote discontent, increased litigation and further lawlessness. But in post-Confucian times the process continued with rise of the powerful Legalistic School, and influence of statesmen-philosophers, Shang Yang, Han Fei-tzŭ and Li Ssŭ, particularly in state of Ch'in. Han Fei-Tzŭ defined law as 'enactments made by gov. with penalties which the people feel sure will be carried out, when approbation is attached to obedience and punishment awaits its violation or disregard'. (Bk. 43). Until mod. times there was no civil code governing rights of contract and of property, which were governed by customary, professional or local rules. Breaches of contract, which could not be settled without recourse to the law courts, were considered as offences against rules of morality and were therefore judged and punished in same way as crimes. Each subsequent dynasty issued its codified penal laws, the most famous being the Manchu code known as the *Ta Ch'ing Lü Li* and promulgated in 18th cent., characterised by its reasonableness, clarity, moderation and conciseness and brevity of its language.

Acc. to Chi. L. the family and relatives of a criminal were held vicariously responsible. Also a prisoner was required to confess his crimes before punishment could be administered. In practice beating and even torture were sometimes used to elicit confession. Although in mod. times, and under W. influence, new penal and civil codes have been promulgated, social pressures upon individual to accept customary morality are so effective that, in gen., only the 'hardened criminal' comes up for judgment in law courts. D.H.S.

E.R.E., VII, pp. 830ff.; J. D. Ball, *Things Chinese*, 5th edn. (1925), pp. 324ff.; Fung Yu-lan, *Hist. of Chinese Philos.*, vol. 21 (1937), pp. 312ff.; Hu Shih, *Development of the Logical Method in Ancient China* (1932), pp. 174ff.

(Japanese) → Shinto has scarcely anything in the nature of a code of L. In anc. Japan there was customary L., unwritten and ill-defined, the community being held together by power of ruler and strength of family system. The oldest code mentioned is the constitution formed by → Shotoku Taishi in CE 604, consisting of 17 articles. During 7th and 8th cents., codes of L. showing marked Chi. influence came into existence, notably the Taiho Code (CE 701) in 11 vols., part of which in revised edition of CE 718 is still extant. During long feudal period individual shoguns issued their own laws. A simple code of 51 articles, known as the *Teiei Shikimoku* was formed in 12th cent. and remained effective till CE 1867. This rejected Chi. influence and was partic. adapted to Jap. feudalism. For a period of some 700 years the Mikado had no real voice in gov., and L. codes were formed and administered by the shogunate. Contact with W. nations and the Meiji restoration led to a criminal code being promulgated in 1882, followed by proclamation of a constitution in 1889 and by a civil code in 1900. Two fundamental principles have from the first characterised Jap. L.: the supreme and divine sovereignty of Mikado and the family system. D.H.S.

E.R.E., VII, pp. 854ff.; B. H. Chamberlain, *Things Japanese* (1905), pp. 278ff.

(Sacred) →→ Canon Law; Torah.

-Lawḥ al-maḥfūẓ (The Preserved Tablet). Qur. lxxxv:21f. says, 'Nay, it is a glorious Qur. in a preserved tablet.' → Trad. and law books develop this. It is doubtful whether 'preserved' qualifies 'tablet' or 'Qur.', but it is gen. taken with 'tablet'; this is explained as the original of Qur. in heaven (*Umm al-kitāb* = mother of the Book). This is the only Qur. ref. In Trad. and the law books, the decrees are all said to have been inscribed with the pen (*qalam*) on the L. The Arabic idiom is that the pen has dried, meaning that nothing remains to be added. J.R.

E.I., III, pp. 19f.; Hughes, p. 285; D. B. Macdonald, *Theology*, p. 335; Wensinck, *Creed*, index (Table); Sweetman, *I.C.T.*, 1, p. 25; II, p. 90; IV, pp. 151, 301.

Laylat al-Qadr (The Night of Power). A night towards end of → Ramaḍān. Qur. xcvii says, 'We caused it (the Qur.) to descend on *Laylat al-Qadr*. Who shall teach you what L. al-Q. is? L. al-Q. excels 1,000 months. In it the angels and the spirit descend by permission of their Lord in every matter, and all is peace till day-break.' The exact night is not known, but → Trad. seems to favour view that it is one of the odd number nights in last ten of Ramadan. Some say it is 27th; it seems that in E. Africa (Tanzania) it is held to be 21st. (→ Retreat). J.R.

E.I., III, p. 1111; Hughes, pp. 282f.; D. B. Macdonald, *Theology*, p. 335; G. S. P. Freeman-Grenville, *The Muslim and Christian Calendars* (1963), p. 84.

Leda In Grk. mythology, the mother of Helen and Polydeuces, whom she conceived through intercourse with → Zeus in shape of a swan. There are many variants of myth; the subject was a favourite one in art. The idea of birth from an → egg may stem from belief in bird-shaped deities. S.G.F.B.

M. P. Nilsson, *Minoan-Mycenaean Religion* (1950²), ch. 10; *O.C.D., s.v.: Kleine Pauly*, III, 531–2.

Left and Right The significance of L. and R. differs in various religs. and folklore. In O.T. and N.T., R. is the better side (e.g. right hand is used in blessing, Gen. 48:17ff.; at → Last Judgment, the blessed are set on R. and damned on L., Mt. 25:31ff.). With Romans, R. was orig. unlucky and L. lucky, whereas Greeks took contrary view. Preference for L. is shown in → magic. Acc. to early Grk. medical theory, the male body was arranged from R. and female from L. S.G.F.B.

*R.G.G.*³, IV, col. 382; *L.R-G.*, II, pp. 357, 424, 457; O. Nussbaum, 'Die Bewertung von Rechts und Links in der römischen Liturgie', *J.f.A.C.*, 5 (1962); S. Morenz, 'Rechts und Links im Totengericht', *Z.Ae.S.A.*, 82 (1957).

Legal alms (Islam) (*Zakāt*). This is a tax levied on property over a certain amount which has been in one's possession for a year. The word *ṣadaqa* is also used, as in Qur. ix:60 (in the pl.), which gives standard list of classes for whose benefit L.-A. is collected: poor and needy; collectors of the tax; people who have been won over; for ransom of slaves; debtors; in God's path (→ Jihād), and for travellers. *Ṣadaqa* came to mean voluntary almsgiving (→ Hospitality); *zakāt*, the legal alms. The Qur. frequently calls believers those who observe the *ṣalāt* (ritual worship → Prayer) and pay the *zakāt*. Details of what should be paid, as given in traditions and law books, suggest a mainly agricultural or pastoral society; but there are regulations about different kinds of property. The tax on animals is heavier for those pastured at large than for those fed at home, the reason obviously being that the owner who has to feed his animals at home is put to greater expense. On same principle, crops which are irrigated are taxed less than those which are dependent on rain. Property excepted is equipment for → *Jihād*, theological books, and various types of articles considered essential to owners. The tax may be paid to collector, or one may pay it directly to members of classes entitled to benefit from it. States now follow west. methods of taxation and do not levy *zakāt;* but many pious Muslims pay it as relig. duty. At the feast after Ramadan it is customary for people, able to do so, to pay what is called the *zakāt* of breaking of fast (*zakāt al-fiṭr*), most commonly by providing food for poor. It is not a statutory tax, but many consider it obligatory. J.R.

E.I., IV, pp. 1202–5; Jeffery, *Vocabulary*, p. 153; Querry, I, p. 133; Levy, *Social Structure*, index; Watt, *Medina*, Excursus I.

Lemuria In Roman relig., days (9, 11, 13 May) on which the *lemures*, hungry and kinless ghosts, were supposed to haunt houses and were appeased and dismissed by ritual feeding. S.G.F.B.

A. Grenier, *Les religions étrusque et romaine* (1948), pp. 118, 132; *O.C.D., s.v.;* U. E. Paoli, *Urbs: aspetti di vita romana antica* (1942), pp. 202ff.

Lentulus, Letter of Document, dating prob. from 13th cent., purporting to give account of physical appearance of Christ, written by L., a Roman official in Judaea at time concerned. The writing, which attr. great physical beauty to Christ, is evidently a pious forgery. Robert Eisler argued that the Letter in its extant form is a Chr. revision of an authentic, but uncomplimentary original. S.G.F.B.

M. R. James, *The Apocryphal New Test.* (1926), pp. 477ff.; R. Eisler, *Iesous basileus ou basileusas*, II (1930), pp. 327ff., *The Messiah Jesus and John the Baptist* (1931), pp. 396ff.

Leontopolis, Jewish Temple Onias, a Jew. priest who fled from persecution of Antiochus Epiphanes, founded a temple at L., Egypt, in 170 BC. Although it contravened the Law that the Jerusalem → Temple was only place for offering sacrifice, little is said in condemnation of temple of Onias in Jew. lit. After fall of → Jerusalem in CE 70, the Romans demolished the L. temple lest it should become centre of Jew. national life. The site was excavated in 1906. S.G.F.B.

Schürer, *G.J.V.*, III, pp. 97ff.; S. G. F. Brandon, *Jesus and the Zealots* (1967), pp. 292ff.; W. M. Flinders Petrie, *Hyksos and Israelite Cities* (1906), pp. 19ff.; G. R. Driver, *The Judaean Scrolls* (1965), pp. 234ff.

Levellers Relig. and political sect in 17th cent. England, opposed to kingship and advocating complete freedom in relig. and manhood suffrage. Their leader was J. Lilburne. The L. were mainly supported by Parliamentary Army; but Oliver Cromwell suspected them, and their leaders were imprisoned for agitation. They disappeared after Restoration (1660). S.G.F.B.

D. B. Robertson, *The Religious Foundations of Leveller Democracy* (1951); J. Needham, 'Land, the Levellers, and the Virtuosi', in *Time: the Refreshing River* (1943).

Leviathan Heb. *liwyāthān*, meaning something 'coiled or twisted', hence a monstrous serpent. Such a monster was common to Semite mythology: acc. to a → Ugarit text, it had 7 heads. It appears as a sea monster (Ps. 104:25–6; Job, 41:1–8), but not serpentine. The L. also was a popular concept with Apocalyptic and Rabbinic writers. In medieval Chr. thought L. was identified with Hell. S.G.F.B.

H.D.B.[3], pp. 578ff.; *R.G.G.*[3], IV, col. 337–8; Brandon, *C.L.*, pp. 120, 153ff.; G. R. Driver, *Canaanite Myths and Legends* (1956), pp. 86ff., 102ff.; E. Mâle, *The Gothic Image* (E.T. 1961), p. 380.

Levirate Marriage (Lat. *levir*, 'husband's brother') Acc. to Mosaic legislation (Deut. 25:5–10), if a married man died leaving no son, his brother should marry the widow and first son of that union should inherit name and estate of the deceased brother. Similar customs occur among other peoples (e.g. in India, Persia), and were prob. designed to ensure an heir who would perform necessary sacrifices in ancestor rites. In Mk. 12:19 the → Sadducees cite L.-M. to ridicule doc. of → Resurrection of dead. L.-M. is forbidden in State of Israel; Reform Judaism dispenses with it. (→ Onanism). S.G.F.B.

H.D.B.[2], pp. 625; J. Pedersen, *Israel*, I–II (1926), pp. 77ff., 91ff.; Ad. Lods, *Israël* (1949), pp. 262ff.; *E.J.R.*, pp. 238–9.

Levites Trad. descendants of Levi, son of → Jacob, whose birth entitled them to act as priests. Their orig. is obscure. The primitive trad. in → Judges 17–8 suggests that L. were a priestly caste of no fixed abode. They seem to have been devotees of → Yahweh, were warlike and had charge of → Ark in battle; they were also concerned with → Urim and Thummin and teaching of → Torah. After Exile, L. lost priestly status to Aaronite caste and became Temple servants. (→→ Aaron; Hierarchy, Heb.). S.G.F.B.

H.D.B.[2], pp. 793–7; *R.G.G.*[3], IV, col. 336–7; *E.J.R.*, p. 239.

Leviticus, Book of The 3rd book of → Pentateuch. Critical opinion divides L. into two parts. The older, chs. 17–26, known as the Code of Holiness, appears to be a distinctive writing containing legislation on ritual and social matters (e.g. →→ Sabbath; Passover; Day of Atonement: marriage, the *Lex Talionis*); it seems to reflect teaching of → Jeremiah and → Ezekiel, and prob. dates *c.* 550 BC. The other part derives from → Priestly trad., *c.* 450 BC. The whole work purports to be revealed by → Yahweh to → Moses. The → Talmud designates L. 'Law of the priests'. (→ Judaism). S.G.F.B.

H.D.B.[2], *s.v.; P.C.*[2], pp. 241ff.; *R.G.G.*[3], IV, col. 339–40.

Li Chinese term denoting a rite, the procedure proper to ceremonies of sacrifice, burial of dead, marriage, etc. Acc. to anc. Confucian doc., welfare of country, fertility of land, peace and prosperity of the people were believed to depend on correct performance of ritual observance by the rulers. Scholars and gentlemen had to be familiar with a huge corpus of ritual rules (some 300 rules of major ritual and 3000 minor observances). The *Li* were embodied in the *Chou Li*, the *I Li*, and notably the → *Li Chi* which became one of the 5 Confucian Classics. *Li* was accepted as one of cardinal virtues of → Confucianism and came to denote the propriety, good manners, courtesy and politeness which should govern all human relationships. It was the outward expression of humanity (*jên*) and righteousness (*i*); it was the feeling of reverence and respect, the external exemplification of eternal principles. D.H.S.

A. Waley, *The Analects of Confucius* (1938), pp. 54ff.; W. A. C. H. Dobson, *Mencius* (1963), p. 194; R. H. Mathews, *Chinese-English Dictionary* (1952), pp. 566–7.

Libations The ritual pouring out of liquid (water, wine, blood) is a widespread relig. practice, and its purpose varies. L. could be offerings made (1) to gods (e.g. effusion of blood in Jew. → Atonement ritual; Grk. custom of pouring a little wine on ground before meals to the Good Daimon or to Zeus) (2) to the dead, who were thought to be thirsty (→ Refrigerium). In anc. Egypt. mortuary ritual, L. of water had both purificatory and revivifying virtues. S.G.F.B.

R.Ae.R-G., pp. 424ff.; *H.D.B.*[2], p. 873; *O.C.D.*, p. 960; A. Parrot, *Le 'Refrigerium' dans l'au-delà* (1937).

Liberation, Hindu Concepts Idea of salvation or liberation in → Hinduism is repr. by variety of terms →→ *mokṣa*, *mukti*, *nirvana*, *kaivalya*, etc. With dominance of belief in → rebirth, it is assumed that liberation involves cessation of rebirth. The self or soul (→→ *atman*, *jiva*, *puruṣa*) attains some kind of transcendental state beyond suffering. However, the nature of the state and means to attaining it vary considerably acc. to teachings of various schools and sects. For → Samkhya-Yoga, soul exists in isolation. For → Advaita, there is no individual existence after liberation, since there is in truth but one Self. For theistic schools and sects, liberation is conceived as some kind of relationship with God, variously described. Different categories of heavenly relationship are: union with God (entering into his body), *sāyujya*; identifying and exercising God's supernatural powers, *sārṣṭi*; having same form as God, *sārūpya*; dwelling in same place as God, *sālokya*; being close to God, *samīpya*. Many → *bhakti* teachers deny first, since it involves too close identification, and so loss of individual identity. Heavenly existence is also goal of man in *Mimamsa*, but without ref. to supreme God to be in communion, etc., with. There is divergence about whether → *jivanmukti* or 'liberation while alive' is poss. In gen. the *bhakti* schools deny it, though not → Madhva; it is more characteristic of schools, such as → Yoga, strongly emphasising practice of inner contemplation. There is also, therefore, diversity of view about means to attainment of liberation. In theistic schools salvation is essentially due to → grace of God (the role of → *karma* being taken care of by belief that it is God who guides and arranges its effects). But operation of grace is conditional upon faith and self-surrender (*prapatti*) of devotee (→→ *Vadagalai, Tengalai*). For Samkhya-Yoga, liberation comes through strenuous practice of meditation, culminating in knowledge of distinction between soul and matter. In case of *Advaita*, liberation likewise accrues essentially upon existential inner knowledge of truth. In theistic schools, place of liberation is God's → heaven, such as Vishnu's blessed realm, Vaikuṇṭha. There are hells or purgatories by contrast; but gen. these are not considered to be permanent abodes of those who suffer in them, so that, except in → Dvaita school, there is belief in everlasting liberation, but not everlasting damnation. Some Hindu theologians have argued for universal liberation (*sarvanmukti*)—e.g. the 16th cent. Advaitin, Appaya Dikṣita: so long as any individual remains unliberated, → *maya* remains; so ultimate conquest of ignorance and illusion involves salvation of all. This doc. has been emphasised in recent times by S. → Radhakrishnan. In interim before universal liberation, already liberated selves are identified with God and his powers, and act on behalf of those still involved in suffering. (→Salvation) N.S.

Li Chi (Book of Rites or Ceremonial). One of the five classics of Confucian canon. Together with the *Chou Li* and *I Li* (compiled in 2nd cent. BC), it collects together teachings of early Confucians concerning ritual. Early in 1st cent. BC Tai Tê produced the *Ta Tai Li*, and this was followed by a 2nd collection of ritual works by his nephew, Tai Shêng, known as the *Hsiao Tai Li*. This latter still retained its orig. name in CE 79; by CE 175 it was called the *Li Chi*. The book contains 46 chapters, some extremely important for study of → Confucianism. Throughout the cents. numerous and voluminous commentaries were produced. It was trans. into Eng. by J. Legge, in *S.B.E.*, 2nd edn. (1899), vols. 27–8. (→ Li). D.H.S.

Lieh Tzŭ (Lieh-tsê, Lieh Yü-k'ou). Chi. Taoist philosopher, reputed author of the *Book of Lieh-tzŭ*. Historicity doubtful. Believed to have lived in 4th cent. BC. The book is variously attr. to 3rd cent. BC and 4th cent. CE. Its main argument contends that life is fleeting and futile, and is ended by death; it is mechanistically determined, and without teleological significance. A hedonistic philos. of life is advocated. The book is full of naive stories of the irrational and marvellous, borrowing much of its material from earlier sources, e.g. → Chuang Tzŭ. D.H.S.

A. C. Grahan, *The Book of Lieh Tzŭ* (1960).

Light and Darkness It is natural for man to prefer L. to D., and this instinctive preference is reflected in his religs. L. is gen. an attribute of superior forms of deity (e.g. sun-gods, → sky-gods), whereas D. is assoc. with → Devil and → demons. In Egypt. relig. → Apophis, dragon of D., nightly threatened → Rē, the sun-god; Iranian → dualism identified → Ahura Mazdah with L., and → Ahriman with D.; in Vedic relig. → Mitra repr. with light-sky and → Varuna the dark-sky; the alternating principles of Chinese cosmology, → Yin and Yang, were identified respectively with D. and L. Death and the underworld were assoc. with D. (e.g. → Sheol; → *kur-nu-gi-a;* → Hades). Conversely → Heaven as assoc. with L. S.G.F.B.

E.R.E., VIII, pp. 47–66; G. Van der Leeuw, *La religion* (1948), pp. 55ff.; E. O. James, *The Worship of the Sky-God* (1963); G. Dumézil, *Mitra-Varuna* (1948), *Les dieux des Indo-Européens* (1952), p. 42.

Limbo Chr. → soteriology, by making faith in Christ essential to salvation, was faced with problem of accounting for *post-mortem* destiny of those who lived before coming of Christ and unbaptised infants, who died in → Original Sin but were innocent of personal sin. Two special departments of → Hell were, accordingly, invented: (1) *limbus patrum*, for O.T. saints, (2) *limbus infantium* for unbaptised infants. In these L.'s, both suffered no pain, but were excluded from → Beatific Vision. (→ Descent into Hades). A vivid account of L. is given by → Dante in *Divina Commedia*, *Inferno*, IV: virtuous pagans also are here accommodated in L. S.G.F.B.

D.C.C., *s.v.; R.G.G.*³, IV, col. 378–80; S. G. F. Brandon, *The Judgment of the Dead* (1967), ch. 5.

Liṅgam The *linga* or *lingam* is main emblem of → Śiva. The discovery of cone-shaped objects, almost certainly *lingams* in → Indus Valley Civilisation indic. that cult is pre-Aryan. In Veda there are disapproving refs. to phallus-worshippers; but by period of classical → Hinduism usage was beginning to be more widely accepted. In Dravidian south erection of ritual posts seemingly was connected with *lingam* cult; it was customary to mount a *lingam* over grave of ascetics. The form of *lingam* most commonly found in temples is short stone cylindrical pillar with rounded top; also there are images in form of a *lingam* with god or goddess sitting inside it. It is also symbol of →

Liṅgāyat sect: each adherent is supposed to wear or carry one. The counterpart of *lingam* is circular object with hole in it, the *yoni*, symbolizing female generative organ. The *lingam* symbolizes Śiva's generative and creative power. N.S.

H. Zimmer, *Myths and Symbols in Indian Art and Civilization* (1962).

Liṅgāyats Import. sect of S. Indian → Śaivism, going back to teacher Basava, who lived in latter part of 12th cent. CE. The sect's docs. are also known as Vīra-Saivism or 'Heroic Śaivism'. Movement's name arises from concentration on → *liṅgam* as one true symbol of divinity; adherents carry *lingam* with them, either round neck or in special box. The cult of images is rejected, and in principle caste system and necessity of priestly offices of → Brahmins are rejected (in practice, however, L. have not remained unaffected by these institutions). Basava's teachings appear to have involved gen. opposition to → Aryan practices, for sacrifices, cremation and prayers for dead were rejected, together with trad. ban on remarriage of widows. Equality between sexes and different castes was part of his teaching. It is poss. that he was influenced by Islam; though there is evidence of earlier Shaivite teachings analogous to those of Vira-Shaivism. The theology of the L. is not unlike that of → Śaiva Siddhanta; but is less dualistic in emphasis, and calls itself a form of qualified non-dualism (→ *Visistādvaita*). By his creative power, Śiva creates out of his own substance world and souls, and it is supreme function of soul to return to its origin. This is achieved by → initiation into order, under guidance of → *guru*, and by continued worship of, and meditation, upon Śiva, as mediated through his symbol, the *lingam*. L. ethics imply that adherent should practice daily worship, follow worldly occupation honestly, support itinerant pastors who preach faith, practice equality with fellow-L., practice commensality and intermarriage with other L., and show humility, as befits servants of Śiva. The pastors (*jaṅgamas*) act as preceptors, and substitute for Brahmins. All L. are also expected to reprove unworthy interpretations of faith and wrong views and feelings about God. They are chiefly to be found in Andhra Pradesh and Mysore. N.S.

H. Bhattacharyya (ed.), *The Cultural Heritage of India*, vol. 4 (1956); S. N. Dasgupta, *A History of Indian Philosophy*, vol. 5 (1962); S. M. Hunashal, *The Lingayat Movement: A Social Revolution in Karnatak* (1947); R. G. Bhandarkar, *Vaishnavism, Shaivism and Minor Religious Cults* (1928).

Literature (Sacred) →→ Avesta; Bible; Bhagavad-Gītā; Brāhmanas; Book of Dead; Books (sacred); Coffin Texts; Gathas; Granth; Qur'ān; Pahlavi Literature; Pyramid Texts; Rig-Veda; Upanishads.
(Buddh.) (Sanskrit) → Sanskrit. T.O.L.
(China–Japan) →→ Tripitaka (Chinese); Tao Tsang; Kojiki; Nihongi. D.H.S.

Liturgical Movement 20th cent. movement, prob. repr. reaction against earlier subjectivism, to restore people's participation in official worship of Church (→ Liturgy). Starting in → R.C. Church and affecting most parts of it, the L.-M. has had its counterparts in → Anglican and other Prot. Churches. S.G.F.B.

*D.C.C., s.v.; R.G.G.*³, II, col. 1773, 1787–8.

Liturgy Grk. *leitourgia*, *ex. leōs*, 'people', and *ergon*, 'work'. L. was orig. used of any kind of public service; in → LXX it partic. denoted services in Jerusalem → Temple. L. has two meanings in current English: (1) to describe all Church services in contradistinction to private devotion; (2) as title of → Eucharist. It is thus commonly used in → E. Church. S.G.F.B.

L. Duchesne, *Christian Worship* (E.T. 1927); G. Dix, *The Shape of the Liturgy* (1954); W. K. L. Clarke (ed.), *Liturgy and Worship* (1932; *D.C.C., s.v.;* N. Zernov, *Eastern Christendom* (1961), ch. 9; *R.G.G.*³, IV, col. 401–23; A. Baumstark, *Comparative Liturgy* (E.T. 1958); T. Klauser, *The Western Liturgy and its Hist.* (E.T. 1953).

Lobha Buddh. term for 'greed', which is regarded as one of the 3 'roots' of the evil condition of human existence, the others being → Dosa and → Moha. Buddh. discipline, moral/meditational, aims at bringing about eradication of L., principally by cultivation of its opposite, viz. generosity, (→ Dāna), which can take practical form, as in giving of one's possession or money or other resources to others for their welfare; it can also be cultivated in its mental form of thinking generously of others. T.O.L.

Logia Grk. = 'sayings'. It has been supposed, largely on a rather vague statement of Papias (*c.* 60–130), that there once existed a collection of sayings of Jesus. N.T. scholars have thought that these L. formed a source from which Gospels of Mt. and Lk. were compiled. This hypothetical source is designated Q = *Quelle* (German, 'source'). L. is sometimes used also for sayings attr. to Jesus, preserved on papyri found at Oxyrhynchus (Egypt). S.G.F.B.

B. H. Streeter, *The Four Gospels* (1924), chs. 7–11; *P.C.*², col. 654b–g; B. P. Grenfell and A. S. Hunt, *ΛΟΓΙΑ ΙΗΣΟΥ*, *Sayings of Our Lord* (1897); H. G. Evelyn-White, *The Sayings of Jesus* (1920); V. Taylor, in *New Test. Studies*, ed. A. J. Higgins (1959), pp. 246ff.; F. G. Downing, 'Towards the Rehabilitation of Q', *N.T.S.*, 11 (1964–5).

Logical Positivism The philosophy of the Vienna Circle inspired by Humean empiricism, scientific method and mathematical logic. In 1929 the members of Circle issued declaration of their aims and methods in the *Wissenschaftliche Weltauffassung der Wiener Kreis* ('the Vienna Circle: its scientific world-conception'). The L. Positivists set out to show that all metaphysical statements are cognitively meaningless, that all metaphysical speculation is pseudo-knowledge. This position was well expressed by Neurath, when he said that with regard to metaphysics one should indeed be silent, but not *about* something. The special terms of metaphysics, they said, were meaningless; by contrast a cognitively meaningful sentence was empirically verifiable.

Critics of L.-P. pointed out that this verifiability principle was not itself empirically verifiable, and so could not be said to be cognitively meaningful. However, this was countered by the L.-P.'s who argued that principle of empirical verifiability was a decision or recommendation or prescription for use of the expressions 'cognitive meaning' and 'understanding'. Even so, it is not clear what the principle claims. At one point, it was understood as a claim that the meaning of a proposition is identified with the operations involved in verifying it. Though they abandoned this clearly fallacious view, some L.-P.'s still insisted that the specification of a method of application is a necessary condition for a concept to have any meaning at all. In 2nd quarter of 20th cent. most of the L.-P.'s explained the notion of verifiability by saying that a statement is verifiable, if it stands in a specified logical relation of some sort to observation; a statement which, acc. to Ayer in 1st edn. of *Language, Truth and Logic*, expressed statements about 'sense contents' and 'sense data'.

The L.-P.'s had no great interest in ethics. In 1930 Schlick published his *Problems of Ethics*, in which he contends that → ethics is primarily a factual, not a normative study. It is primarily concerned with psychology of moral behaviour. However, the application of principle of verifiability to study of ethics will clearly involve rejection of all characteristically ethical language as cognitively meaningless. This was the view put forward so clearly by Ayer in *Language, Truth and Logic*. Similarly, Ayer held that possibility of relig. knowledge had been ruled out by rejection of metaphysics. The theist's assertions are, therefore, neither valid nor invalid: they are indeed not expressions of any genuine proposition. The fact that people have relig. experience, though interesting from a psychological point of view, does not imply that there is such a thing as relig. knowledge, any more than having moral experience implies that there is such a thing as moral knowledge.

The characteristically Positivist view of religion is that relig. language is meaningless or nonsensical. As a result of A. G. N. Flew's writings, the debate about verification became a debate about falsifiability. The question was asked whether there was any conceivable event, the occurence of which would refute theism. Some philosophers and theologians met the challenge of Positivism by pointing out that, so long as → theology did not make any empirical assertions, the Positivists' analysis of religion could be developed. However, most theologians regarded this defence as an attenuation of Christ. theology. J.H.-T.

Primary sources: A. J. Ayer, *Language, Truth and Logic* (1936); A. J. Ayer (ed.), *Logical Positivism;* R. Carnap, *Logical Syntax of Language* (1937; M. Schlick, *Problem of Ethics* (1930); L. Wittgenstein, *Tractatus Logico—Philosophicus* (1922).

Secondary sources: John Passmore, *A Hundred Years of Philosophy* (1957), ch. 16; J. O. Urmson, *Philosophical Analysis* (1956), part 2; G. J. Warmock, *English Philosophy since* 1900 (1958), ch. 4; J. Weinberg, *An Examination of Logical Positivism* (1963).

Logos Grk. = 'Word' or 'Reason'. Heraclitus (*c.* 500 BC) used L. to denote a rational law or principle permeating and governing universe. The concept was adopted and popularised by → Stoics; in → Alexandria it was developed by Platonic thinkers and provided → Philo with useful category in his philosophising of Jew. relig.—with him it became almost an hypostatised intermediary agent between God and World. In early Chr. thought, L. was employed most notably in Gospel of → John (1:1ff.), where it is equated with God from eternity and described as being incarnated in → Jesus of Nazareth. In 2nd cent., the → Apologists exploited L.-idea in seeking to present Christianity as acceptable to Hellenistic philosophy. → Athanasius used concept very effectively in his Christology. The idea of basic law or truth, which is implicit in order and rationality of universe, and on which the moral or social order rests, is anc. and occurs in many religs. (→→ Asha; Maat; Rta; Memph. Theol.; Memra). S.G.F.B.

O.C.D., *s.v.; E.R.E.*, VII, *s.v.; D.C.C.*, *s.v.; R.G.G.*³, IV, col. 434–40; *Th.Wb.*, IV, pp. 69ff.; W. Jaeger, *The Theology of Early Greek Philosophers* (1948), *passim*; R. Reitzenstein, *Die hellenist. Mysterienreligionen* (1927², 1956); Schürer, *G.J.V.*, III, pp. 555ff.; C. H. Dodd, *The Bible and the Greeks* (1954), pp. 115ff., *The Interpretation of Fourth Gospel* (1954), pp.

263ff.; Harnack, *H.D.*, *passim;* A. Grillmeier, *Christ in Christian Tradition* (E.T. 1965), *passim.*

Lohan (Chinese term, derived from Skt. *arhan, arhat;* Jap. and Korean—*rahan, rahat*). Signifies one who has attained Buddh. enlightenment and perfection. The L. are personal disciples and worthies of Buddha. Originally 16 in number, from 10th cent. CE 18 have been gen. recognised in China; their images were intro. into halls of Buddh. temples, where they are regarded as patrons and guardians of → Buddhism throughout world. D.H.S.

For detailed description, E. T. C. Werner, *Dict. of Chinese Mythology* (1932).

Lollards Orig. followers of J. Wycliffe. The name prob. meant 'number of prayers'. L. based their teaching on personal faith, Divine → election, and Bible. They gen. rejected the distinctive doctrines and hierarchy of medieval Church, and propagated their views through 'Poor Preachers'. Starting as academic movement, after 1400 Lollardy became increasingly popular among poorer classes. Despite persecutions, it continued into 15th cent., and prepared way for → Reformation. S.G.F.B.

J. Gairdner, *Lollardy and the Reformation in England*, 4 vols. (1908–13); *D.C.C.*, *s.v.;* G. M. Trevelyan, *England in the Age of Wycliffe* (1925).

Longevity, Search for (Chinese) L. has always been regarded by the Chinese as one of 3 supreme blessings. Man, acc. to Chi. thought, is not composed of a spiritual soul and a material body; but is entirely material. L. is assured so long as constituents of personality, dispersed at death, can be held together. Hence, particularly in → Taoism, the development of techniques for L. or continuous survival. The search for L. followed three main lines: (1) search for the mushroom or herb of L. on P'êng Lai (The Isles of the Blessed); (2) → alchemy to produce drug or elixir of L.; (3) hygiene, dietary restrictions and breath-control to ensure L. The Chi. ideal was *ch'ang shêng pu lao* ('long life without old age'), a life conceived by Taoist adepts as free and unrestricted, the life of a → *hsien* (immortal). The god of L. (Shou Hsing) is a domestic god, univ. worshipped throughout China, and repr. as old man of happy mien, riding on stag with a flying bat above head. He holds a large peach, and attached to his long staff are a gourd and a scroll. The stag and bat repr. happiness; the peach, gourd and scroll are symbols of L. The search for and attainment of L. is a constant theme in Chi. folklore and literature. D.H.S.

H. Maspero, *Le Taoisme* (1950), pp. 83ff.; E. T. C. Werner, *Dict. of Chinese Mythology* (1932).

Lotus Sūtra → Saddharma-Pundarīka. T.O.L.

(Chinese—*Miao Fa Lien Hua Ching*) The L.-S., or the Lotus of the True Doctrine (*Saddharma-pundarīka sūtra*) was first trans. into Chinese by Dharmarakṣa (Fa Hu), who flourished *c.* CE 266–308. With its doc. of the one Buddha-vehicle, which opens way to Buddhahood for all believers, its stress on the eternal and omniscient Buddha, and its wealth of images and parables, it soon became venerated as a fundamental scripture of Chi. Buddhism. Trans. again by → Kumārajīva early in 5th cent. CE, it came to be regarded by the → T'ien T'ai school as highest fulfilment of Buddha's teaching and complete exposition of Truth. It was treasured by most sects of the → Mahāyāna; it is of paramount importance for develop. of a rich Buddh. mythology in China, in which the eternal Buddha-principle, repr. in innumerable forms, is shown as working out purpose of salvation for all suffering humanity. To quote → W. E. Soothill, the L.-S. is 'unique in the world's relig. literature. A magnificent apocalypse, it presents a spiritual drama of the highest order, with the universe as its stage, eternity as its period, and Buddhas, gods, men, devils as its dramatic personae. From the most distant worlds and from past aeons, the eternal Buddhas throng the stage to hear the mighty Buddha proclaim his ancient and eternal Truth. . . . On earth he has assumed human form with all its limitations. Now he reveals himself *sub specie aeternitatis* as the Eternal, Omniscient, Omnipotent, Omnipresent Buddha, creator-destroyer, recreator of all worlds.' D.H.S.

W. E. Soothill, *The Lotus of the Wonderful Law* (1930), p. 13; E. Zürcher, *The Buddhist Conquest of China* (1959), *passim*; D. H. Smith, *Chinese Religions* (1968), pp. 114f., 132f.; K. L. Reichelt, *Truth and Tradition in Chinese Buddhism* (1927), *passim.*

Love (Buddh.) → Metta. T.O.L.

(Chinese) The character *ai* has much the same wealth of connotation as the Eng. word 'love'. It expresses idea of 'taking into the heart' and hence 'affection, to be fond of, to like, to love'. The supreme Confucian virtue *jên*, variously trans. as 'goodness, benevolence, human-heartedness, love' approx. most nearly to Chr. virtue of love as → *agapē*. This close resemblance is revealed in → Confucius' use of term in the → *Analects*. It is 'to love all men'; it is seen in practice of reverence, generosity, sincerity, sagacity and charitableness. It is more import. than life itself. No mean man can possess it, but the courageous, the simple, the modest and the enduring are near to *jên*.

→ Mo-tzŭ taught that *jên* expresses itself in 'universal love' (*chien ai*), which is rooted in Will of Heaven. Because Heaven loves all men impartially, we should do the same. Mo-tzŭ, however, based practice of universal love on utilitarian concept of mutual benefit, whereas the Confucians taught that *jên* is the perfect expression of orig. goodness of one's Heaven-born nature. Mo-tzŭ refused to allow any discrimination in exercise of universal love, on account of close ties of affection which bind us closer to some than others. The Confucians argued that this was contrary to human nature. The clearest expression of Confucian concept of *jên* is found in neo-Confucian philosopher, → Chu Hsi (12th cent.). Acc. to his teaching, *jên* is inherent in mind, it is Principle of Origin, one of the Divine attributes, the positive and active mode of the Supreme Ultimate. It is source of affection, which enables a man to regard others as one with himself. It is mild and gentle, unaffected by poverty or wealth or high or low estate. In its operation there is moral insight, courtesy and judgment. It is sincere and unselfish, and to love others as we love ourselves is to perfect love. D.H.S.

W. T. Chan: art. 'The evolution of the Confucian Concept of "Jên"', in *Philos. East and West*, vol. 4, no. 4 (1955), pp. 295–319; C. B. Day, *The Philosophers of China* (1962), pp. 63–5, 207–9, 304–5.

(Christian) In N.T., two Grk. words are used for L., which is the basic and most distinctive Chr. virtue, denoting both God's love for man and attitude man should have towards God and his neighbour. These words are *philia* and *agapē*. Although in → LXX these words could mean sexual love, the latter is never denoted thus in N.T.; *phileō* ('I love') is used in → John's Gospel interchangeably with *agapaō* for divine love (e.g. 5:20). Paul's exaltation of *agapē* in I Cor. 13:4ff. made it peculiarly the word for Chr. L. The *A.V.* trans. *agapē*, 'Charity'. L., with Faith and Hope, constitute the 'Theological Virtues'. (→ Agape). S.G.F.B.

H.D.B., *s.v.; Th.Wb.*, I, pp. 34ff.; V. Warnach, *Agape* (1951); A. Nygren, *Agape and Eros*, new edn. (1953); *E.R.E.*, VII, pp. 164ff.; *R.G.G.*³, IV, col. 361–9.

Ludlul bel nemeqi Opening words ('I will praise the Lord of wisdom'), often quoted as title of an Akkadian text concerning problem of suffering; it is sometimes referred to as the 'Babylonian Job'. (→→ Job, Book; Mesopot. Relig.). S.G.F.B.

A.N.E.T., pp. 438ff.; W. G. Lambert, *Babylonian Wisdom Literature* (1960), pp. 14ff.; Brandon, *M.D.*, pp. 96ff.; T. Jacobsen, *I.A.A.M.*, pp. 212ff.

Lucifer Lat.: 'light-bearer'. The → Vulgate trans. of epithet for King of Babylon in Is. 14:12. → Jerome and other Fathers, connecting this epithet with Lk. 10:18, used L. as synonym for → Devil. L. was also name of the fiercely anti-Arian bishop of Cagliari (d. 370 or 371). (→ Arian Controversy). S.G.F.B.

D.C.C., p. 826; *R.G.G.*³, IV, col. 464–5.

Luke, Gospel of Known as Third Gospel, L. was prob. written *c.* CE 80–90, and formed first vol. of an account of Christ. Origins, of which → Acts of Apostles is the second. Written in idiomatic Grk., it is consciously a literary composition (1:1ff.). L. uses narrative framework of → Mark's Gospel, → Q., and trads. peculiar to itself (e.g. Birth stories, 1–2). Some scholars think that present L. comprises 'Proto-Luke' (i.e. an orig. and independent draft), which was later interwoven with Markan narrative. The author and place of orig. of L. are unknown. S.G.F.B.

J. M. Creed, *The Gosp. acc. to St. Luke* (1930); B. H. Streeter, *The Four Gospels* (1924); V. Taylor, *Behind the Third Gospel* (1926); *H.D.B.*, *s.v.; P.C.*², pp. 820ff., 763–5.

Lumbini Buddh. place of pilgrimage, and one of the 4 → Holy Places, since, acc. to Buddh. trad., it was place of the Buddha's birth (*Jātaka*, I, 52, 54). The place is described in Buddh. lit. as a park situated in Sakyan tribal territory between Kapilavastu and Devadaha. L. was visited by Buddha during course of his travels; he there delivered to the monks a discourse known now as the *Devadaha Sutta*. The emperor → Ashoka made a pilgrimage there, *c.* 249 BC, a fact which has been confirmed in mod. times by discovery of a commemorative pillar erected by Ashoka and bearing five-line inscription in a dialect of E. India. This was deciphered in 1898, and found to consist of 3 sentences: 'When King Devānampiya Piyyadesi had been anointed twenty years, he came himself and worshipped [this spot] because the Buddha Sakyamuni was born here. [He] both caused to be made a stone bearing a horse [?] and caused a stone-pillar to be set up [in order to show] that the Blessed One [Bhagavan] was born here. [He] made the village of Lumbini free of taxes and paying [only] an eighth share [of the produce]'. The Chinese Buddh. pilgrim, → Fa-hsien, who visited India at begin. of 5th cent. CE, mentions L., but does not appear to have located it nor to have visited it; only the ruins of town of Kapilavastu were then to be seen. Similarly another pilgrim → Hsuang-tsang (*c.* CE 636), visiting Kapilavastu, heard only accounts of a stone pillar in the outlying forest, but was not able to visit spot. The pillar bearing Ashoka's inscription has now been restored; it is located 2m. N. of Bhagavanpura, within territory of Nepal; the place is known as Rumindei. (→ Kapilavatthu). T.O.L.

S. Dutt, *The Buddha and Five After Centuries* (1957), ch. 2.

Lun Yü (*The Analects of Confucius*). One of the Four Books which formed basic texts in Chi. schools for study of → Confucianism, and chief source for our knowledge of Confucius and his teachings. Prob. complied *c.* 400 BC by disciples of Confucius, it received something like its present form in 2nd cent. CE, and from Sung Dynasty, when → Chu Hsi (CE 1130–1200) compiled his ed. and commentary (*Lun Yü Chi Chu*, 1177), the book became basis of all education. It is composed of 20 chapters of unequal value and authenticity, mainly recording in short paragraphs sayings of Confucius. There are many excellent trans. in Eng. and other European languages. D.H.S.

J. Legge, *The Chinese Classics*, 2nd edn. (1893), vol. 1; W. E. Soothill, *The Analects of Confucius* (1910); A. Waley, *The Analects of Confucius* (1938).

Luqmān Legendary figure whose name is used as title of Qur., sura xxxi. It contains a passage (vv:11–8, but 13f. seem misplaced) where L. instructs his son. L. is known in Arab legend. Though mentioned in the Qur., he is not normally considered a prophet. At a later time fables were attributed to him. He has been called an Ethiopian slave, which has led some to connect him with Aesop. He has also been called son of → 'Ād, and entitled 'the man of the vultures' because he was granted the power to live as long as seven vultures. J.R.

E.I., III, pp. 35–7; Hughes, pp. 301f.; A. Roediger (ed.), *Locmani Fabulae* (1839); J. Horovitz, *Koranische Untersuchungen* (1926), pp. 132–6.

Lustration *Ex.* Lat. *lustrum*, a purificatory ritual performed in Rome by censors every 5 years. It took form of procession, prob. of circular movement, in which various magical objects were carried. The word is often used in more gen. sense for any purificatory rites, incl. → baptism. S.G.F.B.

W. Warde-Fowler, *Relig. Experience of the Roman People* (1911), pp. 209ff.; *O.C.D., s.v.*

Luther, Martin (1483–1546) The German Reformer who began the Protestant Reformation, was born at Eisleben in Thuringia, Nov. 10th, 1483, son of Hans and Margaret Luther. His father, a miner, rose to moderate affluence. Martin went to school at Mansfeld, Magdeburg and Eisenach; in April, 1501, he matriculated in the Univ. of Erfurt, where he took the arts course and degrees of B.A. and M.A. In July 1505, without consulting his parents, he entered the relig. order of Eremetical Augustinians at Erfurt. L. was ordained priest in April 1507; his father attended his First Mass. He was selected for advanced theological studies in Erfurt, chiefly under Nominalist theologians. In 1508 he went to new Univ. of Wittenberg to lecture in the Arts Faculty. There, in 1512 he took his degree of D.D., and succeeded his old friend and teacher Johannes von Stauptiz, in the chair of Biblical Theology. He now began a great series of Biblical courses on the *Psalms* (1513–5), *Romans* (1515–6), *Galatians* (1517) and *Hebrews* (1518). These were years of intense Biblical study, during which he also read widely in the Fathers, espec. → St. Augustine. They were also for him a time of spiritual anguish. Easement of mind came to him when he saw that the righteousness, which avails before God, is a divine gift to men, on the sole ground of their commitment in faith to the mercy of God. Meanwhile L. accumulated many duties; he was soon Prior, District Vicar and preacher not only in his monastery but in parish church at Wittenberg, where he exercised immense influence in lucid, simple sermons, shot through with insight, pathos and humour. L. was involved in the educat. revolution of his day, the displacement of → Aristotle in theology, and replacement of the later Schoolmen by Augustine and the Fathers. This programme he succeeded in estab. in Wittenberg in 1516–7. Then, almost unawares, he became entangled in a Church struggle centring on → Indulgences. These were matters of dispute among theologians and moralists, uncertain of their scope and extent. L. protested in 1518 against local indulgences attached to All Saints Church, Wittenberg. In 1517 there was a more obvious scandal in the promulgation of the Jubilee Indulgence in Germany, ostensibly for rebuilding of St. Peter's, Rome; but which was intended also to discharge the huge debts of the young Archbishop of Mainz. L. wrote 95 Theses about Indulgences, posted them on All Saints Church and sent copies to the Archbishop and Bishop of Brandenburg. These Latin theses were turned into German, printed, and swiftly circulated through Germany. Because they had implicitly challenged the papal plenitude of power, they opened a Church struggle centring in L. and in Wittenberg. In 1518 L. had an interview at Augsburg with Cardinal Cajetan, and refused to recant. In 1519 a debate in Leipzig with Cath. theologian John Eck forced him to face the implications of his resistance to authority, and led him to utter a defiance which brought the Papal Bull *Exsurge domine* against him in 1520. To this he replied in a series of theological manifestoes—notably his 'Appeal to the Christian nobility of the German Nation', his 'Babylonish Captivity' (in Latin and denouncing 4 of the 7 → Sacraments) and the 'Liberty of a Christian Man'. The faithful protection of Luther's prince, Frederick the Wise of Saxony, secured him a hearing at

Imperial Diet of Worms, April 1521, where he again firmly refused to recant. His prince hid him away for next months in the historic castle of the Wartburg overlooking Eisenach. Here he dressed as a German knight, bearded, as 'Junker Georg'; but here he also began his trans. of the German Bible. He did not finish the Bible for more than ten years, and enlisted a team of scholars incl. the brilliant Philip Melanchthon; but the German Bible bore the imprint of his own genius and laid a deep hold on the life of the whole German people.

L.'s theology had extensive practical implications, notably his attacks on the → Mass, on Private Masses, on Monastic Vows and on clerical celibacy. During his absence, a radical reformation began in Wittenberg which found its leader in L.'s senior colleague Andrew Karlstadt. His preaching, and the iconoclasticism which arose from it, constituted a dangerous and open defiance of the recent Imperial Diet at Nuremberg; in March 1522 L. returned to Wittenberg and in a brilliant series of sermons redressed the situation. In the next months he had to fight a legalistic puritanism and an enthusiastic spiritualism, of which Thomas Müntzer was the brilliant and violent exponent. When Müntzer took the lead in the Peasants War in Thuringia in 1525, L. violently dissociated himself from what he called 'the murdering and thieving hordes of peasants'. 1525 is the watershed of his career. It marks his wedding with Katherine von Bora, and his controversy with Erasmus.

In 1524 the Eucharistic controversy opened between the Reformers, L. stoutly maintaining the doc. of the → Real Presence against theologians of Switzerland and Strasbourg; the attempt to heal the breach in the colloquy at Marburg 1529 was abortive. The relig. truce of Nuremberg (1532) led to a breathing space for L. During all this time, he continued to pour out an immense flood of writings, hymns (notably *Eyn' Feste Burg*), catechisms, liturgies, sermons and thousands of occasional tracts. Towards end of his life, he witnessed a recrudescence of Papal political and Imperial military power, which account in part for the vehemence of his attack on the → Papacy in his later years, the resilience of which he under-estimated. L. continued to lecture while he had strength; he preached to within a few hours of his death in Eisleben, where he had been born. He died 18 Feb., 1546. L. had limitations and faults; but he had won to himself a band of devoted preachers and reformers, who established the great spiritual communions of Lutheranism, drawing on his work and inspiration. E.G.R.

There is a vast number of German and Scandinavian studies on Luther's life and theology. Among English studies are R. H. Bainton, *Here I Stand* (1951); F. Lau, *Luther* (1964); A. G. Dickens, *Luther* (1967); P. Watson, *Let God be God* (1947); E. G. Rupp, *The Righteousness of God* (1953).

Lü Tsung An import. school of Chi. Buddhism founded by Tao Hsüan (CE 595–667). It is based on the Hinayanist → Vinaya, and more concerned with organisation and gov. of monasteries than with subtleties of doc. The founder believed that morality and discipline lie at basis of the relig. life. The chief monastery of sect is at Pao-hua-shan in Kiangsi province, where only two meals a day are permitted and no drink but tea. D.H.S.

S. Couling, *Encycl. Sinica* (Shanghai, 1917; 1965), p. 318.

M

Mâ Anc. Anatolian fertility-goddess, akin to → Cybele and → Anahita. She was served by priests called *fanatici*, who danced in wild ecstasy and wounded themselves in her honour. M. had warlike attributes; when her cult was brought to Rome, she was identified with → Bellona. S.G.F.B.

Cumont, *R.O.*, pp. 50ff.; E. O. James, *Cult of the Mother-Goddess* (1959), pp. 182ff.

Maat Egypt. word meaning 'truth', 'justice'. M. repr. basic order of universe and of human society, and was assoc. with sun-god → Rē. M. was depicted as seated goddess, daughter of Re: her symbol was a feather. In scenes of → Judgment of Dead in → Book of Dead, the heart of the deceased is weighed against M. or her symbol (→ Psychostasia). S.G.F.B.

R.Ae.R.-G., s.v.; S. G. F. Brandon, *Judgment of the Dead* (1967), ch. 2.

Maccabees, Books of 1st Bk. of M., orig. written in Heb., now surviving only in Grk., relates exploits of Judas Maccabaeus and family in Jew. struggle for relig. and political freedom against Greek (Seleucid) rulers of Syria during 2nd cent. BC. It prob. dates *c.* 100 BC. 2nd Bk. of M. is abridgment of 5 vol. work by Jason of Cyrene, in Grk., *c.* 100 BC. It deals with same struggle, but its narrative is more concerned with the marvellous and miraculous. These two works are incl. in → Apocrypha. 3rd Bk. of M. is a relig. novel written in Grk. by Alex. Jew *c.* 100 BC—CE 100. It deals with Jew. triumph over enemies through divine intervention during reign of Ptolemy Philopator (222–204 BC). 4th Bk. of M. is a kind of sermon on supremacy of pious reason over passions, partic. as evidenced in sufferings of Maccabean martyrs. Written prob. early in 1st cent. CE, it attests exaltation of martyr-ideal. These two works are incl. in → Pseudepigrapha. S.G.F.B.

R. H. Charles (ed.), *A.P.*, I, II (1913); R. H. Pfeiffer, *Hist. of New Test. Times* (1949), pp. 203ff., 215ff., 461ff.; Schürer, *G.J.V.*, III, pp. 139ff., 359ff.; K.-D. Schunck, *Die Quellen des I u. II Makkabäerbuches.*

Macao (Ao Mên). A small peninsula on coast of S. China, near to Canton and Hongkong, it has been occupied by Portuguese since CE 1557; it provided base from which Chr. missionaries entered China, was used as centre for training missionaries and Chi. converts, and place of retreat in time of persecution. D.H.S.

C. Cary-Elwes, *China and the Cross* (1957), *passim.*

Madhva Sometimes transliterated as 'Madhwa': chief exponent of dualistic (→ Dvaita) school of Vedanta. Born in 1197 in Udipi near Mangalore in W. India, he early gained a reputation for effectiveness in doctrinal disputation, during extensive journeys round south and later north India. His chief concern was to refute → Advaita, regarded as dangerously incompatible with → Vaisnavite devotionalism which M. preached. His biography is, however, largely legendary (certain miracles ascribed to him, such as walking on water, have suggested Christ. influences, but these are doubtful). He was regarded as incarnation of → Vayu 'Breath' or 'Spirit', as mediator between God and man. His main works were commentary on *Brahmasutra* and others on principal → Upaniṣads and on → *Bhagavadgita.* He died in 1276. His followers are mainly to be found in S. India, esp. in the Kanara country. N.S.

B. N. K. Sharma, *Hist. of the Dvaita School of Vedanta*, 2 vols. (1960–1); S. Subba Rao (tr.), *Vedanta-Sutras with the Commentary of Sri Madhwacharya* (1936); S. S. Raghavachar (tr.), *Madhva's Srimad Visnu Tattva Vinirnaya* (1959); B. N. K. Sharma, *Madhva's Teachings in his own Words* (1963).

Mādhyamika School of Buddh. philosophy founded by Nagarjuna (*c.* CE 150), the central doc. of which is the negation (*śūñyatā*) of all empirical concepts, such as → *dhammas*, or ultimate constituents of existence, affirmed in the → Abhidhamma of the Theravādins. The notion of *sunyata* was already to be found in the Prajnaparamita literature; it was this which Nagarjuna formulated and expounded in such a way as to make it the basis of a new school of Buddh. philosophy. The criticism levelled by this → Mahāyāna school against the Theravāda was that latter's Abhidhamma method of analysis, while it was true to teaching of Buddha in rejecting notion of a real, eternally-existing self, and in analysing the human individual into → *khandhas*, and the *khandhas* into *dhammas*, failed to carry this method of analysis of concepts to its logical end; the Theravāda stopped short at the *dhammas*, and affirmed reality of these. Acc. to M., this was an arbitrary halting of method of analysis: *dhammas* were also concepts which must be seen as only temporary resting places in the analytical process: Acc. to M., *dhammas* also had no reality; for the real was devoid (*śūñya*) of all conceptual constructions. M. was thus a doc. of an Absolute which is to be realised only through *Prajñā*, i.e. Wisdom, or Intuition; Prajnā is itself the Absolute. The *dhammas* have no nature of their own as the Theravāda affirmed; only the Absolute has this. The M. school held that this was a view which steered between the *ātma*, or self-affirming doc., and the *nairyātma*, or self-rejecting doc. of Theravāda; hence the name '*Middle View*' (*Madhyamaka Darśana*), by which this school came to be known; this designation does not, however, seem to have been used by Nargarjuna or his contemporary and associate → Aryadeva.

There were, acc. to Murti, 3 subsequent stages in develop. of the M. school, after formulation of its central principle by Nagarjuna and Aryadeva. These were: the splitting of M. into 2 schools, the Prāsangika, repr. by Buddhapālita, and the Svātantrika, repr. by Bhāvaviveka; then, in early 7th cent. CE, the re-affirming by Candrakirti of the more vigorous Prāsangika or *reductio ad absurdum* method as the norm for M.; finally a syncretism of M. with the → Yogācara sch., carried out by Śāntaraksita and Kamalaśīla; it was this form of M. which became dominant philosophy of Buddhism of → Tibet. Because of its affirmation (*vāda*) of principle of *śūñya*, the M. school is known also as the *Śūñyavāda*. T.O.L.

T. R. V. Murti, *The Central Philosophy of Buddhism* (1955); E. Conze, *Buddhist Thought in India* (1962), part III, 2; Richard H. Robinson, *Early Madhyamika in India and China* (1967).

Maenads In Grk. mythology, tragedy and art, women inspired to ecstatic frenzy by → Dionysos. In their wild abandon of conventions of ordinary life and fierce expression of primitive instincts, the M. were type-repr. of feminine reaction to orgiastic worship of Dionysos in Thrace. The M. are also called Bacchae and Thyiades. S.G.F.B.

J. Harrison, *Prolegomena*, pp. 388ff.; *O.C.D.*, *s.v.;* E. R. Dodds, *The Greeks and the Irrational* (1963), pp. 270ff.; *Kleine Pauly*, III, col. 899–901.

Magadha Kingdom of N. India at time of the Buddha, notable in Buddh. hist. as region in which Buddhism had its birth. M. was one of four major kingdoms of India in 5th cent. BC (the others being Avanti, Kosala, and kingdom of Vaṃsas), and consisted of area south of the Ganges river, now known as Bihar. During early Buddh. period, M., like the other kingdoms was growing at expense of confederations of tribal societies such as that of the → Vajjis. One of results of growth of monarchy of Magadhan pattern was thus the disruption of tribal life and breakdown of old trads. and *mores*. Part of success of early Buddhism may be attributed to its ability to make available a new corporate life to take place of tribal society, and provide a democratic refuge from increasing autocracy of new kingdoms. Something of basic opposition between the two forms of society, the Buddh. → Sangha and the Magadhan kingdom, may be reflected in hostility of Magadha's king → Ajātasattu towards Buddha, although his father, King → Bimbisāra is repres. as supporter of Buddha. The capital of M. was, in earlier Buddh. period, at Rajagaha; later the royal centre shifted to Pātaliputta (modern Patna). It was from M. that Buddhism spread into other regions of India after third → Buddh. Council at Pātaliputta. By this time, in reign of → Ashoka, M. had become an extensive empire, with considerable natural resources, mineral and agricultural, and an import. international trade. The connection between language spoken in Magadha at time of Buddha, and the → Pali in which discourses of Buddha have been preserved has been a matter of controversy. The Buddh. trad. of → Ceylon affirms that Pali is in fact the language of M. (known as Magadhī or *Māgadhika-bhāsā*) and that, therefore, the Pali version of the discourses preserves the orig. words of Buddha. But modern critical and linguistic studies have suggested that there were notable differences between Māgadhī and Pali; by some scholars it is suggested that the latter was more prob. a dialect of Ujjayinī, a region somewhat to west of M. T.O.L.

Malalasekere, *D.P.P.N.*, vol. 2, pp. 402–4; Sukumar Dutt, *The Buddha and Five After Centuries;* D. D. Kosambi, *Culture and Civilisation of Ancient India* (1965); E. Lamotte, *Histoire du Bouddhisme Indien* (1958).

Magi Grk. *magos*, *ex.* Old Persian *magu*. The orig. of M. is obscure; they seem to have been a Median 'tribe' recognised in Iran as specialists in priestly arts. At some stage they embraced → Zoroastrianism, prob. changing it profoundly from its orig. form (→ Gāthās). In Graeco-Roman world, M. were known as Zoroastrian priests; but name was also given to other oriental exponents of → occultism. S.G.F.B.

E.R.E., VIII, *s.v.;* Zaehner, *D.T.Z.*, pp. 161ff.; R. N. Frye, *The Heritage of Persia* (1962), pp. 75ff.; *R.G.G.*[3], IV, col. 602; J. Bidez and F. Cumont, *Les mages hellénisés*, 2 vols. (1938).

Magic The practice of M. is so anc., widespread

and various in its forms that succinct definition is impossible. M. seems to stem from instinctive miming of what is profoundly desired. The factor of imitation, on principle that 'like begets like', is evident in most forms of M. Paleolithic culture shows two forms of M.: (1) → cave art: animals stuck with darts to cause same to happen in future hunt (2) covering of corpse with red pigment perhaps to revivify it, since red is colour of blood, the life-substance. The same principle is involved in → witchcraft practice of identifying puppet with a person, and then injuring puppet so that person may suffer like injury. Much magical practice has been assoc. with demonology: action is here based on belief that, by esoteric knowledge, → demons can be persuaded or forced to execute commands of magician. → Ritual and M. are very closely connected, involving principle of → *ex opere operato*, i.e. that specific efficacy is generated by actual performance of a ritual action, which often involves recitation of verbal formula. Distinction is usually drawn between 'white' and 'black' magic: the former being socially benevolent (e.g. rain-making), the other malevolent. Distinction is also attempted between relig. and magic; but such attempts gen. rest on *a priori* definitions of the two entities concerned: in practice most religs. exhibit magical features. (→→ Black Mass; Frazer; Ritual Perpet. of Past). S.G.F.B.

E.R.E., VIII, pp. 245–321; *R.G.G.*, IV, 595–601; Frazer, *The Magic Art* (*G.B.*), 2 vols. (1936[3]); C. H. Ratschow, *Magic und Religion* (1955); *S.O.*, 7 (*Le monde du sorcier*, 1966).

(Chinese) Spec. assoc. with → Taoism; but → Buddhism and → Confucianism admit M. theory and a certain amount of practice. M. pervades the popular relig. of China. It aims at an extension of human powers in this and in a post-mortem existence, and seeks control over gods and spirits. It also aims at knowledge of future, and control over the elements (→→ Alchemy, Astrology, Five Elements, Yin-Yang). It makes great use of charms and amulets, and abnormal psychic phenomena. M. plays enormous role in folk-lore and popular literature, and pervades almost every aspect of life. It is based on anc. doc. of the close affinity and mutual interdependence of the spiritual, natural and human spheres.

In anc. China sorcerers and witches were known as *wu*, and performed quasi sacerdotal functions mainly connected with → divination and → exorcism. Their methods included mimetic dancing, drum-beating, chanting mystical formulae and trance-mediumship. They were believed to possess powers of foretelling future, communicating with gods and spirits, invoking good and exorcising evil influences. In gen., Confucianism set its face against M. and sorcery. The functions of the early magicians (*wu*) were largely taken over by Taoist and Buddh. priests. Popular temples of both faiths became, and have remained, centres at which almost every conceivable form of M. is performed: to regulate rainfall, to ensure good harvests, to expel disease and misfortune, to attract good luck, to ensure progeny etc. M. underlies many observances still carried out at popular festivals, and many acts which the family performs for well-being of its members.

Anti-witchcraft clauses are found in penal code of late Manchu Dynasty; severe penalties were inflicted on those found guilty. D.H.S.

E.R.E., VIII, pp. 259ff.; J. J. M. de Groot, *The Religious System of China*, 1892 (1964), vols. 5 and 6; W. B. Dennys, *The Folklore of China*, 1876 (1966), *passim*; H. A. Giles, *Strange Stories from a Chinese Studio* (1880); C. H. Plopper, *Chinese Relig. seen through the Proverb* (1926), pp. 118ff.; S. Couling, *Encycl. Sinica* (1917) 1964, pp. 321–2.

(Japanese) The anc. rituals of → Shinto were not so much prayers as magical formulae and solemn incantations, by which magician-priests compelled the gods to do their bidding. In anc. Shinto the magical element clearly prevails over the relig. sentiment. In purification rituals there is much use of sympathetic or imitative M.; e.g. the magical transfer of sin and guilt to some object which can then be thrown into a river. Mirrors, swords, jewels and scarves are regarded as powerful implements of M. Besides public ceremonies, great use is made of spells and charms, → divination and augury. Persons who had passed certain stages of ascetic training engaged in M., → exorcism and occult practices. Later, after intro. of → Buddhism into Japan, these were combined with and elaborated by Buddh. occultism. There grew up a belief that Buddhism offered superior ceremonial M. for calling down favourable supernatural aid, as witnessed by an almost fanatical devotion to reading of luck-bringing *sūtras*. In particular the → Shingon sect made use of ritual utterances, sacred texts, mystic formulae, symbols, postures, movements etc., to invoke aid of powerful deities. As Buddhism, in popular form, became debased, partic. during 14th and 15th cents., the practice of M., sorcery, exorcism and divination swept over whole of society. Confucian teaching in Japan has had restraining influence on practice of M., and W. and Chr. influence is far from negligible; but in mod. Sinto sects there is still great reliance on exorcism, divination and use of M. in healing of diseases. D.H.S.

E.R.E., VIII, pp. 296ff.; D. C. Holtom, *The National Faith of Japan* (1938), pp. 183–4; W. G. Aston, *Shinto* (1905), pp. 327ff.; M. Anesaki, *Hist. of Japanese Religion* (1930), pp. 46, 234.

(Vedic and Hindu) The dividing line between magical and non-magical sacrificial techniques, etc., in Vedic hymns is hard to draw. Roughly, one can detect increase in magical interests in later Vedic period, stemming from three sources. First, the elaboration of ritual increasingly implied its independent potency, so that propitiation, celebration and persuasion of the gods became less important—this trend culminated in the → Mimamsaka interpretation of Veda. Second, the → Brahmin class assimilated some magical methods of *sudras* and non-Aryans, as is evidenced by material contained in → *Atharvaveda*, much of which is of an incantatory and magical nature; and by growth of interest in → *tapas*, austerities practised in part to generate power. Third, the Upaniṣadic conception of → *Brahman* as basis of reality suggested that esoteric knowledge could give power over the world (though main interest of Upaniṣads was in power which would bring liberation). Though at one time the Brahmin was despised for using his skills to harm enemies, etc., there are a number of such spells in the *Atharvaveda*, as well as all sorts of incantations for warding off evils and promoting good. There are elements of such magic in the *samskaras* or → sacraments, e.g. rites to promote conception, safeguard child in womb, etc. It was, however, yogis and practitioners of → asceticism who gained most formidable reputation for magical power: the ascetic could incinerate his enemies with glance, destroy crops, protect cities, etc. Even the ordinary man could hope to ward off evils by fasting, etc. The practice of medicine, though strongly tied to magical techniques in *Atharvaveda*, developed highly scientific character in classical period, and was known as *Ayurveda* (the most import. exponent being Caraka, 1st cent. CE); but both for poor and rich it existed side by side with magical and semi-magical practices, such as offering of oblations (*homa*) by priesthood for recovery from illness, etc. Recourse to purificatory and auspicious rites has remained a pervasive feature of Hinduism, and has been useful source of livelihood for Brahmanical specialists. The efficacy of repetition of → *mantras* has been reinforced by growth of → Tantric ritualism. Prognostication of future through → dreams, omens, birthmarks, etc., was common in early nad classical India, but largely gave way to → astrology from 4th and 5th cents. CE onwards. Auspicious occasions could be determined astrologically, whether for marriage, pilgrimage, sacred bathing, etc. In add. to above widespread magical beliefs, there are a whole variety of partic. practices in agricultural communities, etc., in various parts of India. N.S.

A. A. Macdonnell, 'Magic (Vedic)', in *E.R.E.;* V. Henry, *La Magie dans l'Inde antique* (1904).

Mahābhārata The 'Great Bharata', one of two great epics of Hindu literature (→ *Ramayana*), trad. ascribed to legendary Vyāsa, the 'Compiler', sometimes treated as partial incarnation (→ *avatara*) of Viṣṇu. The main bulk of it was finalised by 3rd and 2nd cents. BC, though the → *Bhagavadgita* and other interpolations may be rather later. It contains about 90,000 stanzas. The main theme concerns a civil war in kingdom of Kurukṣetra, the area round modern Delhi. The five sons of Pāṇdu, who had been king but who had renounced throne to become relig. hermit, are forced out, on Pandu's death, by their cousins, the sons of Dhṛtarāṣṭra. The Pandavas (sons of Pandu) are, however, helped by friendly chief, → Krishna. Eventually reconciliation between them and the Kauravas, their cousins, is effected and kingdom is divided between them. But Duryodhana, chief of Kauravas, defeats Yudhiṣhira, one of Pandavas, in great gambling contest and wins whole kingdom. The Pandavas go into exile, and eventually, after 13 years, succeed in gathering allies and forces. A huge battle is engaged in Kuruksetra. The Pandavas and Krishna win; Yudhisthira occupies throne, and period of peace and just rule follows, until the five brothers, and their joint wife Draupadī, leave for Himalayas to enter city of the gods. There may be hist. basis for story, going back to a 10th cent. BC war in N. India. There is a great deal of relig. teaching in M., partly because in later stages of its composition it was edited by priests. It has over long period been a main source of popular entertainment and relig. and moral instruction—a factor in the widespread impact of the *Bhagavadgita* on popular Hinduism. The Epics are reckoned to be *itihāsa* (part of → *smṛti*) and, with → *Puranas*, are sometimes counted as the 'fifth Veda'. However, they do not possess full revealed authority of Vedic scriptures, but belong to auxiliary scriptures known as *smṛti* (→ revelation, Hindu). The epic was trans. into Tamil and other Dravidian languages in medieval period, facilitating its use as medium of relig. education in south. N.S.

E. W. Hopkins, *The Great Epic of India* (1920), *Epic Mythology* (1915); M. N. Dutt, *A Prose Translation of the Mahabharata*, 3 vols. (1895–1905); R. C. Zaehner, *Hinduism* (1965).

Mahābodhi Society Buddh. society founded in → Ceylon in 1891 by Ceylonese monk, the Venerable Anagarika Dharmapala. The primary aims of M.S. were, first, restoration of the Mahā Bhodi temple at Buddha-gāya, in N. India (scene of the Buddha's enlightenment); second, the revival of the Buddha-Sāsana in land of its birth. At that time → Buddha-gāya (or Bodh-Gāya) was in province of Bengal, then part of

British-ruled India. The temple was part of the property of a Shaivite (Hindu) landowner, and was in seriously neglected condition. The M.S. called conference at Bodh-Gāya in Oct. 1891 to enlist support of Buddhists of various other countries; in following year began publication of journal *The Maha Bodhi and the United Buddhist World*, which from then on played a not unimport. part in winning sympathy and support from Eng.-speaking people in India and elsewhere, but partic. from Indian intelligentsia. Opposition from both Hindu landowners and British authorities, however, was such that a lengthy process of legal action became necessary, which ended only with India's independence from British rule and the passing by new Government of Bihar of Buddha-Gāya Temple Act in 1949, under terms of which a temple management committee, consisting of 4 Buddh. and 4 Hindu members, was entrusted with care and control of temple. By this time the M.S. had gained considerable support, in India and elsewhere; besides its headquarters in Calcutta, it had estab. other centres at Madras, Kushinagara, Sarnath, Bombay and at → Anuradhapura in Ceylon. The first president of Society, Sir Ashutosh Mookerjee, succeeded in 1908 in intro. study of → Pali at University of Calcutta, thus bringing about revival of study in India of canonical scriptures of → Theravāda Buddhism. Other Indian universities also have, since then, joined in revival of Pali studies. The M.S. has branches at Gaya, Sarnath, New Delhi, Lucknow, Bombay, Madras, Nautanwa and Ajmer; it publ. journal in English, *The Maha Bodhi*, which circulates not only in Asian but also in a number of West. countries. T.O.L.

D. Valisinha, 'The Revival of Buddhism: The Maha Bodhi Society', in P. V. Bapat (ed.), *2,500 years of Buddhism* (1956, repr. 1959).

Mahābodhi-Vamsa Pali Buddh. work, 'the great bodhi-tree chronicle', which tells story of sacred bodhi tree under which the Buddha gained enlightenment. The intro. carries story back to time of a former Buddha Dipankara (→ Buddhas, other than Gotama), and continues narrative to incl. the transplanting of a cutting from the Indian tree at Anuradhapura in Ceylon. The work, which is in prose, is attr. to Upatissa, who composed it from older sources prob. during 1st half of 11th cent. The text was edited by S. A. Strong, and published by the Pali Text Society of London in 1891. T.O.L.

Mahākassapa Thera One of most prominent of disciples of the Buddha, concerning whom there are many refs. in the canonical scriptures. He was highly esteemed by Buddha for his equanimity and ability as teacher and preacher. He is said to have lived to a great age. T.O.L.

Mahāpadāna-Sutta A *sutta* found in the *D.N.* of the Pali canon, which gives details of the 7 Buddhas up to and incl. Gautama. (→ Buddhas other than Gotama). In this *Sutta* a conventional scheme is adopted, whereby details of each of these Buddhas are given under eleven headings: the *Kappa*, or period of world-history in which born; social rank; family or clan; length of life; tree under which Enlightenment was attained; two chief disciples; numbers of → *arahants* present at assemblies held by the Buddha in question; name of personal attendant; name of father; name of mother; birthplace. T.O.L.

Sacred Books of the Buddhists, vol. 2, T. W. and C. A. F. Rhys Davids (trs.), *Dialogues of the Buddha*, part 2, 5th edn. (1966), pp. 1–41.

Mahā-Parinibbāna Sutta Book of Buddh. Pali canon which relates events of last year of the Buddha's life, his death, cremation and distribution of his relics. It is found in the → *Dīgha Nikaya* of the → Sutta Pitaka, and is one of longest of suttas. Much material contained in this sutta occurs elsewhere in Pali Canon with only slight differences; acc. to Rhys Davids as much as two-thirds of *Sutta* can be so identified. The parallel passages are in gen. in books which are the oldest in canon. T.O.L.

T. W. Rhys Davids, *Buddhist India* (1903), ch. 10.

Mahāsanghikas One of the major divisions of early Buddhism, dating from 4th cent. BC (→ Councils, Buddh.; Schools of thought, Buddh.). T.O.L.

Mahāsatipatthāna Sutta An import. constituent of Buddh. Pali canon of scripture. The *Sutta* consists of discourse said to have been addressed by the Buddha to monks of Kammāssadamma on subject of the bases of Mindfulness (*Sati-patthāna*), by means of which → nibbāna was to be gained, and on the → 4 Holy Truths. It is gen. considered one of most import. suttas, has been much trans., and the subject of numerous commentaries. The recital of it is held to partic. auspicious; espec. at time of death, whether it is recited by the dying or heard by him. It is found in the → *Dīgha Nikāya*; also in two separate parts, as the *Satipatthāna Sutta* and *Saccavibhanga Sutta* (the latter dealing with the 4 Holy Truths) in the → *Majjhima-Nikāya*. T.O.L.

Mahāvamsa One of Pali chronicles (*vaṃsa*), the Great (*Mahā*) Chronicle sets out hist. of Buddhism in India to time of its intro. into → Ceylon, and subsequent hist. in Ceylon to time of King Mahāsena (poss. 4th cent. CE). The author of M. is gen. held to be Mahānāma, writer of 6th cent. CE. The M. covers much the same grounds as the → Dīpavamsa, and is prob. based on same earlier source; the M. differs from the Dīpavamsa in that it adds certain amount of new material and is in form of epic poem. It has been described as a 'coherent, refined and enlarged version' of Dīpavamsa. The → Culavamsa forms a supplement and continuation of the M. Like the Dīpavamsa, the M. is valuable source of evidence for hist. of early Buddhism in India and Ceylon. It has been trans. into Eng. by W. Geiger, as *The Mahavamsa, or The Great Chronicle of Ceylon* (1912, repr. 1964). T.O.L.

Mahāvastu Title of import. Buddh. work in Skt. (lit. 'The Great Subject' or 'Great Event'). The work forms part of the → Vinaya-Pitaka of the Lokottaravādin school of the → Mahāsanghikas. The M. consists principally of a biography of the Buddha, told acc. to view of the Lokuttaravādins that Buddhas are 'exalted above the world' (*lokuttara*) and that they only, conventionally and outwardly, conform to this-wordly existence. This is a view which repr. a transitional stage towards that of fully developed → Mahāyāna. The narrative of the M. is interspersed with much material of the → *Jātaka/Avadāna* type, amounting to half the total work; it is thus, acc. to Winternitz, 'especially valuable as a treasure trove of Jātakas'. The date of orig. composition of the M. is difficult to determine; the trend towards Mahāyāna ideas may suggest the very early Christ. period; there are also refs. to the Huns and to Chinese language which suggest date about 4th cent. CE for its final form, although nucleus is prob. older, perhaps as early as 2nd cent. BC. T.O.L.

M. Winternitz, *Hist. of Indian Literature* (1933), vol. 2, pp. 239–47; J. J. Jones (tr.), *Mahavastu*, vol. I (1949), vol. 2 (1952), vol. 3 (1956).

Mahāvīra The 'great hero' (meaning of name), who was re-founder and reformer of → Jainism, and 24th → Tirthamkara, being immediate successor of → Parsva. His personal name was Vardhamāna. Born about 550 BC, he was contemporary of → Buddha and likewise of → *ksatriya* stock; his life acc. to trad. accounts had a not dissimilar pattern to that of Buddha. At age of 30 he left his wife and daughter to become wandering ascetic; and assoc. for time with Makkhali Gosala, the chief founder of the → Ajivikas. After 13 years of austerity and contemplation he gained *kevala* or omniscience, and was accorded the title of *Jina* or 'victor' (from which the terms Jain, Jaina and Jainism are derived). He organised following among those who had allegiance to Jain trad. going back to Parsva, and spent rest of life preaching law and instructing disciples. He died at age of 72, of self-starvation, near Rājagṛha, in Bihar. As Tirthamkara, M. is venerated, but the Jain doc. of → liberation is such that the life-monad (→ *jiva*) at final → nirvāna ascends to summit of cosmos, to remain there changeless and blissful, and unable to enter into transactions with rest of world. Thus there is no questions of communion with, or prayer to, the Tirthamkaras. N.S.

C. Della Casa, *Il Giainismo* (1962); Margaret S. Stevenson, *The Heart of Jainism* (1915); H. Zimmer, *Philosophies of India* (1956).

Mahāyāna One of main distinctive trads. or schools of Buddhism; lit. means 'great' (*mahā*), 'means of salvation' (*yāna*). Various other yānas were distinguished, such as the Śravaka-yana, the →→ Vajrayāna or Mantrayāna; but the school from which the M. was primarily distinguished was the whole of the older, more conservative wing, consisting of at least 18 separate sects, such as the → Theravādins, the → Sarvāstivādins etc. which collectively was described by adherents of the newer way as → '*Hīnayāna*' or 'small' means of salvation. What was meant by the comparison was that Hīnayāna schools set forth a way of reaching salvation that had only limited appeal; it was not universalist in intention or scope, as the M. claimed to be. The date of emergence of M. is difficult to determine, but was somewhere within period 1st cent. BC–1st cent. CE. Its universalist emphasis was reflected in greater place given to virtue of compassion than had been the case in the Hīnayāna school, which was characterised by its emphasis on wisdom. The M. emphasised both equally. Another characteristic feature of M. was much greater place it gave to the → *Bodhisattva*, as the ideal or goal of human life, towards which all men could and should strive. In acc. with more open, universalist character of M., there was from beginning a readiness to engage wholeheartedly in intellectual debates of the time and to use the *lingua franca* of contemporary Indian intellectual class (mainly Brāhmans), viz. → Sanskrit. This took form, however, of a Sanskritised version of language used by Buddhists (Prākrit) (→ *Pāli*), a version which has come to be known by mod. linguists as 'hybrid Sanskrit' or 'Buddh. Sanskrit' (although it is not exclusively Buddh., but a stage in evolution of Indian language). The universalist intention had also effect of rendering M. more flexible, and more ready to incorporate new features of belief and practice, some of which were derived from popular indigenous relig.; others may have reflected the strongly Graeco-Roman influence in N.W. India, where M. developed, such, e.g. as concept of Divine Wisdom or Transcendental Wisdom, *Prajñā-pāramitā*, thought of as a feminine principle, and given popular currency in notion of Prajñā-pāramitā as 'mother' of Buddha, i.e. the eternal Buddha. The M. developed also, as its central philosophy, the doc. of *Śūñyatā*, or 'voidness'. The philosophical school in which this doc. was developed notably by → Nagarjuna (2nd cent. CE) was known as → *Mādhyamika*. In course of develop. of Buddh. thought, this was followed by → Yogācāra school, founded by → Asanga and → Vasubandhu (4th cent. CE). The Yogācāra docs. and practices paved way for a yet greater assimilation of M. to popular Indian relig.; this was last phase of the M. and is usually known as Mantra-yāna or → Vajra-yāna, a form which appears from 8th cent. CE onwards; in a sense this was a new 'yāna', but it is also the ultimate Buddh. product of the M. school. Known also as Tantric Bhm., it had a counterpart in → Tantric Hinduism, into which the Buddh. form eventually, *c.* 12th CE, disappeared. M. however, by reason of its universalist outlook and missionary spirit, had by this time spread into China, Korea and Japan, there developing yet further new forms in the 'Pure Land' or Amida Buddhism, and in Ch'an or Zen. (→ Buddhism in China). T.O.L.

E. Conze, *Buddhist Thought in India* (1962); T. R. V. Murti, *The Central Philosophy of Buddhism* (1955); W. M. McGovern *An Introduction to Mahāyāna Buddhism* (1922).

-Mahdī (The Guided One). The 12th → imām of the Shi'a, Muḥammad al-Muntaẓar is held to have disappeared *c.* 264/878, and to be in occlusion till he returns to revive → Islām and conquer world. This will be followed by period of prosperity till last day comes. The → Isma'ilis hold that Isma'il, son of sixth imam will return as the M. → Sunnis also have a vague belief in the M., but do not emphasise the doc. so much as the Shi'is. Trads. say he will be of → Muḥammad's family, that he will estab. Islam and reign for seven years or more. But gen. Sunnis think of → Jesus as making Islam triumphant before end of world. There is some confusion about roles of Jesus and the M. One trad. attempts to solve this by declaring that there is no M. but Jesus (cf. H. Walter, *The Ahmadiya Movement* (1918), p. 38). There have been claimants to office from time to time. 'Ubaydallah, founder of the → Fatimid dynasty, made such a claim, as did also Ibn → Tūmart, and in more mod. times the M. of the Sudan is the best known. J.R.

E.I., III, pp. 111ff.; Pareja, index; Trimingham, *Ethiopia*, index, *Sudan*, pp. 148ff.; P. M. Holt, *A modern history of the Sudan* (1961), *passim*; F. Rosenthal, *Ibn Khaldun*, index.

Mahinda Buddh. monk of 3rd cent. BC, gen. held to be son of emperor → Ashoka, and leader of Buddh. expedition to → Ceylon which resulted in conversion to Buddh. faith of island's king, Devānam-piya Tissa, and many of people of Ceylon. M. ordained many monks and lived to see the → Sangha firmly estab. in Ceylon. He died at age of 60; at cremation of his body the highest honours were paid to it. A *cetiya* was erected over his remains. His name is still highly esteemed in Ceylon. T.O.L.

W. Geiger (ed.), *Mahāvamsa* (1908, repr. 1958) chs. 12–20, trsl. *Great Chronicle of Ceylon* (1912, repr. 1964).

Maḥmal (Maḥmil). Covered litter carried by tall camel at time of → Pilgrimage, said to have been sent from Cairo since 7th/13th cent. Litters were sent from different centres. Adorned outside, many have held copies of Qur. inside. The litter was a claim to sovereignty. It is a mistake to think that the litter carried covering for the → Ka'ba, although this has often been stated as a fact. After the → Wahhabis gained the Hijaz in 1344/1925, difficulties arose, so practice of sending a M. has ceased. It used to be taken to → 'Arafat during Pilgrimage ceremonies, where places were set apart for different Ms. On return home, the camel was freed from further work. J.R.

E.I., III, pp. 123f.; Pareja, index; Hughes, pp. 306f.; Lane, *Egyptians*, index.

Maitreya (Buddha) → Metteya. T.O.L.

Maitreya-Natha → *Asanga.* T.O.L.

Majjhima Nikāya The *nikāya* (collection, or assembly) of Buddh. Suttas of middle-length (*majjhima*); one of the five *Nikāyas* of the → Sutta Pitaka of Pali Buddh. canonical scriptures, or → Tipitaka. The M.N. comprises 152 suttas in all, arranged in 3 gps. of approx 50 each. Acc. to Pali trad., the transmission of the M.N. suttas was entrusted to an Elder named → Sariputta at 1st Buddh. Council, held immed. after the death of Buddha (→ Councils, Buddh.). The commentary by → Buddhaghosa on the M.N. is entitled Papañca-Sūdanī. The M.N. has been trans. into Eng. by J. B. Horner as *Middle Length Sayings*, 3 vols. (1954–9). T.O.L.

Makkhalī-Gosāla Relig. teacher of anc. India contemporary with the Buddha, and mentioned in Buddh. scriptures (D.N., i, 53). He denied that men had moral responsibility for their actions, and affirmed that men's lives were determined by fate and by their social position and psychological make-up. He is mentioned as one of six teachers of what were, acc. to the Buddha, false doctrines; of these M.'s views are regarded as the most dangerous. His followers were known as the → Ājivakas. T.O.L.

Mālik Name of angel in charge of hell, mentioned in Qur. xliii:77. Those who are sent to hell cry to him wishing that God may make an end of them, and he tells them to stay. Here the word used is Jahannam (→ Hell). lxxiv:27f. speaks of Saqar (→ Hell) over which there are 19 guardians. xl:52 speaks of the guardians of Jahannam. But Mālik is commonly considered to be chief guardian. J.R.

Mishkāt, pp. 966, 1214, 1223, 1270; Hughes, p. 312; Masson, *Coran*, p. 932.

Mālik b. Anas (*c.* 97–179/*c.* 715–95). Belonged to Medina and was first to draw up a law book (*al-Muwaṭṭa'*). It is to some extent based on trads. trace to → Muḥammad; but most trads. are not traced right back, and often M. expresses his own opinion, doubtless based on Medina practice. His followers developed his work, so he was looked on as founder of school called after him (→ Muslim Law, schools of). His pupil Ibn al-Qāsim (132–191/719–806), who studied with him for 20 years is the one through whom M.'s teaching is handed down. His pupil Saḥnūn (160–240/776–854) produced *al-Mudawwana* on the teachings of *al-Muwaṭṭa'*, giving his queries to Ibn al-Qasim with his reply. This is an import. work on Mālikī doc. produced in N. Africa. The Maliki school spread westwards and became predominant in Spain and N. Africa. The theology normally follows → Ash'arite doc. When the → Wahhabis took Medina, they demolished the dome over M.'s tomb along with others. J.R.

E.I., III, pp. 205–9; Hughes, p. 312; Pareja, index (correct Abas to Anas); D. B. Macdonald, *Theology*, index; Wensinck, *Creed*, index; Coulson, *Law*, index; Schacht, *Jurisprudence*, index; Rutter, *Holy Cities*, II, p. 257.

Mammon *Ex.* → Aramaic word for 'riches', prob. derived from Semitic root *'mn*, 'to be firm, reliable'. Since M. in Mt. 6:24 and Lk. 16:13 seems to be personified, the idea developed in Chr. trad. that M. was a Canaanite god of riches; but there is no evidence for it. S.G.F.B.

H.D.B., *s.v.; E.R.E.*, VIII, *s.v.*

Man, Doctrine of All religs. are based on some estimate of human nature and destiny. The burial practices of Paleolithic Man indicate that an evaluation of human nature was already current that envisaged some form of survival of physical death. The earliest literate societies (Egypt and Sumer) believed that a human being was more than a body. Both regarded man as a psycho-physical organism, though they differed in their views of his *post-mortem* destiny (→ Eschatology). Ideas of man among the religs. fall gen. into two categories: (1) of man as a psycho-physical organism, the unity of which → death shatters. Some believe that this situation can be reversed either by ritual-magic (Egypt), or by divine action (i.e. → resurrection), as e.g. in →→ Judaism; Christianity; Islam; Zoroastrianism (2) of man as subject to → metempsychosis, whereby his soul or real self passes through successive → incarnations (e.g. in →→ Hinduism; Buddhism; Orphism; Gnosticism). Metempsychosis is gen. seen as punishment, from which → salvation is sought. Most religs. seek to explain the existent human situation, usually regarded as bad, and the reason of man's life, in terms of a divine or supernatural purpose. (→→ Atman; Ba; Ka; Nephesh; Psyche; Soul). S.G.F.B.

Brandon, *Man and his Destiny in the Great Religions* (1962), bibliographies; C. J. Bleeker (ed.), *Anthropologie religieuse* (1955); *The Intellectual Adventure of Anc. Man*, ed. H. and H. A. Frankfort (1948).

Man (Buddh. view) →→ Anatta; Khandha. T.O.L.

(Chinese view) The problem of human nature (*hsing*), and its relation to morality, was one of major concerns of post-Confucian philosophy. → Confucius' own teachings imply orig. goodness of human nature, as conferred on many by Heaven. → Mo-tzŭ believed that human nature is like pure silk, its goodness and evil being entirely dependent upon what it is 'dyed' with. This idea that man's nature is in itself neither good nor evil was held by Kao-tzŭ, a contemporary of → Mencius. Shih Shīh (*c.* 4th cent. BC) affirmed that human nature is partly good, partly evil. Mencius is famous for his teaching that human nature is orig. good. He was violently opposed by → Hsün-tzŭ who, influenced by Taoist theories that man's nature is result of natural processes of cosmic evolution, insisted that human nature is evil. The → Yin-Yang School developed a dualistic approach to problem of human nature, man being compounded of elemental forces of *Yin* and *Yang*. During Han Dynasty, and largely under influence of Tung Chung-shu (*c.* 179–104 BC), 'nature' was attr. to *yang* and 'feelings' to *yin*.

On the whole, → Buddhism in China was dominated by concept of the Buddha-nature which is univ. and primordially inherent in all living beings, including man.

Orthodox Confucian teaching concerning nature of man finds most complete formulation in works of → Chu Hsi (12th cent. CE). He taught that man's capacity to speak, move, think and act is entirely product of Ether (*ch'i*), within which Principle (*Li*) adheres. This Principle, contained within the Ether, forms the individual human being and is known as his 'nature' (*Hsing*). The expression of Eternal Principle in love, righteousness, propriety, wisdom and sincerity, revealed that human nature is orig. and univ. good; but the mind of man, acted upon by external influences, loses its purity, giving rise to feelings which may be good or bad. But, while the nature of man is wholly good, the feelings may be perverted. D.H.S.

Fung Yu-lan, *Hist. of Chinese Philos.*, 2 vols. (1937, 1953), *passim*; W. T. Chan, *Source Book in Chinese Philos.* (1963), *passim;* J. P. Bruce (tr.), *The Philosophy of Human Nature by Chu Hsi* (1922); C. B. Day, *The Philosophers of China* (1962), *passim*; H. O. H. Stange, in C. J. Bleeker (ed.), *Anthropologie religieuse* (1955).

(Islamic doc.) In pre-Islamic Arabia, perhaps because of hardships of desert life, there was a prevailing fatalism which has had tendency to survive at times within Islam. The Qur. gives no clear guidance on this, for one can choose vv. to prove man is a puppet in God's hands, and others to prove he has → freewill. The Qur. teaches that man is created by God, the details of his procreation being described (lxxv:37f.; xxii:5; xxiii:14). In comparison with God, man is weak (iv:32) and ignorant (xx:109). Nevertheless he has import. position, for God has placed him on earth as his representative (*khalīfa*) (ii:28; vi:165), created him to serve him (li:50) and provided for his needs, making nature subservient to him (xiv:37). God appeals to man by rational arguments to serve him, drawing attention to regularity of natural laws (xiii:3f.; xxxi:27ff.); but man does not always take heed. He is un-ungrateful (c:6; xliii:14), and unbelieving (xxxvii: 12ff.; vii:144). Man's life on earth is temporary (lv:26), but he has to give account of himself after death and receive reward or punishment acc. to verdict (→→ Hell; Paradise; Judgment of the dead). The Qur. speaks both of man's lowly position in relation to God and of high position God has prepared for him in this world and next, if he does God's will. At same time there are vv. suggesting that man's final destiny is dependent on God's arbitrary choice (cf. ii:99; xvi:39, 95).

The → trads. on the whole teach determinism; but on other hand they are so full of instructions on all kinds of matters as to how man should act, speaking of due rewards and punishments acc. to what one does, that they virtually assume that man has freedom to act. Among theologians the doc. that God is altogether different from man is general; but among the → Ṣūfīs the desire for union with God and the almost pantheistic view of some of them run counter to the more gen. accepted doc. It may be said that formally Islam has no real doc. of man, theologians being more concerned with God. One is left to gather from scattered sources prevailing views of man's position and significance. Among the common people there is tendency to fatalism, with the feeling that they are in God's hands, and they must say *al-ḥamdu lillāh*—'Praise be to God' (→ *Ḥamdalah*) whatever happens. Whether good fortune or ill, everything is *min Allah* (from God). At same time they can be as active as anyone in trying to further their interests, though conscious all the while that they can succeed only if God wills it. Among educated classes there is stronger sense of man's ability to act on his own initiative. They believe practically in free-will, and so insist that man can prosper by his efforts. This type of argument has also been put forward by some relig. leaders (→ Rashīd Riḍā). The → Ahmadiyya Movement teaches man's high position as 'the axis or centre of the created universe', which God has created for man's service. Man is to serve as a manifestation of God's attributes. If he fails to do so he suffers; but God is not injured. Man has free choice which makes poss. the attainment of nearness to God. (→→ Prayers for dead; Women, status). J.R.

Nicholson, *Studies*, index II; Wensinck, *Creed, passim*; 'Alī, *Qur'ān*, index; Bashir al-Din, *Intro. to . . . the Holy Quran* (1949), pp. 421ff.; S. G. F. Brandon, *Man and his destiny in the great religions* (1962), ch. VII; F. Rosenthal, *Ibn Khaldun*, index; H. B. Smith, 'The Muslim doctrine of man', *M.W.*, XLIV (1954), pp. 202ff.; J. Macdonald, *Eschatology*, vol. III (1964), pp. 291ff.

(Jap. view) → Shinto regards M. as both, divine and earthly. He is *ame-no-masu-hito*' ('sacred human being increasing infinity'), i.e. a being who, living under blessing of the → *kami*, is destined to prosper in happiness. But he is also described as *ao-hito-gusa* ('green-grass man'), which stresses his earthly nature. His special endowments of tendencies and capacities are received from the *kami*, through direct descent through ancestors. Being a part of divine nature, if man permits his innate disposition to find normal expression, he will spontaneously achieve filial piety, loyalty and love for his fellow man. Jap. concepts of the N. of M. were greatly influenced by → Confucian and → Buddh. teachings, which derived from China. D.H.S.

J. Herbert, *Shinto* (1967), p. 59.

Mana → Melanesian Relig. E.J.S.

Manār Party → Rashīd Riḍā. J.R.

Manāt May be connected with the god of fate, Mᵉni (cf. Isaiah, lxv:11). In pre-Islamic worship M. was female. Her main sanctuary was a black stone on road from Mecca to Medina. Some Medina nobles are said to have had wooden idols of M. in their houses. For condemnation of worship of M. and other two goddesses see Qur., liii, 19f. J.R.

E.I., III, p. 231; *Mishkāt*, p. 1163; Wellhausen, *Reste*, pp. 25ff.

Mandaeans A → Gnostic sect, sometimes known as 'Nasoreans' or 'Christians of St. John', which orig. in E. Jordan in 1st or 2nd cent. CE, and now survives south of Baghdad. Acc. to M. doctrine, man's soul will finally be delivered from imprisonment in body and demonic assault by a redeemer *Manda da Hayyê*, the personification of 'Knowledge of Life', who had conquered the evil powers when on earth. This redeemer seems to reflect some knowledge of Jesus Christ, although the M. are hostile to Christianity. Their chief scripture is the *Ginza* (*c.* 7th or 8th cent.). Since M. practise frequent → baptism and make much of → John the Baptist, their descent from his disciples has been assumed. The problem of their origin remains obscure, despite much specialist discussion. Mandaism and → Manichaeism appear to have been mutually affective. (→→ Harranian Relig.; Sābians). S.G.F.B.

E.R.E., VIII, *s.v.; R.G.G.*, IV, col. 709–72; E. S. Drower, *The Mandaeans in Iraq and Iran* (1937); H. Ch. Puech in *H.G.R.*, III, pp. 67–83, 444–6; *R.A.C.*, I, col. 1169–72; G. Widengren, *Mani and Manichaeism* (E.T. 1965), pp. 15ff.; E. Segelberg, *Maṣbūtā* (1958); K. Rudolph, *Die Mandäer*, 2 vols. (1960–1), *Theogonie, Kosmogonie u. Anthropologie in den mandäischen Schriften* (1965); E. M. Yamauchi, 'Present State of Mandaean Studies', *J.N.E.S.* 26 (1966).

Manes Lat. 'spirits of the dead', prob. derived euphemistically from *manus*, 'good'. The dead were orig. thought of as an undifferentiated mass with a collective divinity, hence called *Di Manes.* It became custom from early Empire to end grave inscriptions with formula: *Dis Manibus Sacrum*, 'sacred to the divine spirits of the dead'. S.G.F.B.

O.C.D., *s.v.;* F. Cumont, *After Life in Roman Paganism* (repr. 1959), pp. 60ff.

Manichaeism A relig., basically dualistic, founded by Mani (*c.* CE 215–75), a native of Seleucia-Ctesiphon, who taught mainly in Persian Empire and was executed (flayed alive) by Sassanian king Bahram I. Mani's system, documented by MSS. found in Egypt and Chinese Turkestan (thus attesting diffusion of M.), was gen. syncretistic, but derived basically from Zoroastrian dualism of cosmic conflict of Light and Darkness. This → dualism was reflected in Gnostic-type doc. of Man, which explained misery of human situation as due to primaeval mishap whereby particles of Light became imprisoned in material bodies. Mani saw himself as successor of →→ Buddha, Zoroaster, and Jesus, sent to save men by revealing esoteric truths necessary to salvation. M. was extremely ascetic in practice, esp. in regard to sex and food (vegetarianism). M. was a missionary faith and spread rapidly east and west; it both competed with and influenced Christianity: → Augustine of Hippo was orig. converted to M., and M. influence has been discerned in →→ Albigenses, Bogomiles, Cathari. (→→ Gnosticism; Mandaeans; Marcion). S.G.F.B.

H. and C. Puech, *Manichéisme* (1949), in *H.G.R.*, III, pp. 88ff.; *E.R.E.*, VIII, *s.v.; R.G.G.*, IV³, col. 714–22; A. Adam, *Texte zum Manichäismus* (1954); G. Widengren, *Mani and Manichaeism* (E.T. 1961); S. Runciman, *The Medieval Manichee* (1955); L. J. R. Ort, *Mani* (1967).

(in China) The first M. pilgrim came to China in CE 694. M. is first mentioned in Chi. lit. in memoires of → Hsüan-tsang. During T'ang Dynasty, M. flourished particularly among the Uighurs in China, and many temples were built. M. monasteries existed at Yangchou, T'ai Yüan, Honan-fu and Hsian. By imperial decree, M. property was confiscated in CE 843 and temples closed; but the faith continued until end of Ming Dynasty, partic. in Fukien Province. Import. M. works were discovered early in 20th cent. at → Tun Huang. (→ Manichaeism). D.H.S.

D. H. Smith, *Chinese Religions* (1968), pp. 149ff.; S. Couling, *Encycl. Sinica* (1917, 1965), pp. 325–6.

Mañjuśrī One of the two most prominent → Bodhisattvas in Mhy. Buddh. belief, the other being → Avalokitesvara, who personifies compassion; M. personifies *prajñā* wisdom. He is not mentioned in Pali canon, nor in earliest Skt. works; he appears prominently in the → *Lankāvatāra Sūtra*, as one of the two main questioners of the Buddha. He is regarded as principal Bodhisattva in the → *Lotus Sūtra*, where the Bodhisattva → Maitreya is repr. as seeking instruction from him. Buddh. iconography repr. him as having in his hands the sword of knowledge and a book, symbolising his wisdom. He became an import. figure in the Bhm. of China, Japan, Tibet, Nepal and Java. Just as the Dalai Lama is regarded in → Tibet as an incarnation of Avalokitesvara, so outstandingly wise rulers have been regarded as incarnations of M. T.O.L.

Mantra A verse, considered sacred, from the → Veda (or more gen. any sacred formula). The most famous M. is the → *Gayatri.* In → Brahmanical Hinduism it has been thought that the M.'s penetrate to nature of the entities which they concern, and so bring control of them. The most basic form of M. has been thought to be the 'seed-formula' or *bīja-mantra*, consisting of one syllable—the most famous and efficacious being the syllable → *Om* (or *Aum*). An esoteric interpr. of the M.'s was characteristic of → Tantrism. In theory, only the disciple can learn true meaning of a sacred formula from mouth of teacher. N.S.

Mantrayāna A later form of Mahāyāna Buddhism, characterised by use of *mantras*, or chants, as a method (*yāna*) of gaining enlightenment. (→ Vajrayāna). T.O.L.

Manu The progenitor of the human race, acc. to Hindu mythology. Each age (→ Time, Hindu views of) has its own M., in a sequence of fourteen, the present one being the seventh, Manu Vaivasvata. M. is hero of a flood story which may have Semitic origins. → Viṣṇu, in his incarnation as fish, warns M. to prepare a great boat, to hold the seven → rishis, animals and plants. The fish, growing to enormous size, ultimately guides the boat to safety when the great flood begins to subside. M. is also supposed to have been given the Vedas, to instruct men; and is credited with origin of Hindu law (→ *dharma*), the most famous of the law books being named after him. N.S.

Maori Religion New Zealand forms the southernmost extremity of Polynesia, and the pre-Christ.

relig. (now extinct) of the indigenous peoples of N.Z. is normally treated as an intrinsic part of → Polynesian Religion. In fact M. relig. shared most of basic presuppositions of P. relig. concerning the sacred, the gods, the spirits, and their interrelations with world of men. Thus, to take only one example, the M. belief in spirits (*atua*), involved belief in a hierarchy of supernaturals, from the great gods of the sky (Io, Rangi), down to the purely local *atua* investing natural phenomena and the powerful *atua* of the departed. The spirit of man was called *atua pore pore* (little spirit. But *atua* could also denote anything falling within sphere of the sacred (cf. use of Sioux word *wakan* in → North American Indian Relig.). Closely assoc. with this was the concept of → *tabu*, or unapproachability—a further common feature of Poly. relig. Nor do M. cultic practices, or their beliefs on subject of nature and destiny of man, differ fundamentally from those once current in rest of Polynesia. Thus, for instance, while the spirits of chiefs and other powerful persons were considered to pass on death into the heavens, the spirits of common people were believed to pass, *via* the north cape of N.Z., into a region called *Te Reinga*, and thence into the various levels of *Po*, the abode of the dead. On the way the spirit had to cross a river, *Wai-ora-tane* ('living water for man'); in cases of recovery from severe illness, the individual's spirit (or free-soul) was thought to have been turned back at river (→ Styx).

Where M. relig. differs most strikingly from Poly. relig. is in richness and scope of its mythology. Best has shown that this mythology prob. existed in two forms: an esoteric, centred on cult of the → High God Io, and restricted to privileged individuals; an exoteric, known to all. Best suggests, further, that common people had in many cases not even heard the name of Io. The myth of Io tells how the self-existent sky-god Io expressed his intention to pervade all space, and then brought into existence light, the heavens (Rangi) and the earth (Papa). Io himself is without images, without an active cult (though not a → *deus otiosus*), and no myths are told concerning his origin; he dwells in uppermost of twelve heavens, and is source of all being, all life and esp. the energy of human procreation. In the 'lower' cycle of myth, interest is centred on the sky-father (Rangi) and the earth-mother (Papa), who were orig. joined together in a perpetual embrace, but were finally separated by their offspring, among them Tane Mahuta (god of forests), Tangaroa (god of ocean) and Tumatanenga (god of mankind). Creation is then described genealogically. In this version the emergence of gods of night precedes that of gods of day; here, too, there is much speculative depth: 'The word became fruitful; it dwelt with the feeble glimmering; it brought forth night: the great night, the long night, the lowest night, the loftiest night, the thick night, to be felt, the night to be touched, the night unseen, the night following on, the night ending in death. . . .' The elaborate mythology of M. relig. forms a superstructure unparalleled, so far as is known, in the religs. of pre-literate peoples. The complex substructure is, however, still essentially that of Polynesia. E.J.S.

R. Taylor, *Te Ika a Maui; or, New Zealand and its Inhabitants* (1870); E. Best, *The Maori* (Memoirs of the Polynesian Society, V, 1924), I–II; R. Pettazzoni, 'Io and Rangi', in *Essays on the History of Religions* (1954), pp. 37–42; C. R. H. Taylor, *A Pacific Bibliography*[2] (1965), esp. pp. 216–21.

Māra (in Buddh. Thought) Māra, the Evil One, is ref. to many times in Buddh. scriptures. (For comprehensive account of refs. in → Pali canon, cf. T. O. Ling, *Buddhism and the Mythology of Evil* (1962), pp. 96–163). Like the → Devil in W. relig. thought, M. is regarded as a demonic being who is arch-enemy of all who seek to live the holy life. Acc. to Buddh. trad., he sought to deflect the Buddha from attaining of enlightenment: the contest between M. and Buddha is ref. to only briefly in Pali texts, but is described in elaborate detail in the Skt. → *Lalita Vistara.* Here, as in subseq. encounters, M. is shown as entirely powerless to influence Buddha in any way; he retires discomforted and dejected (*Sutta Nipāta* 425–49). M. makes appearance again from time to time in course of Buddha's ministry, sometimes assuming human or animal forms as disguise; but always with same complete inability to effect any evil purpose against Buddha, who always sees through the disguise and recognises his adversary. M. is repr. as seeking espec. to disturb Buddha and Buddh. monks and nuns when they are engaged in meditation. A collection of stories about M., found in Pali Canon, is the *Māra-Samyutta* of → *Samyutta-Nikaya.* Another notable appearance of M. occurs in the → *Mahāparinibbāna Sutta*, where he seeks to persuade Buddha that it is time for him to leave this mortal existence and enter *pari-nibbāna*, on ground that he had promised to do so once his preaching of the → Dharma had been successful and his relig. estab. among men, and that these conditions had now been fulfilled. Buddha on this occasion, agrees with M., and declares that in 3 months he will indeed pass into *pari-nibbāna*.

In Indian relig. this concept of an Evil One is peculiar to Buddhism. The figure of M. has features which link it with popular beliefs in demons; but M. is also a being whose nature combines those forces which militate against the holy life, espec. the morally unwholesome quality of greed, hatred and delusion. The name M. means lit. 'the killer' or 'the death-agent'; it indic. by its negative form that the Buddh. emphasis is by contrast a positive one, viz., attainment of life, at a level which Māra cannot reach. In Buddh. → cosmology M. is regarded as dominating lowest of the 3 planes of existence, i.e. the → *kāma* or sensual world. At a more advanced and sophisticated stage of understanding the figure of M. is seen to be but a name for everything that is impermanent (→ *anicca*), evil (→ *dukkha*), and impersonal (→ *anatta*). The role of belief in M. in Buddh. hist. appears to have been to provide transition from popular notions of discarnate evil demons, to the more abstract analysis of the human situation in moral-psychological terms, and a helpful way of understanding resistance to the holy life which a man might experience, but which he is assured can be overcome by following the Buddh. way. T.O.L.

E. Windisch, *Māra und Buddha* (1895); J. Masson, *La religion populaire dans le Canon Bouddhique-Pali* (1942); T. O. Ling (*op. cit.*).

Marabout From *murābiṭ*, literally member of a monastery (*ribāṭ*), or hospice (→ Almoravids). M. is used esp. in N. Africa. M.'s are treated as saints with power to impart blessing (*baraka*). They are consulted on all subjects. Even Barbary corsairs consulted them about most favourable time for a pirate expedition (cf. S. Lane-Poole, *The Barbary Corsairs* (1890), p. 222). But credit must be given to many of the M.'s for taking their share in spread of → Islām in W. Africa. J.R.

Pareja, index; T. H. Weir, *The Shaikhs of Morocco in the XVIth Century* (1904).

Marcion Chr. heretic, native of Sinope in Pontus, who d. *c.* 160. M.'s writings are lost, but it is evident from attacks made on him by many orthodox writers (e.g. → Irenaeus, Tertullian) that his teaching was widely influential. Acc. to M., Christianity is essentially a Gospel of Love, not of Law. He regarded → Paul as alone among → Apostles in understanding true nature of Christianity by his denunciation of Jew. Law. M. rejected O.T., which he saw as revelation of a cruel → Demiurge, wholly different from God of Jesus. Of N.T. writings, M. accepted only 10 Epistles of Paul and an edited version of Gosp. of → Luke; his use of Scriptures influenced formation of orthodox → canon. M.'s → Christology was → Docetic; he attr. Crucifixion to God of O.T. Orthodox reaction was strong; by end of 3rd cent. most Marcionite communities were absorbed into → Manichaeism. S.G.F.B.

A. Harnack, *Marcion* (1921); E. C. Blackman, *Marcion and his Influence* (1948); J. Knox, *Marcion and the New Test.* (1942); *D.C.C.*, *s.v.;* *E.R.E.*, VIII, pp. 407–9; *R.G.G.*[3], IV, col. 740–2; H. Frhr. Von Campenhausen, 'Marcion et les origines du Canon néotestamentaire', *R.H.P.R.*, 46 (1966).

Marcus Aurelius Antoninus (121–80) Roman emperor from 161, notable in hist. of relig. for his *Meditations*, written in Grk., in which he evaluates his experience of life in terms of → Stoicism. The work, not intended for publication, affords invaluable insight into a mind fundamentally sincere and noble, as it struggles with intimations of relig. faith and conclusions of reason. M. was, ironically, led to persecute Christianity as dangerous to well-being of Roman society. S.G.F.B.

The Meditations, ed. and trans. C. R. Haines (Loeb Class. Library, 1930); *E.R.E.*, VIII, *s.v.;* P. B. Watson, *Marcus Aurelius Antoninus* (1884); *O.C.D.*, pp. 124–5; A. S. L. Farquharson, *Marcus Aurelius: his Life and World* (1952[2]).

Marduk Patron-god of → Babylon. M. had no place in orig. Sumerian pantheon, but Babylon's later political hegemony led to his exaltation. The → *Enuma elish* was designed to show how M., repr. as son of → Ea, was accepted by other gods as their lord and how they built for him his great temple of E-sag-il at Babylon. M. is depicted in *Enuma-elish* as creator of world and mankind. S.G.F.B.

Dhorme, *R.B.A.*, pp. 139ff.; H. W. F. Saggs, *The Greatness that was Babylon* (1962), pp. 338ff.; B. Meissner, *Babylonien u. Assyrien*, II (1925), pp. 15ff.; Brandon, *C.L.*, pp. 91ff.

Mārga Sanskrit term for 'path' or 'way'; trad. three main ways are distinguished in → Hinduism, the *karmamarga* or way of (ritual and ethical) works, and this is above all the concern of → *Mimamsa* school, the → *jnanamarga* or way of knowledge, i.e. the gnosis of ultimate reality through philosophical and contemplative knowledge; and the *bhaktimarga* or way of devotion (→ *bhakti*). The term can also be used for path prescribed by a partic. relig. movement, such as the → Buddha's path. The division between the three *margas* is somewhat artificial, since many orthodox expositors would consider *karmamarga* as an essential prerequisite of *jnana*, while some *bhakti* theologians would consider that devotion brings its own kind of *jnana*. N.S.

Mari Tablets Excavations at Mari, on Iraqi border, have brought to light a Sumerian city dating from 3rd mil. BC. 20,000 tablets from archives of king Zimri-Lim (*c.* 1750 BC) provide valuable information on period of Heb. Patriarchs. S.G.F.B.

A. Parrot, *Mission archéologique de Mari*, I (1956), II (1958); G. Dossin *et alii*, *Archives royales de Mari* (1950–60); M. E. L. Mallowan, *Early Mesopotamia and Iran* (1965); *H.D.B.*[2], p. 618; *A.N.E.T.*, pp. 482ff.

Mark, Gospel of Acc. to trad., written in Rome, and gen. regarded as earliest of Gospels, setting pattern for Gospels of → Lk. and → Matt. (→ Synoptic Gospels). Scholars have variously dated it 66–75: there is much reason for placing it just after Flavian triumph in 71 over rebel Judaea. M. uses Palestinian trad. of → Jesus in presenting him as Son of God. M.'s thesis is that Jew. disciples recognised Jesus only as → Messiah of Israel (8:27ff.), and that his divinity was first perceived by Roman centurion, a Gentile, at Crucifixion, when rending of Temple Veil attested obsolescence of Judaism (15:37–9). M. shows anti-Jew. attitude, and shifts responsibility for Crucifixion from Pilate to Jew. leaders. The Gospel, which is written in Grk., ends at 16:8, without describing → Resurrection of Jesus: it is not clear whether this was orig. end or whether orig. MS. became torn at this point. Identity of author is unknown: acc. to trad., Mark is the John Mark of Acts 12:25. S.G.F.B.

V. Taylor, *The Gospel acc. to St. Mark* (1952); *H.D.B.*[2], *s.v.; P.C.*[2], pp. 799ff.; S. G. F. Brandon, 'The Date of the Markan Gospel', *N.T.S.*, 7 (1961), 'The Apologetical Factor in the Markan Gospel', in *Studia Evangelica*, II (1964); *Jesus and the Zealots* (1967), ch. 5 (with bibliogr.).

Marks, 32, of a Great Man (Buddh.) A feature of Buddh. trad. is that there are certain marks, 32 in number, which characterise a great man; or, more properly, a 'superman', and, hence, a Buddha, although the trad. is pre-Buddh. in origin. These 32 marks are listed in the *Lakkhana Sutta* ('Discourse concerning Marks') of the → *Digha Nikāya* (in E.T. by T. W. and C. A. F. Rhys Davids in *Dialogues of the Buddha* part III, pp. 132–67). The possessor of these marks is to be recognised, acc. to brahmin trad., as either a great king or founder of a relig. movement. Rhys Davids comments that 'most of the marks are so absurd, considered as marks of any human, that they are prob. mythological in origin, and three or four seem to be solar'. He points out what appears to be the irony implicit in the Lakkhana Sutta in the contrast it makes between the marks and the noble ethical qualities they are supposed to represent. The 32 marks of the superman are as follows: (1) He has feet with level tread. (2) On soles of his feet appear perfectly shaped wheels, thousand-spoked. (3) He has projecting heels. (4) He has long fingers and toes. (5) His feet are soft and tender. (6) He has hands and feet like a net. (7) His ankles are like rounded shells. (8) His legs are like an antelope's. (9) Standing without bending he can touch his knees with his hands. (10) His male organs are concealed in a sheath. (11) His complexion is the colour of gold. (12) His skin is so delicate that no dust cleaves to his body. (13) The down on his skin grows in single hairs, one to each pore. (14) The down on his body turns upward, every hair of it, in little rings curling to the right, blue-black in colour. (15) He has a frame divinely straight. (16) He has the seven convex surfaces. (17) The front half of his body is like a lion's. (18) There is no furrow between his shoulders. (19) His proportions have the symmetry of the banyan tree. (20) His bust is equally rounded. (21) His taste is supremely acute. (22) His jaws are as a lion's. (23) He has forty teeth. (24) He has regular teeth. (25) He has continuous teeth. (26) His eyeteeth are very lustrous. (27) His tongue is long. (28) He has a divine voice, like the karavika bird's. (29) His eyes are intensely blue. (30) He has eyelashes like a cow's. (31) Between the eyebrows appears a hairy mole, white and soft like cottondown. (32) His head is like a royal turban. All these marks of the superman are said in the Lakkhana Sutta to be result of meritorious actions in former existences. T.O.L.

Marriage (Chinese) Until mod. times, M. in China was essentially a contract between two families, the parties concerned being, in many cases, not even consulted. Marriage between those of same surname was forbidden. Though marriage customs varied enormously in different parts of country, there were three essential conditions: (1) A contract was drawn up and signed by parents and guardians. (2) The acceptance of wedding gifts by bride's family. (3) The acceptance of bride into groom's family. The preliminaries to a bethrothal were conducted through the offices of a go-between. Horoscopes were consulted, after which a formal offer of marriage by groom's parents was assented to in writing by bride's parents. On wedding day, the bride is conducted with great ceremony to bridegroom's home, where the actual ceremonies take place before relatives and friends. The actual time when a woman becomes a man's wife is when they worship before the groom's household gods and ancestral tablets. Then bride and groom drink a mixture of wine and honey from goblets tied together with red thread. A marriage feast is prepared, at which bride and bridegroom kowtow to parents and relatives. Later a visit is paid to bride's family, where groom and bride worship before her ancestral tablets. The bride enters her husband's family to serve his parents and ancestors. Her status immeasurably increases when she gives birth to a male child.

Two closely related marriage customs were prevalent in China until mod. times. If a girl's bethrothed died before the marriage, it somesometimes happened that she went through the marriage ceremony with the dead youth and afterwards entered house of the mother-in-law as a widow. Sometimes, in the case of an unmarried son prematurely dying, his parents, through a go-between, contracted with family of a girl, who had died about the same time, for a marriage ceremony to take place, the coffins afterwards being placed side by side in the ancestral graveyard. (→→ Family, Divorce, Adultery.) D.H.S.

For full description of M. in China see J. Dyer Ball, *Things Chinese*, 5th edn. (1925), pp. 367ff.; J. G. Cormack, *Birthday, Wedding, Funeral and other Customs* (1923), pp. 47ff.

(Hindu) Trad., Hindu marriage has taken a number of forms. Acc. to law books (→→ Manu, Law Books of; *dharma*) there are eight grades of wedlock, ranging from full marriage of two spouses of same class or caste down to seduction scarcely distinguishable from rape. Marriage without dowry and by purchase was trad. quite common; while romantic liaison outside family control, known as *Gāndharva*, played large part in classical literature of Hinduism, the most interesting form being the *svayamvara* or 'own-choice' in which girl chooses man. Polygamy was practised, mainly among wealthier classes; while polyandry is attested in story of the → *Mahabharata*, where the five Pandyas shared Draupadi as common wife. It is evident from law-books that caste endogamy was by no means universal in classical India, and anc. classifications of marriage indicate relatively fluid situation. With hardening of the → caste system it became increasingly difficult for M. to occur outside family and caste control. Never popular from Brahmanical point of view, re-marriage came into increasing disfavour, and the sentiment against found its medieval and mod. expression in the practice of → *sati* (suttee), where faithful wife followed spouse onto the pyre. Widows came to be a depressed class, except in so far as their status gave them opportunity for spiritual search. On the whole, divorce has been strongly discouraged in upper class Hinduism, partly because of poss. of husband's taking a second wife, etc., if suitable male offspring were not forthcoming from first marriage. However, the complexity of Hindu custom has in fact allowed greater variation than allowed for in orthodox law books (e.g. practice of matriarchy in Kerala, etc.). An increased puritanism has characterised late medieval and mod. periods, partly under influence of Muslim purdah. Also in same period there has been increase in system of child marriage. The trad. ceremonials of betrothal and marriage are highly complex, and for high class Hindus repr. one of most import. ritual functions of → Brahmins. Mod. legislation has attempted to curb child marriage and discourage excessive expenditure on marriage ceremonial itself. N.S.

K. M. Kapadia, *Marriage and Family in India* (1958); Anant S. Altekar, *The Position of Women in Hindu Civilization* (1956); J. J. Meyer, *Sexual Life in Ancient India* (1952); A. L. Basham, *The Wonder that was India* (1954).

(Islam) (*Nikāh*). In Islam M. is fundamentally a civil contract in which a woman receives a dower (*mahr*) in return for marital rights (cf. Qur. iv:3f.; xxiv:33; v:7). Those to be married must not be within prohibited degrees (iv:27); they must be agreed; the woman, esp. if she is a virgin, must have a legal guardian (*walī*). If she has no suitable male relative, the → *qāḍī* acts as *walī*. The dower, or portion of it (the remainder being a debt due to wife) must have been paid. There should be two competent witnesses. Formerly it was customary to have no written marriage certificate, but in modern states this is necessary. In earlier times children below age of puberty could be married, though cohabitation did not take place till after it; but some modern states have introduced laws about earliest age for marriage (e.g. 16 for females and 18 for males in Egypt; 14 and 16 respectively in Algeria). Particularly in Ḥanafī (→ Muslim Law, schools of) circles the doc. of marriage equality (*kafā'a*) has been held to ensure that husband is at least in same grade of society as wife, for it was felt that a woman should not marry into a lower grade; nowadays this is not always so carefully observed as formerly. The marriage feast (*walīma*) was from early times considered indispensable. A trad. says there is no marriage without the smoke and tambourine, i.e. the smoke of preparations of feast, and music. A main purpose of the *walīma* was to publicise marriage. It has gen. been held that the Qur. permits a man to have four wives at same time, but the context of the regulation deserves consideration. The verse (iv:3) says that if people are afraid they cannot look properly after orphans they may marry up to four women, but if they cannot act equitably towards them, then only one. Many modern Muslims argue that this v. really teaches monogamy, because no man can act equitably in such circumstances. Though that is an ingenious argument, a more effective one might be to point out that the regulation is not so much a matter of permitting polygamy as of caring for orphans. It may, therefore, be interpreted as a temporary measure, or one to be put in force only in emergency. In fact, the average Muslim has only one wife. The *mu'ta* type of marriage (→ Shi'a) is not recognised by → Sunnis. A Muslim man may marry a Jew. or Christ. woman; but a Muslim woman may marry only a Muslim. J.R.

E.I., III, pp. 912–4; Hughes, pp. 313–27; *Mishkāt*, pp. 658ff.; Querry, I, pp. 639ff., II, 1ff.; Lane, *Egyptians*, ch. VI; Gaudefroy-Demombynes,

Institutions, ch. VIII; E. Westermarck, *Marriage ceremonies in Morocco* (1914) (French trans. 1921); J. N. D. Anderson, *M.W.*, XLI (1951), pp. 113ff., 186ff.; Coulson, *Law*, index; J. Robson, 'Muslim Wedding Feasts', *T.G.U.O.S.*, XVIII (1961), pp. 1ff.; R. B. Serjeant, 'Recent marriage legislation from al-Mukallā with notes on marriage customs', *B.S.O.A.S.*, XXV (1962), pp. 472ff.; Rahman, *Islam*, p. 38.

(Japanese) Ideas and legal regulations concerning M. in Japan passed through 3 different stages: (1) That of the age of Taiho-ryo (CE 701–1192), when Jap. practice was much influenced by Chi. morals and law. (2) That of feudal age (13th cent.–1868) moulded by → Bushido. (3) The mod. age since 1868, much influenced by Christianity and the West. Until the Meiji Restoration (1868), M. was a contract between families, and consent of the parties concerned was not necessary. The Meiji civil code insisted on consent both of contracting parties and of parents. During the Feudal Age, M. between members of nobility needed consent of government. Polygamy was forbidden but not concubinage, which was prevalent among wealthy. A child by a concubine had inheritance rights. In 1882 concubinage ceased to be recognised by law. A second M. was permitted when first was dissolved by divorce or death; but, as in China, re-M. by a widow carried with it social stigma. M., as in China, was arranged by a go-between, and contract ratified by exchange of gifts. The actual wedding ceremonies were similar to those in China. The law required no relig. ceremony; but in modern times many weddings are conducted in Chr. churches and → Shinto temples. Usually the actual ceremony takes place in home of bridegroom, and introductions made to relatives and friends at a M. feast. In gen., the status and position of women in the home was considered inferior. D.H.S.

E.R.E., VIII, pp. 459–60.

(Sacred) The union of the sexes is a fundamental concern of relig., and it has found many forms of expression therein. The earliest → cosmogonies employ sexual imagery to account for origin of deities or cosmic phenomena (e.g. in Egypt: union of → Geb and → Nut; in Mesopot. of → Ti'âmat and Apsu). The concept of the → Great Goddess naturally involved idea of her union with a god, usually a vegetation deity, for promotion of fertility (→→ Ashtart; Cybele; Ishtar). This union was ritually repr. in form of S.-M., sometimes with king and queen, or priest and priestess, impersonating deities concerned. The S.-M. was often part of a → myth-and-ritual complex commemorating the New Year. A text from → Ugarit gives vivid and rather Rabelaisian picture of → El in this connection. Examples of this fertility-form of S.-M. are found in anc. Egypt, Mesopot., Anatolia, Greece and India: a faint memory of it is preserved in European folk-customs of May Queen, Green Man and Maypole. Another form of S.-M. occurs in depictions of the divine births of pharaohs Hatshepsut and Amenhotep III, they being each the offspring of god → Amun and queen concerned. S.G.F.B.

E. O. James, *The Cult of the Mother Goddess* (1959); T. H. Gaster, *Thespis* (1961), pp. 430ff.; S. H. Hooke (ed.), *Myth, Ritual and Kingship* (1958); H. Frankfort, *Kingship and the Gods* (1948); M. Eliade, *Traité d'histoire des religions* (1949), chs. 7–8, E.T. *Patterns of Comparative Religion* (1958), chs. 7–8; *H.G.R.*, I, p. 257.

Mars Among Italian gods, the next after → Jupiter: his name also occurs as Mavors, Mamers, and (Etrusc.) Maris. M. was god of war and agriculture: which was his orig. attribute is unknown. At Rome his festivals were in March and Oct., when the Salii performed war-dances (*arma ancilia mouent*). Before start of a war, the general commanding shook sacred spears of M. M. was identified with Grk. → Ares. S.G.F.B.

O.C.D., *s.v.;* F. Altheim, *Hist. of Roman Religion* (E.T. 1938), pp. 138ff.; A. Grenier, *Les religions étrusque et romaine* (1948), pp. 102ff.; G. Dumézil, *Les dieux des indo-européens* (1952), pp. 111ff.

Martyr *Ex.* Grk. *martus*, 'witness'. In Christianity, term used orig. for → Apostles who witnessed life and resurrection of Christ (Acts 1:8, 22); it later described those who 'witnessed' to their faith by suffering and death during Roman → persecution of Church. From 2nd cent. a M.-cult was estab., the M.'s death being liturgically celebrated at tomb, relics venerated, and acts recorded. Those who suffered for their faith are venerated in many other religs.: (e.g. →→ Judaism, Islam, Buddhism). Pagan Alexandrians also treasured memory of those who suffered resisting Roman government. Many → Zealots died under torture for their faith. (→ Maccabees, Book). S.G.F.B.

D.C.C., *s.v.; R.G.G.*, IV, col. 587–93; T. W. Manson, 'Martyrs and Martyrdom', *B.J.R.L.*, p. 39 (1957); H. Musurillo, *The Acts of the Pagan Martyrs* (1954); W. H. C. Frend, *Martyrdom and Persecution in the Early Church* (1965); *E.J.R.*, p. 252; S. G. F. Brandon, *Jesus and the Zealots* (1967), pp. 57, 143–5, 177.

(Islam) The word Martyr (*shahīd*) occurs in Qur'an in sense of witness, meaning 'to see'. God is spoken of as *al-Shahīd*, the one who sees men's actions. Although word in Qur. does not mean 'martyr', it developed meaning like the Greek *martus*. Fundamentally a M. is reckoned as one killed in → *jihād* against unbelievers. Such M.'s are given high reward in heaven. Some parties hold that they do not require to be washed and shrouded before burial, but should be buried with their wounds apparent. Books of → Tradition and Law give a wider meaning. A trad. given by Muslim says, 'He who is killed in God's path is a M., he who dies in God's path is a M., he who dies of plague is a M., and he who dies of a disease in the belly is a M.' Another trad. in Muslim's collection says, 'If anyone asks God for martyrdom with a genuine purpose, God will bring him to the dwellings of the martyrs even if he dies on his bed.' Other trads. reckon among M.'s women who die in childbed and people who suffer a violent death from robbers, wild beasts, shipwreck, or some other cause. The tomb (*mashhad*) of a M. is liable to become place of pilgrimage. M.'s may even be accepted as intercessors (→ Intercession). →→ 'Āshūrā'; -Ḥusayn; Karbalā. J.R.

E.I., IV, pp. 259–61; Hughes, pp. 327f.; Guillaume, *Life*, index (s.v. Lists); *Mishkāt*, pp. 808ff.

Mary, Cult of The Gospel accounts of Mary as virgin-mother of Christ (Mt. 1:18ff.; Lk. 1:26ff.) naturally made her a major figure of Chr. interest and devotion. Already in 4th cent., M. was called *Theotokos*, 'God-bearer', which was trans. into Lat. as *Mater Dei*, 'Mother of God'. Belief in her perpetual virginity evolved about the same time. Such attributes gave M. unique status, and caused her to be regarded as highest of God's creatures. This theological exaltation was doubtless reinforced by the emotional need, evident in many religs., to venerate the female principle (→ Great Goddess). Thomas → Aquinas taught that *hyperdulia*, i.e. unique and superlative devotion, should be paid to M. Although theologians carefully distinguished between *hyperdulia* and *latria*, 'worship', which was for God alone, popular devotion has often been Mariolatry, i.e. Mary-worship. M. came to be regarded as 'Mediatrix of All Graces'; in medieval → Dooms M. was repr. as interceding with a vengeful Christ for sinful mankind. The doc. of M.'s → Immaculate Conception was defined by Pope Pius IX in 1854, and that of her Corporal Assumption into heaven by Pius XII in 1950. In W. Church six principal feasts of M. are commemorated; her cult flourishes in E. Church, being universally attested by her innumerable → icons. New centres of cult of M. were estab. at Lourdes in 1858 and Fatima, Portugal, in 1917, consequent on her alleged manifestations at these places. The cult ceased in countries that became Prot., but a modified revival has resulted from Oxford Movement in → C. of E. S.G.F.B.

E.R.E., VIII, *s.v.; D.C.C.*, pp. 496, 823, 867ff.; *R.G.G.*, IV, col. 763–6; G. G. Coulton, *Five Centuries of Religion*, I (1923), chs. 9, 10; J. A. MacCulloch, *Medieval Faith and Fable*, ch. 7; N. Zernov, *Eastern Christendom* (1961), p. 234; P. Evdokimov, *La femme et le salut du monde* (1958), pp. 207ff.

Marx, Karl (1818–83) Together with F. Engels, M. produced the political theory of Communism. Son of a German Jew who became a Christian, M. was brought up in a liberal intellectual atmosphere. Although influenced by Hegelian ideas while a student, he criticised → Hegel's philosophy for its uncritical acceptance of contemporary State as present manifestation of absolute Spirit, contending that philosophy should both criticise State and direct its effective reformation in interests of society as a whole. M. took from Hegel both notion of alienation and recognition of dialectical process of reality. Where he considered that he fundamentally differed from Hegel was in his materialism. M. did not deny reality of mind, but asserted priority of material factors in opposition to what he regarded as Hegel's idealism. On the other hand, M. rejected the crude materialism of Feuerbach, who interpreted the processes of reality in terms of a mechanical causality. For M. the dialectical development of history in continual sequence of thesis, anti-thesis and synthesis is controlled by social and economic forces. M. regarded relig. as a human product which reflects man's feeling of alienation. In partic., contemporary relig. reflects the dehumanisation imposed by structure of capitalist society. As 'opium of the people', relig. offers to man in his estrangement an illusory hope of happiness in a life after death which will compensate for real evils of present existence. M. holds that nature of relig. must be exposed, so that men, no longer misled by its false promises, will take action needed to transform political, social and economic life and estab. a communist society, by overthrowing contemporary order based on institution of private property. As the causes of man's estrangement are thereby eradicated, so relig. will disappear. M. did not discuss relig. at great length; he considered that it had been properly condemned by Feuerbach's analysis of relig. doctrines as projections of man's thoughts and ideals about himself. Hegel's explanation of relig. was thus refuted. M. criticised Feuerbach's theory on ground that it failed to recognise the partic. historical forms of relig. are products of partic. social situations. As for the Chr. Church, M. holds that gen. it has identified itself with ruling classes and has produced doctrines that pretend to give divine justification to their status and practices. Even when the Church has attempted some social witness, it has been quite ineffective. M. has contributed to relig. thought by indicating importance of non-theological factors in relig. Although they can be over-emphasised, social and economic considerations are relevant to understanding of any relig. position. M.'s thought about relig. has also tended to separate the socialist movements, which it has inspired, from the Church. The official policy of Communist states is gen. atheistic. Recently, however, there have been signs that some Marxists are interested in entering into dialogue with Christians. The social, political and economic aspects of Marxism do not inevitably imply an atheistic position. (→ Communism). D.A.P.

Marx and Engels, *On Religion* (selections); H. P. Adams, *Karl Marx in His Earliest Writings* (1940); S. Hook, *From Hegel to Marx* (1936).

Mass *Ex.* Lat. *missa.* Term used for → Eucharist in R.C. Church; it prob. derives from words of dismissal at end of the Roman Rite: *Ite, missa est.* St. Ambrose (*c.* 339–97) already used expression '*missam facere*' = 'to perform the Mass'. In the W. Church, High Mass (*Missa solemnis*) has been chief act of worship from earliest times, as Eucharist has been in E. Church. H.M. requires three ministers: the celebrant (a priest), deacon and sub-deacon (→ Hierarchy, Chr.). Where only a priest is available, a Sung Mass (*Missa Cantata*) is custom on Sundays in parish churches. Low Mass is simplified form of M. that grew up in Middle Ages, in consequence of custom for each priest to say M. daily. M. is regarded as the ritual enactment of sacrificial death of Christ (→ Sacrifice of Mass). Cath. churches were primarily designed to provide appropriate setting for performance of M. In Requiem M. the sacrifice is offered for repose of souls of dead. (→ Prayers for Dead). S.G.F.B.

D.C.C., s.v.; E. O. James, *Christ. Myth and Ritual* (1933), ch. 5; J.-A. Jungmann, *Missarum solemnia. Explication génétique de la messe romaine*, 3 vols. (1954).

Maṣṣēbhāh Heb. for stone pillar. There are many refs. to M.'s in O.T.: sometimes they are erected on graves or commemorate events; but often they have cultic significance, being objects of anointing and libations (e.g. Gen. 35:14). M.'s prob. marked place of theophany: they figure also in Canaanite relig. (→ Stones, Sacred). S.G.F.B.

E.R.E., VIII, *s.v.; H.D.B.*, pp. 772ff.

Materialism (Chinese) Until intro. into China during 20th cent. of materialistic philosophies of W. derivation, Chi. philosophical systems cannot fairly be described as materialistic. Though materialistic tendencies are occasionally found, notably in dualistic theories of → Yin-Yang (Yin and Yang being considered by many Chi. philosophers as material substances), and in the Naturalism of → Hsün-tzŭ and Wang Ch'ung, → Confucianism invariably accepted belief in a transcendent Reality. Buddh. philosophy in China was Idealistic; → Taoism rested in belief that Ultimate Reality consisted of absolute, incomprehensible Reality described as → Tao. Though usually agnostic and this-wordly, and often classified as materialistic, Chi. indigenous philosophy might well be described as Organic Naturalism. D.H.S.

Mathurā Important centre of Buddhism in India from time of emperor → Aśoka. In early Buddh. period, the town was situated about 5 m. to S.W. of modern town of Mathurā or Muttra which is on W. bank of the Jumna river about 100 m. S. of Delhi. There are refs. to M. in the Pali canon; the Buddha is said to have visited town and to have commented unfavourably upon place, to effect that the ground there was rough, that there was much dust, that it was beset with fierce dogs and demons, and that alms were to be had only with difficulty. But even in his lifetime there were apparently followers of the Buddha to be found there. After Buddha's death, a monk named Mahā Kaccana stayed there, and was visited by the king, Avantiputta, to whom the monk is said to have delivered a discourse on subject of caste, now known as the Mathurā (or Madhurā) Sutta (*M.N.*, II, 83–90), after which king became a Buddh. Poss. Mahā Kaccana may have been import. agent in the spread of Bhm. in M. By time of → Aśoka, M. had become a prominent centre of Bhm. and after 3rd → Buddh. Council, held at Patna, the → Sarvāstivādins, moving westwards made it their stronghold. It was in M. that use of the → *rupa*, or Buddha-image developed; whether it originated here or in area of Greek influence in → Gandhāra being a matter of controversy. The → Milindapañhā, composed in early years of Christ. era, speaks of M. as one of chief cities of India. The Chinese pilgrim → Fa-Hsien testifies to strength of Bhm. in the M. region when he visited India in 5th cent. CE, as did Hsuan Tsang in 7th cent. (S. Beal, *Buddhist Records of the Western World* (1884), vol. I, pp. 179ff.); acc. to latter, both → Hīnayāna and → Mahāyāna flourished there. M. was plundered by the Muslim invasion under Mahmud of Ghazni (977–1030). The town is sometimes ref. to as Uttara-Mathurā, to distinguish it from the M. in S. India (Madura). T.O.L.

Matsuri The solemn celebrations which take place periodically in every → Shinto temple. Most M. are accompanied by impressive festivities, and the word is gen. trans. into Eng. as 'festival'. But, etym., M. is closely assoc. with verb *Matsuru*—to worship. It is also one of components of *matsurigoto*—government, thus revealing that all important affairs of political and social life are made occasions for worship of the → *kami*, and M. is fundamentally to live in constant attitude of prayer and obedience to the *kami*. D.H.S.

J. Herbert, *Shinto* (1967), pp. 168ff.

Matthew, Gospel of Most Jewish of the Gospels in its interests and outlook. Its author cannot be identified; it was written for Grk.-speaking Jew.-Christ. community, poss. in Alexandria, about CE 85. Its narrative framework is based on Gosp. of → Mark; it also incorporates material from Q. M. differs from Gosp. of → Luke in its acc. of birth of Jesus, and in locating appearances of Risen Jesus in Galilee, instead of Jerusalem. M. was trad. ranked as the first Gospel (→ Synoptic Gospels), and is notable for its acc. of Sermon on the Mount (5–7). In past ages M. was most popular of the Gospels. Mt. 27.25 unforunately provided scriptural authority for Chr. → Anti-semitism. S.G.F.B.

B. H. Streeter, *The Four Gospels* (1924); A. H. McNeile, *The Gosp. acc. to St. Matthew* (1915); E. Klostermann, *Das Matthäusevangelium* (1927²); *P.C.*², pp. 769ff.; *H.D.B., s.v.; R.G.G.*³, II, col. 762–3; W. D. Davies, *The Setting of the Sermon on the Mount* (1964); S. G. F. Brandon, *Jesus and the Zealots* (1967), pp. 284ff.; *Trial of Jesus of Nazareth* (1968), ch. 5.

Māturīdī Māturidites. Abū Mansūr Muḥammad b. Muḥammad al-M. (d. Samarqand, 333/944) is titular head of the M. school of theology in Sunni Islam. Little is known about him personally. He was a Ḥanafī (→ Muslim Law, schools of). His school and the → Ash'arites were equally orthodox, despite some slight differences. Both used → *kalām*. In most areas the Ash'arites came to be considered the defenders of orthodoxy; yet there are M. influences to be found among them. The M.'s, e.g., laid emphasis on actions in which man has choice (*ikhtiyār*), which to many minds has seemed superior to the Ash'arite doc. of *kasb* (→ Acquisition). It may be said that the M.'s were more liberal in some respects. Prob. on this account Ash'arites have tended to be influenced by their docs. without realising it. For E.T. of a Maturidite's articles of belief cf. D. B. Macdonald, *Theology*, 308ff. J.R.

E.I., III, pp. 414f.; Pareja, pp. 635, 700ff.; *G.A.L.*, I, pp. 209, *S.I.*, 346; Wensinck, *Creed*, index; Sweetman, *I.C.T.*, II, p. 8; IV, p. 12; Watt, *Philosophy*, index.

Mawdūdī, Abul A'lā → Jamā'at-i-Islāmī. J.R.

Mawlawiyya → Ṣūfī Orders. J.R.

Mawlid al-nabī (The Prophet's birthplace, or birthday). → Muḥammad's reputed birthplace in Mecca was honoured by a building with dome and minaret. The site was first honoured by Khayzurān, mother of the 'Abbasid Caliph Hārūn al-Rashīd, and it remained place of sanctity till the → Wahhabis took Mecca in 1344/1925. They broke down the dome and minaret and removed all ornaments. This was in keeping with their firm belief that all such repr. a type of idolatry, for they should be assoc. only with worship of God. The celebration of Muhammad's birthday, which takes place on 12th Rabī' I, the third month of lunar year, was a late development opposed by legists and theologians, but grad. adopted in many countries by force of public sentiment. The Wahhabis oppose it on principle. It takes form in different regions of special prayers, recitation of whole Qur., literary compositions called *mawlids*, processions and almsgiving. For trans. of a Turkish *mawlid*, see Pareja, 801–3. J.R.

E.I., III, pp. 419–22; Broadhurst, *Ibn Jubayr*, pp. 111, 166; Rutter, *Holy Cities*, I, pp. 270f.; Pareja, pp. 654f.; Lane, *Egyptians*, ch. xxiv.

Māyā Mother of the Buddha, and wife of → Suddhodana. Acc. to Buddh. trad., M. possessed moral qualities that fitted her to be the mother of Buddha, and had lived a pure life from day of her birth. On day the Buddha-to-be was conceived M. had dream, that she was carried by heavenly beings to the Himālayan mountains, where she was bathed by wives of the gods and dressed in robes of a goddess; then she was taken to a golden palace, where, as she lay on a couch, the Buddha-to-be, in form of a white elephant, entered the right side of her body. This dream is a familiar feature of popular Buddh. legend, and is frequently depicted in murals which decorate temples and pagodas in S.E. Asia.

Towards end of her pregnancy, when birth of the child was imminent, M. set out to visit her own people in neighbouring Devadaha. The child was born while she was on her journey, in the sāla grove of → Lumbini, as M. stood beside a sala tree, holding a branch of it. She died seven days later, and, acc. to trad. was reborn in the → Tusita heaven, where, after his enlightenment, Buddha went to preach to her the Dhamma. It is a feature of Buddh. belief (found in commentarial literature), that the mother of a Buddha dies soon after birth of Buddha-to-be, since it would not be fitting that she who had given birth to a Buddha-to-be should bear any other child. (→ Virgin Birth). T.O.L.

Māyā (Hindu) A key Hindu concept, commonly trans. 'illusion', since it bears this meaning in theology of → Advaita Vedanta. Its orig. meaning is the creative and transforming power of a god or of God. The idea of this quasi-magical capacity changed into that of conjuring or illusionism. In Advaita, the world is not fully real, but is like an illusion, which is created from one point of view by activity of → *Brahman* or ultimate reality in its personal manifestation as → *Iśvara* or Lord, and from subjective point of view by power of → *avidyā*—a primordial spiritual ignorance which causes individuals to see world as something other than *Brahman* and so as independently real. This ignorance has to be broken, if liberation is to be achieved. → Sankara's doc. of *maya* was criticised by → Ramanuja and other opponents of Advaita, partly for theological reasons—for God is 'demoted' in Sankara's system, since Creator shares in illusoriness of world he creates—and partly for philosophical reasons—for doc. of illusion undermines concept of knowledge as ordinarily understood. Sankara used impermanence (*anītya*) as criterion of illusoriness; but it was pointed out that a thing can be both real and impermanent. Mod. Advaitins have tended to modify doc. of *maya*. N.S.

P. Devanandan, *The Concept of Maya* (1950); S. N. Dasgupta, *Hist. of Indian Philosophy*, vol. 2 (1932).

Maya Relig. → American Relig. (ancient). C.A.B.

Mazdahism Movement founded in Persia by Mazdah in reign of Sassanian king Kavad (CE 488–531). Only known from hostile records, M. was a form of relig. communism, advocating sharing of wealth and women: its relation to → Manichaeism is uncertain. The Mazdahites were massacred *c.* 528: the name became pejorative to describe later religio-social movements. S.G.F.B.

E.R.E., VIII, *s.v.;* R. N. Frye, *The Heritage of Persia* (1962), pp. 221ff.; Zaehner, *D.T.Z.*, pp. 188ff.

Mazdayasnian Epithet for worshippers of → Ahura Mazdah. (→ Zoroastrianism). S.G.F.B.

Mean, The (Chinese = *Chung-Yung*). *Chung* means what is central, and *yung* means what is universal and harmonious. The M. is the harmony in human nature which underlies our moral nature, and the harmony which prevails throughout nature and universe. The theory that man and nature form a unity dominates Chi. thought.

The Doctrine of the Mean (*Chung Yung*) is a small book of Confucian school, trad. ascribed to Tzŭ Ssŭ, grandson of → Confucius, and forming ch. 28 of the → *Li Chi*. It was selected by → Chu Hsi (1130–1200), to become one of the Four Books, which became basic texts for the civil service examins. in China from CE 1135 until CE 1905. It is a book of fundamental import. for study of → Confucianism, and deals with such topics as Heaven and Man, human relations, moral virtues, nature and destiny, and the mean and harmony. D.H.S.

E. R. Hughes, *The Great Learning and the Mean in Action* (1942); Fung Yu-lan, *Hist. of Chinese Phil*, vol. 1 (1937), pp. 369ff.; W. T. Chan, *Source Book in Chinese Phil.* (1963), pp. 95ff.

Mecca A town on caravan routes from N., S., E. and W. Arabia, about 48 miles from Red Sea, owed its development to existence of a → *ḥaram*, where people could come in safety. The early story of M. is legendary, speaking of →→ Adam, Abraham, Ishmael and a series of tribes. Though in a barren country, its position led to development of a mercantile community. Qur. cvi, 2 refers to the double caravan of winter and summer. The people traced their lineage to an eponymous ancestor → Quraysh; but although they belonged to the tribe, by → Muḥammad's time difference of wealth and status had developed, and tribal responsibility for all its members was weakening. Business interests were supreme. The rites centred at the → Ka'ba were idolatrous. In such circumstances Muhammad's mission was partly religious, in narrow sense of word, and partly social. He denounced idols and defended rights of poor. Yet he had respect for the Ka'ba; while at → Medina, he received permission to carry out pilgrimage which he was anxious to perform in spite of signs of idolatry all around. When he took M., he purged it of idols and made it centre of → Islām to which pilgrims have ever since gathered annually to the → Pilgrimage from all over world. Its soil is considered so sacred that many pilgrims hope they may have the distinction of dying and being buried there. Accordingly many bring their shrouds with them. J.R.

E.I., III, pp. 437–48; C. Snouck Hurgronje, *Mekka* (1888–9); H. Lammens, *La Mecque à la veille de l'Hégire* (1924); Burton, *Pilgrimage*, part III; Rutter, *Holy Cities*, index; O'Leary, *Arabia*, ch. x; Kamal, *Sacred Journey*, ch. V, and *passim;* Rahman, *Islam*, index.

Mediation/Mediator → Salvation. S.G.F.B.

(Islam) Unless one considers the → Intercession of → Muḥammad for his followers as coming under this head, → Sunnī Islām has no place for mediation. It is different in → Shi'a Islam, for the → *imams* are prominent as mediators in its doc., and not merely intercessors. A trad. credits Muhammad with having said to → 'Alī, 'You and your descendants are mediators for mankind, as they will not be able to know God except through your introduction'. Another tells how during the → *Mi'rāj*, God said to Muhammad, 'I am pleased with you as a servant, beloved, messenger and prophet, and with your brother 'Ali as successor and door. . . . By you, by him and by the *imams* of his descendants I shall show mercy to my servants and handmaidens.' In another, God says, 'Those servants of mine who are dearest to me and most held in honour by me are Muhammad and 'Ali, my beloved and agent. If anyone wishes something from me he should approach me by them, for I will not reject the request of one who asks me by them and by the good ones of their family.' Blessing is also sought at tombs of saints who are regarded as mediators. This occurs even within Sunnī Islām, but chiefly among the common people. J.R.

Donaldson, *Shi'ite*, pp. 344ff.; al-Ḥurr, *Jawāhir*,

pp. 235, 268: see also 267 ('The *imams* after him (sc. 'Ali) who are the means of access to God'), 275, 277, 278, 348; Fyzee, *Creed*, pp. 95f.

Mediator (Chinese and Far Eastern) The concept of M., in sense of one who acts as intermediary between God (gods) and man, derives partly from the → Ancestor cult, in which eldest male heir acted as repr. in presenting the prayers and petitions of family to ancestors; partly from custom of employing a 'middle-man' or 'go-between' in settling disputes, and a powerful advocate in presenting one's petitions to a superior authority. In China, the emperor, by virtue of his unique status as Son of Heaven, was considered alone fitted to be M. between the Supreme God (→→ Shang Ti, T'ien) and man. Through prayers and sacrifices offered by him, the needs and aspirations of all people and nation were conveyed to Heaven, and Heaven's blessings sought. On a lower scale, each provincial and city magistrate performed mediatory functions between tutelary gods of his district and the people. In popular relig., both → Taoist and → Buddh., the services of innumerable lesser deities were sought as M.'s with the Supreme Deity. In partic. Ts'ao Chün, god of the hearth, otherwise known as Ssŭ Ming, master of destinies, mediated between the family and God; though numerous → bodhisattvas of Buddhism carried out mediatory functions. D.H.S.

Medina About 180 miles N. of Mecca, M. was orig. called Yathrib. It came to be called al-Madīna, presumably short for *Madīnat al-nabī* (the city of the Prophet). It was situated in a wide fertile neighbourhood occupied by two principal Arab tribes, Aws and Khazraj, and three tribes of Jew. faith, Qurayẓa, al-Naḍīr, and Qaynuqā'. After agreement with people from Yathrib, → Muḥammad sent followers there and afterwards went also with → Abū Bakr. The members of Aws and Kharzaj who welcomed the → Muslims were called → Helpers. Muhammad grad. estab. his power; when he conquered → Mecca he retained Medina as his capital and home. He died and was buried there; pilgrims still visit his tomb, which the → Wahhabis did not destroy after their conquest. Though Medina is not part of the → Pilgrimage ceremonies, it is considered the second most sacred town by Muslims; therefore it is only natural that those who have come to Mecca for Pilgrimage should wish to visit scene of Prophet's estab. of → Islām, and pay their respects at his tomb. The two first Caliphs, Abū Bakr and → 'Umar were buried alongside Muhammad. → 'Uthmān, the third Caliph also had M. as capital; when → 'Alī succeeded him he removed to Iraq and M. ceased to be capital. But it is so sacred in Muslim eyes that no non-Muslim is allowed to visit it. It is said, however, that when the Medina railway was being built non-Muslim engineers were allowed in town during daytime because of work needing to be done, but were not allowed to stay over night. J.R.

E.I., III, pp. 83–92; Pareja, index; Burton, *Pilgrimage*, part II; Rutter, *Holy Cities*, II, pp. 170ff.; Kamal, *Sacred Journey*, pp. 97ff.; Rahman, *Islam*, index; Watt, *Medina*, *passim.*

Meditation (Buddh.) M. is one of the 3 major components of the Buddh. way, the other 2 being morality, which precedes and must always accompany activity of meditation, and wisdom, which is reached as result of meditation (→ Eightfold Path). The West. reader is liable to misunderstand what the Buddh. means by M., and to imagine that it implies a 'relaxed' or 'inactive' state. But in the Buddh. view M. is an activity, in which one is engaged in subduing discoursive thought, destroying or discouraging unwholesome mental states, and initiating or nourishing wholesome mental states. It is a discipline, i.e., it has to be learned by a disciple from a master; without such personal supervision it cannot properly be undertaken. Herein is one of principle reasons for existence of the Buddh. monastery; it is a school of meditation, where younger monk learns from older or more advanced monk. M. is a highly developed and complicated discipline; of the methods used it is sufficient to say that they have to be learnt personally. Classical texts dealing with M. do exist, notably the → Visuddhimagga of → Buddhaghosa. An intro. to *theory* of subject has been made available to Eng. readers by E. Conze in his *Buddhist Meditation* (1960). (→→ Jhāna; Samādhi). T.O.L.

(School of) (Buddhism) → Zen. D.H.S.

Meekness (China and Far East) Basic to organisation of society in China, Japan and Korea was teaching of humility and submission to others. The people must meekly submit to officials, the clan to its chief, the family to its head, the young to their elders, the wife to her husband. → Confucian teaching concerning M. may be summed up in proverb: 'Heaven, earth, men and spirits all love the humble and not the proud'. → Taoism taught that the virtuous man is humble, like water always seeking the lowest place, requiting injury with kindness, and opposed to strife and non-assertive. → Buddhism had great influence in inculcating virtues of meekness, patience under provocation, the non-requiting of injury, gentleness, forbearance, on grounds that such an attitude led to accumulation of one's store of merit. 'The humble reap advantage; the haughty meet with misfortune.' D.H.S.

Megalithic Culture (Grk. *megas*, 'great'; *lithos*, 'stone'). Name given to culture characterised by tombs and sanctuaries built of large stones. It orig. in E. Mediterranean area, in 3rd mil. BC, and spread W. as far as Orkney and Shetland Is. M.-C. appears to have been inspired by a fertility relig., centred on → Great Goddess, and embodying a cult of dead. The stone temples of Malta are impressive examples of M. sanctuaries; the M. avenues at Carnac (Brittany) and Avebury, and → Stonehenge constitute other forms of sanctuaries. S.G.F.B.

J. Hawkes, *Prehistory*, I (1963), pp. 248ff.; *H.G.R.*, I, pp. 99ff.; J. D. Evans, *Malta* (1959); G. Sieveking, in E. Bacon (ed.), *Vanished Civilizations* (1963).

Megilloth Heb. = 'Rolls'. The name given to five books in latest section of Heb. Bible, which are read at major festivals: *Song of Solomon*, at → Passover; *Ruth*, at Feast of Weeks; *Lamentations*, at anniv. of destr. of → Jerusalem in 586 BC; → *Ecclesiastes*, at Feast of Tabernacles; *Esther* at Feast of Purim (→ Festivals, Jewish). The Midrash on Lament. contains much anc. material. (→ Judaism). S.G.F.B.

R.G.G.[3], IV, col. 829; Oesterley-Robinson, *L.R.M.J.*, pp. 74ff.; *E.J.R.*, p. 346.

Melanesian Religion Melanesia comprises the Solomon Is., the Santa Cruz group, the Banks' Is., New Hebrides, New Caledonia, the Loyalty Is., and Fiji. Indigenous relig. as such is now extinct, following Christianisation of area. The information we possess about relig. beliefs and practices derives largely from late 19th and early 20th cent. observers, who tended to treat area as a whole; mod. scholarship now recognises great diversity of relig. within area. Certain generalisations may be made. Thus the M.s do not seem to have worshipped a Supreme Being, though this is largely an *argumentum e silentio*, and there is some evidence for belief in a Creator (Qat, Tagaro, etc.) who, having created world and spirits, withdrew, and is thus to be classified as a → *deus otiosus*. Deities worshipped can, acc. to Codrington, be divided broadly into two classes: 'spirits', i.e. supernatural beings of an order higher than man; and 'ghosts', i.e. disembodied spirits of departed men, esp. close relatives. In east of area (New Hebrides and Banks' Is.) the former were more prominent; in west (Solomon Is.) the latter. In Banks' Is., a spirit, *vui*, was described thus: 'It lives, thinks, has more intelligence than a man; knows things which are secret without seeing; is supernaturally powerful with → *mana* (see below); has no form to be seen; has no soul, because itself is like a soul.' In Solomon Is. the 'ghost' (*tindalo*) of a great man was revered as link with unseen world, a powerful helper in crises of life, and yet potentially a dangerous enemy (→ Ancestor Worship). Should the deceased have been a warrior, his spirit was worshipped as a *keramo*, or war spirit, an effectual aid in combat. In the case of 'ghosts', worship was responsibility of next-of-kin, and carried out in spec. constructed shrines, containing images and relics of departed; here → sacrifices were offered, partly propitiatory in nature. From these and all other rites women and children were excluded.

Whatever the form of worship, its primary object was always appropriation of supernatural power, *mana*. This M. term, which has come to be a *terminus technicus* in comp. relig., has been frequently misapplied. Although Codrington claimed *mana* to be 'impersonal', he also pointed out that it was 'always connected with some person who directs it; all spirits have it, ghosts generally, some men'. This has led later scholars to question both the fact of its impersonality, and theories based on this assumption. *Mana*, it is now claimed, is a supernatural quality, rather than an impersonal force. *Mana* was never worshipped: only persons and things possessing *mana*. 'All success and all advantage proceed from the favourable exercise of this *mana*; whatever evil happens has been caused by the direction of this power to harmful ends, whether by spirits, or ghosts, or men. In no case, however, does this power operate, except under the direction and control of a person—a living man, a ghost, or a spirit' (Codrington). Deriving power from one of these sources, the individual M. (not a priest: the M. had no priests) can try and manipulate it to his own ends. Natural objects—plants, trees, streams, stones, etc.—were taken to be possessors of power through some supernatural agency (→ Animism), and might be adapted for use in e.g. → Amulets. The corollary of *mana* was the → Polynesian term → *tabu*, which signified, also in M., the quality of unapproachability and danger to anyone insufficiently prepared (→ Holy). A *tabu* was inherent in some places and objects, and might be imposed on others by any person possessing sufficient power (→ Magic). Nuclei of power in M. relig. were the restricted (or secret) societies of men, in which communion with dead was carried on, under strict *tabu* safeguards.

The M. shared belief, common to many preliterate peoples, in a free-soul, which could leave the body in dream or trance, and which could be enticed from body by magic. Loss of vital force was interpreted as loss of soul. On death, this soul proceeded to its own abode, though in some sense still active in or near the grave. The land of dead was conceived in various ways, though commonly as 'an empty continuation of the worldly life'. Mortuary practices varied between inhumation (when normal grave goods were provided), exposure, and (in some cases) cremation. E.J.S.

R. H. Codrington, *The Melanesians* (1891); *E.R.E.*, viii, pp. 529b–38a; F. R. Lehmann, *Mana* (1922); *R.G.G.*[3], iv, cols. 841–3; A. P. Elkin, *Social Anthropology in Melanesia* (1953).

Melqart (Melkart) Phoenician god (name deriv. from *milk* = 'king'; *qart* = 'city'). M. was chief god of Tyre, and, because of Tyre's supremacy, a chief deity of Phoenic. pantheon. M. had similar position in → Carthaginian relig., and his cult was also prominent at Gades. M. was orig. a solar deity; human sacrifices were sometimes made to him. The Greeks identified M. with → Heracles. (→ Moloch; → Phoenic. Relig.). S.G.F.B.

G. Contenau, *La civilisation phénicienne* (1949), pp. 90ff.; D. Harden, *The Phoenicians* (1962), pp. 85ff.; G. and G. Lapeyre and A. Pellegrin, *Carthage punique* (1942), pp. 60ff.; R. Dussaud, 'Melqart, d'après de récents travaux', *R.H.R.*, 151 (1957); O. Eissfeld, *Der Gott Kamel* (1953).

Memphite Theology Term used to describe a → cosmogony (Egypt.) composed by priests of Memphis, making their god → Ptah supreme creator. The M.-T. cleverly demotes the Heliopolitan god → Atum by making him an agent of Ptah, who is repr. as creating by his conceptual knowledge and potent utterance. The text of the M.-T., which dates from 3rd mil. BC, was preserved by king Shabaka (716–695 BC) on a stone now in British Museum (hence the 'Shabaka stone'). S.G.F.B.

S. G. F. Brandon, *C.L.*, ch. 2, with full bibliog.

Mēmrā Aramaic = 'word'. In the → Targums, M. is used in commenting on O.T. passages where it was felt desirable to remove impression that God acted directly and anthropomorphically on specific occasions. A tendency to hypostatise → Yahweh's word (*dābār*) as creative healing entity appears in O.T. (e.g. Ps. 33:6; 107:20), and prob. antedates → Philo's use of → Logos. S.G.F.B.

E.R.E., VIII, *s.v.;* Oesterley-Robinson, *L.R.M.J.*, pp. 48ff.; *E.J.R.*, p. 242.

Mencius (Chinese name—Mêng k'o. *c.* 371–289 BC). Famous Confucian philos. and author of *Book of Mencius*, one of the Four Books which, from Sung Dynasty onwards, became the basis of Chi. education. M. was a native of small state of Tsou (Shantung), and was educated by disciples of Tzǔ Ssǔ (grandson of → Confucius). Little is known of his family or private life. Like Confucius, he was a professional teacher, and sought official position as adviser to several of princes of his day. As a political and social philos. he has exerted an immense influence. Though accepting feudalistic structure of society of his time, M. argued that gov. is primarily for benefit of the people. He exalted gov. by the ideal 'king', who was a 'sage', ruled by moral force or virtue, and followed what he called the 'Kingly Way' (*Wang Tao*). In this, his doctrine has similarity to that of Plato's *Republic*. He opposed despotism and rule by brute force, and maintained that the people had a right to rebel against the tyrant. The divisions of society, between rulers and ruled, exist solely to make cooperative division of labour possible. Acc. to M., rule by Kingly Virtue is poss., because of inherent goodness of human nature. All men possess in germ the four cardinal virtues (love, righteousness, propriety and wisdom). They have innate knowledge of the good and innate ability to do good. All men are potentially capable of becoming 'sages', and it is aim of gov. to stimulate, encourage, educate and train in all people the 'shoots of goodness'. For M., humanity (*jên*) and righteousness (*i*) are guiding principles both in governmental and private life. He bitterly opposed → Mo-tzǔ's doc. of universal love without discrimination, and Yang-tzǔ's doc. of hedonism. He also opposed Mo-tzǔ's utilitarian teaching that virtues should be practised because they are beneficial. For M. virtue is the natural expression of one's human-ness. M. came to be recognised in China as a 'sage' second only to Confucius. His teaching, recognised as orthodox → Confucianism developed along idealistic lines, exercised a profound influence on whole movement of Confucianism over the last mil. D.H.S.

J. Legge, *The Life and Works of Mencius* (1875); W. A. C. H. Dobson, *Mencius* (1963); W. T. Chan, '*Mencius*' in *Encycl. Brit.* (1960), *Source Book in Chinese Philos.* (1963); Fung Yu-lan, *Hist. of Chinese Philos.*, vol. 1 (1937).

Menorah Heb. for seven-branch candelabra that stood in → Temple. It was captured by Romans in CE 70, and is repr. on Arch of Titus in Roman Forum among spoils of conquered Judaea brought in triumph to Rome. The M. is also used in → synagogues; it has become symbol both of → Judaism and modern state of Israel. Its significance has been variously explained: e.g. as deriving from → Tree of Life, or symbolizing life-giving light of God. S.G.F.B.

R.G.G.[3], IV, col. 859; J. Leveen, *The Hebrew Bible in Art* (1944), pp. 16ff.; E. L. Sukenik, *Anc. Synagogues in Palestine and Greece* (1934), pp. 54ff., Pl. XII, XIV; *E.J.R.*, p. 258.

Mercury Roman god of traders, identified with Grk. → Hermes, from whom he prob. derives; his temple on Avertine hill dates from 495 BC. The Gauls and Teutons identified M. with their chief deity: evidence about name used among Gauls is conflicting; the German equation was with Wodan (Odin) (→→ Celtic Relig.; Scandin. Relig.). S.G.F.B.

O.C.D., p. 559; F. Altheim, *Hist. of Roman Religion* (E.T. 1938), pp. 250ff.; J. Vendryès,

Le religion des Celtes (1948), pp. 261ff.; E. Tonnelat, *La religion des Germains* (1948), p. 342; A. Ross, *Pagan Celtic Britain* (1967), s.v. 'Mercury'.

Mercy In the Chr. doc. of God there is a basic tension between the Justice and the M. of God. It finds its most striking expression in the opposing concepts of Christ as merciful Saviour and stern Judge at → Final Judgment (→ Dooms). It led to exaltation of Virgin Mary as embodiment of M. and compassion (→→ Dēisis; Mary, Cult; Osiris). S.G.F.B.

(China and Far East) Pre-eminently an attr. of gods and rulers. The mercy of → Buddha incl. all beings in an all-embracing love. → Kuan Yin (Kwannon), the Goddess or Lord of Mercy, is most popular deity, everywhere worshipped and adored. In Japan, the insignia of the emperor: a mirror, a bead and a sword, symbolize truth, mercy and justice respectively. (→ Names of God, Islam). D.H.S.

Merit (Buddh.) The Pali term for merit is → *Puñña*, popular corruptions of which are used in S.E. Asian Buddh. countries: in → Ceylon, *pin*; in Thailand *boon*; in Burma the notion of merit is more usually ref. to by the word *kutho*, which is the Burmese form of the Pali term *kusala*, meaning good in sense of meritorious. (→ *Puñña*). T.O.L.

(China and Far East) → Buddhism, with its doctrine of → *karma*, intro. into China and Far East the idea that cumulative credit of one's own good deeds would lead to a better rebirth. The idea was taken up by → Taoism, and in popular relig. to become a chief incentive to virtue. The ordinary layman's desire to acquire M. towards some specific personal end led to wide variety of practice. M. could be acquired by charity, by contracting for recitation of Buddha's name, by release of living creatures (*fang shêng*), by devotion to the → Sangha, abstinence, giving up something desirable, making long → pilgrimages etc. Numerous popular tracts assessed merit or demerit of partic. actions. The transfer of M. was an import. feature of Far Eastern Buddhism. A good reserve of M. was deemed not only to affect an individual's future, but to promote well-being of one's deceased ancestors, family, clan and descendants. The recitation of Buddh. formulae in monasteries produced M., which could be transferred to benefit others, or accrue to one's own account in the W. Paradise. Buddh. rites for the dead, were dominated by idea of M., transferred to soul of deceased so as to ensure an early and better rebirth. The boundless stores of M. accumulated by Buddhas and → bodhisattvas were available to assist the faithful. The desire for accumulation of M. provides a strong incentive to benevolence and compassion. (→ Indulgences). D.H.S.

C. H. Plopper, *Chinese Relig. seen through the Proverb* (1926), pp. 224ff.; H. Welch, *The Practice of Chinese Buddhism* (1967), *passim*.

Meru Mount Meru is mythic mountain figuring as axis of world in trad. Hindu → cosmology. 84,000 *yojanas* (leagues) high, it is place where the gods disport themselves. Some descriptions of jewel-bedecked gardens, palaces, celestial musicians, etc., are reminiscent of other paradises in Indian and other traditions (→ Pure Land). M. is north of Himalayas, and is surrounded by four continents. The one to south, and incl. India, is *Jambudvīpa*, 'the island of *jambu* (rose-apple) trees'. M. was used as churning rod when → Vishnu churned the ocean (→ *avataras*). N.S.

Mesopotamian Religion This designation, which implies unified trad. of relig. faith and practice, is frequently used for what were, historically, the religs. of three distinctive peoples who lived in Mesopotamia: the Sumerians, Akkadians or Babylonians, and Assyrians. It is justified because → Sumerian relig. trads. were adopted, with modifications, by the other two peoples. Sumerian continued as the liturgical and learned language long after 1800 BC, when it ceased to be spoken. (→→ Assyrian Relig.; Babylonian Relig.). See Synoptic Index under 'Mesopot.'. S.G.F.B.

Dhorme, *R.B.A.*, pp. 3ff.; H. W. F. Saggs, *The Greatness that was Babylon* (1962), pp. 157ff., 301ff.; D. Diringer, *The Alphabet* (1948), p. 49.

Messiah, Messianism *Ex.* Heb. *māshīaḥ*, 'anointed'. The first kings of Israel, Saul and David, were initiated into their royal office by anointing. Under David, Israel achieved great power and prestige, so that later generations, when faced with misfortune, looked back to him as the ideal king, and longed for a 'son of David' to deliver them from their oppressors and restore glory of past. This longing, after Exile, took form of Messianic hope, i.e. that → Yahweh would send his Anointed (Messiah) to deliver his people and punish their enemies. Since idea of the M. was never officially defined, conceptions varied from a human (e.g. Isa. 45:1) to a super-human being (e.g. Dan. 7:13ff.). At → Qumran, two M.'s were envisaged, a priestly and a royal. In 1st cent. CE, under direct Roman rule, M.-hope became very strong, as both → Josephus and N.T. attest. → Jesus was recognised as M. (Mk. 8:29), as were many others (→ Christ). The M. hope survived disaster of year 70, to flare up again in 132, when → Bar-Kochba, recognised as M., led fierce but unsuccessful revolt against Rome. Many pseudo-M.'s appeared in later → Judaism (down to 18th cent.). Hope of coming of an ideal king and saviour had been current in Egypt long before its appearance in Israel. So-called Messianic movements have appeared in modern times among various depressed peoples, being expressive of their hopes of deliverance. (→→ Cargo Cults; Chiliasm). S.G.F.B.

Schürer, *G.J.V.*, II, pp. 469ff.; S. Mowinckel, *He That Cometh* (E.T. 1959); *H.D.B.*, *s.v.; E.R.E.*, VIII, pp. 570–87; *R.A.C.*, II, col. 1250–4; *R.G.G.*³, IV, col. 895–907; J. Klausner, *The Messianic Idea in Israel* (1956); W. O. E. Oesterley, *Evolution of the Messianic Idea* (1908); J. H. Breasted, *The Dawn of Conscience* (1935), pp. 198ff.; *E.J.R.*, pp. 259ff.; V. Lanternari, *H.R.*, 2 (1962), pp. 52ff.; T. W. Manson, *The Servant-Messiah* (1953).

Metempsychosis *Ex.* Grk. 'transferring of soul (*psychē*) from one body to another': other designations are: 'transmigration of soul'; 'rebirth'; 'reincarnation'. The idea of life as a cyclical process, i.e. of passage of → soul through successive bodies, is a natural deduction made by many primitive peoples from phenomena of birth and death and reproduction of family features in children: it was prob. incl. in cult of → Great Goddess and some → ancestor-cults (e.g. Chinese). As a relig.-philosoph. doctrine it appeared in India *c.* 600 BC (→ Samsāra), and adopted into → Buddhism, which ensured its diffusion throughout Asia. It was taught in Greece in 6th cent. BC by →→ Pythagoreans and Orphics, and accepted into →→ Platonism and → Neoplatonism. Herodotus thought, erroneously, that idea came to Greece from Egypt. Belief in M. was current also in →→ Celtic, Teutonic religs., in → Gnosticism and certain esoteric forms of Judaism. Since M. presupposed cyclic view of → Time, it was ruled out in religs. conceiving of Time as linear (e.g. Judaism, Christianity, Zoroastrianism.) (→ Rebirth). S.G.F.B.

E.R.E., XII, pp. 425–40; *R.G.G.*³, VI, col. 1696–1700; J. Head and S. L. Cranston (eds.), *Reincarnation* (1961); Brandon, *M.D.*, *passim*, *History, Time and Deity* (1965), ch. 4 (with bibliog.).

(China, Japan, Korea) Neither → Confucianism nor → Shinto has any doctrine of M. When → Buddhism came to China, Korea and Japan, the doc. of → *karma* and belief in rebirth, linked to → Mahāyāna ideal of universal fellowship and idea that meritorious actions could be dedicated to assist souls in inferior resorts of M. to progress to better resorts and finally to Buddahood, came to exert an almost irresistible appeal. So long as soul is bound within the karmic process, and not entirely freed from hatred, greed and stupidity, it must inevitably be subject to rebirth in one of resorts of M. (→ Samsāra).

Various modifications of concept of M. were developed in Buddhism, → Tibet. Bhm. and → Taoism; but essential idea is same. Great mural paintings in popular temples repr. the wheel of M., or wheel of birth and life, whilst idea of M. is disseminated in numerous popular works such as the *Yü Li* or *Precious Records*, which depicts in gruesome detail the underworld of Buddhism and Taoism, where all souls go at death for → judgement. The souls of exceptionally virtuous men are reborn as gods; those who have lived a good life return to earth as men or women; some for their sins are reborn as animals, hungry ghosts or denizens of hell.

The Wheel of M. represents six modes of existence: gods, demi-gods or *asuras*, human beings, animals, hungry ghosts and demons. These six primary resorts of M. are again subdivided. All sentient beings are considered to be fettered to wheel of M., until they attain release from karmic process by entering on Buddahood and → Nirvana. D.H.S.

J. Hackin (ed.), *Asiatic Mythology* (1932), pp. 363ff.; C. A. S. Williams, *Outlines of Chinese Symbolism* (1931), pp. 392ff.; M. Anesaki, *Hist. of Japanese Relig.* (1930), pp. 67–8; *E.R.E.*, XII, pp. 429ff.

(Hindu doctrine) The doc. of M. (rebirth, reincarnation, transmigration), together with connected belief in *karma*, has come to be pervasive feature of → Hinduism. It was characteristic feature of unorthodox → Sramanic relig. movements, such as →→ Jainism, the Ajivikas and early Buddhism, but was not part of relig. of Vedic hymns. Its appearance within → Brahmanical relig. dates from → Upanisads (e.g. it is taught by Yājñavalkya as new doc. in the *Bṛhadāranyaka Upaniṣad*). Since the belief was present at least in Jainism at very early date, it is reasonable to conclude that Upanisadic teaching repr. synthesis between Vedic and non-Aryan elements. The spread of belief may have been facilitated by absorption of early → Samkhya, which shared features in common with the sramanic movements. The idea of continuous cycle of life (→ *samsara*) brought with it a more elaborate cosmology. Even gods died, to be reborn, and thus liberation was to be pursued against the backcloth of cosmic processes of immense or infinite duration (→ Time, Hindu attitudes). The belief was combatted by → Carvaka materialists, but otherwise became universal in Indian trad. With exception of Buddhists (and in a sense → Advaitins), the entity undergoing process of rebirth was considered to be the eternal soul (→→ *atman*, *jiva*, *purusa*), which on death is divested of sense-organs, etc., and clad only in sheath of subtle matter. It is then reborn in another gross body, until such time as it may achieve → *moksa* or liberation. The Advaitin interpretation is somewhat different, for there is here only one Atman. The individual is essentially constituted by his empirical ego, and it is this which, in Advaita, transmigrates. Once individuality has been overcome, through Self-realisation, the process of rebirth ceases. During periods of cosmic dissolution (*pralaya*), souls exist in quiescent or latent state, resting so to say. With re-creation of cosmos the karmic forces become operative once more. Since rebirth can occur in various forms, as man, animal, etc., it occurs too in various planes of existence, e.g. in heavens and purgatories. Thus there is a continuum, and a circulation, between all forms of life. The deprivation of the self of its sensory and intellectual faculties, etc., between one life and next implies that typically there is no memory of previous births, though yogis and others are supposed to be able to achieve such memories. Indian folklore also abounds with stories of children, etc., who recognise people and places that they have not previously seen, unless in a previous existence. The instinctive behaviour of children, the supposed spontaneous generation of some insects, etc., have been adduced as empirical grounds for belief, and various philosoph. arguments (e.g. that any proof of eternity of the self implies pre-existence) have been advanced for belief, incl., in recent years, a fairly full treatment of topic by S. → Radhakrishnan. N.S.

L. Renou, *Religions of Ancient India* (1953); S. Radhakrishnan, introduction to his *The Brahma Sutra* (1960); N. Smart, *Doctrine and Argument in Indian Philosophy* (1964).

Methodism Form of Chr. worship and living, developed among organised groups of followers within → C. of E. in 18th cent. by John and Charles → Wesley, which, after their deaths, became a separate denomination. Such separation was alien to the Wesleys' intentions; but the peculiar development of the groups ('Societies') made it inevitable. Wesley's annual Conference of Lay Preachers (from 1744) was legalised in 1784, to secure continuance of orderly government of Societies by 100 members nominated by deed-poll, with provision for their successors: all this being outside constitution of the C. of E. This Conference appointed Preachers to local 'Preaching Houses', whose doctrinal standards were to be Wesley's *Sermons* and *Notes on the N.T.* Prob. Wesley's ordination of Coke as Superintendent of the American Societies was decisive. Wesley had come to believe (through Stillingfleet's *Irenicum*) that the orders of presbyter and episcopus (→ Hierarchy, Christ.) were equivalent, and, therefore, that he (esp. in an emergency where the C. of E. refused to act) had the right, as presbyter, to ordain. Wesley had resisted the administration of Sacraments by his Preachers, his prescription being morning Communion in Parish Church, evening evangelistic service in the Preaching House or open air. But the hosts of converts who had no link with Anglicanism, and growing refusal of clergy to allow the Methodists Communion, led (after Wesley's death) to *Plan of Pacification* (1795), whereby the Conference allowed administration of Sacraments to its own Preachers; in 1836 it adopted ordination by imposition of hands, and separation was complete. The 19th cent. was marked by two main developments: schism within Methodism and increasing alienation from C. of E. The schisms were largely motivated by non-theological factors, such as endeavour to emulate Wesley's authoritarianism by men like Jabez Bunting in an increasingly democratic age, and the development of Wesley's orig. working-class converts, through virtues of honesty and hard work that he inculcated, into a prosperous middle-class which in turn tended to overlook spiritual needs of the 'submerged tenth' of the new age. The largest schism (the 'Primitive Methodists', from 1811) grew to a Church of ¼ million members, its leading figure in later years being the famous Biblical scholar, A. S. Peake (1865–1929). The 19th cent. Oxford Movement in C. of E. sought to recover its Cath. consciousness by renewal of those elements in the pre-Reformation heritage which Wesley had found distasteful. The contempt of Newman and the rest for M. was repaid with interest, and inevitably the Methodists, children of the C. of E., were thrust by reaction into waiting arms of the Free Churches. Hence the curious blend in modern M. of Anglican and Nonconformist trads. of worship, morals, policy. The M. Union (1932) brought together all but a few inconsiderable splinters of the sundered M. bodies, the principal exception being Calvinistic Methodists of Wales. Wesley's rejection of 'double predestination', and the strong flavour of → Arminianism in M. worship and doc., had never carried with it the followers of Whitefield, whose successors are mainly confined to Wales today.

M. in Britain today embraces a membership of ¾ million and a 'community' (children, adherents etc.) of over 2 m. It has been a great missionary church; its anticipation of Anglican evangelism in U.S.A. has led to its present membership there of 15 m. Africa, Asia, the W. Indies, and Brit. Commonwealth complete a total constituency of some 50 m. Methodists in the community of the World Church. Wesley, the 'master-builder', had unwittingly laid foundations of one of the three greatest (non-Roman and Orthodox) Churches in the world. The M. constitution is historically 'pragmatic', and forms series of concentric circles, from the local chapels organised into 'circuits', each with a team of Ministers under the 'Superintendent', the Districts under 'Chairman', and the central authority of the annual Conference of 650 (half Ministers, half Laymen). Wesley's prime institution of local groups or 'Classes', meeting weekly, which formed the orig. cells of M., has largely declined. The basis of membership is 'sincere desire to be saved from sin through faith in Jesus Christ, and evidence of this in life and conduct'. The two Sacraments and the *Book of Offices* are largely Anglican, except for the 'Covenant Service', an innovation of Wesley's, in which other mod. churches (e.g. Church of South India) have shown interest. The worship is trad. dominated by hymns of C. Wesley, which spell out the characteristic M. emphases on salvation through faith, assurance, perfect love, and corporate priesthood. There has always been strong demand for disciplined Chr. living, corporate and individual, and for social welfare, under such leaders as Hugh Price Hughes (1847–1902) and John Scott Lidgett (1854–1953). Conversations with Anglican representatives since 1956 have led to suggested means of reunion in Gt. Britain, which is now under debate. The essence of this scheme is the 'Service of Reconciliation', which would bring back episcopacy into the M. system, thus making intercommunion possible and initiating a process of 'growing together' which may, in time, heal breach that the Evangelical Revival, under the Wesleys, began.

M. in U.S.A., beginning with the famous 18th cent. 'circuit riders', was organised into an independent Episcopal Church as result of Wesley's ordination of Coke and Asbury. The 19th cent. saw numerous schisms. The M. Prot. Church drew away in 1830, abolishing episcopacy and admitting laymen to the governing Conference; in 1844 the Southern Conferences separated on question of slavery. These bodies reunited in 1939 to form the M. Episcopal Church, although many splinter-churches remain. The American Church is more urban and prosperous than Brit. M., and less interested in theological as contrasted with social questions. The Bishops have greater power of visitation and discipline than their Anglican counterparts. Annual Regional Conferences transact the normal administrative work of Church, with triennial National Conferences on major questions of policy. In education, hospitals and children's homes, in missionary work and social evangelism, the American M. Church has played a leading part, and is by far the strongest centre of M. in the world today. (→→ Apostolic Succ.; Bishop). B.D.

Standard *Hist. of Methodism* by W. J. Townsend, H. B. Workman, G. Eayrs (1909); R. E. Davies –E. G. Rupp (eds.), *A Hist. of the Methodist Church in Gt. Britain*, vol. I (1965), with full bibliog.: specially import. are contributions of M. L. Edwards, J. E. Rattenbury, J. S. Simon, F. Hildebrandt. By non-Methodists: M. Piette, *John Wesley in the Evolution of Protestantism* (E.T. 1937); G. C. Cell, *The Rediscovery of John Wesley* (1935); M. Schmidt, *John Wesley, a Theological Biography*, vol. I (1962). On doctrine: H. Lindström, *Wesley and Sanctification* (1950), and works of Rattenbury and Hildebrandt.

Metta Buddh. term for lovingkindness or goodwill; acc. to Buddh. thought, one of the 4 → *Brahma-Vihāras*, or 'spiritual abodes'. T.O.L.

Metteyya (Pali); **Maitreya** (Skt.) Name of the Buddha who is yet to come. This is in acc. with the Buddh. theory that there had been a series of 'Awakened' or 'Enlightened' Ones (Buddhas) prior to → Gotama, who lived in 6th cent. BC, and that there will be others after him. The details of M.'s life story are foretold in many Buddh. works, such as the *Cakkavatti-Sihanāda Sutta* of the → *Digha Nikaya*, the *Anagatavamsa* and *Maitreyavyakarana*; the details agree closely with those of life of Gotama, but with substitution of other personal names, locations etc. This future Buddha is regarded by Buddhists as living at present a supernatural existence in a Tusita heaven, in world of the devas (→ Cosmology, Buddh.). His personal name is held to be Ajita, Metteyya being his *gotra* or clan name, and having ref. to a root which indic. friendship or love. The eschatological hopes inspired by doc. of this future Buddha's coming occasionally lead to forms of → Messianism in Buddh. countries, e.g. parts of C. Asia and Burma. The inscription: 'Come Maitreya, come!', is found carved on rocks in mountains of Tibet and Mongolia. T.O.L.

T. W. and C. A. I. Rhys-Davids, *Dialogues of the Buddha*, part 3 (1921, repr. 1965), pp. 73f.; E. Conze, *Buddhist Scriptures*, 1959. pp. 237-42.

Meykaṇḍa (or Meykaṇḍa-deva). 13th cent. Tamil saint and author of the *Śivajñāna-bodham* ('Realisation of the knowledge of Śiva') a key text in the development of the → Śaiva Siddhanta school. Acc. to somewhat legendary accounts of his life, he is supposed to have been initiated by a teacher (→ *guru*) at age of three and given name Meykanda or 'Discoverer of Truth'. The Truth he discovered was set forth in the *sutras* of *Śivajñānabodham*, and his teacher became in due course his pupil and one of four major saints (→ *acaryas*) of Śaiva Siddhanta, of whom Meykanda is reckoned greatest. A contemporary of his, and another prominent exponent of of Śaivism, Śrīkaṇṭha, has been erroneously identified with him. N.S.

S. N. Dasgupta, *Hist. of Indian Philosophy*, vol. 5 (1961); J. H. Piet, *A Logical Presentation of the Saiva Siddhanta Philosophy* (1952); G. Matthews (tr.), *Siva-nana-bodham* (1948); H. Bhattacharyya (ed.), *The Cultural Heritage of India*, vol. 4 (1956).

Michael, Archangel M. appears in Bible as supernatural champion of men against → Devil (Jude 5:9; Rev. 12:7–9). In early Chr. lit., he is presented partic. as succouring Christians against demonic attack at death. In medieval conception of Last Judgment (→ Dooms), M. had decisive role, presiding over → psychostasia and repelling demonic interference. M. was believed to have appeared on Mt. Gaganus in 5th cent. CE: his cult was popular in Middle Ages and many churches were dedicated to him, often on former pagan sites. Some Coptic and Ethiopic texts seem to indic. connection between M. and → Thoth. (→ Angels). S.G.F.B.

R.A.C., V, col. 243–51; *D.C.C.*, *s.v.; R.G.G.*³, IV, col. 932–3; *E.R.E.*, VIII, pp. 619–23; L. Kretzenbacher, *Die Seelenwaage* (1958), p. 56; S. G. F. Brandon, *Judgment of the Dead* (1967), ch. 6.

Midrash Heb., from root meaning 'to seek out', with ref. to meaning of sacred scripture, signifying result of such search. In Rabbinic lit., it came to mean 'commentary', and was divided into two classes: *M. Halakah*, i.e. commentary on → *Halakah* = 'rule', 'binding law', and *M. Haggadah*, i.e. commentary on → *Haggadah* = 'narration', which became a rich homiletic exposition of scripture. There is a vast M. lit. (→ Judaism). S.G.F.B.

Oesterley and Robinson, *L.R.M.J.*, pp. 57ff.; I. Epstein, *Judaism* (1959), pp. 114ff.; *E.R.E.*, VIII, *s.v.; E.J.R.*, pp. 261ff.

Middle Way (Buddh.) The *Majjhimā-patipadā* (Pali), or *Madhyamā-pratipad* (Skt.), the 'middle way' or 'path' between materialism and sensual indulgence, and rationalism and asceticism, is name used for Buddhism in early period. By avoiding the two extremes, claimed the Buddha, he had 'gained knowledge of that middle path which gives vision, which gives knowledge, which causes calm, special knowledge, enlightenment, nibbāna'. (*Dhammacakkappavattana Sutta*). T.O.L.

Miki (CE 1798–1887) → Tenri-kyō. D.H.S.

Mi Lei Chi. name for → Maitreya, the most powerful → bodhisattva after → Kuan Yin in the Chinese pantheon. He waits in the Tushiti heaven until his advent as the future Buddha, 5,000 years after → Sakyamuni's entrance into → Nirvana. His image, found near entrance to Buddh. temples, is fat and smiling, so that he became known to westerners as the Laughing Buddha. D.H.S.

K. L. Reichelt, *Truth and Tradition in Chinese Buddhism* (1927), pp. 186–7; S. Couling, *Encycl. Sinica* (1917, 1965), pp. 322–3.

Milinda King whose discussions with the Buddh. monk Nāgasena are related in the Pali work → *Milinda-panha*, i.e. 'The Questions of Milinda'. By his Greek name of Menander he was known to classical Gk. historians; by modern authorities, M. is regarded as having ruled in middle of 2nd cent. BC over territory to N.W. of India, which incl. Kabul and → Gandhāra, the Swat valley and poss. part of the west. Punjab. Whether or not he became a Buddh. is unknown. T.O.L.

A. K. Narain, *The Indo-Greeks* (1957).

Milinda-Panha A non-canonical Pali Buddh. work, composed in style of the canonical Suttas, having form of dialogue between Buddh. monk Nāgasena and King → Milinda. The dialogue contains quotations from Pali canonical scriptures and repr. point of view of → Theravāda school. The work has 8 main divisions; in each some 10 or 12 questions are dealt with. These are kind of problems that might present themselves to anyone acquainted with major Buddh. ideas and practices, but who has become aware of what appear to be inconsistencies or uncertainties. The first dilemma, e.g., is why the Buddha, who is regarded as having attained → *nibbāna*, should accept homage from others: if he had fully attained, would he not be indifferent to homage, and, if he received homage (as he did), then could he be regarded as having attained *nibbāna*? I. B. Horner, who has recently made a new trans. of the M. into Eng.; comments that 'the multitude of topics discussed or touched on makes it difficult to think of any Buddh. theme it ignores entirely'. The Buddh. scholar → Buddhaghosa quotes frequently from the M.: it was evidently well-known by his time. The work was composed prob. in India or Kashmir sometime after Milinda's own time, poss. at about begin. of Christ. era. The M. was trans. into Sinhalese in 18th cent CE by a monk named Sumangala. The Pali text, ed. by V. Trenckner, was published in Roman script in 1880 (pts. repr. 1963); it was trans. into Eng. by T. W. Rhys-Davids and publ. as vols XXXV and XXXVI of *S.B.E.* in 1890. A new Eng. trans. by I. B. Horner, making use of more recent advances in Pali studies, was publ. in 2 vols. in 1963–4. T.O.L.

Mīmāṁsā Known also as *pūrvamīmāṁsā* (→ Vedanta) and as *karmamīmaṁsa*, since it deals with sacred works or *karma* relevant to salvation, it is one of six trad. schools of Hindu philosophy. It is chiefly concerned, however, not with philosophical questions but with exegesis of earlier Vedic scriptures (the name *pūrvamīmāṁsā* means 'earlier exegesis' as distinguished from the 'later' constituted by Vedanta, which concentrates on docs. of → Upaniṣads, etc.). The exegesis of M. has largely to do with ritual, and only incidentally is a world-view implied. The earliest extant work of school is the *Mīmāṁsāsūtra*, ascribed to Jaimini, and dating from about beginning of Christ. era in present form. (Like other Hindu *sutras* it must have long prior history.) Two sub-schools came into being after 8th century CE, due to varying commentarial interpretations of Kumārila Bhaṭṭa (8th cent.) and Prabhākara, a younger contemporary. The chief dispute was over epistemology. The main feature of M. is attempt to interpret all Vedic utterances as injunctions rather than statements, and as having their essential meaning in guidance of ritual and, to some extent, conduct. Thus the gods mentioned in Vedic hymns disappear as entities affirmed by scriptures and retain merely this significance—that their names figure in various injunctions about ritual. This reflects way in which in period of → *Brahmanas* concern with ritual itself came to displace concern with objects towards which ritual had been orig. directed. Still, M., to maintain its position, had to presuppose a *Weltanschauung*. E.g. the periodic collapse and re-creation of cosmos (→ cosmology, Hindu), virtually universally held in rest of Hindu trad., was denied, since Veda had to be treated as instrinsically valid, and so eternal and unchanging. M. is atheistic, and until late period retained old Vedic hope of heaven as reward of correct conduct and sacrifice, rather than ideal of liberation (→ *mokṣa*) from rebirth which entered → Brahmanical trad. during Upaniṣadic period. This is sign of antiquity of M. Although coupled with Vedanta, in many respects M. is in conflict with principles of the various schools of Vedanta. N.S.

A. B. Keith, *The Purva Mimamsa* (1921); N. V. Thadani, *The Mimamsa: the Sect of the Sacred Doctrines of the Hindus* (1952); F. Edgerton (tr.), *The Mimamsa Nyaya Prakasa of Apadevi* (1929).

Minerva Italian goddess of handicrafts, identified with → Athena. M. may have been of Etruscan orig., since she first appears at Rome in an Etruscan-like triad with → Jupiter and → Juno. S.G.F.B.

O.C.D., *s.v.;* F. Altheim, *Hist. of Roman Religion* (E.T. 1938), pp. 232ff.; A. Grenier, *Les religions étrusque et romaine* (1948), pp. 104ff.

Mīnīm Designation for persons regarded as obnoxious in → Talmud and Rabbinic lit. About CE 100 R. Gamaliel II added a 12th Benediction to the Shemoneh 'Esreh (the venerable prayer used in Jew. liturgy), condemning M. The identity of the M. has been much debated; it seems gen. agreed that they were, or incl., → Jew. Christians. S.G.F.B.

E.R.E., VIII, *s.v.;* M. Simon, *Verus Israel* (1948), pp. 214ff.; *E.J.R.*, p. 264.

Ming (Fate) Chi. character signifying the appointment, decree, ordinance or will of Heaven, and hence fate or destiny; also decree by which Heaven calls men to life and determines their fate. For → Confucius Heaven was a purposeful Supreme Being, and M. was expression of its purpose. Acc. to → Mencius, 'that which happens without men causing it to happen is from M.' (5b, 6). The → Mohists strongly attacked what they believed to be a fatalistic element in Confucian concept of M. Acc. to Chi. theory, the rise or fall of a dynasty was determined by the M. of Heaven. (→ Fate, or Destiny). D.H.S.

L. Wieger, *Chinese Characters* (1915, 1965), p. 47; Fung Yu-lan, *Hist. of Chinese Philos.*, vol. 1 (1937), *passim.*

Minotaur In Grk. mythology, a bull-headed man, born of → Poseidon and Pasiphaë, wife of Minos. A → labyrinth at Knossos, Crete, was alleged to have been built to house M., who was killed by Theseus. It is thought that idea of M. orig. from bull-cult in → Cretan Relig.; M. P. Nilsson traces it to bull-contests at Knossos. S.G.F.B.

E.R.E., VIII, *s.v.;* M. P. Nilsson, *The Mycenaean Origin of Greek Mythology* (1963 edn.), pp. 176ff.; C. Picard, *Les religions préhelléniques* (1948), *passim.*

Miracles Action implying a superhuman power has naturally been attr. to gods in all religs. Such power has also been ascribed to human beings regarded as enjoying special divine favour (e.g. → Moses, → Heracles, Chr. saints, sacred → kings). Miraculous power may also be acquired by extreme → asceticism (e.g. Hindu ascetics) or by → magic. In Christianity, M. had a basic significance from beginning. In Gospels and Acts, the M. of → Jesus are cited as *sēmeia* ('signs') or *erga* ('works') attesting his Messiahship (e.g. Mt. 11:2ff.; Acts 2:22), the greatest being his Resurrection. Acc. to Acts, the Apostles also worked M. The credibility of Chr. M. became topic of sceptical attack and apologetical defence in 19th cent. The issue is now gen. viewed in wider context of → phenomenology of relig. S.G.F.B.

*H.D.B.*², *s.v.; E.R.E.*, VIII, *s.v.; R.G.G.*³, VI, col. 1831–46; R. M. Grant, *Miracle and Natural Law in Graeco-Roman and Early Christ. Thought* (1952).

(Islam) *Mu'jiza* (baffling) is a miracle wrought by a prophet, and *karāma* (charism) one wrought by a saint. The Qur. word is *āya* (sign), which is also word for a verse of the Qur. The Qur. refers to miracles by Moses, Solomon, Jesus, but claims none for → Muḥammad. He was content to wait when asked for a sign (x:21). It is only by God's permission that a messenger can produce a sign (xxix:49). Even if a sign were granted, there is no guarantee that people would believe (vi:109). God declares he sends no signs because people of earlier times declared them false (xvii:61). The Qur. itself should satisfy the people (xxix:50). Muhammad is content to call himself a warner, and to point to wonders done by God in nature. The supreme miracle is the → Qur., which was brought to him piecemeal by → Gabriel. (→ I'jāz). But

→ Trad. does not hesitate to ascribe M.'s to Muhammad. Portents are recorded regarding his birth, childhood and youth (cf. Guillaume, *Life*, 69, and → Baḥīra). E.g. when there was no water at al-Ḥudaybiya except some Muhammad had in a vessel, he put his hand into it and water poured out between his fingers to supply 1,500 men with enough for drinking and ablution. He said of a secretary of his who had apostatised that the earth would not accept him. The story says that when the man died he was buried several times, but each time was cast up on the surface. Another story tells of suffering caused by drought in Medina. Muhammad prayed, raising hands, and clouds appeared bringing torrential rain which lasted a week. As it was damaging property and drowning animals, appeal was made by Muhammad, and when he prayed the clouds moved away from Medina. Those few examples quoted are given by → Bukhari, or → Muslim or both. A great number of miracles are attr. to Muhammad. It is the same with saints. Their miracles are astonishing, whether performed during lifetime or at their tombs after death. (→ Saints). J.R.

E.I., II, p. 744; III, p. 624; Hughes, pp. 850f.; Pareja, pp. 800ff.; *Mishkāt*, pp. 1271ff. (chs. XXIV, XXV); D. B. Macdonald, *Theology*, index (*karāma* and *mu'jiza*); Wensinck, *Creed*, index (Miracles); Nicholson, *Studies*, index; Sweetman, *I.C.T.*, index to each vol.; F. Rosenthal, *Ibn Khaldun*, index; Miller, *Bāb*, index (*mu'jiza*).

-Mi'rāj Lit. 'the ladder'. Used of the night journey → Muḥammad is said to have made to heaven. After he had gone to Jerusalem (→ *Isrā'*), he mounted → Burāq and entered the various heavens accompanied by → Gabriel. He met prophets and holy men of earlier times in different heavens, no indic. being given why some should be in higher heavens than others. In the highest heaven, he was ordered by God to command his people to pray 50 times daily. On his way down he met Moses who, when he heard what had been commanded, said his people could never observe so much; he must, therefore, go back and ask for a reduction in number of times. Eventually the number was reduced to five. As a good deed gets a tenfold reward (cf. Qur., vi:161), it is held that the five daily times of → prayer are credited as 50. Some have treated incident as a dream; others have interpreted it in terms of journey of soul of deceased to the divine throne of → judgment; → Ṣūfīs have interpreted it in terms of rising of soul through the veils of the sensual to mystical knowledge and the unveiled presence of God. J.R.

E.I., III, pp. 505–8; Hughes, pp. 351f.; *Mishkāt*, pp. 1264ff.; Pareja, pp. 794ff. and index; Guillaume, *Life*, pp. 181–7; W. McKane, 'A manuscript on the Mi'rāj in the Bodleian', *J.S.S.*, II (1957), pp. 366ff.

Mishnah Heb. = 'instruction'. The M. is authoritative collection of Jew. Oral Law, in Heb., forming basis of Palestinian and Babylonian versions of → Talmud. Acc. to trad., it was compiled by R. Judah ha-Nasi (135–*c*. CE 220) from earlier material. The → Pharisees believed that Oral Law was given to → Moses on Sinai, together with Written Law (→ Torah). The M. has exercised a profound influence upon subsequent → Judaism. S.G.F.B.

H. Danby (tr.), *The Mishnah* (1933); H. L. Strack, *Intro. to Talmud and Mishnah* (E.T. 1945); Oesterley and Robinson, *L.R.M.J.*, pp. 97ff.; *R.G.G.*[3], IV, col. 966–8; I. Epstein, *Judaism* (1959), pp. 114ff.; *E.J.R.*, pp. 373.

Missal *Ex.* Lat. *Liber missalis* or *Missale*. Book containing all matter necessary for celebration of → Mass throughout year. The Missale Romanum is official M. of R.C. Church, dating from 1570 but deriving from the *Sacramentarium Gregorianum* (595). S.G.F.B.

D.C.C., *s.v.*

Mission (the Propagation of Religion) Among the great religs. of the world, it is poss. to distinguish between missionary (Lat. *missio*, 'sending') and non-missionary religs. M.-religs. are those which hold their basic tenets to have relevance outside the immediate circle of believers; non-M. religs. make no such claim. A number of factors affect this orientation: those religs. which are closely identified with a specific ethnic group, or which lack any element of prophecy, are normally non-M.; M.-religs. have usually been those based on teachings of a founder, teachings capable of being applied to, or adapted to fit, situations other than that in which they were first propagated. M.-religs. thus claim to be of universal relevance, and take steps to make good that claim. It must, however, be recognised that religs. have often been propagated spontaneously, as result of population movements and cultural contacts, without necessarily involving an active sense of mission.

Non-M. religs. incl. the so-called 'primitive' religs., those of China and Japan, and Hinduism. In last case, however, the activities of individual teachers and groups inside and outside India, partic. since Swāmī Vivekānanda (World's Parliament of Religions, Chicago, 1893) have come to be regarded as mission. But in none of these cases is the concept of mission vital to the ethos of the relig. in question.

Present-day M.-religs., using term in its widest sense, are numerous; but three among them—Buddhism, Islām and Christianity—are worthy of special mention.

In Buddhism, the M. motive was implicit from first, in the Buddha's gathering of a company of disciples. His discovery and teaching of the → *Dhamma*, and his own refusal to enter immediately into → *Nibbāna*, preferring rather to communicate his discovery to those who would listen, provides starting point of Buddh. M.; the *Dhamma* has always been taken to have relevance for whole of mankind. The truth is one; mankind is one. The instrument of M. has normally been the → *sangha*, or monastic community. The proclamation of the *Dhamma* may thus take place irrespective of local conditions. After an initial period of expansion (→ Buddhism, Gen. Survey), the M. of Buddhism stagnated; it has only been taken up again in 20th cent., partly in response to West. and Christ. challenges. The world M. of Buddhism is today acknowledged by virtually all Buddh. groups.

Since Islām and Christianity have both developed out of the Jewish tradition, a word must be said concerning → Judaism and M. Judaism certainly fulfils many of conditions of a M.-relig. There are many passages in the O.T. which have ref. to non-Jews: e.g. Gen. 12:3, '. . . in you all the families of the earth will be blessed'; Isa. 42:6, 'I have given you as a covenant to the people, a light to the nations.' However, Jew. interpretation of these and similar passages has normally been centripetal, rather than centrifugal. The coming of the → Messiah and estab. of his kingdom will indeed be of significance to all men; but the direction of movement will be inward, rather than outward. The nations will come to 'the mountain of the house of the Lord . . . all nations shall flow to it' (Isa. 2:2f.). This, together with the ethnic character of Judaism and its unwillingness, until recently, to adapt, has meant that there has been no true M. activity, other than on a limited scale in Hellenistic times (→ Proselyte).

As in case of Buddhism, the implicit M. basis of Islām is to be found in the postulate of universal significance applied to message of prophet → Muhammad, and partic. his vision of unity of Godhead. Explicit M. passages are found in the Qur'ān: e.g. 'Say to those who have been given the Book and to the ignorant, Do you accept Islām?' (3:19); 'He it is who hath sent His apostle with guidance and the religion of truth, that He may make it victorious over every other religion . . .' (61:9). M. might be accomplished by force, if necessary (→ Jihād). The spread of Islām in early Middle Ages followed closely path of Arab conquests, and M. work was common duty, rather than left to specialist missionaries. The Muslim method has always been that of radical displacement of 'false' relig., and has seldom permitted either theological adaptation or accommodation. At present time, the principal areas of Islamic expansion are in E. and W. Africa, though M.'s are also found in the West. Not all are strictly orthodox; among related movements owing allegiance to radical Islamic vision are the → Ahmadiyya Movement and American → Black Muslims.

Even more clearly than in case of Islām, M. is fundamental to Christianity. Much of basic Chr. vocabulary is virtually incomprehensible apart from the M. dimension: →→ gospel, church, apostle, martyr are cases in point.

Although → Jesus of Nazareth was believed by first followers to be Jew. → Messiah, and, although his own message appears to have been directed first of all to 'the lost sheep of the house of Israel' (Matt. 10:6), within very few years of founding of first church, the message of his death and resurrection was being proclaimed to non-Jews (cf. Acts 11:20). As far as may be gathered from the written records, the first deliberate attempt to spread the Chr. message in Cyprus and Asia Minor was mission of Barnabas and → Paul (Acts 13), during which non-Jews were again approached (v. 46). Within thirty years of death of Christ, Chr. congregations were founded in virtually all chief cities of Mediterranean area, and within three cents., Christianity became state relig. of Roman Empire.

Once the ethnic barrier had been broken, there was no further questioning of universal dimension of work of Christ, though there is reason to believe that some, at least, of the first Christians in Jerusalem rejected this development (→ Jew. Christianity). In → Synoptic Gospels, and partic. in Luke-Acts, the M. implications of work of Christ are clearly stated: 'Thus it is written, that the Christ should suffer and on the third day rise again from the dead, and that repentance and forgiveness of sins should be preached in his name to all nations, beginning from Jerusalem' Lk. 24:46f., cf. Matt. 28:19f., Acts 1:8). The theological implications of this view are developed in Fourth Gospel, in which coming of Jesus is represented as a light—'the true light that enlightens every man' (1:9)—coming into the world. He is, further, 'the Lamb of God, who takes away the sin of the world' (1:29). His work is to be continued in work of his disciples, and the gift of the → Holy Spirit is given in order that this work might be fulfilled: 'As thou didst send me into the world, so I have sent them into the world' (17:18, cf. 20:21–3).

Both in theory and practice, Paul laid foundations on which Chr. M. thought has built ever since. His practice was to found independent congregations, each responsible for its own support, administration and propagation. His theory was complex, but seems to have rested on view that Israel was indeed the people of God; that they had rejected the Messiah; but that, when 'the full number of the Gentiles' had been brought into the kingdom of God, 'all Israel will be saved' (Rom. 11:2).

Undoubtedly one reason for success of the Chr. M. in Hellenistic world was its exclusiveness in an age of eclecticism and tolerance—its conviction that 'there is salvation in no one else' (Acts 4:12). Similar exclusiveness has been a fairly constant feature of Christianity in all periods of expansion; e.g. in early Middle Ages in Europe (when the M. instrument, as in Buddhism, was the monastic community) and in 19th and early 20th cents. in Asia and Africa. Recent developments, esp. in study of non-Chr. religs. and in politics, have, however, brought about certain modifications in this view. At present time, although conservative groups still present Christianity by method of radical contrast, leading to ultimate displacement, a growing consensus is adopting the ideals of 'presence' and 'dialogue' *vis-à-vis* other religs. 19th-cent. views of the Chr. West, transmitting its saving message to non-Christ. East have been abandoned, along with such pejorative terms as 'pagan' and 'heathen'. M. is seen rather as a function of the Church as a whole, over against world as a whole, irrespective of time and place. E.J.S.

(*Literature*) There is no concise comparative treatment of subject as a whole, and little explicit treatment of theme of M. in Buddhism and Islām, though incidental refs. are abundant. For an older view see *E.R.E.*, VIII, pp. 700a–51b. On the Christ. M. see G. H. Anderson (ed.), *The Theology of the Christian Mission* (1961); J. H. Bavinck *An Intro. to Science of Missions* (E.T. 1964); J. Blauw, *The Missionary Nature of the Church* (1963); A. von Harnack, *Expansion of Christianity in First Three Centuries*, I–II (E.T. 1904–5); H. Kraemer, *The Christian Message in a Non-Christ. World* (1938); K. S. Latourette, *A History of Expansion of Christianity*, I–VII (1939–47); S. C. Neill *A History of Christ. Missions* (1964); E. J. Sharpe, *Not to Destroy but to Fulfil* (1965); B. G. M. Sundkler, *The World of Mission* (E.T. 1965); G. F. Vicedom, *Missio Dei* (1958).

Mistletoe Acc. to Pliny (*Nat. hist.*, xvi, 249–51), the Druids regarded M. as sacred and 'the universal healer'; it was cut with a golden sickle and its gathering was marked by sacrifice of two white bulls. M. was also the plant by which Norse god Balder was slain. J. G. → Frazer, in a detailed study, concluded that M. was thought to be the life of the oak; he identified Virgil's 'Golden Bough' (*Aen.* VI, pp. 136ff., 203ff.) with M. (→→ Celtic Relig.; Scandin. Relig.). S.G.F.B.

J. G. Frazer, *Balder the Beautiful* (*G.B.*, XI, 1936 edn.), chs. 9, 12; A. Ross, *Pagan Celtic Britain* (1967), pp. 33, 278.

Mitama *Tama* or *mitama* is the → Shinto term for soul or spirit, *mi* being an honorific. The body is conceived as its temporary dwelling-place. Acc. to Shinto psychology, the M. may be considered under four different aspects: *ara*-M; *nigi*-M; *saki*-M; and *kushi*-M, which in some cases can be separated, and even, after death, be located in different places. The sacred object, in which the M. of the → *kami* dwells and is worshipped is the M-*shiro* or → *shintai*, and is carefully preserved in the temple sanctuary as the supreme object of devotion. D.H.S.

W. G. Aston, *Shinto* (1905), pp. 26ff.; J. Herbert, *Shinto* (1967), *passim*.

Mithra, Mithraism Anc. Indo-Iranian god, whose orig. can be traced back to 2nd mil. BC. In → Rig-Veda, M. is closely assoc. with → Varuna; in pre-Zoroastrian Iran, M. was prob. god of sacrosanct contract (*mithra*) and light. M. is not mentioned in → Gāthās, an omission that has caused much speculation: poss. → Zoroaster's exaltation of → Ahura Mazdah excl. M., or he may have put M. anonymously among → Amesha Spentas. In later Zoroastrianism, M., as the *Mithra Yasht* shows, became important deity. The cult of M. spread W., prob. absorbing Babylonian → astralism *en route*, and also closely assoc. with solar worship ('Sol Invictus', the 'Unconquerable Sun'). M. reached Rome by 67 BC; but it was during Empire period that it attained its greatest success. Appealing to soldiers, it spread along frontiers of Empire from the Danube to Britain. This Roman M. had form of a → mystery religion. The focus of the cave-sanctuaries (*mithraea*) was a sculptured repr. of M. slaying the Cosmic Bull; although the ethos of scene is Persian, the origin of myth concerned is unknown, but it prob. concerned new life and fertility. Acc. to Plutarch, Mithra acted as 'mediator' between → Ohrmazd and → Ahriman, thus indic. that M. was based on Iranian → dualism. The presence in *mithraea* of images of a lion-headed monster, repr. → Zurvan *dareghō-chvadhata*, suggests that Iranian idea of → Time was also prob. incl. in M.-theology. Each M.-confraternity comprised seven grades; → initiation involved severe tests of neophyte's courage and devotion. The triumph of Christianity marked end of M., which had been its strong rival. 'Mithras' was W. form of name. S.G.F.B.

F. Cumont, *Textes et monuments figurés relatifs aux Mystères de Mithra*, 2 vols. (1896, 1899), *The Mysteries of Mithra* (E.T. 1956 edn.); *E.R.E.*, VIII, *s.v.;* J. Duchesne-Guillemin, *Zoroastre* (1948), 'Ahriman et le dieu suprême dans les mystères de Mithra', *Numen*, II (1955); G. Dumézil, *Mitra-Varuna* (1948); Zaehner,

D.T.Z., chs. 2, 4, 5; M. J. Vermaseren, *Corpus Inscriptionum et Monumentorum Religionis Mithriacae* (1956), *Mithras: the Secret God*, E.T. (1963); L. A. Campbell, *Mithraic Iconogr. and Ideology* (1968).

Miya A → Shinto temple. Name commonly employed in Jap. literature to indicate abode of a Shinto deity (→ *kami*). *Mi*—an honorific prefix; and *ya*—house. → also Jinja. D.H.S.

D. C. Holtom, *The National Faith of Japan* (1938), p. 7; J. Herbert, *Shinto* (1967), pp. 128ff.

Miyako Anc. Jap. name for mod. city of Kyoto, which remained capital of Japan from CE 794–1868, and for cents. was centre of Jap. culture and of → Buddhist Church. D.H.S.

Modernism The term is used in various contexts to describe movements within Christianity to relate trad. faith to current thought. The conflict between relig. and science in 19th cent. led many scholars to examine critically the hist. origins of Christianity and philosophical presuppositions of Chr. theology. Their aim was gen. apologetic, but their studies inevitably led to conclusions inconsistent with orthodox trad. Such a movement occurred in R.C. Church in latter part of 19th cent., the most notable leaders being A. Loisy, L. Laberthonnière, A. Fogazzaro, F. von Hügel and G. Tyrrell. The movement was officially condemned by Pope Pius X in 1907. In recent years a more liberal attitude has found a certain qualified expression in R.C. Church. Attempts at reinterpretation of trad. faith have been continuous in Prot. Christianity, notable examples being assoc. with →→ Bultmann, Tillich, and R. Niebuhr. In the → C. of E., the Modern Churchmen's Union (orig. founded 1898) promotes liberal relig. thought by annual conferences and journal (*The Modern Churchman*). A form of M. finds expression in Liberal → Judaism. No comparable movements have yet affected the other great religs., although individual scholars, familiar with W. modes of thought, have attempted some reinterpretation of their trad. faith and practice. It would seem inevitable that all religs. will eventually find it necessary to adjust to the pressures of modern thought about the nature of man and the world in which he lives. (→→ A. Bonhoeffer; Philosophy of Relig.). S.G.F.B.

E.R.E., VIII, *s.v.; D.C.C.*, pp. 910–11; *R.G.G.*[3], IV, col. 1067–8, V, col. 896–903; A. Vidler, *Modernist Movement in Roman Church* (1934); H. Stephan, *Geschichte der deutschen evangelischen Theologie* (1960[2]), chs. IV, V; L. E. Elliott-Binns, *English Thought, 1860–1900. The Theological Aspect* (1956); H. D. A. Major, *English Modernism* (1927); P. Ramsey (ed.), *Religion* (Humanistic Scholarship in America, The Princeton Studies, 1965); A. C. Bouquet, *The Christian Faith and Non-Christian Religions* (1958); *E.J.R.*, *s.v.* 'Reform Judaism'; J. L. Blau, *Modern Varieties of Judaism* (1966), pp. 25ff.

Moggalāna Mahā Moggallāna Thera (i.e. 'the Great', 'the Elder') was a chief disciple of the Buddha, and close friend from childhood of → Sariputta, another principal disciple. The two were converted to the Buddh. way on same occasion, when they heard Buddha preach. They were ordained together, and are regarded in trad. as the ideal disciples. M. was warmly praised by Buddha for his ability as expounder of the Buddh. way to other monks (S.N. iv, 183ff.). He was charged with welfare of the other monks. Several verses among the → *Theragāthā* are attrib. to M., in which he exhorts his fellow monks to holy living. He is mentioned frequently in Suttas of the Pali canon. He died earlier than Buddha as result of a violent attack on him by brigands; these had been hired by heretics, whose followers had diminished as a result of M.'s preaching. T.O.L.

G. P. Malalasekere, *D.P.P.N.*, vol. 2, pp. 541–7.

Moggaliputta-Tissa A Buddh. Thera, or elder monk, said to have acted as president of 3rd Buddh. Council at Patna in reign of emperor → Ashoka (→ Councils, Buddh.), and to have composed the Pali treatise known as *Kathāvatthu* (Points of Controversy), which now forms fifth of the 7 books of the → Abhidhamma-pitaka of the → Theravāda school. Acc. to trad., it was M. who, in 6th year of Ashoka's reign, had ordained the emperor's son Mahinda into the → Sangha; after the 3rd Council, M. organised Buddh. missions into various regions adjacent to India by monks from Magadha, incl. the sending of Mahinda to Ceylon. M. is said to have been 80 years of age at death, which occurred in 26th year of Ashoka's reign; he had been a member of the Sangha for 68 years. T.O.L.

Malalasekere, *D.P.P.N.*, vol. 2, pp. 664–6; H. Oldenburg (ed. and tr.), *The Dipavamsa* (1879); W. Geiger and M. H. Bode (eds. and trs.), *Mahavamsa; or Great Chronicle of Ceylon* (1912, repr. 1964).

Moha Buddh. term meaning 'illusion', or erroneous view of things characteristic of the man whose nature is 'unenlightened'. M. is regarded as one of the 3 'roots' of evil (the others being → Dosa and → Lobha). *Avijja* (Pali), → *Avidyā* (Skt.) = ignorance, is a synonym for M. T.O.L.

Mohism (→ Mo-tzŭ). The organisation which resulted from life and teaching of Mo-tzŭ, presided over by a leader, called Chu-tzŭ, who was regarded as a sage. M. was very influential in China during 4th and 3rd cents. BC. It taught practice of universal love, encouraged hard labour, self-denial and living of a simple life. Though strongly opposed to aggressive warfare, the Mohists were trained in use of arms and tactics of defence. Their asceticism and utilitarianism were too extreme and their doc. of universal love too idealistic for the Chinese, and the movement practically died out by end of 3rd cent. BC. D.H.S.

Fung Yu-lan, *Hist. of Chinese Philosophy*, vol. 1 (1937), chs. 5, 11; W. T. Chan, *Source Book in Chinese Philosophy* (1963), ch. 9.

Moira Grk. = 'fate'. In → Homer, fate appears as an impersonal law, which even → Zeus has to respect. The expression *hyper moron*, 'beyond what is fated', suggests danger of upsetting such law or order. In *Iliad* XXIV, 209f., M. is personified, and repr. as goddess spinning man's fate at birth. In → Hesiod (*Theog*. 216f., 901f.), three Moirai are concerned with allotting of human fate. (→ Fate). S.G.F.B.

O.C.D., p. 357; R. B. Onians, *Origins of European Thought* (1951), pp. 303ff.; Brandon, *M.D.*, pp. 164ff.; E. R. Dodds, *Greeks and the Irrational* (1963), pp. 6ff.; *Kleine Pauly*, III, 1391–6.

Mokṣa Principal term, with *mukti*, for release, liberation or → salvation in Hinduism, coming from a root *muc* 'to free' (i.e. from rebirth, → *samsara*). It is reckoned trad. to be one of four ends or aims of life (→ Ethics, Hindu), together with pleasure, economic gain and virtue (*dharma*). Another term for release is → *kaivalya*. The content of salvation differed considerably, acc. to theologies of various schools and movements, sometimes involving existence in → heaven(s). N.S.

Molech, Moloch Term occurs eight times in O.T. in connection with child-sacrifice. It was formerly interpreted as title for a foreign god derived from *melekh*, 'king', and → Melqart was gen. identified as god concerned. Recent research indicates that M. was a technical term for child-sacrifice. S.G.F.B.

O. Eissfeldt, *Molk als Opferbegriff im punischen u. hebräischen u. das Ende des Gottes Moloch* (1935); *H.D.B.*², *s.v.*

Monasteries, Buddh. Buddh. monasteries of China, Korea and Japan, of Ceylon, and continental S.E. Asia, differ among themselves in varying degrees, but all repr. continuation of a trad. reaching back to early period of Buddhism in the pre-Christ. era. At time of the Buddha and during cent. after his death, members of the Order (→ *Sangha*), were wandering homeless, almsmen (*bhikkhus*), although even in Buddha's day they had use of *ārāmas*, or private gardens given to them by wealthy laymen. Before 2 cents. had passed from Buddha's death, the practice of living together in shelters known as *āvāsas* had developed. These *āvāsas* were orig. places of shelter to which bhikkhus would resort during monsoon season, when travel was difficult or impossible. The *āvāsas* grad. developed into permanent settlements, called *lenas*, each inhabited by its own regular monk-residents, whereas the earlier *āvāsas* had been centres or, as it were, hostels with no regular, fixed body of residents. In the → Vinaya Pitaka, which governs common life of Buddh. Order, 5 different kinds of dwelling are mentioned under collective term *lena*. Of these the 2 most import. are the *vihāra* (house for monks) and the *guhā* (a cave). It was in these 2 forms that the earliest settled monasteries were found. On the plains of N. India it was the brick, or brick and stone free-standing *vihāra* which became the monastic institution; in India south of Vindhya mountains it was the *guhā* or cave-dwelling which became more usual place of habitation for monks. These caves were at first fairly simple; it is not always certain whether they were lived in, or were used merely as secluded places for purpose of meditation. But later they were large and elaborate monastic dwellings, consisting of large complexes of rooms, halls shrines, etc. Since they were less exposed to weather and invading armies than free standing *vihāras* of the plains, many have survived, esp. in the Western Ghats of India. The total number of cave-monasteries which have thus survived is in region of one thousand; the clearing and exploration of these has been a notable feature of archeological work in India since the 1840s. Some of the more import. complexes which have been discovered are → Ajantā, Elephanta, Ellorā, Kanheri, and Karle; there are altogether 44 such centres known at present, scattered throughout S. and W. India. Since some sites are known to have been inhabited for a thousand years, they provide valuable evidence of the develop. of Buddh. art through the cents. A transition from cave, i.e. rock-hewn monasteries, to free-standing, stone-built structures, which succeeded them, can be seen in some places; before Buddhism finally disappeared from India it was the *vihāra* type of monastery which had become normal.

Another change which monasteries underwent in India from about 8th cent. CE onwards was from numerous, small 'parish' monasteries, each of which served as centre of Buddh. teaching and devotion for a village or group of villages, to large, imposing places of learning which more nearly resembled colleges or even universities. Such large monastic centres, → Nālandā, Odantapura (in Bihar), Vikramasilā (in W. Bengal) Amarāvatī, and Nāgārjunakonda (in Andhra Pradesh) were monuments to piety and generosity of kings and rich merchants. The concentration of Buddh. education and learning in such centres was, however, assoc. with decline of smaller, parish-type of monastery, whose life had been oriented much more towards learning 'for faith' rather than 'for knowledge'. By time the Chinese travellers →→ Hsuan-tsang and I-tsing visited

India in 7th cent. CE, many smaller monasteries had already been deserted and were in ruins, soon to be lost in encroaching jungle. The large monastic institutions of N. India were rich, and easy targets for Turkish Muslim invaders of 11th and 12th cents.; by that time few of the older, smaller monasteries were left and by 13th cent. Buddh. monasticism had almost entirely disappeared from India. By this time, however, the monastic institution had become a feature of Ceylon, S.E. Asia, China, Korea, Japan and Tibet. It is even poss. that it may have had some formative influence upon ascetic communities of E. Mediterranean, as there was considerable cultural traffic between India and Mediterranean world in early Christ. cents.

From India those Buddh. monks who were deprived of monasteries by Muslim invasion travelled north and east, esp. to Tibet. The monasteries of Tibet continued to flourish, and provide dominant feature of Tibetan society down to mod. times (→ *Tibetan Buddhism*). A continuous trad. of monastic life from 3rd cent. BC to present can be traced in → Ceylon, and in continental S.E. Asia from about 5th cent. CE. There were monasteries in S.E. Asian archipelago from 7th cent. CE (→ *Indonesia, Buddhism in*); but most of these have not survived to present. Apart from monasteries of Buddh. → China, Korea and Japan, where Buddhism and the monastic trad. underwent developments peculiar to E. Asia, it is in Ceylon and continental countries of S.E. Asia (Burma, Thailand, Cambodia and Laos) that Buddh. monasticism survives in something like early form.

In S.E. Asia today the Buddh. monastery is still, throughout most of region, the local centre of popular relig., and bearer and preserver of → Theravāda form of Buddhism, which places great importance on the Sangha as a community of men dedicated to the holy life. The typical monastery is a group of buildings within compound, enclosed by wall; the surrounding wall ensures necessary degree of seclusion but in no sense isolates M. from surrounding society. It used to be monks who provided entire education of lay people; now this is increasingly undertaken by various national states; but the school will still very often be located within monastic compound, esp. in Thailand.

Within complex of buildings, etc., which together make up the Buddh. M. of S.E. Asia, the most import. items are: (1) shrine room or sanctuary, where there is usually a large → *Buddha-rupa*, and where → *uposattha* devotional services are held, where ordinations take place, and where the → *Patimokkha* is recited by monks; (2) an assembly hall, usually open on all four sides, where other *Buddha-rupas* are housed and where in evening of Buddh. sabbath lay people come to hear sermons by monks, although in some cases, esp. in city monasteries, these may be preached in sanctuary instead; (3) the huts or cubicles in which monks (or guests) are housed, are usually simple wooden rooms with little furniture apart from rolled-sleeping mat, a small shrine and poss. a picture or two; (4) in many monasteries of S.E. Asia, a school-building for the children of the village; (5) one or more → *stupas*, or pagodas, in grounds, usually near sanctuary. The exact number of component features, and size and elaborateness of each item varies from monastery to monastery, and from urban to rural areas. So also does name by which whole complex is known. In Ceylon it is a *vihāra* or *sanghārāma* (see *ārāma*, (above)); in Burma, a *phongyi-chaung*, i.e. a house for monks (*phongyi* ('great glory'), being the popular word in Burma for a monk); in Thailand, it is a *Wat*, a word possibly derived from primitive name of the M., i.e. *āvāsa* (above); in Cambodia and Laos also it is a 'Wat'. T.O.L.

Sukumar Dutt, *Buddhist Monks and Monasteries of India* (1962); R. Gard, *Buddhism* (1961), ch. V; H. K. Kaufman, *Bangkhuad: A Community Study in Thailand* (1960), ch. VI, 'The Wat: its Structure, Economy and Function'; E. Lamotte, *Histoire du Bouddhisme Indien*, 1958, ch. IV; W. Rahula, *Hist. of Buddhism in Ceylon* (1956); J. G. Scott (Shway Yoe), *The Burman: His Life and Notions*, 3rd edn. (1909, repr. 1963), chs. 4, 13.

(Hindu). The estab. of regular monasteries occupied by members of an order is comparatively late development within → Hinduism. Trad., the favoured method of pursuing contemplative life, for upper class Hindu, was through practice of the four → *asramas*, culminating in giving up settled life and becoming as → *sannyasin*. The retreat of the → *vanaprastha*, whither pupils would go for instruction in sacred lore, and more gen. the dwelling places or *ashrams* of → *gurus*, whither disciples would go, had some of properties of monastic life. But unlike →→ Buddhism and Jainism, Hinduism possessed no unified monastic order. In middle ages, esp. in south, orders were founded, with hierarchical structure, and buildings, sometimes within temple complexes, developed for coenobitical living and purposes of preaching and teaching. → Sankara was energetic in spreading an Advaitin order in different parts of India, four centres which he estab. still surviving. Likewise →→ Ramanuja and Madhva promoted M., and phenomenon developed within the → Lingayats. The increase in Hindu M. owed something to decline of Buddhism and Jainism. In mod. times, most import. adaptation of M. has come through the *maṭhs* estab. by → Ramakrishna movement, which have done much for relig. education and social service (as well as missionary work abroad). The typical garb of Hindu monk is a saffron or salmon-coloured robe. N.S.

Monasticism The urge to abandon ordinary domestic life, to concentrate on worship, meditation and sacred study, has found expression in various religs. It has taken form of living solitary life as hermit (e.g. in →→ Hinduism; Taoism; Christianity); but where guidance and instruction are needed, communities have been founded where members live under a common rule. The earliest example of M. is the Buddh. → Sangha. → Philo (*de vita contemplativa*) describes the → Therapeutae, Egypt.–Jew. ascetics, who lived as monastic community nr. → Alexandria in 1st cent. CE. At same period other Jew. ascetics lived similarly at → Qumrân. Chr. M. orig. in Egypt, St. → Antony being regarded as its founder. M. profoundly affected life of Church, both in E. and W., esp. during Middle Ages. At → Reformation, M. was suppressed in Prot. countries: it has been revived in 19th–20th cents. in → C. of E. and in French Evangel. Church at Taizé-les-Cluny. M., both Buddh. and Chr., has been a way of life for both men (monks) and women (nuns). In Buddhism and Christianity, M. has been regarded as higher form of relig. life, esp. since it involves permanent → celibacy. M. also requires personal poverty and community of goods. Chr. M. has been based on threefold vow of poverty, chastity, and obedience (to one's Superior). (→→ Basil, Rule; Benedict; Cistercian Order; Cluny, Order; Dominic; Francis; Jesuits). S.G.F.B.

S. Dutt, *Buddhist Monks and Monasteries of India* (1962); H. Dumoulin, *Hist. of Zen Buddhism* (E.T. 1963); *E.R.E.*, VIII, pp. 781–805; *R.G.G.*[3], IV, pp. 1070–81, I, pp. 1430–2; W. H. Mackean, *Christian Monasticism in Egypt* (1920); R. Draguet, *Les pères du désert* (1949); G. G. Coulton, *Five Centuries of Religion*, 4 vols. (1923–50); C. Dawson, *Religion and the Rise of Western Culture* (1950); D. Knowles, *The Monastic Order in England* (1940), *The Religious Orders in England*, 3 vols. (1948–59); J. Leclercq *et alii*, *Analecta monastica*, 3 vols. (1948–55).

Mongols Name of one of chief ethnographical divisions of Asiatic peoples. Early hist. obscure. Under Jenghis Khan (CE 1162–1227) and his descendants, the M. carved out a vast Asian empire from Russia to China. As the Yüan Dynasty, they ruled China from 1280–1368. Their older religion was → Shamanistic; but during their period of empire they showed remarkable tolerance to all religs., being influenced by → Islam in the W., by → Nestorian Christianity, and by → Buddhism in China. Mongolia itself was only superficially influenced by Buddhism till late 16th cent., when the M. were converted to the 'Lama' form of Mahāyāna Buddhism of → Tibet. From that time onwards, Mongolia was governed by a politico-eccles. authority, the Buddh. monasteries wielding great power. In the 1920s Mongolia became a Peoples' Republic within the Soviet sphere. An intense and bitter campaign against relig. was followed by persuasion and provision of alternative occupations for priests. The number of *lamas* (priests) was reduced from about 100,000 to about 200, and most ex-priests are now married. Several monasteries were brought under State control, and influence of Buddhism has rapidly declined. (→ Altaic Relig.). D.H.S.

Guy Wint (ed.), *Asia: A Handbook* 1965, pp. 117ff.; Arts in *E.R.E.*, VIII and *Encycl. Brit.*, vol. 15; E. D. Phillips, *The Mongols* (1969), *C.H.I.*, V, ch. 7.

Monks, Buddh. → *Sangha*. T.O.L.

Monophysitism *Ex.* Grk. *monos*, 'one'; *physis*, 'nature'. In development of → Christology, it was disputed whether the Incarnate Christ had one single divine nature or a double nature, divine and human. The Monophysite view was condemned at Council of → Chalcedon (451), which made the Dyophysite doc. (two natures) orthodoxy. Ensuing controversies resulted in break between Orthodox Church and M. Churches of the Copts, Abyssinians, Syrian Jacobites, and Armenians, which have continued M. S.G.F.B.

D.C.C., *s.v.*; *E.R.E.*, VIII, *s.v.*; Harnack, *H.D.*, vols. III–VI; A. Grillmeier, *Christ in Christian Tradition* (E.T. 1965).

Monotheism Belief in one personal transcendent God, as opposed to belief in many gods (polytheism) and pantheism (identifying God with universe). The evolutionary view of hist. of relig. (e.g. in E. B. Tylor's → animism) saw relig. as progressing from polytheism to M. This view provoked reaction of those, like W. Schmidt, who sought to show that there was an orig. M., from which polytheism repr. a declension: the concept of a → high god among various peoples was cited as evidence of this *Urmonotheismus*. Much of this debate doubtless stemmed from assumption of European scholars, educated in Heb.-Chr. trad., that M. repr. highest form of relig. Sympathetic study of other religs. reveals that such qualitative distinctions are not relevant in other contexts. Anc. → Egypt. relig. provides a significant and representative example of how, in a polytheistic context, ref. can be made to a single deity, the 'Great God'. (→ Henotheism). Man's concept of deity repr. the deification of sources of power evident to him in universe, and logically leads to polytheism or dualism. M. inevitably entails problem of orig. of Evil, unless good and evil are attr. to one God. Judaism, Islam and Christianity claim to be M., but title of Christianity is disputed by the other two on ground that doc. of → Trinity is tritheism, a charge which Christians strenuously reject. → Zoroastrianism is logically M.; → Sikhism is fifth major monotheistic relig. (→→ Dualism; God). S.G.F.B.

E.R.E., VIII, *s.v.; R.G.G.*, IV, col. 1109–16, VI, col. 1197–9; R. Pettazzoni, *The All-Knowing God* (E.T. 1956); E. O. James, *The Concept of Deity* (1950); G. Van der Leeuw, *La religion* (1948), pp. 155ff.; R. Pettazzoni, 'Das Ende der Urmonotheismus', *Numen*, III (1956).

Monothelitism *Ex.* Grk. *monos*, 'one', and *thelein*, 'to will'. In → Christology, a 7th cent. heresy which maintained that Christ, though having two natures (divine and human), had only one will. M. developed as attempt to reconcile → Monophysites with orthodoxy. After involved controversy, in which Pope Honorius approved of M., the Council of Constantinople (680) condemned M., defining orthodoxy as belief that two wills existed in Christ. S.G.F.B.

D.C.C., *s.v.; E.R.E.*, VIII, *s.v.;* Harnack, *H.D.*, IV, pp. 252ff.; A. Grillmeier, *Christ in Christian Tradition* (E.T. 1965).

Months (Islam) Sacred in pre-Islamic times. During Dhul Qa'da (11th), Dhul Ḥijja (12th), Muḥarram (1st) and Rajab (7th) fighting was banned by mutual consent in N. Arabia in pre-Islamic times. Fairs and pilgrimages were held during these periods; such agreement was prob. reached to leave trading and pious rites undisturbed. But truce was sometimes broken, notably in the *Fijār* (transgression) battles in which → Quraysh and Kināna opposed Hawāzin. → Muḥammad is said to have assisted his uncles in one of the four battles. After going to Medina, Muhammad still retained respect for the sacred months, but allowed retaliation in them against polytheists (cf. Qur., ii:190; ix:36). Sura v:2,97f. refer partic. to period of → pilgrimage to Mecca, and insist on sanctity of time. At an earlier Medina period Muhammad justified fighting in the sacred months, though recognising it as serious, on ground that driving people from the → Ka'ba and Mecca was worse (ii:214). J.R.

E.I., III, pp. 698f. (Muḥarram), p. 1093 (Radjab); Wellhausen, *Reste*, pp. 97ff.; Watt, *Medina*, pp. 8f.

Moon, The Except in → Sumerian relig., the M. has gen. had a subordinate role in relig., the sun invariably taking precedence in deified celestial phenomena. In Sumerian pantheon → Sin, the M.-god, was father of sun-god → Shamash. The M. was early connected with reckoning of time, and its phases have been subject of myths and apotropaic rituals. The M. has also been regarded as both a male and female, and a benevolent and malevolent deity. (→→ Americ. Relig. anc.; Khons; Crescent, Islam). S.G.F.B.

S.O., IV (*La lune: mythes et rites*), 1962.

Mormons Popular designation of 'Church of Jesus Christ of Latter-Day Saints', founded by Joseph Smith in 1830 at Manchester, New York. Smith claimed to have found 'Book of Mormon', its location being revealed by an angel named Moroni. The Book is alleged to be records of a Prophet Mormon, and is accepted as Holy Scripture by M. In 1843 Smith claimed another revelation sanctioning polygamy, a practice that has continued a point of dispute for M. Smith's successor, Brigham Young, estab. headquarters of sect at Salt Lake City, Utah, in 1847. Despite persecution, the M. have increased, and founded communities in English-speaking countries, Norway, Sweden and Switzerland. Ed. Meyer studied orig. of M. in preparation for his great work on Christian origs. (*Ursprung u. Anfänge des Christentums*, 3 vols., 1921–2). S.G.F.B.

E.R.E., XI, pp. 82–90; *R.G.G.*^{3}, IV, col. 1138–41; Ed. Meyer, *Ursprung u. Geschichte der Mormonen* (1912).

Moses The great pivotal figure of Heb. → Heilsgeschichte, where he is repr. as leader sent by → Yahweh to deliver Israel from Egypt. bondage, and through whom Yahweh made his covenant with Israel and delivered his Law on Sinai. Heb. trad. makes M. a native of Egypt, though Heb. by race: his name is prob. of Egypt. orig. Although his historicity is not seriously doubted, it is obvious that later Jew. trad. assigned to M. imaginery exploits and revelations. It would seem that M. presented Yahweh to certain Heb. tribes in some new way (Ex. 3:13ff.) such that, under his leadership, deliverance was achieved from Egypt and settlement effected in Canaan. M. has been important to Christians, being figured in Chr. art from earliest times. (→ Judaism). S.G.F.B.

H.D.B.^{2}, *s.v.; R.G.G.*^{3}, IV, col. 1151–5; H. H. Rowley, *From Joseph to Joshua* (1950), *Men of God* (1963), 'Moses and the Decalogue'; *E.J.R.*, pp. 270ff.; R. Smend, *Das Mosebild von Heinrich Ewald bis Martin Noth* (1959).

(Islam) (Mūsā). Frequently mentioned in the Qur. in both Meccan and Medinan suras. Some passages are quite lengthy, e.g. ii:44–69; vii:101–63; x:76–93; xx:8–98; xxvi:9–68; xxvii:7–14; xxviii:2–43; xxxvii:114–22; xliv:16–32 (here called 'a noble messenger' but not named); lxxix:15–26. Ref. is made to M.'s infancy, his being rescued from ark by pharaoh's family and being entrusted to his sister who takes him to his mother to nurse, his killing the Egyptian, his stay in Madyan (Midian), call at the burning bush, the rod becoming a snake and the hand becoming white, → Aaron being sent along with him, the signs (i.e. plagues), the Red Sea, Sinai, the tablets written by God, M.'s anger on finding people worshipping the calf, the 40 years of wandering, punishment of Korah (Qārūn). While much is known, there are differences from the Bible story. Korah appears in xxix:38; xl:25, along with Haman and Pharaoh, as one of the three to whom M. was sent. xxviii:76–82 tells of the destruction of Korah (cf. Numbers, xvi), but repres. him as a proud, rich man. While M. takes the Children of Israel from Egypt, he is repres. as a messenger to Pharaoh. When his magicians are confounded, they express belief in M.'s God in spite of Pharaoh's threats (vii:118ff.; xx:73ff.). Though M. is angry with Aaron when he learns about the calf, its maker is anachronously called al-Sāmirī (the Samaritan—xx:87, 96). M. is said to have received nine signs to Pharaoh (xvii:103; xxvii:12). When God refused M.'s request to see him, he showed his glory to the mountain which was reduced to powder (vii:139). God gave M. the Book and the *Furqān* (ii:50), a word explained by Bell as from Syriac *purqānā* (salvation). In viii:42 the battle of → Badr is called the day of the *furqān*. The idea of deliverance may apply in both places. In xxviii:8 it is Pharaoh's wife who suggests rescuing the infant M. In → Trad. and in books of stories of prophets there is much legendary material about M. J.R.

E.I., III, pp. 738f. (Mūsā); II, pp. 780f. (Ḳārūn); Hughes, p. 281 (Korah), pp. 356–66 (Moses); J. Horovitz, *Koranische Untersuchungen* (1926), pp. 141–3; J. Walker, *Bible Characters in the Koran* (1931), pp. 84–111; Bell, *Introduction*, index.

Mosque (*Masjid*, place of prostration). The Muslim place of worship. As all prayer must be offered facing the → Ka'ba in Mecca, mosques are orientated so that a wall, in middle of which there is a niche (*miḥrāb*), faces in that direction. On occasion a mosque has had to be built in alignment with other buildings which do not face in required direction, in which circumstance, while the outer walls seem to be wrongly orientated, the inside walls are so arranged that the worshippers face in the proper direction (→ Qibla), e.g. the Moti Masjid in Agra Fort. During public prayer the → *imām* stands facing niche and the worshippers draw themselves up in lines behind him. To right of niche, facing worshippers, there is in large mosques a pulpit from which the Friday sermon (→ Khuṭba) is preached. In many countries the main area of mosque is unroofed, but in others mosques are roofed. In courtyard there is a tank for the → ablution before prayer. Mosques vary from very humble buildings to marvels of architecture. The normal decoration consists of Qur. verses in fine writing; but occasionally one may find floral decorations, the Wazīr Khān mosque in Lahore being notable example. Larger mosques have minarets from which call to prayer (→ Adhān) is made. The minarets in great mosque at Mecca, which includes the Ka'ba, grew to seven; elsewhere four is normally the maximum, and many mosques have only one. Besides being a place for communal, or private, worship, the mosque has often been a school or college (→ Education), in which the teacher takes his place at one of the pillars with his scholars gathered round him. Shoes must be removed when entering mosque; but in many mosques, esp. those which attract sightseers, large shoes are provided for them to wear over their outdoor shoes, and so avoid defiling the sacred place. J.R.

E.I., III, pp. 315–89; Hughes, pp. 329–46; Pareja, index (mosquée); Hitti, *History*, index; K. A. C. Cresswell, *A Bibliography of Muslim architecture in Egypt* (1955); Mez, *Renaissance*, pp. 332ff.

'Mother of the child' (*Umm al-walad*). Technical term for a slave-woman who has borne a child to her master. It early became practice in the legal schools to hold that she must be set free on her master's death. J.R.

E.I., IV, pp. 1012–5; Hughes, p. 655; Levy, *Social Structure*, index.

'Mother of the faithful' (*Umm al-mu'minīn*). Title applied to any of Muhammad's wives. Authority for this is found in Qur. xxxiii:6, 'his wives are their mothers'. This follows statement that the Prophet is the closest relative of the believers. J.R.

Hughes, p. 654.

Mo Tzŭ (Mo Ti; Micius), *fl.* 5th cent. BC. Import. Chi. philosopher, influential during the Warring States period (401–221 BC). His works are contained in 71 chapters (53 extant). Critic of → Confucianism for its partiality, concern for wealth-consuming ceremonies, and belief in Fate → (*Ming*). Pre-eminently a teacher of righteousness and universal love, M. found ultimate sanction for his teaching in Will of a supreme righteous and benevolent God (T'ien), and in existence of supernatural agents with power to reward and punish. Deeply concerned for prosperity of country and people, M. advocated exaltation of the virtuous, taught frugality and opposed aggression. He applied pragmatical and utilitarian tests to all doctrines, basing his teaching on reason and logic. The purity of his own motives, ideals and practice were never in question; but his asceticism and utilitarianism were considered too extreme. M. attracted a following of about 300, who gave him implicit loyalty and obedience. His movement became wide-spread, but after his death split into three rival factions. Weakened by internal dissension and opposed by Confucians, it ceased to be distinctive by the Han dynasty. Interest in Mohism revived in 18th cent. on publication by Pi Yüan of Mo-tzŭ's works with commentary in

1783. Standard Chi. edition and commentary by Sun I-jang, 1894 (rev. ed. 1907). D.H.S.

Y. P. Mei, *The Ethical and Political Works of Mo-tzŭ* (E.T. 1929); A. Forke, *Me Ti des Socialethikers und seines Schüler philosophische Werke* (G.T. 1922); Y. L. Fung, *Hist. of Chinese Philosophy*, vol. 1 (E.T. 1937), pp. 76–105, 246–76; W. T. Chan, *Source Book in Chinese Philosophy* (1963), pp. 211–31.

Mourning (Chinese) In mod. China, in face of Communist anti-relig. propaganda and break-up of anc. familial system, the trad. M. is rapidly being greatly modified or falling into disuse. Anc. M. on which the modern, modified by local usage and practice were based, are given detailed treatment in the → *Li Chi* (*S.B.E.*, vols. 27, 28). The anc. customs were governed by strict regard for status of deceased, degree of relationship, and detailed rules of propriety. Later they were influenced by Buddh. and Taoist eschatological ideas.

Five degrees of mourning were recognised: for parents; grandparents and great-grandparents; brothers, sisters etc.; uncles, aunts etc.; for distant relatives. For a parent the period of mourning was nominally 3 years, actually 27 months, during which period officials had to resign their appointment and retire from public life. Strict regulations governed dress, diet and deportment during period. No special mourning rites were observed in case of children up to age of 15, burial taking place at once without ceremony.

On death of an adult a diviner was called to decide a propitious date for the funeral ceremonies. Sometimes the actual funeral was delayed for months and even years, the coffin being temporarily housed in a suitable place. The body of deceased was washed, dressed, prepared and encoffined, acc. to prescribed rites. It was placed on two stools with head towards the door; at head was placed a table with paper flowers, candles, incense burners, lampstand, and above all the spirit-tablet of the deceased. A period of 7 times 7 days was observed for deep mourning; funeral rites being performed by Buddh. and Taoist priests on each 7th day until the 49th. Intimations were sent to relatives and friends, and days assigned for reception and entertainment of guests.

Customs regarding mourning were very strict. Outer garments were of coarse, white calico, the men wearing headdress of same. Full mourning was worn by younger for their elders, but no M. was obligatory by seniors for juniors, by parents for children, or by husband for wife.

On morning of funeral, priests chanted prayers and the relatives kowtowed to deceased with weeping and wailing. The coffin was then taken out head first and placed on huge catafalque, which had from 32 to 80 bearers. The carriage or car of deceased preceded the catafalque, together with male mourners. The eldest son, as chief mourner, carried a three-tailed banner of paper, on which was inscribed name of deceased. The women followed in carts covered with white calico in strict order of precedence. In procession were men and boys carrying banners, lanterns and paper articles of every description, to be burned at grave. There were also companies of priests and musicians with drums, horns and other musical instruments, which were played as procession moved along. The grave was specially prepared and chosen acc. to → Fêng Shui, and a rigid order of precedence was followed at burial.

On 3rd day after funeral the mourners returned to grave to present food and burn paper money. On 21st, 35th and 49th days food was offered before the spirit-tablet. On 60th day the soul of deceased was supposed to have gone through all the various judgement halls, being judged for deeds done in the body. D.H.S.

J. J. M. de Groot, *The Relig. System of China*, vol. 2 (new ed. 1964); J. D. Ball, *Things Chinese*, 5th ed. (1925), pp. 403ff.; A. Cormack, *Chinese Birthday, Wedding, Funeral and other Customs* (1923), pp. 77–117. (→Funerary Rites).

(Islam) The official period of mourning is short. Friends visit the bereaved, prayers are offered, and the Qur. is recited for a few nights. Visiting graves is allowed; some would prohibit women from this because they are liable to be upset. Trad. tells of → Muḥammad weeping when his son Ibrāhīm died, saying, 'The eye weeps and the heart grieves, but we say only that with which our Lord is pleased, and we are grieved over being separated from you, Ibrāhīm.' But the → trads. condemn excessive weeping and wailing; Muhammad is said to have cursed the wailing woman and the woman who listens to her. In spite of this, wailing is common, but usually only before funeral. There is a certain amount of convention. The present writer has noted that when a death took place, wailing women produced the most disconcerting sounds until body was removed from house, after which the wailing ceased and the women departed silently. (→→ Burial of the dead; Funerary Rites; Prayers for the dead). J.R.

Hughes, p. 366; Pareja, pp. 658f.; *Mishkāt*, pp. 360–70; Lane, *Egyptians*, ch. XXVIII; Dickson, *Arab of Desert*, ch. XIV; Gaudefroy-Demombynes, *Institutions*, p. 171.

Mudrās Symbolic gestures used both in ritual and in iconography in Indian religs. (primarily →→ Hinduism and Buddhism). Several hundred M., signifying moods, gods, circumstances of many kinds, etc., are employed in Indian dance. Use of ritual gestures was import. in → Tantrism; for reasons which are obscure term also ref. to female partner in sexual rite of the 'left-hand' Tantra. The use of symbolic handsigns in Tantric ritual spread widely into popular worship, a common custom being touching of six parts of body (heart, head, forehead, eyes, etc.) with suitable gestures. The understanding of the *M.* is indispensable for appreciating relig. significance of large part of Indian art. N.S.

A. K. Coomaraswamy and G. K. Duggirala, *The Mirror of Gesture, Being the Abhinaya Darpana of Nandikesvara* (1917); R. V. Poduval, *Kathakali and Diagram of Hand Poses* (1930); J. N. Banerjea, *The Development of Hindu Iconography* (1956); D. R. Thapar, *Icons in Bronze* (1961); Tyra de Kleen, *Mudras: The Ritual Hand-Poses of the Buddha Priests and the Shiva Priests of Bali* (1942).

Muezzin (*Mu'adhdhin*). One who makes the call to prayer (→ Adhān). A trad. says that when the Muslims came to → Medina they discussed how people should be summoned to prayer. One suggested using a bell like the Christians; another suggested using a horn like the Jews. → 'Umar suggested sending a man to summon to prayer, and → Muḥammad asked Bilāl, who was the first M., to summon the people. Another trad. tells of a man having vision, in which he was told about use of a M. to call people to prayer. When he informed Muhammad, he said this was a true vision, and so adopted practice recommended. The call, as made by an accomplished M., is very impressive. Yet in earlier times at least, M.s as a class were treated as not being very intelligent, and funny stories were told about their peculiarities. J.R.

E.I., III, pp. 373–5; *E.I.*², I, pp. 187f.; *Mishkāt*, pp. 130–2; Hughes, pp. 366f.; Levy, *Social Structure*, p. 335.

Muftī A jurisconsult recognised as so well versed in details of the relig. law (→ *sharī'a*) that he is consulted on difficult problems. His ruling is called a *fatwā*. Under the Turkish sultanate, the chief interpreter of the law was the Grand Muftī, or Shaykh al-Islam. When his *fatwās* were contrary to the sultan's will, they still took precedence over it. A new civil code became law in Turkey in 1345/1926, and a new criminal code was introduced in 1348/1929. This brought end to privileges of doctors of canon law. Elsewhere the office exists with weakened influence. In past the work of the M. was of great importance, as books of *fatwās* were compiled and acted as guide on matters of law. J.R.

E.I., II, p. 92 (*fatwā*); Hughes, p. 367; Pareja, index; D. B. Macdonald, *Theology*, index; Coulson, *Law*, index (muftī. Look also under names of different countries.).

Muḥammad, the Prophet Born in → Mecca *c.* CE 570. His father, 'Abdallah, had died, and his mother, Āmina, died when he was five or six years old. His grandfather, → 'Abd al-Muṭṭalib, cared for him till his death a few years later, after which Muhammad received protection from his uncle → Abū Ṭālib. Legend has wonderful stories of his birth and youth. (→ Miracles); but little is really known about him till manhood. He is said to have travelled on trading missions to Syria (→ Baḥīra). On one occasion, when 25 years old, he was entrusted with her business affairs in a caravan by → Khadīja, a well-to-do widow; she was so pleased with him and his capability that they married. Muhammad, now in more comfortable circumstances, spent much time in meditation, going frequently to solitude of a cave in Mt. → Ḥirā'. At age of 40, he had vision of a heavenly being who told him to recite. He refused, but the visitant insisted; the words he was told to recite are considered to be those at begin. of Qur. xcvi (→ Muhammad's Call). The experience disturbed him, but Khadīja assured him this was a divine inspiration. During succeeding years Muhammad recited other vv. which now form part of the → Qur. His preaching dealt with → Allah (whom the people acknowledged as chief God) as the only God, with rewards and punishments in life after death, and with need for honesty in business and consideration for poor. M. made some followers, but → Quraysh showed great hostility. About CE 619 both Khadīja and Abu Talib died, and Muhammad was left without the wife who had encouraged him and the uncle who had given him protection. Conditions became difficult and he sought a protector, with no very satisfactory success. Eventually he came in touch with people from Yathrib (→ Medina), *c.* 180 miles N. of Mecca; as result of negotiations, he sent followers there and finally followed with → Abu Bakr in 1/622. This emigration, the → Hijra, was turning point in Muhammad's career, as was early recognised, for not long after his death, the Muslim era was fixed as beginning that year. Hard times still lay ahead, and severe battles had to be fought (→→ Badr, Uḥud), but Muhammad gradually estab. a community which superseded tribal loyalties. A constitution was drawn up which regulated the affairs of the → Muslims and their dealings with neighbouring peoples, Jewish and others. It incl. an article hostile to Quraysh, which suggests it was early. As result of hard fighting against Quraysh and others, Muhammad estab. himself in Yathrib, which came to be called Madīnat al-nabī (the city of the Prophet) and eventually al-Madīna, anglicé Medina. In 6/628 he had set out on pilgrimage to Mecca but was stopped at al-Ḥudaybiya, where he made a peace treaty with Quraysh. About two years later, when his allies,

Khuzā'a, appealed for help, he decided to make a move to Mecca. He set out, with a large army, in 8/630 and offered a general amnesty. As result Mecca was taken with practically no bloodshed. There were still more battles to be fought, but Muhammad had estab. himself in a strong position. Tribes from different regions in Arabia swore allegiance to him. Mecca, cleared of its idols, was made sacred centre of → Islām; but Muhammad returned to stay in Medina. In 10/632 he led what is called the Farewell Pilgrimage. At → 'Arafat he preached a sermon in which he declared the abolition of much which had applied in pre-Islamic times, exhorted the people to treat women reasonably and to follow guidance of Qur. His health was not good at this time, and he died in Medina a few months later, in 11/632.

Muhammad was a man of strong convictions, prepared to stand up for his teaching in spite of persecution and difficulty. To say, as has been done, that his character deteriorated after he settled in Medina, is due to misunderstanding. There he still taught same message of the one God. Leading an army and estab. a state, did not interfere with his fundamental teaching. He had to oppose enemies and estab. the community; all the time he had implicit faith in his choice by God to be his messenger who was in receipt of divine inspiration. Some instances of his treatment of enemies seem cruel, but a more common characteristic was his clemency. It does, however, seem as if Muhammad grad. did tend to magnify himself. The phrase 'God and his messenger', common in Medina suras (cf. ii:279; ix:3; xxiv:49), suggests this, as also the Qur. instruction (xxxiii:56) to invoke blessings on him, and his claims to have a final say in matters of dispute; but it would be fairer to recognise that he considered himself merely as God's representative who issued commands which God had entrusted him to deliver. His attitude is not so presumptuous as it sounds. God's rule affects every sphere of life, and he had appointed Muhammad to deal with men.

Muhammad must have had extraordinary personality and charm, for he bound to himself men of different types and kept their devotion; he made them realise that his call was to something more than allegiance to himself. When many tribes after his death felt that their oath of allegiance no longer applied, there was a nucleus of followers who understood the essential nature of his mission and helped to estab. the relig. he had so persistently proclaimed. His chief service to Arabia was to supply belief in the one God to Arabs, who had never been attracted by Judaism or Christianity. There are many echoes of these religions in the Qur.; but they are not transcriptions. Muhammad evidently learned much from Jews and Christians; but in him we have an orig. presentation of relig. truth produced from his brooding mind. His use of stories of early prophets is somewhat stylised. This usually takes form of telling how the prophet came to a people and proclaimed his message, and how, when he was rejected, the unbelievers were destroyed. Such thoughts must have comforted Muhammad in the difficult days in Mecca. But it is clear that, while Muhammad did have some knowledge of Jew. and Christ. scriptures, it was not at first hand. While he recognised his responsibility as teacher and leader, he made no exaggerated claims for himself. He was merely a warner. He was not the source of the message, but merely its transmitter. It, therefore, followed that Muhammad himself is not essential to Islam, except to extent that he was the one chosen by God to proclaim the message; but while that is so, many of his followers have exalted him to a position which he never claimed, and treated him as something more than human. (→→ Jews; Muhammad's Call; Emigrants; Helpers; Jesus Christ). J.R.

E.I., III, pp. 641–57; Guillaume, *Life*; al-Wāqidī, *al-Maghāzī*, Arabic text ed. Marsden Jones, 3 vols. (1966); Muir, *Life*; Watt, *Mecca*, *Medina*; M. Hamidullah, *Prophète de l'Islam*, 2 vols. (Paris, 1959); L. P. Elwell-Sutton (trans.), *Payambar: the Messenger*, by Zeinolabedin Rahnema, 3 vols. (1964–6); Rahman, *Islam*, ch. 1.

Muḥammad's birthplace/birthday → Mawlid al-nabī. J.R.

Muḥammad's Call It is gen. said that the first revelation in the Qur. is sura xcvi:1–5, where Muhammad is told to read (or, recite). Trad. tells that when the angel came to him on mount → Ḥirā' with the command, and Muhammad replied that he could not read (or, recite), the angel squeezed him. This happened three times, after which Muhammad received the revelation (cf. Guillaume, *Life* and *Mishkāt*). An import. Qur. passage is liii:1–18, which speaks of two visions Muhammad had: one strong in power bringing a revelation, and a second descent by the lote-tree of the boundary. This is commonly held to be a tree in paradise, but the context suggests one near Mecca. The call is usually said to have come through → Gabriel, he being the one Muhammad saw, but Bell has argued that Muhammad at this stage believed he had seen God. Trad. has material supporting this. *Mishkāt*, 1207, quotes a trad. given by → Tirmidhī in which Ibn 'Abbas (→ 'Abdallāh b, al-'Abbās) says Muhammad saw his Lord twice. Qur. lxxxi:15ff. refer somewhat vaguely to the vision. Muhammad 'Ali, in n. 2683 to his Qur. trans., says the 'noble messenger' in v. 21 refers to Muhammad, not to Gabriel. Note 2684 says v.

23 means Muhammad saw himself on the clear horizon, meaning that his light would shine throughout the world, surely a difficult explanation. Whether Muhammad believed at first that God himself came giving him the commission, or whether he believed it was Gabriel, there is no question that he had a strong sense of a call, no less clearly than men like → Amos (vii:15), or → Isaiah (vi:6ff.). JR.

Guillaume, *Life*, pp. 104ff.; *Mishkāt*, pp. 1252ff.; Muir, *Life*, ch. III; Bell, *Introduction*, index (Call), 'Muhammad's Call', *M.W.*, XXIV (1934), pp. 13ff.; Watt, *Mecca*, pp. 39–52. Notes in Sale, *Qurán* and Blachère, *Coran*, on suras liii and lxxxi; Nöldeke, *Geschichte*², I, pp. 78ff.

Muhammad 'Abduh (1267–1323/1849/1905). Prominent as a leader of liberal thought in Egypt, had the conventional education of al-Azhar (→ Education), but developed individual views. He early showed interest in mysticism, then came under the influence of → Jamal al-Din al-Afghani. He supported rising of 'Urabi Pasha, after which he was exiled from Egypt, going first to Beirut, then to Paris, where he joined Afghani and helped with journal *al-'Urwa al-wuthqā*. He visited Tunis, and went back to Beirut, where his teaching was popular. In 1307/1888 he was allowed to return to Egypt, where he held official appointments and became → Mufti in 1317/1899. He argued that canon law must be revised to make it adaptable for mod. conditions. He wished to lead masses to a simplified relig. and a pure observance. He opposed saint-worship and medieval docs. → Islām, in his view, was a relig. of reason, but had been vitiated by blind acceptance of authority. All generations, he held, had right to independent investigation. He deplored the state of Islam in his day. It had given great benefit to Europe in past, its influence through the → Crusades and visitors to Muslim Spain leading to → Reformation. But while Islam had given help to others, Muslim countries were backward because they did not follow the light they had. He held that the indispensable essentials of Islam are to be found in the Qur. and in some trads., and that these sources are to determine matters of belief and practice. Islam is the perfect religion, incl. the essentials of →→ Judaism and Christianity. The supreme function of Islam is to unite all men in the bonds of the one true religion. His teaching, while it was in some respects rather ingenuous, has remained influential, being of far more lasting worth than Afghani's. It has led to changed outlook of average educated Egyptian of present day, and its influence has extended more widely. His arguments have been continued and developed, not always with his understanding. J.R.

E.I., III, pp. 678–80; Pareja, index; Hourani, *Thought*, index; Cragg, *Counsels*, ch, III and index; G. E. von Grunebaum, *Islam, Essays in the nature and growth of a cultural tradition* (1961²), 190ff.; C. C. Adams, *Islam and modernism in Egypt* (1933), *passim*; *G.A.L.*, S III, pp. 315–21; Elie Kedourie, *Afghani and 'Abduh* (1966); Smith, *Modern History*, index; M. 'Abduh, *The Theology of Unity*, E.T. by Isḥāq Musa'ad and K. Cragg (1966).

Muḥarram First month of the Muslim lunar year. For rites celebrated during first ten days, →→ 'Āshūrā and -Ḥusayn. J.R.

E.I. III pp. 698f.; Hughes pp. 407–17.

Muḥtasib An official under → Caliphate who was an inspector and censor of morals. His assistants patrolled markets daily and reported any offence they detected. The M. had duty of seeing that the Friday noon service in the mosque was not neglected, of checking people who persistently failed to attend prayers, or who broke the Ramadan fast, of ensuring that widows and divorced women observed prescribed waiting period (*'idda*) before remarriage. If he found someone about whose qualifications he had suspicion, he could stop him and investigate; he also had duty of rebuking theologians who were guilty of heresy. But he was forbidden to enter private premises to pursue any investigation. The faults he detected must be done publicly. J.R.

E.I., III, pp 702f.; Hughes, p. 418; Pareja, p. 685; Levy, *Social Structure*, pp. 334ff. and index.

Mujtahid (One who exerts himself). Develops meaning of one who has become qualified to give authoritative rulings on relig. and legal matters. The effort made to give authoritative opinion is *ijtihād*. In → Sunni Islam it has long been held that the 'gate' of *ijtihād* was closed early; but there are signs today of a more liberal spirit. In past, since 3rd century of Islam, only a few have been recognised as having right to be considered in the class of M.'s. In → Shi'a Islam there are M.'s who, considered as representatives of the hidden → imam, are recognised as authoritative. J.R.

E.I., II, pp. 448f.; Hughes, pp. 418f.; Pareja, index (*muǧtahid*); Levy, *Social Structure*, pp. 181, 248.

Mūla Buddh. term, meaning lit. 'a root', used in analysis of the human moral condition. Acc. to Buddh. thought, there are 6 M.'s, or moral conditioners: 3 unwholesome, viz. greed, hatred and illusion, or → *lobha*, → *dosa*, and → *moha*; and 3 wholesome, viz. generosity, love and absence of illusion, or *alobha*, *adosa* and *amoha*. These M.'s condition the quality of consciousness and volition, and thus the quality of → *karma*. Syn. for *alobha* is → *dāna*; for *adosa* → *metta*; and for *amoha* → *paññā*. T.O.L.

Mullah Used in Persian, Urdu, Turkish, is a corruption of Arabic *mawlā* (master). It is a title given to one learned in theology and canon law. The M.'s are a conservative class. J.R.

Hughes, p. 419; Pareja, index (*mullā*).

Mummification Anc. Egypt. anthropology envisaged man as a psycho-physical organism (Doc. of → Man), so that preservation of body was essential for *post-mortem* life. As evidence of → Pyramid Texts show, by *c.* 2500 BC attempt was being made to prevent disintegration of corpse. More elaborate means of embalmment were later developed, the whole process taking 70 days acc. to Herodotus. M. was a relig. process, the chemical means of preservation being reinforced by ritual magic. After M., the 'Opening of the Mouth' was performed, whereby the embalmed body was magically re-endowed with ability to see and take nourishment, which was to be regularly provided at tomb, in which it would for ever live. (→→ Egypt. Relig.; →→ Eschatology, Eg.; Funerary Rites, Eg.; Osiris). (→ Inca Relig.). S.G.F.B.

G. E. Smith and W. R. Dawson, *Egyptian Mummies* (1924); E. A. W. Budge, *The Mummy* (1925); Kees, *T.*[2]; *R.Ae.R.-G.*, pp. 482ff.; S. Bjerke, 'Remarks on the Egypt. Ritual of "Opening the Mouth",' *Numen*, XII (1965).

Munkar and Nakīr → Examination in the grave. J.R.

Murji'ites Name applied to a section of Muslims in the early period, from verb *arja'a* (to defer, postpone), because, unlike the → Kharijites, they refused to pronounce judgments on fellow Muslims, treating that as God's prerogative on the day of → judgment. They were not a sect in strict sense; for they did not necessarily all agree on theological matters, their chief characteristic being their hesitation to judge. This meant that they did not declare a serious sinner to be outside community, or a sinful ruler to be unworthy to continue in office. → Abū Ḥanīfa is held to have belonged to this party. He taught that the faith is indelible which involves knowledge of God and confession of him and of → Muḥammad and acknowledges divine revelation. He further held that prayer behind any → *imām* is valid. M. did not judge anyone who claimed faith, even though his deeds did not confirm it. J.R.

E.I., III, pp. 734f.; D. B. Macdonald, *Theology*, index; Wensinck, *Creed*, index (Murdjites, Abū Ḥanīfa); Watt, *Philosophy*, index; Pareja, pp. 692f., 697, etc.; Seale, *Theology*, pp. 87ff.

Muṣaddiq The one who collects *zakāt* (→ Legal Alms). It was custom to appoint such officials in independent states, but nowadays official appointments are rare. Changes in system of taxation have had effect, and even acc. to canon law, one may give his *zakāt* direct to someone who comes within categories of recipients. J.R.

Hughes, p. 422; Watt, *Medina*, pp. 253, 367.

Musaylima b. Habib prophet of the B. Ḥanīfa in Yamāma (Cen. Arabia), contemporary with → Muḥammad. Although he is played down in Muslim literature and ridiculed, as the diminutive form of Maslama applied to him shows, he seems to have been active during Muhammad's lifetime and to have had a considerable following. M. is commonly called 'the liar'. → Ibn Ishaq tells of his sending a message to Muhammad, in which he said they owned half the land between them. Another story tells of a B. Ḥanīfa deputation accepting Islam, but apostatising when they, along with M., returned home. M. is described as an imitator of Muhammad; but he had great influence. He is said to have married Sajāḥ, a prophetess of the Christ. tribe Tamīm, so strengthening his position. → Abū Bakr engaged in war with him, sending → Khalid b. al-Walid as commander after the Muslims had suffered two defeats. A violent battle took place at 'Aqrabā' in 12/633, and M. was killed. J.R.

E.I., III, pp. 745f.; Hughes, p. 422; Guillaume, *Life*, index; Watt, *Medina*, index.

Music The connection between music and religion is so gen. recognised that it is surprising to find how little work has been done, partic. from the side of comp. relig., in relating the phenomenology of the two. The material is vast: musicologists, ethnomusicologists and anthropologists have assembled details of instruments, scales, rhythm, harmony (if any) and performance from many ethnic and relig. areas. But, although so much is known about the practical function of M. in various contexts, little attention has been paid to its significance as an aspect of relig. action. Histories of M., which normally cover more or less the same ground, beginning with 'primitive' M. and proceeding, *via* the anc. civilisations, to M. in Orient and West, frequently tend to overlook the relig. significance of their material. Philosophies of M., on the other hand, are often deficient in hist. sense and synoptic vision. Of modern phenomenologists of relig., only G. van der Leeuw has made a tentative approach to problem of M. in relig.

Clearly, any attempt to evaluate the overall relig. significance of M. must begin with recognition that M. in pre-literate societies is an aspect of cultic action—but only one aspect among many. Others incl. the → dance (cultic action in its purely physical aspect) and the word or *libretto*, in which the action is verbalised and conceptualised (→ Myth and Ritual). The ritual practices of pre-literate peoples (which cannot, without more ado, be taken to repr. those of prehistoric man) can normally be broken down into this threefold pattern of action, word and M. (The → image takes its place in this pattern as an attempt to render permanent either some aspect of the action or some conception of the beyond.) The existence or otherwise of prior stages, in which the conceptual element is missing, must remain a matter for speculation. However, studies of animal behaviour, together with what we know of the rituals of Palaeolithic man (the famous 'Dancing Sorcerer' in the Trois Frères cave is a case in point) would seem to suggest that the link between M. and the dance precedes the further link between words and M. (there is some poss. evidence from the Trois Frères cave of ritual music at this time). The dance as rhythmic motion, often, in pre-literate societies, with direct sexual connotations, would almost certainly be 'accompanied' in some way. The object would be to accentuate rhythm by means of hand-clapping, stamping, beating of improvised percussion instruments, and the like. But the object of the ritual—apart from its immediate magico-relig. purpose—was to bring man into contact with what he understood as being the realm of the sacred. Just as the rhythmic dance was not his normal pattern of physical motion, so the notes which he produced, either by straining his voice outside its common range of expression, or by adapting natural objects to produce sounds, were 'abnormal', and hence potentially sacred. Imitation of sounds of animals and birds, partic. such animals and birds as he felt to be messengers or vehicles of spirits (→ Animism, Totemism), would also be a sacred act, expanding his consciousness beyond bounds of the natural into realm of the supernatural. (→ Dance, Sacred).

The peculiarly emotive quality of highly rhythmical M., partic. when accompanied by rhythmical physical action, is well known. The close connection of M. and the dance with the phenomena of 'spirit possession' (→ Shamanism) in pre-literate societies strengthens the assumption that the role of M. in such societies was, within the ritual as a whole, to mediate contact with spirit world. The spirit world, too, might express itself musically: the Plains Indian, in his quest for personal vision of his guardian spirit, was taught a 'spirit song', which was thought to be the peculiar expression of the spirit (→ North American Indian Religion). It is also common knowledge that use of intensive, rhythmical and repetitive snatches of melody can serve as one means toward attainment of trance and catalepsy —the state *par excellence* of spirit-possession. This is a constant element in the hist. of relig., from the Shaman, beating his drum to summon the spirits, to the practices of the 'Holy Rollers'. Religs. of a fertility character (with which may be classified most of the religs. of pre-literate peoples) are more likely to resort to M. purely for sake of its emotive quality than are those religs. in which rational considerations predominate.

M. as an emotive force is virtually coextensive with relig. in pre-literate societies. The actual techniques practised involve rhythm (often highly complex, as in much trad. African M.), short and symmetrical melodies, and performance with precentor and chorus-response. Music divorced from participation, espec. in the dance, is virtually unknown. Occasionally, the orig. motivation may have changed; for instance, the African 'work-songs' have very little in them today of the sacred. But in every case there is some tendency toward an abnormal state of mind and body. The ritual action as a whole, whatever its setting, is all-important; the vocal and instrumental sounds produced serve to reinforce the action, estab. contact with spirit world for whatever purpose the individual, or group (for music of this order is a social action rather than an individual performance) may have in mind.

The transition from hunting and gathering cultures to settled agrarian cultures saw develop. of M. from spontaneous to a more considered part of ritual. Whereas ritual had previously been determined by purpose, and only incidentally attached to fixed sites (→ Australian Aborigine Religion), it now became centred on the temple, considered as dwelling-place of god or goddess. The emergence of writing *c.* 4th mil. BC rendered more permanent hymns and prayers dedicated to the gods. In Mesopotamia and Egypt, temples were provided with an establishment of musicians and dancers, whose function was to enrich and accompany the cycles of worship, daily and seasonal. Unfortunately, though we have many Egyptian and Mesopotamian reliefs of musicians and their instruments, we know practically nothing of character of the M. performed in these temples. We may, however, infer from later sources that connection between word and M. had already begun, alongside older pattern of M. and dance, to affect role of M. in worship. In the O.T. there is evidence of both: M. was performed in connection with temple-worship in Jerusalem, and esp. in conjunction with the → Psalms; M. and the dance are noted, e.g. in 1 Sam. 10:5f., as being part of trademark of the cultic prophets. The same type of twofold development can be noted in India, where, on one hand, the *Vedas* are known to have been chanted from an early date, while on the other, the purely melodic forms, of which the *rāga* is the best known, might exist independent of cult, although closely linked with social basis of caste system. The dance, again, in → Hinduism is assoc. partic. with the fertility aspect: → Śiva is represented in iconography as lord of the dance. In Greece, tension between the chthonic and Olympian religs. (→ Greek Relig.) is to some extent reflected in musical practice: the anthropomorphism of the Olympic cult led to a devaluation of M. as an emotive factor, while M. and the dance continued to flourish in the → Mystery Cults. This meant, *inter alia*, that the way was left open for a more positive evaluation of sculpture over against the other plastic arts, that the early hymn technique developed into a form of → drama in which the orig. relig. connotation grad. disappeared, and that speculative thinkers in time called in question some more pronounced of the emotive factors of M. The condemnation of the *aulós* (a reed instrument) on account of its use in ecstatic cults (→→ Dionysos, Orphism) is a case in point. It was, however, recognised that the moral and emotional significance of M. was not to be restricted to such crude distinctions: → Plato in partic. based an entire theory of musical education on idea that each mode (a scale with varying proportions of whole- and semi-tones) had its proper and inimitable emotional character. The only comparable theory of M. which we know from the anc. world is that of China. → Mencius stated that 'In music of the grandest style there is the same harmony that prevails between heaven and earth', and that 'Music is an echo of the harmony between heaven and earth' (→ Tao). However, little is known of anc. music of China. (See p. 460).

M. in pre-literate cultures and in anc. civilisations, then, was primarily melodic and rhythmic. It might be emotive, in which case it was inevitably linked with the dance, or it might serve as a vehicle for expression of a text. For the develop. of polyphone (the simultaneous performance of independent melodic lines) and harmony we must look to mod. Western trad.

In hist. of Chr. Church, we see M. being used in three ways: emotive, conceptual and aesthetic. The connection between M. and the dance in W. Church has grown progressively less pronounced since Middle Ages, though experiments in liturgical ballet and mime (with or without M.) have recently been made in Europe. The main line of musical develop. in the Church has been in melodic treatment of liturgical texts. From its early beginnings in worship of → synagogue, in which antiphonal technique was already applied, the line can be followed through work of Ambrose (*c.* 339–97) and Gregory the Great (*c.* 540–604) to the plainsong (still called 'Gregorian') of Middle Ages and later. The antiphonal technique of plainsong was espec. suited to the monastic community, though it has been adapted for congregational use in some churches. About 7th cent. there emerged the practice of *organum* song (parallel fourths or fifths); the process of experimentation which this heralded has gone on unchecked to present day. Polyphonic settings, partic. of the → Mass, grew more and more elaborate (among outstanding composers may be mentioned Machaut, Okeghem, des Prés, Byrd, Tallis and Palestrina), and farther and farther removed from capacities of congregation. This had effect of breaking link between M. and the cult, and intro. the aesthetic element as import. factor; appreciation took place of participation.

The → Reformation redressed balance somewhat, in that congregational singing of psalms and hymns was emphasised (the former in Calvinist trad., the latter in Lutheran) as a means of collective affirmation of Chr. doctrine and experience—a feature later adopted by R. Catholicism and further stressed in successive Evangelical Revivals (→→ Methodism, Wesley). But at same time the trad. of polyphonic settings of Mass and other liturgical texts was extended and developed, reaching its climax in Baroque period with the great Passions, motets and cantatas of J. S. Bach. The refinement of the church organ in 18th cent. led to writing of elaborate chorale preludes and other organ works, all of which took their place in the liturgical context of Lutheran worship: again the name of Bach is outstanding. Churches of Calvinist trad., on the other hand, were long suspicious of use of musical instruments in church. The subjective aesthetic element, although never far removed from M. of Baroque period in Europe (the Masses of Haydn and Mozart, and the Oratorios of Händel are cases in point) became dominant in Romantic movement. Many great romantic composers (Beethoven, Brahms, Bruckner, Mendelssohn and others) wrote 'church M.', with no thought of its liturgical setting. The 19th cent. in Anglican and Orthodox Churches, however, saw composition of innumerable settings of liturgy for use of choirs. In every case, the technical requirements of this M. tended to set performer apart from congregation, which was reduced to passive role of audience (a pitfall avoided by Bach, who interspersed arias and choruses with chorales). The same tendency has persisted into our own day in the West, where advanced church M. has remained a matter for musical specialists.

In recent years there has been a movement to re-establish M. in its ritual context. The → liturgical movement has seen reintroduction of plainsong on a large scale, in Roman, Anglican and some Lutheran Churches (e.g. in Sweden). Simplified settings of liturgy have replaced elaborate polyphonic settings (an example is seen in work of French Jesuit Fr. Gelineau). Carols—relig. folk songs—have attained a new popularity. The aim in each case has been to restore M. to its orig. position as an organic part of self-expression of the worshipping congregation. In the 'young Churches' of Africa and

Asia, indigenous M. has been adapted for use of people, with new spontaneity as a result: a striking example is the *Missa Luba* from the Congo. This work is, however, still at an early stage. E.J.S.

E.R.E., ix, pp. 5–61; *R.G.G.*[3], iv, cols. 1195–224; *Die Musik in Geschichte und Gegenwart* (1949ff.); *The New Oxford History of Music*, I–III (1954–60); R. Aigrain, *La musique religieuse* (1929); B. Wibberley, *Music and Religion* (1934); C. Sachs, *The Rise of Music in the Ancient World* (1943), J. Kunst (ed.), *The Wellsprings of Music* (1962); E. Routley, *The Church and Music* (1950); W. Apel, *Gregorian Chant* (1958); A. M. Jones, *Studies in African Music* I (1959); H. Weman, *African Music and the Church in Africa* (1960); G. van der Leeuw, *Sacred and Profane Beauty* (E.T. 1963); B. Nettl, *Theory and Method in Ethnomusicology* (1964); J. Gelineau, *Voices and Instruments in Christian Worship.*

(Sacred) (China–Japan) Chi. M. was orig. of highly symbolical character, and has occupied prominent place in rituals from Shang and Chou Dynasties. A whole section of the → *Li Chi* (Cf. trans. by J. Legge, *S.B.E.*, vol. 28, 1885, pp. 91ff.) is given over to discussion of M. and its effects in producing inner harmony and virtue. Its symbolical nature is everywhere emphasised. Even forms of many Chinese M. instruments were symbolical: the *shêng* or reed-organ symbolised the phoenix; the 'sonorous stone' typifies carpenter's square or a just and upright life; the guitar resembles moon in shape; the *ch'in* or lute is symbol of matrimonial harmony. The Chi. scale consisted of 5 sounds. The instruments of M. were divided into 8 categories: stone, metal, silk or stringed, bamboo, wood, skin, gourd and clay. The ritual M. used in worship of → Confucius was intro. from Bactria in 2nd cent. BC, and still bears traces of its Greek origin. It is slow and plaintive, and consists of singing and posturing to accompaniment of antique instruments. Buddh. and Taoist priests chant in their services, using gongs and bells to mark rhythm of their prayers, to call attention of gods and spirits, and to disperse demons and malicious influences. A large variety of bells and gongs of different shapes and sizes are in daily use in temples. Every temple of any size has a large bell (without a clapper) and a large drum. Bells in Peking, Osaka, Kyoto and Nara are among largest in world. Almost unique among anc. musical instruments are the stone chimes used in Confucian rituals, consisting of sonorous stones of varying thickness, hung on a large frame. Buddh. priests make great use of the 'wooden fish', hollowed and shaped like a skull and struck by a piece of wood. The 'wind bells' hanging from eaves of temples and pagodas are believed to drive away demons.

Japanese music, in its present form, was intro. from China by Buddh. monks. D.H.S.

C. H. S. Williams, *Outlines of Chinese Symbolism* (1931), pp. 248ff.; J. D. Ball, *Things Chinese*, 5th edn. (1925), pp. 498ff.; Bredon and Mithrophanow, *The Moon Year* (1927), pp. 206ff.; B. H. Chamberlain, *Things Japanese*, 5th edn. (1905), pp. 339ff.; B. Wiant, *The Music of China* (Hong Kong, n.d.).

Muslim One who submits himself to God and belongs to the community of → Islām. J.R.

(b. al-Hajjāi) (*c.* 205–261/820–875). A traditionist of Naysabur whose compilation of traditions, *al-Ṣaḥīḥ* (the sound), is considered by → Sunnis to be one of two most authoritative collections. His collection and → Bukhari's are called the two *Ṣaḥīḥs*. While most consider Bukhari's superior to M.'s, others, esp. in the West, were inclined to favour M.'s. But both are held in high esteem. M. began his collection with a valuable intro. to the science of Tradition. → Ḥadīth). J.R.

E.I., III, p. 756; *G.A.L.*, I, pp. 166–8; *S.* I, pp. 265f.; Pareja, index; Goldziher, *M.S.*, II, pp. 245–8, 252; Guillaume, *Traditions*, index; Siddiqi, *Hadith*, index; J. Robson, 'The transmission of Muslim's Ṣaḥīḥ', *J.R.A.S.* (1949), pp. 46ff.

(Brethren) (*-Ikhwān al-Muslimūn*). Society founded in Ismailiya in 1346/1927 by Ḥasan al-Bannā', a teacher, to uphold and advance Islam. He was a follower of the doc. of → Rashīd Riḍā, but political elements became prominent later in party. The M.B. held that the Qur. is in harmony with scientific knowledge, and wished to unify Egypt on Qur. principles. They desired to improve economic conditions, providing equal opportunity for everyone, both men and women. They engaged in social service and charitable work, instituted schools and started journals. Many branches were started, incl. branches of Muslim Sisters. When Banna' was moved to Cairo in 1352/1933, the movement expanded. They hoped to achieve liberation of Arab countries and achieve Arab unity. The ultimate aim was universal peace and civilisation on Islamic principles, which involved return to → Qur. and → Hadith. They were characteristically Muslim in their combination of relig. and politics. They wanted a one-party Islamic government, for to them the Muslim community was a single party, and they were prepared to fight to attain their goal. Although they were able to extend their activities to other countries such as Syria, Palestine, Jordan, Iraq, the Sudan, they were suspect because of their political activities. Banna' was assassinated in 1369/1949; two years later Ḥasan b. Ismā'īl al-Ḥudaybī was recognised as leader, but in following year there was tension. The brotherhood was dissolved in Egypt in

1374/1954; in Syria four years later. It might have been allowed to continue as a purely relig. movement, but to separate religion and politics is un-Islamic. J.R.

Pareja, index (*-iḫwān . . .*); I. M. Husayni, *The Moslem Brethren* (1956); Cragg, *Counsels*, ch. VII; *M.W.*, xxxv, p. 349; xliv, pp. 151f.; xlv, pp. 206f.

(Law, Schools of) The four schools of law which became predominant among → Sunnis are connected with names of famous men, but the doc. was developed by their followers. The Ḥanafī school was traced to → Abū Ḥanifa of Kufa, and was developed by his pupils Abū Yūsuf (d. 182/798) and al-Shaybānī (d. 189/804). It has commonly been accused of being too much dependent on opinion (*ra'y*); but the accuracy of the charge is questionable. In Medina the Mālikī school was traced to → Mālik b. Anas, who compiled a law book (*al-Muwaṭṭa'*) partially based on trads. traced to → Muḥammad. The doc. of the school owes much to Malik's pupil Ibn al-Qāsim (d. 191/806), whose dictation of teachings from Malik with commentary was collected by Saḥnūn b. Sa'īd (d. 240/854) in *al-Mudawwana*. The Shāfi'ī school goes back to Muḥammad b. Idrīs → al-Shāfi'ī, who, of Hāshimite stock, spent his early days in Mecca. He studied in Medina during last nine years of Malik's life, after which he went to Baghdad where he came in touch with Shaybānī. He is credited with being father of Muslim jurisprudence, and was the one most responsible for emphasis on the → *sunna* of the Prophet. His main career was divided between Baghdad and Fusṭāṭ (Old Cairo), where he died. To → Aḥmad b. Ḥanbal, pupil of Shafi'i, the Ḥanbalī school is traced. He became stricter in his teaching, basing his doct. principally on the →→ Qur. and Tradition. He did not publish his teaching himself; his followers collected his sayings and opinions, and his son collected a large body of trads. which he heard from his father. There were other schools in Sunni Islam which were grad. superseded. Notable among them was that of al-Awzā'ī (d. 156/774) in Syria. The Ẓāhirī (literalist) school, also called the Dāwūdī, is traced to Dāwūd b. Khalaf (d. 270/883). It spread for a time. In Spain its most notable repres. was → Ibn Hazm. The only time it received official recognition in Spain was under the Almohad Ya'qūb b. Manṣūr (580–95/1184–99), who estab. it as the state system. But this strict literalist doc. made no gen. appeal.

The four schools are not to be considered sects. They recognise one another as good Muslims. Their divisions have been not so much doctrinal as geographical; for it was normal practice that one should belong to the school of his district. The Hanafi has been prominent in lands of former Turkish Empire and in Indian subcontinent. The Maliki has mainly been confined to N. Africa. The Shafi'i has applied to S. Arabia, from where it spread to Indonesia, also to Upper Egypt and E. Africa. The Hanbali is confined to the → Wahhābi regions of C. Arabia. In mod. times many countries have modified the system, often choosing what seemed best from different schools. In some respects the schools have been superseded; but only in Turkey has the → *sharī'a* been completely abandoned.

It should be understood that in Islam law ref. to all spheres of life; therefore relig. practices come within the teaching of the schools as much as matters considered legal in the West. Islam makes no distinction between sacred and secular; everything comes under God's law. While Shi'i law depends mainly on the Qur. and their trads., Shi'is hold that any elaboration comes only through the divinely inspired → *imām*. J.R.

E.I., articles on separate schools. Pareja, pp. 632ff.; Goldziher, *Die Ẓâhiriten* (1884); Schacht, *Jurisprudence*, *passim*; Coulson, *Law*, *passim*; Rahman, *Islam*, pp. 81ff.

Muslims, Mutual Responsibilities The Qur. indic. that M. have duties towards one another. v. 3 exhorts them to assist one another to virtuous conduct, not to guilt and enmity. xlviii:29 describes M. as compassionate among themselves. xlix:11f. exhort M., men and women, to avoid mocking others, scoffing at them, calling them by nicknames, prying into their affairs. iv:88 says that when greeted by someone a M. should reply with a better greeting, or at least with one as good as that received. E.g., a very satisfactory reply to greeting 'Peace be upon you' would be 'And upon you be peace, and God's mercy and blessings'. Trad. mentions various duties M. should be able to expect from one another. The M. is said to be one from whose tongue and hand other M.s are safe. Other duties are returning a salutation, → visiting the sick, following funerals (→ burial of the dead), accepting an invitation, saying 'God have mercy on you' when someone sneezes, giving advice when consulted, helping people to fulfil their oaths. (→ Ethics and morality, Muslim). J.R.

Mishkāt, pp. 6, 320; Levy, *Social Structure*, pp. 192–241, *passim*.

Mutakallimūn (Lit. people talking). Came to be used for scholastic theologians (→ Kalām). → Aquinas called them Loquentes. While they differed from the → Mu'tazilites in doc., they learned from them to use rational arguments in their theological doc. (→→ -Ash'arī; Avempace; Averroes; -Māturīdī). J.R.

D. B. Macdonald, *Theology*, index; Wensinck, *Creed*, index (Kalām); Sweetman, *I.C.T.*, IV, *passim*; Maimonides, *The Guide of the Perplexed*:

trans. M. Friedländer, 3 vols. (1881–5), index (Mutakallimim), do. abridged, trans. from Arabic, C. Rabin, comm. by J. Guthmann (1952), index (Mutakallimūn); Rahman, *Islam*, pp. 94ff.

Mu'tazilites The name is connected with the word *i'tazala* (to withdraw), said to have been used by → al-Ḥasan al-Basrī (d. 110/728), when Wāṣil b. 'Aṭā', or 'Amr b. 'Ubayd withdrew from his circle and founded a new school, teaching that a great sinner who claimed to be a believer was in an intermediate state, neither a believer nor an infidel (*al-manzila bayn al-manzilatayn*). This might suggest a political connection with the beginnings of what became an import. party within Islam, as it rejects views of the → Kharijites, who treated all such as infidels, and of the → Murji'ites, who held they were believers. Those most concerned with this argument were the → Umayyads, soon to be superseded by the → 'Abbasids. As time went on, the docs. of the M.'s developed. The chief centres were in Basra, where the discussions began, and in Baghdad. Among chief founders of M. theology were Abul Hudhayl (d. 226/841) and al-Naẓẓām (d. *c.* 231/854) from Basra and Bishr b. al-Mu'tamir (d. 210/825) in Baghdad. The party called themselves the people of unity and justice (*ahl al-tawḥīd wal 'adl*). 'Unity' refers to their insistence on God's unity, as they held that the doc. which says God possesses attributes involves multiplicity. They argued that the attributes were not *in* his essence, but *were* his essence, for he does not possess knowledge, sight, etc. (→ God), to enable him to know, see, etc. 'Justice' indic. their doc. that God must do what is best for his creatures. This involves freewill and man's responsibility for his deeds. They also taught that the Qur. is created (→ al-Qur'ān), a necessary doc. in keeping with their strict insistence on God's unity. They are noted for introducing philosophical methods into theological discussion. The movement had a short period of official favour. Al-Ma'mūn, the Caliph, issued decree in 212/827 declaring that doc. of creation of Qur. is the only true one. There was popular opposition; but in 218/833 an inquisition (*miḥna*) was instituted, a strange instrument in hands of a party which taught freewill. → Ahmad b. Hanbal was an outstanding opponent of the official views; he suffered flogging and imprisonment for his faith. The decree was eventually cancelled by al-Mutawakkil in 234/848, when the doc. of eternity of Qur. became official one, and the M.'s were in their turn persecuted. The movement declined, becoming largely academic in its discussions; but it continued for some cents. in areas removed from centre of Caliphate. J.R.

E.I., III, pp. 787ff.; Pareja, pp. 696ff. and index; D. B. Macdonald, *Theology*, index; Wensinck, *Creed*, index; Watt, *Philosophy*, ch. 7 and index; Sweetman, *I.C.T.*, II–IV, index; F. Rosenthal, *Ibn Khaldun*, index; Seale, *Theology*, Part II; Rahman, *Islam*, pp. 87ff. and index.

Mystery Religions The Greeks used word *mysterion* (pl. *mysteria*) to designate rites of private or secret character, in distinction from public rituals conducted on behalf of state. Whereas all citizens were gen. qualified to participate in latter, a person had to be specially initiated into a M., the purpose of which was to secure some form of personal salvation or beatitude, usually after death. Each M. had a *mythos*, mostly concerning death and resurrection of a divine person. Initiation involved purification, instruction in some secret doctrine, and rites, often simulating death and rebirth. In some M. there were prob. special revelations, ritual marriages and sacred meals. The ceremonies seem often to have been ritual representations of events of *mythos* (→ Ritual Perpetuation of Past). Since initiates were sworn to secrecy and kept their vows, very little direct information survives of actual doctrines and rites of the various M. Greece produced two M.: → Eleusinian M. and → Orphism (→ Dionysos). In Graeco-Roman world many foreign M. flourished, chief among them being those connected with →→ Adonis; Attis; Isis and Osiris; the Kabiri; Mithras. The M. helped to meet personal spiritual needs not catered for by State-cults. Christianity was, technically, a M. Influence of M.R. can be traced in later European culture. (→→ Apuleius; Sabazios). S.G.F.B.

G. Mylonas: *Eleusis and the Eleusinian Mysteries* (1961); W. K. C. Guthrie, *Orpheus and Greek Religion* (1952[2]); N. Turchi, *Fontes historiae mysteriorum aevi hellenistici* (1923); V. Macchioro, *Zagreus* (1930); R. Reitzenstein, *Die hellenistischen Mysterienreligionen* (1927[3]); H. Gressmann, *Die orientalischen Religionen im hellenist.-römischen Zeitalter* (1930); F. Cumont, *R.O.*, and *The Mysteries of Mithra* (E.T., ed. 1956); S. Angus, *The Mystery-Religions and Christianity* (1925); A. D. Nock, *Conversion* (1933); A. Moret, *Mystères égyptiennes* (1923); *R.Ae.R.-G.*, pp. 494ff.; *E.R.E.*, IX, pp. 70–83; *The Mysteries* (Eranos Yearbooks), ed. J. Campbell (1955); A. Loisy, *Les mystères païens et le mystère chrétien* (1914); E. Wind, *Pagan Mysteries in the Renaissance* (ed. 1967); *Kleine Pauly*, III, 1533–42.

Mysticism Evelyn Underhill, a recognised authority on subject, defined M. as 'the name of that organic process which involves the perfect consummation of the Love of God: the achievement here and now of the immortal heritage of man' (*Mysticism* (1930[12]), p. 81). This definition by a Christian, aware of other forms of M., repr. an ideal evaluation, for which much evidence can be cited. The hist. of relig., however, induces caution in accepting such a definition, since there is a vast amorphous mass of phenomena that may fairly be labelled M. Belief that it is poss. for the conscious self to transcend bodily limitations and commune with, or become immerged in, some other form of being occurs in primitive cultures as well as in higher religs. Such experience can be induced by various means: e.g. → Yoga praxis, self-hypnosis, → dancing, and drugs (→ Peyote Cult). The higher forms of M. do not gen. resort to such means: certain approved methods for meditation and contemplation are taught and various stages of the mystical life charted. M. has often been suspect to relig. authorities, since mystics tend to claim spiritual experiences independently of official means of grace, and sometimes insights contrary to orthodoxy. The subject is vast, and, because it concerns subjective experience, difficult to evaluate; it clearly involves the reality of relig. for many people, irrespective of partic. relig. trad. to which they formally adhere. In some of its aspects, M. seems more a subject for psychology or psychiatry. The mystics of many religs. have recorded their experiences in writing, sometimes employing an intensely emotional and even erotic imagery. M. is, in fact, a generic term covering an enormous range and variety of experience from that of the → shaman to those of St. Teresa of Avila (1515–82) or the →→ Ṣūfī Hallaj. All the great figures in hist. of relig. were, basically, mystics. (→→ Ecstasy: Neoplatonism; → Psychology of Relig.). S.G.F.B.

E.R.E., IX, pp. 83–117; *R.G.G.*[3], IV, 1237–62; W. James, *The Varieties of Religious Experience* (1903); G. Van der Leeuw, *La religion* (1948), pp. 482ff.; S. Spencer, *Mysticism in World Religion* (1963); R. Otto, *Mysticism East and West* (E.T. 1957); R. C. Zaehner, *Mysticism, Sacred and Profane* (1957), *Hindu and Muslim Mysticism* (1960); G. Widengren, 'Researches in Syrian Mysticism', *Numen*, VIII (1961); A. Schimmel, 'Yunies Emre', *ibid.*, 'The Martyr-Mystic Hallāj in Sindhi Folk-Poetry', *Numen*, IX (1962); D. Knowles, *What is Mysticism?* (1967).

(Hindu) Mysticism, interp. as quest for inner illumination, union with ultimate reality, etc., is import. feature of Hindu trad., and of Indian trad. in general. It has been nurtured by institution of the → *sannyasin*, one who 'gives up the world' to search for spiritual truth, by practice of → yoga and → *dhyana* or meditation, and, in later times, by → monasticism. → Asceticism has also been important, in symbolizing and promoting aim of indifference to wordly concerns. In add., there is some evidence of 'panenhenic' mysticism—seeing world existentially as unified reality; and of more particularised experiences of rapport with nature, as in early life of → Ramakrishna. In gen. form, Hindu M. has been continuous with that expressed in unorthodox relig. movements, such as →→ Jainism and Buddhism. It has frequently been assoc. with pursuit of → *jñāna* or knowledge (gnosis); typically, knowledge of ultimate reality has been taken to mean an existential experience of it. Thus there is a polarity in trad. between the *jnanamarga* or way of knowledge as exemplified in interior M. and *bhaktimarga* or way of devotion, exemplified in loving adoration of God as personal Being. But the two ways blend. Further factors in interpretation of Hindu M. are part played by sacrificial ritual as in Vedic relig. and that played by analogous, but more diffuse, sacramentalism of → Tantrism. Thus sometimes interior quest could blend with trad. ritualism; sometimes with later sacramentalism. The chief instance of former blend—and one which was to prove highly influential in later Hindu theology—was the → *Brahman-Atman* doc. propounded in some classical → Upaniṣads. The inner meaning of ritualism is *Brahman*, the sacred force pervading universe and sustaining and yet also present in the earthly sacrifice; the inner quest of → yoga is realisation of eternal self. The self and *Brahman* are declared to be one, and the yogi's self-training is seen as itself a form of sacrifice. The ineffable non-dual state achieved by mystic is symbolized as fourth (*turīya*) in the sequence whose first three members are: waking, dreaming and dreamless sleep (*Māndūkya Upaniṣad*), and sometimes significance of sacred syllable → Om is seen as pointing to this higher state of consciousness. Monistic emphases in Upaniṣadic M. may have been reinforced by panenhenic mysticism (as, e.g., R. C. Zaehner has argued). For in → Samkhya-Yoga, which prob. had non-Brahmanical origin, the need to see inner realisation as identification or union with *Brahman*, was not felt; and both for it and → Jainism the highest state is one of wholeness or pure perception of eternal self or life-monad. The liberation accruing was not union with anything, but blissful isolation of soul in a transcendental state, no longer subject to rebirth. The → *Bhagavadgita* recognises poss. of *jnanamarga*, but emphasises much more strongly efficacy of *bhakti*, and thus in its gen. trend is anti-mystical, though it at same time 'laicises' the concept of self-control, which is import. to the pursuit of inner realisation. The most import. later reaffirmation of centrality of *jnana* was that of → Śankara, whose rigorous application of a monistic position (→ *tat tvam asi*) gained some of its persuasiveness from non-duality of mystical experience itself (i.e. no sense of contrast between subject and object characterising ordinary experience). It also showed influence of similar mystically-oriented philosophy, that of → Nagarjuna. But by his doc. of two levels of relig. truth, Sankara reserved place, at lower level, both for Vedic ritualism and *bhakti*. Meanwhile → Tantrism evolved a sacramentalism in which use of formulae and external symbolic acts was held to conduce to unification of individual with divine, and so sacraments came themselves to be seen as means of existential knowledge of ultimate (incl. the ritual breaking of tabus, through meat-eating, sexual intercourse, etc., which symbolized equanimity in regard to worldly values of those who attain truth). Neither sense of isolation of soul as expressed in M. of → Yoga nor identification with ultimate reality expressed in → Advaita were satisfactory for proponents of *bhakti* relig., which held to a differentiation of soul and world from God in accord with sentiments of worship and loving adoration. Nevertheless, *bhakti* relig. also blended with interior yoga. Thus in → Madhva's *Dvaita*, meditation is seen as being directed towards the Lord, with whom yogi can gain union (though not strict identification). Less theologically, but more poetically, the relation between → Krishna and the *gopis*, with whom he sported, was seen as expressing loving relation between God and souls. The mythology served as vehicle for a mysticism of love, in which two become one and yet remain distinct. There were analogous conceptions in Śaivism, e.g. in → *Śaiva Siddhanta*. Sometimes sense of identification with God was transferred to → *guru*, as himself somehow identified with God—a sentiment clearly expressed by, e.g., 13th cent. Maharashtrian saint Jñānadeva. In mod. period, the initial reform and revival movements within Hinduism were rationalistic rather than mystical in spirit; but the → Ramakrishna movement has been import. in widening interest in value of contemplation. Ramakrishna himself practised not only various forms of *bhakti* but was capable of deep meditation or → *samadhi*. The contemplative life also plays central part in teachings of → Aurobindo and other mod. *gurus*. The trend towards subordinating *bhakti* to *jnanamarga* has been assisted by impressive revival of *Advaita Vedanta* in last cent. and half. One of chief attractions of Hindu thought and practice for Westerners has been Hinduism's contemplative techniques, in period when mystical relig. in Christianity has been largely neglected (at any rate, within Protestantism). N.S.

S. N. Dasgupta, *Hindu Mysticism* (1959), *Yoga Philosophy in Relation to Other Systems of Indian Thought* (1930); M. Eliade, *Yoga: Immortality and Freedom* (1958); E. Wood, *Great Systems of Yoga* (1954); P. C. Bagchi, *Studies in the Tantras* (1939); R. Otto, *Mysticism East and West* (1957); K. Sen, *Medieval Mysticism of India* (1936); H. Bhattacharyya (ed.), *The Cultural Heritage of India*, vol. 4 (1956); D. S. Sarma, *The Renaissance of Hinduism* (1944); N. Smart, *The Yogi and the Devotee* (1958); R. C. Zaehner *Mysticism Sacred and Profane* (1958).

Myth and Ritual The origin of M. appears to have been twofold: (1) as a kind of libretto to ritual action. (2) aetiological. Very anc. examples of (1) occur in mortuary ritual in → Pyramid Texts, where various actions in embalming dead are accompanied by utterances, rel. to these actions, addressed to deceased as → Osiris. As example of (2) a Mesopot. text may be cited concerning toothache: before treatment starts, cause of toothache is explained in terms of orig. of worm held to be responsible for it. More elaborate forms of M. (e.g. → Enuma elish, → Yahwist acc. of Fall of Adam) are gen. literary products of theological motivation, or philosophical parables as with → Plato (M. of Er.). Considerable attention has been given by certain scholars to what appears to be a M.-and-R. pattern related to sacred → kingship in anc. Near East. The basic thesis is that king repr. the vegetation god, whose annual cycle of death and resurrection were ritually enacted at New Year festival: a recitation of myth of creation, ritual combat, sacred → marriage, triumphant procession, and decreeing of fates were other constitutive episodes of this M.-and-R. complex. The pattern was assumed to have existed in Egypt, Mesopot., Canaan, Israel, and among Hittites. The M.-and-R. thesis has encountered much specialist criticism. C. G. → Jung formulated a psychological interpretation of M., tracing it to certain archetypal structures of the Unconscious. (→→ Magic; Scandinavian School). S.G.F.B.

J. Harrison, *Ancient Art and Ritual* (1918); S. H. Hooke (ed.), *Myth and Ritual* (1933), *The Labyrinth* (1935), *Myth, Ritual and Kingship* (1958); I. Engnell, *Studies in Divine Kingship in the Anc. Near East* (1943); E. O. James, *Christian Myth and Ritual* (1937), *Myth and Ritual in the Anc. Near East* (1958); H. Frankfort, *Kingship and the Gods* (1948); *R.G.G.*[3], IV, col. 90–1, 1263–82; *O.C.D.*, p. 594; T. H. Gaster, *Thespis* (1961); C. G. Jung, *Symbols of Transformation* (E.T. 1956); F. Fordham, *An Intro. to Jung's Psychology* (1959), pp. 24ff.

Mythology *Ex.* Grk. *mythologia*—'telling of mythic legends', or 'legendary lore'. The term has been loosely and misleadingly used to describe many kinds of relig. phenomena. (→ Myth and Ritual). S.G.F.B.

O.C.D., s.v.; H. W. Haussig, *Wörterbuch der Mythologie* (from 1963); A. Brelich, 'Mitologia', in *Liber Amicorum*: C. J. Bleeker (1969).

N

Nāgārjuna Indian Buddh. philosopher of 2nd cent. CE, founder of → *Mādhyamika* sch. of → Mhy. Buddhism. This N. is to be distinguished from N., the alchemist and exponent of → Tantra, who lived poss. as late as 8th cent. CE, and is known as author of a work on *suvarnatantra* ('gold-magic'), entitled *Rasaratnākara*. The two N.'s are regarded in Tibetan trad. as one and same person. N., the Mādhyamika philosopher, is gen. held to have been of → Brahman family, and from S. India. He spent most of life in S. India, at Srī Parvata or Srī Śailam, a great centre of Mhy. Buddhism from his day onwards. He was close friend of the Satavahana king, Yajnaśri Gautamiputra (CE 166–96). There is reliable evidence connecting him with the great centre of learning in S.E. India (Andhra) which bore his name, viz. → Nāgārjunikonda; also with similar centre in Bihar at → Nālanda. His great work was the *Mādhyamika-kārikā* or *Mādhyamika-śāstra*. Herein was laid the groundwork of school of Buddh. philosophy of which he was founder, and which had many exponents from his time until disappearance of Buddhism from India in 12th cent. CE. The *M-kārikā* has been described as epitome of the Mahāyāna *sūtras*. The school of thought founded by N. was characterised pre-eminently by its use of term *śūñyatā*, for a method of expounding the 'voidness' of any concepts, and even of the ultimate 'elements' or *dhammas* believed in by the → Theravādins. T.O.L.

T. R. V. Murti, *The Central Philosophy of Buddhism* (1955), pp. 87–91; Richard H. Robinson, *Early Mādhyamika in India and China* (1967), pp. 21–70.

Nāgasena A learned Buddh. monk, whose discussion of controversial points of belief and practice with the Greek king Milinda (Menander) are recorded in the Pali work → *Milinda-pañhā*, composed in 1st cent. CE. Acc. to text of this work, N. was born in a village in Himālaya; he was of a → brahman family, but entered Buddh. → Sangha in early manhood, and studied the Buddha-Dhamma at various places, incl. Pātaliputta (Patna), where he is said to have become an → Arahant. Thence he moved to Sāgala (Sialkot), where he met King Milinda. However, the Chinese version of text mentions Kashmir as his place of birth. Although text of Milinda-pañhā claims also that N. was a man of such incredible ability that he mastered whole of the → *Abhidhamma Pitaka* after hearing it once, no other mention of him occurs in contemporary lit., a fact which has led some modern scholars to doubt his historical existence. T.O.L.

I. B. Horner, *Milinda's Questions*, vol. I (1963), translator's Introduction.

Nag[c] Hammâdi Place in Upper Egypt, about 100 kilom. n. of Luxor, where 13 Coptic MSS were found in 1945 or 1946. These MSS date from 3rd–4th cents. CE, and give texts of 49 works of → Gnostic origin, incl. a few → Hermetic tractates. The texts are Coptic trans. of Grk. originals, and prob. belonged to a Chr.-Gnostic community. Among these works was the Gospel of → Thomas, which contains early trads. about Jesus. The find provides direct orig. evidence of → Gnosticism, of which little existed previously. The N.-H. docs. are now in Coptic Museum, Cairo, except for one (the 'Jung Codex') in Zürich. They are sometimes ref. to as the Chenoboskion MSS, from neighbouring anc. Chr. monastery. Trans. of some works are given in books listed below. (→ Thomas, Gospel). S.G.F.B.

W. C. van Unnik, *Evangelien aus dem Nilsand* (1960), *Newly Discovered Gnostic Writings* (1960); J. Doresse, *The Secret Books of the Egyptian Gnostics* (E.T. 1960); F. L. Cross (ed.), *The Jung Codex* (1955); C. J. de Cantanzaro, 'The Gospel acc. to Philip', *J.T.S.*, XIII (1962).

Nakatomi One of 4 priestly classes of → Shinto which emerged at early and unknown dates: the others being the → Imbe (Abstainers), the → Urabe (Diviners), and the Sarume (Musicians and Dancers). The N. (Ritualists) had charge of ceremonies and read the → Norito or state rituals. They formed a hereditary corporation, belonging to the imperial clan. D.H.S.

W. G. Aston, *Shinto* (1905), p. 201; D. C. Holtom, *The National Faith of Japan* (1938), p. 28.

Nālanda A centre of Buddh. learning in N. India,

founded by a Gupta king prob. in 5th cent. CE or just after. N. is often mentioned in the Pali canon, esp. in the → Dīgha Nikāya as place visited by the Buddha and his disciples; it was there, e.g., that → Sariputta is said to have uttered his confession of absolute faith in the Buddha, sometimes ref. to as his 'lion's roar', an incident which is recorded in the Mahā Parinibbāna Sutta (*D.N.*, II, 81ff.). N. had not, however, achieved any great prominence when it was selected by the Gupta king as location for a new monastery; the site was selected as auspicious by an augurer. Some time in 6th cent. CE N., which had by then become monastic seminary for training of monks, was developed into centre of secular as well as relig. learning; from this time onwards it is properly ref. to as a monastic university. As such it acquired international fame. In this respect N. was one of a small number of such centres of higher learning (others being, e.g. Nagarjunikonda, Virkramasila, and Odantapura) which by 8th cent. CE had begun to monopolise the monastic scene; the smaller local monasteries as centres of piety were in many places then in decline. So far as Buddh. learning was concerned, N. became a great centre of → Mahāyāna philosophy. Acc. to the Chinese pilgrims →→ Hsuan-tsang and I-tsing, who visited place during period of its maximum grandeur and prosperity, it housed some 3,000 or more monk-scholars, was of great extent and impressive, even of spectacular appearance; its learned scholars and alumni enjoyed high prestige in Indian society. There was close assoc. between N. and Tibet; such was the continuing prestige of the Indian monastic establishment that a centre of learning was estab. in Tibet in 1351 bearing same name. Acc. to Buddh. historian Tāranātha, the Muslim Turks, who invaded N. India in 12th/13th cents. CE, 'conquered the whole of Magadha and destroyed many monasteries; at N. they did much damage and the monks fled abroad'. Some life was salvaged from the ruins; a few monks maintained a much reduced activity until at some date not exactly known, N. as a monastic centre fell into ruins, some of which still remain. A new monastic centre of learning has in the mod. period been re-estab. at N. The site of anc. N. has been identified with a village 7 miles north of mod. Rajgir (Rajagaha of anc. times). (→ *Monasteries, Buddh.*). T.O.L.

Sukumar Dutt. *Buddhist Monks and Monasteries of India* (1962); S. Beal, *Buddhist Records of the Western World*, 2 vols. (1884).

Nānak First of → Sikh → Gurus, and main founder of community (the two other most import. Gurus being →→ Arjun and Gobind). Born at Nankana, 40 miles from Lahore, in 1469, he married young and worked for time as accountant. However, influenced by → Ṣūfīsm and → *bhakti* movement, he underwent a relig. experience, about age of 30, and became wandering teacher. Like → Kabir, he preached essential unity of God, despite differences between Hindus and Muslims, and travelled widely in subcontinent (he is also said to have made pilgrimage to → Mecca). His hymns came to be incorporated in scriptures of Sikhism (→ *Granth, Adi*). His teaching emphasized formlessness of God (→ God, Sikh conception of), to whom he ref. as *Sat Kartār*, 'True Creator' or *Sat Nām*, 'True Name'; the need for purity of life while living in world (N. was opposed to → asceticism, and lived at home between preaching journeys); importance of calling on name of God in love; equality of men (N. was deeply opposed to → caste system as well as to division between Hindu and Muslim); and function of Guru as reminding men of their divine destiny. In relation to God, N.'s teaching was perhaps more Muslim than Hindu; but he accepted belief in reincarnation and concept of → *māyā*. He had at least two children, one of whom, Sri Chand, was regarded as his successor at his death in 1504, by some of the followers, though Nanak himself nominated Angad, who is recognised as the second in the line of orthodox Sikh succession. By practising inter-relig. and inter-caste equality, N. had succeeded in forming beginning of a distinctive trad., separate both from Hinduism and Islam. He also, through his vernacular hymns, set pattern of a popularly understood faith influential in giving Panjab ultimately a sense of identity. N.S.

Khushwant Singh, *A History of the Sikhs*, vol. 1 (1963).

Naqshabandiyya → Ṣūfī Orders. J.R.

-Nasā'ī Aḥmad b. Shu'ayb (215–303/830–915), was a traditionist b. in Nasā in Khurasan. He travelled widely in search of traditions, and made collection of them which is one of the six books accepted as canonical by → Sunnis. He was highly respected as a traditionist; although he was youngest of the compilers of the six books (→ Ḥadīth), his was the fourth to be gen. recognised. In spite of his distinction he had an unfortunate end. In Damascus he was questioned about the relative superiority of Mu'awiya and 'Alī; when he refused to agree that 'Ali was inferior to Mu'awiya, he was beaten and kicked so violently that he died. It is said his body was carried to Mecca for burial. J.R.

E.I., III, p. 848; *G.A.L.*, I, pp. 170f.; *S.*, I, pp. 269f.; J. Robson, 'The Transmission of Nasa'i's Sunan', *J.S.S.*, I (1956), pp. 38ff.

Nats Term used in Burma for hostile spirit-beings, of whom there are said to be 37 chiefs, or lords. The N. must propitiated in various ways; they are held to be of destructive nature, and must be continually guarded against. The attitude of peoples of Burma (hill tribes as well as plain-dwelling Burmese speakers) are sometimes described in terms of 'worship', but this is not entirely accurate; offerings are made to the N., but largely in order to placate them. Their characteristics are similar to those of the → *Yakkhas* of Pali canon; hence popular Burmese Buddh. attitude towards N. is largely same as that of the canon towards Yakkhas. The N. are regarded as having a king, Tha-gya-min, identified in Burma with → Sakka of Pali canon, king of the spirit-beings. T.O.L.

ShwayZoe (Sir J. G. Scott), *The Burman: His life and notions*, 3rd edn. (1909, repr. 1963); Maung Htin Aung, *Folk Elements in Burmese Buddhism* (1962).

Nature, Worship (Chinese) Chi. relig. has its roots in an → ancestor cult and a primitive → animism which inculcates worship of forces of nature, or rather the spirits which govern natural phenomena; in partic. the gods of the soil and grain. By Han Dynasty, Chi. philosophy had developed a purely naturalistic cosmogony; but in popular relig. an anc. nature-worship has survived, the spiritual world being peopled by innumerable deities assoc. with natural objects and functions, always under control of a Supreme Deity. The air, earth and almost all natural objects are inhabited by spirits, some beneficent but many of them evil. The ubiquitous *t'u ti* or gods of the soil and grain are a principal object of worship as protective deities in the localities over which they exercise control. They are appealed to by people for everything that affects their lives. (→ Cosmogony, Chinese). D.H.S.

J. J. M. de Groot, *The Religious System of China, passim*; W. E. Soothill, *The Three Religions of China* (1923), *passim*; C. H. Plopper, *Chinese Religion seen through the Proverb* (1926), pp. 20ff.

(Jap.). Anc. → Shintō was essentially a cult of nature, and nature-gods constitute almost whole of its pantheon. They remain main subject of its rich mythology, and the main objects of its worship. Almost every natural object and function is deified, from the great sun-goddess, → Amaterasu to goddess of food and gods of plants, animals, wind and rain, mountains and rivers etc. D.H.S.

E.R.E., IX, pp. 233ff.; W. G. Aston, *Shinto* (1905), pp. 121ff.; D. G. Holtom, *The National Faith of Japan* (1938), pp. 180–1.

Nazarene (Nazorean) Term used in several senses. (1) In N.T. of 'Jesus the N.', as native of Nazareth (e.g. Mk. 1:24; but Mt. 2:23 is puzzling). (2) As designation for Christians in Acts 24:5 (in Jew. lit. the form 'Nozri' occurs). (3) Name given by 4th cent. Chr. writers to Jew. Chr. groups in Syria, regarded as heretical. They used an Aramaic version of Gospel known as 'Gosp. acc. to the Hebrews' or 'Gosp. of the N.'s'. (4) The → Mandaeans were called 'Nasoreans' in their earliest lit. (→ Hebrews, Gospel). S.G.F.B.

M. Goguel, *The Life of Jesus* (E.T. 1933), pp. 191ff.; Ch. Guignebert, *Jésus* (1947), pp. 80ff.; M. R. James, *The Apocryphal N.T.* (1926), pp. 1ff.; *B.C.*, V, pp. 386ff.; *R.G.G.*³, IV, col. 1385.

Nazarite *Ex.* Heb. *nāzīr*, 'the separated' or 'consecrated'. Name given to persons in anc. Israel who devoted themselves to → Yahweh by observing certain → tabus: acc. to Jud. 13:4ff., Nu. 6, abstinence from wine and ritually unclean food, leaving hair uncut, avoidance of contact with dead. The abstention from wine has suggested that N. vow repr. primitive reaction of nomads against corrupting civilisation of Canaan, characterised by viniculture. The vow could be taken for varying periods by both sexes; an elaborate ritual marked its completion. It was an act of piety to pay expenses of those discharging vow, as → Paul did (Acts 21:23ff.). S.G.F.B.

*H.D.B.*², *s.v.; E.R.E.*, IX, *s.v.; R.G.G.*³, IV, col. 1308–9 ('Nasiräer'); J. Pedersen, *Israel*, III–IV (1940), pp. 264ff.; A. Lods, *Israël* (1949), pp. 353ff.; *E.J.R.*, p. 282.

Necromancy Term gen. denotes practice of evoking dead for purpose of → divination. N. has been widespread, and implies belief that dead have knowledge of future. Notable examples are: calling up of dead Samuel by so-called 'Witch of Endor' (I Sam. 28:7ff.); Gilgamesh's consulting with dead Enkidu (Epic of → Gilgamesh, Tab., XII); Odysseus's seeking of Teiresias in → Hades, to learn cause of his misfortune (*Od.*, XI, 494); Benevenuto Cellini's experience in Colosseum, Rome (although called necromancy, the undertaking was rather an invocation of demons). Mention might be made of anc. Egypt. 'Letters to the Dead': messages addressed to dead, written on vessels used in mortuary offerings. N. has been gen. regarded as a nefarious practice. (→ Spiritualism). S.G.F.B.

C. J. Gadd, *Ideas of Divine Rule in Anc. Near East* (1948), pp. 88ff.; B. Meissner, *Babylonien u. Assyrien*, II (1925), pp. 66, 197; W. O. E. Oesterley, *Immortality and Unseen World* (1930), pp. 124ff.; E. R. Dodds, *The Greeks and the Irrational* (1963 edn.), pp. 248, 285; *The Life of Benevenuto Cellini* (Phaidon Press, 1949), pp. 120ff.; A. H. Gardiner and K. Sethe, *Egyptian Letters to the Dead* (1928).

(China–Japan) → Magic (China and Japan). D.H.S.

Nembutsu (*Namu-Amida-Butsu*), 'Calling the Name'. The practice, fostered by the → Pure Land Sects, of daily repeating name of → Amida Buddha, accompanied by belief that all, through trust in Amida, will be born in the Buddha's paradise. D.H.S.

Neo-Confucianism → Idealist School of Neo-Confucianism. D.H.S.

Neoplatonism In hist. of relig., N. repr. synthesising of various philosophical trads. of Hellenistic culture to meet relig.-intellectual needs of Graeco-Roman society in autumn of classical civilisation. N. was basically a synthesis of →→ Platonic, Pythagorean, Aristotelian and Stoic elements, to which were prob. added insights from oriental, Jew. and Hermetic relig. thought. Its centre was → Alexandria, metropolis of cosmopolitan culture. Among its chief exponents were Plotinus (*c.* 205–69), Porphyry (*c.* 232–303), → Iamblichus (*c.* 250–330). Such thinkers aimed at constructing a philosophy that was intellectually sound and spiritually uplifting. They assumed that man had capacity for passing beyond limits of his personality to commune with the Absolute or the One (acc. to Plotinus). The conception of such an ascent of the soul, involving → ecstasy, was essentially mystical (→ Mysticism). N. reflected widespread contemporary desire for spiritual emancipation which is evidenced in →→ Gnosticism; Mystery-religions; and Christianity. N. was gen. antagonistic to the last; however, it exercised a great influence on many Chr. thinkers, e.g. → Augustine, and its legacy in writings of → 'Dionysius the Areopagite' on medieval Christianity was very great. S.G.F.B.

E. R. Dodds, *Select Passages illustrating Neoplatonism* (trans. 1923; text 1924); *E.R.E.*, IX, *s.v.; O.C.D., s.v.;* S. Angus, *The Religious Quests of Graeco-Roman World* (1929); A.-J. Festugière, *La révélation d'Hermès Trismégiste*, III (1953), IV (1954); *Les Sources de Plotin* (Fondation Hardt pour l'étude de l'antiquité classique, Entretiens, t.V, 1960); *C.A.H.*, XII (1939), ch. 12, 18; J. Geffcken, *Der Ausgang des griechisch-römischen Heidentums* (ed. 1963); H. Ludin Jansen, 'Die Mystik Plotin', *Numen*, XI (1964); *Cambridge Hist. of Later Greek and Early Medieval Philosophy*, ed. A. H. Armstrong (1967).

Nephesh Heb. word usually trans. 'soul'. It did not, however, mean the inner essential self (→ Soul), but rather the animating factor, i.e. the 'vital breath'. N. was also a gen. term for 'person', and could even denote a dead person or corpse. S.G.F.B.

A. R. Johnson, *The Vitality of the Individual in the Thought of Anc. Israel* (1949), pp. 9ff.; G. Pidoux in C. J. Bleeker (ed.), *Anthropologie religieuse* (1955), pp. 15ff.; Brandon, *M.D.*, pp. 117, 123ff.; D. Lys, *Nèphèsh* (1959).

Nergal Mesopot. god of the underworld; his name derives from orig. title *Ne-iri-gal* = 'Power of the great dwelling'. Although a god of horrific mien and profoundly feared, N. was not Mesopot. → Devil, but recognised as one of the four divine rulers of Mesopot. universe. N.'s orig. cult-centre was Kutu (Cuth in II Kgs. 17:30). S.G.F.B.

Dhorme, *R.B.A.*, pp. 38ff.; B. Meissner, *Babylonien u. Assyrien*, II (1925), pp. 36ff., 184ff.

Nestorianism Chr. heresy affirming existence of two separate Persons, the one divine and the other human, in the incarnate Christ. N. repr. an inevitable phase in process of defining → Christology in terms of current Grk. metaphysics (→→ Monophysitism; Monothelitism). N. took its name from Nestorius, bp. of → Constantinople, and was characterised by rejection of title *Theotokos* ('God-bearer') for Virgin → Mary as being incompatible with full humanity of Christ. N. was condemned at Council of Ephesus (431); Emp. Theodosius II banished him to Upper Egypt, where he died. Many E. bishops rejected decree of C. of Ephesus and organised a separate Nestorian Church, which spread Christianity through Cen. Asia to China. They suffered much from Mongols in 13th–14th cent.; a remnant survives today in Iraq, known as Assyrian Christians. (→ N. in China). S.G.F.B.

E.R.E., IX, *s.v.; D.C.C., s.v.; R.G.G.*[3], IV, col. 1404–6; H. Chadwick, *Eucharist and Christology in the Nestorian Controversy* (1951); A. Grillmeier, *Christ in Christian Tradition* (E.T. 1965), pp. 363ff.; W. A. Wigram, *The Assyrian Church* (1910); J. M. Fiey, *Assyrie chrétienne*, 2 vols. (1965); J. Joseph, *The Nestorians and their Muslim Neighbours* (1961).

(in China) Brought to China by a Syrian monk, A-lo-pen in CE 635, N. was well received by emperor, who gave the monk leave to preach and found a monastery for 21 monks. For about 200 years, N. continued to grow, and numerous monasteries were built. N. suffered in the fierce relig. persecutions of 845; but recovered influence during Yüan (Mongol) dynasty, when great numbers of tribal people of central and E. Asia were converted to faith: Uighurs, Kirghis, Kitans, Keraits, Naimans, Alans. After fall of Yüan Dynasty (1368), the N. church in China died out. Knowledge of Chi. N. came through discovery in 1625 of a famous inscribed stele near Hsi-an, the former capital of China. The stele, with inscriptions in Chinese and Syriac, was erected in 781 and gives brief summary of N. doc., an account of its intro. to China, and progress of faith till 781. The discovery of N. texts at → Tun Huang and archaeological finds at Ch'üan-chou and several other cities have added to our knowledge.

Relations between N. and → Buddhism in China were at first cordial, and the intro. of masses for dead into Buddhism prob. owes much to N. influence. But there is evidence that N. suffered obstruction and persecution from Buddh. rivals. (→ Nestorianism). D.H.S.

D. H. Smith, *Chinese Religions* (1968), pp. 280ff.; P. Y. Saeki, *The Nestorian Monument in China* (1916); A. C. Moule, *Christian in China before the year 1550* (1930).

New Guinean Religion N.G. is the world's second largest island (after Greenland), parts of which are still unexplored. It is imposs. to generalise too extensively about the religs. of the N. Guineans, who are of several different racial groups, and speak a wide variety of languages and dialects. The difficulty of internal communication in N.G. has meant that many tribes have developed in isolation, with distinctive local deities, cults and beliefs. Such overall pattern as can be seen is that common to other pre-literate peoples of Oceania (→→ Melanesian, Polynesian, Australian Aborigine, Maori Religs.). For the N. Guinean the world is inhabited by spirits (→ Animism), the spirits of the departed being esp. venerated and feared (→ Ancestor Worship). → Cannibalism and head-hunting are practised, though not universally, as means of appropriating power of deceased (→→ Magic, Mana). → Fertility rituals, in which propitiation of spirits plays an import. role, are universal. Other common features incl. → initiation rites and other *rites de passage*, forms of → totemism and use of the → bullroarer to repr. voices of the supernaturals. In gen., mortuary practices are similar, both in their ethos and their variety, to those of the other Melanesian and Polynesian islands. See also → Shamanism, → Cargo Cults. E.J.S.

There are few general accounts: *E.R.E.*, IX, pp. 339b–52b; C. G. Seligmann, *The Melanesians of British New Guinea* (1910). A comprehensive list of many specialist studies will be found in C. R. H. Taylor, *A Pacific Bibliography*[2] (1965), esp. pp. 465ff.

New Testament →→ Bible; Canon of N.T.; Covenant.

(Islam) →→ Bible; Injīl. J.R.

Nibbāna (Pali)/**Nirvāṇa** (Skt.) Buddh. term well known, but frequently misunderstood in the West. In its Pali form N. occurs in the most anc. Buddh. texts, such as the → *Sutta Nipāta*; in its Skt. form, N. continued to have import. place in → Mahāyāna, although what it signified varied to some extent between the schools. In its orig. sense and usage, N. was connected with the verb *nibbati*, 'to cool by blowing'; assoc. is the term *nibbuta*, found in the *Sutta Nipāta* more often than N., which is a past participle used in adjectival sense to describe the early Buddh. ideal man, 'he who is cooled'. The 'cooling' here ref. to is a state of being cooled from 'fever' of greed, hatred and delusion, the 3 principal forms of evil in Buddh. thought. In this sense it was apparently used in anc. India as everyday word for being well, or healthy (i.e. not in state of fever). In Buddh. usage N. thus refers to new level of being of man who is *nibbuta;* a level of being into which Buddha, and other early Buddh. who gained enlightenment, were considered to have entered, when they had become free from the defilements, or → *kilesas*, but still continued to live out what remained of mortal life. This 'nibbana-in-principle' was thus known as *kilesa-nibbāna.* When the physical components of this mortal life had reached moment of dissolution, i.e., when the death of body occurred, *nibbāna* was then complete (*pari*) and this was known as *pari-nibbāna.* The events immediately preceding this in case of → Gotama, and the event itself, are described in the → *Mahā-Parinibbāna Sutta.* N. is described in Pali texts as tranquil, pure and deathless. It has sometimes mistakenly been supposed by West. observers of Buddhism to be tantamount to 'extinction' or 'annihilation'; this is due to misunderstanding of idea of *nibbati* (see above), and the notion that it is life, rather than evil passions, which is 'blown out'. The 'annihilationist' view is explicitly rejected by Buddha (→ Uccheda-Vāda).

With develop. of the philosophical schools of Mahāyāna, the term *nirvāṇa* (the Skt. form) was related to concepts of an Absolute which these schools developed; thus N. was equated with → *Śūñyatā*, with the essence of the Buddha → *Dharma-kāya*, and with 'ultimate reality', or *Dharma-dhātu*. In the → Yogācāra school espec., in acc. with view that the illusory world of objects is dependent on real world of consciousness, → Saṃsāra (empirical existence) was held to be but an illusory aspect of N. T.O.L.

Nibbuta Buddh. term for the man who is 'cooled', i.e. from the fever of greed, hatred and illusion which is common to all humanity, and is thus 'healthy', or has attained salvation. The state into which such a man has entered is that of → Nibbana. T.O.L.

Nichiren (CE 1222–82). An outstanding figure in relig. hist. of Japan. A prophet, missionary and reformer, who (1253) founded Buddh. sect called after his name. His early life was spent in search for true doc. of → Buddhism. Disgusted by corruption of Buddh. hierarchy, the divisions between Buddh. sects, and the calamitous state of country, at age of 30, N. came to conviction that true Buddhism is enshrined in the Lotus Scripture (*Saddharma-pundarīka sūtra*).

He denounced → Honen and → Jodo Buddhism, and later attacked other sects; the conservative formalism of disciplinary school of Ritsu and newly intro. meditation school of → Zen. He called on government to suppress false teaching, and be converted to unique truth of the Lotus. With fervent zeal, he preached in temple and marketplace. Persecuted, attacked by mobs, exiled, suffering cold and hunger, he was sustained by his sense of mission. He attracted a large following; his sect continues to the present day.

Three things stand out in his teaching: (1) Utterance of name of Lotus Scripture (*Namu-Myoho-renge-kyō*—'Adoration to the Lotus of Perfect Truth') has mantic power. In a degenerate age, meditation on the formula and its simple repetition are sufficient for attainment of enlightenment. (2) The graphic and symbolical repr. of Supreme Being, who is Buddha in his metaphysical entity, inherent in every being, the oneness of the Buddha-nature and its inexhaustible manifestations. (3) Need to estab. a Holy Centre, a central seat of univ. Buddhism, which is to rule world throughout ensuing ages.

N.'s teaching, which was meant to unify Buddhism, gave rise to most intolerant of Jap. Buddh' sects. D.H.S.

M. Anesaki, *N. the Buddhist Prophet* (1916); *Hist. of Japanese Buddhism* (1930), pp. 191ff.; E. Steinilber-Oberlin, *The Buddhist Sects of Japan* (1938), pp. 238ff.

Niebuhr, Reinhold (1892–   ). One of the most significant of mod. American theologians, whose work has profoundly affected Christ. thought in many lands. Born in Wright City, Mo., U.S.A., N.'s pastorate at Detroit (1915–28) led him to lifelong concern with interrelation of Christ. ethic and politics. Influenced by Dialetical Theology of → K. Barth and reaching his prime during World War II, N. concentrated on the spiritual problems basic to the human situation —his *magnum opus*, embodying his Gifford Lectures is significantly entitled *The Nature and Destiny of Man* (2 vols., 1941–3), and was followed by books of similar concern, e.g. *The Children of Light and the Children of Darkness* (1944), *Discerning the Signs of the Times* (1946), *Faith and History* (1949), *The Irony of American History* (1952), *Christian Realism and Political Problems* (1953), *The Structure of Nations and Empires* (1959).

N., who was Professor of Christ. Ethics at Union Theological Seminary, New York, from 1928 until retirement in 1960, has been intent on showing that relig. liberalism is too unrealistic to cope with facts of human nature and history. For him, Christ. realism meant recognising that human sin makes development of God's Kingdom on earth imposs. Although regarding Christ. dogmas as myths, he defends them as having deeper insight into reality than any other philosophy. The true philosophy of → History, acc. to him, reveals the ultimate meaning of life in death, which proclaims the finitude of man and his institutions: 'It (History) is meaningful because eternal principles are vindicated in both the life which overcomes death in rising civilizations, and in the death which overtakes proud life in dying ones' (*Nature and Destiny of Man*, II, p. 318). N. vigorously rejects any philosophy of life that encourages a sense of man's self-sufficiency. 'Stoicism' is esp. to be condemned: 'Stoic freedom from anxiety is thus involved in both a self-sufficiency, which does not do justice to man's actual dependence upon the world about him, and also in a determinism which does not do justice to the evil in history' (*op. cit.*, I, p. 309). Hence N.'s insistence on the importance of eschatology: 'The idea of a "last" judgment expresses Christianity's refutation of all conceptions of history, acc. to which it is its own redeemer and is able by its process of growth and development to emancipate man from the guilt and sin of his existence, and to free him from judgment' (*op. cit.*, II, p. 303). N.'s theology is in the trad. of → Augustine and → Luther, and it has had profound influence on mod. Christ. thought, partic. in America, confronted as it is with attractions and perils of 'the affluent society', made poss. by mod. science and technology. S.G.F.B.

D. R. Davies, *Reinhold Niebuhr* (1948); E. J. Carnell, *The Theology of R. Niebuhr* (1951); C. W. Kegley and R. W. Bretall, *R. Niebuhr: his Relig., Social and Political Thought* (1956); *R.G.G.*[3], IV, col. 1458–9; H. Shelton Smith, R. T. Handy, Lefferts A. Loetscher, *American Christianity*, II (1963), pp. 455–65, 516–21; P. Ramsey (ed.), *Religion* (Princeton Studies, 1965), index.

Night of Power → Laylat al-qadr. J.R.

Nihongi Chronicles of Japan from earliest times to CE 697. A primary source for knowledge of ancient → Shinto. Completed in 720, in 30 (extant) books, it is attr. to → Shōtoku Daishi. It was composed almost wholly in Chi. language. The early part consists of Jap. myths and legends. The record from *c.* 500 onwards is of highest import. for hist. of Japan. Its pre-eminence as a source of knowledge of Jap. antiquity has seldom been contested. See also → *Kojiki*. D.H.S.

W. G. Aston (tr.), *Nihongi* (1896, repr. 1956).

Nikāya Buddh. term for a 'body' of things, or a collection: thus, (1) a collection of Suttas, or Discourses (usually of the Buddha). Five such *Nikāyas* together make up the → Sutta-pitaka, second of the three constituent parts of Pali canon of scripture, viz. the *Dīgha-N.*, *Majjhima-N.*, *Anguttara-N.*, *Saṃyutta-N.*, and *Khuddaka-N.*; (2) a body of monks; the term N. is used in this sense in → Ceylon to distinguish sects or schools of the → Sangha. T.O.L.

Nimbārka Vaisnavite theologian and founder of the *Sanaka* or *Nimbarka-sampradaya*, his date is uncertain, perhaps early 14th cent. CE. A south Indian, he settled at Brindaban, and incorporated cult of → Radha and → Krishna into his devotions and that of his followers. His theology owed something to → Ramanuja, and it is a form of *bhedābheda* (difference-non-difference, sc. between souls, world and God). Souls are offshoots of God, and even in state of liberation, when they are absorbed into → *Brahman* as energies of God, they remain distinct from him. The supreme Being is identified as Krishna, who in his loving graciousness vouchsafes to some a vision of himself. But this direct knowledge of God requires cultivation, through listening to teacher who himself has had direct experience, pondering teachings and meditating on them until they have attracted complete conviction. Though N. is a *bhakti* theologian, he tended to emphasize concept of *upāsana* or meditative worship. Unlike → Vallabha, another proponent of Radha-Krishna cult, N. stresses works—the five *sādhanas* or practices leading to salvation are work, knowledge, devotion, surrender to God and obedience to → *guru*. He wrote a commentary on the → *Brahmasutra*, known as *Vedantapārijātasurabha* and some poetical works, incl. hymns. The N. sect is mainly found in N. India. His system is sometimes known as *Dvaitadvaita* (Dualism-Non-Dualism), to distinguish it from both →→ *Dvaita* and *Advaita* (most of his criticisms in fact were directed at latter). N.S.

R. Bose, *Vedanta-Parijiatasaurabha of Nimbarka and Vedanta-Kaustubha of Srinivasa*, 3 vols. (1940–43); U. Mishra, *Vedanta School of Nimbarka* (1940); R. Bose Chaudhuri, in H. Bhattacharyya (ed.), *The Cultural Heritage of India*, vol. 3 (1959).

Ninomiya Sontoku (CE 1789–1856). Known as the peasant-sage of Japan, he originated movement known as → Hōtoku. Seeking to bring prosperity to peasants and to country, he believed that moral reformation was basic to improvement in material conditions. Pointing out that all men receive innumerable blessings from the gods, from nature, from emperor and country, from ancestors and society, he taught that all men owed a debt of gratitude, which should be repaid in high moral endeavour, self sacrifice, hard work, frugality and industry. His early efforts at reform of peasant society seemed unavailing; but his devotion and self-sacrifice so impressed the people that increasing numbers gave him their support, and the society of Hōtoku was formed, and has continued its influence to present day. Favouring no one relig. sect, N.S. drew his inspiration from → Confucianism, → Buddhism and → Shinto. Through practical express. of his relig., N.S. had great influence on development of public works, relief of distress, encouragement of new industries and promotion of a national spirit in Japan. D.H.S.

E.R.E., IX, pp. 374–5; R. C. Armstrong, *Just before the Dawn* (*The life and work of Ninomiya Sontoku*) (1912).

Nirvāna → Nibbāna. T.O.L.

Nizārīs → Assassins. J.R.

Noah Acc. to Gen. 5:29, Lamech called his son N. 'saying this same shall comfort us for our work and for the toil of our hands, because of the ground which the Lord (→ Yahweh) hath cursed.' This explanation prob. indicates that N. was orig. a → culture-hero of Heb. folklore who alleviated toil of agriculture by inventing wine (Gen. 9:20). The → Yahwist writer obscures this theme by making N. hero of → Flood (Gen. 6:11ff.); he also uses N.'s blessing and cursing of his sons to justify Israel's seizure of Canaan (Gen. 9:24ff.), thus furthering his philosophy of History. (→ Heilsgeschichte). S.G.F.B.

E. König, *Die Genesis* (1919), pp. 309ff.; G. von Rad, *Genesis* (E.T. 1961), pp. 114ff.; Brandon, *M.D.*, pp. 127ff., *C.L.*, pp. 141ff.

Norito Jap. name for ritualistic prayers which are read by officiating priests before shrine altars of → Shinto. N. is defined as 'words spoken to the → *kami*'. The prototypes of mod. N. are found in those of the → Engi Shiki. The style is archaic and stately, the imagery elaborately figurative. After Meiji Restoration (1868), national law standardized the N. to be used at various grades of shrines and for partic. ceremonies, i.e. New Year festival, spring ceremony of praying for crops, autumn thanksgiving, purification etc. (→ Engi Shiki). D.H.S.

D. C. Holtom, *The National Faith of Japan* (1938), pp. 159ff.

North American Indian Religion The relig. beliefs and practices of the indigenous tribes of the N. American continent present a complex and far from homogeneous picture. The disparate nature of the source material adds to this complexity, as do the variety of approaches which missionaries, explorers, anthropologists, ethnologists and other observers have applied to that material. Further, many early observations can no longer be verified. The systematic settlement of the continent from Europe between the 17th and early 20th cents. brought about the virtual extinction or decimation of many tribes; their orig. cultural patterns, with which relig. belief was so closely assoc., were often completely destroyed, surviving in an attenuated form only in isolated areas and on the reservations. There are no written sources, other than petroglyphs and pictograms, often of uncertain interpretation.

It seems clear, however, that among the hunting peoples of N. America, relig. involved belief in spiritual beings (→ Animism), forming a hierarchy of a Supreme Being, a creative and yet paradoxical → Demiurge, often with characteristics of a → Culture Hero, and a multitude of lesser individual spirits.

The nature of the N. Amer. concept of the Supreme Being, or Great Spirit, has provided matter for much scholarly debate. Schmidt, following Lang, was disposed to see in the Supreme Being of at least some Indian peoples, notable the Algonkians, evidence of primal → monotheism; other scholars hold that figure of Great Spirit is merely a shadow of Christ. missionary teaching, projected on to data of primal relig. In all probability, neither extreme view is correct. The Woodland and Plains Indians seem to have had a clear conception of a Supreme Being living in, or identified with, the sky, before the coming of first Christ. missionaries. Yet this hardly constitutes evidence of primal monotheism. Kitci Manitou of the Algonkian, Tirawa-Atius of the Pawnee, Wakonda or Wakan-Tanka of the Sioux and the Winnebago Earthmaker are such → High Gods. The Supreme Being, whatever his name, is a creator whose power pervades all things and who is concerned with welfare of man. But he does not as a rule intervene directly in human affairs. The Pawnee Tirawa-Atius is said to act through intermediaries: 'It is he who sends help to us by these lesser powers, because they alone can come to us so that we can see and feel them.' He is often a shadowy and indistinct figure, though not altogether a → *deus otiosus*, since tobacco-smoke, dances and prayers can be offered to him. A Dakota Sioux is recorded as having prayed: 'Grandfather Wakan-Tanka! You are first and always have been! Everything belongs to you! It is you who have created all things! You are one and alone!' But the everyday practice of relig. is concerned less with the Supreme Being than with his emissaries.

It should further be noted that the name of the Supreme Being is frequently identical with, or similar to, name given to concept of sacred power, or force, present in all things in proportion as they partake of nature of the sacred. Typical words for this power are the Algonkian *manitou*, the Sioux *wakan* and the Iroquois *orenda*. For the Sioux, *wakan* could denote anything out of the ordinary, or exhibiting quality of the sacred; an unusual child could be described as *wakan*, while the Oglala Sioux called the horse the '*wakan* dog'. The word could be applied to moon and stars, to trees and other natural objects—in fact to anything belonging to sphere of Wakanda. *Manitou*, on other hand, seems to have been used in the gen. sense of 'spirit' rather than merely 'power'. Thus an early missionary was told by a sick man: 'I believe your *manitou* is all-powerful; tell him to cure me, and I will give you ten beavers'. The first white settlers themselves were regarded as *manitou*. No clear distinction seems, however, to have been drawn between the spirits—of which the Great Manitou was chief—and their supernatural power.

Although the Supreme Being is gen. thought of as being a creator, the world in its present form is rather the work of a subordinate being, a Demiurge or Culture Hero. Mischievous and paradoxical, this → 'Trickster' is often theriomorphic—hare, coyote, mink, raven or bluejay. Or he may have more human characteristics, as in the case of the Algonkian Kulōskap (Glooscap), or the Nanabozho of the Great Lakes area. His character, as summed up by Radin, comprises the component elements 'phallic', 'voracious', 'sly' and 'stupid'. The N. Amer. trickster-myths almost all give account of either the creation or transformation of world; their hero is a wanderer, always hungry, for the most part amoral, an inveterate practical joker and highly sexed. He may or may not have divine traits. In Radin's study of the Wakdjunkaga cycle of the Winnebago Sioux of Wisconsin, the following summary of the Trickster's attributes is reported: 'The person we call Wakdjunkaga was created by Earthmaker, and he was a genial and good-natured person. Earthmaker created him in this manner. He was likewise a chief. He went on innumerable adventures. ... Through him it was fulfilled that the earth was to retain for ever its present shape, to him is due the fact that nothing today interferes with its proper functioning. True it is that because of him men die, that because of him men steal, that because of him men abuse women, that they lie and are lazy and unreliable. ... Yet one thing he never did: he never went on the warpath, he never waged war.' In addition the Trickster shares the functions of a Culture Hero in that, in course of his adventures, he creates many objects that man needs, and lays down the customs that he is to observe. He shows man the use of fire, flint and tobacco; he provides him with food; he regulates passage of the seasons, and tames the forces of nature. Whether or not these functions orig. belonged in the content of other exploits of the Trickster is, however, a moot point.

A related N. Amer. Ind. relig. concept is that of the Owner of Animals—an idea which is espec. prevalent among the hunting peoples of the north. Hultcrantz makes the following points: (1) The concept is based on the ideology of the hunting community, in which each group is bound by common allegiance to a leader. (2) It reflects observed fact that animal groups do in fact have leaders. (3) 'The owner of the animals is the guardian soul of an animal collective. . . .' (4) 'The animal guardian owns and rules over the animals in the same way as the Supreme Being rules over human beings, animals and the entire universe. . . .' Each species is thought of as having its own supernatural owner; these owners may be arranged in a hierarchy, expressed either in idea of a separate guardian or owner for the land and sea animals respectively, or in the idea of a supreme owner —bear, buffalo or seal (→ Eskimo). In any case, it was necessary to gain favour of the owner in order to ensure success in hunting; this involved observation of strict → tabus, and careful propitiatory rites, both before and after hunting.

Among agricultural tribes of south and southwest of area, relig. centres less on animal life than on vegetation. The figure of the → earth mother (sometimes with a corresponding sky-father) is the focus of cult, which is seasonal, and aims at maintenance of the natural order. Some tribes (e.g. the Pawnee) carried out → human sacrifices to ensure → fertility of their fields.

A further feature of relig. of more developed N. Amer. hunting tribes is → totemism, or blood relationship, sometimes involving ideas of descent of members of partic. tribe or (more usually) clan from some animal, fish or bird. The Ojibwa had some 40 separate totem clans, members of which were held to be related to persons of same totem, even those belonging to different tribes. The Delaware, Sauk, Menomini and Ottawa Indians traced their ancestry back to totem animals—tortoise, turkey, bear, wolf, eagle, antelope and others. Dances were held in honour of totem, at which appropriate animal-masks were worn. Some clans avoided killing their totem-animal, while others did so only in a ritual setting, and others again would do so freely. Typical is attitude of the bear clan of the Menomini; a hunter might kill a bear only after having asked its forgiveness, and no other member of clan might eat its flesh. The bones of head were later preserved and accorded reverence. Many totem clans practised exogamy. The 'totem poles' of the north-west served mainly as clan and tribal emblems, and were only loosely connected with practice of totemism, which had more social than relig. significance.

In addition to clan-totemism of this kind, some tribes observed what might be characterised as 'individual totemism', or a personal relationship between a man and his (often animal) guardian-spirit. This is closely assoc. with the phenomenon, basic to N. Amer. Ind. relig., of the personal vision. The individual male's quest for a vision was normally begun in early adolescence (sometimes even earlier), and had to be brought to a successful conclusion as a condition of success in life. Various ascetic practices were undertaken (fasting; running to point of exhaustion; repeated cold baths; enemas, etc.), followed by long periods of solitude. These, with their accompanying rites and prayers, were continued until such time as the youth had an espec. vivid dream or other revelation of his guardian-spirit, who taught him a personal 'spirit song' and bestowed power on him. Frequently the spirit was that of an animal or bird—an 'individual totem'. On the Great Plains, quest for a vision could be resorted to repeatedly even after adolescence; in fact, whenever occasion demanded it. Later quests might be accompanied by self-torture (as among the Cheyenne); in such cases the sun was usually involved, and the practice is most clearly seen in connection with the Sun Dance (see below). The ultimate source of the vision among the Sioux was held to be the Supreme Being Wakonda; and the Omaha recognised a hierarchy of visions, beginning with animals, passing through cloud appearances, an eagle-winged human shape, and culminating in mere sound of a voice. The Sioux was advised: 'Walk ye in remote places, crying to Wakonda. Neither eat nor drink for four days. Even though you do not gain the power, Wakonda will aid you. If you are as poor men, and pray as you cry, he will help you.' To have had a vision was the condition of entry into the Midewiwin, or Grand Medicine Society of the Great Lakes area (Ojibwa, Menomini, Winnebago); similar secret societies were also found among the Omaha, the Iroquois and the Pueblo. In every case the purpose of the society was to provide instruction in more advanced shamanistic practices and techniques (→ Shamanism).

Relig. ceremonies varied with means of sustenance of tribes concerned. Hunting rituals involved propitiation of appropriate spirits of animal world. There was, however, little or no blood sacrifice (in sharp contrast to cultures of Mexico, Central and S. America, with their chthonic religs.); reliance was instead placed on capacity of the 'medicine man' or shaman to mediate with spirit world. (→ Americ. Relig. anc.). Common offerings were, however, tobacco smoke (peculiarly the property of Supreme Being), 'prayer sticks' bearing symbols of spirits for whom they were intended, and vegetable matter. The blood sacrifices of the Sioux were an exception. Most rituals involved elaborate dances; hunting communities danced in imitation of actions of animal to be hunted, and sang to its owner (→ Magic; → Music). Since women were regarded as incompatible with successful hunting, strict continence was practised before each expedition. When a large hunt took place the hunters appointed a leader with supernatural power: either a medicine man (Pueblo, Papago, Creek, Paviotso) or some individual who had recently had a vision involving animal to be hunted (Plains Indians, see above). Further rituals took place after hunt. Similar preparations were made in connection with war parties. Spirit-power had to be ensured before, during and after battle. Beginning with a vision, the party fasted, observed sexual continence, and took with them a medicine man; should the latter receive some unfavourable omen, the party returned home (Osage). The killing and scalping of enemies often involved elaborate ceremonies of purification. When peace was to be made, there were further ceremonies to be undertaken, notably smoking of the 'peace pipe' or calumet, and calling on the four winds, the sky and the earth to witness pact.

The most spectacular of dance-rituals was that annual festival which the Dakota called the Sun Dance, the Cheyenne, the New Life Lodge and the Ponca the Sacred or Mystery Dance. Apparently of comparatively late origin, its purpose was renewal of fertility and well-being of earth; it was performed by most tribes every summer, and might involve individual self-torture, though this feature was by no means universal. Among the Cheyenne, the dance was given by a 'Pledger', in obedience to an individual vow. The tribes having assembled, elaborate preparations were made, involving erection of a huge lodge and altar to west of site. After three days the dance began in the lodge, lasting from two to four days. During this time the dancer fasted, and some offered blood sacrifices of their own flesh. The attention of participants was concentrated throughout on sun or centre-pole of the lodge. The final tortures in the Dakota Sun Dance were reserved for those who were seeking a vision, and wished to become shamans; those entering dance enrolled in different grades, involving different tortures, depending on objective of their entry. Without a vision, the dance was incomplete. Apart from its relig. significance, the Sun Dance filled an import. social function as an annual focus of participants' communal life. (→ Dance, Sacred).

N. Amer. Ind. beliefs on subject of nature and destiny of man have been characterised by Hultcrantz as 'predominantly shallow and superficial'; hence their wide variety. Most tribes seem to have believed that man had two separate and distinct souls: (1) a 'free-soul', which might leave body in states of sleep or trance, and which was regarded as course of human consciousness; (2) a 'life-soul', which was sum of those factors expressing physical or psychical activity, and which was looked upon as source of human life. Alternatively, man might be thought of (e.g. by the Sioux) as possessing four or more souls; or as having only one soul. It was widely held that the soul was pre-existent, and belief in reincarnation was not unknown, though seldom carefully formulated. Old age, disease (or other disability) and death were signs of loss of free-soul, even when the state as such was brought about by intrusion of malignant spirits. The free-soul could be lost, or stolen by shamans or other spirit-forces; having once left body, it might only return if it did not stray too near land of dead. On death, 'a state in which the symptoms of life are either entirely absent or else only faintly perceptible', the free-soul was believed to leave body first, followed by life-soul. After death, souls might be distributed in various ways: some returning to other bodies; others becoming ghosts; others again going to land of dead—this last was visualised in a variety of ways, of which the 'Happy Hunting Grounds' was only one. (→ Soul).

Mortuary customs also varied greatly; inhumation, exposure and cremation were all poss. methods of disposal. The normal grave goods were provided. The Ojibwa kindled a fire on grave, where it was kept burning for four days and nights (the length of deceased's journey to land of dead). After death, it was believed that soul (or one of the souls) of deceased embarked on a long and difficult journey; again, details varied considerably from tribe to tribe, respecting both location of land of dead, and the means of reaching it. In one version, the journey involved walking along a narrow path, guided by spirit of a dog or star, until a fork in the path was reached; here the path branched into an easier and a more difficult way. The souls of courageous were able to take the easier and shorter way. Every soul had at one point to cross water: on a narrow bridge, a slippery log (Cherokee, Iroquois) or a great serpent (Algonkian). When all obstacles had been passed, the Happy Hunting Grounds in the sky—an idealized extension and continuation of earthly life—were finally reached. (Simultaneously, however, the individual's other souls might be being reborn or haunting their ancestral homes, there being no logical consistency on this point.) The Ojibwa had a legend concerning a seriously ill hunter, whose free-soul was able to follow this path, and subsequently to return; the return journey was vastly more difficult. The same tribe held that some souls of dead were never able to reach land of dead; but since *post-mortem* existence was vaguely conceived and in any case ethically undifferentiated, their fate was uncertain. At a later date, perhaps under influence of Chr. teachings, some tribes developed a concept of 'hell'.

The impact of Christ. missionary work, as well as leading to decline of many of these beliefs and practices, also produced syncretistic relig. phenomena, the most import. being the → Peyote cult. E.J.S.

Comprehensive bibliographies in A. Hultcrantz, *Conceptions of the Soul among North American Indians* (1953), and R. M. Underhill, *Red Man's Religion* (1965). See also W. Schmidt, *High Gods in North America* (1933); P. Radin, *The Trickster* (1956); Hultcrantz, 'The Owner of the Animals in the Religion of the North American Indians', in (*idem*, ed.), *The Supernatural Owners of Nature* (Stockholm, 1961), pp. 53–64; 'N. American Indian Relig. in the Hist. of Research', in *H.R.*, vols. 6 (1966), 7 (1967); M. L. Ricketts, 'The N. American Indian Trickster', in *H.R.*, vol. 5 (1965).

Nudity, Ritual The uncovering of body in worship, and magical and mourning rituals is anc. and widespread. Sumerian priests ministered completely naked: the reason is not clear, but physical deformity disqualified from priesthood thus suggesting gods enjoyed sight of perfect human body. N., complete or partial, was feature of → Dionysiac festivals and Roman Lupercalia (→ Festivals); Cretan priestesses exposed their breasts, but this was prob. due to secular fashion; in Aztec ritual dances girls exposed their *pudenda*; some Heb. prophets prophesied naked (I Sam. 19:24; Is. 20:2ff.). Christ. → baptism orig. required N. of neophytes, as did → Mithraic initiation. Acc. to Pliny (*hist. nat.* 26:93), a healing ritual connected with → Apollo involved giving of medicaments to naked patient by naked virgin; he also reports belief that storms could be diverted by a woman uncovering herself (*hist. nat.* 28:23). Folk customs among many peoples, incl. Christians, employ both male and female N. in promoting agrian fertility or warding off disease. N. was often required in magical spells, and was frequent in → witchcraft. Mourning rituals often involved N.: Egypt. women bared their breasts; Micah 1:8 indicates primitive Heb. custom. Certain Indian ascetics (e.g. →→ Ajwikas; Digambaras) went naked, so also some Chr. sects (→→ Adamites; Anabaptists), as sign of pre-Fall innocence. Motives for ritual N. are evidently various; in magical rituals it was prob. apotropaic significance of sex organs (e.g. Celtic *sheelagh na-gigs*). A medieval Christ. custom of depicting naked on tombs may also be noted (→→ Dukhobors; Phallic Cults). S.G.F.B.

E.R.E., I, pp. 265, 447, IV, p. 704, V. pp. 60–1, IX, p. 830; C.-F. Jean, *La religion sumérienne* (1931), pp. 205, 212, n. 6; *R.G.G.*³, IV, col. 1294; L. S. S. O'Malley, *Popular Hinduism* (1935), p. 167; J. Z. Smith, 'The Garments of Shame', *H.R.*, 5 (1965); C. Picard, *Les religions préhelléniques* (1948), pp. 75ff.; E. Panofsky, *Tomb Sculpture* (1964), figs. 357, 358, 365.

Numen, pl. **Numina** Lat. designation for manifestation of divine action or function. N. could be used for various actions of a named god (*Juno multa habet numina*, Servius on Aen. 1:8), or an action, e.g., 'going' (old Indian *yāna*) was → Janus, the *numen actionis*. R. Otto used term in his thesis concerning the → Holy. S.G.F.B.

F. Altheim, *Hist. of Roman Religion* (E.T. 1938), pp. 192ff.; W. Warde Fowler, *Roman Ideas of Deity* (1914), pp. 11ff.

Nuns (Buddh.) The *therī*, or female parallel to the Buddh. institution of monkhood → *thera*, was recognised in Buddhism from time of Buddha himself, who gave permission for → ordination of women into such an Order, albeit reluctantly, acc. to account given in the → *Vinaya Piṭaka* (II, pp. 253ff.), and largely because he was persuaded so to do by disciple → Ananda. Some of the *therī* in early period achieved great progress in the Buddh. life, acc. to the Pali canon; a collection of verses (*gātha*) expressive of their relig. zeal and attainments forms part of canon, viz. → the *Therigāthā*. The Order exists now only as a tiny and somewhat insignificant institution in some Asian countries: in Thailand female lay devotees (*upāsikā*), who have not received ordination as *therī*, and who wear white robes, live in permanent quarters attached to certain monasteries where their life is very similar to that of a regular Order of nuns; they are mostly elderly women and are supported by generosity of other Buddh. lay people. T.O.L.

(Chinese) Buddh. nunneries were estab. in China under imperial patronage about mid. of 4th cent. CE, and nuns exerted considerable influence upon court and government. Fo T'u-têng (d. 349) is regarded as having taken initiative in estab. an order of nuns on Chi. soil. The nunneries were small, governed by old and experienced prioresses, usually situated near and under authority of a large monastery, in which the nuns were ordained. Nuns do a great work from a relig. and financial point of view, mainly among devout Buddh. women. It is estimated that, before Communist regime, there were some 225,000 nuns in China. D.H.S.

E. Zürcher, *The Buddhist Conquest of China* (1959), *passim;* K. L. Reichelt, *Truth and Tradition in Chinese Buddhism* (1927), p. 265; H. Welch, *The Practice of Chinese Buddhism* (1967), pp. 412–6.

Nuṣayrīs Extreme → Shi'a sect in N. Syria, named after Muhammad b. Nusayr who (*c.* 245/859) announced he was the *bāb* (door) of 10th Shi'a *imām.* They believe in a triad, *ma'nā* (divine essence), *ism* (name), *bāb* (door), which developed from → Ismā'īlī doc. They identified → 'Ali with the *ma'nā,* → Muḥammad with the *ism,* and → Salmān with the *bāb.* Because of this deifying of 'Ali they were called 'Alawīs when France received the mandate after World War I. They hold women have no souls, but make an exception of → Fāṭima, to whom they give the masc. name Fāṭir (Creator). They believe in → metempsychosis. In worship they have a liturgy. They observe some Christ. festivals and saints' days. There are degrees of initiation, and secrecy is demanded. Because of frequent persecution, they follow the Shi'a practice of *taqiyya* (dissimulation). J.R.

E.I., III, pp. 963ff. (Nuṣairī); Pareja, pp. 844f.; Hitti, *History*, pp. 448f.; Excellent bibliographies in *E.I.* and Pareja.

Nut Egypt. sky-goddess. Acc. to Heliopolitan → cosmogony (Egypt.), N. was daughter of Shu ('sky') and Tefnet ('moisture'); by intercourse with her brother → Geb., earth-god, she produced the deities →→ Osiris and Isis, →→ Set and Nephthys. In art N. is repr. as gigantic woman whose body over-arches earth, and on which sun and stars appear, or as cow whose body is vault of heaven. The creation of world was often depicted in terms of Shu's lifting up of Nut from her primordial embrace with Geb. The image of N. was frequently painted at bottom or on lid of coffin for protection of dead. S.G.F.B.

R.Ae.R-G., s.v.; Brandon, *C.L.*, ch. 2.

Nyāya One of six trad. schools of philosophy of Hinduism (→ Philosophy, Hindu), and closely assoc. with → Vaisesika. It is primarily concerned with logic and rules of argument, and prob. orig. from desire to frame satisfactory rules of disputation in relig. and philosophical matters—disputations being of long-standing importance in Indian trad., as in medieval Europe. By 10th cent. CE or earlier, it had largely coalesced with Vaisesika to form joint school, and agreed upon, among other things, a form of philosophical theism. The chief text is the *Nyāyasūtra*, of about 2nd cent. CE. A sophisticated and highly technical school of logic, known as the *Navyanyāya* ('New Logic') developed around CE 1200. The Nyaya developed classical proofs of God's existence in Indian trad., which were criticised by → Ramanuja. N.S.

A. B. Keith, *Indian Logic and Atomism* (1921); S. C. Vidyabhusana, *A Hist. of Indian Logic* (1921).

O

Oannes Acc. to → Berossos, O. was a fearsome being, half-man and half-fish, who in the primaeval period, taught the people of Babylonia the arts of civilisation. In this late legend a memory of → Ea (Enki) is prob. preserved. S.G.F.B.

Brandon, *C.L.*, pp. 111ff.

Oath The reinforcing of one's affirmation or denial about some issue by an O. is an anc. and widespread practice: its forms of expression have been diverse. The practice prob. derives from a common primitive belief in the magical efficacy of speech: to give verbal expression to a thought endows it with a form of being. This is seen in its crudest form in some such O. as: 'If what I say is not true, may I fall dead.' In such a formula no other power is evoked than that of the utterance itself. O.'s are gen. strengthened by invoking magical power of some object (e.g. relics of saints, holy books), or a deity or supernatural being (saint or demon), on assumption that such powers will punish falsity. S.G.F.B.

E.R.E., IX, pp. 430–8; *R.G.G.*^{3}, II, col. 347–54.

Oaths (Islam) The Qur. has oaths (*aymān*) by natural objects, e.g. lxxxvi:1 (the heaven), lxxxix:1ff. (dawn, etc.), xci:1ff. (sun, moon, etc.); by the Qur., cf. xxxvi:1; xxxviii:1; xliv:1; by angels, cf. xxxvii:1ff.; lxxvii:1ff. If the Qur. is God's eternal, uncreated word, swearing by natural phenomena and angels still to be created seems strange. The subject of O. is treated seriously. ii:225 and v, 91 say God will not take people to account for vain words in an O.; but the first says he will punish them for what their hearts have acquired, and the second speaks of ways of expiating an O. xvi:93 warns against violating O. taken in God's name, verse 96 says they must not be taken with deceitful purpose, and iii:71 speaks of punishment for those who for some small gain do not fulfil their O. (cf. lviii:15, 17, 19). lxvi:2 says God has sanctioned annulling of O. (cf. v:91 above). Though this has a partic. ref., it may be taken as gen. principle. O. should be taken by God, not by anyone or anything else, not even by the → Ka'ba, or → Muḥammad's tomb; but this is not always carried out. Many swear by saints, esp. at their tombs, and some Shi'is swear by → al-Husayn at Karbala, or → 'Alī at Najaf. An Arab in S. Arabia once told writer that, if anyone swore by God, one could not rely on it; but if one swore by a saint, this was absolutely reliable. A trad. says, 'If anyone swears he must swear by God, or keep silent.' Another tells that when Muhammad swore an O. and considered some other course of action better, he made expiation of the O. and followed the better course. His strongest O. is said to have been, 'By him who overturns the hearts.' A favourite one was, 'By him in whose hand my soul is.' To take an O. one must be of age to be responsible for performance of relig. duties (*mukallaf*), and the O. must be deliberately taken, not under duress. In court an O. may be demanded when there is a charge of wounding but not sufficient evidence. The defendant is asked to swear his innocence, and if he does so he is acquitted; otherwise judgment is given in favour of plaintiff. In a murder case 50 O. altogether must be sworn by one or more. The accuser is asked to swear, if he refuses, the accused is asked. The 50 oaths are accepted as settling case. J.R.

E.I., II, pp. 783–5 (ḳasam); Wellhausen, *Reste*, pp. 186ff.; Hughes, pp. 437–9; *Mishkāt*, pp. 727ff.; Levy, *Social Structure*, pp. 258, 347; Blachère, *Coran*, index (serments); Querry, II, pp. 175ff.; 'Alī, *Qur'ān*, index; Schacht, *Jurisprudence*, index.

Obaku One of three sects of Jap. → Zen (→→ Rinzai and Soto) introduced by → Ingen. The name Obaku is Jap. for Huang Po, a famous Chi. → Ch'an master (d. CE 850). O. spread rapidly in 17th cent. In its ascetic practice, it differs but little from → Rinzai. It taught that, though sudden enlightenment is for highly gifted, a more grad. way is open for those with less talent. → Zazen and practice of the → kōan are most useful means for sudden attainment of → satori. The grad. way of enlightenment makes use of calling on name of Buddha, i.e. → nembutsu. → Amida is regarded as the Buddha-spirit in every sentient being, having no existence outside one's own mind. Chi. influence is particularly noticeable in O., reflected in architecture of its temples and relig. ceremonies of sect. Today the sect claims more than 550 temples. D.H.S.

Dumoulin, *Hist. of Zen Buddhism* (1963), pp. 228ff.

Occultism Modern term used imprecisely to denote wide range of phenomena: e.g. →→ divination; magic; mystery-religions; healing-cults; necromancy; spiritualism; witchcraft. Ref. is also made to 'occult sciences', which could incl. any practice just mentioned or investigation of para-normal phenomena such as telepathy, precognition, clairvoyance, apparitions, poltergeists. The term 'occult science' is not, significantly, used to denote abnormal psychology or psychiatry. There allegedly exists a mass of para-normal phenomena which remains scientifically suspect. The basic reason is prob. that evidence cited about it is inherently doubtful, and not of kind that can be reproduced for controlled scientific examination and experimentation. S.G.F.B.

E.R.E., IX, *s.v.; R.G.G.*³, IV, col. 1614–9.

Oho-harahi, Ō-harai (Great purification). → Shinto ceremony which incl. a preliminary lustration, expiatory offerings and recital of → norito, in which the Mikado, by virtue of authority transmitted to him by the sun-goddess, → Amaterasu, declares to his ministers and people absolution of their sins and impurities. The chief ceremony was performed in the capital twice yearly, on last days of 6th and 12th months. In add. to the national purification, there were local and individual celebrations. D.H.S.

W. G. Aston, *Shinto* (1905), pp. 294ff.

Oil, Holy →→ anointing, unction. S.G.F.B.

Old Age (Chinese) Reverence for elders is one of fundamental virtues of → Confucianism, and O.A. is held to be a great honour. Assoc. with wealth and happiness, it is one of the three great blessings. Longevity was principal aim of → Taoist alchemistic and hygiene techniques. Shou Hsing, god of longevity, is worshipped as a domestic god. Orig. a stellar deity, he is now everywhere repr. in human form as an old man of happy mien, riding a stag with a flying bat above his head. He holds a peach, and attached to his long staff are a gourd and a scroll. The stag and bat represent happiness; the peach, gourd and scroll are symbols of longevity. D.H.S.

E. T. C. Werner, *Dictionary of Chinese Mythology* (1932), pp. 431–2.

Old Catholics Designation of small national Churches, comprising Christians who have separated from R.C. Church at various times: (1) Church of Utrecht (1724); (2) German, Austrian and Swiss O.-C., who refused to accept Papal → Infallibility decree of Vatican Council, 1870; (3) small Slav groups, comprising Poles and Croats in U.S.A. and Poland. The O.-C. continue faithful to trad. Catholicism, without accepting Papal authority: they allow marriage of clergy. O.-C. entered into full communion with C. of E. in 1932. S.G.F.B.

*D.C.C., s.v.; R.G.G.*³, I, col. 295–9; C. B. Moss, *The Old Catholic Movement: its Origin and Hist.* (1948).

Old Testament →→ Bible; Covenant.

(Islam) →→ Bible; Psalms; Tawrāt. J.R.

Olmecs → American Relig. (ancient). C.A.B.

Olympian gods Grk. gods who were believed to dwell on Mt. Olympus, highest mt. in Greece, presided over by → Zeus. These deities were of → Indo. European origin, and are contrasted with → chthonian gods of → Aegean relig. (→ Greek Relig.). S.G.F.B.

W. K. C. Guthrie, *The Greeks and their Gods* (1950); Brandon, *C.L.*, pp. 172ff.

Ōm Om or Aum is the most import. sacred sound in Vedic and Hindu trad., used as symbol and expression of → *Brahman*, and as object of meditation (e.g. in → Yoga). There is speculation, in the → Upaniṣads (notably the *Māndūkya*), on its inner significance. Thus the three elements A, U and M are taken to symbolise waking, dreaming, dreamless sleep; and silence thereafter the highest state of mystical consciousness, which is inexpressible. Again, in later works, the three elements stand for trinity of →→ Brahma, Viṣṇu and Śiva. N.S.

Omens →→ Divination; Prodigies and Portents (China–Jap.).

Omphagia Grk. 'eating of raw flesh'. The culminating act of Dionysiac ecstatic dance was tearing to pieces and eating an animal (→→ Dionysos; Maenads). Acc. to Grk. mythology, → Orpheus and Pentheus met this fate; such myths prob. preserve memory of orig. human victims. The O. 'was a sacrament in which God was present in his beast-vehicle and was torn and eaten in that shape by his people' (E. R. Dodds). Similar acts of O. are recorded from Brit. Columbia and Morocco. The Chr. sacrament of Holy → Communion has been compared with O.; there is a phenomenological, but no historical parallel (→ Orphism). S.G.F.B.

J. G. Frazer, *Spirits of the Corn and of the Wild* (*G.B.* 1933), I, pp. 142ff.; E. R. Dodds, *Greeks and the Irrational* (1963 edn.), pp. 274ff.; W. K. C. Guthrie, *Orpheus and Greek Religion* (1952²), pp. 53, 199, 268; R. Benedict, *Patterns of Culture* (1949), pp. 126ff.

Onanism Acc. to Gen. 38:8ff., Onan, to avoid performing the → Levirate marriage, 'spilled the semen on the ground, lest he should give offspring to his brother. And what he did was displeasing in the sight of the Lord (→ Yahweh), and he slew him also'. Onan's masturbation or *coitus interruptus* seems to have incurred divine wrath because of his refusal to do his ritual duty.

O. was not morally reprobated in Anc. World: in Egypt. → cosmogony, → Atum begins cosmic creation by masturbation. S.G.F.B.

Brandon, *C.L.*, pp. 22ff.; H. Licht, *Sexual Life in Anc. Greece* (E.T. 1949), pp. 313ff.

Ophites *Ex.* Grk. *ophis*, 'serpent'. Name of early → Gnostic sect, so-called because they regarded the serpent in Gen. 3:1ff. as saviour of mankind from God of O.T. They reversed orthodox interpretation of → Fall, seeing it as marking man's emancipation from primeval ignorance. There were various sects of O., called Naassenes, Cainites and Sethites. S.G.F.B.

E.R.E., IX, *s.v.;* R. M. Grant, *Gnosticism* (1961), pp. 52ff., 89ff.; J. Doresse, *The Secret Books of the Egyptian Gnostics* (E.T. 1960), *passim*; *R.A.C.*, I, col. 635–43.

Opus Anglicanum English embroidery of the Middle Ages, much used in ecclesiastical vestments and highly prized throughout Europe. I.A.B.

A. G. J. Christie: *English Medieval Embroidery* (1938); *Opus Anglicanum*, Catalogue of Exhib. at Vic. & Alb. Mus., London, 1963.

Oracles Man's desire to know future or have supernatural advice about future action has found universal expression in → divination. O. may be distinguished from divination in that they invoked belief that at certain places knowledge of future could be obtained from deities located there: e.g. at → Delphi, Dodona, Olympia, temple of → Amun in Siwa oasis). The word is sometimes used for divination unconnected with specific deity: e.g. → Oracle Bones. (→→ Sibylline O.; Urim and Thummin). S.G.F.B.

Oracle Bones The mod. discovery (from *c.* 1900 onwards) near An-yang, in Honan Province, China, of large quantities of inscribed scapula bones of sheep, and oxen and tortoise shells, and their subsequent interpretation has revolutionised knowledge of Shang Dynasty, which ruled this part of China between *c.* 1765–1123 BC. The O.B., which belonged to royal archives, were extensively used in → divination. Oval pits were made in the bones, and, when heat was applied, fine cracks appeared on highly polished surface. These were interpreted by priest-diviners. Questions and answers were often written in an archaic Chi. script. Divination was made on questions respecting war, politics, weather, harvests etc. The O.B. reveal that Chinese of 2nd mil. BC possessed an elaborate culture and fully developed writing, and reveal a paramount concern for relig. by the state. D.H.S.

H. G. Creel, *The Birth of China* (1936), *Studies in Early Culture*, 1st series (1938); Chêng Tê-k'un, *Archaeology in China*, vols. 1, 2 (1959).

Ordination (Buddh.) Ordination, in Buddh. context, is initiation into the Buddh. Order (→ Sangha) in presence of witnesses (i.e., members of Sangha), and self-dedication to monastic life. It is not a conferring of priestly rights or powers; it is not necessarily life-long or unrepeatable. There are two kinds of Buddh. O.: the lower (*pabbajjā*), by which a man becomes a *sāmanera* or novice; the higher (*upasampadā*), by which novice becomes monk (*bhikkhu*). The ceremony for O. to *sāmanera* varies from country to country, and acc. to whether novice has intention to remain in Order for several months or years, or whether he is entering for few days only, e.g. for period of 3 to 7 days on occasion of a relative's cremation (practice followed in Thailand). In latter case the candidate has his head shaved, brings two robes (the lower robe, or sabong, or *antaravāsaka*; the upper robe, or *uttarāsangha*; → Dress, Relig. (Buddh.); but not the *sanghāti* or stole, since this is worn only by monks (*bhikkhus*). He also brings incense and candles, and formally asks abbot for permission to join monastery. After reminding him of privilege of being a novice, and merit it will entail for himself and family, the abbot admits him. The more formal ceremony for admission of novice who intends subsequently to become monk consists of candidate's being brought before a chapter of at least 10 monks, headed by abbot or senior monk of at least ten years standing, and taking part in set form for ordaining of novices and monks. This is held in the sanctuary (*vihāra*). The candidate kneels, and asks for admission as novice, handing to abbot 2 yellow robes in which he is to be ordained. The abbot then formally presents to him these robes, reminding him of frailty and impermanence of human body which they are to cover. The candidate receives them, and retires to put them on; as he does so he recites a formula reminding himself that his robes are worn as protection against cold, and heat, against flies and insects, wind and sun and attacks of snakes, and to cover nakedness, and that he wears them in all humility, for use, and not for ornament. He then returns, makes obeisance, and asks to have administered to him the 3 → Refugees, and 10 → precepts. Having received them from abbot, repeating them sentence by sentence, he makes obeisance, seeks forgiveness by his brethren of all faults and declares his wish to share with his brethren any merit he has gained. The *sāmanera* spends his time in monastery learning life of the Sangha, helping with daily chores, and accompanying a *bhikkhu* on his alms round etc. He does not attend recitation, twice monthly, of the → *Patimokkha;* this is attended only by *bhikkhus.*

When a novice subsequently seeks higher ordination (*upasampadā*) as monk, he first goes through form for the ordering of a novice again; this is then followed by further and longer ceremony of O. in course of which candidate must be able to answer satisfactorily a list of questions concerning his status and condition (whether he is free from disease, debt, military service, is 20 years of age, etc.). He is presented by one of his two tutors. On this occasion the three robes, incl. stole, are presented, together with candidate's new alms-bowl, which he will use as a *bhikkhu* for receiving food from lay people each day. These are then ceremonially returned to him by abbot. An address is then given by abbot, or president, in which new *bhikkhu* is reminded of glory of life of a *bhikkhu*, and of high moral standards which are now his, and the chaste, honest, peaceable and humble life he must live.

O.'s are held at any time of year except the 3 months of → Vassa; the actual date is agreed upon in consultation with abbot of monastery where the O. is to be carried out, which is usually in man's home village, and with astrologers in order to settle upon an auspicious day for man concerned. A favourite time is just before Vassa, since it is Vassa period alone which is reckoned in counting years of service as a monk. Those who are entering for a few months only (a custom followed in Thailand esp.) will therefore do so at beginning of Vassa, i.e. in May or early June. In continental S.E. Asia another favourite time is a few months earlier, after end of rice-harvest, when funds are more plentiful, since O. is usually accompanied by considerable festivity, which sometimes lasts for more than one day (→ Festivals, Buddh.). T.O.L.

R. Gard, *Buddhism* (1961), pp. 157–66; H. K. Kaufman, *Banghuad: A Community Study in Thailand* (1960), pp. 123–31; Manning Nash, *The Golden Road to Modernity* (1965) (for Burmese Buddhism), pp. 124–31; K. E. Wells, *Thai Buddhism: Its Rites and Activities* (1959), *passim*.

(Christ.) Term used in Chr. Church for rites prescribed to endow ministers (e.g. deacons, priests, bishops) with spiritual power and authority requisite to their office. The essential ritual act is imposition of hands of bishop and other proper persons on head of candidate. In R.C. Church vessels for → Mass (chalice and paten) are symbolically delivered to ordinand to priesthood (*Traditio* or *Porrectio Instrumentorum*). O. always takes place in assoc. with → Eucharist (→→ Apostolic Succession; Hierarchy, Chr.). Forms of O. are usual in → initiation into hiearchies of other religs. S.G.F.B.

D.C.C., pp. 696, 989; W. K. L. Clarke (ed.), *Liturgy and Worship* (1932), pp. 626ff.

Origen (*c*. 186–*c*. 255), Chr. theologian and Biblical scholar, b. at → Alexandria of Chr. parents, and studied at Catechetical School there under → Clement. His father was killed in persecution of Septimus Severus (CE 202); O. would have volunteered for martyrdom himself, had not his mother hidden his clothes. Later (at 17) he was appointed to succeed Clement, who had fled during the persecution. To this work O. devoted himself with unparalleled ardour and success, adopting extreme asceticism as his rule of life, even to extent of literal self-mutilation (Mt. 19, v. 12)—probably to avoid suspicion of scandal through presence of women at his lectures. To broaden his teaching, he studied pagan philosophy under Ammonius Saccas, founder of → Neoplatonism. His conversion of the wealthy Ambrosius, secured for him shorthand writers and copyists, and he began his vast output of writings. O. visited Rome and heard → Hippolytus preach; he was consulted by the Governor of Arabia and the Emperor's mother, Julia Mammaea; in 230, while in Caesarea, he was ordained priest by his friends, the Bps. of Jerusalem and Caesarea; but Demetrius, Bp. of Alexandria, who had not been consulted, and who had some time looked askance on this over-powerful layman, deposed him from his chair and his priesthood; this had no effect in Caesarea, where O. settled and expanded his work and influence, writing, travelling, converting heretics, expounding Scripture in Church (these 'homiles' were taken down and published), consulted as theological 'arbiter' by great and small. Maximin's persecution (235/7) exiled him to Cappadocia; under Decius (251/1) he was tortured, and died a few years later.

Writings: (1) The *Hexapla* (extant in fragments), a six-column text of O.T., giving in parallel columns the Heb., in original and in Grk. letters, and four current Grk. versions. → Jerome used orig. copy at Caesarea. The object of work was critical: to estab. the wording and meaning of the original Heb., which O. recognised as authoritative. (2) *Commentaries* and *Homilies* on most books of Bible. Many survive, incl. the great Comm. on John, in Grk.: many in Latin trans. by others. (3) *De Principiis*, the first Christian 'Dogmatics', dealing in 4 books with God, the world, human freedom, and Scripture. Only fragments of Grk. orig. survive; it exists almost complete in Latin trans. of Jerome and Rufinus, the latter paraphrastic and unreliable. (4) *Contra Celsum*—8 books of apologetic, answering far-reaching attack on Christianity by Celsus (eclectic Platonist) of 70 years earlier. O. here brings the 2nd cent. Grk. Apologetic trad. to culmination, and anticipates all later work on the theme. (extant in Grk.). (5) Minor writings incl. *Prayer*, *Exhortation to Martyrdom* (extant), *De Resurrectione* (fragments of Lat. version extant). Import. material in the (Greek) *Philocalia*: 27 'choice passages' edited in 4th cent. by Gregory Nazianzus and → Basil.

O. aimed at systemising whole range of Chr. theology, and confronting pagan world with an intellectually formulated *Weltanschauung*, based on Scripture and elaborated in terms of contemporary eclectic and Stoicised Platonism. From this he takes his deep-seated monism, his ideal of an intellectual and ethical 'aristocracy', the immortality and pre-existence of souls, the → (Orphic) *Sōma-Sēma* (creation being punishment for ante-mundane sin), the Stoic emphases on Providence and ethical *apatheia*. Acc. to H. Chadwick (*Celsus*, p. XII), O.'s 'well-known criticisms of the trad. Church doc. of the resurrection of the flesh are in fact nothing more than a slight modification of the arguments used by the Academy against the anthropomorphism of the Epicurean notion of the gods'. Through such spectacles, O. studies and expounds Bible in greater depth and detail than any other before → Luther, educing his peculiar version of Christianity from its text by → *allegory*. For him, Scripture had three meanings: the 'flesh' (literal), 'soul' (moral), 'spirit' (mystical), e.g. *Princ*., IV, 2:4; but all these do not apply to every passage, and in practice O. fused moral and mystical, and often dismissed the literal altogether. Yet he had a firm grasp of central → kerygma: cf. *Princ*., *init*.

In theology, O. was a pioneer, shirking no speculation and often initiating trends which later Church modified or outgrew. The unity and transcendence of God are affirmed at expense of a real or apparent subordinationism—although he achieved a notable development of idea of 'eternal generation' of the Son. The work of the → Holy Spirit is restricted to already 'sanctified' Christians. Souls are created eternally, with ascents and descents into various forms and levels of existence until final → *Apocatastasis* (Universal Restoration). Free-will is the cornerstone of his ethics, and → apotheosis the ultimate destiny, achieved by Chr. → gnosis, and described by O. with a strong tinge of mysticism.

O.'s reputation in lifetime was almost superhuman; but reaction set in with Methodius (d. *c*. 311) and the 4th cent. Antiochenes. Although men like Pamphilus, → Athanasius, Basil, Gregory, defended his teaching, the climax came with → Epiphanius' condemnation (in *Panarion*, *c*. 375), of O. as a heretic, which persuaded Jerome, hitherto O.'s supporter and translator. O. was condemned by a Council of Alexandria (400) and Pope Anastasius I. The controversy lingered until the Emp. Justinian and two Councils of Constantinople (543/553) listed O.'s 'errors', and ordered their rejection throughout Christendom. O., the greatest scholar and theologian of the early centuries, thus paid penalty of the over-sanguine pioneer, the shift of theological fashion, and the personal and eccles. jealousies of 4th and 5th cent. Churchmen. B.D.

The lit. is enormous (→ 'Alexandrian Theology'); full bibliographies (to their dates) in H. Chadwick, *Origen–Contra Celsum* (1953); R. P. C. Hanson, *O.'s Doctrine of Tradition* (1954), *Allegory and Event* (1959). Text almost complete in *G.C.S.*, esp. Koetschan's monumental *De Principiis* (1913) and *Celsus* (1899). Older text of de la Rue (1733 et seq.) reprinted in Migne, *P.G. Philocalia* ed. J. A. Robinson (1893). Recently recovered fragments of *Comm. on Ephesians*, *Rom*., *I Cor*., in *J.T.S.* (O.S.), III, IX, X, XIII, XIV; R. Cadiou, *Commentaires inédits des Psaumes* (1935); J. Scherer, *Entretien d'O. avec Héraclide* (discovered 1941), Cairo (1949). Trans. of *De Princ*.: G. W. Butterworth (1936), *Celsus*, Chadwick (above). E. R. Redepenning, *Origenes* (1841); E. de Faye, *Origène*, 3 vols. (1923–8); J. Daniélou, *Origen* (E.T. 1955); W. Völker, *Das Vollkommenheitsideal des Origen* (1931). Arts. in *D.C.B.*, IV (Westcott), *P.R.E.*, XIV (Preuschen), *D.T.C.*, XI (Bardy).

Original Sin A Christ. doctrine that derives from → Paul's view that 'through one man (Adam) sin entered the world', so that, 'by the trespass of the one the many died' (Rom. 5:12–21). Chr. → soteriology required an explanation of orig. of state of perdition from which Christ saved men. Paul's suggestion was gradually developed into doc. of O.-S., acc. to which, through seminal identity with → Adam, every human being shares in guilt of Adam's → Fall. It was gen. held that guilt was transmitted by concupiscence. Hence the new-born were guilty of O.-S., from which they were cleansed by → baptism. O.-S. is distinguished, theologically, from Actual Sin, which results from personal choice of action, either in commission or omission. Since 18th cent., due to rationalism and natural science, belief in O.-S. has been greatly modified or abandoned by liberal-minded Christians. Other religs. have no comparable doctrine. Jew. Rabbinic thought traced man's tendency to actual sin to Adam's Fall, and explained death thereby. Belief in → metempsychosis usually involves idea that this painful state results from some primeval ignorance or illusion; but questions of guilt do not arise. (→→ Adapa; Hesiod; Avidya). S.G.F.B.

N. P. Williams, *Ideas of the Fall and of Original Sin* (1927); *E.R.E.*, IX, *s.v.; R.G.G.*³, VI, col. 484–94; Harnack, *H.D.*, *passim*; *D.C.C.*, *s.v.; E.J.R.*, p. 141; Brandon, *M.D.*, pp. 224ff.

Orphism The one Grk. relig. movement that had a trad. founder, Orpheus; but in what sense he was its founder is obscure. The myth that Orpheus was killed and dismembered by → Maenads may indic. some orig. identification with → Dionysos-Zagreus (see below). O. emerged in either 6th or 7th cent. BC, and was basically concerned with destiny of → soul (*psychē*). In contrast to Homeric view, the *psychē* was regarded in O. as inner essential self and immortal by nature. The dualism of man's nature was explained in myth of Dionysos-Zagreus, son of → Zeus: evil → Titans, who killed and ate the divine child, were destroyed by Zeus and from their ashes mankind was formed having a dual nature, compounded of divine Dionysian element (the *psychē*) and Titanic material (the body). Thus, acc. to → Plato, Orphics called the body (*sōma*) the tomb (*sēma*) of the soul. O. taught → metempsychosis. So far as its → soteriology can be discerned, O. aimed at delivering soul from successive incarceration in bodies (of all kinds, incl. fish and vegetation). As a → mystery religion, O. had an initiatory ritual, incl. purification, and imparting of secret knowledge: it also involved a discipline of life, incl. vegetarianism. Acc. to texts inscrib. on gold leaves, being prob. of O. orig. and found in graves, the instructed deceased claimed to be of celestial origin and hoped to be freed from the 'sorrowful weary wheel' of reincarnation. O. also had a cosmogony which apparently traced orig. of world from → Chronos, and prob. drew on Iranian concept of → Zurvan. O. had some connection with → Pythagoreanism; it influenced Plato, and prob. → Gnosticism. S.G.F.B.

W. K. C. Guthrie, *Orpheus and Greek Religion* (1952²); V. Macchioro, *Zagreus: studi interno all'Orfismo* (1930); I. M. Linforth, *The Arts of Orpheus* (1941); M. P. Nilsson, *Gesch. d. griech. Relig.*, I (1955²); E. Rohde, *Psyche*, 2 vols. (1898); R. Eisler, *Orpheus, the Fisher* (1921); W. Jaeger, *The Theology of Early Greek Philosophers* (1947), pp. 55ff.; Harrison, *Prolegomena; passim;* N. Turchi, *Fontes*, pp. 1–39; L. Mouliner, *Orphée et l'orphisme à l'époque classique* (1955); S. G. F. Brandon, *History, Time and Deity* (1965), pp. 47ff., 89ff., *The Judgment of the Dead* (1967), ch. IV.

Orthodoxy *Ex.* Grk. 'right opinion', used in Chr. Church in contrast to → heresy. In → E. Church, term also describes those churches in communion with Patriarch of Constantinople. Christianity is distinguished among the religs. by importance attached to holding authorised, i.e. 'right', definition of faith (→ Creeds). S.G.F.B.

E.R.E., IX, *s.v.*

(Hindu) The norm of orthodoxy in → Hinduism, as interpr. by → Brahmins and as in first instance the relig. of the upper classes (→ *varnas*), is recognition of authority of → *Veda*. This is coupled with acceptance of the secondary canon known as → *smrti*. Those schools and relig. movements which do not formally rely upon *Veda*, such as →→ Jainism, Buddhism, the →→ *Ajivikas* and Carvaka materialists are reckoned to be unorthodox or *nāstika*, literally 'it-is-not-ish', in contrast with schools, etc., which are *āstika*, lit. 'it-is-ish'. There is evidence that → Samkhya-Yoga was at one time *nastika*, though by classical period it had come to accept Vedic revelation. Lower-class → *bhakti* movements, e.g. in → Dravidian south, might in fact lay greater store by non-Vedic scriptures, such as the *Prabandham*, in interpretation of relig. and reality; but might yet claim O. by coordinating their teachings to those of Veda. In fact, the achievement of figures such as →→ Ramanuja, Madhva, Caitanya and Vallabha in part lay in their synthesis of Vedic and non-Vedic trad. Some movements, such as → Lingayats, were technically unorthodox, though they gained recognition as part of social fabric of Hinduism—likewise with 'foreign' religs., such as that of the → Parsis, and Mar Thoma (Syrian) Christians (→ Chr. Movements in India). O. did not imply any special set of beliefs, beyond recognition of *Veda*, since in fact the theologies and systems of metaphysics supposedly based on the sacred trad. ranged from → atheism, through theism to absolutism, and had their focus in wide variety of gods or symbolisations of God. N.S.

Osiris Egypt. royal mortuary-god and ruler of dead. Meaning of name (written in hieroglyphs of an eye above a throne) is uncertain, as is also orig. of deity. In art, O. is repr. as mummified corpse, with head exposed wearing double-crown of Upper and Lower Egypt, and hands holding symbols of royalty. In → Pyramid Texts (*c.* 2400 BC), O. was already centre of a complex mortuary ritual based on legend of his death and → resurrection. The dead king was ritually assimilated with O., to achieve immortality. At this stage, O. was essentially hero of a human-divine drama: some scholars believe he was orig. a historical personage. Little ref. is made to O. in Pyr. Texts as vegetation-god; this aspect is prominent later, together with ascription of cosmic (incl. solar) attributes. Gradual democratisation of mortuary cult made O. saviour-god for all persons able to afford burial acc. to Osirian rites. The cult of O. grew in importance in Middle Kingdom (2160–1580), with a mystery-drama at → Abydos. With development of idea of → judgment of dead, O. assumed role of judge; because of his personal significance, he out-rivalled sun-god → Rē. The Osirian mortuary-cult continued into Roman period, until suppression of paganism in 4th cent. CE. A → mystery religion centred on → Isis and O. became popular in Graeco-Roman world, as → Apuleius attests. In terms of → phenomenology of relig., O. anticipates

Christ as dying-rising saviour-god; but O.'s death was not interpreted soteriologically. (→→ Egypt. Relig.; Funerary Rites, Egypt.). S.G.F.B.

E. A. W. Budge, *Osiris and the Egyptian Resurrection*, 2 vols. (1911); *R.Ae.R-G.*, pp. 567ff.; Kees, *T.*², *passim*; S. A. B. Mercer, *Relig. of Anc. Egypt* (1949), chs. 6, 17, 19, 22; R. Reitzenstein, *Die hellenistischen Mysterienreligionen* (1956²), pp. 186ff.; H. Gressman, *O.R.*, pp. 16ff.; Brandon, *M.D.*, ch. 2, 'The Ritual Technique of Salvation in the anc. Near East', in S. G. F. Brandon (ed.), *The Saviour God* (1963), *Judgment of the Dead* (1967), ch. I; S. Morenz, 'Das Werden zu Osiris', *Staat. Mus. z. Berlin: Forsuch. u. Berichte*, I (1957); J. G. Griffiths, *The Origins of Osiris* (1966); E. Otto, *Egypt. Art and the Cults of Osiris and Amun* (E.T., 1968); S. G. F. Brandon, 'Saviour and Judge: Two Examples of Divine Ambivalence', in *Liber Amicorum; for C. J. Bleeker* (1969).

P

Pabbajaka (Pali); **Parivrājaka** (Skt.) A 'homeless one', 'one who has gone forth', (sc., from home) hence, a name in early Buddhism for member of the Buddhist Order. (→ Sangha). T.O.L.

Pacceka-Buddha (Pali); **Pratyeka-Buddha** (Skt.) An 'Isolated' Buddha, is one who does not proclaim the transcendental knowledge he has gained by his Enlightenment (*bodhi*). Whereas disciples gain Enlightenment by hearing the truth (*Dhamma*) proclaimed by the Buddha (i.e. by a 'universal', or *sammā-sambuddha*), the P.-B. attains to transcendental knowledge of the truth independently. Since he does not possess the faculty to proclaim it, he does not rank as a universal-Buddha; the term 'P-B.' is sometimes trans. as 'silent Buddha'. In the *Khaggavisāna Sutta* (part of → *Sutta Nipāta*), the → Buddha (Gotama) is asked by → Ānanda, his disciple, concerning the way the P.-B. attains Enlightenment. The Buddha, after explaining, gives examples of (private) utterances or soliloquies of former P.-B.'s, each of which ends with the refrain 'fare solitary as a rhinocerus'. → Buddhaghosa, in his commentary on *Sutta Nipāta*, gives life-stories of the P.-B.'s named in *Sutta*. The Skt. work, the → *Mahā-vastu* mentions 500 P.-B.'s said to be living near Benares just before appearance of the Buddha Gautama; on hearing of imminent coming of a universal Buddha, they disappeared. T.O.L.

Sutta Nipāta, P.T.S. (1948), tr. by E. M. Hare as *Woven Cadences of Early Buddhists* (1945); trans. of the *Mahāvastu* by J. J. Jones, 3 vols. (1949–56).

Pagoda (Buddh.) A Buddh. sacred shrine or memorial building. The Eng. word is derived from Portuguese *pagode* or *pagoth*, which in turn appears to have been derived by the Portuguese from an Asian word; opinions vary as to what the Asian original was. It was evidently a word encountered by the Portuguese in India and Ceylon; hence the Skt. *bhāgavatha* and the Sinhalese *dāgaba* have both been suggested. Whether derivation from latter is true or not, the word P. usually refers to the kind of Buddh. shrine which in Ceylon is called a *dāgaba*, and which is a develpt. of the anc. Indian → Stupa, which may or may not have contained sacred relics. In Burma this is called a *Hpaya* (object of veneration) or *Zedi* (fr. Pali *cetiya*, a shrine). In Thailand the same kind of structure is called a *Phrayachedi*. T.O.L.

S. Dutt, *The Buddha and Five After Centuries* (1957), ch. 12; J. G. Scott, *The Burman* (1882); Manning Nash, *The Golden Road to Modernity* (1965), pp. 116–24; Kenneth E. Wells, *Thai Buddhism: its rites and activities* (1960).

(China) Chinese *t'a*. First erected in China in 3rd cent. CE, and Buddh. in origin, their primary object was to preserve relics of a Buddha or saint. They are often assoc. with temples or monasteries, and consist of a tower divided into an odd number of stages, usually 7, 9, 11 or even 13. They are a prominent feature on Chi. landscape, with average height of about 170 ft., the highest being at Tingchou in Hopei Province (360 ft.). Made of brick or glazed brick, they are usually octagonal. They came to be regarded as propitious, bringing happiness and prosperity to a district, and are connected mainly with → Fêng Shui. D.H.S.

J. D. Ball, *Things Chinese*, 5th edn. (1925), pp. 440ff.; S. Couling, *Encycl. Sinica* (1917, 1965), p. 417.

Pahlavi Literature A considerable body of documents in Pahlavi or Middle Persian, dating from 8th to 11th cent. CE., provides valuable information, additional to → Avesta, on → Zoroastrianism. Some of it also concerns → Manichaeism. The most important Zoroast. sources are the *Dīnkart*, the → *Bundahishn*, and the *Arṭā-ī-Virāf Nāmah*. Old Eng. trans. exist in the *S.B.E.* S.G.F.B.

E.R.E., VIII, pp. 104–6; *L.R-G.*, II, pp. 209ff.; Zaehner, *D.T.Z.*, pp. 27ff., 341ff.

Pa Kua (The Eight Trigrams). Though attr. to mythical Chi. emperor, Fu Hsi (2852 BC), they were invented in Chou Dynasty, primarily for → divination; with their combinations into 64 hexagrams, they became basis of Chi. philosophical and cosmological speculations. (→ I Ching).

Each of the P.K. is composed of three lines, divided or undivided, thus:

The divided line repr. the → Yin and the undivided, the → Yang; the P.K. together symbolise main constituents of Chi. universe: Heaven, Earth, Fire, Water, Wind, Thunder, Hills, Marshes. They also repr. compass directions, moral qualities etc. They are supposed to contain clue to secrets of universe, and are extensively used in China for divination and geomancy. Plaques made of copper, silver or jade are engraved with the P.K., forming a circle round symbol of creation, and are considered to have power of preserving wearer from misfortune and ensuring prosperity. D.H.S.

Fung Yu-lan, *Hist. of Chinese Philosophy*, vol. 1 (1937), pp. 382ff.; W. T. Chan, *Source Book in Chinese Philosophy* (1963), pp. 262ff.; C. A. S. Williams, *Outlines of Chinese Symbolism* (1931), p. 123ff.

Paleolithic Religion With the first appearance of man (*homo sapiens*) in the archeological record of Upper Paleolithic era (*c.* 30,000 BC), it is evident that a complex of belief and ritual practice of a religio-magical kind already existed. It was centred on three basic concerns: food, birth and death. Paleo. → cave-art was magical, designed to promote successful hunting and fertility of animals. It also indic. practice of mimetic dances in animal disguise, doubtless with magical intent. Carved figures of women with maternal attributes exaggerated, but faces blank, reveal concern with fertility and birth. Male figures are rare, and schematic in form. Burials give evidence of → funerary rites, implying belief in *post-mortem* existence. There is also evidence of a cult of skulls. A sculptured female figure holding a bison's horn (known as the 'Venus of Laussel') appears to have been focus of a rock-sanctuary, and may indicate local cult of goddess as source of life, a prototype of later → Great Goddess. A male anthropoid figure with animal attributes (known as the 'Dancing Sorcerer') in the Trois Frères cave (Ariège) has been interpreted as a divine 'Lord of the beasts'. A curious picture of a bird-headed man, struck down by a wounded bison, in a remote part of the Lascaux caves, may indic. practice of black → magic. Some French prehistorians have recently claimed to discern mythic scenes connected with fertility in cave-art. S.G.F.B.

J. Maringer, *The Gods of Prehistoric Man* (E.T. 1960); Th. Mainage, *Les religions de la Préhistoire: l'age paléolithique* (1921); H. Breuil–R. Lantier, *Les hommes de la Pierre Ancienne* (1951); A. Laming, *Lascaux* (E.T. 1959); P. Wernert, in *H.G.R.*, I, pp. 53–97; E. O. James, *Prehistoric Religion* (1957); S. Giedion, *The Eternal Present: the Beginnings of Art* (1962); A. Laming-Emperaire, *La signification de l'art paléolithique* (1962); G. Clark, *The Stone Age Hunters* (1967); K. J. Narr, 'Approaches to the Religion of Early Paleolithic Man', *H.R.*, 4 (1964); A. Leroi-Gourhan, *Les religions de la Préhistoire* (1964).

Pali Language of canonical texts of → Theravāda Buddhism, which was preserved in → Ceylon orig., and now in Burma, Thailand, Laos and Cambodia also. Opinions differ concerning orig. home of language. Acc. to T. W. Rhys-Davids, it was dialect of Kosala, the tribal territory in what is now Uttar Pradesh, to N.E. of the Ganges; M. Walleser suggested it was the '*Pātali-bhāsā*', lang. of Pātaliputra (Patna) capital of → Magadha. E. Windisch and W. Geiger also regarded P. as poss. a modified form of 'Magadhese', the lang. allegedly spoken by the Buddha, and one which would have served as the *lingua franca* of elite of Magadhan empire. A more recent opinion on subject, expressed by E. Lamotte, is that P. was a lang. of C. India, a 'high middle-Indian' dialect, i.e. one of the old Prākrit languages derived from Sanskrit, but approximating more closely to Vedic form of Sanskrit than to classical. Evidence concerning characteristics of Maghadhese language (or Māgadhī), has come to light in mod. times in connection with inscriptions made by Magadhan emperors, notably → Aśoka; these indic. significant differences between Magadhese and P. The most that can at present be said, therefore, is that P. is lang. of the Theravāda → Tipitaka, the separate parts of which may have come from different regions of India and thus have embodied variety of local linguistic usages; that it was transmitted orally over several cents., and that later stages of transmission, before words were committed to writing, took place in Ceylon. T.O.L.

For a comprehensive account of scholarly work on subject see E. Lamotte, *Histoire du Bouddhisme Indien* (1958), pp. 607–28.

Pandora Acc. to → Hesiod (*Works and Days*, pp. 80ff.), the First Woman, made by the gods to punish mankind for receiving gift of fire from → Prometheus. P. opened a jar containing ills that afflict men; only Hope was restrained from escaping from jar. The myth reflects Hesiod's evaluation of life; but much of its significance is obscure. S.G.F.B.

O. Lendle, *Die 'Pandorasage' bei Hesiod* (1957); W. O. Oldfather, 'Pandora', in *P.W.*, XVIII (3); Brandon, *C.L.*, pp. 177ff.

Panentheism Term orig. used by K. C. F. Krause (1781–1832), which now describes view of God and of his relation to world primarily developed by American philosopher C. Hartshorne (1897–), on basis of A.N. → Whitehead's process philosophy. H. defines God as the adequate object of worship, which implies that he is essentially perfect, and presupposes that God is chief exemplification, not the exception to all ultimate metaphysical principles and so is a proper object of rational investigation. H. rejects, on one hand, the → pantheism which so identifies God with totality of reality that the concept of 'God' becomes a cipher for the 'world'. On the other hand, H. rejects classical theistic concept of God as a wholly unmoved, unchanging absolute who utterly transcends world, actualises all values and is outside temporal process, on grounds that since not all values are compossible, no such being could conceivably exist and that concept rules out the genuine personal existence and reciprocal relationships implied in relig. faith in God as perfect. As perfect being, God's nature is fundamentally that of love. His perfect love means that he is maximally influenced by every concrete entity, in that he experiences everything that occurs without loss as part of own experience (and so incl. world's contingent existence in own being without losing own self-identity over against world). At same time God is maximally influential on world since he is related to every actual entity as ground of its being; although this influence is restricted acc. to his nature as love and his creative purposes, with result that each entity has a limited freedom of its own in determining its actuality. In H.'s view, therefore, God embraces world and cannot exist without a world, but is more than the contingent world which he creates and which has a relative independence. H. describes his panentheistic concept of God as 'dipolar', since he asserts that there is both an absolute, unchanging, eternal, necessary aspect of God's being, and a relative, changing, temporal, contingent aspect. The former aspect describes God's primordial nature or 'existence', in accord. with which his perfection is seen as state of 'unsurpassibility by others'. God is that being whose bare, abstract existence is completely independent of all else and compatible with all possibilities. Whatever else happens to be the case, God must exist in some perfect form, and so his existence is necessary and eternal. The latter aspect describes the consequent nature or concrete 'actuality', in which primordial nature of God is in fact instantiated. Here God's perfection is interpreted as a 'self-surpassibility'; acc. to this, his perfection at any one time is surpassed by his perfection at a later time, if, as must happen in a processive reality, in interval events have occurred and so have added to God's total experience and expression of his love. God's actuality is thus seen as a personal state for which → Time is real, and in which he chooses between non-compossible ways of concretising his perfection. The panentheistic concept of God has been developed and related to Christ. theological concerns by S. M. Ogden, J. B. Cobb and P. N. Hamilton. D.A.P.

C. Hartshorne, *Man's Vision of God* (1941), *The Logic of Perfection* (1962), *A Natural Theology for our Time* (1967); J. B. Cobb, *A Christian Natural Theology* (1965); S. M. Ogden, *The Reality of God* (1967); P. N. Hamilton, *The Living God and the Modern World* (1967).

Pan-Islam The idea that, because Islam is a unity, all Muslims should unite to counter Western domination was advocated by → Jamāl al-Dīn al-Afghānī. In Egypt he was joined by → Muḥammad 'Abduh, who differed from him only in method. Afghani advocated revolution, but 'Abduh preferred peaceful channels for the movement. In 1297/1880 Afghani was exiled from Egypt, and 'Abduh three years later. In Paris they founded a society called *al-'Urwa al-wuthqā* ('the firmest handle', in French 'le lien indissoluble'—cf. Qur. ii:257; xxxi:21), and a short-lived journal of same name to promote Islam. The Khilafat Movement in India (1337–43/1918–24) was another aspect of same outlook. In more recent times many Muslim states have gained independence, but rivalries exist among them. There never has been a unified Islamic state, unless perhaps in the earliest days; even then, of the first four Caliphs → Abū Bakr was the only one who died a natural death. Divisions soon arose and increased greatly under the → 'Abbasids. There still are sentimental ideas of unity; but practical difficulties always seem to hinder their realisation. J.R.

Pareja, pp. 355f. and index (Ğamāl al-Dīn and Muhammad 'Abduh); W. C. Smith, *Modern History*, index (Khilafat, Pan-Islam); Cragg, *Counsels*, index; G. Antonius, *The Arab Awakening* (1938); E. Kedourie, *Afghani and 'Abduh* (1966).

Paññā (Pali); **Prajñā** (Skt.) P., or wisdom, constitutes the 3rd and highest level of the Buddh. life, the other two being *sila* (→ Morality) and *samādhi* (→ Meditation): (→ Eightfold Path). The wisdom ref. to in this term is that which is specifically Buddh. It consists of direct apprehension of transcendent truths, concerning nature of world and human existence, which must at first be accepted in faith, but with intention of verifying these transcendent truths for oneself, experientially. (→ Faith), by living the Buddh. life. The truths thus apprehended are formally set forth as the → Four Holy Truths. P. is also direct apprehension of impermanence (→ Anicca), ill (→ Dukkha), and impersonality

(→ Anatta) of all existence. A synonym of P. is → Vipassanā. Refs. to P. are frequent in the Pali → Suttas. The realisation of transcendent truth is also central concern of → Mahāyāna. P. is one of the most import. single terms in the Skt. Sutras; a body of lit. exists which is devoted entirely to Prajñā-pāramitā, i.e. transcendental Wisdom (→ Prajñā-pāramitā Sūtras). T.O.L.

Nyanamoli, *The Path of Purification* (Visuddhimagga) (1964), pp. 479ff.; D. T. Suzuki, *Studies in the Lankāvatāra Sutra* (1930), pp. 283–7.

Pantheism *Ex.* Grk. *pan*, 'all'; *theos* 'God'. Term, which seems to have been used first by J. Toland in 1705, denotes religs. which identify God with universe. Much early Grk. philosophy and Stoicism were pantheistic; so also are some aspects of →→ Hinduism and Buddhism. In W. thought, B. Spinoza (1632–77) was notable for P. of his formula 'God or Nature'. → Mysticism often verges on P. (→ Monotheism). S.G.F.B.

E.R.E., IX, pp. 609–17; *R.G.G.*[3], V, col. 37–42.

Pao P'u Tzŭ A fundamental treatise on Taoist alchemy, dietetics and magic, by → Ko Hung (CE 317). The book exerted immense influence on development of popular → Taoism in China. Acc. to its teaching, the art of becoming a → *hsien* or Taoist immortal depended on a strict discipline which involved doing of a fixed number of good actions, rhythmic respiratory exercises, care of the sperm, and ingestion of a sufficient dose of drug of immortality. The book, by its lengthy discussion of use of charms, methods of divination, and reciting of prayers and making of offerings to the spirits, gives considerable insight into popular relig. practices in 3rd and 4th cent. China. D.H.S.

Ch'ên Kuo-fu–T. L. Davis (trs.), 'Inner chs. of the Pao P'u Tzŭ', in *Proceedings of American Acad. of Arts and Sciences*, vol. 74 (1941); L. Wieger, *Hist. of Relig. Beliefs and Philos. Opinions in China* (E.T. 1927), ch. 52; H. Welch, *The Parting of the Way* (1957), pp. 127–9.

Papacy (Pope) *Ex.* Grk. *papas*, Lat. *papa*, 'father'. The title *papas* was used orig. in W. Church for any bishop; but it was officially reserved for Bp. of Rome, i.e. the Pope, in 1073, by Pope Gregory VII. The disappearance of Mother Church of → Jerusalem in destruction of city in 70 removed orig. source of authority and trad. for Christianity, and led to predominance of churches in great cities of Roman Empire. It was natural that Church of Rome should acquire unique status through its location in metropolis of Empire; this advantage was reinforced by claim of its bishop to be successor of St. → Peter, chief of Apostles. The developing claims of P. to primacy were greatly assisted by collapse of W. Roman Empire before barbarian attack in 5th cent. Despite much tribulation, P. gradually emerged as unchallenged source of relig. authority and legatee of Roman culture to the new nations of Europe converted to Christianity. Owing to different circumstances, no bishop of → E. Church attained like status; moreover, that Church suffered gravely from attack of Islam. In medieval Europe, the relig. authority of P., often backed with considerable political power and wealth, was supreme: all other ecclesiastics were regarded as deriving their authority from Pope. The → Reformation, essentially a revolt against P., led to its exclusion from many countries; even in Cath. states, from 16th cent. royal power and growing nationalism curtailed Papal power. The decree of Papal → Infallibility in 1870 repr. logical conclusion of Papal claims. In modern world the Pope still commands the most powerful and numerous of the Chr. Churches, and enjoys unique prestige. The influence of P. on Christianity in doctrine, discipline, organisation, learning and culture has been immense. There has been no comparable authority in other great religs. (→→ Catholic; Constantine, Donation; Vatican Council, Second). S.G.F.B.

E.R.E., IX, *s.v.; R.G.G.*, V, col. 51–91; E. Giles, *Documents illustrating Papal Authority, A.D. 96–454* (1952); J. Haller, *Das Papsttum. Idee und Wirklichkeit*, 5 vols. (repr. 1962); T. G. Jalland, *The Church and the Papacy* (1944); C. Espinosa, *Magisterio pontificio* (1964); J. Meyendorf (*et alii*), *The Primacy of Peter in the Orthodox Church* (1963); G. G. Coulton, *Papal Infallibility* (1932); F. Heer, *Aufgang Europas* (1949); W. Ullmann, *Medieval Papalism: the Political Theories of the Medieval Canonists* (1949), *Growth of Papal Gov. in Middle Ages* (1955); G. Barraclough, *The Medieval Papacy* (1968).

Paradise →→ Eschatology; Heaven.

(Islam) Word commonly used in → Qur. for abode of the blessed is *al-janna* (the garden), pl. *jannāt*. The plural is always used when followed by 'Adn (Eden), which occurs eleven times. al-Firdaws (Paradise) occurs only twice (xviii:107; xxiii:11), the former speaking of the gardens of Firdaws, the latter of those who 'inherit Firdaws as everlasting abode. The word Illīyūn occurs in lxxxiii:18f.: there it seems clearly stated to be the record of deeds of the pious; but the view is commonly held that it is a very high, or the highest, part of paradise. The descriptions of the abode of the blessed are in material terms. They dwell in gardens below which rivers flow. xlvii:16f. speak of rivers with water which is incorruptible, rivers of milk with unchangeable taste, rivers of wine pleasant to the drinkers, and rivers of purified honey. iii:127 says the garden will be as large as the heavens and earth. xxxvii: 41ff. speak of the blessed in gardens of delight reclining on couches, being served with pure drink which causes no intoxication, and having beside them large-eyed maidens. They will have purified spouses (ii:23; iii:13). The wives are elsewhere called houris (*ḥūr*, cf. xliv:54; lii:20; lv:72; lvi:22). The blessed will have ornaments and fine clothing (cf. xviii:30; xxii:23; xxxv:30; lxxvi:12, 21). The clothing is silk, satin, or brocade; the colour is green. The life there is everlasting. The → Trads. provide great detail about the pleasures of P.: e.g., both Bukhari and Muslim incl. a trad. which quotes → Muḥammad as saying that in P. a believer will have a tent of a single hollowed pearl, 60 miles broad (or long), with a family in each corner which he will visit in turn. He will have two gardens with silver vessels and two with golden. A trad. given by Tirmidhi says Firdaws, from which the four rivers of P. issue, is the highest of a hundred stages in P., and that above it is the Throne. While the tendency was to treat the life of the blessed after death as simply a luxurious type of life in this world, many have preferred to understand the language as figurative to express more spiritual ideas. There is a better trad., obviously an echo of 1 Cor., ii:9 which is itself indebted to Isaiah lxiv:4, which declares that God has said, 'I have prepared for my righteous servants what eye has not seen, nor ear heard, nor has entered into the heart of man.' J.R.

E.I.[2], II, pp. 447–52; *Mishkāt*, pp. 1196ff.; Wensinck, *Creed*, index; Sweetman, *I.C.T.*, indexes; J. Macdonald, *Eschatology*, *I.S.* (Dec. 1966), pp. 331ff.

Pāramita Term used in → Mhy. Buddhism, ref. to qualities or virtues, the cultivation of which leads to enlightenment. A list of 6 P.'s is given: generosity, morality, patience, vigour, concentration (or meditation) and wisdom. Later this list was expanded to 10, by add. of skill in means necessary to help others; profound resolution to produce enlightenment; the ten powers (→ Bala); and practice of the → Jhānas. Cultivation of these virtues was regarded in Mhy. Buddhism as proper training for a → Bodhisattva. A slightly different list of 10 P.'s is given by → Buddhaghosa in his *Visuddhimagga* (section IX). T.O.L.

E. Conze, *Buddhist Thought in India* (1962), pp. 211–7; R. Gard, *Buddhism* (1961), pp. 145–50; D. T. Suzuki, *Studies in the Lankāvatāra Sutra* (1930), pp. 365–7; Nyanamoli, *The Path of Purification* (1964), pp. 321–53.

Paritta Protective chant, used in Buddhism from earliest period. Such a chant 'whereby both brethren and sisters of the Order, and laymen and laywomen may dwell at ease, guarded, protected and unscathed' occurs in the → Dīgha Nikāya, in the *Āṭānāṭiya Suttanta* (T. W. Rhys Davids, *Dialogues of the Buddha*, part III (1921, repr. 1965), pp. 188–97). It is poss. that in this matter early Buddhism was adapting use of *raksha-mantras* (protective formulae), a practice already current among people of India; it was able to do so because the practice was made consistent with Buddh. principles by making the P. a means of converting hostile forces: 'the agencies whose power to harm is deprecated' were 'blessed with good wishes, and suffused with outgoing love' (Rhys Davids, *op. cit.*, p. 186). A list of 6 such P.'s is given in the *Questions of Milinda*, viz.: (1) the *Ratana* Sutta (found in the → *Khuddakapatha* and → *Sutta Nipāta* (II:1); (2) the *Khanda*, (A.N., II:72; Vinaya Pitaka, II:109, *vide S.B.E.*, 20, p. 76); (3) the Peacock (*Jāt.*, II:159); (4) the Banner Crest (*S.N.*, *vide Kindred Sayings*, I:283); (5) *Āṭānāṭiya* (already mentioned); (6) the *Angulimāla* (Theragatha, *vide Psalms of the Brethren*, W.874–6). The → *Visuddhimagga* of → Buddhaghosa also gives a list of 5 P.'s (ch. XII, para. 31), (i.e. those mentioned above, omitting the Angulimāla), which it describes as 'efficacious'. The ceremonial chanting by monks of such P.'s at request of lay people on specific and auspicious occasions, is a feature of S. Asian Buddhism; in Ceylon the practice is quite frequent and is known as *pirit*. The use of P.'s was, and sometimes still is, employed also in connection with national ceremonies in Buddh. countries. T.O.L.

Parousia Grk. = 'presence', or 'arrival'. Customary term in N.T. study for second coming of Christ. Belief that P. was imminent and would mark end of world profoundly conditioned outlook of first Christians, and its non-achievement greatly affected development of Christianity. (→→ Advent; Eschatology, Christian; De-eschatologisation; Judgment, Last). S.G.F.B.

E.R.E., *s.v.; R.G.G.*[3], V, col. 130–2; A. L. Moore, *The Parousia in the N.T.* (1966).

Parsee, Pārsīs Name, *ex. Pars*, a province of anc. Persia, given to Persian → Zoroastrians who left Persia in 8th cent. to escape → Islam and settled in what is now Bombay and neighbourhood. The P. have preserved chief beliefs and practices of → Zoroastrianism, also the → Avesta and → Pahlavi books. It was the bringing of a P. copy of Avesta to France in 1772 by → Anquetil du Perron that initiated scientific study of Iranian culture and lit. in Europe. (→ Dahmas). S.G.F.B.

E.R.E., IX, *s.v.;* J. J. Modi, *The Religious System of the Parsees* (1885), *Catechism of Zoroastrian Religion* (1911).

Pārsīs Also transliterated 'Parsees', i.e. Persians: the Zoroastrian community, mainly settled in W. India, esp. in Bombay. The P. orig. from migration of Zoroastrians to Diu in Kathiawar in 8th cent. CE in face of Islamic militancy in homeland. Already → Zoroastrianism had been present in India, mainly in north-west, and among traders settled on west coast. This latter fact may have facilitated settlement of community in Kathiawar. A little later the group moved to Sanjān in Gujarat, where local ruler allowed them to settle and continue their relig. practices. From there the P. eventually spread to other areas, a dispersion ultimately reinforced by fall of Sanjan to Muslims. An import. centre was Nausari, near Surat. When latter became chief entrepot for Western traders, the P. began to acquire new prosperity; when focus of trade shifted to Bombay many of them migrated there. In early part of 19th cent., British-style education was intro. to Bombay, and the P. adapted fast to new cultural milieu. They thus acquired outstanding position in trade and manufacturing. During previous period of over 1000 years from migration to India the community had become partly Hinduised in custom, but had retained with astonishing conservatism the rituals of their faith, and had continued to use portions of the → *Avesta* in their liturgy, although much of it was imperfectly understood. The estab. of contacts with the Gabars (the remaining Zoroastrians in Persia) in the 15th cent. increased the literary resources of the P., through bringing in of → Pahlavi literature; but it was also to be occasion of sectarian split in 18th cent., when it was found that Persian and Indian calendars differed, and priesthood in Gujarat split into two parties. The animosities produced by split, however, grad. abated, and schism is no longer significant. Tensions also arose within community in 19th cent., since stress on education was bound to have repercussions on understanding of the trad. The priesthood was ill-educated, and skilled in a complex ritual which did not always seem to correspond to *Avesta* itself, now rediscovered and reinterpreted in light of mod. scholarship. Grad. reform of the faith was accomplished, although community was penetrated at one end by secularism and at other by → Theosophy, which could justify conservatism through allegorical modes of interpretation. Mod. Parsiism has strongly stressed monotheistic character of faith, obscured somewhat by previous ritualism. The central liturgical symbol of God and holiness is → fire, the cult of which is conducted in temples, to which non-Parsis do not have access. The purity of fire, and need to preserve its purity, account for ceremonies of purification which are conducted five times daily in temples by priesthood, and for custom of exposing the dead in the so-called 'Towers of Silence' (→ Dakhmas). Central also to liturgy is fairly elaborate system of offerings or sacrifices, of ghi, → *haoma* (a bitter plant which differs from the original *haoma* or → *soma*), etc. Correct living, acc. to precepts of morality and purity, is summed up as → *asha* (equivalent to Vedic concept of → *rta*; which at the cosmic level is creative order of God hypostatised as Ardibehesht, one of the six aspects of → *Ameshā-Spentās* (holy immortals) of → Ahura Mazdah. The precepts of morality are summed up as *humata*, good thought, *hūkhta*, good word, and *huvarshta*, good deed. Emphasis upon charity has assisted community in its endeavours towards educational and social betterment. In course of its long existence in India, Parsiism has taken on many of properties of → caste (not unlike the Jains, → Jainism), with little intermarriage outside community (but some with Europeans); thus the P. have not proselytised, while few have been converted to other religs. The community numbers over 100,000. N.S.

A. V. W. Jackson, *Zoroastrian Studies* (1928); J. Duchesne-Guillemin, *The Western Response to Zoroaster* (1958); Sir J. J. Modi, *Ceremonies and Customs of the Parsees* (1937); J. N. Farquhar, *Modern Religious Movements in India* (1919); H. Bhattacharyya, *The Cultural Heritage of India*, vol. 4 (1956); M. Haug, *Essays on the Sacred Writings, Languages and Religion of the Parsis* (1907).

Pārśva The Jain → *tirthamkara* preceding → Mahavira, and 23rd in line of *tirthamkaras*. Prob. not just legendary figure, but an historical teacher of → Jainism, in late 9th and early 8th cent. BC. P. is typically ref. to as Parsva*nāth* ('Lord Parsva'), a title applied to other Tirthamkaras. He is said to have been born in → Banaras, and to have given up world after living life of a householder. After attaining omniscience, he preached to others, eventually dying, after month's fast, reputedly at age of 100 years. The pattern of his life thus corresponds to that of Mahavira. N.S.

H. Zimmer, *Philosophies of India* (1956); J. Jaini, *Outlines of Jainism* (1940).

Parthian Religion A tribe of Iranian nomads, known as the Parni, under their leader Arsaces, seized the satrapy of Parthava *c.* 247 BC from the declining Seleucid government. Known in consequence by Greek and Roman writers as the Parthians, they grad. extended their empire until they controlled a vast area of middle Asia, from the frontiers of Syria in the W. to those of Bactria in the E. Parthian rule was finally ended by the Sassanians *c.* CE 227. The orig. native relig. of the P. is obscure. The evidence, mostly archaeological, reveals an extensive syncretism, prob. due to tolerant policy of the Arsacid kings. Although → Zoroastrianism was never fully adopted, → Ahura Mazdah was worshipped, the → Magi were influential, and the cults of the → fravashi and → fire were observed. Greek and Semitic gods were known, and identified with Iranian deities. The Jews, settled in Mesopot. and Babylonia, flourished under the P.; Christianity was estab. in many places; and Buddhism and other Indian cults were known in E. Parthia. P. funerary practice significantly shows divergence from Zoroastrianism: the dead were buried, not exposed. A notable monument of P. syncretism is a relief from temple of → Bel at Palmyra: it depicts Baalshamin in centre, flanked by Aglibol (moon-god) and Malakbel. All wear Hellenistic cuirasses over oriental tunics and trousers. Significant also are the relig. statuary and frescoes found at Dura Europos. P. doubtless assisted greatly in transmission of Iranian and Mesopot. cults to Graeco-Roman world. S.G.F.B.

M. A. R. Colledge, *The Parthians* (1967); R. N. Frye, *The Heritage of Persia* (1962), pp. 178ff.

Passover (Pesach) The most notable of Jew. festivals, held in spring. P. is closely integrated with another, orig. separate, feast: Mazzoth or Unleaven Bread. Acc. to Ex. 12:21ff., the combined festival had a historical origin. On night of Exodus → Yahweh ordered the Israelites to mark their houses with blood of sacrificed lamb lest they should perish when he destroyed the first-born of Egypt. Mazzoth commemorated the fact that, in hastening from Egypt, the Israelites had no time to leaven their bread. These two rites clearly had very different origins. P. was orig. an apotropaic rite practised by pastoral people where sacrifice bought immunity of first-born of man and beast. Mazzoth was orig. an agricultural ritual, designed to prevent transfer of ill from previous year by use of old leaven with new corn. The historicising of anc. rituals, of forgotten origin, occurs in other religs. The → Samaritans still continue to sacrifice a paschal lamb at Nablus (Shechem). (→ Judaism). S.G.F.B.

*H.D.B.*², *s.v.;* A. Lods, *Israël* (1932), pp. 335ff., 505; S. H. Hooke, *Origins of Early Semitic Rituals* (1938), pp. 50ff.; H. Wildberger, *Jahwes Eigentumsvolk* (1960), pp. 43ff.; I. Epstein, *Judaism* (1959), pp. 171ff.; *E.J.R.*, pp. 254, 295ff.; H. H. Rowley, *Worship in Anc. Israel* (1967), pp. 47ff., 87ff., 114ff.; J. B. Segal, *The Hebrew Passover from Earliest Times to A.D. 70* (1963).

Patañjali The author of *Yogasūtra* ('Aphorisms on Yoga') initial literary source for teachings of → Yoga school. He has often been identified with the Patanjali who wrote commentary on work of great grammarian Panini; but author of *Yogasutra* prob. lived several cents. later. P. wrote against background of → Samkhya metaphysics, but alters the practical emphases—e.g. → *asanas*, postures, are substituted for *tarka*, reasoning, as an element in pursuit of higher experience of release. N.S.

M. Eliade, *Yoga: Immortality and Freedom* (1958); S. N. Dasgupta, *Yoga Philosophy in Relation to Other Systems of Indian Thought* (1930), *Yoga as Philosophy and Religion* (1924); J. H. Woods, *The Yoga System of Patanjali* (1914).

Path, Buddhist → Eightfold Path. T.O.L.

Paticca-Samuppāda A Buddh. formula, often trans. as 'Dependent Origination', or 'Chain of Causation', which expresses doc. that all physical and psychical phenomena are conditioned by antecedent physical or psychical factors, and that whole of existence can be shown to be an uninterrupted flux of phenomena. The doc. implies also rejection of idea of any permanently existing entity or ego, human or animal. Twelve terms are used to set forth the doc.: old age and death (*jarā-marana*) are due to antecedent rebirth (*jāti*); rebirth is due to antecedent process of becoming (*bhava*); becoming is due to clinging (to life) (*upādāna*); clinging is due to craving (*taṇhā*); craving is due to feeling (*vedanā*); feeling to sense-impression (*phassa*); sense-impression to the 6 Bases of sense (*āyatana*); the 6 Bases to corporeality (*nāma-rūpa*); corporeality to consciousness (*viññāna*); consciousness to karma-formations (*sankhāra*); and karma-formations to ignorance (*avijjā*). The formula is found in canonical scriptures in the → *Saṃyutta Nikāya* (II, 7), and is expounded by → Buddhaghosa in the → *Visuddhimagga*, ch. XVII (tr. pp. 592ff.). Nyanatiloka, *Guide Through the Abhidhamma-Pitaka* (2nd edn. 1957), pp. 157–73, for refs. to European writing on the subject. T.O.L.

Pātimokkha (Pali); **Prātimokṣa** (Skt.) Moral code of Buddh. monks, consisting of list of more than 200 offences, in descending order of seriousness, recited in assembly of whole company of monks in every monastery on → Uposattha days. A monk who is guilty of any of these offences is required to confess the matter and receive the appropriate penalty. (→ Discipline, Buddh. Monastic). T.O.L.

Patriotism (China–Japan) Until comparatively recent times, the love and loyalty of majority of Chinese were given to family, clan and ruler; not to country or nation as such. The people at large took little or no interest in affairs of government. They were the governed, their chief interests bound up in family and locality. Instances of intense patriotism are found among ruling scholar-class. The rise of nationalism in recent years, and foreign aggression, has resulted in loosening of ties of family and local loyalty and growth of patriotism, inculcated in the schools and army. The result today is a fervid nationalism, a rabid xenophobia and adulation of the charismic leader of the nation. Nevertheless, loyalty to provincial and regional interests often takes precedence over love and loyalty to country as a whole.

The Japanese have always been characterised by intense and even fanatical loyalty and love of country. P. is one of basic elements of → Shinto. With the Meiji Restoration of 1868 and revival of State Shinto, the sun-goddess → Amaterasu became emblem of the ideal cohesion of the state, and centre of loyalty and P. that bind the nation to the throne. In schools, children were taught from infancy to glorify the national trad., and to consider reverence for the gods, love of country and obedience to emperor, as fundamental virtues. D.H.S.

D. C. Holtom, *The National Faith of Japan* (1938), *passim*.

Paul, St. The fact that P.'s Epistles comprise about one quarter of contents of N.T., and that he is the main figure in → Acts, indic. his importance in Chr. Origins. He is presented as the divinely-chosen Apostle of the Gentiles, whose writings were greatly treasured. This gen. impression is strangely contradicted on closer exam. of these same documents. P. is revealed as involved in bitter conflict with powerful opponents who repudiate his authority and contradict his teaching. These opponents were undoubtedly the leaders of the → Jerusalem Church, and incl. the orig. disciples of Jesus. The true nature of this conflict is obscure. It appears most likely that P., not an orig. disciple of Jesus, presented to Gentiles a different version of the faith. Since P. was a Hellenistic Jew, his version was prob. designed to make Jesus intelligible to Gentiles, to whom he would not have been if presented only as → Messiah of Israel. P. reinterpreted the Crucifixion as a divinely-planned means of saving mankind from enslavement to daemonic forces (→ Archons): Jesus was the incarnation of a preexistent divine being, who thus became saviour of mankind (I Cor. 2:7ff.). The logic of this → soteriology meant that both Jews and Gentiles needed salvation, thus depriving Jews of their prized status as God's chosen People. Hence P.'s rejection by Jerus. Christians. P.'s weakness was that he could not deny authority of Jerus. leaders, but they could reject his. The Acts does not record P.'s fate after arriving in Rome as a prisoner. It would seem that the future of P.'s teaching was saved by disappearance of Jerus. Church in Jew. national disaster in 70. The importance of P.'s teaching is fundamental. P. was a seminal thinker, and he laid the foundations of Christianity as a universal salvation-relig. The Jerus. Christians would have kept Christianity confined to Judaism. P.'s letters have been a basic source for subsequent theology, and played influential part in thinking of Prot. Reformers. (→→ Christianity; Epistles (under title), Judaism). S.G.F.B.

A. D. Nock, *St. Paul* (1938); J. Klausner, *From Jesus to Paul* (E.T. 1942); H. J. Schoeps, *Paul*, (E.T. 1961); A. Schweitzer, *Paul and his Interpreters* (E.T. 1912), *The Mysticism of Paul* (E.T. 1931); W. L. Knox, *St. Paul and Church of the Gentiles* (1939); M. Goguel, *La naissance du Christianisme* (1946); W. D. Davies, *Paul and Rabbinic Judaism* (1948); S. G. F. Brandon, *The Fall of Jerusalem and the Christian Church* (1957[2]), *Jesus and the Zealots* (1967); Bruce, *N.T.H.*

Peace, Ideal of (China–Japan) The Chinese, in spite of numerous revolutions and wars which have disturbed their hist., have been regarded as a peace-loving people. The long → Confucian traditions inculcated a profound respect for law and order, and held up ideal of human society being peacefully ordered in perfect accord with cosmic harmony. Revolutionary movements, arising out of corrupt government, semi-relig. in character, were inspired by desire for a Great Universal Peace (e.g. the Yellow Turbans at the close of Han Dynasty, and the T'ai P'ing (Great Peace) rebellion in middle of 19th cent.). In modern times the *Ta T'ung Shu* ('The Book of Great Concord'), written by philosopher-statesman K'ang Yu-wei (1858–1927) has been very influential. In it are combined Confucian ideas, → Buddh. idealism, and mod. West. concepts of internationalism and World Peace, in a utopian vision of whole world as great commonwealth and golden age of universal peace.

The Japanese throughout their hist. have been distinctively warlike. From mid. of 8th cent. CE, → Hachiman, the god of war, has been prominent in → Shinto worship, and there has been a manifest tendency to exalt the military ideal. The sectarian rivalries within → Buddhism, in spite of its teachings of peace and brotherhood, often resulted in organised warfare in which monks engaged. Shinto envisaged universal peace through extension throughout world of the emperor-centred state relig. of Japan. D.H.S.

Pelagianism Pelagius, a British or Irish monk, in early 5th cent. propounded the view that man could himself initiate action towards his own → salvation, and was not wholly dependent on divine → grace. P. as a doc., was concerned to maintain man's moral responsibility against view that man could do nothing good without God's prevenient and supporting grace. P.'s most formidable opponent was → Augustine of Hippo. After much controversy and repeated official condemnation, P. finally disappeared in 6th cent. P. also challenged orthodox doc. of

→ Original Sin, maintaining that Adam's sin affected himself alone and not whole human race. A modified form of P., admitting necessity of grace, and known as Semi-P., flourished in Gaul and was formally condemned by Council of Orange, 529. The defeat of P. signified gen. acceptance of Augustinian view of grace. S.G.F.B.

E.R.E., IX, *s.v.; D.C.C.*, pp. 1040ff., 1239; *R.G.G.*[3], V, col. 206–7; T. Bohlin, *Die Theologie des Pelagius u. ihre Genesis* (1957); J. Ferguson, *Pelagius: a historical and theological study* (1956); P. Brown, 'Pelagius and his Supporters', *J.T.S.*, XIX (1968).

Pentateuch Trad. Chr. name for first five books of O.T. For Jews these books constitute the → Torah, 'Law', being evaluated as authoritative exposition of all individual and social morality. Modern scholars, regarding Book of Joshua as having same sources as P., often incl. it with other five books under title of Hexateuch. The P. is trad. ascribed to → Moses. Modern critical scholarship distinguishes three main sources or traditions underlying present text of P.: the →→ Yahwist (J); Elohist (E); Priestly (P). Two distinct codes of laws are also discerned: the Book of the → Covenant (C), Ex. 21–23; the 'statutes and ordinances' of Deut. 12–26 (D). The composition of P. is thought to extend from 9th to 4th cent. BC. This document-hypothesis has been challenged by → Scandinavian School, who prefer more fluid evolution of tradition. (→ Judaism). S.G.F.B.

H.D.B.[2], *s.v.; R.G.G.*[3], V, col. 211–7; C. R. North, 'Pentateuchal Criticism', in H. H. Rowley (ed.), *The Old Test. and Modern Study* (1951); R. H. Pfeiffer, *Intro. to the Old Test.* (1948), pp. 129ff.

Pentecost Grk. = 'fiftieth day'. The Jew. Feast of Weeks was so-called, since it fell on 50th day after → Passover. Originating from offering of first-fruits of harvest (Deut. 16:9), P. was later held to commemorate giving of → Torah to Moses. In Christ. trad., P. marks descent of → Holy Spirit (Acts 2:1ff.). S.G.F.B.

E.J.R., p. 401; *D.C.C.*, *s.v.*

Perfections (Buddh.) → *Pāramitā.* T.O.L.

Perfection (China, Japan, Korea) The ideal of P.—the perfected man—is prominent in Chi. religs. In → Confucianism it is exemplified in the *Shêng Jên* or Sage, whose life through practice of virtue achieves perfect harmony with Heaven and Earth. In → Taoism, P. is realised by return to the → Tao, unity with the Tao, and complete realisation of the Tao of one's own nature. Though a virtuous life is emphasised, → alchemy, hygiene techniques and mystical contemplation are considered necessary means to achieve this state, for which there are several names: *Shên Jên* or Spiritualised Man, *Chên Jên* or Realised Man, *Chih Jên* or Perfected Man. In Chi. → Buddhism the ideal is the perfect realisation of one's own buddhahood, to become a → bodhisattva (Chinese: *p'u sa*) or perfected spirit. Confucianism is also dominated by ideal of a perfect society, ruled over by a sage-king. Buddhism has always held out hope of eventual P. of all sentient beings in Buddhahood.

Korean and Jap. ideas of P. are mainly derived from the Chinese. D.H.S.

Persecution, Religious Attempts to suppress form of relig. faith and practice regarded as obnoxious are anc. and widespread. Motives vary: the more usual are (1) religious—the persecuted relig. is seen as false and dangerous to relig. of persecutor. (2) Political—a relig. is evaluated as promulgating ideas subversive to state's internal stability or foreign policy. (3) Moral—a relig. is deemed to undermine or pervert trad. moral values. The earliest instance of P. is prob. that by → Akhenaten of cult of → Amun: motives here were a mixture of (1) and (2). Motives are gen. mixed when governments persecute; popular persecution (e.g. → anti-Semitism) is more likely to be inspired chiefly by socio-relig. dislike and fear. Some notable examples of P. are listed here for comparison. Roman P. of Christians seems mainly to have had political and moral motives. Islamic P. of idolatry was relig., as was its P. of → Ṣūfīs. Chr. P. of heretics was gen. relig. in motive, though political factors could also operate (e.g. against →→ Albigenses; Lollards). P. of Protestants by R.C.'s, and *vice versa*, and of Protestants by Protestants in various countries have gen. been inspired by relig.-political motives. Roman P. of → Zealots and → Druids was to suppress nationalist movements inspired by relig. P. of → witches was due to popular fear of black → magic. P. suffered by → Buddhism in various lands has been variously motivated. → Russian communist P. of Christianity has been political. The Nazi P. of Jews seems to have stemmed from racial prejudice. A common feature of P. of relig. is imputation of immorality to those persecuted: often such charges have been baseless, and prob. reflect both superstitious prejudice and unconscious desire for self-justification. P. has taken various forms from civil disabilities to torture and death. P. has rarely been wholly successful, gen. owing to inefficiency in methods and prosecution. The grad. acceptance of Islam by many Chr. peoples in Near East and N. Africa resulted more from advantage of professing the dominant relig. than from active P. Toleration has gen. grown *pari passu* with decline of relig. fervour. (→→ Inquisition; Martyrs). S.G.F.B.

E.R.E., IX, pp. 742–69; *R.A.C.*, II, col. 1159–

1228; W. H. C. Frend, *Martyrdom and Persecution in the Early Church* (1965); H. C. Lea, *The Inquisition of the Middle Ages* (ed. 1963); J. B. Bury, *A Hist. of Freedom of Thought* (n.d.); J. Wach, *Sociology of Religion* (1944); A. A. T. Ehrhardt, *Politische Metaphysik von Solon bis Augustin*, 2 vols. (1959); L. E. Browne, *The Eclipse of Christianity in Asia* (1933); C. Eliot, *Hinduism and Buddhism*, III (1921).

Persephone Prob. pre-Hellenic goddess who became assoc. with → Demeter as her virgin-daughter (→ Korē). Acc. to Homeric Hymn to Demeter, P. was carried off by → Hades, whose queen she became. The subsequent decision of → Zeus that P. was to spend each year partly with Demeter and partly with Hades, has been interpreted as allegory of life of the seed-corn. P. had → chthonian associations, and was assoc. with the → Eleusinian Mysteries. She was also connected with → Orphism as mother of → Zagreus. Pindar (*fr.* 133) speaks cryptically of the dead 'at whose hands Persephone accepts satisfaction for her ancient grief', which may be an allusion to death of Zagreus. S.G.F.B.

O.C.D., *s.v.;* G. E. Mylonas, *Eleusis and the Eleusinian Mysteries* (1961), *passim*; Harrison, *Prolegomena*, pp. 271ff.; C. Picard, *Les religions prehélléniques* (1948), pp. 109ff.; W. K. C. Guthrie, *The Greeks and their Gods* (1950), pp. 282ff.; W. F. Otto in J. Campbell (ed.), *The Mysteries* (1955), pp. 61ff.

Personification →→ Animatism; Animism.

(China–Far East) The indigenous religs. of China and Far East, rooted as they are in primitive → animism, imbued innumerable natural objects and processes with personality, repr. them in human form and deeming them to be possessed of human attributes. The → T'ien (Heaven) of pre-Confucian relig. in China (→ *Shih Ching* and *Shu Ching*) was conceived as an August Deity able to see, hear, taste and smell, omniscient and omnipotent and subject to anger or compassion. The myths of Jap. → Shinto personify the great natural forces: sun, moon, wind and rain, together with innumerable natural objects and processes.

The belief in unity of man with nature, and human and spiritual worlds led, on one hand, to deification of men, and, on other hand, to attribution of human qualities and personality to gods and spirits. But the characterisation of gods was often weak and vague. Their personalities rarely stand out with the distinctiveness of Greek gods. The attributes and functions of various gods are seldom clearly defined, but merge into each other. Even their sex cannot always be determined. Though in earlier times natural objects etc. were conceived of as divinities, with development of relig. personalised gods and spirits came to be thought of as inhabiting or controlling various objects and forces of nature.

→ Buddhism, orig. and philosophically denying the 'self', as it developed in popular forms of Mahāyāna, came to personify many of attributes of Buddha: Infinite light and life as → Amitabha (Amida); grace and compassion as → Kuan Yin (Kwannon); power as → Ta Shih-chih (Daiseishi); wisdom as → Wên Shu (Monju). D.H.S.

J. Hackin, *Asiatic Mythology* (1932), *passim*; W. G. Aston, *Shinto* (1905), pp. 5ff.; D. C. Holtom, *The National Faith of Japan* (1938), pp. 109ff.; K. L. Reichelt, *Truth & Tradition in Chinese Buddhism* (1927), *passim.*

Petavatthu A minor book of Buddh. Pali canon. It is found in 5th, or *Khuddaka, Nikaya* of *Sutta Pitaka.* It is gen. listed 7th among books of the *K.-N.* Like 6th book, the *Vimanavatthu*, the P. deals with fates of departed spirits who do not find rebirth in embodied existence; the *Vimanavatthu* describes the celestial abodes of those *devas* or spirits whose rebirth is happy, though unembodied, because of previous good → *karma.* The V. consists of 83 stories of such *devas*, arranged in 7 chapters. The P. concerns unhappy lot of ghosts who suffer as result of some previous bad *karma*; it contains 51 stories arranged in 4 chapters. Both books are, rel. to other parts of Pali canon, late in origin, poss. 3rd cent. BC and are clearly intended for use in popular moral instruction and exhortation. (→ Dead, State of). T.O.L.

Peter, St. A Galilaean, repr. in Gospels as chief → apostle of Jesus: in → Acts he appears in early chapters as leader of → Jerusalem Church, but is not mentioned again after 15:7–14. Paul witnesses to his prominence, but indic. his subordination to → James, the Lord's brother (Gal. 2:9, 11ff.). 'Peter' was a title (Grk. *petros* = rock, trans. Aramaic 'Cephas'): acc. to Jn. 1:42, the title was given by Jesus to a disciple whose name was Simon. Chr. trad. tells of martyrdom of P. in Rome, prob. about 64. Analysis of N.T. reveals conflicting evidence about P.'s position in Church *vis-à-vis* James, the Lord's brother, who quickly succeeded P. as head of Jerus. Church. I Cor. 1:12 suggests presence of P. at Corinth and formation of a P. party against → Paul. Mk. 8:29–33 indic. that P. recognised Jesus as → Messiah, but not his soteriological role. The author of Gosp. of Matt. (16:18) regarded P. as rock upon which Christ founded his Church. The epithet, 'Barjona', given to P. in Mt. 16:17 is puzzling: it could mean 'extremist' or 'terrorist', i.e., → Zealot. The claim of Pope to be successor of P. effectively contrib. to supremacy of → Papacy. Two Epistles are attr. to P. in the N.T., but their authenticity is doubtful; in →

Apocryphal N.T. there are Acts of P., → Apoc. of P., and Gosp. of P., which are later pseudepigraphic writings. S.G.F.B.

O. Cullmann, *Peter: Disciple-Apostle-Martyr* (E.T. 1953); *H.D.B.*², *s.v.; R.G.G.*³, V, col. 247–9; *D.C.C.*, *s.v.;* S. G. F. Brandon, *Jesus and the Zealots* (1967), *passim.*

Peter, Apocalypse of 2nd cent. apocryphal writing, surviving only in fragments and quots. It takes form of vision of next world and fate of dead granted by Jesus to his Apostles. The work is important for study of Chr. → eschatology: some of its material may derive from → Orphic sources. S.G.F.B.

M. R. James, *The Apocryphal New Test.* (1924), pp. 505ff.; E. Hennecke, *Neutestamentliche Apokryphen*³, II (1964), pp. 314ff.; A. Dieterich, *Nekyia* (1913²); F. Cumont, *After Life in Roman Paganism* (1959 edn.), pp. 173ff.; S. G. F. Brandon, *The Judgment of the Dead*, ch. 6.

Peyote Cult Peyote (*Lophophora williamsii*) is a small cactus, found along the Rio Grande and in Mexico. It contains various alkaloids, incl. the hallucinogen mescaline: when taken in sufficient quantity (either dried or infused), it produces euphoria and trance. Used in relig. context for centuries, first by → Aztecs, and later by → N. American Indian tribes as far north as Wisconsin, P. became in 19th cent. the focus of a distinctive cult. While form of cult is entirely indigenous, with drumming and singing, it incorporates Christian elements (prayer, healing, testimony). In 1941 the cult was incorporated as the Native American Church of Oklahoma; in 1945 as the Native American Church of the United States. E.J.S.

J. S. Slotkin, *The Peyote Religion* (1956); R. M. Underhill, *Red Man's Religion* (1965), pp. 265–9; R. H. Lowie, in *E.R.E.*, IX, pp. 815a–b.

Phallus, Cult of Preoccupation with male and female sexual organs in a relig. or magical context is anc. and widespread. That the P. appears more often in iconography may indic. male predominance or fact that female genitals are more difficult to portray. The repr. of either, apart from the body, suggests symbolic significance: both appear in Paleolithic → cave art. The P. as cult object seems to have been worshipped or venerated in anc. Greece: the god Priapus was essentially a deified P.; the P. was prominent in cult of → Dionysos (e.g. giant P. dedicated to Dionysos at Delos (*Bilderatlas*, 13/14 Lief., Abb. 14); ritual unveiling of P. in fresco of Villa dei Misteri, Pompeii). The veneration of P. is characteristic of cult of → Shiva (→ lingam): the P. of → Osiris had important role in his cult. The assoc. of P. with a specific deity doubtless indic. worship of male generative power: → ithyphallic gods had similar significance. The P. was used as magical object usually to promote fertility in women (there were even medieval Chr. instances, e.g. in cult of St. Foutin at Embrun, France). The P. was also used as apotropaic → amulet against → witchcraft and → evil-eye. It may be noted here that the vulva was depicted in some medieval churches in England and Ireland in the so-called *Sheila-na-gig*, and models of male and female genitals were hung in chapel of St. Fountin at Varailles in Provence in 16th cent. The May-pole was a fertility symbol; it could have phallic significance. (→ Yoni). S.G.F.B.

E.R.E., IX, pp. 815–31; S. Giedon, *The Eternal Present* (1962), pp. 173ff.; G. E. Mylonas, *Eleusis and the Eleusinian Mysteries* (1961), pp. 296ff.; H. Licht, *Sexual Life in Anc. Greece* (E.T. 1932), pp. 120ff., 206ff.; L. S. S. O'Malley, *Popular Hinduism* (1935), pp. 88ff.; *R.Ae.R-G.*, pp. 590–2; J. G. Frazer, *The Magic Art* (*G.B.*), II (1936³), pp. 65ff.; *R.G.G.*³, V, col. 324–6; G. R. Scott, *Phallic Worship* (1941); A. Ross, *Pagan Celtic Britain* (1967), pp. 229, 232; F. Sierksma, *The Gods as We Shape Them* (1960), ill. pp. 8, 33–4, 68, 69.

Pharisees *Ex.* Aramaic, 'separated ones'. The P. were successors of → Hasidaeans, becoming distinguished from 2nd cent. BC for strict observance of → Torah. However, unlike → Sadducees, they valued oral trad. highly (→ Mishnah), and were progressive in theology: they believed in → resurrection, *post-mortem* retribution, angels, human free-will, and divine providence. They were also distinguished for hostility to pagan rulers of Israel (a P. was joint founder of → Zealotism). Most information about P. comes from → Josephus (*Wars*, II, 162f.; *Ant.*, XVIII, 12f.), → Talmud, and N.T. In Gospels, the P. are repr. as opponents of Jesus and incur his condemnation for their legalism; however, it is evident that there was a basic kinship in doctrine (esp. in eschatology), and, acc. to → Acts, many Pharisees joined → Jerus. Church. The P., as a party, disappeared after 70; but their beliefs were incorporated into Rabbinic → Judaism. (→ Hillel). S.G.F.B.

R. T. Herford, *The Pharisees* (1924); L. Finkelstein, *The Pharisees*, 2 vols. (1940); *E.R.E.*, IX, *s.v.;* Schürer, *G.J.V.*, II, pp. 388ff.; W. Förster, *Palestinian Judaism in New Test. Times,* (E.T. 1964), pp. 168ff.; *H.D.B.*², *s.v.; R.G.G.*³, V, col. 326–8; N. N. Glatzer, 'Hillel the Elder in the Light of the Dead Sea Scrolls', K. Standahl (ed.), in *The Scrolls and the New Test.* (1958); *E.J.R.*, p. 299.

Phenomenology of Religion ('Religionsphänomenologie') This designation is often used by Continental scholars for the study customarily called → 'Comparative Religion' ('vergleichende Religionswissenschaft'). P.-R. is distinguished from → Theology (which assumes existence of God) and History of Religion (→ 'Religionsgeschichte'), in being concerned not with validity or origin of relig. belief and practice, but with their existential significance as evidence of man's thought and action. Its aim has been defined as 'studying the action of man in relation to God, not the action of God'. It is basically a humanistic, not a theological, discipline; it is inevitably concerned with the historical data of relig., but it does not seek to study relig. in its historical development. Whether P.-R. is a better designation than 'Comparative Religion', or can rightly be used as a synonym, is debatable. Although the latter is not semantically accurate (it really means the 'comparative study of religion'), it is both an estab. and convenient expression. In practice Comparative Relig. is concerned with the hist. as well as the comparison of relig. phenomena; for the hist. and comparative aspects cannot properly be studied in strict separation from each other. Studies in P.-R. are rarely confined to describing relig. phenomena. S.G.F.B.

R.G.G., V, col. 322–4; G. Mensching, *Vergleichende Religionswissenschaft* (1949); A. Bertholet, *Wörterbuch der Religionen* (1952), p. 402; C. J. Bleeker, 'The Relation of the Hist. of Religions to kindred religious Sciences', *Numen*, I (1954); M. Eliade, 'History of Religions and a New Humanism', *H.R.*, I (1961), *Traité d'histoire des religions* (1948), E.T., *Patterns in Comparative Religion* (1958); G. Van der Leeuw, *La Religion* (1948); J. Wach, *Sociology of Religion* (1944); *The Comparative Study of Religion* (1958); Brandon, *Man and his Destiny in the Great Religions* (1962); Widengren, *R-P.* (1969).

Phi Siamese name for spirit-beings. They are believed to be responsible for causing human sickness and misadventures of all kinds, not because of their inherent evilness but on account of some specific discourtesy or offence by person who suffers the P.'s attack. Like the → Nats of Burma, P. are thought of as inhabiting rivers, mountains, wild places, and esp. trees. They manifest themselves in variety of roles: vampires, will o' the wisps; also as house-guardians, and spirits who cause the rice to grow. The house-guardian spirit is known also as *Phra Phum* (*ex.* Skt. *bhūmi*), the earth thus, 'the earth-spirit', and is given a small 'house' (*sam*) outside almost every Thai home. At this *Sam-Phra-Phum*, raised from ground by short pole, are offered food, flowers, incense and candles. The manufacture of these *Sam-Phra-Phum* is a flourishing craft even in metropolis of Bangkok. Apart from these categories of P., there are spirits of dead persons; these are usually regarded as malevolent, esp. when death was result of violence or accident; it is regarded as imperative that special rites be performed to protect living from their malevolent attacks. (→→ Yakka: Nat). T.O.L.

Philistines A non-Semitic sea-faring people who settled in coastal plain of Palestine *c.* 12th cent. BC. They figure much in O.T. and Assyrian records. They seem to have adopted → Canaanite relig., their chief god being → Dagon. S.G.F.B.

E.R.E., IX, *s.v.; H.D.B.*[2], *s.v.; C.A.H.*, II, pp. 283ff.; *R.G.G.*[3], V, col. 339–41.

Philo (*c.* 20 B.C.–*c.* CE 50) Alexandrian Jewish thinker and exegete, born of rich and influential family, P. had considerable status in Alex.-Jew. community, representing it in an embassy to Rome in 39. His *Legatio ad Gaium*, describing events at this time, is important for hist. of Jew.-Roman relations in 1st cent CE, as is also his *In Flaccum*. P. was educated in Grk. philosophy; in his allegorical interpretations of the O.T. he sought to present Jew. relig. in terms of Grk. metaphysical thought. He made much use of idea of → Logos as intermediary between God and world, though it is uncertain how far he hypostatises the concept. P.'s anthropology was dualistic, being reminiscent of → Orphic *sōma-sēma* form. He regarded soul as preexistent and immortal; he speaks of rebirth ('*palingenesia*'), but not of physical → resurrection. P.'s voluminous works, in Grk., are significant as evidence of extent to which trad. Jew. relig. could be Hellenised; they were preserved by Christians, partic. of → Alexandria, whose thought they greatly influenced. (→ Alexandrian Theology; → Clement of Alexandria). P.'s writings also influenced → Neoplatonism. S.G.F.B.

Most of Philo's works are ed. and trans. in Loeb Classical Library; cf. *Legatio ad Gaium*, ed. and trans. E. M. Smallwood (1961); *In Flaccum*, ed. H. Box (1939); E. R. Goodenough, *The Politics of Philo Judaeus*, with Gen. Bibliography (1938); *An Intro. to Philo Judaeus* (1940); Schürer, *G.J.V.*, III, pp. 487ff.; *E.R.E.*, I, pp. 309ff.; *R.G.G.*[3], V, col. 341–6.

Philosophy, Hindu Although much of Indian philosophy has concerned itself with technical and metaphysical issues arising in and out of epistemology, logic, etc., many systems of thought have been determined essentially by prior relig. concerns. There has been over very long period a lively interplay between schools belonging to different relig. trads.—Hindu, Buddhist, Jain, etc. It is, therefore, somewhat artificial to separate off H.P. from other forms of Indian philosophy. However, it has been trad. to differentiate between *astika* or orthodox schools and *nāstika* or unorthodox schools (→ orthodoxy, Hindu), namely between those which do and those which do not recognise authority of Vedic revelation (→ revelation, Hindu). The *nāstikas* comprise Buddh. schools, the Jains and → Carvaka (Materialists). Trad. the *astika* schools are reckoned to be six in number, and are ref. to as the *saḍdarśana* or 'six viewpoints'. These are coupled in three pairs, namely →→ Sāmkhya and Yoga; Nyāya and Vaiśeṣika, and Mīmāmsā and Vedānta. In fact, within each viewpoint there are sub-schools, most import. in Vedanta (→→ Advaita, Visistadvaita, Dvaita). Of the six, the Nyaya and Vaisesika are least influenced by relig. premisses—the Nyaya being largely devoted to issues in logic and about styles of argument, Vaisesika being largely concerned with systematisation of an atomist account of physical world. Though primary shape of a system may be influenced by relig. concerns, the arguments used to back up elements of a system are relatively independent of relig. presuppositions. For example, the trad. Hindu arguments for and against existence of a personal God (→ *Iśvara*) begin from such premisses as that anything which is composed of parts must have an arranger, and counter-arguments are directed against premiss, etc. Despite the formally orthodox character of the six viewpoints, they vary widely in relig. principles. Thus Samkhya and Mimamsa are atheistic, in denying existence of personal Creator of world; Yoga affirms personal God, but he is not Creator, but rather a unique soul who has never been involved in round of → rebirth and who serves as aid to meditation; Nyaya-Vaisesika is theistic, largely because a Creator is brought in to explain initial combinations of atoms in periods when cosmos is recreated out of chaos (→ Cosmology, Hindu); the Vedanta is divided among schools affirming supremacy of a personal God and those affirming non-personal account of ultimate reality (→ *Brahman*). The most productive period of Indian philosophy was medieval, from 7th to 16th cent. CE, though shape of the systems was by then largely determined through composition of classical *sutras* or aphoristic expositions of viewpoints (the most import. being the → *Brahmasutra*, which served as basis of various expositions of Vedanta). The medieval philosophers wrote extensive commentaries on the *sutras* and other works, and geared their arguments to poss. objections of other schools, giving Indian philosophy an esp. lively, though at the same time rather scholastic, character. The 16th to 18th cents. were rather arid, but there was something of revival in 19th. This was partly because of desire to relate Indian trad. ideas to Western philosophy and seek synthesis between the two (facilitated by analogies between Vedanta and the then fashionable → Hegelianism). At same time, a wider rediscovery of past occurred through editing, translating and printing of anc. texts. The new synthesis tended to favour Advaita; and 20th cent. empiricism has made comparatively little impact on Indian philosophical scene. There has, however, been some revival of interest in earlier Indian materialism, which virtually disappeared in medieval period, though up till then it maintained vigorous challenge to relig. interpretations of reality which have remained dominant. N.S.

S. N. Dasgupta, *Hist. of Indian Philosophy*, 5 vols. (1922–55), *Philosophical Essays* (1941); M. Hiriyanna, *The Essentials of Indian Philosophy* (1951), *Outlines of Indian Philosophy* (1958); S. Radhakrishnan-C. A. Moore (eds.), *A Source Book in Indian Philosophy* (1957); N. Smart, *Doctrine and Argument in Indian Philosophy* (1964); K. Potter, *Presuppositions of India's Philosophies* (1963); E. Frauwallner, *Geschichte der indischen Philosophie*, 2 vols. (1952–6); S. Radhakrishnan-J. N. Muirhead (eds.), *Contemporary Indian Philosophy* (1952).

(Ionian) For hist. of relig., the philosophical speculation that orig. in the Ionian cities in 6th cent. BC marked a new and portentous development in man's attempt to understand his world. Instead of resorting to myth or divine revelation, Thales, Anaximander, Anaximenes, → Xenophanes and Heraclitus, sought to explain world in terms of its constitution from some basic substance and the inherent qualities of that substance. Their interpretations were → pantheistic. (→ Anaxagoras). S.G.F.B.

F. M. Cornford, *From Religion to Philosophy* (1912), in *C.A.H.*, IV, pp. 538ff.; W. Jaeger, *The Theology of the Early Greek Philosophers* (1947); G. S. Kirk-J. E. Raven, *The Presocratic Philosophers* (1960); L. Robin, *La pensée grecque* (1928); *I.A.A.M.*, ch. 12.

(Jain) J.P. has certain distinctive docs. in add. to *Weltanschauung* presented by → Jainism as relig. system. The most import. are a form of relativism (*syādvāda*) and a theory of 'perspectives' (*naya*) by which world is known. Acc. to former, assertions about world must be qualified as tentative, because their truth depends upon context, and so dogmatism is ruled out. This theory was even applied to Jain docs. themselves, and formed basis of an attitude of relig. toleration. Acc. to theory of perspectives, any object can be considered from a number of points of view (as displaying unique characterisation, universal ones, etc.). The main expositions of J.P. are the *Pravacanasāra* ('Essence of Exposition') and the *Tattvārthadhigama-sūtra* ('Aphorisms penetrating to Fundamental Principles'), both written some time after 3rd cent. CE. In medieval period, extensive logical works were composed by Jains; and Hemacandra (12th cent. CE) incl.

among encyclopedic writings works on philosophy, ethics and politics. The Jain philosophers engaged in vigorous disputation with members of other schools, e.g. producing arguments against existence of a personal God (→ Indian arguments about existence of God, p. 305). N.S.

J. Jaini, *Outlines of Jainism* (1940); C. L. Jain, *Jaina Bibliography* (1945); S. Mookerjee, *The Jaina Philosophy of Non-Absolutism* (1944); Dale Riepe, *The Naturalistic Tradition in Indian Thought* (1960).

Philosophy of Religion Definition of P.-R., like that of Philosophy, is difficult if not indeed impossible. Many will feel that most import. lesson to be learned in Philosophy is that clarity is not a simple matter of definition. For this reason we shall do well to begin by noting changes in relations of Philosophy and Theology in the 20th cent. In early years of cent. they were very closely related; the theologian and philosopher preached, as it were, from the same pulpit. The typical attitude of idealist philosophy —which was dominant philosophy of period—is that Philosophy and Theology come to same conclusion about world, namely that reality is spiritual. The realism of Russell and Moore was a reaction against idealism and brought with it a more restricted view of nature of Philosophy. Against idealist speculation the realists argued that Philosophy was more analytical in its method and nearer to common-sense in its standpoint. The extreme of this empiricism was the → Logical Positivism movement which, though it gained few adherents in Britain, was nevertheless very influential. For Logical Positivists theological assertions, like moral assertions, were nonsense. Neither type of assertion was properly a statement, inasmuch as neither stated any verifiable facts, and could therefore have no meaning. So relations of Philosophy to Theology became rather distant in the 1930–40's. Nor were matters much improved by the newer manifestation of empiricist influence—linguistic analysis. It was not until the 1950's that linguistic analysis became an accepted feature of P.-R.; for it was not at first appreciated that this methodology did not imply any rigid theory of meaning like that of Logical Positivists. The linguistic philosopher asked what the functions of theological statements were or what jobs they did. This meant that questions of the meaningfulness of relig. language was not prejudged. This is when a new era began in P.-R., an era in which there could be co-operation between Philosophy and Theology without misleading assumption about the identity of their aims. In different ways both disciplines had undergone changes, and these are reflected in our new understanding of P.-R.

The philosopher of relig. nowadays recognises his task is primarily a critical rather than a creative one. The old method of philosophising led to a more ambitious estimate of P.-R. It set out to furnish proofs—i.e., to prove theological conclusions from non-theological premisses. There are two reasons why this is no longer the way we set about P.-R., both of which could be expressed by saying that the old method presupposed a view of philosophy which has now become old-fashioned. Since some people do not take any kind of fashion seriously, it will be as well to make the two points in a more direct fashion. The first is that, as mentioned above, philosophy is now regarded as essentially a subject which has no direct relation with things, so that the language of philosophy is second-order rather than first-order. This means that, just as the material world is not the direct concern of the philosopher ('Do I see two lamps or one'? can be either a matter of investigation [science] or a matter of reflection [philosophy]), so God is not the philosopher's direct concern. Perhaps both philosopher and theologian now see that theology does not result from metaphysical inquiry, but from direct relations of the relig. man with God. Thus in recent years the theologian has often insisted that theological thinking is an ecclesiastical undertaking, thinking done in and for the community brought into being by the revelation of God. There may have been some philosophers who have lost faith in theology because they looked to philosophy to provide them with some independent way of attaining relig. truths; but philosophy is not another way of learning what revelation teaches us. Its business is to deal with what we may broadly class as logical questions in regard to relig. beliefs; in this sense of the word we can discern a widening of the scope of logic to incl. study of forms of language. So philosophy is spoken of as a linguistic study—this is where it begins, because concepts cannot be studied, described, or criticised except with ref. to the concrete situation in which they are tested. To call philosophy a linguistic study can be very misleading; but it is less misleading to start from such a description than to begin, as some theologians do, by describing philosophy as a study of reality. The philosopher of religion studies relig. language with a view to placing it on the map of language. His first task is that of describing, as carefully and exhaustively as he can, the various forms of relig. discourse so as to bring out their likeness to, and their difference from, other forms of discourse.

This understanding of task of philosophising about theology is less ambitious than the old method, which was an endeavour to prove the truth of theology. This meant that theological conclusions were proved from non-theological premisses; for without such a ref. to an independent source there would be no proof. The abandonment of this method is due to our realisation that in philosophy we do not prove anything. This was put trenchantly by F. Waismann in his paper 'How I see Philosophy': 'No philosopher has ever proved anything. The whole claim is spurious. What I have to say is simply this. Philosophic arguments are not deductive; therefore they are not rigorous; and therefore they don't prove anything. Yet they have force'. ('How I see Philosophy', *Contemporary British Philosophy*). As Waismann went on to say, the difference between logic and philosophy was that philosophy did less and more than logic. It did less than logic because it never establishes anything conclusively; and more, in that, if successful, it effects a change in our whole mental outlook. To call philosophical arguments proofs would be to confuse them with formally valid ones. Such a confusion might lead to an attempt to apply to former the criteria for evaluating latter, and this could only result in rejection of all poss. philosophical arguments as invalid. This would surely be to miss the point of philosophical arguments. Or, again, this confusion of philosophical arguments with logical ones might lead someone to 'tidy up' philosophy and present it as a 'respectable' study by attempting to force philosophical arguments into the deductive mould, in this way making philosophy a formal science. In this case philosophy would have won respectability at cost of becoming an irrelevant game. It is worth stressing that there is one respect in which philosophical arguments are like logical ones: despite fact that they are not rigorous, they have force. They are not compelling, but they do have a bearing on conviction. But, in saying this, we must be clear that the way in which they bear on conviction is often like the way in which poetry bears on our convictions. The philosopher is a strange animal—often he seems to be something like a scientist, often like a logician, and often like a poet. It is where analysis grows into proof, and proof becomes a matter of vision, that philosophy appears. One other point must be mentioned about the old notion of task of P.-R. By seeking to prove the theological position from non-theological premisses, it denies that there is ultimately any difference between theological and non-theological language. This is quite contrary to view that is implied by use of principle that every area of language has its own logic, and that the justification of any proposition has to be done from within its own area. This is the kind of anti-reductionist attitude that has characterised not only moral philosophy (e.g. formulations of the naturalistic fallacy), but even more obviously epistemological theories of perception (the rejection of phenomenalism).

Once again, we are brought back to point that the philosophical theologian (or philosopher of religion) will concern himself with exam. of the many and varied forms of relig. discourse. The first thing that this involves is the classification of different types of language and meaning that appear in religion. Thus, within Christianity, the language of liturgical prayer is not the same as language of Creeds; nor again is language of Creeds the same as language of pulpit. Those parts of the Gospels which seem to have no other function than that of telling a story are to be distinguished from those parts that express the author's faith in Christ. There are thus both descriptive and nondescriptive forms of discourse in the Gospels. Again, the descriptive statements are not homogeneous, because there are historically descriptive statements and non-historical descriptions. In the Fourth Gospel there is a fusion of languages of poetry, of mysticism, of metaphysics, and of history. The philosopher of religion will be concerned to show the logic of such biblical language. In doing this, he resists temptation to proceed as the philosopher usually does, by taking specimen sentences from the language that he investigates, isolating them, and then offering an analysis of them. Otherwise, like so much recent P.-R. we shall be concerned with such bizarre samples of relig. language as 'God exists'. If we are appealing to ordinary language in our exam. of theology, the ordinary language to which we must appeal is biblical language. In philosophising about theology, we are dealing with language about the self-revealing God, and this means that we are dealing with the belief that God has spoken. In so far as the Bible expresses this conviction, and is for all Christians in some sense an authority, it is to the language of Bible that we should turn to find typical use of talk about God and Christ. One reason why analytic philosophers have concerned themselves only with general question of meaningfulness and character of relig. language is that this fundamental notion of revelation in theology brings us into collision with the radical empiricism which has been the attitude characteristic of analytic philosophy. It cannot be anything to do with fact that such philosophy is analytic; for theology is also in many ways a matter of analysis. The cause lies in belief that revelation cannot be called knowledge. It is argued that if anything can be said, then it can be said clearly, and whatever cannot be said clearly cannot be meaningful. So philosophy is described as the dissolution of problems engendered by nuclear language, and the solution of problems which can be clearly stated. But, as G. Marcel has said, a problem is not the same thing as a mystery (*Being and Having*, E.T. 1951, pp. 100–1, 117). A problem is something which can be solved and which ceases to be a mystery for me when I have solved it. Mystery is something fundamentally different. It remains mysterious even when understood, because understanding here is understanding of what is beyond our comprehension. It is the linguistic philosopher's faith that there is no unfathomable mystery that has led him to turn his back on the language of faith as revealed in the Bible. Thus, despite denials of metaphysics, the metaphysical position determining the philosopher's attitude is revealed. This is where P.-R. is involved in the metaphysical debate; for this metaphysics, which had proved destructive of relig. belief, can be countered only by a different metaphysics.

Clearly we cannot accept the criticism that there is no such thing as P.-R., but it is worth considering the criticism for a moment. It is not a clear position, and most often the kind of attitude it expresses is that which regards Philosophy and Theology as entirely unrelated disciplines. There have not been wanting in the hist. of thought expressions of the view classically expressed by Tertullian in his *De Praescriptione Haereticorum*, ch. 7—'What is there in common between Athens and Jerusalem? What between the Academy and the Church? . . . Away with all projects for a "Stoic", a "Platonic" or a "dialectic" Christianity! After Christ Jesus we desire no subtle theories, no acute enquiries after the gospel.' We have seen that there is no sense in which we can put the question of the relation between Philosophy and Theology as a choice between them. The philosopher must be concerned with the language of religion, just as much as the theologian must concern himself continually with philosophical questions. The import. of a philosophical style or attitude for a theologian is very clear in the case of Karl → Barth, whose early develop. owes much to his struggle with Idealism. P.-R. is as much a part of Philosophy as the Philosophy of Science and the Philosophy of Morals. The claim that there is no such thing as P.-R. can only be made by philosophers, if they forget this. Equally the claim can only be supported by theologians who succumb to temptation to think of Philosophy as some entity outside the Church, and Theology as some purely domestic entity within Church. Tracing the influence of great metaphysical systems on develop. of relig. doctrine is itself part of task of the philosopher of religion. Christianity, to take but one example, has a most interesting history of developing doctrine precisely because of the trad. of Christian Philosophy. Not only is it true, as → Whitehead said, that it is a religion perennially in search of a metaphysic, but it is also a religion perennially coming to terms with different metaphysics.

The question of truth or falsity of relig. belief is tied up with adoption of metaphysical positions. Therefore, merely describing various forms of relig. language, and showing their natural habitat, does not exhaust P.-R. This could not be true in any case, since to show the logic of relig. language will involve showing not only its domestic logic but also its foreign logic. That is, we need to ask how this language is related to other languages. We must show the connection between statements of faith and those of history, science and common-sense. It is obvious that, with some very few exceptions, there are no relig. words. Relig. language is ordinary language used religiously. The philosopher must ask whether this is a valid use. Furthermore, useful though the concept of 'game' is in elucidating language, we cannot say that relig. language is a mere game. We must ask whether the statements the relig. man makes are true or false. In describing the various forms of Christ. language, for instance, we must distinguish between those sentences which are statements of fact and those which are not assertions at all. There are so many examples of latter in Christ. language that we must distinguish several sub-species of them, and this is why it is pointless to characterise relig. language as emotive language. There are exclamations, petitions, thanksgiving, and vows to be found in the broad class of liturgical language; the Bible is also rich in examples of precepts, exhortations, promises, and aspirations. But, ultimately, the interest of these forms of language derives from the meaningfulness and truth of assertions in relig. language. Many import. things can be said about religion which are interesting even if religion is not true; but, in the end, we take religion seriously because we are convinced of its truth. Religion is very much a matter of belief, and the relig. man is not content with meaningful statements but only with what is true. In various ways the question of truth poses a task that the modern philosopher of religion tends to avoid. Nevertheless, this is a question which not only the very nature of Philosophy but even intellectual integrity demands that we should answer. Professor John E. Smith has pointed out how in this way P.-R. is advantageous to both Philosophy and Theology. 'On the one hand', he says, 'religion and theology must not be kept in a separate compartment safe from all criticism at the hands of philosophy, and, on the other, philosophy must not attempt to shield itself from dealing with those difficult questions about the nature of things and the status of man in reality that have ever been the concern of religious faith' (*Philosophy of Religion*, p. 25).

One of the ways in which P.-R. in past sought to fulfil this responsibility of pronouncing on truth of relig. belief was the develop. of a natural theology. The first natural theologian was probably → Plato, Book Ten of whose *Laws* deals with problem of the rational bases of theology. The term was invented by Varro, but its modern use derives from Raymond de Sébonde. Great care is needed in use of this term 'natural theology', as it is not obvious what contrast we wish thus to make. In 20th cent. natural theology has been the object of Karl → Barth's blistering attack. Partly because of this and partly because of philosophical scepticism as to possibility of any such enterprise, natural theology has become the 'sick man of Europe', and many theologians and philosophers would be quite happy to see it die. However, we ought to ask whether it is as theologically reprehensible and philosophically indefensible as it is assumed to be. The difficulty is that in past natural theology has been understood as a rational preface to docs. which are otherwise known. This model of the two roads is clearly indefensible; and it does not require any great subtlety to see that this does not so much answer as raise the problem of knowing God. Even if we abandon this fallacious model of a road going only so far, and then a new road taking us on from there, we still have to face problem of how we start on this quest. The special task of a natural theology is to show the grounds for the Christ. (or Buddh. or Hindu) picture of the world, and this is not a simple matter of proving the existence of God.

The mention of natural theology and proofs of existence of God lead to what is perhaps the main problem of P.-R.—what do we mean by the idea of God? The discussion of the proofs of God's existence will always be an essential part of P.-R. For it is by no means obvious why the existence of God cannot be proved. The theistic arguments can be classified as belonging to one of two types—the *a priori* and the *a posteriori*. An *a priori* argument moves from considerations, whose truth is independent of or logically prior to experience—i.e., it is a purely logical proof. As *a posteriori* argument is one whose premiss or premisses are known to be true only by experience. The only *a priori* argument is the Ontological Argument, which has been formulated in different ways by → Anselm (who was its first formulator) Descartes and the Idealists. The most subtle formulation was that of St. Anselm, who in the second chapter of his *Proslogion* defines God as 'that than which a greater cannot be conceived', and then argues that this entails that God exists. His argument is that, if God exists only in thought, we can imagine an existing God, and this would be a greater. This situation cannot exist, and so God must exist. Ever since → Kant, the argument has usually been dismissed because it is alleged that it fallaciously regards existence as a predicate. Recently, however, there has been considerable debate about it, and it has been vigorously defended by Charles Hartshorne in his *Logic of Perfection* and *Anselm's Discovery*. The other two arguments—the Cosmological and the Teleological—are *a posteriori* arguments. The former argues from the contingency of things in world to the necessary existence of God or, as it is sometimes put, to the existence of a First Cause. Various fallacies are involved here (and once again Kant is the most import. critic), the main one being that the sense in which things are contingent—a term more properly used of propositions—does not imply that there must be a necessary existence and that, once started on a causal regress, we cannot stop at a *First* Cause. The Teleological Argument argues from evidence of design to existence of a Designer. This is the most empirical of the arguments, and so the most vulnerable. The most telling criticism was that of Hume—which was that the argument was not properly an analogical argument because it dealt with the unique case of the world. The detailed analysis of the three classical theistic arguments, and others such as the various forms of the Moral Argument, will show that between these arguments and the conclusion there is, as → Kierkegaard put it, a leap. So the arguments cannot be regarded as coercive logical demonstrations; but they do show the kinds of considerations that lead one to believe. Also they reveal what kind of concept is that of the God in whom we believe. If this is the case, then to make relig. belief identical with proof is misleading, despite the fact that the proofs do articulate an ontological insight which is at the root of relig. commitment.

One of the results of an analysis of theistic proofs is the clarification of idea of God. The task of characterising God is one of the most difficult in Theology, and this part of theological language presents any philosopher of relig. with one of the most complicated of his problems. If the predicates used of God are true, then there must be some empirical anchorage for such descriptions. But it is clear that the empirical anchorage for such descriptions does not offer a straightforward test of these descriptions. In a word, we have the old problem of analogy. Acc. to the classical doc. of → analogy, no statement concerning God, with the exception of negative statements, is literally true. Yet these statements do not reveal an ambiguous use of their terms, and so we may say that we predicate these concepts of God analogically. All statements concerning God must make use of language which in the first instance is used to describe the world, and so all descriptions of God are analogical. If we use such analogical language successfully of God, this means that we are able to indicate quite clearly that the language is no longer to be understood in its primary sense. That is to say, the way of analogy presupposes the way of negation, and so relig. language always moves back and forth between affirmation and negation. And here we see, not only how every concept which we may want to use to describe God has to be balanced by another concept which has a different, perhaps even a contrasting, emphasis; but also the way in which theology is very much like metaphysics, which also has its paradoxes and negative concepts. It is easy to see from hist. of theology how it has absorbed into itself from time to time certain metaphysical notions such as the absolute, being, and nonbeing. This kind of borrowing, however, is always done to further a theological purpose. The fascinating plundering of metaphysical treasures has tended to make theologians blind to the very different purpose to which these concepts were then put. By the analysis and criticism of the whole range of predicates, P.-R. systematically studies the complex of beliefs which is the theology of whatever faith we are examining, and in the same way it discusses the relation of these doctrines to the information given by the sciences and the visions expressed by the artists. J.H.-T.

A. G. N. Flew–A. MacIntyre, *New Essays in Philosophical Theology* (1955); J. Hick, *Philosophy of Religion* (1963); H. D. Lewis, *Philosophy of Religion* (1965); T. H. McPherson, *Philosophy of Religion* (1965); Basil Mitchell, *Faith and Logic* (1957); N. Smart, *Reasons and Faiths* (1958), *Historical Selections in the Philosophy of Religion* (1962); F. R. Tennant, *Philosophical Theology*, 2 vols. (1937).

Phoenician Religion The Phoenicians were Canaanites inhabiting certain cities of Syria (most notably Tyre, Sidon, and Byblos). Hence their relig. was basically → Canaanite relig. The chief god of Tyre, the leading city, was → Melqart; Sidon's god was → Eshmun. P.-R. was spread by colonisation: → Carthaginian Relig. (→→ Astarte; Dagon; Moloch; Ugarit). S.G.F.B.

D. Harden, *The Phoenicians* (1962), ch. 7; Dussaud, *Les religions*, livre II; G. Contenau, *La civilisation phénicienne* (1949), chs. 2 and 4; *E.R.E.*, IX, pp. 887–97 (pre-Ugaritic evidence); Clemen, *P.R.*

Phongyi-Chaung Burmese name for a Buddh. monastery (*Phongyi* = monk; *chaung* = house or building). (→ Monasteries, Buddhist). T.O.L.

Phylacteries Jew. amulets (Heb. *tephillin*), comprising small leather cases, attached by straps to forehead and left forearm by male Jews at weekday divine service. Each case contains pieces of parchment on which are written the passages: Ex. 13:1–10, 13:11–6; Deut. 6:4–9, 11:13–21, each of which contains relevant injunction for the custom. Reform → Judaism has dropped use of wearing them. S.G.F.B.

E.J.R., p. 380; *H.D.B.*[2], p. 770 Y. Yadin, *Tefillin from Qumran* (1969).

Pilgrimage A relig. custom that is both anc. and widespread. P. involves three factors: a holy place; attraction of individuals or crowds to this place; a specific aim, i.e. to obtain some spiritual or material benefit. The custom of P. was known in anc. Egypt; e.g. to tomb of → Osiris at Abydos. P. occur in all the major religs.: in → Islam, P. to Mecca is a relig. duty, and is highly organised. Jews made P. to Jerusalem → Temple until its destruc. in 70 CE; the 'Wailing Wall', a portion of substructure of Temple area later became place of P. P. was often imposed as penance in medieval Christianity. Places of P. are various: tombs of holy personages (e.g. Holy Sepulchre, Jerusalem, tomb of St. Thomas Becket, Canterbury); location of a holy object or relic (e.g. → Ka'ba at Mecca; relics of Cosmic → Egg at Hermopolis; tooth of → Buddha at Candy); places connected with miraculous healing (e.g. Epidauros, Lourdes). Besides hope of spiritual benefits or healing, P. often held social attractions, as is evident from Chaucer's *Canterbury Tales*; they gen. brought material advantages to places concerned. P.-shrines became rich with offerings of pilgrims, and economic benefits extended to many persons, e.g., makers of silver-shrines for Artemis of Ephesus (Acts 19:23f.). Chr. pilgrims wore distinctive dress or sign. S.G.F.B.

E.R.E., X, pp. 10–28; *S.O.*, IV (1960), *'Les Pèlerinages'; D.C.C., s.v.; R.G.G.*[3], VI, col. 1537–42; V. and H. Hell, *The Great Pilgrimages of the Middle Ages* (1966); *E.J.R.*, pp. 302, 402.

(China) Earliest known centres of P. in anc. China were the 5 sacred mountains: T'ai-shan in Shantung; Hua-shan in Shensi; Hêng-shan in Shansi; Nan-yu-shan in Hunan; and Sung-shan in Honan. Both → Taoism and → Buddhism built monasteries and temples on these mountains, which grad. became enormously popular centres of P., attracting hosts of pilgrims from far and wide. In add., Buddhism succeeded in creating great new centres of P.: monasteries and temples dedicated to honour of powerful and miracle-working Buddhas and → bodhisattvas. Particularly famous are P'u-t'o-shan, an island off the coast of Ningpo; Chiu-hua-shan in Anhwei; Wu-t'ai-shan in Shansi and O-mei-shan in

Szechuan. Besides these, there are enormous number of holy places which attract thousands of P. every year. As a rule, it is special circumstances, such as sickness, poor harvests, failing business, etc., which send men on P. But grievous sins, which brought calamity to a home, may be atoned for by P. Often P. are undertaken as a result of vows being made. Occasionally they grow out of real relig. need and spiritual aspiration.

The usual season for P. is autumn. After suitable acts of worship, and choosing of a lucky day by divination, the pilgrims of a neighbourhood will set out together under a chosen leader. They wear special clothing, with red or yellow waistcoat, red being worn by those who are going to expiate sins. The pilgrims, carrying bowls with sticks of incense, move forward in groups of 10–50 in silent meditation, except when leader calls for prayer. They eat only vegetarian food, and mark their long and arduous journey by many penances. On arrival at destination, having bathed and purified themselves, they proceed to main temple hall for worship. On return the same rules, acts of worship and asceticism are observed until they arrive home.

From CE 4th cent. onwards, it became common for Chi. Buddh. monks to travel westward on pilgrimages to India and other Buddh. countries, some even reaching as far as Ceylon. The purpose was to study at fountain-head of Buddh. learning, to bring back sacred scriptures and Buddh. relics. Among most famous Chi. pilgrims are → Fa Hsien (*c.* 399); Sung Yün (518); I Ch'ing (634–713) and → Hsüan-tsang (629–45). The P. of these men had a profound influence on development of Buddhism in China.

It has also been customary for hundreds of Chi. Muslims every year to make the P. to → Mecca, and also to other sacred Muslim shrines such as tomb of the Prophet's uncle at Canton. D.H.S.

K. L. Reichelt, *Truth and Tradition in Chinese Buddhism* (1927), *passim*, *Religion in Chinese Garment* (1951), *passim* (espec. ch. 9); H. Welch, *The Practice of Chinese Buddhism* (1967), pp. 305–10, 370–5; K. Schipper, 'Les pèlerinages en Chine: montagnes et pistes', *S.O.*, III (1960).

(Hindu) The practice of P. was already well developed by period of classical Hinduism. With Aryanisation of whole of sub-continent and construction of Hindu temples, the number of places to visit multiplied; by medieval period it was common for pilgrims to travel great distances—e.g. to Cape Comorin in south, to Orissa in east, to Kathiawar in west and to the Himalayas, which had over long period developed special sanctity, as being most auspicious region for retreats and → ashrams of holy men, etc. The trad. of wandering mendicants (*sadhus*, → *sannyasis*) may have been import. factor in encouraging lay pilgrimages also, and certainly helped in transmission of relig. ideas from one part of country to another. Early Hindu temples developed rest houses for travellers and provisions for feeding pilgrims. The larger centres, such as → Banaras and Puri, have developed commercially as consequence of regular influx of pilgrims. As well as sacred cities, large temples and hermitages, rivers and esp. junctions of rivers, are import. places to visit, and it is esp. auspicious to bathe in sacred waters at certain times. Thus practice of P. is coordinated with complex system of → festivals, such as the *kumbha mela* at Prayaga (Allahabad), when millions of pilgrims may congregate. Even lesser festivals or times of auspicious bathing, etc., will attract large numbers in big centres: an influx of 200,000 is not unusual at Banaras. Apart from bathing, a common rite is circumambulation of sacred object or shrine; and this can extend to wide circuit of whole sacred area, such as the holy road circling Banaras—the so called *Panchkosī*, which has about 600 shrines to visit, and extending some 50 miles. Since P.s bring merit or wipe out sins, they are also occasion for special austerities. It has been characteristic of more import. relig. teachers in Hindu trad., such as →→ Śankara, Ramanuja, Vallabha, Ramakrishna, etc., to travel extensively to holy places; in medieval period this was not merely a means of diffusing new docs., but occasion for learned disputation with philosophers and theologians in import. centres (since holy places and large temples tended to attract scholars—some centres turning in effect into university towns, such as Banaras). N.S.

H. Bhattacharyya (ed.), *The Cultural Heritage of India*, vol. 4 (1956); C. H. Buck, *Faiths, Fairs and Festivals of India* (1917); C. Jacques, 'Les pèlerinages en Inde', *S.O.*, III (1960).

(Islam) The rites performed in Mecca are known as the '*umra* (lesser P.), and may be performed at any time. The *ḥajj*, which is the P. prescribed as a duty to be performed once in a lifetime by those who are adult, sane, in good health, and have sufficient means to perform the journey and to support the family during their absence, can be performed only on specified days in Dhul Ḥijja, the last month of the Muslim year. In pre-Islamic times the '*umra* appears to have been a purely Meccan ceremony observed by → Quraysh, but the *ḥajj*, which is fundamentally to places outside Mecca, was attended by Arabs from all parts of the Hijaz and from farther afield. Fairs were held during preceding month at 'Ukāẓ and Majanna, and during the first eight days of Dhul Hijja at Dhul Majāz. Arms were deposited with a member of Quraysh (→ Months, sacred . . .), and the Quraysh merchants of

Mecca found markets of value to their trade.
When visiting Mecca an *'umra* should be observed, no matter what the purpose of the visit or time of year. An *'umra* is also observed preparatory to the *ḥajj*. The pilgrim must don the → *iḥrām* at one of the appointed stations outside Mecca, and repeat often throughout the P. the cry, 'At thy service, O God, at thy service, at thy service. Thine are the praise, the grace and the kingdom. Thou hast no partner.' The *'umra* consists of rites at and near the → Ka'ba. After ablution and expression of intention, the pilgrim circles the Ka'ba (the *ṭawāf*) seven times, counting from opposite the → Black Stone, which should traditionally be touched or kissed; but when crowd is too large for one to get near, a wave towards it suffices. The circuits are made counter clockwise, three at quick pace, then four at slower one. The pilgrim then goes to certain spots for prayers, after which he goes out to run between the hillocks al-Ṣafā and al-Marwa (the *sa'y*) seven times. This is held to repres. Hagar's searching for water. The *iḥram* may then be removed. Certain Qur. verses and prayers should be recited at special places during rites. As pilgrims cannot be familiar with all the prayers, suitable guides are appointed to direct and lead their devotions; but if one cannot hear, it is allowable to pray what one chooses in one's own language.

On the 7th of Dhul Ḥijja a sermon is preached about the *ḥajj*; on the 8th the pilgrims go to Minā, to E. of Mecca, and spend the night in the valley. Next day, or during night if it is in the hot season, they go to → 'Arafat about 13 miles from Mecca. There they stand on or around a hill from after midday till sunset. This standing (the *wuqūf*) is supreme act of the P. Whether or not one is able to hear the sermon which is preached, the standing is essential. Trad. says the greatest sinner is the one who stands at 'Arafat and thinks his sins have not been forgiven. Without the *wuqūf* no P. is complete. After sunset pilgrims stampede to Muzdalifa (the *ifāda*, or *nafra*) where they pray the sunset and night prayers, then search for pebbles to take to Minā. In the valley of Mina there are three pillars (*jamras*) said to repres. devil who is reputed to have tempted → Ishmael three times to run away when → Abraham intended to sacrifice him. Seven stones are thrown at each *jamras* on three days. Then an animal should be sacrificed (→ *'Id al-aḍḥā*), after which the pilgrim has his hair cut. Men commonly have the head shaved, but women have only a few hairs clipped. Now the pilgrim changes to ordinary clothing; but the restrictions of the *iḥram* remain till another series of circuits of the Ka'ba is made. A visit for purpose may be made on any of the three days at Mina. Finally, before leaving Mecca, a farewell circuit of the Ka'ba is made, after which one should drink some → Zamzam water, a practice also followed during the *'umra.*

The rites have been taken over from pre-Islamic practice and purified. Idols were destroyed, and performing the *ṭawāf* naked was forbidden. Many rites are by Muslim trad. assoc. with Abraham, whatever their orig. significance may have been. Women may attend the P., but must be accompanied by husband, or a male relative. For their *iḥrām*, → *iḥrām*. If they have their courses while in *iḥrām*, they may not perform *ṭawāf* or say the daily prayers till purified, but they may repeat other prayers which do not involve prostration. They may attend the *ḥajj* ceremonies outside Mecca and perform the *'umra* when purified.

It is allowable for one who is not able to perform the P., although he possesses the means, to appoint another to perform it in his name. He must pay all expenses of his substitute, but the substitute acquires no merit for himself. One who has performed the P. acquires the title of *ḥājjī* (or *ḥājj*). J.R.

E.I., III, pp. 31–8; *Mishkāt*, pp. 535ff.; Kamal, *Sacred Journey*; Burton, *Pilgrimage*, appendix, I; Rutter, *Holy Cities*, I, pp. 104ff.; Querry, I, pp. 216ff.; Wellhausen, *Reste*, pp. 68ff.; Gaudefroy-Demombynes, *Institutions*, pp. 81ff., *Le Pèlerinage à la Mecque* (1923); Levy, *Social Structure*, pp. 161f.; F. Rosenthal, *Ibn Khaldun*, index; *M.W.*, XLV (1955), 'Pilgrimage prayers', 269ff., LIII (1963), 'Speech by King Su'ud and Conference', pp. 74–6.

(Japan) The mountains of Japan are the homes of gods, and over the cents. scores of mountain shrines have become centres of P. Relig. P. began with consecration of many mountain peaks as places of Buddh. worship in CE 8th cent. During 9th and 10th cents., definite series of pilgrim itineraries were estab. From 15th cent., P.s to 33 sanctuaries of → Kwan-On were undertaken by P. bands, wearing white robes, on which they received stamps of various sanctuaries, chanting hymns, performing penances and subsisting on alms. Some of these mountain-P. were in nature of initiatory ceremonies for young people entering on adult life; the P.s being guided and directed by trained leaders. Besides great mountain peaks, there were several purely Buddh. or → Shinto centres of pilgrimage, as e.g. the temple at Ise dedicated to the supreme Deity of Shinto. To this centre almost all Japanese aspired to go at least once in a lifetime. The habit of making P. to far distant shrines, led to formation of clubs, in which contributions were made monthly to a P. fund, those going each year on P. being chosen by lot, with a member acting as leader.

In mod. times the mountain-P. have taken on more and more a festive and holiday nature, the relig. aspect being less emphasised than formerly. D.H.S.

E.R.E., X, pp. 27–8; W. G. Aston, *Shinto* (1905), pp. 237–8; M. Anesaki, *Hist. of Japanese Religion* (1930), *passim*; C. Blacker, 'Initiation in the Shugendo', in *Initiation* (1965), pp. 96ff.; S. Usaku, 'Les pèlerinages au Japon', *S.O.*, III (1960).

Pi-hsia Yüan-chun → Taoist goddess, the Princess of the Motley Clouds. Known and worshipped throughout China under many names: T'ien Hsien, the Heavenly Immortal; Niang-niang-Sung-tzǔ, the Lady who brings children; Shêng Mu, the Holy Mother; Yü Nü, the Jade Maiden; T'ai-shan Niang-niang, the Lady of Mt. Tai etc. She is often repr. as daughter of God of the Eastern Peak. Her cult can be traced back as far as the Han Dynasty. She is honoured as protectress of women and children, giver of children who presides over childbirth. She is also patron of foxes. She is usually depicted accompanied by two assistants, and attended by train of lesser divinities. D.H.S.

E. T. C. Werner, *Dictionary of Chinese Mythology* (1932); H. Maspero, 'The Mythology of Modern China', in J. Hackin (ed.), *Asiatic Mythology* (1932, repr. 1963).

Pillars of Practical Religion (*Arkān al-Islām*). They are the five duties: profession of faith (*shahāda*), 'There is no deity but God; Muhammad is God's messenger'; prayer, or worship (*ṣalāt*); legal alms (*zakāt*); fasting (*ṣawm*); pilgrimage to Mecca and neighbouring sites. Some have added *jihād*. See entries under each item. J.R.

Pillar Saints Designation for type of Christ. ascetic who lived on top of a pillar; they are known also as *Stylites* from the Grk. word *stulos*, 'pillar' (but not to be confused with the 'pillar' (*stuloi*) apostles of → Jerusalem Church to whom → Paul ref. (*Gal.* ii:9). The first of the P.S. seems to have been St. Simeon Stylites (*c.* 390–459), who lived major part of life on pillar (grad. increasing height), near Antioch (Syria). He attracted crowds of pilgrims and had many imitators in Syria, Mesopot., Egypt and Greece. The practice continued until 10th cent. This form of austerity may be comp. with those of Hindu ascetics (→ Asceticism, Hindu). Poss. pillars were chosen as providing station between heaven and earth. S.G.F.B.

D.C.C., pp. 1257, 1299; *R.G.G.*³, IV, col. 1076.

Pious Foundations (Islam) (*Awqāf*, pl. of *waqf*). These are properly real estate given as endowment, the usufruct of which is used for specific lawful purpose. The owner must be in his right mind, free, and have right of disposal. P.F. may be of public or private nature, devoted to such purposes as mosques, schools, public works, or for people in need. They require administrators who are paid a salary. The first is appointed by donor of endowment, and, except among the Mālikīs (→ Muslim Law), he may appoint himself. The → *qāḍī* has right of supervision, and appoints or dismisses administrators. Acc. to the → *sharīʿa*, such property may not be sold; in Egypt in mod. times P.F. have come under political control. In Morocco the term *ḥubus* or *ḥubs* is used. In 1342/1924 a law in Turkey abolished the Evkaf Ministry and transferred its affairs to a directory subordinate to premier. J.R.

E.I., IV, pp. 1096–103; Hughes, p. 664; Querry, I, pp. 575ff.; Pareja, index (*waqf*); Levy, *Social Structure*, index (*awqāf*).

Pirque Aboth Heb. = 'Chapters of the Fathers'. Collection of sayings of sixty Jew. sages concerning life as evaluated by Rabbinic piety. The work, dating *c.* CE 70–170, is highly varied and is incl. in → Mishnah. (→ Judaism). S.G.F.B.

H. Danby, *The Mishnah* (1933); C. Taylor, *The Sayings of the Jewish Fathers* (1900²); Oesterley-Box, *L.R.M.J.*, pp. 91ff.; *E.J.R.*, *s.v.* 'Avot'.

Piśāca Anc. Indian term for a spirit-being, or demon—since the P. are usually regarded as evil, or hostile to men. As such they are mentioned in Buddh. Pali Canon at various places, in connection with contemporary popular beliefs. As with → *yakkhas*, it is poss. that belief in P. has origin in idea of 'man-eating demons', i.e. cannibals, in certain parts of India. A tribe bearing name P., among whom cannibalism was practised, is known to have existed in N.W. India; the tribe, on account of its cannibalism, may however have derived its name from that of the demons, if this was already current. T.O.L.

G. Grierson, 'Pisaca = Homophagoi', *J.R.A.S.* (1905).

Pistis Sophia Title, misleadingly given by first modern editors, of Coptic MS. containing text of two works of Gnostic origin, *c.* 3rd cent. CE. The 1st work concerns revelation allegedly made by Jesus to disciples 12 yrs. after Resurrection, about fate of the → aeon Pistis Sophia, and questions asked by disciples, preeminently by Mary Magdalene, of Jesus and his answers. The 2nd work has form of post-Resurrection prophecy of Jesus about punishment of sinners after death. The → Gnosticism revealed is of popular kind. The → Nag Hammadi writings help to elucidate background of P.-S. S.G.F.B.

E.R.E., X, *s.v.*; *R.G.G.*, V, col. 386–8; J. Doresse, *The Secret Books of the Egyptian Gnostics* (E.T. 1960), pp. 64ff. E.T. by G. Horner (1924).

Plato (427–347 BC) One of the greatest names in hist. of philosophy, P. has also great importance for hist. of relig. It is succinctly expressed in the advice given by Socrates (it is difficult to distinguish here Plato's views from those of his master): 'to take care of the soul' (*epimeleisthai tēs psychēs*). P.'s tractate *Phaedo* is devoted to proving the → soul's intrinsic immortality. In the *Phaedrus* a complete doc. of → Man is attempted, which reflects → Orphic influence. A primordial state is envisaged in which souls, by nature divine and immortal, cannot all maintain their orig. elevation, and sink down to find solid resting places in material bodies. From this results → metempsychosis in both human and animal bodies, which causes contamination of soul, which has to be expiated. This situation will be understood by the wise man (philosopher), who will also know how to free his soul from such a fate and restore it to its former state. P.'s theory of Ideas as the perfect essential Forms of reality, of which this phenomenal world is the imperfect reflection, was an inspiring interpretation. Thus God was conceived in noble and pregnant imagery as the Form of the Good. P.'s philosophy, preserved in a number of attractively presented Dialogues, has exercised a formative influence on much subsequent relig. thought. → Philo was profoundly affected by it, and it provided basis of → Neoplatonism. Christ. theology was largely moulded by thinkers educated in Platonic metaphysics (→→ Clement of Alexandria; Origen, Augustine). P.'s influence continued through Middle Ages, even though eclipsed for a while by that of → Aristotle. The Renaissance marked revival of interest in P., whose influence was great in 17th cent. Eng. theological thought as existence of the 'Cambridge Platonists' testifies. S.G.F.B.

Texts and trans. of Plato's works are conveniently presented in Loeb Classical Library. *E.R.E.*, X, *s.v.; R.G.G.*³, V, col. 407–15; B. Russell, *Hist. of Western Philosophy* (1946); L. Robin, *La pensée grecque* (1928); E. Caird, *The Evolution of Theology in the Greek Philosophers*, 2 vols. (1904); A.-J. Festugière, *La révélation d'Hermès Trismégiste*, II (1949), III (1953), IV (1954); Harnack, *H.D.*, 7 vols.; G. Leff, *Medieval Thought* (1958); E. R. Dodds, *The Greeks and the Irrational* (1951); E. Wind, *Pagan Mysteries in the Renaissance* (1967).

Plymouth Brethren Chr. relig. body, founded by J. N. Darby, at Plymouth, England, in 1830. Their teaching combines elements of → Calvinism and Pietism, and is much concerned with the Millennium (→ Chiliasm). They have no organised ministry, observe the Breaking of Bread each Sunday as appointed representation of Christ's death, and are conservative in interpret. Bible. Their principle of complete autonomy of each local church has tended to sub-divide the movement. Though numerically weak, the P.-B. exist in many parts of the world and are active in missionary work. S.G.F.B.

E.R.E., II, pp. 843–8; *D.C.C., s.v.; R.G.G.*³, II, col. 40–1 ('Darbysten').

P'o → Hun and P'o. D.H.S.

Poimandres Grk. = 'Shepherd of Men'. Title of 1st book of → Hermetic Lit., and of semi-divine being, under whose guidance the revelation is received. P. is also called 'the Mind of the Sovereignty'. See bibliog. to Hermetic Lit. S.G.F.B.

Polygamy (Islam) Qur. iv:3 allows two, three, or four wives if people are having difficulty in the care of orphans, but only if they are treated equitably; otherwise only one wife is allowed, or such slavewomen as one may possess. Although there is here a qualified recognition of P., it is the exception rather than rule; for most people are unable for economic reasons, if for no other, to maintain more than one wife. But among certain classes there has been throughout the cents. an assumption that a man has right to up to four wives at same time. Some people, however, are now arguing that the Qur. verse really advocates monogamy, because no one can avoid partiality (→ Marriage). In Muslim countries, where education has become more common than formerly, there is feeling in favour of monogamy; it is normal practice. Sometimes a clause is even incorpor. in marriage settlement to effect that husband will not contract second marriage during existence of first. In Pakistan some years ago there was great outcry among women when a minister of state married second wife. In Indonesia there is a gen. feeling among Muslims against P. In Tunisia a law came into effect in 1376/1957 (1st Jan.) abolishing P. (*M.W.*, XLVIII (1958), 263). J.R.

Mishkāt, Book XIII, *passim*; Pareja, pp. 459, 548, 677, 724, 731f.; Hughes, pp. 462–4; Gaudefroy-Demombynes, *Institutions*, p. 130; Levy, *Social Structure*, index; Rahman, *Islam*, p. 38.

Polynesian Religion Polynesia extends from Hawaii in N. to New Zealand in S., and incl. the Samoa, Tonga, Tahiti, Society and Marquesas groups of islands (→ Hawaiian Religion and → Maori Religion are treated separately.) The indigenous relig. of P. is no longer practised, following intensive Christ. missionary work in 19th and 20th cents., though elements survive in folk-lore. P. deities were numerous. The greatest was Tangaroa (Samoa: Tangaloa; Tahiti: Ta'aroa), a → High God assoc. with celestial phenomena, ancestor of all other gods, and origin of everything. One form of P. creation myth tells how Tangaroa emerged from a shell, made earth out of a new shell, and then created gods and spirits; a variant tells of Tangaroa drawing up islands with a fish-hook. Tangaroa appears sometimes to have been regarded as a → *deus otiosus*, unconcerned with his creation (on the Ellice Is. his name might not be spoken, → Yahweh); elsewhere he even degenerated into a sea-god. Other great gods incl.: Tane ('man'), primordial ancestor; Tu, war-god; Rongo, god of peace and plenty; Hiro sun-god; and Hina, moon-goddess. The functions of these gods, who were more import. in mythology than in cult, varied greatly from island to island. Beneath them in rank were the spirits, some of which were deified ancestors (→→ Animism, Ancestor Worship, Melanesian Religion). The relig. practices of P. were twofold: an exoteric form, concerned with spirits, their praise, propitiation and manipulation; an esoteric form, centred on worship of the great gods, the province of priests and aristocracy. This latter form was cultivated in secret societies (*areoi*). A similar dualism was found in beliefs concerning destiny of man after death. The soul of departed was believed to pass to western paradise of the gods only as reward of rank; the common people could look forward to nothing more than a shadowy after-life in *Po* (region above sky and below floor of ocean), followed by ultimate annihilation. In neither case were moral considerations significant. The soul of a chief or other great man might become a lesser god, and receive worship at a cult centre (*marae*), though ancestor worship as such was less prominent than in Melanesia. P. mortuary practices varied greatly, at least among chiefs, though common people practised only simple inhumation; a dead chief might be buried in a canoe or vault, exposed on a tree or platform, or set adrift. Occasionally the head of a chief might be recovered and preserved.

A P. term which has passed into the vocabulary of comp. relig. is → *tabu*, signifying a quality of unapproachability and danger inherent in the sacred (→ Holy); a *tabu* person, object or site might not be approached or touched by anyone who was insufficiently prepared. Thus kings, chiefs and the dead were *tabu*, as were all with whom they came into contact; women were *tabu* during pregnancy and menstruation; sites of ritual activity and known abodes of spirits were *tabu*. A temporary *tabu* might be placed on anything or anyone by a king, chief, priest, medicine-man or other person having sufficient power (→ *Mana*).

Having power over spirits, the P. priest or medicine-man might turn this power to good or evil ends. In former case, he functioned as seer (interpret. → oracles), healer and mediator with spirit-world; he offered → sacrifices on behalf of group or individual to secure co-operation of the spirits. In latter case, he might practice black → magic or sorcery. As sorcerer (*tahutahu*), he worked through his familars (*ti'i*), often using methods of contagious magic, curses and drawing out of soul of his victim. Counter-measures involved many techniques known from → shamanism. E.J.S.

E.R.E., X, pp. 103b–12a; *R.G.G.*³, V, cols. 449–51; R. W. Williamson, *Religious and Cosmic Beliefs of Central Polynesia*, I–II (1933), *Religion and Social Organization in Central Polynesia* (1937); M. Brillant–R. Aigrain (eds.), *Histoire des Religions*, i (n.d.), pp. 285–90.

Polytheism Recognition and worship of many gods. P. has been variously explained: (1) as primitive form of relig. out of which → monotheism evolved: (2) as degeneration from primordial monotheism. Phenomenologically, P. reflects man's experience of universe as manifesting diverse forms of superhuman power. P. is gen. assoc. with primitive forms of culture, but not necessarily so: e.g. → Marcus Aurelius could use both sing. and pl. of *theos* ('god') as synonyms in the same sentence, indic. a conception of deity to which categories of P. and monotheism were irrelevant. S.G.F.B.

*R.G.G.*³, IV, col. 1109–16; G. Vander Leeuw, *La religion* (1948), *passim*; E. O. James, *The Concept of Deity* (1950), pp. 31ff.; A. Brelich, 'Politeismo a Soteriologia', in S. G. F. Brandon (ed.), *The Saviour God* (1963), 'Der Polytheismus', *Numen*, VII (1960).

(China-Far East) Popular relig. in all Far Eastern countries is incurably polytheistic. Though a supreme Deity is usually recognised, he rules over hierarchy of innumerable gods and divine beings, drawn, as case may be, from the mythologies of → Taoism, → Buddhism, → Shinto etc. P. seems to have developed out of the → polydaemonism of a primitive nature-worship. D.H.S.

Pontius Pilate Roman governor of Judaea (CE 26–36), who sentenced → Jesus of Nazareth to death for sedition. An inscription found at Caesarea in 1961 shows that his title was 'Praefectus' of Judaea. The portrait of P. in the → Gospels differs seriously from that given by →→ Philo and Josephus. There is much reason for thinking that both Jew. and Christ. accounts of P. have been distorted by apologetic considerations. P. figured much in Chr. legend. His wife, named Procla, was → canonised in E. Church: P. is a saint and martyr in → Ethiopian Church. S.G.F.B.

S. G. F. Brandon, 'Pontius Pilate in History and Legend', *R.A.H.*, ch. 17, *Jesus and the Zealots* (1967), *The Trial of Jesus* (1968)—with bibliogs.; J. Blinzler, *Der Prozess Jesu* (1969), pp. 260ff.

Poseidon Grk. god of earthquakes and water, esp. sea. Although evidently a native Grk. deity, P.'s orig. is obscure: his most significant titles are *enosichthōn* ('earthshaker') and *gaiēochus* ('possessor of earth'). In Grk. mythology, P. and → Zeus were brothers, and in division of universe, consequent on overthrow of → Kronos, their father, P. received dominion of the sea. P. was also called Hippios, 'Lord of Horses', poss. from his cult among horse-breeding Thessalians. P. was never assoc. with any significant relig. or ethical ideas. His most famous temple was on Cape Sounion. S.G.F.B.

H. J. R. Rose, *Handbook of Greek Mythology* (1928), pp. 63ff.; *O.C.D.*, *s.v.;* W. K. C. Guthrie, *The Greeks and their Gods* (1950), pp. 94ff.

Possession → Demons.

Prajñā-Pāramitā Sūtras Lit. 'the Wisdom-Perfection', (i.e. Perfect Wisdom), is name given to type of literature in → Mahāyāna Buddhism, the central teaching of which is the doc. of → Śūñyatā, which, says Murti, 'revolutionised Buddhism'. It is knowledge of *Śūñyatā* which constitutes the 'Perfect Wisdom'. The *P.-P. Sutras* vary in length from the '100,000 verses Sutra' (*Śata-sāhāsrikā Sūtra*), to the → Heart Sūtra (*Hṛdaya Sūtra*), which is only a few lines in length. Between these extremes, 9 others are known and published, of which the best known and most import. is the Diamond-cutter Sūtra (*Vajracchedikā*). The *P.-P. Sūtras* are reckoned to be among earlier productions of Mahāyāna School; in form they stand fairly close to the dialogues of Pali canon. The Buddha (here the 'Lord', or Bhagavan) is repr. as engaging in discourse with his disciple Subhuti, whereas in other Mahāy. Sūtras he more usually discourses with another → Bodhisattva. It is thought that the *P.-P. Sūtras* had origin in S. India; thence spread to N. The great Mahāy. teachers →→ Nagarjuna, Vasubandhu and Asanga wrote substantial commentaries on these sūtras; these commentaries were trans. into Chinese, in which form only they are now extant. T.O.L.

M. Winternitz, *Hist. of Indian Literature*, vol. 2 (1933), pp. 341ff.; T. R. V. Murti, *The Central Philosophy of Buddhism* (1955), pp. 83f.; E. Conze, *Buddhist Wisdom Books* (1958), *Perfect Wisdom* (1961).

Prakṛti Also transliterated *prakriti*; Sanskrit term for 'nature', considered as unitary substance, and distinguished in → Samkhya from → *purusas* or eternal souls implicated in nature and therefore in round of → rebirth. It is sometimes identified with → *maya*, as magical creative power and creation of God; and with → *śakti*. Thus, mythically, nature is repr. as the female (Durgā, → Kali, etc.), the consort of Śiva. In Samkhya it is considered to be endowed with a teleological drive so that, through its transformations, it ultimately assists souls towards → liberation. N.S.

Pratyeka-Yāna → *Yāna*. T.O.L.

Prayer (General) P. is a universal relig. phenomenon, because it stems from the natural human disposition to give verbal expression to thought and emotion. As man naturally communicates by speech with his fellows, so he instinctively addresses the supernatural powers of his belief through the same medium. It has been suggested (e.g. by J. G. → Frazer) that man at first thought to force supernatural beings by magic to do his will, and resorted to soliciting (praying to) them when he found that magic did not work. Such a development from → magic to P. cannot be substantiated by existant data, and is improbable as a theory. Primitive forms of P. certainly appear often to have form or intent of incantation or spell (such use can be found even in higher religs.: e.g. the mechanical use of the Lord's Prayer (*Pater Noster*), often repeated, for apotropaic purposes). The earliest evidence of P. (e.g. in → Pyramid Texts and Sumerian tablets) reveal variety of approach similar to that in ordinary communication, i.e. petition, supplication, cajolery. From earliest period also examples of both private and public P. are found: the latter conducted by a recognised relig. authority, e.g. → divine king or priest. Although P. was doubtless orig. extempore in origin, it soon acquired set forms, which were often committed to writing—such forms soon acquired trad. sanctity and became estab. in liturgical worship (e.g. Jew. Shemoneh Esreh; Chr. → Eucharist). Chr. scholars have formulated a theology of P., and distinguish many kinds: e.g. vocal P., mental P., liturgical P., extempore individual P., contemplative P. (→ Worship). S.G.F.B.

E.R.E., X, pp. 154–205; *D.C.C.*, *s.v.;* F. Heiler, *Prayer* (E.T. 1932); *R.G.G.*³, II, col. 1209–34.

(China) Chi. relig., from earliest recorded time, has been permeated with desire and need to seek communion with spiritual powers, whether conceived as gods or ancestor-spirit. In the state-cult of → Confucianism, P. occupied central place in the elaborate rituals. It became customary for prayers to be carefully composed, written down, at first on bamboo or wood and later on silk or paper, and read in silence before altar whilst all worshippers were reverently kneeling. The prayers were then presented on altar, and later either burnt or carefully preserved in or near the shrine. Though petitions for blessings, often of a material nature, were a chief concern, P.'s often contained all elements of worship and adoration, confession, invocation, petition, intercession and thanksgiving. There is little evidence of P. in orig. → Taoism, but later in Taoist relig. a chief duty of priests consisted of petitionary prayers on behalf of clients, partic. at times of sickness, misfortune or calamity. From CE 8th cent. onwards, both

Buddh. and Taoist priests engaged in offering masses for souls of dead. In Mahāyāna → Buddhism of China innumerable prayers are offered to Buddhas and → bodhisattvas, espec. → Amitābha and → Kuan Yin. → Tibetan Buddhism, common in N. China, makes use of prayer-wheel, whilst everywhere scrolls, flags, streamers and inscriptions carry petitions and invocations. Prayer is an integral part of the → ancestor-cult carried out in family, whilst devout Buddh. have recourse to silent meditation and petition in nearest temple at all times of special need. D.H.S.

E.R.E., X, p. 170; W. E. Soothill, *The Three Religions of China* (1923), pp. 133–47, 233, 243; K. L. Reichelt, *Truth & Tradition in Chinese Buddhism* (1927), *passim*.

(Islam) The Arabic word (*ṣalāt*), used for what is commonly called the five times of daily prayer is better trans. 'worship'. The word *du'ā'* (supplication) rather repres. idea of prayer, at least in sense of petition. The five times of worship: shortly after sunset; when night has closed in; a little before sunrise; some time after midday; in afternoon, are obligatory on all who take their relig. seriously. After ceremonial → ablution, one should express intention (*nīya*) regarding the P.'s one is about to perform, whether voluntary or obligatory, and how much one intends to do. It has normally been practice for men to observe P. with head covered; but many nowadays who have adopted European dress pray bareheaded. It is imposs. to put forehead on ground in prostration when wearing hat with brim. When the fez was banned in Turkey after Kemal's revolution, many relig. Turks took to wearing cap with brim turned to back, thus making it possible to touch ground with forehead while head was covered.

Worship is divided into → *rak'as* (*ex.* root 'to bow'); each time of P. has a precise number, 3 after sunset, 4 at night, 2 at dawn, and 4 each after midday and in afternoon. In add. supererogatory *rak'as* are recommended: 2 after sunset, 2 after night prayer, 2 before dawn, 4 before and 2 after midday, but 4 before and 4 after the noon worship on Friday. All P. must be offered facing towards → Ka'ba in Mecca. The worship consists of praise of God, recitation of some Qur. verses, and P. for blessings on → Muḥammad. The *Fātiḥa* (sura i) and other Qur. portions are recited. Different postures are adopted in course of worship: standing with hands at sides while expressing intention; with thumbs on lobes of ears and fingers spread out when uttering the initial 'God is most great'; standing with right hand on left below navel when expressing God's praise and reciting Qur.; bowing with hands on knees (*rukū'*) while expressing God's greatness; standing with hands at sides when expressing assurance that God hears him who praises him; prostrating oneself with forehead touching ground when extolling God's holiness; sitting on one's heels while saying 'God is most great', again prostrating and declaring God's greatness. The first *rak'a* ends with worshipper standing with thumbs on lobes of ears. At end of every two *rak'as* and at close of prayer one sits on heels and says, 'God is most great'. One should then declare that his words and deeds are for God's sake, followed by invocation of blessings on Muhammad. The index-finger of right hand is then raised while declaring that God is the only deity and Muhammad is his servant and messenger. Then comes a P. for blessing on Muhammad and his family as God blessed → Abraham and his family, followed by P. for blessing in this world and next and deliverance from hell. Then turning head right and left one says, 'Peace be upon you'. This is addressed to those on either side; but also to angels and spirits of departed, for the practice is followed even when one prays alone. This ends ritual; if one has special petitions to offer, he may now make them holding his hands open in front with the palms upward.

The daily worship may be observed anywhere, alone or in company. The obligatory worship, when said in mosque or elsewhere with an → *imām*, is said by all at same time; but people can begin voluntary P.'s when they choose. Extra P.'s may be offered for special needs, e.g. in time of trouble (*Ṣalāt al-ḥāja*), when seeking success in an undertaking (*Ṣ. al-istikhāra*). An odd number of *rak'as* may be said after night prayer (*Ṣ. al-witr*), and 20 *rak'as* are a common observance after the night prayer in Ramaḍān (*Ṣ. al-tarāwiḥ*).

It had always been customary for people to say P.'s in Arabic (but → Ibn Tūmart). In Turkey the P.'s have now for some time been said in Turkish. The use of Arabic is not compulsory in *du'ā'* for people whose language is not Arabic. Kamal, *Sacred Journey*, says with regard to certain P.'s offered at different sites during → Pilgrimage, that people may either use the recommended prayer in Arabic, or offer prayers in own language, presumably extempore. J.R.

E.I., IV, pp. 96–105; Hughes, pp. 464–71; Guillaume, *Life*, pp. 112–4; Pareja, pp. 641–5; *Mishkāt*, Book IV; Querry, I, pp. 49ff.; Wensinck, *Creed*, index (*Ṣalāt*); Gaudefroy-Demombynes, *Institutions*, pp. 71–6; Donaldson, *Shi'ite*, index (Prayers); Cragg, *Minaret*, ch. 4; F. Rosenthal, *Ibn Khaldun*, index.

(Japan) The → Norito of Shinto are ritualistic P.'s, read by officiating priests before shrine altars. They are more in nature of magical formulae than P.'s as we understand them, prompted by desire for material and temporal blessings, and with no purpose of moral and spiritual development. As in China, → Mahāyāna Buddhism brought to Japan not only techniques of spiritual meditation, but such faith in the saving efficacy of compassionate Buddhas and → bodhisattvas as to call forth in Buddh. devotees the most ardent prayers of adoration, penitence, petition, intercession and thanksgiving, prayers primarily directed to attainment of salvation. Buddhism has had a profound influence on mod. sectarian Shinto. P., as spiritual communion with eternal and divine source of all good, is fundamental in doc. and practice of many of most influential of mod. Shinto sects. D.H.S.

E.R.E., X, pp. 189ff.; W. G. Aston, *Shinto* (1905), pp. 232ff.; D. C. Holtom, *The National Faith of Japan* (1938), *passim.*

Predestination In terms of comparative study, P. finds two forms of expression in relig., both obviously stemming from logically incompatible premisses. (1) the attrib. of omnipotence and omniscience to a supreme deity logically implies that he has ordained the future or fate of every person. The obvious inequality of human fortune has, accordingly, to be ascribed to the deity, which causes him to appear capricious and unjust. At a primitive stage of theological thought this conclusion is accepted by stressing divine omnipotence and inscrutability of purpose: →→ Yahweh, Zeus, Allah notably appear in this guise. (2) More acute is problem in those religs. which repr. God as the morally good, as well as the omnipotent and omniscient Creator, against whom man sins and deserves perdition. The ques. inevitably arises as to whether God, in making man, predestinated him to sin and so to be damned. The situation is further complicated in → Christianity and → Islam (to a lesser degree in → Zoroastrianism) by belief that God has planned for man's → salvation, but that man also has freedom of will to accept or reject this salvation. The fact that many reject the opportunity of salvation, when presented to them, led to belief among certain Christians, and in Islam, that God has predestinated a minority to salvation and the rest to damnation. (→→ Augustine, St.; Calvin; Election; Fall of Man; Fate; Man; Original Sin). S.G.F.B.

E.R.E., X, *s.v.;* Harnack, *H.D.*, III–VII; N. P. Williams, *The Ideas of the Fall and of Original Sin* (1927); K. E. Kirk, *The Vision of God* (1932²); *R.G.G.*³, V, col. 479–81; H. W. Robinson, *The Christian Doctrine of Man* (1913); W. M. Watt, *Free Will and Predestination in Islam* (1948); Zaehner, *D.T.Z.*, *s.v.* 'Free-will'; W. C. Greene, *Moira, Fate, Good and Evil in Greek Thought* (1944); R. B. Onians, *The Origins of European Thought* (1951), Pt. III; Brandon, *M.D.*, *History, Time and Deity* (1965).

(Buddh.) The B. attitude to any doc. of divine P. of human affairs, such, e.g. as is found in orthodox Islamic theology, is closely akin to the Bdm. attitude to → Determinism. The theistic-P. view was known to early Buddh. as that of the Issarakārana-vādins, 'those who say that the agent in all that happens is Ishwara (i.e. God)'. This view is refuted in the → *Jātaka* literature (*Jat*, V, 238), where it is argued that doc. that God is agent in human activity implies that man has, therefore, no responsibility for his actions, or that man has no freedom of moral choice. Since the premise from which Buddh. thought on this matter begins is that man has such freedom, and a theistic P. conflicts with this, P. is rejected. Another argument, put forward elsewhere in the *Jātakas*, is that the view that God is responsible for all that happens involves his being the author of injustice. (*Jat*, VI, 208). This, clearly, is in itself not a disproof of the doc. of theistic P. so much as an objection to it on moral grounds. T.O.L.

K. N. Jayatilleke, *Early Buddhist Theory of Knowledge* (1963), pp. 410–1; Piyadassi Thera, *The Buddha's Ancient Path* (1964), pp. 63–4.

(China) → Fate (China). D.H.S.

(Islam) → Free Will and Predestination (Islam). D.H.S.

Pre-Islamic Period →→ Ethics and morals (Pre-Islamic); Idolatry (Islam); -Jāhiliyya. J.R.

Presbyterianism The term describes those Calvinist churches reformed in faith and ruled by elders. 120 independent denominations compose the World Alliance of Reformed Churches with Presbyterian government, numbering 47 million members. These churches repr. the mod. successors of the Swiss Reformation founded by → Zwingli and → Calvin. The theology of the sect is always written in a confession or catechism, adhering to the Calvinism summarised by the *TULIP* of the Synod of Dort (1618–9), i.e. Total depravity: the Fall has left man in state of corruption and helplessness; Unconditional election: election is founded upon God's purpose before foundation of world; Limited atonement: the efficacy of Christ's atonement extends to the elect only; Irresistible grace: regeneration is in word of God; Perseverence of the saints: God preserves the elect, ever renewing them so that, in spite of their sins, they do not fall from grace. Similar doctrinal views are to be found in the Westminster Confession, the second Helvetic Confession, and the Heidelberg Catechism of 1563. While these anc. creeds are held in honour, new confessions are being composed by younger churches. The United P. Church in the U.S.A., the largest single unit in the World Alliance, (3,200,000) composed a new confession in 1967. The government of Reformed-P. Churches is composed of locally elected lay representatives, who are ordained as ruling elders upon acceptance of tenets of the written confession and the laws of Church order (The Book of Discipline). The ruling elders constitute, along with the teaching elders (ministers), a Session, the lowest court in a series of judicatories. The lay leader of the local congregation is the Clerk of Session. The principal court is the Presbytery (Classis, Colloquy, etc.), consisting of all teaching elders (ministers) and one representative elder from each congregation within a prescribed area. This court has function of a → Bishop. It holds authority over all the real property of constituent congregations, ordains ministers, and has sole power to initiate or dissolve the call of a minister to a church. The actions of Presbytery may be appealed to the higher judicatory of Synod (several presbyteries), or to the highest court of the General Assembly. The pattern of government is a reflection of the 17th cent. Swiss city-state. The government of the U.S.A. is an example of a secular form of Presbyterian polity.

The Reformed-P. movement sought to return to rule and faith of Church apparent in the N.T. It affirmed Holy Scripture to be 'only infallible rule of faith and life', as distinguished from Bishop or Pope. Zwingli (1484–1531) of Zürich, a chaplain to Swiss Papal mercenaries, initiated the Swiss reformation. His ideas spread quickly in all directions and found enthusiastic acceptance among divers European groups. His leadership was cut short by his untimely death in battle of Cappel. The most eminent reformer was the French Jean Calvin (1509–64), who composed the first edition of his *Institutes of the Christian Religion* before entering on his career in Geneva. His doc. of the → Eucharist differed from Zwingli's symbolic interpretation, by asserting that Christ was real and present in the Eucharist, when received by the faithful believer. John Knox of Scotland (*c.* 1505–72), pastor of the Eng. refugee congregation in Geneva, returned to his native land to lead a reform after pattern of Calvin's Geneva. His principal work is the *History of the Reformation of Religion within the Realm of Scotland*, which describes his struggle with Mary, Queen of Scots. The French Huguenots were constituted as a P. Church at Synod of Paris (1559). More than 5,000 were slaughtered in Massacre of St. Bartholomew's Eve (23–24 Aug. 1572). However, the Huguenots were granted relig. freedom by Edict of Nantes (13 Apr. 1598), which was revoked by Louis XIV (18 Oct. 1685), causing a new wave of persecution. The Waldenses of the Italian Piedmont, followers of Peter Waldo (d. 1217), entered the P. movement at Synod of Chanforans (1532), under guidance of G. Farel (1489–1565), Calvin's predecessor and associate in Geneva. The Constituent Assembly of Debreezen (1565) marks affirmation of Reformed tenets by many Hungarians, who had been followers of John Hus (d. 1415). The present Magyar Church (2,000,000 members) is second largest in the Alliance.

The Reformed-P. church is world-wide in scope, with more than half of the representatives in the Alliance from the 'younger' nations. The Church in Brazil (110,000 members), abortively founded by Huguenots in 1555, is currently among the most rapidly expanding churches in world. The churches in Korea, Formosa and Philippines have recently developed into leading Chr. groups in Far East. Among most recent additions to the Alliance have been churches in the Upper Nile and Iran. There has always been a strong interest in missionary endeavour among Calvinists, who have estab. hospitals and universities in assoc. with their churches. Universities are essential for training of teaching-elders (ministers) in a sect which has always held high academic standards as a value. Presbyterians have led in the → ecumenical movement. Their members are gen. from the middle class; attempts have been made to connect sect with rise of capitalism. J.M.F.

J. T. McNeill, *The Hist. and Character of Calvinism* (1954); J. Kennedy, *Presbyterian Authority and Discipline* (1960); J. Moffatt, *The Presbyterian Churches* (1928). Information Secretary, World Alliance of Reformed Churches, 150 Route de Forney, 1211 Geneva 20, Switzerland.

Preserved Tablet → -Lawḥ al-maḥfūẓ. J.R.

Priest(s) → Hierarchy; → Ordination.

(China) The earliest priesthood in China consisted of → shaman-diviners (*Wu*) of both sexes, who were deemed to exercise extraordinary powers over spiritual world. Their functions appear to have been threefold: invocation of spirits of dead; foretelling future; and exorcism of evil. Beside them were a body of officials who performed rites and ceremonies of a state relig. In the state relig., as it developed from Han Dynasty onwards, the emperor, or his delegates, performed functions at all levels, but were regarded, not as priests but as state officials. → Confucianism never possessed a distinctive priesthood. → Buddhism in China was organised monastically; till at least the CE 4th cent., the monks or priests were foreigners. Chi. monks were trained and ordained in monasteries, but needs of laity led to rise of a large body of priests to serve temples of popular relig. The Buddh. clergy are celibate, have shaven heads, and wear distinctive dress. → Taoist priests derived most of their functions from anc. shaman-diviners; in their monastic foundations, the training, ordination and organisation of their priesthood, they borrowed from Buddhism. The Taoist priests live in their own homes, marry, and wear ordinary dress except when celebrating their rites. Many are itinerant, deriving their livelihood from selling charms, fortune-telling, and practising exorcism, astrology and alchemy. The priesthood in China has always been closely controlled by the state. Ordination diplomas need state ratification, and numerous edicts sought to control growth of clergy. With many noted exceptions, priests of Buddhism and Taoism in China have had a poor reputation. D.H.S.

E.R.E., X, pp. 290ff.; J. J. M. de Groot, *The Religious System of China*, 6 vols. (new edn. 1964), *passim.*

(Japan) →→ Nakatomi; Imbe; Urabi; Kannushi; Priest-Buddh. D.H.S.

Priestly Code (P) A literary source, trad. or editorial commentary, which O.T. scholars recognise as final factor in composition of extant text of → Pentateuch. P. conceives of Israel as a → theocracy, and is concerned to show how → Yahweh achieved this through → Moses and Joshua, and the covenanted legislation given to regulate Israel's life as Elect People of God. P. dates from *c.* 5th cent. BC, and embodies ideals of → Ezekiel. S.G.F.B.

R. H. Pfeiffer, *Intro. to the Old Test.* (1948), pp. 188ff.; *H.D.B.*^{2}, pp. 746ff.; *P.C.*^{2}, pp. 169ff.; *R.G.G.*^{3}, V, col. 215–7; C. R. North, in H. H. Rowley (ed.), *The Old Testament and Modern Study* (1951), pp. 48ff.

Prodigies and Portents (China-Japan) The Chi. belief in P.-P., omens and signs resulted in early development of large class of specialists in arts of → divination by the milfoil, tortoise-shell, → Pa Kua, bamboo sticks etc.; they were adepts in recording and interpreting all strange and unusual phenomena so as to predict future. The theory that human affairs are intimately bound up and mutually related to natural and spiritual worlds carried with it firm conviction that Heaven (T'ien) manifests its will by means of P.-P. Though → Confucius deprecated belief in P., in the *Doctrine of the Mean* (24), we are told that 'when a nation (or a family) is about to flourish, there are sure to be happy omens; when it is about to perish, there are sure to be unhappy omens'. Portents incl. every kind and class, even to such trivial things as spluttering of a lamp wick, hoot of an owl, unusual flight of birds. The most important P.'s incl. shooting stars, comets, eclipses (espec. of sun), earthquakes, floods, rebellions. These usually portend national disaster or fall of dynasty.

By art of divination, as known and practised in anc. → Shinto by the → Urabe, the will of the → *kami* could be determined. Any unusual event was taken as a good or bad omen, and interpreted and dealt with in prescribed rituals. Chi. beliefs regarding P.-P. were assimilated by Japanese, so that Buddh. and Shinto priests practised arts of divination and were considered adepts at interpretation of all unusual phenomena and occurrence in nature. (→→ Divination; Oracle Bones).MD.H.S.

Profession (of Islam) This is fundamentally utterance of statement of belief (*shahāda*): 'There is no deity but God; Muhammad is God's messenger.' The statement is valuable, being simple and easily understood. It asserts that there is only one God, a statement commonly strengthened by holding up index finger of right hand. In asserting that → Muḥammad is God's messenger one is stating not only that Muhammad was a prophet, but that he is the medium of God's final revelation. Sir Thomas Arnold, in his *The Islamic Faith* (1928), strikingly shows how much these words mean to the Muslim when he says: 'It is whispered in the ear of the new-born babe; it is one of the first sentences the growing child is taught to utter; on all possible occasions the pious Muslim loves to repeat it, and these should be the last words on the lips of the dying.'

Six articles of belief are commonly assoc. with this → 'pillar': Belief in (1) God's unity; (2) angels; (3) sacred books, said to be 104–60 to Seth, 30 to Abraham, 10 to Moses before the → Torah, the Torah, the Psalms, the Gospel and the Qur.; (4) prophets, incl. messengers (*rusul*) and mere prophets (*anbiyā'*), 315 messengers and 124,000 prophets being claimed, the five most import. in order being →→ Muhammad, Abraham, Moses, Jesus, Noah, 25 being mentioned in the Qur.; (5) the last day when God will judge mankind; (6) predestination, which has been prevailing view as against → freewill, but which does not necessarily lead to fatalism. (→ Creed, Islam). J.R.

Hughes, p. 63; D. B. Macdonald, *Theology*, p. 293; Wensinck, *Creed*, index (Confession of faith), and pp. 197ff.; Gaudefroy-Demombynes, *Institutions*, pp. 49ff.

Prometheus A mysterious but significant figure of Grk. mythology: the name means 'forethinker'. P. was by nature a → Titan. → Hesiod presents P. as the benefactor of men, stealing for them fire from heaven, which → Zeus had withheld, and also arranging that men should retain best parts of a sacrificed animal. In revenge, Zeus sent → Pandora to plague mankind. Prometheus was also horribly punished by Zeus. In later art and lit., P. appears as creating men out of clay. S.G.F.B.

O.C.D., s.v.; L. Séchan, *Le mythe de Promethée* (1951); Brandon, *C.L.*, ch. 5.

Prophecy, Prophets (Hebrew; Christ.) The Grk. word *prophētēs* has a twofold meaning: of one who 'tells forth' a divinely inspired message, and, since such a message often concerns the future, of one who 'foretells' the future. In one sense all → revelation, i.e. knowledge deemed to come from a supernatural source, is 'prophecy': as such P. would incl. →→ augury, divination, oracles (→→ Delphi oracle; Sibylline Oracles). The term, however, is usually limited to type of phenomena gen. designated P. in the O.T., i.e. where revelation is received personally, without use of artificial means as in divination. Such P. implies special personal relationship between prophet and deity. Often the message is received when prophet is in state of → ecstasy: a notable non-Heb. instance is recorded in Egypt. story of Wen-amon (11th cent. BC). Heb. lit. shows ecstatic prophecy long antedating canonical prophets (e.g. I Sam. 10:5ff., 19:24). The word used for 'prophet' was gen. *nābī'*; *rô'eh* denoted 'seer'. Acc. to I Sam. 9:9, *rô'eh* was formerly used for one then called *nābī'*. There were professional prophets; 'false prophets' were also known. The canonical P.'s were gen. non-professional (e.g. Amos). In anc. Israel a Yahwist prophetic trad. can be discerned, which was concerned to proclaim → Yahweh as unique God of Israel; stress was laid upon his moral character and his special providence for Israel. The preservation of this trad. in writing had decisive influence on develop. of → Judaism, and also Christianity. Although the canonical record ends with Malachi, the prophetic trad. continued into the CE, and both → John the Baptist and → Jesus may be described as P.'s. The N.T. contains many refs. to P., but of a kind more concerned with prediction (e.g. Acts 11:27–8, 21:10–11). (→→ Glossolalia; Qumrân; Shamanism: → Muhammad; Zoroaster). S.G.F.B.

E.R.E., X, *s.v.; H.D.B.*[2], *s.v.*, *R.G.G.*, V, col. 608–38; *E.J.R.*, pp. 310ff.; A. Guillaume, *Prophecy and Divination* (1938); A. Lods, *Les prophèts d'Israël* (1935); *R.Ae.R-G.*, 'Prophezeiung'; H. H. Rowley, 'The Nature of O.T. Prophecy in the Light of Recent Study', *The Servant of the Lord* (1965); G. Guariglia, 'Prophetismus u. Heilserwartungsbewegungen bei den niedrigen Kulturen', *Numen*, V (1958); J. Lindblom, *Prophecy in Anc. Israel* (1962).

(China-Japan) → Inspiration (China–Japan). D.H.S.

Prophet(s) (Islam) The Qur. uses words *rasūl* (messenger), pl. *rusul*, and *nabī* (Prophet), pl. *anbiyā'*, the former considered a higher grade, as being sent to a special community with scripture containing a law, whereas P. merely preached a message. But a messenger is also a P., although P. are not all messengers. A trad. says there have been 124,000 P., among whom were 315 messengers. The Qur. mentions a number, most of whom were Biblical characters. → Abraham was father of the faithful. Noah, Lot, →→ Ishmael, Moses, Shu'aib (Jethro), → Hūd, → Ṣāliḥ and → Jesus stand high among the messengers. P. mentioned are Idris (Enoch), the Patriarchs, Aaron, David, Solomon, Elijah, Elisha, Job, Jonah, John the Baptist and his father Zechariah. Joseph has a whole sura devoted to him (xii). Messengers have message in idiom of their people (xiv:4). Some were given preference over others (ii:254). Each community has messenger (x:48), and each messenger will be questioned about those to whom he was sent (vii:5; cf. v:108). It is worthy of note that some Muslims object to 'apostle' being used to trans. *rasūl*, as is often done, because that word in Eng. suggests disciples of Jesus who became apostles, a rank much inferior to that of *rasūl*. The disciples are mentioned in the Qur. as *al-Ḥawāriyyūn* (iii:45; v:111f.; lxi:14). Though Muslims later came to believe in sinlessness of P., this doc. has no place in Qur., or the classical trad., but miracles are commonly attr. to them. J.R.

E.I., III, pp. 802f.; Wensinck, *Creed*, index; Nicholson, *Studies*, index (Miracles); Sweetman, *I.C.T.*, indexes; Blachère, *Coran*, index, Masson, *Coran*, index; M. 'Abduh, *Theology of Unity* (tr. Musa'ad and Cragg) (1966), chs. 7ff.; F. Rosenthal, *Ibn Khaldun*, index (prophecy).

Proselyte Grk., meaning 'stranger' or 'foreign sojourner'. In N.T., P. denotes a convert to Judaism. The N.T. distinguishes between P. and 'God-fearers': the essential distinction seemingly being that P. underwent → circumcision. Two other conditions for admittance to full membership were → baptism and sacrifice. Acc. to Rabbinic ruling, 'God-fearers' had to decide after one year whether they would be circumcised. After formal conversion, a P. ranks as full member of the Jewish people. P. is often used in wider sense of convert to any relig. or sect. S.G.F.B.

H.D.B.[2], *s.v.; E.R.E.*, X, *s.v.;* Schürer, *G.J.V.*, III, pp. 102ff.; *E.J.R.*, pp. 312ff.

Prostitution, Sacred The custom of obliging women, often virgins, to prostitute themselves to strangers in temple of a goddess was widespread in anc. Near East (Mesopotamia, Syria, Canaan, Anatolia, Cyprus, Greece). The goddesses concerned were →→ Ishtar, Astarte, Ma, Anaitis, Aphrodite. Acc. to Herodotus (I:199), at → Babylon and in Cyprus money so earned was sacred. S.-P. apparently had two forms: (1) As a sacrifice that every woman had to make once in her life to the goddess; (2) as a regular institution in certain temples staffed by sacred prostitutes. The Heb. *Qadeshah* was of this kind (e.g. Deut. 23:17). In India the *devadāsī* ('temple prostitute') served a god, being a member of his harem and contributing to treasury of temple by her earnings. The exact purpose of S.-P. is obscure: it was doubtless connected with ritual promotion of fertility. S.G.F.B.

J. G. Frazer, *Adonis, Attis, Osiris* I (1936[3]), pp. 36ff.; H. W. F. Saggs, *The Greatness that was Babylon* (1962), pp. 349ff.; Dhorme, *R.B.A.*, pp. 213, 219; A. L. Basham, *The Wonder that was India* (1954), pp. 184ff.; H. Licnt, *Sexual Life in Anc. Greece* (E.T. 1949), pp. 388ff.; *E.R.E.*, VI, *s.v.* ('Hierodouloi'), pp. 671–6; X, pp. 406–8; J. Gray, *The Canaanites* (1964), pp. 124, 228–9.

Protected Peoples (*Ahl al-dhimma*). Name applied to Jews, Christians and other non-Muslims who live in a state subject to Islamic law. A member of these peoples is called a *dhimmī*. Such people are given liberty to practise their relig. but not to propagate it, and are offered protection. In return they have to pay a poll-tax (→ *jizya*), which is taken from freemen, varying in amount acc. to their financial position. Women, minors, monks and people unable to work because of physical or mental illness were exempted. *Dhimmīs* had to submit to certain indignities regarding dress; they were not allowed to build their houses higher than those of neighbouring Muslims. They had to give way to Muslims on the road. Being P.-P., they were not subject to military service unless they wished to volunteer. In Ottoman Turkey the tax was abolished when gen. conscription was intro. in mod. times. While *dhimmīs* were gen. given liberty, though treated as second-class citizens, there was often danger of mob violence which the authorities found it difficult to control. On other hand, *dhimmīs* often rose to influential positions in state. J.R.

E.I.[2], II, pp. 227–31; Pareja, pp. 666f. and index (*d̲imma*); Tritton, *Non-Muslims*; Levy, *Social Structure*, index (*dhimmīs*); Gaudefroy-Demombynes, *Institutions*, pp. 122ff.

Psalms (Islam) The Book of P. is called in the Qur. *al-Zabūr* (iv:161; xvii:57; xxi:105), where it is conceived of as revelation given to David. The third passage above gives a direct quotation from Ps. xxxvii:29, 'My upright servants will inherit the earth'. In Arabic lit. quotations are also made as from the Book of P.; but while some are recognisable, most would be difficult to find. Later lit. had advantage of knowledge of some Jew. and Christ. converts which was not so available to → Muḥammad. J.R.

E.I., IV, pp. 1184f.; Hughes, pp. 439ff., 698.

Pseudepigrapha Term used for writings attr. to famous persons, to endow them with authority. Such false attribution was an accepted convention in anc. Judaism, and not gen. regarded as reprehensible. The term is usually employed for Jew. relig. writings not incl. in → canon of O.T.: e.g. Book of → Enoch, Assumption of Moses (→ Apocalyptic Lit.). S.G.F.B.

Psychē Grk. = 'soul'. In → Homer, the P. was the principle of animal life, which at death descended to → Hades as shadowy replica of living person, and was then known as the *eidōlon*: it was distinguished from the *thymos*, the conscious self. By 6th cent. BC this distinction was dropped, and P. became term for the inner essential self or → soul, regarded in → Orphism, and by → Plato, in → Neoplatonism, and → Gnosticism, as preexistent and immortal. In N.T., P. is used both in sense of Heb. → nephesh and as immortal soul: → Paul called latter *pneuma*, making P. principle of animal life. In Grk.-speaking Chr. theology P. became accepted term for immortal soul.
S.G.F.B.

R. B. Onians, *The Origins of European Thought* (1951); E. Rohde, *Psyche*, 2 vols. (1898); Brandon, *M.D.*, chs. 5, 6.

Psychic Powers (Buddh.) → *Iddhi*. T.O.L.

Psychology of Religion It is virtually impossible to give a brief definition of P.R. While its main area of reference is taken to be the relig. experience of the individual or social unit, much depends on the presuppositions with which this area is approached. Some psychologists claim that there is no such thing as P.R., or at most that P.R. is purely an aspect of general psychology, directed towards an area of doubtful validity. Others, more reasonably, allow that relig. is a sufficiently well-defined area of experience to permit the distinctive approach which the term P.R. implies. But as W. H. Clark points out, 'the psychology of religion has never enjoyed a wholly respectable academic status' (*Approach*, p. 5). It is gen. agreed that P.R. is a boundary discipline, and cannot exist in isolation from general psychology, the →→ history, phenomenology and sociology of religion, and (in some cases) theology. This fundamental uncertainty as to status and terms of ref. is reflected in the short history of the discipline.

Although P.R. has, in some sense, existed as long as men have found it necessary to reflect on the bases of their relig. faith, and can thus be traced back to Classical Antiquity, its scientific origins do not go back much beyond the 1890s. In its beginnings, P.R. was largely a product of N. American empiricism; it aimed at approaching the phenomena of relig. experience (partic. such things as conversion, prayer, etc.) by careful exam. and assessment of individual cases, assembled from autobiographies, journals, and answers to questionnaires. Among the Amer.

pioneers, four names in partic. are worthy of mention: G. S. Hall, J. H. Leuba, E. D. Starbuck, W. James. Hall founded in 1889 *The American Journal of Psychology*, which has been called the first scientific forum of P.R. He also directed attention of pupils to the individual phenomena of Amer. revivalism. Leuba published his first import. art., 'A Study in the Psychology of Religious Phenomena', in 1896 (*A.I.P.*, vol. 7); in 1912 appeared his most influential work, *A Psychological Study of Religion*. Leuba was basically a rationalist, and approached his subject from the biological point of view, claiming that relig. is called forth by the individual's search for 'moral harmony'. The first comprehensive handbook in P.R. was Starbuck's *The Psychology of Religion* (1899), in which the author was concerned mainly to analyse the phenomena of relig. conversion. This book was instrumental in shaping William James' Gifford Lectures, *The Varieties of Religious Experience* (1902), a work which is still read today, though less as a textbook in P.R. than as a relig. classic. Among the avenues opened up by James we may note his distinction between 'the religion of healthy-mindedness'—optimistic, unconcerned with the problem of evil, exemplified by → Christian Science and the 'mind-cure' movements —and 'the religion of the sick soul'—pessimistic, obsessed by evil and the problems of sin and forgiveness, exemplified by 'Calvinism'. James drew many of his examples from relig. pathology (extreme cases produced for clarity of illustration). While remaining agnostic on poss. of divine revelation, he suggested that, should there be such a thing as revelation, the pathological state of mind might well provide the optimum condition for its reception.

The type of approach and method exemplified for all time by James has continued to exercise a certain influence in the English-speaking world. It was purely individualistic; social relig. phenomena were regarded of being of secondary significance. It was purely inductive, its object being to proceed from the partic. case to the gen. principle. And it was ultimately rationalist; what purported to be an interpret. of relig. experience often took form of a pragmatic explaining-away of that experience. It had little awareness of role of tradition in shaping the individual's experience. Nor did it concern itself with collective experience of social unit. Its material was drawn almost entirely from Prot. revivalism, which in N. Amer. had developed in a highly individual direction. It was thus, despite its initial clarity, gravely deficient in import. psychological areas.

In early years of present cent., a two-pronged attack on the Amer. school came from Germany and France. In England, the influence of the Americans was considerable, since dominant schools of relig. and anthropology worked along similarly individualist lines. The German attack was spearheaded by W. Wundt, in his monumental *Völkerpsychologie* (1900ff.); in this work, as well as attacking the Americans and their European imitators, Wundt advanced anthropological reasons for treating problems of P.R. in a collective, rather than individual, way. Wundt's work was little read outside Germany. More widespread influence was exercised by the French sociological school, led by Durkheim. For some years there had existed in France a flourishing school of experimental psychology, whose most outstanding repr. had been J. M. Charcot; his assoc. of mysticism with hysteria was esp. well known. The sociologists, however, concentrated—for what now appear to have been *a priori* reasons—on the collective aspect of P.R., to the virtually total exclusion of the individual. Durkheim, following Comte, saw in relig. the apotheosis of the social unit, having no validity outside sphere of the collective. 'The sacred'—that which for man (esp. primitive man) is vested with ultimate authority—is none other than the group acting on, and on behalf of, its constituents. Durkheim's views, expressed definitively in *Les formes élémentaires de la vie religieuse* (1912) had considerable implications for P.R., since they postulated three well-defined stages in the evolution of relig. apprehension—mythological, metaphysical and scientific—each of which is characterised by its own modes of thought. Lévy-Bruhl went further than Durkheim in stressing pre-logical character of primitive relig. thought: his theory of 'primitive mentality' was influential for a time, but was later retracted.

A reaction involving rehabilitation of experience of individual as sole formative basis of relig. in assoc. with names of Nathan Söderblom and Rudolf Otto. Both made use of the categories of → 'the holy' and 'holiness'. Söderblom's contribution antedates that of Otto, but it was the latter's book *Das Heilige* (1917, E.T. *The Idea of the Holy*, 1923), which brought before an international public the term 'numinous', with which this approach is partic. associated. The concern of both men was to emphasise the *sui generis* character of relig. experience; the adjective 'numinous' (from Lat. → *numen*) is used to denote the simultaneous attraction and repulsion felt by *homo religiosus* in face of the unknown. While Otto's theory had its widest application in field of primitive relig., Söderblom worked independently on problems of sanctity and mysticism, widening the term 'mysticism' to embrace the relig., experience of e.g. → Luther: this he called 'the mysticism of personality' as contrasted with 'the mysticism of the infinite'. However, Söderblom was never concerned with P.R. as an independent discipline. His successor Tor Andrae went further along this partic. line, with good results. Another disciple of Söderblom, Friedrich Heiler, known above all for his work on prayer, *Das Gebet* (1918), should be mentioned in this connection. → Mysticism was from first a fruitful field for students of P.R. Among the more noteworthy books published before World War I which expressly took up the individual viewpoint were W. R. Inge, *Christian Mysticism* (1899); F. von Hügel, *The Mystical Element of Religion*, I–II (1908); Evelyn Underhill, *Mysticism* (1911) and *The Mystic Way* (1913).

Between the wars, scholars working in P.R. attempted to consolidate position of discipline by production of handbooks, in which developments of previous quarter-century were summed up and evaluated. The most outstanding of these was perhaps the American J. B. Pratt's *The Religious Consciousness* (1920). Among Pratt's achievements was formulating of one of most widely-accepted summary definitions of religion: 'Religion is the serious and social attitude of individuals or communities toward the power or powers which they conceive as having ultimate control over their interests or destinies.' In Pratt can also be seen the working of the widening process in which material from other relig. trads. was brought in to elucidate states and trends previously illustrated largely from Christ. and 'primitive' sources.

The most import. development of these years was, however, the emergence of depth-psychology—partic. the schools of → Freud and → Jung—and its influence on P.R.

Freud's methods of psycho-analysis, centred on interpret. of dreams (*Traumdeutung*) as means of access to the sub-conscious and his gen. attitude to relig. as an illusion, produced in response to experiences in infancy, have been widely caricatured; but they incl. elements which have proved valuable in P.R. The concept of repression, by which impulses and images are removed from the conscious to the unconscious mind, and the formative influence of early and forgotten (or deliberately repressed) experiences are cases in point. What Freud failed to see is that his categories are equally applicable to anti-relig., as to relig. attitudes. His own negative attitude to relig., expressed e.g. in *Die Zukunft einer Illusion* (1927, E.T., *The Future of an Illusion*, 1949), may very well be explained in 'Freudian' terms. The energy with which he, as an atheist, returned again and again to relig. questions can be described, in Allport's term, as a 'reaction formation'—a situation which, as Sundén has pointed out, is common in so-called atheists and anti-clerical polemists. There is no denying that Freud gave import. impulses to psychological study of relig.; among the anthropologists whose work was influenced by Freud should be mentioned Malinowski. However, the theoretical basis of the Freudians' work in P.R. was often too weak to bear the vast edifices that they attempted to erect on it.

C. G. Jung, orig. a disciple of Freud, was forced by nature of his discoveries and interprets. to dissent from extreme individualism of his master. In dreams and fantasies of his patients he encountered recurring images and patterns, which he claimed to correspond closely to inner structure of 'primitive' → mythology and relig.—for instance to the *mandalas* of certain forms of → Mahāyāna Buddhism. In light of these discoveries, Jung was led to work out a theory of the symbolical structure of dreams. In this theory he postulated existence of two layers of the unconscious: one individual; the other (deeper) collective. The patterned dreams in question proceed from the 'collective unconscious', and from dispositions common to all men in all ages, which he calls 'archetypes'. The archetypes may be seen in three aspects: the 'archaic image', which is the symbolical form in which the archetype is coupled to the conscious mind; the archetype itself; and the 'engram', which is the physiological basis of the archetype.

The great virtue of Jung's system is that it permits the scholar to treat formation of mythology as something living, since the impulses themselves are still part of the human makeup. It also allows for more positive attitude to relig. symbolism than has often been case in comparative relig. It has, in fact, been claimed that Jung's contribution to P.R. is the most import. thing to have happened in the discipline this century. The alliance between Jungian psychology and comparative relig., which is to be found e.g. in the *Eranos Jahrbuch*, has been of great benefit to both fields. Among leading figures in present day comparative relig. who have been influenced by school of Jung, pride of place must go to the Rumanian phenomenologist Mircea Eliade. Although it has been objected that in Jung himself speculation sometimes took upper hand over objective research, his real import. is to be seen in avenues of research he opened up for others.

Although work of Freud and Jung is not, properly speaking, the latest develop. within P.R., little has happened since then to erase their impression from the discipline. Recent progress has been rather a matter of refinement of technique than of radically new departures. At present time, a number of alternative approaches may be noted. Once more it should be stressed that choice of approach is still bound up with convictions of individual student.

(1) The analysis of individual phenomena of spiritual life, using the classical techniques of James, modified in accordance with develops. in psych. since Freud. This involves exam. of theory of personality, often in light of received categories—body, soul, spirit, etc.—and may well concentrate on such 'classical' factors as sin, guilt, forgiveness and the like. It is, however, no longer poss. to treat questions of individual P.R. in isolation from their social implications.

(2) The analysis of social phenomena of the relig. life, following the sociological approach. The sociologist concentrates on such factors as role of trad., and the transmission of trad., within social unit; questions of responsibility, ethics and law; the family, clan, tribe, society, nation, denomination, sect or church as formative influences on develop. of relig. life; and class as a relig. factor. It goes without saying that the individual is still studied, though in rel. to the group or groups of which he is a member. In both these first approaches, the material may be taken as given, without being subject to experimental control (→ Sociology of Relig.).

(3) Detailed study of relig. behaviour of individuals and groups, using methods of experimental psychol., with or without evaluation.

(4) Exam. of relig. as factor in mental hygiene, the primary concern being mental health of individual. Among well-known writers who have approached P.R. from this angle are Maeder, Fromm and Frankl. Their concern stems directly from schools of psychoanalysis, and is often centred on problems of psychiatry and abnormal psychology.

(5) Often linked with this approach, though operating within framework of a Christ. society and theological system, is pastoral psychology (sometimes known more specifically as pastoral counselling or clinical theology). Pastoral psychol. differs from P.R. in that its ultimate aim is neither descriptive nor analytical, but therapeutic, acc. to the interpret. placed upon that idea by the theol. system within which it is practised. It can, and does, make extensive use of methods and findings of P.R. gen., and psychotherapy in partic., though it goes far beyond either of these in the normative character it claims for its optimum state. The present trend is, however, to discourage dilettantism in pastoral psychol., and to urge on pastors the need to cooperate with psychotherapists whenever poss. in treatment of individual cases.

(6) The place of P.R. within relig. phenomenology and comparative relig. gen. is still unclear—partly because few have the specialised clinical psychol. training necessary for accurate evaluation. The advance made by followers of Jung in this field, and theories put forward by the Swedish scholar H. Sundén in his recent work *Religion och rollerna*[2] (1960), in which he interprets relig. in terms of 'role-taking', are, however, encouraging signs. The immense complexity of the material is recognised, and the relative uncertainty experienced by the investigator in dealing with unsystematically collected material is taken into account. Yet there remain vast possibilities. Among the phenomena which still call for thorough psychol. study may be mentioned: heredity and environment as formative factors in relig. life of individual; the vexed question of the relig. 'instinct' or *Anlag*; the nature of relig. experience as it affects the behaviour and decision-making capacities of individual in isolation or within the group; relig. conversion (and its opposite, the abandonment of relig.); expressions of relig. life of individual, incl. prayer, and culminating in 'sanctity' and various forms of mysticism. A partic. pressing need in connection with this latter point is the analysis of effects of so-called psychedelic drugs (mescalin, LSD, etc.) in rel. to mystical experience (an analysis undertaken from the R.C. point of view by R. C. Zaehner in *Mysticism Sacred and Profane*, 1957). The phenomena of spirit-possession, inspiration and ecstatic utterances also have their place here. On the institutional level, myth, ritual and worship must be treated together, as aspects of essentially the same complex of ideas and behaviour-patterns. Attention must be paid at same time to occurrence of 'religious' phenomena in 'secular' movements, such as Communism. The role of the charismatic leader—king, priest, prophet—has received considerable attention from phenomenologists of late, and might be further elucidated by P.R. The list could be prolonged indefinitely, since there is no aspect of comparative relig. which is not susceptible to psychol. analysis.

But it must be remembered, finally, that P.R. has nothing whatsoever to say on question of relig. truth. Its task is descriptive and analytical; it can in no circumstances become normative. The existence or otherwise of a deity or ultimate reality, to which relig. expression refers, is not a question which P.R. can presume to answer. The investigator brings to his investigations certain presuppositions. These have not always been admitted. But if P.R. has any role to play as a discipline, its non-normative character must be recognised, and its claims modified accordingly. (→ Philosophy of Religion). E.J.S.

The main authorities are cited in text. See also: G. W. Allport, *The Individual and his Religion*

(1951); *The Nature of Prejudice* (1954); T. Andrae, *Die Frage der religiösen Anlage* (1932); C. Baudouin, *Psychologie analytique et religion* (1953); E. Berggrav, *Kropp och själ* (1933); W. H. Clark, *The Psychology of Religion* (1958); M. Eliade, *The Sacred and the Profane* (E.T. 1959), *Myths, Dreams and Mysteries* (E.T. 1960); V. E. Frankl, *Der unbewusste Gott* (1948); E. Fromm, *Psychoanalysis and Religion* (E.T. 1950); L. W. Grensted, *The Psychology of Religion* (1952); S. Hiltner, *Pastoral Counseling* (1949); A. Huxley, *The Doors of Perception* (1954); A. Maeder, *Ways to Psychic Health* (E.T. 1953); C. R. Rogers, *Client-Centered Therapy* (1951); H. N.-R. W. Wieman, *Normative Psychology of Religion* (1935).

Psychostasia Grk. = 'weighing of souls'. In anc. Egypt. → eschatology idea first appears of weighing heart of deceased against symbol of → Maat. The motive was prob. to obtain impartial assessment. The idea, involving souls (*kēres*), not hearts, appears in → Homer. The P., as a form of → judgment of dead, occurs in the following religs.: Greek, Christianity, Islam, Zoroastrianism, Hinduism, Buddhism. Its most notable expression is in the medieval → Doom. (→→ Michael, Archangel). S.G.F.B.

S. G. F. Brandon, *The Judgment of the Dead* (1967), 'The Weighing of the Soul', in Eliade, *F-S.;* L. Kretzenbacher, *Die Seelenwaage* (1958).

Psychopompos Grk. = 'conductor of souls'. A supernatural being (sometimes orig. a death-god) figures in many religs. as summoner or conductor to underworld of those fated to die: e.g. in Egypt. relig. → Anubis; Gr. relig. → Hermes or → Charon; Etruscan relig. → Charun; early Christianity → Michael; Mesopot. relig., cf. Epic of → Gilgamesh, VII, 17f. S.G.F.B.

Ptah God of Memphis, repr. in human form, in closely fitting garment, holding sceptre. In → Memphite Theology, P. is presented as orig. creator-god, →→ Atum, Horus and Thoth being attributes of him. As Ta-tenen, P. was identified with Egypt as it arose from primaeval chaos of Nun; he was also regarded as artificer-god, whom Greeks identified with → Hephaistos; he was assoc. with Sokaris, Memphite mortuary-god. S.G.F.B.

Sandmann-Holmberg, *The God Ptah* (1946); S. A. B. Mercer, *The Religion of Anc. Egypt* (1949), pp. 148ff.; *R.Ae.R-G.*, pp. 614–9; Brandon, *C.L.*, pp. 29ff.

Puberty, Rites of (China) → Initiation (Chinese). S.G.F.B.

Pudgala-Vādins Buddh. sect that appeared about 200 years after death of Buddha, i.e. at begin. of 3rd cent. BC. A brahman named Vatsiputra, who had been converted to Buddhism, put forward theory that while the → *anatta* doc. denied existence of an enduring individual soul, nevertheless *something* endured; this was the *pudgala*, or 'person'. He claimed that Buddha, in his discourses, had made use of notion of *pudgala*, and had thus indic. real existence of the person. The majority of Buddh.s monks demurred from this opinion; it was pointed out that use of term *pudgala* in Buddha's discourses was merely a concession to everyday usage. V., however, won a number of monks to his view, since the *pudgala*-theory appeared to satisfy demands of justice better than the *anatta* doc. For, if there is no enduring entity which transmigrates from existence to existence, there could be no proper basis for retributive justice operating through → *karma*; hence incentive to responsible moral action was lost. The monks who opposed the *pudgala-vādins* did so because it seemed that notion of a *pudgala*, which transmigrated, was the reappearance, under another name, of rejected notion of the → *atta* (*ātman*). Nevertheless, the P. sect continued to grow, and as late as 7th cent. CE the Chi. pilgrim → Hsuan-tsang recorded that there were 66,000 P. monks: approx. a quarter of total no. of Buddh. monks in India at that time. The P.'s were known also as Vatsīputrīyas, after name of originator of doc. They themselves became divided on minor points into four subsects; the differences between them are now obscure, since the lit. of these sects is virtually non-existent. T.O.L.

A. Bareau, *Les sectes bouddhiques du petit vehicule* (1955); E. Conze, *Buddhist Thought in India* (1962), pp. 121–31.

Puñña (Buddh.) Term used in B. trad. and usually trans. 'merit'. The task of merit-making is primary for great majority of Buddh.s, whether monks or laymen; it is regarded as the production of wholesome → Karma, which will secure an entail of spiritually more mature existence, or, in popular parlance 'a good rebirth'. P. has 3 aspects: (1) → Dāna or generosity, as a corrective to tendencies to egoism; (2) → Sila or keeping of the moral precepts; (3) Bhāvanā or meditational development. For monks who are spiritually more advanced (3) is their major concern; although (1) and (2) are still important; for those less spiritually advanced (1) and (2) are still their major concern. For majority of laymen emphasis is predominantly on (1) and (2), in the giving of food, robes, money or land (primarily for support of monks), and the keeping of the 5 moral precepts; when poss. also (3) (→ Sila). More spiritually advanced laymen, or *upāsakas*, will also acquire merit by meditating. In B. countries of S.E. Asia and Ceylon, merit-making under aspects (1) and (2) is thus basis of popular relig. and the concern of the majority. T.O.L.

D.N., 33; Itivuttaka, 60; *A.N.*, VIII:36; Michael

M. Ames, 'Magical Animism and Buddhism: a Structural Analysis of the Sinhalese Religious System', in *J.A.S.* (1964).

Purāṇas The P. or 'Ancient Stories' are part of auxiliary scriptural canon of Hinduism (→ *smrti*), and contain wealth of mythological material. The P. gen. recognised are of eighteen, and date from Gupta period onwards, though much of material in them is considerably older. In part they are product of → *bhakti* movement, and in theory they subscribe to synthesis between →→ Brahma, Śiva and Viṣṇu as the three great manifestations of the ultimate (→ *trimurti*), six P. being in principle devoted to each of the three great gods. Often, however, the P. are clearly sectarian in spirit. In add. to the eighteen great P., there are lesser P. subsidiary to them and known as *upapuranas*. Trad. the P. are ascribed to Vyasa, legendary author of the → *Mahabharata* and compiler of Vedic hymns. Written in poetry, they theoretically conform to a fixed pattern (in fact they do not) in which each P. sets forth in sequence the topics of creation, destruction, etc., of world; the genealogy of gods and heroes; successive reigns of different → Manus; and dynasties. These topics are roughly followed in the P. as we have them. Following their absorption into auxiliary canon, they were held to serve function of popularising and concretising teachings of → Upaniṣads for benefit of ordinary people. Certainly philosophical and theological ideas are woven into the P., esp. in sections dealing with creation. There is fairly extensive use made of → Samkhya-Yoga categories, and the gen. trend is towards a modified monism or *bhedābhedavada* (doc. of difference and non-difference, sc. between God, the world and souls → *Visistadvaita*). The most import. of the P. is the *Bhāgavata Purāṇa* (also called the *Srīmad-Bhāgavata*), which gave rise to large number of commentaries. Also import. are the *Viṣṇu P. Śiva P.*, *Agni P.* and *Kūrma P.*, a portion of which containing relig. and philosophical teachings is called the *Īśvaragītā* ('Song of the Lord'). The P. present classical shape of Hindu mythology, and in partic. the attitudes to → Time, the creation and destruction of universe, etc., characteristic of developed Hindu → cosmology. The term *purana* is also found in the *Upaniṣads* and elsewhere (i.e. before composition of the P.) to ref. to anc. lore, and the importance attached to transmission of anc. legend helped in recognition of the P. as part of *smrti*. N.S.

V. R. Ramachandra Dikshitar, *The Purana Index*, 3 vols. (1951–5); H. H. Wilson, *The Vishnu Purana*, 5 vols. in one (1961); M. N. Dutt, *A Prose Translation of Srimadbhagavatam* (1896); R. C. Hazra, *Studies in the Upapuranas* (1958); S. N. Dasgupta, *Hist. of Indian Philosophy*, vol. 3 (1940).

Pure Brethren → Ikhwān al-Ṣafā'. J.R.

Pure Land School (Chi. Buddh.) In Chinese—Ching T'u: prob. oldest and least philosophical of sects of → Mahāyāna Buddhism in China. → Hui Yüan is considered to have founded P.L. in 402 CE, calling it the White Lotus sect; name was changed later to P.L. when a revolutionary society adopted it. Hui Yüan and successors accepted the orthodox Buddh. teaching that life is sorrow and disillusionment, governed by → karma and rebirth, but directed mind to the infinite host of → Buddhas and → bodhisattvas who offered believer the assistance which only infinite grace, power and merit could give. They took as principal scripture the Greater Sukhāvatī-vyūha sūtra (*Wu-liang-shou ching*), which proclaimed doc. of salvation by faith in Amitabha Buddha (→ Amida), and contains vivid descriptions of the P.L. or Western Paradise, ruled over by Amitabha, assisted by the two great bodhisattvas, → Kuan Yin and Ta Shih Chih.

One of greatest exponents of P.L. was Shan-tao (613–81 CE), who taught that men, steeped in ignorance and evil desire, have little power to save themselves. They must place their reliance on faith in Amitabha alone, who guarantees to all who sincerely believe in him salvation and entrance upon the P.L. His saving grace, mercy and infinite merit are freely offered to all who simply call upon his name in faith. This emphasis on saving faith and devotion to all the Buddhas and bodhisattvas may be compared to the → bhakti developments in Hinduism.

When, at close of T'ang Dyn., the hard divisions betw. various sects of Buddhism in China tended to be obliterated, the P.L. sects came to exert a pervasive and dominating influence in Chi. Buddhism; they remain the most effective relig. force among Chi. Buddhists in mod. times. The teachings of P.L. are condensed in the famous *Ch'i Hsin Lun* (Awakening of Faith in the Mahayana); E.T. by D. T. Suzuki (1900), and T. Richard (1910). (→ Jodo). D.H.S.

K. L. Reichelt, *Truth & Tradition in Chinese Buddhism* (1927), ch. 5; D. H. Smith, *Chinese Religions* (1968), pp. 125ff.

Purgatory Adjustment of Chr. → eschatology caused by delay of → Parousia, led to invention of idea of P. for accommodation of dead after Immediate Judgment until → Last Judgment. In P. the souls of dead, not guilty of unrepented mortal sin, expiated their venial sins. Although in a disembodied state, there was a strong tendency to envisage the dead as suffering physically in P. The Papal institution of → Indulgences was designed to give remission from pains of P. to the 'poor souls'. The medieval conception of pains of P. often differed scarcely from those of Hell, except that latter were eternal. The rejection of P., by the Reformers, mainly owing to abuse of Indulgences, left Prot. eschatology with awkward problem about condition of dead awaiting Last Judgment. The Buddh. Hells are really Purgatories, since souls expiate sins before next reincarnation. (→ Judgment of the Dead). S.G.F.B.

D.C.C., *s.v.; R.G.G.*³, II, col. 665–80; J. A. Fischer, *Studien u. Todesgedanken in der alten Kirche*, I (1954); A. Stuiber, *Refrigerium Interim: die Vorstellungen vom Zwischenzustand u. die frühchrist. Grabeskunst* (1957); G. G. Coulton, *Five Centuries of Religion*, I (1923), ch. 5; J. A. MacCulloch, *Medieval Faith and Fable* (1932), ch. 12; S. G. F. Brandon, *Judgment of the Dead* (1967), chs. 6, 9.

Purification(s) (Islam) In add. to → ablution before worship, Islam has regulations about a number of special circumstances where P. is required. Bathing (*ghusl*) whole body is necessary after certain impurities, such as sexual intercourse and nocturnal emission. A trad. says that, if one lies on one's wife without having intercourse, it is still necessary to bathe. Women must bathe on purification after their monthly courses and after childbirth. While in these states of uncleanness they cannot engage in ritual worship. It is customary, but not compulsory, to bathe before Friday noon prayer, before festival prayers, and after coming in contact with something unclean, such as dead body. A vessel from which a dog laps is rendered unclean and must be washed seven times. Otherwise impurity affecting clothing, etc. is removed by sprinkling water or using sand. A trad. tells of a Bedouin passing water in the Medina mosque, whereupon → Muḥammad administered a gentle rebuke and gave orders that a bucket of water be poured over the place. The tooth-stick (*miswāk*) for purifying the mouth is said to be pleasing to God. After relieving oneself, it is necessary to wipe oneself three times. (→ Clean, Unclean). J.R.

E.I., IV, p. 608; *Mishkāt*, Book III; Hughes, p. 477.

Puritans Designation for more extreme Eng. Protestants who sought to purify Church of supposedly unscriptural objects and practices (e.g. vestments, sign of cross, marriage ring) left untouched by settlement estab. by Queen Elizabeth I. Their theology was Calvinist (→ Calvin). They played an influential part in relig. and politics of 17th cent. England. The term 'Puritan' had no precise connotation and ceased to be applicable after 1660. For the hist. of religs., the P. who migrated to America are of particular interest. In New England they endeavoured to set up communities based on covenant with God, after pattern of the idealised Israel of the O.T. S.G.F.B.

E.R.E., X, pp. 507ff.; E. S. Morgan, *Visible Saints: Hist. of a Puritan Idea* (1963); R. C. Simmons, 'Early Massachusetts', *History Today*, XVIII (1968).

Puruṣa Sometimes transliterated *purusha;* lit. means 'man'; the term is used in → Samkhya-Yoga to ref. to the eternal soul, which is distinct from material nature, though typically entangled in it, in the round of → rebirth, until such time as individual can gain release (→ *kaivalya*). The term is also used for Cosmic Man in → *Rgveda*, X:40, the *Puruṣasukta* or 'Hymn of Man'. He comprises the world and heaven, and it is through his being sacrificed that universe and the variety of living creatures are formed. N.S.

Pyramids The P. evolved from an early tomb-form known as the mastaba, a plateau-like stone structure over burial pit. The earliest P. is the Step P. of Zoser (*c.* 2815 BC) at Sakkara, its architect being → Imhotep. P. were built as tombs for pharaohs of 3rd–7th dynasties (to *c.* 2294 BC), and for many of Middle Kingdom (to *c.* 1777 BC). Pyramidal tombs were used by kings of Meroe and Napata in the Sudan (*c.* 300 BC–CE 350). P. were also used for burial of queens and nobles in Egypt. The royal Egypt. P. had a complex of subsidiary buildings, incl. a mortuary temple. The pyramidal shape has been variously explained: as a ladder up to heaven; as a repr. of rays descending from sun (→ Pyramid Texts). S.G.F.B.

I. E. S. Edwards, *The Pyramids of Egypt* (1947); *R.Ae.R-G.*, pp. 619ff.

Pyramid Texts Collections of religious texts, in hieroglyphic characters, inscribed on interior walls of pyramids at Sakkara of pharaohs Unis (5th Dyn.), Teti, Pepi I, Merenrē, and Pepi II (6th Dyn.). Additional texts are found in pyramids of Oudjebeten, Neit and Apouit, queens of Pepi II, and of Ibi, obscure king of 7th Dyn. The P.-T., dating from *c.* 2350–2175 BC, constitute oldest corpus of relig. writings. In their present form, they incorporate even older material, some of it evidently predating union of Upper and Lower Egypt, *c.* 3000 BC. The P.-T. were collected and arranged by priests of → Heliopolis, to enable the dead kings, in whose pyramids they were inscribed, to be raised from death and reach the next world in safety. In composing the P.-T., the priests drew on trad. material, incl. funerary rituals, rituals of embalmment, myths, hymns, magical spells; incantations, and prayers. Some material reveals a primitive state of culture: the so-called Cannibal Hymn attests former practice of ritual cannibalism. The Heliopol. priests used P.-T. to exalt god of

Heliopolis, → Atum-Rē, as supreme deity and divine father of the kings. Atum-Rē is set forth as original creator-god (→ Cosmogony (Egypt.)). Despite their evident desire to present after-life of kings as eternal beatitude in company of Atum-Rē, the priestly editors had to admit another mortuary trad. into P.-T. This trad. was centred on → Osiris, with whom each dead king was ritually assimilated, to be united to Osiris in resurrection. The P.-T. are invaluable source of information about earliest phase of → Egypt. religion. Ref. is made in them to many other gods, and to various relig. beliefs and practices. Material from the P.-T. appears in later Egypt. mortuary literature, namely, →→ Coffin Texts and Book of the Dead. (→ Funerary Cult, Egypt). S.G.F.B.

K. Sethe, *Die altägyptischen Pyramidentexten*, 4 vols. (1908–22, repr. 1960); K. Sethe, *Übersetzung u. Kommentar z. d. altäg. Pyramidentexten*, 4 vols. (n.d.); L. Speelers, *Les Textes des Pyramides égyptiennes*, 2 vols. (1923–4); S. A. B. Mercer, *The Pyramid Texts*, 4 vols. (1952); S. A. B. Mercer, *Literary Criticism of the Pyramid Texts* (1956); *R.Ae.R-G.*, pp. 619–23; I. E. S. Edwards, *The Pyramids of Egypt* (1949); A. Piankoff, *The Pyramid of Unas* (1968).

Pythagoreanism Relig.-philosophical movement founded by Pythagoras (*fl.* 531 BC) at Croton, S. Italy. Pythagoras was already a legendary figure in 4th cent. BC, and little certain is known of him. He had reputation for spiritual power and learning, believed in → metempsychosis and that soul was of divine origin but imprisoned in body; he interpreted world in terms of numbers. The relig. society which P. estab. in Croton, lived acc. to a strict discipline, involving silence and abstention from flesh. It was suppressed *c.* 425 BC. P. prob. had some orig. kinship with → Orphism. A revived form of P. (Neopythagoreanism) flourished in Rome and → Alexandria from 1st cent. BC. S.G.F.B.

O.C.D., s.v.; E.R.E., X, *s.v.;* W. Jaeger, *The Theology of the Early Greek Philosophers* (1947); L. Robin, *La pensée grecque* (1928), pp. 57ff.; G. S. Kirk-J. E. Raven, *The Presocratic Philosophers* (1957), ch. 7; J. Carcopino, *La basilique pythagoricienne de la Porte Majeure* (1943).

Q

Q Symbol for German word *Quelle* = 'source', used in N.T. study for hypothetical collection of sayings of Jesus, embodied in Gospels of Matt. and Lk. (→ Synoptic Problem). S.G.F.B.
B. H. Streeter, *The Four Gospels* (1924), pt. II, chs. 9, 10; V. Taylor, in A. J. B. Higgins (ed.), *New Testament Studies* (1959), pp. 246ff.; *P.C.*², pp. 654b–g; F. G. Downing, 'Towards the Rehabilitation of Q', *N.T.S.*, 11 (1964–5).

Qadarites → Free-will and Predestination. J.R.

Qāḍī Muslim judge in a → *sharī'a* court. He should be a Muslim of high character, who is versed in sacred law and has sound sight and hearing. Women are not eligible for office. While in theory the Q. is responsible for dealing with both civil and criminal cases, his jurisdiction has mainly been restricted to matters of family law and inheritance, marriage and divorce, the care of widows and orphans, → pious foundations, etc. He should also deal with matters in which the *sharī'a* specifies a punishment laid down by God (→ *ḥadd*). This being God's ruling, the Q. should try anyone suspected of breaking such a law, and, if he is convicted, see that he suffers proper penalty. There was no appeal from the Q.'s judgment, but in fact such judgments were often overturned by governors. In mod. times systems of appeal have been intro. in most countries. Egypt and Tunisia have abolished the *sharī'a* courts; elsewhere the position of the Q. has changed. J.R.
E.I., II, pp. 606f. (*ḳāḍī*); Pareja, pp. 683ff.; Levy, *Social Structure*, pp. 338ff.; Coulson, *Law*, index; Mez, *Renaissance*, ch. 15.

Qādiriyya → Ṣūfī Orders. J.R.

Qarmaṭians (Carmathians) A sect of the → Ismā'īlīs. An insurrection was begun by Ḥamdān Qarmaṭ near Wāsiṭ in 288/900. He built place of security called *Dār al-hijra* (Abode of retirement), where meetings were held and a community was developed. His followers had to pay various contributions, not least of which was a fifth of their income. In add. to other contributions, there was a measure of communism. The initial rising was unsuccessful, but eventually the movement became strong in al-Aḥsā in the E. of modern Saudi Arabia. Raiding was carried on in Lower Mesopotamia, and pilgrim routes were cut. Mecca was taken in 317/930 and the → Black Stone was taken away. It remained in Q. hands till 340/951, when it was returned by order of the Fatimid Caliph. Elsewhere the movement had little success, but the centre in E. Arabia remained a source of trouble to the → 'Abbasids.

The Q. doc. denied all divine attributes, holding that the divine essence has given forth light by which various forms of intelligence and matter have been created; but created beings have no real individuality. The divine essence, which was alone at beginning, will be alone in the end. A course of initiation through various degrees was demanded, initiates being required to make firm promises not to reveal secrets. They were taught to use speculative philosophical reasoning, as a result of which doubts were raised about the systems of relig., including Islam. At same time they were taught to believe in authority of the hidden → *imām*, the infallible teacher, whence → Ghazālī calls them Ta'līmites, from *ta'līm* (teaching). Massignon credits them with considerable influence on philosophy and mysticism.

The Q. were also one of the influences towards the develop. of trade guilds. They have usually been described as a violent party causing death and havoc in neighbouring countries; but Nāṣir-i Khusraw (6th/11th cent.) gives an interesting account of their trading and treatment of workers. They advanced money to people in need, expecting payment only of the capital. This is sound Muslim economics, a return to which is advocated by many at present day, for interest is looked on as → usury. People who had suffered from some calamity were helped from public funds. J.R.
E.I., II, pp. 767–72 (Ḳarmaṭians); Pareja, index (Qarmaṭes); Nāṣir-i Khusraw, *Safar-nāma*, ed. and tr. C. Schefer (1881), pp. 226ff.; D. B. Macdonald, *Theology*, index; Sweetman, *I.C.T.*, II, p. 88; Hitti, *History*, index; Mez, *Renaissance*, pp. 304ff.

Qibla The direction towards which Muslims pray, commonly said to be Mecca, but more accurately the → Ka'ba, partic. the space between the spout (*mīzāb*) and the W. corner. Mosques are orientated so that the *miḥrāb* (niche, → Mosque) faces in correct direction. Elsewhere a calculation of the direction must be made. In Mecca Muhammad may have prayed facing Ka'ba, but with the → Hijra he faced Jerusalem during first 16 or 17 months; then the direction was changed to its present one. Qur. ii:109 says: 'To God belong the E. and the W.; whatever way you turn, God's face is there.' Bell in his trans. adds note saying this is a hint of coming change of Q. Blachère, *Coran* has a fuller note. It would appear that, since Muhammad obviously felt a Q. necessary, this v. is not so much a statement, as might appear on surface, that it does not matter where one faces, as an assurance of God's greatness and omnipresence. Later in same sura vv. 136ff. speak of change of Q., 139 saying, 'Turn your (i.e. Muhammad's) face in direction of the Sacred Mosque, and wherever you (pl.) are, turn your faces in its direction.' This desire to localise God is not peculiar to Islam. J.R.

E.I., II, pp. 985–9; Hughes, pp. 480f.; Pareja, index; Levy, *Social Structure*, index.

Quirinus God of Sabine orig., who formed third member of Roman divine triad with →→ Jupiter and Mars. Little is known of Q., but → Dumézil has argued that he was god of peace and fecundity, who completed the 'magical omnipotence of Jupiter' and 'the martial power of Mars'. S.G.F.B.

O.C.D., *s.v.;* G. Dumézil, *Jupiter, Mars, Quirinus* (1941[2]); A. Grenier, *Les religions étrusque et romaine* (1948), pp. 105ff.

Qumrân A location N.W. of Dead Sea; name appears in Wadi Qumrân, which flows into D. Sea from the W., and in Khirbet Qumrân, a ruined building complex from Hellenistic-Roman period on a rocky shelf N. of the wadi. The derivation of Qumrân is uncertain; it cannot (*pace* F. de Saulcy and others) be identified with Gomorrah. The identification of site of Khirbet Qumrân with the City of Salt (Heb. *'îr hammelaḥ*), mentioned as a Judaean frontier post in Josh. 15:62, was first suggested by M. Noth (*Josua*, 1938, p. 72); it has been confirmed by discovery of an Iron Age II settlement beneath Hellenistic-Roman foundations. To this earlier period belongs a circular cistern (cf. II Chron. 26:10), subsequently incorporated in water system which served later building complex.

Between 1947 and 1956 there were discovered in eleven caves in vicinity remains of over 500 documents, dated palaeographically to the two or three cents. preceding CE 70. With excavation of Khirbet Qumrân in 1951–6, it became apparent that these documents had belonged to library of a relig. community of Jews which had its head-quarters in this building complex for about 100 yrs. (*c.* 130–30 BC); then, after absence of some 30 yrs., for further phase of between 60 and 70 yrs., until Jewish War of CE 66–73. Between Khirbet Qumrân and the D. Sea lies the community cemetery, containing over 1,000 burials. The community cannot have numbered more than a few hundred at any time, although it may have had sympathisers in other parts of Palestine. While we must not assume that all the documents reflect beliefs and practices of community to which they belonged, the evidence of those which are most clearly 'community documents' combines with archaeological evidence, yielded by excavation of Khirbet Qumrân, to provide coherent picture of hist. and character of community.

Manuscript discoveries: Of the documents recovered from Qumrân caves, about 100 are biblical texts. The others incl. commentaries on biblical texts, liturgical and calendrical texts, prescriptions for community life, apocalyptic treatises and so forth. Very few are in anything like perfect condition; the great majority are fragmentary. Most are inscribed on skin. The predominant language is Hebrew, but some are written in Aramaic and a few in Greek. The 'Rule of the Community' gives valuable information on the members' way of life. So does the 'Zadokite Document', two early mediaeval copies of which were discovered in the *genizah* of the Old Cairo synagogue towards end of 19th cent.; it can now be assoc. closely with the Qumrân community, but belongs to a different stage in community's development from that repr. by the 'Rule of the Community'. (→ Damascus Fragment).

One import. aspect of these MS discoveries is that they present us with Heb. biblical texts 1,000 yrs. earlier than the earliest previously known to be extant, and in at least three different textual types: Babylonian (proto-Massoretic), Egyptian (the → LXX *Vorlage*) and (for → Pentateuch) popular Palestinian, closely akin to the Samaritan recension. But equally import. is the fresh information which they supply about a relig. movement in → Judaism contemporary with the later inter-Testamental period and the earlier N.T. period. Whereas Albert Schweitzer at beginning of 20th cent. knew of no 'general eschatological movement' which could serve as background for ministry of → John the Baptist and Jesus (*The Quest of the Historical Jesus*, 1910, p. 368), the Qumrân texts provide adequate evidence of precisely such a movement.

Origin of Qumrân Community: The *ḥasîdîm* (→ Hasidaeans), who bore brunt of persecution which followed Antiochus IV's decrees against continued practice of Jew. relig. (168–164 BC) and regarded the → Hasmonaean resistance as affording but 'a little help' (Dan. 11:34), looked for deliverance by divine intervention. The success of the Hasmonaeans was not the bringing in of everlasting righteousness, on which their hopes were fixed. Bewildered and unhappy, they felt like blind men groping for right way until a leader arose in whom they recognised a God-given 'Teacher of Righteousness', one who showed them how God's purpose would unfold and what their part was in its unfolding. Under his guidance, they betook themselves to the wilderness of Judaea, where they were organised as the true remnant of Israel. Special care was taken to maintain the priestly and levitical orders within the community. They disowned the Hasmonaean high-priesthood as illegitimate, since in their eyes the sons of Zadok alone could function as high priests. The last Zadokite high priest had been deposed by Antiochus IV in 171 BC. They, therefore, took no part in → Temple worship while it was defiled by unworthiness of the priests; but they themselves constituted a 'living Temple' to God, as the community of 'Israel and Aaron'—'Israel', i.e. the laity, being the 'holy place', and 'Aaron', i.e. the priesthood, being the 'holy of holies'.

Organisation and life: The nucleus of the community with which the Teacher of Righteousness started was fifteen: twelve laymen and three priests. In later days, when community had grown much larger, each group of ten, into which it was divided for various practical purposes, had to incl. one priest. In the new age, to which they looked forward, the priesthood would play a dominant part; the head of state himself would be a priest, superior even to the prince of the house of → David (the influence of → Ezekiel's blueprint for the new commonwealth of post-Exilic days is evident here). Those who entered community were called to be 'volunteers for holiness'. No one was obliged to enter; those who applied for admission were subjected first to a searching novitiate, and, when that was satisfactorily concluded, to a stern and lifelong discipline. During first probationary year, novices retained their personal property; during second year it was deposited with community treasurer; if, at end of that time, a candidate was admitted to membership, it was merged with the common fund. A stern penalty was imposed on anyone who 'knowingly deceived with regard to property'. The organisation of the community was hierarchical: there were priests, → Levites, elders, and the rank and file, commonly called 'the many'. At times a gen. assembly or 'session of the many' was held. Standing orders governed conduct of the meeting, incl. precedence in sitting down and decorum in addressing assembly and listening to others addressing it. The community was divided into 'camps', with an inspector in charge of each; a chief inspector was charged with maintenance of discipline over whole community. Activities by day and night were so arranged that some members, relieving each other by relays, were continuously engaged in reading and expounding sacred scriptures or in listening to their reading and exposition. The repeated ablutions and weekly eating of the shewbread, prescribed in the levitical law for the priests of Israel, were practised by whole community of Qumrân. Communal worship and communal consultation, organised in groups of ten (one of whom must be a priest), were regular features.

It is difficult to suppose that the strict regimentation of members' daily life could have left any room for marriage and family life. On the other hand, the Qumrân cemetery contained some female burials, and some community documents make provision for wives and children. It may be that, in course of time, strictness of discipline was to some degree relaxed; and prob. a distinction must be made between those men who embraced the full rigour of wilderness-asceticism, and those who sympathised heartily with basic tenets of community but continued to live 'in the world', in cities and villages of Palestine. The existence of such 'associate members' would not only account for evidence of family life but would also ensure congenial hospitality for full members, if they had to journey on community business. We may compare Jesus' injunction to his disciples to 'find out who is worthy', in any place they visit and stay with him until they leave it (Matthew 10:11).

Qumrân Theology: The Teacher of Righteousness imparted to his followers an interpret. of the Law (→ Torah) stricter than that of the strictest Pharisaic school. At Qumrân indeed the → Pharisees were viewed as intolerably lax, 'seekers after smooth things' or 'givers of smooth interpretations' (a phrase drawn from Isa. 30:10). The 'Teacher' also imparted to them a new and orig. interpret. of Heb. prophecy, acc. to which, they were now living on threshold of fulfilment of all that the prophets had foretold. It was their special function, by their devotion to the Law of God and their insight into his purpose, to be his instrument in winding up present age and inaugurating the age to come. While the present age, the 'epoch of Belial', was running its course, they had to endure privation and persecution for righteousness' sake; but their endurance would not only secure their own acceptance before God but would also make atonement for the land of Israel, polluted as it was by misdeeds of its rulers. But the time was fast approaching when they would be the executants of divine vengeance on the ungodly, espec. on the Gentile oppressors of Israel; thus would be realised the vision of → Daniel, in which he saw judgment given to 'the saints of the Most High' (Dan. 7:22). The form in which they envisaged this vengeance is spelt out in detail in the 'Rule of War', an outline of forty years' eschatological struggle (with a cessation of fighting every seventh year). In the first campaign (of six years' duration) the Kittim (prob. the Romans, as in Dan. 11:30) are attacked and wiped out; at end of the forty years evil is annihilated and the new age of righteousness decisively established. The end of present age and dawn of new age would be marked, they believed, by appearance of three personages foreseen by the prophets: a great prophet or second → Moses (the prophet of Deut. 18:15ff.), a great priest or second → Aaron, and a great warrior-king or second David. The last two are sometimes called 'Messiahs' (of Aaron and Israel respectively); where the title → Messiah occurs in the singular, it is the coming Davidic king that is meant. It does not appear that the Teacher of Righteousness was identified with any of these figures; he was rather a preparer of way for Messianic age than a Messianic personage himself. One feature of the new age would be restoration of an acceptable ritual in a purified Temple in a new Jerusalem, under a worthy priesthood.

The community literature attaches great importance to right knowledge—in partic., to knowledge of the mysteries of divine purpose, attainable through correct interpret. of the prophetic writings. The characteristic features of later → Gnosticism are absent. Qumrân anthropology was dualistic and may reflect Iranian influence; men belong either to dominion of prince of light or to that of prince of darkness, and their lot in this regard is determined in advance. Yet this dualism is subordinated to Jew. monotheism; it is God who foreordains men to one dominion or the other. (→ Dualism).

Community History: From earliest days the community had to face opposition and attempts at repression. Their principal opponent, during lifetime of Teacher of Righteousness, is ref. to as the 'Wicked Priest'. The epithet 'wicked' may mean primarily 'illegitimate', because non-Zadokite. While every high priest of Jerusalem after 171 BC was 'wicked' in this sense, the refs. to the Wicked Priest are best understood of one individual. He has been identified with a wide variety of historical characters, ranging from Menelaus (high priest 171–161 BC) to Eleazar, captain of Temple in CE 66; but is best identified with one of the Hasmonaeans, prob. with Jonathan, who succeeded his brother Judas Maccabaeus as insurgent leader in 160 BC and was high priest from 152 to his death in 143 BC. (→ Maccabees). The Teacher of Righteousness survived assaults of his enemies; this is implied by the application to him in one of the Qumrân commentaries of the words of Psalm 37:14f., 32f., to effect that he and his companions are delivered from the enemy, who is instead given over to the Gentiles for judgment. Jonathan fell into hands of the Seleucid regent Trypho, who put him to death; later the community (like the author of the 'Psalms of Solomon') saw in the overthrow of the Hasmonaean dynasty by the Romans divine nemesis on that dynasty as a whole for its persecution of the Teacher and his successors. At one time, perhaps, it was expected that the final dénouement would come within the Teacher's lifetime. When, however, he died (or, in Qumrân idiom, 'was gathered in'), his followers revised their time-schedule and reckoned that a last probation of forty years might intervene between his death and the ultimate judgment (compare the Christ. counterpart to this reckoning, based on Psalm 95:10, in Ep. Hebrews 3:7ff.). The Roman occupation of → Judaea in 63 BC was taken as sure sign that the end was imminent. This appears from a Qumrân commentary on Habakkuk, where Habakkuk's 'Chaldaeans' are interpreted as the Kittim (i.e. the Romans), who are sent by way of retribution against the wicked rulers in Israel, but who themselves act with such rapacity as to merit divine retribution in their turn. The régime of the Romans, however, lasted longer than was orig. expected. The Qumrân lit. (to judge by what has been published thus far) reflects conditions of the pre-Herodian cent. rather than those of last century of community's existence. Why the Qumrân centre was abandoned for thirty years towards end of first century BC we cannot be sure; the Parthian invasion (40 BC), or the fighting in which Herod made good his royal title (37 BC), or the earthquake of 31 BC which gravely damaged the buildings, or some unidentifiable circumstance, may have been the cause. Neither can we be sure if the reoccupation of the centre about 4 BC was accompanied by any modification of community's earlier outlook or way of life. Archaeological evidence suggests that the attack on and destruction of the centre about CE 68 by the Romans (who thereupon occupied part of it as military outpost) involved the overcoming of resistance. This resistance may have been offered by members of the community; it may have been offered by → Zealots who had commandeered the centre; the community may have made common cause with the Zealots. Even if events did not develop as had been forecast in the 'Rule of War', now was the time for all good men to march to the help of Yahweh against the mighty. The enigmatic 'Copper Scroll', found in Qumrân Cave 3, with its inventory of hidden treasure—temple property confiscated and stored away to serve as sinews of war?—may be related to this situation. As it was, the 'sons of darkness' triumphed and those 'sons of light' who survived were dispersed. If some of them joined forces with refugees from the → Jerusalem Church, that could account for some features which in following generations distinguish the Jewish-Christian → Ebionites from their fellow-Christians elsewhere (Gentile and Jewish alike).

Relation to other groups: The relation of the Qumrân community to other Jew. relig. groups is much debated. The → Therapeutae in Egypt, described by → Philo (*de vita contemplativa*), present several close resemblances; but they were a lay, rather than a priestly, community. The Pharisees, like the Qumrân community, prob. traced their spiritual ancestry back to the *ḥasîdîm* of early 2nd cent. BC; but, although their very name means 'separatists', they did not go nearly so far in their separation as the men of Qumrân did. They did not withdraw into wilderness, and, for all their differences with the → Sadducees and chief-priestly families, they did not refuse to take part in the Temple services. A similarity has naturally been recognised between the Zadokite sympathies of the Qumrân community and the designation of the Sadducean party, but this can be little more than fortuitous. It is not certain that 'Sadducee' has anything to do with the name Zadok; in any case, the Sadducees of history figure as partisans of the Hasmonaeans and of the high priests of Herodian and Roman periods, all of whom were repudiated by the men of Qumrân precisely because they usurped the office which belonged by right to the house of Zadok alone. More prob. is some assoc. between the Qumrân community and the → Essenes. The resemblances between the beliefs and practices of the Essenes, as described by Philo, Pliny, → Josephus, and → Hippolytus, and those of the Qumrân community, as reconstructed from the cave documents and archaeological findings at Khirbet Qumrân, suggest that the Qumrân community was one of several groups of Jew. nonconformists sharing the gen. designation 'Essene'. These resemblances do not amount to complete identity, but this may be due partly to fact that the Qumrân community was a somewhat eccentric Essene group and partly to the fact that the data of the Qumrân texts belong to an earlier stage of develop. than that reflected by our authorities for the Essenes. Outstanding points of resemblance are the long novitiate, strict discipline, ceremonial washings, common meals, hierarchical organization, respect paid to priesthood, community of goods, rigorous sabbath rules, study of prophecy and the exacting standard of righteousness. A suggested identification with the Zealot followers of Judas the Galilaean and his descendants is unconvincing; but it is prob. wrong to think of the Essenes and Zealots as sharply opposed. Hippolytus, indeed, speaks of one branch of Essenes distinguished as 'zealots' (*Philosophumena* ix:21).

If no direct contact between the Qumrân community and the early Christians can be estab., in part perhaps because of gaps in our evidence, yet both movements share a common heritage of Jew. nonconformity and the Qumrân material supplies a new and welcome background against which many parts of the N.T. can be read with greater understanding. Closer connection has been sought in → John the Baptist and in the devout community of Damascus with which → Paul was assoc. immediately after his conversion. F.F.B.

J. M. Allegro, *The Dead Sea Scrolls* (1956); H. Bardtke, *Die Handschriftenfunde am Toten Meer*, 2 vols. (1952, 1958); M. Black, *The Scrolls and Christian Origins* (1961); H. Braun, *Qumran und das Neue Testament*, 2 vols. (1966); F. F. Bruce, *Biblical Exegesis in the Qumran Texts* (1960); M. Burrows, *The Dead Sea Scrolls* (1955), *More Light on the Dead Sea Scrolls* (1958); F. M. Cross, *The Ancient Library of Qumran* (1958); G. R. Driver, *The Judaean Scrolls* (1965); A. Dupont-Sommer, *The Essene Writings from Qumran* (1961); A. R. C. Leaney, *The Rule of Qumran* (1966); E. Lohse, *Die Texte aus Qumran* (1964); J. T. Milik, *Ten Years of Discovery in the Wilderness of Judaea* (1959); K. Stendahl (ed.), *The Scrolls and the New Testament* (1958); R. de Vaux, *L'Archéologie et les Manuscrits de la Mer Morte* (1961); G. Vermes, *The Dead Sea Scrolls in English* (1962); *Revue de Qumran*, ed. J. Carmignac (Paris, 1958ff.): C. Burchard, *Bibliog. zu den Handschriften vom Toten Meer*, 2 vols. (1965); Y. Yadin, 'The Temple Scroll', *B.A.*, XXX (1967).

-Qur'ān Sacred book of Islam, roughly size of the New Testament. The orthodox doc. holds it to be the eternal, uncreated word of God, inscribed on the Preserved Tablet (→ *-Lawḥ al-maḥfūẓ*) in heaven. This is the archetype (*umm al-kitāb*, lit. mother of the book) from which the Q. was revealed piecemeal to → Muḥammad by → Gabriel. The name comes from *qara'a* (to read, or, recite). Muslims often call the book *-Furqān* (cf. ii:181), feeling that the word is a title. For different suggestions see *E.I.*², II, pp. 949f.; Jeffery, *Vocabulary*, pp. 225ff.; Bell, *Introduction*, pp. 136ff. and → Moses. Some hold that Muhammad was responsible for arrangement of Q. in its 114 suras, but this is questionable. The conventional story is that after battle in which → Musaylima was killed → 'Umar was troubled because many Q. readers had been killed, and advised → Abū'Bakr to have the various portions of Q. collected into a volume. After some hesitation, he gave Zayd b. Thābit the task. Later, in → 'Uthman's Caliphate, it was found that different readings existed in various parts of expanding empire, and Zayd was again employed, this time to draw up authoritative version which should supersede all others. This 'Uthmanic Q. is the version which is authoritative to present day. It is said that other versions were destroyed; but → Ibn Mas'ūd.

The suras are headed 'Meccan' or 'Medinan', meaning that they belonged to period before or after the → Hijra; but some Meccan suras have Medina vv. and *vice versa*. Except for number of shorter ones, the suras are not units; the subject changes, sometimes abruptly. No. xii is exceptional, for all but the last 10 of its 111 vv. deal with story of Joseph. No. lv has a refrain running throughout. In some others there are groupings of stories of prophets. In gen., except for first, the suras are arranged with longest at beginning and shortest at end. The shortest are 103, 108, 110 with three vv. each; the longest is No. 2 with 286 vv. Each one, except No. 9, begins with 'In the name of God, the Merciful, the Compassionate'. Some have a few separate letters at beginning, but no satisfactory explanation of them has been found. They have been called names of God and are used in → charms.

The fundamental teaching is that God, Creator of all things, is One, that he demands obedience, and that he will judge mankind on day of Judgment, rewarding faithful with → paradise and consigning the unbelievers to → hell. The Meccan suras have accounts of → early prophets, obviously to encourage Muhammad, for they tell of prophets who brought message which was rejected; in consequence unbelievers were destroyed. The Medina suras have many regulations to guide new community, e.g. laws regarding food, marriage, divorce, inheritance, condemnation of wine and gambling. There are also refs. to incidents in fighting with Meccans and instructions regarding fighting with infidels. The style of Medina suras is more matter-of-fact, as gen. rule, than that of the Meccan; but the fundamental docs. are still emphasised. One feature is a growing ref. to Muhammad's person and authority. Verses throughout normally have a rhyme, though not acc. to strict rules of rhyme in poetry. The assonance is of great help in recitation; one feels that the form of language is often determined by exigencies of the rhyme. For devotional purposes some divisions are made. There are 30 juz' (pl. *ajzā'*, portions) for reading Q. in a month. There are 60 *ḥizb* (pl. *aḥzāb*, divisions) with the quarter, half and three-quarters marked. These portions are marked in margin. There are also seven *manzil* (pl. *manāzil*, stages) for reading Q. in a week, but these are not normally marked in margin. The margin also contains indications of points where it is appropriate to prostrate oneself (→ sajda). Translators do not indic. these divisions.

The question of translating the Q. has caused considerable dispute. Because it is God's uncreated word many have argued that it is untranslatable, for by its very nature a trans. is different from the original. Some felt that there was no harm in a trans. if the Arabic text was printed alongside. There are many trans. in various languages, by Muslims and non-Muslims, some with, but most without the Q. text in Arabic. While Muslims may feel there is no harm in trans.: the Q., they would still hold that the trans. may give the meaning of the Q., but is not the Q. itself. What follows is a selected list of trans. G. Sale, *The Qurán*, ed. E. M. Wherry, 4 vols., London, 1896; E. H. Palmer, *The Koran*, World's Classics; J. M. Rodwell, *The Koran*, Everyman's Library; R. Bell, *The Qur'ān*, 2 vols., Edinburgh, 1937, 1939; A. Yusuf Ali, *The Holy Qur-an, Text, Trans. and Commentary*, Lahore, 1934 and later edns; Muhammad Ali, *The Holy Qur'ān*, Lahore, 1953⁵; M. Pickthall, *Meaning of the Glorious Koran*, London, 1930; Bashir al-Din (under auspices of), *The Holy Quran with Eng. trans. and comm.*, Rabwah, 1955; A. J. Arberry, *The Koran Interpreted*, 2 vols., London, 1955; R. Blachère, *Le Coran*, 2 vols., Paris, 1949, 1950 (suras arranged in a chronological system); shorter edn., in one vol., Paris, 1957, gives the suras in normal order; D. Masson, *Le Coran*, Paris, 1967; R. Paret, *Der Koran*, Stuttgart, 1963–6. While giving the suras in the normal order, Bell tries to separate different elements within the suras, suggesting dates for them.

The Q. is valued, not only for its teaching, but also as something sacred in itself. Sura lvi:78, speaking of the Q., says, 'Only the purified shall touch it'. A good Muslim should, therefore, be ritually pure before even touching a copy of the Q. J.R.

H. Hirschfeld, *New Researches into composition and exegesis of the Qur'ān* (1902); Nöldeke, *Geschichte*²; A. Jeffery, *The Qur'ān as Scripture* (1952); Bell, *Introduction;* H. U. W. Stanton,

The Teaching of the Qur'ān (1919); F. Rosenthal, *Ibn Khaldun*, index; Rahman, *Islam*, ch. 2; Pareja, ch. 11.

Qur'ān, verse numbering Since Flügel's edition of the Q. and his Concordance (1842) most West. translators have followed his verse numbering, a system which is not acceptable among Muslims. The numbering of the standard Egypt. Q. has gained favour in Muslim circles, though there are other oriental recensions with some differences. In this Dictionary Flügel's numbering has been followed in giving Q. refs. because so many trans. use it. Blachère and Paret in their trans. give both systems of numbering. Masson gives the Egypt., but supplies comparative tables on pp. 983ff. Palmer, Rodwell, Bell and Arberry all keep to Flügel's numbering. Bell, *Introduction*, ix, x gives 'Table of Differences' between the two systems. In many places the two coincide, but a slight difference frequently occurs, amounting in two instances to as many as 7 vv. See also Bell, *Introduction*, p. 58. J.R.

Quraysh Tribe, named after eponymous ancestor, of which → Muḥammad was member. About mid. 5th cent. CE, under their leader Quṣayy, they took from → Khuzā'a the sacred territory round the → Ka'ba, and developed Mecca as mercantile centre. As members of Q. became custodians of Ka'ba, their influence was doubly great. They opposed Muhammad when they thought he was undermining their ascendancy; but after the Conquest of Mecca they realised that their influence still counted. It was long a dogma of most → Sunnis that the → Caliph should be descended from Q., and the Shi'a → *imāms*, except 'Alī, were all descendants of Muhammad. J.R.

E.I., II, pp. 1122–6; Guillaume, *Life*, pp. 52–61 and *passim*; Hughes, p. 483; Watt, *Mecca*, *passim*, *Medina*, *passim*; Levy, *Social Structure*, index.

R

Rabbi(s) Heb. = 'my master'. The term orig. in Palestine (it was current in 1st cent. CE) for person expert in Jew. law and thus qualified to give decisions. Through the centuries the office has increased in importance and acquired official status, with recognised preparatory training. Today the R. is a communal official, concerned with educational, social and pastoral as well as relig. matters. Rabbinic lit. chiefly comprises commentary and exposition of → Torah, embodied in → Talmud (→→ Judaism; Mishnah; Targums). S.G.F.B.

E.J.R., pp. 319–20; Oesterley-Box, *L.R.M.J.*

Rābi'a al-'Adawiyya (*c.* 99–185/717–801). Famous Muslim woman ascetic, mystic and saint of Basra. She believed firmly in God as the One, and held that to put anyone or anything beside him was polytheism. When asked if she loved → Muḥammad, she replied that she did, but that she had been turned away by love of the Creator from love of his creatures. Though she believed in God's greatness, she held that the soul could come into union with him. Purification was essential to attain this, so everything which might detract from contemplation of God should be put aside. A characteristic doc. of hers was love of God without desire of reward, or because of fear of punishment. By such love she felt that union would be attained. Throughout her life she practised strict asceticism; she was held in such respect that miracles were attributed to her. (→ Asceticism, Islam). J.R.

E.I., III, pp. 1089–91; Margaret Smith, *Rābi'a the mystic* . . . (1928), *Early Mysticism*, pp. 185ff., 218ff. and index, *Ghazālī*, index; Ibn Khallikān, p. 215.

Radhakrishnan, S. Sarvepalli Radhakrishnan, a S. Indian → Brahmin, has been an influential interpreter of Hinduism and Indian philosophy. As well as holding various university posts, incl. King George V Chair of Philosophy in Calcutta, and Spalding Chair of Eastern Religions and Ethics at Oxford, he has been successively Vice-President and President of Republic of India. He has expounded a moderate and universalistic version of → Vedanta, playing down somewhat the doc. of → *maya* in Advaita; and has over long period urged unified view of Indian trad., in which the different schools of philosophy and different relig. movements have delineated different aspects of one ultimate reality. Considering that many of present sufferings of men are due to materialism and relig. and other divisions, he has propounded an idealistic Vedanta as means of perceiving unity of relig. and true destiny of mankind. He has also edited and trans. with commentary some of the more import. texts of Indian trad., incl. the *Dhammapada* (1948); *The Bhagavadgita* (1948); *The Principal Upaniṣads* (1953); and *The Brahma Sutra* (1960). These trans. are useful in presenting both text and trans., though the commentary is often more homiletic than exegetical. R.'s principal writings are: *The Hindu View of Life* (1927); *An Idealist View of Life* (1932); *Eastern Religions and Western Thought* (1939); *Indian Philosophy*, 2 vols. (1923–7). He has also helped to edit various works, incl., with C. A. Moore, *A Source Book in Indian Philosophy* (1957). N.S.

P. A. Schilpp (ed.), *The Philosophy of Sarvepalli Radhakrishnan* (1952), which incl. bibliography of R.'s writings by T. R. V. Murti.

Rādhā Soāmī Movement The Radha Soami Satsang is a movement with Sikh and Hindu affinities orig. in teachings of Shiv Dayal (1818–78), a banker in Agra, who was much influenced by teachings of *Adi* → *Granth*, though brought up as Vaisnavite. The name of group signifies union between Radha, symbolizing the soul, and Soami (Swami), the Master (i.e. God); and identity also repeated between → guru and God and between disciple and guru. Shiv Dayal taught a form of → yoga, known as *śabd yoga*, concentrating on the *sabd* or creative word emanating from supreme Being. The movement divided after Shiv Dayal's death, one centre continuing at Agra under succession of *gurus*, the other (now more vigorous one) on river Beas, near Amritsar, the first of this line of *gurus* being a Sikh. The Beas Radha Soamis attracted fair amount of interest and support among Sikhs, Hindus and others. Though opposed to principle of the *Khalsa* (→ Sikhism), Beas gurus have remained outwardly *kesadhari*, but there are strong differences from orthodox Sikhism. First, the *guru* plays import. role, and in effect replaces the *Granth* (though teachings of first five Sikh Gurus are recognised); it is the *guru* who performs initiation into group; second, the Radha Soamis do not recognise Sikh initiation, and more gen. claim to be movement which adherents of all religs. can follow; third, the account of supreme Being and structure of universe is more elaborate than that typically expressed by Sikhism. Save for initiation, the movement is not ritualistic. N.S.

J. N. Farquhar, *Modern Religious Movements in India* (1919); Radha Soami Satsang (publishers), *Radha Soami Colony, Beas and its Teachings* (1960).

Rāhula Son of Gotama → the Buddha. Acc. to Pali texts, R. was born at → Kapilavatthu about time that Gotama left his home in search of enlightenment. Later, Gotama visited Kapilavatthu, when R. was still a child, and the boy was ordained a → *samenera* or novice of the Buddh. order. Thereafter he was recipient of much of Buddha's teaching, acc. to the canon; a number of → Jātaka stories and Suttas are trad. regarded as having been addressed by the Buddha to Rāhula. The collection of verses known as the → *Theragāthā*, (the Pslams of the Brethren) incl. some attr. to R. (vv. 295–8). He is said to have pre-deceased the Buddha. T.O.L.

Rājagaha (Pali)/**Rājagṛha** (Skt.) City in anc. India of import. in early hist. of Buddhism. It was capital of kingdom of Magadha during earlier period, until Pātaliputta (Patna) took its place. It was situated to S. of the Ganges, and a little S. of present town of Rājgir. In Buddh. hist. its chief import. is that it was scene of → Council said to have been held immediately after death of the Buddha, for purpose of agreeing on authentic version of discourses of Buddha (→ Suttas) and the monastic Discipline-code (→ Vinaya). At that time, acc. to → Buddhaghosa's commentary on the Vinaya Pitaka, the Samantapāsādikā, there were 18 large monasteries in R. One of these was the first *ārāma*, or permanently enclosed ground, to be donated to the → Sangha, viz, the *Veluvana* or 'Bamboo-grove', given to Buddha and his monks by King → Bimbisāra. (→ Monasteries, Buddh.). By time the Chi. pilgrim → Hsuan-tsang visited place in 7th cent. CE, R. was largely in ruins, with jungle closing in on the ruined buildings, and a small surviving village. T.O.L.

Malalasekere, *D.P.P.N.*, vol. II, pp. 721–4; S. Beal, *Buddhist Records of the Western World* (1884), vol. 2, pp. 161–7; J. Marshall, 'Rajagriha and its Remains', *Archaeological Survey of India, Report* (1905–6), pp. 86–106.

Rak'a Word from root meaning 'to bow', which is used as name for a section of the prayers. (→ Prayer, Islam). J.R.

Rāma The seventh *avatara* of → Viṣṇu, and, next to → Krishna, the most important. Hero of → *Ramayana*, he may have been an historical person, poss. a local chief in region of Ayodhya or Banaras (his father-in-law, Janaka certainly existed, and is mentioned in → Upaniṣads). R. was esp. popular in N. Indian Vaisnavism in late medieval period, and his name (as 'Ram') became common name for God. R. is taken as supreme example of justice, patience in adversity, faithfulness and gentleness. N.S.

Ramaḍān 9th month of the Muslim lunar year, when the annual fast is observed (→ Fasting, Islam). It was during this month that Muḥammad is reported to have received first Quranic revelation (→ Laylat al-Qadr). J.R.

E.I., III, p. 1111; Hughes, pp. 533–5.

Ramakrishna Properly Rāmakṛṣṇa, and also titled Śri Rāmakṛṣṇa Paramahaṃsa, the Bengali saint after whom the → Ramakrishna Movement (Mission, Math) is called, and who provided initial source of inspiration. He has thus been a seminal figure in mod. Hindu renaissance. Born of Brahmin family in Hooghly district of W. Bengal, he early showed signs of religiosity and capacity for mystical ecstasy. In 1856, at age of 20, he became chief priest of → Kali temple at Dakshineshwar on outskirts of Calcutta. He increasingly was susceptible to visions of Kali, and performed rigorous meditative exercises. Under influence of Tota Puri, an Advaitin monk, he came to interpret his experiences from standpoint of → Advaita or Non-Dualism. However, his position was a 'realistic' one, i.e. not committed to illusionism (→ *maya*) which characterised medieval Advaita: he regarded world and Absolute (*Brahman*) as equally real. Religiously, he combined approaches of → *bhakti* and meditative knowledge (→ *jnana*). This synthetic approach to Hindu trad. itself was carried over to other faiths; R. attempted to explore through living practice the faiths of Islam and Christianity, and claimed to have experiences of Allah and Christ. During such periods of exploration he dressed and acted as Muslim and Christian. This relig. experimentalism is at basis of followers' claim that there is a universal truth present in different religs. Though no intellectual, he attracted great attention from a group of mainly Bengali intellectuals, among whom he made conversions: the most notable was → Vivekananda, who proved to be the organising genius and principal ideologist of new movement. R., as well as attempting to transcend relig. divisions, also went beyond caste feelings which had at one time been strong in him, because of his upbringing. His character had a sweetness, sim plicity and charismatic quality which made him renowned as saint. His teachings were typically cast in form of parables, stories and similes. Many of these have been preserved, though he wrote nothing. He died in 1886. N.S.

M. Gupta (ed.), *The Gospel of Sri Ramakrishna* (1947); R. Romain, *The Life of Ramakrishna* (1954); Swami Saradananda, *Sri Ramakrishna, the Great Master* (1951).

(Movement) Stems from teachings of → Ramakrishna, consolidated by intellectual and organising ability of → Vivekananda. It was first formally organised as Ramakrishna Mission in 1897; and reorganised in 1909, so that educational, charitable and missionary side of work could be separated, for legal purposes, from monastic side, known as the Math. Henceforth comprehensive name for movement has been the R. Math and Mission. Apart from head monastery at Belur Math, there are branch monasteries in major cities of India and in some smaller centres. The Mission has huge new headquarters at Gol Park, Calcutta. There are R. Vedanta Centres in N. and S. America (New York, Boston, Chicago, Los Angeles, San Francisco, Buenos Aires, etc.) and in Europe (London, Gretz in France, etc.); while educational and charitable work is carried out in Fiji, Mauritius, Malaysia, Burma, etc., where there are Indian communities. As well as running schools and hostels for students, movement has done much, through publishing, lecturing, etc., to disseminate Vedantin heritage. In stressing universal character of Hinduism and adapting itself to social needs of a society in transition, the movement has been one of factors in the mod. Hindu renaissance. N.S.

Swami Gambhirananda, *History of the Ramakrishna Math and Mission* (1957).

Rāmānanda A seminal figure among N. Indian reforming → *bhakti* movements which attempted to synthesise best in Hinduism and Islam, R. (? 1299–1410) was a → Brahmin of Prayaga (Allahabad) and pupil of Rāghavānanda, an → *acarya* or leader of the Sri Vaiṣṇava sect of → Ramanuja, living in → Banaras. At first a follower of → Advaita, R., influenced by Raghavananda's Vaisnavism, eventually founded his own sect, which emphasised equality of all castes before God. Though his theology did not differ substantially from that of → Visistadvaita as expounded by Ramanuja, R. was socio-relig. revolutionary, and incl. among chief disciples, twelve in number, Brahmins, a Muslim, a Panjabi peasant (Jat), a leather-worker or Chamar (thus an outcaste), a soldier and two women. Thus he effectively estab. an egalitarian movement, which was to have profound effects. One disciple, → Kabir, was not only an ancestor of → Sikhism but also of the Kabīrpanthī sect, while two others founded less import. sects. Beyond Kabir, there was Dadu, who was founder of the → Dadupanthis. It was characteristic of these movements to urge caste-equality and a *bhakti* devoted to single Lord, often without recourse to worship of images. The relig. of R. leaned on cult of → Rama, and a later import. figure in promoting this type of Vaisnavism was → Tulasi Das, interpreter of → Ramayana in the N. Indian vernacular. The consonance of R.'s preaching with some of ideas of Indian → Sufis helped to spread movement towards inter-relig. understanding, esp. among lower classes, less committed to Brahmanical understandings of Vaisnavism. The followers of R. are known as Ramanandis or Ramavats. N.S.

R. G. Bhandarkar, *Vaisnavism, Saivism and Minor Religious Sysyems* (1913); G. A. Nateson (ed.), *Ramananda to Ram Tirath: Lives of the Saints of Northern India* (1947); J. C. Oman, *Mystics, Ascetics and Saints of India* (1903).

Rāmānuja Hindu philosopher and → Vaisnavite theologian, and chief exponent of → Visistadvaita (Qualified Non-Dualism) school of Vedanta. He is trad. held to have been born in CE 1017, but prob. later; he died in ? 1137. R. came from Bhūtapurī in S. India and studied sacred knowledge in Kanci and Srirangam, under Yāmuna, whose teachings foreshadow those of pupil. Though he married, R. gave up world at age of 30, to become a → *sannyasin.* He preached in both N. and S. India. He was primarily concerned to combat docs. of → Advaita, which seemed to him incompatible with relig. of → *bhakti.* On returning to Srirangam, he suffered some persecution from ruler and moved to Hoysala country; eventually, however, he was able to return to Srirangam, where he died. His chief writings were his commentary on the → *Brahmasutra*, a commentary on the → *Bhagavadgita*, the *Vedāntadīpa* ('Lamp of Vedanta'), the *Vedāntasamgraha* ('Epitome of Vedanta') and the *Vedāntasāra* ('Essence of Vedanta'). His achievement was not merely literary; for in writing systematically a synthesis of Tamil bhakti relig. (→ Alvars) and Sanskrit Vedantin trad., he gave new shape to S. Indian Vaisnavism and came to be venerated as its foremost saint. His emphasis on devotion led to strong account of work of God's grace, and his followers, the Srī Vaiṣṇavas, divided into two main schools, the → Vadagalai and → Tengalai, who differed on interpr. of role of human effort in attainment of salvation. N.S.

S. N. Dasgupta, *Hist. of Indian Philosophy*, vol. 2 (1932); B. Kumarappa, *The Hindu Conception of Deity as Culminating in Ramanuja* (1934); G. Thibaut (tr.), *The Vedanta-Sutras with the Com-*

mentary of Ramanuja, Max Müller (ed.), *S.B.E.*, vol. 48 (1904); J. A. B. van Buitenen, *Ramanuja on the Bhagavadgita* (1953); M. R. Rajagopala Ayyangar, *Vedanta Sangraha of Sri Ramanuja*; N. B. Narasimha Ayyangar (tr.), *Vedantasara* (1953).

Rāmāyaṇa One of two great epics of Hindu literature (→ *Mahabharata*); was prob. completed by 1st cent. BC (though first and last of its seven books are later). Trad., it is ascribed to the sage Vālmīki. It is more homogeneous than *Mahabharata*, and much shorter (24,000 stanzas). It appears to have orig. in Kosala, in N. India, and much of action takes place in capital of that kingdom, Ayodhyā. The hero of epic, as its title ('Career of Rama') is → Rama, who came to be treated as an → *avatara* of Viṣṇu. (In first book he is described as such, an indication of its later composition.) The story mainly concerns vicissitudes of Rama and his wife Sītā, when latter is carried off by Rāvaṇa, demon king of Lankā (Ceylon). Previously, Rama, who had married Sītā after demonstrating his strength at her father's court (he being king of Videha), had been impelled to give up succession to own father's throne and had lived with wife as a hermit. He had helped to clear forest of Daṇḍaka of many demons plaguing ascetics dwelling there. Ravana, therefore, decided to take revenge, on behalf of his fellow-demons. He comes to hermitage disguised as ascetic, and seizes unsuspecting Sita. She is then born off in Ravana's aerial carriage to Lanka. Rama and his half-brother Lakṣmaṇa search for her, and get help of monkey king Sugrīva, who entrusts his best adviser Hanumant (Hanuman) with job of finding Sita. He discovers her in Lanka, and returns to gather army of monkeys, who form bridge across sea from India to Ceylon. After great battle, culminating in duel between Rama and Ravana, the latter is slain, and Rama appoints a new king of Lanka. However, he no longer accepts Sita as wife, because of doubts as to her innocence in captivity. She defies his suspicions by throwing herself on a pyre, but firegod → Agni refuses to consume her. Rama and Sita now joyfully return together to Ayodhya, where he is crowned king. In last book, there is a less happy ending. The people of Kosala murmur against Sita, being unconvinced of her innocence. Rama gets Lakṣmaṇa to take Sita away and abandon her. She finds her way to Valmiki's hermitage, there giving birth to twins. After they have grown up. Rama recognises them as own, and Sita asks earth to swallow her to demonstrate her utter innocence. Duly she is so swallowed up. Not long thereafter Rama gives up kingdom to the twins, and resumes his place in heaven as → Viṣṇu. Among vernacular versions of story of Rama, the most influential was that of Tulasī Dās (or Tulsi Das) (? CE 1532–1623), whose *Rāmacaritamānasa* is Hindi rendering of it, in many respects different in sentiment and plot from *Ramayana* itself, and stressing very strongly relig. of *bhakti* which Tulasi Das wished to teach. N.S.

H. P. Shastri (tr.), *The Ramayana of Valmiki*, 3 vols. (1952–9); R. C. Dutt, *The Ramayana and the Mahabharata* (1910); W. D. P. Hill, *The Holy Lake of the Acts of Rama* (1952).

Rashīd Riḍā (d. 1354/1935). Born in Tripoli (Lebanon), studied in Cairo, and became follower and later biographer of → Muhammad 'Abduh. He founded the journal *al-Manār* in 1315/1898, carrying it on till his death. His purpose was to foster social, relig. and economic reforms, to prove Islam is suitable for mod. conditions, to uphold divine law as instrument of government, to remove superstition, devotion to saints, and practices not in keeping with orig. Islam, to counteract false doc. and → Ṣūfī practices, and to promote education. He had earlier advocated importance of a → Caliph who would be head of a relig. society, with independent rulers in different countries; but when Turkey abolished Caliphate, he turned towards → Wahhābī docs. with which he had much in common. He and his associates are commonly called the *Salafiyya*, indic. a doc. of return to orig. Islam free from accretions, or the *Manār* Party. Among their interests have been equal rights of education for boys and girls, disapproval of → polygamy, and advocacy of women's rights. R.R. began a Quranic commentary in *al-Manār* in which he tried to show the Qur. has message for every age. He allowed allegorical interpretation, but would not admit that Qur. could be infallible only in relig. and moral matters, though not necessarily in matters historical and scientific. The influence of movement's teachings is still felt. J.R.

C. C. Adams, *Islam and Modernism in Egypt* (1933), index; *G.A.L.*, S, III, pp. 321–3; G. Antonius, *The Arab Awakening* (1938), pp. 109, 159f.; Pareja, index; A. Hourani, *Thought*, index; Cragg, *Counsels*, index.

Rē Egypt. sun-god and chief state-god. Rē is → Coptic word for sun; Greeks rendered it 'Ra'. R. was gen. assoc. with patron-gods of ruling dynasties. His earliest assoc. was with → Horus Harachte, a falcon-deity. At → Heliopolis R. was identified with → Atum. The Heliopol. → Pyramid Texts solarises king's *post-mortem* destiny. The shifting of government to Thebes in Middle and New Kingdom led to R.'s assoc. with → Amun; → Akhenaten's substitution of → Aten for Amun was aimed, *inter alia*, at strengthening solar element in state-cult. During New

Kingdom (1580–1090 BC), many of R.'s attributes were usurped by → Osiris, who tended to eclipse him as Egypt's chief god (→ Scarab). S.G.F.B.

S. A. B. Mercer, *The Religion of Anc. Egypt* (1949), ch. 7; *R.Ae.R-G.*, pp. 626ff.

Rebirth → Metempsychosis.

(Buddh.) →→ Samsāra; Death, Buddh. view; Paticca-Samuppada. T.O.L.

(China–Japan) → Rebirth (Buddh.). D.H.S.

Recluse (Chinese) Assoc. in China with both → Taoism and → Buddhism. There is mention of R. in anc. literature, e.g. → *Analects* 18:6–7, where they seem to have turned their backs on world in order to maintain their personal purity and integrity. Throughout course of Chi. hist. it was not unusual for Confucian scholars, espec. in periods of turmoil, to hide their talents and go into retirement in order to preserve their moral integrity and cultivate union with nature. Both Taoism and Buddhism in China had their R., 'old men in the mountains', who in caves and solitary mountain hermitages practised meditation, thaumaturgy and → shamanism. Many devoted themselves to trance and asceticism, and stirred popular imagination by their alleged supernatural powers. A famous example is the dhyāna-master, Po Sêng-kuang (d. *c.* 397 at the age of 110), who lived for 53 years in his mountain hermitage, remained in trance for 7 days at a stretch and was believed to have regular contact with ferocious beasts, mountain spirits and Taoist immortals. Whilst aim of Confucian R. was to keep clear of an official career and preserve his moral integrity, and that of Taoist was to seek after immortality, the Buddh. R. kept himself from entanglements of world in order to strive for emancipation of all beings. D.H.S.

E. Zurcher, *The Buddhist Conquest of China* (1959); H. Welch, *The Practice of Chinese Buddhism* (1967), pp. 318ff.

Reformation, The A relig. revolution which took place in 16th cent.; it broke unity of medieval Christendom, giving place to the new Protestant Churches, and a renewed Catholicism. That unity had always been more apparent than real: the twin authority of Pope and Emperor was source of continual tension, while the attempt to reform Church by Councils, in 15th cent. had floundered on rock of nationalism. By 16th cent., the cry 'Reform the Church in Head and Members' was centuries old, and at every level of society there was resentment at a Church 'legalised, externalised, institutionalised to a degree which would have horrified the Apostles' (Lortz). There had been saints and doctors and movements of renewal during 15th cent.; but not enough to move against inertia of vested interest. The humanists had turned attention to Bible (e.g. the Erasmus New Testament, 1516; the Complutensian Polygot, 1522), seeking truer texts, based on better manuscripts, and using more accurate exegesis.

In many universities there was tension between the humanist theological programme, based on Bible and the Fathers, and that of the later Schoolmen. Such was Wittenberg, where from 1512 Martin → Luther was Prof. of Biblical Studies, as well as Prior and District Vicar of order of Eremetical Augustinians. In 1517 a Jubilee Indulgence was promulgated in German lands under authority of young Archbishop of Mainz; on Oct. 31st 1517 Luther wrote him, protesting against → Indulgences and enclosing copy of 95 Theses about Indulgences, which that same day (the Eve of All Saints Day) he nailed to door of the collegiate church of All Saints, Wittenberg. The Latin theses were soon turned into German, printed and widely circulated before end of year. Slowly repressive authority began to move. In 1518 Luther was summoned before the Thomist Cardinal Cajetan at Augsburg, but refused to recant. In 1519 a debate with theologian John Eck forced him to face the implications of his repudiation of papal power. In 1520 the Papal Bull *Exsurge Domine* condemned him. To this he replied in a succession of writings, appealing to all classes of the German people and awakening lively response. At the Imperial Diet at Worms in April, 1521, Luther appeared before young Emperor Charles V, and resolutely refused to withdraw. Under protection of his prince, Frederick the Wise, Luther went into hiding in historic castle of the Wartburg, where he began the trans. of Bible into German, a work of genius which was to lay deep impress on language, life and relig. of his nation. Luther's theological statements, notably about the → Mass, about private masses, → celibacy, monastic vows, (→ Monasticism), had practical implications, during his absence, owing to activities of others, notably his senior colleague Andrew Karlstadt, who proclaimed an iconoclastic programme of legalistic Puritanism. Luther was forced to come from hiding and returned to Wittenberg in March 1522, redressing situation in a brilliant series of sermons. Luther had henceforth to fight on two fronts: against → Papacy, and against the new radical ferment which had grown up in Thuringia. The latter was led at first by Thomas Müntzer, (→ Anabaptists), a gifted but violent preacher of anti-clerical war, who led the Thuringian Peasants to disaster in war of 1525. Luther vigorously dissoc. himself from movement in his 'Against the murdering, thieving hordes of peasants'.

By 1525 other patterns of R. were emerging, in

cities of Switzerland and South Germany, and in England, France and Scotland. But Wittenberg remained a centre of powerful propaganda. Here Luther found help in genius of Philip Melanchthon, whose humanistic educational programmes earned him the title 'Praeceptor Germaniae'. Important, too, was John Bugenhagen, who became parish Priest of Wittenberg and organiser of reform in N. Germany and in Scandinavia. Luther and his colleagues lectured and preached in Univ. of Wittenberg, whence there went a stream of Lutheran influence into many cities of Germany, Austria, Hungary and Scandinavia. Luther's hymns, liturgies ('German Mass, 1526'), and Catechisms helped to nourish the Lutheran Churches. By 1526 there was political support for Luther by a group of princes, and concessions were made by the Catholics, which were withdrawn in 1529. The 'Protestants' against this withdrawal, a group of princes and of 14 Imperial cities, gave to Protestantism its abiding name. In 1530 at Diet of Augsburg, these Prots. put forward the Augsburg Confession, the work of Melanchthon, and this became normative for Lutheranism. In Denmark the Augsburg Confession and Lutheran faith were adopted 1536–7; its Church order came from John Bugenhagen. Reform was imposed in Norway, by Danish Crown at same time, and, after a prolonged and bloody struggle, upon Iceland. In Sweden the R. owed most to the ruler, Gustavus Vasa, the Archdeacon Laurentius Andreae, and the brothers Olaus and Laurentius Petri. In the Swedish R. the → apostolic succession was kept. In Finland a former Wittenberg student, Mikael Agricola translated much of Bible into Finnish. There was a considerable Lutheran infiltration into Poland, Bohemia and Austria; but in E. Europe gen. Lutheranism found its strongest hold in Hungary.

Another pattern of R. emerged in the cities, which with their self-contained community life, and their structure of guilds and councils, created a planned reformation in which preachers and the 'godly magistrates' worked hand in hand. Ulrich → Zwingli (1483–1531) was a thorough Swiss and former army chaplain. As preacher at the Gross Münster in Zürich, he led the R. there, defending a public protest against the Lenten fast in city in 1522. Two public Disputations (Jan., Oct. 1523) won over authorities and much public opinion to side of reform. Not until 1525 were the Mass and images abolished, and Zwingli able to intro. the most simple and radical of R. liturgies. By this time a group of young Zwinglians, led by Conrad Grebel and Felix Manz, who had repudiated Zwingli's reliance on 'godly magistrate', pressed for radical reform and began to baptise adults (1525). They were at first exiled, and then treated with increasing severity from Prot. and Cath. authorities. This Anabaptist movement spread rapidly and widely, despite severe persecution. Zwingli's noble dream of a Chr. commonwealth led him to try to build a civic league of Prot. cities, which led in end to war with the Cath. cantons and his death on disastrous field of Cappel, Oct. 1531. Other cities had undertaken planned reform on similar lines: Basle under leadership of humanist scholar, John Oecolampadius; St. Gallen under Vadianus, Berne by group of laymen incl. the artist and dramatist Manuel. In Strasbourg, a band of gifted men, Martin Bucer, Wolfgang Capito, Matthew Zell had to fight hard for reform in a city which seemed to have magnetic attraction for a series of radical adventurers. But it was in French-speaking Switzerland, and in the genius of John → Calvin, that this emerging pattern found its habitation. Calvin (1509–63), a Frenchman, had come to Geneva in exile from one of the fierce flurries of persecution in France. He was trained in law, and vastly learned in theology and espec. in Bible and the Fathers. In 1538 the R. movement in Geneva was checked, and with his ebullient associate, William Farel, Calvin went into exile. In next three years, in Strasbourg he learned much from reformation there. In 1541 he returned to Geneva at request of city, which accepted his celebrated *Ordonnances Ecclesiastiques*. Thenceforth he dominated city with his preaching, liturgies, catechisms, and a moral oversight, accepted with great earnestness by his followers. Geneva became a city of refuge for Prots. from France, and a training ground for pastors of Reformed Church. Calvin's famous *Institutes* (begun 1536, final edition 1559) provided theological arsenal for the new Protestantism, a synthesis of Bible, the Fathers, Luther and Swiss R. In France, which seemed natural ground for Calvin's R., the R. became involved in political and military ploys between Crown and nobility. The first generation of humanist reformers was soon scattered into exile by Francis I; but the new faith spread quickly to all levels of society, and soon had powerful friends at court. Despite constant and watchful attention of Calvin, and his assistant and successor Theodore Beza, consolidation of Reformed Church in France was an indigenous affair. The political and military entanglements of Protestantism and Catholicism in France led to various compromises which bade fair to make former an import. state within the state, while bloody reprisals, and notably the Massacre of Saint Bartholomew (1572) only strengthened Prot. resistance. Finally, the 'politiques', who cared more for peace and political unity than for relig. war, triumphed in the compromise peace of the Edict of Nantes (1598).

In Holland, there were fierce persecutions in a land which was under direct rule of Spanish Emperor. There was a swift development of radical Anabaptist movement, culminating in the debacle at Munster in Westphalia (1535), which permitted develop. of a more peaceful Biblical pietism under Mennoz Simmons. Meanwhile, both Lutheran and Calvinist influences were current. In 1561 the confession of faith (*Confessio Belgica*) was published. Now Protestantism became involved in struggle for Dutch Independence under William the Silent, which continued after his assassination in 1584, and ended in estab. of Dutch Republic, when for a half-century Dutch art and Dutch theology were preeminent. In Scotland, too, the Reformed church triumphed, after twenty years of struggle, under leadership of John Knox and Andrew Melville. The Scots Confession (1560) is one of most forthright Prot. confessions. Calvinism also infiltrated into E. Europe, in Poland, Austria, and espec. in Hungary.

In England, the relig. R., which linked the humanists at Oxford and Cambridge with survival of medieval → Lollardy, was soon entangled in matrimonial troubles of King Henry VIII. These involvements resulted in a national Church, and breaking of all ties with Papacy. Scholars like Tyndale and Cranmer produced an English Bible and English liturgy in reign of Edward VI. Queen Mary I attempted to bring country back to Catholicism; but, despite heavy persecution, the Prot. cause grew and reached a certain stability in the reign of Elizabeth I.

The radicals of the R. ranged from organised sects of Anabaptists to individual thinkers and spiritualists, among whom were Hans Denck, Sebastian Franck, Caspar Schwenckfeld. Spain and Italy were most difficult areas for Prot. R. Certain exiled Italian reformers, who turned from mysticism to rationalism, led way to anti-Trinitarian and Socinian theology (→ Unitarianism). These relig. movements, which constituted the Prot. Churches and the R., were interwoven with political and sociological conditions which, in increasing momentum of European life, saw birth pangs of modern world. E.G.R.

T. M. Lindsay, *History of the Reformation*, 2 vols. (1906–7); B. J. Kidd, *Documents Illustrating the Continental Reformation* (1911); J. Lortz, *Die Reformation in Deutschland*, 2 vols. (1939); H. J. Grimm, *The Reformation Era* (1954); E. G. Léonard, *Histoire Générale du Protestantisme*, 3 vols. (1961–); G. H. Williams, *The Radical Reformation* (1963); E. G. Rupp (chs. 3–4), N. K. Anderson (ch. 5), R. R. Betts and F. C. Spooner (ch. 6), G. R. Elton (ch. 7) in *The Cambridge New Modern History*, II (1958).

Refrigerium In anc. Egypt. → eschatology the dead were imagined as thirsty, and assurance of refreshment is a reiterated theme of mortuary texts and iconography (e.g.: 'may Osiris give thee water'). This idea of parched condition of dead occurs in many religs. of anc. Near East (it finds expression in N.T., Lk. 16:24). *Post-mortem* refreshment (*refrigerium*) was also a theme of early Chr. eschatology. S.G.F.B.

A. Parrot, *Le 'Refrigerium' dans l'au-delà* (1937); A. Stuiber, *Refrigerium Interim: die Vorstellungen von Zwischenzustand u. die frühchrist. Grabeskunst* (1937).

Refuges, The Three (Buddh.) → Tri-ratna. T.O.L.

Regeneration The idea occurs in two different forms in hist. of relig. The Grk. word *palingensia* ('born again') was used in → Stoicism with ref. to cyclic theory of → Time, acc. to which, after a cosmic conflagration, world-order is reborn and repeats itself again. This idea occurs in N.T. (Mt. 19:28). R. was used in a mystical sense in → mystery religions. Rituals of → initiation often signified that neophyte died to former self and was reborn to new life. Paul's doc. of → Baptism in Romans, 6:1ff. is the most notable example of such R. R. can be used in the quite different context of → metempsychosis. S.G.F.B.

E.R.E., X, *s.v.;* A. D. Nock, *Conversion* (1933), *s.v.* ('Rebirth'); G. Wagner, *Das religionsgeschichtliche Problem von Römer* 6, 1–11 (1962); *H.D.B.*², *s.v.*

Reincarnation →→ Metempsychosis; Rebirth.

Relics The preservation of objects, believed to contain beneficial virtue because of former associations, is very anc. Fragments of skulls, apparently used as cups, from Paleolithic sites may indic. belief that some virtue of dead owner might thus be imbibed: there are modern ethnological parallels. The cult of R. flourished in Egypt: e.g. head of → Osiris was venerated at → Abydos; frags. of cosmic egg were shown at → Hermopolis. Greece provides many examples, deriving from → hero-cult (bones of Theseus at Athens, shoulder-bone of Pelops at Elis): possession of such R. ensured a city's reputation and safety. The Chr. cult of R. began early in connection with remains of → martyrs. Belief in efficacy of such R. led to division of remains among many churches and persons, and to eager search for R. connected with Biblical persons. Such demand inevitably resulted in invention of R. and attr. of various magical virtues to them. Almost every conceivable item connected with O.T. heroes, Christ and the saints, was exhibited somewhere (often in more than one place): e.g. frags. of Cross, Christ's shroud, Moses' rod, feathers from Gabriel's wings, the Virgin's milk, and even the prepuce of Christ. Miracles were claimed for R., and more famous became objects of → pilgrimage. The cult of R. has flourished in → Buddhism (remains of the Buddha are treasured in many places), in → Jainsim and → Islam. S.G.F.B.

E.R.E., X, pp. 650–62; Brandon, *C.L.*, p. 49; *O.C.D.*, *s.v.; D.C.C.*, *s.v.; R.G.G.*[3], V, col. 1042–7; J. A. MacCulloch, *Medieval Faith and Fable* (1932), ch. 9; B. Kötling, *Der frühchristliche Reliquienkult und die Bestattung im Kirchengebäude* (1965); J. Walsh, *The Shroud* (1964).

(Buddh.) It is claimed by Buddh. that some relics of Gotama the Buddha are still enshrined in the great pagodas; e.g. a tooth, in Temple of Sacred Tooth at Kandy, in → Ceylon; some hairs, in the Shwe Dagon Pagoda at Rangoon, in Burma. In this matter Buddhism is distinguished from the other Indian religs. of → Hinduism and → Jainism, which do not inculcate showing of reverence to relics of a human body. On the other hand, → Islam, which, like early Buddhism, had no recognised object of worship, has developed this feature. It is poss. that it was customary in N. India at time of Buddha to build cairn over bones of a great man, and give honour to them, and that this is origin of Buddh. use of the → *stupa*, in which relics not only of Buddha, but of other Buddh. saints are said to be enshrined. Another of Buddha's relics, which it is claimed has been preserved, is his alms-bowl or *patra*, which, comments Eliot, 'plays a part somewhat similar to that of the Holy Grail in Christian romance'. Acc. to the → *Mahāvaṃsa*, the emperor → Ashoka sent it to Ceylon. Various legends are concerned with its subsequent travels. Acc. to Marco Polo, it was taken from Ceylon to China by order of Kublai Khan in 1284, although acc. to other legends, it is in Persia, Kandahar. (→→ Buddha, The; Gotama; Mahā-Parinibbāna Sutta). T.O.L.

Mahāvaṃsa; Da Cunha, *Memoir on the History of the Tooth Relic of Ceylon* (1875); C. Eliot, *Hinduism and Buddhism* (1921, repr. 1957), III, pp. 22–8.

(China–Far East) Though Japan, Korea and Siam seem to care little for R. properly so-called, when → Buddhism became firmly estab. in China, one of main purposes of numerous → pilgrimages to India and the W. was to bring back holy R. of the Buddha and Buddh. saints, by possession of which great monasteries enhanced their prestige. From Han Dynasty onwards, there are well-attested discoveries of anc. seals and other regalia, amulets, inscribed stones, jade or bronze objects which were regarded as auspicious objects and tangible proofs of the ruler's virtue. Their finding was often marked by miraculous happenings, luminous emanations and other supernatural phenomena. Buddhists, wishing to prove early existence of Buddhism on Chi. soil, record at least nine discoveries of 'Aśoka-relics' (→ Aśoka) during 4th cent. CE. The numerous → pagodas were primarily memorials erected over R. of Buddh. saints. In CE 819, the emperor Hsien-tsung, a devout Buddh., proposed to bring a celebrated R., a finger-bone of Buddha, to the capital, to be lodged in imperial palace for three days and afterwards exhibited in various temples. A famous Confucian scholar, Han Yü, used occasion to write a memorial to the throne condemning Buddhism, and advising that the relic should be destroyed by fire and water, and the pernicious cult exterminated. For this he was demoted and banished. D.H.S.

E. Zürcher, *The Buddhist Conquest of China* (1959), *passim*; C. P. Fitzgerald, *China* (rev. edn. 1950), pp.352–5.

(Islam) R. of Muhammad are preserved in a number of mosques and elsewhere, incl. hairs and teeth. The most common relic is his footprint, of which there is example at rock in Jerusalem from which he ascended to Paradise (→ Mi'rāj). The words used for relics are *athar sharīf* (noble relic, pl. *āthār sharīfa*) and *dhakhīra* (treasure). J.R.

E.I., II, pp. 604f. (*ḳadam sharīf*); *E.I.*,[2] I, p. 736 (*athar*); *E.R.E.*, X, p. 662; Goldziher, *M.S.*, II, pp. 356–68; Mez, *Renaissance*, pp. 337–9.

Religion, Origin of This subject, closely related to that of origin of idea of → God, has been abundantly discussed. Many theories have been advanced in explanation, Most start from a preconceived theory: e.g. E. B. Tylor's → animism; S. Freud's Oedipus' myth; R. Otto's idea of the → Holy. Sounder conclusions are to be drawn by investigating earliest evidence of human culture which archeology has provided. What might be termed → Paleolithic Relig. reveals man's preoccupation with the three basic issues of food, birth (fertility) and death. In dealing with these he resorted to actions that, rationally, had no apparent practical value. By so doing, man evidently believed that he could utilise or invoke powers beyond those which he himself naturally possessed. How he conceived of such power(s) is obscure; his magical practices suggest some idea of a power that could be utilised by ritual-miming of thing desired. It is possible that some conception of the → Great Goddess, as source of life, was already current, and perhaps that of a 'Lord of the Beasts', who owned the animals man hunted. In such → ritual actions the same proleptic motive operated as in other activities, e.g. tool-making, namely to seek security by anticipating future needs. In other words, relig. appears to have been essentially assoc. with man's time-consciousness as was also his material culture. His time-consciousness made man aware of his mortality, thus causing sense of fundamental insecurity and prompting quest for *post-mortem* security. In Paleolithic era this quest found expression in → funerary rites designed to secure and provide for p.m. existence of dead. (→ Time). S.G.F.B.

L. H. Jordan, *Comparative Religion* (1905); *E.R.E.*, X, pp. 662–93; H. Pinard de la Boullaye, *L'étude comparée des religions*, 2 vols. (1925); G. van der Leeuw, *La Religion* (1948); M. Eliade, *Traité d'histoire des religions* (1949), E.T., *Patterns of Comparative Religion* (1958); 'Quest for the "Origins" of Religion', *H.R.*, IV (1964), 'Crisis and Renewal in Hist. of Religions', *H.R.*, V (1965); J. Wach, *The Comparative Study of Religions* (1958); E. O. James, *The Origins of Religion* (1948); E. Cassirer, *An Essay on Man* (1944); A. N. Whitehead, *Religion in the Making* (1927); P. A. Ashby, 'The Hist. of Religions', in P. Ramsey (ed.), *Religion* (The Princeton Studies, 1965); *R.G.G.*[3], V, col. 966–7, 986–94; J. Maringer, *The Gods of Prehistoric Man* (E.T. 1960); S. Giedon, *The Eternal Present: the Beginnings of Art* (1962); G. Clark, *The Stone Age Hunters* (1967); Brandon, *M.D.*, chs. 1, 12, *History, Time and Deity* (1965), 'Ideas of the Origin of Religion', in *D.H.I.*

Religions, Comparative Numbers The following are the estimated strengths of the major religs. given for 1966 in the *Britannica Book of the Year* (1967), p. 668: Christian (969,591,000); Muslim (478,885,000); Buddhist (168,389,000); Hindu (416,863,000); Jewish (13,382,000); Confucian (365,008,000); Taoist (53,362,000); Shinto (69,115,000); Zoroastrian (150,000). It must be emphasised that these can only be very approx. estimates; they repr. rather the numbers of those brought up within the cultural traditions denominated. S.G.F.B.

R.G.G.[3], V, 'Karte der Religionen u. Missionen der Erde'.

Religionsgeschichte Expression used by German-speaking scholars for field of study designated in English 'History of Religions'. The use of the (Eng.) plural 'Religions' is significant, because it emphasises fact that each relig. is to be treated as a distinctive historical phenomenon. To speak of 'History of Religion' (sing.) might imply *a priori* assumptions about the nature of Religion such as to preclude objective consideration of specific groups of relevant data in their historical context. R. is, thus, carefully distinguished by some scholars from → Comparative Religion and → Phenomenology of Religion. In practice, however, it is difficult to investigate historical data of any relig. without some measure of interpretation that inevitably involves ref. to the other two disciplines. R. is, nevertheless, of basic importance, because the historical data of any relig. must be properly ordered and studied before its wider significance can be evaluated. R. has been used comparatively in Biblical studies (e.g. C. Clement, *Religionsgeschichtliche Erklärung d. N.T.*, 1924). S.G.F.B.

See bibliographies to Comparative Relig. and Phenomenology of Relig. *R.G.G.*[3], V, col. 986–94; A. Bertholet, *Wörterbuch der Religionen* (1952), *s.v.*; E. Lehrmann in *L.R-G.*, II, pp. 1ff.; H. Stephan, *Gesch. d. deut. evang. Theologie* (1960[2]), pp. 276ff.; M. Eliade, *H.R.*, 5 (1965), pp. 1ff.; M. Brillant et R. Aigrain (ed.), *Histoire des Religions*, 5 vols. (1953–6); M. Gorce et R. Mortier (ed.), *Histoire générale des religions*, 5 vols. (1948–52); G. van der Leeuw (ed.), *De Godsdiensten der Wereld*, 2 vols. (1949); G. Widengren, *Religions Värld* (1953[2]); N. Turchi, *Storia delle religioni*, 2 vols. (1954); P. T. Venturi (ed.), *Storia delle religioni*, 2 vols. (1954[4]); R. Pettazzoni, *Manuali di storia delle religione*, *Numen*, I (1954); M. Eliade-J. M. Kitigawa, *The Hist. of Religions: Essays in Methodology* (1959).

Resurrection (1) The idea of R. of the dead occurs in religs. where man is regarded as a psycho-physical organism. Acc. to this evaluation, the physical body is as essential as → soul to personal life. Consequently a significant afterlife demands R. of body as well as survival of soul. R. is not necessary in religs. that regard soul as inner essential self, which migrates from body to body (→→ Metempsychosis; Buddhism; Hinduism; Orphism). In anc. Egypt. → funerary ritual was designed to resurrect body as → Osiris had been resurrected. Belief in R. was estab. in → Judaism by 2nd cent. BC (→ eschatology, Jew.); it was inherited by → Christianity and → Islam. Ultimate R. is also envisaged in → Zoroastrianism (→ eschatology, Iranian). In its orig. form in these religs. R. was conceived as a re-animating of physical body. However, in Christianity and Zoroastrianism it was believed that resurrected body would be made physically perfect and of an appropriate age.

(2) The R. of Christ, although it authorises Chr. hope of personal R., is a unique instance: it has some phenomenological parallels with R. of Osiris. The nature of the N.T. records preclude reliable knowledge of orig. of belief in R. of Christ: the belief seems to have stemmed from conviction of certain disciples, preeminently → Peter, that they had seen Jesus after his death; this orig. conviction was later elaborated in accounts stressing physical reality of his R. (e.g. Lk. 24:37ff.; Jn. 20:24ff.). However, despite his

resuscitation in his crucified body, Christ, like Osiris, did not resume his earthly life; he ascended to heaven. Acc. to → Paul's doc. of → baptism (Rom. 6:3ff.), baptised Christians are assimilated to Christ, and begin a new risen life in their risen Saviour.

The R.'s of Osiris and Christ are distinguished from R.'s of vegetation deities such as →→ Adonis, Attis, Tammuz by their historicised presentations. S.G.F.B.

A. T. Nikolainen, *Der Auferstehungsglauben in der Bibel und ihrer Umwelt*, 2 vols. (1944); G. Thausing, *Der Auferstehungsgedanke in aegyptischen religiosen Texten* (1943); *R.G.G.*[3], col. 688–702; Brandon, *M.D.*, chs. 2–8; *Judgment of the Dead* (1967), chs. 2, 4, 6–8; *D.C.C.*, pp. 1157–8; *R.A.C.*, I, col. 919–38; Ch. Guignebent, *Jésus* (1947), pp. 601ff.; M. Goguel, *La naissance du Christianisme* (1946), pp. 41ff.; R. Elkund, *Life between Death and Resurrection acc. to Islam* (1941); J. D. C. Parry, *The Zoroastrian Doctrine of a Future Life* (1929); *E.J.R.*, p. 331.

(Islam) The Qur. speaks of a day when all dead will be resurrected and judged. It is variously called the Day of R. (*yawmul qiyāma*, e.g. ii:79, 107); Day of Decision (*yawmul faṣl*, e.g. xxxvii:21; lxxvii:14); Day of Judgment (*yawmul din*, e.g. i:3; xxxvii:20); Day of Reckoning (*yawmul hisāb*, e.g. xxxviii:15; xl:28); Day of Upraising (*yawmul ba'th*, xxx:56); the Hour (*al-sā'a*, e.g. vii:186; xvi:79; xxi:50). There are many refs. to awful nature of the day. The R. is to be in bodily form. 'From it (sc. the earth) we created you, into it we shall return you, and from it we shall bring you forth a second time' (xx:57). The Meccan unbelievers could not accept idea of bodily R. They are quoted as saying, 'What! when we die and become dust and bones, shall we be raised up?' (xxiii:84, cf. xiii:5; xxvii:69; lxxix:10f. etc.). The Qur states clearly that God the Creator has power to bring dead back to life (xlvi:32). When unbelievers ask who will give life to dead bones they are told that it is God who gave them life at first and who has all power (xxxvi:78ff.). Men will rise at the summons. 'When he gives you a summons, lo, from the earth you will come forth' (xxx:24). Sinners will imagine they have been no longer than an hour in their graves (xxx:54f.; xxiii:114ff.). In xxxix:68 ref. is made to two blasts of trumpet. After first blast all swoon, but some whom God excepts, and after the second all stand up looking (cf. lxxix:6f.). Then judgment begins. It is to be noticed that the blast is for 'all who are in the heavens and in the earth'. → Bukhari and → Muslim have a trad. traced to → Abu Hurayra in which Muḥammad says that between the two blasts there will be forty, but when questioned Abu Hurayra refused to say whether Muhammad meant days, months, or years. Then God will send down water which will make men sprout. The only thing in man which does not decay is the tail-bone (*'ajb al-dhanab*), from which the frame will be reconstituted on the day of R. Trad. speaks of various signs before last day (→ Hour). The reconstitution of old body presented difficulty to later scholars. There was the problem that a body became dust which was changed into vegetation which nourished another man, so all bodies are not distinct from one another. → Ghazali said the body with which man rises need not be identical with the orig. → Averroes (Ibn Rushd) held that philosophical proof cannot make immortality known; revelation is needed. Another aspect is question whether soul is immortal. If that is so, it involves allegorical interpretation of R. as meaning that immortal soul is joined to a spiritual body (cf. 1 Cor., xv:35ff.). J.R.

E.I., II, pp. 1048–51; Hughes, pp. 537–44; Wensinck, *Creed*, index; H. U. W. Stanton, *The Teaching of the Qur'ān* (1919), p. 103; Van den Bergh, *Tahāfut*, index; G. F. Hourani, *Averroes*, p. 53; J. Macdonald, 'Eschatology', *I.S.* (June 1966), pp. 129ff. See also index to Qur'ān trans. by Arberry, Bell, Blachère, Masson, Muhammad 'Ali. *Mishkāt*, pp. 1165ff.; Sweetman, *I.C.T.*, I, II, IV, index.

Retaliation (Islam) In Muslim law R. (*qiṣāṣ*) applies to killing and injuries which are not fatal. Qur. xvii:35 (Meccan) makes it clear that, while next of kin has right to take vengeance for a death, he must not be extreme, which may mean that no more than a life for a life is to be exacted. ii:173 (Medinan) specifies like for like in R. and adds that this may be waived in return for payment, which makes a final settlement. In iv:94f. distinction is made between accidental and intentional killing of a believer. Death is not to be penalty for accidental killing, but certain punishments are prescribed; punishment for intentional killing of a believer is Jahannam (→ Hell) presumably, though not stated here, after execution for murder. R. is applicable for non-fatal injuries, Qur. v:49 being quoted in justification. Here the Qur. seems to accept O.T. law of an eye for an eye, etc., but adds that one may remit punishment as a gift. The → trads. give specific instances of killing or maiming with treatment prescribed. One, e.g., given by both →→ Bukhari and Muslim, tells how a woman had broken a girl's front tooth. The matter was taken to → Muḥammad and he ordered R. to be taken. Protest was made, and when the girl's family said they were prepared to accept a fine, this received Muhammad's approval. The schools have varied in matters of detail regarding carrying out of R., but they have recognised the practice.

In mod. times modifications have taken place. The individual may not now act on his own in R. The one who is charged must be proved to have committed the offence before punishment is justified. J.R.

E.I., II, pp. 822–8 (ḳatl), pp. 1038–41 (ḳiṣāṣ); Hughes, pp. 481f. (qiṣāṣ); Guillaume, *Traditions*, pp. 107–10; *Mishkāt*, Book XV; Querry, II, pp. 541ff.; Coulson, *Law*, Part III, and index (codes, criminal law, homicide).

Retreat (Islam) R. (*i'tikāf*), is used of period spent in a mosque during which one engages in certain devotions accompanied by fasting. During period one may go out only for necessary purposes. → Muḥammad is said to have observed such a R. during last ten days of → Ramaḍān, in which part of the month → *Laylat al-Qadr* is believed to occur. Trad. says that during a R. Muhammad would visit an invalid, going direct to his house and not allowing any interruption. Another says the → sunna is that one who is observing a R. should not visit an invalid, attend a funeral, embrace his wife, or go out for anything but necessary purposes. → Abū Dāwūd records both. J.R.

E.I., II, p. 564; Hughes, p. 222; Wensinck, *Handbook*, p. 206; *Mishkāt*, pp. 444f.; Querry, I, pp. 210ff.; M. Smith, *Early Mysticism*, index.

Revelation Most religs. claim to embody supernatural truths that have been divinely revealed. The means of such revelation are various. The following examples are representative: Egyptians believed that ch. 30 of → Book of Dead had orig. been found under statue of → Thoth; → Yahweh revealed → Torah to Moses and his will on specific occasions through → prophets; Christians believe both life and teaching of → Jesus constitute divine revelation; the → Qur'ān embodies revelation of Allah to → Muhammad; the *Gāthās* purport to record revelations of → Ahura Mazdah to → Zoroaster; many → Upanishads are *śruti* ('revealed literature') assoc. with renowned sages; the doctrines of Buddhism are presented as revelations of the → Buddha. Supernatural guidance on specific issues was also sought through → divination, → necromancy, and oracles (→→ Delphi, Sibylline Or.). The psychology of R. is complex. In essence, R. purports to be knowledge about the divine purpose and will which could not be known by ordinary means of investigation or ratiocination. Such R. is usually evaluated as authorising the peculiar claims of the relig. concerned. (→ Dreams). S.G.F.B.

G. Van der Leeuw, *La religion* (1948), pp. 412ff.; *R.G.G.*³, IV, col. 1597–1613; S. Morenz, *Aegyptische Religion* (1960), pp. 32ff.; *E.R.E.*, X, *s.v.;* S. Radhakrishnan, *The Principal Upaniṣads* (1953), pp. 22ff.; *H.D.B.*², pp. 847–9; *E.J.R.*, p. 332.

(Hindu) So far as there is a conception of R. in Hindu trad., it is that of *śruti*, lit. 'what is heard', taken to ref. to Vedic hymns together with the works (→→ *Brahmanas*, *Aranyakas*, Upaniṣads) appending thereto. This corpus is collectively the → Veda. Paradoxically, what is prob. the most relig. influential book in Hindu trad., the → *Bhagavadgita*, does not belong to *śruti*, but rather to corpus of auxiliary writings having some authority known as → *smṛti*, lit. 'what is remembered'. This auxiliary corpus is typically taken to comprise the *dharmaśāstras* or law books, notably Law Books of → Manu (the *Manusmrti*), → *Puranas* and *itihāsa* or Epics, the last, of course, incl. *Bhagavadgita*. However, despite theoretical supremacy of Veda, many later expositions of *bhakti* relig. put as much emphasis on works lying outside both trad. *śruti* and *smṛti*, such as hymns, etc., of the → Alvars, and various scriptures (*āgamas*) of Saivite pietism. As to *śruti*, it has been trad. considered that it was heard or delivered to seers or → rishis of anc. past. But there have been varying views as to ultimate provenance of this revealed Veda. For → Yoga school, it is essentially result of intuition of the rishis considered as yogis. Thus truth of R. is accessible to yogic intuition. For → Sankara the higher truth contained in R. is likewise result of inner realisation, in this case the non-dual intuition of identity of → *Brahman* and → *Atman;* but the scriptures have function of pointing to this experience. For → Nyaya-Vaisesika, the scriptures orig. from God, and derive validity from him, as one who is omniscient. On other hand, the → Mimamsa, being atheistic, could not validate scriptures thus, and regarded them as eternal. They, therefore, denied the periodic collapse and re-creation of universe, a belief virtually universal among other Hindu schools, since belief would call in question eternity of scriptures. The Advaitin view of *śruti*, which has analogues in → Mahayana Buddhism, amounts to view that essential meaning or import. of scripture is what scripture ref. to, i.e. it is a 'non-propositional' view of revelation. In Indian philosoph. discussions, import. part is played by concept of testimony (*śabda*) as a source of knowledge about reality, since it was function of *śruti* as a form of testimony to acquaint people with truth about transcendental realm. N.S.

J. N. Farquhar, *Outline of the Religious Literature of India* (1920); M. Bloomfield, *The Religion of the Veda* (1908); R. C. Zaehner (tr.), *Hindu Scriptures* (1966); B. D. Basu (ed.), *The Sacred Books of the Hindus* (1909–29); S. K. Murthy, *Revelation and Reason in Advaita Vedanta* (1959).

(Islam) →→ Inspiration; -Qur'ān. J.R.

(Jain) As → Jainism is atheistic there is no question of its deriving teachings from divine R. Nevertheless, the teachings handed down orally from time of → Mahavira are authoritative, though it is not clear how far these are fully repr. in Jain canon. In early 2nd cent. BC, the schism between → Digambaras and → Svetambaras is supposed to have begun, and with it, disagreement about canon. It was considered that full knowledge of orig. oral trad. was lost. But the Svetambaras reconstructed scriptures and reduced them to final form at council in 5th cent. CE. They consist of eleven sections (*angas*), and are in *ārdhamāgadhī* ('semi-Magadhi', i.e. dialect of Magadha, where Mahavira preached), but influenced by later Maharashtrian dialect. Despite disagreements, the shape of Svetambara and Digambara docs. is so close that antiquity of the teachings contained in canon, even though it was finalised so late, can be accepted. However, though the anc. teachings are in this sense authoritative, they are not regarded as having essentially derived from Mahavira. The latter, as → Tirthamkara, attained omniscience; and he thus gained perfect knowledge of nature of reality; but this was known in principle before his time, back to time of → Parsva and beyond. N.S.

G. Della Casa, *Il Giainismo* (1962); H. Jacobi, art. 'Jainism' in *E.R.E.*; and tr. *Gaina Sutras*, Max Müller (ed.), *S.B.E.*, vols. 22 and 45 (1884, 1895).

Ṛgveda The 'Royal Veda' or 'Royal Knowledge' (also transliterated *Ṛig* and *Ṛig Veda*), most import. of four collections (*saṁhitās*) of Vedic hymns. Composed over longish period up to *c*. 900 BC, the hymns were used in sacrificial ritual of → Vedic relig. Hymns drawn from R. are rearranged in another of the collections, the → *Samaveda*. As part of orthodox Hindu canon (→ Revelation, Hindu), they are treated as eternally valid expressions of transcendental truth, etc., though the → Upaniṣads in fact came to have greater importance theologically. There are 1028 hymns in the R., addressed to various gods, the most important being →→ Indra, Agni, Varuna, Soma. Lesser gods later to assume great significance were → Viṣṇu and → Rudra (→ Śiva). Goddesses were not prominent. The hymns increasingly displayed kathenotheistic tendencies, ascribing attributes of other gods to the one being addressed and raising him, within framework of given hymn, to supreme status. Growing interest in problem of creation of world brought out monotheistic tendencies, and exaltation of → Prajapati, together with speculations such as those contained in 'Hymn of Creation' and the → *Purusasukta* (*Ṛgveda*, x:40, 129). The collection also contains the → Gayatri, used in daily prayer. The language is a precursor of classical Sanskrit, and not all of it is perfectly understood. N.S.

Max Müller and H. Oldenberg (trs.), *Vedic Hymns*, 2 vols., in Max Müller (ed.), *S.B.E.*, vols. 32 and 46 (1891–7); F. Geldner (tr.), *Der Rig.-veda*, 3 vols. (1951); A. A. Macdonell, *Hymns from the Rig Veda* (1922).

Righteousness (China–Japan) The import. Chinese character *i*, usually translated R. has implicit within it the idea of restoring harmony and concord after disagreement, by giving satisfaction to the interested parties. Hence *i* is what is just, right, equitable, proper. R. is recognised as one of the four cardinal virtues of → Confucianism. Regarded as an attribute of → T'ien and the sage-kings of former times, it is mark of the superior man (*chün-tzŭ*). It was → Mencius who raised R. to highest level of moral values, and taught that R. is a true expression of man's orig. nature, to be prized more than life itself. R. in the ruler, not only justice in a legal sense, but uprightness, integrity and love of the people, is basis of well-being and prosperity of the state.

→ Shinto has no recognised ethical code. The more specific virtue of R. (*seigi* or *nahoki-koto*) is incl. in basic individual virtue of sincerity (*makoto*), which is a life-attitude of sincerity, faithfulness, loyalty, gratitude and love, stemming from awareness of the divine. It is following the Way of the → Kami (*kannagara-no-michi*). The Japanese, from intro. of → Confucianism in 5th cent. CE, were greatly influenced by the Confucian ethic, with its concept of R. as a universal law to which all beings should conform; also by the Buddh. ideal of R. as embodied in the → *arhat* or perfected saint. (→ Ethics). D.H.S.

L. Wieger, *Chinese Characters* (new edn. 1965), p. 179; W. T. Chan, *Source Book in Chinese Philosophy* (1963), pp. 50ff.; Jean Herbert, *Shinto* (1967), pp. 68ff.

Rinzai (Chinese: Lin-chi). Founded by the Chi. Buddh. Lin Chi or I-hsüan (d. CE 867), and intro. into Japan by → Eisai (1141–1215), R. became one of the two major schools of → Zen, distinguished from → Sōtō by unorthodox means employed to attain sudden enlightenment, i.e. striking and shouting, the use of nonsensical language and paradox, and the → koan exercises. It flourished in the Kamakura period; its great temples became centres of great cultural and artistic achievement. The great R. master, → Hakuin (1685–1768) laid foundation for mod. development of Zen. D.H.S.

H. Dumoulin, *Hist. of Zen Buddhism* (1963); D. T. Suzuki, *Studies in Zen* (1955).

Rishi Or ṛṣi, a Vedic sage or seer. The R.'s were supposedly composers of revelation (*śruti*) comprising the Vedic hymns. The term was more widely used of anc. sages in Hindu trad., and is sometimes applied honorifically to mod. figures claiming special insight into divine reality. The primary R.'s were seven in number: Gautama, Bharadvāja, Viśvamitra, Jamadagni, Vasiṣṭha, Kaśyapa and Atri (acc. to the *Śatapatha* → *Brahmana*—later works give different lists). Acc. to theory of world-ages (→ Time, Hindu view of), each different epoch has different set of R.'s. Of special importance among R.'s outside primary seven are → Bṛhaspati, founder of astronomy/ → astrology; and → Manu, lawgiver and teacher of → Sanskrit to mankind. Manu also had cosmic significance, since each → *kalpa* is divided into 14 *manvantaras* or 'Manu-reigns' presided over by a Manu. N.S.

Rites and Rituals (Chinese) From earliest recorded times R. have played a dominant role in China, not only in relig., but in organisation of social and political life. It was in 1st Mil. BC, during the Chou Dynasty, that a detailed corpus of R. grew up to govern the mutual relationships of a feudalistic society, to ensure meticulous performance of those ceremonies by which the gods and ancestor spirits were worshipped, and to provide detailed prescriptions for correct procedure in all major events of life, such as birth, marriage, death and mourning. The scholar-class, through whose agency China was governed, were trained in R., for which → Confucius himself evidenced a profound concern. Though regarding R. as fundamental in all harmonious relationships and as chief means of beautifying life, Confucius insisted that R. must never be divorced from sincerity (*ch'êng*), and was outward manifestation of benevolence (*jên*) and → righteousness (*i*). R. was regarded as one of the four cardinal virtues.

Once China had become unified under a supreme ruler, the empire came to be regarded as an organic structure in which every person, from emperor to meanest peasant, each had his appropriate duties and functions, and harmony and well-being of the whole depended upon meticulous performance of the rituals of a state cult, whilst the life of everyone from cradle to grave was controlled by R. An over-emphasis on R. resulted in a hide-bound conservatism, and a measure of artificiality and even hypocrisy pervading human relationships. (→→ Li; Li Chi).

Our chief source for the R. & R. of Confucianism is the *Li Chi*, vols. 27 and 28 in the *S.B.E.* For the detailed R. of Buddh. monastic life in China, see H. Welch, *The Practice of Chinese Buddhism* (1967). D.H.S.

(Japanese) Our chief source for the R. & R. of → Shinto is the → Engishiki, which gives a minute description of official Shinto R., as performed in 10th cent. The most solemn and import. of these R.'s was the *Ohonihe* or Great Food Offering, performed soon after accession of a Mikado to throne. The successive phases of nearly all Shinto rituals were: (1) the purification of participants and of place where the rites were to be performed; (2) the summoning of the → Kami; (3) the presenting of symbolic offerings, songs and dances to the *kami*; (4) the chanting of the → norito (prayers); (5) divination; (6) withdrawal of offerings and inviting the *kami* to retire; and (7) a sacred communal feast. The primary interest of the early public R.'s of Shinto was to safeguard the food supply, to ward off calamity, to obtain numerous offspring, to secure prosperity and permanence of throne, and to effect purgation for ceremonial and moral impurity.

The monastic R.'s of Buddhism in Japan were similar to those of the → Pure Land and → Ch'an sects of China. The highly complicated and detailed rituals of → Zen Buddhism came to exert great influence over many aspects of Jap. life—e.g. the → tea ceremony, archery, flower arrangement etc. D.H.S.

D. C. Holtom, *The National Faith of Japan* (1938), p. 27; W. G. Aston, *Shinto* (1905), pp. 268–326; J. Herbert, *Shinto* (1967), pp. 147ff.

Ritual The Grk. word for 'rite' was *dromenon*, 'a thing done'. Ritual was prob. magical in origin, taking form of mimetic action to reproduce what was mimed. Such solemnly intentioned action was deemed to generate efficacy on principle of → *ex opere operato*, i.e. by the very fact of its enactment. Ritual action would often be accompanied by recitation of words, both invocatory and explanatory in intent (→ Myth and Ritual). The innate conservatism of human mind has operated to ensure punctilious repetition of such action, and to invest it with status of sacred tradition. The → Pyramid Texts, the earliest corpus of relig. texts (*c.* 2400 BC) reveal existence of an elaborate mortuary ritual. S.G.F.B.

J. E. Harrison, *Ancient Art and Ritual* (1935); S. H. Hooke, *Myth and Ritual* (1933), ch. I; E. O. James, *Comparative Religion* (1938), ch. 3; *R.G.G.*³, V, 1127–8; G. Van der Leeuw, *La religion* (1948), pp. 364ff.; A. N. Whitehead, *Religion in the Making* (1927), pp. 10ff.; Brandon, 'Idea of Ritual', in *D.H.I.*

(Bronzes) (Chinese) The Shang Dynasty (*c.* 1500–1027 BC) employed a superb mastery of bronze technique for production of ornamental ritual vessels of great variety of shapes and usage, and unique in their concepts of design, shapes and purpose. The excellence of these Shang Dynasty R.B. has never been surpassed. They were made for actual use at ancestral sacrifices, and, as inscriptions show, were often made in honour of partic. individual ancestors. The production of R.B. was continued in early Chou Dynasty, which inherited the rituals and sacrificial system of the Shang, and the use of these vessels in sacrifices was eventually codified in the → *Li Chi* and the *Chou Li*. In early Chou Dynasty it also became customary to record the award of honours in inscriptions cast on bronze vessels; more rarely to commemorate an event or a victorious campaign. These inscriptions have great hist. interest.

The R.B. reflect an elaborate ritual, in which food and wine were offered to ancestral spirits. Hence the R.B. comprise vessels for cooking, containing and serving food; for preparing, pouring and drinking wine; together with basins and ewers for water. Though many fanciful theories have been propounded, the complex, stylised zoomorphic and geometrical designs with which the vessels are decorated, though obviously of symbolic import., have not been satisfactorily interpreted. Of a comparatively small number of motifs, the most common are those of the → dragon and the monster-mask (→ T'ao T'ieh). (→ Ancestor Cult). D.H.S.

W. Willetts, *Chinese Art*, vol. 1 (1958); B. Karlgren, Arts, in *BMFEAS*, vols. 9, 16, 18, 23 (1937–51); P. Ackerman, *Ritual Bronzes of Ancient China* (1945).

Ritual Perpetuation of Past The principle involved has found widespread expression; it stems from natural tendency to commemorate a past event by miming it, so that its benefits might be reproduced or perpetuated. The most anc. example occurs in Egypt. mortuary ritual: the embalming and resurrection of → Osiris were ritually represented on behalf of deceased to reproduce their efficacy in him. Numerous other examples can be cited; the most notable being the ritual perpetuation of Christ's death in each celebration of the → Mass. S.G.F.B.

J. Harrison, *Ancient Art and Ritual* (1935); S. G. F. Brandon, 'The Ritual Perpetuation of the Past', *Numen*, VI (1959), 'The Ritual Technique of Salvation in the Anc. Near East', *The Saviour God* (1963), *History, Time and Deity* (1965), ch. 2.

Roman Religion Rome, starting as small city-state (8th cent. BC) became metropolis of Mediterranean world. Its relig. underwent a corresponding transformation. In its orig. form, R.-R. was essentially utilitarian, being concerned with physical needs: food, prosperity of family and state in peace and war. The concept of deity lacked distinctive personification; the → numen characterised native Roman theology. In contrast to → Grk. relig., R.-R. was poor in mythology. Its rituals, which were many and diverse, were basically magical. Apart from certain priesthoods (→→ Arvales; Hierarchy (Roman)), the trad. celebrant of relig. rites was the *paterfamilias* and magistrates. This family and civic aspect of relig. persisted to end of Roman state. The chief Roman deities were of Italian or Etruscan orig. (e.g. →→ Jupiter; Mars; Quirinus; Juno, Minerva; Venus). R.-R. became increasingly nationalist as Rome pursued its imperial career: the Roman triumph significantly culminated with sacrifice to Jupiter Capitolinus; the nationalist aspect also finds dramatic expression in Virgil's *Aenid*. The intention of R.-R. was essentially that of maintaining peace with the gods, whose rights were meticulously defined and respected: hence importance of → divination on critical occasions. R.-R. was not concerned with spiritual needs of individuals; these were met from 3rd cent. BC by gradual influx of Grk. and oriental cults and philosophies (e.g. →→ Pythagoreanism; Cybele; Bacchanalia; Mithraism; Mystery Religions; Stoicism). In Imperial period, the political element in R.-R. became concentrated in cult of Emperor and Roma, genius of the state. The Emp. Augustus endeavoured to strengthen the trad. relig. and mores of Roman people. The triumph of → Christianity in 4th cent. found political expression in Imperial patronage. The change was resisted by Roman aristocracy, and the issue significantly centred on statue of Victory in the Curia, to which Senate offered homage: Gratian ordered its removal in 382. R.-R. disappeared with suppression of pagan sacrifices by Theodosius I in 391 and destr. of pagan sanctuaries in 399. See Synoptic Index under 'Rome'. S.G.F.B.

W. Warde Fowler, *The Religious Experience of Roman People* (1911), *Roman Ideas of Deity* (1914), *E.R.E.*, X, *s.v.;* W. R. Halliday, *Lectures on Hist. of Roman Religion* (1922); F. Altheim, *A Hist. of Roman Religion* (E.T. 1938); A. Grenier, *Les religions étrusque et romaine* (1948); P. Fabre, *H.G.R.*, II, pp. 303ff.; H. J. Rose, *Anc. Roman Religion* (1948); F. Cumont, *R.O.*, *After Life in Roman Paganism* (1922); J. Carcopino, *La basilique pythagoricienne de la Porte Majeure* (1943); K. Latte, *R-G.L.*, 5 (1927²), *Römische Religionsgeschichte* (1960); G. Dumézil, *Jupiter, Mars, Quirinus* (1941²); *Les dieux des Indo-Européens* (1952); E. M. Hooker, 'The Significance of Numa's Relig. Reforms', *Numen*, X (1963); G. Dumézil, *La religion romaine archäique* (1966).

Rosaries Device, consisting of string of knots or beads, for aiding memory in relig. exercises, which involve repetition of divine names or formulae. Its use appears to have orig. in Brahmanic India, and is current in cults of → Vishnu and → Shiva. From Hinduism, the R. was adopted by Buddh.s of all lands. R. are also used by → Sikhs and → Muslims; among Jews R.

have a psychological, not relig. use. The Chr. use of R. has been explained as orig. from Muslim custom adopted during → Crusades; but there is evidence of earlier use. The present R.C. R. has 150 beads, with cross or crucifix attached: the size of beads and their arrangement are related to a specific plan of devotion. The R.C. Church keeps Feast of the Holy Rosary on 7 Oct. S.G.F.B.

E.R.E., X, *s.v.; D.C.C.*, *s.v.; R.G.G.*³, V, col. 1184–5.

Rosary (Islam) While → Wahhabis consider the R. (*subḥa*) an innovation for which no allowance may be made, its use is long estab. Ref. to it occurs at least as early as late 2nd/early 9th century; but theologians looked on it with disfavour. In earlier times, it seems, no objection was made to using pebbles as a help to counting prayers, or counting on one's fingers. Use of a R., which some consider to have been intro. from India, is an understandable development. It seems most commonly used in earlier times among → Sufis. Trad. gives the 99 names of God, but does not seem to speak of repeating them. It does, however, speak of some ejaculations which may be used a certain number of times. E.g., the following, said after every prescribed prayer, will save one from disappointment: 'Glory be to God' 33 times; 'Praise be to God' 33 times; 'God is most great' 34 times, making up 100 repetitions. These phrases 33 times each, followed by statement of God's unity and power, guarantee forgiveness no matter how numerous one's sins are. A R. of 100 beads is usual. This enables one to enumerate the 99 names of God along with the word Allah, or count any number of 100 repetitions of ejaculations. Lane speaks of pilgrims bringing home R.'s as presents from Mecca, and tells of ceremony using a R. of 1,000 beads, each the size of a pigeon's egg, in which Qur. passages and prayers were recited after a death in order to guarantee the deceased felicity. For a Shi'a practice → Karbalā. (→ God, Concept, 99 names). J.R.

E.I., IV, p. 492; Hughes p. 546; *Mishkāt*, pp. 196–8; 489f.; Mez, *Renaissance*, pp. 328ff.; Goldziher, 'Le rosaire dans l'Islam', *R.H.R.*, xxi, pp. 295ff.; Lane, *Egyptians*, pp. 80f., 443, 531f.

Ṛta Sometimes transliterated *rita*: the cosmic and moral order maintained by → Varuṇa. As sky-god, Varuṇa maintained regular processes by which universe is governed, and these were assimilated to moral, ritual and relig. order which men must obey. R. is, therefore, the right order which Varuṇa imposes upon universe as its creator. It is through this order that sacrifices have their effects. It has been seen as germ of idea of → *karma*, but though it has some analogy, *karma*-doc. seems to have entered later Vedic thought from outside sources. The opposite of *ṛta* is *anṛta* (*anṛtam*), a common expression for 'untruth'. The idea of the moral and relig. law was later summed up as → *dharma* (→ Arta). N.S.

Rudra Rudra, god of → *Rgveda*, is early form of great god → Śiva. Name has been variously interpr. as meaning 'howler', 'red one', 'lord of tears'; it may be of non-Indo-European origin, esp. if it is correct to think that a proto-Śiva was present in → Indus Valley civilisation. R. is repr. in Vedic hymns as fearsome and destructive, whose arrows bring plague (yet he is also patron of healing herbs). In → Upaniṣads, notably *Śvetāśvatara*, he is elevated to role of supreme object of worship. Lesser spirits were also given name of *rudras*: these were messengers of Rudra-Śiva. N.S.

Rukū' A posture during Muslim → prayer, with head bowed and palms of hands placed on knees. J.R.

Ruler Worship (China–Japan) In China the ruler performed sacral functions, his person was regarded as sacred and inviolable, his title being 'Son of Heaven', but he was never regarded as a God to be worshipped in this life. He owed his mandate (→ *ming*) to rule from Heaven, owed implicit obedience to Heaven, and in the sight of Heaven appeared abject and humble. Only after death was he worshipped as a divine ancestor spirit, and given status within a spiritual hierarchy under Heaven.

In Japan, the ruler was thought of and worshipped as direct descendant of supreme sun-goddess, → Amaterasu. The position of the emperor in Japan is best summed up in the words of Etsujirō Uyehara: 'He (the Japanese emperor) is to the Japanese mind the Supreme Being in the cosmos of Japan, as God is in the universe of the pantheistic philosopher. From him everything emanates, in him everything subsists. . . . He is supreme in all temporal affairs of the state as well as in all spiritual matters.' The emperor is Heaven-descended, divine and sacred; he is preeminent above all his subjects. He must be reverenced and is inviolable. (→ King, Divine). D.H.S.

D. H. Smith, 'Divine Kingship in Ancient China', *Numen*, vol. 4 (1957); J. Herbert, *Shinto* (1967), pp. 389ff.

Rūpa Buddh. term for (1) 'corporeality' (2) a visible object. In former sense it occurs in conjunction with other terms, such as *loka* (realm or world) to denote one of three realms in Buddh. → cosmology, i.e. realm of pure form (without material substance). In this sense also it denotes first of the 5 → *khandhas*, or groups of constituent factors which make up the human 'individual'; in this case it denotes the whole physical aspect as distinct from psychological aspects, repr. by the other 4 khandhas. In second sense, it is used espec. of representations of the Buddha used in Buddh. devotions, often ref. to in the West as 'Buddha-images' or 'Buddha-statues'. The use of *Buddha-rūpa* appears to have developed in India in 1st cent. BC or CE. Before, symbols to repr. Buddha had been used, such as the → Bo-tree, and → *stupa* or mound. It is uncertain whether the Buddha-R. orig. in India, from use of the *vigraha* or representation of the god in → *bhakti* devotion, or whether it was feature of Hellenistic relig., intro. into N.W. India from Hellenised → Gandhāra or Bactria. Strong claims have been made for both theories. The claim that this was an indigenous develop. on Indian soil usually takes form that it was in region of Mathurā (on Jumna river, south of mod. Delhi), a stronghold of the → Sarvāstivādins, that this occurred. There is evidence of use of the Buddha-R. in both Gandhāra and in the Mathurā area within roughly same period. The import. point of difference is that the form developed at Mathurā was distinctively more Indian in character, while the Gandharan form was obviously indebted to Greek influence; in latter case the representation of Buddha resembles the Greek god of later antiquity. Seckel, *op. cit.*, p. 163. In course of transmission through India and Buddh. lands of S.E. Asia, the style of the Buddha-R. continued to be modified acc. to local conventions, assuming different characteristic forms in Ceylon, Burma, Thailand, China and Japan. T.O.L.

A. K. Coomaraswamy, *Hist. of Indian and Indonesian Art* (1927); B. Rowland, *The Art and Architecture of India* (1953); Dietrick Seckel, *The Art of Buddhism* (1964), part II, ch. 3.

Russia, Religion in The Communist Revolution of 1917 meant dominance of party committed to materialistic and anti-relig. philosophy of Marxism (→ Marx). The Orthodox Church, closely assoc. with Czarism, lost its privileged position, and suffered persecution in various forms. Although public worship was not legally forbidden, anti-relig. propaganda was officially encouraged. The Church's support of the national war effort against Germany led to some amelioration. In 1943 the Holy Synod was allowed to elect successor to Patriarchate, vacant since 1924. In the post-war period the real situation has been obscure. Russian Christians are understandably discreet in their contacts with other Christians, and are instinctively patriotic. → Baptists seem to have suffered from Government pressure; and Jews cannot migrate to Israel. S.G.F.B.

D.C.C., *s.v.* (bibliog); R. Conquest (ed.), *Religion in the U.S.S.R.* (1967), *Religion und Atheismus heute* (East Berlin, 1966); M. Bourdeaux, *Religious Ferment in Russia* (1968).

Ryōbu (Dual) Shintō An attempt to fuse the two great faiths of mediaeval Japan, worked out by priests of the → Shingon sect of Buddhism. R. is attr. to → Kobo Daishi (774–835), who taught the principles which formed R. in 12th cent., and which were developed vigorously in 13th cent., to become dominant form of → Shinto, highly influenced by Buddhism. Joint Shinto-Buddh. sanctuaries were served by amalgamated priesthood (*shasō*), and Buddh. rites were conducted in Shinto shrines. Through R. the ethical content and philosophical outlook of Shinto were deepened. During course of Tokogawa shogunate, R. met with relentless attack from advocates of Pure Shinto; early in the Meiji era the forced separation of Buddhism and Shinto was effected, so that R. practically disappeared as a system of doctrine and ceremony. D.H.S.

D. C. Holtom, *The National Faith of Japan* (1938), pp. 36–8; W. G. Aston, *Shinto* (1905), pp. 36ff.; M. Anesaki, *Hist. of Japanese Religion* (1930), pp. 136ff.

S

Sabbath Heb. *shabbāth*, *ex* verb *shābbath*, 'to desist'. The word S. could be applied to any sacred season requiring cessation of work. The orig. of the S., as such an occasion occurring every 7th day, is obscure. A Babylonian orig., though often suggested, cannot be proved. The earliest O.T. refs. to S. indic. that it was a day sacred to → Yahweh: the reason given in Gen. 2:2–3 (P), connecting it with the Creation, is post-Exilic. After Exile, observance of S. was increasingly elaborated, so that it became a distinctive Jew. practice. The first Christians kept the S.; but its observance was grad. dropped, the 1st day of week becoming Chr. holy day in memory of Christ's Resurrection. The S. continues as a treasured rest-day in → Judaism. S.G.F.B.

E.R.E., X, pp. 885–94; *H.D.B.*³, *s.v.; D.C.C.*, *s.v.; E.J.R.*, pp. 336ff.

Sabazios A Thracio-Phrygian god, identified by Greeks with → Dionysos. S. seems orig. to have been a → chthonian deity, connected with agriculture and fertility; he was repr. bearded and in Phrygian dress. Private associations for cult of S. existed at Athens in late 5th cent. BC; but it was in Imperial period that he became god of a syncretistic → mystery-relig. S. was identified with → Yahweh as *Kyrios Sabaōth*, and was called *Theos Hypsistos* ('God Most High'). His cult was notable for use of votive models of hands, making the *benedictio Latina* and decorated with cult symbols, partic. snakes. The 3rd cent. CE-frescoes on sarcophagus of Vincentius, Rome, graphically depict the mysteries of S. (→ Syncretism). S.G.F.B.

W. O. E. Oesterley, 'The Cult of Sabazios', in S. H. Hooke (ed.), *The Labyrinth* (1955); Cumont, *R.O.*, pp. 60ff.; Gressmann, *O.R.*, pp. 110ff.

Ṣābians A people who are not to be confused with pre-Islamic S. Arabian Sabaeans. They are mentioned three times in the Qur. (ii:59; v:73; xxii:17). The first two passages mention them along with Jews, Christians, believers in the Last Day, and doers of good, all of whom will be rewarded. The third mentions Magians and polytheists as well as Jews, Christians and S., saying God will distinguish between them on Day of Resurrection. They are most prob. the → Mandaeans, wrongly called Christians of St. John, still found near the Euphrates and Tigris. Baptism is a frequent and import. rite, so running water is necessary. In Ḥarrān there were star-worshippers who called themselves Ṣ., presumably for no other reason than to persuade the 'Abbasid Caliph they were among peoples deserving protection. They incl. famous learned men, notably astronomer Thābit b. Qurra and his followers, who trans. many Greek mathematical and astronomical works. They flourished till brought to an end by the Mongols in 7th/13th cent. The Mandaeans still follow their old relig., their chief centre being the marsh lands of Iraq; but some have moved into towns, having a quarter of their own in Baghdad. The Amarah silversmiths who have been well-known for their hereditary work in silver belong to Mandaeans. (→ Harranian Relig.). J.R.

E.I., IV, pp. 21f.; Hughes, p. 551; Bell, *Introduction*, p. 13; Blachère, *Coran* (ii:59); Hitti, *History*, index.

Sacraments Lat. *sacramentum* orig. meant soldier's oath of allegiance; it was used in Lat. N.T. for Grk. word *mysterion.* In Chr. theology, a S. is 'the visible form of invisible grace' (→ Augustine); since Peter Lombard's (*c.* 1100–60) ruling, seven S. have been recognised in W. Church: →→ Baptism, Confirmation, Eucharist, Penance (→ Confession), Extreme → Unction, Holy Orders (→ Hierarchy, Chr.), Matrimony. Baptism and the Eucharist are regarded as the greater S. Acc. to Cath. theology, a S. consists of the 'matter' (*materia*), (e.g. in Baptism, water), and the 'form' (*forma*), i.e. a specific formula (e.g. in the Eucharist, Christ's Words of Institution). The right 'form' and 'matter', used with right 'intention', guarantees validity of S.; their specific grace is conveyed → *ex opere operato*, i.e. independently of moral worthiness of officiating minister. The C. of E. officially recognises Baptism and Eucharist as the 'two Sacraments ordained of Christ our Lord'. The E. Church administers the same seven S. as R.C. Church, calling them 'mysteries'. Prot. Churches have gen. retained, with varying forms of administration and interpretation, Baptism and the Lord's Supper (Eucharist). S. are repudiated by → Quakers and → Salvation Army. The sacramental principle, i.e. the mediation of some kind of spiritual grace or benefit by material means (e.g. eating sacrificial victim, →→ amulets, relics), is anc. and widespread among mankind and is closely connected with 'contagious' → magic. S.G.F.B.

E.R.E., X, pp. 897–915; *D.C.C.*, *s.v.*; G. Van der Leeuw, *La religion* (1948), pp. 356ff.; O. C. Quick, *The Christian Sacraments* (1927); *R.G.G.*³, V, col. 1318–29; J. W. C. Wand, *The Development of Sacramentalism* (1928); N. Zernov, *Eastern Christendom* (1961), pp. 238ff.; B. Leeming, *Principles of Sacramental Theology* (1956).

(Hindu) Orthodox Hindu sacraments are the *saṁskāras* or ceremonies which punctuate career of a person, from before birth (e.g. rites to promote conception and ensure welfare of baby in womb), to after death → funeral customs, Hindu), and incl., importantly, →→ initiation and marriage. Total number of such rites is about forty. The use of outer signs and actions to promote inner spiritual effects was prominent feature of → Tantrism, shading off into magic at one end and → yoga at other. The eating of food offered to a god (the *prasada*) has some sacramental properties; and sometimes the eating of communal meal (e.g. in early → Sikhism) was means of breaking down caste barriers. The notion of 'real presence' of a god in the elaborately sanctified image and the poss. of worshipper's identifying with god is widespread in Hindu theory of worship. The concept of such ritual identification is central to Tantrism. N.S.

Sacred Cities (Hindu) Among variety of sacred places in Indian trad., seven cities are deemed esp. sacred and worthy of → pilgrimage: → Banaras (Kāsī), Ayodhyā, Mathurā, Māyā (Hardwar), Kāñci (Conjeeveram) and Dvāravatī (Dwarka). Also import. are Prayāga (Allahbad), Madurai and Purī. Ayodhya and Mathura (with nearby Brindaban) are assoc. respectively with → Rama and → Krishna. N.S.

Sacred Places (China and Far East) In China the most anc. of sacred places were the ancestral temples and earth → altars for worship of the spirits of the land and grain. But throughout Far East innumerable places, where people believed there were mysterious and peculiar manifestations of spiritual power, came to be regarded as sacred, and were marked by erection of temples and shrines. Long before the Christian era certain great mountains were regarded as places of exceptional sanctity: in China, the five sacred mountains of T'ai shan, Hua shan, Hêng shan, Nan-yoh shan and Sung shan; in Japan, → Fujiyama. D.H.S.

(Islam) One might imagine that Islam, which worships Creator rather than creature, would have no specially S.P., but human nature seems to need such spots, whatever one's relig.; Islam has many →→ Mecca, Medina, Jerusalem, in this order of merit among towns. Mecca which has the → Ka'ba, God's house, was a centre of worship before Islam and is now the most sacred spot. For other S.P. in vicinity → Pilgrimage. Medina has Muhammad's tomb. Jerusalem, capital of people among whom the O.T. prophets arose, was also the spot from which → Muḥammad is reported to have made his midnight ascent to heaven (→ Mi'rāj); for a time was the → *qibla*. Popular Islam has many S.P., mainly tombs of saints. Relics of tree worship are still to be found; but when sites of trees are honoured, they are interpreted as having connection with saints. The → Wahhabis, who emphasise necessity of avoiding every suggestion of idolatry, destroyed a number of domes over S.P. when they took the Hijaz, incl. what was held to be Muhammad's birthplace, his praying place, and → Fatima's birthplace in Mecca. They removed all monuments in anc. cemetery of al-Baqī' at Medina, levelling to ground mementos of, among others, the Caliph 'Uthman, Muhammad's daughter Fatima, and her son al-Hasan. In → Shi'a Islam there is no doubt about value of honouring S.P. They have a number of such to which pilgrimage is made, incl. → 'Ali's tomb at Najaf, → al-Husayn's shrine at Karbala, 'Ali al-Riḍā's shrine at Mashhad (Meshed), the shrine of al-Kāẓimayn (the two Kāẓims, the 7th and 9th imams) near Baghdad, and shrine of the 'Askariyyayn (10th and 11th → imams) at Sāmarrā. For sacred soil → Karbalā (→ Saints). J.R.

Donaldson, *Shi'ite*, index; Pareja, pp. 828–31.

Sacrifice(s) The custom of offering something to a deity is anc. and widespread; it doubtless stems from an instinct deeply rooted in human nature. The Biblical story of Cain and Abel (Gen. 4:3ff.) may be cited as illustrating the two main forms of S.: the animal victim and the bloodless food-offering. Similarly the story of S. of Isaac (Gen. 22:1ff.) indicates that Hebrews were aware of custom of → human S. and of its substitution by animal S. (→ Moloch). The various types of sacrifice may be grouped acc. to their purposes: (1) S. was often intended as food for the gods: e.g. acc. to Mesopot. trad., mankind was created to serve the gods by offering S. and building temples; (2) S. were often offered to propitiate an offended deity: 'Shall I give my first-born for my transgression?' (Micah 6:7). Such propitiatory S. were gen. also vicarious: → Paul succinctly witnesses to this aspect both in Judaism and Christianity when he says: 'Christ our paschal lamb is sacrificed for us'; (3) S. could effect → communion with a deity by the eating of victim (→ omophagy); (4) S. could be made for maintenance or renewal of life, e.g. the Aztec custom of offering hearts of human victims (→ Americ. relig. anc.); (5) → Divination in Mesopot., Etruria and Rome involved inspection of entrails of victim; (6) S. was used to confirm a covenant; e.g. → Yahweh's covenant with Israel at Sinai (Ex. 24:4ff.); (7) S. was used apotropaically to ward off evil, e.g. in → Passover ritual the blood of sacrificed lamb marking door-posts protected Israelite homes from divine destruction visited on Egyptians. (8) S. has often been made to, or for, the dead: e.g. in funerary rites of Patroklos in *Iliad*, XXIII: 166ff. The burning of victim was obvious way of conveying S. to the gods: in Vedic India → Agni, the fire-god, was regarded as priest of the gods (→ altars). Priests often lived on what was offered to gods. The idea of vicarious S. is fundamental to Christianity, and in → Catholicism S. of Christ is perpetually re-presented in → Eucharist. In → Brahmanic Hinduism, S. was believed to generate cosmic power. The fact that word 'sacrifice' derives from Lat. *sacer*, 'holy', and *facere*, 'to make', indic. wide variety of forms of S. beyond those defined here: e.g. offering of → incense and flowers before image of a god could be regarded as S. (→→ Atonement, Day; Blood; Foundation S.; Prostitution, Sacred; Sacrifice of Mass; Scapegoat). S.G.F.B.

E.R.E., XI, pp. 1–39; E. O. James, *The Origins of Sacrifice* (1933), *The Nature and Function of Priesthood* (1955), ch. 5; *R.G.G.*³, V, col. 1637–58; G. Van der Leeuw, *La religion* (1948), pp. 341ff.; *H.D.B.*³, *s.v.; O.C.D.*, *s.v.; R.Ae.R-G.*, pp. 547–60; Dhorme, *R.B.A.*, ch. 9; *E.J.R.*, pp. 338ff.; H. H. Rowley, *Worship in Ancient Israel* (1967), *passim*; E. O. G. Turville-Petre, *Myth and Religion of the North* (1964), pp. 251ff.; A. Ross, *Pagan Celtic Britain* (1967), *passim*; J. Chelhod, *Le sacrifice chez les Arabes* (1955); G. Rendtorff, *Studien zur Gesch. des Opfersinn Alten Israel* (1967); Th. P. van Baaren, 'Theoretical Speculations on Sacrifice', *Numen*, XI (1964).

Sacrifice (Chinese) S., propitiatory rather than expiatory, was an import. element of Chi. worship from earliest times, and the principal method of approach to gods and ancestor spirits. Its purpose was to induce supernatural protection and blessings. It came to be firmly integrated into → Confucian system, and into elaborate state rituals, which were carried out at appropriate times throughout year until abolition of monarchy in 1912. In every family it was an integral part of the → ancestor cult. Agnostic and humanist scholars (e.g. → Hsün-tzŭ) sought justification for practice of S. as a purely secular function, by regarding it as a means of beautifying life, and cultivating moral values of filial piety, loyalty, gratitude, etc. In anc. times human S. was not uncommon, but by time of Confucius the practice had almost died out, effigies of straw being substituted. The materials of S. were numerous and varied: domestic animals, grain, various kinds of food, fermented liquor, silk, jade, etc. The animals chosen had to be of one colour and without blemish. S. was made to Supreme God (→ T'ien or → Shang Ti), to the host of deities who exercised spiritual control over various aspects of life, and to spirits of deceased ancestors. In the elaborate state ritual, only king offered S. to Shang Ti, and thus asserted his claim to imperial office of *pontifex maximus*. S. to Shang Ti by anyone else was tantamount to rebellion. In add., at appropriate seasons of year, the king made sacrifices to earth, the four quarters, the mountains and rivers, the household gods and the deceased ancestors.

Part of the administrative duties of officials was to offer S. to gods who enjoyed gov. recognition, and knowledge of S. was a part of their intellectual equipment. 19th cent. Chi. law stipulated that it was duty of prefectural and county magistrates to officiate at the S. to gods of earth and grain, mountains and rivers, winds, clouds, thunder and rain, and to spirits of sage monarchs, brilliant princes, loyal officials and heroic martyrs, whose temples lay within their districts. These sacrifices took place at beginning of spring and autumn. Times of special need or danger, i.e. eclipses, floods, epidemics, droughts, famine, etc., were marked by appropriate S.

Each family or clan performed its own S. to ancestors. In its simplest form S. consisted of daily burning of → incense before the ancestral tablets. More elaborate offerings of food and drink were made on 1st and 15th of month, on festive days and on anniversary of death of a deceased member of family. The great clan S. at ancestral temples followed anc. practice, the actual S. being offered by head of clan, and the ritual being guided by a master of ceremonies. The S. rites were followed by clan feast, and to share in the S. meat was evidence of clan membership. D.H.S.

J. Legge, *S.B.E.*, vol. 3, vols. 27–8 (1885); W. E. Soothill, *The Three Religs. of China* (1923), *passim*; C. K. Yang, *Religion in Chinese Society* (1961), *passim*.

(Hindu) The central ritual of → Vedic relig. was sacrifice (*yajna*). By period of → *Brahmanas*, S.

had become highly elaborate, and were presided over by various categories of priests (→ Hierarchy, Hindu), who alone had esoteric knowledge and technical skill to perform them and control the sacred power (→ *Brahman*) implicit in sacred utterances (→ *mantras*) and actions. One common offering was libation of → Soma, a sacred and intoxicating juice; there were animal S., the most spectacular being the → *asvamedha.* The sacrificial performances were held to bring blessings and material benefits to those on whose behalf they were conducted. As consequence of increased importance of these rituals, the idea of S. came to be used as key to explaining creation and continuance of whole universe; hence centrality of idea of *Brahman* in Upaniṣadic speculation. In post-Upaniṣadic period the sacrificial system remained important, but rise of temple-worship brought about changes in functions of priestly class. The administration of temple rites, which had analogies to those of householder, came to have greater prominence. The upper class (→ Twice-born) householder was enjoined to perform the five great S. (the recitation of *mantras* as S. to *Brahman*; libation of water and giving of offerings to ancestors; pouring ghee on sacred fire, as a S. to gods; the offering of grain to living beings; and reverence for men, through hospitality). Also of continuing importance were S. performed at rites-of-passage (marriage, funerals, etc.). There was a grad. decline through classical and medieval times of animal S. in Brahmanical ritual, though other forms of animal S. were performed among some Shaiva sects, typically involving decapitation of animal (goat, cockerel, buffalo, etc.) in front of icon of god or goddess. Such a rite is still practised in Bengal, but most orthodox Hindus disapprove of custom. Animal S. have rarely been performed among → Vaisnavites. Ritual suicide, such as → *sati* (suttee), has also been counted as form of S., and theoretically in anc. and medieval India execution of criminals was a S. The dominance of temple worship has led to decline of Brahmanical S. in mod. India; but for special occasions large sacrificial halls (impermanent structures) are still put up. N.S.

J. A. Dubois, *Hindu Manners, Customs and Ceremonies*, 3rd edn. (1928); Margaret Stevenson, *Rites of the Twice-Born* (1920); C. G. Diehl, *Instrument and Purpose* (1956).

(Japanese) In anc. times the Japanese, as with most primitive peoples, offered S. to supply material needs of the gods and ancestor spirits, and only later were S.'s merely symbolical in character. In → Shinto, food, clothing, habitations, weapons, and implements and vessels of all kinds were objects of S. Great care was taken to avoid all pollution. Sometimes objects of S. were duplicated, so as to escape all possibility of blemish. S. was offered to propitiate gods or ancestors, and also as thank-offerings for services rendered, or in hope of future blessings. An expiatory S. (*aga-mono*—things of ransom) was deemed to cleanse from ritual impurity. In gen. the individual worshipper made his offerings at a temple or shrine; but the S. of great state rituals assumed a collective character, and were assumed to result in benefit to whole nation. Though in anc. times, as in China and Korea, human sacrifice was practised, the moral development of people led to substitution of animal victims or effigies. The simple daily offerings to household gods consisted of rice, salt and water. On special occasions other kinds of food and drink were offered. The → Gohei is symbolic of the anc. offering of clothing.

Buddhism in Japan follows the univ. Buddh. practice of avoiding all animal S. → Incense, lighted candles and flowers are offered on → altar. By such S. the Buddh. believe that they acquire merit, either for themselves or for others. D.H.S.

E.R.E., XI, pp. 21ff.; J. Herbert, *Shinto* (1967), pp. 168ff.

(Islam) → 'Id al-Aḍḥā. J.R.

Sacrifice of Mass From an early period the → Eucharist was regarded as being in some way a → sacrifice: Christ's words at → Last Supper have a sacrificial connotation. From Middle Ages increasing emphasis was laid on propitiatory aspect of S.-M., and → Masses were said with special intentions for both living and dead (requiem mass). The abuses of this belief and practice was a contributory cause of → Reformation. The doc. of S.-M. was affirmed by Council of Trent (→ Counter Reformation). The S.-M. has been much studied by mod. Cath. theologians, concerned to explain its relation to sacrificial death of Christ on → Calvary. S.G.F.B.

B. J. Kidd, *The Later Medieval Doc. of Eucharistic Sacrifice* (1898); M. de La Taille, *Mysterium Fidei* (1921); F. C. N. Hicks, *The Fulness of Sacrifice* (1930); W. Spens, in E. G. Selwyn (ed.), *Essays Catholic and Critical* (1926), pp. 430ff.

Saddhā Buddh. term for → Faith. T.O.L.

Saddharma-Pundarīka Sūtra 'The Lotus of the True Law' Sutra, one of most import. Buddh. Skt. texts of the → Mahāyāna school, and prob. the best known. The text purports to be the teaching of the transcendent Buddha, who is here repr. as a god above the gods, a being infinitely exalted and eternal, who can say 'I am the father of the world, the self-existent (*svayambhū*)'. Unlike the → Buddha of Pali scriptures, he does not go from place to place preaching message, but announces it from hill where he sits surrounded by a vast number of monks and nuns, → Bodhisattvas, gods and demi-gods. The teaching reflects a transitional stage between that of the → Hīnayāna and Mahāyāna; the former is here said to have been an accommodation of the transcendental Buddha's message to suit needs of men of lower intelligence and ability. Winternitz comments that the spirit of this *Sutra* is very like that of the Hindu → *Purānas*, and espec. the → Bhagavad-Gītā: the words of the Buddha here bear strong resemblence to those of the Lord → Kṛṣna in the Gītā. A similar doc. of the Buddha's manifesting himself is also found: out of pity for men and their weaknesses, he appeared as a man and 'pretended' to become enlightened and enter *nirvāṇa*. The work is in 27 chapters, partly in Skt. prose, partly in Buddh. Skt. verse. It contains material of mixed date; the nucleus is regarded as belonging to 1st cent. CE, some of which is quoted by → Nagarjuna. It was trans. into Chinese *c.* CE 223, and is highly regarded by Chinese and Japanese Buddh. T.O.L.

M. Winternitz, *Hist. of Indian Literature*, vol. II (1933), pp. 295–305.

Sadducees Jew. politico-relig. party, orig. in 2nd cent. BC, and poss. named after high priest Zadok (2 Sam 8:17). Politically the S. were mainly members of priestly aristocracy, and in 1st cent CE cooperated with Roman gov., since their interests were vested in stable social and political order. Hence their action to suppress → Jesus. In relig., the S. opposed the → Pharisees, in accepting written → Torah only and rejecting oral trad. They also rejected doc. of → resurrection, → angels and spirits (Acts 23:8). The S. disappeared in Jew. disaster of 70 CE (→ Judaism). S.G.F.B.

J. W. Lightley, *Jewish Sects and Parties in Time of Jesus* (1925), pp. 19ff.; *H.D.B.*², *s.v.; E.R.E.*, XI, *s.v.;* Schürer, *G.J.V.*, II, pp. 406ff.; J. Klausner, *Jesus of Nazareth* (E.T. 1929), pp. 216ff.; J. Jeremias, *Jerusalem z. Zeit Jesu* (1958²), II, pp. 95ff.; *Th.Wb.*, VII, pp. 35ff.; S. G. F. Brandon, *Jesus and the Zealots* (1967), *passim*; *E.J.R.*, pp. 339ff.; Bruce, *H.N.T.*, pp. 69ff.

Ṣaḥīḥ (Sound = genuine, reliable). Ṣ., used gen. with the meaning given, is employed in technical sense of the most reliable class of traditions → *Ḥadīth*). It is also used as title of collections of trads. by → Bukhari and → Muslim, commonly called *al-Ṣaḥīḥān* ('the two sound works'). Ṣ. is also used frequently as title for → Tirmidhi's collection of trads. J.R.

Saichō → Dengyō Daishi. D.H.S.

Saints (Buddh.) → Bodhisatta. T.O.L.

(China–Japan) The distinction between S. and → hero-god is not clearly drawn either in the popular relig. of China or in → Shinto. → Buddhism, in both countries, recognised as S.'s those who through numerous rebirths attained enlightenment. The Chi. term *Shêng Jên*, often trans. 'S.; holy man', originally meant a 'sage' or a 'wise man'; one who had attained such perfection of wisdom and virtue that he completely fulfilled his destiny as a human being, was perfectly in harmony with cosmic law and thus formed a trinity with Heaven and Earth. The stress is laid as much on intellectual as moral attainment. Such perfection of life entitles the S. to veneration. → Confucius held up, as supreme ideal, the sages or holy kings of anc. times. Though he himself never laid claim to be a *shêng jên*, he came to be regarded as China's greatest S. and the books attr. to him were regarded as 'holy teaching'. The deification of men of renowned virtue continued throughout Chi. and Jap. hist., and both in Buddhism and Taoism hagiographies of famous men were produced, miracles attr. to them and temples erected for their perpetual veneration. D.H.S.

E.R.E., XI, pp. 51, 61.

(Christ.) →→ Canonisation; Indulgences.

(Islam) The commonest Ar. word is *walī* (friend), pl. *awliyā'*, from root meaning 'to be near'. Qur. X:63 says, 'There is no fear to God's friends, nor do they grieve.' The cult of saints became prevalent, and still is so, in spite of much condemnation. Saints' tombs are visited by suppliants seeking some blessing; a saint has an annual → *ziyāra* at his tomb when people gather from great distances to do him honour and make petitions, after which time is spent in merrymaking. The qualification of sainthood is that miracles (→ *karāmāt*) should have been performed by saint in lifetime, or have taken place at his tomb. These are on different level from miracles (*muʿjizāt*) of → prophets, being merely a personal distinction given saint, unlike evidential miracles of prophets. But though prophets, esp. → Muḥammad, are superior to saints, the saints mean more to common people. There are different grades of saints. The highest is the *ghawth* (refuge, help), followed by the *quṭb* (mystical pole). Some transpose the order, and one meets the two words together for same man. It is also said that the *ghawth* is the *quṭb* when recourse is had to him. The *nuqabā'* (spiritual chiefs), 3 in number, survey the universe. The four *awtād* (pillars) are responsible for four cardinal points of world. There are 7 *abrār* (pure ones) always travelling in 7 climes of world to spread Islam. Through the 70 *abdāl* (substitutes), of whom 40 are in Syria and 30 elsewhere, God maintains world in existence. When one dies, he is immediately replaced. While *ghawth* and *quṭb* are often applied to specific men, the people in the other classes are gen. unknown. Besides them there are many connected with different *ṭarīqas* (→ Ṣūfī orders), or with separate localities, not all associated with a particular *ṭarīqa*. All have quality of imparting *baraka* (blessing). This is prominent among the so-called → marabouts of N. Africa. J.R.

E.I., IV, pp. 1109–11; Pareja, pp. 777ff.; *E.R.E.*, II, pp. 64ff.; Nicholson, *Studies*, index (miracles), *Mystics*, ch. 5; Arberry, *Doctrine*, ch. 26; D. B. Macdonald, *Attitude*, index; M. Smith, *Early Mysticism*, index; Mez, *Renaissance*, pp. 293ff.; Trimingham, *Sudan*, pp. 126ff., *Ethiopia*, pp. 247ff.; M. Lings, *A Moslem saint of twentieth century* (1961); F. Rosenthal, *Ibn Khaldun*, index; J. Robson, 'Some Arab saints', *T.G.U.O.S.*, V, pp. 62ff.

Sáiva Siddhanta The Sáiva Siddhanta ('Shaivite Doctrine') is a S. Indian system of theology, based on belief in → Śiva. Its gen. form is not unlike that of → Dvaita, though it is not a school of Vedanta. The docs. were given their main shape by → Meykanda (13th cent. CE) in his *Śivañānabodham*, in which he gave philosophical form to teachings of Tamil Saivism as expressed in poetry of Mānikkavāchagar (9th cent. CE) and of the → Alvars. Reality is analysed as being comprised of Pati (the Lord, i.e. the personal Creator), *paśu* (souls, lit. 'animals') and *pāśa* (the bond, i.e. matter). The Lord guides the soul into communion with him and operates *karma* with total justice and love. Nature is the → *māyā* of God: but here the term does not mean 'illusion' (as in → Advaita, etc.), but rather the creative substance which is acted on by God's energy (*śakti*, personified also as the consort of Śiva), and so transformed into the material world and the psychophysical organisms in which souls have their earthly locus. Salvation accrues upon long reliance on Śiva as saviour, and on acceptance of discipline under a guru who reflects Śiva's nature and is in a sense an incarnation of the Lord. The S.S. is influential in Tamil-speaking areas, incl. N. Ceylon. N.S.

V. Paranjoti, *Saiva Siddhanta* (1954); G. U. Pope, *The Tiruvācagam* (1900); T. M. P. Mahadevan, *The Idea of God in Saiva-Siddhanta* (1955); G. Matthews, *Sivananabodham of Meykanda* (1948); N. Smart, *Doctrine and Argument in Indian Philosophy* (1948).

Śaivism The worship of → Śiva; also transliterated 'Shaivism', from *Śaiva*, 'follower of Śiva' or 'to do with Śiva'. Ultimately to become, with → Vaisnavism, one of two great modes of symbolising and worshipping supreme Being in Hinduism, S. prob. has roots in pre-Aryan culture of → Indus Valley Civilisation. The cult of → Rudra/Siva is of no special importance in Vedic hymns, though there are indications of Siva's non-Aryan character in epithets bestowed on him. S. emerged as import. cult in post-Upaniṣadic period, side by side with growing importance of cults clustering round figure of → Viṣṇu, and by medieval period was a strong force both in S. India and N. The renaissance brought about by influential teachings and missionary activity of → Sankara and successors gave S. an ideology interpr. through medium of → Vedanta, though in Tamil country there emerged form of theology very different from Sankara's, being essentially dualistic, namely → *Saiva Siddhanta*. This was more oriented to → *bhakti* than → Advaita (even though latter gave place to it, at lower level of truth than the higher non-dual experience of *Brahman*). The fact that Sankara's Saivism was monistic was in part due to greater stress in S. on practice of yoga and interior → mysticism, partly because of Siva's status as the Great Yogi (*mahayogi*, → Siva). On average, S. was less inclined to *bhakti* than schools of Vaisnavism. The *Saiva Siddhanta* was mainly dependent upon Tamil scriptures, composed by the *Nayanars*, hymnodists dating mainly from 7th to 10th cents. CE, and corresponding to Vaisnavite → *Alvars*. The theology so produced was strongly monotheistic, esp. since S. did not, on whole, subscribe to elaborate theory of → *avataras* characteristic of Vaisnavite piety in medieval period. However, the other main form of Saivite theology, that of Kashmir S., also called *Trika* or 'Threefold', because of its acceptance of threefold scripture drawn from non-canonical *Agamas*, conforms much more closely to non-dualism expounded by Sankara, though it makes use of much of terminology characteristic of *Saiva Siddhanta* (e.g. such allegorical terms as *paśu* or 'animal' to symbolize soul—Siva being Paśupati or 'Lord of beasts', and *mala*, a force making for the bondage of soul. Kashmir S. was influential and widely discussed during medieval period, and repr. a form of *bhedabheda* or 'difference-in-non-difference-doctrine', such as may have lain behind the → *Brahmasutra* and which bifurcated into non-dualism of Advaita and qualified non-dualism of theistic → Visistadvaita → Ramanuja). Another import. Saivite movement was the Vira-Saivism or 'heroic Saivism' expounded by Basava in 12th cent., which is basis for belief among → Lingayats. One consequence of teaching of Sankara who, though a Saiva nevertheless also paid reverence to Viṣṇu, has been diffusion of those who accept his Advaitin docs. but in principle recognise both Siva and Visnu, within framework of law laid down for upper classes, etc., in the → *smrti* (in partic. the *Kalpa Sutra*, →→ *dharma*, Manu, law books of). These observers of both orthodoxy and the great cults are termed → *Smārtas* (followers of *smrti*).

Before and during medieval period, growing importance attached to cult of goddesses (often with origins in fertility rites), and whereas Visnu was scarcely able to attract any potent consorts (though Laksmi came to be popular, as goddess of fortune, though without any substantial temple rite), S. expanded its popularity and scope through increase of worship of mother-goddesses, esp. in Bengal. The cults of → Kali, Durga, Parvati and others coalesced with those of Siva, so that → Śaktism (worship of female aspects of the divine Being) reinforced the Saivite side of Hinduism. The female creative power, *śākti*, was symbolised by this form of worship, and was quite closely bound up with → Tantrism, a kind of universal sacramentalism reaching beyond restricted ritualism of Brahmanical relig. The concerns of Tantrism, in postulating ritualising of identity between worshipper and God, coincided with non-dualism of Saivite theology (other than the *Saiva Siddhanta*, etc.). The wide spread of S. in medieval times is indic. by distribution of the more import. Saiva temples and centres of → pilgrimage—the Paśupatinātha shrine in Nepal; great temple of Rameswaram on S. tip of India; the Visvanatha temple in → Banaras and temple of Somnāth in Kathiawar. The decay of → Buddhism left way open for absorption into S. of Buddh. Tantra and other motifs. A notable example was widespread mythology assoc. with figure of Gorakhnath, prob. an historical figure (though credited with fantastic magical powers) of 9th cent. CE or later, who synthesised Saivite Pasupata trad. with Tantrism and → Yoga. The cult focused on 84 *siddhas* or perfect ones (yogis), whose folklore is widespread in N. India. The yogis of movement are called the Kānphaṭa or 'Split-ear' yogis, since initiation involves insertion of large ring in ear. Other ascetics on fringes of S. are the Aghorīs, successors of the Kāpālika, who eat from human skulls, etc. (→ Asceticism, Hindu). S. has very extensive literature, incl. Puranic material and *āgamas* or scriptures both in Sanskrit and in Dravidian languages. of *Saiva Siddhanta* literature the two most import. works are the *Sivananabodham* of → Meykanda and the *Tiruvāchaka* of Māṇikkavachakar. Saivite ascetics and others are distinguished by horizontal streaks painted on foreheads (distinguished from the usually vertical marks of Vaisnavism), while most import. emblem of Siva is the → *lingam*, which plays central role for → Lingayat sect. N.S.

R. G. Bhandarkar, *Vaishnavism, Shaivism and Minor Religious Systems* (1928); J. E. Carpenter, *Theism in Medieval India* (1921); S. Shivapadasundaram, *The Saiva School of Hindusim* (1934); F. Kingsbury and G. E. Phillips (trs.), *Hymns of the Tamil Saivite Saints* (1921); T. M. P. Mahadevan, *The Idea of God in Saiva-Siddhanta* (1955); Mohan Singh, *Goraknath and Medieval Hindu Mysticism* (1937); S. N. Dasgupta, *Hist. of Indian Philosophy*, vol. 5 (1962); S. B. Dasgupta, *Obscure Religious Cults as Background to Bengali Literature* (1946).

Sajāḥ A prophetess who took part in rising against → Abū Bakr after Muhammad's death. Her father belonged to tribe Tamīm and her mother to Taghlib, many of whom were Christians. She had little success, and withdrew to -Yamāma, where she is said to have married → Musaylima. Her doc. is unknown. Later she went to Basra and accepted Islam. J.R.

E.I., IV, pp. 44f.; Muir, *Caliphate*, index; Watt, *Medina*, pp. 139–41.

Sajda Act of prostration (*sujūd*), kneeling with forehead touching ground, the forearms resting on ground with hands open. It is one of attitudes adopted in course of worship (*ṣalāt* → Prayer). If in course of prayer one is doubtful how many → *rak'as* have been performed, or if one has been inattentive, two *sajdas* should be made (*sajdat al-sahw* = s. of forgetfulness). If one has received some blessing, a S. should be performed, accompanied by words praising God (*S. al-shukr* = S. of thankfulness). Copies of the Qur. mark in margin places where it is suitable to perform a S. in course of reading. They are usually at vv. containing word from this root. J.R.

E.I., IV, p. 45; Hughes, p. 556.

Sakadāgāmin Term used in Buddhism for one who is regarded as highly advanced in spiritual progress and will return only once more (*sakadāgāmin*, once-returner) in course of cycle of rebirth, then as an → *anāgāmin*; after that he will achieve → nibbāna; i.e. in his next birth but one he (or she) will be an → arahant. The S. is said by Buddha to be one who has reduced moral imperfections of → lobha → dosa and → moha to a minimum. T.O.L.

D.I., I, p. 156; T. W. Rhys Davids, *Dialogues of the Buddha*, part I, pp. 200ff.

Sakīna Appears six times in Medina suras of the Qur. (ii:249; ix:26, 40; xlviii:4, 8, 26). As an orig. Ar. word it means 'tranquillity', and Jeffery notes that in places it indic. heavenly assistance. Bell uses 'assurance' in all but ii:249, which is the difficult occurrence. It speaks of sign of Saul's kingship being that 'the ark will come to you containing a S. from your Lord'. One feels that here at least is a suggestion that → Muḥammad had heard of Jew. conception of the → Shechina and misunderstood it. It is something contained in the → ark. Curiously this is the one occurrence which is indefinite.

Elsewhere one finds 'the S.', or ref. to God's sending 'his S.'. A trad. given by →→ Bukhari and Muslim tells of a man tethering his horse and reciting sura xviii. A cloud began to approach, and the horse became afraid. Muhammad was told about the incident and said, 'That was the S. which came down by reason of the Qur.' Here it seems clearly to be used of divine visitation of some nature. Tranquillity cannot apply here, esp. so far as the horse is concerned. J.R.

E.I., IV, p. 78; Hughes, pp. 560f.; Sale, *Qurán*, I, p. 380; Masson, *Coran*, II, p. 248n; Jeffery, *Vocabulary*, p. 174; *Mishkāt*, p. 448.

Sakka Name used in Buddh. Pali canon for the *devānam indo*, or chief of the *devas* (i.e. heavenly beings), who in Buddh. → Cosmology rules over the lowest but one of the heavens in the *deva*-world. The → *devas* are repr. as fighting against the → *asuras*, or demons, under the leadership of S. A section of the → Saṃyutta Nikāya, the *Sakka-Saṃyutta*, consisting of 25 short suttas, is devoted to exploits of S. He is said to be devoted to Buddha and his relig. T.O.L.

Śakti Hindu concept of 'power', i.e. creative power of God. It is typically conceived as female and is repr. mythically through figures of consorts of the gods, esp. in → Saivism, where → Kali (Durga, etc.) is dynamic counterpart of → Siva. S. is also identified with → *prakrti* or nature, a concept figuring prominently in → Samkhya, and used in elaboration of Vaisnavite and Saivite cosmology and docs. of → cosmogony. In its formed and visible state, it is also identified with → *maya*. The cult of S. as personified is known as → Saktism, and it plays prominent part in → Tantrism. The first major expression of concept is found in the *Śvetāśvatara Upaniṣad*. (→ *Upaniṣads*). N.S.

Śāktism Name given to cult of female manifestations of ultimate reality in Hinduism, esp. prevalent in Bengal and Assam. Term derives from → *śakti* 'power': the power of divine Being is conceived as female. Hence typically major Hindu gods have goddess consorts. Where female becomes central focus of piety, there is S., and the most notable cults are those of Durga and → Kali. S. is sometimes rather confusingly identified with → Tantrism, partly because scriptures of the *Śāktas* belong to class known as → *Tantras*. The cult of → mother goddesses is strong in S. India, where Śaktic elements have been incorporated into → Saivism. N.S.

Sākyas The tribe in which → the Buddha Gotama was born. The tribe inhabited the Himalayan foothills in what is now Nepal. Their chief town was → Kapilavatthu, the Buddha's home in childhood and early manhood. Their form of government was that of an assembly (*sangha*) of elders, often ref. to by modern writers as republican. The affairs of government were conducted in the Mote-Hall (Santhāgāra) at Kapilavatthu. They appear to have practised endogamy to a considerable degree, although they do appear also to have intermarried with the Koliyans, a neighbouring tribe. Many of the Sākyan tribe are said to have entered the Buddh. Order when Buddha returned to Kapilavatthu after his enlightenment. One of these was the barber Upāli, who was ordained first, and was thus theoretically senior to others, who formerly had been his social superiors. (*Vin.*, II, pp. 181f.). A large number of S. were later massacred, during lifetime of Buddha, by king of Kosala in revenge for an insult. T.O.L.

Sākyamuni Title sometimes given to → Gotama, the Buddha, meaning the sage (*muni*) of the *Sākya* clan, a clan who inhabited the foothills of the Himālaya in region of present-day Nepal. T.O.L.

Salafiyya → Rashīd Riḍā. J.R.

Ṣāliḥ A prophet sent to and rejected by → Thamūd in N. Arabia, is frequently mentioned in the Qur., e.g. vii:71ff.; xi:64ff.; xxvi:141ff.; xxvii:46ff. Ṣ. gave a she-camel as a sign and asked the people to leave it to pasture freely; but the camel was hamstrung and killed, and the people were destroyed by a severe storm and earthquake. J.R.

E.I., IV, pp. 107f.; Hughes, pp. 562f.; Watt, *Mecca*, pp. 28, 129.

Salmān *The Persian.* A somewhat legendary character who is said to have been a → Magian, then a Christian before coming in touch with → Muḥammad in Medina, where he was a slave and accepted Islam. He is repres. as a seeker who travelled in his search for truth. The digging of the Trench as a protection when the Meccans came against Medina in 5/627 is said to have been suggested by him. His name occurs among transmitters of → Trads. and he himself is mentioned in some. → Shi'a trad. quotes his authority freely. One trad. names him as one of three of whom → paradise is desirous. In another, → 'Ali quotes Muhammad as saying every prophet has seven eminent men as guardians, but he has been given 14, whom he names, S. being in their number. S. has been called one of the founders of → Sufism. His tomb near Madā'in is visited by Shi'is returning from Karbalā; but there is difference of opinion about his place of burial. He is the *bāb* of the → Nusayris. → Sunnis venerate him, but Shi'is do so to a much greater extent. Among his distinctions is that he is patron saint of barbers. J.R.

E.I., IV, pp. 116f.; Pareja, pp. 838, 844; *Mishkāt*, index (Proper Names; Isnād); Guillaume, *Life*, pp. 95–8; J. Horovitz, *Salmān al-Fārisī*, in *D.I.*, XII, pp. 178–83; Donaldson, *Shi'ite*, p. 267.

Salutations (Islam) Qur. iv:88 says: 'When you receive a S., reply with a better one, or return it.' The common greeting among Muslims is *al-salām 'alaykum* ('peace be upon you'), to which one may reply *wa-'alaykum al-salām* ('and upon you be peace'), or add to this *wa-raḥmat Allāh wa-barakātuhu* ('and God's mercy and blessings'). → Trad. has various instructions, e.g. 'One who is riding should salute one who is walking, one who is walking should salute one who is sitting, and a small company should salute a large one.' But all one needs to say in reply to People of the Book (→ Protected Peoples) is, 'The same to you.' A trad. says that the one who is first to give a salutation is free from pride. The daily periods of worship are ended by saying with head turned first to right, then to left, 'Peace be upon you and God's mercy'. (→ Prayer). J.R.

E.I., IV, pp. 89ff.; Hughes, pp. 563f.; *Mishkāt*, pp. 968ff.; Pareja, p. 643; Lane, *Egyptians*, ch. 8, pp. 203ff.; Dickson, *Arab of Desert*, ch. 17.

Salvation S., in some form, figures in almost every relig.: it can often simply mean divine deliverance from disease and material misfortune. In what are termed 'salvation-religions', S. involves a soteriology (*ex* Grk. *sōtēria* 'salvation'), which gen. envisages men as being in some spiritually perilous or doomed situation, from which they need to be saved (→ Man, doc. of). Thus, in → Egypt. relig. S. was from complete disintegration of body and personality in death; in →→ Christianity, Islam, Zoroastrianism, S. is from divine perdition; in →→ Hinduism, Buddhism, Orphism, Gnosticism, from → metempsychosis. In these religs., S. has involved a saviour, i.e. a god or divine hero, who provides the means of S., of which man is otherwise incapable. These means of obtaining S. are various: e.g. → Osiris, by ritual participation in his resurrection; → Christ, by defeating daemonic powers enslaving mankind or propitiating offended God; → Buddha, by revealing truth of human situation; → Mithras, by releasing new life in slaying Cosmic Bull. To qualify for S. in these religs., faith in the saviour is essential, which in turn involves acceptance of various doctrines, ritual and moral disciplines. These religs. gen. imply a dichotomy of mankind into 'saved' and 'damned', each condition being variously conceived in imagery derived from the trad. hopes and fears of the cultures concerned. In → Judaism S. gen. meant deliverance of Israel from foreign oppression. (→ Atonement; → Mystery Religions; → Tenri-kyō). S.G.F.B.

E.R.E., XI, pp. 109–51; S. G. F. Brandon (ed.), *The Saviour God* (1963); *R.G.G.*³, II, col. 584–600; G. Van der Leeuw, *La religion* (1948), pp. 96ff., 409ff.; C. J. Bleeker (ed.), *Anthropologie religieuse* (1955); Brandon, *M.D.*, *History, Time and Deity* (1965).

(Chinese) → Confucianism has little teaching to offer concerning either S. from troubles and ills of this life, or S. conceived in terms of a transformed humanity, or S. as a blissful *post-mortem* existence. Confucianism, predominantly this-worldly and conservative, held forth the ideal of a perfect state which would result from restoration of a 'golden age', ruled over by sage-kings of distant past. Such a perfect state could only be poss. under rule of a sage-king, and by acceptance of ethical standards of Confucianism by everyone from king to peasant.

→ Buddhism in China, offered a satisfactory cosmological explanation of universe, with an ethical interpretation of world, thus providing a total solution for human frailties and social ills. It was also designed to transform suffering humanity into perfect beings in a W. Paradise. (→→ Amitabha, Kuan Yin, Pure Land). Its doc. of universal S. was readily accepted by the Chinese. It was copied by → Taoism; but latter was always more concerned with offering panacea for ills and misfortunes of life by magico-relig. techniques.

The sectarian relig. societies which sprang up in China, usually at times of acute crisis and political instability and disorder, often centred in a charismic leader with messianic pretensions, who claimed to be mediator between the gods and humanity and sought to estab. a 'kingdom of universal happiness and peace', justifying his claims by miracles, magic and faith-healing.

The hist. of religs. in China reveals that popular imagination was, throughout the cents., profoundly stirred by the mythological constructions of Buddhism and Taoism in respect of an after-life, in which the consequences of human frailty and sin were mitigated by compassionate intervention of gods, Buddhas and → bodhisattvas. But the this-worldly and pragmatical influence of Confucian ethics has remained so strong that, even when Confucianism came to be discarded, as in modern Communist China, the ideal of national S. remains, with belief in poss. of estab. on earth of a 'perfect' society. D.H.S.

W. E. Soothill, *Three Religs. of China* (1923), *passim*; C. K. Yang, *Relig. in Chinese Society* (1961), pp. 229–32; D. H. Smith, *Chinese Religions* (1968), *passim*.

(Hindu concept) Strictly, the notion of S., closely geared to Judaeo-Christ. ideas, does not occur in → Hinduism, because of difference of sentiment and milieu. However, there are undoubted analogies. The major term used in classical Hindu writings for achievement of a transcendental or eternal state is → *moksa*; related to it is *mukti*—both derive from root meaning 'to free'. Hence it is useful to use the term → liberation to designate analogue of salvation in Hinduism. Other terms used incl. → *nirvana*, also used in →→ Jainism and Buddhism. Since some Hindu conceptions of S. involved existence in → heaven, the concept of liberation has to be related to trad. → cosmology. A further import. Hindu idea has been that of 'living liberation' or *jivanmukti*; one attaining such state is *jivanmukta*, exempt from law of → *karma*, etc., and serene; but living out life in this state until death claims him. Also, whereas S. in Christ. trad. implies S. from *sin*, it has been more typical in Indian context to conceive ignorance (→ *avidya*) as major obstacle to the higher life (→ *Bhagavadgita*), but → Sin, Hindu concept. N.S.

Salvation Army World-wide Chr. movement, organised on military basis (with 'General' at its head), devoted to evangelistic and social work: it was founded in 1865 by William Booth. Its theology is strictly evangelical: → sacraments are rejected: its technique of conversion is based on emotional, rather than intellectual, appeal. S.G.F.B.

R. Sandall, *The Hist. of the Salvation Army*, 3 vols. (1947–55); *E.R.E.*, XI, *s.v.; R.G.G.*³, III, col. 185–7.

Samādhi, Buddh. term, meaning lit. 'concentration'. The term is used in connection with practice of → meditation, and refers to fixing of attention on a single object, thus discouraging discursive thinking. 3 degrees of intensity are distinguished: (1) preparatory concentration (*parikamma-samādhi*); (2) Neighbourhood or access concentration (*upacāra-samādhi*), where the state of → *jhāna* is being approached; (3) Attainment concentration (*appana-samādhi*), i.e. the degree of S. which is present when the state of *jhāna* has been attained. T.O.L.

Samādhi Basic term used in Hindu (also Buddh., etc.) meditation, for the state of concentration or higher trance. It constitutes eighth element in path of classical → Yoga (as also of → Buddhism). Yoga distinguishes two forms—one where higher state of consciousness is fixed on some object or idea (*samadhi* 'with support'); the other where there is pure consciousness, without object (*samadhi* 'without support'), the latter being the superior state. Long practice can give yogi the capacity for S. at will. The attainment of higher consciousness brings existential knowledge of the self or of ultimate reality, and the fruit is → liberation. Thus term S. is also applied to final decease of a saintly yogin: what externally is death is final realisation of the absolute and liberation from body. N.S.

M. Eliade, *Yoga: Immortality and Freedom* (1958).

Sāmanera (Pali); **Śrāmanera** (Skt.) Buddh. novice-monk. (→ Ordination, Buddh.). T.O.L.

Samaritans Name, derived from capital of N. kingdom of Israel, of religio-ethnic Heb. sect. The orig. of the S. is obscure; Jew. lit. emphasises non-Heb. element among them (II Kgs. 17:29), but they were prob., in the main, descendants of northern Israelites. Vicissitudes of fortune experienced by S. and Jews after 586 BC led to deep enmity between them. The S. refused to recognise Jerusalem → Temple as covenanted sanctuary of God, asserting instead the claims of their own temple on Mt. Gerizim. The S. accept → Pentateuch only as holy Scripture; its text differs slightly from Heb. version. Jew.-S. antipathy is reflected in N.T. (→ Simon Magus). The S. have shrunk to a small community living at Nablus. S.G.F.B.

E.R.E., XI, *s.v.; H.D.B.*³, *s.v.;* J. E. H. Thomson, *The Samaritans* (1919); M. Gaster, *The Samaritans* (1925); W. O. E. Oesterley and T. H. Robinson, *Hist. of Israel*, II (1932), ch. 11; H. H. Rowley, 'Sanballat and the Samaritan Temple', *Men of God* (1963); *R.G.G.*³, V, col. 1350–5; *E.J.R.*, pp. 341ff.; J. Macdonald, *The Theology of the Samaritans* (1964); D. Winton Thomas (ed.), *Archaeology and O.T. Study* (1967), pp. 343ff.

Sāmaveda Second of four collections (*saṁhitās*) constituting the Vedic hymns. It consists of verses, nearly all taken from → *Rgveda*, arranged for liturgical purposes; and was assembled between completion of *Rgveda* collection and the → *Yajurveda*. Its name derives from term *sāman*, a melody, and the work is intended as anthology of verses chanted or sung during the → *soma* sacrifice. The verses are addressed chiefly to Soma, but also to → Indra, the great consumer of *soma*. Because collection is essentially a re-arrangement of elements of *Rgveda* for musical purposes, there is little independent literary or relig. value in the S. (→ Veda). N.S.

R. T. H. Griffith, *The Hymns of the Samaveda* (1893).

Sambhoga Kāya → Buddha-Kāya. T.O.L.

Sāṁkhya One of the trad. six schools of Hindu philosophy (the so-called *saddarsana*); the name lit. means 'enumeration', perhaps because of school's tendency to enumerate categories. It is commonly coupled with → Yoga, which in effect serves as practical technique of → liberation worked out against background of a metaphysical cosmology supplied by S., though there are minor metaphysical differences between the two schools. S. depicts universe as made up of innumerable souls (*puruṣas*), on the one hand, and nature (*prakṛti*) on the other. Typically souls are embedded in nature and pursue the round of → rebirth until such time as they attain liberation. The psychophysical organism, incl. the intellect (*buddhi*), is regarded as part of material nature, and the conscious functioning of the individual occurs through association of a soul with a psychophysical organism. The soul transmigrates through innumerable lives, incarnated in human, animal and other forms of life. In the state of liberation, which accrues upon an existential realisation of the fundamental distinction (*viveka*) between itself and nature, the soul is no longer capable of suffering, which characterises all material existence. Like nearly all other trad. Indian schools, S. envisages the periodic collapse and re-formation of the cosmos. The emergence of the cosmos out of chaos at beginning of each cycle is explained through an evolutionary theory. Nature is composed of three strands or qualities (→ *gunas*), in tension. These are *sattva* (essence), *rajas* (energy) and *tamas* (mass). The equilibrium between the three is disturbed at end of a period of chaos because the → *karma* of souls demands it: they have in the meantime had a period of rest. The first *guna* to predominate when the equilibrium is disturbed is *sattva*; by an evolutionary interplay there emerge various forms of 'mental' life, such as *buddhi*. This distillation out of more refined forms of matter sets off interplays between the other *gunas* resulting in formation of material objects, organisms, etc. The whole process is explained without ref. to a personal Creator—a feature which S. shares with early unorthodox schools of thought, such as → Jainism. This may indic. that S. belongs essentially to the non-Aryan, non-Vedic side of early Indian relig. Despite its atheism, however, S. principles were used in exposition of Vaisnavite cosmology: the description of how God creates and guides the periodic formation of universe absorbed the theory of *gunas*. N.S.

A. B. Keith, *The Samkhya System*, 2nd edn. (1949); S. S. Suryanarayana Sastri (tr.), *The Sankhya-karika of Isvara Krishna* (1948); N. Smart, *Doctrine and Argument in Indian Philosophy* (1964); E. H. Johnston, *Early Samkhya* (1937); S. N. Dasgupta, *A History of Indian Philosophy*, vol. 1 (1922).

Saṁsāra (Budd.) Term used in Buddhism for transmigration; lit., moving about continuously, coming again and again (i.e. to rebirth), the term refers to notion of going through one life after another. The endlessness and inevitability of S. are described in *S.N.*, II, p. 178. It is claimed by Buddh. that to appreciate properly the Buddh. truth of the → *dukkha* or suffering entailed in all existence, it is not enough to consider one single lifetime, wherein *dukkha* may or may not be immediately apparent; one must have in view the whole frightful unending chain of rebirth and the sum of misery entailed therein. S. refers not only to round of rebirth in human forms; the whole range of sentient beings is incl., from the tiniest insect to man, and forms an unbroken continuum. Only at stage of human existence, however, can S. be transcended, and release, or → Nibbana, attained. (→ Metempsychosis). T.O.L.

(Hindu concept) The cycle or stream of existence, involving rebirth, as conceived in → Hinduism and also →→ Jainism and Buddhism. The idea gen. went with cycle view of the universe (→ Cosmogony, Hindu concepts), a cosmology involving immense computations of scale of both → time and space, and sense of unsatisfactoriness of the impermanent. The nature of S. is repr. by a wheel, and the revolutions of cycle of individual existence parallel those of cosmos. S. is also repr. as a stream, and great teachers who can transport men to other side (to → liberation) are seen as makers of fords (→ *Tirthamkaras*). S. is also realm of God's magical creative power or → *maya*; and in → *Advaita* is overcome through seeing it as illusion (so that one who knows non-illusory higher reality of → *Brahman* is no longer subject to S.). (→ Metempsychosis, Hindu). N.S.

Samurai Warrior class of mediaeval Japan, formed in 12th cent. CE, whose members inherited the Confucian ethic, cultivated the supreme virtues of fidelity and contempt of death, and received a strict physical, mental and moral training to inculcate simplicity of life, endurance of hardship, strict truthfulness and devotion to one's own lord. In a rigidly stratified society, their lives were governed by rigid discipline, ceremonial and a code of rules. (→ Bushido). Under the Tokugawa shogunate they became a ruling class of ministers, advisers and administrators. D.H.S.

G. B. Sansom, *Japan* (1931, rev. edn. 1946); M. Anesaki, *Hist. of Japanese Religion* (1930); *E.R.E.*, VII, p. 486.

Saṃyutta-Nikāya Third of 5 → *Nikāyas* which together make up → Sutta Pitaka of Buddh. Pali canon. The name *saṃyutta* indics. method of arrangement of Suttas used for the Nikaya, viz., that of 'yoking together' suttas dealing with same main topic. Thus first section or chapter (*vagga*) of S.-N. is made up of suttas dealing with → Devas, or heavenly beings (*Deva-Saṃyutta*), with Kosala (*Kosala-Saṃyutta*), with → Māra, the Evil One (*Mara-Saṃyutta*), with nuns, or *therī* (*Therī-Saṃyutta*), with → Brahma, Hindu deity (*Brahma-Saṃyutta*), with → Yakkas (*Yakka-Saṃyutta*), with chief of the gods → Sakka (*Sakka-Saṃyutta*) and, similarly, various other subjects. One of most famous suttas contained in S.-N. is the → *Dhamma Cakkappavattana Sutta* (*S.N.*, V, pp. 420ff.), which sets out what is held to be first sermon of Buddha after attaining enlightenment. The S.-N. contains altogether 2,889 suttas. These are arranged in 56 Samyuttas, which in turn are arranged in five main sections or chapters (*vagga*). The S.-N. has been trans. into Eng. under title *Kindred Sayings*: the first *vagga* as vol. I (1917, repr. 1950); the 2nd as vol. II (1922, repr. 1952) by C. F. Rhys Davids; the remaining 3 *vaggas* by F. L. Woodward as vols. III, IV and V (1955, 1956, 1956). T.O.L.

San Ch'ing (The Three Pure Ones). Chinese name for supreme triad of → Taoist deities who dwell in highest of 36 heavens, and rule over universe. The first, Yüan-shih T'ien-tsun (Primordial Heaven-Honoured One), abdicated rule of world to the second, → Yü Huang (The Jade Emperor), who in turn will abdicate the rule to third, → Chin-ch'üeh Yü-ch'ên T'ien-tsun ('The Celestial Honoured One of the Jade Dawn of the Golden Gate'). D.H.S.

E. T. C. Werner, *Dictionary of Chinese Mythology* (1932); H. Maspero, *Le Taoïsme* (1950), p. 134; Holmes Welch, *The Parting of the Way* (1957), p. 137.

Sangha (or Samgha) Third of the 'three jewels' (→ Tri-Ratna) of Buddhism: the Order of *bhikkhus*, or monks. The word S. means 'assembly' and was term used in N. India at time of → Buddha for assemblies, by means of which contemporary tribal republics or confederations managed their affairs. The republican assemblies are brought into connection with the Buddh. community at beginning of → *Mahāparinibbāna Sutta*, where the Buddha is repr. as saying: 'As long as the Vajjians foregather thus often, and frequent the public meetings of their clan, so long may they be expected not to decline but to prosper.' Certain conditions governing way they should assemble are then mentioned in the *Sutta*; the whole saying is then repeated word for word, with same conditions, in respect of Buddh. S. It is clear from this discourse, preserved by Buddh. S. at time when the Vajjian republic had been overthrown by advancing monarchy, that the Buddh. S. was to be successor to old tribal republics, poss. even providing refuge from conditions of life under new autocratic rule.

The members of the Buddh. S. were those followers of Buddha who, having heard and received the → *Dhamma*, were prepared to leave behind life of household or family and become wandering almsmen (*bhikkhus*). The bhikkhu was also known as *pabbajaka*, one who had gone forth (from home). Their own name for community appears to have been 'the Bhikkhu-sangha'; whereas by non-Buddh. S. they were at first known as *Sākya-puttiya-samanas*, i.e. wanderers (*samanas*) of (him of) the → Sākya clan, viz. Gotama. The term *samana* was in common use in anc. India to distinguish wandering ascetic type of relig. man from the → brahman; thus 'Samanas and Brahmans' was a way of ref. to the two main and contrasting types of relig. life.

The transition from the wandering life to that of settled community of almsmen appears to have been connected with practice such wanderers had of gathering together during the 3 months of monsoon rains (approx. July–September) in a common shelter, simply as a matter of convenience. Other *samanas* besides Buddh. followed this practice; but only in case of followers of Buddha did the rains-retreat develop into permanent, settled community life. The reasons for this are still not altogether clear: the characteristically Buddh. doc. of selflessness (→ *anatta*) may have had, as its reverse side, an emphasis on a wider community of being where notion of *anatta* could be strengthened, and where a common life could be enjoyed which reduced need for personal possessions, and hence personal identity, to a minimum. The member of the → S. was allowed to possess only minimum of personal belongings: his robes and alms-bowl (in which he received food from donor-householders); these were outward sign of his dedicated relig. life, and distinguished him in eyes of ordinary householders from the mere vagabond; in add. to these he was allowed needle (to repair his robes), → rosary (for use in meditation), razor for shaving head every → *Uposattha* day, and filter through which to pour drinking water, in order to save the lives of any small insects which might be contained in it. In principle these are still the only possessions allowed to monk in → Theravāda countries, although in practice he may receive gifts of various kinds from lay people; these will, however, usually be justifiable in view of some special need—e.g. a typewriter or fountain pen for monk who is a writer—and will be regarded in theory as property of S.

The code of discipline which regulated behaviour of members of the S. was embodied in the → Patimokkha. In add. there were various rulings and prescriptions concerning nature and conduct of S. life, which together formed the Vinaya, or Discipline; they were gathered and arranged in trad. form which came to be known as the → Vinaya Pitaka. In earliest period of Buddh. hist. the way of life was summed up in the twofold 'Dhamma-Vinaya', or Doctrine and Discipline. The earliest disagreements within S. arose over infringements of monastic discipline and were occasions of 2nd Buddh. → Council: the outcome was secession of the → *Mahāsanghikas* from orthodox Sthavira body of the S. Various other divisions within the S. have taken place from time to time; doc. differences, however, have not necessarily been a serious cause of separation; in anc. India even → Mahāyāna and → Hīnayāna monks could be found in same monastery. In Theravāda countries today the S. is divided into several sects, or *nikāyas* (→→ Burma; Ceylon; Thailand).

The S. is, in its gen. structure, democratic. In varying degrees, however, a certain measure of authority has come to be vested in chief monk, or abbott of local monastery. In countries where the King is also Protector of the S. (Thailand, Cambodia, Laos) a hierarchical structure of the national S. has resulted, with various grades of monkhood conferred by King. In some cases these may depend also on qualifications gained in study of → Pali. The S. has a recognisable social role; it is not a body of men withdrawn from ordinary world and its affairs. It has an import. place in society of Buddh. countries, based on reciprocal relationships between monks and laymen. The former are preservers, transmitters and teachers of the Buddha's doc. (→ Dhamma) and are in many ways, spiritual and practical, counsellors of the laity; the latter, in return, provide for material needs of monks by providing them with food, robes and monastic buildings. (→ Monasteries Buddh.). The main purpose of life in S. is, in theory, the opportunity it provides for life of meditation, and hence of improving one's spiritual status. In practice, however, meditation is not always emphasised. Membership of S. is not necessarily life-long. A man may take → ordination for certain limited period. Such temporary monks, however, are not so highly respected by lay people as those whose intention it is to remain life-long members of Order. In some Theravada countries it is customary for boys to spend a few months as members of S. before 'coming of age'; those who do so enjoy, subsequently, a higher prestige than those who have not. Very often such short-term membership is undertaken during the 3 months of → Vassa, the rainy season, or 'Buddh. Lent'. For the various grades of monks, (novices, monks, abbotts) → Ordination, Buddh. (→→ Patimokkha; Vinaya-Pitaka). T.O.L.

Bigandet, P., 'Notice on the Phongyies, or Buddhist Monks' in *Life or Legend of Gaudama the Budha of the Burmese* (*sic*) 1866; D. P. Chattopadhyaya, *Lokāyata* (1959); Sukumar Dutt, *The Buddha and Five After Centuries* (1957), part; and *Buddhist Monks and Monasteries of India* (1962); R. Gard, *Buddhism* (1961), ch. V; Phra Khāntipalo, *The Patimokkha* (1966); E. Lamotte, *Histoire du Bouddhisme Indien* (1958), pp. 58–94.

Sanhedrin *Ex* Grk. *synedrion*, 'council', term adopted by Jews for their supreme court of justice until fall of → Jerusalem, CE 70. Although Rabbinic trad. traced S. back to → Moses, its hist. orig. prob. dates from 2nd cent. BC. Its hereditary head was the high priest: by 1st cent. CE its → Sadducean element was counter balanced by → Pharisees. Under Roman rule, the S. exercised civil and relig. jurisdiction over Palestinian Jews: it could apparently pronounce capital sentences, but Roman confirmation was required for their execution. There is much obscurity about constitution and powers of S., since later Rabbinic trad. presented it in idealistic form. (→ Judaism). S.G.F.B.

E.R.E., XI, *s.v.; H.D.B.*², *s.v.;* Schürer, *G.J.V.*, II, pp. 188ff.; J. Jeremias, *Jerusalem z. Zeit Jesu* (1958²), I, pp. 85ff., II, pp. 87ff.; P. Winter, *On the Trial of Jesus* (1961), *passim*; *E.J.R.*, pp. 343ff.; J. Blinzler, 'Das Synedrium von Jerusalem und die Strassprozessordnung der Mischna', 52 (1961).

Śankara (Shankara) Chief exponent of the Hindu theology known as → Advaita Vedanta (non-dualistic Vedanta). S. was born at Kaladi in what is now Kerala State in S.-W. India, about 788 CE. He was the main figure in the revival of Hinduism, at end of period when Buddhism had been a powerful rival to orthodoxy. He packed much into a short life (he died in CE 820). Apart from his extensive writing, he travelled round the Indian sub-continent reforming relig. and founding monastic orders based on Dvaraka in Kathiawar, Puri in Orissa, Badri in N. India and Sringeri in the South. His most import. philosophical-theological work was the commentary on the → Brahmasutra; other writings incl. expositions of principal → Upaniṣads and a commentary on the → *Bhagavadgita*. He also composed some devotional works. His original re-presentation of the essence of Brahmanical relig., which owed something to his teacher Govinda, a pupil of → Gaudapada, was in part influenced by → Madhyamika Buddhism; and S. was accused of being a *pracannabauddha* or 'crypto-Buddh.'. This accusation stemmed from recognition that S.'s distinction between 'higher' truth and 'everyday' truth was revolutionary, in that the bulk of the Vedic texts, which formed basis of orthodox interpretations of relig., were consigned by S. to the lower level of truth. The distinction enabled S., however, to give a highly consistent exegesis of conflicting passages in the Upaniṣads and other sacred texts. Passages referring, for instance, to a personal God as supreme reality were consigned to the lower level; texts expressing the essential identity of the self and → Brahman (the so-called 'identity-texts', such as → *tat tvam asi*) were seen as indic. the experience of supreme realisation. S. started from an exegetical basis, but he backed up his interpretations by acute philosophical arguments. The systematisation of Vedanta achieved by him made a lasting imprint on Indian philosophy and Hindu theology. He attracted substantial criticism; but the Advaitin school gained considerable impetus from his writings, and has proved the dominant ideology in mod. re-interpretation of the Hindu heritage achieved since the mid-19th cent. His system has been compared to Absolute Idealism as expressed by Western philosophers such as → Hegel and Bradley. N.S.

Swami Nikhilananda (tr.), *Self-Knowledge* (*Sankara's Atmabodha*) (1946), *Sankara's Commentary on the Brahma-Sutra*, *S.B.E.* (1890, 1896), vols. 34, 38; Sacchidananda K. Murty, *Revelation and Reason in Advaita Vedanta* (1959); M. Govindagopal, *Studies in the Upanisads* (1960); R. Otto, *Mysticism East and West* (1932).

Sannyāsin (Also transliterated *saṃnyāsin*). One who has moved on to last of four stages of life in classical Hinduism (→ *asramas*) and become wandering holy man. This state of having given up world is called *sannyāsa*. Although in theory it supervened upon stages of being householder and then 'forest-dweller' or *vanaprastha*, it was not uncommon for people to become *S.* at early age. The term is also used more gen. for Hindu holy men (*sadhus*); though technically it is only the → twice-born who can, acc. to the law-books (→ *dharma*), properly become *S.* The *S.*, having broken ties with world and ordinary social duties, counts as outcaste; but, unlike those who are born as outcastes or → untouchables, he has always been treated with greatest respect. The typical garb of the *S.* is rags, and he carries begging-bowl, water-pot, staff and few other meagre possessions. (→ Asceticism, Hindu). N.S.

G. S. Ghurye, *Indian Sadhus* (1953); J. C. Oman, *The Mystics, Ascetics and Saints of India* (1903); J. Auboyer, *Daily Life in Ancient India* (1961).

Sanskrit, Buddhist Language and Literature Sanskrit, an Indo-European language intro. into Indian sub-continent by → Aryan tribes, who began to enter from N.W. in mid. 2nd mil. BC, developed in India from the early (Vedic) form in which it was intro. (the language of → Ṛg-Veda), to the 'classical' or later form. It was primarily the → brāhman priests who were bearers and preservers of S.; because of this, it was language of intellectual discourse in India and enjoyed unique prestige. In gen. it was in the N.W. and W. of India that influence of S. was greatest in early Buddh. period; hence its use by Buddh. S. begins from period when there was an expansion of Buddh. community from lower Ganges valley westward, into region around → Mathura, where the S. trad. of the brahmans was stronger than in the E. A sect of the → Mahāsanghikas, the Lokottaravādins, produced a work in mixed Sanskrit, the → *Mahāvastu* which has survived to mod. times and was, acc. to text itself, part of the → *Vinaya Piṭaka* of this school. Buddh. S. works of various kinds were produced from this period onward, but no complete S. canon of Buddh. scripture has survived. Fragments of the → Sarvāstivādin canon are extant, notably the *Prātimoksa Sūtra* (→ *Pātimokkha*), and quotations from Sarvāstivādin S. canon occur in other works such as the → Divyāvadāna, and → Lalita-vistara. These later S. works are extremely numerous; some are known only from Chinese and Tibetan trans. which were made from them and which have survived, the orig. S. texts having been lost in decay and destruction of many monasteries of N. India. The most import. of these, to which refs. are made elsewhere in this volume are: →→ *Mahāvastu* (already mentioned); *Lalita-vistara; Buddha Carita; Avadāna; Divyāvadāna; Saddharma-pundarika Sūtra; Prajnā-paramitā Sūtras*, esp. the →→ Heart Sutra and Diamond Sutra; →→ *Lankāvatāra Sūtra* and the *Abhidharma-Kośa*. T.O.L.

E. Lamotte, *Histoire du Boudhisme Indien* (1958); M. Winternitz, *History of Indian Literature*, 25, 2 vols. (1933).

Sanskrit Sacred language of → Hinduism, evolving out of that of the Vedic hymns (which stands to classical S. somewhat as Homeric Greek stands to classical Greek); it was also main vehicle of literature and administration over long period of Indian history. The Hindu scriptures (→ revelation, Hindu) are written in S., while those of →→ Buddhism and Jainism are in Prakrits—orig. vernacular and non-literary forms of language. Many → Mahāyāna texts became heavily sanskritized and are deemed to be written in 'Buddh. Hybrid Sanskrit'. The rules of language were explored and set out scientifically by ancient grammarians Panini and → Patanjali. Trad., it was thought that there was an eternal primeval language, perceived by → Manu, who taught it to men, and that S. most nearly corresponds to this orig. divine language, other tongues being corruptions of it. (→ Veda). N.S.

T. Burrow, *The Sanskrit Language* (1955).

Sanūsiyya → Ṣūfī Orders. J.R.

Saoshyans (Sôshyans) In later → Zoroastrianism, the 'Saviour', whom at the end, will raise the dead (→ resurrection). In the → *Gāthās*, the S. is really Zoroaster himself, not an eschatological figure; in later belief S. was regarded as the posthumous son of Zoroaster. S.G.F.B.

Zaehner, *D.T.Z.*, pp. 58ff., 317ff.; *E.R.E.*, XI, pp. 137b–8a; G. Widengren, in *Numen*, I (1954), pp. 42ff.; S. G. F. Brandon, *Judgment of the Dead* (1967), pp. 162ff.

Sarapis (Lat. Serapis) God of Graeco-Roman Egypt. Although both anc. and mod. scholars have traced origins of S. outside Egypt, it now seems estab. that cult derived from that of → Apis-bulls at Memphis. Oserapis was title of dead Apis-bull identified with → Osiris. Ptolemy I (305–282 BC) seems to have promoted cult in form designed to unite his Greek and Egypt. subjects. In art S. was repr. like trad. figure of → Zeus, but with attributes of Osiris; phenomenologically, he was a saviour and god assoc. with after-life, fertility and oracles; through assoc. with → Aesculapius (→ Imhotep), he was also a god of healing. S. became chief god of → Alexandria, his Serapeum being one of sights of city; his cult also assumed aspect of → mystery relig. As Osiris, S. was assoc. with → Isis and Harpocrates (→ Horus); although his cult spread outside Egypt, it tended to be eclipsed by that of Isis. S.G.F.B.

R.Ae.R.G., *s.v.; O.C.D.*, *s.v.;* H. I. Bell, *Cults and Creeds in Graeco-Roman Egypt* (1953); E. Bevan, *Hist. of Egypt under Ptolemaic Dynasty* (1927), pp. 41ff.; *Bilderatlas*, 9–11 Lief. (1926); Cumont, *R.O.*, ch. IV; R. Stiehl, 'The Origin of the Cult of Sarapis', *H.R.*[3] (1963)—argues for a Babylonian origin.

Sariputta/Sariputra Chief disciple of → Gotama, the Buddha, and a Thera (Elder Monk) of Buddh. → Sangha. S. was his 'religious' name as monk; his personal name is given as Upatissa (*M.N.*, I, p. 150). A → brahman by birth, he had 3 younger brothers and 3 sisters; these also became Buddh. monks and nuns. He was highly esteemed by Buddha for his wisdom, and acc. to trad., was an accomplished preacher and expounder of Buddh. doc. There was a specially close relationship between S. and → Ānanda, Buddha's personal attendant, → Rāhula, Buddha's son, and → Moggallāna, all of whom were among his most prominent disciples. Acc. to the *Saṃyutta Nikāya* (V, p. 161), S. died of an illness a few months before the Buddha. After cremation of his body, the relics were taken to Sāvatthi. Ānanda was profoundly disturbed at news of his death; the Buddha took the occasion to remind him of the impermanence of all things. T.O.L.

Sārnāth → Isipatana. T.O.L.

Sarvāstivādins Name of Buddh. sect in anc. India, belonging to the → Hinayana trad. (see p. 168). They constituted one of 2 main divisions of the → Sthavira wing of the Buddh. Sangha, the other being the Vibhajyavādins, or 'Analysers'. The differences between them were over question whether present mental events (*dhammas*) only have reality, as the Vs. maintained, or whether past and future mental events could also be said to have a real existence, as the S.'s believed. Their name indicates this view: *sarva* (all—past, present, and future) *asti* (exists). They had become sufficiently numerous body by time of → Asoka (3rd cent. BC) for the dispute to necessitate calling of the Council of Pātaliputta (Patna). (→ Councils, Buddh.). After Council, the S.'s withdrew from lower valley of Ganges, N.W.wards to → Madhura which became a stronghold of their school. They used → Sanskrit rather than (as the Theravādins did) Pali, and are regarded as constituting a transitional stage between the older, conservative schools of Buddhism and → Mahāyāna. T.O.L.

Sāsana The word most commonly used in Buddh. countries of S. Asia to refer to what in West. languages is called the '*religion*' of the Buddha (or Buddhism). The Pali word carries sense of both 'doctrine' or 'teaching', and also 'rule of life'. Thus, the authentic way of ref. to what European languages call 'Buddhism' is 'Buddha-Sāsana'. T.O.L.

Satan, Satanism In the O.T. the word S. orig. meant 'adversary'; it is first used of a distinctive being in → Job, chs. 1–2, where S. is one of the 'sons of God', and specially concerned with observing deeds of men and reporting their sins to God. In non-canonical Heb. lit., S. gradually becomes the → Devil, and as such he appears in N.T., being identified also with the Serpent of Gen. 3. During Middle Ages and later → witches and → heretics were often accused of Satanism, i.e. worshipping S. (→ Black Mass). Satanism has also been affected by esoteric groups in modern times. (→ Dualism). S.G.F.B.

H.D.B.[2], *s.v.; E.R.E.*, XI, *s.v.;* Ch. Guignebert, *Le monde juif vers le temps de Jésus* (1935); Père B. de Jésu-Marie (ed.), *Satan* (1951); H. T. F. Rhodes, *The Satanic Mass* (1954); M. Summers, *Witchcraft and the Black Art* (1945), pp. 192ff.; M. A. Murray, *The God of the Witches* (1931); *E.J.R.*, pp. 344ff.; T. Ling, *The Significance of Satan* (1961). (→ Spirits/Demons, Islam).

Satī Often transliterated 'suttee'; lit. a 'good woman', and hence in partic. one who dies on husband's funeral pyre. Thus 'suttee' came to be used to mean rite itself. The custom, fairly anc. in → Hinduism, is analogous to that found in number of cultures where relatives, ministers and servants of king are supposed to die with him. The status of widow in orthodox Hinduism was scarcely favourable, since those of upper classes were expected to shave heads and devote themselves to relig. exercises, etc.; thus there was some motive for the higher sacrifice. The custom was condemned by → Sikhs (notably the Guru Amar Das) and by some other groups; there was agitation for reform from missionaries and from leading Hindu reformers, notably Ram Mohan Ray; the practice was banned in British India in 1829, and a little later in princely states. N.S.

Sati Patthāna Sutta → Mahā-Satipatthāna Sutta. T.O.L.

Satori Jap. term for Buddh. 'illumination' or 'enlightenment'. In → Zen, it is the state of consciousness of the Buddha-mind, pure consciousness, without mental discrimination, seeing into one's own Buddha-nature, essential wisdom (*prajnā*). If the experience can be characterised, either mentally or emotionally, it is not S. S. is an experience beyond description and altogether incommunicable. Basically, it is the integration or realisation of man in his psychic totality, the liberation of the unconscious forces of the human psyche. D.H.S.

H. Dumoulin, *Zen Buddhism* (1963), pp. 273ff.; E. Wood, *Zen Dictionary* (1962), pp. 114–5; C. Humphreys, *A Buddhist Students' Manual* (1956); D. T. Suzuki, *Essays in Zen Buddhism*, 2 (1933), pp. 32, 62ff.

Saturn, Saturnalia Saturn, Roman god assoc. with seed-corn and sowing, is of obscure origin: he may have derived from → Etruscan relig., and ultimately from Greece; he was identified with Grk. → Kronos. His festival (Saturnalia), on Dec. 17, was time of merry-making, when presents were exchanged and slaves had temporary liberty. It also incl. custom of mock-king or Lord of Misrule (→ Abbot of Unreason), in which some scholars have discerned primitive rite of mock-king who was subsequently killed as a → scapegoat. Saturn survived in medieval → astrology, to be transformed at Renaissance into Father Time. S.G.F.B.

O.C.D., *s.v.;* J. G. Frazer, *The Scapegoat* (*G.B.* 1933[3]), pp. 306ff.; W. Warde Fowler, *The Relig. Experience of Roman People* (1911), *passim;* A. Grenier, *Les religions étrusque et romaine* (1948), pp. 114ff.; P. Seznec, *La survivance des dieux antiques* (1940), *passim*; E. Panofsky, *Studies in Iconology* (1962 edn.), ch. 3.

Sautrāntika Buddh. philosophical school of → Hīnayāna trad. characterised by rejection of the → Abhidhamma, which adherents of school held to be no part of authentic doc. of Buddha. For them only the Sutras were authoritative, and were the 'end' or *anta* of the doc.: hence the name in Skt., *Sūtra-anta*; like the → Sarvāstivādin school, from which they emerged (see p. 168), somewhere in early part of 2nd cent. BC, the S.'s used Sanskrit. Their views were not unlike those of the → *Pudgalavādins*; for, in rejecting notion found in Abhidhamma, of separate, instantaneous, non-continuous *dhammas*, they posited 'the continuous existence of a very subtle consciousness' as basis of human life; it was this, in their view, which progressed to → Nirvāṇa. They differed from Pudgalavādins in maintaining that it is not the whole 'person' which transmigrates, but only *one* of the 5 → skandhas which go to make up a 'person', viz., a subtle form of *consciousness*. They placed less importance on philosophical terminology and concepts repres. by such terminology, which were, they held, but 'fruitful fictions'. Their ideas may have contributed in some measure to those of Mhy. school of → *Yogācāra*. T.O.L.

E. Conze, *Buddhist Thought in India* (1962), pp. 141ff.; P. S. Jaini, 'The Sautrāntika theory of bīja', in *B.S.O.A.S.*, vol. 22 (1959), pp. 236–49.

Sayyid (Lord). Title given to descendants of Muhammad through 'Ali and Fāṭima (→ Sharīf). In some districts, notably Pakistan and India, the Hijaz and S. Arabia, the title is applied only to descendants of → al-Ḥusayn. Many from S. Arabia have gone to Malaya and Indonesia. In Ḥadramawt partic. S.'s are shown great respect, receiving regular gifts and acting as arbitrators. They dress in white and keep themselves separate from rest of community. The word S., often spelt *sidi*, is used sometimes, esp. in N. Africa, for a → saint. In many countries it is used as an everyday form of address. The Pakistani and Indian spelling of the word, when transliterated, is normally Syed. S.'s incl. both →→ Sunnis and Shi'is. J.R.

E.I., IV, p. 76; Pareja, p. 782; Levy, *Social Structure*, p. 367.

Scandinavian Religion Repr. northern form of Germanic, or Teutonic, relig., which in turn goes back to Indo-European (abbr. I.-E.) sources: (there is a wealth of illustrative material from other branches of the I.-E. (→ Aryans) family of religs.). The relig. of the S. Germanic peoples is very imperfectly known from occasional refs. in classical writers (notably Caesar and Tacitus) and what can be deduced from secondary sources; but the pre-Christ. relig. of the N. Germanic peoples can be reconstructed in considerable detail. The basic unity of Germanic relig. is evident, though there is a vast difference between the observations of Tacitus (*Germania*, 2, 3, 9, 10, etc.) and the complex mythology given in Snorri's *Edda*. More than 1,000 years separate the two, during which time the southern tribes had been subject to various influences, classical and Christ.; Scandinavia, on the other hand, remained in almost complete isolation until Viking period (*c.* CE 800–1050). It has been argued that S.R. was by that time already moribund, and enjoyed a temporary new lease of life in confrontation with Christianity.

Our earliest sources of information concerning relig. in the north. countries are purely archaeological. In Neolithic period, megaliths, called in Danish *dysser* and in Swedish *gånggrifter*, provide evidence of a cult of dead, in which the entire family was involved, and at which common meals were eaten. It has been suggested that the → Megalithic Culture orig. in the E. Mediterranean, and that it involved some form of sun-worship. In all S. examples, entry to the collective burial-chamber is on south side, implying belief in the north as realm of the dead. These practices, and the grave-goods provided, estab. belief in continued existence after death.

Sun-worship would also appear to be key to understanding of Bronze Age rock-carvings (Sw. *hällristningar*) of coasts of Sweden and Norway. These carvings, which are now believed to be products of a mixed race, including by this time I.-E. elements, date from 2nd mil. BC. They are 'schematic, allusive, narrative' (Bibby), and incl. ships, ploughs, leaves, men, animals, footprints, and sun-symbols. It is clear from the dancing figures, the *lur*-players, and what seem to be representations of a *hieros gamos* (→ Marriage, Sacred), that their orig. context was cultic. New carvings were added at intervals, hence their unsystematic character. They reflect a fertility relig., in which worship of sun played prominent part. An import. piece of corroborative evidence is the model of a solar chariot, found in 1902 at Trundholm in Denmark, dating *c.* second half of 2nd mil. BC. It has six wheels, is drawn by horse, and surmounted by gold-plated sun-disc. The chariot of which this is a model, and the ploughs and ships repr. on the carvings, were certainly used in Bronze Age in context of annual fertility rites. Little can be said about the deities worshipped in these rites; no positive identification is possible, though attributes of the great triad of Nordic gods—Odin (spear, horse), Thor (sun, axe, hammer) and Frey (phallus and other fertility symbols)—are already in evidence. Burial practices in Bronze Age varied between inhumation and cremation, though no extensive conclusions can be drawn from this; increasingly elaborate grave-goods were provided, partic. among aristocracy.

The settlement of Iceland, after CE 874, by political refugees from Norway, and subsequent careful transmission of a highly developed lit. and hist. trad. on the island, have provided scholars with an extensive body of source material illustrative of S. relig. beliefs and practices during late Iron Age (Vendel and Viking Periods, *c.* 550–1050). The main Norwegian–Icelandic sources are as follows: (1) pre-Christian skaldic verses; (2) The *Verse Edda*, parts of which may date from 7th cent.; (3) Snorri's *Prose Edda*, a handbook of mythology and poetic technique, dating from early 13th cent.; (4) The Sagas, esp. Snorri's *Heimskringla* and incl. the *Landnámabók*; (5) Codes of law; (6) Runic inscriptions. Additional material is found in certain non-Scandinavian writers, incl. the Arabic authors Ibn Rusteh and Ibn Fadlān, and Latin authors Rimbert (*Vita Anskarii*, *c.* 870), Adam of Bremen (*Gesta Hammaburgensis ecclesia pontificum*, *c.* 1075) and Saxo Grammaticus (*Gesta Danorum*, *c.* 1210). As far as Iceland is concerned, the period is divided by the official adoption of Christianity by the *Althing* in 1000; it is consequently recognised that the relig. of the written sources may have been subject to Chr. influence. Some settlers came to Iceland *via* the British Isles, where, apart from Christianity, Celtic motifs (in art as well as mythology and relig.) were still current. So, while the import. of the lit. sources cannot be overestimated, they should be complemented whenever possible by evidence of archeology, place-names, folk-lore and the like.

In the S. pantheon, three gods in partic. stand out as *foci* of worship. Adam of Bremen wrote that in the great temple of Uppsala, 'the people worship the statues of three gods in such wise that the mightiest of them, Thor, occupies a throne in the middle of the chamber; Wotan and Frikko have places on either side . . .' (*Gesta*, 4:26). These three gods, Odin, Thor and Frey (Icel. Oðinn, Þórr, Freyr), repr. the three 'functions' of I.-E. society—authority, power and fertility (Dumézil). The primacy of Thor in the Migration and Viking Ages (400–1050) reflects the import. of the warrior ideal, partic. among the common people: 'To Odin come/the battle-slain earls,/but Thor has the tribe of thralls' (*Hárbarðsljód* 24, tr. Branston).

Odin is the god of supreme cosmic authority, powerful and terrible. His name corresponds to the Skr. Vāta. He is the All-father, king of the gods, wise, master of magic power, inventor of runes and ruler of the hall of dead warriors, Valhalla. There are a number of myths telling how Odin gained his great power and wisdom: one tells how he laid one of his eyes in the well of Mimir in exchange for wisdom (*Völuspá* 28); another refers to Odin's self-sacrifice in the same quest: 'I know that I hung/on the windy tree/all of nine nights,/wounded by weapons/and offered to Odin,/myself to myself/ on that tree/ which no one knows/whence its root springs' (*Hávamál* 138). Odin's consort is the → earth-mother Frigg; his animals the eight-footed horse Sleipnir and the ravens Huginn and Muninn; and his weapon the spear.

Thor is a warrior-god and god of thunder, a parallel to the Vedic → Indra. Like Indra, he wields the thunderbolt (cf. Skr. *vajra*), symbolised by his weapon the hammer (called *Mjöllnir*). Like Indra, too, he is a great drinker of intoxicants. Others of his attributes incl. a belt and iron gauntlets. He is repr. as a red-bearded giant, and myths tell of his feats in overcoming powers of chaos; from the violence of the passing thunderstorm comes his appellative Thor the Driver. He had a fertility aspect as lord of the air: 'Thor, they say, presides over the air, which governs the thunder and lightning, the winds and rains, fair weather and crops' (Adam, *Gesta* 4:26).

A similar function is filled by the one-handed Tyr (Icel. Týr), of whom Snorri says: 'He is the boldest and most courageous of gods, and victory in battle depends upon him; it is good for brave men to call upon him' (*Edda*, 24). In Viking times, Tyr was little more than this; however, there is reason to believe that he was orig. a → high god, similar to, if not formally identical with, Grk. → Zeus, Lat. → Juppiter and Skr. → Dyāus pitar. From this position he was grad. ousted by Odin.

The most typical of the gods of fertility is Frey, who occupied third place in the Uppsala temple, where he was repr. *cum ingenti priapo*. He is the son of Njord and the sister of Freya. Frey 'rules over rain and sunshine, and thus also over growing plants, and it is good to call on him for the crops and for peace' (Snorri, *Edda*, 23). His attributes incl. a ship, *Skiðblaðnir*, and a golden boar, *Gullinborsti*, swifter than a horse, on which he rode to the funeral of Balder (see below). The import. of Frey is attested by his epithet *veraldargoð*, 'god of the whole world'.

Frey's sister Freya is most prominent of S. goddesses. She is a type of the great → earth-mother, repr. in S. relig. by a number of fertility goddesses, incl. Frigg. Idun and Trud (cf. Nerthus, in Tacitus *Germania*, 40). Although the tales told of her are piecemeal, there is clear evidence of belief in her absence from earth during autumn and winter—a common element in I.-E. fertility myths. Otherwise, she is sexually promiscuous, and is said to have had relations with all male members of the pantheon. She is also concerned with fate of dead: 'She possesses the hall in heaven called Fólkvangr, and wherever she rides in battle, she gets half of the dead, while Odin gets the other half' (Snorri, *Edda*, 23). This ambivalence is again typical of chthonic goddesses (cf. e.g. the Hindu → Kalī).

Frey and Freya, with Njord their father, belong to the category of *vanir*, a group of gods contrasted in some texts with the *aesir*—gods of the earth, broadly speaking, as against gods of the sky. The acceptance of the *vanir* into the pantheon took place, acc. to the myths, only after battle and reconciliation.

Among many gods and goddesses not known by any partic. cult devoted to them, two, Loki and Balder, are worthy of mention. In S. relig., the paradoxical figure of Loki repr. the forces of evil—'the scourge of the gods, some call him: the originator of all treachery and the bane of all gods and all men . . . pleasant and handsome to look upon, but evil-minded and most unreliable in his habits' (Snorri, *Edda*, 32). In the ambiguity of his character, he is reminiscent of the → Trickster of → North American Indian Religion: helpful when it suits his purposes, and blood-brother of Odin, but dangerous at all times. Thus, while Loki gave Odin his spear and ring, Frey his ship and boar, and Thor his hammer (all cult-objects), he gave birth to Hel, the goddess of death, and the wolf Fenris. His greatest act of treachery was in bringing about death of Balder.

Balder (Icel. Baldr), son of Odin and Frigg, was most beautiful and wisest of the gods, and is a S. version of the → dying-rising god of vegetation; the possibility of Christ. influence on the myth of Balder cannot be ruled out. Acc. to Snorri *Edda*, 48), Balder 'had great and terrible dreams concerning his life', which he revealed to the gods. Frigg, therefore, made all things swear never to harm her son, overlooking only the → mistletoe. The gods then amused themselves by proving Balder's immunity, until Loki persuades the blind Höðr to throw a mistletoe branch at him. The branch pierces him; he dies, 'and that is the greatest misfortune that has befallen gods and men'. Another of Odin's sons, Hermod, is sent to try and procure Balder's release from Hel, Hel agrees, on condition that all things in the world weep for him. A giantess, Þökk, refuses to weep, and Balder remains below. Finally in the myth comes Loki's imprisonment and punishment: bound beneath a poisonous serpent, the venom dripping in his face, he will remain until Ragnarök.

The cosmogony of S. relig. is both subtle and complex; its complexity is increased by fact the post-Christ. date of one of the main sources, Snorri's *Edda*. The question of the extent of Christ. influence on the myths of origin and destruction has never been settled; here we can only note the possibility. The other main source, the *Völuspá* (first poem in *Poetic Edda*), is older, but cryptic; occasional refs. elsewhere add details to picture, which may be reconstructed as follows:

In the beginning was a yawning gulf (*Ginnungagap*), bounded in north by the intense cold of *Niflheimr* and in south by the intense heat of *Múspellsheimr*. The cold and heat meet to form a giant, *Ymir*, and a cow, *Auðumla*. The cow sustains Ymir with her milk, and, by licking the salty stones of Ginnungagap, produces another being, *Búri*. Buri and Ymir's daughter Bestla have a son, Borr, who becomes father of Odin, Vili and Vé. These three destroy Ymir and his progeny, all but one of his sons, Bergelmir, who fathers a new race of giants. Ymir's corpse is then taken by Odin and his brother, and from it they make the earth: his blood becomes seas, lakes and rivers; his bones mountains; his skull the heavens. This they call Midgard (*Miðgarðr*). Then man is created: 'As the sons of Borr walked along the sea-shore, they found two tree-trunks and took them and from them created man; the first (son) gave them life and breath, the second sense and movement, the third form and speech and hearing and sight. They gave them clothing and names: the man they called Askr (ash) and the woman Embla (elm). And from them was born the human race, which was made to dwell in Midgard' (Snorri, *Edda*, 8). This account of creation of man from growing plants has an interesting parallel in the Iranian *Bundahishn*, 15.

At centre of the world stands a tree called Yggdrasill—a type of cosmic tree or world tree, found in many cosmologies as agent of coherence and focus of sacred power. We have already mentioned myth of Odin's self-sacrifice in quest for power; his act in hanging himself on the cosmic tree estab. it as a tree of knowledge. It is also a type of the actual cosmos, assailed by evil powers, but concealing beneath its roots a sacred spring, called the Well of Urðr (*Urðarbrunnr*), at which the gods have their judgment seat. The tree is in fact 'the agency by which the fabric of universe is maintained' (Branston). While some scholars have seen in Yggdrasill a reflection of the Christ. cross, and in the sacrifice of Odin a reflection of the crucifixion, both motifs are well attested from pre-Christ. sources. A *Scholion* (138 or 134) on Adam of Bremen's *Gesta* reads, ref. to the Uppsala temple: 'Near this temple stands a very large tree with widespreading branches, always green winter and summer. What kind it is nobody knows. There is also a spring at which the pagans are accustomed to make their sacrifices . . .'. Since it is known that sacrifice in pre-Christ. times was often by hanging, the cultic context of myth seems clear. (→ Cross).

The home of the gods was called Asgard (*Āsgarðr*), a fortress or mountain at heart of Midgard, with separate halls for various deities and heroes. One of the halls is Valhalla (*Valhöll*), which is not, despite Wagner, a synonym for 'heaven'; we shall return to this idea later.

There is a period set to the world of men and gods. In fulness of time, all things are doomed to destruction in that universal cataclysm which *Völuspá* calls *Ragnarök* (the doom of the gods), but which is elsewhere called Ragnarökkr (the twilight of the gods, *Götterdämmerung*). The former is more appropriate, since this is an expression of the fate which neither man nor god can escape. First comes a dreadful winter—three winters with no summer, heralded by three years of moral dissolution. The wolf Fenrir swallows the sun; earth and mountains heave and crack; the wolf runs wild, destroying all he meets; the heavens split; the horn of Heimdallr sounds; Yggdrasill trembles; and the gods go forth to their last great battle, before fire consumes all things. In time, there will emerge new heavens and a new earth, but the details given are sketchy. In the myth of Ragnarök there are parallels to both I.-E. and Christ. eschatologies; the account in *Völuspá* would appear to be a composite 'vision', drawn from these and other sources, but elaborated in post-Christ. times.

The subject of → eschatology in S. relig. is thus a complex one, and S. beliefs in the destiny of man share in this complexity. Funerary customs of Bronze and Iron Ages bear witness to belief in continued existence of the dead in the grave-mound; sacrifices could be made to them, and their possessions were laid beside them. But there was no absolute consistency of practice: cremation and ship-burials would both seem to indicate belief in a journey to the land of the dead—a belief bound up in some way with the aristocratic cult of Odin. In both *Eddas*, Valhalla is ruled over by Odin, who chooses a number of those killed in battle on earth to join him there (others may be taken by Freya). The hall is a warrior's paradise, lined with shields and armour. The fortunate dead are conducted to Valhalla by the Valkyries, the female 'choosers of the slain'. The heroes there spend their days in eating, drinking and combat—'that is their sport' (Snorri, *Edda*, 48). But the majority of dead go, not to Valhalla, but to *Hel*. This word signifies two things: first, a goddess, daughter of Loki and queen of underworld; and secondly, the underworld itself. 'The road to Hel leads downward and northward' (Snorri, *Edda*, 48)—nine days' ride through deep, dark valleys, across a → bridge (*Gjallarbrú*), and thence to the gates. But the sources use *hel* to signify simply 'death':

Icel. *fara til heljar* = to die; *drepa mann til heljar* = to slay. And, while it is certainly used to denote the abode of the dead, its use is vague, and it seems to signify the place of the dead in general rather than a particular location. Little is said about the state of the dead. It is partic. import. to note that, although the journey to Hel was believed to be difficult and dangerous, there seems to have been no clear conception of a *post-mortem* → judgment. Selection for Valhalla was on basis of courage and manner of death, and not bound up with any other moral consideration. In theory, the dead might return (cf. myth of Balder), and there was some measure of commerce between the world of the living and world of the dead (→ Shamanism); but this belongs rather to the lower levels of S. relig. than to its developed mythology.

There is little that can be said concisely about these lower levels. So much is clear, however, that the mythology of the *Eddas* repr. an 'aristocratic' relig., while the common people lived in a world peopled by supernatural beings who controlled every aspect of their daily lives. Tales abound of fairies, elves, trolls, giants and other denizens of wood and stream, forest and mountain—all of whom were potentially dangerous, and had to be constantly propitiated. Private rites were carried out in connection with birth, marriage and death, while regular rituals of the house were concerned mainly with the *álfar* (elves), who governed fertility and may have been spirits of departed ancestors. Sacrifice to these beings (*álfablót*) was held in winter; it is thought likely that the pre-Christ. festival of Yule (cf. Sw. *Jul.* A.-S. *guili*, Goth. *fruma jiuleis*) was devoted to the *álfar*. Many mod. Scandinavian Christmas customs can be traced directly back to this source.

The cultic aspect of S. relig., whether carried out in family or in public, was seasonal, and centred on maintenance of the natural order, principally by means of sacrifice (*blót*). Originally, as Tacitus points out, the Germanic tribes had no temples, deeming it inconsistent with divine majesty to 'imprison their gods within walls' (*Germania*, 9), and worshipped in the open, in enclosed cult places (Icel. *hörgr*). By Viking times, temples (Icel. *hof*) were in use, of which the greatest was the temple at what is now Gamla Uppsala, Sweden. Each prominent family had its private *hof*, of which the head of family was priest (*goðe*). Horses, pigs and dogs were among sacrificial animals; blood was spread on altar and walls, and sprinkled on participants. → Human sacrifice also took place. 'It is customary ... to solemnise at Uppsala, at nine-year intervals, a general feast of all the provinces of Sweden. ... The sacrifice is of this nature: of every living thing that is male, they offer nine heads, with the blood of which it is customary to placate gods of this sort. The bodies they hang in the sacred grove that adjoins the temple. ... Even dogs and horses hang there with men' (Adam, *Gesta*, 4:27). Connected with the sacrifice was a cultic meal, designed to promote fellowship between men and the gods.

Little can be said with certainty about the psychology of S. relig.; but it would seem to have rested on foundations of sacrifice to the gods, fear and propitiation of the dark powers of surrounding world, trolls and the like, and a firm belief in fate. The concept of fate is of espec. significance, since it was believed that in the last resort, even the gods themselves were unable to escape its workings. Fate was personified in S. mythology as the three Norns (*Urðr, Verðandi, Skuld*), female beings who control human destiny from cradle to grave (cf. Grk. Eumenides). As is common, belief in fate went hand-in-hand with highly developed techniques of augury and divination. On personal level, each individual was thought to possess a guardian spirit, or 'fortune' of his own; the commonest names for this were *hamingja* and *fylgja*—not identical concepts, but with similar import. The idea of free will was practically unknown in S. relig.; hence there was no moral code comparable to that found in prophetic relig. The Nordic virtues were bound up with the family unit, and with personal honour: the breaking of any link in family chain, esp. by violence, demanded vengeance (a constant theme of the Sagas). The individual who lost his honour, for any reason whatever, was excl. from society. In this code, dominated by ideals of courage, strength and virility, the gods participated to the full. In fact, the world of the gods was in many ways analogous to, and closely bound up with, the world of men. E.J.S.

The literature is enormous. The following works may be mentioned:
1. *General. Handwörterbuch des deutschen Aberglaubens*, I–X (1927–42); J. Grimm, *Deutsche Mythologie*[4] (new edn. 1953), E.T. *Teutonic Mythology* (1880–8); W. Mannhardt, *Wald- und Feldkulte*, I–II (1875–7); E. Mogk, 'Germanische Religion', in *Bilderatlas*, 1 Lief. (1924); F. Cornelius, *Indogermanische Religionsgeschichte* (1942); J. A. Mac-Culloch. *The Celtic and Scandinavian Religions* (1948); B. Branston, *Gods of the North* (1955); G. Dumézil, *Les dieux des Germains* (1959); J. de Vries, *Altegermanische Religionsgeschichte*[2], I–II (1956–7) (an especially valuable work, with comprehensive bibliography); E. O. G. Turville-Petre, *Myth and Religion of the North* (1964).
2. *Special Studies.* H. M. Chadwick, *The Cult*

of Othin (1899); J. G. Frazer, *Balder the Beautiful* (1914); D. Strömbäck, *Sejd* (1935); E. Birkeli, *Fedrekult i Norge* (1938); H. Ljungberg, *Den nordiska religionen och kristendomen* (1938), *Tor* (1947); W. Baetke, *Das Heilige im Germanischen* (1942); H. R. Ellis, *The Road to Hel* (1943); G. Dumézil, *Loki* (1948); H. Celander, *Förkristen jul enligt norrönä kallor* (1955); A. B. Rooth, *Loki in Scandinavian Mythology* (1961).

Scandinavian School of History of Religions The term S.-S. (or Uppsala S.) is really a misnomer, since it is, strictly speaking, neither exclusively Scandinavian nor a precisely defined school. Its general position is shared by a number of non-S. scholars, and use of term must not be taken to imply either an overall consensus among S. historians of relig. or a lack of openness toward other approaches and methods. Broadly speaking, representatives of the S.-S. stress the following points: (1) Scientific religio-historical method based on philological and thematic treatment of source materials; (2) Drawing of clear distinction between historical, phenomenological, and psychological approaches to hist. of relig.; (3) Extreme scepticism toward evolutionism in hist. of relig.; (4) Recognition of belief in, and worship of, → High Gods at an early level of relig. development; (5) General (though not uncritical) acceptance of findings of → Myth and Ritual school. The term 'S.-.S' should be taken to denote an approach to problems of hist. of relig. favoured by certain S. scholars, mainly (but not exclusively) within field of anc. Near East. religs. Forerunners of S.-S. outside Scandinavia include A. Lang, W. Schmidt, R. Pettazzoni, A. Jeremias, A. B. Cook, S. H. Hooke and A. M. Hocart. The focus of S.-S. is in Sweden, and partic. in the University of Uppsala, where influential chairs are at present occupied by G. Widengren (the most outstanding repr. of S.-S.), S. Wikander, H. Riesenfeld and H. Ringgren. Danish and Norwegian scholars have not participated to same extent in Uppsala approach; nor have representatives of hist. of relig. in Lund and Stockholm. Import. contributions have, however, been made by the Danes J. Pedersen and E. Nielsen, and the Norwegian S. Mowinckel. As already mentioned, the S.-S. is concerned to a great extent with religs. of anc. Near East, and esp. with problem of cultural patterns in relig. Hence considerable attention has been paid to complex problems connected with kingship, cult and tradition. In biblical exegesis, which is an organic part of Near East. field of study, S. scholars have developed the 'traditio-historical method' (*R.G.G.*[3] refers to *Kultgeschichtliche Methode*), which aims at a synthetic approach, formulated partly in conscious opposition to methods of literary criticism and form-criticism. The aim of this approach is to take full account of totality of relig. trad. and its transmission, with as little reliance as poss. on *a priori* theories. The priority of oral over written trad. is generally allowed. In N.T. studies, emphasis is placed on this same complex of trad. and transmission within cultural framework of late → Judaism, its ideas and concepts; particular attention has been paid of late to problem of nature and transmission of the Gospel tradition. E.J.S.

General: G. Widengren, 'Die religionsgeschichtliche Forschung in Skandinavien in den letzten zwanzig Jahren', in *Zeitschr. f. Rel. -u. Geistesgesch* (1953), pp. 193–222, 320–34; H. Ringgren and Å. V. Ström, *Religionerna i historia och nutid*[2] (1959); I. Engnell and B. Reicke, 'Traditionshistorisk metod', in *Svenskt Bibliskt Uppslagsverk*[2] (1963), ii, cols. 1254–64.
Evolutionism: G. Widengren, 'Evolutionism and the Problem of the Origin of Religion', in *Ethnos* (1945), pp. 57–96.
Phenomenology: G. Widengren, *Religionens värld*[2] (1953); German trans. *Religionsphänomenologie* (1969).
Ancient Near East and O.T.: J. Pedersen, *Israel*, I–IV (E.T. 1926–40); G. Widengren, *The Accadian and Hebrew Psalms of Lamentation*[2] (1937), *Hochgottglaube im alten Iran* (1938), *Mani and Manichaeism* (E.T. 1961), *Sakrales Königtum im Alten Testament und im Judentum* (1952); I. Engnell, *Studies in Divine Kingship* (1943), *Gamla Testamentet* (1945); H. Ringgren, *Word and Wisdom* (1947), *The Prophetical Conception of Holiness* (1948), *Israel's Religion* (E.T. 1966); S. Mowinckel, *Religion und Kultus* (G.T. 1953), *He That Cometh* (E.T. 1956), *Prophecy and Tradition* (1946), *The Psalms in Israel's Worship* (E.T. 1962); E. Nielsen, *Shechem*[2] (1959), *Oral Tradition*[5] (1960); G. W. Ahlström, *Aspects of Syncretism in Israelite Religion* (1963); R. A. Carlson, *David, the Chosen King* (1964).
N.T.: H. Riesenfeld, *Jésus Transfiguré* (1947); K. Stendahl, *The School of St. Matthew* (1954); B. Gerhardsson, *Memory and Manuscript* (1961).

Scapegoat The best known example of ritual-S. is in Day of → Atonement ritual (Lev. 16), where sins of Israel were transferred to a goat which was then driven into desert (in N.T. times it was thrown over precipice). A similar ritual-transference of ill occurs in purification of leper (Lev. 14:53), where a bird was released sprinkled with blood of another ritually infected with the disease. S.-rituals were also known in Greece, Ionia and Massilia. In Athens, at the Thargelia, two S. (*pharmakoi*), one repr. men, the other women, were driven from city and prob. stoned to death. In Ionia the *pharmakos* was beaten on his genitals with squills before being burned: this custom has been interpreted as indic. that victim had some fertility significance. The ritual-transference of evil occurs in various forms elsewhere. (→ Azazel). S.G.F.B.

J. G. Frazer, *The Scapegoat* (*G.B.* 1933[3]); *E.R.E.*, XI, *s.v.; O.C.D.*, *s.v.* ('Pharmakos'); H. H. Rowley, *Worship in Anc. Israel* (1967), pp. 92ff.

Scarab Anc. Egypt. → amulet in form of beetle. The Egypt. word for the S.-beetle was *khepre(r)*, which also meant 'to be' or 'to become'. Since Sun-god → Rē was regarded as self-existent creator, the S.-beetle became popular symbol for him; moreover, its habit of rolling ball of dung suggested a divine S.-beetle rolling sun across sky. Carved of various materials, the S. was widely used as symbol of eternal renewal of life. In → funerary ritual, a S., engraved on base with ch. 30 of → *Book of Dead* was placed in mummy-wrappings for use at → judgment of dead. (→ Heart). S.G.F.B.

E. A. W. Budge, *The Mummy* (1925), pp. 280ff.; *E.R.E.*, XI, *s.v.;* W. M. Flinders Petrie, *Scarabs and Cylinders* (1917); *R.Ae.R.G.*, pp. 297ff., 720ff.

Schleiermacher, Friedrich Daniel Ernst (1768–1834) Apart from a few years at Halle as student and professor, S. spent most of academic life in Berlin where he became Professor of Theology in 1810. Under influence of Spinoza and Schlegel, S. regarded the Enlightenment's rationalist approach to reality as seriously inadequate—especially in relig. matters. The concentration on reason resulted in an ignorance of the reality disclosed by intuition. In these views, S. reveals his indebtedness to the Romantic movement, but he considered that aesthetic concerns of Romanticism needed to be completed by relig. His views on nature of relig. first appeared in *On Religion, Speeches to its Cultured Despisers* (1799) and *Monologen* (1800). In 1821 he published *The Christian Faith*, a comprehensive and systematic account of his theological views which has become a classic of Prot. theology. For S. relig. is based on the 'feeling of absolute dependence'. The term 'feeling' is an unfortunate one, for by it S. was not refer. to a subjective emotion; although, starting with → Hegel, this is the way he has often been misinterpreted. The term 'feeling' denotes a kind of intuition, by which an individual has an immediate awareness of the divine. The divisions of subject and object and of finite and infinite are overcome in this feeling; for in it the finite individual is conscious of himself as essentially related to the infinite and absolute ground of his being. The dependence is both causal and teleological, since it concerns both origin and goal of life. Theology is the explication of significance of this feeling. The concept of God, for instance, does not ref. to a separate, supernatural person but to the correlate of our consciousness of absolute dependence. The attributes of God are expositions of the content of that consciousness. The doctrine of the → Trinity provides a comprehensive expression of the Christian's basic self-awareness. Whether or not these views mean that S. was a pantheist is still a debated question. Since authentic relig. is based on an immediate awareness of the divine which underlies every aspect of daily life, it neither needs nor finds guarantees in supernatural, miraculous interferences. Thus S. avoids conflict between scientific rationalism and faith. Eternal life is not a future event, but a present state of consciousness of unity with God. The different historical religs. are derived from different apprehensions of this God-consciousness. In → Jesus the consciousness of unity with God achieved perfection; this is the clue to understanding his Christological status. → Sin is interpreted as division between man's potential and his actual God-consciousness: it is a universal state of mankind which has only been overcome by Jesus. The soteriological status of Jesus rests on his being the archetype or representative man who is able, with our consent, to create the same total God-consciousness in us. S. thus based faith on what is given in the existential self-understanding both of the individual and of the community of believers. Although often criticised, S.'s views have exercised a fundamental influence on most subsequent Prot. theology. His system offers, on the basis of a kind of relig. experience, a poss. way of holding together modern thought and Chr. belief. D.A.P.

F. D. E. Schleiermacher, *On Religion, Speeches to its Cultured Despisers; Soliloquies; The Christian Faith:* R. B. Brandt, *The Philosophy of Schleiermacher* (1941); R. R. Neibuhr, *Schleiermacher on Christ and Religion* (1964).

Scholasticism Word used to describe work of Chr. scholars during Middle Ages aimed at explaining the → revelation contained in Holy Scripture in terms of current philosophical thought. Such exegesis had begun with the Grk. and Lat. Fathers of Early Church; but medieval S. was equipped with a dialectical technique, based on method of *pro* and *contra*. S. assumed that faith could be harmonised with reason, and an estab. system of logic ensured rationally demonstrated conclusions. The theoretical foundations of S. were laid by → Augustine and Boethius. In 9th cent., John Scotus Erigena defined carefully distinction between *auctoritas* (Holy Scripture) and *ratio* (reason). The transmission of works of → Aristotle, chiefly through Arabic trans., provided a new and effective impetus. Chief representatives of S. are →→ Anselm, Abelard, Albertus Magnus, and Thomas Aquinas. The

Summa Theologica of the last was the supreme achievement of S.; it remains a chief subject of study for R.C. priests and scholars. Christian S. is paralleled by a similar movement in Islam: →→ Mu'tazilites; Averroes; Avicenna.

S.G.F.B.

E.R.E., XI, pp. 239ff.; *D.C.C.*, *s.v.;* R. L. Poole, *Medieval Thought and Learning* (1932); E. Bréhier, *La Philosophie du Moyen Age* (1949); G. Leff, *Medieval Thought* (1958); E. R. Fairweather (ed.), *A Scholastic Miscellany: Anselm to Ockham* (1956).

Schopenhauer, Arthur (1788–1860) Son of a Danzig merchant, who preferred to become philosopher than follow in family business. S. was greatly influenced by → Kant, espec. concerning phenomenal nature of reality as known; but he rejected Kant's moral affirmation of God. Although also influenced by the Idealists, in particular by Schelling's doctrine of the will, S. regarded his own philosophy as a condemnation of Fichte, Schelling and → Hegel. His egoism and sarcastic remarks about other philosophers did not endear him to academic world. His books were not widely sold and his ideas were largely unnoticed until last decade of his life. Although he held that reason is primarily concerned with practical needs of life, he considered that man has developed to point where he can turn at times to disinterested aesthetic and philosophical contemplation. In 1813 S. was introduced by F. Mayer to Indian philosophy. He retained an interest in Oriental thought throughout his life, expressing great admiration for the → Buddha. He held that his understanding of reality was basically the same as Indian doctrine of → Māyā, in which individual subjects and objects are regarded as appearances. S.'s basic claim is that reality of any object consists of its appearing to, or being perceived by, a subject: e.g., the reality of a chair as perceived by me is limited to what I perceive it to be. From this S. concluded that a percipient subject is correlative with any object, and so the real world is a unity of perceiver and perceived. Behind all appearances is the fundamental thing-in-itself. S. holds that since introspection of our own bodies and actions shows us that the body is in fact objectified will, so this fundamental thing-in-itself is to be considered as 'Will'—a single Will, for there can be only one such reality. All phenomena are manifestations of this Will—a Will which appears to be, on the one hand, a blind, unknowing impulse; on the other hand, always a 'Will to live'. This Will is endlessly striving and never fulfilled. In men it is experienced as a never satisfied demand for happiness and self-assertion. The world is an arena where each individual strives for mastery. The evil, suffering and cruelty of world are thus expressions of fundamental nature of reality. While men may combine, espec. in form of states, to ease suffering and to check evil, ultimately they cannot be eradicated since they express the nature of the thing-in-itself behind all phenomena. S. thus repudiates optimism of Hegelian idealists, who assert the 'rational' character of even the dark side of life, and thus justifies his title as 'the philosopher of pessimism'. There are two ways of escape from evil of life. A temporary escape is offered by aesthetic contemplation, where man becomes a disinterested observer and is freed from demands of his desires. A lasting escape is offered by → asceticism and self-negation. → Salvation is thus achieved by renunciation of fundamental will to live. Here S. identifies his philosophy with Indian thought about blessedness of resignation. S. rejects both theism and pantheism as childish and unable to face reality of evil. His writings aroused in Germany considerable interest in Oriental thought and relig. —e.g. in Paul Deussen. His thought partic. influenced Nietzsche, Wundt, Vaihinger and von Hartmann—in art, Wagner and Thomas Mann. D.A.P.

A. Schopenhauer, *The World as Will and Idea; Selected Essays:* F. C. Copleston, *Arthur Schopenhauer, Philosopher of Pessimism* (1946); V. J. McGill, *Schopenhauer, Pessimist and Pagan* (1931).

Schweitzer, Albert (1875–1965) German theologian (b. at Kaiserberg, Alsace), whose writings and personal example have profoundly influenced Chr. thought. His *Von Reimarus zu Wrede* (1906, E.T. *The Quest of the Historical Jesus*, 1910) intro. a new epoch in N.T. study. In this work, after a critical survey of earlier studies of → Jesus, S. set forth his 'konsequent-eschatologische Auffassung' ('Consistent-Eschatological Interpretation'). He argued that career and teaching of Jesus are only intelligible in terms of contemporary Jew. → Apocalyptic: that Jesus, when his hope of eminent end of world failed, decided to save his people from final tribulation by self-sacrifice. S. applied his eschatological thesis also in interpr. → Paul's teaching (*Paul and his Interpreters*, E.T. 1912; *The Mysticism of Paul the Apostle*, E.T. 1931). In 1913 S. abandoned a distinguished academic career to devote himself as missionary doctor to natives at Lambaréné (Equatorial Africa). S. was also an accomplished musician and authority on J. S. Bach. In his non-Biblical writings, he set forth his philosophy as 'reverence for life'. He was awarded Nobel Peace Prize, 1952, and British Order of Merit, 1955. S.'s eschatological thesis was extended to interpret. of early Chr. doc. by his friend Martin Werner (→ De-eschatologisation). Although S.'s interpretation met much opposition, it has left its mark on N.T. study. S.G.F.B.

R.G.G.[3], V, pp. 1607–8 (bibliog.); H. Stephan, *G.D.E.T.*, index; S. Neill, *Interpretation of the N.T.* (1964), pp. 191ff.; Werner, *Die Entstehung d. chr. Dogmas* (1941[4]).

Scriptures, Hindu Strictly the canon of Hindu → revelation consists in the → Veda, though there is auxiliary canon consisting in law books (→ *dharma*), the epics (→ *itihasa*) and → Puranas. However, the S. which in fact have been appealed to in evolution of classical and medieval Hinduism, among → *bhakti* cults and → Tantrism, have been much wider in scope, incl. writings known as *Tantras*, sectarian Upaniṣads (later than classical → Upaniṣads forming part of Veda) and collections of hymns of Dravidian hymnologists (e.g. → Alvars). It became not unusual to treat *Puranas* as a fifth Veda (i.e. additional to four anc. collections of hymns, etc.), and to treat *Tantras* as of equal validity with Veda. Nevertheless the Vedic writings have continued as norm of → orthodoxy, even if their prescriptions and teachings sometimes have merely theoretical relationship to Hinduism as practised. (→ Books, Sacred). N.S.

Seal (of Prophecy) This was a growth on → Muḥammad's shoulders. One trad. compares it to a pigeon's egg in size. Another says it was a collection of moles like warts at end of Muhammad's left shoulder-blade. Another, given by both →→ Bukhari and Muslim, says it was between Muhammad's shoulders and like a button on a bride's pavilion. Ibn Isḥāq tells story of the monk → Baḥīrā, who recognised Muhammad as the expected prophet, when in youth he had come to Buṣrā in Syria with a mercantile expedition. Baḥira is said to have had a book in his cell which described the seal, which corresponded with the growth between Muhammad's shoulders and showed he was the expected prophet. Ibn Hishām, Ibn Isḥāq's editor, said seal was like imprint of a cupping-glass. J.R.

Guillaume, *Life*, p. 80; Muir, *Life*, pp. 529f.; Watt, *Mecca*, p. 37; *Mishkāt*, pp. 96, 738, 1239f.

(of the Prophets) (*khātam al-nabiyyīn*) This phrase is used of Muhammad in Qur. xxxiii:40, and is understood to mean that he is the final prophet who has brought God's last revelation to mankind. Paret, in a brief n. on verse, suggests alternatively that it may mean he is the one who confirms his predecessors. Muḥammad 'Alī, in n. 1994 to his trans. of the Qur., says phrase means that Muhammad is final prophet because the perfect law of Qur. is the final manifestation of God's will in laws to guide humanity. But to this he adds that title involves further that 'certain favours bestowed on prophets were for ever to continue among his followers'. This did not mean that perfect law meant God had nothing more to say to mankind; for 'it is recognised by Islām that the Divine Being speaks to his chosen ones now as He spoke in past, but such people are not prophets in real sense of word'. (→ Ahmadiyya Movement). J.R.

Secret Societies (Chinese) Have flourished in China since days of the Red Eyebrows who overthrew Wang Mang in CE 25. Since Ming Dynasty, S.S. have led at least eight rebellions against central government, two of which, the White Lotus Rebellion (1356–69) and the T'ai P'ing Rebellion (1854–67) almost succeeded. S.S. have been a perennial factor in rebellion and revolution. In times of political weakness and social disruption they have proliferated. The authoritarian gov. of China has always feared heterodoxy, and whilst legally recognising → Buddhism and → Taoism, exercised strict control over them and persecuted all forms of deviation, thus forcing sectarian movements underground and leading to rise of numerous S.S.

S.S. attracted those who lacked support of a strong familial organisation, the poor and underprivileged peasants and urban labourers. They are the most strongly organised groups in Chi. society outside the kinship system. Some had primarily a political and economic interest, using relig. as a means to inculcate loyalty and group solidarity. Others were predominantly relig. in character, drawing their inspiration from Buddhism and Taoism, and, in more recent times (e.g. the I Kuan Tao or Way of Pervading Unity), accepting teachings of all the major religs.—Confucianism, Buddhism, Taoism, Islam and Christianity, and worshipping images of all their respective gods or prophets. The relig. element is particularly prominent in their initiation rites; but most encourage various forms of asceticism, reduction of desires and control of mind, and inculcate belief in magic, talismans and incantations.

The S.S. of China are too numerous to detail. Among most prominent are the White Lotus, the White Cloud, the White Sun, the Red Sun, the Dragon Flower, the Big Swords, the Red Spears, the Unity Sect. Even as late as 1955, the Communist gov. has had to campaign and take strict measures against 'reactionary' S.S. (→ Sects, Chinese). D.H.S.

E.R.E., XI, pp. 309ff.; J. J. M. de Groot, *Sectarianism and Relig. Persecution in China*, 2 vols. (1903–4); H. Welch, *The Parting of the Way* (1957), p. 157; C. K. Yang, *Relig. in Chinese Society* (1961), *passim*; B. Favre, *Les Sociétés Secrètes en Chine* (1933).

Sects (Chinese) Lack of central authority and organisation in → Taoism and Chinese → Buddhism resulted in growth of numerous S., usually perpetuating influence and teaching of some distinguished Master. Though in each case the number of parent S. was small, each larger community had many offshoots which frequently took other names. Taoism divided into a N. and two S. schools; but altogether some 86 S.'s have been enumerated. At time when Buddhism reached peak of its influence in T'ang Dynasty, there were some 10 major S. or schools; but sectarian differences did not play a major role, except in case of heterodox secret S. By time of Sung Dynasty, a process of syncretism practically eliminated main sectarian differences, and → Pure Land and → Ch'an predominated.

Islam in China was differentiated into Old S. and a New S.; later a New New S. arose to emphasise a return to Muslim orthodoxy. Christianity brought to China its sectarian differences. The distinction between R.C. and Protestantism was strongly emphasised. In 20th cent. a movement towards union of Prot. denominations gathered increasing momentum.

→ Confucianism, closely linked to state and scholar class, frowned upon heterodoxy; its various schools of interpretation can hardly be designated by term S. (→ Secret Societies). D.H.S.

E.R.E., XI, pp. 309ff.; J. J. M. de Groot, *Sectarianism and Relig. Persecution in China* (1903–4). For a classification of the main Buddh. S., cf. K. L. Reichelt, *Truth and Tradition in Chinese Buddhism* (1927), pp. 306ff. For Taoist S., cf. H. Welch, *The Parting of the Way* (1957), pp. 145ff.

(Japanese) The tendency to form S. has operated as a powerful formative influence in Jap. relig. through hist. In → Shinto a distinction is made between State Shinto and S. Shinto; in the Meiji era 13 Shinto S. received official recognition, about half of which came into existence after 1868. These Shinto S. owed their origin to popular need for relig. expression, and to influence of inspired popular teachers. Three most influential of these Shinto S. are →→ Kurozumikokyo, Tenrikyo and Konkokyo. Since World War II, there has been a great revival of sect. Shinto, which has resulted in proliferation of new S., many of an eclectic or syncretistic nature and owing much to Buddhism and Christianity.

For about 70 years after the introduction of Buddhism into Japan there were no sect. differences. In 7th and 8th cents. CE six S. were introduced, namely Sanron, → Jojitsu, → Hosso, Kusha, Kegon and Ritsu. Of these only Hosso remains influential today. The great → Tendai and → Shingon S. were intro. early in 9th cent. CE; but it was not till great awakening of 12th and 13th cents. that the great Jap. Buddh. S. of →→ Jodo, Zen, Shin and Nichiren arose through inspired work of great leaders.

Trad. Jap. Buddhism is divided into 12 S. Those which died out have been replaced by two small S., Yudzu Nembutsu and Ji, and by division of Zen into →→ Rinzai, Soto and Obaku. D.H.S.

E. Steinilber-Oberlin, *The Buddhist Sects of Japan* (1938); D. C. Holtom, *The National Faith of Japan* (1938), pp. 67–70, 189–286; R. Hammer, *Japan's Relig. Ferment* (1962).

Secularization (Chinese) The roots of S. in China may be traced back to the humanistic and atheistic philosophies of anc. times, notably → Hsün-tzŭ (4th cent. BC) and Wang Ch'ung (1st cent. CE). Many Confucian and Taoist scholars throughout history accepted a S. and non-relig. interpretation of human life and destiny. With 20th cent., and partic. after World War I, under influence of W. science and philosophies, and later of Communism, there has been a large-scale turning away from relig. beliefs and piety, the growth of scepticism and atheism, and increasing S. of society. Attempts to elevate → Confucianism into a state relig. proved abortive. Violent attacks were made on Christianity, → Buddhism and → Taoism as being outmoded, anachronistic and pre-scientific. The Confucian system, incl. its ethics, came under intense criticism. Nothing short of complete S. of society would suffice. For trad. justification of power in name of Mandate of Heaven was substituted its justification in name of rights of man. The sacrificial rituals of an official cult were abandoned. An increasing proportion of social and economic organisations were transformed into purely secular bodies by abandoning their patron deities and cultic practices. Temples and monasteries were sequestered for secular use, Chr. churches closed, and priests and monks condemned as wealth-consuming and unproductive members of society. The educ. system was purged of all relig. influence. Though relig. freedom is guaranteed under present constitution, government policy in China is anti-relig. and aims at complete S. D.H.S.

C. K. Yang, *Relig. in Chinese Society* (1961), pp. 342–51, 363–77.

(Japan) No nation in Asia has progressed farther than the Japanese in using purely material means, scientific and technological, for human improvement. With abolition of state → Shinto and cult assoc. with a divine emperor, Japan has become a secular state. Yet, apart from small percentage of intellectuals who have imbibed scientific humanism and materialistic philosophies from the W., the vast majority of

Jap. people accept a relig. interpretation of human life and destiny. Sectarian Shinto and → Buddhism exert strong and pervasive influence. Since World War II there has been revived interest in relig., partic. manifest in emergence of numerous syncretistic → sects claiming millions of adherents. D.H.S.

Self-Immolation (Buddh. Monks) The practice of self-immolation by Buddh. monks, notably in Vietnam in recent times, appears to have been derived from Mhy. Buddhism of China, where it is known from at least 5th cent. CE. There would seem to be some inconsistency between this practice and the Buddh. prohibition against taking life, incl. one's own. Moreover, in the → Cakkappavattana Sutta the Buddha is repres. as saying in his first sermon that monks should avoid the two extremes of self indulgence and self mortification; self-immolation would appear to be a case of latter. However, justification for cult of self-sacrifice by burning, which grew up among Mhy. Buddh.s, is found in approval given by Buddha to suicide of a monk named Godhika, who, after attaining state of spiritual release through meditation (*samadhika-ceto-vimutti*) six times in succession and then falling away from it, committed suicide the seventh time he attained it, in order not to fall away from it again (*S.N.*, I, pp. 120f.); also in practice of burning a light in honour of Buddha, which is regarded as meritorious act. The cult of self-immolation is explicitly countenanced in Skt. treatise, → *Saddharma-pundarika Sūtra*; the story is related of a → Bodhisattva who, after eating incense and drinking oil for 12 years, bathed himself in perfumed oil and set fire to himself as act of self-offering to the Buddha. Although the Sutra goes on to say that realisation of the truth of the → Dharma is more meritorious than such acts of self-sacrifice, nevertheless the cult of self-immolation seems to have developed among Chinese Mhy. Buddh.s, among whom this Sutra (trans. into Chinese in early 3rd cent. CE) was very popular.

It is this anc. practice, of which there are a number of examples in Chi. Buddh. hist. between 5th and 10th cents., which has been revived by Buddh.s of Vietnam. The motive in this revival has been devotion to Buddha, his teaching and relig., which appeared to Vietnamese Buddh.s to be threatened by those whom they regarded as persecutors of their faith. A Theravādin monk of Ceylon (the Ven. Dr. Walpola Rāhula) commenting on these recent cases, and observing that practice is alien to → Theravāda Buddhism, and 'not in keeping with the pure and original teaching of the Buddha', nevertheless adds (no doubt with use of napalm in Vietnam in mind) 'it is better to burn oneself than to burn others' (*The Guardian*, London, 18 Oct, 1963). T.O.L.

Seppuku → Harakiri. D.H.S.

Septuagint (LXX) Grk. trans. of anc. Heb. scriptures. Name derives from legend that Ptolemy Philadelphus (285–246 BC) arranged for Heb. Bible to be trans. into Grk. by 72 translators. The S. was prob. made in 2nd cent. BC by several Alexandrian Jew. translators. It incl. writings (→ Apocrypha) not in → canon of Heb. O.T., from which it also differed in other ways. The S. was gen. regarded by Christians down to late 4th cent. as authentic version of O.T. S.G.F.B.

*H.D.B.*², pp. 347ff.; *D.C.C.*, *s.v.; R.G.G.*³, V, col. 1704–7.

Seraphim Acc. to their only mention (Is. 6:2ff.) in O.T., the S. were supernatural adorants and ministers at court of → Yahweh: they had six wings, and, apparently genital organs. The word *saraph* = fiery serpent (e.g. Nu. 21:8), and in → Enoch (I. 20:7), the S. were serpentine. Christians have identified S. with → angels, relating them to the → Cherubim. S.G.F.B.

H.D.B., *s.v.; R.A.C.*, V, col. 78–80, 172–5, 177–80; *D.C.C.*, *s.v.; E.J.R.*, p. 349.

Sermon, Buddha's First → *Dhamma Cakkappavattana Sutta*. T.O.L.

Sermon (Islam) → Khutba. J.R.

Serpents, Serpent-worship The religs. and folklore of many peoples witness to fascination and fear that S. have evoked. The swift sinuous movements and deadly power of S. suggest mysterious evil: anc. Heb. mythology explains enmity between men and S. as consequence of → Fall (Gen. 3:14f.). The S.'s habit of sloughing its skin suggested that it knew secret of perpetual rejuvenation: the *Epic of → Gilgamesh* tells how S. gained this at expense of man (i.e. Gilgamesh); in Heb. acc. of Fall, S. is responsible for Adam's loss of immortality. Prob. because S. live in holes in ground, they have been assoc. with → chthonic deities and the dead (e.g. in Greece and Rome). The cult of S. has been widespread (e.g. Egypt, Crete, Canaan, Israel, India, Mexico). The S. has figured much in fertility-cults, and its identification with the phallus (→ Phallic Cults) has assoc. it with women in mythical imagery: conception has often been attr. to S., also menstruation; the suckling of S. by women is a frequent motif, and in medieval → Dooms S. attack breasts of women. In Chr. thought the → Devil was identified with 'that ancient serpent' (Rev. 12:9); the 'worm that dieth not', tormenting damned in Hell, was depicted as S. (→→ Aesculapius, Ophites). S.G.F.B.

E.R.E., XI, pp. 399–423; *R.G.G.*³, V, col. 1419–20; *R.A.C.*, IV, col. 226–50; J. G. Frazer, *Folklore of Old Test.* (1923), pp. 18ff.; M. Eliade,

Patterns in Comparative Religion (E.T. 1958), pp. 164ff.; *R.Ae.R-G.*, pp. 681–5; J. Ph. Vogel, *Serpent Worship in Anc. and Mod. India* (1924); *H.D.B.*², pp. 897–8; S. G. F. Brandon, *The Judgment of the Dead* (1967), p. 234, n. 139; E. C. Dimock, *H.R.*, 1 (1961), pp. 307ff.; 3 (1963), pp. 300ff.

Servant Songs, The Designation used for passages in Isaiah (42:1–4; 49:1–6; 50:4–9; 52:13–53:12) concerned with mission, sufferings, death and (apparent) resurrection of a 'Servant' of → Yahweh. The Servant is anonymous, except in 49:3, where he is called Israel; he appears to suffer vicariously. The S.-S. were early regarded as predictions of → Jesus (e.g. Acts 8:28ff.). The meaning of the S.-S. and identity of 'Servant' continue to be discussed by scholars. S.G.F.B.

H. H. Rowley, *The Servant of the Lord and Other Essays on the Old Test.* (1952); *H.D.B.*², pp. 898–9; *E.J.R.*, p. 350; M. D. Hooker, *Jesus and the Servant* (1959).

Set (Seth) Anc. Egypt. god. S. appears in → Pyramid Texts as 'Lord of Upper Egypt' and brother of → Osiris, whom he kills. Cast in role of murderer of Osiris, S. was grad. regarded as god of evil, assoc. with red desert, storms, and other forms of ill. The favour accorded his cult by the hated Hyksos invaders of Egypt added to S.'s evil reputation. In Osirian mythology, S. is repr. as persecuting → Isis and her son → Horus: the latter later contends with S. to avenge his father and secure his patrimony. In iconography S. is shown with head of mysterious animal, perhaps an okapi. In Grk. version of Osirian myth, S. was identified with Grk. monster Typhon. It is likely that S. was connected in → Gnosticism with Seth, son of Adam, after whom a Gnostic sect was named. There is an element of → dualism in the conflict of Set and Horus. S.G.F.B.

R.Ae.R-G., *s.v.;* S. A. B. Mercer, *The Relig. of Anc. Egypt* (1949), chs. 3, 5; *Ae.R.T.B.*, I, *passim*; J. Doresse, *The Secret Books of the Egyptian Gnostics* (E.T. 1958), pp. 104ff.; H. te Velde, *Seth: God of Confusion* (1967).

Sex, attitude to → Fertility. S.G.F.B.

(attitude) (China) The Chi. attitude to S. has been dictated by a strong familialism, the prudery of → Confucianism and inferior status and economic dependence of women. From the → *Shih Ching* and the → *Ch'un Ch'iu Tso Chuan* there is ample evidence to show that in early feudal period the relation betw. sexes was much freer and sexual code far less strict than in later times when Confucian morality became gen. accepted. Many Odes of the *Shih Ching* are frankly licentious. Confucian morality devised, and the familial system demanded, the strictest code of rules to regulate relation betw. sexes in home, and insisted on partial seclusion of women. Courtship and romantic love were deemed to be no fit preparation for marriage. The procreation of children was a first duty of filial piety, and bearing of children a chief function of wife. Celibacy was considered to be unnatural. Though unchastity on part of wife was severely punished, extramarital relationships on part of husband were condoned by society so long as they were conducted with due discretion. Concubinage for rich, and resort to courtesans and prostitutes was common means of sexual gratification. The popular romantic novels, considered by strict Confucian moralists as licentious and depraved, usually had as main theme some extramarital liason. In mod. Communist China the breakdown of old Confucian familialism and equal status accorded to women have resulted in much freer attitude to S. D.H.S.

R. H. van Gulik, *Sexual Life in Ancient China* (1961); J. D. Ball, *Things Chinese*, 5th edn. (1925), pp. 367ff., 588ff.; C. P. Fitzgerald, *China* (1935, rev. edn. 1950), pp. 47–8.

(Japan) → Shinto does not seem to be concerned about problems of S. Premarital and extramarital relationships are discouraged. Sexual intercourse is deemed to cause temporary uncleanness, demanding ritual purification. Virgins were often selected as priestesses and dancers before the gods; but this did not entail vows of perpetual chastity. During Yedo Period (1615–1868), Chinese notions of absolute subjection and seclusion of women made great progress. The first duty of wife was to be faithful and obedient to husband, and second marriages of widows were frowned upon. Though chastity in both men and women was considered a virtue, prostitution was socially recognised; it was deemed permissible, and even obligatory, for a girl to allow herself to be sold into prostitution to support her destitute parents. A feature of Jap. social life is the professional dancing and singing girl, known as Geisha. Training of the Geisha often began as early as her seventh yr.; after apprenticeship, she contracts with her employer for a number of yrs., and is seldom able to reach independence except by marriage. → Buddhism exerted a great influence in Japan in promoting ideals of continence, chastity and celibacy. D.H.S.

J. Herbert, *Shinto* (1967), p. 75; W. G. Aston, *Shinto* (1905), pp. 248ff., *Japanese Literature* (1899), pp. 232f.

Sha'bān (*Middle Night of*). This night, known in Persia, Pakistan and India as *Shab-i-barāt*, is held by many to be occasion when God ordains all actions people are to perform during ensuing year. In some countries it is occasion for a festival; in others the night is spent in prayer and mosques are lit and well attended. In some countries the prayers are in commemoration of dead; elsewhere people believe that such attendance to prayer during night may result in good being ordained for them, failing to note inconsistency that they could not have spent night in prayer if it had not been ordained for them. On this night the waters of → al-Kawthar are believed to flow into well → Zamzam. J.R.

E.I., III, p. 1111, IV, p. 239; Hughes, p. 570; Pareja, p. 655; Lane, *Egyptians*, pp. 476–8.

-Shādhiliyya → Ṣūfī Orders. J.R.

-Shāfi'ī, Muḥammad b. Idrīs (150–204/767–820), had a most import. influence on Muslim jurisprudence. He belonged to tribe of → Quraysh, and was descended from Hāshimī section to which the Prophet Muḥammad belonged. He was brought up in Mecca, and he studied under → Mālik b. Anas in Medina during last nine years of Mālik's life. For a time Sh. taught in Baghdad, but having spent some time earlier in Egypt, he returned there in 200/816 to stay. He was buried at foot of al-Muqaṭṭam, and his tomb has remained place of pilgrimage. Sh. had great influence in the recognition of *ijmā'* (→ *Sharī'a*) as a basis of law, widening it beyond consensus of Prophet's → Companions. He held that the →→ Qur. and Ḥadīth were the fundamental bases, but that *ijmā'* and *qiyās* (→ *Sharī'a*) were applicable in absence of guidance from the two fundamental bases. But he argued that if a trad. previously unknown were found and authenticated, and differed from something decided by *ijmā'* or *qiyās*, it must take precedence. J.R.

E.I., IV, pp. 252–4; Hughes, pp. 570f.; D. B. Macdonald, *Theology*, index; Wensinck, *Creed*, index; Schacht, *Jurisprudence*, *passim*; Coulson, *Law*, index (Muḥammad ibn-Idrīs); Rahman, *Islam*, index; *G.A.L.*, I, pp. 188–90 *S.*I., pp. 303–5.

-Shahrastānī, Muḥammad b. 'Abd al-Karīm (*c.* 469–548/1076–1153). He was b. at Shahrastān in Khurasan, studied at Jurjāniyya, Naysabur and elsewhere. He is perhaps best known for his *Kitāb al-milal wal niḥal* (Book on religions and sects), in which he discusses many Muslim sects, also dealing with parties belonging to other religs., and with philosophers. Another import. work is his *Summa Philosophiae* (*Nihāyatu'l-iqdām fī 'ilmi'l-kalām*), ed. with abridged trans. by A. Guillaume (1934). Here he deals with older theologians and also with philosophers, and shows individuality of approach to questions discussed in earlier generations. J.R.

E.I., IV, pp. 263f.; *G.A.L.*, I, pp. 550f.; *S.*I., pp. 762f.; Ibn Khallikān, II, pp. 675–7; *Kitab al-milal wal niḥal*, Arabic text, ed. Cureton (1846); D. B. Macdonald, *Theology*, pp. 291–3; Watt, *Philosophy*, pp. 126f. and index; Sweetman, *I.C.T.*, I–IV, index of authors.

Shakers Name for members of 'The United Society of Believers in Christ's Second Appearing', or 'The Millennial Church'. The S. stemmed from a Quaker (→ Friends, Society) revival in England in 1747. The most notable leader was Ann Lee, known as Mother Ann, who was regarded as 'The female principle in Christ'. To escape persecution, the S. migrated to America in 1774. The movement embodied communistic and pacifist principles, and greatly esteemed celibacy. Its members affected a common dress, ate together, abstained from alcohol, and practised faith-healing. The name 'S' derived from their shaking when in state of spiritual exaltation. Their numbers have greatly declined. (→ Communism). S.G.F.B.

E.R.E., III, pp. 781ff.; *D.C.C.*, *s.v.;* H. Desroches, *Les Shakers américains. D'un néo-christianisme à un pre-socialisme?* (1955).

Shamanism The word 'shamanism' is derived from the Tungusian *šamān*, 'priest, medicine man'. S. proper is indigenous relig. of Ural-Altaic peoples in N. Asia and Europe, from Lappland in W. to Bering Straits in E. The word S. is also used, somewhat more loosely, to describe a type of relig. practised, *inter alia*, in N. America (→→ North American Indian Religion; Eskimo Religion) and Oceania (→ Australian Aborigine Religion), in which certain of phenomena of S. are prominent. S. belongs in cultural context of hunting peoples; it also presupposes belief in a multiplicity of spirits (→ Animism) and in continued existence, after death, of individual soul (→ Ancestor Worship). The most distinctive features of S. have to do with choice, initiation and techniques of those specialists in mediation between the world of spirits and the world of men, who are called shamans. The office of S. may be hereditary, or acquired by, or bestowed upon, a suitably endowed person after period of intensive training. The S. may be an epileptic, or otherwise predisposed to fits and trances; in his training he is subjected to severe austerities under guidance of an older S., to establish communion with his familiars. On initiation, he is given authority over certain spirits, and invested with his dress and equipment. A S.'s dress is elaborate and symbolical, while his indispensable instrument is the drum (or tambourine), ornamented with esoteric symbols, in which the spirits gather at his call. Thereafter his functions are priestly, oracular and medicinal. He offers sacrifices, foretells future, and cures diseases, in each case with help of the spirits. Disease, being regarded as loss of individual's free-soul, the S. pursues the departed soul, gains control over it, overcomes its enemies, and returns it to sick man. All this is done in state of trance. The power of the S. to project his own soul into realm of the spirits is his most distinctive attribute. The spirits themselves may be good or evil, and thus may provide assistance or opposition to work of the S. A special category is provided by supernatural rulers of nature (waters, mountain ridges, forests, species of animals, birds, fishes, etc.), the cooperation of which was most necessary to wellbeing of hunting peoples. Beyond these were the supreme deities, organised hierarchically under a → High God, called by the Evenks *Amaka sheveki* (*amaka* = grandfather), and living in a graded series of heavens. The S. could, it was believed, penetrate into these spirit-worlds acc. to range of his powers. When undertaking e.g. to expel a spirit of disease, the S. had special tent made for him by people he served, the centre-pole of which represented the cosmic tree; he also undertook his 'spirit-flight' with encouragement and help of his people. During (or after) his ecstatic labours, singing and beating his drum, he described in detail what he saw and experienced, and might even communicate his ecstasy to people around him. Finally he danced and fell into a cataleptic state, as the spirits were brought under control. In his spirit-flight he might be represented by an animal-double; the Evenks believed that the animal-double (*khargi*) was sent by S. on his behalf to spirit-world to fulfil his commands. Parallel phenomena have been noted among certain N. Amer. Ind. tribes and the Eskimos, where there are striking similarities of technique. S. as a religion is now practically extinct (e.g. in Lappland), though certain shamanistic beliefs persist in popular folk-lore. (→ Altaic Religion). E.J.S.

E.R.E., XI, pp. 441a–6b; *R.G.G.*³, V, cols. 1386–8; U. Harva, *Die religiösen Vorstellungen der altaischen Völker* (1938); M. Eliade, *Le chamanisme* (1951); A. Friedrich and G. Buddruss (eds.), *Schamanengeschichten aus Sibirien* (1955); H. Findeisen, *Schamanentum* (1957); H. N. Michael (ed.), *Studies in Siberian Shamanism* (1963).

Shamash Anc. Mesopot. sun-god. S. was regarded as son of moon-god → Sin; his chief cult-centres were at Larsa and Sippar. S. was guardian of laws; he is repr. on Code of Hammurabi, enthroned and worshipped by king. S. had a relatively inferior place in Mesopot. pantheon. Sumerian names: Utu, Babbar. S.G.F.B.

M. Jastrow, *Aspects*, pp. 108ff.; B. Meissner, *Babylonien und Assyrien*, II (1925), pp. 18ff.; Dhorme, *R.B.A.*, pp. 60ff.

Shang Ti Chinese term for the Supreme God, syn. with → T'ien. In anc. China, S.T. was the primaeval ancestor-spirit (→ Ti). He was conceived of in personal and anthropomorphic terms. As Supreme God, he was worshipped in the state relig., and sacrifices and prayers were offered to him by the emperor.

Later Prot. Christianity in China used the term S.T. to designate the Chr. God; whilst R.C. preferred the term 'T'ien Chu' ('Lord of Heaven'). D.H.S.

Sharī'a, or *Shar'* (path) is technical term for canon law of Islam. It is considered to be divinely estab. and not developed by man's experience or reasoning. Its bases are (1) the Qur., (2) → Tradition, (3) *Ijmā'* (consensus), (4) *Qiyās* (analogical reasoning on basis of above). The first two are the fundamental bases. *Ijmā'* gets its authority from a trad. which says: 'My people will never agree on an error'. But it is not always clear whose consensus is acceptable, or how one realises that it has been reached; for Islam has never had councils compared to those of early Christ. Church. The Sh. governs whole of life and strictly ought to be followed by orthodox Muslims; but in many countries *'āda* (customary law) has held a place alongside the Sh. (s.v. art. *'āda* in *E.I.*², I, pp. 170–4). But in mod. times the Sh. has suffered considerably. In 1346/1927 Turkey abandoned it, adopting Swiss family law, and in more recent times Egypt and Tunisia have abolished Sh. courts (→ *Qāḍi*).

Although the Sh. is intended to govern all aspects of life, dealing with relig. doc. and practice, general behaviour, politics, it has not claimed to be able to deal with inward belief, judging wholly on basis of outward action. Actions are divided into five classes: (1) Obligatory (*farḍ, wājib*); (2) Recommended (*mandūb*); (3) Prohibited (*ḥarām, maḥẓūr*); (4) Disapproved (*makrūh*); (5) Legally indifferent (*mubāḥ*). Even in earlier times a ruler could overturn the verdicts of Sh. courts. Nowadays modifications have been made in some countries to accommodate it to mod. conditions. In many respects West. influence has led to changes; but on whole the family law has normally kept to provisions of the Sh. Among the → Shi'a the Qur. is held as principal basis of law. They have their own trads. which come through → 'Ali's family. Their interpretation of these sources, however, does not always agree with that of the → Sunnis. The hidden → *imām* is still ultimate ruler, and government of the day and the → *mujtahids* are merely repres. him during his 'occlusion'. J.R.

E.I., IV, pp. 320–4; Hughes, pp. 285–92; Pareja, pp. 636ff.; Schacht, *Jurisprudence, passim*; J. N. D. Anderson, *Islamic law in the modern world* (1959), *Recent developments in sharī'a law*, 9 arts. in *M.W.*, XL–XLII, *Islamic law in Africa* (1954); N. Safran, 'The abolition of the Sharī'a courts in Egypt', in *M.W.*, XLVIII (1958), pp. 20ff., 125ff.; Cragg, *Counsels*, index; Coulson, *Law*, index; Rahman, *Islam*, ch. 6 and index.

Sharīf Pl. *ashrāf*, meaning 'noble'. At one time applied to members of → 'Abbasid branch of family of Hāshim as well as to descendants of Muḥammad through → 'Ali and his daughter Fāṭima: it was later restricted to Muhammad's descendants, and in some districts only to those descended from 'Ali's son al-Ḥasan, descendants of → al-Ḥusayn being called → *sayyids*. But often both titles are used indiscriminately. In Egypt *Ashrāf* formerly wore green turbans. *Ashrāf* are to be found in all classes of society, but while all were shown respect in past because of their ancestry, this is not so common nowadays. Members of this family held sway in Mecca for many cents. till ousted by Ibn Sa'ūd. Now Husayn in Jordan and sultan of Morocco are the only rulers of Sharifian family left. Ashrāf have strong sense of their dignity as descendants of Prophet; they do not allow their daughters to marry anyone but a *sharīf*. J.R.

E.I., IV, pp. 324–9; Pareja, pp. 303, 782; Levy, *Social Structure*, pp. 65–8, 72f.; T. H. Weir, *The shaikhs of Morocco in the xvith century* (1904).

Shaykh (Lit. 'old man', i.e. over 50 years old). Commonly used as title. It was traditionally used of chief of a tribe; it has come to be applied to people of standing in relig., political, or social circles, irrespective of age, often being merely courtesy title. Shaykh al-Islam was title of chief → *muftī*. In the Sufi orders it repres. an import. function (→ Ṣūfī). Elsewhere it is used of headman of town or village (*Shaykh al-balad*). In India and Pakistan it is used by people who claim descent from one of first two Caliphs, or from Muḥammad's uncle → al-'Abbās. In Lebanon members of import. Maronite families are given title. J.R.

E.I., IV, p. 275; Hughes, p. 571; Pareja, index (šayḫ al-islām); Levy, *Social Structure*, index; Dickson, *Arab of Desert*, pp. 52f., 116f.; S. and N. Ronart, *Concise Encyclopaedia of Arabic Civilisation*, Djambatan-Amsterdam (1959), pp. 484f.

Shê-Chi Chinese gods of the soil and grain, worshipped from most anc. times. Their altars, mounds of earth under the open sky, (*shê-chi-t'an*), were symbolic of territorial jurisdiction. Sacrifices to the S.-C. of the whole land, in spring and autumn, were the exclusive privilege of emperor; but every territorial division had its own S.-C. Small shrines, 4′–5′ square, are numerous throughout China to cater for popular worship of the gods of soil and grain. Within them are two small images, now regarded as man and wife, but originally repr. the S.-C. D.H.S.

E. T. C. Werner, *Dictionary of Chinese Mythology* (1932); M. Granet, *La Religion des Chinois* (1951), pp. 59ff.

Shekinah Heb. = 'that which dwells', 'indwelling'. Word used in Jew. lit., but not O.T., denoting manifestation of Divine Presence. The term was apparently developed to avoid idea of localisation of God in an anthropomorphic sense. Hence the Jerusalem → Temple, though regarded as dwelling place of Yahweh, was ref. to as 'the house of the S.'. The concept was closely assoc. with glory, light and fire, which in O.T. were often forms of Divine manifestation: e.g. Ex. 24:16; I Kgs. 8:11. In Chr. Ep. to Hebrews, 1:3, Christ is 'the effulgence of the glory'. In rabbinic lit. the S. denotes manifestation of God's Presence in human life (it brings peace and blessing to home, *Sot.* 17a), and principle of Divine immanence in creation. (→ Sakīna). S.G.F.B.

H.D.B.[2], *s.v.; E.J.R.*, *s.v.*

Shên Chinese term, usually rendered as spirit, divine, god. In anc. China, two characters denoted the disembodied spirits, → *kuei* and *shên*, often placed in apposition. The *kuei-shen* comprised the whole host of spiritual beings, incl. nature spirits and the *post-mortem* spirits of men. The *kuei* dwelt on or under the earth, often repr. as malevolent; the *shên* rose above and were beneficent spirits. S. came to denote the *animus*, intellectual, moral and spiritual energy within man. In later times S. signified gods as opposed to *kuei*—demons; and '*shên kuei hsien fo*' (gods, demons, immortals and Buddhas) repr. whole range of divine beings. It is incorrect to use S. to repr. God in the Chr. sense. D.H.S.

Sheol Heb. name for place of dead, conceived variously as immense pit below foundations of earth or city with walls and gates, immersed in dust and darkness. Although early Hebrews did not believe in immortality, they thought that something of the living person (→ Soul) descended to S. at death, to lead a wretched existence there, beyond care of → Yahweh: it was the common fate for good and bad, great and small. Later, S. was grad. transformed into place of retribution (e.g. in Book of → Enoch). S.G.F.B.

H.D.B.[2], *s.v.;* A. Lods, *Isräel* (1932), pp. 253ff.; R. H. Charles, *A Critical History of the Doctrine of a Future Life* (1913), pp. 33ff., 215ff.; Brandon, *The Judgment of the Dead* (1967), ch. 4.

Shī'a (Division, sect). Applied, fundamentally as a nickname, to a smaller branch of Islam than the

→ Sunnis. There are two main groups of the Sh., the Imāmīs and the → Ismā'īlīs, with various sub-divisions. The movement began as a political one, holding that → 'Ali should have been first → Caliph. As time passed, theological dogmas developed (→→ -Ḥusayn; Mediation). The imamate is fundamental (→ Imām). The *imāms* are not only of true descent from Muḥammad through 'Ali and → Fatima, a light has been transferred to them successively starting from Muhammad. The Imāmīs, who form main body of the Sh., believe that this light gives the imams a partial divinity, though still mortal. The → Zaydīs merely hold that they are rightly guided and have no element of divinity. Other sections believe in varying degrees of divinity. Love of the imams is essential for safe crossing of → -*Ṣirāṭ*; for those whose answers are unsatisfactory will be hurled into hell. The hidden imam is the → Mahdi, who will come to rule. → Jesus will come and pray behind him. The Qur. is accepted as God's word, but opinions differ about its being uncreated. Shi'is have their own collections of trads. (→ Ḥadīth). It is believed that Muhammad gave 'Ali special instructions. Shi'is make greater allowance for freewill than Sunnis, holding that God has foreknowledge of men's deeds, but does not compel them. They have → *mujtahids*, a class with right to form opinions on matters of law. They are the hidden *imam's* agents acting under his guidance; so their decisions take the place *ijmā'* and *qiyās* hold among Sunnis (→ Sharī'a). They have slight differences in the call to prayer (→ Adhān), and also in the → prayers themselves. By what is called *taqiyya* (dissimulation) they are allowed to dissemble their beliefs if danger arises from making them known. It is held that belief is in the heart, so concealment is justified to avoid suffering. They allow a kind of marriage called *mut'a*, in which a contract is drawn up in proper fashion, but incl. a date for the termination of marriage. Ladies of better classes do not enter into such marriages. Authority for this type of marriage is claimed to be based on Qur. iv:28; Sunnis do not agree with such an interpretation.

Since 908/1502 the Sh. faith has been official relig. of Persia. Elsewhere the largest community of Imamis is to be found in Uttar Pradesh in India, with centre at Lucknow. Communities occur in Iraq and elsewhere. J.R.

E.I., IV, pp. 350–8; Hughes, pp. 572–9; Mez, *Renaissance*, ch. 5; Pareja, index; Miller, *Bāb*; Donaldson, *Shi'ite*; Fyzee, *Creed;* H. Corbin, *Sur la notion de 'walāyat' en Islam Shî'ite*, in Charney, *Normes*, pp. 38–47; Levy, *Social Structure*, index; Watt, *Philosophy*, index; F. Rosenthal, *Ibn Khaldun*, index.

Shih Ching (Classic of Poetry). One of the 5 Confucian classics, and a chief source for knowledge of relig. customs and beliefs of pre-Confucian China. It comprises 305 poems in 4 books, the first, *Kuo Fêng*, being a collection of local songs classified by States, whilst the other three books, *Hsiao Ya*, *Ta Ya* and *Sung*, are for most part songs of a ritual character. Trad. attr. selection of the poems to → Confucius; they were so interpreted by Confucian scholars as to inculcate morality, social duties and a concern for ritual. Destroyed in the 'Burning of the Books' by Ch'in Shih-huang Ti (246–209 BC), an attempt at restoration was made in Han Dynasty when four versions appeared, of which only one made by Mao Ch'ang has survived, with explanations hist., moral and symbolic. The classic became, and remained, an invaluable basis for Confucian education. There are numerous trans. and studies of the S.C. in Eng. and other European languages. D.H.S.

S. Couvreur, *Cheu King* (1926); M. Granet, *Festivals and Songs of Ancient China* (E.T. 1932); A. Waley, *The Book of Songs* (1937); J. Legge, *The Chinese Classics*, vol. 4, 2nd edn. (1893); B. Karlgren, *The Book of Odes* (1950).

Shingon Jap. Buddh. sect of highly mystical and syncretistical nature, founded in CE 806 by → Kōbo Daishi. The deities and demons of various religs. are interpreted as manifestations of Mahā-Vairocana Buddha (Jap. Dainichi), whose body comprises the whole cosmos. Cosmic mysteries are repr. and symbolised in visible and tangible forms. The postures, movements and utterances of an elaborate ritual evoke mysterious powers. The cosmos is graphically repr. in diagrams called *mandala*, which symbolise two aspects of universe: its ideal or potential entity, and its vitality or dynamic manifestations. Shingon = Chinese 'Chên Yen' (True Word), itself a trans. of Skt. *mantra*. D.H.S.

M. Anesaki, *Hist. of Japanese Buddhism* (1930), pp. 124ff.; E. Steinilber-Oberlin, *The Buddhist Sects of Japan* (1938).

Shinran (1173–1263). A follower of → Honen, S. proclaimed → Amida as the Buddha of Infinite Light and Boundless Compassion. He founded the → Jodo-Shinshu (The True Sect of the Pure Land), largest and most import. sect of Jap. Buddhism. By discarding monastic robes, marrying and living an ordinary family life, S. sought to show that secular life was no bar to Buddh. salvation. He purged → Jodo Buddhism from its assoc. with trad. mysteries and methods of spiritual exercises, and related it to common life of the people, seeking to annul distinction between relig. and secular. The Buddha's grace was a free gift, appropriated neither by virtue nor by wisdom but by faith. S. sought obscurity and shunned publicity; but his following grew, and by 15th cent. had been formed into a powerful eccles. organisation. D.H.S.

A. Lloyd, *Shinran and his works* (1913); M. Anesaki, *Hist. of Japanese Religion* (1930), pp. 181ff.; E. Steinilber-Oberlin, *The Buddhist Sects of Japan* (1938), pp. 198ff.

Shinshū → Jodo, → Shinran. D.H.S.

Shinshu-kyō (Divine-healing teaching). An import. → Shinto sect, founded by Yoshimura Masamochi (b. 1839), after Meiji Restoration of 1868. He became its first superintendent priest. Its sacred texts are the → *Kojiki* and → *Nihongi*, as interpreted by Yoshimura. It seeks to preserve anc. Shinto orthodoxy, emphasising purification rituals and food taboos. Its teachings are esoteric, with great emphasis on ceremonial and meditation. Two rites, which have attracted widespread attention, are the Fire-walking ceremony and rite of purification by boiling water. Various other rites of purification and expurgation are performed, to cleanse from inner spiritual defilement and drive away all kinds of evil. Other rites are observed to induce the divine spirit to enter and 'possess' body of the individual. D.H.S.

D. C. Holtom, *The National Faith of Japan* (1938), pp. 233ff.

Shintai (Pronounced go-shintai). From *shin*—divine, and *tai*—substance. A sacred object, usually of little intrinsic value, which is kept in the → honden of a Shinto temple, and regarded by priests and people as symbolic repr. of the deity or as object in which deity is enshrined. It is regarded with such awe and reverence that it is usually enveloped in a number of precious cloths and caskets, to which more are added as previous ones show signs of wear. S. may be mirrors, stones, sacred texts, anc. swords etc. The S. of the great imperial shrine of Ise is a mirror, a sun-symbol. D.H.S.

W. G. Aston, *Shinto* (1905), *passim*; D. C. Holtom, *The National Faith of Japan* (1938), pp. 10–1; J. Herbert, *Shinto* (1967), *passim.*

Shintō (Derived from Chinese *shên-tao*, 'the way of the gods'). The native relig. of Japan. Anc. S. was a primitive cult of nature-worship. From *c.* 5th cent. CE, this was reinforced with → Confucian ideas of social morality, filial piety and → ancestor-worship. S. mythology ascribed creation of Japan to the gods, from whom emperor and people were descended. The Jap. emperor was thought of as direct descendant of → Amaterasu. (→ *Kojiki* and → *Nihongi*). By 8th cent., Buddh. influence predominated in Japan, and a syncretism between → Buddhism and Shinto led to → Ryobu-S. A revival in 17th cent. of Pure S. led to a gov. sponsored formulation of national ethics, a programme of patriotic rites and cult of loyalty to nation, known as State-S. (→ *Jinja-S.*). At Meiji restoration (1882), State-S. was separated from Sectarian-S. (Kyoha-S.), which flourished among the common people, who also practised simple rites of Domestic-S. in their homes. S. is polytheistic. It possesses neither creed, code nor authoritative canon of scriptures. Concerned with ceremonial purity, its teachings concerning sin and salvation are rudimentary. Ideas concerning an after-life are vague, and S. is without an eschatology. Some modern S. sects tend towards monotheism through Chr. influence. (→ Sects, Jap.). D.H.S.

D. C. Holtom, *The National Faith of Japan* (1938); W. G. Aston, *Shinto* (1905); R. Hammer, *Japan's Religious Ferment* (1962); J. Herbert, *Shinto* (1967).

Shu'ayb A prophet mentioned in Qur. vii:83ff.; xi:85ff.; xxix:35f.; and xxvi:176ff. In first three he goes to people of Madyan (Midian); in the other to the people of the thicket. xv:78f. speak of people of thicket as being punished without ref. to a prophet. Sh. has popularly been identified with Jethro (Reuel), father-in-law of Moses. xxix:35f. tell how he warned people of the last day and evil of working mischief. They disbelieved and were destroyed by earthquake. The other passages contain exhortation to give full measure and just weight in business dealings. J.R.

E.I., III, p. 104; IV, pp. 388f.; Sale, *Qur'án*, II, pp. 222–4, 362–4; III, pp. 20f., 231f.; Hughes, pp. 58f.; J. Horovitz, *Koranische Untersuchungen* (1926), pp. 119f.; Bell, *Introduction*, p. 122; Watt, *Mecca*, p. 129.

Shu Ching (Classic of History or Book of Documents). One of the 5 Confucian Classics, being records made by court chroniclers in pre-Confucian China. The book, whose editing is trad. ascr. to → Confucius, was destroyed in 213 BC by Ch'in Shih Huang-ti; in the Han Dynasty it was partially reconstituted by Fu Shêng and a later descendant of Confucius, K'ung An-kao, and now comprises a total of 58 sections. The authenticity has been subject of endless discussion. There is gen. agreement that at least 7 chapters are founded on anc. trad., and contain vital material bearing on Chi. civilisation in anc. pre-Confucian times. D.H.S.

J. Legge, *The Chinese Classics*, vol. 3, 2nd edn. (1893); S. Couvreur, *Chou King* (1927).

Shushi School (→ Chu Hsi) Orthodox Confucian School in Japan, adopted by Iyeyasu (d. CE 1616), founder of Tokugawa shogunate, as accepted system of morality. Intro. in 14th cent. by → Zen monks, it sought for realisation of the Way or Reason of Heaven in human life. The great leader of S. school was Hayashi Razan (1583–1657), who advocated → Shinto as foundation of national life, and → Confucianism as basis of the social order. The school emphasised the gradation of classes, and subordination of individual to the social order; taught virtues of obedience to superiors, of benevolence and justice and observance of propriety. S. had great influence on Jap. educated class (as → Chu-Hsi's teachings in China), and provided firm ethical basis for organisation of political and social life. D.H.S.

M. Anesaki, *Hist. of Japanese Religion* (1930), pp. 223ff.

Sibylline Oracles Grk. and Rom. lit. tells of inspired women called Sibyls who made notable prophecies. They existed in various places: ten are listed, the earliest ref. being to the S. at Erythrae (Asia Minor); the S. of Cumae is well known from Virgil's acc. (*Aeneid*, VI). A collection of such prophecies or oracles was kept at Rome, until destroyed in CE 405, and was officially consulted at times of crisis. The idea of such oracles, gen. written in Grk. hexameters, caused Jew. writers to compose pseudo-S.-O. (from *c.* 2nd cent. BC) as propaganda against paganism and Roman Empire. These Jew. S.-O. were later adapted for Chr. purposes. 15 books of S.O. are known, of which 12 survive. They constitute invaluable source of information about Jew. and Chr. reaction to pagan culture and Roman imperialism. S.G.F.B.

Trans. in: Charles (ed.), *A.P.*, II (1931); E. Kautzsch (ed.), *A.P.*, II (1900). *E.R.E.*, XI, *s.v.; O.C.D.* ('Sibylla'); *D.C.C.*, *s.v.; R.G.G.*², VI, col. 14; Schürer, *G.J.V.*, III, pp. 421–50; A. Peretti, *La Sibilla babilonese nella Propaganda ellenistica* (1943); P. Dalbert, *Die Theologie der hellenist—jüd. Missions-Literatur* (1954), pp. 106ff.; R. H. Pfeiffer, *Hist. of New Test. Times* (1949), pp. 226ff.

Sigālovāda Sutta A discourse of the Buddha found in the → *Dīgha Nikāya* of the Pali canon. Sigāla was a young householder of Rājagaha whom the Buddha saw worshipping the 4 quarters of compass, together with the nadir and zenith. Buddha then taught him a better form of devotion—social duties towards the six directions: parents, teachers, wife and children, friends, workpeople and relig. teachers. The *Sutta* thus provides complete account of social duties of a lay Buddh. Acc. to trad., Sigāla became a follower of Buddha. The *Sutta* is also known as the *Gihivinaya* (householder's discipline). (→ Family and Social Duties, Buddh.). T.O.L.

Sikhism The Sikhs (literally 'Disciples'), though belonging orig. to movement designed to see unity between best in Islam and best in Hinduism, have evolved a distinctive relig. and culture of their own. The teachings of Muslim → Kabir was main pioneer in spread of an inter-relig. → *bhakti* in N. India; also import. in genesis of a unified faith were → Sufi orders, one member of which was Farid (?13th cent.), some of whose hymns are incl. in Sikh scriptures (→ *Granth, Adi*) and who settled at Pak Pattan in Panjab, ultimately to be most import. Sufi centre in region. The tendencies towards unified devotionalism were crystallised in life and teachings of → Nanak, first of the ten → Gurus, or leaders of Sikh community. He preached unity of God (→ God, Sikh conception), centrality of devotion (*bhakti*), summed up in repetition of divine name, equality of men of different → castes, evils of image-worship, importance of brotherly love and need of a guru as guide. None of these elements was precisely orig. to Nanak, but his achievement was two-fold: first, he combined these sentiments into coherent scheme, which had ready appeal to both educated and uneducated folk; second, he started institutions to carry on way of life which he propounded. He did not set himself up as a divine incarnation, but considered himself to be servant and teacher of new community. The latter grew as separate organism partly because of commensality practised by Nanak and followers, thus breaking with an import. aspect of inter-relig. and caste division. Nevertheless, the Sikhs as yet did not differ substantially from other groups, such as the *Kabirpanthis*, followers of the 'Kabir path', likewise rejecting social divisions in name of devotional relig. On Nanak's death in 1539, Angad took over as next Guru, rather than Sri Chand, Nanak's son. Some of Nanak's followers were loyal to latter, and formed community of Udasis, who remained Sikhs in principle, though they were not later to take on the outward badges (beards, turbans, etc.) which came to differentiate main Sikh body. Angad, whose leadership lasted till 1552, collected Nanak's poems, setting in train process to culminate in formation of the *Granth*; to him is attr. invention of the *gurmukhi* script, used in Panjab. Further consolidation of movement occurred under leadership of third Guru (d. 1574), the gentle Amar Das. He insisted that visitors to him should eat with disciples, and organised system of parishes. He also brought about reforms in ceremonial designed to replace use of → Brahmanical rites at births, marriages, etc., by specifically Sikh ones; he attacked practices of purdah and → satī (*suttee*). He was succeeded by son-in-law Ram Das (d. 1581), who effectively promoted missionary activities. More import., however, in evolution of community and faith was his youngest son, fifth Guru, → Arjun, builder of the Harimandir (Golden Temple) at

Amritsar, compiler of first authoritative canon of scriptures (→ *Granth, Adi*) and himself a gifted writer. The Sikhs, having received fairly favourable treatment under → Akbar, were regarded as dangerous by latter's successor Jehangir, esp. as Arjun was reported as sympathetic to Khusrao, who had started rebellion against his father Jehangir. Arjun was captured and tortured. He died in 1606, to be succeeded by son Hargobind (d. 1644). It was during his leadership that Sikhs effectively started to transform themselves into martial community, partly to protect themselves against pressure of Jehangir and his successor as Mughal Emperor, Shah Jehan. However, Hargobind's forces were no match for those of Mughal's in the plains, and he withdrew to Kiratpur, in Himalayan foothills. Likewise his successor Har Rai (d. 1661) spent most of his leadership away from main centres of Sikh loyalty. The five-year old Hari Kishen succeeded, but died at 8, while at the court of Aurangzeb. He nominated uncle Tegh Bahadur (d. 1675) as ninth Guru. He acquired strong popular following, being modest and yet firmly resistant to persecution of Sikhs in Panjab. He was finally arrested and executed in Delhi. It was his son → Gobind, tenth and last Guru, who completed revolution, turning Sikhs into distinctive and militarily effective body. This was in main a consequence of persecutions they had suffered, which showed that they required strength and solidarity to protect themselves. Gobind's chief work was to weld followers into new community, the *Khalsa*, with its own initiation and outer badges or five 'k's: *kes*, wearing the hair and beard unshorn; *kaṅghā*, the comb required to keep the hair tidy (and typically covered by turban); *kach*, knee-length breeches, as were worn by soldiers; *kaṛā*, steel bracelet worn on right wrist; and *kirpān*, dagger. The members of community were forbidden to take alcohol or tobacco, or to eat meat killed acc. to Muslim manner (by bleeding). The scriptures were finalised, and assigned by Gobind status of Guru. Thus, at his death, succession of leaders came to an end. Gobind's measures involved something of social revolution, as well as bifurcation of community—the former because many of local leaders of Sikhs were → *ksatriyas* and → *vaisyas*, unwilling to make absolute break with Hinduism implied by Gobind's reforms, so that power in new community passed to the *jats*, who were chiefly peasant cultivators. Because those who did not adopt new emblems nevertheless maintained link with the *Khalsa*, two main types of Sikhs emerged, *kesādhārīs* (unshaven Sikhs) and *sahajdhārīs* (those who take time to adopt full forms of faith). A certain fluidity at edges of the *Khalsa* has characterised the Sikhs since that time, esp. as administration of the → *gurdwaras* (temples) was over long period in hands of *udasis*, whose relig. lineage went back to Sri Chand and belonged to *sahajdhārī* group. The century following estab. of *Khalsa* was confused one in Panjab, which was scene of struggle for power between Afghans and disintegrating Mughal empire. However, Sikh military dominance was estab. under Ranjit Singh (1780–1830), who drew on forces of Panjabi nationalism. The Sikh kingdom was nevertheless destroyed after two wars by British, and wound up in 1849. The reign of Ranjit Singh increased fluidity at edges of the community, for the prestige of Sikhs induced an increasing number of Hindus to adopt tenets and worship of Sikhism, without however undergoing Sikh initiation (into *Khalsa*) or formally breaking with Hinduism. Such *sahajdhārī* Sikh families might incl. a son or two brought up as *kesādhārīs*. Among such groups are the Nirankaris, formerly strong in Kasmir, founded by Dyal Das (d. 1855). Also at fringes of orthodox Sikhism are the → Radha Soamis. In latter part of 19th cent., reform movements arose, partly to combat proselytising activities of → Arya Samaj and Christ. missionaries, partly to restore morale of Sikhism, somewhat shattered by British conquest, and these expressed themselves in such organisations as the Singh Sabha, which did much to promote education in schools created by the *Khalsa*. Such activities checked drift of Sikhs back into Hinduism, and even recruited new converts from within Hinduism. Meanwhile a major problem was restoration of control of → *gurdwaras* to the *khalsa*, since they were mainly administered by *udasis*, whose loyalties were semi-Hindu. This restoration was achieved through militant policy of the *Akali Dal* (among others)—a radical group formed in 1920s. After independence (1947), the Akalis and others agitated for separate Sikh state in Panjab, ultimately conceded by gov. of India. The notable tendency in 20th cent. for *sahajdhārī* Sikhs to become reabsorbed in resurgent Hinduism is one main reason for concern to promote separate *Khalsa* identity among the *kesādhārīs*. In that respect, there is some justification for logic of Gobind's reforms. Because of fluidity of Sikh allegiance outside *Khalsa*, the distinction is sometimes made between Singhism and Sikhism—the former ref. to practices of the 'Singhs', i.e. members of *Khalsa* inaugurated by Gobind, whose male members took surname 'Lion' or Singh. The theology of S. has remained relatively unchanged through hist. of faith, emphasising belief in one God, and incorporating the Hindu doc. of → rebirth. Ethical attitudes have not been unaffected by transition from pacifist relig. following to militant community. N.S.

Khushwant Singh, *A History of the Sikhs*, 2 vols. (1963–6); M. A. Macauliffe, *Sikh Religion*, 6 vols. (1903); Jogendra Singh, *Sikh Ceremonies* (1941); J. C. Archer, *The Sikhs in Relation to Hindus, Moslems, Christians, and Ahmadiyyas* (1946).

Sīla Buddh. term for 'virtue' or 'morality' (→→ Morality (Buddh.); Eightfold Path). T.O.L.

Simon Magus Mysterious wonder-worker and relig. charlatan (cf. →→ Alexander of Abonoteichos; Apollonius of Tyana) who figures much in early Chr. lit. Acc. to Acts 8:9–24, a magician called Simon, practising in Samaria, tried to buy spiritual power from the Apostles. In 2nd cent., → Justin Martyr tells of a 'Simon of Samaria', a magician who was deified at Rome and honoured by a statue (Justin prob. misread an inscription to Semo, a Sabine god); he was assoc. with a certain Helena, regarded as emanation of his 'first idea' (I *Apol.* 26). Justin does not, curiously, identify this S. with the S. of Acts. Other Chr. writers regard this S. as founder of a → Gnostic sect; but Justin groups him with pretenders to divine status. Legend also told of S.'s encounters with St. → Peter in Rome. It has been suggested that in → Ebionite trad. (→ Clementine Lit.) S.M. is a hostile disguise for → Paul in his conflict with Peter. S.M. is trad. regarded as first heretic (→ heresy), and sin of 'Simony' has been named after him. S.G.F.B.

E.R.E., XI, *s.v.;* P. Carrington, *The Early Christian Church*, 2 vols. (1957), *passim*; J. McL. Wilson, *The Gnostic Problem* (1958), pp. 99ff.; *D.C.C.*, *s.v.;* H. J. Schoeps, *Theologie u. Gesch. des Judenchristentums* (1949), pp. 425ff.

Sin (anc. Near East) S. is interpreted here to mean actions that offend deity: such actions may be of a relig. or moral character. Anc. Egypt. texts provide earliest evidence of assoc. of deity with maintenance of moral law. Tomb inscriptions of *c.* 2400 BC reveal that moral transgressions were regarded as concern of sun-god → Rē, who embodied → *Maat*, i.e. 'order', 'truth'. As the 'Declarations of Innocence' in → *Book of the Dead* show, S. incl. both moral and relig. offences (e.g. blasphemy as well as murder). In Mesopot. texts, S. seems to be conceived more in terms of ritual offences. The Heb. → Decalogue, contains both moral and ritual injunctions. The development of belief in → Yahweh as moral god caused emphasis on moral probity instead of ritual perfection (e.g. Micah 6:6–8). In Greece and Rome the social character of relig. meant that S. incl. both ritual and moral offences: Ignorance was often regarded as cause of S. Acc. to eschatology of → Orphism and → Eleusinian Mysteries, the uninitiated were punished as sinners in Hades. In → Zoroastrianism wilful non-alignment with → Ahura Mazdah against → Ahriman was S. S.G.F.B.

E.R.E., XI, pp. 528ff.; *R.G.G.*[3], VI, col. 474–84; Brandon, *Judgment of the Dead* (1967), chs. 1–4, 7.

(Buddh.) → Ethics (Buddh.). T.O.L.

(Chinese) In pre-Confucian China, S. was conceived as a crime or an offence against divine cosmic order ordained by Will of Heaven. Moral and spiritual delinquency were recognised as meriting judgment of Heaven, which meted out punishment in this life by means of agents who had received Heaven's appointment. To this idea was added concept of S. as transgression from the → mean or norm. Acc. to Confucian morality, man's Heaven-born nature is perfect and he is naturally formed for virtue. Every man can be a Sage; but he is prone to err, and deviate from the norm. Such deviation demands reformation, education, guidance and example rather than penitence and appeals for remission of punishment. → Confucianism recognises as great sins, theft and robbery, murder, perverseness, mendacity, vindictiveness and vacillating weakness; but the greatest S. is unfilial conduct.

Three principal terms are used for S. *Tsui*, the most commonly accepted term for S., means crime, punishment, penalty, to give occasion for blame, a violation of decorum or a breach of etiquette. In use of this term, S. and its consequences are imperfectly discriminated, and term covers such a breadth of meaning as to lose much of its ethical content. *O* means evil, vicious, bad; and *Kuo* means to transgress or overstep the mark. These terms are often used in conjunction, e.g. *tsui o*, *tsui kuo*.

→ Buddhism brought to the Chinese a vivid concept of an after-life, and a doc. of future punishment for sins committed in this life, and idea that present sufferings are result of past S. It taught that future retribution for S. could be avoided by accumulation of → Merit by such means as chanting liturgies, repentance, meritorious actions, asceticism and the like. It intro. a soteriology by its doc. of transferred merit. Buddhas and → bodhisattvas had accumulated infinite stores of merit; by appealing to them in penitence and faith, the consequences of S. could be wiped out and a blissful future life guaranteed. These Buddh. ideas exercised a profound influence on Confucians and Taoists alike, and on popular beliefs. D.H.S.

E.R.E., XI, pp. 535ff.; W. E. Soothill, *Three Religs. of China* (1923), ch. 10.

(Christ.) In N.T., S. connotes offences against

both God and Man. Although emphasis is laid on intention rather than on act (Mt. 15:18–9), disbelief in Christ or improper reception of → Eucharist (I Cor. 11:27–9) were sinful. The concept of S. became a basic factor in Chr. soteriology. Acc. to doc. of → Original Sin, every child inherited → Adam's guilt and a nature prone to S. This guilt was removed by → baptism. Post-baptismal S. was a problem, and early Christians held that it could not be forgiven. Chr. theology gradually developed a doc. of S., espec. in connection with sacrament of Penance (→ Confession). Besides Original S., two other forms were distinguished: (1) Mortal S., which merited eternal damnation; (2) Venial S., which did not involve loss of God's sanctifying → grace. Chr. hymns and devotional lit. attest preoccupation with S., and its relation to death of Christ. → Eschatology is essentially connected with S.: S. is expiated in → Purgatory and eternally punished in → Hell. (→→ Judgment of Dead; Salvation). S.G.F.B.

E.R.E., XI, pp. 538ff.; *D.C.C.*, *s.v.; R.G.G.*[3], VI, col. 484–506; *H.D.B.*[2], *s.v.;* J. F. Bethune-Baker, *Intro. to Early Hist. of Christ. Doctrine* (1903), pp. 301ff.; Harnack, *H.D.*, 7 vols. (*passim*); Brandon, *M.D.*, ch. 6, *The Judgment of the Dead* (1967), ch. 5.

(Hindu concept) The dominant motif in Indian trad. is that → salvation or → liberation is ultimately achieved by knowledge (though evolution of → *bhakti* schools modified or altered emphasis); consequently, the root of suffering to which men are bound in round of → *samsara* is ignorance (→ *avidya*) of a primordial kind, rather than sin as such. However, notions of both ritual and moral sin (*pāpa*) and its opposite, merit (*puṇya*) have played large part in working out of → *karma*-theory and in application of sacrificial techniques to overcome sin. An elaborate system of relig. penances was worked out in the law-books (→ *dharma*) to expiate pollutions arising from different offences; in principle secular punishments were considered as penitential and expiatory in character. Pollution itself might not be due to fault of individual or individuals—e.g. pollution arising from a death in family—and methods of purification were used to wipe it out. The moralising of early ideas of sin was seen in hymns to → Varuna, the upholder of cosmic moral law (→ *rta*), and in elaboration of *karma*-theory. The → *Bhagavadgita* emphasis on renunciation of fruits of one's actions implied ultimately a psychological account of overcoming of consequences of sin; and this approach was given special application in → Tantrism, where under controlled conditions the breaking of moral taboos could itself lead to liberation. In →→ Yoga, Advaita and other schools emphasising existential gnosis, sinfulness is obstacle to such knowledge: thus calmness, self-control, etc., are regarded by → Sankara as conditions which need to be fulfilled before the desire arises to know → *Brahman*. On other hand, the *bhakti* schools looked to God's grace as cause of liberation; but this faith, which could in principle have antinomian consequences, was typically accompanied by strong sense of humility and sinfulness on part of devotee. In popular relig., various exercises have been considered meritorious and useful in removing consequences of past evil deeds—such as → pilgrimages and bathing in sacred places, listening to scriptures (e.g. the → *Puranas*), repetition of sacred names of gods (God), etc., though such attention to external performances brought criticism from →→ Kabir, Nanak and others among reforming devotional teachers of medieval period. The strong emphasis on purificatory techniques in Hinduism and the complex possibilities of ritual pollution have played import. role in shaping and preserving → caste system. N.S.

E. W. Hopkins, *Ethics of India* (1924); S. Rohde, *Deliver Us from Evil: Studies on the Vedic Ideas of Salvation* (1946); C. von Fuerer-Haimendorf, *Morals and Merit* (1964).

(Islam) Islam is not so much interested in sin as in sins; but, mainly in → Ṣūfī circles, there is a sense of sinfulness requiring cleansing. Elsewhere the emphasis is chiefly on S.'s committed which need to be forgiven. The Qur. refers to → Adam's S. (cf. xx:118ff.; vii:18ff.), for which he and Eve were expelled from heavenly garden. Islam is usually said to reject doc. of → Original S., saying only that man is created weak (cf. Qur. iv:32), which is not quite the same as Orig. S. But mankind has suffered Adam's fate of being exiled from the garden because of his S. In xx:121, where the dual is used in telling Adam and Eve to go down from garden, the plural is used immediately afterwards about being enemies to one another, which surely refers not just to first parents, but to their descendants. The Qur. declares clearly that S. will be punished both in this world and next (cf. xxiv:18f., 23; v:37); but it has much to say of God's forgiveness. He forgives the penitent one who believes and does what is good (cf. xx:84; viii:29; iii:129); but the S. of assoc. anything with God is unforgiveable (iv:51, 116). The Qur. has several names which speak of God's mercy (→→ God, 99 names, Nos. 1, 2, 32, 34, 79, 83). v:99 ('Know that God is severe in requital and that God is forgiving and compassionate') combines punishment and pardon. The greatness of God's forgiveness is clearly expressed in xxxix:54, which says he forgives totally; but iv:22 denies acceptance of a deathbed repentance. The Qur. speaks of major S.'s (cf. iii:9; viii:54; xci:14), but distinction between major and minor was mainly the work of traditionists and theologians. A trad. gives following list of seven major S.'s: polytheism, magic, unlawful manslaughter, spending orphans' money, usury, desertion in battle, slandering chaste but careless believing women. S. is gen. repres. as disobedience to God's commands rather than as transgressing some standard. While God demands obedience and is ready to forgive, it is held that he is unaffected by man's deeds. It would make no difference to him, if all unbelievers became believers and all the believers unbelievers. This involves conception that there is no absolute standard of right and wrong, for to believe that would be to set up an authority alongside God. It is he who has commanded what should be done and prohibited what should be avoided. (→→ Intercession; Kharijites; Murji'ites). J.R.

E.I., II, pp. 925ff. (Khaṭī'a); Hughes, pp. 594f.; Wensinck, *Creed*, index; Jeffery, *Vocabulary*, pp. 123f.; M. Smith, *Ghazali*, index; Sweetman, *I.C.T.*, II, IV, index; *E.R.E.*, XI, pp. 567–9.

(Japanese) Two words are used of almost identical meaning, *tsumi* and *aku*. *Tsumi* means both sin and disaster, and incl. immoral behaviour, misfortune, or ritual mistakes. These involve pollution, which needs to be destroyed by ritual purification. A distinction is made between *ama-tsu-tsumi* ('heavenly sins') and *kuni-tsu-tsumi* ('terrestrial sins'). The former incl. destructive acts harmful to agriculture; the latter inflicting deadly injury, immodest actions, killing domestic animals, using magic, leprosy, etc. The occurrence of moral evil was regarded in → Shinto as caused by evil spirits beyond man's control. There is nothing in Shinto comparable to doc. of → original sin. The sinner is regarded as one who has ceased for a while to be a member of world of goodness and happiness, to which, either by warnings or by punishment, he is encouraged to return. D.H.S.

J. Herbert, *Shinto* (1967), pp. 77–8.

Sin (deity) Anc. Mesopot. moon-god; also called Nanna = 'man of the sky'. In art S. is depicted as enthroned bearded figure, wearing tiara, surmounted by crescent moon. His chief cult-centre was Sumerian city of Ur; another import. centre was Harran. S. was regarded as 'lord of the month', and maintained justice at night. In Mesopot. pantheon S. was father of sun-god → Shamash and → Ishtar. S.G.F.B.

Dhorme, *R.B.A.*, pp. 54ff.; Jastrow, *R.B.*, *passim*; B. Meissner, *Babylonien u. Assyrien* (1925), II, *passim*; M. Lambert in *S.O.*, V (1962), pp. 71ff.

Sin-eating A curious custom once current in Wales and borderlands of eating food brought in contact with corpse, whereby its sins were assumed: a special 'sin-eater' usually undertook this office. The eating of food touched by dead at funerals has been a widespread funerary practice (e.g. England, Wales, Bavaria, India). The custom has been explained as transformed survival of primitive corpse-eating to absorb virtues of deceased. The European customs would seem more prob. to derive from pagan funerary feasts and mortuary offerings (→ Refrigerium). S.G.F.B.

E.R.E., XI, *s.v.;* A Parrot, *Le 'Refrigerium' dans l'au-delà* (1937); F. Cumont, *After Life in Roman Paganism* (1959 edn.), pp. 53ff.

-Ṣirāṭ (Lit. the road). A bridge, finer than a hair and sharper than a sword, suspended over hell. All will have to attempt the crossing. Believers will cross like lightning, but unbelievers will fall into hell. This idea, seemingly borrowed from Zoroastrian sources (→ Chinvat Bridge), is explanation of → Tradition and later Islam, but has no basis in the Qur. There Ṣ. is used as an ordinary path (vii:84), or as God's path (cf. xlii:53; xiv:1; xxxiv:6; xxii:24). xxxvii:23 speaks of path to fierce fire (al-jaḥīm); but there is no suggestion that it is a bridge over hell. Very common is 'the straight path' (→ *-Ṣirāṭ al-mustaqīm*). (→ Bridges.). J.R.

Hughes, p. 595; Pareja, pp. 719, 723, 799; D. B. Macdonald, *Theology*, index; Wensinck, *Creed*, index (Bridge); N. A. Faris, *The foundations of the articles of Faith*, trans. with notes of a book of Ghazali's *Ihyā'* (1963), p. 94, and index.

-Sirāt al-mustaqīm (The straight path). A phrase which occurs 30 times in Qur., with or without the definite article. Compare phrases 'God's path' (xlii:53) and 'the path of the Mighty', 'the Praiseworthy' (xiv:1; xxxiv:6). It repres. the true relig. In the first sura it occurs with explanatory addition, 'the path of those to whom thou hast shown favour'. J.R.

Hughes, pp. 595f.; Masson, *Coran*, p. 779 says cf. Ps. xxv:4; xxvii:11; lxxxvi:11. If this suggests the phrase is a borrowing from the language of Psalms, it is difficult to support it. The second passage uses Heb. *mīshōr* (level) along with 'path' (*ōraḥ*); but other two passages merely speak of God's path. When the Qur. speaks of God's path it normally uses word *sabīl* (→ Jihād). (Christianity was 'the Way' (*hē hodos*) in → Acts (9:2)).

Śiva (Also transliterated 'Shiva'). Lit. 'Auspicious One'; with → Viṣṇu, one of the two great gods of → Hinduism, and focus of worship in → Saivism. In form of → Rudra, S. was present in → Vedic relig., but his ancestry is prob. even more anc., since there is evidence of a god having Śiva's characteristics in → Indus Valley Civilisation. It was in post-Upaniṣadic period, however, that S.'s elevation to supreme Being occurred, through relig. movement known as *Pāśupatas*, who worshipped S. under title of Paśupati or 'Lord of Beasts'. Gen. speaking, there has been no Saivite doc. of → *avataras* or incarnations of S., except in few sects imitative of → Vaisnavism. The name S. arose from concern to propitiate a dangerous god through lucky and benevolent-sounding name; it has been characteristic of iconography and mythology of S. to depict him as fierce and the destroyer (he is among other things the personification of → Time, which brings decay). At same time S. is the *Mahāyogī* or Great Yogi, and patron of → yoga, who generates great power through austerities (→ *tapas*); his body is covered with ashes and hair is matted—both marks of Hindu ascetic. From his hair there flows the sacred → Ganges, as it descends from the Milky Way. The austere, yogic side of S. is complemented by his assoc. with generation and fertility. Thus most import. emblem of S. is the → *lingam*. His exuberance is expressed in his repres. as the *Naṭarāja*, king of the dance, through which he dances out the creation and ultimately the destruction of universe. S. is also repr. as great teacher. Thus various contradictory and complementary aspects are welded together in iconography of S.: he is both creative and destructive, austere and exuberant, self-controlled and orgiastic, benevolent and fierce, good and evil. Similar remarks apply to various spouses with whom he is united → Kālī, Durgā, Pārvatī. In → Saktism, some of worship and devotion directed to S. was diverted to the goddess, notably under form of Kali. The goddess tends to be taken as personification of creative force (*śakti*) of S.; the union between the passive and active, male and female aspects of divine being is symbolised by S. as hermaphrodite (Ardhanarīśvara). Apart from *lingam*, the most import. symbols assoc. with S. are snakes and the bull Nandi. N.S.

A. Danielou, *Hindu Polytheism* (1964); J. N. Banerjea, *The Development of Hindu Iconography* (1956); H. Zimmer, *Myths and Symbols in Indian Art and Civilization* (1962); A. K. Coomaraswamy, *The Dance of Siva* (1957).

Skandha (Skt.) Buddh. term for a component of human personality. (→ *Khandha*). T.O.L.

Sky Gods Deification of sky, usually in personified form, is anc. and widespread. It is significant, however, that no evidence has yet been found that this occurred in → Paleolithic relig. The earliest literate societies provide examples of S.-G.: →→ Anu in Sumer; Horus in Egypt (the sky was also deified as goddess → Nut); →→ Yahweh in Israel; Zeus in Greece; Varuna in India; T'ien or Shang-ti in China; Ahura Mazdah in Iran. S.-G. are often cosmic creators, omnipotent and omniscient; frequently they are thought to be withdrawn from world. Sometimes the S.-G. has been related to → Earth Goddess (acc. to Aeschylus (*Danaids*, fr. 44), 'the rain, dropping from the husband Heaven impregnates Earth, and she brings forth for men pasture for flocks and corn, the life of man'). S.-G. have been cited as attesting a primeval monotheism (→ High Gods). S.G.F.B.

See bibliography to 'High Gods'.

Slavery (Islam) In the →→ Qur. and Ḥadīth the right to possess slaves is recognised. In Muhammad's time slaves were normally captives taken in course of fighting. Male captives were sometimes put to death; but they could be set free if they accepted Islam on field of battle, or they could be enslaved. Women were made slaves and their masters had right of sexual relations with them. But while S. is recognised, the Qur. commands that kindness be shown to slaves (cf. iv:40). Allowance is made for manumission of slaves (cf. xxiv:33). This may be done by master telling slave that he (or she) is free either on the spot, or as a promise in future, esp. after master's death; by an agreement that slave may purchase freedom over a period; or by a woman slave who had borne a child to her master being free on his death (→ Mother of the child). Some breaches of law required freeing of a slave as punishment (cf. iv:94; lviii:4). Male and female slaves might be married to one another, but a slave could have no more than two wives. On master's death slaves, who have no claim to manumission, become property of his heirs. Though there has been much cruelty through slave-raiding and ill-treatment by harsh masters, many slaves had reason to be content with their position. It was even poss. for some slaves to rise to positions of authority, notably, e.g. in the Mamlūk (slave) dynasties in India and Egypt. S. has continued in some districts into mod. times, but it is grad. dying out. On 6 November 1962 H.R.H. Amir Faysal, President of the Council, Saudi Arabia, announced abolition of S. in kingdom. Acknowledging difficulty of observing Islam's stipulation about their treatment, he announced the 'absolute abolition of S. and the manumission of all slaves', and promised compensation to those to whom it was due. J.R.

*E.I.*², I, pp. 24–40; Hughes, pp. 596–600; Lane, *Egyptians*, index; W. Arafat, 'The attitude of Islam to slavery', *I.Q.*, X, pp. 12–18; Rutter, *Holy Cities*, II, pp. 90–4; Trimingham, *Sudan*, index, *Ethiopia*, index, *West Africa*, index; Dickson, *Arab of Desert*, ch. 39; Cheragh 'Ali, *A critical exposition of the popular 'Jihād'* (1885), appendix B; N. Daniel, *Islam, Europe and Empire* (1966), index.

Slavic Religion Since the Slavic peoples were Christianised between the 8th and 12th cents., our information about their former relig. beliefs is sparse, being derived almost entirely from later Russian, Czech, German and Danish sources. There are no pre-Christ. Slavic written sources. Some additional information comes from folk-lore and archaeology. The S. were of Indo-European stock, and appear to have had a complex pantheon, headed by a → High God of Indo-Eur. type. Procopius (*De Bell. Got.*, iii:14) wrote: 'They (the E. and S. Slavs) worship one god whom they conceive to be creator of the thunder and maker of all things; to him they sacrifice cattle and other victims'. One of the names of this god was Perun. A sun-god, Dažbog, was also worshipped, together with a god of fire, Svarožic. The most prominent deity in the W. was Svantevit, whose temple at Arkona (Rügen) has been found and excavated; his image was said to have been four-headed, and among his attributes were a sword, bridle, saddle, and a white horse, by means of which omens were taken; he also had an establishment of 300 man-at-arms and horses (*vide* Saxo Grammaticus, *Historia Danica*, xiv). It seems that Svantevit was basically a war-god. Names of other deities vary greatly, though divine attributes and functions appear to follow the general Aryan pattern. Thus, apart from the great gods, there were numerous minor gods and goddesses, and many spirits: '. . . they reverence rivers, nymphs and other spirits, and sacrifice to them all' (Procopius). Names of the spirits included *beregyni*, *vila* and *rusalka*. S. relig. was characterised, *inter alia*, by worship in temples, a cult of fire, a priesthood, the practice of augury and periodic sacrifices (→ Scandinavian Religion). S. beliefs on subject of nature and destiny of man incl. the following elements: (1) Belief in continued existence of human soul after death; (2) Belief in the simultaneous possibility of *post-mortem* existence in or near grave, and in a land of the dead; (3) Either inhumation or cremation as means of disposal of dead, in each case with grave goods, and occasionally with human sacrifice (→ *satī*); (4) Traces of → Ancestor Worship. E.J.S.

E.R.E., XI, pp. 587a–95b; *R.G.G.*[3], VI, cols. 105–7; B. O. Unbegaun, *La religion des anciens Slaves* (1948); V. Pisani, 'Il paganesimo balto-slavo', in P. T. Venturi (ed.), *Storia delle Religioni*[4] (1954), II, pp. 55ff.; H. Ringgren and Å. V. Ström, *Religionerna i historia och nutid*[2] (1959), pp. 392–5; A. Brückner, *R-G.L.*, 3 (1926).

Smārtas Followers of → Sankara and adherents of a relatively non-sectarian Hinduism, though with a bias towards → Saivism. Term is derived from → *smrti*, the trad. or auxiliary canon containing the → *Puranas*, Epics and law-books. The term implies that the S., as well as being orthodox and thus accepting Vedic → revelation (and in partic. the → Advaitin interpretation of Vedanta), recognises →→ Śiva, Viṣṇu and Brahma (→ *trimurti*) as celebrated in *Puranas*, etc., together with sacred law binding upon upper-class Hindus as prescribed in the *sutras*. The chief centre of S. is the Sringeri *math* (monastery) in Mysore, whose head (*Jagadguru* 'World-*guru*') stands in line of succession from Sankara. S. are enjoined primarily to worship deities Visnu, Siva, Durga (→ Sakti), Sūrya (the Sun) and → Ganesa. The gen. temper of S. relig., combining Advaita and synthesis, has been highly influential in statement of mod. Hinduism. N.S.

Smṛti (Also transliterated *smriti*). The auxiliary canon in orthodox → Hinduism, supplementing Veda (→ revelation, Hindu). Lit. 'memory' or 'what is remembered', S. incl. the → *Puranas*, the Epics (*itihasa*) and the law books (→ Manu, *dharma*). S. not only defined rules of living in society, but contained mine of mythological and spiritual instruction available to lower classes, to whom Veda was not accessible. In south, by medieval period, collections of relig. poetry (→ *Alvars*) came to play similar role to that of S. Those Hindus who adhere to laws of S. and who follow → Sankara, are known as the → *Smārtas*. N.S.

Sneezing-yawning → Bukhari gives a trad., traced through → Abu Hurayra, that → Muḥammad said: 'God likes S. but dislikes Y. So when one of you sneezes and praises God it is the duty of every Muslim who hears him to say, "God have mercy on you!" But Y. comes only from the devil, so when one of you yawns he should restrain it as much as possible, for when one of you yawns the devil laughs at him.' Another trad. from same source says one who sneezes should say, 'Praise be to God!'; one who hears him should say to him, 'God have mercy on you!', to which he should reply, 'God guide you and give you wellbeing!' A trad. from → Muslim says that one who yawns should hold hand over mouth, lest the devil enters, a belief not confined to Islamic circles. J.R.

Hughes, pp. 600f., 695; *Mishkāt*, pp. 990ff.; Lane, *Egyptians*, p. 210.

Social Duties (Buddh.) → Family and Social Duties (Buddh.). T.O.L.

Sociology of Religion S.R. is, or perhaps ought to be, at least as much about sociology as it is about religion. In other words, S.R. starts in gen. context of examin. of persons acting and interacting in society rather than from within framework of theology or comparative relig. It is here that the S.R. can be distinguished from what is sometimes called 'religious sociology', a study which usually implies some prior commitment on part of investigator (e.g. a concern for the mission of Church in a secular society), and which usually incorporates wider sociological findings only where they can be used in the partic. problem under investigation. Too sharp a division between the two kinds of investigation should not be made, however. Relig. sociology will, as has been said, make use of gen. sociological findings, methods or theories and the sociologist of relig. often obtains useful data (e.g. on demographic aspects of relig. practice) from work of relig. sociologists.

One implication of this distinction is that S.R. should have a relationship of reciprocal exchange with other areas of sociological investigation and the gen. body of sociological theory. Familiar concepts such as 'role', 'status', 'elite' and 'authority' may be used as much by sociologists studying relig. as by those studying other areas. Relig. organisations (churches, sects, denominations) have their place in the gen. context of organisation theory; e.g. Etzioni has incorporated relig. bodies into his comparative analysis of complex organisations. Another example of fruitful overlap in sociological investigations is provided by Weber's use of concept of 'charisma'. While the term was origin. taken from theological writings and has been most specifically applied to relig. leaders, the concept is more usefully seen, from point of view of sociologist, in the context of Weber's discussion of types of authority. Here charismatic authority, where the legitimacy of that authority resides in personal claims of an extraordinary individual, repr. a certain 'ideal type' of authority, alongside bureaucratic and trad. types. Most existing kinds of authority will, of course, comprise a mixture of all three types. The role of prophet is an example of personal charisma, while the role of priest repr. a case of 'charisma of office' (charisma residing in priestly office rather than in individual occupant), often mixed with trad. and bureaucratic elements. It is clear that this kind of discussion has implications beyond field of S.R., in, e.g., the field of political sociology.

In this short article it is proposed to examine specifically the contributions of two sociologists of the S.R.: namely E. Durkheim and M. Weber. While both theorists made relig. an import. focal point of their investigations, it can be stated that neither were excl. sociologists of relig. Their approaches to relig. can only be fully understood in context of their wider approaches to society and social action.

Simmel has argued that 'the S.R. must make a basic distinction between two types of relig. organisation'. In the first case (he instances many primitive religions), a common god grows out of the 'togetherness' of a unified group. In second case, and here he suggests Christ. sects provide good example, it is the concept of the god itself which unites members who may indeed have little else in common. It is perhaps useful, as a first approximation, to suggest that Durkheim attended primarily to the first kind of relig. organisation, while Weber was chiefly concerned with second. Durkheim wished to lay bare the fundamental basis of relig., to find relig. in its purest form unobscured by 'popular mythologies and subtle theologies'. He found this elementary form of the relig. life in the → totemism of Australian aborigines, members of a society which, he felt, was surpassed by no other in its simplicity (→ Austr. Aborig. Relig.). He assumed that among these clans it was poss. to explain their relig. without ref. to any other form of relig. Here, Durkheim argued, rituals and ritual attitudes were directed towards the totem, a repres. of some species ascribed to all members of a given clan and the source of that clan's identity. This was not a case of animal-worship; animals and plants derived their sacredness from fact that they were used as totemic objects rather than totems deriving their sacred character from the totemic species. The totem was a repres. of something else, a power greater than itself which Durkheim calls the totemic principle or god. This principle was, in its turn, society itself. In worshipping the totem and observing → taboos concerning the totemic object, the clansmen were re-affirming their collective sense of belonging. Society, Durkheim stressed here as elsewhere, is essentially a moral force; it is external to us and instils in each a sense of obligation. To Durkheim, society, morality and relig. were three major elements of a closed and interacting system. The circularity in Durkheim's analysis was not seen as a weakness in his argument; rather, it emphasised that relig. was not being 'reduced' to the 'merely social', for 'the social' was the most fundamental reality of all.

How far can Durkheim's approach be extended to mod. pluralistic societies? Clearly, there are difficulties in the direct application of Durkheim's model espec. if we equate a society with a mod. nation. For, in and between mod. nations, relig. is as likely to be a force for division as a basis for unity; and, even where relig. conflicts are absent or subdued, it is not always easy to assert that relig. can be basis of unity embracing so many different classes, ethnic groups, moral codes and sub-cultures, espec. where relig. preferences appear to be assoc. with these other classification. Durkheim's approach may, however, be relevant in two ways. In first case, we extend the term 'religion' to incl. phenomena not usually classified as such, a procedure in accord. with Durkheim's statement that 'there are relig. phenomena that belong to no determined religion'. Thus it might be poss. to examine ideologies, nationalism or patriotism in Durkheim's terms. Herberg attempts something of this nature, when he examines the identification of the three basic relig. groupings in the U.S.A. (Prot., Cath. and Jew) with what he calls 'the American way of life'. In U.S.A., Herberg argues, we have a civic relig. characterised by 'pervasive secularism amid mounting religiousity'. This very gen. patriotic relig. is supported by and supports the three main sources of relig. identification. Similarly, we may examine the role of national or local rituals (perhaps funerals of leading statesmen) in affirming or maintaining underlying collectively held values. Lloyd Warner has studied the role played by a formally secular ceremony, the Memorial Day Celebration, in a New England town. He sees the ceremony as a 'cult of the dead', serving to unite various relig. and ethnic groups and expressing shared underlying values. While this ceremony is studied at local level, the symbols brought into play (e.g. Lincoln's Gettysburg's address) often coincide or overlap with national symbols. We need more detailed analyses of ceremonies and ideologies on lines suggested by Warner and Herberg; but, at same time, differences *within* the societies or communities under examin. should not be overlooked. Working-class → Baptists and Middle-class Episcopalians may partake in certain common ceremonies, but the *meaning* of their participation may be very different for each partic. grouping.

The second way in which Durkheim's analysis might be applied is in examin. of sub-cultures or relig. bodies *within* mod. societies. Thus it might be poss. to examine or re-examine the Jew. ghetto, a relig. sect, a communistic society or the → Black Muslim movement in these terms. Again, it can be shown that presence of certain symbols, the performance of rituals and adherence to prohibitions re-affirm and sustain a faith, which is seen as entering all areas of social and personal life. Each aspect of social life may be seen as impinging on others; adherence to rules of endogamy, e.g., can be seen as presenting safeguards against dilution of the faith, and, reciprocally, relig. practice can be seen as maintaining the domestic unit. However, there is one factor common to all these cases which is missing from Durkheim's primitive society. That is the fact that they all, to varying degrees, exist in a society where they are faced with hostility, discrimination or a wordly indifference. The unity of these collectivities is maintained, to some degree, *against* the rest of society, the white society, the Gentile society or the worldly secular society. Again we are brought up against the fact that conflict and division are characteristics of society, and that these are as import. as unity or cohesion. Durkheim's approach may take us some way in examin. of relig. in contemporary world, but it does not take us all the way.

Implicitly, Weber supplies two elements missing from a purely Durkheimian approach. Firstly, he shows relig. and society interacting in different ways and at different levels, thereby providing a more appropriately pluralist approach. Secondly, he intro. notion of subjective 'meaning': in this context, the meaning of relig. belief and practice for actors in a relig. context, and the way in which these shape the actor's perception of world in which he lives. Thus society is not only plural in that it consists of many groups and interests, but also in that it contains many different perspectives of that society. People see society and social goals in many ways, and these different orientations are *in part* influenced by overall relig. values. At one level Weber considers various ways in which relig. provides answers to fundamental problems of 'meaning', such as problem of evil and senseless suffering. (There is a danger here, of course, that relig. may be seen purely as something which supplies 'answers', and not also something which asks 'questions'. As Durkheim writes in a slightly different context: 'men do not weep for the dead because they fear them; they fear them because they weep for them'.) The answers to these basic questions also shapes the actor's attitude towards what may gen. be described as the 'world', i.e., all those aspects of political, economic, sexual and aesthetic life which today, to varying degrees, lie outside immediate ambit of the major world religions. Weber suggests two polar extremes here: the withdrawal from world of the mystic, and the positive engagement in world, an orientation which he calls 'active asceticism'.

Such an approach might remain at level of individual psychology were it not for fact that Weber intro. an import. intervening variable between these relig. orientations to world and religions as a whole, namely the '*stand*' or status group. Relig. activity is organised in society within status groups, groups clustering around allocation of prestige in society and having certain styles of life in common. It is well known, e.g., that preferences in favour of one denomination or another are not randomly distributed throughout a community, but are, to varying extents, assoc. with a person's socio-economic status. Weber sees inter-relationships between relig. and society working through status groups in various ways. At one very gen. level he sees the major world religions as being shaped by status groups of their leaders. Thus Weber identifies the following 'primary carriers' of the world religions: 'In Confucianism, the world-organising bureaucrat; in Hinduism, the world-ordering magician; in Buddhism, the mendicant monk wandering through the world; in Islam, the warrior seeking to conquer the world; in Judaism, the wandering trader; and in Christianity, the itinerant journeyman.' Weber recognises that this is a 'formula', and it is one which needs to be subjected to detailed critical scrutiny. However, this simple formulation reminds us that religs. are not shaped by *all* the followers of a partic. faith (each adherent carrying, as it were, equal weight), but that certain groups are partic. strategic at certain times and under certain circumstances.

Furthermore, economic and social position of status groups shapes orientations that the members of these groups have towards world. Thus, crudely speaking, low status groups see relig. as providing compensations for that status and adopt attitude of passive resignation or active opposition to world. High status groups, on other hand, see relig. as playing a role legitimising their superior status and fortune, and world is not seen in fundamental opposition to their relig. In this respect, Weber has much in common with → Marx. However, Weber goes much further in opening up problem of *variation* in the role of relig. at same social level. Thus groups occupying roughly the same under-privileged status may, in their relig. withdraw from world, actively oppose world or seek to minimise tension between themselves and world, with their relig. perhaps serving to assist social mobility or the inculcation of dominant values. Using the perspective adopted by Weber, we may see relig. and society interacting at all levels in most complex ways.

It is in the context of this kind of discussion that we may view Weber's much debated work on relationship between Protestantism and capitalism. Weber's central concern was to examine relationship between ideas and social action, and his discussion of role of → Calvinism and the development of capitalism may be seen as a case-study here. Weber was, therefore, seeking to supplement what had come to be identified as the Marxian view of relig., a view which tended to see relig. as an epiphenomenon, a reflection of social and economic forces. But, on other hand, Weber did not see ideas as free floating elements to be adopted at random by whosoever chose to reach for them. It was not, he stated clearly, his intention to substitute a one-sided idealistic interpretation of history for a one-sided materialistic interpretation. Ideas existed in a social context—indeed, it was not ideas as such that interested Weber, but ideal (and material) *interests* as these were organised in status groups. The impact of Calvinism cannot be isolated from social and economic position of leading Calvinists; consequently one must recognise that impact of Calvinism was likely to be very different at different times and places. Thus Tawney was correct to point out that both an individualistic capitalism and a collectivist socialism could be derived from Calvinist doc. Weber was, however, not so concerned with this point; rather he was concerned with demonstrating that relig., as a major source of orientation to world, can have an impact on society which is separable from and not reducible to social and economic status of its believers. If the relig. factor were excl. from our analysis of a social situation, then the outcome of that investigation might be very different.

G. Lenski adopts Weber's approach in his study of Detroit, where he considers the impact of relig. on attitudes to family, economic life, politics and education. He finds that in many situations relig. can be seen as making an impact even where such factors as social class are taken into account. Whether or not one is a Prot. or a Cath. may help to predict a person's attitudes towards, e.g., social mobility. One of Lenski's import. theoretical contributions is in making distinction between the 'communal' and the 'association' aspects of relig., the former focussing on networks of relationships and patterns of residence among relig. adherents, the latter examining their degree of involvement in the church as a specific institution for worship. In the first we are looking at extent to which believers choose their spouses or friends from among other members of same socio-relig. community; in the second we are looking at indices such as frequency of worship. Jews, e.g., are seen as having a high communal involvement, but low associational involvement. In making this distinction, Lenski has provided a useful tool for developing our exam. of relationship between relig. and society.

Lenski's distinction between the communal and associational aspects of relig. perhaps brings us back to our starting point, the consideration of contributions made by Durkheim and Weber. At associational level, the varying degrees of interaction between relig. and society can be examined by using and developing theoretical tools and orientations suggested by Weber. The communal approach, focussing upon intimate interconnections between relig., the family and the community (always recognising that these exist in a wider socio-cultural framework) brings us up against the kinds of problems studied by Durkheim and his successors. And, finally, we may investigate ways in which these communal aspects shape and modify the associational, and ways in which the association provides focus for the community. A consideration of the approaches of Durkheim and Weber shows that they provide useful analytical tools, and also that there is much work to be done.

The picture presented so far of the S.R. is incomplete in several ways. In examin. approaches of Durkheim and Weber, we have looked at interaction between society and relig., the central concern of the sociologist in this field. Two models of this interaction have been suggested; the first presenting picture of functional interdependence between society and relig., and the second presenting more complex pattern of interaction at many levels. These models leave out two import. concerns for the sociologist of relig. The first is the exam. of the kinds of relig. structure that exist; the second is concerned with the gen. culture in which relig. belief and practice take place. This second concern in partic. focusses on secularisation.

In this first area, discussion has tended to revolve around distinction between a church and a sect, an orig. formulation by Troeltsch which has been subjected to considerable criticism and modification. The typology has been expanded to incl. other varieties of relig. organisation such as the cult, the denomination, and the institutionalised sect. Distinctions between kinds of sects have been made, and E. Troeltsch's assumption that the sects are intimately connected with lower classes in society has been challenged. It has been argued that distinction is based largely on experience of Christ. churches and that it is one that does not necessarily have universal applicability. Certainly not all relig. phenomena (→ cargo-cults are a case in point) can be readily subsumed under this kind of distinction.

The value of the church/sect typology lies not merely in its use as basis for classification, but more in the fact that it postulates existence of certain relationships within relig. organisations. E.g., when we talk about a sect, we are postulating that a world-rejecting or -devaluing orientation is functionally linked with a small, relatively unstructured organisation demanding a high degree of personal commitment. These relationships are seen as functional in that, it may be argued, the high degree of personal participation (perhaps a stress on 'priesthood of all believers') serves to sustain a sense of hostility to or removal from world. The precise nature and strength of this hypothesised relationship is, of course, a matter for empirical research. More detailed investigation is also required into dynamic aspects of church/sect typology. Sects are seen often as breaking away from the more estab. churches; the relationship between the two is, in these initial stages, one of mutual hostility. Cohn, e.g., has described some medieval millenarian movements partly in terms of economic and relig. estrangement of certain sections of society from the official Cath. Church. The process, whereby a sect-type structure moves towards a less exclusive and more 'accommodating' denomination, has also been documented for some relig. bodies. It is likely that a more precise delineation of the theoretical and dynamic issues, which lie behind the simple church/sect typology, will provide some powerful tools for the exam. of interplay between relig. and society.

The discussion of church/sect typology does not exhaust the account of relig. organisations. Special attention must also be paid to question of relig. *leadership*. Weber's gen. discussion of sources of authority is of great value here. In addition to looking at nature of the relig. leader's *authority*, sociologists may also look at the *role* of such a leader. What, e.g., is a priest expected to do? How do the expectations of different groups of people (e.g., expectations of laity as against expectations of fellow priests) differ or come into conflict? Finally, relig. leaders may be examined in the extent and ways in which they constitute an *elite*. How far does this elite remain specific to church (clerical celibacy may play a part here), or how far does it merge into other elites in society? These are just some of the questions raised by an exam. of relig. leadership, and must form part of a discussion of relig. organisations as a whole.

Finally, it is necessary to pay brief attention to concept of secularization, a term which appears to be used in two senses. In first place, it refers to something which happens within, and to, a specific relig. organisation. The orig. sect, e.g., becomes 'diluted' with worldly or secular values, perhaps as result of its very success in attracting adherents in its early stages. → Wesley's often quoted remark about the feared effect of wealth (acquired as a result of development of frugal and abstemious habits) on true relig. is relevant here. But the term secularisation, as more often used, refers to a process happening to relig. as a whole. We are dealing with such phenomena as declining frequency of participation in relig. activity, together with the more long-term process whereby number of areas of life, over which relig. has effective influence, dwindle. These two processes need not take place together, as Herberg's analysis of the United States demonstrates. Here he argues that rising relig. participation is coupled with belief that relig. should be separate from political or economic life.

The S.R., in conclusion, is seen as having three foci of interest. The approaches of Durkheim and Weber serve to outline some of the major patterns of inter-relationship between relig. and society. Secondly, the organisational framework, within which and through which these inter-relationships take place, must be considered. Finally, discussion of the processes of secularisation indic. the cultural background against which that analysis is placed. It is unlikely that all investigators will give equal weight to all three problem areas; but it is doubtful whether a full analysis can take place in absence of any one of them. D.H.J.M.

E. Durkheim, *The Elementary Forms of the Religious Life* (1954); W. Herberg, *Protestant, Catholic, Jew* (1960); G. Lenski, *The Religious Factor* (1963); L. Schneider (ed.), *Religion, Culture and Society* (1964); W. Lloyd Warner, *The Living and The Dead* (1959); M. Weber, *The Protestant Ethnic and the Spirit of Capitalism* (1930), *The Sociology of Religion* (1965); K. H. Wolff, *The Sociology of Georg Simmel* (1964) (not primarily concerned with the sociology of religion).

Soma Sacred plant, and also a god, in → Vedic relig., with alcoholic or other hallucinatory effects. It was same as the Iranian → *Haoma*, though herb identified as *Haoma* by mod. → Parsis and used in ritual does not seem to correspond with anc. plant, the juices of which were made into a beverage. It has been argued that S. cannot have been alcoholic, since it was processed into beverage during performance of Vedic sacrificial ritual (hence no time for fermentation). It was prepared by crushing between stones; the plant itself may have been type of fleshy creeper. It was favourite drink of → Indra, giving him boisterousness in fights against the enemy, etc. S. as god figures prominently in 9th book of → Rgveda, and is repr. as healer of illness, etc., and identified with moon (Candra). Though import. in Vedic relig., S. had little role in classical and later Hinduism, partly because Vedic relig., as mediated by → Brahmins, only formed one element in new complex, and partly because of loss of techniques of producing the liquor itself. N.S.

A. A. Macdonell, *Vedic Mythology* (1897); A. Danielou, *Hindu Polytheism* (1964).

Son of Man This essentially Heb. or Aramaic expression was frequently used by → Jesus, seemingly with ref. to himself, acc. to → Gospels; it is used only once elsewhere in N.T. (Acts 7:56). Its meaning has been much discussed by N.T. scholars. It could have been used in two ways: (a) as a synonym for 'man'; (b) apocalyptically, as in Dan. 7:13 and → Enoch 37–71. Its apocalyptic use can also be variously interpreted: as an expression for → Messiah or for the Elect Community, the true Israel. The impossibility of determining the authenticity of any single recorded saying of Jesus inevitably precludes any certain conclusion. It would seem prob. that Jesus did frequently use the expression; the fact that he was certainly regarded by many as the Messiah suggests that he used it apocalyptically with ref. to himself. (→ Christology). S.G.F.B.

S. Mowinckel, *He That Cometh* (E.T. 1956), pp. 346; *H.D.B.*[2], pp. 141(d)ff.; *D.C.C.*, *s.v.; R.G.G.*[3], IV, col. 874–6; *E.J.R.*, p. 249; J. A. Emerton, 'The Origin of the Son of Man', *J.T.S.*, IX (1958); Bruce, *N.T.H.*, pp. 123ff., 165ff.

Sotapanna Buddh. term meaning lit. 'the stream-enterer'; i.e. one who has entered the stream in order to cross to the 'further shore', viz. → Nibbana. In most gen. sense, term means a 'convert' to the way of Buddha. To have become a S. means that one is excl. from further rebirth in hell (→ Cosmology, Buddh.), or as an animal, a spirit or *peta* (→ Petavatthu), and is guarantee of attainment of enlightenment (→ Bodhi), not necessarily in same life, but certainly in some future life (→ Samsara). The further progress of the S. is regarded as following a scheme which is set forth in a conventional form in the Buddh. scriptures as 'once-returner' (→ Sakadāgāmin), then 'non-returner' (→ Anagamin), and finally → Arahant. T.O.L.

Soteriology *Ex* Grk. *sōteria* = salvation. Term used for teaching or belief about → salvation. S.G.F.B.

Sōtō (Chinese, *Ts'ao-tung*). One of two main streams of → Zen Buddhism, founded in China by Tung-shan (807–869) and Ts'ao-shan (840–901). Its fundamental concept was that of oneness of the Absolute and the relative-phenomenal. Training, concentrating on a cross-legged sitting in meditation (→ Zazen), followed a system of five stages, called the five relationships, leading from recognition of a higher or 'real' self, overshadowing the 'seeming' self, up to realisation of complete oneness with absolute reality. Enlightenment came through silent illumination. S. was introduced into Japan by → Dogen (1200–53), and popularised by Kei-zan (1268–1325). Mod. S. tends towards quietism. D.H.S.

H. Dumoulin, *Hist. of Zen Buddhism* (1963); E. Wood, *Zen Dictionary* (1962); D. T. Suzuki, *Studies in Zen* (1955).

Soul (Spirit) The idea that human nature is compounded of a physical body and a non-physical entity, i.e. the soul, prob. arose among primitive peoples from experience of dreams, breath, death, etc. as E. B. Tylor supposed in his theory of → animism (→ animatism). Among earliest literate peoples there is evidence of variety of idea about this non-physical entity. The Egyptians had a complicated anthropology, involving concepts of → *ba* and → *ka*. Acc. to Mesopot. and Heb. anthropology man was a psycho-physical organism; the non-physical element was closely assoc. with breath (→ *nephesh*), and was prob. imagined as a horrific wraith after death of the body. Homeric anthropology distinguished two non-material parts of human nature: the *thymos*, i.e. the conscious self; the → *psyche*, the animating principle of life, which alone survived death as an unconscious wraith. By 6th cent. BC, in certain circles (→→ Orphism; Plato; Pythagoreanism) the *psyche* alone came to be regarded as inner essential conscious self, that pre-existed and survived the body. This Grk. concept of the S. found expression in doc. of → metempsychosis, and was similar to Hindu idea of the → *atman*, although it was not identified with principle of cosmic reality as was the *atman*. → Buddhism, in its classic form, rejected Hindu concept of *atman* as the essential immortal self, though it taught doc. of → *saṃsāra*. In → Zoroastrianism two non-material entities were identified: the *urvan*, which survived body and was apparently regarded as S., and the *daēnā*, a mysterious entity approx. to the conscience (→ *fravashi*). Chinese anthropology distinguished two kinds of soul which were related to alternating cosmic principles of → *yin* and *yang*. No clear idea of S. emerges in the *Qur'ān*; later Muslim thinkers propounded a highly metaphysical concept of it. The N.T. reveals two different trads. about S. The Jew. view of man as a psycho-physical organism was accepted by the orig. Jew. Christians, and found expression in belief in physical → resurrection. The letters of → Paul show influence of Orpheo-Platonic conception of S. as the essential immortal self. These two trads. have been incorportated into the Chr. doc. of Man: thus, while the S. is not regarded as pre-existent, it is intrinsically immortal and survives body, which is ultimately to be raised again to life. In medieval art, the soul was depicted as tiny nude human figure that departed from the mouth at death. Prob. mindful of findings of mod. psychology and psychiatry, Chr. theologians now appear to be hesitant about defining orig. and nature of the S. (→→ Man, Doctrine of; Eschatology; 'plural souls', p. 474b). S.G.F.B.

E.R.E., XI, pp. 125–55; C. J. Bleeker (ed.), *L'anthropologie religieuse* (1955); Brandon, *M.D.*, *passim*, *R.A.H.*, ch. 5, 6.

(Buddh.) →→ Anatta; Pudgala-Vadins.

(China–Japan) *China* → Hun and P'o.

Japan: The concept of *tama* or → *mitama* is nearest → Shinto equivalent to what we call the S. From anc. times it was believed that body is only a temporary dwelling-place of S., even during life. Many folk-lore stories speak of the *tama* leaving body for a period of time. Another concept is that of *tamashii* or the 'spirit of the S.', prob. a higher aspect of *tama*. Everyone is given and possesses his own *tamashii*, which will live on after body is dead, ever growing into higher dimensions. It is that aspect of *tama*, which, acc. to some authorities, becomes a → kami.

The idea that S. consist of two elements is common, and may be derived from China. One is the *kumi-tama*, which governs unconscious movements of body, and appears at conception. The other is *wake-mitama*, derived from parents and entering child at birth. Death results from disharmony betw. these two elements. The *tama*, being the essential part of man, is also conceived as essential part of other animals and even plants.

→ Shinto has no developed → eschatology. In early Shinto, the human S. was prob. thought of as going to a Land of Gloom (Yomotsu-kuni) or the Plain of High Heaven (Takama-no-hara); but legends speak only of future life for the S. of deities and great men. D.H.S.

J. Herbert, *Shinto* (1967), pp. 59ff.

(Islam) It is sometimes difficult to separate these terms in Arabic. While one may say *nafs* is soul and *rūḥ* is spirit, the distinction between the terms is not hard and fast, for both may be defined as soul, spirit, or vital principle. The Qur. indic. that the *nafs* repres. the individual's true self. Indeed, the word is commonly trans. as 'self'. Qur. iii:24 speaks of a day when every *nafs* will be fully paid what it has earned. xxxix:43 says God takes souls at time of their death, and those who have not died, in their sleep. This suggests the *nafs* is the permanent individuality. Lane, *Lexicon*, s.v. *nafs*, notes that when one sleeps God takes the *nafs*, not the *rūḥ*. The question of pre-existence of S. does not arise in the Qur., unless one may explain in this way vii:171, which speaks of God taking from loins of children of Adam their descendants and making them bear witness that he is their Lord. The verse is difficult to explain, but one feels an explanation on basis of pre-existence is not satisfactory. In poetry, and among mystics, idea of pre-existence appears, not only that of → Muḥammad and → *imāms* as in → Shi'a Islam. → Avicenna has a poem which speaks of S. coming down from loftiest abode as a dove and longing for time of its return. 'Abd al-Karīm b. Ibrāhīm al-Jīlī (765–*c.* 813/1365–*c.* 1410) taught that the *nafs* is created from light of attributes of Lordship. God created Muhammad's *nafs* from his own (the *nafs* of a thing being its essence), then he created Adam's *nafs* as a copy of Muhammad's. Abū Sa'īd b. Abul Khayr (357–440/967–1049) declares God created the S. 4,000 years before he created bodies, kept them by him and shed a light on them. Ibn al-Fāriḍ (577–632/1182–1235), famous → Ṣūfī poet, speaks of the S. being intoxicated with wine of divine love during its pre-existence before being joined to body. Orthodox Islam does not accept belief in such pre-existence, but attributes immortality to the *nafs*. The *rūḥ* is sometimes spoken of as vital principle; sometimes as the breath, for after it departs man ceases to breathe. There are times when one might trans. *rūḥ* as spirit and *nafs* as flesh; for one speaks of the *nafs* which prompts to evil (*al-nafs al-ammāra bil sū*— xii:53). Other aspects of the *nafs* are the animal (*hayawāniyya*) S., which governs body, the rational (*nāṭiqa*) S. (the inspired soul led by God to do good), the self-reproaching (*lawwāma*) S. (Qur. lxxv:2) which turns to God in penitence, and the S. tranquil at rest with God (*muṭma'inna*, lxxxix:27). When the Qur. speaks of God breathing into man, it is always from his *rūḥ* (cf. xv:29; xxxviii:72). The *rūḥ* is considered something created; in add. to being the spirit, it may also be an angel (→ Holy Spirit). A missionary in E. Arabia once travelled displaying the words in John iv:24, 'God is spirit', and caused great offence; for in the form *Allāh rūḥ* it seemed to imply the blasphemous doc. that God is created. J.R.

E.I., III, pp. 827–30; Hughes, pp. 604ff.; Lane, *Lexicon*, s.v. *nafs* and *rūḥ*; D. B. Macdonald, *Theology*, index; Nicholson, *Studies*, index; Arberry, *Doctrine*, pp. 52f.; Sweetman, *I.C.T.*, I, II, IV, index; J. Macdonald, *Eschatology*, in *I.S.*, IV, pp. 150–63; F. Rosenthal, *Ibn Khaldun*, index.

Souls, Festival of (China) → Festivals (Chinese). D.H.S.

Spirits (Buddh.) →→ Yakkha; Pisaca; Nat; Phi. T.O.L.

Spirits and Spiritism (China) Belief in and fear of spirits has stronger hold on Chinese than any other relig. idea. The spirit world, inhabited by spirits of every degree and kind, is believed to influence human life in all its aspects. Good fortune and ills of life are alike attributed to gods, spirits of the dead and demons. This has resulted in elevation of Spiritism to be most distinctive feature of popular relig. in China. In earliest recorded times, the *wu* or shaman-diviners, both male and female, purported to be able to communicate with spirits of dead and receive intelligent messages from spirit-world. Their function was largely taken over by Taoist practitioners, Buddhist priests and professional mediums. To-day, popular temples of → Buddhism and → Taoism are often centres of spirit-cults in which priests engage in communication with spirits of dead by all the well-known means of seances, trance, spirit-possession, dreams, clairvoyance, clairaudience, automatic writing and the like. As the Chinese believe that spirits are ubiquitous, Spiritism is favoured as means to ward off or appease malignant spirits, and to communicate with deceased ancestors and favourable spirits to promote good fortune and happiness. In gen., → Confucianism has frowned upon spirit-cults, and laws proscribing activities of mediums and witches were frequently promulgated. D.H.S.

N. B. Dennys, *Folklore of China* (1876), *passim*; C. H. Plopper, *Chinese Relig. seen thr. the Proverb* (1926), pp. 101ff.; A. J. A. Elliott, *Chinese Spirit and Medium Cults in Singapore* (1955), *passim*. See also J. J. M. de Groot, *The Relig. System of China*, 5 vols. (new edn. 1964); H. Dore, *Chinese Superstitions*, 15 vols. (1914–29).

Spirits and Demons (Islam) Muḥammad accepted a certain amount of belief in S. benignant and malevolent common to thought-world of pre-Islamic Arabia, as can be seen from the Qur. Popular Islam has accepted still more. Those which appear frequently in Qur. are the → *jinn*. Other names are applied to types of S. *'Ifrit* occurs in Qur. xxvii:39. In popular thought this is a violent type. *Ghūl* is a type which can assume any form and often tries to mislead travellers. *Si'lāt* is a female, prob. ugly, for term can be used of an ugly old woman. Devils are known as *shayāṭīn* (sing. *shayṭān*, → Satan), a word frequently used in Qur. Iblīs (from root *diabolos*) is their chief. Qur. xviii:48 speaks of him as being among the *jinn*; but elsewhere we read of the angels, with exception of Iblīs, obeying God's command to do obeisance to → Adam (cf. ii:32; vii:10; xv:30f.; xxxviii:73f.). vii:11 represents Iblīs as saying God has created him of fire, which would connect him with the *jinn* rather than → angels. Though some mod. Muslims attempt to explain away old belief in malevolent S., the common people still believe in a world peopled by S. mainly malevolent. Their favourite haunts are trees and open spaces. J.R.

Wellhausen, *Reste*, pp. 148ff.; Doutté, *Magie*, *passim*; *E.R.E.*, I, pp. 669f., IV, 615–9; Canaan, *Aberglaube*, pp. 6ff.; Hughes, pp. 84, 137f., 196; A. S. Tritton, 'Spirits and demons', *J.R.A.S.* (1934), pp. 715ff.

Spiritualism (The term 'spiritism' is often preferred for beliefs and practices gen. designated S.). Anc. practices purporting to estab. communication with the dead are dealt with under → Necromancy. Modern S. (its exponents would reject term 'necromancy' as pejorative) dates from occult experiences claimed by an American family named Fox in 1848. Since then the movement has become widespread, and it understandably attracts many people suffering from bereavement. Various means are used for making contact with dead: e.g. mediumistic trance, table-turning, automatic writing. Mediums, i.e. persons claiming special powers of communication with dead, have often gained considerable reputations, even for ability to 'materialise' the dead. Scientific investigation of what is termed 'para-normal phenomena' or 'extra-sensory perception' (ESP) has been undertaken by various institutions (notably by British Society for Psychical Research). The gen. conclusions of such research seems to be that instances of telepathy and pre-cognition can occur, but that mediumistic communication with dead is not proven. 'ESP' phenomena are prob. traceable to mental processes not yet fully understood. Some Christians attrib. spiritualistic phenomena to demons (→ Occultism). S.G.F.B.

There is an immense Spiritualistic lit. of doubtful value. Ref. should be made to *Proceedings of the Society for Psychical Research* (from 1882), and its *Journal* (from 1884), and *Journal of the American Society for Psychical Research* (from 1907), *E.R.E.*, XI ('Spiritism'); *R.G.G.*[3], VI, col. 251–3 ('Spiritismus'); A. R. Osborn, *The Superphysical* (1937); W. Carrington, *Matter, Mind and Meaning* (1949); G. N. M. Tyrrell, *The Personality of Man* (1947); J. B. Rhine, *New Frontiers of the Mind* (1950); J. R. Smythies (ed.), *Science and E.S.P.* (1967).

Spring rites (China–Japan) The prime object of agricultural rites of China and Japan is to guard ripening crops against disease, pests, storms, floods, etc., and to ensure abundant harvests. Among numerous festivals of lunar yr., the S.R. were of utmost importance.

In China one of the great imperial rites was performed in spring at the Shê Chi T'an, an altar and group of buildings to S.W. of palace. There the emperor worshipped and made sacrifices to the gods ruling the land (*shê*) and those controlling grain crops (*chi*). An import. sacrifice was also made to patron god of agriculture, Hsien Nung, at beginning of farming season. This was followed by the 'imperial ploughing', when emperor made six furrows in a sacred field with an ox-drawn plough. The grain sown in this field was carefully tended; when harvested it served as offerings at imperial sacrifices. At same time of yr., the empress sacrificed to divine patron of silkworms. Among popular S.R. was → Ch'ing Ming, when people sacrificed at ancestral graves and repaired the tombs. (→ Ancestor Worship).

Of the numerous agricultural festivals of Japan, the *ta-asobi* rites are enacted at very beginning of yr. The *ta-asobi* (*ta*- rice fields; *asobi*—play) is a sort of pantomime in which whole process of rice cultivation is enacted from beginning to end, to obtain a bountiful harvest. The *haru* (spring) *matsuri* is held everywhere in spring to pray for an abundant harvest. Also there is a group of S.R. connected with blossoming of cherry trees, symbols of purity. Early in spring the festival of *nana kusa* is held, when seven kinds of herbs are offered to the → *kami* to welcome spring, and rice-gruel, boiled with seven species of herbs, is eaten.

Most of anc. festivals of China and Japan are seasonal and rural, connected with cycle of vegetation. A concern for → fertility is seen in link betw. these spring and autumn rites and rituals of betrothal and marriage. D.H.S.

S.B.E. (1885, repr. 1966), vol. 28, p. 239; M. Granet, *Festivals and Songs in Anc. China* (1932), pp. 147ff.; Bredon and Mitrophanow, *The Moon Year* (1927), pp. 63f., 214ff.; J. Herbert, *Shinto* (1967), pp. 168ff.

Śramaṇa (Sramanic) The term *śramaṇa*, often coupled in Indian texts with *brāhmaṇa* (brahmins), ref. to the non-Brahmanical type of holy man, usually a wandering mendicant and ascetic, who might also function as a relig. teacher. Such ascetics were common at time of rise of Buddhism. The coupling of sramanas with Brahmins implies both a certain contrast and a recognition that in a religiously plural society both groups played in the same league, as relig. leaders. → Jainism, the → Ajivakas, to some extent Buddhism and perhaps other movements later to be absorbed within classical Hinduism, such as the → Samkhya-Yoga school, have a gen. similar pattern of belief (living beings implicated in cycle of rebirth, the possibility of release, typically by *gnosis* and austerity, lack of primary concern with gods and sacrificial ritual, an elaborate cosmology): hence their sometimes being grouped as 'sramanic' movements in contrast to orthodox Brahmanism. N.S.

L. de la Vallée Poussin, *Indo-Européens et Indo-Iraniens* (1936); H. Zimmer, *Philosophies of India* (1956); M. Eliade, *Shamanism* (1965); A. L. Basham, *History and Doctrines of the Ajivikas* (1951).

Sraosha (Srōsh) In → Zoroastrianism, 'obedience' to God's will. By uniting man to God, S. came to be hypostatized as mediator between God and man, and was accorded an eschatological role as judge and guide of righteous to heaven. S.G.F.B.

Zaehner, *D.T.Z.*, pp. 94ff.; J. D. C. Pavry, *The Zoroastrian Doctrine of a Future Life* (1929), pp. 12ff.

Śravaka-Yāna → *Yāna*. T.O.L.

Śri 'Beauty' or 'Fortune'; one of titles of consort of → Visnu, known also as Lakṣmī. Sometimes she is mythically treated as coeternal with Visnu; but also she is repr. as having emerged from waters of ocean, during churning of ocean (→ *avataras*). She is repr. iconically as seated on lotus; her images are favourite decoration of homes. In Sri → Vaisnavism, the → Vadagalai regard Laksmi as much the saviour as Visnu; but among the → Tengalai she is merely a mediatrix (having role analogous to that of → Virgin Mary). Just as Visnu becomes incarnate as →→ Krishna, Rama, etc., so Sri/Laksmi becomes incarnate in their spouses, Sītā and Rādhā. The term 'Sri' is also widely used as honorary prefix in addressing people (like 'Mr' or 'Esquire'). N.S.

A. Danielou, *Hindu Polytheism* (1964); J. Dowson, *A Classical Dictionary of Hindu Mythology and Religion* (1961).

Sthaviras Name given to more traditionalist wing of Buddh. monks in their disputes with the → Mahāsanghikas and others in the cents. immediately following death of the Buddha. (→→ *Councils, Buddh.; Schools of Thought, Buddh.*). T.O.L.

Stoicism Zeno of Citium founded a philosophical school, *c.* 300 BC, which was named after the Stoa Poikile, Athens, where he and his successors taught. S., the philosophy assoc. with this school, gave philosophical expression to the pessimistic evaluation of human life inherent in the classical trad. of Grk. relig. thought. The Stoic interpretation of the universe was realistic: the trad. gods were regarded as cosmic forces, and the cosmic pattern was held to conform to a basic → logos or reason. Man's superiority to other creatures was due to his rational mind (*nous*), and it was his duty to 'live acc. to practical acquaintance with the processes of Nature' (Chrysippus, 280–207 BC). The rational order of universe was regarded as divine providence (*pronoia*), and evil was seen as a necessary feature of the constitution of things, of which the wise man would take account, carefully controlling his reaction to it. Stoic physics provided no sanction for belief in personal survival of death, and Stoic eschatology viewed → Time as cyclical process that continuously repeated the same pattern of phenomena. S. demanded resolution of character in denying man's basic instinct for ultimate personal significance. As a philosophy of life, it appealed to many Greeks and Romans; the writings of → Epictetus and → Marcus Aurelius reveal outlook of those who sought earnestly to live acc. to its principles. (→ Greek Relig.). S.G.F.B.

E.R.E., XI, pp. 860–4; *O.C.D.*, *s.v.; R.G.G.*³, VI, col. 382–6; V. Goldschmidt, *Le systeme stoicien et l'idee de temps* (1953); A.-J. Festugière, *La révélation d'Hermès Trismégiste*, II (1949), pp. 260ff.; L. Robin, *Le pensée grecque* (1928), pp. 409ff.; *C.A.H.*, XI, pp. 690ff.; G. Murray, *Stoic, Christian and Humanist* (1940), ch. 2; G. Mancini, *L'Etica stoica da Zenone a Crisippo* (1940).

Stonehenge Most famous monument of → megalithic culture, situated on Salisbury Plain, England. Archaeological research has shown that S. reached present form in three stages (*c.* 1900–1400 BC); there is evidence of some deliberate destruction *c.* 50–400 CE, which may be due to Roman action. The monument incl. circle of blue stones, brought from Prescelly Mountains, Wales, thus attesting some special significance (→ Stones, Sacred). A carved representation of a dagger suggests relations with Aegean area (Mycenae), *c.* 1600–1500 BC (→ Aegean Relig.). The relig. significance of S. has not yet been determined: it was prob. connected with sun-worship, and perhaps with a mortuary ritual. There has been much speculation of connection of S. with older megalithic sanctuary at Avebury and huge artificial hill of Silbury, both in near neighbourhood. S.G.F.B.

R. J. C. Atkinson, *Stonehenge* (1956), 'Silbury Hill', *Antiquity*, XLI (1967); J. Hawkes, 'God in the Machine', *ibid* (discussion of recent astronomical theory).

Stones, Sacred A typical and vividly presented example of a S.S. and its cult occurs in Gen. 28:18ff.: the stone is the focus of Jacob's numinous experience, it is ritually anointed, and its location named 'Bethel' = 'House of God'. The cult of S.S. is very anc.: e.g. the 'blue stones' at → Stonehenge which were prob. sacred since they were brought there from Wales, *c.* 1700 BC (→ Megalithic Relig.). The cult of S.S. was also widespread: e.g. in Egypt, Greece, Canaan, Arabia (→ Ka'ba), India. The selection of particular S. as sacred was prob. due to various causes: peculiar shape or position, origin (e.g. meteorites); sometimes they may orig. have been commemorative (e.g. marking tomb of hero). Of peculiar interest in this connection are the faceless stone images of a goddess (? Persephone) found in Libya (cf. A. Rowe, *Cyrenaican Expeditions of Univ. of Manchester*, 1955–7 (1959), plates 27–9). (→→ Herme; Delphi; Massebhah). S.G.F.B.

E.R.E., XI, *s.v.; O.C.D.*, *s.v.; R.G.G.*, VI, pp. 348–50; *H.D.B.* ('Pillar'); R. J. C. Atkinson, *Stonehenge* (1956).

Store-Consciousness Name given to Mahāyāna Buddh. doc. (*ālaya-vijñāna*). (→ Yogācāra). T.O.L.

Stūpa (Skt.); **Thūpa** (Pali) A 'tope', or dome, i.e. hemispherical mound of stone and earth, or brick and earth, which, in lay Buddhism from time of → Ashoka (or poss. earlier), has served as focus for popular piety. The S., stone or brick-built, was a develop. from earlier form earth-mound, or tumulus, known in India as *cetiya* (from *ci*, to heap up). These simple mounds were a feature of folk-religion in India prior to rise of Buddhism; during early Buddh. period the folk-cult of the *cetiya* developed into Buddh. cult of the S. The latter was justified, from Buddh. point of view, on grounds that the S. was a memorial, either to Buddha, or to an early Buddh. saint. The develop. prob. took place in context of lay Buddhism rather than monastic; it has remained primarily a feature of lay Buddh. devotion. Acc. to the → Mahā Parinabbāna Sutta, the Buddha himself commended building of S., as places for enshrinement of relics; this was, acc. to the Sutta, in answer to question raised by → Ananda, of what were to be done with Buddha's remains after death. (*D.N.*, II, pp. 141ff.; Rhys-Davids, *Dialogues of the Buddha*, part II, pp. 154ff.). Over remains of Buddha, and of other great Buddh.s S. were to be raised, to which reverence was to be paid. It is pointed out by Sukumar Dutt that this idea is not altogether easy to reconcile to other aspects of early Buddh. doc., such as the impermanence of all compounded things (→ *anicca*) and unreal nature of so-called individual (→ *anatta*). Nor does assumption that S.'s were built *in order* to house relics of Buddh. saints find corroboration in the S.'s themselves, since not all anc. S.'s, discovered in India, appear to be relic-chambers. This suggests that cult of S. is a develop. of folk-cult of tumulus or *cetiya*.

The building of S.'s was a notable feature of the Buddhism of Ashoka's time. At first, the S. appears to have been simple hemisphere of stone, surrounded by railing to emphasise its sanctity; later, the railing was elaborated and became massive balustrade, inside which a processional pavement was provided. Survivals of this type of S. are to be seen in India: (1) In C. India, at Sānchi, Bhilsā and Bārhut; (2) In S. India, on banks of the Krishna and Godavari rivers in Madras State, on sites of the ancient → Amarāvati and Nāgārjunikonda. Trad. the work of S.-building is that of kings and wealthy laymen, who are held to gain great merit thereby. Outside India a most magnificent example of a S. is the Shway Dagon pagoda on outskirts of Rangoon, said to house some hairs of Buddha. This pagoda, which has remained in continual use down to present day, and is focus for devotion of thousands of Burmese Buddh., who visit it weekly, provides good example of what the S.'s of anc. India may have been in more expansive days of Indian Buddhism. (→→ Dagaba and Pagoda). T.O.L.

Sukumar Dutt, *The Buddha and Five After Centuries* (1957), chs. 12–14.

Styx, The In Grk. → eschatology, a river of underworld across which the dead were ferried by → Charon to reach their final destination. The crossing of the S. constituted a kind of test: only those dead who had been properly buried could cross; those not thus qualified lived wretchedly between lands of living and dead. The idea of crossing water after death is anc. It is found in → Pyramid Texts and Mesopot. texts. The Chinvat Bridge in Iranian eschatology and → Sirat Bridge in Islam (→ Bridges) also suggest passage across river to next world. If idea of Isles of the Blessed derives from → Cretan relig., as seems prob., passage across sea by dead would be implied in pre-Hellenic eschatology. There is some evidence also of a transmarine Celtic Elysium, and Saxon and Norse ship-burials are significant. The origin of idea is obscure. In Egypt it may have arisen from fact that dead were gen. transported across Nile to W. side for burial. The occurrence of idea in other folklores may stem from feeling that a definitive barrier existed between lands of living and dead. S.G.F.B.

R.Ae.R-G., pp. 333–4, 831–3; A. Lesky, *Thalatta* (1947), pp. 71ff.; F. Cumont, *After Life in Roman Paganism* (1922), pp. 75ff.; *E.R.E.*, II, p. 689, XI, p. 904; J. G. Frazer, *Balder the Beautiful*, II (1936), pp. 294ff.; *M.A.W.*, p. 98; A. Ross, *Pagan Celtic Britain* (1967), pp. 39, 332; E. O. G. Turville-Petre, *Myth and Religion of the North* (1964), pp. 271ff.

Suddhodana Father of → the Buddha, Gotama. S. was a chieftain of the N. Indian → Sākya tribe. His wife was → Māyā, who died 7 days after giving birth to Gotama. It was predicted of the child Gotama by soothsayers that he would become either a universal monarch or a Buddha. S., therefore, sought to protect the boy from any experience of unpleasant aspects of human life, such as illness, old age and death, and to surround him with pleasures. It was, in spite of this protection, that Gotama is said in trad. to have seen in one day a disease-ridden man, an old man, and a corpse, and thus to have been brought to reflection upon meaning of phenomenal human existence. When news of Gotama's having attained enlightenment reached S., the latter sent messengers inviting the Buddha to come to → Kapilavatthu. The messengers, however, hearing Buddha preach, were converted and entered the → Sangha without delivering their message. This happened repeatedly until 10th time, when message reached Buddha. On his visiting Kapilavatthu and conversing with S., the latter became a → *sotapanna*. Some years later, when S. was dying the Buddha visited him;

after hearing his discourse, S. became a lay → arahant, and died soon after. T.O.L.

Śūdras Lowest of four classes (→→ *varnas*; caste system) in Vedic society. Orig. they were drawn from peoples conquered by invading → Aryans, and were partly assimilated into Vedic society. Their rights, however, were circumscribed and they did not have access to Vedic → revelation nor to initiations open to → twiceborn, i.e. the upper three classes, Mostly they had servile occupations, but some groups came to engage in skilled crafts, business, etc. The distinction between S. in gen. and outcastes was blurred in classical → Hinduism, but they repr. in effect different waves of partial assimilation of dominated populations under relig. and social elite. Although S. might not learn → Veda, other relig. writings were open to them, such as → *Puranas* and the *itihasa* or Epics, together with later vernacular hymns, etc. Some of impetus of → *bhakti* relig. came from its appeal to the S. and other relig. underprivileged groups. N.S.

J. Auboyer, *Daily Life in Ancient India* (1961); R. S. Sharma, *Shudras in Ancient India* (1958).

Suffering → Evil, Origin of. S.G.F.B.

(in Buddh. thought) → Dukkha; Four Holy Truths. T.O.L.

(problem) (China) Recognising S. as an inescapable fact of human experience, → Confucianism attr. it mostly to human failure and error. Acc. to its doc. of perfectability of human nature by education, training and example, most S. could be eliminated by personal cultivation of virtuous life, regulation of all human relationships, and estab. of a just society. → Mencius taught that 'calamity and happiness are in all cases of men's own seeking' (2a:4); yet he suggests that Heaven uses S. as discipline: 'When Heaven is about to confer a great office on anyone, it first exercises his mind with S., and his sinews and bones with toil; it exposes his body to hunger, and subjects him to extreme poverty; and it confounds his undertakings. In all these ways it stimulates his mind, hardens his nature and supplies his incompetences' (6b:15). Confucianism recognised, however, that S. is also result of cosmic disharmony, or of spiritual agencies beyond man's control. In such cases, man must stoically accept the decrees of Fate. The mod. Confuc. scholar, K'ang Yu-wei (1858–1927) analyses causes of S. under 9 spheres of distinction, such as race, family, class, occupation, etc. He argues that S. can only be finally eliminated when such distinctions are abolished and whole world becomes a unity.

→ Taoism explained S. as due to departure from the → Tao, in which the modes of quiescence and activity are always perfectly balanced, natural and spontaneous. S. is eliminated by getting rid of all artificial activity and a return to the Tao of one's own nature.

→ Buddh. teaching that all life is S., and can only cease by negation of Self, went counter to life affirming spirit of the Chinese. Yet to millions of Chinese, who found life an intolerable burden, the doc. that S. is result of ignorance, stupidity and greed, an inevitable concomitant of the karmic process, was attractive, esp. as Buddhism provided way of escape from S. in promise of salvation for all sentient beings.

Popular relig. in China attributed S. to activities of host of spiritual beings. To interfere with these activities, except through magico-relig. techniques of skilled practitioners, was fraught with danger. This fear of interfering with spiritual agencies or with → Fate has given impression that the Chinese are callous and indifferent to S. But Buddhism, in particular, encouraged compassion for S. of all creatures, and all Chinese religs. are optimistic in holding belief in human perfectibility, with S. finally eliminated. D.H.S.

J. Legge, *The Life and Work of Mencius* (1875), pp. 171, 342; W. T. Chan, *Source Book in Chinese Philos.* (1963), pp. 729–36.

Ṣūfī, Sufism Ṣ. is derived from ṣūf (wool), from the coarse woollen garments worn by ascetics, as the movement developed from → asceticism. Sufism is often trans. as → 'mysticism'; but while there are many contacts with beliefs in other religs., it is essentially related to the →→ Qur. and Muḥammad, although some exponents seem to have overstepped Islamic limits, e.g. Abū Yazīd of Bisṭām (d. 261/875), who ejaculated 'Glory be to me! How great is my majesty', and → Ḥallāj, crucified in 309/922 for his statement: 'I am the Truth', which his judges took to be a claim to divinity, although he did not. The developed Ṣ. doc. distinguishes between what is called 'station' (*maqām*) and 'state' (*ḥāl*), the former repres. the Ṣ.'s efforts on the Path, the latter being divine gifts. The chief stations have been detailed as repentance, abstinence, renunciation, poverty, patience, trust in God, and satisfaction; the first, however, commonly called a divine gift. The states have been called meditation, nearness to God, love, fear, hope, longing, intimacy, tranquillity, contemplation, certainty. A director (→ *shaykh*), who must be absolutely obeyed, is necessary for one starting on the Path. One who has, under this direction, gone through the stations is invested with the Ṣ.'s patched cloak. The Ṣ. seeks union with God, and this is attained through → ecstasy. The words *fanā'* (passing away) and *baqā'* (remaining) indic. the necessary preparation and goal. By *fanā'* one passes from passions and desires and finally reaches cessation of conscious thought; by *baqā'* one has arrived at stage of unity where one is conscious of continuous survival in unity with God. There have been pantheistic tendencies within Sufism, but the normal Ṣ. is faithful to his Islamic theology, however difficult it may be to reconcile idea of union with God with Islamic doc. that God is altogether different from his creation. Among famous Ṣ.'s were al-Muḥāsibī (d. 243/837) who settled in Baghdad, → Dhul Nūn of Egypt, → Junayd, Muḥāsibī's pupil, who had more comprehensive view of mystical thought and experience than many of his predecessors. Later → Ghazālī made Ṣ. thought acceptable to orthodoxy. J.R.

Trans of S. works: R. A. Nicholson, *Kashf al-maḥjūb* by Hujwīrī, Gibb Mem. Ser. (G.M.S.), 1911 (repr. 1959), *Mathnawī* of → Jalāl al Dīn Rūmī; A. J. Arberry, Kalābādhī's *Ta'arruf* (The Doctrine of the Sufis) (1935), Niffarī's *Mawāqif* and *Mukhāṭabāt*, G.M.S. (1935); M. Smith, Muḥāsibī's *Ri'āya*, G.M.S. (1940).

E.I., IV, pp. 681–5; Hughes, pp. 115ff., 608ff.; Pareja, pp. 747ff.; *E.R.E.*, XII, pp. 10ff.; Mez, *Renaissance*, pp. 280ff.; R. A. Nicholson, *Mystics*; Massignon, *Hallaj*; A. J. Arberry, *Sufism* (1950); D. B. Macdonald, *Attitude*, index; C. Rice, *The Persian Sufis* (1964); F. Rosenthal, *Ibn Khaldun*, index; Rahman, *Islam*, chp. 8.

(Orders) *Ṭarīqa* (road), developing meaning of a rule of life, is used of a Ṣ.O. The orders developed in 6th/12th cent. The first, related to → 'Abd al-Qādir al-Jīlānī, became widespread in Muslim world, esp. in India. The Suhrawardiyya, traced to Shihāb al-Dīn al-Suhrawardī (d. 630/1234), spread mainly in Afghanistan and India. The Shādhiliyya, traced to 'Alī b. 'Abdallah al-Shādhilī (d. 651/1258) of Tunis, has been widely spread esp. in N. Africa and Egypt. The Mawlawiyya (Turkish, Mevleviya) goes back to → Jalāl al-Dīn Rūmī, entitled *Mawlānā*. It was widely spread in Turkish Empire under the Ottomans, and known popularly as the whirling dervishes. The Naqshabandiyya in C. Asia traces descent to Muhammad al-Naqshabandī (d. 791/1389). The Bekṭāshiyya is traced to a saint Bekṭāsh, whose biography is legendary. This order was assoc. with the Janissaries in Turkey; after suppression of the orders in Turkey in 1344/1925, their centres were mainly in Albania and Egypt. The Tijāniyya order, traced to Aḥmad al-Tijānī (d. 1230/1815) spread through N. Africa, esp. the French colonies, and largely displaced the Qādiriyya, one of four orders Aḥmad had earlier joined. The Sanūsiyya in Cyrenaica has been partly military and partly relig. It was estab. by Muḥammad al-Sanūsī (d. 1276/1859). The orders and their sub-divisions are very numerous. For list see *E.I.*, IV, pp. 667ff., art. Ṭarīḳa. The orders have centres, or convents (*ribāṭ*, *khānaqa*); the members are divided in classes: (1) those who spend lives in worship and possess a hierarchy (→ Saints), the closest approach in Islam to clergy; (2) members who live ordinary life, but join in acts of worship in community. The orders are orthodox, but have different rituals which they observe. They hold regular → *dhikrs* in add. to observing the five daily times of prayer. Something is found in special worship within the membership which people feel lacking in the stated prayers. J.R.

E.I. and *E.I.*[2] (so far as it has gone) give arts. on separate orders with bibliog.; Hughes, pp. 117ff.; Pareja, ch. 15; D. B. Macdonald, *Aspects*, pp. 145–209, *Attitude*, pp. 162ff.; Arberry, *Sufism*, ch. 8, etc.; J. S. Trimingham, 'Formative stages of the Isl. relig. orders', *T.G.U.O.S.*, XVIII (1961), pp. 65ff., *Ethiopia*, pp. 233ff., *Sudan*, pp. 187ff.; J. A. Subhan, *Sufism, its saints and shrines*, rev. edn. (1960); Rahman, *Islam*, ch. 9; J. K. Birge, *The Bektashi Order of Dervishes* (1937); J. M. Abun-Nasr, *The Tijaniyya* (1965) (excellent bibliography); A. W. Sadler, 'Islam: The parish situation', *M.W.*, LI (1961), pp. 201ff.; H. B. Barclay, 'A Sudanese religious brotherhood', *M.W.*, LIII (1963), pp. 127ff.; A. M. M. McKeen, 'The Ṣūfī-Qawm Movement', *M.W.*, LIII (1963), pp. 212ff.

Suhrawardiyya → Ṣūfī Orders. J.R.

Suicide (China) S. in China is fairly common, though accurate statistics are not available. The most frequent causes are 'loss of face', anger and revenge. There is a commonly held belief that S. will bring dishonour and lack of public esteem to one's enemy or oppressor, poss. involve him in legal action, and cause him to be harassed by visitations from a vengeful ghost. S. is more common among women, either to avoid a hateful or dishonourable marriage, or to protest against oppression and ill-treatment within old marriage system. In imperial China, ministers and officials who had been condemned to death were sometimes allowed to commit S. as act of clemency, in place of dying under hand of public executioner. A general, defeated in war, found in S. an alternative to disgrace. Among other motives for S. were loyalty to deceased master, grief for death of father, husband or son, and shame for action deemed to tarnish family's honour. The most frequent means of S. were hanging, drowning, or taking of excessive doses of opium or other poisons. D.H.S.

E.R.E., XII, p. 26; S. Couling, *Encycl. Sinica* (1917, 1964), pp. 530–1; J. D. Ball, *Things Chinese*, 5th edn. (1925), pp. 622–7.

(Japan) (→ Harakiri). S. is common in Japan.

In anc. times custom required S. of loyal servant on death of his lord. Later, clay images were substituted for bodies of attendants and favourite animals; but custom known as *junshi* was revived in feudal period as a voluntary act, and was regarded as praiseworthy. During Yedo period (1615–1868), the custom of unhappy lovers committing S. (*shinju* or *aitaishi*) was so common that special regulations were devised to forbid it. The chief causes of S. are mental disease and physical pain; but S. as result of poverty, jealousy, remorse, family troubles, business failures, etc. have always been common. Hanging, drowning and taking of poison are chief means of S. D.H.S.

E.R.E., XII, pp. 35–7.

(Religious) It is significant that S. has been officially condemned by the three → monotheisms: Judaism, Christianity, Islam; whereas forms of relig. or ritual S. occur in other religs. in which doc. of → metempsychosis is a fundamental datum: →→ Buddhism, Hinduism; → Shinto provides special case in → Harakiri. However, examples of S., inspired by relig. motives are known in the monotheistic religs., and were often approved. E.g. in Judaism the S. of Samson (*Judges* xvi:28–31) and the → Zealot garrison of Masada. → Augustine of Hippo discussed question whether S. was justifiable for woman to avoid violation and decided no; but he recognised poss. instances in which it might be justified, as in case of certain Christ. martyrs. Evidence has been found at the Djebel Nif-en-Nser (N. Africa) indic. practice of ritual S. among Donatists (→ Donatism). Mass S.'s of Russian Christians, who opposed the reforms of Patriarch Nikon, took place in 1672 and 1691. Certain deities committed S. (→→ American Religs., anc.; Jataka); or like Yama, Hindu god of death, found way to land of dead. (→→ Sāti; Self-Immolation, Buddh.). S.G.F.B.

E.R.E., XII, pp. 21–40; *R.G.G.*[3], V, pp. 1675–6; A. Berthier, *Les vestiges du Christianisme antique dans la Numide Centrale* (1942); *History Today*, XVIII (1968), p. 612.

Sujūd → Sajda. J.R.

Sumatra (Buddhism) → *Indonesia* (Buddhism). T.O.L.

Sumatra and Java, Hinduism in For approx. a thousand years, from the 7th to 16th cent., Hindu culture was a feature of the islands of Sumatra and Java. Indian influence, while it may have been present earlier, seems to have increased from about the 7th cent., when S. assumed a new importance owing to increase at that time in sea-borne trade between Persia, India and China, an increase which was due to improved economic situation in China and the vigorous condition of Persian civilisation in early Islamic period. This Indian influence was felt most strongly in S.E. Sumatra, and then in Java. In S. the Indianised state of Shrivijaya had emerged by 7th cent. As in other areas of S.E. Asia, the cultural and relig. influence was primarily, as van Leur has said, 'an affair of the royal court and the hierocracy'. The prestige of the great kingdoms of India was shared by the relig. cults assoc. with them →→ Shaivism, Vaishnavism and Buddhism—the rulers of Sumatran and Javan kingdoms therefore adopted the relig. ritual practices of their Indian royal exemplars. In van Leur's words, there was relatively little influence at level of folk-culture; Hindu influence on these islands 'had to do only with things sacral—relig. rites and ritual, and also literature and government techniques, which had a consecrated, magical character' (*Indonesian Trade and Society*, p. 251). It was a matter of Brahmanisation: the process which was going on in S. India was making way from there by the now busy sea routes to these islands. In S. the initial Brahmanisation was succeeded by a strong influx of Buddhism, as the latter, in its → Mahāyāna form, became dominant relig. and cultural force in India. By end of 7th cent., S. possessed own great centres of Mahāyāna Buddhism, evidence of which is found in account of Chinese pilgrim I Tsing's travels in S., which he visited on his journey between China and India in 671, and where he stayed between 685 and 695. In central Java also, initial period of Brahmanization was seen in emergence of Shailendra dynasty in mid-8th cent., assoc. with cult of Shiva. This was followed by adoption of Buddhism; this adherence of kingdom of central J. to Buddhism caused shift of Shaivite Hindu cult to E. of island. This was followed by resurgence of Shaivism in central J. in latter part of 9th cent. A group of temples at Prambanam in central J., built prob. in early 10th cent., has temple of Shiva as central feature, while another of the central group is a temple of Durga, the consort of Shiva. Stories of Hindu epic, → *Ramayana*, are illustrated in reliefs which decorate the galleries. As in Khmer kingdom (→ Cambodia, Hinduism in), so here also the temple had function of a mausoleum, in which king, earthly representative of Shiva, would be entombed after death, together with other members of royal family, each in own temple-mausoleum, and each identified with a Hindu deity. Although east. part of J. had a more continuous history of Shaivite devotion, Hinduism appears to have been even more superficial there than in central J.; indigenous cults were scarcely disturbed, but continued under guise of Shaivism. A notable feature in hist. of Hindu trads. in J. was trans. of epic poem → *Mahabharata* into Javanese prose in reign of Dharmavamsa (? 985–1006); this, the first Javanese literature, made lasting impression on popular culture, and is still a prominent theme in Javanese drama. Shaivite and Buddh. forms of relig. co-existed harmoniously, both in S. and J., and in later stage of development of Mahāyāna, i.e., the Tantric form, a synthesis of → Tantric Buddhism and Shaivism emerged, with adherence to Shaivism forming initiation into more advanced Tantric practices. By middle of 14th cent. in S., Indianised ruling classes were practising form of Tantric Buddhism with strong admixture of Shaivite elements. But just as in India this Tantric cult was displaced by the advance of → Islam, so too in S. and J.; as the Hindu rājas of India were succeeded by Muslim sultans and emperors, the Indonesian islands again followed Indian example in relig. The penetration of Islam into Indonesia was more complete than that of Hindu cults had been; it affected not only rulers but peasants and tradesmen, and became more deeply rooted. Only in island of Bali, to east of J., has Hinduism survived to present day; it is, however, a Hinduised culture peculiar to Bali, which incorp. a good deal of popular, indigenous, pre-Hindu religion. (→ *Hinduism: Introduction into S.E. Asia*). T.O.L.

G. Coedès, *Les États Hindouisés d'Indochine et d'Indonésie*, 3rd edn. (1964); D. G. E. Hall, A. History of South-East Asia (1964); J. C. van Leur, *Indonesian Trade and Society* (1955).

Sumerian Religion The relig. of the Sumerians, a non-Semite people who dwelt in area n. of Persian Gulf, provided basic pattern of → Mesopot. relig. S.R., which is documented by texts dating from 3rd mil. BC, was polytheistic, with a well-ordered pantheon. This latter feature is remarkable since it does not reflect the political situation: the struggle for hegemony among S. city-states, each with its patron-deity, did not affect precedence of these deities, and → An, god of heaven, remained head of pantheon (→→ Babylon, Marduk). Other chief S. deities were Enki (→ Ea), → Enlil, Inanna (→ Ishtar), → Sin, Dumuzi (→ Tammuz). These deities were served by professional priesthoods in temples which constituted the most important edifices in the deities concerned: a notable feature of S. temple was the *ziggurat*, a large tiered tower. Worship consisted esp. of sacrifice, the 'food of the gods'. S.R. was rich in mythology, particularly about creation. Magic and divination were practised. S. → eschatology was pessimistic, offering no prospect of happy afterlife. (→ Cosmog., Mesop.). S.G.F.B.

C.-F. Jean, *La religion sumérienne* (1931); S. N. Kramer, *Sumerian Mythology* (1944), in *M.A.W.*, pp. 93ff., *A.N.E.T.* (for trans. of Sumerian relig. texts); Dhorme, *R.B.A.*, *passim*; T. Fish, 'Some Ancient Traditions concerning Men and Society', *B.J.R.L.*, 30 (1946); H. Frankfort, *Kingship and the Gods* (1948); R.-R. Jestin, 'La conception sumérienne de la vie post-mortem', *Syria*, XXIII (1956); Brandon, *C.L.*, ch. 3; A. Falkenstein and W. von Soden, *Sumerische u. akkadische Hymnen u. Gebete* (1953); M. Lambert, 'Polythéisme et monolatrie des citès sumeriennes', *R.H.R.*, 157 (1960).

Sunna (Sunnīs) Indic. not only custom, but something which is a standard of behaviour. In Islam it came to mean specially → Muḥammad's S., i.e. what he laid down either by word or deed, or by tacit approval of matters which took place in his presence. The main body of Muslims are called *ahl al-sunna wal jamā'a* (the people of the S. and the community). They are often called Sunnīs, but some object to this term. They claim to be followers of Muhammad's S., and to be the real community. Some trads. speak of serious nature of unfaithfulness to the community. One says Muslims will divide into 73 sects, 72 of which will go to hell. The other is the *jamā'a*, and it will go to the garden (Abū Dāwūd, *Sunna*, 1). The other main body of Muslims is the → Shī'a. J.R.

E.I., IV, pp. 555–7; Hughes, pp. 622f.; Schacht, *Jurisprudence*, general index; D. B. Macdonald, *Theology*, index; Watt, *Philosophy*, index; Rahman, *Islam*, index.

Śūnya, Śūñyatā, Śūnyavāda → *Mādhyamika*. T.O.L.

Śūñyatā (Skt.) 'Emptiness', term used in Buddh. philosophy to denote the emptiness of ultimate reality and permanency which characterises all concepts (→ Madhyamika). T.O.L.

Sura (Pl. *suwar*). Name given to each of the 114 sections of the → Qur. They vary greatly in length. No very satisfactory derivation has been found. The Hebrew *shūrāh* (a row) has been suggested, indic. a series of passages; but this is difficult to justify. Bell has suggested the Syriac *ṣūrtā* (writing, text of Scripture). He admits that 'the laws which govern the interchange of consonants in Arabic and Syriac are against that derivation', but defends it on the ground that 'in words directly borrowed, these philological laws do not necessarily hold'. Whatever the derivation, the word is used for a passage of Scripture. J.R.

E.I., IV, pp. 560f.; Nöldeke, *Geschichte*², I, pp. 30f., II, 30ff.; H. Hirschfeld, *New Researches* (1902), p. 2; Bell, *Introduction*, index; Hughes, p. 623.

Susa-no-wo-no-Mikoto ('The impetuous male deity'). The rain-storm-god of → Shinto. The → *Kojiki* and → *Nihongi*' accounts of him are vague and contradictory. He is repr. in Shinto mythology as boisterous, ever raging and weeping and stirring up trouble. He was offspring of → Izanagi-Izanami, or as produced from washing of Izanagi's nostrils, when latter was purifying himself after his return from underworld. He was assigned to rule over world; but his repeated acts of violence and suffering caused to the sun-goddess, → Amaterasu, led to his expulsion by the gods to subterranean world. He is the arch-offender of Jap. mythology; but several of his acts have an unmistakably beneficial character. D.H.S.

W. G. Aston, *Shinto* (1905), pp. 96ff., 136ff.; D. C. Holtom, *The National Faith of Japan* (1938), pp. 109–11, 126–7; S. Elieev, 'The Mythology of Japan', in J. Hackin (ed.), *Asiatic Mythology* (1932, 1963), pp. 391ff.; J. Herbert, *Shinto* (1967), *passim.*

Sūtra (Skt.); **Sutta** (Pali) The basic unit of Buddh scripture. From root meaning 'to sew', *sutra* has as primary meaning a 'thread', hence a 'thread' of discourse, a dialogue of the Buddha upon a partic. subject. Sometimes the subject of discourse is indic. by the title, e.g. '*Samaññaphala Sutta*', the S. concerning the fruits of the relig.; sometimes the title indic. place or occasion of the S.'s being delivered, e.g. *Kosambiya*-S., the discourse delivered to monks at Kosambi; sometimes the person to whom the discourse was addressed, e.g. *Kutadanta* S., a dialogue with the brahman named Kutadanta. The word S. is used also to refer to an anc. verse, or quotation, or to a rule or clause of the → Patimokkha, or code of monastic discipline. (→ Sutta-Pitaka). T.O.L.

Sūtras (Hindu) In orthodox Hindu trad, the S. is an aphoristic exposition (there is more extended use of term in → Buddhism). S. concerned ritual observances, family customs and rituals of → twice-born, law, and philosophy, etc. Need for such manuals arose in → classical period of Hinduism. The *Śrautasūtras* concerned Vedic ritual; the principles underlying these were formulated in the *Mīmāṃsāsūtra* (→ Mimamsa). Similar works formulated basic tenets of other philosophical schools, i.e. →→ Samkhya-Yoga; Nyaya, Vaisesika; Vedanta. The basic document of last is the important → *Brahmasutra* or *Vedantasutra* (as it is also called). The obligations of householder were expressed in the *Gṛhyasūtra* (→ *Grhastha*), while orthodox law or *dharma* was summed up in *dharmasūtras* (→ Manu, Law Books of). Expansions of the S. material were often ref. to as *śāstras*. S. and *sastras* covered main aims of life for orthodox Hindu, viz. pleasure, → *kāma*, economic gain, *artha*, virtue, → *dharma* and →→ liberation, *mokṣa*. In theory the philosophical treatises were mainly oriented to last of these aims. The composers of S. rejoiced in brevity with which they could express theses, one reason for necessity of extended commentaries of the S. The most import. of these have been the commentaries on *Brahmasūtra* by leading exponents of Vedanta, esp. →→ Sankara, Ramanuja and Madhva. N.S.

M. Winternitz, *History of Indian Literature*, 2 vols. (1927–33).

Sutta-Nipāta Name of book contained in the 5th or *Khuddaka-Nikāya*, of the Sutta-Pitaka, of the Pali Buddh. canon of scripture. By gen. agreement of modern scholars this is one of most anc. sections of Buddh. canonical lit.; it provides valuable evidence of some earliest forms of Buddh. ideas and teaching. It consists of an anthology, largely of verse, arranged in five chapters: (1) The chapter of the snake; (2) The minor chapter; (3) The great chapter; (4) The chapter of 'eights'; (5) The way to the beyond. Of these (4) is sufficiently old to possess a commentary which is also a book of the canon, the *Niddesa* (in the *Khuddaka-Nikāya*). Since the *Niddesa* comments only upon the 4th chapter, this evidently existed in separate form at an early date. A commentary on the complete S.-N. was composed by → Buddhaghosa, entitled *Paramattha-jotikā*. The Pali text of S.-N. was published in Roman script in 1913 by the PTS. Trans. into Eng. have been made by Sir Muttu Cumaraswamy (of 30 sections only), entitled *Sutta-Nipāta, or Dialogues and Discourses of Gotama Buddha* (1874); by V. Fausboll, *The Sutta-Nipāta, A Collection of Discourses* (1880), as vol. X of the *S.B.E.* (rev. 1898); by Lord Chalmers, *Buddha's Teachings* (Harvard Oriental Series, vol. 37, 1932); by E. M. Hare, *Woven Cadences of Early Buddhists* (1945, 2nd edn. 1948). T.O.L.

Sutta-Piṭaka One of the three major divisions, or Piṭakas ('baskets'), of Buddh. canon of scripture, consisting of → Suttas, i.e. discourses or dialogues, as distinct from other two divisions of canon: the → Vinaya-pitaka (the code of discipline governing life of Sangha), and the → Abhidhamma-pitaka (a systematic arrangement of essential propositions and formulae). The S.-P. is made up of 5 collections or *Nikāyas:* → *Dīgha-Nikāya;* → *Majjhima-N.;* → *Anguttara-N.;* → *Khuddaka-N.* Some books contained in the S.-P. are not strictly of sutta type, e.g. the → *Jātaka*, and → *Dhammapada*. The sutta proper is characterised by a formal intro. consisting of the words 'Thus have I heard' (these being attr. to the disciple → Ananda, who, acc. to trad., recited the suttas at Council of Rajagaha immediately after Buddha's death. (→ Councils, Buddh.), and statement of circumstances in which the sutta or discourse was delivered, viz. place, occasion, who was present, who was thus addressed, or question raised. The style of material in the S.-P. is clearly popular and intended for apologetic and teaching purposes: similes, parables, allegories and lengthy repetitions for sake of emphasis abound. The S.-P. in Pali is fullest collection extant; a Chinese collection exists which contains 4 *āgamas*, corresponding to first, 4 *Nikāyas* of Pali S.-P. (→ Tipitaka, Buddh.). T.O.L.

Śvetāmbara The *Svetambaras* or 'White Clad Ones' are, with the → *Digambaras*, one of two major sects or divisions of → Jainism; deriving name from fact that they favour wearing of white garments by monks (in contrast to nudism favoured by *Digambaras*). The schism between sects occurred in part through migration of Jains in early 3rd cent. BC to Deccan, to form *Digambara* wing. Apart from issue of nudism (largely a theoretical issue since it is rarely practised in public today), chief points distinguishing the S. are their canon, finalised at council in Kathiawar in 5th cent. CE (→ revelation, Jain), and details of their temple cults. In 15th cent., in Gujarat, a group, known as the *Sthānakavāsis*, broke away from S. over the use of images in worship. N.S.

Synagogue *Ex.* Grk. *synagōgē* = 'assembly'. The S. became a Jew. institution some time after Babylonian Exile (6th cent. BC), doubtless to meet needs of those who could not worship in Jerusalem → Temple, i.e. the majority of Jews. By 1st cent. CE, as the N.T. testifies, S.'s existed in Jew. communities both in Palestine and → Diaspora. S.-worship was non-sacrificial, and consisted chiefly of readings from Law and Prophets, with prayers, canticles and, sometimes, a sermon. The S. contained an 'Ark', i.e. a cupboard, in which sacred rolls of Scripture were kept. A minimum of ten males was necessary to constitute a S. for worship. The organisation and upkeep of a S. was undertaken by various officials. The earliest known Palestinian S. was recently excavated at Masada; S.'s of 2nd and 3rd cent. have been unearthed in Greece. The S. continues as characteristic institution of → Judaism. S.G.F.B.

*H.D.B.*², *s.v.; R.G.G.*³, VI, col. 557–9; Schürer, *G.J.V.*, II, pp. 427ff.; W. O. E. Oesterley and G. H. Box, *The Relig. and Worship of the Synagogue* (1907); E. L. Sukenik, *Anc. Synagogues in Palestine and Greece* (1934); Y. Yadin, *The Excavation of Masada*, 1963/4 (1965), pp. 76ff.; *E.J.R.*, p. 369.

Syncretism Term orig. used by Plutarch (*de fraterno amore*, 19) for fusion of relig. cults which occurred in Graeco-Roman world, 300 BC–200 CE. The process was gen. spontaneous, but it could be product of official action as in institution of cult of → Sarapis. Few religs. were wholly immune from some degree of S.; even → Judaism, despite its monotheistic trad. was affected, and → Christianity from its beginnings, as Paul's letters show, combined many different relig. ideas and rituals. (→→ Gnosticism; Hermetica; Mystery Religions). Although term is gen. used in connection with Graeco-Roman culture, S. is to be found in all places where there has been contact between religions. S.G.F.B.

E.R.E., XII, *s.v.;* S. Angus, *The Religious Quests of Graeco-Roman World* (1929), *The Mystery Religions and Christianity* (1925); Cumont, *R.O.*; Gressmann, *O.R.; R.G.G.*³, VI, col. 563–6; J. Geffcken, *Der Ausgang des griechisch-römischen Heidentums* (1963 edn.).

Synoptic Problem Description given to problem inherent in fact that Gospels of →→ Mt., Mk., Lk. contain many passages similar in content and sometimes in phraseology. The gen. accepted solution of problem is that Mk. is the oldest Gospel and provided narrative-framework for Mt. and Lk. Further, that non-Markan accounts of teaching of Jesus common to Mt. and Lk. were derived from a lost source designated → Q. In addition to Markan and Q material, Mt. and Lk. each contains matter peculiar to itself, e.g. in the Infancy and Resurrection Narratives. A further elaboration of this solution of S.P. is the Proto-Luke theory, first advanced by B. H. Streeter, acc. to which Lk. had already written a Gospel when a copy of Mk. reached him, parts of which he incorporated into his existent work. Certain scholars, mostly R.C., maintain that Mt. was earliest Gospel. (→→ Formgeschichte; Logia). S.G.F.B.

B. H. Streeter, *The Four Gospels* (1924); F. C. Grant, *The Gospels: their Origin and Growth* (1957); *P.C.*², pp. 748ff.; *H.D.B.*², pp. 341ff.; V. Taylor, *Behind the Third Gospel* (1926); *R.G.G.*³, II, col. 753–69.

T

Tabu (Taboo) Word of Polynesian orig. designating some person or thing regarded as dangerous, with whom, or with which, relations are forbidden (→ Polynesian Rel.). The 'danger' is invariably of a 'holy' kind, assoc. with the idea of mana. To prevent profane contact with such an object, which might be disastrous for person concerned and for his community, rules are promulgated forbidding contact or prescribing safeguards where contact is necessary. The idea and praxis of T. are anc. and occur in most religs. The Bible provides many instances of consequences of infringing T. (e.g. Jos. 6:17–7:26; II Sam. 6:6ff.). (→→ Clean and Unclean; Holy, The). S.G.F.B.

J. G. Frazer, *Taboo and the Perils of the Soul* (*G.B.* 1936); *E.R.E.*, XII, *s.v.*; F. Steiner, *Taboo* (1956); *R.G.G.*[3], XII, col. 598–600.

Ta Hsüeh (The Great Learning). With the → *Analects*, → Mencius and the → *Chung Yung*, it formed the Four Books of Confucianism, basic documents in the educational system of China for the past 800 years. It was orig. ch. 42 of the → *Li Chi*. It was attr. to Tsêng-tzŭ, disciple of → Confucius, and gives in succinct form the teaching of Confucius on education, morals and political ideals. It claims as its purpose 'to exemplify illustrious virtue, to love the people and to rest in the highest good'. It teaches that starting-point of moral and social life lies in thorough investigation of things, from which follow extension of knowledge, sincerity of will, rectification of the mind, cultivation of personal life, regulation of family, national order and universal peace. Not much attention was paid to the T.H. till time of Ssŭ-ma Kuang (CE 1019–86), who wrote commentaries upon it and popularised its teachings, which have had enormous influence in China ever since.

There are several excellent trans. in Eng., notably those of J. Legge, E. R. Hughes, Lin Yu-t'ang and W. T. Chan. D.H.S.

Fung Yu-lan, *Hist. of Chinese Philosophy*, vol. 1, pp. 361ff.; W. T. Chan, *Source Book in Chinese Philosophy* (1963), pp. 84ff.

T'ai Chi ('The Great Ultimate'). Chinese term for final cause of all things. It is mentioned in 3rd appendix of the → *I Ching:* In the beginning there was T'ai Chi (the Great Ultimate). It engenders → *yin* and *yang*, which produced the four emblems, which in turn produced the eight trigrams. The term was used by → Taoists to express the underlying Unity, which does nothing but accomplishes everything. The term was borrowed by Chou Tun-I (1017–73), who composed the *T'ai Chi T'u* or Diagram of the Supreme Ultimate, to depict the process of universal creation through interaction of movement and quiescence. For the neo-Confucians T'ai Chi was the transcendent first cause, through which all things come to be. It contains the Principle or *li* essential to all 'being', and may be equated with → Tao. D.H.S.

For a full discussion, see Fung Yu-lan, *Hist. of Chinese Philosophy*, vol. 2 (1953), var. refs. under 'Supreme Ultimate'.

T'ai I ('The Great Unity'). Chinese Taoist term, synonymous with → Tao, → T'ai Chi ('the Great Ultimate') and T'ai Ho ('the Great Harmony'). Philosophically T'ai I repr. the Chi. attempt to find a unity underlying diversity of universe, and antedating creation. The concept, borrowed from the → Taoists, influenced the → neo-Confucians of Sung Dynasty. By the Taoists, T'ai I was worshipped as a supreme deity. As early as 2nd cent. BC, Han Wu Ti (140–86 BC), under influence of a Taoist magician, Miu Chi, instituted worship of and sacrifices to T'ai I. Soon afterwards T'ai I was assoc. with T'ien I (The Heavenly Unity) and Ti I (The Earthly Unity), in a supreme triad of Taoist gods. Gradually, with development of Taoist pantheon, T'ai I gave place to → Huang-Lao Chün, who in turn was succeeded by → Yü Huang (The Jade Emperor) as head of the pantheon. D.H.S.

E. T. C. Werner, *Dict. of Chinese Mythology* (1932); H. Welch, *The Parting of the Way* (1957), pp. 102ff.

Taiwan (Formosa) An important island of nearly 14,000 sq. miles situated in W. Pacific and separated from the Fukien Province of China by the Formosa straits, some 90 miles wide. Its aboriginal inhabitants, animists and head-hunters, were related in culture and language to the Indonesians. They now number only about

200,000 out of total population of 11 m., composed almost entirely of Chi. immigrants from S. parts of mainland. The language and culture are Chinese; the religs. are → Confucianism, → Taoism and → Buddhism, with a strong minority of Christians. Hist. dates only from 17th cent. CE. Before that time there were sporadic raids from China and Japan. In 16th cent. Spanish and Portuguese attempted to estab. settlements. Spanish navigators gave the name 'Formosa' on account of island's outstanding beauty. In 1624 the Dutch built a fort and maintained a settlement for 37 years, being driven out by a Chi. sea-lord, Chên Ch'êng-kung (Koxinga), who ruled the island from 1662–83. T. then came under rule of Chi. Manchu dynasty, and process of colonisation continued throughout succeeding centuries. It became a Chi. province in 1885, was ceded to Japanese after the Sino-Jap. war of 1894–5, and ruled by them till end of World War II, when it was returned to Nationalist China. Since 1949, the capital city Tapei has been the seat of Chinese National Government under Chiang Kai-shek, with military and financial aid from U.S.A. T. has become militarily strong and economically prosperous. There is a high degree literacy, a strong emphasis on trad. Chi. culture, and freedom of relig. belief is guaranteed by the constitution. D.H.S.

Guy Wint (ed.), *Asia, a Handbook* (1965); M. Mancall (ed.), *Formosa Today* (1964).

T'ai Shan Most revered of the five sacred mountains of China, honoured alike by Confucians, Buddhists and Taoists. The → *Li Chi* records that Chou Dynasty (*c.* 1022–221 BC) rulers made → pilgrimages to mountain to sacrifice, a custom continued throughout hist. times by Chi. emperors. It became a chief centre of pilgrimage; in early spring the Chinese in their thousands make pilgrimages to the Holy Mountain to worship at the numerous Taoist and Buddh. temples. In → Taoism and popular relig. of China, the god of T.S. is greatest of terrestrial gods, belonging to a group of mountain gods known as the Gods of the Five Peaks who, since beginning of 11th cent. have been given title of Shêng Ti (Holy Emperor). The god of T.S. was entrusted by the Jade Emperor (→ Yü Huang) with control over human life and destiny. He appoints birth and death; in early centuries of our era he became Lord over infernal regions and judge of the dead. Souls went forth from T.S. to be born and returned thither after death. Under control of god of T.S., a whole hierarchy of spiritual beings directs all aspects of terrestrial life: birth, death, destiny, honours, fortune, posterity etc. → Pi-hsia Yüan-chün ('The Princess of the Motley Clouds') is his daughter, known and worshipped as the Lady of T'ai Shan. Her temple on mountain is the most popular. T.S. is rich in hist. situations, recorded on innumerable rock inscriptions, and round it, through the ages, has gathered a vast store of legend, mythology and relig. lore. D.H.S.

E. Chavannes, *Le T'ai Chan* (1910); H. Dore, *Chinese Superstitions*, vol. 9 (1914–29); E. T. C. Werner, *Dict. of Chinese Mythology* (1932); H. Maspero, 'The Mythology of Modern China', in J. Hackin (ed.), *Asiatic Mythology* (1932 and 1963), pp. 279ff.

Ta'līmites → Ismā'īlīs. J.R.

Tammuz Hebrew name for Mesopot. vegetation god, known in → Sumerian relig. as Dumuzi. T. was a typical → dying-rising deity, and was assoc. with → Ishtar, the fertility goddess, as her lover. A Sumerian text makes Inanna (Ishtar) responsible for T.'s death. The Akkadian myth of Ishtar's descent into underworld has a concluding passage concerned with ritual commemoration of → resurrection of T. That death and res. of T. were annually celebrated by women is attested by Ez. 8:14. T. had important role in Mesopot. relig., and figured with Ishtar in healing rituals; but he did not become a *post-mortem* saviour like → Osiris owing to pessimistic nature of Mesopot. eschatology. S.G.F.B.

M. Jastrow, *Aspects*, pp. 343ff.; S. N. Kramer, *Sumerian Mythology* (1961 edn.), pp. 101ff.; *From the Tablets of Sumer* (1956), pp. 185ff.; C. and F. Jean, *La religion sumérienne* (1931), pp. 67ff.; M. Meissner, *Babylonien u. Assyrien*, II (1925), pp. 24ff.; Dhorme, *R.B.A.*, pp. 115ff.; A. Moorgat, *Tammuz: der Unsterblichkeitsglaube in der altorientalischen Bildkunst* (1949); T. Jacobsen, 'Toward the Image of Tammuz', *H.R.*, I (1962); O. R. Gurney, 'Tammuz Reconsidered: some recent developments', *J.S.S.*, 7 (1962); E. M. Yamauchi, 'Additional Notes on Tammuz', *J.S.S.*, XI (1966).

Tantric Buddhism → *Vajrayāna*. T.O.L.

Tantrism (Hindu) T. is form of sacramental ritualism, often with esoteric and magical aspects, characterising certain forms of →→ Buddhism and Hinduism, and going back to about 4th cent. CE or earlier. The term *tantra* derives from root meaning 'to expand' or 'extend', i.e. knowledge; and is used more narrowly for class of scriptures in which Tantric ideas are expounded. These *Tantras* claim same authority as → Veda, and are intended to reinvigorate relig. in declining days of the *kaliyuga* (→ Time, Hindu). The origins of movement lie largely in N. India and in Assam, i.e. in least Hinduised regions, and repr. one wave of resurgence of non-Aryan elements. Ritualism thereby is widened beyond that controlled by trad. → Brahmanical relig. T. penetrated both into →→ Saivism and Vaisnavism, though it was stronger in former, since cult of female deities (→ Saktism) played import. role in T., and they are more prominent in Saivite piety. A coalescence between Tantric ritualism and yogic practices, analogous to interiorisation of Vedic ritual in Upaniṣadic period, gave T. an esoteric dimension, so that later Tantra is largely inspired by homology between the microcosm and macrocosm. Though much in movement was anti-ascetic and seemed to give easy road to → salvation, through initiation into the mysteries, Tantric → yoga experimented with new forms of → asceticism, through sublimation of sexual union as symbol of union →→ between Śiva and Śakti. Thus the so-called 'lefthand' Tantra (*vāmācāra*) practised the breaking of → tabus under ritual conditions, indulging in the five M.'s (*makāras*), *madya* or alcohol, *māṁsa* or meat, *matsya* or fish, *mudra* or symbolic gestures (but term also referred to female partner) and *maithuna* or sexual intercourse. These rites were conducted in a sacred circle, *maṇḍala*, and involved people of different castes. This esoteric T. in theory was ascetic in sense that only those who had proper detachment and initiation could use it as liberating technique, though it merged into and in part grew out of orgiastic fertility cults. Both actually and in imagery sexual union was a prominent symbol in much of Tantric speculation, since it signified union of Siva and Sakti, and reintegration of primordial polarity which has given rise to world of multiplicity. Also import. was use of → *mantras* (sacred utterances), *dhāraṇīs* (protective spells) and *yantras* (diagrammatic devices). The use of *mantras* is found in → Vedic relig., together with use of such sacred sounds as → Om: and T. evolved complex and esoteric theory of potency of sounds as having sacramental and magic efficacy. The visual equivalents of *mantra* is *yantra*, which provides a schematised representation of some force, aspect or element in universe. Through correct use of *yantra* one gains power over, or identification with, the force, etc. For instance, the *yantra* called 'remover of desire' gives power over → *Kāma*, desire (esp. sexual desire). The theory of identification was applied to worship. The only person fit to worship a deity is a deity, and so worshipper goes through purifications through → breath-control, repetition of *mantras*, etc., to identify with self of the god. Extensive use of sacred utterances in T. had, as in Veda, the corollary that user had to understand inner meaning of what was being said; Tantric texts are often hard to follow because of ref. to secret meanings. Typically, the follower of Tantra is required to be initiated (→ initiations, Hindu) by → *guru*. The literature of the Tantras is vast, much of it having been edited and publ. in last fifty years. The revival of interest in T. has not had marked effect on mod. relig. and philosoph. thought in India, though there are strong Tantric elements in work of → Aurobindo. N.S.

Sir John Woodroffe (Arthur Avalon) *et. al.* (eds.), *Tantrik Texts Series*, 20 vols. (1913–); Sir John Woodroffe, *Shakti and Shakta* (1959), *Serpent Power* (1958), *The World as Power* (1957), *The Garland of Letters* (1955); S. K. Das, *Sakti or Divine Power* (1934); M. Eliade, *Yoga: Immortality and Freedom* (1958).

Tao A central concept both in Confucian and Taoist thought. The word does not appear, on the → Oracle Bones, but is used on early Chou Dynasty bronze inscriptions in sense of 'A Way, a Road', and as a proper name. 44 instances of its use in pre-Confucian literature have been recorded, signifying a road, way, to conduct, to guide, to tell, a course of action. In the → *Analects* of → Confucius, it is twice as frequent, usually with an ethical content as 'The Way' i.e. the Way in which an individual, a ruler or a state *ought* to go, the Way which Heaven has made regulative for human conduct. In → Taoism, e.g. the → *Tao Tê Ching*, the word acquires metaphysical meaning. It is a first and all-embracing principle, whereby all things are produced. It is the unchanging Unity underlying the shifting plurality of phenomena, the impetus giving rise to every form of life and motion. It is that which exists of itself. It is formless, yet complete, existing before Heaven and Earth, without sound, substance or change, all-pervading and unfailing. Though nameless, we call it *Tao*. Its action is spontaneous. It is not a thing as Heaven, Earth and all phenomena are things, and may be spoken of as 'non-being' (*wu*). But it is no mere nothingness, having brought the universe into being. It is impalpable, immeasurable and latent in all forms. The aim of the Taoist philosopher was to seek realisation of Tao, and perfect accord with the Tao of one's own nature and of universe. D.H.S.

Fung Yu-lan, *Hist. of Chinese Philosophy*, vol. 1 (1937), numerous refs., espec. pp. 177ff.

Taoism Taoism is a relig. indigenous to China wh. grew out of an amalgam of early shamanistic and magical cults with the mystical elements in the philos. of → Lao Tzŭ and → Chuang Tzŭ. In its early stages it aimed at the realisation of perfect happiness and the indefinite prolongation of life. T. taught that these aims could be achieved by unity with → Tao, by practising → wu wei or non-activity, by non-interference, humility and quietude, eschewing force, pride and self-assertion. Techniques were taught to assist men to become T. immortals (→ hsien). These included alchemy, asceticism, hygiene and dietary rules, a form of Chinese → yoga, magic and petitionary prayers to various powerful deities.

In the Han Dyn. (*c.* CE 2nd cent.) T. developed

as a popular religion (→ Chang Ling), spreading rapidly throughout China with a cultic organisation and a priesthood. During subsequent centuries T. vied with → Buddhism both for popular support and imperial favour. Between the two religs. there was considerable hostility, but also extensive mutual borrowings. T. peopled the universe with innumerable gods to match the Buddhas and → bodhisattvas of Buddhism. It established monasteries and nunneries patterned on Buddhist models, and took over many Buddhist ideas and ritual practices.

T. flourished in the T'ang Dyn., when many emperors were ardent supporters and patrons. Emperor Hsüan Tsung (CE 712–56) ordered a T. temple to be built in every city, and every noble family should possess a copy of the → *Tao Tê Ching*. By the time of the Sung Dyn. (CE 960–1280) the main patterns of T. relig. were fully established. → Yü Huang was recognised as supreme T. deity. The reputed descendant of → Chang Ling was given the title 'celestial master' and recognised by the government as titular head of the T. faith. The extensive T. Canon (→ Tao Tsang) was catalogued and published in CE 1019. T. was divided into numerous sects: some 86 have been recorded. But it followed two main divisions: an eremitic and monastic T. characterised by withdrawal from the world, asceticism, meditation and relig. study; and by the T. of hereditary temples, served by priests who married and handed on their relig. status and functions to their children. These priests moved about among the masses, performing relig. ceremonies, selling charms and amulets, telling fortunes, casting horoscopes. They gained reputation for sorcery and magic by which they communicated with spirit-world, to cure sicknesses and ward off misfortune.

Relig. T. has, in gen., been despised as gross superstition by Chi. scholar-class. As an influence inspiring → secret societies it has been feared. It has always lacked cohesion and centralised authority, each temple and monastery being autonomous. The philos. basis of T. maintains a perennial appeal. In mod. times, largely thr. lay societies, T. has encouraged temperance, frugality, almsgiving, meditation and study of T. writings. The Chi. gov. actively discourages relig. T. as an anachronistic superstition. At same time the first national T. organisation of a represent. character in entire hist. of the relig. was set up in 1953 under direction of Bureau of Relig. Affairs. T. continues to flourish among the Chi. diaspora, e.g. in → Taiwan, where there are estimated to be some 2,000 T. temples. D.H.S.

Holmes Welch, *The Parting of the Way* (1957); H. Maspero, *Le Taoïsme* (1950); D. H. Smith, *Chinese Religions*, chs. 6, 9, 13 (1968); W. Eichhorn. 'Taoism' in *Concise Encycl. of Living Faiths*, ed. R. C. Zaehner (1959); L. Hodous. 'Taoism' in *Gt. Religs. of Modern World*, ed. E. J. Jurji (1946). See also bibliogs. to Chinese Religs.; Fang Shih; Hsüan-hsüeh; Huang-Lao Chün; Ko Hung; Tao Shih.

Tao Shih Chinese term used for Taoist priests from 4th cent. CE. They live in villages or in nearby T. monasteries (*kuan*); unlike their Buddh. counterparts, they marry and their office is usually hereditary. Some are itinerant, wandering about countryside with small bands of disciples, selling charms and practising astrology, fortune telling, magic, exorcism, interpretations of dreams and cure of sickness. D.H.S.

Tao Tê Ching ('Classic of the Way and its Virtue'). A small Chinese classic of about 5,250 words, attr. to → Lao-tzŭ, and chief source book for study of philosophical → Taoism. It has had perennial influence in China; about 350 commentaries on it are still extant. There are over 40 E.T. It combines philosophical speculation with mystical reflection. Its literary style is abstruse, terse, and its meaning often vague and cryptic, making interpretation difficult. The book is chiefly concerned with → Tao, the eternal, unchanging principle, effortless and spontaneous in its workings, which lies behind phenomenal universe; and the power or virtue of Tao, which is called *Tê* and is the principle of individuality in things. A. Waley assigns work to an anonymous Quietist *c.* 240 BC, who directed a polemic attack against the Realists or Legalists (Fa Chia) of his time, and also against → Confucianism. Many mod. Chi. scholars accept the trad. 6th cent. BC date. D.H.S.

A. Waley, *The Way and its Power* (1934); J. J. L. Duyvendak, *Tao Tê Ching* (1954); W. T. Chan, *Source Book in Chinese Philosophy* (1963), ch. 7.

T'ao T'ieh Ogre mask; monster mask. (The Chi. characters suggest gluttony.) Appears as frequent motif in designs on Shang and Chou dynasty → ritual bronzes, and reveals import. of animal imagery in relig. experience of ancient China. It seems to be a compound of more than one kind of animal, but feline characteristics predominate. A conventionalised and highly stylised animal-mask is repr. in full face, with huge protruding fangs and the body doubled on either side of the face. Speculation as to its origin and meaning is inconclusive. To some it suggests gluttonous ogre, whose wide-open jaws indicate an all-powerful and all-consuming storm-god. Carl Hentze sees in T.T. evidence of a magico-mystical concept of birth and death, light and darkness, indicative of a dualistic world-view. In view of fact that, throughout hist. times in China, the guardian spirits of graves have been repr. in form of grotesque animals, and door-gods, which protected the Chi. home, are depicted as fearsome warriors, it may be that primary purpose of the T.T. was to frighten away evil influences which had designs on sacrifices offered to ancestral spirits, and upon corpses in the graves. D.H.S.

W. Willetts, *Chinese Art*, vol. 1 (1958), pp. 161–2, 186–9; C. Hentze, *Tod, Auferstehung, Weltordnung: Das mythische Bild in altesten China* (1955); D. H. Smith, 'Chinese Religion in the Shang Dynasty', in *Numen*, VIII (Leiden, 1961).

Tao Tsang The Taoist Canon, a collection of 1120 volumes, compiled over period of some 15 cents. The books form a heterogeneous collection, their date and authorship unknown. Many of them make use of an esoteric language, meant only for initiates. Taoist writings were collected together in CE 745 to form basis of future Canon, published, *c.* 1444–7 (acc. to L. Wieger, 1506–21). Only two copies of the vast collection survived to mod. times, one in Peking and one in Tokyo. A modern edn. was printed in Shanghai, 1924–6, comprising 1,057 works of orig. Ming Dynasty edn., and 63 from a 1607 supplement. D.H.S.

L. Wieger, *Le Canon Taoiste* (1911); H. Maspero, *Le Taoisme* (1950), pp. 73ff.; H. Welch, *The Parting of the Way* (1957), pp. 88–9.

Tapas Lit. 'heat', but ref. more partic. to practice of austerity in →→ Hinduism and Jainism, where it plays prominent part. Through → asceticism the → yogi is supposed to be able to generate magical heat, which can be both creative and destructive. Thus in → *Rgveda* Prajapati creates world through T. (→ Cosmogony, Hindu concepts); while there are numerous accounts in Hindu mythology of ascetics burning up opponents. T. is productive of god-like power. The practice of sweating, as means towards shamanistic ecstasy, is attested elsewhere; and prominent type of ascetic practice in Hinduism was sitting among the 'five fires', viz. fires built to north, west, south and east, together with sun above. In → *Upaniṣads* T. is treated as means, though inferior means, to realisation of → *Brahman*; but not too much should be made of contrast between it and → *jnana* or gnosis; for it as characteristic of Indian yoga to employ ascetic methods in service of direct existential knowledge of ultimate reality, the self, etc. N.S.

M. Eliade, *Yoga: Immortality and Freedom* (1958).

Targum Designation, meaning 'interpretation', given to → Aramaic trans. or paraphrases of O.T. T.'s became necessary when Hebrew ceased to be gen. understood by Jews. Originating in oral explanations in → synagogue, the famous T.'s of Onkelos on → Pentateuch and Jonathan on the Prophets were already in use in 3rd cent. CE (→ Judaism). S.G.F.B.

Oesterley and Box, *L.R.M.J.*, pp. 39ff.; *E.J.R.*, *s.v.*

Ta Shih Chih (The Most Mighty). Chinese name for → bodhisattva Mahāsthāna prāpta who, with → Kuan Yin, assists → Amitabha to rule the Western Paradise. By his power he is able to break influence of → *karma* and release soul from cycle of rebirths. D.H.S.

K. L. Reichelt, *Truth and Tradition in Chinese Buddhism* (1927), p. 186; S. Couling, *Encycl. Sinica* (1917 and 1965), p. 322.

Tat Tvam Asi Lit. 'That art thou' or 'That thou art'; most famous of identity texts in → Upaniṣads (*Chāndogya Upaniṣad* 6.8.7 and following sections). It sums up teaching of Uddalaka to his son Śvetaketu, and implies that true essence of universe and true essence of the person are same. It was taken in sense of a strict identity by → Sankara and other → Advaitins; while for → Ramanuja it means that individual self has same essential properties as God. → Madhva dealt with text somewhat summarily by suggesting different reading. The prefix *a-* in Sanskrit means 'non-' or 'un-'. As full text was *sā ātmā tat tvam asi*, and words are not separated from one another in Devanagari (Sanskrit) script, it was poss. for Madhva to suppose that an *a-* before *tat* had coalesced with the preceding *ā* of *sā*, to read 'Non-that thou art'. This enabled him to give a strictly dualistic (→ *Dvaita*) interpretation. N.S.

Tathāgata Buddh. term, frequently used by the Buddha when ref. to himself; the meaning is lit., either 'he who has thus (*tathā*) come or arrived (*āgata*), or, 'he who has there (*tathā*) gone (*gata*)'; but reason for use of term is uncertain. → Buddhaghosa offers eight different explanations in his commentary on the → Dīgha Nikāya; this indic. that there was no agreed explanation, and that he was in doubt. It is applied to → Arahants; since non-Buddhists were apparently expected to understand what it meant; it may have been a pre-Buddh. usage. It seems, however, to have been given a Buddh. meaning; it is said that the T. cannot be 'discovered', i.e. known empirically, even during lifetime, i.e. when still associated with corporeal and mental phenomena; much less so, therefore, after death. (→ *Sutta Nipata*, XXII, 85f.). T.O.L.

Taurobolium →→ Cybele; Criobolium. S.G.F.B.

Tawḥīd (Declaration of Unity). An Islamic doc. subject to different interpretations. The most gen. acceptable meaning is that it asserts God is without partner or equal; that he alone must be worshipped (cf. Qur. cxii). The → Mu'tazilites explained it in ref. to God's nature being a unity, denying that he possessed attributes, for that suggested multiplicity. T. may also mean that God is the only real existing one; cf. No. 51 of God's 99 names, *al-Ḥaqq* (the Real). Qur. xxviii:88 (everything perishes but his face), and

lv:26f. (everyone upon it passes away, but the face of your Lord, the Lord of glory and honour, remains) strengthen the view. 'Face' is used in sense of 'person'. This may mean that a time will come when all contingent existence will disappear and God will remain in solitude. Or, as in → Ṣūfī circles when emphasis is laid on *waḥdat al-wujūd* (unity of existence), it may develop into → pantheism, acc. to how the phrase is interpreted. (→→ God (Islam); God, names of). J.R.
E.I., IV, p. 704; *E.R.E.*, II, p. 190; IX, p. 243; Wensinck, *Creed*, index; D. B. Macdonald, *Theology*, index; Sweetman, *I.C.T.*, I, II, IV, index (God, unity of); Osman Yahia, *Aspects intérieurs de l'Islam*, in Charnay, *Normes*, pp. 31ff.

Tawrāt From Heb. → Torah, is mentioned 18 times in the → Qur. in Medina suras as a book revealed to Moses. A Meccan sura (liii:37) ref. to the scrolls of Moses, and refs. to him occur in Meccan suras, e.g. lxxix:15ff.; xliv:16ff.). The T. contains God's word, by light of which prophets, masters and rabbis gave judgment (v:47f.). God taught the T. to → Jesus (v:110) who confirmed it in the → Injīl (v:50). It refers to → Muḥammad (vii:156). Jews are accused of displacing vv. (iv:48; v:16, 45) and of forgetting or concealing part (v:16; iii:64; vi:91). Like an ass carrying books (lxii:5), they are unaware of contents. In gen. the Qur. has no direct knowledge of → Pentateuch; but v., 49 gives details of → retaliation similar to Exodus xxi:23f. → Trads. have many refs. which bear little resemblance to Pentateuch; but later writers showed acquaintance with Jew. Scriptures, and trans. were made. The most knowledgeable and severest critic of the Tl was → Ibn Ḥazm. J.R.
E.I., IV, pp. 706f.; Hughes, pp. 339f., 629f.; Goldziher, *Z.D.M.G.*, XXXII, pp. 341ff.; R. Bell, *Introduction*, index, 'Muhammad's knowledge of the O.T.', *Studia Semitica et Orientalia* (1945); Sweetman, *I.C.T.*, III, pp. 178ff.

Taxes (Islam) → Jizya; Kharāj. J.R.

Taxila (Taksasilā) → Gandhāra. T.O.L.

Tê An import. Chinese character, usually trans. 'virtue'. In its earliest usages it signified the 'power' or 'potential' of personality, an attribute of the Supreme Being, a quality which in a great man enables him to subdue his enemies, gain a following, impose his authority and influence over his fellow men. This 'power' or 'force' might work alike for good or evil; might manifest itself in benevolence or wrath. During Chou Dyn., the concept of T. became charged with new ethical meaning. It was divine or kingly power used for good of people and land. It was what made a man acceptable in sight of Heaven. It resulted in prosperity, peace and blessing. T. came to be used for moral conduct, conduct beautiful and admirable in itself, apart from its consequences. D.H.S.
L. Wieger, *Chinese Characters* (1915 and 1965), p. 37; A. Waley, *The Way and its Power* (1934), pp. 31f.; D. H. Smith, *Chinese Religions* (1968), pp. 24f.

Tea Earliest mention of T. in China is CE 350, though it is said to have been imported there by an ascetic from N. India in 543. Its use as a beverage spread through China and Japan under patronage of Buddh. monks. By 9th cent., it was in gen. use throughout China as a national beverage. Lu Yu (d. 804) is author of the 'Tea Classic' (*Ch'a'Ching*), and is worshipped in China by tea planters as their tutelary deity. Its intro. into Japan is attr. to → Kōbō Daishi (774–835), and was employed to keep Buddh. monks wakeful during midnight devotions. → Eisai (1141–1215) is regarded as father of Jap. tea culture, and Shukō (1442–1502) as the founder of the tea ceremony (*ch'a-no-yu*), intimately associated with → Zen Buddhism. The tea ceremony seems to have begun as a ritual, in which Zen monks successively drank tea out of bowl before image of → Bodhidharma. With Jap. aristocracy it developed into luxurious social institution, in which tea was prepared and drunk acc. to elaborate ritual and code of rules. Always assoc. with Zen, it inculcated intimacy, respect, purity, tranquillity, simplicity and judgment. The tea house in Japan is one of most socially import. institutions. D.H.S.
K. Okakura, *The Book of Tea*, 2nd edn. (1958); J. D. Ball, *Things Chinese*, 5th edn. (1925); B. H. Chamberlain, *Things Japanese*, 5th edn. (1905); H. Dumoulin, *Hist. of Zen Buddhism* (1963), pp. 190–2, 212–24.

Teilhard de Chardin, P. (1881–1955) French Jesuit, whose book *The Phenomenon of Man*, publ. in E.T. (1959) with intro. by Sir Julian Huxley, biologist and agnostic, made him known to a wide public as new thinker-prophet of Christianity. His training in theology and natural science (geology and palaeontology) enabled him to interpret cosmic evolution in terms of a neo-Christology, very ingeniously and imaginatively presented. The fact that T. had encountered opposition of his relig. superiors, together with his own personality, contributed much to the attraction of his work. To Chr. theologians, disheartened by impersonal nature of the cosmic process as presented by mod. science, T.'s book provided hope of rehabilitating the trad. Chr. *Weltanschauung*. Hence a cult of T. has developed; his other writings have been published and eagerly studied and discussed. The thought of T. and its current appreciation are symptomatic of present climate of Chr. thinking. Time will doubtless prove what is of abiding significance in T.'s achievement. S.G.F.B.

P. Teilhard de Chardin, *The Phenomenon of Man* (E.T. 1959); *Le Milieu Divin* (E.T. 1964); N. M. Wildiers, *An Intro. to Teilhard de Chardin* (E.T. 1968).

Templars (Knights Templar) Military order founded in 1118 to defend Jerusalem, captured by → Crusaders in 1099. The T. adopted form of → Cistercian Rule, and were essentially a monastic order devoted to exercise of arms in service of Church. New members underwent an impressive → initiation. The order was organised in four ranks: knights, chaplains, sergeants, and craftsmen. In Jerusalem, their mother house was close to site of Solomon's Temple (hence their name). This connection was commemorated in their churches elsewhere, which were circular (e.g. Temple Church, London). The T.'s stay in Palestine ended with Muslim capture of Acre, at which the Master of the T. was killed. The T. had acquired extensive properties in Europe. Their wealth and the rivalry of the → Hospitalers led to their ruin. King Philip the Fair of France, aided by Pope Clement V, caused the leading T. to be tried for immorality, heresy and superstition. Using torture, their condemnation was secured. The order was officially suppressed by Clement V in 1312. The gen. innocence of the T. of charges brought against them is now widely recognised. S.G.F.B.

G. A. Campbell, *The Knights Templars, their Rise and Fall* (1937); J. Charpentier, *L'Ordre des Templiers* (1944); G. Lizerand, *Le dossier de l'affaire des Templiers* (1928); *D.C.C., s.v.*; E. Simon, *The Piebald Standard* (1959).

Temple (Jerusalem) → David's bringing of → Ark of Yahweh to captured Jebusite fortress of → Jerusalem was prob. designed to provide both a political and relig. centre for Israel. The policy was completed by Solomon's building of Temple there, doubtless on site now known as the *Haram esh-sharîf*. An account of this T. is given in Kgs 6:1ff. It was primarily designed to be dwelling place of → Yahweh, the Ark being the *locus* of his presence. After existing some 350 years, this T. was destroyed by Nebuchadrezzar, 587–586 BC. A second and more modest T. was built under Zerubbabel in 516 BC. This T. was rebuilt on magnificent scale by Herod the Great, being finally completed a few years before its destr. in CE 70 by the Romans under Titus. The estab. of Jerusalem as Israel's holy city and acceptance of T. as only covenanted sanctuary of Yahweh meant that the catastrophe of 70 marked end of both Israel's national life and the sacrificial cultus of Yahweh. Jew. relig. life thereafter came to be centred on study of → Torah and in worship in → synagogue. But memory of T. has ever since been a powerful emotive factor in Jew. mind: it found concrete expression in pilgrimage to the Wailing Wall, a surviving portion of sub structure of T.; its idealised reconstruction was also a favourite topic of Rabbinic study and speculation. In plan, the various T.'s consisted of open courts surrounding the 'house', a structure containing the 'holy of holies'. Altars for burnt-offerings and incense, the → menorah and 'table of showbread' were chief furniture for conduct of cultus. The T. was also the national treasury, controlled by the priestly aristocracy. In 1967, for first time since year 70, Israel gained possession of Jerusalem and its holy places. The Temple area (i.e. the *Haram-esh-sharîf*) also contains two of the holiest shrines of Islam: the Dome of the Rock (on trad. site of Mt. Moriah) and the Mosque of Al-Aqsa. S.G.F.B.

Josephus describes Herodian T. and its destr. in *Jew. War*, V, 184–247, VI, 71ff.; cf. S. G. F. Brandon, *Jesus and the Zealots* (1967), *passim*, A. Parrot, *The Temple of Jerusalem* (E.T. 1957); F. J. Hollis, *The Archaeology of Herod's Temple* (1934); *H.D.B.*², *s.v.*; L. H. Vincent and A. M. Steve, *Jérusalem de l'Ancien Testament*, II, *Le Temple* (1954); M. Join-Lambert, *Jerusalem* (E.T. 1958); *Brief Guide to the Dome of the Rock and al-Haram al-Sharif* (Supreme Awqaf Council 1965); Schürer, *G.J.V.*, II, pp. 224ff.; J. Jeremias, *Jerusalem zur Zeit Jesu* (1958²), *passim*; *E.J.R.*, pp. 378ff.; K. M. Kenyon, *Jerusalem* (1967).

Temples, Hindu Use of T. and images in → Hinduism is post-Upaniṣadic: rites of Vedic period were conducted outside or in temporary structures. Indeed no free-standing buildings for Hindu worship are found before 4th cent. CE; but these were prob. preceded by fairly long period in which clay and wooden buildings were used to house images, but of which, being in perishable materials, we have no trace. The major period for T.-building was from 7th cent. onwards, and two main styles developed—the N. Indo-Aryan and S. Dravidian. The main difference is in rounding of the towers, etc., in north, contrasting with rectangular pyramidal style of south. The usual plan of full-size T. incl. central room to house chief image (*garbhagṛha*), joined to worship-hall (*maṇḍapa*) and porch. This complex is set in courtyard, and enclosed by walls and gateways. A common feature is bathing tank. The image-room is surmounted by tower, and often gateways are surmounted by towers, esp. in → Dravidian style, where the entrance tower (*gopuram*) may be more ornate and high than that at centre. Very often a T. has, as part of complex, bathing tank, with steps leading down to it. The T. itself is often raised on platform (but Golden Temple at Amritsar was built below ground level, to symbolise contrast in attitude of pious → Sikh). Much of N. Indian T. architecture was destroyed by Muslims, so that major architectural glories are found in south (and in Orissa). A few big T. have been built in recent times, notably in Delhi and at Banaras Hindu University. Degree of access to T. varies. Recent legislation, following → Gandhi's campaign on behalf of untouchables, has in principle thrown open T. (but usually not the image-room) to all; but some T. are operated by societies as private property, to maintain exclusiveness. The main function of the T. is for *pūjā* (→ Worship, Hindu); but congregational worship is not typical. Though the orig. function of the → Brahmins was performance of sacrificial ritual, which had nothing to do with the T. cult, they came to dominate administration of T. and the carrying out of increasingly elaborated rituals directed towards the god. N.S.

Stella Kramrisch, *The Hindu Temple*, 2 vols. (1946); P. Brown, *Indian Architecture*, *Buddhist and Hindu* (1949).

Temptation, in Buddh. Thought → *Mara*. T.O.L.

Tendai School of Jap. Buddhism (→ T'ien T'ai). Intro. into Japan by → Dengyō Daishi (b. CE 767), when he returned from China in 805 with scriptures and treatises of → T'ien T'ai school of Chi. Buddhism. He emphasised universality of salvation or attainment of Buddha-hood. He estab. a great T. centre on Mt. Hiei, near Kyoto; for centuries it remained greatest centre of Buddh. learning in Japan. With → Shingon, T. was leading force of relig. faith and philosophical thought in Japan. Its teachings were based principally on the → *Lotus Sūtra* (Jap. *Hokke-kyō*).

Acc. to T. the Buddha is hist. manifestation of the universal and primordial Buddha-nature, which can and will appear at any time on earth to further purpose of universal salvation. As a hist. person, Buddha attained full truth of existence; he is Tathāgata—the 'Truth-Winner'. But he is simply a manifestation of Dharmatā, the fundamental nature of universe; which, as Dharmakāya (Jap. Hosshin), the 'Truth-Body', is the universal Buddha-soul in which all participate; as Nirmānakāya (Jap. Wo-jin), the 'Condescension-Body', he is the concrete object of faith; and as Sambhogakāya (Jap. Hō-jin), the 'Bliss-Body', he reveals his wisdom and power in blissful glories of celestial existence. Since T. taught that the Buddha-nature is inherent in all existences, its ideal aim consists in full realisation in oneself of Buddha-nature and participation in Buddha's purpose and work. Both moral striving and contemplation are in vain, unless founded on and aiming at faith in Buddha. This faith means not only adoration of Buddha and dependence on his teachings, but identification with and participation in the universal Buddha-soul; i.e. to live life of the universal self. D.H.S.

M. Anesaki, *Hist. of Japanese Religion* (1930), pp. 111ff.

Tengalai One of two sub-sects, with the → Vadagalai, of the → Sri Vaisnavas, followers of → Ramanuja. They were effectively formed into separate sub-sect by Piḷḷai Lokācārya, elder contemporary of → Venkatanatha of the Vadagalai school. Not only do the T. emphasise very strongly action of divine grace in → salvation, espousing the 'cat-principle' (→ Vadagalai), but they rely chiefly on non-Vedic scriptures known as the *Prabandham*, being a collection of poems of the → Alvars. Lokacarya wrote sixteen treatises expounding T. teachings, which became normative for interpretation of the scriptures. Though his work was decisive in formation of school, Lokacarya is not regarded as greatest saint of the T.: this place is occupied by Maṇavāla or Varavara Muni (1370–1443), regarded as → *avatara* of Ramanuja. His cult became popular, and teachers whom he had appointed carried on the T. docs. to many parts of S. India. The T. is sometimes ref. to as the 'southern' school in contrast to the Vadagalai or 'northern' school, being stronger in southern parts of S. India, and having headquarters at Tirunelveli. N.S.

J. E. Carpenter, *Theism in Medieval India* (1921); M. N. Paul (tr.), *The Vedanta Tattva-Traya* of Pillai Lokacarya (1904); S. N. Dasgupta, *Hist. of Indian Philosophy*, vol. 3 (1961); H. Bhattacharyya (ed.), *The Cultural Heritage of India*, vol. 4 (1956).

Tenri-kyō (Relig. of Heavenly Reason). The most widespread and enduring of → sects of mod. → Shinto. Within less than 100 years of its founding, it grew into society of 5 million, with 10,000 local churches and a working staff of over 60,000 men and women. It is a strong missionary faith, and has developed extensive educational and social work. Its great national centre is in Tamba Ichi, where lies the unfinished → altar, whose completion awaits the cleansing of mankind. T. began in teachings of two remarkable women, who believed themselves to be inspired by a supreme, omnipotent creator God. The first was a peasant woman named Kino (1756–1826), who, at the age of 46, was inspired to proclaim that all existing religs. were incapable of saving sinful humanity. She deemed herself to be the saviour, transmitting final message of God, whose motive was love and whose purpose was universal salvation. She seems to have been influenced by Jap. Christianity of 16th and 17th cents. When she died, there remained a considerable following, mainly peasants, who having recorded her sayings, faithfully recited them at the meetings. They withstood persecution, and organised themselves into three orders of monks, nuns and tertiaries.

The real foundation of T. is ascribed to Miki

(1798–1887), whose childhood and early married life were marked by piety and devotion to Buddh. → Jodo sect. In 1838 she had experience of trance which completely changed her life. She believed herself to be possessed by the Lord of Heaven, who commanded her family to dedicate everything to his cause for sake of suffering humanity. Against great opposition, she sold all her property for relief of poverty and suffering. She suffered mockery and ridicule, persecution and imprisonment; but her ardent faith and powers of healing drew to her a following which rapidly spread throughout Japan.

The chief teachings of the sect are embodied in 4 texts, regarded as sacred writings. The sect has great similarities to → Christian Science, stressing import. of mental and spiritual health and divine healing, and need to be fully and sincerely surrendered to the divine will. The soul of man is part of omnipresent spirit of God. Man himself creates good and evil fate, and T. is way to overcome fate by turning evil to good. The process is the T. scheme of → salvation, which opens up channel between man and God. The purification and revitalization of its members will lead to reformation of human society. T. exalts dignity of labour, and inculcates daily unselfish service of others. A year after Miki's death, T. was given a measure of legal recognition, and gained complete legal and institutional independence in 1908. D.H.S.

D. C. Holtom, *The National Faith of Japan* (1938), pp. 267–86; M. Anesaki, *The Hist. of Japanese Religion* (1930), pp. 311–5; 371–2.

Teraphim Heb. term prob. meaning images of household gods in human shape (I Sam. 19:13). Orig. connected with → ancestor worship, T. seem later to have denoted representation of → mother goddess, used by women as aids to fertility and child-bearing. In Hos. 3:4, T. are assoc. with the → ephod. S.G.F.B.

*H.D.B.*², p. 413; *R.G.G.*³, VI, col. 690–1.

Teutonic Relig. → Scandinavian Relig. S.G.F.B.

Thailand, Buddhism in Mod. Thailand is a predominantly Buddh. country; approx. 94% of its population regard themselves as Buddhists. The form of the relig. which prevails (as in rest of continental S.E. Asia apart from Vietnam) is the → Theravāda. The earliest evidence of Buddhism in the territory now called Thailand is from *c.* 6th cent. CE. This is of an archaeological kind, from various places in the central plain of T., notably Nakhon Pathom (or Phra Pathom) about 30 m. W. of Bangkok), and Lopburi, about 60 m. N. of Bangkok. The oldest and largest *chedi* or → *stupa* in T. is at Nakhon Pathom. The evidence from these places in the central plain is from period when region was part of a kingdom of the Mon people, whose centre was at Thaton in lower Burma. S. T. at that time formed the Mon kingdom of Dvārāvatī; the kind of Buddhism in kingdom in early period seems to have been predominantly → Hīnayāna. From about 8th to 13th cent. the region came under power of Sri Vijaya kingdom of Sumatra (→ Indonesia), when the → Mahāyāna form of Buddhism seems to have been more prominent; evidence of this exists in Buddha- → rupas which have been discovered, dating from this period. Between 11th and 14th cents. large parts of what is now T. came under power of the Khmers, a people to E. (in what is now Cambodia), and whose relig. was much more strongly Hindu. In 14th cent. the hist. of the Thai nation proper may be said to begin, with the setting up by the Thais (a people related to Chinese, ethnically and linguistically, who were then moving southwards from Yunnan) of a kingdom with its capital at Sukhodhaya (about 150 m. N. of modern Bangkok). During 14th cent. the reputation of Sinhalese Buddhism (after reforms carried out by Parakamma Bahu I, the 12th cent. king of Ceylon), attracted Siamese monks to → Ceylon, who then returned to T. to spread the Sinhalese reforms. From this time onward Theravada Buddhism predominated in T. In mid. 14th cent. the capital was moved southwards from Sukhodhaya (or Sukhothai) to Ayodhaya (or Ayuthia), about 50 m. N. of the mod. Bangkok. When this was destroyed by Burmese in 1767, a new dynasty founded yet another capital, first at Dhonburi, on west bank of Chao Phya river, then on opposite east bank at what is now Bangkok. The 4th king of this dynasty, Mongkut, or Rāma IV was, at his accession in 1851 at age of 47, a Buddh. monk; his 17 years reign as king was one of most import. in the hist. of T.; it was he who laid foundations of mod. T., and initiated a reform movement within the Buddh. Order; this was seen in a reformed, more strictly disciplined sect of the → Sangha, known as the *Dhammayutika-nikāya*; this has continued to be a powerful influence in Thai Buddhism to present day; co-existing on friendly terms with main sect, or *Mahā-nikāya*, of Buddh. Order. Each has its large Bangkok monastic headquarters: Wat Bovornives (of the Dhammayutika-nikāya) and Wat Mahāthat (of the Mahā-nikāya); in each there is a large educational institution (*Mahā-Vidyālaya*) for training of monks. King Mongkut was succeeded by his son Chulalongkorn, or Rāma V (1868–1910), who also played import. role as a Buddh. ruler; during his reign an extensive modernisation of T. was carried out, largely owing to his initiative. Among other contributions which he made to vitality of Buddhism in T. was publication of the Pali → Tipitaka, or canon of scripture, in European volume-form, with text printed in Thai characters. During the six cents. since the Sinhalese Theravāda form of Buddhism was intro., it has had a deep reaching influence on whole of Thai life; in the words of G. Coedès, 'the entire population is steeped in Buddhism'; the country has enjoyed a modest but sufficient standard of living, with remarkably little social unrest. Since second World War, however, there has been an increasing adoption of West. ways and standards, in metropolitan area of Bangkok at least; although in rural areas, where majority of population live, Theravāda Buddhism still provides the basis of belief, culture and behaviour. (→→ *Festivals; Holy Days; Political Power; South-East Asia*). T.O.L.

Prince Chula Chakrabongse, *Lords of Life: A History of the Kings of Thailand*, 2nd edn. (1967); G. Coedès, *The Making of South East Asia* (1966); H. K. Kaufman, *Bangkhuad* (1960); A. L. Moffatt, *Mongkut, the King of Siam* (1961); R. S. le May, *Buddhist Art in Siam* (1967); J. E. de Young, *Village Life in Modern Thailand* (1955); K. E. Wells, *Thai Buddhism: its Rites and Activities* (1959).

Thailand and Burma, Hindu influence on These two countries, which together make up W. half of Indochinese peninsula, have been less affected by influence of Hindu cults than Cambodia and Indonesia, although latter are geographically farther from India. The reason lies in nature of Indian relig. influences upon S.E. Asia in early cents. of Christ. era and partic. in fact that the *Mon* peoples who inhabited area mostly to W. of the Chao Phya (Menam) river very early became Buddh., while the *Khmers* (→ Cambodia, Hinduism in), who inhabited E. side of peninsula, inherited from India Hinduised cults of divine kingship.

The Mons in early cents. of Christ. era inhabited the low-lying south. and cent. regions of what is now Burma, and parts of S. and W. of what is now Thailand, esp. the lower river valley of the Chao Phya. Their chief city was Suddhammavati (present-day Thaton, on E. coast of Gulf of Martaban) until about 9th cent. CE, after which it shifted to Pegu. Because of proximity to India, the land inhabited by Mons appears to have been first in S.E. Asia to be affected by Indian influence. Earliest evidence of Indian culture in Burma are fragments of Buddh. → Pali canon found in Irrawaddy valley near present town of Prome; these date from about 5th cent. CE. The earliest influence from India in region would therefore seem to be Buddh.; evidence of Hindu influence is lacking for earliest period, but this cannot be taken as proof that there was none. By 7th cent. the Pyus, who preceded Burmese as immigrants from Tibetan region, had estab. a kingdom known as Shrikshetra, at Hmawza (near modern Prome) in lower Irrawaddy valley. Among stone sculptures found at Hmawza, belonging to period, are repres. of Hindu god → Vishnu, and of various Mahāyāna Buddh. → *bodhisattvas*. The Burmese entered Irrawaddy valley a cent. or so later, and estab. capital at Pagan. A Mon king, Makuta, was brought captive by Burmese to Pagan, and allowed to settle there; the Nanpaya shrine, which he then built there (mid 11th cent.) shows Hindu deities among other, Buddh., figures in reliefs that decorate interior. Beyond such examples as this of Hindu influence intermixed with Buddh., there is nothing of more positive character which would suggest Hinduisation of court life such as characterised early kingdoms of E. Indochina, viz, Fu nan, and Champa (→ *Cambodia, Hinduism in*). Such slight Hindu influences as there were in Burma are much less import. than the predominantly Buddh. influence which Mon civilisation exhibited, and which the Mons, conquered though they were by Burmese, and, later by Thais, passed on their conquerors.

The Thais, who moved into area now known as Thailand, from N. (i.e. from S. China) during 12th and 13th cents., inherited two trads. First, there was that of Mons, of whose Buddh. culture there is considerable archaeological evidence in lower Chao Phya (Menam) plain, and esp. at sites in W. part of plain such as Nakon Phatom (Phra Phatom); second there was the Indo-Khmer civilisation which had deeply affected area to E. of Chao Phya plain, and all of which had formed part of Hinduised empire of Kambuja (→ *Cambodia, Hinduism in*).

When, in 15th cent. the Thais overthrew Khmer kingdom and thus expanded territory eastwards, they once again absorbed much of culture of area into which they moved, an area which had been saturated for cents. with Hindu-Khmer culture. From the Mons they had inherited → Theravada Buddhism, as a monastic relig. with roots in life of the people; now they inherited from the Khmers royal rituals and statecraft, which they adapted to meet requirements of Buddh. relig.; modes of art and architecture; Sanskrit language and lit.; astrology, and some popular Hindu festivals.

Laos, like Thailand, did not receive any direct Hindu influence from India; as part of Khmer kingdom from time of conquest by Jayavarman I (late 7th cent.), some Hindu influence was mediated into region through Khmer culture. The Lao belong to Thai group of peoples who moved S. from China into Indochinese peninsula in increasing numbers in 13th cent., and entered largely into area of Hindu Khmer culture. Like Thais, the Lao have, since 14th cent., counted themselves a Theravada Buddh. people; their culture, however, exhibits same admixture of popular elements, some indigenous, some derived from Brahmanism. → Astrology is perhaps most widespread Brahman feature of popular culture of these three Theravada Buddh. countries. Its practitioners were formerly almost always → Brahmins, but now in some places Buddh. monks have mastered Brahman lore and assumed role. The astrologers are frequently consulted by all classes of society in these countries in connection with fixing of dates for public ceremonies, import. enterprises, house building, weddings, and other *rites de passage*. The festivals of Hindu origin which are widely celebrated are *Sankranti* (New Year's Day), in April; First Ploughing Ceremony; and Festival of Lights, in November. T.O.L.

G. Coedès, *Les États Hindouises d'Indochine et d'Indonesie* (1964); D. G. E. Hall, *A History of South-East Asia* (1964); H. K. Kaufman, *Bangkhuad: A Community Study in Thailand* (1960); H. M. Nash, *The Golden Road to Modernity: Village Life in Contemporary Burma* (1965).

Thamūd An anc. Arabian people mentioned in inscription of Sargon (715 BC), by classical writers, and in → Qur. (cf. xi:64ff.; liv:23ff.; xci.11ff. etc.). They are said to have lived at al-Ḥijr, the mod. Madā'in Ṣāliḥ, in the Hijaz. They were destroyed because of their treatment of their prophet → Ṣāliḥ. Thamudic graffiti have been discovered. J.R.

E.I., IV, p. 736; Bell, *Introduction*, index; Hitti, *History*, index.

Theft (Islam) (*Sirqa*). Qur. v:42 prescribes cutting off hand of male or female thief, without making distinction regarding small and large thefts. Muhammad 'Ali in his trans., n. 693, suggests it may be metaphorical, or maximum penalty; but the legal schools thought differently. They vary about value of stolen article for which maiming is administered, some saying at least 10 dirhams and others 3. Some would amputate right hand for first offence, and left foot, left hand and right foot in that order for subsequent offences. Shafi'is and Malikis prescribe imprisonment for fifth offence; but it is difficult to see how one could commit a fifth one. Hanafis, Zaydis and Shi'is imprison for third offence, but Shi'is prescribe death for fourth. There is no maiming for articles of trifling value, for stealing such things as fruit or milk which can quickly go bad, for stealing wine, stringed musical instruments, chess sets, crosses, for such are not lawful for a Muslim. Freemen and slaves may both be amputated for T., but there is no amputation for stealing a free-born infant, as he is not property; but there is for stealing infant slave. This punishment can be administered only to adult of sound mind who has not stolen under compulsion from another. Nowadays (→ Ḥadd) amputation has prob. ceased to be administered everywhere. If it exists, it must be very rare. (→ Muslim Law). J.R.

E.I., IV, p. 173; Hughes, pp. 284f.; *Mishkāt*, pp. 766ff.; Querry, pp. 514ff.; I. Guidi and D. Santillana (trs.), *Sommario del diritto Malechita di Ḫalīl*, 2 vols. (1919), II, pp. 724ff.

Theism (Chinese) Though Chi. relig. remained incurably polytheistic, there was in pre-Confucian China a strong tendency towards T.; → T'ien or → Shang Ti was regarded as supreme being, the source of all that is and object of worship. This T.-tendency continued within state relig. From time of → Confucius, however, the gen. trend of Chi. philos. thought was agnostic and may be defined as an organic-naturalism, in which a single unitary principle (→ Tao) is equated with all that exists. The *Tao* was conceived as absolute, unconditioned being. A monism underlies the duality of → Yin and Yang, which, acc. to Chi. theory, produce all things by spontaneous action. Philos. → Buddhism reinforced this anti-T. and monistic trend. But Chi. → Mahāyāna Buddhism manifests strong theistic tendency, and in popular cults → Amitabha or → Yü Huang came to be worshipped as a supreme God. (→ Monotheism). D.H.S.

D. H. Smith, *Chinese Religions* (1968), *passim*; W. E. Soothill, *Three Religs. of China* (1923), pp. 115ff.

(Japan) Monism rather than T. is the philos. basis of Jap. religs. The idea of one great principle of life or spirit underlies polytheism of → Shinto, and worship of innumerable Buddhas and → bodhisattvas in Jap. Buddhism. Tendencies towards T. are seen in singling out of one deity (e.g. → Amaterasu) and regarding it as absorbing functions and worship of all the rest. The tendency to T. is partic. noticeable in so-called theistic sects of modern Shinto; this may be largely due to Christ. influence. (→ Monotheism). D.H.S.

D. C. Holtom, *The National Faith of Japan* (1938), pp. 40ff., 236–7; W. G. Aston, *Shinto* (1905), pp. 66ff.

Theocracy The earliest definition of T. is given by → Josephus: 'Could there be a finer or juster polity than one that sets God as governor over all things, assigning to the priests generally the administration of the most important affairs, and entrusting to the high priest the leadership of the priests' (*c. Apion.*, II, 185). Josephus is describing the ideal form of government for → Israel, implied in the Torah, for which the → Maccabees and → Zealots fought. Theocratic government has been attempted elsewhere (e.g. pharaonic Egypt; Mesopot. city-states; Islam; Tibet; in concept of Christendom). Medieval Christendom provides significant evidence of basic difficulty of T. in the constant conflict between Pope (→ Papacy) and Emperor of Holy Roman Empire for precedence. S.G.F.B.

E.R.E., XII, *s.v.;* J. Wach, *Sociology of Religion* (1944), *passim*; H. Frankfort, *Kingship and the Gods* (1948); C. J. Gadd, *Ideas of Divine Rule in Anc. Near East* (1948); F. Heer, *Aufgang Europas* (1949); E. Troeltsch, *The Social Teaching of the Christian Churches*, 2 vols. (E.T. 1931); A. A. T. Ehrhardt, *Politische Metaphysik von Solon bis Augustin*, 2 vols. (1959).

Theology *Ex.* Grk. *theologia*, lit. 'discourse about God'. The word was prob. invented by → Plato (*Rep.* II, 379a). Acc. to W. Jaeger, 'the creation of that new word sprang from the conflict between the mythical tradition and the natural (rational) approach to the problem of God'. The word was adopted into Christianity for systematic study and presentation of topics relating to God. The subject being so vast and many-sided, Chr. theologians have distinguished a number of special topics or departments of T.: e.g. dogmatic; Biblical; moral; ascetical; mystical; symbolic; sacramental; apologetical; pastoral; philosophical; liturgical; natural. The term T. can also be used to describe the systematic study and presentation of doctrines of other religions. S.G.F.B.

E.R.E., XII, *s.v.; R.G.G.*³, VI, col. 754–839; W. Jaeger, *The Theology of the Early Greek Philosophers* (1947); Harnack, *H.D.*, 7 vols.; F. R. Tennant, *Philosophical Theology*, 2 vols. (1928–30); F. H. Smith, *The Elements of Comparative Theology* (1937); C. Welch, 'Theology', in *Religion*, ed. P. Ramsey (The Princeton Studies, 1965).

(Far East) Both in its narrower etym. meaning denoting 'discourse of doctrine concerning God', and in its wider connotation as systematic and scientific study of relig., T. was a discipline practic. unrecognised in Far East until intro. of W. education. The application of scientific method to study of E. religs. was first made by W. scholars. In mod. times many distinguished Chinese and Japanese scholars have made notable contributions to T. The works (in English) of the following scholars are significant: F. K. L. Hsü; C. K. Yang; Y. C. Yang; K. Ch'ên (Chinese), and M. Anesaki; J. M. Kitagawa; D. T. Suzuki (Japanese). D.H.S.

Theosophy *Ex.* Grk. *theos*, 'God'; *sophia*, 'wisdom'. The term, although embodying the word 'God', usually denotes forms of relig. faith based on → pantheism or nature-mysticism, and gen. claiming esoteric knowledge. T. could be used to designate, e.g., → Buddhism, → Gnosticism, → Hermeticism. Modern T. is usually assoc. with the Theosophical Society (founded 1875), of which the great exponent was Mrs. Annie Besant. It claims to embody truths basic to all religs.; but it draws much on Hinduism, accepting → metempsychosis and idea of → karma. It naturally rejects the distinctive claims of the theistic religs. of →→ Judaism, Christianity, Islam. S.G.F.B.

E.R.E., XII, *s.v.; R.G.G.*³, VI, col. 845–7.

Theosophy (in India) The sophical movement, formally inaugurated through founding of Society in 1875 in America, was initially largely dominated by Madame Helena Petrovna Blavatsky (1831–91). Beginning with → spiritualism, she and her associates wished to create synthesis of the esoteric truth of all religs., and were antagonistic to Christ. exclusivism. → Occultism, Egyptology and other elements were woven together in her *Isis Unveiled* (1877). The Theosophists, despite these unpromising beginnings and various scandals generated by claims to miracle-working and by unconventionality of sexual relationships and attitudes among some of their leaders, became a moderately import. force in India, mainly through energy and magnetism of Annie Besant (1847–1933); she was mainspring of movement after death of Madame Blavatsky, and was in forefront of Indian nationalist politics, being elected President of Congress Party. Under her leadership, the Society, which had estab. headquarters in Adyar, a suburb of Madras, in 1882, became strongly devoted to reinterpretation of and defence of trad. Hindu values, and was a factor in resurgence of Hindu ideology in mod. period. To some extent the occultist and spiritualistic elements in T. were played down, or refashioned in light of ideas drawn from Hinduism. At first Mrs. Besant's attitudes to Hindu institutions were not noticeably reforming, though she criticised child marriage; but later on the Society placed greater emphasis on social work. A notable achievement was Mrs. Besant's establishment, in 1898, of Benares Central Hindu College, which was shaped on principle of a missionary college. Relig. instruction in Hindu and Theosophical values was part of curriculum (other Indian-founded institutions of time had not incl. this relig. element in teaching). This was later to form nucleus of well-known Banaras Hindu University, though Mrs. Besant lost control of College, on account of resistance to some of her later teachings, etc. Though there have been sectarian splits, notably outside India, and esp. through defection of Rudolf Steiner (1861–1925), founder of the Anthroposophical Society, T. has remained fairly cohesive in India, appealing to eclectic Hindus chiefly. Mrs. Besant's attempt to intro. a messianic element into the faith, cause of much of the dissension, came adrift when the young Krishnamurti, groomed for office, effectively broke away and taught a moderate and unsectarian spirituality. The movement does quite a lot to publish Hindu classics, etc., and, though its main function in India in encouraging self-confidence about trad. Hinduism, is obsolescent, it continues as one of vehicles of mod. inter-relig. → syncretism. The teachings of T. involve belief in a universal Spirit, reincarnation as part of an evolutionary process, idea of various planes of reality and existence of a hierarchy of perfected beings (the White Brotherhood, the Mahatmas, etc.), who supervise processes of the world. The investigation of occult phenomena is encouraged, together with → comparative religion (usually seen as showing unity of religs., but not always very scientifically conducted). The movement emphasises a higher gnosis, mediated by → rishis or adepts from hierarchy. N.S.

Annie Besant, *Annie Besant: An Autobiography* (1908); H. Bhattacharyya (ed.), *The Cultural Heritage of India*, vol. 4 (1956); J. N. Farquhar, *Modern Religious Movements in India* (1915); H. P. Blavatsky, *Key to Theosophy* (1893); C. W. Leadbeater, *Spiritualism and Theosophy* (1928); J. Krishnamurti, *Commentaries on Living*, 2 vols. 1956–8).

Thera (Pali); **Sthavira** (Skt.) Term used in Buddhism for *senior* monk. In the → Vinaya Pitaka distinction is made between a *thera bhikkhu* and a *nava bhikkhu*, i.e. a senior, as distinct from a junior (lit. 'new') monk. (*Vin.*, I, 47; p. 290). In the → *Dīgha Nikāya*, however, 3 grades are distinguished: *thera bh.*, *nava bh.*, and *majjhima* (or intermediate) *bh.* (*D.*, III, p. 125). A bhikkhu was regarded as *thera* either by reason of number of years he had spent in → sangha or, (even though junior in years) because of eminence in wisdom and learning and in spiritual attainments. Corresponding grade among nuns was indic. by Pali term *theri.* (→ Sthaviras). T.O.L.

Theragāthā; Therīgāthā The Theragāthā consists of collection of verses (*gāthā*) attr. to 264 of senior (i.e. → *thera*) monks, of early Buddhism, renowned for their spiritual attainments and virtue. Similarly the Therīgāthā is collection of verses attr. to 'senior' (*therī*) nuns of same period. The 2 collections form part of the → Khuddaka Nikāya, which is part of the → Sutta Pitaka of Buddh. Pali canon. The vv. are held by mod. scholars to contain authentic compositions of earliest Buddh. period, although some parts appear to be work of later redactors on basis of fragments of reminiscence (Geiger, *Pali Literature and Language* (1956), p. 21). The verses are attr. to partic. monks or nuns by name; such ascriptions may not in every case be trustworthy, but in many there may be sound hist. trad. behind ascription. Like other early Buddh. lit., they are of value for reconstructing anc. Indian social hist. The Theragāthā has total of 1,279 verses; the Therīgāthā 522. These have been trans. into Eng. by C. A. F. Rhys-Davids; the former as *Psalms of the Brethren* (2nd edn. 1937, repr. 1964); the latter as *Psalms of the Sisters* (1909, repr. 1964). T.O.L.

Therapeutae Monastic community of Egypt. Jew. ascetics living near → Alexandria. Described only by → Philo (*De vita contemplativa*), who compared them with → Essenes. Eusebius erroneously took them for a Chr. sect. The T. have acquired new significance through the → Qumrân Covenanters. (→ Monasticism). S.G.F.B.

E.R.E., XII, *s.v.;* Schürer, *G.J.V.*, III, pp. 535ff.; M. Black, *The Scrolls and Christian Origins* (1961), pp. 45ff.

Theravāda Name of one of principal schools of Buddhism, now repr. mainly in Ceylon, Burma, Thailand and Cambodia. The first major division of Buddh. → Sangha was between the → Mahāsanghikas, or Great Sangha party, and those who upheld stricter observance of monastic code of discipline, who claimed to be in true trad. of the 'elders', and were known therefore as → Sthaviras. The controversy between the two groups was occasion for 2nd Buddh. Council (→ Councils, Buddh.). The Sthaviras subsequently divided into the 'Personalist' school or → *Puggalavādins*, and the *Vibhajyavādins*, name which means poss. 'the analyzers', or 'those who make distinctions' (sc., between reality of present events and past/future events). The → Sarvāstivādins broke away from Vibhajyavādins after 3rd Buddh. Council at Patna; it was sometime after this that differentiation began to be made among Vibhajyavādins between those who became known as the Mahīsasakas, and those who assumed the name Theravādins. Acc. to Bareau, the difference between them was at first only geographical: the Theravādins being those Vibhajyavādins who were found in India south of Deccan and in Ceylon, while the Mahīsasakas were those in other parts of India. Grad. slight divergences of scriptures and doc. developed. The Theravādins claimed that theirs was the authentic and orig. form of the Buddha's teaching, as it had been contained in canon of scripture received by Sangha at 1st Buddh. Council at Rājagaha immediately after decease of Buddha; thus they applied name Theravāda, i.e. 'the Teaching of the Elders' (*Dīpavaṃsa IV*, 6, 13; *Mahāvaṃsa* iii:40). The Theravādins also divided into 3 groups in Ceylon, viz. the Mahāvihārika, the Abhayagirika, and the Jetavaniya, terms which ref. to different great monastic centres in Ceylon. (see Fig. p. 168). All of these schools, into which the early Sthaviras thus developed, were regarded by adherents of the → Mahāyāna, or 'great way to salvation', as teaching and practising only a 'lesser way to salvation', or → Hīnayāna. The latter term is sometimes used by Westerners as though it were interchangeable with Theravāda; this is not so, since the Th. was only one of the Hīnayāna schools. It is even more incorrect to ref. to Buddhism of S.E. Asia as Hīnayāna, even though it is the Theravādin form which flourishes and is predominant. Traces of Mahāyāna, are still to be found in S.E. Asia, not merely in archeological remains, but also in beliefs and practices. T.O.L.

A. Bareau, *Les sectes bouddhiques du petit vehicule* (1955); P. V. Bapat, 'Principal Schools and Sects of Buddhism' in P. V. Bapat (ed.), *2500 years of Buddhism* (1956, repr. 1959).

Thomas Christians Christians living in coastal area of S.W. India, near Travancore and Cochin (hence also called Malabar C.). They claim to be descended from converts of St. Thomas the Apostle, who is supposed to have visited these parts. It is more likely that they originate from Syrian Christians who settled here in 6th cent., being adherents of the → Nestorian form of Christianity. Under Portuguese influence, many formally joined R.C. Church at Synod of Diamper (1599). In 1930 others came into communion with Rome as the Malankarese Uniat Church. Syriac is used in their liturgies. S.G.F.B.

E.R.E., XII, pp. 178ff.; *D.C.C.*, pp. 844ff.; L. W. Brown, *The Indian Christians of St. Thomas* (1956). (→ Chr. Movements in India).

Thomas, Gospel Title given to Coptic document found at → Nag Hammadi, comprising 114 → *logia* or 'sayings of Jesus'. It dates *c.* CE 400, and is prob. Coptic trans. of Grk. orig. of *c.* CE 140. The *logia* are repr. as 'secret words which the Living Jesus spoke, and Didymos Judas Thomas wrote'. The G.T. seems to be → Gnostic; but it may preserve an early trad. stemming from Syria, independent of canonical → Gospels. It notably exalts → James, bro. of Jesus. S.G.F.B.

A. Guillaumont *et al.* (eds.), *The Gospel acc. to Thomas* (1959); R. M. Grant and D. M. Freedman, *The Secret Sayings of Jesus* (1960); W. C. van Unnik, *Evangelien aus dem Nilsand* (1960); B. Gärtner, *Theology of Gosp. of Thomas* (E.T. 1961); R.McL. Wilson, *Studies in Gosp. of Thomas* (1960); W. H. C. Frend, 'The Gosp. of Thomas: is Rehabilitation Possible?', *J.T.S.*, XVIII (1967).

Thoth Anc. Egypt. god of wisdom and art of writing. T. is gen. depicted with head of ibis, and holding scribe's pen and palette. In → judgment of dead, T. recorded verdict of weighing of heart. His cult-city was Chmunu, which Greeks called Hermopolis, thus indic. their identification of T. with → Hermes. As the 'Thrice-great Hermes', T. is the source of divine revelation in → Hermetic Lit. S.G.F.B.

P. Boylan, *Thoth, the Hermes of Egypt* (1922); *R.Ae.R.-G.* ('Thot'); S. A. B. Mercer, *The Relig. of Anc. Egypt* (1949), pp. 140ff.; S. G. F. Brandon, *Judgment of the Dead* (1967), ch. 2; *C.L.*, pp. 33ff., 44ff.

'Thracian Rider' God Numerous stelae have been found in the Balkans, partic. Bulgaria, showing in carved relief male figure, mounted on horse, pursuing an animal (e.g. boar, goat, stag). Often human attendants are shown behind him. The monuments belong gen. to 2nd–3rd cent. CE. The mounted figure recalls Grk. tomb sculptures of mounted figure of deceased; but the Thracian monuments are not sepulchral. They often bear Grk. and Lat. inscriptions, giving name of divinity concerned: the most frequent name is 'Heros' or 'Heron'. Sometimes the name is → Apollo or → Asklepios; but these are clearly only approx. identifications. There has been much specialist discussion of identity and nature of the T.R. It has been thought that the deity came to Thrace from Phrygia; since the T.R. is sometimes shown with several heads or faces, it has also been suggested that the deity was orig. a sun god. S.G.F.B.

G. I. Kazarow, *Die Denkmäler des thräkischen Reitergottes in Bulgarien* (1938); R. Pettazzoni, *The All-Knowing God* (E.T. 1956), pp. 178ff.; C. Picard, *R.H.R.*, 150 (1956), pp. 1–26.

Three Gems, or Jewels → Tri-Ratna. T.O.L.

(Marks of Existence) (Buddh.) → *Tilakhana*. T.O.L.

Thupavaṃsa Pali Buddh. book, attr. to writer named Vācissara of 13th cent. CE. The work is in prose, and is compilation of material drawn from older commentaries and chronicles of Pali Buddhism. As its title shows, it is a chronicle (*vaṃsa*) concerning the → stupas (*thupa*) or reliquary mounds, venerated by Buddhists, and deals partic. with one at Anuradhapura in Ceylon. T.O.L.

Ti Anc. Chinese term for apotheosised rulers. → Shang Ti = the first ancestor, the highest ruler, God. The character first appears on inscriptions of Shang Dynasty (2nd mil. BC) → Oracle Bones, where word is used as name for a sacrifice, and then for the divine ancestor to whom sacrifice was made. With the Chou Dynasty, the practice of applying 'Ti' to dead kings fell into oblivion, though Shang Ti continued as the Supreme Deity and was synonymous with → T'ien. The term came to be applied as title of respect to kings in this world, as well as to divine beings. The 5 legendary emperors were known as the 'Wu Ti' (Five Emperors). In 3rd cent. BC the title 'Ti' began to be assumed by reigning kings, and acquired political significance. The first emperor of China gave himself title Ch'in Shih-huang-ti, or 'The First Supreme Ruler Ch'in'. D.H.S.

Derk Bodde, *China's First Unifier* (1938), pp. 124ff.; D. H. Smith, 'Divine Kingship in Ancient China' in *Numen*, vol. 4 (1957).

Ti'âmat (Mummu Ti'âmat) Personification of sea in the → *Enuma elish*, whom → Marduk slays and from its body forms world. T. is often ref. to as a dragon; the text does not sanction this (although there is some poss. iconographic support): the epithet used for T. is *ku-bu*, which E. A. Speiser trans. 'monster' (*A.N.E.T.*, p. 67). (→ Cosmogony, Mesop.). S.G.F.B.

Brandon, *C.L.*, pp. 94ff.; P. Garelli and M. Leibovici, *La Naissance du Monde*, *S.O.*, I (1959), pp. 119ff.

Tibetan Buddhism The hist. of T. Buddhism may be conveniently divided into two main periods, the first being from 7th to 12th cents. when the relig. was being imported as something new from India and Nepal; the second from 13th to 20th cents. when it was fully integrated with T. social life. The final eclipse of → Buddhism in India at the end of 12th cent. provides the effective dividing line; for T. monks and scholars were regular visitors at the various Buddh. establishments, large and small, of medieval India right up to time of their destruction by the Moslem invaders. Thus the Tibetans became, thanks to their extraordinary zeal and determination, the chief inheritors of the later forms of Indian Buddhism, the →→ *Mahāyāna* and *Vajrayāna*. Indeed it is mainly from T. sources that we are able to gain some idea of the great variety, wealth and complexity of Indian Buddh. teachings and practices from the 8th to 12th cents. The Buddhism of this period is usually passed over in a few sentences in histories of Indian relig. as being so corrupt as to be scarcely worthy of mention. The evidence of the Tibetan trans. of this very period prove, however, that the great philosophic and doctrinal trads. of Mahāyāna Buddhism were still very much alive in Bihar and Bengal under the Pāla kings (8th to 12th cents.), although ritual and iconography, as well as ways of meditation and personal devotion were strongly affected by tantric theories, of which more below. Right up to 12th cent., distinguished Indian Buddh. teachers, of which most famous were Atīśa and Śākya-śrī, visited Tibet, while the continual high standard of trans. from Sanskrit to Tibetan achieved by Indian scholars and Tibetan translators over whole range of Indian Buddh. lit. is sufficient proof of vitality of Buddh. philosophy and relig. during this period, often misleadingly referred to as the 'twilight' of Buddhism in India.

In Tibet a few small Buddh. chapels were constructed in and around Lhasa during reign of King Srong-brtsan-sgam-po (d. CE 650), who came subsequently to be regarded by T. Buddh. historians as first of Tibet's great relig. (i.e. Buddh.) kings. However this king, like most of his successors, seems to have followed the relig. practices of his ancestors and was certainly buried acc. to non-Buddh. rites (→ Bon and Tibetan pre-Buddh. relig.). During reign of his descendent, King Khri-srong-lde-brtsan, who ruled throughout second half of 8th cent., the first T. monastery was founded at bSam-yas and the first seven T. monks ordained. The prime mover was the famous Indian teacher Śāntarakshita; later accounts (unrecorded until 14th cent.) give credit to great yogin magician Padmasambhava, although there is no certainty that he was even an historical person. About 792 a great debate was held at bSam-yas in order to judge between relative merits of Indian and Chinese forms of Buddhism. The Indian party, lead by teacher Kamalaśīla, disciple of Śāntarakshita, triumphed. The new relig. was largely a court interest; but it held its own or was merely tolerated side by side with the indigenous relig. cults with which it prob. began to come to terms. During this period the Tibetans were more concerned with holding their Asian empire than with practising new forms of relig. However, two sucessors of Khri-srong-lde-brtsan, namely Sadna-legs and esp. Ral-pa-can, regarded as the third of the great relig. kings, sponsored the new doc. More chapels were built and methods of trans. were systematized. Also Buddh. monks began to make their appearance, still rare, however, as ministers. The murder of Ral-pa-can (836) led to fierce reaction against state-sponsored Buddhism, and in turmoil of political disruption it disappeared from Tibet until 978. In this year some Buddh. teachers returned from E. Tibet where serious Buddh. practisers seem to have been taking refuge. About same time an enthusiastic line of Buddh. kings in W. Tibet, actually descendents of old royal line at Lhasa, began to sponsor foundation of temples and monasteries, the training of scholars and trans. of texts throughout their domains, which stretched from Mt. Kailas westwards to Ladakh and southwards to Indian frontier. Their nearest sources for Buddh. teachers, texts, architectural styles and the rest, were Kulu and Kashmir, where Buddhism still flourished. The most famous Tib. scholar and translator of this period was Rin-chen-bzang-po (958–1055).

From now on T. monks and scholar-travellers from C. Tibet began to go to India in increasing numbers. Esp. noteworthy are 'Brog-mi (992–1072) and Mar-pa (1012–96), who became fountain-heads respectively of the *Sa-skya* and *bKa-rgyud-pa* orders of T. Buddhism. *'Brog-mi* studied one year in Nepal, then 8 years at Vikramashīla (Bihar), while Mar-pa spent more than 16 years at hermitage of his chosen teacher Nāropa at Phullahari (Bihar). In 1042 the great Indian teacher Atīśa, who had previously even visited Sumatra at invitation of its Buddh. rulers, arrived in Tibet at instance of rulers of W. Tibet. However he moved on to C. Tibet, where he remained until death at Nye-thang in 1054. His personal influence was enormous; there can have been few T. relig. leaders of the day who were unaffected by his personal example. His favourite disciple was 'Brom-ston (1008–64), who founded the monastery of Rva-sgreng (1056) and the relig. order of the *bKa'-gdams-pa*, lit. 'Bound by command'. However, the strictness of its ordinances did not appeal to most Tibetans, who clearly preferred freer and more colourful forms of relig.

In 1053 the monastery Sa-skya was founded by a disciple of 'Brog-mi, and this soon became centre of a new and powerful relig. order. Chief of Mar-pa's disciples was the gentle ascetic Mi-la Ras-pa, renowned as much for his songs as his magical powers. He transmitted his teachings to sGam-po-pa (1079–1153), whose direct disciples estab. six famous schools, all based on his teachings and within the gen. relig. order of the *bKa'-rgyud-pa*, lit. 'Transmitted Word'. These six were the Phag-mo-gru, Karma-pa, mTshal, 'Bri-khung-pa, sTag-lung-pa and 'Brug-pa. Some of these schools chose their head-lamas by the reincarnation system, as subsequently adopted in the case of the Dalai Lamas.

With the estab. of these schools T. Buddhism began to come into its own, and, as by this time the bulk of Indian Buddh. lit. had been trans. into Tibetan, the Indian connection became ever less important. Also T. villagers and herdsmen were by now as ready to accept the services of Buddh. monks as of their more familiar Bon priests, and Buddhists and Bon-pos practised often quite amicably side by side. Bitter animosities sometimes developed between the various Buddh. orders, not on doctrinal but on political grounds. Many of these orders and their individual monasteries were closely connected with noble families and so became involved in their rival ambitions.

While Moslem invaders were laying waste the great relig. establishments of N. India, the → Mongols led by Genghiz Khan, who became chief in 1206, were slaughtering the inhabitants of N. China as first stage of their ruthless conquest of a huge Asian empire. Thus T. monks and lamas, now that India was lost to them as a land of religion, soon began to find scope for missionary activity amongst the Mongols, a relig. task which brought great material advantages esp. when Kublai Khan became Emperor of China. The grand lama of Sa-skya thus became a kind of vassal-ruler of Tibet and this arrangement lasted until 1354, when Byang-chub rGyal-mtshan of Phag-mo-gru overcame Sa-skya and won Mongol recognition. After 130 years of rule the Phag-mo-gru were forced out by the Rin-spungs princes, and they in turn by the rulers of gTsang. These different families all represented rival relig. interests, and throughout whole disturbed period there was a complex interplay of alliances between noble families and monastic centres. Buddhism was by now fully integrated with T. society and internal politics. Despite holiness and genuine learning of some monks and prelates, the outward worldliness of the estab. relig. orders seems to have resulted in reaction in favour of a new reformed order which had its beginnings in life and teachings of the great relig. figure Tsong-kha-pa (1357–1419). Known as the *dGe-lugs-pa*, lit. 'Model of Virtue', this new school grew rapidly in popularity and influence under guidance of his able successors. The Mongol (Yüan) dynasty of China was succeeded by the Ming, a nationalist dynasty, but T. lamas seem to have maintained links with certain Mongol clans. The head lamas of the dGe-lugs-pa order involved themselves with one of these, whence they received the title *Ta-le*, written as Dalai by Westerners. In 1642, thanks to the Mongol chief Gu-shri Khan, the Fifth Dalai Lama overcame his rivals, and from that time dates predominance of dGe-lugs-pa (nicknamed 'Yellow Hat') order in Tibet and the political eclipse of all older orders, although some of them have managed to keep their relig. life intact up to present day. Mongol and Chinese interference in Tibet in time of Sixth Dalai Lama resulted from 1721 onwards in a vague kind of Chinese suzerainty over Tibet, readily accepted by the great dGe-lugs-pa prelates in so far as the Manchu Emperors (until end of their dynasty in 1911) remained generous patrons of T. Buddhism.

No comprehensive canon of Mahāyāna and Vajrayāna Buddhism ever existed in India; but, by trans. into Tibetan in course of some six cents. all canonical, quasi-canonical works, as well as commentarial and independent writers of Indian Buddh. teachers that they could find, the Tibetans grad. built up their own canon, which had assumed by 13th cent. more or less its present form. Chief credit for this goes to the great scholar and encyclopaedic writer Bu-ston (1290–1364). It was divided into two parts: the canon proper known as the *Kanjur* ('Translated Word'), containing works attrib. to the 'historical' → Buddha Śākyamuni, to various transcendent Buddhas and to tantric divinities identified as Buddhas; secondly the Commentaries known as the *Tanjur* ('Translated Treatises') containing trans. writings of Indian scholars and teachers. The *Kanjur* comprises 100 or 108 printed volumes (depending on the ed.), and the *Tanjur* comprises 225 volumes. These vast collections of Indian Buddh. lit. provide the doctrinal basis for T. relig. The most significant parts are the texts on

Monastic Discipline (Skr. → *Vinaya*), the 'Perfection of Wisdom' literature (Skr. → *Prajñāpāramitā*), the great *Mahāyāna-Sūtras* and lastly the Tantras representing the Vajrayāna. The texts on Monastic Discipline are those of the Indian Buddh. School known as Mūlasarvāstivādin; in context they correspond closely with the *Vinaya* texts of the → Theravādin. The 'Perfection of Wisdom' texts provide philosophical basis of T. Buddhism and are prob. the most revered of all relig. books in Tibet. It would be a poor temple indeed which did not contain the 18 volumes of this partic. set. However, the works which are the chief inspiration of T. Buddh. practice are the → *Tantras*, with their descriptions of the great divinities and of sets of divinities arranged as 'mystic circles' (Skr. *maṇḍala*), their collections of spells (Skr. *mantra*) by which the divinities are invoked, their refs. to consecration-rituals and to symbolic ritual of sexual union, their teachings of essential identity of microcosm of human body with macrocosm of universe, and their conviction that Buddhahood can be gained in course of a single life by those who know how. The essence of the Vajrayāna is the symbolic use of imagined divine forms, which repr. at one and same time the five components (→ *skandha*) of human personality, the five points of space (the centre and the four quarters), the five evils (stupidity, wrath, desire, malignity and envy) and the five wisdoms (pure absolute, mirror-like, discriminating, undifferentiated and active) usually repr. by the five Buddhas named Illuminator, Imperturbable, Jewel-Born, Boundless Light and Infallible Success. These five-fold sets, which stand for human personality and the infinite universe on the one hand, and the perversity of phenomenal existence and the purity of Buddhahood on the other, are the basic assumptions around which all tantric practice revolves. The main purpose of temple ceremonies is to bring a specified set of divinities face to face with the worshippers to gratify them with sacrificial offerings (e.g. lights, incense, sacrificial cakes, consecrated alcohol etc.), to receive their empowering blessings, and to dismiss them when they came. Such a set of divinities, already well known to the participants from their earlier training in meditation upon them, act as 'integrators' of the human personality, strengthening it in its aspirations towards the perfection of Buddhahood. Watching a community of T. monks performing such a ceremony, one observes that each individual, unaware of his fellows, reverts to a form of individual meditation with his eyes fixed before him and his mind on the symbolic gestures, e.g. the miming of hand-gestures or the offering of universe in form of individual heaps of rice-grains.

T. monks and religious, perhaps numbering as many as half a million out of poss. total population of three million, repr. a large variety of relig. and social interests. From 8th cent. onwards there were always those who were scholars, usually translators and interpreters up to 12th cent.; thereafter commentators and instructors who worked entirely through medium of Tibetan, once cultural contacts with India were at an end. Despite achievement of their own vast canon and ever growing quantities of indigenous exegetical lit., oral trad. remained strong; even in 20th cent. many monk-scholars of the great dGe-lugs-pa monasteries around Lhasa might be highly skilled in philosophical and logical debate while still barely able to write their own name. In Tibet lit. scholarship has remained preserve of a minority of specially gifted individuals. Another import. minority has been concerned with methods of meditation and techniques of → yoga, derived ultimately from Indian yogins and monks of 10th and 11th cents., the peak period of T. interest in mediaeval Buddh. India. The older orders of T. Buddhism trace their origins back to the more illustrious of the Eighty-Four Magicians (*mahāsiddha*), many of whose works are preserved in tantric section of T. canon. The dGe-lugs-pa (Yellow Hat) order may be seen as reform movement in that its founder and his successors insisted upon strict monastic discipline and encouraged philosophical studies, thus turning away from freer ways of thought and of living allowed to those who claim to follow tantric yoga. While the older orders never abandoned normal monastic discipline, in many of their establishments, their docs. and practices were always at the disposal of married householders, who by their professional skill and knowledge might become 'lamas' in their own right, and also of those who contracted out of the limited responsibilities of cenobitic life, living as solitary ascetics and hermits. The most famous of these two categories are prob. the translator Mar-pa, who lived as ordinary householder, and, by contrast, his foremost pupil and successor Mi-la Ras-pa, who led a life of self-inflicted hardship and solitary meditation. However, the great majority of T. monks, whether belonging to older orders or the dGe-lugs-pa, have been content with normal round of easy-going monastic life, playing a full part in temple ceremonies or performing rituals on request in laymen's homes, doing a turn of polishing or marketing, preparing their own simple meals and beloved buttered tea, or going out on excursions with friends.

The term for an ordinary monk is *grva-pa* (pronounced 'trapa'), and *dge-slong* (pronounced 'gélong'), which trans. in early lit. the Skr. word *bhikṣu*, now ref. to a monk who has taken upon himself full set of monastic vows (corresponding to Skr. *pratimokṣa*). The term 'lama' (*bla-ma*) means 'superior', but may be used out of politeness for any venerable monk or village priest. (It corresponds to Catholic use of title 'father'). From 13th cent. onwards certain establishments, notably the Karma-pa, began to find their chief lamas when still children by making use of the regular Buddh. theory of → rebirth. Thus a successor was sought in an infant showing signs indic. that he was a reincarnation of a deceased head- ama. The orig. of idea is prob. to be found in the series of Indian yogins gen. ref. to as the Eighty-Four Great Magicians; for several of these had been conceived of as reincarnations of their predecessors. This reincarnation system was adopted by the dGe-lugs-pa order at end of 15th cent. in case of their own grand-lama, and thus the succession of Dalai Lamas (Dalai represents a Mongolian title meaning 'ocean') came into existence; the 14th in this series now lives as exile in India. The idea spread to many other relig. establishments, and by 20th cent. there were more than two hundred head-lamas in Tibet who had been discovered as 'reincarnations' in their early years. Other establishments, which chose not to adopt this system, continued to elect their abbots on their personal merits. In case of the great Sa-skya order succession was hereditary, usually from uncle to nephew.

Over the cents. the Tibetans have developed an extraordinary devotion for their relig. in all its outward forms. They have depended upon their monks and lamas in times of sickness and in order to ensure prosperity. Ceremonies and relig. pageants have added colour and interest to their lives, much as was case in mediaeval Europe. The layfolk themselves often show great personal devotion, visiting temples, reciting invocations, making numerous prostrations, and going on long pilgrimages as holiday excursions. T. Buddhism has absorbed much T. pre-Buddh. relig. (→ Bon) in form of local divinities, now accepted into Buddh. pantheon, oracles and divination, horoscopes and fortune-telling which play so large a part in life of Tibetans of all classes. D.L.S.

Sir Charles Bell, *Tibet Past and Present* (1924); Bu-ston, *History of Buddhism* (E.T. 1931–2); D. L. Snellgrove, *Buddhist Himālaya* (1957); *The Hevajra-Tantra* (1959); *Four Lamas of Dolpo* (1967); W. Y. Evans-Wentz, *Tibet's Great Yogi Milarepa* (1928); *Tibetan Yoga and Secret Doctrines* (1935); *The Tibetan Book of the Dead* 3rd edn. (1959); sGam-po-pa, *Jewel Ornament of Liberation* (E.T. 1959); G. Tucci, *Tibetan Painted Scrolls* (1949); L. A. Waddell, *The Buddhism of Tibet* (1958[2]); R. A. Stein, *La Civilisation tibétaine* (1662); H. E. Richardson and D. L. Snellgrove, *A Cultural History of Tibet* (1968).

T'ien Chinese term. Apart from cases where T. means 'the sky', it corresponds with our word 'Heaven', in sense of Providence, Nature, God. The character seems to have orig. as a pictogram repr. an anthropomorphic concept of deity; but later explained in the *Shuo Wên* Dictionary (*c.* CE 200), in abstract terms, as that which is above men. The deity T. had no part in Shang Dynasty relig., and was prob. intro. by the Chou Dynasty (*c.* 1000 BC) into relig. of China as a supreme sky god. The term was used in close apposition to → Shang Ti for Supreme Deity. → Confucius used the term T. almost exclusively for the Overruling Providence. He honoured T. as source of goodness (*Ana.* 8:19), acknowledged his dependence on T. (*Ana.* 6:26), understood T.'s will for him (*Ana.* 2:4), and believed that T. approved him (*Ana.* 14:37). T. cannot be deceived (*Ana.* 9:11), guides men's lives (*Ana.* 11:8) and cares (*Ana.* 9:5; 7:22). → Mo-tzŭ taught that T. is righteous and loving. Later (e.g. with → Hsün-tzŭ), T. came to be conceived of in purely naturalistic terms. The worship of T. in Chi. relig. was the supreme act of worship, performed by ruler on an altar, never enclosed in a temple but under open sky, and round to symbolise Heaven. The emperor was Son of Heaven (T'ien Tzŭ), and owed his mandate to rule from T. In popular relig. T., conceived anthropomorphically, was recognised as Supreme Deity under the title Lao T'ien Yeh ('The Venerable Ancient T.').

The R.C. church in China took the term T'ien Chu (Lord of Heaven) as name for God, whilst Protestants preferred the term Shang Ti. D.H.S.

H. G. Creel, *Studies in Early Chinese Culture*, 1st Ser. (1938), p. 51; D. H. Smith, 'Divine Kingship in Ancient China', in *Numen*, vol. 4 (1957); A. Waley, *The Analects of Confucius* (1938), pp. 41ff.

T'ien T'ai (→ Tendai). The most influential Chi. sect of → Buddhism during T'ang Dynasty. Founded by Chih I or Chih K'ai (538–97), in a famous monastery on the T'ien T'ai mountains of S.E. China, its basic text is the → *Lotus Sūtra*, in which is to be found the quintessence of Buddhism: → Sakyamuni Buddha is but an earthly manifestation of the Eternal Buddha. Chih I relied extensively on theories of → Nāgārjuna. He emphasised idea of totality, the whole and its parts being identical. The whole cosmos and all the Buddhas were present in a grain of sand. Absolute Mind embraces universe in its entirety. In its substance Absolute Mind is the same; in its functioning it is differentiated. In T.T. the practical expression of relig. was linked to spiritual cultivation and pursuit of wisdom by concentration (*chih*) and insight (*kuan*). A remarkable spirit of toleration pervaded T.T.; for all interpretations of Buddha's teaching found place in its grand scheme. It divided teachings of Buddha into five periods, regarded not as contradictory but as progressive, leading up to the *Lotus Sūtra*, the crown, quintessence and plenitude of Buddhism. The school is not only import. for its doctrines; but for great monastic foundations which flourished during the T'ang Dynasty until great persecution of 845, from which time forward T'ien T'ai rapidly declined in China. It was also influential in → Korea, and was intro. into Japan early in 9th cent. D.H.S.

K. L. Reichelt, *Truth and Tradition in Chinese Buddhism* (1927), pp. 49ff.

-Tijanīyya → Ṣūfī Orders. J.R.

Ti-Lakkhaṇa (Pali); **Tri-Laksana** (Skr.) Buddh. term for the 3 aspects or characteristics of all phenomenal existence. These characteristics are: (1) → *anicca* (Pali)/*anitya* (Skt.), impermanence; (2) → *dukkha* (Pali)/*dukkha* (Skt.), ill or imperfection; and (3) → *anatta* (Pali)/*anātman* (Skt.), lit. 'soullessness' or impersonality. T.O.L.

Tillich, Paul Johannes (1886–1965) Born in Prussia, educated in Germany, Tillich began his career in Berlin; he held chairs in Philosophy and Theology in German universities before emigrating to U.S.A., where he completed his life work. His theology reveals influence of → Kierkegaard, Schelling, Heidegger and the liberal theology in which he was grounded. The strong strain of liberalism in his thought is evident in his opposition to the neo-orthodox insistence that the Bible is only source of theology. Theology is for him both kerygmatic and apologetic. That is, the theologian must express eternal truth of Gospel in terms which are the cultural currency of his partic. generation. The theologian must both be involved in different forms of culture, and work within 'the theological circle' as member of Chr. Church. Theology is an essent. rational activity proceeding by careful definition and strict inference, and developing systematic thought. It is necessarily correlated with philosophy, and elicits answers to questions concerning man's situation which philosophy raises. The language of theology and religion is entirely symbolical, though there are exceptions to this. Originally, T. made only one exception—the definition of God as Being itself, but he later spoke of other exceptions. To assert God's existence is for T. the only real atheism. The trad. arguments for God's existence are, he thinks, an expression of the *question* of God implied in human finitude. Thus they show ways in which reason actually seeks revelation. Turning to → Christology, T. regards it as answer to man's existential situation of sin. Sinful man is estranged from ground of his being and from his own essential being. This is the universal character of existence, and the structures of evil drive man to despair. Jesus Christ reveals God in such a way that whole of human life has been changed. Though the → Incarnation was a fact, we have no account of → Jesus' life which is a purely historical record. Historical criticism has 'no direct relevancy for the doc. of the Christ'. This doc. is that Christ brings new Being into world because in him essential manhood comes into existence. Certainty concerning the Incarnation comes to the Christian through his experience as member of Church, a society of faith and love. The being of the Church is paradoxical, in sense that there are two valid and equally necessary ways of looking at it: the theological and the sociological. So T. rejects suggestion that there is an invisible Church as well as a visible. On question of meaning of history, T. says Chr. answer is given in symbol of Kingdom of God. This expresses the ultimate fulfilment, in which contrast between essence and existence is overcome universally and completely. The Kingdom does not belong entirely to another world. We can discern in history the fragmentary victories of Kingdom of God, which point to non-fragmentary side of Kingdom of God 'above' history, which is the 'end' of history. J.H.-T.

Tillich's main works are: *Systematic Theology* (3 vols.), *Protestant Era*, *The Interpretation of History*, *The Courage To Be*.

Cf. J. L. Adams, *Tillich's Philosophy of Culture* (1965); K. Hamilton, *The System and the Gospel* (1963); J. Heywood-Thomas, *Paul Tillich—An Appraisal* (1963); Kegley and Bretall (ed.), *The Theology of Paul Tillich* (1952); D. H. Kelsey, *The Fabric of Paul Tillich's Theology* (1967); B. L. Martin, *Tillich's Doctrine of Man* (1966).

Time (basic significance) Man's awareness of T. causes within him a sense of fundamental insecurity: he knows that he is subject to change, decay and death. This sense of insecurity is a basic motivating force in his relig., and finds various forms of expression. Five forms may be distinguished: security from T. has been sought by ritual magic (e.g. in Egypt); T. has been deified (e.g. in India, Iran, → Mithraism); in → metempsychosis, T. is the 'sorrowful weary wheel' of existence in the phenomenal world, which is mistaken for reality; in Heb. relig., T. is revelation of God's purpose for Israel; in Christianity, T. is interpreted teleologically as the unfolding and achievement of the divine plan for → man's slavation. The fundamental significance of T. for understanding man and his relation to the universe is now becoming increasingly appreciated. (→→ Religion, Origin; Zurvan; Americ. Relig. anc.) S.G.F.B.

S. G. F. Brandon, *History, Time and Deity* (1965)—extensive bibliography; J. T. Fraser (ed.),

The Voices of Time (1966); E. Vogelin, *Anamnesis* (1966).

(Chinese views) The doc. of relativity of both T. and space, taught by Taoist philosophers →→ Lao-tzŭ and Chuang-tzŭ was subject of discussion by the Dialecticians of 4th cent. BC. It may be summed up in famous paradox of Hui Shih (*c.* 380–305 BC) 'one goes to the state of Yüeh today and arrives there yesterday'.

A cyclical interpret. of history is attr. to → Mencius, who taught that periods of order succeeded to period of chaos, and that every 500 years a sage would emerge to put world in order (Mencius 2b:13; 7b:38). A cyclical theory of T. exercised tremendous influence in Han Dyn. (206 BC–*c.* CE 200), and continued to dominate Chi. philos. thought throughout history. On basis of unity of man and nature, the operation of cycles was deemed to be a universal pattern controlling human affairs and nature alike. The great Buddh. scholar Sêng Chao (384–414), argued that since the past is not found in the present, nor present in past, T. is unreal. Motion, too, is illusory since motion depends on T. The neo-Confucian Shao Yung (1011–77) attempted to form a metaphysical theory of history. He argued that past, present and future are due to our subjective point of view. He regarded history as an infinite number of cycles, and held that one revolution consist of 12 generations or 360 years; an epoch consists of 30 revolutions or 10,800 years; a cycle consist of 12 epochs or 129,600 years. The first three epochs in a cycle give birth to heaven, earth and man successively. By end of 6th. epoch → Yang has reached height of its influence and begins to give way to → Yin; this results in decline until eventually, after 129,600 years, the cycle ends and another begins. This arbitrary scheme was evidently influenced by Buddh. concepts of T. and idea of an infinite series of worlds. The mod. Confucian scholar K'ang Yu-wei (1858–1927), greatly influenced by W. thought, attempted to bring a linear view of T. within scope of trad. Confucian thought with its cyclical view. He conceived T. as an evolutionary process from chaos, through a period of approaching peace to a final period of great peace and unity.

The Chinese were always greatly concerned with recording of T. Tremendous importance was given to the calendar, promulgated annually by emperor with the assistance of the Board of Astronomy. Two methods were employed in recording T. One was the cycle of 60 years. This sexagenary cycle was formed from two sets of characters: the 12 Earthly Branches and 10 Heavenly Stems. Combined together in sets of two, they recorded the years. The other method employed was to record the years of a reign or part of reign, as the reign-name was often changed during the life-time of a monarch. Until mod. times the Chinese followed a lunar year, dividing each month into periods of 10 days. By use of intercalary months the lunar year was adjusted to a solar time-scale, the commencement of the year being determined by the sun. The 24 hours of day and night were divided into 2 hourly periods. All seasonal activities and festivals of the Chinese were regulated by the calendar. (→ Ages of World). D.H.S.

W. T. Chan, *Source Book in Chinese Philos* (1963), *passim*; J. D. Ball, *Things Chinese*, 5th edn. (1925), pp. 661ff.; J. Needham, in J. T. Fraser (ed.), *Voices of Time* (1966).

(Hindu Views) The history of the universe, acc. to classical Hindu cosmology, is made up of recurring periods of creation and dissolution (only one of the orthodox schools, the → Mimamsa, denies this periodicity). Each period of creation is a *kalpa*, and corresponds to a day in the life of → Brahmā; at end of such a period the universe relapses into a dissolved state (a night of Brahmā). A kalpa lasts 4,320 million terrestrial years. A life of Brahmā lasts 100 years, a total cycle of over 300 million million earthly years; then there is a period of quiescence until a new Brahmā comes into existence. Thus the mythic cosmology of Hinduism (like that of Buddhism, which influenced classical Hinduism in this matter—the Vedic cosmology was much more modest in its scope) involves a cyclical view of universe. Within a kalpa, there is also a schematism of history—the period being divided into 14 *manvantaras* (→ Manu). Each of these comprises 71 *mahāyugas* (aeons), each of which is divided into 4 *yugas* (ages), viz. Kṛta, Tretā, Dvāpara and Kali, of diminishing lengths. During the mahayuga, virtue and happiness progressively diminish. Acc. to Vaisnavite trad., there is some periodic restoration, due to intervention of → *avatāras*; but these only arrest the decline, till coming of last avatara of the age, Kalki, who will usher in a new age, or at least the transition to the next mahayuga. The cyclical account of cosmos, with its immensities of epochs, contrasting so strikingly with the short-term view of history implicit in O.T. cosmology, fits in with belief in → rebirth and the suggestion in Hindu thinking that progress to liberation is an immense and arduous affair (except for those who have faith in the way of → *bhakti*). Another motif in the classical trad. is that Time is destructive—thus it is symbolised most clearly by → Kālī, the consort of Śiva (her name is a feminine form of word for time in Sanskrit); likewise Time is described in the *Bhagavadgita* as destroyer of the worlds. By contrast, true liberation is often thought of as consisting in a timeless, changeless state, beyond the power of decay and destruction.

Somewhat at variance with these notions is the mod. evolutionary doctrine of → Sri Aurobindo: here the ongoing of Time brings new spiritual potentialities, as though we are at the beginning of an epoch, rather than moving towards its end. (→→ Ages of World; Liberation). N.S.

S. G. F. Brandon, *History, Time and Deity* (1965); S. J. Samartha, *The Hindu View of History* (1959); A. Danielou, *Hindu Polytheism* (1964).

Tipiṭaka The canon of Buddh. scripture in Pali, regarded as authoritative by the → Therāvada; it is earliest form of Buddh. teaching available and the most complete. The name Ti-pitaka means 'three baskets'. These are (1) → Vinaya-pitaka; (2) → Sutta-pitaka; (3) → Abhidhamma-pitaka. (1) consists of narratives concerning estab. of the Buddh. → Sangha, and the rules governing its life. (2) consists of the *Suttas* or 'threads (of discourse)', i.e., dialogues of the Buddha and some of his disciples with various contemporaries, and is arranged in 5 collections, or *nikāyas* viz. →→ *Dīgha Nikāya; Majjhima-N; Anguttara-N; Samyutta-N; Khuddaka-N.* The Abhidhammapitaka consists of seven books, in which the doc. contained in popular, apologetic form in the *Suttas* is abstracted, condensed and systematised in numerical lists and under topic-headings. The Ti-pitaka is the form of Buddh. scripture which is regarded as authoritative in Theravada Buddh. countries of S. Asia, viz. Ceylon, Burma, Thailand, Cambodia and Laos; it is this, more than any other one single factor, which constitutes their unity as a group. Acc. to trad., compilation of this canon began immediately after death of Buddha, at Council held at Rajagaha (→ Councils, Buddh.). The canon was further developed at 2nd Council (at Vesāli), and was in all import. respects, incl. addition of the latest section, the Abhidhamma-pitaka completed by time of 3rd Council, held during reign of → Ashoka (at Patna). Ashoka, who holds so honoured a place among Theravādin Buddhists, is not mentioned in the canonical lit.; he is in the post-canonical Pali chronicles. The assumption is therefore that composition of canon had been completed and settled before time of Ashoka (3rd cent. BC). Distinction must be made, however, between fixing of canon in verbal trad., and its being committed to written form; the latter took place, acc. to evidence of chronicle entitled → *Dipavaṃsa*, in reign of King Vattagamini, i.e. during latter part of 1st cent. BC (*Dipavaṃsa* 20:20–1). The text of Pali T., which until 1855 remained in ms. form, in palm-leaf collections preserved mainly in Ceylon, Burma and Thailand, began to be printed as result of interest of European scholars, notably George Turnour of Ceylon Civil Service, who in 1837 had published part of non-canonical work *Mahāvaṃsa*, and of Fausboll, Oldenberg and T. W. Rhys-Davids. Since 1855 practically the entire text of T. in Pali has been trans. into Roman script and published by Pali Text Society of London. Most of text of the 5 *Nikāyas*, which make up the T. has also been trans. into Eng. and published as: *The Book of the Discipline* (Vinaya-pitaka) 5 vols. (1938–52) (vol. VI to follow); *Dialogues of the Buddha* (*Dīgha Nikāya*), 3 vols. (1899–1921); *Middle Length Sayings* (*Majjhima-N.*), 3 vols. (1954–9); *The Books of the Gradual Sayings,* (*Anguttara-N.*), 5 vols. (1932–6); *The Book of Kindred Sayings* (*Samgutta-N.*), 5 vols. (1917–30); various books of the *Khuddaka-N.* separately as follows: *Khuddaka-patha and Dhammapada* (Minor Anthologies, vol. I) (1931); *Udāna and Itivuttaka* (Minor Anthols., vol. II) (1935); *Sutta-nipāta* (*Woven Cadences*) 2nd edn. (1948); *Vimāna vatthu and Petavatthu* (Minor Anthols., vol. IV) (1942); *Theragāthā* (*Psalms of the Brethren*) (1913), (*Psalms of the Sisters*) (1909, repr. 1964); *Jataka Stories*, 6 vols. (1895–1907) (repr. as 3 vols. 1956); *Buddhavaṃsa and Cariva-piṭaka* (Minor Anthols., vol. III) (1938). The books of the Abhidhamma-pitaka, published in trans. by the Pali Text Society are: *Puggala-paññantii* (*A Designation of Human Types* (1922); *Kathā-vathu* (*Points of Controversy*) (1915); *Dhātukathā* (*Discourse on Elements*) (1962). (→ Tripitaka). T.O.L.

-Tirmidhī Abū 'Īsā Muḥammad b. 'Īsā (d. 279/892), noted traditionist from Tirmidh on the Amu Darya. He travelled to learn → trads. and was a pupil of → Bukhari. T. was credited with remarkable powers of memorising. His collection of trads., called *Jāmi*' (comprehensive), is one of the six → Sunni canonical works. He discusses each trad. using technical terms to indic. its value, and ends with ch., unfortunately incomplete, giving explanation of his terminology. His classification is import. in develop. of criticism of trads.; but only after considerable delay did the community recognise his work at its true value. J.R.

E.I., IV, pp. 796f.; *G.A.L.*, I, pp. 169f., *S.*I., pp. 267ff.; Goldziher, *M.S.*, II, pp. 252f. etc.; J. Robson, 'Transmission of T.'s Jāmi'', *B.S.O.A.S.* (1954), xvi/2, pp. 258ff.

Tīrthaṁkaras Title of the 24 great teachers of → Jainsim, the last being → Mahavira. Lit. word means 'one who makes a ford', sc. across stream of existence. Only the last two, → Parsva and Mahavira, can be counted as historical figures. Trad. Jain mythology schematises succession of T., the years between one teacher and next descending proportionately. Thus the gap between the first, Ṛṣabha, and second, Ajita, is 37,760 million million years; while that between Parsva and Mahavira is only 250. The T. are objects of veneration in Jain temple-cult; but strictly they, as liberated life-monads (→ *jiva*), motionless at summit of cosmos (→ cosmology, Jain), can have no transactions with rest of existence, so they are not deities who aid worshipper on path towards → salvation. A list of the T. and their characteristics is found in J. Jaini, *Outlines of Jainism* (1940). N.S.

Titans → Hesiod (*Theog.* 424) refers to 'the former Titan gods', whom he repr. embattled against the Olympian gods (→ Greek Relig.). The Olympian gods signify the good order of (Grk.) universe; the T. monstrous forces of disorder. The struggle between them may reflect memory of Olympian relig. ousting → Aegean relig. In → Orphism, the T. kill and eat → Zagreus. S.G.F.B.
E.R.E., XII, *s.v.;* Brandon, *C.L.*, pp. 173ff.

Toledoth Yeshu (Heb. = 'History of Jesus') A medieval anti-Christ. account of Jesus written in Hebrew; it dates from 13th cent., but poss. derives from earlier Aramaic work. It repr. Jesus as illegitimate son of Mary by a Roman soldier Panthera, a calumny dating back to 2nd cent. The miracles of Jesus are ascribed to black magic. The work is to be evaluated primarily as a Jew. response to Christ. propaganda and persecution. J. Klausner, *Jesus of Nazareth* (E.T., 1929), pp. 47ff. S.G.F.B.

Tolerance (China–Japan) Though Chinese in gen. are extremely tolerant of a man's personal relig. beliefs, from time that → Confucianism was estab. as supreme orthodoxy of the state, a strict administrative control over relig. sought to guard interests of ruling power against any poss. subversive influence of heterodoxy. Any relig. belief or activity divergent from state orthodoxy might be regarded as heterodox and an object of intolerance by authority and law. → Taoism and → Buddhism were accorded legal right to exist; though regarded by Confucian scholars as heterodox, the essence of their teaching was blended with Confucianism, and their gods, Buddhas, temples and priesthoods officially recognised.

T. varied from time to time acc. to proclivities of emperor and his advisers. At times intense persecution broke out, motivated by political and economic rather than relig. considerations. The emperor always maintained a strict monopoly over performance of rituals for worship of Heaven. T. was not granted to heretical, sectarian and secret relig. societies, which were rigorously persecuted. Behind this intolerance shown to heterodoxy lay concern for the three basic relationships of sovereign and minister, father and son, husband and wife; the maintenance of the five Confucian virtues; and fear of competitive centres of political power.

The numerous foreign communities in China were allowed to practise their own religs. and were accorded considerable measure of T. so long as their practices were not inimical to public morality and state interest. Proselytism was gen. frowned upon. In 19th cent., T. was forced upon the Chi. gov. in respect of Christianity, which was regarded with suspicion as an agent of W. imperialistic designs. When the Chi. Republic was proclaimed, freedom of relig. belief was made an article of new constitution and so remains, though present attitude of Communism to all religs. is intolerant.

The close assoc. of → Shinto with state and with nationalistic spirit of the Japanese has resulted in periodic displays of intense intolerance of other faiths, though the Japanese throughout hist. times have been prone to accept and assimilate relig. and cultural ideas from outside. Japan owes an immeasurable debt both to Chi. culture and to Buddhism. For 1,000 years Shinto and Buddhism developed in reasonable T. side by side with mutual borrowings. (→ Ryobu Shinto). From early 17th cent. onwards, during Yedo period (1615–1868), a period of intense persecution of Christians and expulsion of foreigners was followed by nationalistic revival of Shinto, and attempts to undermine pervasive influence of Buddhism. Relig. intolerance again reached peak in years immediately preceding World War II, when rigid state control over relig. expression was imposed and all activities deemed inimical to national aspirations were rigorously suppressed. (→ Attitude to other religs., China–Japan →→ Heresy; Orthodoxy; Persecution). D.H.S.
C. K. Yang, *Relig. in Chinese Society* (1961), ch. 8.

Toleration (Islam) → Protected Peoples. J.R.

Toltecs → American Relig. (ancient). C.A.B.

Tombs (Islam) Acc. to strict Muslim teaching structures should not be erected over graves, a rule not gen. observed. Most countries have elaborate T. of import. persons; some fine examples of architecture, to mention only the Taj Mahal at Agra, erected by Shah Jahan in honour of his wife Mumtaz Mahal, witness that strict doc. cannot control everyone. The → Wahhabis have expressed strong disapproval of sepulchral monuments and have destroyed many; but they have not interfered with Muḥammad's tomb at Medina. Where they have authority, they have destroyed → saints' tombs. J.R.
Hughes, pp. 635–9; Wensinck, *Handbook*, pp. 89f.; Gaudefroy-Demombynes, *Institutions*, pp. 172 f.

Torah Heb. word meaning 'teaching', 'instruction', 'guidance'. In → Judaism it came to designate revelation of Yahweh's law for Israel in → Pentateuch, which is consequently called the T. The term sometimes has other connotations, e.g. to distinguish Biblical legislation from that of → Rabbis. S.G.F.B.
E.J.R., p. 387.

Torii, Tori-wi A distinguishing feature of → Shinto temples. Consists of sort of gate-frame composed in its simplest form of two vertical posts supporting two horizontal ones. Symbolically they are supposed to repr. bird-perches, as, acc. to Shinto mythology, the singing of birds assisted to invoke return of → Amaterasu, the sun-goddess, when she had withdrawn into a cave and deprived world of her light. Orig. made of unpainted tree-trunks, mod. T. are often more elaborate, sometimes made of concrete or bronze, and often painted in bright red and black. Each main Shinto temple usually has three T., the first one marking entrance to sacred precinct, the others spaced on main road to the → *honden.* T. are sometimes used to mark sacred character of some natural or man-made object. D.H.S.

J. Herbert, *Shinto* (1967), pp. 95ff.

Totemism Name, adopted from Ojibwa Indians, for a complex of ideas and practices, both anc. and widespread, connecting men with animals. → Paleolithic relig. provides evidence of sense of kinship with animals, and the cultures of primitive peoples in both anc. and mod. world attest continuance of this sense. T. is not a relig., but it finds relig. expression in widespread worship of animals. It has been esp. influential in social institutions, partic. marriage. (→ N. Americ. Indian Relig.). There is much doubt today about the validity of applying concept of T. to relig. phenomena formerly identified as such; the symbolic factor has been stressed. S.G.F.B.

J. G. Frazer, *Totemism and Exogamy*, 4 vols. (1935[5]), suppl. 1937; *E.R.E.*, XII, *s.v.; R.G.G.*[3], VI, col. 954–6; Ad. E. Jensen, *Mythos u. Kult bei Naturvolkern* (1951); E. O. James, *Prehistoric Religion* (1957), pp. 234ff.; A. Laming, *Lascaux* (E.T. 1959); G. van der Leeuw, *La religion* (1948), *passim*; M. Eliade, *Patterns of Comparative Relig.* (E.T. 1958), *passim*; C. Lévi-Strauss, *Le totémisme audjourd'hui* (1962).

Tradition (Islam) → Ḥadīth. J.R.

Transcendentalism T. (or New England T.) was an American relig. and philos. theory, having roots partly in European romantic idealism (esp. Goethe, Coleridge and Carlyle) and partly in New England → Puritanism. Intensely individualistic, T. combined relig. liberalism with political democracy in a framework of literary romanticism. It involved a pantheistic view of God and nature, an insistence on freedom of conscience, self-reliance and the absolute personal value of the moral law. T. emerged in 1830s and 1840s in writings of a group of New England authors, notably Ralph Waldo Emerson (1803–82) and Henry David Thoreau (1817–62). Emerson was → Unitarian minister, but resigned after refusing to administer the Eucharist. His characteristic teachings were expressed in his only book, *Nature* (1836), and in his many essays, poems and lectures, among which his address on *The American Scholar* (1837) and *Harvard Divinity School Address* (1838) are deserving of mention. All express, in some form, the conviction that the inner life of man parallels life of nature ('the law of correspondence', derived in part from Emanuel Swedenborg), and that each individual is unique: his advice to divinity students was to 'go alone . . . refuse the good models . . . cast behind you all conformity'. Emerson was primarily a theorist: Thoreau a man of action. Thoreau is best known for experiment in solitary living recorded in his masterpiece *Walden* (1854); he was an early exponent of the theory and practice of civil disobedience.

Both Emerson and Thoreau were deeply, if uncritically, interested in Oriental literature; there are many traces of Hindu docs. in their writings. Deliberate, though often far from accurate, statements of docs. of →→ *karma* and *maya* are found in Emerson (see e.g. essay on 'Compensation'), and he never explicitly rejected doc. of → *samsara.* He and Thoreau read all trans. of Hindu, Buddh., Chinese and Islamic scriptures then available, but not for their own sake; their object was to find teachings which supported, or seemed to support, own views. In Thoreau's words: 'While the commentators and translators are disputing about the meaning of this word or that, I hear only the resounding of the ancient sea and put into it all the meaning I am possessed of, the deepest murmurs I can recall, for I do not in the least care where I get my ideas, or what suggests them.' But although the Transcendentalists were thus interested in Oriental religs. only from their own thoroughly eclectic viewpoint, they were indirectly instrumental in stimulating interest in Comp. Relig. in America. One of the impulses which eventually issued in the 1893 World's Parliament of Religions in Chicago came from New England.

These elements in T.—individualism, romanticism, puritanism, eclecticism—have all passed in various ways into fabric of Amer. relig., over against dominant orthodoxies. T. was in many ways America's declaration of intellectual and spiritual independence. In Emerson's own words, spoken in 1837: 'We will walk on our own feet; we will work with our own hands; we will speak our own minds.' E.J.S.

The literature of T. is vast, and growing, and selection is practically imposs. An outstanding gen. work is F. O. Matthiessen, *American Renaissance* (1941). See also A. Christy, *The Orient in American Transcendentalism* (1932); H. Shelton Smith, R. T. Handy and Lefferts A. Loetscher, *American Christianity* (1963), II, ch. 14; W. S. Hudson, *Religion in America* (1965), pp. 173ff.

Transmigration of Souls →→ Metempsychosis; Rebirth.

Transubstantiation, Doctrine of This doc. was elaborated in Middle Ages to account for change of bread and wine consecrated at → Eucharist into Body and Blood of Christ, acc. to orthodox belief. The doc. was based on a metaphysical analysis of objects into 'substance' (i.e. the inner essential nature) and 'accidents' (i.e. the external and variable form of manifestation). Acc. to doc. of T., at Eucharist the 'substance' of the bread and wine, changed into Christ's Body and Blood, while retaining their outward ('accidental') form of bread and wine. The Lateran Council of 1215 defined belief in T. as *de fide.*; the Council of Trent (→ Counter Reformation), reaffirmed this position against Prot. rejection of doc. S.G.F.B.

E.R.E., V, pp. 555ff.; Harnack, *H.D.*, VI, pp. 46ff., 232ff.; J. F. Bethune-Baker, *Intro. to Early Hist. of Christ. Doctrine* (1903), col. 393ff.; *R.G.G.*[3], I, pp. 26–8.

Trees, Sacred The cult of T. is anc. and widespread. T. have often been identified with a deity or regarded as its dwelling place: Egypt. and → Indus Valley art show goddesses within trees; the → *ded*-column, identified with → Osiris, may have been a tree; T. appear in Cretan relig. scenes. The Grk. dryads were tree-spirits; Grk. mythology assoc. many deities with T. (e.g. → Apollo with laurel (metamorphosis of Daphne), → Athena with the olive, → Attis with the pine and almond). The maypole prob. repr. a vegetation deity (→ Phallus, cult). T. with supernatural qualities also figure in many religs. The → Yahwist creation story tells both of T. of Life and a 'T. of Knowledge of Good and Evil' (Gen. 2:9, 15:3.1ff.). A T. or plant that 'makes the old man as the young man' appears in the Epic of → Gilgamesh. Rev. 22:1–2 describes a T. of Life in the New Jerusalem. In Norse mythology the ash-tree Yggdrasil supports the world. Islamic eschatology knows of a T. of Zaqqūm, which has bitter fruit. There are legends about the T. from which Christ's → cross was made; in Chr. folklore the yew symbolised immortality, and the Glastonbury thorn stemmed from staff of Joseph of Arimathaea. So far as a common factor can be discerned, behind such variety of faith and practice, it would seem to be man's awe for another order of life, often manifest in strange and impressive forms. It is doubtful whether cult of T. stems from feeling of kinship with nature, as has been suggested. S.G.F.B.

E.R.E., XII, pp. 448–57; *R.Ae.R.-G.*, pp. 82–7; *O.C.D.*, *s.v.*; Brandon, *C.L.*, pp. 132ff.; V. Cornish, *The Churchyard Yew and Immortality* (1946); J. G. Frazer, *The Magic Art*, II (*G.B.* 1936), chs. IX–X; M. Eliade, *Patterns in Comparative Relig.* (E.T. 1958), ch. 8; L. S. Lewis, *St. Joseph of Arimathaea at Glastonbury* (1937), pp. 21ff.; E. O. James, *The Tree of Life* (1966).

Tribal Religion, India A wide variety of tribal groups, lying outside main fabric of Hindu society, is found in Indian subcontinent. The pattern of tribal relig. was at one time even more complex, but in course of time many tribal groups got themselves assimilated into → caste structure. The economies of groups vary widely, from settled cultivation, through cattle-raising to hunting. There are also some criminal castes or tribes. The total number of tribes is 250; but some are well on the way to assimilation, partly under impact of mod. administration and education, encouraging more general adoption of patterns of settled agriculture. The tribal population is about 30 million, at 1951 census. Among import. tribes and others which have been subject of detailed anthropological study are: the Nagas (divided into five major groups) of N.E. Assam; the Garo (Assam); the Ho (Munda-speakers: the Chota Nagpur plateau); the Bhils (Rajasthan); the Gond and Bhumia (Madhya Pradesh); the Thakurs (Maharashtra); the Mer (Gujarat); the Saora (Orissa); the Chenchu (Andhra Pradesh); the Toda (Nilgiri Hills, Madras); the Kadar (Cochin, Madras). Also import. are the Vedda (Ceylon). It is not poss. to generalise about religs. of the groups, though typically there is belief in ancestral spirits, village deities, demonic forces and a supreme deity; the characteristic Hindu belief in → *karma* and rebirth is largely absent. N.S.

Dept. of Anthropology, Govt. of India, *Tribal Map of India* (1956); A. V. Thakkar *Tribes of India*, 2 vols. (1950–1); J. P. Mills, *The Rengma Nagas* (1937); R. Burling, *Rengsanggri: Family and Kinship in a Garo Village* (1963); D. N. Majumdar, *The Affairs of a Tribe: A Study in Tribal Dynamics* (1950), *A Tribe in Transition* (1937); Y. V. S. Nath, *Bhils of Ratanmil: An Analysis of the Social Structure of a Western Indian Community* (1960); L. N. Chapekar, *Thakurs of the Sahyadri* (1960); H. R. Trivedi, *The Mers of Saurashtra: An Exposition of their Social Structure and Organization* (1961); V. Elwin, *The Religion of an Indian Tribe* (1955); U. R. Ehrenfels, *The Kadar of Cochin* (1952); W. H. R. Rivers, *The Todas of the Nilgiri Hills* (1906); C. von Furer-Haimendorf, *The Aboriginal Tribes of Hyderabad*, 3 vols. (1943–8); C. G. and B. Z. Seligman, *The Veddas* (1911); W. J. Culshaw, *Tribal Heritage* (1949); H. Bhattacharyya, *The Cultural Heritage of India*, vol. 4 (1956).

Trickster The name 'T' was first given to a figure meriting description found in → N. American Relig. A similar character has since been distinguished in →→ African, Australasian, and

Polynesian Religs.; it is also found in → Greek Relig. (→ Prometheus tricked Zeus over parts of sacrificed animal reserved to gods), and Loki in → Scandinavian Relig. The 'T' appears in many diverse guises: deceiver, thief, parricide, cannibal, inventor, creator, benefactor, magician, perpetrator of obscene acts. Many attempts have been made to explain idea of 'T'; but none has been gen. accepted. The variety of form of 'T' may reflect mythological portrayal of a kind of surd-factor, of diverse manifestation and common occurrence in human experience. S.G.F.B.

L. Makarius, 'Le mythe de "Trickster"', *R.H.R.*, 175 (1969), pp. 17–46 (with bibliog.).

Tri-Kāya Doctrine (Buddh.) → Buddha-Kāya. T.O.L.

Trimūrti 'Having three forms/aspects': conception of God in classical → Hinduism as being threefold, in persons of →→ Brahma, Viṣṇu and Śiva, respectively creator, preserver and destroyer of universe. The threefold symbolism was taken over into art. The attempt has been made to identify a seal-carving of → Indus Valley Civilisation with the T., but this is doubtful. The three aspects of the divine Being were identified with the → *gunas*. The T. was a means of synthesising major cults and the → Brahmanical trad., but tended to be somewhat theoretical, since in fact relig. sentiment tended either to be sectarian or, as in case of the → Smartas, focused on more than three deities of the T. (since → Ganesh and Sūrya were added). Iconographically, the threefold representation of God, esp. Śiva, was not uncommon, the most famous instance being the T. statue at Elephanta, near Bombay, symbolising Śiva as Uma (his → *śakti*), Mahesvara, preserver of world, and the destructive Bhairava. (→ Trinity). N.S.

J. N. Banerjea, *The Development of Hindu Iconography* (1956); Sir J. Marshall, *Mohenjo-daro and the Indus Culture*, 3 vols. (1931); H. Zimmer, *Myths and Symbols in Indian Art and Civilization* (1962).

Trinity, Doctrine of That there is One God existent in Three Persons is the central dogma of Chr. theology. Although the doc. is not definitively stated in N.T., certain passages could be cited as authorising it: e.g. Mt. 28:19. The deification of Jesus made such a doc. theologically necessary, since → monotheism was a basic axiom which Christianity inherited from its Jew. origins (→ Christology). Because the → Holy Spirit was also regarded as a distinct entity, a formula had to be found which guarded against apparent belief in three Gods, yet avoided conceiving of Father, Son and Spirit as merely aspects of one divinity. The Grk. word *trias*, 'trinity', had been used by Theophilus of Antioch (*c.* 180); but there was much bitter controversy (→ Arianism) before doc. was finally estab. by Council of → Constantinople (381). The doc. of the T. is regarded by Christians as a mystery known through → revelation, not by unaided human reason, though it is held not to be contrary to reason. Triads of deities are known in other religs. (e.g. → Osiris-Isis-Horus in Egypt; the → Trimūrti in Hinduism); but these conceptions are not true parallels to Chr. T., which is essentially a subtle metaphysical composition, occasioned by peculiar orig. and development of Christianity. (→ 'Filioque' Clause). S.G.F.B.

Harnack, *H.D.*, 7 vols. *passim.*; A. E. Rawlinson (ed.), *Essays on the Trinity and Incarnation* (1928); L. Hodgson, *The Doc. of the Trinity* (1943); *E.R.E.*, XII, pp. 457–64; J. N. D. Kelly, *Early Christian Creeds* (1950); C. Welch, *The Trinity in Contemporary Theology* (1953).

Trinity (Islam) Islam denies Christ. doc. of the → Trinity, cf. Qur. iv:169, 'Believe in God and his messengers and do not say "Three"'; v:79, 'The Messiah, son of Mary, is only a messenger ... and his mother was a faithful woman'; v:116, where God asks Jesus if he told people to take himself and his mother as gods, and Jesus denies it. Islam has tended to think the T. is Father, Mother, Son. Mod. Muslim propaganda often treats the T. with ridicule, but medieval Muslim apologists discussed it more seriously. J.R.

Hughes, pp. 646f.; Bell, *Introduction*, pp. 141, 165; Sweetman, *I.C.T.*, index to each vol.

Tripiṭaka (Chinese) The collection of Buddh. scriptures, trans. into Chi. and known as the *San Tsang*, or Chi. T., is recognised as a most import. source for study of → Buddhism; partic. the → Mahāyāna of China and Japan. From earliest days of Buddhism in China, emphasis was laid on trans. of Skt. texts. Great schools of translators worked under guidance of Buddh. scholars such as → Kumarajiva, Paramartha, and → Hsüan-tsang, and produced a voluminous Buddh. literature. Already, by time of Tao-an (CE 374), the need arose for catalogues of Buddh. scriptures. The most famous of early catalogues is that known as the *K'ai Yüan*, completed in 730. In CE 1883 Bunjiu Nanjio, a Jap. scholar, published a definitive catalogue of extant Buddh. scriptures in Chi. (Oxford: and repr. in 1929); an edn. of the Chi. T., compiled by J. Takakusu, was published in 85 vols., between 1924 and 1932, known as the Taisho ed. Only a small proportion of this vast collection has been trans. into Eng.

The name *San Tsang* or T. is a misnomer, as besides the → Sūtra, the → Vinaya, and the → Abhidharma, there is a 4th sect. of miscellaneous works, incl. many orig. Chi. Buddh. writings, such as the *Sūtra of Hui-nêng*, the *Huang-Po Doctrine of Universal Mind*, and many other → Ch'an (Zen) writings.

In the *Sūtra Pitaka*, though most of works are Mahāyānist, incl. the great works of the → *Prajñāparamitā*, there are also → *Nikayas* by the → Theravadins and → *Agamas* by the → Sarvastivadins. In the same way the *Vinaya Pitaka*, and the *Abhidharma Pitaka* contain both Hinayānist and Mahāyānist works.

In all, the Chi. T. is estimated to be about 70 times the length of the Chr. Bible. Many of the works, preserved by various schools of Chi. Buddhism, are highly repetitive and differ very little from each other in essentials. But the Chi. reverence for the written word has allowed little to be discarded throughout the cents. (→ Tipitaka, Buddh.). D.H.S.

S. Beal, *Catena of Buddhist Scriptures from the Chinese* (1871); E. Conze *et al.*, *Buddhist Texts* (1954), pp. 271ff.; C. Humphreys (ed.), *A Buddhist Students' Manual* (1965), pp. 159, 178, 249ff.

Tri-Ratna The 'Three gems' or *Tri-ratna* are the 3 principal features of Buddh. relig., viz., the → *Buddha*, → *Dhamma* (Skt. *Dharma*) and → *Sangha*. Throughout S.E. Asia, Buddh. devotions, incl. those of lay people, always begin after ascription of honour to Buddha, with chant in which the devotee affirms his dependence on these three: '*Buddham saraṇaṃ gacchāmi; Dhammam saraṇaṃ gacchāmi; Sangham saraṇaṃ gacchāmi*,' i.e. 'I go for refuge to the Buddha; . . . to the Dhamma; . . . to the Sangha.' They are therefore known also as the '3 refuges'. Ref. to devotional practice of taking refuge in these 3 is found in Pali canon, in the → *Saṃyutta Nikāya* (E.T., *Kindred Sayings*, vol. I, p. 283). In the → *Mahā-parinibbāna Sutta* the Buddha is repres. as saying that he who steadfastly trusts in virtues of the 3 gems has already 'entered the stream', i.e. is a → *sotappana*, one who has set out on way to enlightenment.

The three are regarded as interrelated and interdependent, and from early refs. to three as a conventional formula, it is clear that affirmation of all three constitutes the bare minimum of Buddh. relig.; thus a system which affirmed the Buddha and his doc. only, without affirming also necessity of the relig. Order, the Sangha, would not properly be called Buddh. (→→ Devotions, Buddh.). T.O.L.

Tri-Yāna → *Yāna*. T.O.L.

Ṭulayḥa b. Khuwaylid al-Asadī came to Medina in 9/630 with some of his tribe and submitted to Muḥammad, but rebelled following year. In 11/632 he was defeated by → Khālid b. al-Walīd at Buzākha. He escaped and later accepted Islam. He had claimed to be a prophet, so the diminutive form of his real name, Ṭalḥa, is used in ridicule, cf. → Musaylima. Ṭ. fought with distinction in Iraq and Persia. Why he claimed to be prophet is not clear, as little or no record is left of his teaching. He was prob. a dissident tribal leader rather than prophet. J.R.

E.I., IV, pp. 830f.; Muir, *Life*, index, *Caliphate*, index (Ṭoleiḥa); Watt, *Medina*, index.

Tun Huang For over 1000 years, one of most import. Buddh. centres in China. From Han Dynasty (206 BC–CE 220), an import. stage-post at the E. end of the 'silk-road' to C. Asia, it became a great Buddh. centre and place of → pilgrimage. In 366 the first of the Buddh. cave-temples was begun; the construction of temples and grottoes continued throughout the next mil., until close of Yüan Dynasty (1368). At height of its fame, it boasted 1000 grottoes, of which only 480 remain, in which have been preserved thousands of sculptures and murals, recording the triumphs of Buddh. art in China. The earliest murals (386–581), revealing considerable foreign influence, present adaptations of anc. Chi. mythology and legends, together with stories from Buddh. scriptures. With the Sui Dynasty (581–618), the sculptures and paintings became more realistic and distinctively Chi., opening the way to the highly developed art of T'ang Dynasty (618–907), in which what is ostensibly relig. art depicting the ideal Buddh. paradises becomes excuse for a fascinating social commentary on the times. During Sung Dynasty (960–1279), when flames of war spread to T.H., the monks of the cave temples, before taking flight, sealed up their scriptures, scrolls and documents in one of the caves. These were accidentally discovered by a Taoist priest in 1900; in 1907 Sir Aurel Stein, and later Paul Pelliot, brought thousands of these scriptures, pictures and scrolls to the W., where their study has immeasurably enriched our understanding of Chi. relig. and culture. D.H.S.

P. Pelliot, *Les Grottes de Touen-Houang*, 6 vols. (1920); A. Waley, *A Catalogue of Paintings from Tun Huang* (1931).

Tutelary gods and spirits (China) As in China the family is unit rather than individuals of which it is composed, the T. gods worshipped are guardians of home and its lands, rather than gods attached to individual persons for their protection. In anc. China the most import. and universally worshipped guardian spirits were the *chung liu*, protector of the home, and the *shê* or spirit of the soil or earth. As the *Book of Rites* (→ *Li Chi*) says: 'The Lord of the home is Chung Liu, and the Lord of the country is Shê' (3:5). Assoc. with the *chung liu*, whose sacred place was directly under a hole in the roof thr. which the smoke of the hearth-fire escaped, were four other guardian deities of the home, presiding over the stove, well, outer gates and inner doors. Assoc. with the *shê* was *chi*, the god of millet who gave protection to crops. In later times *tsao-chün*, the god of the stove or the kitchen god, came to be universally worshipped throughout China as guardian of home, exercising power over all its members, determining length of their lives, and distributing riches or poverty at will. Annually he reported to the supreme God on conduct of family. Almost every home was also protected by door-gods, whose images were pasted on outer doors and whose function was to drive away demons and all evil influences.

Shrines to protective gods of rural places, known as *t'u ti*, are seen everywhere in China, in villages, along roads, on banks of canals etc. Incense is burned to them by those seeking their aid. These 'earth-gods' are under gen. protection of the T. god of city, the guardian king of walls and moats, whose name is *ch'êng wang*. Every city had its 'Ch'êng Wang' temple, to whom the magistrate and his officials periodically went to make their report, offering worship and sacrifice on behalf of all inhabitants. In times of plague, drought, floods etc. an image of Ch'êng Wang would be taken in procession from temple to scene of disaster, and there implored to exert his good influences to restore prosperity. D.H.S.

H. Doré, *Recherches sur les Superstitions en Chine* (1914–29), vol. 11, *passim*; C. B. Day, *Peasant cults in China* (1940), pp. 59ff.; E. T. C. Werner, *Dict. of Chinese Mythol.* (1932) *passim.*

(Japan) In Japan, as in China and all Far Eastern countries, a whole host of deities are worshipped mainly because of their guardian and protective functions. The gods of hearth, hall door and kitchen stove watch over home, whilst the numerous gods of vegetation are venerated as protectors of food. Inari, the god of rice, brings aid in all difficulties of life and is god of prosperity in every form. Protective gods of roads and highways form an import. group in → Shinto mythol. A T. god protecting a definite area, whether large or small, is *chingu-no-kami*, who must be propitiated when any encroachment is made on his territory such as the building of a house or temple or digging of a well. Shinto always gave great prominence to tribal and local T. deities, the so-called *ubusuna-no-kami* or guardian deities of one's birthplace. The newly-born child is taken to temple of the T. god for presentation, and ever afterwards his person is under that god's protection. By many Japanese Hachiman, the war-god, is considered as a great protective deity, assoc. and even identified with T. gods of local shrines. Soldiers often carry on their persons a relic from his shrine in belief that they will be under his protection in battle. D.H.S.

J. Hackin (ed.), *Asiatic Mythol.* (1932), pp. 385ff.; D. C. Holtom, *The National Faith of Japan* (1938), pp. 176, 203, 244; J. Herbert, *Shinto* (1967), *passim.*

Twice-Born The three upper classes of trad. Hindu society (→→ *varnas*, caste system) are counted as 'T-B.' or *dvija*, since they undergo full initiation into community figured as a rebirth, when they are invested with the sacred thread (→ Initiations, Hindu). Thus a line is drawn between them and the → *sudras* (and still more, the → untouchables). Since not everyone among the →→ *ksatriyas* and *vaisyas* underwent initiation in later Hinduism, the term *dvija* came increasingly to ref. to → Brahmin class. N.S.

Tychē Grk. 'fortune', 'chance'. In Hellenistic times T. was personified as goddess, and as *Agathē Tychē*, 'Good Fortune', was patroness of various cities. The historian Thucydides uses T. to denote situations that men could not anticipate or control. In philosophy, T. came to signify 'chance'. Polybius called T. 'that mighty *kainopoiousa*' ('revolutionary'). In Grk. romances T. was usually regarded as malicious. S.G.F.B.

O.C.D., *s.v.;* Brandon, *M.D.*, pp. 174ff.

U

Uccheda-vāda Buddh. term for the doc., repudiated as false, of *uccheda*, or annihilation, i.e. that no life of any sort continues after death of the body. In the *Brahma-jala Sutta*, the Buddha distinguished 7 diff. sorts of such annihilation doc. over against which he set the higher truth *D.N.*, i, 34). The doc. of the Annihilationists is sometimes referred to as *uccheda-diṭṭhi*, or the 'annihilation-illusion', which, together with *atta-diṭṭhi*, or the 'soul-illusion', constitute the 2 illusions, or false views, regarding personality. T.O.L.

T. W. Rhys-Davids (tr.), *Dialogues of the Buddha*, Part I (1956), pp. 46–9.

Udāna Book of Buddh. Pali canonical scriptures, the 3rd book of the → *Khuddaka-Nikāya*. It consists of collection of 80 solemn utterances (*udāna*) of the Buddha, each of which is preceded by a prose or prose and verse narrative indicating occasion for the solemn utterance. Under title *Verses of Uplight*, the U. was trans. by F. L. Woodward and pub. as *Minor Anthologies*, vol. 2 (1935), of the *Sacred Books of the Buddhists*. T.O.L.

Ugarit Name of anc. city found at Ras Shamra, on N. Syrian coast in 1928. Since that date excavation has revealed a Canaanite city that had trading relations with Egypt, Mesopot., and Aegean world (*c.* 1400–1250 BC). Most notable among rich finds are tablets inscribed with relig. texts in a language variously called 'Proto-Canaanite', 'Proto-Phoenician', 'Ugaritic'. These texts are of greatest value as evidence of relig. faith and practice of Canaanites at this period, and also for Semitic philology. Texts also have been found in Egyptian, Sumerian, Akkadian, Hittite, and Hurrite. The U. texts are of great importance for O.T. study; U. iconographic data and evidence of funerary practice are also very significant. (→ Canaanite Relig.). S.G.F.B.

C. F. A. Schaeffer, *The Cuneiform Texts of Ras Shamra-Ugarit* (1939), *Ugaritica*, 4 vols. (1939–62); R. de Langhe, *Les textes de Ras Shamra-Ugarit et leurs rapports avec le milieu biblique de l'Ancien Testament*, 2 vols. (1945), *Myth, Ritual and Kingship* (ed. S. H. Hooke, 1958), ch. V; G.-R. Driver, *Canaanite Myths and Legends* (1956); *R.G.G.*[3], VI, col. 1091–106; J. Gray, *The Krt Text in the Lit. of Ras Shamra* (1955); P. Fronzaboli, *Leggenda di Aqhat* (1955); A. S. Kapelrud, *The Ras Shamra Discoveries and the O.T.* (E.T. 1963).

Uḥud Mountain *c.* 3 miles N. of Medina. In 3/625, a year after their defeat at → Badr, the Meccans came seeking vengeance. Once again their numbers were greatly superior; though they had some success in the battle, they were unable to push their advantage home, and returned disappointed. → Muḥammad was wounded, but although he recognised a measure of set-back, it was explained as God's method of testing the Muslims (cf. Qur. iii:166, 172f.). J.R.

E.I., III, pp. 970f.; Guillaume, *Life*, pp. 370–426; Watt, *Medina*, pp. 21–9; Rutter, *Holy Cities*, II, pp. 242, 247f.

'Ulamā' (commonly spelt Ulema); pl. of *'ālim* (a learned man). This learning has to do with →→ Qur., Hadith and bases of Islamic law. The 'U., versed in such knowledge, have been able to give → *fatwas* on that basis, or administer the law, or guide regarding orthodox belief and practice. It is not a priestly class, but a class who have studied under learned men from whom they received acknowledgment of qualifications, and so entered this body. The 'U. are usually conservative. Although without stated authority, they have been welcomed as advisers, and their views have carried weight; but rulers who consulted them often acted independently. Attempts were made to control the 'U. by giving them official salaried positions; on the whole this has not influenced their expression of opinion. They have continued, whether recognised or not, to exert influence. Mod. adaptations of law and the estab. of separate states suggest the decline of their influence, but one should not underestimate the import. of popular aspect for them. J.R.

E.I., IV, p. 994; Hughes, p. 650; D. B. Macdonald, *Theology*, index; Schacht, *Jurisprudence*, index (Scholars); Levy, *Social Structure*, index; Watt, *Philosophy*, p. 38; Cragg, *Counsels*, index; Rahman, *Islam*, index.

'Umar b. al-Khaṭṭāb Second → Caliph (13–23/634–644). Hostile to → Muḥammad at first, he accepted the new relig. a few years before the → Hijra, and became an ardent follower. Muhammad later married his daughter Ḥafṣa. A man of strong views, 'U. has been credited by some with being Muhammad's mentor. During his Caliphate the empire was greatly extended. He changed title of office from *Khalīfa* (successor) to *Amīr al-mu'minīn* (commander of the faithful). A strict disciplinarian, he controlled his commanders as well as the populace. He estab. the calendar, starting from year of the Hijra. He set up a *dīwān* (register) of those entitled to state pensions, intro. certain extra prayers during → Ramadan (→ Prayer), expelled non-Muslims from Arabia, instituted office of → *qāḍī* and enforced strict punishments for misdemeanours. His life was austere, although his armies were acquiring great wealth by their conquests. He was assassinated by a Christ. slave and buried beside Muhammad and → Abū Bakr. J.R.

E.I., III, pp. 982ff. (critical account); Hughes, pp. 650ff. (conventional account); Pareja, index (Omar); Muir, *Caliphate*, pp. 82ff.; Watt, *Mecca*, index, *Medina*, index; Hitti, *History*, index.

Umayyads A Caliphate (40/41–132/661–750) estab. by Mu'āwiya, governor of Syria, after → 'Ali's assassination and → al-Hasan's abdication. Its capital was Damascus. Mu'awiya's son Yazīd had to deal with → Husayn's rising, but was unable to deal with 'Abdallah b. al-Zubayr who set himself up as Caliph in the Hijaz, gained influence in other parts of Arabia, and even in Syria and Iraq. He and his son had short reigns, then rule changed to another branch of family under Marwān. In Caliphate of his son 'Abd al-Malik, Ibn al-Zubayr was defeated and killed. 'Abd al-Malik became Caliph in 65/685 and reigned 20 years. Under him, and four sons who succeeded him, the domain of Islam spread to its widest limits, from Atlantic in W. to borders of China in E. 'Abbasid historians have accused the U., with one exception, of being irreligious and turning Caliphate into a kingdom, but this is not wholly justifiable. As result of 'Alid and 'Abbasid subversion the U. were eventually overthrown. Damascus capitulated, but U. rule was established in Spain, and later, the Amīr, 'Abd al-Raḥmān III, after being in office from 300/912, assumed title of Caliph in 317/929. But while this Caliphate remained in name till 423/1031, its glory departed when second Caliph, al-Ḥakam II, was succeeded by a 12 year old son. He and succeeding Caliphs were under power of military leaders. The capital was Cordova, chief centre of culture and learning in Europe at time. J.R.

E.I., IV, pp. 998–1012; Pareja, index (Umayyades-Andalus and U. -Syrie); Levy, *Social Structure*, index; Rahman, *Islam*, index.

Umma (People, community). In the Qur., U. commonly has relig. undertone, but not always. Yet chief idea speaks of a relation to God. Each U. received a messenger (x:48; xvi:38; xxiii:46, etc.) who was rejected and accused of falsehood, though not by all. Judgment will befall unbelievers (iv:45; xxviii:75). x:20 says mankind was orig. one U., but people went different ways; xvi:95 says if God had willed, he would have made of mankind one U.; but he leads astray and guides whom he wills. Muslims are the best U. (iii:106); but sections of Jews and Christians also deserve title, e.g. iii:109f.; v:70; vii:159.

→ Muḥammad instituted an U. in Medina, with constitution drawn up not long after the → Hijra. It incl. believers of → Quraysh and Yathrib, those who follow them, are attached to them, and fight along with them as a single U. It calls itself a document between → Emigrants and → Helpers, containing treaty and covenant with the Jews. One article says the B. 'Awf are an U. along with the believers, followed by a statement that Jews and Muslims each have their own relig. The wording is a little vague, poss. meaning that they are separate U.'s; united by treaty. Disputes are to be ref. to Muhammad, who claims to speak in God's name as leader. An import. point is that the U. is not constituted on tribal basis. The Muslims are an U., whose basis is relig., but this does not prevent it from working alongside an U. with a different religion. J.R.

E.I., IV, pp. 1015f.; Pareja, p. 70; Jeffery, *Vocabulary*, p. 69; J. Horovitz, *Koranische Untersuchungen* (1926), p. 52; Watt, *Medina*, pp. 221–50 and index; Rahman, *Islam*, index.

Ummī In the Qur. Muḥammad is called the U. prophet (cf. vii:156, 158). Muslims normally understand this to mean 'illiterate'; but though this enhances value of → Qur., there is reason to question it. The Qur. also uses the plural (cf. ii:73; iii:69; lxii:2), where it must mean something like Gentiles, or perhaps natives. Some suggest 'heathen'; but if sing. and pl. have same meaning, it is difficult to think of Muhammad being called a heathen prophet. lxii:2 says he was sent a messenger to the *ummiyyūn*, which might indicate he was raised in a heathen community. The chief point seemed to be that his people had previously had no prophet with an inspired book. A suitable word is hard to find, so one feels that 'gentile' raises fewest objections. It cannot mean 'illiterate', for Muhammad was brought up in a mercantile community and seems to have been a good business man, if the story of his successful conduct of → Khadīja's business is correct. One would expect this to involve ability to keep accounts. Arberry trans. 'the prophet of the common folk'; Blachère 'le Prophète des Gentils'; Paret has 'heidnisch' for *ummī*. Bell has 'the native prophet' with footnote "Belonging to the community", perhaps also implying lack of Scriptures.' J.R.

E.I., IV, p. 1016; Bell, *Introduction*, pp. 17–20; Wensinck, *Creed*, p. 6; Horovitz, *Koranische Untersuchungen* (1926), pp. 51–3; 'Ali, *Qur'an*, notes 117, 454, 950; Blachère, *Coran*, notes on iii:69; vii:156.

Unbelievers (Islam) Most general Ar. term is *kāfir* (pl. *kāfirūn*), which comes from root meaning to be ungrateful, but develops meaning of infidel. *Mushrik* is one who believes in more gods than one, a polytheist. *Mulḥid* (lit. one who deviates) has different meanings, sometimes as strong as 'atheist', or gen. equivalent to 'heretic'. It is applied to → Isma'ilis, who hold to esoteric meaning of Qur. *Dahrī* is a materialist who believes in eternity of matter, an atheist. *Dahriyya* applies to party holding such beliefs. *Zindīq*, pl. *zanādiqa*, derived from Iranian sources, is commonly said to be an U. who makes a show of belief. It has a connection with → Manichaeanism and with heretical teaching, and *zindīqs* were sought and persecuted. The word is commonly applied to all suspected unbelievers. J.R.

E.I., II, pp. 618–20: IV, pp. 378–80, 1228; Wensinck, *Creed*, index (Infidel); Hughes, p. 207; Sweetman, *I.C.T.*, I, II, IV, index of Arabic words.

Unction The ritual use of oil is ancient. In Egypt cult-statues of deities were anointed in daily toilet ritual; the dead were anointed, and so were officials on induction to office; it is not certain whether king was anointed at coronation, but it is prob. Three motives underlie such U.: cleansing, healing, transference of power. U. was used in Mesopot. and by Hittites for ritual and magical purposes. There is much evidence of U. in O.T. (e.g. Jacob anoints stone at Bethel (Gen. 28:18); Saul was anointed as king, I Sam. 10:1). The → Messiah was → Yahweh's Anointed (→ Christ). In Cath. Church, U. is used at → Baptism, → Confirmation, and royal coronations. Following the injunction of Ep. of James 5:14ff., the sick are anointed, and U. became one of the 7 → Sacraments. Anointing of the very sick came to be regarded as preparation for death; hence the term Extreme U. (for those *in extremis*). Prot. Churches reject U.; C. of E. uses it at Coronations and for sick, if desired. S.G.F.B.

E.R.E., XII, *s.v.; D.C.C.*, *s.v.; R.G.G.*[3], V, col. 1330–4; *R.Ae.R-G.*, pp. 647–9; B. Meissner, *Babylonien u. Assyrien*, II (1925), *passim*; *H.D.B.*[2], p. 35; W. K. L. Clarke (ed.), *Liturgy and Worship* (1932), *passim*; N. Zernov, *Eastern Christendom* (1961), p. 253; H. B. Porter, 'Origin of Medieval Rite for Anointing Sick and Dying', *J.T.S.*, VII (1956); W. Ullmann, 'Thomas Becket's Miraculous Oil', *J.T.S.*, VIII (1957).

Underworld A subterranean location for abode of the dead doubtless derived from burial of the dead, the grave being regarded as an entrance to this place (→→ Hades; Hell; *Kur-nu-gi-a*; Sheol). The anc. Egyptians believed that the sun-god passed through U. each night. Cremation did not notably change belief in subterranean abode of dead. (→ Eschatology). S.G.F.B.

E.R.E., XII, *s.v.;* H. Kees, *Totenglauben u. Jenseitsvorstellungen der alten Aegypten* (1956[2]), pp. 59ff.; E. Bendann, *Death Customs* (1930), pp. 162ff.

Uniat Churches Designation for E. Churches in communion with Rome, but retaining certain distinctive customs and institutions (e.g. rites, → baptism by immersion, marriage of clergy). The term was first used in 1595. S.G.F.B.

D.C.C., *s.v.; R.G.G.*[3], VI, col. 1128–36; N. Zernov, *Eastern Christendom* (1961), pp. 148ff., 195ff.

Unitarianism As a system of Chr. thought and relig. observance, derives name from central doc. of the single personality of God the Father, in contrast with the Trinitarian conception of threefold being as Father, Son and Holy Spirit. The significance of movement, however, is imperfectly indic. by name; its true importance lies in an undogmatic approach to relig. questions and in its teachings concerning God, man, the nature and work of Jesus Christ, and the sources of relig. belief. Unitarians have been conspicuous throughout their hist. for devotion to reason in matters of relig. and to civil and relig. liberty, and for their exercise of tolerance to all sincere forms of relig. faith. In United States, and to much less extent in British Isles, there is a 'humanist' element in U., which lays great stress on man's spiritual autonomy. A spiritual theism, however, is characteristic of movement in its widest manifestations. Unitarians are to be found mostly in Brit. Isles, United States, Canada, Hungary and Transylvania. In such countries as France, Holland and Switzerland, Liberal Chr. ministers and congregations are organised within the various Prot. churches, the name U. rarely being used.

The greatest single influence which led to orig. and growth of U. Christianity in England and Europe was free and independent study of Bible in → Reformation and post-Reformation period. Criticism of orthodox doc. of → Trinity was voiced in 16th cent. and later by a few advanced thinkers. Most notable of these was the Spanish physician Michael Servetus (1511–33), put to death for his heretical opinions at instigation of John → Calvin; John Biddle

(1616–62), 'the father of English Unitarianism'; the Italian, Faustus Socinus (1539–1604).

In Eng., U. church life had beginnings among dissenting ministers and congregations, for whom chapels were built consequent on Toleration Act of 1689. Invariably orthodox at start, many of these chapels came to adopt U. opinions during 18th cent. As such chapels had been founded on principle of non-subscription to human → creeds, there were no doctrinal barriers to adoption of freer and more tolerant form of Christianity. Approx. one third of congregations in Brit. Isles (now numbering 318) have continuous hist. from last quarter of 17th cent. The most characteristic movement of thought was that in which 'Arian' or 'Socinian' views of person of Christ developed into acceptance of him as a purely human figure, though still central to spiritual and devotional life. At same time, many trad. doctrines of orthodox Christianity, such as the Trinity, inherited guilt, eternal punishment and vicarious atonement, were either abandoned or regarded as non-essential to the Chr. life. This process took place mainly in chapels that were called → Presbyterian. At beginning of 19th cent., U. Christianity was, broadly speaking, a biblical relig., accepting miracles, rejecting creeds (which were regarded not as incredible but non-biblical), resting its hopes on an external revelation, and attaching little importance to what it regarded as the uncertain influences and promises of 'natural religion'. This position was radically changed by develop. of scientific knowledge and of biblical and historical criticism during 19th cent., aided by influence of new thinkers and teachers. As result of work in United States of W. E. Channing, Theodore Parker and R. W. Emerson, and, in England, of J. J. Taylor, J. Hamilton Thom, and, preeminently, James Martineau, U. became a spiritual relig., finding its supreme authority in relig. history and experience interpreted by reason and conscience of mankind, welcoming results of modern biblical criticism, and seeking to understand and co-operate with non-Christ. religions.

U. in N. America followed essentially same develop. as in England, although in early stages → Arminianism rather than anti-Trinitarianism was dominant factor. → Arianism gave way to a purely humanitarian view of Jesus Christ, and mod. faith is based on large-minded acceptance of results of scientific and comparative study of all religions. The influence of U. in United States has been out of all proportion to size of movement, and has been chiefly exercised through gen. culture and impulse given to literary creation by freedom and breadth of the U. spirit. The most outstanding develop. of 20th cent. has been formation of the U. Universalist Association (1961), a union of the American U. Association and the Universalist Church of America, and comprising over 1,000 churches and fellowships.

No official statement of belief binding upon adherents of U. and Free Christian Churches has ever been issued. The principle of nonsubscription to creeds and exercise of private judgment in matter of faith and morals are steadfastly maintained. Church members are, however, bound together by a community of spirit, and the vast majority of U. would give their support to a concise statement of purpose which has been freely adopted by many congregations: 'In the love of truth, and in the spirit of Jesus Christ, we unite for the worship of God and the service of man.' Brief statements of belief drawn up from time to time lay emphasis upon conception of God as universal spirit indwelling in man, the essential worth and dignity of individual, the leadership and spiritual authority of Jesus Christ, the achievement of salvation by service and sacrifice, and the conviction of eternal life here and hereafter. One of consequences of their toleration is the U. reverence for great leaders of major non-Christ. religions of world, and their readiness to act in fellowship with representatives of other forms of faith. F.K.

E. M. Wilbur, *A History of Unitarianism*, vol. I (*Socinianism and its Antecedents*), vol. 2 (*In Transylvania, England and America*) (1946, 1952); R. V. Holt (ed.), *A Free Religious Faith* (1945); K. Twinn (ed.), *Essays in Unitarian Theology* (1959); D. McL. Greeley, *A Free Church in a Changing World* (1964).

Untouchables Modern name given to lowest classes of Hindu society, lying in social scale below → *sudras* (though distinction with latter was somewhat fluid, since many of latter were regarded as excluded or impure). If creation of the *sudra* class repr. first phase of assimilation of conquered populations by the → Aryans, the U., outcastes or 'fifth' class (*pañcama*) repr. the next. Fear of ritual pollution among upper classes contributed to segregate and humiliate this servile population, and by classical period it was regarded as polluting even to set eyes on them, esp. the *caṇḍālas*, whose chief function was carrying and cremating corpses: the term came to be used more widely for untouchables. Certain occupations were peculiarly unclean: sweepers, tanners, sellers of alcohol, fishers, etc., partly because of growth of → *ahimsa* sentiments. A caste (*jati*) hierarchy developed within the 'fifth' class. Also excluded from participation in Aryan society were tribal groups and *mlecchas* or foreigners, who were technically untouchable, though they were sometimes given class status. Similarly some non-Hindu groups, notably →→ Jains and Parsis, were not regarded as untouchable and were fitted within caste structure. In mod. times the campaign to improve lot of the outcaste culminated in work of → Gandhi, who gave them honorific name of 'Harijans' (sons of God) and Dr. Ambedkar, the untouchable leader who with many of his followers adopted Buddhism. The Indian constitution, adopted in 1951, outlawed practice of untouchability, and favoured educational treatment is provided for lower castes. N.S.

L. Dumont, *Homo Hierarchicus* (1968); S. Fuchs, *The Children of Hari* (1951); M. Singh, *The Depressed Classes* (1947); Hazari, *I was an Outcaste* (1957); D. Keer, *Dr. Ambedkar: Life and Mission* (1954).

Upagupta → Divyāvadāna. T.O.L.

Upali A barber, of the → Sākya tribe, who was ordained into Buddh. → Sangha in time of the Buddha. T.O.L.

Upaniṣads The U. (also transliterated 'Upanishads') are the last section of → Veda. The classical or principal U. were prob. composed between 800 and 400 BC. A large number of later works are also called U., some dating from as late as 15th cent. CE; but they do not have canonical status (→ Revelation, Hindu; → *śruti*): collections of them differ as to how many should be incl. under the title—over a hundred are commonly listed. But usually when ref. is made to the U., what is meant is collection of thirteen principal U. The older of these were in prose, some of later in verse. The name means lit. 'sitting next to' or 'session', i.e. the session of pupil or pupils with the Vedic teacher or, less lit., it means 'secret instruction', since what was imparted was esoteric knowledge. They orig. in part from instructions given by forest-dwelling teachers (→→ *vanaprastha*, *asramas*), who having partly withdrawn from world tended to be instructors of young in Vedic lore. The U. repr. the → Vedanta, the last part of Veda, and as such were concerned with penetrating meaning of highly complex ritual activities, etc., of Vedic relig., as prescribed in → *Brahmanas*, etc. Thus they were much concerned with identifying nature of → *Brahman*, the sacred power implicit in sacrifice and to be seen as underlying processes of whole world. Though thus concerned with the force essentially manipulated ritually by the → Brahmins, there is in some passages an anti-Brahmanical tendency. Trad. commentators have quite understandably attempted to see complete unity of theme in the writings; but in fact there is variety of tendencies expressed in them. Most import. is the identification of *Brahman* with the self or → *atman* as summed up in various formulae, above all → *tat tvam asi*; but some U. are more overtly personalistic in their account of ultimate reality, notably the *Kaṭha* U., the *Śvetāsvatara* and the *Īśa*. The doc. of → rebirth is first explicitly taught, within orthodox Vedic trad., in the U.; and greater prominence is attached to → yoga and contemplation. By a process of 'interiorisation', sacrifices are treated psychologically, so that contemplation becomes form of sacrifice, and by turning inwards, to realise the *atman*, one can also penetrate to *Brahman*. Though later interpretation by → Sankara emphasised illusoriness of world as → *maya*, this conception is scarcely prominent, though some texts, e.g., the *Māṇḍūkya U.*, in expressing a strongly monistic doc. might be taken to imply it. There are elements of what was later systematised as → Samkhya in the U., notably the idea of → *gunas* and that of the → *purusa* or eternal soul. In the *Svetasvatara*, Rudra (→ Śiva) is given prominence, an anticipation of later → *bhakti* cults focusing on Siva. Among import. teachers cited is Yājñavalkya. Later theologians and philosophers commented extensively on the U. and on the → *Brahmasutra*, which was supposed to be an aphoristic summary of teachings of Vedanta. In this connection, a distinction is trad. made between the U. and the earlier part of Vedic corpus. The latter concerns action, in partic. ritual action, such as performance of sacrifices. It is the 'action-portion' of Veda, for those concerned in the *karmamarga*. The U. have to do essentially with way of gnosis or knowledge (→ *jnanamarga*). In giving knowledge, they bring ultimate → liberation. The distinction demarcates the schools of →→ Mimamsa and Vedanta. The trans. of the U. in 19th cent. had some philosoph. influence in West, notably on → Schopenhauer. The principal U. are as follows. The *Bṛhadāraṇyaka* (also transliterated *Brihadaranyaka*), a long prose U., is an adjunct to the *Śatapathabrahmana*. A substantial part of it is devoted to teachings of Yajnavalkya, about the Self. An import. part of his doc. is that the Self within is the Self indwelling whole universe. It is described as unseen, incomprehensible, etc., since one cannot see the seer of seeing, the thinker of thought, etc. Only in a state where there is no duality between subject and object can this Self be grasped. It is to be spoken of as *neti neti* 'Not thus, not thus'. By grasping this teaching one gains immortality. Yajnavalkya's teachings are preceded by some miscellaneous matter, incl. some accounts of creation and a dialogue between Ajātaśatru, king of Banaras (and so a → *ksatriya*), and the Brahmin Gargya, in which former gives instruction in secret doc. of the Self as the real of the real (*satyasya satyam*), perhaps the strongest instance in the U. of a non-Brahmin taking on role typically reserved for → Brahmins. The *Chāndogya*, another long prose U., of the Tāṇḍin school of → *Samaveda*, and begins with praise of, and teachings about, the syllable → Om, this being most sacred and powerful of sounds used in chants (*sāmāni*). A central passage is dialogue between Śvetaketu and his father Uddālaka, in which latter propounds secret doc. of the Self, culminating in formula → *tat tvam asi* ('That art thou'). This is followed by long exposition of doc. of the Infinite and attainment of the eternal; together with a dialogue in which Prajāpati the creator instructs → Indra. The main conclusion is that the one who will attain → liberation, no longer to be reborn, is one who has obeyed Vedic ordinances, etc., and concentrated his faculties on the Self. Here there is a coalescence between ritual and social duty and practice of → yoga. The *Taittirīya*, a shorter, mainly prose, U. takes name from school of the *Yajurveda*. It incl. teaching of → Varuṇa to his son Bhṛgu, through which latter, by practice of → *tapas* comes to see that highest aspect of → *Brahman* is bliss (*ananda*). There is also an identification of *Brahman* with food. Another prose U., the *Kauṣītakī*, takes name from a school of the → *Rgveda*, and begins with instruction by the Brahmin Citra to Svetaketu's father on path the individual takes in next world. He goes successively to the moon and other mythic planes of existence, finally penetrating to seat of → Brahma. Brahma questions him as to identity, and the right reply is 'What thou art, that am I': Brahma himself being the real of the real. Among other topics treated there is an extended account of fundamental nature of consciousness. The work concludes with another dialogue in which Ajatasatru has the better of a Brahmin. The *Kena* is a short U. of the Talavakara school of *Sāmaveda*, the first part in verse and second in prose. The first part expounds a doc. of the Self similar to that of Yajnavalkya in the *Brhadaranyaka*. The second part incl. myth exalting → Indra, first god to recognise *Brahman*. The *Īśa*, a very brief verse U. belonging to → *Atharvaveda* trad., expresses a panentheistic position, in which supreme Being is the Lord (*Īśa*). The relatively late verse *Kaṭha*, of the Kāṭhaka school of *Yajurveda*, is the most unified and artistic of classical U. It comprises a dialogue between the young Nāciketas and Yama, the Lord of Death. Yama's teaching tends to subordinate the impersonal *Brahman* to the Lord; and there is strong emphasis on practice of *yoga*. Through this immortality is won, and the Self discriminated from that which embodies it and binds it to world. However, the emphasis upon Yoga tends to obscure the theistic elements in *Kaṭha* (which may in any case have been exaggerated by some Western commentators). The relatively late *Śvetāsvatara* (it is unclear as to which school of Vedic transmission it belongs) is much more explicitly theistic; it is a poem of moderate length and incl. intense praise of Rudra (→ Siva) as supreme Lord, origin of Veda, etc. Also late, the *Muṇḍaka*, of the *Atharvaveda*, a fairly short verse U., is also theistic in spirit; those who practise yoga will pass close in eternal life to the supreme Person. By contrast the *Māṇḍūkya*, a short prose work but prob. rather late, is strongly monistic in emphasis. It expounds inner meaning of sound → Om, divided into four elements, A, U, M and the silence after it. The last symbolises non-dual mystical experience of identity with ultimate reality. Likewise the *Aitareya*, of similar length and also in prose, and belonging to school of that name of → *Rgveda* trad., expounds creation of world by the Self, and identifies latter with everything in world. The long *Maitri U.*, chiefly in prose and somewhat in style of the *Bṛhadāraṇyaka*, etc., but prob. fairly late, expounds syncretistic theism (identifying Brahma, Viṣṇu and Śiva among others), gives full account of → *karma* doc. and, *inter alia*, applies early → Samkhya categories, notably the doc. of → *gunas*, to creation. The short *Praśna*, mainly prose, U., and annexed to *Atharvaveda*, is account of questions (*prasna*) addressed to teacher Pippalāda, on variety of topics, culminating in exposition of the *turiya* or 'fourth' state of consciousness, i.e. non-dual mystical experiences. As well as these principal U., a list of nearly a hundred lesser and later works in same genres can be found in S. N. Dasgupta (see below), p. 28. N.S.

S. N. Dasgupta, *Hist. of Indian Philosophy*, vol. 1 (1922); R. C. Zaehner, *Hindu Scriptures* (1966); R. E. Hume, *The Thirteen Principal Upanishads* (1962); S. Radhakrishnan, *The Principal Upaniṣads* (1953); P. Deussen, *The Philosophy of the Upanishads* (1906); L. Renou, *Religions of Ancient India* (1953); K. N. Jayatilleke, *Early Buddhist Theory of Knowledge* (1962).

Upāsaka Term used in Buddhism for devout layman (or laywoman—*upāsikā*). U. indic. one who 'follows', 'serves', 'attends', or 'accords honour'. The Pali texts ref. to existence of large numbers of these U. (e.g. *D.N.*, III, 148; Rhys Davids, *Dialogues of the Buddha*, III, p. 142). The term is in current use in S. Asian Buddh. countries to describe laymen of pious disposition who on → holy days keep the 8 moral precepts, fasting from midday, and poss. engaging in meditation. These are usually more elderly members of laity, though not exclusively so. T.O.L.

Uposatha (Buddh. sabbath) → Holy Days, Buddh. T.O.L.

Urabe (Diviners). A hereditary corporation of

priests in anc. → Shinto, whose duty was to divine by means of deer's shoulder-blade or tortoise-shell. D.H.S.

W. G. Aston, *Shinto* (1905), p. 203.

Urim and Thummin A form of → divination used in Heb. relig. in pre-Exilic period (e.g. I Sam. 14:41ff.); the institution seems to have been of an oracular kind (→ Oracles), being regarded as means of revealing → Yahweh's will. Despite much discussion, the meaning of the words U. and T., and the mode of operation involved remain obscure. (→ Ephod). S.G.F.B.

*H.D.B.*², *s.v.; R.G.G.*³, VI, col. 1193–4; *E.J.R.*, *s.v.* ('Oracle').

Urmensch German term meaning 'Primordial Man', used in hist. and compar. study of relig. The idea of an U. occurs in many religs. (sometimes a primordial pair, male and female, is envisaged, e.g. Adam and Eve). The U. appears in various roles. He may be first human being and progenitor of mankind, e.g. → Adam (and Eve); Mâshya (and Mashyôî) in Iran; poss. → Adapa; → Izanagi (and Izanami) in Japan; poss. → Deucalion and Pyrrha in Greece. The U. may be a supernatural prototype of man, e.g. →→ Gayomard (Iran); → Purusha (India); Christ as → Logos (Jn. 1:1ff.); Anthropos in → Gnosticism. In Indo-Iranian mythology, → Yama (→ Yima) is a type of U. who becomes first man to die and be transformed into ruler of dead. In I Cor. 16:45 → Paul briefly draws parallel between First Adam and Last Adam, i.e. Christ. The thesis, advanced by R. Reitzenstein, that a *U-mythos* was once current in anc. East, has not been gen. accepted. S.G.F.B.

*R.G.G.*³, VI, col. 1195–7; R. Reitzenstein, *Die hellenistischen Mysterienreligionen* (1927), pp. 168ff., 177ff.; Brandon, *C.L., passim.*

Ushabti Anc. Egypt. meaning 'the answerer'. Name given to statuettes, made of various materials, which were placed in Egypt. tombs. The figure has form of → mummy, with face and hands exposed: it holds two hoes, or hoe and mattock, and has rope basket suspended over shoulder. On the body is inscribed Chap. VI of → *Book of Dead*, to effect that the U. will answer, if its owner is called on to work in next world. U.'s first appear in Middle Kingdom (*c.* 2052–1778 BC); they are found in great abundance and witness to Egypt. resort to → magic in mortuary cultus. S.G.F.B.

E. A. W. Budge, *The Mummy* (1925), pp. 251ff.; *R.Ae.R.-G.*, pp. 849–53.

Usury (China–Japan) There does not seem to have been much moral or relig. objection to U. in China and Far Eastern countries, though literature is full of protests against rapacious landlords and money-lenders. The misfortunes of poor usually led to recourse to money-lenders, rich landlords or usurious townsfolk who charged interest rates of 2–5% per month, and who also invested in pawnshops, a favourite form of investment for the wealthy until rise of mod. banking and commerce. In Japan traders would often attach themselves to a monastery, ostensibly to supply commodities, but in reality to engage in U. because they found ecclesiastical prestige useful in enforcing debts. In China many attempts were made to combat U. The most successful were the mutual loan societies organised on a cooperative basis. D.H.S.

A. H. Smith, *Village Life in China* (1900), pp. 152ff.; G. B. Sansom, *Japan* (1946) *passim.*

(Islam) U. (*Ribā*). Condemned in Qur. ii:276–81; iii:125 and in → Tradition. The legal schools have developed details regarding what constitutes U. In dealing with commodities which can be weighed and measured, like for like must be given if goods are homogeneous. Interest on money lent must not be taken. Some mod. Muslims would like to see system of interest abolished; many who are due interest from a bank either refuse to take it, or employ it on some form of benevolence. → Muhammad 'Abduh caused a furore when he declared it was lawful to invest money in the Post Office Savings Bank. J.R.

E.I., III, pp. 1148–50; Hughes, pp. 656f.; Pareja, p. 679; *Mishkāt*, pp. 602ff.; V. Berger-Vachon, 'Le Ribâ', in Charnay, *Normes*, pp. 81–100; A. I. Qureshi, *Islam and the theory of interest* (1967²).

'Uthmān b. 'Affān 3rd Caliph (23–35/644–56), member of → Umayya family in Mecca, married Muḥammad's daughter Ruqayya, and after her death her sister Umm Kulthūm. He was pious and easy-going, but caused resentment through favouring relatives. A rising took place and he was assassinated. In his period the official Qur. text in use ever since was drawn up. J.R.

E.I., III, pp. 1008ff.; Nöldeke, *Geschichte*², index; Jeffery, *Materials*, introd.

'Uzzā Mentioned in Qur. liii:19, was goddess worshipped at Nakhla near Mecca, her symbol being a tree. When Abu Sufyan went to attack → Muḥammad in 3/625, he had with him the symbols of 'U. and → al-Lāt, the former being a patron goddess of Mecca. J.R.

Wellhausen, *Reste*, pp. 34–45; *E.I.*, IV, pp. 1–69; Hughes, P. 658, cf. p. 285; *Mishkāt*, p. 1163.

V

Vaḍagalai One of sub-sects of the → Sri Vaiṣṇavas and followers of → Ramanuja. They are distinguished from other sub-sect, the → Tengalai, over doc. of grace and other matters. Both schools emphasise importance of God's grace for → salvation, but disagree over role of the *prapatti* or self-surrender which is human response to grace. According to the V., human effort in *prapatti* is condition of grace, while the Tengalai consider grace to come unconditionally. The V. account is known as *markaṭa-nyāya* or 'monkey principle', in contrast to the *mārjāra-nyaya* or 'cat principle'. The baby monkey needs to hold on to mother when latter transports it from A to B: likewise devotee has to make some effort in being transported to salvation. However, the mother-cat simply transports her young by scruff of neck, and the kitten does nothing. In practice, the effort required acc. to V. *prapatti* doc. incl. the fulfilment of Vedic and other duties. It is by striving hard for salvation through performance of duty that one ultimately comes to realisation of emptiness of such means (*upāyaśūnyatā*) and throws oneself on God. The V. is in consequence more conservative about relig. duties and retains central place for Vedic revelation (while the Tengalai rely more or less exclusively on the Tamil *Prabandham*, → Alvars), and is more oriented towards 'upper-class' (→ twice-born) relig. Further, the V. assign great prominence to → Sri or Lakṣmī, consort of Viṣṇu, as co-equal saviour. There are other minor differences, such as use of different sectarian marks, etc. However, polemics between two schools have sometimes been strong, partly because of rivalries over temple administration, etc. The V. are sometimes known as the 'northern' school (though both belong to south) because its main centre in Mysore. It has a succession of → Acaryas traced back to Ramanuja. The most import. teacher of school was → Venkatanatha. (→ Grace). N.S.

T. A. Gopinath Rao, *History of Sri Vaisnavas* (1923); J. E. Carpenter, *Theism in Medieval India* (1921); S. N. Dasgupta, *Hist. of Indian Philosophy*, vol. 4 (1940); H. Bhattacharyya (ed.), *Cultural Heritage of India*, vol. 3 (1956).

Vaiśeṣika One of the six schools of trad. Hindu → philosophy. It expounds an atomistic account of universe, whose matter is formed by everlasting atoms formed in various combinations. It was primarily a proto-scientific approach to metaphysical problems, rather than relig. one. However, in course of its evolution it assoc. more and more closely with the → Nyaya school. In period of coalescence, in 10th cent. CE and earlier, it expounded metaphysical theism. God was used to explain combination of atoms at end of a period of cosmic dissolution; he is thus periodic Creator. The classical arguments for existence of God within Indian trad. were systematised in the Nyaya-Vaisesika, notably by Udayana (10th cent. CE). The basic text of V. is the *Vaisesikasutra*, of about CE 100, and attr. to Kaṇāda. N.S.

J. Sinha, *Indian Realism* (1938); D. Riepe, *The Naturalistic Tradition in Indian Thought* (1961); G. Bhattacharyya, *Studies in Nyaya-Vaisesika Theism* (1961). (→ Atomic Theory).

Vaiṣṇavism The cult of → Viṣṇu; also spelt 'Vaishnavism' (while some authors prefer to use 'Vishnuism'); and derived from *Vaiṣṇava*, 'follower of Visnu' or 'to do with Visnu'. V. arose out of coalescence of cults (→→ Vasudeva, Krishnə, etc.) during post-Upaniṣadic period and has been characterised through history by emphasis on → *bhakti*, coupled with belief in → *avataras* (descents or incarnations of Visnu). Its most import. literary product was the → *Bhagavadgita*, but there is also an extensive literature of myths, etc., contained in → *Puraṇas*, while in medieval period V. theology flourished (→→ Ramanuja, Madhva, Caitanya, Vallabha). The growth of → Saivism at approximately same time resulted in dominance of the two forms of piety as alternative manifestations of Hindu theism, and most Hindus are either Saivas or Vaisnavas. This dominance was achieved by middle ages; but not without some friction—there was, e.g., some persecution of V.'s in S. India (→ Ramanuja). Medieval V. created synthesis between Vedantin theology and relig. of the Tamil poets (→ Alvars), but itself divided into sects or *sampradayas*. The most import. was the *Śrī-sampradāya*, of which Ramanuja was head or →

acarya; this divided into two sub-schools after his death, the →→ *Tengalai* and *Vadagalai*, differing over doc. of → grace, and leaning respectively heavily upon vernacular and Sanskrit texts. Other import. sects are the *Brahmasampradaya* of Madhva, the *Sanaka-sampradaya* of → Nimbarka and the *Rudrasampradaya* of → Vallabha. In late medieval period there was growth in cult of → Rama (hitherto unimportant) in N. India, where also V. came into fruitful interplay with Islamic → Sufism, resulting in teachings of →→ Kabir, Nanak and others (and issuing in the creation of → Sikhism). North Indian Vaisnavism divided into number of sects, stemming chiefly from trad. of Rāmānanda, Kabir's teacher. The use of vernacular in teaching and the egalitarian anti-caste tendencies of V. in this period facilitated its rapid growth. Import. among centres of V. pilgrimage is Brindaban, Vṛndavana, scene of → Krishna's activities. Pious Vaisnavites differentiate themselves by placing sectarian marks on foreheads, etc. (e.g. two vertical white streaks and red transverse streak; or two perpendiculars and yellow dot, etc.—roughly, Vaisnavite marks involve some vertical lines, while Saivite ones are horizontal). N.S.

J. Gonda, *Aspects of Early Vishnuism* (1954); R. G. Bhandarkar, *Vaishnavism, Shaivism and Minor Religious Systems* (1928); H. H. Wilson, *Religious Sects of the Hindus* (1958); J. E. Carpenter, *Theism in Medieval India* (1921); H. Raychaudhuri, *Materials for the Study of the Early History of the Vaishnava Sect* (1936).

Vaiśyas Lowest of three upper or 'twice-born' classes (→ *varnas*) in Vedic and classical → Hinduism. Orig. they were chiefly cultivators, etc.; they supplied labour and resources off which the →→ *ksatriyas* and Brahmins lived. With incorporation of a fourth or servile class, the → *sudras* and spread of → Aryan dominance over new centres of cultivation, etc., the strength of V. class increased, and by classical period many of them were landowners, merchants, highly skilled craftsmen, etc. Expansion of trade enabled them to build up powerful guilds, and many V. attained import. posts in state service. Many became Buddhists, since Buddh. beliefs were more open and favourable to activities of this rising middle class. N.S.

L. Dumont, *Homo Hierarchicus* (1968); J. Auboyer, *Daily Life in Ancient India* (1961).

Vajji Name of tribal republic of N. India at time of Buddha, mentioned several times in early Buddh. lit. The name V. indic. both a geographical region and its people, consisting of confederate tribes. During life-time of Buddha, the V. were a peaceful and prosperous community; soon after his death they were conquered by King Ajātasattu, and absorbed into kingdom of → Magadha. Ref. is made to the V. in the → Mahāparinibbāna Sutta, where Buddha draws parallel between the V., with their republican form of government, and the Buddh. → Sangha. The implication of this for the monks may have been that, after destruction of old republican form of society by new expanding monarchies, the Sangha was only preserver of old democratic order. T.O.L.

T. W. Rhys-Davids, *Buddhist India* (1903), *Dialogues of the Buddha*, Part II (1966[5]), pp. 78–85.

Vajrayāna Name given in Indian Buddhism to last phase of develop. of the → Mahāyāna, of which V. is the continuation, although by its name it is designated as a separate '*yāna*' or means to salvation. An alternative name, used more esp. of earlier stage of develop., is → *Mantra-yāna*. The → Yogācāra school, which arose in 4th cent. CE, had emphasised practical importance of meditational methods and disciplines; the Mantrayāna developed this still further, and gave prominent place to use of *mantras*, or sacred chants, the use of which, in combination with mystical symbols and gestures of various kinds, was held to be most potent method of achieving more advanced spiritual states. Much material for such practices was taken over from popular, indigenous Indian relig., e.g. magical spells similar to those contained in the Hindu *Atharva-Veda*. Systematisation of use of this material is the stage of develop. known as V. The aim of system was infinitely enhanced psychic experience here and now, rather than distant goal of → *nirvaṇa* after countless rebirths; hence V. entailed much greater concern with the occult, with magical transformations and miracles, than earlier forms of Buddhism. One region of its greater strength was E. India (i.e. modern Bihar, Orissa and Bengal); the great Buddh. monastic centre or university of Vikramaśīla was stronghold of V., from whence it was carried to Tibet, notably by Padmasambhava, where too it became dominant form of Buddhism, and where it was preserved to mod. times (→ Tibetan Buddhism). T.O.L.

D. Snellgrove, *Buddhist Himālaya* (1957).

Vallabha Vallabha or Vallabhācārya (→ *Acarya*) (? 1481–1533: the dates may be slightly late) was a Telugu Brahmin and virtually founder of Vallabhacari sect (a branch of the *Rudrasampradaya*, going back to Viṣṇusvāmin in 14th cent.), who was the proponent of doc. known as *Visuddhādvaita* or pure non-dualism (very different however from → Sankara's non-dualism, for Vallabhacaris reject doc. of illusion, treating → *maya* as God's real creative activity). Relig. and intellectually precocious, V. early won wide reputation as teacher of → Vaisnavism. He travelled extensively, and ultimately settled in →

Banaras, where he married, having two sons. Shortly before death he became a → *sannyasin*, though he did not in his teachings encourage → asceticism. His theology was panentheistic, with strong emphasis upon → *bhakti* and the all-sufficiency of God's grace in bringing about → liberation. However, we can enjoy bliss in this life, participating, through *bhakti*, in joy of God and his creation, and this state is even superior to → *mokṣa*. Prominent in V.'s relig. was the cult of Rādhā and → Krishna: the union between the lovers is like union in bliss of soul and God. The most import. work attr. to him, the *Anubhāṣya*, was in part composed by his son Viṭṭhala. The Vallabhacaris became quite influential in W. India. The eroticism of cult of Radha and Krishna and the antinomianism liable to follow from V.'s repudiation of works as conducive to → salvation gave movement a not altogether unjustified reputation for licence in 19th cent. It is strong mainly in W. India. An import. figure in movement is that of aristocratic woman hymn-writer, Mira Bai (1498–1573). N.S.

S. N. Dasgupta, *Hist. of Indian Philosophy*, vol. 4 (1961); N. A. Thooti, *The Vaishnavas of Gujarat* (1935); J. G. Shah, *A Primer of Anu-Bhashaya* (1960); H. von Glasenapp, *Doctrines of Vallabhacharya* (1959).

Varṇas The four *varṇas* (lit. 'colours') or classes (→→ Brahmins, *ksatriyas*, *vaisyas*, *sudras*) repr. theoretical division of society in →→ Vedism and Hinduism. They thus provide framework for what was later elaborated into Hindu → caste system. Practice did not always follow theory, and from very early time main divisions of society were five or even six in number, since outside the four classes were those who did not come within purview of the → *dharma* (even *sudras* had few rights and did not belong to → Aryan society): notably there were the 'low-born', predecessors of the → untouchables of mod. period. Also foreigners (*mlecchas*) did not fit into framework of *V.*, though they could be given status corresponding to one of lower three classes, acc. to occupation or prestige. The top three classes were counted as the → twiceborn (*dvija*), since they underwent full → initiation (a rebirth), and had access to →→ revelation or *śruti*. *Sudras* in classical times had access to →→ *Puranas*, Epics, and *Tantras*. The fifth class, outside *V.* were given some recognition by law, in that questions about relig. purity and need to frame expiations, etc., in relation to contact with them necessarily arose. N.S.

J. Auboyer, *Daily Life in Ancient India* (1961); L. Dumont, *Homo Hierarchicus* (1966).

Varuṇa Next to → Indra, V. was most import. of gods of the → *Rgveda*, but despite exalted status he largely disappeared from popular imagination in period of classical → Hinduism. The name is prob. connected with Uranus (Ouranos); ascription to him of title *Asura* (→ *asuras*), term otherwise used for antigods, suggests connection with Iranian → Ahura Mazdah. Both were certainly → sky-gods (as also Dyaus, in Vedic hymns, who was, however, eclipsed by V.). V. is repr. as having strong ethical concern, and he is above all the one who maintains and guards → *rta*, the cosmic order which also, *via* moral rules, regulates behaviour of men. His ethical functions are reinforced by his being a king and preserver of justice. His omniscience (for he sends messengers everywhere) enables him to oversee deeds of men. He punishes sins severely, whether ritual or moral. In hymns to V. there is strong sense of humility and sinfulness of men. In later times, V.'s functions declined, and he was assoc. with control of waters and was bringer of dropsy. N.S.

A. Danielou, *Hindu Polytheism* (1964).

Vassa (Buddh. Lent) → Holy Days, Buddh. T.O.L.

Vasubandhu Buddh. writer of fourth cent. CE. Born at Purusapura (Peshawar) in → Gandhara, capital of Kanishka's kingdom, he entered Buddh. monkhood. At first a → Hīnayānist of school of the → Sarvāstivadā, V. composed compendium of the Abh. teaching of this school, his → *Abhidharma-Kosá*. This came to be considered most authoritative treatise of Sarvāstivadā. His conversion from the Sarvāstivāda school to the → Mahāyāna is trad. attr. to efforts of his brother, → Asanga. His life story is related by 6th cent. writer Paramartha. This was trans. into Eng. in 1904 by Takakusu (in *T'oung Pao*, Serie II, vol. V, pp. 269–96). This translator raised question whether the biographer Paramartha had confused material appertaining to separate V.'s, thus merging two figures into one. The view that there were 2 V.'s was argued by E. Frauwallner in 1951. In his view there was a Sarvāstivādin writer of name in 4th cent. ('the elder V'.) and brother of Asanga, who was converted to Mhy., and wrote an import. Vijnānavāda (Mhy.) work. There was another Sarvāstivādin in 5th cent. ('the younger V.'), who the author of the *Abhidharma-kośa*. Doubt was thrown on Frauwallner's theory in 1958 by P. S. Jaini, who presented new evidence to uphold trad. view that writer of the *Kosá* was converted by his brother Asanga to the Mhy., and subsequently composed at least one import. work of the Vijñānavāda sch. S. Dutt, in 1960, inclined to theory of 2 V.'s, and maintained that author of the *Kosá*, 'in spite of his intellectual leanings to Mahāyānism, was not a Mahāyānist, but a Vaibhāsika of the Kashmirian school'. It is to the second, younger V. that Dutt attr. the three treatises on logic, *Vāda-hṛdaya*, *Vāda-vidhi*, and *Vāda-vidhāna*,

('Heart of Dispute', 'Method of Dispute', and 'Rule of Dispute') trad. attr. to writer of the Kosa. This younger V., in Dutt's view, was author of the Mhy. *śāstras*, a learned monk who lived at imperial capital, Ayodhya and had the Gupta King Skandagupta as his patron. T.O.L.

J. Takakusu (tr.), 'Paramartha's Life of Vasubandhu', in *T'oung Pao*, Serie II, vol. V (1904), pp. 269–96, 'The Date of Vasubandhu', in *Indian Studies in honour of Charles Rockwell Lanman* (1929); E. Frauwallner, *On date of Buddhist master of the law Vasubandhu*, Serie Orientale, Roma III (1951); P. S. Jaini, 'On the theory of two Vasubandhus', in *B.S.O.A.S.*, vol. XXI (1958); S. Dutt, *Buddhist Monks and Monasteries of India* (1962), pp. 280–5.

Vatican Council, Second The Second Vatican Council was opened by Pope John XXIII in St. Peter's, Rome, on Oct. 11th, 1962. It was closed on 8 Dec. 1965, by Pope Paul VI. It had met for four sessions in the autumn of each year for two months, but commissions and sub-commissions were busily at work throughout the three years that the C. sat.

The originator of the C. was Pope John XXIII, who announced his intention early in 1959, a few months after his election to succeed Pius XII. The idea of a C. had been mooted both under Pius XII and Pius XI; for the last General C. (the First Vatican) only sat for seven months between Dec. 1869 and July 1870. Nearly a century had elapsed, of great growth of the R.C. Church outside Europe. Instead of 700 bishops in 1870, some 2,700 arrived in 1962; and, for first time in hist. of Church, Mediterranean and European bishops were in a minority to those from other continents, N. and S. America each sending some 500, and Africa, Asia and Australasia another 700. A number of abbots-president and other heads of import. relig. orders took part. Representatives from other Chr. churches were invited to observe.

A great deal of preparatory work had been done by different commissions, in which the departments of the Curia, who divide between them all the business of the Church, were heavily represented. The first sign that the C. was determined to have a mind of its own came at the very outset on Saturday, 13 Oct. On the initiative of Cardinal Frings of Cologne and Cardinal Lienart of Lille, the Conciliar Fathers refused to accept names suggested by Curia for the different commissions to which the agenda was to be entrusted. The C. insisted on making its own elections and appointments to these commissions, in which the serious work of preparing the different decrees and constitutions went on. The First Session was mainly taken up with reform of → Liturgy, which it was hoped would be reasonably harmonious. The question of the sources of Revelation, the relations between Scripture and Tradition, was also raised in first weeks, and disclosed sharp differences of opinion which Pope John endeavoured to harmonise by creating a special commission with two presidents: Cardinal Ottaviani of the Holy Office and Cardinal Bea, the German Jesuit who had been placed at head of newly created Secretariat for Christian Unity. Those working for Christian Unity, partic. strong among the Germans who were anxious to build bridges with Lutherans, wanted the C. to reaffirm pre-eminence of Scripture rather than Tradition: the Council of Trent had treated Scripture and Tradition as two co-equal sources.

The health of Pope John began to fail early in 1963; he died in June of that year, to be succeeded by Cardinal Montini of Milan, whom he had plainly indicated as the man he would like to carry through the work of the C. There is a good deal of evidence that Pope John had envisaged the C. as only lasting for one session, sufficient to open long-closed windows, let in fresh air, and start a general process of spring-cleaning and bringing Catholic thought and practice up to date. In his last months Pope John was made very anxious by the realisation of what strong and often conflicting convictions were present among the bishops of the world, and still more among their experts or '*periti*' who accompanied them.

Pope Paul made it plain that he would respect independence of C. as fully as Pope John had done, seldom attending in person, but introducing modifications in procedure. Orig. there had been 12 presiding Cardinals, heads of Commissions, sitting acc. to business in hand, but no limit on speeches, all in Latin. Cardinal Cushing of Boston wanted to install simultaneous translation, but it was found that there were no interpreters who had been trained with Latin as one of their languages. Pope Paul appointed 4 Cardinals as moderators who took charge of the business: Doepfner, of Munich, Suenens of Malines-Brussels, Lercaro of Bologna, and Agagianian of Propaganda Fidei, the Curial body in charge of the Missions.

The C. met at 9 every morning, and, after celebration of Mass by a different prelate and sometimes in a different rite, sat through morning gen. hearing 12 to 15 speeches, with the cardinals, who all sat together, taking precedence, but being expected to conform to general rule that speeches should not exceed 10 minutes. There were bars in St. Peters' for coffee; the speeches were varied by taking of votes, the Fathers being enabled to vote without leaving their stalls in the nave of St. Peters' through an electronic voting device.

The labours of the C., slow in gathering momentum, got into their stride in 3rd and 4th

Sessions, and 1964 may be taken as the decisive session. The 2nd Session was dominated by discussions on Collegiality, the doc. that supreme gov. of Church is the whole episcopate, and that every bishop has a double responsibility, to his own diocese, but equally to Church in general. The champions of this doc. claimed that First Vatican C. intended a decree affirming it, had that C. not been abruptly terminated by the imminent fall of Rome to the House of Savoy. It is intended to counter-balance, without diminishing, the special prerogatives of the Pope as Vatican I had affirmed them. As consequence of this wider sense of episcopal responsibility, Pope Paul instituted a Synod of Bishops in numbers about a tenth of C., whose first meeting took place in Oct. 1967.

By 2nd Session it had become abundantly clear that intellectual leadership of C. lay with bishops of Europe, i.e. German, French, Dutch, Belgian, who were strongly ecumenical and determined to change the trad. image of Church and to get rid of what Bishop de Smet of Bruges, an outstanding orator, termed 'Triumphalism'. The bishops of N. America, like those from Brit. Isles, had at first expected to follow lead of Curia, and it was some little time before they re-orientated themselves. But when they did, the great majority supported what came to be known as the Progressives, as did most bishops from S. America, from Australasia and from Asian and African mission-fields. The result was a general pattern of voting by which most decrees were approved by majorities of 2,000, with only about 100 bishops saying 'Non placet'.

The great achievements of C. were the Decrees passed in 3rd and 4th Sessions. The main document of C. on nature of the Church, hailing the laity as the People of God, seeks to get away from older idea of the teaching Church, comprising bishops and priests, with the Pope at their head, and the taught, the great majority, namely, the laity, who were also looked on as the flock tended by their shepherds. The conception of the People of God was embodied in the Liturgical Decree, authorising great changes in celebration of Mass. It was designed to ensure more active participation by laity by putting much of Mass into the vernacular and calling for much more response.

Equally far-reaching was the changed emphasis of Church expressed in decrees on Ecumenism, and in Declaration on Religious Freedom. The first recognised other Chr. bodies as channels of grace, where previous teaching, while allowing presence of grace in lives of individuals belonging to these other bodies, had not given theological recognition to their collective Chr. character. This Decree is intended as Roman Church's contribution to new respect as well as charity between Chr. churches to prepare ground for an eventual unity, healing the unhappy hist. legacy of division. (→ Ecumenical Movement). The Declaration on Religious Freedom went much further than most Cath. theologians had been willing to go in past. It has always been Cath. teaching that a man must obey his conscience, even an erroneous conscience, while Church had duty to affirm that there is an objective revealed truth which can be known and recognised. The Declaration placed new emphasis on freedom of conscience, as incl. right of a man not only to hold out but to spread his own beliefs. There was much debate in C. whether this would not be seized on by revolutionary political movements, to the embarassment of civil governments. But the Decree was adopted, the American bishops being foremost in fight for it.

The 3rd and 4th Sessions saw the conservatives, still strong in Curia, accepting their defeats quietly. Of the 16 decrees and declarations which the C. issued, many said very little, though they say enough to give the C.'s authority to far-reaching changes if the Pope should choose to make them. There were decrees on Mass Media, on Chr. Education, Priestly Training, and Priestly Life, on Missionary activity, and on relations of Church with Oriental Christians and with non-Chr. religions. But the decree that commanded most outside interest was on the Pastoral Constitution of Church in Modern World. This called for more Cath. Action against poverty, and for peace, though it did not come out clearly against nuclear war as one school of thought had hoped.

The Pope reserved to himself whether there should be any variation in teaching on old and new methods of preventing pregnancy as a topic unsuitable for public discussion. The C. began in secrecy, but with each session its proceedings became more public, and in 3rd and 4th Sessions, journalists, if properly vouched for, could be present at full morning sessions in St. Peters', though not at the Commissions where the real work was done. It may be added that some half of bishops present, were, with their experts or secretaries, guests of the Holy See, and that the cost of C., though it has never been disclosed, was certainly exceedingly large. Histories of the Four Sessions have been published in French by Father Wenger, editor of *La Croix*; in Eng. by an American priest writing as Xavier Rhynne, (*Vatican Council II*), *The Second Session* (1964), *The Third Session* (1965), *The Fourth Session* (1966). There is a good succinct account of whole Council, unfortunately titled *Vatican Politics*, by George Bull (1966). The different Decrees are published separately by Catholic Truth Society; in one volume, with a commentary, by Geoffrey

Chapman Ltd., and by Paulist Press (U.S.A.). Among numerous commentaries may be mentioned two by E. Schillebeecks, O.P., trans. under title of *Vatican II: a Struggle of Minds* (dealing with first two sessions (Dublin, 1963); *Vatican II: the Real Achievement*, covering 3rd and 4th Sessions, (1967); see also *Theological Highlights of Vatican II*, by Joseph Ratzinger (The Paulist Press, 1966). D.W.

Vatsīputrīyas A school of Buddh. thought, founded by Vatsiputra (3rd cent. BC), which, unlike the orthodox, affirmed the reality of a human 'person', which transmigrated from one existence to another. (→ Pudgala-Vādins). T.O.L.

Vāyu God of wind in → *Rgveda*, who pervades atmospheric realm, and in later writing sometimes considered as 'spirit' indwelling all life. Though of some importance in Vedic period, V. faded somewhat in classical → Hinduism; but in → Madhva's Vaisnavism he played import. mediating role between God and men; only through him can → salvation be achieved; he was regarded as being incarnated in Madhva himself. N.S.

Veda The *Veda* (lit. 'Knowledge') is the sacred literature (→ revelation, Hindu) of Brahmanical → Hinduism. The earliest part consists in collections of Vedic hymns—the →→ *Ṛgveda*, the *Samaveda* and *Yajurveda*, together with more magically oriented work, the → *Atharvaveda*. To these collections were added expository works, known as → *Brahmanas* and 'forest treatises', the → *Aranyakas*. Overlapping with these latter categories of writings, there are the → Upaniṣads. These constitute last part of Veda (→ Vedanta). Later than the classical Upaniṣads are number of lesser Upaniṣads not recognised as forming part of sacred canon. Students who studied the V. under teacher were also expected to become proficient in number of subsidiary sciences, the *Vedāngas* or 'limbs of the Veda', namely sacrificial technique, phonetics, prosody, etymology, grammar and → astrology. Over long period the V. was handed down orally, in remarkably conservative and efficient manner. The essentials of Upaniṣadic teaching were later summed up in the → *Brahmasutra*. N.S.

Vedānta Vedanta, lit. meaning 'the end of the Veda', is one of the six schools of trad. Hindu → philosophy, though it comprises within itself viewpoints of widely differing character. The usual adjective is 'Vedāntin', but occasionally one has 'Vedantist' in mod. English. V. expounds later part of Vedic scriptures, namely the → *Upaniṣads*; and is in principle based on summary of Upanisadic teaching contained in → *Brahmasutra*. Sometimes 'Vedanta' is used more narrowly to ref. to 20th cent. versions of → Advaita Vedanta, as found in writings of → Vivekananda and exponents of the 'perennial philosophy' (e.g. Aldous Huxley). Trad. V., as the *uttaramimāṁsā* or 'later exegesis' of the Veda, is coupled with → Mimamsa or *purvamīmāṁsā*, the 'earlier exegesis' of the Veda. In fact, however, the two schools have very different assumptions, and V. is, moreover, much more concerned with systematic metaphysical thinking. The main schools within V. are →→ Advaita (Non-Dualism), Visistadvaita (Qualified Non-Dualism) and Dvaita (Dualism). These differ radically on such issues as relation between self and ultimate reality (→ *Brahman*) and nature of God. Thus essentially V. is a group of systematised viewpoints with common subject-matter, viz. the nature of *Brahman* as in first instance expounded philosophically and theologically in Upaniṣads. The main phases of development of V. have been: first, period leading to distillation of Upaniṣadic teaching in *Brahmasutra*; second, period up to Gaudapāda and → Sankara (late 8th, early 9th cents. CE), who created Advaita V. as a system, drawing in part on → Mahayana Buddh. ideas, esp. the → *Śūnyavāda*); third, post-Sankara period, which saw not only further development of Advaita, but reaction against it expressed by →→ Ramanuja, Madhva and others; fourth, late medieval period, up to European colonial incursion (16th cent. CE); finally, mod. period. The fourth period was quite lively, but not as creative as predecessors, since it involved largely variations on earlier-estab. themes. The final period has seen restatements of V. in light of new cultural situation brought about by estab. of Western-style higher education in British India and by challenge of Christ. missionary activities. The synthesis between trad. Vedantin (esp. Advaitin) ideas and Western philosophy was facilitated by dominance of Absolute Idealism among Western philosophers in latter part of 19th cent. Two influential figures in expression of a mod. V. to the West have been →→ Vivekananda and S. Radhakrishnan. The adaptation of V. to an evolutionary account of history of world was undertaken by → Sri Aurobindo. N.S.

S. Radhakrishnan, *The Brahma Sutra* (1960); S. N. Dasgupta, *Hist. of Indian Philosophy*, vols. 1–3 (1922–40); S. D. Sarma, *The Renaissance of Hinduism* (1844); N. Smart, *Doctrine and Argument in Indian Philosophy* (1964); M. Hiriyanna, *The Essentials of Indian Philosophy* (1951); Paul Devanandan, *The Concept of Maya* (1950).

Vedic Religion The expressions 'Vedic religion' and 'Vedism' are sometimes used to ref. to relig. of Vedic hymns; sometimes more broadly to relig. of total corpus of → Veda, down to the → Upaniṣads, and therefore incl. the → *Brahmanas*, etc. It is convenient here to use broader sense. Vedism reprs. an evolution out of relig. of →

Aryan invaders of India into a more syncretistic theology and cultus, affected by a millennium of symbiosis between Aryan tribes and indigenous population whom they conquered, incl. the → Indus Valley Civilisation and various village cultures of N.W. India, comprising Munda-speaking, perhaps → Dravidian-speaking and other elements. Although invaders had in most respects inferior cultural development compared with that of Indus civilisation, highly urban and centralised, they were superior in warfare, and already possessed sophisticated sacrificial cultus, together with a pantheon related to that of anc. Iran. The cultus is repr. indirectly in hymns of Veda, which were used in connection with rites administered by the priestly (→ Brahmin) class, whose dominance grew during the millennium of Vedism, Early Western interpreters of Veda, such as Max Müller, diagnosed it as form of nature-worship; certainly many of the gods do have a relationship to natural phenomena (such as → Indra, wielding thunderbolts, → Agni, god of fire, Sūrya the sungod, etc.). However, this is to overlook some other import. motifs. Thus Indra in his battles against demonic forces reflects Aryans' struggle against orig. masters of the Panjab (much if obscurely, can be inferred from hymns about conquest of region). But, more importantly, a great deal of mythology and language of hymns needs to be understood against background of the sacrificial ritual. E.g. the importance of Agni, and features of his mythology, have to do with part played by fire in rites. Further, Vedic mythology richly indics. interplay of the invaders' beliefs and cultus with that of those they conquered, together with earlier strata of conflict. Thus the gods recognised in anc. Iran, and presumably during transition of Vedic Indians into India, viz. the → *asuras*, are treated largely as 'antigods'. A considerable number of hymns in → *Rgveda* are addressed to the aggressive Indra, who is repr. not merely as an atmospheric deity but as warrior assisting Aryans in overthrowing the *dasyus* and destroying their fortified towns. Also in Vedic hymns there are numerous refs. to → *Brahman*, the sacred force implicit in ritual. Hence it is reasonable to conclude that, though natural phenomena interpreted mythologically played some part in evolution of Vedic pantheon, reflection in the divine sphere of human events and rituals was at least as import. This analogy between ritual and action here on earth and events of higher realm ultimately issued in the *Brahman-Atman* identification in Upaniṣads; but only after infiltration into Vedic relig. of ideas drawn from non-Aryan sources, primarily belief in → rebirth and eternity of the → self (→ *atman*). Further, increasing elaboration of cultus itself led to necessity of contextual writings to supplement hymns themselves. These →→ *Brahmanas* and *Aranyakas* formed bridge to → *Upaniṣads*. The concentration upon details and meaning of the ritual both enhanced and was symptom of prestige of priestly class; and was supplemented by incorporation of folk-magic and incantatory formulae as expressed in the → *Atharvaveda* into Vedic collection. There was thus some shift from direct interest in the gods to the sacred and magical performances occurring here at earthly level. On other hand, the sacrifice itself could be seen as a cosmic event, as in the *Puruṣasūkta* (→ *puruṣa*); and later hymns of *Rgveda*, e.g., contain some profound speculations about origin of universe. The emergence of creators such as Prajāpati signalised certain drift towards monotheistic belief; while it was characteristic of many hymns to heap the attributes of other gods upon the god addressed within a hymn, thus elevating a given god to supreme place within the context (kathenotheism). The most elevated of such deities was → Varuna, though later he was to lose much of his importance; and assoc. with him was concept of cosmic, moral and ritual order, → *rta*. The later functional creator gods, such as Prajāpati, Viśvakarman, etc., did not seem to have cultic and mythic power to displace other gods; nor did any of earlier import. deities, such as →→ Indra, Varuna, Agni, etc., succeed in estab. a recognised predominance over all others (as did → Zeus, e.g., in Greek pantheon). To some extent way towards more unified conception of divinity was through process of identification, as in famous verse (*Rgveda*, i, 164, 46): 'They call it Indra, Mitra, Varuna, Agni; or again the celestial bird Garutman; the one reality the sages call by various names. They call it Agni, Yama, Mātariśvan.' In another respect, identification became increasingly import.: the homology between sacrificial ritual and spheres of reality, which it controlled, led to search for true identification of sacred power, *Brahman*. This was rationale of much Upaniṣadic speculation. Knowledge of *Brahman* gave power; and knowledge of its identity gave power over sphere of reality identified with *Brahman*. The search for such knowledge was ultimately synthesised with yogic gnosis (search for self) in formula → *tat tvam asi* and other identity statements. However, though this came to be import. motif in later Vedic relig., it was not only one (e.g. there is the theism of *Kaṭha* and *Śvetāśvatara* → *Upaniṣads*). It was task of later → *sutra* writers and commentators to evolve unified view of Upaniṣadic thought as summit of Vedic relig. By consequence earlier Vedic hymns and *Brahmanas*, etc., were interpreted from standpoint of later synthesis, and thus to large extent trad. Hindu views of Veda differ from account given above and of mod. scholarly investigations of evolution of Vedic polytheism. Vedic relig. differs from classical → Hinduism in a number of respects. First, the characteristic and dominant cults of classical Hinduism have been those of →→ Viṣṇu and Śiva. Both gods are present in Vedic hymns, but relatively unimportant. Moreover, the hymns make hostile refs. to phallus-worshippers (evidently cult of → *lingam* assoc. with Śiva). Second, the cult of → images and temple worship do not appear in Veda. Third, there are only foreshadowings of later → *bhakti* relig. Fourth, the division into → *varnas* or classes was present, but not fully-fledged → caste system of later Hinduism. Fifth, only in Upaniṣads is there the almost all-pervasive belief, of Hinduism, in → rebirth. Sixth, centre of relig. is the sacrificial cultus, which later played smaller and smaller actual part in fabric of Hinduism. On other hand, Vedic religion set certain patterns which have maintained themselves. First, dominance of Brahmin class was well estab. by mid-Vedic times. Second, upper-class patterns of → initiation and domestic ritual have continued with relatively little change, considering time-span involved. Third, Upaniṣads have retained dominant position scripturally and have remained normative for expositions of → Vedanta. Fourth, pattern of identifying one divinity with another, etc., has been followed in later Hinduism in task of synthesising variety of cults (e.g. in identification of Brahma, Śiva and Viṣṇu). Fifth, many gods of Vedic pantheon have persisted into later Hinduism, even if they have been less import. cultically than they once were. Sixth, an import. factor in unity of Indian culture has been Aryanisation and Sanskritization of literary and administrative structures of subcontinent in classical and medieval times—something which grew out of culture repr. by Vedic writings as mediated by priesthood recognising Vedic writings as revelation (→ *śruti*). But at same time incorporation of a supplementary canon (→ *smṛti*) and influence in medieval times of vernacular relig. poetry (→ *Alvars*), *Tantras* and other texts, has in practice greatly modified interpretation of Veda. Thus Vedic relig. has complex relationship to Hinduism; in theory, constituting its origin and norm; in fact, being one of factors entering into wider relig. and cultural synthesis. N.S.

M. Bloomfield, *Religion of the Veda* (1908); A. B. Keith, *Religion and Philosophy of the Veda and Upanishads*, 2 vols. (1925); L. Renou, *Religions of Ancient India* (1953); M. Müller, *The Vedas* (1956); L. Renou, *Bibliographie Vedique* (1931); R. N. Dandekar, *Vedic Bibliography* (1946); A. A. Macdonell and A. B. Keith, *Vedic Index of Names and Subjects*, 2 vols. (1958); A. A. Macdonell, *Vedic Mythology* (1897); F. Edgerton, *The Beginnings of Indian Philosophy* (1964), 'The Upaniṣads: What do they seek and why?', *J.A.O.S.*, vol. 49 (1929), pp. 97ff.; M. Winternitz, *History of Indian Literature*, vol. 1 (1927).

Veṅkaṭanātha Hindu theologian of medieval period (dates: ?1268–?1369), and one of main exponents of → Visistadvaita. His life was spent mainly in composing relig. works and in → pilgrimages. His chief writings were commentary on → Ramanuja's commentary on the → *Brahmasutra* and works on practical life of → Brahmin and on logic. He also wrote a relig. drama about → Krishna. He was leading theologian of → Vadagalai school of post-Ramanuja Vaisnavism. He is also known as Vedānta Desika. N.S.

S. N. Dasgupta, *Hist. of Indian Philosophy*, vol. 3 (1940); S. Singh, *Vedanta Desika: His Life, Works and Philosophy* (1958); S. M. Srinivasa Chari, *Advaita and Visistadvaita* (1961).

Venus Italian goddess of obscure orig. It is poss. that V. was orig. the → *numen* of 'charm, beauty'; it is not certain whether a fertility factor was included. At unknown date V. was identified with → Aphrodite, and in classical Rome assumed her attributes. Since Venus Genetrix was claimed as mother of the *gens Iulia*, the cult of V. in this form became important in Empire period. S.G.F.B.

H. J. Rose, *Roman Religion* (1949), pp. 92ff.; A. Grenier, *Les religions étrusque et romaine* (1948), *passim*; E. Giovannetti, *La religione di Cesare* (1937), *passim*.

Vesak (Vesākha, Pali/**Vaiśākha,** Skt.) →→ Holy Days (Buddh.); Festivals (Buddh.). T.O.L.

Vesāli (Pali); **Vaiśālī** (Skt.) In early Buddh. period an import. city of N. India, to N. of Pataliputta (Patna) between the Ganges and Himālaya. Between V. and the Himālaya there extended uninterruptedly a natural forest. The city was visited by Buddha on several occasions and various discourses (→ *Suttas*) are reputed to have been first uttered there. It was also stronghold of the Nigantha sect (known as → Jains); they regarded Buddhists as their rivals, and on occasions of Buddha's visits to V. are alleged to have made considerable efforts to prevent their own followers from coming under his influence. It was a place said to have been greatly admired by Buddha, who, on his last visit, 3 months before death, took a long deliberate final look at the familiar scene. About a cent. later it was at V. that the 2nd Buddh. → Council was held, to decide points at issue between → the Sthaviras and their critic Vajjiputtaka. By time the Chi. pilgrim → Hsuan-tsang visited place in 7th cent. CE, V. had suffered great decline and was a small insignificant place, apart from its hallowed assoc. for Buddhists. It is identified with village of Basrah in Muzafferpur district. T.O.L.

Vesta, Vestal Virgins V. was Roman hearth-goddess, in whose circular shrine in the Forum, the sacred fire of the city's hearth burned perpetually. The annual opening of the shrine's mysterious *penus* and cleaning of building were days of ill-omen. The sacred fire was tended by V.V. chosen by the *Pontifex Maximus*. They had many privileges, but were strictly controlled by the *Pontifex*: unchastity was punished by entombment alive. S.G.F.B.

O.C.D, *s.v.;* F. Altheim, *Hist. of Roman Relig.* (E.T. 1938), *passim*; A. Grenier, *Les religions étrusque et romaine* (1948), *passim.*

Vestments The wearing of special clothes in worship or other relig. exercises is a frequent but not universal custom; there are instances of absence of clothes (→ Nudity, Ritual). Paleolithic 'shamans' prob. wore animal disguises (→ Paleo. Relig.). The regalia of Egypt. king had relig. significance; of the clergy only the *sem*-priest wore a special vestment (leopard-skin). The Jew. high-priest had elaborate V., which were carefully prescribed (Ex. 39). Chr. eccles. V., developed out of ordinary dress, grad. became elaborate and ornate; they vary acc. to rites (e.g. special V. for → Eucharist) and to status of clergy. The regalia and V. cf Chr. kings have usually had relig. significance, as did also V. of Chinese Emperor. Paintings at Dura-Europas show Iranian priests with special V.; masks relating to sacred offices were worn in → Mithraism; distinctive clothing was worn by → Druids, Aztec priests (→ Amer. relig. Anc.), and still is in → Shinto. Besides liturgical or ritual V., special dress or insignia are worn by monastic orders (Chr., Buddh.), and by Muslim pilgrims to Mecca (→ Islam), and was by crusaders, and medieval Chr. pilgrims. Behind such multifarious practice, and in view of absence of special V. in certain religs., it is difficult to discern any common factor. There is some evidence that professional priesthoods have tended to adopt distinctive dress, although anc. Egypt provides a notable exception. The monastic habit seems to have a twofold purpose: it distinguishes those who have adopted monastic life, and constitutes form of discipline. Later symbolical explanations are sometimes given (e.g. in Chr. Church) of V., whose origs. are not known. S.G.F.B.

E.R.E., V, pp. 65–6; *D.C.C.*, *s.v.; R.G.G.*[3], III, 1646–8.

Vietnam Composed of two great deltas of the Red River in the N. (formerly Tongking), and the Mekong River in the S. (formerly Cochin-China), and the narrow coastal plain between (Annam). Little is known hist. before 111 BC, when the Chi. Han Dynasty annexed Red River delta and coastal plain, which became a province of the Chi. empire known as Nan-Yüeh (Nam-Viet). It remained an integral part of China for 1,000 years, during which the V. people adopted Chi. religs., philosophy, writing, social and administrative patterns etc. In CE 939, V. gained independence under native rulers, and, except for short period (1413–27) under Ming Dynasty, remained independent, though acknowledging Chi. suzerainty, till French conquest in latter half of 19th cent. The Japanese took over control during World War II. In 1954 the country was divided into two zones, Communist in N., and Nationalist in S., since when the country has been bitterly divided by civil war. The combined population of N. and S. V. is about 33 m. The religs. are → Buddhism, → Taoism and → Animism, with about 1 million Christians in the S. D.H.S.

Guy Wint (ed.), *Asia: a Handbook* (1965); B. R. Pearn, *Hist. of S.E. Asia* (1963).

Vihāra Lit. 'an abode', 'a dwelling place'; in Buddh. usage, a large building where *bhikkhus* (monks) resided, hence, a monastery. In → Ceylon and → Thailand word is now used to ref. to large hall or sanctuary which contains the → *Buddha-rupa.* The name of mod. Indian state, Bihar, (where Buddhism originated) is another form of word. T.O.L.

Vijñāna-Vāda Alternative name for Buddh. school of → Yogācāra, meaning 'those who affirm' (*vāda*) 'consciousness' (*vijñāna*), i.e., as the ultimate reality. T.O.L.

Vimānavatthu → *Petavatthu.* T.O.L.

Vinaya-Piṭaka First of the 3 *piṭakas* or 'baskets' of Buddh. scriptures, i.e. the → Ti-piṭaka (Skt. Tripiṭaka). The V.-P. is the 'discipline' *piṭaka*, i.e. its contents are concerned principally with rules governing life of the Buddh. → Sangha or Order of monks. A number of different versions of V.-P. are known: that of the → Theravādins, in Pali; of the → Mahāsanghikas, the Mahīśāsakas, the Dharmaguptakas, and the → Sarvāstivādins, preserved in various Chinese versions, in Tibetan, and in Buddh. hybrid Skt. The gen. scheme of contents is same in each case: (1) Section dealing with the Patimokkha rules for monks, or bhikkhus; this is called the bhikkhu-division (*bhikkhu-vibhanga*, Pali; *bhikśu-vibhanga*, Skt.); (2) Similar section for nuns, or bhikkhunīs (3) A section called 'the groups' (*khandhakas*), each 'group' dealing with a special aspect of life of Sangha, such as ordination, the → *Uposattha*, meeting-rules concerning dress, robes, medicine, food, dwellings, furniture, etc. In the Pali V.-P. of the Theravādins, these groups are arranged in two series: the first is called the Great Chapter (*Mahāvagga*); the second, the Lesser Chapter (*Cullavagga*). The rulings in the *Vibhanga* and *Khandhaka* sections are given a narrative setting; the occasion on which an offence occurred or practice began to be followed is described, together with the Buddha's decision on subject given on that occasion. The rules regarding ordination, in the *Mahāvagga* of the *Khandhaka*, are given in context of founding of the Order, after Buddha's enlightenment. In case of the V.-P. of the Sarvāstivādins and Mahāsanghikas, the *Khandhakas* section is intercalated between the *Bhikkhu-vibhanga* and *Bhikkhunī-vibhanga*. In all extant V.-P.'s, except those of the Mahīśāsakas and the Mahāsanghikas, various additional items have been appended, at a time after compilation of main work; some of these appendages are as late as 1st cent. BC. Prob. the oldest material which now comprises the V.-P. is the → *Patimokkha*, list of offences which is recited on *Uposattha* days by the monks in assembly and confession made by a monk of any offence of which he is guilty (→ Discipline, Buddh. Monastic). In the *Bhikkhu-vibhanga* this *Patimokkha* list of offences is amplified by addition of a commentary on basic text. T.O.L.

The *Bhikkhu-vibhanga*, or *Suttavibhanga* has been trans. into Eng. by I. B. Horner in 3 vols. as *The Book of the Discipline*, vols. I, II and III (1938, 1940, 1942); the *Mahāvagga* of the *Khandhaka* as vol. IV (1951); the *Cullavagga* of the *Khandhaka* as vol. V (1952).

Viññāna (Pali); **Vijñāna** (Skt.) Term used in Buddh. analysis of human existence; usually translated 'consciousness', the most import. of the 5 constituent groups (→ Khandhas), that make up human individual. It is V. which is regarded as the regenerative force, that which passes on, at termination of one human individual existence, to form another. V. is incl. in the 'chain of causation' (→ Paticca-Samuppada), as the 3rd link. T.O.L.

Vipassanā (Pali)/**Vipaśyanā** (Skt.) Buddh. term, usually trans. 'inward vision', 'insight'. V. is one of the 2 principal factors in attainment of enlightenment; the other is *samatha*, or quietening of the mind. V., in sense of transcendental insight into, or analysis of, the nature of things, is regarded as the second and more import. It is by V. that the Buddh. truths concerning the suffering (→ Dukkha), impermanence (→ Anicca), and impersonality (→ Anatta) of all existence are seen and acknowledged. The pair of terms *samatha-vipassanā*, are regarded as synonymous with *samādhi-pannā* (meditation) and wisdom (→→ Samadhi; Panna). The develop. of this pair of factors, mental quiescence and transcendental insight, is connected very closely with cultivation of the absorptions (→ Jhāna). → Meditation, Buddh. T.O.L.

Virgin Birth The idea of a woman, usually a virgin, giving birth without sexual intercourse is anc. and widespread. Among some primitive peoples, poss. owing to biological ignorance, conception has been attrib. to variety of other causes. Grk. mythology provides numerous instances of V.B., in which a deity fathers child in some extraordinary way (e.g. → Zeus by impregnating Danaë in form of shower of gold). Such myths were usually concerned to explain divine parentage of heroes, both legendary and real (e.g. Alexander the Great). The Egypt. pharaohs claimed to be offspring of → Atum or → Amun through the god's intercourse with their mother (→ Kingship, Divine). The → Buddha was believed to be virgin-born. The V.B. of → Jesus is recorded in two Gospels only (Mt. 1 : 18ff.; Lk. 1.26ff.): it is not mentioned elsewhere in N.T.; Paul's silence about V.B. is strange, since it would have provided powerful support for his advocacy of virginity. The orig. of belief is obscure: the idea of V.B. was un-Jewish, yet the two accounts concerned are distinguished for their Jew. setting. It is poss. that belief arose out of need to rebut an early Jew. accusation that Jesus was born of an illicit union. In later Chr. belief, the V.B. became theologically necessary in view of doc. of → Original Sin, which was held to be transmitted through carnal conception. (A logical consequence of this view was later doc. of → Immaculate Conception of Virgin Mary). S.G.F.B.

E.R.E., XII, *s.v.; R.G.G.*[3], III, 1068–9; E. Norden, *Die Geburt des Kindes* (1924); Ch. Guignebert, *Jesus* (E.T. 1935), pp. 115ff.; J. Klausner, *Jesus of Nazareth* (E.T. 1929), pp. 232–3; C. Clemen, *Religionsgeschichtliche Erklärung des N.T.* (1924), pp. 114ff.; R. Bultmann, *Die Geschichte d. synoptischen Tradition* (1957[3]), pp. 316ff., *Ergänzungsheft* (1958), p. 44; E. Stauffer, *Jesus* (E.T. 1960), pp. 23ff.; L. Leaney, 'The Birth Narratives in St. Luke and St. Matt.', *N.T.S.*, 8 (1962–3); H. H. Oliver, 'The Lucan Birth Stories and the Purpose of Luke-Acts', *N.T.S.*, 10 (1963–4); H. Frhr. von Campenhausen, *Die Jungfrauengeburt in der alten Kirche* (1962). D. Flusser in *C.C.*, p. 229, cites some poss. Jew. Ils.

Viśiṣṭādvaita V. ('Qualified Non-Dualism') is major form of → Vedanta teaching. Its chief exponent was → Ramanuja, whose aim was to present theistic account of ultimate reality (→ *Brahman*). Also import. in development of teachings of school were Pillai Lokacarya (→ Tengalai) and → Venkatanatha. As name of school indicates, it teaches a kind of monism or non-dualism, but one in which nevertheless a vital difference is maintained between God, on one hand, and world and souls on other. This difference between God and souls, etc., was necessitated by importance attached by Ramanuja and successors to → *bhakti* and loving dependence on → Viṣṇu. The tension between two aspects of V. was resolved chiefly through analogy between soul-body relationship and God-world relationship. A person is a unitary being, even though eternal self can be distinguished from psycho-physical organism (body). Likewise God and world constitute a unity, but God is nevertheless distinguishable from world, which functions as his 'body' and subserves his purposes. Whereas human bodies are not totally subservient to intentions, etc., of the self, the world is totally the instrument of God's will. Likewise soul-body relationship is in some sense mirrored in God's relationship to individual selves: he functions as their *antaryāmin* or 'inner controller'. This model of the Lord (→ *Isvara*) as Self of world enabled Ramanuja to emphasise human dependence on God, and to make sense of → grace, a corollary of *bhakti* devotionalism, since destiny of individual's eternal self depends upon action of the Lord. However, Ramanuja's successors came to be divided on problem of precise way in which grace operates, and in partic. about whether human effort conduces to salvation (→→ Vadagalai, Tengalai). The released self attains god-like state in relationship with Lord, sharing in his bliss and possessing kind of omnipotence, for no desire of self is now left frustrated. But, though in these respects the liberated self is like God, it does not share latter's capacities of creation and destruction, nor his power to bring about → salvation. The essential likeness between the self and God enables the Qualified Non-Dualists to explain the text → *tat tvam asi* and other 'identity' texts in scriptures as meaning that self is one with *Brahman*, in sense that they share same essential nature. Philosophically, V. adopted a realist position, in contrast to doc. of illusion (→ *maya*) featuring so prominently in → Advaita Vedanta. The latter was criticised for confusing impermanence and illusoriness, and thus denying proper status to common-sense knowledge. Thereby, moreover, belief in personal Lord and Creator was relegated to realm of 'lower' (ultimately illusory) knowledge. Though V. was centered on faith in a personal God, a powerful and subtle critique of trad. philosoph. 'proofs' of God's existence was offered by Ramanuja in his commentary on the → *Brahmasutra*. The source of knowledge of God lies in God himself, and does not spring from formal arguments. V. cosmology owed much to → Samkhya, only, of course, latter's categories are seen against theistic background: thus nature (→ *prakrti*), out of which articulated world as we know it has evolved is seen as God's 'body' in its subtle form. Qualified Non-Dualism is most import. systematic presentation of Vaisnavite theology (though see also → Dvaita); but in mod. times it has been much less influential in restatement of Hindu belief than Advaita. N.S.

J. Estlin Carpenter, *Theism in Medieval India* (1921); S. M. Srinivasa Chari, *Advaita and Visistādvaita* (1961); J. A. B. van Buitenen (ed. and tr.), *Ramanuja's Vedarthasamgraha* (1957); Max Müller (ed.), *S.B.E.*, vol. 48 (1904); N. Smart, *Doctrine and Argument in Indian Philosophy* (1964).

Visiting the sick Muslim trad. treats this as an import. duty which Muslim, can expect from one another (→ Muslims mutual responsibilities). Blessing descends on one who visits his sick Muslim brother. A trad., given by → Muslim, is based on Matthew xxv:42ff., beginning with rebuke for failing to visit the sick. Another quotes → 'Abdallah b. al-'Abbas as saying a short visit and making little noise when visiting an invalid is part of the → *sunna* (q.v.). (→ Retreat). J.R.

Hughes, p. 658; *Mishkāt*, pp. 320ff.; Wensinck, *Handbook*, p. 214.

Viṣṇu Also transliterated 'Vishnu', one of two great gods of → Hinduism, with → Śiva. V. was of no outstanding importance in the → *Rgveda*, being one of number of solar deities addressed in hymns. In post-Vedic period, however, he steadily rose in importance, partly because his cult merged with that of Vasudeva and → Krishna. This syncretic tendency was assisted by development of conception of various incarnations (→ *avataras*), through which V. manifests himself and restores true relig. The parallel emergence of Śiva to a supreme position brought about synthesis in which they and → Brahmā, the creator, formed kind of → trinity, or alternative representations of ultimate reality (→ *trimurti*). At human level, this involved relatively peaceful (but not always so) coexistence of →→ Vaisnavism and Saivism. The iconography and mythology of V. are complex. He is most often repr. as dark, with four arms, bearing various emblems, or as asleep on serpent Śeṣa, repr. primeval ocean. In latter state, V. is quiescent, before beginning of next period of creation (→ cosmogony, Hindu). From his navel there emerges Brahma, who acts agent in creative process. The emblems wielded in his hands, in other representation of him, incl. a conch, disc, lotus, bow and mace (disc symbolizes sun, mace his power to destroy, etc.). The steed of V. is magical bird Garuḍa, maybe relic of a theriomorphic cult which early Vaisnavism absorbed. His consort is Lakṣmī, also ref. to as → Srī, goddess of fortune. She plays import. role in domestic worship and is focus of an annual pan-Indian festival. V. as creator of world and restorer of → *dharma*, etc., is treated as more benevolent deity than Śiva; sometimes the contrast is made between V., the preserver, and

Siva, the destroyer,—though both gods in principle have both functions, though V.'s folding up of created world is portrayed in mythologically more gentle way, for he falls asleep. His benevolence towards men is depicted in story of his 'three strides': he gains dominion of world from → *asuras*, by taking on form of dwarf (→ *avataras*), whom king of *asuras* promises as much land as he could cover in three strides. V.'s strides take him across whole universe. As far as cult and devotion go, V. gets less, in a sense, than Siva; for it is primarily the persons of his *avataras* who are focus of → *bhakti*, etc. However, salvation is typically described in terms of communion with V. in his heaven, Vaikuntha (→ heaven, Hindu conceptions of). Other titles than Vasudeva, etc., ascribed to V. are Nārāyaṇa and Hari. N.S.

A. Danielou, *Hindu Polytheism* (1964); J. N. Banerjea, *The Development of Hindu Iconography* (1956); H. Zimmer, *Myths and Symbols in Indian Art and Civilization* (1962).

Visuddhimagga Title of one of most import. books of post-canonical Pali lit. of the → Theravāda. Its author, → Buddhaghosa was instrumental in restoring some of prestige which Pali as a language for Buddh. writing had lost to Sanskrit by 5th cent. CE. The title of work is usually trans. as 'Path of Purification'; it indic. primary concern of book, viz., a thorough description and exposition of the Buddh. life. This is reflected in the 3 main divisions of book: morality (*sīla*), meditation (*samādhi*), and wisdom (*paññā*), i.e. the threefold description of the Buddh. life (→ Eightfold Path). The first section, on morality, consists of 2 chs.; the section on meditation, or concentration, contains nine chapters (III–XI), setting out various methods, in partic, the 40 poss. objects which may be used to aid develop. of concentration; some of these are physical objects, some mental. Still on subject of meditation, chs. XII and XIII describe its rewards. The third section, concerned with wisdom or understanding (*paññā*), contains 10 chs. (XIV–XXIII). Of these, XIV–XVII provide theoretical analysis of experience, after manner of the → Abhidhamma (q.v.) lit. The 4 following chs.; XVIII–XXI, are entirely practical, and show how the meditator's own experience may be analysed in terms of theory set out in XIV to XVII. Ch. XXII sets out nature of truths which are directly perceived as climax of the Buddh. life, and ch. XXIII, as a parallel to XII and XIII in the previous section, sets out benefits of transcendental wisdom. A new transl. from Pali into Eng. has been made by Bhikkhu Nyānamoli, *The Path of Purification* (1964). T.O.L.

Vivekananda Narendra Nath Datta, who later took relig. name of Vivekananda, was born of high class Calcutta family in 1863; after meeting → Ramakrishna, by whom he was converted to a living faith, he was increasingly drawn to life of renunciation. He and number of other disciples became → *sannyasins* after Ramakrishna's death in 1886, and estab. themselves in a house-monastery. V. and the others undertook extensive trips round in India. In 1893 funds were collected to send V. to the Parliament of Religions in Chicago, being held in conjunction with World Fair; he made a strong impression. The publicity launched him on lecturing tours in America and England; this formed beginning of overseas missionary work of the → Ramakrishna movement, which was formally organised as Ramakrishna Mission in 1897. It was devoted to monastic living, teaching and service of the poor and sick, and soon had *maths* in import. centres up and down India. Later, in 1909, for legal purposes, the charitable and teaching side of organisation was split off from monastic side, and so movement is now known as Ramakrishna Math and Mission. V. took further trip to Europe and U.S. in 1899–1900. He died in 1902. His teachings emphasised unity of relig., the various rituals, myths and docs. of the different faiths merely being secondary details: so that, in respect of these modes of expressing the one truth, there is no call to insist upon universal uniformity. Inspiration for this view was derived from Ramakrishna's experimentation in treading paths of different religions. His teachings were expressed in a modified → Advaita Vedanta, and stressed relig. humanism. Relig. is 'the manifestation of the Divinity that is already in man'. Thus V. preached meditative practices as means of realising this divinity, and was critical of notions of dependence on an external God. Western relig. in over-emphasising man's fallen nature had militated against right kind of spiritual self-reliance. A prolific writer and lecturer, V. provided an intellectual expression to homely and parabolic teachings of his master. N.S.

Swami Gambhirananda, *History of the Ramakrishna Math and Mission* (1957); Swami Vivekananda, *The Complete Works of Swami Vivekananda*, 7 vols. (1924–32); Swami Nikhilananda, *Vivekananda, a Biography* (1953).

Void, Doc. of (Buddh.) → *Mādhyamika*. T.O.L.

Voodo Form of devil-worship brought by Negro captives from Gold Coast (Africa) to America and West Indies (partic. Haiti). Name derives from Ewe word *vudu* meaning 'gods' (→ Africa, West, Religion). Orig. the chief sacrifice in V. was a girl-child, ref. to as 'the goat without horns'. In more recent times a white kid acts as substitute. Candidates for V. priesthood have to undergo horrible and disgusting tests (they are credited with supernatural powers). Worship is of

orgiastic kind, and incl. snake-dances. S.G.F.B.
G. Parrinder, *African Ideas of God* (ed. E. W. Smith, 1950), p. 231; M. Deren, *Divine Horsemen: the Living Gods of Haiti* (1953); A. Métreau, 'Sorcellerie, magie blanche et médicine dans la religion du vodou', *R.H.R.*, 144 (1953).

Vows (General) V. are gen. solemn promises, voluntarily undertaken, to a deity, to perform some specified action beyond one's normal obligations. Sometimes V. may be made to, or between, human beings (e.g. Marriage V.), and reinforced by invocation of deity as witness. Basically V. are bargains with deity, made in hope of divine succour or reward. The custom of making V. occurs in most religs. The O.T. has many examples (cf. Gen. 29:20–2; I Sam. 1:11; → Nazarites). Likewise the N.T. (e.g. Acts 19:23 I Cor. 7). Grk. and Lat. lit. abound with instances (e.g. Agamemnon's V. to Artemis which resulted in sacrifice of his daughter Iphigenia; Octavian vowed temple to Mars Ultor for victory). A notable instance of V. in Chr. Church are the threefold V. of poverty, chastity and obedience in → Monasticism. → Canon law distinguished between 'simple' and 'solemn' V., with implication of irrevocability of latter. In Middle Ages V. were frequently connected with building church, giving some specified ornament for church, making → pilgrimage. Psychologically V. express natural reaction to intense personal need, by making a high bid for divine help. S.G.F.B.
E.R.E., XII, pp. 644–60; *D.C.C.*, *s.v.; R.G.G.*^{3}, II, col. 1321–5.

(China) It was a common custom in anc. China for princes and great officers of feudal states to make solemn V. on great public occasions such as ratification of treaties of peace or alliances. Sacrifices of animals were made (oxen and pigs by princes, dogs by officials, fowls by common people); blood of sacrificed animal was smeared on lips of those making the V. The covenant was written in blood on a tablet, which was buried with the sacrifice. In the *Ch'un Ch'iu Tso Chuan* are numerous instances of such solemn V. being taken and soon broken, so that anc. moralists protested that formal V. were detrimental to sound morals.

Frequent in China were V. of eternal brotherhood made betw. friends and ratified by mingling of their blood, which was supposed to create a bond equiv. to blood relationship. The numerous → secret societies and brotherhoods in China bound their initiates by solemn V. to provide mutual aid, protection and friendship. Elaborate ceremonies were devised to emphasise solemnity and binding force of V. taken. The most famous example of such is the celebrated V. of the Peach Garden, (a theme of romance and drama), when the three heroes, Liu Pei, Kuan Yü and Chang Fei (2nd–3rd cents.) bound themselves to fight together for preservation of the Dyn. against the Yellow Turban rebellion. The ceremony took place in Peach Garden of Chang Fei; it was ratified by sacrifice of a black ox and white horse.

Relig. V. are common in → Buddhism and → Taoism, and are taken by both monks and laymen, those of former being stricter and more comprehensive. In Chi. Mahāyāna Buddhism, the 48 'bodhisattva V.' are detailed in the *Wu-liang-shou sūtra*, and may be summed up in the V. never to rest until salvation of all sentient beings is achieved. Buddh. monks, on reception into the order, take numerous V.; the four great V.: (1) To seek salvation of world; (2) To root out from self all evil and passion; (3) To study law of Buddha; (4) To attain to perfection of Buddhahood are taken by monks and devout laymen alike. In gen., Taoism copied Buddhism in practice of taking V.

A common practice in China, in cases of severe sickness etc., is to make a V. (*hsü yüan*) to offer gift to a god or temple, to do some act of merit, to fast, or to go on → pilgrimage. D.H.S.
J. Legge, *The Chinese Classics* (1861–72), vol. 5, *passim*; H. Welch, *The Practice of Chinese Buddhism* (1967), pp. 285ff., 361ff. For a full discussion and numerous refs. see *E.R.E.*, XII, pp. 646ff.

(Islam) (*Nudhūr.*) Are assoc. with → oaths. Qur. lxxvi:7 says, 'Fulfil vows', and xxii:30 has something similar about V. regarding → Pilgrimage rites. ii:273 says God knows the V. people make. A trad. says V. have no effect against fate, obviously meaning that one's predestined term of life cannot be extended to enable one to fulfil a V. But another tells of a son who informed Muhammad his mother had died without fulfilling a V., and he told son to fulfil it. Naturally it is laid down that one must not make a V. to commit some wrongdoing. J.R.
E.I., III, pp. 806–8 (*nadhr*); Wensinck, *Handbook*, pp. 244; → Bibliog. at Oaths.

Vulgate Lat. version of Bible (*editio vulgata*), made by → Jerome, on order of Pope Damasus, and publ. in complete form *c.* 404. Its orig. purpose was to produce authoritative version in place of conflicting text of Old Lat. MSS. Jerome used orig. Heb. version for much of O.T. Jerome's text was subject to increasing corruption in later reproduction. Pope Sextus V issued a definitive text in 1590; a corrected ed. followed in 1592; a new revision, initiated by Pius X in 1907, is still proceeding. S.G.F.B.
H.D.B.^{2}, *s.v.; D.C.C.*, *s.v.*

W

Wahhābīs Name commonly applied to members of movement which owed its origin to Muhammad b. 'Abd al-Wahhāb (1115–1206/1703–92), native of N. Arabian town 'Uyayna. He had early in life been a → Sufi, but his later studies in various centres brought him under influence of doc. of → Ibn Taymiya, and he returned to 'Uyayna to preach his message. The degeneracy of popular relig. depressed him. He denounced idolatry of visiting → saints' tombs, invoking prophets, saints and angels and seeking their intercession, and making vows to anyone but God. To him the → Qur., the → Sunna and necessary application of reason were only right sources of knowledge. He upheld doc. of predestination and denounced allegorical interpretation of Qur. He further demanded that faith should be proved by works. Attendance at public prayer was made obligatory, the → rosary was forbidden, mosques must be devoid of ornament. Smoking tobacco was not only forbidden, but punished by not more than 40 stripes. He had to leave 'Uyayna; but found supporter in Muhammad b. Su'ūd at Dar'iyya. The new sect soon became involved in warfare and its fortunes rose and fell. The W. empire expanded all over N. Arabia and into Syria and Iraq till overthrown in 1234/1818. The movement seemed doomed, but in 1320/1902 'Abd al-'Azīz, known in the W. as Ibn Saud, captured Riyāḍ and grad. extended his influence till he captured the Hijaz containing holy cities of Mecca and Medina by 1344/1925. In 1331/1912 he had instituted agricultural colonies whose residents were called *Ikhwān* (brethren), indic. that the relig. tie superseded the tribal. They were to cultivate the land to produce wealth and were given arms for relig. warfare. With this nucleus Ibn Saud spread his power. In more recent times the state has profited greatly from sale of oil concessions. Though the theology of movement may seem to some reactionary, its purpose is to restore a pure Islam like that in Prophet's time. It is still puritanical; but there is no hesitation about using the results of Western science. The movement's chief contribution is its effort to get rid of practices which are considered idolatrous, and to oppose the medieval teachings which were not part of the original Islam. J.R.

E.I., IV, pp. 1086–90; Pareja, index; J. L. Burckhardt, *Notes on the Bedouins and the Wahabys* (1831); H. St. J. Philby, *Arabia of the Wahhabis* (1928), *Sa'udi Arabia* (1955); H. C. Armstrong, *Lord of Arabia, Ibn Saud* (1934) (French trans., 1935); Dickson, *Arab of Desert, passim;* Rutter, *Holy Cities, passim*; K. S. T. Twitchell, *Saudi Arabia*, 2nd edn. (1953); Rahman, *Islam*, index; G. Rentz, 'The Wahābīs' in *Religion in the Middle East*, II (1969).

Walāya (*friendship*) This may apply to all believers in so far as God is pleased with them; but is more normally applied to → saints, who are brought into closer fellowship with God. In → Shi'a Islam, word is used of period of the imamate, which succeeded period of prophethood concluded in → Muḥammad. Here it seems to combine the two ideas of friendship and supremacy, or government. The hidden → imam, who is in occlusion, is both near to God and in control of affairs. The form more usual for supremacy, or government is *wilāya*. J.R.

O. Yahia, 'Aspects intérieurs de l'Islam,' in Charnay, *Normes*, p. 18; H. Corbin, 'Sur la notion de walâyat en Islam shî'ite, in Charnay, *Normes*, pp. 38ff.; Arberry, *Doctrine*, p. 61.

Wang Yang-ming (Personal name Shou-jên): 1472–1529. Born into noble and scholarly family in Chekiang Province, he commenced his official career at age of 28, and distinguished himself in several import. governmental posts, and by success in suppressing rebellions. His forthright personality, attacks on → Confucian orthodoxy and his own novel teachings incited enmity of rulers and conservative officials, and from 1521–7 he lived in virtual retirement in his native place. He was greatest exponent of → Idealist School of neo-Confucianism, which after his death continued to exercise great influence in China and Japan. His *Enquiry on the Great Learning* contains all his fundamental doctrines—that the mind is one with Universal Principle (*li*); that the highest good is inherent in the mind; that the sage forms one body with all things; that extension of innate knowledge through action is way to perfect moral life. D.H.S.

W. T. Chan, *Source Book* in *Chinese Philosophy* (1963); Fung Yu-lan, *Hist. of Chinese Philosophy*, vol. 2 (1953), pp. 596–620; W. T. Chan (tr.), *Instructions for Practical Living and other neo-Confucian Writings of Wang-ming* (1963).

War, attitude (China) In anc. China sacrifice and war were reckoned to be greatest affairs of state, and there was almost continual internecine strife betw. states and W. with barbarian tribes. The gods were always invoked before going to W. The two most solemn ceremonies connected with W. were the *lei* and *ma* sacrifices. The *lei* sacrifice was offered to supreme God by sovereign himself; the *ma* sacrifice was offered on field of battle.

Opposition to W. was voiced by many of early → Confucians and → Taoists; partic. by → Mo-tzŭ, who condemned rapacious aggression of feudal lords as an unmitigated evil, opposed to will of a righteous Heaven, and destructive of people's livelihood.

The first classical treatise on art of W. was written by Sun Wu of Ch'i *c.* 500 BC.

Confucianism accepted theory that the sovereign, being supreme ruler, could have no enemy of equal status with himself, therefore, any W. on which he was engaged was virtuous and repr. righteous punishment of rebels and offenders. Socially, soldiers were ranked in lowest grade of social structure, being regarded as necessary evil. Yet throughout Chi. hist., great military leaders were deified, and → Kuan Yü came to be universally worshipped as God of W. D.H.S.

E.R.E., XII, pp. 692–4.

(Japan) The Japanese, throughout their hist., have exalted the military ideal. Devoted loyalty to one's lord expressed itself in military service. The spirit of → bushido was cultivated among the → Samurai. War heroes were deified and → Hachiman, the god of war, was one of most popular deities. Even Buddh. monasteries, in 11th and 12th cents., formed small standing armies of monks and men who worked on their estates, and made W. on civil rulers and even among themselves. The spiritual exercises of → Zen not only gave guidance to warriors in their spiritual aspirations, providing a relig. basis for their sense of honour and virtue of courage; they also promoted their practical training in arts of W. In mod. times the great military shrine in Tokyo, honouring spirits of those who had died in W., was second only in import. to great imperial shrines. W., until after traumatic experience of World War II, was always considered a legitimate instrument of political policy and national aggrandisement. D.H.S.

G. B. Sansom, *Japan* (1946), *passim*; M. Anesaki, *Hist. of Japanese Relig.* (1930), pp. 13, 210–2.

War (Holy) Among early peoples W. was instinctively regarded as an activity in which the gods of the combatants were also involved. A ceremonial palette of the pharaoh Narmer (*c.* 3000 BC) shows king, assisted by hawk-god (→ Horus), destroying his enemies; the Sumerian 'Stele of the Vultures' attests a similar view. Evidence abounds of sacred character of W., gen. finding ritual expression and assumption of divine approbation, with most anc. peoples: e.g. Greeks, Romans, Etruscans, Celts, Germans, Scandinavians, Aztecs. The Israelite god → Yahweh was essentially a war-god, and Hebrew lit. contains abundant evidence of idea of the H.W.: the conquest of Canaan was conducted under the aegis of Yahweh. Among the Dead Sea Scrolls was one of the 'War of the Sons of Light against the Sons of Darkness'. (→→ Qumran; Maccabees; Zealots) The H.W. is a fundamental concept of Islam (→ Jihād). The → Crusades provide the most notable Chr. example of H.W. (→ Sikhs). S.G.F.B.

G. v. Rad, *Der heilige Krieg im alten Israel* (1958[2]), H.D.B.[2], pp. 1029ff.; *R.G.G.*[3], III, col. 62–73; Y. Yadin, *The Scroll of the War of the Sons of Light etc.* (1962); S. G. F. Brandon, *Jesus and the Zealots* (1967).

(Islam) → Jihād. J.R.

Wat Siamese name for Buddh. monastery (*ex* → *āvāsa*); → Monasteries, Buddh. T.O.L.

Wealth, attitude (China) The Chinese regarded W., along with happiness and longevity, as one of the three greatest blessings. Ts'ai Shên, the god of W., is universally worshipped; a shrine or pictures of him are found in almost every home. His temples are numerous; he is the special patron of merchants. Apart from renunciation of W. by → Buddhists and some → Taoist priests, there is no gen. relig. condemnation of economic acquisitiveness as sin of avarice. Yet, acc. to orthodox → Confucian doc., growing rich by trade was considered morally incompatible with virtue and benevolence. The mercantile class was morally despised, socially degraded, and sometimes politically suppressed. Chi. relig. sought to mitigate oppressiveness of rich by giving supernatural sanction to qualities of generosity and benevolence. Worship of numerous gods of W. was deemed to assist in attainment of W., but at same time committed one to justice and generosity in its dispensation. D.H.S.

C. K. Yang, *Relig. in Chinese Society* (1961), pp. 76ff.

Wên Ch'ang Chi. God of Literature. Named Chang Ya, he was born during T'ang Dynasty in mod. Chekiang, and went to live in Ssŭch'uan (W. China), where he was subsequently worshipped as a god. He was a brilliant writer, held appointment in the Board of Rites; after his sudden disappearance and death, he was canonised, and later (1314) apotheosised, taking his place among the gods of China. In → Taoist mythology he has as many as 17 reincarnations, ranging over 3000 years, being identified with star-god, Tzŭ-t'ung, patron of literature, enthroned in the star-palace of the Dipper or Great Bear. He received imperial recognition, and numerous temples were built in his honour. D.H.S.

E. T. C. Werner, *Dictionary of Chinese Mythology* (1932); H. Maspero, 'The Mythology of Modern China', in J. Hackin (ed.), *Asiatic Mythology* (1932), pp. 311ff. (→ Deification).

Wên Shu Chi. name for the → bodhisattva Manjusri, who is personification of thought and knowledge. He is repr. as riding on lion, and holding in his hands a sword and book. The Chinese regard the holy mountain, Wu-t'ai-shan, as his chief resting place. D.H.S.

S. Couling, *Encycl. Sinica* (1917, 1965), p. 326.

Wên and Wu The posthumous titles given to founders of Chou Dynasty in China (*c.* 11th cent. BC). They are constantly ref. to in Chi. literature, and regarded as supreme examples of kingly virtue. D.H.S.

Wesley, John and Charles John (1703–91) and Charles (1707–88), 15th and 18th children of Samuel Wesley (1662–1735), rector of Epworth (Lincs.). Educ. Christ Church, Oxford, J. proceeded to fellowship at Lincoln Coll. At Oxford, the brothers gathered round them a group of Chr. students (incl. George Whitefield), who, from their devotions and practical good works, based on planned living, were nicknamed 'Methodists'. After ordination, the brothers sailed (1735) on a mission to Georgia, where C. became secretary to the Governor (Oglethorpe); the mission was a failure. Their friendship with Peter Böhler, and J.'s visit to Moravian colony at Herrnhut, was speedily followed by their 'conversion' (1738): their faith, hitherto conformist and conventional, took fire and impelled them to life-long crusade of evangelism. Their intention was to revivify the → C. of E., which, with its rigid parish system and distrust of → 'enthusiasm', was failing to measure up to relig. needs of a growing, changing country. Finding many parish churches closed to him, J. betook himself to field-preaching. His success led him to organise 'Societies' of devout laymen everywhere (on model of the Oxford student groups) for active worship and work in parishes. From 1742 J. became a travelling evangelist, averaging 8000 miles a year on horseback, bringing the Gospel to a whole new constituency of farm labourers, fishermen, and the multitudes of workers whom the Industrial Revolution bred in cities of the North and Midlands. For them J. provided and published a Christian Library; he integrated them by constant letter-writing, personal supervision, and strict control of local lay leaders, into a body that slowly grew apart from parent Church, little as he and still less as C. wished it. The work spread to Ireland and Scotland and (from 1760) America, where growth of 'Methodism' caused J. to ordain Thomas Coke and (through him) Francis Asbury as 'Superintendents' (1784)—or Bishops, as they regarded themselves. J. laboured to day of death, within a week of which he wrote his celebrated letter to William Wilberforce against the 'execrable villainy' of the slave-trade. High-Churchman, sacramentalist, the 'Master-Builder' and almost unparalleled preaching evangelist, J. merits inclusion among the Saints of the Church. C., mellower than J., and, unlike him, blessed with a happy marriage, was likewise an itinerant preacher, but on a far lesser scale; his unique contribution are his Hymns. He was prob. the world's greatest hymn-writer, both in quantity (estimates vary from 5000 to 7000) and quality, and his finest hymns are used universally—'Jesu, Lover of my Soul', 'Love Divine, all loves excelling', and hymns for the Chr. year, from 'Hark the herald-angels sing' to 'Christ the Lord is Risen today', and 'Hail the Day that sees Him rise'. (→ Methodism). B.D.

J. Wesley's *Journal* and *Sermons*: there are many modern Eng. and American edns. Standard lives by Southey (1820), Tyerman (1870), and J. S. Simon (5 vols., 1921 *et seq.*). C. Wesley's *Journal*, ed. T. Jackson (1849); *Life*, by T. Jackson (1841); mod. works by F. L. Wiseman (1933), and F. C. Gill (1964), both entitled *Charles Wesley*. R. E. Davies and E. G. Rupp (eds.), *A Hist. of the Methodist Church in Gt. Britain*, vol. I (1965); contains best modern summary, with full bibliog.; M. Schmidt, *John Wesley, a Theological Biography*, vol. I (1962).

Whitehead, Alfred North (1861–1947) Born at Ormsgate, son of Anglican clergyman, W. was educated at Trinity College, Cambridge, where he became a Mathematics Fellow. Beginning as mathematician, W. collaborated with B. Russell in production of *Principia Mathematica.* Leaving Cambridge in 1910, he became Professor of Science and Technology at University College, London. During this time his interests became more philosophical, and he developed a philosophy of nature in a series of works—notably in the *Concept of Nature* (1920). In 1924 he joined the Depart. of Philosophy at Harvard University, retiring in 1937. His Gifford Lectures, given at Edinburgh in 1927 and 1928 (publ. in 1929 as *Process and Reality*) expound his philosophy of organism. This philosophy, W. said, was a recurrence of pre-Kantian modes of thought, but a recurrence transmitted by mod. scientific and humanistic thought. *Process and Reality* was a sustained effort of constructive thought, for which

W. thought the time was ripe, since the new physics, on one hand, and sociology, on the other, had provided the necessary incentive and material for the new philosophy.

W.'s system is certainly the most imposing metaphysical production in mod. British philosophy. He called his system the philosophy of organism; what he proposes is a social doc. of being. The world is a non-growing complex of real things which act upon each other within patterns set by primordial order; it is a continuing process of events driven on into novelty by blind, undifferentiated creativeness. In its onward course, selected possibilities from the domain of eternal bodies are capitalised, since to come to be as event is to acquire characteristics. What completes the system is the concept of God. God is a necessary part of W.'s system; but the term does not occur in the statement of the categorical scheme. Nor is the concept of God immediately deducible from the scheme taken by itself. It is, in fact, an explanatory concept in the scheme. The concept of God is intro. in the course of W.'s answer to problem of origin of the subjective importance of a temporal actual entity. If some actual entities have beginnings in time, then we have the problem of how these actual entities can satisfy the categorical demand of subjective unity. W.'s solution is the argument for 'a principle of concretion'. His ontological principle implies that the only reasons are actual entities. So, if some novel possibility is relevant to every partic. temporal situation, the best of these relevancies must be some fact in the constitution of primordial and everlasting actual entity. This non-temporal actuality can, W. thinks, be called God, because the qualities generated by its apprehension are precisely the sense of refreshment and companionship which is essentially a feature of relig. experience. W. distinguishes between the primordial and the consequent beings of God. The primordial aspect of His Being is His envisaging the realm of possibility in its abstraction from two particular matters of fact. The consequent nature of God refers to God's concreteness, as He is related to the world and as the world's events are objectified in Him. God receives from world the effects of the world's action; but He receives them in His own way as subject. The content of the divine experience changes with the happenings in the world. J.H-T.

Whitehead's most import. works are: *Process and Reality*, *Adventures of the Mind*, *Science and the Modern World* and *Religion in the Making*. Cf. W. A. Christian, *An Interpretation of Whitehead's Metaphysics* (1959); D. M. Emmett, *Whitehead's Philosophy of Organism* (1932); I. Leclerc, *Whitehead's Metaphysics: An Introductory Exposition* (1958); I. Leclerc (ed.), *The Relevance of Whitehead* (1961); W. Mays, *The Philosophy of Whitehead* (1959); P. A. Schilpp (ed.), *The Philosophy of Alfred North Whitehead* (1941).

Wills (Islam) → Inheritance and wills. J.R.

Wine, for intoxicants (China–Japan) Neither → Confucianism nor → Shinto had any relig. prohibitions regarding use of W. W. or fermented liquor was used at sacrificial feasts and offered to gods and ancestor spirits as libations. The 'Hygiene Sch.', which developed in → Taoism taught that the 'interior gods' detest smell of wine and meat, and Taoist adepts must in consequence avoid their use. But other Taoists, e.g. the Sch. of Pure Conversations, developed in 3rd. cent. CE, actually encouraged drinking of wine. Some modern Taoist sects forbid use of W. as an encouragement to → asceticism. → Buddhism in China and Japan forbad use of W. to monks, but did little to discourage its use among laity. W. is forbidden to Muslims in China, and by some Christ. sects both in China and Japan. In both countries drunkenness is common, but is usually confined to feasts where large quantities of W. are consumed. A social stigma attaches to over indulgence in W. only when it results in impropriety or breach of peace. D.H.S.

Wisdom (Buddh.) → *Paññā*. T.O.L.

(Books) (Buddh.) → *Prajnā-Pāramitā Sūtras*. T.O.L.

(Literature) Designation for class of Heb. lit. dealing with practical issues of life within context of belief in divine government of world: → Job, Proverbs, → Ecclesiasticus, Wisdom of Solomon are usually incl. in this class. W-L. was a well estab. *genre* of Egypt. and Mesop. lit.; its products predate the Heb. and prob. influenced some of it. S.G.F.B.

*H.D.B.*², pp. 1039–40; *E.R.E.*, XII, pp. 742–6; W. O. E. Oesterley and T. H. Robinson, *Intro. to the Books of the O.T.* (1937), pp. 150ff.; M. Noth and D. Winton Thomas (eds.), *Wisdom in Israel and in Anc. Near East* (1955); *A.N.E.T.*, pp. 405ff.; W. G. Lambert, *Babylonian Wisdom Lit.* (1960); J. A. van Dijk, *La sagesse suméro-accadienne* (1953); Fr. W. Freiherr von Bissing, *Altaegypt. Lebenswissheit* (1955).

Witchcraft The Shorter Oxford English Dictionary defines witchcraft as 'the exercise of supernatural power supposed to be possessed by persons in league with the devil'. This is based upon ideas about medieval and Renaissance witchcraft; but comparable ideas are almost worldwide and mod. anthropologists have made broader definitions. Gen. W. is now distinguished from sorcery or bad magic, and many peoples who believe in it make this distinction. It is held that → magic may be good or bad, public or private. The magician uses either suggestive or palpable means of harming his victim, such as casting spells, or sticking pins in an image. But the witch normally uses no apparatus and affects victim by psychic influences. The witch is commonly, though not always, believed to be female, and she is thought to turn into a vampire or bird, or accompany an animal familiar, flying through the air to a 'coven' of her fellows, where they feed on human flesh provided by one of their number. Witches are accused of cannibalism, but also of other troubles: unnatural disasters, blight, hailstorms, barrenness, impotence, sickness and death. The witch may have no apparatus, but can be accused of practising harmful magic as well. That magicians poison their enemies may be true; but clearly witches cannot do many things for which they are blamed, and strictly have no existence. People are accused of W. when much of it is fanciful; while there are real witch-doctors, there are no witches, only people accused of this imaginary offence.

Belief in W. was known in classical times; there is little trace of it in Bible, because theory of a separable soul was not congenial to Hebrews. The 'witch' of Endor (so-called only in the A.V. page headings) was properly a spiritualistic medium, and the few other Biblical refs. are to harmful magic and poisoning. There are occasional refs. to W. in European Chr. writers; but it was not made a heresy till 1484 by Pope Innocent VIII. Then the Inquisitors got to work and made holocausts in many parts of Europe. The theory that W. was a relic of Druidic religion or anc. fertility cults, popularised by M. Murray, has not been accepted by historians or anthropologists, despite her attempt to show that every king of England down to Charles I was sacrificed to make a witches' holiday. Anc. superstitions continued for centuries after the formal conversion of Europe to Christianity, and old festivals were preserved in mummers' plays; but these were not W., which ref. to the night-flying of cannibalistic hags, arising from the imagination and added to fantasies of incubi and succubi.

The social background of the great European witch craze was medieval malaise; espec. the Black Death, which swept Europe almost every ten years from 14th cent. and drastically reduced its population. Scapegoats were found in Jews, →→ Cathari heretics, Knights' Templar, and finally in witches. Jews had been accused of devouring unbaptised children and others in their Sabbaths and Synagogues; the same charge and terms were used of witches. High infant mortality continued to bring accusations against any poss. culprits: midwives, mothers, mothers-in-law, neighbours and old widows.

In 9th cent. a council at Ancyra declared that night-flying was illusory; but in 15th cent. there was said to be a new sect in league with → Satan, to whom women had flown at a Sabbath. The Bull of Pope Innocent VIII in 1484 declared that it had 'lately come to our ears . . . that many persons of both sexes . . . have abandoned themselves to devils . . . and have slain infants yet in the mother's womb'. The → Inquisition had already been at work; in trials at Arras in 1459 accused witches were burnt under the name of Vaudois or Waldensians. Although the French Parlement later annulled the sentences, all but one of the accused had been executed. Innocent's Bull gave new power to Inquisitors, and their leaders in Germany, Kramer and Sprenger, produced an infamous handbook of procedure, *Malleus Maleficarum*, the 'Hammer of Witches'. This demanded torture to produce confessions, encouraged children to denounce parents, criminals to give evidence, and defending lawyers to betray their clients. Witches condemned by church courts were handed over to secular arm to be burnt alive. It is not known how many people were killed, but the bishop of Bamberg alone claimed to have burnt 600 witches. C. and N. Europe were particularly afflicted for over 200 years, during which time scores of thousands perished. But in Spain, home of the Inquisition, officials were more critical of popular accusations. In 1611 the Inquisitor Salazar Frias examined 1800 accused people and concluded that there was no evidence that any of them had committed an act of W. Not all Inquisitors were so enlightened; but accusations were carefully checked, and Spain, like Britain, never saw the mass burnings for imaginary witchcraft that disgrace C. Europe.

Reformed England, soon beyond Innocent's Bull, allowed no legal torture and had no Inquisition; but continental ideas slowly exerted influence, and in 1563 a statute promised death to people practising W., enchantment, or sorcery resulting in destruction of another person. The reign of Elizabeth I saw greatest number of executions as it was a time of unrest. James I published his *Daemonologie*, in which he attacked the adoration of devil, and the damnable opinions of Reginald Scot, a Kentish squire who had boldly ridiculed witchcraft ideas. The reigns of Charles I and the Commonwealth were milder; but there was a trial of Lancaster witches or gypsies in 1612; in 1644 a self-appointed witch-finder, Matthew Hopkins, spread terror in south-east for three years till the Long Parliament investigated the matter. The last official execution in England was in 1684; the law was amended in 1736 to forbid hangings, though popular opinion was still often agitated about W.

American settlers, of most relig. denominations, took with them witchcraft-beliefs that were current in Europe. There were occasional executions of suspects, and a final outburst at Salem in Massachusetts in 1692. A new governor from England, Sir William Phipps, instituted inquiries into W. accusations, and the Harvard theologian Cotton Mather supported him in belief that the devil was active through annoyance at losing his American territories which he had ruled through the old Indian religion. Twenty people and two dogs were executed, and hundreds were imprisoned or fled. The governor was recalled, the agitation subsided, and most people, except Mather, repented their cruelty.

Belief in W. in Europe declined among educated classes, and improved health and lower rates of infant mortality removed some causes of the mania. Nowadays small groups sometimes claim to practice W.; 'white witches' working for good or indulging in private ceremonies, but they have no connection with medieval W. belief, which was based upon notions of evil people practising the reverse of good, with Black Masses and cults of the devil (→ Satanism). There is little evidence that this was ever done, for the records come solely from prejudiced Inquisitors who attributed to witches their own fantasies, and, even where confessions were given freely or extracted by torture, they were written down by the Inquisitors. The true successors to witch-hunts are the mod. persecutions of Jews, Negroes, or any deviant minorities. Nazis and Ku Klux Klan continue the pattern of terror in search for scapegoats to bear the ills of society.

Similar beliefs to those of European W. are found in many parts of world, though with variations acc. to culture. Popular beliefs in India still hold that witches meet at night at cremation or burial grounds, and chant incantations in state of nakedness. They are distinguished from exorcists, whose services can be used to drive away evil spirits. Witches and sorcerers work only evil in secret, making spells, using the evil eye, and preparing images of their victims in which nails and thorns are stuck to give them pains in same places. Magical flight is believed in almost universally; the same magical powers are credited to holy yogis and fakirs, or evil witches and sorcerers. The shamanic priests of Siberia and N. America are believed to fly, often changing into birds so that they fly off in freedom of ecstasy (→ Shamanism). But whereas holy men may cover great distances in ecstasy, or more moderately practise levitation, witches and sorcerers are thought to be engaged in nefarious raids upon the life-stuff of their victims, enhancing their own powers and prolonging their lives at expense of others.

African W.-beliefs have been espec. closely studied by mod. anthropologists. Most African languages distinguish the witch, who works at night by psychic means, from the sorcerer who uses tangible apparatus. The witch is different from the witch-doctor, who heals those who have been bewitched, and is a public and respected figure. Many of the 'secret societies', male initiation and ancestral organisations, have as one function the control or extirpation of W. There are frequent mod. witch-hunting movements in which new leaders and methods appear, additional to the local and traditional witch-doctors. The Bamucapi witch-hunters spread across C. Africa in the 1930's, and the Atinga were active in W. African countries in the 1950s. Thousands of people, mostly women in W. Africa, were accused of witchcraft and purged by ordeals and fines. There were few deaths, since mod. laws forbid capital punishment for this offence. Many W. charms were surrendered; but, despite accusations of cannibalism, outside observers saw no evidence of this.

African W.-belief is as complex as European. There is the idea of the separable soul which leaves body in dreams; the prowling witch may catch an innocent wandering soul and take it away to the cannibalistic orgy. But, even though women have confessed to this crime, it has been said that they do not eat the physical body, but only 'the soul of the flesh'. W. explains the high infant mortality, and other sudden and unaccountable diseases, such as poliomyelitis. Similar explanations are given for unnatural phenomena, blighted crops or floods in one field and not another. Family organisation encourages suspicion of strange women: wives who come from a distant group, rival wives, barren women, mothers whose children die, mothers-in-law, old women who live abnormally long, all may be subject to accusation. Improvement in health services will contribute to decline in witch-belief; though it is said that there is an increase of belief due to modern insecurity, there is no evidence of the comparative incidence of the belief in past centuries in tropical countries. Pagan temples have generally been healing shrines for the bewitched, and with decline in their power this function has been transferred to the many independent churches and new cults. Orthodox churches tend to deny or ignore the witch-fears; but the proliferation of new sects shows need for exorcists and new style witch-doctors. Where there is continued family or social unrest, outlets for emotions will be directed against old witches or new public enemies, all of them scapegoats for the ills of society. E.G.P.

E. E. Evans-Pritchard, *Witchcraft, Oracles and Magic among the Azande* (1937); C. L'Estrange Ewen, *Witch Hunting and Witch Trials* (1929); M. J. Field, *Search for Security* (1960); H. C. Lea,

Materials towards a History of Witchcraft (1939); M. A. Murray, *The Witch-cult in Western Europe* (1921); W. Notestein, *A History of Witchcraft in England* (1911); L. S. S. O'Malley, *Popular Hinduism* (1935); E. G. Parrinder, *Witchcraft, European and African* (1963).

(China–Japan) → Demons and Demonology. D.H.S.

Women (China–Japan) →→ Marriage, Divorce, Adultery. D.H.S.

(Islam) The → Qur. produced a distinct advance on the pre-Islamic position of W. Much of sura iv devotes space to discussion of subject, and the Qur. deals with it frequently elsewhere. W. have rights of → inheritance, receiving half the amount a male heir receives. When two male witnesses cannot be found, one man and two women may give evidence in court, for, if one errs, the other may be able to refresh her memory (ii:282). Husbands must maintain their wives and in gen. the husband is superior. If he fears his wife may be refractory, he has authority to admonish her, keep away from her bed and chastise her. If she becomes obedient, all is well; but if a breach is feared, the matter should be settled by arbiters, one from each family (iv:38f.). While husbands rank superior to wives, and have better right to take a wife back during the '*idda* period (→ Divorce), ii:228 says W. have 'the same rights as those exercised over them.' W. must cover themselves and not display ornaments, letting them be seen only by husbands, male relatives within prohibited degrees, slaves, aged servants, or children (xxiv:31); this does not apply to older women (xxiv:59). If any women commit indecency to which 4 witnesses testify, they are to be confined to their houses till death, or till God provides some way of dealing with them (iv:19). During her courses, a W. being unclean, cannot engage in the prayers, or observe the fast. The prayers do not require to be made up, but omitted days of fasting must, when she is purified. It has sometimes been said erroneously by people in the W. that W. have no place in → paradise. The Qur. speaks of various classes of men and W. for whom God has prepared forgiveness and a mighty reward (e.g. xxxiii:35). In some regions the → '*Ulamā*' still look with disfavour on W. praying in mosques; but in many countries they do, though in separate lines from men. An import. institution was right of W. to hold property over which their husbands had no control. In mod. states, W. are freed from some regulations which restricted them and have rights not previously available, such as entry into professions and public life. On 1 Jan. 1957 W. in Tunisia were granted the franchise at 20 on condition that they abandoned the veil. In 1963 W. in Iran were given the franchise. (→→ Divorce; Ḥarīm; Marriage; Mother of the child; Polygamy, Rashīd Riḍaā). J.R.

Lane, *Egyptians*, index; Pareja, p. 459; Gaudefroy-Demombynes, *Institutions*, ch. 8; Levy, *Social Structure*, index; Coulson, *Law*, *passim*; Cragg, *Counsels*, index; Rahman, *Islam*, p. 38; N. Daniel, *Islam, Europe and Empire* (1966), index; *M.W.*, XLVIII (1958), 'Tunisia', p. 263; N. Asaf, 'Woman in Islam', *I.L.* (Oct. 1967), pp. 5–24.

Worship → Ritual. Subject is dealt with in most articles on specific religions. See Synop. Indices.

(Buddh.) →→ *Devotions; Holy Days; Pagoda; Stupa.* T.O.L.

(China) Several Chi. terms are roughly equiv. to Eng. word W., having gen. significance of 'to salute with reverence', 'to salute acc. to appropriate rites'. The clearest expression of Confucian idea of W. is to be found in the *Book of Rites* (→ *Li Chi*), which forms one of the 5 Confucian Classics. It opens with the words: 'Always and in everything let there be reverence', and emphasises need for reverence in all ceremonies which regulate intercourse of men with gods and ancestors, and esp. in W. of Supreme God. Though great emphasis is always placed on meticulous performance of rituals of W., → Confucius was insistant on import. of sincerity. Without inward sincerity, worship is vain. → Confucianism also related true service of God with proper cultivation of one's own nature and preservation of moral values. The motive of W. was to honour spiritual beings; but in doing so material, moral and spiritual blessings were deemed to accrue to worshipper and those whom he represented. W. in → ancestor cult was justified on grounds that it fostered in the living feelings of love, reverence and duty towards family and state. Though acts of W. by common people consisted mainly of simple offerings, prostrations and prayers before household gods and ancestor tablets, in the state cult W. was conducted with great ceremonial, dignity and solemnity. The rituals followed a prescribed pattern. Trad. relig. music was used. Specially composed prayers were written on tablets, recited, presented at altar and ritually burned. Numerous sacrifices and libations were made. Distinguished scholars assisted emperor in performing the state W.; a Master of Ceremonies guided and directed the proceedings. Much of Chi. W. was connected with mortuary rites for deceased ancestors, which played a basic role in Confucian relig. Their main purpose was 'to express gratitude to the originators and recall the beginnings', to cultivate moral values, and to foster refinements of human relationships.

In Chi. Buddhism, apart from small number of learned monks and mystics, → Buddhas and →

bodhisattvas are objects of W. for all devout Buddhists. This is esp. true of → Amidist or Pure Land sects. The recitation halls in monasteries of these sects, dominated by images of → Amitabha and his two great assistants, are devoted to W., known as 'honouring the Buddha's name'. The reason given for this W. is a desire to save all sentient life, and to become a Buddha. In gen., however, the laity worship in both Buddh. and Taoist temples for more mundane reasons such as cure of sickness, desire for prosperity and success in business, birth of a son etc. Wieger (*op. cit.*) describes Amidism in China as a 'real theism, Amitabha having approx. attributes of God, → Avalokitesvara those of saviour (not redeemer) and rebirth in the Pure Earth being eternal salvation'. In respect of W. of devout Buddhists, he writes 'They pray lengthily, humbly, ardently, from the bottom of the heart, with attitudes so natural and touching that all suspicion of simulation must be laid aside'. D.H.S.

E.R.E., XII, pp. 959ff.; J. Legge (tr.), *S.B.E.*, vols. 27 and 28, *passim*; L. Wieger, *Hist. of Relig. Beliefs and Philos. Opinions in China* (1927), p. 591; D. H. Smith, *Chinese Religions* (1968), *passim*; H. Welch, *The Practice of Chinese Buddhism* (1967), *passim*.

(Christ.) →→ Eucharist; Liturgy; Mass.

(Hindu) The practice of worship in → Vedic relig. was bound up with performance of sacrifice (*yajna*) and with domestic rituals. The latter have remained import. in → Hinduism, but the old Brahmanical sacrificial techniques have faded in significance. The emergence of classical Hinduism put emphasis on → *bhakti*, while in the early cents. of Christian era use of → temples and → images became widespread, resulting in present situation, where sacred buildings and festivals proliferate. Worship or *pūjā* (term which may be of → Dravidian origin) became norm in approaching the gods, whether in domestic shrines or in temples, etc. The simplest form of *puja* involves repetition of god's name, or recitation of formula such as the → *gayatri*. At other extreme are elaborate ceremonials directed to the gods by officiants (*pūjāris*), when the deity is given homage and entertained as though human (being roused, washed, fed, etc.), or, at great festivals, taken out in procession. Mostly, H.W. has not been congregational, and attendance at temple is individual act, though congregational worship developed in some *bhakti* sects. In course of temple rites, offerings are made to god, either by priesthood or worshippers. Commonly offerings of food (*prasada*) are made, to be consumed by faithful. Animal sacrifices are now relatively rare (→ sacrifices, Hindu). The growth of → Tantrism affected forms of worship, through evolution of mixed Vedic-Tantric ritual used by many *pūjāris*, and adaptation to individual use of forms of yoga posture (→ *asanas*) and meditation as preliminary to paying homage to god. The worshipper, in purifying himself thus, can identify with essence of deity (though this account is less applicable to → Vaisnava *bhakti*). In add. to great temples, there is large number of local shrines, devoted to village-gods (*gramadevata*, → gods, Hindu) and other sacred entities. On whole, temple-worship, though import., is not necessary part of Hinduism, in sense that worship can be practised anywhere, and esp. at home. The Hindu in visiting temple is visiting home of the god, just as on other occasions he will go to pay homage to a holy man in his → ashram, etc. In medieval India use of hymns became popular in worship (though not yet in congregational worship); and hymnodists of S. India (→→ Alvars, Saivism) had marked impact on development of *bhakti* faith. The hymn (*kīrtana*) extolling deity (the term lit. is any sort of laudatory recital) was later adapted by → Caitanya into the *sankirtana* or congregational hymn. The practice of such collective relig. singing became extremely popular, esp. in Bengal, and was accompanied by scattering of votive offerings (*prasada*) for the faithful to scramble for. *Sankirtana* influenced the → Brahmo Samaj, which adopted the style, as have Christ. congregations. Dancing has also been common feature of temple ceremonial. The old Vedic *yajna* still is sometimes performed; but it is largely in domestic or social rites, such as marriages among upper classes, that Vedic ritual has survived as living force. On the whole yogic *dhyana* or meditation cannot be counted as form of worship, though some forms of it (e.g. in teaching of → Madhva) involve meditating upon God as supreme object of worship. (→ Festivals, Hindu). N.S.

Mrs. S. Stevenson, *The Rites of the Twice-Born* (1920); C. G. Diehl, *Instrument and Purpose* (1956); S. Kramrisch, *The Hindu Temple*, 2 vols. (1946); H. Bhattacharyya, *The Cultural Heritage of India*, vol. 4 (1956); L. S. S. O'Malley, *Popular Hinduism* (1935).

(Jain) As far as is known there was no significant practice of worship in early → Jainism. A major tenet of J. is that there is no Creator God; but other gods, as inhabitants of universe were not denied. However, way to → liberation lies not through prayer, etc., but through practice of austerity and meditation, typically within J. order of monks. At one time, though it died out, J. possessed cult of → *stūpas*, as in Buddhism; and reverence was paid to the → Tirthamkaras, who showed way to emancipation. Partly under influence of classical → Hinduism, J. evolved temple-cults, where respect was paid to Tirthamkaras. This eventually took on much of air of

Hindu worship, and spread of temples was assisted by relative prosperity of the J. community, who saw in endowment of places of worship a sign of piety. There was, in later medieval period, some resistance to use of idols, esp. in Gujarat. Hindu priests are used as officiants in → Svetambara temples; but officiants are J. in → Digambara ones. From strict point of view there can be no transaction between Tirthamkara and devotee, as former exists on a changeless plane, so that use of images tends to be explained as way of keeping Tirthamkaras vividly in mind, since reflection on perfection of their life-monads (→ *jiva*) in the liberated condition is conducive to striving to emulate the ideal. N.S.

J. Jaini, *Outlines of Jainism* (1940); Mrs. M. Stevenson, 'Worship (Jain)', *E.R.E.*

(Japan) Acc. to → Shinto mythol., the Jap. people are descendants of the gods, and all Japanese have deep and continuous sense of having direct relationship with their ancestors, human and divine. The term W. applies both to respect for human beings and reverence for the gods. The Shinto term for W. is *matsuru*, which means to live in attitude of constant prayer and obedience to the → *kami*. Consequently, their protection should be besought. W., therefore, plays considerable role in daily life, both before family altars and in temples. The daily W. (*nikku*), when offerings and prayers are made to household gods, consists of simple ceremony before the → *kamidana*. Solemn W. (*matsuri*) takes place periodically in every Shinto temple. The objects of W. are the emperors, great national and local heroes, nature deities and functional gods.

The purpose of W. is: (1) To report all significant happenings to the *kami*; (2) To express gratitude for blessings received; (3) To offer to the *kami* praise and prayer; (4) To discover will of the *kami*, and to seek their protection and blessing. Private individual prayers are seldom mentioned in anc. Shinto records; but there are abundant examples of official liturgies or → *norito*, containing mainly petitions for material blessings. Shinto temples are always open throughout day for direct, personal approach to the *kami* on part of worshippers; on festival occasions they are open day and night, when elaborate rituals of W. are celebrated by Shinto priests.

The acts performed in W. by individual worshippers are simple: a symbolic purification, the clapping of hands, a brief prayer or meditation with bowed head, and an offering.

For Buddh. W. in Japan → Worship (Buddh.). D.H.S.

E.R.E., XII, pp. 802ff.; D. C. Holtom, *The National Faith of Japan* (1938), pp. 163ff.; W. G. Aston, *Shinto* (1905), ch. 10; J. Herbert, *Shinto* (1967), chs. 6 and 7.

Wu Hsing Chi. name for the 5 elements or natural forces; wood, fire, earth, metal and water, of which, acc. to anc. Chi. theory, the universe is composed. Their combination is source of everything; they are mutually productive and destructive of each other in rotation. When properly united, they create peace and prosperity.

In anc. China stress was laid on interaction between ways of nature and human affairs, and the theory of the W.H. was used for magic and divination. During period 403–221 BC, the W.H. formed basis of a unified system of cosmology. To Tsou Yen (*c.* 305–240) is attr. the combining of this theory with that of → Yin-Yang, and a cyclical interpretation of nature and history. This theory exercised tremendous influence during Han Dynasty (206 BC–CE 220), espec. over Tung Chung-shu (*c.* 179–104 BC); it had great impact on Chi. ethical and social teaching, encouraging view that all things are mutually related and in constant flux and transformation. The number 5 (*wu*) was considered to have a cosmological and mystical significance, and the W.H. were thought to correspond with the 5 primary colours, tones of music, tastes, directions, sense organs, virtues, feelings, social relations, etc. (→ Alchemy). D.H.S.

Fung Yu-lan, *Hist. of Chinese Philosophy*, vol. 1 (1937), pp. 41–2, 159ff., 275–6; E. T. C. Werner, *Dictionary of Chinese Mythology* (1932).

Wu Ti → Kuan Ti. D.H.S.

Wu Wei Chi. term meaning 'non-activity'. A concept of early → Taoist philosophy, which taught that at centre of all movements, transformations and spontaneous action of nature was the immovable, inactive, perfectly quiescent → Tao, which 'makes complete without acting and obtains without seeking'. This spontaneity of nature centred in the inactivity of Tao should be, they taught, the model of all human behaviour, individual, social and governmental. The individual must seek return to his natural self, and, discarding power, ambition and man-made moral standards, seek to cultivate a *wu wei* of the mind. Applied to government, the ruler utilises free and spontaneous activity of the people, guiding and controlling events, acc. to Tao, and influencing them by his power and virtue (→ Tê). The more perfect his government, the more inactive he will be. The doc. of W.W. was a Taoist protest against coercion, either by military force, multiplicity of laws, or Confucian moral standards, which, acc. to Taoism, only increased lawlessness, aggression and human misery. D.H.S.

H. Welch, *The Parting of the Way* (1957), pp. 19ff., 83–6; Fung Yu-lan, *Hist. of Chinese Philosophy* (1937), vol. 1, pp. 331–4.

Y

Yahweh (Yahveh) Personal name of god of Israel, usually trans. into English as 'the Lord' (sometimes transliterated 'Jehovah'). The name in Heb. was written in consonants only: YHVH; its orig. vowels are unknown, since the sacred name was not pronounced and expressions such as *Adonai* ('My Lord') used instead. 'Yah' and 'Yahu' appear at end of some personal names, and prob. preserve a form of sacred name. The orig. meaning of Y. is obscure: it is interpreted in Ex. 3:14 as 'I will be as I will be'; it was prob. connected with verb 'to be', and was poss. an assertion of the effective reality of the deity. There is evidence that Y. was orig. god of the Kenites, a nomadic people, and was prob. known also among the Aramaeans of N. Syria. Heb. trad. reveals that Y. had not always been god of Israel (Ex. 3:1ff., 6:2ff.; → Covenant). Y. seems orig. to have been a desert god, assoc. with war, storm and fire (→→ Yahwist; Judaism). S.G.F.B.

H. H. Rowley, *From Joseph to Joshua* (1950), pp. 148ff., *Worship in Anc. Israel* (1967), pp. 8ff.; *P.C.*², 89f., 179c; M. Noth, *Hist. of Israel* (E.T. 1960)², pp. 92ff.; W. F. Albright, *From the Stone Age to Christianity* (1946), pp. 197ff, *Yahweh and the Gods of Canaan* (1968); A. Lods, *Isräel* (1949), pp. 150ff., 370ff.; H. Wildberger, *Jahwes Eigentumsvolk* (1960); D. K. Andrews, 'Yahweh the God of the Heavens', in W. S. McCullough (ed.), *The Seed of Wisdom* (1964); *R.G.G.*³, III, col. 515–16; *E.J.R.*, pp. 407ff.

Yahwist (J.) The word has a twofold use: (1) It designates writer(s) or literary trad. distinguished by use of → Yahweh in Genesis and Exodus (also prob. throughout → Pentateuch, or → Hexateuch). This source (often abbrev. 'J'), dating *c.* 900–750 BC, has been described as 'both an epic and a drama' (R. H. Pfeiffer). It does in fact present a philosophy of → history, tracing development of Yahweh's providence from → Fall of Adam to Settlement of → Israel in Canaan. It is designed to give the various tribes that became Israel a sense of unity from a common past and cult of Yahweh. (2) This purpose of J. was the literary expression of policy of a party devoted to estab. Yahweh as god of Israel. The O.T. provides evidence of grad. success of this Y. policy. (→ Heilsgeschichte). S.G.F.B.

R. H. Pfeiffer, *Intro. to Old Test.* (1948), pp. 142ff.; *H.D.B.*², pp. 745ff.; C. R. North, *The Old Test and Modern Study* (ed. H. H. Rowley, 1951), pp. 48ff., 84ff.; O. Eissfeldt, *Geschichtsschreibung im Alten Testament* (1948); M. Noth, *Hist. of Israel* (E.T. 1960²), pp. 110–38; *R.G.G.*³, III, col. 516–7; S. G. F. Brandon, *History, Time and Deity* (1965), ch. 5.

Yajurveda The third of four collections (*saṁhitās*) constituting Vedic canon, and compiled some time after the → *Rgveda.* It consists largely in sacrificial formulae (*jayus*, sing.) incl. prose utterances together with stanzas; while the *Rgveda* arranges hymns in acc. with gods addressed, the Y. arranges them (or rather stanzas from them) in order to be used in ritual. The Y. illustrates growth of ritualism and concentration upon acts themselves, rather than upon gods, which tended to transform → Vedic relig. The Y. was handed down in two main forms, the Black and the White. The White Y. incl. its detailed expositions of rubrics accompanying ritual actions in a separate → *Brahmana*, the *Śatapatha Brāhmana*, while the Black Y. interweaves its rubric and commentarial material with the formulae themselves. The White Y. is a little later than Black, and both date from *c.* a cent. or two after *Rgveda.* The instructions contained in them are designed for the *adhvaryu* or priest involved in manual part of ritual (→ Hierarchy, Hindu). N.S.

A. B. Keith (tr.), *The Veda of the Black Yajus School, Entitled Taittiriya Samhita*, 2 vols. (1919); R. T. H. Griffith (tr.), *The Texts of the White Yajur Veda; Translated with a Popular Commentary* (1899); M. Winternitz, *History of Indian Literature*, vol. 1 (1927).

Yakkha Class of supernatural beings mentioned in Buddh. Pali canon; in some cases the Y.'s appear to be semi-divine spirit-beings possessing supernatural powers but morally neutral; in other cases Y.'s are repr. as wicked beings, hostile esp. towards human beings who seek to live a holy life. Buddh. etymology explained the term Y. as being derived from root *yaj*, to sacrifice. Even though etymology may be incorrect, it indic.

that in early Buddh. times Y.'s were beings to whom sacrifices were sometimes offered. They are certainly ref. to in Pali texts as 'flesh devourers'; in many cases the ref. appears to be to the Y.'s eating human flesh. This has led to suggestion that idea of wild demonic beings inhabiting lonely places (characteristic of Y.'s in Pali canon) may have been orig. from existence of cannibal tribes in certain parts of anc. India. On other hand, Y.'s are also assoc. with disease, and idea may have its roots in the 'flesh devouring' aspect of certain diseases, held to be work of Y.'s. The horrific character of the Y.'s finds expression in Buddh. texts mainly in refs. to loud noises made by Y.'s at night or in lonely places, to disturb or frighten monk or nun engaged in meditation. T.O.L.

J. Masson, *La Religion Populaire dans le Canon Bouddhique Pali* (1942), ch. 9; T. O. Ling, *Buddhism and the Mythology of Evil* (1962), pp. 15–19.

Yama (Buddh.) Lord of death, in Buddh. trad., Y. repr. element of anc. popular Indian belief which Buddhism has preserved and given its own features. Old age, illness, punishment and approaching death are his messengers, sent as warnings to men not to live careless and immoral lives. At death men are examined as to whether they have heeded these messengers; if they have not, they are despatched to various appropriate hells. (*M.N.*, III, pp. 179f.). Y. thus repr. in popular, mythological terms, Buddh. idea that a man's moral actions inevitably bring their appropriate rewards or penalties. In the *Mahāsamaya Sutta* of the → Digha Nikaya, 'twin Yamas' are mentioned, which Rhys-Davids takes to be conception similar to that of Castor and Pollux. (*D.N.*, II, p. 259; cf. Rhys-Davids, *Dialogues of the Buddha*, II, p. 290). (→ Yen Wang). T.O.L.

J. Masson, *La Religion Populaire dans le Canon Bouddhique Pali* (1942), ch. 5.

Yāna Term occurring in Buddhism (Pali, Skt, and Buddh. Hybrid Skt.), signifying a means of attaining Enlightenment. In course of Buddh. history various Y.'s came to be distinguished, each characterised by different methods and scope from others. The use of these terms began with rise of the self-styled 'Great' means to salvation, the → Mahā-yāna. Adherents of this form distinguished the way of those known as Śrāvakas, who heard the teachings of the Buddha and followed his way, but were unconcerned about Enlightenment of others, as the Śrāvaka-yāna. Those rare individuals who discover the way to Enlightenment without hearing the teaching of Buddha, and without being concerned for Enlightenment of others were described as 'private' or 'pratyeka'—buddhas, and their way to Salvation was known as the Pratyeka-yāna. The way of those who are destined to become enlightened, but who postpone their final full Enlightenment for sake of assisting others on the way were known as → Bodhisattvas, and their way was the Bodhisattva-yāna. It was this which was called also the Mahā-yāna, while the Śrāvaka-yāna and the Pratyeka-yāna were together regarded as the two-fold way, Dvi-yāna, which was also → Hīna-yāna or a 'Lesser' means to Enlightenment—'lesser' that is, in sense that it was less widely embracing, less inclusive than Māha-yāna; not that it was necessarily an inferior method. Since Hīna-yāna was characterised as two-fold (Dvi-yāna), the Mahāyāna was also characterised as Eka-yāna (single). Occasionally the Hīnayāna and Mahāyāna, (i.e. the Dvi-yāna and Eka-yāna) are together spoken of as the Three-fold means, the Tri-yāna, in some Mhy. texts (see D. T. Suzuki, *Studies in the Lankavatara Sutra*, 1930, pp. 358–61). A further yāna was that which developed in India during period CE 500–1000, which made great use of symbolism and sacred chants, and was known as → Vajra-yāna or Mantra-yāna. This is sometimes referred to as Tantric Buddhism. T.O.L.

Yang → Yin-Yang. D.H.S.

Yazīdīs (Yezidīs) Kurdish sect, mainly in Mosul neighbourhood, with some around Aleppo, often called devil worshippers, but calling themselves worshippers of God. Their relig. has →→ Zoroastrian, Manichaean, Jew., Christ. and Muslim elements. They believe in → transmigration of souls. Their own language is used in worship, but their two sacred books, *Kitāb al-jilwa* (The Book of Revelation) and *Maṣḥaf Rāsh* (Black Book), are in Arabic. They are reserved for a partic. class. God is the only Creator, but Malak Ṭā'ūs (Peacock Angel), the active aspect of God's being, carries out his will. Bronze and iron peacocks, called *sanjaq* (pl. *sanājiq*), are fashioned, connected with 7 angels who assisted in creation. Six are carried round Y. districts annually. Only by birth can one become a Y. Malak Ta'us is invoked in prayer. Sunrise prayer is conducted facing sun. A three days' fast is observed in December. Shaykh 'Adī b. Musāfir (d. *c.* 557/1162), a → Ṣufī held in gen. respect by Muslims, is considered by the Y. to have become divine. Pilgrimage is made to his tomb in September, assoc. with ritual ablutions, processions, hymns and dances. The Y. observe → baptism and → circumcision, the latter being optional. There is something of a caste system; distinction between clergy and laity, the chief → shaykh being considered infallible in matters of belief. Monogamy is practised, but the amīr may have several wives. Marriage outside sect is forbidden. Divorce is poss., but difficult to obtain. The punishment for adultery is death. J.R.

E.I., IV, pp. 1163–70; *E.I.*², I, p. 195 ('Adī b. Musāfir); Pareja, pp. 853–5; C. Brockelmann, *History of the Islamic people*, (E.T., 1949), p. 106; G. Furlani, 'Yezidī villages in N. Iraq', in *J.R.A.S.* (1937), pp. 483–91; *M.W.*, XXXIV (1944), 'An account of the Yezidīs', pp. 304ff.; *E.R.E.*, XII, *s.v.*; A. Mingana, 'Devil Worshippers', *J.R.A.S.*, July 1916; T. Bois, *Les Yézidis* (1961).

Yeisai → Eisai. D.H.S.

Yellow Spring (Chinese: Huang Ch'uan). Term often used in China to denote Hades, ruled over by → Yen Wang, and deemed to be situated down in the earth. D.H.S.

Yen Wang (or Yen-lo Wang). Chi. name for → Yama, who was orig. the chief of the ten kings of hell; he was degraded to become ruler of the fifth hell, because he was considered to be too compassionate towards criminals who came before him for judgement. → Buddhism borrowed this god and his functions from → Brahmanism; he is adopted also by → Taoism. He alone of kings of hell is depicted with a dark face. D.H.S.

Yima Anc. Iranian → *Urmensch* and counterpart of Vedic → Yama. Acc. to earliest trad., his reign of 1,000 years was a primeval Golden Age. Advised by → Ahura Mazdah of coming evil, Y. excavated underground paradise for himself and the best of men, animals and plants; thence he will emerge in last days to re-people the earth. Y. appears as a semi-divine being. In his reform of Iranian relig., → Zoroaster imputes to Y. original sin of slaying the ox and causing men to eat it (*Yasna* 32:8), prob. in some ritual for immortality. Acc. to R. C. Zaehner, Zoroastrians replaced Y. by → Gayomart, Mashyē and Mashyanē. S.G.F.B.

Zaehner, *D.T.Z.*, pp. 132ff.; G. Widengren in *Numen* I (1954), pp. 45ff.; J. Duchesne-Guillemin, in C. J. Bleeker (ed.), *L'Anthropologie religieuse* (1955), pp. 98ff.

Yin-Yang Chi. theory that all life and phenomena in universe result from interaction of two opposite and complementary Primary Modes or Creative Agents gained prominence during latter centuries of Chou Dynasty: it gave rise to the Y-Y. School, attr. to Tsou Yen (*c.* 305–240 BC). The theory, developed by Han Dynasty philosophers (notably Tung Chung-shu, *c.* 179–104 BC), came to have extensive influence over all aspects of Chi. civilisation: metaphysics, cosmology, government, art; it was fundamental in → Fêng Shui.

The characters Yin and Yang orig. meant the dark and bright sides of a sunlit bank; but by time of → Confucius, they had acquired a philosophical significance as two aspects of a duality which Chi. thinkers perceived in all things. The Yin was Earth, negative, passive, dark, feminine, destructive; the Yang was Heaven, positive, light, masculine, constructive. They are supposed to have proceeded from the Great Ultimate (→ T'ai Chi); in perpetual interplay, as the influence of one increases that of the other decreases. The theory helped to develop view that all things are mutually related and in constant process of transformation. It also explained the unity of man and nature, and gave a cosmological basis for ethical and social teachings. (→ Dualism). D.H.S.

W. T. Chan, *Source Book in Chinese Philosophy* (1963), pp. 244–9; E. T. C. Werner, *Dictionary of Chinese Mythology* (1932).

Yoga This term (lit. 'yoking' or 'harnessing', sc. one's mental and physical powers) is used in three senses. Most typically it refs. to methods of self-contol and meditation, taking various forms in Indian trad.; in this sense one can speak of Hindu, Buddh., Jain, etc., yoga. More narrowly term refs. to the methods and docs. of one of six orthodox schools of philosophy in → Hinduism, namely the → Yoga school. The term is also used very widely (notably in the → *Bhagavadgita*) to mean method or discipline leading to → salvation: thus in *Gita* distinction is made between *karmayoga*, discipline of dutiful action in world —which, if undertaken without regard for karmic fruits of action—can lead to release; and *jñānayoga*, here ref. to discipline of knowledge, as attainable acc. to precepts of → Samkhya-Yoga. Also, there is method of → *bhakti*, or *bhaktiyoga*. When used alone and not in compounds, word is most likely to ref. to methods of self-control and meditation, one set among which are those propounded by Yoga school. There is reason to think that yogic practices orig. in India primarily in non-Aryan cultural milieu. There are refs. to ascetics of various kinds in Vedic hymns, but the central conceptions of Vedic relig. did not focus on yogic techniques. But in period of the →→ *Brahmanas* and *Upaniṣads*, sacrificial relig. and yoga coalesced up to a point through interiorisation of idea of sacrifice and the matching of microcosmic psycho-physical processes with processes of the macrocosm. Ascetic (→ *tapas*) and shamanistic elements in Vedic relig. also lent themselves to synthesis between sacrificial ritualism and yogic self-control. The famous identification of → *Brahman* and → *atman* (→ *tat tvam asi*) is culmination of this synthesis between 'outer' and an 'inner' approach to ultimate reality. However, when Samkhya-Yoga school emerged in its classical form, it owed little to Upaniṣadic synthesis; its description of reality has more in common with unorthodox relig. ideas (e.g. those of → Jainism and the → Ajivikas) than with Brahmanical thinking. However, synthesising tendencies in Hindu culture led to eventual incorporation of motifs from Samkhya-

Yoga in → Vedanta; and yogic methods of meditation were an import. element in contemplative self-control necessary for attainment of knowledge, and therefore of → liberation, in → Advaita Vedanta. Another application of yoga was in → Tantrism. In mod. times various movements incl. → Ramakrishna movement have modified yogic methods to mod. conditions, while → Sri Aurobindo urged practice of an 'integral yoga' in which contemplation and self-discipline is integrated into this-wordly moral and cultural life. N.S.

M. Eliade, *Yoga: Immortality and Freedom* (1958); S. Dasgupta, *Yoga as Philosophy and Religion* (1924), *Hindu Mysticism* (1959).

(School) One of six traditional schools of view points within Hindu → philosophy, and closely assoc. with → Samkhya, from which it draws main features of its picture of universe. This picture supplies background and *rationale* for practice of techniques of → Yoga. The only substantial difference in ontology between Yoga and Samkhya is that former postulates existence of a God, the one soul never to undergo the processes of → *samsara* and rebirth and one who serves as aid to meditator in his striving towards → liberation. The latter state, however, does not, in Yoga, consist in union or communion with God, but in perfect isolation (→ *kaivalya*) and freedom from suffering (*duḥkha*). Also, Samkhya prescribes knowledge or discrimination (*viveka*) as cause of liberation, while Yoga emphasises purification of consciousness through various physical and psychological techniques. However, difference is more real than apparent, for knowledge here, as typically elsewhere in Indian trad., involves kind of existential insight into nature of reality and does not accrue simply from pure philosophising. Yoga proposes methods of meditation to bring about purification of consciousness, in such way that nature of underlying soul (*puruṣa*) will be apparent; so the individual will see essential otherness of soul from material nature, thereby gaining release from latter's bonds. The methods of Yoga are divided between Hatha Yoga and Raja ('Royal') Yoga: the former is concerned with physiological side; latter with higher processes of contemplation. The distinction is somewhat artificial in that in principle two sides are interdependent, with physiological exercises being preliminary to the others. The classical account of Yoga is found in the *Yogasūtra* of → Patanjali. The practices comprise eight elements (*angas*): namely restraint (*yama*), disciplines (*niyama*), postures (→ *asana*), → breathing control (→ *pranayama*), elimination of perception of outer objects (*pratyāhāra*), concentration (*dhārana*), meditation (→ *dhyāna*) and absorption (→ *samādhi*). The first two ref. to moral discipline, incl. list of precepts not unlike those of → Buddhism, banning taking of life (→ *ahiṃsā*), lying, stealing, sexual activity and avariciousness. The practice of postures and breathing control belong to Hatha Yoga; the final three elements of Yogic practice involve attainment of *ekāgratā* (single-pointed-ness), i.e. concentration of consciousness, and meditation on various symbols, such as fire, the heart, God, etc. Finally, the Yogin can gain state where the soul's essential nature is perfectly reflected in consciousness. The practice of Yoga is supposed to bring about, as side-effect, acquisition of miraculous powers (*siddhis*), such as power to become invisible, to know moment of one's death, etc. Thus the Yogin possesses powers which may threaten and surpass those of gods. There is also in Yoga well-developed occult physiology, centering on the snake-like interior energy, coiling upwards from base of trunk to the top of the spine, known as → Kundalini. N.S.

M. Eliade, *Yoga: Immortality and Freedom* (1958); J. H. Woods, *Yoga System of Patanjali* (1927); S. N. Dasgupta, *Yoga as Philosophy and Religion* (1924), *A History of Indian Philosophy*, vol. 1 (1922).

Yogācāras Name of those Mhy. Buddhists who professed doc. of → Asanga and his brother → Vasubandhu. The doc. was known also as Vijñānavāda, and the adherents as Vijñānavādins. The name of doc. ref. to its central idea: that *vijñāna* (consciousness) alone is real, whereas objects of consciousness are not. The doc. was a reaction to, and to some extent directed against, views of the → Mādhyamika, acc. to which both subject and object in consciousness are unreal (in characteristic Mādhyamika form, reality is → *śūñyatā*). Acc. to the Y., occurrence of *illusion* demonstrates that consciousness can have 'content', 'without there being a corresponding object outside'. This shows 'the self-contained nature of consciousness', (Murti); for the so-called object or 'content' of consciousness is result of an inner modification of consciousness. On other hand, the doc. was a reaction to, and was directed against, the extreme rigour of → Theravādin Abhidhamma School, with its assertion that there is a certain fixed number of ultimately real → *dhammas*, or psychic 'atoms', of which all existence is made up. This, acc. to the Y., is to attr. reality to ultimate non-entities; consciousness alone is real, and it is the *yogācāra*, the man deep in meditation, who alone realises the truth: 'The yogācāra sees what is as it really is.' It was emphasis upon the practical clearing and purifying of consciousness by means of *yoga* which led to alternative name Y., by which school of the Vijñāna-vādins was known. Thus, the title V. refers to the *speculative*, and the name Y. to the *practical* aspect of this school. Since *vijñāna* alone exists, it alone receives false impressions and makes false constructions, and has to be cleansed of its false dualisms and illusions. As Conze points out, adherents of this school have no special or superior right to the title Yogācāra, 'practitioners of Yoga'; the name is given them largely because it occurs in title of one of Asanga's chief writings, the *Yogācāra-bhūmi Śāstra.*

To some extent the Y. were developing ideas found in earlier Buddhism, incl. poss. those of the → Sautrantikas, who taught that of the 5 → skandhas it is vijñāna alone which transmigrates from rebirth to rebirth. The Y. developed the doc. of → ālaya-vijñāna, or 'store-consciousness', by which was meant pure consciousness, before it particularises itself as substratum of a human mind or consciousness. This is a concept somewhat similar to that of Hindu idea of the universal → Brahman; there was, however, another closer affinity within Buddhism itself, viz, with the → *Lankāvatāra Sūtra.* This 'store-consciousness' thus performs role of a permanent 'self', although the Y., in accordance with their Buddh. tenets, denied existence of a self. In this respect they have been accused of attempting to reconcile the irreconcilable. (Conze, *Buddhist Thought in India,* pp. 133f.).

However, the Y. had also a practical, indeed, relig. concern. Against the excessively intellectualist, extremist and negative analysis taught by the → *Mādhyamika,* they sought to recover importance of meditational practice and restore this to its proper place in Buddh. system. The Mādhyamika was a critique of phenomenal existence based on logic, whereas the Vijñānavāda was critique based on psychology, i.e. Buddh. psychology, and in this respect it constituted return to attitude and methods of early Buddhism.

Vijñānavāda is sometimes given credit for formulation of doc. of the three Bodies of Buddha (→ *Tri-kāya*); but in this also → Asanga and his followers were but giving systematic shape to ideas found in earlier Buddhism. The Tri-kāya doc. worked out by Asanga corresponded with Y. view of the three kinds of truth. The first is 'conventional truth' (*parikalpita*), i.e., concepts based on sense-perception, which are not really inherent in what is perceived, but are due to the perceived. The second is examined truth, concepts as they are examined concerning their cause, that out of which they have originated, and the conditions of their decay. This second kind of truth (*paratantra*) thus goes deeper than conventional truth. The third is final or highest truth (*parinispanna*), which is without origin or decay, changeless, and devoid of distinction of subject and object. The 3 'Bodies of the Buddha' were understood in similar fashion. The *nirmāna-kāya* was like conventional truth, purely imaginary; it was held that the Buddha-nature made an appearance of ordinary human existence. The *sambhoga-kāya* was akin to second kind of truth, while the *dharma-kāya* was the eternally true nature of Buddha. Different Buddhas may have differing *nirmāna* bodies or even *sambhoga* bodies, but all constitute the one eternal *dharma-kāya,* which like highest kind of truth, is unknowable, except in so far as it can be realised by the Buddha within himself.

While the Y. made explicit ideas which they had derived from earlier stages in development of Buddh. thought, they also provided basis for further develops., notably that of the → *Vajrayāna,* or tantra. With its combination of ritual, worship and yoga in context of absolutist ideas, its double aspect as both relig. and metaphysics, and its aim of transmuting human personality by mystic institution with the Absolute, Vajrayāna would appear to owe not a little to system of Y. school. There is a great deal of Y. lit. (→→ *Asanga, Vasubandhu*); but most is in Tibetan or Chinese trans. (i.e. from Sanskrit). T.O.L.

T. R. V. Murti, *The Central Philosophy of Buddhism* (1955), ch. 13; E. Conze, *Buddhist Thought in India* (1962), Part III, chs. 1 and 3.

Yogi A practitioner of → *yoga*; term is sometimes transliterated *yogin,* and feminine form is *yoginī.* There may have been yogis in → Indus Valley Civilisation; but certainly they have been part of Indian relig. scene since very early times. The god → Śiva in his form as 'Great Lord' (*Maheśvara*) is mythically regarded as patron of yogis, and as the Great Yogi (*Mahāyogī*). Just as term *yoga* can be used in wide sense to incl. both Hindu and non-Hindu (e.g. →→ Jain and Buddh.) practices, so likewise *yogi.* N.S.

Yomei School (→ Shushi school). A Jap. school of → Confucianism, which based itself on teachings of → Wang Yang-ming (1472–1528). Its pioneer in Japan was Nakaye-Toju (1608–48), known as the sage of Ōmi. He laid emphasis on spiritual culture and training, and on devotion to the Cosmic Soul, the 'Prime Conscience', of which man is the image, often obscured and distorted—a microcosm, whose purpose is to cultivate the orig. purity of the soul and manifest universal will to love. The school had few followers, but exerted a widespread influence. D.H.S.

M. Anesaki, *Hist. of Japanese Religion* (1930).

Yüan-shih T'ien-tsün → San Ch'ing D.H.S.

Yü Huang Yü Ti, Yü Huang Shang Ti: 'The Jade Emperor'). Chief god of → Taoist pantheon, and incorp. into → Buddh. pantheon in an inferior position to Buddha. In Chi. popular relig., Yü Huang is ruler over all Buddhas, gods, spirits and kings of Hades, and metes out justice to mortals. Though Chi. literati attr. the 'invention' of Y.H.

to Sung Dynasty emperor Shên-Tsung (998–1022), he was already, by T'ang Dynasty, a supreme god of popular belief. His palace is in the highest heaven, where, on analogy of the Chinese empire, he is surrounded by a huge court of celestial ministers, guards, officials and minor functionaries, to whom he delegates administration of various departments of universe. (→ San Ch'ing). D.H.S.

Yüan Chwang → Hsüan Tsang. D.H.S.

Z

-Zabūr →→ Bible; Psalms (Islam). J.R.

Zagreus In Grk. mythology the son of → Zeus and → Persephone, whom → Titans killed and ate. Zeus slew the Titans with his levin-bolts, and from their ashes mankind was born. This myth helped to explain → Orphic view that man's nature was compounded of Titanic and divine (Zagreus) elements. Behind the myth doubtless lay a complicated and obscure evolution of belief and ritual practice. Z. is a mysterious figure who may derive from anc. Cretan → chthonian god, with whom his devotees sought communion by eating raw flesh of a bull. This Z. came to be identified with → Dionysos, and was thus assoc. with the Dionysian and → Orphic mysteries (→ Mystery Religs.; → Omophagia). S.G.F.B.

W. K. C. Guthrie, *Orpheus and Greek Relig.* (1932²), pp. 111ff.; Harrison, *Prolegomena*, pp. 478ff.; V. Macchioro, *Zagreus* (1930), *passim*; E. Rohde, *Psyche* (1898), II, pp. 116ff.

Ẓāhirites → Muslim Law, Schools of. J.R.

Zakāt → Legal Alms. J.R.

Zalmoxis (Zamolxis) → Chthonian god or *daimon* (→ demonology) of the Getae of Thrace. Acc. to Herodotus (IV, 94–6), the Getae believed that they went to Z. at death, and periodically they sacrificed a man as messenger to him. He also reports tale that Z., orig. a slave of → Pythagoras, returned home and imposed upon his people by promising them a happy afterlife. He convinced them by withdrawing for three years into underground chamber and re-appearing thence. The tale seems an → Euhemerist explanation of a cultus in some way reminiscent of Pythagoreanism. E. R. Dodds has discerned affinities with → shamanism. S.G.F.B.

A. D. Nock, *C.R.*, XL (1926), pp. 184ff.; E. R. Dodds, *The Greeks and the Irrational* (1963 edn.), pp. 144, 165–6; E. Rohde, *Psyche* (1898), II, pp. 7, n. 3, 28ff.

Zamzam A well within courtyard of sacred mosque at Mecca, reputed to be that revealed to → Hagar when abandoned with Ishmael in desert by Abraham and anxiously seeking for water. (→ 'Abd al-Muṭṭalib). A building has been erected around it, with door in E. wall opening into chamber about 15 ft. sq., lined with marble. A marble tank is kept filled with water so that pilgrims can drink during absence of those who draw water. The water, greatly valued, is credited with healing virtues. Pilgrims commonly bring their shrouds to soak them in Z. water. Bottles of it are carried home. Visitors say water is brackish; some have found it unpleasant to taste. J.R.

E.I., IV, pp. 1212f.; Hughes, p. 701; Wellhausen, *Reste*, p. 76; Rutter, *Holy Cities*, I, pp. 261f.; Burton, *Pilgrimage*, index; Lane, *Egyptians*, index.

Zaydīs A branch of the → Shi'a, with docs. not far removed from those of → Sunnis. They are traced to Zayd, grandson of → Husayn, who had risen against the → Umayyads and was killed *c.* 122/740. The Z. have never been numerous; but two states have been estab., one S. of the Caspian for some 250 years to *c.* 520/1126, the other in the Yemen from before end of 3rd/9th cent. till the present day. Z. insist on an → imam who is descendant of Muḥammad, but they do not insist on his being from one partic. branch. Their imam should be learned and able to lead his forces to fight. They reject doc. of hidden imam; unlike other Shi'is (Imāmīs), they do not consider →→ Abu Bakr and 'Umar usurpers. In theology they have connections with → Mu'tazilite doc. In worship they follow common Shi'i differences from Sunnis (→ Prayer). They reject all ascriptions of semi-divinity to → 'Ali, and idea of a divine light descending on imams. Their imam is held to be human being whom God guides. They believe in *ijmā'* (consensus, → Shari'a), but only that of their own scholars. They do not allow *mut'a* marriage (→ Shi'a), and reject → Sufism. Their present situation is obscure. J.R.

E.I., IV, pp. 1196ff.; Pareja, index; E. Griffini, *Corpus juris di Zaid ibn 'Ali* (1919); A. S. Tritton, *The rise of the imams of Sanaa* (1925); Watt, *Philosophy*, index; Coulson, *Law*, index; R. B. Serjeant, 'The Zaydīs' in *Religion in the Middle East*, II (1969).

Zazen → Zen meditation while sitting in an approved posture, hallowed by Buddh. trad. The body is maintained upright, the legs crossed, the breathing regulated, whilst the mind is freed from all attachments, desires, concepts and judgements.

The aim of Z. is → Satori, to enter the 'dharma gate of great rest and joy'. D.H.S.

H. Dumoulin, *Hist. of Zen Buddhism* (1963), pp. 159ff.; E. Wood, *Zen Dictionary* (1962), p. 157.

Zealots, The Jew. sect founded by Judas of Galilee in CE 6, to resist incorporation of Judaea into Roman Empire. The Z. opposed payment of tribute to Rome and recognition of Rom. Emperor as *despotēs* ('lord') as constituting apostasy, since → Yahweh was Israel's lord and the resources of Judaea were his. After suppression of revolt and death of Judas, the Z. maintained guerilla resistance against Rome and Jew. collaborators until revolt in 66. During siege of → Jerusalem, the Z. held the → Temple. After fall of Jerus. in 70, some Z. reached Egypt and tried to raise revolt among Jews there: they were arrested and died after torture, refusing to recognise Caesar as 'lord'. At Masada, 960 Z., incl. women and children, held out until 73, when they chose suicide rather than surrender to Romans. Recent research and excavation of Masada have led to re-assessment of Z., after long acceptance of → Josephus's prejudiced account of them. The essentially relig. character of Zealotism is now recognised. This reassessment makes necessary a new evaluation of relations of Jesus and Jew. Christians to the Zealots: one of Jesus' disciples was a Z., and it is prob. that he was crucified between two Z. The name 'Z.' is Grk. trans. of *Kannā'im* (pl. 'zealous'), which prob. derived from Phinehas, who 'was zealous for his God' (Num. 25:6ff.). An extremist group of Z. were called 'Sicarii' ('dagger-men'). S.G.F.B.

M. Hengel, *Die Zeloten* (1961); Y. Yadin, *Masada: Herod's Fortress and the Zealots' Last Stand* (1966); S. G. F. Brandon, *Jesus and the Zealots* (1967), with extensive bibliography.

Zen (→→ Rinsai, Obaku, Sōtō). A form of → Buddhism developed in China as → Ch'an, which, transplanted to Japan, became one of most import. and influential of Buddh. schools, and unique in hist. of relig. It upholds the direct, mystical experience of Reality through maturing of an inner experience. It claims to transmit the essence and spirit of Buddhism directly, without reliance on scriptures, words and concepts, and the reasoning based on them. It seeks inner spiritual enlightenment, and encourages practice of meditation or contemplation, teaching that man's orig. nature is the Buddha-nature, unrealised through ignorance.

Z. has had profound influence on Jap. culture, inspiring finest works of art and literature. Its principles were applied to military arts of Judo and Kendo (fencing), and in the → tea ceremony, flower arrangement, landscape gardening etc. Z. monasteries are usually places of great aesthetic appeal, marked by quiet, order, cleanliness and strict relig. discipline. In life of the monks, meditation, worship and energetic manual labour alternate. There is no great stress on ascetic practices. Self-realisation and one's Buddha-nature are equally found in practical affairs and in meditation.

The intro. of Z. to the W., notably by D. T. Suzuki, has led to keen interest, resulting in many import. studies; but also to Z. cults which are often a caricature rather than a true expression of Z. Buddhism. D.H.S.

Of many important works in Eng., the reader will find those of D. T. Suzuki, A. Watts, C. Humphreys and Chang Chên-chi interesting. See espec. H. Dumoulin, *Hist. of Zen Buddhism* (1963), which contains an adequate bibliography.

Zeus Grk. sky-god and head of Olympian pantheon (→ Grk. Relig.). Z. was of Indo-European orig. and akin to Roman → Jupiter, Vedic Dyaus pita, and Germanic Ziu. The name signifies 'sky', and Z. was assoc. with meteorological phenomena, partic. thunder and lightning. By → Homer, Z. is styled 'Father of gods and men'; but epithet is meant to present him as the divine *pater familias*, not divine Creator. Z. was regarded as embodying cosmic order, which meant in turn upholding moral laws deemed basic to stability of Grk. society (→→ Moira; Maat; Re). In Grk. mythology, Z. has many liaisons with mortal women: such tales prob. reflect conditions of heroic Mycenaean age. Like other → sky-gods, Z. tended to be a remote deity. The → Stoics identified Z. with fire, supreme principle in their cosmology: the *Hymn of Cleanthes* nobly presents this conception. In art Z. was repr. as a well-developed man of majestic bearing, bearded, with emblems of sovereignty, and often accompanied by eagle. His chief cult-centre was Olympia. The myth of birth of → Z. in Crete, his deliverance from his father → Kronos, whom he eventually dethrones, as recorded by → Hesiod, may reflect memory of displacement of Aegean gods by Olympian gods (→ Aegean Relig.) or orig. from a Hittite cosmogonic myth (→ Hittite Relig.). The Greeks gen. identified chief god of other peoples with Z. (e.g. →→ Amun; Hadad; Yahweh). S.G.F.B.

A. B. Cook, *Zeus*, 3 vols. (1914–30); H. J. Rose, *Handbook of Greek Mythology* (1928), pp. 43ff.; W. K. C. Guthrie, *The Greeks and their Gods* (1950), pp. 35ff.; M. P. Nilsson, *The Mycenaean Origin of Grk. Mythology* (1932), *Greek Folk Religion* (1940), *passim*; W. F. Otto, *The Homeric Gods* (E.T. 1954), *passim*; F. W. Beare, 'Zeus in the Hellenistic Age', in *The Seed of Wisdom*, ed. W. S. McCullough (1964); E. O. James, *The Worship of the Sky-God* (1963), pp. 114ff.; Brandon, *C.L.*, pp. 166ff.; M. H. Jameson in *M.A.W.*, pp. 247ff.

Ziyāra (visit) Applied partic. to visiting Muḥammad's tomb at Medina and tombs of → saints. Certain prayers should be said. Saints' days are celebrated with a Z., the celebration beginning with procession in which the saint's flags, normally kept at → tomb, are paraded. A new covering for tomb may be brought, and men cut or pierce themselves with daggers. Light relief may be added by clowns who engage in mock fight. Afterwards the people may enter shrine to pray. To the majority, however, saints' days become a fair with amusements and camel races. → Shi'a Muslims believe that Z.'s to shrines of → imams at Meshed, Karbala, Najaf and Kazimayn rank with the → Pilgrimage (Ḥajj). J.R.

E.I., IV, p. 1234; Hughes, pp. 713–5; Burton, *Pilgrimage*, I, ch. 16; Lane, *Egyptians*, pp. 246f.; Rutter, *Holy Cities*, II, pp. 191ff.; Levy, *Social Structure*, p. 250.

Zoroaster, Zoroastrianism 'Zoroaster' is the Grk. rendering of 'Zarathustra', name of one who left the impress. of his inspiration on → Iranian relig. Specialist opinion inclines to date Z.'s birth *c.* 570 BC. Since he is known only through his own utterances, preserved in the → *Gāthās*, Z. remains essentially an obscure figure: he has been regarded as a kind of → shaman, a mystic and a prophet. He certainly assumed for himself a special relation with → Ahura Mazdah, whom he exalted as Supreme Deity. Z. repr. the world as divided between two contending 'primal spirits', identified severally with Good and Evil; the relation of these spirits with Ahura Mazdah is obscure, except that Ahura is at one with the Good. Mankind has to choose between these spirits, and their choice affects their eternal destiny. After his death, Z.'s relig. was adapted to incl. certain anc. deities rejected by him, notably → Mithra and → Anahita; the → Magi prob. effected this adaptation. This form of Zoroastrianism remained essentially dualistic; it became the estab. faith of Iran, and, through many vicissitudes, continued until its gradual extinction after Islamic conquest of Iran in 7th cent. CE, except for a surviving remnant of believers in Iran (the Gabars) and the → Parsis of India. The influence of Z. was immense: it is traceable in →→ Judaism; Mithraism; Gnosticism; Manichaeism. (See Synoptic Index under Iran). S.G.F.B.

Zaehner, *D.T.Z.*; J. H. Moulton, *Early Zoroastrianism* (1913); W. B. Henning, *Zoroaster: Politician or Witch Doctor?* (1951); J. Duchesne-Guillemin, *Zoroastre* (1948); *Ormazd et Ahriman* (1953), *The Hymns of Zarathustra* (E.T. 1952), *The Western Response to Zoroaster* (1958), *Symbolik des Parsismus* (1961); *E.R.E.*, XII, *s.v.*; G. Widengren, 'Stand und Aufgaben der iranischen Religionsgeschichte', *Numen*, I (1954), II (1955); M. Molé, 'Une histoire du mazdéisme est-elle, possible?', *R.H.R.*, p. 162 (1962); R. N. Frye, *The Heritage of Persia* (1962); Brandon, *M.D.*, ch. 8 (bibliog.); J. Bidez and F. Cumont, *Les Mages hellénisées*, 2 vols. (1938); K. Rudolph, 'Zarathustra: Priester u. Prophet', *Numen*, VIII (1961); I. Gershevitch, 'Zoroaster's Own Contribution', *J.N.E.S.*, 23 (1964).

-Zuhrī Muḥammad b. Muslim Ibn Shihāb (*c.* 50–124/670–742), an import. Muslim traditionist. He has been accused of inventing a trad. about the three mosques, Mecca, Medina, Jerusalem, deserving → pilgrimage, because the → Umayyads were troubled by Ibn al-Zubayr's anti-Caliphate in Mecca and wished to make Jerusalem substitute place of pilgrimage. The story is doubtful, because of Z.'s youth at time; although a version has his name as transmitter, another occurs without his name. The canonical books do not hesitate to incl. the trad. as genuine. Some criticised Z. for accepting patronage at Umayyad court in Damascus; but this did not conflict with his import. services to → Tradition. Z. ardently searched for trads., and while he is said to have disliked writing trads., his vast material could hardly have been preserved without writing. Besides being an import. authority among traditionists, he is the authority most frequently quoted by → Ibn Ishaq. J.R.

E.I., IV, pp. 1239f.; Goldziher, *M.S.*, II, index; J. W. Fück, 'Die Rolle des Traditionalismus im Islam', *Z.D.M.G.*, XCIII (1939), pp. 4f.; Siddiqi, *Hadith*, index; Abbott, *Papyri*, index; J. Robson, 'Ibn Ishaq's use of isnād', *B.J.R.L.*, 38 (1956), pp. 449ff. and *passim*.

Zurvān (Zervan) Anc. Iranian god of → Time. The name has been traced back to 12th cent. BC; but first certain evidence of Iranian interest in Time is provided by Eudemus of Rhodes (4th cent. BC); the earliest Iranian lit. ref. to Z., in *Vidēvdāt* (→ Avesta), implies anc. trad. associating Z. with eschatology. Iranian sources show that Time was deified in two forms: Zurvān *akarana*, i.e. 'Infinite Time'; Zurvān *dareghō-chvadhāta*, i.e. 'Time of the Long Dominion' or 'Finite Time'. This latter Z. was to last for 12,000 years, and ruled human life in this world, bringing old age and death. Owing to identification of → Ahura Mazdah with principle of Good in later → Zoroastrianism, Z. *akarana* came to be regarded as Creator of → Ohrmazd (i.e. Ahura Mazdah) and → Ahriman. During Sassanian period (CE 226–652), this Zurvanite form of Zoroastrianism competed with trad. form. Z. was an important deity in → Mithraism, and, as Z. *dareghō-chvadhāta*, was repr. by image of lion-headed monster, with signs of zodiac, in the *mithraea*. S.G.F.B.

R. C. Zaehner, *Zurvān: a Zoroastrian Dilemma*

(1955), *D.T.Z.* (1961); G. Widengren, *Hochgottglauben in alten Iran* (1938), pp. 266ff.; J. Duchesne-Guillemin, *Zoroastre* (1948), 'Ahriman et le dieu suprème dans les mystères de Mithra', *Numen*, II (1955); U. Bianchi, *Zaman i Ohrmazd* (1958); S. G. F. Brandon, *History, Time and Deity* (1965), ch. 3; W. Culican, *The Medes and Persians* (1965), p. 27, pl. 4.

Zwingli, Ulrich (1484–1531) Swiss Reformer, b. in Alpine country of Toggenburg; after schooling in Bern and Basle, attended Universities of Vienna and Basle. Z. had training in theology and became an ardent Erasmian. In 1516 he accepted the living of Einsiedeln, where he withstood successfully the sale of → Indulgences by Samson. He became a papal pensioner for some years, attending Swiss soldiers as chaplain on two Italian campaigns. In 1518 he became 'people's priest' in the Gross Münster in Zürich and began a notable ministry of prophetic preaching, applying interpret. of Scripture to public and international as well as private matters. A near approach to death during Plague in 1519 seems to have deepened his religion, which was more than a rational humanism ascribed to him by 19th cent. historians. Like other forward-looking contemporaries, Z. much admired → Luther's defiance of Church authority, though he claimed to have made his own rediscovery of Biblical teaching on justification by Faith. The opening of Reformation in Zürich was when a group of citizens, in the presence of Z., broke the Lenten fast in house of Zürich printer Froschauer. The subsequent events in city set the pace for other cities and showed how the constitutional machinery of a great city, the guilds and Councils, could be used to carry through reformation of church life, worship and oversight of public morals. In Zürich, too, a public Disputation, from being an academic occasion, became an appeal to public opinion, and challenge to magistrates for decision. The first Disputation took place in the Gross Münster, 29th January 1952[3], when the reforming party sat behind open Bibles, and when the Catholic party was taken off guard, despite able manoeuvring of John Faber, Vicar General of Bishop of Constance. After iconoclastic riots in autumn, there was a further disputation concerning → images and → Mass. By end of year, the city had broken with diocesan authority, and next summer organs, relics and images were removed from churches. Z. himself produced new liturgies (1523 and 1525), which are among most drastically simplified of Reformation. Notable achievements were the Bible Conferences for pastors, held in the Gross Münster and known as 'Prophesyings', and the Zürich version of Bible which resulted from them and collaboration of ten other Zürich scholars, Pellikanos and Leo Jüd. Throughout, Z. paid deference to the 'godly magistrates', and was content to let them set pace and time for public reform. In 1528 he went so far as to leave to magistrates the power of excommunication. This roused fierce opposition from a group of his brighter young men, headed by the patricians' son, Conrad Grebel, who attacked his deference to magistrate, and accused him of stalling Reformation. They became the Swiss Brethren who are now regarded by historians as first → Anabaptists. Although other cities, notably Bern and Basle were on way to Reformation, Z. became more and more concerned at isolation of Zürich between Catholic Cantons and strove to build up a Christ. civic league of Reforming cities, including Strassburg. This involvement in politics brought threat of war in 1529, and the reality in 1531. Z. and 23 other chaplains fell on battlefield at Cappel. Heinrich Bullinger, who succeeded him as Antistes of Zürich consolidated the Zwinglian trad. by abandoning Z.'s military and foreign policy. (→ Reformation). E.G.R.

The definitive biography is by O. Farner, 4 vols. (1943–60). Cf. W. Köhler, *U. Zwingli* (1952); J. Rilliet, *Zwingli* (E.T. 1966); J. V. Pollet, *Huldrych Zwingli* (1963). Selections from his writings in *Library of Christian Classics*, vol. XXIV, 1953, *Zwingli and Bullinger*, ed. Bromiley. See also 'Zwingli' and 'Zwinglianisme', in the *Dict. Théol. Catholique*.

SYNOPTIC INDEX

Buddhism
Abhidhamma
Abhidhamma-Pitaka
Abhidhammika
Abhidhammatha-Sangaha
Abhidharma-Kosa
Abhidharma-Pitaka
Abhinna
Abode
Abortion
Absolute
Acarya
Access concentration
Adi-Buddha
Adultery
Afghanistan
Agama
Ages of the World (Chi. and Jap.)
Ajanta
Ajatasattu
Ajirckas
Alaya-Vijnana
Alcohol
Almsgiving
Alobha
Altar (Jap.)
Amarapura
Amaravati
Amida
Amida (Jap.)
Anagamin
Anagarika
Anagarika Dharmapala
Ananda
Anathapindaka
Anatta
Ancestor Worship (Chi. and Jap.)
Anger
Angel (Chi. and Jap.)
Anguttara-Nikaya
Anicca
Annihilation
Annihilationist-view
Anuruddha
Anuradhpura
Anussati
Arahant
Arama
Architecture (Chi. and Jap.)
Ariya-sacca
Art
Arupa-loka
Arya-deva
Asanga
Asava
Asceticism (also under Chi. and Jap.)
Ascetism (Hindu)
Asoka
Asuras
Asvaghosa
Atheism (Chi. and Jap.)
Atheism (Indian)
Atman (Hindu)
Atthakatha
Atthasalini
Attitude to other religs. (Chi. and Jap.)
Avadana
Avalokitesvara
Avasa
Avidyā (Avijja)
Avidyā (Hindu)
Ayatana
Bala
Banāras
Barlaam and Joseph
Bhikkhu (see Ordination and Sangha)
Bhumi
Bimbisara
Blest, Abode (Chi. and Jap.)
Bodhi
Bodhidharma
Bodhi Tree
Bodhisatta
Bon and Tibetan pre-Buddh. relig.
Brahma-cariya
Brahma-vihara
Buddha, as generic title
Buddhas, other than Gotama
Buddha, Gotama
Buddha, Gotama, Historicity of
Buddhacarita
Buddhism in China
Bodies of the Buddha
Buddha-Kaya
Buddha-Gaya
Buddhadatta
Buddhaghosa
Buddha-sasana
Buddha-vamsa
Buddhism, general survey
Buddhist scriptures
Burmese Buddhism
Burial (Chi.)
Burial (Jap.)
Bu-ston
Cakkappavattana Sutta
Canon of Scripture
Cambodia
Caste-Buddhist attitude
Causation, chain of
Ceylon, Buddhism
Cetiya
Ch'an
Chinese Religions
Chronology
Citta
Communism
Compassion
Conceit
Conception (i)
Conception (ii)
Cosmology
Cosmogony (Jap.)
Consciousness
Councils
Craving
Creator
Creed (also under Chi. and Jap.)
Cremation (also under Chi. and Jap.)

Synoptic Index (Buddhism)

Culavamsa
Culavagga
Dagaba
Daibutsu
Dainichi
Dalai Lama
Dana
Dead, disposal of
Dead, state of (Chi. and Jap.)
Death, Buddhist view of
Death, Personification of
Death, Recollection of
Defilement
Demonology
Dengyō Daishi
Departed, spirits of
Desire
Destiny (Chi. and Jap.)
Determinism
Deva
Devadatta
Deva-duta
Devanampiyatissa
Devil
Devotee, lay
Devotions
Dhamma
Dhamma Cakkappavattana Sutta
Dhammasangani
Dhammapada
Dharma (Hindu)
Dharmapada
Dharma-Kaya
Dhatu
Dhatu-katha
Dhatu-vamsa
Dhyana
Dhyana (Hindu)
Diamond Sutra
Digha Nikaya
Dipankara
Dipavamsa
Discipline, Monastic
Discipline, Relig. (Chi. and Jap.)
Disease (also under Chi. and Jap.)
Ditthi
Divyavadana
Dogen
Doctrine
Dosa
Dōshō
Drama (Chi. and Jap.)
Dress, Religious (also under Chi. and Jap.)
Dukkha
Dvi Yana
Ego
Eightfold path
Eisai
Eka-yana
Elders
Emptiness
Enlightenment
Ennin
Envy
Eschatology (also under Chi. and Jap.)
Eternity
Ethics (also under Jap.)
Evil (also under Chi. and Jap.)
Excommunication
Exercises, spiritual
Extinction
Fa Hsien
Faith (also under Chi. and Jap.)
Family and Social Duties
Fanaticism (Chi. and Jap.)
Fasting
Fatalism
Fate (Chi.)
Feeling
Festivals (also under Chi. and Jap.)
First sermon
Fo
Food rules
Four Holy Truths
Free will
Gandhabbas
Gandhara
Gaya
Genshin
God, concept of (Chi. and Jap.)
God, Indian arguments about existence
Gods
Good Life
Gotama
Grasping
Greed
Hachiman
Hakuin
Happiness
Hatred
Heart Sutra
Heaven
Hell
Heresy (also under Chi. and Jap.)
Hetu
Hinayana
Hinduism
Honen
Holy, concept of
Holy days
Holy places
Holy truths
Hossō
Hua Yen
Hui Yüan
Idolatry (Chi. and Jap.)
Ignorance
Iddhi
Image
Immolation
Immortality (also under Chi.)
Incense (Chi. and Jap.)
India
Indian Religions
Indo-China
Indonesia
Indriya
Influxes
Ingen
Initiation (also under Chi.)
Insight
Ippen
Isipatana
I Tsing
Japan and Jap. Relig.
Jataka
Java
Jhana
Jinjō
Jodo
Jojitsu
Kalpa
Kama
Kamma
Kaniska
Karma (Hindu concept)
Karuna
Kapilavatthu
Kaya
Katha Vathu
Kegon School
Khandha
Khuddaka Nikaya
Kilesa
Kings, Buddhist
Kōan
Kōbō Daishi
Korea
Kosa
Koyasan
Ksatriyas
Kuan Yin
Kumarajiva
Kusha School
Kushinagara
Kwan-On
Laos
Lalita-Vistara
Lanka
Lankavatara-Sutra
Literature, Buddhist, Pali
Literature, Buddhist, Sanskrit
Lobha
Lohan
Lotus Sutra
Love
Lumbini
Lü Tsung
Madhura
Madhymika
Magadha
Magic (Chi. and Jap.)
Mahabodhi Society
Mahabodhivamsa
Mahakassapa
Mahapadana Sutta
Mahaparinibbana Sutta
Mahasatipatthana Sutta
Mahasanghikas
Mahavamsa
Mahavastu
Mahayana
Mahinda
Maitreya (Buddha)

Synoptic Index (Buddhism)

Synoptic Index (China)

Chinese Cults and Philosophies

Shang Ti
Shê-Chi
Shên
Shih Ching
Shu Ching
Sin
Soul
Souls, Commemorative Festival of
Souls, Transmigration of
Spirits and Spiritism
Spring Rites
State of the Dead
Suffering, problem of
Suicide
Ta Hsüeh
Ta Shih Chih
T'ai Chi
T'ai I
T'ai Shan
Taiwan
Tao
Taoism
Tao Shih
Tao Tsang
Tao Tê Ching
T'ao T'ieh
Tê
Tea
Theism
Theology (Far East)
Ti
T'ien
T'ien T'ai
Time
Tolerance
Tripitaka
Tun Huang
Tutelary Gods and Spirits
Usury
Vietnam
Vows
Wang Yang-ming
War, Attitude to
Wealth, Attitude to
Wên Ch'ang
Wên Shu
Wên and Wu
Wine
Witchcraft
Women, Status of
Worship
Wu Hsing
Wu Ti
Wu Wei
Yang
Yellow Springs
Yen Wang
Yü Huang
Yüan Chwang
Yüan-shih T'ien Tsun
Yin-yang

Christianity

A and Ω
Aaronic blessing
Abba
Abbess
Abbot
Abbot of Unreason
'Abd al-Jabbār
Abelard, Peter
Abercius, Inscription of
Abgar, Legend of
Ablutions
Abomination of Desolation
Abrahamites
Abraham's Bosom
Abraham, Testament of
Abraxas, or Abrasax
Absolution
Absolution of the Dead
Abstinence
Abuna
Acacian Schism
Acacius
Accaophori
Acceptilation
Accident
Accidie
Acolyte
Act of Supremacy
Acts of the Apostles
Acts of the Martyrs
Actual Sin
Adalbert of Bremen
Adam
Adamites
Adamnan, St.
Adeste Fideles
Adoptianism
Adoptionism
Adoration
Adultery
Advent
Adventists, Second
Advocatus Diaboli
Aelia Capitolina
Agapē
Agapetai and Agapetoi
Agatha, St.
Ages of the World
Agnes, St.
Agnus Dei
Agrapha
Alb
Albertus Magnus
Albigenses
Alcuin
Alexander VI (Pope)
Alexandria, Church of
Alexandrian Theology
Alleluia (Hallelujah)
All Saints' Day
All Souls' Day
Almsgiving
Altar
Amana Society
Ambo
Ambrose, St.
Ambrosian Rite
Ambrosiaster
Amen
Amice
Amish
Ammonius Saccas
Amyraldists
Anabaptists
Analogy
Analogy of Religion, The
Anamnesis
Anaphora
Anathema
Anchorite; Anchoress
Andrewes, Lancelot
Andrew, St.
Andrew St., Acts of
Angel
Angel (Chi. and Jap.)
Anglican Communion
Anglicanism
Anglo-Catholicism
Anne, St.
Anno Domino
Anselm, St.
Antichrist
Antinomianism
Antioch
Antiochene Theology
Antony, St.
Apollinarianism
Apocalyptic Literature
Apocatastasis
Apocrypha
Apocryphal New Testament
Apollonius of Tyana
Apollos
Apologetics
Apologists
Apostasy
Apostle
Apostolic Age
Apostolic Fathers
Apostolic Succession
Aquinas, St. Thomas
Arcana Discipline (arcani disciplina)
Arianism
Aristeas, Letter of
Ark (of Noah)
Armageddon
Arminianism
Art (sacred)
Ascension of Christ
Ascetical Theology
Asceticism
Ashes
Ash Wednesday
Asperges
Assumption of Virgin Mary
Astral Religion
Athanasian Creed
Athanasius
Atonement
Augustine, St.
Azymites

Synoptic Index (Christianity)

High Church
Hippolytus
Holy Spirit
Hospitallers, or Knights Hospitaller
Host
Icon(s)
Ignatius, St.
Immaculate Conception of Virgin Mary
Impassibility of God
Incarnation
Index Librorum Prohibitorum
India, Christian Movements
Indulgences
Infallibility, Papal
Injīl
Inquisition, The
Irenaeus, Bp. of Lyons
-Islām
Isrā'
James, brother of Jesus
Japanese Religion
Jehovah's Witnesses
Jerome, St.
Jerusalem
Jerusalem, Church of
Jesuits
Jesus Christ (in Islam)
Jesus of Nazareth
Jewish Christianity
Joachim of Fiore
John, Gospel of
John, Revelation of
John the Baptist
Josephus, Flavius
Judaising
Judas Iscariot
Judgment of the Dead
Justin Martyr
Kerygma
King, Divine
Kublai Khan
Kyrie Eleison
Labarum
Lambeth Conferences
Last Supper
Lateran Basilica
Lentulus, Letter of
Levellers
Leviathan
Limbo
Liturgical Movement, The
Liturgy
Logia
Logos
Lollards
Love (Christian)
Lucifer
Luke, Gospel of
Luther, Martin
Macao
-Mahdī
Mammon
Mandaeans
Marcion
Mark, Gospel of
Martyr
Mary, Cult of
Mass
Matthew, Gospel of
Mercy
Messiah
Methodism
Michael, Archangel
Mînîm
Miracles
Miracles (Islam)
Missal
Mission
Modernism
Monasticism
Monophysitism
Monotheism
Monothelitism
Mormons, The
Moses
Mystery Religions
Mysticism
Nag Hammadi
Nazarene (Nazorean)
Neoplatonism
Nestorianism
Nestorianism in China
New England Transcendentalism
New Testament
Niehbuhr, R.
Nudity, Ritual
Old Catholics
Old Testament
Ophites
Opus Anglican
Ordination
Origen
Original Sin
Orthodoxy
Panentheism
Papacy (Pope)
Parousia
Paul, St.
Pelagianism
Pentecost
Persecution, Religious
Peter, St.
Peter, Apocalypse of
Phallus, Cult of
Pilgrimage
Pillar Saints
Pistis Sophia
Plymouth Brethren
Pontius Pilate
Prayer
Presbyterianism
Puritans
Q (Quelle)
The Reformation
Refrigerium
Regeneration
Relics
Religionsgeschichte
Resurrection
Revelation
Ritual Perpetuation of Past
Rosaries
Russia, Religion
Sabbath
Sacraments
Sacrifice
Sacrifice of Mass
Sadducees
Salvation
Salvation Army
Satan, Satanism
Schleiermacher, Friedrich Daniel Ernst
Septuagint (LXX)
Seraphim
Servant Songs, The
Scholasticism
Schweitzer, Albert
Shakers
Shang Ti
Sibylline Oracles
Simon Magus
Sin (Christian)
Son of Man
Soul
Spiritualism
Synagogue
Syncretism
Synoptic Problem
Teilhard de Chardin, P.
Temple (Jerusalem)
Templars (Knights Templar)
Time
Toledoth Yesu
Transcendentalism
Transubstantiation, Doctrine of
Trees, Sacred
Trinity, Doctrine of the
Unction
Uniat Churches
Unitarianism
Urmensch
Vestments
Virgin Birth
Vows
Vulgate
War, Holy
Wesley, John and Charles
Zealots, The

Egypt

Abydos
Adultery
Ages of the World
Akh
Akhenaten (Amenhotep IV)
Alchemy
Almsgiving
Altar
Amarna Tablets
Amun (Amen, Amon)
Ancestor Cults
Andjty (or Anzti)

Synoptic Index (Egypt; Gnosticism; Greek)

Ankh
Anubis
Apophis
Apotheosis
Astral Religion
Aten (Aton)
Atum
Ba
Bastet
Bes
Book of the Dead, the
Book of Life
Bull, Apis
Canopic Jars
Chronology
Circumcision
Coffin Texts, The
Confession
Cosmogony, Egypt.
Ded-column
Demons (Egypt)
Descent into Hades
Devil, The
Dualism
Egyptian Religion
Eschatology, Egypt
Festivals
Funerary Rites (Egypt)
Geb
Hathor
Heart
Heliopolis
Hermes Trismegistos, Hermetic Literature
Hermopolis
Hierarchy, Egypt
Horus
Iamblichos
Imhotep
Isis
Judgment of the Dead
Ka
Khons(u)
Khnum
King, Divine
Maat
Marriage, Sacred
Memphite Theology
Monotheism
Mummification
Myth and Ritual
Nudity, Ritual
Nut
Osiris
Persecution, Religious
Phallus, Cult of
Pilgrimage
Rē
Refrigerium
Relics
Resurrection
Revelation
Ritual Perpetuation of Past
Salvation
Sarapis (Lat. Serapis)
Scarab
Serpents, Serpent-worship
Set (Seth)
Sin (anc. Near East)
Sky Gods
Soul
Stones, Sacred
Styx, The
Theocracy
Therapeutae
Thoth
Time
Trees, Sacred
Trinity, Doctrine of the
Unction
Underworld
Ushabti
Vestments
Virgin Birth
Wisdom-Literature

Gnosticism

Abraxas, or Abrasax
Aeon(s) Grk. *Aiōn*
Albigenses
Alexandria, Church of
Astral Religion
Barbelo-Gnostics
Bardesanes
Basilides
Carpocrates
Cerdo
Cerinthus
Demiurge
Dualism
Docetism
Elkesaites
Encratites
Gnosticism, Gnostics
Hermes Trismegistos, Hermetic Literature
Irenaeus, Bp. of Lyons
Nag Hammadi
Neoplatonism
Ophites
Orphism
Pistis Sophia
Poimandres
Salvation
Set (Seth)
Simon Magus
Syncretism
Theosophy
Thoth
Urmensch

Greek

A and Ω: (alpha and omega)
Academy
Actaeon
Adonis
Adultery
Adyton
Aegean Religion
Aegis
Aeon(s) Grk. *Aiōn*
Aeschylus
Aesculapius
Agathos Daimon
Ages of the World
Agnostos Theos
Alexander of Abonutichos
Alexander the Great
Alexandria (in Egypt)
Allegory, Allegorical Interpretation
Almsgiving
Altar
Amazons
Ambrosia
Amenhotep (or Amenophis)
Amphiaraos
Amphictionies
Anaxagoras
Ancestor Cult
Anthesteria
Aphrodite
Apollo
Apollonius of Tyana
Apotheosis
Apotropaic
Archōn (pl. Archontes)
Ares
Aretalogies
Ariadne
Aristotle, Aristotelianism
Artemis
Astral Religion
Astrology
Ate
Athena
Atomic Theory
Attis
Axe, Double
Bacchae
Bacchanalia
Bacchus
Baubo
Bilocation
Bogomiles
Butterfly
Bucranion
Britomartis
Brimo-Brimos
Bouphonia
Cabiri
Cecrops
Cereberus
Ceres
Chaldaeans
Chance
Charites
Chaos
Charon

Hinduism

Synoptic Index (Hinduism; Iran; Islam)

Iran

Islam

Synoptic Index (Islam)

Synoptic Index (Islam; Jainism)

Jainism

Synoptic Index (Japan)

Synoptic Index (Judaism)

Synoptic Index (Judaism; Mesopotamia; Rome; Sikhism)

Mesopotamia

Rome

Sikhism

GENERAL INDEX

General Index

General Index

General Index

Dhul Khalaza → Idolatry
Dhul khimar → -Aswad
diabolos → Devil, The
Dialectical Materialism → Atheism (Western: anc. and mod.)
Diamond-cutter Sutra → Prajna-Paramita Sutras
Dido → Aeneas
Dievas → Balts, Religion
Diffusionist School → Anthropology
Digha-Nikaya → Nikaya
Diktynna → Britomartis
Dilthey, W. → Existentialism
Di Manes → Ancestor Cults (Roman)
Din → Judaism
Dindshenchas → Celtic (Pagan) Religion
Dinkart → Pahlavi Lit.
Diodore of Tarsus → Antiochene Theology
Diogenes of Sinope → Cynics
Dionysius Exiguus → Anno Domino
diptychs → Funerary Rites (Christian)
Dirghagama → Agama
Dirghagama (Skt.) → Dighanikaya (Pali)
Dithyramb → Dance, Sacred
divali → Alcohol (Hindu attitude to)
divination (Chi.) → Oracle bones
divination (Chi. and Jap.) → Prodigies and Portents (Chi. and Jap.)
divination (Jap.) → Rites and Rituals (Jap.)
divorce (India) → Marriage (Hindu)
Djamar → Australian Aborigine Religion
Djangawwul → Australian Aborigine Religion
Doddridge, Philip → Congregational Church
Dodona → Oracles
Dogon → Africa, West
von Dohm, W. → Judaism
dola → Festivals (Hindu)
Dome of the Rock → Haram
Dome of the Rock → Jerusalem
Dome of the Rock → Temple (Jerusalem)
Domini canes → Dominic, St.; Dominican Order
Don → Celtic (Pagan) Religion
Donatus → Donatism
door-keepers → Hierarchy, Christian
Dorobo → Africa, East
Double Procession of the Holy Ghost → *Filioque* Clause
dove → Aphrodite
Dragon-boat festival → Dragon
Dragon-boat festival → Festivals (Chinese)
dreams → Psychology of Religion
Dream Time → Australian Aborigine Religion
dromenon → Ritual
dropsy → Varuna
Drsti (Skt.) → Ditthi (Pali)
drugs → Food (Islam); Peyote Cult; Psychology of Relig.
Druids → Celtic (Pagan) Religion
Druids → Mistletoe
Druj → Angra Mainyu
Druj → Demons (Iranian)
Druj Nasu → Funerary Rites (Zoroastrian)
drums → Africa, East
dryads → Trees Sacred
Duhkha (Skt.) → Dukkha (Pali)
duhkha → Kaivalya
dulia → Adoration
Dumuzi → Sumerian Religion
Dumuzi → Tammuz
Duns Scotus → Acceptilation
Duns Scotus → Adoptianism
Dura Europos → Parthian Religion
Durga → Festivals (Hindu), God (Hindu concepts); Kali; Saivism; Sakti; Saktism; Siva; Smartas
Durkheim, E. → Anthropology
Durkheim, E. → Psychology of Religion
Durkheim, E. → Sociology of Religion
Dvaita → Caitanya
Dvaitadvaita → Nimbarka
Dvapara → Time (Hindu views)
Dvaraka → Krishna (Krsna)
Dvaravati (Dwarka) → Sacred Cities (Hindu)
Dvesa (Skt.) → Dosa (Pali)
Dvi-yana → Yana
Dyaus → Varuna
dysser → Scandinavian Religion
Deva-raja → Cambodia (Hinduism)

Eastern Peak → Death, Personification of (Chi.)
Ecclesiasticus → Apocrypha
École Biblique → Dominic, St.; Dominican Order
Edda → Scandinavian Religion
Eddy, Mark Baker → Christian Science
Edesius of Tyre → Ethiopic Church
Edict of Nantes → The Reformation
eidolon → Eschatology, Greek
Eight Immortals → Hsian
Eight Trigrams → Cosmogony-Cosmology (Chi.)
Eighty-Four Magicians → Tibetan Buddhism
Eisler, Robert → Lentulus, Letter of
Eka-yana → Yana
Ekottarikagama → Agama
El → Canaanite Religion
Eliade, Mircea → 'Death of God'
Eliade, Mircea → Psychology of Religion
Elijah → Judaism
Elijah, Gaon of Vilna → Judaism
Elijah Muhammad → Black Muslims
Elioun → Elyon
Elipandus → Adoptianism
elixir → Alchemy
elixir of immortality → Fang Shih
Elizabeth I → Church of England
Elizabeth I → Reformation
Ellora → Caves
El Shaddai → El
elves → Scandinavian Religion
emandwa → Africa, East
Embla → Scandinavian Religion
embroidery → Opus Anglicanum
Emerson → Transcendentalism
Encyclopaedists → Deism
endogamy → Caste System (Hindu)
Endo → Africa, East
Enk Ai → Africa, East
Enkidu → Bestiality
Enkidu → Descent into Hades
Enkidu → Gilgamesh, Epic of
Eno → Hui Neng
Eostre → Easter
Ephesia → Diana of the Ephesians
Epidauros → Aesculapius
Epidauros → Healing, Divine
Epidauros → Pilgrimage
Epiphanes → Carpocrates

General Index

General Index

General Index

General Index

General Index

General Index

Moctecuzoma → American Religions (ancient)
Moggallana → Sariputta/Sariputra
Mongols → Altaic Religion
Mongols → Tibetan Buddhism
Monju → Personification
monkey-principle → Vadagalai
'monkey trial' → Fundamentalism
monogamy → Marriage (Islam)
Mons (see end of M's)
Moore → Philosophy of Religion
Moral Argument → Philosophy of Religion
Moral Philosophy → Christian Ethics
moran → Africa, East
Morgan, Lewis H. → Anthropology
Mormon, Book of → Mormons, The
Moses → -Mi'raj
Moses ibn Ezra → Judaism
Moses Isserles → Judaism
Moses Maimonides → Judaism
Mot → Canaanite Religion
Mother Ann → Shakers
Mothes of God → Mary, Cult of
Mo Ti → Mo Tzu
Mount Meru → Cosmology (Hindu)
Mousterian Man → Burial
Mouth, Opening of the → Mummification
Mozart → Music
mTshal → Tibetan Buddhism
Mu'awiya → Umayyads
Mughals → Arjun
Muhammad, light of → -Haqiqat
Muhammad al-Muntazar → -Mahdi
Muhammadiyya → Islam in Indonesia
Muharram → 'Ashura'
Mulhid → Unbelievers (Islam)
muladhara → *Kundalini*
Mulasarvastivadin → Tibetan Buddhism
Müller, F. Max → Comparative Religion
Müller, F. Max → Henotheism
Mundaka Up. → Upanisad
mundus → Ancestor Cults (Roman)
Mungan-ngaua → Australian Aborigine Religion
Muninn → Scandinavian Religion
munis → Asceticism (Hindu)
Munkar → Examination (Islam)
Muntzer, Thomas → Anabaptists
Muntzer, Thomas → Reformation
Muratorian Fragment → Canon of New Testament
Mushaf Rash → Yazidis
Mushrik → Unbelievers (Islam)
Muslim → -Islam
Muspellsheimr → Scandinavian Religion
Mut → Amun (Amen, Amon)
mut'a → Shi'a
Muwahhidun → Druzes
myrtle → Aphrodite
myrtle → Bona Dea
Mystery Plays → Drama, Religious
mythology (psychology) → Psychology of Religion
Meru, Mt. → Cambodia (Hinduism)
Mons → Thailand and Burma (Hindu)

Naassenes → Ophites
nabi → Prophets (Islam); of Judaism (*navi*)
Naciketas → Upanisads
nafs → Soul, Spirit (Islam)
Nagarjuna → Madhyamika
Nagarjunakonda → Monasteries, Buddhist
Nagarjunkonda → Nalanda
nagas → Gods (Hindu)
Nagas (tribe) → Tribal Religion (India)
Nagasena → *Milinda*
nahoki-koto → Righteousness (Chi. and Jap.)
Na'ila → Idolatry
Nakir → Examination
Nalayiram → Alvars
Nam Dev → Granth, Adi
nama → Khandha (Pali)/Skandha (Skt.)
nama-rupa → Paticca-Samuppada
Nammalvar → Alvars
Nanabozho → North American Indian Religion
nana-jusa → Spring Rites (Chi. and Jap.)
Nanautzin → American Religions (ancient)
Nandi → Cow; Siva
Nanna → Sin (deity)
Nanpaya shrine → Thailand and Burma (Hindu)
Nan-yoh shan → Sacred Places (Chi. and Jap.)
Nan-yu shan → Pilgrims and Pilgrimages (Chi.)
Nara → Daibutsu
Naraka → Cosmology (Hindu)
narakas → Afterlife, Hindu; Hells (Hindu)
Narayana → Visnu
Narmer → War, Holy
Nasafi → Creed (Islam)
Nasa'i → -Hadith
Nasoreans → Mandaeans
Nasr → Idolatry
nastika → Atheism (Indian); Hinduism; Orthodoxy (Hindu); Philosophy (Hindu)
nataraja → Cosmogony (Hindu)
nataraja → Siva
Nathan → Judaism
Nathan the Wise → Judaism
Native American Church → Peyote Cult
Nats → Burma, Buddhism in
Natural Law → Christian Ethics
Natural Theology → Philosophy of Religion
Nauruz → Festival(s)
nava bhikkhu → Thera (Pali)/Sthavira (Skt.)
navi → Judaism
Navyanyaya → Nyaya
Ndembu → Africa (South), Religious cults
Neanderthal Man → Burial
Nebed → Demons (Egypt)
Nebuchadnezzar → Jerusalem
Nebuchadnezzar → Temple (Jerusalem)
Nechepso → Astral Religion
Nectar → Ambrosia
Nefertiti → Akhenaten (Amenhotep IV)
Nehemiah → Judaism
Neith → Cosmogony, Egypt
Neolithic Revolution → Agriculture
Nerthus → Scandinavian Religion
Nestorius → Nestorianism
neti neti → Upanisads
Newton, Isaac → Boehme, Jacob
New Year → Festivals (Chinese)
Ngewo → Africa, West
Niang-niang-Sung-tzu → Pi-hsia Yuan-chun
Nicene Creed → Creeds
Nicodemus, Gospel of → Descent into Hades
Niddesa → Sutta-Nipata

General Index

General Index

Ruhanga → Africa, East
Rukmini → Krishna (Krsna)
Rule of War → Qumran
rupa → Khandha (Pali)/Skandha (Skt.)
Ruqayya → ‘Uthman
Russell → Philosophy of Religion
Russia, Church of → Eastern Church
Ruth → *Megilloth*
Rva-sgreng → Tibetan Buddhism

Saadia Gaon → Judaism
Sabbatical year → Almsgiving (Israel)
sabda → Revelation (Hindu)
sabd yoga → Radha Soami Movement
Saccavibhanga Sutta → Mahasatipatthana Sutta
saccidananda → Advaita Vedanta; God (Hindu concepts)
Sacramentarium Gregorianum → Missal
Sacred Heart → Heart
sacred thread → Agni
sacrificial victims → Bon and Tibetan Pre-Buddhist Religion
sa'd → Idolatry
saddarsana → Darsana
Saddikim → Judaism
sadhanas → Nimbarka
sadhus → Asceticism (Hindu); Pilgrimage (Hindu)
Sad-na-legs → Tibetan Buddhism
saeculum → Ages of the World (Grk. and Rom.)
Safed → Judaism
Safwan, Jahm B. → Jahmites
Sarasvati → Festivals (Hindu)
Sarasvati (river) → Ganges
Sarekat Islam → Islam in Indonesia
Sarekat Merah → Islam in Indonesia
Sarekat Rayah → Islam in Indonesia
Sariputta → Ananda
Sarmatians → Altaic Religion
sarsti → Liberation
Sartre → Existentialism
Sarume → Nakatomi
sarupya → Liberation
sarvamukti → Liberation
Sa-skya → Tibetan Buddhism
Sastras → Sutras (Hindu)
Satanael → Bogomiles
Sata-sahasrika Sutra → Prajna-Paramita Sutras
Satipatthana Sutta → Mahasatipatthana Sutta
Sat Kartar → God (Sikh concepts)
Satmi → Descent into Hades
Sat Nam → God (Sikh concepts)
Saturnalia → Festival(s)
satyagraka → Gandhi
Satyrs → Dionysos
Saul → Judaism
Saul → Messiah
Saule → Balts, Religion
Savitr → Gayatri
Savoy Declaration → Congregational Church
sayujya → Caitanya
sayujua → Liberation
Schammai, R. → Hillel; Judaism
Schechter, S. → Judaism
Scheduled Classes → Buddhism, General Survey
Schelling → Existentialism
Schelling → Tillich, Paul Johannes
Schmidt, Wilhelm → Anthropology
Schmidt, Wilhelm → Monotheism
Scholastica, St. → Benedict, St.
Scholasticism → Aquinas, St. Thomas
Scholem, G. → Judaism
Schoolcraft, H. R. → Anthropology
Schweitzer, A. → Qumran
Scopes, J. T. → Fundamentalism
Scot, Reginald → Witchcraft
Scythians → Altaic Religion
Sebonde, Raymond de → Philosophy of Religion
sectarian marks (Hindu) → Vaisnavism
Sed-Festival → Festival(s) (Egypt.)
Sedna → Eskimo Religion
sedu → Cherubim
sedu → Demons (Mesopot.)
Sefer Hasidim → Judaism
seigi → Righteousness (Chi. and Jap.)
se'irim → Demons (Hebrew)
sag-did → Funerary Rites (Zoroastrian)
sagunam Brahman → Advaita Vedanta; Guna
sahajdharis → Sikhism
Sahihs → -Hadith
Sahihs → Muslim b. al-Hajjaj
Saicho → Dengyo Daishi
Saiva Siddhanta → Darsana
Sakka/Sakra → India
Sakkai → Judaism
Sakyamuni → Buddha (The), Gotama (Gautama-Skt.)
Sakya-sri → Tibetan Buddhism
Saladin → Crusades
Saladin → Fatimids
Salafiyya → Rashid Rida
salat → Prayer
Salathiel Apocalypse → Esdras, Book of
Salem → Witchcraft
Salii → Mars
Salisbury, John of → Abelard, Peter
salokya → Liberation
Salt-goddess → American Religions (ancient)
salvation-religions → Salvation
samadhi → Breathing control
samanera → Ordination, Buddhist
samanas → Sangha (or Samgha)
Samantapasadika → Literature, Buddhist (Pali)
Sambhoga-kaya → Buddha-Kaya
Sam-Phra-Phum → Phi
Samson → Suicide
Samuel → Divination
Samuin → Celtic (Pagan) Religion
Samurai → Bushido
Samyuktagama → Agama
Samyutta-Nikaya → Nikaya
Sanaka-sampradaya → Vaisnavism
sanatana dharma → Hinduism
Sande → Africa, West
Sangharaja → Buddhism in South-East Asia
sangharama → Monasteries, Buddhist
sanghati → Ordination Buddhist
sankhara → Khandha (Pali)/Skandha (Skt.)
sankhara → Paticca-Samuppada
sankirtana → Caitanya
sankirtana → Worship (Hindu)
Sankranti → Thailand and Burma (Hindu)
sanna → Khandha (Pali)/Skandha (Skt.)
San Salvador → American Religions (ancient)

Songhay → Africa, West
Sons of Zadok → Damascus Fragments, The
Sophia → Barbelo-Gnostics
sorcerers (Chinese) → Magic, Chinese
sorcery (African) → Africa, East; South; West
sortes sanctorum → Divination
soteriology → Salvation
Sothis → Calendar, Religious Origins
Sothis → Festival(s)
soul-substance → Blood
Spencer, H. → Ancestor Cults (Introductory)
Spengler, O. → History, Philosophy of
Sphinx → Dreams
Split-ear yogis → Saivism
Spinoza, B. → Pantheism
spirit-tablet → Burial (Chinese)
spirit-tablet → Confucianism
spirit-tablet → Mourning Customs (Chi.)
spit → Africa, East
spring festival (Chinese) → Ch'ing Ming
Srautasutras → Sutras (Hindu)
Sravaka-yana → Mahayana
Sravaka-yana → Yana
Sri Chand → Sikhism
Srihavsa → Advaita Vedanta
Srikantha → Meykanda
Srimad-Bhagavata → Puranas
Srong-brtsan-sgam-po → Tibetan Buddhism
srsti → Cosmogony (Hindu)
Ssu-ma Kuang → Ta Hsueh
sTag-gzigs → Bon and Tibetan Pre-Buddhist Religion
sTag-lung-pa → Tibetan Buddhism
Starbuck, E. D. → Psychology of Religion
Steiner, R. → Anthroposophy
Stele of Vultures → War, Holy
Step Pyramid → Architecture (Religious)
sterilisation → Birth Control
Sthanakavasis → Svetambara
Sthavira (Skt.) → Thera (Pali)/Sthavira (Skt.)
Sthaviras → Buddhist Schools of Thought
Sthaviras → Theravada
Sthenno → Gorgo(n) or Medusa
Stigmata → Francis of Assisi, St., Franciscan Order
Stonehenge → Architecture (Relig.)
Stonehenge → Megalithic Culture
Stonehenge → Stones, Sacred
store-consciousness → Alaya-Vijnana
store consciousness → Hosso
Strasbourg → Reformation
Levi-Strauss → Anthropology
Suarez → Adoptianism
sub-deacons → Hierarchy, Christian
Subh-i Azal → Babis
Subhuti → Prajna-Paramita Sutras
subintroductae (Lat.) → Agapetai and Agapetoi
subjective-creationist school → Advaita Vedanta
Subrahmanya → Gods (Hindu)
substance → Transubstantiation, Doctrine of
sucellos → Celtic (Pagan) Religion
Sudras → Caste System (Hindu)
Suetonius → Jesus of Nazareth
Sugriva → Ramayana
suicide (African) → Africa, East
suicide (Jain) → Ethics, Jain
sukha → Happiness, Buddhist concept of
Sukhavati → Amida
Sukkoth → Judaism
Sukkoth → Festival(s)
Sumana → Ceylon, Buddhism in
Sumangala-vilasini → Literature, Buddhist (Pali)
Sumerian King list → Chronology
Sunday → Holy Days, Buddhist
Sunden, H. → Psychology of Religion
suneisaktoi (Grk.) → Agapetai and Agapetoi
Sung-shan → Pilgrims and Pilgrimages (Chi.)
Sung shan → Sacred Places (Chi. and Jap.)
Sunyata → Sunya; Sunyata; Sunyabada
Sunyavada → Madhyamika
Sunyavada → Sunya; Sunyata; Sunyavada
Supper, Last → Eucharist
Suresvara → Advaita Vedanta
Surya → Agni; Smartas
Susa-no-wo → Izanagi-Izanami
susumna → *Kundalini*
Suttee → Sati
Sutra of Brahma's Net → Discipline, Religious (Chi. and Jap.)
Suwa' → Idolatry
Suzuki, D. T. → Zen
svabhavavada → Carvaka
Svantevit → Slavic Religion
Svarozic → Slavic Religion
Svatantrika → Madhyamika
svayamvara → Marriage (Hindu)
Svetaketu → Upanisads
Svetasvatara Up. → Upanisads
Swami Vivekananda → Mission (the Propagation of Religion)
swastika → Cross
Swazi → Africa (South); Religious Cults
Sweden → Scandinavian Religion
Sweden → Reformation
Swedenbourg → Transcendentalism
swing festival → Festivals (Hindu)
Swiss Brethren → Zwingli, Ulrich
Synod of Diamper → Thomas Christians
star-worshippers → Sabians

Ta Shih-chih → Personification
Ta Shih Chih → Pure Land School (Buddhist also Jodo)
Ta Tai Li → Li Chi
Ta T'ung Shu → Peace, Ideal of (Chi. and Jap.)
Ta'aroa → Polynesian Religion
ta-asobi → Spring Rites (Chi. and Jap.)
table of showbread → Temple (Jerusalem)
table-turning → Spiritualism
Tacitus → Jesus of Nazareth
T'ai Chi → Five Elements (Chi.)
T'ai Miao → Altar (China)
T'ai Miao → Architecture (Chi. and Jap.)
T'ai P'ing → Fanaticism (Chi. and Jap.)
T'ai P'ing → Peace, Ideal of (Chi. and Jap.)
T'ai P'ing Rebellion → Secret Societies (Chinese)
T'ai P'ing T'ien Kuo → Hung Hsiu-ch'uan
T'ai-shan → Pilgrims and Pilgrimages (Chi.)
T'ai shan → Sacred Places (Chi. and Jap.)
t'ai-shan Niang-niang → Pi-hsia Yuan-chun
Tailtiu → Celtic (Pagan) Religion
Taittiriya Up. → Upanisads
Taizé-les-Cluny → Monasticism
Taj Mahal → Tombs (Islam)

General Index

Toleration → Persecution, Religious
Toltec → American Religions (ancient)
Tome of Pope Leo → Chalcedon, Council of
Tonalpouhalli → American Religions (ancient)
Tonatiuh → American Religions (ancient)
tool-making → Religion, Origin of
Tooth relic → Ceylon, Buddhism in
Tooth, Sacred → Relics (Buddhist)
Torah → Judaism
Tortoise (Kurma) → Avatara
Tosaphists → Judaism
totem poles → North American Indian Religion
towers of silence → Dakhmas
Toynbee, A. J. → History, Philosophy of
Tozi → American Religions (ancient)
traditores → Donatism
mediumistic trance → Spiritualism
transtheism → Atheism (Indian)
Trappists → Cistercian Order
Tree of Knowledge of Good and Evil → Trees, Sacred
Tree of Life → Trees, Sacred
Treta → Time (Hindu views)
Trickster → Scandinavian Religion
trickster myths → North American Indian Religion
Tri-kaya → Buddha-Kaya
tritheism → Monotheism
Trito-Isaiah → Deutero-Isaiah
Trito-Isaiah → Isaiah, Book of
Tri-yana → Yana
Troeltsch, E. → Sociology of Religion
trolls → Scandinavian Religion
Trophonios → Chthonian Deities
Troy → Labyrinth
Trsna (Skt.) → Craving (Tanha, Pali)
truce → Months (Islam)
Trud → Scandinavian Religion
Truth of Causality → Destiny (Chi. and Jap.)
Ts'ai Shen → Wealth, attitude to (Chi.)
Tsao Chun → Kitchen God
Tsao-Chun → Tutelary gods and spirits (Chi.)
Ts'ao-tung → Soto
Tso Chuan → Ch'un Ch'iu
Tsuina → Demons and Demonology (Jap.)
Tsuki-yomi → Izanagi-Izanami
Tu → Polynesian Religion
T'u Ti → Death, Personification of (Chi.)
T'u ti → Nature, Worship of (Chi.)
T'u ti → Tutelary gods and spirits (Chi.)
Tuatha De Danann → Celtic (Pagan) Religion
Tübingen School → Baur, Ferdinand School
Tuchilcha → Etruscan Religion
Tulasi (Tulsi) Das → Ramayana
Tulip → Presbyterianism
Tung-lin monastery → Hui Yuan
Turan → Etruscan Religion
Turks → Altaic Religion
Tu-shun → Hua Yen
Tusi → -Hadith
Tusita → Bodhisatta (Pali)/Bodhisattva (Skt.)
T'u-teng → Nuns, Chinese
Twelvers → Imam
Tyche → Chance
Tylor, E. B. → Animism
Tylor, E. B. → Anthropology
Tylor, E. B. → Comparative Religion
Tyndale → Reformation
Typhon → Set (Seth)
Tyr → Scandinavian Religion
Tyrrell, G. → Modernism
Tzu Ssu → The Mean
Tzu-t'ung → Wen Ch'ang

'Ubaydallah → Fatimids
'Ubaydallah → -Mahdi
ubusuna-no-kami → Tutelary gods and spirits (Jap.)
uccheda-ditthi → Annihilation (Buddhist)
Udasis → Sikhism
Udayana → God (Indian arguments); Vaisesika
Uddalaka → Tat Tvam Asi; Upanisads
Udgitr → Hierarchy (Hindu)
Udzat-eye → Evil Eye
Uganda → Africa, East
Uga-no-mitama → Inari
Uggae → Death
Uke-mochi → Inari
Ukko → Finna-Ugric Religion
Ukupanipo → Hawaiian Religion
Ulrich of Augsburg → Canonisation
Uma → Gods (Hindu), Kali; Trimurti
'umra → Pilgrimage
Underhill, Evelyn → Psychology of Religion
untouchables → Buddhism, General Survey
untouchables → Caste System (Hindu)
Upadana → Grasping
upadana → Pattica-Samuppada
Upagupta → Divyavadana
Upali → *Sakyas*
upanayana → Initiation (Hindu)
Upapuranas → Puranas
upasampada → Ordination, Buddhist
upasika → Nuns, Buddhist
Uppsala → Scandinavian Religion
Ur → Funerary Rites (Mesopot.)
Ur → Sin (deity)
Urabe → Nakatomi
Uranus → Varuna
Urartu → Armenia, Armenians
Urash → Adultery (Babylon)
Urðarbrunnr → Scandinavian Religion
Uriah → David
urigallu → Hierarchy, Mesopotamian
Urmonotheismus → Monotheism
Urshanabi → Charon
urvan → Soul
Uta → Shamash
Utanapishtim → Flood, The
Utanapishtim → Gilgamesh, Epic of
Utrecht, Church of → Old Catholics
uttaramimamsa → Vedanta
uttarasangha → Ordination, Buddhist
Uzzah → Clean and Unclean

Vacaspati Misra → Advaita Vedanta
Vadianus → Reformation
Vahanian, G. → 'Death of God'
Vaikuntha → Visnu
Vaisali (Skt.) → Vesali (Pali)/Vaisali (Skt.)
Vaisesika → Darsana
Vaisyas → Caste System (Hindu)
Vajjiputtaka → Vesali (Pali)/Vaisali (Skt.)
Vajracchedika → Prajna-Paramita Sutras
Valhalla → Scandinavian Religion

General Index

General Index